Carpentry

AND BUILDING CONSTRUCTION

FIFTH EDITION

Carpentry
AND BUILDING CONSTRUCTION
FIFTH EDITION

John L. Feirer • Gilbert R. Hutchings • Mark D. Feirer

Glencoe McGraw-Hill

New York, New York   Columbus, Ohio   Woodland Hills, California   Peoria, Illinois

Glencoe/McGraw-Hill

*A Division of The **McGraw·Hill** Companies*

Copyright © 1997 by Glencoe/McGraw-Hill. Previous copyright © 1993 by Glencoe/McGraw-Hill; previous copyrights © 1986, 1981, 1976 by John L. Feirer and Gilbert R. Hutchings. All rights reserved. Except as permitted under the United States Copyright Act, no part of this publication may be reproduced or distributed in any form or by any means, or stored in a database or retrieval system, without prior written permission from the publisher.

Printed in the United States of America.

Send all inquiries to:
Glencoe/McGraw-Hill
3008 W. Willow Knolls Drive
Peoria, IL 61614-1083

ISBN 0-02-838699-X

4 5 6 7 8 9 10 027 02 01 00

Cover photography by Ted Mashima.

Cover and interior design by Seventeenth Street Studios.

Preface

This new edition of *Carpentry and Building Construction* builds on the updated information presented in the previous edition. The text retains its strong focus on the many new tools, materials, and techniques now being used in the residential construction industry. For example, the text provides information on metal framing connectors, glulams and wood I-beams, pneumatic nailers and staplers, plate joiners, ceramic tiles, and mechanical systems. School-to-work activities are now included at the end of many units. New appendices provide information on metric construction, math concepts, science concepts, employability skills, and communications skills.

This book has been designed as a basic text for students in wood technology classes at the high school, vocational school, and community junior college levels. It will also be helpful to those in apprenticeship training and to do-it-yourselfers who wish to undertake building or remodeling projects. The text emphasizes careful work habits and attention to building codes.

Building a house calls for the use of a great variety of materials. This book includes discussions of many of them—in particular, poured concrete, brick-veneer, and concrete masonry units. However, wood remains the basic material for most homes built in the United States. For this reason, *Carpentry and Building Construction* includes a wealth of detailed information on this subject.

In revising this text, the authors have reviewed courses of study from schools, trade unions, and public agencies to determine what should be included. They have also carefully reviewed technical materials from companies and other organizations involved in building construction. Finally, they have drawn upon professional experience in the building trades and many years of teaching.

Students who carefully study this text should achieve the following behavioral objectives:

➤ To be able to identify career opportunities in the building trades.

➤ To be able to demonstrate competency in the use of the materials and hand and power tools used in building construction.

➤ To be able to understand the building codes used in residential building construction.

➤ To be able to read the prints and technical materials used in building a home.

➤ To be able to demonstrate skills meeting or exceeding recognized standards.

The many companies and individuals who have contributed to this work are recognized in the Acknowledgments.

Acknowledgments

PERSONAL

Susan M. Hutchings
Daniel W. Irvin
John Polderman
William K. Purdy
Walter C. Schwersinske

COMMERCIAL, PROFESSIONAL, AND GOVERNMENTAL

The Abitibi Corporation
Acorn Products Company
Allied Chemical, Barrett Division
Alsco, Incorporated
Aluminum Company of America
American Concrete Institute
American Forest Products Industries, Incorporated
American Hardboard Association
American Ladder Institute
American Olean
American Optical Corporation
American Plywood Association
American Society of Heating, Refrigerating, and Air-Conditioning Engineers
Amerigo
Andersen Corporation
Armstrong Cork Company
Atlas
Automated Building Components, Incorporated
Baker-Roos, Incorporated
Benjamin Moore and Company
Berger Instruments
Berry Industries, Incorporated
Bethlehem Steel
Billings
Bird and Son, Incorporated
The Black & Decker Manufacturing Company
Boice-Crane Company
Bostitch, Incorporated
Boston Chamber of Commerce
Bowater Board Company
British Columbia Lumber Manufacturers Association
Bruce Oak Flooring
Buck Brothers, Incorporated
California Redwood Association
Canadian Wood Council
Caterpillar Tractor
The Celotex Corporation
Clark Equipment
Clausing Corporation
Condon-King Company, Incorporated
Consumers Power Company
Continental Homes
Copper Development Association
Council of the Forest Industries of British Columbia
Crawford Door Company
Curtis Companies, Incorporated
E. I. du Pont de Nemours and Company, Incorporated
Delta
Desa Industries, Incorporated
De Walt
Dexter Lock Company
Disston Saw Company
The Donley Brothers Company
Douglas Fir Plywood Association
Dow Chemical Company
Engelhard Corporation
Feather-Lite Manufacturing Company
Federal Pocket Door Frame Company
The Flintkote Company
Formica Corporation
General Electric Company
Georgia-Pacific Corporation

Grand Rapids Sash and Door
   Company
Greenberg-May Prod. Inc.
Greenlee Brothers and Company
Harr, Hedrich-Blessing
H C Products Company
Heart Truss and Engineering
Home Planners, Inc.
Independent Nail and Packing
   Company
Inland Steel Company
International Conference of
   Building Officials
International Harvester Company
Irwin
The I-XL Furniture Company,
   Incorporated
Johns-Manville
Johnson-Howard Lumber Company
Kemper Brothers, Incorporated
Kohler Co.
Koppers Company, Incorporated
Lennox Industries, Incorporated
The Lietz Company
Los Angeles Building and
   Construction Trades Council
Macklanburg-Duncan Co.
Manor House Cupolas
Manpower Magazine
Maple Flooring Manufacturers
   Association
Marvin Windows
Masonite Corporation
McKee Door Company
Memphis Moldings, Incorporated
Metric Monitor
Miller Lumber Company
Millers Falls Company
Millwork Supply Company
Minnesota & Ontario Paper
   Company
Mobile Home Manufacturers
   Association
Modernfold Industries
Morgan Company
Mueller Brass Company
Mutschler Brothers Company
National Association of Home
   Builders Research Foundation,
   Incorporated
National Forest Products
   Association
National Gypsum Company

National Hardwood Lumber
   Association
National Lumber Manufacturers
   Association
National Manufacturing Company
National Oak Flooring
   Manufacturers Association
National Research Council
National Woodwork Manufacturers
   Association
Nautilus Industries, Incorporated
Nord
Nordahl Sliding Door Pockets
Norton Company Construction
   Products Division
Nu-Wood Sheathing
Oliver Machinery Company
Overhead Door Corporation
Owens Corning Fiberglas Corp.
Paslode Company
Patent Scaffolding Company
Frank Paxton Lumber Company
Pease Company
Permabilt Manufactured Homes,
   Incorporated
Pittsburgh Plate Glass Company
Porta-Table Corporation
Porter-Cable Machine Company
Portland Cement Association
Powermatic, Incorporated
Raynor Manufacturing Company
Red Cedar Shingle & Handsplit
   Shake Bureau
Redman Industries, Incorporated
Remington Arms Company,
   Incorporated
Republic Steel Corporation
Research Products Corporation
Reynolds Aluminum Company
Rock Island Millwork
Rockwell Manufacturing Company
Rolscreen Company
Russell Jennings
Safway Steel Products, Inc.
St. Regis Paper Company, Panelyte
   Division
Sanford Roof Trusses
H. J. Scheirich Company
Scholz Homes, Incorporated
Scovill, Caradco Division
Sears Roebuck and Company
Senco Products, Incorporated
Shakertown Corporation
The Sherwin-Williams Company

Shopmate
Simonds Saw and Steel Company
Simplex Products Group
Simpson Timber Company
Southern Pine Association
Spotnail, Incorporated
Stanley Iron Works, Incorporated
Stanley Tools
Sterling Homes, Incorporated
Structural Clay Products Institute
Textron Company
Timber Engineering Company
Trus-Joist Corporation
United States Department of
   Agriculture
United States Department of
   Commerce, National Bureau of
   Standards
United States Forest Service,
   Forest Products Laboratory
United States Gypsum Company
United States Plywood
   Corporation
United States Savings and Loan
   League
United States Steel Corporation
The Upson Company
Van Mark Products Corporation
Vega Industries, Incorporated
Weiser Company
Western Electric Company
Western Red Cedar Lumber
   Association
Western Wood Moulding and
   Millwork Producers
Western Wood Products
   Association
Westinghouse
Weyerhaeuser Company
David White, Inc.
Woodbridge Ornamental Iron
   Company
Wood Conversion Company
Wood-Mode Kitchens
Wood-Mosaic Corporation

Contents

SECTION IV: FOUNDATIONS — 213

1 Introduction

1

Careers in Construction

THE CONSTRUCTION INDUSTRY

The construction industry is one of the largest and most important industries in the United States. In 1988, for example, it accounted for $\frac{1}{10}$ of the entire gross national product, or $325 billion. The industry employs millions of workers in a wide variety of occupations. Figs. 1-1a,b. Many of these workers are skilled craftspeople. Construction is divided into four major divisions:

➤ Residential construction.
➤ Nonresidential construction.
➤ Highway and heavy construction.
➤ Municipal utilities construction.

Residential construction is the largest of these categories. It accounts for approximately one-third of the total dollar volume of the industry. It includes both single-family homes and multiple-family buildings.

Nonresidential construction includes everything from churches and small commercial buildings to schools, large industrial buildings, and shopping centers. Highway and heavy construction includes roads and other large excavation projects. Municipal utilities construction includes such activities as water-supply and sewer construction, power line construction, and other municipal service construction.

Another way of describing the construction industry is to divide it into *light* construction and *heavy* construction.

1-1a. *Framing walls.*

1-1b. *Installing insulation.*

Light construction typically includes houses, small residential buildings, and small commercial buildings. These structures are often built with frameworks of wood or light-gauge metal. Heavy construction includes large commercial buildings, highways, dams, and other structures.

Being a part of the construction industry is a challenging career. Many of these jobs give you a chance to work actively on construction projects. Variety, usefulness, vitality—these are the rewards, along with good pay and varied working conditions, for the individuals who make a career in construction.

Every construction project is a team effort requiring people of varied educational backgrounds and skills. These include architects, contractors, and workers in the crafts, and business people who supply the materials.

A great deal of light building construction is now done in the factories. There is increased use of prefabricated components such as trusses, prehung doors, and many other items that are built in the factory and installed as complete units at the job site. Even more important, many complete homes (modular form) are now produced in the factory. Such homes have plumbing, heating, and electrical work already installed and are ready for moving to the site.

INDUSTRY TRENDS

According to the Bureau of Census, the construction industry is expected to add 760,000 jobs before 2000. Construction employment is expected to grow approximately 15%. Table 1-A. Overall, this represents a steady expansion during the 1990s. However, the construction industry is subject to periodic economic downturns. For example, the 1991 recession made it difficult for many people in the skilled crafts to get jobs. Most people who have been in the industry for a long time expect it to experience periods of growth and decline. Important factors that affect the growth of the industry include mortgage interest rates, the availability of construction financing, government spending, and business investment.

CAREER LEVELS

In construction there are three career levels that require special training and education: craft, technical, and professional.

Craft

Workers in the building crafts represent the largest group of skilled workers in the United States labor force. Altogether, more than 5.1 million were employed in 1988.

There are more than two dozen skilled building trades. Several major trades—carpenter, painter, plumber, bricklayer, and construction electrician—each had more than 100,000 workers in a recent year. Carpenters alone numbered over 1,100,000 making them by far the largest group of skilled workers employed in the building trades.

Many skilled workers in the construction industry are self-employed. They run small businesses, often employing just a few people.

Table 1A. *Percent Change in Employment, 1988-2000.*

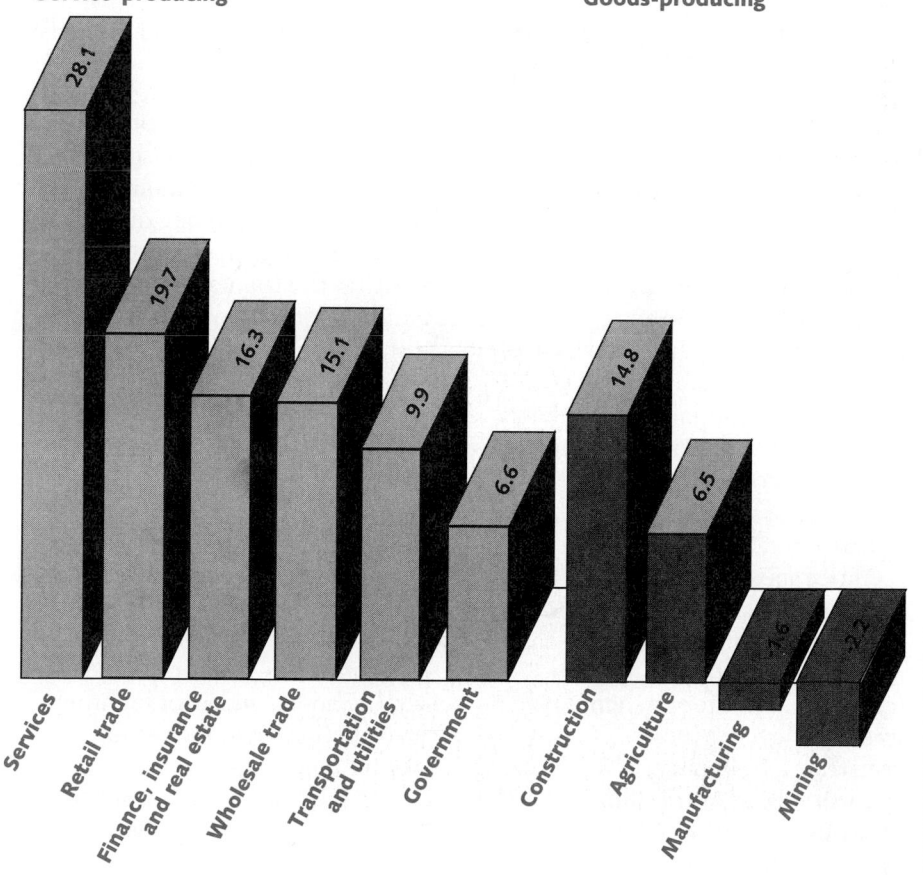

Service-producing: Services 28.1, Retail trade 19.7, Finance, insurance and real estate 16.3, Wholesale trade 15.1, Transportation and utilities 9.9, Government 6.6

Goods-producing: Construction 14.8, Agriculture 6.5, Manufacturing 1.6, Mining 2.2

1-2. *Bricklayers must work with various masonry materials.*

Building trades workers are employed mainly in the construction, maintenance, repair, and alteration of homes and other buildings, highways, airports, and similar structures. Because construction materials and skills are so varied, specialization of work operations has occurred. Thus, building trades workers who use essentially the same materials or skills have tended to become identified with distinct trades. For example, bricklayers and stonemasons both work with

1-3. *This roofer is installing asphalt shingles.*

masonry materials. Fig. 1-2. Although operating engineers do not work with particular materials, they have related skills that enable them to operate equipment for excavating, grading, and hoisting.

The building trades consist primarily of workers who generally have a high level of skill and a sound knowledge of assembly and construction operations. Many of these workers are union members. In unions, a worker in the crafts is often called a *journeyman*. These workers often are assisted by apprentices, tenders, and laborers.

The work of journeymen may be grouped into three broad classifications: structural, finishing, and mechanical. However, some—carpenters, for example—may do finishing as well as structural work. Generally, each building trade is classified in one of these three categories, as follows:

Occupations mainly concerned with *structural* work are carpenter, operating engineer (construction machinery operator), bricklayer, structural ironworker, ornamental ironworker, cement mason, reinforcing ironworker (who puts reinforcing steel in concrete forms), rigger and machine mover, stonemason, and boilermaker.

Occupations mainly concerned with *finishing* work are lather, plasterer, marble setter, tile setter, terrazzo worker, painter, paperhanger, glazier, roofer, and floor covering installer. Fig. 1-3.

Occupations mainly concerned with *mechanical* work are plumber, pipefitter, construction electrician, sheet-metal worker, elevator constructor, and millwright.

Since most of the work in this book is directly related to carpentry, a more detailed description of this occupation follows. Carpenters are employed in almost every type of construction activity. They erect the wood framework of the building, including subflooring,

sheathing, partitions, floor joists, studding, and rafters. When the building is ready for trimming, they install molding, wood paneling, cabinets, window sash, doorframes, doors and hardware, as well as build stairs and lay floors. Carpenters, when doing finish work, must concern themselves with appearance as well as structural accuracy of the work.

Carpenters also install heavy timbers used to build docks, railroad trestles and similar structures. They build the forms needed to pour concrete decks, columns, piers, and retaining walls used in the construction of bridges, buildings, and other structures. They erect scaffolding and temporary buildings at the construction site.

Carpenters saw, fit, and assemble plywood, wallboard, and other materials. They use nails, bolts, wood screws, or glue to fasten materials. Carpenters use hand tools such as hammers, saws, chisels, and planes, and power tools such as portable power saws, drills, and rivet guns.

As mentioned earlier, because of the wide scope of the work performed in the trade, some carpenters specialize in a particular type of carpentry. For example, some carpenters specialize in erecting the framework of a building; others specialize in the installation of millwork and finish hardware (trimming), laying hardwood floors, or building stairs. Specialization is more common in the large cities; in small communities carpenters often do many types of carpentry. In rural areas, carpenters may do the work of some other crafts, particularly painting, glazing, or roofing. However, as a general rule carpenters stay in a particular field such as home, bridge, or highway construction, or in industrial maintenance.

For individuals who want to enter construction through trades, apprenticeship training programs have been established to prepare for journeyman work. Apprentices in the building trade are generally required to be between 18 and 25 years of age and in good physical condition. These programs, which are three to four years in length, combine on-the-job training with basic instruction in tools and procedures of the trade. In many cases, the apprentice will actually go to school one day each week for practical classroom and shop instruction. In every instance, whether on the job or in the class, the apprentice receives a regular hourly wage which is a percentage of the journeyman's rate. A good way to get started in an apprenticeship is to have a good background in carpentry and building construction in your high school classes or in a vocational school.

1-5a. *The architect must be a creative person. He or she must also understand construction practices and be a good business manager to be successful.*

1-5b. *A career in building construction offers a wide variety of opportunities. There are many ways to learn more about these occupations, including interviewing a person in the field. This student (left) is talking to a successful interior designer.*

Technical Careers

There are many careers in building construction that require additional preparation in a technical institute or community junior college. A technician is one who works on a team with engineers, architects, contractors, and people in the skilled trades. Technical specialists in construction go where they are needed. In the field, at construction sites or in the architect's office, the technician has the knowledge and technical skill to do work that lies in an occupational area between the craftsperson and the architect or engineer. Some of the common two-year technician programs are in drafting and general building construction. Fig. 1-4. These programs provide a good background in design, construction practices, and procedures. They may include such courses as surveying, architectural drafting, plan reading, basic estimating, business administration, and building techniques.

1-4. *A two-year associate of arts degree in architectural drafting is an excellent way to get into the building construction industry.*

Professional Careers

If you are planning to go on to college, there are many opportunities for professional careers related to construction. Some of the most important include architect, interior designer, industrial education teacher, and landscape engineer. Figs. 1-5a,b.

All of these professional opportunities require a knowledge of building construction.

OTHER CONSTRUCTION CAREERS

Because the construction industry is so large, there are many opportunities for employment in businesses that serve the industry. Many people either sell or service

1-6. *People who sell or service tools must know how those tools are used. Thus, they must understand building construction.*

tools and equipment. Fig. 1-6. Many others supply or fabricate building materials such as lumber or millwork. Fig. 1-7. Still others are employed by manufacturers to test and evaluate new products for the construction industry. Fig. 1-8. Whatever specific subject you are interested in, you can find a place for it in the construction industry.

1-7. *A working knowledge of wood helps those who work for lumber or millwork suppliers. This supplier specializes in millwork for Victorian-style houses.*

1-8. *This person works for an independent research laboratory. He is testing the performance of vapor-barrier paint.*

THE ENTREPRENEUR

Most large businesses started as small businesses. This is true of some of the largest corporations. The building of a business requires skill and hard work. It can be difficult to imagine the energy needed to start a business. Anyone starting a small business faces a variety of tasks. He or she first must have the money needed. (This money may have to be borrowed.) He or she also must have a product or service that can be sold at a profit. He or she must have a way of distributing the product or service to the public. The smaller the business, the more of these jobs the owner-operator may have to do. In some small businesses, the owner-operator has all of these responsibilities. In larger businesses, such duties are divided. For example, one person (or one department) may be in charge of making the product. Another may be in charge of advertising it. A third may be in charge of delivering the item. Usually, the larger the business, the greater the number of people needed for each of these duties.

The person who starts a business is usually an *entrepreneur.* An entrepreneur is anyone who organizes and manages a business. This person also assumes the risks of the business. This means that the entrepreneur is responsible for paying the business expenses. All responsibility for the success of the business rests with the entrepreneur.

All entrepreneurs face four similar problems. These problems are:
- ➤ Identifying a *need.*
- ➤ Finding a *product* to satisfy the need.
- ➤ *Financing* the business.
- ➤ *Selling* the product.

Let's look at each of these concerns.

All successful businesses have one thing in common. They were started because someone noticed that people needed or wanted an item or service. Once an entrepreneur has noticed a need, he or she can then find an item or a service to fill this need.

Starting a business is not easy. Succeeding in business is even harder. Anyone who starts a business is an entrepreneur. But not all entrepreneurs are successful. For an entrepreneur to be successful, his or her business must be successful. The success of an entrepreneur's business depends on the entrepreneur's success in solving the problems that every business faces.

YOUR FUTURE IN CONSTRUCTION

There are countless opportunities for promotion in the construction industry. The individual who begins as a carpenter with a journeyman's license can continue to a position such as superintendent. The technical school or community college graduate may start as a drafter and become an assistant engineer, job superintendent, or project manager. College graduates may start as assistant architect, or assistant engineer, and work up to full professional status, eventually becoming a partner or owner of a business.

If you are interested in a career in carpentry or related work, here are some sources you can contact for information:
- ➤ Local union of the United Brotherhood of Carpenters and

Joiners of America.
➤ Local carpentry contractors or general contractors.
➤ Local joint union-

management apprenticeship committee.
➤ Local office of state employment service or state

apprenticeship agency.
➤ Bureau of Apprenticeship, U.S. Department of Labor.

QUESTIONS

1. List several typical construction projects and tell whether they are light or heavy construction.

2. Describe the three levels of careers in construction.

3. What is the largest group of workers in the building trades? How many are employed in this craft?

4. What are the three broad classifications of journeyman work in the building trade?

5. Explain how you can become a carpenter through an apprenticeship program.

6. The building industry offers job opportunities as a technician for those desiring to be an assistant engineer, a job superintendent, or a project manager. Name two other job opportunities.

ACTIVITIES

1. Language Arts. *Journeyman* is a term used in Unit 1. Look up the derivation of this word in a college dictionary. How does the original meaning of this word relate to its present usage?

2. Social Studies. *Unions* are referred to several times in this unit. Where and when was the first carpenter's union formed in the United States? Use an encyclopedia for your research. In a paragraph, briefly describe the development of carpenter's unions. Be sure to include the date, the names of the people responsible, and their motives.

3. Social Studies. As was pointed out in this unit, "Specialization is more common in the large cities; in small communities carpenters often do many types of carpentry." Are you from a small town or a large city background? On the basis of your personal experiences, can you think of four reasons why carpentry is more specialized in large cities?

4. Social Studies. You are concerned about the local employment possibilities in carpentry. Using the Yellow Pages of your area phone book, locate the address of the nearest carpenter's union. Write a short letter to the local union requesting information about the future of employment in carpentry.

5. Math. If the working population in the United States is 125 million and 15% of these workers are in the construction industry, how many construction workers are there?

6. Social Studies. Review the material in an *Occupational Outlook Handbook* or visit with a building engineer, technician, or craftsperson. Correlate the scientific knowledge differences required for each occupational category. Determine if educational experience correlates with advanced salaries.

THE SCHOOL-TO-WORK CONNECTION

Skilled tradespeople such as carpenters, masons, and electricians are the ones who actually build a house, but many others are involved in the general construction process. Most of these people have to know something about how a house is built, even though they might not know how to use construction tools. For example, an appraiser may determine the value of the land on which a house will be built. To do this, the appraiser must know something about the types of foundations that are typically used.

1. Make a list of all the people involved in building a house. Try to think of as many people as you can who are involved before construction actually starts. Write a short paragraph about how much each one has to know about construction. Then contact one person and interview him or her.

2 Planning, Design, and Building Codes

One of every six United States families looks for a new place to live every year. A family looking for housing has three main choices: to *rent*, to *buy* an existing home (including mobile homes and condominiums); or to *build*. If the choice is either of the last two, then an understanding of building construction is very important. Fig. 2-1. If the family decides to build a home, a great deal of planning must precede the actual construction. Fig. 2-2 and Table 2-A. Some of the major decisions are as follows.

2-1. *A knowledge of good construction is valuable to many people—those in the building industry, those in real estate, and anyone who buys a new or existing home.*

DETERMINING WHAT TO SPEND

The amount to spend for housing depends on the family's requirements and financial situation. A general rule is that the cost of housing should not exceed 2½ times the average annual income of the family. Not more than 25% of monthly income should be spent for all housing expenses, including mortgage payments, utilities, and repairs. However, some families want to spend more on housing, expecting that their income will rise, and also that it would cost more to buy a home in the future, because of inflation. Others find that due to other heavy expenses it is prudent to spend less. Also, banks are often unwilling

2-2. *A scale model can be built to help in the planning stages of house construction.*

Table 2-A. *A Checklist of Products and Services in Constructing a New Home.*

Items	Are we going to have this?	Amount budgeted	Approximate date to order	Arrangements made
Lot Cost				
Attorney Fees or Legal Expenses				
Survey				
Building Permit				
Insurance				
Excavating—Skin, Backfill and Grading Basement Footing, Wall and Post Footing, Windows and Tarring				
Footing Drain or Tile				
Step and Porch Footing				
Garage Footing and Wall				
Garage Floor				
Basement Floor				
Cement Porches and Walks				
Gravel or Concrete Drive				
Brick Veneer				
Planters—Exterior				
Chimney, Fireplace Flashing				
Subfloor				
Beam, Post, Stairs				
Basic House				
Interior Trim				
Insulation				
Flooring and Underlayment				
Floor Finish				
Kitchen Cabinets				
Kitchen Countertops				
Interior Planters, Dividers and Bookshelves				
Paneling				
Complete Carpenter Labor				
Built-Ins				
Dry Wall or Plaster				
Plumbing with Water Heater				
Heating—Complete				
Electric Wiring and Fixtures				
Linoleum and Tile Floors				
Slate and Ceramic Tile Floors				
Wall Tile				
Sump Pump				
Well or Water Hook-Up				
Septic System or Sewer Hook-Up				
Gas Hook-Up				
Gutter and Drains				
Painting—Interior				
Painting—Exterior				
Storm Windows and Doors—Installed				
Vanities—with Top				
Bath Accessories				
Window Wells				
Landscaping—Trees, Seed, etc.				
Clean-Up—Building, Yard, Windows				
Heat				
Power				
Interest or Loan Expense				
Closing Costs				
Miscellaneous Extras				

2-3. *This house uses photovoltaic panels to generate electricity from the sun. The panels are mounted near the ridge of the roof.*

2-4. *This community has good access to recreational facilities.*

to lend as much money as the borrower needs to buy the house he or she wants.

Of the total available for building, approximately 12 to 15% should be budgeted for the lot and the remainder for the house and landscaping.

Selecting and Purchasing a Lot

There are many factors involved in selecting and purchasing a lot that will be suitable for a particular house. Usually it is necessary to look for a lot in a new development or an individual lot in a built-up neighborhood. The following are points to consider:

➤ Solar access. Is it possible to use the sun

2-5. *These materials had to be delivered by helicopter because the building site was on a small island. The house was built with milled logs.*

to supply part of the heating and electrical needs of the house? Trees, hills, and nearby houses can obstruct the sun, making it difficult to heat air or water with a solar system. They can also obstruct photovoltaic electrical panels. For this reason, some communities even have restrictions that prevent one house from shading another house. Fig. 2-3.

➤ Convenience. Are jobs, schools, community services, and recreational facilities nearby? Will the lot be served by municipal water and sewer systems? If water and gas lines, sewers, and streets are not yet installed, find out if there will be an assessment for them later. Fig. 2-4.

➤ Lot shape and contour. Is the lot wide enough and deep enough for the house? Is it contoured up or down so that it will require a specially designed home, unlike the average home that can be built on a flat lot? How easy will the lot be to build on? Some lots can be difficult to reach with all the materials and equipment needed for construction. Fig. 2-5.

➤ Future prospects of the neighborhood. Is it likely to remain relatively stable, or will the nature of the area change as the city grows? Since the home is the largest single investment for most families, it is important to protect it through careful planning.

➤ Local zoning restrictions. Every city or area is divided into various zones, generally in the following order: single-family dwellings, multiple-family dwellings, apartments (cooperatives or condominiums), light commercial, heavy commercial, light industrial, and heavy industrial. Most families want a lot in a neighborhood that is restricted to single-family dwellings.

➤ Deed restrictions. Within any zoning area there may be individual deed restrictions on the lot. These may specify the minimum size house that can be built on the lot, the setback allowance from the street to the first solid wall of the home, the distance from either lot line in which a house cannot be built, and similar points. These are all limiting factors that affect the size and shape of the house that can be placed on a particular lot.

Legal Documents

The terms *real property* and *real estate* refer to land and the buildings on it. To buy such property it is necessary to be concerned with at least three legal documents.

➤ The *survey*, which shows the boundaries of the property.

➤ The *deed*, which is evidence of ownership, and by which ownership is transferred.

➤ The *abstract of title*, a history of the deeds and other papers affecting the ownership of the property, usually for the most recent 60 years.

Before buying a piece of real property, the purchaser should have a survey made to make certain that the property meets building needs. An abstract is usually prepared by a company that specializes in tracing the ownership of property through legal

documents. Real estate agents often help the purchaser to obtain the necessary legal papers. Also, buyers and sellers often hire lawyers to examine the abstract and other legal papers connected with the transfer of real property.

When the property is finally purchased, the buyer should retain a copy of the official survey, the abstract, and the deed. All of these are needed to secure financing and building permits.

Selecting House Plans. There are several methods of obtaining house plans for the lot. The method you choose can have a significant effect on the final price of the house.

One popular way to get house plans is to purchase them from a company that specializes in designing *stock plans*. These are standard plans that can fit many different lots. Such companies usually have plan books that show floor plans and drawings of what the finished house would look like. These drawings are called *elevations*. Once a suitable house plan is picked out, complete working drawings, materials lists, and specifications can be purchased. This is the least expensive way to find a house plan. Other good sources are magazines and other publications devoted to such plans. The purchaser looks through the designs until he or she finds one that is suitable. The

2-6a. *This award-winning modular house features many interesting wood details.*

purchaser can then buy several copies of the complete set of working drawings, materials lists, and specifications. This is the least expensive way to find a house plan.

House plans can also be obtained from local building dealers who have limited architectural service. If the purchaser agrees to buy all the necessary materials from the dealer, he will gladly help the purchaser in selecting and doing some simple redesigning of the house plan. However, if the house is to be completely and individually designed, an architect must be employed. The fee usually ranges from 5 to 10% of the total building cost, depending on whether the architect only designs the house or also supervises its construction.

Still another way to choose house plans is through a company that specializes in precut material. The company will then supply all the precut materials and a contractor to build the house. It is also possible to purchase an entire prefabricated home or a modular home which can be moved to the site. Fig. 2-6a.

The style of a house should be carefully considered during a search for house plans. Certain styles fit better in some parts of the country than in others. Also, some styles can involve extra expense if the materials and labor needed to build them are not commonly available. Figs. 2-6 b, c, d, e.

2-6b. *This house has white cedar log walls.*

2-6c. *A contemporary house.*

2-6d. *A brick house.*

2-6e. *A Spanish-style house with a clay tile roof.*

FINANCIAL ARRANGEMENTS

After deciding on the house and the plans, the next step is to ask for contractors' bids on the cost of construction. To get a rough idea of how much the house should cost, find out the average cost per square foot of residential building in your area. Then multiply this figure by the number of square feet

in the plans. Fig. 2-7. However, this cost will vary greatly according to such features as fireplaces, built-ins, and other refinements that may be included in the home. Figs. 2-8a,b,c. The only way to get an accurate price estimate is to ask contractors to bid on the cost of construction. It is usually desirable to get two or three bids and to talk to contractors in detail about their bids before deciding who is to build the home. Often the contractor and the architect work in close cooperation, or the contractor and the building and supply company may work together.

After a contractor has been chosen, it is usually necessary to obtain financing from a bank or savings and loan company. If the arrangements meet with the approval of the lending agency, financing up to a certain percent of the total cost can be obtained. This percentage varies, but 80% is not an unusual amount. Fig. 2-9. The borrower must have the down payment from savings or an equivalent value in a house lot. The bank or savings and loan company will arrange a mortgage

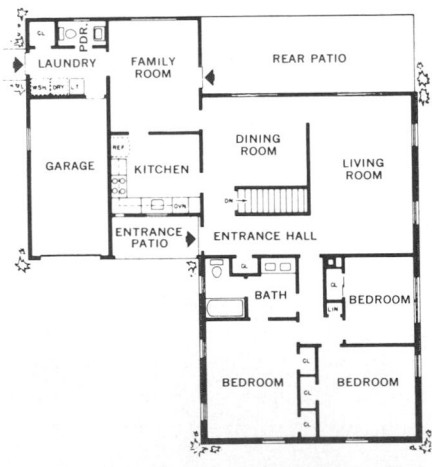

2-7. *A reasonable estimate of the cost can be found by checking the number of square feet in the layout and multiplying by the average cost of building (per sq. ft.) in your locality.*

2-8a. *Outdoor amenities can increase the cost of a house, but make it a nicer place to live.*

2-8b. *The type and quality of interior features such as cabinets and appliances can also affect the cost of a house.*

2-8c. *Some features, such as wood stoves, can be added later to reduce the initial cost of a home.*

loan which is really a *lien* on the property: this means that the lender is given some security for the repayment of the money. Usually the lender can claim the property itself if the borrower does not make payments. Typically a mortgage may run from 12 to 40 years, at the prevailing interest rate. This rate varies. Often the interest cost alone on a mortgage over the years will equal or exceed the actual building cost of the house. The mortgage will often include money for *closing costs*—charges for paper work and similar items needed to make the loan transaction. Mortgages are often arranged so that the monthly payment includes not only amounts for principal and interest on the loan but also amounts for insurance and taxes on the property. The lender holds these funds *in escrow*, for payment when the tax and insurance bills are due.

Once financing has been arranged, contracts must be signed for the construction. From this stage on, it is the responsibility of the contractor and/or architect to make sure that the building goes as planned. The contractor will usually obtain a building permit

2-9. *When making final plans for the building, some people hire a lawyer. He or she can take care of the legal aspects of contract signing, closing procedures, and taking possession. The lawyer can also work with the bank officials to discuss mortgage arrangements.*

from the city or county, have the lot cleared of trees and the grading done, and install a temporary electrical hook-up which can be used when building.

Contractors are usually paid a certain portion of the construction cost before the home is started. They are paid again at certain stages of construction, such as when the rough framing is done and the roof is on, and when the exterior is completed. They get their final payment when the house is completed.

BUILDING CODES

Building codes establish minimum standards of quality and safety in housing. Each code is actually a collection of regulations that governs the details of construction. A builder can construct a house that surpasses the code requirements, but he or she cannot construct a house that falls short of the code requirements. It is important to note that any code identifies a *minimum* level of construction. Many builders go beyond the codes because they want higher-quality houses.

Types of Building Codes

There is no one building code that covers the entire nation. Instead, various regions are covered by different building codes. This means that a house constructed in Texas, for example, might be built to different standards than a house built in Maine or California. This is partly due to the fact that such things as climate and the availability of building materials vary from region to region. The major regional codes include the Uniform Building Code (prevalent in the west), the Basic Building Code (prevalent in the midwest

and east) and the Standard Building Code (prevalent in the south). Some rural areas are not covered by any code.

In addition to the various regional building codes, each state, county, and city can develop its own codes. These cannot be less stringent than the regional code, but they can be more stringent. For example, some cities in the western U.S. have codes intended to encourage water conservation. These are more stringent than codes in areas where the availability of water is not a problem.

Also, mortgage and loan associations, as well as some federal agencies, establish certain requirements for home construction. These standards must be met in order to get a certain type of mortgage on the home.

Finally, there are codes that cover particular parts of the construction. These include plumbing codes and electrical codes. The National Electrical Code, for example, is the primary electrical code used throughout the United States.

Inspections and Permits

In areas that are covered by building codes, it is usually necessary to get a permit to begin construction of a house. This is done by submitting a full set of working drawings to the local building department (usually a branch of the city or county government). The building department will examine the plans to ensure that they meet the local building codes. If they do, the builder is issued a permit to begin construction. This permit must be kept on the building site at all times.

At key points during construction, a city or county building inspector will visit the job site to examine the work. The types of inspections required vary from town to town, but often include an inspection of footing trenches and foundation formwork, framing, wiring, plumbing, and insulation. The builder must call the building department to schedule an inspection when each part of the job is complete. When he or she visits, the inspector can require that work be done over or replaced if it does not meet the building codes.

When the house is complete, one last inspection will be made. If there are no problems, a Certificate of Occupancy will be issued. This certifies that the house is ready to be lived in.

QUESTIONS

1. How many families each year look for a new place to live?

2. What are the three common ways of finding permanent housing?

3. In terms of annual income, what is the maximum that should be spent on housing?

4. List several points that should be checked before purchasing a lot.

5. Approximately how much of one's total building budget should be spent on a lot?

6. Are all local building codes uniform? Explain.

7. Describe what a deed is.

8. Why is it important to have a survey made?

9. What is an abstract of title?

10. Name three ways of obtaining house plans.

11. What is the range in cost for architectural services? Explain why these costs vary.

12. At what stages of construction are inspections usually required?

13. What is a Certificate of Occupancy?

ACTIVITIES

1. Math. A family has a monthly income of $3,200.

a. What is their annual income?

b. Using the guidelines presented in this unit, what is the maximum amount they should spend per month for housing including mortgage, utilities, and repairs?

c. They really like a house listed for $89,900. Is this price within the general guidelines for cost of housing in this unit? Discuss with a friend what more you would like to know before deciding if this family could buy this house.

2. Science. Visit a local greenhouse or plant nursery to determine which annuals and perennials would be best for landscaping the east and south sides of a new home. Also, determine which deciduous and which coniferous trees would be the fastest growing and most suitable for your proposed building area.

3. Social Studies. The text mentions that one of every six American families moves each year. Research the inventions and developments that have evolved from the Industrial Revolution that have allowed our society to become so mobile.

After you have listed as many developments and inventions you can, pick out the three that you feel were most significant in influencing our society's mobility. Briefly explain why you believe they are the most important.

THE SCHOOL-TO-WORK CONNECTION

Before starting to design a house, an architect or builder must know the particular codes that apply to the area in which the house will be built.

1. Imagine that you are going to remodel the kitchen in the house or apartment that you live in. The design of the new kitchen calls for relocating one wall, installing one new electrical outlet, and changing the location of the sink. Find out what codes you'll have to follow. Check with the building and zoning department or with the housing department or town clerk.

Reading Prints

The ability to read and understand drawings, prints, and plans is basic to all construction. Sketches, drawings, and prints are a kind of language. They tell you everything you need to know to build something, including the materials needed. Fig. 3-1. By means of *lines*, *symbols*, and *dimensions*, the ideas of the designer or architect are conveyed to you. To be a good builder you must be able to interpret correctly the sketch, drawing, or print so you can visualize the size and shape of the product to be built. Fig. 3-2a.

A *sketch* or *drawing* of something to be built is the way original ideas are put on paper. A simple drawing is called a *shop sketch*. A *print* is an exact copy of the drawing. In the building industry most prints are called *blueprints*. The paper originally used for blueprints had a dark blue background, with white lines that represented the drawing. More commonly a blueprint has dark blue lines on a white background. Blueprints are commonly used in house construction and other building trades because they do not fade when exposed to sunlight.

An architect, designer, or drafter usually has the responsibility for making the original drawing. Many carpenters also have the ability to make a good sketch. They must often take measurements "on the job" and then make sketches which are sometimes used to do the

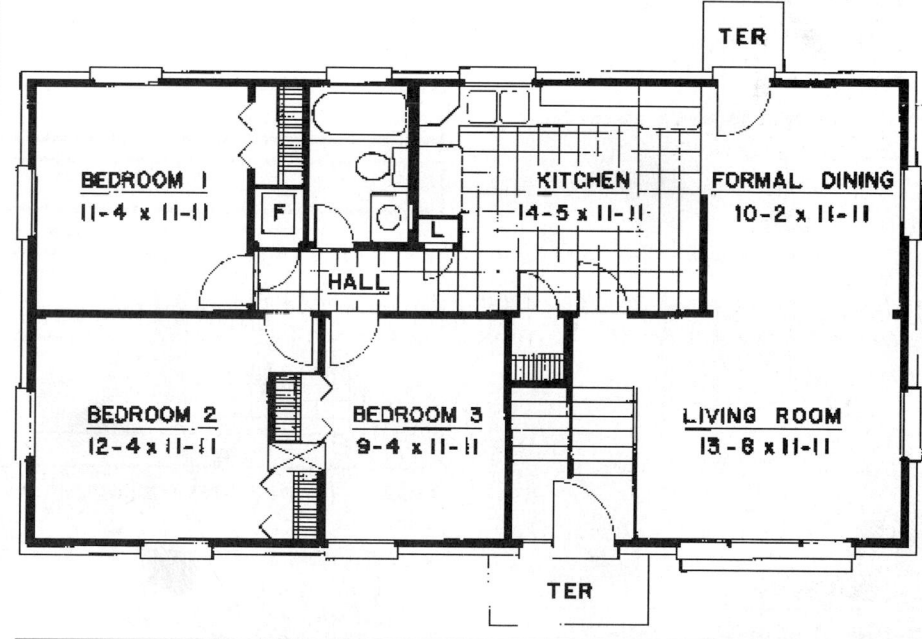

3-1. *This floor plan is just one of the many drawings you would have to understand if you were to build a home.*

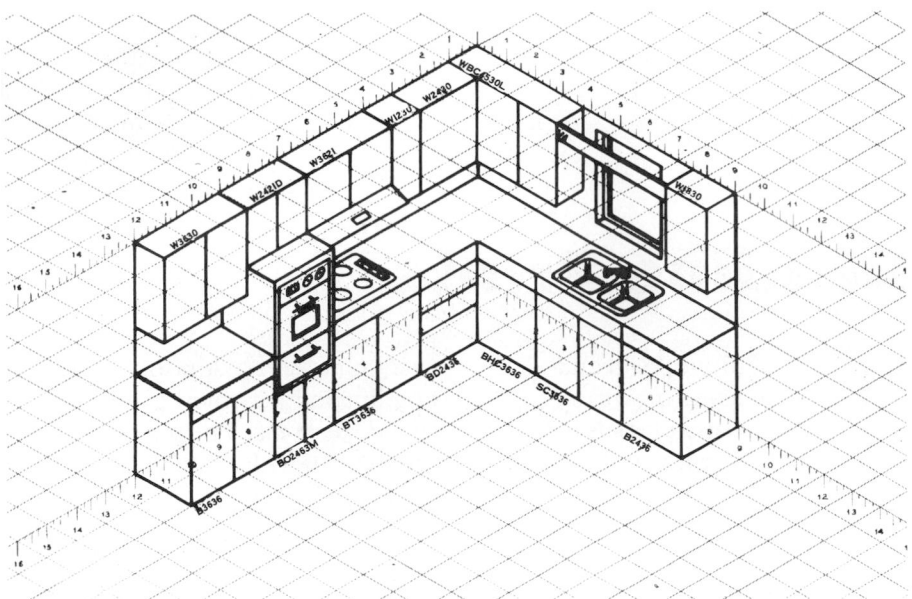

3-2a. *Sometimes isometric sketches are made so that the consumer can get a better picture of what an object or a room will look like.*

Another advantage is that estimating software can be combined with drawing software to produce materials lists directly from the drawings. Fig. 3-2b.

METHODS OF MEASUREMENT

Two common systems of measurement are used worldwide. The United States currently uses the customary (English) system of measurement while all of the other industrial nations in the world use the metric system. The United States is moving toward the metric system; so you should be acquainted with it. The three common units of measure used are those for *length, liquid measure,* and *weight.* Fig. 3-3a.

In the customary (English) system, lengths are given in inches, feet, yards, and miles. In the metric system, lengths are given in millimetres, centimetres, metres, and kilometres. Fig. 3-3b. A metre, which is the basic unit of length, is slightly longer than a yard (39.37"). Since the entire metric system is based on units of ten, the

building or remodeling. At other times the sketches are reviewed, refined, and then made into a set of drawings and prints. Pictorial sketches are sometimes used.

Computer-aided drafting and design (CADD) is frequently used to create site plans, floor plans, elevation drawings and even perspective drawings of a house. Using a variety of software packages, a drafter can create these drawings on a computer screen. The drafter can then send them electronically to a printer or a plotter (a plotter has pens of various colors). One advantage of using the computer as a drawing tool is that the drawings can easily be revised, without the time-consuming erasures needed when the drawing is first made on paper.

3-2b. *A plotter or printer is required for computer-generated architectural drawings.*

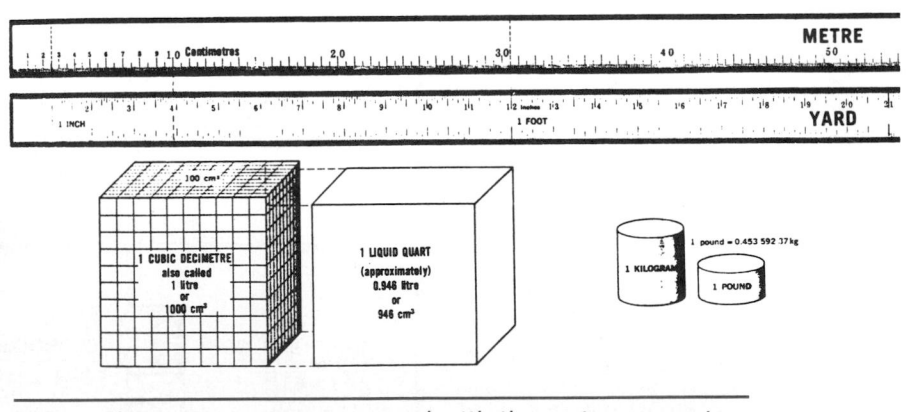

3-3a. *The metric system compared with the customary system.*

3-3b. *Note that one inch is approximately 25 mm.*

millimetre is equal to $\frac{1}{1000}$ of a metre and a centimetre is $\frac{1}{100}$ of a metre. A kilometre is 1000 times a metre. Actually l" is equal to 25.4 millimetres. The two common length measures used in the customary system for buildings are the inch and the foot, while the only two length measurements used in the metric system are the millimetre and the metre. It is easy to convert from one to the other as you can see in Table 3-A. In building construction all millimetre measurements are rounded off to the closest full measurement. For example, 1" is equal to 25 millimetres.

The *liquid* measure in the customary system is in quarts and gallons, while in the metric system it is in litres. A litre is about 5% more than a quart. Liquid measure for finishing materials including paints is normally given in litres, half-litres and quarter-litres. *Weight* measure in the customary system is given in pounds, while in the metric system it is in kilograms. A kilogram is approximately 2.2 pounds.

In metric countries, particularly Britain, a standard module is 300 millimetres, which is very close to one foot. In architectural drawings, all building measurements are given in millimetres and all site measurements in metres and fractions of a metre.

To get better acquainted with both systems of measurement, it is a good idea to use measuring tools marked both in inches and feet and in millimetres, centimetres, and metres. Some rules are numbered in centimetres, with ten small divisions (millimetres) between each one. However, most rules

Table 3-A. *Conversion Table for Woodwork.*

Customary (English)	Actual	Metric Accurate Woodworkers' Language	Metric Tool Sizes	Lumber Sizes Thickness	Lumber Sizes Width
$\frac{1}{32}$ in	0.8 mm	1 mm bare			
$\frac{1}{16}$ in	1.6 mm	1.5 mm			
$\frac{1}{8}$ in	3.2 mm	3 mm full	3 mm		
$\frac{3}{16}$ in	4.8 mm	5 mm bare	5 mm		
$\frac{1}{4}$ in	6.4 mm	6.5 mm	6 mm		
$\frac{5}{16}$ in	7.9 mm	8 mm bare	8 mm		
$\frac{3}{8}$ in	9.5 mm	9.5 mm	10 mm		
$\frac{7}{16}$ in	11.1 mm	11 mm full	11 mm		
$\frac{1}{2}$ in	12.7 mm	12.5 mm full	13 mm	12 mm	
$\frac{9}{16}$ in	14.3 mm	14.5 mm bare	14 mm		
$\frac{5}{8}$ in	15.9 mm	16 mm bare	16 mm	16 mm	
$\frac{11}{16}$ in	17.5 mm	17.5 mm	17 mm		
$\frac{3}{4}$ in	19.1 mm	19 mm full	19 mm	19 mm	
$\frac{13}{16}$ in	20.6 mm	20.5 mm	21 mm		
$\frac{7}{8}$ in	22.2 mm	22 mm full	22 mm	22 mm	
$\frac{15}{16}$ in	23.8 mm	24 mm bare	24 mm		
1 in	25.4 mm	25.5 mm	25 mm	25 mm	
$1\frac{1}{4}$ in	31.8 mm	32 mm bare	32 mm	32 mm	
$1\frac{3}{8}$ in	34.9 mm	35 mm bare	36 mm	36 mm	
$1\frac{1}{2}$ in	38.1 mm	38 mm full	38 mm	38 mm (or 40 mm)	
$1\frac{3}{4}$ in	44.5 mm	44.5 mm	44 mm	44 mm	
2 in	50.8 mm	51 mm bare	50 mm	50 mm	
$2\frac{1}{2}$ in	63.5 mm	63.5 mm	64 mm	64 mm	
3 in	76.2 mm	76 mm full		75 mm	75 mm
4 in	101.6 mm	101.5 mm		100 mm	100 mm
5 in	127.0 mm	127 mm			125 mm
6 in	152.4 mm	152.5 mm			150 mm
7 in	177.8 mm	178 mm bare			
8 in	203.2 mm	203 mm full			200 mm
9 in	228.6 mm	228.5 mm			
10 in	254.0 mm	254 mm			250 mm
11 in	279.4 mm	279.5 mm			
12 in	304.8 mm	305 mm bare			300 mm
18 in	457.2 mm	457 mm full	460 mm		
24 in	609.6 mm	609.5 mm			
36 in	914.4 mm	914.5 mm			
48 in—4'	1219.2 mm	1220 mm or 1.22 m			
96 in—8'	2438.4 mm	2440 mm or 2.44 m			

Panel Stock Sizes
1220 mm or 1.22 m width
2440 mm or 2.44 m width

show measurements in millimetres only. Whenever possible, use a rule that is numbered in millimetres since these are easier to read. There will be less chance of error.

In architectural layouts, the general practice is to show all residential drawings in millimetres. Site plans are dimensioned in metres.

Building materials come in standard sizes, and most homes are built according to certain dimensional design standards. When the building industry converts to metrics, new standards will replace the customary ones. The design module for building materials will be 100 mm, which is slightly less than four inches.

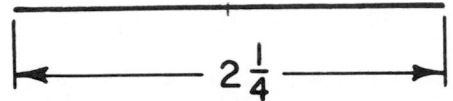

3-4b. *Use a rule to measure this line.*

length. Measurements are usually given in feet, inches, and parts of an inch. You should not find it hard to measure feet in exact inches. You already know that there are twelve inches in a foot and three feet, or thirty-six inches, in a yard.

Let's take a look at the chart shown in Fig 3-4a. It is in the English system. The distance between 0 and 1 represents one inch. At line A you see that the inch is divided into two equal parts. Each half represents ½". On a rule this ½" division line is the longest line between the inch marks. At line B the inch is divided into four equal parts. The first line is ¼"; the second line is 2⁄4" or ½"; the third line is ¾". At line C you will notice that the inch is divided into eight equal parts so that each small division is ⅛". Two of these divisions make 2⁄8" or ¼" (as shown on line B). Four of these divisions make 4⁄8" or 2⁄4" or ½". At line D the inch is divided into sixteen parts. This is usually the smallest division on rules used in drawing. Notice again that 4⁄16" is equal to 2⁄8" or ¼". One line past ¼" is equal to 5⁄16". You will see on your rule that between the inch marks, the ½" mark is the longest one. The ¼" mark is the next longest, the ⅛" mark the next, and the 1⁄16" mark is the shortest.

To read a part or fraction of an inch, count the number of small divisions beyond the last inch mark. For example, when measuring the line in Fig. 3-4b, you will find that it is 2" plus four small divisions. This is

2⁴⁄₁₆", which is the same as 2²⁄₈" or 2¼". One small division past ½" would be 9⁄16" (8⁄16" + 1⁄16").

SCALE

Drawings must often be reduced from actual size so they will fit on a piece of paper. Care is taken to make such drawings according to *scale*, that is, exactly in proportion to full size. Fig. 3-5. For example, an architect can represent any size of building on a single piece of paper by drawing it to a certain scale. The scale is not a unit of measurement but represents the ratio between the size of the object as drawn and its actual size. If the drawing is exactly the same size as the object itself, it is called a full-size or full-scale drawing. If it is reduced, as most scale drawings are, it will probably be drawn to one of the following common scales.

Customary Scales

6" equals 1' (read "six inches equals one foot"): half size.

3" equals 1': one-fourth size.

1½" equals 1': one-eighth size.

1" equals 1': one-twelfth size.

¾" equals 1': one-sixteenth size.

½" equals 1': one twenty-fourth size.

⅜" equals 1': one thirty-second size.

¼" equals 1': one forty-eighth size.

3⁄16" equals 1': one sixty-fourth size.

⅛" equals 1': one ninety-sixth size.

A scale of ¼" equals 1' is often used for drawing buildings and rooms. Detail drawings, which show how parts of a product are made, are prepared to scales of ⅜", ½", ¾", or 1¼" equal 1'.

READING AN ENGLISH (INCH) RULE

Rules used in carpentry are one foot (twelve inches) or multiples of one foot up to one hundred feet, in

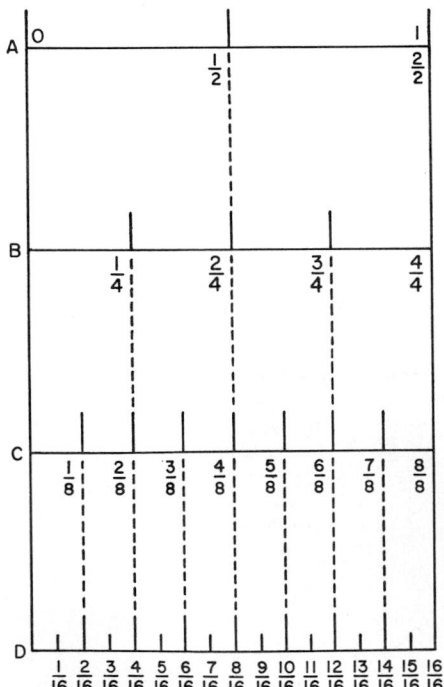

3-4a. *Divisions of an inch.*

Metric Scales

The preferred metric scales are as follows :

1 equals 1: full size
1 equals 2: half size
1 equals 5
1 equals 10
1 equals 20
1 equals 50
1 equals 1250
1 equals 2500

ELEMENTS OF DRAWING

-A drawing consists of lines, dimensions, symbols, and notes. *Lines* show the shape of a product and include many details of construction. Fig. 3-6. *Dimensions* are numbers that tell the sizes of each part as well as overall sizes. The craftsman must follow these dimensions in making the materials list and the layout. *Symbols* are used to represent things that would be impractical to show by drawing, such as doors, windows, electrical circuits, and plumbing and heating equipment. Figs. 3-7a,b,c,d. Some drawings also contain *notes* or written information to explain something not otherwise shown. Frequently in these notes *abbreviations* are given for common words.

Lines

The lines described below are used for all drawings.

Centerlines. These are composed of long and short dashes, alternately and evenly spaced with a long dash at each end; at intersections the short dashes cross. Very short centerlines may be broken if there is no confusion with other lines.

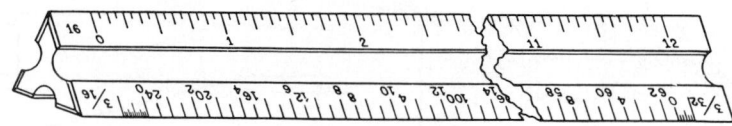

ARCHITECTS' SCALE

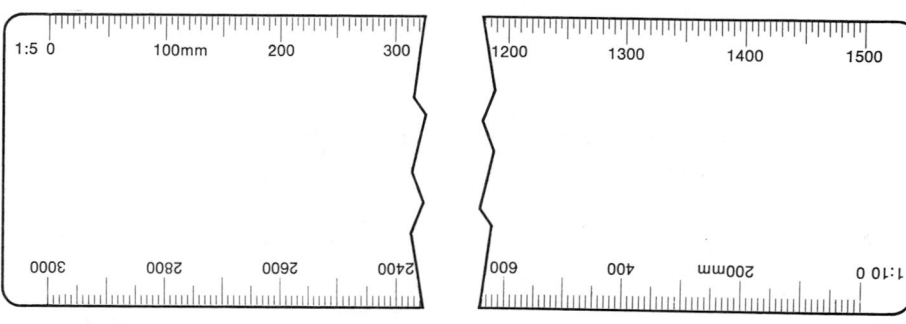

METRIC SCALE

3-5. *Two types of tools for making scale drawings—the architect's scale (for customary measurements) and the metric scale.*

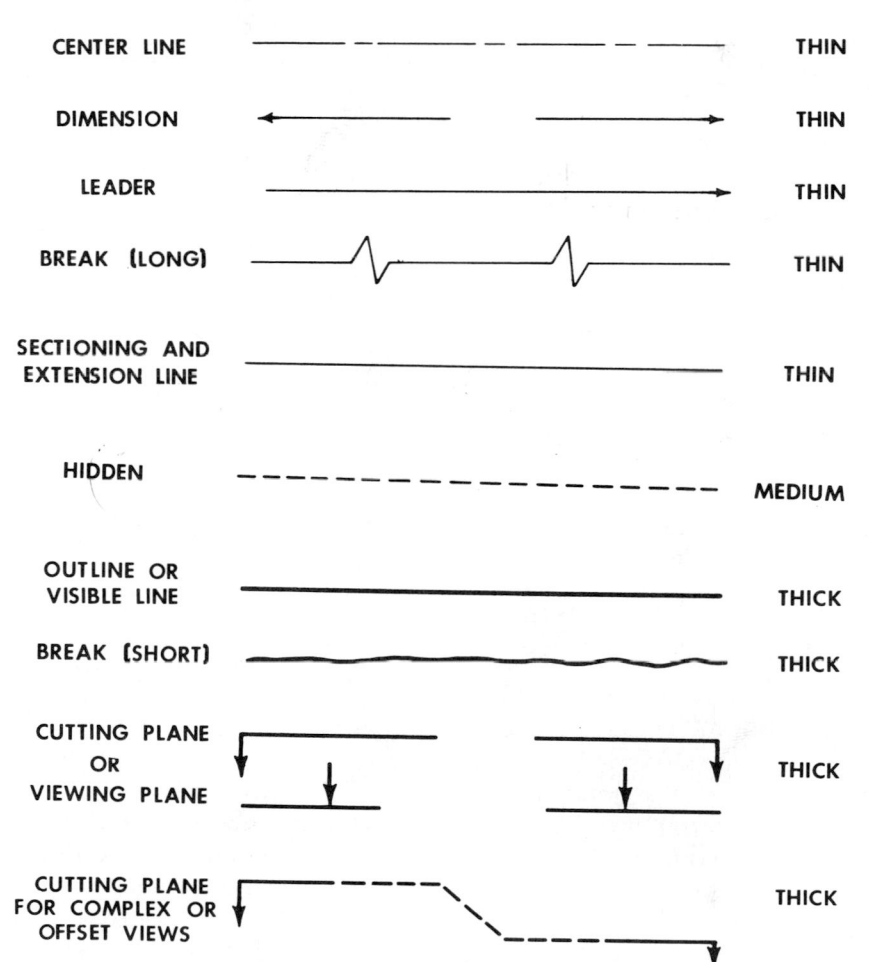

CENTER LINE	THIN
DIMENSION	THIN
LEADER	THIN
BREAK (LONG)	THIN
SECTIONING AND EXTENSION LINE	THIN
HIDDEN	MEDIUM
OUTLINE OR VISIBLE LINE	THICK
BREAK (SHORT)	THICK
CUTTING PLANE OR VIEWING PLANE	THICK
CUTTING PLANE FOR COMPLEX OR OFFSET VIEWS	THICK

3-6. *Alphabet of lines.*

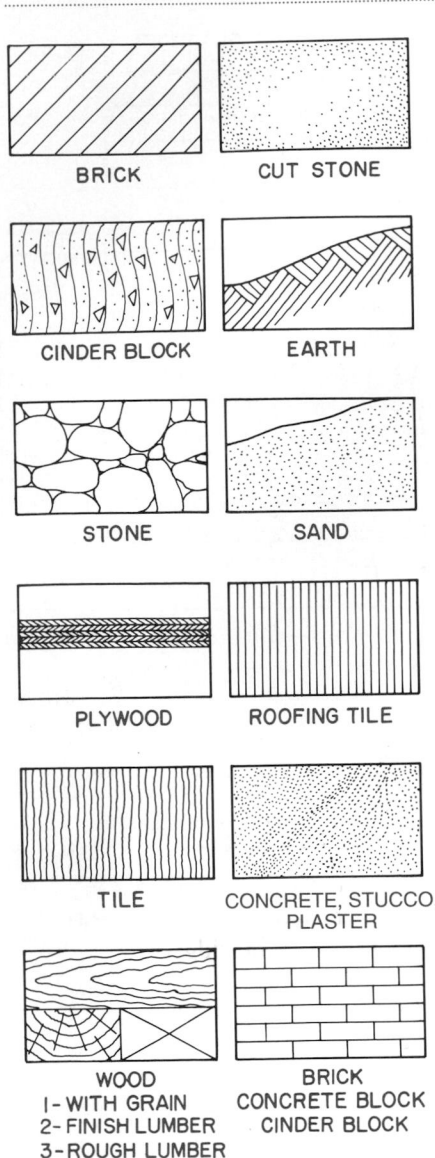

3-7a. *Symbols for building materials.*

Materials shown in figure: BRICK, CUT STONE, CINDER BLOCK, EARTH, STONE, SAND, PLYWOOD, ROOFING TILE, TILE, CONCRETE, STUCCO, PLASTER, WOOD (1- WITH GRAIN, 2- FINISH LUMBER, 3- ROUGH LUMBER), BRICK CONCRETE BLOCK CINDER BLOCK

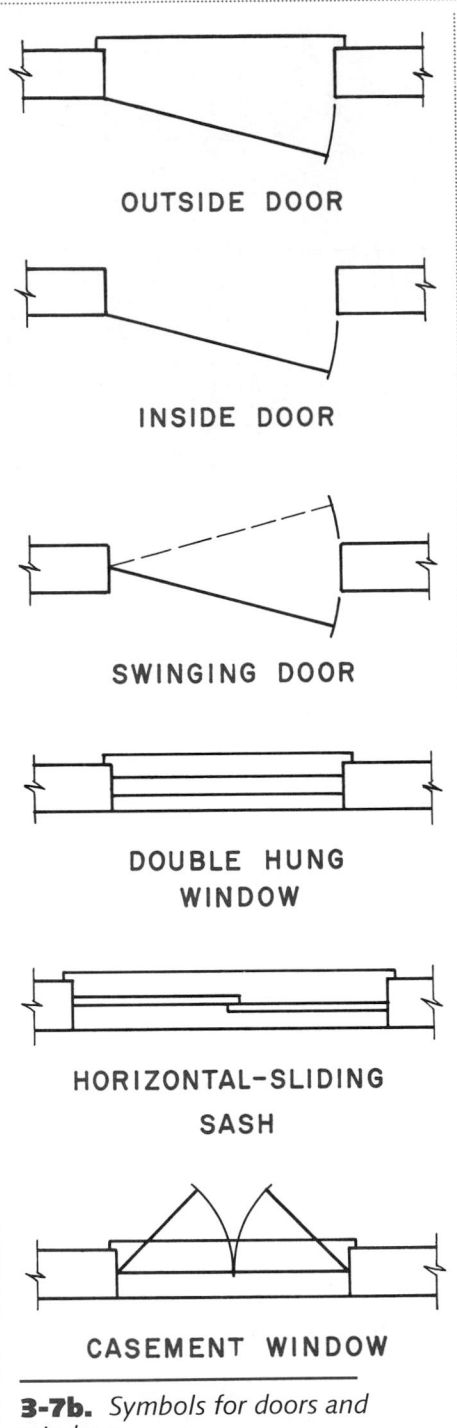

OUTSIDE DOOR

INSIDE DOOR

SWINGING DOOR

DOUBLE HUNG WINDOW

HORIZONTAL-SLIDING SASH

CASEMENT WINDOW

3-7b. *Symbols for doors and windows.*

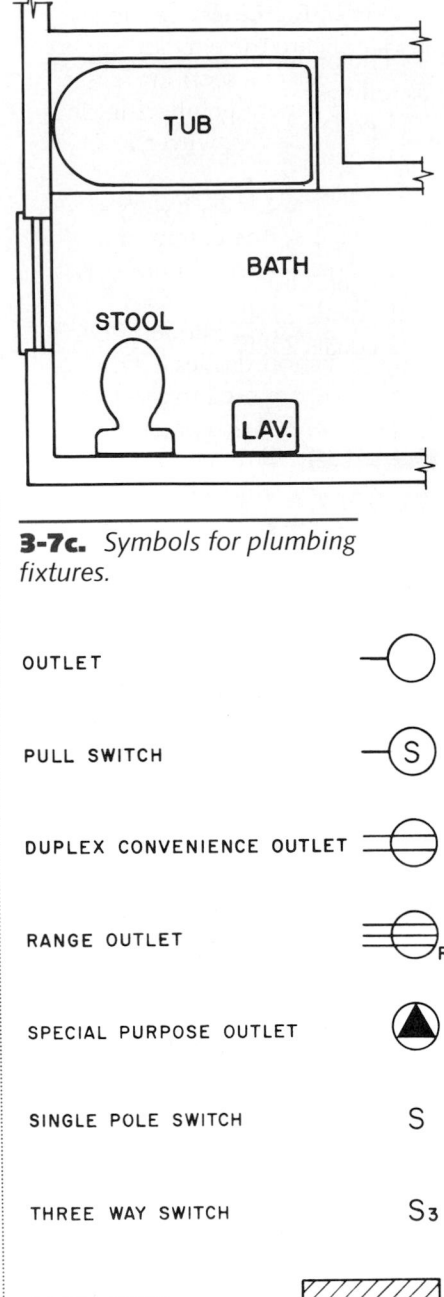

TUB

BATH

STOOL

LAV.

3-7c. *Symbols for plumbing fixtures.*

OUTLET

PULL SWITCH

DUPLEX CONVENIENCE OUTLET

RANGE OUTLET

SPECIAL PURPOSE OUTLET

SINGLE POLE SWITCH

THREE WAY SWITCH

POWER PANEL

3-7d. *Symbols for electrical wiring.*

Leader Lines. These lines are used to indicate a part or portion to which a note or other reference applies. They terminate in an arrowhead or a dot. Arrowheads should always terminate at a line; dots should be within the outline of an object. Leaders should terminate at any suitable portion of the note, reference, or dimension.

Dimension Lines. Dimension lines terminate in arrowheads at each end. On construction drawings they are unbroken. On production drawings they are broken only where space is required for the dimension.

Break Lines. Short breaks are indicated by solid, freehand lines. Full, ruled lines with freehand zigzags are used for long breaks.

Sectioning Lines. Sectioning lines indicate the exposed surfaces of an object in a sectional view. They are generally full, thin lines, but they may vary with the kind of material shown.

Extension Lines. Extension lines indicate the extent of a dimension and should not touch the outline.

Hidden Lines. Hidden lines consist of short dashes evenly spaced and are used to show the hidden features of a part. They always begin with a dash in contact with the line from which they start, except when such a dash would form the continuation of a full line. Dashes touch at corners. Arcs start with dashes at the *tangent* points (where they touch each other).

Outline or Visible Lines. The outline or visible line represents those lines of the object which can actually be seen.

Cutting Plane Lines. These lines show where a section has been taken from the building drawings for detail representation.

ARCHITECTURAL WORKING DRAWINGS

Architectural drawings, Fig. 3-8, are prepared as *presentation drawings* or as *working drawings*. Presentation drawings require techniques of pictorial drawing, such as perspective (showing depth) and shading. A construction drafter is not concerned with presentation drawings. He or she prepares architectural working drawings consisting of plans, elevations (which show heights), sections and details (close-up views), and isometric views. (Isometrics are constructed around three basic lines that form 120° angles. See Fig. 3-2a.) The plan drawings in Fig. 3-8 were originally drawn on sheets of 24" × 36" paper. Most of the drawings were drawn to a scale of ⅜" = 1'-0". The drawings were reduced in size to fit on the pages of this book. Thus, the drawings cannot be scaled directly.

Structural Members

In working with architectural drawings, you will find the following structural members referred to often. Therefore you will need to be familiar with them. Here they are classified according to use.

Footings. Footings rest on soil material and transmit their received load onto the soil. The natural material on which a footing rests is called the *foundation bed*. Footings support columns, piers, pilasters, walls, and similar loads. Usually, footings are made of concrete, although wood or timber may be used.

Vertical Members. Vertical members are in compression; that is, they support loads acting downward at the top. Columns, posts, studs, and piers are those most often encountered.

➤ *Columns.* Columns may be steel, timber, or concrete. They rest on footings and are the principal load-carrying vertical members.

➤ *Piers.* Piers are of concrete, timber, or masonry construction. They rest on footings and support horizontal or vertical members. In bridge construction, a pier is an intermediate support for the adjacent ends of two bridge spans.

➤ *Studs and posts.* Studs are vertical members used in wood-frame construction, spaced close together in walls. Posts are heavier vertical members used in wood-frame construction, usually at corners.

Horizontal Members. Those most frequently encountered are:

➤ *Joists.* These are framing members typically spaced 16" or 24" from the center of one to the center of the next. Joists take the load directly.

➤ *Beams.* Beams, like joists, take the load of the floor directly, but they are generally spaced wider than four feet on center.

➤ *Girders.* Girders take the load of either joists or beams and are generally the heaviest horizontal members in a structure.

➤ *Lintels.* Lintels are beams which span door or window openings and carry the structure above those openings.

Roof Members. Those most frequently encountered are:

➤ *Common rafters.* Those members that run square with the top plate and extend to the ridge board.

➤ *Hip rafters.* Those that extend from the outside angle of the plates toward the apex of the roof.

➤ *Jack rafters.* Those that are square with the top plate and intersect a hip rafter.

➤ *Valley rafters.* Those that extend from an inside angle of the plates toward the ridge.

➤ *Cripple rafters.* Those that cut between valley and hip rafters.

➤ *Purlin.* A timber that supports several rafters at one or more points, or one that supports the roof sheathing directly.

➤ *Trusses.* Structural members that connect together to span the space between the walls of a building. They support the roof load or floors.

Flooring

Subflooring is laid atop joists or trusses. Building paper is put between subflooring and finished flooring where required.

Sheathing, Siding, and Roofing

Structural members are covered with suitable materials to form the

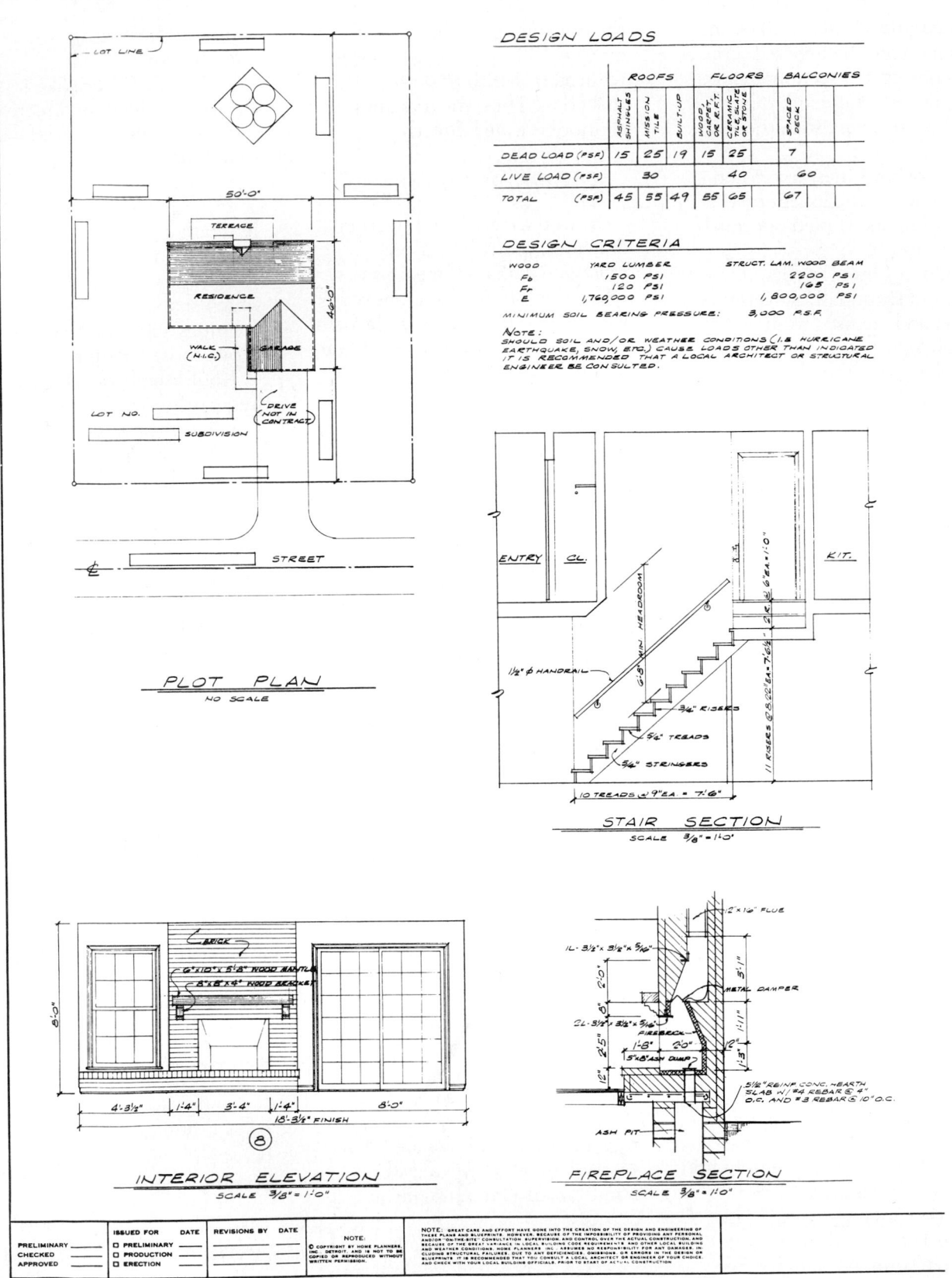

3-8a. *A complete set of working drawings for building a home.*

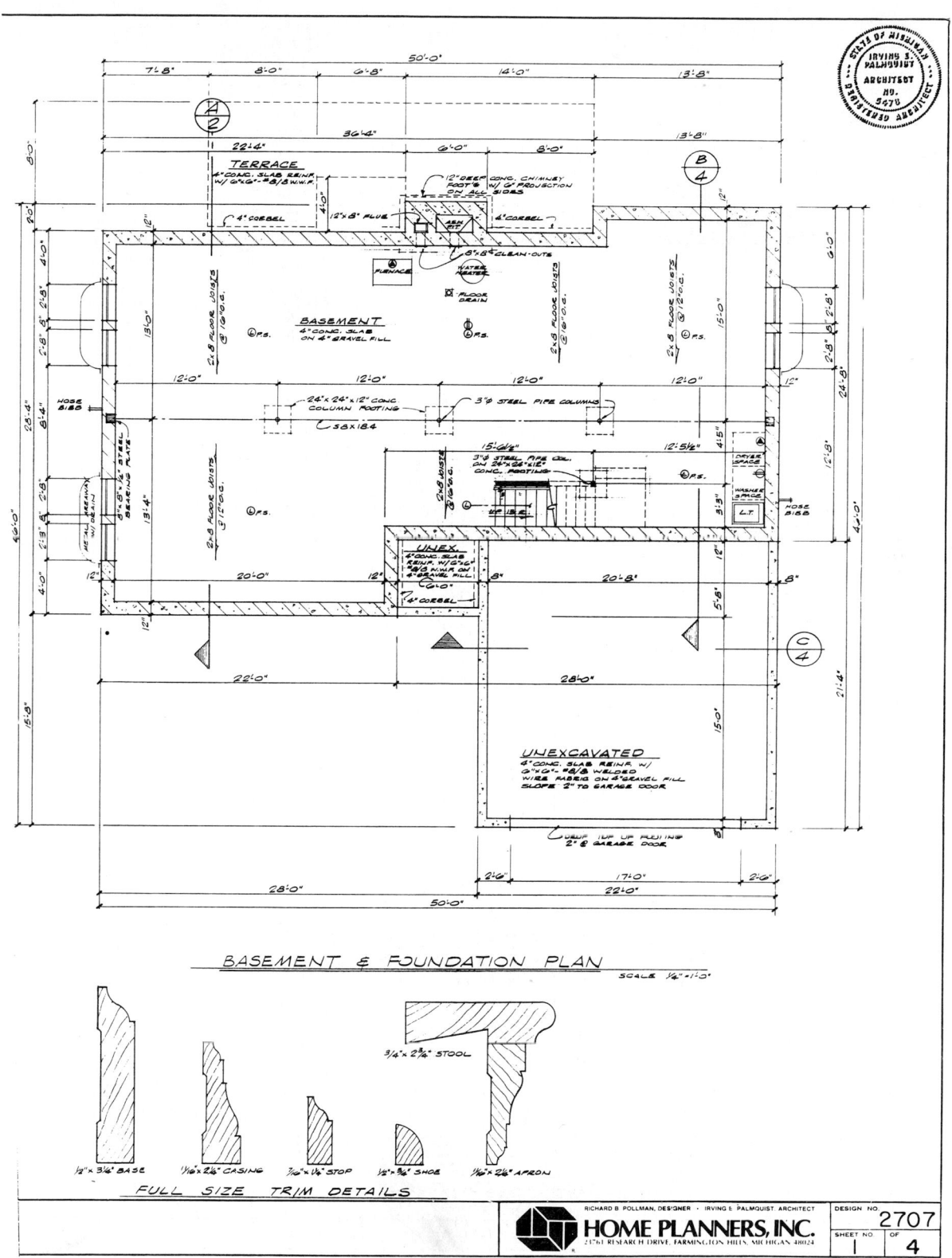

BASEMENT & FOUNDATION PLAN

SCALE 1/4"=1'-0"

3/4" x 2 3/4" STOOL

1/2" x 3 1/4" BASE   11/16" x 2 1/4" CASING   3/16" x 1 1/2" STOP   1/2" x 3/4" SHOE   11/16" x 2 1/4" APRON

FULL SIZE TRIM DETAILS

RICHARD B. POLLMAN, DESIGNER • IRVING E. PALMQUIST, ARCHITECT

HOME PLANNERS, INC.
23761 RESEARCH DRIVE, FARMINGTON HILLS, MICHIGAN 48024

DESIGN NO.	2707
SHEET NO.	OF
1	4

(© Home Planners, Inc.)

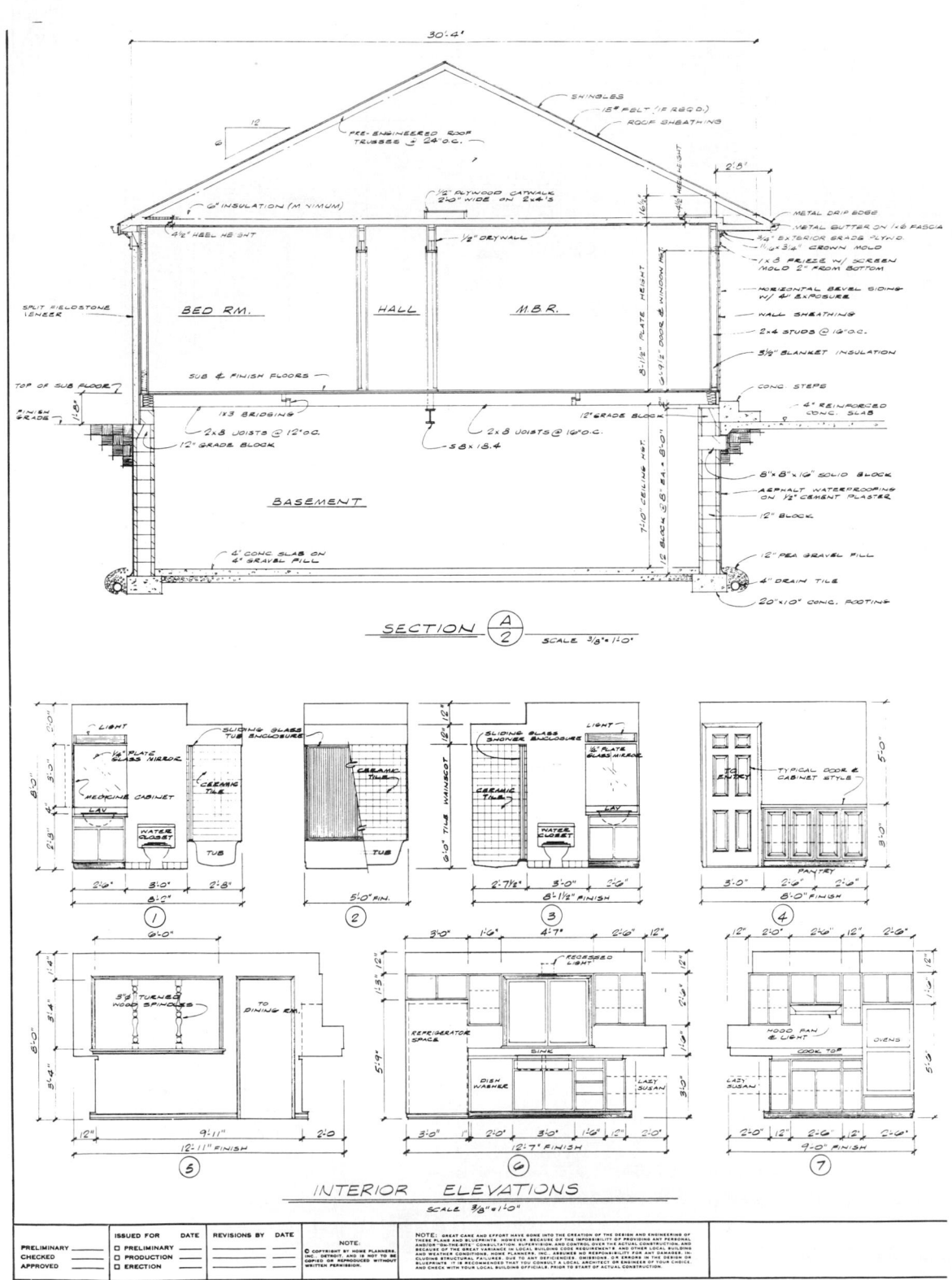

SECTION $\frac{A}{2}$ SCALE 3/8"=1'-0"

INTERIOR ELEVATIONS

SCALE 3/8"=1'-0"

(© Home Planners, Inc.)

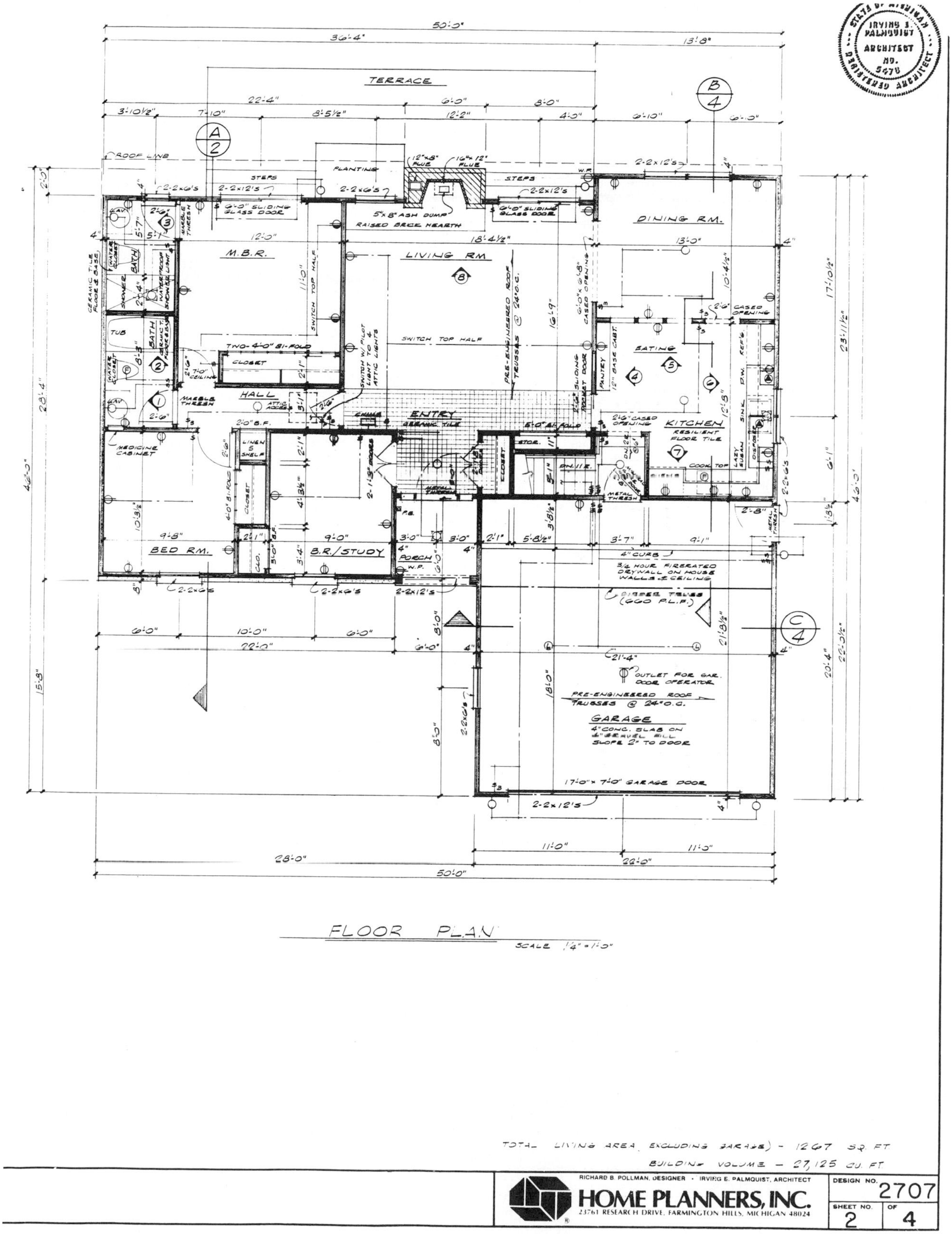

FLOOR PLAN

TERRACE

M.B.R.

LIVING RM.

DINING RM.

EATING

KITCHEN
RESILIENT FLOOR TILE

HALL

ENTRY
CERAMIC TILE

BATH

TUB

CLOSET

LINEN & SHELF

MEDICINE CABINET

BED RM.

B.R./STUDY

PORCH

GARAGE
4" CONC. SLAB ON
4" GRAVEL FILL
SLOPE 2" TO DOOR

PRE-ENGINEERED ROOF
TRUSSES @ 24" O.C.

OUTLET FOR GAR.
DOOR OPERATOR

17'-0" x 7'-0" GARAGE DOOR

SCALE 1/4" = 1'-0"

TOTAL LIVING AREA (EXCLUDING GARAGE) – 1267 SQ. FT.
BUILDING VOLUME – 27,125 CU. FT.

RICHARD B. POLLMAN, DESIGNER · IRVING E. PALMQUIST, ARCHITECT
HOME PLANNERS, INC.
23761 RESEARCH DRIVE, FARMINGTON HILLS, MICHIGAN 48024

DESIGN NO. 2707
SHEET NO. 2 OF 4

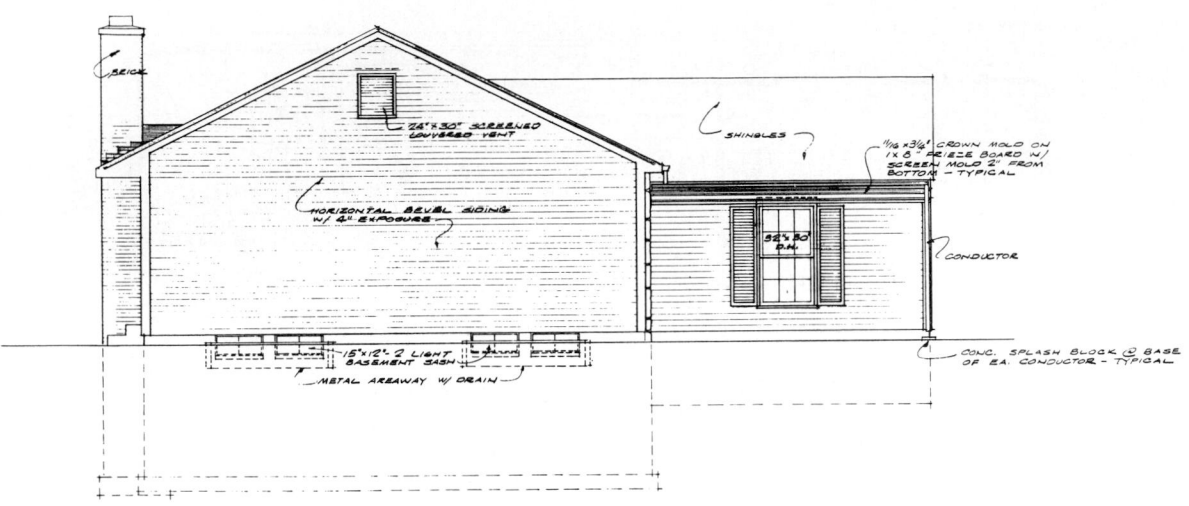

LEFT SIDE ELEVATION

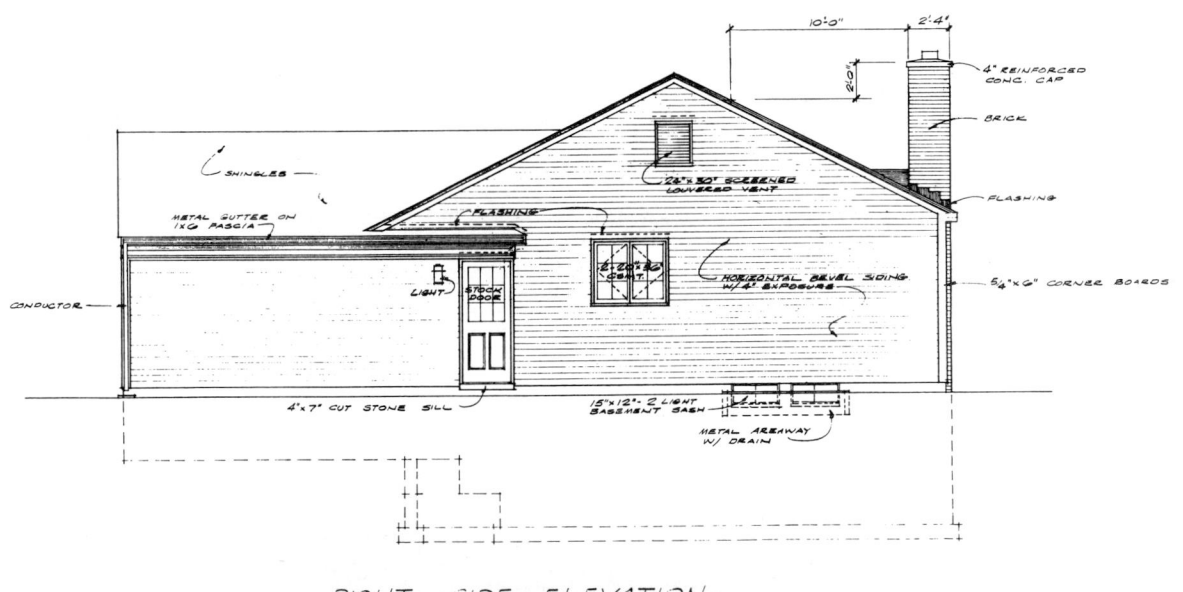

RIGHT SIDE ELEVATION

(© Home Planners, Inc.)

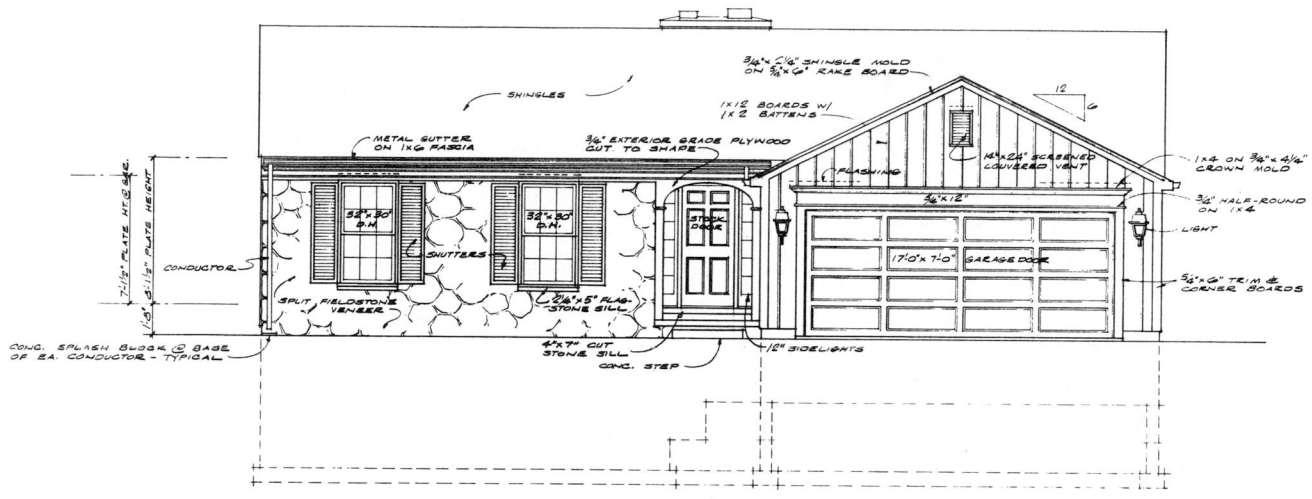

SHINGLES

3/4"x 2 1/4" SHINGLE MOLD
ON 3/4"x 6" RAKE BOARD

1X12 BOARDS W/
1X2 BATTENS

12

METAL GUTTER
ON 1X6 FASCIA

3/4" EXTERIOR GRADE PLYWOOD
CUT TO SHAPE

1 1/2"x 24" SCREENED
LOUVERED VENT

1X4 ON 3/4"x 4 1/4"
CROWN MOLD

FLASHING

3/4" HALF-ROUND
ON 1X4

3/4"x 12"

LIGHT

32"x 30"
D.H.

32"x 30"
D.H.

STEEL
DOOR

SHUTTERS

17'0"x 7'0" GARAGE DOOR

5/4"x 6" TRIM &
CORNER BOARDS

CONDUCTOR

7 1/2" PLATE HT @ GAR.

8 1/8" PLATE HEIGHT

1'-6"

SPLIT FIELDSTONE
VENEER

2"x 5" FLAG-
STONE SILL

4"x 7" CUT
STONE SILL

12" SIDELIGHTS

CONC. SPLASH BLOCK @ BASE
OF EA. CONDUCTOR - TYPICAL

CONC. STEP

FRONT   ELEVATION

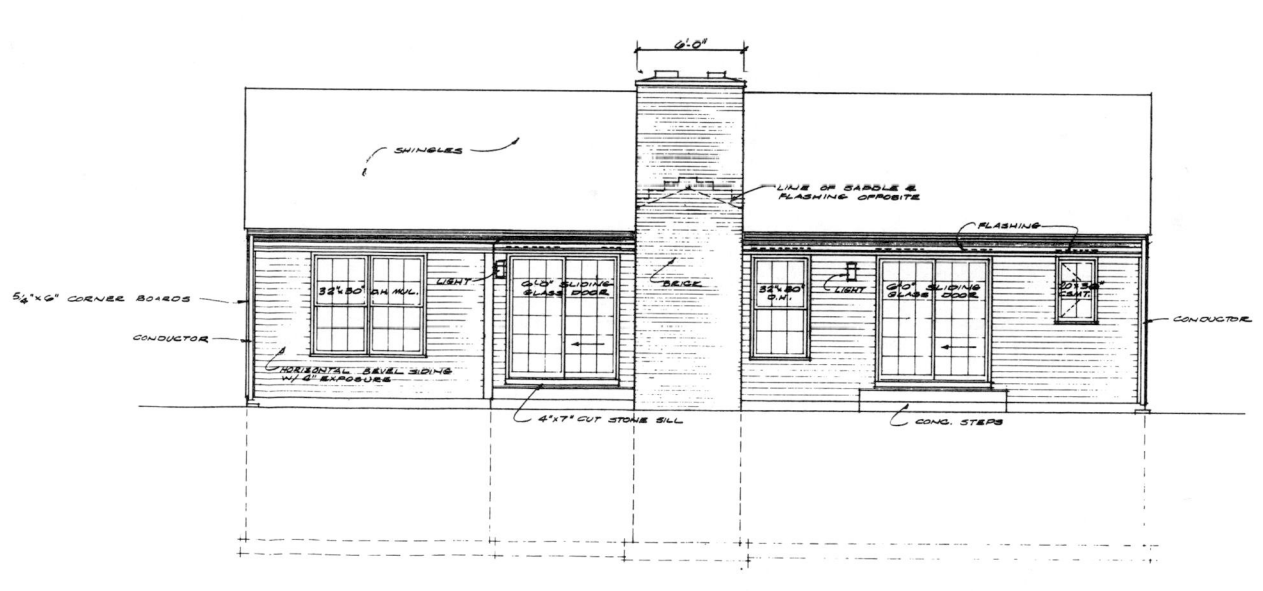

6'-0"

SHINGLES

LINE OF GABBLE &
FLASHING OPPOSITE

FLASHING

5/4"x 6" CORNER BOARDS

32"x 30" D.H. MUL.

LIGHT

6'0" SLIDING
GLASS DOOR

BRICK

32"x 30"
D.H.

LIGHT

6'0" SLIDING
GLASS DOOR

20"x 54"
CASE.

CONDUCTOR

CONDUCTOR

HORIZONTAL BEVEL SIDING
W/ 4" EXPOSURE

4"x 7" CUT STONE SILL

CONC. STEPS

REAR   ELEVATION

RICHARD B. POLLMAN, DESIGNER · IRVING E. PALMQUIST, ARCHITECT

HOME PLANNERS, INC.
23761 RESEARCH DRIVE, FARMINGTON HILLS, MICHIGAN 48024

DESIGN NO. 2707

SHEET NO 3 OF 4

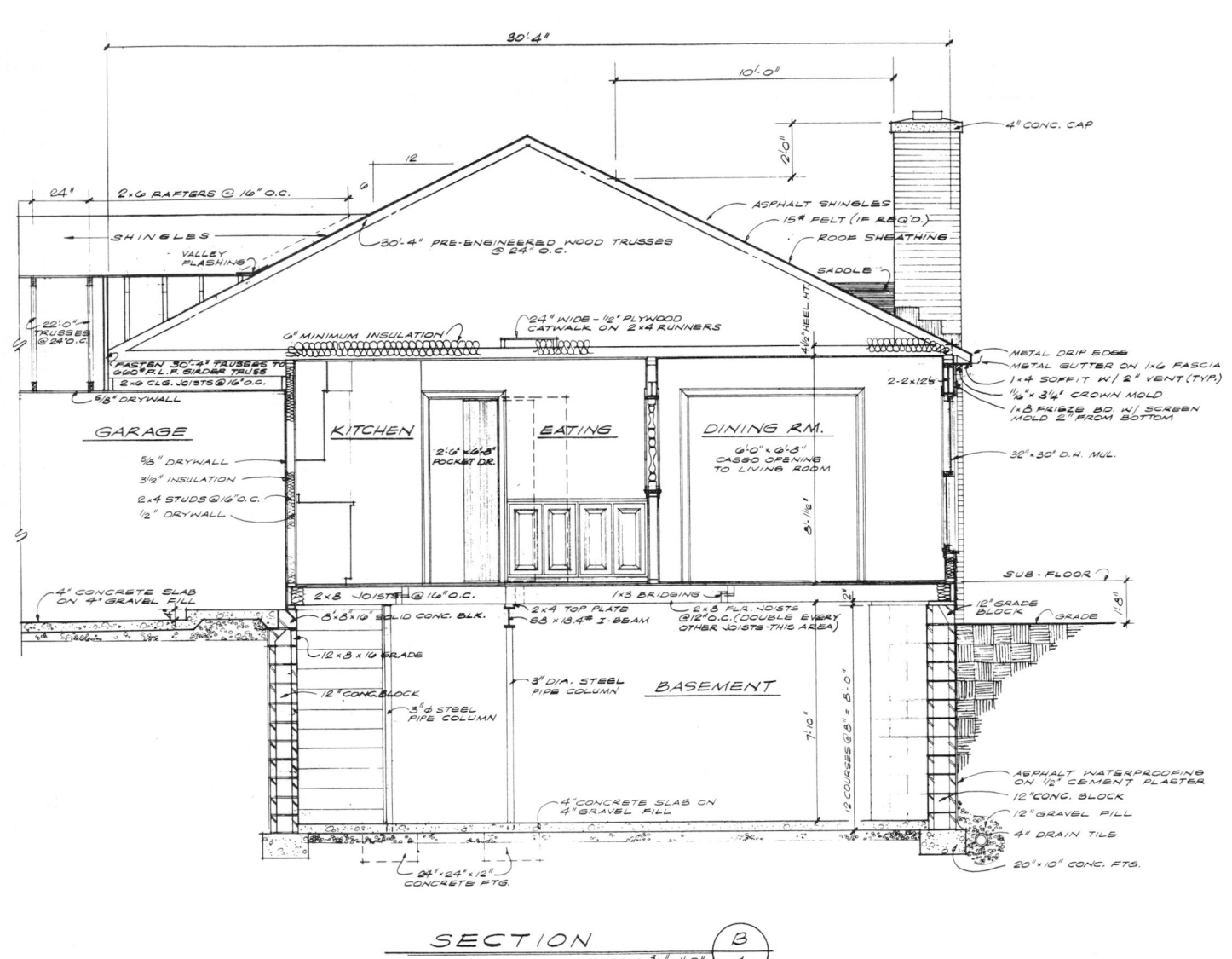

30'-4"

10'-0"

12

4" CONC. CAP

24"   2×6 RAFTERS @ 16" O.C.

ASPHALT SHINGLES
15# FELT (IF REQ'D.)
ROOF SHEATHING

SHINGLES

VALLEY
FLASHING

30'-4" PRE-ENGINEERED WOOD TRUSSES
@ 24" O.C.

SADDLE

22'-0"
TRUSSES
@ 24'O.C.

0" MINIMUM INSULATION

24" WIDE - 1/2" PLYWOOD
CATWALK ON 2×4 RUNNERS

FASTEN 30'-4" TRUSSES TO
660# P.L.F. GIRDER TRUSS
2×6 CLG. JOISTS @ 16" O.C.

5/8" DRYWALL

METAL DRIP EDGE
METAL GUTTER ON 1×6 FASCIA
1×4 SOFFIT W/ 2" VENT (TYP.)
11/16" × 3 1/4" CROWN MOLD
1×8 FRIEZE BD. W/ SCREEN
MOLD 2" FROM BOTTOM

2-2×12's

GARAGE

KITCHEN

EATING

DINING RM.

5/8" DRYWALL
3 1/2" INSULATION
2×4 STUDS @ 16" O.C.
1/2" DRYWALL

2'-6" × 6'-8"
POCKET DR.

6'-0" × 6'-8"
CASED OPENING
TO LIVING ROOM

32" × 30" D.H. MUL.

4" CONCRETE SLAB
ON 4" GRAVEL FILL

2×8 JOISTS @ 16" O.C.

1×3 BRIDGING

SUB-FLOOR

8"×8"×16" SOLID CONC. BLK.

2×4 TOP PLATE
S8 × 18.4# I-BEAM

2×8 FLR. JOISTS
@ 12" O.C. (DOUBLE EVERY
OTHER JOISTS -THIS AREA)

12" GRADE
BLOCK

GRADE

12 × 8 × 16 GRADE

3" DIA. STEEL
PIPE COLUMN

BASEMENT

12" CONC. BLOCK

3"Ø STEEL
PIPE COLUMN

ASPHALT WATERPROOFING
ON 1/2" CEMENT PLASTER
12" CONC. BLOCK
12" GRAVEL FILL
4" DRAIN TILE
20"×10" CONC. FTG.

4" CONCRETE SLAB ON
4" GRAVEL FILL

24"×24"×12"
CONCRETE FTG.

SECTION
SCALE 3/8"=1'-0"

B
4

DESIGN LOADS	ROOFS			FLOORS		BALCONIES
	WOOD OR ASPHALT SHINGLES	MISSION TILE	BUILT-UP	WOOD, CARPET OR R.F.T.	CERAMIC TILE, SLATE OR STONE	SPACED DECK
DEAD LOAD (PSF)	15	25	19	15	25	7
LIVE LOAD (PSF)	30	30	30	40	40	60
TOTAL (PSF)	45	55	49	55	65	67

DESIGN CRITERIA	YARD LUMBER		STRUCT. LAM. WD. BM.	
	Fb =	1,500 PSI	Fb =	2,200 PSI
	Fv =	120 PSI	Fv =	165 PSI
	E =	1,760,000 PSI	E =	1,800,000 PSI

MINIMUM SOIL BEARING PRESSURE = 3,000 PSF

NOTE: SHOULD SOIL AND/OR WEATHER CONDITIONS (IE. HURRICANE, EARTHQUAKE, SNOW ETC.) CAUSE LOADS OTHER THAN INDICATED, IT IS RECOMMENDED THAT A LOCAL ARCHITECT OR STRUCTURAL ENGINEER BE CONSULTED.

NOTE: GREAT CARE... THESE PLANS AND... AND/OR "ON-THE-SIT... BECAUSE OF THE GR... AND WEATHER CON... CLUDING STRUCTUR... BLUEPRINTS. IT IS R... AND CHECK WITH TO...

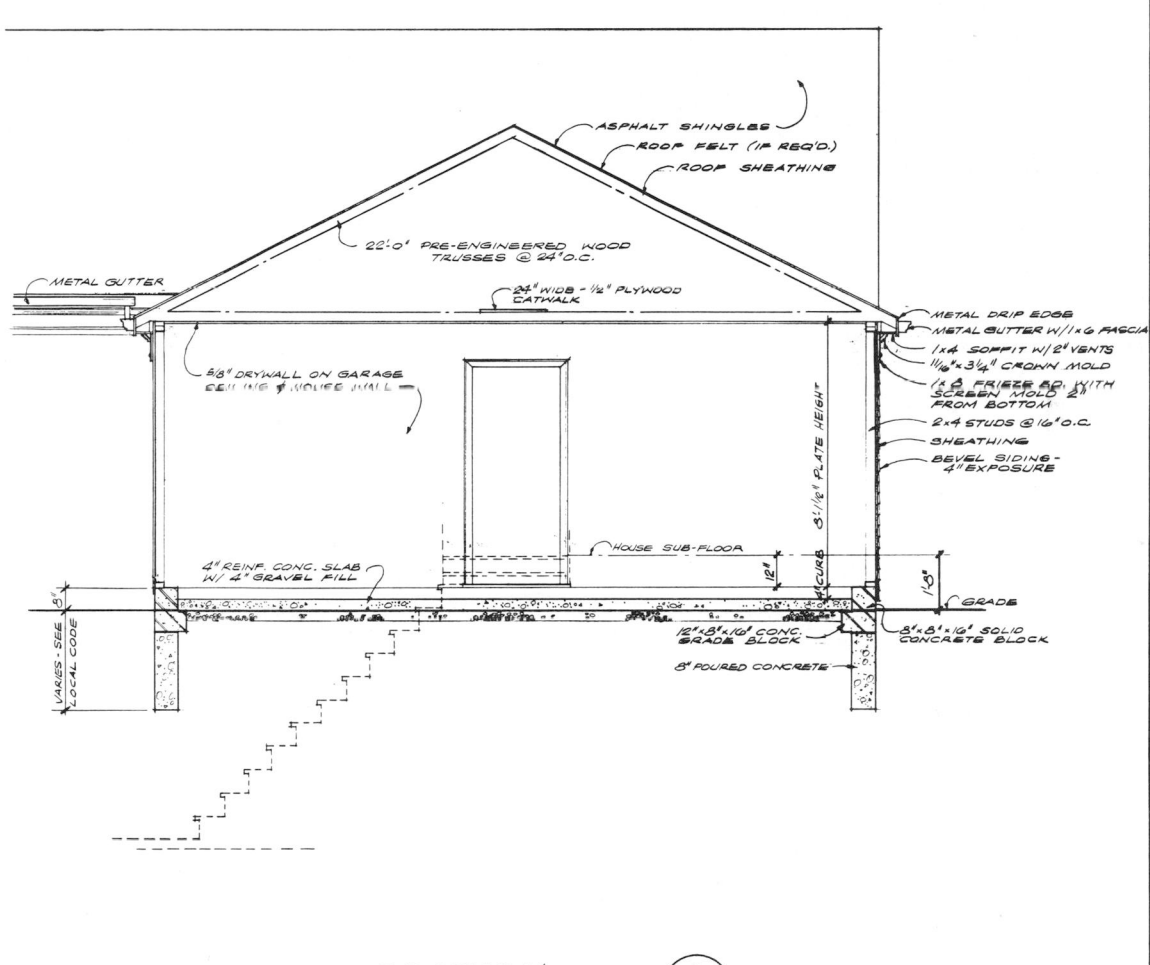

ASPHALT SHINGLES
ROOF FELT (IF REQ'D.)
ROOF SHEATHING

METAL GUTTER

22'-0" PRE-ENGINEERED WOOD TRUSSES @ 24" O.C.

24" WIDE - 1/2" PLYWOOD CATWALK

METAL DRIP EDGE
METAL GUTTER W/ 1×6 FASCIA
1×4 SOFFIT W/ 2" VENTS
11/16" × 3 1/4" CROWN MOLD
1×6 FRIEZE BD. WITH SCREEN MOLD 2" FROM BOTTOM
2×4 STUDS @ 16" O.C.
SHEATHING
BEVEL SIDING - 4" EXPOSURE

5/8" DRYWALL ON GARAGE CEILING & HOUSE WALL

8'-1 1/2" PLATE HEIGHT

4" REINF. CONC. SLAB W/ 4" GRAVEL FILL

HOUSE SUB-FLOOR

12"

8'-0"

VARIES - SEE LOCAL CODE

12"×8"×16" CONC. GRADE BLOCK

8"×8"×16" SOLID CONCRETE BLOCK

8" POURED CONCRETE

CURB

1'-8"

GRADE

SECTION
SCALE 3/8" = 1'-0"
C
4

IRVING E. PALMQUIST, ARCHITECT

HOME PLANNERS, INC.
23761 RESEARCH DRIVE, FARMINGTON HILLS, MICHIGAN 48024

DESIGN NO. **2707**

SHEET NO. **4** OF **4**

DESIGN #2707 © HOME PLANNERS, INC.

3-8b. *The finished house shown in the preceding drawings.*

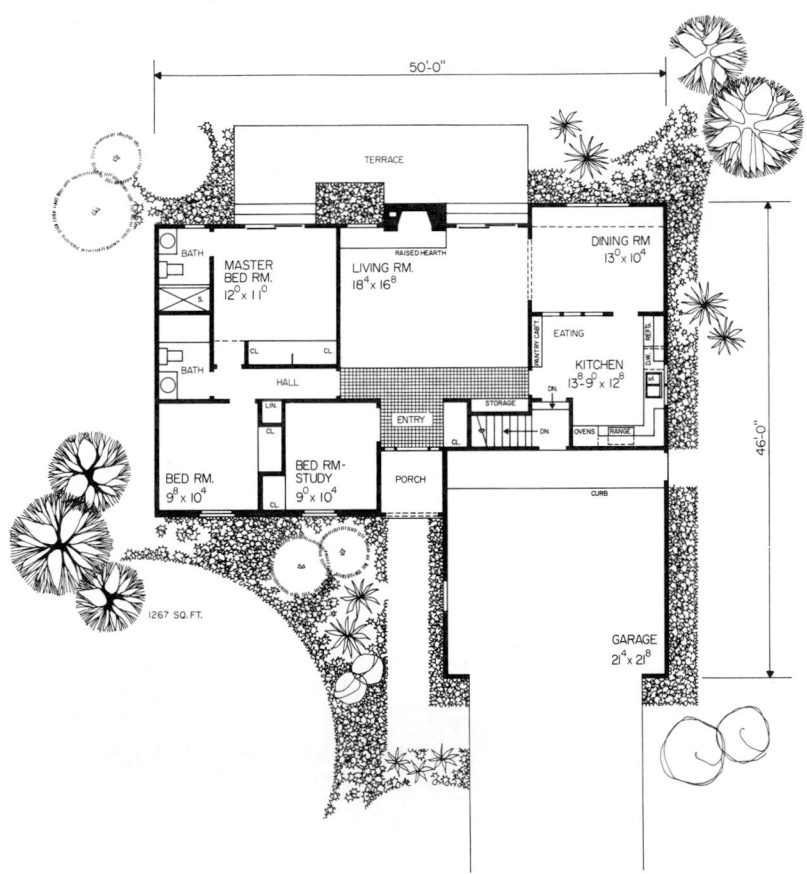

Home Planners, Inc.
23761 RESEARCH DRIVE, FARMINGTON HILLS, MICHIGAN 48024

outside walls and the roof. Insulation is placed between sheathing and interior materials.

Utilities

Heating, air conditioning, wiring, and plumbing are the utilities or mechanical systems of a building. They are represented by drawings.

Finishing and Painting

Glazing, plastering, finish trim, and painting complete the building.

PRINCIPLES OF CONSTRUCTION DRAWING

Construction drawings are based on the same general principles as are all other technical drawings. The shape of a structure is described in *orthographic* (multiview) drawings, made to scale. Its size is described by *figured dimensions*, whose extent is indicated by dimension lines, arrowheads, and extension lines. Overall relationships are shown in *general drawings* similar to assembly drawings. Important specific features are shown in *detail drawings* usually drawn to a larger scale than the general drawings. Additional information about size and material is furnished in the specific and general *notes*. If you are familiar with other types of working drawings, you will find obvious similarities in construction drawings. However, there are certain terms and uses of drawings that are found only in the construction field. Chiefly these are related to the materials and methods of construction and the conventional practices of construction drawing.

Views in Construction Drawings

The views of a structure are presented in general and detail drawings. General drawings consist of plans and elevations; detail drawings are made up of sectional and specific detail views.

Plans. A plan is a top view—a projection on a horizontal plane. Plan views are used for specific purposes, such as site plans, foundation plans, and floor plans.

Site Plan. A site plan, also called a *plot plan*, shows the building site with boundaries, contours, existing roads, utilities, and other physical details such as trees and buildings. Site plans are drawn from notes and sketches based upon a survey. The layout of the structure is superimposed on the contour drawings, and corners of the structure are located by reference to established natural objects or other buildings.

Foundation Plans. A foundation plan is a top view of the footing or foundation walls, showing their area and location by (1) distances between centerlines and (2) distances from reference lines or boundary lines. Foundation walls are located by dimensions from the corner of the building to the wall itself. All openings in foundation walls are shown.

Floor Plan. Floor plans, commonly referred to as plan views, are cross-section views of a building. The horizontal cutting plane is placed so that it includes all doors and window openings. A floor plan shows the outside shape of the home; the arrangement, size, and shape of rooms; types of materials; thickness of walls and partitions; and the types, sizes, and locations of doors and windows for each story. A plan may also include details of framework and structure, although these features are usually shown on separate drawings called framing plans.

Elevations. Elevations are external views of a structure; they may be drawn to show views of the front, rear, and right or left side. They correspond to front, rear, and side views in orthographic projections on vertical planes. An elevation is a picturelike view of a building that shows exterior materials and the height of windows, doors, and rooms. It may also show the ground level surrounding the structure, called the *grade*.

Framing Plans. Framing plans show the size, number, and location of the structural members constituting the building framework. Separate framing plans may be drawn for the floors, walls, and roof. The floor framing plan must specify the sizes and spacing of joists, girders, and columns used to support the floor. Detail drawings are added, if necessary, to show the methods of anchoring joists and girders to the columns and foundation walls or footings. Wall framing plans show the location and method of framing openings and ceiling heights so that studs and posts can be cut. Roof framing plans show the construction of the rafters used to span the building and support the roof. Size, spacing, roof slope, and all necessary details are shown.

Floor Framing. Framing plans for floors are basically plan views of the girders and joists. The unbroken double-line symbol is used to indicate joists which are drawn in the positions they will occupy in the completed building. Double framing around openings and beneath bathroom fixtures is shown where used.

Wall Framing. Wall framing plans are *detail drawings* showing the locations of studs, plates, sills, and bracing. They show one wall at a time. Usually they are elevation views.

Roof Framing. Framing plans for roofs are drawn in the same manner as floor framing plans. A drafter should imagine that he or she is looking down on the roof before any of the roofing material (sheathing) has been added. Rafters are shown in the same manner as joists.

Sectional Views. Sectional views, or sections, provide important information as to height, materials, fastening and support systems, and concealed features. They show how a structure looks when cut vertically by a plane. The cutting plane is not necessarily continuous but, as with the horizontal cutting plane in building plans, may be staggered to include as much construction information as possible. Like elevations, sectional views are vertical projections. Being detail drawings, they are drawn to large scale. This facilitates reading and provides information that cannot be given on elevation or plan views. Sections may be classified as *typical* and *specific*.

Typical Sections. Typical sections are used to show construction features that are repeated many times throughout a structure.

Specific Sections. When a particular construction feature occurs only once and is not shown clearly in the general drawing, a cutting plane is passed through that portion. The cutting plane is indicated by lines on the general drawing. These lines, which sometimes have an arrow at each end, are identified with letters or numbers or both. See, for example, A-2 on the floor plan drawing on page 24. In this case, the cutting plane lines show the relationship between the floor plan drawing and the section drawing.

Details. Details are large-scale drawings showing the builders of a structure how its various parts are to be connected and placed. Details do not use a cutting-plane indication, but they are closely related to section drawing because sections are often used as parts of detail drawings. The construction at doors, windows, and eaves is customarily shown in detail drawings. Such drawings are also used whenever the information provided in elevations, plans, and sections is not clear enough for the mechanics on the job. They are usually grouped so that references may be made easily from general drawings.

Dimensioning Construction Drawings

Plan views are dimensioned both outside and inside the building lines. Outside dimensions describe changes and openings in the exterior wall in addition to overall dimension. Inside measurements locate partitions relative to each other and to exterior walls. All horizontal dimensions are shown in a plan view.

Notes in Construction Drawings

Notes in a set of construction drawings are clear, direct statements regarding such matters as materials, construction, and finish. They are included wherever necessary to provide information not clearly indicated by the dimensions. There are two kinds of notes—specific and general.

All notes on the drawings themselves are *specific*. Such notes may add to the dimensioning information or they may explain a procedure or material standard. When more than one line of

explanatory notes is placed on a drawing, lower case lettering is used. Titles and subtitles are always in upper case letters. Many terms frequently used on construction drawings are abbreviated to save space.

General notes are usually grouped according to material of construction in a tabular form called a *schedule*.

The notes with a set of construction drawings are so extensive that they cannot all be placed on the drawings themselves. All of the general notes and many specific notes are made into a separate list called the *specifications*. These notes tell the manner in which work will be performed, designate what materials and finishes are to be used, and establish the responsibility of the unit performing the work.

Although it is not a drafter's or a carpenter's job to prepare specifications, these workers should be familiar with such notes. This is because the specifications give detailed instructions regarding materials and methods of work and are therefore an important source of information related to the drawings.

A drafter experienced in preparing construction drawings can be of assistance to the specifications writer. Specifications should be written clearly and briefly. Fig. 3-9.

Bill of Materials in Construction Drawings

A bill of materials is a table of information that tells the requirements for a given project. It shows the item number, name, description, quantity, kind of material, stock size, and sometimes the weight of each piece. Table 3-B.

SPECIFICATIONS

The house is to be built for _____ Owner,

residing at (Number) _____ (Street) _____

_____   _____   _____
(City or Town)   (County)   (State)

and is to be built upon the Owner's property located as described below:

_____

_____

LOCATION OF HOUSE ON LOT — The location of the house shall be as shown and dimensioned on the Plot Plan included in the Working Drawings.

GENERAL CONDITIONS OF THE SPECIFICATIONS

GENERAL DESCRIPTION OF THE WORK—The Contractor shall supply all labor, material, transportation, temporary heat, fuel, light, equipment, scaffolding, tools and services required for the complete and proper shaping of the work in strict conformity with the Drawings and Specifications. All work of all trades included in the Specifications shall be performed in a neat and workmanlike manner equal to the best in current shop and field practice.

BIDS—In receiving bids for the work specified herein, the Owner incurs no obligations to any bidder and reserves the right to reject any and all bids.

CONTRACT DOCUMENTS—The Contract Documents consist of the Drawings, Specifications, Plot Plan and the Agreement. The Contract Documents are complementary and what is called for by one shall be as binding as if called for by all. The intent and purpose of the Contract Documents is to include all labor, material, equipment, transportation and handling necessary for the complete and proper execution of the work.

PERMITS AND INSPECTIONS—The Contractor shall give all notices, secure and pay for all permits and inspections and shall comply with all laws, ordinances and regulations governing construction, fire prevention, health and sanitation bearing on the conduct of the work.

PROTECTION—The Contractor shall fully and continuously protect all parts of the work from damage, and shall protect the Owner against all loss or injury arising in connection with the execution of the Contract. He shall protect adjacent property as required by law, and shall provide and maintain all passageways, guard fences, lights and other facilities for protection as required by public authority or local conditions. The Contractor shall protect all trees, shrubs, walks and curbs from damage during building operations. The Owner shall provide adequate fire and tornado insurance during construction.

CONTRACTOR'S LIABILITY INSURANCE—The Contractor shall insure himself against claims under Workmen's Compensation Acts and from all other claims for damage for personal injury, including death, which may arise from operations under this Contract, whether such operations be by himself or by any Sub-Contractor or by anyone directly or indirectly employed by either of them. Certificate of such insurance shall be furnished and shall be subject to the Owner's approval for adequacy of protection.

CASH ALLOWANCES—All cash allowances specified shall be included in the Contract sum. If the Owner's selections total more or less than the allowances specified, the Contract sum shall be adjusted accordingly.

EXTRA WORK—Work shall not be started on any item not included in the Plans, Specifications and Contract until the Owner and Contractor agree in writing to the specific quantity and quality intended and to the cost of the extra work. Owner and Contractor shall operate in strict conformity with this requirement for their mutual protection.

CLEANING—The Contractor shall at all times keep the premises free from accumulations of waste materials and rubbish, and at the completion of the work all rooms and spaces shall be left broom clean.

WORK NOT INCLUDED—The following items of work are excluded from the Contract, however, may be included if noted under "Special Items Included."

Blasting	Furniture and Furnishings
Sub-soil Drain	Venetian Blinds
Waterproofing	Window Shades
Driveways and Walks	Refrigerator
Finished Grading, Planting	Cooking Range
and Landscaping	Bathroom Accessories
Fences	Weatherstripping

EXCAVATION AND GRADING

The General Conditions of the Specifications apply to this Section.

WORK INCLUDED—The work under this Section shall consist of furnishing all equipment and performing all necessary labor to do all excavating and rough grading work shown or specified. Excavate to dimensions one foot greater in size than the outside dimensions of the masonry and to the depth required or to solid formation suitable for the foundation. The top soil removed from the excavation shall be stored on the site. Sufficient excavated materials shall be retained to bring the grade up to the necessary level to receive the top soil. If additional earth is required for the rough grading, the Contractor shall furnish it as specified under Special Items Included. Excavation shall be kept free from standing water at all times.

BACK FILLING—The Contractor shall back fill against all walls to the grade line with clean earth well tamped and wetted.

MASONRY

The General Conditions of the Specifications apply to this Section.

WORK INCLUDED—The work under this Section shall consist of furnishing and installing all material and equipment and performing all necessary labor to do all masonry work shown or specified.

FOOTINGS—Footings shall be of concrete mixed in the proportion of 1 part Portland cement, 3 parts of clean, coarse, sharp sand free from loam or vegetable matter, and 5 parts of ¾" gravel. Concrete shall be machine mixed with clean water to the proper consistency and shall be placed immediately after mixing and thoroughly puddled into the forms. Contractor shall check bearing power of soil in all cases and construct footings of sufficient size to conform to local soil requirements and building code.

3-9. *Specifications for a house. This is the first of four pages. Other main topics covered are Miscellaneous Iron, Framing and Carpentry, Sheet Metal, Lath and Plaster, Painting and Finishing, Electric Wiring, Plumbing, and Heating.*

Table 3-B. *Part of the Materials List for a House.*

Item	Grade & Species	Pcs.	Lumber Size	Length	F.B.M.	Price	Amt.
Framing							
Posts	#1 D.F.	3	6 × 6	14'0"	126		
	"	3	2 × 4	10'0"	20		
	"	1	4 × 4	10'0"	14		
Girders	"	6	2 × 8	16'0"	128		
	"	3	2 × 8	8'0"	32		
1st Floor Joists	"	4	2 × 8	14'0"	75		
	"	30	2 × 8	12'0"	480		
	"	22	2 × 8	10'0"	294		
1st Floor Joist Headers	"	2	2 × 8	16'0"	43		
	"	3	2 × 8	12'0"	48		
	"	2	2 × 8	10'0"	27		
	"	3	2 × 8	8'0"	32		
Flower Pot Support	"	1	1 × 6	16'0"	8		
	"	1	2 × 12	14'0"	28		
	"	1	2 × 2	14'0"	5		
	"	1	2 × 10	4'0"	7		
Ceiling Joists	"	8	2 × 4	12'0"	64		
	"	6	2 × 4	10'0"	40		
	"	3	2 × 4	4'0"	8		
Rafters	"	3	2 × 8	20'0"	80		
	"	15	2 × 8	18'0"	360		
	"	10	2 × 8	16'0"	214		
	"	10	2 × 8	14'0"	187		
	"	15	2 × 8	12'0"	240		
Studs—Exterior	#2 D.F.	94	2 × 4	10'0"	627		
	"	33	2 × 4	8'0"	176		
Studs—Partition	"	5	2 × 6	10'0"	50		
	"	134	2 × 4	10'0"	893		
Plates	"	1	2 × 6	14'0"	14		
	"	9	2 × 4	16'0"	96		
	"	9	2 × 4	14'0"	84		
	"	21	2 × 4	12'0"	168		
	"	12	2 × 4	10'0"	80		
	"	9	2 × 4	8'0"	48		
Lintels (Wdo. & Door)	#1 D.F.	6	2 × 6	14'0"	84		
	"	2	2 × 6	12'0"	24		
	"	5	2 × 4	8'0"	27		
Diagonal Braces	#3 P.P.	4	1 × 4	12'0"	16		
	"	2	1 × 4	14'0"	9		
Stair Horses	#1 D.F.	3	2 × 10	12'0"	60		
Bsmt. Stair Treads	"	3	2 × 10	12'0"	60		
Handrail	"	2	2 × 4	10'0"	13		
Grounds	#3 P.P.	1220 L'	1 × 1	Random	102		
Bridging	"	380 L'	1 × 3	"	95		
Sheathing							
Sub-Flooring	#2 D.F. Shiplap		1 × 8	Random	940		
Wall Sheathing	#3 P.P. Shiplap		1 × 8	"	1456		
Roof Sheathing	"		1 × 8	"	1267		

QUESTIONS

1. Why is it important to learn to read prints?

2. What is a blueprint?

3. Define scale.

4. Describe the basic elements of drawing.

5. Name some of the common lines.

6. Name the common views needed in a construction drawing.

7. What is an elevation?

8. What are framing plans?

9. Why are sectional views shown?

10. What are detail drawings and what is their purpose?

11. What are specifications?

12. Define a bill of materials.

ACTIVITIES

1. Social Studies. This unit describes the differences between the metric measurement system and the English system. Historically, the United States has, until recently, used the English system. Why do you think that it has been difficult to switch to an all-metric system in the United States?

2. Social Studies. Why does the English measuring system use terms such as *feet*, *inch*, and *yard*? Use either a college dictionary or world history book to find out.

3. Language Arts. Scan the floor plans and architectural drawings in this unit. Select five labels that you are unfamiliar with. For example, you may not understand the term "flashing." Determine the meanings of these unfamiliar words by studying the diagram or looking for their meanings in the index. If either of those methods fail, refer to a dictionary. Share the definitions with the other members of your class.

4. Math. If the scale on a drawing of a garage is ¼" = 1'-0" and the segment representing the length of the garage is 6½" long, how long will the garage be?

5. Math. From the house plans contained in this unit determine:

a. how many windows there will be in the basement.

b. which of the two bedrooms is the larger. Discuss with a friend how you determined this.

THE SCHOOL-TO-WORK CONNECTION

Permits and inspections are two ways of enforcing building codes. A permit is a license that gives you permission to do the work. You'll need a permit if remodeling work is extensive or if you will be building a new house. When you apply for the permit, you will usually have to provide working drawings of the project. After you submit the drawings, they will be reviewed by building officials.

1. Photocopy Fig. 3-8b (page 30). Show it to a building official in your community. Find out what types of drawings he or she would expect from you if you wanted to build this house. If this house was already built and you wanted to expand the dining room by extending it 4' towards the back yard, what drawings would you need? Finally, what drawings would be needed if you wanted to install a skylight (36" long and 14 1/2" wide) above the bedroom/study. What drawings would be required if the skylight was 48" wide?

2. Whenever construction work requires a permit, you may have to schedule time for a building inspector to examine the work. He or she will check to see that the work meets or exceeds the building codes. On small projects the inspector might come out only for a final inspection. On a larger project there might be several intermediate inspections before a final inspection. It is your job to call for the inspection. Show the photos on pages 46A-H to a local building official. Find out when inspections would be necessary.

Energy Efficiency

About one-fifth of our total national use of energy is for climate conditioning of houses, apartments, condominiums, mobile homes, and other living units. Energy is needed for heating, air conditioning, humidifying, dehumidifying, and air cleaning. As the cost of energy rises, it becomes increasingly important to make all types of living units more energy efficient. Anyone planning to build or remodel a house must consider every possible way of reducing energy needs. Also, this must be done without adding too much to the cost of construction. There are energy-saving materials and devices available that are not too expensive and save enough energy to justify their cost.

Energy is used in daily living in a wide variety of ways. Precious energy is consumed in almost everything we do, such as cooking a meal, switching on a light, watching television, taking a shower, or washing clothes. When the weather turns cold or hot, energy is consumed to compensate for these conditions.

Of the many factors that influence internal temperature, the most important is outside weather. If it is cold outside, heat is lost through the living unit in many ways:

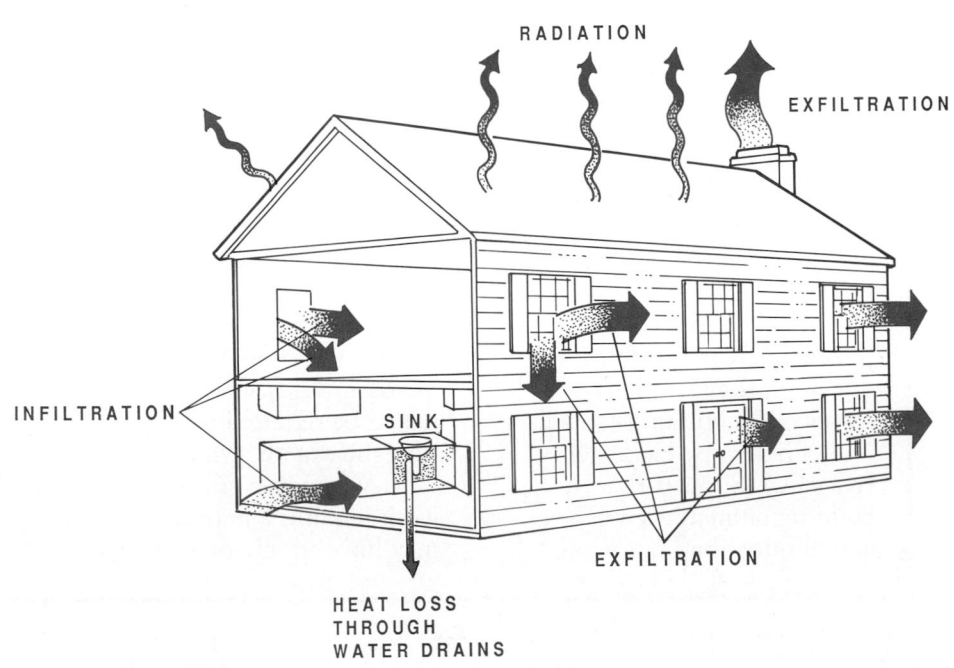

4-1. *Types of heat loss.*

➤ By *exfiltration*, the leakage of warm air to the outside through cracks in windows, walls, and doors.

➤ By *infiltration*, the leakage of cold outside air into the house.

➤ By *radiation*, in which warmth is lost to the sky and the surroundings. (A warm body tends to lose its heat by infrared radiation.)

➤ By *conduction*, the transfer of heat through solid materials.

➤ By *heat loss through water drains*. Energy is used to heat water. As the hot water goes down the drain, this energy is lost from the home. Fig. 4-1.

It has been estimated that nearly 40 percent of heat loss is due to exfiltration and infiltration.

Heat is generated and gained in living quarters by appliances, electric lights, and people. Some heat is also gained through solar energy, even in the standard home. Fig. 4-2. In cold weather, the difference between heat loss and heat gain must be made up by some type of heating unit to maintain a comfortable temperature range of 68 to 78 degrees F. (20 to 26 degrees C). Fig. 4-3. In addition, energy is used to clean the air and to add humidity for comfort.

In warm weather, many of the same factors are at work. When the outside temperature is greater than the indoor temperature, heat tends to flow into the house (infiltration). To maintain comfort, an air conditioner is often used to remove this excess heat. Excess moisture is removed from the air by a dehumidifier.

There are three ways construction can aid in energy conservation:

1. Existing homes can be made more energy efficient with such improvements as additional insulation, storm doors and windows, careful caulking, weatherstripping, and the addition of energy-efficient appliances. In cooling climates, dark-colored roofing can be replaced with light-colored roofing to reduce solar heat gain.

2. New homes can be designed to take advantage of the latest materials for saving energy. These can include insulated sheathing, radiant barriers, super-efficient heating and cooling systems, and insulating windows.

3. New homes can gather heat and electricity through the use of nontraditional techniques, including solar heating/cooling,

4-2. *Typical sources of heat gain.*

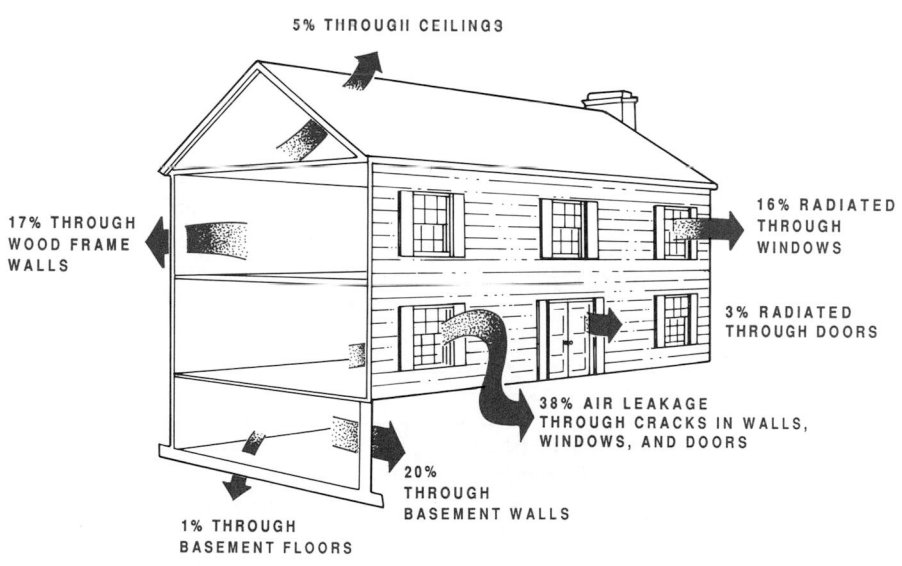

4-3. *The amount of heat lost through a house insulated to current standards.*

wind-generated electricity, and photovoltaic electricity. These sources reduce the need for heat and electricity produced by traditional sources.

In planning any structure to include energy-saving devices, the following must be given careful consideration:

➤ Will the device or material save sufficient energy to pay for itself within a reasonable period? This is called the "payback" period. The payback period usually varies from one to fifteen years.

➤ Will the structure be within current construction capabilities and local building codes?

➤ Will the structure be acceptable from an architectural standpoint? For example, will tiny windows sparsely placed be acceptable?

➤ Will the design drastically change the lifestyle of the residents? In the years ahead, most living units must be smaller and more space efficient. For example, it may not be desirable to have both a living room and a family room. Many current house plans call for a *great room* as an all-purpose living area. Today, fewer homes have separate dining rooms, and bedrooms are smaller.

CAULKS AND SEALANTS

One of the easiest and least expensive ways to reduce energy consumption is to seal the house to prevent air leakage. This is typically done with caulking. Caulking is inexpensive and easy to apply. Joints should be caulked where air leakage can be expected, such as around the casings of windows and doors. Fig. 4-4. If considerable movement of a joint is expected, a sealant is the best material to use. Sealants are similar

to caulks, but they are generally more flexible and more expensive. Because of their flexibility, sealants are often applied to the joint between two dissimilar materials. The joint between brick and wood trim is an example of where a sealant would be appropriate. Fig. 4-5.

Caulks and sealants come in various forms. Most commonly, however, they come in a sealed

cartridge for use in a caulking gun. Fig. 4-6.

Applying Caulks and Sealants

For caulks and sealants to work properly, they must be applied properly.

The materials to be caulked should be clean, dry, and free of

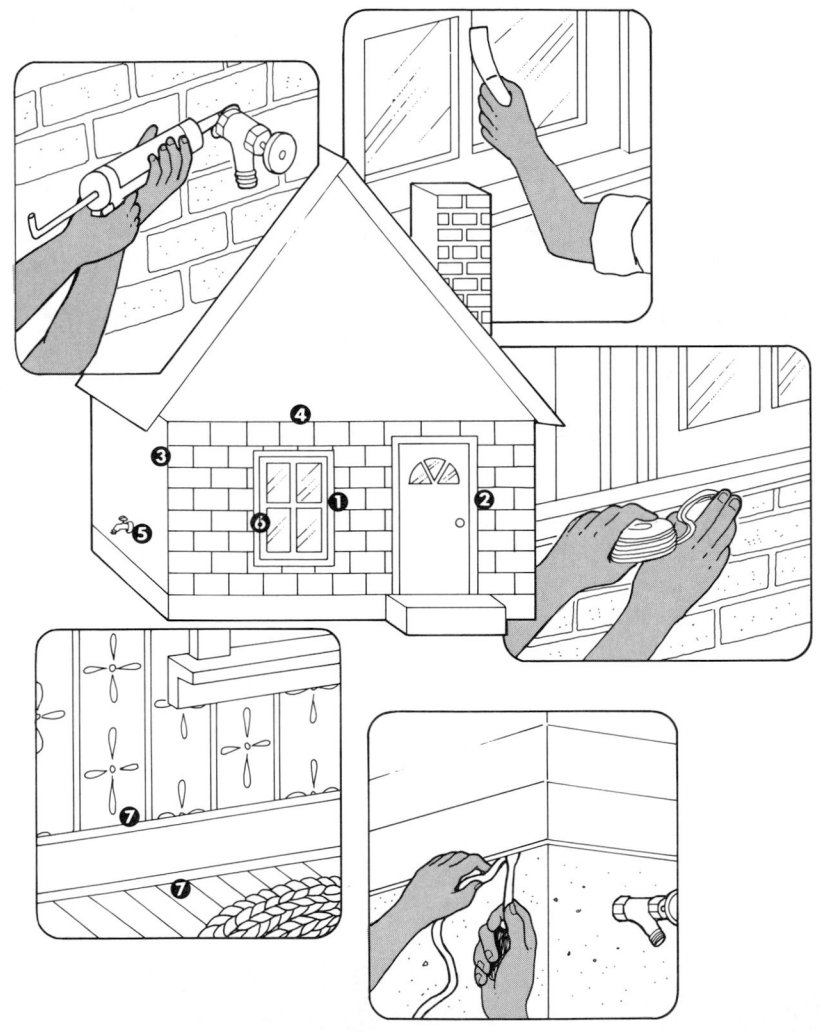

4-4. Caulks or sealants should be applied: 1. around the window where the frame meets brick, siding, or sheetrock; 2. along the top and sides of the door where the frame meets brick, siding, or sheetrock; 3. where wall meets wall; 4. where wall meets roof overhang; 5. around water faucets, using tube-type caulking and a caulking gun; 6. around window panes and frames, using glazing compound where glass meets frames; 7. where baseboard meets wall, with a ribbon-type caulk.

dust, grease, or other residue. Concrete and other masonry should be dry and thoroughly cured. Aluminum, bronze, or galvanized steel should first be wiped with a solvent such as methyl ethyl ketone. This will remove any protective coating on the metal. Glass and ceramic tile should be washed with soap and water, rinsed, and dried. Wiping

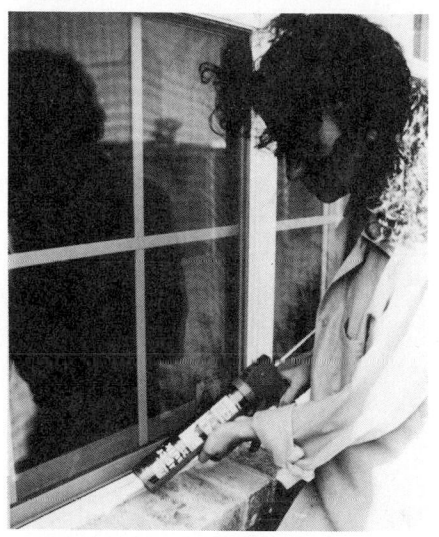

4-5. Caulking or sealing the joints between materials prevents air infiltration.

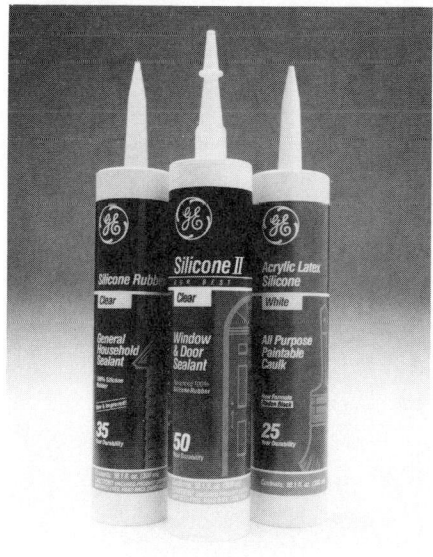

4-6. Caulks and sealants usually come in disposable tubes.

the cleaned surfaces with a solvent such as isopropanol will remove any traces of soap.

When using a caulking gun, hold it at a 45 degree angle to the surface and squeeze with steady pressure. Keep the rear of the caulking gun slightly slanted toward the direction you are moving. Slowly draw it along so that the sealant not only fills the crack, but also overlaps the edges. Move the gun with a pulling, not a pushing, motion. To get a smooth bead, fill a single seam in one stroke.

The temperature of the material to be caulked should be at least 45 degrees F. Lower temperatures prevent the caulk from adhering properly. The best time to apply caulk to an exterior joint is in the spring or fall. At those times the width of the joint will be halfway between its seasonal extremes. If caulk is applied when the joint is at its smallest dimension, expansion later in the year might open up the joint.

Most caulks and sealants should be tooled after application. This means that they should be pushed into the joint and smoothed over. Many builders wipe the joint with a wet finger, but this is generally not a good idea because many caulks and sealants contain toxic chemicals. Also, some caulks and sealants can be difficult to remove from the skin. Instead, the joint should be tooled with a plastic spoon or similar device.

Choosing a Caulk or Sealant

It is important that the builder select the correct kind of caulk or sealant for each particular purpose and follow the instructions of the manufacturer. The durability of these materials varies depending on their exposure to weather. As a

guide to choosing the correct material, Table 4-A lists caulks and sealants appropriate for residential construction.

Wall Sheathing

More and more builders are choosing sheathings designed specifically for energy conservation. Each sheathing material has certain advantages and disadvantages that must be considered in making the best selection for each job.

These sheathings are nonstructural, meaning that they cannot be used without some other material to make walls and roofs rigid. Plywood sheathing can be used in combination with insulating sheathings to improve the rigidity of the structure. Another technique is to install sheet-metal let-in braces beneath the insulating sheathing.

These are T-shaped sheet metal braces that can be installed diagonally across either the outside or the inside of a wall. Fig. 4-7. A shallow, narrow kerf (gain) must be cut into each stud to insert the sheet metal brace. The brace is nailed in place with the cross section of the T nailed to the outside of the studs. Siding must be nailed directly to the studs using long, thin siding nails because the insulating sheathing cannot serve as a nailing base.

There are various types of insulating sheathing now used in residential construction. All of them are types of plastic. All of them must be covered with a fire-rated material. One advantage of insulating sheathings is that they pack a lot of R-value into a relatively thin package. Unlike fiberglass batt insulation, insulating sheathings reduce the amount of heat conducted through wall studs. This is because they completely cover the framing. Fig. 4-8.

While insulating sheathing is fairly moisture resistant, this can sometimes cause problems. For example, if insulating sheathing is applied to the exterior of the studs and covered directly with painted wood siding, moisture can become trapped between the two materials. This sometimes results in paint blistering or peeling away from the wood. Some builders prevent this problem by installing the siding over furring strips. The furring lifts the siding away from the insulating sheathing by about ⅜" and allows ventilation behind the siding.

There are four basic types of insulating sheathing used most often in residential construction.

Expanded polystyrene (EPS) is made of a material similar to that used in making coffee cups and

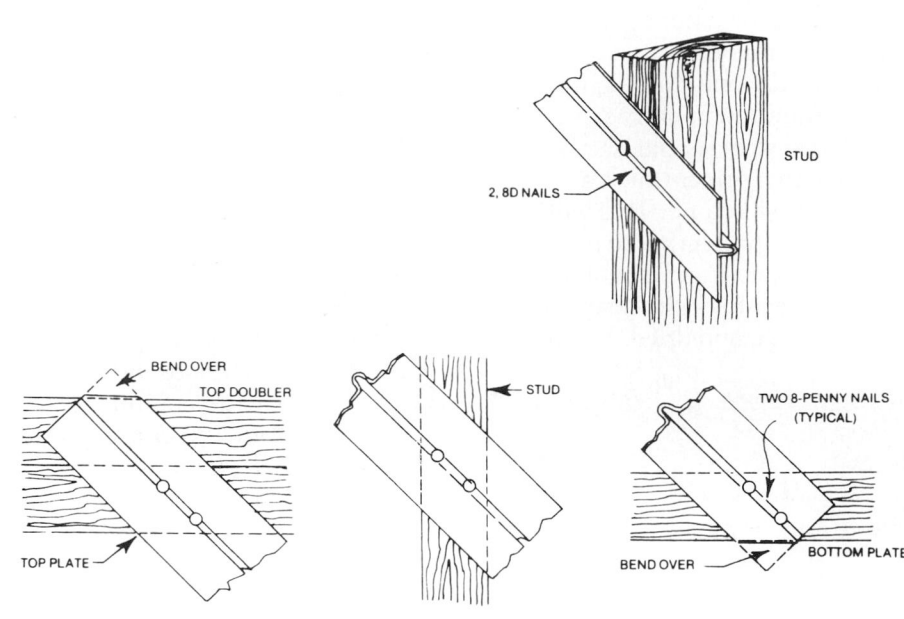

4-7. *Sheet metal let-in braces must be used with nonstructural insulating sheathing.*

Table 4-A. *Characteristics of Caulks and Sealants.*

Caulk/Sealant	Approximate Lifespan Used Outdoors (Years)	Flexibility	Adhesion	Compatible Paints	Other Characteristics
Oil-Base	1-2	Fair	Good	• Latex • Solvent-base	• Least expensive
Butyl Rubber	5-15	Good	Good	• Latex • Some solvent-base	• Never hardens completely
Styrene Butadiene Rubber	3-10	Fair to Good	Fair	• Latex	• Adheres to damp surfaces • Adheres to treated lumber
Polyvinyl Acetate	1-3	Fair	Fair to Good	• Latex • Solvent-base	• Adheres to damp surfaces • Can be used as a light-duty adhesive
Vinyl Acrylic	5-20	Good	Good to Very Good	• Latex • Solvent-base	• Adheres to damp surfaces • Sometimes includes a fungicide
Solvent Acrylic	5-20	Good	Very Good	• Latex • Solvent-base	• Not recommended for indoor use
Kraton	5-15	Good	Good	• Latex • Solvent-base	• Adheres to asphalt
Polysulfide	10-25	Very Good	Good	• Latex • Solvent-base	• Resists chemicals
Polyurethane	5-15	Very Good	Fair to Good	• Latex • Solvent-base	• Often used in commercial construction
Silicone	20 or more	Outstanding	Fair to Good	• Alkyd	• Sometimes includes a fungicide

(Rows for Polyvinyl Acetate, Vinyl Acrylic, and Solvent Acrylic are grouped under "Latex.")

4-8. *Insulating sheathing applied horizontally as sheathing.*

inexpensive ice chests. It is manufactured in large blocks which are sliced into sheets for use in construction. Unlike most other insulating sheathing, EPS is not made with the chemicals that damage the earth's ozone layer. Its R-value equals 3.6 to 4.2 per inch.

Extruded polystyrene (XEPS) is similar to EPS. The material is made by forcing plastic molecules through a die. It is less susceptible to damage than EPS and less likely to absorb moisture. This is why it is often used to insulate foundations. Its R-value equals 5 per inch.

Polyisocyanurate is an insulating panel that is faced on both sides with foil. Its R-value equals 5.6 per inch.

Polyurethane is similar to polyisocyanurate, and is also faced on both sides with foil. It differs from polyisocyanurate, however, in that it is less expensive and stronger. Its R-value equals 5.6 per inch.

STANDARD HOME CONSTRUCTION

Many things can be done to improve the energy efficiency of the standard home. Some of these things can be done at small cost; others are expensive.

➤ Limit the size of the living unit (in square feet) by redesigning the living quarters. If each area can be made more flexible (have several uses), the original cost of construction can be reduced and energy efficiency improved.

➤ Use the correct kind of sheathing. Installation of energy-efficient sheathing instead of standard materials provides great fuel savings.

➤ Add proper insulation in walls, ceilings, and floors and around the perimeter of the building.

➤ Add proper, well-fitted storm windows and doors and double-glazed windows.

➤ Install the correct type of weather stripping around all doors and windows.

➤ Add caulking around all windows and doors where the frame meets the siding and around all other possible openings. Caulking should be applied around an outside faucet, between the basement and floor framing, the drip cap and siding, the corners formed by siding, where pipes and wires penetrate the ceiling, below an unheated attic or chimney, and where chimney and masonry meet siding.

➤ Add attic ventilation. Attics with a ceiling vapor barrier must be ventilated with one square foot of vent area for each 300 square feet of ceiling. Attics without a ceiling vapor barrier must be ventilated with one square foot of vent area for each 150 square feet of ceiling. The vents may be in the roof, soffit, or gable. One of the most efficient venting systems is that installed in the ridge of the roof.

➤ Insulate duct work. Duct work may be insulated by adding insulating tape around each joint and furnace opening. Also, batt insulation completely covering all exposed duct work can be installed.

BUILDING ENERGY-EFFICIENT HOMES

The standard homes being built in the 1990s are generally more energy efficient than homes built at any time previously. This is partly due to changes in building codes that require more efficiency and less energy use. It is also due to programs that discourage the waste of energy and encourage conservation.

Several well-known national and regional programs are designed to help builders build and market homes that are very energy-efficient. Several of the programs have extensive training and marketing manuals for builders to use. These programs include:

➤ The Home Builder's Design and Education Program. Developed by the Florida Solar Energy Center, the program has a strong emphasis on reducing cooling costs.

➤ The Super Good Cents Home Program. This program, particularly strong in the Pacific Northwest, has spread to various parts of the country.

➤ The Alaska Craftsman Home Program. This program encourages super-insulated homes in cold climates.

➤ The Arkansas Plan. Sponsored by the U.S. Department of Housing and Urban Development, the training materials are based on a demonstration house built in Little Rock, Arkansas. This was one of the earliest programs. Some of its recommendations have since been modified.

➤ The R-2000 Home Program. This is a Canadian program sponsored in part by the Canadian Home Builders' Association.

Because houses built under these programs often provide excellent examples of energy-efficient construction, three of them will be summarized in the following pages.

These programs are The Home Builder's Design and Education Program (houses for hot, humid climates), The Arkansas Plan (houses for moderate climates), and The Alaska Craftsman Home Program (houses for cold climates).

Energy-Efficiency for Hot, Humid Climates

Much of the southern portion of the U.S. is characterized by hot, humid weather. In such a climate, builders are less concerned with reducing heating costs than they are with reducing cooling costs. Design and construction of a house in this climate, therefore, depends on two basic strategies:

➤ Site the house properly. This will reduce the amount of heat gain and will increase the amount of natural ventilation.

➤ Use construction materials and techniques appropriate for the climate.

Both of these basic strategies are intended to reduce the need for air conditioning, which consumes a lot of energy. When air-conditioning must be used, the installation of a high-efficiency air conditioner will reduce operating expenses.

Siting considerations. Shade trees can block solar radiation and prevent it from overheating the house. They should be saved whenever possible. This is particularly important when the trees are on the south, east, or west side of the house. Careful excavation of the site will prevent damage to the root systems of shade trees. If utility lines must pass close to a tree, they should be tunneled beneath the tree, rather than be placed in trenches that would damage the tree's root system. Fig. 4-9.

The house should be located so that major areas of glass face north or south. Glass on the north is shaded by the house itself. Glass on the south can be protected by overhanging eaves that block the heat of the sun when it is high on the horizon. When the sun is in the east or west, it is fairly low on the horizon, so eaves cannot easily block it. This is why glass should be minimized on the east and west sides of a hot climate house. Fig. 4-10.

Every building site is exposed to a certain pattern of winds. This

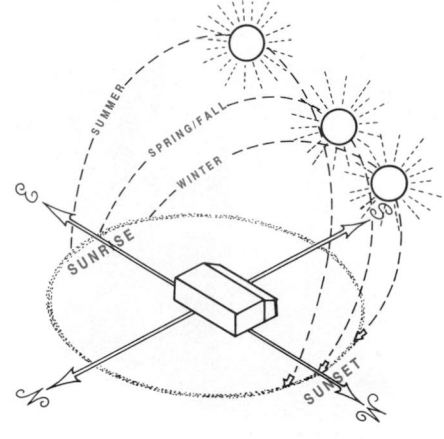

4-10. *Windows on the east and west sides of a house in a hot climate should be minimized. It is difficult to protect them from the sun.*

pattern may change from season to season, but the prevailing breezes are fairly predictable. A house in a hot climate should be sited to take best advantage of these breezes. A special map called a wind rose shows the prevailing breezes for selected locations. Fig. 4-11.

Construction details for hot, humid climates.
Foundations. The recommended foundation is the slab-on-grade foundation. This type of foundation is easy to construct. Its mass can be used for passive solar heating in the winter. Because a slab floor tends to stay cooler than the outside air in the summer, it is an excellent floor in hot climates.

There are two types of slab-on-grade foundations. The most simple type is called a monolithic slab-on-grade. This means that the floor slab and the footings are poured together and form one unit. The second type of foundation is called a stem wall foundation. Both types of foundations have similar construction details. Fig. 4-12.

With both foundations, all slab penetrations must be carefully sealed to prevent the entry of radon

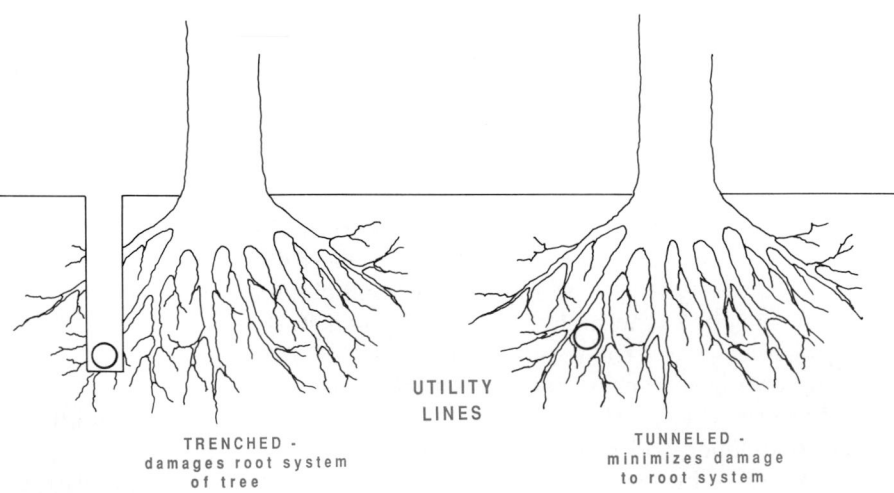

UTILITY LINES

TRENCHED - damages root system of tree

TUNNELED - minimizes damage to root system

4-9. *To protect the roots of shade trees from damage during construction, nearby utility lines should be tunneled beneath the tree or routed around it.*

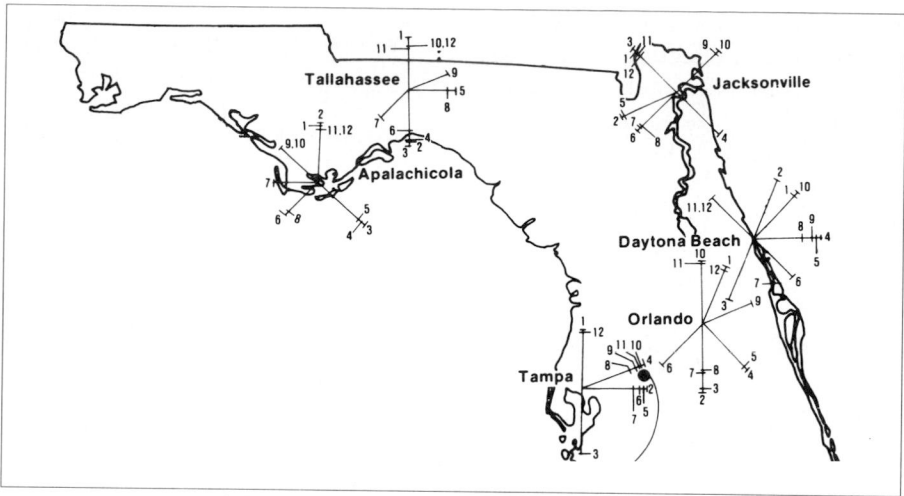

4-11. *A wind rose map shows the direction and intensity of prevailing winds. It can be used to determine the best placement for a house on a lot.*

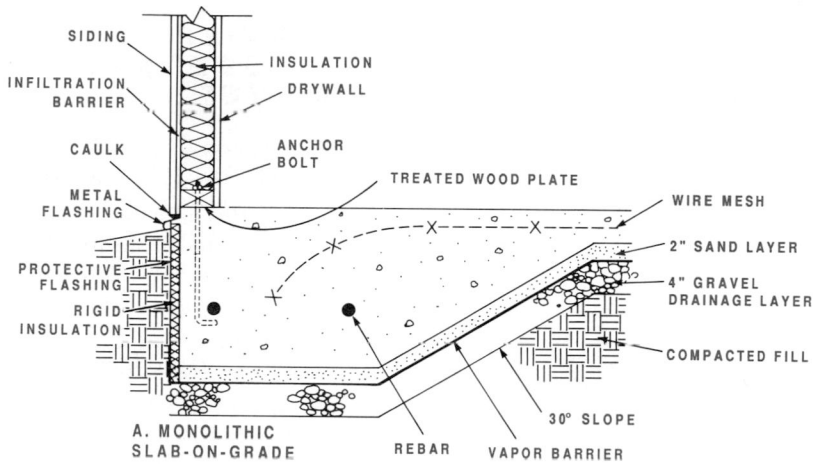

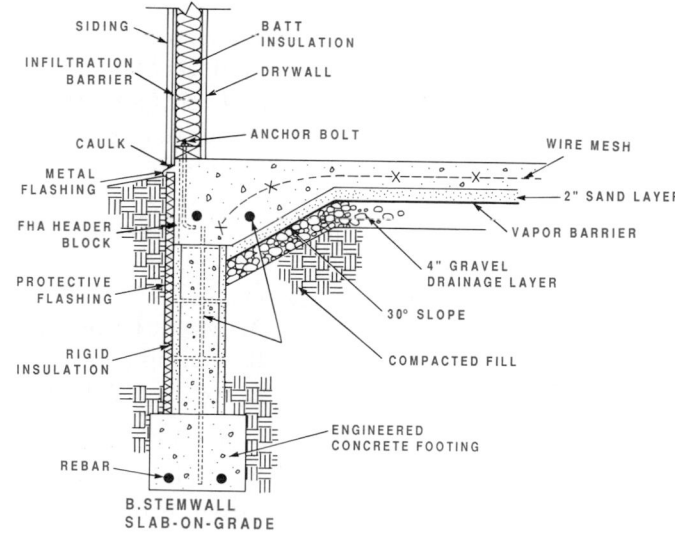

4-12. *Slab-on-grade foundations for a hot climate.*

into the house. A wire mesh layer placed in the middle of a standard 4" slab will help to prevent cracking. The perimeter of the slab should be shaded with shrubs or other vegetation to prevent the sun's heat from being conducted into the living space. Rigid insulation placed around the perimeter of the foundation reduces heat loss in the winter and heat gain in the summer.

An energy-efficient slab floor should be finished with a conductive floor finish. This will help the floor to feel cool in warm weather. Carpeting and vinyl tend to minimize this cooling effect. Ceramic tile is a very conductive finish floor, though it can be expensive. As an alternative, some builders stamp decorative patterns into the concrete before it has cured. Concrete colorants can be added at that time. The resulting floor is both cost-efficient and energy-efficient.

Walls and roofs. Recommended wood-frame wall and roof construction is similar in many respects to techniques recommended for energy-efficient buildings elsewhere in the country. Such recommendations include:
➤ Reducing the number of framing members to reduce heat conduction.
➤ Carefully insulating walls and ceilings.
➤ Routing wiring along the soleplates instead of through the middle of wall cavities to keep the insulation from being compressed.
➤ Sealing the house to prevent unwanted air infiltration.
➤ Installing light-colored siding and roofing to reflect solar radiation away from the house.
➤ Installing continuous soffit vents and ridge vents.

Radiant barriers. One energy conservation technique that is unique to hot climates is the use of radiant barriers in walls and roofs.

While not yet a widespread technique, radiant barriers show promise for reducing heat gain in a house.

A radiant barrier is a layer of aluminum foil installed within a roof, ceiling, or wall. Because foil reflects up to 95% of the thermal radiation striking it, it reduces heat transfer through wall and ceiling assemblies. For this process to work, however, the foil must face an airspace. Radiant barriers have been used successfully in a number of states. Fig. 4-13.

In new construction, the radiant barrier is most effective (and easiest to install) in a roof system. It can be draped over the roof rafters before the roof decking is installed. It is applied so that it droops slightly between the rafters; this creates the necessary airspace between the foil and the decking. Fig. 4-14.

A radiant barrier can also be installed in a wall, but the construction detailing is more involved than when it is placed in a roof. Fig. 4-15.

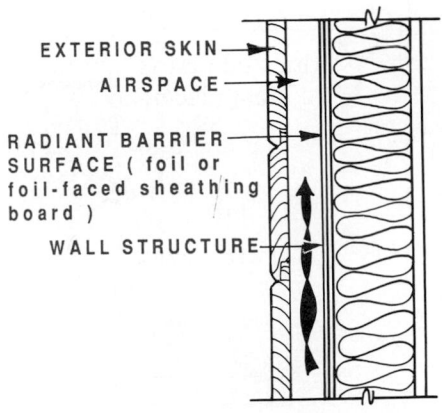

4-15. *A radiant barrier in a wall.*

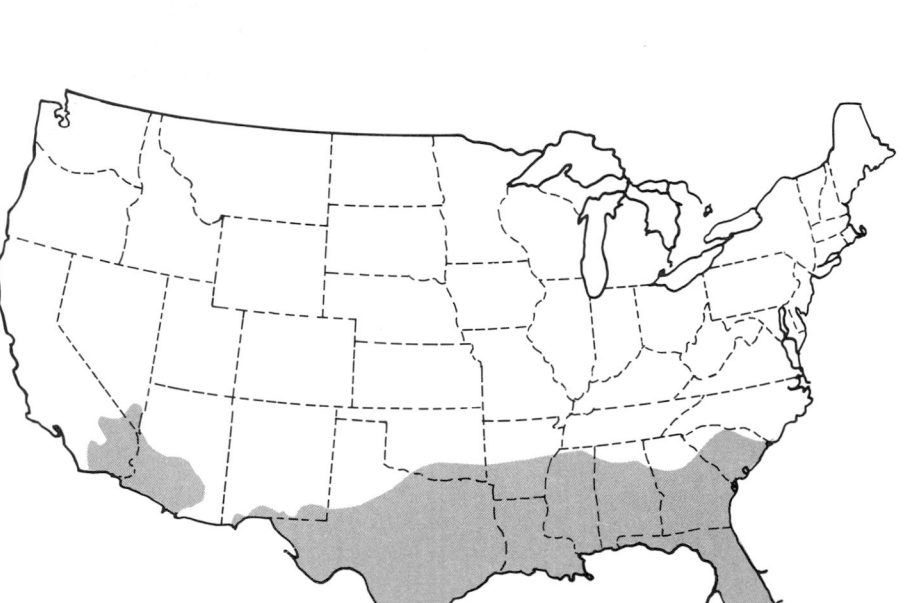

4-13. *Areas in which radiant barriers are most effective.*

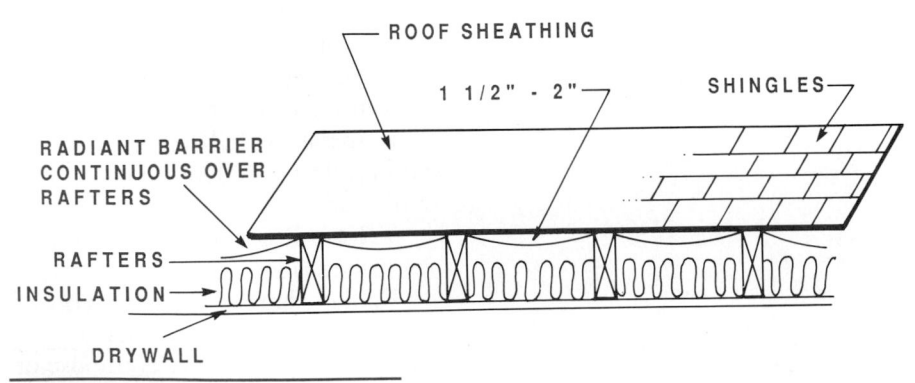

4-14. *A radiant barrier in a roof.*

ENERGY-EFFICIENCY FOR MODERATE CLIMATES

An energy-saving home was sponsored by the U.S. Department of Housing and Urban Development and built in Little Rock, Arkansas. It has become known as the *Arkansas Plan* or *Arkansas Home*. Fig 4-16. Basically, this home involved the redesigning of wall and ceiling construction to allow for 6 inches of insulation in walls and 12 inches in ceilings. The design also called for smaller windows equipped with storm windows, metal exterior doors with insulation cores and magnetic weather stripping, power attic ventilation, humidifier, dehumidifier, and air filtration equipment. Figs. 4-17, 18, and 19. Specifications include the following, most of which are shown in Fig. 4-17:

1. Vapor barriers covering walls, ceilings, and floors.

2. Windows that have storm windows and are caulked.

3. Metal exterior doors 1¾"thick with urethane core.

4. Attic space with power roof ventilators and eave vents.

5. Inspection catwalk.

6. Wiring and piping installed to permit correct placement of insulation.

7. Humidifier.

8. Dehumidifier.

9. Air filtering device.

10. Sill and window flashing.

11. Wall studs (2" × 6") spaced 24" on center.

12. Window headers.

13. Proper structural support.

14. Tie plates and drywall back-up clips.

15. Insulated ducts.

16. Centrally located climate conditioning equipment.

17. Partition walls of 2" × 3" studs.

18. Construction strength that is soundly engineered.

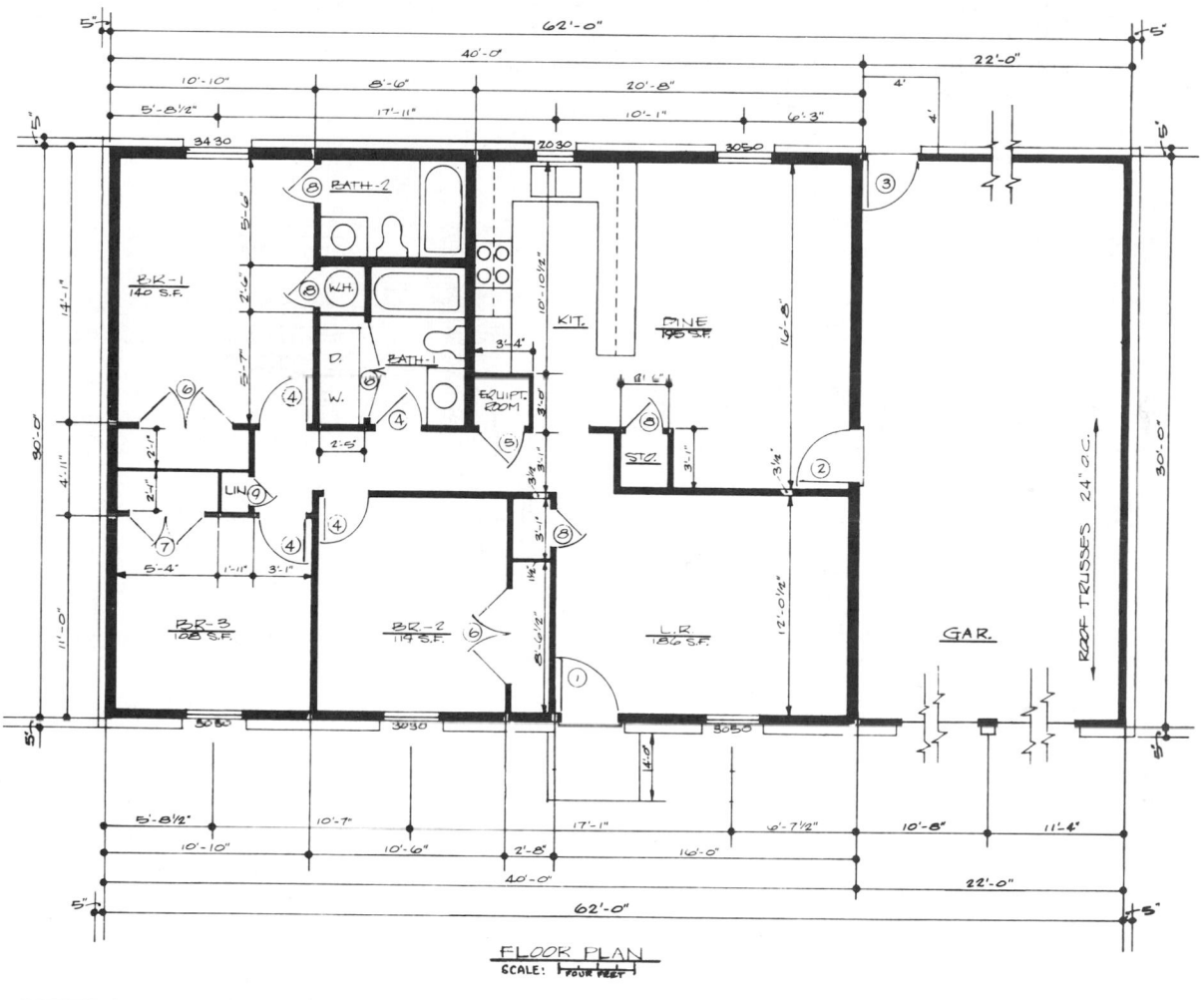

FLOOR PLAN
SCALE: ⊢ FOUR FEET ⊣

	DOOR SCHEDULE	
1.	3-0 × 6-8 × 1¾"	THERMA-TRU
2.	2-8 × 6-8 × 1¾"	THERMA-TRU
3.	2-8 × 6-8 × 1¾"	H.C. EXT.
4.	2-6 × 6-8 × 1⅜"	H.C. INT.
5.	2-6 × 6-8 × 1⅜"	H.C. INT. W/LOUVER
6.	2-6 × 6-8 × 1⅜"	H.C. INT. PAIR
7.	2-0 × 6-8 × 1⅜"	H.C. INT. PAIR
8.	2-0 × 6-8 × 1⅜"	H.C. INT.
9.	1-6 × 6-8 × 1⅜"	H.C. INT.
10.	9-0 × 7-0	O.H. GAR. DOOR

4-16. *Floor plan. Most rooms have one small window. The bathrooms have no windows. All plumbing runs are on inside walls. Full insulation, therefore, can be installed in the outside walls.*

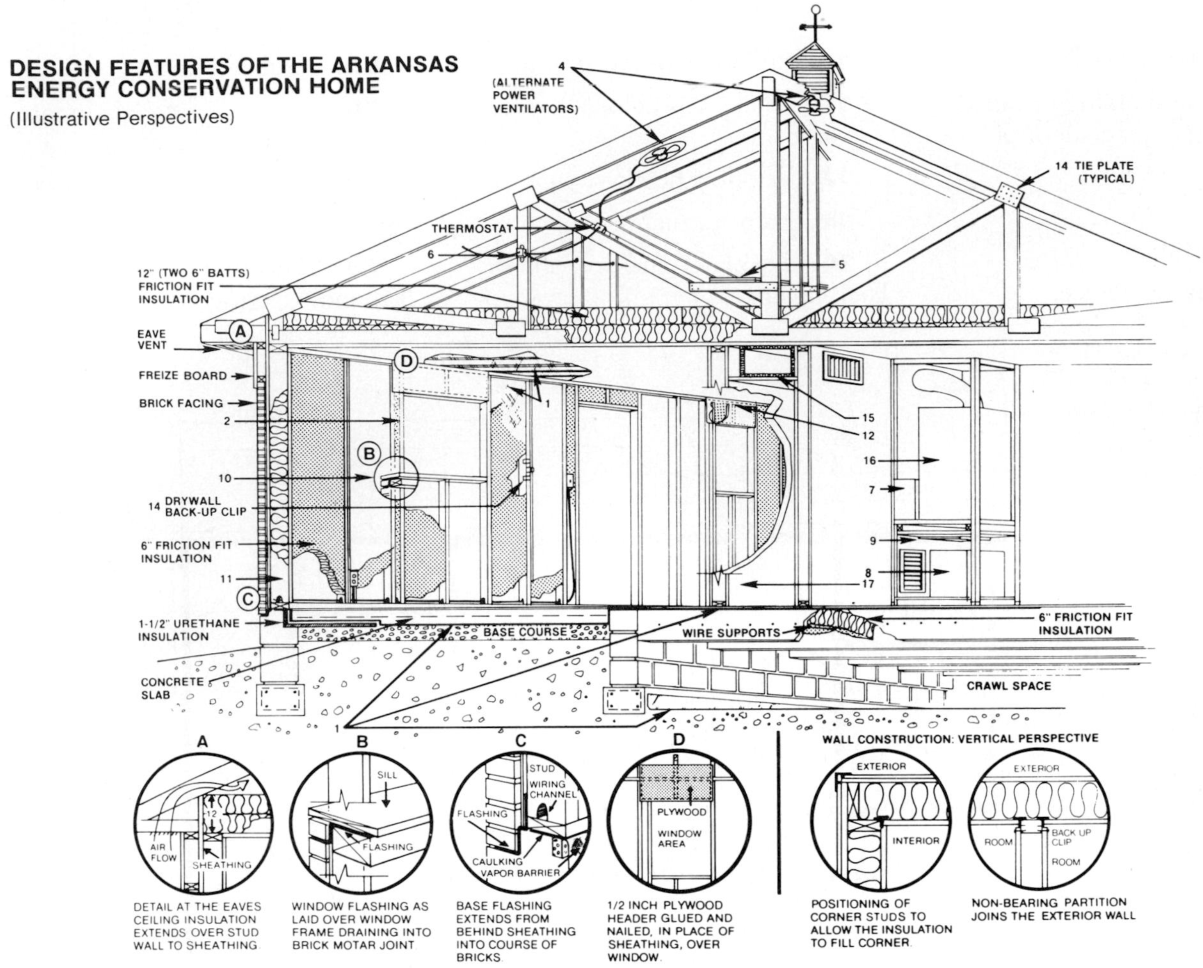

DESIGN FEATURES OF THE ARKANSAS ENERGY CONSERVATION HOME
(Illustrative Perspectives)

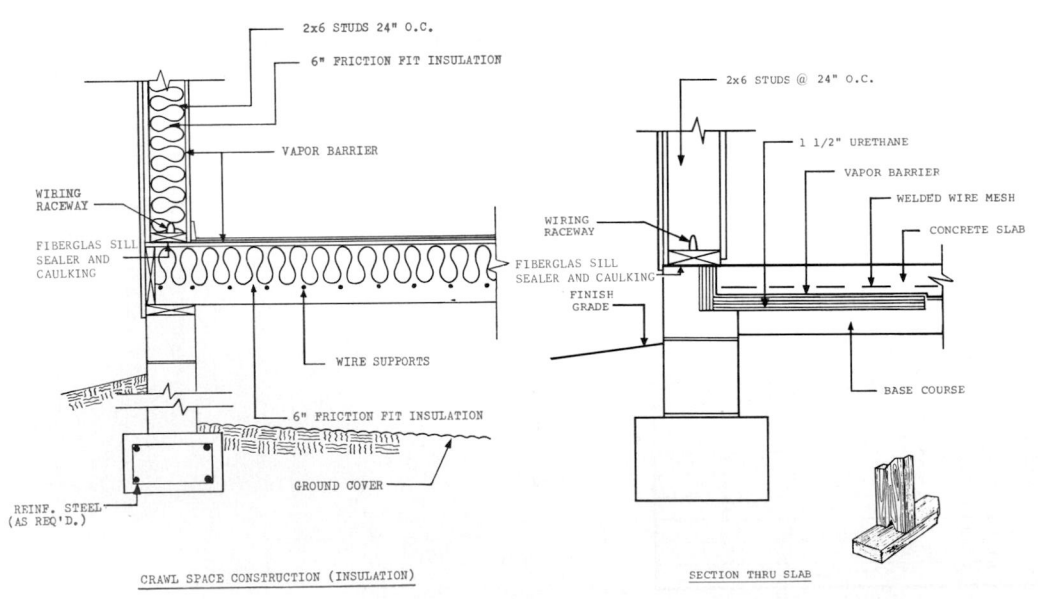

4
(ALTERNATE POWER VENTILATORS)

14 TIE PLATE (TYPICAL)

THERMOSTAT
6

5

12" (TWO 6" BATTS) FRICTION FIT INSULATION

EAVE VENT

FREIZE BOARD

BRICK FACING
2

10

14 DRYWALL BACK-UP CLIP

6" FRICTION FIT INSULATION
11

1-1/2" URETHANE INSULATION

CONCRETE SLAB

A
D
1
B

15
12

16
7

9
8
17

BASE COURSE

WIRE SUPPORTS

6" FRICTION FIT INSULATION

CRAWL SPACE

C

1
1

A — DETAIL AT THE EAVES CEILING INSULATION EXTENDS OVER STUD WALL TO SHEATHING.
AIR FLOW / SHEATHING

B — WINDOW FLASHING AS LAID OVER WINDOW FRAME DRAINING INTO BRICK MOTAR JOINT
SILL / FLASHING

C — BASE FLASHING EXTENDS FROM BEHIND SHEATHING INTO COURSE OF BRICKS.
STUD WIRING CHANNEL / FLASHING / CAULKING VAPOR BARRIER

D — 1/2 INCH PLYWOOD HEADER GLUED AND NAILED, IN PLACE OF SHEATHING, OVER WINDOW.
PLYWOOD WINDOW AREA

WALL CONSTRUCTION: VERTICAL PERSPECTIVE

POSITIONING OF CORNER STUDS TO ALLOW THE INSULATION TO FILL CORNER.
EXTERIOR / INTERIOR

NON-BEARING PARTITION JOINS THE EXTERIOR WALL
EXTERIOR / ROOM / BACK UP CLIP / ROOM

4-17. *Design features of the Arkansas Home.*

2x6 STUDS 24" O.C.
6" FRICTION FIT INSULATION
VAPOR BARRIER
WIRING RACEWAY
FIBERGLAS SILL SEALER AND CAULKING
WIRE SUPPORTS
6" FRICTION FIT INSULATION
GROUND COVER
REINF. STEEL (AS REQ'D.)

CRAWL SPACE CONSTRUCTION (INSULATION)

2x6 STUDS @ 24" O.C.
1 1/2" URETHANE
VAPOR BARRIER
WELDED WIRE MESH
CONCRETE SLAB
WIRING RACEWAY
FIBERGLAS SILL SEALER AND CAULKING
FINISH GRADE
BASE COURSE

SECTION THRU SLAB

4-18. *Section of crawl space, floor, and wall. Note the notch at the bottom of all exterior studs to form a wiring raceway. This eliminates the need to drill holes in the studs and allows full insulation in the walls without any obstruction.*

Stages in House Construction

1. The empty lot. *The construction of every new house begins with an empty lot. Location, topography, solar access and views can determine the value of a buildable lot.*

2. Foundation layout. *After the approximate location of the house has been cleared of excessive vegetation, the builder can stake out the foundation. Sometimes stringlines running between the stakes are used to identify where digging will be required.*

3. Excavation begins. *Depending on the depth and volume of excavation, various types of heavy equipment may be needed. This could include loaders, backhoes, or bulldozers. Topsoil should be removed and piled for later reuse. Other excavated materials should be used elsewhere on the site for fill if possible. This will reduce the expense of trucking and disposal.*

4. Foundation depth. *The earth should be excavated to a depth below the local frostline. This could range from 6" to 4' or more. Proper depth of footings will ensure that the foundation will not be displaced or damaged by the movement of freezing and thawing soil.*

5. Checking the excavation. *During all stages of rough sitework, the depth of the excavation should be monitored carefully. Here the builder is using a transit to check the depth of a footing trench.*

6. Forming footings. *When the excavation is complete, formwork for the foundation can be installed. In this case, concrete will be placed in the footing forms to support masonry foundation walls. When the foundation walls are concrete, the walls and the footing are often formed and placed at the same time.*

7. Foundation slabs: placement. *Many houses, particularly those in mild climates, have a concrete slab foundation. In such cases, the edges of the foundation are formed first. Then water and electric lines can be roughed in and the concrete can be placed. Note the use of wire mesh slab reinforcement.*

8. Foundation slabs: screeding. *When a section of the slab has been poured, the concrete is screeded level using boards to strike off the excess concrete. Screeding progresses section by section as the slab is completed. This worker is wearing protective boots while working in the concrete.*

10. Basement construction. *In basement construction, foundation walls of concrete or masonry must accommodate vents, beam pockets, and other structural details. The exterior surfaces should be dampproofed up to grade level with some type of foundation coating. In this photo, the black coating has already been applied to some of the walls.*

9. Foundation slabs: finishing.
*Once the entire slab has been screeded and floated, it can be troweled smooth.
On small slabs troweling can be done by hand, but on larger slabs it is more efficient to use a power trowel like the one shown in this photo. Troweling consolidates the top surface of the slab into a smoother, stronger surface.*

11. Partition and floor framing. *When the foundation walls are complete, a basement slab can be poured between them. Basement walls can then be framed. In this photo, a structural wall running the length of the house supports the center span of floor trusses. Note that the trusses run the entire width of the house. This is a very efficient structural system.*

12. Framing walls. *Once plywood, OSB, or T&G lumber decking has been nailed to the floor structure, carpenters have a solid surface on which to frame walls. The studs and wall plates are generally laid out and assembled flat on the deck. Some carpenters also apply sheathing to the walls at this point.*

13. Erecting walls. *Framed walls are tipped into place after assembly. When walls are as long as this one, sheathing is often applied after the wall is up to make the wall easier to lift. Note how wood bracing secures the previous wall in several locations.*

14. Checking the plans. *As work progresses, the plans are checked frequently to ensure the accuracy of the framing. Proper wall bracing is critical to ensure the safety of the job site. Note braces in the background of this photo.*

15. Training and safety. *The best time to teach a new employee about construction safety is when he or she first arrives on the job. Proper attire, including a hardhat, is important to maintaining a safe work site.*

16. Setting roof trusses. *As walls are completed, roof framing can begin. Many builders prefer to use roof trusses (shown here) because this speeds construction. Care should be taken to install the trusses properly, and to brace each one as it is erected.*

17. Sheathing. *Energy-efficient houses often feature insulating sheathing. This material is applied directly to the studs, and forms a tight envelope around living areas of the house. This reduces heating and cooling requirements.*

18. Interior framing details. *Interior framing becomes increasingly detailed as construction continues. This photo shows the rough framing for an L-shaped stair with landing. The framing in the foreground indicates that the floor level will drop a step, perhaps to a sunken living area.*

19. Exterior finish. *When the house has been fully framed and sheathed, scaffolding is placed in preparation for roofing installation. The scaffolding should have safety rails around all platforms. Also note the temporary electrical meter to the right of the house. This provides electricity until permanent service can be provided.*

20. Roofing. *Scaffolding permits the roofers to apply shingles around the perimeter of the roof, and in other areas that would be difficult to reach otherwise. Roof flashing can also be installed at this time.*

21. Setting windows. *The delivery of windows should be timed to coincide with the completion of sheathing. This reduces the likelihood of glass breakage during storage. Windows should be plumbed and squared carefully to ensure proper operation.*

22. Siding. *With the windows in place, panel or lap siding can be applied to the house. This photo shows horizontal wood siding being cut to length with a radial arm saw. Tables on either side of the saw support long lengths of siding. Usually one worker cuts siding while other workers install it.*

23. Installing mechanicals. *Plumbing, HVAC, and electrical systems can be installed once the house has been closed in. This work is usually done by contractors with special training. This contractor is cutting metal ducts for the heating system.*

24. Installing insulation. *Before finished wall and ceiling surfaces are installed, insulation and vapor barriers should be installed. This worker is placing fiberglass insulation batts in a ceiling cavity. Safe installation includes wearing a dust mask, gloves, and a long-sleeved shirt.*

25. Installing drywall. *Interior wall and ceiling surfaces are commonly formed by drywall. This material can be handnailed in place. A stronger installation can be made by screwing the drywall into place. This calls for the use of an electric screwdriver or screw gun.*

26. Finishing drywall. *Seams and edges of a drywalled room must be covered with a special tape embedded in joint compound. To ease the taping or texturing of ceilings, a worker sometimes wears drywall stilts. These allow him access to the entire ceiling without requiring him to move scaffolding frequently.*

27. Installing ceiling tile. *In some houses, dropped ceilings are installed instead of drywall ceilings. Lightweight squares of acoustical tile are installed within a grid of metal supporting rails. Other interior finish materials can be installed at this time.*

28. Electrical system. *The installation of the electrical system is completed in several stages during construction. After the rough-in, an electrician can complete the wiring of the service panel. Sometime later permanent power will be brought to the house. Then outlets, switches, and lighting fixtures can be installed.*

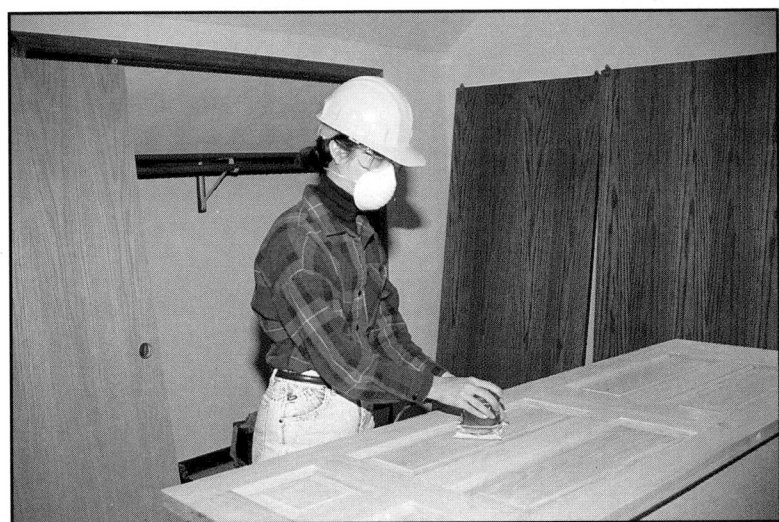

29. Finishing woodwork. *The installation of doors is one of the last tasks to be completed. Some doors are prefinished by the manufacturer. Generally, however, the doors receive a finish at the jobsite. This worker is using an electric palm sander to sand a panel door prior to finishing.*

30. Landscaping. *When all the tradespeople have completed their work, heavy equipment is again brought to the site to finish the rough grading and replace topsoil removed earlier. Then the landscapers can begin work. Here they are rolling out strips of sod for the new lawn.*

The design of the house is unique in many ways. The home has 1200 square feet of living space. It was designed with windows and doors on the front and rear walls only, with no windows or doors on either the left or the right side of the house. As a result, there is only one small window in each major room of the house. This necessitates the use of air conditioning in almost every location in the country in which the house is built.

This home reduced the heat loss 66% over a typical standard home of exactly the same size (1200 square feet) built to FHA standards. Both homes were built without a basement, but with a crawl space for heating ducts. Conservation in the *energy-saving house* was achieved as follows:

➤ Windows/doors—32.2%. Achieved by using metal doors with urethane cores, magnetic weather stripping, and double-glazed windows. The windows were limited to an area of not more than 8% of the floor area

➤ Flooring—18.2%. Achieved with floor insulation over crawl space and around the slab perimeters.

➤ Duct loss—18.4%. Achieved by using special insulation on the heating and air-conditioning ducts.

➤ Walls—7.7%. Achieved by using 2 × 6 studs on 24"centers, instead of the standard construction 2 × 4 studs on 16" or 24" centers. Six inches of insulation (R-l9) were put into the walls.

➤ Ceiling—7.5%. Achieved by using 12 inches (R-38) of insulation in the ceiling and by adding attic fans.

➤ Infiltration—15%. Achieved by using friction fit batts and polyethylene vapor barriers for walls, floors, and ceilings instead of the batts with integral vapor barriers used in standard construction.

Energy-Efficiency for Cold Climates

Where winter temperatures are particularly cold, extra care must be taken to reduce the loss of heat from houses. The Alaska Craftsman Home Program promotes voluntary energy-efficiency standards for new construction and retrofit construction. Houses meeting these standards:

➤ Meet a rigorous thermal requirement for the shell of the house.

➤ Minimize air leakage.

➤ Provide adequate air quality by using a mechanical ventilation system.

➤ Include energy-efficient lighting and appliances.

➤ Assure that safety standards are maintained.

Though there are various ways to meet these standards, one of the most interesting involves superinsulation techniques. The term "superinsulation" describes a variety of techniques that add unusually high levels of insulation to the house. Walls, for example, are typically insulated to between R-30 and R-40. Ceiling insulation ranges from R-40 to R-65. The proper and careful placement of vapor barriers is critical when superinsulating a house. Maintaining a steady supply of fresh air is also very important. Fig. 4-20.

Most superinsulated houses are built with wood-frame construction. Some of them have *strapped* walls. After the walls have been insulated, a continuous vapor barrier is stapled to the inside edges of the studs. Then 2 × 2 or 2 × 3 strapping is nailed horizontally to the studs. Additional insulation is then placed between the straps. Fig. 4-21.

By installing the straps horizontally, the two layers of insulation run at right angles to

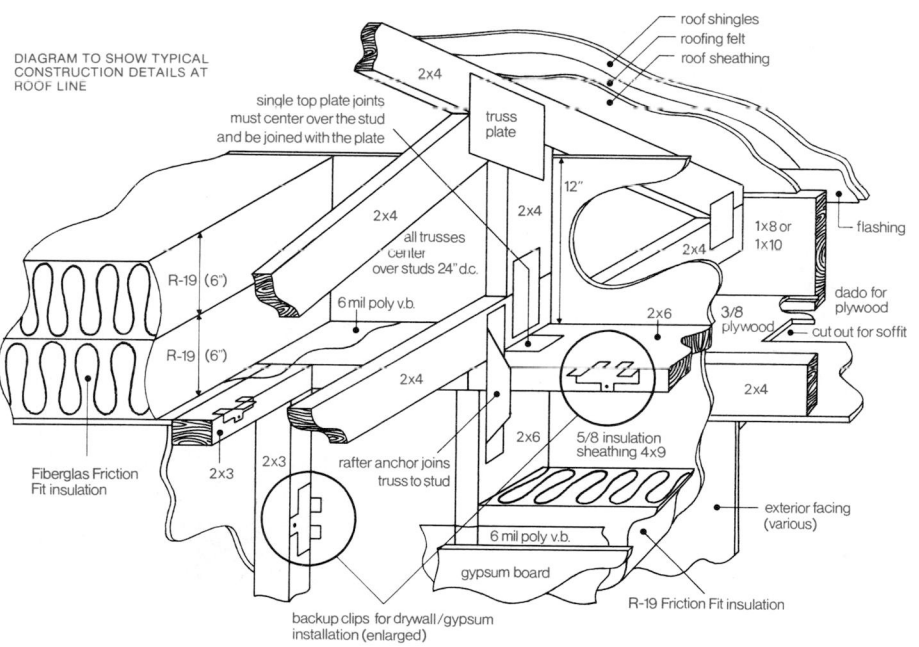

DIAGRAM TO SHOW TYPICAL CONSTRUCTION DETAILS AT ROOF LINE

4-19. *Typical construction details at the roof line.*

4-20. *A superinsulated house has thick walls to accommodate extra insulation. This photo shows a second stud wall built inside the exterior bearing wall. Note also that there is a space between the two walls. This is called a thermal break.*

each other. This minimizes thermal bridging through the studs. One advantage of a strapped wall is that wiring and plumbing runs can be installed without puncturing the continuous vapor barrier. However, one disadvantage is that the thicker walls make framing around doors and windows more difficult.

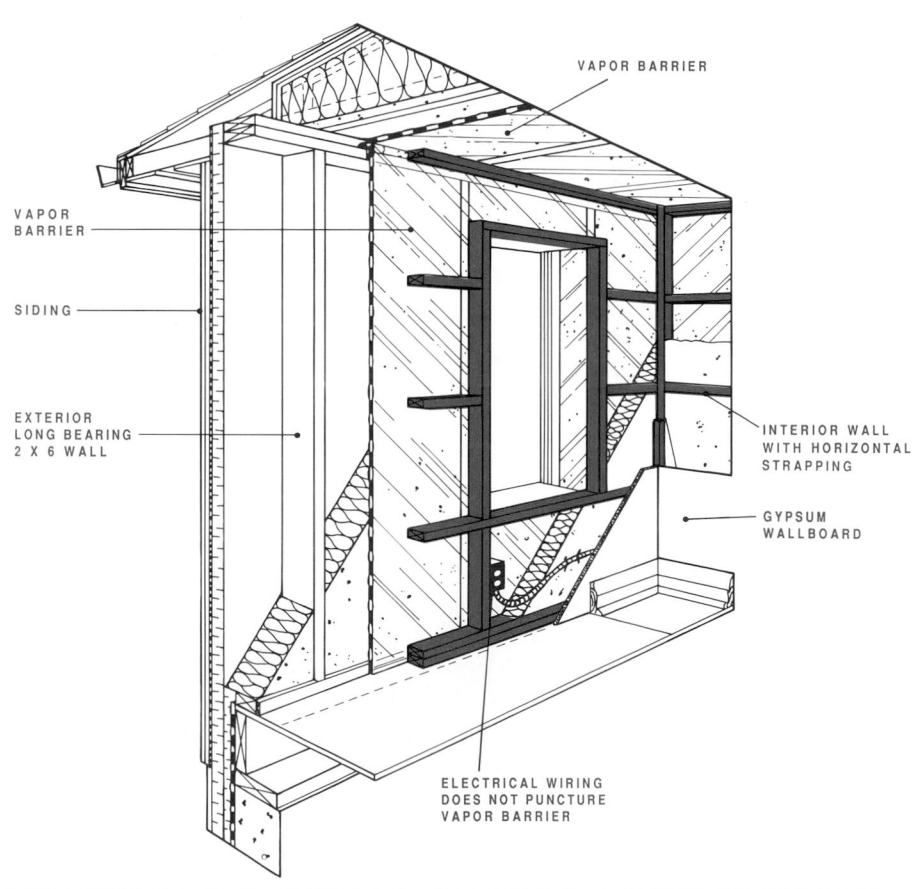

VAPOR BARRIER

VAPOR BARRIER

SIDING

EXTERIOR LONG BEARING 2 X 6 WALL

INTERIOR WALL WITH HORIZONTAL STRAPPING

GYPSUM WALLBOARD

ELECTRICAL WIRING DOES NOT PUNCTURE VAPOR BARRIER

4-21. *One type of superinsulated wall. Horizontal wood straps are nailed to the walls to create additional space for insulation.*

SOLAR HOMES

There are two basic types of solar heating systems: active and passive. An active system makes use of large solar collecting panels, usually on the roof of the house. Fig 4-22. A heat storage unit is located apart from the collector. Heated liquid or air is transferred from the collector to the storage unit and then to the living spaces by mechanical means. A complex system of pumps, fans, pipes, and ducts is needed to transfer the heat. With a passive system, the building itself collects and stores solar heat. Fig. 4-23. Large south-facing windows act as collectors. Thick walls or floors store the heat. Heat is transferred to living spaces through natural, rather than mechanical, means.

The Active System

For the builder of an active solar system, the major problems are posed by the collector and the storage unit. Most active solar energy systems specify flat plate collectors installed in or on the roof. The builder must use a roof design that accommodates these panels. Many of the collectors are built into the roof itself. Others are

4-22. *A home equipped with an active solar energy system.*

free-standing units on or over a roof. In a few homes, the solar collectors are designed as a unit separate from the house itself. The builder must also provide a piping system from the collector to the storage unit and on to the heating and air conditioning units.

The homeowner must decide whether an active solar energy system is worth its cost. The combined cost of the equipment, construction, and servicing of the system may be greater than the energy savings over a ten-to-fifteen-year period.

The Passive System

A passive solar system is less expensive because it has little or no mechanical equipment. Many homeowners, therefore, prefer the passive system.

There are five basic elements in a complete passive system.

➤ *Collector.* The collector is the large glass or plastic area through which sunlight enters the structure. Fig. 4-24. The collector must face true south, or at least within fifteen degrees either way of south. The collectors must not be shaded by buildings or trees from 9:00 A.M. to 3:00 P.M each day during the heating season. Fig. 4-25.

➤ *Absorber.* The sunlight passing through the collector is absorbed by the hard, darkened surface of the storage element. The surface is dark because dark colors absorb more heat.

➤ *Storage.* The storage element is usually either a thick masonry structure (such as a wall, floor, or room divider) or large containers of water. Both water and masonry store heat effectively. The storage unit is sometimes referred to as a thermal mass. The absorber and the storage unit are often the same wall or floor. *Absorber* applies only to the exposed surface. *Storage* refers to the material below or behind the surface. Fig. 4-26.

➤ *Distribution.* In a passive system, heat circulates from the

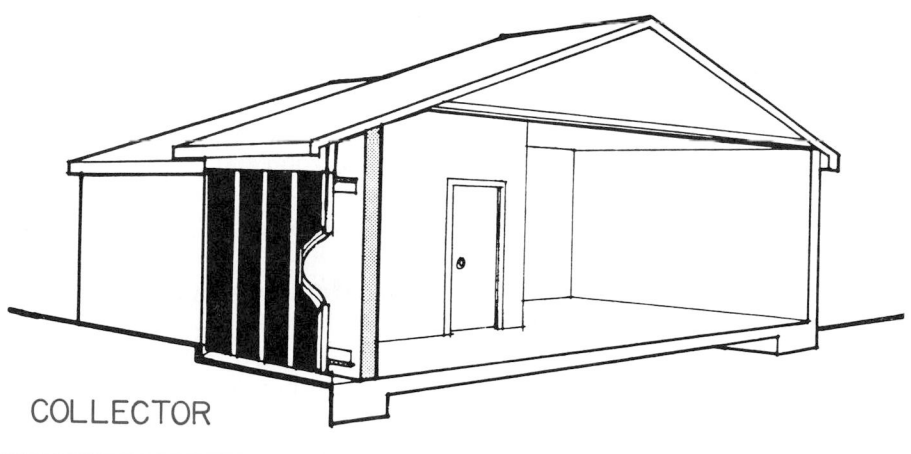

4-23. *A passive and active solar home with large windows facing south.*

COLLECTOR

4-24. *The collector must be a large area of glass or plastic.*

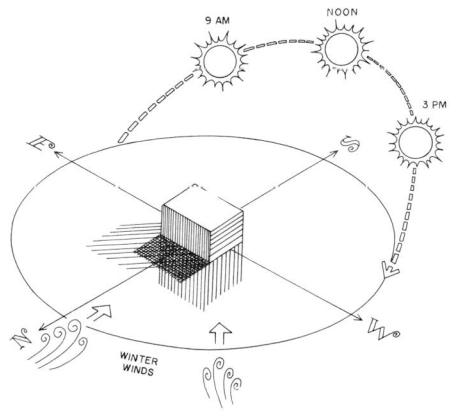

4-25. *To make the best use of sunshine and to protect against cold north winds, solar collectors should face within 15° of true south.*

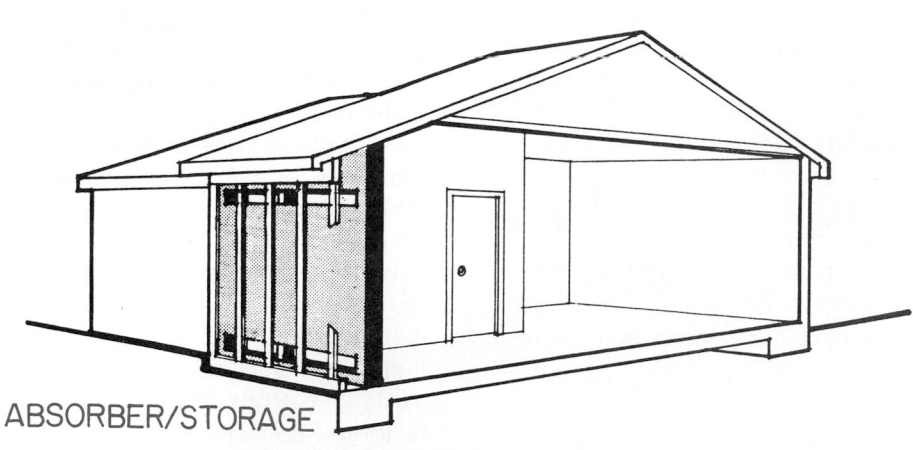

ABSORBER/STORAGE

4-26. *In many systems, the solar energy is absorbed and stored by heavy walls.*

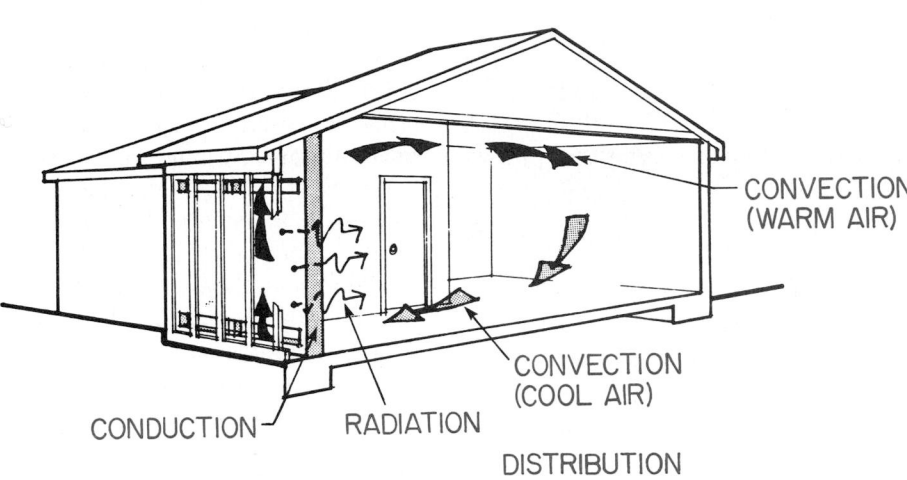

CONVECTION (WARM AIR)

CONDUCTION

RADIATION

CONVECTION (COOL AIR)

DISTRIBUTION

4-27. *Most passive solar energy systems use natural means of distributing the heat.*

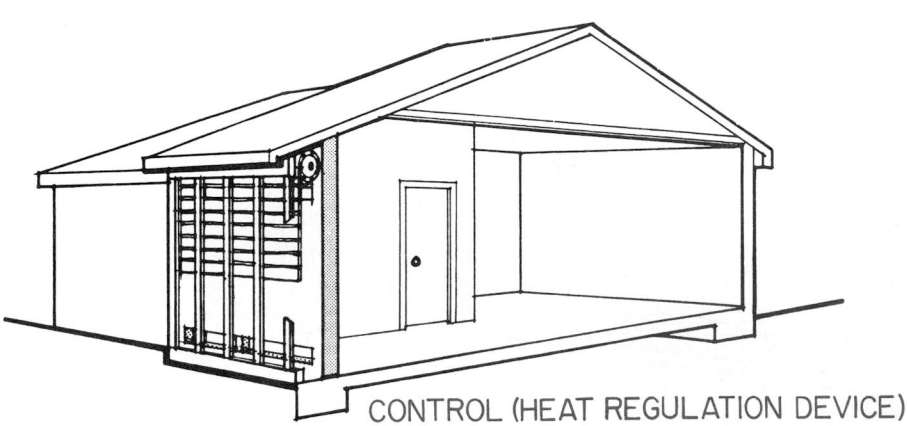

CONTROL (HEAT REGULATION DEVICE)

4-28. *Shutters or heavy curtains keep the heat from escaping during the night.*

storage unit to the living spaces by three methods: *conduction, convection,* and *radiation.* Fig. 4-27. *Conduction* refers to heat moving through solid objects. For example, a spoon placed in a cup of hot coffee conducts heat up its handle. *Convection* refers to the motion of hot air or water. Passive solar systems make use of the fact that warm air rises to create currents to heat rooms. *Radiation* is heat moving as a wave similar to light. A warmed surface inside a home will emit heat (infrared radiation) that will travel towards cooler areas. In addition to these natural means, fans and ducts are sometimes used to distribute heat.

➤ *Controls.* Controls include the insulating methods used to prevent heat loss back through the collector at night. Fig. 4-28. Curtains and shutters are normally used. Roof overhang or awnings that shade the collector in the summer and prevent overheating are also controls. Fig. 4-29. Sometimes fans, vents, and dampers are part of the control system.

Direct gain systems. There are three types of passive solar energy systems: direct gain, indirect gain, and isolated gain. With a direct gain system, sunlight heats the living spaces directly. Sunlight enters through a south-facing window and heats the air in the room. It is also absorbed in masonry walls or floors, which are typically 4" to 6" thick. At night, as the air in the room begins to cool, the walls and floor radiate the stored heat into the room. Fig. 4-30.

Indirect gain systems. With an indirect gain system, sunlight does not directly heat the living spaces. Rather, it heats a thermal mass that in turn heats the living spaces. A Trombe wall is a good example of an indirect gain system.

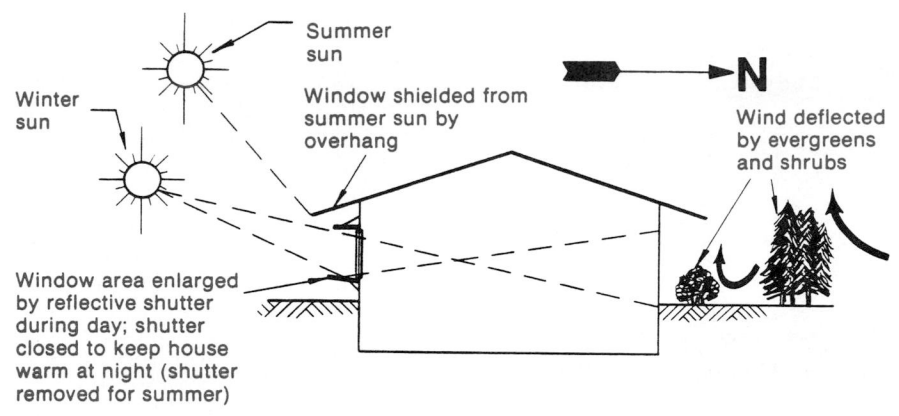

4-29. *Note how the angle of the sun changes from season to season.*

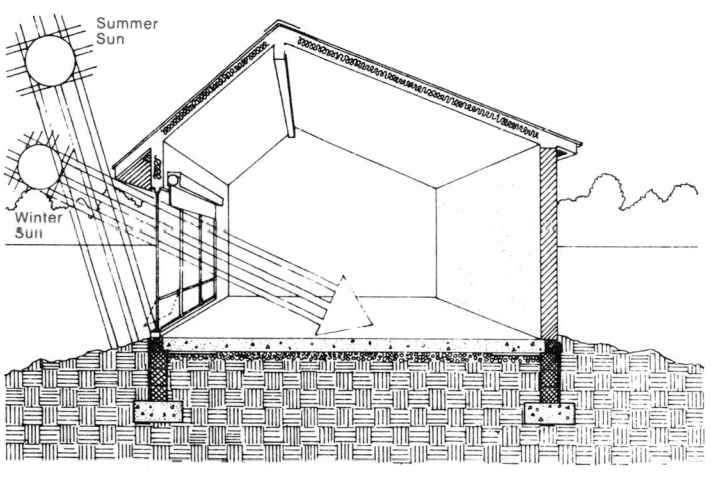

4-30. *In the direct gain system, sunlight passes through the window to heat the air in the room and to be absorbed by the walls and floors.*

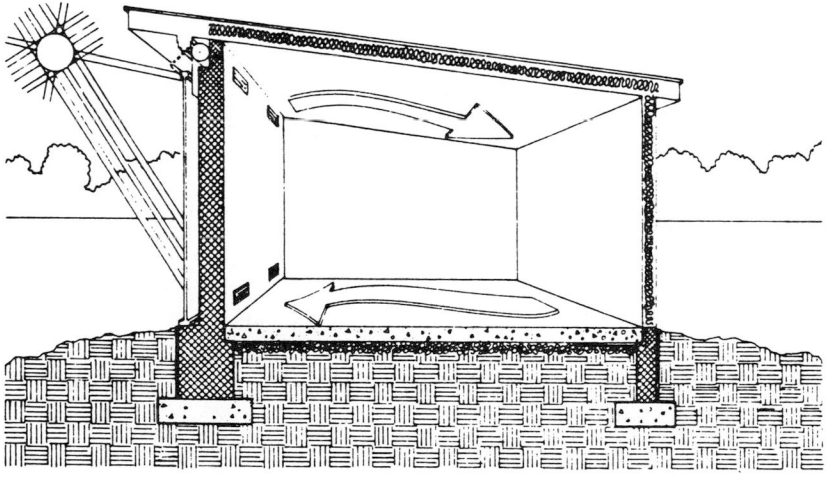

4-31. *The indirect gain system places a heat-storage mass between the windows and the room. This system reduces the problems of excessive glare and too rapid heating that often occur with direct gain systems.*

Fig. 4-31. It is a solid masonry wall 8" to 16" thick on the south side of the house. It is often made of concrete blocks that have been filled with concrete. Glass or plastic glazing is mounted about 4" in front of the wall's surface. Sunlight passes through the glazing and heats the air between the glazing and the masonry wall. Some of the heat is absorbed by the wall, passes through it by conduction, and radiates into the room on the opposite side of the wall. There are usually also vents in the Trombe wall at the top and the bottom. As the air between the wall and the glazing is heated, it rises and passes through the upper vents into the opposite room. This warm air is replaced by cooler air being drawn through the lower vents from the room. As the air is warmed by the sun, it continues to rise and pass into the room. This convection current is used to heat the living spaces opposite the Trombe wall.

The water wall is a variation of the Trombe wall. Fig 4-32. In place of a masonry wall, large containers of water are located between the living spaces and the glazing. The water absorbs the sunlight and slowly radiates the heat into the living area.

Isolated gain systems. An isolated system is one built apart from the area being heated. One such system is a solar greenhouse built as part of a house. Solar heat is collected through the greenhouse glazing. It is absorbed and stored by masonry or containers of water. The stored heat is transferred to the house by convection and radiation. Fig. 4-33.

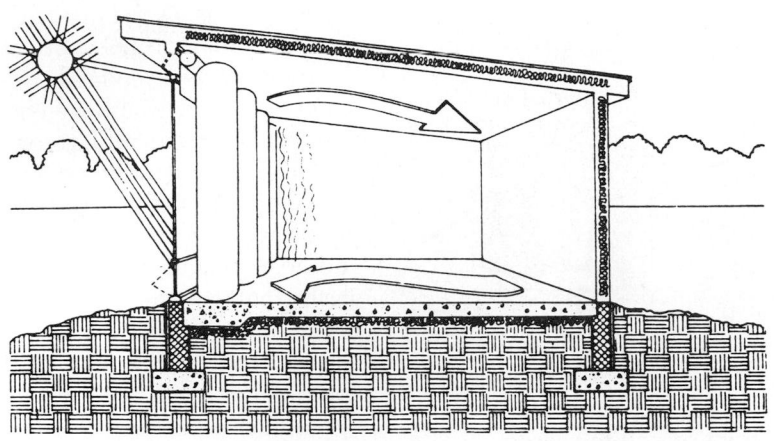

4-32. *A water wall serves the same purpose as the Trombe wall in an indirect gain system.*

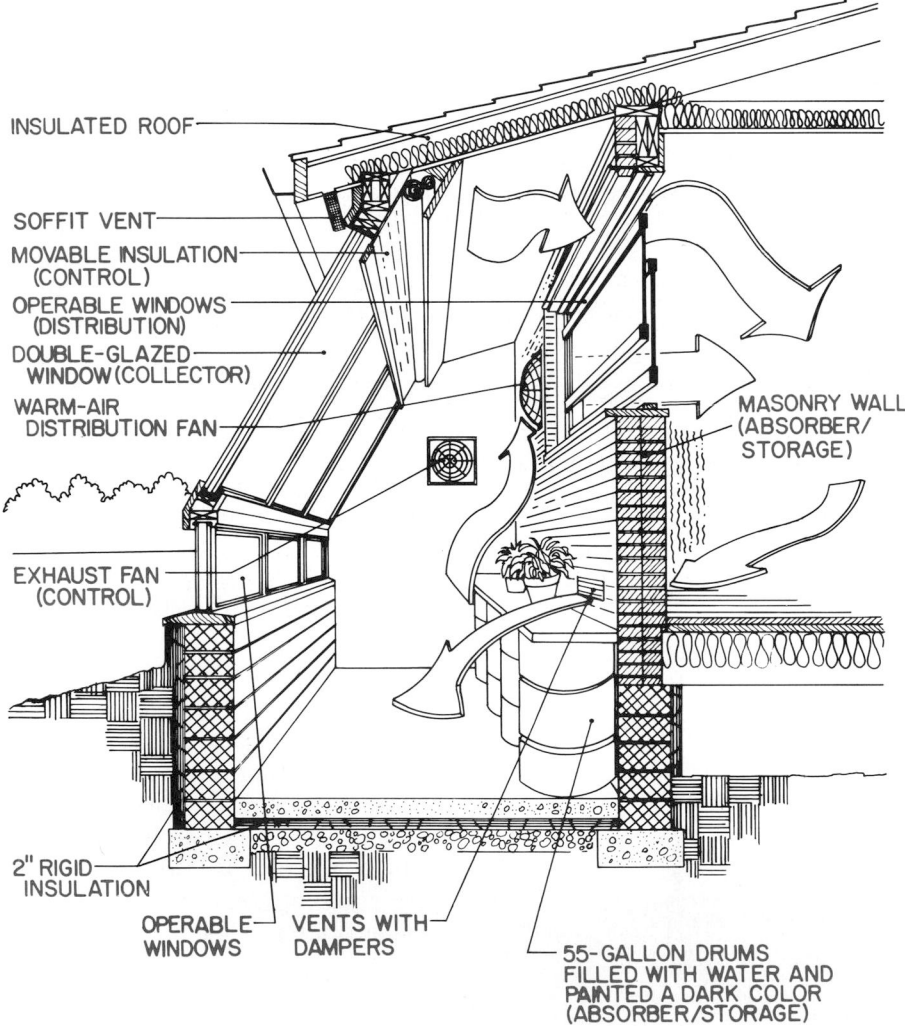

INSULATED ROOF

SOFFIT VENT

MOVABLE INSULATION (CONTROL)

OPERABLE WINDOWS (DISTRIBUTION)

DOUBLE-GLAZED WINDOW (COLLECTOR)

WARM-AIR DISTRIBUTION FAN

EXHAUST FAN (CONTROL)

MASONRY WALL (ABSORBER/STORAGE)

2" RIGID INSULATION

OPERABLE WINDOWS

VENTS WITH DAMPERS

55-GALLON DRUMS FILLED WITH WATER AND PAINTED A DARK COLOR (ABSORBER/STORAGE)

SOLAR GREENHOUSE

4-33. *The solar greenhouse is the most popular type of isolated gain system. It is the easiest to add to an existing home.*

Insulation

A high insulation level is important to a solar energy system. Basements should have two inches of rigid insulation between the wall and the ground, and if possible, three inches above the grade line. If a permanent wood foundation is used, the stud cavities should be well insulated. For slab-on-grade construction, the footings and walls should be insulated along the entire perimeter from two to four feet from the exterior walls. In cold climates, it is a good idea to insulate under the entire slab with rigid insulation.

Walls should be built with 2 × 6 studs, which will increase the amount of insulation that can be installed. No wiring or plumbing runs should go through outside walls. Use wiring raceways at the bottom of the walls. Fig 4-18.

There should be adequate insulation in the roof and the attic. Batts at least 5½" thick should be installed between 2 × 10 rafters. The floor of the attic should also be well insulated. A vapor barrier of 6-mil polyethylene should be carefully overlapped with the plastic sheet used in the wall. In hot, humid climates the roof or attic must be ventilated in the summer.

All exterior doors and windows should be insulated and should fit tightly. Double- or triple-pane insulated glass should be used. Fig. 4-34. Caulking and weather-stripping are extremely important throughout the house.

SOLAR ELECTRICITY

In recent years, much progress has been made in using the sun to provide electricity directly to a house. Many homeowners now use solar electricity systems to provide *some* electricity. With a properly designed system, however, *all* the electrical needs of a house can be met. This means that houses can be built in remote sites that are not served by utility companies. Such sites are known as being "off the grid," meaning that the house is not connected to a regional network of electrical supply lines.

The chief component of a solar electricity system is a collection of solar cells called a *photovoltaic panel*. These panels produce electricity directly from sunlight. They have no moving parts and produce no pollution as a byproduct of operation.

4-35a. *A photovoltaic panel.*

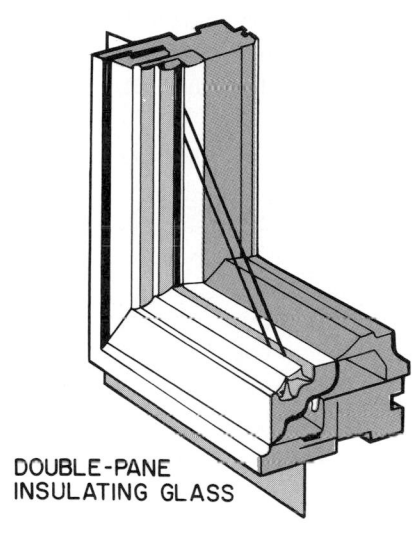

DOUBLE-PANE
INSULATING GLASS

4-35b. *Photovoltaic panels are mounted on this house just below the chimney.*

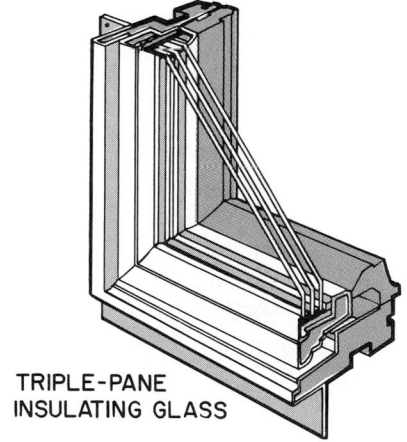

TRIPLE-PANE
INSULATING GLASS

4-34. *Double- or triple-pane windows are necessary for an effective passive solar energy system.*

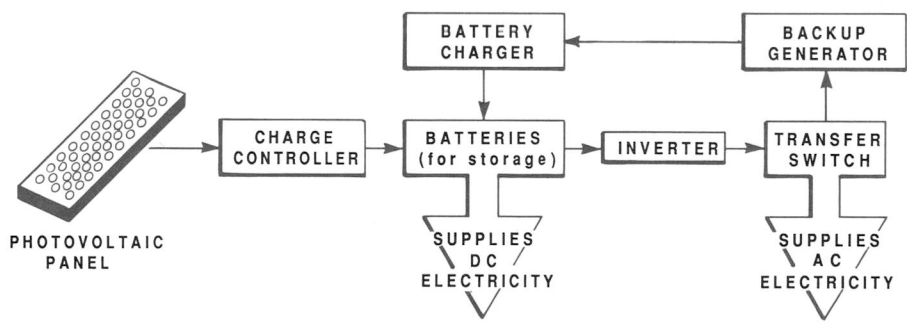

4-36. *Schematic drawing of a photovoltaic system that provides AC and DC electricity.*

Maintenance requirements are minimal. Photovoltaic panels are typically mounted on a roof. The roof should support the panels at an angle and in a direction that maximizes solar gain. Fig. 4-35.

Electricity gathered by a photovoltaic panel must be converted into a form that is usable by standard light fixtures and appliances. It must also be stored for use in periods when the sun is not shining, such as nights and cloudy days. The panels are therefore connected to a system that can provide AC and DC power on demand. Fig. 4-36.

QUESTIONS

1. What is the most important factor influencing internal temperature?

2. Name three considerations in planning an energy-efficient house.

3. Name three types of energy-efficient wall sheathing.

4. Name four things that can improve the energy efficiency of a standard house.

5. How does the framing in the Arkansas Home differ from that in a standard house?

6. What are the two main types of solar energy systems?

7. Name the five basic elements in a passive solar energy system.

8. What are three important characteristics of a superinsulated house?

9. What is a photovoltaic panel?

ACTIVITIES

1. Math. The heating and air conditioning costs for a given house for a year are $650 and $250 respectively. By spending $450 in energy conservation measures, heating costs would decrease by 15% and air-conditioning costs would decrease by 10%.

a. Assuming constant energy costs, how many years will be required to recover the costs of these conservation measures?

b. Assuming a 10% increase in energy costs each year, how much will be saved in five years by the conservation measures?

c. Discuss with a friend what this would mean over the lifetime of the house.

2. Language Arts. Imagine building a home in the year 2035. Based on everything you have read in this unit, describe how you think homes will be built in 2035. Realistically consider a typical home's size, the materials that will be used, the conservation needs, and the construction methods. Use your imagination, but base your "vision" on the factual information that was presented in this unit.

3. Social Studies. Read carefully the information under the heading "Standard Home Construction" in this unit. Write down at least three ways you could improve the energy efficiency of your home.

THE SCHOOL-TO-WORK CONNECTION

The type and quality of windows are major factors affecting the energy efficiency of a house. Window construction has changed to improve energy efficiency. One of the biggest improvements in window energy efficiency relates to glass (or glazing). Advances in glass manufacturing technology have resulted in advanced glazing types that reduce heat loss (in heating climates) or heat gain (in cooling climates). The effectiveness of window glass is usually expressed in terms of its R-value.

1. Write to three window manufacturers, requesting a catalog of their most energy-efficient windows. Once you have all three catalogs, find the windows in each that have the greatest R-value and compare them. Which window is the most energy-efficient?

UNIT
5

Wood as a Building Material

For all-around utility, wood has few if any equals as a building material. Fig. 5–1. Wood's advantages are numerous:

➤ Wood is a renewable resource.

➤ Wood is light in weight. It is easily shipped and handled.

➤ Wood is easily worked into various shapes.

➤ Wood is easily fastened with nails, staples, bolts, connectors, screws, or glue.

➤ Wooden buildings are easily altered or repaired. Openings can be cut and additions made without difficulty.

➤ Wood makes a smooth, sanitary interior, holds a decorative coating, and lends itself well to preservative treatments. (See Appendix for information on finishing wood.)

➤ Wood is strong. Pound for pound, certain common framing woods are actually as strong and stiff as fairly good steel, and stronger than cast iron.

➤ Wood has low heat conductivity, which helps keep buildings warm.

➤ Wood resists rust, acids, salt water, and other corrosive agents better than many other structural materials.

➤ Wood has high salvage value compared with original cost.

➤ Wood combines well with other materials.

TREE GROWTH

A tree is a woody plant having one main self-supporting stem or trunk, at least 10 feet tall at maturity, crowned by leafy boughs. Like human beings, trees require food. They need water. They cannot grow without the sun's rays. Fig. 5–2.

The growing, "working," parts of a tree are the *tips of its roots*, the *terminal buds*, the *leaves*, and a layer of cells just inside the bark, called the *cambium*. It is the cambium layer which produces new wood. Inside the cambium is the sapwood, which carries sap from the roots to the leaves. At the center is the heartwood which is not living, but which gives strength and rigidity to the tree. Water from the soil enters a tree through its roots. The water

5-1. *Wood is the basic building material used in most of the homes built in the United States.*

travels upward through the sapwood into the leaves where it is combined with carbon dioxide from the air. Through a marvelous process called *photosynthesis*, the energy of light transforms these substances into food to nourish the whole tree. The food is carried from the leaves back down to the branches, trunk, and roots through the inner bark.

After a tree is harvested, its life story can be read in the rings on the stump. In the temperate zone one ring is added for each year of growth. Most annual rings consist of a light band formed in the spring (early wood), and a dark band formed in the summer (late wood). When growth conditions are favorable and food and water abundant, the rings are wide. When drought or other adverse conditions occur, growth slows down and the rings are narrow.

The annual rings are also visible when you look at the end grain of lumber. Fig. 5–3. Experienced builders sometimes look at the rings on framing lumber to determine the suitability of the lumber for certain uses.

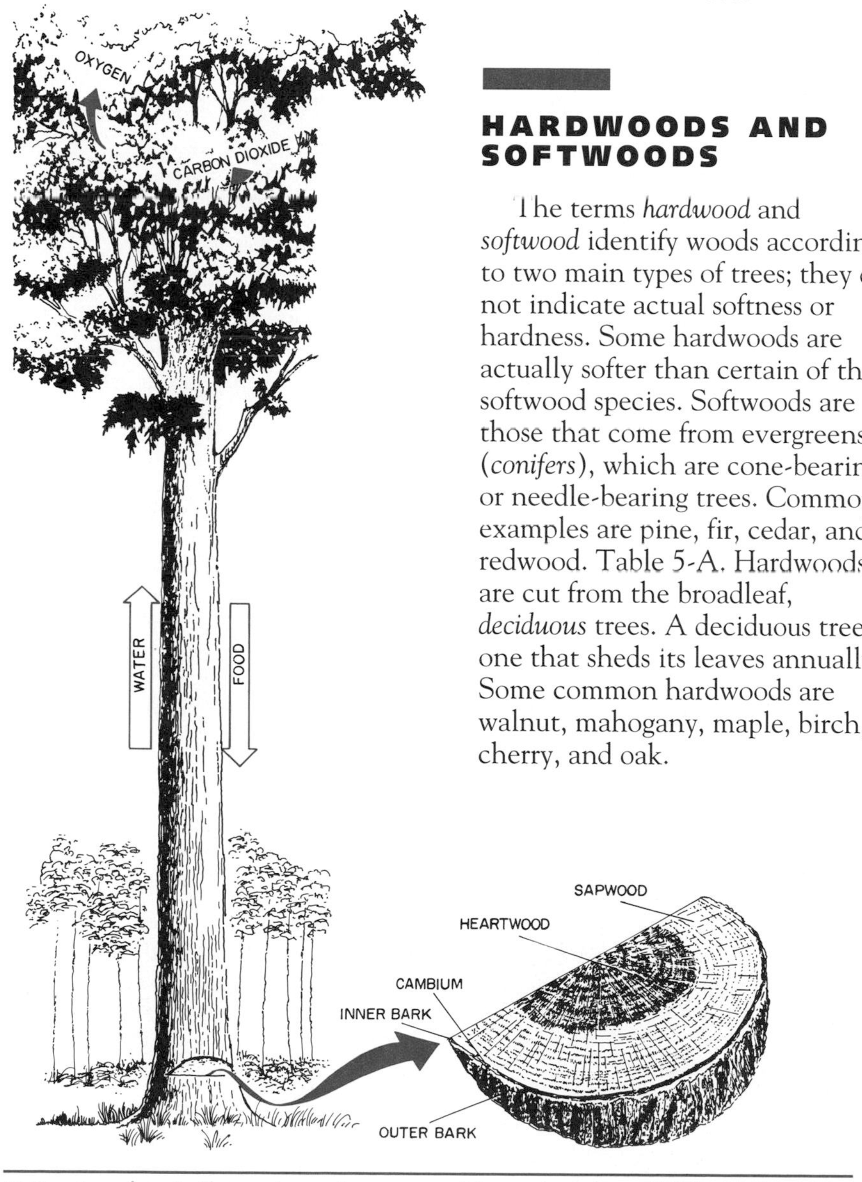

5-3. *Growth rings are evident in the end grain of lumber.*

HARDWOODS AND SOFTWOODS

The terms *hardwood* and *softwood* identify woods according to two main types of trees; they do not indicate actual softness or hardness. Some hardwoods are actually softer than certain of the softwood species. Softwoods are those that come from evergreens (*conifers*), which are cone-bearing or needle-bearing trees. Common examples are pine, fir, cedar, and redwood. Table 5-A. Hardwoods are cut from the broadleaf, *deciduous* trees. A deciduous tree is one that sheds its leaves annually. Some common hardwoods are walnut, mahogany, maple, birch, cherry, and oak.

METHODS OF CUTTING BOARDS FROM LOGS

There are two common ways of cutting boards. Fig. 5–4. The first is called *plain sawn* (when it is hardwood) or *flat grained* (when softwood). The log is squared and sawed lengthwise (tangent to the annual growth rings). The second method is called *quarter saw* (when hardwood) or *edge grained* (when softwood). This lumber is not cut parallel to the grain, but sawed so that its rings form angles of 45° to 90° with the surface.

Plain-sawn lumber is usually cheaper, and its defects extend through fewer boards. It is also easier to kiln dry and produces greater widths. However, it has a high tendency to shrink and warp.

Quarter-sawn lumber has a low tendency to warp, shrink, and swell, provides a more durable surface, does not tend to twist or cup, and holds paints and finishes better.

SEASONING

When a tree is cut down, the wood may contain from 30 to 300% more moisture than it will after drying. For example, a cubic foot of oak may contain as much as 14 quarts of water. Fig. 5–5.

OXYGEN

CARBON DIOXIDE

WATER

FOOD

SAPWOOD

HEARTWOOD

CAMBIUM

INNER BARK

OUTER BARK

5-2. *Lumber is the only major renewable material available for building.*

Table 5-A. *Commercial Names of the Principal Softwoods.*

Commercial Names for Lumber	Official Common Tree Names	Botanical Names
Cedar:		
Alaska Cedar	Alaska-cedar	Chamaecyparis nootkatensis
Incense Cedar	incense-cedar	Libocedrus decurrens
Port Orford Cedar	Port-Orford-cedar	Chamaecyparis lawsoniana
Eastern Red Cedar	eastern red cedar	Juniperus virginiana
	southern red cedar	J. silicicola
Western Red Cedar	western red cedar	Thuja plicata
Northern White Cedar	northern white-cedar	Thuja occidentalis
Southern White Cedar	Atlantic white-cedar	Chamaecyparis thyoides
Cypress	bald cypress	Taxodium distichum
	pond cypress	T. distichum var. nutans
Fir:		
Balsam Fir	balsam fir	Abies balsamea
	Fraser fir	A fraseri
Douglas Fir	Douglas-fir	Pseudotsuga menziesii
Noble Fir	noble fir	Abies procera
White Fir	subalpine fir	Abies lasiocarpa
	California red fir	A. magnifica
	grand fir	A. grandis
	noble fir	A. procera
	Pacific silver fir	A. amabilis
	white fir	A. concolor
Hemlock:		
Eastern Hemlock	Carolina hemlock	Tsuga caroliniana
	eastern hemlock	T. canadensis
Mountain Hemlock	mountain hemlock	Tsuga mertensiana
West Coast Hemlock	western hemlock	Tsuga heterophylla
Juniper:		
Western Juniper	Alligator juniper	Juniperus deppeana
	Rocky Mountain juniper	J. scopulorum
	Utah juniper	J. osteosperma
	western juniper	J. occidentalis
Larch:		
Western Larch	western larch	larix occidentalis
Pine:		
Jack Pine	jack pine	Pinus banksiana
Lodgepole Pine	lodgepole pine	P. contorta
Norway Pine	red pine	P. resinosa
Ponderosa Pine	ponderosa pine	P. ponderosa
Sugar Pine	sugar pine	P. lambertiana
Idaho White Pine	western white pine	P. monticola
Northern White Pine	eastern white pine	Pinus strobus
Longleaf Yellow Pine	longleaf pine	Pinus palustris
	slash pine	P. eliottii
Southern Yellow Pine	loblolly pine	Pinus taeda
	longleaf pine	P. palustris
	pitch pine	P. rigida
	shortleaf pine	P. echinata
	slash pine	P. eliottii
	Virginia pine	P. virginiana
Redwood:	redwood	Sequoia sempervirens
Spruce:		
Eastern Spruce	black spruce	Picea mariana
	red spruce	P. rubens
	white spruce	P. glauca
Engelmann Spruce	blue spruce	Picea pungens
	Engelmann spruce	P. engelmannii
Sitka Spruce	Sitka spruce	Picea sitchensis
Tamarack	Tamarack	Larix laricina
Yew:		
Pacific Yew	Pacific yew	Taxus brevifolia

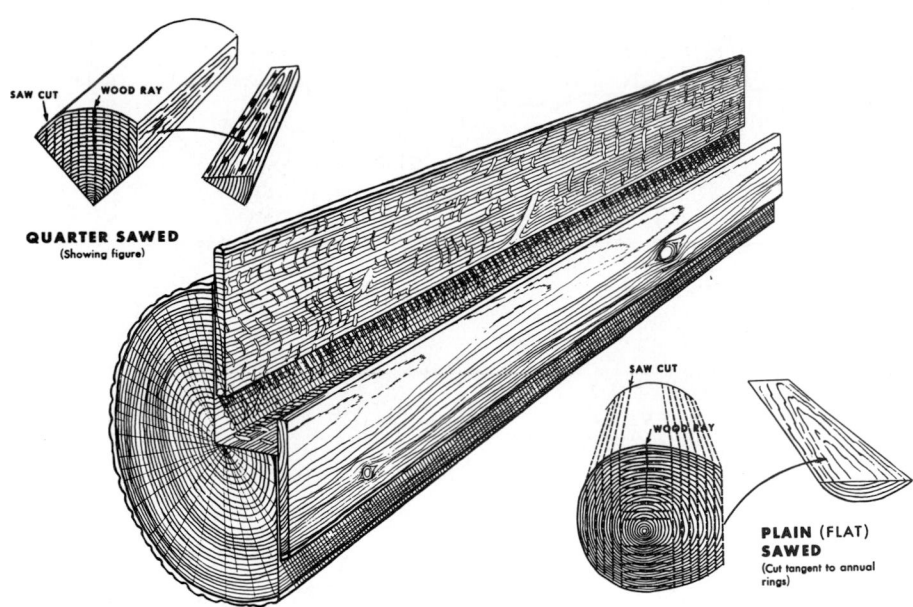

5-4. *Common methods of cutting lumber.*

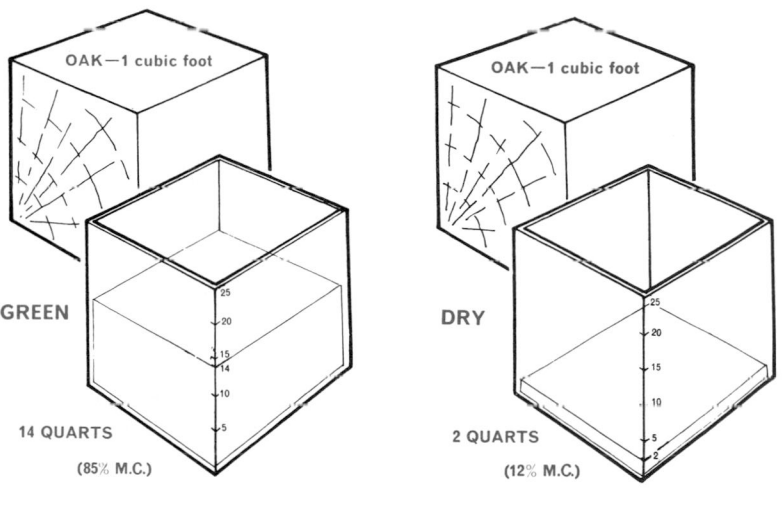

5-5. *Compare the amounts of water in green and dried lumber.*

There are two methods of seasoning or drying wood: *air drying* and *kiln drying*. Air drying, or seasoning, is done out of doors. The rough lumber is stacked either on edge at an angle or in layers separated by crosspieces called *stickers*. The wood is allowed to remain stacked usually from one to three months and sometimes longer. After correct air drying, the wood should have an average moisture content of 19% or less.

In kiln drying, the lumber is stacked in piles also with stickers between the boards. It is then placed in a *kiln*—an oven in which moisture, air, and temperature are carefully controlled. Steam is applied to the wood at low heat; then the steam is reduced and the heat increased. As the heat increases, moisture is taken out of the wood. Properly kiln-dried lumber has less than 10% moisture content. Green, 1" lumber can be dried to 6 to 12% moisture content in three or four days in a modern kiln. Moisture content can be checked during the drying process with a moisture meter.

In both kinds of drying, seasoning causes some defects that downgrade the quality of the lumber. Among the most common are checks, honeycombs, warps, loosening of knots, and cracks caused by unequal shrinkage.

MOISTURE CONTENT

Moisture content (M.C.) is a measure of the amount of water contained in wood. M.C. is expressed as a percentage of the oven-dry weight of the wood—the lower the percentage, the drier the wood. For interior woodwork, the recommended moisture content varies with the part of the country. Fig. 5–6.

In the drying process lumber tends to shrink, both in width and length. However, shrinkage in length is normally so small that in almost all species it is not considered a problem.

Water exists in green wood in two conditions: *free* in the cell cavities, and *absorbed* in the cell walls. When the cell walls have absorbed all the water they can hold, but there is no water in the cavities, the wood is at the *fiber-saturation point*. Water in excess of this amount cannot be absorbed by the cell walls. Therefore, it fills the cell cavities. Removal of this free water has no apparent effect upon the properties of wood except to reduce its weight. However, as soon as any water in the cell walls is removed, wood begins to shrink. Since the free water is the first to

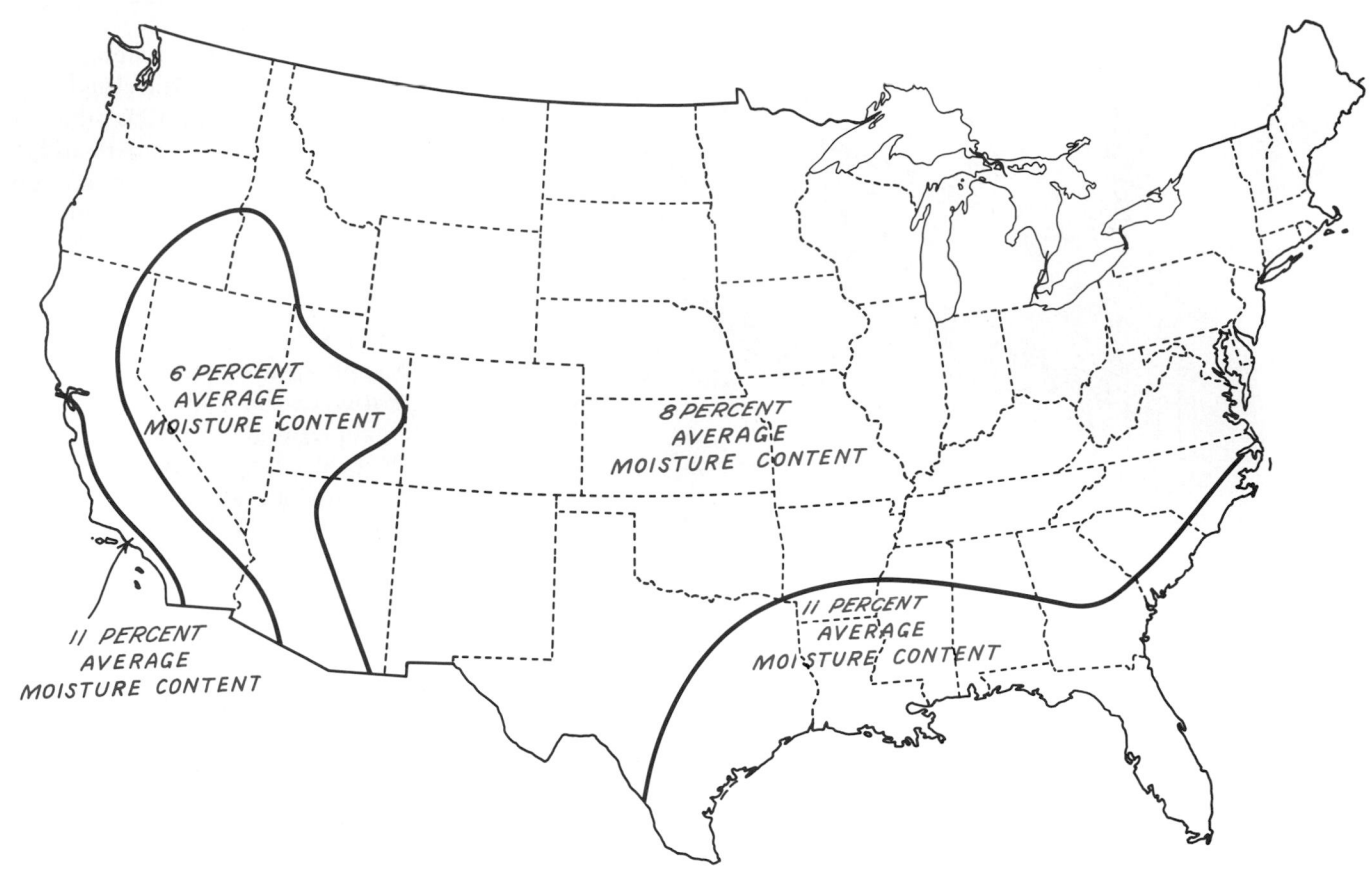

5-6. *Recommended average moisture content for lumber to be used for interior woodwork in buildings in various areas of the U.S. In Canada the recommended moisture contents are as follows: Vancouver, 11%; Saskatoon, 7%; Ottawa, 8%; Halifax, 9%. (These cities represent four major geographical areas.)*

be removed, shrinkage does not begin until after the fiber-saturation point is reached.

The fiber-saturation point varies from about 23 to 30% moisture content but, for practical purposes, it can be taken as approximately 28% for most woods. Therefore reductions in moisture from natural or green condition down to roughly 28% do not result in shrinkage. The desired moisture content of lumber depends on its use. Fig. 5–7.

After the fiber-saturation point has been passed and the cell walls begin to give up their moisture, they shrink in all directions and not uniformly. Shrinkage is actually the contraction of cell walls. This process causes a certain amount of shrinkage across the face of wood that is edge grained

(vertical) or quarter sawed and about twice as much in plain-sawed lumber. Even though lumber is dried to a certain percentage it will continue to pick up or give off water, depending on the condition of the air. If the air is damp, dry wood will swell, causing many problems. If the air is very dry, the wood will shrink. When the moisture content is in balance with the humidity of the surrounding air and neither gains or loses moisture, the wood is said to have *equilibrium moisture content*. Fig. 5–8.

Checking Moisture Content

There are two common ways of determining moisture content. One is by oven-drying methods, and the

other is by using a moisture meter.

Use of a moisture meter is the more common method. Fig. 5–9. While the meter readings do not show the same accuracy as those obtained with an oven sample, they are good enough for building construction. These meters provide the only means of checking moisture content rapidly. This is often necessary when lumber is being processed through a manufacturing plant, as in the production of mass produced housing or in on-site home building.

There are two types of moisture meters. One has needles which pierce the lumber and measure the electrical resistance of current flow through the wood. The other is a capacity-type that measures the

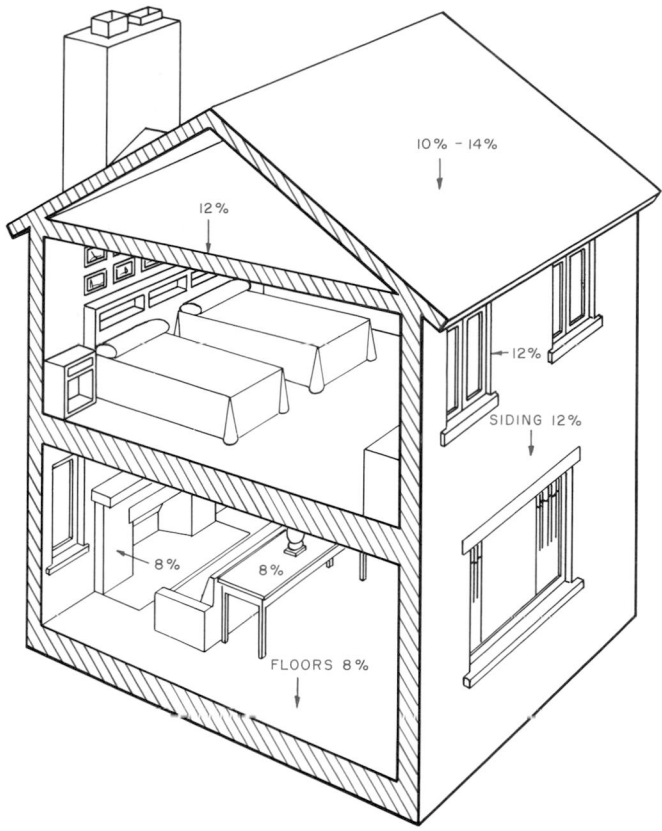

5-7. *Best moisture content of lumber for various uses.*

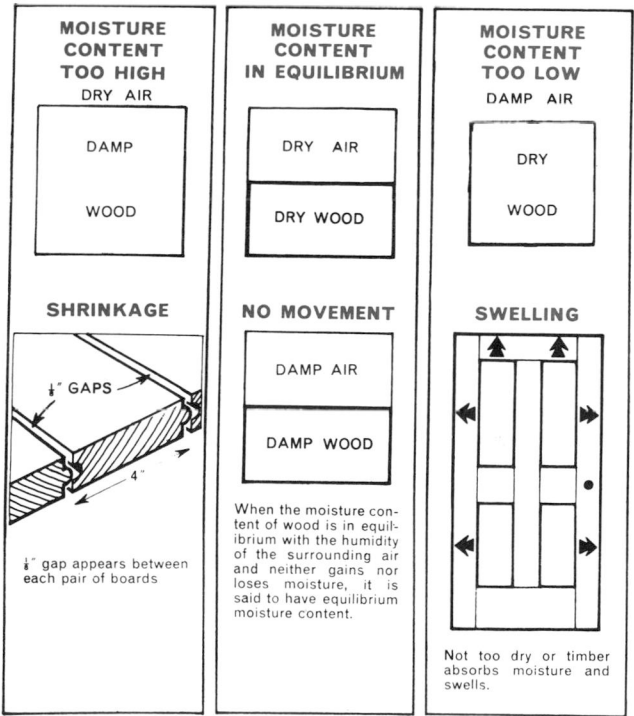

5-8. *Wood at the correct moisture content reduces swelling and shrinkage to a minimum.*

relation between moisture content and a constant setting. This second type can be recognized by the plates or shoes which are applied to the lumber surface.

The accuracy of most meters is within the range of plus or minus 1% of the true figure—assuming that moisture content is uniform throughout the thickness of the board. However, moisture is not always uniform. For example, when lumber is dried rapidly in a kiln, higher moisture is found in the center of the piece than on the outside. Therefore a more accurate reading can be obtained by cutting off the end of a board and inserting the needles in the end grain near the center of the piece. Meters should never be used on foggy days or when the air is excessively humid. Top boards or outside pieces that have been exposed to the weather for some time may be

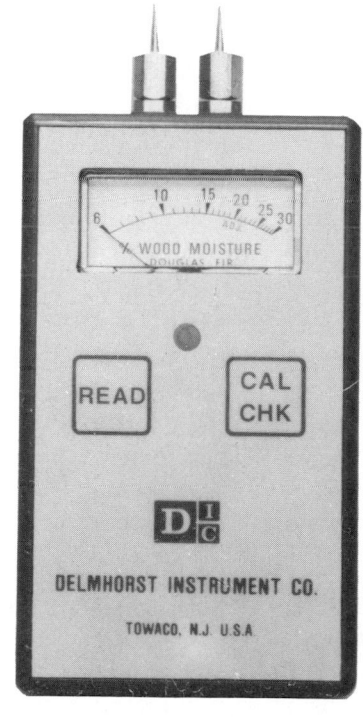

5-9. *Electronic moisture meters give a reading of the moisture content of wood.*

above or below the average of the lumber pile.

In house construction, such things as the prevention of plaster cracks and the fitting of drawers and doors depend on the use of lumber with proper moisture content.

GRADES OF LUMBER

A tree grows much like an onion, adding a new layer each year. When the tree is small, the limbs are low to the ground. As it grows larger, the lower limbs drop off and additional material fills out the tree's diameter. In the growing process, many defects develop in wood that lower its quality. For example, each limb that drops causes a knot to form, but as a tree increases in diameter, the growth covers these knots. Because of this, the best quality lumber is found in the lower part of the trunk near the outside.

So that the purchaser can know the quality of the wood he or she buys, lumber is classified in grades, according to the defects in it. In the grading process, a lumber piece must meet the lowest requirements for its grade. Wide differences in quality are found in the same grade because some lumber is much better than the minimum for its grade, but not quite good enough for a higher classification. In the lumberyard, the sawer (or *sawyer*) attempts to cut each log into pieces of the best possible grade. The actual grading is done by specialists either manually or electronically (using computers).

Defects in Standard Grades

Defects in lumber are the faults which detract from the quality of the piece, either in appearance or utility. Fig. 5–10. About twenty-five characteristics and conditions which occur in softwood lumber are used when grading. These terms and their definitions are found in any set of grading rules. Some of the more common terms and definitions used by the woodworker are:

Check. Lengthwise grain separation, usually occurring through the growth rings as a result of seasoning.

Decay. Disintegration of wood substance due to action of wood-destroying fungi.

Knot. Branch or limb embedded in the tree and cut through in the process of lumber manufacture; classified according to size, quality, and occurrence. To determine the size of a knot, average the maximum length and maximum width unless otherwise specified.

Pitch. Accumulation of resin in the wood cells in a more or less irregular patch.

Pitch-pocket. An opening between growth rings which usually contains or has contained resin, bark, or both.

Shake. A lengthwise grain separation between or through the growth rings. May be further classified as ring shake or pitch shake.

Split. Lengthwise separation of the wood extending from one surface through the piece to the opposite or an adjoining surface.

Stain. Discoloration on or in lumber other than its natural color.

Summerwood. Denser outer portion of each annual ring, usually without easily visible pores, formed late in the growing period, not necessarily in summer.

Torn grain. Part of the wood torn out in dressing.

Wane. This is bark or lack of wood from any cause on the edge or corner of a piece.

Warp. Any variation from a true or plane surface; includes bow, crook, cup, or any combination thereof.

Bow. Deviation flatwise from a straight line from end to end of a piece, measured at the point of greatest distance from the straight line.

Crook. Deviation edgewise from a straight line from end to end of a piece, measured at the point of greatest distance from the straight line; classified as slight, small, medium, and large. Based on a piece 4" wide and 16' long, the distance for each degree of crook shall be: *slight crook* = 1"; *small crook* = 1-1½"; *medium crook* = 3"; and *large crook* = over 3". For wider pieces it shall be ⅛" less for each additional 2" of width. Shorter or longer pieces may have the same curvature.

Cup. Deviation flatwise from a straight line across the width of a piece, measured at the point of greatest distance from the line; classified as slight, medium, and deep. Based on a piece 12" wide, the distance from each degree of cup shall be: *slight cup*, ¼"; *medium cup*, ⅜"; *deep cup*, ½". Narrower or wider pieces may have the same curvature.

The poorest quality piece permitted in each grade is specified by the grading rules. As assurance to the purchaser, many manufacturers of softwood lumber stamp the grade on the end, edge, or face of the piece.

Hardwood Lumber Grading

Hardwoods are available in three common grades, *firsts* and *seconds* (FAS), *select*, and *No. 1 common*. Generally, firsts and seconds are used for built-ins and paneling.

Grading rules for hardwood lumber have been established by the National Hardwood Lumber Association. Each different kind of hardwood lumber has a slightly different grading standard.

Relatively little hardwood is used in building construction, but it is used where particular beauty or durability is important. Places where hardwoods are sometimes used include door and window

5-10a. *Round knot hole through two wide faces.*

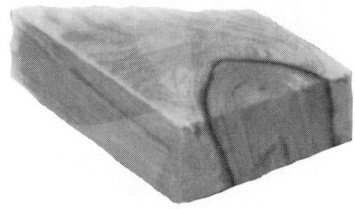

5-10b. *Sound, encased knot through two wide faces.*

5-10c. *Sound, star-checked, intergrown knot through two wide faces.*

5-10d. *Sound, intergrown knot through two narrow faces.*

5-10e. *Sound, intergrown knot through all four faces.*

5-10f. *Sound, intergrown knot through three faces.*

5-10g. *Wane is the presence of bark or lack of wood from any cause on the edges or corners of a piece of lumber.*

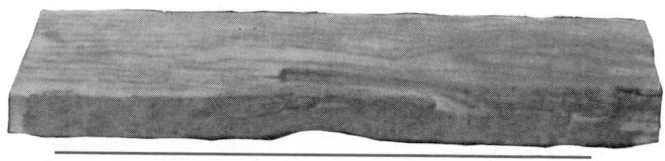

5-10i. *White Speck and Honeycomb are caused by a fungus in the living tree. White Speck is small white pits or spots. Honeycomb is similar but the pits are deeper or larger. Neither is subject to further decay unless used under wet conditions.*

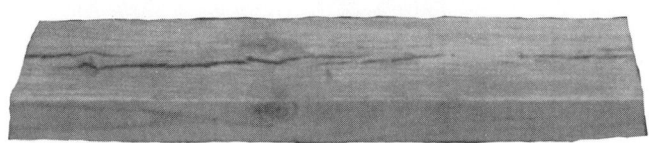

5-10h. *Shake is a lengthwise separation of the wood which usually occurs between or through the annual growth rings.*

5-10j. *Decay is a disintegration of the wood substance due to action of wood-destroying fungi. It also may be called dote, rot or unsound wood.*

5-10k. *Splits are similar to checks except the separations of the wood fibers extend completely through a piece, usually at the ends.*

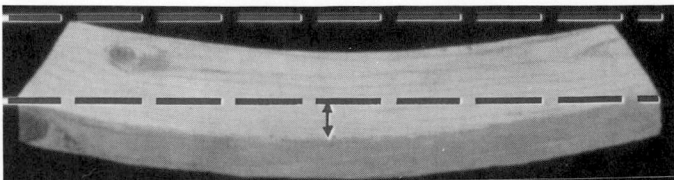

5-10l. *Bow is a deviation from a flat plane of the wide face of a piece of lumber from end to end.*

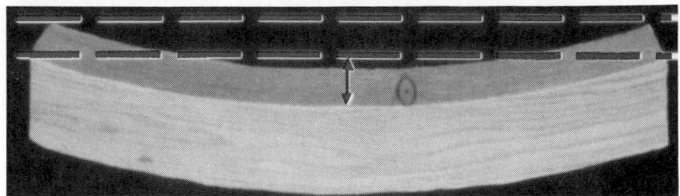

5-10m. *Crook is a deviation from a flat plane of the narrow face of a piece of lumber from end to end.*

5-10n. *Twist is a deviation from the flat planes of all four faces by a spiraling or torsional action, usually the result of seasoning.*

Table 5-B. *Standard Thicknesses and Widths of Common Softwood Lumber.*

Nominal			Minimum Dressed						
				Dry			Green		
	Exact	Rounded		Exact	Rounded		Exact	Rounded	
inches	mm	mm	inches	mm	mm	inches	mm	mm	
1	25.4	25	¾	19.1	19	25/32	19.8	20	
1¼	31.8	32	1	25.4	25	1 1/32	26.2	26	
1½	38.1	38	1¼	31.8	32	1 9/32	32.51	33	
2	50.8	50	1½	38.1	38	1 9/16	39.7	40	
2½	63.5	63	2	50.8	50	2 1/16	52.4	52	
3	76.2	75	2½	63.5	63	2 9/16	65.1	65	
3½	88.9	90	3	76.2	75	3 1/16	77.8	78	
4	101.6	100	3½	88.9	89	3 9/16	90.5	90	
5	127.0	125	4½	114.3	114	4 5/8	117.5	117	
6	152.4	150	5½	139.7	140	5 5/8	142.9	143	
7	177.8	175	6½	165.1	165	6 5/8	168.3	168	
8	203.2	200	7¼	184.1	184	7½	190.5	190	

casings, stair treads, balusters and handrails, and cabinetry. For more detailed information on hardwood grading, consult the text *Cabinetmaking and Millwork*, also by Dr. John L. Feirer.

Softwood Lumber Grading

Grading rules for softwood lumber are outlined in the bulletin "Voluntary Product Standard PS20-70." This standard was developed by the National Bureau of Standards (NBS) in cooperation with producers, distributors, and users of softwoods. Major lumber organizations and many governmental agencies, including the Forest Products Laboratory of Madison, Wisconsin, contributed to these standards.

According to this voluntary standard, lumber is divided into two basic groups: *green* or *unseasoned* lumber (with moisture content in excess of 19%), and *dry* or *seasoned* lumber (19% or less M.C.). Table 5-B. Based on this standard, each major lumber association has developed a complete set of grading rules. Since these grading rules are extensive and vary somewhat for each association, it is best for the builder who uses primary lumber from one section of the country to secure a complete set of grading rules from the organization in that area. For example, if most of the building lumber comes from the western

---

Table 5-C. *Lumber Abbreviations.*

AD—Air-dried
ADF—After deduction freight
ALS—American Lumber Standards
AVG—Average
AW&L—All widths and lengths
BD—Board
BD FT—Board feet
BDL—Bundle
BEV—Bevel
BH—Boxed Heart
B/L, BL—Bill of lading
BM—Board Measure
B&S—Beams and Stringers
BSND—Bright Sapwood no defect
BTR—Better
CB—Center beaded
CF—Cost and freight
CIF—Cost, insurance and freight
CIFE—Cost, insurance, freight, exchange
C/L—Carload
CLG—Ceiling
CLR—Clear
CM—Center matched
CS—Caulking seam
CSG—Casing
CV—Center V
DET—Double end trimmed
DF—Douglas Fir
DF-L—Douglas Fir-Larch
DIM—Dimension
DKG—Decking
D/S, DS—Drop siding
D&M—Dressed and matched
E—Edge or modulus of elasticity
EB1S—Edge bead one side
EB2S—Edge bead two sides
E&CB2S—Edge & center bead two sides
EV1S—Edge vee one side
EV2S—Edge vee two sides
E&CV1S—Edge & center vee one side
E&CV2S—Edge & center vee two sides
EE—Eased edged
LGTH—Length
LIN—Lineal
LNG—Lining
LP—Lodgepole pine
M—Thousand
M. BM—Thousand (ft.) board measure

MC—Moisture content
MG—Mixed grain
MLDG—Molding
MOE—Modulus of elasticity or "E"
MOR—Modulus of Rupture
MSR—Machine Stress Rated
NBM—Net board measure
N1E—Nose one edge
PAD—Partly Air Dried
PARA—Paragraph
PART—Partition
PAT—Pattern
PET—Precision end trimmed
PP—Ponderosa pine
P&T—Posts and Timbers
RC—Red Cedar
RDM—Random
REG—Regular
RGH—Rough
R/L, RL—Random lengths
R/S—Resawn
R/W, or RW—Random widths
R/W, R/L—Random width, Random length
SB1S—Single bead one side
SDG—Siding
SEL—Select
SG—Slash or flat grain
S/L, or SL—Shiplap
STD. M—Standard measure
SM—Surface measure
SP—Sugar pine
SQ—Square
STK—Stock
STPG—Stepping
STR—Structural
S&E—Side and edge
S1E—Surfaced one edge
EG—Edge (vertical) grain
EM—End matched
ES—Englemann spruce
f—Allowable fiber stress in bending (also Fb)
FAS—Free alongside (vessel)
FG—Flat or slash grain
FLG—Flooring
FOB—Free on board (Named point)
FOHC—Free of heart center
FRT—Freight
Ft—Foot

FT.BM—Feet board measure (also FBM)
FT.SM—Feet surface measure
H.B.—Hollow back
HEM—Hemlock
H&M—Hit and miss
H or M—Hit or miss
IC—Incense cedar
IN—Inch or inches
IND—Industrial
IWP—Idaho white pine
J&P—Joists and Planks
JTD—Jointed
KD—Kiln-dried
L—Larch
LBR—Lumber
LCL—Less than carload
LF—Light Framing
LFVC—Loaded full visible capacity
LGR—Longer
S2E—Surfaced two edges
S1S—Surfaced one side
S2S—Surfaced two sides
S4S—Surfaced four sides
S1S&CM—Surfaced one side and center matched
S2S&CM—Surfaced two sides and center matched
S4S&CS—Surfaced four sides and caulking seam
S1S1E—Surfaced one side, one edge
S1S2E—Surfaced one side, two edges
S2S1E—Surfaced two sides, one edge
TBR—Timber
T&G—Tongued and grooved
VG—Vertical (edge) grain
WDR—Wider
WF—White fir
WT—Weight
WTH—Width
WRC—Western Red Cedar
WWPA—Western Wood Products Association
SYMBOLS
"—Inch or inches
'—Foot or feet
x—By, as 4 x 4
4/4, 5/4, 6/4, etc.—nominal thickness expressed in fractions

states, then the grading rules published by the Western Wood Products Association should be used. These are available in a reference entitled *Western Woods Use Book*. Similar grading books are available from such associations as the *Southern Pine Inspection Bureau*, *West Coast Lumber Inspection Bureau*, *Redwood Inspection Service*, *Northeastern Lumber Manufacturers Association*, and *Northern Hardwood and Pine Manufacturers Association*.

Basic Selection Factors. Attention to the following points, and familiarity with common lumber abbreviations, will simplify the selection and specifications of softwood lumber. Table 5-C.

Product Classification. Identify product names for clarity. Examples: paneling, structural decking, joists, rafters, studding, beams, and siding. Table 5-D.

Species. Include all suitable species. With more species to choose from, you may be able to lower your costs. Check with your local supplier.

When wood color, grain, durability or other special characteristics are important, select and specify the species accordingly.

Grade. Specify standard grades as described in the official grading rules. Consider all grades suitable for the intended use. For economy,

it is recommended that the lowest suitable grade be specified.

Stress Rating. When strength is a factor, specify the stress rating requirements without reference to grades. There are two methods of assigning stress value—visually and by machine. (More detail is given later in this unit, under *Stress-Grade Lumber*.)

Grade Stamps. Specify grade-stamped framing lumber, sheathing, and other construction items. Finish lumber and decking may also be grade-stamped on ends or backs where the stamp will not be visible in use and may be so specified if desired.

Size. For standard products such as boards and framing, specify the nominal size by thickness and width in full inches. Example: 1×6, 1×8, 2×4, 2×6. Table 5-E. (Nominal sizes are larger than actual or dressed sizes. For example, a nominal 2 by 4 is $1\frac{1}{2}$ by $3\frac{1}{2}$ dressed.)

Surface Texture. Indicate whether lumber is to be smooth surface (surfaced) or rough surface (rough).

Seasoning. Specify "seasoned" lumber to assure long-range product quality, stability, increased nail-holding power, improved paintability, and workability. "Seasoned" covers both major methods of drying lumber—air dried or kiln dried.

Stress-Grade Lumber

Stress-grade lumber is structural lumber that has been scientifically graded with electronic devices and stamped with information to indicate the specific load it will support.

To understand stress grades it is necessary to know something about loads and strength properties of wood. The home and each of its parts are subject to a variety of external forces or loads. These loads can be classified as either dead or live.

Dead load is the weight of the material used in the structure. It is its own weight plus its share of the total weight of the remainder of the structure. For example, a dead roof load includes the rafters, or trusses, and all of the roofing material.

Live load, on the other hand, refers to the weight or forces *applied* to the house. Live loads may be static, repetitive, or impact.

Static loads are those which are applied slowly and remain constant, or are repeated relatively few times. The furniture in a house is a static load.

Loads that are applied a large number of times are called *repetitive* or *fatigue* loads. People walking across the floor illustrate this type.

Impact loads are sudden or instantaneous forces. A high wind or a tree falling against the roof is an impact load.

Table 5-D. *Product Classifications of Western Lumber.*

	Thickness in.	Width in.		Thickness In.	Width in.
Board Lumber	1"	2" or more	**Posts & Timbers**	5" x 5" and larger	not more than 2" greater than thickness
Light Framing	2" to 4"	2" to 4"	**Decking**	2" to 4"	4" to 12" wide
Joists & Planks	2" to 4"	6" and wider	**Siding**	thickness expressed by dimension of butt edge	
Beams & Stringers	5" and thicker	more than 2" greater than thickness	**Moldings**	size at thickest and widest points	

Standard lengths of lumber generally are 6 feet and longer in multiples of 1'

Table 5-E. *Common Materials Used in Home Construction (Dimensional Data/Nominal, Dressed).*

	Product Description	Nominal Size		Dressed Dimensions		Length Ft.
		Thickness In.	Width In.	Thicknesses and Widths In.		
				Surfaced Dry	Surfaced Unseasoned	
Framing	S1S1E, S1E or S4S	2	2	1 ½	1 ⁹⁄₁₆	6 ft. and longer in multiples of 1'
		3	3	2 ½	2 ⁹⁄₁₆	
		4	4	3 ½	3 ⁹⁄₁₆	
		6	6	5 ½	5 ⅝	
		8	8	7 ¼	7 ½	
		10	10	9 ¼	9 ½	
		12	12	11 ¼	11 ½	
		Over 12	Over 12	Off ¾	Off ½	

			Thickness In.	Width In.		
Timbers		5 and Larger	½ Off Nominal			Same

	Product Description	Nominal Size		Dressed Dimensions Surfaced Dry		
		Thickness In.	Width In.	Thickness In.	Width In.	Lengths Ft.
Decking	S2S, CM, EV1S, D&M	2	4	1 ½	3	
		3	6	2 ½	5	
		4	8	3 ½	6 ¾	Same
			10		8 ¾	
			12		10 ¾	
Selects and Commons S-Dry	S1S, S2S, S4S, S1S1E, S1S2E	⁴⁄₄	2	¾	1 ½	
		⁵⁄₄	3	1 ⁵⁄₃₂	2 ½	
		⁶⁄₄	4	1 ¹³⁄₃₂	3 ½	
		⁷⁄₄	5	1 ¹⁹⁄₃₂	4 ½	
		⁸⁄₄	6	1 ¹³⁄₁₆	5 ½	Same
		⁹⁄₄	7	2 ³⁄₃₂	6 ½	
		¹⁰⁄₄	8 and wider	2 ⅜	¾ Off nominal	
		¹¹⁄₄		2 ⁹⁄₁₆		
		¹²⁄₄		2 ¾		
		¹⁶⁄₄		3 ¾		
Flooring	(D&M), (S2S & CM)	⅜	2	⁵⁄₁₆	1 ⅛	
		½	3	⁷⁄₁₆	2 ⅛	
		⅝	4	⁹⁄₁₆	3 ⅛	Same
		1	5	¾	4 ⅛	
		1 ¼	6	1	5 ⅛	
		1 ½		1 ¼		

	Product Description	Nominal Size		Dressed Dimensions		
		Thickness In.	Width In.	Thickness In.	Width In.	Lengths Ft.
Rustic and Drop Siding	(D&M) If 3/8" or 1/2" T&G specified, same over-all widths apply.	⅝	4	⁹⁄₁₆	3 ⅛	
		1	5	²³⁄₃₂	4 ⅛	
			6		5 ⅛	Same
			8		6 ⅞	
			10		8 ⅞	
	(Shiplapped, ³⁄₈-in. lap)	⅝	4	⁹⁄₁₆	3	
		1	5	²³⁄₃₂	4	Same
			6		5	
	(Shiplapped, ³⁄₈-in. lap)	⅝	4	⁹⁄₁₆	2 ⅞	
		1	5	²³⁄₃₂	3 ⅞	
			6		4 ⅞	Same
			8		6 ⅝	
			10		8 ⅝	
			12		10 ⅝	
Ceiling and and Partition	(S2S & CM)	⅜	3	⁵⁄₁₆	2 ⅛	
		½	4	⁷⁄₁₆	3 ⅛	
		⅝	5	⁹⁄₁₆	4 ⅛	Same
		¾	6	¹¹⁄₁₆	5 ⅛	

Table 5-E (cont.). *Common Materials Used in Home Construction (Dimensional Data/Nominal, Dressed).*

	Product Description	Nominal Size		Dressed Dimensions		Length Ft.
		Thickness In.	Width In.	Thicknesses and Widths In.		
Bevel Siding Grades	Bevel Siding	½	4	7/16 butt , 3/16 tip	3 ½	Same
		9/16	5	15/32 butt , 3/16 tip	4 ½	
	Western Red Cedar Bevel Siding available in ½", 5/8", ¾" nominal thickness. Corresponding thick edge is 15/32", 9/16" and ¾".	5/8	6	9/16 butt , 3/16 tip	5 ½	
		¾	8	11/16 butt , 3/16 tip	7 ¼	
		1	10	¾ butt , 3/16 tip	9 ¼	
			12		11 ¼	
	Wide Bevel Siding (Colonial or Bungalow)	¾	8	11/16 butt , 3/16 tip	7 ¼	
			10		9 ¼	
			12		11 ¼	
Finish and Boards S-Dry	S1S, S2S, S1S2E	3/8	2	5/16	1 ½	3' and longer. In Superior grade, 3% of 3' and 4' and 7% of 5' and 6' are permitted. In Prime grade. 20% of 3' to 6' is permitted.
		½	3	7/16	2 ½	
		5/8	4	9/16	3 ½	
		¾	5	5/8	4 ¼	
		1	6	¾	5 ½	
		1 ¼	7	1	6 ½	
		1 ½	8 and wider nominal	1 ¼	¾ off	
		1 ¾		1 3/8		
		2		1 ½		
		2 ½		2		
		3		2 ½		
		3 ½		3		
		4		3 ½		
Factory and Shop Lumber	S2S*	1 (4/4)	5	25/32 (4/4)	(See Rough Sizes Below)	6 ft. and longer in multiples of 1'
		1 ¼ (5/4)	and	1 5/32 (5/4)		
		1 ½ (6/4)	wider	1 13/32 (6/4)		
		1 ¾ (7/4)	(4" and wider in 4/4 No. 1	1 19/32 (7/4)		
		2 (8/4)	Shop	1 13/16 (8/4)		
		2 ½ (10/4)	and 4/4 No. 2	2 3/8 (10/4)		
		3 (12/4)	Shop)	2 ¾ (12/4)		
		4 (16/4)		3 ¾ (16/4)		

* These thicknesses also apply to Tongue & Groove (T & G)
See coverage estimator chart above for T & G widths.

Minimum Rough Sizes   Thicknesses and Widths Dry or Unseasoned All Lumber (S1E, S2E, S1S, S2S)
80% of the pieces in a shipment shall be at least 1/8" thicker than the standard surfaced size, the remaining 20% at least 3/32" thicker than the surfaced size. Widths shall be at least 1/8" wider than standard surfaced widths.
When specified to be full sawn, lumber may not be manufactured to a size less than the size specified.

Abreviations

Abbreviated descriptions appearing in the size table are explained below.	S4S—Surfaced four sides.	D & M—Dressed and matched.
S1S—Surfaced one side.	S1S1E—Surfaced one side, one edge.	T & G—Tongue and grooved.
S2S—Surfaced two sides.	S1S2E—Surfaced one side, two edges.	EV1S—Edge vee on one side.
	CM—Center matched.	S1E—Surfaced one edge.

To handle these loads, wood and other materials used in the home must have certain strength properties. Fig. 5–11. Loads cause stress in a piece of wood. *Stress* refers to a force acting on a piece of material and tending to change the shape of the piece. The most common stresses are tensile, compressive, and shear.

Tensile (or *tension*) stress occurs when forces tend to elongate the piece. *Compressive* (or *compression*) stress is a result of squeezing or crushing. *Shear stress* is caused by opposite forces that meet head on, like the blades of a pair of shears. For example, when a floor joist is under a load it develops three kinds of stress. Compression develops along the upper edge of the joist, tension along the lower edge, and horizontal shear through the middle. Fig. 5–12. There is also a vertical shear where the joists rest on the foundation.

A load or a weight on the ends of joists, beams, and similar pieces of lumber causes stress that tends to compress the fibers. A load that causes the joist to bend produces tension in the extreme fibers on the face farthest from the applied load. It also causes compression in the extreme fibers along the face nearest to the applied load.

The *modulus of elasticity* is a measure of the stiffness of material or a measure of resistance to deflection (bending). A piece may deflect slightly or a great deal depending on the size, span, load, and modulus of elasticity for the particular species. Each species of wood and each grade of lumber within that species has its own strength properties. For example, Douglas fir has a higher modulus of elasticity (stiffness) than western cedars. Southern yellow pine has greater compressive strength endwise than ponderosa pine. The National Lumber Manufacturers Association and other trade associations such as the Western Wood Products Association compile tables that indicate the strength properties of all the common species and grades.

Saw mills also produce some lumber that is stress-rated and marked with a grade stamp that gives exact information about the strength properties of that particular piece of wood. The rating may be done on the basis of

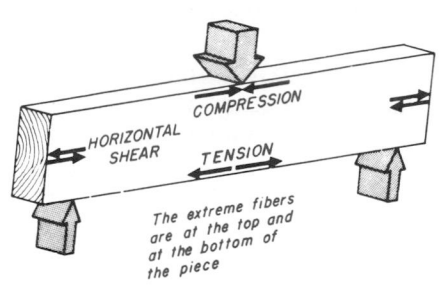

5-12. *Note how the various forces act on a floor joist.*

appearance (visual stress-rated lumber) or it may be done mechanically (machine stress-rated lumber). Most retail lumberyards do not handle stress-rated lumber. The typical retail yard stocks only *yard lumber*, which is adequate for average house construction. A house built of the proper-size yard lumber for joists, beams, and rafters will be of adequate strength. However, for certain items, when strength properties are critical, the architect may specify stress-rated lumber of a certain species and grade. For example, manufacturers of roof trusses will often use stress-grade lumber since these parts are so important to the strength of the home.

STORING LUMBER

In Lumberyards. Lumber stored in yards should be indoors under covered sheds. If stored outdoors it should be protected by covering with plastic or waterproof paper. Fig. 5–13. If the sides, top, and ends of a piece of lumber are properly covered, it will not absorb too much moisture outdoors even in damp, rainy, or humid weather. In indoor storage, moisture content can be controlled by regulating the temperature in the storage shed.

On the Job. Lumber received on the job for house construction should be stored carefully to prevent shrinking and swelling. It should be off the ground and piled carefully with stickers between each layer. It should then be covered with waterproof material until used.

Lumber kept indoors will pick up or lose moisture until it reaches a balance with the moisture of air in the room. Fig. 5–6 is a map of the United States which shows the proper moisture content for wood to be used in the interior parts of heated buildings. If lumber, when delivered, has a lower moisture content than was ordered, it will pick up additional moisture until it balances with that in the air. Even paint does not keep wood from absorbing moisture, since it does not completely seal the wood.

FIGURING BOARD FEET

Sizes of softwood or building construction lumber have been standardized for convenience in ordering and handling. Building materials sizes run 6, 8, 10, 12, 14, 16, 18, and 20 feet in length, 2, 4, 6, 8, 10, and 12 inches in width, and 1, 2, and 4 inches in thickness.

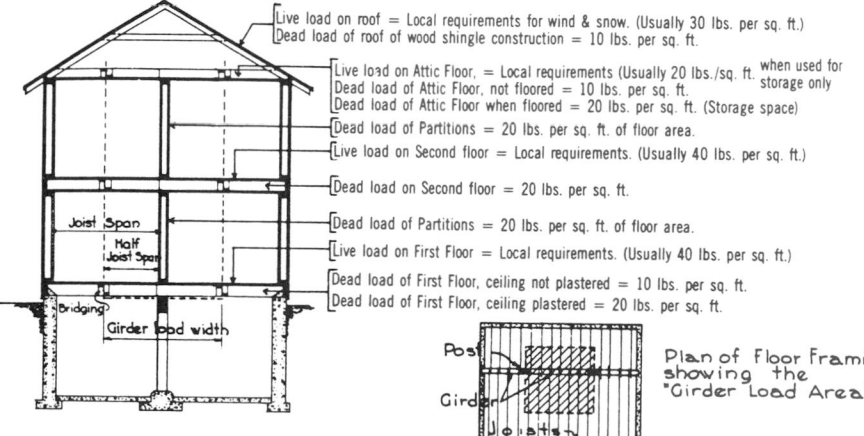

Diagram Showing Method Of Figuring Loads For House Framing

Live load on roof = Local requirements for wind & snow. (Usually 30 lbs. per sq. ft.)
Dead load of roof of wood shingle construction = 10 lbs. per sq. ft.

Live load on Attic Floor, = Local requirements (Usually 20 lbs./sq. ft. when used for storage only
Dead load of Attic Floor, not floored = 10 lbs. per sq. ft.
Dead load of Attic Floor when floored = 20 lbs. per sq. ft. (Storage space)

Dead load of Partitions = 20 lbs. per sq. ft. of floor area.

Live load on Second floor = Local requirements. (Usually 40 lbs. per sq. ft.)

Dead load on Second floor = 20 lbs. per sq. ft.

Dead load of Partitions = 20 lbs. per sq. ft. of floor area.

Live load on First Floor = Local requirements. (Usually 40 lbs. per sq. ft.)

Dead load of First Floor, ceiling not plastered = 10 lbs. per sq. ft.
Dead load of First Floor, ceiling plastered = 20 lbs. per sq. ft.

Joist Span
Half Joist Span
Bridging
Girder load width

Post
Girder
Joists

Plan of Floor Framing showing the "Girder Load Area".

5-11. *Live and dead loads.*

As mentioned briefly earlier, the actual width and thickness of dressed lumber are considerably less than the standard, or nominal, width and thickness. For the relative differences between standard and actual sizes of construction lumber, see Table 5-E. Hardwoods which have no standard length or width run ¼, ½, 1, 1¼, 1½, 2, 2½, 3, and 4 inches in thickness. Plywoods run from 4 feet in width to 8 feet in length, and vary in thickness from ⅛ to 1 inch. Stock panels are usually available in 48-inch widths and in lengths varying in multiples of 16 inches up to 8 feet. Panel lengths run in 16-inch multiples because the accepted spacing for studs and joists is 16 inches. The amount of lumber required is measured in board feet. A *board foot* is a unit of measure representing a piece of lumber having a flat surface area of 1 square foot and a thickness of 1 inch nominal size. The number of board feet in a piece of lumber can be computed by the arithmetic method or by the tabular method.

Arithmetic Method

In order to determine the number of board feet in one or more pieces of lumber, the following formula is used:

$$\frac{\text{Pieces} \times \text{Thickness (in.)} \times \text{Width (in.)} \times \text{Length (ft.)}}{12}$$

Example 1: Find the number of board feet in a piece of lumber 2" thick, 10" wide and 6' long. Fig. 5-14.

$$\frac{2 \times 10 \times 6}{12} = 10 \text{ bd. ft.}$$

Example 2: Find the number of board feet in 10 pieces of lumber 2" thick, 10" wide and 6' long.

$$\frac{10 \times 2 \times 10 \times 6}{12} = 100 \text{ bd. ft.}$$

If all three dimensions are expressed in inches, the same formula applies except the divisor is changed to 144.

Example: Find the number of board feet in one piece of lumber 2" thick, 10" wide, and 18" long.

$$\frac{1 \times 2 \times 10 \times 18}{144} = 2\frac{1}{2} \text{ bd. ft.}$$

Tabular Method

The standard Essex board measure table found on the back of the blade of the framing square is a quick and convenient aid in computing board feet. Fig. 5–15. In using the table, all computations are made on the basis of 1" thickness. The inch markings along the outer edge of the blade represent the width of a board 1" thick. The third dimension, length, is provided in the vertical column

5-13. *It is a good idea to purchase lumber that has been properly stored at the lumberyard.*

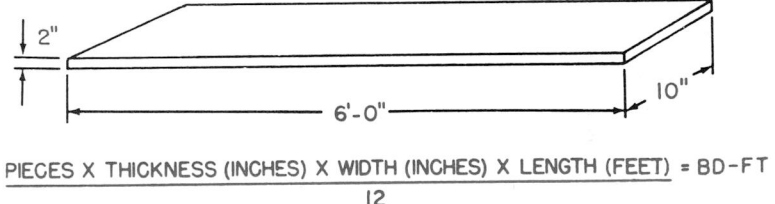

$$\frac{\text{PIECES} \times \text{THICKNESS (INCHES)} \times \text{WIDTH (INCHES)} \times \text{LENGTH (FEET)}}{12} = \text{BD-FT}$$

$$\frac{1 \times 2 \times 10 \times 6}{12} = 10 \text{ BD-FT}$$

5-14. *Figuring board feet, using common arithmetic.*

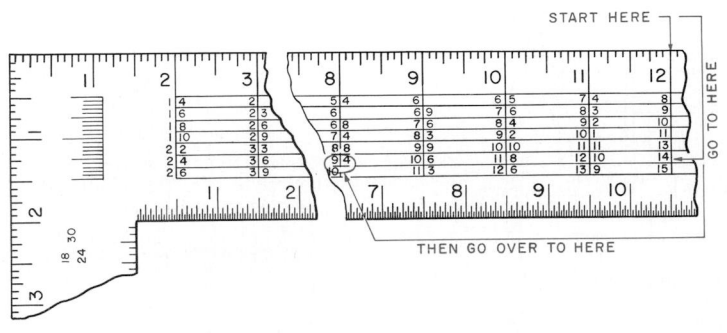

5-15. *Essex board measure table.*

Table 5-F. *Estimating Board Feet.*

Width	Thickness	Board feet
3"	1" or less	¼ of the length
4"	1" or less	⅓ of the length
6"	1" or less	½ of the length
9"	1" or less	¾ of the length
12"	1" or less	Same as the length
15"	1" or less	1 ¼ of the length

of figures under the 12" on the outer edge representing a 1" thick board that is 12" wide.

To compute the number of board feet in a piece of lumber 4" thick, 8" wide, and 14' long, find number 14 in the vertical column under the 12" mark on the outer edge. Follow the guideline under figure 14 laterally to the left across the blade until it reaches the figure on that line directly under the inch mark corresponding to the width of the piece. Under the 8" mark on the guideline indicated by the 14, the figures 9 and 4 appear. The figure to the left represents feet and that on the right represents inches. In this case, these figures mean that there are $9\frac{4}{12}$ or $9\frac{1}{3}$ board feet in a piece of lumber 14' long, 8" wide, and 1" thick. Remember, however, that we were checking a board 4" thick. Therefore we must still multiply by 4, for a final answer of $37\frac{1}{3}$ board ft.

Rapid Estimation

Rapid estimation of board feet can be made by the use of Tables 5-F and 5-G.

METRIC LUMBER MEASURES

Most major wood-producing countries cut lumber into the customary (English) sizes with thicknesses and widths in inches and lengths in feet. However, lumber to be shipped to most foreign countries is marked with metric sizes. Millimetres (mm) are used to indicate thickness and width, and metres (m) for length. The common sizes of lumber are almost identical in either system of measurement. For example, the basic thickness is 1" or 25 mm, and nominal width is 100 mm or 4". The metric lengths range from 1.8 m, which is approximately 6', and

Table 5-G. *Board-Foot Measure.*

Nominal size (in.)	Actual length in feet								
	8	**10**	**12**	**14**	**16**	**18**	**20**	**22**	**24**
1 x 2		1⅔	2	2⅓	2⅔	3	3⅓	3⅔	4
1 x 3		2½	3	3½	4	4½	5	5½	6
1 x 4	2⅔	3⅓	4	4⅔	5⅓	6	6⅔	7⅓	8
1 x 5		4⅙	5	5⅚	6⅔	7½	8⅓	9⅙	10
1 x 6	4	5	6	7	8	9	10	11	12
1 x 7		5⅚	7	8⅙	9⅓	10½	11⅔	12⅚	14
1 x 8	5⅓	6⅔	8	9⅓	10⅔	12	13⅓	14⅔	16
1 x 10	6⅔	8⅓	10	11⅔	13⅓	15	16⅔	18⅓	20
1 x 12	8	10	12	14	16	18	20	22	24
1¼ x 4		4⅙	5	5⅚	6⅔	7½	8⅓	9⅙	10
1¼ x 6		6¼	7½	8¾	10	11¼	12½	13¾	15
1¼ x 8		8⅓	10	11⅔	13⅓	15	16⅔	18⅓	20
1¼ x 10		10⁵⁄₁₂	12½	14⁷⁄₁₂	16⅔	18¾	20⅚	22¹¹⁄₁₂	25
1¼ x 12		12½	15	17½	20	22½	25	27½	30
1½ x 4	4	5	6	7	8	9	10	11	12
1½ x 6	6	7½	9	10½	12	13½	15	16½	18
1½ x 8	8	10	12	14	16	18	20	22	24
1½ x 10	10	12½	15	17½	20	22½	25	27½	30
1½ x 12	12	15	18	21	24	27	30	33	36
2 x 4	5⅓	6⅔	8	9⅓	10⅓	12	13⅓	14⅔	16
2 x 6	8	10	12	14	16	18	20	22	24
2 x 8	10⅔	13⅓	16	18⅔	21⅓	24	26⅔	29⅓	32
2 x 10	13⅓	16⅔	20	23⅓	26⅔	30	33⅓	36⅔	40
2 x 12	16	20	24	28	32	36	40	44	48
3 x 6	12	15	18	21	24	27	30	33	36
3 x 8	16	20	24	28	32	36	40	44	48
3 x 10	20	25	30	35	40	45	50	55	60
3 x 12	24	30	36	42	48	54	60	66	72
4 x 4	10⅔	13⅓	16	18⅔	21⅓	24	26⅔	29⅓	32
4 x 6	16	20	24	28	32	36	40	44	48
4 x 8	21⅓	26⅔	32	37⅓	42⅔	48	53⅓	58⅔	64
4 x 10	26⅔	33⅓	40	46⅔	53⅓	60	66⅔	73⅓	80
4 x 12	32	40	48	56	64	72	80	88	96

increase in steps of 300 mm (or 0.3 m) to 6.3 metres. Note that 300 mm is close to but slightly shorter than a foot. Table 5-H.

The metric size of panel stock such as plywood is 1220 mm (or 1.22 m) by 2440 mm (or 2.44 m), which is, for all practical purposes, the same as a 4' × 8' sheet. In countries "going metric" a 1200 × 2400 mm size is used, based on a 100 mm building module. As in customary lumber measurement the S2S (surfaced on two sides, or planed) lumber will always measure less than the rough sawn (nominal) size. An allowance should be made for this when stating required sizes.

PRESERVATIVE-TREATED LUMBER

To increase the durability of wood, it can be treated with liquid preservatives soon after being milled into lumber. Preservative-treated wood is often used outdoors, or where wood is in contact with concrete or masonry, because it is resistant to decay and termites. In one treating process,

Table 5-H. *Standard Range of Sizes for Sawn Softwood (in Metric). Thickness and width are given in millimetres (mm) and length in metres (m).*

mm	75	100	125	150	175	200	225	250	300
16	x	x	x	x					
19	x	x	x	x					
22	x	x	x	x					
25	x	x	x	x	x	x	x	x	x
32	x	x	x	x	x	x	x	x	x
36	x	x	x	x					
38	x	x	x	x	x	x	x		
40	x	x	x	x	x	x	x		
44	x	x	x	x	x	x	x	x	x
50	x	x	x	x	x	x	x	x	x
63		x	x	x	x	x	x		
75		x	x	x	x	x	x	x	x
100		x		x		x		x	x
150				x		x			x
200						x			
250								x	
300									x

Lengths: 1.8 to 6.3m × 0.3 m   Allow: 4mm for planning

the wood is dipped into vats of preservative chemicals, and then allowed to air-dry. In another process, the chemicals are forced deep into the wood under pressure. In a third process, the chemicals are injected into wood. Various species of wood can be successfully treated with preservatives, but fir, spruce and pine are most commonly treated. Depending on the process and the chemicals used, treated wood will range in color from natural wood tones to various shades of green or brown. Some treated wood can be painted or stained.

The amount of preservative used to treat wood can be adjusted to provide varying levels of protection against decay. Wood that will be used in direct contact with the ground (fence posts or structural posts, for example) should receive the highest level of treatment available. As with standard lumber, preservative-treated lumber is graded and stamped with identifying marks that indicate its suitability for various uses. Fig. 5–16.

Because of the chemicals used in the preservative treatment of lumber, it is important to handle the material properly. Treated wood should not be burned under any circumstances—toxic chemicals may be produced as a part of the smoke and ash. When sawing or machining treated wood, wear a dust mask to avoid breathing the sawdust. Wear eye protection also. Whenever possible, such operations should be done outdoors to avoid indoor accumulations of airborne sawdust. After handling the wood, wash your hands thoroughly, particularly before eating.

Though preservative-treated wood has a wide variety of uses in building construction, it should not be used where it might come in contact with food (the top of a picnic table, for example). Only treated wood that is visibly clean and free of surface residue should be used for decks and walkways. Though there is some debate about the suitability of preservative-treated wood for use inside the house, there is little doubt concerning its suitability for use outdoors.

5-16. *Chemically-treated wood is used for a wide variety of purposes outdoors, including decks, stairs, railings, and retaining walls.*

1. List five advantages of wood as a building material.

2. Describe the difference between early wood and late wood.

3. Name the two common methods of cutting boards from a log.

4. Tell how much moisture a typical tree may contain when it is first cut down, as compared with the moisture in dried lumber.

5. Describe what is meant by *fiber saturation point*.

6. Describe the two methods of drying lumber.

7. Define moisture content.

8. Name two ways of checking the moisture content of lumber.

9. List several defects in standard grades of lumber.

10. What are the three types of warp?

11. What organization handles hardwood lumber grades?

12. Why is it necessary to secure a complete set of grading rules for detailed help on selecting lumber?

13. When is *stress-grade lumber* used?

14. Tell how lumber should be stored for on-the-job building.

15. Define the term "board-foot."

16. How many board feet are in a piece of lumber 2" × 8" × 10'?

17. What unit is used for the thickness and width of lumber in the metric system?

18. Name the woods most commonly treated with preservative chemicals.

19. In what locations is it most important to use preservative-treated lumber?

ACTIVITIES

1. Math. A house has 1,800 square feet of roof. When the house was built, the local regulations required a dead load capacity of 30 lbs./sq. ft. (See Fig. 5-11.)

a. How many tons will the roof support if it was built to minimum standard?

b. The weather forecast is for 2' of snow. If the snow weighs 18 lb./cubic foot, will the roof hold?

2. Math. Using Table 5-F, one can estimate the board feet for boards of width 3", 4", etc., by taking a fraction of the length.

a. If the board is 6" wide, what fraction of the length should one use?

b. If the board is 8" wide, what fraction of the length should one use?

c. If the board is 10" wide, what fraction of the length should one use?

3. Social Studies. Locate those states in the United States where lumber is one of the primary economic resources. Find out what type of lumber they produce.

4. Science. Secure several pieces of thin wood such as would be used for model building. These are meant to simulate floor joists and rafter members. Place some roof members over a 10" span on edge (thickness size). Place other roof members over a 10" span on the face side (width size). Using a gentle one- or two-finger pressure against the edge span and against the face span, recognize the deflection differences. Correlate the deflection differences with tension and compression stresses as explained in this unit. Scientifically define why floor joist and rafter members are placed in a building on edge.

THE SCHOOL-TO-WORK CONNECTION

One way to reduce the demands on our forests is to use wood more efficiently.

1. Many trade associations in the construction industry publish brochures that describe how to use wood efficiently. Write to the following association requesting a free list of their publications: The Western Wood Products Association. You can obtain the address from your public library.

Plywood

Plywood is a most versatile building material. Fig. 6-1. It can be used in nearly every step of home building, including:

➤ Roof decking, where plywood adds strength and rigidity.

➤ Gable ends and soffits, where plywood provides a smooth, clean, easy-to-paint surface.

➤ Subfloors and underlayment. Plywood makes a firm, smooth base for flooring.

➤ Interior walls. Plywood has warmth of real wood.

➤ Base for tile, cork, and decorative walls. Plywood is smooth, flat, and durable.

➤ Built-ins. These can be planned for beauty, convenience, and need.

➤ Sheathing, to produce walls that are strong and rigid.

➤ Fences, windbreaks, and patio screens, to provide privacy and comfort.

➤ Exteriors. Smart and modern plywood exteriors can be arranged to fit any home styling.

➤ Concrete forms. Plywood used this way can be reused for sheathing.

WHAT PLYWOOD IS

Plywood consists of glued wood panels made from layers and/or plies of veneer or veneer and wood.

6-1a. Plywood is a versatile material. Here it is used for the roof sheathing, as well as for the webs of the wood I-beam rafters.

6-1b. Plywood is being used as the underlayment for this wood floor.

The grain of each layer is at an angle, usually a right angle, to the grain of the nearest layer on each side. The grain of the outer plies always runs in the same direction. The outer plies are called *faces*, or *face* and *back*. The center ply is called the *core*. The ply or plies between the core and the faces are called *crossbands*.

Veneer is a very thin sheet of wood that is sawed, peeled, or sliced from a log. Construction and industrial plywoods (formerly called softwood plywoods) are made entirely of veneer of three, four, five, six, or seven plies. Hardwood plywoods may be made entirely of veneer (in which case they are called *veneer-core* plywoods), or of veneer bonded to a core of glued-up lumber, (called *lumber-core* plywood). Sometimes hardwood plywood has a particleboard core. Fig. 6-2.

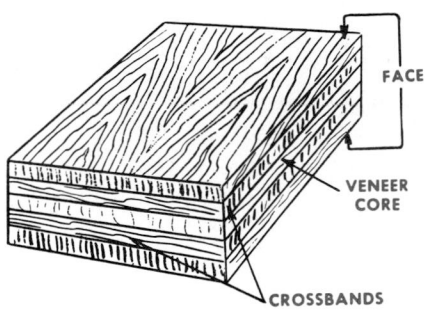

6-2a. *Veneer core. The core is made of thick wood veneer.*

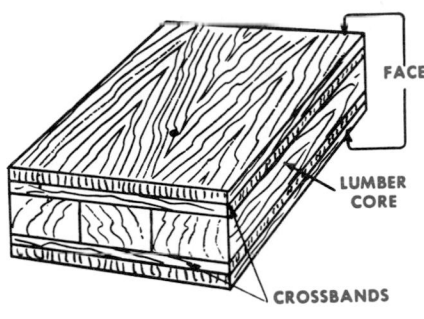

6-2b. *Lumber core. The core consists of strips of lumber bonded together. Good woods for lumber-core plywood are basswood and chestnut.*

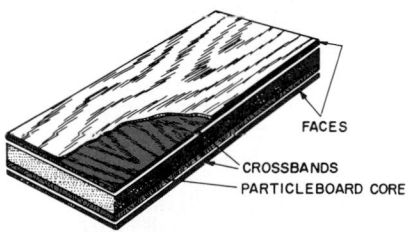

5-PLY WITH PARTICLEBOARD CORE

6-2c. *Particleboard core. The core is made of particleboard, a wood composition material sometimes referred to as chipboard. This kind of plywood is commonly used for cabinet doors because it is very stable.*

MANUFACTURE OF CONSTRUCTION AND INDUSTRIAL PLYWOOD

This unit deals primarily with construction and industrial plywood because that material, rather than hardwood plywood, is used most in construction. An examination of how this material is made will help you to understand the properties which make it so important in the building construction industry. Fig. 6-3.

Only selected logs qualify as plywood "peelers"—logs from which veneers for plywood are cut.

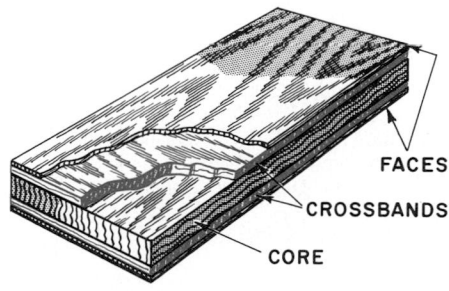

5-PLY WITH VENEER CORE

6-3. *Cutaway view of a typical piece of plywood.*

Such veneers are generally cut from the lower, larger portion of the trunk where the wood is mature and strong, with the clearest grain. The log comes from the forest and goes first into the storage pond. Next it is cut to lathe size, and then it moves into the plywood factory and through the debarker. Now it's a peeler "block"—pick of the forest crop—ready to become plywood.

Huge tongs from an overhead crane lift it into the lathe. Metal gripper chucks clamp both ends and the block begins to spin, revolving swiftly against a long, keen, razor-sharp blade of steel.

The blade bites in. A continuous strip of thin wood is peeled off—unwound from the log like paper from a roll.

This is *veneer*, not plywood. The lathe cuts it to an exact and specified thickness—from ⅛" to ⁵⁄₁₆"—and sends it streaming over conveyors to the clipping machine.

Giant knives, controlled by a skilled operator, cut the veneer to proper width for full utilization. It passes on into long mechanical dryers, where the moisture content of the wood is scientifically reduced to provide for greatest panel stability and best glue bond.

Next comes patching. Wood is never perfect; so the natural defects are cut out, to be replaced with solid wood or synthetic patching materials, carefully glued into place.

Next, some of the sheets go through the glue spreader, where large rollers cover both sides with a uniform thickness of adhesive. These glue-covered pieces are stacked alternately with dry veneers, to make up panels of the desired thickness. This is called the *lay-up* process.

Always there is an *odd* number of layers (3, 5, or 7). And, as mentioned earlier, there is always a cross-graining of layers. The grain of each layer is placed at *right angles* to that of adjacent layers. (Some plywood has two plies glued together with the grain parallel to form one layer.) The result is a balanced panel of cross-laminated wood veneers—strong, rigid, split proof, able to resist great impact.

Several important steps remain before the panel is finished. After lay-up, panels go into presses where the wood and glue are bonded into one homogeneous material. Two important variations are made here.

If the panel is to be *exterior-type* plywood, for permanent outdoor or marine use, the glue must be completely waterproof. Also, heat as well as pressure is required on the press. The result is a highly durable bond.

If the panel is to be *interior-type* plywood—for ordinary indoor and construction use—the adhesives are not waterproof, and may be cured with or without heat. Even these glues, however, are highly resistant to moisture. The interior panel can be produced more economically than the exterior type.

From the press, panels move through machines which trim them to exact, precision-squared sizes and sand them down to proper thickness. Then comes inspection, repair of blemishes in face plies, and final grading.

CONSTRUCTION AND INDUSTRIAL PLYWOOD

Construction and industrial plywood is manufactured under U.S. Product Standard PS 1-74 replacing the previous standard PS 1-66 for *softwood plywoods*. The standards are different from old regulations in such areas as the use of hardwoods. Also, common softwood panels are now constructed of an even number of

Table 6-A. *Exterior Type Grades (a).*

Panel Grade Designations	Minimum Veneer Quality			
	Face	Back	Inner Plies	Surface
Marine, A-A, A-B, B-B, HDO, MDO[b]				Sanded 2 sides
Special Exterior, A-A, A-B, B-B, HDO, MDO[c]				Sanded 2 sides
A-A	A	A	C	Sanded 2 sides
A-B	A	B	C	Sanded 2 sides
A-C	A	C	C	Sanded 2 sides
B-B (concrete form)[d]				
B-B	B	B	C	Sanded 2 sides
B-C	B	C	C	Sanded 2 sides
C-C Plugged	C Plugged	C	C	Touch-sanded
C-C	C	C	C	Unsanded(e)
A-A High Density Overlay	A	A	C Plugged	—
B-B High Density Overlay	B	B	C Plugged	—
B-B High Density Concrete Form Overlay	B	B	C Plugged	—
B-B Medium Density Overlay	B	B	C	—
Special Overlays	C	C	C	—

(a) Available also in Structural I and Structural II classifications.

(b) Marine grades shall meet the requirements of Exterior type and shall be of one of the following grades: A-A, A-B, B-B, High Density Overlay, or Medium Density Overlay.

(c) Special Exterior—An Exterior type panel that may be produced of any species covered by this Standard. Except in regard to species, it shall meet all of the requirements for Marine panels (see b) and be produced in one of the following grades: A-A, A-B, B-B, High Density Overlay, or Medium Density Overlay.

(d) B-B concrete form panels—Face veneers shall be not less than B grade and shall always be from the same species group. Inner plies shall be not less than "C" grade. This grade of plywood is produced in two classes and panels of each class shall be identified accordingly. Panels shall be sanded two sides and mill-oiled unless otherwise agreed upon.

(e) Except for decorative grades, panels shall not be sanded, touch-sanded, surface textured, or thickness sized by any mechanical means.

Table 6-B. *Interior Type Grades.*

Panel Grade Designations	Minimum Veneer Quality			
	Face	Back	Inner Plies	Surface
N-N	N	N	C	Sanded 2 sides
N-A	N	A	C	Sanded 2 sides
N-B	N	B	C	Sanded 2 sides
N-D	N	D	D	Sanded 2 sides
A-A	A	A	D	Sanded 2 sides
A-B	A	B	D	Sanded 2 sides
A-D	A	D	D	Sanded 2 sides
B-B	B	B	D	Sanded 2 sides
B-D	B	D	D	Sanded 2 sides
Underlayment	C Plugged	D	C & D	Touch-sanded
C-D Plugged	C Plugged	D	D	Touch-sanded
Structural I C-D [a]				Unsanded [b]
Structural I C-D Plugged, Underlayment[a]				Touch-sanded
Structural II C-D [a]				Unsanded [b]
Structural II C-D Plugged, Underlayment [a]				Touch-sanded
C-D	C	D	D	Unsanded [b]
C-D with exterior glue	C	D	D	Unsanded [b]

(a) Structural panels—These panels are especially designed for engineered applications such as structural components where design properties, including tension, compression, shear, cross-panel flexural properties and nail bearing may be of significant importance.

(b) Except for decorative grades, panels shall not be sanded, touch-sanded, surface textured, or thickness sized by any mechanical means.

plies, and a grade trademark change has been made from DFPA to APA. These standards affect the *use of plywood* in building construction and the *way in which materials are ordered.*

Types. Plywood panels have traditionally been divided into two major categories: interior plywood and exterior plywood. Now, however, there are a variety of designations that allow builders a more precise understanding of the materials' suitability in construction. The various grades of exterior plywood are listed in Table 6–A. The various grades of interior plywood are listed in Table 6-B.

Plywood panels are often classified according to their resistance to weathering or moisture. *Exterior* panels are made with waterproof glue. They are intended for full and continued exposure to the weather. Such panels would include siding plywood. *Exposure 1* panels are also made with waterproof glue. They are suitable for areas of high moisture content, but they are not as weather-resistant as exterior panels. They could, for example, be used for soffits but not for siding. *Exposure 2* panels are made with water-resistant glue. They are appropriate for brief, noncontinuing exposure to the weather. Sheathing plywood fits into this category. *Interior* panels are made with glues that are not necessarily water-resistant. They should be used indoors only.

In addition to the standards of moisture resistance, plywood may be designated as *structural.* These panels are designed for special engineering uses where strength and stiffness are of maximum importance. Grades of structural panels are listed in Table 6-C.

Foundation-grade plywood includes panels that have been treated with preservative chemicals. These are designed to be used where the wood will be permanently installed below grade.

Veneer Quality. Top quality is N. The quality of the others ranges from A to D. D is the lowest quality. Table 6-D.

Species. Plywood is manufactured from seventy different species of wood including native and imported hardwoods. However, most plywood will continue to be produced primarily of softwoods such as Douglas fir. On the basis of stiffness and other factors, these species are divided into five groups. The strongest woods are found in Group 1. Table 6-E.

Plywood Construction. Plywood is constructed of three, four, five, six, or seven plies. A *ply* is a sheet of veneer cut to various thicknesses ranging from as thin as $\frac{1}{16}$" to as thick as $\frac{5}{16}$". Note that an even number of plies can be used to make up the thickness. However, the number of *layers* used in panel construction is always odd, such as three, five, or seven. Table 6–F. This is possible because two of the

Table 6-C. *Structural Panels.*

Grade	Glue Bond	Species
Structural I C-D [a] C-D Plugged [a] Underlayment [a]	Exterior	Face, back and all innerplies limited to Group 1 species
Structural II C-D [a] C-D Plugged [a] Underlayment [a]	Exterior	Face, back and all inner plies may be of any Group 1, 2 or 3 species
Structural I All Exterior grades	Exterior	Face, back and all inner plies limited to Group 1 species
Structural II All Exterior grades	Exterior	Face, back and all inner plies may be of any Group 1, 2 or 3 species

(a) Special limitations applying to Structural (C-D, C-D Plugged, Underlayment) grade panels are:
— In D grade veneers white pocket in any area larger than the size of the largest knothole, pitchpocket or split specifically permitted in D grade shall not be permitted in any ply.
— Sound tight knots in D grade shall not exceed $2\frac{1}{2}$" measured across the grain.
— Plugs, including multiple repairs, shall not exceed 4" in width.

Table 6-D. *Veneer Quality.*

N	Intended for natural finish. Selected all heartwood or all sapwood. Free of open defects. Allows some repairs.
A	Smooth and paintable. Neatly made repairs permissible. Also used for natural finish in less demanding applications.
B	Solid surface veneer. Repair plugs and tight knots permitted. Can be painted.
C	Sanding defects permitted that will not impair the strength or serviceability of the panel. Knotholes to $1\frac{1}{2}$" and splits to $\frac{1}{2}$" permitted under certain conditions.
C plugged	Improved C veneer with closer limits on knotholes and splits. C plugged veneers are fully sanded.
D	Used only in interior type for inner plies and backs. Permits knots and knotholes to $2\frac{1}{2}$" in maximum dimension and $\frac{1}{2}$" larger under certain specified limits. Limited splits permitted.

Table 6-E. *Species of Wood from Which Plywood is Manufactured.*

Group 1	Group 2		Group 3	Group 4	Group 5
Apitong (a) (b)	Cedar, Port Orford	Maple, Black	Alder, Red	Aspen	Basswood
Beech, American	Cypress	Mengkulang (a)	Birch, Paper	Bigtooth	Fir, Balsam
Birch	Douglas Fir 2 (c)	Meranti, Red (a)(d)	Cedar, Alaska	Quaking	Poplar, Balsam
Sweet	Fir	Mersawa (a)	Fir, Subalpine	Cativo	
Yellow	California Red	Pine	Hemlock, Eastern	Cedar	
Douglas Fir 1 (c)	Grand	Pond	Maple, Bigleaf	Incense	
Kapur (a)	Noble	Red	Pine	Western Red	
Keruing (a) (b)	Pacific Silver	Virginia	Jack	Cottonwood	
Larch, Western	White	Western White	Lodgepole	Eastern	
Maple, Sugar	Hemlock, Western	Spruce	Ponderosa	Black (Western	
Pine	Lauan	Red	Spruce	Poplar)	
Caribbean	Almon	Sitka	Redwood	Pine	
Ocote	Bagtikan	Sweetgum	Spruce	Eastern White	
Pine, Southern	Mayapis	Tamarack	Black	Sugar	
Loblolly	Red Lauan	Yellow Poplar	Engelmann		
Longleaf	Tangile		White		
Shortleaf	White Lauan				
Slash					
Tanoak					

(a) Each of these names represents a trade group of woods consisting of a number of closely related species.

(b) Species from the genus Dipterocarpus are marketed collectively; Apitong if originating in the Philippines; Keruing if originating in Malaysia or Indonesia.

(c) Douglas Fir from trees grown in the states of Washington, Oregon, California, Idaho, Montana, Wyoming, and the Canadian Provinces of Alberta and British Columbia shall be classed as Douglas Fir No. 1. Douglas Fir from trees grown in the states of Nevada, Utah, Colorado, Arizona and New Mexico shall be classed as Douglas Fir No. 2.

(d) Red Meranti shall be limited to species having a specific gravity of 0.41 or more based on green volume and oven dry weight.

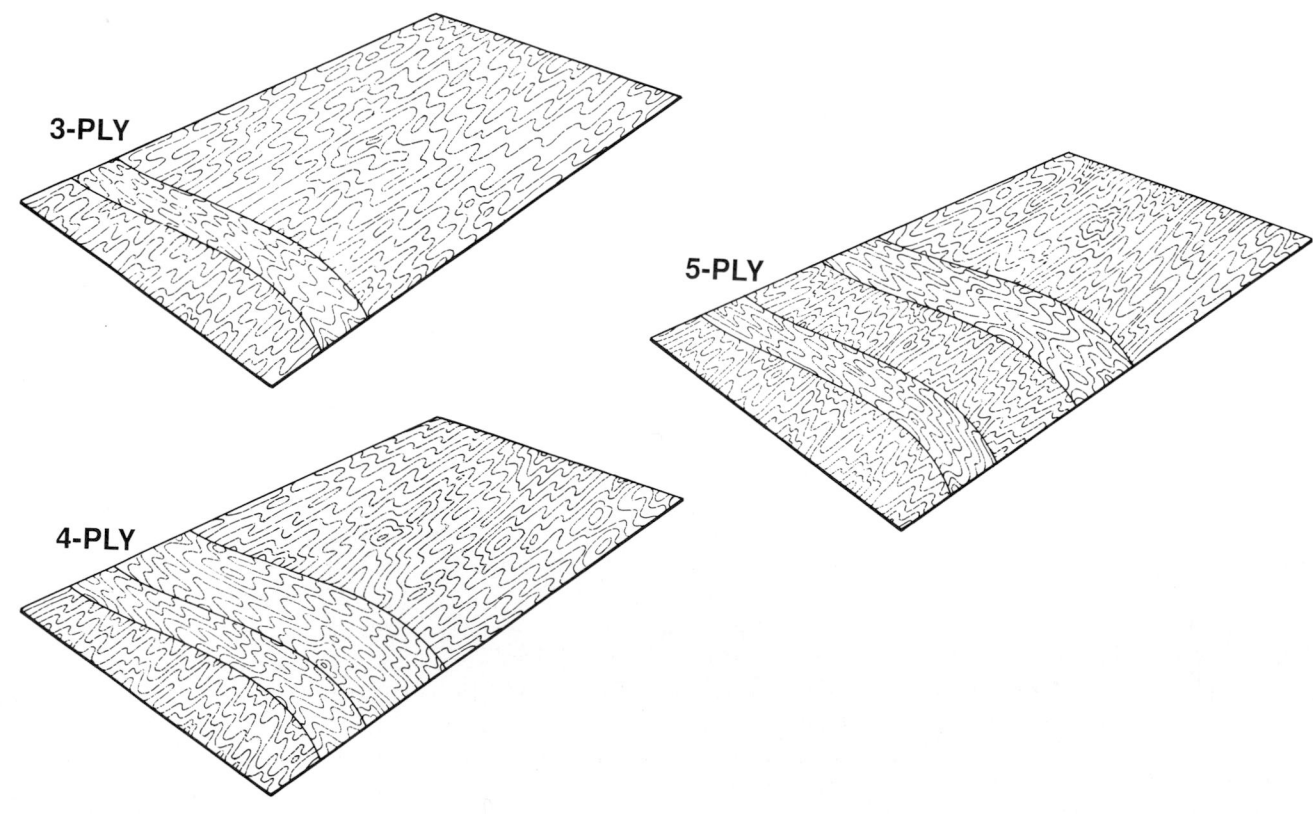

6-4. *Types of panel construction.*

Table 6-F. *Panel Constructions.*

Panel Grades	Finished Panel Nominal Thickness Range (inch)	Minimum Number of Plies	Minimum Number of Layers
Exterior Marine Special Exterior B-B concrete form High Density Overlay High Density concrete form overlay	Through ⅜ Over ⅜, through ¾ Over ¾	3 5 7	3 5 7
Interior N-N, N-A, N-B, N-D, A-A, A-B, A-D, B-B, B-D Structural I (C-D, C-D Plugged and Underlayment) Structural II (C-D, C-D Plugged and Underlayment) **Exterior** Structural I and Structural II A-A, A-B, A-C, B-B, B-C Medium Density and special overlays	Through ⅜ Over ⅜, through ½ Over ½, through ⅞ Over ⅞	3 4 5 6	3 3 5 5
Interior (including grades with exterior glue) Underlayment **Exterior** C-C Plugged	Through ½ Over ½, through ¾ Over ¾	3 4 5	3 3 5
Interior (including grades with exterior glue) C-D C-D Plugged **Exterior** C-C	Through ⅝ Over ⅝, through ¾ Over ¾	3 4 5	3 3 5

Note: The proportion of wood based on nominal finished panel thickness and dry veneer thickness before layup, as used, with grain running perpendicular to the panel face grain shall fall within the range of 33 percent to 70 percent. The combined thickness of all inner layers shall be not less than 1/2 of panel thickness based on nominal finished panel thickness and dry veneer thickness before layup, as used, for panels with 4 or more plies.

inner plies may be glued together with the grain parallel to form one inner layer. Fig. 6-4. The grain of all layers must be perpendicular to the grain of the adjacent layer. For example, plywood that is ½" thick can be constructed of four plies. The two inner plies are glued together with the grain parallel to form the inner layer. A face and a back veneer are glued to the center layer at right angles. The result is plywood of four plies made up of three layers.

The same ½" plywood could be manufactured of three plies with three layers. In this construction the center ply would be much thicker than in the four-ply construction.

Thickness and Size. Thickness of standard plywood ranges from ¼" to 1¼" and greater in ⅛" increments. The standard thickness of unsanded panels ranges from 5⁄16" to 1¼", in increments of ⅛" for thicknesses over ⅜".

Plywood is available in panel widths of 36", 48", and 60" and in lengths ranging from 60" to 144" in 12" increments. Plywood 48" wide by 96" long (a typical 4' × 8') and 48" wide by 120" long (4' × 10') are most commonly available.

Grade Markings. Grade marks are stamped on the face and edge of all plywood that meets the American Plywood Association's standards. Typical grade trademarks are shown in Figs. 6-5 and 6-6 together with notations of what each element means.

Sheathing Panels. Certain grades of plywood panels are used for subflooring, interior and exterior wall sheathing, and roof decking. These include grade trademarks of C-C, C-D, structural C-C, and structural C-D.

When these panels are used for sheathing purposes, they must include an identification as shown in Table 6–G. A careful study should be made of this information since it is important in selecting the correct sheathing for certain kinds of construction.

Note that the sheathing is identified by the group of wood species used, the type as indicated by interior, exterior and structural, and the nominal thickness of the panel. The index numbers, as you will note, are particularly useful when panels are used for subflooring and roof sheathing to describe the recommended maximum span in inches under nominal conditions. Fig. 6-6. The left-hand number refers to the spacing of the roof framing and the right-hand number refers to the spacing of floor framing.

For example, suppose you wish to select a ⅜" thickness of plywood sheathing to use on a roof in which the joists are spaced 24". Under these conditions any one of several different grades in Group 1 and 2 could be used. Table 6-G. For example, you could select a panel made of Group 1 wood species with an exterior grade of C-C.

Again, suppose you need to select a sheathing panel for subflooring in which the joists are 16" on center. You could select any sheathing grade in ½" thickness in the first column, ⅝" thickness in the second column and ¾" thickness from the third column. Table 6-G. As you can see, a thinner panel made of wood in the stronger wood species can be used in place of a thicker panel in the weaker wood species. For example, for this use you may select a ½" thick Group 1 *interior* C-D type or a ¾" thick Group 4 *interior* C-C type to do the same job.

Ordering. To order plywood you should designate the species, number of pieces, width, length, number of plies, type, grade, and finished thickness, in that order. A typical order might be as follows: Group 2 plywood: 100 pcs. 48 inch by 96 inch, 3-ply interior type, A-D grade, sanded two sides to ¼" thickness.

The above order means that you want 100 pieces of 4' × 8' plywood made up of three plies with a face of the second highest veneer quality and a back of the lowest veneer quality, sanded on both sides to a finished thickness of ¼". The material would be suited for all interior work.

Another typical order might be:

Group 3 plywood: 100 pcs. 48 inch by 96 inch, 3-ply exterior type, A-A grade, sanded two sides to ⅜" thickness (add further special requirements).

For more detailed information concerning all plywood, obtain a copy of U.S. Product Standard PS 1-74 for Construction and Industrial Plywood with typical APA Grade-Trademarks from the American Plywood Association, Tacoma, Washington.

Sanded Grades

Grade of veneer on panel face
Grade of veneer on panel back

A-C (APA)

Species Group number — **GROUP 2**
Designates the type of plywood — **EXTERIOR**
Product Standard governing manufacture — **PS 1-74 000**

(Also available in Groups 1, 3, and 4)

Unsanded Grades

Grade of veneer on panel face
Grade of veneer on panel back

C-D (APA)

Identification Index — **32/16**
Designates the type of plywood — **INTERIOR**
Product Standard governing manufacture — **PS 1-74 000**
Type of glue used — **EXTERIOR GLUE**
Mill number

Concrete Form

Grade of veneer on panel face
Grade of veneer on panel back

B-B PLYFORM (APA)

Registered grade trademark of American Plywood Association for B-B (Concrete Form)
Class of production — **CLASS I**
Designates the type of plywood — **EXTERIOR**
Product Standard governing manufacture — **PS 1-74 000**
Mill number

(Also available in Class II and HDO)

Specialty Panels

303 SIDING 16 oc

Species Group Number — **GROUP 3** (APA)
Designates the type of plywood — **EXTERIOR**
Product Standard governing manufacture — **PS 1-74 000**
Mill number

(Also available in Groups 1, 2, and 4)

Grade of veneer on panel face
Grade of veneer on panel back
Designates the type of plywood Exterior or Interior   Product Standard governing manufacture

A-B · G-1 · EXT·APA · PS 1-74 000

Species Group number   Mill number

6-5. *Typical grade markings. The top four show how these appear as back stamps while the lower one shows on edge marking.*

C-D (APA)
32/16
INTERIOR
PS 1-74 000
EXTERIOR GLUE

STRUCTURAL I
C-D (APA)
24/0
INTERIOR
PS 1-74 000
EXTERIOR GLUE
(Also available as Structural II. Both made only with exterior glue)

C-C (APA)
32/16
EXTERIOR
PS 1-74 000

6-6. *Typical grade markings on sheathing panels.*

Table 6-G. *Identification Index Table for Sheathing Panels (a).*

Species of Face and Back		Grade		
Group 1 (b)		C-C, Str. I C-C, C-D, Str. II C-C, C-D (c), C-D		
Group 2 (d)		C-C, Str. II C-C, C-D, C-D	C-C, Str. II C-C, C-D, C-D	(b)
Group 3			C-C, Str. II C-C, C-D, C-D	(b) (b)
Group 4 (d)			C-C, C-D	C-C, C-D (b)

	Nominal Thickness			
	5/16	20/0	16/0	12/0
	3/8	24/0	20/0	16/0
Nominal Thickness	1/2	32/16	24/0	24/0
	5/8	42/20	32/16	30/12
	3/4	48/24	42/20	36/16
	7/8		48/24	42/20
	(e)			

(a) Identification Index refers to the numbers in the lower portion of the table which are used in the marking of sheathing grades of plywood. The numbers are related to the species of panel face and back veneers and panel thickness in a manner to describe the bending properties of a panel. They are particularly applicable where panels are used for subflooring and roof sheathing to describe recommended maximum spans in inches under normal use conditions and to correspond with commonly accepted criteria. The left-hand number refers to spacing of roof framing with the right-hand number relating to spacing of floor framing. Actual maximum spans are established by local building codes.

(b) Panels of standard nominal thickness and construction.

(c) Panels manufactured with Group 1 faces but classified as Structural II by reason of Group 2 or Group 3 inner plies.

(d) Panels conforming to the special thickness and panel construction provisions.

(e) Panels thicker than 7/8" shall be identified by group number.

WORKING WITH PLYWOOD

Storage to Avoid Warpage. The best method of storing plywood is to lay the sheets flat. If this is not possible, they should be stored on edge with the sheets supported in a vertical position. Never lay plywood at an angle, especially the thinner panels, as it will warp.

Cutting to Avoid Splintered Edges. When hand sawing, always place plywood with the good face up and use a saw that has at least 10 to 15 points to the inch. Make sure that the panel is supported firmly so it will not sag. Hold the saw at a low angle when cutting and, if possible, place a piece of scrap stock underneath. When using a circular saw, install a special plywood blade or a sharp combination blade. The blade should be adjusted so that the teeth just clear the top of the stock. When cutting plywood on a table saw, always place the good side of the plywood up. When cutting with a portable, power handsaw, place the good face down.

Using Nails and Screws. Nails or screws do not hold well in the edges of plywood. It is important to remember this, especially when attaching hinges. Whenever possible, hinges for plywood doors should be the kind that attach to the face rather than to the edge.

When nailing plywood, always choose nail size in terms of panel thickness. Nails should be selected as follows: for 3/4" plywood, 6d casing nails or 6d finishing nails; for 5/8", 6d or 8d finishing nails; for 1/2", 4d or 6d; for 3/8", 3d or 4d; and for 1/4", use 3/4" or 1" brads. For very careful installations, predrill to keep the nails from splitting out at the edge. The drill should be slightly smaller in diameter than the nail. Space nails about 6" apart for most work. Closer spacing may be necessary only when nailing thin plywood to avoid buckling between the joints. Nails and glue together produce a strong joint. Flathead wood screws are needed when nails will not provide adequate holding power. Glue should also be used whenever possible.

The following gives plywood thicknesses, diameter, and the length of the smallest screws recommended:

3/4" plywood—No. 8—1 1/2"
5/8" plywood—No. 8—1 1/4"
1/2" plywood—No. 6—1 1/4"
3/8" plywood—No. 6—1"
1/4" plywood—No. 4—3/4"

(Use longer screws when the work permits.)

Screws or nails should be countersunk and the holes filled with wood dough, putty, or plugs. Apply filler until it is slightly higher than the plywood surface, then sand it level after it is dry.

Drilling. If the back side of plywood is going to show, chipped edges can be avoided by placing a wood block under the back when drilling.

HARDWOOD GRADE STANDARDS

Hardwood plywoods are used primarily for interior paneling, built-ins, cabinets and similar finish carpentry applications. A complete description of this material can be found in the textbook, *Cabinetmaking and Millwork*, also written by John L. Feirer and published by Glencoe/Macmillan-McGraw-Hill.

1. Explain the steps in the manufacture of plywood.

2. List six uses for plywood in building construction.

3. Explain how exterior-type plywood differs from interior plywood.

4. Explain some of the precautions that must be taken in working with plywood.

1. **Science.** Conduct a strength test for screw-holding power in plywood edges versus plywood faces. This test can be accomplished using cabinet hinge placement and forcing down the side opposite the hinges. Face-holding or edge-holding screws should reveal a difference in support rendered.

2. **Language Arts.** How does the word *plywood* relate to the way the material is made? When answering, use the word *plies*.

3. **Language Arts.** Study Table 6-F and Fig. 6-4. If you were building a home, which ply of plywood would you purchase? Explain your choice in a short paragraph.

4. **Math.** Discuss with a friend why the number of layers (not plies) must always be odd. (Hint: What would happen to the faces if there were an even number?)

5. **Math.** Plywood is available in various widths. (36", 48", 60") and lengths (60", 72", 84", 96", 108", 120", 132", 144").

   a. If there are three widths and eight lengths as noted above, how many different sizes with the same thickness are available? How many of these does your local supplier carry?

   b. How many times bigger is the largest than the smallest of these?

THE SCHOOL-TO-WORK CONNECTION

Plywood uses wood very efficiently. It is strong, performs predictably, and can be used to cover large areas quickly. These characteristics are the reason that plywood is used so extensively in the construction industry, particularly in residential construction. For plywood to perform properly, however, it must be stored correctly. Water and sun can damage plywood.

1. Visit a local lumberyard. Ask to see how they store the various types of plywood. Some yards carry pressure-treated plywood and hardwood plywood, as well as standard construction plywoods and paneling. Are there any differences in how various types of plywood are stored?

2. Imagine that you are a builder who is remodeling a house. Ten sheets of hardwood plywood will be delivered to the jobsite tomorrow, but you won't be there to receive them. Write instructions to someone on your crew, telling that person how to store the plywood.

UNIT 7

Composition Panels— Hardboard, OSB, and Others

For many years, solid wood was the only wood used in residential construction. It was used for sheathing, siding, and finish floors. The introduction of plywood panels for sheathing, subflooring, and siding significantly changed the construction of homes. Now a number of other panel products, called composition panels, are available in addition to plywood. Fig. 7-1.

Unlike plywood, which is made from layers of wood veneer, composition panels are made from pieces of wood. These may range in size from small fibers to large (1" by 3") flakes. Fig. 7-3. The individual pieces are mixed with an adhesive and formed under pressure into uniform sheets. The most common panel size is 4' × 8', but panels up to 8' wide by 16' long are available. The panels are often (though not always) made from sources that would not be used otherwise. These include:

➤ Tree species not appropriate for veneer production.

➤ Trees that are too small for lumber production.

➤ Portions of trees that would otherwise go unused, such as stumps and limbs.

Though composition panels are most often used for sheathing and subflooring, they can also be used for cabinetry, furniture, and paneling. Fig. 7-2. The most common types of composition panels are oriented-strand board (OSB), hardboard, particleboard, and medium-density fiberboard (MDF). Table 7-A.

7-1. *Composition panels. From left to right: oriented-strand board (OSB), particle board, medium-density fiberboard, hardboard, and T & G oriented-strand board. Panels most often come in 4 x 8 sheets.*

ADHESIVES

Perhaps the most important ingredient of a composition panel is the adhesive used to bond the wood pieces or particles. Phenolic-formaldehyde resins and urea-formaldehyde resins are the adhesives generally used in making composition panels.

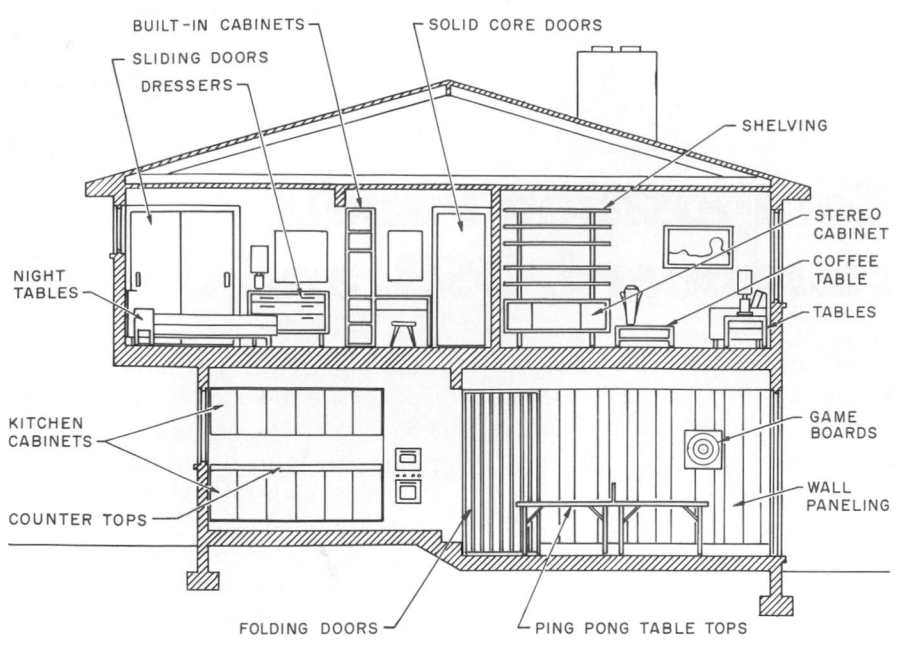

7-2. *Composition panels can be used for sheathing and subflooring, as well as these specialty uses.*

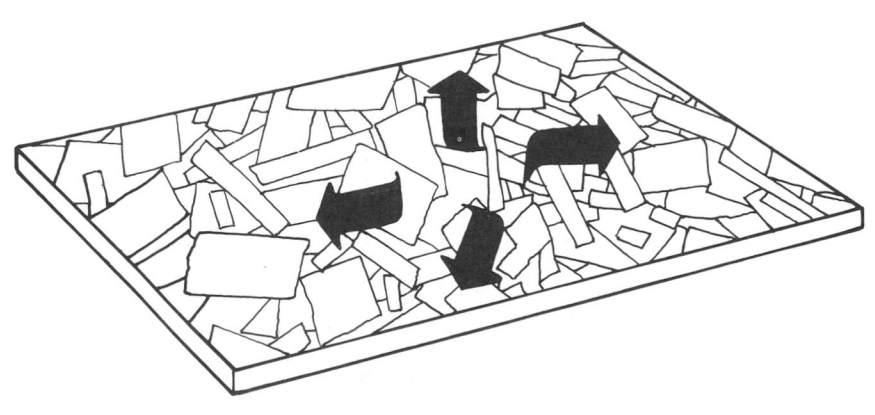

7-3. *Waferboard is one type of composition panel. Note that waferboard flakes have a nondirectional, or random alignment. Note also that this type of composition board is composed of chips, rather than sheets on veneer.*

Phenolic resins are waterproof. That is why they are used for exterior structural applications such as sheathing. Urea resins are less expensive than phenolic resins. They are water-resistant, not waterproof. This makes them appropriate for use in cabinet construction and other indoor applications.

Adhesives and Health

Formaldehyde is a widely used chemical. Unfortunately, some people are very sensitive to airborne formaldehyde. The chemical can cause eyes to water, or it may lead to breathing problems. This can be a significant problem with products that "off-gas" formaldehyde (meaning that formaldehyde is released into the air). When these products are used in tightly-sealed houses, the chemical can accumulate to unhealthy levels.

Urea-formaldehyde resins are a particular problem in this regard. Because of the manufacturing process, urea resins off-gas more formaldehyde than phenolic resins do. The U.S. Department of Housing and Urban Development has issued standards that limit the amount of formaldehyde that is acceptable within housing.

ORIENTED-STRAND BOARD

Oriented-strand board (OSB) has been available since the early 1980s. It is now considered to be similar to plywood in strength and utility. OSB is used primarily for sheathing and subflooring. The panels are made from reconstituted wood strands bonded with adhesive under heat and pressure. Though a variety of wood species can be used, those most often used are aspen, southern pine, and various medium-density hardwoods. The strands in an OSB panel are directionally oriented in layers that are perpendicular to each other. Panels will usually have three or five layers. The most common adhesive used to bond the strands is phenol-formaldehyde. Fig. 7-4.

It is available with square edges or with T&G edges. Common thicknesses range from $\frac{3}{8}$" to $1\frac{1}{8}$". Though OSB is generally made with a waterproof adhesive, the panels are not suited to long-term exposure to the weather. Sheathing should be covered as soon as practical. To increase the moisture resistance of OSB panels, the edges are coated with a factory-applied sealant.

OSB is also available as panel siding. The panels are manufactured with a weather-resistant overlay that should be painted or stained.

Like most wood products, OSB will shrink or swell slightly with changes in humidity. Sheathing and subfloor should be installed with a ⅛" gap between the ends of adjacent panels, and ¼" at the sides. OSB will also swell if exposed to water.

Handling OSB

Oriented-strand board is more susceptible to thickness swelling than plywood. If the edge seal is damaged during storage or installation, moisture can sink into the panel and swell its edges. Panels should not be stored directly on the ground. Instead, they should be stacked on a level platform supported by 4" × 4" stringers or other blocking. OSB panels should be covered loosely with a waterproof tarp as soon as they arrive at a job site. The tarp should be arranged so as not to trap ground moisture beneath it. Steel banding that secures the panels during delivery should be cut soon after panels arrive at the job site. This will prevent the edges from being damaged if the stack of panels swells.

Waferboard

Many people confuse OSB with *waferboard* because the products look similar. The main difference is that waferboard is made with flakes of wood that are randomly aligned throughout the panel, instead of oriented in particular directions. Though this makes waferboard equally strong in all directions, it is not as strong as OSB overall. To span a given distance, a sheet of waferboard will have to be thicker than an otherwise comparable sheet of OSB. Fig. 7-5.

HARDBOARD

Hardboard is an all-wood panel manufactured from wood fibers. Logs are cut into small wood chips which are reduced to fibers by steam or mechanical processes. These fibers are refined, then compressed under heat and pressure in giant presses to produce a sturdy, quality building material.

Some of the advantages of hardboard are:
➤ It has superior wear resistance.
➤ It does not split, crack, or splinter.
➤ It has high abrasive resistance.
➤ It is easy to work with ordinary tools.
➤ It is easy to fasten and bend.

Hardboard has many uses for interiors and exteriors of new and

Table 7-A. *Characteristics of Composite Panels.*

Material	Primary Uses	Resin	Wood Component
OSB	Sheathing, subflooring, siding	Phenol-formaldehyde	Wafers or flakes
Hardboard	Siding, paneling	Phenol-formaldehyde	Fibers
Particleboard	Underlayment, cabinet carcasses, substrate for plastic laminate	Urea-formaldehyde (phenol-formaldehyde available)	Particles
Medium-density Fiberboard	Cabinets, cabinet doors, furniture	Urea-formaldehyde	Fibers

7-4. OSB. The strands are directionally oriented.

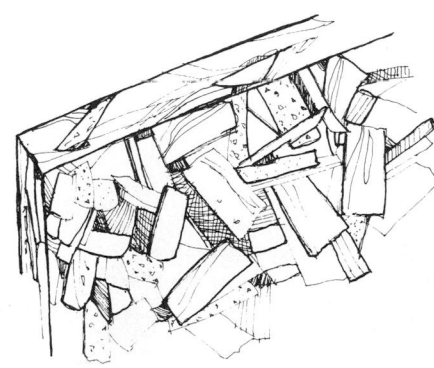

7-5. Waferboard. Note that the wafers are not aligned.

7-6a. *A major advantage of using panel stock—uniformity of size and shape—is illustrated in these stacks of standard-size hardboard.*

7-6b. *Decorative exterior hardboard such as this V-grooved panel simplifies construction.*

remodeled homes. About half of all hardboard is used in building construction for siding, interior paneling, underlayment, kitchen cabinets, and similar purposes. Fig. 7-6.

Types and Sizes of Hardboard

Hardboard is made in three basic types: *standard, tempered,* and *service.* Standard hardboard is given no additional treatment after manufacture. This board has high strength and good water resistance. It is commonly used in cabinetwork because it has a very smooth surface and finishes well. Tempered hardboard is standard board to which chemical and heat-treating processes have been applied to improve stiffness, hardness, and finishing properties. Service hardboard has somewhat less strength than standard. It is used where low weight is an advantage. It does not have quite as smooth a surface as standard.

Hardboard is manufactured with one or both sides smooth. One side smooth is known as S1S and two sides smooth is S2S. Hardboard is available in thicknesses from $\frac{1}{8}$" to $\frac{3}{8}$", the common thicknesses being $\frac{1}{8}$", $\frac{3}{16}$", and $\frac{1}{4}$". The standard panel size is 4' × 8', but widths up to 6' and lengths to 16' are also available.

Specialty Hardboards. Because hardboard is manufactured, it can be made in shapes, sizes, and surfaces to meet varying needs of the building industry. The following paragraphs list a few of the many kinds available.

Perforated hardboard has very closely spaced holes punched or drilled in the surface. The openings may be round, square, or diagonal and can be fitted with metal hooks, holders, supports, or similar fittings. Fig. 7-7. Such hardboard is in common use not only in homes, but in stores for display and storage.

Embossed patterns are available in simulated leather, wood grain, and basket weave.

Acoustical hardboard has perforations which improve its

7-7. *Perforated hardboard can be useful in storage areas of a house.*

properties for controlling sound. It makes an excellent covering for ceilings and walls.

Wood-grain hardboard is printed with grain to match the color and texture of oak, walnut, mahogany, and many other woods. It is popular for interior paneling. Many other types of hardboard panels are designed for building construction.

Hardboard exterior siding is available in both horizontal lap and vertical panel style, fully prefinished or factory-primed. Lap siding, which is made in widths of 6" to 12" and up to 16' in length, is applied horizontally as clapboard. The vertical panel siding is available in 4' widths and in lengths up to 16'. Some lap and panel sidings are embossed with wood grain or other textures. Panel sidings come with V-grooved surfaces or in plain panels for board-and-batten style application.

Filigree hardboard panels are decorative items. They are made of tempered hardboard, smooth on both sides, and die-cut to provide the filigree patterns. They are normally ⅛" thick and available in sizes up to 4' × 8'. They are used in cabinet doors, room dividers, folding screens, sliding doors, and as accent wall panels, among others.

Hardboard underlayment is service-grade hardboard, planed to a uniform thickness. Though it is used relatively infrequently for this purpose (most builders prefer particleboard underlayment), it is still available in some areas. It comes in 3' × 4' and 4' × 4' sizes. These sheets are nailed (with ringed underlayment nails) or stapled over subflooring or old finish to serve as a uniform base for floor tile, linoleum, and carpeting. Fig. 7-8. Panels should be fitted in staggered fashion, spaced about ¹⁄₃₂" apart. Joints should not coincide with those on the subfloor. Use 4"

7-8. Both hardboard and particleboard, shown here, make excellent underlay material for finish flooring.

spacing between fasteners across the entire area of the panel. Hardboard manufacturers have their own instructions for applying underlayment, which should be followed.

Other special-purpose hardboard products include ceiling blocks, attractive ceiling beams, and barn siding, among others. There is also a wide range of accessories to simplify the use of hardboards. Examples of accessories are metal, wood, vinyl, or hardboard moldings, color-matched to the prefinished paneling; color-matched nails; and special adhesives for nail-free applications.

PARTICLEBOARD

Particleboard is made by combining wood flakes or particles with resin binders, and hot-pressing them into panels. The panels range from ¼" to 1½" thick, from 3' to 8' wide, and up to 24' in length. Almost any dimension may be obtained by cutting or gluing segments together. In the manufacturing process, the

composition and properties of each panel are carefully controlled.

There are two basic types of particleboard—*extruded* and *mat-formed*. Panels made by the extrusion process are generally used by the manufacturer that produced them. Mat-formed wood particleboard is sold for a wide variety of uses in the building and woodworking trades. In addition to these basic kinds of particleboard, the product comes in ten different grades and in three different densities (high, medium, and low). Table 7-B.

Uses in Architecture and Home Building

Particleboard is an important material for providing flat, true surfaces which are needed in most homes. Uses for this material in home building include nearly all types of counters; cabinets; drawers; shelving; vanities; sliding, folding, solid-core, or accordion doors; room dividers, and many other kinds of built-ins.

One of the largest uses of particleboard in the home is in the construction of kitchen counters, sink tops, and cabinets. Fig. 7-9. Components made with particleboard may be purchased

7-9. Applying plastic laminate to a particleboard core for counter tops.

from cabinet and counter top manufacturers or built on the site. Many cabinet and sink top manufacturers use particleboard because of its smooth, grain-free surface, which is a good base for high-pressure laminates. Also, doors made of particleboard are warp-free, requiring a minimum of on-site adjustment.

Counter tops and cabinets of particleboard can be built on the construction site. Often this is done with panels veneered with popular kitchen cabinet woods. These are commonly available through lumber and building materials dealers. Particleboard also makes good shelving, which can be painted easily.

The largest single use of particleboard in the construction industry is for floor underlayment. It provides a smooth, stable base for resilient tile or carpeting.

Selecting and Specifying Particleboard

A wide choice of particleboard products is available. This is partly because there are many manufacturers and they use different raw materials and processes. Another reason for the variety is that since particleboard is a man-made product, it can be produced in different forms to meet specific needs. Table 7-C.

To select the right particleboard product for a specific job, be sure to read the manufacturers' descriptions of their materials. Such descriptions will tell you the specific characteristics of each product. Also you will need to know the requirements for the job you are doing.

For example, one type of particleboard may have very high stiffness; it would be best suited for use as a core material for very large table tops, large folding partitions or wall panels, or for use where intermediate supports are limited. However, another type with lower stiffness might be just as good if adequately supported or overlaid.

Besides stiffness, there are other properties—machinability, edge-finishing characteristics, hardness, surface smoothness—which are important in selecting a specific panel. It is important to know how these and other properties vary from one type of panel to another.

There are certain variables which can be controlled during the

Table 7-B. *Types and Uses of Particleboard.*

1. Corestock	Products of flakes or particles bonded with urea-formaldehyde or phenolic resins with various densities and related properties.	For furniture, casework, architectural paneling, doors and laminated components.
2. Wood Veneered Particleboard	Corestock overlaid at the mill with various wood veneers.	For furniture, panels, wainscots, dividers, cabinets, etc.
3. Overlaid Particleboard	Particleboard faced with impregnated fiber sheets, hardboard or decorative plastic sheets.	For applications such as furniture doors, wall paneling, sink tops, cabinetry and store fixtures.
4. Embossed Particleboard	Surfaces are heavily textured in various decorative patterns by branding with heated roller.	For doors, architectural paneling, wainscots, display units and cabinet panels.
5. Filled Particleboard	Particleboard surface-filled and sanded ready for painting.	For painted end-products requiring firm, flat, true surfaces.
6. Exterior Particleboard	Made with phenolic resins for resistance to weathering.	For use as an exterior covering material.
7. Toxic-Treated Particleboard	Particleboard treated with chemicals to resist insects, mold and decay producing fungi.	For tropical or other applications where wood products require protection against insect attack or decay.
8. Primed or Undercoated	Factory painted base coat on either filled or regular board—exterior or interior.	For any painted products.
9. Floor Underlayment	Panels specifically engineered for floor underlayment.	Underlay for carpets or resilient floor coverings.
10. Fire-Retardant Particleboard	Particles are treated with fire retardants.	For use where building codes require low flame spread material, as in some schools, office buildings, etc.

manufacturing process to produce a certain type of panel. These variables include density, flake or particle shape, amount and type of resin, and moisture content.

Density. Stock panels range in density from 24 to 62 pounds per cubic foot. Ordinarily, a panel with high density will also have greater strength and a smoother, tighter edge than a low-density panel.

Particles Used. Two strong influences on the properties of board products are:
➤ The size and shape of individual flakes and particles.
➤ The ratio of resin to particles.
Particle shape and resin content can be controlled to create a given set of physical properties. The size, type, and position of the particles also will influence a panel's surface smoothness.

Resin. Two types of resin, urea-formaldehyde and phenol-formaldehyde, are used in the manufacture of particleboard. Urea-formaldehyde is the most common and is suitable for interior use. Phenol-formaldehyde is used where the panel is subjected to extreme heat or humidity or for exterior applications.

Moisture Content. It is especially important to control the moisture content of those particleboard panels which are to be overlaid. This is because the core material and the overlay material must have nearly equal moisture content. Panels normally are shipped from the mill at a moisture content of 7 to 9% unless otherwise specified.

Special Properties. Panels can be given special finishes or treatments at the mill. They may be filled or primed for easy painting, or embossed for decorative, textured surfaces. The edges of panels may be banded with lumber, cut to size, or given special sanding or overlays. Laminating and/or edge-gluing is done to make panels of unusual sizes.

Working with Particleboard and Hardboard

These materials are free from the cracks and other imperfections commonly found in wood. They present none of the problems related to grain in wood. Table 7-C.

Generally, particleboard and hardboard are worked with standard woodworking tools. These materials can be sawed, routed, rabbeted, shaped, and drilled cleanly, with good edges and corners. Fig 7-10. Since these

Table 7-C. *Typical Working Characteristics of Manufactured Board.*

	Thick Panels—¼"—1½"		Thin Panels—⅛"—⅜"		
	Flake Board 42 # cu. ft.	**Particleboard 40 # cu. ft.**	**Hardboard**		
			Standard	**Tempered**	**Specialties**
Bending	Fair	Fair	Good	Excellent	Good
Drilling	Excellent	Good	Good	Excellent	Excellent
Hardness	High	Medium	Medium	High	High
Laminating	Excellent	Good	Good	Excellent	Excellent
Nailing	Good	Good	Fair	Good	Good
Painting	Unfilled—Good Filled—Excel.	Unfilled—Fair Filled—Good	Fair	Excellent	Excellent
Punching	Fair	Fair	Fair	Excellent	Good
Routing	Excellent	Good	Fair	Excellent	Good
Sanding	Excellent	Good	Fair	Excellent	Good
Sawing	Excellent	Good	Fair	Excellent	Good
Screw Holding	Excellent	Good	Fair	Good	Good
Shaping	Excellent	Good	Fair	Excellent	Good
Water Resistance	Interior or Exterior	Interior or Exterior	Interior	Exterior	Interior or Exterior

7-10. *There is no chipping or splintering when cutting hardboard or particleboard.*

boards are made to exact thicknesses and finish-sanded at the mill, there is little need for further surface preparation. (For information on finishing these materials, see Appendix.)

All types of joints usually employed in casework or used with architectural assemblies are readily made with particleboard. Architectural panels may be butted or V-grooved, splined, or the joint emphasized with a batten or decorative molding. In cabinetry, joint types include ordinary miter, splined or lockmiter, dowel, mortise and tenon, dovetail, and tongue and groove.

The absence of voids gives these boards a full, uniform contact surface for glued joints. This assures strong glued butt joints, permitting short lengths to be glued into longer sections for a minimum of waste.

MEDIUM-DENSITY FIBERBOARD

Medium-density fiberboard (MDF) is a composition panel similar to particleboard. However, it is made from individual wood fibers instead of wood particles. The fibers are mixed with urea-formaldehyde resin. Because of the uniformity of the fibers used in the manufacturing process, MDF panels are uniform throughout their thickness and have an extremely smooth surface. This makes them ideal for use where the end product will be painted. This includes door panels and cabinetry. MDF is also used as a substrate for plastic laminates.

MDF can be worked with standard cutting tools, but carbide-tipped saw blades render the best results. Because the sawdust is extremely fine, it is important to wear appropriate dust protection when cutting or sanding the material.

QUESTIONS

1. What are the advantages of manufactured building board products?

2. List five manufactured building boards.

3. List five specialty hardboards and several uses of each.

4. How is particleboard made?

5. What are the two basic types of particleboard?

6. What is one of the largest uses of particleboard in the home?

7. What is the primary difference between oriented-strand board (OSB) and waferboard?

8. Name the two most common types of resins used in the manufacture of composition panels.

ACTIVITIES

1. Science. With a friend, list five reasons why the building boards described in this unit, as well as many other building materials, are rectangular.

2. Science. Particleboard is manufactured with a range of densities. You decide to use ¾" particleboard for a sheathing project. You can choose either 24 lb./cubic foot or 40 lb./cubic foot board. If there are 1,800 square feet to cover, what is the difference in weight of the sheathing required using these two different densities? Is the weight difference important?

3. Social Studies. Compare the building materials that go into today's homes with the materials that went into pioneers' log cabins. What types of materials used in today's homes were considered a luxury in a log cabin?

Framing Connectors and Engineered Wood

The homebuilding industry generally relies on materials and techniques that have been proven over the years. New ideas sometimes take hold slowly. Builders are conservative for good reason. It takes considerable time and money to build a house, and mistakes can be costly. The industry has, however, accepted several new materials and products in recent years. Among them are several important structural products. These products are:

➤ Laminated-veneer lumber (including wood I-beams).

➤ Glue-laminated beams.

➤ Metal connectors for wood framing.

These products can be found on residential job sites. They are used to solve a variety of framing problems. The products can replace or supplement more conventional materials. For example, wood I-beams can be used instead of dimension lumber for floor joists and rafters. Glue-laminated beams can be used in place of timber or steel to span large openings. Metal joist hangers can replace simple toenailed connections.

As builders gain more experience with these products, more uses will be found for them. This unit will provide a basic understanding of the products.

LAMINATED-VENEER LUMBER

The term *laminated-veneer lumber* describes a family of products made with wood veneer as the basic element. Fig. 8-1. These products are used primarily for beams, headers, joists, and rafters in both residential and commercial construction. The products are predictable in performance and available in lengths of 60' or more. They are lightweight, rigid, and cost-effective. They also shrink and swell less than solid lumber. Fig. 8-2.

Manufacturing LVL

Laminated-veneer lumber (LVL) products are manufactured in plants around the United States and Canada. Bundles of ⅒" thick veneer are delivered to the plant. Fig. 8-3. Veneer from any species of

8-1. *Laminated-veneer products include solid headers (right) and wood I-beams (left).*

8-2. *One advantage of LVL I-beams is that they are light in weight. Care should be taken, however, not to let an I-beam flex back and forth too much prior to installation.*

wood may be used, though Douglas fir is most commonly used. Southern yellow pine is also used frequently. The sheets of veneer pass via conveyor belt through large, open-ended drying ovens. This dries the veneer to a uniform moisture content. As each sheet exits the drying oven, it is ultrasonically graded and checked for quality.

The veneer is then fed into an automatic glue-spreader, which coats the top of each veneer sheet with a uniform layer of adhesive. The adhesive is a phenol-formaldehyde resin that is waterproof, resistant to heat, and very strong. As the glued sheets are assembled, the highest-grade veneers are placed at the top and bottom of the layup. This increases the overall strength of the finished product. The sheets are then fed continuously into a machine that uses heat and pressure to cure the adhesive. The resulting *billet* may be 80' long. Billets are then cut into stock for headers, beams, or for the chords of wood I-beams.

Finished LVL products are shipped to materials dealers by truck or railcar in 60' lengths. When a builder orders LVL products, the dealer cuts them to approximate length and delivers them to the job site. The builder is usually responsible for cutting them to exact length on the job.

Structural Performance

A cross-section of laminated-veneer lumber (LVL) looks similar to a cross-section of plywood. Fig. 8-4. However, there is an important difference between the products. Plywood is cross-laminated. This means that the grain of each layer runs perpendicular to the grain of

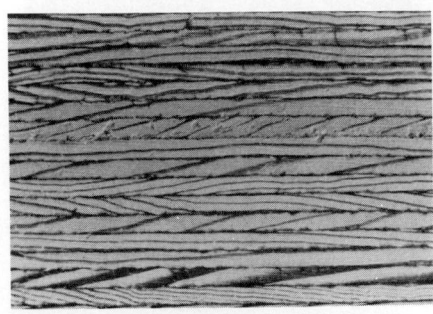

8-4. *A cross-section of LVL stock.*

adjoining layers. In contrast, the grain of every layer in laminated-veneer lumber runs in the same direction. This is called *parallel-lamination*. This process produces a material that is more uniform than would be found in a like thickness of material produced by cross-lamination. It also means that the end grain of each veneer layer is exposed only at the very ends of LVL products.

Because each piece of stock is so uniform, LVL products are very predictable in their performance. For the architect or engineer, this means that the structural performance of the building can be carefully controlled. For the builder, this means that each piece of LVL will behave exactly like the other pieces in a load. If there is any swelling, for example, all the pieces will swell by the same amount. In contrast, each piece of dimension lumber may shrink or swell differently after leaving the mill. Laminated-veneer lumber leaves the mill typically at 8% moisture content.

LVL I-Beams

One of the most common laminated-veneer lumber products is the I-beam (also called an I-joist). Fig. 8-5. It is most often used in floor construction as a joist, but can also be used in place of rafters in roof construction. Fig. 8-6. The top and bottom chords of the I-

8-3. *Bundles of veneer awaiting conversion into LVL products.*

8-5. *Wood I-beams come in various sizes. Prescored circular knockouts along the length of each one can be removed to provide access for plumbing and electrical lines.*

beam are made from continuous lengths of laminated-veneer lumber. The web is made from sections of structural ⅜" plywood or oriented-strand board (OSB). Waterproof adhesive is used to attach webs to chords. No nails or staples are used. Wood I-beams are available in depths ranging from 9" deep to 32" deep. An I-beam chord

8-6a. *Wood I-beam floor systems are quickly installed.*

8-6b. *An I-beam roof.*

is commonly 1¾" or 2⁵⁄₁₆" wide.

I-beams have several advantages over solid lumber. Because they are available in lengths of 60' or more, a single I-beam can run the entire width of a house. This speeds installation of an I-beam floor. Relatively few pieces of stock must be handled, which saves time. A wood I-beam is lighter in weight than an equal length of solid lumber. For example, a wood I-beam 26' long and 9½" deep weighs about 50 pounds. A solid length of lumber 2" × 10" of the same length weighs about 96 lbs. Its light weight makes a wood I-beam relatively easy to handle and install.

Installation Details. The web of an I-beam is not in the same plane as its chords, so care must be taken when cutting the product. The easiest method is to use a radial arm saw for crosscutting. However, some cutting with a circular saw is inevitable. To do this safely, the shoe of the saw must be prevented from lodging against a chord during the cut. This is done by placing a wood block against the web and between the chords. The I-beam may then be cut with ease.

Wood I-beams used in floor construction are installed in similar fashion to dimension lumber joists. They can be nailed to the plate (by toenailing through the lower flange) or secured by metal joist hangers. They can be braced with solid blocking, I-beam blocking, or metal cross-bracing.

When joist hangers are used, several considerations must be kept in mind. Joist hangers are generally nailed to the I-beam with 10d common nails. Nails should never be driven sideways (parallel to the laminations) into an I-beam chord. This tends to split the laminations, reducing the strength of the product. Instead, nails should be driven into the chord at a 45-

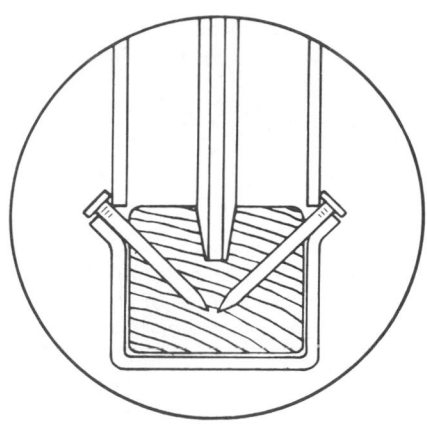

8-7. *Nails should always be driven through an LVL chord at a 45° angle to avoid splitting the stock.*

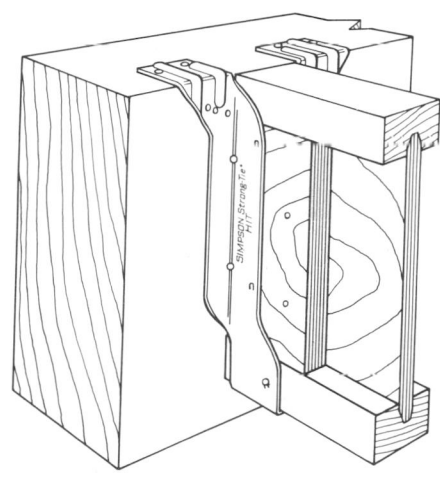

8-8. *Bearing blocks fit between the joist hanger and the I-beam. They prevent the web from buckling at stress points.*

degree angle. Fig. 8-7. In some instances, slender blocks of wood should be permanently installed against the web on either side of the I-beam. These are called web stiffeners or bearing blocks. They reinforce the chord against cross-grain bending. They also prevent the web from buckling at points of high stress. Fig. 8-8. Web stiffeners should also be installed where an I-beam crosses a mid-span support such as a floor girder. Fig. 8-9. Where two I-beams intersect, backing blocks should be used

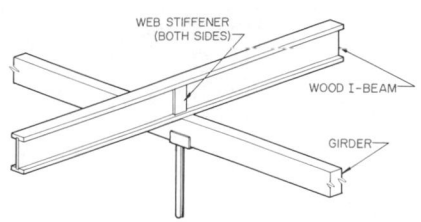

8-9. *Web stiffeners should be installed on both sides of the I-beam where it crosses a support.*

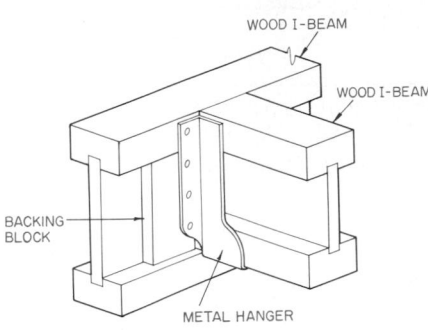

8-10. *Recommended detail where two I-beams intersect.*

behind the joist hanger to give it solid bearing. Fig. 8-10.

Wood I-beams can be doubled up to form a header, but they should not be tripled. The expense of such an assembly would typically exceed other options, such as a glue-laminated header. Also, metal hangers are not recommended for use with tripled I-beams.

The web of a wood I-beam has 1½" diameter pre-scored knockouts located approximately 12" on center along its entire length. Fig. 8-5. These can be punched out with a hammer to create passages for plumbing and electrical lines. This eliminates the need for time-consuming drilling or notching. Additional 1½" diameter holes can be cut anywhere along the length of the web. Larger round or square holes may be cut, but only according to the manufacturer's recommendations. The chords of an I-beam should never be notched or drilled. This could weaken the

8-11. *Laminated-veneer header stock.*

product to the point of failure.

Unlike solid lumber, wood I-beams are made in different ways and to different specifications by individual manufacturers. Therefore, you must contact the manufacturer of the specific product you intend to use in order to get span tables and other details.

LVL Headers

Laminated-veneer headers and beams can be used in place of solid wood or built-up wood headers. Fig. 8-11. The product consists of many layers of veneer laminated together into a solid material with a rectangular cross-section. When the product has been properly installed, the layers of veneer will be perpendicular to the ground. LVL header and beam stock comes in various thicknesses. Stock with a thickness of 1¾" is most common in residential work. Stronger stock can be made by nailing two or more layers of LVL together. Use three rows of 16d nails spaced 12" on center. Common depths of LVL headers and beams range from 5½" to 18". Table 8-A.

Cutting and nailing these products is no different than working with solid lumber. Fig. 8-12. Some builders, however, feel that the nail-holding ability of LVL headers

8-12. *An LVL beam can be secured to intersecting stock with a metal hanger.*

Table 8-A. *Common Dimensions for LVL Headers and Beams.*

Depth*	Thickness
5½", 7¼", 9½", 11⅞", 14", 16"*, 18"*	1¾"

* 16" and 18" beams should be used only in multiple thicknesses.

and beams is considerably greater than that of solid lumber. Holes must not be cut in LVL headers or beams.

Care and Handling

All laminated-veneer products are produced using waterproof adhesives. This allows them to withstand normal exposure to moisture during installation. But as with plywood and other manufactured wood products, LVL should not be exposed unnecessarily to moisture. LVL beams and headers are more sensitive to moisture damage than I-beams. All LVL products are wrapped in protective material for transport to the job site. This

wrapping should not be removed until the materials are ready to be installed.

LVL products should be stored on edge prior to installation. This is particularly important for I-beams because they are relatively weak in lateral strength. The chords of an I-beam are continuous lengths of laminated-veneer lumber, but the web is not a continuous length of material. Storing an I-beam on its side or allowing it to flex back and forth could break the glued butt joint that joins individual sections of web. This would severely weaken the product.

GLUE-LAMINATED BEAMS

When layers of solid sawn lumber are glued together, the strength and rigidity of the resulting material is greater than solid timber of equal dimension. This is the principle behind glue-laminated beams. Until recently,

8-14. *Glulam beams are ideal for situations in which considerable distances must be spanned.*

these beams, called *glulams*, were used only in commercial and heavy construction. The ability of a glulam to take various forms and to span great distances made it a very useful material. Fig. 8-13. These same characteristics, on a smaller scale, are what make glulams increasingly useful in residential construction. Large rooms and open floorplans are popular with home buyers. Glulam construction is sometimes more cost effective than using steel or solid timber to span such distances. Glulam beams can also be used for garage door headers, patio door headers, window headers, and even exposed structural stair stringers. Fig. 8-14.

Glulam beams have significant resistance to fire. A glulam is difficult to ignite, and burns slowly if it does catch fire. In some fires where an unprotected steel beam may fail completely, a glulam beam will retain significant strength.

Fabrication

Glulam beams are made by laminating lengths of dimension lumber using structural adhesives. The individual layers of the beam are adhered face to face, clamped together, and allowed to cure at room temperature. The grain of all

8-13. *Glulam beams can be made in many forms, as shown by this dramatic series of structural arches.*

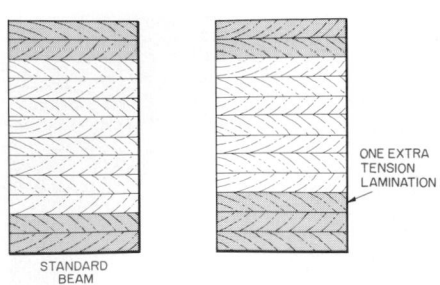

STANDARD BEAM

ONE EXTRA TENSION LAMINATION

8-15. *The layers of a glulam beam.*

laminations is approximately parallel along the length of the beam. Each layer is no more than 2" thick. Woods most commonly used in the construction of glulams are Southern yellow pine and Douglas fir.

As with laminated-veneer lumber, the best quality material is used in the top and bottom layers of a glulam. This improves the strength of a glulam by nearly 100% as compared to random layering. When a fire rating is required for the glulam, the arrangement of layers is altered slightly to put additional high quality lumber on the bottom of the beam. Fig. 8-15.

Glulams are often cambered. *Camber* is a slight upward curve in the beam, like the crown in a piece of lumber. When the beam is in place and fully loaded, the curve straightens out. Beams that are not cambered may sag slightly when they are fully loaded.

Grades

Three grades of glulams are available. The differences between the grades are purely visual. There are no differences in strength or method of manufacture. The grades are:
- ➤ Industrial.
- ➤ Architectural.
- ➤ Premium.

Industrial grade is suitable for areas in which appearance is not of

particular importance. Voids may appear on the exposed edges of the glulam. The beam is surfaced only on the sides.

Architectural grade is used where appearance is somewhat more important. Some voids are permitted, but any voids over ¾" in diameter will be filled. All exposed faces are surfaced and the exposed edges of the beam are eased.

Premium grade is appropriate where appearance is of primary importance. All knot holes and voids are filled. All exposed faces are surfaced and the exposed edges are eased.

Specifying Glulams

When ordering or specifying glue-laminated beams, width and depth are the factors to pay attention to. Because glulams are planed after lamination, the end product is not as wide as the original pieces. Typically, information about the loads expected is given to the lamination fabricator, who probably has an engineer on staff. The engineer will calculate the stresses and identify a beam configuration that will work.

Glulams used as beams can be ordered in nearly any size and length. Glulams used for standard headers are typically 3½" or 5½" wide. They come in depths that range from 7½" to 18".

Installation Details

Care must be taken to install glulams properly. They should not be notched or drilled in any way unless this has been accounted for in the design of the glulam. Heavy-gauge metal framing connectors are often used to secure glulams. Common glulam connection details are shown in Fig. 8-16.

METAL FRAMING CONNECTORS

In the early days of wood frame construction, all wood-to-wood connections were secured only with nails. While this ensured that the connection would hold, it could be time consuming. Also, because of differences in nailing technique between individual carpenters, the strength of the connections varied

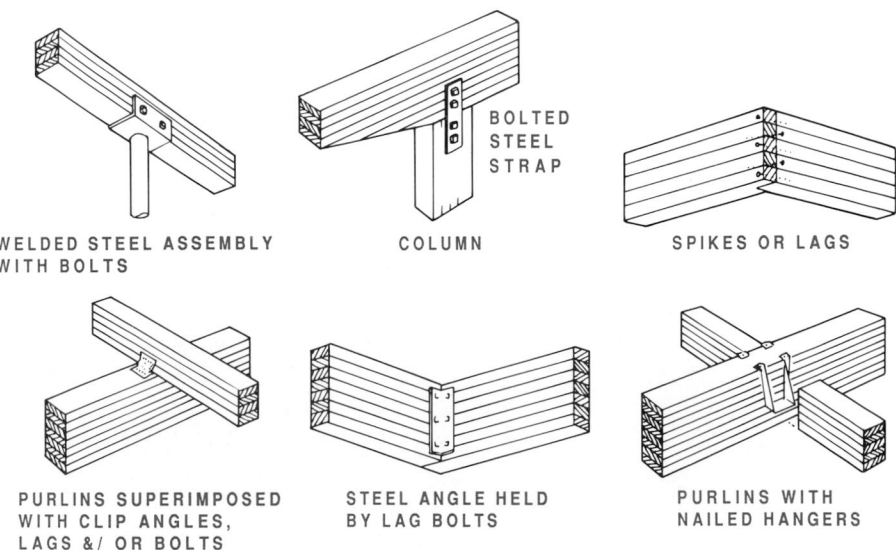

WELDED STEEL ASSEMBLY WITH BOLTS

BOLTED STEEL STRAP

COLUMN

SPIKES OR LAGS

PURLINS SUPERIMPOSED WITH CLIP ANGLES, LAGS &/ OR BOLTS

STEEL ANGLE HELD BY LAG BOLTS

PURLINS WITH NAILED HANGERS

8-16. *Common connections for use with glulam beams.*

Table 8-B. *Galvanized Steel. The thickness of metal used for framing connectors.*

GALVANIZED STEEL

Gauge	In Decimals[2]	In Approximate Fractions
3	—	—
7	—	—
10	0.138" (3.5 mm)	1/8"
11	0.123" (3.1 mm)	1/8"
12	0.108" (2.7 mm)	3/32"
14	0.078" (2.0) mm)	3/32"
16	0.063" (1.6 mm)	1/16"
18	0.052" (1.3 mm)	1/16"
20	0.040" (1.0 mm)	1/32"
22	0.034" (0.8 mm)	1/32"

1. Actual steel dimensions will vary from nominal dimensions according to industry tolerances.
2. mm=millimetres

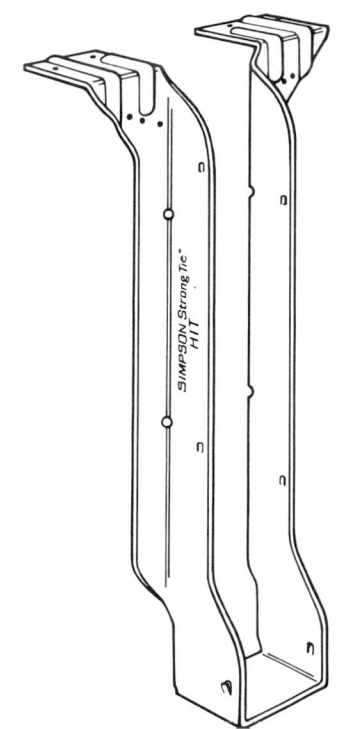

8-17a. *A joist hanger.*

8-17b. *These joist hangers are aligned with the bottom of an intersecting beam.*

considerably. Metal framing connectors speed framing and improve the uniformity of connections.

A metal connector is a formed or stamped metal bracket designed to make wood-to-wood, wood-to-masonry, or wood-to-concrete connections. Some are intended to remain exposed: these are called ornamental connectors. However, most will never be seen after the building is completed. These connectors are made from various gauges of galvanized steel. Table 8-B.

A very wide variety of connectors is available to the builder and carpenter. The following information is intended to be a general overview of the products, not a comprehensive discussion. The best source of detailed application information comes from manufacturers of metal connectors. You should consult their product literature. Also, you should check the building codes for your area to make sure that the specific connectors you wish to use are approved for that application.

Hangers

Perhaps the most common metal connector is the joist hanger. Fig. 8-17a. These sturdy brackets are used where floor or ceiling joists intersect another framing member, such as a beam. The standard hangers are made from 16-gauge galvanized metal. They are typically installed with 10d nails. However, using 16d nails will improve the strength of the connection. Joist hangers are available in sizes to fit most common framing situations. Headers, for example, may be doubled and hung from a joist hanger. Even stock as large as glulam beams and large solid timbers may be used with joist hangers.

Joist hangers are often used when the top edge of the joists must be at the same level as the top edge of the intersected beam. The hanger is nailed both to the beam and to the joist. They are also common when the bottom edges of

the intersecting members must be flush. Fig. 8-17b.

Installing a joist hanger is simple. Typically, the hanger is nailed first to the beam. Then the joist is slipped into place and nailed. However, some carpenters find that it is sometimes easier and more efficient to secure the hanger first to the end of the joist. They then put the joist in position and nail the hanger to the beam. This is also done when the carpenter finds that the joist stock varies slightly in depth from piece to piece. This may be due to uneven drying, or it may be the result of a mixed load of lumber.

For proper installation, the hanger must be flush with both intersecting members. If the sides of the hanger are spread out too wide, the joist will be raised slightly above the header. This will cause a lump in the floor sheathing. If the seat of the hanger is "kicked out" from the beam, settling later on may cause the floor to squeak. Fig. 8-18.

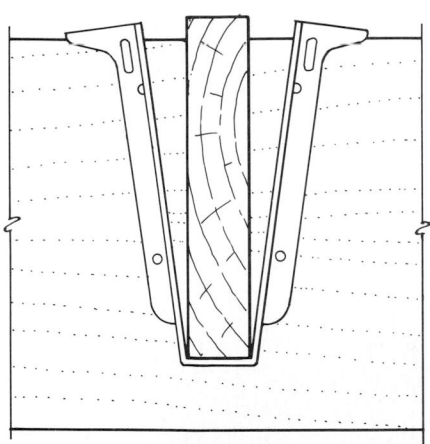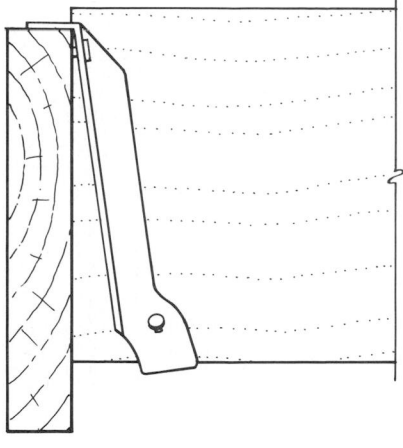

8-18. Common mistakes when installing joist hangers. An overspread hanger will raise the height of the joist (left). If the hanger is "kicked out" from the header (right), the floor may squeak later.

8-20a. Railing ties are first connected to the post. Galvanized screws may be used because the connection is not load bearing.

The most common mistake made when installing joist hangers is to use too few nails. The connection depends on nails for shear strength. Thus, undernailing could cause it to fail when loads are placed on the floor. Check the manufacturer's literature carefully. Use all the nails recommended. Table 8-C shows one manufacturer's nailing recommendations for standard joist hangers.

Ties

Metal framing ties are also used on job sites. The most common form of tie is a flat strap. The strap can be used wherever it is necessary to hold pieces of wood together. The straps are perforated so that they can be nailed in place without drilling. They may also be bent to fit various angles. Fig. 8-19.

Another type of tie is formed into an angular shape. It can be used in unobtrusive locations to join wood members at right angles. Such ties do not carry structural loads. Instead, they simply hold the pieces of wood together. An example is the tie that connects deck railings to deck posts. Fig. 8-20. The post holds the railing up; the tie simply holds them together. An advantage of this particular connection is that it eliminates the need for surface-nailing the connection. It also reduces the chance that water will penetrate the area around the nails.

Table 8-C. Sample Nailing Recommendations for Standard Joist Hangers.

Joist Size	Recommended Nail	Number of Nails Required
2 x 4	10d x 1½"	2
2 x 6, 2 x 8		4
2 x 10, 2 x 12, 2 x 14		6
2 x 14, 2 x 16		8

8-19. Metal ties are being used here to connect sections of a top plate.

8-20b. *Screws are then run into the underside of the railing. This eliminates surface nailing and reduces the chances for rot.*

Other Metal Connectors

The wide variety of metal connectors makes them useful from foundation to roof. Metal post bases can be embedded within concrete slabs or piers. The base holds the wood post slightly above the level of the concrete to reduce the possibility of rot. When the post is bolted to the post base, it is securely tied to its foundation. Fig. 8-21.

8-21. *A post base holds the wood slightly above the top of the pier to reduce rot.*

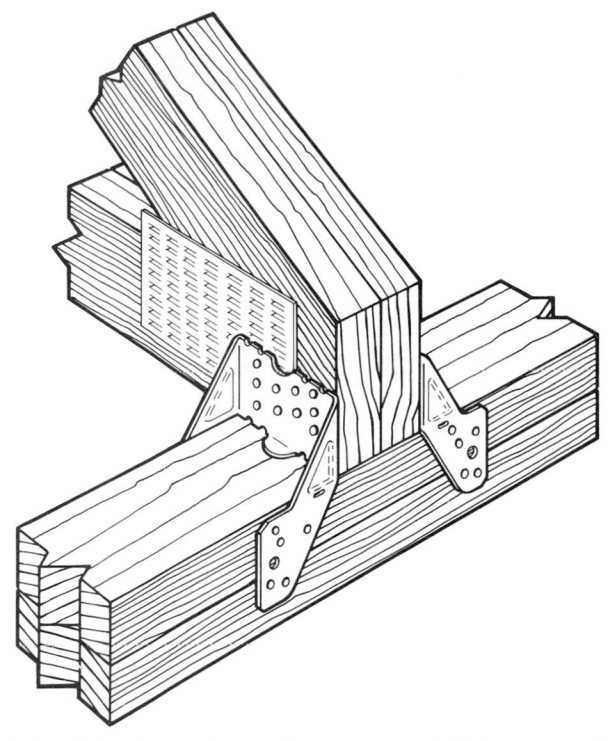

8-22. *These metal connectors are being used to improve the connection between a truss and a double top plate.*

Rafters and trusses can be tied securely to the top plate with various types of metal clips and brackets. Fig. 8-22. In areas prone to earthquakes or fierce weather,

8-23. *By strengthening the connection between rafters and the top plate, these hurricane clips help the structure of a house to resist severe weather.*

metal connectors are sometimes required in residential construction. For example, metal hurricane clips connecting top plates to rafters will prevent the roof from lifting off in extremely high winds. Fig. 8-23.

Fasteners for Metal Connectors

Most structural framing connectors are used in situations where the nails used to fasten them are exposed to shear stresses, rather than withdrawal forces. In other words, the nail is loaded perpendicular to its length. It is extremely important that the fasteners used to secure metal connectors be able to withstand shear stress. Otherwise, the connection may fail.

Some builders use drywall screws to secure connectors because the screws penetrate wood quickly and resist withdrawal. *Drywall screws do not have much shear strength. They should never be used to secure metal framing connectors. Only nails should be used with most framing connectors. In some instances, bolts are appropriate.*

The appropriate length of nail varies with the type of connection. Manufacturer's literature should be consulted for nail schedules. However, when 16d nails are specified, this generally refers to common nails, not 16d sinkers. Sinkers are slightly thinner and shorter than commons. Some manufacturers provide special nails, sometimes called "joist hanger nails," for use with their connectors. The increased diameter of these nails, compared to standard nails of similar length, improves shear strength.

QUESTIONS

1. List three advantages of laminated veneer lumber.

2. List three advantages of I-beams over solid lumber.

3. What is the resistance of a glulam beam to fire?

4. How are glulam beams fabricated?

5. What is the most common metal connector?

ACTIVITIES

1. Language Arts. Write a short report in which you explain the history of lamination as it applies to construction materials. In your report, discuss the advantages that led to the rapid acceptance of laminated materials among members of the building trades.

THE SCHOOL-TO-WORK CONNECTION

Metal framing connectors are readily available at most lumberyards and home centers. However, there is such a wide variety of connectors that not all of them are available at every store. Connectors that may be difficult to find are those for joining engineered wood products such as laminated-veneer lumber and glue-laminated beams.

1. Locate a catalog from a manufacturer of framing connectors. See if you can find a connector suitable for securing 2 x 10 joists to the side of a beam. The joists intersect the beam at a 45-degree angle.

Tools and Machines

Safety

In building construction, safety is regarded as an important part of the total operation for at least two reasons. One is the natural concern for people's welfare. Another is financial. Building contractors know that injuries to employees are costly since they reduce the efficiency of the working force and may result in expensive medical bills and lawsuits. Therefore many contractors have safety programs which are intended to protect employees.

Safety is of prime importance in the operation of the power tools you will be using in building construction. Therefore you should not just read but *really learn* the safety rules for any job you do, and put the rules into practice. Do this for each piece of equipment you use. Learn to make safety a habit as you develop your skills.

Builders and carpenters who have been interviewed after being injured often say something like, "I knew it was a dumb thing to do, but I just went ahead anyway." Many of these tradespeople could remember a moment before their accident when they suspected danger. Those who ignored that warning later wished they had not.

With common sense and an understanding of basic safety precautions, you have a good chance of avoiding injury on the job site. The following information will acquaint you with basic safety precautions.

WHO IS AT RISK?

Construction work is hazardous. This is partly because of the great number of tools used and the wide variety of working conditions. Building a house is not like building radios in a

9-1. *This man is wearing eye protection and a hard hat. What other safety device could he have used?*

factory. The working conditions on a typical job site are difficult to control. For that reason, workers in construction must take extra responsibility to guard their own safety *and* the safety of other workers. Fig. 9-1.

Falling is the most common cause of injury on a job site. Anyone who works above ground—carpenters, masons, roofers, painters, and others—should take extra care while working. For example, stairwells should have a safety railing around them at all times. Temporary openings in a roof, such as skylight framing, should be covered with a sheet of plywood when not being worked on. Roof jacks or other scaffolding should be used whenever necessary (see Unit 22). The following points are true about construction injuries in general.

➤ Younger workers are more likely to be injured than older workers. This might be because older workers have more experience.

➤ New employees have a higher accident rate than long-time employees. This could be due to their unfamiliarity with the job.

CRAFTSMANSHIP AND SAFETY

Many builders feel that there is a direct relationship between craftsmanship and safety. They feel that workers who take the time to do a job carefully are safer workers. One reason for this is that it takes a lot of concentration to do a job right. By concentrating on the job, a worker is less likely to be distracted by other workers and thus less likely to be injured. Another reason is that a high degree of craftsmanship slows the pace of construction. Some builders find that the number of injuries increases when workers move too fast.

9-2. *Whenever possible, materials should be moved by machine.*

HANDLING MATERIALS SAFELY

Many materials are required to build a house. Proper handling of these materials makes any job site safer. Whenever possible, stacks of material should be lifted by equipment specially designed for this task. This prevents workers from exhausting work, and also shortens the delivery time. Fig. 9-2.

A carpenter is more likely to get a back injury caused by lifting improperly than to be injured by a power tool. In fact, back injuries are the most common injury suffered by carpenters. Masons are prone to this injury, too. Back injuries can be prevented if you remember this: "Lift with your knees, not with your back." This means that when lifting most

weights, you should bend your knees while keeping your back straight. Fig. 9-3. Long pieces of material should be carried by two people.

Many building materials become very slippery when wet or frosty. This is particularly true of plastic, plywood, and housewraps. Be sure to dispose of scraps properly. Make this a habit: never step on any material that is not nailed down.

Proper support while cutting materials is important. Whenever possible, the material should be held securely at a comfortable height. Portable workbenches that can be moved around the site are useful. Fig. 9-4. In some situations, special clamps can be attached to jigs in order to secure a workpiece and keep it from slipping while being cut. Fig. 9-5.

HEALTH HAZARDS

Some injuries are not obvious because they develop over a long period of time. Repeated contact with chemicals or dust is one example. Some chemicals take a

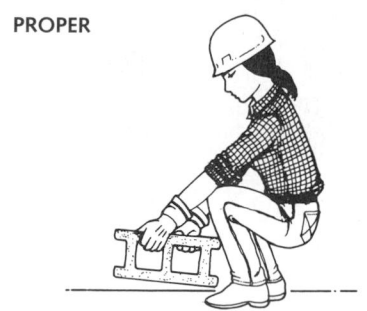
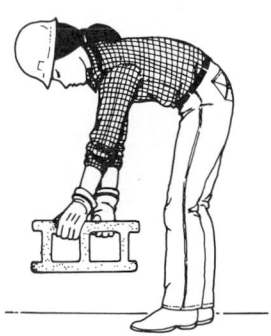

9-3. *Lifting properly will reduce the possibility of back injury.*

9-4. Portable workbenches can be used to position materials at the right height for cutting. This one has built-in clamps.

9-6. Some power tools, like this sander, are equipped with dust bags. This reduces airborne dust.

9-7. Safety information should be displayed at the job site.

long time to affect a worker's health. When a worker finally realizes the problem, his or her health may already have been damaged. This is why it is important to wear protective clothing, including a dust mask or respirator when appropriate. A dust mask can filter out particles, but cannot protect you against fumes. To protect yourself against chemical fumes, you should wear a respirator. Many tools can also be equipped with dust collection systems. Fig. 9-6.

Manufacturers of various chemicals found on construction sites can provide Material Safety Data Sheets (MSDS) to workers. These sheets explain the hazards associated with those chemicals. Fig. 9-7.

Another kind of long-term illness occurs when parts of the body are gradually damaged over time. This can come from doing a repetitive task that causes minor irritation to nerves and tissues. A carpenter, for example, can develop a problem in one wrist after years of using a hammer. This is due to frequent movement of the wrist in a certain way. Hammering with a minimum of wrist movement can help carpenters avoid this problem.

Other workers, such as trim carpenters and tilesetters, work a lot while on their knees. Special kneepads can protect knees from injury. Fig. 9-8.

AVOIDING SAW KICKBACK

Kickback is one of the most common risks of using portable circular saws, table saws, and radial-arm saws. It occurs when the stock being cut is thrown back at the operator at high speed, or when the saw itself is unexpectedly

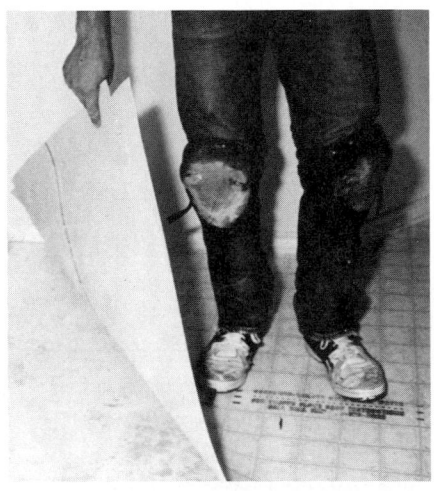

9-8. Kneepads are useful for tradespeople who work on the floor, such as trim carpenters and tile setters.

9-5. Lever clamps such as these can be used to secure materials during cutting. They can be screwed to jigs.

propelled towards the operator. Kickback can be prevented with a few simple precautions.

Portable Circular Saw

With a portable circular saw, kickback occurs when the saw itself is thrown back at the operator. Whenever you feel the need to force the saw into the cut, something is wrong. Shut off the saw and find out what it is. The problem might be a saw kerf closing in and pinching a blade. It might be a dull blade or a difficult knot.

Table Saw

Table saw kickback can be caused by the workpiece getting pinched between the blade and the fence. It can also be due to the saw kerf closing up behind the blade. In each case, the workpiece can be hurled *towards the operator* at great speed. To avoid the danger, take the following precautions:

➤ Make sure the fence is exactly parallel to the blade.

➤ Never tilt the sawblade towards the fence.

➤ Feed stock straight through the blade; crooked cuts are dangerous.

➤ Never stand directly behind the blade. If stock is kicked back, this is the path it will take.

Radial-arm Saw

Radial-arm saw kickback can take two forms. A portion of the stock can be thrown away from the operator at high speed. This portion could bounce off another object and strike the operator. A more dangerous event is when the saw suddenly "climbs" the stock being cut and moves towards the operator.

When using the saw to crosscut, pull it forward only enough to make the cut. Be sure the stock

9-9. A ground fault circuit interruptor (GFCI) attached to an extension cord protects workers against electrical shock.

rests firmly against the fence, and pull the saw slowly and steadily through the stock. Keep a good grip on the control handle, not a casual one.

Because compound miter saws are similar in operation to radial-arm saws, these precautions should also be taken with them.

ELECTRICAL SAFETY

Electrical tools have become very important on the job site. Electrical safety should be equally important. Very little electricity is required to injure or kill a worker.

Electricity flows from a point of origin and returns to that point of origin through a conductor. Moisture can turn many materials into good conductors. A person can become part of this loop by touching both wires in a circuit or by touching the hot wire and the ground. You can also become part of the loop if the metal tool you are using comes in contact with a wire carrying electricity. Double-insulated tools reduce these possibilities, but they do not eliminate them.

Make sure all power tools are grounded. A properly grounded electrical system is essential. If a person ever becomes part of the hot

circuit, electricity will flow through the ground wire, not through that person. Any break in the grounding system makes the entire system useless.

Circuit breakers and fuses help to prevent shocks. A *ground-fault circuit interruptor* (GFCI) is a fast-acting circuit breaker that can protect people from electrical shock. Fig. 9-9. A GFCI can be attached to a cord supplying electricity to a power tool. Such a safety device is particularly important whenever moisture is present.

DRESS

➤ Wear safety glasses whenever your work involves a threat to your eyes. (Sometimes this is required by law.) Fig. 9-10.

➤ Clothing should be suitable for the prevailing weather conditions.

➤ In a shop or on a job site, you

9-10. Always wear adequate eye protection for the job to be performed. Sometimes it is necessary also to wear a mask for operations such as spray painting.

9-11. *Supervisory and sales personnel should never enter the job site without wearing a hard hat and eye protection.*

will probably work harder and safer in clothes you are not afraid to get dirty. If at all possible, as you enter the shop each day you should exchange your regular clothing for coveralls or other accepted working attire.

➤ Avoid wearing pants or overalls that are too long. Cuffs made by turning up the legs of pants tend to catch heels, causing falls.

➤ To avoid catching on nails, keep the sleeves of shirts or jackets buttoned.

➤ Keep hair cut short or keep long hair in place with a visor or hair net.

➤ To protect feet from protruding nails, wear shoes with thick, sturdy soles.

➤ To protect feet from falling objects, wear safety shoes or boots with steel toe caps.

➤ Wear a hard hat when exposed to overhead work or whenever there is danger from falling objects. Fig. 9-11.

➤ Remove neckties, rings, wristwatches, neck chains, and all other jewelry.

AVOID FALLS

➤ Check scaffolding and temporary walkways before walking on them. Be sure the supports are strong and secure.

➤ Use only ladders which are in good condition and set up properly.

GENERAL SAFETY

The following is a list of general safety rules to be used in the shop or on the job site as you work on and around machines and construction. These rules will help to protect you and others who are near you while you work.

➤ Always walk—do not run.

➤ Never talk to or interrupt anyone who is working on a machine.

➤ Remove power plug or turn off power supply to a machine when changing cutters or blades.

➤ Never leave tools or pieces of stock lying on the table surface of a machine being used.

➤ When finished with a machine, turn off the power and wait until the blade or cutter has come to a complete stop before leaving.

➤ Always carefully check stock for knots, splits, metal objects, and other defects before machining.

➤ Do not use a machine until you understand it thoroughly. Any tool can cause serious injury if mishandled.

➤ Use guards on power equipment. It should be understood that using guards does not necessarily prevent accidents.

PRACTICE GOOD HOUSEKEEPING

➤ Materials and equipment should be stacked straight and neat.

➤ Keep aisles and walkways clear of tools, materials, and debris.

➤ To prevent fires and reduce hazards which cause accidents, dispose of scraps and rubbish daily.

➤ Whenever you see protruding nails, remove them or bend them down immediately.

➤ When working above other people, place tools and materials where they will not fall and cause injuries.

Guards must be used correctly if they are to provide fullest protection. Also, it is impossible to do some operations, especially on the table saw, with the regular guard in place. Therefore there are times when special guards should be used.

➤ Always keep your fingers away from the moving cutting edges. An accident is often caused by trying to run too small a piece through a machine.

➤ Keep the floor around the machine clean. The danger from falling or slipping is always great.

➤ Make all adjustments with the power off and the machine at a dead stop.

➤ Always use a brush to clean the table surface.

➤ Always keep your eyes focused on where the cutting action is taking place.

➤ Always use sharp tools.

➤ When using tools for set-up work on a machine: (1) Select the right tool for the job. (2) Keep it in safe condition. (3) Keep it in a safe place.

➤ Report strange noises or faulty operation of machines to your instructor or supervisor.

➤ Follow the suggestions for each machine given in this book.

The Congress of the United States in April of 1971 made the Federal Occupational Safety and Health Act (OSHA) an official part of the national labor law. The purpose of this law is "…to assure so far as possible every working man and woman in the nation safe and healthful working conditions and to preserve our human resources." This law affects all employees who are working in the building trades where one or more workers are employed. As an individual employed in the building trades, it is just as important to develop safe work attitudes and habits as outlined by this law as it is to develop the skills of your trade.

Building trades employers will be looking for men and women with these traits for their benefit and welfare as well as yours as a skilled trade worker. Thus it is important to know and follow safety rules.

Since its beginning, OSHA has monitored thousands of workplaces, including construction sites. As agents of the federal government, OSHA inspectors have the legal right to inspect any construction site for safety violations. If inspectors find violations, a fine may be imposed on the builder.

9-12. *Whenever this drawing of a guard appears with an illustration, a guard must be used for the operation shown.*

GENERAL SAFETY RULES FOR PORTABLE POWER TOOLS

The following are general safety rules. We strongly advise you to check the manufacturer's manual for any special safety instructions.

➤ Never use portable power tools in contact with water, including rain, or if any part of your body is in contact with moisture. Be sure the power plug is removed before making any adjustments.

➤ Portable power tools should be properly grounded with a three-prong grounded plug. If a grounded receptacle is not available, use a three-to-two prong adapter plug which has been properly grounded.

➤ Always wear approved eye protection.

➤ Always disconnect the power plug when the work is completed.

➤ Be sure the switch is in the "off" position before connecting the power plug.

➤ Always use the recommended extension cord size. Table 9-A.

NOTE: In the following units on tools and machines, many illustrations show dangerous operations being performed on machines without guards. The guards have been removed so that the photographs will show the operations more clearly. *Whenever a drawing of a guard appears with an illustration, **a guard must be used** for the operation that is shown.* Fig. 9-12.

Table 9-A. *Recommended Extension Cord Sizes for Use with Portable Electric Tools.*

Name-plate Amperes	Cord Length in Feet																			
	25	50	75	100	125	150	175	200	225	250	275	300	325	350	375	400	425	450	475	500
1	16	16	16	16	16	16	16	16	16	16	16	16	16	16	16	16	16	16	16	14
2	16	16	16	16	16	16	16	16	16	16	14	14	14	14	14	12	12	12	12	12
3	16	16	16	16	16	16	14	14	14	14	12	12	12	12	12	12	10	10	10	10
4	16	16	16	16	16	14	14	12	12	12	12	12	12	10	10	10	10	10	10	10
5	16	16	16	16	14	14	12	12	12	12	10	10	10	10	10	8	8	8	8	8
6	16	16	16	14	14	12	12	12	10	10	10	10	10	8	8	8	8	8	8	8
7	16	16	14	14	12	12	12	10	10	10	10	8	8	8	8	8	8	8	8	8
8	14	14	14	14	12	12	10	10	10	10	8	8	8	8	8	8	8	8		
9	14	14	14	12	12	10	10	10	8	8	8	8	8	8	8	8	8			
10	14	14	14	12	12	10	10	10	8	8	8	8	8	8	8	8				
11	12	12	12	12	10	10	10	8	8	8	8	8	8	8	8					
12	12	12	12	12	10	10	8	8	8	8	8	8	8	8						
13	12	12	12	12	10	10	8	8	8	8	8	8	8							
14	10	10	10	10	10	10	8	8	8	8	8	8								
15	10	10	10	10	10	8	8	8	8	8	8									
16	10	10	10	10	10	8	8	8	8	8										
17	10	10	10	10	10	8	8	8	8											
18	8	8	8	8	8	8	8	8	8											
19	8	8	8	8	8	8	8	8												
20	8	8	8	8	8	8	8	8												

Notes: Wire sizes are for 3-CDR Cords, one CDR of which is used to provide a continuous grounding circuit from tool housing to receptacle. Wire sizes shown are A. W. G. (American Wire Gauge). Based on 115V power supply; Ambient Temp. of 30° C, 86° F.

QUESTIONS

1. Why is safety so important to the building contractor?

2. Why should students wear some form of work clothes for building construction?

3. What features should you look for when buying shoes to be used for working on a job site?

4. Do guards prevent accidents on power machines? Explain.

5. Why should portable power tools be grounded?

6. Explain why it is important to wear proper eye protection at all times, even when you are not operating equipment.

7. Describe the proper way to lift heavy objects.

8. What can a respirator do that a dust mask can't?

ACTIVITIES

1. Language Arts. Many safety precautions concerning dress are discussed in this unit. Pick three of them. Discuss two negative consequences for each if an employee ignored the precaution.

2. Social Studies. Why is it as important for an individual to develop safe working habits as it is that he or she develop job skills?

3. Social Studies. Why do you think that the Congress of the United States developed the Federal Occupational Safety and Health Act in 1971? Do you think that it is necessary for the government to mandate safety precautions? Write a three-paragraph persuasive essay arguing either for or against safety rules and federal mandates.

4. Math. Carol's Construction Company and Bill's Building Group both employ fifteen workers full-time. Carol has a 1% loss of work time due to injuries. Bill has a 7% loss rate for injuries.

a. Using a forty-hour work week and a standard pay rate for a local skilled worker, compute the difference in lost wages for the two construction crews for a week.

b. Figure the difference in the lost wages for a year for the two crews.

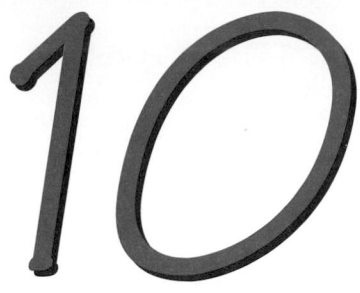

Hand Tools

LAYOUT, MEASURING, AND CHECKING DEVICES

Tool	Description	Uses
Bench Rule Fig. 10-1.	A 12-inch or one foot (or 300 mm) rule. One side is divided into eighths, the other into sixteenths. A metric rule is divided into centimetres or millimetres.	**1.** To make simple measurements. **2.** To adjust dividers. *Caution.* Never use as a straightedge.

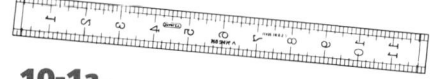

10-1a.

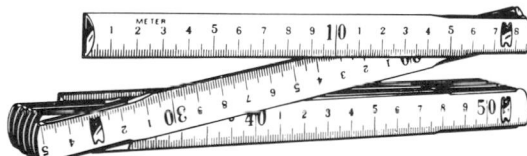

10-1b.

| **Zig-Zag Rule** Fig. 10-2. | A folding rule of six- or eight-foot (or 2 m) length. | **1.** To measure distances greater than 2' (600 mm), place the rule flat on the stock. **2.** To measure less than 2' (600 mm) it is better to use the rule on edge. (This instrument is good for inside measurement, since the reading on the brass extension can be added to the length of the rule itself.) |

10-2.

| **Flexible Tape Rules** Fig. 10-3. | A flexible tape that slides into a metal case. Comes in a variety of lengths from 6' to 100' or 2m to 50m. The steel tape has a hook on the end that adjusts to true zero. | **1.** To measure irregular as well as regular shapes. **2.** To make accurate inside measurements. (Measurement is read by adding 2" (50 mm) to the reading on the blade.) |

10-3a.

10-3b.

Tool	Description	Uses
Try Square Fig. 10-4.	A squaring, measuring, and testing tool with a metal blade and a wood or metal handle.	**1.** To test a surface for levelness. **2.** To check adjacent surfaces for squareness. **3.** To make lines across the face or edge of stock.
Combination Square Fig. 10-5.	Consists of a blade and handle. The blade slides along in the handle or head. There is a level and a scriber in the handle.	**1.** To test a level or plumb surface. **2.** To check squareness—either inside or outside. **3.** To mark and test a 45-degree miter. **4.** To gauge-mark a line with a pencil.
Sliding T Bevel Fig. 10-6.	A blade that can be set at any angle to the handle. Set with a framing square or protractor.	**1.** To measure or transfer an angle between 0 and 180 degrees. **2.** To check or test a miter cut.
Dividers Fig. 10-7.	A tool with two metal legs. One metal leg can be removed and replaced with a pencil. To set the dividers, hold both points on the measuring lines of the rule.	**1.** To lay out an arc or circle. **2.** To step off measurements. **3.** To divide distances along a straight line.
Framing or Rafter Square Fig. 10-8.	A large steel square consisting of a blade, or body, and a tongue.	**1.** To check for squareness. **2.** To mark a line across a board. **3.** To lay out rafters and stairs.

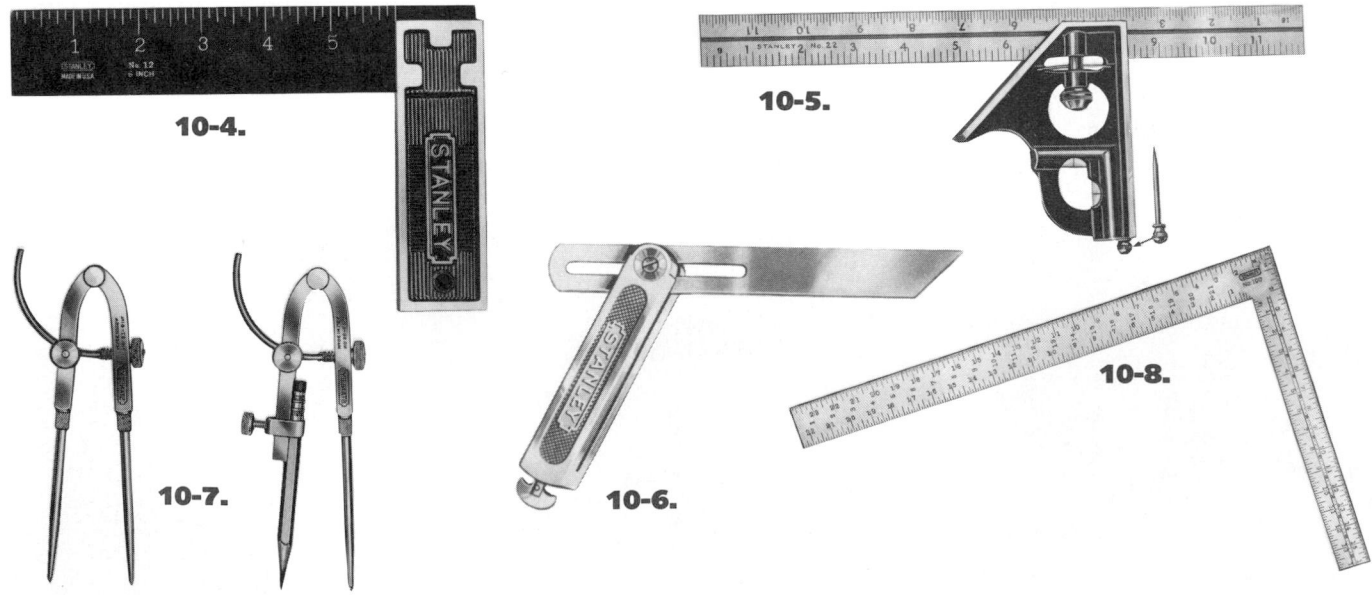

10-4.

10-5.

10-7.

10-6.

10-8.

Tool	Description	Uses
Carpenter's Level Fig. 10-9.	A wood, metal, or plastic frame with several glass leveling vials. Some levels measure electronically instead.	To check whether a surface is level or plumb.
Marking Gauge Fig. 10-10.	A wood or metal tool consisting of a beam, head, and point.	To mark a line parallel to the grain of wood.
Scratch Awl Fig. 10-11.	A pointed metal tool with handle.	**1.** To locate a point of measurement. **2.** To scribe a line accurately.
Trammel Points Fig. 10-12.	Two metal pointers that can be fastened to a long bar of wood or metal.	**1.** To lay out distances between two points. **2.** To scribe arcs and circles, larger than those made with dividers.
Chalk Line and Plumb Bob Fig. 10-13.	A combination tool used as a plumb bob and chalk line. It is a lead weight with a pointed end. The opposite end has a hole for attaching a cord that measures perpendicularly.	**1.** To determine the corners of buildings. **2.** To establish a vertical line.
Electronic Calculator Fig. 10-14.	A portable, solar-powered calculator that computes measurements directly in feet and inches.	Calculates volumes and areas, converts decimals to fractions, and helps to solve various framing layout problems.

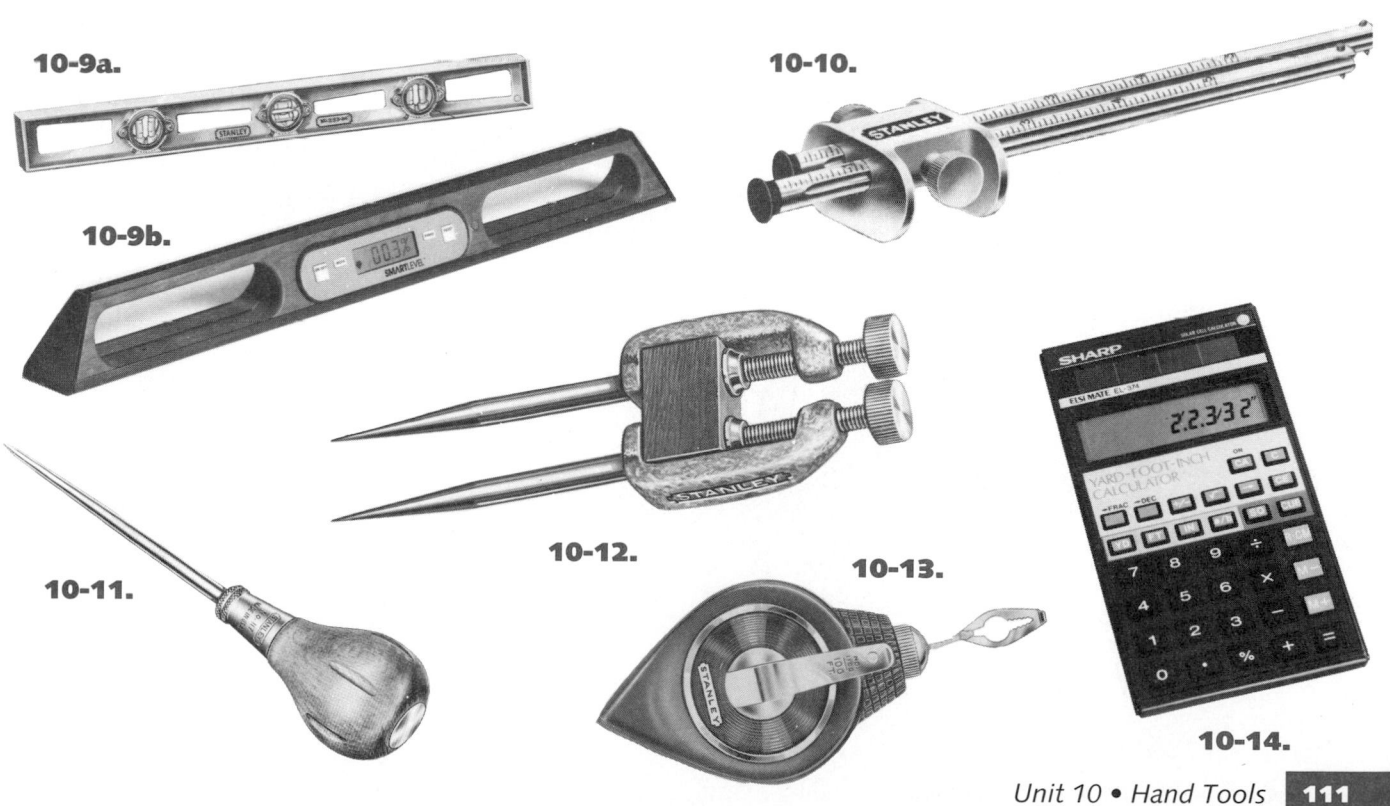

10-9a.

10-9b.

10-10.

10-11.

10-12.

10-13.

10-14.

SAWING TOOLS

Tool	Description	Uses
Back Saw Fig. 10-15.	A fine-tooth crosscut saw with a heavy metal band across the back to strengthen the thin blade.	**1.** To make fine cuts for joinery. **2.** To use in a miter box.
Crosscut Saw Fig. 10-16.	A hand saw in lengths from 20" to 26" with from 4 to 12 points per inch. A 22", 10-point saw is a good one for general purpose work.	**1.** To cut across grain. **2.** Can be used to cut with the grain. *Caution:* Never cut into nails or screws. Never twist off strips of waste stock.
Rip Saw Fig. 10-17.	A hand saw in lengths from 20" to 28". A 26", 5 ½-point saw is good for general use.	To cut with the grain. *Caution:* Support the waste stock. Never allow end of saw to strike the floor.
Compass Saw Fig. 10-18.	A 12" or 14" taper blade saw.	**1.** To cut gentle curves. **2.** To cut inside curves.
Keyhole Saw Fig. 10-19.	A 10" or 12" narrow taper saw with fine teeth.	To cut small openings and fine work.

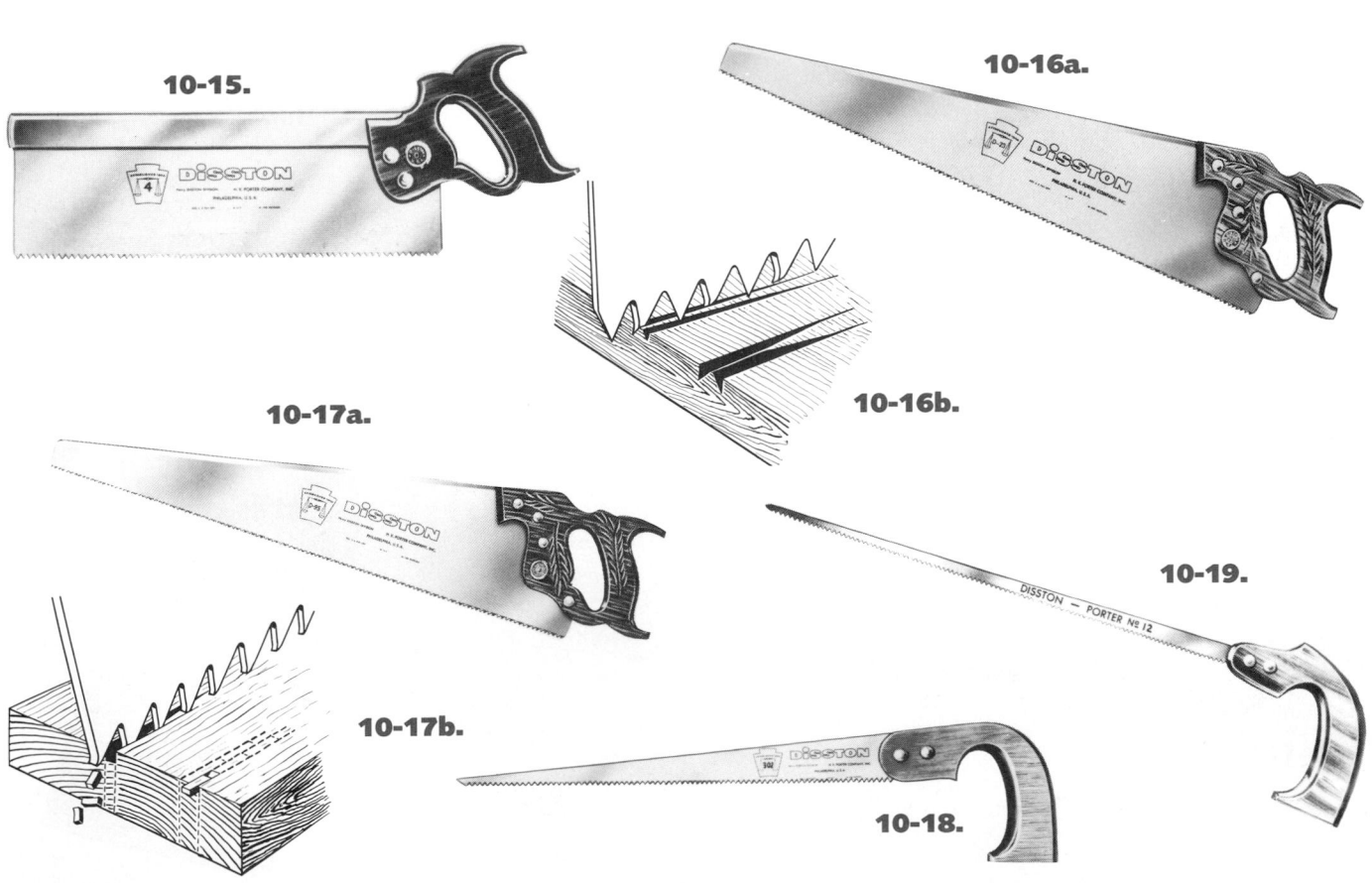

10-15.   10-16a.   10-16b.   10-17a.   10-17b.   10-18.   10-19.

Tool	Description	Uses
Miter Box Saw Fig. 10-20.	A longer back saw (24" to 28").	Used in a homemade or commercial miter box for cutting miters or square ends.
Coping Saw Fig. 10-21.	A U-shaped saw frame permitting 4 ⅝" or 6 ½" deep cuts. Uses standard 6 ½" pin-end blades.	**1.** To cut curves. **2.** To shape the ends of molding for joints. **3.** For scroll work.
Dovetail Saw Fig. 10-22.	An extremely thin blade with very fine teeth.	For smoothest possible joint cuts.

EDGE-CUTTING TOOLS

Tool	Description	Uses
Smooth Plane Fig. 10-23.	A 7" to 9" plane.	**1.** For general use. **2.** For smaller work.
Jack Plane Fig. 10-24.	A 14" or 15" plane.	**1.** Ideal for rough surface where chip should be coarse. **2.** Also used to obtain a smooth, flat surface.

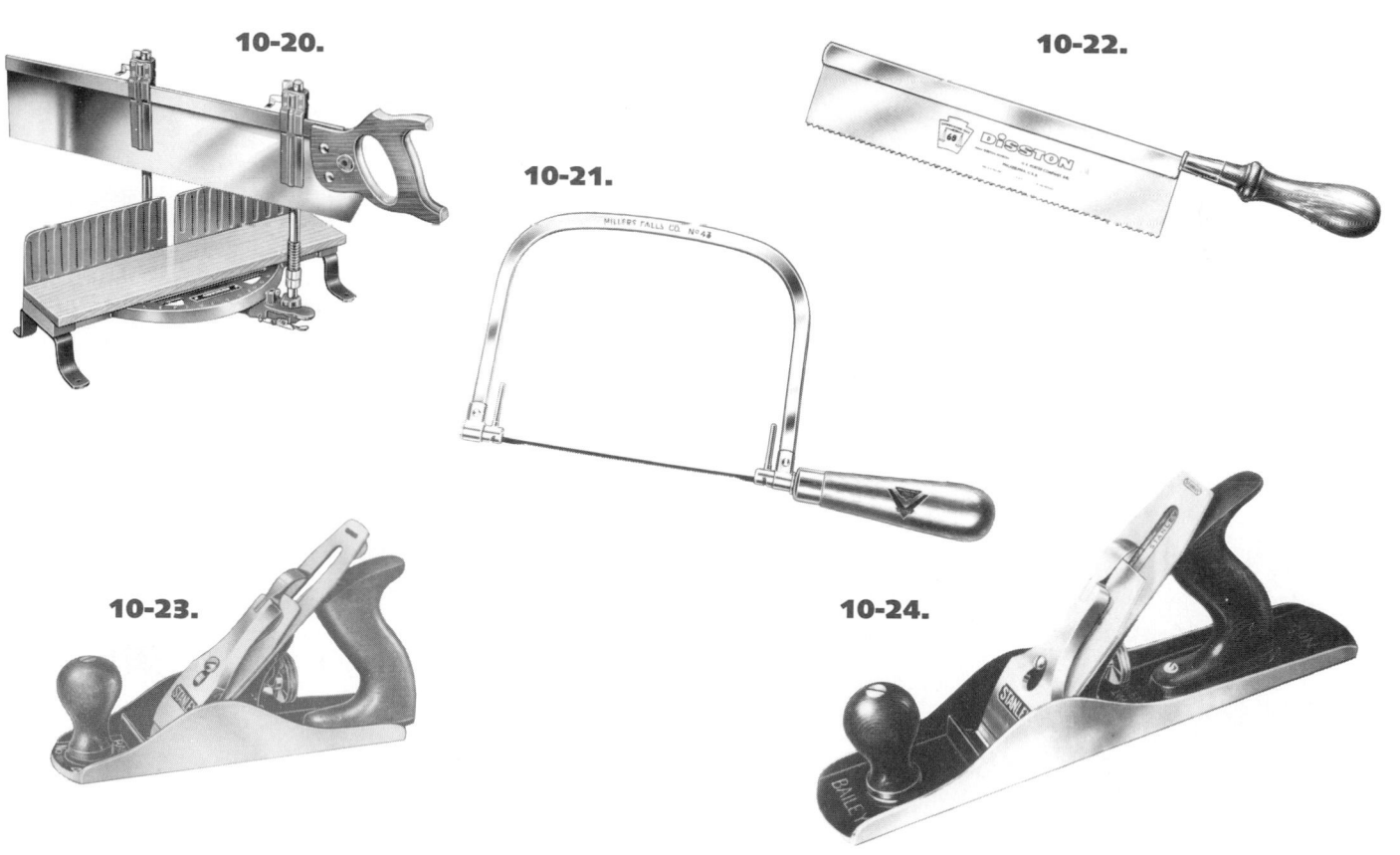

10-20.

10-21.

10-22.

10-23.

10-24.

Tool	Description	Uses
Fore Plane Fig. 10-25.	An 18" plane.	For fine flat finish on longer surfaces and edges.
Jointer Plane Fig. 10-26.	A 22" or 24" plane.	**1.** To smooth and flatten edges for making a close-fitting joint. **2.** For planing long boards such as the edges of doors.
Router Plane Fig. 10-27.	A cutting tool with several cutters.	To surface the bottom of grooves and dadoes.
Block Plane Fig. 10-28.	A small plane with a single, low-angle cutter with the bevel up.	**1.** To plane end grain. **2.** For small pieces. **3.** For planing the ends of molding, trim, and siding.
Wood Chisels Fig 10-29.	A set usually includes blade widths from ⅛" to 2".	To trim and shape wood.
Surform Tool® Fig. 10-30.	Available in plane file type. Also round, or block-plane types. A blade with 45-degree cutting teeth.	For all types of cutting and trimming.

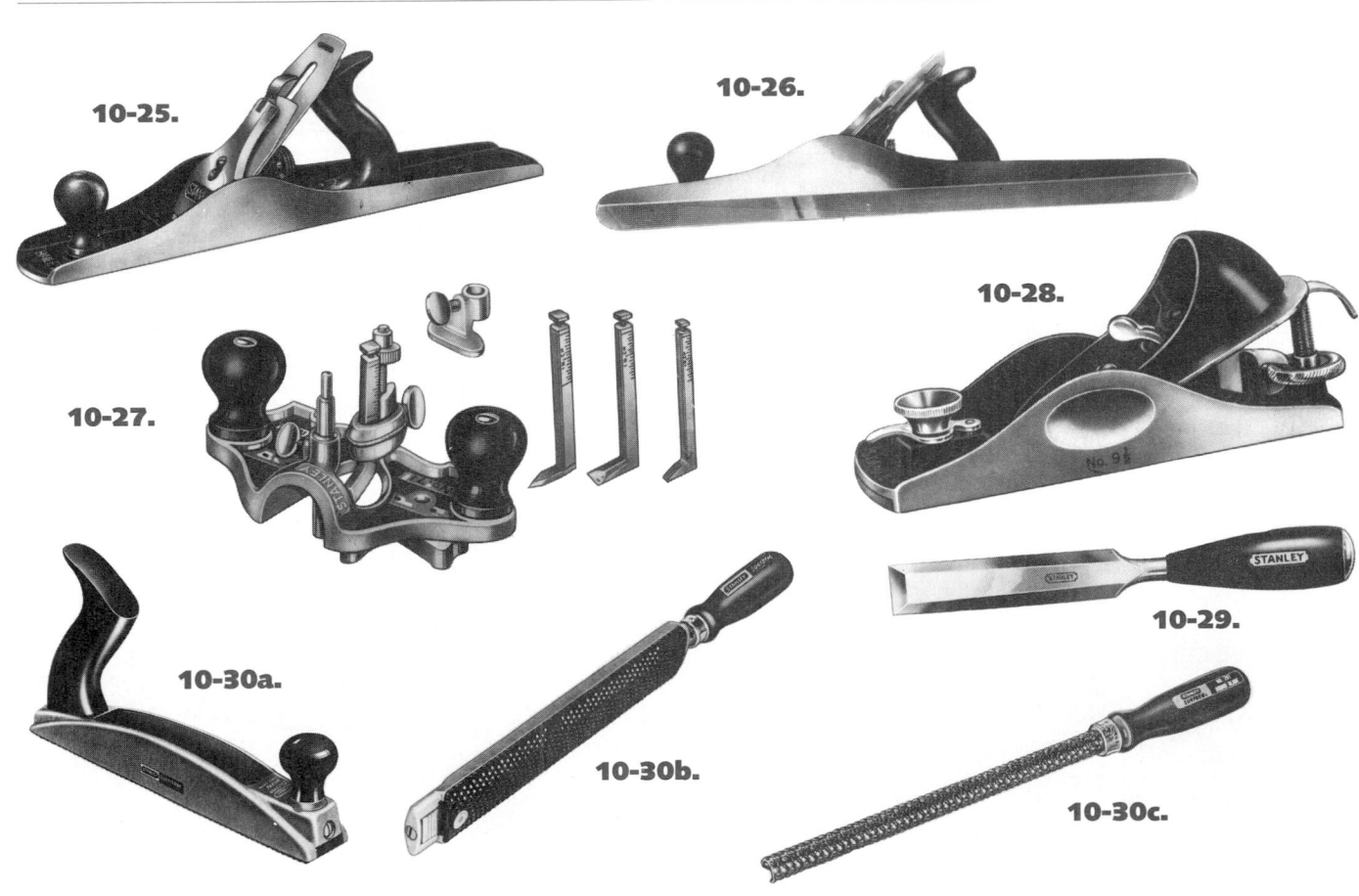

10-25.

10-26.

10-27.

10-28.

10-29.

10-30a.

10-30b.

10-30c.

Tool	Description	Uses
Hatchet Fig. 10-31.	A cutting tool with a curved edge on one side and a hammer head on the other. Has hammer-length handle.	To trim pieces to fit in building construction. For nailing flooring.
Utility Knife Fig. 10-32.	An all-purpose knife with retractable blade.	**1.** To cut and trim wood, veneer, hardboard, and particleboard. **2.** To make accurate layouts.

FASTENING AND ASSEMBLY TOOLS

Tool	Description	Uses
Vise Fig. 10-33.	Metal vise has replaceable wooden faces to protect wood. Larger vises attach permanently to work bench. Others clamp to table or counter.	Holds work for sawing, planing, sanding, and many other jobs.
Claw Hammer Fig. 10-34.	Has curved claw. Heads weigh from 5 to 20 ounces. Face may be flat, bell, or checkered. Handle may be of wood, steel, or fiberglass.	For driving or removing nails. Use 16-ounce head with flat or bell face for general construction. Steel or fiberglass handles are better than wood.
Rip Claw Hammer Fig. 10-35.	Has wedge-shaped claw.	For prying apart pieces that have been nailed together.
Mallet Fig. 10-36.	Heads with two striking surfaces, often made of wood, rubber, or plastic.	Used for striking blows where steel hammers would mar or damage the surface.

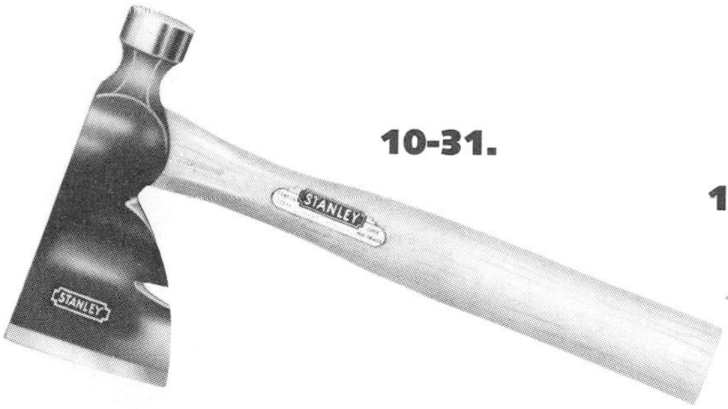

10-31.

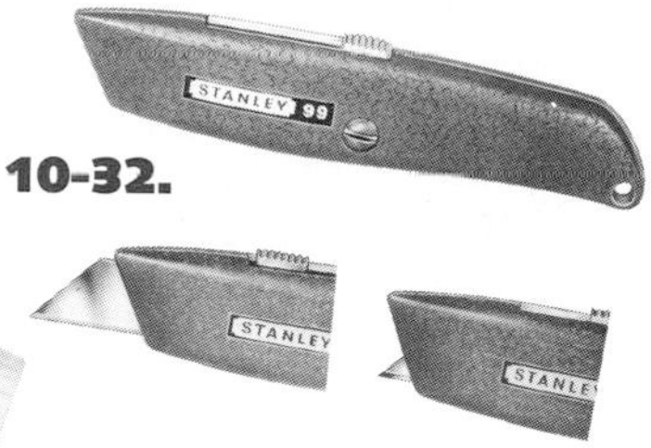

10-32.

10-33.

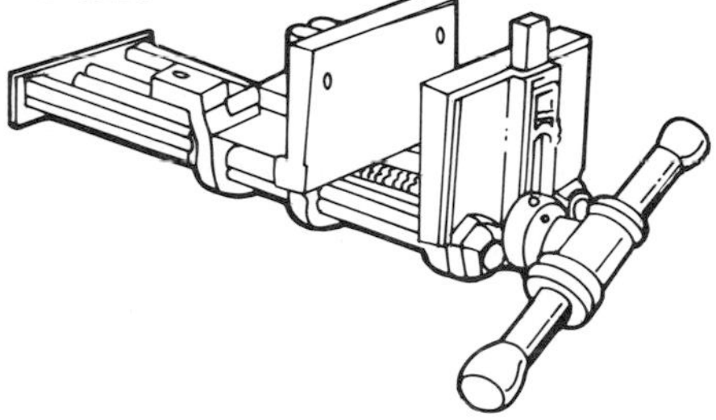

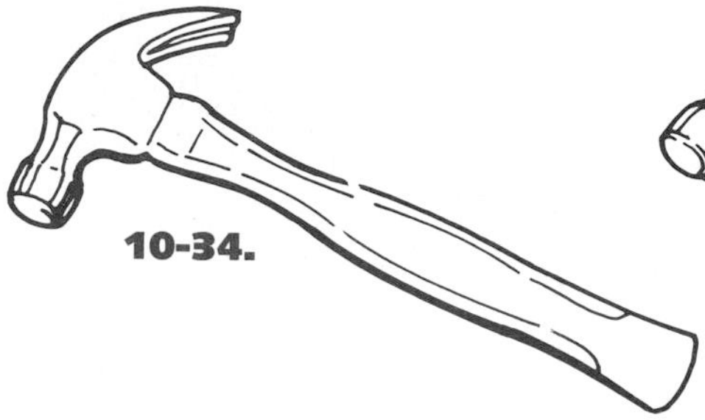

10-34.

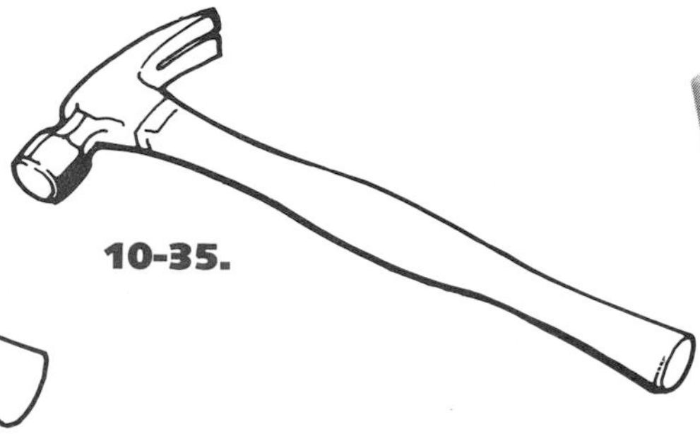

10-35.

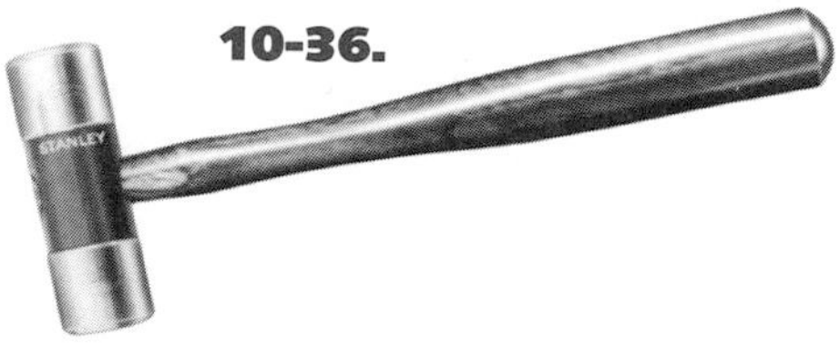

10-36.

Tool	Description	Uses
Ripping bars Fig 10-37.	Available in lengths up to 8'. Three-foot bar is suited for general use.	For pulling large nails and for removing old materials during renovation.
Nail Set Fig. 10-38.	Concave tip will not slip from nail head. Tip diameter from 1/32" to 5/32".	For driving nails below the surface on interior trim. Nail holes can then be filled.
Screw Drivers Fig. 10-39.	For slotted and Phillips head screws. Standard slotted head widens from tip to shank. Cabinet slotted head is a uniform width to reach recessed screws.	Select head width that most closely fits screw slot. Use No. 1 Phillips for screw gauges 0-4, No. 2 for gauges 5-9, No. 3 for gauges 10-16, and No. 4 for gauges 17 and larger.
Stapler Gun Fig. 10-40.	Heavy-duty models drive up to 9/16" staples with spring-driven plungers. Some require use of hammer or mallet.	For attaching ceiling tile, insulation, screen, and other soft or thin materials.
Hammer Tacker Fig. 10-41.	Quickly drives staples.	For attaching insulation, roofing felt, and building paper.

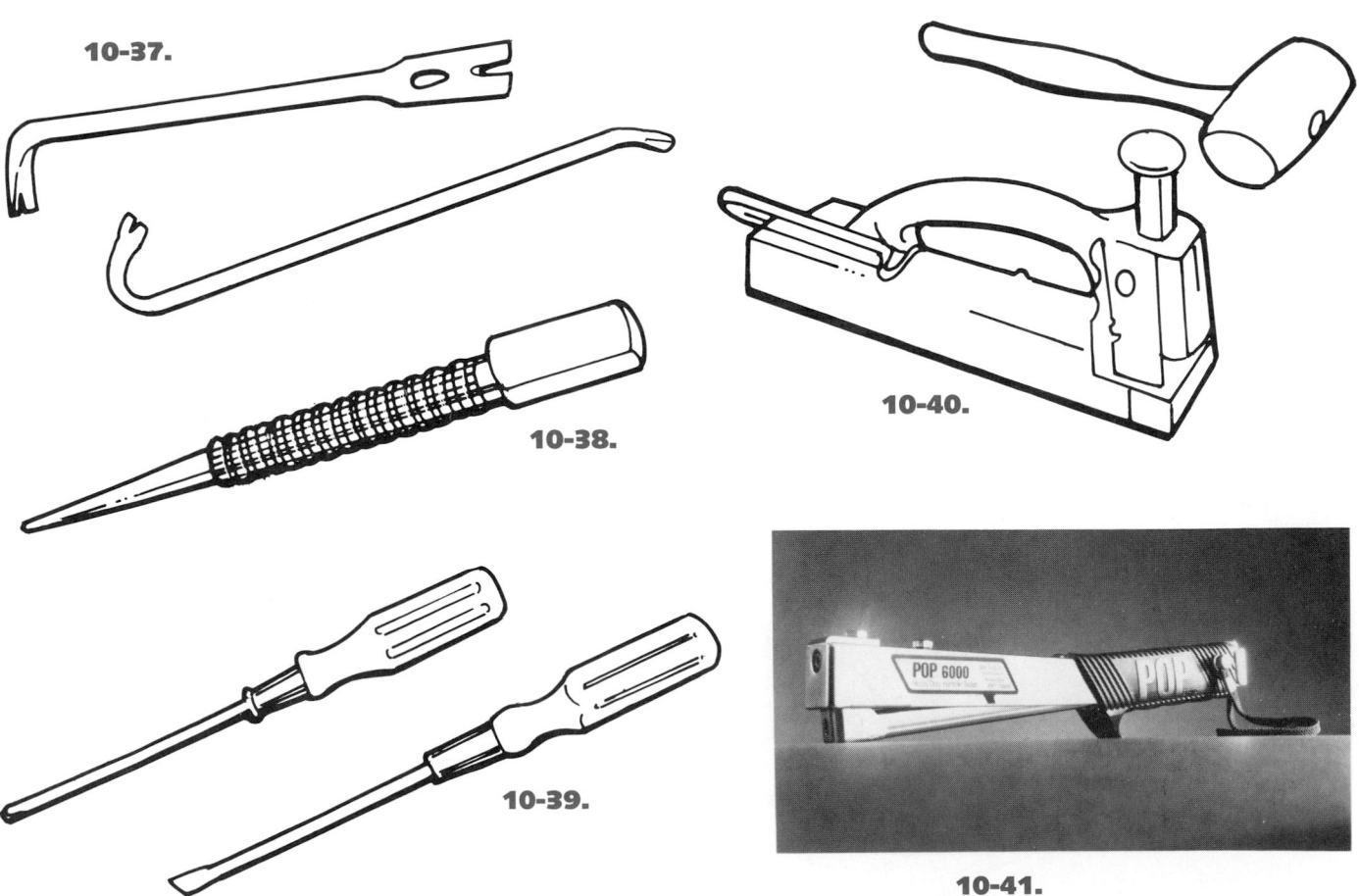

10-37.

10-38.

10-39.

10-40.

10-41.

DRILLING AND BORING TOOLS

Tool	Description	Uses
Auger Bit Fig. 10-42.	May be either single-twist or double-twist bit. Comes in sizes from No. 4 (1/4") to No. 16 (1").	**1.** To bore holes 1/4" or larger. **2.** Single twist bit is better for boring deep holes.
Dowel Bit Fig. 10-43.	A shorter bit with a sharper twist.	To bore holes for making dowel joints.
Expansion Bit Fig. 10-44.	A bit that holds cutters of different sizes. Sometimes this tool is called an expansive bit.	**1.** To bore a hole larger than 1". **2.** One cutter will bore holes in the 1" to 2" range. **3.** A second cutter will bore holes in the 2" to 3" range.
Brace Fig. 10-45.	Two common types—the plain for a full swing, and the ratchet for close corners.	To hold and operate bits.
Foerstner Bit Fig. 10-46.	A bit with a flat cutting surface on the end.	**1.** To bore a shallow hole with a flat bottom. **2.** To bore a hole in thin stock. **3.** To bore a hole in end grain. **4.** To enlarge an existing hole.
Bit or Depth Gauges Fig. 10-47.	Two types—onc is a solid clamp, the other a spring type.	To limit the depth of a hole.

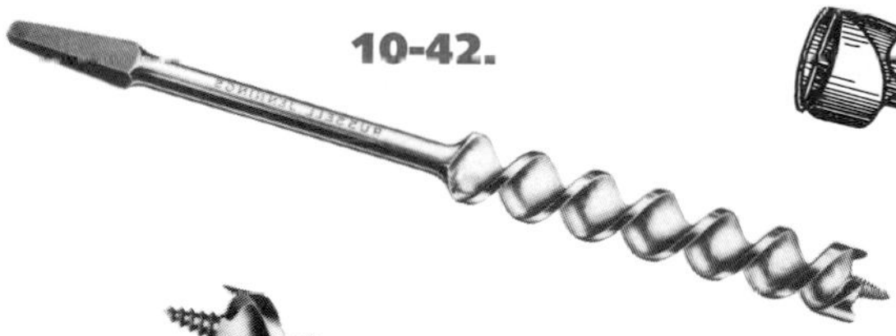

10-42.

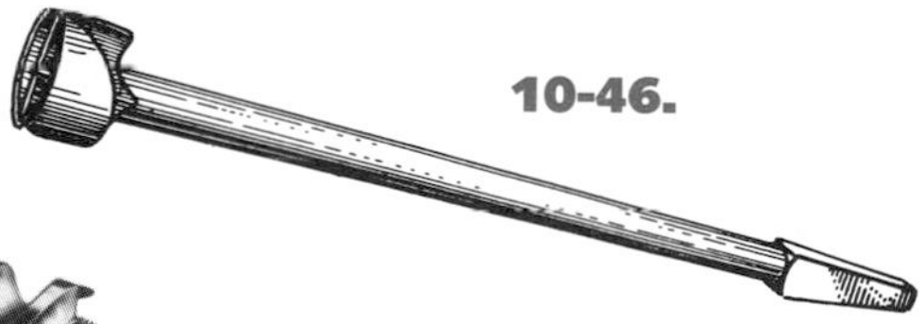

10-46.

10-47a.

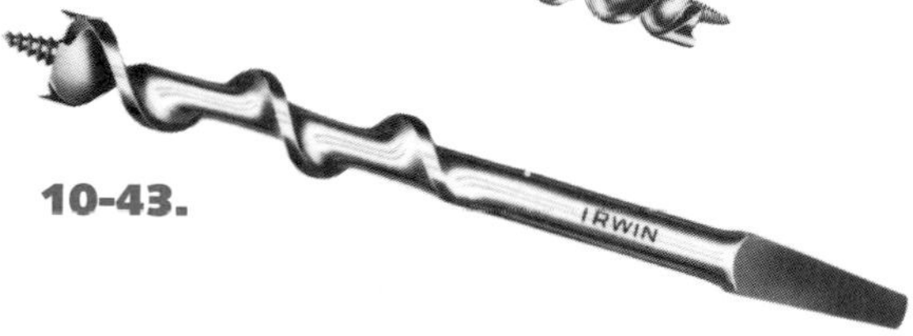

10-43.

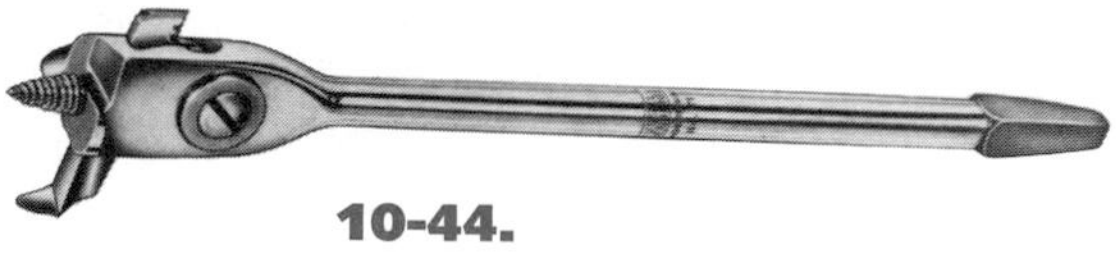

10-44.

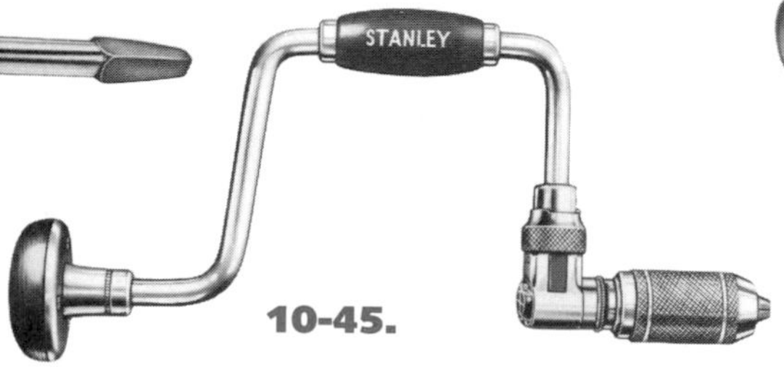

10-45.

10-47b.

Tool	Description	Uses
Twist Drill Bit Fig. 10-48.	A fractional-sized set from $\frac{1}{64}$" to $\frac{1}{2}$" is best.	To drill small holes for nails, screws, etc.
Hand Drill and Bit Fig. 10-49.	A tool with a 3-jaw chuck.	For use in a brace.
Automatic (Push) Drill Fig. 10-50.	A tool with drill points and handle. Drill point sizes: #1 = $\frac{1}{16}$" ; #2 = $\frac{5}{64}$" ; #3 = $\frac{3}{32}$" ; #4 = $\frac{7}{64}$" ; #5 = $\frac{1}{8}$" ; #6 = $\frac{9}{64}$" ; #7 = $\frac{5}{32}$" ; #8 = $\frac{11}{64}$".	To drill many small holes without need of electricity.

METALWORKING TOOLS*

Tool	Description	Uses
Hacksaw Fig. 10-51.	A U-shaped frame with handle. Uses replaceable metal-cutting blades.	To cut all types of metal fasteners, hardware, and metal parts.
Cold Chisel Fig. 10-52.	A tool-steel chisel with cutting edge especially hardened and tempered for cutting metal. Angle between bevel surface is about 60 degrees.	**1.** To cut off a rivet or nail. **2.** To get a tight or rusted nut started.

*In building construction, many metalworking tools are needed to set up and adjust machinery and to work with metal hardware and fasteners.

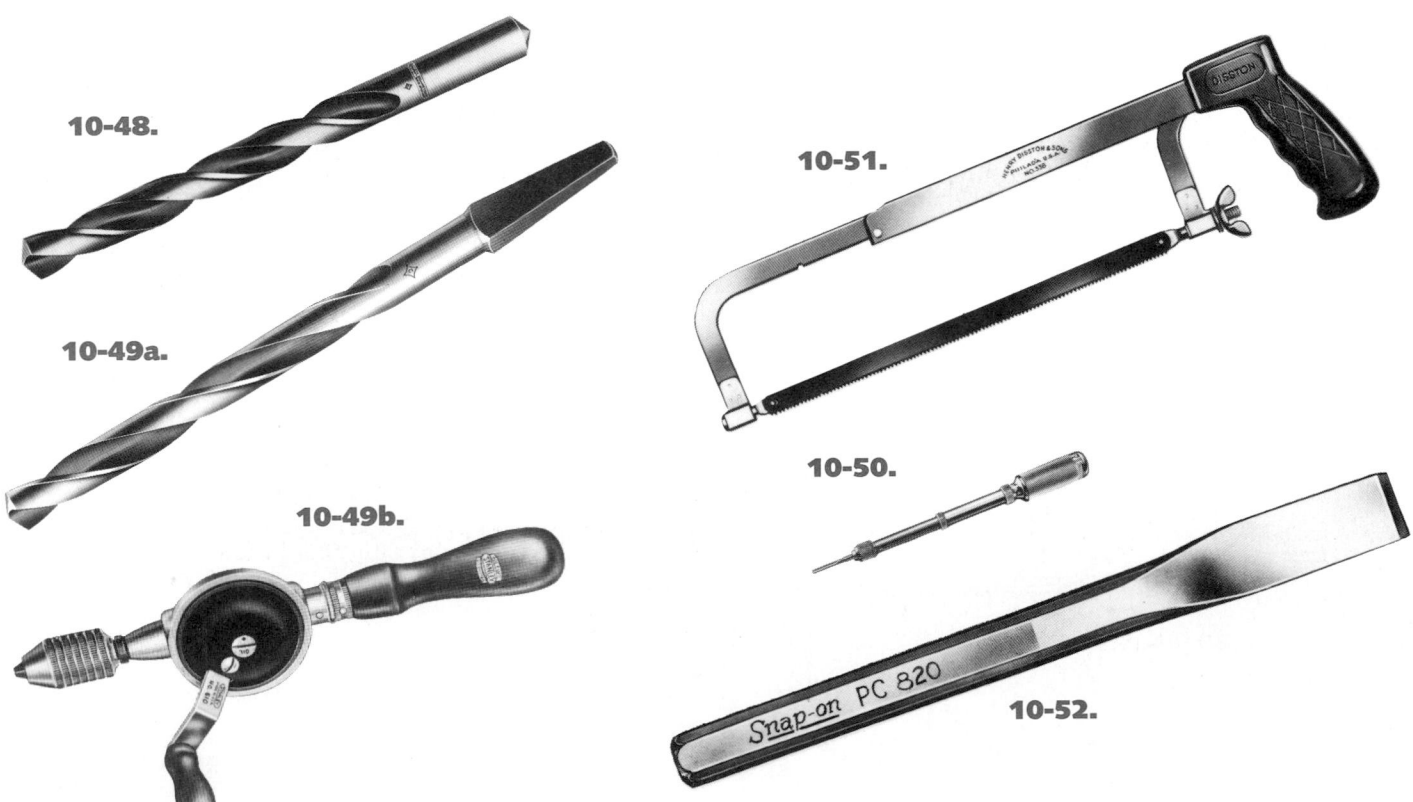

10-48.

10-49a.

10-49b.

10-51.

10-50.

Snap-on PC 820   10-52.

Tool	Description	Uses
Adjustable Wrench Fig. 10-53.	An extra-strong, lightweight, thin-jawed tool with one adjustable jaw. Wrench develops greatest strength when hand pressure is applied to the side that has the fixed jaw.	**1.** To make adjustments on machines, when there is plenty of clearance. **2.** To install and replace knives and blades.
Open-end Wrench Set Fig. 10-54.	A series of nonadjustable wrenches with accurately machined openings on their ends. Sizes of openings are stamped on each tool. For variety of work, a complete set is needed.	**1.** To make adjustments on machines where there is plenty of clearance. **2.** To install and replace knives and blades.
Box Wrench Fig. 10-55.	A metal wrench with two enclosed ends. Heads are offset from 15 to 45 degrees.	To make adjustments where there is limited space for movement.
Socket Wrench Set Fig. 10-56.	A series of sockets using a variety of handles.	To assemble and disassemble machinery. Fits many sizes of bolts and nuts.
Vise-grip Wrench Fig 10-57.	An all-purpose tool with double-lever action that locks the jaws on the work.	Used as a substitute for a vise, clamp, pipe wrench, fixed wrench, or adjustable wrench.
Pipe Wrench Fig 10-58.	A tool with hardened, cut teeth on the jaws.	Used on pipes and rods, never on nuts or bolts.

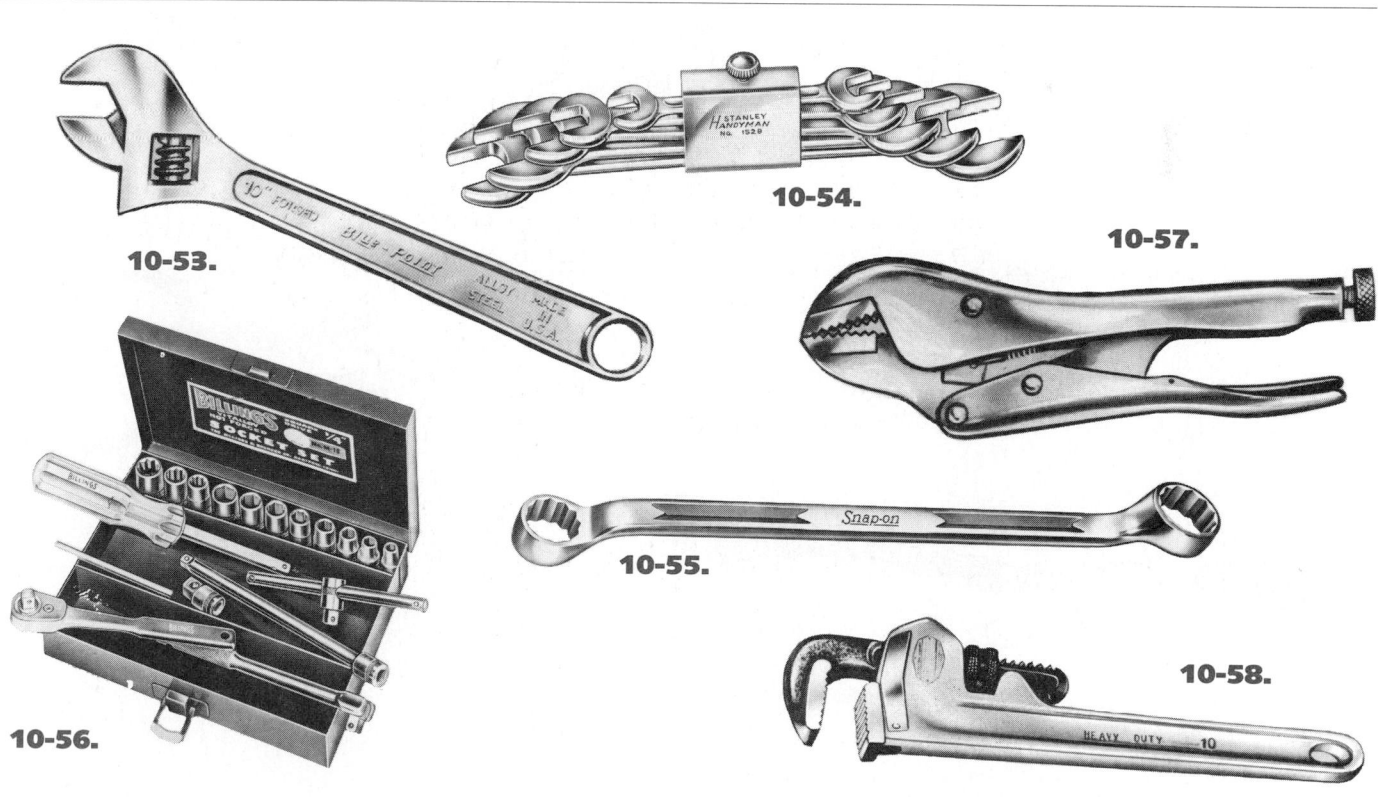

10-53.

10-54.

10-57.

10-55.

10-56.

10-58.

Tool	Description	Uses
Allen Wrenches Fig. 10-59.	Hexagonal steel bars with bent ends.	To tighten and loosen set screws that are often used to hold jointer and planer knives in cutterhead.
Combination Pliers Fig. 10-60.	An all-purpose, slip-joint adjustable pliers.	To hold and turn round pieces. Never used on heads of nuts or bolts.
Long, Flat-nose Pliers Fig 10-61.	Pliers with long, thin, flat nose.	To hold and bend thin wire and metal fittings.
Box-joint Utility Pliers Fig 10-62.	A larger pliers with a slip joint at four positions.	To hold and turn large, round parts.
Tin Snips Fig. 10-63.	Available with jaws from 2" to 4" in length.	For cutting sheets of metal, plastic, asphalt, and other construction materials.

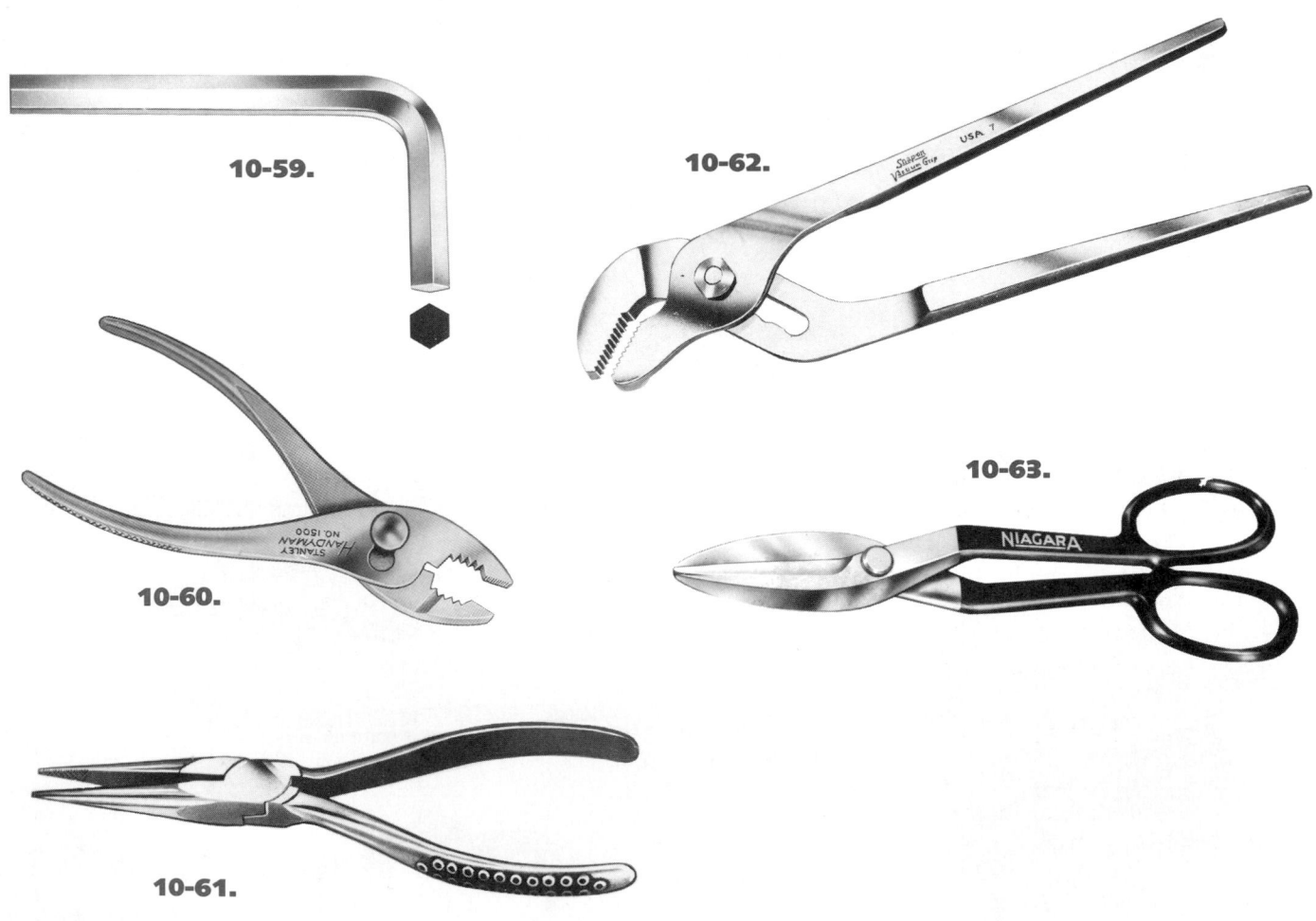

10-59.

10-62.

10-60.

10-63.

10-61.

1. Name several kinds of common rules.

2. What are four uses for the combination square?

3. Why are flexible tapes useful measuring tools?

4. What is the difference between a crosscut saw and a rip saw? Describe their teeth.

5. Name the hand saws that are used for cutting irregular curves.

6. The back saw has relatively few teeth. Name some other differences between the back saw and the dovetail saw.

7. Arrange the following planes in order of length: (a) fore, (b) jack, (c) jointer, (d) smooth.

8. What kind of plane is used to clean out the bottoms of grooves and dadoes?

9. Name two types of metal hammers and explain how their uses differ.

10. When would you use a mallet instead of a claw hammer?

11. How would you determine what size Phillips screw driver to use?

12. Name the tool used for operating bits. For operating drills?

13. Describe several uses for the Foerstner bit and the device that is used to limit the depth of a hole.

14. Why are metalworking tools needed in a wood shop?

15. Should a pipe wrench be used on bolts and nuts?

16. Name several common kinds of pliers.

ACTIVITIES

1. Science. A lever is a simple machine used to increase mechanical advantage. With reference to nail hammers, the head is shaped differently for some (curved claw versus straight claw). Handle length for finish hammers is different from that for framing hammers. Conduct nail-pulling tests between curved-claw and straight-claw hammers. Likewise, lengthen the handle for a fiberglass-handled framing hammer. Determine if the mechanical advantage is increased over the shorter handle.

2. Science. Go through the entire list of categories of hand tools listed in this unit. How many of those tools rely on electricity for power? How would carpentry be different today had it not been for the development and harnessing of electricity?

3. Math. You see an advertisement in a trade magazine for a set of twist drills in sizes from 1/16" to 1/4" with 1/64" between sizes. How many drills are there in this set?

4. Math. A friend asks you to drill a hole in some material so that a nonstandard-sized pin with a diameter of $\frac{3}{5}$" will slide in with as little excess space as possible. You have drills sizes $\frac{1}{2}$", $\frac{5}{8}$", $\frac{3}{4}$", $\frac{9}{16}$", and $\frac{11}{16}$". Which size should you use?

5. Science. Discuss with a friend why drills with adjustable chucks have three-jaw chucks rather than two or four or five-jaw chucks.

THE SCHOOL-TO-WORK CONNECTION

Though most hand tools for building construction are fairly familiar, some come in a wide variety of shapes, sizes, and models. Hammers are an example. There are differences in handle types (straight or hatchet), handle materials (wood, fiberglass, steel), and head weights (from 10 oz. to 32 oz.).

1. Carpenters in one part of the country might prefer one type of hammer, while carpenters in another part might prefer another type. If your school has access to the Internet (an electronic network linked by computers and phone lines), see if you can use it to gather information about these regional preferences. One way to do this would be to search by the keyword "carpenter" for forums (groups of people) who are interested in that subject. Then try to locate framing carpenters in southern California and in New England. Ask them about their preferences for type and weight of framing hammer. Write up your findings in a short essay that describes why you think these preferences have developed.

11

Portable Circular Saw

SAFETY

The following are general safety rules. We strongly advise you to check the manufacturer's manual for any special safety instructions.

➤ Make sure the teeth of the blade are sharp and set correctly.

➤ Never make an adjustment on a saw when it is running.

➤ Don't stand directly in line with the saw blade. If the blade binds, it may kick the saw back out of the cut. If this happens, turn off the switch immediately.

➤ Always keep the guard in place and the blade adjusted for the correct depth of cut.

➤ Use the correct blade for the work to be done.

➤ Disconnect the power source to change a blade. Make sure that the teeth are pointing in the direction of rotation and that the arbor nut is tightened properly.

➤ Allow the saw to reach full speed before starting a cut.

➤ Always keep your hands clear of the cutting line.

➤ When finished with a cut, release the switch and wait until the blade comes to a dead stop before setting the saw down.

➤ Always support the work in such a way that one part will fall away from the blade when the cut is complete.

A portable circular saw is one of the most important tools on any job site. It has replaced the handsaw as a carpenter's first choice for cutting framing lumber.

It is equally useful for cutting panel products such as plywood and OSB. Fig. 11-1. With the proper kind of blade, even materials such as plastic laminate, masonry, and nonferrous metals can be cut.

Circular saws vary considerably in size, shape, and power. Generally, however, they are classified according to the diameter

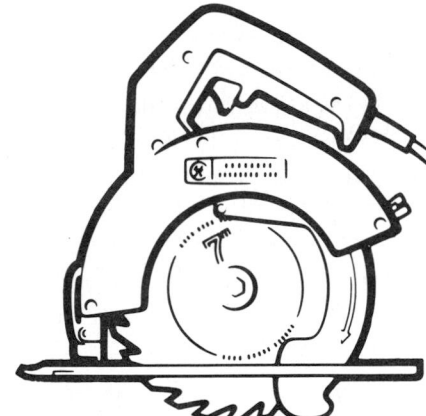

11-1. *A portable circular saw being used.*

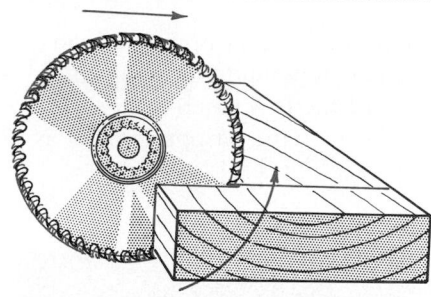

11-2. *The cutting action of the portable circular saw is different from that of the table saw. The portable saw cuts from the bottom up.*

of the blade. A 7¼" saw, for example, has a 7¼" diameter blade. Circular saws range in size from 3⅜" to 25 3/16". The smallest saws are used for trim work. The largest saws, which may require two people to operate, are used for cutting large timbers.

Because the blade cuts from the bottom of the material, it will leave a smoother cut at the bottom than at the top. Fig. 11-2. This is why plywood used for cabinetry or siding should be cut with the good side facing down. It is not important to do this when cutting sheathing.

TYPES

Two basic types of circular saws are the contractor's saw (sometimes called a sidewinder) and the worm-drive saw.

11-3. *A 7 ¼" contractor's saw (also called a sidewinder).*

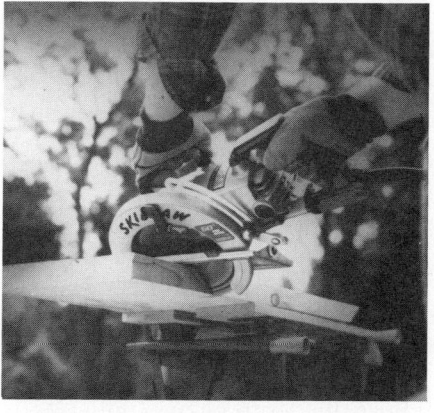

11-4. *A worm-drive saw. Notice that the saw has two handles. This improves operator control.*

A contractor's saw has a motor that is perpendicular to the blade. Fig. 11-3. The blade is usually mounted on the right side of the motor and is driven by a spindle connected directly to the motor.

A worm-drive saw has a motor that is parallel to the blade. Fig. 11-4. The blade is on the left side of the motor. Power from the motor is transferred to the blade through two gears mounted at right angles to each other. This arrangement generally results in slower blade speed but higher torque.

PARTS

The saw consists of a motor, a handle, a baseplate or shoe, a fixed and a movable guard, a blade, and a

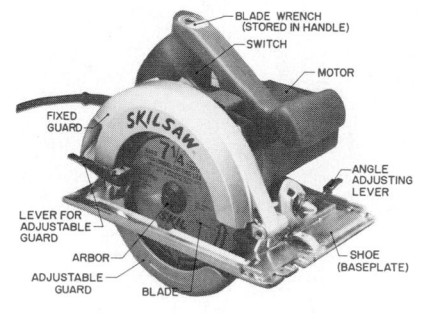

11-5. *Main parts of a portable circular saw.*

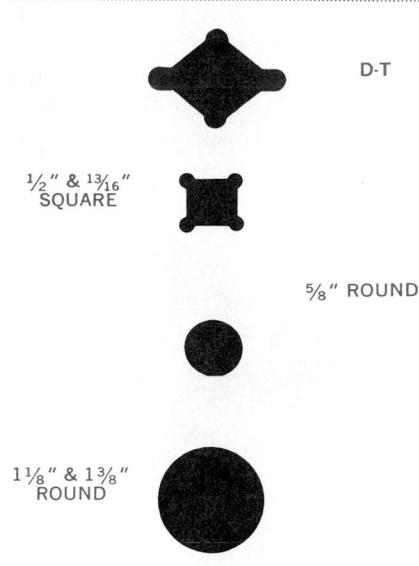

11-6. *Arbor hole bore sizes and shapes for portable circular saw blades.*

switch. Fig. 11-5. Blades used are the same type as for the table saw. Be certain that the blade is of the correct diameter and that the arbor hole in the blade is of the right size and shape for the saw. Fig. 11-6.

Saw handles can be of two different types, or a combination of both. A saw handle behind the saw motor is called a push handle, while a saw handle above the motor is called a top handle.

Portable circular saws come with an accessory rip fence. The fence is a metal guide attached to a flat bar, which slips into slots in the front of the saw's shoe. The rip fence can be adjusted to control the width of a cut.

When doing remodeling work, or when cutting certain materials, it is helpful to control dust created during sawing operations. Some saws can be fitted with a bag that collects sawdust or they can be connected to a vacuum hose. Figs. 11-7a and 11-7 b.

Because circular saws are so portable, they are used all over a job site. Saws can be damaged, however, if they are dropped or abused. A damaged power tool is dangerous, so some manufacturers make saws with parts that can easily be replaced. Fig. 11-8.

Saw guards are particularly susceptible to damage. They should be examined periodically to ensure that they are working correctly.

11-7a. *Circular saw with dustbag.*

11-7b. *A vacuum hose will remove excess dust.*

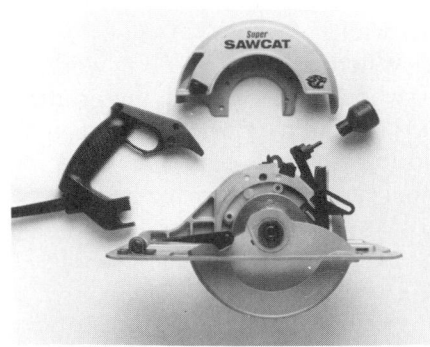

11-8. *The modular design of some saws makes replacement of damaged parts easy.*

CROSS CUTS

1. Mark the cutoff line on the right-hand end of the board whenever possible. This will give better support as the cut is made. Place the work over the saw horses or support it securely in some other way so that the cut line is clear.

2. Loosen the nut or clamp to adjust the depth of cut. Only about ⅛" of the blade should show below the stock. Fig. 11-9. Place the baseplate, or shoe, on the work with the blade in line with the layout line. Turn on the switch and allow the saw to come up to full speed. Guide the saw across the board firmly but without too much pressure, following the layout line. Fig. 11-10. A guide like the ones in Fig. 11-11 will make crosscutting much more

11-9. *Adjusting the saw for the depth of cut.*

accurate. A long ripping cut can be made freehand following the layout line. It is much better, however, to use a ripping fence as shown in Fig. 11-12.

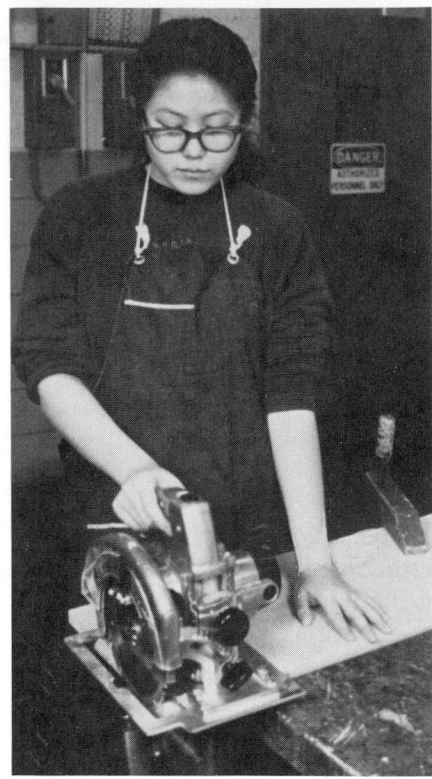

11-10. *Crosscutting. Notice that the guard covers nearly all of the blade that is not in contact with the workpiece.*

11-11. *Using a protractor guide for cutting. This can be adjusted to any angle to make miter cuts.*

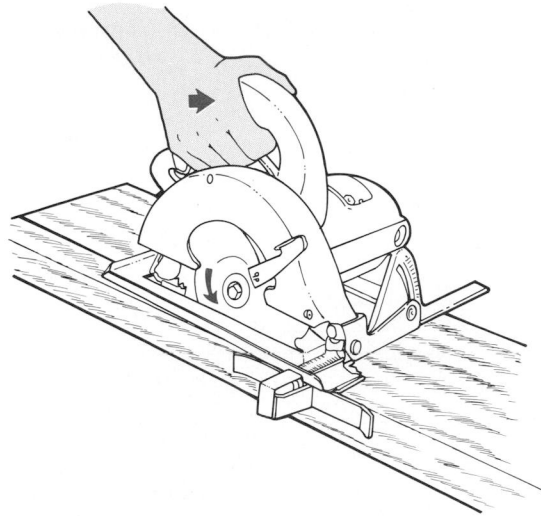

11-12. *Ripping with a fence. When ripping a long board, either walk slowly with the saw or stop the saw and pull it back in the kerf a little way, taking a new position to finish the cutting.*

MITER CUTS

Angle or miter cuts can be made freehand except that it is more difficult to start the cut on the layout line. A protractor attachment is ideal to use for making miter cuts. This device is marked in degrees and can be set to cut any angle by moving the projecting arm to the correct degree. To use this attachment, the shoe is lined up with the protractor straightedge. Then saw the same as for any cut.

BEVEL CUTS

On most saws the shoe can be adjusted between 45 and 90 degrees. Loosen the wing nut or handle and tilt the shoe to the desired angle. Then retighten the wing nut or handle. Adjust the saw for the correct depth of cut. Make the bevel cut freehand or use a jig to guide the saw. Fig. 11-13.

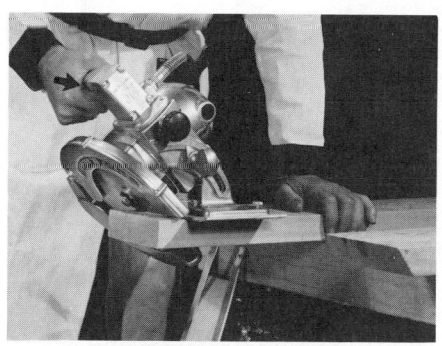

11-13. *Making a bevel cut.*

COMPOUND ANGLE CUTS

A compound angle cut can be made by tilting the saw blade and using a protractor guide. Fig. 11-14.

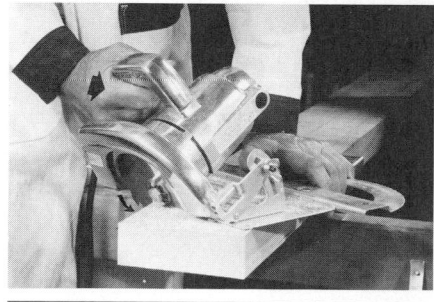

11-14.

POCKET CUTS

Internal or pocket cuts can be made in a panel or in solid lumber. An example of this operation is cutting the opening in a counter top for a sink. Swing the saw guard out of the way and keep it there. Place the front edge of the saw base on the work. Start the saw and let it come to full speed. Then, using the front edge of the saw base as a pivot, slowly lower the blade into the work at the guide line. Fig. 11-15.

11-15. *Starting a pocket cut. Notice that the guard must be held out of the way. Be sure to release the switch and let the blade come to rest before lifting the saw out. Clean out the corners with a hand saw.*

CUTOFF TABLE

To provide a firm, convenient surface for making crosscuts, angle cuts, and bevel cuts, a portable metal table is available for use with the portable power saw. Figs. 11-16a and 11-16b. This table can be helpful to builders working with aluminum, vinyl, wood, or composition siding.

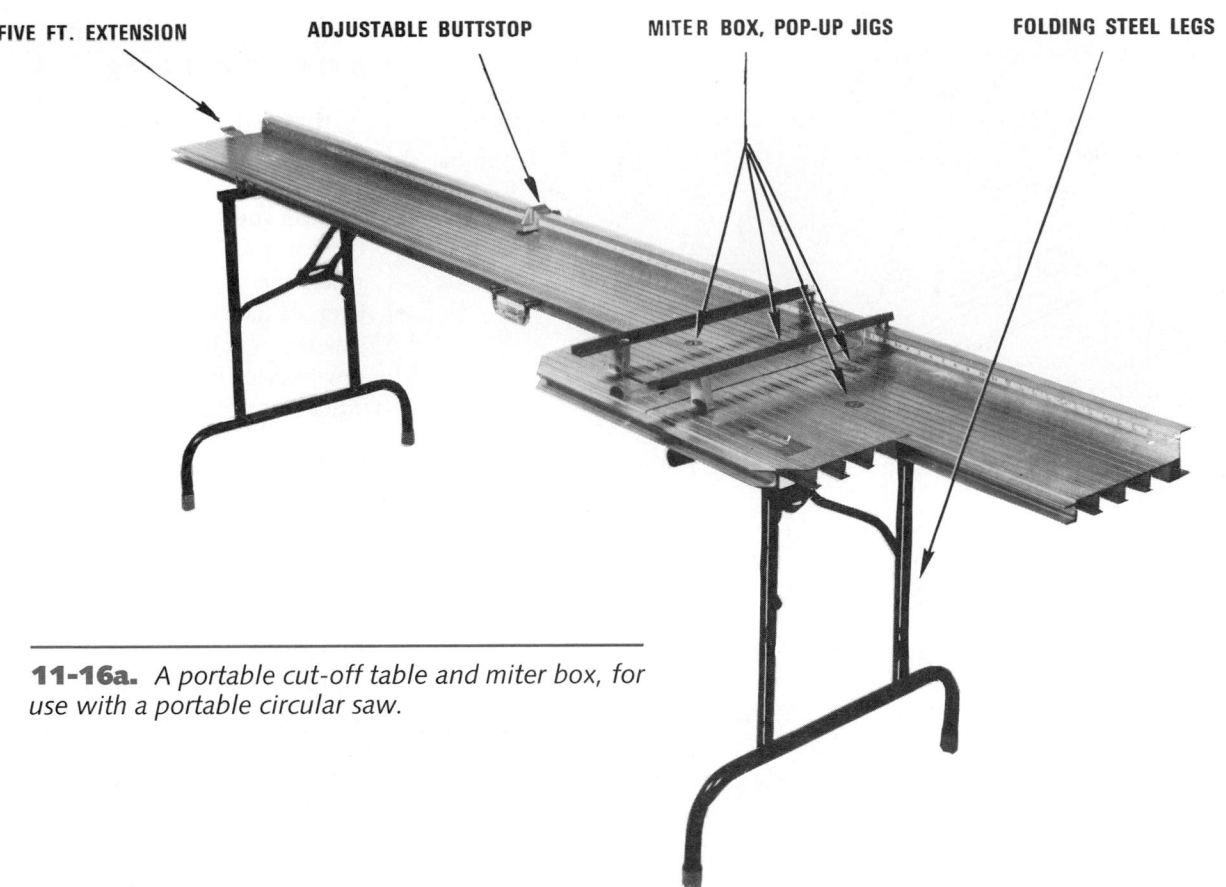

FIVE FT. EXTENSION   ADJUSTABLE BUTTSTOP   MITER BOX, POP-UP JIGS   FOLDING STEEL LEGS

11-16a. *A portable cut-off table and miter box, for use with a portable circular saw.*

The table also has a stop block which clamps to the fence or to the cutoff extension, providing consistently accurate repeat cuts.

Miter stops pop up from the table surface to hold the stock in position. This makes a flat miter cut possible with minimum set-up time. Fig. 11-17. Edge miters are made by tilting the saw to the proper angle and proceeding as in crosscutting. Fig. 11-18.

11-16b. *The cut-off extension is self-storing. When used, it is pulled out and clamped into position. The piece to be cut off butts against the stop at the end of the extension.*

11-17. *Cutting flat miters, using the pop-up miter stops as a guide.*

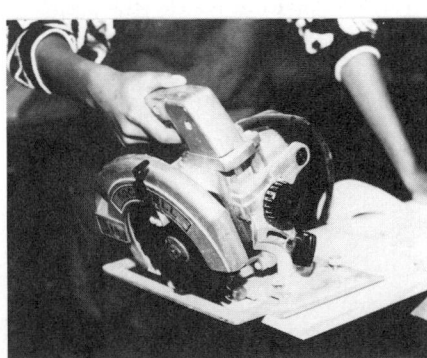

11-18. *Edge miters are cut by tilting the portable circular saw to the desired angle.*

1. List three safety rules for the portable power saw.

2. What are portable power saws normally used for?

3. When making straight cuts with a portable power saw, how deep should the saw blade be set?

4. Describe two methods of making miter cuts.

5. Describe how a bevel can be cut.

6. What is a pocket cut?

1. Social Studies. The saw is an ancient tool. The portable circular saw is a fairly recent development in the technology of tools. Using library resources, research the history of the saw. Organize your findings in a brief written report.

THE SCHOOL-TO-WORK CONNECTION

The portable circular saw is one of the most important tools on a jobsite. The saw is used for a variety of work that calls for crosscutting and rip-cutting lumber. Fitted with a suitable blade, the circular saw can also be used to cut masonry, cabinet plywood, and even countertop stock with a plastic laminate surface. Some blades are even designed specifically for remodeling work. These blades are designed to minimize the tooth damage that would otherwise occur if a blade accidentally cut through a nail.

Choosing the correct blade for the job is very important. For example, using the wrong blade to cut through plywood will severely splinter the edges of the face veneer. You probably won't mind if this occurs when you are cutting sheathing plywood because the cut edges will be covered by another material such as shingles or siding. But if you are making a built-in cabinet out of plywood, the cut edges must be smooth and splinter-free. Using the correct blade will help you accomplish this. Blades available for a circular saw are similar to those available for a table saw, except that they are smaller in diameter.

1. Imagine that you have been hired to work on a project to build an addition to a house. You will do all the carpentry on the project, including cutting into one of the existing walls, framing the addition, and installing cedar lap siding. What blades do you think you will need?

2. Your supervisor has asked you to find a local source for 7-1/4 20-tooth carbide-tipped circular saw blades. Consult the phone book to locate stores that sell this blade. Obtain prices from three sources. Find out if the price per blade will change if you buy more than one. Then write a paragraph that summarizes your findings. Recommend to your supervisor which store to purchase from and why.

12

Table Saw

SAFETY

The following are general safety rules. We strongly advise you to check the manufacturer's manual for any special safety instructions.

➤ Make all fence adjustments when the power is off and the blade has stopped revolving.

➤ Always adjust the saw blade so it protrudes just enough above the stock to cut completely through.

➤ Never reach over a spinning saw blade; instead, bring the cut piece back around the side of the machine.

➤ Keep your fingers away from the saw blade at all times.

➤ Unplug the saw before changing blades.

➤ Always keep the guard and splitter in place unless this is impossible for the kind of cut you are making.

➤ If the cut you are making doesn't permit use of the regular guard, use a feather board or a special guard.

➤ When crosscutting with the miter gauge, never use the fence for a stop unless a clearance block is used.

➤ Always push the stock through with a push stick when ripping stock that cannot be fed safely by hand.

➤ Never stand directly behind the blade.

➤ Always use a sharp blade.

➤ When ripping, place the jointed edge against the fence.

➤ Keep the saw table clean. Remove all scraps with a brush or push stick, *never with your fingers*.

➤ Remove rings, watches and other items that might catch in the saw. Wear garments with short or tight sleeves.

➤ Use the proper saw blade for the operation being performed.

➤ Always hold the stock firmly against the miter gauge when crosscutting and against the ripping fence when ripping.

➤ Be certain the fence is clamped securely.

➤ When a helper assists you, he or she should not *pull* the stock. The helper only *supports* the stock.

➤ Do not saw warped material on the table saw.

➤ If stock must be lowered onto the revolving blade for certain cuts, use stops and guards. Never have your hands in line with the blade.

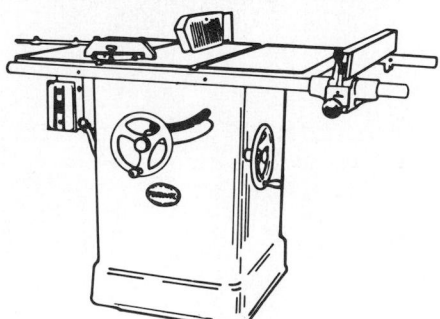

PARTS

Study the parts of the table saw, as shown in Fig. 12-1. Notice that this is a tilting arbor saw. The table top has two grooves cut in it into which the miter gauge fits. These are parallel to the saw blade. The

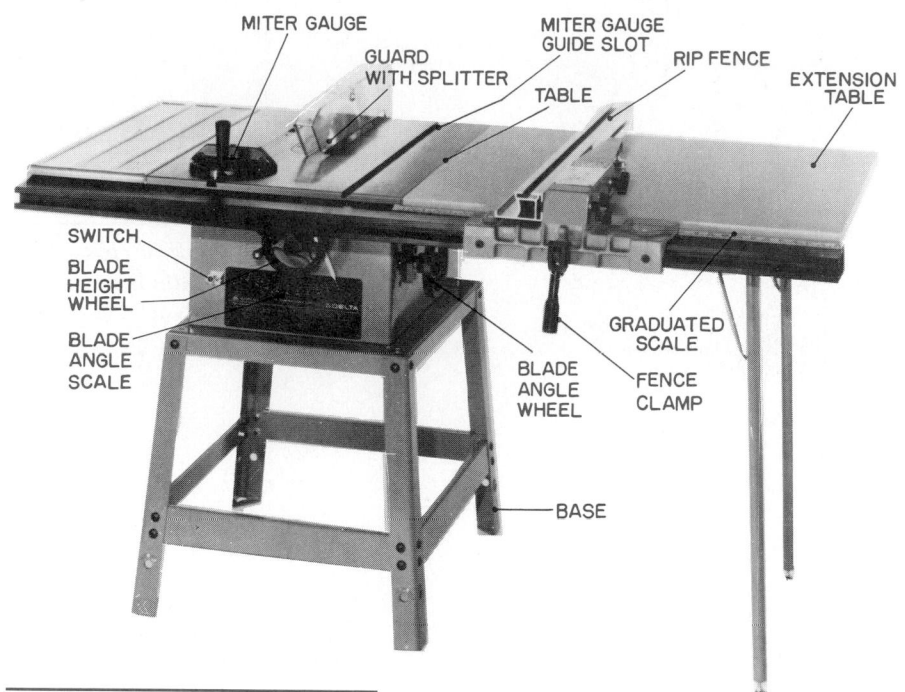

12-1. *Parts of a 10" table saw.*

miter gauge sometimes comes equipped with a stop rod which can be adjusted in length for cutting duplicate parts. A fence clamps to the table for all ripping operations. Also available are table extensions which can be fastened to the sides of the table top. These are especially convenient when cutting long or large stock such as a sheet of plywood. An opening in the center of the table is covered by a throat plate. A guard, which drops over the blade, is always fastened to the back or side of the table.

The guard should be kept in place whenever possible. (There are some operations for which regular guards cannot be used; a special guard or a feather board should then be used.) There is also a splitter which fits directly behind the saw blade and is slightly thicker than the blade. It keeps the saw kerf open as the cutting is done.

Many fundamental woodworking operations can be done with the table saw. It can be used not only for cutting stock to size but also for cutting many joints.

SIZE

The size of the table saw is determined by the largest diameter blade it is designed to take. Most table saws used on a job site or in a shop are 10" saws, but smaller and

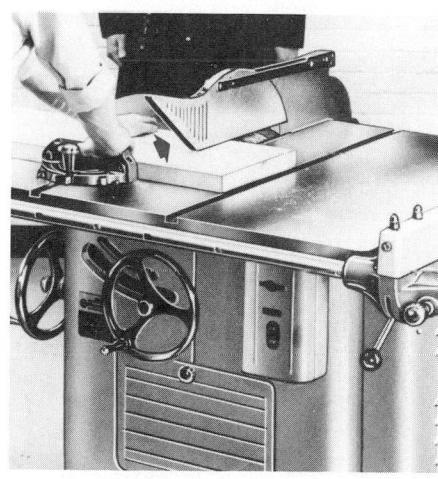

12-2. *The table saw is frequently found on the job site. The operator should always closely follow the recommended safety procedures in its use.*

12-3. *Portable table saws are often used for finish carpentry tasks because they can be moved from room to room. This one is being used to rip a board.*

larger saws are available. There are three kinds of table saws commonly used in building construction. Fully-enclosed stationary saws are heavy and have enclosed bases to collect sawdust. They are typically used in shops. Open-base table saws, sometimes called contractor's saws, rest on a metal framework that makes them light enough to move from job site to job site. Fig. 12-2. Portable table saws, also called benchtop saws, are light enough for one person to carry from room to room. They are typically used for finish carpentry. Fig. 12-3.

Most table saws feature a fixed, horizontal table and a blade that can be raised, lowered, and set at an angle. A miter gauge or a ripping fence is used to guide the wood through the blade.

BLADES

There are many kinds of saw blades. In selecting a blade, make sure that you secure one with the correct diameter arbor hole size. Never attempt to install a blade that has too large a hole.

The most common kinds of blades are:

➤ The *cutoff* or *crosscut* blade. This has teeth similar to the hand crosscut saw and is used primarily for trimming stock to length and squaring. Fig 12-4a.

➤ The *hollow-ground* (or *planer*) blade. This is used for fine cabinetwork. Fig. 12-4b. The teeth of this blade are not set (bent). The necessary side clearance is ground in the body of the blade as the cross section drawing shows. (Most saws have some teeth that are bent to the right and others to the left. The teeth are bent this way to make the kerf, or saw cut, slightly wider than the blade. This provides clearance so the blade will not stick in the kerf.)

➤ The *ripsaw* blade. This has chisel-like teeth and is used for ripping operations. Fig. 12-4c.

➤ The *combination* blade. This has a combination of ripping and crosscut teeth and is used for a great variety of cutting. Several styles of teeth are available, and each has a particular application. Fig. 12-4d.

➤ The *plywood* blade, as the name indicates, is a special blade for cutting plywood. It cuts with a minimum of chipping and leaves an extremely smooth edge. The steel is specially tempered to give the teeth a longer life for cutting through the many glue lines in plywood. Fig. 12-4e.

Blades for the table saw are available with or without carbide-tipped teeth. Carbide is an extremely hard material that is brazed onto each tooth of the blade. Fig. 12-4f. A carbide-tipped blade is generally more expensive than an equivalent steel blade, but it lasts much longer, particularly when it is used to cut materials such as particleboard and plywood. The tooth configuration of carbide-tipped blades varies

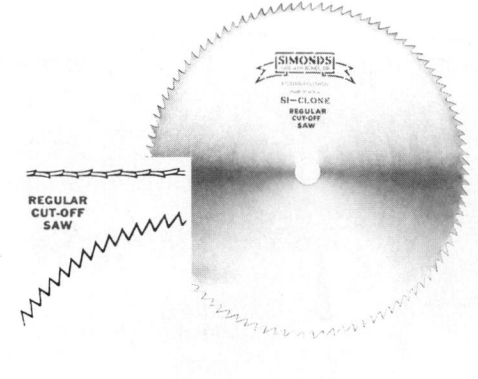

12-4a. *Cutoff or crosscut blade. This blade is designed for cutting only across the grain of the lumber.*

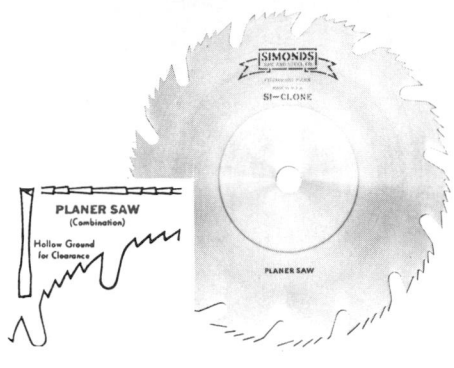

12-4b. *Hollow-ground, or planer, blade. It should be used only where a smooth finish cut is needed.*

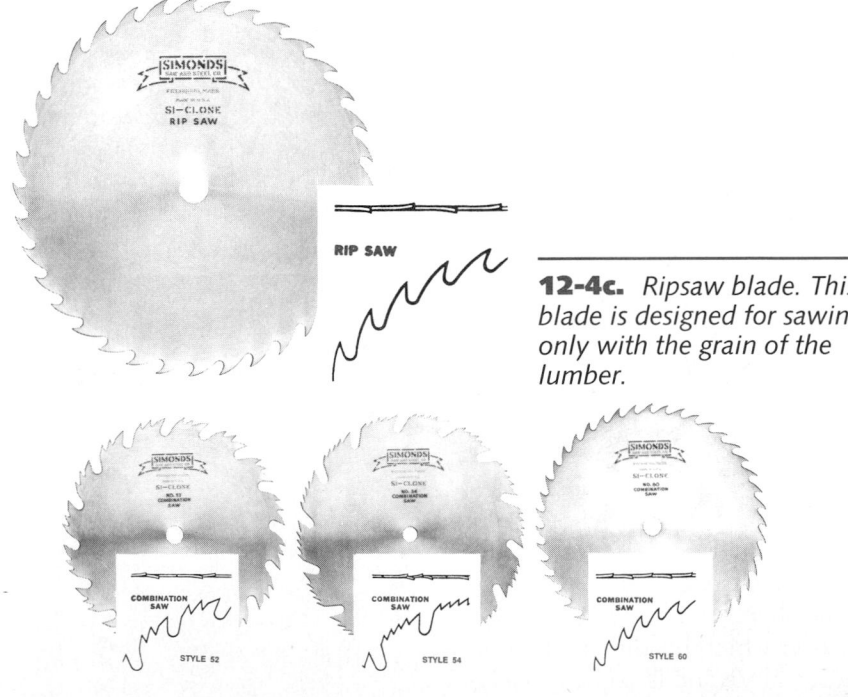

12-4c. *Ripsaw blade. This blade is designed for sawing only with the grain of the lumber.*

12-4d. *Combination blades. These blades are designed to be used for either ripping or crosscutting, and are convenient when it is impractical to change blades frequently. Style-52 teeth are recommended for bench saws that require a fine cut. Style-54 teeth are recommended for radial-arm saws. Style-60 teeth are the fastest cutting of the various combination saws and are recommended for use on all types of machines.*

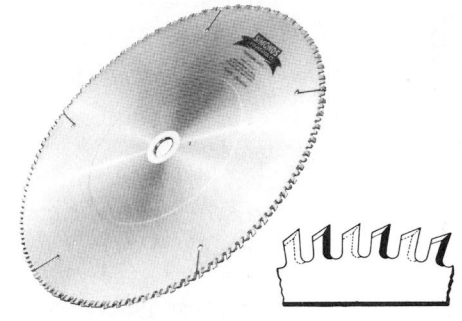

12-4e. *Plywood blade. This blade is designed for cutting across the grain and can be used for either hard or soft woods, or plywood. When used for plywoods, the finer tooth saws are recommended.*

12-4f. *Carbide-tipped blades are designed for longer blade life.*

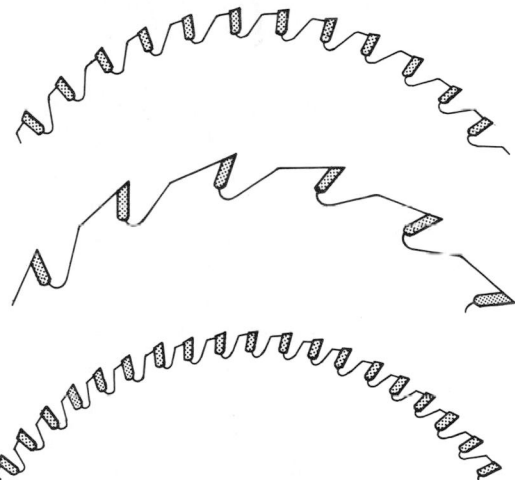

12-4g. *Carbide-tipped blades can have various tooth configurations. Shown here are three possibilities.*

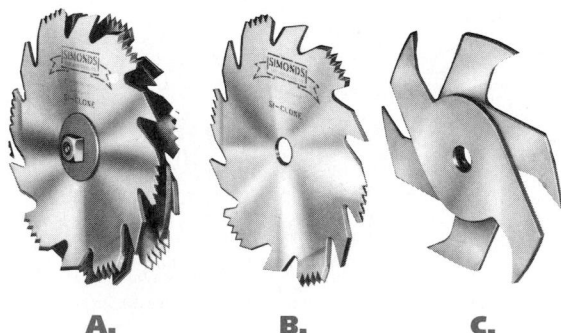

A.   **B.**   **C.**

12-4h. *A. An assembled dado head. B. An outside cutter. C. Chippers or inside cutters.*

according to the type of cutting for which the blade will be used. Fig. 12-4g.

Dado Head

In addition to standard equipment, a *dado head* can be purchased that will cut all common widths of grooves or dadoes. Fig. 12-4h. This will be described later.

ADJUSTMENTS

Installing or Removing a Saw Blade

1. Unplug the saw to prevent accidental startup.

2. Remove the throat plate. This usually snaps in and out of position.

3. Select a wrench to fit the arbor nut. On some saws the arbor has a left-hand thread and must be turned clockwise to loosen. However, some saws have a right-hand thread. If so, you must turn it counterclockwise to remove. Always check the thread before loosening. A good rule to remember is that the nut always loosens by turning it in the direction the teeth are pointing (direction of blade rotation). If the nut doesn't come off easily, hold a piece of scrap wood against the blade to keep the arbor from turning. Fig. 12-5.

4. Remove the nut and the collar, and take off the old blade.

5. Replace the blade in the correct position, with the saw teeth pointing in the direction of blade rotation. Replace the collar and nut. Tighten it firmly, but not too tight. The nut tightens against the rotation and will not come off. Replace the throat plate.

12-5. Hold the blade with a piece of scrap wood. The nut will loosen if turned in the direction in which the teeth are pointing.

Raising the Saw Blade

There is a wheel or lever on the front of the machine to raise or lower the blade. Often, in addition, there is a lock that must be loosened when making this adjustment. To raise the blade to the proper position, hold the workpiece near the side of the blade and carefully turn the wheel until the top saw tooth is at the correct height. For most cutting, the top of the blade should extend no more than ⅛" above the stock. On many joint cuts, however, the blade must be set for the exact depth of cut.

Tilting the Saw Blade

A lever or handle on the side of the machine tilts the blade. A pointer or scale on the front indicates the degree of tilt. There is usually a lock to hold the blade in position when it is tilted.

Adjusting the Fence

A ripping fence is fastened to the table for all ripping operations and for many other cutting jobs. It is usually placed to the right of the

12-6. Adjusting the fence for the correct width of cut. Make a small test cut on the workpiece. Measure it to double-check the setup before making the complete cut.

blade. To adjust the fence to the correct position, first move it to an approximate location. Hold a rule or a tape measure at right angles to the fence and carefully measure the distance from the fence to the nearest edge of one tooth. Fig. 12-6.

On some machines there is a pointer on the fence and a scale on the front of the table to indicate the width of cut. This should be checked frequently to make sure it is accurate. Each time the blade is changed, this scale will have to be checked, because the amount of set in the saw blade will affect the distance between the fence and the saw kerf. It is a good practice to use this scale for rough setups only. Accurate setups should be made by making a test cut and checking it with a rule or by superimposing (mock assembly of parts).

Adjusting the Miter Gauge

The miter gauge, which is used for crosscutting operations, can be used in either groove of the table but usually is placed in the groove to the left of the blade. There is a pointer and scale on the miter gauge for setting it to any degree right or left. Most gauges have automatic stop positions at 30, 45, 60, and 90 degrees.

RIPPING

Install a ripping or combination blade for these operations:

Cutting Wide Stock to Width

1. When the width of the board to be cut is 6 inches or more, this is considered a wide cut. Adjust the fence and blade accordingly.

2. Turn on the machine. Place the board over the table. Push the board against the fence with the left hand, and push the board forward with the right. If the board is longer than 6 or 8 feet, have a helper stand behind the saw to hold the piece up after it passes the blade. If a helper is not available, use a roller stand as shown in Fig. 12-7.

3. Feed the stock at an even speed into the blade about as fast as it will cut. Be careful not to overload the saw. Hold your right hand close to the fence as you push the end of the board through the saw. Fig. 12-8a.

4. If extremely thick or hard wood is being cut, it is often necessary to cut partway through the board, then turn the board over and complete the cut.

ROLLER - 2 DIA.

¾ PLYWOOD

8

2 x 4 BLOCKS
2 x 4 STOCK

#10 x 2 FL. HD.
WOOD SCREWS

½ x 4 CARRIAGE
BOLT, WITH
FLAT WASHER,
& WING NUT

30

¾ PLYWOOD

25

2 x 4 STOCK

FOOT SPAN - 18"

12-7. *A roller stand used to support long stock when ripping.*

12-8a. *Ripping on the table saw.*

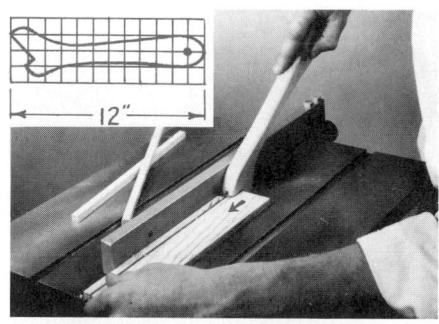

12-8b. *Using a push stick in ripping narrow stock.*

Cutting Narrower Stock to Width

1. When cutting stock narrower than 6 inches, observe the same general practices as in starting the cut on wide stock.

2. As the end of the board reaches the front of the table, use a push stick to do the work you began with your right hand, guiding the board between the blade and the fence. Fig. 12-8b. *Never under any circumstances cut narrow stock without a push stick.* It is good practice to hang the push stick conveniently at the side of the saw so that you don't take a chance and cut without it.

3. If very narrow stock is being cut, it may be a good idea to cut half the length of the stock, pull it back out, reverse it, and complete the cut from the other end. Fig. 12-9.

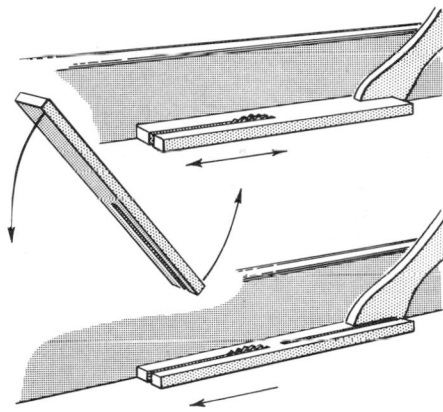

12-9. *Another method of ripping narrow stock. Saw halfway through and then move the stock back out of the saw. Turn the stock end for end and complete the cut.*

CROSSCUTTING

Install a crosscutting, hollow-ground, or combination blade. Use the miter gauge for most crosscutting operations. For added support of the workpiece some operators like to fasten permanently a long support board to the miter gauge. Always remove the ripping fence for crosscutting, except when using stop blocks. See Fig. 12-16. Carefully mark a line on the edge of the stock nearest the blade. (You must be able to see the mark easily, so you can begin the cut accurately.) Be sure the miter gauge is set to cut the correct angle. It is also a good practice to use the stop rod as an aid to prevent the stock from moving while the cut is made.

Cutting Short Boards

Place the gauge in the groove in the side toward the longest portion of the board. Fig. 12-10. Hold the stock firmly against the gauge and advance it slowly into the blade. Never drag the cut edge back across the blade.

Cutting Long Pieces

If the board is longer than 6', have a helper support the other end.

12-10. Crosscutting narrow pieces.

Cutting Plywood

Because of its construction and often because of its size, plywood presents special cutting problems. Since grain directions of alternating plies are at right angles to each other, there is a tendency to split out the ends of cross-grain layers, no matter what the direction of the cut. The glue lines are also a problem in that they dull the blade. Finally, since plywood is glued up in large sheets, the workpiece is often too large to fit conveniently on the table of a table saw.

To reduce these problems to a minimum, adjust the blade so it will barely clear the top of the plywood, and place the stock with the good side up. Fig. 12-11. Then use one of the three following methods to guide the stock:

➤ The miter gauge can be reversed in the table groove to cut a piece of plywood that would be too wide to crosscut normally (in most cases, this would be 8" or more). Hold the stock against the miter gauge and slide the gauge backward to make the cut.

12-11. Plywood should be cut with the good face up. Use a combination, crosscut, or plywood blade.

12-12. Starting a cut on a piece of plywood with the miter gauge reversed.

Fig. 12-12. Use this technique only when you can complete the entire cut without moving the miter gauge to a different position.

➤ Another suggestion for sawing plywood is to clamp a straightedged board on the underside of the plywood. This will act as a guide against the edge of the table. Fig. 12-13.

➤ The ripping fence can be used as a guide in cutting large pieces of plywood, including full-size sheets. Before starting the cut, adjust the blade to the proper height. Also, make sure that the workpiece and any waste will be fully supported as

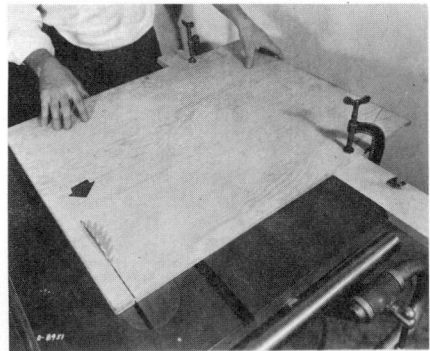

12-13. Clamp a piece of scrap stock, with a straight edge, to the underside of a piece of plywood to act as a guide when cutting.

12-14. *Using the rip fence on a table saw to cut grooves on the bottom of a plywood panel.*

12-17. *Using a stop block on an auxiliary board fastened to a miter gauge for cutting pieces to identical length.*

they leave the top of the table saw. Turn on the saw, and then rest the leading edge of the plywood on the front of the saw table. Push the plywood forward, while at the same time applying pressure to keep it against the ripping fence. Fig. 12-14. As you complete the cut, make sure you push the workpiece *and the waste* free of the blade.

Cutting Identical Pieces to Length

There are many ways of cutting identical pieces to length:

➤ For cutting many short pieces, clamp a stop block to the ripping fence in front of the cutting edge of the blade. Adjust the fence to cut the proper length of stock. By placing the end of the board against this stop, you can cut the correct length and there will be plenty of clearance between the fence and the finished pieces to prevent kickback. Fig. 12-15.

➤ A second method is to adjust the stop rod on the gauge for the correct length of the cut. Fig. 12-16.

➤ A third method is to clamp a stop block to the auxiliary board fastened to the miter gauge. Fig. 12-17.

➤ A fourth method is to clamp a stop block to the table. Fig. 12-18.

12-15. *This method is recommended for cutting several short pieces of the same length from a long piece of stock.*

12-16. *Using the stop rod on the miter gauge is a quick, accurate way of cutting several pieces to the same length. Remember to square one end of each piece first.*

12-18. *Using a stop block clamped to the table.*

SPECIAL CUTS

Cutting a Bevel or Chamfer with the Grain

Tilt the blade to the correct angle for the chamfer or bevel. Place the fence on the table so the blade tilts away from the fence. Adjust the height of the blade to clear the top of the board slightly. Hold the work firmly against the fence as the cut is made. Fig. 12-19.

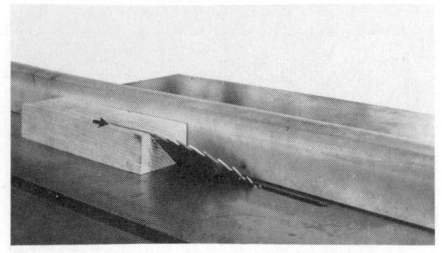

 12-19. *Cutting a bevel with the grain.*

Cutting a Bevel or Chamfer Across Grain

Adjust the blade to the correct angle and place the miter gauge in the groove on the side toward which the blade tilts. Hold the stock firmly against the gauge to make the cut. Sometimes it's a good idea to clamp the stock to the gauge for making this kind of cut. Fig. 12-20.

JOINT CUTS

All cuts for making joints should be done with a crosscut, hollow-ground, or combination blade, since it is important to have a very smooth cut.

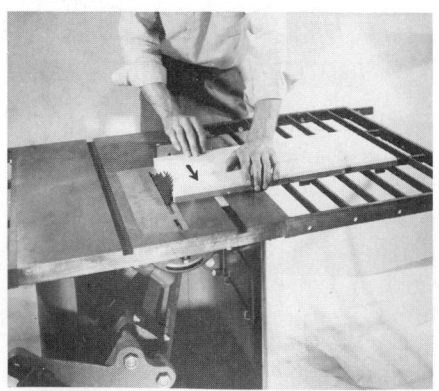

 12-20. *Cutting a chamfer across grain by tilting the saw blade to 45 degrees.*

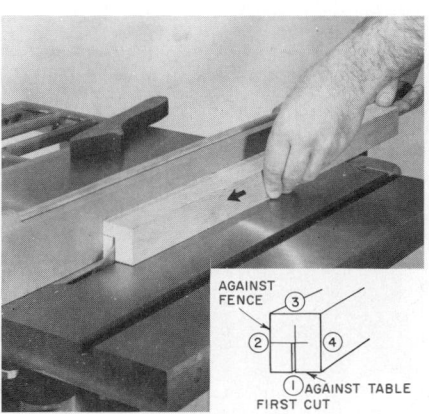

12-21. *Making the first cut of a rabbet with the grain. After the cut has been started, hold the work against the fence with your left hand and push it along with a push stick. Notice that side No. 1 is against the table and side No. 2 is against the fence.*

Cutting a Rabbet

There are two common methods of cutting a rabbet on the table saw:

Method A. Making two cuts with a saw blade. Lay out the width and depth of the rabbet on the end or edge of stock so that the lines can be easily seen during the cutting. Adjust the saw blade to a height equal to the depth of the rabbet. If the rabbet is cut with the grain, place the stock face down on

 12-22. *Making the first cut of a rabbet across the grain.*

12-23. *Making the second cut of a rabbet with the grain. With this method the waste stock falls away from the blade without binding or kickback. Notice that side No. 2 is against the table and side No. 3 is against the fence.*

the table, with the edge against the fence, and make the first cut. Fig. 12-21. If the rabbet is cut across grain, place the stock face down and hold it against the miter gauge with the end firmly against the fence. Fig. 12-22. For the second cut, adjust the blade to a height equal to the width of the rabbet and adjust the fence with the saw blade just inside the waste stock. Fig. 12-23. Hold the surface away from the rabbet firmly against the fence and carefully make the second cut. If the surface or edge of the board that was on the table for the first cut is held against the fence when the second cut is made, the strip of wood which is cut out will kick back with considerable force.

Method B. Using a dado head. Set up the dado head as described on page 138. Take a piece of wood about the size of the ripping fence and clamp it to the fence. Keep the clamps up off of the table so they will not interfere with the stock during the cut. Set the fence for the desired width of cut, and adjust the height of the dado head for depth of cut. Take care to hold the stock firmly on the table to avoid an uneven cut. Fig. 12-24.

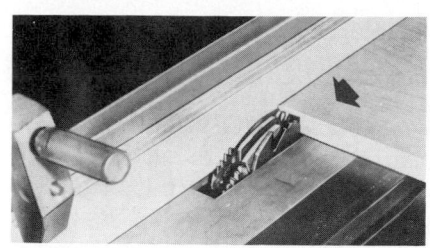

 12-24. *Cutting a rabbet with a dado head. Hold the workpiece firmly on the table to insure an even cut.*

Cutting a Miter

Miter cuts are commonly made at a 45 degree angle, because wood is often joined to form 90 degree corners. If other corner angles are required, however, you must find the correct angle for the miter cuts. To do this, divide 180 degrees by the number of sides; then subtract that answer from 90. The result will be the number of degrees for each miter cut. For example, to make cuts for a five-sided figure:

$$180 \div 5 = 36$$
$$90 - 36 = 54$$

Make the cuts at a 54-degree angle.

Making a flat miter cut: With the saw blade set for 90 degrees, adjust the miter gauge to the correct angle to be cut. Make a test cut first to verify the proper angle. Check the cut with a try square or an adjustable bevel square. Then hold the workpiece firmly against the miter gauge. Cut the miter from the inside edge of the workpiece to the outside edge. Fig. 12-25.

Making a miter on edge: Tilt the saw blade to an angle of 45 degrees and set the miter gauge at 90 degrees. Place the miter gauge in the groove so the blade tilts away from it. Adjust it to the correct height, and make the miter cut as shown in Fig. 12-26.

 12-25. *Making a flat miter cut. With wood screws a piece of scrap stock is fastened to the miter gauge. This prevents "tear out" as the blade cuts through the edge of the molding.*

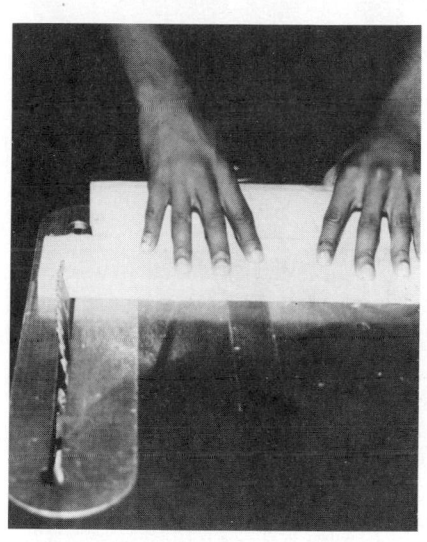

 12-26. *Making an edge miter.*

Cutting a Groove

A groove is a rectangular opening cut with the grain of wood. There are three simple ways of doing this operation.

Method A. Making two or more cuts with a standard blade. Adjust the blade to a height equal to the depth of the groove. Adjust the fence so the blade will remove stock to form

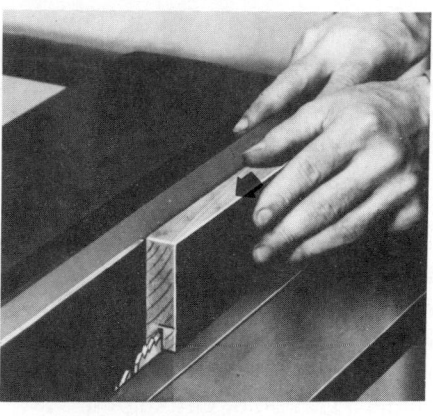

 12-27a. *Cutting a groove.*

```
          STOCK TO BE GROOVED
    FENCE          PROTECTIVE
                      STRIP
        A      B          B      A

                     FENCE


              SAW TABLE
            SAW BLADE
```

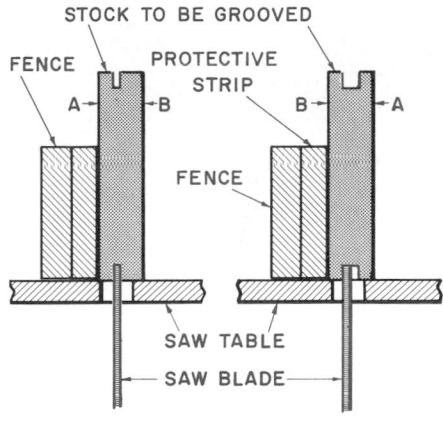 **12-27b.** *Here are the steps for cutting a groove with a single saw blade.*

one side of the groove. Make the first cut. Turn the stock around so the second face is against the fence and make the second cut. This will insure that the groove will be in the center of stock. When the two outside cuts have been made on all the pieces, move the fence over, if necessary, and make cuts as needed to clean out the remaining stock. Figs. 12-27a and 12-27b.

Method B. Using wobble washers. Wobble washers replace the regular washers that hold the blade on the arbor. They can be set so the blade wobbles once the saw is started. The blade then cuts a groove of a specific width. The resulting groove is fairly rough. *This technique is somewhat dangerous because the blade does not run smoothly. This technique is not recommended.*

Method C. Using a dado head. This is the safest and fastest method of cutting grooves. A dado head consists of two outside cutters with chippers placed between them. Fig. 12-28. Unplug the saw,

then remove the throat plate and the saw blade. Place one of the dado head blades on the arbor and then put on the correct number of chippers for the desired width of groove. Finally, add the second blade. (Usually the blades and cutters are ⅛₆", ⅛" and ¼" wide, making it possible to cut a groove of any standard width.)

Turn the chippers until the points are evenly spaced and the swaged (enlarged) cutting edge of

the chipper is in the gullet of the outside cutter. Fig. 12-29. For example, if three cutters are used, they should be set 120 degrees apart. This makes the dado head operate smoothly. Install a throat plate of the type made specially for a dado head. Fig. 12-30. Adjust the dado head and the fence as required, and proceed with the cut. Fig. 12-31.

Adjustable Dado Head

The adjustable dado head is easy to use and will give a clean cut. Fig. 12-32. The width can be set by

12-28. *With this dado head set you can cut grooves from ⅛" to ¹³⁄₁₆" in intervals of ¹⁄₁₆".*

12-29. *The dado head mounted on the saw arbor. The swaged ends on the chippers must be set in the gullet of the outside cutters, because of the additional thickness. This thickness will clean up the bottom of the cut when paper or cardboard shims are used if the dado head must be set to an interval of less than ¹⁄₁₆".*

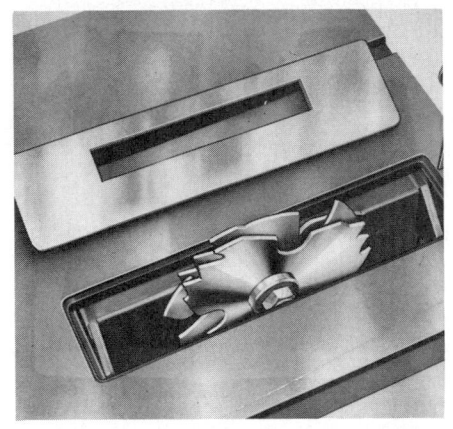

12-30. *A special throat plate is needed for installing a dado head.*

12-31. *Cutting a groove, using a dado head.*

12-32. *Using the adjustable dado.*

12-33a. *An adjustable dado head.*

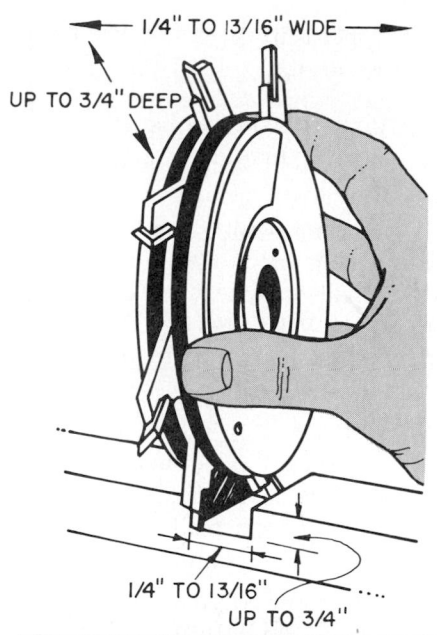

1/4" TO 13/16" WIDE

UP TO 3/4" DEEP

1/4" TO 13/16"
UP TO 3/4"

12-33b. *Drawing of an adjustable dado head. Note that the depth, as well as the width of cut, is adjustable.*

loosening the arbor nut and rotating the center section of the head until the width mark on this part is opposite the desired dimension. Fig. 12-33a. The cut can be easily and accurately varied to any width from ¼" to ¹³⁄₁₆". Fig. 12-33b.

Cutting a Stopped Groove

A stopped groove is not cut along the entire length of the stock. Such grooves are usually toward the center of the stock. Fasten hand screws to the fence to control the length of the cut. Turn on the machine. Hold one end of the stock against the first clamp, and lower it into the saw. Push the stock along until it strikes the second clamp. Carefully raise the stock. Fig. 12-34.

12-34. *Cutting a stopped groove. Notice the use of hand screws as stop blocks to control the length of cut.*

 12-35. *Cutting a plain dado.*

Cutting Dadoes

Plain dado. A dado is a groove cut across grain. It can be done in any of the ways described for cutting a groove. The fence can serve as a stop block while the work is held against the miter gauge. When cutting a regular dado, pass the stock completely across the cutter, then remove the

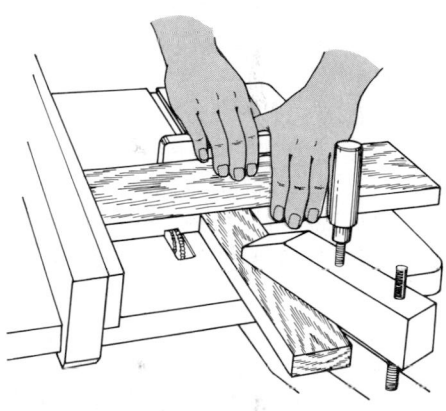

12-36. *Cutting a blind or stop dado. A stop block clamped to the table controls the length of cut.*

stock. Fig. 12-35. Do not draw the board back across the dado head. *This is a very important precaution when using the dado head.*

Blind dado. A blind dado or gain is cut only partly across the board. Clamp a stop block to the fence to control the length of the dado. Cut the dado as before until the board hits the stop block. Fig. 12-36. Then slowly raise the board or turn off the machine and remove the board.

1. Name five kinds of blades that can be used on a table saw.

2. Name the two devices that are used to guide stock when cutting on a table saw.

3. Tell how to remove a saw blade.

4. Explain two ways of supporting long stock for ripping.

5. In ripping narrow stock, what safety device should be used?

6. What safety precaution should you take before removing a saw blade?

7. When cutting plywood, should the good side be up or down?

8. Briefly tell when and why a stop block should be used.

9. How many cuts are necessary to make a rabbet on a table saw with a single saw blade?

10. Tell how to cut a groove with a single saw blade.

11. Describe how to assemble a dado head for cutting a $^{13}\!/_{16}$" groove.

12. What is a stop groove?

13. What is another name for a blind dado?

ACTIVITIES

1. Language Arts. Assume that you have to show another person how to cut a piece of plywood. Prepare yourself to teach this task by writing down the directions in a clear step-by-step fashion. Use transitional terms such as "first," "second," "next," "at the same time" and "consequently." Be sure to include in your directions the type of saw blade to be used and all pertinent safety precautions.

2. Language Arts. There are some slight differences in the meanings of *chamfer* and *bevel*.

Look up both words in a college dictionary. Explain how they differ.

3. Math. Owning and maintaining circular and radial arm saws are essential to a career carpenter. What type of financial investment is required? Find out the typical prices of the two tools.

4. Science. Collect wood shavings (sawdust) made by three different saw blade types (crosscut, rip, and combination). View the differences in appearance of the three sawdust types. A magnifying glass may help in viewing the differences. Correlate the shape of the sawdust grains with the tooth shape of the different blades.

5. Math. Assuming a saw blade cuts a $^1\!/_8$" kerf, how many cuts with a standard blade would be needed to cut a $^9\!/_{16}$" groove?

THE SCHOOL-TO-WORK CONNECTION

A table saw is usually the most important power tool in cabinetmaking and general woodworking shops, but it is not always found on a construction jobsite. This is partly because its size makes it difficult to move to and from the jobsite. Also a capable carpenter can do so much with a portable circular saw. On large projects, however, a table saw can be very important, particularly if a lot of casework will be built on site.

1. For you to be able to work safely on a table saw, it must be adjusted properly and the guard must be in place. Moving the saw from jobsite to jobsite can throw it out of adjustment, and the guard can be damaged. Assume you are the supervisor on a jobsite. Prepare a written list of instructions for setting up and adjusting a table saw after it has been delivered to your jobsite. Be sure to include suggestions about where the saw should be set up, and on what surfaces.

2. To use your time efficiently as a supervisor, you will have to minimize repetitive tasks wherever possible. Figure out a way to avoid having to write out setup instructions every time the table saw moves to a new jobsite.

13

Radial-Arm Saw

SAFETY

The following are general safety rules. We strongly advise you to check the manufacturer's manual for any special safety instructions.

➤ Always keep the safety guard and the anti-kickback device in position.

➤ Make sure the clamps and locking handles are tight.

➤ When crosscutting, adjust the anti-kickback device (sometimes called "fingers") to clear the top of the work by about ⅛". This acts as a guard to prevent your fingers from coming near the revolving saw.

➤ Make sure the stock to be cut is held tightly against the fence.

➤ For crosscutting, dadoing, and similar operations, pull the saw into the work.

➤ Return the saw to the rear of the table after each cut.

➤ For ripping, make sure that the blade is rotating upwards toward you. Use the anti-kickback device to hold work firmly against the table. Feed the stock from the end opposite the anti-kickback device.

➤ Keep your hands away from the danger area—that is, the path of the saw blade.

➤ Be sure the power is off and the saw is *not* rotating before making any adjustments.

➤ Always use a sharp saw or cutter.

➤ Allow the saw to reach full speed before making a cut.

➤ Hold the saw to prevent it from coming forward, before turning on the power.

➤ This saw tends to feed itself into the work. Therefore it is necessary to regulate the rate of cutting by holding back the saw. Otherwise it will feed faster than it can cut, causing the motor to stall.

➤ Use a brush or stick to keep the table clear of all scraps and sawdust.

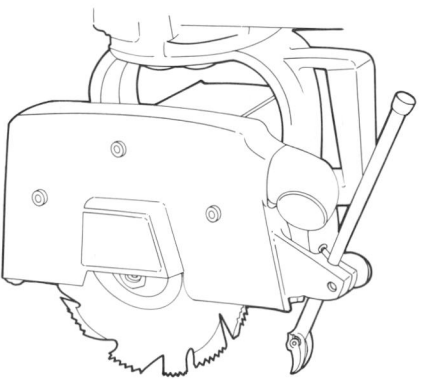

The basic parts of the radial-arm saw are shown in Fig. 13-1.

The radial-arm saw, Fig. 13-2, is a very versatile machine. It can be used for ripping, dadoing, grooving, and various combinations of these cuts. Many of these operations can be performed more easily on the radial-arm saw than on any other machine. For instance, a long board can be cut into shorter lengths easily because the board remains stationary on the table while the saw is pulled through the

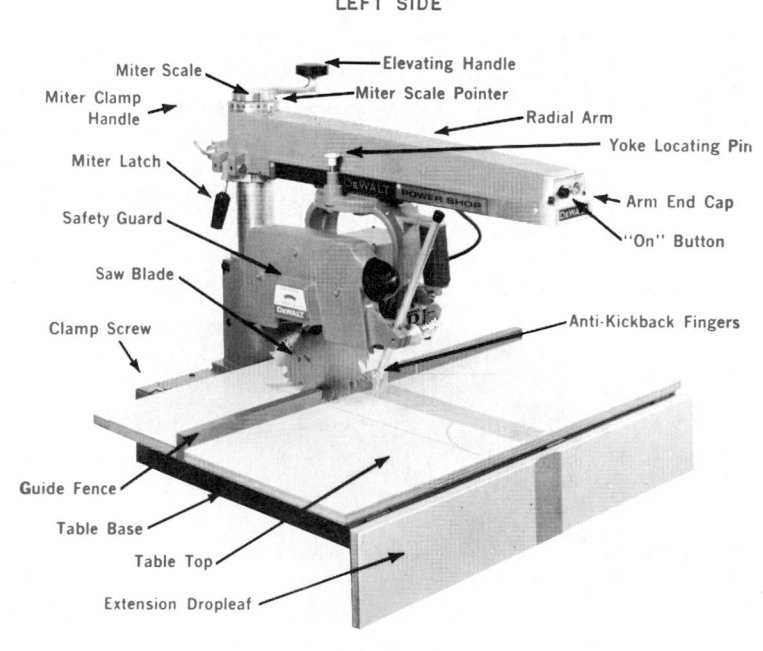

RADIAL-ARM CONTROLS RIGHT SIDE

- Rip Pointer
- Rip Scale
- "Off" Button
- Rip Lock
- Line Cord
- Column
- Key Switch
- Yoke Clamp Handle
- Dust Spout
- Motor Restart
- Yoke Handle
- Motor
- Yoke
- Right-Hand Motor Arbor
- Bevel Locating Pin
- Space Boards
- Bevel Scale
- Bevel Clamp Handle

13-1a. *Study the names of the parts and controls. You must know them to follow directions for making adjustments and cuts. See Fig. 13-1b.*

RADIAL-ARM CONTROLS LEFT SIDE

- Miter Scale
- Elevating Handle
- Miter Clamp Handle
- Miter Scale Pointer
- Radial Arm
- Miter Latch
- Yoke Locating Pin
- Safety Guard
- Arm End Cap
- Saw Blade
- "On" Button
- Clamp Screw
- Anti-Kickback Fingers
- Guide Fence
- Table Base
- Table Top
- Extension Dropleaf

13-1b. *Radial-arm controls on the left side.*

13-2a. *A 10" radial-arm saw is the standard-size saw found on most job sites.*

stock. Another advantage is that the saw blade is on top of the work so that when dadoes, grooves, and stop cuts are made, the cut is always in sight.

A radial-arm saw is usually described by the size of its blade. The smallest radial-arm saws have an 8¼" diameter blade, while heavy-duty saws might have a 16" blade. The most common radial-arm saw used on a construction site has a 10" blade.

INSTALLING THE SAW BLADE

Remove the guard by removing the wing nut on top of the motor housing. Fig. 13-3. Raise the blade so it will clear the table top when it is removed.

To remove the arbor nut, hold the arbor with one wrench and turn the nut clockwise with a second wrench. Fig. 13-4.

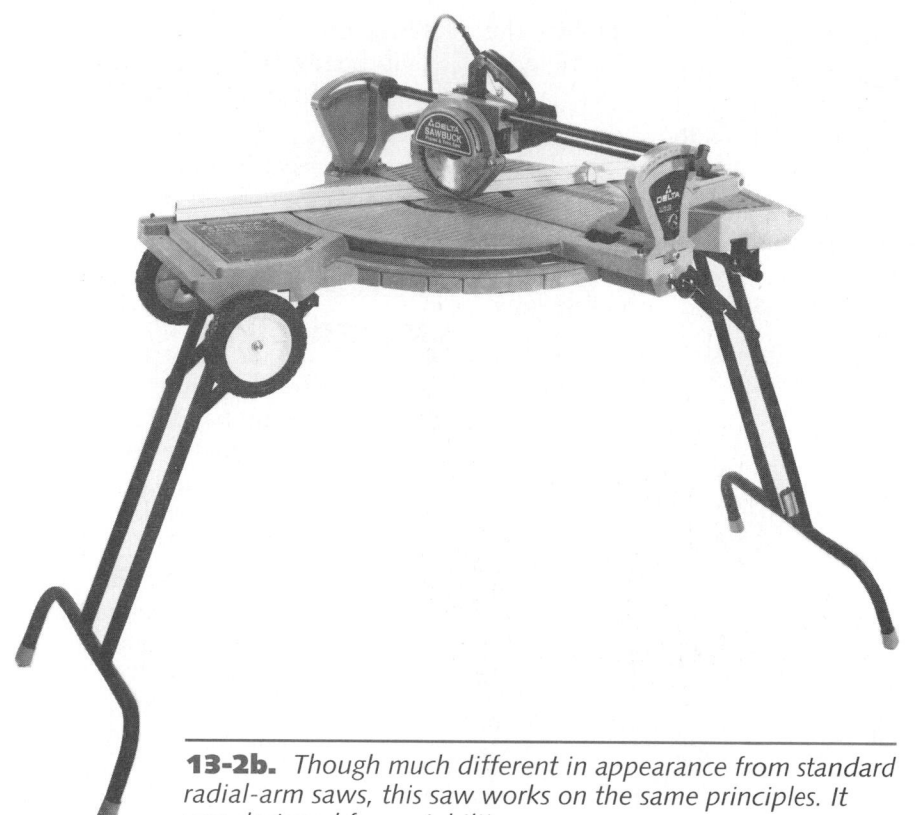

13-2b. Though much different in appearance from standard radial-arm saws, this saw works on the same principles. It was designed for portability.

13-3. The guard is held firmly on the motor housing by a wing nut.

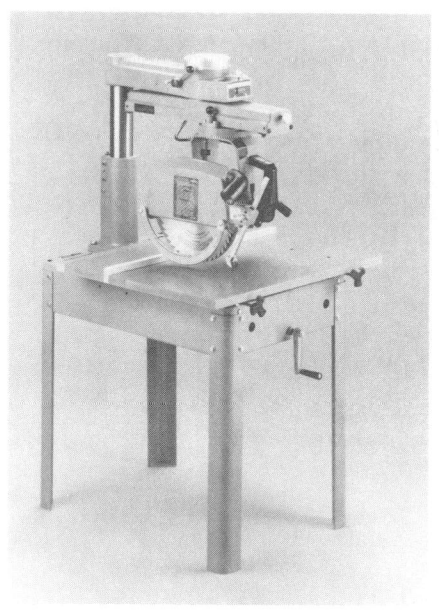

13-2c. A 12" radial-arm saw.

13-2d. The smallest true radial-arm saws have an 8¼" blade and are portable.

13-4. The arbor is held in place with a hex wrench. On some machines the arbor is held by using an open-end wrench on a flat area between the blade and motor housing. Use the correct size wrench to turn the arbor nut.

13-5. *The teeth on the bottom of the saw blade point away from the operator and toward the column. Not all blades will have an arrow to show the direction of rotation.*

Do not attempt to hold the blade with a block of wood while you loosen the nut. If you do, the saw will climb onto the block and be forced out of alignment.

Place the blade on the arbor. Make certain the teeth at the bottom are pointing away from you and toward the column. Replace the collar, recessed side against the blade. Replace and securely tighten the nut. Then replace the guard. Fig. 13-5.

CROSSCUTTING

1. Mount a crosscutting or combination saw blade on the arbor.

2. Adjust the radial arm to zero (at right angles to the guide fence) and set the motor so that the blade will be at right angles to the table top. Lock the radial arm with the miter clamp handle.

3. Turn the elevating handle down until the teeth are about 1/16" below the surface of the wood

table. (The blade should follow the saw kerf already cut in the table.)

4. Adjust the anti-kickback fingers about 1/8" above the work surface.

5. With one hand, hold the work on the table firmly against the guide fence. The layout line should be in line with the path of the saw.

6. Turn on the power and allow the saw to come to full speed.

13-6a. *When cutting stock to length, place the workpiece against the fence and slowly pull the saw into the stock. (Note the guard printed over this caption. This means that a guard must be used for this operation.*

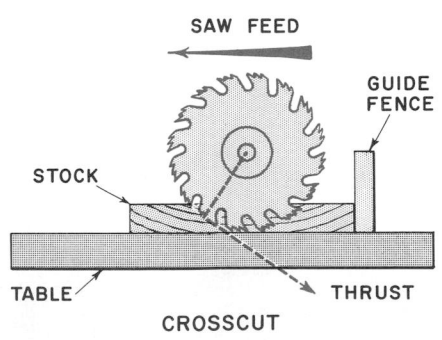

13-6b. *In crosscutting, the saw's thrust is downward and to the rear, thus holding the stock firmly against the guide fence.*

Grasp the motor yoke handle and pull the saw firmly but slowly through the work. Fig. 13-6.

7. When the cut is completed, return the saw behind the guide fence. Then turn off the power.

MITER CUTS

Flat miter. For miter cuts, loosen the miter clamp handle and lift the miter latch. Swing the arm to the desired angle. Reclamp and make the cut as described under crosscutting. Fig. 13-7. The flat miter can also be cut by clamping or nailing a piece of stock on the table top at the required angle.

Edge miter (bevel). To make an edge miter, loosen the bevel clamp handle and pull out the bevel locating pin. Tilt the motor to the desired angle and reclamp. The saw will have to be elevated so the blade will clear the table top when the motor is tilted. Proceed with the cut as described under crosscutting. Fig. 13-8.

Compound miter (double bevel). To cut the compound miter, the arm is set as described under flat miter cuts and the motor is tilted as for edge miters. The correct settings for the arm and motor can be determined by referring to Table 13-A. Many rafter cuts are compound miters. These cuts require special saw settings, which are shown in Table 13-B. The cut is then made as described under crosscutting. Fig. 13-9.

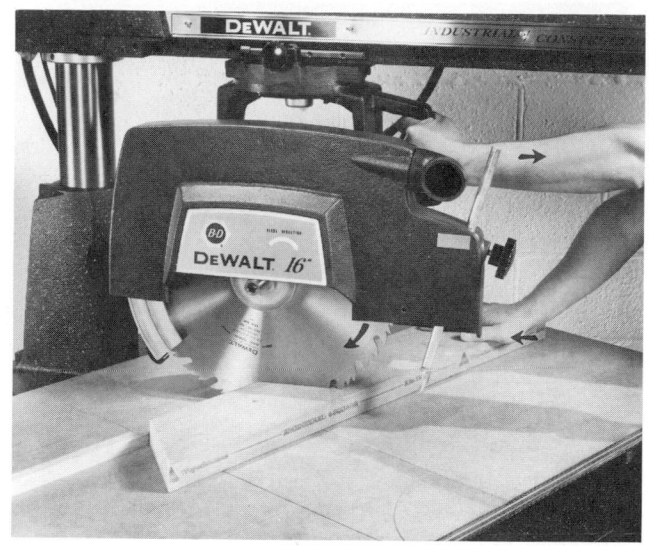

13-7. Cutting a flat miter. The workpiece is held firmly against the fence and the saw is pulled slowly into the stock as in crosscutting.

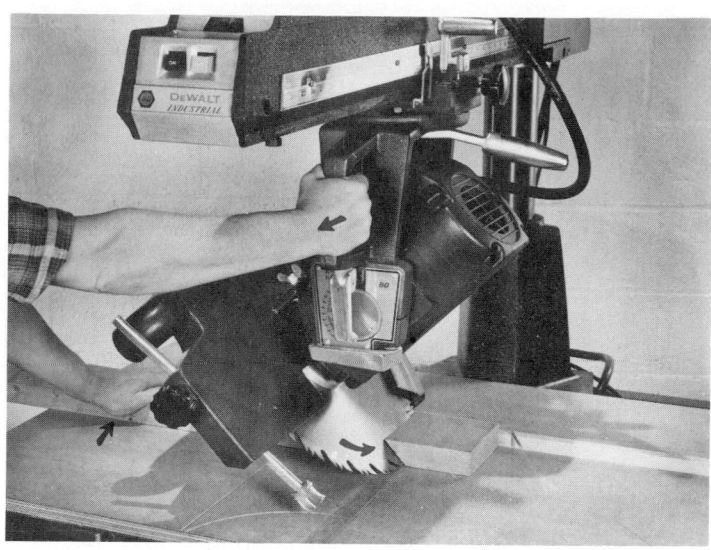

13-8. To make an edge miter (bevel), hold the workpiece with the left hand and pull the saw into the work with the right hand.

Table 13-A. Compound Angles. Table of compound angles for use on the radial-arm saw. Note that angles are given for both butt and miter joints. NOTE: The track arm angle given in the table is the number of degrees off 90°. A four-sided box with mitered corners and with the sides tilted 25° requires a track arm setting of 23° off 90° (90° - 23° = 67°). The track arm is set at 67°.

The figures in the table below are degrees to nearest quarter-degree, and are for direct setting of track-arm and blade tilt. Taper per inch given in second column applies only to front elevation and only to a four-sided figure.

Tilt of Work	Equivalent Taper per Inch	4-Side Butt		4-Side Miter		6-Side Miter		8-Side Miter	
		Blade Tilt	Track-Arm	Blade Tilt	Track-Arm	Blade Tilt	Track-Arm	Blade Tilt	Track-Arm
5°	.087	½	5°	44 ¾	5°	29 ¾	2 ½	22 ¼	2
10°	.176	1 ½	9 ¾	44 ¼	9 ¾	29 ½	5½	22	4
15°	.268	3 ¾	14 ½	43 ¼	14 ½	29	8¼	21 ½	6
20°	.364	6 ¼	18 ¾	41 ¾	18 ¾	28 ¼	11	21	8
25°	.466	10	23	40	23	27 ¼	13 ½	20 ¼	10
30°	.577	14 ½	26 ½	37 ¾	26 ½	26	16	19 ½	11 ¾
35°	.700	19 ½	29 ¾	35 ¼	29 ¾	24 ½	18 ¼	18 ¼	13 ¼
40°	.839	24 ½	32 ¾	32 ½	32 ¾	22 ¾	20 ¼	17	15
45°	1.000	30	35 ¼	30	35 ¼	21	22 ¼	15 ¾	16 ¼
50°	1.19	36	37 ½	27	37 ½	19	23 ¾	14 ¼	17 ½
55°	1.43	42	39 ¼	24	39 ¼	16 ¾	25 ¼	12½	18 ¾
60°	1.73	48	41	21	41	14 ½	26 ½	11	19 ¾

13-9. *When making a compound miter cut, the arm or track and motor unit must be carefully set to the correct angles as shown in Table 13-A.*

13-10. *When ripping, adjust the "fingers" on the anti-kickback device to project about 1/8" below the surface of the workpiece. As the work is fed, the "fingers" will ride up on the surface of the work. Always use a push stick to feed the workpiece past the saw blade as the cut is finished.*

Table 13-B. *Conversion Table—Fractional Pitches into Degrees and Minutes. Rafters can be cut accurately with the radial-arm saw by setting the saw according to this table. To use the table, locate rise in inches per foot of run (first column) or fractional pitch of roof (second column). Read across the column for the rafter to be cut and read angle for saw setting. With saw blade set at 90° to table surface, swing the arm to the right and set it at angle indicated. To complete "bird's-mouth" and make plumb and tail cuts, swing saw to the left 90° from first setting.*

| Rise in Inches per Foot of Run | Fractional Pitch | Pitch in Degrees & Minutes | Commons | | Hips and Valleys | | Jacks | | |
			Seat & Plumb Cut on Framing Square	Seat Cut in Degrees[1]	Side Cut on Framing Square	Side Cut in Degrees[2]	Side Cut on Framing Square	Side Cut in Degrees[2]	Seat Cut for Hip or Valley[1]
2	$1/12$	9° - 30'	12" & 2"	9° - 30'	12" $11^{15}/_{16}$	44° - 45'	12" $11^{13}/_{16}$	44° - 35'	6° - 45'
3	$1/8$	14°- 5'	12" & 3"	14° - 5'	12" $11^{13}/_{16}$	44° - 30'	12" $11^{5}/_{8}$	44° - 5'	10° - 0'
4	$1/6$	18° - 25'	12" & 4"	18° - 25'	12" $11^{11}/_{16}$	44° - 15'	12" $11^{3}/_{8}$	43° - 20'	13° - 15'
5	$5/24$	22° - 40'	12" & 5"	22° -40'	12" $11^{1}/_{2}$	43° - 50'	12" $11^{1}/_{16}$	42° - 40'	16° - 25'
6	$1/4$	26° -35'	12" & 6"	26° - 35'	12" $11^{5}/_{16}$	43° - 20'	12" $10^{3}/_{4}$	41° - 45'	19° - 25'
7	$7/24$	30°- 15'	12" & 7"	30° -15'	12" $11^{1}/_{16}$	42° - 40'	12" $10^{3}/_{8}$	40° - 45'	22° - 25'
8	$1/3$	33° -40'	12" & 8"	33° - 40'	12" $10^{7}/_{8}$	42° - 10'	12" 10	39° - 45'	25° - 10'
9	$3/8$	36° - 55'	12" & 9"	36° - 55'	12" $10^{5}/_{8}$	41° - 25'	12" $9^{5}/_{8}$	38° - 45'	27° - 55'
10	$5/12$	39° - 50'	12" & 10"	39° - 50'	12" $10^{3}/_{8}$	40° - 50'	12" $9^{1}/_{4}$	37° - 40'	30° - 30'
11	$11/24$	42° -30'	12" & 11"	42° - 30'	12" $10^{1}/_{8}$	40° - 5'	12" $8^{7}/_{8}$	36° - 30'	32° -55'
12	$1/2$	45°	12" & 12"	45°	12" $9^{7}/_{8}$	39° - 25'	12" $8^{1}/_{2}$	35° - 15'	35° - 15'
13	$13/24$	47° - 15'	12" & 13"	47° - 15'	12" $9^{5}/_{8}$	38° - 45'	12" $8^{1}/_{8}$	34° - 10'	37° - 25'
14	$7/12$	49° - 25'	12" & 14"	49° - 25'	12" $9^{3}/_{8}$	38°	12" $7^{13}/_{16}$	33°	39° -30'
15	$5/8$	51° -20'	12" & 15"	51° - 20'	12" $9^{1}/_{16}$	37°	12" $7^{1}/_{2}$	32°	41° - 25'
16	$2/3$	53°- 10'	12" & 16"	53° - 10'	12" $8^{3}/_{4}$	36° - 10'	12" $7^{3}/_{16}$	30° - 55'	43° - 15'
17	$17/24$	54° - 45'	12" & 17"	54° - 45'	12" $8^{1}/_{2}$	35° - 20'	12" $6^{15}/_{16}$	30° - 5'	45° -0'
18	$3/4$	56° - 20'	12" & 18"	56° - 20'	12" $8^{1}/_{4}$	34° -30'	12" $6^{11}/_{16}$	29° - 15'	46° - 40'

1: Bevel scale setting for cutting "bird's-mouth" with the setup shown in Fig. 9-2. To set up for the plumb or tail cut on a common rafter, set the angle of the arm at the difference between 90° and the angle shown in this column.

2: Angle of arm with saw set at 45° on the bevel scale.

Ripping

1. Mount a combination or ripping blade. Pull the entire motor carriage to the front of the arm. Pull up on the locating pin above the yoke. Rotate the yoke 90 degrees *clockwise* until the blade is parallel to the guide fence. The motor should be "outboard" (that is, away from the column) so it will not obstruct the cutting. Fig. 13-10. When ripping wide panels, it is necessary to rotate the yoke counterclockwise so the motor will be "inboard" (that is, toward the column). This will increase the ripping capacity. Fig. 13-11. Always remember to set the guards properly for maximum protection.

2. Move the motor assembly along the radial arm until the correct width is shown on the rip scale. Tighten the *rip clamp* (on opposite side of radial arm from locating pin). Lower the saw until the blade just touches the wood table.

3. Adjust the guard so that the infeed end clears the work slightly (about ⅛"). Adjust the anti-kickback device so that the points are ⅛" below the surface of the workpiece. Fig. 13-12.

4. Turn on the power. Make sure the saw is rotating upwards toward you. Hold the work against the guide fence and feed it into the blade as shown in Fig. 13-13. Never feed the work from the anti-kickback end. Use a push stick to complete the cut. Fig. 13-14.

13-11. The ripping capacity can be increased by rotating the saw counterclockwise and ripping with the blade "outboard" (away from the column).

13-12. For your safety and the safety of others working around you, always set the guards properly for maximum protection.

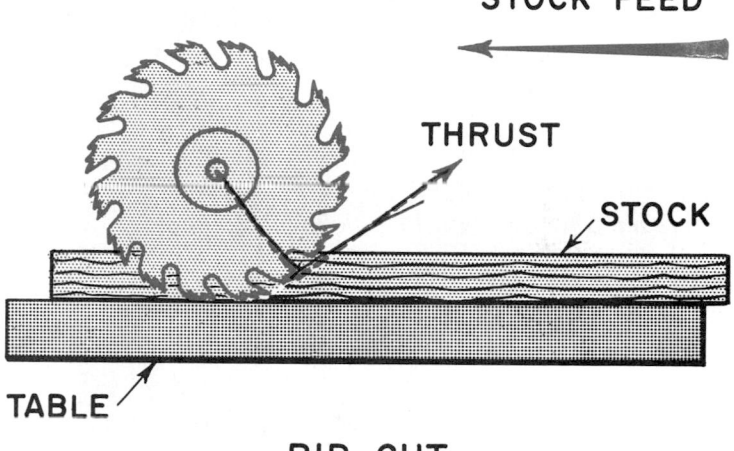

STOCK FEED

THRUST

STOCK

TABLE

RIP CUT

13-13. When ripping stock, always feed it into the rotation of the blade as shown here.

13-14. Use a push stick to complete the cut. Push the stock about 2" beyond the saw. Then pull the stick directly back.

Ripping Angles

The motor is positioned as described in ripping. Then the saw is elevated and the motor is tilted in the yoke to any desired angle from the horizontal to the vertical position. Lower the saw until the teeth are 1/16" below the wood table. Make the cut as described under ripping. Several cuts of this type are shown in Figs. 13-15a, b, c, d.

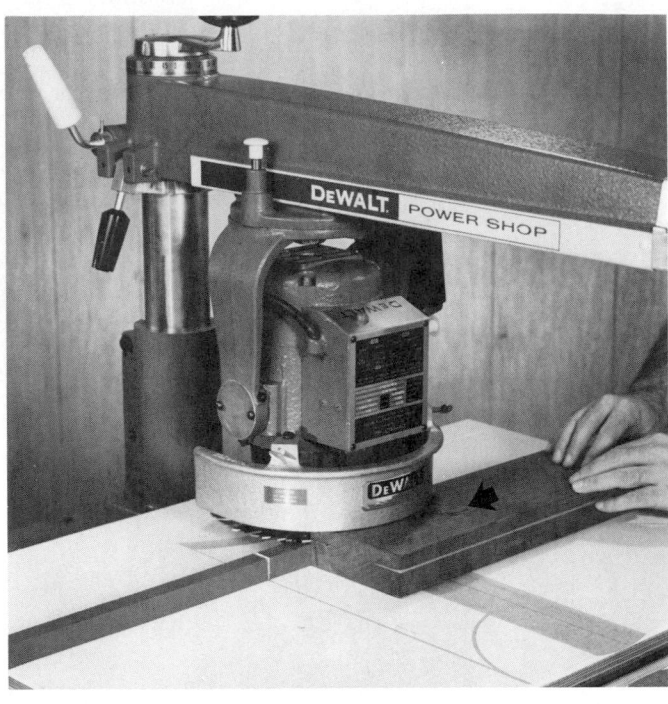

13-15c. *A groove can be cut on the edge of a piece of stock by rotating the motor unit to a vertical position. Notice the use of the special guard.*

13-15a. *Ripping a bevel.*

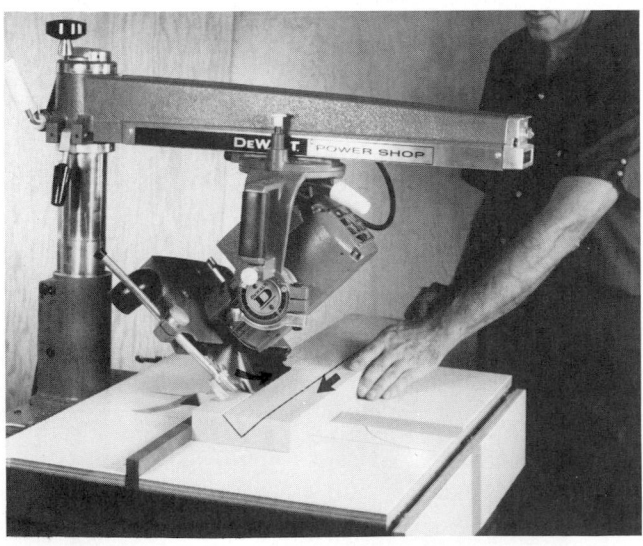

13-15b. *A V-block can be made by making two bevel rip cuts to a set depth.*

13-15d. *A rabbeted edge can be made on an angle by making the first cut as shown in Fig. 13-15c and then setting the saw as shown here to complete the cut.*

USING A DADO HEAD

The same types of dado heads which are used on the circular saw can be used on the radial-arm saw. Be sure the arbor hole is the correct size. Mount the dado head as described on page 138. Make certain the saw teeth next to the table top are pointed back toward the column, the same as when mounting a saw blade. Fig. 13-16. Replace the guard and rotate the dado head by hand to make sure it turns freely.

Plain dado. A dado is cut across the grain of the wood. Mount the correct combinations of cutters for the desired width of cut. Take a piece of scrap stock of the same thickness as your finished stock, and lay it on the table top. Lower the blade until it just touches the surface of the scrap stock. Remove the scrap piece. On most radial arm saws, one revolution of the elevation crank lowers the blade $\frac{1}{8}$". If a $\frac{1}{4}$"-deep cut is desired, turn the elevating crank two complete turns; then proceed with the cut as you would for crosscutting. Fig. 13-17.

Blind dado. Place a clamp stop on the radial arm to limit the travel of the saw and insure that all dadoes will be the same length. Should you want the dado to be blind on both ends, raise the saw by turning the elevating handle. Clamp the stock in place. Locate the saw over the point where the cut is to begin and turn on the machine. Lower the blade by turning the elevating handle to the desired depth. Then pull the saw until the carriage hits the front clamp stop. Turn the power off, then raise the saw and push it back against the rear clamp. Fig. 13-18.

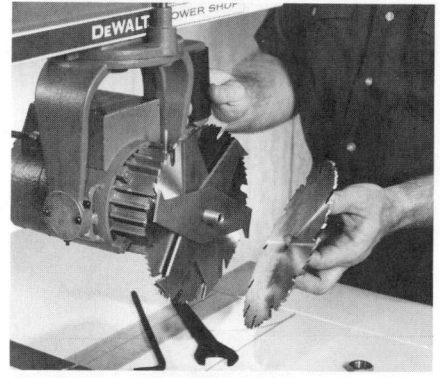

13-16. *Mounting the dado head. Note how the chippers are placed an equal distance apart.*

13-17. *Cutting a plain dado.*

13-18. *Cutting a blind dado. Notice the use of two clamps on the arm to limit the travel of the saw.*

Grooves

Install the dado head as described on page 138 and rotate the motor unit counterclockwise as for ripping. Clamp the rip lock and set the depth of cut. Proceed as in ripping. Fig. 13-19. *Be sure that the direction of feed is as shown in Fig. 13-13.*

To cut a groove on the edge of a piece of stock, loosen the yoke clamp handle, pull the yoke locating pin, turn the yoke 90 degrees *counterclockwise*, reset the yoke pin, and tighten the yoke clamp handle. Raise the radial arm about 2" by turning the elevating handle. Then loosen the bevel clamp handle, pull the bevel locating pin, and pivot the motor to the vertical position. Lower the radial arm so that the saw is the correct height off the table top. Place the yoke in the correct position and tighten the rip lock. Be sure the blade is properly guarded. Again, refer to Fig. 13-13 to see the direction of feed. Fig. 13-20.

13-19. *Making a groove with a dado head. This cut is sometimes called ploughing.*

Rabbet

Install the dado head, set up the saw, and make the cut the same as for cutting a groove. Fig. 13-21. The end rabbet can be made with a combination saw blade. Raise the radial arm about 2", loosen the bevel clamp, pull the bevel pin, and turn the motor unit to the vertical position. Push the pin in, tighten the clamp, and lower the saw to the desired height. The material to be cut should be placed on a wooden auxiliary table, so the guard will clear the table top. Figs. 13-22 and 13-23. The shoulder cut is made with the saw in the regular crosscutting position. Adjust the saw blade to the correct depth of cut. Fig. 13-24.

13-21. *Cutting a rabbet.*

13-20. *Cutting a groove with a dado head. Note the plywood placed over the table so the groove just clears the guide fence.*

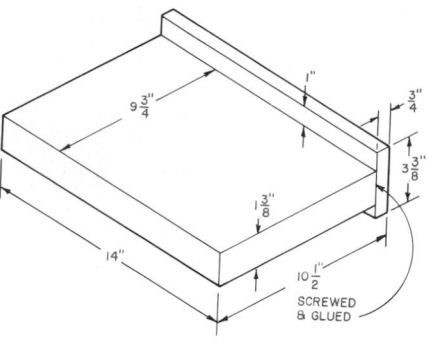

13-22. *Auxiliary wood table for horizontal cutting. This table is installed in place of the standard guide fence. To do this, release the clamp screws, lift out the guide fence, slide in the auxiliary table, then retighten the clamp screws.*

13-23. *To make an end rabbet, place the stock flat against the auxiliary table and fence (Fig. 13-22). Then make the first cut with the saw in the horizontal position.*

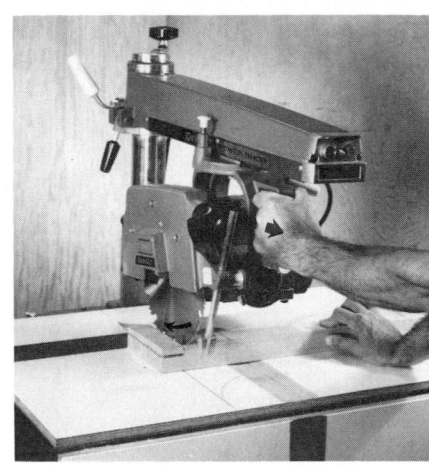

13-24. *The second cut for an end rabbet is a simple crosscut with the blade set for correct depth.*

1. Describe the main safety precautions to follow in operating a radial-arm saw.

2. Tell how to do crosscutting on a radial-arm saw.

3. In ripping stock on a radial-arm saw, does the work or the saw move? Explain the action.

4. What are the fundamental operations of the radial-arm saw?

5. Explain why it is easier to cut a blind dado on the radial-arm saw than on the circular saw.

6. Describe the procedure for cutting a rabbet on the radial-arm saw.

1. **Language Arts.** Examine furniture in your home or apartment. Which pieces do you think could be the product of a radial arm saw? How do you know? Write a short paragraph identifying those features of the furniture that you think were created by a radial arm saw. Look for features such as rabbeted edges, grooves, and dadoes.

2. **Language Arts.** Create a safety manual for use with the radial arm saw. Write your precautions so they are easy to read and remember. Your manual should be prepared neatly so that it is suitable for use in the workplace. Diagrams can be included.

3. **Language Arts.** Look up the word *dado* in a college dictionary. What is the original meaning of this word? How does the meaning relate to its use in carpentry?

4. **Math.** In doing some finish work at a job, you plan to use a radial arm saw to rip an exceptionally fine piece of hardwood. The nominal size of the piece you have is 1" by 6" by 8'. You need three pieces 7' long and 1¾" wide. Can the pieces be cut from the one given piece? If they can be, how much will be left over? Did you consider the wood removed by the saw blade?

Though it can be used to rip stock, the best use of a radial-arm saw is for crosscutting. For this reason it is sometimes called a cutoff saw. This saw is quite effective when properly adjusted, but it is more prone than other saws to getting out of adjustment. This is partly due to the way in which the saw motor is mounted. It is also due to the fact that the saw is often used to cut through heavy stock such as 4 x 4 posts. A radial-arm saw that is out of adjustment makes accurate cuts difficult to achieve. It is also a safety hazard. Make it a habit to check the saw periodically to make sure it is cutting square to the fence. Check also to see that the blade is square to the table. Each saw is adjusted differently, however. Consult the owner's manual for specific instructions. To encourage users to make routine adjustments, keep the owner's manual near the saw.

1. Can you locate the owner's manual for the radial-arm saw at your school? If not, write to the manufacturer to ask for one. You'll need to know the model number of the saw and its size. If you know approximately how old the saw is, include that information. Most of this information is located on a metal plate attached to the saw. When you receive the manual, devise a method for keeping it near the saw. The manual should be accessible, but should not interfere with the use of the saw.

Power Miter Saw

SAFETY

The following are general safety rules. We strongly advise you to check the manufacturer's manual for any special safety instructions.

➤ Be sure to follow manufacturers' instructions. Some miter saws have a different cutting operation than others.

➤ Do not disable the blade guard.

➤ Make any adjustments to the saw only after the blade has stopped moving.

➤ Unplug the miter saw before changing blades.

➤ The stock to be cut should be supported along its entire length and on both sides of the blade.

➤ Wear safety glasses—wood chips and sawdust can be ejected from the machine at high speed.

➤ Some miter saws operate with a high-pitched whine. Wear hearing protection.

➤ Make sure the stock is solidly supported by the saw table. Do not lift stock into the blade.

➤ The saw should be equipped with either a manually-operated blade-brake or an automatic blade-brake. This allows the blade to be stopped quickly after the cut has been made.

➤ Review general safety rules for the use of electric tools.

THE POWER MITER SAW

The power miter saw (sometimes called a power miter box) has become an important tool on the job site. Fig. 14-1. Though some frame carpenters use the tool for cutting 2" × 4" stock, it is very useful to finish carpenters for cutting moldings. This is because it makes a clean cut that is very accurate. The tool is portable and easy to set up. Some power miter saws can even make compound cuts in one pass. Fig. 14-2.

The machine may be set up to cut miters either right or left. Most saw tables contain positive (locked) stops at 90 degrees and 45

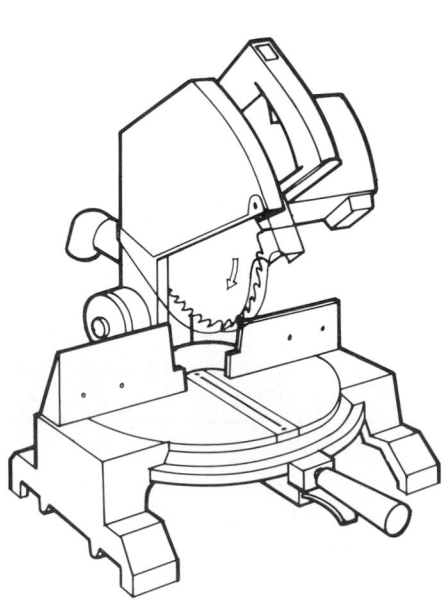

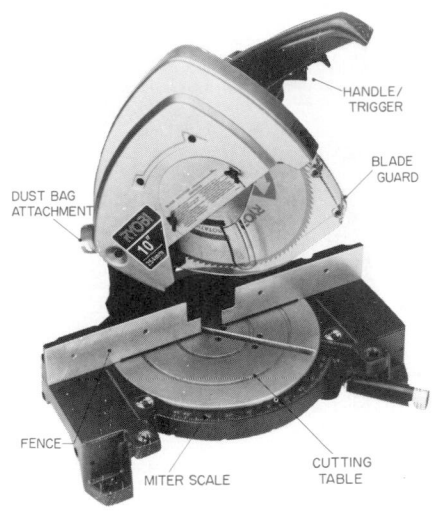

14-1. *A 10" power miter saw.*

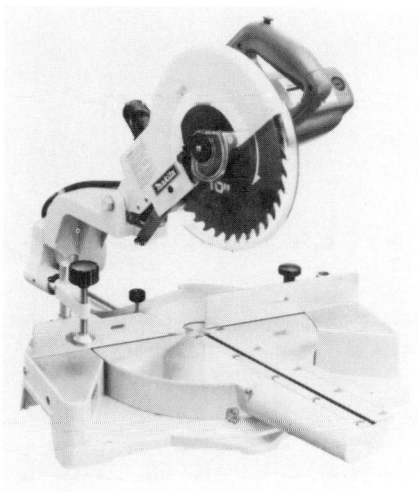

14-2. *This power miter saw can make compound cuts.*

degrees. Some saw tables also contain positive stops at 15 degrees, 22.5 degrees, and 30 degrees. A variety of materials can be cut on the saw, including plastic, wood, and light-weight metal extrusions. An appropriate blade must be used in each case. Figs. 14-3a, b, c.

One of the few disadvantages of the tool is that it cannot be used to rip stock. It is used only for crosscutting.

14-3a. *Cutting stock to length.*

14-3b. *Cutting a 2"x 4" at a 45° angle.*

14-3c. *Cutting soft aluminum extrusions. When cutting aluminum, a stick wax should be applied to the side of the blade.*

Saw Blades

Most power miter saws use blades that range between 8" and 16" in diameter. The most common blade sizes are 8", 8¼", 8½", and 10". These blades are available either in standard or carbide-tipped versions. As in any cutting operation, the blade should be sharp.

Removing the Blade

To remove the saw blade from the power miter saw, first disconnect from the power source. Then place the hex wrench in the hex slot in the end of the arbor, to hold the arbor stationary. Fig. 14-4. Remove the arbor nut with an open-end wrench by applying pressure on the wrench in the direction of the blade rotation. Remove the nut, the collar, and the blade. To install a blade, place it on the arbor. Make certain the teeth at the bottom are pointing away from you and toward the fence. Replace the collar, with the recessed side against the blade. Replace and securely tighten the nut.

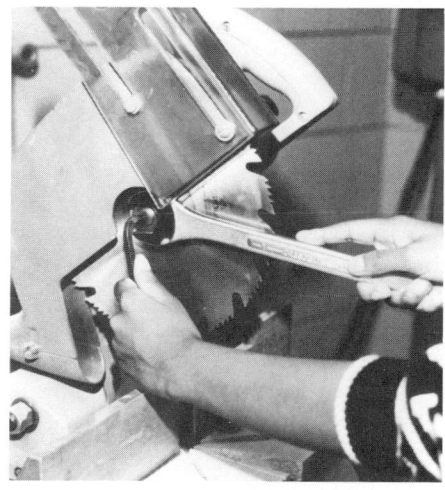

14-4. *Removing saw blade.*

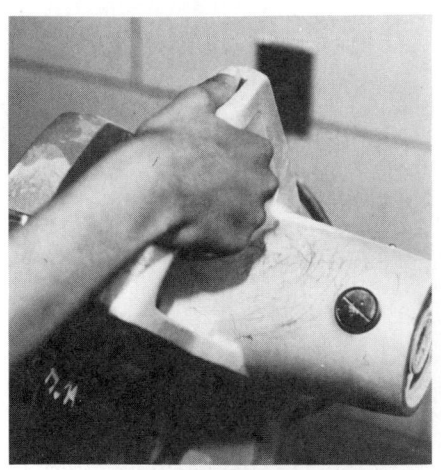

14-5. To stop the machine, release the trigger on the grip and press down on the brake button with your thumb.

Operating the Power Miter Box

To turn on the saw, pull the switch trigger. Fig. 14-5. Make the cut by pivoting the saw down into the wood. As soon as the cut is completed, release the switch trigger, return the cutter-head to the up position, and press down on the brake button. Many power miter saws have automatic blade brakes. On such saws, the blade will stop immediately after the trigger is released. This is an excellent safety feature.

Crosscutting with the Power Miter Saw

When cutting flat pieces, first check to see if the material is bowed. If it is, make sure the material is positioned on the table as shown in Fig. 14-6. If the material is positioned as shown in Fig. 14-7, the material will pinch the blade near the completion of the cut.

To make angle cuts, release the friction clamp or the cam lock, as shown at arrow #1. Fig. 14-8. Move the indicator to the angle to be cut

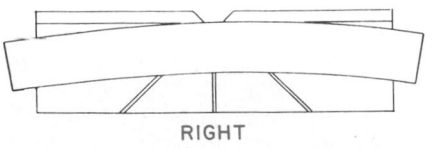

RIGHT

14-6. When cutting flat bowed pieces, examine the piece first. The concave side is the side with the "dish" in it. The convex side is the opposite side.

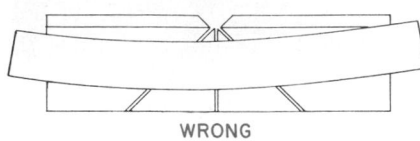

WRONG

14-7. Material positioned as shown here will pinch the blade.

14-8a. To change the angle of the saw cut, release the cam lock (arrow #1). Move the indicator to the proper angle and reclamp. When setting the saw to cut at 90° or 45°, release the cam lock and depress the positive lock (arrow #2) until it engages the desired stop on the machine; then re-engage the cam lock.

and reclamp the cam lock. When making 45 degree or 90 degree angle cuts, release the cam lock (#1). Depress the positive lock as shown at arrow #2 in Fig. 14-8a and 14-8b. Move the handle over until the positive lock (#2) makes contact with the stop on the machine; then re-engage the cam lock (#1).

Two methods can be used to cut crown moldings (trim where walls meet ceiling). For one method,

14-8b. Cutting a piece of base molding at a 45° angle.

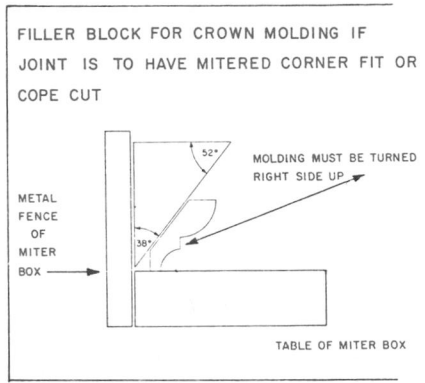

14-9a. Using a filler block to hold the crown molding in the correct position for sawing miters for outside corners, or for sawing to provide an outline for coping an inside corner.

construct a filler block as shown in Fig. 14-9a. Fasten the filler block to the fence by drilling two holes in each side of the fence and securing the block to the fence with roundhead wood screws from the rear. When the filler block is installed in this way, the crown molding will be on the table of the miter saw in the same position as it would be when nailed between the ceiling and the wall.

14-9b. To miter crown molding on a standard power miter saw without using a filler block, turn it upside down, and angle it to the fence as shown. Cut at a simple angle.

14-9c. To miter crown molding on a compound-miter saw, lay the molding flat on the table. Set the saw for the appropriate bevel and miter angle. Cut at this compound angle.

The inside corner joint in crown molding is often coped instead of mitered. A power miter saw can be used to make the first cut in the piece to be coped, without the need for an angled filler block. First, the molding is placed at an angle to the saw's fence and its table, as if it were being installed. But the edge that would normally go against the ceiling should go against the table; the other edge should go against the fence. Think of the molding as being "upside down" in the miter saw and you will understand its position. Fig. 14-9b.

Once the molding is in position, a 45-degree miter cut should be made. This exposes the profiled edge of the molding. The profile can then be back-cut with a coping saw. When placed at 90 degrees to another length of molding, the coped piece will fit against it exactly.

COMPOUND-MITER SAW

The blade of a standard power miter saw is always perpendicular to the saw's table. This allows the saw to be used to make simple crosscuts. The blade of a compound-miter saw is mounted so that it can be tilted. Fig. 14-10. This allows the saw to be used to make compound crosscuts as well as simple crosscuts. A compound cut is made when the blade cuts the stock at a miter angle and at a bevel angle at the same time. Fig. 14-11.

A compound-miter saw is very useful for cutting crown moldings, handrails, and other trim that requires compound angle cuts. Fig. 14-9c. When mitering 45-degree crown molding, for example, the saw should be set at a 30-degree bevel angle and a 34.5-degree miter angle.

14-10a. The blade of a compound-miter saw can be tilted away from a vertical plane. This allows it to make a miter cut and a bevel cut at the same time.

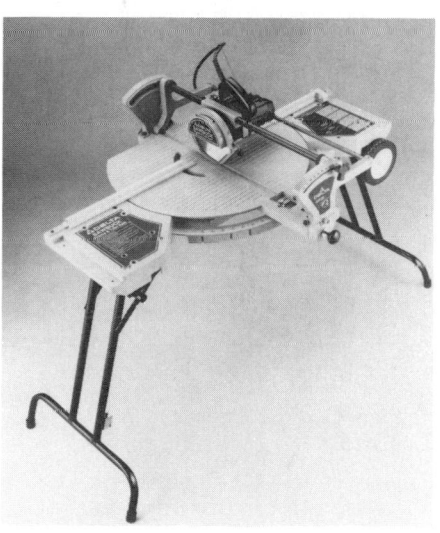

14-10b. This compound-miter saw was designed for portability. When the legs are folded up, the saw can be pulled to the next location.

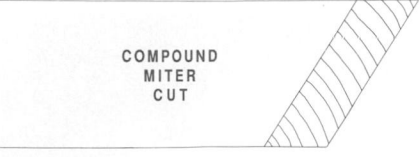

14-11. *A compound miter cut (top) compared with a standard cut (below).*

14-12. *This saw is being used to make a compound cut on 2 x 4 stock.*

The motor of some compound-miter saws is mounted on steel tubes that allow the saw head to slide back and forth across the table. Fig. 14-12. Such saws can be fitted with dado sets. They can cut dadoes only across the grain, however. They cannot cut lengthwise dadoes.

QUESTIONS

1. Why do finish carpenters find the power miter saw useful?

2. How should stock be supported while it is being cut on the power miter box?

3. Why is a blade brake important?

4. How is a standard power miter saw different from a compound-miter saw?

ACTIVITIES

1. Social Studies. The text discusses the uses of the portable power saw in the carpentry industry. However, there are other fields where portable power saws also are used. Identify two fields other than carpentry that use these saws. Describe not only how they are used, but also how they benefit that field.

THE SCHOOL-TO-WORK CONNECTION

Unlike a radial-arm saw, a power miter saw is very portable and can be moved easily from room to room in a house under construction. Most major tool manufacturers offer this tool, but designs can differ considerably. This can make it difficult to decide which saw to purchase.

1. Obtain tool catalogs from several sources. One way of finding tool manufacturers is to look through the advertisements in a construction trade magazine. (You can find names of these magazines by checking with the reference librarian at your local library.) Once you have at least three catalogs, compare the specifications of the tools to identify the saw that could crosscut the widest board.

15

Portable Electric Drill

SAFETY

The following are general safety rules. We strongly advise you to check the manufacturer's manual for any special safety instructions.

➤ Review general safety rules for use of portable electric tools.

➤ Disconnect the power plug before installing or removing drill bits.

➤ Make certain the drill bit is clamped securely in the chuck.

➤ Be sure the chuck key has been removed.

➤ Do not force the drill—use an even, steady pressure.

➤ Never use a bit with a square, tapered tang in an electric drill. The drill's chuck will not hold this kind of bit securely.

➤ When laying the drill down, always have the point away from you, even when it is "coasting" to a stop.

➤ Never drill through cloth.

➤ Always clamp small pieces; do not hold them with your fingers when drilling.

The portable electric drill is an extremely versatile power tool. With the right bit it can drill holes in nearly any material. Fitted with various accessories, it can remove finishes, install screws, mix paints, and do many other jobs.

The major parts of the tool are the housing, a handle, a motor, and a chuck. Fig. 15-1. Most drills have a key-type chuck, but some drills have a keyless chuck that can be tightened by hand. Fig. 15-2. The most common shape for an electric drill is the pistol-grip drill, but there are other configurations as well. Fig. 15-3. The most common sizes of electric drills used in construction are ¼", ⅜", and ½". These dimensions refer to the largest diameter of drill bit shank that the chuck can hold.

Some drill housings are made of metal, but many are made of plastic to reduce the danger of electrical shock. These plastic housings are called double-insulated housings.

Some electric drills operate at only one speed. Others, called variable speed drills, can be operated at various speeds. Control of the speed is important when drilling certain types of materials and when using the drill to start or remove screws.

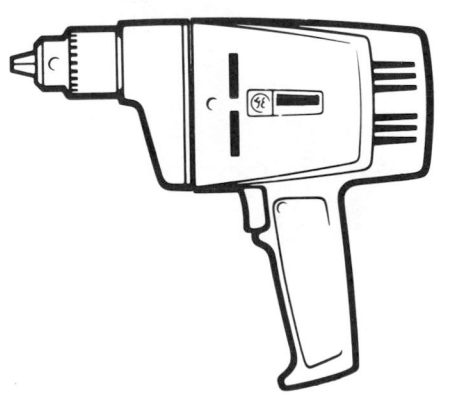

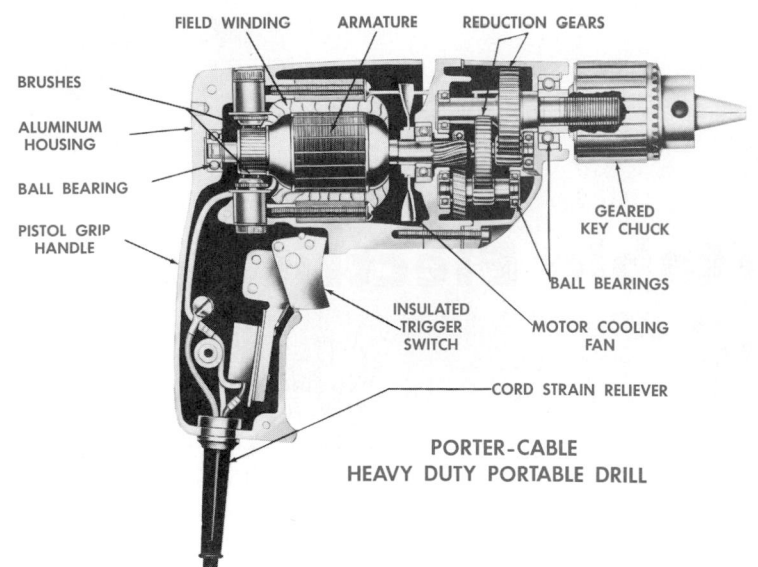

15-1. *Parts of a ¼" portable drill.*

15-2. *An electric drill with a keyless chuck.*

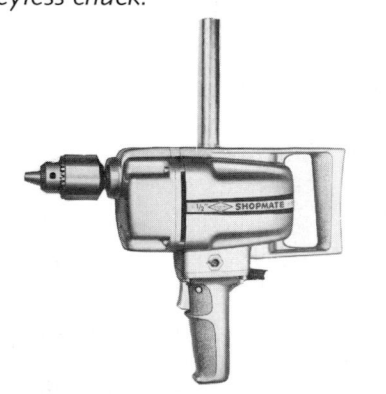

15-3. *The ½" capacity electric drill with spade handle.*

15-4a. *A cordless drill.*

15-4b. *A cordless drill and battery charger. A twist bit is in the drill's chuck.*

CORDLESS DRILLS

Many manufacturers now offer a range of electric drills powered by rechargeable nickel-cadmium (ni-cad) batteries. These drills are particularly useful where long lengths of extension cord would be undesirable, or where electrical power is not available. Fig. 15-4a.

The batteries of a cordless drill are housed in a plastic battery pack that is usually mounted inside the handle of the drill. To charge the batteries, the battery pack is removed from the drill and placed in a charger. The charger is plugged into regular household current and restores full battery strength in approximately one hour. Fig. 15-4b.

OTHER TYPES OF DRILLS

In addition to the standard drill models, several variations of the tool have been designed for particular building trades.

Hammer drills are used to drill holes in masonry materials. These durable drills usually have a ⅜" or ½" chuck. While the chuck revolves, a mechanism within the drill creates a rapid, hammer-like reciprocating action. This helps to drive a spinning masonry bit into the material. Fig. 15-5a. Rotary hammers work on a similar principle, but are used for heavy-duty drilling applications, such as core drilling in masonry. Fig. 15-5b.

Screw guns, also called electric screwdrivers, are ¼" electric drills that have a nosepiece instead of a standard chuck. The nosepiece holds a screwdriver tip, and sometimes a mechanism for holding a screw on the tip. These tools are not intended to drill holes; their main use is the

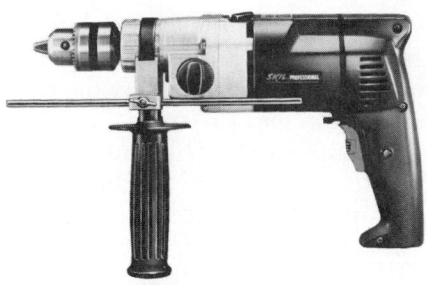

15-5a. *A ½" hammer drill.*

15-5b. *A rotary hammer.*

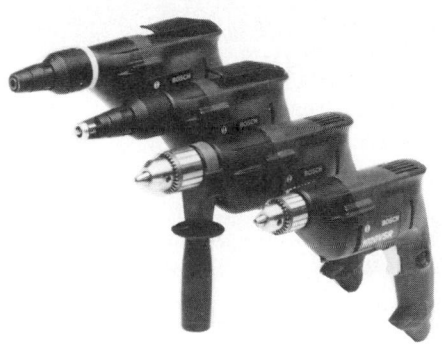

15-6. *Screw guns (in back) compared to electric drills.*

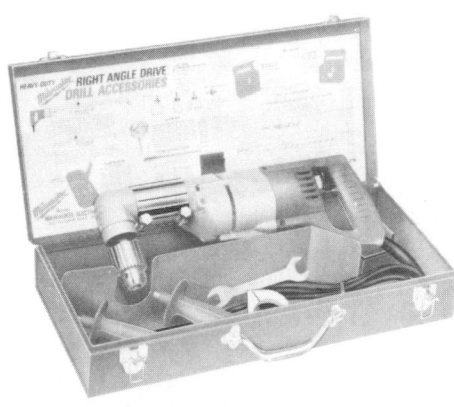

15-7. *A right-angle drill.*

repeated driving of screws. They are particularly useful for fastening drywall to wood or metal studs. They are also used to install subflooring and decking. Screw guns can be fitted with tips for slotted-head and Phillips-head screws, and with bits that allow the tool to drive socket head fasteners and hex head fasteners. Fig. 15-6.

Right-angle drills are often used by electricians and plumbers. A ⅜" or ½" chuck is turned 90 degrees to the body of the drill. This allows drilling in tight spaces, such as through studs 16" on center. Fig. 15-7.

DRILL BITS

One of the reasons for the versatility of electric drills is that many types of bits and cutters are available for the tool. Twist bits and spade bits are the bits most commonly used on a job site.

Twist bits are available for cutting wood or metal at high speeds. Common sizes range from ⅛" diameter to ½" diameter in increments of ¹⁄₆₄". A metal case that holds a group of twist bits is called an index. Most twist bits are made from high-speed steel (HSS). Fig. 15-4b.

Spade bits are used primarily to bore holes in wood. A large spur point guides the bit, and horizontal cutting surfaces remove stock. Spade bits are relatively inexpensive. Fig. 15-8.

Hole saws are technically not drill bits, but they are used on electric drills to cut holes. A hole saw is a cylindrical metal sleeve with sawtooth edges. Hole saws are used to cut large diameter holes. They fit on a mandrel that is chucked into the electric drill. Fig. 15-9.

Brad point bits have a center spur that prevents the drill bit from

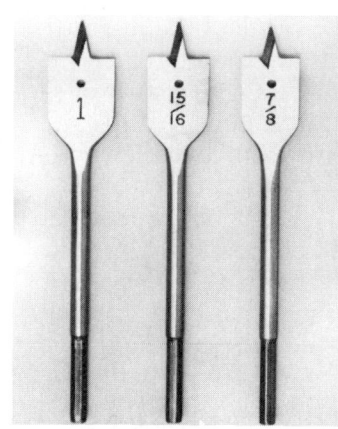

15-8. *Spade bits.*

15-9. *Hole saws.*

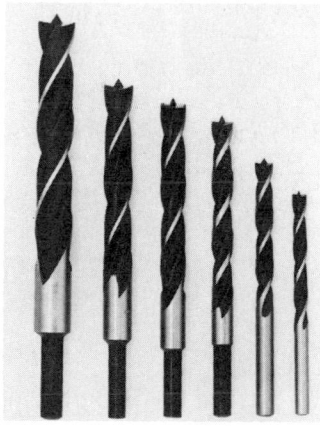

15-10. *Brad-point bits.*

"walking" as the hole is started. Sharp cutting edges at the perimeter of the bit cut smooth, clean holes in wood with a minimum of splintering. Fig. 15-10.

Foerstner bits have a brad point and are intended for boring smooth holes that have flat bottoms. Such holes can be used as mortises. Another feature of Foerstner bits is that they can be used to drill through any grain, including end grain. Fig. 15-11.

Masonry bits should be used on brick, concrete, and other masonry materials. They have a beveled tip and wide flutes that carry grit and dust away from the cut. Fig. 15-12.

Step bits are used primarily in the electrical trades and sheet metal working. Each bit can drill several different sizes of holes; each hole is deburred by the cutting layer above. These bits can also be used to cut some plastics. Fig. 15-13.

Hex shank bits are used for heavy-duty drilling in metal, wood and plastic. The hexagonal shank of the bit reduces slippage. Fig. 15-14.

Auger bits are designed to cut deep holes quickly through wood. The screw point pulls the bit through the wood, and the deep flutes help to remove chips efficiently. Fig. 15-15.

Self-feed bits are designed to bore large diameter holes. They are pulled into the wood by a center screw point. Radially-mounted straight cutting blades are replaceable and remove stock quickly. Fig. 15-15.

Glass/tile bits have special tips that bore through difficult-to-cut materials such as glass, ceramic tile, and mirror. Fig. 15-16.

A **combination drill and countersink** is a convenient tool for inserting woodscrews. It is always necessary to drill the correct size holes for woodscrews to prevent splitting the workpiece and to get the maximum holding power. This is usually a three-step procedure if the screw is to be

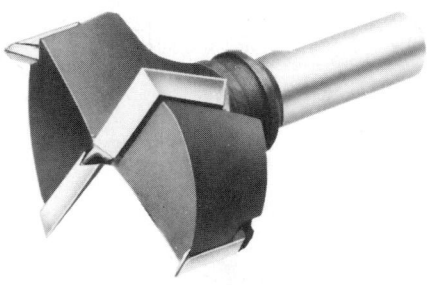

15-11. A Foerstner bit.

15-12. A masonry bit.

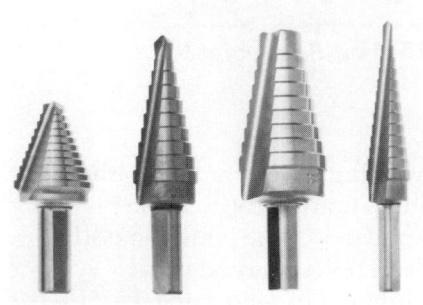

15-13. Step bits.

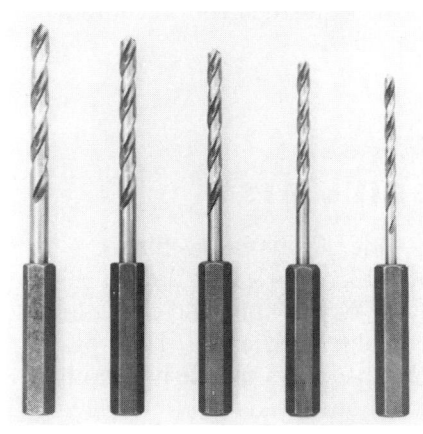

15-14. Hex shank bits.

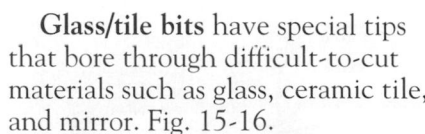

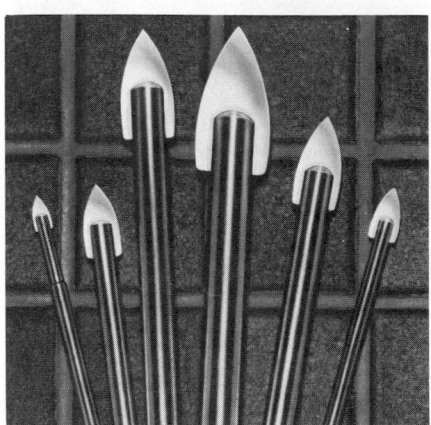

15-16. Glass/tile bits.

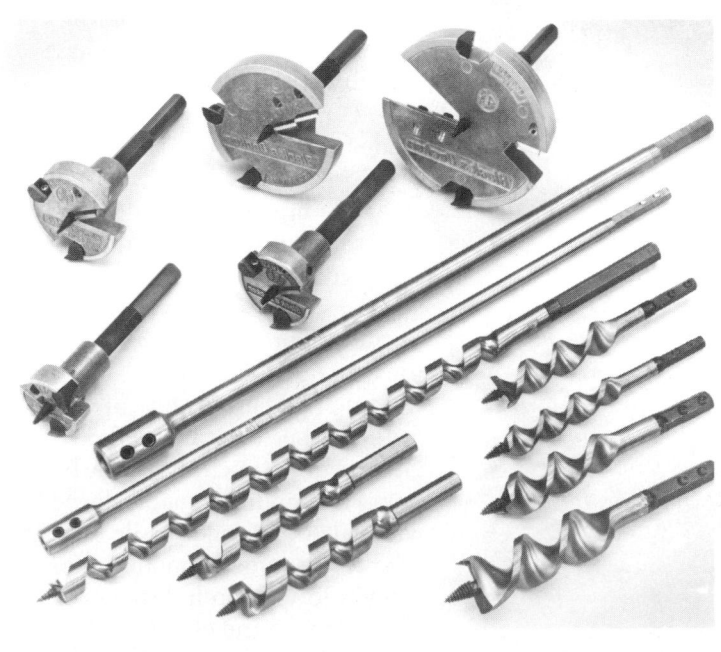

15-15. Self-feed bits (at top), drill bit extensions, and auger bits (at bottom).

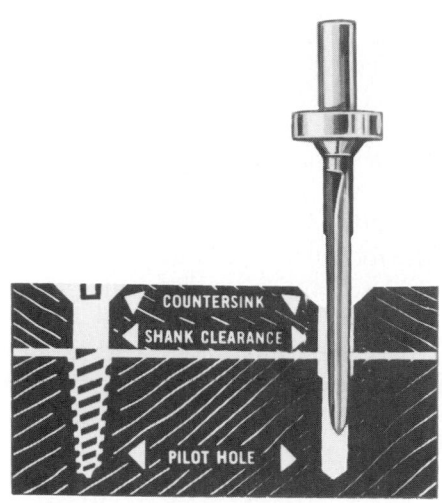

15-17. *Combination drills are available in most of the common woodscrew sizes. For example, if a 1" #8 woodscrew is used, a 1" #8 combination drill should be used.*

15-18. *Always tighten the chuck securely to prevent the bit from slipping.*

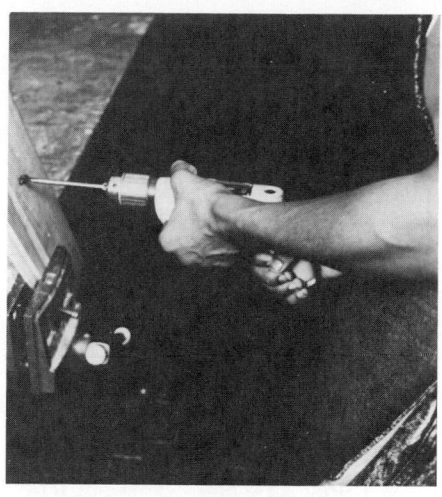

15-19. *Drilling a hole in flat stock. Be sure to hold the tool at right angles to the workpiece.*

countersunk. The combination drill, however, will drill the pilot hole, shank, hole, and countersink, all in one operation. Fig. 15-17.

INSTALLING A BIT

Before inserting a bit, make sure that it has a straight shank. Turn the drill chuck by hand until the jaws are open wide enough to take the desired size bit. Insert the bit shank in the chuck as far as possible, then close the jaws by hand. Next, tighten the chuck by inserting the key wrench in each of the key holes in succession. Use all three holes to avoid slippage as much as possible. Fig. 15-18. To release the bit, only one hole needs to be used. Remember, always unplug the drill when changing bits.

DRILLING HOLES

Always use the correct bit or accessory. See Table 15-A. Make sure the bit is sharp. Apply just enough pressure to the drill to keep it cutting. Too little pressure will make the bit dull; too much pressure may cause it to stall or break. To prevent break-through splintering, clamp a piece of scrap wood behind the piece being drilled. Always clamp the wood in a vise, or hold it securely with a clamp. Hold the tool at right angles to the work when drilling a straight hole. Fig. 15-19. This can be checked by using a try square to align the tool.

DRILLING HOLES FOR WOOD SCREWS

Select the correct size drill for the wood screws. The pilot hole is for the threaded portion of the screw. In hardwood, it is good practice to bore the pilot hole the same size as the root diameter. (Consult Fig. 15-20 under heading *Root Diameter*.) In softwood, drill the pilot hole about 15 percent smaller.

Drill the pilot hole through the first piece and into the second piece to the desired depth. Drill the

Table 15-A. *Suggested Drilling Speeds.*

Material or Job	Bit or Accessory	Suggested Speed	
		¼" Drill	⅜" Drill
Wood	Twist Drill	High	High
Wood	Spade Bits	High	High
Wood	Auger Bits	Med. to Low	High to Med.
Wood	Hole or Dial Saw	Med. to Low	Medium
Heavy Metal	Twist Drill*	Medium	High
Light Metal	Twist Drill*	High	High
Plastics	Twist Drill	Medium	High
Driving Screws	Driver Bit	Low	Low

* Only high speed twist drills should be used for drilling in metal.

BORING CHART FOR WOOD SCREWS

NO. OF SCREW	MAXIMUM HEAD DIAMETER	SHANK DIAMETER BASIC DEC. SIZE	SHANK DIAMETER NEAREST FRACTIONAL EQUIVALENT	ROOT DIAMETER AVERAGE DEC. SIZE	ROOT DIAMETER NEAREST FRACTIONAL EQUIVALENT	THREADS PER INCH	NO. OF SCREW
0	.119	.060	1/16 OVERSIZE .002	.040	3/64 OVERSIZE .007	32	0
1	.146	.073	5/64 OVERSIZE .005	.046	3/64 BASIC SIZE	28	1
2	.172	.086	3/32 OVERSIZE .007	.054	1/16 OVERSIZE .008	26	2
3	.199	.099	7/64 OVERSIZE .010	.065	1/16 UNDERSIZE .002	24	3
4	.225	.112	7/64 UNDERSIZE .003	.075	5/64 OVERSIZE .003	22	4
5	.252	.125	1/8 BASIC SIZE	.085	5/64 UNDERSIZE .007	20	5
6	.279	.138	9/64 OVERSIZE .002	.094	3/32 BASIC SIZE	18	6
7	.305	.151	5/32 OVERSIZE .005	.102	7/64 OVERSIZE .007	16	7
8	.332	.164	5/32 UNDERSIZE .007	.112	7/64 UNDERSIZE .003	15	8
9	.358	.177	11/64 UNDERSIZE .005	.122	1/8 OVERSIZE .003	14	9
10	.385	.190	3/16 UNDERSIZE .002	.130	1/8 UNDERSIZE .005	13	10
11	.411	.203	13/64 BASIC SIZE	.139	9/64 OVERSIZE .001	12	11
12	.438	.216	7/32 OVERSIZE .003	.148	9/64 UNDERSIZE .007	11	12
14	.491	.242	1/4 OVERSIZE .008	.165	5/32 UNDERSIZE .009	10	14
16	.544	.268	17/64 UNDERSIZE .002	.184	3/16 OVERSIZE .003	9	16
18	.597	.294	19/64 OVERSIZE .003	.204	13/64 UNDERSIZE .001	8	18
20	.650	.320	5/16 UNDERSIZE .007	.223	7/32 UNDERSIZE .004	8	20
24	.756	.372	3/8 OVERSIZE .003	.260	1/4 UNDERSIZE .010	7	24

No. 0
No. 1
No. 2
No. 3
No. 4
No. 5
No. 6
No. 7
No. 8
No. 9
No. 10
No. 11
No. 12
No. 14
No. 16
No. 18
No. 20
No. 24

15-20. *Drill Size Selection Chart. Root diameters are average dimensions measured at the middle of the threaded portion. Shank diameters are shown as a decimal in thousandths of an inch. To use this chart, read down either of the columns headed Number of Screw to the screw size used. For example, if a No. 5 woodscrew is used, the shank diameter of the screw will require a 1/8" hole. The pilot hole will need to be 5/64". Note that the pilot hole is 0.007" undersized. This is about right for softwood. In hardwood the next larger drill size, 3/32", should be used. The column at right shows actual woodscrew shank sizes. To determine the size of a screw visually, lay the screw shank on the silhouette.*

shank hole through the first piece. For flathead screws, use an 82-degree, rose-type countersink to enlarge the end of the shank hole. If the screw is to be covered with a plug, bore the hole for this first, then the shank hole, and finally the root diameter hole.

A second method of drilling holes for screws is to drill the shank hole first. Then hold the first piece over the second and mark the location for the pilot hole with a scratch awl.

DRIVING SCREWS

If the drill is equipped with a variable speed control and a reversing switch, it can be used as a powerful screwdriver. A slotted or Phillips screwdriver bit is placed in the chuck instead of a drill bit. Fig. 15-21.

Using an electric drill to drive screws takes some practice, but it is not difficult. Start the screw slowly, increase the speed as the screw moves into the stock, and finish by slowing the drill to a stop. To prevent damage to the wood surface, the screw can be driven in

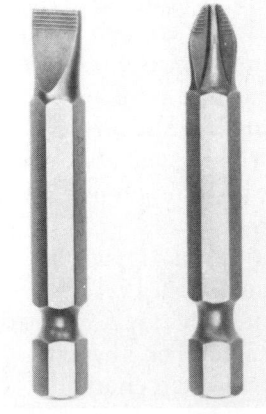

15-21. *Power screwdriving bits.*

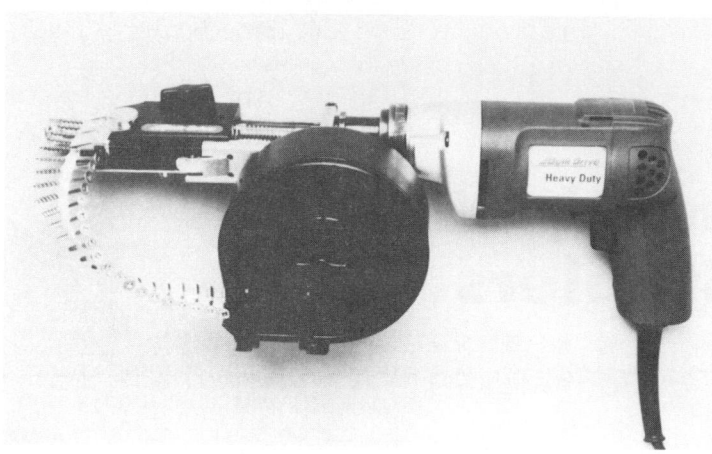

15-22. A self-feeding screw gun.

partway and then finished with a standard screwdriver. A Phillips bit is easier to use than a slotted bit because it is less likely to slip off the screw.

Attachments are available for some electric drills that allow them to drive a great number of screws in a short period of time. These attachments use coils of screws and automatically feed each screw to the tip of the drill. This is useful for such repetitive tasks as screwing subflooring in place. Fig. 15-22.

QUESTIONS

1. List three safety rules that should be observed when using the portable electric drill.

2. Why are some portable electric drill housings made of plastic?

3. Why is it necessary to drill the correct size hole for wood screws?

4. When drilling holes for wood screws, what is the advantage of a combination drill?

5. How far should the drill bit be inserted in the chuck?

6. When drilling a hole, what should be done to prevent splintering the workpiece as the hole is completed?

7. What is the purpose of a pilot hole?

8. The shank hole should have the same diameter as what part of the wood screw?

9. What kind of hole does a Foerstner bit leave?

10. What kind of battery powers a cordless drill?

ACTIVITIES

1. Social Studies. The text discusses safety measures to follow while using drills. Years ago, when factories were first equipped with large machines, safety measures were not strictly observed. What are some specific examples of hazardous conditions that existed for American workers in early factories?

2. Math. You are to drill a hole in a piece of hardwood so that a pin with a diameter of .391" will slide in with as little excess as possible. You have available a set of bits from $\frac{1}{16}$" to $\frac{1}{4}$", with $\frac{1}{64}$" between sizes. You have another set with bits from $\frac{1}{4}$" to $\frac{1}{2}$", with $\frac{1}{16}$" between sizes.

a. How many bits are in these sets?

b. Which bit should you use?

c. How much oversize is the hole in thousands of an inch?

THE SCHOOL-TO-WORK CONNECTION

There are more models of electric drills on the market than any other power tool.

1. Your supervisor has asked you to plan a fence construction project. The work calls for drilling two holes each in forty-five 4 x 4 posts. The fence will be about 250' from the nearest electrical outlet. In one paragraph, give your supervisor two options for accomplishing this work. Recommend one of the options. Explain your choice.

Pneumatic Nailers and Staplers

SAFETY

The following are general safety rules. We strongly advise you to check the manufacturer's manual for any special safety instructions.

When using a pneumatic nailer or stapler, always take the following precautions:

➤ Always wear eye protection when using a nailer. Hearing protection also is recommended.

➤ Never try to clear a jammed nailer while it is still connected to an air supply. Disconnect the tool from the air supply before performing any maintenance on it.

➤ Never fire the nailer unless the nosepiece is in contact with the workpiece to be nailed.

➤ Never carry a nailer with your finger on the trigger. If you should accidentally bring the nose of the nailer in contact with an object (including another person or yourself), a nail could be fired accidentally.

➤ Never use bottled gases to power the tool. The driver blade of a nailer sometimes makes a spark when it hits a nail. Thus, running a nailer on oxygen could cause an explosion. Also, carbon dioxide and other gases are bottled at far higher pressures than are safe for a nailer.

➤ Air-driven nails sometimes ricochet. Keep bystanders away from the immediate work area.

➤ Never operate a nailer at a pressure higher than it was designed to handle. Check the pressure gauge of the compressor periodically.

➤ If you are using a belt-driven compressor, make sure that the belts are protected by a cover.

➤ Before transporting a compressor, release the pressure in the tank. Secure the compressor so it does not roll around in the back of the truck.

➤ The hoses connected to a nailer should be in good condition. Never step on a hose. This prevents premature wear, and reduces tripping dangers. Pay particular attention to hoses while using nailers on a roof.

➤ Make sure the nailer is pointing down when you connect a pressurized air hose to it. Air entering suddenly can cause the tool to fire.

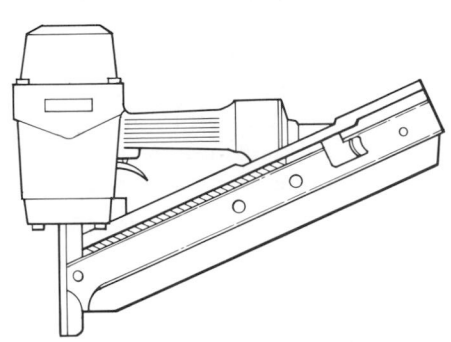

A *pneumatic nailer* or *stapler* is a tool that uses compressed air to drive fasteners into wood. Fig. 16-1. Both tools are connected to a long, flexible high-pressure hose. The other end of the hose is connected to an air compressor. Similar pneumatic tools are available to drive pins, corrugated fasteners, and other fasteners.

16-1a. *A pneumatic framing nailer. Safety glasses should always be worn when using pneumatic tools.*

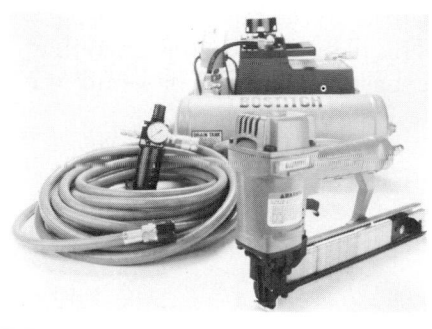

16-1b. *A pneumatic stapler with air hose and compressor.*

The use of air-powered nailers at construction sites has greatly improved the process of fastening materials. These tools install nails faster than hand nailing, and with less worker fatigue. In addition, they are quite useful in confined situations where it is difficult or impossible to swing a hammer. The use of air-powered staplers has introduced staples as alternatives to nails in many applications such as attaching sheathing and roof shingles.

NAILERS

Pneumatic nailers are also called nailers or air-nailers. They come in a variety of sizes because they must fit the type of nail being driven. For example, a nailer designed to drive 16d nails will not be able to drive brads. When choosing a nailer for a particular job, first determine the type and size of nail needed. Then find a nailer that will drive that nail. Finally, find a compressor to suit the chosen nailer.

16-3. *A coil-fed nailer.*

There are two basic types of nailers:
- ➤ Strip-fed nailers. These nailers hold a row of nails in a spring-loaded magazine. The magazine can either be angled away from the nose of the tool or not. Fig. 16-2.
- ➤ Coil-fed nailers. These tools are shorter than strip nailers because they hold the nails in a coil behind the head of the tool. Fig. 16-3.

Strip nailers are more common on job sites than coil nailers. Some builders prefer strip nailers because the narrow shape of the tool fits into tight spaces. Toenailing studs is a situation in which a strip nailer is somewhat easier to use. The width of the nail coil sometimes prevents a coil nailer from being used where space is tight, even though the tool is shorter than a strip nailer. A coil nailer generally holds more nails than a strip nailer, however. This means that it can be used longer without the need for reloading.

Most nailers and staplers work on the same basic principles. Air under high pressure is fed to the tool through a high-pressure hose linked to a compressor. The head (and sometimes the handle) of a

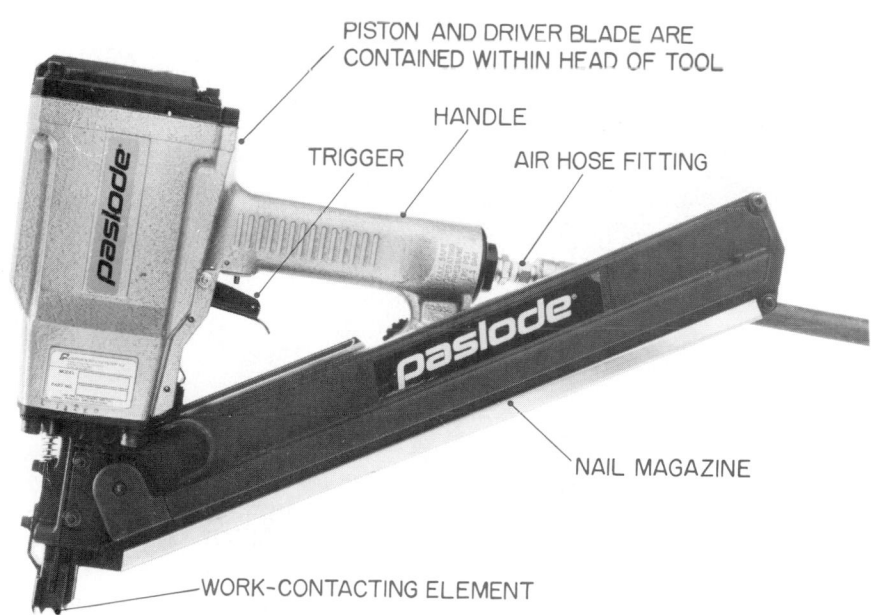

PISTON AND DRIVER BLADE ARE CONTAINED WITHIN HEAD OF TOOL

HANDLE

TRIGGER

AIR HOSE FITTING

NAIL MAGAZINE

WORK-CONTACTING ELEMENT

16-2. *The parts of a pneumatic strip nailer. This one has an angled magazine.*

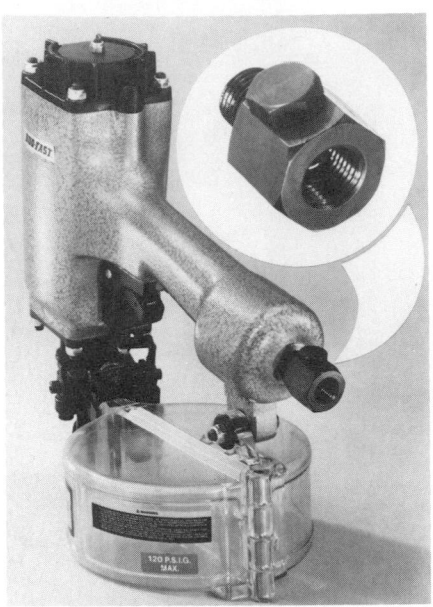

16-4. *This coil-fed nailer is equipped with a pressure relief valve that prevents excess air pressure from damaging the tool.*

16-5. *Using a nailer to fasten a subfloor.*

nailer holds a charge of compressed air. When the trigger is pulled, this air is released against a piston in the head of the tool. This piston is attached to a driver blade. When the piston is forced downward by the compressed air, it pushes the driver blade, which strikes a fastener. The fastener is then driven into the wood at high speed. After a fastener has been driven, pressurized air forces the piston back into place, pulling the driver blade with it. The spring-loaded magazine pushes another fastener into place. The tool is then ready to fire again.

Some nailers are equipped with a pressure relief safety valve. This device is attached to the air hose fitting at the back of the tool. It is designed to release excess air pressure before it reaches the tool. This will prevent damage to the nailer if the air pressure reaches a level that is higher than the tool can handle. Fig. 16-4.

Operating a Nailer

All nailers and staplers employ a two-step firing sequence. This is an important safety feature. The trigger must be pulled *and* the nose of the tool must be pressed against the workpiece before the tool will fire. The trigger will not work otherwise. This helps to prevent the tool from being fired accidentally.

A nailer is typically held in one hand and pressed firmly against the workpiece. Because of the striking force of the driver blade, the nailer will recoil somewhat. With practice, you will be able to prevent this recoil from marring the wood being nailed. Fig. 16-5.

There is another reason for practice-firing a nailer when first using it. The nosepiece sometimes obscures the exact position of the nail. This can make it difficult to place the nail exactly where it is needed. This is more important when doing finish work such as nailing trim.

Some nailers exhaust air through a plate in the top of the nailer. This plate can be adjusted so that exhaust air does not blow into the face of the operator.

Most nailers operate on about 80 psi to 120 psi. The operating pressure appropriate for the tool is found in the owner's manual.

16-6. *This framing nailer is powered by a small internal-combustion engine located in the head of the tool. It does not require a compressor or hoses, which makes it very portable.*

No-compressor Nailers

The majority of air nailers are operated with air supplied by an air compressor. A relatively new type of nailer is considerably different. The force that pushes the driver blade into the fastener is supplied by a very small internal combustion engine located in the head of the tool. A special butane fuel, supplied by the manufacturer in disposable canisters, is injected into a chamber above the piston. The fuel is ignited by a spark from a rechargeable battery. The piston/driver blade is forced down to strike the fastener. Because the tool is entirely self-contained, hoses and a compressor are not required. This makes the nailer particularly useful in remote locations, or in places where air hoses and a compressor would be awkward to use. Fig. 16-6.

STAPLERS

Pneumatic staplers are very similar to nailers, both in the way they work and in the way they are used. These tools are used primarily for installing sheathing, subflooring, and roofing. Fig. 16-7. However, they can also be used to fasten framing, trim, and wood flooring.

Operating a Stapler

Staplers, like nailers, incorporate a two-step firing sequence as a safety feature. This requires that the stapler be held against the workpiece before the trigger will operate.

Staples should be driven flush with the surface of the wood. They should not be countersunk because this reduces the effective thickness of the wood. Building inspectors sometimes look for this when inspecting the sheathing. An

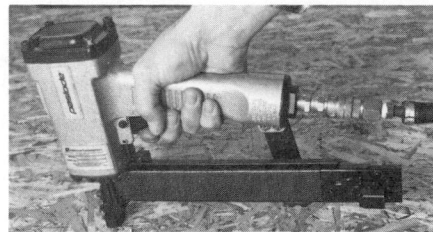

16-7. A pneumatic stapler.

inspector can call for repairs if the effectiveness of the sheathing has been reduced by countersunk staples. To avoid overdriving a staple, the crown of the staple should be kept perpendicular to the grain of the wood. This "locks" the wood fibers into place beneath the fastener.

When fastening trim, some builders prefer to install the staple parallel to the grain of the wood because the fastener is less visible when installed this way. However, this is not the preferred installation method.

Factors that lead to overdriving the staple include excessive air pressure, a driver blade that is too long, or a worn bumper. (A bumper is a part inside nailers and staplers that stops the piston at the end of its travel.) The operator should inspect installed staples periodically to be sure that they are being driven properly.

Using a Stapler to Install Roofing

Properly driven staples can speed the application of asphalt and wood shingles. Most building codes

Table 16-A. *Minimum Staple Leg Lengths Applicable to Most Roofing Jobs.*

Thickness of Wood Deck	Minimum Staple Leg Length	
	With First Layer of Shingles	With Second Layer of Shingles
3/8"	1"	1 1/4"
1/2"	1 1/8"	1 3/8"
5/8" and Thicker	1 1/4"	1 1/2"

NOTES:
1. Lengths allow for up to 1/8" of roofing felt(s).
2. Lengths assume single thickness strip shingles (not laminated or multi-thickness) of maximum 1/8" thickness per shingle for new and any old layers. Longer lengths are necessary for laminated or multi-thick shingles.

accept roofing staples on a one-for-one basis. This means that if a shingle is normally installed with four nails, it will require four staples. This guideline applies to new construction as well as re-roofing applications.

Staples used to install asphalt or fiberglass roofing must be galvanized. They must be made from 16-gauge wire or thicker. The crown width must be at least 15/16". Roofing staples should penetrate the sheathing at least 3/4". If the sheathing is thinner than 3/4", the staple should penetrate the sheathing at least 1/8". Table 16-A.

Proper driving of staples is important when installing shingles. Improperly-driven staples can cause leaks. Staples that are overdriven, or that tear the shingle, should be sealed with asphalt roofing cement. Another staple should then be driven nearby. Fig. 16-8.

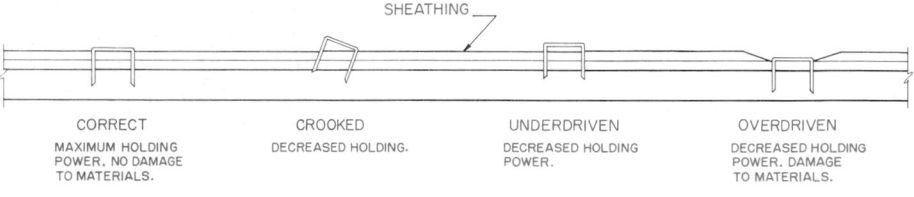

SHEATHING

| CORRECT | CROOKED | UNDERDRIVEN | OVERDRIVEN |
| MAXIMUM HOLDING POWER. NO DAMAGE TO MATERIALS. | DECREASED HOLDING. | DECREASED HOLDING POWER. | DECREASED HOLDING POWER. DAMAGE TO MATERIALS. |

16-8. Staple application.

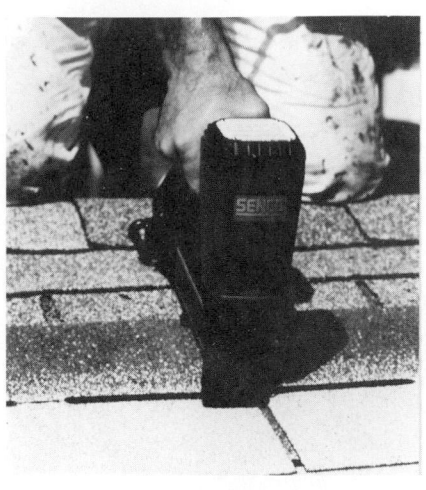

16-9. *New shingles being installed over old ones. Note that the staple is being placed below the asphalt sealing strip, not in it.*

Roofing staplers often have a shingle gauge built into the underside of the magazine as an aid in gauging shingle exposure. Staples should be placed ⅝" above the shingle cutout, and just below the factory-applied self-sealing adhesive strip. Fig. 16-9. Staples that run through the adhesive strip can prevent the strip from sealing properly. The crown of the staple should be parallel to the length of the shingle. This improves the ability of the shingle to resist wind uplift.

NAILER AND STAPLER MAINTENANCE

Nailers and staplers are not difficult to maintain. One of the most important tasks is making sure the tools are properly lubricated.

Various gaskets within air nailers and staplers prevent the tool from leaking air. These gaskets should be lubricated on a regular basis. One way to do this is to put a few drops of tool oil into the air intake of the nailer, just before hooking the tool up to the hose. Another method is to attach a line lubricator to the compressor. A line lubricator is a device that automatically adds small amounts of lubricant into the air hose, which then conveys the lubricant to the tool. The line lubricator is usually mounted downstream from the air filter.

To clean the magazine, spray it with WD-40 and then wipe it clean. The work-contacting element of a pneumatic tool should be cleaned periodically as well. This is particularly important if the tool is used frequently for installing roofing. The asphalt sealing strips on shingles will foul the tip of the tool. Use a putty knife to clear away excess asphalt. Solvents are sometimes used for cleaning, but they can damage O-rings within the tool. Check with the manufacturer for cleaning recommendations.

COMPRESSORS

Most compressors used on residential job sites are portable units. They can easily be moved around the site to be close to the

16-10. *Parts of an air compressor.*

16-11a. *This compact device is called a pancake compressor. Compare its parts to those in Fig. 16-10.*

work being done. Portable compressors are usually powered by electric motors, but large compressors can be powered by gas engines. The major parts of a compressor include a pump, a motor, an air-storage tank, a tank pressure gauge, a line-pressure gauge, and a regulator. Fig. 16-10.

The motor usually drives the air pump by way of a belt connected to a flywheel. Some compressors are gear-driven, however, and others are direct-drive. Electric motors typically range from ½ hp to 2 hp. Inside the pump, one or more pistons compress air into a small chamber. Most pumps on construction compressors are called *single-stage* pumps. This means they pump the compressed air directly into a

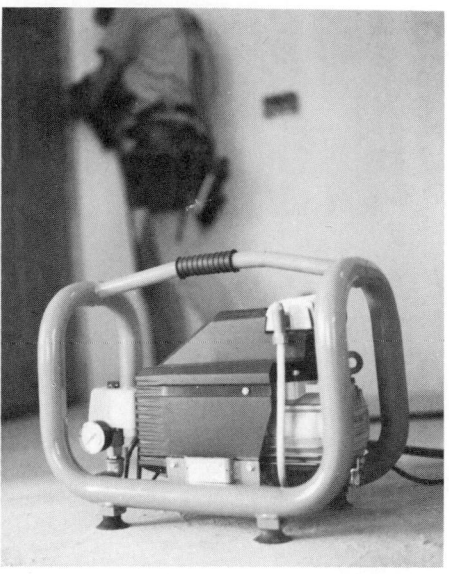

16-11b. *This innovative direct-drive compressor serves various roles. In the photo at right, it supplies air to finish nailers and small staplers. (The air supply is in the frame.) The photo on the left shows it connected to a twin-tank assembly, where it has enough air to supply heavy duty pneumatic tools.*

Sizing a Compressor

An air compressor must supply a steady supply of compressed air to a tool. Symptoms of a deficient air supply include air leakage on the tool, fasteners not set deep enough, and skipped shots.

The amount of air used by various types and sizes of pneumatic tools varies considerably. A framing nailer can use as much as 15 times more air to drive a framing nail than a smaller nailer uses to drive finish nails. Generally, pneumatic tools that drive larger fasteners require more air per fastener than those that drive smaller fasteners.

The rate and frequency of use will determine the air consumption. A compressor supplying air to nailers used to fasten underlayment will have to work harder than one used to drive framing nails. This is because fastening underlayment is repetitive work that calls for a lot of fasteners to be driven quickly. A framing nailer is typically used more slowly. Some workers find that they can fire fasteners faster than a compressor can supply air. This usually means that the compressor is undersized.

The air compressor must be sized to accommodate all the demands placed upon it. One manufacturer of pneumatic tools suggests the following formula for sizing a compressor:

Multiply the cubic feet of free air used per operation by the number of operations per minute. Add a 15% safety factor. The total figure will equal the cubic feet of free air required from the compressor to operate the tool.

storage tank. Fig. 16-11.

The storage tank is usually a cylinder that holds 1 gallon to 10 gallons of air. The advantage of a larger tank is that it makes more air available to the nailer at any given moment. The disadvantage is that a larger tank makes the compressor heavier and harder to move around. A pressure gauge allows the pressure within the tank to be monitored.

The regulator is a valve that controls the amount of air pressure reaching the nailer. The line-pressure gauge monitors the pressure in the hose leading to the air tool. This is important because the pressure in the tank may be different than the pressure in the hose.

Compressor Maintenance

Proper maintenance of an air compressor is not complicated. The oil level in the compressor pump should be maintained at the proper level. Air stored in the tank should be released at the end of each day. This helps to clear out any moisture that may have accumulated inside the tank. (Moisture can rust a tank from the inside.)

The air intake filter on the pump should be cleaned regularly. A filter will trap dirt, moisture, and other contaminants. If these contaminants reached the nailer, they could lead to excessive tool wear. Removing moisture keeps the air lines from freezing in cold temperatures. It also reduces the chance for corrosion.

Check all the fittings on the compressor periodically and tighten them as needed. The vibration of a compressor can loosen these fittings over time. Replace the drive belt if it looks frayed or damaged.

A properly-working regulator is crucial for the nailer to work properly. Improper pressure keeps the nailer from setting nails completely into the wood. Excess pressure is hard on the tool and increases wear considerably.

HOSES

The hose supplying air to a pneumatic nailer or stapler should have a minimum working pressure rating that is 50% higher than the maximum pressure delivered by the compressor. This allows a margin of safety in case the compressor malfunctions. An air hose should have a minimum inside diameter of $\frac{5}{16}$". Hoses 25' long to 50' long should have an inside diameter of $\frac{1}{2}$". Hoses longer than 100' should not be used. Table 16-B.

An air hose should always be as short as possible. One reason for this is that air moving through a hose is slowed by friction. The longer the hose, the harder the compressor must work to overcome the friction. Also, long lengths of hose present a tripping hazard.

Keep the outside of the hoses clean. This helps to avoid premature wear. Keep the snap-on fittings at each end of the hose out of the dirt. Dirt and sawdust can clog the fittings, making it difficult to attach them to a nailer or stapler. Dirt-caked fittings can introduce dirt into the pneumatic tool.

FASTENERS

Nails

Air nailers are not loaded with individual nails. Instead, they are loaded with either strips or coils of nails. Fig. 16-12. In either case, the manufacturer collates the nails for use in the nailer. This means that each nail is connected to an adjacent nail, generally with plastic or paper strips. These fastening materials are released from each nail as it is driven. Sometimes a small piece of plastic or paper is driven into the hole with the nail.

Table 16-B. *Recommended Inside Diameters of High-Pressure Hoses.*

Hose Length	Recommended Inside Diameter
25' - 50'	$\frac{3}{8}$"
51' - 100'	$\frac{1}{2}$"
Over 100'	Do Not Use

16-12a. *These stainless steel nails come in coil form and stick form. The stick nails have a modified D-head.*

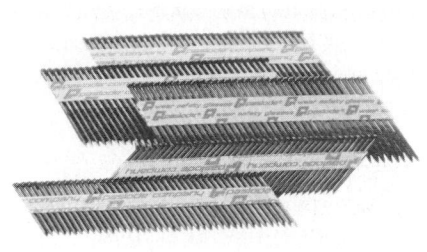

16-12b. *These nail strips are collated with paper.*

This is generally not a problem, but can affect some interior finishes.

Strip nails and coiled nails allow the nailer to be self-feeding. As soon as one nail is driven, another nail is pushed into place behind it. There are generally more nails in a coil than in a strip.

When air nailers were first introduced to the construction industry, the selection of nails was limited. Now, however, many types of nails are available. They come in a variety of shapes, metal types, and head types. Galvanized nails also are available. Nails are described by the type of shank, type of head, and length.

Nail Shanks. The *shank* of a nail is the portion below the head. The shape of the shank determines how well the nail will hold in various types of wood. Several shapes are available for air nailers.

Smooth-shank nails are commonly used for general construction purposes. The smooth shank provides good holding power in a variety of woods. Included in this category are most framing and roofing nails. Fig. 16-13.

Screw-shank nails have more holding power than smooth-shank nails. They have a spiral shape that is particularly useful for nailing hardwoods. Fig. 16-13.

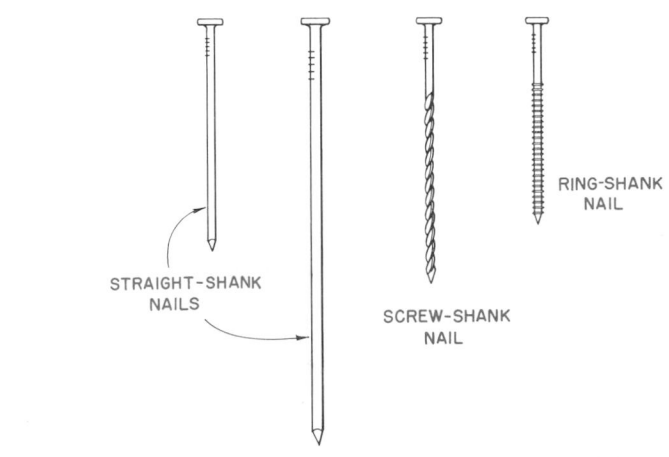

STRAIGHT-SHANK NAILS

SCREW-SHANK NAIL

RING-SHANK NAIL

16-13. *The basic types of nails for pneumatic fastening.*

Ring-shank nails have a series of ridges or "rings" running from the point nearly to the head. These nails are best for applications that require extra holding power, such as nailing wood that has a high moisture content. Ring-shank nails are sometimes used to nail subfloors because they can reduce the occurrence of squeaky floors. Fig. 16-13.

Nail Heads and Lengths.
Nails for air nailers now come in almost as many varieties as do standard nails, including finish head, round head, and duplex head. One type of head that is found only with air nailers is the modified D-head. The shape of this head allows nails to be packed close together on nail strips. Fig. 16-14.

Nails range in length from ½" brads to 5" spikes.

Staples

Staples for pneumatic tools are typically categorized by length, width of crown, wire size, and type of point. Fig. 16-15. Staples are generally available from ⅛" long to 2½" long. The width of the crown is the overall width of the staple, including both legs. The crown can be categorized as narrow, intermediate, or wide. The wire size can be heavy or fine. Choosing the correct staple depends on the work

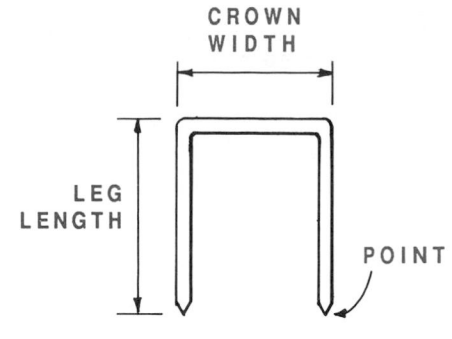

16-15. A staple for pneumatic application.

to be done. For example, a fine-wire, narrow crown staple is appropriate where holding power is not critical and where the staple must be unobtrusive. Heavy-wire, wide crown staples are appropriate for asphalt roofing and other applications where extra holding power is needed.

Staples are also available with various points. Chisel-point staples and blunt-point staples are the most common on job sites. The legs of these staples penetrate the wood in a straight line, and are suitable for most applications. Divergent-point staples have opposing bevels on each leg. When the staple enters the wood, each leg splays out in a different direction. This offers particularly strong holding power in soft woods. Fig. 16-16.

Finally, staples can be made of various materials, including steel, galvanized steel, stainless steel, aluminum, and bronze.

Application of Staples. The placement and number of staples used when installing framing generally follows standard nailing schedules. (See Section V, "Framing.") Where a 16d nail would be used, a 14-gauge staple 3" long can be used instead. Where an 8d nail would be used, a 14-gauge staple 2⅜" long can be used instead. Table 16-C.

In general, plywood wall sheathing can be fastened with either a 14-gauge staple, a 15-gauge staple, or a 16-gauge staple. Staples used to install wall sheathing should penetrate the framing at least 1". For example, ½" plywood wall sheathing calls for staples 1½" long. Table 16-D.

The fastening schedule for stapling plywood subfloor and roof sheathing is shown in Table 16-E.

Table 16-C. Staples for Framing.

If This Nail Would Be Used	It Can Be Replaced By This Staple*
8d	14-gauge staple 2⅜" long
16d	14-gauge staple 3" long

*Staples must have a crown at least 7/16" wide.

Table 16-D. Staples for Plywood Wall Sheathing.

Sheathing Thickness	Staple Gauge	Minimum Staple Length*
⅜"	14 gauge	1 ⅜"
½"	15 gauge	1 ½"
⅝"	16 gauge	1 ⅝"

*Staples must have a crown at least 7/16" wide.

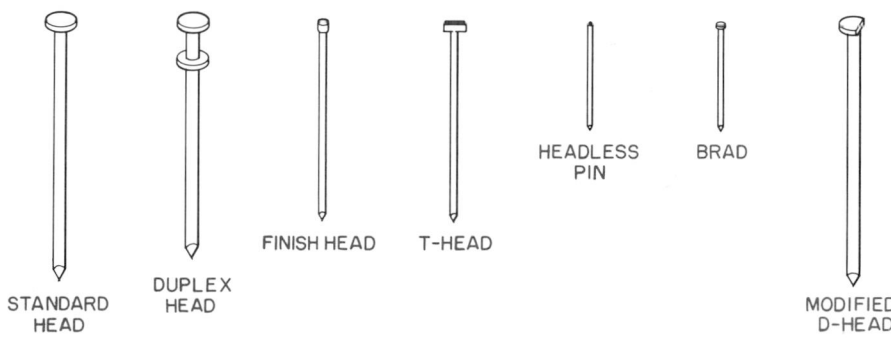

16-14. Nail heads for pneumatic fastening.

STANDARD HEAD   DUPLEX HEAD   FINISH HEAD   T-HEAD   HEADLESS PIN   BRAD   MODIFIED D-HEAD

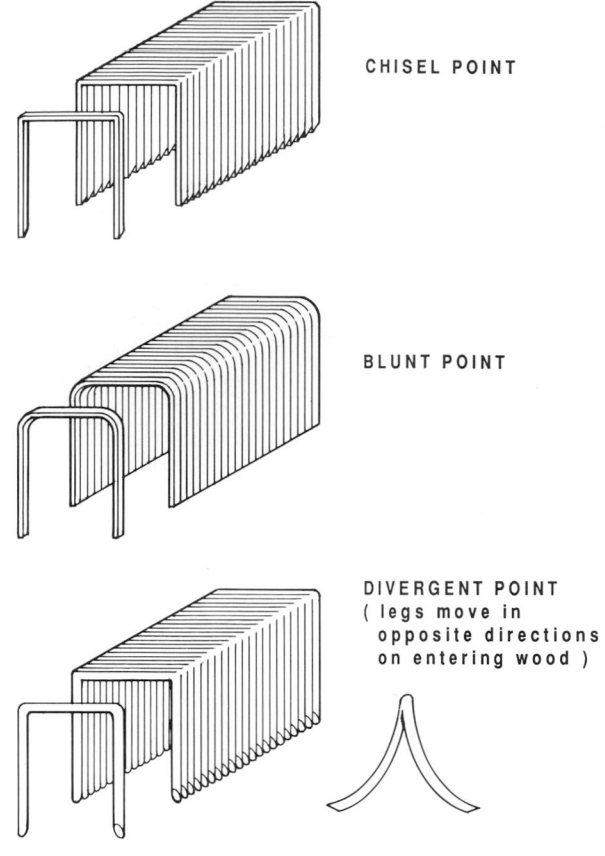

CHISEL POINT

BLUNT POINT

DIVERGENT POINT
(legs move in
opposite directions
on entering wood)

16-16. *Common staple points.*

Other Fasteners

Pneumatic tools can be used to install a variety of special fasteners in addition to nails and staples. Some air tools can drive corrugated fasteners. These are usually installed across a wood joint. As the fastener enters the wood, it draws both sides of the joint together. This makes a corrugated fastener excellent for assembling picture frames. Some builders install a pair of heavy-duty corrugated fasteners to butt-join wall top plates and other framing members. Fig. 16-17.

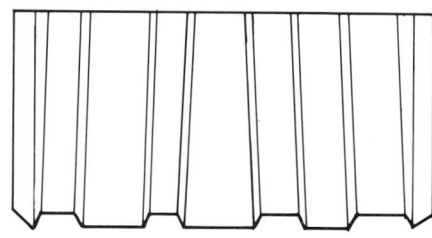

16-17. *Corrugated fastener.*

Table 16-E. *Staples for Plywood Roof Sheathing and Subfloors.*

Description Attached Material	Attached Material Nominal Thickness	Spacing Specifications (In Inches)			Fastener Specifications[1-2]	
		Edges	Intermediate		Min Leg Length (In Inches)	Fastener Style[3]
			Roof	Floor		
Plywood	$^5/_{16}$ - $^1/_4$ - $^3/_8$	6	12	10	1 $^3/_8$	No. 14 Gauge Staple
						No. 15 Gauge Staple
					1$^5/_8$	No. 16 Gauge Staple
	$^1/_2$	6	12	10	1$^1/_2$	No. 14 Gauge Staple
						No. 15 Gauge Staple
Subfloor					1 $^3/_4$	No. 16 Gauge Staple
	$^5/_8$	6	12	10	1 $^7/_8$	No. 14 Gauge Staple
					2	No. 15 Gauge Staple
& Roof					2 $^1/_4$	No. 16 Gauge Staple
Sheathing[4]		6	12	10	2	No. 14 Gauge Staple
	$^3/_4$				2 $^1/_8$	No. 15 Gauge Staple
		6	10	8	2 $^3/_8$	No. 16 Gauge Staple

[1] Staples shall have a 7/16" minimum O.D. Crown Width.
[2] Fasteners exposed to weather shall be zinc coated by hot dip galvanizing, mechanically deposited or electro-deposited.
[3] Nails may have T-heads, modified round heads, or standard round heads.
[4] Where subfloor spans 48 inches or more, fasteners shall be spaced six inches on center at all supports except where a closer spacing is indicated.

1. Name the three basic elements of a pneumatic fastening system.

2. What should you do first before clearing a jammed nailer?

3. Name the two basic kinds of air nailers. Name one advantage of each.

4. What part of a nailer or stapler actually contacts the fastener and pushes it into the workpiece?

5. Describe the two-step firing sequence of a nailer.

6. What is the pressure range that most air nailers operate on?

7. Why should air-driven staples not be countersunk?

8. What is the minimum crown width appropriate for a roofing staple?

9. Name two ways of lubricating a pneumatic tool.

10. What is a regulator?

11. What length and gauge of staple is generally used in place of a 16d nail?

12. When staples are used to apply plywood wall sheathing, how deeply should they penetrate the framing?

1. Language Arts. Pneumatic tools are a fairly recent development. Trace the historical development of pneumatic tools.

2. Language Arts. Using a dictionary, research the meaning of the word *pneumatic*. From what foreign word or words does the meaning of the term derive?

THE SCHOOL-TO-WORK CONNECTION

Working on a construction jobsite is a very active endeavor. Not only must you maneuver unwieldy materials from place to place, but you also have to lift them into position and fasten them securely. Much of the work is repeated over and over again, which can strain muscles and joints.

1. After working on a jobsite for several months, you begin to notice occasional numbness in your fingers, sometimes accompanied by swelling or tenderness. The problem seems to occur after you have been using a pneumatic nailer for long periods. One of your co-workers suggests that this sounds like "carpal tunnel syndrome." Another co-worker says you should just ignore the problem and it will go away.

Contact the physical therapy department at your local hospital and see if they have any information on carpal tunnel syndrome. If not, investigate the topic at your library. Write a paragraph explaining what this malady is. Describe what types of construction activities might lead to it.

Router

The following are general safety rules. We strongly advise you to check the manufacturer's manual for any special safety instructions.

➤ Routers generate a lot of noise and sawdust. Wear hearing protection and a dust mask.

➤ When inserting a bit, slide it into the chuck until it bottoms out, then back it off slightly and tighten the chuck. A bit resting against the bottom of the chuck can vibrate loose.

➤ Be sure to lubricate the sliding mechanisms of plunge routers to ensure smooth operation.

➤ Review general safety rules for use of portable electric tools.

➤ Make certain the fence or guide is securely clamped.

➤ When using the power tool, keep both hands on the handles.

➤ Feed in the correct direction.

➤ Always lay the power tool down with the cutter pointing away from you and be alert to the coasting cutter.

➤ Always hold onto the power tool when it is turned on.

➤ Make certain the workpiece is securely clamped.

➤ Make adjustments only when the cutter is at a dead stop.

➤ Be certain the power switch is off before connecting the power plug.

➤ When installing or removing cutters, be sure the power plug is disconnected.

The *router* is a portable tool that is used primarily for shaping the surfaces and edges of stock and for cutting joints. With accessories, a router can also be used to cut mortises, trim plastic laminate, and cut circles. Some builders feel that a router is the most versatile tool available. Fig. 17-1.

The router comes in a variety of shapes and sizes. Light-duty routers

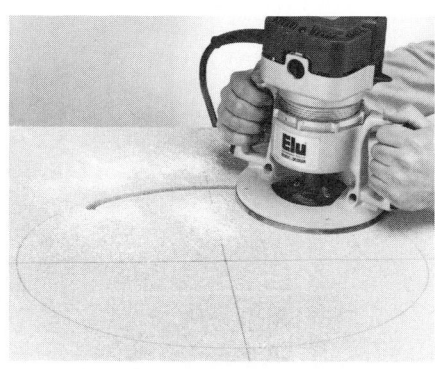

17-1. *This router is being used freehand to cut an opening for a sink.*

17-2. A plunge router.

17-3a. D-handle router.

have motors of less than 1 horsepower, while heavy-duty routers have motors approaching 4 horsepower. Standard routers have a motor that screws into a base. Fig. 17-1. By unlocking the motor and turning it one way or another, the bit can be raised or lowered. Other routers, called plunge routers, have motors mounted on vertical metal posts. The motor slides up and down on the posts, allowing the spinning bit to be "plunged" into

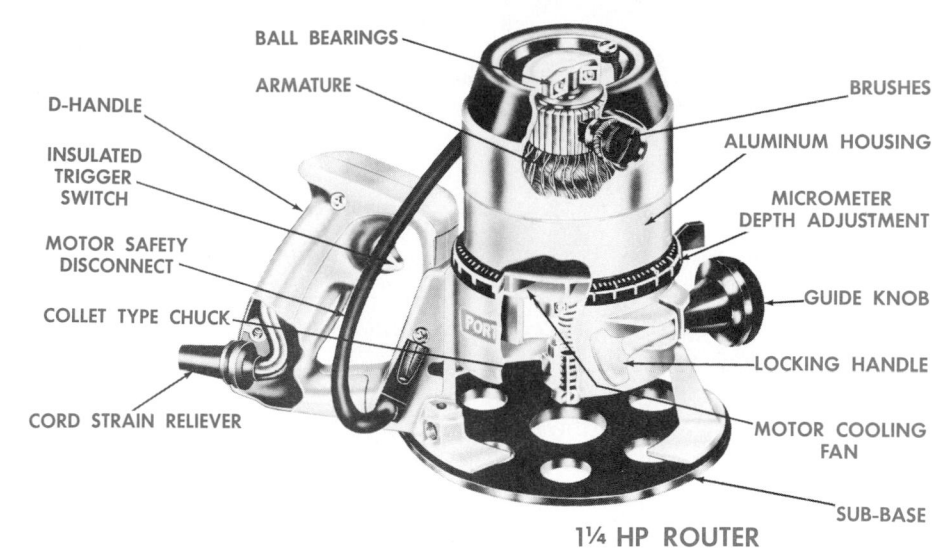

BALL BEARINGS
ARMATURE
D-HANDLE
BRUSHES
INSULATED TRIGGER SWITCH
ALUMINUM HOUSING
MOTOR SAFETY DISCONNECT
MICROMETER DEPTH ADJUSTMENT
COLLET TYPE CHUCK
GUIDE KNOB
LOCKING HANDLE
CORD STRAIN RELIEVER
MOTOR COOLING FAN
SUB-BASE

1¼ HP ROUTER

17-3b. Portable router with parts named.

the workpiece Fig. 17-2.

Some routers have what is called a "D" handle. Fig. 17-3. The handle contains the trigger. Some like this type of handle because it allows the router to be used with one hand.

ROUTER BITS

These bits come in many shapes for doing grooved or decorative work in the surface or edge of stock. Some of the common ones are straight,

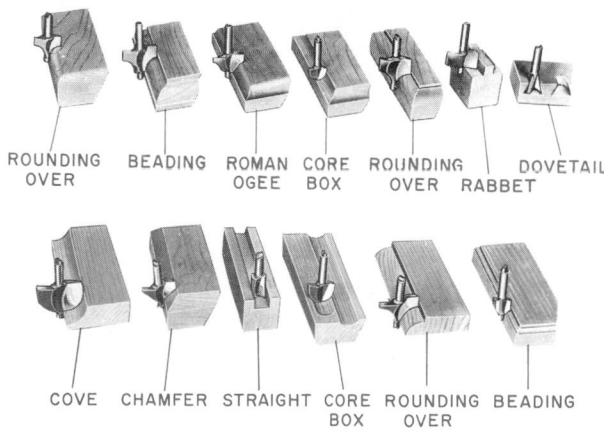

ROUNDING OVER   BEADING   ROMAN OGEE   CORE BOX   ROUNDING OVER   RABBET   DOVETAIL

COVE   CHAMFER   STRAIGHT   CORE BOX   ROUNDING OVER   BEADING

17-4. A few of the hundreds of router bits available.

rounding-over, beading, cove, and chamfer bits. Fig. 17-4. In addition, a dovetail bit is needed for cutting a dovetail joint. The shank of a router bit typically comes in diameters of ¼", ⅜", or ½".

Most router bits have cutting edges on their sides, rather than on their ends. One important exception is the plunge-cutting bit. This bit has cutting surfaces on its edges and on its end. With a plunge-cutting bit in place, a router can "drill" a pilot hole and then cut or trim material starting from that hole.

Router bits are available either with high-speed steel cutting edges or with carbide-tipped cutting edges. The carbide-tipped bits are generally more expensive, but they last longer before needing sharpening.

It is common to add a ball-bearing collar to router bits. These collars can be used to change the profile, width, or depth of a

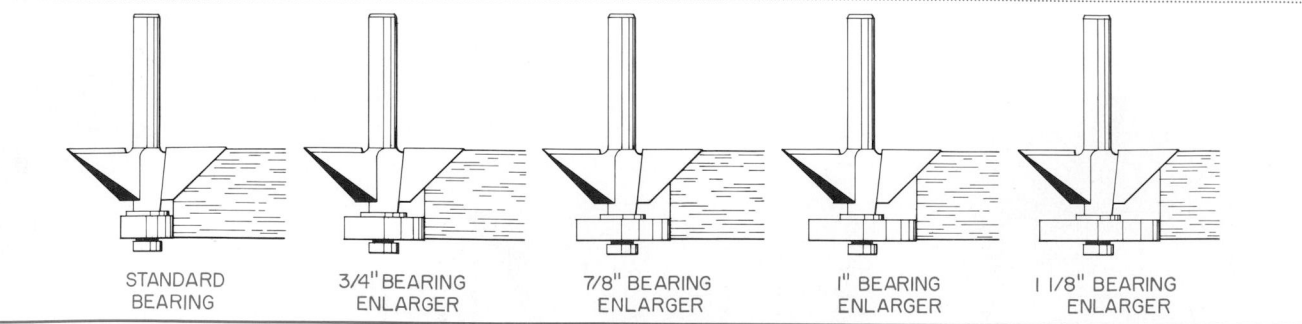

STANDARD BEARING 3/4" BEARING ENLARGER 7/8" BEARING ENLARGER 1" BEARING ENLARGER 1 1/8" BEARING ENLARGER

17-5. *Ball-bearing collars space the router bit away from the work. Changing the size of the collar changes the depth or profile of the cut.*

given router bit. Fig. 17-5. If the collar is mounted on the shank side of the bit, the combination is called a bearing-over bit. If the collar is mounted on the other end of the bit, the combination is called a bearing-under bit. Fig. 17-6.

The depth and direction a router can cut may be controlled in many ways. For example, the router can be guided by a straightedge, a circle guide, or a pilot edge beneath the bit. It can also be used freehand. Fig. 17-7.

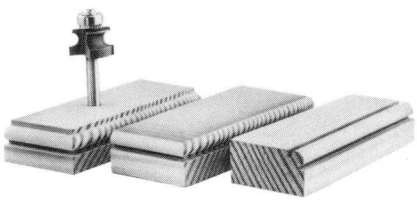

17-6. *This beading bit has a bearing collar mounted opposite the shank. This configuration is called a "bearing under" bit.*

17-7a. *The amount the router can move sideways can be controlled in various ways. As shown here, a straightedge can be clamped to the stock and the router base held in contact with it.*

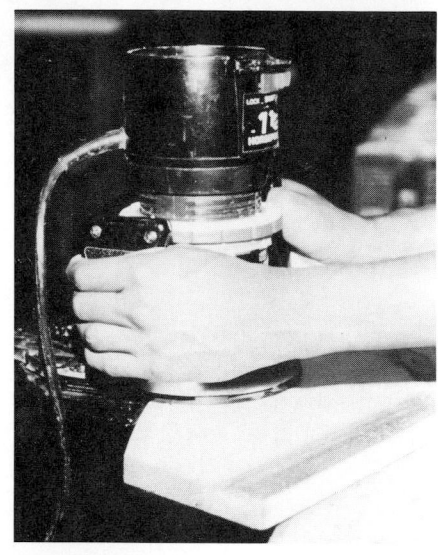

17-7b. *A straight or circular guide can be attached to the base to control the lateral movement. A guide is used here to make a cut near the edge of a round table top.*

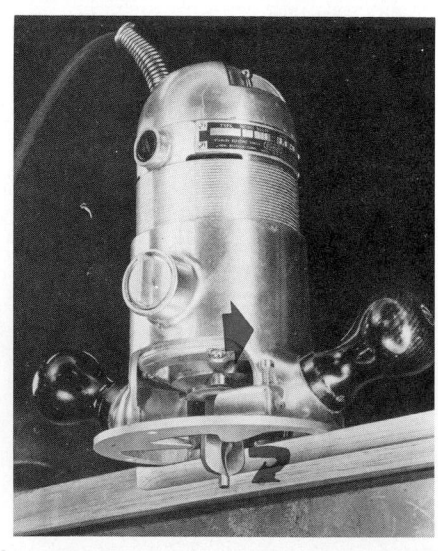

17-7c. *Many bits have pilot edges to control the amount of cut.*

Installing Cutters

1. Disconnect the power plug.

2. Lock the shaft or hold it with a wrench, depending on the kind and size of router.

3. Insert the shank of the bit into the chuck at least ½".

4. Tighten the chuck with a wrench.

5. Unlock the shaft.

6. Adjust the depth of cut by moving the motor unit up and down in the base.

7. Make a test cut in scrap stock. *Hold onto the router when turning on the power, to overcome the starting torque of the motor.*

Feed Direction

Always feed against the direction of motor rotation. When making a cut on a straightedge, feed from left to right. When cutting on circular stock, feed in a counterclockwise direction. Fig. 17-8.

Your judgment of how fast to feed will have to be developed by practice. The speed at which the best cut is made will depend on the size cut to be made and on the hardness of the wood. Most routers run at speeds of about 21,000 rpm. This is the speed without a load. The motor will slow down when under a work load. If the router is fed too fast, the motor will slow down too much, causing a poor cut. If the router is fed too slowly, the bit will get hot, possibly drawing

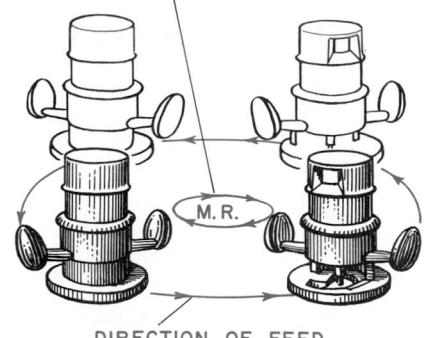

DIRECTION OF MOTOR ROTATION (M.R.)

M.R.

DIRECTION OF FEED

17-8. *The router bit revolves clockwise. Therefore, when cutting straight edges, move the router from left to right. When making circular cuts, move the router counterclockwise.*

the temper from the cutting edge or burning the wood. Don't force the cut; allow the bit to cut freely. Listen to the motor for an indication of whether it is working at its most efficient speed.

USING A ROUTER

Cutting Grooves, Dadoes, Gains, or Mortises

To make these cuts, fasten a straight router bit in the chuck. Adjust the router bit so that it extends the desired depth beyond the base. Attach a guide to the base to control the cut. Lay out the cut and locate the guide. Start at one side or end and move the router along to make the cut. Fig. 17-9.

Cutting Decorative Edges

As mentioned, bits of many shapes are used for cutting decorative edges. Many of these have a pilot tip which does not cut but merely rides against the uncut

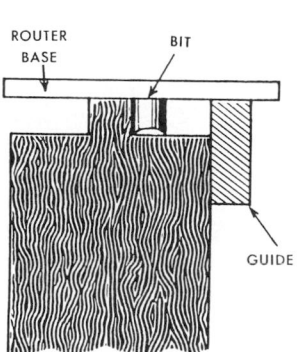

ROUTER BASE   BIT

GUIDE

17-9a. *Cutting a groove in the edge of a board. Notice the extra piece of wood attached to the guide. This will give the router added support when riding on the narrow edge of the workpiece. (In the photograph, a previous cut removed much of the stock.)*

17-9b. *Cutting a dado.*

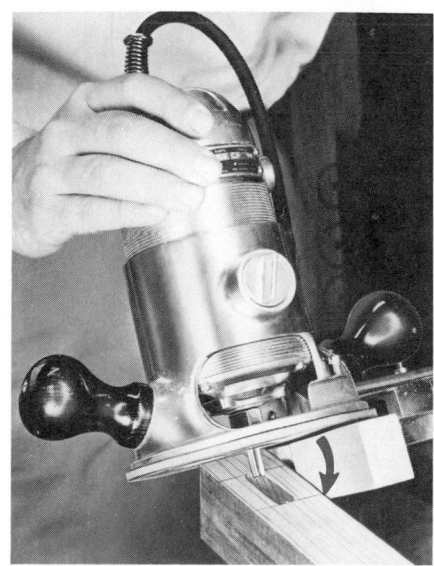

17-9c. *Cutting a mortise.*

edge of the wood. Attach the bit in the machine and adjust for depth. Secure a piece of scrap the same thickness as the finished stock and clamp it to the top of a bench. Hold the router firmly against the top of the work and move the cutter into the stock. Check to see that the desired shape is being cut. Fig. 17-7c. The shape can be changed by moving the motor up and down in the base. Fig. 17-5.

Freehand Routing

Signs and decorations are sometimes made freehand with the router. Carefully lay out the areas to be removed. Secure a bit of the desired diameter and fasten it into the router. Clamp the work to the tabletop, then lower the router into the design. Move the router along to follow the outline.

Dovetail Joint

The best joint for most drawer construction is the dovetail. This joint is sometimes used for other wooden "box" construction as well. It is a difficult joint for some to make by hand but simple with a router and dovetail attachment.

1. Clamp the dovetail attachment to a bench or table. Square up the stock to be used for the front and sides of the drawer or box. Fasten a template guide to the base of the router and install a dovetail bit. Adjust the dovetail bit to extend below the base the desired amount. This amount can usually be determined by making a trial cut and readjusting the router to the exact depth.

2. Select a board which will be one side of the box or drawer. Clamp it face side in against the front of the base and protruding ½" or more above the top surface of the base. This is shown as board B, Fig. 17-10a.

3. Clamp board A, which will be the front or back of the drawer or box, inner side up. Make sure that it is in full contact with board B. It should be set flush with the top end of B. Both boards must be in contact with the locating pins. See arrow "C" on Fig. 17-10b.

4. Place the dovetail template over the two pieces of stock and clamp in place. Fig. 17-10c.

5. Make a trial cut, being sure that the template guide follows the template. Fig. 17-10d. If the trial joint is too *loose*, adjust to make a *deeper cut*. If the trial joint is too *tight*, adjust for a *shallower cut*. Fig. 17-10e and f.

6. Figure 17-11a shows a drawer side which does not fit far enough into the front. When this happens, turn *in* the template adjusting nut (D in Fig. 17-10b). This allows a deeper cut into the drawer front. If the drawer side fits in too deeply, Fig. 17-11b, turn the template adjusting nut *out*. Be sure these adjusting nuts on both ends of the fixture are set the same.

7. The completed dovetail should appear as in Fig. 17-11c.

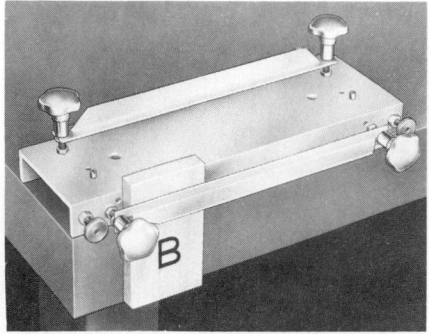

17-10a. *Clamp side in place.*

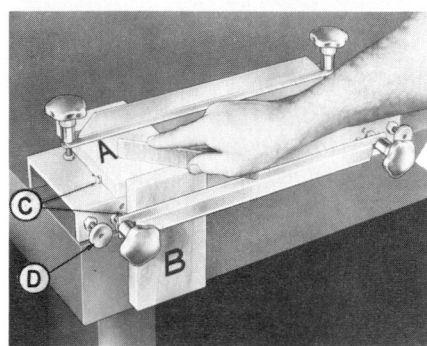

17-10b. *Clamp front or back in place.*

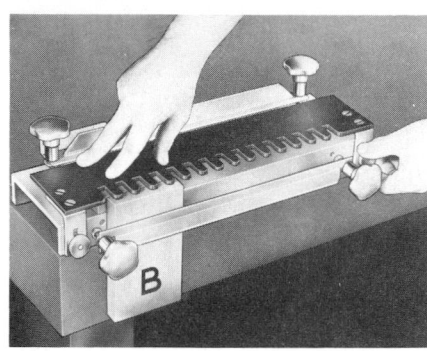

17-10c. *Place template over piece.*

The left end of the fixture is used for cutting the right front of the drawer and the left rear corner. The left front and right rear corner are cut on the right end of the dovetail fixture.

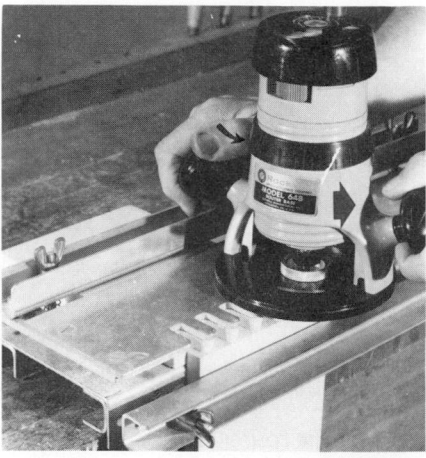

17-10d. *Cutting the dovetail.*

17-10e. *Drawer front and side are held on the outside of the fixture, in the same position in which they were cut.*

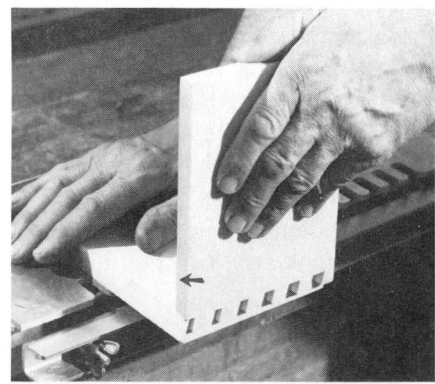

17-10f. *Back of drawer side is tipped up and the front of the joint is checked.*

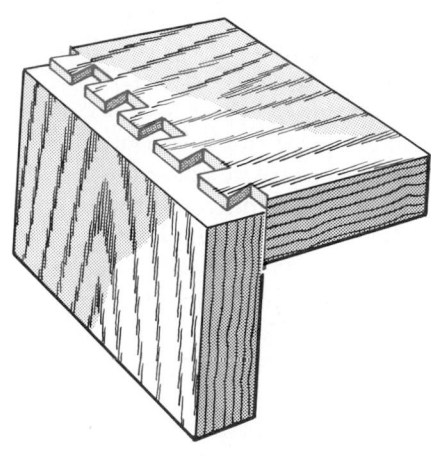

17-11a. *If the drawer side does not fit far enough into the front, turn the template adjusting nut in to allow a deeper cut in the drawer front.*

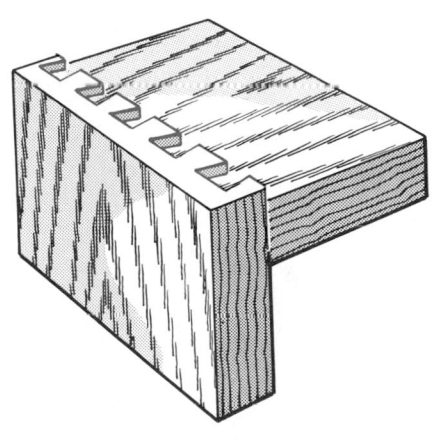

17-11b. *If the drawer side fits too deeply into the cuts in the front, turn the template adjusting nut out. (Note, however, that sometimes the side will be set low intentionally. This allows for clearance between the drawer side and the cabinet. If this is done, complete the joint by cutting a rabbet on the inside of the drawer front equal to the depth of the projection.)*

17-11c. *The dovetail joint is found in the finest drawer construction.*

Dovetail Dado

The dovetail dado is a good joint to use where extra strength is needed, because the joint will pull the two pieces together and hold tightly. It is an ideal joint for fastening a drawer side to a front when the front "lips over" the cabinet sides. Fig. 17-12.

Install the dovetail bit in the router and attach the guide. Adjust the depth of cut and set the guide for the first cut. Fig. 17-13a. If the slot is to be cut in a drawer front, it will not be necessary to clamp a piece of wood on either side of the work to support the router. When the first cut has been completed, set the second piece in the vise with a piece of scrap stock on each side. The scrap pieces should be at least ¾" thick and both the same thickness. Leave the depth of cut set the same as for the slot, and readjust the guide so one cut is made on each side to form the tenon. The width of the tenon is cut to fit the slot by adjusting the guide. Fig. 17-13b. It is recommended that a trial cut be made in scrap stock of the same thickness to insure a good fitting joint.

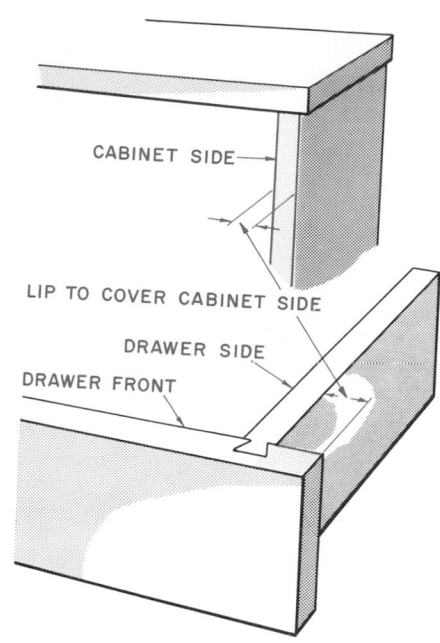

17-12. *The dovetail dado joint is an excellent joint to use for drawer construction on contemporary furniture. This joint is also recommended for attaching the sides of a cabinet to the top, when the cabinet top overhangs the side panels.*

17-13a. *Cutting the dovetail mortise or slot. Note that in the picture it is cut in the edge of the workpiece. For a drawer front or cabinet top, the cut would be made on a surface.*

17-13b. *Cutting the dovetail tenon or stub. A cut is made on each side, leaving the tenon in the center.*

17-14. *Cutting a hinge mortise on a door. If a square corner hinge is used, the corners of the cut must be squared with a chisel. However, hinges are available with round corners so they fit directly into the opening. After gains or mortises are cut on the door, the template guide can be transferred to the doorframe for cutting hinge mortises on the jamb.*

Hinge Butt Routing

A special template is available for hinge butt routing. Because the bits leave a slight curve at the corner of the cut, it is necessary to chisel the corner square for some hinges. Figure 17-14 shows a metal template in position on a door. This guides the router so that the hinge mortises are cut easily and quickly, in the proper location, to uniform size and depth.

ROUTER ACCESSORIES

One reason that routers are so versatile is that there are a number of accessories available to fit them. A guide fence is very useful. The edge of the fence rides against the edge of the stock, guiding the router in making a cut parallel to the edge. Fig. 17-15. An adjustable circle-cutting jig works like a trammel to guide the router. Fig. 17-16. A dust collection hose, connected to a shop vacuum cleaner, removes chips and dust. This allows the operator to see the cut more

clearly. It also helps to prevent chips from flying at the operator, which increases safety. Fig. 17-17.

Some woodworkers mount a router upside-down beneath a plywood or particleboard top, so that the bit can extend through the top. When a simple fence is added, this "router table" becomes a tool that operates much like a shaper.

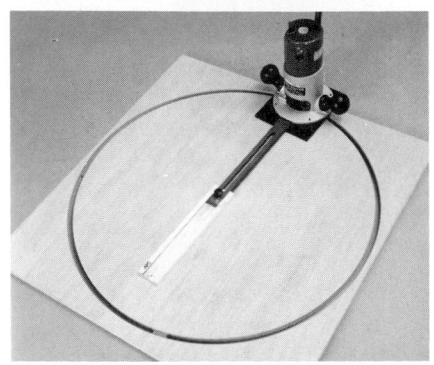

17-16. *A router with a circle-cutting jig.*

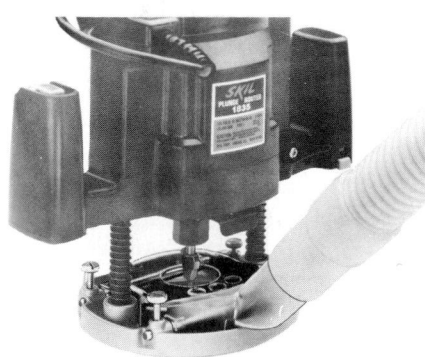

17-17. *A dust collection hose can be connected to a router and a vacuum cleaner.*

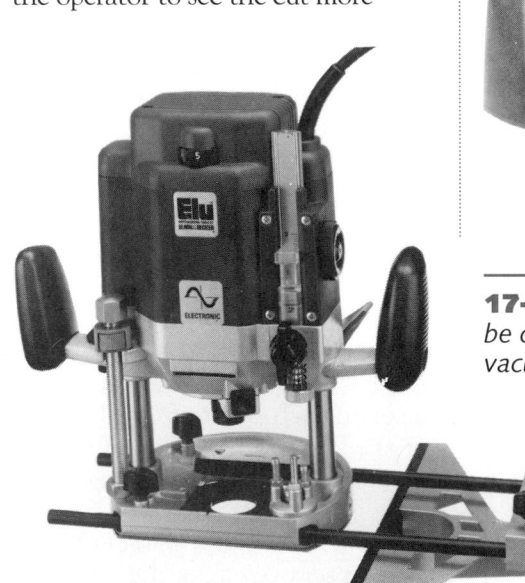

17-15. *A plunge router with a guide fence.*

1. Besides using the router for shaping surfaces and edges, describe what other operations can be performed by using a router and accessories.

2. Name six common kinds of router bits.

3. What kind of bit has cutting surfaces on the bottom of the bit as well as on the sides?

4. What accessory is necessary for cutting a groove parallel to the edge of stock?

5. When making a cut along the outside edge of a piece of stock, in which direction should the router be fed?

6. What accessory is necessary to cut a dovetail joint with a router?

7. How is a plunge router different from a standard router?

ACTIVITIES

1. Language Arts. *Dovetail joint* is an interesting and colorful term. Why is this joint called "dovetail"?

2. Science. Inspect some of the drawers in your own furniture. See if they are constructed with dovetail or dovetail dado joints. Next try to find a drawer that does not use dovetail joint construction. Assess the construction of the different drawers. Which type do you feel is better built? Explain your findings and assessment in a short descriptive paragraph.

THE SCHOOL-TO-WORK CONNECTION

A router is an extremely versatile tool. Of the two types of routers, plunge models are more versatile than fixed-base models. The motor moves up and down on spring-mounted posts so the bit can be lowered, or "plunged," into the workpiece.

1. One of the things that makes a router so versatile is the wide variety of bits available for it. Carpenters prefer carbide-tipped bits to high-speed steel bits, even though carbide bits are more expensive. This is because carbide holds a sharp edge longer than high-speed steel. One drawback to carbide, however, is that it is brittle. The cutting edge of a carbide bit can easily be nicked if it bangs against other metal surfaces. For this reason, carbide bits should be protected when they are not being used. Some carpenters keep bits in the plastic containers that 35mm film comes in. Think of two other ways you might protect bits. Test your theories.

2. You should get in the habit of inspecting a bit before each use. Check it for nicked or dull edges. One way to check a bit edge for sharpness is to brush it lightly across your fingernail. If the cutting edge won't "grab" when you do this, it's dull. Anyone with lots of router experience probably has his or her own way of gauging the sharpness of bits. Find as many of these people as you can and collect their tips. Describe the tips in a short essay. Which tips are the safest, and why? If you have access to the Internet, you might be able to contact experienced router users.

3. Like the motor in most portable power tools, the electric motor in a router is a universal-type motor. One type of maintenance you might encounter is the need to change brushes. These are actually small blocks of carbon that conduct electricity to the motor's commutator. Brushes eventually wear down because the commutator spins at high speed whenever the tool is running. If a router fails to start when you turn it on, or if it sputters, the brushes are probably ready for replacement. Brushes are typically located near the top of the router beneath a black plastic cap (see Fig. 17-3B). Replacement brushes are made for specific tools. Use the phone book to locate a source of replacement brushes for a router. Call the source and obtain a price for a pair of brushes. (Brushes should always be replaced in pairs.)

18

Saber Saw

SAFETY

The following are general safety rules. We strongly advise you to check the manufacturer's manual for any special safety instructions.

➤ Review general safety rules for use of portable electric tools.

➤ Select the correct blade for the work and properly secure it in the chuck.

➤ Be certain the material to be sawed is properly clamped.

➤ Keep the cutting pressure constant. Do not force the cut.

➤ When finished, turn off the power switch and allow the saw to come to a dead stop before setting the saw down.

➤ Hold the base down securely on the work when cutting.

The *portable jig* (also called *saber* or *bayonet*) *saw* is the best choice for an on-the-job cutting tool for straight or irregular cutting. This tool can do the same cutting as a floor-type jig or band saw, with the

added convenience of a hand tool. A larger jig saw can cut through material 2" thick. It also can cut through a 2" × 4" piece in less than 15 seconds. It will cut metal, wood, plastic, and many other materials. Most hand jig saws use orbital action (cutting the material on the up stroke and moving away from it on the down stroke). Because of this, cutting speed is greatly increased and the saw cuts with a cleaner edge.

PARTS

The design of this tool varies with the manufacturer. However, all of these tools consist of a motor, a handle, a mechanism to change rotary action into up-and-down action, and a baseplate or shoe. Figs. 18-1 and 18-2. Select the correct blade. Table 18-A. At least three teeth must be on the cutting surface at all times. To install the blade, loosen the set screws or clamp, and slip the blade into the slot under the chuck cover until you are sure it is tightly seated. Then tighten the set screw or clamp.

OPERATIONS

Straight and Irregular Cutting

Mount the work so it is held rigid. Fig. 18-3. Make a layout line that can be followed. Set the shoe

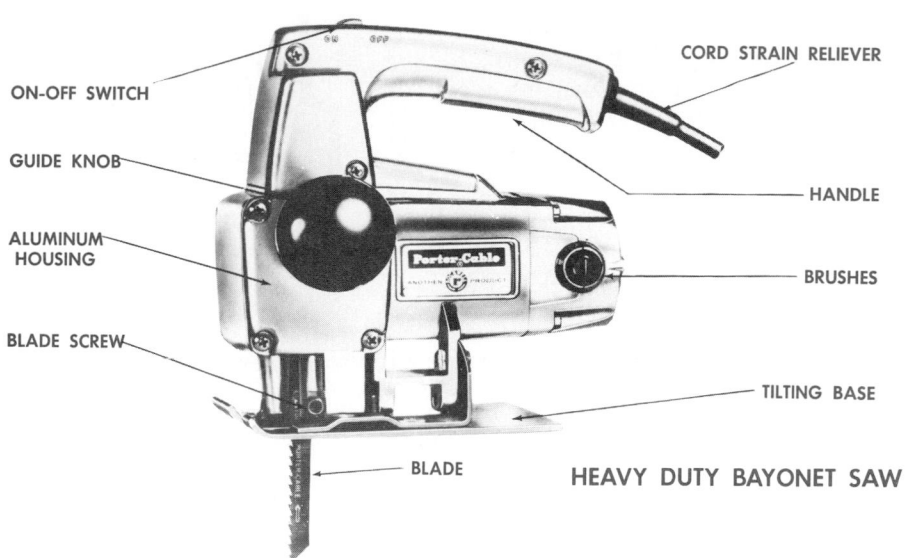

ON-OFF SWITCH

GUIDE KNOB

ALUMINUM HOUSING

BLADE SCREW

BLADE

CORD STRAIN RELIEVER

HANDLE

BRUSHES

TILTING BASE

HEAVY DUTY BAYONET SAW

18-1. Parts of the bayonet, saber, or hand jigsaw.

18-2. Saber saws can have various handle shapes and styles.

18-3. Cutting a curve. Notice how the work is clamped to the table.

18-4a. Straight cutting.

Table 18-A. Blade Selection. Guide for selecting the correct blade.

Heavy cuts 2" x 4" at 45°	6 teeth per inch
General Cutting	7,10
Smooth Cuts	12
Plywood	12
Hardboard	12
Cardboard	Knife
Leather	Knife

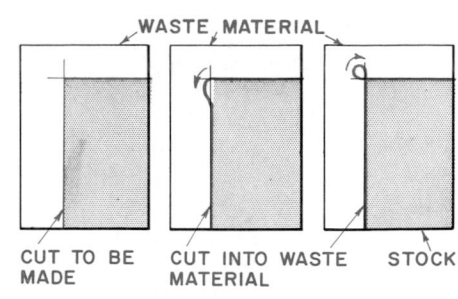

WASTE MATERIAL

CUT TO BE MADE

CUT INTO WASTE MATERIAL

STOCK

18-4b. Two methods of cutting an exterior corner. One way is to make a slightly curved cut at the corner; then trim this off with a second cut. Another method is to make a complete circle in the waste stock.

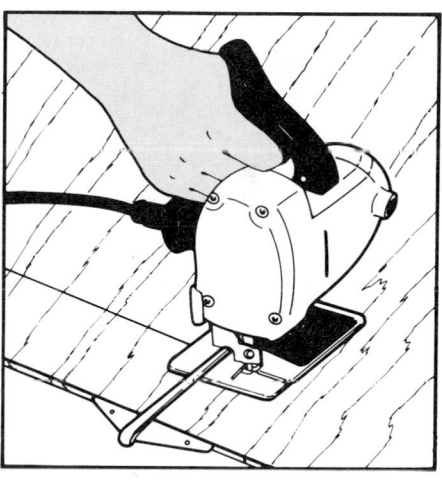

18-5. Using a fence to do crosscutting.

of the tool on the work. Start the motor and allow it to come up to full speed. Then move the saw along slowly. Fig. 18-4. Don't force the cutting. Use only enough pressure to keep the saw cutting at all times. The tool is always held in one hand. The other hand can hold the work or steady the saw. For more accurate straight cutting, a ripping fence can be installed. Fig. 18-5. The ripping fence can also be used for cutting circles. A nail or peg must be driven into the center of the circle.

Plunge or Internal Cutting

The portable jigsaw can be used to cut out an internal area without first drilling a hole. This is called plunge cutting. With a pencil, mark out the area to be cut. Choose a convenient starting place inside the waste stock. Tip the tool forward with the shoe resting on the surface of the material and the top of the blade clear of the work surface. Fig. 18-6a. Turn on the power. When the blade reaches full speed, slowly lower the back of the machine until the blade cuts through the material to the full depth. Then cut out the opening. Fig. 18-6b.

Bevel Cutting

The shoes of some saws can be adjusted from 0 to 45 degrees for bevel cutting. Fig. 18-7. Such cutting can be done freehand, as shown in Fig. 18-8, or with a guide.

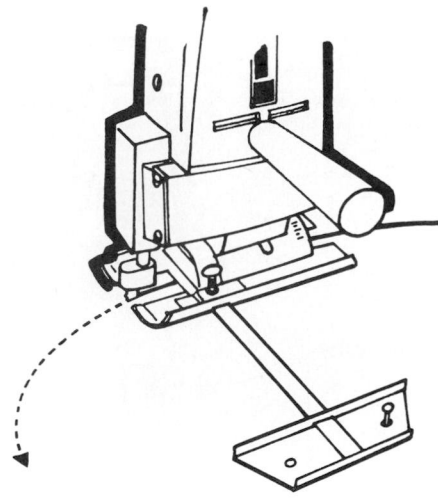

18-9. *Making a circle cut.*

Circle Cuts

For circle cuts, remove the guide and turn it over. Set the guide into position for the radius desired and tighten it. Make a pocket cut or drill a pilot hole on the circumference of the desired circle and insert the saw blade. You will find it very difficult to make perfect circles starting from the edge of the board. With the blade on the circumference of the circle, locate the center of the circle and drive a small nail through the hole in the guide at that point. Now begin the cutting, but do not force the saw. Let it do the cutting and you will have a perfect circle. Fig. 18-9.

Reciprocating Saw

Another type of all-purpose saw operates with a back-and-forth movement, like a hacksaw without a frame. This saw is most commonly used for remodeling or cabinetwork, since it can cut wood, plastic, metal, ceramics, and many other materials. Fig. 18-10.

Reciprocating saws take blades that are similar to saber saw blades, but they are longer and wider. Fig. 18-11. Blades are available to cut

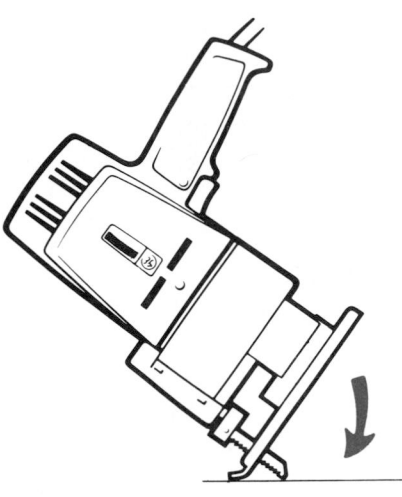

18-6a. *Tip the saw up on the front of the baseplate. Turn it on and allow it to come to full speed before lowering the blade into the workpiece.*

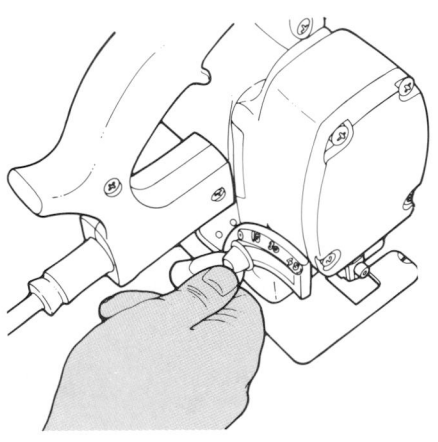

18-7. *Adjusting the shoe, or baseplate, for bevel cutting.*

18-6b. *Making an internal cut.*

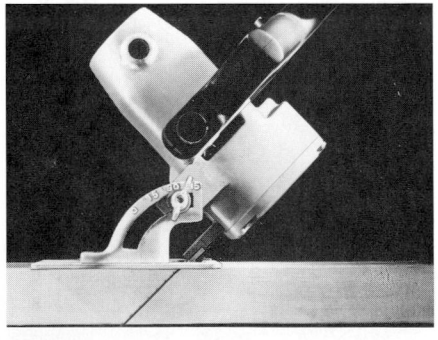

18-8. *Cutting a bevel with the saber saw.*

wood, plastic, metal, and reinforcing bar. If the reciprocating saw is to be used on a remodeling project, it is a good idea to equip it with blades designed for cutting nail-embedded wood. These blades are less likely to snap if they hit a hidden nail.

18-10a. *Reciprocating saws.*

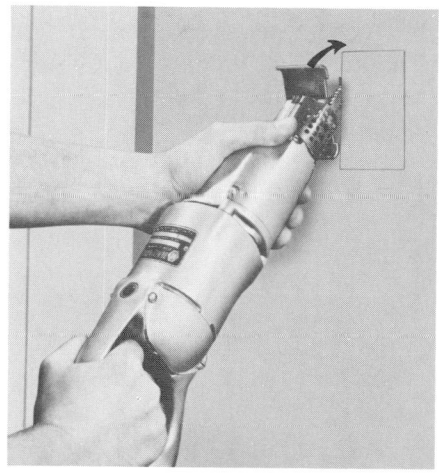

18-10b. *Making a plunge cut with a reciprocating saw.*

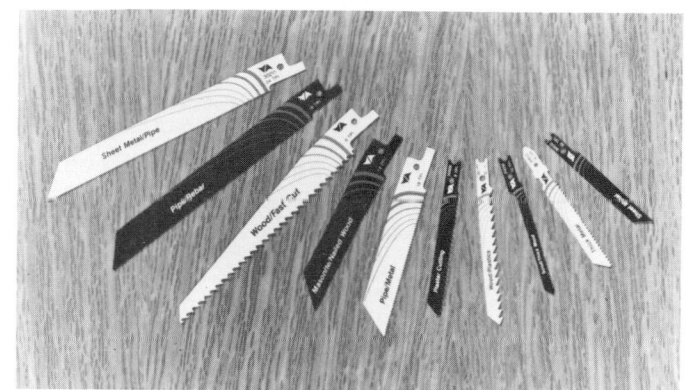

18-11. *The wide blades are for reciprocating saws. The smaller blades are for saber saws.*

QUESTIONS

1. List three safety rules that should be observed when using a saber saw.

2. By what other names is the saber saw sometimes known?

3. What materials can be cut with a portable electric jig saw?

4. When using the saber saw, at least how many teeth should be on the cutting surface at all times?

5. How much pressure should be used when cutting with the saber saw?

6. What is meant by plunge cutting?

7. Describe how circles can be cut with the saber saw.

ACTIVITIES

1. Language Arts. Using the *Readers' Guide to Periodical Literature*, look up consumer-buying articles on jigsaws. Write a brief report detailing the brand names and prices of the jigsaws that are highly recommended.

2. Language Arts. How does a jigsaw differ from a circular saw? List at least ten differences.

3. Science. Correlate the blade size of a portable saber saw and a portable circular saw. Explain why portable saber saws are used for both straight and irregular cuts, whereas a portable circular saw is used only for straight cuts. Correlate the blade shapes with the sawdust shavings produced.

19

Portable Sanders

SAFETY

The following are general safety rules. We strongly advise you to check the manufacturer's manual for any special safety instructions.

➤ See general safety rules for operation of portable electric tools.

➤ Be sure the abrasive is in good condition and that its grit is correct for the work to be done.

➤ Be sure the abrasive belt is installed with the correct tension and is tracking properly.

➤ Keep your hands away from abrasive surfaces.

➤ Never touch the edge of a belt or disc while the sander is in use.

➤ Be sure there are no nicks or tears in the edge of a disc or belt.

➤ Disconnect the power plug when changing abrasives.

➤ Make certain the switch is in the "off" position when plugging in the power cord.

In recent years, portable electric sanders have become more common in construction. They are used for tasks ranging from heavy stock removal to delicate final sanding of finish woodwork. There are several kinds of sanders. The most common sanders on a job site are the belt sander and the finishing sander.

There are many different types of sandpaper. Fig. 19-1.

19-1. *Sandpaper comes in a variety of forms, including sheets and belts.*

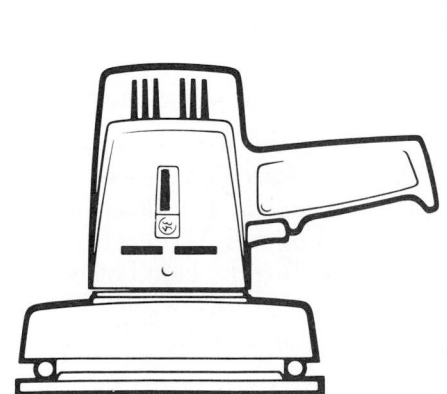

PORTABLE BELT SANDER

The *portable belt sander* operates in a manner similar to the floor-model belt-sanding machine, except that the revolving belt is placed on the work instead of the work against the belt. Fig. 19-2. The size of the machine is determined by the width of belt. To increase safety and reduce the

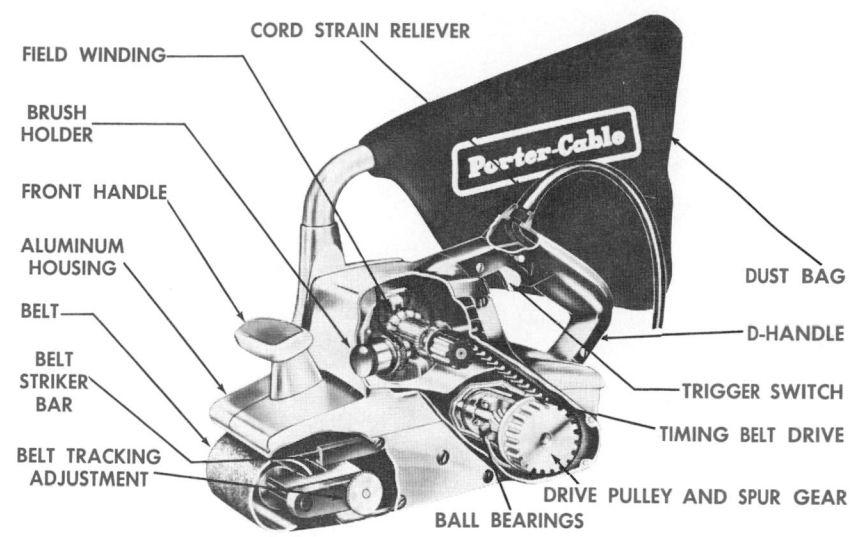

FIELD WINDING
CORD STRAIN RELIEVER
BRUSH HOLDER
FRONT HANDLE
ALUMINUM HOUSING
BELT
BELT STRIKER BAR
BELT TRACKING ADJUSTMENT
DUST BAG
D-HANDLE
TRIGGER SWITCH
TIMING BELT DRIVE
DRIVE PULLEY AND SPUR GEAR
BALL BEARINGS

19-2. *Parts of a portable belt sander.*

19-3. *This heavy-duty 4" belt sander includes a dust collector.*

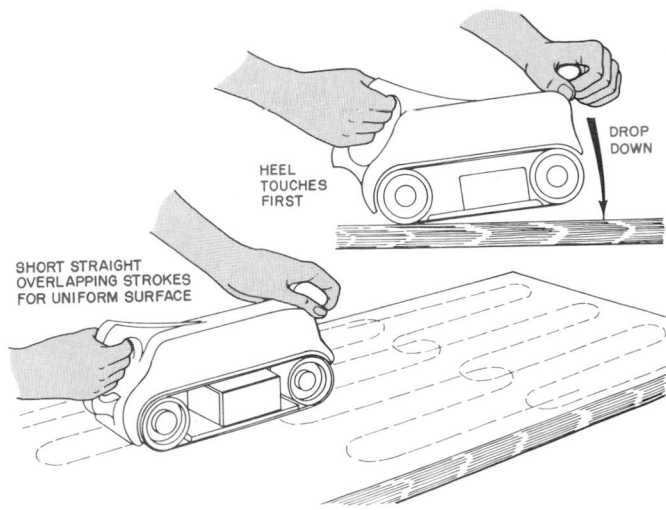

DROP DOWN
HEEL TOUCHES FIRST
SHORT STRAIGHT OVERLAPPING STROKES FOR UNIFORM SURFACE

19-4. *Lower the sander slowly to the surface. Move the machine in the pattern shown.*

amount of dust in the air, some belt sanders have a dust collector bag. Fig. 19-3.

Installing the Belt

Install the belt so that the arrow on the inside of the belt points in the same direction as the arrow on the side of the sander. When the belt has been placed on the pulleys, it can be made to run straight by adjusting the tracking screw. The

belt should not be allowed to rub against the left side of the machine.

Using a Portable Belt Sander

The proper technique is to put the cord over your right shoulder, hold the machine with both hands, turn the machine on, and lower the back of it slowly onto the wood. Then do the sanding by moving the machine back and forth, and at the same time moving it slowly from one side to the other. Fig. 19-4.

FINISHING (OR PAD) SANDER

There are many kinds of finishing sanders. Parts of a typical one are shown in Fig. 19-5. All of these sanders operate on one of the three basic principles shown in Fig. 19-6. Those with straight-line action are the least likely to leave cross-grain scratches. The size of this machine is determined by the size of the abrasive sheet used. *Finishing sanders* are primarily used for fine finish-sanding after the project is assembled. To replace a sheet of abrasive, first cut a sheet of paper to the required size. The paper is held on the pad at either end and pressure keys are used to lock the paper in place. Release the pressure keys at either end. Fasten the paper in one end and lock the key at that end. Pull the paper tightly over the pad, slip the loose end under the other clamp, and tighten this lock. The exact method of fastening the paper to the pad will vary with different sanders.

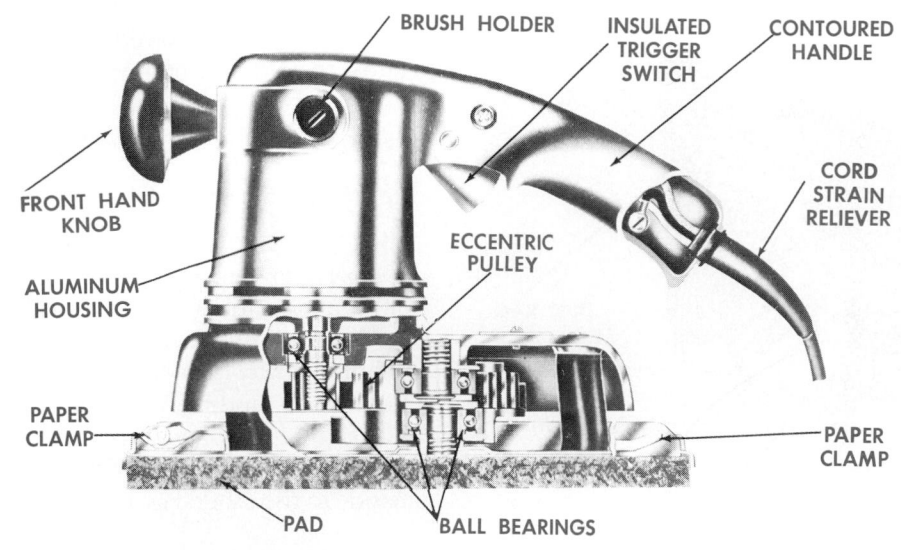

19-5. *Parts of a half-pad finishing sander.*

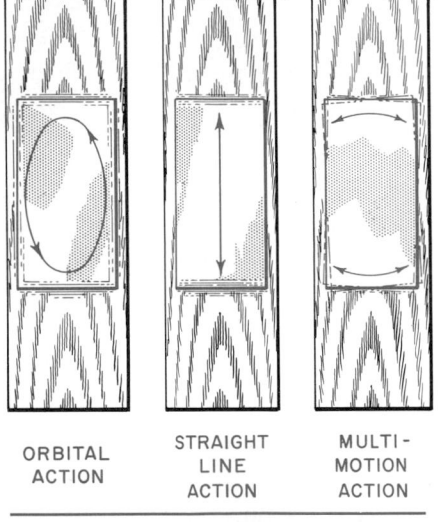

ORBITAL ACTION   STRAIGHT LINE ACTION   MULTI-MOTION ACTION

19-6. *Three kinds of action in finishing sanders. Orbital and multi-motion action may cause some cross-grain scratches. Straight-line action is like hand sanding and results in the best surface.*

Using a Finishing Sander

The finishing sander should rest evenly on the stock. Apply a moderate amount of pressure and move the sander back and forth, working from one side to the other. Fig. 19-7.

19-7. *Using a finishing sander.*

OTHER SANDERS

There are several other kinds of sanders that might be used on a construction job site. The *random orbital sander* can be used to remove stock quickly or for finish sanding. It is best used for sanding broad, flat areas. Fig. 19-8. *Pad sanders* are the smallest sanders commonly available. They are used in finishing work to sand places that would be inaccessible to larger sanders. Fig. 19-9. Air-driven (pneumatic) tools are now common in construction. Some pneumatic sanders are available as well. Fig. 19-10.

19-8. *Random orbital sander.*

19-10. *This sander is powered by air supplied by a compressor.*

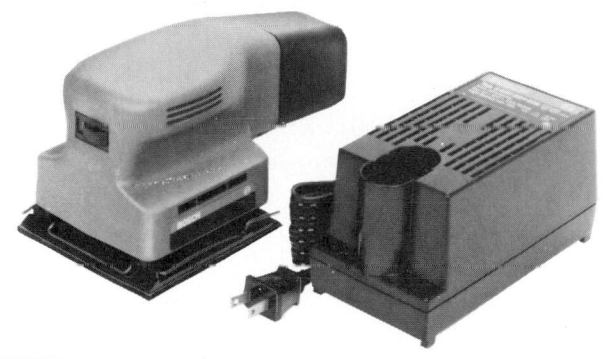

19-9. *This cordless pad sander, with charger, can be used where electrical outlets are unavailable.*

QUESTIONS

1. List three safety rules that should be observed when using the portable sander.

2. How is the size of a portable belt sander determined?

3. When installing a belt on a portable electric sander, in which direction should the arrow on the inside of the belt point?

4. Describe the proper technique for using a portable belt sander.

5. Finishing sanders have three kinds of actions. Name them.

6. Describe the proper technique for using a finishing sander.

ACTIVITIES

1. Math. The pad on a pad sander measures 7 ⅜" by 3 ⅝". You have a supply of sheets of abrasive. Each sheet is 11" by 9".

a. How many sheets of the appropriate size for the sander can be cut from each of these sheets?

b. How much waste will there be? (Have you considered how much will be needed so that the sheet can be clamped into place?)

2. Social Studies. Find out when industry began mass-producing furniture. What inventions had to be developed before this became a reality? What were the first pieces of furniture to be mass produced?

Jointers, Planers, and Electric Planes

Carpenters and builders now use a number of tools that were once found only in woodworking shops. These tools include jointers, planers, and combination jointer/planers. In recent years, power tool manufacturers designed small, portable versions of their woodworking shop tools. The portability of these tools makes them easy to bring to the job site. Also, some builders find that converting rough stock to finished stock on site is sometimes less costly than purchasing finished stock from a lumberyard.

This unit will describe these tools, along with electric planes. An electric plane does much the same job as a jointer.

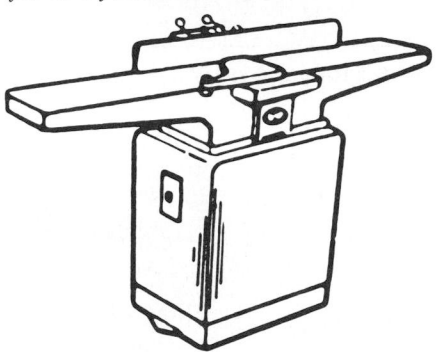

JOINTER SAFETY

The following are general safety rules. We strongly advise you to check the manufacturer's manual for any special safety instructions.

➤ *Always keep the knives of the jointer sharp.* Dull knives tend to cause kickback and also result in poor planing.

➤ *The fence should be tight.* Never adjust the fence while the jointer is running.

➤ Adjust the depth of cut before the jointer is turned on.

➤ *See that the guard is in place and operating easily.* If the regular guard is removed, a special guard must be provided.

➤ *Always allow the machine to come to full speed before using it.*

➤ Check the stock for knots, splits, metal particles, and other imperfections before jointing. Defective stock may break up or be thrown from the jointer.

➤ *Keep the left hand back from the front end of the board when feeding.*

➤ *Stand to the side of the jointer, never directly behind it.* In case of kickback, you will be out of the way.

➤ *Cut with the grain, never against it.*

➤ *Always use a push stick or push block.*

➤ *Do not try to take too heavy a cut.*

➤ *Use common sense in determining when stock is too thin or too short to joint safely.*

➤ Never apply pressure to the board with your hand directly over the cutterhead.

➤ Use a brush to clean shavings off the table. Never use your hand.

➤ Be sure that portable jointers will not tip over during use. They should be secured temporarily to the subfloor or to a workbench.

Although the jointer is not used for a great variety of operations, it is one of the most frequently used machines for preparing stock. Common uses of the jointer are for surfacing a board and for planing an edge or an end. It can also be used for cutting a rabbet, bevel, chamfer, or taper.

The *jointer* has a cylindrical cutterhead which usually has three or four blades (or knives). The blades rotate, shearing off small chips of wood, thus producing a smooth surface on the workpiece.

SIZE

The size of a jointer is indicated by the length of the knives. Since most jointing operations are performed on the edge of stock, a 6" or 8" jointer is most common. Fig. 20-1.

20-1a. *A 6" jointer.*

20-1b. *This 6 1/8" benchtop jointer is very portable.*

The length of the bed also affects the usefulness of the jointer, since a longer bed provides better support for jointing longer pieces.

PARTS

The *frame* or *base* of the jointer has two tables—the *front* or *infeed table* and the *rear* or *outfeed table.* Fig. 20-2. On most machines, both of these tables are adjustable, although there are some on which only the infeed table can be raised or lowered.

The *cutterhead* is the heart of the jointer. As mentioned, it consists of the head itself and three or more knives. This assembly usually operates on two roller bearings. Fig. 20-3.

The *fence* provides support for the work while it is fed, on edge or on end, through the machine. The fence can be adjusted to various angles, usually up to 45 degrees both ways from the vertical position.

The *guard* is a protective device covering the cutterhead. It either swings out of the way or lifts up. Most operations, except rabbeting on some jointers, and certain tapering, should be done with the guard in place.

A jointer operates from about 4,000 rpm to as much as 16,000 rpm. Some jointers are equipped with a variable speed control. This allows the operator to adjust the speed to fit the type of material being cut.

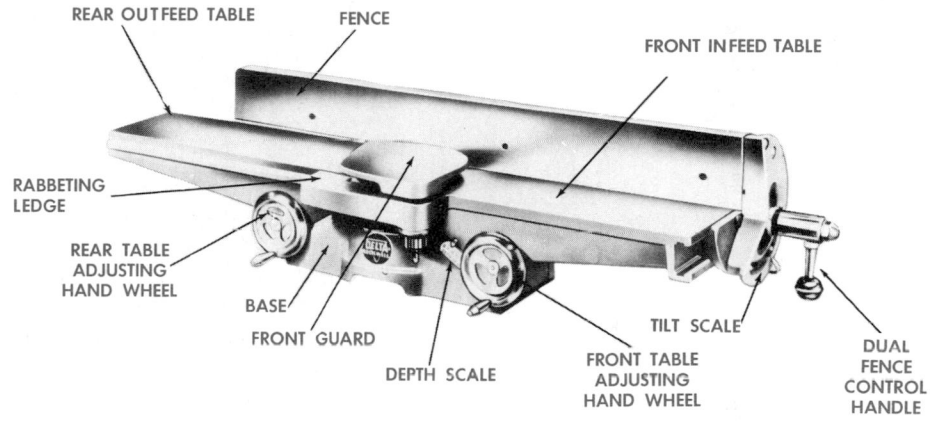

20-2. *A 6" jointer with the parts named.*

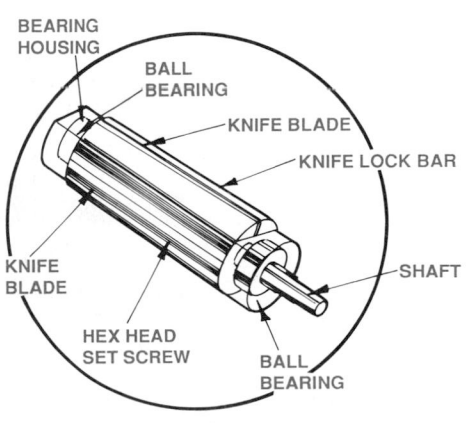

20-3. *A 6" cutterhead with the parts named.*

ADJUSTMENTS

Aligning and Adjusting the Outfeed Table

The top of the outfeed table must be at exactly the same height as the knife blades at their highest point of revolution. If the table is too low, the board will drop down onto the knives as it leaves the infeed table. This will cause a recess to be cut at the end of the board. If the table is too high, the board will be slightly tapered. Figure 20-4 shows correct and incorrect cuts.

To align the knives with the table as just mentioned, turn the cutterhead until one blade is at its highest point. Release the table locking screw on the side of the jointer. Lower the outfeed table until it is below the blade; then place a straightedge on the outfeed table with one end projecting over the blade. Fig. 20-5. Turn the table up slowly until it is in line with the knife at the highest point. Turn the cutterhead over slowly by hand until there is very light contact between the knives and the bottom of the straightedge. Tighten the lock nut. Once the outfeed table is set, it does not require changing except for certain cuts such as stop chamfers and bevels, and recess cuts. If the outfeed table is the fixed kind, raise or lower the cutterhead until the knives are even with the outfeed table.

Adjusting the Infeed Table

The distance the infeed table is below the knives determines the depth of cut. The depth of cut to be taken will depend on:

➤ The width of the surface being jointed.

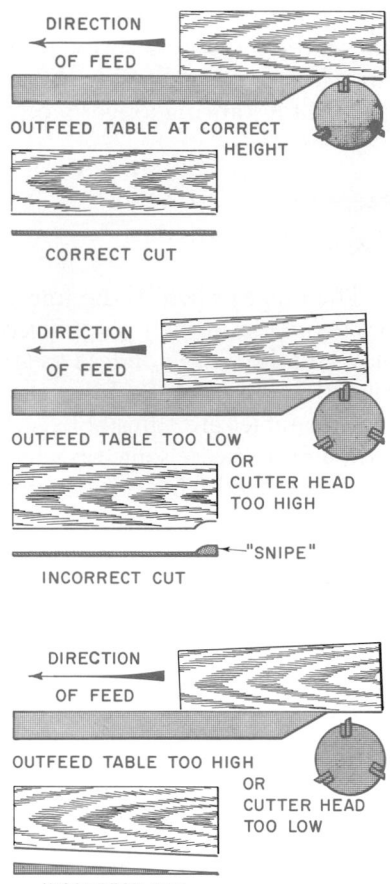

20-4. The jointer must be adjusted so the outfeed table is at exactly the same height as the cutterhead knife at its highest point. Otherwise a taper or a recess will be cut. (A recess is sometimes called a "snipe.")

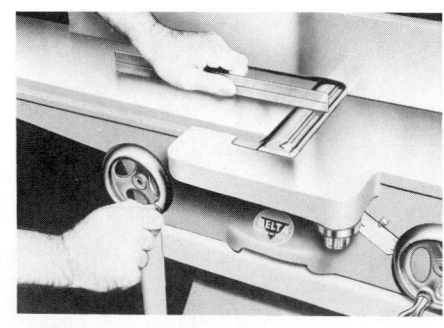

20-5. Adjusting the outfeed table. Raise the table slowly until the straightedge rests evenly on the table and the knife. Always replace the guard after making this adjustment.

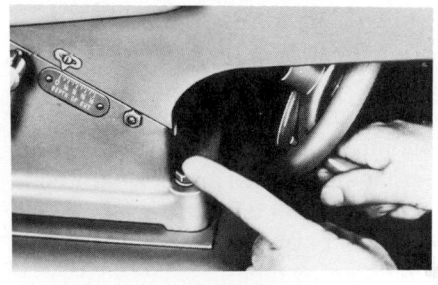

20-6. Always check the depth of cut before making a cut on the jointer.

➤ The kind of wood and grain pattern.

➤ Whether you are making a rough or finish cut.

Loosen the lock on the side of the infeed table, then turn the handle beneath the table to raise or lower it. There is a pointer and scale, indicating the depth of cut, which must be checked periodically for accuracy. Fig. 20-6.

Adjusting the Position of the Fence

For most operations it is desirable to have the fence at an exact right angle to the table. To adjust the fence, loosen the knob or lever that holds it in position; then set the fence at a 90-degree angle to the table. To check that the angle is correct, hold a square against the table and fence. Fig. 20-7. The fence can be moved in or out. When cutting, never expose any more of the blade than necessary.

The fence can also be *tilted* 45 degrees to right or left. This can be set on the tilt scale and checked with a protractor head of a combination square set or a sliding T bevel. There is a pointer and scale to indicate the tilt. Fig. 20-8.

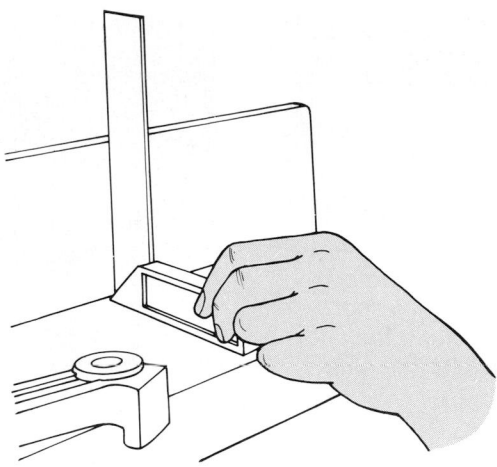

20-7. *Use a try square to make sure the fence is set at right angles to the table.*

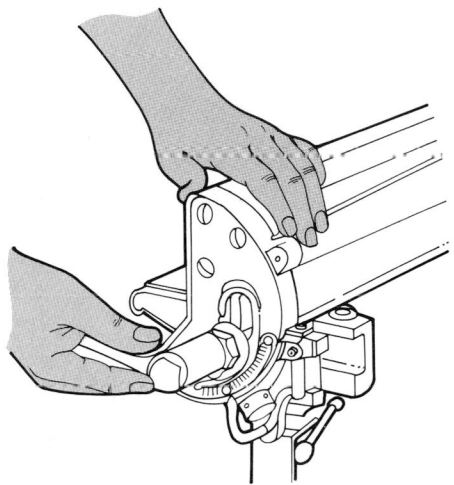

20-8. *Loosen the fence control handle to adjust for the angle of cut. The fence can also be moved in and out to distribute the wear on the knives, especially for edge jointing.*

BASIC PROCEDURES

1. Check the fence for squareness and the infeed table for depth of cut before turning on the machine. If the jointer has been used for some other operation, make a trial cut after resetting it.

2. Adjust the *depth of cut* with these things in mind:

➤ The amount of stock to be removed. Take a light cut for such operations as face planing or end planing and a slightly heavier cut for edge planing.

➤ The kind of wood. A light or heavy cut may be made on soft woods; a light cut is best on hard woods.

➤ The kind of planed surface. Take a heavier cut for removing stock and a lighter cut for finishing.

3. Change the position of the fence periodically to distribute the wear on the jointer knives.

4. When duplicate parts are needed, do the jointing operations

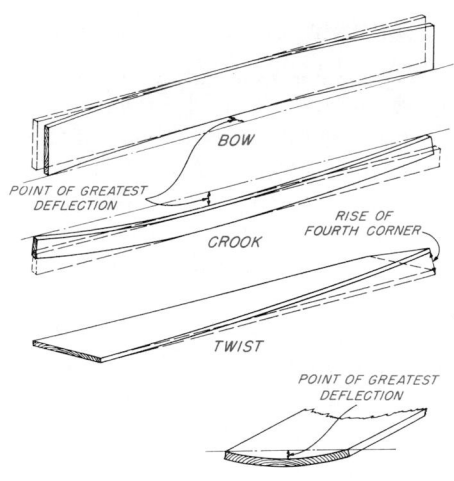

20-9. *Common kinds of warp that can be removed on the jointer.*

first; then cut the stock into the desired smaller pieces.

5. If you are right-handed, stand to the left of the jointer with your left foot forward and right foot back and beneath the infeed table. Move your body along as you do the planing operation.

6. Always check a board for warp and wind first. Fig. 20-9. Place a concave surface down for the first cuts. If the board has twist, balance it on the high corners to take the first cuts.

Planing a Surface

1. Check the board for warp and for direction of grain. Be certain the jointer is correctly adjusted.

2. Hold the board firmly on the infeed table with your left hand toward the front of the board and your right hand on the push block. This is the proper position if you are using a one-handed push block. Fig. 20-10. The push block is hooked on the end of the board that is over the infeed table. If a two-handed push block is being used, apply equal pressure on it with both hands. Fig. 20-11.

3. Turn on the machine and allow it to come to full speed.

4. Move the stock forward, keeping your left hand back of the cutterhead. When about half to two-thirds of the board has passed the cutterhead, move the left hand to the board over the outfeed table. Fig. 20-12.

5. After most of the board has passed over the cutter, move the right hand to the portion of the board over the outfeed table to finish the cut. *Never place your hand directly over the cutterhead.* Fig. 20-13.

20-10a. *Using the one-handled push block.*

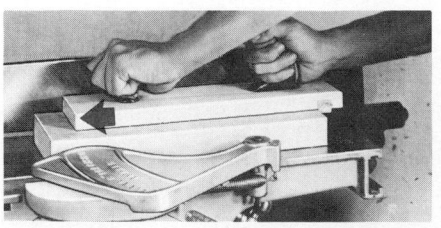

20-11a. *Using a two-handled push block to do facing on short stock. The knob is held in the left hand and the handle in the right.*

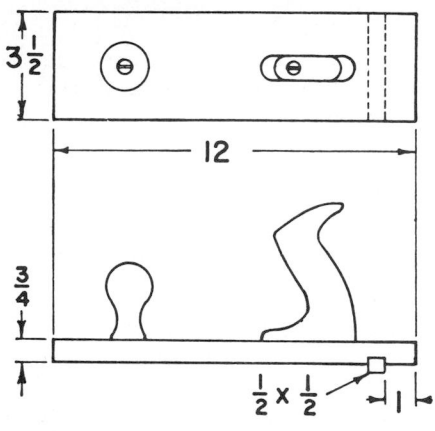

20-11b. *Drawing of a two-handled push block. This one has a knob and handle from a hand plane.*

20-12. *Face planing or surfacing on an 8" jointer. Note how the left hand is kept back from the front edge of the board.*

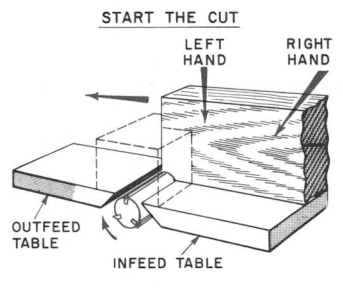

START THE CUT

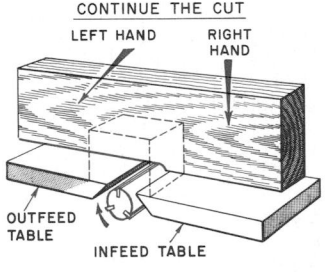

CONTINUE THE CUT

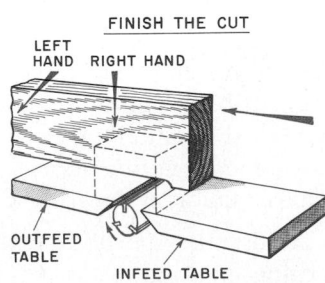

FINISH THE CUT

20-13. *Correct method of feeding when the hands are moved as stock passes across the cutterhead. The danger area is shown in color.*

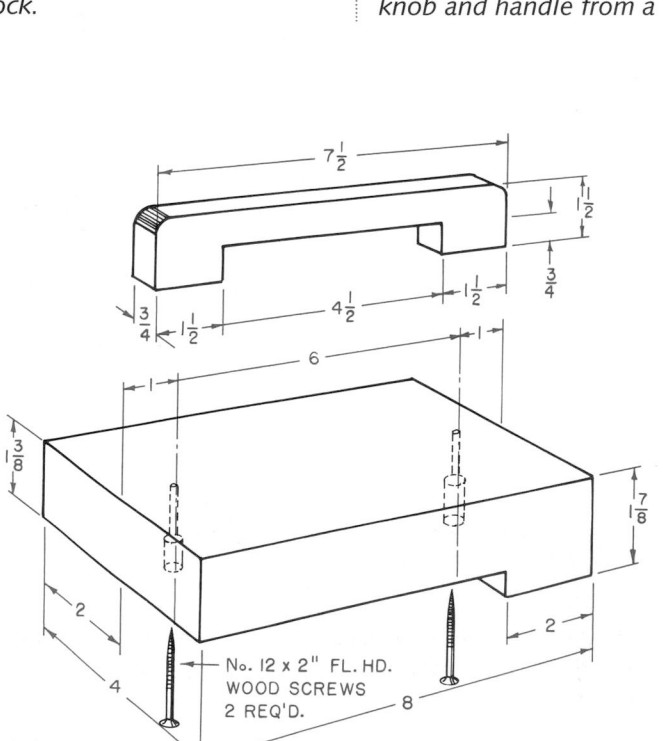

20-10b. *A drawing of a one-handled push block.*

Planing an Edge

The most common use for the jointer is planing or jointing an edge. Fig. 20-14a. An edge is said to be jointed when it is at right angles to the face of the board and is true along its entire length. Fig. 20-14b.

1. Check the fence for squareness. Generally, for safest operation, it is best to set the fence as close as possible to the left side of the machine.

2. Select the best edge and determine the grain direction.

3. Adjust for proper depth of cut. To insure parallel edges on the stock, rip to width and allow just enough extra stock to joint off the sawn edges.

4. Hold the stock firmly against the infeed table and the fence. The

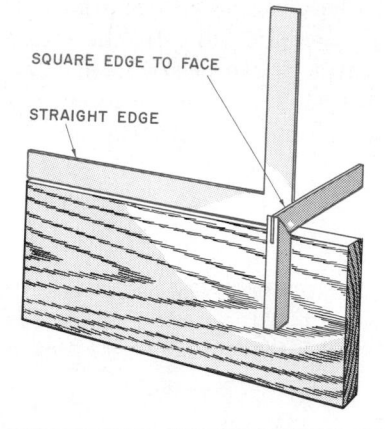

20-14b. *A properly jointed edge is straight along its entire length and forms a 90° angle with the working face.*

jointed or planed surface of the board should be against the fence.

5. For the right-handed person, the left hand is a guide and the right hand pushes the stock across the cutterhead. Move the left hand along with the board until the major portion of the board is over the outfeed table; then

move the right hand to the other side of the cutterhead, to the stock over the outfeed table. Do not push the board too fast, as this will make a rippled edge.

Cutting a Rabbet

One of the best ways to cut a rabbet with the grain is on the jointer.

1. Adjust the fence so that the distance between the end of the knives and the fence is equal to the width of the rabbet.

2. Lower the infeed table an amount equal to the depth of the rabbet. If the rabbet is quite deep, it may be necessary to cut it in two passes. In that event, the table is lowered an amount equal to about half the depth of the rabbet for the first pass, then lowered again to the desired depth to complete the cut.

3. Remove the guard, if necessary. Hold the stock firmly on the infeed table and move it along slowly. Fig. 20-15.

Many types of simple moldings can be rabbeted in this way.

20-14a. *Jointing the edge of a board.*

20-15. *Cutting a rabbet. On some machines it is not necessary to remove the guard, as must be done here.*

PLANER SAFETY

➤ Never run used lumber through the planer. The blades can be damaged if they hit a hidden nail or staple. Repairs are time consuming and expensive.

➤ Never stand directly behind the planer. If stock kicks back, this is the path it will take.

➤ Do not force stock into the planer; let the infeed roller pull the stock through. Do not pull stock out of the planer; support it on the tips of your fingers as it leaves the machine.

➤ Take a successive series of shallow cuts rather than one deep cut. This is particularly important when planing hardwoods. A cut that is too aggressive can damage the stock and overload the planer.

➤ To be cut safely, a board must engage both the infeed roller and the outfeed roller. Therefore, the board must be several inches longer than the distance between these two rollers.

➤ Get in the habit of examining every board that will be fed through the planer. Check for loose or large knots, warped surfaces, and other flaws that might be a problem.

➤ You can tell a lot about a planer by listening to it. If the machine suddenly makes any unusual noise, shut it off immediately and find the problem.

The purpose of a planer is to reduce the thickness of a board, smooth its surface, and make one side parallel to the other. Only recently have portable models been available for job site use.

Like a jointer, a planer has a cylindrical cutterhead mounted with three or four blades. As the cutterhead rotates, the knives make many small cuts in the surface of the board.

Planers range in size from 7" to 52". The size indicates the widest board that can be surfaced. The most common sizes for job site use are 12" and 13" planers.

Parts and Controls

Unlike a jointer, the cutterhead of a planer is mounted *above* the bed of the machine. Fig. 20-16. The cutterhead and several other key parts are contained in a metal housing.

20-16a. *Parts of a planer.*

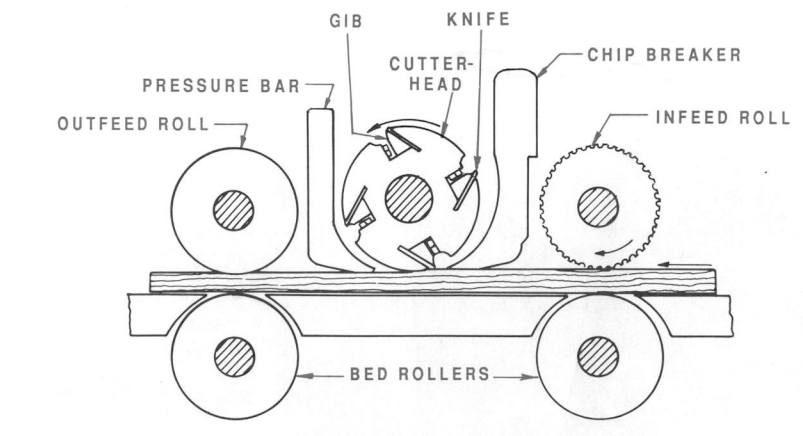

20-16b. *Chief operating parts of a planer.*

20-16c. *This 12" portable planer can be moved easily around the job site.*

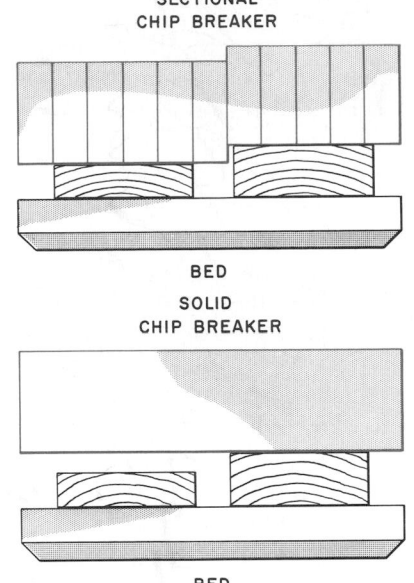

20-18. *Note the advantage of a sectional chip breaker when surfacing two or more pieces of slightly different thickness. If a solid chip breaker is used, there is no pressure on the thinner stock. As a result, the cutterhead tears the grain.*

The infeed roll moves the stock into the cutterhead. It is corrugated and usually made in sections. Fig. 20-17. With a sectional infeed roll, several pieces of slightly different thickness can be fed into the machine at the same time. Between the infeed roll and the cutterhead is a *chip breaker* that is also usually made in sections. Fig. 20-18. The edge of the chip breaker is set fairly close to the knives and can be adjusted up and down slightly. This device keeps the stock firmly pressed to the bed and prevents torn grain. If there were no chip breaker, the stock would tend to tear or split off in long slivers.

The *cutterhead* itself is cylindrical. It has three or more knives which smooth the upper surface of the board and cut it to uniform thickness. Just beyond the cutterhead is the *pressure bar*, which holds the stock firmly to the bed after the cut is made. Finally, the board passes the smooth *outfeed roll*. This helps to move the stock out of the machine. Some planers include additional rollers directly beneath the infeed and outfeed rollers. These are called bed rollers. They also help to move stock through the machine.

The kind and number of controls on a surfacer vary somewhat with its size. There is a switch to turn the power on and off. All machines have an elevating handwheel that moves the bed up and down to control the depth of cut. There is sometimes a feed control that determines the rate at which the stock moves into the cutters. On some larger machines a speed control is available for changing the rpm of the cutterhead. The two common adjustments, however, are to raise and lower the bed and to adjust the feed. The feed rate should be varied with the width of stock, the kind of wood, and the desired quality of the surfaces. Fairly wide, hard pieces of wood should be fed at relatively slow speed, and narrower pieces of softer wood at a higher feed rate.

Operating Procedure

1. If long stock is to be surfaced, it is a good idea to get someone to help at the other end. If no one can help, place a roller stand at the "out" end of the planer to support the stock.

2. Before planing a warped board, true one face on the jointer.

3. If possible, determine the grain direction of each piece and feed *with* the grain. Place the pieces conveniently near the infeed table with the grain in the proper direction.

4. Measure the thickness of the stock and adjust the machine to remove *about* $\frac{1}{16}$" to $\frac{1}{8}$". Generally a piece is surfaced in from one to three cuts. For example, if stock measures 1" and you wish to reduce it to $\frac{13}{16}$", adjust the planer so that the first cut will be $\frac{1}{8}$". Then the second cut should be $\frac{1}{16}$".

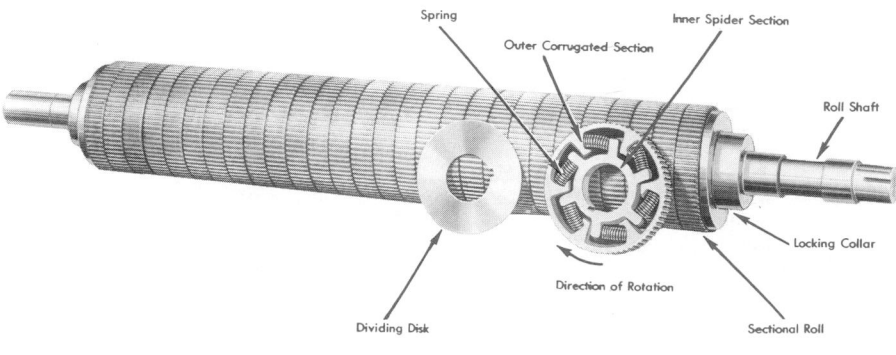

20-17. *Upper infeed roll.*

20-19. *Surfacing stock that has been glued up.*

5. Turn on the power and allow the planer to come to full speed. To avoid injury from kickback, stand to one side, *never directly behind the stock.* Feed the stock into the infeed rolls and, as soon as it takes hold, remove your hands from the stock. Never let your fingers get under the edges.

6. If the wood starts into the machine slightly crooked, a tap on the edge will straighten it. If the stock sticks, turn off the machine immediately and lower the bed.

7. If large amounts of stock must be removed, always take some off both faces. If this is not done, the board will tend to *cup* because it has slightly more moisture toward the center than it does at the outside.

8. When stock has been glued up to make a larger surface, it is impossible to true or face it on the jointer. To do it on the planer, first remove all the glue from the surface. Then adjust the machine to a slow feed and a light cut. Fig. 20-19. Place the best face on the bed of the planer and true one side. Then reverse the stock, readjust for thickness, and plane.

Squaring Up Stock

A common use for the planer is to square up stock for stair balusters and other finish work. When the stock has been rough cut to size, joint two adjacent sides on the jointer. Mark number 1 on the end grain of the working face and number 2 on the working edge. To square up the stock and reduce it to correct size, adjust the machine to about 1⁄16" over finish size. Place the working face against the bed and the working edge to the right, and feed all pieces through the machine. Return all stock to the front of the machine and place it on the bed in the original position. Then turn each piece a quarter turn to the right and repeat the surfacing. Adjust the machine for the second cut and surface the stock to the final size.

Planing Thin Stock

If very thin stock must be planed, it is a good idea to use a backing board. This is true for all stock 3⁄8" or less in thickness. Make sure that the backing board is true, smooth, and at least 3⁄4" thick.

20-20. *A jointer/planer uses one motor to drive both cutterheads.*

COMBINATION MACHINES

There are machines available that combine the job of a planer and a jointer into one machine. Fig. 20-20. These machines are called jointer/planers. There is a separate cutterhead for the jointer portion of the machine and the planer portion, but both cutterheads are driven by one motor.

Some builders find that a jointer/planer offers a good compromise between portability and versatility. Also, such machines can cost less than two separate machines.

PORTABLE ELECTRIC PLANE

The following are general safety rules. We strongly advise you to check the manufacturer's manual for any special safety instructions.

➤ Be sure that the blades are sharp. Dull blades result in a poor cut that can be difficult to control.

➤ The workpiece should not be allowed to move or vibrate. Secure it with clamps. Doors should be placed in a door buck or otherwise secured.

➤ Make adjustments to the plane only when the cord has been disconnected from a power source.

➤ Use two hands to guide the plane. Stand in such as way that you can guide the tool over the stock to be cut with an uninterrupted motion.

➤ Do not put an electric plane down until the motor has come to a complete stop.

➤ Wear suitable protection for your eyes and ears.

Sometimes called a power plane, this tool greatly reduces the time and labor involved in planing by

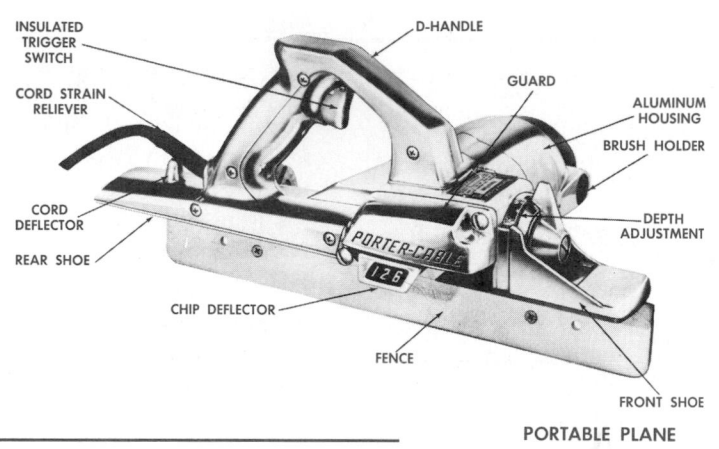

20-21. *Parts of a portable electric plane.*

20-22. *The arrow on the motor housing of this electric plane indicates the direction in which the cutterhead turns.*

20-23. *Using a portable electric plane to surface the edge of a door.*

hand. It is particularly useful for installing and trimming doors and paneling because it will make a smooth, accurate cut. It can also be used to straighten lumber or trim siding.

Parts of an Electric Plane

The electric plane is a portable tool. A cylindrical cutterhead similar to the one in a planer or a jointer is the actual cutting device. It is mounted above the fence and protected by a housing. Fig. 20-21. The cutterhead of many electric planes is fitted with three straight blades. Some cutterheads, however, have curved blades mounted in a spiral configuration. These are more difficult to sharpen than straight blades, but they make a very smooth cut. In both cases, the cutterhead revolves towards the front of the tool. Fig. 20-22.

The cutter must be set at zero before setting for depth of cut.

Move the depth adjustment lever (located at the front of the plane) to the zero position and turn the plane over. To the left of the handle and directly behind the motor bracket is a cutter-adjusting lever. Turn this lever toward the rear of the plane and lay a straightedge across the cutter so that it rests on both the front and rear shoes. Turn the cutter by hand until it lifts the straightedge. Then adjust the lever until the tip of the cutting edge just touches the straightedge when it (the straightedge) rests evenly on both shoes. Now the desired depth of cut can be set by rotating the depth-adjustment lever.

To use, place the plane on the work, with the front shoe and fence held firmly against it. Fig. 20-23. Turn on the power. Then apply steady, even pressure as you do the planing. Never overload or push the plane too hard. When working on thick plywood or hardwoods, do not attempt to cut as fast as for softer woods. The plane can also be set for outside bevel cuts from zero to 45 degrees. In planing the edges of plywood, there is danger of breaking out the cross-grain plies at a corner. The best way to prevent this is to clamp a piece of scrap wood at the end of the plywood before the cut is made. As you near the edge, move the plane very slowly.

1. What function do rotary cutters on a jointer perform?

2. How is the size of a jointer indicated?

3. How is the depth of cut adjusted on a jointer?

4. What happens if the outfeed table of a jointer is too low?

5. What happens if the outfeed table of a jointer is too high?

6. List five safety rules for operating a jointer.

7. What three factors should be considered in adjusting for depth of cut?

8. When should a push block be used?

9. Indicate the most common use for a jointer.

10. Describe the proper procedure for cutting a deep rabbet on the jointer.

11. List three safety rules for operating a planer.

12. Where is the cutterhead mounted on a planer?

13. When using a planer, how much stock should be removed on each pass?

14. Name three uses for a portable electric plane.

ACTIVITIES

1. Math. The jointer removes wood from the stock and turns it into shavings (waste). What percentage is wasted with each pass over the jointer?

a. In each of the following calculate the percentage of the wood removed if the jointer cuts $\frac{1}{16}$" from one face of the stock.
  i.   1" by 6" by 8",
  ii. 1" by 4" by 10',
  iii. 1" by 8" by 16',
  iv. 2" by 6" by 8',
  v.   2" by 4" by 10'.

b. From your answers in **a**, predict what percentage of the wood is removed if the stock is 1" by 12" by 16' or 2" by 10" by 20'.

2. Social Studies. A jointer is one of many machines used by skilled carpenters. Figure 20-2 shows the parts of a jointer. Those parts are standardized. If they need to be replaced, you need to replace only a specific part and not the entire machine. Research the concept of standardized parts. Who was responsible for applying it in industry? Relate the concept of standardized parts to assembly line production.

THE SCHOOL-TO-WORK CONNECTION

A shop planer is typically a large, stationary tool that is used to surface rough stock prior to subsequent woodworking operations. Lighter weight planers, such as the one in Fig. 20-16c, are more likely to be found on a construction jobsite. These portable units can't surface stock that's as wide or as thick as stock commonly put through a shop planer. Portable planers are better suited to working with the type of lumber typically used at the later stages of a construction project, particularly 1x and 2x softwoods.

1. The chief advantage of a portable planer over larger units is that it can be easily brought to the jobsite and moved from place to place. This portability has one disadvantage, however. A portable planer does not come with a cabinet that lifts the controls and table to a convenient height. Design a simple stand for a portable planer that will support it at a convenient height. For this exercise, assume that you will have to build the stand on site using common construction tools and materials. The stand must be strong enough to support the portable planer. It must be stable enough so that you can feed lumber through the planer without tipping the unit over. In addition, the stand must hold the planer securely, yet you should be able to disengage the two when it comes time to move to another jobsite. Explain your design with a rough sketch. Be sure to include the basic dimensions of height, width, and depth.

21

Plate Joiners

SAFETY

These are general safety rules. We strongly advise that you also refer to the manufacturer's manual.

➤ Most workers are unfamiliar with the use of a plate joiner. Several practice cuts should be made on scrap stock to familiarize the user with the operation of the tool.

➤ A plate joiner ejects dust and chips at a high rate of speed. Keep your face away from the dust ejection chute. Wear safety glasses at all times.

➤ Never cut a slot in a small piece of wood that is hand-held.

➤ Most plate joiners are noisy. Wear ear protection.

➤ Failure to retract the blade fully after a cut may allow it to contact the workpiece prematurely during the next cut. This is likely to cause kickback.

➤ Clamp any workpiece that is likely to move during the cut.

➤ Keep hands away from the blade area when making plunge cuts.

➤ Chips and dust ejected from the machine may cause a slipping hazard. Consider connecting the machine to a dustbag or a vacuum system.

➤ Do not disable the antikickback points on the faceplate of the plate joiner. Make sure the points engage the workpiece.

➤ Unplug the power cord when changing blades or performing routine maintenance on the tool.

➤ Be sure that the blades are sharp. Sharp blades improve the cutting action and minimize the possibilities for kickback.

➤ Check the operation of the guard base before using the tool. It should close smoothly over the blade.

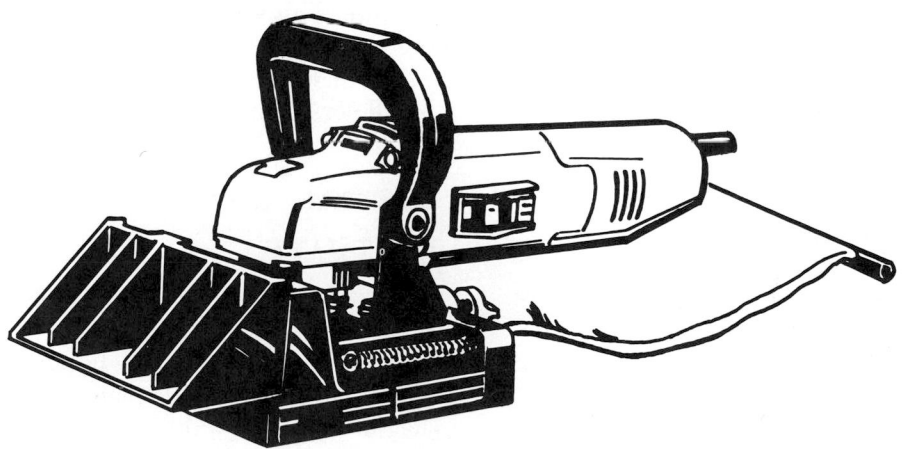

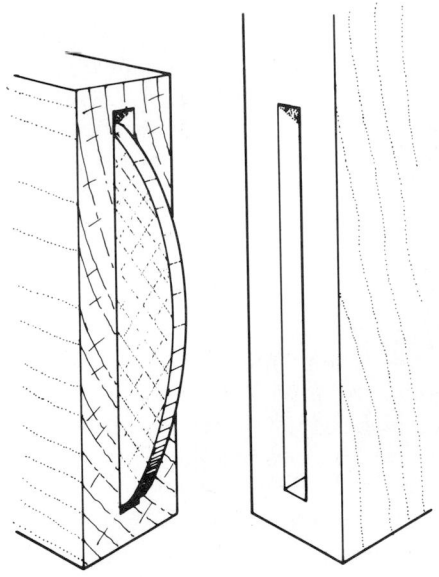

21-1. *A plate joint ready to be assembled.*

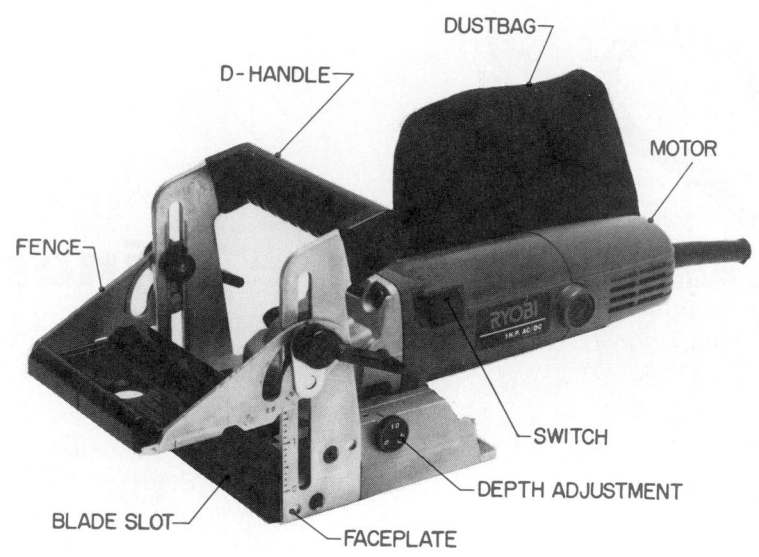

21-2. *Parts of a plate joiner.*

A *plate joiner* is a portable power tool that cuts crescent-shaped grooves in the edge of wood stock. Small wood splines, called "plates" or "biscuits," are then glued into the grooves. Fig. 21-1. The stock can then be joined with other stock in which matching grooves have been cut. The biscuits strengthen the joint and help to register the pieces accurately. Plate joiners are commonly found in woodworking shops. Trim carpenters, however, are beginning to use the tool for such tasks as assembling casing and joining shelves to site-built cabinetry. The tool can also be used for such things as butt-joining custom wood flooring that is not end-matched.

PARTS

The basic plate joiner weighs between 6 lbs. and 8 lbs. and has a 4-amp or 5-amp motor. Fig. 21-2. The motor is connected to the arbor or a 4" diameter blade by way of gears or by a flexible, toothed

belt. At the front of the tool is a metal faceplate. Small metal antikickback pins or rubber pads on the lower portion of the faceplate help to keep the tool from sliding as the blade is plunged into the workpiece. An adjustable fence is used to position the joiner against the workpiece. The typical fence moves up and down, but some joiners have fences that can be angled as well. Fig. 21-3.

The depth of cut on some joiners may be controlled with a small adjusting knob at the side of the tool. This knob sets the cut for the three different sizes of biscuits. The joiner most often has a D-handle or T-handle grip.

BISCUITS

Plate joinery calls for the use of small, football-shaped wood plates. The plates are die-cut from beech blanks. The grain of the plate runs diagonally to the width of the plate. This helps the plate to resist shear stresses across the completed

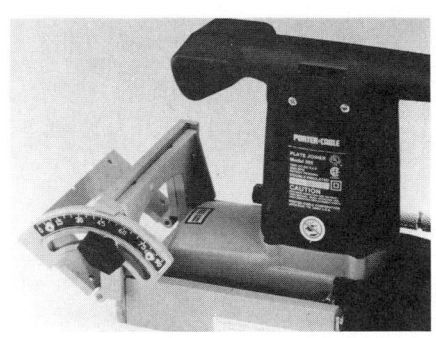

21-3a. *The adjustable fence of this plate joiner is set up to make a cut in angled stock.*

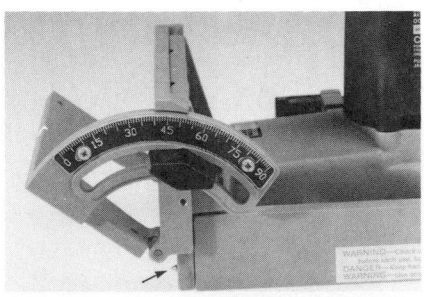

21-3b. *Detail of the plate joiner shown in Fig. 21-3a. Note the anti-kickback pin at the bottom of the faceplate.*

joint. The plates are compressed during manufacture. When a plate is placed in a glued joint, it absorbs moisture from the glue and expands slightly. This makes it fit the joint tightly as the glue dries. White glue or carpenter's glue may be used.

Plates come in three standard sizes:
➤ Number 0 (approximately ⅝" wide by 1¾" long).
➤ Number 10 (approximately ¾" wide by 2⅛" long).
➤ Number 20 (approximately 1" wide by 2½" long).

Plates are most often used to join solid wood and composition-wood panels. However, plastic plates are available for joining synthetic countertop materials such as Corian®. Because plastic plates do not absorb moisture from adhesives, they will not expand within the joint. Plastic plates are used primarily to speed assembly and to help the joint resist shear.

BASIC PROCEDURES

The procedure for cutting plate joints is similar no matter what the application. As an example, assume that two 1" × 6" boards must be edge-joined to create shelf stock for a built-in cabinet. Place the boards edge to edge. Then mark small lines across the joint with a pencil. The lines should be 8" to 10" on center.

Adjust the joiner's depth of cut for the size of plate you are using. Then adjust the joiner's fence to center the cut in the thickness of the board. Clamp one board at a time to a workbench or set of sawhorses. Press the faceplate of the joiner against the stock, using a centerline marker on the tool to align it with the layout lines on the board. Turn the joiner on and push it towards the board. This will plunge the blade into the stock.

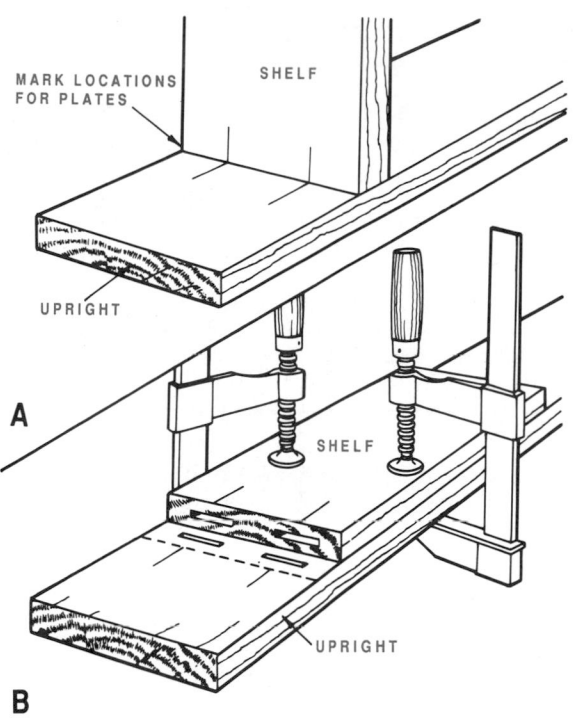

21-4. *Joining shelves to uprights.*

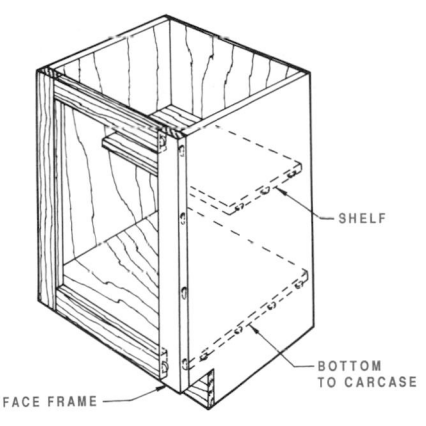

21-5. *Plate joints in cabinetry.*

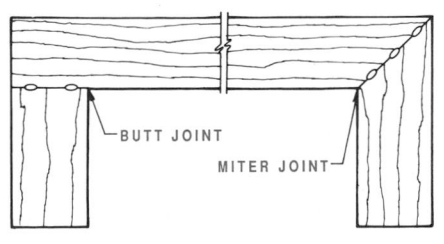

21-6. *Plate joints in closet shelving.*

After the cut is complete, pull the joiner away from the stock and line it up with the next layout mark. Continue to make cuts in this manner. After turning off the tool, clamp the second board in place and make those cuts.

To assemble the boards, use glue to lightly coat the inside of each cut in one board, then insert the plates. Apply additional glue to the exposed portions of the plates and the edges of the boards, then press the boards together and clamp them.

To plate-join a shelving unit, mark the plate locations on the ends of each shelf and on the uprights. Fig. 21-4. The shelf can then be clamped to the upright to serve as a fence to guide the joiner. When the grooves have been cut, glue and assemble the unit.

Other common plate joint applications are shown in Figs. 21-5, 21-6, and 21-7.

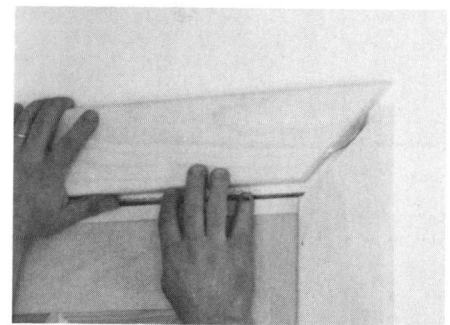

21-7. *Plate joints can also be used for joining baseboards and casing.*

1. What may happen if the blade of the plate joiner is not fully retracted after each cut?

2. What wood is used in the making of joiner plates?

3. Plates for biscuit joinery come in three sizes. What are they?

4. Name several applications for plate joinery in residential construction.

1. Language Arts. As discussed, the plate joiner allows two pieces of wood stock to be joined along the edge. In your view, would a plate shaped like a triangle or a rectangle lend as much strength as a plate shaped like a circle or an ellipse?

THE SCHOOL-TO-WORK CONNECTION

The plate joiner is yet another power tool that was first used by shop woodworkers. Like the router, it is showing up more often on construction jobsites, particularly when the project calls for high-quality finish work. Many carpenters and builders, however, are not familiar with the plate joiner. They may have seen advertisements for one in trade magazines, or they may have noticed the tool in the catalog of a power tool manufacturer.

There is a good chance, however, that they have not used the tool. One way in which someone becomes acquainted with a new tool is by seeing someone else use it. Another way is by asking questions of someone who is familiar with the tool.

1. Imagine that you are the owner of a small construction company. One of the carpenters who works for you thinks a plate joiner might be a useful tool to have on site, but doesn't know much about the tool. You have never used a plate joiner, either, but you decide to investigate. Write down a list of questions that you would like to ask about the tool. Then try to locate someone who has used the tool on a construction jobsite. Start by asking friends and classmates. You might also contact a store that sells plate joiners to ask if they can refer you to a builder who has purchased the tool. Who else can you ask? Once you find someone who has used the plate joiner, interview them by phone. See if they can answer your questions.

2. Assume that you've decided to buy a plate joiner. Find at least three retail sources for this tool. Compare prices. If you only expected to use the tool once in a while, which tool would you purchase? Write a brief explanation of your decision.

22

Scaffolds and Ladders

SCAFFOLDS

A *scaffold* is a temporary or movable platform to stand on when working at a height above the floor or ground. The scaffold must also support the weight of the worker's tools and materials. Scaffolds make it possible to work safely, in a comfortable and convenient position, with both hands free.

Scaffolding is of two general types:
➤ Wood scaffolding, constructed on the job.
➤ Manufactured scaffolding.

Wood Scaffolding

The *Occupational Safety and Health Administration (OSHA)* is the federal agency that develops regulations regarding safe construction techniques. OSHA has determined that job site scaffolding is one of the leading causes of accidents in the construction industry. It is important, then, that scaffolding be set up properly. This is particularly important for wood scaffolding built on the job site. Such scaffolding is not usually tested for strength before use.

A fall from any height can lead to serious injury or death. If you ever doubt the safety of wood scaffolding, do not use it.

When constructing wood scaffolding, select clear straight lumber for maximum strength. Fig. 22-1. Use adequate bracing and nail securely using a duplex head nail. Fig. 22-2. These nails can be driven in tightly and still be easily pulled when dismantling.

The horizontal wood pieces on which you stand are called scaffolding planks. To ensure that they will not snap beneath you, extra care must be taken in choosing these planks. Plank material should span relatively short distances. It should be free of knots, splits, and other imperfections. Because of their predictable performance and extra strength, laminated wood planks made specifically for scaffolding are used by some builders. Other builders use aluminum planks. Either type of plank is better than lumber planking.

Manufactured Scaffolding

Manufactured scaffolding is designed to be readily assembled or dismantled. Figs. 22-3 and 22-4. The scaffold planks may be set at various heights for comfort and safety. For interior use, casters are installed for easy movement. The end frames may be assembled in a staggered position, making it possible to work off a stairway. Fig. 22-5. Where additional height is necessary, the units may be stacked.

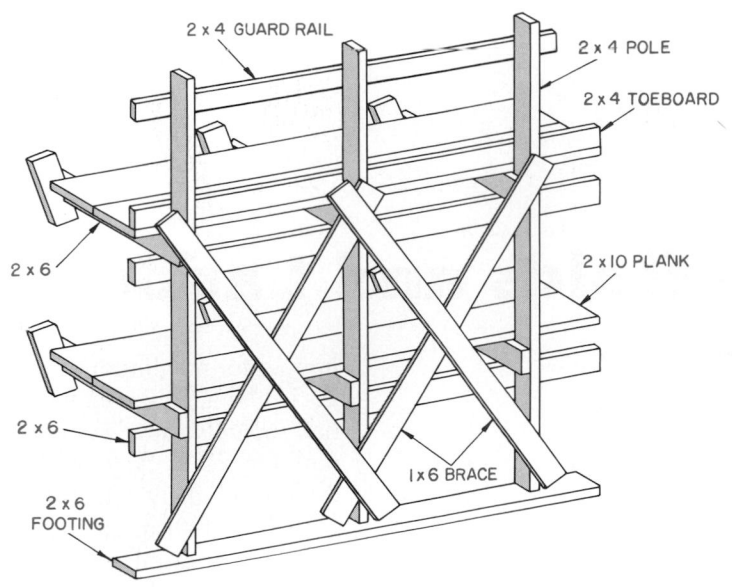

22-1. *A scaffold must be safe. Use adequate supports and bracing. Note the blocks at the large arrows. These blocks are attached to the building. They are notched to receive the 2" x 6" boards.*

22-2. *A duplex head nail.*

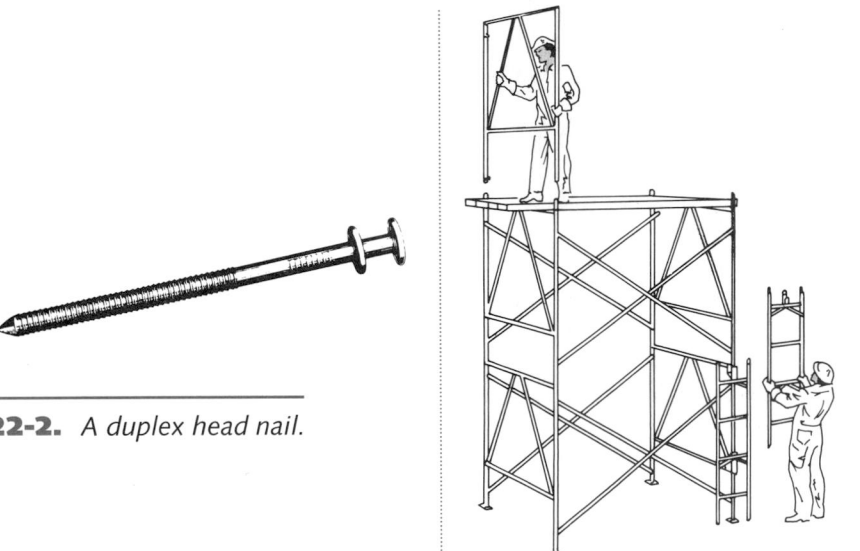

22-4. *Assembling manufactured scaffolding. Note that the ladder is a part of the unit.*

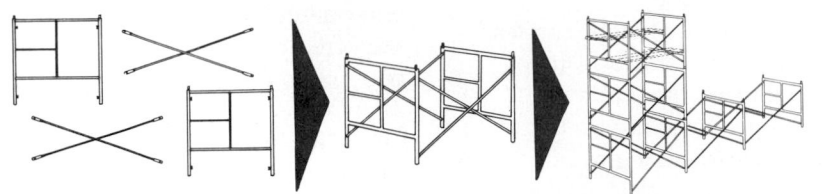

22-3. *Manufactured scaffolding components may be assembled in a variety of sizes and shapes, depending on the job requirements.*

SCAFFOLDING SAFETY

The following are general safety rules. *We strongly advise you to check the manufacturer's manual for any special safety instructions.*

➤ All scaffolding should be plumb and level. Use adjusting screws, not blocks, to adjust to uneven grading conditions.

➤ Adequate support should be provided. Use base plates, making sure that they rest firmly on the ground.

➤ All braces should be fastened securely.

➤ Cross braces should never be climbed. Access to scaffolds should be by stairs or fixed ladders only.

➤ Wall scaffolds should be securely anchored.

➤ Free-standing scaffold towers must be secured by guying (attaching guy ropes or wires) or other means.

➤ Proper guard rails should be provided. Add toe boards when required on planked or staged areas.

➤ Ladders or makeshift equipment should never be used on top of the scaffold.

➤ A scaffold should never be overloaded. Inspect the scaffolding assembly regularly.

➤ Lumber used for scaffold planks must be properly inspected and graded for that purpose. Both ends of planks must be cleated to prevent planks from sliding off supports. If planking is to be continuous, it should have at least a 12" overlap, and should extend at least 6" beyond the center of the support. Also do not extend the plank too far beyond the supports because such planks tend to be unstable.

➤ Whenever necessary for stability, planks should be nailed or clamped to the scaffold.

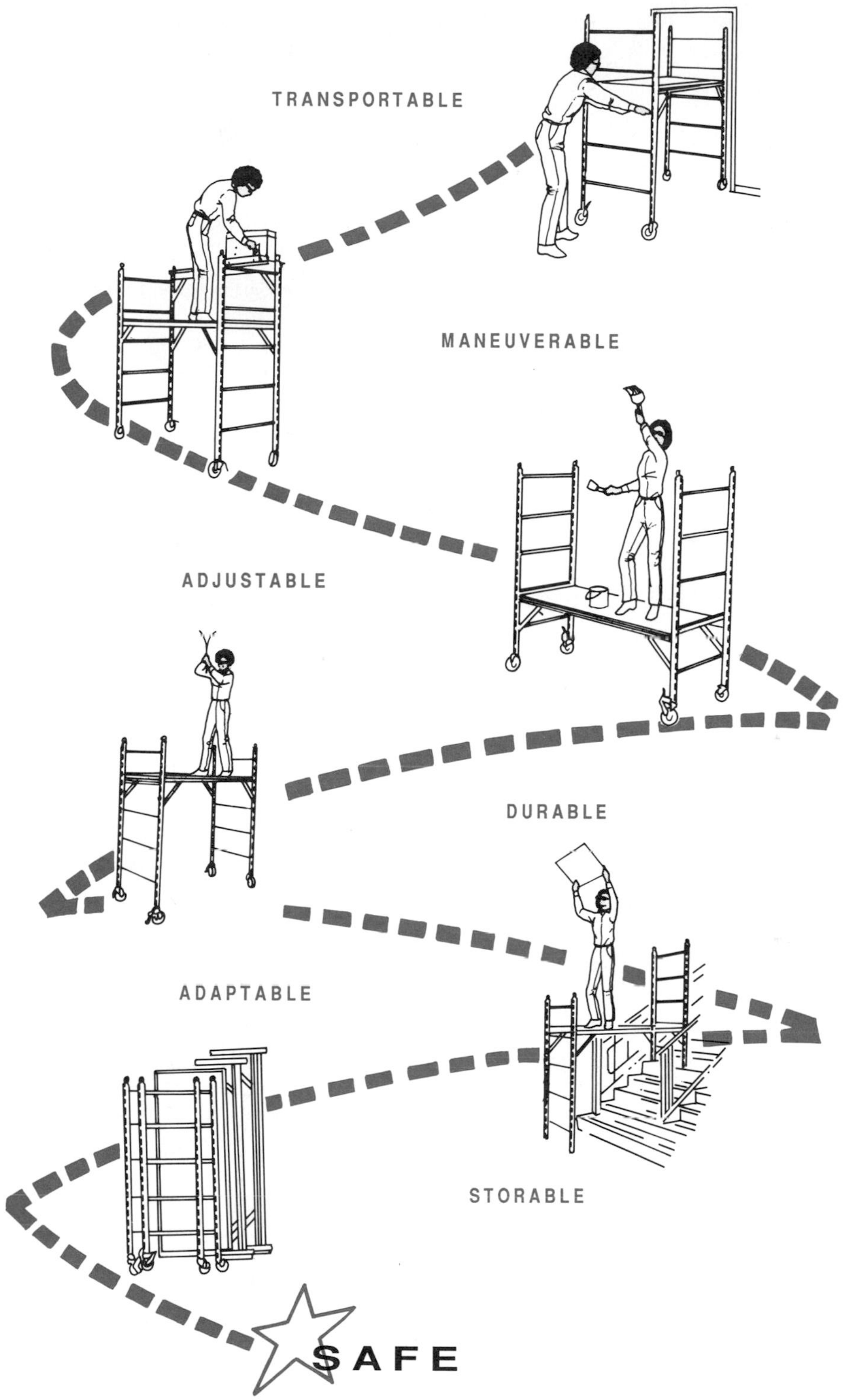

TRANSPORTABLE

MANEUVERABLE

ADJUSTABLE

DURABLE

ADAPTABLE

STORABLE

★SAFE

22-5. *Manufactured scaffolding is versatile equipment.*

BRACKETS, JACKS, AND TRESTLES

Brackets

Scaffold planks may be supported by special brackets which are available for sidewall and roof installations. There are various styles of *sidewall* and *corner brackets*. Some are nailed to the studs while others are bolted or hooked directly around the studding. Fig. 22-6. The nail-attached wall and corner brackets are secured to the wall with 20d nails driven at an angle into the wall stud through the tapered holes in the bracket.

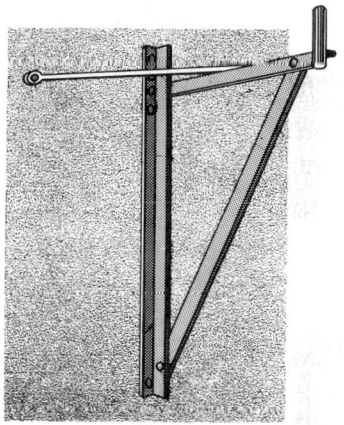

22-6a. *A nail-attached wall scaffold bracket.*

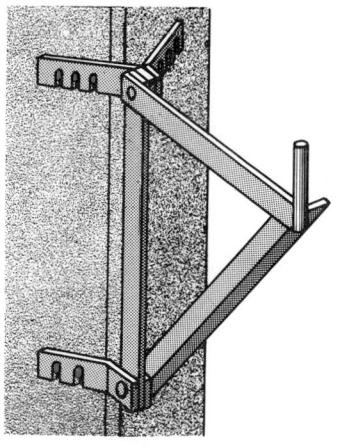

22-6b. *A nail-attached corner scaffold bracket.*

22-6c. *A studding bracket. The scaffold plank support on this bracket hooks around a stud (see the insert).*

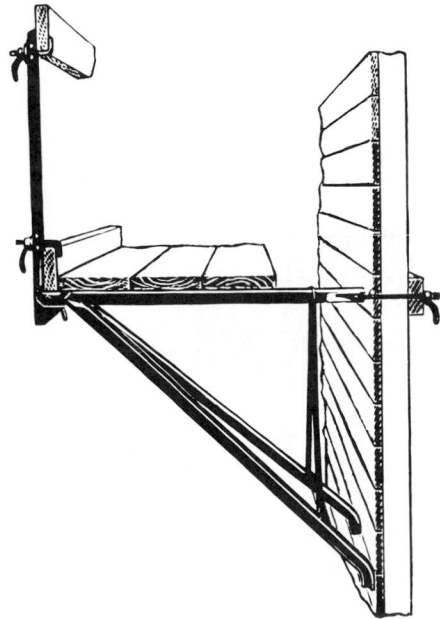

22-6d. *Bolt-attached brackets. Note the guard rail used with this bracket. This rail can also be used with other types of brackets.*

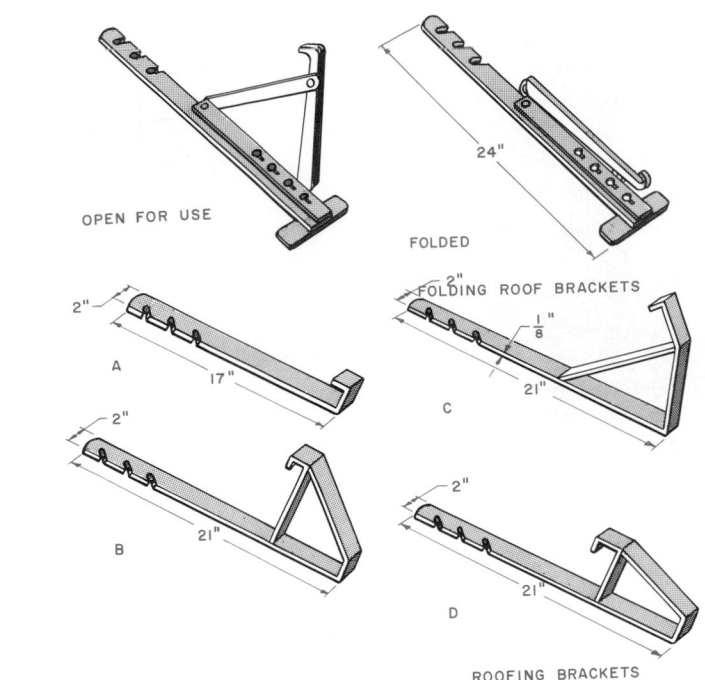

22-7a. *Roofing brackets. The folding roof bracket adjusts to various roof pitches, from 90 degrees to level walkways. It is ideal for use on steep roofs and will handle planks as large as 2" x 10". A. This roofing bracket holds a 2" x 4" or 2" x 6" flat against the roof. B. This bracket supports a 2" x 6" at a right angle to the roof. C. This bracket positions a 2" x 6" so that it provides a level walkway. D. This bracket supports a 2" x 4" at a right angle to the roof.*

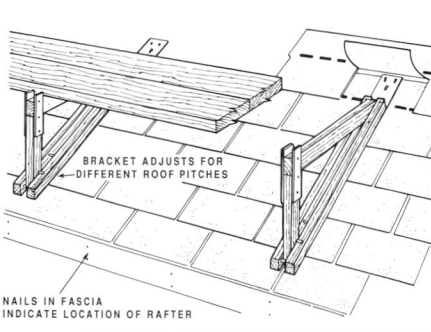

22-7b. *Roof brackets should be nailed through the roof and into the rafters.*

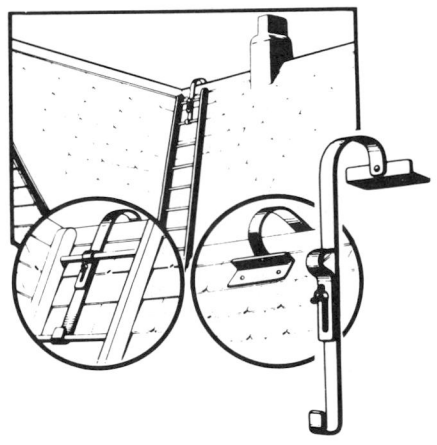

22-7c. *A ladder hook is used to support a ladder for use on a very steep roof.*

The brackets may be easily removed without pulling the nails. Any nails remaining after brackets are removed are driven flush.

Many styles of *roofing brackets* are available for various applications. Roofing brackets are attached with nails through the roof sheathing and into the rafters. They can be removed without pulling the nails. When they are removed, the nails are driven flush with the roof, and the shingles cover the nails that had held the bracket in place. One style holds a 2" × 4" or 2" × 6" flat against the roof. Others will hold the 2" × 4" or 2" × 6" on edge at right angles to the roof. A third type positions a 2" × 6" so that it provides a level walkway on a roof. Fig. 22-7.

Ladder Jacks

A *ladder jack* is a device for hanging a scaffold plank from a ladder. A jack can be used over or under any ladder that has rungs rather than steps. It has two hooks at the top and two at the bottom which fit close to the ladder siderails, preventing excessive loads on the ladder rungs. The ladder jack adjusts to the pitch of the ladder and can be hooked over the rungs with one hand. Fig. 22-8. The scaffold plank is then placed onto the horizontal projection to provide a convenient work platform so you do not have to move the ladder frequently. Fig. 22-9.

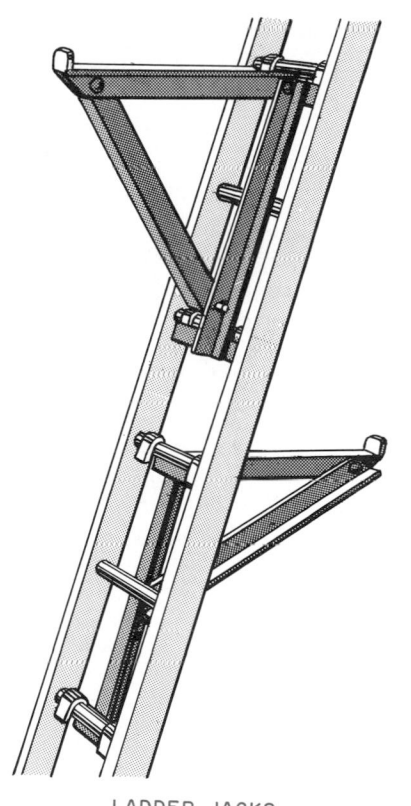

LADDER JACKS

22-8. *Ladder jacks may be used over or under any ladder with rungs.*

22-9. *A ladder jack mounted under the ladder with a scaffold plank in place.*

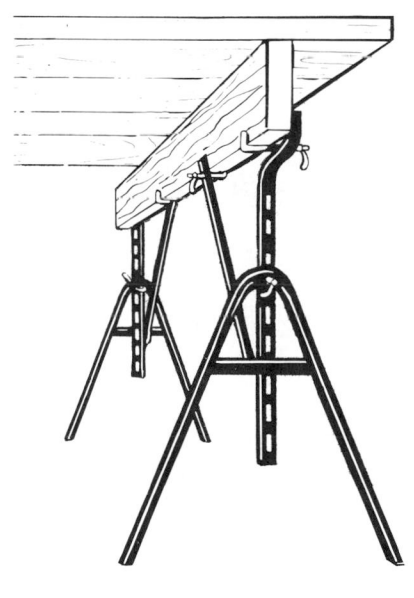

22-10. *Trestles used to support scaffolding.*

Trestles

A *trestle* consists of two jacks as shown in Fig. 22-10. Trestles are available in a wide range of sizes, from 16" to 12', each with height adjustments at approximately 3" intervals. Timber is used as a *ledger* (a stationary support) between the jacks to support the scaffold. This type of scaffold is sometimes used by plasterers and gypsum dry-wall applicators for working on ceilings. The scaffolding is set up over the entire floor area, on trestles about 18" to 20" high. The workers then can work continuously without stopping to take the scaffolding apart, move it, and set it up again.

Pump Jacks

Pump jacks are commonly used to gain access to the sidewalls of a house during siding or painting operations. *Pump jacks* are metal devices that slide up and down along vertical posts made from doubled 2 × 4s. The pump jacks carry horizontal planks that support the worker. They have foot pedals that allow the worker to "pump" each jack upwards along the posts. To reverse the direction, the worker turns a hand crank on each jack, which gradually lowers the assembly. Fig. 22-11.

Each post must rest on a wood pad that provides solid support (a short length of 2 × 8, for example). It must also be anchored to the house at least every 10 ft. by metal stand-offs nailed into the underlying studs. The posts should be made from solid, knot-free lumber. The pieces should be nailed securely to each other. The poles should be no more than 30 ft. high.

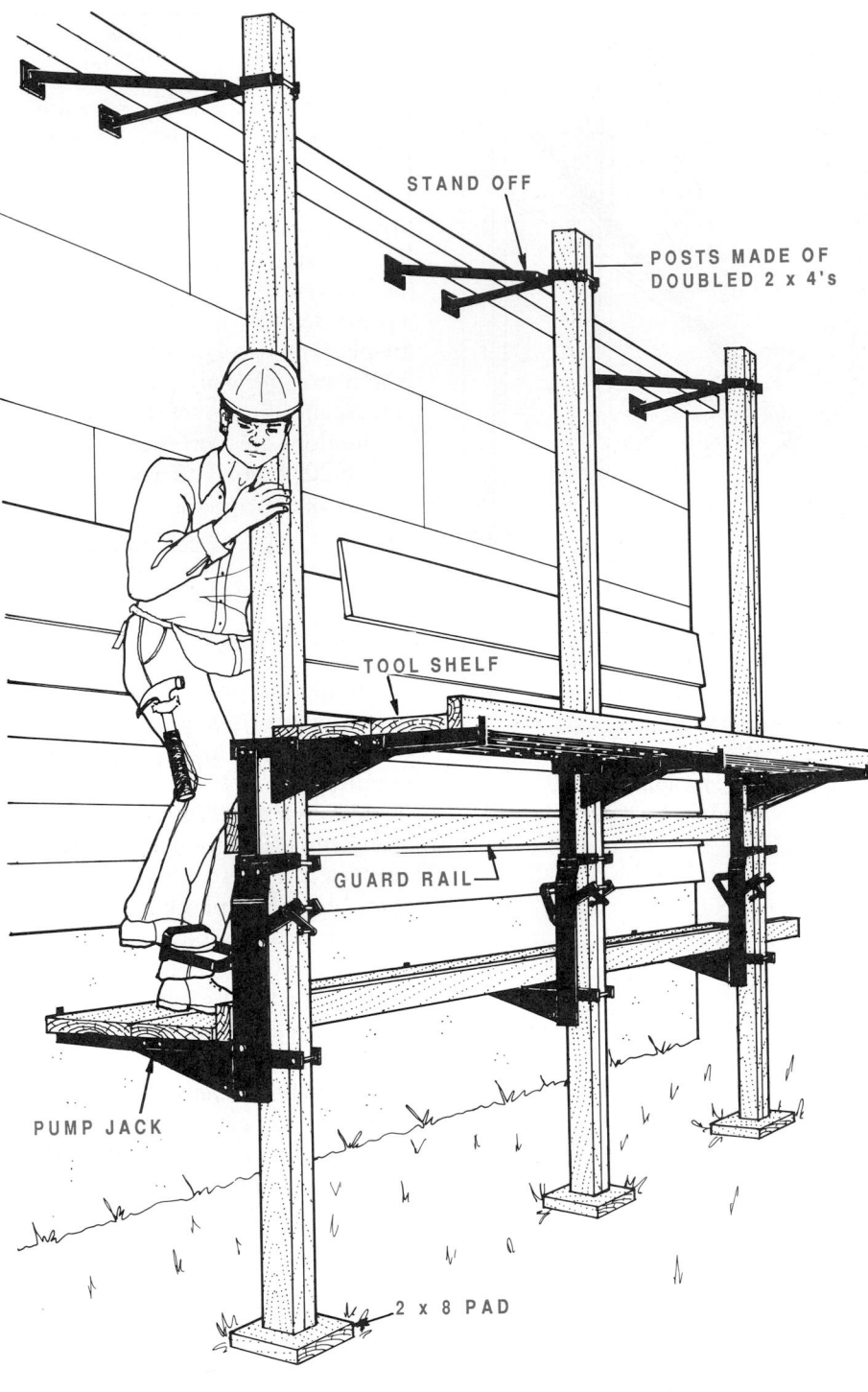

STAND OFF

POSTS MADE OF
DOUBLED 2 x 4's

TOOL SHELF

GUARD RAIL

PUMP JACK

2 x 8 PAD

22-11. *Pump jacks can be raised or lowered to any height along the sidewall of a house.*

LADDERS

Carpenters often must use ladders for high work. Ladders are usually made of wood, aluminum, or fiberglass, and they come in many sizes. Commonly they are made in lengths from 3' to 50', with special three-section ladders available for reaching greater distances. Table 22-A.

There are three basic types of ladders (Fig. 22-12):
- Folding (stepladder).
- Straight.
- Extension.

To set up a straight or extension ladder, place the lower end against a base so it cannot slide. Then grasp a rung at the upper end with both hands. Raise the top end and walk forward under the ladder, moving your hands to grasp other rungs as you proceed. Fig. 22-13. When the ladder is erect, lean it forward to the desired position. Check the angle, height, and stability at top and bottom. Fig. 22-14.

When using a stepladder, always be certain that the four legs are firmly supported and that the spreaders are straight and level. Never stand on the top step of the

Table 22-A. *Determining the Correct Ladder Length for Safe Working Conditions.*

If Vertical Height	Minimum Working Length
12 ft.	16 ft.
14 ft.	18 ft.
16 ft.	20 ft.
20 ft.	24 ft.
24 ft.	28 ft.
28 ft.	32 ft.
32 ft.	36 ft.
34 ft.	40 ft.
38 ft.	44 ft.
44 ft.	50 ft.

For heights of 50' and over, three-section ladders are available. Table measurements allow for overlap required in two-section ladders.

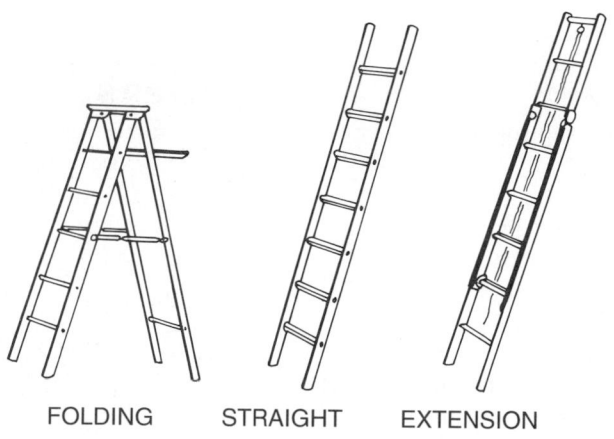

22-12. *The three types of ladders: folding, straight, and extension.*

FOLDING   STRAIGHT   EXTENSION

22-13. *To raise an extension ladder, walk forward under the ladder as shown, moving the hands to grasp other rungs as you proceed.*

ladder. The ledge on the back of the ladder is for holding tools and materials. Do not use it as a step.

When working from a ladder, set it where the work can be reached with ease. Never lean out far to one side. Relocate the ladders as necessary so the work area can be reached without much leaning.

When going up or down, grip the ladder firmly and place your feet squarely on the rungs. Make certain your shoes and the rungs are free of mud and grease. While working, it is recommended that

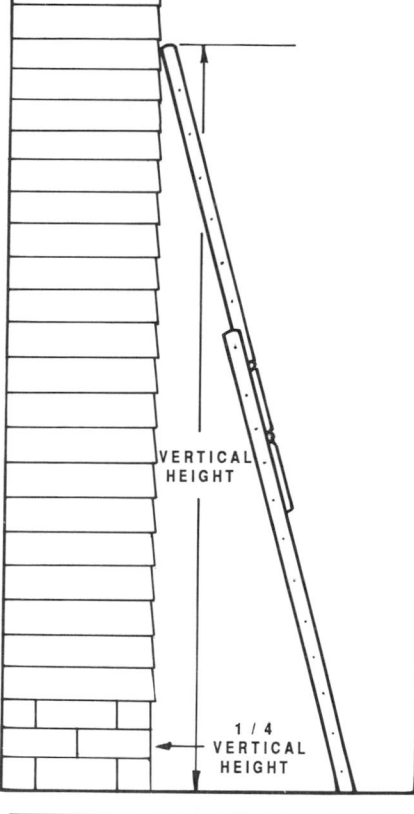

22-14. *For safety on a ladder, the pitch or angle should be such that the horizontal distance at the bottom is one-fourth the working length of the ladder.*

VERTICAL HEIGHT

1/4 VERTICAL HEIGHT

one leg be wrapped around a rung. When using a ladder for access to a roof, the ladder should extend above the edge of the roof by at least 3'. Fig. 22-15.

22-15. *The top of the ladder should extend above the edge of the roof at least three feet.*

LADDER SAFETY

In using any ladders or scaffolding, it is extremely important to follow all safety rules. Be sure to read and follow the safety rules presented in this unit. *Read and follow also the instructions in any literature that accompanies the ladder or scaffolding. Such literature may include special safety instructions.*

➤ Inspect ladders carefully. Keep nuts, bolts, and other fastenings tight. Lubricate moving metal parts frequently. Do not allow makeshift repairs. Never straighten or use a bent metal ladder.

➤ Ladders must stand on a firm, level surface. Always use safety feet with non-slip bases.

➤ Face the ladder when climbing up or down.

➤ Always place the ladder close enough to the work to avoid dangerous overreaching.

➤ Keep your weight centered between both side rails.

➤ Keep steps and rungs free of oil, grease, paint, or other slippery substances.

➤ Be sure that stepladders are fully open and the spreader straight.

➤ Never stand or climb on the top, pail rest, or rear rungs of a stepladder.

➤ Never place ladders in front of doors or openings unless appropriate precautions are taken.

➤ Always insure that the working length of the ladder will reach the support height required. It should extend at least 3' above a roof or other elevated platform. Never stand on the top three rungs.

➤ To keep a ladder from shifting, lash or tie it as close to the upper (top) support point as you can.

➤ Position the ladder so the horizontal distance of the ladder foot from the top support is one-fourth the working length of the ladder (75 degree angle). (*Working length* is the distance from the ground to the top support.) Always make sure that both side rails are fully supported top and bottom.

➤ Read and follow manufacturer's instructions when using an extension ladder. Most extension ladders have the extension section on the front, but some ladders have the extension on the rear of the base section.

➤ Make sure all locking devices are secure.

➤ Overlap extension-ladder sections by the following amounts: 3' for total extended lengths up to 36'; 4' for total lengths of 36' to 48'; and 5' for total lengths of 48' to 60'.

➤ Be sure all locks on extension ladders are securely hooked over rungs before climbing.

➤ Adjust the height of an extension ladder only when standing at the base of the ladder.

➤ Metal and water conduct electricity. *Do not use metal, metal-reinforced, or wet ladders where direct contact with a live power source is possible.* Provide for temporary insulation of any exposed electrical conductors near the place of work.

➤ A ladder is intended to carry only one person at a time. Do not overload.

➤ Never use ladders in a horizontal position.

➤ Store ladders in dry, cool, ventilated places. Fig. 22-16.

➤ Never use ladders after prolonged immersion in water or exposure to fire, chemicals, or fumes that could affect their strength.

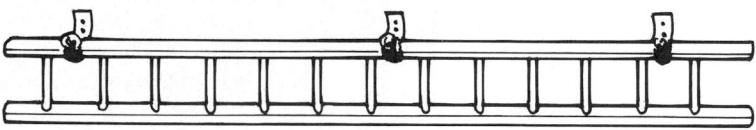

22-16. *A ladder should be stored horizontally on supports to prevent sagging. Never store ladders exposed to weather or near heat.*

QUESTIONS

1. What is a scaffold?

2. What are the two types of scaffolds?

3. What is a duplex head nail?

4. List several kinds of scaffold brackets.

5. What is a ladder jack?

6. List the three basic types of ladders.

7. Describe the method of setting up an extension ladder.

8. At what angle should an extension ladder be set against a building?

9. How much should the sections of an extension ladder overlap when working at a height of 39'?

10. What is a pump jack?

ACTIVITIES

1. Language Arts. Explain how scaffolding was used on the Statue of Liberty when it was renovated several years ago. How old is this historical landmark and from whom or what nation did the United States acquire this magnificent art piece? How much scaffolding was used and what renovations had to be made?

2. Language Arts. The triangle occurs in many of the devices noted in this unit. Why?

3. Science. With a friend, make a triangle and a rectangle from pieces of scrap lumber or cardboard by fastening the ends together with one nail or paper fastener. Test for strength. What characteristics does the triangle have that the rectangle does not have and vice versa?

IV Foundations

23

Locating the House on the Building Site

Most city building regulations require that a plot plan be a part of the house plans, to show the location of the building on the lot. Before the exact location of the house is determined, check local codes for minimum setback and sideyard requirements. The location of the house is usually affected by such codes. Sometimes the setback is established in accordance with existing houses on neighboring property.

After the site is cleared, the location of the outer walls of the house is marked out. Usually the surveyor will mark the corners of the lot after making a survey of the plot of land. Sometimes the surveyor will also be asked to do a rough marking of the corners of the building.

There are two basic ways of accurately determining the location of the proposed building on the property:

➤ By measuring from an established reference line.

➤ By using an instrument such as a level or a transit.

LAYING OUT FROM A REFERENCE LINE

Sometimes a building or excavation may be planned to parallel an identifiable line, such as a street or property line. Such a line can then be used as a guide or *reference point*. This makes it possible to stake out the site without using a transit level or an optical level. When working in this way, it is best to make a drawing of the property before attempting to stake out the site itself. Figure 23-1 shows such a drawing. In that illustration, rectangle ABCD represents the property lines, and boundary AB is the identifiable line. Refer to the drawing as you study the following paragraphs. The letters in the following paragraphs refer to points and lines on the drawing. They will help you to understand the actual operation of staking out the site. To stake out, proceed as follows:

1. Check the plot plan to find the setback distance. Along boundaries AC and BD measure this distance back from front line AB. The setback is shown by segments AO and BO.

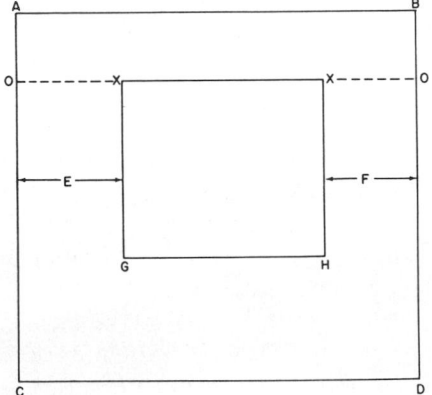

23-1. *Staking out a rectangular building without the use of an optical or transit level.*

2. Stretch a line tightly between the points marked O. This line shows where the front of the building will be.

3. On line OO, locate the front corners of the building. There are two ways to do this. You can obtain the measurement from the plot plan to see how far the corners will be from the side boundaries. Then along line OO measure in the indicated distances from AC and BD. Or, if the building is to be centered between the side boundaries, you need not refer to the plot plan. Instead, subtract the length of the building from the length of OO, then measure in half this distance from each end of OO. (An X represents each front corner of the building on Fig. 23-1.) Measure the distance between the two points marked X and check this distance with the plans. The distance XX represents the length of the building and it must be accurate.

4. Check the plans to learn the depth of the project (how far back it will extend from the front corners). Mark off the depth by extending lines back from the two points marked X. If the boundary lines of the lot form a 90 degree angle at the corners, these lines should be parallel to AC and BD. Note that E is the same as OX, and F the same as XO. Thus E and F show the distance between sides of the building and the side boundary lines of the lot. Points G and H are used to represent the rear corners of the building.

If the boundary lines of the lot are not at right angles to each other, make certain that when the building is located on the site the minimum front and sideyard requirements are established at the building's closest point to the boundary line. Under these circumstances the building lines will probably not be parallel to the boundary lines of the lot. Therefore it will be necessary to establish the corner of the building which will be closest to the boundary line and then lay out the building from this point by using the method described on page 217, "Laying Out a Right Angle." Also see "Laying Out a Simple Rectangle" on page 218.

5. Establish a line to indicate the rear of the building. (This is shown by GH on the drawing.)

6. If the building is not rectangular, divide it into smaller rectangles. Then follow the steps just given to find the front, back, and sides of each smaller rectangle. In other words, more lines such as OO will have to be established to indicate the front of each rectangular area of the building. You can get the necessary information from the plans. Then Steps 3, 4, and 5 are carried out for each rectangle. The result will be a group of adjoining rectangles which will show the total outline of the building.

23-2. *A level, or optical level, also called a builder's level or a dumpy level.*

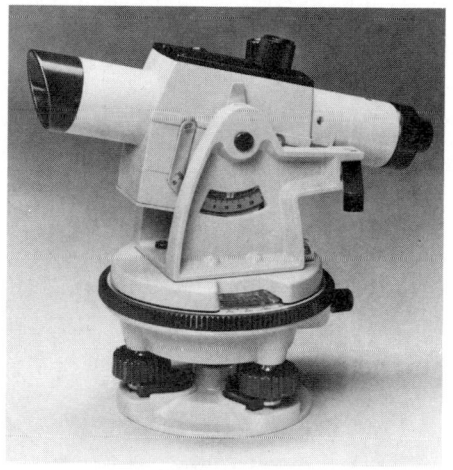

23-3. *A transit level.*

LAYING OUT WITH A TRANSIT OR LEVEL

The Instruments

Two basic kinds of levels can be used to lay out a building site or check portions of the construction for level.

➤ The *level*, or optical level, sometimes called the dumpy level or builder's level. Fig. 23-2.

➤ The *transit level*, often called simply a transit. Fig. 23-3.

Both types of levels sit atop a tripod. Fig. 23-4. The basic difference between a level and a transit is that the telescope of the level is fixed in a horizontal position. It can be used only for measuring horizontal angles

23-4. *Using a transit level.*

because it cannot be tilted up and down. The telescope of the transit can be moved up and down as well as sideways. Because of this, a transit can do everything a level can do. It can also measure vertical angles and determine if a wall is plumb.

One type of level, called a *laser level*, transmits an invisible, infrared reference plane across a job site. Fig. 23-5a, b. A single crew member can set up the laser level. He or she can then move to another portion of the site and determine level by holding an electronic detector against a leveling rod. When the detector senses the reference plane, it signals the crew member with a light or with an audible tone.

One type of transit, called an electronic transit, reads angles electronically and displays them on an LCD screen. It is used when extremely accurate measurements are required. Fig. 23-6a. A device called an electronic field book can be attached to such a transit to store information. Fig. 23-6b.

Most of the basic layout procedures described on the following pages can be carried out with either a level, a transit, a laser level, or an electronic transit.

23-6b. *This surveyor is entering information into an electronic transit.*

Reference Points

To lay out a building by means of a transit or a level you must have a basic starting point. This point is usually called the *bench mark*. It is a reference point from which measurements can be made.

In built-up areas the surveyors will often have provided a bench mark. It may appear as a mark, or point, on the foundation of a nearby building. More often it is a stone marker in the ground at a designated location. Sometimes the level of a nearby sidewalk, street, or curbing is used as the bench mark.

The bench mark may appear on the architect's drawings. If so, the plans will usually be oriented to that point.

Another key reference point is the *grade line*, which will be discussed later.

Setting Up a Level

Figure 23-7 shows a typical location for setting up a transit or level in relation to a building site. The point over which the level is directly centered (point A in the

23-5a. *A laser level allows measurements to be taken by one person.*

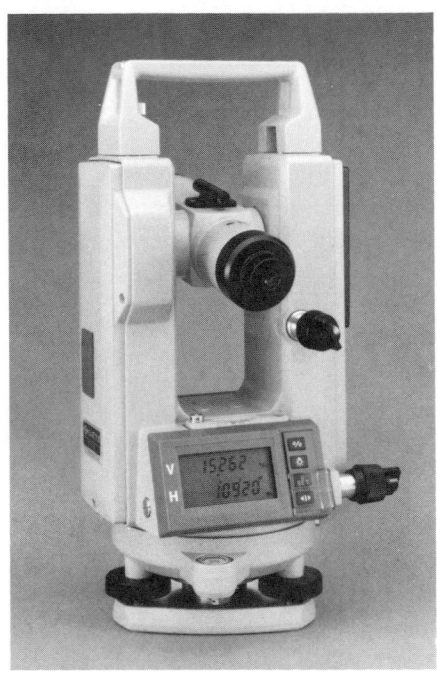

23-6a. *An electronic transit.*

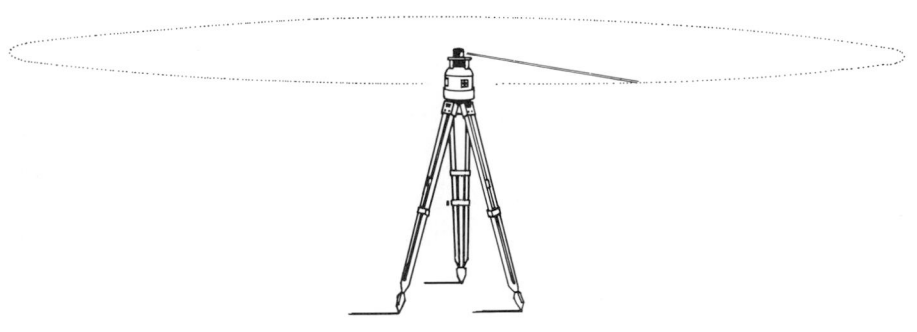

23-5b. *A laser level projects a horizontal reference plane across the job site.*

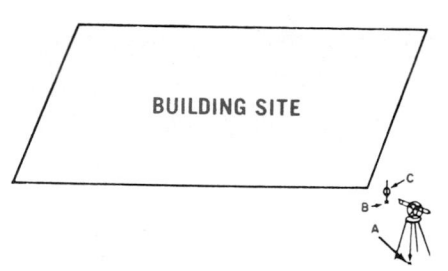

BUILDING SITE

23-7. *Laying out a building site with a transit level or optical level.*

drawing) is called the *station mark*. This is the point from which the layout is to be sighted (or shot). It may be a bench mark or a corner of the lot. In Fig. 23-7 point B is the bench mark.

Set up the level where the area of the plot can be conveniently sighted. (If the bench mark and the station mark are not the same, you should also be able to sight the bench mark conveniently.) Under the head of the level there is a hook. A plumb bob suspended from the hook is used to center the level directly over the station mark. Adjust the tripod so that it rests firmly on the ground, with the sighting tube at eye level.

To level the head of the instrument, loosen the horizontal clamp screw (Fig. 23-8, arrow 1)

and turn the telescope until the bubble (arrow 2) is in line with two opposite leveling screws (arrow 3). Grip the screws with the thumb and forefinger of each hand. Loosen one screw as you tighten the other the same amount. Do this by moving your thumbs toward or away from each other. Keep the screws snug on the foot plate. Do not overtighten them. Continue to adjust the screws until the bubble is centered. Then rotate the telescope 90 degrees so that it is over the other two leveling screws and repeat the previously described leveling procedures. Return the telescope to the first position. Check the bubble, and readjust if necessary. Recheck the second position. Continue to alternately check the bubble between the two positions until the bubble is within one graduation on either side of center in the bubble tube.

Once the level is properly set up, *be careful not to move or jar the tripod.*

Establishing Points on a Line

For this operation you must use a transit level. With a plumb bob, level the instrument and center it accurately over a point on the line.

Sight the telescope on the most distant visible known point of that line. Lock the horizontal motion clamp screw to keep the telescope on line. Then adjust the tangent screw to place the vertical cross hair exactly on the distant point. Now, by tipping the telescope in the vertical plane (up or down), you can determine the exact location of any number of stakes on that same line. Fig. 23-9.

Laying Out a Right Angle

Using a plumb bob, set up an optical level or a transit level directly over the line at the point where the right angle is to be. This is shown as point A in Fig. 23-10. Sight a reference point on that line and set the 360 degree scale at zero. (B is the reference point in Fig. 23-10.) Turn the telescope until the scale indicates that an arc of 90 degrees has been completed. Establish a leveling rod (Fig. 23-11a, b) in position along this line of sight at the desired distance. (D in Fig. 23-10 indicates this distance.) A line from the rod to the point from which the sighting was taken will be perpendicular to the base

23-8. *Operating a level. The parts used to adjust the level are: (1) the horizontal clamp screw, (2) the bubble, and (3) the leveling screws.*

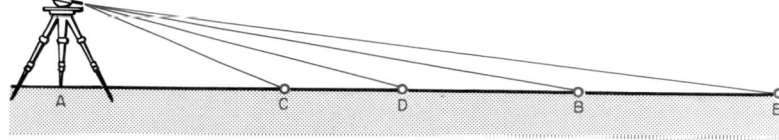

23-9. *Establishing points on a line with a transit.*

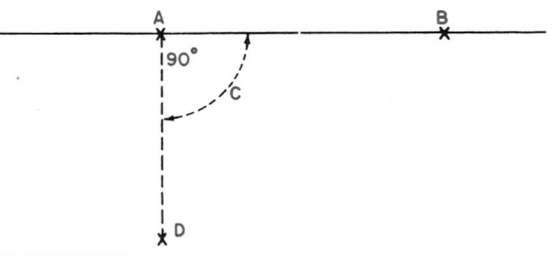

23-10. *Laying out a right angle with a transit or a level.*

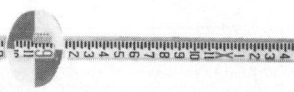

23-11a. *A leveling rod with target. Note that the rod is divided into feet, inches, and eighths of an inch.*

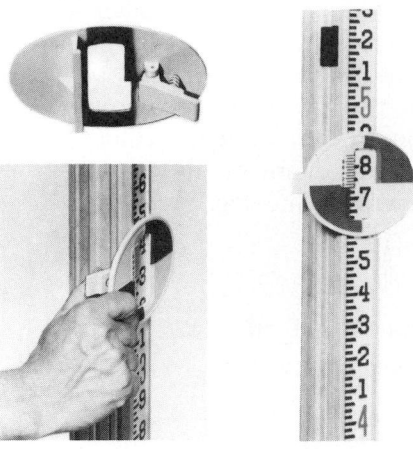

23-11b. *The target on the leveling rod can be moved up or down by releasing the clamp on the back of the target. Shown here is an engineer's leveling rod. It is divided into whole feet, tenths, and hundredths of a foot.*

line. Thus a right angle will be formed where the lines intersect. (This would be at point A of Fig. 23-10.)

Staking Out the Building

When the location and alignment of a building have been determined, a rectangle comprising the exterior dimensions of the structure is staked out. If the building is to be a simple rectangular structure, the staked-out area will follow the exact exterior of the foundation line. (Layout of an irregular building is discussed later.)

Laying Out a Simple Rectangle

To perform this operation you work from an established line such as a road or street line, a property line, or other reference line. This line is shown as AB in Fig. 23-12. Locate the point which represents the lateral (side) limit for a front corner of the project (C in Fig. 23-12).

Still referring to Fig. 23-12, set up the optical or transit level at point C. Sight point E, turn the telescope 90 degrees, and establish point D, a front corner of the project. Then move the instrument and set it up at point E. This should be a greater distance along line AB from point C than the intended length of the project. Set a stake at F by sighting C and turning the telescope 90 degrees. Point F should be the same distance from AB as D. The distance between points C and D will be equal to the distance between points E and F.

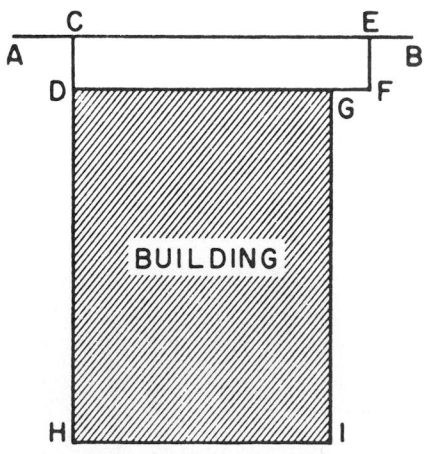

23-12. *Laying out a regular square or rectangle building with an optical level or a transit level.*

The front line of the building is established by marking off the length of the project (DG) along line DF. The two front corners of the building are located at D and G. (This is assuming that the building is to be parallel to the established line, such as a road or property line. If it is not, check the architect's plans or the plot plan for the correct setback and establish the two front corners of the building accordingly.)

Now return the instrument to point C and set it up. Sight point E, then swing the instrument 90 degrees and sight along this position to establish H, a rear corner of the building.

Now move the instrument and set up at G; sight D and swing the sight tube 90 degrees and identify I, the other rear corner of the building.

To prove the work (that is, check its accuracy) measure distance IH. If IH is equal to DG, the work is correct; if not, the work must be repeated.

Laying Out an Irregularly Shaped Building

Where the outline of the building is other than a rectangle, the procedure in establishing each point is the same as described for laying out a simple rectangle. However, more points have to be located, and the final proving of the work is more likely to reveal a small error. When the building is not to be regular in shape, it is usually best first to lay out a large rectangle which will comprise the entire building or the greater part

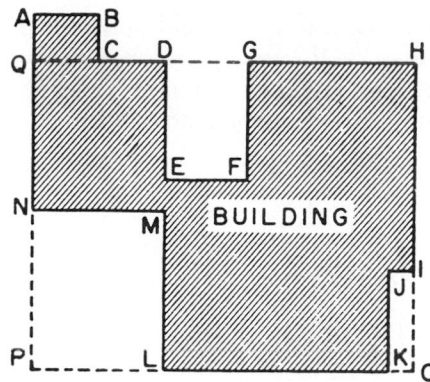

23-13. *Laying out an irregular building made up of a series of squares and rectangles with an optical level or a transit level.*

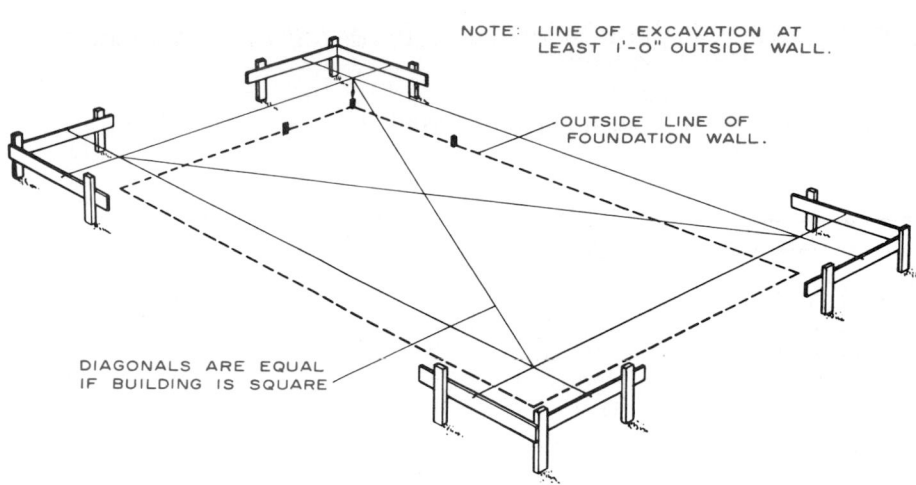

NOTE: LINE OF EXCAVATION AT LEAST 1'-0" OUTSIDE WALL.

OUTSIDE LINE OF FOUNDATION WALL.

DIAGONALS ARE EQUAL IF BUILDING IS SQUARE

23-14. *Using batter boards to establish the outline and height of the foundation wall. The top edge of the batter board represents the heights of the foundation wall.*

of it. This is shown in Fig. 23-13 as HOPQ. Having once established this accurately, the remaining portion of the layout will consist of small rectangles, each of which can be laid out and proved separately. These rectangles are shown as LMNP, ABCQ, DEFG, and IJKO in Fig. 23-13.

Batter Boards

The next step, after the corners of the house have been established, is to determine lines and grades as aids in keeping the work level and true. *Batter boards* are horizontal boards fastened to small posts and placed near where the corners of the building will be located. Use of these boards is one method of locating and marking the outline of the building. Fig. 23-14. The height of the boards is sometimes established to conform to the height of the foundation wall.

To set up batter boards, the first step is to locate the corners of the building precisely by one of the methods previously discussed in this unit. Nails are driven into the tops of the stakes to indicate the outside line of the foundation walls. To be certain that the corners are square, measure the diagonals of the completed layout

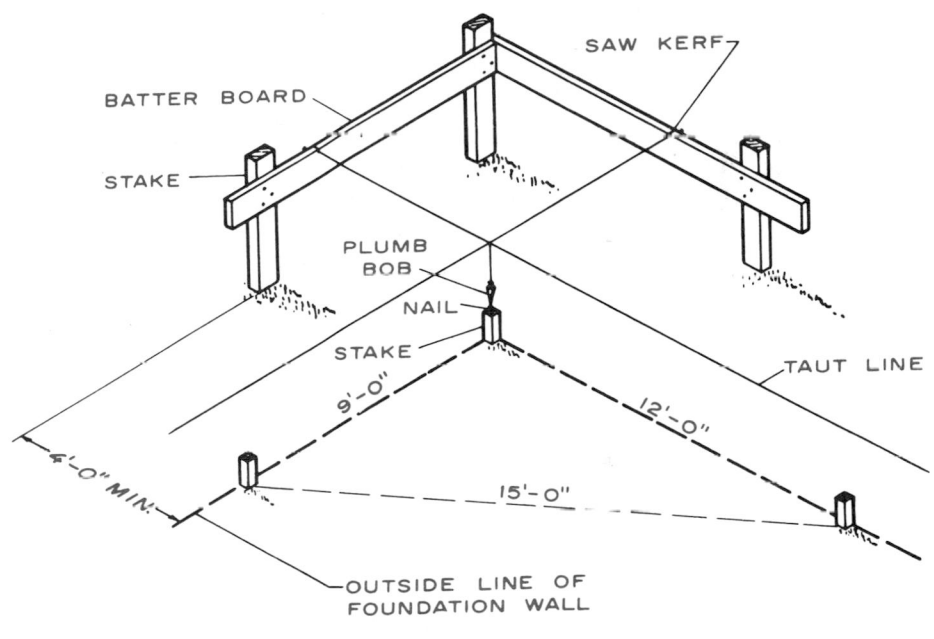

SAW KERF

BATTER BOARD

STAKE

PLUMB BOB

NAIL

STAKE

9'-0"

12'-0"

4'-0" MIN.

15'-0"

TAUT LINE

OUTSIDE LINE OF FOUNDATION WALL

23-15. *Checking the corners of the house layout to make certain they are square, using the 3-4-5 system. In this drawing, a multiple of 3, 4, 5 was used—9, 12, and 15—which is three units of each: 3 x 3 = 9, 3 x 4 = 12, and 3 x 5 = 15.*

to see if they are the same length. The corners can also be squared by using the *3-4-5 system.* This is done by measuring along one side a distance in 3' units such as 6, 9, 12, and along the adjoining side the same number of 4' units (8, 12, and 16). The diagonals will then measure the equal of 5' units (10, 15, and 20)

when the unit is square. Thus a 9' distance on one side and a 12' distance on the other should result in a 15' diagonal measurement for a true 90 degree corner. Fig. 23-15.

The batter boards are set up after the corners have been located. Three 2" x 4" or larger stakes of suitable length are driven at each location 4' (minimum) beyond the lines of the foundation; then 1" × 6" or 1" × 8" boards are nailed horizontally so the tops are all level and are all the same distance from the grade line. Next, twine or stout string (carpenter chalkline) is held across the tops of opposite boards at two corners and adjusted so it will be exactly over the nails in the corner stakes at either end. A plumb bob is handy for setting the lines. Saw kerfs at the outside edge are cut where the lines touch the boards so that they may be replaced if broken or disturbed. After similar cuts are located in all eight batter boards, the lines of the house will be established. Check the diagonals again to make sure the corners are square. The area for an L-shaped building, for example, can be divided into rectangles, treating each separately or as an extension of one or more sides.

Grade Line

Another important reference point from which measurements are made is the grade line. This is found on the architect's plan and refers to the level of the ground where it will touch the foundation of the completed building. The grade line must be established accurately because it is used for making important measurements. From the grade line you can find the depth of the excavation and also establish certain elevations such as floor and foundation levels.

Sometimes the bench mark is used as a reference point for establishing the grade line. At other times this line may be located in relation to the level of an existing street, sidewalk, or curbing. The grade line is indicated on a stake driven into the ground outside the excavation area.

Establishing Elevations

Check the architect's plan to see which elevations are to be determined. Set up and level the instrument as previously described. Be certain that the locations of the elevations can be seen through the telescope. Place a leveling rod (sometimes called a measuring rod) upright on any point to be checked. Then sight through the telescope at the leveling rod. Take a reading by means of the horizontal cross hair in the telescope. Then move the rod to the second point to be established. Raise or lower the rod until the reading is the same as for the first point. The bottom of the rod is then at the same elevation as the original point.

In accurate work a spirit level (carpenter's level) may be attached to the leveling rod to check if the rod is being held plumb. The rod can also be kept plumb by aligning it with the vertical cross hair in the telescope. The person at the telescope can tell the rod holder which way to move the top of the rod. An assistant should hold the leveling rod, and should move the target on the rod up or down until the crossline on the target comes in line with the cross hair sights in the sighting tube.

Measuring Difference in Elevation

To learn the difference in elevation between two points, such as A and B in Fig. 23-16, set up and level either a transit level or an optical level at an intermediate point. With the measuring rod held on point A, note the reading where the horizontal cross hair in the telescope crosses the graduation marks on the rod. Then with the rod held on point B, sight on the rod and note where the horizontal cross hair cuts the graduations on the rod. The difference between the reading at A (5') and the reading at B (5'6") is the difference in elevation between A and B. Thus the ground at point B is 6" *lower* than the ground at point A.

Sometimes it is not possible to sight two points from a single point between them. A high mound can

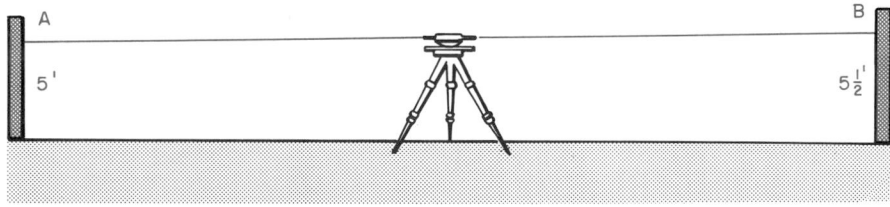

23-16. *Obtaining the difference in elevation between two points that are visible from an intermediate point.*

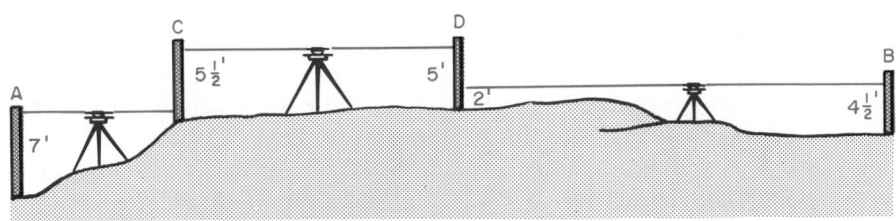

23-17. *Obtaining the difference in elevation between two points not visible from a single intermediate point.*

cause this difficulty. To solve this problem, one or more additional intermediate points (such as C and D) must be used for setting up the instrument, as shown in Fig. 23-17.

HEIGHT OF FOUNDATION WALLS

The proposed height of the foundation walls above grade determines the depth of the excavation. The excavation is dug to a depth which will give the foundation walls the correct height above grade. To determine this depth it is common practice to use the highest elevation on the perimeter of the excavation as the reference point. Fig. 23-18. This is true for graded and ungraded sites. This method will insure good drainage if sufficient foundation height is allowed for the sloping of the finish grade. Fig. 23-19. (When the grading is completed, the level of the ground is referred to as *finish grade*.) Foundation walls at least 7'4" high are desirable for full basements, and 8' walls are commonly used.

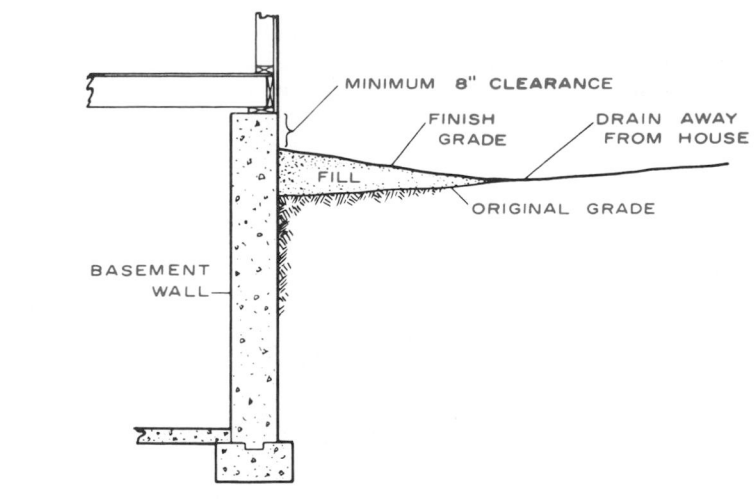

23-19. *If necessary, add fill to bring the finish grade above the original grade and insure drainage away from the house.*

Foundation walls should be extended above the finish grade around the outside of the house. This is done so that the wood finish and framing members will be adequately protected from soil moisture and will be well above the grass line. Thus, in termite-infested areas, there will be an opportunity to observe signs of termites between the soil and the wood. Protective measures can then be taken before damage develops.

The top of the foundation wall should usually be at least 8" above the finish grade at the wall line. The finish grade at the building line (perimeter of the building) will often be 4" to 12" above the original ground level. In lots sloping upward from front to rear, this increase may amount to more than 12". In very steeply sloped lots, a permanent retaining wall at the rear of the wall line is often necessary.

Enough height should be provided in crawl spaces to permit inspections for termites, and also to install soil covers. Such covers reduce the effect of ground moisture on framing members. Ordinarily there should be at least 18" between the undersides of the joists and the highest point of ground enclosed by the foundation walls.

If the interior ground level is excavated or is otherwise lower than the outside finish grade, measures must be taken to assure good drainage. Figure 23-19 shows one method of dealing with this problem. Installing a drainage system would be another possibility.

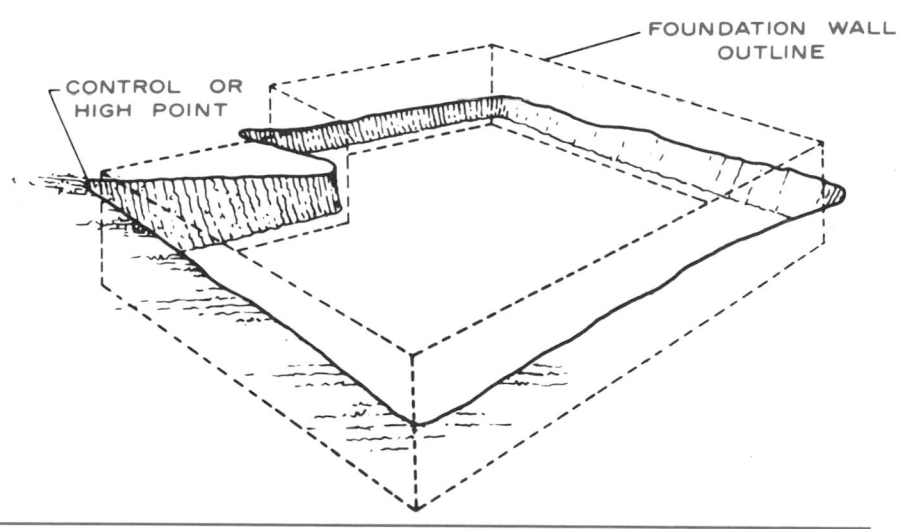

23-18. *To establish the depth of the excavation, use the highest elevation of the excavation as the control point.*

EXCAVATION

Before excavating for a new home, determine the subsoil conditions by test borings or by checking existing houses constructed near the site. A rock ledge may be encountered, requiring costly removal; or a high water table may require design changes from a full basement to crawl space or concrete slab construction. If there has been a landfill on the building site, the footings should always extend through to undisturbed soil. Any variation from standard construction practices will increase the cost of the foundation and footings. Thus it is good practice to examine the types of foundations used in neighboring houses. This might influence the design of the house you are building.

Excavation for basements may be accomplished with one of several types of earth-moving equipment. Topsoil is often stockpiled by bulldozer, grader, or front-end loader for future use. Fig. 23-20. Excavation of the basement area may be done with a front-end loader, power shovel, or similar equipment.

Power trenchers are often used in excavating for the walls of houses built on a slab or with a crawl space, if soil is stable enough to prevent caving. This eliminates the need for forming below grade when footings are not required.

It is best to excavate only to the top of the footings or the bottom of the basement floor, because some soil becomes soft upon exposure to air or water. Thus it is advisable not to make the final excavation for footings until nearly time to pour the concrete unless form boards are to be used.

Excavation must be wide enough to provide space to work. This can involve not only

23-20. A grader being used to strip the topsoil from a building site in preparation for excavating the basement.

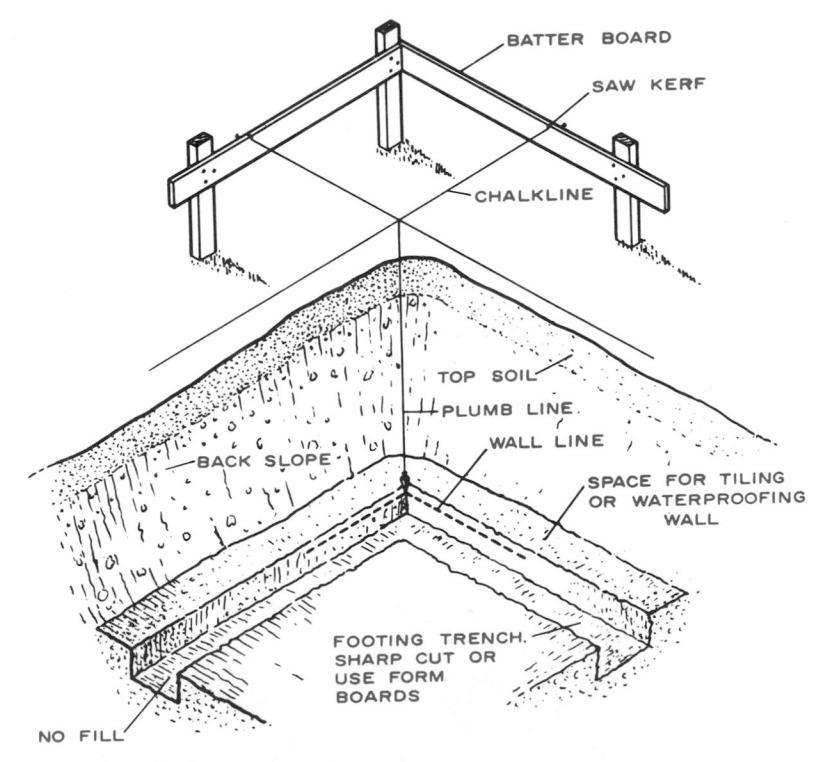

23-21. The excavation of the basement area is back-sloped to eliminate cave-ins. Note the use of the batter board and chalk line to drop the plumb line for accurately locating the foundation wall line.

constructing the walls, but possibly also waterproofing them and laying drain tile, if these operations are necessary, as in poor drainage areas. Fig. 23-21. The steepness of the back slope of the excavation is determined by the subsoil encountered. With clay or other stable soil, the back slope can be nearly vertical. When sand is encountered, an inclined slope is required to prevent cave-ins.

When excavating for basements, some contractors roughstake only the perimeter of the building for the removal of the earth. When the proper floor elevation has been reached, the footing layout is made and the earth is removed. After the concrete is poured and set, the building wall outline is established on the footings and marked for the formwork or concrete block wall.

Estimating Excavation

Excavation costs are based on the total cubic yards of earth to be removed. Using the house plan in Fig. 23-22, figure the earth to be removed for the excavation for the basement area. To determine the volume of material to be removed, multiply the length times the width times the depth. This is usually done in feet and decimals of a foot rather than in feet and inches. Table 23-A. When the length, width, and depth of the excavation are in feet, the volume will read in cubic feet.

In the example, Fig. 23-22, multiply 7' (depth of excavation) × 28' (26' width of house + 2' clearance between the excavation and the outside of the foundation wall) × 42' (40' length of house + 2' clearance). The answer is 8,232 cubic feet.

To convert this to cubic yards, divide by 27 (because there are 27 cubic feet in 1 cubic yard):

$$\frac{8,232}{27} = 304.8$$

Thus, in even numbers, approximately 305 cubic yards of

Table 23-A. *A Conversion Table of Inches to Decimal Fractions of a Foot.*

Inches	Feet
1	0.083
2	0.167
3	0.250
4	0.333
5	0.417
6	0.500
7	0.583
8	0.667
9	0.750
10	0.833
11	0.916
12	1.000

Table 23-B. *Excavation Factors. To use this table, use as an example an excavation 24' x 30' and 6' deep. 24' x 30' – 720 square feet. In the table, the 6' depth shows 0.222 cubic yards for each square foot. The total amount of the excavation is figured: 720 square feet (total area of excavation) x 0.222 (cubic yards per square foot for a 6' depth) = 159.84 cubic yards of material to be excavated. (Another example is given in the text.)*

Depth	Cubic Yards per Square Foot
2"	0.006
4"	0.012
6"	0.018
8"	0.025
10"	0.031
1'0"	0.037
1'6"	0.056
2'0"	0.074
2'6"	0.093
3'0"	0.111
3'6"	0.130
4'0"	0.148
4'6"	0.167
5'0"	0.185
5'6"	0.204
6'0"	0.222
6'6"	0.241
7'0"	0.259
7'6"	0.278
8'0"	0.298
8'6"	0.314
9'0"	0.332
9'6"	0.350
10'0"	0.369

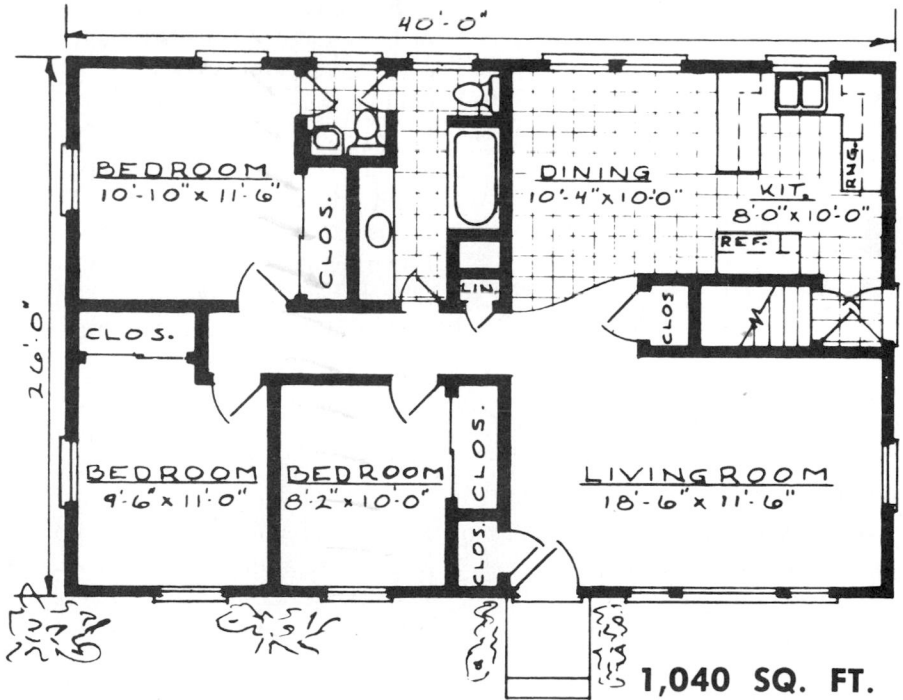

40'-0"
26'-0"

BEDROOM 10'-10" x 11'-6"
CLOS.
CLOS.
DINING 10'-4" x 10'-0"
KIT. 8'-0" x 10'-0"
RNG.
REF.
CLOS
BEDROOM 9'-6" x 11'-0"
BEDROOM 8'-2" x 10'-0"
CLOS.
CLOS.
LIVING ROOM 18'-6" x 11'-6"

1,040 SQ. FT.

23-22. *With a 7' deep excavation, the basement for this house will require the removal of 305 cubic yards of material.*

material will have to be excavated.

Table 23-B provides another way of determining the cubic yards of material to be removed. It can be used if the depth of the excavation is one of the standard ones shown on the table. Refer again to Fig. 23-22. The excavation needed for this house is 28' wide and 42' long, and is to be dug 7' deep. Multiplying the width by the length, you find that the area of the excavation is 1,176 square feet. Referring to Table 23-B you see that for an excavation 7' deep, 0.259 cubic yards of material are removed for each square foot. Thus by multiplying 1,176 by 0.259 you find that approximately 305 (actually 304.5) cubic yards of material will be removed.

Trench excavations, such as those that might be dug for utilities, can be figured by using Table 23-C. For example, if a trench is to be 42" deep and 18" wide, Table 23-C shows that 19.4 cubic yards of material will be removed for every 100 lineal feet. Such a trench might be dug for a house with a 30' setback. To determine how much material would be removed, divide 19.4 by 0.30 (since 30' is 0.30 of 100'). The answer is that 5.82 cubic yards of material would be removed.

Table 23-C. *Trench Excavations— Cubic Yard Content per 100 Lineal Feet.*

Depth in Inches	Trench Width in Inches						
	12	18	24	30	36	42	48
6	1.9	2.8	3.7	4.6	5.6	6.6	7.4
12	3.7	5.6	7.4	9.3	11.1	13.0	14.8
18	5.6	8.3	11.1	13.9	16.7	19.4	22.3
24	7.4	11.1	14.8	18.5	22.2	26.0	29.6
30	9.3	13.8	18.5	23.2	27.8	32.4	37.0
36	11.1	16.6	22.2	27.8	33.3	38.9	44.5
42	13.0	19.4	25.9	32.4	38.9	45.4	52.0
48	14.8	22.2	29.6	37.0	44.5	52.0	59.2
54	16.7	25.0	33.3	41.6	50.0	58.4	66.7
60	18.6	27.8	37.0	46.3	55.5	64.9	74.1

QUESTIONS

1. Explain how it is possible to locate a house on a site without the use of either an optical level or a transit level.

2. The level is also called an optical level. What is the difference between an optical level and a transit level?

3. What is an electronic transit?

4. Explain how a laser level works.

5. Explain briefly how to learn the difference in elevation between two points.

6. What is the procedure for laying out an irregularly shaped building?

7. Why are foundation walls extended above the finish grade around the outside of the house?

8. Why are test borings taken of the subsoil conditions before excavating for a new home?

9. Why doesn't the excavator remove the soil for the footings at the same time the soil is removed for the basement?

10. Why is the excavation for a basement somewhat larger than the outside dimensions of the foundation wall?

ACTIVITIES

1. Math. An excavation 5' deep is needed to build a house that is to be 26' by 32'.

a. How many cubic yards of material will need to be removed if a 1' clearance is needed outside the foundation walls?

b. How much more must be removed if the builder requires 2' of clearance?

2. Math. What would be the entry in the second column of Table 23-B if the depth was

a. 5'3"?

b. 10'2"?

3. Science. Obtain literature on a large piece of earthmoving equipment. This could be a crawler tractor, hydraulic backhoe, excavator, motor grader, wheel loader, or dump truck. Identify at least six examples of simple machines (lever, wheel and axle, pulley, inclined plane, screw, and wedge) used to create the large piece of complex earthmoving equipment.

4. Language Arts. Visit a site where a house is being built. Pick a construction site where the stakes have just been put up. Try to visit the site every day. For two weeks, keep a journal of what you see. Drawings of the site may be included.

Concrete and Footings

CONCRETE

One of the most important construction materials is concrete. It is a *synthetic* material—that is, it is made from other materials. Specifically, it is made by mixing cement, fine aggregate (usually sand), coarse aggregate (usually gravel or crushed stone), and water in the proper proportions. The product is not concrete unless all four of these ingredients are present. Without coarse aggregate, a mixture of cement, sand, and water is mortar or grout.

The fine and coarse aggregate in a concrete mix are called the *inert ingredients*, while cement and water are the *active ingredients*. The inert ingredients and the cement are thoroughly mixed together first. As soon as the water is added, a chemical reaction between the water and the cement begins. It is this reaction (called *hydration*) that causes the concrete to harden.

Notice the difference between hydration and dehydration. In dehydration a drying out takes place. This is not what happens when concrete hardens. In fact, concrete will harden just as well under water as in air. This shows that hydration is truly a reaction between the water and the cement, not just a drying out of the concrete. Actually, rather than drying out, concrete must be kept as moist as possible in the early stages of hydration. Drying out would cause the water content to drop below the amount needed for satisfactory hydration.

Concrete Ingredients

Concrete used for residential construction consists of portland cement, water, and fine and coarse aggregate. It is important to use good-quality ingredients.

Cement is measured by the sack. One sack of portland cement weighs 94 lbs. and is equal to 1 cu. ft. by volume. Cement should be stored in a dry place to prevent lumps from forming. Lumps that cannot be pulverized by squeezing in the hand should not be used.

The water used to mix concrete must be clean and free from oil, alkali, or acid. A good rule to follow is that the water must be suitable to drink.

Fine aggregate consists of sand or other suitable materials up to ¼" in diameter. Coarse aggregate consists of gravel, crushed stone, or other suitable material larger than ¼". All aggregates should be clear and free of loam, clay, or vegetable matter, which would reduce concrete strength.

The size of the aggregate should vary, depending on the kind of work for which the concrete is to be used. In walls, the largest pieces of aggregate should not be more than one-fifth the thickness of the finished wall section. For slabs, the aggregate should not be more than approximately one-third the thickness of the slab. The largest piece of aggregate should never be larger than three-fourths the width of the narrowest space through which the concrete will be required to pass during pouring.

Admixtures

Ingredients other than cement, water, and aggregates are sometimes added to concrete. These ingredients, called *admixtures*, change such characteristics as the workability or strength of concrete. They can be added before or during the mixing process. Here are some common admixtures.

➤ Air-entraining admixtures introduce microscopic bubbles into the concrete. These bubbles increase the durability of concrete that is exposed to moisture and frequent freeze/thaw cycles. They also improve the workability.

➤ Retarding admixtures make the concrete set up at a slower rate. This is useful in hot weather, or when it will be difficult to finish the concrete before it would normally set up.

➤ Accelerating admixtures increase the rate at which concrete gains strength. This can be important if the concrete must be put into service quickly.

➤ Water-reducing admixtures make it possible to reduce the amount of mixing water without reducing the workability of the concrete. This makes the concrete stronger.

➤ Superplasticizing admixtures generally can do one of two things. They can make the concrete flow very easily or they can significantly increase its strength.

Proportions

Strength, durability, watertightness, and wear resistance of the concrete are controlled by the amount of water per sack of cement.

A large amount of concrete is supplied by ready-mix plants, even in rural areas. Concrete in this form is normally ordered by the number of bags of cement per cubic yard of concrete, in addition to aggregate size and water-content requirements. Five-bag mix (that is, five bags per cubic yard) is considered minimum for most work; where high strength is needed or where steel reinforcement is used, six-bag mix is commonly specified.

When concrete is mixed on the job site, the quantities of cement and aggregate must be figured separately for each cubic yard of concrete. Table 24-A shows the number of bags of portland cement and the cubic feet of aggregates required to produce 1 cu. yd. (27 cu. ft.) of mixed concrete for several suggested trial mixes. Table 24-B shows the amount of water to

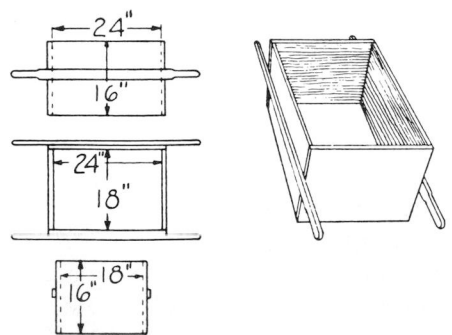

24-1. *A 4 cubic-foot measuring box used for accurate proportioning of concrete.*

Table 24-A. *Suggested Mixtures for Trial Batches and the Materials Necessary for a Cubic Yard of Concrete with Various Maximum Sizes of Aggregate.*

Proportions for Various Trial Mixes of Concrete		Cement	Aggregates	
		bags**	Fine Cu. Ft.	Coarse Cu. Ft.
With 3/4" maximum size aggregate	Mixture for 1 bag trial batch*	1	2	2¼
	Materials per cu. yd. of concrete	7¾	17 (1550 lbs.)	19.5 (1950 lbs.)
With 1" maximum size aggregate	Mixture for 1 bag trial batch	1	2¼	3
	Materials per cu. yd. of concrete	6¼	15.5 (1400 lbs.)	21 (2100 lbs.)
With 1½ " maximum size aggregate (preferred mix)	Mixture for 1 bag trial batch	1	2½	3½
	Materials per cu. yd. of concrete	6	16.5 (1500 lbs.)	23 (2300 lbs.)
With 1½" maximum size aggregate (alternate mix)	Mixture for 1 bag trial batch	1	3	4
	Materials per cu. yd. of concrete	5	16.5 (1500 lbs.)	22 (2200 lbs.)

*Mix proportions will vary slightly depending on gradation of aggregates. A 10 percent allowance for normal wastage has been included in the above figures for fine and coarse aggregate.
**One bag of cement equals 1 cu. ft.

Table 24-B. *Trial Mix Proportions for Sand of Various Moisture Contents. This table also specifies the amount of water to be added to the mix depending on the climate exposure.*

Trial Mix Proportions	Gallons of water added to 1-bag batch if sand is:				Suggested mixture for 1-bag trial batches[4]		
	Dry	Damp[1]	Wet[2]	Very Wet[3]	Cement bags (Cu. ft.)	Aggregates (Cu. ft.) Fine	Coarse
For mild exposure 1½" max. size aggregate	7	6¼	5½	4¾	1	3	4
For normal exposure 1" max. size aggregate	6	5½	5	4¼	1	2¼	3
For severe exposure 1" max. size aggregate	5	4½	4	3½	1	2	2¼

[1] "Damp" describes sand that will fall apart after being squeezed in the palm of the hand.
[2] "Wet" describes sand that will ball in the hand when squeezed but leaves no moisture on the palm.
[3] "Very wet" describes sand that has been subjected to a recent rain or recently pumped.
[4] Mix proportions will vary slightly depending on gradation of aggregates.

Table 24-C. *Water Proportions for Mixing Small Batches of Concrete. Pints of Water to Add to Mixer for Batches using ½, ¼, ⅕ and ¹⁄₁₀ Sacks of Cement.*

Size of Batch	Pints of mixing water to add			
	Very wet sand	Wet sand	Damp sand	Dry sand
5 Gal. Water Per Sack of Cement				
½ sack	14	16	18	20
¼ sack	7	8	9	10
⅕ sack (18.8 lb.)	5⅗	6⅖	7⅕	8
¹⁄₁₀ sack (9.4 lb.)	2⅘	3⅕	3⅗	4
6 Gal. Water Per Sack of Cement				
½ sack	17	20	22	24
¼ sack	8½	10	11	12
⅕ sack	6⅘	8	8⅘	9⅗
¹⁄₁₀ sack	3⅖	4	4⅖	4⅘

use in trial mixes with sand of varying moisture content.

Measuring Materials. For accurate proportioning of materials, a bottomless measuring box may be used. This device is a frame made of l" or 1½" material with a capacity of not less than 1 cu. ft. If larger, it should be of 2, 3, or 4 cu. ft. capacity. These frames should be marked on the inside to show levels at which the volume will equal certain amounts, such as 1 cu. ft., 2 cu. ft., or smaller batches. Handles on the side of the box make it easier to lift after the material has been measured. Fig. 24-1.

To measure the materials, the box is placed on the mixing platform and filled with the required amount of material. The box is then lifted and the material remains on the platform. Pails are often used for proportioning materials. Fig. 24-2. For example, a batch of concrete could be measured by using one pail of portland cement, two pails of sand, and three pails of gravel or crushed stone. (This would be called a *1:2:3 batch*.) Measuring can also be done with shovels or wheelbarrows, depending on the amount of material required. Suggested trial mixes are shown in Tables 24-A, 24-B, and 24-C.

All concrete should be thoroughly mixed until it is uniform in appearance and all materials are uniformly distributed in the mixture.

Testing the Mix

Once the various ingredients have been mixed, the consistency of concrete can be described by referring to its *slump*. Slump can easily be measured at the job site or at the ready-mix plant. A slump test should be done whenever the consistency of the concrete is of critical importance. Such tests are often done in commercial construction. They are sometimes done in residential construction.

24-2. *Using a pail for proportioning concrete materials.*

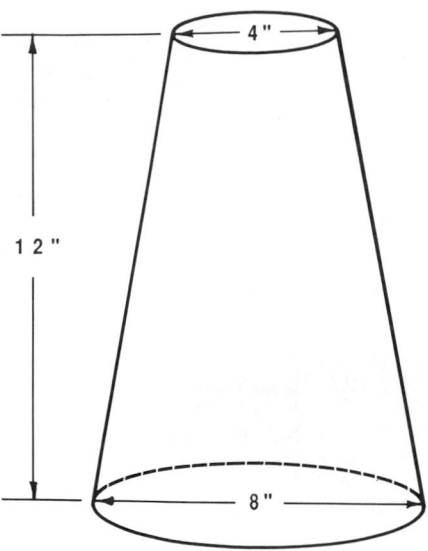

24-3. *A slump test cone.*

24-4. *When the mold is removed from the concrete, the resulting "slump" can be measured.*

In a slump test, concrete straight from the mixer is poured into a small sheet-metal cone of specific dimensions. Figs. 24-3 and 24-4. Once this concrete has been rodded (consolidated), the cone is removed. A measurement is then taken of how much the unsupported mass of concrete loses its conical shape, or "slumps." The greater the slump, the wetter the concrete.

Placing Concrete

Concrete should be placed continuously wherever possible and kept practically level throughout the area being placed. All vertical joints should be keyed to hold the parts together. *Spade* or *vibrate* the concrete to remove air pockets and force the concrete into all parts of the forms. Fig. 24-5.

For concrete to gain full strength, it must be cured properly. If maximum strength is important, the concrete should be covered with material that will slow its loss of moisture. To help the curing process, builders sometimes cover the concrete with polyethylene sheets, wet burlap, or wet straw.

In hot weather, protect concrete from rapid drying. It should be kept moist for several days after pouring. Rapid drying lowers its strength and may damage the exposed surfaces of sidewalks and drives.

In very cold weather, keep the temperature of the concrete above freezing until it has set. The rate at which concrete sets is affected by temperature, being much slower at 40 degrees F and below than at higher temperatures. In cold weather, the use of heated water and heated aggregate during mixing is good practice. In severe weather, insulation or heat is necessary until the concrete has set.

Concrete can usually be delivered directly from the concrete truck. On a steep or heavily wooded site, however, it is sometimes impossible for the truck to get near enough to deliver the concrete by chute. In such cases, the concrete can be pumped from the truck to where it is needed through long, flexible pipes.

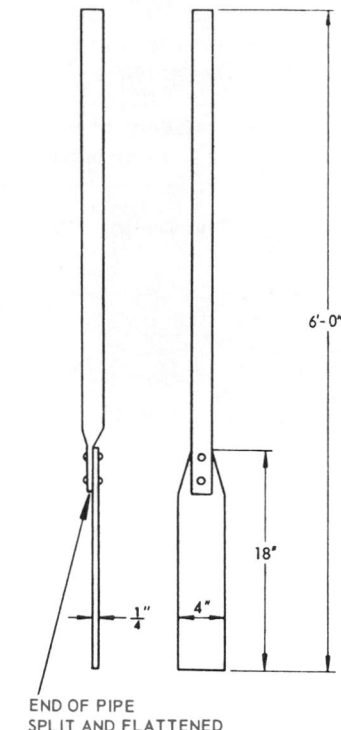

END OF PIPE
SPLIT AND FLATTENED

24-5a. *Spading tool.*

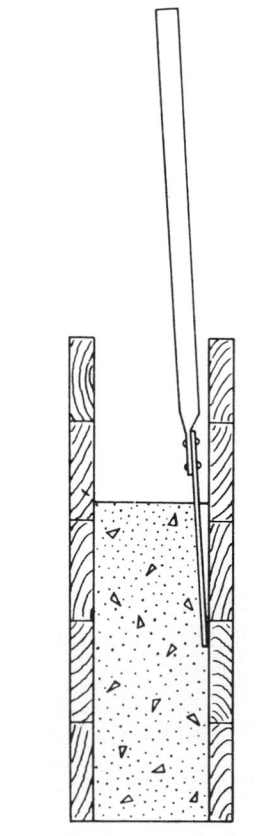

24-5b. *Spading tool in use.*

24-5c. *Using a vibrator to insure that the concrete will be consolidated.*

REINFORCEMENT OF CONCRETE

Reinforcement refers to embedding steel bars or welded-wire fabric in concrete to increase its tensile strength. Concrete has great strength in compression, which means that it can support huge loads placed directly upon it. Steel has excellent tensile strength, which is the resistance to forces that bend and pull a material. When concrete and steel are used together, the resulting material, called reinforced concrete, has the characteristics of both materials. Reinforced concrete has excellent compression strength and good tensile strength. Concrete footings, slabs, and walls are often reinforced with steel.

Types of Reinforcing Steel

Reinforcing steel can be purchased in the form of reinforcing bars, known as *rebar*, or as welded-wire fabric. Rebar is used most often in footings and walls, while welded-wire fabric sees most use in slabs.

Rebar comes in 20' lengths that can be cut or bent on the job site. A hacksaw or a cutting torch can be used to cut rebar, but a rebar cutter makes the job easier. Fig. 24-6. Lengths of rebar usually have a deformed surface that helps the concrete grip the steel. Fig. 24-7. The diameter of rebar needed varies according to the amount of tensile force the concrete needs to carry. Table 24-D.

Welded-wire fabric is really not a fabric at all. It is an open mesh of wires running perpendicular to each other. Fig. 24-8. The most common welded-wire fabric on a residential job site has wires spaced 6" apart in two directions. When used to reinforce a slab, the wire is rolled out first. It is then pulled up into the concrete as the slab is being poured. An alternative (and more accurate) technique is to first place the welded-wire fabric on wire *chairs* that hold it slightly above grade.

Steel reinforcement of any kind must be covered by enough concrete to be effective. The steel must also be protected from rusting. If the steel reinforcement is allowed to rust, the concrete will be damaged. Table 24-E.

FOOTINGS

Foundation walls are enlarged at their base to provide a larger bearing surface against the soil beneath. These enlarged bases are called *footings*.

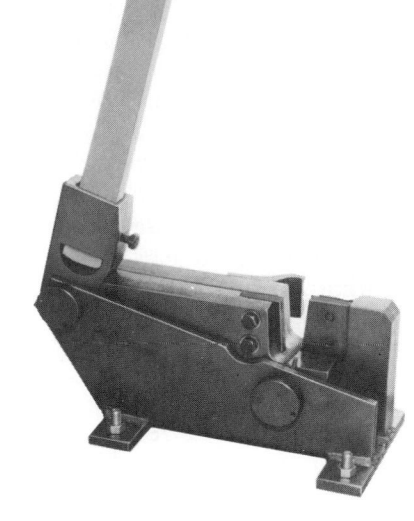

24-6. *A rebar shear can be used to cut rebar to length.*

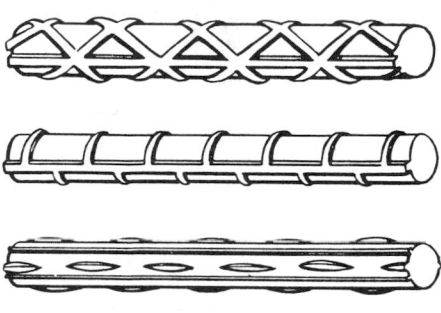

24-7. *Several types of steel reinforcing bars. The pattern helps the concrete grip the bar.*

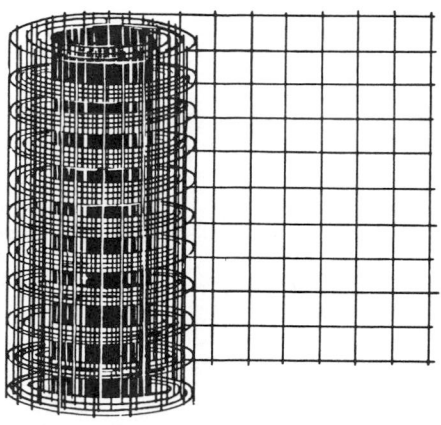

24-8. *Welded-wire fabric.*

Footings are an important part of the foundation, so particular attention should be paid to their size and shape. Footing details will generally be specified on the architectural plans. The FHA Minimum Property Standards specify footing sizes based on soil of average bearing value. Approximately 2,000 lbs. per sq. ft.

or better is used as a guide. These minimum footing sizes are shown in Table 24-F.

Local codes will specify the type and size of footings suitable for the soil condition. In cold climates the footings should be far enough below ground level to be protected from frost. Local codes usually establish this depth, which is often

4' or more in northern sections of the United States, but maybe only 12" elsewhere.

Poured concrete footings are more dependable than those of other materials. Thus they are recommended for use in house foundations. Where fill has been used, the foundations should extend below the fill to undisturbed earth. In areas where irregular settlement of the foundation and the building it supports are likely to occur, local practices that have been successful should be followed.

Table 24-D. *Size, Cross-Sectional Area, and Weight of Reinforcing Bars. This table gives the size, cross-sectional area, and weight for each bar number. Bar numbers are multiples of ⅛".*

Bar number	Bar diameter, in.	Bar area, sq. in.	Approximate weight of 100 ft.
2	¼	0.05	17
3	⅜	0.11	38
4	½	0.20	67
5	⅝	0.31	104
6	¾	0.44	150
7	⅞	0.60	204
8	1	0.79	267

Table 24-E. *Concrete Protection for Reinforcement.*

Members	Minimum concrete protection
Footings	3 in.
Concrete surface exposed to weather	2 in. for bars larger than No. 5, 1½ in. for No. 5 bars and smaller
Slabs and walls	¾ in.
Beams and girders	1½ in.
Joists	¾ in.

Source: American Concrete Institute ACI 318, *Building Code Requirements for Reinforced Concrete.*

Table 24-F. *FHA Minimum Footing Sizes as Specified in the Minimum Property Standards for One and Two Living Units.*

Number of stories	Frame		Masonry or masonry veneer	
	Min. thickness (inches)	Projection each side of wall (inches)	Min. thickness (inches)	Projection each side of wall (inches)
One story:				
No basement	6	2	6	3
Basement	6	3	6	4
Two story:				
No basement	6	3	6	4
Basement	6	4	8	5

Wall Footings

Well-designed wall footings are important in preventing settling or cracks in the wall. One rule for determining the size of wall footings is based on the proposed wall thickness. This two-part rule, which is often followed for normal soils, states:

➤ The footing thickness should be equal to the wall thickness. Fig 24-9.

➤ The footing should project beyond each side of the wall one-half the thickness of the wall. Thus the total width of the footing would be twice the wall thickness.

This is a general rule which may have to be varied. For example, if the soil is of low load-bearing capacity, wider reinforced footings may be required. Also, local regulations often set certain requirements for wall footings as well as column and fireplace footings.

A few rules that apply to footing design and construction are:

➤ Footings must be at least 6" thick (8" or more is preferable).

➤ If footing excavation is too deep, fill with concrete—never replace with dirt.

➤ Use formboards for footings where soil conditions prevent sharply cut trenches.

➤ Place footings *below* the frostline.

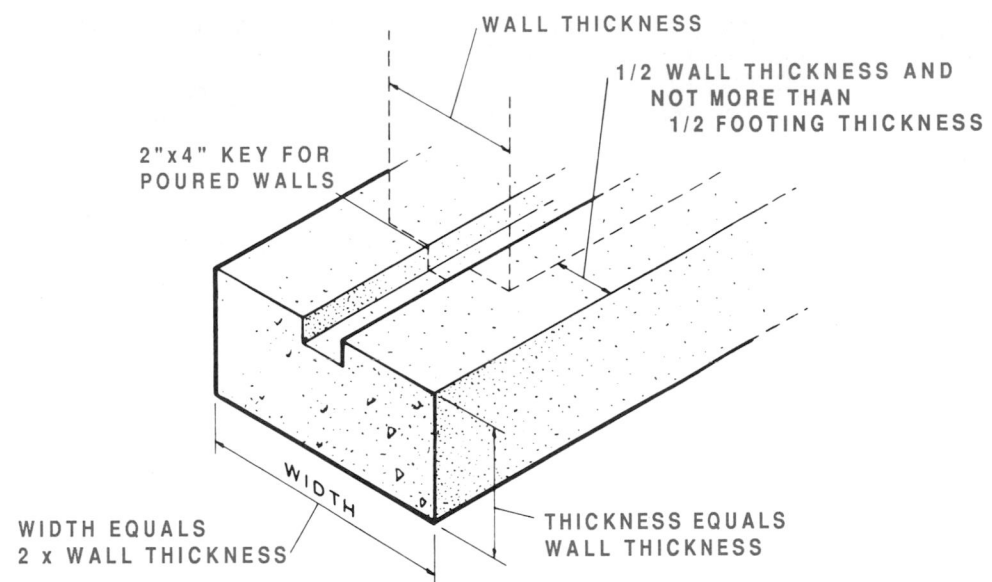

WALL THICKNESS

1/2 WALL THICKNESS AND
NOT MORE THAN
1/2 FOOTING THICKNESS

2"x4" KEY FOR
POURED WALLS

WIDTH

WIDTH EQUALS
2 x WALL THICKNESS

THICKNESS EQUALS
WALL THICKNESS

24-9. *A foundation wall footing.*

➤ Reinforce footings with steel rods where they cross pipe trenches.

➤ Use key slot for better resistance to water entry at wall location. Figs. 24-9 and 24-14.

Footing Forms. A common type of wall footing form is shown in Fig. 24-10. The sides of the footing are molded by boards (called *haunch boards*). The bottom is natural soil. Set the footing form boards (haunch boards) level and nail the spreaders in place with duplex head nails. Fig. 24-11. For many footings, artificial form work is not used at all; the footing is cast with bottom and sides against the natural earth.

Pier, Post, and Column Footings

A footing for a *pier*, a *post*, or a *column* should be square. It sometimes includes a *pedestal*—a raised area on which the member will bear. To anchor a wood post, a protruding steel pin or a metal bracket is sometimes set in the pedestal. Fig. 24-12. At other times, steel posts are set directly on the

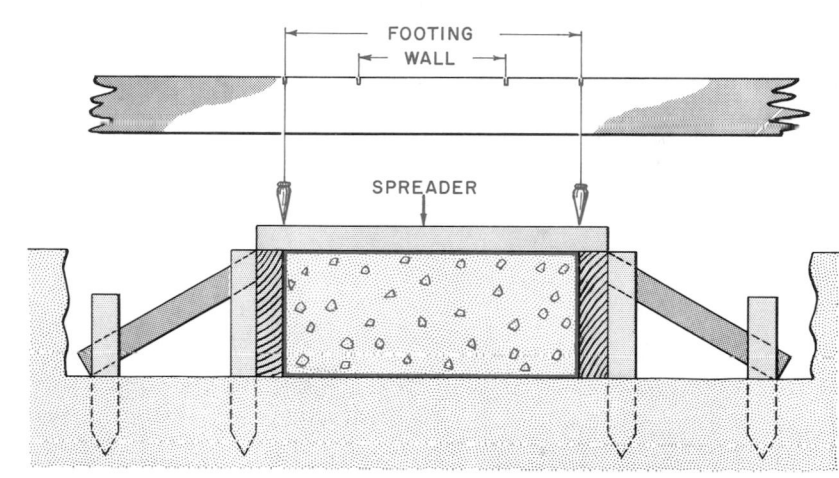

FOOTING

WALL

SPREADER

24-10a. *Footing form detail. Note the notches in the batter board, from which the plumb bobs are hung. These designate the footing width and wall thickness.*

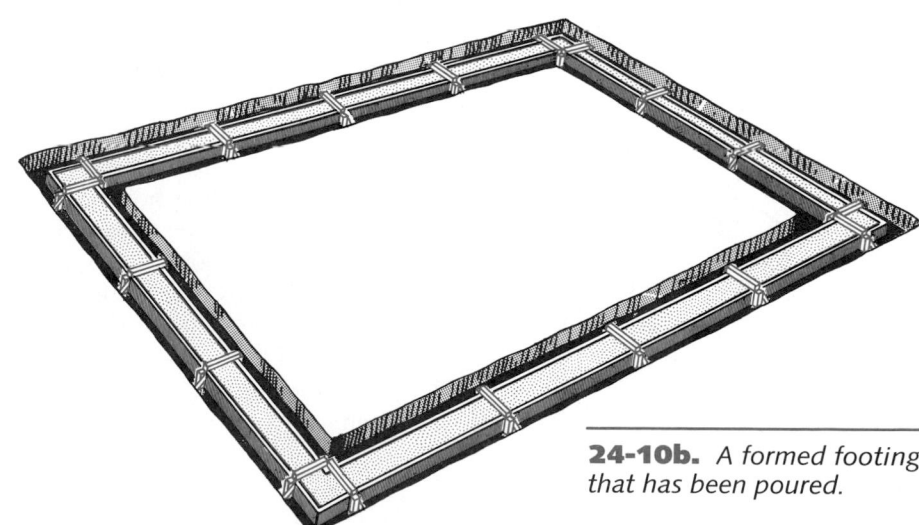

24-10b. *A formed footing that has been poured.*

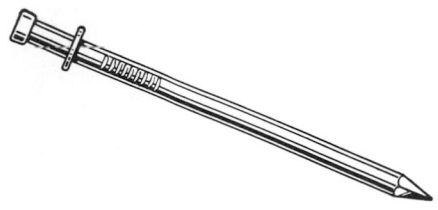

24-11. *A duplex-head nail is used when fabricating forms. This enables the forms to be securely nailed but allows the nail to be easily pulled when the forms are to be removed.*

footing and the concrete floor poured around them.

Footings vary in size, depending on the weight the soil will support and the spacing of the piers, posts, or columns. Common sizes are 24" × 24" × 12" and 30" × 30" × 12". The pedestal is sometimes poured after the footing. The minimum height should be about 3" above the finish basement floor and 12" above finish grade in crawl-space areas.

Footings for fireplaces, furnaces, and chimneys should ordinarily be poured at the same time as other footings.

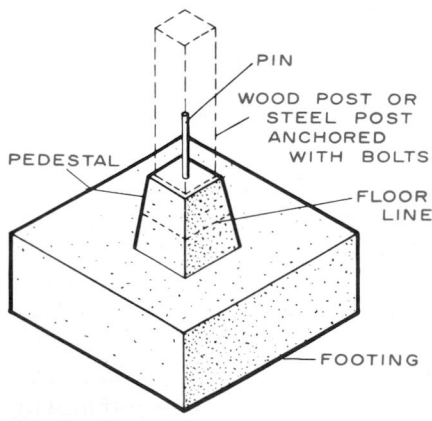

24-12. *Post footing.*

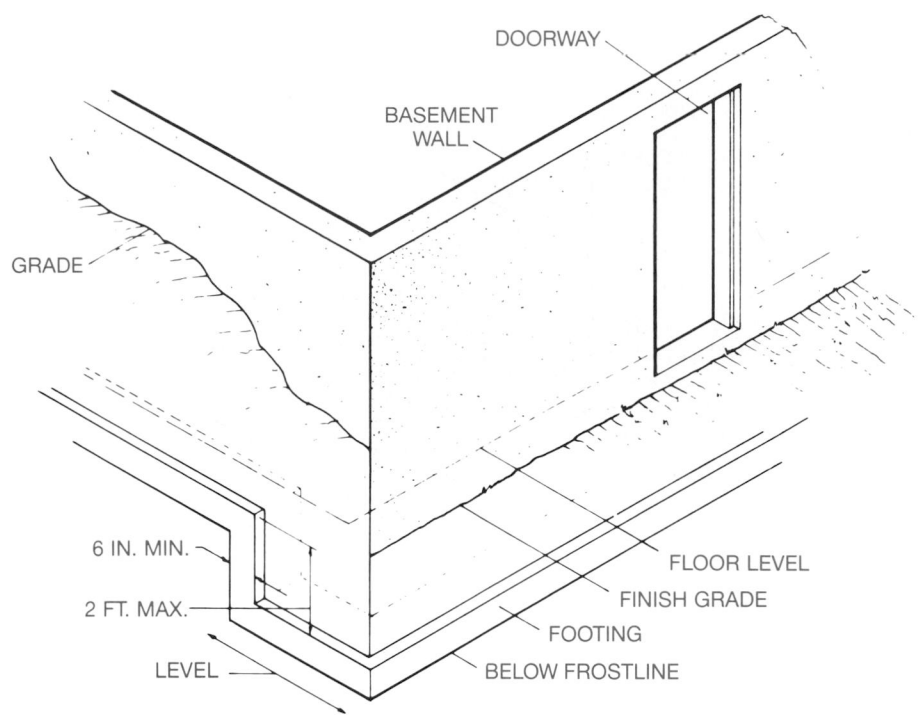

24-13. *Stepped footing details.*

Stepped Footings

Stepped footings are often used where the lot slopes to the front or rear and the garage or living areas are at basement level. The vertical part should be poured at the same time as the rest of the footing. The bottom of the footing is always placed on undisturbed soil below the frostline. Each run of the footing should be level.

The vertical step should be at least 6" thick and the same width as the rest of the footing. Fig. 24-13. The height of the step should not be more than three-fourths of the adjacent horizontal footing. On steep slopes, more than one step may be required. It is good practice, when possible, to limit the vertical step to 2'. In very steep slopes, special footings—perhaps larger and/or reinforced—may be required.

FOOTING DRAINS

Foundation or footing drains must often be used around foundations which enclose basements or rooms which people will occupy below the outside finish grade. Fig. 24-14. These may especially be needed in sloping or low areas or any location where it is necessary to drain away subsurface water. This precaution will help prevent damp basements and wet floors. The use of drains is often necessary where basement rooms are to be occupied or where houses are located near the bottom of a long slope subjected to heavy runoff.

Drains are installed at or below the area to be protected. Clay drain tile, 4" in diameter and 12" long, is sometimes placed at the bottom of the footing level on top of a 2" gravel bed. Fig. 24-14. Tiles are placed end to end and spaced about ⅛" apart. The tops of the joints between the

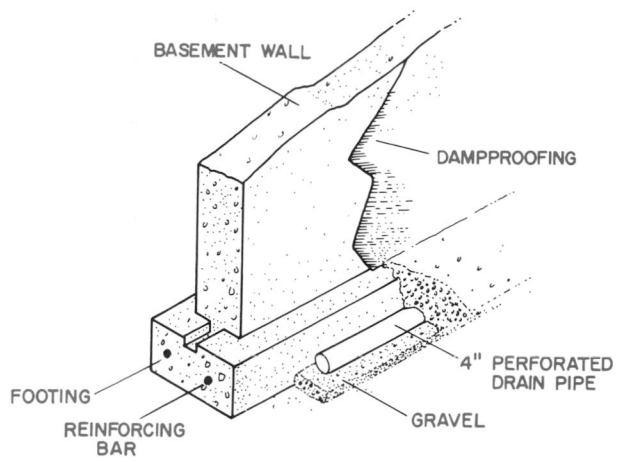

BASEMENT WALL

DAMPPROOFING

FOOTING

REINFORCING BAR

4" PERFORATED DRAIN PIPE

GRAVEL

24-14. *Footing drains are frequently used around foundations. Notice that the bottom of the wall is keyed to the footing. This will tie the wall and footing together.*

tile are covered with a strip of asphalt-saturated felt or a building paper. Then gravel is placed over the tile.

Most new houses use plastic drain pipes for the footing drains. These pipes, typically 3" or 4" in diameter, are placed at the base of the footing. They are usually connected directly to sump pumps or storm sewers. There are many small holes along the bottom edge of each pipe. When water rises into the pipes, it is conveyed away from the house. Fig. 24-14. To maintain proper movement of the water, the pipes should be sloped towards the drain at least ⅛" per foot. Once the pipes are in place, the area can be backfilled with gravel. Some builders line the drainage area with filter

fabric (also called geotextile fabric or landscaping fabric). This fabric is made of polyester or polypropylene fibers. While it allows water to pass through, it prevents tiny particles of soil (called *fines*) from getting into the drainage system and clogging it.

Local building regulations vary. They should be consulted before you start to construct a drainage system.

ESTIMATING

Concrete

As mentioned earlier, concrete is measured and sold by the cubic yard (27 cubic feet). To calculate the amount of concrete required for a job, figure the volume of the forms in cubic feet (thickness × width × length) and divide by 27 to obtain the total number of cubic yards. For example, to pour a 4" thick driveway which is 20' wide and 40' long, calculate the cubic footage by multiplying the thickness, 4" (or ⅓ of a foot) times 20' (width) times 40' (length). This multiplies out to 266⅔ or 267 cubic feet. Converting this to cubic yards, $^{267}/_{27}$ = $9\,^{24}/_{27}$ or 10 cubic yards of concrete are needed to complete the driveway.

Table 24-G provides a shortcut which can be used in estimating amounts of concrete. For the 4" × 20' × 40' driveway, read down the left column of the table to the depth of the concrete in inches, which is 4". Reading across you find that one cubic yard at that depth will fill 81 sq. ft. The area of the driveway is 800 sq. ft. (which you learn by multiplying the width times the length—20' × 40'). Next divide the total sq. ft. (the area) by the number of square feet covered by one cubic yard of cement:

Table 24-G. *Concrete Estimating. This table indicates the area in square feet that 1 cubic yard of concrete will fill for a variety of thicknesses. For example, 1 cubic yard of concrete will fill a form area of 40 square feet for a wall 8" thick.*

Thickness in.	Sq. ft.	Thickness in.	Sq. Ft.	Thickness In.	Sq. ft.
1	324	4¾	68	8½	38
1¼	259	5	65	8¾	37
1½	216	5¼	62	9	36
1¾	185	5½	59	9¼	35
2	162	5¾	56	9½	34
2¼	144	6	54	9¾	33
2½	130	6¼	52	10	32.5
2¾	118	6½	50	10¼	31.5
3	108	6¾	48	10½	31
3¼	100	7	46	10¾	30
3½	93	7¼	45	11	29.5
3¾	86	7½	43	11¼	29
4	81	7¾	42	11½	28
4¼	76	8	40	11¾	27.5
4½	72	8¼	39	12	27

$$\frac{800}{81} = 9.88$$

Thus you can see that roughly 10 cubic yards of concrete will be needed for the driveway.

This method of calculating concrete requirements will provide the necessary information for ordering ready-mix concrete or for estimating a job. However, if the concrete is to be mixed on the job site, the amount of aggregate and cement will have to be figured. Do this by using the information provided in Table 24-A. If a 6-bag mix is desired, read across the line of the chart under "Cement bags." Note that a 6-bag mix requires 1500 lbs. of fine aggregate and 2300 lbs. of coarse aggregate for each cubic yard of concrete. Applying this to the driveway in the example, multiply these figures by 10 (yards required for the driveway) to obtain the total requirements of cement and aggregate.

Footings

Materials. To determine the amounts of materials required to pour the footings in a home, figure the volume of the forms as described under "Estimating Concrete" (page 233). Table 24-G may be used as an aid.

To see how this works, calculate the footing requirements for the house plan in Fig. 24-15. Note that the foundation measures 42' by 24'. Thus the perimeter—the total of the four sides—is 132 lineal feet. Assuming that the footing size will be 8" × 12", consult Table 24-H. This shows that for 8" × 12" footings, 2.5 cubic yards of concrete are needed for 100 lineal feet. However, the footings in the example are longer than 100', so additional calculations are necessary. The problem now is: If 2.5 cubic yards of concrete will fill 100', how many will be needed for 132'? Divide 132 by 100. The answer is 1.32. This indicates that the house footings are 1.32 times larger than 100. Therefore by multiplying 1.32 × 2.5 you can find out the total amount of concrete needed. The final answer is 3.3 cubic yards.

Labor for Excavation

The labor for excavation of the footings can also be determined by referring to Table 24-H. For the footing size in the previous example (8" × 12"), the table shows it will take 5 hours to excavate 100 lineal feet. Because the perimeter is 132 lineal feet, allowance must be made for the excess over 100. Thus again you divide 132 by 100 and get 1.32. Multiplying 1.32 × 5, you arrive at a final answer of 6.6 hours of labor. In other words if it takes 5

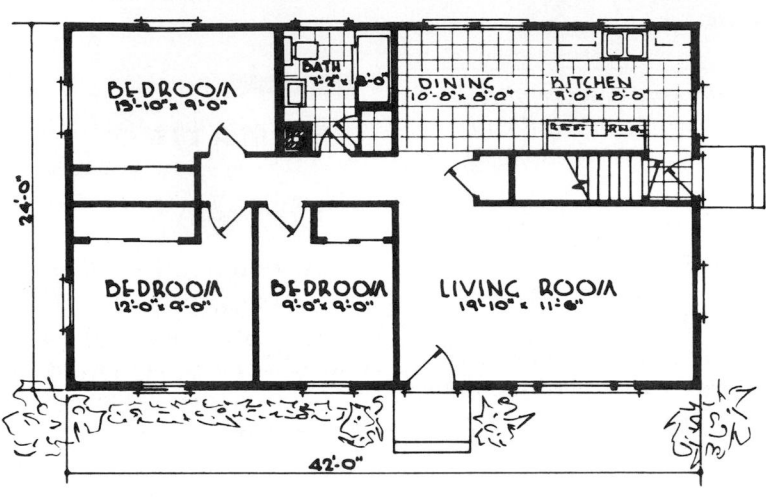

24-15. *House plan for use in calculating materials and labor for footings. (See examples in text.)*

Table 24-H. *Estimating the Material and Labor Needed for Footings.*

Footings	Material			Labor	
Size	Cubic Feet Concrete Per Linear Foot	Cubic Feet Concrete Per 100 Lin. Feet	Cubic Yards Concrete Per 100 Lin. Feet	Excavation Hours per 100 Linear Feet	Placement Hours per Cubic Yard
6 x 12	0.50	50.00	1.9	3.8	2.3
8 x 12	0.67	66.67	2.5	5.0	2.3
8 x 16	0.89	88.89	3.3	6.4	2.3
8 x 18	1.00	100.00	3.7	7.2	2.3
10 x 12	0.83	83.33	3.1	6.1	2.0
10 x 16	1.11	111.11	4.1	8.1	2.0
10 x 18	1.25	125.00	4.6	9.1	2.0
12 x 12	1.00	100.00	3.7	7.2	2.0
12 x 16	1.33	133.33	4.9	9.8	2.0
12 x 20	1.67	166.67	6.1	12.1	1.8
12 x 24	2.00	200.00	7.4	15.8	1.8

Note: Excavation—Reduce hours by 1/4 for sand or loam.
Soil—Increase hours by 1/4 for heavy clay soil.
Placement Labor based on ready-mixed concrete.

hours to excavate 100 lineal feet, it will take 6.6 hours for the excavation of 132 lineal feet.

Labor for Placing Concrete

Table 24-H also provides information for figuring the labor of placing the concrete in the forms, based on the use of a ready-mixed concrete. Using the house in Fig. 24-15, which required 3.3 cubic yards of concrete, calculate the labor for placing the concrete. The table shows that for an 8" × 12" footing, it will take 2.3 hours to place one cubic yard of concrete in the form. To figure the total time, multiply 2.3 (placement hours per cubic yard) × 3.3 (total amount of concrete to be placed) = 7.59 hours or 7.6 hours of labor. This also includes the time for forming the footings. These items may have to be corrected depending on the nature of the soil, as noted at the bottom of Table 24-H.

QUESTIONS

1. What are the active ingredients in concrete?

2. Explain hydration.

3. To mix 1 cubic yard of 6¼-bag-mix concrete, how many pounds of fine aggregate are required?

4. When proportioning materials for mixing concrete, what does 1:2:3 represent?

5. What purpose does concrete reinforcing serve?

6. Name two kinds of reinforcing steel.

7. What is the purpose of a footing?

8. What are the common sizes of footings for piers, posts, and columns?

9. How is concrete measured and sold?

ACTIVITIES

1. Science. The process of hydration is described in this unit. Explain why this process enables people to use cement in a variety of ways other than for footings or driveways.

2. Language Arts. Stepped footings are described in this unit. In a residential neighborhood, look for three houses that require this type of footing. In a short descriptive paragraph, describe the appearance of the footings. Be sure to describe the type of house, where the footing is placed, and how many vertical steps there are.

3. Math. Assume you are building a house. Draw a rough plan of your house as shown in Fig. 24-15. Next, using Table 24-G, try to estimate the material needed for the footings. Show your drawing to another person in the class, but do not show this person your estimate. Ask the person to make an estimate, and see if he or she comes up with the same figure you did.

4. Math. For a 1:2:3 batch of concrete:

a. how many pounds of fine aggregate and coarse aggregate are needed if there are 300 pounds of cement?

b. how many pounds of cement and coarse aggregate are needed if there are 400 pounds of fine aggregate?

5. Math. A building with outside dimensions of 32' by 60' has a footing that is 12" thick and 24" wide.

a. How many cubic yards of concrete are needed?

b. Estimate the hours required to dig the footing.

c. Estimate the hours required to place the concrete.

d. Determine how many bags of cement were used for the footing if the concrete was a six-bag mix.

e. If you referred to Table 24-G to find answers to a, b, and c, discuss with a friend which of these table entries can be determined from the basic dimensions given and which entries are from work experience.

6. Science. Place several pieces of fruit or vegetables (apples, oranges, potatoes, yams, etc.) into two clean half-pint milk cartons. Weigh the ingredients in each carton. Record the weight results. Add enough water to cover the ingredients in one of the cartons. Add water to this carton on a periodic basis to compensate for evaporation. Allow the other carton to be air exposed.

Weigh the carton contents every twenty-four hours for a five-day period. Be sure to record the results. Based on the weight changes, explain which carton's contents are dehydrating and which carton's contents are more closely hydrating as concrete does.

25

Poured Concrete Foundation Walls

Foundation walls form an enclosure for basements or crawl spaces. Also they carry wall, floor, roof, and other building loads. The two types of walls most commonly used are *poured concrete* and *concrete block* (which is discussed in Unit 26 of this book).

The job of forming and pouring concrete foundation walls and footings is usually *subcontracted*. This means that the building contractor hires another contractor—one who specializes in this type of work. These specialists have the necessary tools, materials, and equipment. Therefore the purpose of this unit is mainly to make the reader familiar with the general procedure and requirements for poured concrete foundation walls, as well as the terms commonly used.

POURED CONCRETE FOUNDATION WALLS

Wall thickness and types of construction are ordinarily controlled by local building regulations. Thickness of poured-concrete basement walls may vary from 8" to 10". Fig. 25-1.

Clear wall height should be no less than 7' from the top of the concrete basement floor to the bottom of the joists. Greater

25-1. *Poured concrete foundation walls with anchor bolts.*

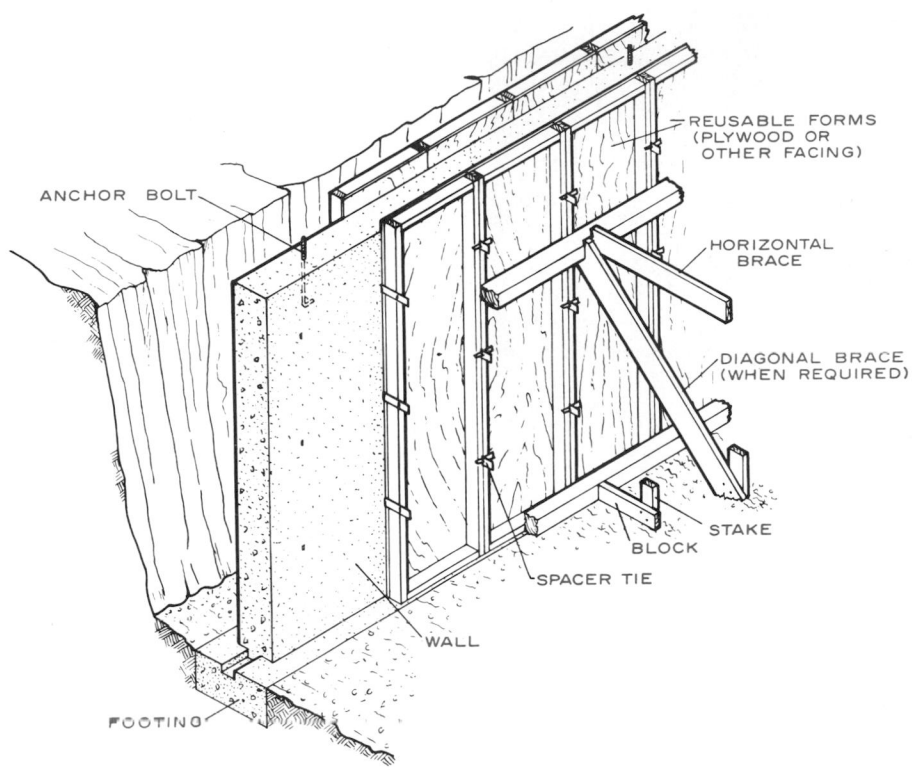

ANCHOR BOLT

REUSABLE FORMS
(PLYWOOD OR
OTHER FACING)

HORIZONTAL
BRACE

DIAGONAL BRACE
(WHEN REQUIRED)

STAKE

BLOCK

SPACER TIE

WALL

FOOTING

25-2. *Form for a poured-concrete foundation wall.*

25-3. *These concrete forms have been plumbed and braced on the outside. Metal snap ties will secure the inner surface of the forms.*

clearance is usually desirable to provide headroom under girders, pipes, and ducts. Many contractors pour walls that are 8' high above the footings. This provides a clearance of 7' 8" from the top of the finished concrete floor to the bottom of the joists.

The forms for poured-concrete walls must be tight. They must also be braced and tied to withstand the forces of the pouring operation and the fluid concrete.

Poured-concrete walls should be *double-formed* (formwork constructed for each wall face). Reusable forms are used for most poured walls. Panels may consist of wood framing with plywood facings. Fig. 25-2. Such panels are fastened together with clips or other ties. Thin metal rods called snap-ties are commonly used to hold foundation wall forms together. The rods extend through the foundation. Metal brackets attached to the rods prevent the forms from spreading. Fig. 25-3. Once the concrete is poured and the forms are stripped, the protruding ends of each rod are snapped off.

Frames for cellar windows, doors, sleeves for utilities, and other openings are set in place as the forms are erected. This is also true of forms for the beam pockets which are located to support the ends of the floor beam. Fig. 25-4.

As mentioned above, forms must have sufficient blocking and bracing to keep them in place during pouring operations. For reusable forms the use of horizontal bracing members is usually sufficient. Forms constructed with vertical studs and waterproof plywood or lumber sheathing require horizontal whalers and bracing. (Whalers are lumber used to stiffen concrete forms.)

Level marks of some type, such as nails along the form, should be used to assure a level foundation top. This will provide a good level sill plate and floor framing.

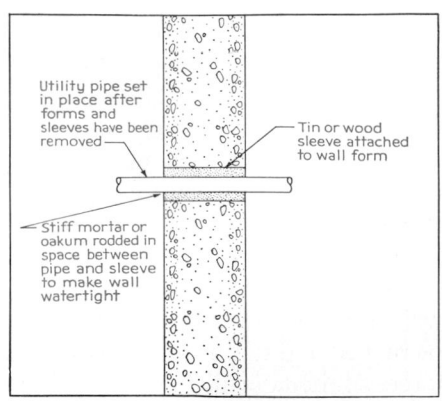

25-4a. Insert a tin or wood sleeve to provide openings through the basement wall for utilities.

25-4b. Openings such as those for foundation vents can be cast into the concrete when the walls are poured.

25-4c. A coating of tar or asphalt prevents seepage of water through the foundation walls.

Concrete should be poured continuously, without interruption. It should be constantly worked to remove air pockets and to get the material under window frames and other blocking. Such working is called *puddling*. Anchor bolts for the sill plate should be installed very soon after the concrete has been placed.

Freshly placed concrete should be protected and possibly heated when temperatures are below freezing.

Forms should not be removed until the concrete has hardened and acquired sufficient strength to support loads imposed during early construction. At least two days (and preferably longer) are required

when temperatures are well above freezing, and perhaps a week when outside temperatures are below freezing.

Poured concrete walls can be *dampproofed* with one heavy cold or hot coat of tar or asphalt. Fig. 25-4c. The coat should be applied to the outside from the footings to the finish grade line. Such coatings are usually sufficient to make a wall watertight against ordinary seepage (such as may occur after a rainstorm), but should not be applied until the surface of the concrete has dried enough to assure good adhesion. In poorly drained soils, a waterproof membrane of roofing felt or similar material can be applied, with shingle-style laps of 4" to 6" over the tar or asphalt coating. A hot coating of tar or asphalt is then commonly applied over the membrane. This covering will prevent leaks if minor cracks develop.

Masonry Construction for Crawl Spaces

In some areas of the country, the crawl-space house is often preferred to those constructed over a basement or on a concrete slab. Three important points in such construction are:

➤ A good soil cover must be used under the house.

➤ The crawl space must be ventilated.

➤ There must be adequate insulation to reduce heat loss through the floor.

More will be said about these points in later units.

One of the primary advantages of the crawl-space house as compared with the full-basement house is the reduced cost. Little or no excavation or grading is required except for the footings and walls. In mild climates, the footings are located only slightly below the finish grade. However, in the northern states where frost penetrates deeply, the footing is often located four or more feet below the finish grade. This, of course, requires more work and increases the cost. The footings should be poured over undisturbed soil and never over fill unless special piers and grade beams are used.

The construction of a masonry wall for a crawl space is much the same as that required for a full basement except that no excavation is required within the walls. Waterproofing is normally *not* required for this type of construction. Common minimum thicknesses for walls in single-story frame houses are 8" for hollow concrete block and 6" for poured concrete.

For crawl-space houses, the minimum footing thickness (depth) is 6"; minimum widths are 12" for concrete block and 10" for the poured foundation wall. However, well-constructed houses usually have 8" walls and 16" × 8" footings.

Poured-concrete or concrete-block piers are often used to support floor beams in crawl-space houses. They should extend at least 12" above the ground line. The minimum size for a concrete block pier should be 8" × 16" with a 16" × 24" × 8" footing. Solid blocks are used for the top course. Poured concrete piers should be at least 10" × 10" with a 20" × 20" × 8" footing.

Unreinforced concrete piers should be no greater in height than 10 times their least dimension. Concrete block piers should be no higher than four times the least dimension.

When exterior wall beams and interior girders are set at right angles to the floor joists, the spacing of piers should not exceed 8' on center. Under exterior wall beams set parallel to the floor joists, the spacing of piers should not exceed 12' on center. Exterior wall piers should not extend above grade more than four times their least dimension unless supported laterally (on the sides) by masonry or concrete walls. As for wall footing sizes, the size of the pier footings should be based on the load they must bear and the capacity of the soil. Review "Footings," page 229.

Sill Plate Anchors

In wood-frame construction, the *sill plate* should be securely fastened to the foundation. Most builders use ½" diameter L-shaped bolts called anchor bolts. These are embedded in the concrete immediately after the pour and spaced about 8' apart. Other builders use metal straps that are embedded in the concrete. Figs. 25-5a and b. The plates should be pressure-treated wood or some other decay-resistant wood. In some regions sill plates are fastened with masonry nails. This method, however, does not provide the uplift resistance of anchor bolts or metal straps. In high-wind and storm areas, well-anchored plates are very important. A *sill sealer* is often placed under the sill plate on poured walls to smooth any irregularities which might have occurred during curing of the concrete. Anchor bolts should be embedded 8" or more in poured concrete walls and 16" or more in walls made of blocks with concrete-filled cores. A large plate washer should be used at the head end of the bolt for the block wall. If termite shields are used, they should be installed under the plate and sill sealer.

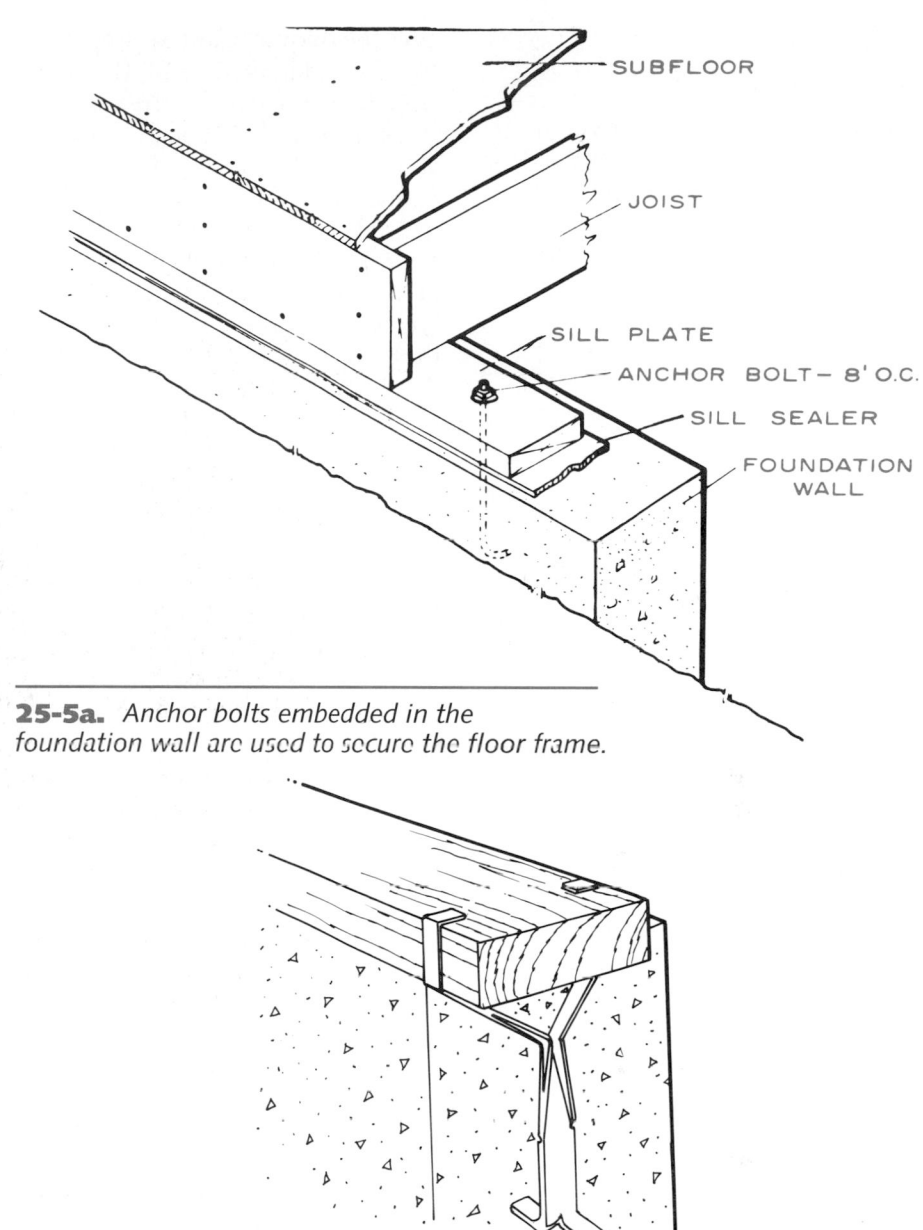

25-5a. *Anchor bolts embedded in the foundation wall are used to secure the floor frame.*

25-5b. *Some builders use metal straps embedded in the concrete.*

SUBFLOOR

JOIST

SILL PLATE

ANCHOR BOLT— 8' O.C.

SILL SEALER

FOUNDATION WALL

Reinforcing Poured Walls

Poured concrete walls need to be reinforced with steel , especially over windows and door openings located below the top of the wall. This type of construction requires that a properly designed steel or reinforced-concrete *lintel* be built

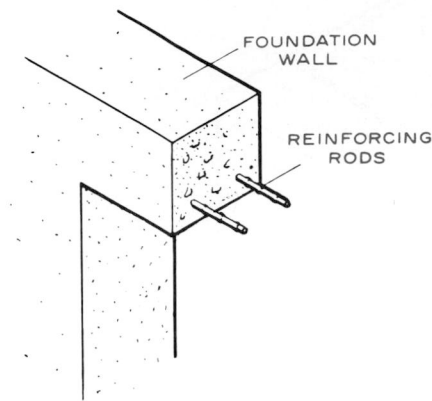

25-6. *Foundation walls must be reinforced over window and door frames.*

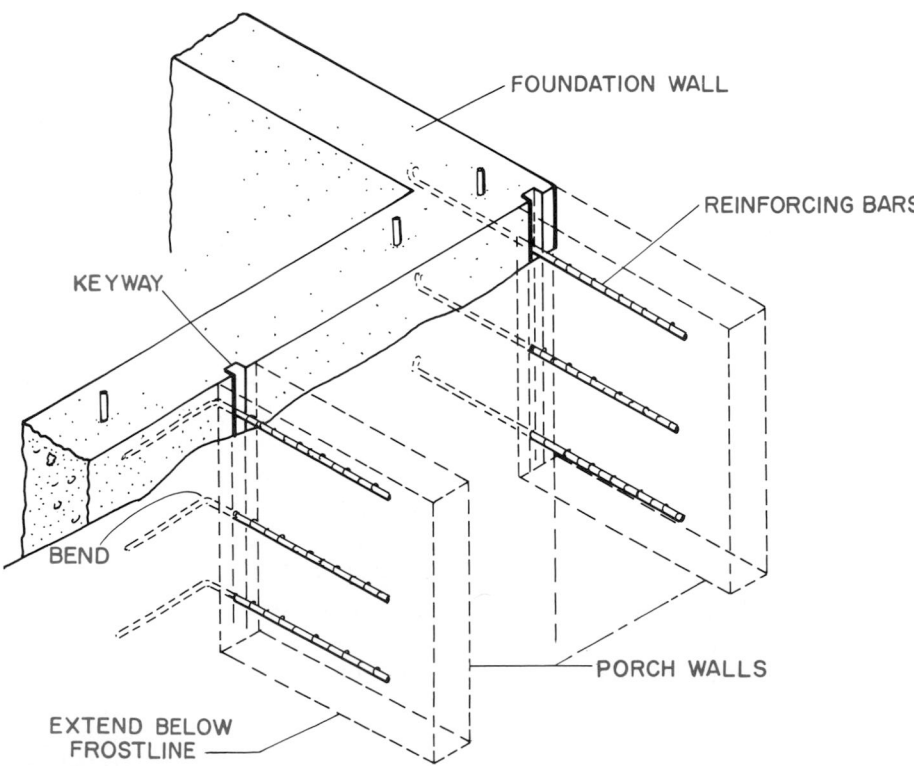

25-7. *Connecting walls are tied to the main foundation wall by reinforcing bars. The bars are placed first in the main foundation walls.*

over the door or window opening. Fig 25-6. In poured walls, the rods are laid in place while the concrete is being poured so that they are about 1½" above the opening. Frames should be prime painted or treated before installation to minimize the absorption of moisture from the concrete. For concrete block walls, a similar lintel of reinforced poured concrete or a precast lintel is commonly used.

Where concrete work includes a connecting porch or garage wall not poured with the main basement wall, it is necessary to provide reinforcing bar (rebar) ties. Fig. 25-7. The rebar is placed during pouring of the main wall. Depending on the size and depth, at least three lengths of ½" rebar should be placed at the intersection of each wall. The deformation provides maximum holding power. Keyways may also be used to resist lateral movement

by forming an interlock between the walls. Such connecting walls should extend below normal frostline and be supported by undisturbed ground.

Masonry Veneer over Frame Walls

If *masonry veneer* is used for the outside finish over wood-frame walls, the foundation must include a supporting ledge or offset about 5" wide. Fig. 25-8. This results in a space of about 1" between the masonry and the sheathing for ease in laying the brick. A base flashing is used at the brick course below the bottom of the sheathing and framing. Fig. 25-8. The flashing should be lapped with sheathing paper. *Weep holes* (to provide drainage) are also located at this course and are formed by eliminating the mortar in a vertical joint. Corrosion-resistant metal ties—spaced about 32" apart horizontally and 16" vertically—should be used to bond the brick veneer to the framework. Where other than wood sheathing is used, secure the ties to the studs. Brick masonry walls are discussed fully in Unit 45.

Brick and stone should be laid in a full bed of mortar; avoid dropping mortar into the space between the veneer and sheathing. Joints that will be exposed to moisture should be tooled to a smooth finish to get the maximum resistance to water penetration. (Tooling is discussed in detail on page 253.)

Masonry laid during cold weather should be protected from freezing until after the mortar has set.

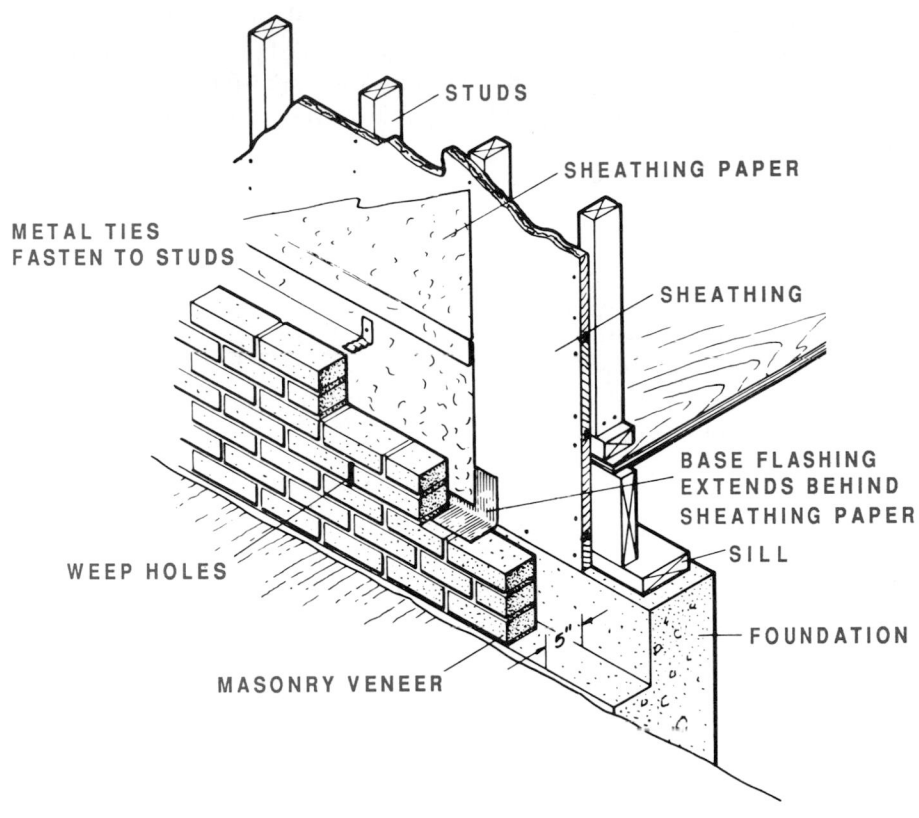

STUDS

SHEATHING PAPER

METAL TIES
FASTEN TO STUDS

SHEATHING

BASE FLASHING
EXTENDS BEHIND
SHEATHING PAPER

SILL

WEEP HOLES

5"

FOUNDATION

MASONRY VENEER

25-8. *A foundation wall under a wood-frame house must include a supporting ledge if a masonry veneer is to be applied.*

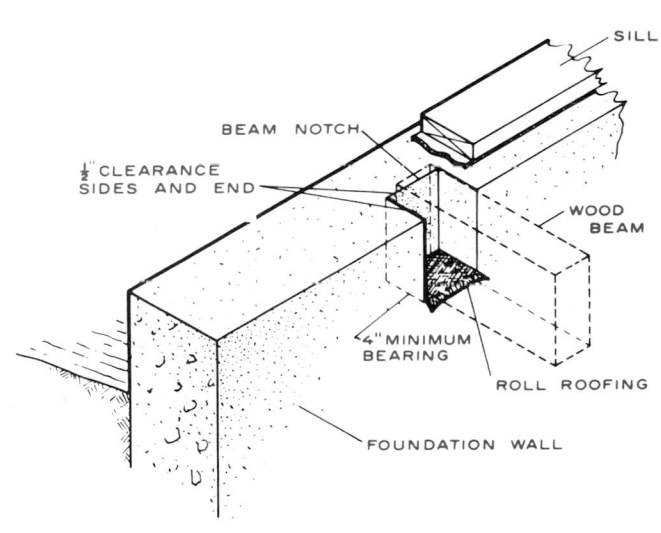

SILL

BEAM NOTCH

½" CLEARANCE
SIDES AND END

WOOD
BEAM

4" MINIMUM
BEARING

ROLL ROOFING

FOUNDATION WALL

25-9. *A beam notch in a foundation wall.*

Notch for Wood Beams

A wall notch or pocket is needed for wooden basement beams or girders. The notch should be large enough to allow at least ½" of clearance at sides and ends of the beam for ventilation. Fig. 25-9. Unless the wood is treated, there is a decay hazard if beams and girders are so tightly set in wall notches that moisture cannot readily escape. A waterproof membrane, such as roll roofing, is commonly applied under the end of the beam to minimize moisture absorption.

Protection against termites. Certain areas of the country, particularly the Atlantic Coast, Gulf States, Mississippi and Ohio Valleys, and southern California, are infested with wood-destroying termites. In such areas, wood construction over a masonry foundation should be protected by one or more of the following methods:

➤ Poured concrete foundation walls.

➤ Masonry foundation walls capped with reinforced concrete.

➤ Metal shields made of rust-resistant material. (Such shields are effective only if they extend beyond the masonry walls and are continuous, with no gaps or loose joints.)

➤ Wood-preservative treatment. (But, this method protects only the members treated.)

➤ Treatment of the soil surrounding the house with chemicals. Some consider this approach to have significant health hazards, so it must be undertaken with considerable care.

See Unit 56 for further details on protection against termites.

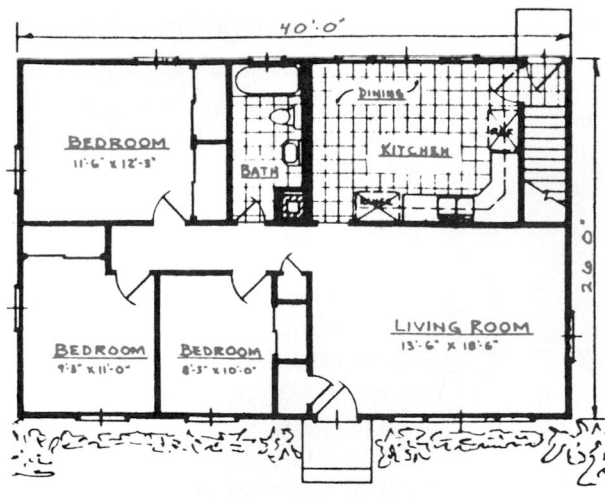

25-10. *A foundation wall 8" thick and 8' high for this home will require 26¼ cubic yards of concrete.*

ESTIMATING

Forming

The foundation wall forms are set on the footings after the footings have cured adequately. Using the house plan in Fig. 25-10, which measures 40' × 26', determine the total foundation wall area, assuming the wall to be 8' high. Multiply 8' (height of foundation wall) × 132' (the perimeter of the building). The answer is 1056 sq. ft. Assuming a wall thickness of 8", refer to Table 25-A. Read down under the column headed "Wall Thickness" to 8". Then read across to the column headed "Forming." Remember, the wall is to be 8' high. The chart shows that the wall will require 7.75 hours per 100 square feet of wall area.

Next, calculate the total time for installing the forms as follows:

Since you know it will take 7.75 hours for each 100 sq. ft., divide the total square feet by 100 and multiply by 7.75.

$$\frac{1056 \text{ (total sq. ft.)}}{100 \text{ (sq. ft. installed in 7.75 hours)}} = 10.56$$

$10.56 \times 7.75 = 81.8$ hours to install forms for the wall in the example.

Next figure the time needed to remove the forms. Consulting Table 25-A, you see that 3 hours will be needed to remove forms for 100 sq. ft. of a high wall. Thus it can be readily seen that more than 30 hours will be needed to remove forms for 1056 sq. ft. The precise calculation is as follows:

$$\frac{1056 \text{ (total sq. ft.)}}{100 \text{ (sq. ft. removed in 3 hours)}} = 10.56$$

$10.56 \times 3 = 31.68$ (or approx. 31⅔ hours total labor time for removing the forms).

Material

The amount of material needed for a concrete foundation wall can be figured using Table 25-A. As an example, take the same wall used in figuring for the forms in the preceding paragraphs. That wall, you remember, was 8" thick and had 1056 sq. ft. of total area.

Find the 8" thickness in the column at left. Reading across, under "Material" you find that 2.47 cubic yards of concrete will be needed for every 100 sq. ft. of wall. Therefore you must divide the total area by 100 (to see how many *hundreds* of square feet there are in the area of the wall) and then multiply by 2.47.

$$\frac{1056 \text{ (total sq. ft. of wall area)}}{100} = \frac{10.56 \text{ (wall area expressed in hundreds of sq. ft.)}}{}$$

10.56×2.47 (cubic yards per 100 sq. ft.) = 26.08 (cu. yds. of concrete for total wall).

For estimating, round off to the next larger ¼ cu. yd.; so a total of 26¼ cu. yds. of concrete would be needed.

Table 25-A. *Estimating Table for Concrete Foundation Walls.*

Walls	Material		Forming			Concrete Placement
	Per 100 Square Feet Wall		Hours per 100 Square Feet			Hours Per Cubic Yard
Wall Thickness	Cubic Feet Required	Cubic Yards Required	Place 0'4'	4'8'	Remove	
4"	33.3	1.24	4.7	7.13	2.0	
6"	50.0	1.85	4.7	7.75	Varies	Average
8"	66.7	2.47	5.0	7.75	as to	3.25
10"	83.3	3.09	5.0	7.90	Height	Hours
12"	100.0	3.70	5.0	7.90	3.0	

Labor

To place concrete in the forms for the wall, Table 25-A shows that it takes an average of 3.25 hours for 1 cubic yard. Multiply the total cubic yards of concrete by the time required to pour 1 cubic yard. This will tell you the total time required for placing the concrete.

In the preceding example, 26¼ cubic yards of concrete were required for the foundation walls. Therefore: 26¼ (cu. yds. of concrete) × 3.25 (hours to place 1 cu. yd.) = 85.31 or, rounded off, 85⅓ hours labor.

QUESTIONS

1. What are the purposes of foundation walls?

2. What are the common thicknesses and heights of a basement foundation wall?

3. What is meant by double-formed?

4. What is meant by dampproofing?

5. What is the maximum height recommended for an 8" x 16" block pier?

6. What is the purpose of a sill plate anchor?

7. How is masonry veneer secured to a wood-frame wall?

8. Why is ventilation required at the end of a wood beam or girder when it rests on a concrete wall?

9. What areas of the country are most troubled with termites?

10. For the home in Fig. 25-10, a foundation wall 8" thick and 8' high will require 26¼ cubic yards of concrete. For a front exterior of brick veneer, the thickness of the foundation wall would have to be increased to 10". Calculate the additional amount of concrete required.

ACTIVITIES

1. Science. Find out whether the foundations of the Sears Building in Chicago and the Empire State Building were constructed from concrete blocks or poured cement walls. Then tell why one type of foundation is preferred over another when erecting huge skyscrapers. While researching, find out the name of the architect responsible for the development of the first skyscraper.

2. Science. The text identifies the need to protect concrete while curing if the temperature is below freezing. Since concrete has as a principal ingredient the same ingredient as ice cubes, explain why curing concrete must be protected from freezing. If temperature is a determiner for concrete hardness, explain what other factor determines concrete hardness as well.

THE SCHOOL-TO-WORK CONNECTION

The foundation is a critical part of the house. If the foundation is improperly designed or the form work poorly built, walls won't be square or level. Cracks can appear in the finished walls. Foundation problems are permanent.

Foundations are often formed, poured, and finished by contractors who specialize in this work. A foundation contractor works on the project as a subcontractor. It typically charges the builder a flat price.

1. Use the phone book to locate several foundation contractors. If you had to hire one company to install the foundation for a house you were about to build, how would you choose one? If you were especially interested in a high-quality foundation, and cost was a secondary factor, what five questions would you ask? List those questions.

Concrete Block Foundation Walls

Concrete block construction is one of the most popular methods for building a foundation. This is because the job does not require formwork, the blocks are relatively inexpensive, and the resulting foundation is adequate for residential construction. Also, work on a block foundation can proceed as time permits—a concrete foundation is generally poured all at once. Fig. 26-1.

GENERAL CONSIDERATIONS

Any hollow masonry unit (or block) is called concrete block. The most common type is made with portland cement, a fine

26-1. *Concrete blocks should be stacked near where they will be used. The L-shaped blocks in this photo will be used at the corners of the building.*

aggregate, and water. Concrete blocks are available in many shapes and sizes for a large variety of applications. Those that are most widely used are 8", 10", and 12" wide. Fig. 26-2. Modular (standard-size) blocks allow for the thickness and width of a standard ⅜" mortar joint; thus they are usually about 7⅝" high by 15⅝" long. This results in blocks which measure 8" high and 16" long from centerline to centerline of the mortar joints.

In addition to the standard types of block, there are specialty blocks for specific purposes. Split-faced blocks have one rough face that looks something like stone. These blocks are sometimes used for the exposed portions of concrete block walls. Fig. 26-3a. Insulating blocks come in various forms, including one that is made from portland cement, sand, polystyrene beads, and chemical additives. Fig. 26-3b.

The thicknesses of concrete block walls vary from 8" to 12" depending on story heights and the lengths of unsupported walls. In cold climates, such walls are customarily constructed of 11 or 12 courses above the footings, with a 4" solid cap-block. This leaves about 7' 4" between the joists and the basement floor.

Concrete block walls require no formwork. Block courses start at the footing and are laid up with about ⅜" mortar joints, usually in a *common bond.* This is the overlapping arrangement shown in Fig. 26-4. Joints should be tooled smooth to resist water seepage.

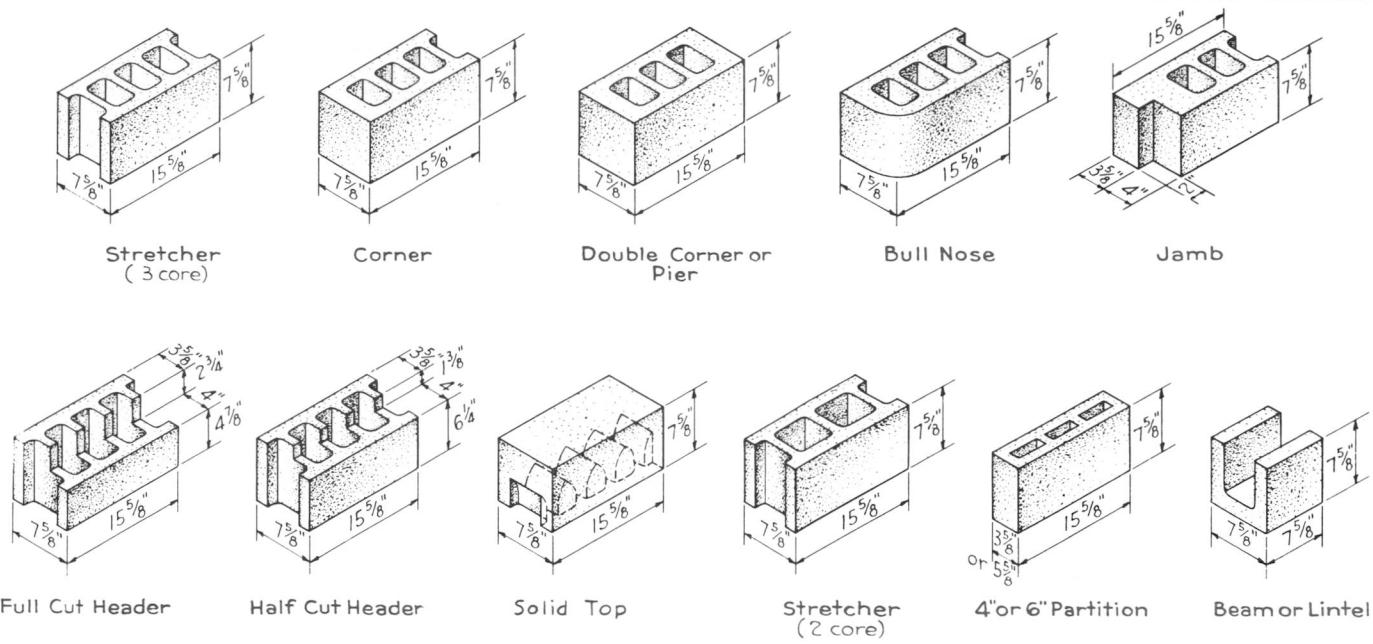

26-2. *Typical shapes and sizes of concrete masonry units. Dimensions shown are actual unit sizes. A 7⅝" x 7⅝" x 15⅝" unit is commonly known as an 8" x 8" x 16" concrete block. Half-length units are usually available for most of the units shown. Check local suppliers to learn what is available in your area.*

Mortar should be spread fully on all contact surfaces of the block. (Such spreading is called *full bedding* of mortar.)

Pilasters are columnlike projections which may be used to strengthen a wall, as by supporting a beam or girder. Some building codes require them. Pilasters are placed on the interior side of the wall and are constructed as high as the bottom of the beam or girder they support. Basement door and window frames should be set with keys for rigidity and to prevent air leakage. Fig. 26-4.

When exposed block foundation is used as a finished wall for basement rooms, the *stack bond pattern* (Fig. 26-4) may be employed for a pleasing effect. This is done by placing blocks directly above one another, resulting in continuous vertical mortar joints. (Vertical joints are called *head* joints. Horizontal joints are called *bed* joints.) However, when this system is used, it is necessary to add some type of joint reinforcement at every second course. This usually consists of small-diameter steel rods arranged in a grid pattern.

26-3b. *This concrete block is 60% polystyrene beads, which increase its insulating value. The slots can be filled with rigid insulation.*

The common bond does not normally require this reinforcing, but when additional strength is desired, it is good practice to use this bonding system.

Freshly laid block walls should be protected in temperatures below freezing. Freezing of the mortar before it has set will often result in low adhesion, low strength, and joint failure.

26-3a. *Split-faced block is sometimes used for decorative effect in exposed locations. This job site is in a warm climate, so the footing is not very deep.*

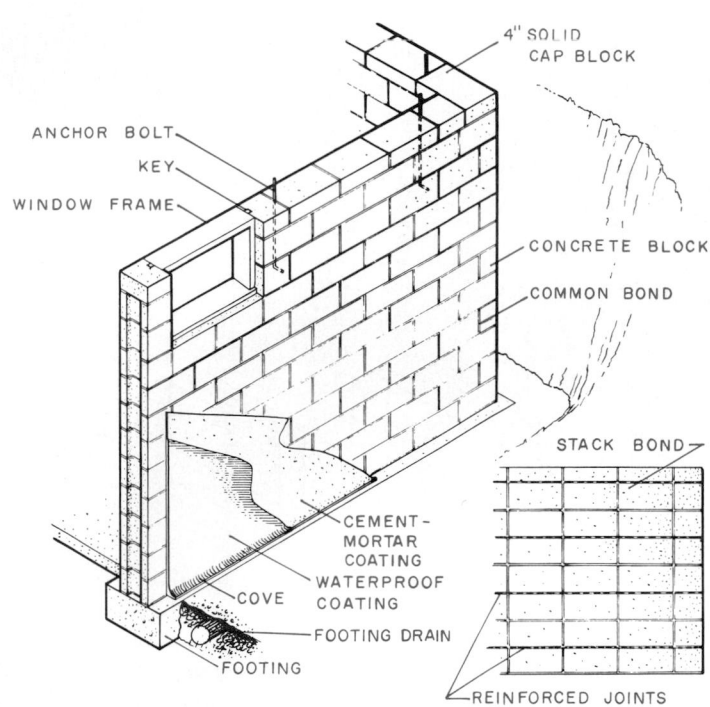

26-4. Concrete block walls.

Labels in figure:
- 4" SOLID CAP BLOCK
- ANCHOR BOLT
- KEY
- WINDOW FRAME
- CONCRETE BLOCK
- COMMON BOND
- STACK BOND
- CEMENT-MORTAR COATING
- WATERPROOF COATING
- COVE
- FOOTING DRAIN
- FOOTING
- REINFORCED JOINTS

26-5. This mason is applying asphalt waterproofing with a long-handled roller.

To provide a tight, waterproof joint between footing and wall, an elastic caulking compound is often used. The wall is waterproofed by applying a coating of mortar or cement plaster over the block and forming a cove where the wall joins with the footing. Fig. 26-4. When the mortar is dry, a coating of asphalt or other waterproofing is applied to the exterior of the wall. Fig. 26-5. This, along with a properly designed footing drain, will normally assure a dry basement.

Sometimes added protection is needed, as when wet soil conditions may be encountered. A waterproof membrane of roofing felt or similar material, with shingle-type laps of 4" to 6", can be applied over the coating. Hot tar or hot asphalt is commonly used over the membrane. This covering will prevent leaks from minor cracks that develop in the blocks or joints between the blocks.

MIXING MORTAR AND TRUCKING THE BLOCK

To build a strong, solid wall you need good mortar. The strength of the mortar bond depends on such items as:

➤ The type and quantity of mortar.
➤ The workability or plasticity of the mortar.
➤ The surface texture of the mortar bedding areas.
➤ The rate at which the masonry units absorb moisture from the mortar.
➤ The water retention of the mortar.
➤ The quality of workmanship in laying up the units.

Standard mortar is a mixture of portland cement, lime, sand, and water. Mortar mixes for various purposes are shown in Table 26-A. Mortar can also be made from masonry cement, sand, and water. Masonry cement is classified as Type N (the average strength for most general masonry work) or Type M (a much stronger mix).

Masonry walls subject to severe frost or stress require mortars that are stronger and more durable than walls exposed to ordinary conditions. Mortar should be mixed in power mixers except for very small jobs where it may be mixed by hand. To avoid damage to your skin, avoid prolonged contact with wet mortar. To prevent such contact, it is a good idea to wear protective clothing. Skin areas that have been exposed to wet mortar should be thoroughly washed with water.

Mortar will stiffen on the mortar board because of evaporation or hydration. When evaporation occurs, the mortar can be retempered to restore its workability by thorough remixing and by the addition of water as

Table 26-A. *Recommended Mortar Mixes—Proportions by Volume.*

Type of service	Cement	Hydrated lime	Mortar sand in damp, loose condition
For ordinary service	1—masonry cement* or	—	2 to 3
	1—portland cement	1 to 1¼	4 to 6
Subject to extremely heavy loads, violent winds, earth-quakes or severe frost action. Isolated piers.	1—masonry cement* plus 1—portland cement	—	4 to 6
	or 1—portland cement	0 to 1/4	2 to 3

* ASTM Specification C91, Type II

26-8. *Care should be taken to protect concrete blocks from the weather prior to laying them.*

required. Fig. 26-6. Mortar stiffened by hydration (setting) should be discarded. When unused mortar stiffens, it is not easy to tell whether evaporation or hydration is the cause. However, a judgment can usually be made on the basis of time elapsed after initial mixing. Mortar should be used within 2 ½ hours after original mixing when air temperature is 80 degrees F. or higher, and within 3 ½ hours when air temperature is below 80 degrees F. Mortar not used within these time limits should not be used.

Mortar must be sticky so that it will cling to the concrete block when it is laid into the wall. When taking a trowel full of mortar from the mortar board, shake the trowel with a quick vertical snap of the wrist to make the mortar stick to the trowel and shake off the excess. This also keeps the mortar from falling off the trowel when it is applied to the edges of the block. Block and mortar should be placed on the scaffold near final position to minimize your movements. Fig. 26-7.

Care must be taken to keep blocks dry on the job. They should be stockpiled on planks or other supports, with the edges free from contact with the ground, and covered for protection against wetting. Fig. 26-8. *Concrete block must not be allowed to get wet just before or during laying in the wall.*

LAYING THE BLOCK

First Course

The hollow cores in concrete blocks are larger at one end than at the other. Blocks should be laid so that the surfaces with the smaller holes are up. This provides a larger mortar-bedding area.

After locating the corners, place the blocks for the first course in position *without mortar* in order to check the layout. A chalked snap-line can be used to mark the footing and help to align the block accurately. A full mortar bed is then spread with a trowel. Make sure there is plenty of mortar along the footing in which to place the bottom edges of the blocks. Fig. 26-9. The corner block should be laid first and carefully positioned.

26-6. *Add water and thoroughly remix to restore the workability of mortar which has begun to dry out.*

26-7. *Distribute the blocks and the mortar to the areas in which they will be used.*

26-9. *Be certain to get a full bed of mortar on the footing when setting the first course.*

26-10. *Push the block downward into the mortar bed and against the previously laid block.*

26-11. *Use the level as a straightedge along the faces of the block to check the alignment.*

26-12. *The level is used to check the top edge for levelness.*

For vertical joints, only one end of the block is covered with mortar. By placing several blocks on end, you can apply mortar to the ends of three or four blocks in one operation. Each block is then brought over its final position and pushed downward into the mortar bed and against the previously laid block. Fig. 26-10.

After three or four blocks have been laid, use the mason's level as a straightedge to assure correct alignment of the block. Fig 26-11. Blocks are then carefully checked with the level and brought to proper grade. Fig 26-12. They are made plumb by tapping with the trowel handle. Fig. 26-13. The first course of concrete masonry should be laid with great care to make sure it is properly aligned, leveled, and plumbed. This will assist you in laying other courses and in building a straight, true wall.

After the first course is laid, apply mortar to the top of the face shells of the block. This is called *face shell mortar bedding*. A face shell is the side wall of a concrete block. Fig. 26-14. Mortar for the vertical joints can be applied to the ends of the next block or to the ends of the block previously laid. Some masons apply mortar to the ends of both blocks to insure well-fitted joints.

The corners of the wall are built first, usually four or five courses higher than the center of the wall. As each course is laid at the corner, check it with a level for alignment, Fig. 26-15, for level, Fig. 26-16, and for plumb, Fig. 26-17. Check each block carefully with a level or straightedge to make certain that the faces of the block are all in the same plane. Fig. 26-18. This is necessary to insure true, straight walls.

A *story pole* or *course pole* is simply a board with markings 8" apart. The use of such a pole provides an accurate method of positioning the top of the masonry

26-13. *The level is used to be certain the outside surface is plumb.*

26-14. *Mortar bedding the face shell in preparation for laying up additional courses.*

26-15. *Check the alignment of the blocks frequently.*

26-16. *Build the corners up first. Be sure to check the blocks for levelness as the work progresses.*

26-17. *After the corners have been built up, be sure to check the corner for plumb before continuing.*

26-18. *Use the level as a straightedge to check the faces of the block, making sure they are all on the same plane.*

26-19. Using a story pole or course pole.

26-20. If the blocks have been stepped back correctly, the alignment can be checked by holding a level or straightedge diagonally across the corners of the block.

for each course. Fig. 26-19. Mortar joints for concrete masonry should be ⅜" thick. Each course in building the corners is stepped back a half block. Check the horizontal spacing of the block by placing the level diagonally across the corners of the block. Fig. 26-20.

Between Corners

When filling in the wall between the corners, a mason's line is stretched from corner to corner for each course. The top, outside edge of each block is laid to this line. Fig. 26-21.

The way the block is handled or gripped is important and is learned with practice. Tipping the block slightly toward yourself, you can see the upper edge of the course below; thus you can place the lower edge

26-21. After the corners have been built up, stretch a mason's line from corner to corner for each course. Between the corners, set the blocks so their top edges align with the mason's line.

26-22. Set the block down carefully, making sure to align it with the block previously laid.

of the block directly over the course below. Fig. 26-22.

By rolling the block slightly to a vertical position and shoving it against the adjacent block, it can be laid to the mason's line with minimum adjustment. *All adjustments to final position must be made while the mortar is soft and plastic. Any adjustments made after the mortar has stiffened will break the mortar bond.* By tapping lightly with the trowel handle, each block is leveled and aligned to the mason's line. Fig. 26-23. The use of the mason's level between corners is limited to checking the face of each block to keep it lined up with the face of the wall.

To assure good bond, mortar should not be spread too far ahead of actual laying of the block or it will stiffen and lose its plasticity. As each block is laid, excess mortar at the joints is cut off with the trowel. Fig. 26-24. If the work is going well, the excess mortar can be applied directly to the end of the block just laid. Fig. 26-25. Should there be a

26-23. The block can be tapped into position with the handle of the trowel.

26-24. Cut off the excess mortar with the trowel.

26-25. Sometimes the mortar that has been cut from the joints can be applied to the ends of the block just laid.

26-26. Well-filled joints will result if mortar has been applied to the vertical joints of the block already in the wall and also to the block being set.

26-27. These blocks have a full mortar bed—that is, mortar has been applied to the cross webs as well as to the tops of the face shells.

delay long enough for the mortar to stiffen on the block, the mortar should be put back on the mortar board and reworked. The application of mortar to the vertical joints of the block already in the wall and to the block being set ensures well-filled joints. Fig. 26-26. "Dead" mortar that has been picked up from the scaffold or from the floor should not be used.

In some localities, a full mortar bed may be specified on all concrete block construction. Fig. 26-27.

Closure Block

The block which fills the final gap in a course between corners is called the *closure block*. To install this block, spread mortar on all edges of the opening and all four vertical edges of the block itself. Fig. 26-28. The closure block should be carefully lowered into place. Fig. 26-29. If some of the mortar falls out leaving an open joint, the closure block should be removed, fresh mortar applied, and the operation repeated.

26-28. When installing the closure block, mortar is applied to all four vertical edges of the opening as well as to the closure block.

26-29. *The closure block is carefully placed in position.*

26-30. *A metal tiebar is placed in the mortar joint to tie an intersecting wall to the main wall.*

26-31a. *Be sure to embed the ends of the tiebar in cores filled with mortar or concrete.*

26-31b. *Notice in Fig. 26-31a that a piece of metal lath has been placed under the tiebar. When the core is filled with mortar or concrete as in this picture, the lath will support the filling.*

26-32. *Metal lath placed across the joint used to tie a nonbearing intersecting wall to the main wall.*

Intersecting Bearing Walls

Bearing walls built of intersecting concrete blocks should not be tied together in a masonry bond, except at the corners. Instead, one wall should terminate at the face of the other wall, with a *control joint* at that point. (This is a joint which controls movement caused by stress in the wall. For more details see page 255.) For lateral support, bearing walls are tied together with a metal tiebar ¼" thick, ¼" wide, and 28" long, with 2" right angle bends on each end. Fig. 26-30. These tiebars are spaced not over 4' apart vertically. The bends at the ends of the tiebars are embedded in cores filled with mortar or concrete. Fig. 26-31a. Pieces of metal lath placed under the cores support the concrete or mortar filling. Fig. 26-31b.

If the control joint at the intersection of the two bearing walls is to be exposed to view or the weather, it should be constructed and sealed with a caulking compound as described on page 255.

Intersecting Nonbearing Walls

For tying nonbearing block walls to other walls, strips of metal lath or ¼" mesh galvanized hardware cloth are placed across the joint between the two walls. Fig. 26-32. The metal strips are placed in alternate courses in the wall. When one wall is constructed first, the metal strips are built into the wall and later tied into the mortar joint of the second wall.

Where the two walls meet, the vertical mortar joint is raked out to a depth of ¾" if it is exposed to view in the finished building. Caulking compound is then packed into this recess, as described on page 255.

Tooling

Weathertight joints and neat appearance of concrete block walls depend on proper tooling. After a section of the wall has been laid and the mortar has become "thumbprint hard" (so that the thumb makes no indentation), the mortar joints should be tooled. The tooling operation compacts the mortar and forces it tightly against the masonry on each side of the joint. Proper tooling also produces joints of uniform appearance, with sharp, clean lines. Unless otherwise specified on the plans, all joints should be tooled either concave or V-shaped.

The jointer for tooling horizontal joints should be at least 22" long, preferably longer, and upturned on one end to prevent gouging the mortar. A suitable handle should be located approximately in the center for handling ease. For concave joints, a tool made from a ⅝" round bar is satisfactory. Fig. 26-33. For V-shaped joints, a tool made from a ½" square bar is generally used. Fig. 26-34. Tooling of the head joints should be done first, using a small S-shaped jointer. Fig. 26-35. Tooling of the bed joints should follow. This will form a continuous horizontal joint. After the joints have been tooled, a trowel is used to trim off mortar burrs flush with the face of the wall. Fig. 26-36. Burrs can also be removed by rubbing with a burlap bag.

CAUTION: Do not move or straighten the block in any manner once the mortar has stiffened, or even partly stiffened. Final positioning of the block must be done while the mortar is soft and plastic. Any attempt to move or shift the block after the mortar has stiffened will break the mortar bond and allow the penetration of water. Fig. 26-37 shows such a break.

26-33. A jointer for concave joints can be made from a piece of ⅝" round bar.

26-34. A jointer for V-shaped bed joints can be made from a ½" square bar.

26-35. A small S-shaped jointer is used for striking the head joints.

26-36. Remove any mortar burrs with a trowel.

26-37. Never attempt to move or shift the block after the mortar has stiffened. This will break the mortar bond and permit water seepage.

Finishing Foundation Walls

Foundation walls of hollow concrete block must be capped with a course of solid masonry to help distribute the loads from floor beams and to act as a termite barrier. Solid-top blocks, in which the top 4" is of solid concrete, are available in some areas. Fig. 26-38. When stretcher blocks are used, a strip of metal lath wide enough to cover the core spaces is placed in the mortar joints under the top course. Fig. 26-39. The cores are then filled with concrete or mortar

and troweled smooth. Fig. 26-40. Sometimes 4" solid units are used to cap concrete block foundation walls. Fig. 26-41. All vertical joints must be completely filled, and slushing of the joints should not be permitted. That is, mortar should not be thrown into the joint with the trowel. The mortar must be placed on the end of the block before it is set in place. Building codes in some parts of the country require that block walls include a steel-reinforced bond beam of poured concrete at every fourth course in the wall.

Installing Anchor Bolts

Wood plates on which the house framing bears are fastened to the top of concrete block walls. This is done by means of anchor bolts ½" in diameter and 18" long, spaced not more than 4' apart. These anchor bolts are placed in cores of the top two courses of block, with the cores filled with concrete or mortar. Pieces of metal lath are placed in the second horizontal mortar joint from the top of the wall and under the cores to be filled. Fig. 26-42. The lath will support the concrete or mortar filling. The threaded end of the bolt should extend above the top of the wall. Fig. 26-43. When the filling has hardened, the wood plate can be securely fastened to the wall.

26-38. A solid-top block is often used for the top course.

26-39. When stretcher blocks are used for the top course, place a strip of metal lath in the mortar joint below.

26-40. With metal lath in place, the cores of the top-course blocks can be filled and troweled smooth.

26-41. Sometimes 4" solid blocks are used to cap a wall.

26-42. Place a piece of metal lath under the core to be filled. This will support the concrete or mortar.

26-43. Fill the core with concrete or mortar and insert the bolt so that the threads extend above the top of the wall.

Control Joints

Stress in masonry walls causes movement which must be controlled. Control joints are one method of solving this problem. These joints are used to control cracking resulting from unusual stresses. The joints are built into the wall in a way that permits slight wall movement without cracking the masonry. They are continuous from the top of the wall to the bottom. To keep control joints from being too noticeable, care must be taken to make them plumb and of the same thickness as the other mortar joints. When a control joint cannot be concealed or when it will be exposed to weather, it should be sealed with caulking compound, following the manufacturer's directions.

Unless a control joint is to be caulked, it should be laid the same as other vertical joints. For a joint to be caulked, make a recess for the caulking material by raking out mortar to a depth of about ¾". Do this after the mortar is quite stiff. Fig. 26-44.

The spacing and location of control joints will depend on a number of factors:
  ➤ The length of the wall.
  ➤ Architectural details.

➤ Local experience about such joints.

Control joints should be placed at the junctions of bearing as well as nonbearing walls, at places where walls join columns and pilasters, and in walls weakened by openings. In long walls, control joints are ordinarily spaced at approximately 20' intervals, again depending on local experience.

26-45. *Precast lintels set in place over openings.*

Lintels

Precast concrete lintels are often used over door and window openings. For modular window and door openings, precast concrete lintels are designed with an offset (or recessed area) on the underside. Fig. 26-45. Steel angles (pieces of steel bent at right angles) are also used for lintels to support block over openings. To fit modular openings, the steel lintel angles must be installed with an offset on the underside. Fig. 26-46.

RELATED OPERATIONS

Cutting Block

Concrete masonry units usually are available in half-length as well as full-length units. However, to fit special job conditions it is sometimes necessary to cut a block with a brick hammer and chisel. The block is scored on both

26-44. *Mortar is raked out of a vertical joint to provide a recess for caulking material.*

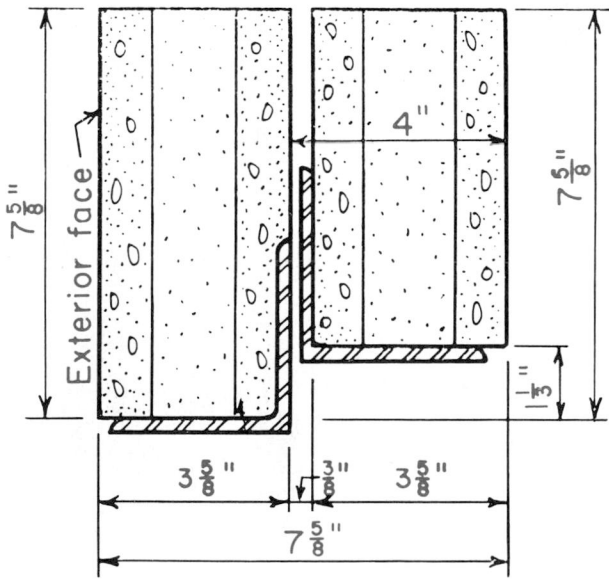

26-46. *Steel angles are sometimes used to support block over openings.*

26-47. *For a clean break, score the blocks along both sides with a chisel.*

26-48. *A masonry saw used for cutting block is fast and accurate.*

sides to make a clean break. Fig. 26-47. For fast, neat cutting, masonry saws are often used. Fig. 26-48.

Patching and Cleaning Block Walls

Any patching of the mortar joints or filling of defects in the blocks should be done with fresh mortar. Particular care should be taken to prevent smearing mortar onto the surface of the block.

26-49. *Remove mortar droppings with the trowel after they have dried slightly.*

26-50. *Rubbing with a small piece of block will remove dry mortar from the surface of the wall.*

26-51. *After the wall has been cleaned with the trowel or a piece of block, brush it for a final cleaning.*

Mortar smears will mar the appearance of the finished wall. Once hardened they cannot be removed. Acid wash should not be used to remove smears or mortar droppings from concrete block walls. Therefore care should be taken to keep the wall clean during construction. Any mortar droppings that stick to the block wall should be allowed to dry slightly before removal with a trowel. This keeps them from smearing the wall. Fig. 26-49. The mortar may smear if removed while too soft. When dry and hard, most of the remaining mortar can be removed by rubbing with a small piece of block. Fig. 26-50. Brushing the rubbed spots removes practically all of the mortar. Fig. 26-51.

Protection

Boards, building paper, or tarpaulins are used to cover the tops of unfinished block walls at the end of the day's work. This will prevent rain or snow from entering the cores. Fig. 26-52.

26-52. *At the end of each day, cover the walls to prevent water from getting on surfaces where blocks will be laid.*

ESTIMATING

Number of Blocks

The number of blocks necessary for a building can be determined by the area of the wall to be built. Nine 8" × 8" × 16" blocks will make eight sq. ft. of vertical wall area. Therefore take the total number of square feet in the wall and divide it by eight. Multiply the result by nine and you will have a good estimate of the number of blocks necessary for the wall.

$$\frac{\text{sq. ft. wall area}}{8} \times 9 = \text{No. of blocks}$$

For example, consider a house with a 25' × 40' foundation and a 7'-high finished basement. The simplest way to find the total sq. ft. of wall area is to multiply the perimeter times the depth. The perimeter is the length of the four walls added together. In this instance the perimeter is 130' (25' + 25' + 40' + 40' = 130'). Multiply this times 7' (the depth of the basement) and you find that the total area of the four basement walls is 910 sq. ft.

Now apply the formula given above:

$$910 \div 8 = 113.75$$
$$113.75 \times 9 = 1,023.75$$

Rounded off, your answer would be 1,024. This, however, is not the number of blocks needed. One further step is necessary. Because the courses overlap or interlock at the corners, subtract ½ block for each corner of each course. The wall in the example would be 11 blocks high; therefore subtract 5½ blocks for each corner or 22 blocks. This shows that a total of 1,002 blocks would be needed. This number would be reduced somewhat more to allow for

windows or other openings.

The number of concrete blocks necessary for a wall can also be determined by referring to the chart in Table 26-B. In the left column, find the size of the block used. If you select an 8" × 8" × 16" block, the chart indicates 110 concrete blocks for each 100 sq. ft. of wall. The walls in the example, you will recall, had an area of 910 sq. ft. Divide this by 100 to find the number of sq. ft. expressed in hundreds.

$$\frac{910 \text{ (total sq. ft.)}}{100} = 9.1 \text{ (hundreds of sq. ft.)}$$

The chart shows that 110 blocks are needed for each 100 sq. ft. Therefore by multiplying 9.1 times 100, you find the total number of blocks needed.

$9.1 \times 110 = 1,001$ total blocks needed

Note that some adjustment may still be necessary if there are openings in the wall. However, the chart allows for the overlapping of blocks at the corners, so it is not necessary to subtract for this as in the previous example.

Note also that the answer is not precisely the same as when calculated by the method given

previously. However, the estimates are very close, which shows that both methods are reliable.

Amount of Mortar

The number of cubic feet of mortar needed for a block wall can also be determined from Table 26-B. For the walls in the preceding example, the chart shows that 3.25 cu. ft. of mortar would be needed for every 100 sq. ft. of wall area. You will recall that there were 9.1 hundreds of sq. ft. in the walls. Thus by multiplying 9.1 times 3.25 you find the total amount of mortar needed to lay up the walls.

$9.1 \times 3.25 = 29.5$ cu. ft. of mortar

Labor Costs

To determine labor costs for laying up the walls, again consult Table 26-B. You will see that 8" × 8" × 16" blocks are laid at a rate of 18 per hour. Taking the figure 1,001 for the total number of blocks, you can divide that number by 18 to learn the number of hours needed for laying the block.

$$\frac{1,001}{18} = 55.6 \text{ hours}$$

Table 26-B. *Estimating Table for Masonry Blocks.*

Masonry Blocks		Material For 100 Square Feet of Wall					Labor
	Wall Thickness	Concrete Block		Lightweight Block			
Size		No. of Units	Mortar Cubic Feet	No. of Units	Mortar Cubic Feet		Blocks Per Hour
8 x 4 x 12	4"			146	4.0		24
8 x 4 x 16	4"			110	3.25		22
12 x 4 x 12	4"			100	3.25		30
8 x 6 x 16	6"			110	3.25		21
8 x 8 x 16	8"	110	3.25				18
8 x 10 x 16	10"	110	3.25				16
8 x 12 x 16	12"	110	3.25				13

Note: Mortar quantities based on ⅜" mortar joints, plus 25% waste. For ½" joints add 25%.

Multiply the hours needed by the hourly rate of pay for laying block. This will give you the labor cost.

SURFACE BONDING OF CONCRETE BLOCK

A material that eliminates the need for conventional mortar above the first course in concrete block walls is available. This material is a mixture of specially formulated alkali-resistant glass fibers ½" long, hydrated lime, portland cement, and a water-resistant agent. The glass fibers provide strength by acting like steel mesh does in reinforced concrete. There are no epoxies or resins in this surface bonding mix. This fiberglass reinforced mortar is applied to the wall surface after the blocks have been stacked dry (with the exception of the base course).

The material is designed to surface-bond concrete masonry blocks to form above-grade (not exceeding two floors or 25 ft.) and below-grade walls, load bearing and nonbearing, in residential and light commercial construction.

In tests conducted by the National Concrete Masonry Association and in actual field installations, surface bonding provided greater flexural strength than conventionally mortared walls.

Since individual block joints are not mortared, users of this material realize important labor savings. Other significant benefits include:
➤ Moisture protection without additional treatment.
➤ Finishing flexibility; walls can be painted, faced, or left as is.
➤ Do-it-yourself homeowners find it easier to lay up block walls.

Layout

The layout of the running bond for the first course is very important because it helps determine whether it will be necessary to cut an odd-sized block for the closure.

The corner units should be laid first, leveled, and aligned. Then the first course should be laid with great care because it will assist you in laying succeeding courses and in building a straight, plumb wall. Fig 26-53.

Once three or four units have been laid, use a level to check them for alignment, grade, and plumbness. Fig. 26-54.

26-53. Lay the first course in a full mortar bed on the footings. The head joints should be butted tightly withour mortar.

26-54. Level and plumb every third or fourth course.

In laying the first course, place a full mortar bed on the foundation, the full thickness of the wall. It is not necessary to apply mortar to the head joints.

Stacking

Once the first course is set in mortar, stacking of block may begin. The corners are usually laid up about four courses high, stepping back each course by one-half a unit length.

The wall is then filled in between these stepped corners. Stretch a mason's line tightly from corner to corner at each third course to assist you in laying the top outside edge of each block to proper line and grade. Fig. 26-55. Blocks should be tightly butted together.

Smoothing the top of the block by scraping the surface of two blocks together eliminates any excess material or burrs. This will aid in the stacking procedure. Block may be stacked to a height not exceeding 10 ft. before applying the reinforced mortar.

26-55. Use a mason's line to assure proper line and grade every third course.

26-56. *Joints are shimmed where necessary to insure a plumb and level wall.*

Shimming

Since there are variations in block from different producers and different areas, keeping the walls level and plumb may require shimming. If shimming is necessary, use sand, sheet metal, or mortar to level and align. Fig. 26-56. The use of ground block will eliminate any variability found in standard block and allow stacking without shimming.

Anchoring Intersecting Walls

Intersecting masonry walls should be anchored with metal straps as in conventional construction. However, since there is no mortar joint, the webs of the block must be notched to accept the anchor. Fig. 26-57.

26-57. *The metal strap anchor in place. The block has been notched (see arrow) to accept the anchor.*

Table 26-C *Control Joints. Control joint locations.*

Wall Location	Length of Wall		
	0'-25'	**26'-59'**	**Over 60'**
Below Grade	No Control Joints Required		Control Joint Every 50'
Above Grade	No Control Joints Required	Use Length to Height Ratio of 3, with a Maximum Length of 50' between Control Joints, regardless of Height.	

Control Joints

Build control joints into the wall as you would in a conventional mortared block wall. See "Control Joints," page 255. The control joints must extend through the reinforced mortar surface coating and, on an exterior wall, must be watertight. Table 26-C.

1.
Determine rough opening dimension required.

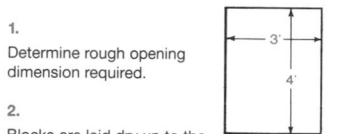

2.
Blocks are laid dry up to the bottom of the window sill. Note: If proper height is not attained in natural coursing, a solid masonry unit can be placed under the sill. Also, the sill unit can be laid in mortar or reinforced mortar if additional height is required. (See Step 5)

3.
Mark the window and door width dimensions on the bottom sill course previously laid up.

4.
Lay up the leads for the openings at these marks.

5.
Fill in each course with block as the walls require. A cut block may be necessary to complete each course. If necessary, place solid masonry units under sill to obtain proper height. If a metal masonry window or door is used, install the metal frame, then place lintel on top of opening. If wood casement windows are specified, follow Step 5 with the exception of installing window casement.

Window and Door Placement

Doors and windows are placed in walls in the same manner as with conventional mortared block walls. Because surface bonding eliminates the need for placing mortar in the joint between the blocks, the rough opening of windows and doors will be altered. To compensate for this dimension difference when installing windows, use steps 1-5 in Fig. 26-58. When installing doors, omit Step 2.

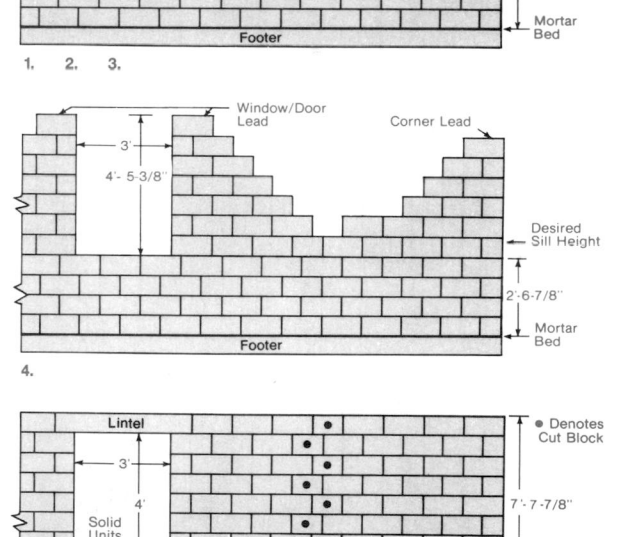

26-58. *Compensating for rough opening dimension differences.*

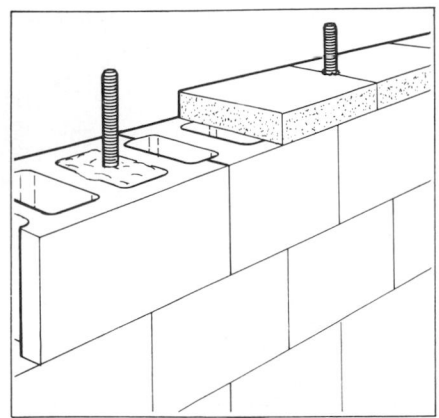

26-59. *Notch the solid blocks for the anchor bolts.*

The Top Course

The top course of dry-stacked concrete block walls must be constructed to insure adequate distribution of vertical loads. The top course construction for surface bonding is the same as with conventional mortared walls. If solid top masonry units and anchor bolts are specified, notch these units to allow clearance for the bolts Fig. 26-59.

Changes in Wall Thickness

When changing wall thicknesses, cap the lower portion in the same manner as a top course. The first course of the new wall thickness must then be started in a mortar bed. Fig. 26-60.

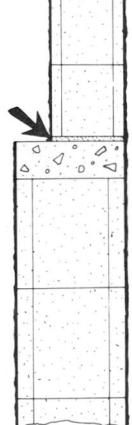

26-60. *Changing the thickness of a wall. Note that a conventional mortar bed is indicated at the arrow.*

Mixing Fiberglass Reinforced Mortar

Mix according to the manufacturer's instructions. Use a clean mortar mixer and make sure the water is clean. Blend the mortar for one to two minutes or until all materials are thoroughly wetted. Additional water may be added to achieve a consistency similar to mortar.

Excessive mixing can cause lumps to form and should be avoided. Total mixing time should not exceed five minutes.

Tools

Standard masonry tools are used with the fiberglass reinforced mortar. To speed application and reduce lines, it is recommended that the corners of the mason's trowel be rounded to a ⅜" radius.

A sheet metal device called a joint guide is used when the application is interrupted for more than an hour. Place the joint guide over the last course of laid block and apply the reinforced mortar up to the straight edge. Fig. 26-61.

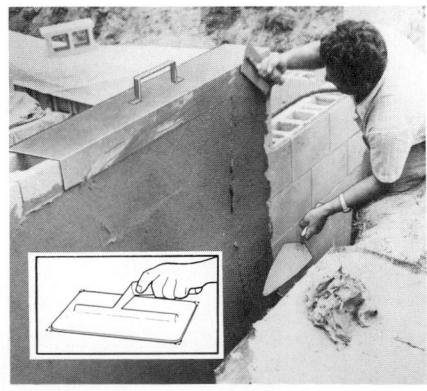

26-61. *Use a joint guide when application is to be stopped for more than one hour. Insert: Round the corners of a conventional trowel for use when applying the reinforced mortar.*

Application of Reinforced Mortar

The wall must be free of dirt, oil, paint or other foreign matter. It must be thoroughly wetted down prior to fiberglass mortar mix application. Fig. 26-62.

The mix should be troweled smoothly on both sides of the wall to a minimum thickness of ⅛". Press firmly to ensure a good bond. Fig. 26-63.

Fiberglass reinforced mortar that has begun to "set," or which is not used within 1½ hours after initial

26-62. *Wet down the wall prior to the application of the surface bonding material.*

26-63. *Trowel the reinforced mortar on both sides of the wall to a thickness of ⅛".*

mixing, should be discarded. Fiberglass reinforced mortar that has stiffened due to evaporation within a 1½ hour period can be retempered to restore its workability.

When it is necessary to discontinue application of the surface bonding for more than one hour, the joint in the reinforced fiberglass mortar must not coincide with the joints in the block. In addition, for the best appearance, the stoppage or discontinuance at vertical joints should occur at a corner, pilaster, or control joint. In this way one day's work can be blended into the next.

Finishing

Various conventional finishes can be applied to fiberglass reinforced mortared walls. Walls that will receive a second treatment such as stucco can be left with a rough finish that will serve as the base coat. The finish coat may be either hand- or spray-applied. Furring strips for supplemental surfaces may be attached to the wall by any conventional method, including nailing and adhesives.

Walls that will be left exposed can be given a smooth finish by taking extra time and care in troweling. These walls can be painted with any standard masonry paint.

Curing

Within 24 hours after application of the reinforced mortar, the wall should be dampened with a water mist when temperature is above 40 degrees F. This prevents premature drying. Depending on the temperature and humidity, surface bonding applications can be wetted down earlier than 24 hours.

26-64. *Freshly applied reinforced mortar should be covered in the event of heavy rain.*

In the event of heavy rain, freshly applied reinforced mortar should be protected with a waterproof covering until it has cured for at least eight hours. Fig. 26-64.

Backfilling

Avoid backfilling the foundation walls before the first floor is in place, or brace the walls by some means until the first floor is installed. A completed wall must cure 48 hours before backfilling and 24 hours before structural work is begun. Avoid standing on the walls during this period. If high compaction is required or mechanical compacting equipment is to be used, the surface bonding must be allowed to cure at least two weeks prior to beginning such work.

The finished grade should be sloped away from the foundation walls for good surface drainage.

Settlement of backfill material should be anticipated. Operating heavy equipment any closer to a wall than a distance equal to the height of this fill should be avoided.

26-65. *Remove a 2" section of reinforced mortar around a damaged area. Then reapply reinforced mortar to patch the damage.*

Repairs

If a block is knocked out of alignment after application of the fiberglass reinforced mortar, or if cracks appear as a result of foundation settlement, repairs can be made by removing a 1" strip on either side paralleling the damage. If the reinforced mortar is still workable, scrape it off. If it has set, chip the area clean and reapply as indicated in the application section. Fig. 26-65.

Other Construction Details

The following construction techniques are the same as with conventional mortared block walls.

➤ Bracing for above- and below-grade walls.
➤ Vertical and horizontal reinforcement.
➤ Wall footings and drainage construction.
➤ Wall thicknesses.
➤ Lintel and sill installation (apply reinforced mortar over lintel faces).
➤ Electrical and plumbing installation.
➤ Pilasters.
➤ Beam pockets.

ESTIMATING

Because mortar joints are eliminated in dry-stack construction, more block is needed per square foot of wall area.

The number of concrete masonry units and amount of surface bonding required can easily be calculated for each 100 square feet of wall by using Table 26-D.

Wall dimensions, door openings, windows and wall heights should be checked to compensate for the elimination of all mortar joint thickness except the bed layer (see Table 26-E). Using full-sized block (full 8" × 8" × 16" dimensions) where available will eliminate this situation.

Table 26-D. *Estimating Table.*

Actual Height of Units, Inches	No. of Units per 100 sq. ft.	Bags per 100 sq. ft. of Wall*
7⅝ (Modular)	121	2
3⅝ (Modular)	255	2
8 (Nonmodular)	115	2

* Includes application to both sides 100 sq. ft. wall.

Table 26-E. *Standard 8" Block.*

No. Block	Length of Wall	Height of Wall
1	1' 3⅝"	8"
2	2' 7¼"	1' 3⅝"
3	3'10⅞"	1'11¼"
4	5' 2½"	2' 6⅞"
5	6' 6⅛"	3' 2½"
6	7' 9¾"	3'10⅛"
7	9' 1⅜"	4' 5¾"
8	10' 5"	5' 1⅜"
9	11'3⅝"	5' 9"
10	13'0¼"	6' 4⅝"
11	14'3⅞"	7' 0¼"
12	15'7½"	7' 7⅞"
13	16'11⅛"	8' 3½"
14	18'2¾"	8'11⅛"
15	19'6⅜"	9' 6¾"

QUESTIONS

1. What is the actual size of most concrete blocks?

2. What is the standard height of a concrete block basement wall? How many courses is this?

3. Describe a stack bond pattern.

4. Name three factors that determine the strength of mortar.

5. When laying a concrete block foundation wall, which block should be laid first?

6. What is a good method to insure that the top of each masonry course is exactly 8" high?

7. When laying concrete blocks, which end is laid face up? Why?

8. What is a closure block?

9. What is a good test to determine when the joints should be tooled?

10. What is a control joint?

11. Why should mortar droppings that stick to the wall be allowed to dry slightly before they are removed?

ACTIVITIES

1. Language Arts. Assume that you are a contractor. You are dealing with a customer who is complaining that you are laying the block for her home too slowly. Explain why it is a slow process. Explain the concept of *mortar bond*.

2. Language Arts. In a comparison/contrast essay, explain the advantages of surface bonding compared with conventional mortared walls.

3. Language Arts. Based upon previous discussions of pressure as a force per unit of area, explain why two stretcher blocks will not support as much as three stretcher blocks, even though the outside measurements of each are the same.

4. Math. A house 26' by 40' will have an 11-course foundation wall. Estimate how many blocks 8" × 8" × 16" will be needed.

27

Slab and Flatwork

Concrete flatwork consists of flat areas of poured concrete, usually 5" or less in thickness. Examples are concrete floor construction for no-basement houses, basement floors, driveways, and walks.

CONCRETE FLOOR SLABS ON GROUND

The number of new one-story houses with full basements has declined steadily, particularly in the warmer areas of the United States. This is due in part to lower construction costs of houses without basements and an apparent decrease in the need for the basement space. For residences without basements or for unexcavated portions under houses, concrete floors on the ground are an excellent type of construction. Fig. 27-1.

Two types of concrete floor construction are the *combined* (or *unified*) *slab and foundation* and the *independent slab and foundation*.

Combined Slab and Foundation

Sometimes referred to as the thickened-edge slab or monolithic floor this construction is useful in warm climates where frost

27-1. *Floor slabs are common examples of concrete flatwork. This slab shows how rough plumbing lines are cast into the floor during pouring.*

penetration is not a problem and where soil conditions are especially favorable. It consists of a footing poured over a vapor barrier with the slab thicker and reinforced at the edges. Fig. 27-2. The bottom of the footing should be at least 1' below the natural grade line and supported on solid, unfilled, well-drained ground.

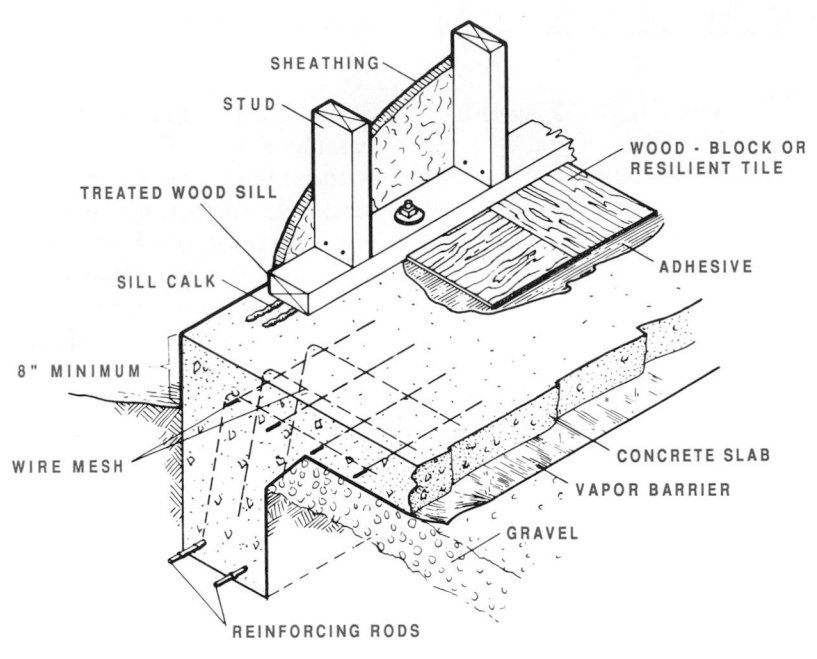

27-2. *A concrete floor and foundation combination (thickened-edge slab).*

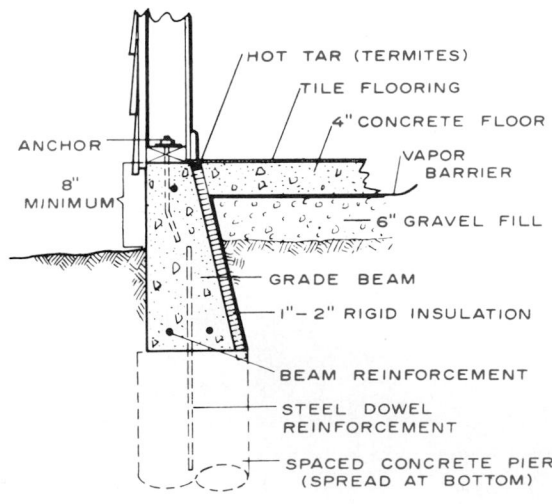

27-3. *A reinforced grade beam used to support a concrete floor. The grade beam spans the area between the concrete piers which are located below the frostline.*

Independent Concrete Slab and Foundation Walls

In areas where ground freezes fairly deep during winter, the walls of the house must be supported by foundations or piers which extend below the frostline to solid bearing on unfilled soil. In such construction, the concrete slab and foundation walls are usually separate. Three typical systems are suitable for such conditions. Figs. 27-3 through 27-5.

CONCRETE FLOOR SLAB REQUIREMENTS

To provide a satisfactory concrete floor slab, the following basic construction requirements should be met:

➤ The finish floor level should be high enough above the natural ground level so that finish grade around the house can be sloped away for good drainage. Top of slab should be no less than 8" above the ground and the siding no less than 6".

➤ Topsoil should be removed. Sewer and water lines are installed, then covered with 4" to 6" of gravel or crushed rock well tamped in place.

➤ A vapor barrier consisting of a heavy plastic film such as polyethylene should be put under the concrete slab. Joints should be lapped at least 4" and sealed. The barrier should be strong enough to resist puncturing during placing of the concrete.

➤ A permanent, waterproof, nonabsorbent type of rigid insulation should be installed around the perimeter of the wall. Insulation may extend down on the inside of the wall vertically or under the slab edge horizontally.

➤ The slab should be reinforced

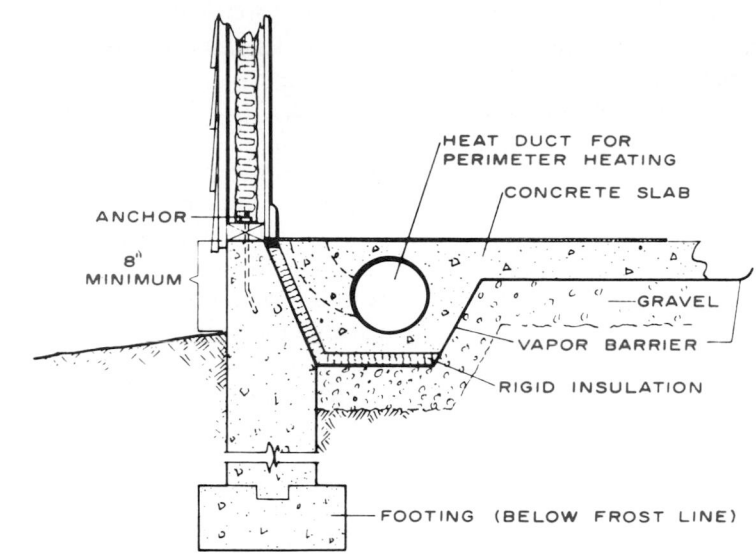

27-4. *Installation details for perimeter heating in a concrete floor.*

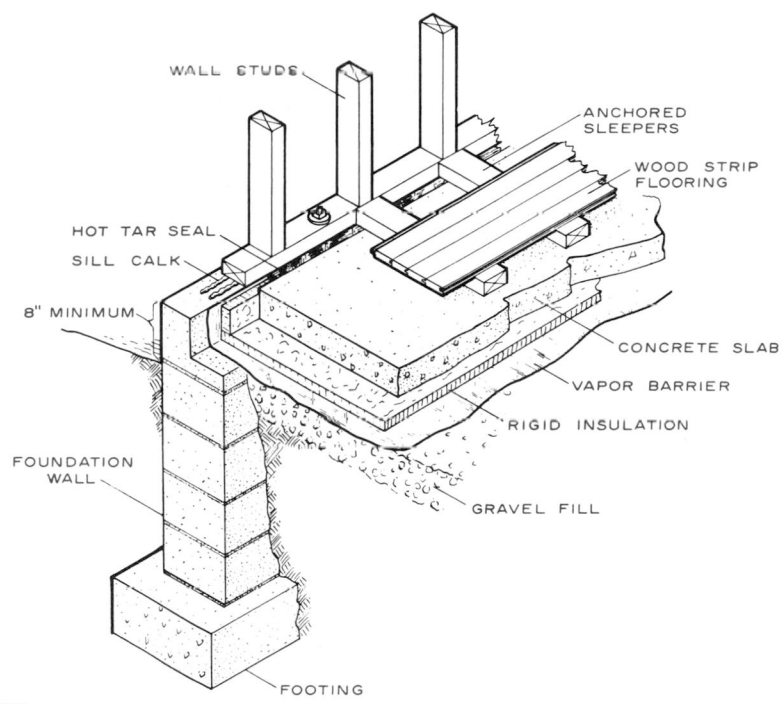

27-5. *An independent concrete floor and wall. The concrete block foundation wall is supported on a footing which is below the frostline.*

with 6" × 6" No. 10 wire mesh or other effective reinforcing. The concrete slab should be at least 4" thick. A thickened-edge slab is preferred in termite areas. Fig. 27-2.

➤ After leveling (as by screeding) the surface should be smoothed with wood or metal floats while it is still plastic. (Screeding and floating equipment and operations are discussed on pages 267-269.) If a smooth, dense surface is needed for the installation of wood or resilient tile with adhesives, the surface should be given a final smoothing with a steel trowel.

CONSTRUCTING A CONCRETE FLOOR SLAB*

Subgrade

It is important that the *subgrade* (the earth below the slab) be well and uniformly compacted to prevent any unequal settlement of the floor slab.

All organic matter such as sod and roots should first be removed and the ground leveled off. Any holes or other irregularities in the subgrade and any trenches for utilities should be filled in layers not exceeding 6" deep and thoroughly tamped. Material for fill should be of uniform character. It should not contain large lumps, stones, frozen chunks, or material which will rot.

The entire subgrade should be rough-graded to an elevation slightly above the finished grade and then thoroughly compacted by tamping or rolling. The finished subgrade should be carefully checked for elevation and profile.

Soil cannot be properly compacted if it is too wet or too dry. A rough idea of the proper moisture content of ordinary soils, except very sandy ones, may be obtained by squeezing some in the hand. With proper moisture content the soil will cling together but will not be plastic or muddy. If the soil is too dry, it should be sprinkled with water and mixed before compacting. If the soil is too wet, it must be allowed to dry. If there is any question that sandy soil may be too dry, water should be added, since an excess of water in such soil does not prevent compacting.

---

* Adapted from material provided by courtesy of the Portland Cement Association.

27-6. *Compacting coarse granular fill before the application of a grout coat.*

Granular Fill

A coarse fill should be placed over the finished subgrade. The fill should be brought to the desired grade and then thoroughly compacted. A small area of fill can be compacted by hand. Fig. 27-6. If the area is large, however, a mechanical tamper should be used. This tool, which is powered by a gasoline motor, is guided by hand over the area to be compacted. This granular (grainy) fill should consist of coarse slag, gravel, or crushed stone, preferably ranging from ½" to 1" in diameter. The fill material particles should be of uniform size to insure a maximum volume of air space in the fill. If

necessary, the material should be screened to remove any *fines* (finely crushed or powdered material). The large volume of air space will keep subsoil moisture from being absorbed.

A perimeter drain line should be placed around the outside edge of the exterior wall footings. The line is connected to drains to help keep ground moisture out of this granular fill. Fig. 27-7. Drain lines are not necessary where the floor is to be located on relatively high ground, where subsoil is well drained, or in a dry climate.

Provisions for Mechanical Trades

Ducts for heating systems as well as supply and waste plumbing lines can be placed under the granular fill. Water service supply lines, if placed under the floor slab, should be installed in trenches of the same depth as those outside the building. This will prevent damage from freezing if the building is not occupied during cold weather. Connections to these utilities can be brought to a point above the finished concrete floor level prior to concreting. The electric supply line and all distributing lines for

electricity and plumbing are carried in the walls or partitions.

Dampproofing

After the granular fill has been compacted and graded, a stiff grout coat should be placed over it. This will provide a smooth surface for installing a membrane-type material for dampproofing. The stiff grout should consist of one part portland cement and three parts sand. This should be at least ½" thick and should be broomed or floated in place.

The grouted surface, when hardened and dried, should be mopped with hot asphalt. The tops of any bearing partition footings should also be mopped. As the mopping proceeds, a layer of 15-pound asphalt saturated roofing felt should be placed on the hot asphalt with edges of felt well lapped. (This felt is the dampproofing membrane mentioned earlier.) Two layers of roofing felt are recommended, with hot asphalt mopped between layers and also on top of the second layer. Fig 27-8. This membrane dampproofing should be continuous over the entire floor area and carried up on the inside of the foundation walls to a point 1" or more above the finished floor level. Fig. 27-7. Workers must

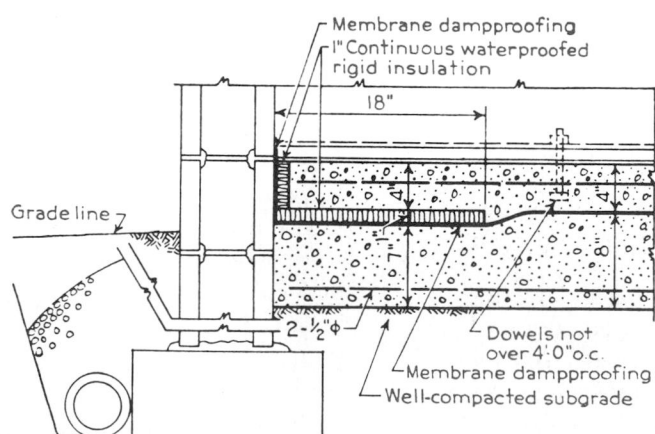

27-7. *Construction details of a concrete floor showing dampproofing and insulation requirements.*

27-8. *Applying dampproofing over the grout coat in preparation for a concrete floor slab.*

be cautioned against puncturing the membrane when placing the concrete floor.

Reinforcement

Metal reinforcement is often placed in a concrete slab to increase its tensile strength and minimize cracking. This reinforcement can consist either of reinforcing bars (called rebar) or welded-wire "fabric" (a grid of horizontal and vertical wires fabricated into a roll). In a 4" thick slab, the reinforcing should be placed 1½" from the top surface. Any reinforcement should be in place before the concrete is poured. Contractors sometimes roll welded-wire fabric over the excavation. They then use a rake or a hook to pull it upwards into the concrete during the pour. However, this makes it difficult to tell exactly where the reinforcement will end. For a more detailed discussion of metal reinforcement of concrete, see Unit 24, "Concrete and Footings."

Insulation

In cold climates, rigid insulation is placed between the foundation walls and the edge of the floor slab. Studies have indicated that this edge insulation is very important in limiting the amount of heat lost by conduction. In addition, rigid insulation may sometimes be placed beneath the slab and on the exterior face of the foundation walls. In warm climates, rigid insulation is generally not needed.

Concrete

Concrete for the floor slab and bearing partition footing should be made with durable, well-graded aggregate. The concrete should contain not more than 6 gallons of water for each sack of cement,

including the moisture contained in the aggregate. If the sand is average-moist, do not add more than 5 gallons of water per sack of cement. The mix should consist of one part portland cement to approximately 2¼ parts of fine aggregate well graded from ¼" down, and three parts of coarse aggregate well graded in size from ¼" up to 1".

The concrete should be workable, so it can be placed without honeycombing or developing excess water on the surface. If necessary, the proportion of fine and coarse aggregate should be adjusted to obtain a mix of desired workability. After placing, the concrete should be thoroughly consolidated by vibrating or by tamping and spading. Then it should be finished. The subsequent steps in finishing the concrete surface will depend upon the floor finish specified.

After finishing, the concrete should be kept moist for at least two days. This improves its strength considerably. However, when the finished floor is to be exposed concrete, at least five days of moist curing are required. Moist burlap or canvas or a waterproof concrete curing paper may be used to cover the floor slab during this period. Curing should begin as soon as the concrete is hard enough to prevent damage. If burlap or canvas is used, it should be kept wet by sprinkling with water.

FINISHING CONCRETE

A horizontal concrete surface, such as a floor, driveway, or sidewalk slab, must be finished. Fig. 27-9. The finish will depend on the use. A good, non-slippery finish is best for sidewalks; a coarse, scored surface for driveways; and a smooth-troweled finish for porches

27-9. *After a slab is poured, it is finished to give it a surface appropriate for its final use.*

and basement floors. A stiff, coarse broom is useful in giving the surface a scored finish. The broom is run crosswise to the slab. Smooth finishes are produced with a steel trowel.

Screeding. The first step in finishing a slab is called *screeding*. A hand-operated screed and the method of using it are shown in Fig. 27-10. The chief purpose of screeding is to level the surface of the slab by striking off (removing) the excess concrete. The concrete is struck off just after it is placed in the forms. The screed rides on the edges of the side forms or on wood or metal strips set up for the

27-10. *Screeding a concrete slab.*

27-11. *A power screed.*

27-12. *An edger.*

purpose. Two people move the screed along the slab. The movement should be like that of a saw.

Screeding may also be done by means of mechanical equipment. Fig. 27-11.

Edging and Jointing. When all water and water sheen has left the surface and the concrete has started to stiffen, other finishing operations can be done. Edging, if necessary, can be done at this time. This operation produces a rounded edge on the slab to prevent chipping or damage. The edger should be run back and forth until a finished edge is produced. The cement mason should be careful that all coarse aggregate particles are covered. Fig. 27-12.

Immediately following edging, the slab is jointed (or grooved). This means that a jointing tool is used to cut *control* or *contraction* *joints* about ¾" deep in the slab. The purpose of these joints is to control cracking. Sometimes shrinkage stresses are present in the slab as a result of temperature changes or dryness. These stresses can cause the concrete to crack. However, where the joints are cut, the thickness of the slab is reduced.

Thus cracks are likely to occur only at these intentionally weakened points. When the concrete shrinks, these joints open slightly, thus preventing irregular and unsightly random cracks. Fig. 27-13.

In sidewalk and driveway construction, the tooled joints are usually spaced at intervals equal to the width of the slab, but not more than 20' intervals. As mentioned, for control joints the jointer should have a ¾" bit. However, if the slab is to be grooved only for decorative purposes, jointers with shallower bits may be used.

It is good practice to use a straight 1" × 8" or 1" × 10" board as a guide when making the groove in the concrete slab. If the board is not straight it should be planed true. The tooled joints should be perpendicular to the edge of the

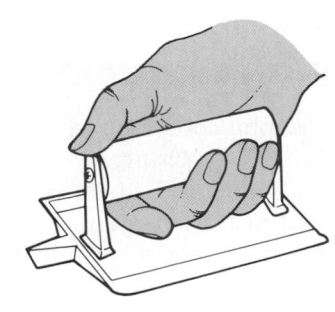

27-13. *A jointer.*

slab. The same care must be taken in running joints as in edging, for a tooled joint can add to or detract from the appearance of the finished slab.

Floating. Screeding leaves a level surface with a fairly coarse finish. When a smoother finish is desired, screeding is followed by *floating.* The wood float is used in making an even gritty surface, as for sidewalks. Fig. 27-14. The wood float is also used to fill up the hollows and to compact the concrete.

Floating is done shortly after screeding, while the concrete is still plastic enough to allow mortar to be brought to the surface. However, the concrete should not be too plastic. Premature floating brings an excess amount of fines and moisture to the surface. This will cause fine "hair" cracks (crazing) or the appearance of a powdery material (dusting) at the surface. Only enough floating should be done to remove defects and to bring up enough mortar to

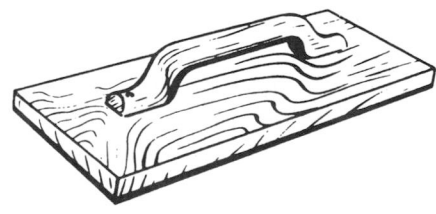

27-14a. *A wood float.*

27-14b. *Floating a concrete slab.*

produce the desired finish. If floating is to be the last step in finishing, it may be necessary to float the surface a second time after the concrete has hardened slightly.

Troweling. For a dense, smooth finish, floating is followed by *steel troweling*. Fig. 27-15. For large areas, a power trowel is convenient. Fig. 27-16. Troweling is not begun until the concrete has hardened enough to prevent fine material and water from being worked to the surface. In fact, troweling should be delayed as long as possible. A surface which is troweled too early lacks durability, whereas one which is troweled too late is too hard to finish properly.

Troweling should leave the surface smooth, even, and free of marks and ripples. A fine textured surface may be obtained by following the first troweling

immediately with a second one. In this second operation the trowel, held flat, is passed lightly and with a circular motion.

For a *hard steel-troweled finish*, the second troweling should be delayed until the concrete has become hard enough to make a ringing sound under the trowel. In hard steel-troweling the trowel is tilted slightly, and heavy pressure is applied to compact the surface.

Kneeboards. When troweling or floating a large surface, kneeboards

(or kneeling boards) may be used. Fig. 27-17. These boards, which measure about 12" × 24", are placed on the concrete to support the weight of the finisher. One board supports the knees, while the second board is placed on the concrete just behind to support the feet of the finisher. As it becomes necessary to move from one area to another, the finisher stands on the rear board. He then places the kneeboard in another area requiring troweling, steps onto the kneeboard, and repositions the second board. The finisher is now in position to continue the floating and troweling operations without having stepped directly onto the fresh concrete.

COMPLETING THE CONSTRUCTION

Construction cannot continue until the concrete has cured enough to withstand foot traffic. When curing is complete the *sleepers* are installed. These are heavy wooden members which lie flat on the concrete slab. They are attached by means of metal clips

27-15a. *A metal trowel.*

27-15b. *Hand troweling a concrete slab.*

27-16a. *A power trowel.*

27-16b. *Power troweling a concrete slab.*

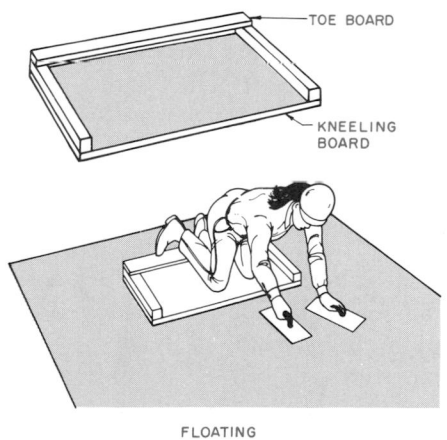

27-17. *Using kneeboards (or kneeling boards) to support the weight of the concrete finisher.*

27-18. *A completed floor slab. Note the metal clips for attaching wood sleepers.*

27-19. *The bottom plates for the partitions are attached to the floor slab. Note the plumbing installed in the partitions.*

which were embedded earlier. Fig. 27-18. The sleepers will provide support for the wooden floor. Next the wall plates are laid out on the slab. They are attached with anchor bolts which were also embedded in the concrete earlier.

When wood flooring is to be installed over the slab, the subfloor and finish floor are installed over the sleepers. After the wallplates have been laid out and attached, plumbing is installed in the partitions. Fig. 27-19. Wall framing can then proceed as will be discussed in Unit 30.

Floor Finishes

The most common coverings for concrete floors on ground are terrazzo, concrete tile, ceramic tile, asphalt tile, wood flooring, linoleum, and wall-to-wall carpeting. When linoleum, asphalt tile, or similar resilient-type flooring material is to be applied, the concrete surface should be given a smooth, steel-troweled finish. When other types of floor covering are contemplated, it is recommended that the manufacturer's advice be obtained as to their suitability and the methods of application.

Some concrete floors are troweled smooth in their natural color and may be sealed, then waxed and polished.

Color can be added to concrete floors by incorporating pure mineral oxide pigments as the concrete is placed. After the concrete has hardened and dried, the colored surface should be waxed and buffed. Color can also be produced by using commercial stains. Stains can generally be obtained from local paint or hardware dealers and should be applied as the manufacturer recommends.

DRIVEWAYS, SIDEWALKS, AND BASEMENT FLOORS

A new home is not complete until driveways and walks have been installed, ready for landscaping. Because the automobile is an important element of life, the garage is usually a prominent part of house design. This in turn establishes the location of driveways and walks.

Concrete and bituminous (blacktop) pavement are most commonly used in the construction of walks and drives, especially in areas where snow removal is important. In some areas of the country, a gravel driveway and a flagstone walk are satisfactory and reduce the cost of improvements.

Basements are normally finished with concrete floors of some type. These floors are poured after all improvements such as sewer and waterlines have been connected. Concrete slabs should not be poured on recently filled areas.

Driveways

The grade, width, and radius of curves in a driveway are important to consider when establishing a safe entry to the garage. Driveways that have a grade more than 7% (7' rise in 100') should have some type of pavement to prevent wash. Driveways that are long and require a turn-around need especially careful design. Fig. 27-20 shows a driveway and turn-around which allow the driver to go forward to the street or highway. In areas of heavy traffic, this is much safer than having to back into the roadway. A double garage should be serviced by a wider entry and turn-around.

Steep driveways should have a near-level area from 12' to 16' long in front of the garage for safety.

The most common type of concrete driveway is the full-width slab driveway. Fig. 27-21. It is particularly practical when the driveway is long or steep. The concrete should be given a finish to prevent cars and people from slipping. The concrete can also be given a color, a pattern, or a texture. It can be given a combination of all three to make it look like other surfaces, such as brick. This is done after the concrete has been placed but before it has cured. The pattern comes from metal stamps that are

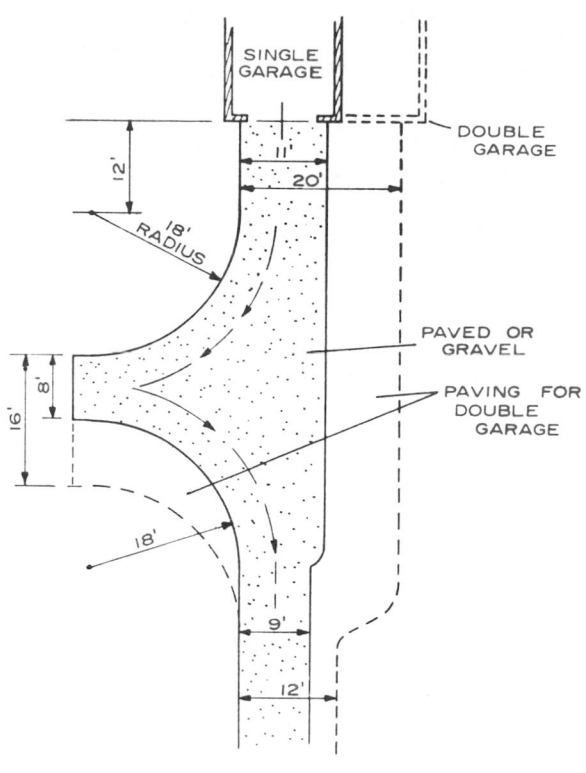

27-20. *Recommended dimensions for a single-slab driveway turnaround.*

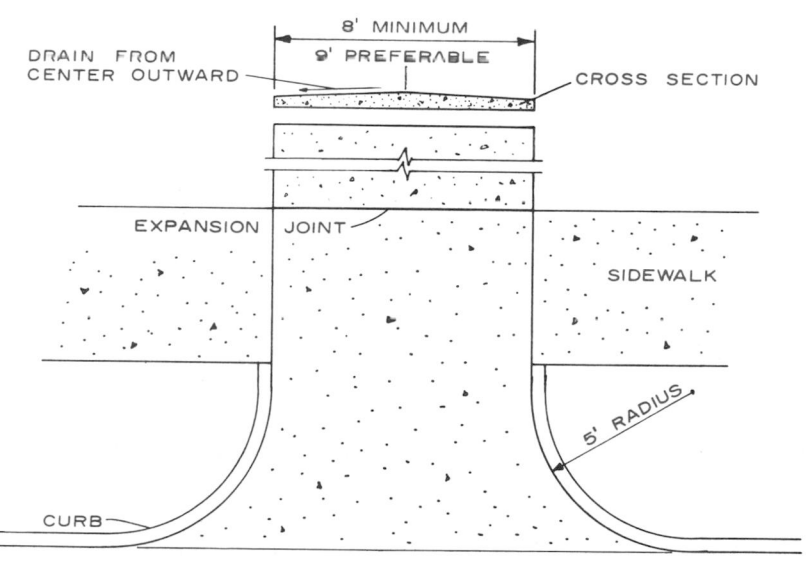

27-21. *Single-slab driveway details. A concrete slab should drain from the center outward.*

27-22. *This concrete driveway was colored and given a pattern to make it look as if it was made of another material.*

pressed into the wet concrete. Fig. 27-22.

The width of the single-slab drive should be 9', although 8' is often considered the minimum. When the driveway is also used as a walk, it should be at least 10' wide to allow for a parked car as well as a walkway. The width should be increased by at least 1' at curves. The radius of the drive at the curb should be at least 5'. Relatively short double driveways should be at least 18' wide, and 2' wider when they also serve as a walk from the street.

Pouring a concrete driveway over an area that has been recently filled is poor practice unless the fill, preferably gravel, has settled and is well tamped. A gravel base is not ordinarily required on sandy, undisturbed soil but should be used on all other soils. Concrete should be about 5" thick. Side forms are often built of 2" × 6" boards. These members establish the elevation and alignment of the driveway and are used to support the strike board for striking off the concrete.

Under most conditions, the use of steel reinforcing is good practice. Steel mesh, 6" × 6", will normally prevent or minimize cracking of the concrete. Expansion joints with asphalt-saturated felt strips should be used where the driveway joins with the public walk or curb, at the garage slab, and about every 40 feet on long driveways. A 5- or 5½-bag commercial mix concrete is ordinarily used for driveways. However, a 5½- to 6-bag mix containing an air-entraining mixture should be used in areas having severe winter climates. Concrete made with these cements contains tiny, well-distributed and completely separated air bubbles that help the concrete to resist damage during freeze/thaw cycles.

Blacktop driveways, normally constructed by paving contractors, should also have a well-tamped gravel or crushed rock base. The top should be slightly crowned for drainage.

Sidewalks

Main sidewalks should extend from the front entry to the street, to a front walk, or to a driveway leading to the street. A 5% grade is considered maximum for sidewalks; any greater slope usually requires steps. Walks should be at least 3' wide.

Concrete sidewalks are constructed much the same as concrete driveways. They should not be poured over filled areas unless the fill is settled and very well tamped. This is especially true of areas near the house after basement excavation backfill has been completed.

Minimum thickness of concrete over normal undisturbed soil is usually 4". As described for concrete driveways, contraction joints should be used and spaced on 4' centers.

When slopes to the house are greater than a 5% grade, stairs or steps should be used. For gentler slopes, other construction may be acceptable, such as a ramp sidewalk, a flight of stairs at a terrace, or a continuing sidewalk. Fig. 27-23. Steps should have 11" treads and 7" risers when the stair is 30" or less in height. When the total rise is more than 30", the tread should be 12" and the riser 6". For a moderately uniform slope, a stepped ramp may be satisfactory. Fig. 27-24. Generally, the rise should be about 6" to 6½", with enough space between risers for two or three normal paces.

Walks can also be made of brick, flagstone, or other types of stone. Brick and stone are often placed directly over a well-tamped sand base. However, this system is not completely satisfactory where the soil freezes. For a more durable walk in cold climates, the brick or

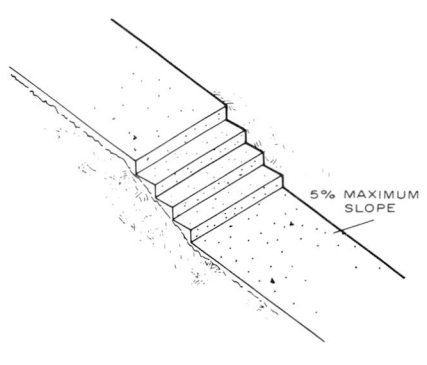

27-23. *Sidewalks placed on a grade should have a 5% maximum slope.*

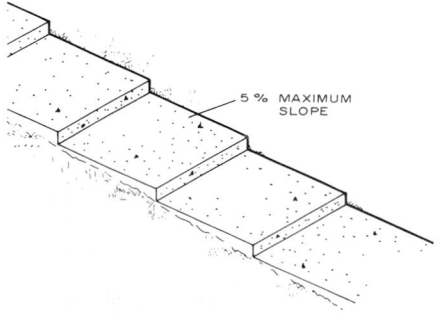

27-24. *A stepped ramp is sometimes used on a moderate grade.*

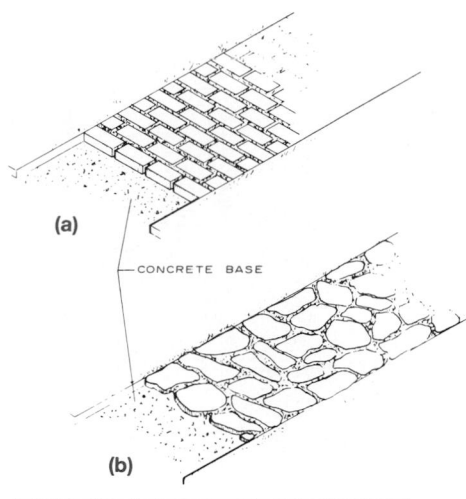

27-25. *Masonry paved walks: A. Brick. B. Flagstone.*

stone topping should be embedded in a freshly laid reinforced concrete base. Fig. 27-25.

As mentioned earlier for blacktops, all concrete sidewalks and curbed or uncurbed driveways should have a slight *crown* for drainage—that is, the center should be slightly higher than the edges. Joints between brick or stone may be filled with a cement mortar mix or with sand.

Basement Floors

Basement floor slabs should be no less than 3½" thick and sloped toward the floor drains. A 2" × 4" (3½" wide) is often used on edge for form work. There should be at least one drain in a basement floor, and for large floors two are more satisfactory. One should be located near the laundry area.

To assure a dry basement floor, a polyethylene film or similar vapor barrier can be installed under the concrete slab. However, basement areas or multilevel floors used only for utility or storage do not usually require a vapor barrier. When finished rooms have concrete floors, the use of a vapor barrier is normally required.

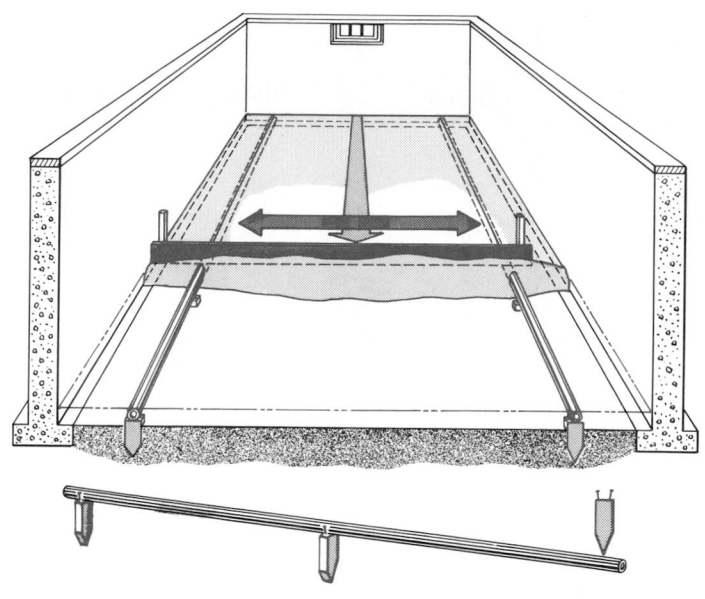

27-26. *A pipe screed used as a guide for the straightedge when leveling a basement floor. Workers should pull the screed toward them by the handles shown at the right and left ends. The arrows indicate the movement of the board. Note that it moves from side to side as well as toward the workers.*

Pipe-Screed Strips. When concrete is poured in an enclosed area, forms are not necessary. A basement floor is an example. The foundation walls serve as forms to confine the concrete. However, such a surface still must be screeded for correct thickness and levelness. This is done by means of rail-like devices on which a screed will ride. The rails are made of sections of 1" pipe set on stakes which are driven into the subgrade. Fig. 27-26. A board with a straight edge can be used as the screed. The pipes used as rails are called *screed strips.* The stakes are driven deep enough so that when the pipes are set on them, the tops of the pipes will be at the level desired for the surface of the slab. After screeding, the pipes and stakes are removed; a float is used to pack concrete in the resulting voids.

ESTIMATING

Material

To calculate the amount of material required for the basement floor for the home shown in Fig.

27-27, first figure the area of the slab. The house measures 26' × 40', so the total area of the basement slab will be 1,040 square feet.

Assume the floor to be 4" thick. Consulting Table 27-A, you see that 81 square feet of area 4" thick can be placed with one cubic yard of concrete. To calculate the total amount of concrete required, divide the total slab area (1,040 square feet) by the square feet from one cubic yard (81).

$$\frac{1040}{81} = 12.84 \text{ cubic yards.}$$

Rounding this off to the next quarter of a yard, you will need an estimated 13 cubic yards of concrete.

Labor

Forms and Screed Strips. To calculate the amount of labor involved in placing the screed strips for the basement floor in the example, refer again to Table 27-A. Here you see that an average of 30 linear feet of screed strips can be set in place per hour.

For the basement in the example, assume a screed strip down each of the long walls and a

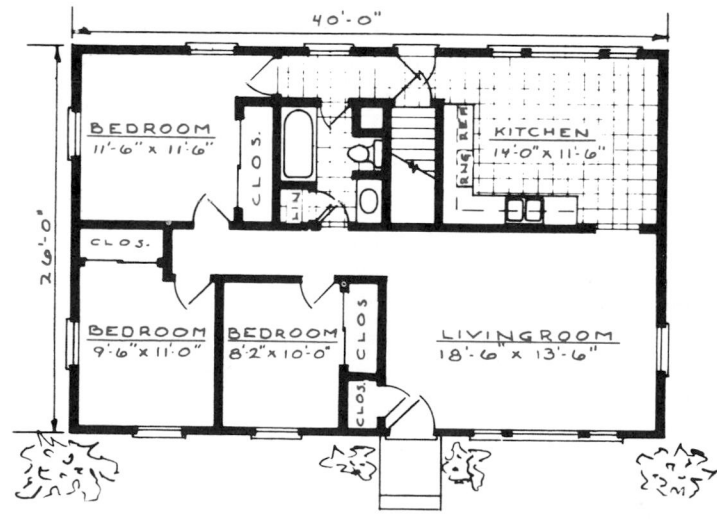

27-27. *Floor plan for the estimating examples given in the text.*

center screed strip. This makes a total of 3 screed strips, each 40' (the length of the building), for a total of 120'. To calculate the time required, divide the total length of screeds (120') by the average linear feet of screed strips that can be placed in an hour (30').

$$\frac{120}{30} = 4$$

Thus you see that four hours will be needed to set the screed strips.

Placement of Concrete.
Next, determine the labor for the placement of the concrete for the basement floor in the example. Referring to Table 27-A, under the heading "Labor" you see that 100 square feet of surface can be placed on the average in 3.6 hours. Divide the total slab area (1,040 square feet) by 100, to get the area as expressed in hundreds of square feet.

$$\frac{1040}{100} = 10.40$$

Next multiply by the time required to place 100 square feet of surface (3.6 hours).

$$10.40 \times 3.6 = 37.44 \text{ hours}$$

Rounding off, you will have to allow for approximately 37½ hours to place and finish the basement floor in the example.

Table 27-A. *Estimating Table for Concrete Slabs.*

| Slabs | Material | | Labor | |
| | Per Square Foot | | | |
Thickness	Cubic Feet of Concrete	Square Feet from One Cubic Yard	Forms and Screeds 100 Linear Ft.	Placement 100 Sq. Ft. of Surface
2"	0.167	162		
3"	0.25	108	Average 30 Linear Feet Per Hour	Average 3.6 Hours
4"	0.333	81		
5"	0.417	65		
6"	0.50	54		

Note: Placement includes finishing with topping. If topping omitted deduct 1.2 hours.

QUESTIONS

1. How deep should the footing be on a combined slab and foundation?

2. When constructing a concrete floor slab, what is the purpose of the granular fill over the subsoil?

3. How is concrete compacted?

4. Describe how the concrete slab is cured.

5. What types of floor coverings require a steel-troweled finish?

6. What is screeding?

7. What problems will occur if floating is done prematurely?

8. What is the purpose of troweling?

9. What is a kneeboard?

10. What is meant by a 6% grade?

11. At what intervals should expansion joints be used on driveways?

12. How thick should a basement floor slab be?

ACTIVITIES

1. Math. It is 50' from the front of a house to the sidewalk by the street. There is a 40' drop in this distance. Will a sidewalk, without any steps, from the house to the sidewalk by the street meet the 5% guideline discussed in this unit?

SECTION V

Framing

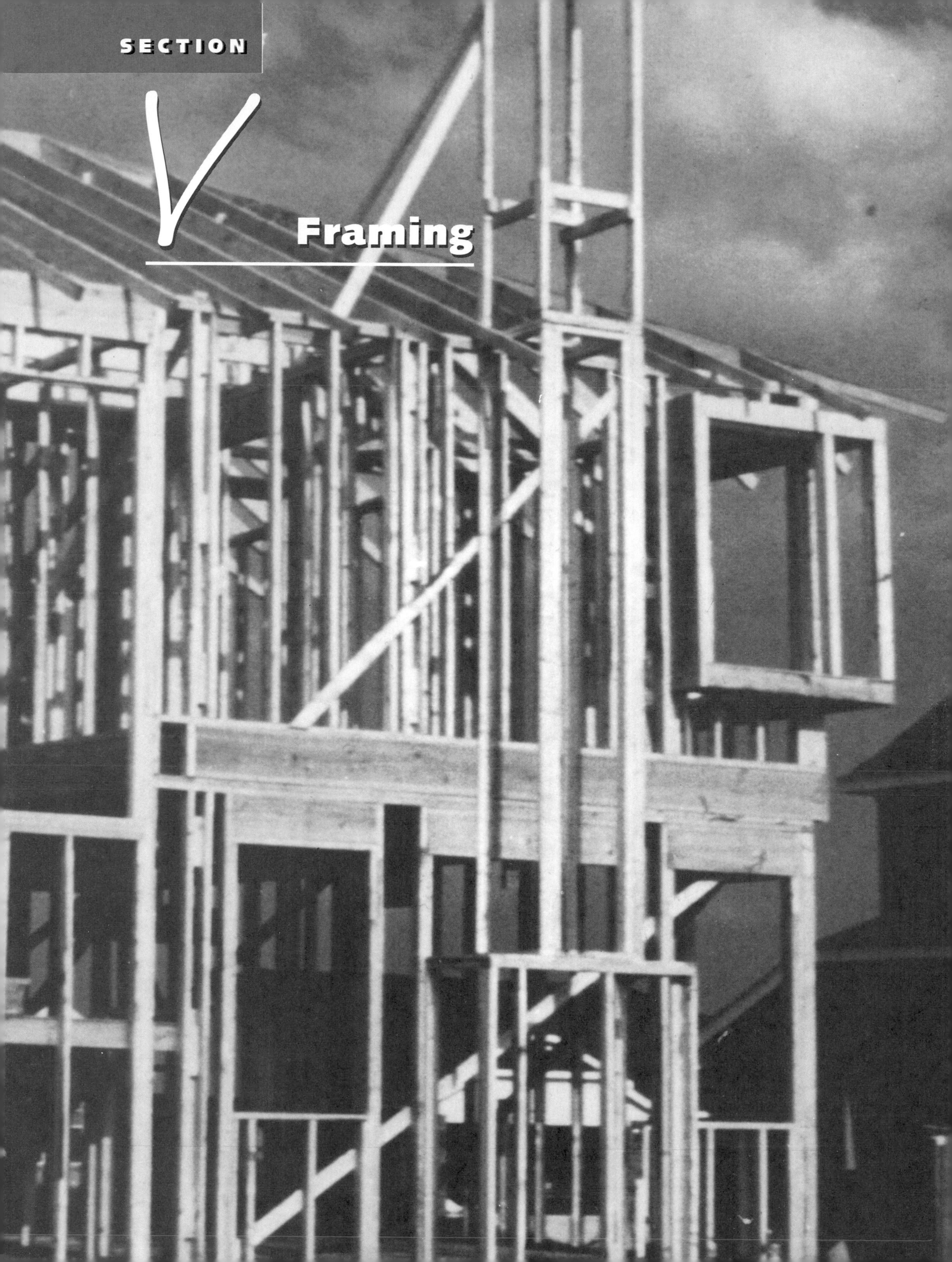

28

Framing Methods

Most homes in the United States and Canada are of wood-frame construction. Many are covered with wood siding; other common coverings include wood shingles, composition shingles or siding, brick veneer, and stucco.

Wood-frame houses have several important advantages. In general, frame construction costs less than other types. It provides more house for a given price and better insulation, thereby increasing comfort to the occupants and reducing heating and air-conditioning costs.

Wood is easily worked and is suitable for use with a wide variety of exteriors. This flexibility allows architects and builders to produce nearly any architectural style.

A well-built wood-frame home is very durable. Some of the oldest buildings in North America are Paul Revere's house in Boston, built in 1677, and the "House of Seven Gables" in Salem, Massachusetts, constructed in 1668. Fig. 28-1.

28-1. *Paul Revere House. This is the oldest home in Boston, built around 1677. Revere left from here on his historic ride to Lexington. The house is open to the public as a museum.*

TYPES OF WOOD FRAMING

Buildings framed of lumber usually belong in one of two main classes:

➤ *Multiple-member assemblies*, often called *conventional framing* or *stick framing*.

➤ *Post-and-beam framing*, which consists of heavier members, more widely spaced.

Each of these framing methods has its advantages, which will be discussed.

Conventional Framing

Conventional framing consists of multiple small members (joists, studs, and rafters) so joined that they act together and share the loads in supporting the structure. When assembled and sheathed, these members form complete floor, wall, and roof surfaces. Two common types of conventional framing are *platform* and *balloon*.

Platform-Frame Construction. As the name indicates, in this type of construction the floors are complete platforms, independent of the walls. The subfloor extends to the outside edges of the building and provides a platform upon which exterior walls and interior partitions are erected. Platform construction is generally used for one-story houses. It is also used alone or in combination with balloon construction for two-story structures. Building techniques in most parts of the United States have been developed almost entirely around the platform system. Fig. 28-2. This book will therefore concentrate on platform-frame construction.

Compared with balloon framing, platform construction is easier to erect because at each floor level it provides a flat surface on which to

work. It is also easily adapted to various methods of prefabrication. Each level of a two-story house is constructed separately. With a platform-framing system, it is common practice to assemble the wall framing on the floor and then tilt the entire unit into place.

Balloon-Frame Construction. The feature which identifies balloon-frame construction is that the studs are continuous from sill to top plate. Fig. 28-3. Studs and first-floor joists rest on the anchored sill. Second-floor joists bear on 1" × 4" ribbon strips which have been let into the inside edges of the studs.

In this type of construction there is less cross-grain wood framing than in conventional construction. Wood expands and contracts across the grain but is relatively stable with the grain. Therefore balloon-frame construction is less likely to be affected by expansion and contraction than conventional construction. This is an advantage for certain types of buildings. Specifically, balloon framing is good for two-story buildings on which the exterior covering is of brick veneer, stone veneer, or stucco. With such buildings, movement of the wood framing under the masonry veneer can be a serious problem.

If exterior walls are of solid masonry, it is also desirable to use balloon framing for interior bearing partitions. Again, this is because there is relatively little cross-grain wood framing. This minimizes dimensional changes in the walls and reduces variations in settlement which may occur between exterior walls and interior supports.

In balloon framing, blocks are placed between the joists to serve the dual purpose of solid bridging and fire stopping. Solid bridging holds the joists' ends in line; fire

stopping prevents the vertical and horizontal spaces from acting as flues in the event of fire. Fig. 28-4.

Balloon-frame construction is rarely used today. The longer framing members required for this type of construction are not readily available, and they cost more than the materials used in platform-frame construction. Therefore balloon framing construction techniques will not be discussed in detail in this book.

Post-and-Beam Construction

In the post-and-beam method of framing, subfloors and roofs are supported by a series of beams spaced up to 8' apart. The ends of the beams are supported by posts or piers. The roof sheathing and the subfloor may consist of planks, usually with a 2" nominal thickness, or structural T&G plywood that is 1⅛" thick. Wall spaces between posts are provided with supplementary framing as needed for attachment of exterior and interior finish. This extra framing and its covering also provide lateral bracing for the building.

Conventional framing uses joists, rafters, and studs spaced 12" to 24" on centers; the post-and-beam method calls for fewer and larger-sized pieces, spaced farther apart.

There are many advantages to be gained through the use of the post-and-beam system of framing. One of the best points is the architectural effect provided by the exposed post-and-beam ceiling. In this type of construction, the roof plank serves as the ceiling, which provides added height to the living area at no additional cost. Generally, the planks are selected for appearance; therefore no further ceiling treatment is required except

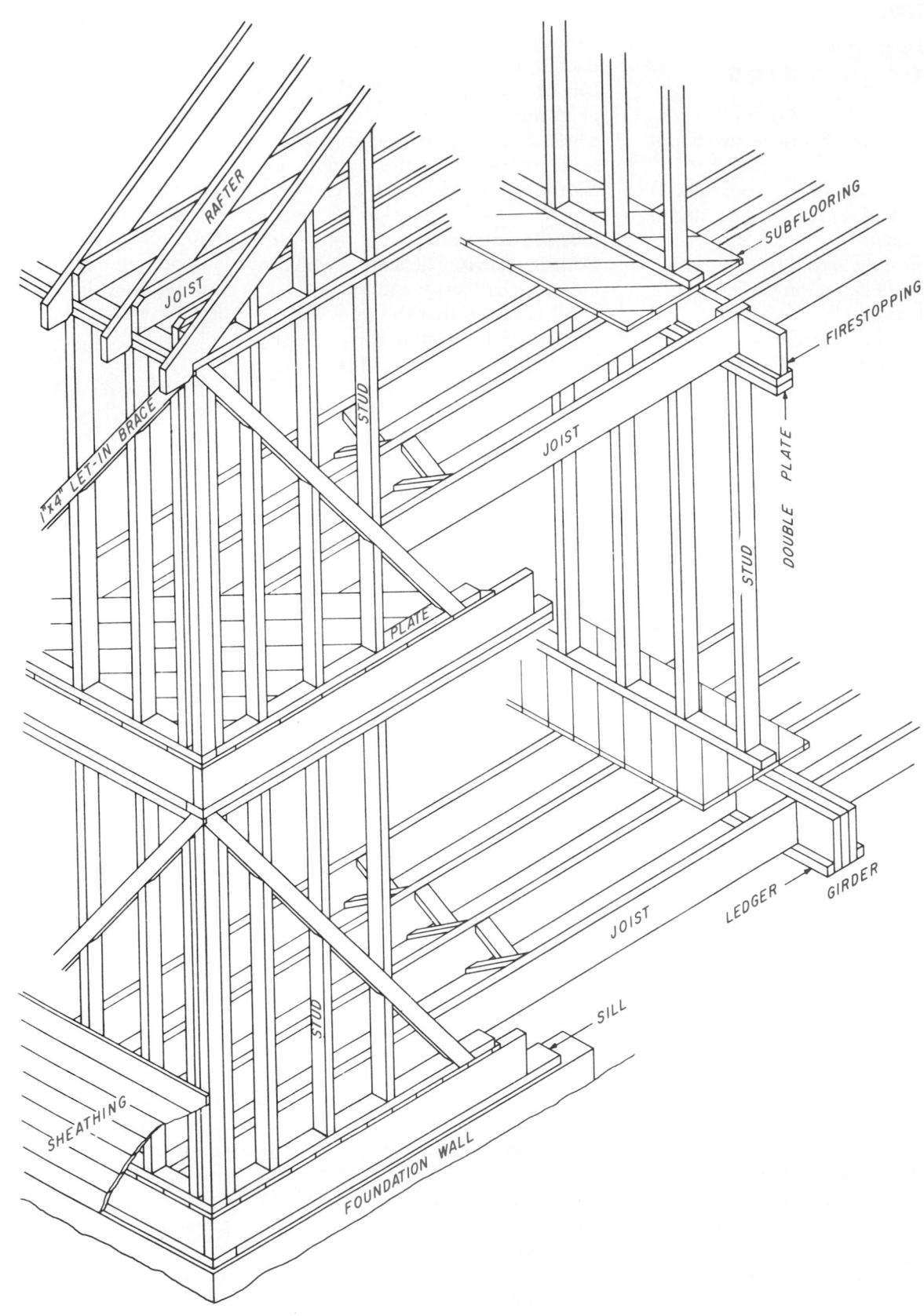

28-2. Platform-frame construction.

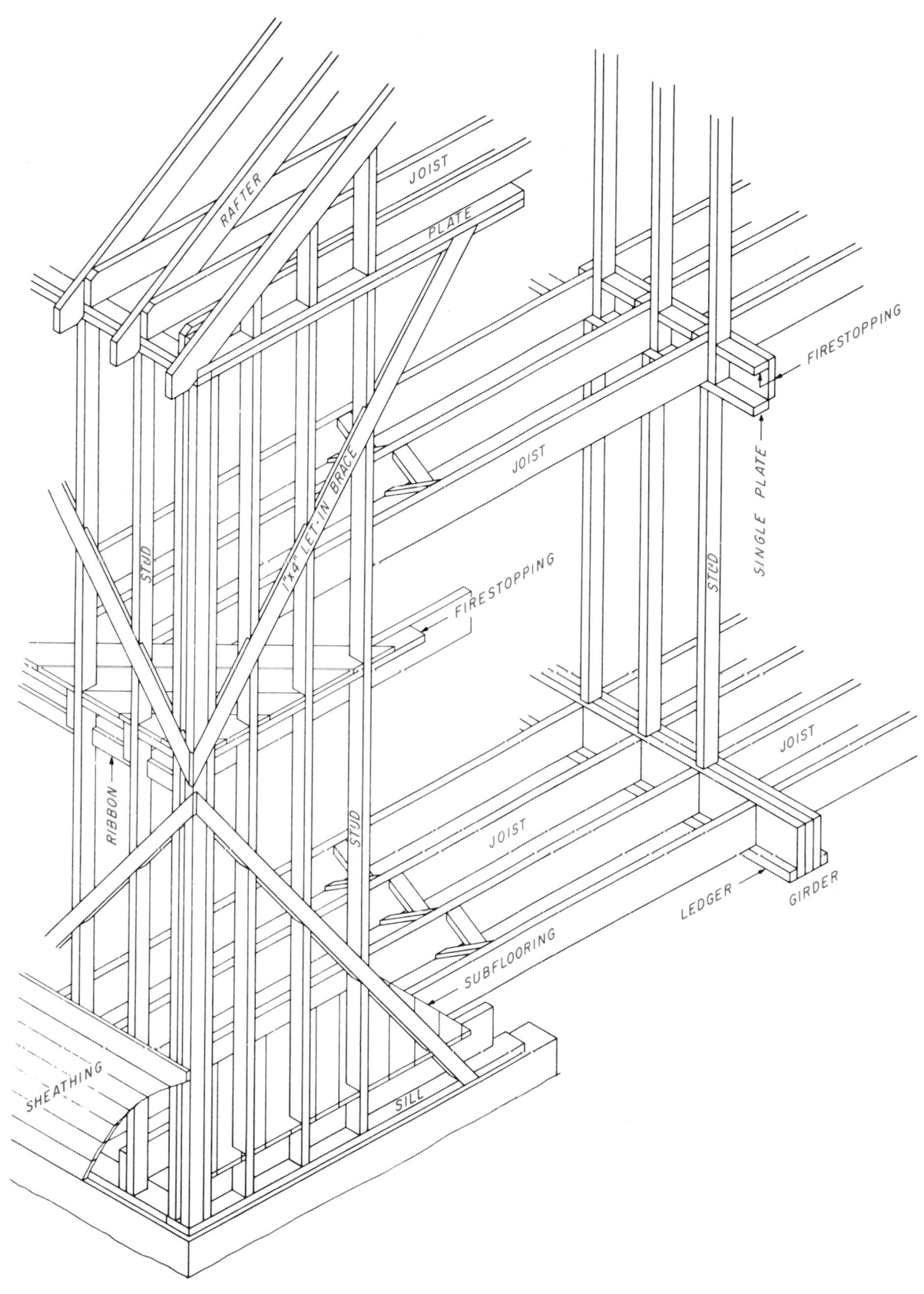

28-3. Balloon-frame construction.

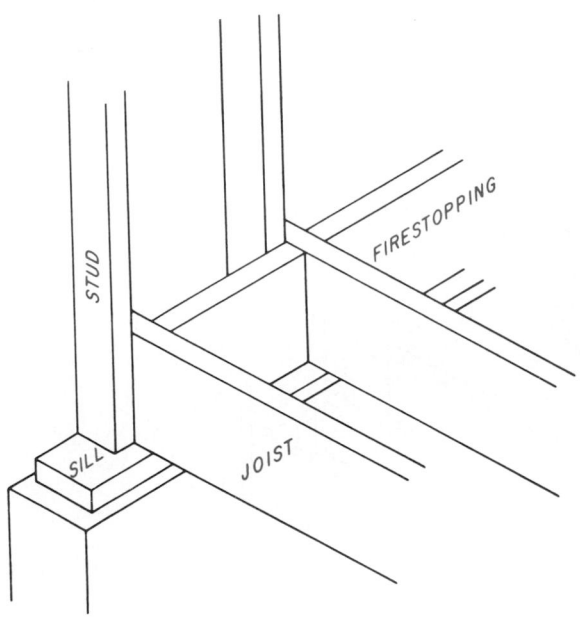

28-4. *First-floor framing at exterior wall—balloon-frame construction.*

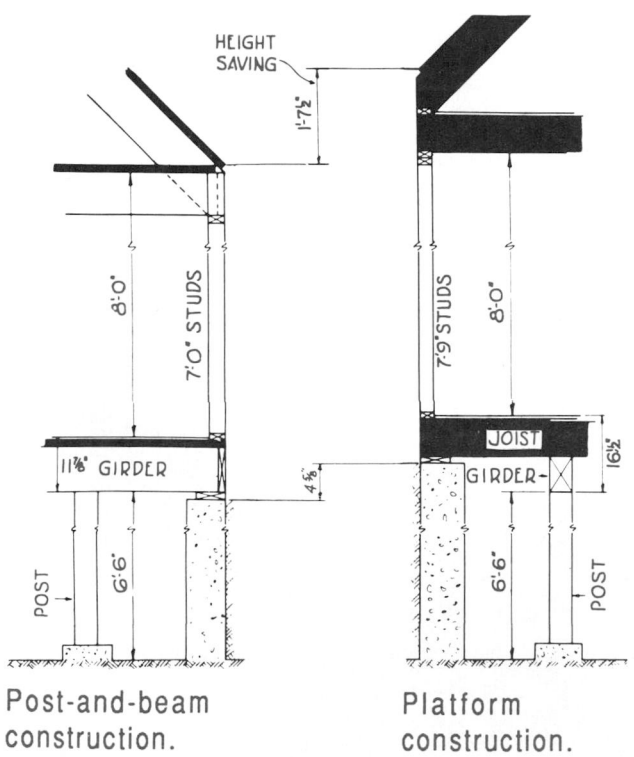

Post-and-beam construction.

Platform construction.

28-5a. *Comparison of height of post-and-beam house with conventionally framed house.*

the application of a finish.

In a well-planned post-and-beam framed structure, there are important savings in labor. As mentioned, the pieces are larger, and there are fewer of them than in conventional framing. The cross-bridging of joists is eliminated, and larger and fewer nails are required. This results in a substantial reduction of labor on the job site.

In post-and-beam framing, the ceiling height is measured to the underside of the plank, but in conventional construction it is measured to the underside of the joists. The difference between the thickness of the plank and the depth of the joist gives the building a smaller volume and also reduces the height of the interior walls.

Figure 28-5a compares the height of a post-and-beam house with that of a conventionally framed house. Figure 28-5b compares the two framing methods.

METAL FRAMING

Metal framing members, sections, and accessories are factory-fabricated for easy job-site assembly. Structural members, such as columns, beams, joists, plates, studs, corner posts, partition tees, window and door members, truss members, and fascia are all available for framing with this system. The most common use of metal framing in residential construction, however, is for non-bearing interior partitions. Metal framing has several advantages. It is not prone to rot or decay, and it does not warp or twist. It will not shrink or swell with changes in moisture inside the house. In some parts of the country, it is actually less expensive than wood framing. Metal framing can also be produced in a variety of lengths that are not available with wood framing.

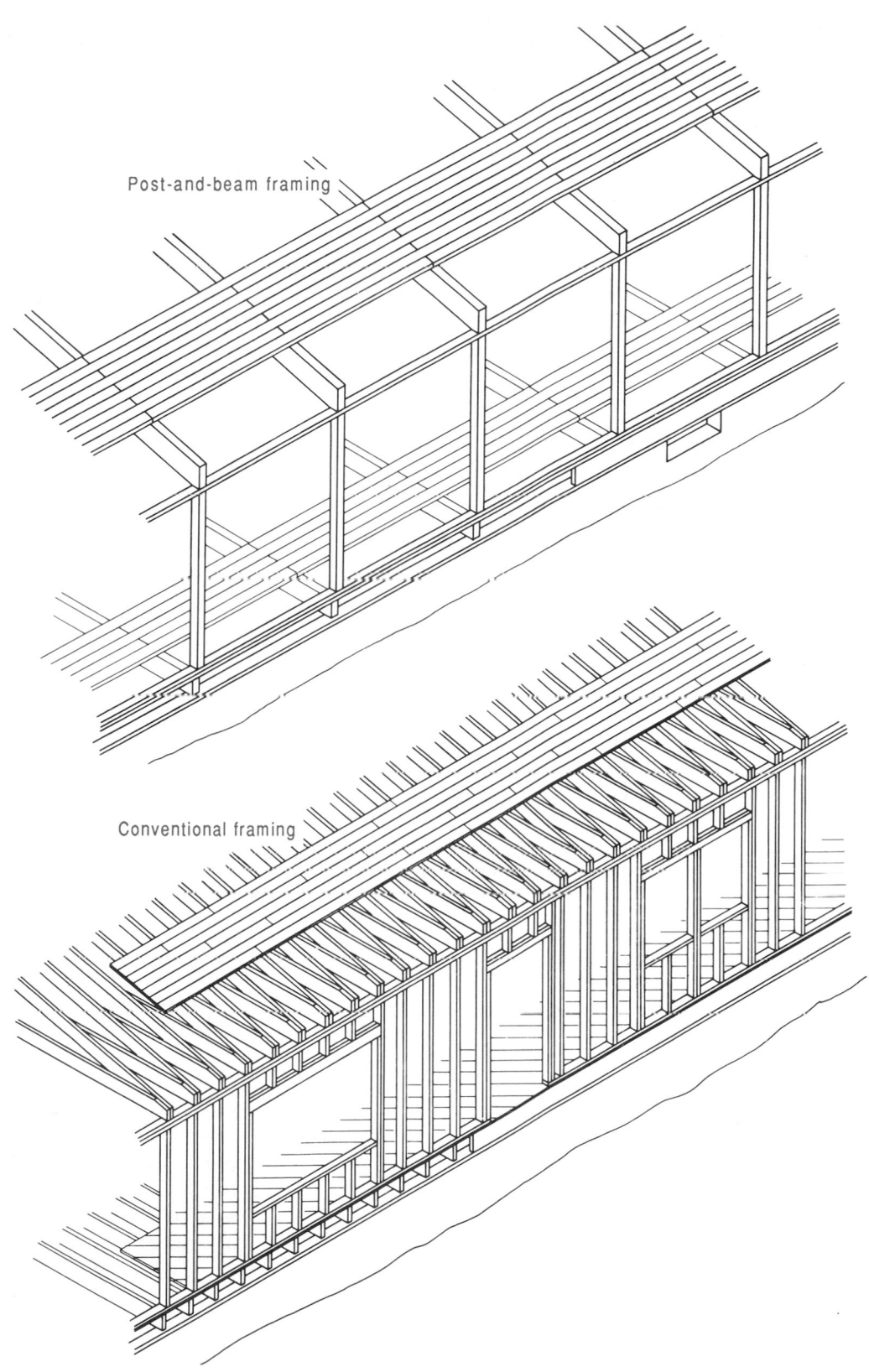

Post-and-beam framing

Conventional framing

28-5b. *Comparison of post-and-beam system with conventional framing.*

Non-bearing Partitions

The parts of a metal-framed partition wall are similar in function to those of a wood frame partition wall. Fig. 28-6. Studs spaced 16" or 24" on center connect top and bottom plates (called runners). Openings in the partitions are framed with horizontal sills and non-structural headers. The framing members are assembled with power screwdrivers using self-drilling, self-tapping panhead screws ½" long. These screws have a Phillips head that keeps the screwdriving bit from slipping under power.

Wiring can be run through the partitions through prepunched holes in the studs. These holes may be lined with rubber grommets to prevent the metal from abrading any wiring. Drywall is then applied to the partitions and screwed to the metal framing.

Structural Framing

Metal framing for exterior walls and other building components is rare in residential construction. However, it is common in light commercial construction.

Walls are assembled in a fashion similar to partition framing, but heavier-gauge metal is used for the components.

Doorframes for both the interior partitions and exterior walls are integral with the system. They are prepainted and come complete with hinges, lock, rubber stops, and weather stripping as necessary. The windows are also integral parts of the system, prefabricated and painted. These units include the interior and exterior trim which is designed to accept ½" drywall and ½" sheathing plus siding on the outside.

The plumbing is installed in the prepunched stud webs. The wiring is passed through insulated grommets which are inserted in the prepunched webs of the studs and plates. Wall and ceiling fixtures are mounted by attaching wood blocking spaced between the flanges of the wall studs or trusses. Friction-tight insulation is installed by placing the batts (bundles of insulating material) between the studs on the exterior walls. Studs are spaced 2' on center, providing adequate space for the installation of heating and air-conditioning ducts.

Roof trusses are set in place and roof sheathing is attached in the same manner as described previously for the subfloor. After the sheathing is in place, roofing, such as shingles, is then installed in a conventional manner.

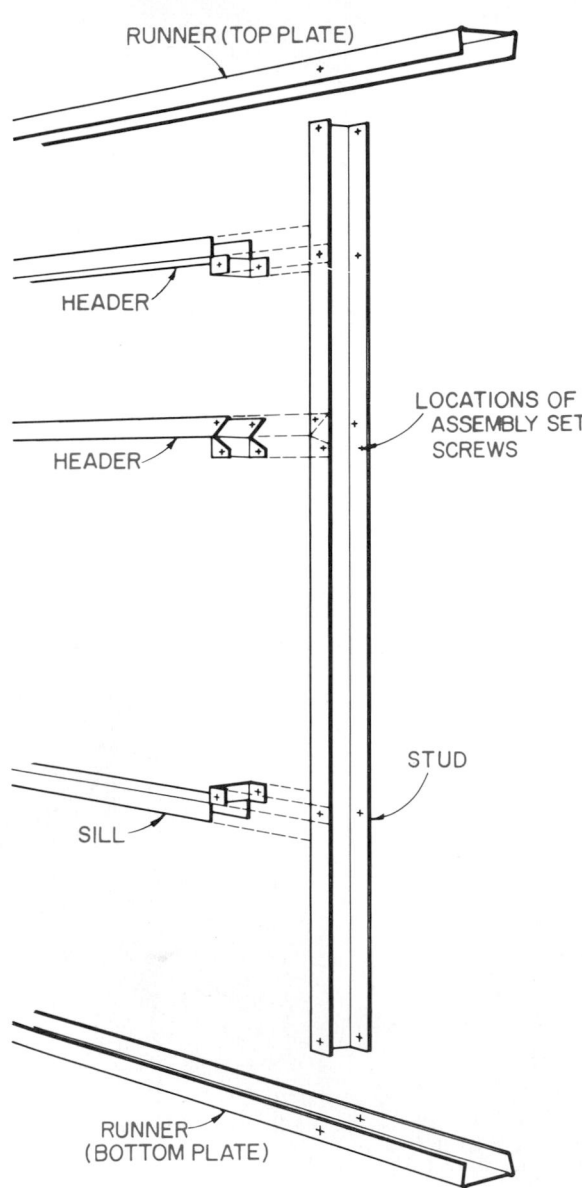

RUNNER (TOP PLATE)

HEADER

HEADER

LOCATIONS OF ASSEMBLY SET SCREWS

STUD

SILL

RUNNER (BOTTOM PLATE)

28-6. *Parts of a metal-framed partition.*

OTHER FRAMING METHODS

Conventional wood-frame construction is the most common structural system used for houses. Other systems can be used, however. Some of these are relatively new on the construction scene. Others are time-honored systems that have recently regained some popularity.

Foam-core Panels

Foam-core panels are sometimes used to form the shell of a house. These panels are built in a factory and delivered to the job site, where they are fastened together. The panels most often consist of 3½" thick rigid insulation sandwiched between sheets of exterior plywood or oriented-strand board (OSB). Panels range in size from 4' × 8' to 8' × 28', and they can be structural or non-structural. Structural foam-core panels can take the place of studs and other framing members. Fig. 28-7.

There are several advantages to building a house with foam-core panels. First, the shell of the house can be erected very quickly. Some foam-core panels also have an inside skin of drywall, which saves time and effort in completing the interior of the house. The panels

28-8a. *The individual pieces of a timber frame are fastened with interlocking wood joinery.*

are energy efficient because they allow very little cold air to leak into the house. On the other hand, it can be difficult to run wiring through the panels. Also, a crane is required for heavier panels.

Conventional framing techniques are still required for interior partitions. Floors and roofs are most often framed conventionally.

Timber Framing

A timber frame is a structural skeleton of posts and beams that is connected with wooden joinery. The use of timbers to frame buildings is a technique with a very long history. In recent years, there has been a revival of interest in timber framing techniques, particularly where forests are readily available to provide the timber stock. Fig. 28-8.

A timber frame is a free-standing structural system that rests on a foundation. The timbers are dimensioned and surfaced. They can be made from hardwood or softwood. Like post-and-beam framing, the supporting members are relatively far apart, compared to conventional framing. The individual parts of a timber frame are connected by interlocking joinery secured by wooden pegs. In order for the many pieces of a frame to fit together properly, a high degree of woodworking skill is required. Some joints are quite complicated, but most are a variation of the mortise and tenon.

28-8b. *The structure of a timber-frame house is often exposed to the interior of the house.*

28-7. *Foam-core panels in place.*

1. List several advantages of wood-framed houses.

2. How does platform-frame construction differ from balloon construction?

3. How does post-and-beam construction differ from platform-frame construction?

4. Can you think of some advantages of metal framing?

5. List some similarities between post-and-beam framing and timber framing.

ACTIVITIES

1. **Math.** The amount of framing needed for the outside of a house is dependent upon the perimeter of the house. A rectangular house that has a depth and width of 26' and 40' has a perimeter of 2(26) + 2(40) = 132'. Houses with dimensions of 24' by 42' or 28' by 38' also have perimeters of 132'.

a. Give the dimensions of ten more houses that also have a perimeter of 132'.

b. Compute the area, in square feet, for each of the above three examples and the ten houses you identified.

c. Do all have the same area? If they do, give the area. If they do not, which has the largest area? Which has the smallest area?

d. Give reasons why you would or would not build the house with the largest area.

2. **Language Arts.** Research Paul Revere's house or the House of Seven Gables. Find out how old each house is. Note any building methods or interesting architectural details. Write a short report on your findings. Don't forget to document the source of your information.

3. **Science.** Balloon framing, as indicated in this unit, is rarely used today. Several disadvantages are mentioned. What type of framing is used today with brick or stucco exteriors? Talk to a builder and find out.

4. **Science.** Contrast the environmental working conditions of wall framers who "stick build" on site with the working conditions of those who assemble metal framing members within factories.

THE SCHOOL-TO-WORK CONNECTION

Most single-family home construction in the United States and Canada uses the platform-frame construction system. Solid lumber and manufactured wood panels (such as plywood and OSB) are the materials typically used to build a platform frame house. The result is a strong building that is relatively easy to construct.

There are other systems and other materials that can be used to build a house. For example, metal framing could be used to build a platform-framed house. The framing system and materials used on a project depend partly on the cost and availability of materials.

The cost of metal framing for residential construction tends to be fairly stable. It is not subject to great swings in price. In contrast, the cost of framing lumber can vary considerably. Sometimes it is less costly to use then metal framing, and sometimes it is more costly.

1. When you have a small project to build, you generally purchase lumber by the piece. In other words, you purchase exactly the number of studs that you need. On a large project it would not be realistic to purchase lumber this way. The construction of an entire house requires a large volume of lumber that would be delivered to the jobsite in large bundles. Find out from a local lumberyard how many 2 x 4 studs are in each bundle. What is this bundle called and what does it cost?

2. Calculate the cost of a 2 x 4 stud if purchased as part of a "bundle." How does this compare with the cost of a stud purchased individually?

29

Floor Framing

Floor framing consists of posts, girders, sills, joists, and subflooring. All members are tied together with nails (and sometimes with construction adhesives) to support the rest of the house. Fig. 29-1.

Materials used for floor framing have changed considerably over the years. The biggest changes have come in joists and subflooring. Nominal 2" lumber is still the most common material for floor joists, but floor trusses, laminated-veneer lumber, and wood I-joists are used with increasing frequency. These materials offer the advantages of light weight, consistent strength, and long lengths. Fig. 29-2. For more information about these products, see Unit 8.

Subflooring was once commonly made from nominal 1" shiplap boards or nominal 1" T&G boards. These were laid diagonally across the joists. On modern job sites, however, it is far more common to find subflooring of plywood or oriented-strand board (OSB). For more information on plywood, see Unit 6; OSB is described in Unit 7.

Another development in floor framing (as well as in roof framing) is the widespread use of metal connectors. These products are designed to strengthen the connection between various wood members and speed construction. The most common metal connector used in floor framing is the joist hanger. Fig. 29-1 and 29-2a.

The majority of this unit describes standard floor framing with conventional lumber. Construction details for floor trusses and wood I-beams are given at the end of this unit.

29-1. *Floor framing. Note the use of metal joist hangers to connect floor joists to a girder.*

POSTS

A *post* is a wooden or steel member which supports girders. A wood post must be solid and not less than 6" × 6" in size. It should

29-2a. *Wood I-joists are often used where predictable stiffness and long lengths are required.*

29-2b. *Parallel-chord trusses are part of the floor framing for this house.*

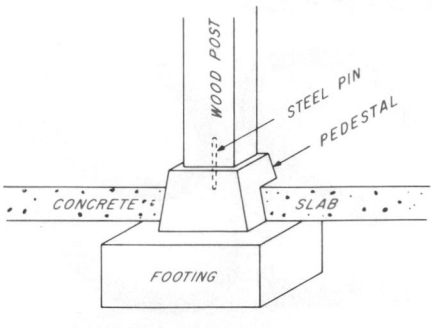

29-3a. *The foundation and pedestal for a basement or cellar post. If the post is wood, a steel pin must be set into the pedestal to secure the post.*

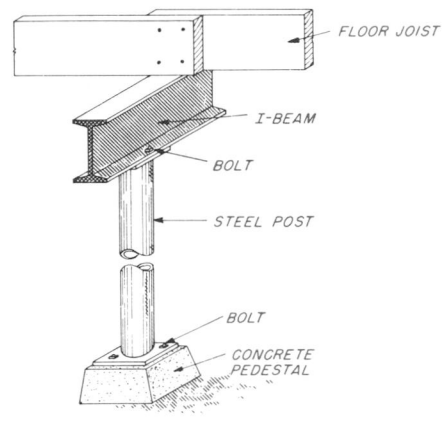

29-3b. *A steel post used with a steel I-beam. A wood beam may also be used with a steel post. Notice the flanges, welded onto each end of the post, for bolting the post into position.*

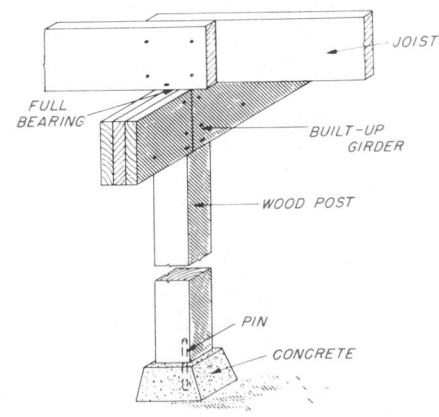

29-4a. *A wood post under a built-up girder. Notice that the joint in the girder is over the support.*

rest on the top of a masonry pedestal that is at least 3" above the floor. Fig. 29-3a. Steel posts may be H-sectional, I-sectional, or round. They have steel bearing plates at each end. Fig. 29-3b.

Wood posts should be square at both ends and securely fastened to the girder. Fig. 29-4. When necessary, a bearing plate should be placed between a wood post and a steel girder. Fig. 29-5. Posts are generally spaced 8' to 10' on center depending on the size and strength of the girder in relation to the load it must support.

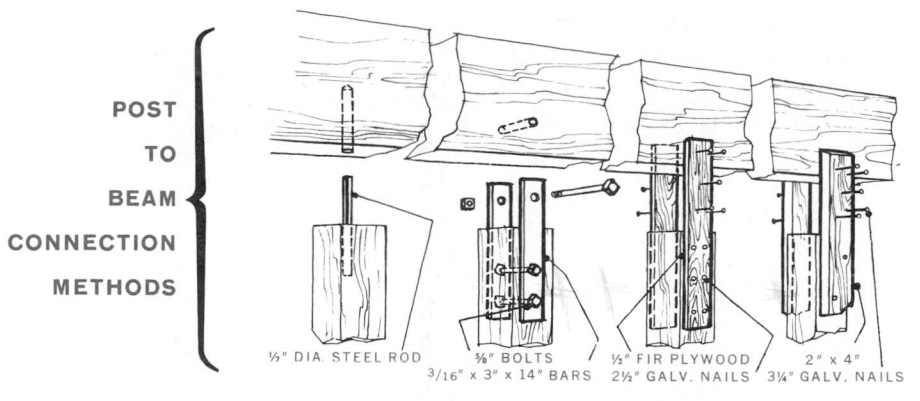

POST TO BEAM CONNECTION METHODS

½" DIA. STEEL ROD ⅝" BOLTS ½" FIR PLYWOOD 2" x 4"
3/16" x 3" x 14" BARS 2½" GALV. NAILS 3¼" GALV. NAILS

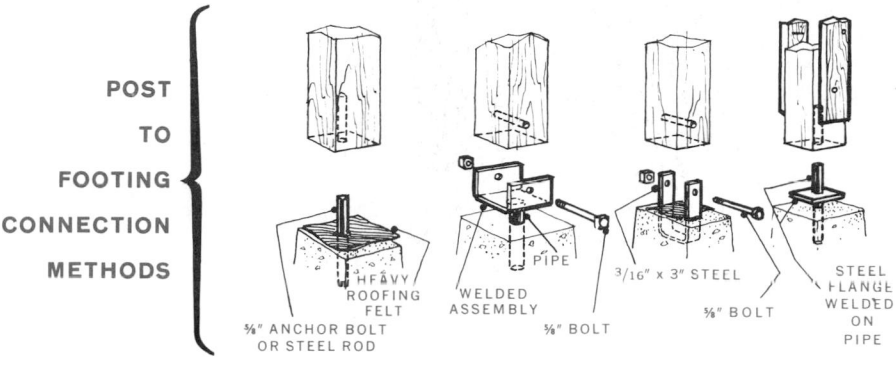

POST TO FOOTING CONNECTION METHODS

HEAVY ROOFING FELT PIPE 3/16" x 3" STEEL STEEL FLANGE WELDED ON PIPE
⅝" ANCHOR BOLT OR STEEL ROD WELDED ASSEMBLY ⅝" BOLT ⅝" BOLT

29-4b. Methods of connecting the post.

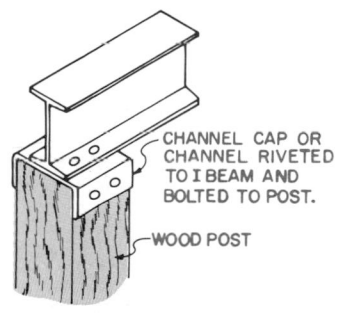

CHANNEL CAP OR CHANNEL RIVETED TO I BEAM AND BOLTED TO POST.

WOOD POST

29-5. If a wood post is used with a steel girder, a cap should be provided for bolting the post in position.

GIRDERS

Girders are large principal beams used to support the floor joists. They may be of wood or steel. An advantage of steel is that it does not present the problem of shrinkage that wood does. One advantage of wood girders is that they are lighter and therefore easier to install. Also, connections are easier to make with a wood girder.

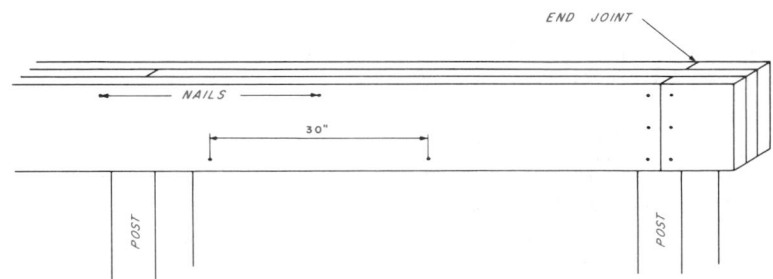

END JOINT

NAILS

30"

POST POST

29-6. A built-up wood beam. The nails in the nailing pattern are 20d.

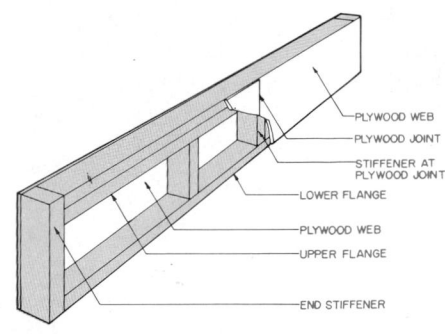

PLYWOOD WEB
PLYWOOD JOINT
STIFFENER AT PLYWOOD JOINT
LOWER FLANGE
PLYWOOD WEB
UPPER FLANGE
END STIFFENER

29-7. Parts of a box beam girder. Properly built, such girders are much lighter for the load they will carry.

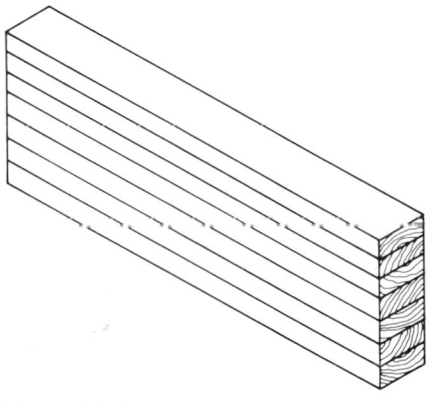

29-8. Glue-laminated beams consist of layers of lumber glued together.

Common types of wood girders include *solid*, *built-up*, *hollow*, and *glue-laminated*. Built-up wood girders consist of planks nailed together with two rows of 20d nails. The nails in each row should be spaced about 30" apart with the end joints over the supports. Fig. 29-6. Table 29-A can be used when determining material requirements for a girder. Hollow beams resemble a box made of 2 × 4s, with plywood webs. They are often called *box beams*. Fig. 29-7. Glue-laminated beams are built in a factory and delivered to the job site. They consist of layers of solid lumber glued together. Fig. 29-8.

The ends of wood girders should bear at least 4" on masonry walls or pilasters. A ½" air space should be provided at each end and at each side of a wood girder framed in masonry. (When steel bearing plates are placed at ends of girders between the masonry and the girder, they should be of full bearing size.) Fig. 29-9. Tops of wood girders should be level with tops of sill plates on foundation walls unless there are ledger strips or notched joists. Fig. 29-10.

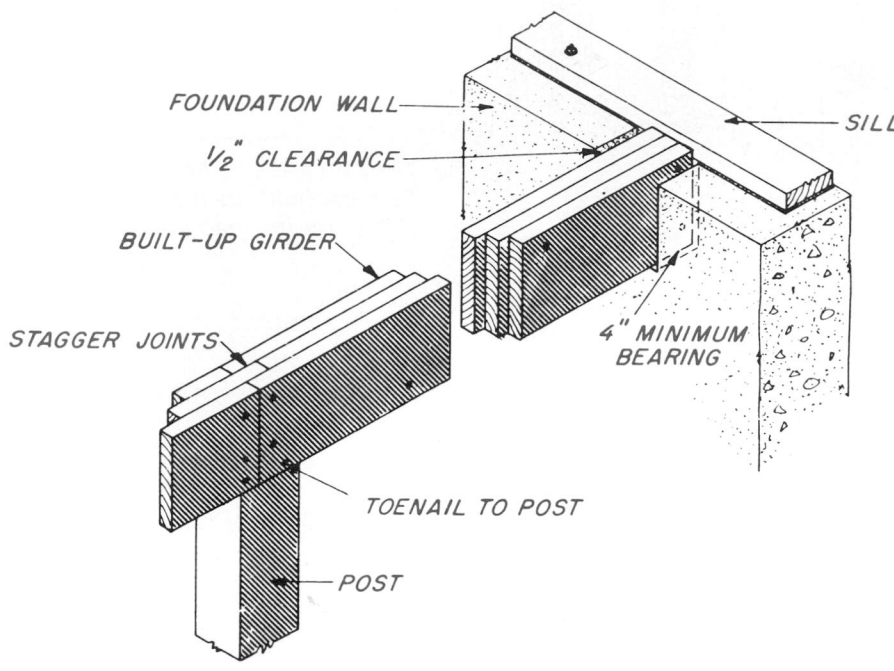

29-9. *A built-up girder set into a masonry pocket. It is best to put a metal bearing plate under the girder.*

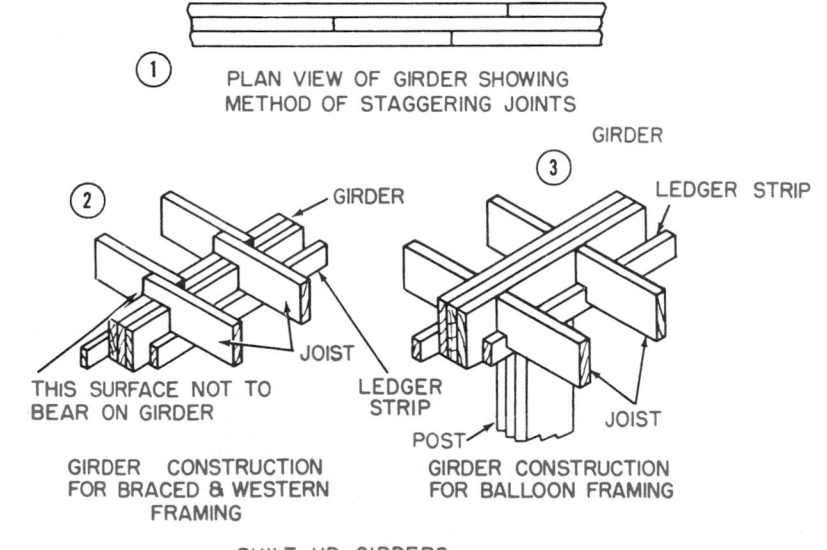

29-10. *When the top of the girder is not set even with the top of the sill plate, it is necessary to install a ledger strip and notch the joists at the girder.*

Table 29-A. *Built-Up Girders. This table can be used for determining the amounts of lumber and nails necessary for a built-up girder. A 4' x 6' girder 20' long contains 43 board feet of lumber (20 x 2.15 = 43).*

Size of Girder	Bd. Ft. per Lin. Ft.	Nails per 1000 Bd. Ft.
4 x 6	2.15	53
4 x 8	2.85	40
4 x 10	3.58	32
4 x 12	4.28	26
6 x 6	3.21	43
6 x 8	4.28	32
6 x 10	5.35	26
6 x 12	6.42	22
8 x 8	5.71	30
8 x 10	7.13	24
8 x 12	8.56	20

Installing a Girder or Beam

If the beam or girder is of metal, it may be installed in one of three locations:

➤ The top of the beam may be flush with the plate to act as a bearing for the joists. Fig. 29-11.

➤ A wood plate may be placed on top of the metal beam to carry the joists. Fig. 29-12.

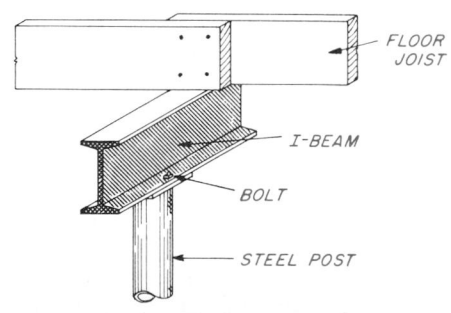

29-11. *This method of running the floor joists over the girder usually requires 2" x 4" spacing blocks between the joists to prevent movement on the beam.*

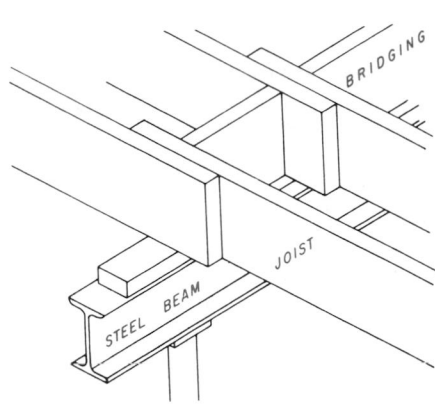

29-12. *This is the method used most frequently to install framing on a steel beam. Fasten a wood sill plate to the beam so that the joists can be nailed to the plate. Note the solid bridging which holds the joist ends vertical.*

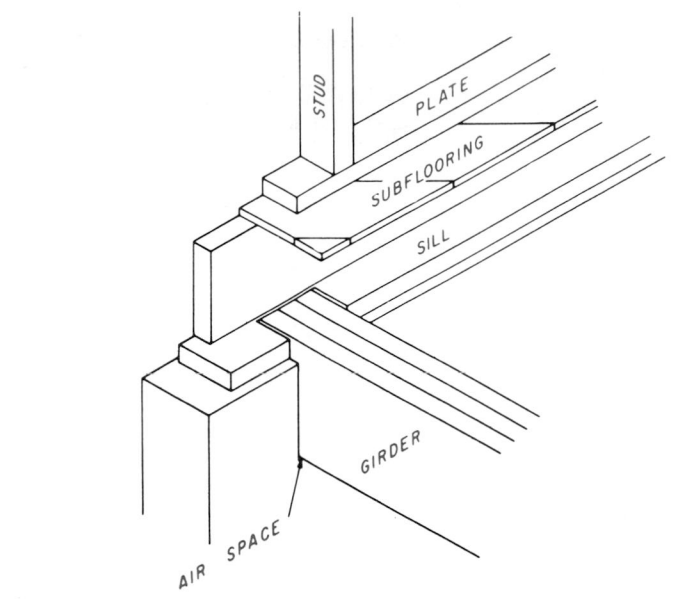

29-14a. *First-floor framing at the girder and exterior wall in platform-frame construction. Note that the girder is flush with the top of the sill.*

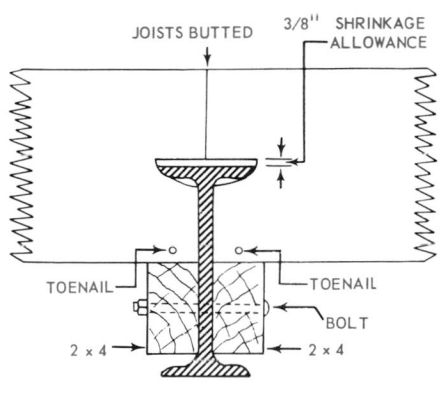

29-13. *A method of notching the joist into a steel girder.*

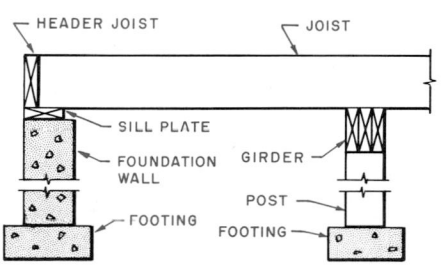

29-14b. *Another view of the construction shown in Fig. 29-14a. Note the placement of the joist.*

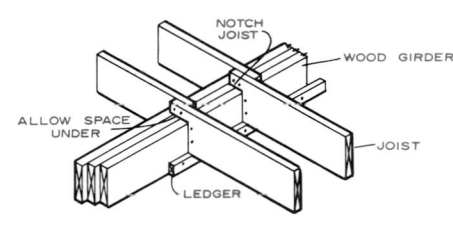

29-15a. *More headroom in the basement is gained by notching the joists and using a ledger strip for support on the girder.*

► When the top of the beam is set slightly higher than the wall sill plate, the joist is framed into the beam. Fig. 29-13.

Whether the beam is wood or metal, make sure that it is aligned from end to end and side to side. Also make sure that the length of the bearing post under the girder is correct so that it will properly support the girder.

Installing Joists Over Girders

In the simplest floor and joist framing, the joist rests on top of the girder. In Fig. 29-14, the top of the girder is aligned with the top of the sill plate. This method is used where basement height provides adequate headroom below the girder. The main disadvantage is that shrinkage is greater than when ledger strips are used. If more clearance is wanted under the

girder, ledger strips are securely nailed to each side of the girder to support the joist. The joists are toenailed to the wood girders and nailed to each other where they lap over the girder. Care should be taken to obtain full bearing on the tops of ledger strips. Fig. 29-15.

Spaced Girders. To provide space for heat ducts in a partition supported on the girder, a spaced girder is sometimes installed. Solid

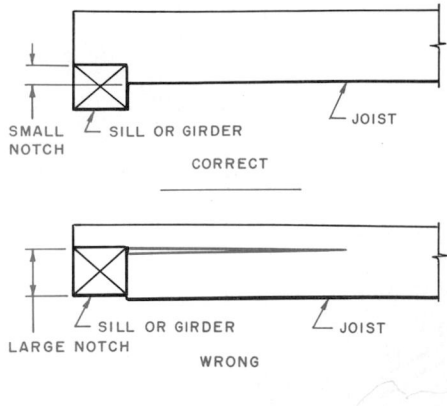

29-15b. When using the method shown in Fig. 29-15a, do not notch the joist more than one-third of its depth.

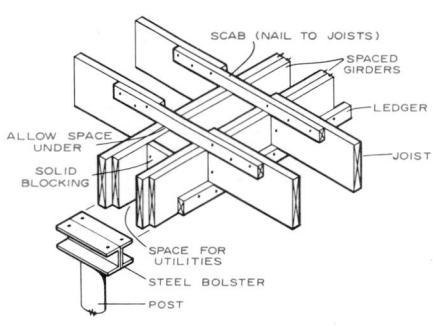

29-16. Spaced girder. The space is used for running plumbing or heating pipes. A piece of wood called a scab is used to span the opening above the girder.

blocking is used at intervals between the two members. Fig. 29-16. A single post support for a spaced girder usually requires a brace, preferably of metal, with a span sufficient to support the two members.

WOOD-SILL CONSTRUCTION

There are two types of wood-sill construction over foundation walls—one for platform construction and one for balloon-frame construction.

The *box sill* is usually used in platform construction. It consists of a sill or sill plate anchored to the foundation wall for supporting and fastening the joists, with a header (band) at the ends of the joists resting on the foundation wall. Fig. 29-17.

Balloon-frame construction also has a sill plate upon which the joist rests. The studs also bear on this plate and are nailed both to the floor joist and to the plate. Fig. 29-18.

The *sill* or *sill plate* is the lowest member of the frame structure that rests on the foundation. Insulation material and a metal termite shield can be placed under the sill, if desired. Fig. 29-19. The sill should consist of one thickness of 2" lumber placed on the foundation walls to provide a full and even-bearing surface. Fig. 29-20. Sills should be anchored to the foundation with ½" bolts spaced approximately 6' to 8' apart, with at least two bolts in each sill.

At one time a thin bed of mortar was spread on top of the foundation to provide a solid bed for the sill. This also was intended to reduce the infiltration of cold air into the building. A better technique is to use sill sealer instead of mortar. Fig. 29-20. Sill sealer comes in a roll. It is usually made from dense but flexible fiberglass or foam that is rolled out on the foundation just before the sills are bolted in place. The weight of the building packs the fiberglass in place to reduce air infiltration.

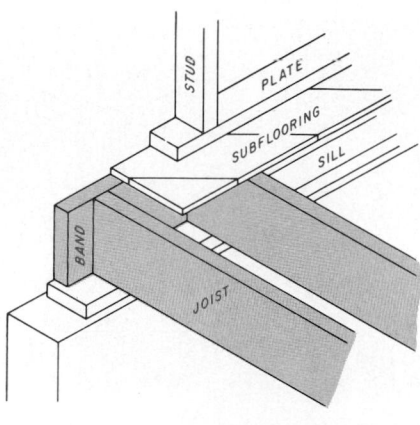

29-17. First-floor framing at the exterior wall in platform-frame construction.

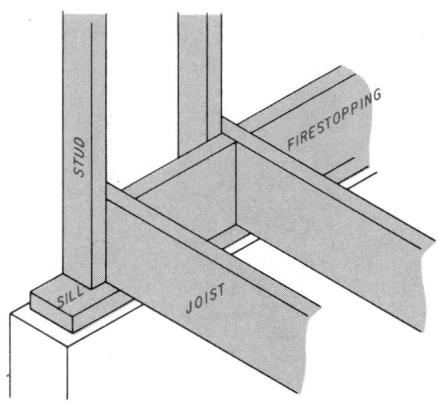

29-18. First-floor framing at the exterior wall in balloon-frame construction.

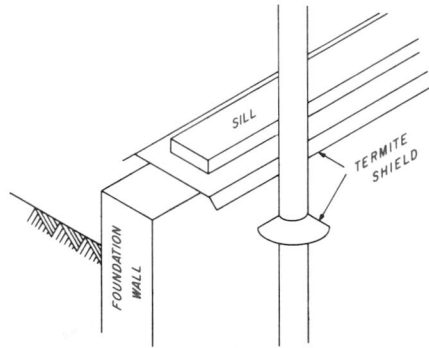

29-19. Termite shields should be not less than 26-gauge galvanized iron, aluminum, or copper. They should be installed on top of all foundation walls and piers, and around pipes. The outer edges should be bent down slightly.

29-20. *Sill sealer should be applied to the foundation before the plates are installed. It reduces air infiltration.*

Installing Sills or Plates on the Foundation

Establish the building line points at each of the corners of the foundation. Pull a chalk line very tight at these established points and snap a line for the location of the sill. Square up the ends of the sill stock. Then place the sill on edge and mark the location of the anchor bolts. With a square, extend these marks across the width of the sill. The distance "X" in Fig. 29-21a shows how far from the edge of the sill to bore the holes. Locate the midpoints between the lines representing the bolt locations and bore holes. If the sheathing is to rest on the foundation walls, allow for this by subtracting the sheathing thickness from the distance "X." Locate and bore holes as previously explained. If termite shields are used, bore holes at the same locations in the insulation and shields. Place the shields over the anchor bolts. Fig. 29-21b. Then place the sill on top. Start at the high point of the foundation and check the sill for level. Shim up as necessary. Add a washer and then tighten the nut to the sill.

In hillside construction where there is a step foundation, short sills are placed on each of the steps and then a longer sill is placed in the highest position for the entire length of the building. Cripple studs are then set onto the short sills and cut to a length which will support the longer sill in a level position to carry the floor joists.

Floor Joists for Platform Construction

Check the house plans to determine the size and direction of the joists. If the sizes for joists are not specified on the plans, consult Table 29-B and Table 29-C to determine the appropriate sizes. On the sill or wall plate lay out the desired joist spacing. Fig. 29-22. If there is to be a double joist under the outside wall, place a ¾" spacer block between the first and second joists. All other joists should be 16" on center (unless the plan calls for 24" on center).

Lay out a double joist under each cross partition. (A *cross partition* is one which runs parallel to the floor joists.) Fig. 29-23. If the cross partition is to be used for plumbing or heating pipes or ducts, place a solid spacer block between the double joists to allow pipes to run between them. Fig 29-16. Transfer the joist spacing marks from the sill onto a story pole and set it aside for later use. Place the header joist on edge, making sure it is aligned with the outside edge of the sill. Toenail the header joist in

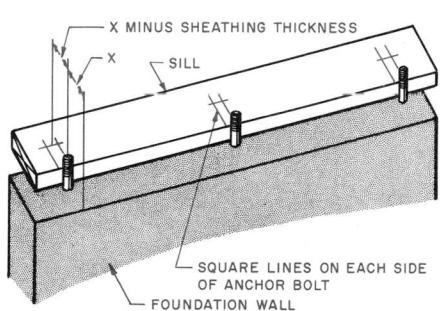

29-21a. *Laying out the location of the bolt holes on the sill.*

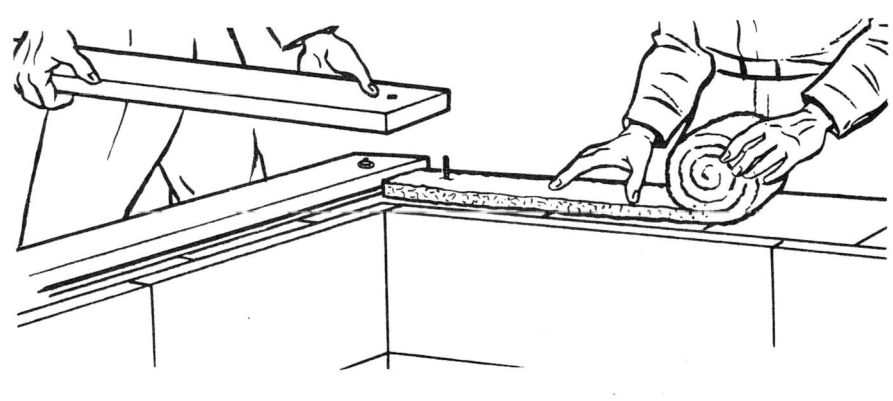

29-21b. *Roll out a strip of fiberglass sill sealer on the foundation wall just before laying the sill plate. The insulation will compress under the weight of the building. This fills irregularities and helps keep out dirt. It also keeps out drafts and reduces heat loss.*

Table 29-B. *Allowable Spans for Floor Joists Using Nonstress-Graded Lumber. The group classifications in this table refer to the species and minimum grades of nonstress-graded lumber. See Table 29-C.*

Size Of Floor Joists (Inches)	Spacing Of Floor Joists (Inches)	Maximum Allowable Span (Feet and Inches)							
		Group I		Group II		Group III		Group IV	
		Plastered Ceiling Below	Without Plastered Ceiling Below	Plastered Ceiling Below	Without Plastered Ceiling Below	Plastered Ceiling Below	Without Plastered Ceiling Below	Plastered Ceiling Below	Without Plastered Ceiling Below
2 x 6	12	10-6	11-6	9-0	10-0	7-6	8-0	5-6	6-0
	16	9-6	10-0	8-0	8-6	6-6	7-0	5-0	5-0
	24	7-6	8-0	6-6	7-0	5-6	6-0	4-0	4-0
2 x 8	12	14-0	15-0	12-6	13-6	10-6	11-6	8-0	8-6
	16	12-6	13-6	11-0	11-6	9-0	10-0	7-0	7-6
	24	10-0	11-0	9-0	9-6	7-6	8-0	6-0	6-6
2 x 10	12	17-6	19-0	16-6	17-6	13-6	14-6	10-6	11-6
	16	15-6	16-6	14-6	15-6	12-0	13-0	9-6	10-0
	24	13-0	14-0	12-0	13-0	10-0	10-6	7-6	8-6
2 x 12	12	21-0	23-0	21-0	21-6	17-6	19-6	13-0	14-6
	16	18-0	20-0	18-0	19-6	15-6	16-6	12-0	13-0
	24	15-0	16-6	15-0	16-6	12-6	13-6	10-0	10-6

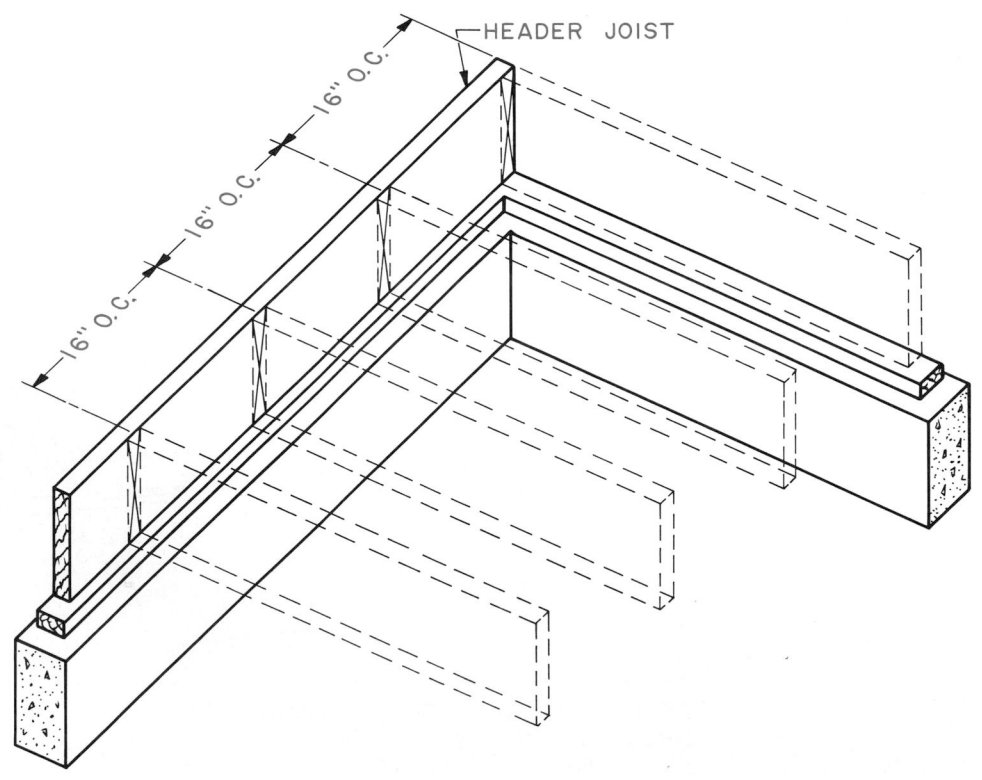

29-22. *Notice that the 16" spacing is measured from the outside edge of the first joist to the center of the second joist and then to the centers of the other joists.*

Table 29-C. *Group Classification—Nonstress-Graded Lumber.*

Species	Minimum Grade	Uniform Building Code Standard Number
Group I		
Douglas Fir & Larch[1]	Construction	25-3, 25-4
Group II		
Bald Cypress (Tidewater Red Cypress)	No. 2	25-2
Douglas Fir (South)[1]	Construction	25-4
Fir, White	Construction	25-3, 25-4
Hemlock, Eastern	No. 1	25-5
Hemlock, West Coast & Western[1]	Construction	25-3, 25-4
Pine, Red (Norway Pine)	No. 1	25-5
Redwood, California	Select Heart	25-7
Spruce, Eastern	No. 1	25-8
Spruce, Sitka	Construction	25-3
Spruce, White and Western White	Construction	25-4[2]
Group III		
Cedar, Western	Construction, West Coast Studs	25-3
Cedar, Western Red and Incense	Construction	25-4
Douglas Fir & Larch[1]	Standard, West Coast Studs	25-3, 25-4
Douglas Fir (South)[1]	Standard	25-4
Fir, Balsam	No. 1, Standard	25-8
Fir, White	West Coast Studs	25-3, 25-4
Hemlock, Eastern	No. 2, Standard	25-5
Hemlock, West Coast & Western[1]	West Coast Studs	25-3, 25-4
Pine, Ponderosa, Lodgepole, Sugar, Idaho White	Construction	25-4
Redwood, California	Construction	25-7
Redwood, California (studs only)	Two Star	25-7
Spruce, Engelmann	Construction, Standard	25-4
Spruce, Sitka	West Coast Studs	25-3
Spruce, White and Western White	Standard	25-4[2]
Group IV (See Section 2501 (e) Uniform Bldg. Code)		
Cedar, Western	Utility	25-3
Cedar, Western Red & Incense	Utility	25-4
Douglas Fir & Larch	Utility	25-3, 25-4
Douglas Fir (South)	Utility	25-4
Fir, White	Utility	25-3, 25-4
Hemlock, West Coast & Western	Utility	25-3, 25-4
Pine, Ponderosa, Lodgepole, Sugar, Idaho White	Utility	25-4
Redwood, California	Merchantable	25-7
Redwood, California (studs only)	One Star	25-7
Spruce, Engelmann	Utility	25-4
Spruce, Sitka	Utility	25-3
Spruce, White and Western White	Utility	25-4[2]

1) Two-inch by 4-inch only.
2) Spruce (White and Western White) shall be graded under the requirements of Section 25.409 of U.B.C. Standard No. 25-4.

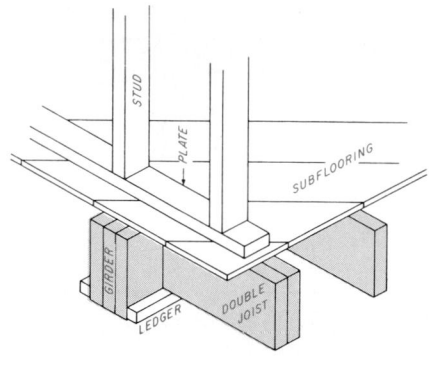

29-23. *Floor joists are doubled under nonbearing partitions.*

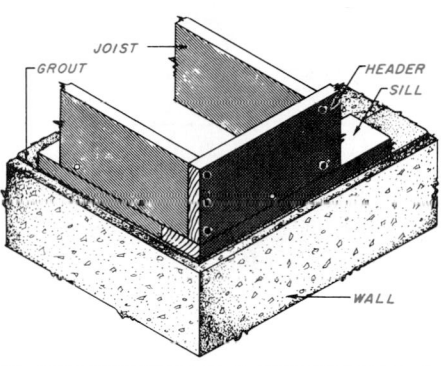

29-24. *Box-sill construction. The header joist is nailed to the other joists with 20d nails. Three nails are driven into the end joist and two into the others. The outside joist and header joist are toenailed to the sill on 16" centers.*

place, nailing as required by code. Now hold the outside joist in a 90-degree vertical position to the header joist along the outside edge of the sill. Spike through the header joist into the end of the outside joist to form the corner. Fig. 29-24.

Any joists having a slight bow edgewise should be so placed that the crown is on top. A crowned joist will tend to straighten out when subfloor and normal floor loads are applied. The largest edge knots should be placed on top since knots on the upper side of a joist are on the compression side of the

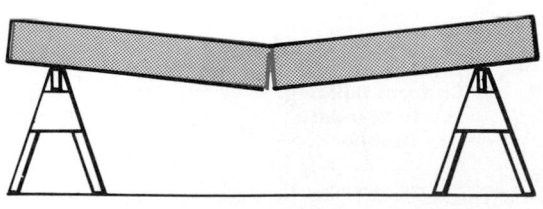

SAW CUT FROM BOTTOM OF BOARD OPENS UP.

29-25a. *With a saw cut at the bottom, the same as with a knot or other defect, the board will open up and break.*

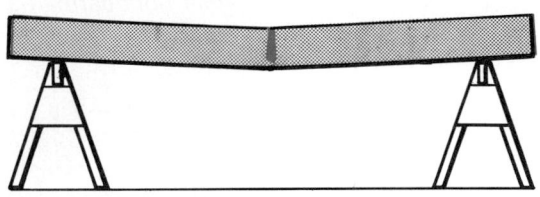

SAW CUT AT TOP OF BOARD BINDS ON THE SAW.

29-25b. *A saw cut at the top of the board will close up (compress). Thus the board will retain more strength than the example in Fig. 29-25a.*

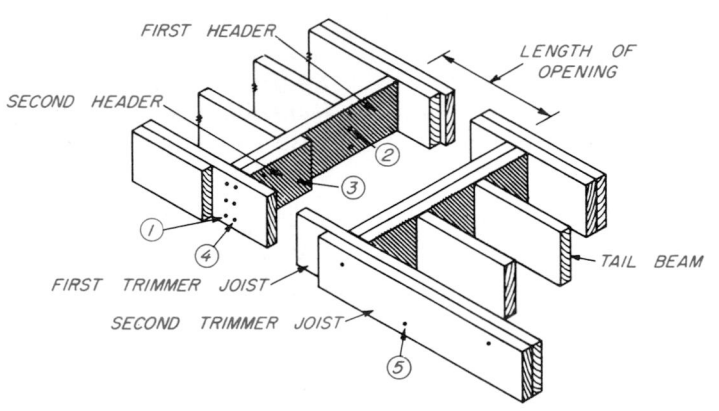

29-26. *Nailing procedure for framing floor openings. 1. First trimmer is nailed to first header with three 20d nails. 2. First header is nailed to tail beams with three 20d nails. 3. Second header is nailed to first header with 16d nails spaced 6" apart. 4. First trimmer is nailed to second header with three 20d nails. 5. Second trimmer is nailed to first trimmer with 16d nails spaced 12" apart.*

member. Fig. 29-25. Place the joists on the sills and securely nail through the header into the ends of the joists. Now lay the story pole (made earlier) across the tops of the joists, near the center and at right angles to the joists.

After the story pole is laid parallel to the joist header, nail it to each of the joists, using the spacing marked to obtain the correct spacing of the joists. Leave this strip in place until the subfloor is laid.

After nailing through the header joist (band) into the ends of the joists, pull a line tight along the top edge to check it for alignment. When the band has been properly aligned, nail the other ends of the joists to the girder and to the joists from the other side of the building. Lay out and frame the floor openings and install the bridging as required. The subfloor may then be laid and nailed in place.

Framing Floor Openings

When framing for large openings such as stairwells, fireplaces, and chimneys, the joists and headers framing the opening should be doubled. Fig. 29-26. The proper method of nailing is also shown in Fig. 29-26. Place the first trimmer joist in position. Lay out on this joist the location of the double header. Cut the first header to length and nail it in position. Lay out on this header the position of the tail beams, using regular spacing.

Place the tail beams in position and nail through the header into these joists, using three 20d nails in the end of each joist. Cut and place the second part of the double header in position, nailing it to the first header. Also nail through the first trimmer joist into the end of the second header. Now add the

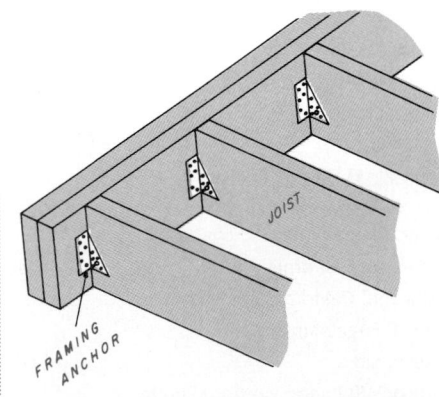

29-27a. *Using framing anchors to secure the tail joists to the header.*

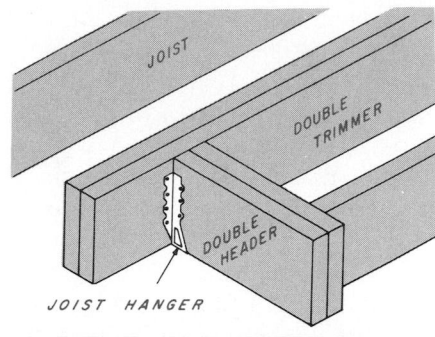

29-27b. Using a joist hanger to secure a header joist to a trimmer joist. Double trimmers and double headers are used around floor openings.

second trimmer joist and nail the two trimmer joists together, keeping the top edges even. Joist hangers are often used as joist supports for the larger openings. Fig. 29-27. For further details of stairwells see "Stairs," Unit 52.

Floor Framing at Bay-Window Projections

The framing for a bay window or similar projection should be arranged so that the floor joists extend beyond the foundation wall.

29-28b. When wall sheathing is nailed into place, it will tie the wall framing to the floor framing.

This allows them to carry the necessary loads. Fig. 29-28. This extension should normally not exceed 2 feet. The joists forming each side of the bay and the header for the bay should be doubled. Nailing, in general, should conform to that for floor openings. The subflooring is extended to the outer framing member and sawed flush with that member. Ceiling joists should be carried by a header framed over the window opening in the projected part of the structure. Fig. 29-29.

Bridging

When joists are placed over a long span, they have a tendency to sway from side to side. To help solve this problem, a bracing method called *bridging* is commonly used.

Floor frames are bridged in order to:
➤ Stiffen the floor frames.
➤ Prevent unequal deflection (bending) of the joists.
➤ Enable an overloaded joist to receive some assistance from the joists on either side of it.

Bridging is of two kinds, horizontal (solid) bridging, Fig. 29-30, and cross (diagonal) bridging. Cross bridging is more generally used since it is very effective and requires less material. Lumber 1" × 3" or 2" × 2" is usually used for cross bridging. Fig. 29-31a and 29-31b. Rigid metal cross bridging with nailing flanges may also be used. Fig. 29-31c. If the joists are over 8' long, one row of bridging is installed at the center of the joist span. For joists 16' and longer, install two rows of bridging equally spaced on the joist span.

Cutting and Installing Diagonal Bridging. Use the framing square to lay out diagonal bridging. The tongue of the square represents the width of the joists; the blade represents the space between the joists. Place a piece of bridging stock across the square as shown in Fig. 29-32, and mark the angle to be cut along the outside edge of the tongue. Cut the piece off at the marked angle. Place this cut on the body of the square at the 14½" mark (for 16" O.C. joist spacing). Lay the other end of the piece of bridging across the 9¼" mark (for a 10" joist) and scribe a mark on the outside edge of the tongue. Cut the bridging to the finished length and try it between two joists for fit.

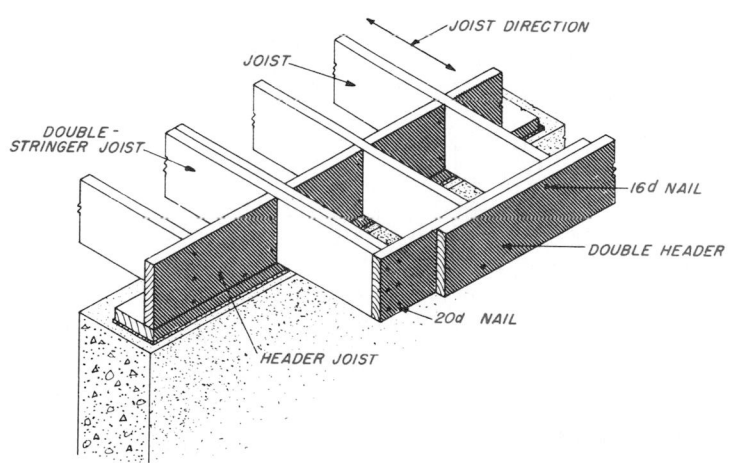

29-28a. Floor framing for a bay window. Nailing procedure: Second header is nailed to first header with 16d nails spaced 6" apart. First header is end-nailed to each member of double-stringer joist with three 20d nails.

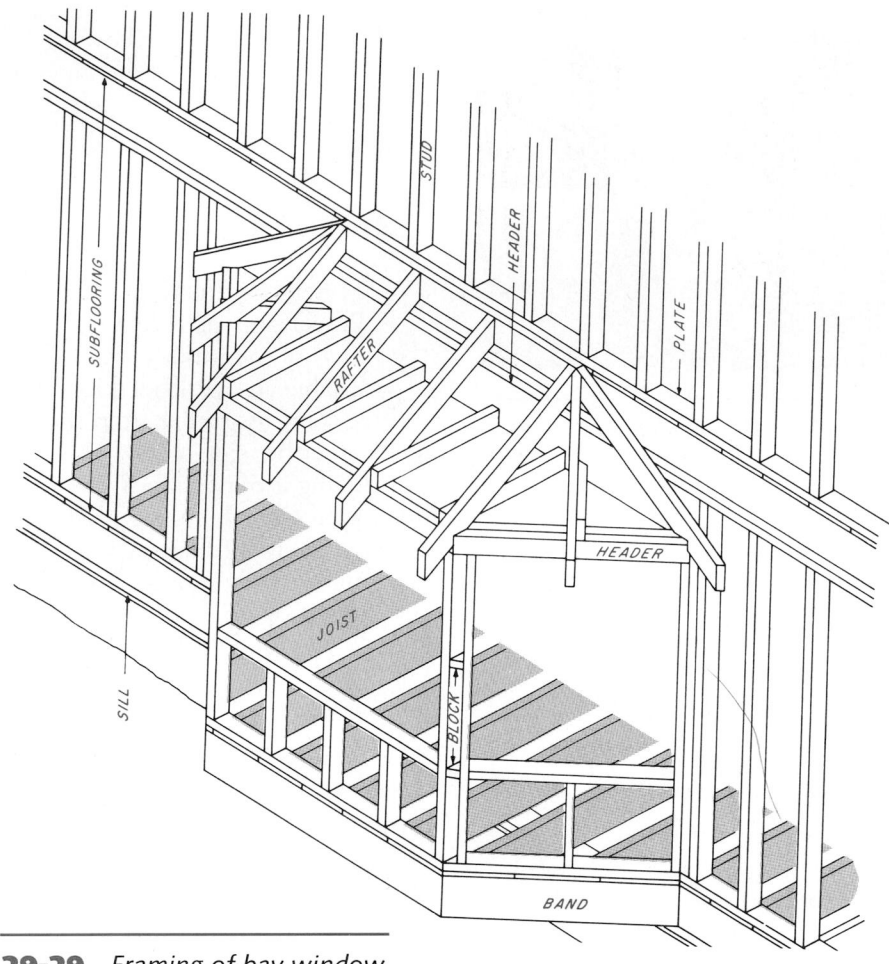

29-29. Framing of bay window.

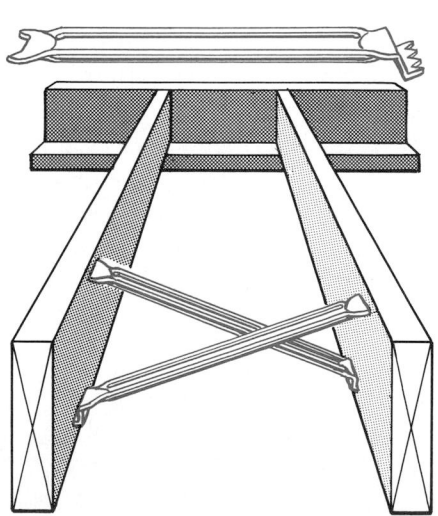

29-31b. Wood diagonal bridging.

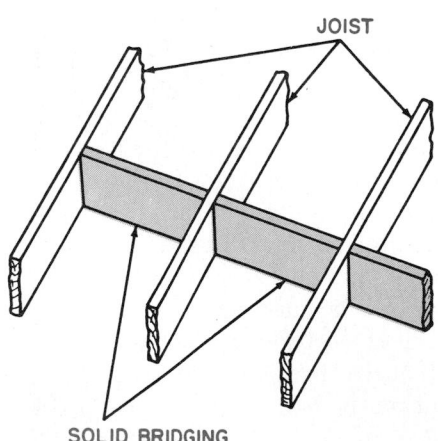

29-30. Horizontal or solid bridging. Nailing is easier if the bridging is offset by the width of the stock. Nails can then be driven directly through the joist into the end of each piece of bridging.

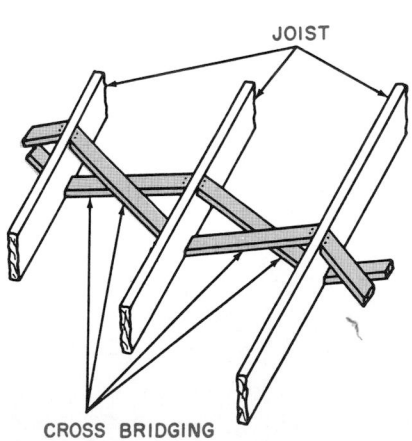

29-31a. Cross, or diagonal, bridging.

29-31c. Metal diagonal bridging.

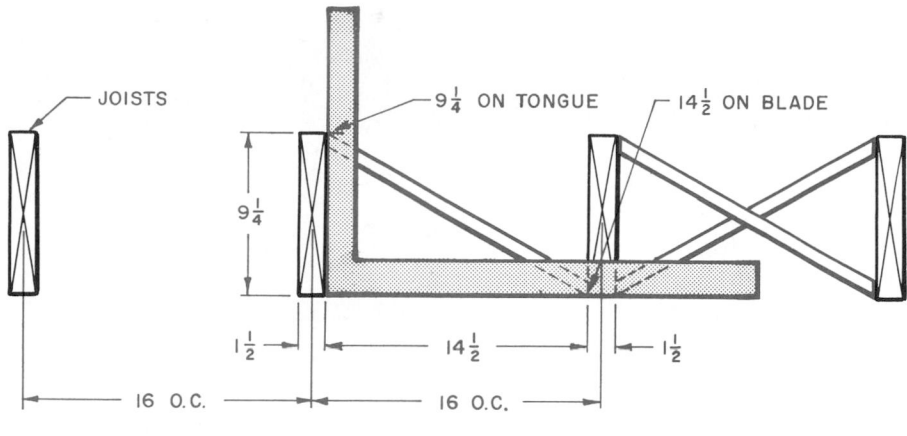

29-32. *Laying out a piece of bridging. (Shown are 2" x 10" joists 16" on center.)*

JOISTS

9¼ ON TONGUE   14½ ON BLADE

9¼

1½   14½   1½

16 O.C.   16 O.C.

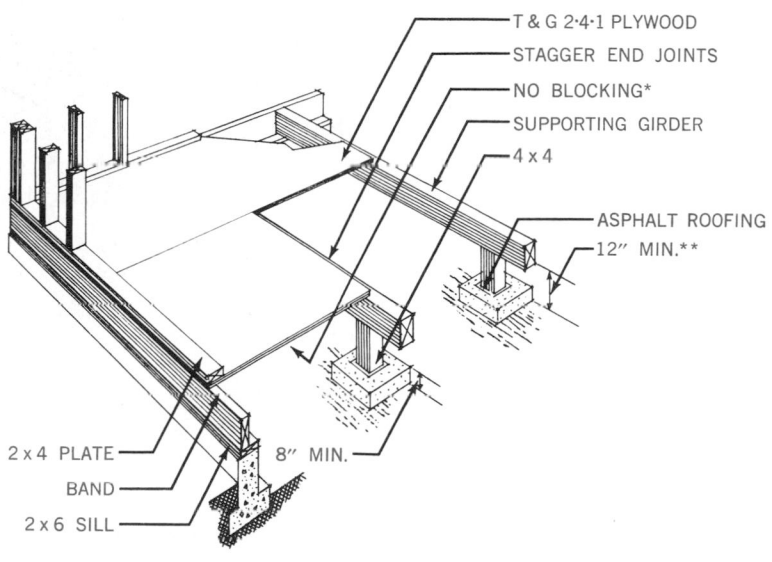

T & G 2·4·1 PLYWOOD
STAGGER END JOINTS
NO BLOCKING*
SUPPORTING GIRDER
4 x 4
ASPHALT ROOFING
12″ MIN.**
2 x 4 PLATE
BAND
2 x 6 SILL
8″ MIN.

29-33. *Girder construction with box-sill framing. The asphalt roofing keeps the wood from contacting the pier. *If square-edge panels are used, blocking is required at unsupported edges. **In areas of termite infestation or under conditions of adverse ground moisture, use 18" minimum.*

Cut the first piece for a template and use as a pattern for the other pieces. For one row of bridging, locate the center of the span and snap a chalk line across the top of the joists. Before installation, drive two 8d nails at each end of the bridging pieces. Drive the nails until the points just show through.

Start at a wall and nail one piece of bridging in position. Continue by placing one row of bridging on each side of the chalk line on the joist. Complete the nailing at the top of the bridging; however, do not nail the bottom until the subfloor has been laid. This permits the joists to adjust themselves to their final positions. The bottom ends of bridging may then be nailed, forming a continuous truss across the whole length of the floor and preventing any overloaded joist from sagging below the others.

GIRDER FLOOR FRAMING

The girder method of floor framing is widely used in warm climates where homes without basements are built. It is much faster than joist-frame construction, but requires heavier or built-up material for the girders. Fig. 29-33. The correct girder size has to be figured on the basis of the load it is to support, the span, and the type of material used. This information is found on the building plans or by checking with the local building department for maximum spans of girders. Girder spacing is usually four feet on center, with the maximum spacing of girder posts usually five feet on center. Steel girders are often used for fairly long spans.

Houses may have 4" × 6" girders set on 4" × 6" posts. First, the building foundation walls and footings are poured. The locations of the piers are established, and the holes for the pier footings are dug. Fig. 29-34. Depending on the soil

29-34. *The footing hole is dug and the precast concrete pier is ready for setting into the hole.*

29-35. The piers are set in place on the footings.

29-36. The foundation wall with the anchor bolts set for the sill. The piers are ready for the posts.

29-37. The sill is bolted in place. The girders are laid and ready for installation.

and local restrictions, these footings may require a built-up form.

The concrete is poured into the cavity provided for the footing, and the piers are set in place. Fig. 29-35. The piers should be in a reasonably straight line, but the height is not critical because the posts will be cut individually to the correct length for supporting the girders. Fig. 29-36. The sill is then cut to size and bolted in place. Fig. 29-37.

The bearing posts must be cut accurately to length to provide a level floor. Pull a line tight from opposite sill plates over the piers. Make certain the line is down tight on the plates. Measure the distance from the line to the top of the pier cap or redwood block on top of the concrete pier. Record this distance, usually on each pier cap or redwood block. Repeat this operation for each line of piers until the height of each bearing post has been determined and recorded. Square one end and cut the bearing posts to length. Care should be taken with material of this size to cut it square with two of its adjacent surfaces.

Treat the end of the post for termites, fungus, and similar problems. Toenail the treated end to the pier cap with two 8d nails on each side (a total of 8 nails). Fig. 29-38. Next square one end of the girder, cut it to length, and toenail it to the posts. Fig. 29-39. If a low house profile is desired or if the finished floor is to have a stepdown area, the tops of the girders in this area are set flush with the top of the sill. When this is done, a special metal hanger must be installed to support the girder end. Fig. 29-40. Two other methods of setting the top of the girder flush with the top of the plate are shown in Fig. 29-41.

When there is a step (two levels) in the floor, the ends of the girders must be headed off to

29-38. The posts are cut to the correct height and toenailed to the wood pad which is set into the precast pier.

29-39. The girders are nailed to the posts. The step in the girders is for a step-down area of the building.

29-40. When the top of the girder is to be even with the top of the sill, a metal hanger is used to support the girder.

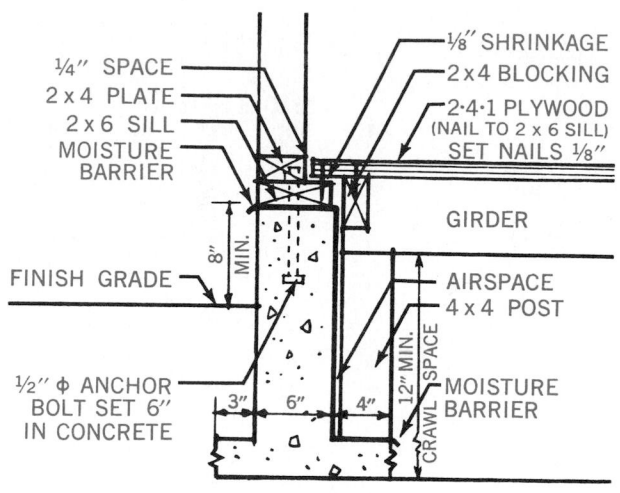

¼" SPACE
2 x 4 PLATE
2 x 6 SILL
MOISTURE BARRIER
⅛" SHRINKAGE
2 x 4 BLOCKING
2·4·1 PLYWOOD (NAIL TO 2 x 6 SILL) SET NAILS ⅛"
GIRDER
FINISH GRADE
8" MIN.
AIRSPACE
4 x 4 POST
12" MIN. CRAWL SPACE
MOISTURE BARRIER
½" φ ANCHOR BOLT SET 6" IN CONCRETE
3" 6" 4"

29-41a. *The girder may be supported on a post set on the footing.*

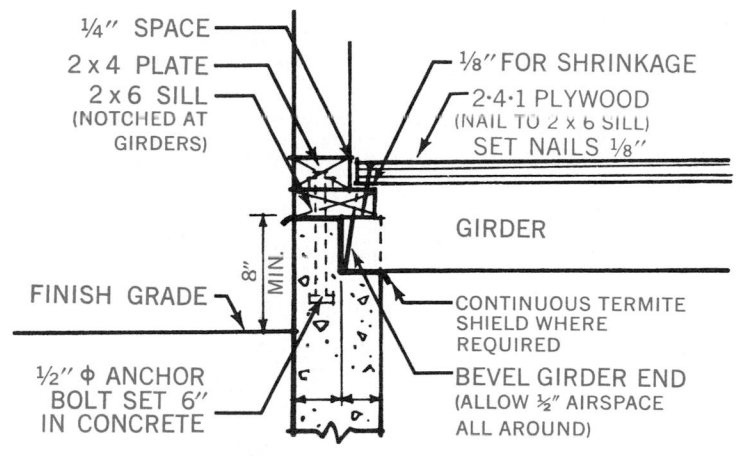

¼" SPACE
2 x 4 PLATE
2 x 6 SILL (NOTCHED AT GIRDERS)
⅛" FOR SHRINKAGE
2·4·1 PLYWOOD (NAIL TO 2 x 6 SILL) SET NAILS ⅛"
GIRDER
FINISH GRADE
8" MIN.
CONTINUOUS TERMITE SHIELD WHERE REQUIRED
½" φ ANCHOR BOLT SET 6" IN CONCRETE
BEVEL GIRDER END (ALLOW ½" AIRSPACE ALL AROUND)

29-41b. *The girder may be supported by a pocket in the foundation.*

29-42. *The girder ends are boxed in for the step in the floor.*

29-43. *The heating and air conditioning ducts are installed. They are wrapped with fiberglass insulation, and the joints are taped. Notice that the 2" x 4" boards which support the duct will also support the flooring around the cutout for the register.*

support the subfloor. A 2" × 6" is used with 4" × 6" girders. Fig. 29-42.

In framing for a fireplace or other openings in the floor, the tail beams and headers are of the same structural material as the girders.

Small openings for heating or air conditioning ducts will require only 2" × 4" boards laid flat. Fig. 29-43. Because working space under the girders is small, the plumbing and heating are "roughed in" before the floor is applied. Fig. 29-44. The subfloor is then cut and nailed in place. The surface is now ready for layout and erection of the sidewalls.

ESTIMATING FLOOR FRAMING

Determining the Number of Joists

The number of joists necessary for a building may be determined by dividing the length of the floor (in

29-44. *Plumbing is roughed in after the girders are in place.*

Table 29-D. *Number of Wood Joists Required for Any Floor and Spacing.*

Length of Span	Spacing of Joists									
	12"	16"	20"	24"	30"	36"	42"	48"	54"	60"
6	7	6	5	4	3	3	3	3	2	2
7	8	6	5	5	4	4	3	3	3	2
8	9	7	6	5	4	4	3	3	3	3
9	10	8	6	6	5	4	4	3	3	3
10	11	9	7	6	5	4	4	4	3	3
11	12	9	8	7	5	5	4	4	3	3
12	13	10	8	7	6	5	4	4	4	3
13	14	11	9	8	6	5	5	4	4	4
14	15	12	9	8	7	6	5	5	4	4
15	16	12	10	9	7	6	5	5	4	4
16	17	13	11	9	7	6	6	5	5	4
17	18	14	11	10	8	7	6	5	5	4
18	19	15	12	10	8	7	6	6	5	4
19	20	15	12	11	9	7	6	6	5	5
20	21	16	13	11	9	8	7	6	5	5
21	22	17	14	12	9	8	7	6	6	5
22	23	18	14	12	10	8	7	7	6	5
23	24	18	15	13	10	9	8	7	6	6
24	25	19	15	13	11	9	8	7	6	6
25	26	20	16	14	11	9	8	7	7	6
26	27	21	17	14	11	10	8	8	7	6
27	28	21	17	15	12	10	9	8	7	6
28	29	22	18	15	12	10	9	8	7	7
29	30	23	18	16	13	11	9	8	7	7
30	31	24	19	16	13	11	10	9	8	7
31	32	24	20	17	13	11	10	9	8	7
32	33	25	20	17	14	12	10	9	8	7
33	34	26	21	18	14	12	10	9	8	8
34	35	27	21	18	15	12	11	10	9	8
35	36	27	22	19	15	13	11	10	9	8
36	37	28	23	19	15	13	11	10	9	8
37	38	29	23	20	16	13	12	10	9	8
38	39	30	24	20	16	14	12	11	9	9
39	40	30	24	21	17	14	12	11	10	9
40	41	31	25	21	17	14	12	11	10	9

One joist has been added to each of the above quantities to take care of extra joist required at end of span. Add for doubling joists under all partitions.

feet) by the joist spacing (in feet), and adding one for the end joist.

Conventional joist spacing is 16" (1⅓') on center. Dividing by 1⅓ is the same as multiplying by ¾. Therefore for joists 16" on center, simply take ¾ the length of the building and add one.

For example, consider a building that is 40' long. Multiply ¾ × 40. The answer is 30. Add one, for a total of 31 joists.

Note, however, that the joists may not extend from wall to wall. Let's say that the building in our example is 20' wide and that we are using 10' joists. The joists will extend only from one wall to a center girder. Another 31 joists will be needed to cover the span from the girder to the opposite wall. Thus a basic total of 62 joists would be needed to span the complete floor area of the building. Also one extra joist must be added for each partition for which double joists are specified.

Table 29-D may also be used to determine the number of joists. In the column headed "Length of Span" find the length of the building (40' in our example). Read across to the spacing of the joists in the example (16") and you find the number of joists required (31). Again, this will have to be doubled if the joists extend only to a center girder, and extra joists must be added for partitions, as specified.

Determining the Material Cost

An accurate cost estimate can be figured by multiplying the number of joists required by the cost per joist. Sometimes, however, the builder will not make up a complete bill of materials, but will want only a rough cost estimate. This can be figured without knowing the exact number of pieces needed. First find the area of the floor by multiplying the length times the width of the building *for each level*. For example, a one-story building 20' wide and 40' long has a floor area of 800 sq. ft. (20 × 40 = 800).

The number of board feet for joists required for a building can be

Table 29-E. *Boardfeet, Nails, and Labor.*

Floor Joist	Material				Nails	Labor
	Board Feet Required for 100 Sq. Ft. of Surface Area				Per 1000 Bd. Ft.	Board Feet per Hr.
Size Of Joist	12"O.C.	16"O.C.	20"O.C.	24"O.C.	Pounds	
2x6	128	102	88	78	10	65
2x8	171	136	117	103	8	65
2x10	214	171	148	130	6	70
2x12	256	205	177	156	5	70

found by using Table 29-E. Again use the example of a building with 800 sq. ft. of floor area. According to the table, if the joists are 2" × 6" and 16" on center, there are 102 board feet of lumber for each 100 square feet of floor surface area. Divide the total floor area by 100, and multiply by the number of board feet which you learned from the table. The answer to the example problem is 816 board feet ($800 \div 100 = 8$; $8 \times 102 = 816$).

By multiplying the cost per board foot of lumber by the number of board feet required, you can obtain a rough cost estimate.

Table 29-E also has information for determining the number of nails necessary. For the floor in the example, the table shows that 10 pounds of nails are needed for each 1,000 board feet. The floor, you will recall, has only 800 board feet; so it will require about eight pounds of nails. Multiply the pounds needed by the cost per pound to find the total cost of the nails.

Determining the Labor Cost

The labor cost for framing a floor can be found by using Tables 29-E and 29-F. First you must know the joist size. Usually this can be learned from the building plan. In the example we have been using, the joists are 2" × 6" × 10'. Refer to Table 29-E, which indicates the number of board feet in lumber of standard sizes. The table shows that

Table 29-F. *Board Feet Content.*

Size of Timber in Inches	Length of Piece in Feet							
	10	12	14	16	18	20	22	24
1 x 2	1 $^2/_3$	2	2 $^1/_3$	2 $^2/_3$	3	3 $^1/_3$	3 $^2/_3$	4
1 x 3	2 $^1/_2$	3	3 $^1/_2$	4	4 $^1/_2$	5	5 $^1/_2$	6
1 x 4	3 $^1/_3$	4	4 $^2/_3$	5 $^1/_3$	6	6 $^2/_3$	7 $^1/_3$	8
1 x 5	4 $^1/_6$	5	5 $^5/_6$	6 $^2/_3$	7 $^1/_2$	8 $^1/_3$	9 $^1/_6$	10
1 x 6	5	6	7	8	9	10	11	12
1 x 8	6 $^2/_3$	8	9 $^1/_3$	10 $^2/_3$	12	13 $^1/_3$	14 $^2/_3$	16
1 x 10	8 $^1/_3$	10	11 $^2/_3$	13 $^1/_3$	15	16 $^2/_3$	18 $^1/_3$	20
1 x 12	10	12	14	16	18	20	22	24
1 x 14	11 $^2/_3$	14	16 $^1/_3$	18 $^2/_3$	21	23 $^1/_3$	25 $^2/_3$	28
1 x 16	13 $^1/_3$	16	18 $^2/_3$	21 $^1/_3$	24	26 $^2/_3$	29 $^1/_3$	32
1 x 20	16 $^2/_3$	20	23 $^1/_3$	26 $^7/_3$	30	33 $^1/_3$	36 $^2/_3$	40
1 $^1/_4$ x 4	4 $^1/_6$	5	5 $^5/_6$	6 $^2/_3$	7 $^1/_2$	8 $^1/_3$	9 $^1/_6$	10
1 $^1/_4$ x 6	6 $^1/_4$	7 $^1/_2$	8 $^3/_4$	10	11 $^1/_4$	12 $^1/_2$	13 $^3/_4$	15
1 $^1/_4$ x 8	8 $^1/_3$	10	11 $^2/_3$	13 $^1/_3$	15	16 $^2/_3$	18 $^1/_3$	20
1 $^1/_4$ x 10	10 $^1/_3$	12 $^1/_2$	14 $^1/_2$	16 $^2/_3$	18 $^2/_3$	20 $^5/_6$	22 $^5/_6$	25
1 $^1/_4$ x 12	12 $^1/_2$	15	17 $^1/_2$	20	22 $^1/_2$	25	27 $^1/_2$	30
1 $^1/_2$ x 4	5	6	7	8	9	10	11	12
1 $^1/_2$ x 6	7 $^1/_2$	9	10 $^1/_2$	12	13 $^1/_2$	15	16 $^1/_2$	18
1 $^1/_2$ x 8	10	12	14	16	18	20	22	24
1 $^1/_2$ x 10	12 $^1/_2$	15	17 $^1/_2$	20	22 $^1/_2$	25	27 $^1/_2$	30
1 $^1/_2$ x 12	15	18	21	24	27	30	33	36
2 x 4	6 $^2/_3$	8	9 $^1/_3$	10 $^2/_3$	12	13 $^1/_3$	14 $^2/_3$	16
2 x 6	10	12	14	16	18	20	22	24
2 x 8	13 $^1/_3$	16	18 $^2/_3$	21 $^1/_3$	24	26 $^2/_3$	29 $^1/_3$	32
2 x 10	16 $^2/_3$	20	23 $^1/_3$	26 $^2/_3$	30	33 $^1/_3$	36 $^2/_3$	40
2 x 12	20	24	28	32	36	40	44	48
2 x 14	23 $^1/_3$	28	32 $^2/_3$	37 $^1/_3$	42	46 $^2/_3$	51 $^1/_3$	56
2 x 16	26 $^2/_3$	32	37 $^1/_2$	42 $^2/_3$	48	53 $^1/_3$	58 $^2/_3$	64
2 $^1/_2$ x 12	25	30	35	40	45	50	55	60
2 $^1/_2$ x 14	19 $^1/_6$	35	40 $^5/_6$	46 $^2/_3$	52 $^1/_2$	58 $^1/_3$	64 $^1/_6$	70
2 $^1/_2$ x 16	33 $^1/_3$	40	46 $^2/_3$	53 $^1/_3$	60	66 $^2/_3$	73 $^1/_3$	80
3 x 6	15	18	21	24	27	30	33	36
3 x 8	20	24	28	32	36	40	44	48
3 x 10	25	30	35	40	45	50	55	60
3 x 12	30	36	42	48	54	60	66	72
3 x 14	35	42	49	56	63	70	77	84
3 x 16	40	48	56	64	72	80	88	96
4 x 4	13 $^1/_3$	16	18 $^2/_3$	21 $^1/_3$	24	26 $^2/_3$	29 $^1/_3$	32
4 x 6	20	24	28	32	36	40	44	48
4 x 8	26 $^2/_3$	32	17 $^1/_3$	42 $^2/_3$	48	53 $^1/_3$	58 $^2/_3$	64
4 x 10	33 $^1/_3$	40	46 $^2/_3$	53 $^1/_3$	60	66 $^2/_3$	73 $^1/_3$	80
4 x 12	40	48	56	64	72	80	88	96
4 x 14	46 $^1/_3$	56	65 $^1/_3$	74 $^2/_3$	84	93 $^1/_3$	102 $^1/_2$	112

2" × 6" × 10' boards have 10 board feet. For a building with 62 joists, as in our example, there would be a total of 620 board feet of joists (10 bd. ft. × 62 = 620 bd. ft.).

Now you can refer to Table 29-E to find the labor cost. The last column shows that one worker in one hour can frame 65 board feet of 2" × 6" joist material. To find the total hours needed, divide the total board feet by the number framed in one hour. The answer is 9.5 hours (620 ÷ 65 = 9.5). Next multiply the hours by the hourly rate.

SUBFLOORING IN JOIST CONSTRUCTION

A subfloor is a wood floor laid over the floor joists, under the finished floor. Ordinarily a subfloor is nailed directly to the floor joists. In conventional joist construction, sound subflooring is virtually a "must." Most modern building codes specify subfloors. Their omission usually is poor economy, even if the finish floor is of strong, durable oak.

Purposes Served by Subflooring

Subflooring serves several important purposes. It lends bracing strength to the building. It provides a solid base for the finish floor, making floor sag and squeaks very unlikely. By acting as a barrier to cold and dampness, subflooring helps keep the building warmer and drier in winter. In addition, it provides a safe working surface for building the house.

Selection and Nailing of Subfloor Boards

If strip flooring is to be used for the finish floor, it is generally recommended that the subflooring

consist either of softwood plywood or of good quality boards about ¾" thick and not more than 6" wide. Wider boards are likely to expand and contract too much.

Square-edge boards generally are preferred to tongue-and-groove boards. This is because snug joining usually is not desirable in subflooring. This is particularly true of houses in moist climates and summer homes which are not heated in the winter. Square-edge boards are more economical too. Boards should be thoroughly dry. The use of green subfloor boards frequently causes squeaks and cracks.

Subfloor boards may be applied diagonally or at right angles to the floor joists. When subflooring is at right angles to the joists, the finish floor should then be laid at right angles to the subfloor. However, it is best to lay the subflooring diagonally. This arrangement permits the finish strip flooring to be laid in any direction. For a home of two or more stories, it is best to have the subfloor boards run in opposite diagonal directions on alternate floors. Diagonal subflooring also provides better bracing and stiffness to the building.

Laying a Diagonal Subfloor

When laying diagonal subfloor, lay a relatively long board first. The short cuttings may then be used as you approach a corner and the length decreases. Work can then proceed on both sides of this first diagonal length.

To lay out the first piece, begin at a corner of the building (B in Fig. 29-45) and measure equal distances along the header joist and the first joist (points A and C). Snap a chalk line along the top of the joists between these two points to form a 45-degree angle. Lay the first board along this line, cut it to

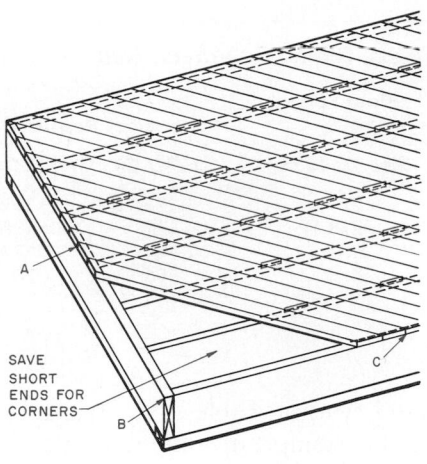

29-45. *Laying out diagonal subfloor.*

fit, and nail it at each joist with two 8d nails, not more than ¾" from the edge.

Often two or more pieces of subfloor board will have to be used to make up one diagonal strip. Ends of these pieces are nailed so they butt together on the top of a joist, forming a joint. Do not allow two of these joints to come side-by-side on the same joist; there should be at least two boards between joints. Generally, the shortest pieces of board should be long enough to span three joists—that is, start from one joist, cross another, and be fastened to a third. Of course, shorter pieces will have to be used in the corners. Fig. 29-46. Many carpenters will use an 8d nail to space between the edges of the subfloor boards. This allows for drainage and buckling which can be caused by swelling if the floor gets wet during construction. Tongue-and-groove boards should have holes at intervals to allow rainwater to drain off.

Laying a Straight Subfloor

Check the plans to determine the way the finish floor is to be laid in relation to the direction of the

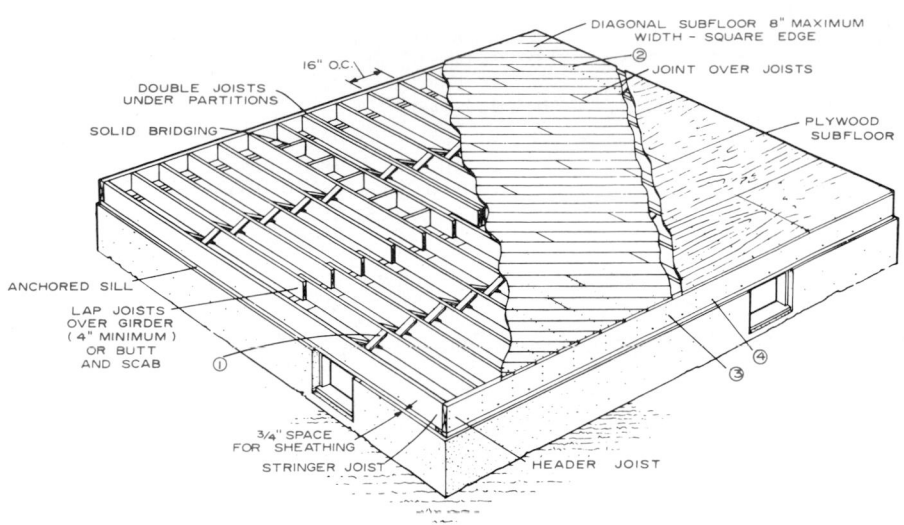

29-46. *Floor framing nailing procedure. 1. Bridging (1" x 3") nailed at top and bottom with 8d nails. 2. Subfloor board nailed with two or three 8d nails (plywood subfloor also shown as alternative). 3. Header joist end-nailed to corner joists and intermediate joists with these 20d nails. 4. Header joist toenailed to sill with 10d nails 16" on center.*

floor joists. If the finish floor is to run parallel to the joists, a straight subfloor may be laid. Begin by laying the first piece of subfloor at one end or edge of the building, at right angles to the joists. Make the joints over the centers of the joists. Laying and nailing are then done generally as for a diagonal subfloor.

29-47. *These girders are set flush with the sill in preparation for the subfloor. Notice the ventilation openings in the foundation wall. These openings are needed in this method of framing.*

Laying a 2" Tongue-and-Groove Subfloor

Some local building codes permit the use of 2" tongue-and-groove (T&G) subfloor over girder floor framing. This eliminates floor joists. When the girder is set into a pocket or hung with a bracket, care should be taken to insure that the top of the girder is even with the top of the sill plate. Fig. 29-47. Sometimes the girders are set on top of the sill, giving the building a high profile; the tongue-and-groove

29-48. *Girder construction with 2" x 6" tongue-and-groove flooring.*

flooring is cut even with the outside of the framing and nailed on top of the girders. Fig. 29-48. Use 16d nails to toenail at the tongue and to face-nail at a joint on all girders. This type of construction requires vents in the foundation.

Panel Subfloors

Plywood and oriented-strand board produce a smooth, solid, stable base for finish flooring. These panels reduce the amount of time it takes to build a floor system. There are two basic approaches to laying a panel subfloor. The floor system can be either a single-layer floor or a double-layer floor. Either one can be glue/nailed or nailed only. However, glue/nailing increases the stiffness of either type of subfloor and reduces the chances of developing squeaks later on.

Single-Layer Systems. This type of floor system was designed specifically for use beneath wall-to-wall carpeting and carpet pad. Single panels are fastened to joists or girders. The carpeting and pad are later applied directly to this surface. This is considered a single-layer floor because it has only one structural layer. (The carpeting is non-structural.) The single layer is, in effect, a combined subfloor and underlayment. Panels should be rated for this kind of use. Ratings are stamped on the back of each plywood or OSB panel manufactured by members of the American Plywood Association.

The advantage of a single-layer floor system is that it is inexpensive and quick to install. Figures 29-49, 29-50, and 29-51 show single-layer floors over various joist and girder configurations. Consult Table 29-G for fastening details. Note in the table that when panels are glued and nailed, fewer nails are required (compared to nailing only). If square-edged panels are used, any

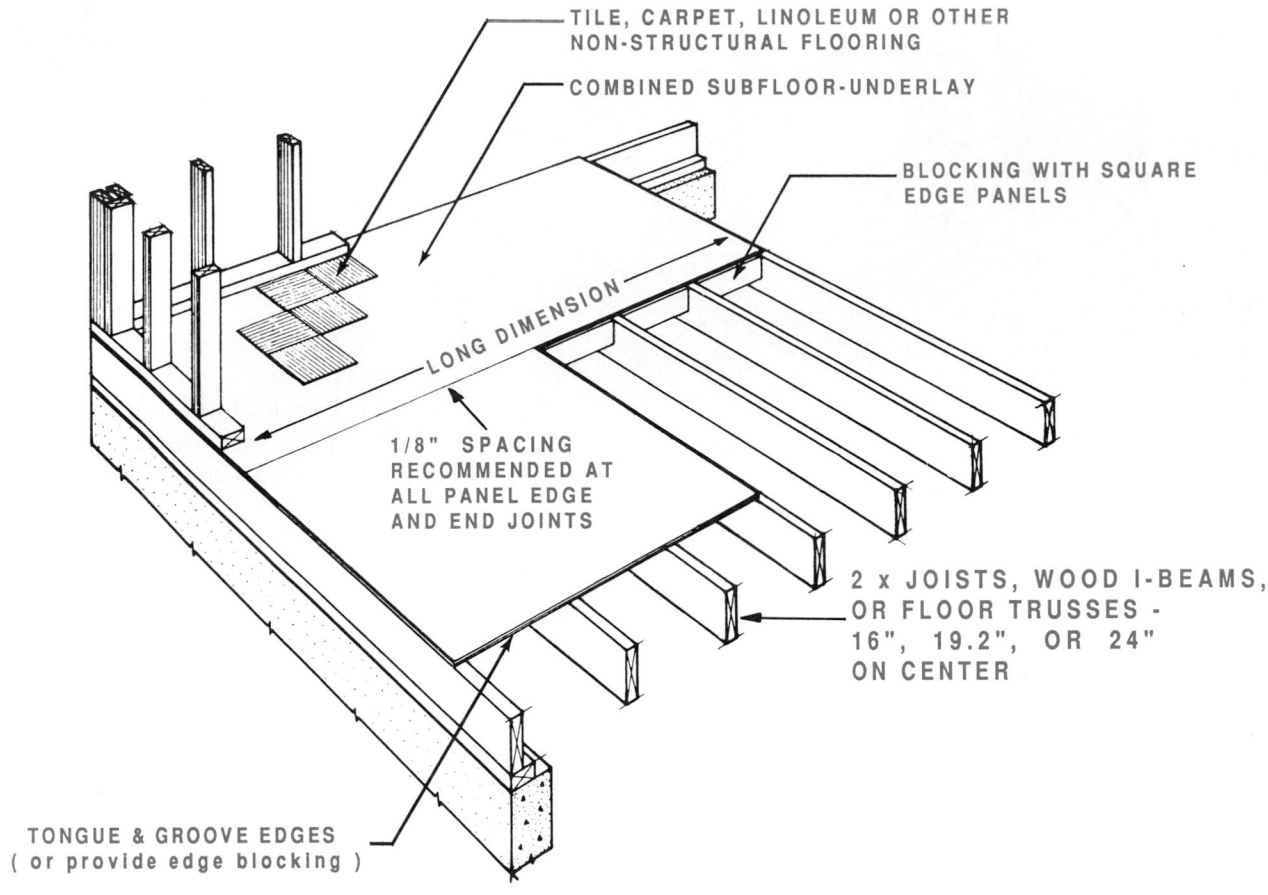

TILE, CARPET, LINOLEUM OR OTHER
NON-STRUCTURAL FLOORING

COMBINED SUBFLOOR-UNDERLAY

BLOCKING WITH SQUARE
EDGE PANELS

LONG DIMENSION

1/8" SPACING
RECOMMENDED AT
ALL PANEL EDGE
AND END JOINTS

2 x JOISTS, WOOD I-BEAMS,
OR FLOOR TRUSSES -
16", 19.2", OR 24"
ON CENTER

TONGUE & GROOVE EDGES
(or provide edge blocking)

29-49. *Single-layer floor over supports 16", 19.2", or 24" O.C.*

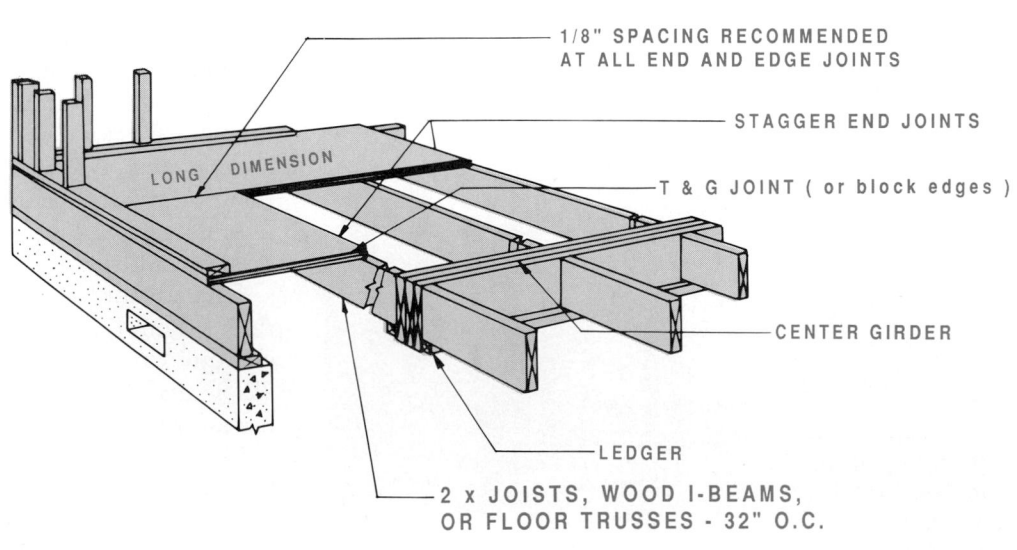

1/8" SPACING RECOMMENDED
AT ALL END AND EDGE JOINTS

STAGGER END JOINTS

LONG DIMENSION

T & G JOINT (or block edges)

CENTER GIRDER

LEDGER

2 x JOISTS, WOOD I-BEAMS,
OR FLOOR TRUSSES - 32" O.C.

29-50. *Single-layer floor: combined subfloor and underlayment over supports 32" O.C.*

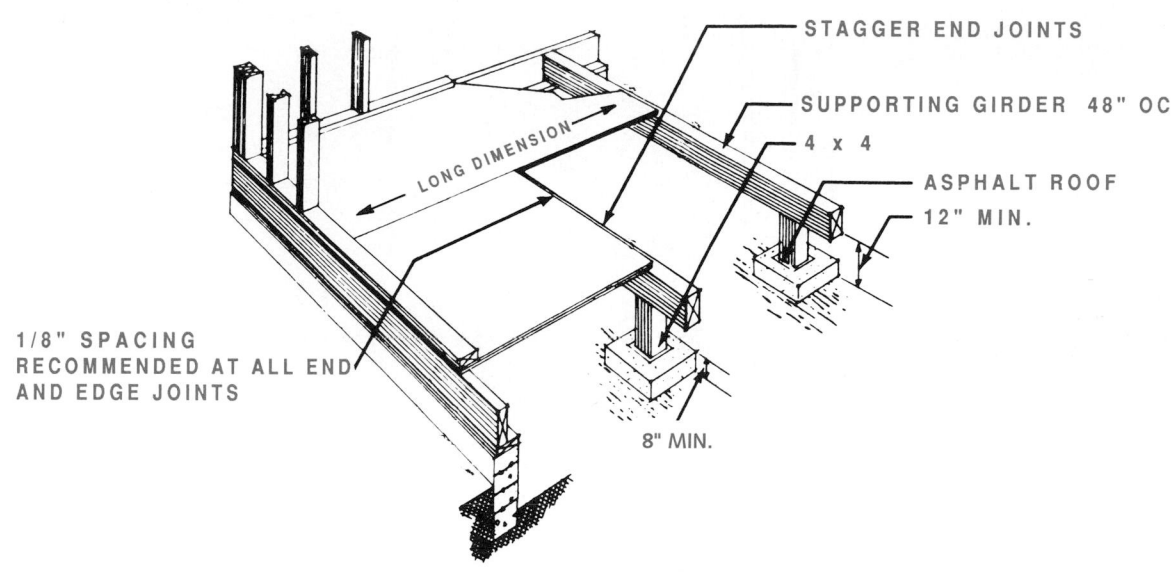

STAGGER END JOINTS

SUPPORTING GIRDER 48" OC
4 x 4

ASPHALT ROOF
12" MIN.

LONG DIMENSION

1/8" SPACING
RECOMMENDED AT ALL END
AND EDGE JOINTS

8" MIN.

29-51. *Single-layer floor over supports 48" O.C.*

Table 29-G. *APA Rated Sturd-I-Floor[a]. Specifications for single-layer floors (combined subfloor and underlayment.)*

Span Rating (Maximum Joist Spacing) (In.)	Panel Thickness[b] (In.)	Fastening: Glue-Nailed [c]			Fastening: Nailed Only		
		Nail Size And Type	Spacing (In.)		Nail Size And Type	Spacing (In.)	
			Supported Panel Edges	Intermediate Supports		Supported Panel Edges	Imtermediate Supports
16	$19/32$, $5/8$, $21/32$	6d ring-or screw-shank[d]	12	12	6d ring-or screw-shank	6	12
20	$19/32$, $5/8$, $23/32$, $3/4$	6d ring-or screw-shank[d]	12	12	6d ring-or screw-shank	6	12
24	$11/16$, $23/32$, $3/4$	6d ring-or screw-shank[d]	12	12	6d ring-or screw-shank	6	12
	$7/8$, 1	8d ring-or screw-shank[d]	6	12	8d ring-or screw-shank	6	12
32	$7/8$, 1	8d ring-or screw-shank[d]	6	12	8d ring-or screw-shank	6	12
48	1 $1/8$	8d ring-or screw-shank[e]	6	(f)	8d ring-or screw-shank[e]	6	(f)

(a) Special conditions may impose heavy traffic and concentrated loads that require construction in excess of the minimums shown.
(b) As indicated above, panels in a given thickness may be manufactured in more than one Span Rating. Panels with a Span Rating greater than the actual joist spacing may be substituted for panels of the same thickness with a Span Rating matching the actual joist spacing. For example, 19/32-inch-thick Sturd-I-Floor 20 oc may be substituted for 19/32-inch-thick Sturd-I-Floor 16 oc over joists 16 inches on center.

(c) Use only adhesives conforming to APA Specification AFG-01, applied in accordance with the manufacturer's recommendations. If non-veneered panels with sealed surfaces and edges are to be used, use only solvent-backed glues; check with panel manufacturer.
(d) 8d common nails may be substituted if ring- or screw-shank nails are not available.
(e) 10d common nails may be substituted with 1-1/8-inch panels if supports are well seasoned.
(f) Space nails 6 inches for 48-inch spans and 12 inches for 32-inch spans.
(g) Applicable building codes may require 10" oc nail spacing at intermediate supports for floors.

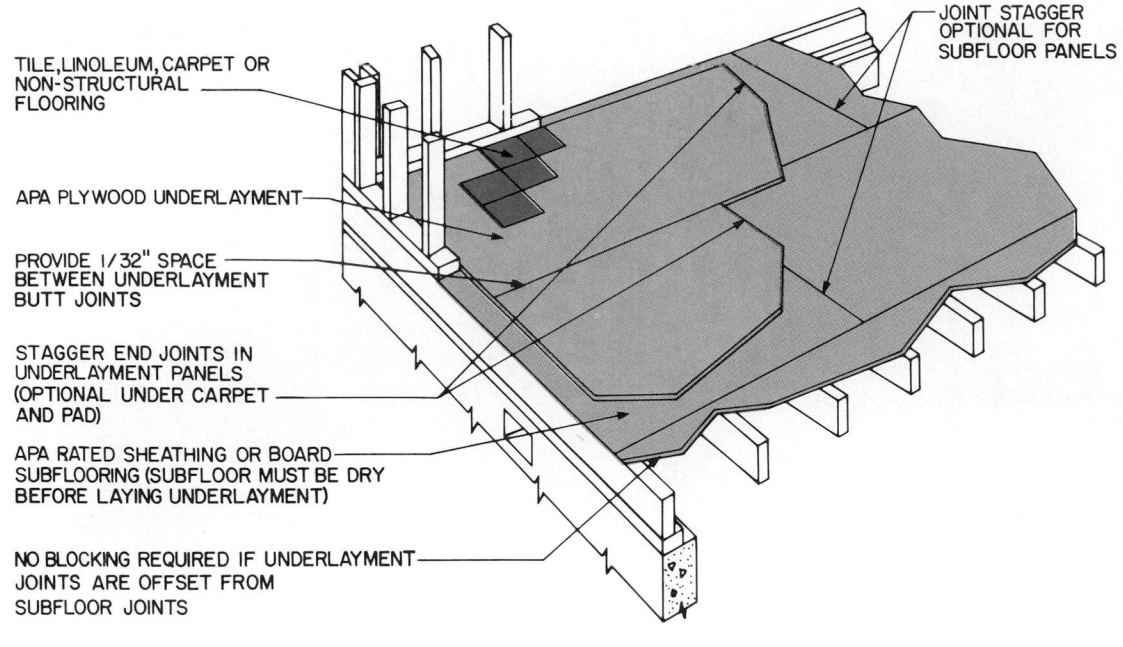

TILE, LINOLEUM, CARPET OR NON-STRUCTURAL FLOORING

APA PLYWOOD UNDERLAYMENT

PROVIDE 1/32" SPACE BETWEEN UNDERLAYMENT BUTT JOINTS

STAGGER END JOINTS IN UNDERLAYMENT PANELS (OPTIONAL UNDER CARPET AND PAD)

APA RATED SHEATHING OR BOARD SUBFLOORING (SUBFLOOR MUST BE DRY BEFORE LAYING UNDERLAYMENT)

NO BLOCKING REQUIRED IF UNDERLAYMENT JOINTS ARE OFFSET FROM SUBFLOOR JOINTS

JOINT STAGGER OPTIONAL FOR SUBFLOOR PANELS

29-52a. *Double-layer floor: plywood underlayment over panel subfloor.*

Table 29-H. *APA Plywood Underlayment(a). Specifications for plywood underlayment.*

Plywood Grades (a)	Application	Minimum Plywood Thickness (in.)	Fastener Size and Type(e)	Fastener Spacing (in.) (b) Panel Edges	Intermediate
APA UNDERLAYMENT APA C-C Plugged EXT. APA RATED STURD-I-FLOOR (19/32" or thicker)	Over smooth subfloor Over lumber subfloor or other uneven surfaces.	1/4 11/32	3d ring-shank nails(c) 3d ring-shank nails (c)	3 6	6 each way 8 each way
Same grades as above, but species Group 1 only.	Over lumber floor up to 4" wide. Face grain must be perpendicular to boards.	1/4	3d ring-shank nails (c)	3	6 each way

(a) In areas to be finished with thin floor coverings such as tile or sheet vinyl, specify Underlayment, C-C Plugged or STURD-I-FLOOR with "sanded face." Underlayment A-C, Underlayment B-C, Marine EXT or sanded plywood grades marked "Plugged Crossbands Under Face," "Plugged Crossbands (or Core)," "Plugged Inner Piles" or "Meets Underlayment Requirements" may also be used under thin floor coverings.

(b) Space fasteners so they do not penetrate framing.
(c) Use 3d ring-shank nails for 1/2 inch panels and 4d ring-shank nails for 5/8 inch or 3/4 inch panels.
(d) For underlayment recommendations under ceramic tile refer to Table 29-J.
(e) Other code-approved fasteners may be used.

unsupported edges must be blocked with nominal 2" lumber. Panels with T&G edges need not be blocked.

Double-Layer Systems.

When a separate subfloor and underlayment are used, this is considered a double-layer floor. A subfloor panel is first fastened to joists, and a plywood underlayment panel is later applied to the subfloor. The underlayment is installed immediately before the application of the finish flooring. It covers any minor construction damage to the subfloor and provides a smooth substrate for the finish flooring. The system is used beneath finish floors such as tile or sheet vinyl, which is then installed. Fig. 29-52. Consult Table 29-H for fastening details.

Underlayment plywood has a touch-sanded surface. This means that it is sanded at the mill just enough to ensure uniform thickness. The inner plies of underlayment plywood resist dents and punctures from concentrated loads such as furniture. To improve the stiffness of the floor, the face grain of the underlayment should be placed perpendicular to supports. The edges of the underlayment should be offset at least two inches from the edges of the subfloor panels. This is usually done automatically because the subfloor extends beneath the wall plates, while the underlayment does not. Fig. 29-52.

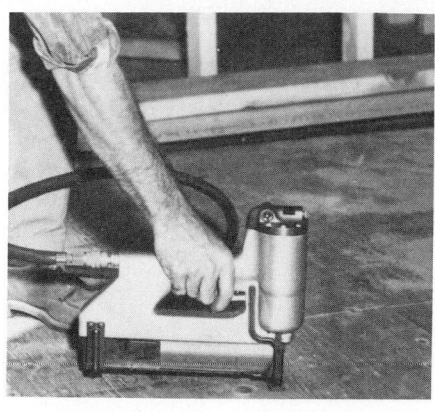

29-52b. *Using a pneumatic stapler to attach plywood subflooring.*

Systems for Wood Flooring and Tile. Wood strip finish flooring may be applied to the subflooring system shown in Fig. 29-53. The flooring may be applied in either direction. If the wood strips are at least ¾" thick, the long

edges of the subflooring do not need to be blocked. The use of T&G panels improves the stiffness of the floor. Consult Table 29-I for fastening details.

Ceramic tile should be installed over a floor system as recommended in Table 29-J.

Laying a Panel Subfloor

Begin laying the plywood subfloor by placing a full sheet even with one of the outside corners of the joist framing. The grain of the plywood should run at right angles to the joists. Drive just enough nails to hold the panel in place. Place the next full panel in position at the end of the first panel. Be sure the joint is centered over the joist, and leave about ½" space between panels.

Begin the second row of panels

at the end of the building, alongside the first panel laid. Cut a panel in half, lay the end flush with the outside of the building, and nail the half panel to the joists. If the joists are running at right angles to the grain direction of the plywood panel, measure and cut the panel so that the joint will be on the fourth joist. Fig. 29-53. Continue to lay and nail panels in this row. The next (third) row of panels is started with a full panel. This will stagger the joints and provide the strongest floor. Continue to lay, driving just enough nails in each panel to hold it in position until all panels are laid. Then complete the nailing as required. Fig. 29-54.

Tongue-and-Groove Plywood Floors. Standard-size T & G panels measure 4' × 8' on

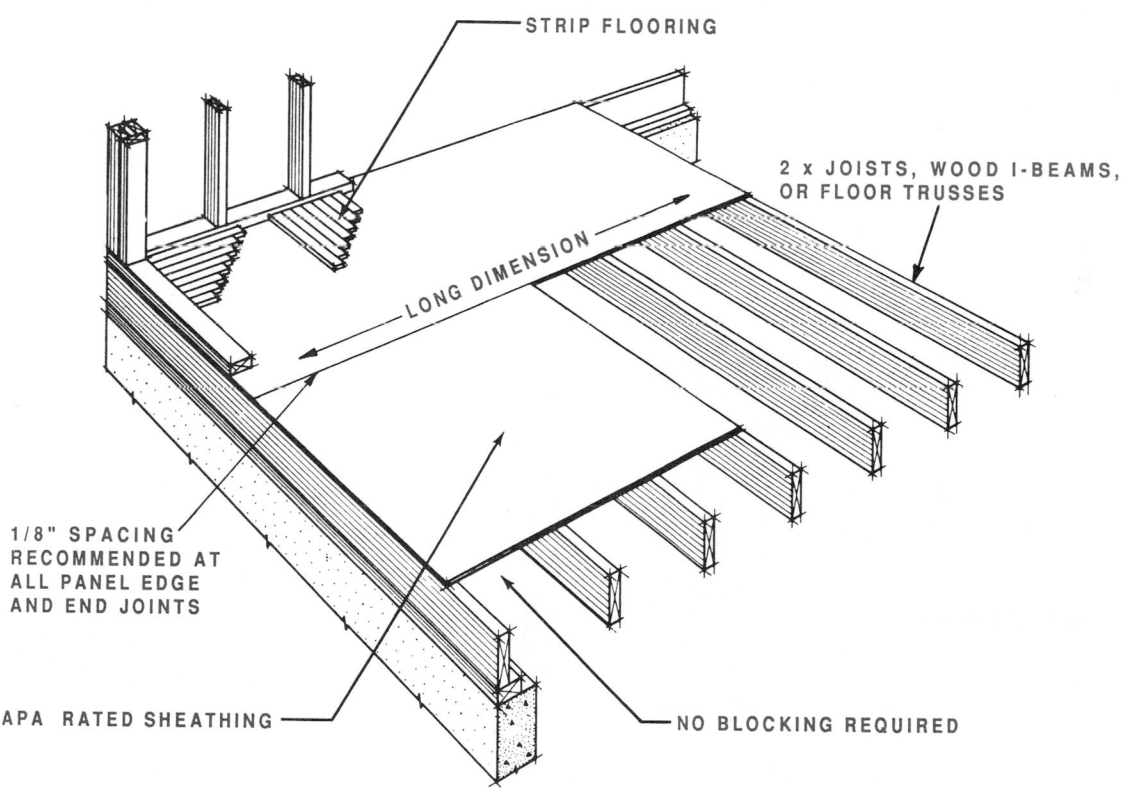

STRIP FLOORING

2 x JOISTS, WOOD I-BEAMS, OR FLOOR TRUSSES

LONG DIMENSION

1/8" SPACING RECOMMENDED AT ALL PANEL EDGE AND END JOINTS

APA RATED SHEATHING

NO BLOCKING REQUIRED

29-53. *Panel subflooring under wood strip flooring.*

Table 29-I. *APA Panel Subflooring*[(a)]. *Specifications for panel subflooring under wood strip flooring.*

Panel Span Rating (or Group Number)	Panel Thickness (In.)	Maximum Span (In.)	Nail Size & Type [(g)]	Nail Spacing (In.)	
				Supported Panel Edges	Intermediate Supports [(f)]
24/16	7/16	16	6d common	6	12
32/16	5/32, 1/2, 5/8	16[(b)]	8d common[(c)]	6	12
40/20	9/16, 19/32, 5/8, 3/4, 7/8	20[(d)]	8d common	6	12
48/24	23/32, 3/4. 7/8	24	8d common	6	12
1 1/8" Groups 1 & 2 [(e)]	1 1/8	48	10d common	6	6

(a) For subflooring recommendations under ceramic tile, refer to Table 29-J. For subflooring recommendations under gypsum concrete, contact manufacturer of floor topping.
(b) Span may be 24 inches if 3/4-inch wood strip flooring is installed at right angles to joists.
(c) 6d commom nail permitted if panel is 1/2-inch or thinner.
(d) Span may be 24 inches if 3/4-inch wood strip flooring is installed at right angles to joists, or if a minimum 1 1/2-inches of lightweight concrete is applied over panels.
(e) Check dealer for availability.
(f) Applicable building codes may require 10" oc nail spacing at intermediate supports for floors.
(g) Other code-approved fasteners may be used.

Table 29-J. *APA Plywood Systems for Ceramic Tile Flooring. (Based on ANSI Standard A108 and Recommendations of the Tile Council of America.) Subfloor and underlayment beneath ceramic tile flooring.*

Joist Spacing (In.)	Minimum Panel Thickness (In.)		Tile Installation
	Subfloor[(a)]	Underlayment[(b)]	
Residential			
16	15/32	(d)	"Dry-Set" mortar; or latex – Portland Cement mortar
16	19/32	—	Cement mortar (3/4" - 1 1/4")
16	19/32	11/32	Organic adhesive
16	19/32	15/32[(e)]	Epoxy mortar
16	19/32 T&G [(c)(e)]	—	Epoxy mortar
Commercial			
16	15/32	(d)	"Dry-Set" mortar: or latex – Portland Cement mortar
16	19/32	—	Cement mortar (3/4" - 1 1/4")
16	19/32	19/32 [(c)(e)]	Epoxy mortar

(a) APA RATED SHEATHING with subfloor Span Rating of 16" o.c. (15/32" panel) or 20" o.c. (19/32" panel), except as noted.
(b) APA Underlayment or sanded Exterior grade, except as noted.
(c) APA RATED STURD-I-FLOOR with 20" o.c. Span Rating.
(d) Bond glass mesh mortar units to subfloor with latex – Portland Cement mortar, prior to spreading mortar for setting ceramic tile.
(e) Leave 1/4" space at panel ends and edges: trim panels as necessary to maintain end spacing and panel support on framing. Fill joints with epoxy mortar when it is spread for setting tile. With single-layer residential floors, use solid lumber blocking or framing under all panel end and edge joints (including T&G joints).

29-54. *The subfloor can be nailed with a pneumatic nailer.*

the face, with additional allowance for the tongue. Fig. 29-55.

Tongue-and-groove subfloor should be started with the tongue toward the outside of the building. Thus any pounding required to close the joints between the panels can be done on a scrap block against the groove. When the panels are nailed in place, the face grain of the panel should run across the main beams, and wherever possible, cover two openings. End joints should be staggered.

If the panels are square edged, 2 × 4 blocking is required under the edges between beams. If both the sides and ends of the panel are tongue-and-grooved, drive the side joints tight first. Then, drive end joints tight. When the floor covering is of the thin, resilient type, fill any cracks 1/16" or wider and sand the joints lightly if they are not absolutely flush.

To achieve the greatest resistance to nail popping, and the maximum in withdrawal strength, use 8d common ring-shanked or helically threaded nails. Space the nails 6" O.C. at all bearing points. However, 10d common smooth-shanked nails may be substituted if desired. Under resilient tile when the beams are not fully seasoned, set all nails 1/8" but do not fill. (*Setting* means driving the heads below the wood surface.) Set the nails just before laying the resilient

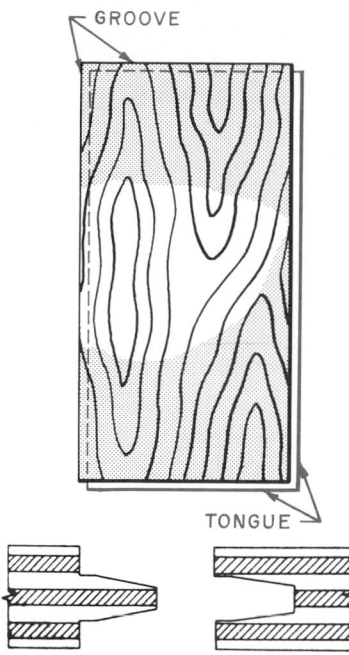

29-55. *A plywood panel 1⅛" thick with a groove on an end and an edge, and a tongue on the other end and edge. The surface is a full 4' x 8' with an additional allowance for the tongue.*

flooring. This lets you take advantage of the beam seasoning that has taken place. When the panels are tongue-and-grooved at the ends, one line of nails can be used to secure them. Drive the nails through both panels at a point near the middle of the tongue as shown in Fig. 29-56a. Figure 29-56b shows T&G plywood applied over box-sill framing.

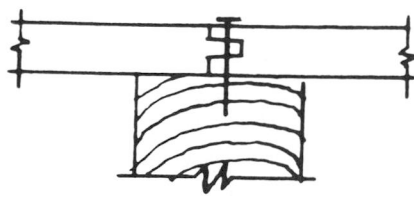

29-56a. *With tongue-and-groove plywood, a single row of nails at the joint is all that is necessary to nail the two panels together and to the girder.*

29-56b. *The T&G plywood may be applied over box-sill framing, as shown. It may also be laid directly on sills and girders which are supported in special brackets.*

ESTIMATING SUBFLOORING

Material

Figure the square feet of floor area in the building. A one-story building 28 feet by 50 feet will contain 1,400 square feet (28' × 50' = 1,400 sq. ft.). To figure the amount of lumber required, use Table 29-K.

In the first column find the type of material to be applied, for example, S4S. Then read across to the second column for the size, for example, 1 × 8. The third column will tell you the board feet per square foot of area. In our example this is 1.15. Multiply the floor area of the building (1,400) by this factor (1.15) to determine the amount of material required for the building. For the building in this example, 1,610 board feet of S4S, 1" × 8" boards will be needed: 1.15 × 1,400 = 1,610.

To figure the number of plywood sheets necessary for the building in the example, divide the floor area of the building by the area of one sheet of plywood. A 4' × 8' sheet of plywood contains 32 sq. ft. (4' × 8' = 32 sq. ft.). Therefore the floor

Table 29-K. *Estimating Subflooring.*

Type	Size	Bd. Ft. per Sq. Ft. of Area	Lbs. Nails Per 1000 Bd. Ft.			
			Spacing of Framing Members			
			12"	16"	20"	24"
T&G	1x4	1.32	66	52	44	36
	1x6	1.23	43	33	28	23
	1x8	1.19	32	24	21	17
	1x10	1.17	37	29	24	20
Shiplap	1x4	1.38	69	55	46	38
	1x6	1.26	44	34	29	24
	1x8	1.21	32	25	21	17
	1x10	1.18	37	29	25	20
S4S	1x4	1.19	60	47	40	33
	1x6	1.15	40	31	26	22
	1x8	1.15	30	23	20	17
	1x10	1.14	36	28	24	19

area in the example will require 43.75 sheets of plywood.

$$\frac{1,400 \text{ sq. ft. of floor area}}{32 \text{ sq. ft.}} = 43.75$$

This is rounded off to 44 sheets.

To determine the quantity of nails required, use Table 29-K. In the column headed "Lbs. nails per 1,000 bd. ft." find the spacing of the framing members for the type and size material to be applied. For our example, if the floor joists are spaced 16" on center, the chart shows that 23 lbs. of nails are required per 1,000 board feet of lumber. Therefore 37.03 or 37 lbs. of nails will be needed ($1,610 \div 1,000 = 1.61$; $1.61 \times 23 = 37.03$).

Labor

To figure the labor for the application of the subfloor, use the information in Table 29-L. For our example, the chart shows 75 board feet of subflooring can be laid each hour. Therefore it will take 21.5 hours to lay 1,610 board feet of lumber ($1,610 \div 75 = 21.46$, or 21.5 hours).

FLOOR TRUSSES

Special trusses can be used in place of lumber joists where long spans are required. These trusses are made in a factory to the specifications of the job. Fig. 29-57.

There are several advantages to using floor trusses. Because they are available in a nearly infinite variety of lengths and depths, they can fit a variety of loading conditions. The most common depths are 14" and 16". The open webs of a truss allow heating ducts, water and drain lines, and other mechanicals to be passed through with ease. Floor trusses are

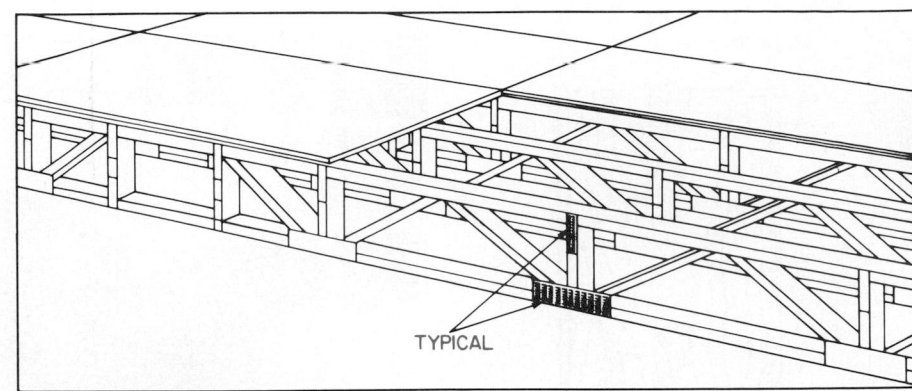

29-57a. *A wood web truss.*

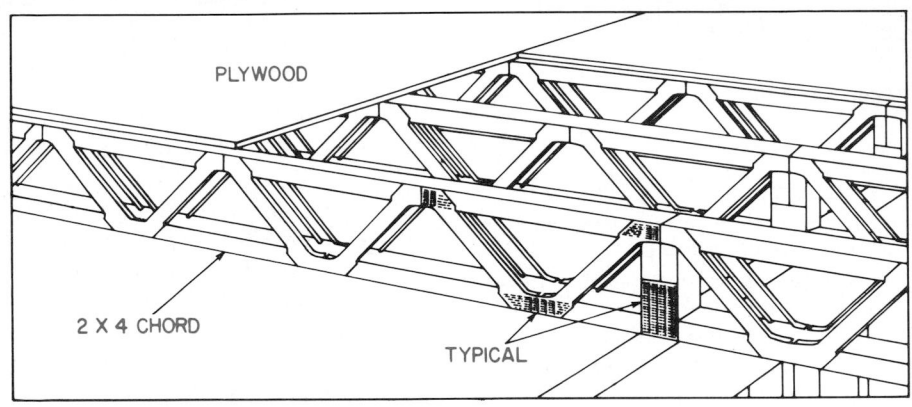

29-57b. *A metal web truss.*

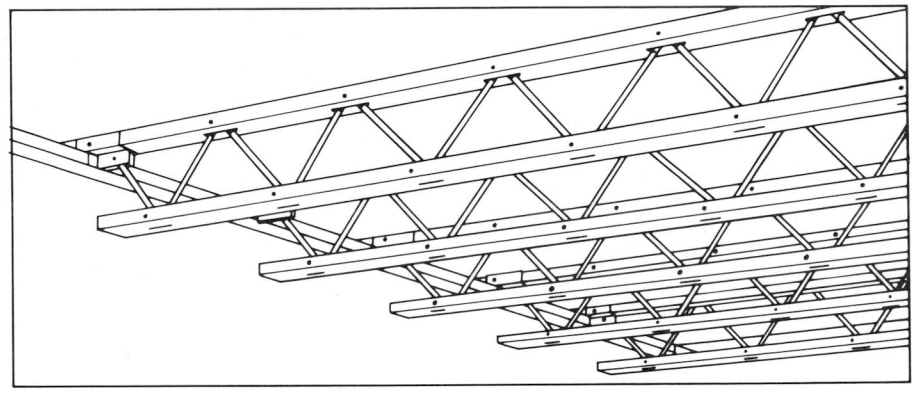

29-57c. *A pipe web truss.*

typically stronger than a lumber joist of the same depth. Finally, a floor truss can be built in lengths that allow it to reach from one side of the house to the opposite side. This speeds construction because fewer pieces of material must be handled.

Table 29-L. *Estimating Subflooring Labor Time.*

Type of Subfloor	Bd. Ft. Installed per Hour
Straight	75
Diagonal	65
Tongue and Groove	55
Plywood	100

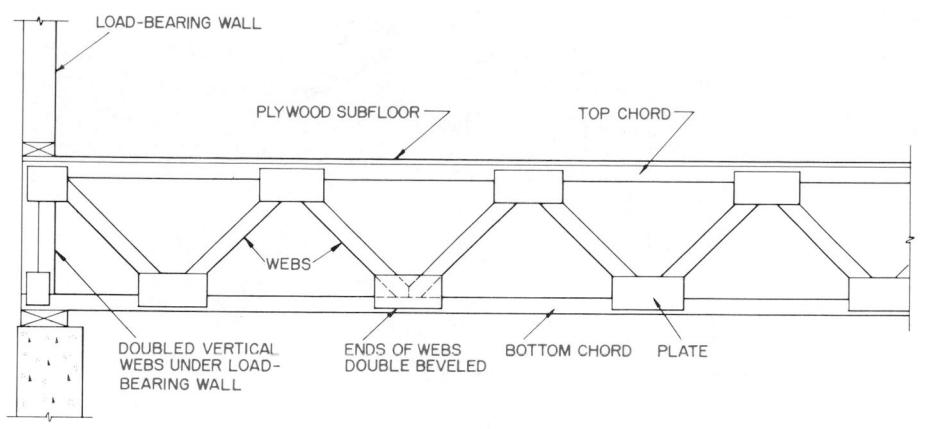

29-58. *Parts of a floor truss.*

Parts of a Floor Truss

A parallel-chord floor truss has only three basic parts. Each part, however, is carefully designed to fit with the other parts. The basic parts are chords, webs, and connector plates. Fig. 29-58.

Chords. The most common type of floor truss in residential construction is called a *4 × 2 parallel-chord floor truss*. Its top and bottom chords are parallel to each other. The top chord and the bottom chord are parallel to each other over the length of the truss. The designation 4 × 2 (pronounced "four by two") means that the chords are made from 2 × 4 lumber with the wide surfaces facing each other. With the chords in this configuration, the truss bears solidly on wall plates and is fairly rigid side to side.

Most floor trusses are designed to bear on the bottom chord. Some, however, can bear on the top chord. Fig. 29-57. Trusses that bear on the top chord are used when the height of the building must be limited. Chords are usually made from machine stress-rated (MSR) lumber. This ensures consistent strength.

Webs. Webs connect the top and bottom chords. They can be made of wood or galvanized metal. Diagonal webs are typically positioned at a 45-degree angle to the chords. Vertical webs are positioned at a 90-degree angle to the chords. When the webs are made of wood, each diagonal piece is double-beveled at both ends to make a tight joint with the vertical webs. The centerlines of intersecting webs and chords must meet at one point. This point is called the *panel point.* Fig. 29-58.

Connector Plates. The connector plate is the part of a truss that holds webs and chords together. In early trusses, the connector plates were made of plywood that was nailed in place. Plates are now made from 16-gauge, 18-gauge, or 20-gauge galvanized metal. During the manufacturing process, the metal plates are punched to create many teeth on one side of the plate. These teeth grip the wood when the plate is pressed into the wood under high pressure. Fig. 29-59.

Installation Details

Techniques required for working with floor trusses are not much different than those required for lumber joists. When the trusses are delivered to the job site, they should be carefully inspected to ensure that they conform to the design specifications. Webs, chords, and plates should be checked at the same time to make sure they were not damaged during transport.

When handling floor trusses, care must be taken to ensure that webs and chords are not damaged. Trusses should always be stored, carried, or lifted in an upright position. A truss lifted with its width parallel to the ground will be stressed in such a way that connector plates could loosen.

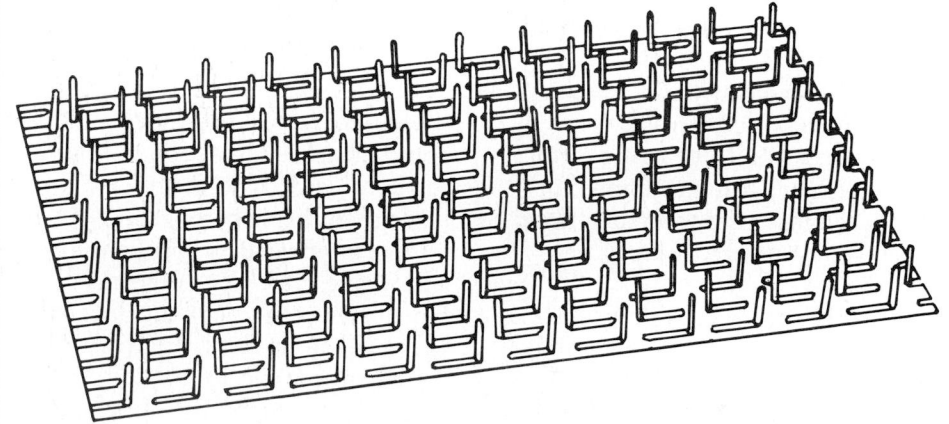

29-59. *Metal connector plates hold the pieces of a truss together.*

As the trusses are being put into place, be sure each one is right-side up. A truss that is installed upside-down could fail. The truss fabricator will sometimes deliver the trusses with a truck that has a small crane attached. If the walls are already in place, the trusses can be lifted into position directly from the truck. This saves a considerable amount of time. Otherwise, the trusses must be lifted into place by hand.

It is important to brace floor trusses as they are being installed. This will increase the safety of workers installing the subfloor. This will also prevent the trusses from being damaged by sideways movement prior to the installation of the subfloor. Generally, lengths of 2 × 4 stock are nailed to the trusses. This bracing is nailed along the center of the truss, perpendicular to its span. The bracing is located so as not to interfere with subflooring or ceiling finish. The truss fabricator can provide detailed bracing instructions. Trusses can be secured to wall plates by toe-nailing them. Subflooring is installed as described earlier in this unit. Fig. 29-60.

WOOD I-BEAMS

Many builders frame residential floors using wood I-beams (sometimes called I-joists) instead of solid lumber joists. These products have many of the same advantages of floor trusses. However, wood I-beams are lighter in weight and can be trimmed or cut to length on the job site (floor trusses must not be altered). Fig. 29-61.

Another advantage of wood I-beams is that they can be obtained without special order. Lumber dealers generally stock wood I-beams in 60 ft. lengths. They cut

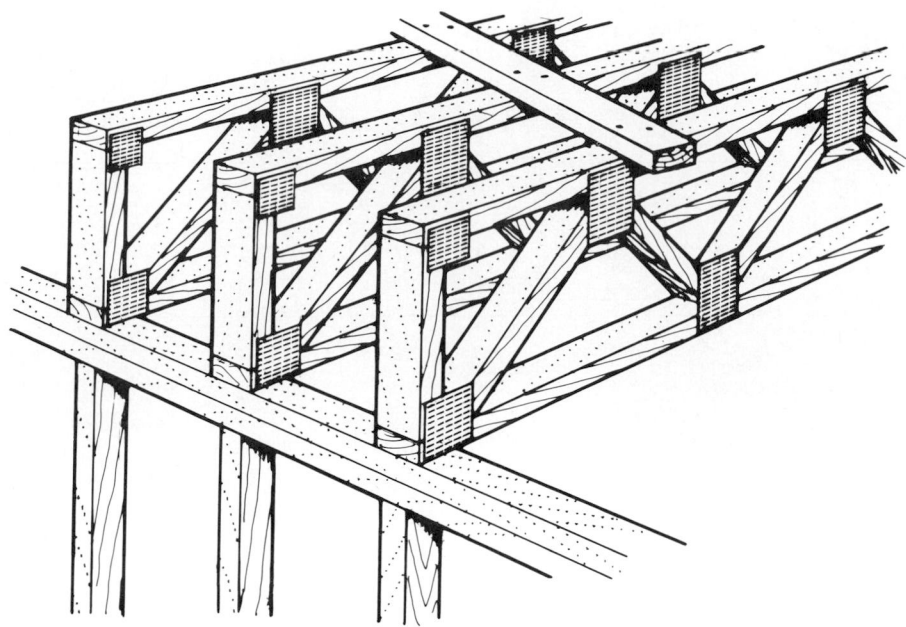

29-60. *Floor trusses are secured to wall plates by toenailing. They are braced temporarily with 2 x 4 stock.*

29-61. *Wood I-beams are often used for floor framing.*

29-62a. *Pre-scored knockouts can be removed for plumbing and wiring runs.*

these long pieces into the approximate lengths required by the contractor. The contractor trims them to exact length.

To provide access for plumbing and wiring runs, wood I-beams have pre-scored knockouts located every 12" along their length. A 1½" diameter hole can be created simply by removing the knockout with a hammer. Fig. 29-62.

Storage

Wood I-beams need little in the way of specialized care once they arrive on the job site. Even though they are made with waterproof glue, wood I-beams should be protected from the weather as much as possible. Any protective wrapping should not be removed until the products are installed. If the protective wrapping is missing,

29-62b. *The knockouts in wood I-beams are located every 12" lengthwise. Note the wood laminations in the I-beam chords.*

I-beams should be covered with a waterproof tarp until installation. The bottom of the tarp should be loose to prevent ground moisture from being trapped beneath it.

A wood I-beam is fairly weak in lateral strength, so it should be stored on edge. Storing it flat could crack the joints that join individual lengths of the web material.

Installation Details

Because the cross-section of a wood I-beam is not rectangular like that of a lumber joist, extra care must be taken in cutting it. To prevent the shoe of a circular saw from getting hung up in a crosscut, scrap stock should be placed against the web as shown in Fig. 29-63. An alternate technique is to make crosscuts with a radial arm saw.

When wood I-beams are used as floor joists, the rim joists can be solid lumber, wood I-beams, plywood, or laminated-veneer lumber. Fig. 29-64. Toenailing should follow the manufacturer's specifications. (For more

information on laminated-veneer lumber, see Unit 8.)

Metal joist hangers are available for use with wood I-beams. The width of the hanger should match the width of the I-beam. A block, called a *web stiffener*, should be added to both sides of the I-beam to improve the fit. Fig. 29-65.

Where a wood I-beam runs continuously over a support, web stiffeners should be added to both sides to improve the bearing characteristics. This can also provide additional bearing surface for lumber or I-beam blocking. Fig. 29-66.

29-64a. *Wood I-beam floor joists can be used with a rim joist of laminated-veneer lumber.*

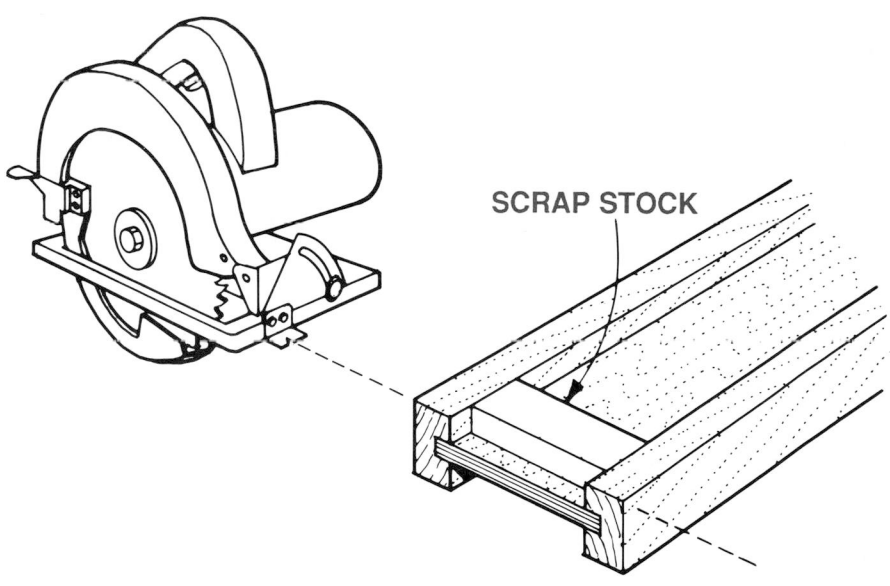

SCRAP STOCK

29-63. *To cross-cut a wood I-joist, place a length of scrap stock against the web. This will prevent the saw's shoe from getting caught by the I-beam flange.*

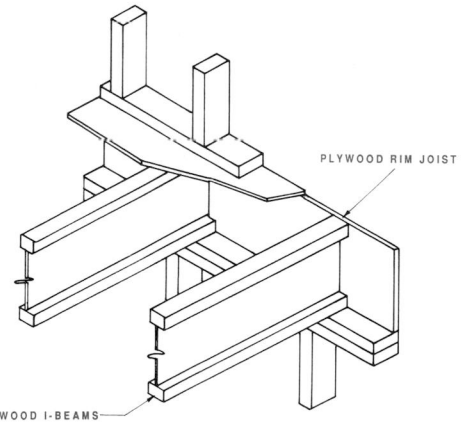

PLYWOOD RIM JOIST

WOOD I-BEAMS

29-64b. *Rim joist details.*

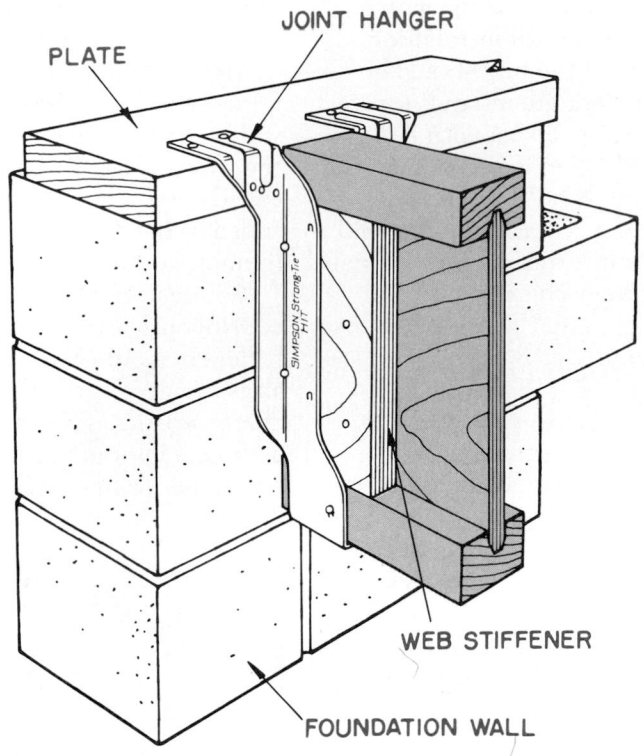

29-65. *A metal joist hanger for wood I-beams. The web stiffener is fastened to both sides of the I-beam.*

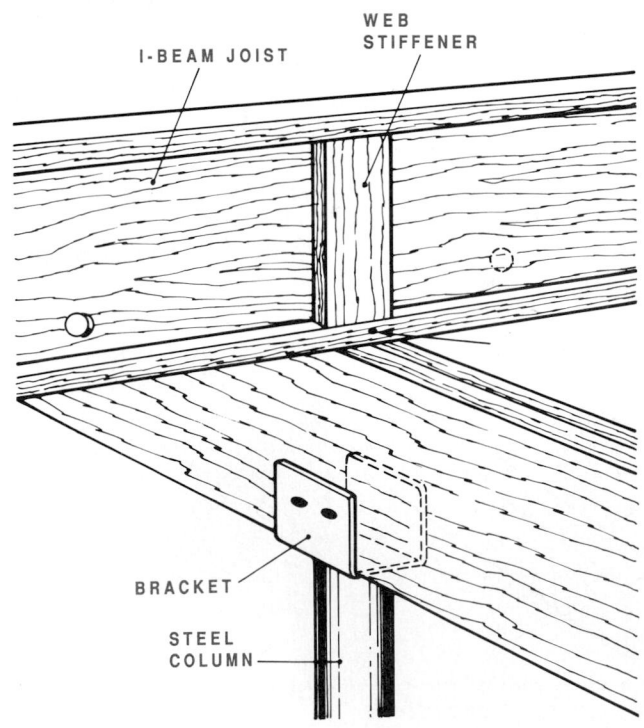

29-66. *Web stiffeners should be installed on both sides of a wood I-beam where it crosses a support.*

1. List the names of the floor framing parts.

2. What is the purpose of a post?

3. What is considered the best method of framing the joist and girder?

4. How is a sill plate attached to a foundation wall?

5. How is the header joist checked for alignment?

6. What is the purpose of bridging?

1. Math. In Table 29-K it indicates that if one uses S4S 1" by 6" stock, 1.15 board feet are needed to cover 1 square foot of area. Why? (Recall what a board foot is.) Discuss with a friend and give at least two reasons why more than one board foot is required to cover one square foot.

2. Social Studies. Research different styles of homes, such as ranch, Cape Cod, and split foyer. Geographically, where did each of these home styles evolve?

3. Science. All nonstress graded lumber species listed in Table 29-C are softwoods (coniferous trees). The species are grouped I, II, III, IV. Table 29-B identifies allowable spans for floor joists with regard to the four groups. Classify four softwoods as high density and four softwoods as low density based on allowable span lengths for various species.

THE SCHOOL-TO-WORK CONNECTION

Lumber is carefully graded so that it will perform predictably. This helps designers and engineers use standardized span charts when working out the design of a residential floor system. All of these factors make floor system design relatively straightforward in new construction.

Many people in the construction industry, however, are involved in remodeling houses, not building new ones. It is quite possible, particularly if a house is old, that some of the floor joists will have weakened over the years. Maybe a small flaw in the wood turned into a large crack. Whatever the reason, damaged joists must be repaired before any remodeling work can proceed. One way to repair and reinforce an existing joist is by attaching another equal-size joist alongside. This is called sistering. The new lumber must be as long as the existing joist and be supported in the same locations. Maneuver the new joist into position, push the old joist back where it belongs, and then nail the two together with 16d nails.

1. Locate several local companies that specialize in remodeling. Call a supervisor to find out what kind of joist damage is most commonly found. Find out what joist repair solutions they have used. Then consult your local building codes to find out if the code has anything to say about joist repairs. Report your findings to the class, using sketches to describe the repair techniques.

2. A floor joist such as a 2 x 10 x 14 is an unwieldy piece of lumber. Moving this material calls for some thought. Always lift heavy materials by bending your knees and keeping your back straight. This may feel awkward at first, but it reduces stress on your lower back. Always get help moving long pieces of lumber. Increasingly, however, wood I-beams are replacing lumber joists in residential construction. Write to a manufacturer of wood I-beams. Request guidelines for moving and handling the product on a jobsite. Summarize these guidelines in a short essay. Note which of the guidelines might apply also to lumber joists.

30

Wall Framing

The exterior walls of a wood-frame house normally consist of *studs, interior and exterior coverings, windows and doors,* and *insulation.* The wall-framing members used in conventional construction are commonly 2" × 4" studs spaced 16"

30-1a. *Walls framed with 2" x 4" or 2" x 6" studs are built in all regions of the country.*

on center. Fig. 30-1. However, 2" × 6" studs spaced 16" or 24" on center are increasingly used in cold climates. The extra thickness of the resulting walls allows space for more insulation. In areas that have very cold winters or unusually long winters, even thicker walls are framed.

Exterior walls and, in some designs, interior walls normally support the roof load. They will also serve as a framework for attaching interior and exterior coverings. When roof trusses spanning the entire width of the house are used, the exterior sidewalls carry both the roof and ceiling loads. Interior partitions then serve mainly as room dividers. When ceiling joists are used, interior partitions usually sustain some of the ceiling loads. Fig. 30-2.

The requirements for wall-framing lumber are *stiffness, nail-holding power, freedom from warpage,* and *ease of working.* Species and

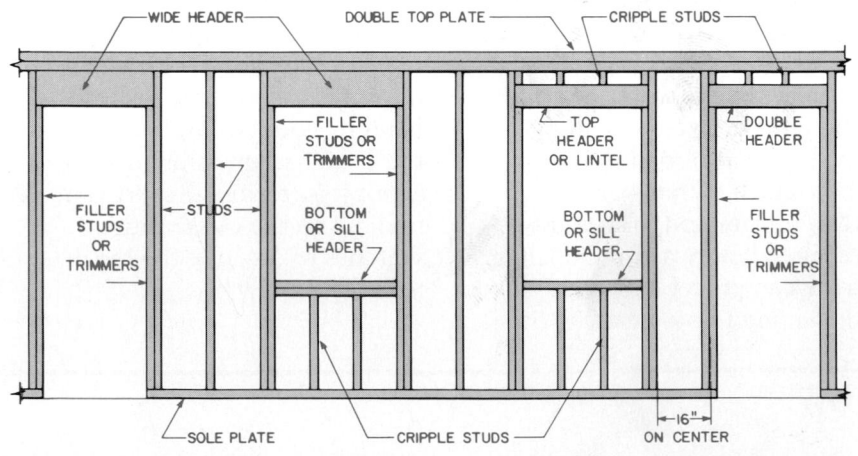

30-1b. *Parts of a framed wall section. (Filler studs are also called jack studs.)*

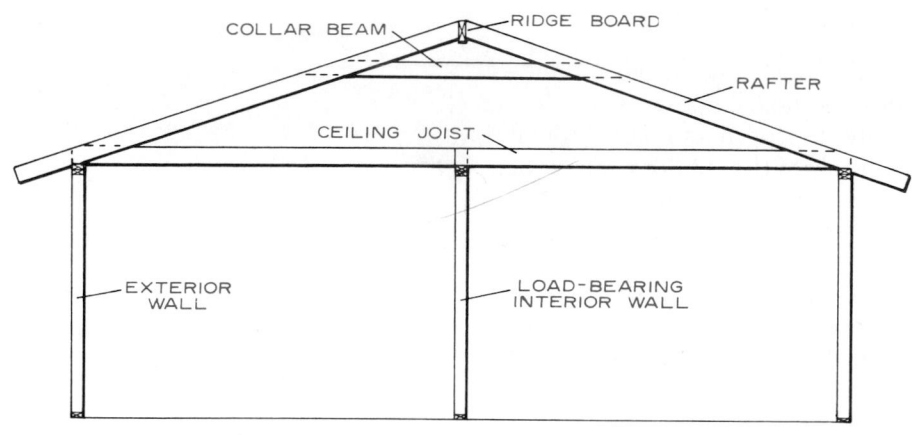

30-2. *Conventional framing requires an interior wall to support the ceiling joists.*

30-3. *Laying out on the subfloor. Use a steel tape to measure from the corner to the centerline of all openings and intersecting partitions.*

grades used for wall framing may, in general, follow those used for floor-framing materials—for example, Douglas fir, the hemlocks, and southern yellow pine. Also commonly used for studs are spruce, pine, and white fir. No. 1 and No. 2 grades are most often used. Moisture content of framing members usually should not exceed 19% for on-site construction and 12% if shop fabricated.

The length of general framing lumber comes in increments of 2'. The vertical members, called studs, come in a standard length of 92⅝". This is called a "precut stud." In some parts of the United States, precut studs are 92¼" long.

As with floor construction, there are two general types of wall framing—*platform construction* and *balloon-frame construction.* The platform method is nearly always used by builders throughout the United States and Canada. This is primarily because platform construction is fairly simple and it lends itself to a great many architectural designs. With the platform method the floor framing should be complete, with subfloor securely fastened in place, before wall framing begins. The first step in wall framing is to lay out the wall locations on the subfloor.

LAYING OUT WALL LOCATIONS

The carpenter responsible for the layout of a building is one of the most important people on the job. Accuracy of layout is most important to the final overall quality of the building. Knowledge of the structural members of the building is also essential. The carpenter must also be aware of special framing requirements for other skilled workers such as plumbers, electricians, and plasterers.

The layout is usually done by two people, a carpenter and an apprentice. The carpenter is responsible for all the measuring and marking. The apprentice observes and learns while holding the end of the measuring tape or chalk line. It is possible for the carpenter to lay out alone, using an awl to hold the end of the tape or chalk line. The area to be laid out must be swept clean. All objects that might be in the way must be removed. This will help make it possible to make a clear, solid chalk line to which the plates are aligned later.

The carpenter must study the plans for the building and have a thorough understanding of them before layout begins. During the actual layout the carpenter should refer to the plans as needed to "pick-off" dimensions.

A steel tape is used to locate the interior partitions and exterior walls. Fig. 30-3. A chalk line is pulled taut on these marks and snapped to indicate the exact location and alignment for the full length of an edge of the sole plate. The carpenter then marks an ✗ on the subfloor to show on which side of the line the plate will be located. After the location of the plates is laid out on the subfloor, the various wall members are cut to size in preparation for assembly of the wall sections.

WALL FRAMING

A 2" × 4" wall system is used to illustrate most of the wall framing techniques in this unit. Construction of walls using 2" × 6" studs is increasingly popular because it allows more insulation to be placed in the walls. Interior partitions are framed in the same fashion no matter what system is used for the exterior walls.

There are various ways to lay out and erect a framed wall. Years ago, carpentry techniques were considerably different than they are now. In those days, carpenters often erected walls using the corner post method or the tilt-up method.

Corner Post Method

With this technique, sole plates were cut to length and nailed securely to the subfloor. Built-up lumber posts were then nailed to the sole plates at all corners of the building, and the posts were plumbed and braced. The sole plates were marked for the locations of studs and other wall elements. Studs were then toenailed to the sole plates. A top plate was installed to tie the tops of the studs together. Finally, the sheathing was installed. Fig. 30-4.

Tilt-up Method

To improve upon the corner post method, carpenters cut all sole plates to length and nailed them securely to the subfloor. They then marked the plates with layout information. Top plates were cut and laid out to match. Studs were cut to length and nailed to the top plate. The wall was then lifted into place on top of the sole plate and braced to hold it in position. The bottom of each stud was then toenailed to the sole plate with four 8d nails. Sheathing was installed as the last step. Fig. 30-5.

Modified Tilt-up Method

There may still be some carpenters who prefer one of the layout and assembly approaches

30-5a. *Plates and headers laid out on the subfloor in preparation for the wall assembly. Notice the use of the solid 4" header.*

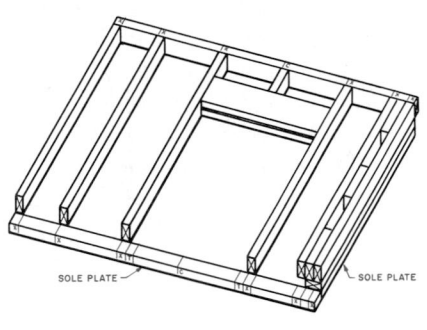

30-5b. *Studs of the assembled wall pushed up against the sole plate opposite the marks where they are to be nailed.*

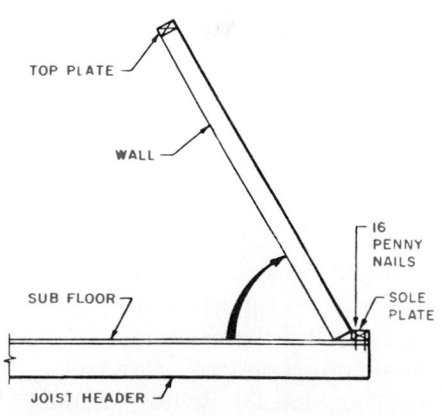

30-5c. *The wall is raised to the vertical position. The ends of the studs are then toenailed to the sole plate.*

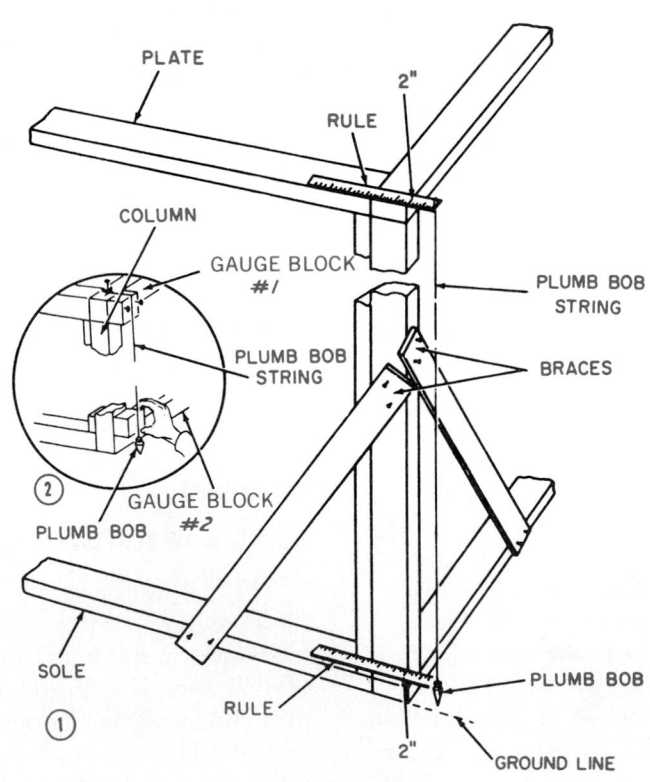

30-4. *Plumbing the post.*

noted above. However, most use a modified tilt-up method that is very efficient. It is easier to build because sheathing is installed while the wall framing is laying flat on the subfloor. Another advantage is that the wall is relatively rigid and absolutely square when it is lifted into place. Here is a summary of the basic layout and assembly steps used today:

30-6. *Most carpenters today lay out, frame, and sheath walls on the subfloor. Walls are then lifted into place.*

➤ Cut sole plate and the two top plates to length for one exterior wall at a time.

➤ Align the sole plate with the top plate and lay out the location of studs, windows, partitions, etc. on the edges of both plates simultaneously.

➤ Spread the top and bottom plates apart.

➤ Place the required number of precut studs between the plates.

➤ Nail studs to the sole plate and top plate by driving nails through plates and into the end of each stud. Install cripples, headers, and other parts of the framing. The doubled top plate is sometimes installed at this point.

➤ Square the wall.

➤ Install panel sheathing (plywood or OSB).

➤ Lift the wall into place. Fig. 30-6.

➤ Install temporary braces to keep the wall in place.

➤ Repeat the process for adjacent walls.

The following text describes the various parts of the interior and exterior walls in platform construction. The layout techniques are appropriate for the modified tilt-up method outlined above. However, they can be applied to other wall assembly and erection approaches.

Sole Plate

All partition walls and outside walls are supported by a piece of material corresponding to the thickness of the wall, usually a 2" × 4". Laid horizontally on the subfloor, this member carries the bottom end of the studs. Fig. 30-7. This 2" × 4" is called the "sole," the "sole plate," or the "bottom plate." Once the framed wall is in position, the sole plate will be nailed into the floor framing. The plate is sometimes located in from the outside of the building at a distance equal to the thickness of the sheathing. Thus when the sheathing is applied it will rest on the subfloor. Building codes often require that the sheathing extend past the sole plate to cover the header joist (also called the rim joist). When the sheathing is nailed both to the wall framing and to the header joist, it ties walls to the floor system. Fig. 30-8. This is a particularly important framing detail in parts of the country that experience earthquake activity. To properly frame this detail, the header joist must be set in from the edge of the foundation a distance that equals the thickness of the sheathing. (The outside surface of the sheathing will be flush with the outside surface of the foundation wall.) Then the sole plate is set flush with the outside edge of the subfloor. Siding or flashing will

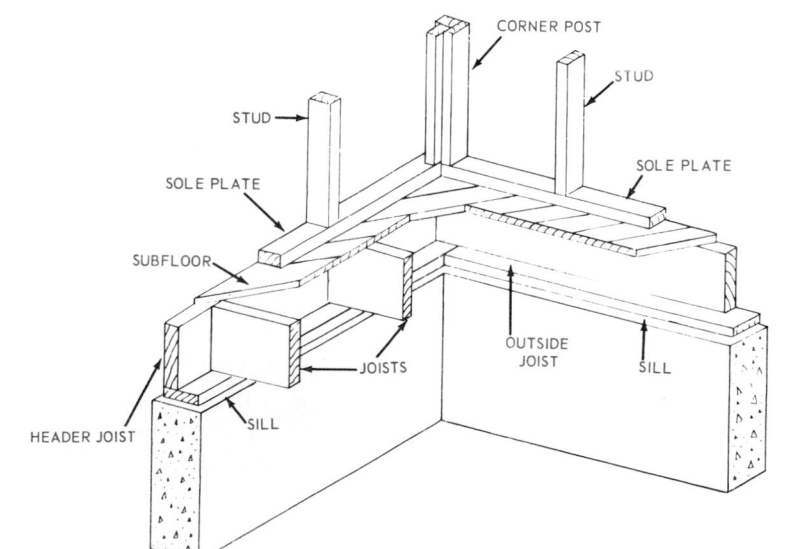

30-7. *The box-sill assembly showing the sole plate as a link between the floor and wall units.*

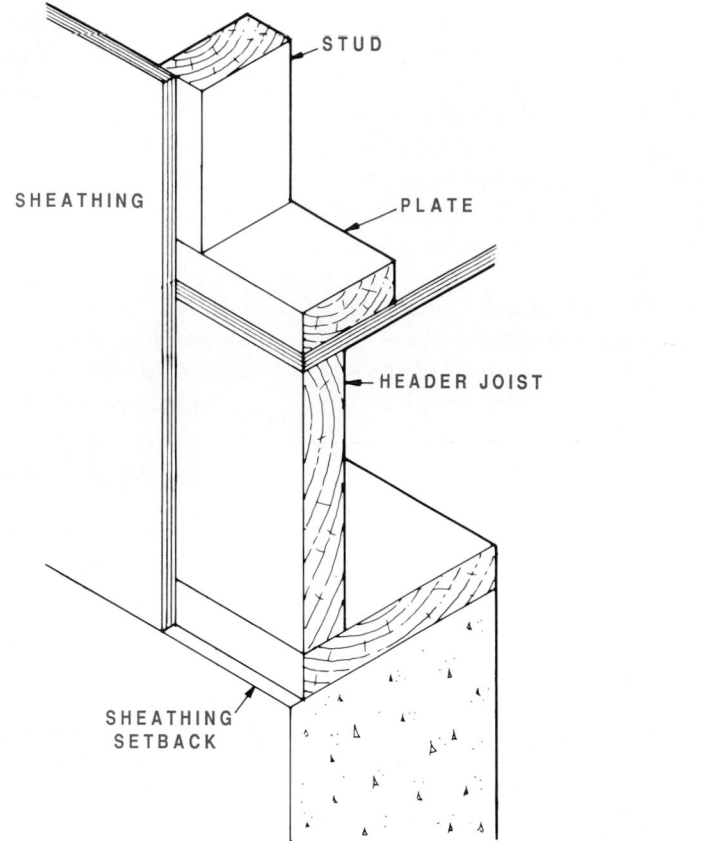

30-8. *Sheathing that extends over the header joist ties the wall system to the floor system.*

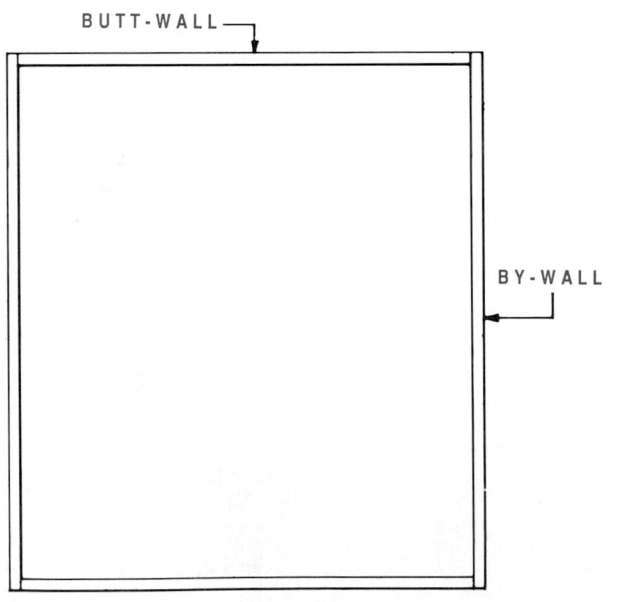

30-9. *To begin layout of the plates, decide which walls will be by-walls and which will be butt-walls. The top and bottom plate of a given wall will be the same length. The doubled top plate of each wall will be longer or shorter by the thickness of the adjoining walls.*

cover the joint between the sheathing and foundation.

Laying Out the Plates. Once the layout for the exterior walls and interior partitions has been snapped out on the subfloor (or the slab), cutting and layout of the plates can begin. As with many carpentry techniques, the procedure for cutting and laying out the plates varies from region to region. For example, some carpenters prefer to calculate the plate lengths and measure the dimensions out on rough stock before cutting the plates to length. Other carpenters simply lay the rough stock over the layout on the subfloor and "eyeball" the cuts. Some carpenters install the double top plate after the walls have been tilted into place, others install it before this happens. The basic concepts of cutting the plates and laying them out are the same, however. The sole plate and the top plate should be laid out at the same time.

Before the plates can be cut to length, the carpenter must decide which walls are "butt-walls" and which are "by-walls." A *by-wall* runs from the outside edge of the subfloor to the outside edge of the opposite end of the subfloor. Fig. 30-9. These walls are typically framed first and tipped up into position. *Butt-walls* are framed next. They fit between the by-walls. Fig. 30-9. The doubled top plate ties butt-walls and by-walls together.

To begin layout of the plates, tack the top and bottom plates together temporarily with 8d nails. The edges of the plates usually face up. Fig. 30-10. Begin measuring from one end of the plates. Use a carpenter's pencil to mark the locations of door and window openings, partitions, studs, and other parts of the wall. The studs that are designated where openings

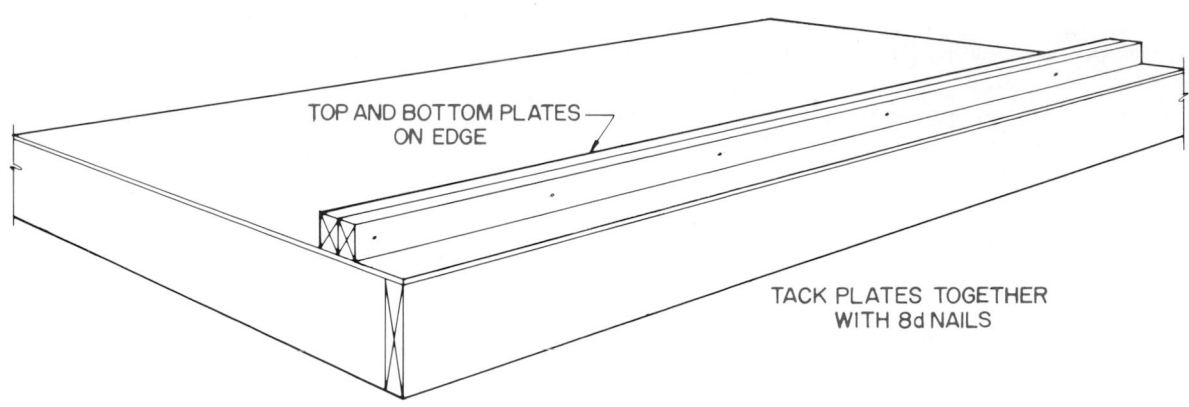

30-10a. *Top and bottom plates are placed together on edge and tacked together. The layout will be marked on the edges.*

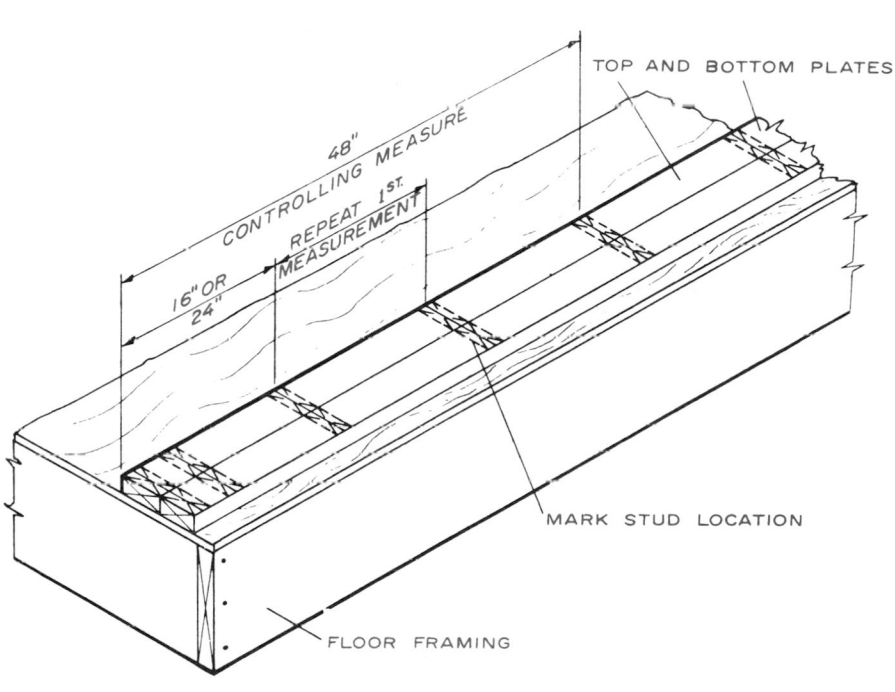

30-10b. *Plates can also be laid out side to side. This drawing shows measuring to the centers of the stud locations. In actual layout a carpenter will mark only the left edge of the stud and then place an X to the right of this line. The line can then be seen along the edge of the stud for alignment.*

30-10c. *The outside wall plates have been nailed together temporarily, and the studs are being laid out with a homemade layout template. This template is 4' long, the standard width of wall sheathing. The template has four fingers, 1½" wide and 16" O.C., representing four stud markings. The fingers are attached to a piece of aluminum angle stock, so that the template works like four try squares at once.*

30-10d. *Laying out the plates for a partition wall. Note the use, in a different position, of the template described in Fig. 30-10c.*

30-10e. *Plates may also be laid out with various types of metal squares.*

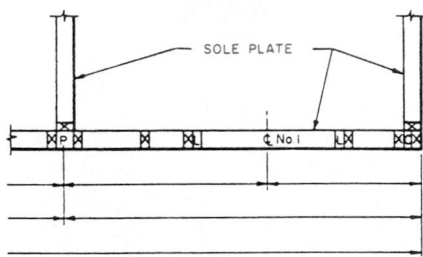

30-11a. *Centerlines of wall openings and intersecting walls are located on the plate by measuring from an outside corner. The locations of the wall members are marked for identification so other carpenters can assemble and erect the walls later.*

occur can then be marked as "cripples." The mark usually used is an O. The full-length studs are usually marked with an X. Other special studs which will be discussed later should also be marked. Corner studs are marked with a C, partition studs with a P, and trimmer or lap studs with an L or S.

Begin the plate layout by referring to the plans to find the distance from the corner of the building to the center of the first opening. Measure off this distance and square a line across the plate at this point. Mark the line with a centerline symbol ⌀ and an identification letter or number for reference when cutting other parts for this opening.

Continue around the outside wall to lay out and mark for identification all of the other openings. Now from the outside corners lay off the centers of all partitions and mark them with a P. Fig. 30-11.

Wall Openings

Studs around wall openings require special treatment. Allowances must be made for framing in doors and windows. These allowances, when added to the size of the finished openings, make up what is called a "rough opening." The rough opening is the distance between the trimmer studs. Fig. 30-12. Most window and door schedules will provide the rough opening (R.O.) size for framing. If not, the following allowances can be used for door and window rough opening widths and heights:

➤ Double-Hung Window (Single Unit):
Rough opening width = glass width + 6".
Rough opening height = total glass height + 10".
➤ Casement Window (Two Sash):
Rough opening width = total glass width + 1¼".
Rough opening height = total glass height + 6⅜".
➤ Doors:
Rough opening width = width of door + 2½".
R.O height = height of door + 3".

Laying Out Wall Openings.
After the wall openings have been located on the plate, on each side of the centerline of each opening

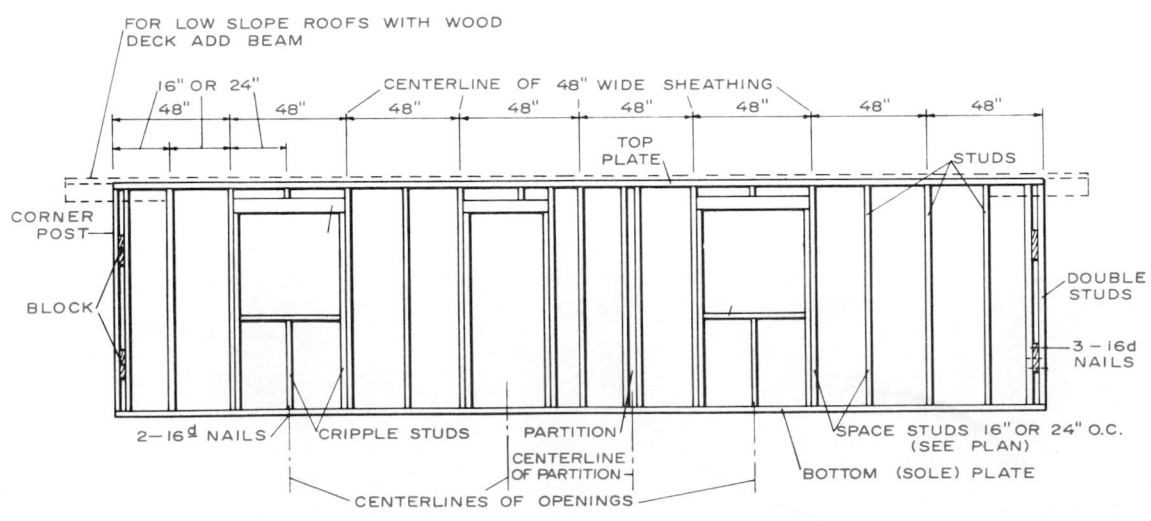

30-11b. *A typical framed wall layout.*

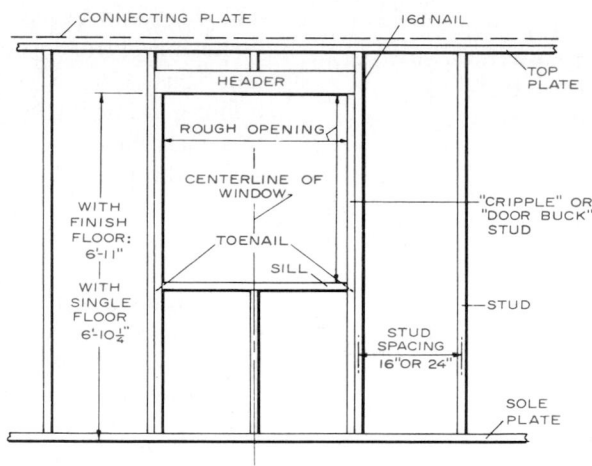

30-12. *Rough framing for a window opening.*

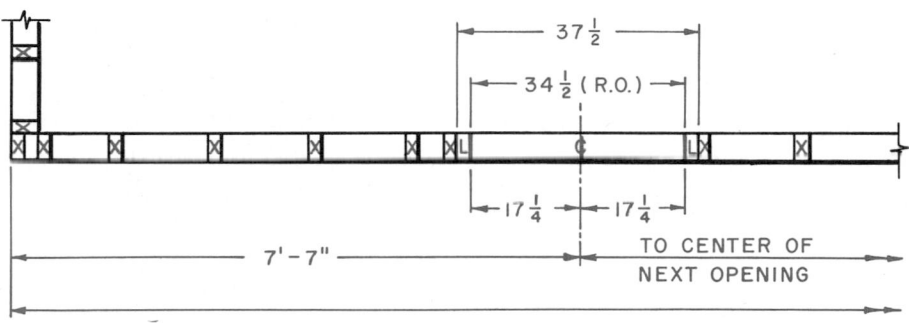

30-13a. *The centerline of a door opening is marked on the sole 7'7" from the outside corner. One-half the R.O. (17 ¼") is then laid off on each side of the centerline. The thickness of the trimmer stud is laid off on each side of this. The header will rest on top of the trimmers and between the full studs marked with an X.*

lay off one-half the rough opening size. Fig. 30-12. For example, for a 2'8" door, the distance between the full-length studs is 37½"—that is, 32" for the door plus 5½" for the side jambs, wedges, and *trimmer studs* (which support the header). Fig. 30-13.

After all openings and partitions have been laid out, proceed by laying out all regular and cripple studs.

Top Plate

The top plate (Fig. 30-14) has the following purposes:
► Ties the studding together at the top.
► Forms a finish for the walls.
► Furnishes a support for the lower ends of the rafters.
► Serves as a connecting link between wall and roof, just as sills and girders are connecting links between floors and the walls.

The plate is made up of one or two pieces of material of the same size as the studs. When placed on top of partition walls, the plate is sometimes called the *cap*. Where the plate is doubled, the first plate or bottom section is nailed with 16d nails to the top of the corner posts and to the studs. The connection at the corner is made as in Fig. 30-15a. After the single plate is nailed securely, the cap plate is nailed to the top plate with 10d nails, spaced 16" O.C.

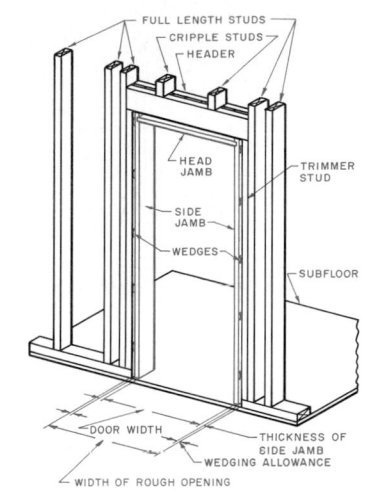

30-13b. *Door framing allowance for rough opening.*

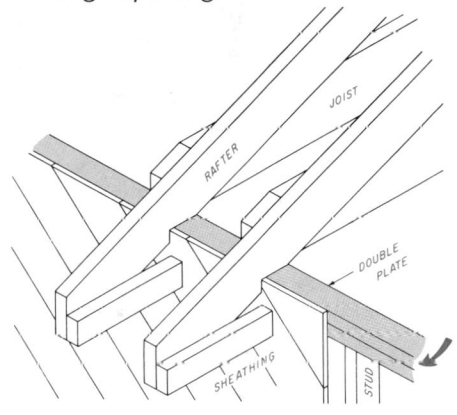

30-14. *The top plates are shown at the arrow. The double or rafter plate sometimes is not fastened until the walls have been erected, plumbed, and straightened.*

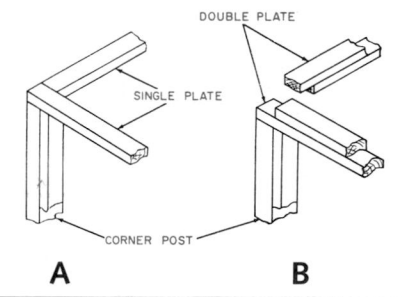

30-15a & b. *Plate construction at a corner.*

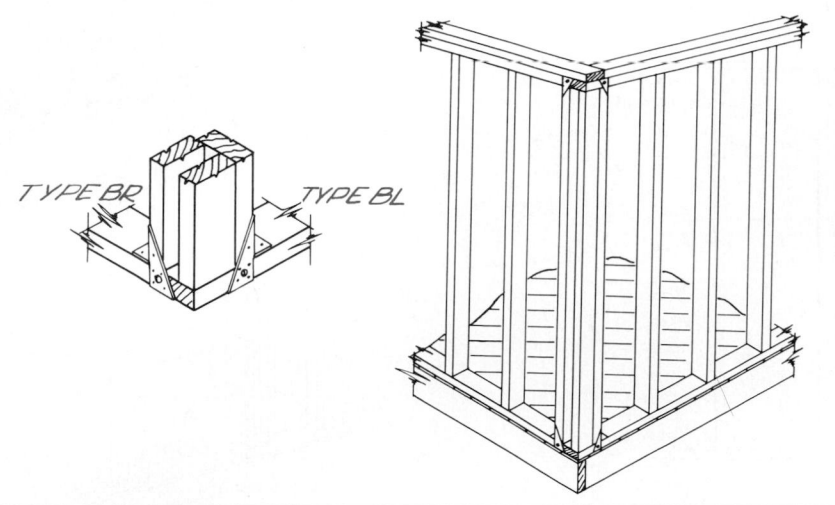

30-15c. *Metal framing anchors may also be used to attach the corner posts to the sole and top plate. Note that these brackets are made in lefts and rights. One of each is necessary.*

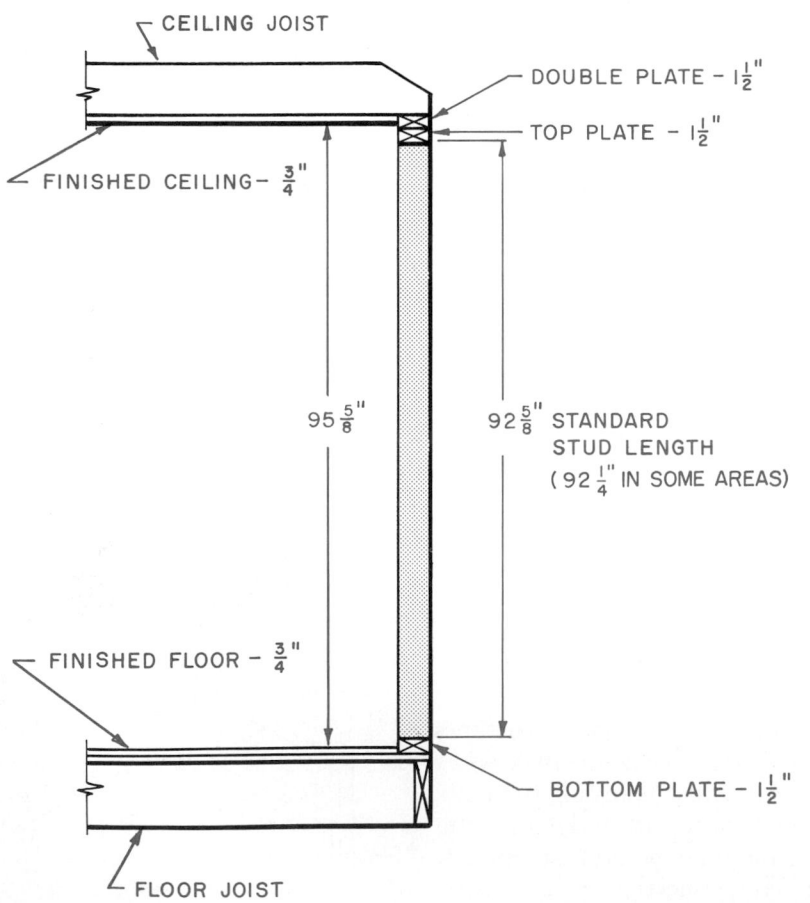

30-16. *A standard stud is 92 ⅝" long (92 ¼" in some parts of the United States). This stud length will provide a 95⅝" ceiling height with a ¾" finished floor and a ¾" finished ceiling. Some studs are now being cut 93" for a 96" (8') ceiling.*

The edges of the top plates should be flush and the corner joints lapped as in Fig. 30-15b. Metal framing anchors may also be used to attach the corner posts to the sole and top plate.

Studs

Studs are a series of slender wood members placed in a vertical position as supporting parts of a wall or partition. Studs should be 2" × 4"s or 2" × 6"s for one- and two-story buildings. As mentioned earlier, short studs that are sometimes added above or below the header of doors and windows are called *cripple studs* or *cripples*. Studs which support headers are sometimes called *trimmer studs*.

The number of full studs, trimmers, and cripples can be determined by counting the layout marks on the wall plates. The lengths of these pieces can be found on the story pole or master stud pattern, as will be explained later. Standard studs can also be purchased precut to finished length. Fig. 30-16.

The stud locations are laid out on the sole and top plate, usually 16" or 24" O.C. Begin the layout on the front wall. Measure the first 16" from the outside-corner edge of the corner post to the center of the first stud. From that point on, measure 16" O.C. for each of the studs.

When beginning the layout of the first stud on an end wall, the center of the first stud is measured from the outside of the sheathing line on the front wall. Fig. 30-17. The same is true for any wall parallel to an end wall, as when there is an offset in the building. The layout of the stud locations on the back wall and all parallel walls should begin from the same end of the building as the layout of the front. By using a common measuring point, the studs will bear over the floor joists, while the

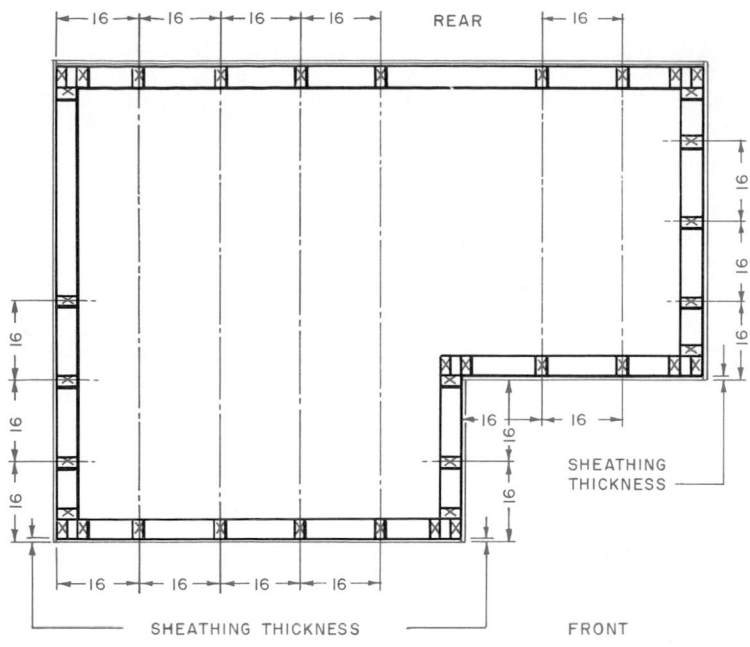

30-17a. *When laying out stud locations, allow for the thickness of the sheathing at the corners. Note that all layout dimensions begin from the left end of the building as one stands in front. This will line up the studs on the front and rear walls.*

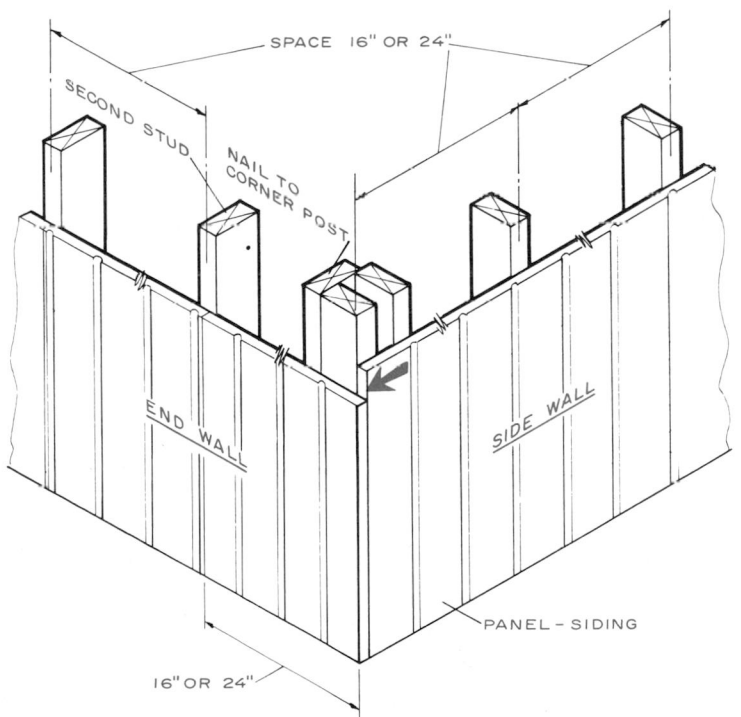

30-17b. *The application of panel-siding or sheathing to a stud wall. Notice the center of the first stud on the side wall is measured from the outside of the corner post. However, the first stud on the end wall is measured from the outside surface of the wall covering material to the center of the first stud. This will permit the wall covering material to lap properly at the corner. See arrow.*

ceiling joists and rafters will bear over the studs. This alignment creates a direct bearing of the rafter right down through to the foundation wall of the building. Fig. 30-18. This alignment of structural members will not occur when studs are spaced 16" O.C. and floor joists are spaced 24" O.C., however. When that happens, the double top plate will distribute the weight of joists that fall between the studs.

Each stud is nailed with two 16d nails through the top and bottom plates (4 nails in all). An alternate fastening technique is to toenail each stud into the plate with four 8d nails, two on each side of the stud. When a particularly strong connection is required between the studs and the plates, metal anchors can be used. Fig. 30-19. This is sometimes done in regions of the country exposed to high winds or seismic activity.

Story Pole and Master Stud Pattern. A *story pole* is a full-size layout of a cross section of a wall. A *master stud pattern* is the same for a portion of the wall. One or the other of these layout devices should be developed for any wall-framing job, as a quick reference for use by all the carpenters. The use of such a device speeds construction and helps eliminate costly errors. This is particularly true when there are many carpenters on a single job or when a building contractor is supervising several jobs.

The story pole will show floor level (or levels if the structure is a multi-story or split level), ceiling height, window and door elevations, and thicknesses of many materials used in construction. Usually, however, only a portion of the wall section is laid out full-size. This portion would be from the top of the subfloor to the bottom of the ceiling joist. In a two-story building it would be the distance between the finished floors. As mentioned,

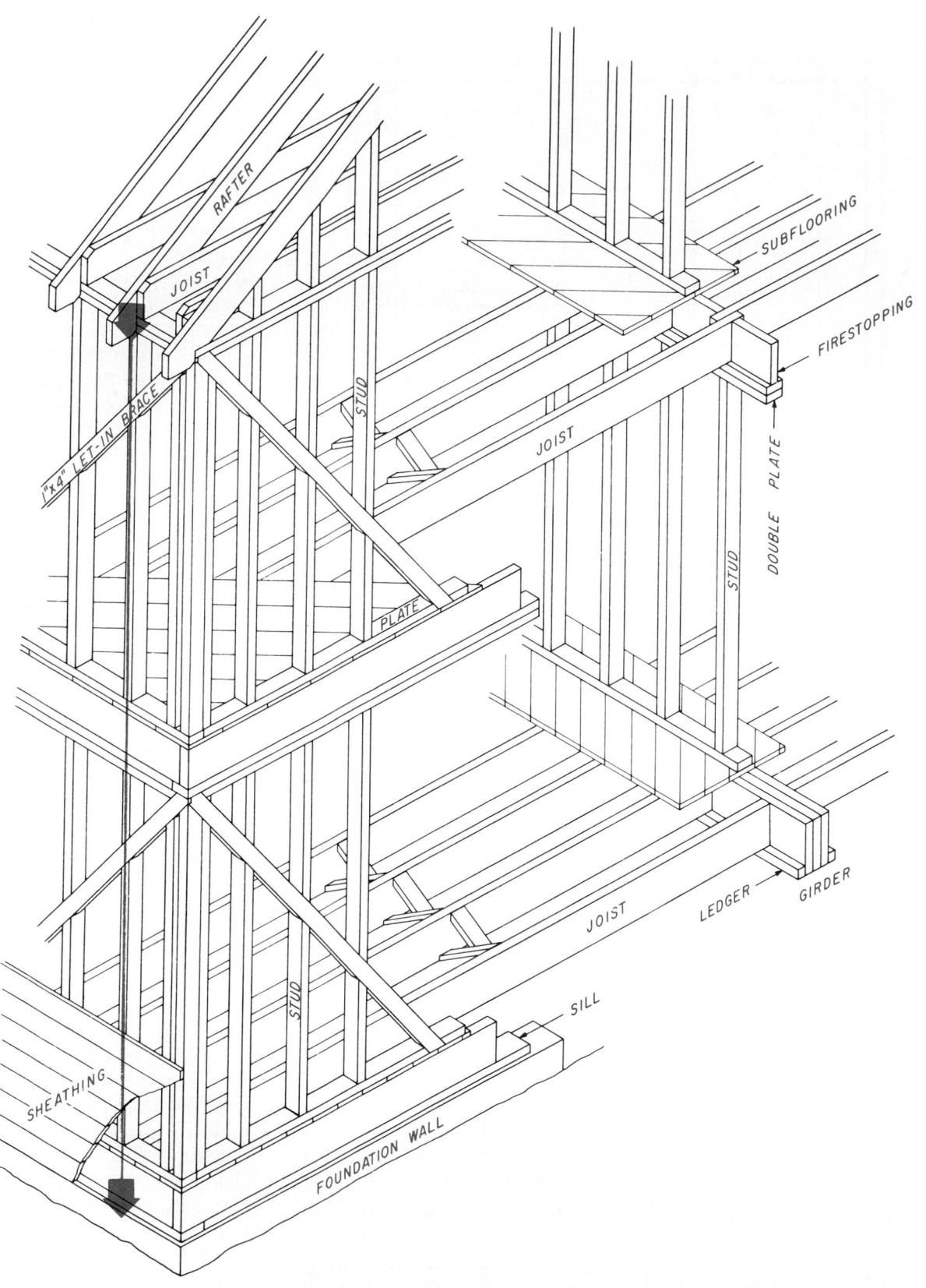

30-18. *The layout of the stud locations ideally coincides with the joist layout. Later the rafters can be laid out directly over the studs and joists. This creates a direct bearing from the roof right down to the footings of the building. Although this alignment is not required when a double plate is used, it is recommended.*

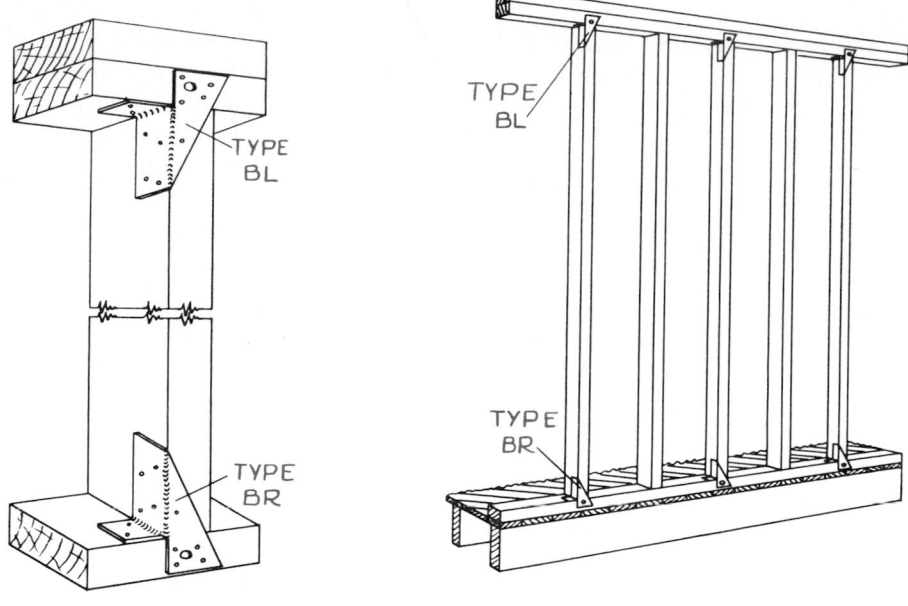

30-19. *Metal framing anchors may be used either inside or outside to attach the studs to the sole and to the top plate. These brackets are normally used only on alternate studs.*

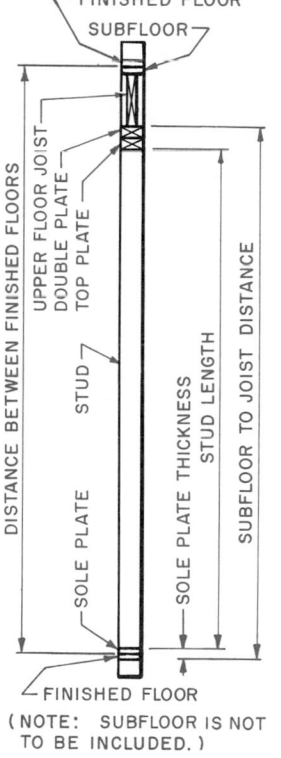

30-20a. *A master stud pattern for a two-story dwelling. Additional information may be included on this layout, as is shown in Fig. 30-20b.*

this drawing of a portion of the wall is called the master stud pattern. It includes information about the location and size of the window headers, sills, door headers, the heights of various openings above the subfloor, and the thicknesses of the ceiling and the finished floor. Fig. 30-20. If there are several different heights to mark off above the subfloor, it may be necessary to avoid confusion by making additional master stud

patterns, labeling them for the various rooms or areas.

Corner Post. A corner post must form an inside corner and an outside corner. The inside corner will provide two good nailing bases for inside wall covering. The outside corner will provide two good nailing bases for outside wall sheathing. Studs at the corners of the frame construction are usually built up from three or more ordinary studs to provide greater strength. Corner posts may be made in several different ways.

Two of the more common methods are shown in Figs. 30-21a and b. The number of corner posts required can be determined by counting the number of places on the plan where two walls intersect at right angles. Corner posts are nailed together with 10d and 16d nails. They are distributed on the subfloor where they will be used for assembly of the wall sections. The short pieces of 2" × 4"s shown at the base of the corner post in Figs. 30-21a and b are installed after the wall erection to provide places for nailing the corner ends of the baseboard. In areas of the country where energy-efficiency is important, other corner assemblies are used. These will be described later in this unit.

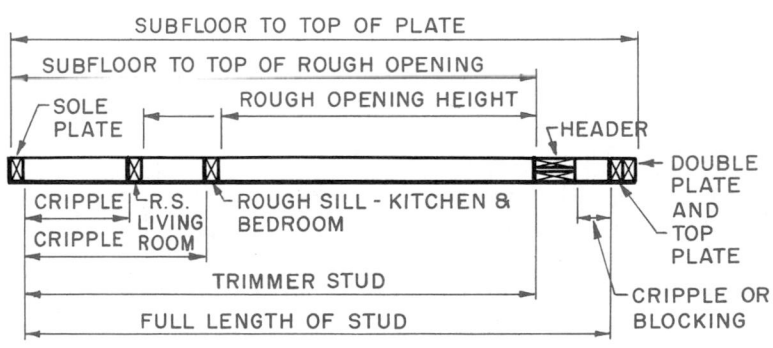

30-20b. *A master stud pattern for a one-story building. Select a clean, straight piece of 1" × 4" or 2" × 4" stock and lay it out full size. The information for this layout is taken from the building plans.*

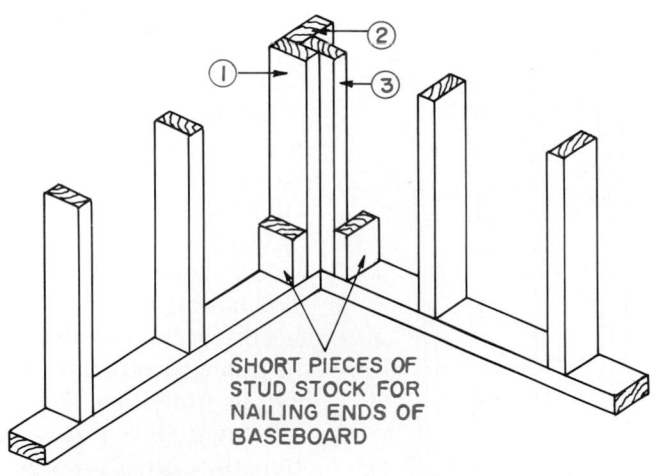

30-21a. *The simplest type of corner post. The pieces numbered 1, 2, and 3 are selected straight standard studs. This is an energy efficient post because it allows insulation to reach the outer edge of the building.*

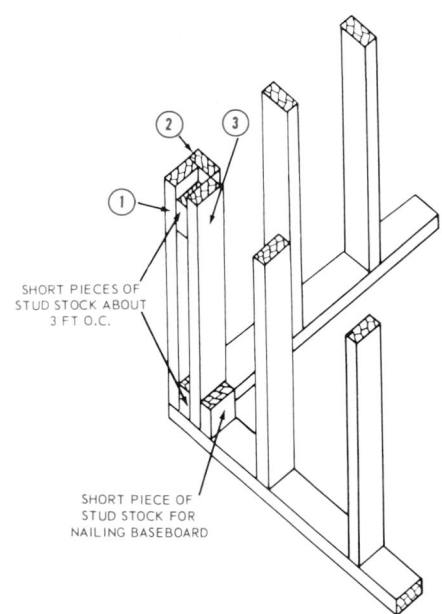

30-21b. *This is the corner post most commonly used. The pieces numbered 1, 2, and 3 are selected straight standard studs. The short blocks are usually 10 or 12 inches long. Studs 1 and 3 are nailed to the blocks with 10d nails. Stud 2 is then nailed to the assembly of 1 and 3. Care should be taken to keep all ends and outside edges flush and even.*

Partition Corner Post. Studs should be arranged at a point where a partition ties into a wall between the corners. Three common types of partition post assemblies are shown in Fig. 30-22a, b, and c. In the type shown in Fig. 30-22a, the regular spacing of the outside wall studs is interrupted by double studs at the point where the partition ties in. The double studs are set 3" apart. This interval allows the partition end stud (which is 3⅝"

wide) to lap the others just enough to permit nailing, while leaving most of the inner edges of the others clear to serve as nailing bases for inside wall covering. A variation of the method in Fig. 30-22a is shown in Fig. 30-22b. This method will give more nailing surface for the inside wall covering.

In another type of partition corner assembly, the regular spacing of the outside wall studs is maintained. Fig. 30-22c. The cross blocks are made of stud stock, with the exception of the bottom block, which is made of wider stock to provide a solid nailing base for ends of baseboard.

The number of partition corners can be counted from the plan. The partition corner posts are nailed together with 10d and 16d nails and distributed to their locations on the subfloor for wall assembly.

Cripple Studs. Cripple studs are those studs which, because of an opening in the wall, do not extend from the sole plate to the top plate. These studs are installed over window, door and fireplace headers and below window sills. Fig. 30-11b. They are located in the same place that a full stud would normally be placed if there

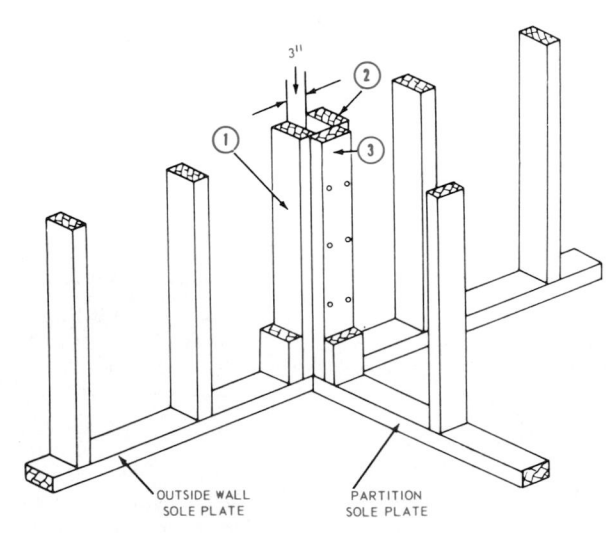

30-22a. *Double-stud partition corner assembly.*

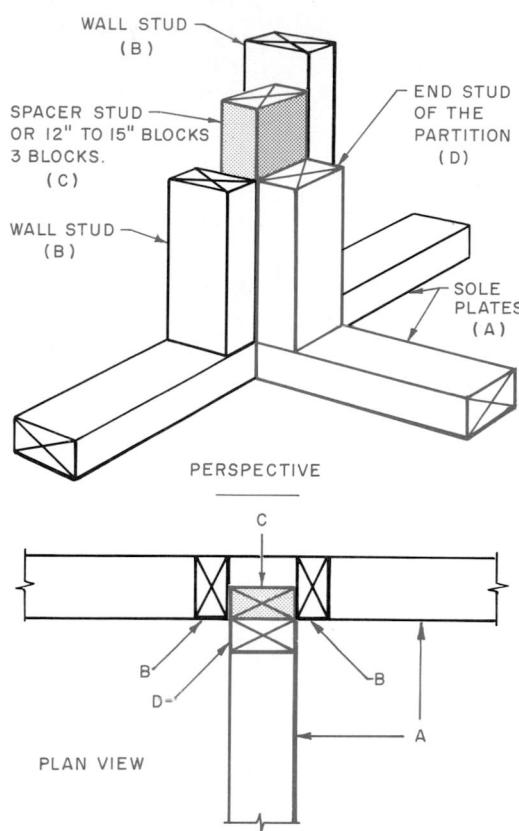

WALL STUD (B)

SPACER STUD OR 12" TO 15" BLOCKS 3 BLOCKS. (C)

END STUD OF THE PARTITION (D)

WALL STUD (B)

SOLE PLATES (A)

PERSPECTIVE

PLAN VIEW

30-22b. *This partition corner assembly is the one most commonly used. It will give more nailing on the inside corners than does the one shown in Fig. 30-22a. Nail the two wall studs to the spacer with 10d nails. The end stud of the partition can be nailed to these studs at this time. Or, it can be nailed up as part of the partition wall and then attached to the spacer at the time the partition is erected.*

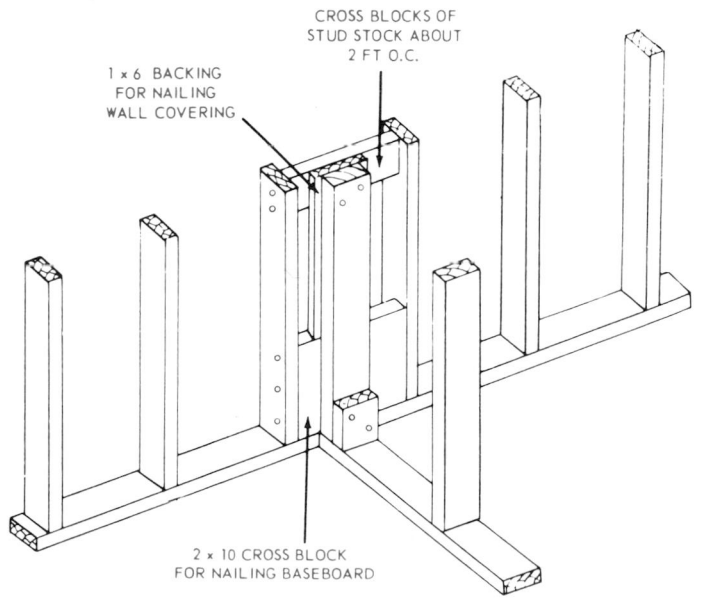

CROSS BLOCKS OF STUD STOCK ABOUT 2 FT O.C.

1 x 6 BACKING FOR NAILING WALL COVERING

2 x 10 CROSS BLOCK FOR NAILING BASEBOARD

30-22c. *Partition corner assembly with wall studs at regular intervals.*

were no opening. Cripples are necessary for nailing outside sheathing and inside wall covering. The lengths of the various cripples can be determined by referring to the master stud pattern. These studs are usually precut to length and distributed with the door and window headers in readiness for the assembly of the wall sections.

Trimmer Studs. As mentioned earlier, trimmers are studs which support the header over an opening. They are shorter than standard studs, and are sometimes called cripples. Fig. 30-23. Sometimes they are also called *double studs* or *lap studs*. These studs are nailed to a regular stud under the ends of the header. To hold them in place, 10d nails are used, spaced 16" apart and staggered as shown in Figs. 30-23 and 30-24. Notice that the trimmer or double stud for a door may extend from the header to the subfloor and does not rest on the sole plate. If this method is used, the sole plate must be cut away between the full studs before the trimmers can be installed. Trimmers should be cut to fit snugly under the header so that they will support it properly. If a header settles, cracks in the plaster or drywall may develop and doors may fit improperly. The double studs in a door opening also form solid supports when the door is slammed (on the latch side) and for the weight of the door (on the hinge side).

Headers

Where windows or doors occur in outside walls or partitions, parts of some studs must be cut out. It is necessary, therefore, to install some form of header over the doorway to support the lower ends of studs that have been cut. Likewise, at the bottom of a window opening the "rough sill" supports the upper ends of studs

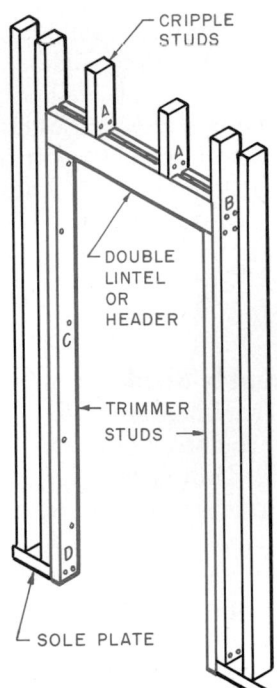

30-23a. *Door opening in a wall or partition. The cripple studs (A) are nailed with four 8d nails, two on each side. The standard studs (B) are nailed to the header with four 16d nails on each side and toenailed to the sole plate with two 8d nails. Or the full stud (B) could be nailed from the bottom up through the plate, with two 16d nails if the sole is attached before the wall is erected. The trimmer is nailed with 10d nails at C and staggered 16" O.C. Two 10d nails are driven into the end of the sole at D.*

SINGLE HEADER MAY BE USED FOR A NONBEARING WALL USE A DOUBLE HEADER WITH SPACERS FOR A BEARING WALL AND OUTSIDE WALLS.

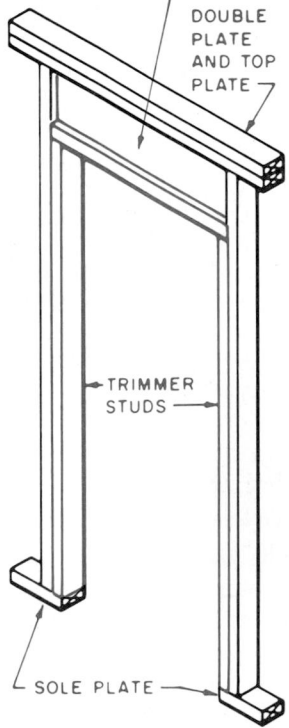

30-23b. *Alternate method of framing a door opening.*

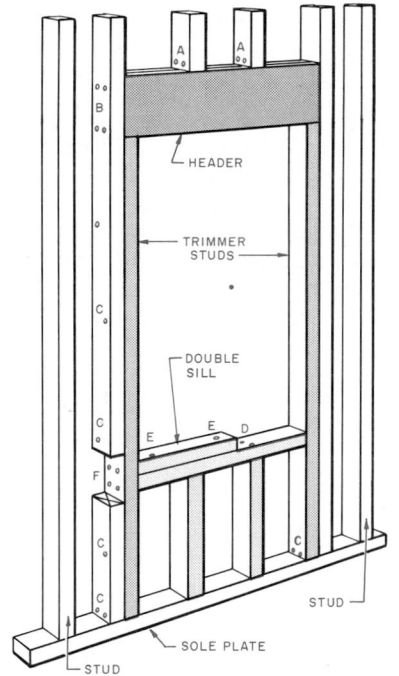

30-24. *Window opening. The cripple studs at A are toenailed with four 8d nails, two on each side. The full stud is nailed to the header at B with four 16d nails and to the trimmer (double stud) at C with 10d nails 16" O.C. It is toenailed to the sole at the bottom. The lower part of the double sill is nailed with two 10d nails into the ends of the cripples at D. The upper part of the sill is nailed to the lower with 10d nails 8" O.C. and staggered.*

that have been cut. Fig. 30-11b. The width of a header is determined by the length of the opening it must span. This information will be available from the building plans or local code requirements. Table 30-A.

Headers are sometimes 4" stock rather than two pieces of 2" material nailed together. This saves work and also allows the thickness of the header to be exactly the same as the width of a 2" × 4" stud. (When two 2" members are used for a header, the total thickness is only 3". This requires a ½" spacer to give the header the full 3½" width of the stud.) Fig. 30-25a, b, and c.

Framing wide openings such as double garage doors which require headers 16' to 18' long can be done with plywood box beams, solid lumber, laminated-veneer lumber, parallel-chord trusses, or even steel I-beams.

The ends of headers in wall framing should be supported on studs

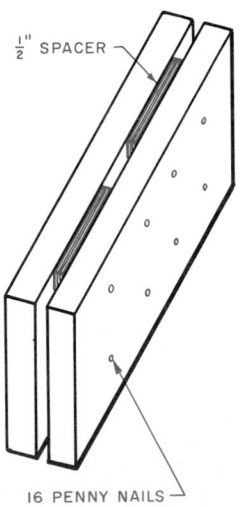

30-25a. *A header built up of two 2" members with ½" spacers to bring the total thickness out to 3½". The members are nailed with 16d nails staggered on 16" centers. Plywood makes a good spacing material.*

Table 30-A. *Maximum Spans for Lintels. These header widths (lintel spans) may be used for most residential buildings.*

Nominal depth of lintels made two thicknesses of nominal two-inch lumber installed on edge	Interior Partitions or Walls				Exterior Walls		
	Limited attic storage	Full attic storage, or roof load, or limited attic storage plus one floor	Full attic storage plus one floor, or roof load plus one floor, or limited attic storage plus two floors	Full attic storage plus two floors, or roof load plus two floors	Roof, with or without attic storage	Roof, with or without attic storage, plus one floor	Roof, with or without attic storage, plus two floors
4 in.	4 ft.	2 ft.	Not permitted	Not permitted	4 ft.	2 ft.	2 ft.
6 in.	6 ft.	3 ft.	2 ft. 6 in.	2 ft.	6 ft.	5 ft.	4 ft.
8 in.	8 ft.	4 ft.	3 ft.	3 ft.	8 ft.	7 ft.	6 ft.
10 in.	10 ft.	5 ft.	4 ft.	3 ft. 6 in.	10 ft.	8 ft.	7 ft.
12 in.	12 ft. 6 in.	6 ft.	5 ft.	4ft.	12 ft.	9 ft.	8 ft.

* Supported loads include dead loads and ceiling.

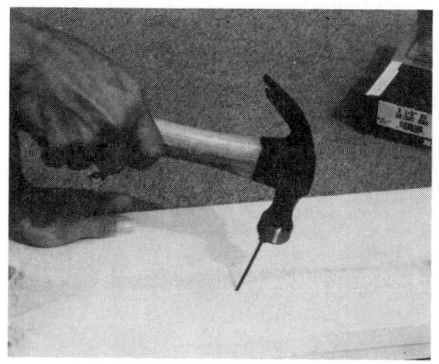

30-25b. *Nails should be driven into the header at an angle.*

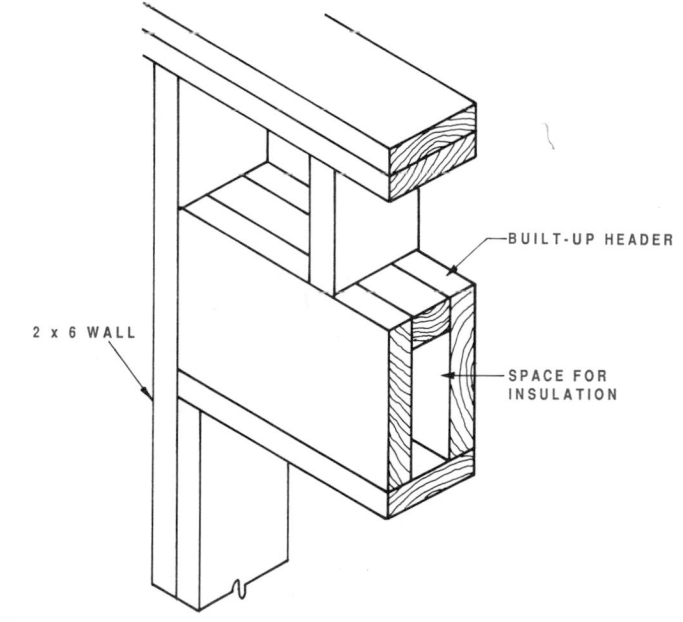

30-25c. *This type of header is sometimes used because it allows insulation above openings.*

2 x 6 WALL

BUILT-UP HEADER

SPACE FOR INSULATION

or by framing anchors, depending on the local code requirements. Figs. 30-26 and 30-27. The header lengths are obtained by measuring the layout of the bottom wall plates. The header is measured between the full studs. Fig. 30-12. In the case of the header for the door shown in Fig. 30-13a, the header length would be 37¾".

It is best to number the openings (such as windows, doors, and fireplaces) for identification and then make a cutting schedule for all headers. One person can cut these to length and, if 2" material is used, nail them together. Use 16d nails, two near each end, and stagger the others 16" apart along the length of the header. Don't forget to use ½" spacers between the 2" members where the nailing occurs. Headers are then distributed to their locations on the subfloor in readiness for the assembly of the wall sections.

EXTERIOR WALLS, ASSEMBLY AND ERECTION

Several procedures can be used when assembling wall sections. Whichever method is used, the order in which the exterior walls are assembled and erected must first be determined. Usually the front and rear walls (the longest sections) should be set up first, and the side walls then erected in between. Fig. 30-28. The wall members can be assembled on the subfloor, the wall squared, sheathing applied, windows installed, and even siding applied before the wall is erected. Fig. 30-29.

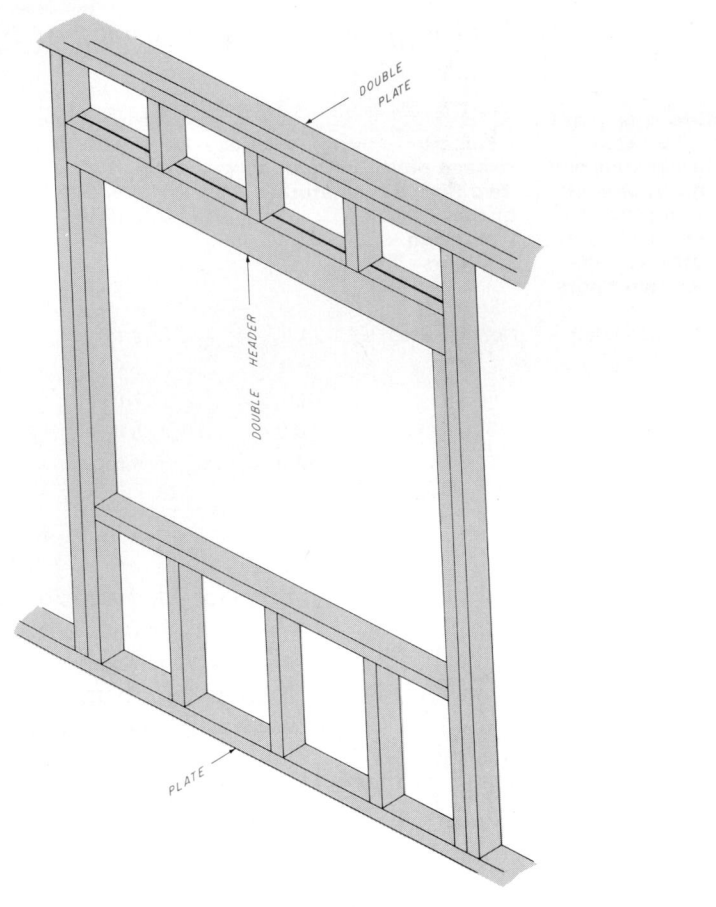

30-26. *Window framing with trimmer studs used to support the header.*

In the most common method of assembling walls, the studs, cripples, trimmers, headers, corners and partition corners are all precut to length. Then they are distributed to the area on the subfloor where they will be assembled. (Some preassembly of wall members may have been done.) Fig. 30-30.

The wall sections are assembled on the subfloor. Fig. 30-31. Begin the assembly by removing the premarked top plate from its temporary nailing on the sole plate. Lay the top plate on edge on the subfloor about 8' out from the sole plate. Face the marks on the top plate toward the sole plate. Lay a stud at each mark and place the header so that the rough sill, cripples, and trimmers are in position. Also place the preassembled corners and partition corners at the marked locations. Beginning at one end of the top plate, nail these members at the locations marked. Drive two 16d nails through the plates into each member. Fig. 30-32. Be careful to

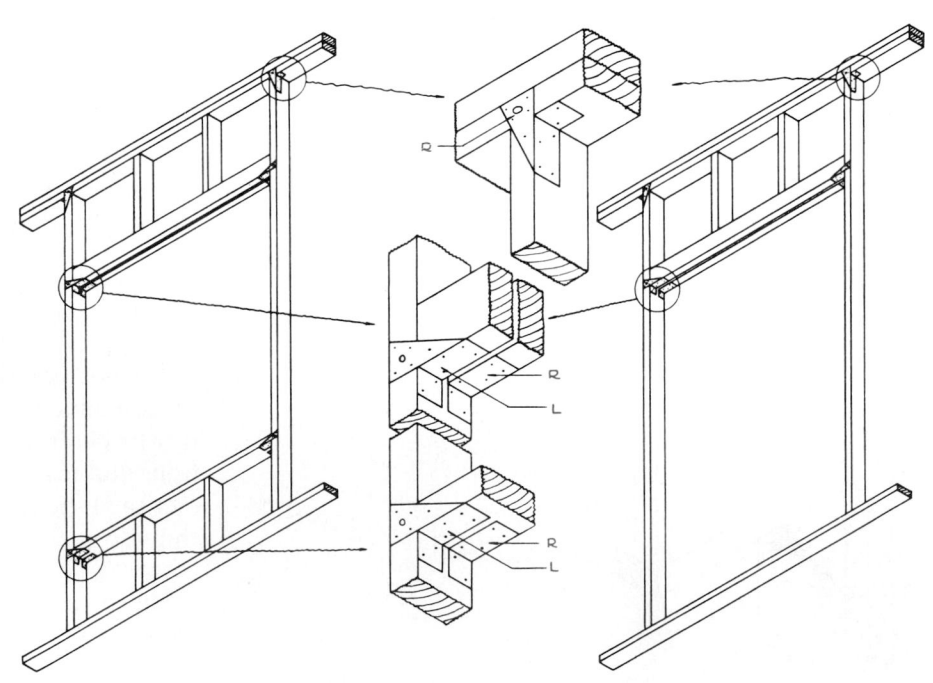

30-27. *Window framing with framing anchors used to support the header, sill, and studs.*

30-28. *Tilting up a long stud wall. In this case, the sheathing will be applied after the wall is in place.*

30-29. *Nailing prefinished paneling on an exterior wall before erection.*

30-30. *The rough sill and cripples have been preassembled and laid with the header for wall assembly later.*

30-31. *Assembling the wall sections on the subfloor in preparation for erection. This man is nailing the window trimmer in place.*

30-32a. *This carpenter is nailing the sole plate to the ends of the studs before the wall is raised.*

30-32b. *Nailing the top plate. Note that the joint in the top plate will be made over the solid header. This is a good practice.*

keep the edges of the members flush with each other. This is necessary for a smooth application of the interior and exterior wall covering later.

When a wall has been fully assembled on the subfloor, it must be squared. Fig. 30-33. This is done by running a tape measure across diagonally opposite corners. If the measurements between all corners are the same, the wall is square. The sheathing can be nailed to the studs while the walls are still on the subfloor. If preferred, the wall framing can be set up, squared, and braced. The sheathing can be applied later. Fig. 30-34. When the sole plate is nailed to the other wall members before erection, chalk line is snapped on the subfloor to show the exact location of the plate. The sole is straightened as it is nailed in position alongside the chalk line. The bottom plate is fastened to the floor framing with 16d nails spaced 16" apart and staggered when practical. The wall can now be plumbed and temporary bracing added to hold it in place in a true vertical position.

30-33. *Checking the assembled wall section for squareness by measuring diagonally across the corners. The two diagonal measurements must be equal.*

30-34. *Another variation of assembly is being used here. Both plates have been nailed to the studs while the wall was lying on the subfloor. After the wall is set up, the window framing will be installed either as a preassembled unit or a piece at a time.*

30-35a. *The exterior walls should be plumbed after being lifted into place. The wall should be braced immediately for safety reasons.*

Temporary Bracing

Temporary bracing may consist of 1" × 6" members nailed to one face of a stud and to a 2" × 4" block which has been nailed to the subfloor. The wall braces may also be nailed to wood stakes driven into the ground outside the perimeter of the foundation. Fig. 30-35. Care should also be taken not to project the ends of the temporary braces above the top plate. Otherwise, the braces could interfere with ceiling and roof framing and would have to be removed. Moving these braces at this time would disturb the plumbed and straightened walls. Use enough nails to hold the wall section securely, but do not drive the nails in all the way. The nailhead should project enough to allow easy withdrawal for removal later. The temporary bracing is left in place until the ceiling and the roof framing are completed and sheathing is applied to the outside walls.

PLUMBING AND STRAIGHTENING THE WALL SECTIONS

As noted earlier, framed walls may be lifted into position with or without sheathing already applied. If the sheathing has not been applied, the walls must be plumbed and straightened. This is done after all the framed walls are in position. Either a level or a plumb bob may be used to plumb the wall sections.

Using a Plumb Bob

To plumb a corner with a plumb bob, first attach to the bob a string long enough to extend to or below the bottom of the corner post. Lay a rule on top of the post so that 2" of the rule extends over the post on

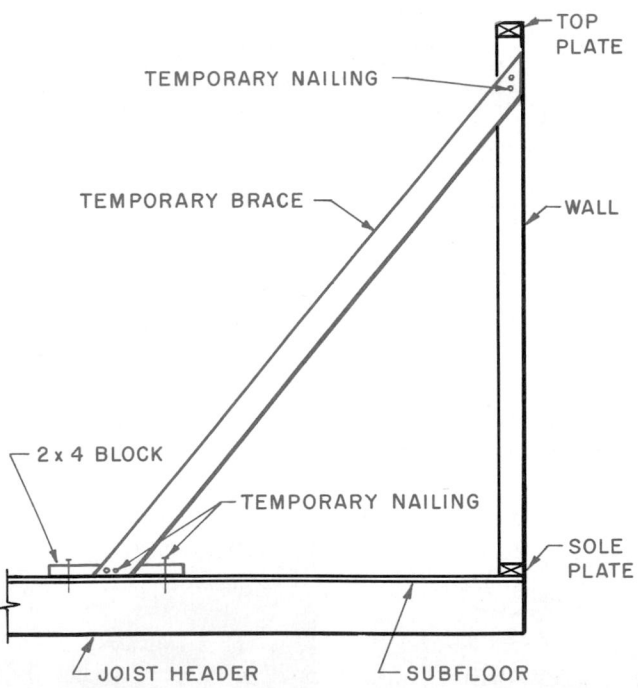

30-35b. *The wall is held in a vertical position while a worker nails the temporary braces.*

the side to be plumbed. Then hang the bob line over the rule so that the line is 2" from the post and extends to the bottom of it. Fig. 30-4 (1). With another rule, at the bottom of the post measure the distance from the post to the line. If the distance is not 2", the post is not plumb. Move the post inward or outward until the distance from the post to the line is exactly 2". Then nail the temporary brace in place. Repeat this procedure from the other outside face of the post. The post is then plumb. This process is carried out for the remaining corner posts and partition posts.

An alternate method of plumbing a post is shown in Fig. 30-4 (2). Attach the plumb bob string securely to the top of the post to be plumbed. Make sure that the string is long enough to allow the plumb bob to hang near the bottom of the post. Use two blocks of wood identical in thickness as gauge blocks. Tack one block near the top of the post between the plumb bob string and the post (gauge block No. 1). Insert the second block between the plumb bob string and the bottom of the post (gauge block No. 2). If the entire face of the second block makes contact with the string, the post is plumb.

Using a Level

To plumb a corner with a level, do not place the level directly against a stud, because the face or edge of the stud is likely to be irregular in shape. Instead, make a long straightedge. Fig. 30-36 and 30-37. The straightedge should have a couple of lugs, for placing against the stud, and an edge on which to place the level. Check the straightedge for trueness by placing it on a level surface and checking with the builder's level. To increase accuracy when plumbing the walls, hold the level

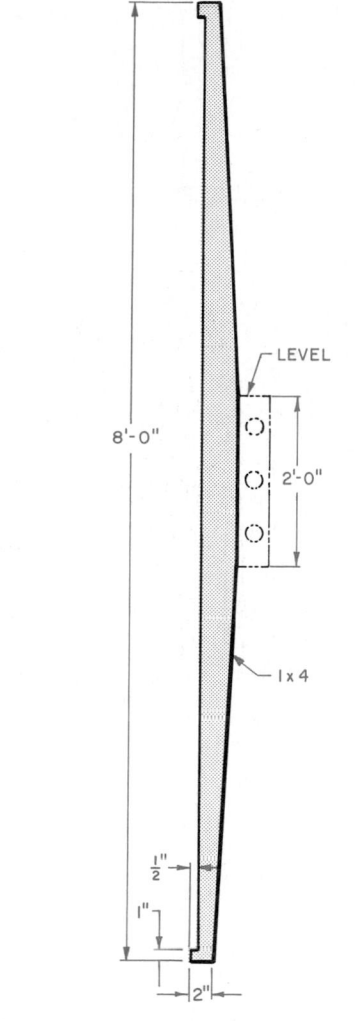

30-36. A straightedge can be made to use with a small level for plumbing the posts.

in such a position that you can look straight in at the bubble. While one worker uses the level, another should be ready to nail the brace to the block on the subfloor as soon as the correct position is found. This nailer works the end of the brace back and forth on signal from the worker with the level. When the nailer gets the word that the bubble is centered, he nails the end of the brace to the block.

Outside corners must be plumbed and braced both in and out and side to side. After all exterior corners have been plumbed and braced, the

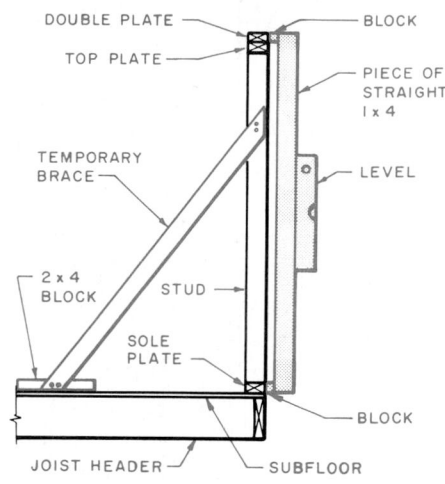

30-37. The straightedge can simply be a piece of 1" x 4" stock. Make sure the edge on which the level is placed is parallel to a line drawn between the two blocks nailed on the ends.

intersecting interior partition posts are plumbed and braced. The partition posts need to be plumbed in one direction only (in and out). This will plumb the exterior wall at the point of intersection. If the top and bottom plates have been correctly cut and laid out, the partition corners will be plumb from side to side after the exterior corner posts are plumbed. After all exterior and partition corner posts have been plumbed and nailed in place with temporary bracing, the wall sections between the posts should be straightened. If necessary, they should be held with additional temporary bracing.

Straightening Walls

To straighten walls, fasten a chalk line to the outside of one of the corner posts at the top. Stretch the line to the corner post at the opposite end of the building, and fasten the line to this post in the

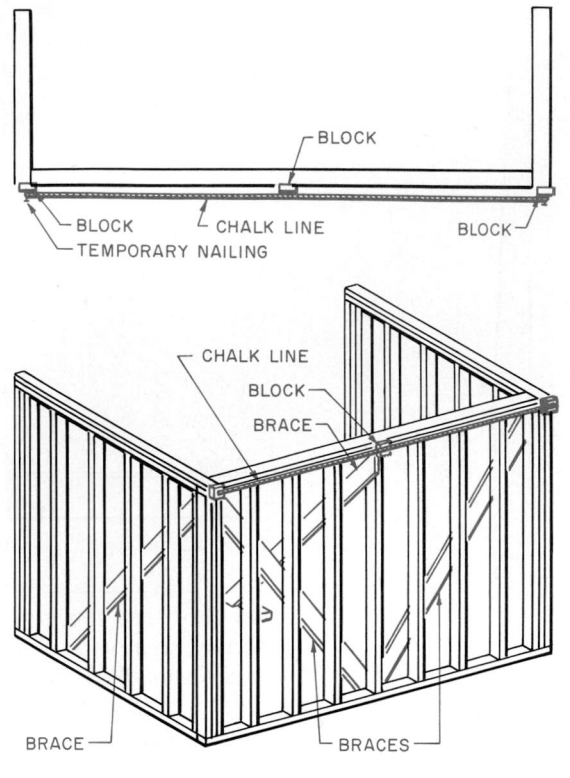

30-38. Using a chalk line as a reference to straighten the walls.

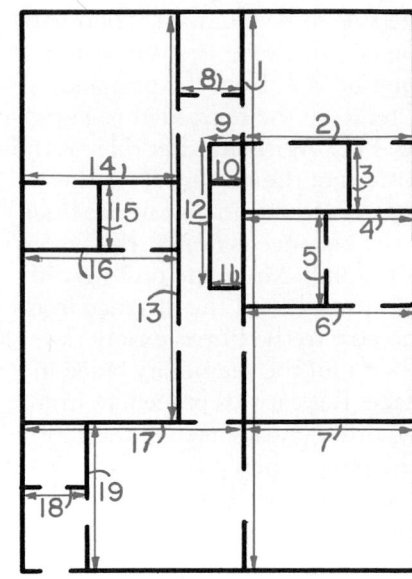

30-39. Sequence of assembling and erecting interior partitions. After reading the text you will understand why the sequence was suggested. There are other possible sequences that would be worth considering. Can you suggest one that might have its own advantages?

same manner as for the first post. Place a small wooden block, ¾" thick, under each end of the line to give clearance. Fig. 30-38. Place additional temporary braces at intervals close enough to hold the wall straight. When the wall is far enough away from the line to permit a ¾" block to slide between the line and the plate, the brace is nailed. This procedure is carried out for the entire perimeter of the building. Inside partition walls should be straightened later in the same manner.

PARTITIONS—ASSEMBLING AND ERECTING

Partition walls divide the inside space of a building. These walls in most cases are framed as part of the building. Partition walls are of two types—*bearing* and *nonbearing*. A bearing wall supports ceiling joists, while a nonbearing wall supports only itself. Partition walls are framed in the same manner as outside walls. After all the exterior walls are set up, plumbed, braced and the sole plate securely nailed, the interior walls (partitions) are assembled and erected. The top and bottom plates for the partitions are cut and laid out in the same way as described for exterior walls. The sizes of the various partition parts (such as headers, trimmers, and cripples) can be learned from the master stud pattern and the building plans. These parts are cut to size, marked for identification, and then distributed to the areas on the subfloor where they are to be assembled. Assembly of the partitions is also the same as described for outside walls. Careful

planning of the order in which the partitions are assembled and erected is very important. A floor plan with a suggested sequence of assembly and erection is shown in Fig. 30-39. The next two paragraphs will explain some of the reasons for the order in which the steps are carried out.

The first operation is to raise, fasten, and temporarily brace the longest center partition. Work then proceeds from one end of the building to the other and from the center wall out to the exterior walls. To save time and effort, operations in one area are completed before moving to the next area.

Still referring to Fig. 30-39, notice that partition 2 helps support the center partition and connects it to the previously plumbed exterior wall. The third partition is at right angles to the second, and the fourth is at right

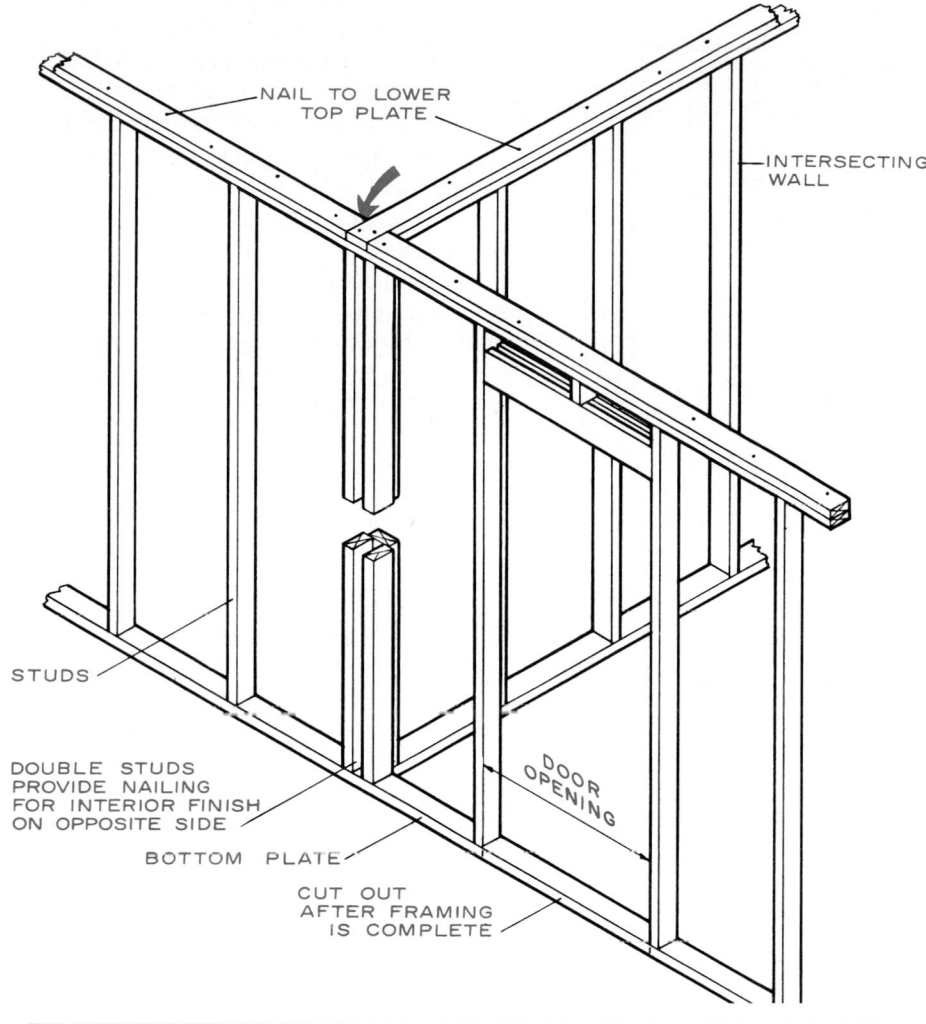

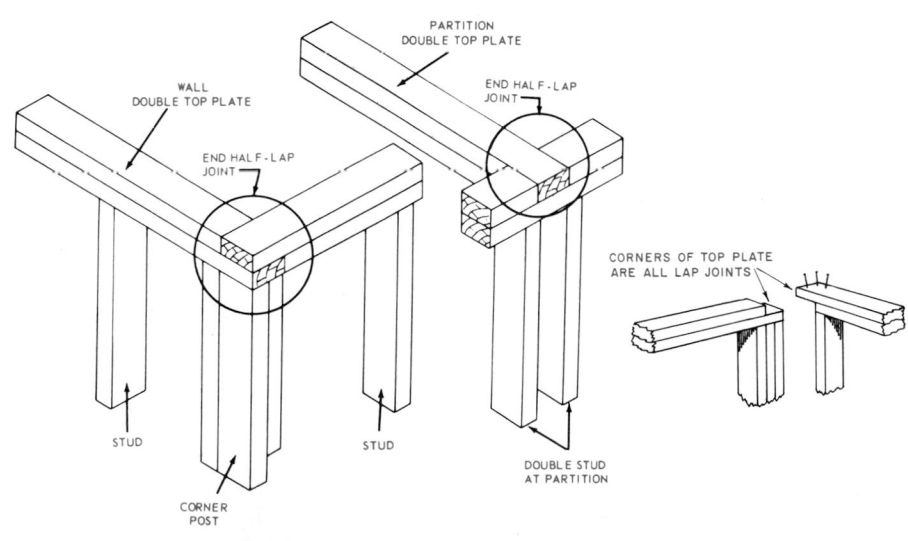

30-40. The top plate is usually fastened in place after the walls have been pumbed and straightened. Ten penny nails are used in the nailing pattern to attach the double plate.

30-41. The double top plates are joined together with half-lap joints.

angles to the third. This pattern continues to the rear of the building. This is better than erecting two parallel partitions (such as 2 and 4) and then having to work in a confined area to erect the connecting partition (3).

The Double Plate or Rafter Plate

The double plate or rafter plate is applied over the top plate. Fig. 30-40. The same kind of material is used as for the top plate. The pieces must be cut accurately to length. This can be done either at the same time when the sole and top plates are cut or after the walls are erected. Note, however, that the rafter plates are not cut exactly the same length as the other two plates. Since one of the primary purposes of this plate is to tie the walls together at the top, the rafter plate laps over the joint formed at a corner of intersecting wall. Fig. 30-41. On a long wall, if joints are necessary in the rafter or double plate, they should be at least 4' from any joint in the top plate. Fasten the double plate with 10d nails spaced 16" O.C. End laps between adjoining plates are nailed with two 16d nails on each lap. (See arrow, Fig. 30-40.)

LET-IN BRACING

When the walls are sheathed with plywood or other panel products, this provides enough rigidity to prevent the walls from racking (shifting) back and forth. If the walls will not be sheathed with panel products, they must be made rigid by adding let-in bracing.

Bracing stiffens framed construction and makes it rigid. Good bracing keeps corners square and plumb. It also prevents warping, sagging, and shifting. Without bracing, the shape changes in the frame would cause badly fitting doors and windows and cracked plaster.

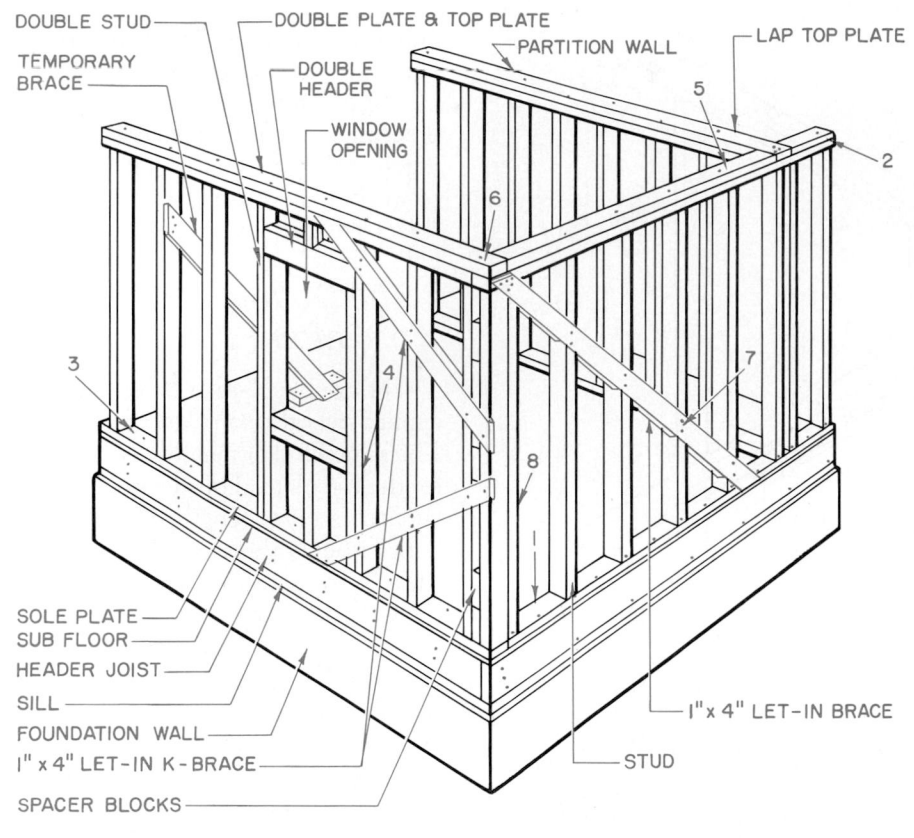

30-42. *The bracing is let-in and securely nailed to the framing.*

DOUBLE STUD
TEMPORARY BRACE
DOUBLE PLATE & TOP PLATE
DOUBLE HEADER
PARTITION WALL
WINDOW OPENING
LAP TOP PLATE
SOLE PLATE
SUB FLOOR
HEADER JOIST
SILL
FOUNDATION WALL
1" x 4" LET-IN K-BRACE
SPACER BLOCKS
1" x 4" LET-IN BRACE
STUD

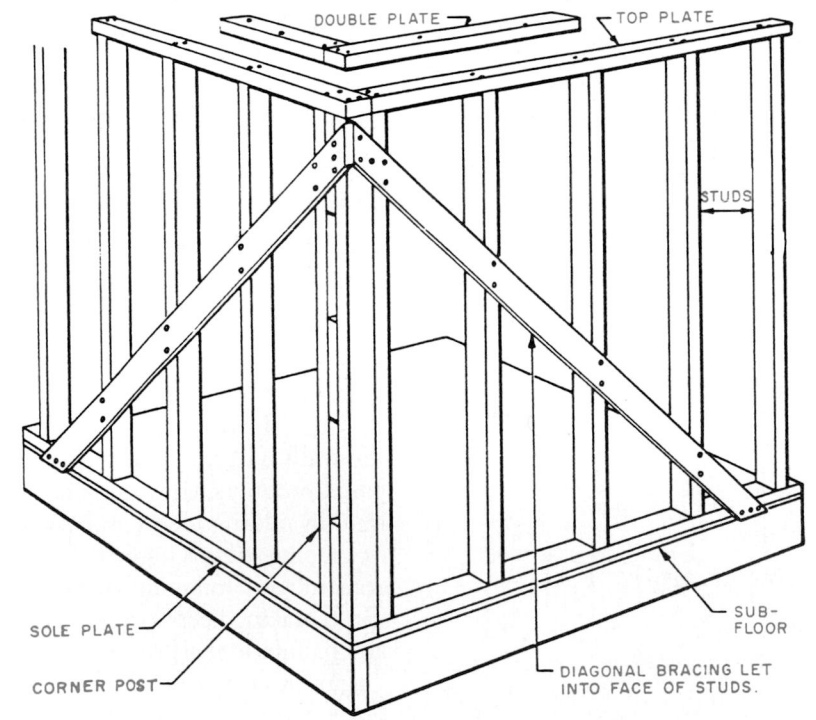

30-43. *Diagonal bracing at the corner. Note the nailing pattern.*

DOUBLE PLATE
TOP PLATE
STUDS
SOLE PLATE
CORNER POST
DIAGONAL BRACING LET INTO FACE OF STUDS.
SUB-FLOOR

It is important to have the frame properly nailed together. The bracing is then securely nailed to hold the framing rigid. Fig. 30-42 provides a review of correct nailing procedure and shows the bracing in place: (1) The sole plate is nailed to a joist or header joist with 16d nails spaced 16" O.C. (2) The top plate is end-nailed to the studs with two 16d nails. (3) Studs are toenailed to the sole plate with two 8d nails on each side. (4) Doubled studs are nailed together with 10d nails 16" O.C. (5) Top plates are spiked together with 10d nails 16" O.C. (6) The top plates, laps, and intersections are nailed together with two 16d nails. (7) A one-inch brace is nailed to each stud and plate with two 8d nails. (8) Corner studs and multiple studs are nailed with 10d nails 12" O.C. Other joints should be nailed to provide proportional strength.

Frame walls may be braced at the corners by diagonal members (usually 1" × 4") set in gains cut into the plates, studs, and corner posts. Fig. 30-42. To lay out these gains, place the bracing members in position against the framing members. Then score (mark) the outline on each stud or plate with a scratch awl. Diagonal braces must be properly nailed at each crossing stud with not less than two 8d nails and at the ends with three 8d nails. Fig. 30-43. A single diagonal extending from floor line to ceiling line should cross at least three stud spaces. When a wall opening makes this impossible, a K-brace is installed. Fig. 30-44.

Sometimes diagonal bracing gains are laid out and cut into the framing before the walls are erected. Then the braces are also nailed to the pole plate before wall erection. Fig. 30-45. When the wall sheathing provides adequate corner bracing, diagonal bracing may be omitted. Diagonal-laid wood sheathing or plywood is usually considered adequate

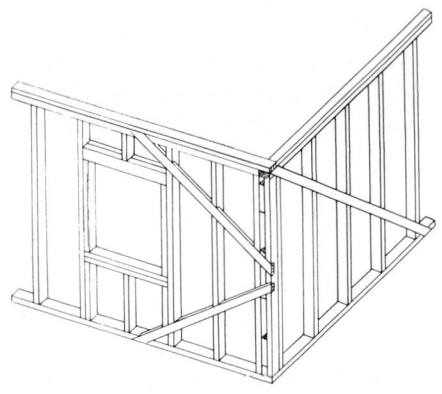

30-44. *A diagonal brace should reach from the double plate to the sole plate and cross three stud spaces. If this is not possible because of an opening, a K-brace should be used. Note the trimmer studs at the window. Instead of being continuous from the sole plate to header, they are broken by the bottom or sill header. There are advantages and disadvantages to each method. Check with the local building inspector to make sure the method you select is approved in your area.*

30-45. *The brace is nailed securely at the bottom only (near top of photo). All other nails are just started. After the wall is set up and plumbed all the nails are driven home to hold the wall plumb.*

bracing. Fig. 30-46. When other sheathing materials are used, a sheet of plywood is sometimes fastened to each side of each corner instead of diagonal bracing.

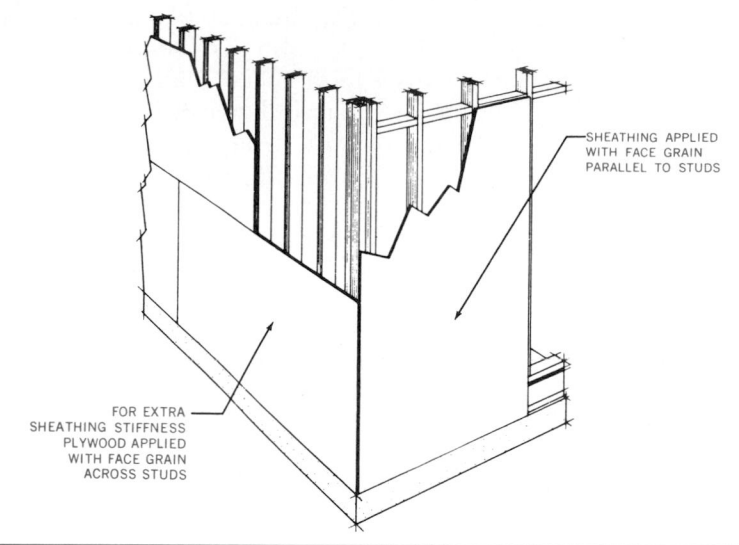

30-46. *Plywood used as sheathing eliminates the need for diagonal bracing.*

30-47. *Using plywood for corner bracing because of a lack of room. Notice the diagonal bracing on the side wall.*

Also if there is not enough room to brace adequately because of an opening in the exterior wall, a sheet of plywood will provide the necessary strength for the corner. Fig. 30-47.

SPECIAL FRAMING

Special framing includes such operations as providing openings for heating vents and plumbing pipes, adding support for heavy items (such as bathtubs), and

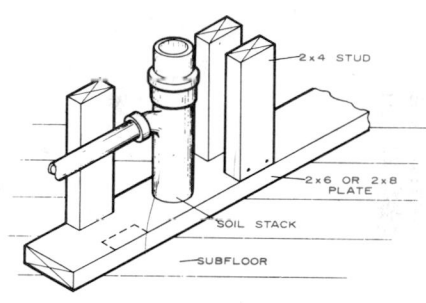

30-48. *A piece of material somewhat larger than 2" x 4" is used for a sole plate to provide room for a 4" soil pipe. The 2" x 4" studs are then installed flatwise.*

providing bases for nailing paneling or other covering materials. Such framing makes a carpenter's job easier and faster in the finishing stages and adds strength and quality to the construction.

Plumbing Stack Vents

Plumbing stack vents are usually installed by using a nominal 2" × 6" plate and placing the studs flatwise at each side. Fig. 30-48. This provides the needed wall thickness for the bell (large end) of a 4" cast-iron soil pipe, which is larger than

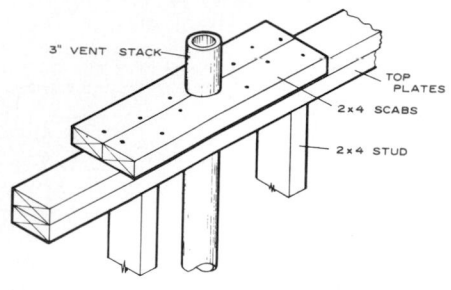

30-49. *A 3" vent stack will fit in a standard 2" × 4" stud wall. The top plate, however, will have to be reinforced as shown here.*

the thickness of a 2" × 4" stud wall. It is also possible to fur out several studs to a 6" width at the soil stack, rather than thickening the entire wall. In areas where building regulations permit the use of 3" vent pipe, a 2" × 4" stud wall may be used, but it requires reinforcing scabs at the top plate. Fig. 30-49. Use 12d nails to fasten the scabs.

Bathtub Framing

The floor joists in the bathroom which support the tub or shower

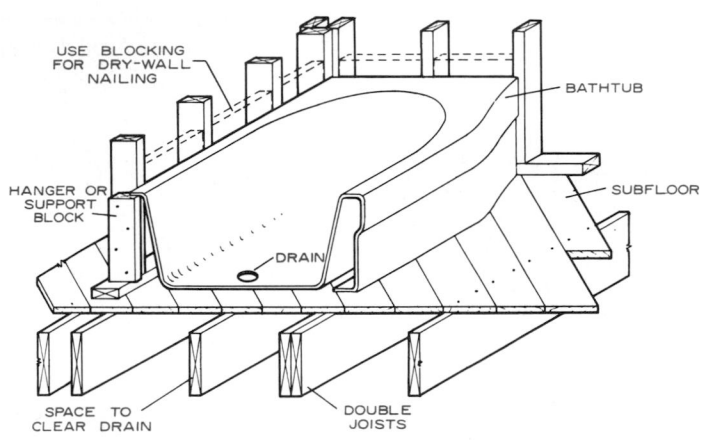

30-50. *Framing for a bathtub.*

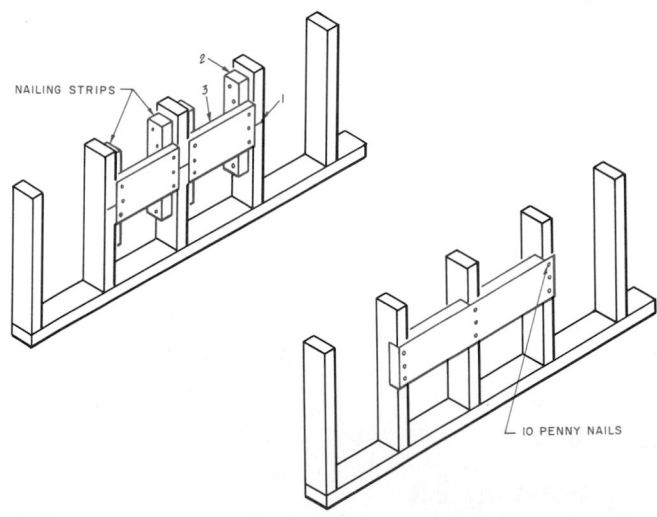

30-51. *Blocking for hanging plumbing fixtures: 1. Determine the height of the fixture and mark the location. 2. Nail a block on the side of the stud, back from the edge a distance equal to the thickness of the backing material. 3. Cut the backing to fit between the studs and nail it in place. Note: The backing material could be gained into the studs (see "Corner Bracing") at the correct height and face-nailed with 10d nails.*

should be arranged so that no cutting is necessary in connecting the drainpipe. This may require only a small adjustment in spacing the joists. Fig. 30-50. When joists are parallel to the length of the tub, they are usually doubled under the outer edge. Tubs are supported at the enclosing walls by hangers or woodblocks. The wall in which the fixture plumbing is located should also be framed to allow for a small access panel.

Plumbing Fixtures

The weight and eventual use of plumbing fixtures requires a secure anchorage. This backing is provided at the necessary locations as shown in Fig. 30-51.

Cabinets and Utility Boxes

Special support and blocking must also be provided for most cabinets. Some cabinets are designed to fit between studs 16" O.C. and flush with the wall covering. These are usually designed to be fastened from the inside of the cabinet, through the sides, directly into the studs. Backing must be provided at the top and bottom of the cabinet for nailing the wall covering.

Bathroom vanities, kitchen cabinets, and other projecting cabinets must be securely fastened. Thus they require special blocking. The location of this blocking can be determined by studying the building plans. One method of blocking for cabinets is shown in Fig. 30-52. In some cases it is advisable to install an extra full-length stud or even a 2" × 6" flatwise in the wall. This is especially true in kitchens in which upper and lower cabinets are to be installed.

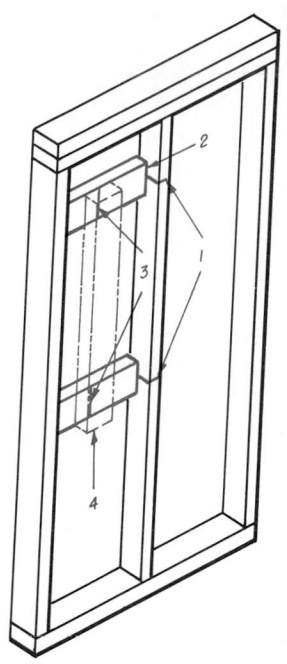

30-52. *Blocking for hanging cabinets: 1. Mark the top and bottom of the cabinets on the studs. 2. Fasten blocks between the studs for attaching the cabinet backing. These blocks must be back from the edge of the studs a distance equal to the thickness of the cabinet backing. 3. Mark the position of the cabinet backing on the blocks. 4. Fasten the cabinet backing to the blocks on the location marks.*

Trim Backing

Baseboard, chair rail, ceiling, and other moldings require additional backing for nailing at the ends. Without additional backing the nails must be driven very near the ends of the molding and usually at a slight angle to anchor into the corner posts. This often results in splitting the ends of the molding. Backing such as shown in Figs. 30-21 and 30-22 will permit correct nailing procedures.

Backing for Accessories

Towel bars, shower curtain rods, soap dishes, tissue-roll holders and similar items should be supported by backing. These items do not

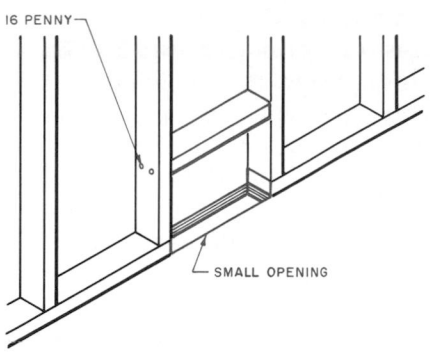

30-53. *Recommended framing for a small heating duct opening.*

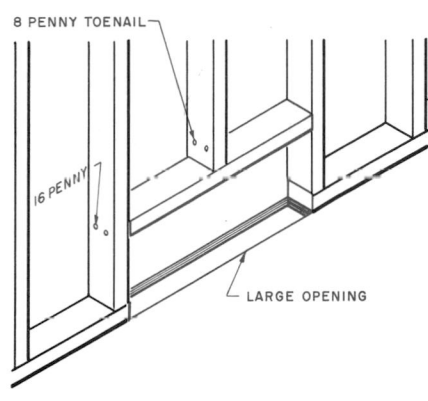

30-54. *Recommended framing for a large heating duct opening.*

require backing as heavy as that for cabinets or plumbing fixtures. Usually a piece of 1" × 4" material located and fastened as in Fig. 30-51 will provide much better support than the wall covering alone.

Heating Ducts

Heating ducts require openings in the ceiling, floor, or wall. Backing must therefore be provided for fastening the covering material. Fig. 30-53. An opening in the wall larger than the distance between the studs will require cutting off one or more studs. It also requires a header to support the shortened stud, which serves as a nailing surface for the wall covering. Fig. 30-54.

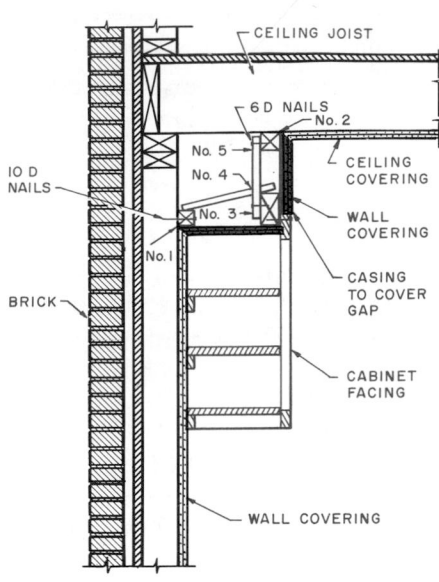

30-55. *Soffit construction details for flush-mounted cabinets.*

Cabinet Soffits

The cabinet soffit is sometimes called a *bulkhead*. There are two common types. The first allows the cabinet to be constructed flush with the front of the soffit. Fig. 30-55. This type is used mainly when the cabinets are built on the job. In the second type, the cabinets are set back about 2". This method, which is more common, is used with prefabricated cabinets. Such cabinets are usually not installed until after the interior painting is completed. Details can be seen in Fig. 30-56.

Constructing Soffits for Flush-Mounted Cabinets. Snap a chalk line along the wall studs to represent the bottom edge of the soffit. (Arrow #1, Fig. 30-55.) This line will usually be 84" plus the thickness of the lath and plaster or dry wall above the finished floor. With 10d nails, nail a 2" × 2" along the top edge of this line into each wall stud.

Assume the shelves are to be 11¼" deep. Snap a chalk line along the underside of the ceiling joists

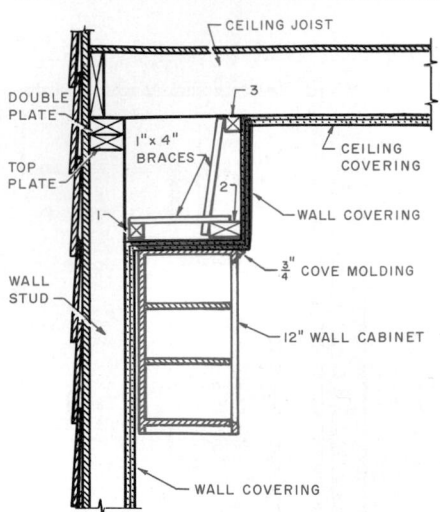

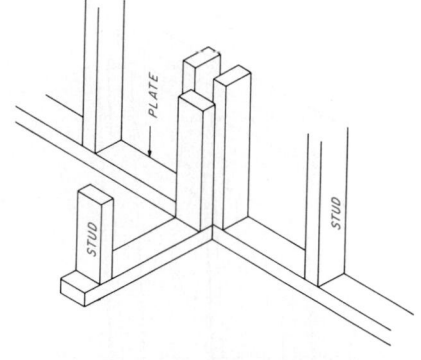

30-56. *Construction details for a conventional soffit.*

11¼" out from the double plate. (Arrow #2.) This allows ¾" for the lath and plaster to be applied later. With 10d nails fasten a 2" × 2" along this chalk line into the bottom edge of each ceiling joist.

(If the ceiling joists run the same direction as the soffit, a ladder-type construction, similar to that used when installing nonbearing partitions, will have to be used. The upper 2" × 2" for the bulkhead is nailed to the underside of the 2" × 4" ladder construction.)

Cut the 2" × 4" for the front bottom edge of the soffit to finished length. Nail 1" × 4" × 12" pieces to the back (Arrow #3) and top edge (Arrow #4) of the 2" × 4". Temporarily tack the 2" × 4" in position by nailing it with 6d nails to the top 2" × 2". (Arrow #5.) With a level make sure that the 2" × 4" is level along its length and that its bottom edge is level with the bottom edge of the 2" × 2" nailed to the wall.

When the 2" × 4" is in position, use 6d nails to fasten the 1" × 4" pieces securely to the two 2" × 2"s. Additional 2" × 4" blocking may be required along the face or bottom edge of the soffit in order to join cabinets or install electrical outlet boxes.

Constructing the Conventional Cabinet Soffit.

This type of soffit framing is used when the cabinets are prefabricated and installed later. Two 2" × 2" boards are installed, one on the wall (Fig. 30-56, arrow 1) and the second on the ceiling (arrow 3). These are positioned and nailed in place as in the previous method. The differences are that the 2" × 2" along the ceiling is positioned 14" from the face of the wall studs to the outside edge of this 2" × 2", and the 2" × 4" at the bottom corner is turned flat rather than on edge (arrow 2). After the wall covering has been applied and painted, the cabinets are attached to the wall and to the bottom of the soffit. The top front edge of the cabinet is securely attached to the 2" × 4" laid flat in the soffit. Since prefabricated cabinets are usually 12" deep, this allows a 2" overhang of the soffit at the front edge. A piece of cove or quarter-round molding may be used to close the joint between the cabinet and the bulkhead.

Wall and Ceiling Finish Nailers

Wall and ceiling finish nailers are horizontal or vertical members to which paneling, dry wall, rock lath, wall board, or other covering materials are nailed. These pieces are installed at the interior corners of walls and at the junction of the wall and ceiling. The vertical nailers located at the interior corners of the walls may be made up of studs placed where they will make a good base for nailing. Fig. 30-57. This method of construction also provides a good tie between walls.

A second method of installing a vertical nailer at the interior wall corners is provided by a 2" × 6" nailed to the stud of the intersecting wall. In this method, a header nailed between the studs of

30-57. *This assembly of studs where a partition meets a wall will provide adequate nailing for the wall finish material.*

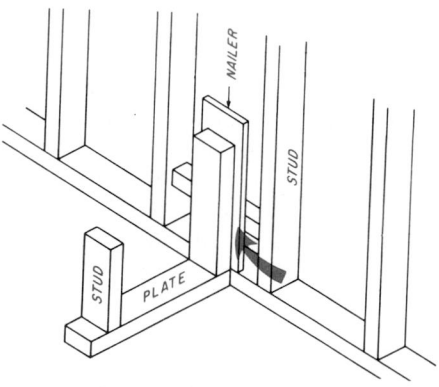

30-58. *Attach a 6" board to the back of the last 2" × 4" and the wall partition to provide adequate nailing for the wall finish material. Note that a header is nailed between the wall studs so that the partition wall may be toenailed through the nailer into the header to secure the partition wall to the main wall.*

the main wall is necessary to back up the nailer. Fig. 30-58.

At the junction of a wall and ceiling, doubling of the ceiling joists over the wall plates provides a nailing surface for the interior wall finish. Fig. 30-59. The walls are tied to the ceiling framing by toenailing through the ceiling joists into the wall plates.

Another method of providing nailing at the ceiling line is similar to that used on the walls. A 2" × 6"

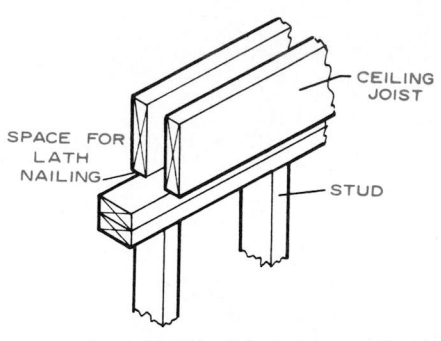

30-59a. *Nailing for the ceiling finish is provided by doubling the ceiling joists at each side of the wall plate.*

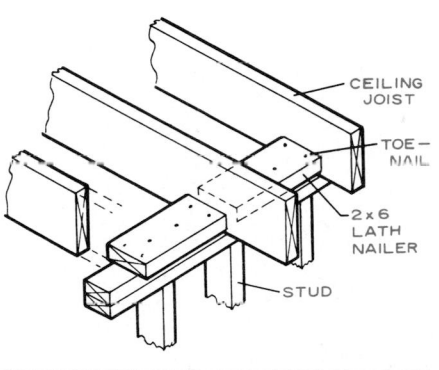

30-59b. *Horizontal lath nailers at ceiling for a stud wall at right angle to joist.*

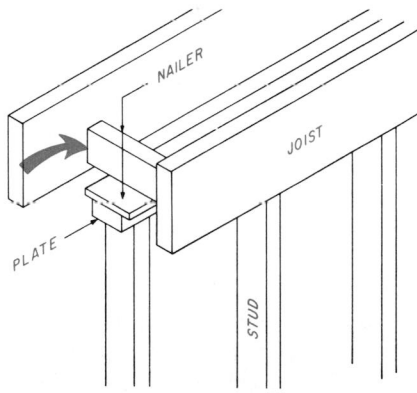

30-60. *A nailer attached to the top of the wall plate. The header nailed between the joists (arrow) can then be toenailed into the top of the nailer to secure the partition to the ceiling.*

nailer is nailed to the top of the wall plate. Fig. 30-60. A header is nailed between the ceiling joists and then toenailed to the wall plate through the nailer.

Nailers need not be continuous. Several short pieces of 2" × 6" can be used rather than new material. Nailers should be firmly secured with 16d common nails so that they will not be hammered out of position when the wall finish is nailed in place. If nailers are out of position, the wall finish material will be out of square at the corner.

Schedule for Special Framing

Usually there is a need to enclose a building quickly, to protect it from the weather. However, special framing is time consuming. Therefore during the regular framing stage a builder will take time to do only those special framing operations which must be done at that time. The rest of the special framing often is done as fill-in work during slack periods in later construction stages. The climate, other projects, and available manpower affect the scheduling of special framing.

MULTILEVEL FRAMING

The use of platform-frame construction simplifies the framing of multilevel structures. The first level of the two-story house is constructed in the same manner as for a one-story home. However, the ceiling joists of the first story become the floor joists of the second story. Therefore these joists must be wider to support the additional load.

A subfloor is applied to the top of the joists, the second-story floor plan is laid out, and the walls are

constructed and raised in the same way as for the first floor. Fig. 30-61. Some architectural designs require an overhang of the second floor joists beyond the first story walls. The framing of the floor joists can be seen in Fig. 30-62.

Split levels and other variations of architecture require a slightly different treatment of the wall framing. After consulting the sectional elevations in the building plans, make a master stud pattern for each level. This pattern will show the true lengths of the studs for the stub walls found in split-level homes. Keep in mind that each floor platform is supported by a wall section. Thus, a second-level floor platform is supported by the walls which enclose the rooms of the lower level. Fig. 30-63.

Bay-window framing is sometimes associated with multilevel homes. Fig. 30-64. A bay-window projection requires that the floor also be framed out beyond the foundation wall, as for a second-floor overhang. Fig. 30-62.

ESTIMATING WALL FRAMING

Materials and Their Costs

The number of 16" O.C. studs required for a building may be roughly estimated by figuring one for each linear foot of wall. This allows for doubling at openings and at corners. If only the material cost is to be estimated, use Tables 30-B (page 347) and 30-C (page 348). For example, consider a building with an exterior wall 20' long and 8' high, framed with 2" × 4" studs 16" O.C. Such a wall will require 168 board feet of material.

To arrive at this answer, first determine the number of square

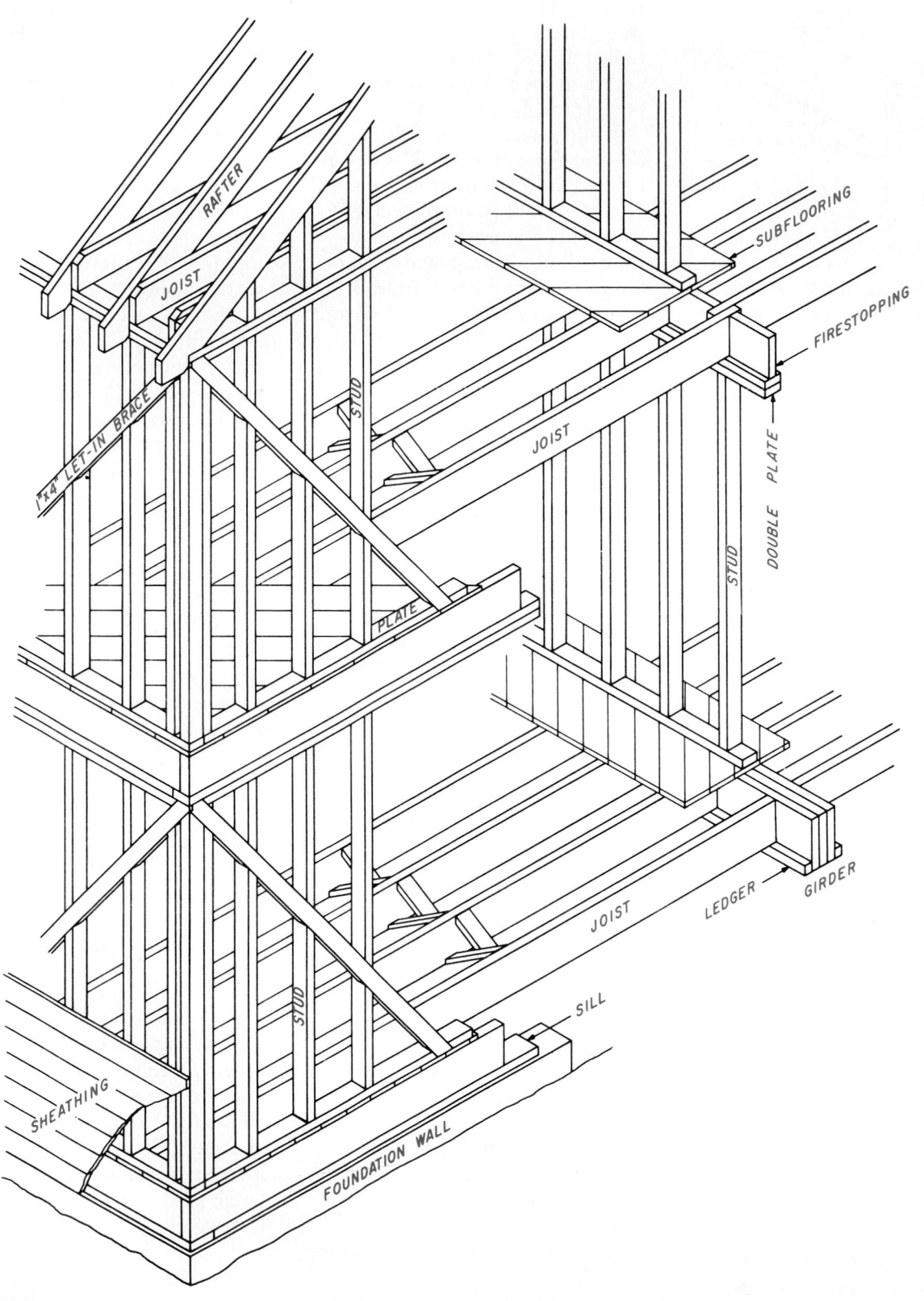

Labels within figure: RAFTER, JOIST, SUBFLOORING, FIRESTOPPING, 1"x4" LET-IN BRACE, STUD, DOUBLE PLATE, JOIST, STUD, PLATE, JOIST, LEDGER, GIRDER, STUD, SILL, SHEATHING, FOUNDATION WALL

30-61a. *Platform-frame construction in a two-story house. This is just two one-story houses built one on top of the other under a single roof. Remember, however, that because of the additional weight of the second level larger support members are needed to carry the load.*

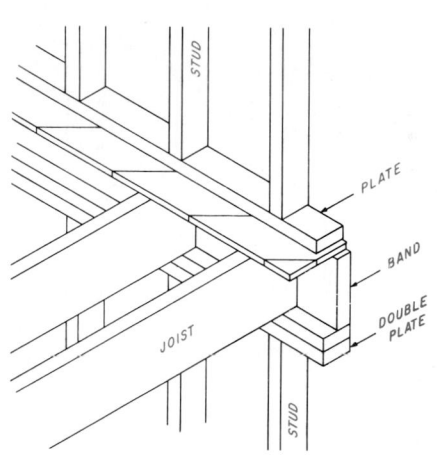

30-61b. *Detail of the second-floor framing at the exterior wall.*

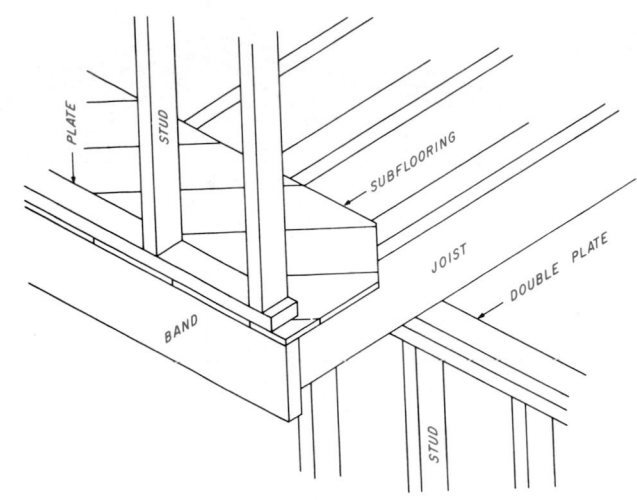

30-62a. *Second-floor overhang on an exterior wall. Since these joists run at right angles to the wall below, they can just be extended.*

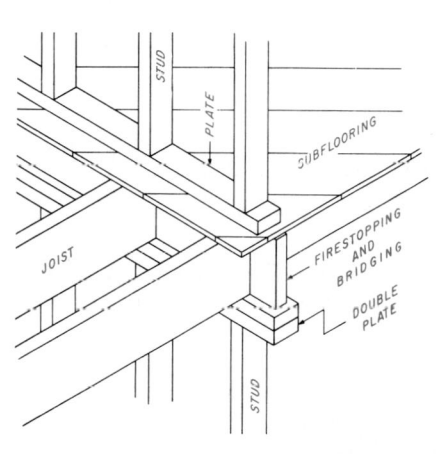

30-61c. *Detail of the second-floor framing over a bearing partition.*

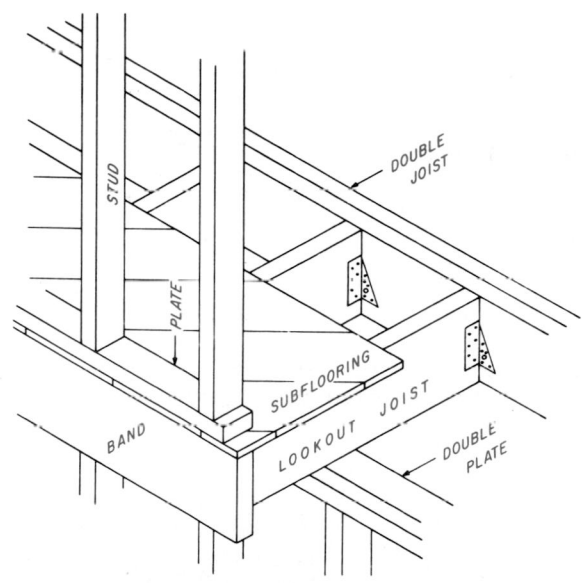

30-62b. *Second-floor overhang with wall parallel to the joists. Lookout joists are used and must be attached to a double joist. The double joist should be located a distance of twice the overhang back from the lower wall.*

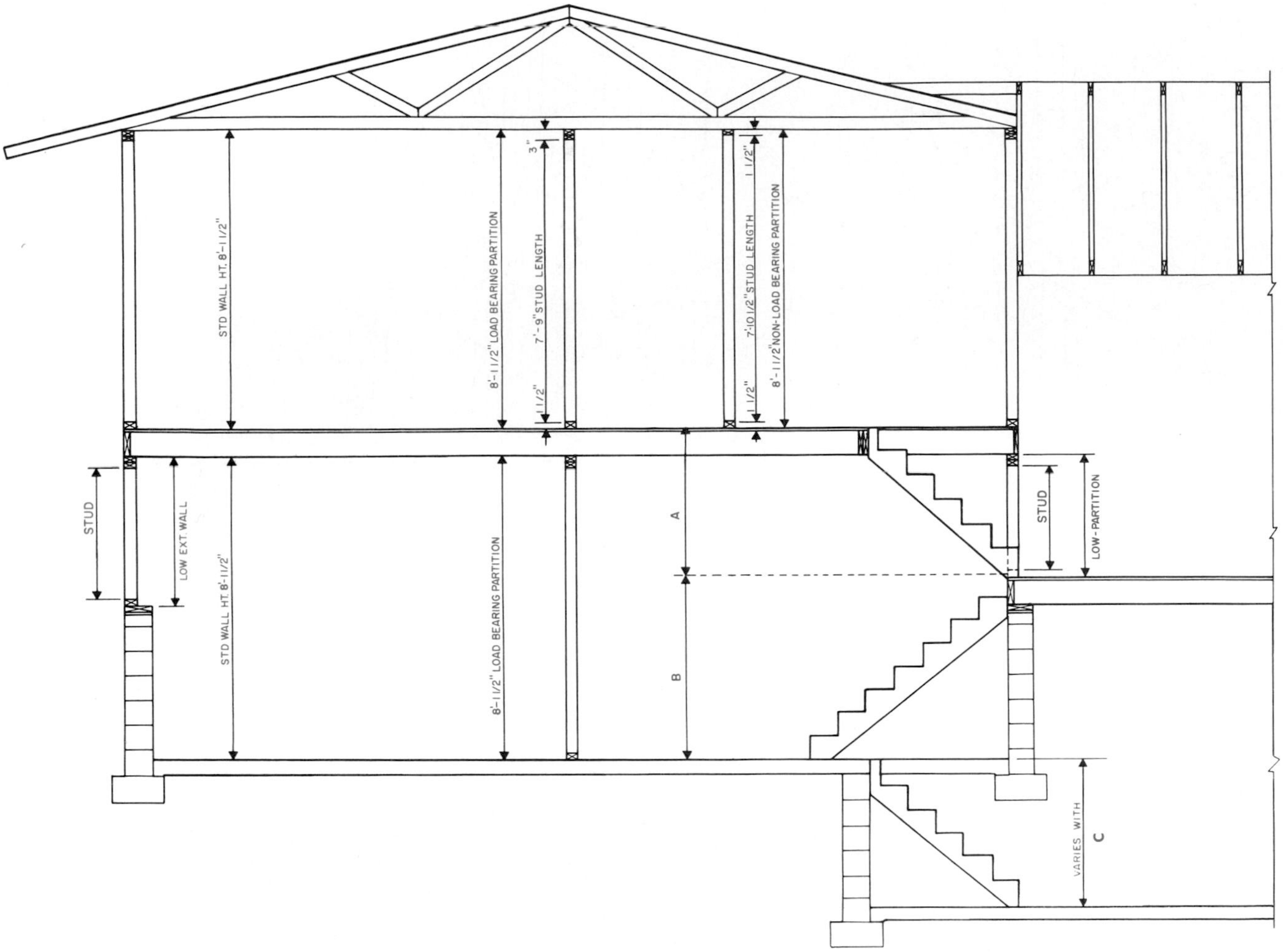

30-63a. Split-level framing. In this drawing the dimension at A is constant. The dimension at B may vary depending on whether 2" x 8" or 2" x 10" floor joists are used. The dimension at C will vary depending upon the number of blocks used in the foundation wall.

30-63b. Floor girders are framed in for the first level. The stub wall is framed in and will help to support the floor framing for the second level of this split-level home.

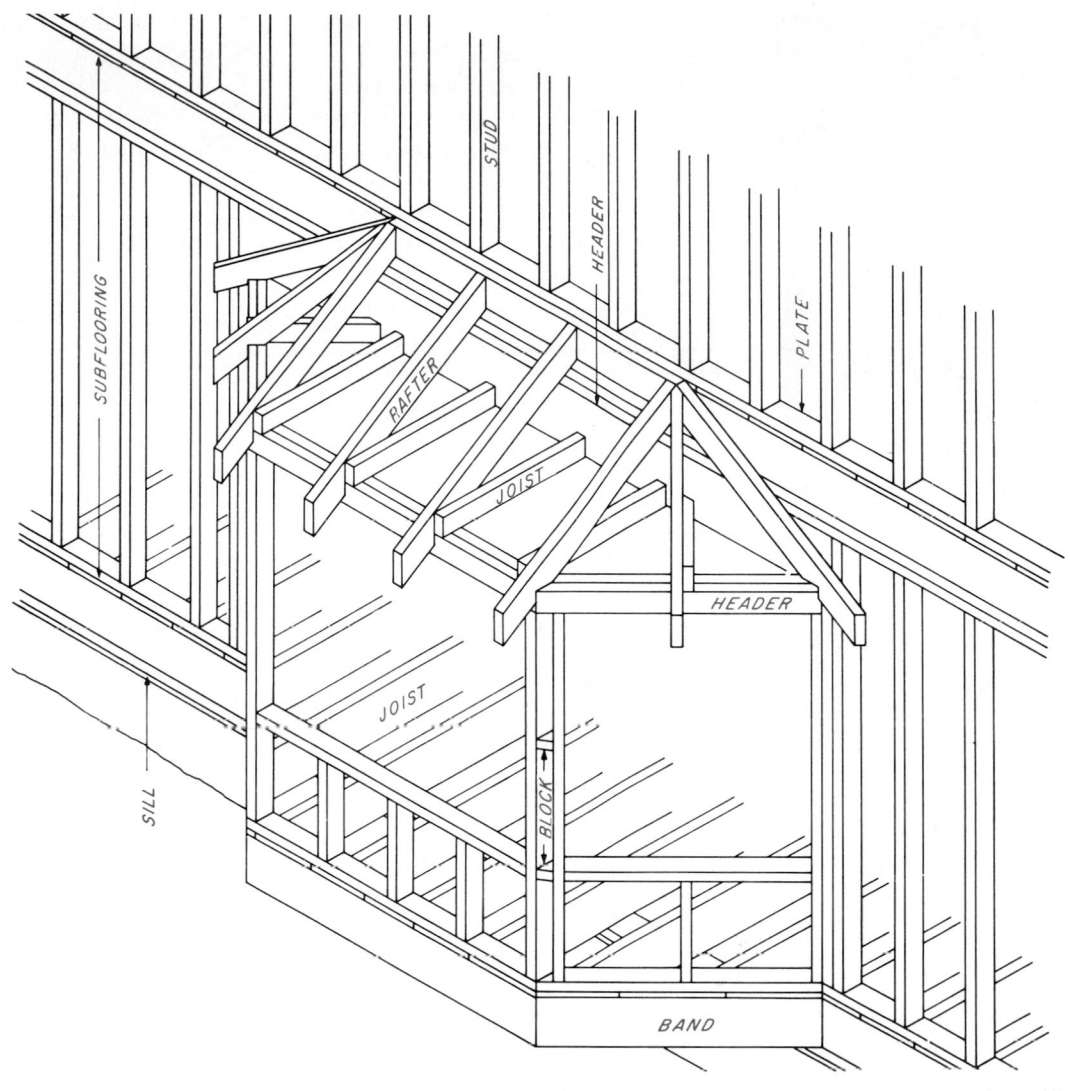

Labels on figure: SUBFLOORING, STUD, HEADER, PLATE, RAFTER, JOIST, HEADER, JOIST, SILL, BLOCK, BAND

30-64a. *Bay window framing. The ceiling joists in the framing of this bay are set on top of the window headers. The top of a bay window should be kept in line with the other windows and doors in the room. Therefore the wall header will not be a standard header height. It will have to be raised so that its bottom is in line with the bottom of the bay ceiling joists.*

Table 30-B. *Exterior Wall Studs. This tells you how you can figure the number of board feet and nails for exterior wall framing.*

Size of Studs	Spacing on Centers	(Studs Including Corner Bracing.)	
		Bd. Ft. per Sq. Ft. per Area	Lbs. Nails per 1000 Bd. Ft.
2"x3"	12"	0.83	30
	16"	0.78	
	20"	0.74	
	24"	0.71	
2"x4"	12"	1.09	22
	16"	1.05	
	20"	0.98	
	24"	0.94	
2"x6"	12"	1.66	15
	16"	1.51	
	20"	1.44	
	24"	1.38	

30-64b. *The framing for this bay window includes built-up headers over the window and a laminated-veneer header over the main opening.*

feet in the wall (20' × 8' = 160 sq. ft.). Refer to Table 30-B. Find "Size of Studs" in the left column (2" × 4" for our example) and read across to the column "Spacing on Center" (16"). In the third column opposite the 16", find the factor for the board feet per square foot of area (1.05 for our example). Multiply this factor by the wall area. Thus 1.05 × 160 = 168 board feet of lumber for the wall. Figure the lumber costs by multiplying the cost per board foot by 168, the amount of lumber required for the wall.

To determine the amount of material for a partition wall, use Table 30-C (for board feet) or Table 30-D (for exact number of studs) and follow the procedure just given.

With Table 30-B you can also figure the number of nails needed.

For an exterior wall built with 2" × 4" studs, 22 lbs. of nails are needed for each 1,000 bd. ft. The wall in the example contains 168 bd. ft. and will require about 3.7 lbs. of nails:

$$\frac{168 \text{ (bd. ft.)}}{1,000} \times 22 \text{ (lbs.} = 3.7 \text{ pounds per } 1,000 \text{ ft.)}$$

The size of the header for each opening will be found on the building plan. Make a list of headers and their sizes for use during construction as a cutting list. From this list determine the number of board feet of lumber, and figure the cost as described in Unit 29, "Floor Framing."

The amount of plate material must also be figured and added to the material list. To determine the number of lineal feet of top and bottom plates for walls having double top plates, multiply the length of the wall by three. Other materials such as gable-end studs, corner braces, fire stopping, and wall backing must also be listed. The number of board feet of lumber can be figured from this list. The total cost is determined by multiplying the total number of board feet by the cost of one board foot of lumber.

Labor Costs

The information in Table 30-E can be used to determine the approximate labor cost in the same manner as described in Unit 29.

Table 30-C. *Partition Studs. With this table you can figure the board feet of lumber needed for partition studs. In addition to giving the amount of material for the partition construction, this table also gives consideration to the need for extra lumber for headers, trimmers, and other special framing.*

	(Studs Including Top and Bottom Plates)		
Size of Studs	Spacing on Centers	Bd. Ft. per Sq. Ft. per Area	Lbs. Nails per 1000 Bd. Ft.
2"x 3"	12"	0.91	
	16"	0.83	25
	24"	0.76	
2"x 4"	12"	1.22	
	16"	1.12	19
	24"	1.02	
2"x 6"	16"	1.48	16
	24"	1.22	

Table 30-D. *Partition Studs. With this table you can find the number of partition studs needed for a job. The factors in the last four columns are used for figuring the number of feet of lumber. In this table they are close to the actual needs for building a partition, without consideration for special framing.*

Number of Feet of Lumber Required Per Sq. Ft. of Wood Stud Partition Using 2" x 4" Studs.

Studs spaced 16" on centers, with single top and bottom plates.

Length Partition in Feet	No. Studs Required	Ceiling Heights in Feet			
		8'0"	9'0"	10'0"	12'0"
2	3	1.25	1.167	1.13	1.13
3	3	0.833	0.812	0.80	0.80
4	4	0.833	0.812	0.80	0.80
5	5	0.833	0.812	0.80	0.80
6	6	0.833	0.812	0.80	0.80
7	6	0.833	0.75	0.75	0.80
8	7	0.75	0.75	0.75	0.70
9	8	0.75	0.75	0.75	0.70
10	9	0.75	0.75	0.75	0.70
11	9	0.75	0.70	0.70	0.67
12	10	0.75	0.70	0.70	0.67
13	11	0.75	0.70	0.70	0.67
14	12	0.75	0.70	0.70	0.67
15	12	0.70	0.70	0.70	0.67
16	13	0.70	0.70	0.70	0.67
17	14	0.70	0.70	0.70	0.67
18	15	0.70	0.70	0.67	0.67
19	15	0.70	0.70	0.67	0.67
20	16	0.70	0.70	0.67	0.67
		0.13	0.11	0.10	0.083

For dbl. plate, add per sq. ft
For 2"x 8" studs, double above quantities.
For 2"x 6" studs, increase above quantities 50%.

Table 30-E. *Estimating Labor for Wall Framing.*

Item	Size or Kind	Est. Labor Performance	Item	Size or Kind	Est. Labor Performance
Partition plates and shoe		50 b.f. per hour	Outside wall plates and shoe	2x4	40 b.f. per hour
Partition studs		50 b.f. per hour		2x6	50 b.f. per hour
Wall backing		50 b.f. per hour	Outside studs	2x4	40 b.f. per hour
Grounds		85 lin. ft. per hour		2x6	50 b.f. per hour
Knee wall plates	2x4	40 b.f. per hour	Headers for wall openings	2x4	40 b.f. per hour
	2x6	40 b.f. per hour		2x6	50 b.f. per hour
Knee wall studs	2x4	40 b.f. per hour	Gable-end studs		50 b.f. per hour
	2x6	50 b.f. per hour	Fire-stopping		50 b.f. per hour
			Corner braces		50 b.f. per hour

1. What is the purpose of the exterior side wall in a structure?

2. What are the requirements for wall framing lumber?

3. Which of the two general types of wall framing is used most often in the United States?

4. With the platform method, the floor framing is complete before wall framing begins. Using this as a clue, what is the basic difference between platform framing and balloon framing?

5. List the names of several parts used in wall framing.

6. What is meant by a rough opening?

7. The width of a rough opening is measured between what two wall members.?

8. What is the purpose of the top plate?

9. When laying out stud locations, why is it important for the carpenter to begin from the same side on the back and front of the house.

10. What is a story pole?

11. What is the purpose of a header?

12. Which method of wall assembly would you prefer and why?

13. Describe how the carpenter can determine when the exterior wall is straight.

14. What is the difference between a bearing and a nonbearing wall?

15. List several examples of special framing.

16. Describe briefly the difference between the two types of cabinet soffits.

17. With the platform method, floor framing is complete before wall framing begins. Would you think that platform framing would simplify the framing of multilevel structures?

ACTIVITIES

1. Social Studies. Wall framing methods in colonial America were very different from those employed today. Research colonial wall framing methods. Briefly describe them. Note how wall framing then differs from the procedures used today. You might also consider the reasons why wall framing is much more complex today.

2. Math. Suppose that a two-foot level is accurate enough to measure with $1/16''$ of true level in the two-foot span. In trying to make an 8' wall plumb (vertical), how much might the wall vary from true plumb? (Hint: Use proportions and similar triangles.)

3. Math. As shown in Fig. 30-33, the measurement diagonals is used to check for squareness. With a friend, use a long tape measure to measure the diagonals of at least four rectangles to see if they are square. You might, for example, measure the floor of a room or the wall of a room.

THE SCHOOL-TO-WORK CONNECTION

There are several methods of estimating construction costs. One method is called a "materials take-off." Working from building plans, the estimator lists all the systems in a house. He or she then determines how many parts are in each system. For example, a wall system that is 24' long will contain a certain number of studs, plates, sheets of plywood, electrical boxes, sheets of drywall, etc. After doing a materials take-off for an entire house, the estimator will know exactly how many studs, electrical boxes, and sheets of plywood will be required.

1. Estimators are usually employed at larger construction companies. Use your phone book to locate a residential construction company you think might employ an estimator. Call the company and get the name of its president or its owner. Then write a letter to this person. Briefly describe the program you are in. Ask if a company estimator might be available to speak to your class about estimating techniques the company uses on residential construction projects.

31

Structural Wall Sheathing

Exterior coverings over wall framing commonly consist of a sheathing material to which is added finish siding, brick, stone, or other exterior wall material. The inner layer of the outside wall covering on a frame structure is called the *sheathing*. The outer layer is called the *siding*. Siding, because it is not a structural element, is considered a part of the exterior finish. The sheathing, because it strengthens and braces the wall framing, is considered a structural element. It is therefore a part of the framing. Sheathing forms a flat base upon which the siding is applied and adds strength to the house. If the type of sheathing used does not provide stiffness and rigidity, diagonal corner bracing should be used. Insulating sheathings fall into this category. Because they are not strictly structural products, they will not be discussed thoroughly in this unit. For more detailed information regarding insulating sheathing, see Unit 46.

TYPES OF SHEATHING

The most common structural sheathings used in residential construction are panel sheathing and solid wood sheathing. In addition, gypsum sheathing has been used in some areas of the country.

Panel Products

Plywood. Plywood wall sheathing covers large areas fast and adds great strength and rigidity to the structure of the house. Fig. 31-1.

31-1. *Plywood sheathing is the most common structural sheathing in residential construction.*

A plywood-sheathed wall is twice as strong and rigid as a wall sheathed with diagonal boards. Therefore let-in corner bracing is not needed with plywood wall sheathing. Plywood also holds nails well and makes a solid nailing base for the finished siding. Plywood sheathing comes in sheets 4' wide and 8' or more long and is square-edged. It may be applied either vertically or horizontally. Fig. 31-2. Plywood siding is also used as exterior coverings without sheathing, but grades, thicknesses, and types vary from normal sheathing requirements. This phase of wall construction will be discussed in Unit 45, "Exterior Wall Coverings."

Another panel product that is used for structural sheathing is oriented-strand board (OSB). Though it is a considerably different type of panel in terms of manufacture, it is generally used as a direct replacement for plywood

sheathing. Nailing and installation details for OSB sheathing are similar to those for plywood. Fig. 31-3.

Wood. Wood sheathing consists usually of 1" × 6" or 1" × 8" boards, but thicker and/or wider stock is sometimes used. Boards may be square-edged for ordinary edge-butt joining, or they may be shiplapped or dressed-and-matched. Fig. 31-4. *Dressed-and-matched* is simply a term which is used instead of *tongue-and-groove* with reference to sheathing, siding, or flooring.

Gypsum. Gypsum sheathing consists of a treated gypsum filler faced on both sides with lightweight paper. Gypsum sheathing comes in 2' × 8' sheets which are applied horizontally. Sheets are usually dressed-and-matched, with V-shaped grooves and tongues. This makes application easier and adds a small amount of tie between sheets.

31-3. *Oriented-strand board is often used instead of plywood for wall sheathing.*

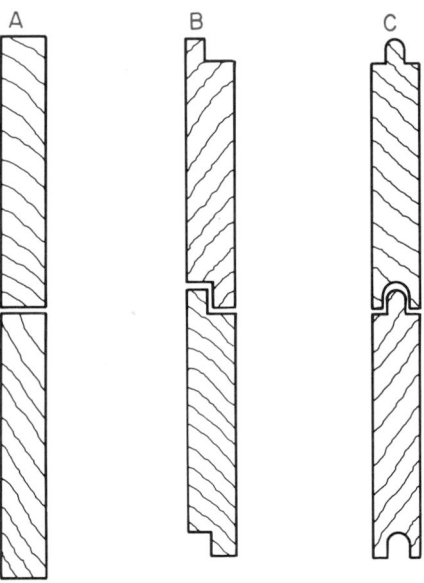

31-4. *Types of edges on wood sheathing: A. Square. B. Shiplap. C. Dressed and matched.*

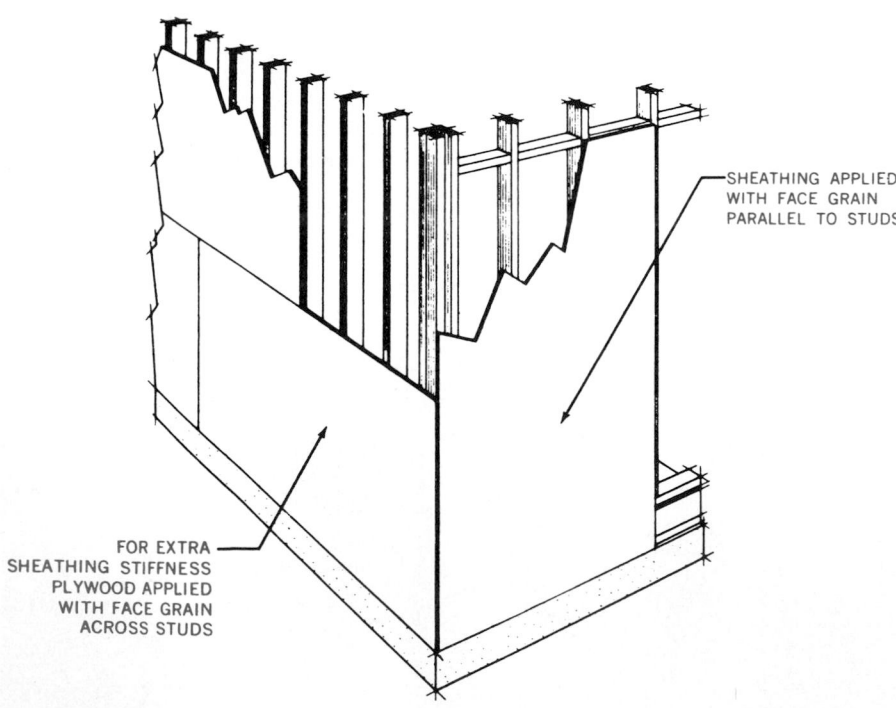

SHEATHING APPLIED WITH FACE GRAIN PARALLEL TO STUDS

FOR EXTRA SHEATHING STIFFNESS PLYWOOD APPLIED WITH FACE GRAIN ACROSS STUDS

31-2. *Plywood sheathing may be applied either horizontally or vertically. When applied horizontally, additional blocking should be included at the horizontal joint between the studs as a base for nailing.*

APPLICATION OF SHEATHING

Sheathing may be applied at any one of several stages during construction:

➤ When the wall is lying on the subfloor, completely framed and squared. The advantage in applying the sheathing at this time is that it can be nailed in place while the wall sections are lying flat, thus

31-5. *Short walls are often framed and sheathed "on the deck." They are then tipped into position.*

eliminating ladders or scaffolding. The disadvantage is the added weight that must be lifted when erecting the walls. Fig. 31-5.

➤ When the wall frames have been erected, plumbed, and braced.

➤ When the ceiling joists have been installed and the wall frames plumbed and braced.

Most carpenters apply the sheathing as soon as possible because it adds strength and rigidity to the structure. Walls that have been covered with sheathing provide a more solid structure for the ceiling and roof members.

Wood

Wood sheathing may be applied either horizontally or diagonally. Fig. 31-6. Horizontal sheathing is more often used because it is easy to apply and there is less lumber waste than with diagonal sheathing. However, horizontal sheathing requires diagonal corner bracing in the wall framework. Diagonal sheathing is applied at a 45-degree angle. This method of sheathing adds greatly to the rigidity of the wall and eliminates the need for corner bracing. There is more lumber waste than with horizontal sheathing because of

angle cuts. As stated, the application is somewhat more difficult. The building specifications will state whether horizontal or diagonal application is required.

With either method of application, 6" or 8" boards should be nailed with two 8d nails at each stud crossing. Wider boards should be nailed with three 8d nails. Unless boards are end-matched (shaped on the ends for tongue-and-groove joining), end joints must lie on the centers of studs. End joints must be broken, meaning that no two end joints may lie next to each other on the same stud. Fig. 31-7. If end-matched boards are used, end joints

may lie in the spaces between studs. However, end joints in adjacent courses (each strip of sheathing is called a course) must not lie in the same stud space.

Before nailing, each board should be driven tightly against the board already in place. Boards at openings should be laid or cut to bring the boards exactly flush with trimmers, headers, or subsills. Sheathing should normally be carried down over the outside floor framing members. This provides an excellent tie between wall and floor framing. Fig. 31-8.

Gypsum

Gypsum sheathing is nailed with 1¾" or 2" galvanized roofing nails. When the exterior finish to be used is one in which siding nails carry through into the studs, the roofing nails for the sheathing may be spaced either 7" on center or 4 nails for every 2' of height. Otherwise, nails should be spaced

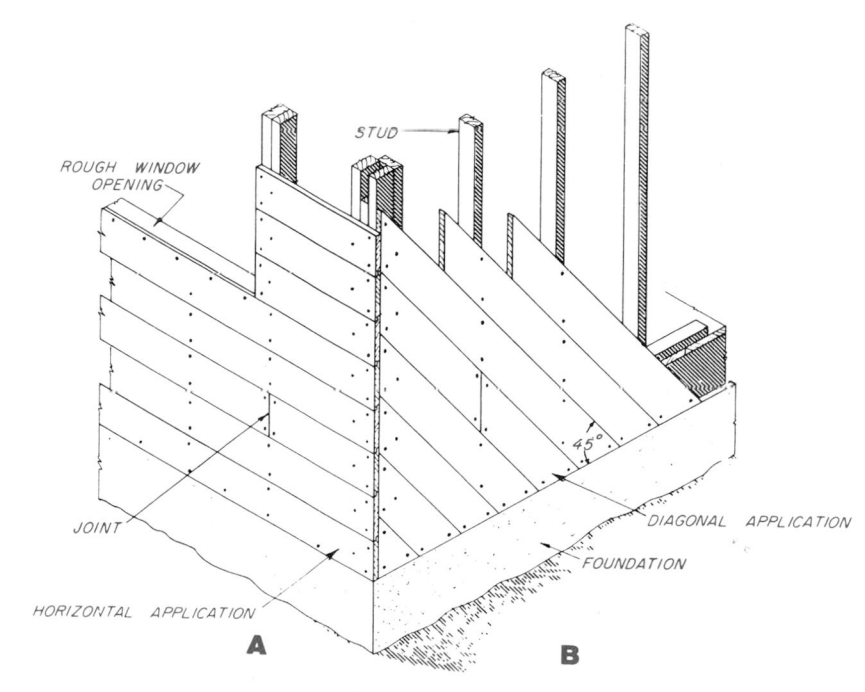

31-6. *Wall sheathing application: A. Horizontal. B. Diagonal.*

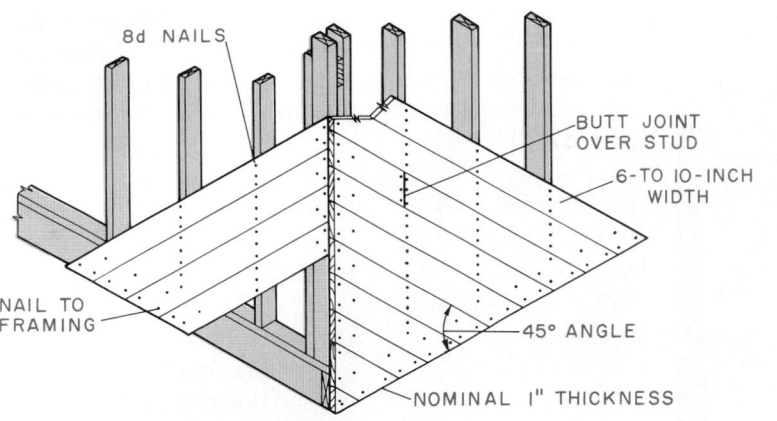

31-7. *Diagonal wall sheathing is applied at a 45° angle. It is nailed with 8d nails to the framing. Note that the pieces are joined at the center of the stud.*

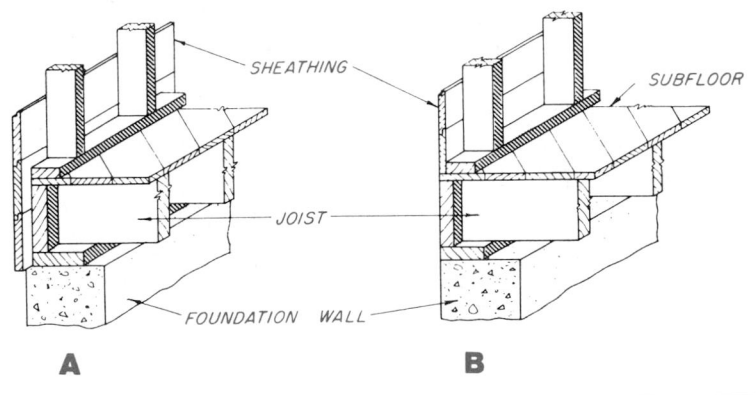

31-8. *Location of sheathing: A. Sheathing may be set on the foundation wall. B. Sheathing may be set on the subfloor.*

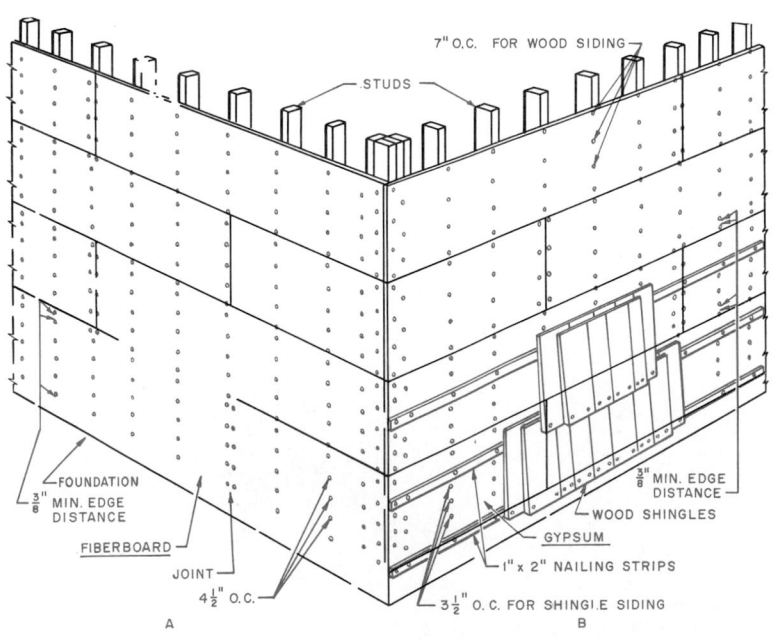

31-9. *Horizontal application of 2' x 2' gypsum sheathing.*

3½" on center (7 nails in 2' height). Fig. 31-9.

Plywood

Plywood used for sheathing is usually in 4' × 8' sheets and should be a minimum of 5/16" thick for studs spaced 16". Fig. 31-10. Six-penny nails should be used, spaced not more than 6" apart on edge members and 12" on intermediate members. Table 31-A and 31-B.

Plywood is usually applied vertically, using perimeter nailing with no additional blocking. Fig. 31-11. When the sheathing is started at the foundation wall rather than the subfloor, use a 2" × 4" nailing strip between the studs for backing. Fig. 31-12.

Plywood can also be applied horizontally. Blocking is desirable at the horizontal joint between studs as a base for nailing.

When finish siding requires nailing between studs (as with wood shingles), the plywood should be 3/8" thick. If 5/16" plywood is used for sheathing, the wood shingles must either be nailed to stripping or attached with barbed nails.

31-10. *Stapling plywood sheathing.*

31-11. Installing plywood sheathing vertically.

BUILDING PAPER

Building paper is applied between the sheathing and the siding. It prevents the passage of air through the walls, but it is of relatively little value as a heat insulator because of its thinness. Building paper should not be confused with house wraps.

Building paper should be used behind exterior stucco finish and also over wood sheathing. It should be provided whether or not the sheathing is tongued and grooved.

In general, the soft, porous, relatively thick machine-finished building papers should be avoided in favor of asphalt-saturated paper or paraffined paper. These papers usually have sufficient water and air tightness and can usually stand handling in all kinds of weather. Building paper should be

Table 31-A. *Plywood Wall Sheathing Application Details.*
Wall sheathing (1)

Panel Identification Index	Minimum Thickness (in.)	Maximum Stud Exterior Covering Nailed to:		Nail Size (2)	Nail Spacing (inches)	
		Stud	Sheathing		Panel Edges (when over framing)	Intermediate (each stud)
12/0, 16/0, 20/0	$^5/_{16}$	16	16(3)	6d	6	12
16/0, 20/0, 24/0	$^3/_8$	24	16, 24(3)	6d	6	12
24/0, 32/16	$^1/_2$	24	24	6d	6	12

Notes: (1) When plywood sheathing is used, building paper and diagonal wall bracing can be omitted.
(2) Common smooth, annular, spiral thread, galvanized box or T-nails of the same diameter as common nails (0.113" dia. for 6d) may be used. Staples also permitted at reduced spacing.
(3) When sidings such as shingles are nailed only to the plywood sheathing, apply plywood with face grain across studs.

Look for these APA grade-trademarks on wall sheathing.

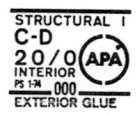

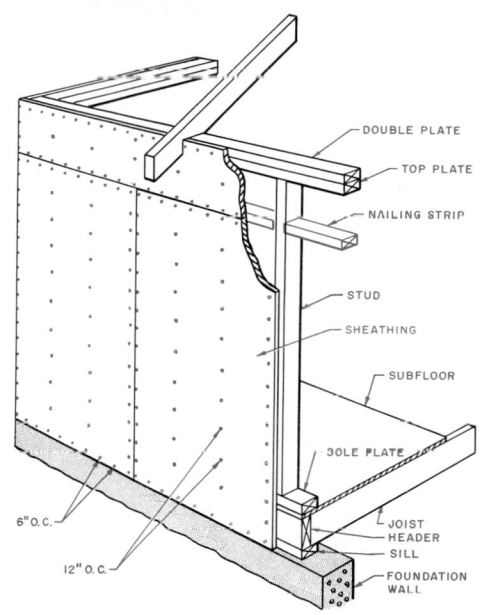

31-12. *Plywood sheathing started at the foundation wall will require a nailing strip along the top joint.*

Table 31-B. *Stapling Schedule.*
Recommended minimum stapling schedule for plywood. All values are for 16-gauge galvanized wire staples having a minimum crown width of $^3/_8$".

Plywood wall sheathing / Without diagonal bracing

Plywood Thickness	Staple Leg Length	Spacing Around Entire Perimeter of Sheet	Spacing at Intermediate Members
$^5/_{16}$"	1 $^1/_4$"	4"	8"
$^3/_8$"	1 $^3/_8$"	4"	8"
$^1/_2$"	1 $^1/_2$"	4"	8"

water-resistant but not vapor-resistant. Vapor-resistant paper might trap moisture between the walls.

The paper should be applied smoothly, and the joints should be lapped and nailed without bulges or cracks through which the air could find its way. Care should be taken around window and door openings to close all cracks.

Building paper should be applied horizontally, starting at the bottom of the wall. Succeeding layers should overlap about 4" and should cover strips previously applied around openings. Strips about 6" wide should be installed behind all exterior trim of exterior openings.

HOUSE WRAPS

House wraps are similar to standard building papers. They reduce air infiltration and protect the sheathing from any moisture that might get behind the siding. However, instead of being made from paper, house wraps are typically made from spun-bonded high-density polyethylene fibers. These fibers interlock in such a way that they allow water vapor to pass through. However, they stop the passage of liquid water. This is called "vapor permeability." The result is that water vapor produced inside the building will not be trapped in the wall cavities. Fig. 31-13.

A house wrap has several advantages over standard building papers. Because of its light weight, it can be installed using rolls 9' wide. This speeds installation considerably. Also, a house wrap is difficult to rip, so it is less likely to be damaged during installation. House wraps are stapled over the wall sheathing before windows and doors are installed.

31-13. *A house wrap is applied between the sheathing and the siding. It reduces air infiltration.*

ESTIMATING

Materials

To determine the amount of wall sheathing required for a structure, first figure the exterior wall area. On a building with walls 8' high and front and rear walls 40' long, the front wall area is 320 sq. ft. (8 × 40). The front and rear walls thus have a total area of 640 sq. ft. (2 × 320). If the end walls are 8' high and 20' long, they contain 160 sq. ft. each (8 × 20), for a total of 320 sq. ft. (2 × 160). The entire structure contains 960 sq. ft. of exterior wall area (320 + 640).

For a house with a hip roof this would be the exterior wall area. For a house with a gable roof, the gable ends have to be figured and added to this amount. To find the area of one gable, multiply the height of the gable by one-half the width of the bottom. Multiply this area by the number of gables to determine the total gable area.

A 4' × 8' sheet of plywood contains 32 sq. ft. The number of plywood sheets required to sheathe the house is 30:

$$\frac{960 \text{ (total exterior wall area)}}{32 \text{ (sq. ft. in 1 plywood sheet)}} = 30 \text{ sheets}$$

The amount of fiberboard or gypsum sheathing is estimated in the same way.

Refer to Table 31-C if lumber is used for sheathing. For example, let us say that 1 × 6, S4S material is to be used and applied horizontally. Read down the left column headed "Type" to S4S and across from size 1 × 6. The column "Board Feet per

Table 31-C. *Sheathing and Subflooring (Horizontal Application). Estimating lumber sheathing and nails for horizontal applications.*

Type	Size	Bd. Ft. per Square Feet of Area	Lbs. Nails Per 1000 Bd. Ft			
			Spacing of Framing Members			
			12"	16"	20"	24"
T & G	1 x 4	1.32	66	52	44	36
	1 x 6	1.23	43	33	28	23
	1 x 8	1.19	32	24	21	17
	1 x 10	1.17	37	29	24	20
Shiplap	1 x 4	1.38	69	55	46	38
	1 x 6	1.26	44	34	29	24
	1 x 8	1.21	32	25	21	17
	1 x 10	1.18	37	29	25	20
S4S	1 x 4	1.19	60	47	40	33
	1 x 6	1.15	40	31	26	22
	1 x 8	1.15	30	23	20	17
	1 x 10	1.14	36	28	24	19

Square Foot of Area" indicates a factor of 1.15. Multiply this factor by the exterior wall area, which in this example is 960 sq. ft. A total of 1,104 board feet of S4S, 1 × 6 material is needed to sheathe the structure (960 × 1.15).

The number of nails required for applying this sheathing can also be determined from Table 31-C. If the wall studs are spaced on 16" centers, 31 pounds of nails are required for each thousand board feet of material. For our example, 34 pounds of nails would be required.

$$\frac{1,104 \text{ (bd. ft. of sheathing)}}{1,000} = 1.104 \text{ (amount of sheathing expressed in thousands of bd. ft.)}$$

1.104 x 31 (lbs. of nails per 1,000 bd. ft.) = 34.2 lbs.

The cost of the material can be figured by multiplying the unit cost times the amount needed.

Labor

Tables 31-D and 31-E can be used as guides in estimating labor time for sheathing application.

Table 31-D. *Wood Sheathing (Diagonal Application). Estimating labor time for wood sheathing.*

Size	Estimated Labor Performance
1" x 6"	65 bd. ft. per hour
1" x 8"	70 bd. ft. per hour
1" x 10"	75 bd. ft. per hour

Table 31-E. *Other Types of Sheathing. Estimating labor time for gypsum and plywood sheathing.*

Type of Sheathing	Size	Estimated Labor Time per 100 sq. ft.
Gypsum board	48" x 96"	2.2 hours
Plywood panels	48" x 96"	1.8 hours

QUESTIONS

1. Why is wall sheathing considered a structural element and a part of the framing?

2. List the two most common types of sheathing.

3. Why isn't let-in corner bracing required when plywood wall sheathing is used?

4. Wall sheathing is usually applied at one of three stages of construction. At which stage would you apply wall sheathing? List reasons.

5. Why is building paper applied between sheathing and siding?

6. Which of the various kinds of building papers available is recommended for application between the sheathing and the siding? Why?

ACTIVITIES

1. Math. In your job working for a contractor, you have been asked to estimate sheathing materials and time for exterior sheathing for a 26' by 42' one-story house with 8' walls and studs 16" O.C. Estimate the following:

a. The number of sheets of 4' by 8' plywood required.

b. The time required to apply the plywood sheets.

c. The number of board feet of S4S 1 × 6 stock required.

d. The time required to apply the S4S 1 × 6 sheathing.

e. The difference in cost using local costs of materials and hourly rates.

2. Social Studies. This unit discusses various types of sheathings for houses (wood, plywood, fiberboard, and gypsum.) As a cultural comparison describe the building materials that go into home construction in China. What similarities and differences could you find?

3. Science. Figure 31-6 shows horizontal and diagonal wood sheathing applications. Which application method would you utilize? Support your answer in scientific terms.

32

Ceiling Framing

When the wall framing has been completed, it is ready to be tied together with the roof framing. There are two basic methods of roof framing for platform-frame construction: trussed roof construction and conventional roof construction.

Trusses are prefabricated assemblies placed on the building and attached as a unit. Fig. 32-1. The lower chords in the trusses form the ceiling of the room and support the ceiling finish. Since trusses are the completed roof frame, they will be discussed in a separate unit (Unit 38).

In conventional roof construction, the *ceiling joists* and *rafters* are laid out, cut, and fastened one piece at a time to the building. Fig. 32-2. *Ceiling joists* are the parallel beams which support ceiling loads. They are supported in turn by larger beams, girders, or bearing walls. *Rafters* are the inclined members of a roof framework. They support the roof loads. Conventional roof framing requires ceiling joists which serve as a tie between the exterior walls and the interior partitions. The ceiling joists also serve as floor joists for an attic or a second story. Fig. 32-3.

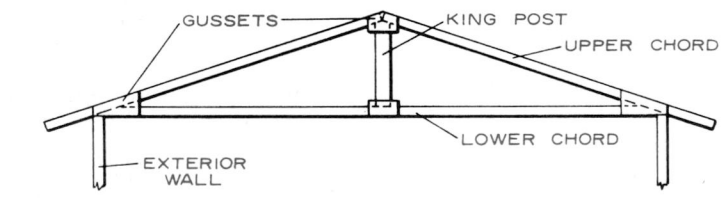

32-1. *Trussed rafter assembly.*

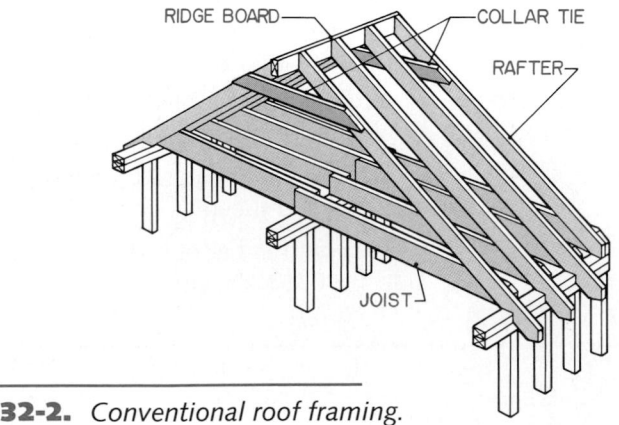

32-2. *Conventional roof framing.*

32-3. *Ceiling framing often serves as support for a second floor. This house in Texas shows various types of ceiling framing.*

CEILING JOISTS

Size

The size of the ceiling joists is determined by the distance they must span and the load they must carry. The species and grade of wood are also factors to be considered. The correct size for the joists will be found on the building plans as recommended by the building code. As a general reference, Table 32-A shows the joist sizes and the spacing and span limitations. Be sure to confirm these with the local building code.

Table 32-A. *Allowable Spans for Ceiling Joists Using Nonstress-Graded Lumber.*

Size of Ceiling Joists (Inches)	Spacing of Ceiling Joists (Inches)	Maximum Allowable Span (Feet and Inches)			
		Group I	Group II	Group III	Group IV
2 x 4	12	11-6	11-0	9-6	5-6
	16	10-6	10-0	8-6	5-0
2 x 6	12	18-0	16-6	15-6	12-6
	16	16-0	15-0	14-6	11-0
2 x 8	12	24-0	22-6	21-0	19-0
	16	21-6	20-6	19-0	16-6

Layout

Ceiling joists are usually located across the width of the building and parallel to the rafters. The ends of the joists which rest on the exterior wall plates next to the rafters will usually project above the top edge of the rafter. These ends must be cut off on a slope that is equal to the roof pitch. Fig. 32-4.

The spacing of the joists is usually 16" or 24" on center, depending on the building specifications. Installation is begun at one end of the building and continued across the structure. Extra joists, if needed, are placed without altering the spacing of the prime joists. The first joist is located at the inside edge of the plate on an end wall. This provides edge nailing for the ceiling finish. Fig. 32-5. The second joist is usually located over the stud in the side wall. The distance between the first two joists will thus be less than 16" or 24", depending on the center spacing used. Fig. 32-6. Each succeeding joist is spaced 16" or 24" on center.

If the layout of the ceiling joists places a joist over a stud and the

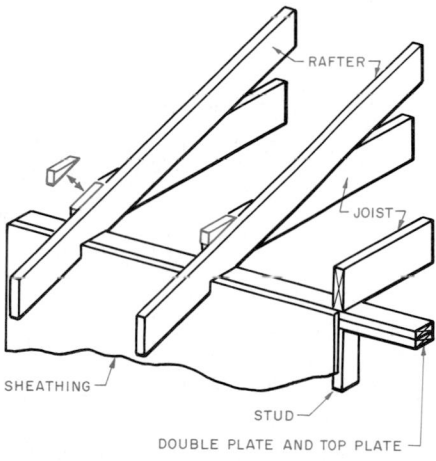

32-4. *The ends of the ceiling joists must be cut off on a slope equal to the roof pitch. It is best to cut them off about ⅛" below the top edge of the rafter.*

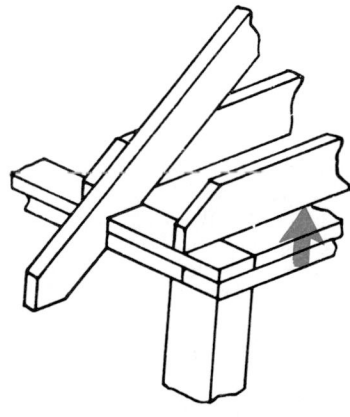

32-5. *The first ceiling joist is set on the inside edge of the end wall to permit nailing of the material for the ceiling surface.*

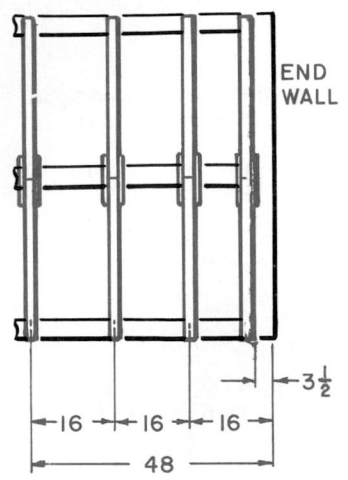

32-6. *The distance between the first two joists is less than 16". The joists shown here are butted end to end on the bearing wall. The butt joint must be reinforced.*

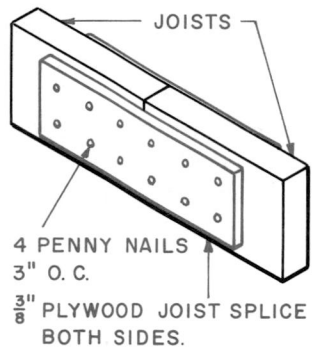

JOISTS

4 PENNY NAILS 3" O. C.

⅜" PLYWOOD JOIST SPLICE BOTH SIDES.

32-7a. *Ceiling joists butted end to end must be spliced together for strength. When lumber is used instead of plywood for a splice, it must be ¾" thick and at least 24" long.*

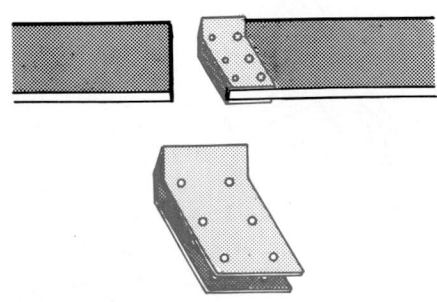

32-7b. *A metal connector may be used to reinforce the butt end joint of the ceiling joists.*

studs for the two sidewalls have been laid out from the same end of the building, the ends of the joists will butt against each other over the bearing wall. Fig. 32-6. The total length of the two joists will equal the width of the building and the ends that butt will have to be squared and cut off to length. Since each of the joist ends will be resting on just half of the partition wall plate, a plywood joist splice should be nailed securely to both sides of the joists. Fig. 32-7a. Metal connectors are also available for this purpose. Fig. 32-7b.

An alternate method of joist layout is to offset the joists 1½" on the two outside walls so that they lap each other when they join over the bearing partition. Fig. 32-8. This lap is face-nailed with three 16d nails, and the joists are toenailed to the bearing partition wall plate with two 10d nails. Nonbearing partitions which run parallel to the ceiling joists are nailed to blocks installed between the joists. Fig. 32-9.

Installation

Sight down the edge of the joist to determine the crown and place the crown, or camber, up. When attaching the ceiling joist to the exterior wall plate, keep the end of the joist even with the outside edge of the plate. Fasten this end of the joist first. Toenail three 10d nails through the joist into the plate or use a metal bracket and the special nails furnished with the bracket. Fig. 32-10. Make sure the walls are straight along the top edge and plumb. Fasten the joists together where they join and then to any other double plates they may cross over. This will tie the building together at the top and make it ready for the roof framing or the sheathing.

Special Framing. When framing a low-pitched hip roof, the

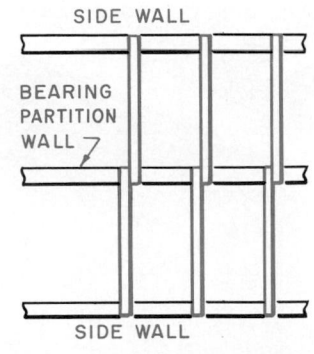

SIDE WALL

BEARING PARTITION WALL

SIDE WALL

32-8. *Ceiling joists lapped on the bearing wall.*

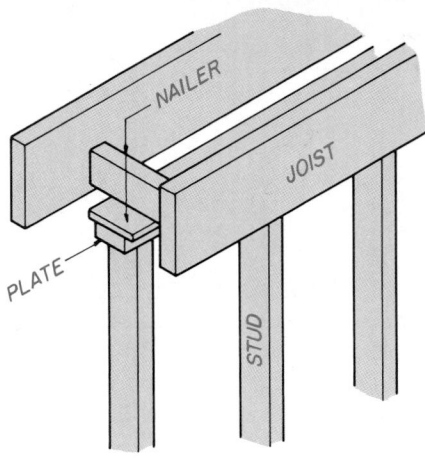

NAILER

JOIST

PLATE

STUD

32-9. *A nonbearing partition wall is fastened to a block which has been nailed between the joists. Notice the backing which has been attached to the top of the partition for nailing the ceiling material.*

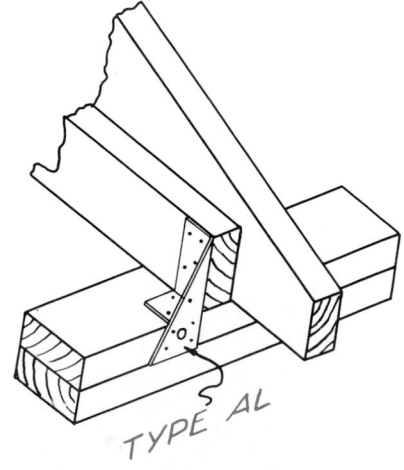

TYPE AL

32-10. *A metal connector used to fasten the ceiling joist to the double plate.*

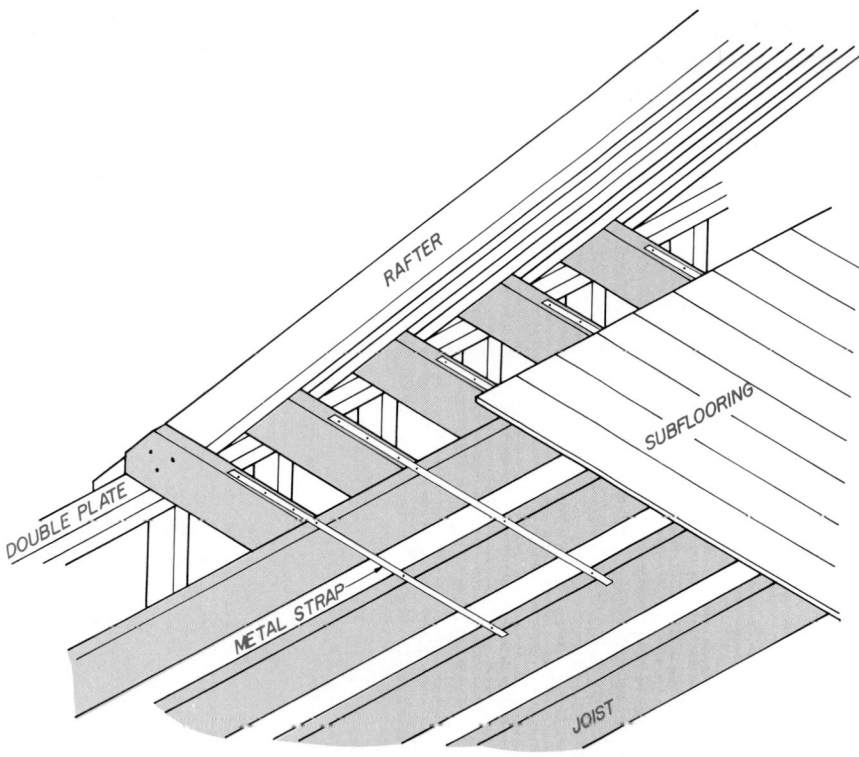

32-11a. *Stub joists are securely anchored to the regular joists with metal straps.*

first ceiling joist will interfere with the bottom edge of the rafters. Stub joists installed at right angles to the regular joists will correct this situation. Fig. 32-11. Space the stub 16" on center for attaching the finished ceiling. Locate them so that the rafters, when installed, may be nailed directly to the side of the stubs.

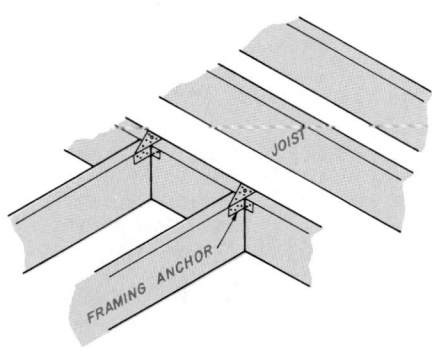

32-11b. *A metal framing anchor may be used in place of the metal straps to secure the stub joists to the regular joist.*

Openings in the ceiling that are larger than the spacing between the joists are often necessary. They may be needed for a chimney or for access to the attic area. An enlarged opening will require the cutting of one or more joists. Such joists will need to be supported and framed as described earlier in the section "Framing Floor Openings" in Unit 29.

Framing For Flush Ceiling Area. A living-dining-kitchen group or kitchen-dining-family room group is often designed as one open area with a flush ceiling throughout. When trusses are used, there is no problem because they span from one exterior wall to the other. However, if ceiling joists and rafters are used, some type of beam is needed to support the interior ends of the ceiling joists.

This support can be provided by a flush beam. A flush beam is usually built up from the same stock used to frame the rest of the ceiling. It can also be made of solid timber or glue-laminated lumber. Joists are fastened to the beam with joist hangers. Fig. 32-12. These hangers are nailed to the beam with 8d nails and to the joist with nails furnished with the hangers. Hangers are perhaps most easily fastened by nailing them to the end of the joist before the joist is raised into place.

On a long span with a continuous joist, the joists sometimes need additional support. In this case, a ceiling joist strongback is constructed. Fig. 32-13. The joists should be aligned and properly spaced where they pass under the strongback before they are blocked and nailed.

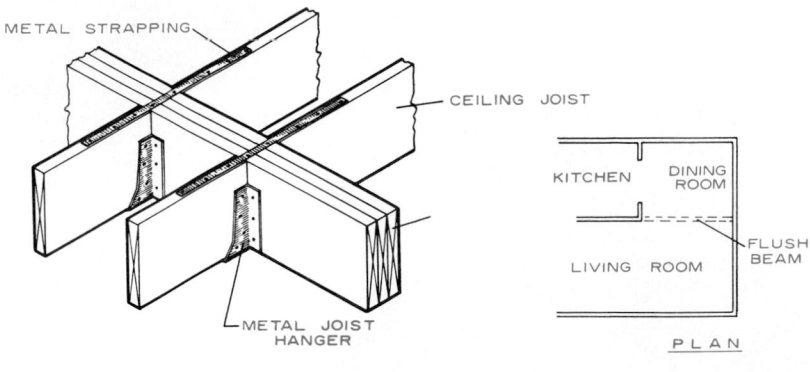

32-12. *Ceiling joists are fastened to a flush beam with joist hangers.*

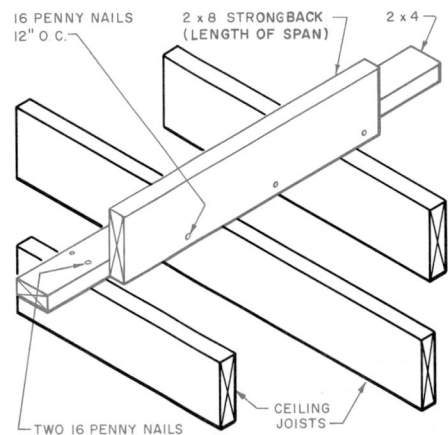

32-13. *A strongback is used to give long joists additional support.*

ESTIMATING

Determining the Number of Joists

One way to determine the number of joists necessary for a building is to divide the length of the floor (in feet) by the joist spacing (in feet), and add one for the end joist. Then multiply by two.

For joists on 16" centers, take three-fourths of the length of the building, add one, and multiply the total by two. For example, if a building is 40' long, 31 joists will be required to span from the front exterior wall to the bearing partition wall (¾ × 40 = 30; 30 + 1 = 31). Another 31 joists will be needed to span from the partition to the rear exterior wall. The total number of joists will be 62 (31 × 2).

If the building is 20' wide and has a bearing partition wall at the center, each joist should be 10' long. Thus, for a building 20' × 40', 62 ten-foot joists will be required. Add to this amount extra joists for openings for which trimmer joists are specified.

Determining the Material Cost

An accurate estimate of the cost can be figured by multiplying the number of joists required by the cost per joist. Sometimes the builder will not make up a complete bill of materials, but will want a rough cost estimate. Without knowing the exact number of pieces needed, this estimate can be made by first finding the area of the ceiling. The area of the ceiling is the length of the building times the width of the building for each level. For example, a one-story building 20' wide and 40' long has a ceiling area of 20 × 40, or 800 square feet.

The number of board feet required for the joists of a building can be found in Table 32-B. Use the building in the example, which contains 800 sq. ft. of ceiling area. According to the table, if the joists are 2" × 6" and 16" on center, there are 88 board feet of lumber for each 100 sq. ft. of ceiling surface area. Divide the total ceiling area by 100 and multiply by the factor in the table:

$$\frac{800 \text{ (ceiling area)}}{100} = 8 \text{ (ceiling area expressed in hundreds)}$$

8 × 88 (bd. ft. per 100 sq. ft. of surface) = 704 bd. ft.

Table 32-B also has information for determining the number of nails necessary. For the ceiling in the example, 13 pounds of nails are needed for each 1,000 board feet. Since the ceiling in the example has 704 board feet, the

Table 32-B. *Material and Labor Requirements for Ceiling Joists.*

Ceiling Joist	Material				Nails	Labor
	Board Feet Required For 100 Sq. Ft. of Surface Area				Per 1000 Bd. Ft. Board Feet per Hr.	
Size of Joist	12"O.C.	16" O.C.	20" O.C.	24" O.C.	Pounds	Board Ft.
2 x 4	78	59	48	42	19	60
2 x 6	115	88	72	63	13	65
2 x 8	153	117	96	84	9	65
2 x 10	194	147	121	104	7	70
2 x 12	230	176	144	126	6	70

ceiling will require about nine pounds of nails:

$$\frac{704 \text{ (bd. ft. of material)}}{1,000} = 0.704 \text{ (material expressed in thousands)}$$

0.704 x 13 (lbs. of nails per 1,000 bd. ft.) = 9.152, or 9 lbs. of nails.

Determining the Labor Cost

The labor cost for framing a ceiling can be found by using the information in the column headed "Labor" in Table 32-B. To use this table, it is necessary to know how many board feet of joist material are required for a ceiling. This can be determined as described earlier in "Determining Material Cost." A more accurate method is to find the number of board feet in one joist and then multiply by the total number of joists in the building.

Use the same example described earlier: a single-story building 20' wide × 40' long. Table 32-C can be used to determine the board feet

Table 32-C. *Board Feet Content.*

Size of Timber in Inches	Length Of Piece In Feet							
	10	12	14	16	18	20	22	24
1 x 2	1⅔	2	2⅓	2⅔	3	3⅓	3⅔	4
1 x 3	2½	3	3½	4	4½	5	5½	6
1 x 4	3⅓	4	4⅔	5⅓	6	6⅔	7⅓	8
1 x 5	4⅙	5	5⅚	6⅔	7½	8⅓	9⅙	10
1 x 6	5	6	7	8	9	10	11	12
1 x 8	6⅔	8	9⅓	10⅔	12	13⅓	14⅔	16
1 x 10	8⅓	10	11⅔	13⅓	15	16⅔	18⅓	20
1 x 12	10	12	14	16	18	20	22	24
1 x 14	11⅔	14	16⅓	18⅔	21	23⅓	25⅔	28
1 x 16	13⅓	16	18⅔	21⅓	24	26⅔	29⅓	32
1 x 20	16⅔	20	23⅓	26⅔	30	33⅓	36⅔	40
1¼ x 4	4⅙	5	5⅚	6⅔	7½	8⅓	9⅙	10
1¼ x 6	6¼	7½	8¾	10	11¼	12½	13¾	15
1¼ x 8	8⅓	10	11⅔	13⅓	15	16⅔	18⅓	20
1¼ x 10	10⅓	12½	14½	16⅔	18⅔	20⅚	22⅚	25
1¼ x 12	12½	15	17½	20	22½	25	27½	30
1½ x 4	5	6	7	8	9	10	11	12
1½ x 6	7½	9	10½	12	13½	15	16½	18
1½ x 8	10	12	14	16	18	20	22	24
1½ x 10	12½	15	17½	20	22½	25	27½	30
1½ x 12	15	18	21	24	27	30	33	36
2 x 4	6⅔	8	9⅓	10⅔	12	13⅓	14⅔	16
2 x 6	10	12	14	16	18	20	22	24
2 x 8	13⅓	16	18⅔	21⅓	24	26⅔	29⅓	32
2 x 10	16⅔	20	23⅓	26⅔	30	33⅓	36⅔	40
2 x 12	20	24	28	32	36	40	44	48
2 x 14	23⅓	28	32⅔	37⅓	42	46⅔	51⅓	56
2 x 16	26⅔	32	37½	42⅔	48	53⅓	58⅔	64
2½ x 12	25	30	35	40	45	50	55	60
2½ x 14	29⅙	35	40⅚	46⅔	52½	58⅓	64⅙	70
2½ x 16	33⅓	40	46⅔	53⅓	60	66⅔	73⅓	80
3 x 6	15	18	21	24	27	30	33	36
3 x 8	20	24	28	32	36	40	44	48
3 x 10	25	30	35	40	45	50	55	60
3 x 12	30	36	42	48	54	60	66	72
3 x 14	35	42	49	56	63	70	77	84
3 x 16	40	48	56	64	72	80	88	96
4 x 4	13⅓	16	18⅔	21⅓	24	26⅔	29⅓	32
4 x 6	20	24	28	32	36	40	44	48
4 x 8	26⅔	32	17⅓	42⅔	48	53⅓	58⅔	64
4 x 10	33⅓	40	46⅔	53⅓	60	66⅔	73⅓	80
4 x 12	40	48	56	64	72	80	88	96
4 x 14	46⅓	56	65⅓	74⅔	84	93⅓	102½	112

content of a single joist. To use this table, the length of the piece must be known. The length of the joists will be found on the building plan. The building in the example is 20' wide with a bearing partition centered in the building to support the ceiling joists. The ceiling joists will be 2" × 6" × 10' long.

Find 2" × 6" in the left column of Table 32-C. Read across to the column headed "10" for a ten-foot joist. There are 10 board feet in one 2" × 6" × 10' piece of lumber. The ceiling in the example has 62 joists. If one joist contains 10 board feet, 62 joists contain a total of 620 board feet of joist material (62 × 10).

Refer to Table 32-C. The column headed "Labor" shows that a worker can frame 65 board feet of joists per hour. The number of hours required to frame the ceiling in the example is 9.5 (620 ÷ 65). Multiply this by the hourly rate to determine the labor cost.

QUESTIONS

1. What are the functions of the ceiling joists?

2. When laying out the ceiling joists, why are the first two ceiling joists less than 16" on center?

3. Describe an alternate method of joist layout over the partition plate.

4. What must be done to the building before the joists are nailed together where they join to the partition plates?

5. What is a ceiling joist strongback?

6. How many joists are needed for a building 48' long if the joists are spaced 16" o.c.?

ACTIVITIES

1. Math. As discussed in this unit, there are two basic methods of framing: trussed roof construction and conventional roof construction. Because trussed roofs are prefabricated, it could be assumed that this method might be cheaper than conventional roof

construction. Find out if this is true by consulting a builder or calling a lumber company that sells trussed roofs.

2. Math. A house has outside dimensions of 26'10" by 42'3".

a. Determine the minimum number of ceiling joists necessary if they are 16" o.c.

b. Choose the minimum size of joist acceptable using Group II stock. See Table 32-A.

THE SCHOOL-TO-WORK CONNECTION

Walls can be framed on the floor deck and tipped into position. However, the working conditions while installing a ceiling are not so convenient. Carpenters often have to "walk" the top plates to install the ceiling framing. Such a slender walkway is problem enough, but as an added hazard the plates may be unsteady. This is because the walls may not have been stiffened by sheathing when the ceiling framing is being installed. For these reasons,

successful ceiling framers have to work thoughtfully and eliminate unnecessary motions. One way in which they do this is to minimize trips up and down ladders. For example, a team of two carpenters will often work with a helper. The carpenters stay on the plates while the helper feeds material up to them.

1. The ends of ceiling joists sometimes have to be trimmed to match the slope of the rafters, as shown in Fig. 32-4. Carpenters sometimes call this

"clipping" the joists. Assume that you are assisting two carpenters to install ceiling framing. To keep up with their steady installation pace, you have to make and clip each joist before you hand it up to them. You don't have time to measure each cut. Devise a simple jig that will speed your work and allow you to mark each cut quickly without using a tape measure.

Roof Framing

The primary function of a roof is to protect the house in all types of weather with a minimum of maintenance. Roof construction should be strong in order to withstand snow and wind loads. Roofing members should be securely fastened to each other to provide continuity across the building, and they should be anchored to exterior walls. Many roofs call for a combination of framing techniques. Fig. 33-1.

A second consideration is appearance. Besides being practical, a roof should add to the attractiveness of the home. Various roof styles are used to create different architectural effects. A carpenter must understand and be able to frame these various styles. Fig. 33-2.

ROOF STYLES

The basic roof styles used for homes and small buildings are as follows:
- Flat.
- Shed.
- Gable.
- Gable with dormer.
- Gable and valley.
- Hip.
- Hip and valley.

Variations of these roofs are associated with architectural styles

33-1. *Roof trusses in place.*

of different countries or geographic regions. Some of these variations include the following. Fig. 33-3.

- ➤ Gambrel.
- ➤ Mansard.
- ➤ Dutch hip.

33-2a. *The gable roof is a common roof style in homebuilding.*

33-2b. *The hip roof presents a slope on all sides of the building.*

33-2c. *In this house, the mansard roof allows full use of the second story.*

Flat Roof

Roof joists for flat roofs are laid at a slight slope for drainage. Sheathing and roofing are applied to the top of the joists, which in this case serve as rafters. The ceiling material is applied to the underside. Fig. 33-3.

Shed Roof

Sometimes called a lean-to, this roof slopes in one direction only. The shed roof is used for contemporary homes and for additions to existing structures. When it is used as an addition, the roof may be attached to the side of the existing structure or to the existing roof. Figs. 33-3 and 33-4.

Gable Roof

The gable roof is the most common. It has two roof slopes which meet at the top, or ridge, to form a gable at each end. For variation, the gable may include dormers which add light and ventilation to second-floor rooms. Fig. 33-3.

Hip Roof

The hip roof slopes at the ends of the building as well as at the two sides. This slope to all sides makes possible an even overhang all around the building. The low appearance of this roofline and the fact that it minimizes maintenance (there is no siding above the eaves) make it a popular choice. Fig. 33-3.

Mansard Roof

The mansard is a variation of the hip roof. It has steep slopes on all four sides but these do not meet at the center as in a hip roof. Partway up on each side a second slope is developed. The second slope is almost flat and continues toward the center of the building, where it meets with the slopes from the other sides. The mansard roof style was brought to this continent by the French when they settled in Quebec. Fig. 33-3.

Gambrel Roof

The gambrel roof is a variation of the gable roof. It has steep slopes on two sides. Partway up a second slope is developed, which continues toward the center of the building. There it meets with the roof from the other side. This roof style was first used in the United States by German settlers in New York and Pennsylvania. Fig. 33-3.

Dutch Hip Roof

The Dutch hip roof is a hip roof with a small gable at each end of the ridge. Like a hip roof, it has an even overhang around the entire building. This protects the walls from rain. Like a gable roof, portions of a Dutch hip roof are formed by two roof slopes which meet at the ridge. A Dutch hip roof is common on single-story houses. Fig. 33-3.

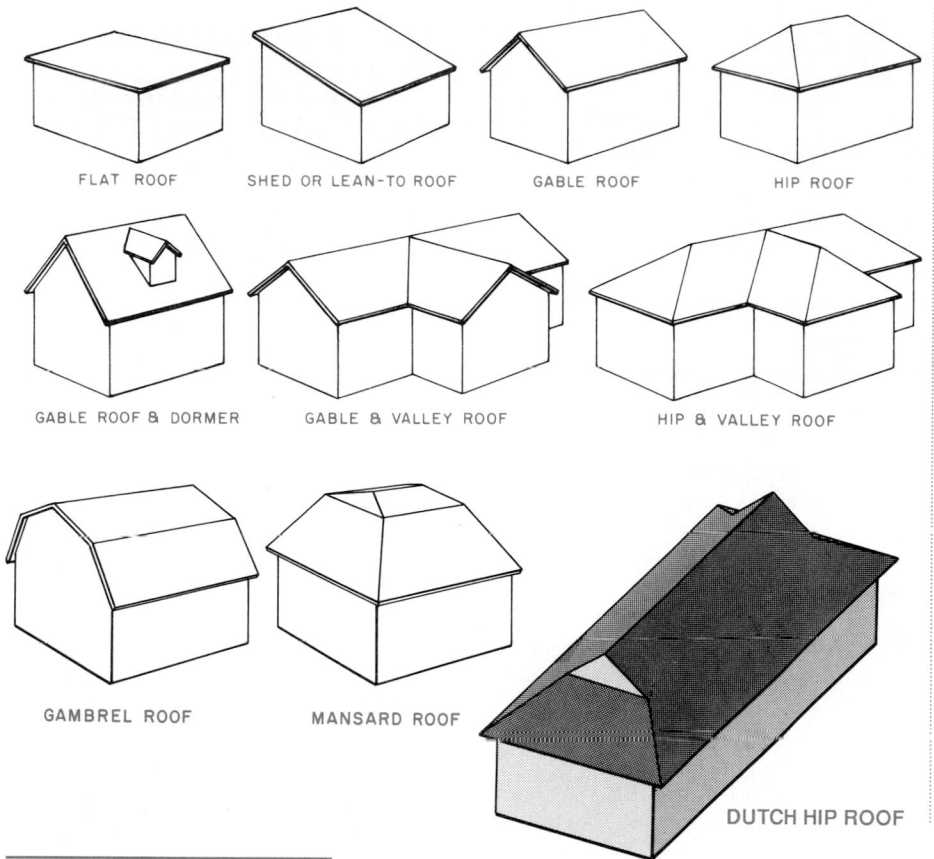

FLAT ROOF   SHED OR LEAN-TO ROOF   GABLE ROOF   HIP ROOF

GABLE ROOF & DORMER   GABLE & VALLEY ROOF   HIP & VALLEY ROOF

GAMBREL ROOF   MANSARD ROOF   DUTCH HIP ROOF

33-3. *Common roof styles.*

ROOF FRAMING TERMS

Span. The distance between the outside edge of the double plates. It is measured at right angles to the ridge board. Fig. 33-5.

Run. One-half the span distance (except when the pitch of the roof is irregular). Fig. 33-5.

Unit of run. One unit of run is equal to 1', or 12", of run. Fig. 33-6.

Measuring line. An imaginary line running lengthwise from the outside wall to the ridge. Fig. 33-5.

Rise. The vertical distance from the top of the double plate to the upper end of the measuring line. Fig. 33-5.

Unit rise. The number of inches that a roof rises for every foot of run (unit of run). Fig. 33-6.

Pitch. The angle which the roof surface makes with a horizontal

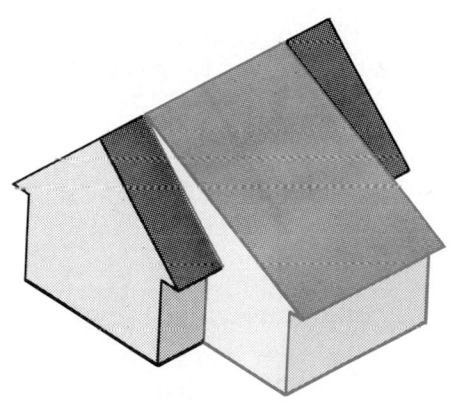

33-4. *A shed roof is an addition tied into the main roof of the existing structure.*

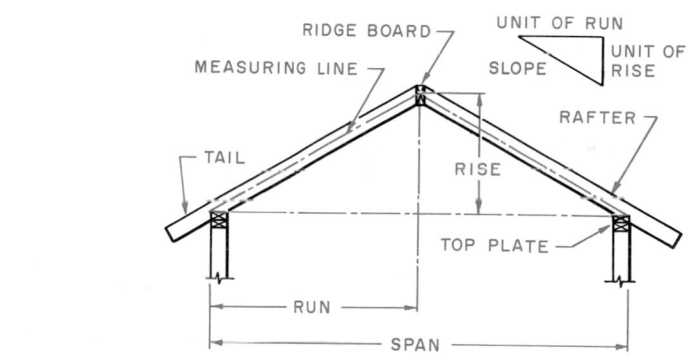

33-5. *Terms used in roof framing.*

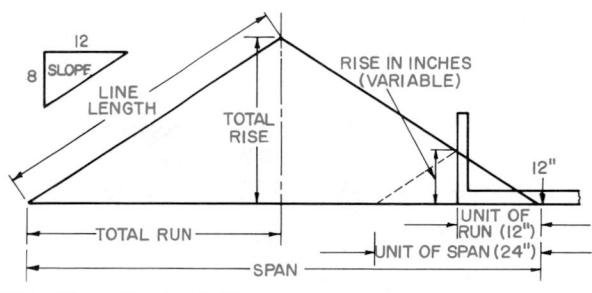

33-6. *A comparison of total and unit terms. The unit of run is always 12". Therefore the unit of span is always 24". The rise in inches is variable, depending on the pitch assigned to the roof. In the example shown here, there are 8" of rise per (foot) unit of run.*

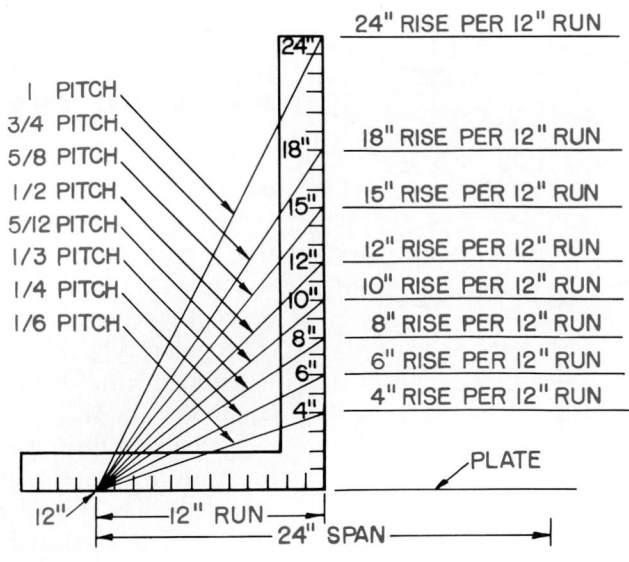

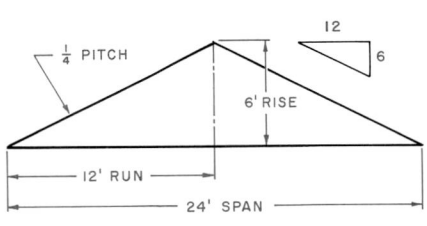

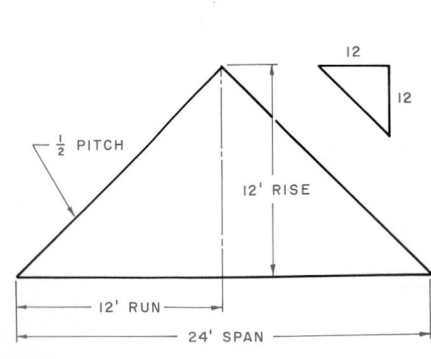

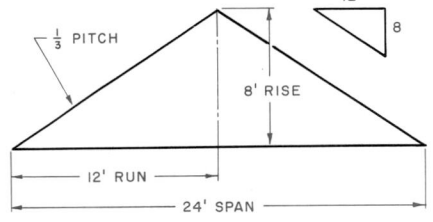

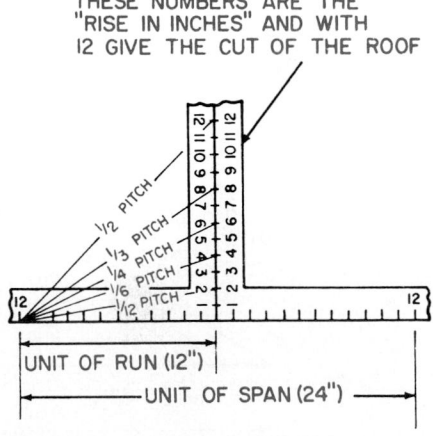

33-7. *A comparison of the two methods of expressing the pitch.*

33-8. *This roof has a ¼ pitch, or 6" to the foot.*

33-10. *A roof with a ⅓ pitch, or 8" to the foot.*

33-9. *A roof with a ½ pitch, or 12" to the foot.*

33-11. *Pitch can be expressed as the rise in inches per unit of run.*

plane. It is the ratio of the rise to the span. Fig. 33-7.

For example, a roof may have a rise of 6' and a span of 24'. Fig. 33-8. Such a roof has ¼ pitch:

$$\frac{6' \text{ (rise of rafter)}}{24' \text{ (span of building)}} = ¼ \text{ pitch}$$

A ½ pitch roof rises one-half the distance of the span. For a 24' span, the rise of a ½ pitch roof would be 12'. Fig. 33-9. The common roof pitches are ¼, ½, and ⅓. Figs. 33-8, 33-9, and 33-10.

Cut of a roof. The rise in inches and the unit of run. It is used when referring to the roof pitch. Fig. 33-11. For example, the cut may be 6-12 (6" of rise per foot of run), 8-12 (8" of rise per foot of run), or 12-12 (12" of rise per foot of run). Figs. 33-8, 33-9, and 33-10.

Slope. The incline of a roof. Slope is the inches of vertical rise in twelve inches of horizontal run. It is expressed sometimes as a fraction (×/12), but typically as "× in 12." For example, a roof that rises at the rate of 4" for each foot (12") of run is designated as having a 4-in-12 slope (or ⁴⁄₁₂). The triangular symbol above the roof in Fig. 33-8 conveys this information.

Plumb and level lines. These terms refer to the direction of a line on a rafter, not to any particular rafter cut. Any line that is vertical when the rafter is in its proper position is called a plumb line. Any line that is level when the rafter is in its proper position is called a level line. Fig. 33-12.

Ridge board. The horizontal piece that connects the upper ends of the rafters. Fig. 33-13.

Tail. The portion of the rafter which extends beyond the wall of the building to form the overhang or eave. Fig. 33-13, arrows.

Rafters. The inclined members of the roof framework. They serve

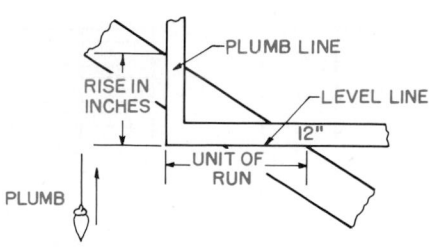

33-12. *The framing square is used to lay out the plumb and level lines on a rafter. The plumb line is drawn along the tongue of the square and the level line along the body (sometimes called the blade).*

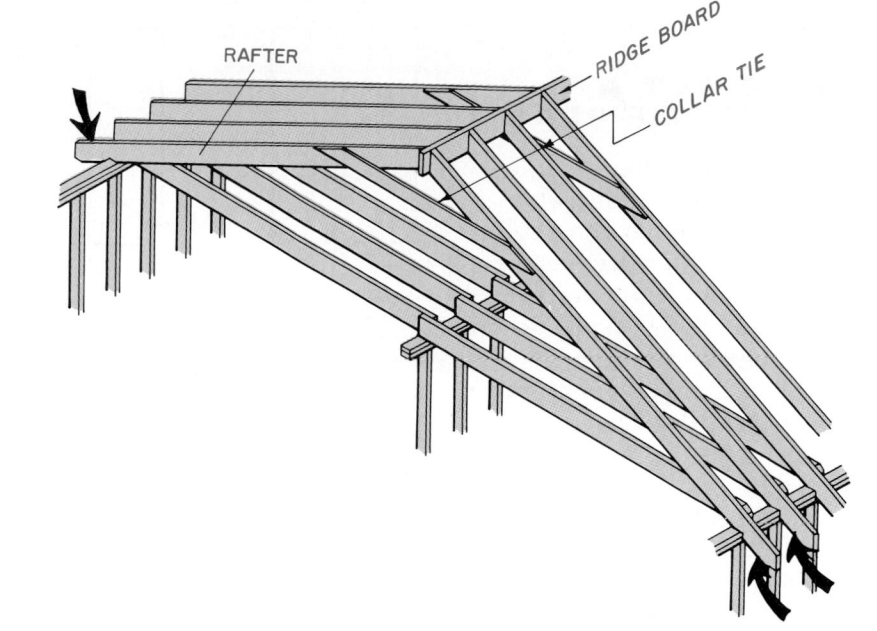

33-13. *The ridge board fastens the upper ends of the rafters together and maintains the correct spacing between them. The rafter tails are shown at the arrows.*

the same purpose in the roof as joists in the floor or studs in the wall and are usually spaced 16" or 24" apart. They vary in width depending on their length, the distance they are spaced apart, their slope, and the kind of roof covering to be used. Rafters sometimes extend beyond the wall of the building to form eaves and protect the sides of the building.

Wood members used for roof framing should normally not exceed 19% moisture content. There are several kinds of rafters necessary for framing the many different roof styles.

Common rafters extend from the plate to the ridge board at 90 degrees to both. Fig. 33-14.

Hip rafters extend diagonally from the corners formed by the plate to the ridge board. Fig. 33-14.

Valley rafters extend diagonally from the plates to the ridge board along the lines where two roofs intersect. Fig. 33-14.

Jack rafters never extend the full distance from the plate to the ridge board. There are three kinds of jack rafters: hip jacks extend from the plate to a hip rafter, valley jacks extend from the ridge to a valley rafter, and cripple jacks extend between a hip rafter and a valley rafter or between two valley rafters. Fig. 33-14.

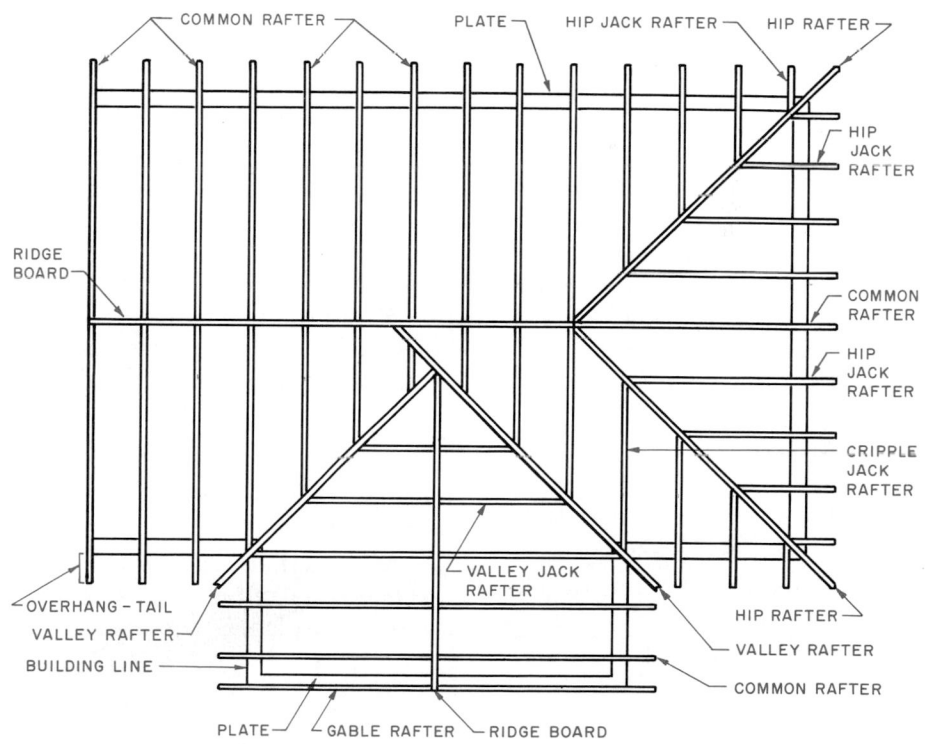

33-14. *The parts of a roof frame.*

LAYING OUT A ROOF FRAME PLAN

Before cutting rafters, the carpenter must determine what kinds are necessary to frame the roof. A roof framing diagram may be included among the working drawings; if not, you should lay one out for yourself.

There are four types of roofs which will usually be of concern to the carpenter:

➤ Gable.
➤ Gable and valley.
➤ Hip.
➤ Hip and valley.

The lean-to or shed roof is one-half of a gable roof. It extends from ridge board to plate on one side only. The gambrel roof plan is the same as for a gable roof. The mansard roof is a combination of a hip and a flat roof or two hip roofs. The first hip off the plate has a steep slope and the second is either flat or has a very low slope.

Always make a roof frame plan to determine the kinds of rafters that will be needed for framing. If the plan is drawn to scale, the exact number of each kind of rafter can also be determined. However, the actual length of each rafter should be figured from the dimensions taken directly off the building. The roof frame plan for each of the more common roof styles can be made as follows:

Gable Roof

1. Lay out the outline of the building. A, Fig. 33-15.

2. Determine the direction in which the rafters will run and draw the center line at right angles to this direction. B, Fig. 33-15.

3. The center line determines the location of the ridge line. C, Fig. 33-15.

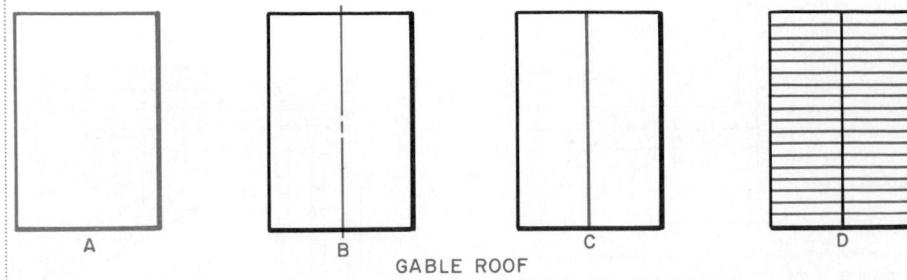

33-15. *Frame plan for gable roof. The frame plan for a shed roof would be one-half of this.*

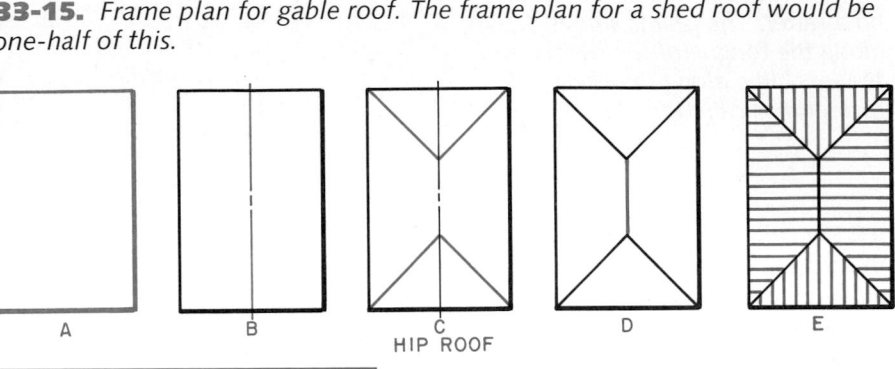

33-16. *Frame plan for hip roof.*

4. Determine the distance between the rafters and lay out the roof frame plan. D, Fig. 33-15.

Hip Roof

1. Lay out the outline of the building. A, Fig. 33-16.

2. Locate and draw a center line. B, Fig. 33-16.

3. At each corner, draw a 45 degree line from corner to center line. This establishes location of hip rafters. C, Fig. 33-16.

4. Draw the ridge line between the intersecting points of the hip rafters. D, Fig. 33-16.

5. Determine the distance between the rafters and lay out the roof frame plan. E, Fig. 33-16.

Gable and Valley Roof

1. Lay out the outline of the building. A, Fig. 33-17.

2. Draw the center line of the larger rectangle. B, Fig. 33-17 (arrow 1).

3. Draw the center line of the smaller rectangle. B, Fig. 33-17 (arrow 2).

4. Draw a line at 45 degrees between the interior corners of the building outline and the ridge line. C, Fig. 33-17.

5. Draw in the ridge lines. D, Fig. 33-17.

6. Determine the distance between the rafters and lay out the roof frame plan. E, Fig. 33-17.

Hip and Valley Roof

1. Lay out the outline of the building. A, Fig. 33-18.

2. Outline the largest possible rectangle inside the building outline. B, Fig. 33-18.

3. Draw center lines for each

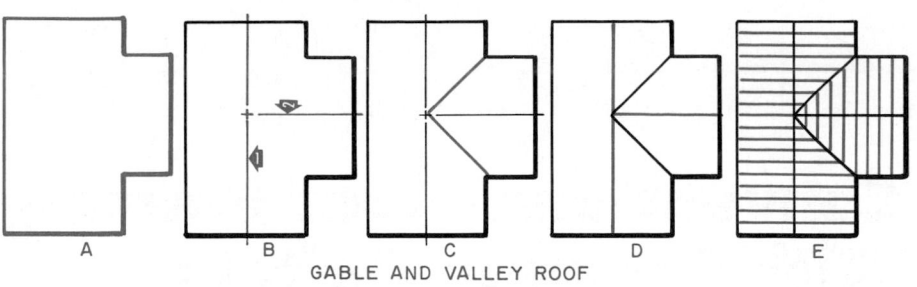

33-17. *Gable and valley roof frame plan.*

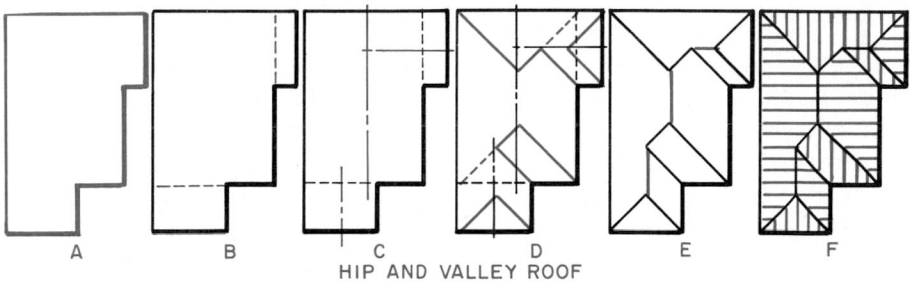

33-18. *Hip and valley roof frame plan.*

rectangle formed inside the building outline. C, Fig. 33-18.

4. Draw a line at 45 degrees from each corner both inside and outside, and extend these lines to intersect with the center lines drawn in C. The solid lines indicate the location of the hip rafters on outside corners and valley rafters on inside corners. D, Fig. 33-18.

5. The center lines drawn in C connect the hip and valley rafters. Draw these in as solid lines to indicate the location of the ridges. E, Fig. 33-18.

6. Figure distance between rafters and lay out roof frame plan. F, Fig. 33-18.

QUESTIONS

1. What is the main purpose of a roof?

2. List several roof styles.

3. What is the ridge board's function?

4. What pieces in the roof serve the same purpose as joists in the floor?

5. What is the difference between a hip rafter and a valley rafter?

6. What is the purpose of a roof frame plan?

ACTIVITIES

1. Math. If a roof has a ⅓ pitch and the span is 22', what is the rise?

2. Math. If the run of a roof is 14'6" and the rise is 7'3", what is the pitch?

3. Math. If a roof has a ⅙ pitch and the rise is 6', what is the span?

THE SCHOOL-TO-WORK CONNECTION

Roof styles are often a matter of regional preference. For example, a hip roof is structurally quite strong. For this reason, a hip roof may be preferred where wind-driven storms are common.

1. Imagine that you are a house designer. You decide to see what housing styles are typical in town. Visit a neighborhood and make a list of every type of roof you see. (The type of roof covering does not matter for this survey.)

34

Conventional Roof Framing With Common Rafters

There are two methods of roof framing for the pitched roof styles discussed in the previous unit: conventional and trussed roof construction. In conventional roof construction, the carpenter builds the roof with ceiling joists and rafters, a piece at a time, on the building's walls. Fig. 34-1. In trussed roof construction the trusses are usually prefabricated and are attached to the building as units. These two framing methods are used most often for roof slopes of 4 in 12 (⅙ pitch) and greater. The framing of a low-pitched or flat roof will be discussed later.

In this unit the layout and cutting procedures for framing a conventional roof will be discussed. The procedure for constructing a pitched roof using trusses will be discussed in Unit 38.

The joist and rafter method is known by most carpenters and therefore is used frequently. Common types of sheathing and finish materials are used. Insulation is easily installed between the joists, and the roof load is carried on the walls without causing the ceiling to deflect.

There are some disadvantages to this type of construction. It takes longer, and the building is therefore exposed to the weather longer. Also, the carpenters

34-1. A conventionally framed roof is installed piece by piece.

building a roof with joists and rafters must stand on scaffolding and ceiling joists.

In conventional roof construction, the rafters should not be erected until the ceiling joists have been fastened in place. The ceiling joists act as a tie and prevent the rafters from spreading and pushing out on the exterior walls.

LAYING OUT COMMON RAFTERS

The rafters are the skeleton of the roof and must be carefully made and fitted if they are to support the roof weight. The top of the rafter rests against the ridge board and is called a top or plumb cut. The bottom of the rafter rests on the plate; this is a level or seat cut. Fig. 34-2. These cuts must be made

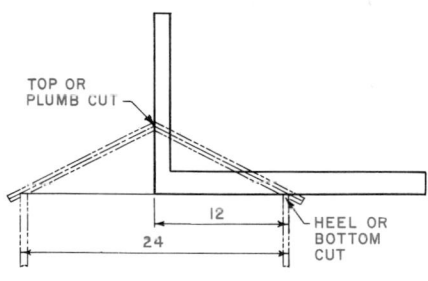

34-2. This framing square was enlarged to show its relationship to the roof and to the top and bottom cuts.

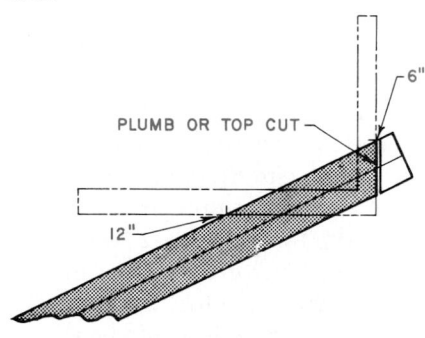

34-3. This plumb line has been drawn for the top cut on a roof with a 6" unit rise (¼ pitch roof).

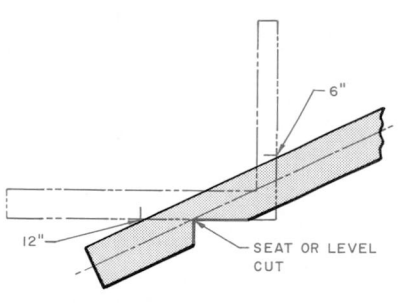

34-4. A level line drawn for the seat cut of a bird's mouth. This cut is made for a roof with a 6" unit rise.

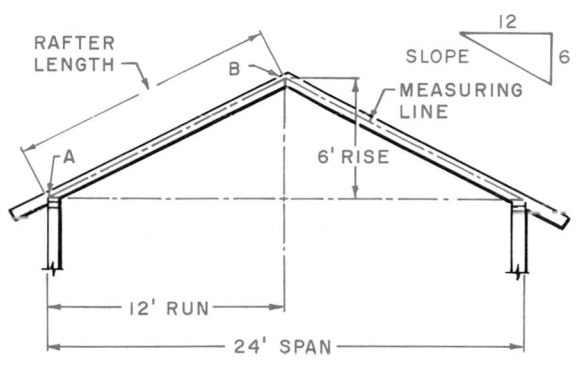

34-5. The theoretical rafter length is from point A to point B.

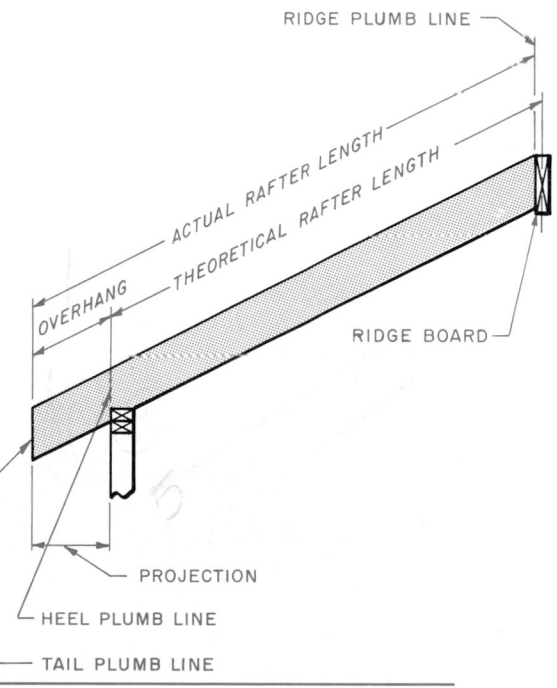

34-6. Actual and theoretical length of common rafter.

accurately if the rafter is to fit properly.

A plumb cut line is drawn with the framing square as a guide. The unit run (12" mark) on the body of the square is aligned with the edge of the rafter. The unit rise on the tongue of the square (number used will correspond to the slope of the roof) is aligned on the same edge of the rafter. The plumb line is then drawn along the edge of the tongue. Fig. 34-3. A level line is drawn for the same roof pitch with the square in the same position on the rafter except that the line is drawn along the body of the framing square. Fig. 34-4.

The theoretical length of a common rafter is the shortest distance between the outer edge of the plate (A) and a point where the measuring line of the rafter comes in contact with the ridge line (B). Figs. 34-5 and 34-6. This length is found along the measuring line and may be calculated in several ways:

➤ By using the Pythagorean theorem.

➤ By applying the unit length obtained from the rafter table on the framing square.

➤ By stepping off the length with the framing square.

➤ By entering rise and run into a calculator specifically designed for solving construction problems.

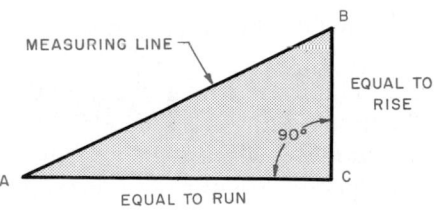

34-7. *The measuring line is the hypotenuse of the right triangle and represents the length of the rafters.*

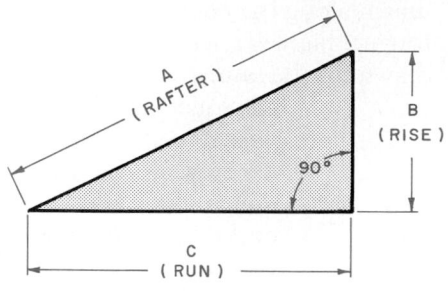

34-8. *The Pythagorean theorem states that the length of the hypotenuse (A) will be the square root of the sum of the squares of the other two sides ($\sqrt{B^2 + C^2}$).*

Pythagorean Theorem Method

The Pythagorean theorem states that the square of the hypotenuse of a right triangle is equal to the sum of the squares of the other two sides ($A^2 = B^2 + C^2$). The rise, the run, and the rafter of a roof form a right triangle, with the rafter as the hypotenuse. Fig. 34-7. The length of the rafter (A) can thus be calculated from the rise (B) and the run (C). Fig. 34-8.

Unit Length Method

The unit length is the hypotenuse of a right triangle with the unit of run (12") as the base and the unit rise (rise in inches per foot of run) as the altitude. Fig. 34-9a. The unit length is found on the rafter table of the framing square. Fig. 34-9b. The inch markings along the top of the table

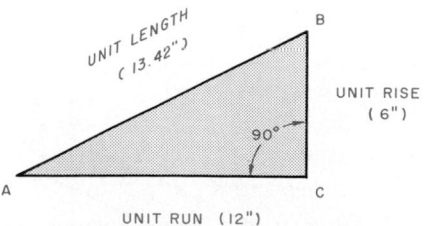

34-9a. *The rafter is represented by the line AB. The length of this line can be found in the rafter table on the framing square.*

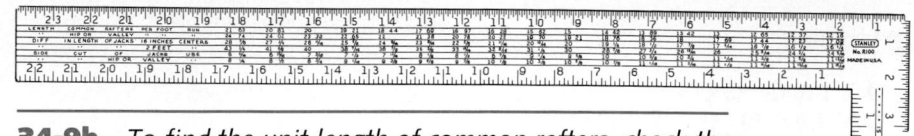

34-9b. *To find the unit length of common rafters, check the rafter table on the face of the steel square (Enlarged portion above).*

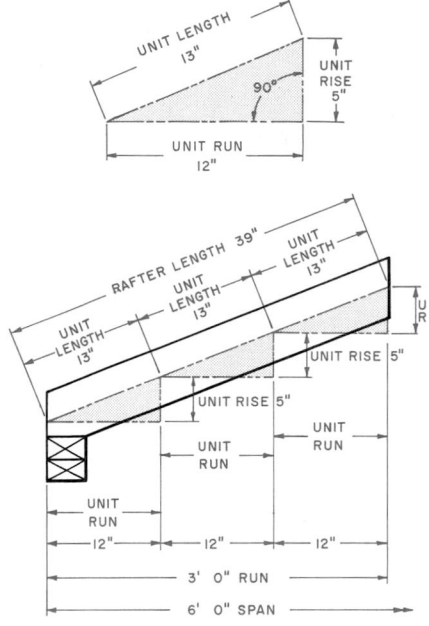

34-10. *The total length of a rafter is the total run times the unit length. In this example the total run is 3' and the unit length is 13". Therefore the theoretical length of the rafter is 39".*

represent unit rise. The top line of the table reads: "Length Common Rafters per Foot Run." If you follow across the top line to the figure under 6 (for a unit rise of 6"), you will find the figure 13.42. This is the unit length for a roof triangle

with a unit run of 12" and a unit rise of 6".

Let's figure the total length of a rafter for a small building with a unit rise of 5", a span of 6', and a run of 3'. Look at the rafter table to obtain the unit length. Fig. 34-9b.

For a unit rise of 5", the unit length is 13" per unit of run (one foot). The total length is the unit length times the total run. The total run of the building in this example is 3'. Therefore the total length of the common rafters is 39". Fig. 34-10.

13 (inches per unit of run) × 3 (units of run) = 39"

Step-Off Method

A third method for finding the theoretical rafter length is by using the framing square to "step off" the length. Fig. 34-11. Place the square on the rafter with the tongue on the plumb cut. Step off the cut of the roof (for example in Fig. 34-11, 6" on the tongue and 12" on the blade) on the rafter stock as many times as there are feet in the total run. In this case, it would be three times.

Often the run of a building will not come out in even feet. For

FULL LENGTH OF RAFTER INCLUDES OVERHANG,
BUT LESS HALF OF RIDGE BOARD THICKNESS.

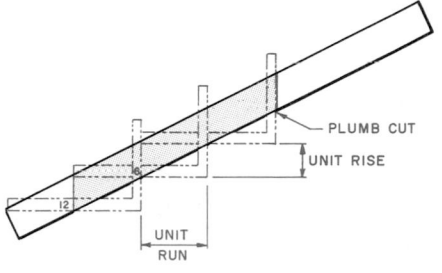

34-11. *Stepping off the length of a common rafter.*

34-12. *A construction calculator is often used to solve roof framing problems. Dimensions can be entered in feet and inches.*

example, the run might be 3'4".
The extra 4" is taken care of in the
same manner as the full foot run.
With the square at the first step
position, draw a line along the edge
of the tongue to represent the
center line of the ridge board. At
the 4" mark of the blade, make a
mark on the rafter along the level
line—not along the edge of the
rafter. Fig. 34-13. Then, as in Fig.
34-11, step off the cut three more
times, for a total run of 3' 4". This
is the theoretical length of the
rafter. The ridge board thickness
and overhang can now be figured
and laid out.

Calculator Method

Small, easy-to-use construction
calculators are becoming common
on job sites. Numbers can be
entered directly into the calculator
in feet and inches, including
fractions. This makes them very
useful for solving roof framing
problems. If you know the rise and
the run of a common rafter, you
can easily determine its length by
entering these figures into the
calculator. You can also use the
tool to calculate cuts for hip rafters
and valley rafters. Fig. 34-12.

CUTTING COMMON RAFTERS

Common Rafter Ridge Allowance

The theoretical length does not
take into account the thickness of
the ridge board or the length of the
overhang, if there is one. To cut a
rafter without an overhang to its
actual length, you must deduct
one-half the thickness of the ridge
board from the ridge end. Fig.
34-14. For example, if 2" material is

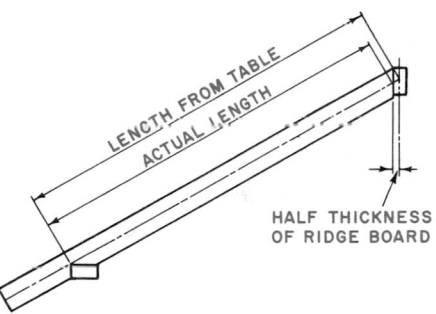

34-14. *Subtract one-half the actual thickness of the ridge board from the theoretical length of the rafter to obtain the rafter's actual length. If there is to be an overhang, this will be added later.*

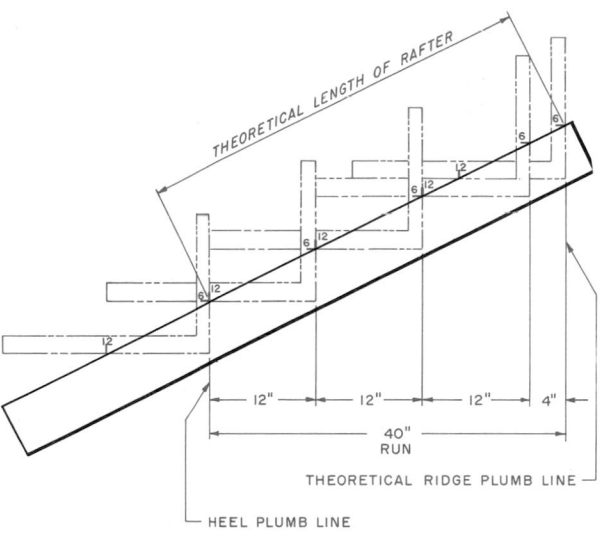

34-13. *Stepping off the rafter when the run is not an even number of feet.*

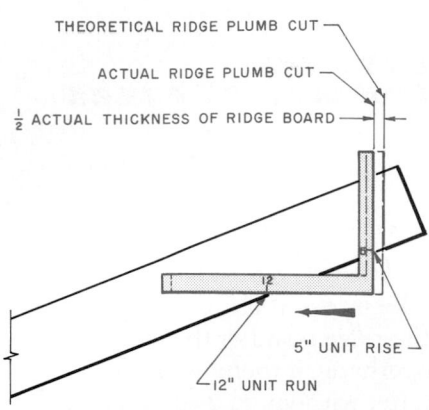

34-15. *Lay off one-half the thickness of the ridge board at right angles to the tongue of the square (along the level line). Do not lay it off along the edge of the rafter.*

used for the ridge board, the actual thickness is 1½". One-half of this is ¾". The ¾" is laid off along the level line, and the line for the actual ridge plumb cut is made. Fig. 34-15.

Common Rafter Overhang

A roof may or may not have an overhang. If not, the rafter must be cut so that its lower end is even with the outside of the exterior wall. Fig. 34-16. The portion of the rafter which rests on the plate is called the seat. To lay out the seat, place the tongue of the framing square on the heel plumb line with the rafter edge intersecting the correct seat width on the blade. Fig. 34-17. Draw a line from the heel plumb line along the blade.

A roof with a wide overhang at the cornice and the gable ends not only enhances appearance but also provides protection to side and end walls. Thus even in lower-cost houses, when style and design permit, wide overhangs are desirable. Though it adds slightly to the initial cost, future savings on maintenance usually merit this type of roof extension.

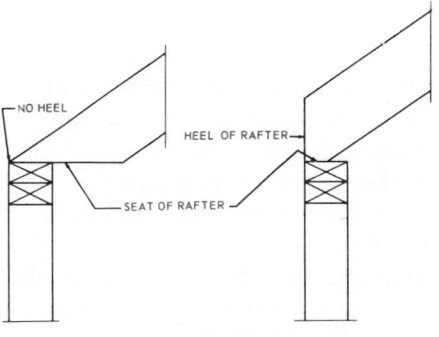

34-16. *The rafter without an overhang may rest on the exterior wall plate with or without a heel. Which do you think would be stronger?*

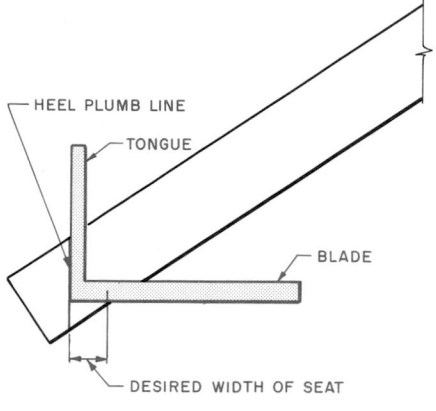

34-17. *Laying out the rafter seat.*

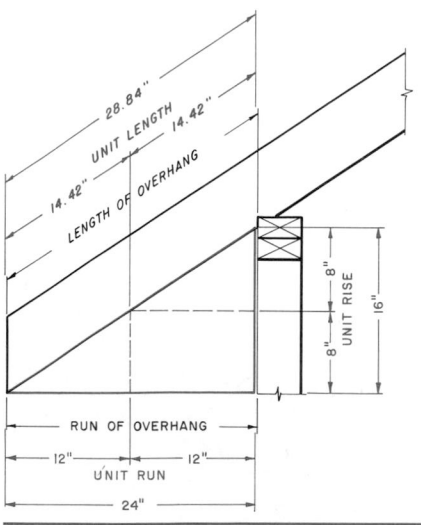

34-18. *The length of the rafter overhang may be found by using the rafter table on the framing square.*

If the roof does have an overhang, or eave, the overhanging part of the rafter is called the tail and must be added to the length of the rafter. The length of the tail may be calculated as if it were a separate little rafter. Any of the methods used for finding rafter length may be used to find the length of the tail. Suppose the run of the overhang (sometimes called the projection) is 2' and the unit rise of the roof is 8". Fig. 34-18. Look at the rafter table and find the unit length for a common rafter with a unit rise of 8". Fig. 34-9b. The unit length of the rafter is 14.42". Since the total run of the overhang is 2', the tail (length of overhang) is 28.84", or 28 $^{27}/_{32}$":

14.42 (inches per unit of run) × 2 (units of run) = 28.84"

Another way to lay off the overhang is with the framing square. Suppose the run of the overhang is 10". Fig. 34-19. Start the layout by placing the tongue of the square along the heel plumb line and setting the square to the cut of the roof. In Fig. 34-19, the square is set to a unit rise of 8" and a unit run of 12". Move the square in the direction of the arrow in Fig. 34-19 until the 10" mark of the blade is on the heel plumb line. Draw a line along the tongue. This will be the tail cut.

Many carpenters do not cut the tail to the finished length until after the rafters have been fastened in place. The length of the tail is calculated, and a sufficient amount of material is left beyond the bird's-mouth for the overhang. Fig. 34-20. All other cuts except the tail plumb cut are made. After the rafters are fastened in place, the exact length of the tail is marked on the end rafters. A chalk line is snapped on the top edge of all the rafters. A tail plumb line is then drawn down from this chalk line on each rafter and the tail is cut along the line.

34-19. *Laying-out the run of the overhang directly on the rafter with the framing square.*

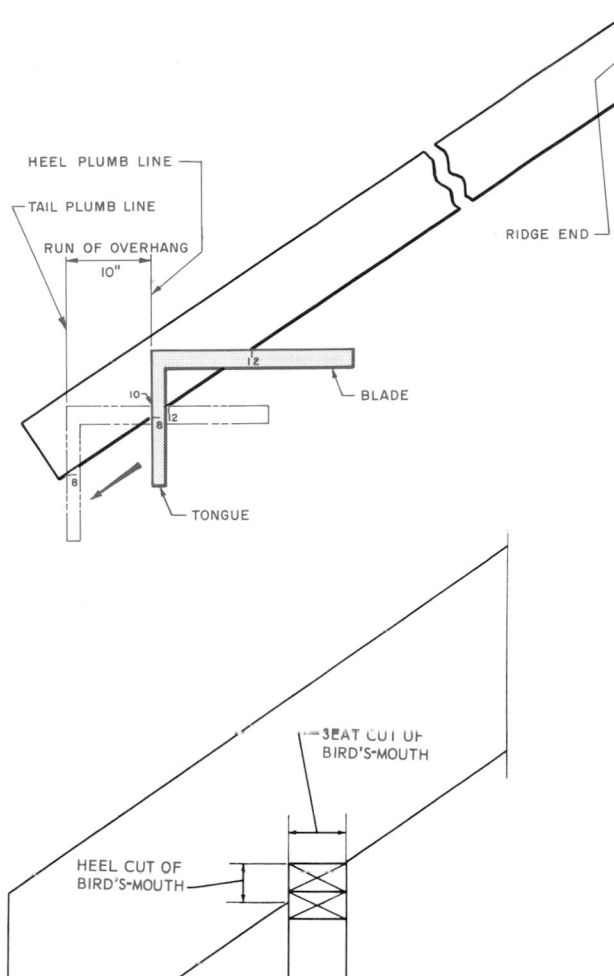

34-20. *The bird's mouth on a rafter with an overhang.*

34-21. *Using the square to lay out a bird's mouth. For a common rafter on a gable roof, the depth of the heel cut is laid out along the heel plumb line. This completes the layout of the bird's mouth. The length of the line at arrow #1 will be the important dimension when laying out the bird's mouth for a hip and valley rafter, as you will learn later.*

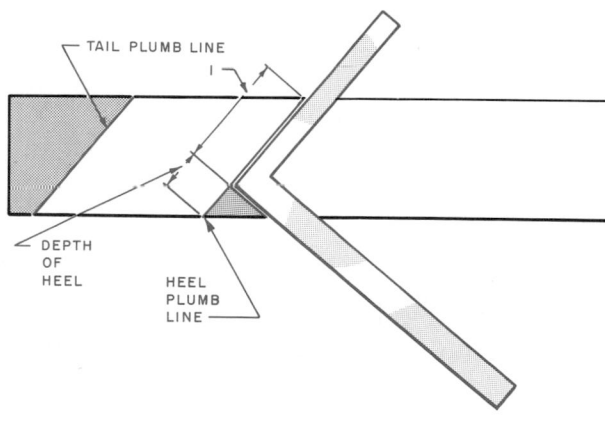

Bird's-mouth

A rafter with an overhang has a notch in it called a bird's-mouth. Fig. 34-20. The plumb cut of the bird's-mouth, which bears against the side of the rafter plate, is called the heel cut. The level cut, which bears on the top of the rafter plate, is called the seat cut.

The size of the bird's-mouth for a common rafter is usually stated in terms of the depth of the heel cut rather than the width of the seat cut. The bird's-mouth is laid out much the same way as the seat on a rafter without an overhang. Measure off the depth of the heel on the heel plumb line, set the square, and draw the seat line along the blade. Fig. 34-21.

Common Rafter Pattern

Calculate the actual length of a common rafter and lay one out on a piece of stock. When laying out rafters, remember to use the crown of the rafter member for the top edge. Carefully cut out the rafter. Use this rafter as a pattern for cutting a second rafter.

Try the two rafters on the building with the ridge board or a scrap piece of the same size material as the ridge board between to see how the heel cut and the top cut fit. If they are all right, use one of these rafters as a pattern to cut all others needed. Distribute the rafters to their locations on the building. The rafters are usually leaned against the building with the ridge cut up. The workers on the building can then pull them up as needed and fasten them in position. A framed-in gable roof is shown in Fig. 34-22.

34-22. *A portion of a framed-in gable roof. The rafters were leaned against the building and pulled up as needed. It is best to have three workers when framing a roof: one at the ridge and one at each plate where the rafters are to be fastened. The rafters are erected alternately: one from the front, then one from the back.*

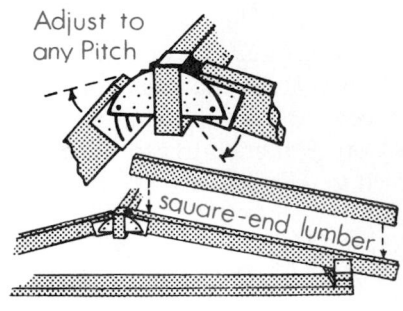

34-23a. *Framing a roof using saddle braces.*

34-23b. *Square-end lumber is used with the saddle brace, which will adjust to any pitch.*

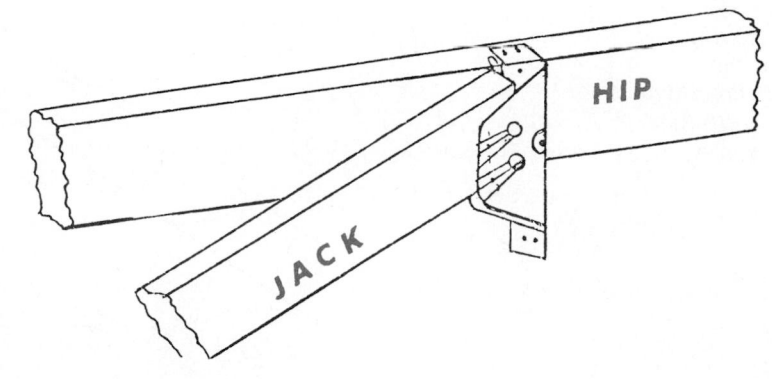

34-24. *Saddle braces may also be used for framing hip and jack rafters.*

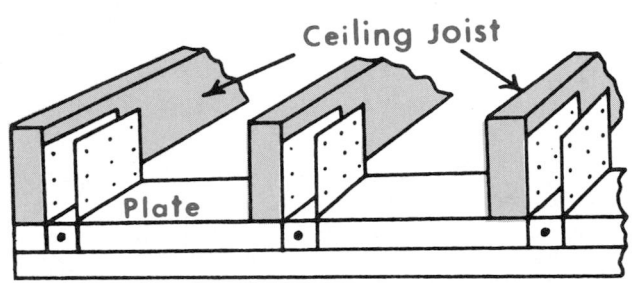

34-25. *Anchor brackets are used to attach the rafters to the ceiling joists and the double plate.*

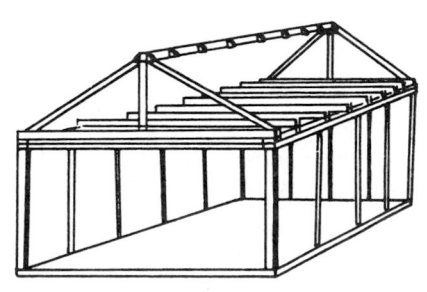

34-26. *The ridge is set in place ready to receive the rafters. Brackets are installed over the ridge.*

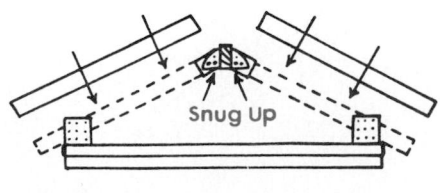

34-27. *Place the rafter in the saddle brace at the ridge and the anchor bracket at the plate. Push it up firmly against the ridge.*

SADDLE BRACE ROOF FRAMING

A metal bracket used for roof framing permits the use of square-end lumber for rafters, eliminating both the plumb cut at the ridge and the bird's-mouth at the plate. This bracket will adjust to any pitch. Fig. 34-23. Hip and jack rafter brackets are also available. Fig. 34-24. This "saddle brace" produces a strong roof which exceeds regulations of federal, state, and local building codes. To use the metal brackets on a gable roof, follow this procedure:

1. Lay out the rafter spacing on the top plates and nail the anchor brackets to the top plates with two nails specifically used for installing metal brackets.

2. Install a ceiling joist

alongside each anchor bracket. Fig. 34-25.

3. Set the ridge in the center of the building at the right height for the required pitch. Fig. 34-26.

4. Lay out the rafter spacing on the ridge board and install the brackets over the ridge. Fig. 34-26. Nail each bracket in place with three roofing nails.

5. Insert a square-end lumber rafter into the saddle brace plate anchor and ridge bracket. Fig. 34-27. Make sure the rafter is pushed firmly against the ridge.

6. With the rafter and ceiling joist in place at the plate, drive a 16d nail from the ceiling joist side through to the rafter. Drive another 16d nail from the rafter side through to the ceiling joist. Fig. 34-28.

7. Make sure the bottom of the saddle brace at the ridge is snug against the bottom of the rafter. Nail each rafter face through the ridge bracket with two roofing nails. Fig. 34-29.

8. After installing all rafters, attach a collar tie to every fourth rafter if the spacing is 16" on center and every third rafter if the spacing is 24" on center. This is a minimum standard. Local building codes may vary. Fig. 34-30.

Attaching a Shed Roof

A shed roof may be attached to an existing building by using these metal brackets. Cut the saddle brace in half at the ridge strap and bend the strap up. Nail it against the existing wall. Fig. 34-31.

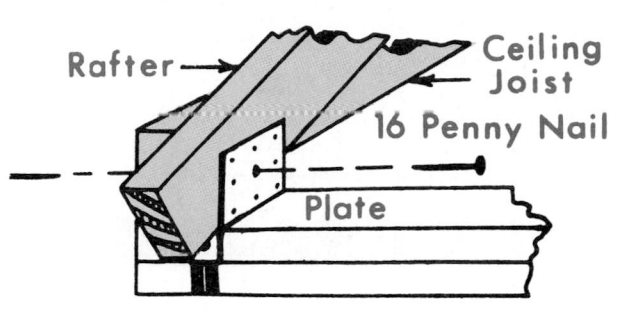

34-28. Nail through the anchor plate into the rafter from one side. From the other side, nail through the ceiling joist into the rafter.

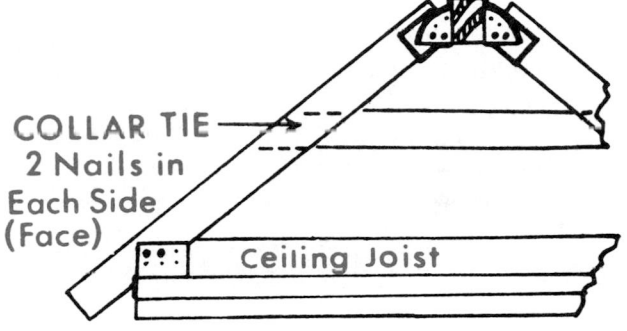

34-30. Installing the collar tie.

34-29. Nail the rafter to the ridge bracket with two nails to each side.

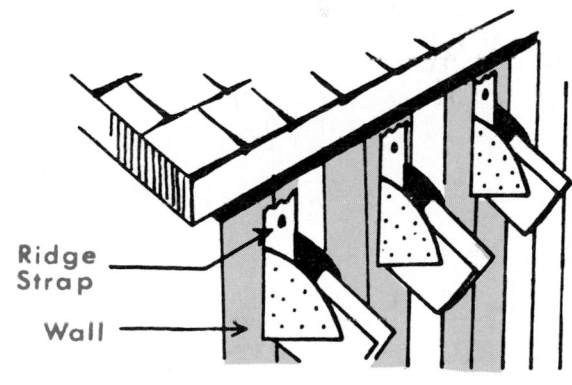

34-31. Using the saddle brace to attach a shed roof to an existing building.

1. What are some of the disadvantages of conventional roof framing?

2. What prevents the rafters from spreading and pushing out on the exterior walls?

3. What is the cut at the top of the rafter called?

4. What is the name of the cut that rests on the plate?

5. When laying out the rafter, what line is drawn along the edge of the tongue on the framing square?

6. What are four ways that the length of a common rafter can be calculated?

7. A building is 24' wide and has a ⅓ pitch. What is the theoretical length of a common rafter?

8. Describe the step-off method for finding the length of a rafter.

9. What is meant by ridge allowance?

10. What is the bird's-mouth?

11. What is a saddle brace?

ACTIVITIES

1. Language Arts. A rafter with an overhang has a notch in it called a bird's mouth. Explain why this notch was given its name.

2. Math. For a house with a slope of 7 in 12 and a span of 26', find the theoretical rafter length for a common rafter.

3. Science. Using the basic information for first, second, and third class levers as simple machines, explain why the rafters are placed against the wall at a steep angle with a large portion of the rafter extending above the top of the wall. Demonstrate what is difficult when the rafters are placed at less steep angles with less of the rafter extending above the wall.

THE SCHOOL-TO-WORK CONNECTION

The most common application for conventional roof framing is the gable roof. However, conventional roof framing is also used in the construction of dormers called "shed" dormers. A shed dormer has a single, flat roof that is pitched at a shallower angle than that of the surrounding roof. Inside, the dormer ceiling can be flat or can follow the upward slope of the rafters. Contractors often build a shed dormer when remodeling an attic into living space. Some shed dormers run the length of the house. Because it is such a visible feature, however, a shed dormer should be compatible with the style of the house. To help it blend in, the dormer should have the same roofing and siding as the rest of the house. Dormer windows should match the style and type of those in the rest of the house.

Preparation for building a shed dormer involves cutting through the existing roofing and sheathing and removing some of the rafters. The dormer is built within the confines of a large, rectangular hole cut into the roof. Essentially, this hole is the rough opening for the dormer. The walls of the dormer are usually framed with 2 x 4 lumber, 16" on center. Framing details are the same as those on a regular exterior wall.

1. Consult a building code book. Read what it has to say about dormer construction.

2. To gain the maximum amount of headroom in a shed dormer, the roof is usually pitched at the shallowest angle possible. Imagine that you have been hired to build such a dormer. The existing roofing material is asphalt shingle. Consult product literature from asphalt roofing manufacturers to find the minimum pitch suitable for that product.

35

Hip and Valley Rafters

The hip rafter is a roof member that forms a raised area or "hip" in the roof, usually extending from the corner of the building diagonally to the ridge. Fig. 35-1a and b. The valley rafter is similar, but it forms a depression in the roof instead of a hip. Fig. 35-1a and c. Like the hip rafter, it extends diagonally from plate to ridge.

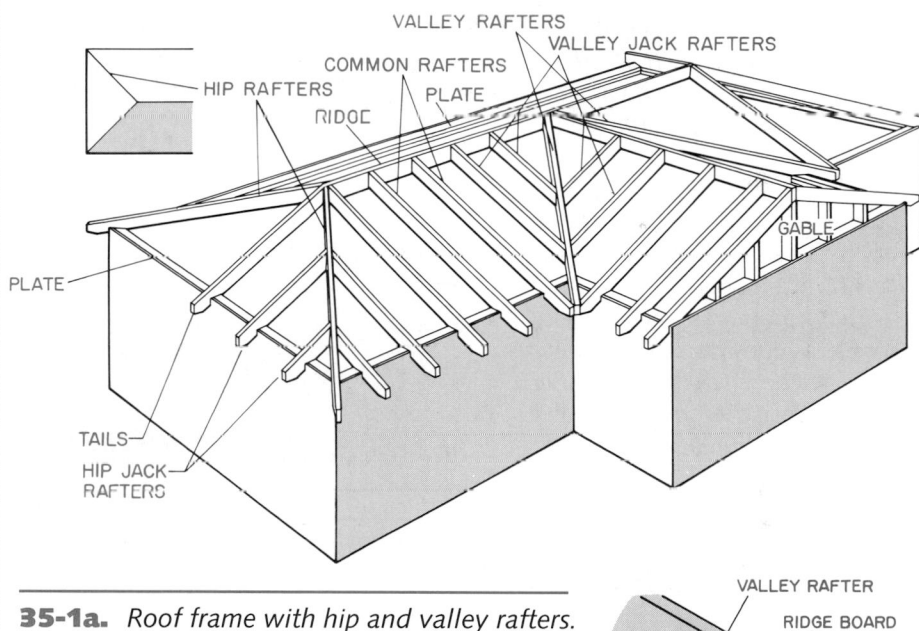

35-1a. Roof frame with hip and valley rafters.

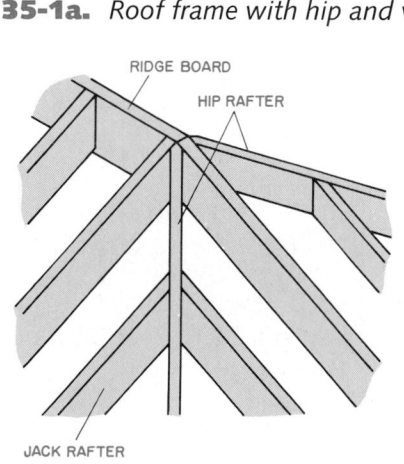

35-1b. Hip rafters framing at the ridge.

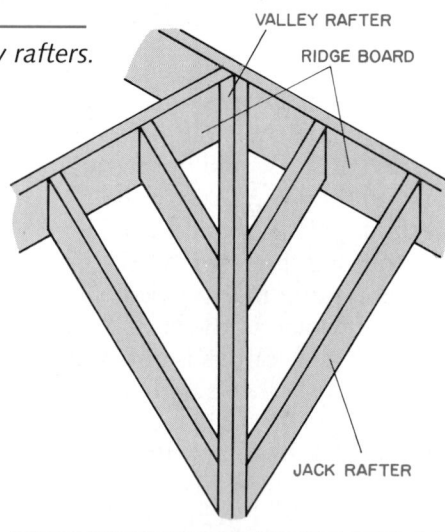

35-1c. Valley rafter framing at the junction of two ridges.

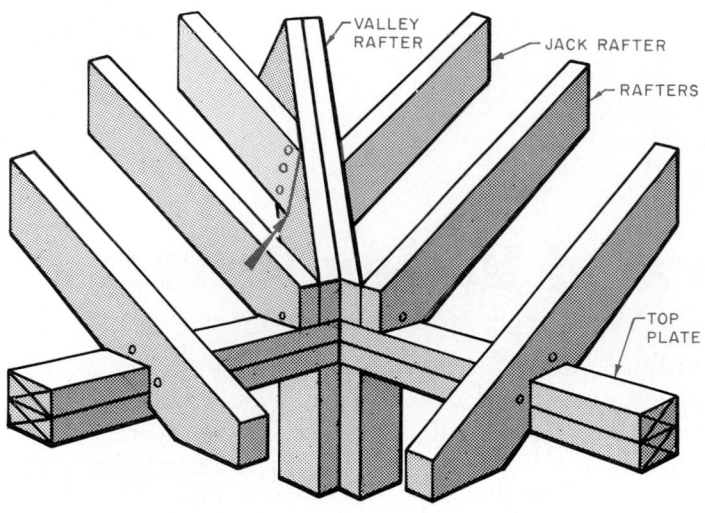

35-2. *Because the beveled cut on the ends of jack rafters creates a longer cut (see arrow), the hip and valley rafters must be 2" deeper than common rafters to permit a full bearing surface. The doubled valley rafter in this drawing has been cut off at the plate. Normally it is extended to become part of the overhang. Doubled valleys are sometimes used to provide more bearing for the roof sheathing.*

The total rise of hip and valley rafters is the same as that of common rafters. Fig. 35-1a. Hip and valley rafters may be the same thickness as common rafters, but they should be 2" deeper to provide full bearing for the beveled end of the jack rafter. Fig. 35-2.

HIP RAFTER LAYOUT

The length of a hip rafter, like the length of a common rafter, is calculated on the basis of the unit run and unit rise and/or the total run and total rise. Any of the methods previously described for determining the length of a common rafter may be used. However, some of the basic data for hip and valley rafters is different.

Figure 35-3 shows part of a roof framing plan for a hip roof. On a hip roof framing plan, the lines which indicate the hip rafters (EC, AC, KG, and IG in Fig. 35-3) form 45-degree angles with the building

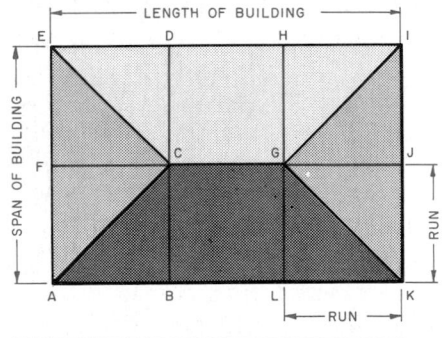

35-3. *Hip roof framing diagram.*

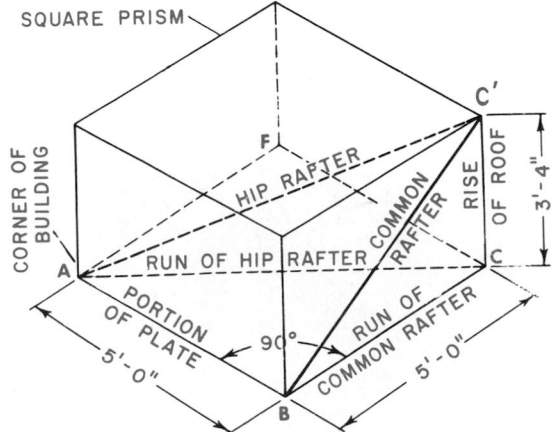

lines. A line which indicates a rafter in the roof framing diagram corresponds to the total run (not length) of the rafter it represents. You can see from the diagram that the total run of a hip rafter is the hypotenuse of a right triangle, with the shorter sides each equal to the total run of a common rafter. Fig. 35-3. In Fig. 35-4 one corner of the roof framing plan (ABCF in Fig. 35-3) has been drawn in perspective to show the relative position of the hip rafter to the common rafter.

The unit run of a hip rafter is the hypotenuse of a right triangle with the shorter sides each equal to the unit run of a common rafter. Fig. 35-5. The unit run of a common rafter is 12". By the Pythagorean theorem, the unit run of a hip rafter is the square root of $12^2 + 12^2$, which is 16.97", or 17. Fig. 35-6. The unit run of a valley rafter is also 17".

Like the unit length of a common rafter, the unit length of a hip rafter may be obtained from the rafter table on the framing square. In Fig. 34-9b, the second line in the table is headed "Length Hip or Valley per Foot Run." This means "per foot run of a common rafter in the same roof." Another way to state this would be "per 16.97" run of hip or valley rafter." For example, the unit length for a unit rise of 8" is 18.76". To calculate the length of a hip rafter, multiply the

35-4. *The relative position of a hip rafter to a common rafter is shown in this perspective drawing of a corner from the roof framing diagram in Fig. 35-3.*

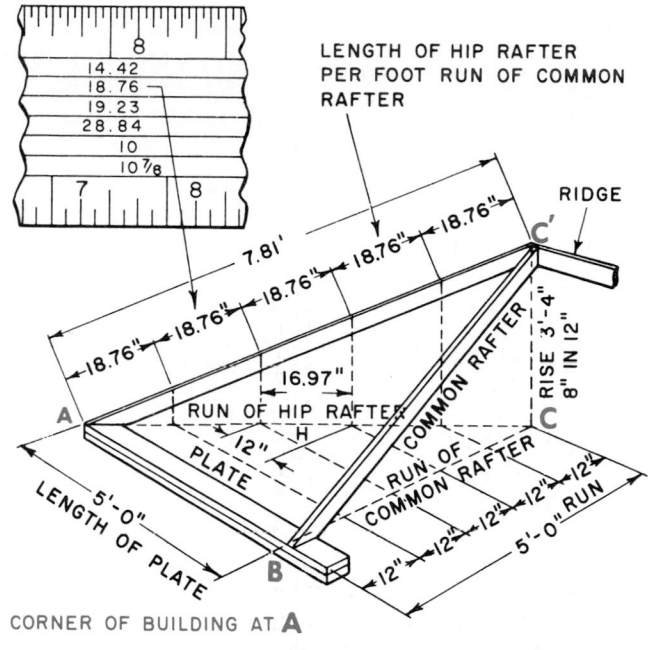

35-5. *The relationship between the unit run of a hip rafter and the unit run of a common rafter.*

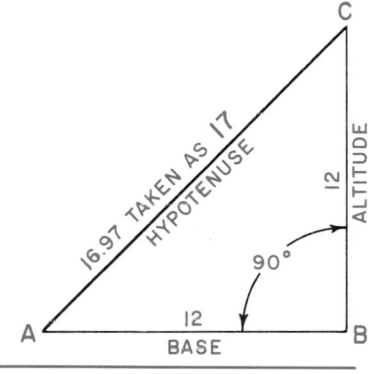

35-6. *The hypotenuse of a right triangle whose shorter sides each equal 12" is 16.97". This can be rounded off to 17".*

unit length by the number of feet in the total run of a common rafter.

In Fig. 35-5, the corner of the building from Fig. 35-3 is shown. In this example the run of a common rafter is 5'. The unit rise is 8" and the unit length of the hip rafter for this unit rise is 18.76". The unit length multiplied by the total run in feet is the length of the hip rafter in inches (18.76" × 5 = 93.8", or 7'9 $^{13}\!/_{16}$"). As in the case of common rafters, this is the theoretical length. To obtain the actual length, the ridge board

shortening allowance and the rafter tail will have to be calculated and laid out.

Plumb and Level Lines

The plumb and level lines on a hip or valley rafter are also referred to as the top and bottom cuts. The top cut is the plumb line and the bottom cut is the level line. To obtain the top and bottom cuts of the hip or valley rafters, set off 17" on the body of the square. On the tongue set off the rise per foot of common rafter run. A line drawn along the body will be the level or seat cut, and a line drawn along the tongue will be the plumb or top cut. Fig. 35-7.

Ridge Allowance

As is the case with a common rafter, the theoretical length of a hip rafter does not take into account the thickness of the ridge board. The ridge-end shortening allowance for a hip rafter depends on the manner in which the ridge end of the hip rafter is joined to the other structural members. The ridge end of the hip rafter may be framed against the ridge board or against the ridge end of common rafters. Figs. 35-8 and 35-9.

If the hip rafter is framed against the ridge board, the shortening allowance is one-half the 45-degree thickness of the ridge piece. The 45-degree thickness of a piece of stock is the length of a line laid at 45 degrees across the thickness of the stock. If the hip rafter is framed against the common rafters, the shortening allowance is one-half the 45-degree thickness of a common rafter.

To lay off the shortening allowance, set the tongue of the framing square to the theoretical ridge plumb cut line. Measure off the shortening allowance along the blade. Fig. 35-10a. Set the square at

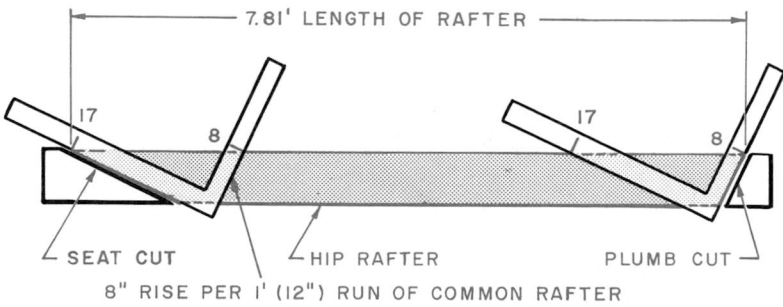

35-7. *Marking the top (plumb) cut and the seat (level) cut of the hip rafter.*

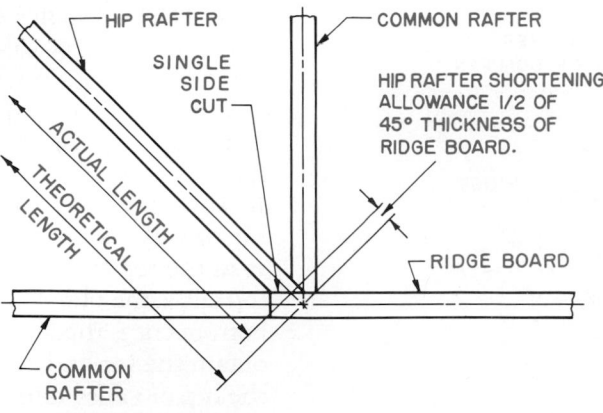

35-8. *A hip rafter framed against the ridge board requires a single side cut. However, the end common rafter must have a 45° angle cut for framing against the side of the hip rafter.*

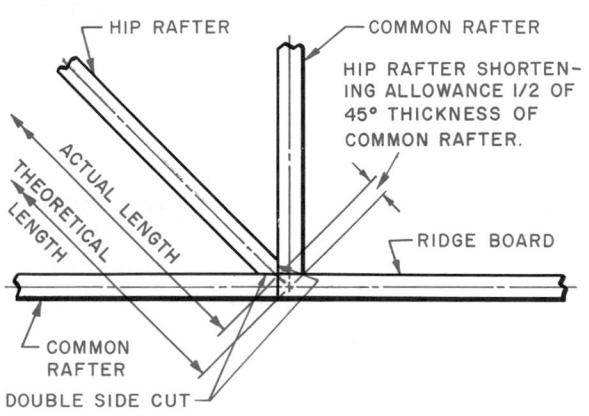

35-9. *A hip rafter framed against the ridge-end common rafters requires a double side cut.*

the mark to the cut of the rafter (unit rise and unit run) and draw the actual ridge plumb cut line. Fig. 35-10b. Remember that the cut of the common rafter is based on a 12" unit run whereas the unit run of the hip or valley rafter is 17". Therefore, to set the square at the cut of the hip rafter, the tongue is set at the unit rise and the blade is set at the 17" mark.

Side Cuts

Since a common rafter runs at 90 degrees to the ridge board, the ridge end of a common rafter is cut square, or at 90 degrees to the lengthwise line of the rafter. A hip rafter, however, joins the ridge piece or the ridge ends of the common rafters at an angle. The ridge end of a hip rafter must therefore be cut to a corresponding angle. This cut is called a *side cut*. Figs. 35-8 and 35-9. The side cut may be laid out in one of two ways.

One method is illustrated in Figs. 35-11 and 35-12. Place the tongue of the framing square along the actual ridge plumb cut line and measure off one-half the thickness of the hip rafter along the blade

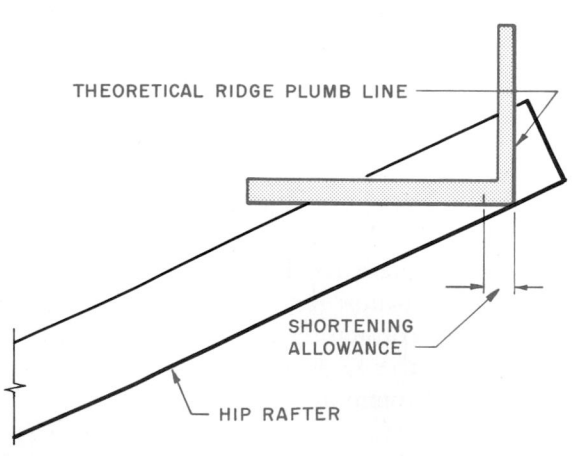

35-10a. *To lay off the shortening allowance, place the tongue of the square along the theoretical ridge plumb cut line and measure off the shortening allowance along the blade of the square (level line).*

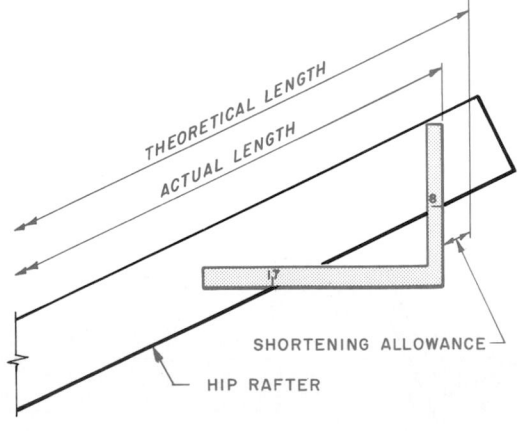

35-10b. *Set the square to the cut of the roof (8" unit rise for this example) with the tongue on the shortening allowance mark. Draw the actual ridge plumb line along the edge of the tongue.*

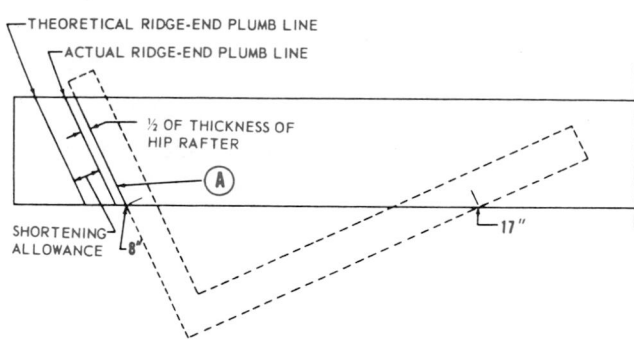

35-11. To lay out the side cut at a right angle to the ridge plumb cut line, measure off one-half the thickness of the hip rafter from the actual ridge plumb cut line.

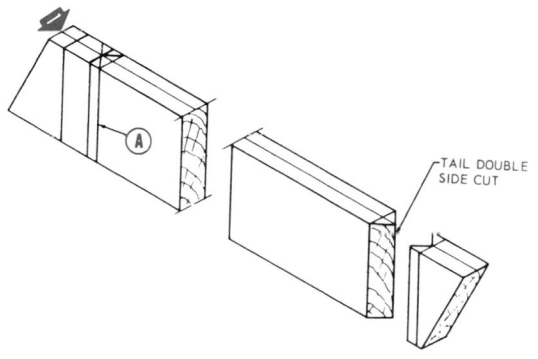

35-12. Draw a centerline on the edge of the rafter (arrow 1). Extend the plumb lines from the face of the rafter to intersect the centerline at 90°. The side cut line is drawn from line A through the intersection of the centerline and the actual ridge-end plumb line.

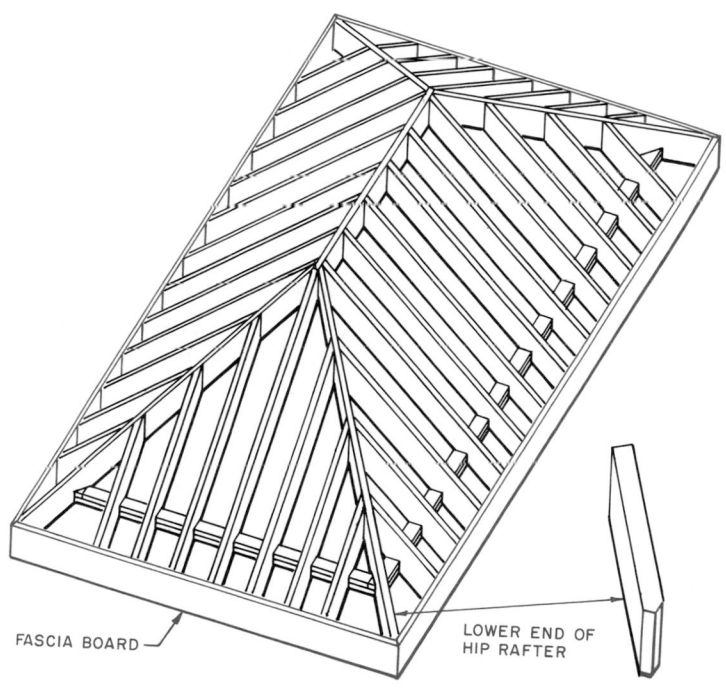

35-13. Hip roof framing. The end of the hip rafter has a double side cut. The fascia boards from the side and end will be fastened along the ends of the rafters and mitered to form an outside corner at the hip rafter. See Fig. 35-12 for detail of hip rafter tail double side cut.

(level line). Shift the tongue to the mark, set the square to the cut of the rafter (17" and 8" in this example), and draw the plumb line. A, Fig. 35-11. Turn the rafter edge up, draw an edge center line, and draw in the angle of the side cut. Fig. 35-12. For a hip rafter which is to be framed against the ridge piece, there will be only a single side cut. Fig. 35-8. For a hip rafter which is to be framed against the ridge ends of the common rafters, there will be a double side cut. Fig. 35-9. In either case, the tail of the rafter must have a double side cut at the same angle, but in the reverse direction, to allow attachment of the fascia board. Fig. 35-13.

A second method of laying out the angle of the side cut on a hip rafter is by referring to the rafter table on the framing square. In Fig. 34-9b, the bottom line of the table is headed "Side Cut Hip or Valley Use." Follow this line over to the column headed by the figure 8 (for a unit rise of 8"). The number shown is 10 7/8. Place the framing square face up on the rafter edge, with the tongue on the ridge-end plumb cut line. (This is line A in Fig. 35-12.) Set the square to a cut of 10 7/8" on the blade and 12" on the tongue. Draw the side cut angle along the tongue. Fig. 35-14.

Overhang

A hip or valley rafter overhang, like a common rafter overhang, is figured as a separate rafter. The run of the overhang, however, is not the same as the run of a common rafter overhang in the same roof. The run of the hip or valley rafter overhang is the hypotenuse of a right triangle whose shorter sides are each equal to the run of a common rafter overhang. Fig. 35-15. If the run of the common rafter overhang is 2' for a roof with an 8" unit rise, the length of the

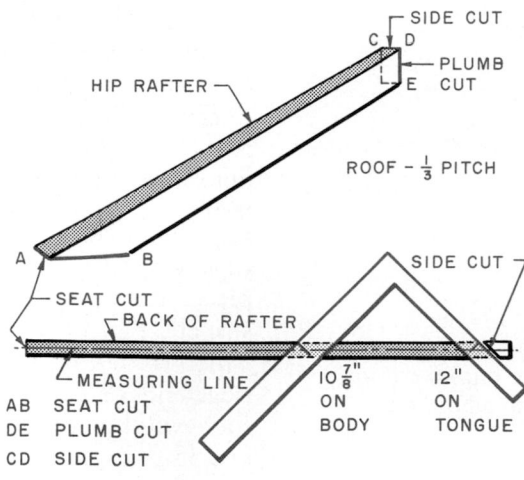

35-14. *Framing square in position on the back edge of the hip rafter for a unit rise of 8". A single side cut will be made for framing against the ridge board.*

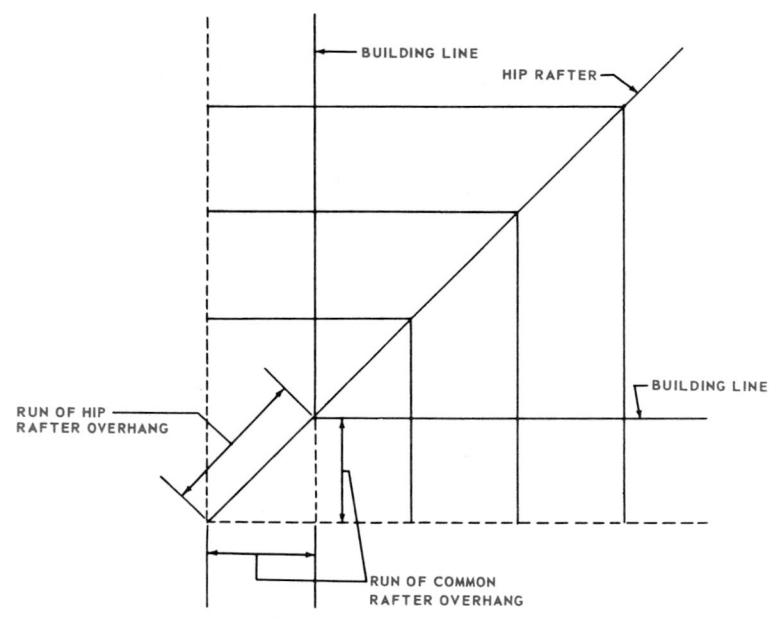

35-15. *Run of hip rafter overhang. For each unit of run (12") of a common rafter, the unit of run for the hip rafter is 17". Therefore if the run of the common rafter overhang in this drawing is 2' (24"), the run of the hip rafter overhang will be 34" (2 x 17).*

hip or valley rafter tail is figured as follows:

1. Find the unit length of the hip or valley rafter on the framing square. Fig. 34-9b. For this roof it is 18.76".

2. Multiply the unit length of the hip or valley rafter by the run of the common rafter overhang:

18.76" (unit length of hip or valley rafter) × 2 (feet of run in common rafter overhang) = 37.52", or 37 ½"

3. Add this product to the theoretical rafter length.

The overhang may also be stepped off as described in Unit 34 for a common rafter. When stepping off the length of the overhang, set the 17" mark on the blade of the square even with the edge of the rafter. Set the unit rise, whatever it might be, on the tongue even with the same rafter edge.

Bird's-mouth

Laying out the bird's-mouth for a hip rafter is much the same as for a common rafter. However, there are a couple of things to remember. When the plumb (heel cut) and level (seat cut) lines are laid out for a bird's-mouth on a hip rafter, set the body of the square at 17" and the tongue to the unit rise (depending on the roof pitch). Fig. 35-7. When laying out the depth of the heel for the bird's-mouth, measure along the heel plumb line down from the top edge of the rafter a distance equal to the same dimension on the common rafter. Fig. 35-16. This must be done so that the hip rafters, which are usually wider than the common rafters, will be level with the common rafters.

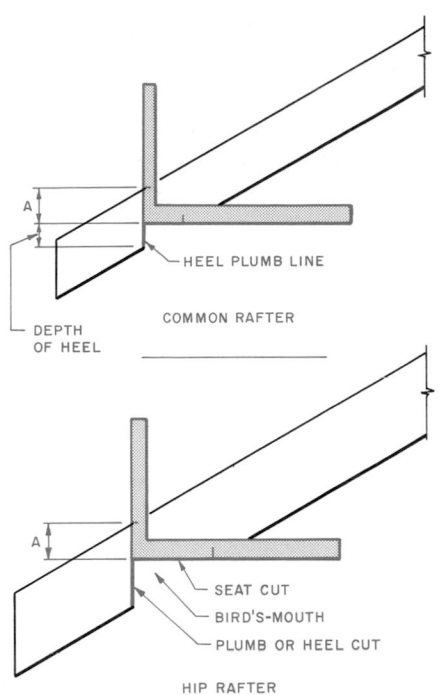

35-16. *When laying out the bird's-mouth on a hip rafter, measure down from the top edge. Dimension A in the drawing must be the same for common and hip rafters so that the tops of all the rafters will be in line for the application of sheathing.*

Backing or Dropping a Hip Rafter

If the dimension above the bird's-mouth is exactly the same on a hip rafter as on a common rafter, the edges of the hip rafter will extend above the upper ends of the jack rafters and interfere with the application of the sheathing. A, Fig. 35-17. This can be corrected by either backing or dropping the hip rafter. *Backing* means to bevel the upper edge of the hip rafter. B, Fig. 35-17. *Dropping* means to deepen the bird's-mouth so as to bring the top edge of the hip rafter down to the upper ends of the jacks. C, Fig. 35-17.

The amount of backing or drop required is calculated as shown in A of Fig. 35-18. Set the framing

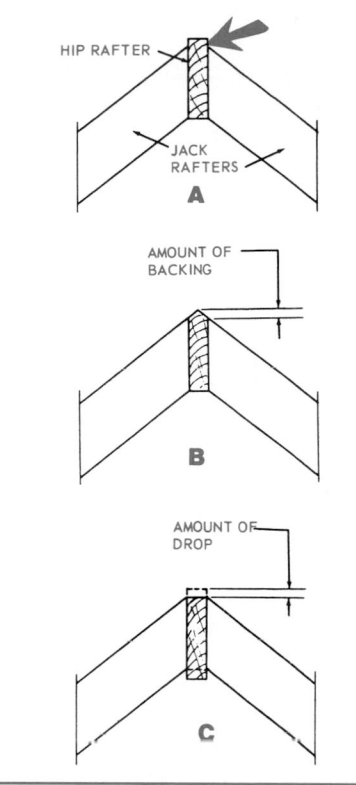

35-17. *A. The edge of a hip rafter may extend above the upper ends of the jack rafters. B. Backing a hip rafter. C. Dropping a hip rafter.*

square to the cut of the rafter (8" and 17" in this example) on the upper edge, and measure off one-half the thickness of the rafter from the edge along the blade (arrow 1). A backing line drawn through this mark, parallel to the edge, will indicate the bevel angle, if the rafter is to be backed. B, Fig. 35-18. The perpendicular distance between the backing line and the edge of the rafter will be the amount of drop (arrow 2). A, Fig. 35-18. This is the amount by which the depth of the hip rafter bird's-mouth should exceed the depth of the common rafter bird's-mouth. C, Fig. 35-18.

VALLEY RAFTER LAYOUT

A valley rafter follows the line of intersection between a main roof surface and a gable roof addition or gable roof dormer surface. Most roofs which contain valley rafters

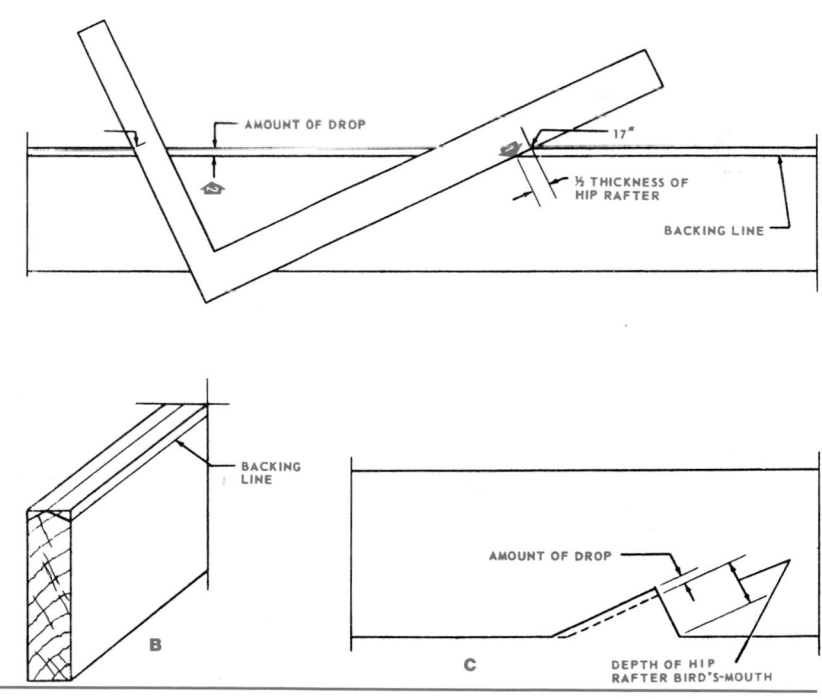

35-18. *Backing or dropping a hip rafter: A. Determining amount of backing or drop. B. Bevel angle for backing the rafter. C. Deepening the bird's-mouth for dropping the rafter.*

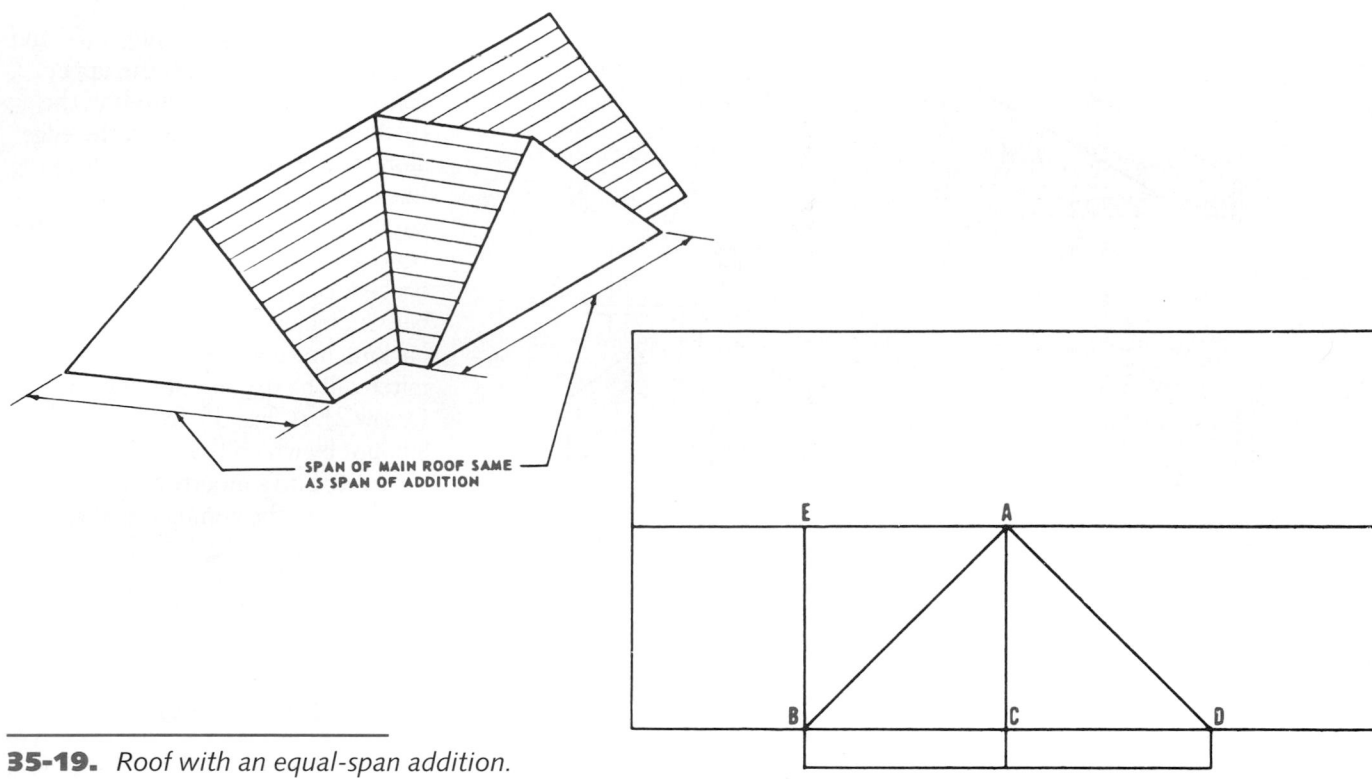

35-19. *Roof with an equal-span addition.*

are equal-pitch roofs; that is, the pitch of the addition or dormer roof is the same as the pitch of the main roof. In an equal-pitch roof the valley rafters always run at 45 degrees to the building line and the ridge boards.

Framing an Equal-Span Roof Addition

In equal-span framing, the span of the addition is the same as the span of the main roof. Fig. 35-19. When the pitch of the addition roof is the same as the pitch of the main roof, equal spans bring the ridge pieces to equal heights.

Look at the roof framing diagram in Fig. 35-19. The total run of a valley rafter (indicated by AB and AD in the diagram) is the hypotenuse of a right triangle whose shorter sides are each equal to the total run of a common rafter in the main roof. The unit run of a valley rafter is therefore 16.97", the same as the unit run for a hip rafter. Figuring

the length of an equal-span addition valley rafter is thus the same as figuring the length of a hip rafter.

The ridge-end shortening allowance for an equal-span addition valley rafter is one-half the 45-degree

thickness of the ridge board. Fig. 35-20. Side cuts are laid out as they are for a hip rafter. The valley rafter tail has a double side cut, like the hip rafter tail, but in the reverse direction, since the tail cut on a

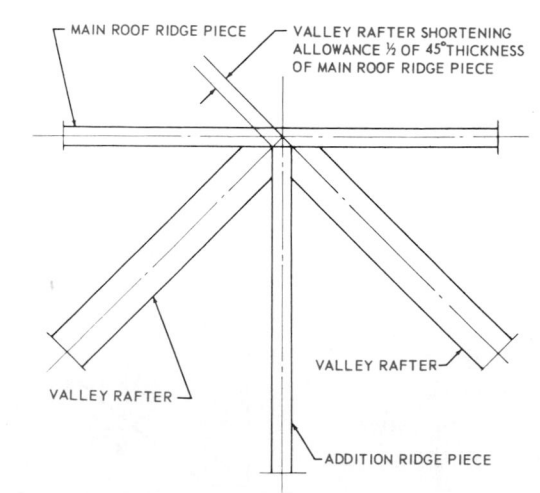

35-20. *Ridge-end shortening allowance for an equal-span addition valley rafter.*

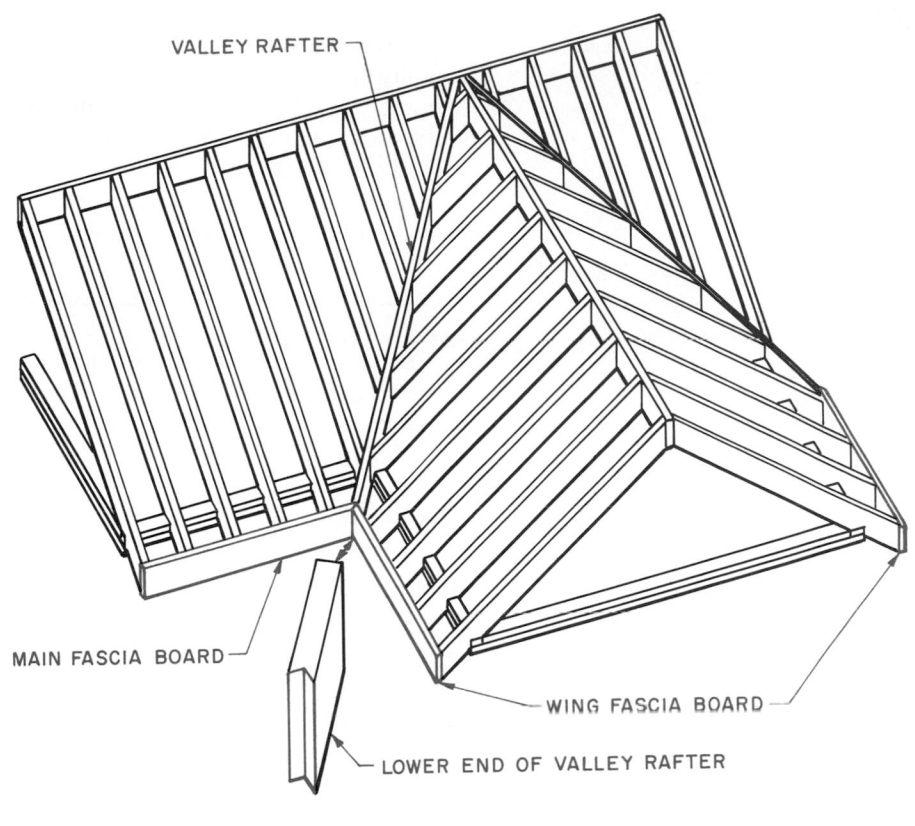

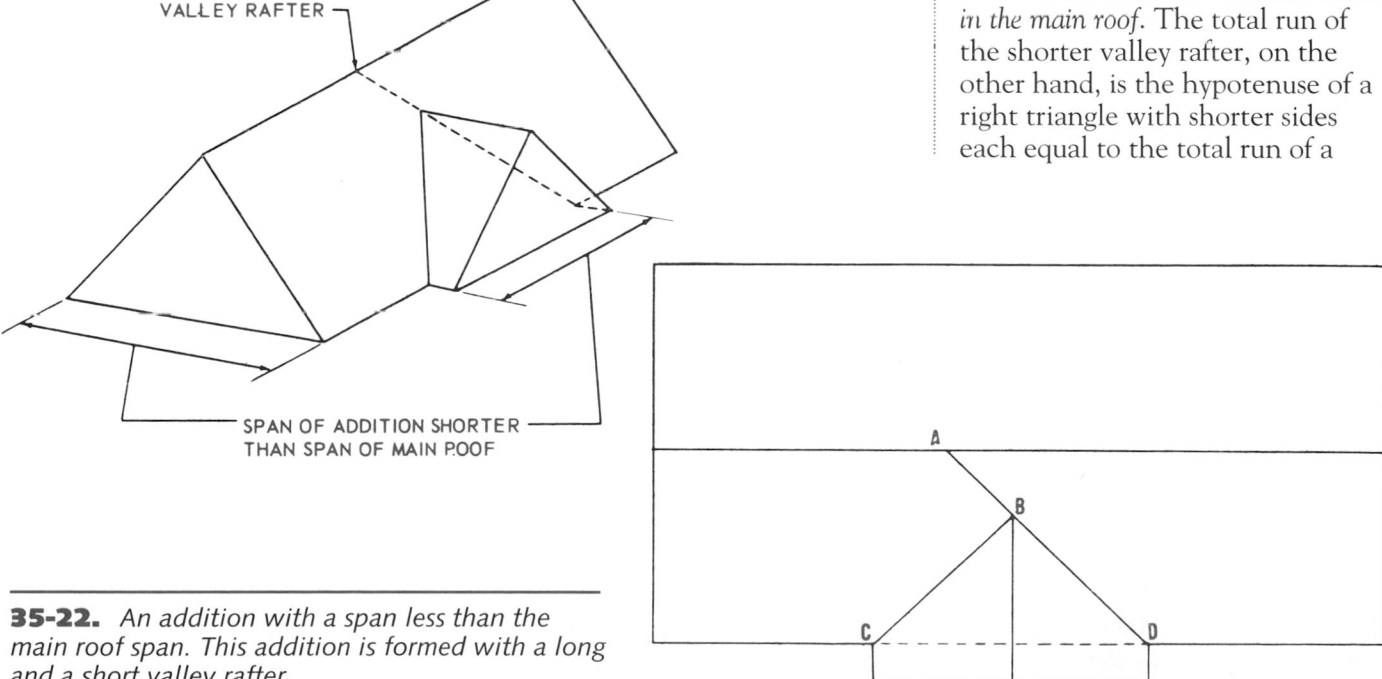

VALLEY RAFTER

MAIN FASCIA BOARD

WING FASCIA BOARD

LOWER END OF VALLEY RAFTER

35-21. *Valley rafter framing. Notice the inside corner formed by the fascia boards.*

FULL-LENGTH VALLEY RAFTER

SPAN OF ADDITION SHORTER THAN SPAN OF MAIN ROOF

35-22. *An addition with a span less than the main roof span. This addition is formed with a long and a short valley rafter.*

valley rafter must form an inside rather than an outside corner. Fig. 35-21. The overhang, if any, and the bird's-mouth are figured just as they are for a hip rafter. A valley rafter, however, does not require backing or dropping.

Framing an Unequal-Span Roof Addition

Sometimes the span of the roof addition is shorter than the span of the main roof. Fig. 35-22. When the pitch of the addition roof is the same as the pitch of the main roof, the shorter span of the addition brings the addition ridge board down to a lower level than that of the main roof ridge board.

There are two ways of framing an addition of this type. In one method, a full-length valley rafter (AD in Fig. 35-22) is framed between the rafter plate and the ridge board, and a shorter valley rafter (CB in the figure) is then framed to the longer one. The total run of the longer valley rafter is the hypotenuse of a right triangle whose shorter sides are each equal to the total run of a common rafter *in the main roof*. The total run of the shorter valley rafter, on the other hand, is the hypotenuse of a right triangle with shorter sides each equal to the total run of a

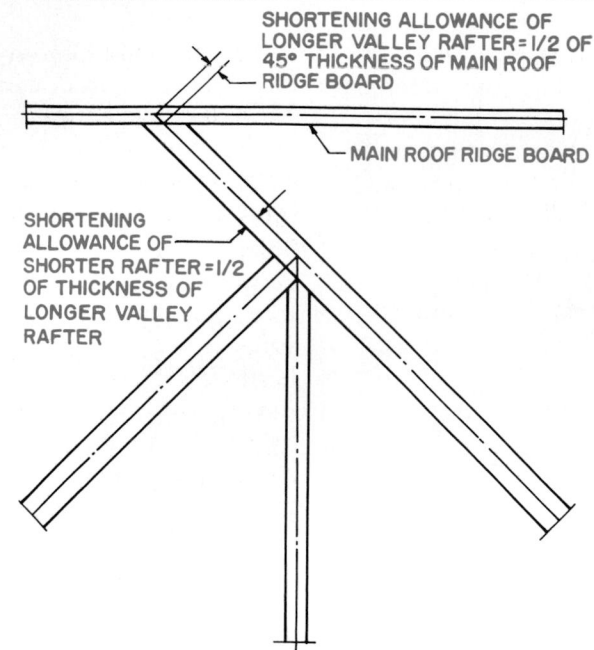

SHORTENING ALLOWANCE OF LONGER VALLEY RAFTER=1/2 OF 45° THICKNESS OF MAIN ROOF RIDGE BOARD

MAIN ROOF RIDGE BOARD

SHORTENING ALLOWANCE OF SHORTER RAFTER=1/2 OF THICKNESS OF LONGER VALLEY RAFTER

35-23. *Long and short valley rafter shortening allowances.*

common rafter *in the addition.* The total run of a common rafter in the main roof is equal to one-half the span of the main roof. The total run of a common rafter in the addition is equal to one-half the span of the addition.

Determining the Length of a Valley Rafter. When the total run

of any rafter is known, the theoretical length can be found by multiplying the unit length by the total run. Suppose, for example, that the addition in Fig. 35-22 has a span of 30' and that the unit rise of a common rafter in the addition is 9". The rafter table in Fig. 34-9b shows that the unit length for a valley rafter in a roof with a common rafter unit

rise of 9" is 19.21". To find the theoretical length of the valley rafter, multiply its unit length by the number of feet in a common rafter of the roof to which it belongs. The total run of a common rafter is equal to one-half the span. Therefore the length of the longer valley rafter in Fig. 35-22 would be 19.21" times one-half the span of the main roof. The length of the shorter valley rafter would be 19.21" times one-half the span of the addition. Since one-half the span of the addition is 15', the length of the shorter valley rafter is 19.21" × 15, or 288.15". Converted to feet, this is 24.01'.

The shortening allowances for the long and short valley rafters are shown in Fig. 35-23. Note that the long valley rafter has a single side cut for framing to the main roof ridge board, while the short valley rafter is cut square for framing to the addition ridge board.

A Second Method of Framing an Unequal-Span Addition

Another method of framing an equal-pitch, unequal-span addition

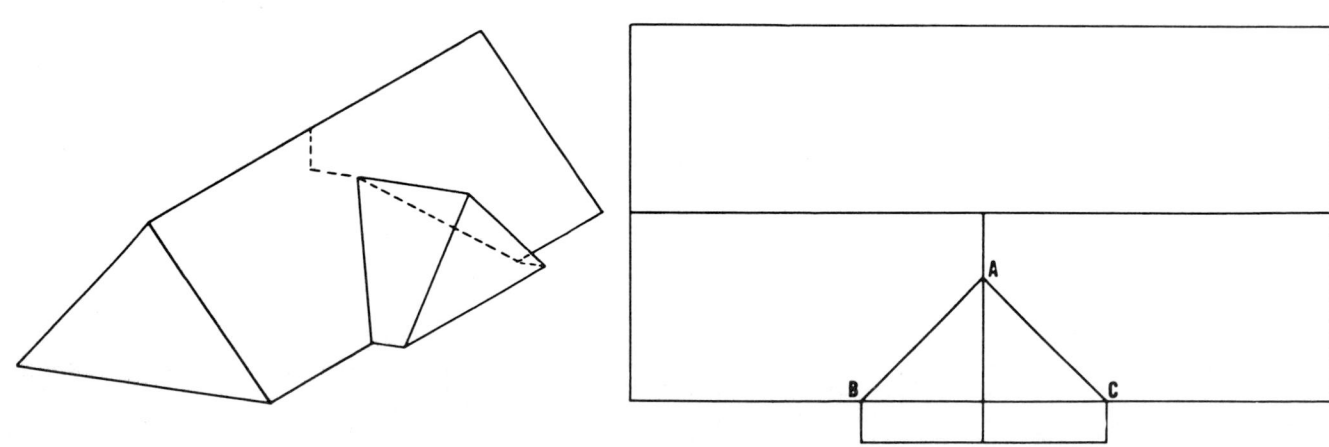

35-24. *Another addition with a span less than the main roof span. This addition is framed with the addition ridge board suspended from the main roof ridge board. The two valley rafters (AB and AC) are the same length.*

is to nail the inboard end of the addition ridge board to a piece of stock which hangs from the main roof ridge board. Fig. 35-24. This method calls for two short valley rafters, each of which extends from the rafter plate to the addition ridge board. The total run of each of these valley rafters is the hypotenuse of a right triangle whose shorter sides are each equal to the total run of a common rafter in the addition.

The shortening allowance for each short valley rafter is one-half the 45-degree thickness of the addition ridge board. Fig. 35-25. Each rafter is framed to the addition ridge board with a single side cut.

Framing a Gable Dormer without Side Walls

When a gable dormer without side walls is framed, the dormer ridge board is fastened to a header set between a couple of doubled main roof common rafters. Fig. 35-26. The valley rafters are framed between this header and a lower header. The total run of a valley rafter is the hypotenuse of a right triangle whose shorter sides are each equal to the total run of a common rafter in the dormer.

The arrangement and names of framing members in this type of dormer framing are shown in Fig. 35-27. Note that the upper edges of the headers must be beveled to the cut of the main roof.

In this framing method, the shortening allowance for the upper end of a valley rafter is one-half the 45-degree thickness of the inside member in the upper doubled header. Fig. 35-28. The shortening allowance for the lower end is one-half the 45-degree thickness of the inside member in the doubled common rafter. Each valley rafter has a double side cut at the upper and the lower end.

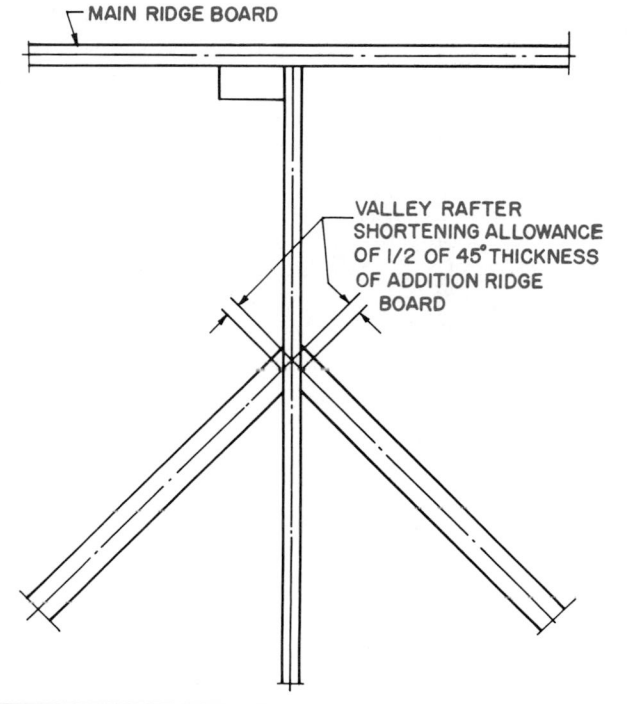

35-25. *Shortening allowance of valley rafters in suspended-ridge method of additional roof framing.*

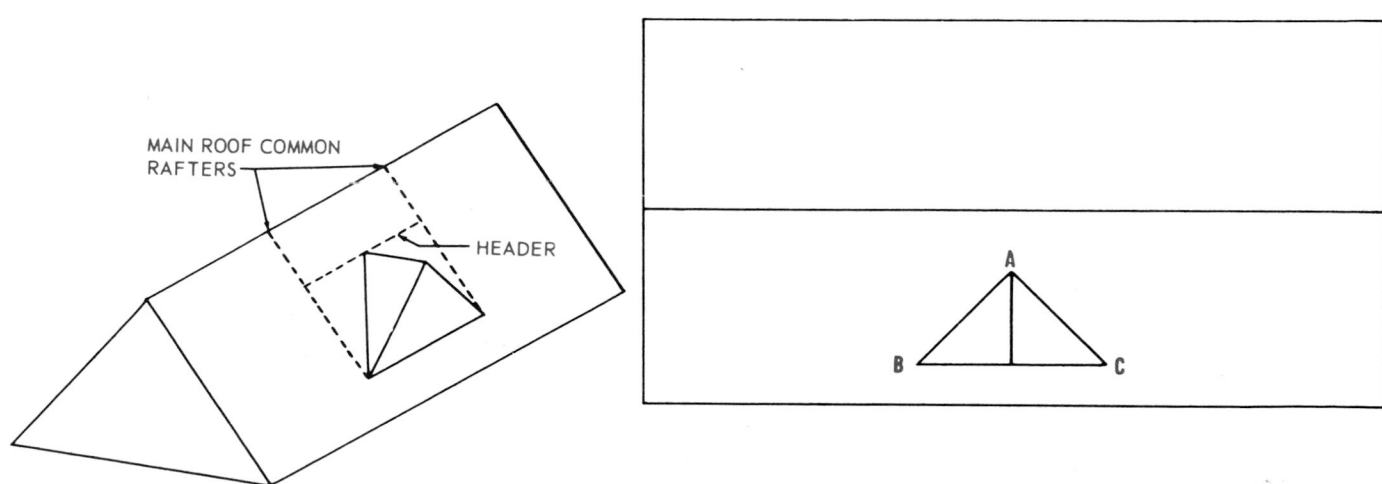

35-26. *Framing a dormer without side walls.*

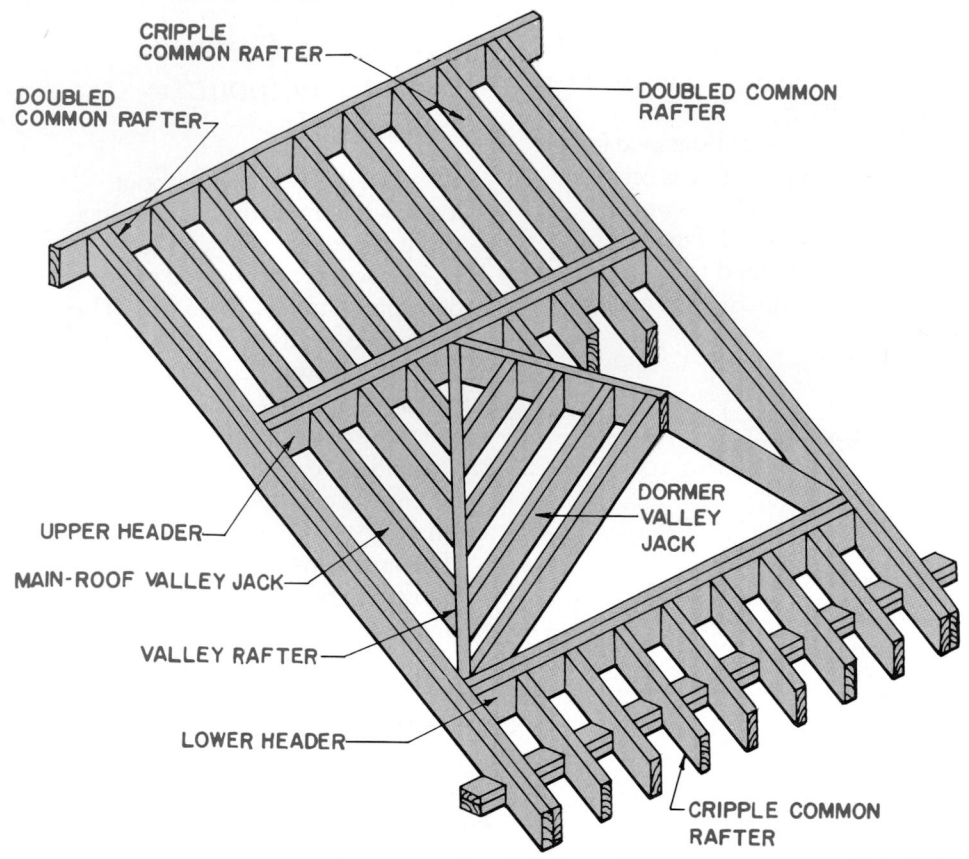

35-27. *Arrangement and names of framing members for a dormer without side walls.*

Framing a Gable Dormer with Side Walls

A method of framing a gable dormer with side walls is illustrated in Fig. 35-29. As indicated in the framing diagram, the total run of a valley rafter is again the hypotenuse of a right triangle whose shorter sides are each equal to the run of a common rafter in the dormer. Figure the lengths of the dormer corner posts and side studs just as you do the lengths of gable-end studs (see p. 407). Lay off the lower-end cutoff angle by setting the square to the cut of the main roof. The valley rafter shortening allowances for this method of framing are shown in Fig. 35-30.

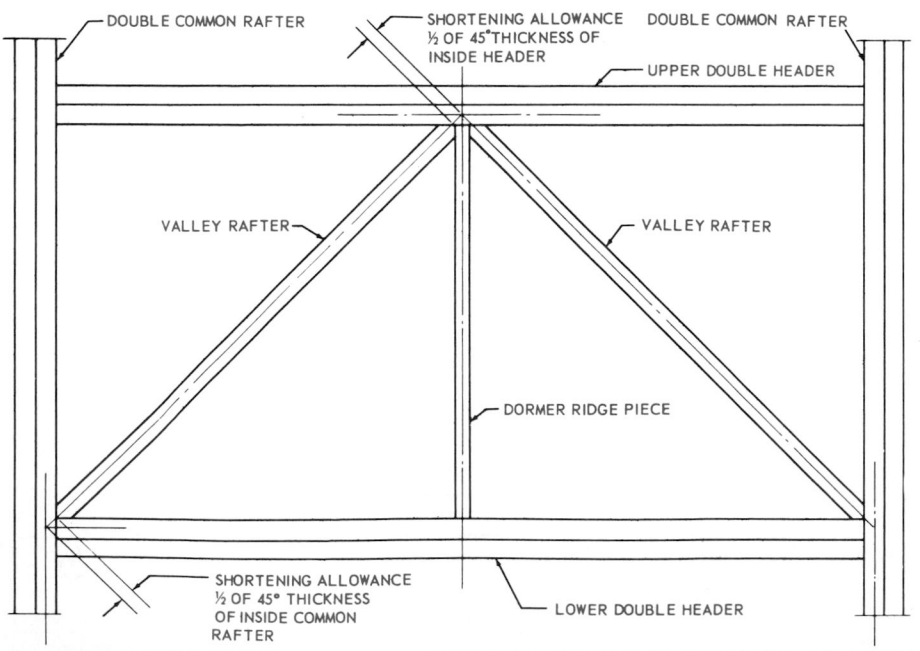

35-28. *Valley rafter shortening allowances for a dormer without side walls.*

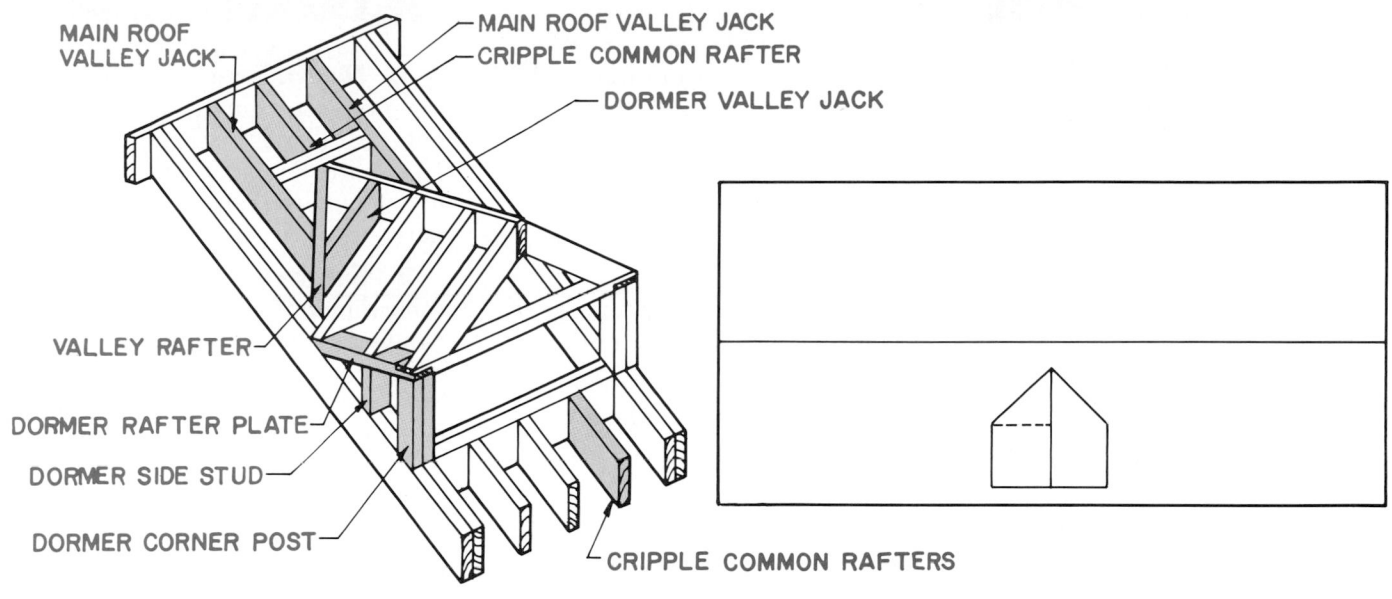

35-29. *Framing a gable dormer with side walls.*

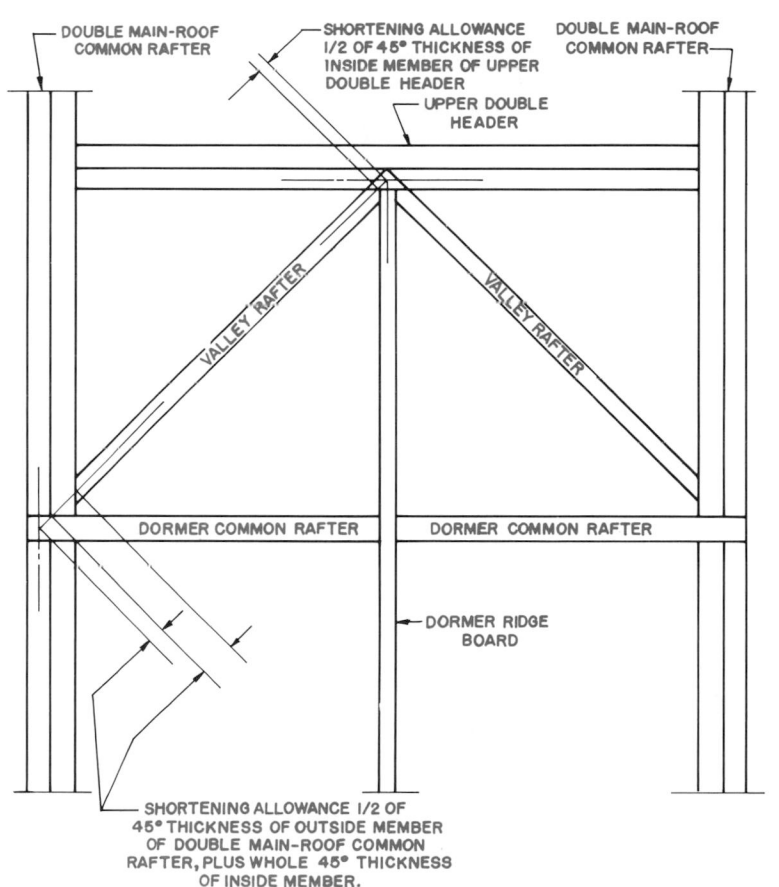

35-30. *Valley rafter shortening allowances for a dormer with side walls.*

1. What is a hip rafter?

2. What is a valley rafter?

3. Explain why the unit run of a hip rafter is 16.97 when the unit run of a common rafter is 12.

4. What number is used on the body of the square when making a cut for a hip or valley rafter?

5. What is the shortening allowance at the ridge for a hip rafter when the ridge end is framed against the ridge board?

6. Why is the run of a hip rafter overhang greater than the run of a common rafter overhang in the same roof?

7. When laying out the depth of the heel for the bird's-mouth on a hip rafter, why must you measure down from the top edge of the rafter a distance equal to the same dimension used on the common rafter?

8. Why must the upper edge of the hip rafter be beveled or the bird's-mouth cut deeper?

9. Describe two methods of framing an unequal-span roof addition.

10. In a right triangle, what is the side opposite the right angle called?

1. **Math.** For a house with a hip roof, if the run of a common rafter is 14' and the slope is 5 in 12, use the Pythagorean theorem to compute the run of a hip rafter.

2. **Science.** Using at least three different materials that are easily obtainable, construct a model roof top that includes a hip and valley portion. Materials could be aluminum foil, package wrapping material, newspaper, cardboard, or clay.

Determine which material is easiest to use in constructing this. Base your findings on such factors as ease of use, workability, strength, and actual representation of a hip and a valley roof.

A gable dormer is sometimes added to an existing house. Because the proportions of a gable dormer restrict its size, gable dormers are used mostly to gain light and ventilation, not to increase usable floor space in an attic remodel.

Determining the size of an add-on dormer is important. It should be in proportion to the house. A large dormer on a small roof will make the house look top-heavy, while a dormer that's too small won't bring much light into the attic. Many builders size the dormer to accommodate a particular window, particularly if it complements other windows in the house. The width of the dormer should be at least 6" wider on each side than the rough opening of the window. This will provide strength at the dormer's corners.

1. Imagine that you are designing a remodeling project to convert an attic into a bedroom. You have decided to build two dormers in the roof. Find out if the dormer windows have to be big enough to serve as emergency exits. A window used in this fashion is called an "egress" window. Check with local building officials, or consult a

building code book.

2. Prior to designing a dormer, many builders or designers will look through photos of dormers for ideas on style, proportion, and construction detailing. Start a file on gable dormers by collecting pictures of various styles and designs. One of the best sources of pictures will be remodeling and homeowner do-it-yourself magazines. Photocopy pictures as you find them. On the back of each photocopy, write any details from the article that might help you to build a similar dormer.

Jack Rafters

A *jack rafter* is a shortened common rafter that may be framed to a hip rafter, a valley rafter, or both. This means that in an equal-pitch framing situation, the unit rise of a jack rafter is always the same as the unit rise of a common rafter.

TYPES OF JACK RAFTERS

A *hip jack* rafter extends from a hip rafter to a rafter plate. Fig. 36-1.

A *valley jack* rafter extends from a valley rafter to a ridge board. Fig. 36-1.

A *cripple jack* rafter does not contact either a plate or a ridge board. There are two kinds of cripple jack rafters: (1) the *valley cripple jack* extends between two valley rafters in the long-and-short-valley-rafter method of addition framing and (2) the *hip-valley cripple jack* extends from a hip rafter to a valley rafter. Fig. 36-2.

LENGTHS OF HIP JACK RAFTERS

A roof framing diagram for a series of hip jack rafters is shown in Fig. 36-3. The jacks are always on the same spacing as the common

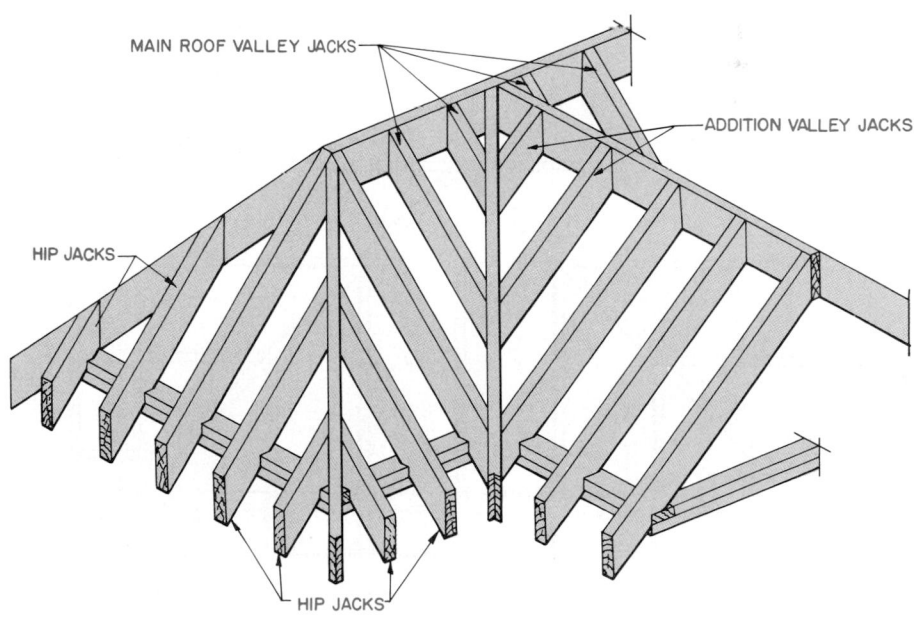

MAIN ROOF VALLEY JACKS

ADDITION VALLEY JACKS

HIP JACKS

HIP JACKS

36-1. *Hip and valley jack rafters.*

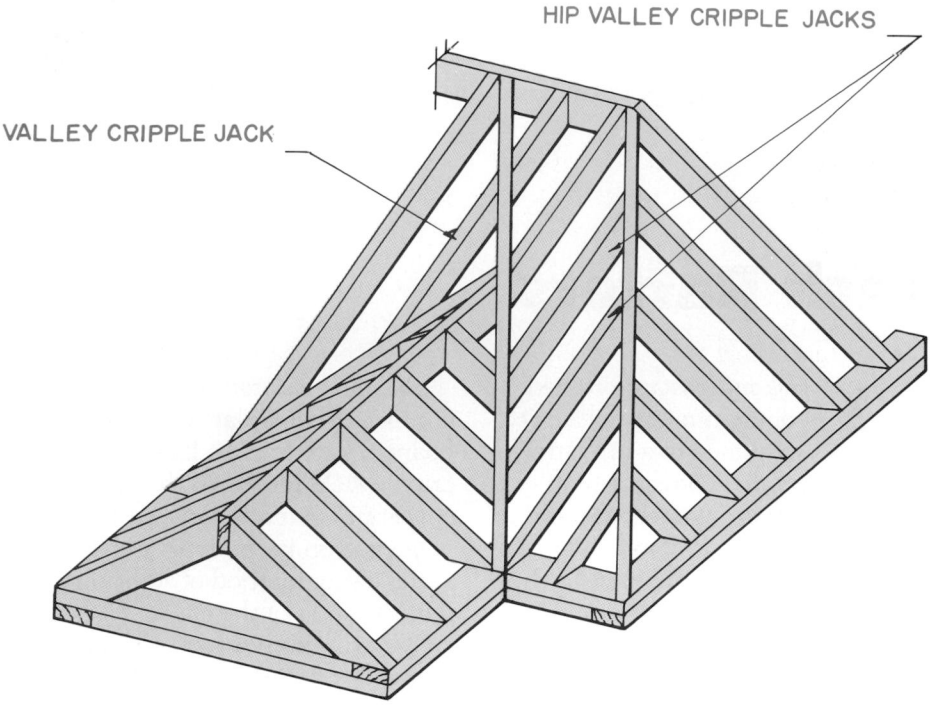

36-2. *Valley cripple jack and hip-valley cripple jacks.*

rafters. The spacing in this instance is 16" on center. You can see from the arrow in the diagram that the total run of the shortest jack is also 16".

Suppose the unit rise of a common rafter in this roof is 8" per 12" of run. The jacks have the same unit rise as a common rafter. The unit length of a rafter is the hypotenuse of a right triangle with the unit run as base and the unit rise as height. The unit length of a jack rafter in the example is therefore the square root of $(12^2 + 8^2)$, or 14.42. This means that a jack is 14.42" long for every 12" of run.

The theoretical total length of the shortest jack rafter can now be calculated:

$$\frac{12" \text{ (unit run)}}{14.42" \text{ (unit length)}} = \frac{16" \text{ (total run)}}{x \text{ (total length)}}$$

$$x = 19.23"$$

This is the length of the shortest hip jack when the jacks are spaced 16" on center and the unit rise is 8". It is also the *common difference* of these jacks. This means that the next hip jack will be $2 \times 19.23"$ long, the one after that $3 \times 19.23"$ long, and so on.

The common difference for hip jacks spaced 16" on center and for hip jacks spaced 24" on center can be found in the rafter table on the framing square. Fig. 34-9b. The third line of the table reads "Difference in Length of Jacks 16 Inches Centers." Follow this line to the column headed 8 (for a unit rise of 8") to find the length of the first jack rafter and the common difference, 19 ¼".

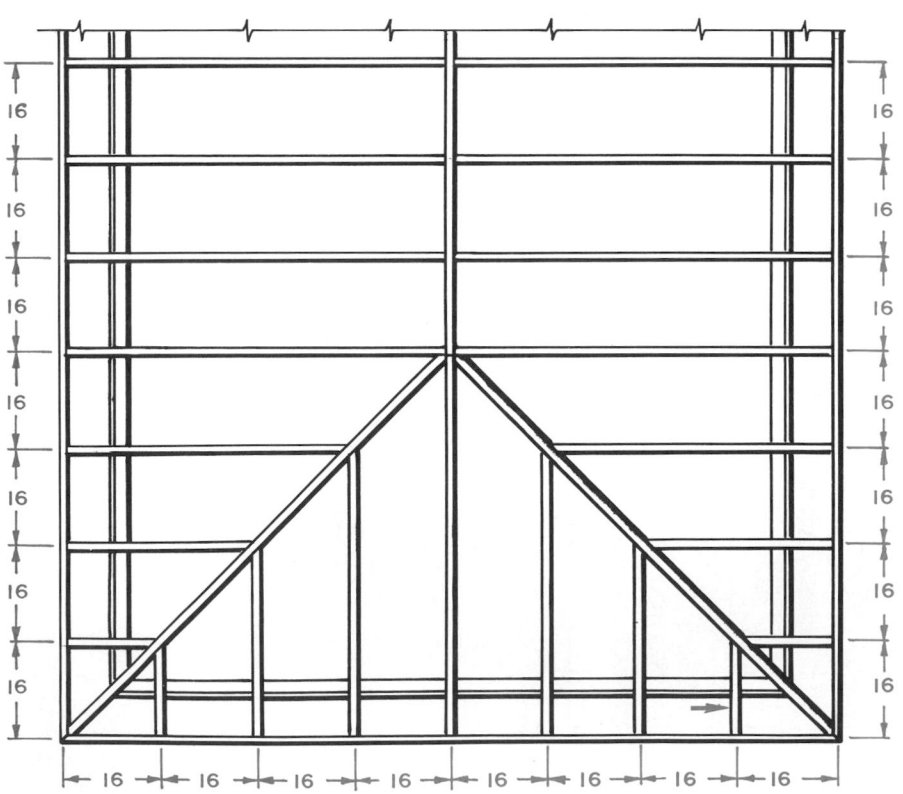

36-3. *Hip jack framing diagram.*

LENGTHS OF VALLEY AND CRIPPLE JACKS

The best way to figure the total lengths of valley jacks and cripple jacks is to lay out a framing diagram. Fig. 36-4 shows part of a framing diagram for a main hip roof with a long-and-short-valley-rafter gable addition. By studying the diagram you can figure the total lengths of the valley jacks and cripple jacks as follows:

The run of valley jack No. 1 is the same as the run of hip jack No. 8, which is the shortest hip jack. The length of valley jack No. 1 is therefore equal to the common difference of jacks.

The run of valley jack No. 2 is the same as the run of hip jack No. 7, and the length is therefore twice the common difference of jacks.

The run of valley jack No. 3 is the same as the run of hip jack No. 6. The length is therefore three times the common difference of jacks. The run of hip-valley cripple No. 4, and also of hip-valley cripple No. 5, is the same as the run of valley jack No. 3. The length of these rafters is thus the same as the length of No. 3.

The run of valley jack No. 9, and also of valley jack No. 10, is equal to the spacing of jacks on center. Therefore the length of each of these jacks is equal to the common difference of jacks. The run of valley jacks Nos. 11 and 12 is twice the run of valley jacks Nos. 9 and 10. The length of each of these jacks is therefore twice the common difference of jacks.

The run of valley cripple No. 13 is twice the spacing of jacks on center, and the length is therefore twice the common difference of jacks. The run of valley cripple No. 14 is twice the run of valley cripple No. 13, and the length is therefore twice the common difference of jacks.

JACK RAFTER SHORTENING ALLOWANCES

A hip jack rafter has a shortening allowance at the upper end consisting of one-half the 45-degree thickness of the hip rafter. Fig. 36-5. A valley jack rafter has a shortening allowance at the upper end, consisting of one-half the thickness of the ridge board (Figs. 35-11 and 35-12) and another at the lower end, consisting of one-half the 45-degree thickness of the valley rafter. Fig. 36-5. A hip-valley cripple has a shortening allowance at the upper end, consisting of one-half the 45-degree thickness of the hip rafter, and another at the lower end, consisting of one-half the 45-degree thickness of the valley rafter. A valley cripple has a shortening allowance at the upper end, consisting of one-half the 45-degree thickness of the long valley rafter, and another at the lower end, consisting of one-half the 45-degree thickness of the short valley rafter.

JACK RAFTER SIDE CUTS

The side cut on a jack rafter can be laid out by the method illustrated in Fig. 35-11 and 35-12 for laying out the side cut on a hip

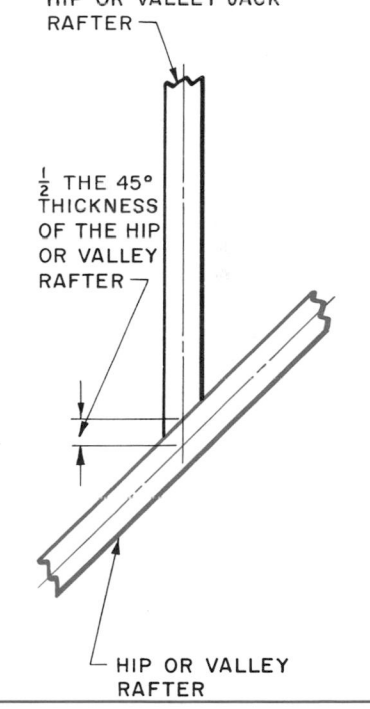

36-5. The shortening allowance for the upper end of a hip jack or the lower end of a valley jack rafter is one-half of the 45° thickness of the hip or valley rafter, whichever the jack rafter intersects.

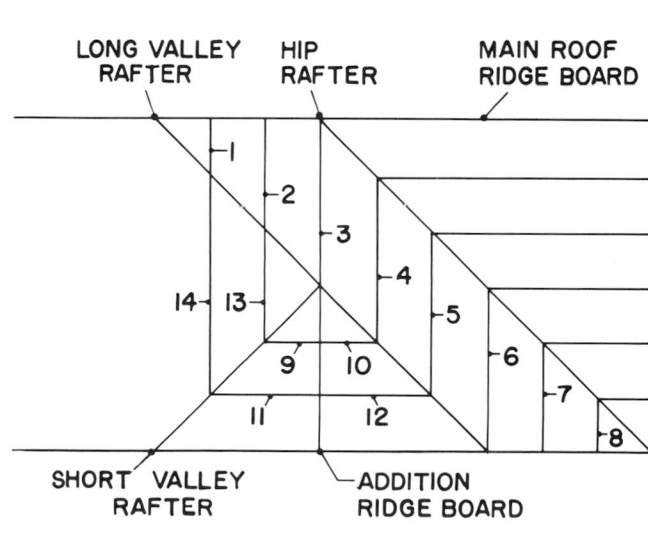

36-4. Jack rafter framing diagram for a hip roof with a gable addition.

rafter. Another method is to use the rafter table on the framing square. Fig. 34-9b. Find the line headed "Side Cut of Jacks Use" and read across to the figure under the unit rise. For a unit rise of 8, the figure given is 10. To lay out the side cut on a jack with this unit rise, set the square face-up on the edge of the rafter to 12" on the tongue and 10" on the blade. Draw the side cut line along the tongue, as was described earlier for side cuts on hip rafters. Fig. 35-14.

JACK RAFTER BIRD'S-MOUTH AND OVERHANG

A jack rafter is a shortened common rafter. Consequently the bird's-mouth and overhang on a jack rafter are laid out just as they are on a common rafter. See Unit 34.

JACK RAFTER PATTERN

Lay out and cut the longest jack rafter first. Be careful to calculate and make all necessary allowances to determine the actual length. Set the rafter in place on the

building and check the fit of all the cuts. See that the spacing between the centers of the rafters is correct.

When everything is correct, use this rafter as a pattern. On the top edge of the rafter, measure down the center line from the ridge end a distance equal to the common difference measurement (found on the framing square rafter table).

This is the length of the second longest jack rafter. Continue to mark the common difference measurements along the top edge until the lengths of all the jacks have been laid out. Fig. 36-6. Using this pattern, mark off all the jack rafters. When all the rafters have been cut, the pattern is used as a part of the roof frame.

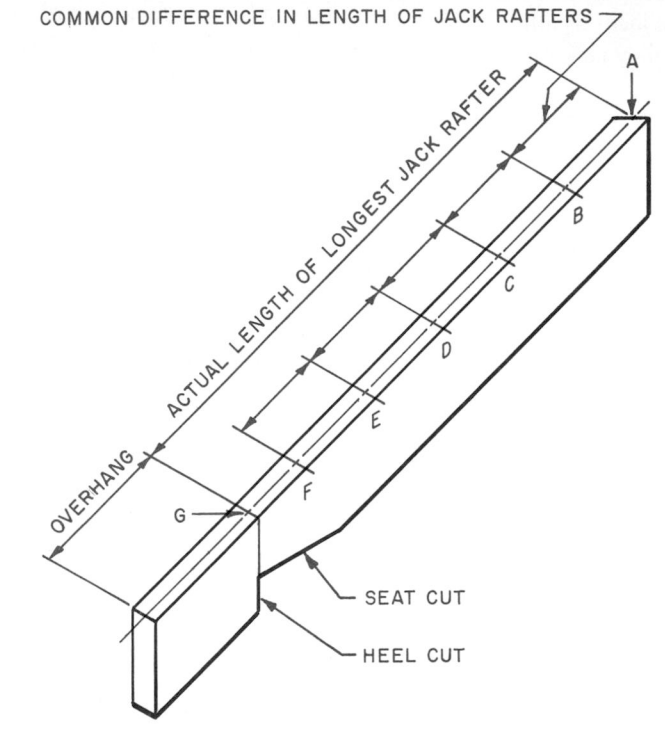

COMMON DIFFERENCE IN LENGTH OF JACK RAFTERS

ACTUAL LENGTH OF LONGEST JACK RAFTER

OVERHANG

A
B
C
D
E
F
G

SEAT CUT
HEEL CUT

36-6. Use the longest jack rafter as a pattern. The second jack rafter is BG, the third jack rafter is CG, and so on.

QUESTIONS

1. What is a jack rafter?

2. What is a hip jack rafter?

3. What is a valley jack rafter?

4. What is a cripple jack rafter?

5. If the shortest hip jack rafter is 19¼" long, how long will the third hip jack rafter be?

ACTIVITIES

1. Math. For a house with a hip roof, the run of a common rafter is 14', the slope is 6 in 12, there is a 2' overhang, and the rafters are 16" O.C.

a. How many different lengths of jack rafters are needed? (Hint: Use a diagram such as that shown in Fig. 36-3.)

b. Figure the length of the two shortest hip jack rafters.

37

Layout and Erection of the Roof Frame

When the building has been framed, plumbed, and squared and the ceiling joists are in place, the structure is ready for roof framing. Lay out and cut two common rafters for trial purposes as discussed in Unit 34. With a scrap piece of material the same thickness as the ridge board, set the two common rafters on the building and check all the cuts to make certain the rafters fit properly. If necessary, make corrections on the trial rafters. When they fit properly, use one as a pattern and cut the required number of common rafters for the roof frame. Lean the rafters in position against the building with the ridge end up. Calculate and lay out the actual length of the ridge board. Then lay out the rafter locations on the double plates and ridge board in preparation for the roof frame erection.

LAYING OUT THE RIDGE BOARD

Gable Roof

Laying out the ridge piece for a gable main roof presents no particular problem, since the theoretical length of the ridge piece is equal to the length of the building. The actual length would include any overhang. Fig. 37-1.

Hip Roof

For a hip main roof, the ridge piece layout requires a certain amount of calculation. In an equal-pitch hip roof, the theoretical length of the ridge piece amounts to the length of the building minus twice the total run of a main roof common rafter. The actual length, however, depends upon the way in

37-1. *Framing a gable roof with an unequal-span addition and a Dutch hip on the front of the addition. The workers are framing the overhang on the gable end.*

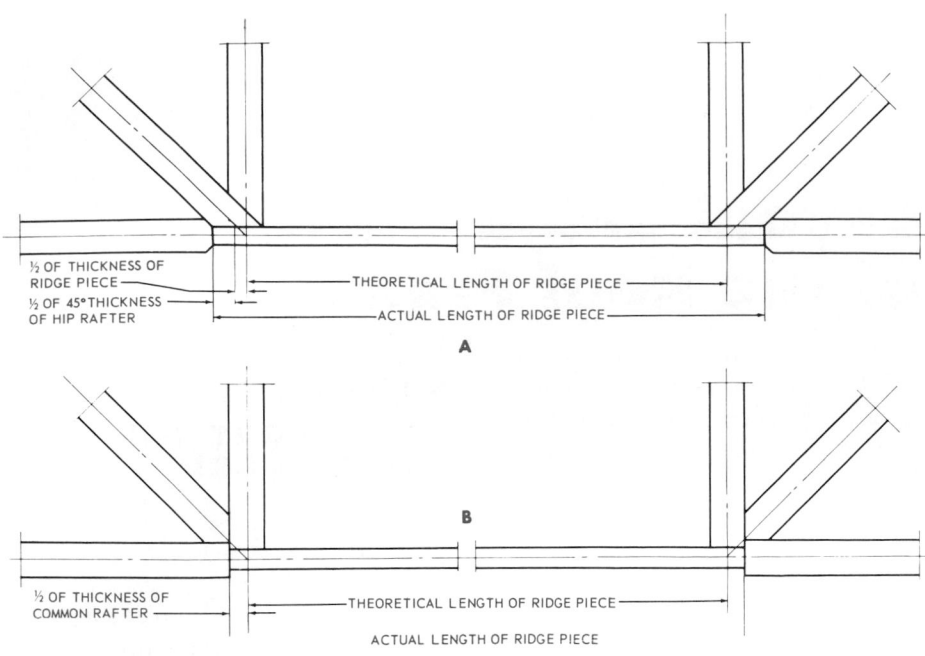

½ OF THICKNESS OF RIDGE PIECE
½ OF 45° THICKNESS OF HIP RAFTER
THEORETICAL LENGTH OF RIDGE PIECE
ACTUAL LENGTH OF RIDGE PIECE

A

½ OF THICKNESS OF COMMON RAFTER
THEORETICAL LENGTH OF RIDGE PIECE
ACTUAL LENGTH OF RIDGE PIECE

B

37-2. *Theoretical and actual lengths of hip roof ridge boards. A. Hip rafter framed against ridge board. B. Hip rafter framed between common rafters. In this drawing the ridge board is 1" material. Usually it is 2", the same as the ridge-end common rafters, and the side cuts on these rafters (A) are not needed.*

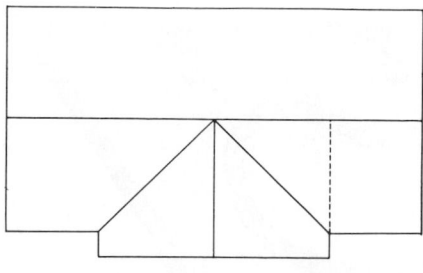

37-3. *Determining the length of a ridge board for an equal-span addition.*

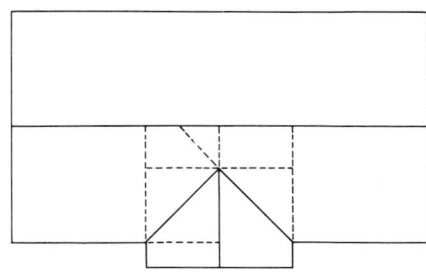

37-4. *Determining the length of a ridge board for an unequal-span addition.*

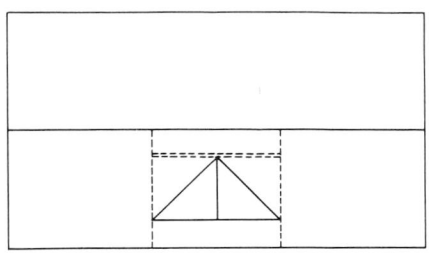

37-5. *Determining the length of a ridge board on a dormer without side walls.*

which the hip rafters are framed to the ridge.

The theoretical ends of the ridge board are at the points where the ridge center line and the hip rafter center lines cross. Fig. 37-2. If the hip rafter is framed against the ridge board, the actual length of the ridge board exceeds the theoretical length, at each end, by one-half the thickness of the ridge board plus one-half the 45-degree thickness of the hip rafter. A, Fig. 37-2. If the hip rafter is framed between the common rafters, the actual length of the ridge board exceeds the theoretical length, at each end, by one-half the thickness of a common rafter. B, Fig. 37-2.

Equal-Span Addition

For an equal-span addition, the length of the ridge board is equal to the length the addition projects beyond the building, plus one-half the span of the building, minus the

shortening allowance at the main roof ridge. The shortening allowance amounts to one-half the thickness of the main roof ridge piece. Fig. 37-3.

Unequal-Span Addition

The length of the ridge board for an unequal-span addition varies with the method of framing the ridge piece. Fig. 37-4. If the addition ridge board is suspended from the main roof ridge board, the length is equal to the length the addition projects beyond the building, plus one-half the span of the main roof.

If the addition ridge board is framed by the long-and-short-valley-rafter method, the length is equal to the length the addition projects beyond the building, plus one-half the span of the addition, minus a shortening allowance consisting of one-half the 45-degree thickness of the long valley rafter.

If the addition ridge piece is framed to a double header set between a couple of double main roof common rafters, the length of the ridge piece is equal to the length the addition projects beyond the building, plus one-half the span of the addition, minus a shortening allowance consisting of one-half the thickness of the inside member of the double header.

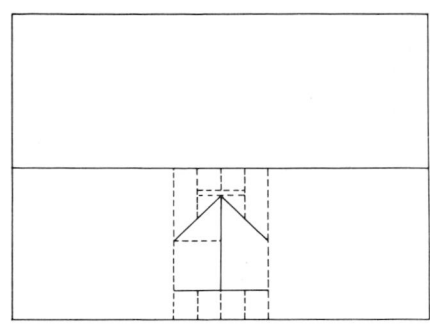

37-6. *Determining the length of ridge board on dormer with side walls.*

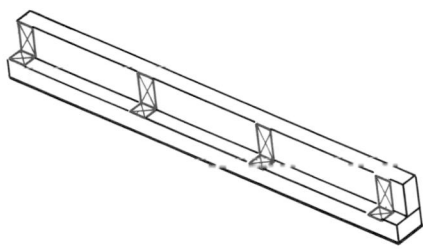

37-7. *Lay the ridge board on edge on the top plate and extend the layout lines from the plate onto the ridge board.*

Dormer without Side Walls

The length of the ridge piece on a dormer without side walls is equal to one-half the span of the dormer, less a shortening allowance consisting of one-half the thickness of the inside member of the upper double header. Fig. 37-5.

Dormer with Side Walls

The length of the ridge board on a dormer with side walls amounts to the length of the dormer side-wall top plate, plus one-half the span of the dormer, minus a shortening allowance consisting of one-half the thickness of the inside member of the upper double header. Fig. 37-6.

LAYING OUT THE RAFTER LOCATIONS

The layout of the rafter spacing on the wall plates and ridge board is determined by checking either the building plans or the roof frame plan. Rafter locations are laid out on plates, ridge board, and other rafters with the same lines and X's used to lay out stud and joist locations. (See Units 30 and 32.) In most cases the rafters are located next to the ceiling joists. The rafters can then be fastened to the side of the joists to tie the building together.

Gable Roof

For a gable roof the rafter locations are laid out on the top plates first. The locations are then transferred to the ridge piece by matching the ridge board against a top plate. Fig. 37-7.

On a gable roof the first rafters on each end are usually set even with the outside wall to permit a smooth unbroken surface for the application of the sheathing. Since the first ceiling joist was set on the inside edge of the wall, it will be necessary to place a spacer block between the first rafter and the first ceiling joist. Fig. 37-8. The other rafters are fastened to the side of the joists along the length of the building.

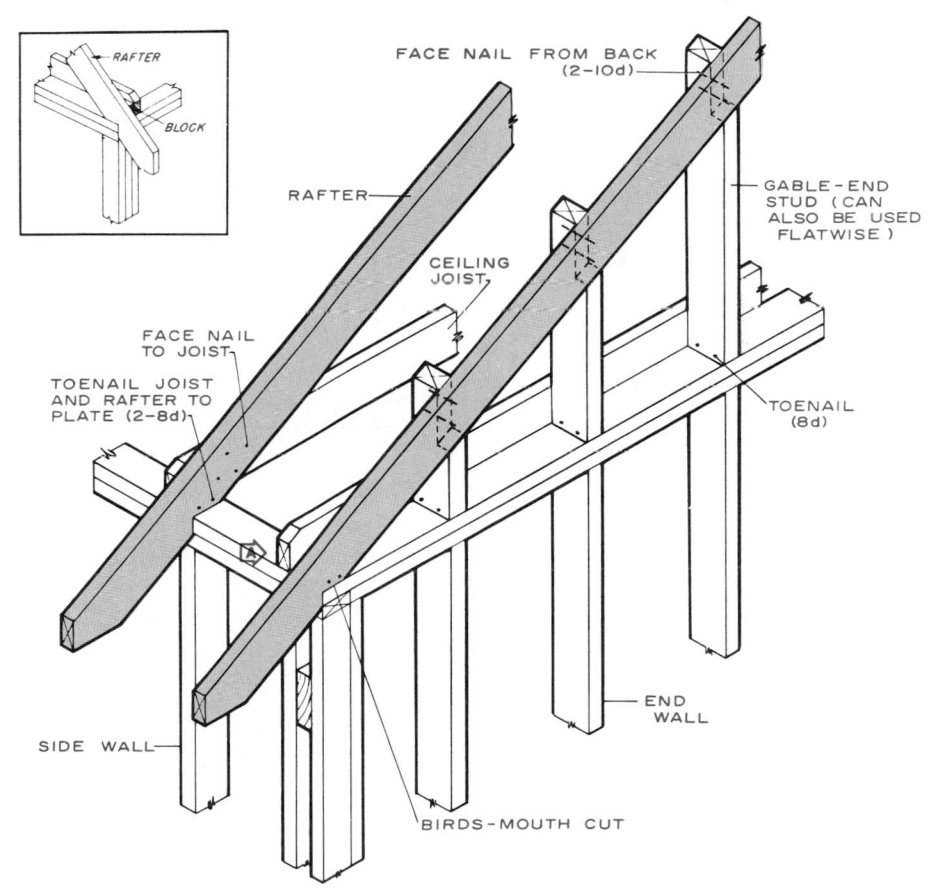

37-8. *Gable roof rafter locations.*

If the rafters are on 24" centers and the ceiling joists are on 16" centers, the first rafter will be placed as shown in Fig. 37-8. The second rafter will rest on the plate between the second and third joists. The third rafter will fasten to the side of the fourth joist. The rafters will continue to alternately rest on the plate between two joists and fasten to the side of a joist along the remaining length of the building. Fig. 37-9.

Always begin the rafter layout on the plates from the same end of the building for the two opposite walls, and continue along the length of the building. Fig. 37-10. This will insure direct bearing down through the walls to the foundation wall. It will also make the rafters butt directly opposite each other on the ridge board. Fig. 37-11.

Hip Roof

The top plate locations of the ridge-end common rafters in an equal-pitch hip roof measure one-half of the span (or the run of a main roof common rafter) away from the building corners. These locations, plus the top plate locations of the rafters lying between the ridge-end common rafters, can be transferred to the ridge board by matching the ridge board against the top plates. Fig. 37-12.

Addition Roofs

In an equal-span addition the valley rafter locations on the main roof ridge board lie alongside the addition ridge board location. In Fig. 37-13 the distance between the end of the main roof ridge board and the addition ridge piece location is equal to distance A plus distance B, distance B being one-half the span of the addition. In Fig. 37-14 the distance between the

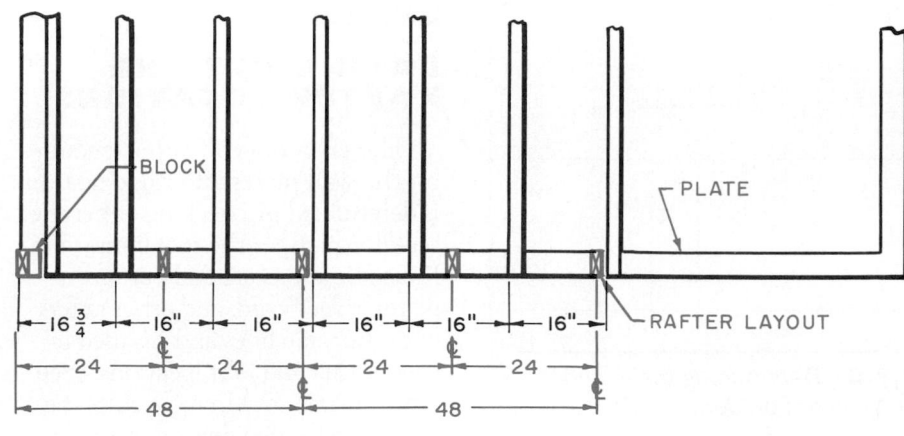

37-9. *Layout of a building with the rafters on 24" centers and the ceiling joists on 16" centers.*

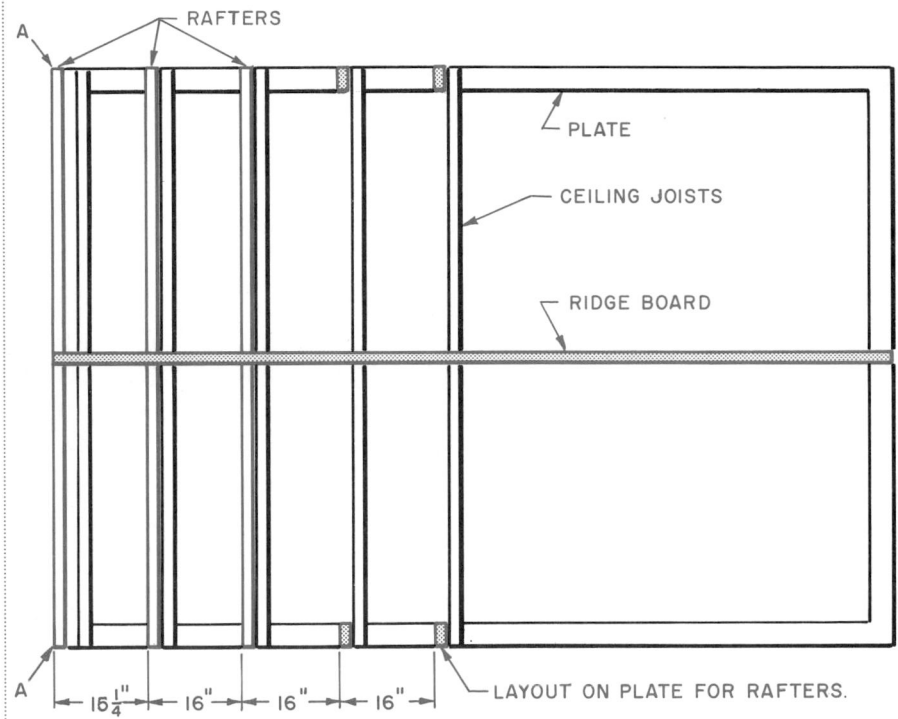

37-10. *Begin the layout of the rafters from the same end of the building as the layout of the floor joists, wall studs, and ceiling joists. In this drawing, the layout for each phase began at arrow A on the two side walls.*

theoretical end of the main roof ridge board and the addition ridge board location is the same as distance A.

In an unequal-span addition, if framing is by the long-and-short-valley-rafter method, the distance from the end of the main roof ridge board to the upper end of the longer valley rafter is equal to distance A plus distance B, distance B being one-half the span of the main roof. Fig. 37-15. The location of the inboard end of the shorter valley rafter on the longer valley rafter can be determined as follows:

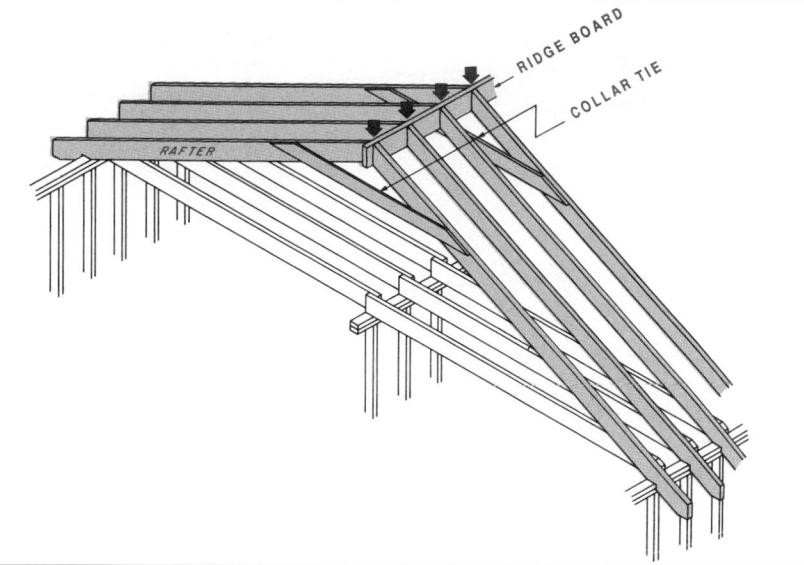

37-11. *The rafters are fastened to the side of the ceiling joists over the wall studs. Note (arrows) that the rafters butt directly opposite each other on the ridge board.*

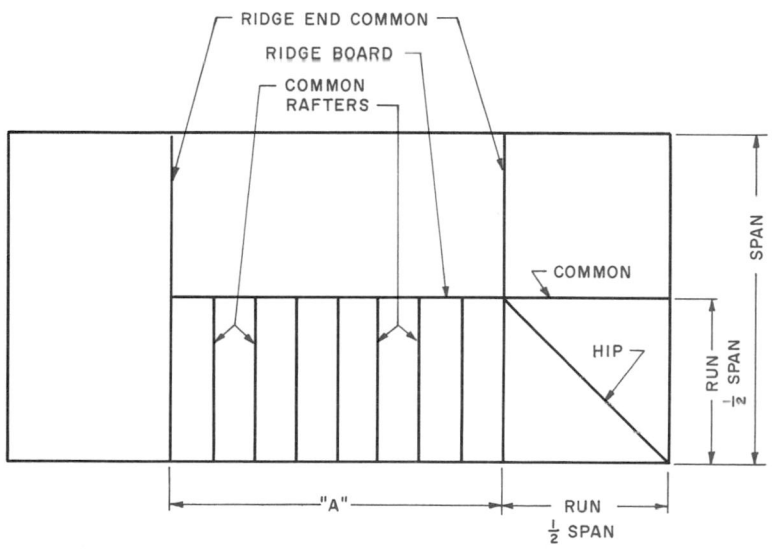

37-12. *The locations of the rafters in area "A" are transferred to the ridge board from the top plate.*

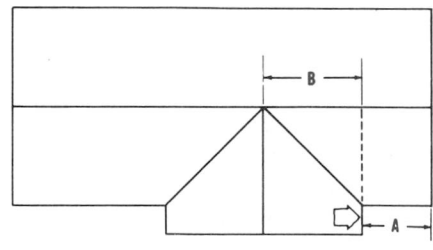

37-13. *Ridge board location for equal-span addition on a gable roof.*

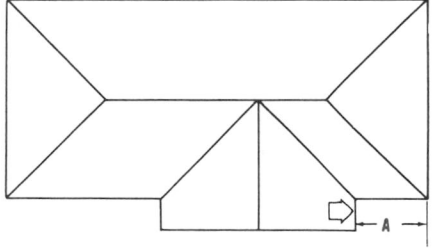

37-14. *Ridge board location for equal-span addition on a hip roof.*

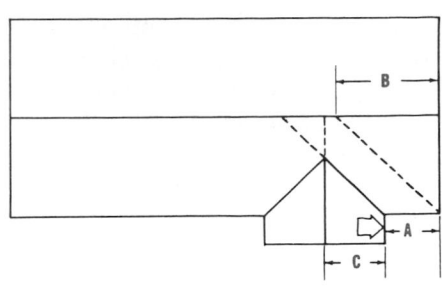

37-15. *Ridge board and valley rafter locations for unequal-span addition.*

➤ Obtain the unit length of the longer valley rafter from the rafter table. Fig. 34-9b. Suppose that the common rafter unit rise is 8". In that case the unit length of a valley rafter is 18.76".

➤ Between the point where the shorter rafter ties in and the top plate, the total run of the longer valley rafter is the hypotenuse of a right triangle whose shorter sides are each equal to the total run of a common rafter in the addition. The total run of a common rafter in the addition is one-half the span. Suppose the addition is 20' wide; the run of a common rafter would be 10'. C, Fig. 37-15.

➤ You know that the valley rafter is 18.76" long for every foot of common rafter run. The location mark for the inboard end of the shorter valley rafter on the longer valley rafter can thus be calculated:

18.76 (in. per ft. of run) × 10 (ft. of run) = 187.6"; 187.6" = 15.63', or 15' 7 %6"

This is the distance from the heel plumb cut line of the longer valley rafter to the location mark.

If framing is by the suspended-ridge method, the distance between the suspension point on the main roof ridge board and the end of the main roof ridge piece is equal to distance A plus distance C. Fig. 37-15. Distance C is one-half the span of the addition. The distance between the outboard end of the addition ridge board and where the valley rafters (both short in this method of framing) tie into the addition ridge board is equal to one-half the span of the addition plus the length of the addition side-wall top plate.

ERECTING THE RIDGE BOARD

Many carpenters raise the ridge board and the gable-end rafters all at one time. Each member supports the other. However, with the gable-end rafters nailed in place, it is difficult to make adjustments.

It is possible to put the ridge board in place before raising any rafters. Nail uprights on the walls and cross partitions below the center line of the ridge board for support. Erect the ridge board, level and align it, and nail it in place. Fig. 37-16a. The ridge board should also be braced longitudinally to prevent the roof from swaying. This is particularly important on a gable roof. Fig. 37-16b. After the ridge board is nailed in position, begin the erection of the rafters.

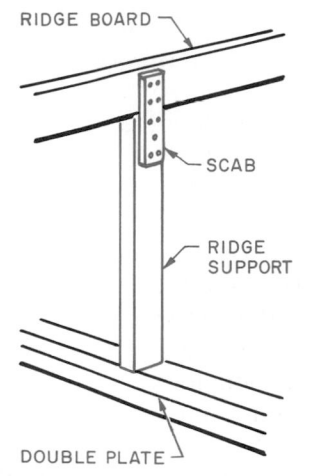

37-16a. *An upright (leg) supports the ridge board in position for the rafter erection.*

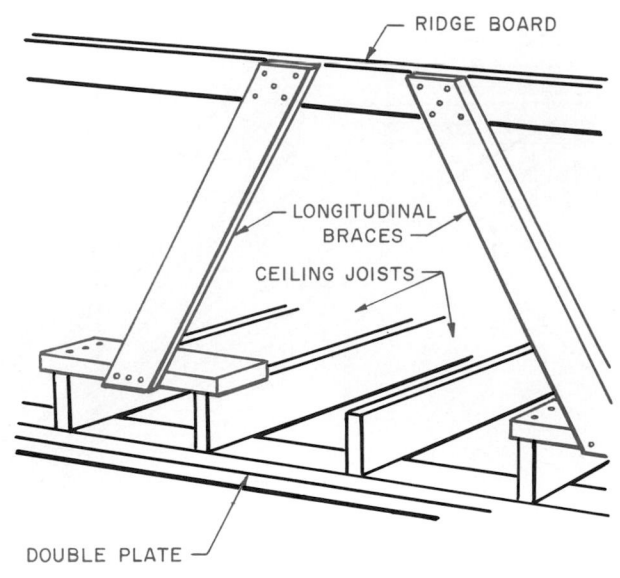

37-16b. *Longitudinal bracing for the ridge board.*

ERECTING THE RAFTERS

Roof framing should be done from a scaffold with planking not less than 4' below the level of the main roof ridge board. The usual type of roof scaffold consists of diagonally braced, two-legged horses, spaced about 10' apart and extending the full length of the ridge piece.

If the building has an addition, as much as possible of the main roof is framed before the addition framing is started. All types of jack rafters are usually left out until after the headers, hip rafters, valley rafters, and ridges to which they will be framed have been installed.

Gable Roof

For a gable roof the two pairs of gable-end rafters and the ridge piece are usually erected first. Two people, one at either end of the scaffold, hold the ridge board in position, while a third person sets the gable-end rafters in place and toenails them at the top plate with

8d nails, two on one side and one on the other side. Make certain the person standing at the ridge pulls the rafter up so that the (plumb) heel cut of the bird's-mouth is tight against the side of the building when the rafter is nailed at the plate.

Each worker on the scaffold then end-nails the ridge piece to one of the rafters with three 10d nails driven through the ridge piece into the end of the rafter. The other rafter is toenailed to the ridge piece and to the first rafter with four 8d nails, two on each side of the rafter.

If the ridge board has not been previously erected and braced, temporary braces like those for a wall should be installed at the ridge ends to hold the rafters approximately plumb, after which the rafters between the end rafters should be erected. Figs. 37-17, 18, and 19. The braces should then be released, and the pair of rafters at one end should be plumbed. The braces are then reset and left in place until enough sheathing has been installed to hold the rafters plumb.

Ceiling-joist ends are nailed to adjacent rafters with four 10d nails,

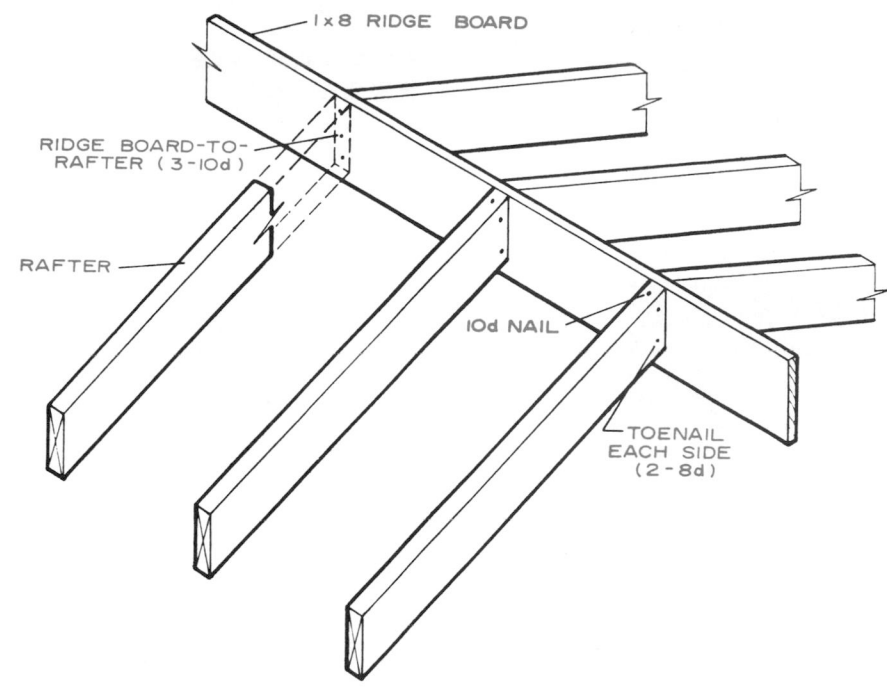

37-17. Rafter nailing procedure at the ridge board.

1 x 8 RIDGE BOARD

RIDGE BOARD-TO-RAFTER (3 -10d)

RAFTER

10d NAIL

TOENAIL EACH SIDE (2-8d)

37-18. Toenailing a rafter to the ridge board and to the rafter opposite it.

two to each side. Metal brackets may also be used to attach the rafters to the plate. Fig. 37-20.

Hip Roof

On a hip roof the ridge board and the common rafters extending from the ridge ends to the side walls are erected first, in about the same manner as for a gable roof. The intermediate common rafters are then filled in. After that, the ridge-end common rafters extending from the ridge ends to the mid-points on the end walls are erected. The hip rafters and hip jacks are installed next.

The common rafters in a hip roof do not require plumbing. If the hip rafters are correctly cut, installing the hip rafters and the common rafter which projects from the end of the ridge board to the end wall will bring the common rafters plumb.

Hip rafters are toenailed to plate corners with 10d nails, two to each side. At the ridge board, they are toenailed with four 8d nails. After the hip rafters are fastened in place, partially drive a nail in the center of the top edge of the hip rafter at the ridge end and at the plate end. Pull a line taut between these nails and as the hip jacks are nailed to the hip rafter, keep the string centered on the top edge of the hip rafter to insure a straight hip line.

The hip jacks should be nailed in pairs, one opposite the other. *Do not nail* all the jacks on one side of the hip and then all the jacks on the opposite side as this would push the hip out of alignment and cause a bow. Hip jacks are toenailed to hip rafters with 10d nails, three to each jack, and to the plate with 10d nails, two to each side.

37-19. *Face-nailing a jack rafter through the ridge board.*

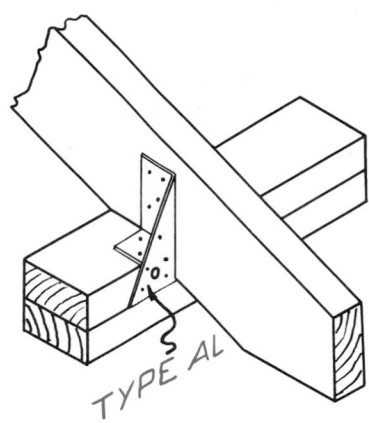

37-20. *Metal brackets are sometimes used to fasten the rafter to the plate. These brackets are fastened with special nails (11 gauge-1¼" long) which are furnished with the bracket.*

Additions and Dormers

For an addition or dormer the valley rafters are usually erected first. Valley rafters are toenailed to ridge boards and headers with three 10d nails. Ridge boards and ridge-end common rafters are erected next, then other addition common rafters, and last, valley and cripple jacks. As with hip rafters, pull a line along the top edge of the

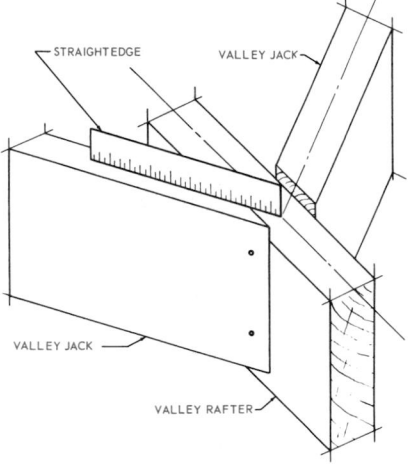

37-21. *Correct position for nailing a valley jack rafter.*

valley rafter and nail the jacks in pairs. A valley jack should be held in position for nailing as shown in Fig. 37-21. When properly nailed, the end of a straightedge laid along the top edge of the jack should contact the center line of the valley rafter as shown.

COLLAR TIE FRAMING

Gable or double-pitch roof rafters are often reinforced by horizontal members called *collar ties*. In a finished attic the collar ties also function as ceiling joists.

The length of a collar tie is calculated on the basis of the height of the tie above the level of the side-wall top plates. The theoretical length of a tie in feet is found by dividing this height in inches by the unit rise of a common rafter in the roof, and subtracting twice the result from the span of the building. For example, in the roof shown in Fig. 37-22, the collar tie is 3' 6", or 42", above the rafter plate. The unit rise of a common rafter in the roof is 10. Forty-two divided by 10 is 4.2, and twice 4.2 is 8.4. This is subtracted from the span of the building: 16-8.4 = 7.6', or about 7' 7³⁄₁₆", which is the theoretical length of the tie.

To bring the ends of the collar tie flush with the upper edges of the common rafters, you must add to the theoretical length of the tie, at each end, an amount equal to the *level width* of a rafter minus the width of the rafter seat cut. The level width is obtained by setting the square on the rafter to the cut of the roof, drawing a level line from edge to edge, and measuring the length of this line.

Lay out the end cuts on a collar tie by setting the framing square on the tie to the cut of the roof. Fig. 37-23.

Collar ties are nailed to common rafters with four 8d nails to each end of a one-inch tie. If two-inch material is used for the ties, they are nailed with three 16d nails at each end.

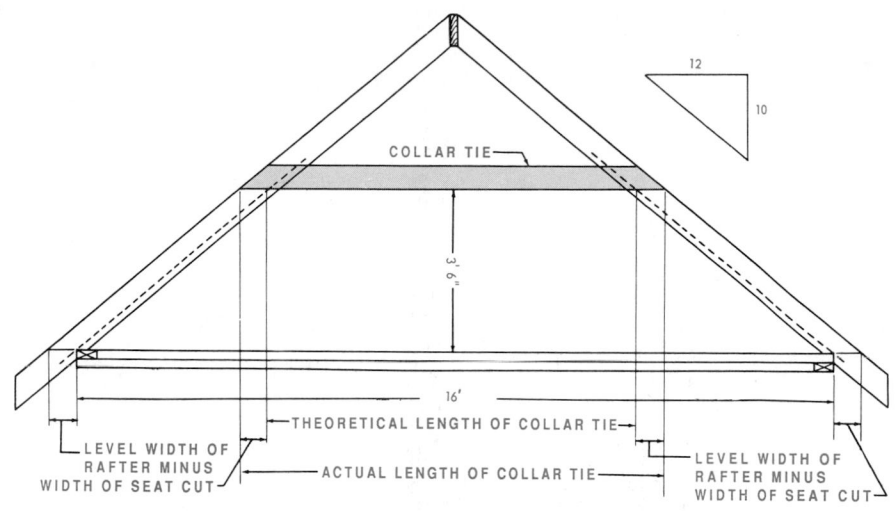

37-22. *Laying out a collar tie.*

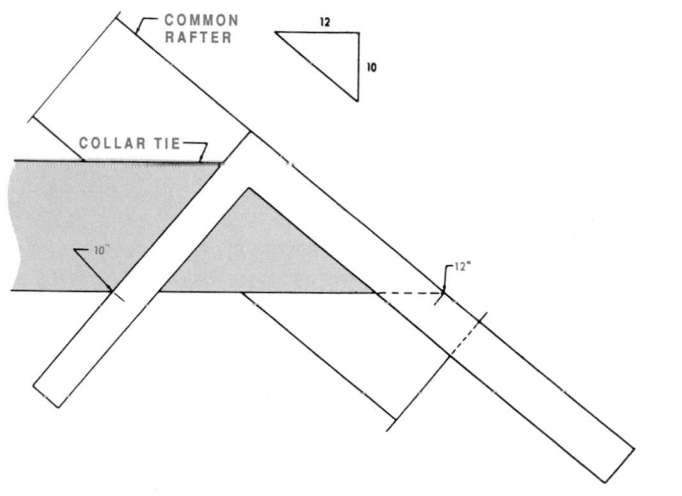

37-23. *Laying out the end cut on a collar tie for a roof with a unit rise of 10".*

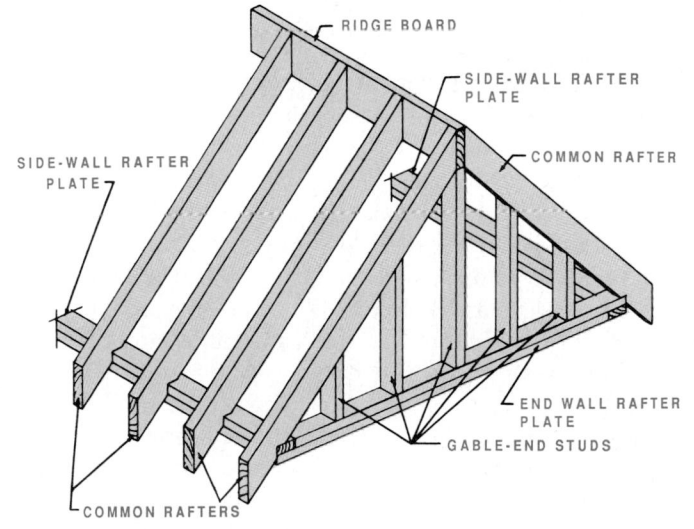

37-24a. *Gable roof framing without a gable overhang.*

GABLE-END FRAMING

Gable-end studs are members which rest on the top plate and extend to the rafter line in the ends of a gable roof. Fig. 37-24a and 37-24b. They may be placed with the edge of the stud even with the outside wall and the top notched to fit the rafter (Fig. 37-24c), or they may be installed flatwise with a cut on the top of the stud to fit the slope of the rafter.

The position of the first gable-end stud is located by making a mark on the double plate directly above the wall stud nearest the ridge line. A, Fig. 37-25. Plumb the gable-end stud on this mark and mark the stud where it hits the bottom of the rafter. B, Fig. 37-25. Mark the cut of the roof across the edge of the gable stud and notch the stud to a depth equal to the thickness of the rafter. C, Fig. 37-25.

The lengths of the other gable studs will depend on the spacing. For studs 24" on center, the line DE in Fig. 37-25 represents 2 units of run (one unit is 12"). For a roof with a unit rise of 6" and studs 24" O.C., the second gable stud will be 12" shorter.

The common difference in the length of the gable studs may be figured by the following method:

$$\frac{24" \, (\text{O.C. spacing})}{12" \, (\text{unit run})} = 2$$

$$2 \times 6" \, (\text{unit rise}) = 12" \, (\text{common difference})$$

A common difference of 12" means that each stud will be 12" shorter than the first, the third stud 24" shorter than the first, the fourth stud 36" shorter, and so on. If the studs are spaced 16" O.C. for the same roof, the common difference in length is 8":

$$\frac{16" \, (\text{O. C. spacing})}{12" \, (\text{unit run})} = 1 \, 1/3$$

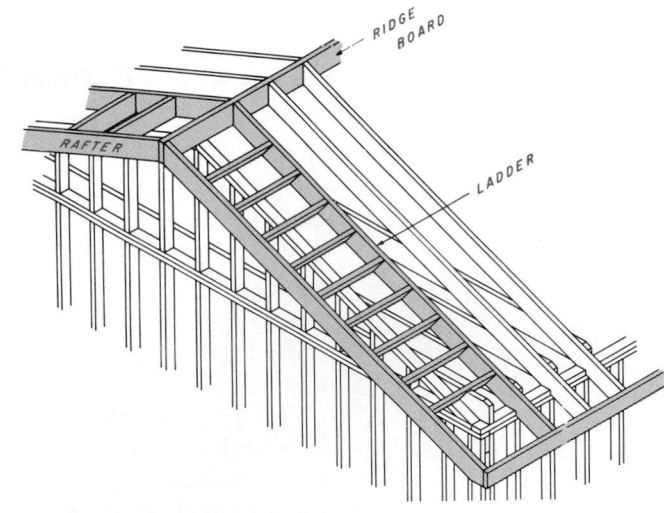

37-24b. *Roof framing for overhang at gable end.*

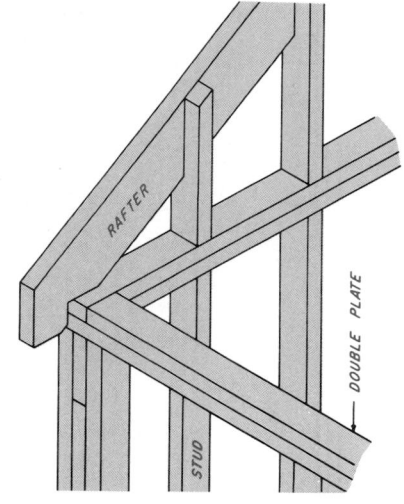

37-24c. *Gable-end studs notched to fit the rafter.*

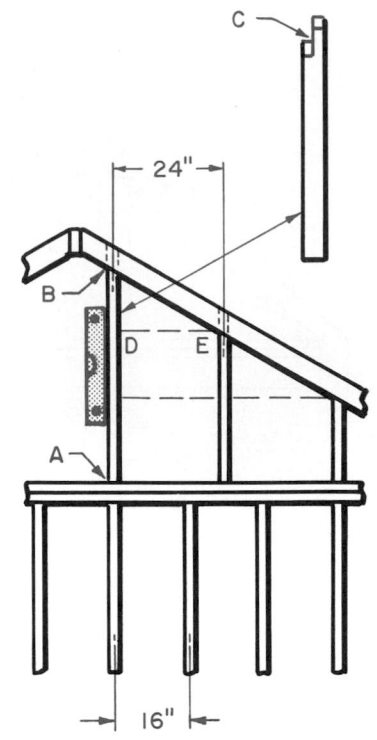

37-25. *Locating the position of the gable-end studs and determining the common difference in length.*

$1\frac{1}{3} \times 6"$ (unit rise) = 8" (common difference)

The common difference in the length of the gable studs may also be laid out directly with the framing square. Fig. 37-26. Place the framing square on the stud to the cut of the roof (6 and 12 for this example). Draw a line along the blade at A. Slide the square along this line in the direction of the arrow at B until the spacing desired between the studs (16 for this example) is at the intersection of the line drawn at A and the edge of the stud. C, Fig. 37-26.

Read the dimension on the tongue which is aligned with the same edge of the stud. This is the common difference (8" for this example) between the gable studs.

Toenail the studs to the plate with two 8d nails from each side. Fig. 37-8. As the studs are nailed in place, care must be taken not to force a crown into the top of the rafter.

FRAMING A GAMBREL ROOF

The gambrel roof is a gable roof with two slopes. It has the advantage of providing additional space for rooms in the attic area. It also minimizes the roof area exposed to snow loads. The framing of this roof style is simply a combination of two common rafters, the lower one having a steep pitch and the upper one a low pitch. If the pitches are known, the rafters may be laid out in the same manner as any common rafter.

The roof may also be laid out full size on the subfloor. Use the run of the building (AB) as a radius and draw a semicircle. Fig. 37-27. Draw a perpendicular line from point A to intersect the semicircle at E. This locates the ridge line. Find the height of the partition walls from

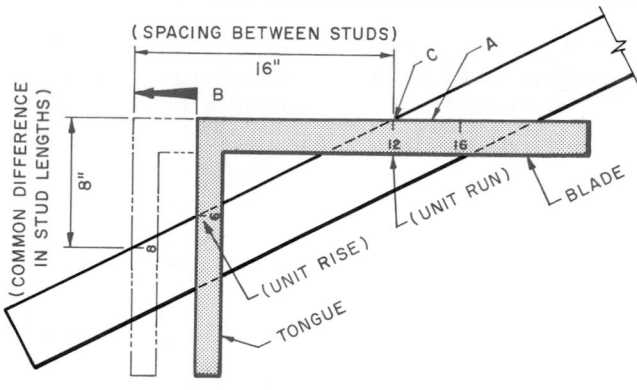

37-26. *Using the framing square to determine the common difference in the length of gable-end studs.*

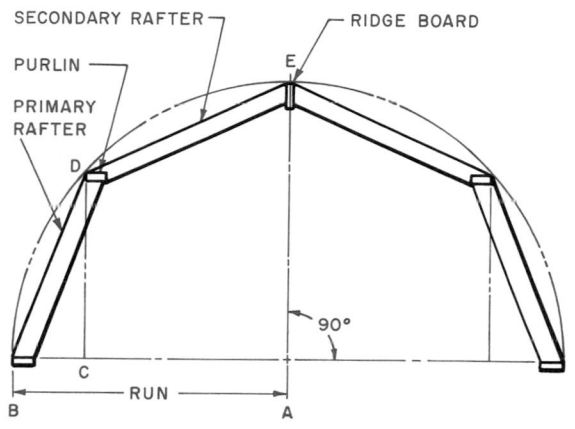

37-27. *The patterns for the rafters in the gambrel roof may be made by laying the roof out full-size on the subfloor.*

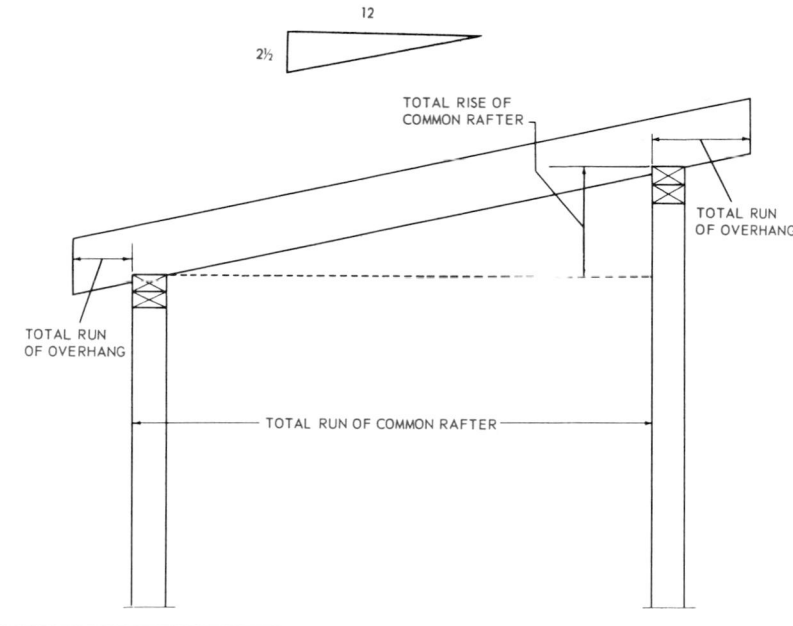

37-28. *Shed roof framing.*

the plans. Draw a perpendicular line this length, between the plate and the semicircle. Line CD, Fig. 37-27. Connect the points B and D and the points D and E. This gives the location and pitch of the primary rafter BD and the secondary rafter DE. From this layout the rafter patterns can be made and cut for trial on the building.

FRAMING A SHED ROOF

A shed roof is essentially one-half of a gable roof. Like the full-length rafters in a gable roof, the full-length rafters in a shed roof are common rafters. However, the total run of a shed roof common rafter is equal to the span of the building *minus the width of the top plate on the higher rafter-end wall.* Fig. 37-28. Also, the run of the overhang on the higher wall is measured from the inner edge of the top plate. With these exceptions, shed roof common rafters are laid out like gable roof common rafters. A shed roof common rafter has two bird's-mouths, but they are laid out just like the bird's-mouth on a gable roof common rafter.

For a shed roof, the height of the higher rafter-end wall must exceed the height of the lower by an amount equal to the total rise of a common rafter.

FRAMING A SHED DORMER

When framing a shed dormer (Fig. 37-29), there are three layout problems to be solved:
➤ Determining the total run of a dormer rafter.
➤ Determining the angle of cut on the inboard ends of the dormer rafters.

► Determining the lengths of the dormer side-wall studs.

To determine the total run of a dormer rafter, divide the height of the dormer end wall, in inches, by the difference between the unit rise of the dormer roof and the unit rise of the main roof. For example, suppose the height of the dormer end wall is 9', or 108". A, Fig. 37-30. The unit rise of the main roof is 8; the unit rise of the dormer roof is 2½. The difference between them is 5½. The total run of a dormer rafter is therefore 108 divided by 5½, or 19.63 feet. Knowing the total run and the unit rise, you can figure the length of a dormer rafter by any of the methods already described.

The inboard ends of the dormer rafters must be cut to fit the slope of the main roof. B, Fig. 37-30. To get the angle of this cut, set the square on the rafter to the cut of the main roof. C, Fig. 37-30. Measure off the unit rise of the dormer roof from the heel of the square along the tongue. Make a mark at this point and draw the cut-off line through this mark from the 12" mark.

The lengths of the side-wall studs on a shed dormer are determined as follows: Suppose a dormer rafter rises 2½" for every 12" of run and a main roof common rafter rises 8" for every 12" of run. A, Fig. 37-30. If the studs were spaced 12" O.C., the length of the shortest stud (which is also the common difference of studs) would be the difference between 8" and 2½", or 5½". This being the case, if the stud spacing is 16", the length of the shortest stud is the value of x in the proportional equation $12 : 5½ :: 16 : x$. Thus $x = 7\frac{5}{16}$. The shortest stud will be $7\frac{5}{16}$" long. The next stud will be $2 \times 7\frac{5}{16}$" long, or $14\frac{5}{8}$", and so on.

A second method of determining the length of the shortest stud (the common difference of the studs) is to make the layout directly on a stud with the framing square. Fig. 37-31. The difference in the rise of the two roofs is 5½". Find the 5½" mark on the tongue of the square and place it on the edge of a stud. Place the 12" mark of the body of the square on the same edge of the stud. Draw a line along the body of the square onto the stud. Slide the square along this line until the 16" mark (the on-center spacing between the

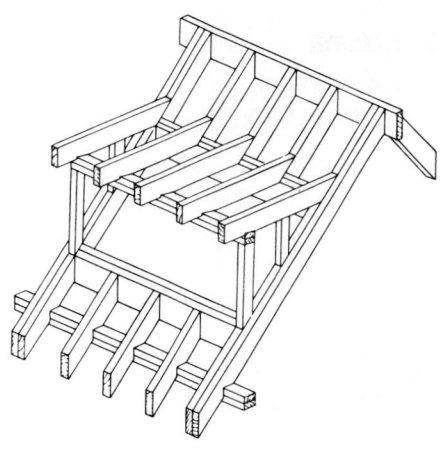

37-29. *Framing a shed dormer.*

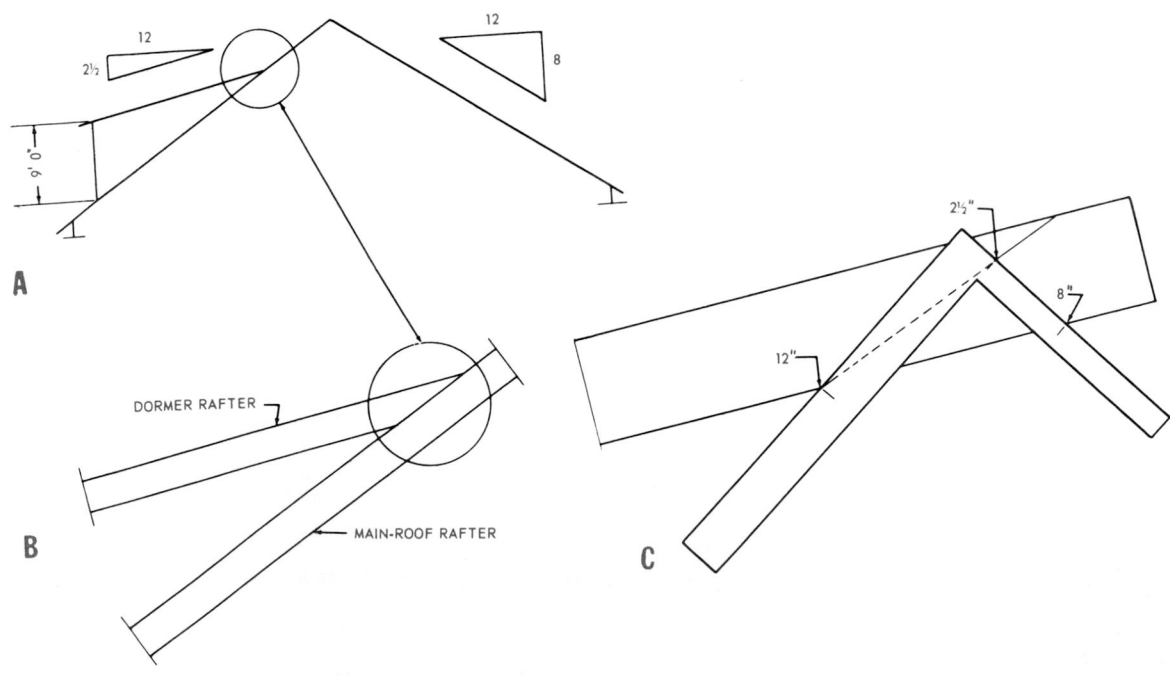

37-30. *Laying out the top cut on a rafter for a shed dormer.*

SPACING BETWEEN STUDS
(16")
3 1/2
12
16
COMMON DIFFERENCE
IN LENGTH OF STUDS

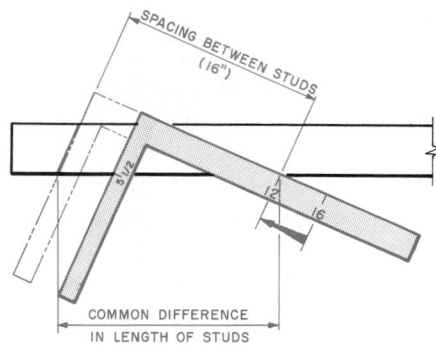

37-31. *Determining the common difference in the length of dormer side-wall studs by direct layout.*

studs) is over the point of the 12" mark. Draw a line along the tongue of the square. This completes the layout for the shortest stud; the second stud will be twice as long, and so on.

To get the lower-end cut-off angle for studs, set the square on the stud to the cut of the main roof. To get the upper-end cut-off angle, set the square to the cut of the dormer roof.

FRAMING A FLAT OR LOW-PITCH ROOF

The two basic types of roofs—flat and pitched—have numerous variations. The so-called flat roof may actually have some slope for drainage. As discussed earlier, the slope is generally expressed as the inches of vertical rise in 12 inches of horizontal run. For purposes of definition, flat roofs might be classed as those having less than a 3-in-12-slope. Fig. 37-32.

Post-and-beam construction is frequently used with flat or low-slope roofs. Fig. 37-33. In conventional stud wall framing for buildings with flat or low-slope roofs, the rafters or roof joists usually serve as ceiling joists for the space below.

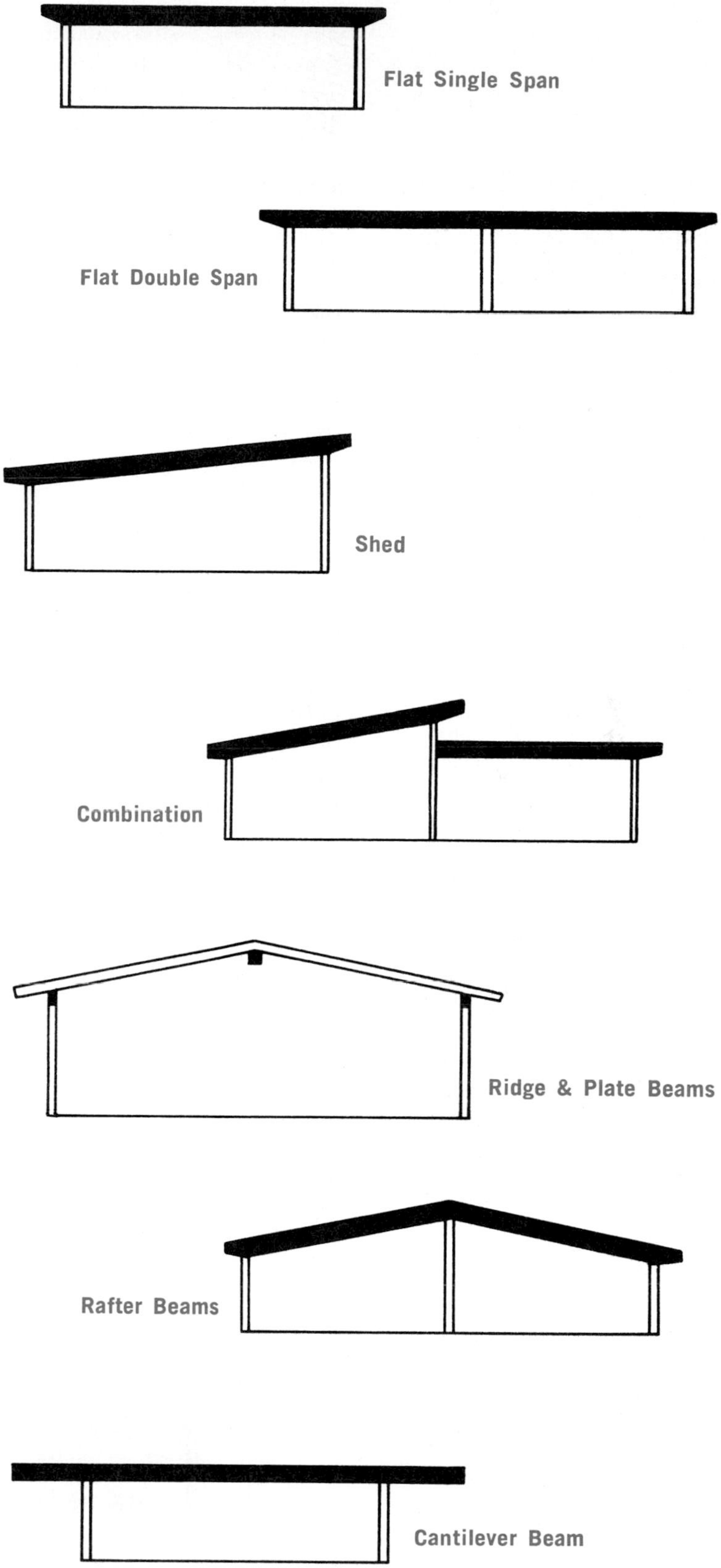

Flat Single Span
Flat Double Span
Shed
Combination
Ridge & Plate Beams
Rafter Beams
Cantilever Beam

37-32. *Variations of flat roof styles.*

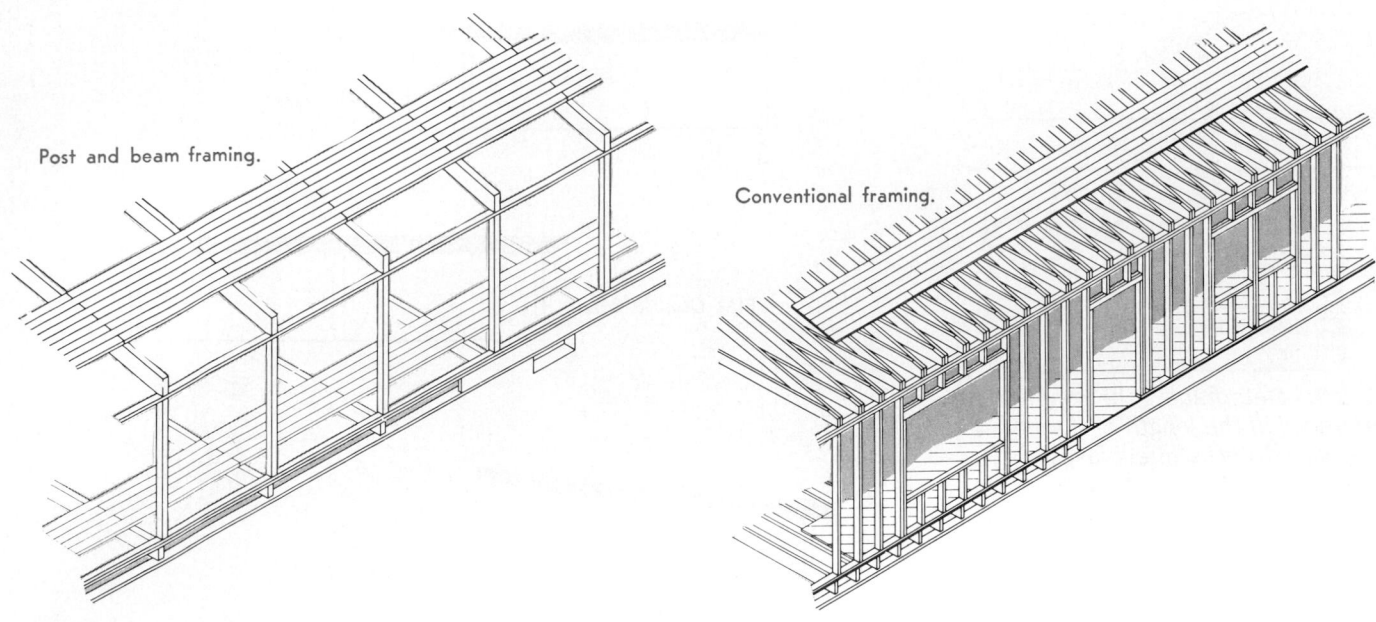

Post and beam framing.

Conventional framing.

37-33. *Comparison of post-and-beam system with conventional framing.*

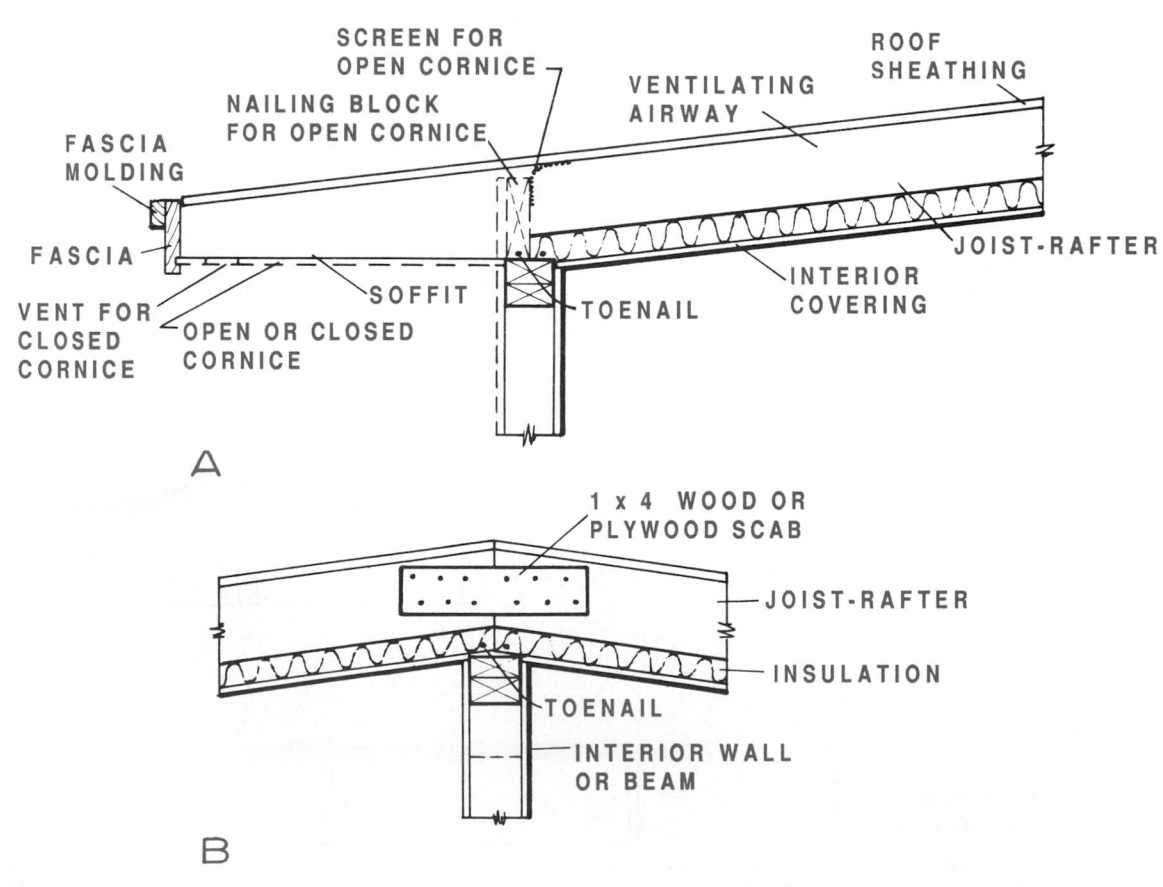

SCREEN FOR
OPEN CORNICE

NAILING BLOCK
FOR OPEN CORNICE

ROOF
SHEATHING

VENTILATING
AIRWAY

FASCIA
MOLDING

FASCIA

JOIST-RAFTER

VENT FOR
CLOSED
CORNICE

OPEN OR CLOSED
CORNICE

SOFFIT

TOENAIL

INTERIOR
COVERING

A

1 x 4 WOOD OR
PLYWOOD SCAB

JOIST-RAFTER

INSULATION

TOENAIL

INTERIOR WALL
OR BEAM

B

37-34. *Rafter-joist construction for a flat roof: A. Detail at exterior wall. B. Detail at interior wall.*

The flat or low-slope roof sometimes combines ceiling and roof elements in one system. This system serves as an interior finish, or as a fastening surface for the finish, and as an outer surface for application of the roofing. Fig. 37-34. In mild climates flat or low-pitch roofs may be built with 2" matched planks for roof sheathing supported on large beams spaced about 6' apart. The planking and beams are exposed on the underside. Fig. 37-35. The exposed material may be dressed smooth and finished with varnish or otherwise decorated.

The structural elements can be arranged in several ways by the use of ceiling beams or thick roof decking which spans from the exterior walls to the ridge beam or center bearing partition. Fig. 37-36. The roof is generally covered with a fiberboard insulation, and this in turn with a composition roof.

Roof joists for flat roofs are commonly laid level, with roof sheathing and roofing on top and with the underside utilized to support the ceiling. Sometimes a slight roof slope may be provided for roof drainage by tapering the joist or adding a cant strip (a triangular piece of lumber) to the top. Insulation may be added just above the ceiling, and the space above the insulation should be ventilated to remove hot air in the summer and to provide protection against condensation in the winter.

Flat and low-pitch roofs generally require larger-sized rafters than pitched roofs, but the total amount of framing lumber required is usually less. In flat roof construction where rafters also serve as ceiling joists, the size of the rafters is based on both roof and ceiling loads. The size is given on the plans or determined from rafter span tables.

When there is an overhang on all sides of the house, lookout rafters are ordinarily used. Fig. 37-37. The

37-35a. *In this home the ceiling is extended beyond the exterior wall to become the overhang.*

37-35b. *The planking and beams are exposed on the underside of the roof.*

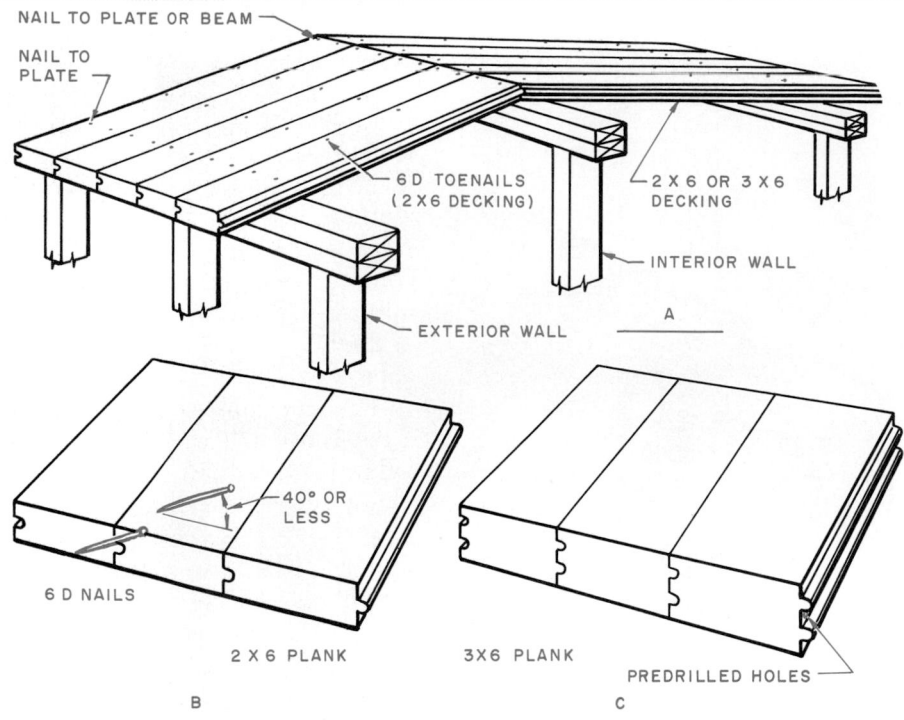

37-36. *Wood-deck construction: A. Installing wood decking. B. Toenailing horizontal joint. C. Edge-nailing 3" x 6" solid decking.*

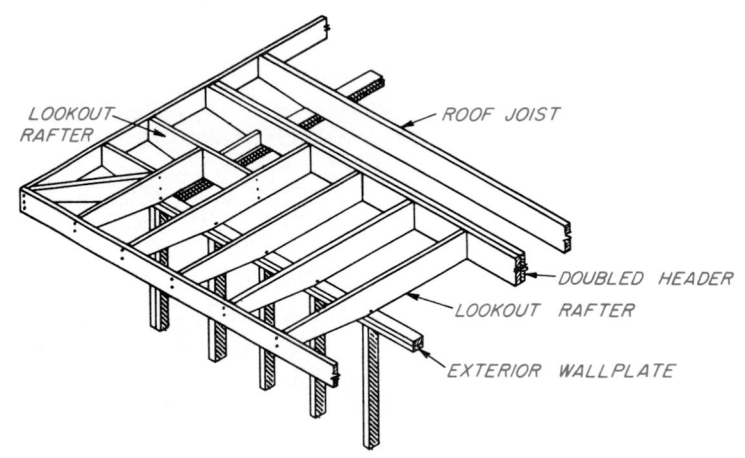

37-37. *Typical construction of flat roof with overhang.*

lookout rafters are nailed to a double header and toenailed to the wall plate. The distance from the double header to the wall line is usually twice the overhang. Rafter ends may be finished with an outside header, which will serve as a nailing surface for trim.

ROOF OPENINGS

Roof openings are those which require interruption of the normal run of rafters or other roof framing. Such openings may be required for a ventilator, chimney, skylight, or for dormer windows. Fig. 37-38.

Roof openings, like floor openings, are framed by headers and trimmers. Double headers are used at right angles to the rafters, which are set into the headers in the same manner as joists in floor opening construction. Just as trimmers are double joists in floor construction, they are double rafters in roof openings.

CHIMNEY SADDLE

The chimney saddle sheds water and snow and prevents ice from building up behind the chimney on the roof. The saddle may be constructed on the roof. If the chimney span and roof pitch are known, it can also be fabricated on the ground and the completed assembly nailed to the roof framing. Fig. 37-39.

The valley strips are 1" × 4" or 1" × 6". The length is determined in the same way as for a valley rafter. Use the framing square to lay out the valley strips. Lay out the top and bottom cuts along the tongue of the square. When measuring off the length of the strip, use the unit length of a common rafter from the roof on which the saddle is to be framed.

For example, a roof with a unit rise of 5" has a unit length of 13". Fig. 34-9b. To lay out the valley strip, position the square with the 13" mark of the tongue and the 12" mark of the blade on the edge of the strip. Draw a line along the tongue for the top cut. Fig. 37-40. Measure and lay off the length of the valley strip. With the square set the same as for the top cut, place the edge of the blade on the length mark and draw a line along the blade for the bottom cut.

The end of the ridge rests on the valley strips. A, Fig. 37-39. This cut is the same as the seat cut for a

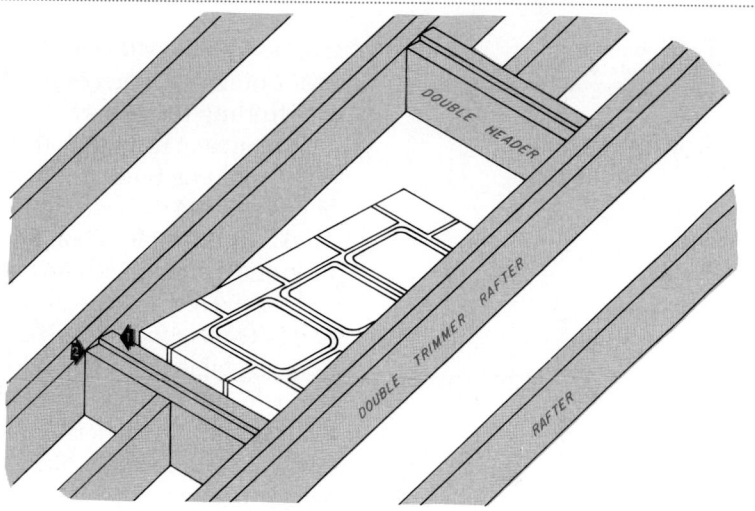

37-38. *Roof framing around the chimney. The top edges of the headers are kept below the top edge of the rafter (arrow 1). The lower edges of the headers are kept even with the top edge of the rafter (arrow 2).*

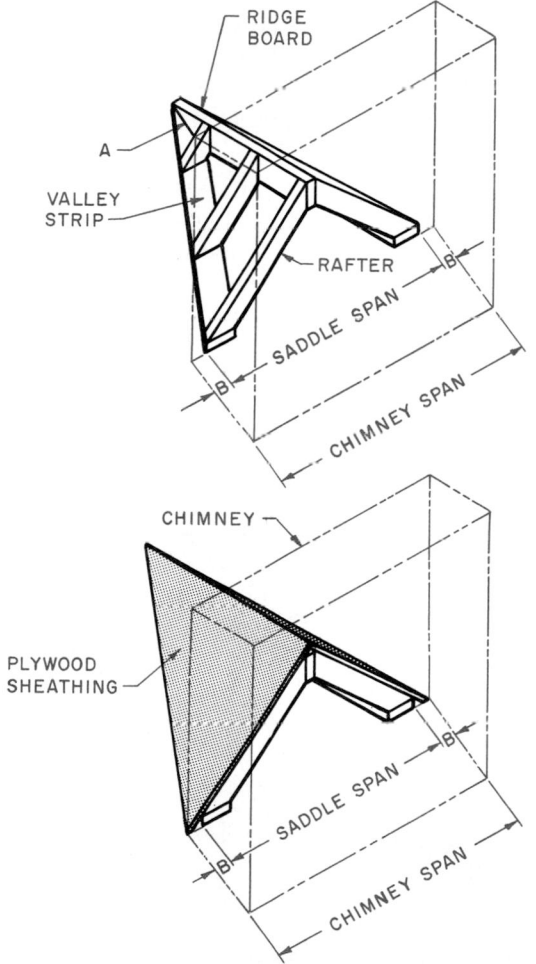

37-39. *The saddle span is less than the chimney width, as shown at "B" in the drawing. This distance ("B") must be subtracted from each side of the chimney width to obtain the actual saddle span. When the sheathing is applied to the saddle rafters, it will project beyond the valley strip.*

common rafter in the main roof. Place the square on the ridge board for the cut of the roof (5" on the tongue and 12" on the blade for the example), and draw a line along the blade. The length of the ridge is equal to the run of the common rafter in the saddle span minus the allowance for the drop of the ridge which is approximately ¾".

The length of the longest rafter is determined by multiplying the saddle run (half the saddle span) by the unit length of the common rafter. Fig. 37-39. Deduct the ridge shortening allowance to obtain the actual length. The top and bottom cuts are the same as for a common rafter in the main roof. However, there is a side cut on the bottom where the rafter rests on the valley strip. This cut is the same as for regular valley jacks. On the rafter table of the framing square, the side cut figure for a valley jack in a roof with a 5" unit rise is 11½". Fig. 34-9b. Lay out and make the cut as described on pages 397-398 for jack rafters.

The cuts are the same for all the rafters in the chimney saddle. However, the rafter lengths differ. The difference in the length of the rafters can be found on the rafter table of the framing square under "Difference in Length of Jacks." For rafters 16" on center in a roof with a unit rise of 5", the second rafter will be 17 5/16" shorter than the first rafter. Fig. 34-9b. The third rafter will be 34 5/8" (2 × 17 5/16) shorter than the first rafter, and so on. When the saddle framing is complete, the sheathing, flashing (to prevent water seepage), and roofing are applied.

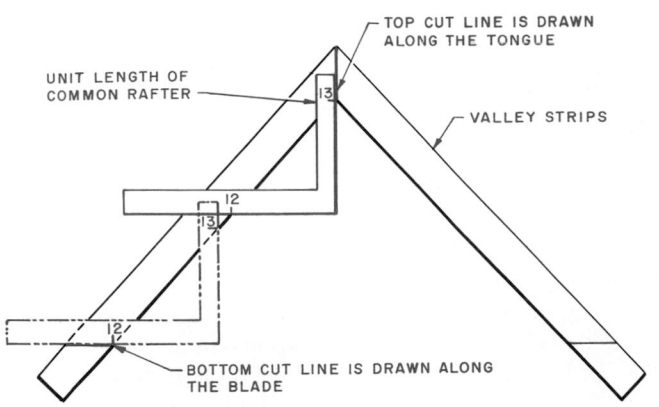

UNIT LENGTH OF COMMON RAFTER

TOP CUT LINE IS DRAWN ALONG THE TONGUE

VALLEY STRIPS

BOTTOM CUT LINE IS DRAWN ALONG THE BLADE

37-40. *Using the framing square to lay out the top and bottom cuts on the valley strips.*

ESTIMATING

Number of Rafters

The number of rafters necessary for a building may be counted directly from the roof framing plan. The number of rafters may also be obtained in the same way the number of floor joists is estimated. For rafters on 16" centers, take three-fourths of the building's length and add one. For example, if

a rectangular building is 40' long, 31 rafters will be required for each of the longer sides (¾ × 40 = 30; 30 + 1 = 31). A total of 62 rafters would thus be needed. Add to this amount extra rafters for the required trimmers and any other special framing.

Material Cost

An accurate estimate of the cost can be figured by multiplying the number of rafters required by the cost per rafter. Sometimes the builder will not make up a complete bill of materials, but wants a rough cost estimate. This

can be figured without knowing the exact number of pieces needed by first finding the area of the roof.

The area of the roof is the length of the building times the width of the building times the factor from Table 37-A. For example, a building 20' wide and 40' long with no overhang will have a roof area of 20 times 40, or 800 (square feet), times the factor from the table. For a roof with a unit rise of 5", the factor is 1.083. The area of the roof, then, is 800 × 1.083, which equals 866.4, or 867 square feet of roof area.

The number of board feet of material for rafters, ridge board, and collar beams required for a building is next determined. Use the same dimensions of the building from the previous example, which contained 867 square feet of roof area, and refer to Table 37-B. If the rafters are 2" × 6" and 16" on center, the chart indicates 102 board feet of lumber for each 100 square feet of roof surface area. Divide the total roof area by 100 and multiply by the factor in the table:

$$\frac{867 \text{ (total sq. ft. of roof area)}}{100} = \frac{8.67 \text{ (roof area expressed in hundreds of sq. ft.)}}{}$$

8.67 × 102 (bd. ft. per sq. ft.) = 884.3 bd. ft.

Table 37-A. *Obtaining Roof Area from Plan Area. When a roof has to be figured from a plan only, and the roof pitch is known, the roof area may be fairly accurately computed from the table. The horizontal or plan area (including overhangs) should be multiplied by the factor shown in the table opposite the rise, which is given in inches per horizontal foot. The result will be the roof area.*

Rise	Factor	Rise	Factor
3"	1.031	8"	1.202
3½"	1.042	8½"	1.225
4"	1.054	9"	1.250
4½"	1.068	9½"	1.275
5"	1.083	10"	1.302
5½"	1.100	10½"	1.329
6"	1.118	11"	1.357
6½"	1.137	11½"	1.385
7"	1.158	12"	1.414
7½"	1.179		

Table 37-B. *Estimating Materials and Labor for Roof Framing.*

Rafters	Board Feet Required 100 Square Feet Surface Area			Nails	Labor
	12" O.C.	16" O.C.	24" O.C.	Per 1000 Board Feet	Board Feet Per Hour
2 x 4	89	71	53	17	
2 x 6	129	102	75	12	See
2 x 8	171	134	112	9	Table
2 x 10	212	197	121	7	Below
2 x 12	252	197	143	6	

Note: Includes common, hip and valley rafters, ridge boards and collar beams.

Rafters	Labor					
	Common	Hip	Jack	Valley	Ridge	Collars
Board Feet Per Hour	35	35	25	35	35	65

Multiply this figure by the cost per board foot to find the total cost of lumber for the roof.

Table 37-B also has information for determining the number of nails necessary. For the roof in the example, 12 pounds of nails are needed for each 1,000 board feet. The roof in the example has about 884 board feet, requiring about 10½ pounds of nails:

$$\frac{884 \text{ (bd. ft. of material)}}{1,000} = 0.884$$

(material expressed in thousands of bd. ft.)

0.884 x 12 (lbs. of nails per 1000 bd. ft.)=10.6 or 10½ lbs. of nails

The cost of the nails for the roof framing is determined by multiplying the cost for one pound by the total number needed.

Labor Cost

The cost of labor for framing a roof can also be found by using the information in Table 37-B. To use this table it is necessary to know how many board feet of rafter material are required for a roof. Use the same examples as previously described: a building 20' wide and 40' long with a gable roof having a unit rise of 5". Find the number of board feet in one rafter and then multiply this by the total number of rafters in the building.

Table 37-C can be used to determine the board feet content of a single piece. To use this chart the length of a piece must be known. To find the length of the rafter for figuring board feet, refer to Table 37-D. The roof in the example has a unit rise of 5" and the building width is 20'. Table 37-D indicates the rafter will be approximately 10' 10" long.

A 2" × 6" rafter, 10' 10" long, would be cut from a 2" × 6" × 12' member. Find 2 × 6 in the left column of Table 37-C and read across to the column headed 12, for a 12' piece. There are 12 board feet in one 2" × 6" × 12' piece of lumber. The roof in the example has 62 rafters (see "Number of Rafters"). Therefore, if one rafter contains 12 board feet of material, 62 rafters contain 62 × 12, or 744 board feet of rafter material.

The cost of framing a roof can be found by using the factor from Table 37-B. There are 744 board feet of common rafter material in the building used for the example. The table shows a worker can frame 35 board feet of common rafters per hour. The number of hours required to frame the roof is 744 divided by 35, or 21.2 hours. To find the cost of labor, multiply the number of hours by the hourly labor rate.

Table 37-C. *Board Feet Content.*

Size of Timber in Inches	Length Of Piece In Feet							
	10	12	14	16	18	20	22	24
1 x 2	$1\frac{2}{3}$	2	$2\frac{1}{3}$	$2\frac{2}{3}$	3	$3\frac{1}{3}$	$3\frac{2}{3}$	4
1 x 3	$2\frac{1}{2}$	3	$3\frac{1}{2}$	4	$4\frac{1}{2}$	5	$5\frac{1}{2}$	6
1 x 4	$3\frac{1}{3}$	4	$4\frac{2}{3}$	$5\frac{1}{3}$	6	$6\frac{2}{3}$	$7\frac{1}{3}$	8
1 x 5	$4\frac{1}{6}$	5	$5\frac{5}{6}$	$6\frac{2}{3}$	$7\frac{1}{2}$	$8\frac{1}{3}$	$9\frac{1}{6}$	10
1 x 6	5	6	7	8	9	10	11	12
1 x 8	$6\frac{2}{3}$	8	$9\frac{1}{3}$	$10\frac{2}{3}$	12	$13\frac{1}{3}$	$14\frac{2}{3}$	16
1 x 10	$8\frac{1}{3}$	10	$11\frac{2}{3}$	$13\frac{1}{3}$	15	$16\frac{2}{3}$	$18\frac{1}{3}$	20
1 x 12	10	12	14	16	18	20	22	24
1 x 14	$11\frac{2}{3}$	14	$16\frac{1}{3}$	$18\frac{2}{3}$	21	$23\frac{1}{3}$	$25\frac{2}{3}$	28
1 x 16	$13\frac{1}{3}$	16	$18\frac{2}{3}$	$21\frac{1}{3}$	24	$26\frac{2}{3}$	$29\frac{1}{3}$	32
1 x 20	$16\frac{2}{3}$	20	$23\frac{1}{3}$	$26\frac{2}{3}$	30	$33\frac{1}{3}$	$36\frac{2}{3}$	40
1¼ x 4	$4\frac{1}{6}$	5	$5\frac{5}{6}$	$6\frac{2}{3}$	$7\frac{1}{2}$	$8\frac{1}{3}$	$9\frac{1}{6}$	10
1¼ x 6	$6\frac{1}{4}$	$7\frac{1}{2}$	$8\frac{3}{4}$	10	$11\frac{1}{4}$	$12\frac{1}{2}$	$13\frac{3}{4}$	15
1¼ x 8	$8\frac{1}{3}$	10	$11\frac{2}{3}$	$13\frac{1}{3}$	15	$16\frac{2}{3}$	$18\frac{1}{3}$	20
1¼ x 10	$10\frac{1}{3}$	$12\frac{1}{2}$	$14\frac{1}{2}$	$16\frac{2}{3}$	$18\frac{2}{3}$	$20\frac{5}{6}$	$22\frac{5}{6}$	25
1¼ x 12	$12\frac{1}{2}$	15	$17\frac{1}{2}$	20	$22\frac{1}{2}$	25	$27\frac{1}{2}$	30
1½ x 4	5	6	7	8	9	10	11	12
1½ x 6	$7\frac{1}{2}$	9	$10\frac{1}{2}$	12	$13\frac{1}{2}$	15	$16\frac{1}{2}$	18
1½ x 8	10	12	14	16	18	20	22	24
1½ x 10	$12\frac{1}{2}$	15	$17\frac{1}{2}$	20	$22\frac{1}{2}$	25	$27\frac{1}{2}$	30
1½ x 12	15	18	21	24	27	30	33	36
2 x 4	$6\frac{2}{3}$	8	$9\frac{1}{3}$	$10\frac{2}{3}$	12	$13\frac{1}{3}$	$14\frac{2}{3}$	16
2 x 6	10	12	14	16	18	20	22	24
2 x 8	$13\frac{1}{3}$	16	$18\frac{2}{3}$	$21\frac{1}{3}$	24	$26\frac{2}{3}$	$29\frac{1}{3}$	32
2 x 10	$16\frac{2}{3}$	20	$23\frac{1}{3}$	$26\frac{2}{3}$	30	$33\frac{1}{3}$	$36\frac{2}{3}$	40
2 x 12	20	24	28	32	36	40	44	48
2 x 14	$23\frac{1}{3}$	28	$32\frac{2}{3}$	$37\frac{1}{3}$	42	$46\frac{2}{3}$	$51\frac{1}{3}$	56
2 x 16	$26\frac{2}{3}$	32	$37\frac{1}{2}$	$42\frac{2}{3}$	48	$53\frac{1}{3}$	$58\frac{2}{3}$	64
2½ x 12	25	30	35	40	45	50	55	60
2½ x 14	$29\frac{1}{6}$	35	$40\frac{5}{6}$	$46\frac{2}{3}$	$52\frac{1}{2}$	$58\frac{1}{3}$	$64\frac{1}{6}$	70
2½ x 16	$33\frac{1}{3}$	40	$46\frac{2}{3}$	$53\frac{1}{3}$	60	$66\frac{2}{3}$	$73\frac{1}{3}$	80
3 x 6	15	18	21	24	27	30	33	36
3 x 8	20	24	28	32	36	40	44	48
3 x 10	25	30	35	40	45	50	55	60
3 x 12	30	36	42	48	54	60	66	72
3 x 14	35	42	49	56	63	70	77	84
3 x 16	40	48	56	64	72	80	88	96
4 x 4	$13\frac{1}{3}$	16	$18\frac{2}{3}$	$21\frac{1}{3}$	24	$26\frac{2}{3}$	$29\frac{1}{3}$	32
4 x 6	20	24	28	32	36	40	44	48
4 x 8	$26\frac{2}{3}$	32	$17\frac{1}{3}$	$42\frac{2}{3}$	48	$53\frac{1}{3}$	$58\frac{2}{3}$	64
4 x 10	$33\frac{1}{3}$	40	$46\frac{2}{3}$	$53\frac{1}{3}$	60	$66\frac{2}{3}$	$73\frac{1}{3}$	80
4 x 12	40	48	56	64	72	80	88	96
4 x 14	$46\frac{1}{3}$	56	$65\frac{1}{3}$	$74\frac{2}{3}$	84	$93\frac{1}{3}$	$102\frac{1}{2}$	112

Table 37-D. *Rafter Length for Some of the More Common Roofs.*

Rise of Rafter	Building Width (In Feet)											
	10	12	14	16	18	20	22	24	26	28	30	32
3"	5'2"	6'2"	7'3"	8'3"	9'3"	10'4"	11'4"	12'4"	13'5"	14'5"	15'6"	16'6"
4"	5'3"	6'4"	7'5"	8'5"	9'6"	10'7"	11'7"	12'8"	13'8"	14'9"	15'10"	16'10"
5"	5'5"	6'6"	7'7"	8'8"	9'9"	10'10"	11'11"	13'0"	14'1"	15'2"	16'3"	17'4"
6"	5'7"	6'8"	7'10"	9'0"	10'1"	11'2"	12'4"	13'5"	14'6"	15'8"	16'9"	17'11"

Note: Tables accurate only to nearest inch.

QUESTIONS

1. Why is the ridge board for a hip roof shorter in length than for a gable roof?

2. The rafter locations on the ridge board should be laid out exactly from the top plate because it will ensure direct bearing down through the walls to the foundation walls. What is another reason that the rafter locations should be placed in this way?

3. Why is it best to erect the ridge board in its proper position before beginning the installation of the rafters?

4. When nailing the common rafters in place, why must the rafter be nailed at the bird's-mouth first?

5. When erecting the rafters for a hip roof, which rafters are erected first?

6. Why must hip jack rafters be installed in pairs?

7. What special treatment is required around roof openings?

8. What is a collar beam?

9. Describe the two methods of installing gable-end studs.

10. How does a gambrel roof differ from a gable roof?

11. When figuring the length of the rafters for a shed roof, how do they differ from the rafters for a gable roof?

12. Why is a flat or a low-slope roof usually less expensive to construct than a pitched roof?

13. What is the purpose of a chimney saddle?

ACTIVITIES

1. Math. If a roof has a 5" rise for each 12" run and the common rafters have nominal dimensions of 2" by 8", find the level width of a rafter by:

a. Drawing a diagram (full size) very carefully and measuring it.

b. Using the Pythagorean theorem. How many inches of rise would there be for each 12" of run if the level width and plumb width were the same?

2. Math. A house with outside dimensions of 26' by 44' has a gable roof with rafters 16" O.C. The roof has a 6" rise for a 12" run. There is no overhang.

a. If there are no special features in the roof, how many rafters will be required?

b. Estimate the roof area in square feet.

3. Science. This unit identifies procedures for framing around the chimney. Chimneys are either of a masonry type or a metal fabrication. For either material, the primary concern is resistance to flammability.

Geology is a scientific study of the earth's origin, history, and structure. It is often referred to as a study of "rocks." Investigate some of the various "rocks" used to construct masonry fireplace chimneys. State if they are igneous, sedimentary, or metamorphic.

38

Roof Trusses

Much modern roof framing of residential and commercial buildings is done with roof trusses. The *simple truss* is an assembly of members forming a rigid framework of triangular shapes. Fig. 38-1. The basic parts of a roof truss are shown in Fig. 38-2. These 2" × 4" members are usually connected at the joints by rectangular connector plates made of metal. Each connector plate has many stamped teeth. The plate is pressed into the wood under hydraulic pressure to splice the joint. Fig. 38-3. Connector plates are fastened to each side of the joint. Most trusses are made in factories and delivered to the job site by truck. Fig. 38-4. They can also be built on the job site. In such cases, the connector plates are replaced by plywood gussets which are nailed and glued into place. Most builders buy commercially made trusses, however.

The roof truss is capable of supporting loads over long spans. Fig. 38-5. Because every part of the truss has been specifically designed to do a particular job, *a truss must never be cut or altered on the job site.* Though most common trusses are

38-1. *Fastening roof trusses in place.*

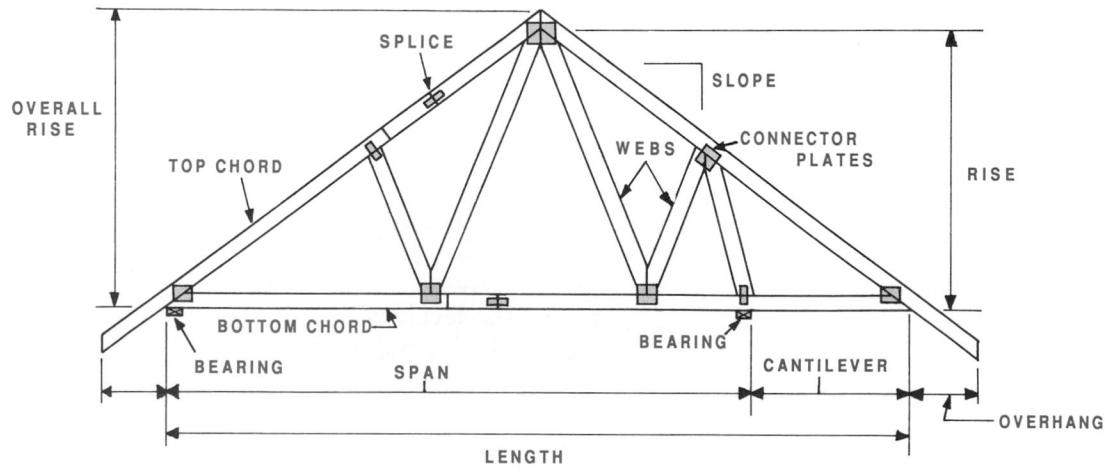

38-2. *The main parts of a roof truss.*

38-3. Toothed metal connector plates are used to fasten the joints of a truss.

38-4. These trusses are bundled in sets with ¾" steel bands for transporting to the building site.

38-5. Through the use of trusses, this barn has a clear span of 80'.

38-6a. These roof trusses have a curved bottom chord.

38-6b. These lumber trusses have doubled top and bottom chords.

38-6c. These tapered trusses form the roof of a small shopping center.

triangular in shape, they can also take other shapes. Fig. 38-6. Trusses can also be built from materials other than 2" × 4" stock, including metal and timber. Fig. 38-7.

Roof trusses save material and on-site labor costs. It is estimated that a material savings of about 30% is made on roof members and ceiling joists. The double top plate on interior partition walls and the double floor joists under interior bearing partitions are not necessary. Roof trusses can also eliminate interior bearing partitions because trusses are self-supporting.

Trusses can be erected quickly, and therefore the house can be enclosed in a short time.

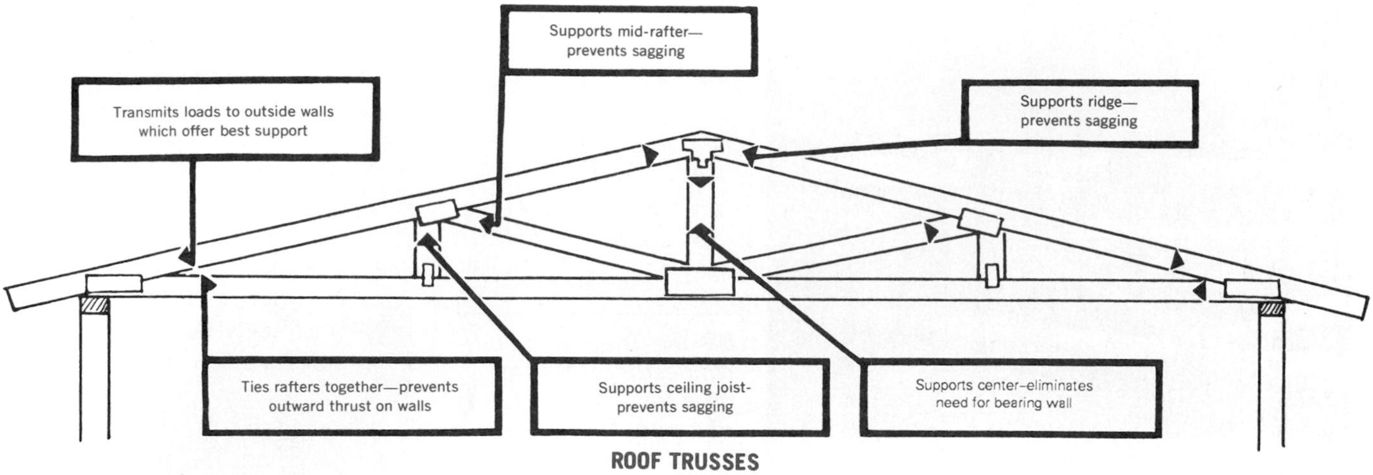

ROOF TRUSSES

Supports mid-rafter—prevents sagging

Transmits loads to outside walls which offer best support

Supports ridge—prevents sagging

Ties rafters together—prevents outward thrust on walls

Supports ceiling joist-prevents sagging

Supports center–eliminates need for bearing wall

ROOF TRUSSES

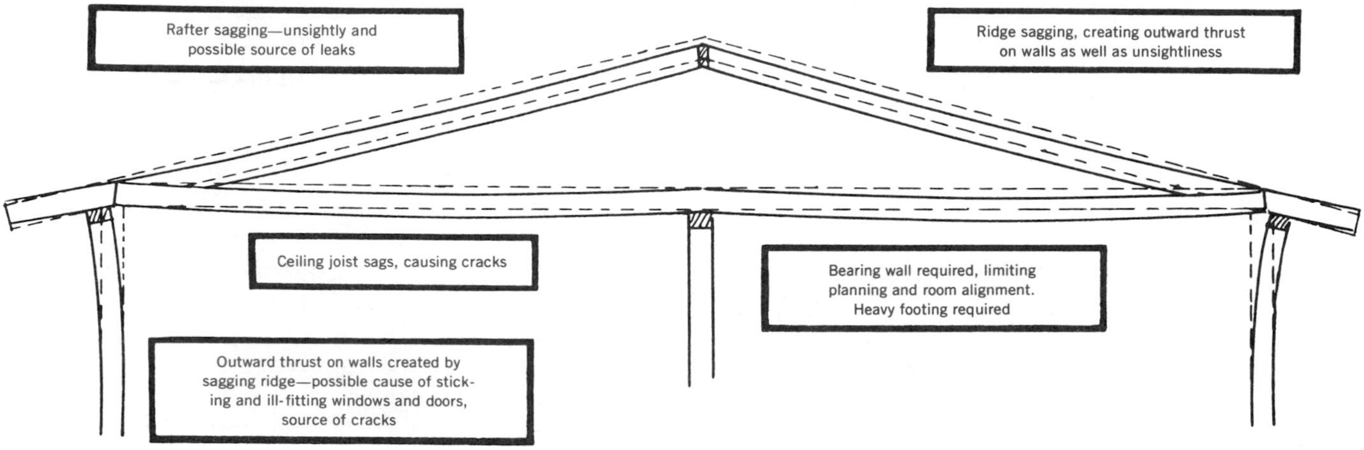

Rafter sagging—unsightly and possible source of leaks

Ridge sagging, creating outward thrust on walls as well as unsightliness

Ceiling joist sags, causing cracks

Bearing wall required, limiting planning and room alignment. Heavy footing required

Outward thrust on walls created by sagging ridge—possible cause of sticking and ill-fitting windows and doors, source of cracks

CONVENTIONAL ROOF FRAMING

38-7a. *Roof truss manufacturers claim many advantages over conventional roof framing methods.*

38-7b. *These lumber trusses were fabricated on the job site and lifted into place with a crane.*

Trusses are usually designed to span from one exterior wall to the other with lengths of 20' to 32' or more. Because no interior bearing walls are required, the interior of the building becomes one large workroom. This allows increased flexibility for interior planning, since partitions can be placed without regard to structural requirements. Fig. 38-7.

Roof trusses come in a wide variety of shapes to solve nearly any problem. Fig. 38-8. The following wood trusses are the ones most commonly used for houses. Fig. 38-9.

➤ King-post.
➤ Fink (also called W-truss).
➤ Scissors.

38-7c. *Once in place, these trusses were left exposed.*

38-7d. *These scissor trusses have lumber chords and tubular steel webs. They span approximately 70".*

These and similar trusses are most adaptable to rectangular houses because the constant width requires only one type of truss. However, trusses can also be used for L-shaped houses. For hip roofs, hip trusses can be provided for each end and valley area. Fig. 38-10.

Trusses are commonly designed for 24" spacing. This spacing requires somewhat thicker interior and exterior sheathing or finish material than is needed for conventional joist and rafter construction using 16" spacing.

KING-POST TRUSS

The king-post is the simplest form of truss used for houses. It consists of upper and lower chords and a center vertical post. B, Fig. 38-9. Allowable spans are somewhat less than for the Fink truss when the same size members are used because of the unsupported length of the upper chord. Furthermore, the grades of lumber used for the two types might also vary.

For short and medium spans, the king-post truss is probably more economical than other types because it has fewer pieces and can be fabricated faster. However, local prices and design load requirements (for snow, wind, etc.) as well as the span should govern the type of truss to be used.

FINK TRUSS

The Fink truss, also called a W-truss, is perhaps the most popular and most widely used of the light wood trusses. A, Fig. 38-9. Its design includes the use of three more members than the king-post truss, but distances between connections are less. This usually

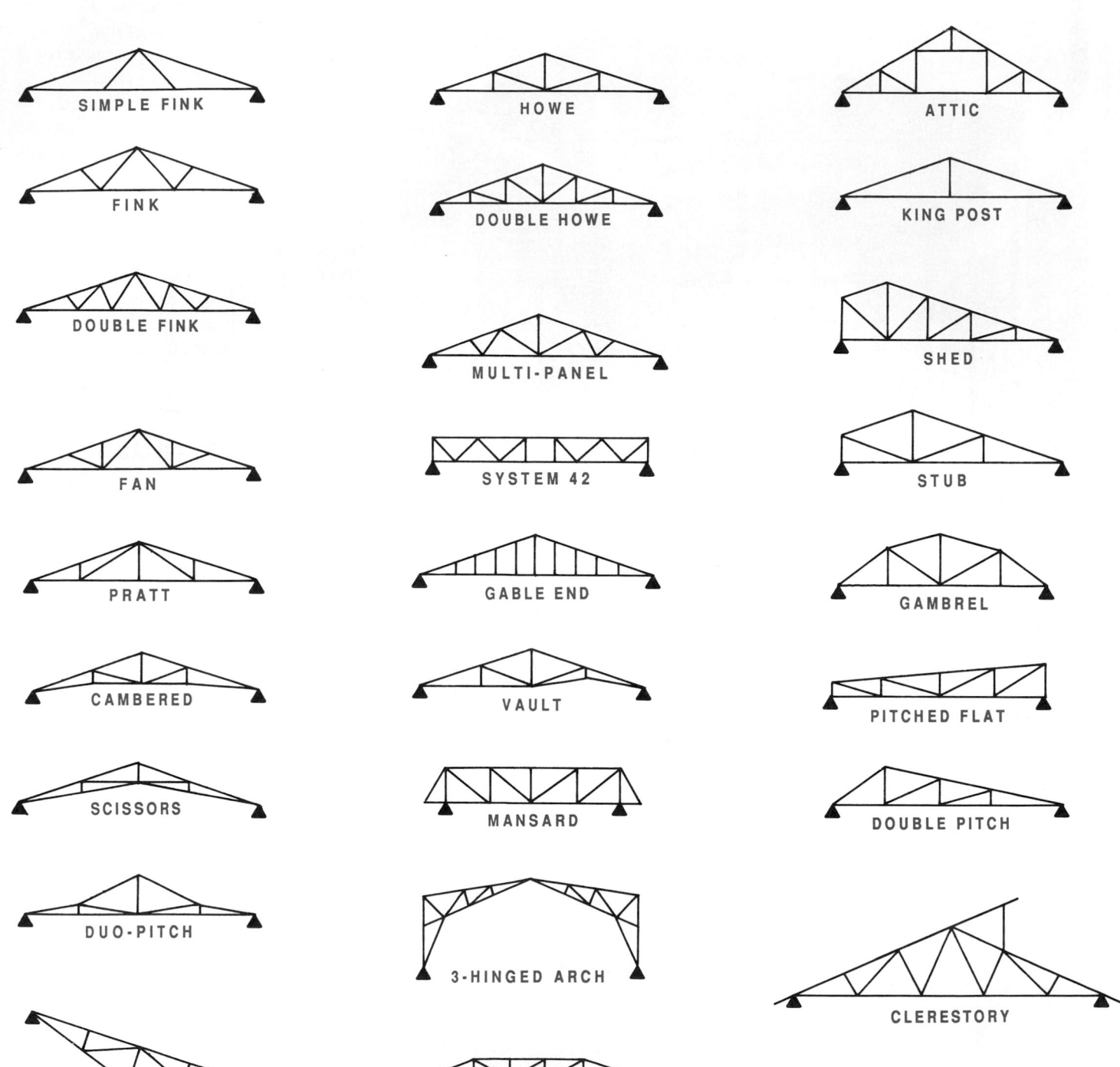

38-8. *Types of trusses.*

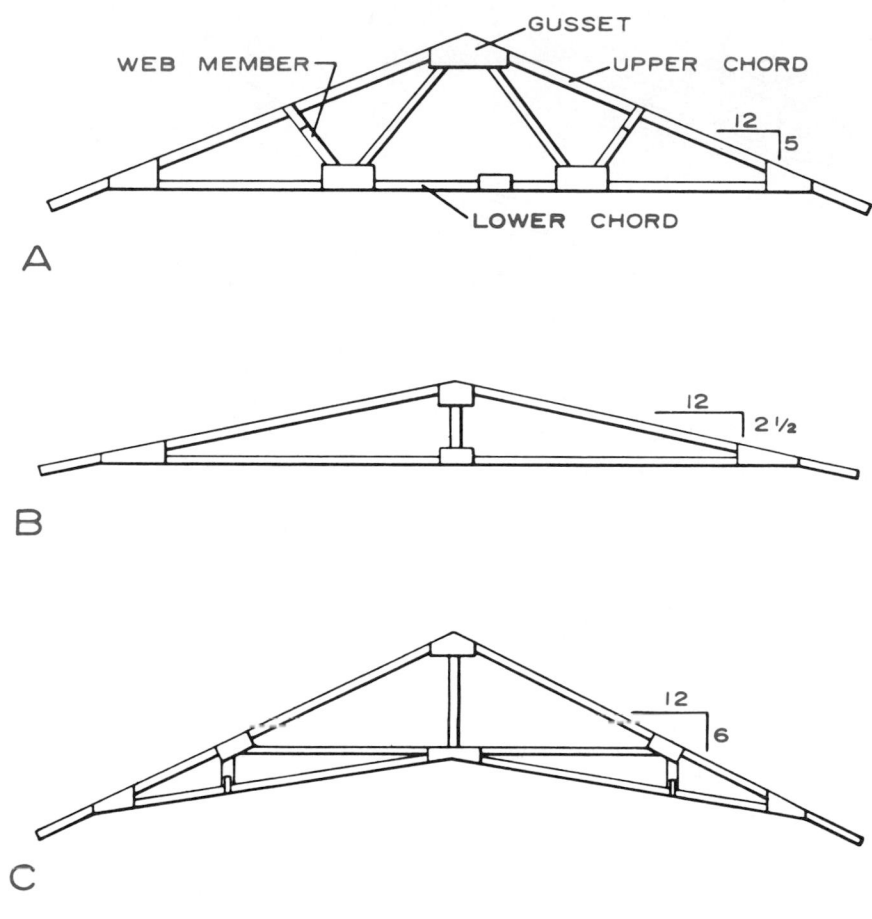

WEB MEMBER — GUSSET — UPPER CHORD

12 5

A

LOWER CHORD

12 2½

B

12 6

C

38-9. *Light wood trusses: A. Fink. B. King-post. C. Scissors.*

allows the use of lower grade lumber and somewhat greater spans for the same member size.

SCISSORS TRUSS

The scissors truss is used for houses with a sloping living room ceiling. C, Fig. 38-9. Somewhat more complicated than the Fink truss, it provides good roof construction for a "cathedral" ceiling with a saving in materials over conventional framing methods.

DESIGN

Plans for the fabrication of trussed rafters must include the preparation of an engineered design. Some building codes require approval and a certificate of inspection on trussed rafters.

The design of a truss includes consideration of not only snow and wind loads but of the weight of the roof itself. Design also takes into account the slope of the roof. Generally, the flatter the slope, the greater the stresses. Flatter slopes therefore require larger members and stronger connections in roof trusses. Hip and valley areas require special trusses. Fig. 38-10.

A great majority of the trusses used are fabricated with metal connector plates. Fig. 38-11. Others are assembled with split-ring connectors. Fig. 38-12. Some trusses are designed with a 2" × 4" soffit return at the end of each upper chord to provide nailing for the soffit of a wide box cornice.

Many lumber dealers are able to provide the builder with completed trusses ready for installation. Often, however, the builder orders trusses directly from a company specializing in manufacturing them. To order a series of trusses, the builder will need to supply a precise description of what he or she wants. Much of the information is on a typical set of plans. It would include the following:

Nominal span. Generally, this is the length of the bottom chord.

Overhang length. The horizontal distance from the end of the bottom chord to the bottom edge of the rafter.

Quantity. How many trusses are required? Be sure to include gable-end trusses.

End cut of rafter. Specify plumb cut, square cut, or untrimmed.

Roof pitch. The vertical rise per 12" run.

Type of truss. See Fig. 38-8 for types of trusses.

Design parameters. This would include information about the loads expected.

Special requirements. Anything unusual about the truss, such as the need for it to cantilever away from a wall or the need to accommodate unusual amounts of insulation.

SITE-BUILT TRUSSES

Sometimes a builder may need to build a roof truss on site. This is sometimes done to stiffen a rafter system. Such trusses use plywood

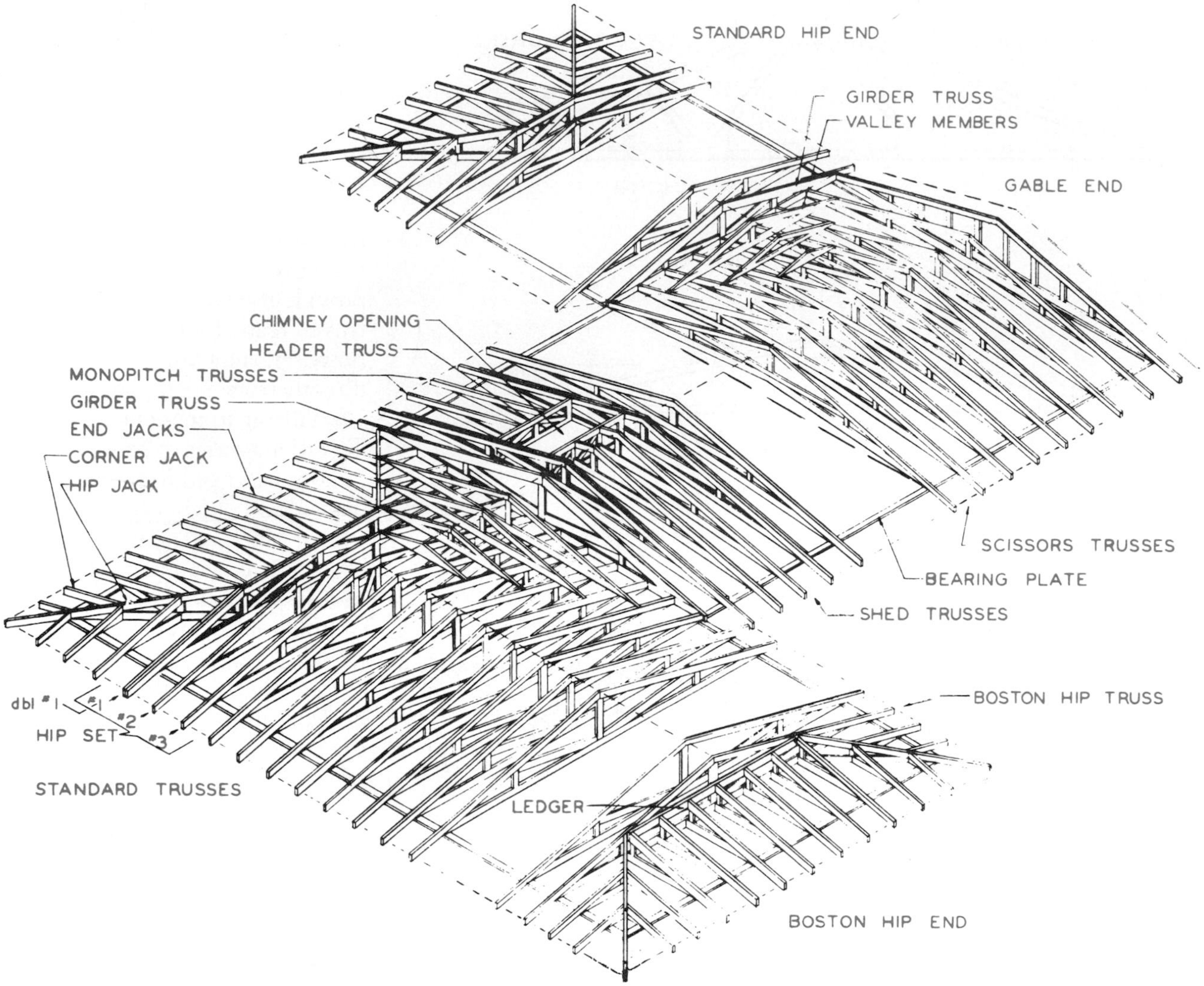

STANDARD HIP END

GIRDER TRUSS
VALLEY MEMBERS

GABLE END

CHIMNEY OPENING
HEADER TRUSS
MONOPITCH TRUSSES
GIRDER TRUSS
END JACKS
CORNER JACK
HIP JACK

SCISSORS TRUSSES
BEARING PLATE
SHED TRUSSES

BOSTON HIP TRUSS

dbl #1 #1 #2 #3
HIP SET

STANDARD TRUSSES

LEDGER

BOSTON HIP END

38-10. *Special trusses are available for hip and valley areas.*

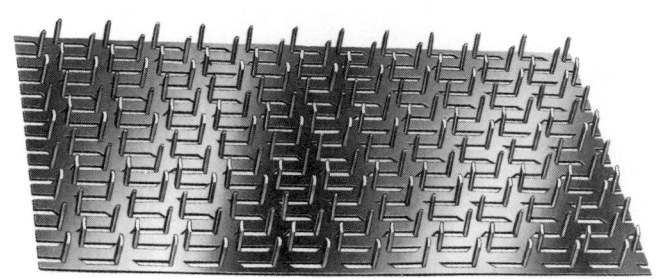

38-11a. *Metal connector plate.*

38-11b. *This jig holds the truss firmly in place during application of the metal connector.*

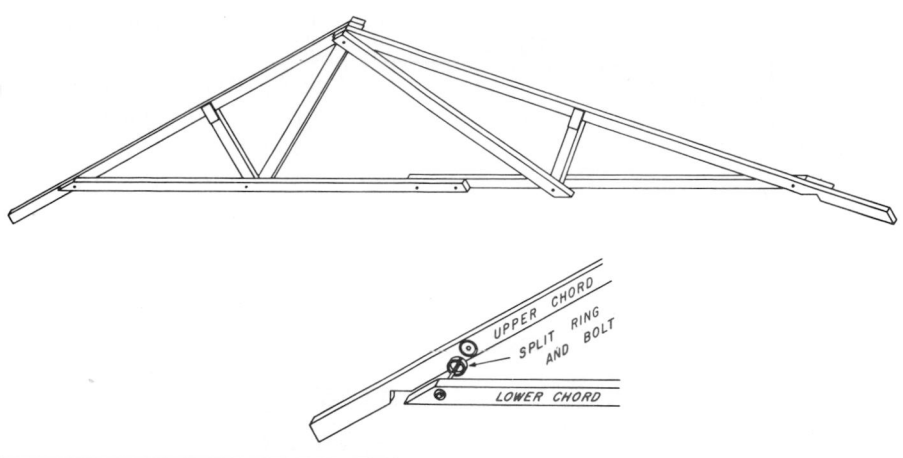

38-12a. *Truss assembled with split-ring connectors.*

gussets or split-ring connectors to secure the joints. Figs. 38-12 and 38-13.

The lumber members of site-built trusses must be cut precisely so that the joints are tight. The plywood gussets are then nailed and glued over both sides of each joint. The face grain of the plywood should run as shown in Fig. 38-14. When cutting gussets from a sheet of plywood, an efficient cutting pattern should be developed to minimize waste. Fig. 38-15. Each completed truss should be set aside immediately after assembly. It

38-12b. *Cutting a hole for a split ring connector.*

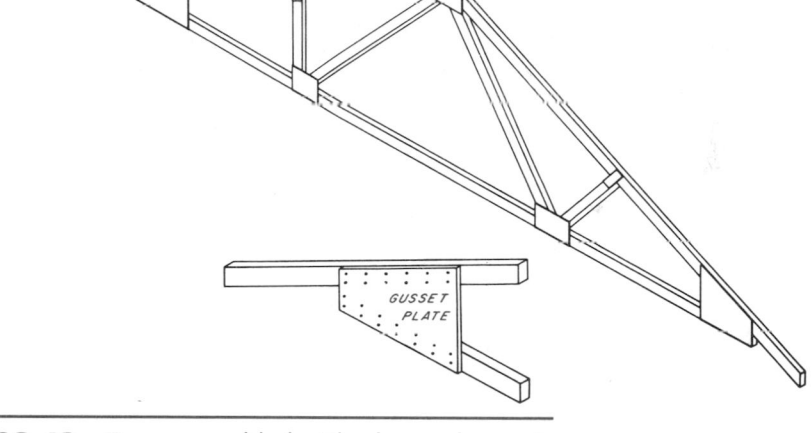

38-13. *Truss assembled with plywood gussets.*

38-12c. *Assembling the truss on the job using the split-ring connector.*

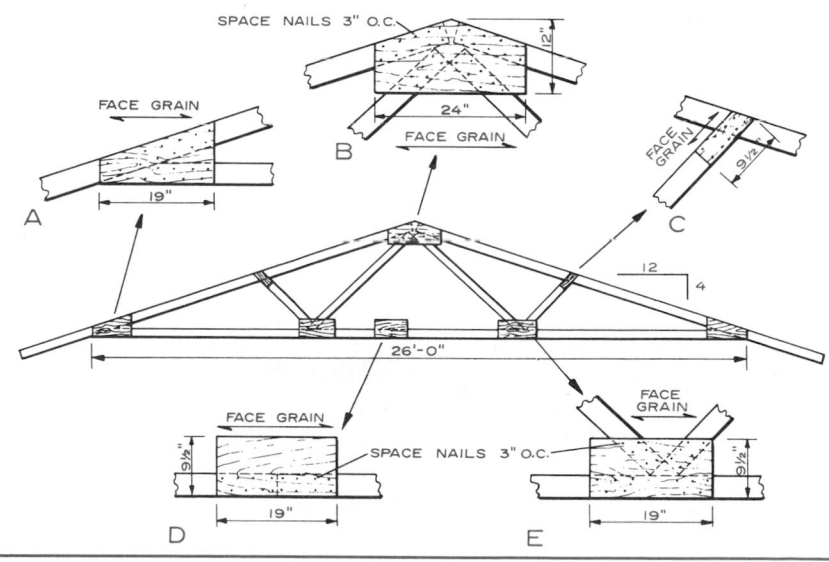

38-14. *Construction details of a 26' W-truss: A. Beveled heel gusset. B. Peak gusset. C. Upper chord intermediate gusset. D. Splice of lower chord. E. Lower chord intermediate gusset.*

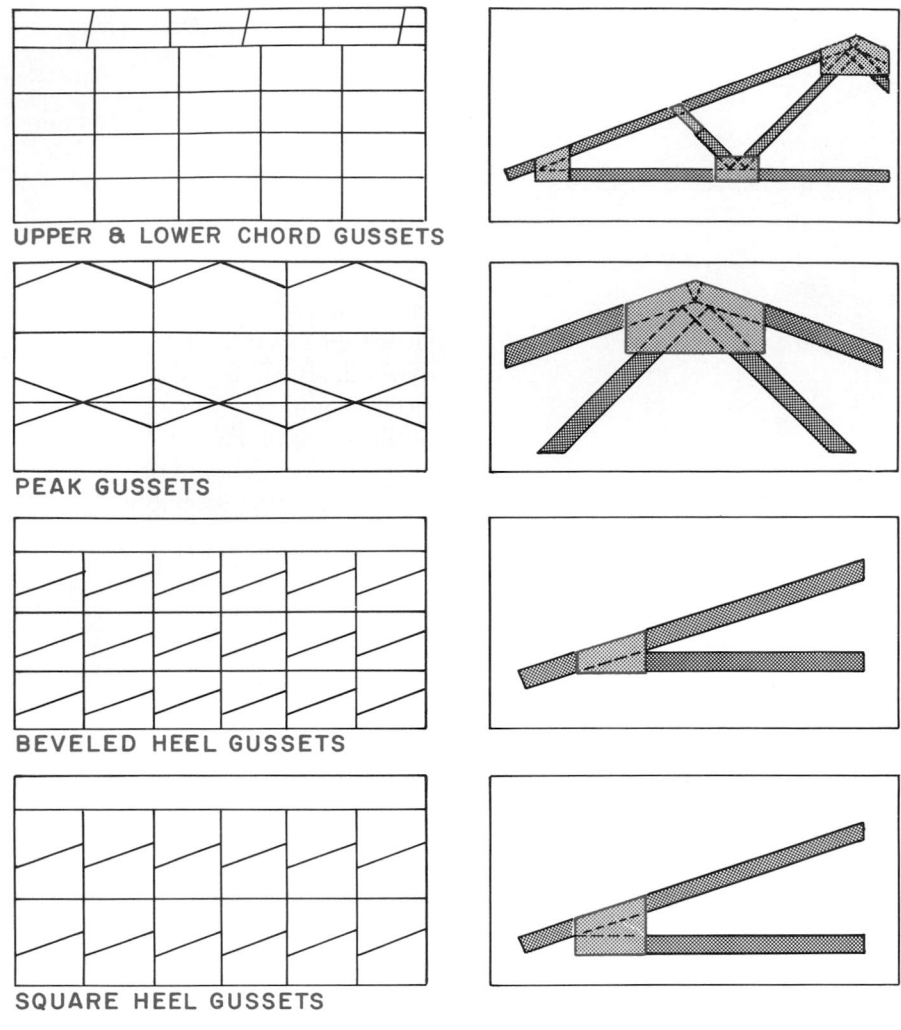

UPPER & LOWER CHORD GUSSETS

PEAK GUSSETS

BEVELED HEEL GUSSETS

SQUARE HEEL GUSSETS

38-15. *Plywood gusset cutting layouts. Make sure the grain of the plywood runs parallel with the lower chord, except for the upper chord intermediate gusset. For this gusset the grain should run parallel to the compression web.*

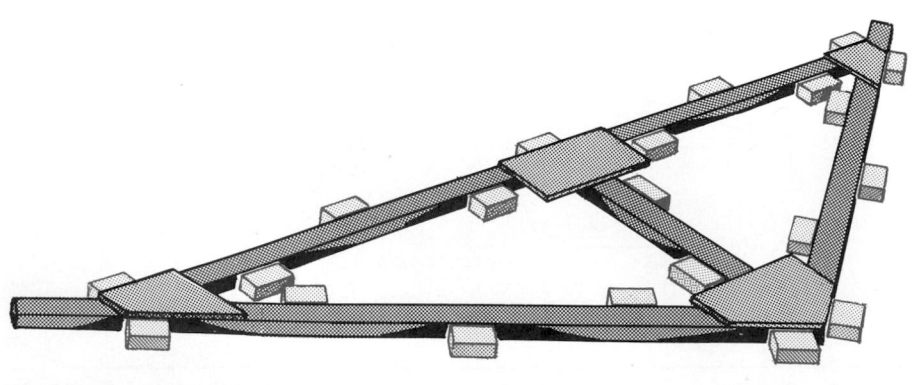

38-16. *A king-post truss laid out and blocked on an assembly table.*

should not be disturbed until the glue has set.

Truss manufacturers often build trusses on specially designed assembly tables that can be adjusted to fit various sizes and styles of trusses. This concept can be used successfully to ensure the accuracy of site-built trusses. Fig. 38-16.

TRUSS ERECTION

Handling

In handling and storage of completed trusses, avoid placing unusual stresses on them. They were designed to carry roof loads in a vertical position, and it is important that they be lifted and stored upright. If they must be handled in a flat position, enough support should be used along their length to minimize bending deflections. Never support the trusses only at the center or only at each end when they are in a flat position.

If the trusses will be stored for more than a week, they should be supported above the ground to protect them from ground water. A tarpaulin should cover the trusses to prevent rain from damaging them. Trusses must be properly supported if it is necessary to store them flat. If the trusses are stored vertically, it is important to prevent them from tipping. This is an important safety consideration: a falling load of trusses can cause serious injury to nearby workers. The steel bands that secure trusses in bundles can be under considerable tension—stand well to the side while cutting these bands. The bands should not be cut or removed until just before the trusses are ready to be erected.

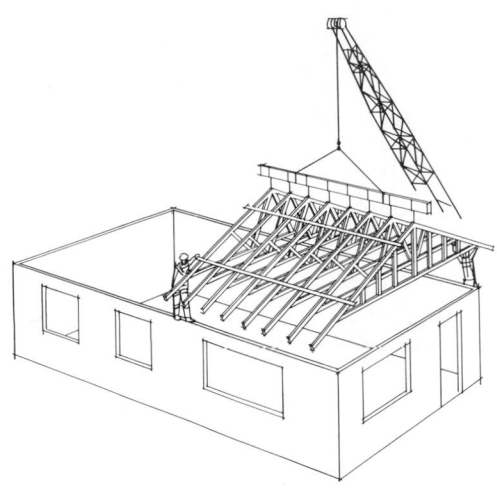

38-17. *Lifting roof trusses into place with a crane.*

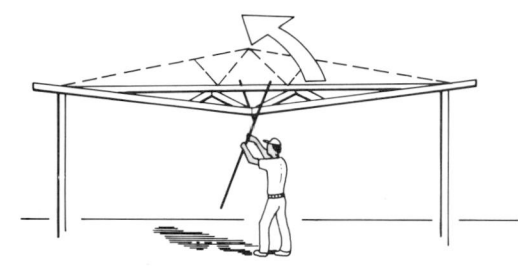

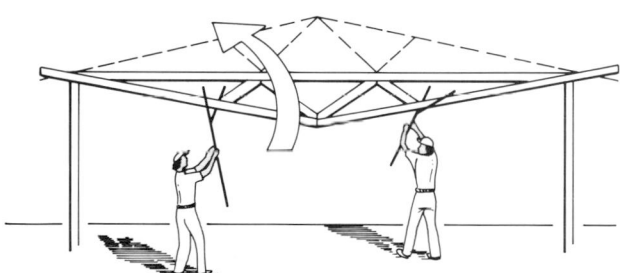

38-18a. *Tipping roof trusses into place. Note the "Y" shaped lifting poles.*

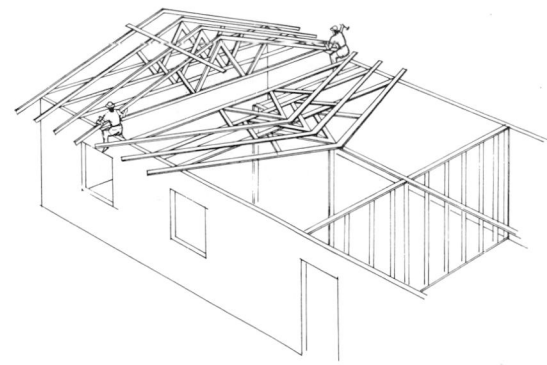

38-18b. *Roof trusses may be nailed in place as they are tipped up.*

Raising Trusses

Completed trusses can be raised in place by hand or by crane. Because a large assembled truss can be quite heavy, cranes are commonly used to set them in place. Fig. 38-17. When a crane is used, it is important to take great care to secure the truss properly as it is being lifted. A rope guide line can be attached to each truss so that a worker on the ground can keep the truss from swinging wildly.

When raising small trusses by hand, considerable care is necessary to avoid damage to the trusses and accidental injury to workers. One by one, the trusses should be placed across the building upside down and swung up into place. Fig. 38-18. Lifting poles shaped like a Y should be used to ensure a good grip on the trusses. Smaller trusses can be tipped up by one person, but larger trusses should be tipped up by two or more workers. Another worker should be at the roof level to brace the trusses as they are tipped into place.

Bracing Trusses

Trusses should be braced temporarily while they are being installed. After trusses are in place, permanent bracing should be installed to make the entire roof structure rigid.

Temporary bracing of trusses is very important. Not only does this help to maintain precise spacing of the trusses during installation, but it also prevents them from tipping over. Nominal 2" lumber is best for bracing. The most important truss to brace is the first one on the building. This is usually a gable-end truss. The truss should be braced with lumber standoffs anchored to stakes driven into the ground. Fig. 38-19. Once this truss is secure, all remaining trusses will be braced to it.

As each new truss is put into place, it should be braced temporarily to the adjacent truss with a length of nominal 2" lumber. The lumber should be secured to the top chord of each truss with two 16d nails. This bracing can be removed as the roof sheathing is installed.

Permanent truss bracing ties the individual trusses into a rigid structural system. Continuous lateral bracing consists of 2" × 4" or wider stock that is nailed to the web of each truss. Fig. 38-20. The exact location of the lateral bracing is usually specified as part of the truss design. The Truss Plate Institute, a truss industry trade group, recommends that diagonal bracing also be installed as shown in Fig. 38-21. This helps to distribute unequal loading to adjacent trusses and stabilizes the lateral bracing.

It is sometimes necessary to permanently brace the bottom chords of the trusses. On trusses with long spans, this prevents the bottom chords from moving as the ceiling finish is applied. Nominal 2" lumber is nailed to the top edge of the bottom chord, and runs the length of the building. Fig. 38-22. Once all the permanent bracing is in place, the roof should be sheathed as soon as possible. Temporary bracing can be removed once the roof structure is secure.

Fastening Trusses

When fastening trusses, resistance to uplift stresses as well as thrust must be considered. Trusses are fastened to the outside walls with nails or framing anchors. The ring-shank nail provides a simple connection which will resist modest wind uplift forces. Toenailing is sometimes done, but this is not always the most satisfactory method. Metal connector plates are located at the

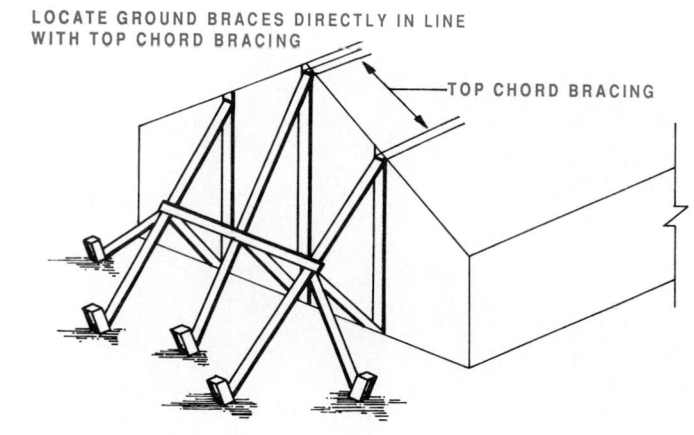

38-19. *The gable end truss should be securely braced.*

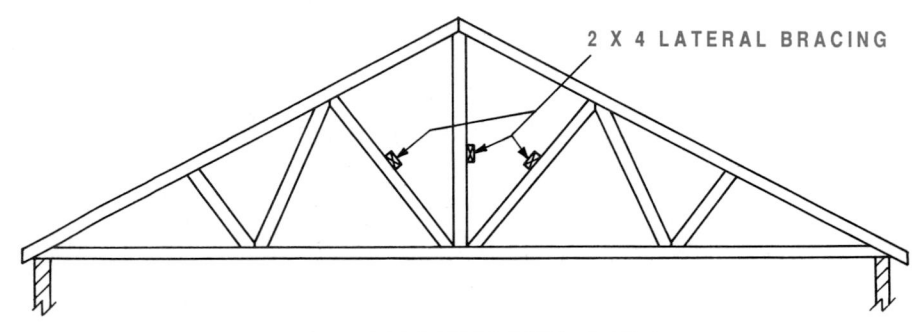

38-20. *Lateral bracing runs the length of the building.*

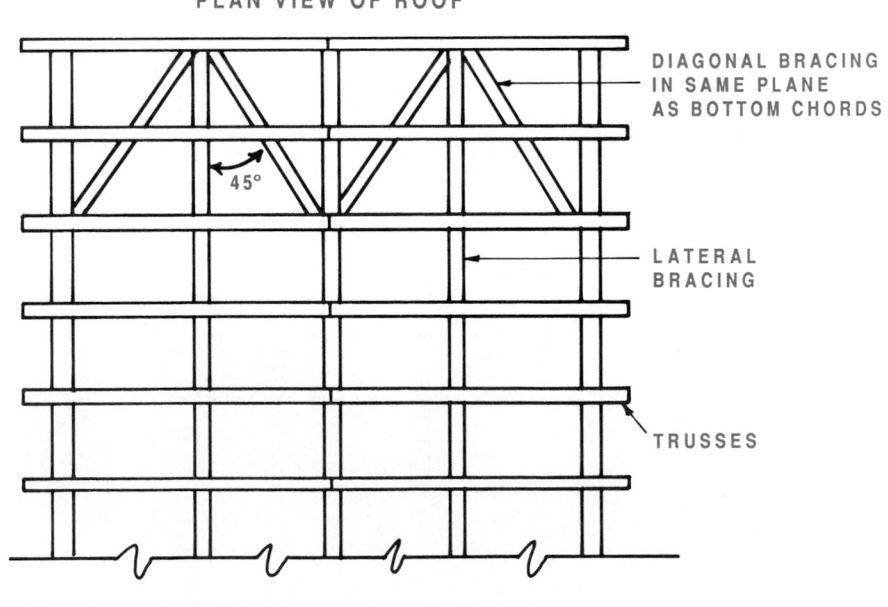

38-21. *Diagonal bracing is placed as needed.*

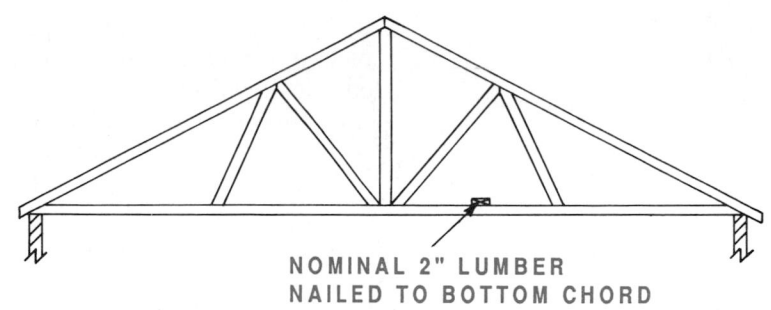

NOMINAL 2" LUMBER NAILED TO BOTTOM CHORD

38-22. *Bottom chord bracing.*

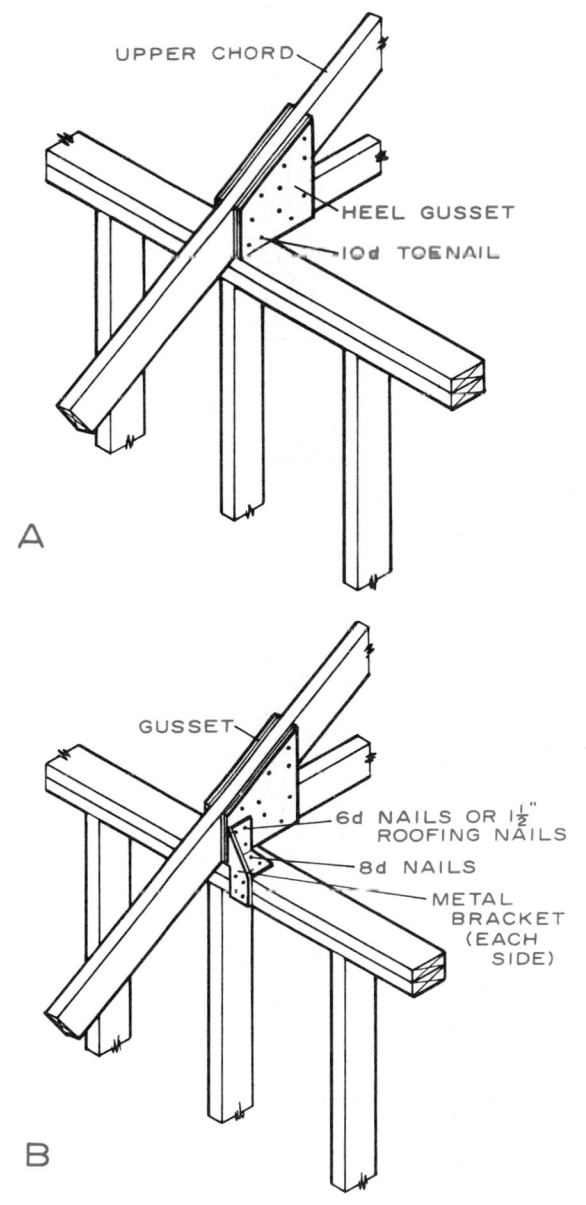

UPPER CHORD

HEEL GUSSET

10d TOENAIL

A

GUSSET

6d NAILS OR 1½" ROOFING NAILS

8d NAILS

METAL BRACKET (EACH SIDE)

B

38-23. *Fastening trusses to the wall plate: A. Toenailing. B. Metal bracket.*

wall plate and make toenailing difficult. However, two 10d nails on each side of the truss can be used in nailing the lower chord to the plate. Fig. 38-23. Predrilling may be necessary to prevent splitting. Because of the single-member thickness of the truss and the presence of gussets at the wall plates, it is usually a good idea to use some type of metal connector to supplement the toenailings.

A better system of fastening trusses involves the use of a metal connector or bracket to replace toenailing entirely. These brackets are available commercially. Fig. 38-24. The brackets are nailed to the wall plates at side and top with 8d nails and to the lower chords of the truss with 6d nails. Fig. 38-23.

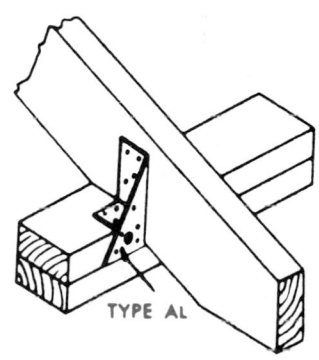

TYPE AL

38-24a. *Sheet-metal brackets are ideal for attaching the roof truss to the wall plate.*

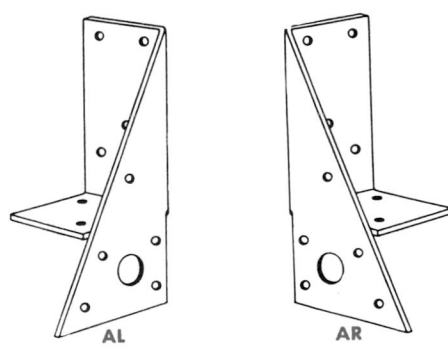

AL

AR

38-24b. *Left-hand and right-hand sheet-metal brackets are available for installation on both sides of the roof truss.*

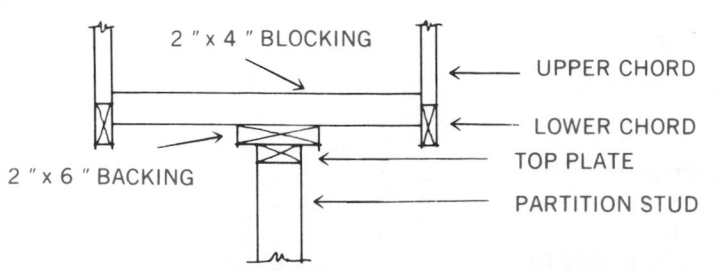

38-25. *Construction details for partitions that run parallel to the roof truss.*

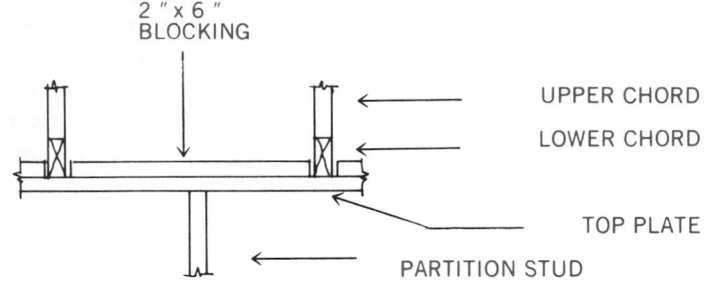

38-26. *Construction details for partitions that run at right angles to the roof truss.*

INTERIOR PARTITION INSTALLATION

Where partitions run parallel to but between the bottom truss chords and the partitions are erected *before* the ceiling finish is applied, install 2" × 4" blocking between the lower chords. Fig. 38-25. This blocking should be spaced not over 4' on center. Nail the blocking to the chords with two 16d nails in each end. To provide nailing for lath or wallboard, nail a 1" × 6" or 2" × 6" continuous backer to the blocking. Set the bottom face level with the bottom of the lower truss chords.

When partitions are erected *after* the ceiling finish is applied, 2" × 4" blocking is set with the bottom edge level with the bottom of the truss chords. Nail the blocking with two 16d nails in each end.

If the partitions run at right angles to the bottom of the truss chords, the partitions are nailed directly to lower chord members. A 2" × 6" backer for the application of the ceiling finish is nailed on top of the partition plates between the trusses. Fig. 38-26.

ESTIMATING

Materials

Most builders buy trusses ready-made. A manufacturer may be able to fabricate a roof truss, deliver it to the job site, and set it on the rafter plate with a crane, ready for the worker to tip it into place, for less than the cost of the material alone in conventional framing.

Labor

Installing the roof trusses on an average size home, with attached garage, containing about 2,000 square feet of ceiling area will take 3 workers about 2 hours. This includes laying out the locations, setting up, and attaching the roof trusses to the rafter plates.

1. What are some of the advantages of using roof trusses in residential construction?

2. What three types of trusses are most commonly used for residential building?

3. Which of the three types of trusses used in building construction is the most popular and extensively used?

4. What is a truss connector plate?

5. What is the best method of attaching the truss to the wall plates?

6. Describe two types of bracing used to secure trusses.

ACTIVITIES

1. Math. You work for a lumber yard. You have been asked to determine the length of each piece needed for a W-type truss which will span 24'. The total rise is 6' and there will be no overhang. The bottom chord has a length of 24'.

a. Sketch a diagram of the truss using the guidelines for where the long and short web intersect the top and bottom chord.

b. Determine the length of the top chord.

c. Determine the length of the long web.

2. Science. In all of the truss designs, one sees many triangles. Why is the triangle a common form in trusses?

THE SCHOOL-TO-WORK CONNECTION

A great deal of research and engineering goes into the design of a roof truss. A truss uses a minimum of materials. Thus, every part has to be carefully considered as part of a system. The parts—lumber and connecting plates—have to perform predictably and consistently. Truss manufacturers generally have at least one, and sometimes several, engineers on their permanent staff. They develop the calculations that describe the strength of a truss. An engineer's stamp on the truss plans is your assurance that the truss has been carefully designed.

1. Locate a truss manufacturer in your area. If you don't find any listings in the phone book, check with a local lumberyard or building materials dealer to see if they supply roof trusses. They may serve as an outlet for the truss manufacturer. Contact the truss company. Find out what information you would have to give them when you order trusses. Ask if they will send you a guideline for storing and erecting trusses. Add it to a file you start on trusses.

2. In the reference section of your library you will find a directory of trade associations. Use it to find a trade association that represents the manufacturers of truss plates. Write to this association, requesting any free publications they might have on the history of truss plates.

39

Roof Sheathing

Roof sheathing covers the rafters or roof joists. The roof sheathing, like the wall sheathing and the subflooring, is a structural element. Therefore applying it is a part of the framing process. Sheathing provides a nailing base for the finish roof covering and gives rigidity and strength to the roof framing. Plywood, oriented strand board (OSB), or lumber roof sheathing is most commonly used for pitched roofs. Lumber or laminated roof decking is sometimes used in homes with exposed ceilings.

LUMBER ROOF SHEATHING

Lumber roof sheathing was once the most common form of sheathing. It is sometimes still used in new construction and remodeling. However, builders in many parts of the country now prefer panel sheathing such as plywood or OSB.

Roof sheathing boards are usually 1 × 4, 1 × 6, or 1 × 8 boards. They can have either a square edge, a T&G edge, or a shiplap edge. The grade is generally No. 3 common or better. The most common species used are Douglas fir, pine, hemlock, spruce, and larch. If the roof is to be covered with asphalt shingles, it is important that thoroughly seasoned material be used for the sheathing. Unseasoned wood will dry out and shrink in width. This shrinkage will cause buckling or lifts of the shingles which may extend along the full length of the board.

Nominal 1" boards are used for both flat and pitched roofs. Where flat roofs are to be used for a deck or a balcony, thicker sheathing boards will be required. Board roof sheathing, like board wall sheathing and subflooring, may be laid either horizontally or diagonally. Fig. 39-1. Horizontal board sheathing may be either closed (laid with no spaces between the courses) or open (laid with spaces between the courses). In areas where wind-driven snow conditions prevail, a solid roof deck is recommended.

39-1. *Roof board sheathing laid horizontally.*

Lumber roof sheathing is sometimes used along with plywood roof sheathing. Open soffits expose the underside of roof sheathing at the eaves, so some builders install lumber sheathing in these areas to provide a decorative effect. The rest of the roof is then sheathed with plywood. This is a particularly effective technique when beveled-edge T&G boards are used to sheath the soffit area. There can be a slight difference in thickness between the two sheathing types, however. If this is the case, the edge of the plywood can be shimmed upwards slightly where it meets the board sheathing. Fig. 39-2.

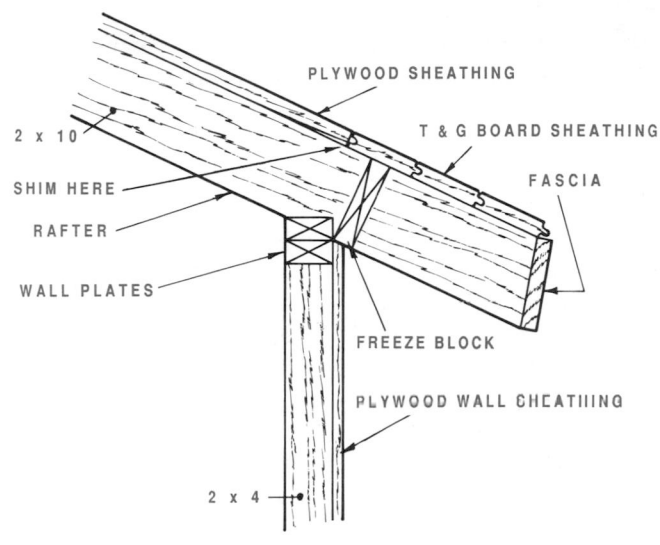

39-2. *Board sheathing is sometimes used where the underside of the roof sheathing will be exposed, as at open soffits. Where the plywood sheathing meets the board sheathing, the edge of the plywood can be shimmed to match the thickness of the boards.*

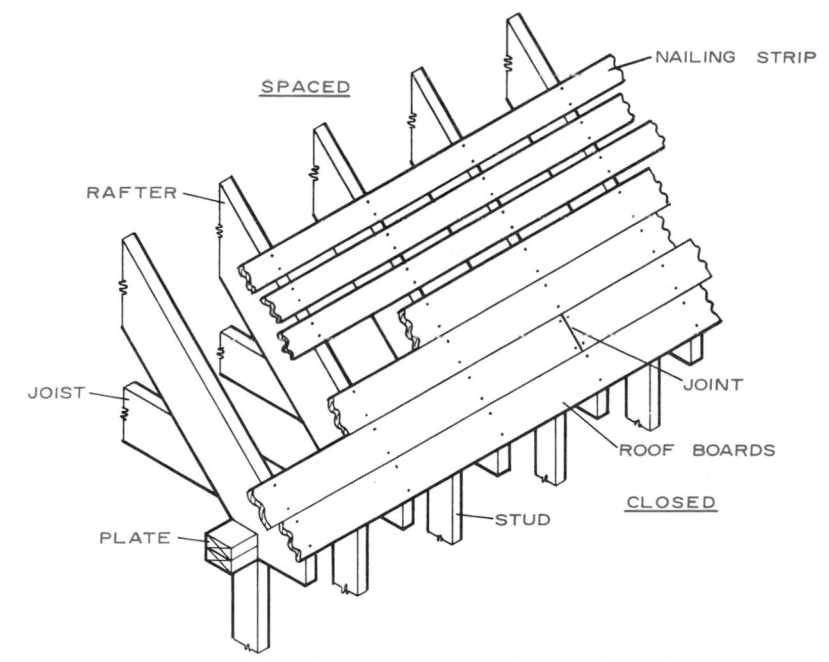

39-3. *Installation of board roof sheathing, showing both closed and spaced types.*

Installation

Closed Sheathing. Roof boards used for sheathing under materials that require solid and continuous support—such as asphalt shingles, composition roofing, and sheet-metal roofing—must be laid closed. Fig. 39-3. Closed roof sheathing may also be used for wood shingles.

Open Sheathing. Open sheathing (sometimes called skip sheathing) is used under wood shingles or shakes in blizzard-free areas or damp climates. Open sheathing usually consists of l" × 4" strips with the on-center spacing equal to the shingle weather exposure but not over 10". (A 10" shingle which is lapped 4" by the shingle above it is said to be laid 6" to the weather.) When applying open sheathing, the boards should be laid up without spacing to a point on the roof above the overhang. Fig. 39-3.

Nailing

Lumber roof sheathing is nailed to each rafter with two 8d nails. Joints must be made on the rafters, just as wall sheathing joints must be made over studs. When end-matched boards are used, joints may be made between rafters, but in no case should the joints of adjoining boards be made over the same rafter space. Each board should bear on at least two rafters.

PLYWOOD ROOF SHEATHING

Many different roof forms are possible with plywood construction. Plywood offers flexibility in design, ease of construction, economy, and durability. Fig. 39-4.

39-4. *Both the roof and sidewalls of this large home are sheathed with plywood.*

It can be installed quickly over large areas and provides a smooth, solid base with a minimum of joints. A plywood deck is also equally effective under any type of shingles or built-up roofing. Waste is minimal, contributing to the low in-place cost. It is frequently possible to cut costs still further by using fewer rafters with a somewhat thicker panel for the sheathing. Plywood and trusses are often combined in this manner. For recommended spans and plywood grades, see Table 39-A.

Installation

Plywood roof sheathing should be laid with the face grain perpendicular to the rafters. Fig. 39-5. Square-edged plywood graded CDX is generally used. This designation means the plywood has one "C" face and one "D" face, and the plies are adhered with exterior-grade (waterproof) glue. End joints should occur over rafters, and rows of panels should be staggered. Unsupported edge joints can be strengthened with metal panel clips that tie the joints together. Fig. 39-6.

A plywood panel will shrink or swell slightly as its moisture content changes. Because of the way it is manufactured, plywood can have a low moisture content as it leaves the mill. If panels are butted tightly during installation, they may buckle as they expand. To prevent buckling, the American Plywood Association recommends that all plywood panels used for roof sheathing be spaced ⅛" apart (the width of a 10d box nail), *unless otherwise recommended by the manufacturer.* This spacing should be followed at all edge joints and end joints. Some panel clips are constructed in such a way that they automatically space panels the proper distance apart. Proper ventilation of the roof will also help to prevent the plywood panels from buckling.

Plywood roof sheathing should have no surface or edge directly exposed to the weather. To reduce handling costs and help the worker apply plywood roof sheathing, a roof platform may be constructed. Fig. 39-7. This platform supports a small supply of plywood sheathing on the roof that is readily accessible to the worker. Another aid which may be constructed is a plywood ladder. It will eliminate the need for a second person to hand the plywood up to the one on the roof.

Table 39-A. *Recommended Uniform Roof Live Loads for APA Panel Sheathing with Long Dimension Perpendicular to Supports [c]. (APA Rated Sheathing and APA Structural I Rated Sheathing.)*

Panel Span Rating	Panel Thickness (in.)	Maximum Span (in.) With Edge Support [a]	Maximum Span (in.) Without Edge Support	Allowable Live Loads (psf) [d] Spacing of Supports Center-to-Center (in.) 12	16	20	24	32	40	48	60
12/0	5/16	12	12	30							
16/0	5/16, 3/8	16	16	55	30						
20/0	5/16, 3/8	20	20	70	50	30					
24/0	3/8, 7/16, 1/2	24	20 [b]	90	65	55	30				
24/16	7/16, 1/2	24	24	135	100	75	40				
32/16	15/32, 1/2, 5/8	32	28	135	100	75	55	30			
40/20	9/16, 19/32, 5/8, 3/4, 7/8	40	32	165	120	100	75	55	30		
48/24	23/32, 3/4, 7/8	48	36	210	155	130	100	65	50	35	
48oc [e]	1⅛	60	48				375	205	100	65	40

(a) Tongue-and-groove edges, panel edge clips (one between each support, except two between supports 48 inches on center), lumber blocking, or other.
(b) 24 inches for ½-inch panels.
(c) When roofing is to be guaranteed by a performance bond, check with roofing manufacturer for minimum thickness, span and edge support requirements.
(d) 10 psf dead load assumed.
(e) Span Rating applies to APA RATED STURD-I-FLOOR "2-4-1."

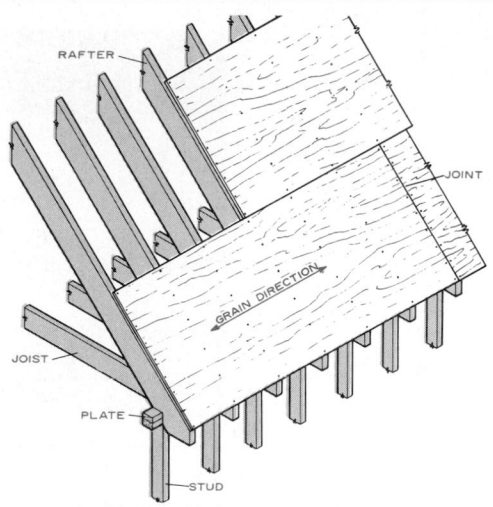

39-5. *The grain of plywood sheathing should be at right angles to the supporting members.*

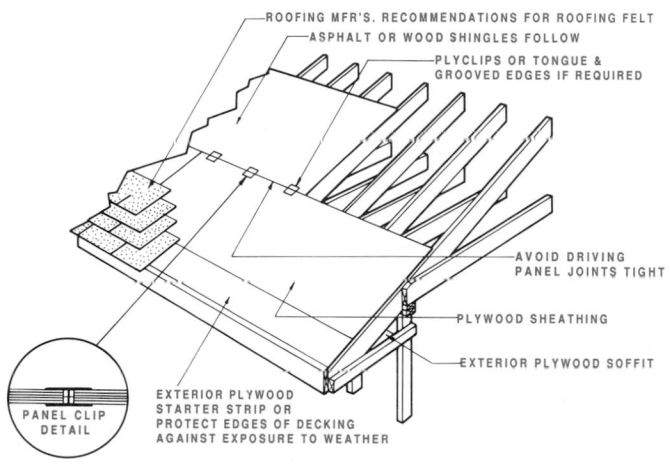

39-6. *Plywood roof sheathing details.*

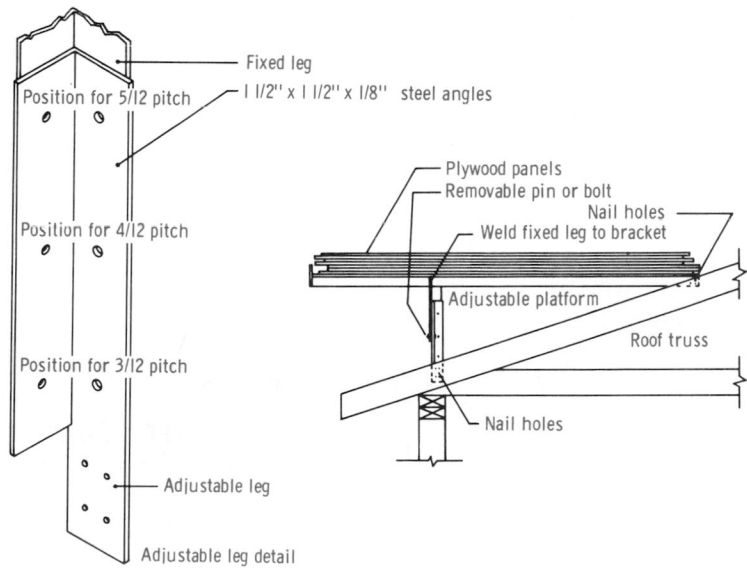

39-7a. *Details for adjustable roof platform.*

39-7b. *Having the sheathing readily available on the roof increases efficiency.*

Figs. 39-8 and 39-9. This ladder is leaned against the building in the normal position of a ladder. The plywood sheets are then set on end on the ⅜" plywood gusset. From there they can be pulled onto the roof as needed for application.

Spans

Depending largely upon its thickness, plywood sheathing can be used to span various distances. Table 39-A shows the most common combinations. Many panels are stamped to indicate their suitability for particular spans. The stamp includes a pair of numbers separated by a slash mark, such as 32/16 or 12/0. The number in front of the slash indicates the maximum spacing of supports when the panel is used for roof sheathing. The number following the slash refers to the maximum spacing of supports beneath panels used for subflooring. Both numbers assume that the long dimension of the

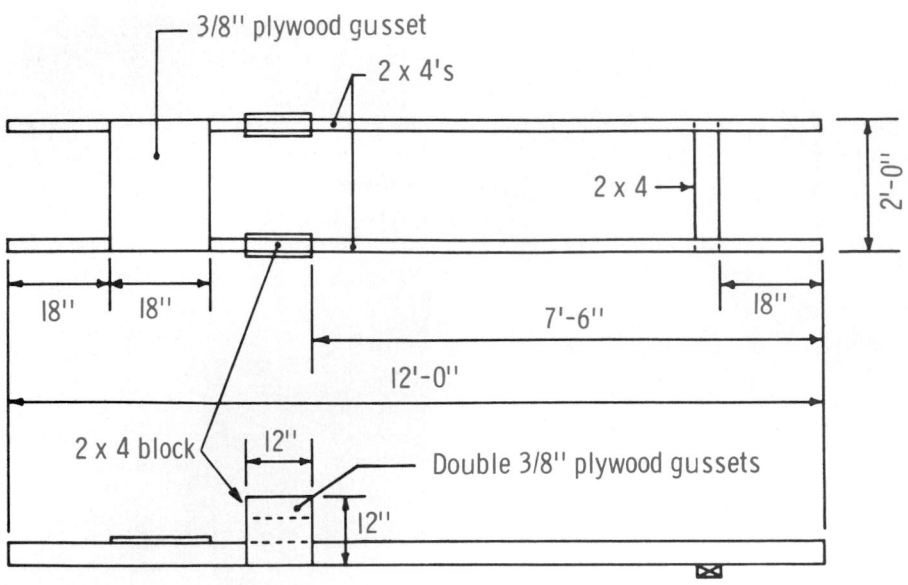

39-8. *Plywood ladder detail.*

3/8" plywood gusset

2 x 4's

2 x 4

2'-0"

18"   18"

7'-6"

18"

12'-0"

2 x 4 block

12"

Double 3/8" plywood gussets

12"

39-10. *Power-driven fasteners speed plywood installation.*

39-9a. *This ladder is made from scrap plywood nailed to a pair of 2 x 4s. A worker can load this ladder before getting on the roof.*

39-9b. *When applying the sheathing, the worker can pull it from the ladder onto the roof.*

panel will span at least three supports. When one of the numbers is a zero, this means that the panel is unsuitable for that particular use. Note that greater spans are generally allowed for sheathing.

Fastening. Nails should be spaced 6" at the panel edges and 12" apart at intermediate supports except where the spans are 48" or more. Then the nails should be spaced 6" on all supports. Use 6d common smooth, ring-shank, or spiral thread nails for plywood ½" thick or less. For plywood l" thick or less, use 8d common smooth, ring-shank, or spiral thread nails. Table 39-B (page 442).

To install plywood roof sheathing, many builders use air-driven staples instead of nails. The staples should be 16-ga. galvanized wire with a minimum crown width of ⅜". They should be spaced 4" apart at panel edges and 8" apart at intermediate supports. Fig. 39-10.

ORIENTED STRAND BOARD SHEATHING

Since the early 1980s, other sheet products have been increasingly used for roof sheathing. The most common of these is oriented strand board

(OSB). OSB is made from "strands" of wood fibers that have been bonded together with water-resistant or waterproof adhesives. Like plywood, it can be installed quickly over large areas.

Installation

Oriented strand board is manufactured to standards set by the American Plywood Association. Because the strands are aligned with the long dimension of the sheet, OSB is strongest in this direction. This is why OSB roof sheathing should be laid with the face "grain" perpendicular to the rafters.

It is very important to space OSB sheets properly. There should be a ¼" space along the edges of adjoining panels, and a ⅛" space at the ends. Metal edge clips can be used to strengthen unsupported edges of OSB sheets.

Fastening. The fastening details that apply to plywood generally apply to OSB as well. Panels should be nailed 6" on center at the edges and 12" on center in the field. Staples should be placed 4" apart at the edges and 8" apart in the field.

DECKING OR PLANKING

Roof decking provides a solid permanent roof deck and an attractive ready-to-finish interior ceiling. It serves as an excellent base for any roofing material. Decking, with tongue-and-groove edges and decorative face patterns, is a standard building product for residential, commercial, and institutional construction. Fig. 39-11. Although known and used as roof decking, its load bearing capacities also make it useful as floor decking. This material is available in grades, patterns, and

39-11. *Decking with tongue-and-groove edges and decorative face patterns provides a durable roof and an attractive ceiling for residential and commercial buildings.*

sizes suitable for both residential and commercial construction.

Grades. The *commercial* grade is designed for use in buildings where appearance and strength requirements are not a prime factor. The *select* grade decking is ideally suited for homes, schools, churches, motels, and restaurants, or wherever an attractive surface appearance is important.

Patterns. Lumber roof decking with a double tongue and groove is available in several patterns. Some of the more common are the regular V-joint, grooved, striated, and eased joint (bullnosed) patterns. Single tongue-and-groove

decking in nominal 2" × 6" and 2" × 8" sizes is available with the V-joint pattern only. Fig. 39-12.

Sizes. Decking comes in nominal widths of 4" to 12" and in nominal thicknesses of 2" to 4". The 3" and 4" roof decking is available in random lengths of 6' to 20' or longer (odd and even).

Decking is also available laminated. It comes in six different species of softwood lumber: Idaho white pine, inland red cedar, Idaho white fir, ponderosa pine, Douglas fir, larch, and southern pine. Because of the laminating feature, this material may have a facing of one wood species and back and interior laminations of different woods. It is also available with all laminations of the same species. For all types of decking, make sure the material is the correct thickness for the span by checking the manufacturer's recommendations.

Installation

Roof decking that is to be applied to a flat roof should be installed with the tongue away from the worker. Roof decking that is being applied to a sloping roof should be installed with the tongues up. The butt ends of the pieces are cut at approximately a 2 degree angle. This provides a bevel cut from the face to the back to insure a tight joint when the

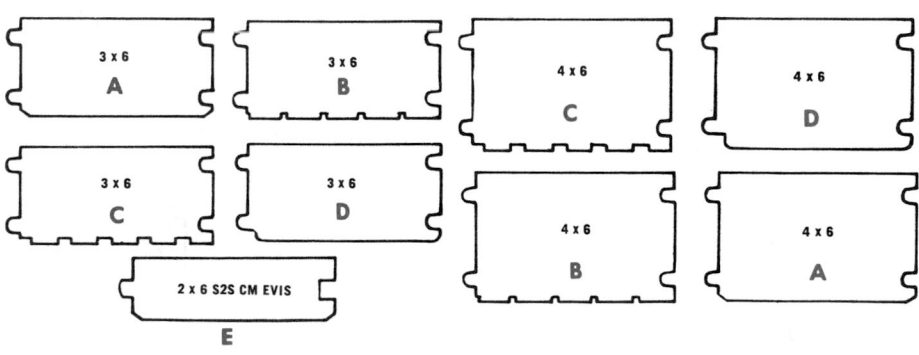

39-12. *Some lumber roof decking patterns and sizes: A. Regular V-jointed. B. Striated. C. Grooved. D. Eased joint (bullnosed). E. Single tongue-and-groove V-joint.*

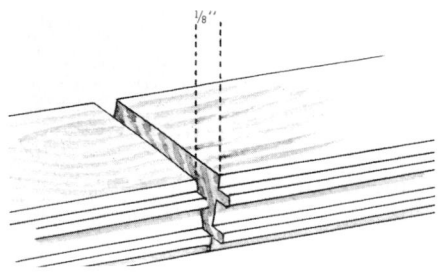

39-13. *The ends of lumber decking are cut at a 2° angle to insure a tight face joint on the exposed ceiling.*

decking is laid in a random length pattern. Fig. 39-13. If there are three or more supports for the decking, a controlled random laying pattern may be used. Fig. 39-14. This is an economical pattern because it makes use of random plank lengths, but the following rules must be observed:

➤ Stagger the end joints in adjacent planks as widely as possible and not less than 2'.

➤ Separate the joints in the same general line by at least two courses.

➤ Minimize joints in the middle one-third of all spans, make each plank bear on at least one support, and minimize the joints in the end span.

The ability of the decking to support specific loads depends on the support spacing, plank thickness, and span arrangement. Although two-span continuous layout offers structural efficiency, use of random-length planks is the most economical. Random-length double tongue-and-groove decking is used when there are three or more spans. It is not intended for use over single spans and it is not recommended for use over double spans. Fig. 39-14.

Nailing. Fasten the decking with common nails twice as long as the nominal plank thickness. For widths 6" or less, toenail once and

face-nail once at each support. For widths over 6", toenail once and face-nail twice. Decking 3" and 4" thick must be predrilled and toenailed with 8" spikes. Fig. 39-15. Some manufacturers provide the 3" and 4" thick roof decking with predrilled nail holes on 30" centers. Bright common nails may be used, but dipped galvanized common nails have better holding power and reduce the possibility of rust streaks. End joints not over a support should be side-nailed

within 10" of each plank end. Metal splines are recommended on end joints of 3" and 4" material for better alignment, appearance, and strength.

SHEATHING AT THE ENDS OF THE ROOF

Where the gable ends of the roof have little or no extension other than the molding and trim, the

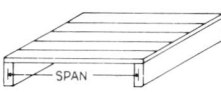
A — SIMPLE SPAN

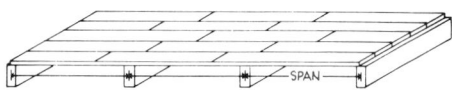
D — CANTILEVERED INTERMIXED SPAN

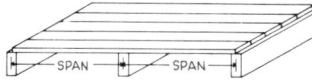
B — TWO SPAN CONTINUOUS

E — CONTROLLED RANDOM PATTERN

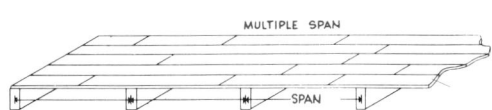

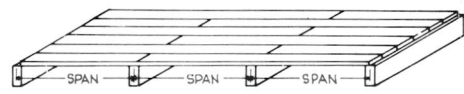
C — MULTIPLE SPAN (A & B)

39-14. *Lumber decking span arrangements.*

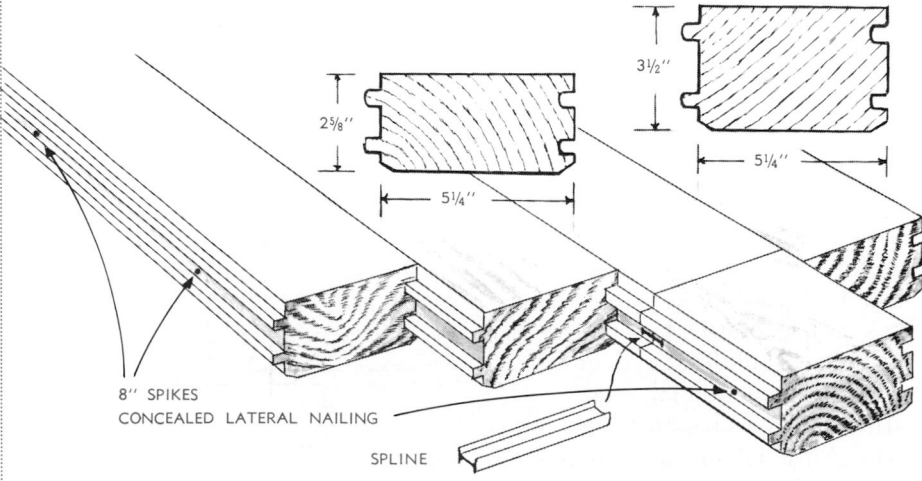

39-15. *Nailing details for lumber decking.*

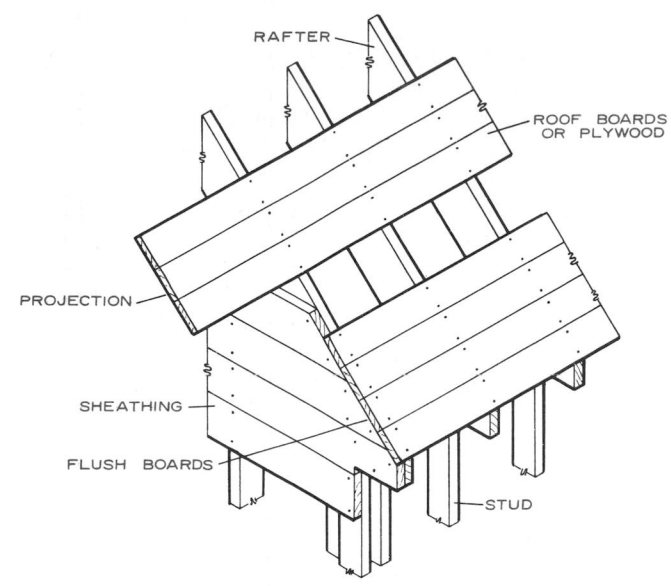

39-16. *Board sheathing at the ends of a gable roof.*

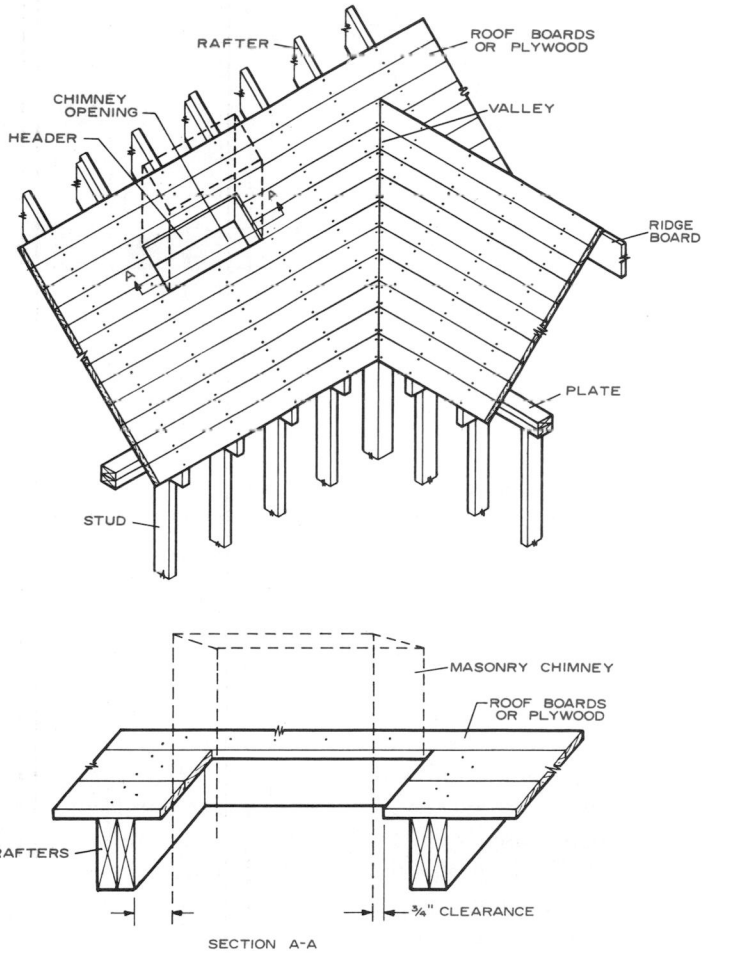

39-17. *Sheathing details at the valley and at the chimney opening. Section A-A shows the clearance between the masonry chimney and the wood structure.*

roof sheathing is usually sawn flush with the outer face of the side wall sheathing. Cuts should be made even so that the trim and molding can be properly installed. See Unit 42, "Roof Trim." Board sheathing that projects beyond the end walls should span not less than three rafter spaces to insure proper anchorage to the rafters and to prevent sagging. Fig. 39-16. In general, it is desirable to use the longest boards at overhangs to secure good anchorage.

SHEATHING DETAILS AT CHIMNEY OPENINGS

Where chimney openings occur in the roof structure, the roof sheathing should have a clearance of ¾" from the finished masonry on all sides. Fig. 39-17. Framing members should have a 2" clearance for fire protection. The sheathing should be securely nailed to the rafters and to the headers around the opening.

SHEATHING AT VALLEYS AND HIPS

The sheathing at the valleys and hips should be fitted to give a tight joint. It should be securely nailed to the valley or the hip rafter. Fig. 39-17. This will give a solid and smooth base for the flashing.

ESTIMATING

Material

Determine the total area to be covered. To figure the roof area without actually getting on the roof and measuring, find the dimensions

Table 39-B. *Recommended Minimum Fastening Schedule for APA Panel Roof Sheathing.*

| Panel Thickness (in.) | Size | Nailing[c] | | Leg Length (in.) | Stapling[a][b] | |
| | | Spacing (in.) | | | Spacing (in.) | |
		Panel Edges	Intermediate		Panel Edges	Intermediate
5/16	6d	6	12	1¼	4	8
3/8	6d	6	12	1⅜	4	8
7/16, 15/32, ½	6d	6	12	1½	4	8
19/32, 5/8, 23/32, 3/4, 7/8	8d	6	12[d]	—	—	—
1⅛, 1¼	8d or 10d	6	12[d]	—	—	—

(a) Values are for 16-gal galvanized wire staples with a minimum crown width of ⅜ inch.
(b) For stapling asphalt shingles to 5/16 inch and thicker panels, use staples with a ¾ inch minimum crown width and a ¾ inch leg length. Space according to shingle manufacturer's recommendations.
(c) Use common smooth or deformed shank nails with panels to 1 inch thick. For 1⅛ inch and 1¼ inch panels, use 8d ring or screw-shank or 10d common smooth-shank nails.
(d) For spans 48 inches or greater, space nails 6 inches at all supports.

Table 39-C. *Determining Roof Area from a Plan. When a roof has to be figured from a plan only and the roof pitch is known, the roof area may be computed from the table below.*

Rise	Factor	Rise	Factor
3"	1.031	8"	1.202
3½"	1.042	8½"	1.225
4"	1.054	9"	1.250
4½"	1.068	9½"	1.275
5"	1.083	10"	1.302
5½"	1.100	10½"	1.329
6"	1.118	11"	1.357
6½"	1.137	11½"	1.385
7"	1.158	12"	1.414
7½"	1.179		

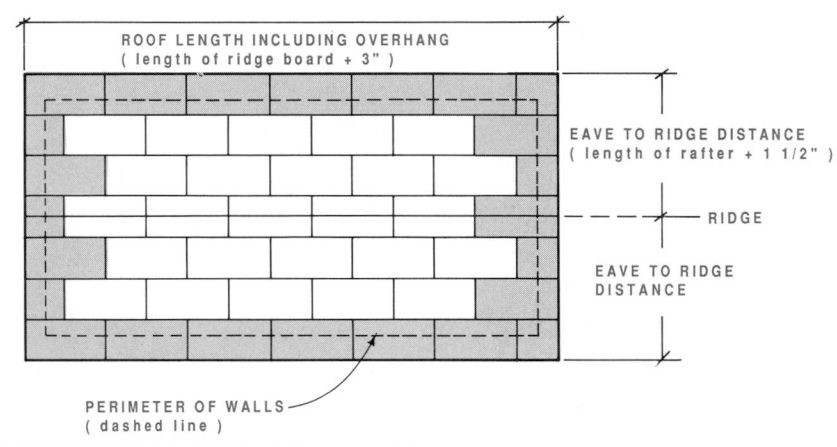

ROOF LENGTH INCLUDING OVERHANG
(length of ridge board + 3")

EAVE TO RIDGE DISTANCE
(length of rafter + 1 1/2")

RIDGE

EAVE TO RIDGE DISTANCE

PERIMETER OF WALLS
(dashed line)

39-18. *A roof sheathing plan for plywood.*

of the roof on the plans. Multiply the length times the width of the roof, including the overhang. Then multiply by the factor shown opposite the rise of the roof in Table 39-C. The result will be the roof area.

For example, assume that a home is 70' long and 30' wide including the overhang and that the roof has a rise of 5½". 70' × 30' = 2,100 sq. ft. For a rise of 5½", the factor on the chart is 1.100. Table 39-C. 2,100 sq. ft. × 1.100 = 2,310 sq. ft. Use this total area for figuring roofing needs, such as sheathing, felt underlayment, or shingles.

Lumber Sheathing. First figure the total area to be covered. Determine the size boards to be used and refer to Table 39-C. Multiply the total area to be covered by the factor from the chart. For example, if 1" × 8" tongue-and-groove sheathing boards are used, the total roof area is multiplied by 1.16. To determine the total number of board feet needed, add 5% for a trim and waste factor.

Panel Sheathing. To estimate the number of plywood or OSB panels required, determine the total roof area to be covered and divide by 32 (the number of square feet in one 4' × 8' sheet). This will give the number of sheets required for covering the area. Be sure to add 5% for a trim and waste allowance.

Another estimating technique is to draw a roof sheathing plan. This is a scale diagram of the roof that shows where individual plywood or OSB panels will be installed. Fig. 39-18. This technique is especially useful when the roof requires the use of more than one kind of panel. An example of this would be when a house has open soffits and decorative plywood will be used in those locations.

Table 39-D. *Roof Board Sheathing Specifications.*

	Nominal Size	Width Dress	Face	Area Factor
Shiplap	1 x 6	5 $^7/_{16}$	4 $^{15}/_{16}$	1.22
	1 x 8	7 $^1/_8$	6 $^5/_8$	1.21
	1 x10	9 $^1/_8$	8 $^5/_8$	1.16
	1 x12	11 $^1/_8$	10 $^5/_8$	1.13
Tongue and Groove	1 x 4	3 $^7/_{16}$	3 $^3/_{16}$	1.26
	1 x 6	5 $^7/_{16}$	5 $^3/_{16}$	1.16
	1 x 8	7 $^1/_8$	6 $^7/_8$	1.16
	1 x 10	9 $^1/_8$	8 $^7/_8$	1.13
	1 x 12	11 $^1/_8$	10 $^7/_8$	1.10
S4S	1 x 4	3 $^1/_2$	3 $^1/_2$	1.14
	1 x 6	5 $^1/_2$	5 $^1/_2$	1.09
	1 x 8	7 $^1/_4$	7 $^1/_4$	1.10
	1 x10	9 $^1/_4$	9 $^1/_4$	1.08
	1 x 12	11 $^1/_4$	11 $^1/_4$	1.07

Table 39-E. *Area Factors for Estimating Decking.*

Size	Area Factor
2" x 6"	2.40
2" x 8"	2.29
3" x 6"	3.43
4" x 6"	4.57

Waste allowance not included in above factors.

Table 39-F. *Labor Time for Roof Sheathing.*

1 x 6 boards S4S	65 b.f. per hour
1 x 6 center match	55 b.f. per hour
1 x 8 shiplap	60 b.f. per hour
1 x 10 shiplap	75 b.f. per hour

Decking or Planking.
Determine the area to be covered. Then refer to Table 39-E, and read in the left column the size planking to be applied. For example, if 2" × 6" material is selected, the factor given is 2.40. Multiply the area to be covered by this factor and add a 5% trim and waste allowance to arrive at the amount of material required.

Labor

To estimate labor costs, refer to Table 39-F.

QUESTIONS

1. What are the most commonly used sheathing materials for pitched roofs?

2. Why is it important that lumber roof sheathing be thoroughly seasoned when used with asphalt shingles?

3. When installing plywood roof sheathing, in which direction should the grain run in relation to the rafters?

4. What is the minimum thickness of plywood that may be used for roof sheathing under asphalt shingles with a rafter spacing of 16"?

5. What are some of the patterns of decking or planking in contemporary architecture?

6. What clearance is recommended between roof sheathing and finished masonry, such as a chimney?

ACTIVITIES

1. Math. A house with a gable roof and outside dimensions of 32' by 56' is to have an 18" overhang on all sides. The rise is 7 $^1/_2$" for each 12" run.

a. Estimate the roof area.

b. Determine the number of 4' by 8' sheets of plywood needed to cover this area.

2. Science. This unit lists recommended roof sheathing boards as either pines, firs, and/or spruces. Botanically speaking, all of these are softwoods. Prepare a comparison/difference table for the three types of species with regard to needle (leaf) structure, bark description, general size (butt width and tree height), suggested uses, and geographic location for large forests.

Roof Coverings*

The roof covering, or roofing, is a part of the exterior finish. It should provide long-lasting waterproof protection for the building and its contents from rain, snow, wind and, to some extent, heat and cold. Materials used for pitched roofs include shingles of wood, asphalt, and fiberglass. Tile and slate are also popular. Sheet materials such as roll roofing, galvanized iron, aluminum, copper, and tin are sometimes used. For flat or low-pitched roofs, composition or built-up roofing with a gravel topping or cap sheet are frequent combinations. Built-up roofing consists of a number of layers of asphalt-saturated felt mopped down with hot asphalt or tar. Other products that are very useful for low-pitched or flat roofs are called single-ply membranes. These materials are rolled out and attached to the roof deck.

The choice of materials and method of application is influenced by cost, roof slope, expected service life of the roofing, wind resistance, fire resistance, and local climate. Due to the large amount of exposed surface, appearance is also important. Figs. 40-1 and 40-2. Shingles, for example, add color, texture, and pattern to the roof surface. All shingles are applied to roof surfaces in some overlapping fashion to shed water. Therefore they are suitable for any roof with enough slope to insure good drainage.

ROOFING TERMINOLOGY

Square. Roofing is estimated and sold by the square. A square of

40-1. *This shingled roof was an important part of the design of this house.*

---

* Some of the material from this unit was adapted from *Construction: Principles, Materials & Methods* by courtesy of the American Savings & Loan Institute Press.

40-2. *This heavyweight shingle, called an architectural shingle, increases the visible texture of a roof.*

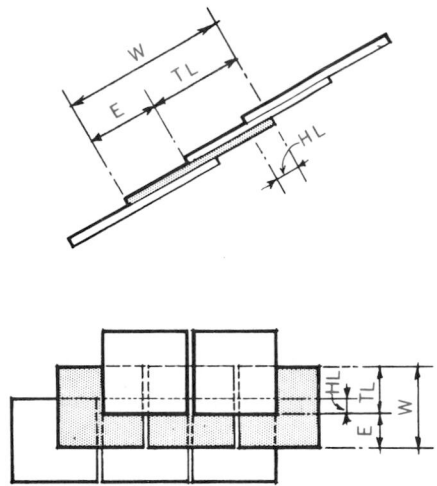

40-3. *Terminology used in roofing: E=exposure, TL=toplap, HL=headlap, W=width of strip shingles or length of individual shingles.*

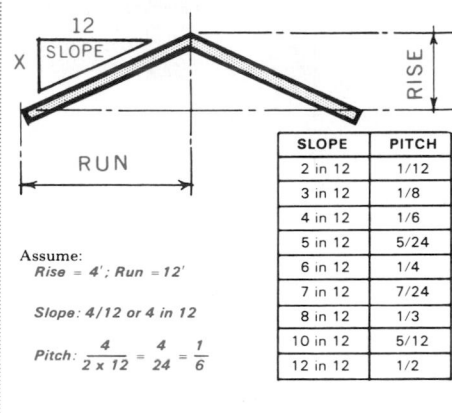

SLOPE	PITCH
2 in 12	1/12
3 in 12	1/8
4 in 12	1/6
5 in 12	5/24
6 in 12	1/4
7 in 12	7/24
8 in 12	1/3
10 in 12	5/12
12 in 12	1/2

Assume:
Rise = 4'; Run = 12'

Slope: 4/12 or 4 in 12

Pitch: $\frac{4}{2 \times 12} = \frac{4}{24} = \frac{1}{6}$

$Slope = \frac{Rise}{Run};$ $Pitch = \frac{Rise}{2 \times Run}$

40-4. *Slope and pitch.*

roofing is the amount required to cover 100 sq. ft. of roof surface.

Coverage. This term indicates the amount of weather protection provided by the overlapping of shingles. Depending on the kind of shingle and method of application, shingles may furnish one (single coverage), two (double coverage), or three (triple coverage) thicknesses of material over the surface of the roof.

Shingles providing single coverage are suitable for reroofing over existing roofs. Shingles providing double and triple coverage are used for new construction, both having increased weather resistance and a longer service life.

Exposure. The shortest distance in inches between exposed edges of overlapping shingles. Fig. 40-3.

Toplap. The shortest distance in inches from the lower edge of an overlapping shingle or sheet to the upper edge of the lapped unit in the first course below (that is, the width of the shingle minus the exposure). Fig. 40-3.

Headlap. The shortest distance in inches from the lower edges of an overlapping shingle or sheet to the upper edge of the unit in the second course below. Fig. 40-3.

Side- or Endlap. The shortest distance in inches by which adjacent shingles or sheets horizontally overlap each other. Fig. 40-3.

Shingle Butt. The lower exposed edge of the shingle.

Slope and Pitch

These terms are often incorrectly used synonymously when referring to the incline of a sloped roof. Both are defined here. Fig. 40-4 also compares some common roof slopes to corresponding roof pitches.

Slope. Slope indicates the incline of a roof as a ratio of vertical rise to horizontal run. It is expressed sometimes as a fraction but typically as X in 12. For example, a roof that rises at the rate of 4" for each foot (12") of run is designated as having a 4-in-12 slope. The triangular symbol above the roof in Fig. 40-4 conveys this information.

Pitch. Pitch indicates the incline of a roof as a ratio of the vertical rise to *twice* the horizontal run. It is expressed as a fraction. For example, if the rise of a roof is 4' and the run 12', the roof is designated as having a pitch of ⅙ ($\frac{4}{24}$ = ⅙).

ROOFING ACCESSORIES

In addition to the shingles, many accessory materials are required to prepare the roof deck and to apply the shingles. These accessories include: underlayment, flashing, roofing cements, eaves flashing, drip edge, and roofing nails or fasteners. With some kinds of shingles, other accessories may be required, such as starter shingles and hip and ridge units. Regardless of the type of shingle to be installed, always check the instructions and recommendations of the shingle manufacturer to insure proper performance.

We will assume in this unit that the roof is correctly and adequately

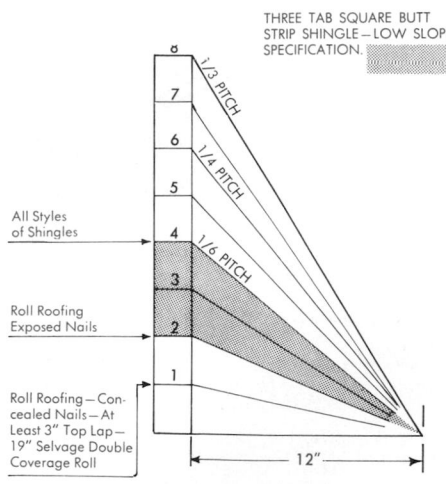

40-5. *Minimum pitch requirements for asphalt roofing products.*

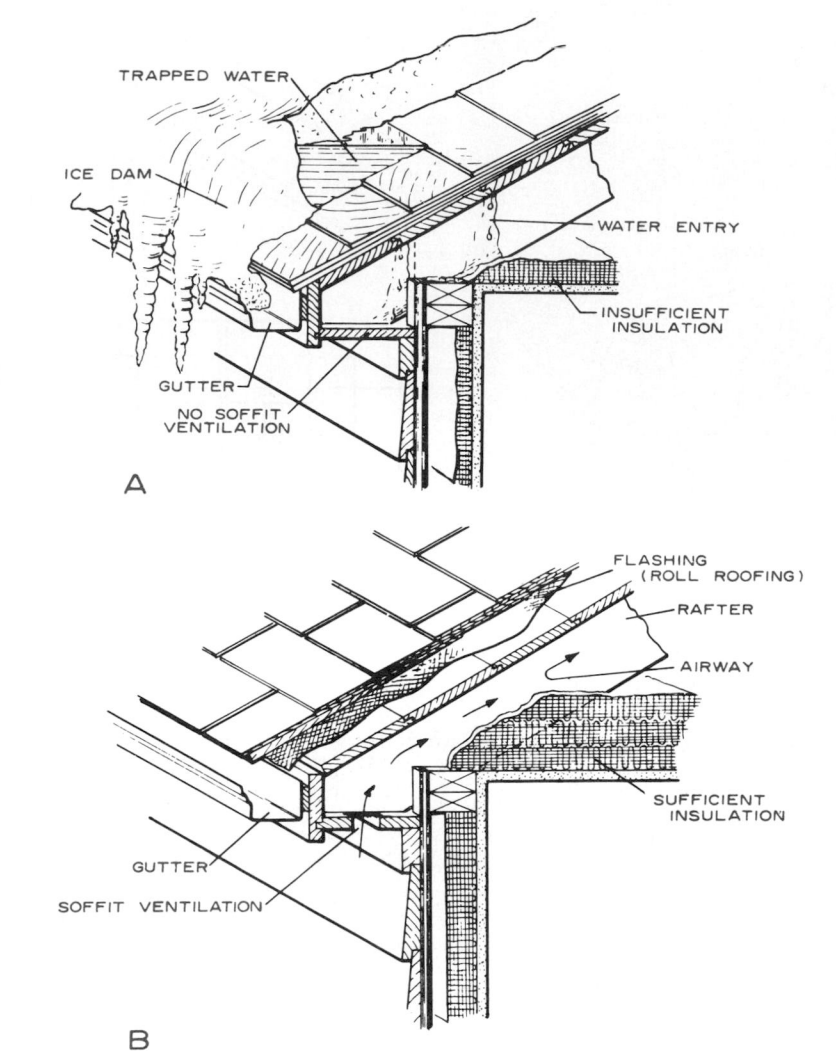

40-6. *A. Snow and ice dams can build up on the overhang of roofs and gutters, causing melting snow to back up under shingles and under the fascia board of closed cornices. Damage to interior ceilings and walls and to exterior paint results from this water seepage. B. Protection from snow and ice dams is provided by eave flashing. Ventilation of the cornice by means of vents in the soffit and sufficient insulation will minimize the melting.*

ventilated. See Unit 41 for prevention of water vapor condensation. When applying shingles, the exposure distance is important. This distance depends mostly on roof slope and shingle type. Fig. 40-5. The minimum slope on main roofs is 4 in 12 for wood, asphalt, and slate shingles. For built-up roofs the maximum slope is 3 in 12.

Underlayment

Underlayment is normally required for asphalt and slate shingles and for tile roofing, but it may be omitted for wood shingles. In areas where snow is common and ice dams occur (melting snow freezes at the eave line), it is a good practice to apply one course of 55-pound smooth-surfaced roll roofing at the eaves. Fig. 40-6. Roof underlayment generally has three purposes:

➤ It protects the sheathing from moisture absorption until the shingles can be applied.

➤ It provides important additional weather protection by preventing the entrance of wind-driven rain below the shingles onto the sheathing or into the structure.

➤ In the case of asphalt shingles, it prevents direct contact between the shingles and resinous areas in wood sheathing which may be damaging to the shingles because of chemical incompatibility.

Underlayment should be a material with low vapor resistance, such as asphalt-saturated felt. Do not use materials such as coated felts or laminated waterproof papers which act as a vapor barrier. These allow moisture or frost to accumulate between the underlayment and the roof sheathing. Underlayment requirements for different kinds of shingles and various roof slopes are shown in Table 40-A.

Installing Underlayment. Apply the underlayment as soon as the roof sheathing has been completed. For single underlay, start at the eave line with the 15-pound felt. Roll across the roof with a toplap of at least 2" at all

Table 40-A. *Summary of Underlayment Recommendations for Shingle Roofs.*

Type of Roofing	Sheathing	Type of Underlayment	Normal Slope		Low Slope	
Asphalt Shingles	Solid	No. 15 asphalt saturated felt	$^4/_{12}$ and up	Single layer over entire roof	$^2/_{12}$ to $^4/_{12}$	Double layer over entire roof[1]
Wood Shakes	Spaced	No. 30 asphalt saturated felt (interlayment)	$^4/_{12}$ and up	Underlayment starter course; interlayment over entire roof	Shakes not recommended on slopes less than $^4/_{12}$ with spaced sheathing	
	Solid[2,4]	No. 30 asphalt saturated felt (interlayment)	$^4/_{12}$ and up	Underlayment starter course; interlayment over entire roof	$^3/_{12}$ to $^4/_{12}$[3]	Single layer underlayment over entire roof; interlayment over entire roof
Wood Shingles	Spaced	None required	$^5/_{12}$ and up	None required	$^3/_{12}$ to $^5/_{12}$[3]	None required
	Solid[4]	No. 15 asphalt saturated felt	$^5/_{12}$ and up	None required[6]	$^3/_{12}$ to $^5/_{12}$[3]	None required[5]

1. Square-Butt Strip shingles only; requires Wind Resistant shingles or cemented tabs.
2. Recommended in areas subject to wind driven snow.
3. Requires reduced weather exposure.

4. May be desirable for added insulation and to minimize air infiltration.
5. May be desirable for protection of sheathing.

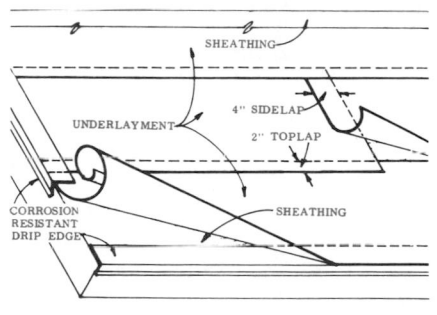

40-7a. *Details for applying the underlayment for single coverage.*

40-7b. *Stapling the underlayment into place.*

horizontal joints and a 4" sidelap at all end joints. Fig. 40-7. Lap the underlayment over all hips and ridges 6" on each side. A double underlay can be started with two layers at the eave line, flush with the fascia board or molding. The second and remaining strips have 19" headlaps with 17" exposures. Fig. 40-8. Cover the entire roof in this manner, making sure that all surfaces have

double coverage. Use only enough fasteners to hold the underlayment in place until the shingles are applied. Do not apply shingles over wet underlayment.

Flashings

Flashing is a special construction of sheet metal or other material used to protect the building from

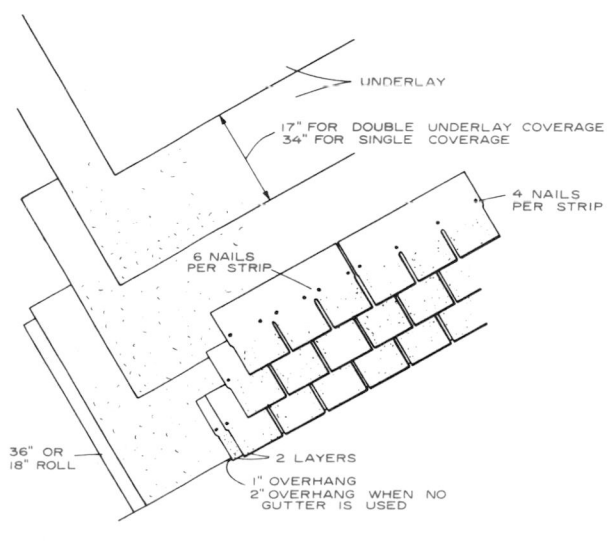

40-8. *Details for double coverage of underlayment.*

water seepage. Flashing must be made watertight and water-shedding. Metal used for flashing must be corrosion-resistant. It should be galvanized steel (at least 26-gauge), 0.019" thick aluminum, or 16 oz. copper.

Flashing is required at the point of intersection between roof and soil stack or ventilator, in the valley of a roof, around chimneys, and at the point where a wall intersects a roof.

Soil Stacks. Apply the roofing up to the stack, cutting it to fit. Fig. 40-9. Then install a corrosion-resistant metal sleeve which slips over the stack and has an adjustable flange to fit any roof slope. Figs. 40-10 and 40-11. A piece of 55-pound roll roofing can also be used. For roll roofing, lay out and cut an opening for the stack as shown in Fig. 40-12. Slip this flange in place over the stack and apply a roof cement 2" up on the stack and 2" out on the flange. Continue shingling over the flange. Cut the shingles to fit around the stack, pressing them firmly into the cement. Fig. 40-13.

Valleys. The open or closed method may be used to construct valley flashing. A valley underlayment strip of No. 15 asphalt-saturated felt, 36" wide, is applied first. Fig. 40-14. The strip is centered in the valley and secured with enough nails to hold it in place. The horizontal courses of underlayment are cut to overlap this valley strip a minimum of 6". Where eaves flashing is required, it is applied over the valley underlayment strip.
Open Valleys. Open valleys may be flashed with metal or with 90 lb. mineral-surfaced asphalt roll roofing in a color to match or to contrast with the roof shingles. The method is illustrated in Fig. 40-15. An 18" wide strip of mineral-surfaced roll roofing is placed over

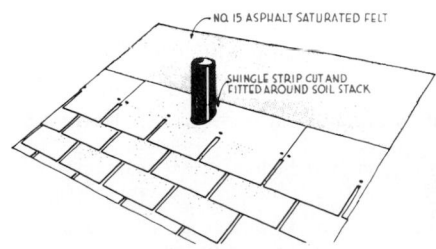
40-9. The shingles are cut to fit around the stack.

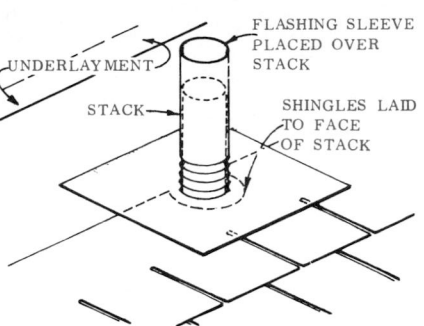
40-10. Place the adjustable metal flashing sleeve over the stack.

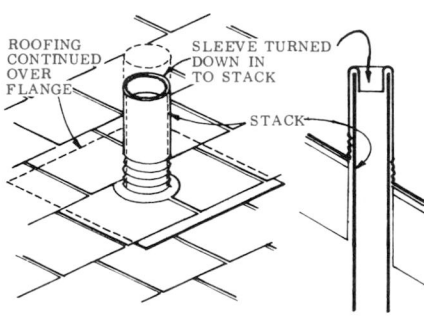
40-11. Lay the shingles over the flange. Turn the top of the sleeve down into the stack to complete the installation.

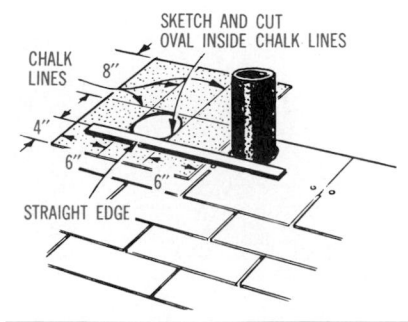
40-12. Laying out a flange of roll roofing for a soil stack.

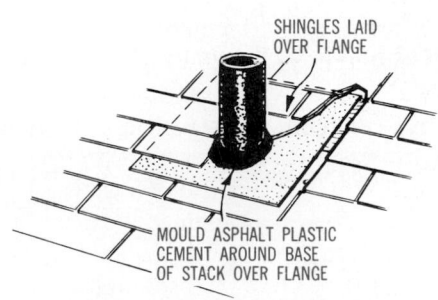
40-13. Completing the installation of the flange. Lay shingles over the flange, fit them around the stack, and press the shingles firmly into the cement.

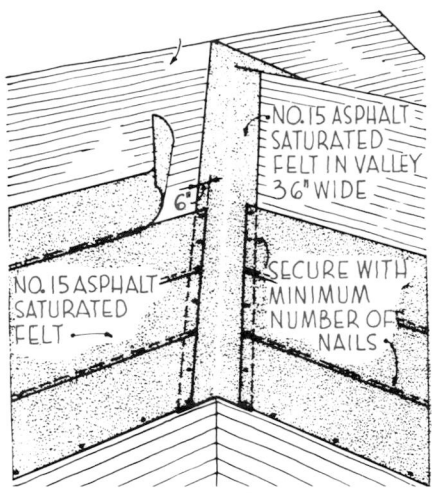
40-14. Applying the underlayment in the valley.

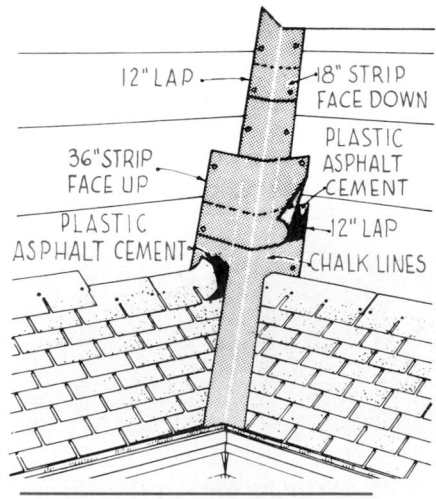
40-15. Open valley flashing details using roll roofing.

the valley underlayment. It is centered in the valley with the surfaced side down and the lower edge cut to conform to and be flush with the eaves flashing. When it is necessary to splice the material, the ends of the upper segments are laid to overlap the lower segments 12" and are secured with asphalt plastic cement. Only enough nails are used in rows 1" in from each edge to hold the strip smoothly in place.

Another strip, 36" wide, is placed over the first strip. It is centered in the valley with the surfaced side up and secured with nails. It is lapped if necessary the same way as the underlying 18" strip.

Before shingles are applied, a chalk line is snapped on each side of the valley for its full length. The lines should start 6" apart at the ridge and spread wider apart (at the rate of 1/8" per foot) to the eave. The chalk lines serve as a guide in trimming the shingle units to fit the valley, insuring a clean, sharp edge. The upper corner of each end shingle is clipped to direct water into the valley and prevent water penetration between courses. Fig. 40-16. Each shingle is cemented to the valley lining with asphalt cement to insure a tight seal. No exposed nails should appear along the valley flashing.

Closed Valleys. Closed (woven) valleys can be used only with strip shingles. This method has the advantage of doubling the coverage of the shingles throughout the length of the valley, increasing weather resistance at this vulnerable point. A valley lining made from a 36" wide strip of 55-pound (or heavier) roll roofing is placed over the valley underlayment and centered in the valley. Fig. 40-17.

Valley shingles are laid over the lining by either of two methods:

➤ They may be applied on both roof surfaces at the same time, with each course in turn woven over the valley.

➤ Each surface may be covered to the point approximately 36" from the center of the valley and the valley shingles woven in place later.

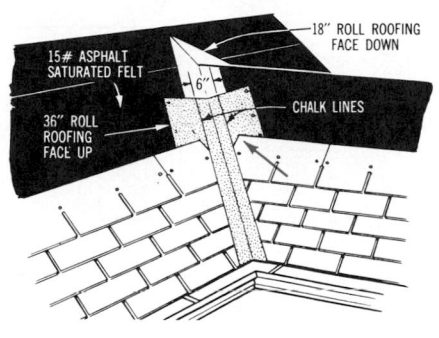

40-16. *Begin laying each course at the chalk line in the valley. Clip the top corners of the shingles as shown at the arrow to prevent water penetration.*

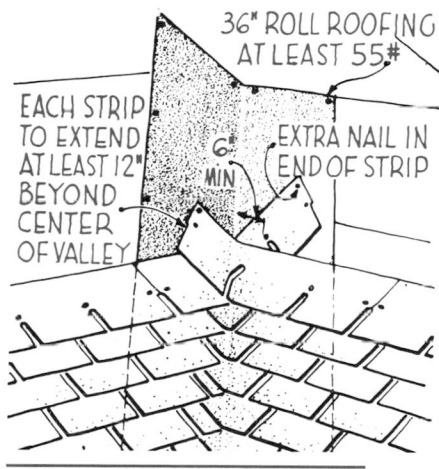

40-17. *Closed valley flashing using woven strip shingles.*

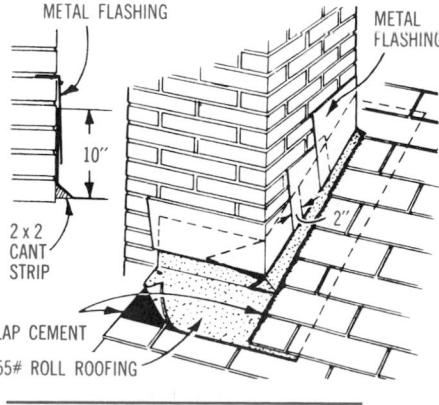

40-18. *Flashing the chimney.*

In either case, the first course at the valley is laid along the eaves of one surface over the valley lining and extended along the adjoining roof surface for a distance of at least 12". The first course of the adjoining roof surface is then carried over the valley on top of the previously applied shingle. Succeeding courses are then laid alternately, weaving the valley shingles over each other.

The shingles are pressed tightly into the valley and nailed in the usual manner (see "Fastening Strip Shingles," page 454) except that no nail should be located closer than 6" to the valley center line and two nails are used at the end of each terminal strip. Fig. 40-17.

Chimneys. Apply the shingles over the felt up to the chimney face. If 90-pound roll roofing is to be used for flashing, cut wood cant strips and install them above and at the sides of the chimney. Fig. 40-18. The roll roofing flashing should be cut to run 10" up the chimney. Working from the bottom up, fit metal flashing over the base flashing and insert it 1½" into the mortar joints. Refill the joints with mortar or roofing cement.

Wall Intersections. Start at the eave line and work upward. Apply the metal flashing over the felt and up onto the wall sheathing, but under the roofing and the siding. The siding should be cut so that it clears the roof by at least ¾". Fig. 40-19.

Roofing Cements

Roofing cements are used for installing eaves flashing, for flashing assemblies, for cementing tabs of asphalt shingles and laps in sheet material, and for roof repairing. There are several types of cement, including plastic asphalt

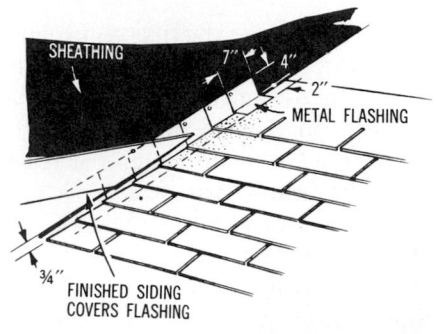

40-19. *Flashing the intersection of a roof and wall.*

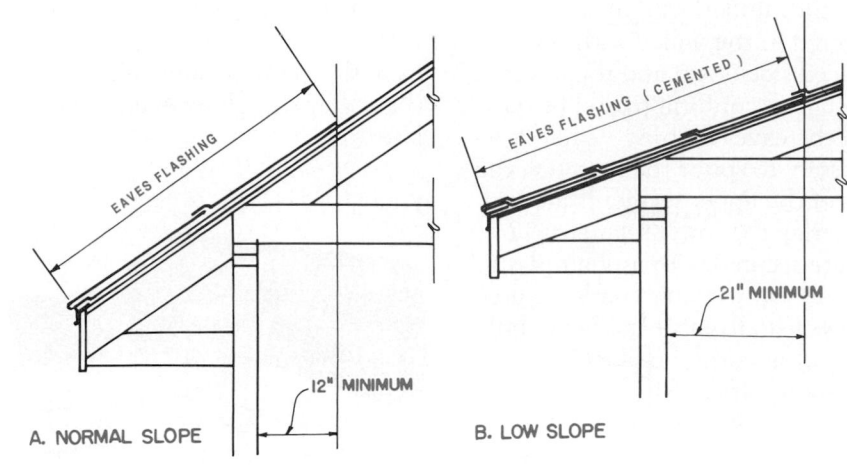

40-20. *Eaves flashing: A. Normal slope. B. Low slope.*

cements, lap cements, quick-setting asphalt adhesives, roof coatings, and primers. The type and quality of materials and methods of application on a shingle roof should be those recommended by the manufacturer of the shingle roofing.

Eaves Flashing

Eaves flashing is recommended in areas where the temperature goes below 0 degrees F, or wherever there is a possibility of ice forming along the eaves. This ice forms a dam which allows water to back up under the shingles.

Eaves flashing is usually formed by an additional course of underlayment or roll roofing applied over the underlayment. For normal slopes this extends up the roof to cover a point at least 12" inside the interior wall line of the building. A, Fig. 40-20.

For low slopes or in areas subject to severe icing, eaves flashing is formed by cementing an additional course of underlayment over the first underlayment as for normal conditions. However, it extends up the roof to cover a point at least 24" inside the interior wall line of the building. B, Fig. 40-20 and Fig. 40-21.

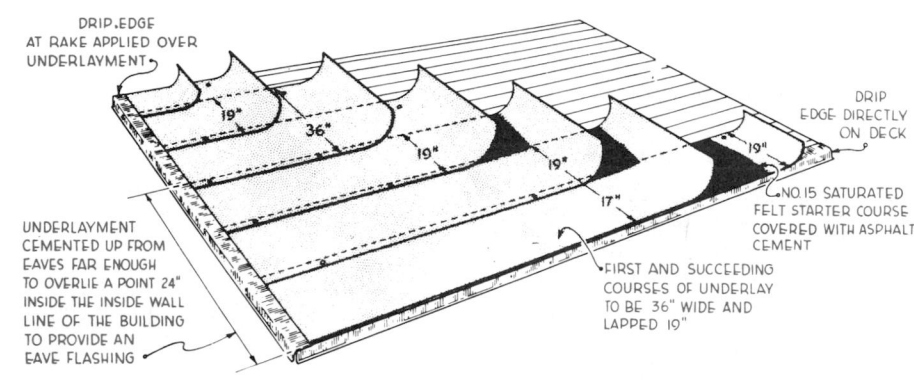

40-21. *Details for applying the underlayment for a low slope.*

Drip Edge

Drip edges are designed and installed to protect the edges of the roof. They prevent leaks at this point by causing water to drip free of underlying eave and cornice construction. Some shapes of preformed drip edges are shown in Fig. 40-22. A drip edge is recommended for most shingle roofs. It is applied to the sheathing and under the underlayment at the eaves, but over the underlayment at the rake. Fig. 40-23.

Roofing Nails

No single step in applying roof shingles is more important than proper nailing. Suitability is dependent on several factors:

➤ Selecting the correct nail for the kind of shingle and type of roof sheathing. Fig. 40-24.

➤ Using the correct number of nails.

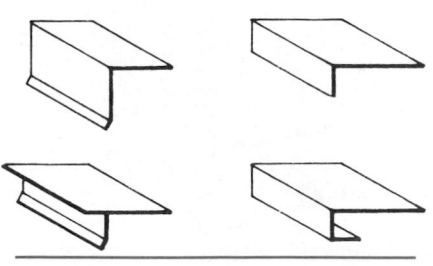

40-22. *Various drip edge shapes.*

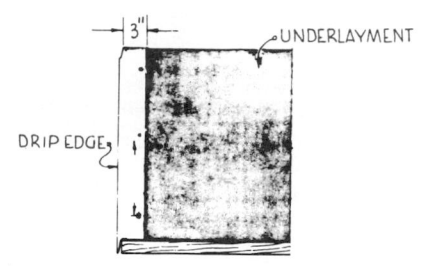

A RAKE

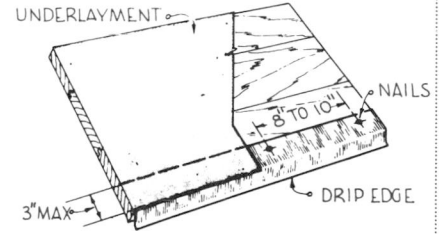

B EAVE

40-23a. *Drip edge application: A. Along the rake. B. At the eave. Note that the underlayment goes under the drip edge at the rake and over the drip edge at the eave.*

40-23b. *Using a pneumatic stapler to install the metal drip edge at the rake.*

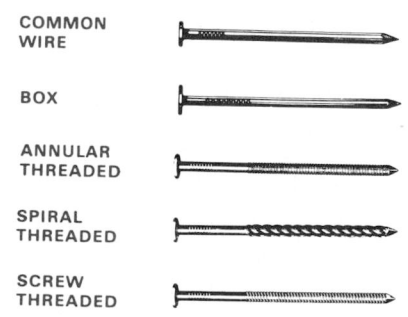

40-24. *Types of smooth and threaded shank nails recommended for the application of shingle roofing.*

➤ Locating them in the shingle correctly.

➤ Choosing nail metal compatible with metal used for flashing.

Roofing nails should be long enough to penetrate through the shingle and through the roof sheathing. They should penetrate at least l" into plank decking. Nails for applying shingles over plywood sheathing should have threaded shanks.

Specific recommendations for the type, size, number, and spacing of roofing nails are given later in conjunction with the information on asphalt and wood shingles and wood shakes.

ASPHALT SHINGLES

Asphalt roof shingles are manufactured in three basic kinds of units. Table 40-B.

➤ Strip shingles of the square-butt or hexagonal type.

➤ Individual shingles of the interlocking or staple-down type.

➤ Giant individual shingles for application by either the American or Dutch lap methods.

In areas where high winds prevail, wind resistant strip shingles with factory-applied adhesive or integral locking tabs are recommended.

Shingles are laid so that they overlap and cover each other to

shed water. Before applying shingles make sure that:

➤ The underlayment, drip edge, and flashings are in place.

➤ The roof deck is tight and provides a suitable nailing base.

➤ The chimney is completed and the counter flashing installed.

➤ Stacks and other equipment requiring openings in the roof are in place with counter flashing where necessary.

Strip Shingles

On small roofs strip shingles may be laid from either rake. Figs. 40-25 and 40-26. On roofs 30' and longer, shingles should be started at the center and applied both ways from a vertical line. This will assure more accurate vertical alignment and will provide for meeting and matching above a projection such as a dormer or chimney. To assure accurate alignment of shingles, use horizontal and vertical chalk lines.

The first course of shingles, called the *starter* course, is applied over the eaves flashing strip and even with its lower edge along the eave. The starter course may be a 9" wide (or wider) starter strip of mineral-surfaced roll roofing of a color to match the shingles. A row of inverted shingles may also be used for the starter course. Fig. 40-27. Fasten the starter strip with roofing nails placed about 3" or 4" above the eave edge and spaced so

40-25. *Shingles laid out on a roof. Some of them have been opened up in preparation for the roofer, who will staple the shingles in place.*

Table 40-B. *Asphalt Roof Shingles.*

	Shingle Type*	Shipping Weight Per Square	Packages Per Square	Length	Width	Units Per Square	Sidelap	Toplap	Headlap	Exposure
STRIP SHINGLES	2 & 3 Tab Square Butt	235 Lb	3	36"	12"	80	—	7"	2"	5"
	2 & 3 Tab Hexagonal	195 Lb	3	36"	11 ⅓"	86	—	2"	2"	5"
INDIVIDUAL	Staple Lock	145 Lb	2	16"	16"	80	2 ½"	—	—	—
GIANT INDIVIDUAL	American	330 Lb	4	16"	12"	226	—	11"	6"	5"
	Dutch Lap	165 Lb	2	16"	12"	113	3"	2"	—	10"

40-26. *This ladder is equipped with an electric hoist used to raise bundles of shingles and other materials up to the roof.*

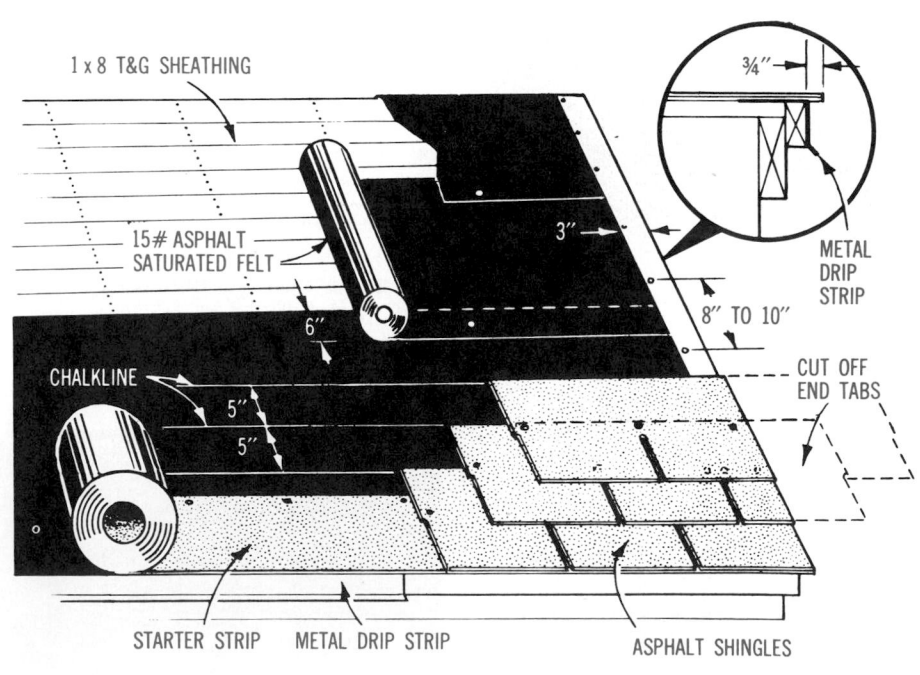

1 x 8 T&G SHEATHING

15# ASPHALT SATURATED FELT

CHALKLINE

6"

5"

5"

3"

¾"

8" TO 10"

METAL DRIP STRIP

CUT OFF END TABS

STARTER STRIP   METAL DRIP STRIP   ASPHALT SHINGLES

40-27a. *Laying asphalt strip shingles.*

40-27b. *This staple gun is equipped with a guide which is placed at the lower edge of the row of shingles previously laid. This positions the shingle being installed for the correct exposure while the shingle is held in position with the left hand.*

40-27c. *After the shingle is located in position, it is stapled from left to right, with four staples.*

that the nailheads will not be exposed at the cutouts between the tabs on the first course. If square-butt strip shingles are used as a starter strip, cut off 3" of the first inverted starter course shingle to be laid at the rake. Then the first course laid right side up is started with a full shingle. Succeeding courses are started with full or cut strips depending upon the pattern desired. Three variations for laying

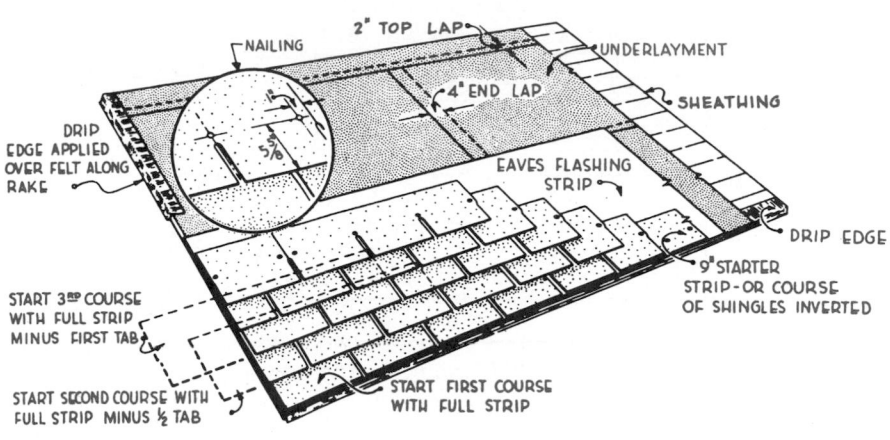

40-28. *Laying asphalt square-butt strip shingles with the cutouts breaking joints on halves.*

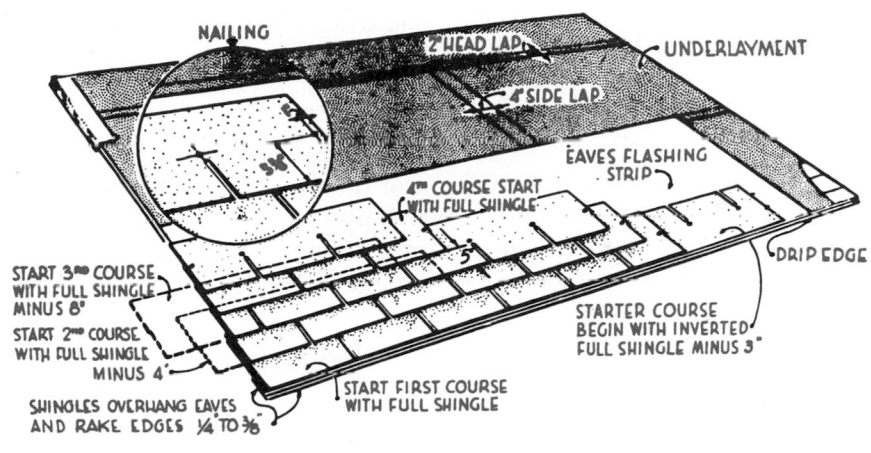

40-29. *Laying asphalt square-butt strip shingles with the cutouts breaking joints on thirds.*

square-butt strip shingles are as follows:

➤ *Cutouts breaking joints on halves.* When the cutouts break the joints on halves, the second course is started with a full shingle cut 6" short (half a tab). The third is started with a full shingle minus the entire first tab. The fourth is started with 1½ tabs cut from the shingle, and so on, causing the cutouts to be centered on the tabs of the course below. Fig. 40-28. This pattern can also be made with less cutting by starting a third course with a full shingle.

➤ *Cutouts breaking joints on*

thirds. When the cutouts break the joints on thirds, the second course is started with a full shingle cut 4" short (⅓ of a tab). The third course is started with a full shingle cut 8" short (⅔ of a tab), and the fourth with a full shingle. Fig. 40-29.

➤ *Random spacing* is achieved by removing different amounts from the starting tab of succeeding courses in accordance with the following general principles:

1. The width of any starting tab should be at least 3".

2. Cutout centerlines of any course should be located at least 3"

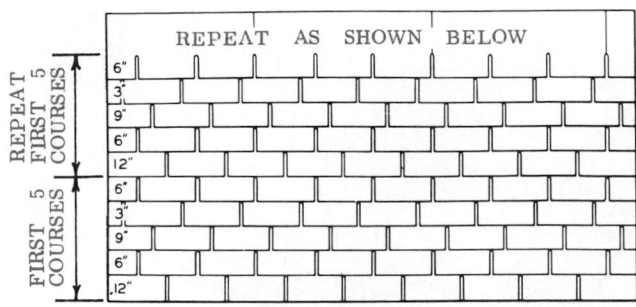

40-30. *Random spacing of asphalt square-butt strip shingles. The first course was started with a full-length strip.*

laterally from the cutout centerlines in both the course above and the course below.

3. Starting tab widths should be varied sufficiently so that the eye will not follow a cutout alignment. Fig. 40-30.

Regardless of the laying pattern, each succeeding course of shingles is placed so that the lower edges of the butts are aligned with the top of the cutouts on the underlying course.

Fastening Strip Shingles.

Nails for applying asphalt roofing should be corrosion-resistant. Hot-dipped galvanized steel or aluminum nails with sharp points and flat heads that are $3/8$" to $7/16$" in diameter are recommended. Shanks should be 10- to 12-gauge wire and may be smooth or threaded. Threaded nails are preferred because of their increased holding power. Aluminum nails should have screw threads with approximately a $12\frac{1}{2}$ degree thread angle. Fig. 40-31. Galvanized steel nails, if threaded, should have annular threads. Nail lengths typically required are given in Table 40-C.

The number and the placement of nails are important for good roof application. Nailing should start at the end nearest the shingle last applied and proceed to the opposite end. To prevent buckling be sure each shingle is in perfect alignment before driving any nail. Drive the nail straight to avoid cutting the shingle with the edge of the nailhead. The nailhead should be driven flush, not sunk below the surface of the shingle.

If the shingles are laid in windy areas, they will require additional protection. A spot of quick-setting cement about 1" square for each tab

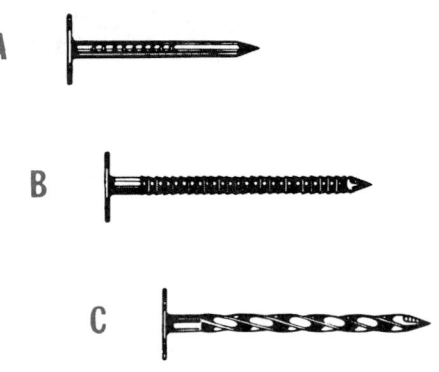

40-31. *Asphalt shingle nails: A. Smooth. B. Annular threaded. C. Screw threaded.*

is applied on the underlying shingle with a putty knife or caulking gun. The free tab is then pressed against the cement. Fig. 40-32.

Three-tab square-butt shingles require four nails for each strip. When the shingles are applied with a 5" exposure, the four nails are placed $5/8$" above the top of the cutouts and located horizontally with one nail 1" back from each end, and one nail on the center line of each cutout. Fig. 40-28. Two-tab square-butt shingles are nailed in a similar manner.

Hexagonal Strip Shingles.

Hexagonal strip shingles permit no spacing variations as do square-butt strips. Application begins with a roll roofing starter course or with inverted shingles. The first course starts with a full strip. The remaining courses begin alternately

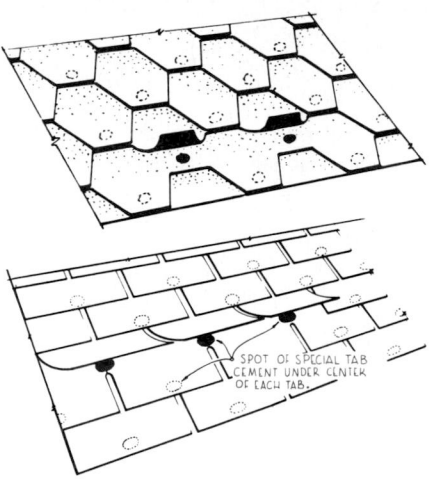

40-32. *Shingle tabs are cemented down for wind protection.*

Table 40-C. *Asphalt Shingle Nail Lengths.*

Application	1" Sheathing	3/8" Plywood
Strip or Individual Shingle (new construction)	1 1/4"	7/8"
Over Asphalt Roofing (reroofing)	1 1/2"	1"
Over Wood Shingles (reroofing)	1 3/4"	—

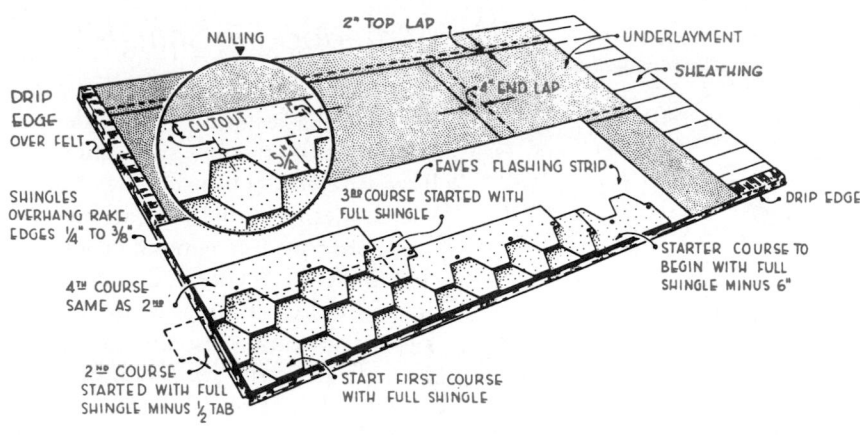

40-33. *Laying two-tab hexagonal strip shingles.*

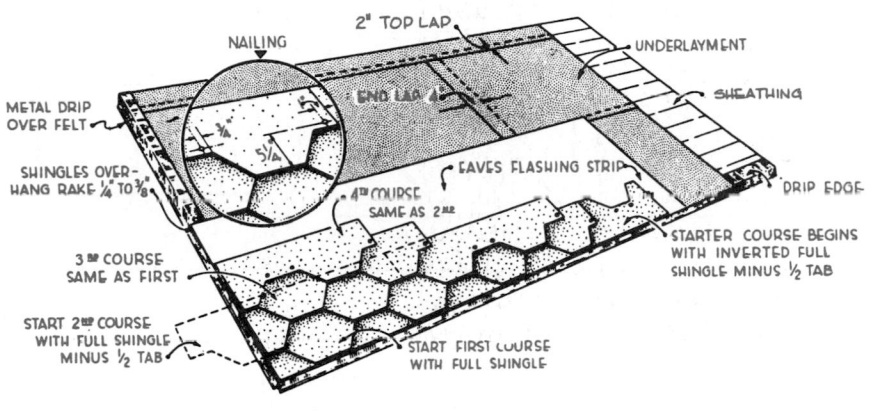

40-34. *Laying three-tab hexagonal strip shingles.*

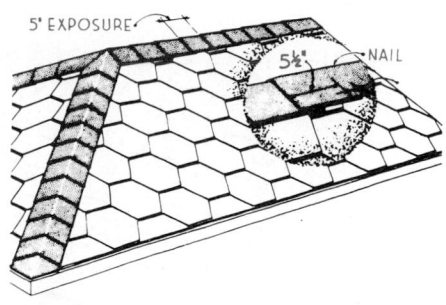

40-35. *Applying hip and ridge shingles.*

with a full strip minus ½ tab and then a full strip. Figs. 40-33 and 40-34. Each course is applied so that the lower edge of the tabs is aligned with the top of the cutouts on the preceding course.

Two- and three-tab hexagonal shingles require four nails per strip located in a line 5¼" above the exposed butt-edge and horizontally as follows:

➤ For two-tab shingles, one nail l" back from each end of the strip and one nail ¾" back from each angle of the cutouts. Fig. 40-33.

➤ For three-tab shingles, one nail l" back from each end and one nail centered above each cutout. Fig. 40-34.

Hips and Ridges. Hips and ridges may be finished by using hip and ridge shingles furnished by the manufacturer or by cutting pieces at least 9" × 12" either from 12" × 36" square-butt shingle strips or from mineral-surfaced roll roofing of a color to match the shingles. They are applied by bending each shingle lengthwise down the center with an equal amount on each side of the hip or ridge. Proper alignment can best be maintained by snapping a chalk line down one side of the ridge on which the edge of the shingle is aligned as it is nailed in place.

Apply the hip and ridge shingles by beginning at the bottom of a hip

or one end of the ridge. Use a 5" exposure. Each shingle is secured with one nail at each side 5½" back from the exposed end and l" up from the edge. Fig. 40-35. When laying the shingles on the ridge, always lay the exposed edge away from the prevailing winds.

Valleys. Valley treatment may be open or closed. See pages 448-449 for details about shingle application at the valleys.

Strip Shingles on a Low-Pitch Roof

Square-tab strip shingles may be used on roof slopes less than 4 in 12 but not less than 2 in 12. Low-slope application methods require:

➤ Double underlayment.

➤ Cemented eaves flashing strip.

➤ Shingles provided with factory-applied adhesives. Or, each free tab of square-butt shingles should be cemented. Fig. 40-32. Application of strip shingles over double underlayment and cemented eaves flashing is shown in Fig. 40-36. Any shingle laying pattern described under normal slope application may be used.

SHEATHING
2 PLY UNDERLAYMENT
PLASTIC ASPHALT CEMENT
DRIP EDGE DIRECTLY ON DECK
19"
36"
4 NAILS PER STRIP
STARTER STRIP OF 90 LB. MINERAL SURFACED SHEET OR SHINGLES REVERSED
UNDERLAYMENT CEMENTED TOGETHER THROUGHOUT EAVES FLASHING AREA
SHINGLES LAID AT 5" EXPOSURE
4 NAILS PER STRIP
ALL TABS CEMENTED DOWN

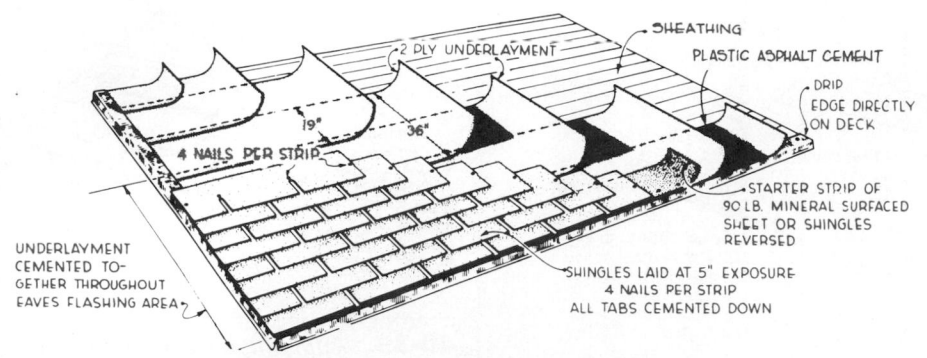

40-36. *Applying strip shingles on a low slope over a double underlayment.*

Interlocking Shingles

Interlocking (lock-down) shingles are designed to provide resistance to strong winds. They have integral locking devices that vary in detail but which can be classified into five general groups. A, Fig. 40-37. Types 1, 2, 3, and 4 are individual shingles while Type 5 is a strip shingle usually having two tabs per strip. Interlocking shingles do not require use of

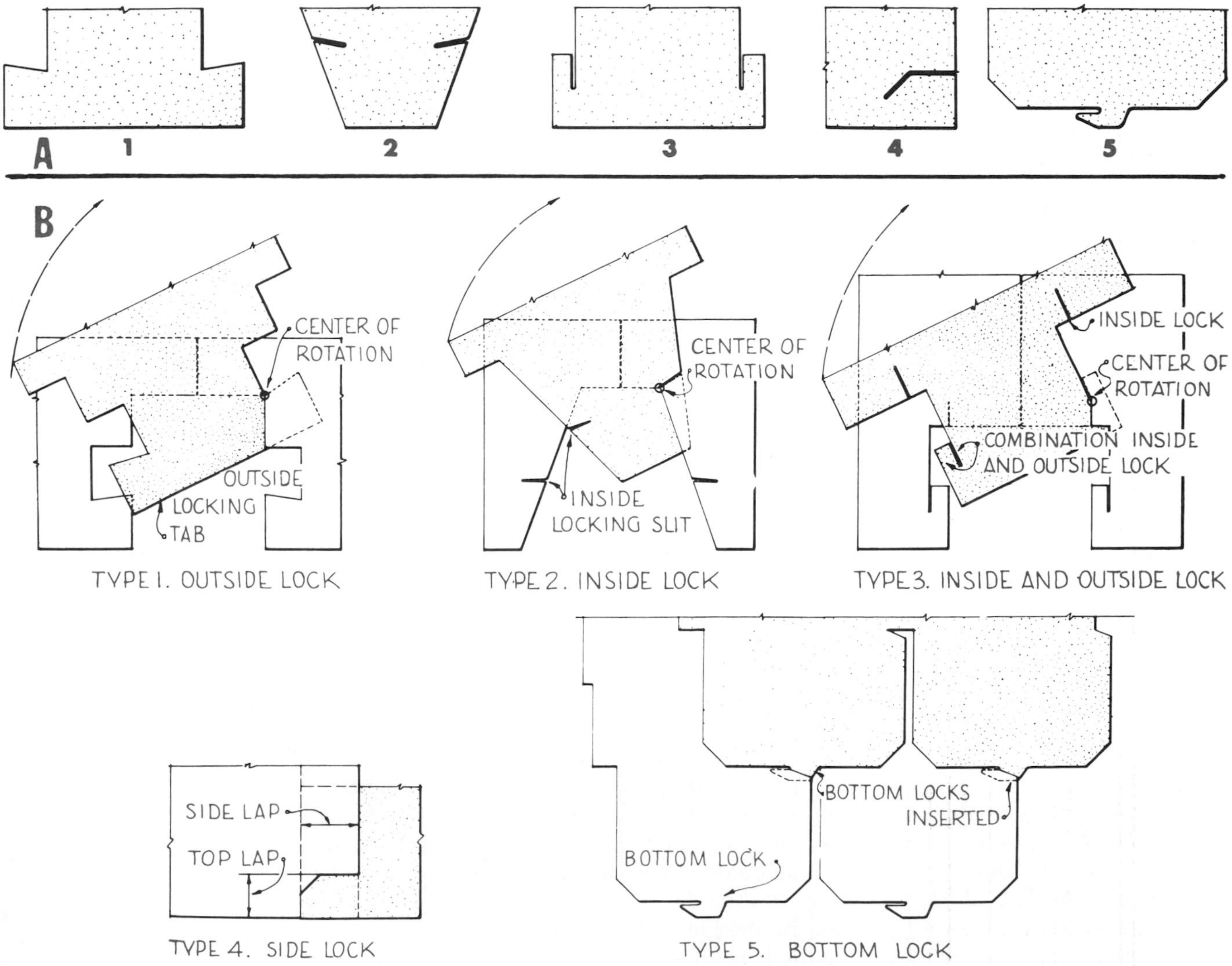

A
1
2
3
4
5
B
CENTER OF ROTATION
OUTSIDE LOCKING TAB
TYPE 1. OUTSIDE LOCK
CENTER OF ROTATION
INSIDE LOCKING SLIT
TYPE 2. INSIDE LOCK
INSIDE LOCK
CENTER OF ROTATION
COMBINATION INSIDE AND OUTSIDE LOCK
TYPE 3. INSIDE AND OUTSIDE LOCK
SIDE LAP
TOP LAP
TYPE 4. SIDE LOCK
BOTTOM LOCKS INSERTED
BOTTOM LOCK
TYPE 5. BOTTOM LOCK

40-37a. *Interlocking shingles: A. Various styles of interlocking shingle tabs. B. Methods of locking shingles.*

40-37b. *Nailing the courses of shingles.*

Table 40-D. *Grades of Red Cedar Roof Shakes.*

Grade	Length and Thickness	Description
No 1. Handsplit & Resawn	15" Starter-Finish 18" x 1/2" Mediums 18" x 3/4" Heavies 24" x 3/8" 24" x 1/2" Mediums 24" x 3/4" Heavies	These shakes have split faces and sawn backs. Cedar logs are first cut into desired lengths. Blanks or boards of proper thickness are split and then run diagonally through a bandsaw to produce two tapered shakes from each blank.
No 1. Tapersplit	24" x 1/2"	Produced largely by hand, using a sharp-bladed steel froe and a wooden mallet. The natural shingle-like taper is achieved by reversing the block, end-for-end, with each split.
No. 1 Straightsplit	18" x 3/8" 24" x 3/8"	Produced in the same manner as tapersplit shakes except that by splitting from the same end of the block, the shakes acquire the same thickness throughout.

* All weights and dimensions are APPROXIMATE.

adhesives, although cement may occasionally be needed along rakes and eaves where the locking devices may have to be removed. The roof slope should not be less than the minimum specified by the shingle manufacturer. The individual shingles (Types 1 through 4) are intended for roof slopes of 4 in 12 and greater.

Installing Interlocking Shingles. Due to the number of designs available, the manufacturer's instructions should be studied carefully. Interlocking shingles are self-aligning but are sufficiently flexible to allow for a limited amount of adjustment to save time, especially on long roofs. It is recommended that the roofs be laid out with horizontal chalk lines to provide guides for the meeting, matching, and locking of courses above dormers and other projections through the roof. The locking devices should be engaged correctly. B, Fig. 40-37.

The proper location of nails is essential to the performance of the locking device. The shingle manufacturer's instructions will specify where the nail should be located to insure the best results.

The procedure for finishing hips and ridges is the same as for strip shingles. Fig. 40-35.

WOOD SHAKES

There are three types of wood shakes: handsplit-and-resawn, tapersplit, and straightsplit. Shakes are produced in three lengths: 16", 18", and 24". Table 40-D. The maximum exposure recommended for double coverage on a roof is 13" for 32" shakes, 10" for 24" shakes, and 7½" for 18" shakes. A triple coverage roof can be achieved by reducing these exposures to 10" for 32" shakes, 7½" for 24" shakes, and 5½" for 18" shakes. Table 40-E.

Shakes are recommended on slopes of 4 in 12 or steeper. By taking special precautions, installations may be made on slopes as low as 3 in 12. These precautions are:

➤ Reduce the exposure to provide triple coverage.

➤ Use solid sheathing with an underlayment of No. 30 asphalt-saturated felt applied over the entire roof with a No. 30 asphalt-saturated felt interlayment between each course.

Shakes may be applied over either spaced or solid sheathing depending on climate conditions. See "Roof Sheathing," Unit 39.

Eaves Flashing

In areas where the outside design temperature is 0 degrees F or colder, or where there is a possibility of ice forming along the eaves and causing a backup of water, eaves flashing is recommended. Fig. 40-38. In these areas shakes should be applied over solid sheathing.

On slopes 4 in 12 or steeper, eaves flashing is formed by applying an additional course of No. 30 asphalt-saturated felt over the underlayment starting course at the eaves. The eaves flashing should extend up the roof to cover a point at least 24" inside the exterior wall line of the building. When the eave overhang requires flashing to be wider than 36", the necessary horizontal joint is cemented and located outside the exterior wall line of the building. A, Fig. 40-20.

For slopes 3 in 12 to 4 in 12 or in areas subject to severe icing, eaves flashing may be formed as described for 4 in 12 slopes except that a double layer of No. 30 asphalt-saturated felt underlayment is cemented together with a continuous layer of plastic asphalt cement. Cement is also applied to

Table 40-E. *Roof Coverage of Shakes at Various Weather Exposures.*

Shake Type, Length and Thickness	Approximate coverage (in sq.ft.) of one square, when shakes are applied with ½" spacing, at following weather exposures, in inches [h];					
	5 ½"	7 ½"	8 ½"	10	11 ½"	16
18" x ½" Handsplit-and-Resawn Mediums [a]	55 [b]	75 [c]	85 [d]	100	—	—
18" x ¾" Handsplit-and-Resawn Heavies [a]	55 [b]	75 [c]	85 [d]	100	—	—
24" x ⅜" Handsplit	—	75 [e]	85	100 [f]	115 [d]	—
24" x ½" Handsplit-and-Resawn Mediums	—	75 [b]	85	100 [c]	115 [d]	—
24" x ¾" Handsplit-and-Resawn Heavies	—	75 [b]	85	100 [c]	115 [d]	—
24" x ½" Tapersplit	—	75 [b]	85	100 [c]	115 [d]	—
18" x ⅜" True-Edge Straight-Split	—	—	—	—	—	112 [g]
18" x ⅜" Straight-Split	65 [b]	90	100 [d]	—	—	—
24" x ⅜" Straight-Split	—	75 [b]	85	100	115 [d]	—
15" Starter-Finish Course	Use supplementary with shakes applied not over 10" weather exposure					

(a) 5 bundles will cover 100 sq. ft. roof area when used as starter-finish course at 10" weather exposure. 6 bundles will cover 100 sq. ft. wall area at 8 1/2" exposure. 7 bundles will cover 100 sq. ft. roof area at 7 1/2" weather exposure; see footnote (h).
(b) Maximum recommended weather exposure for 3-ply roof construction.
(c) Maximum recommended weather exposure for 2-ply roof construction.
(d) Maximum recommended weather exposure for single-coursed wall construction.

(e) Maximum recommended weather exposure for application on roof pitches between 4-in.-12 and 8-in.-12.
(f) Maximum recommended weather exposure for application on roof pitches of 6-in. -12 and steeper.
(g) Maximum recommended weather exposure for double-coursed wall construction.
(h) All coverage based on 1/2" spacing between shakes.

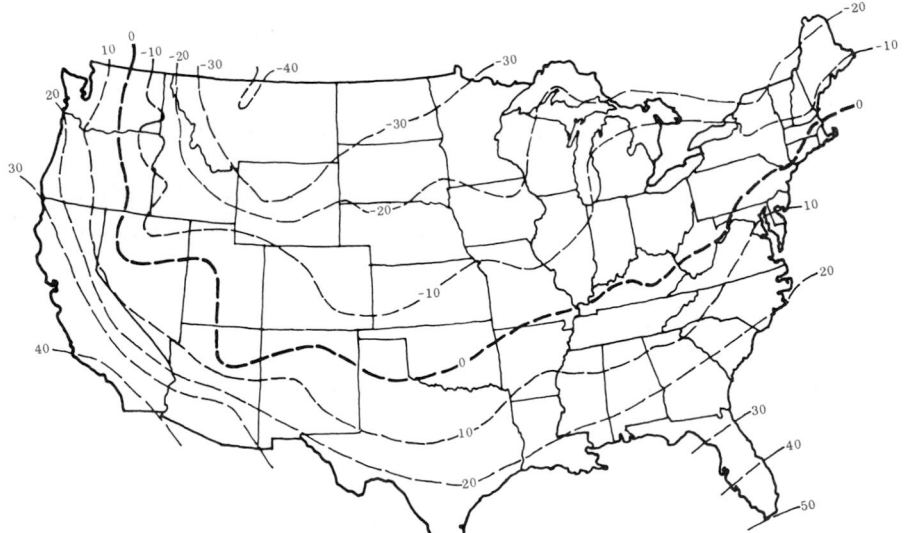

40-38. *Outside design temperatures.*

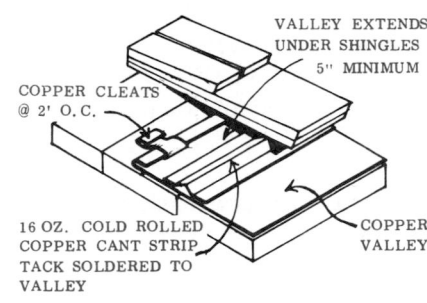

40-39. *A special cant strip is available to minimize the surface contact of copper with red cedar.*

the 19" underlying portion of each succeeding course which lies within the eaves flashing area, before applying the next course of asphalt felt.

Drip Edge

Wood shakes should extend out over the eave and rake a distance of l" to 1½" to form a drip. To align this drip edge, nail a shingle at each end of the roof line and allow it to project. Attach a chalk line to the butt edge, and pull it taut between the two shingles. The butt edge of each wood shingle applied as a drip edge can then be aligned to the chalk line.

Flashing

Unless special precautions are taken, copper flashing materials are not recommended for use with red cedar shakes. Fig. 40-39.

For valley flashing, the *open method* (roofing, felt, and sheet metal) or the *closed method* (hand-fitted shakes) may be used. The open method is highly recommended for longer service life. Open valleys are first covered with a valley underlayment strip of No. 30 asphalt-saturated felt at least 20" wide. The strip is centered in the valley and secured with enough nails to hold it in place. Metal flashing strips 20" wide are then nailed over the underlayment. If the flashing is galvanized steel, it should be preferably 18-gauge, but not less than 26-gauge. Flashing that is center crimped and painted on both surfaces is preferred. The valley edges should be edge crimped to provide an additional water stop. This is done by turning the edges up and back approximately ½" toward the valley center line. The shakes laid to finish at the valley are trimmed parallel with the valley to form a 6" wide gutter.

Closed valleys are first covered with a 1" × 6" wood strip. This strip is nailed flat into the saddle and covered with roofing felt as specified previously for open valleys. Shakes in each course are edge trimmed to fit into the valley, then laid across the valley with an undercourse of metal flashing having a 2" headlap and extending 10" under the shakes on each side of the saddle.

Application of Shakes

Apply a starter strip of No. 30 asphalt-saturated felt underlayment 36" wide over the sheathing. The starter course of shakes at the eave line should be doubled, using an undercourse of 24", 18", or 15" shakes. The latter is made expressly for this purpose.

After each course of shakes is applied, an 18" wide strip of No. 30 asphalt-saturated felt interlayment should be applied over the top portion of the shakes extending onto the sheathing. Fig. 40-40. The bottom edge of the interlayment should be positioned at a distance above the butt edge of the shake equal to twice the exposure. For example, if 24" shakes are being laid at 10" exposure, the bottom edge of the felt should be

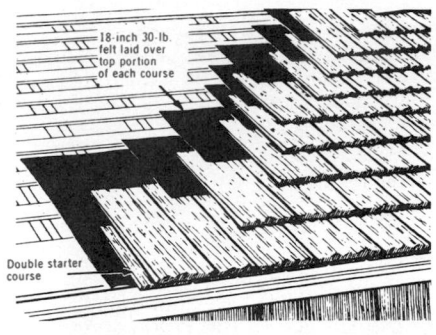

40-40. An 18" wide strip of No. 30 asphalt-saturated felt interlayment is applied over the top portion of the shakes between each course.

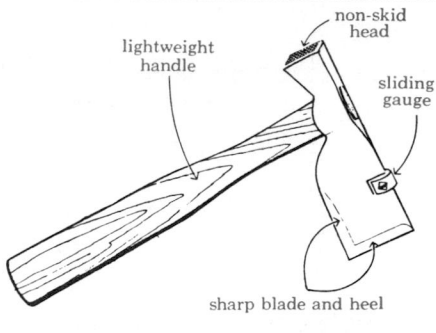

40-41. Shingler's hatchet with an adjustable gauge for setting the exposure.

positioned at a distance 20" above the shake butts. The 18" felt strip will then cover the top 4" of the shakes and extend 14" onto the sheathing.

Individual shakes should be spaced approximately ¼" to ⅜" apart to allow for possible expansion due to moisture absorption. The joints between shakes should be offset at least 1½" in adjacent courses. The joints in alternate courses also should be kept out of direct alignment when a three-ply roof is being built.

When straightsplit shakes, which are of equal thickness throughout, are applied, the froe-end of the shake (the smoother end from which it has been split) should be laid undermost. The application of shakes can be speeded by use of a shingler's or lather's hatchet. Fig. 40-41. The hatchet is used for nailing. It also carries an exposure gauge and has a sharpened heel that can be used for trimming.

Nailing. Only two nails should be used to apply each shake, regardless of its width. Shakes should be attached to the roof deck with either rust-resistant, hot-dipped galvanized or aluminum nails. The nails should be placed

approximately 1" in from each edge and from 1" to 2" above the butt line of the succeeding course. Nails should be driven until their heads meet the shake surface but no farther. Fig. 40-42.

Nail lengths typically required are 6d (2") for shakes with ¾" to 1¼" butt thickness and 5d (1¾") for shakes with ½" to ¾" butt thickness. Nails two-penny (2d) sizes larger should be used to apply hip and ridge units. The nail should always be long enough to penetrate through the sheathing by ½".

Hips and Ridges. The final shake course at the ridge line, as well as shakes that terminate at hips, should be secured with additional nails. This final shake course should also be composed of smoother textured shakes. A strip of No. 30 asphalt-saturated felt, at least 12" wide, should be applied over the crown of all hips and ridges, with an equal exposure of 6" on each side.

Prefabricated hip and ridge units can be used, or the hips and ridges can be cut and applied on the site. In site-construction of hips, shakes approximately 6" wide are sorted out. Two wooden straightedges are tacked on the roof 6" from the center line of the hip, one on each

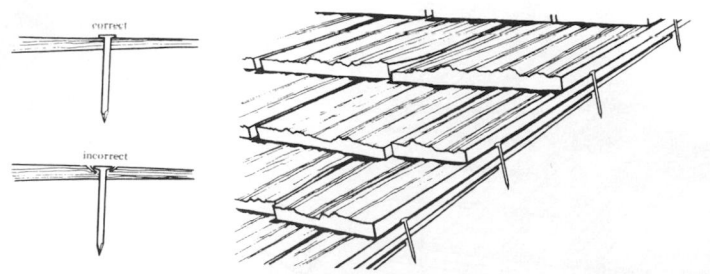

40-42a. *Nails should be driven flush with the surface of the wood shake but no farther. Place the nails from 1" to 2" above the butt line of the succeeding course.*

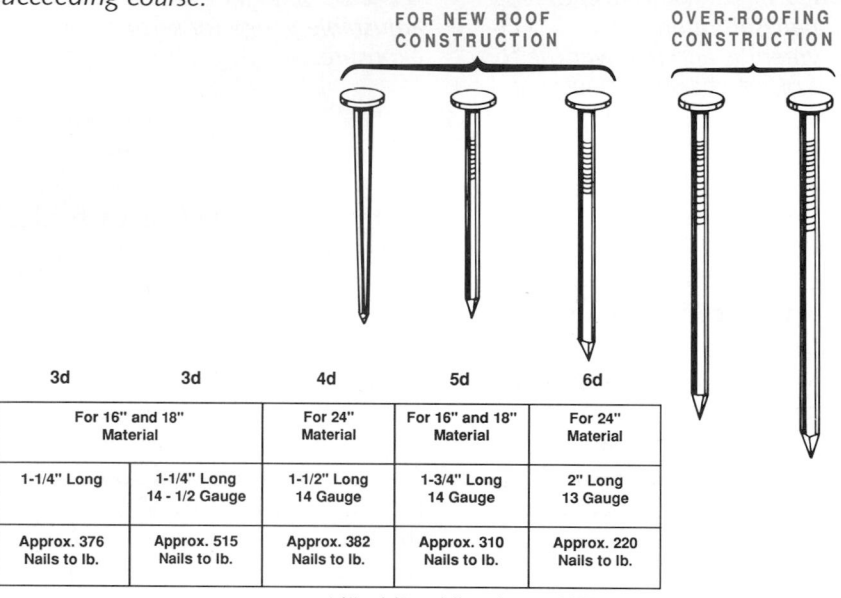

FOR NEW ROOF CONSTRUCTION				OVER-ROOFING CONSTRUCTION
3d	3d	4d	5d	6d
For 16" and 18" Material		For 24" Material	For 16" and 18" Material	For 24" Material
1-1/4" Long	1-1/4" Long 14 - 1/2 Gauge	1-1/2" Long 14 Gauge	1-3/4" Long 14 Gauge	2" Long 13 Gauge
Approx. 376 Nails to lb.	Approx. 515 Nails to lb.	Approx. 382 Nails to lb.	Approx. 310 Nails to lb.	Approx. 220 Nails to lb.

* All weights and dimensions are APPROXIMATE.

40-42b. *Recommended nail sizes for application of shingles and shakes.*

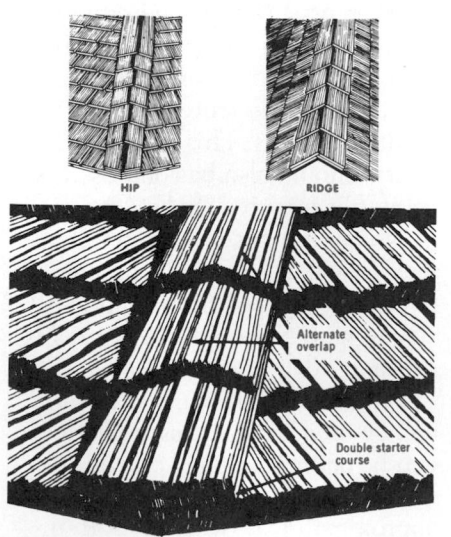

40-43. *Hip and ridge construction using wood shakes.*

side. The starting course of shakes should be doubled. The first shake on the hip is nailed in place with one edge resting against the guide strip. The edge of the shake projecting over the center of the hip is cut back on a bevel. The shake on the opposite side is then applied and the projecting edge cut back to fit. Shakes in the following courses are applied alternately in reverse order. Fig. 40-43.

Ridges are constructed in a similar manner. Exposure of the hip and ridge shakes normally is the same as the shakes on the roof. Ridge shakes are laid along an unbroken ridge that

terminates in a gable at each end. They should be started at each gable end and terminate in the middle of the ridge. At that point, a small saddle is face-nailed to splice the two lines. The first course of shakes should always be doubled at each end of the ridge.

Gable Rakes. Dripping water may be eliminated by inserting a single strip of bevel siding the full length of each gable rake with the thick edge flush with the sheathing edge. The inward pitch of the roof surface will then divert the water away from the gable edge.

Alternate Application Methods.

➤ **Graduated exposures.** By reducing the exposure of each course from eaves to ridge, a variation in roof appearance may be achieved with handsplit shakes. This requires shakes of several lengths. Fig. 40-44.

➤ **Staggered lines.** Irregular and random roof patterns can be achieved by laying shakes with butts placed slightly above or below the horizontal lines governing each course. Fig. 40-45. For an extremely irregular pattern, longer shakes may be interspersed over the roof with their butts several inches lower than the course lines.

WOOD SHINGLES

Wood shingles are manufactured in 24", 18", and 16" lengths conforming to three grades: #1, #2, and #3. Table 40-F. Preformed, factory-built hip and ridge units are available.

The exposure of wood shingles is dependent on the slope of the roof. Standard exposures of 5", 5½", and 7½" for shingle lengths of 16", 18", and 24" respectively are used on slopes 5 in 12 or greater. On 4-in-

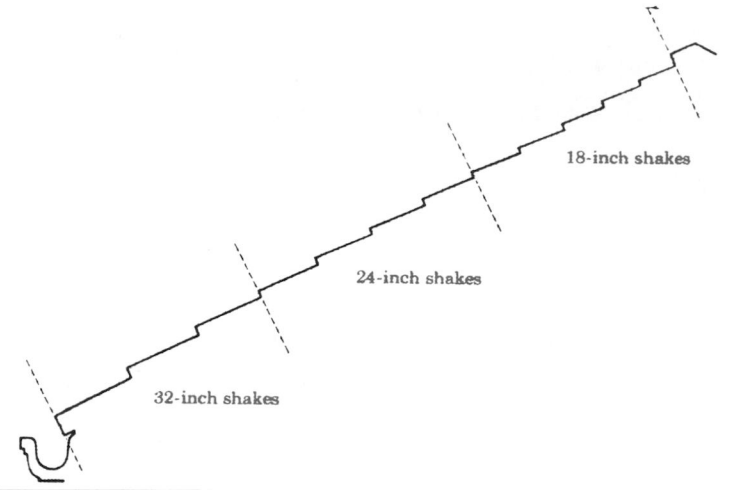

40-44. *A roof with graduated exposure is created by using all three shake sizes.*

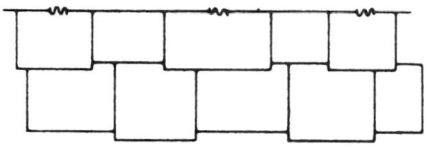

40-45. *Irregular roof patterns can be made by laying the shakes with butts slightly above or below the horizontal lines.*

12 slopes, exposures should be reduced to 4½", 5", and 6¾" for 16", 18", and 24" shingles respectively. On 3-in-12 slopes they should be reduced further to 3¾", 4¼", 5¾" for 16", 18", and 24" shingles respectively. This will assure four layers of shingles over the roof area. Table 40-G. Wood

shingles are not recommended on slopes less than 3 in 12.

Underlayment

Underlayment is not usually used between shingles on spaced or solid sheathing. However, it may be desirable for the protection of sheathing and to insure against air infiltration. For underlayment, No. 15 asphalt-saturated felt may be used.

Drip Edge

Wood shingles should extend out over the eave and rake a distance of 1" to 1½" to form a drip. This edge is aligned in the same manner as described for wood shakes.

Eaves Flashing

In areas where the outside design temperature is 0 degrees F or colder, or where there is possibility of ice forming along the eaves and causing a backup of water, eaves

Table 40-F. *Grades of Red Cedar Roof Shingles.*

Grade	Length	Thickness (at Butt)	No. of Courses Per Bundle	Bdls/Cartons Per Square	Description
No. 1	16" (Fivex) 18" (Perfections) 24" (Royals)	.40" .45" .50"	20/20 18/18 13/14	4 bdls. 4 bdls. 4 bdls.	The premium grade of shingles for roofs and sidewalls. These top-grade shingles are 100% heartwood. 100% clear and 100% edge-grain.
No. 2	16" (Fivex) 18" (Perfections) 24" (Royals)	.40" .45" .50"	20/20 18/18 13/14	4 bdls. 4 bdls. 4 bdls.	A good grade for many applications. Not less than 10" clear on 16" shingles, 11" clear on 18" shingles and 16" clear on 24" shingles. Flat grain and limited sapwood are permitted in this grade.
No. 3	16" (Fivex) 18" (Perfections) 24" (Royals)	.40" .45" .50"	20/20 18/18 13/14	4 bdls. 4 bdls. 4 bdls.	A utility grade for economy application and secondary building. Not less than 6" clear on 16" and 18" shingles, 10" clear on 24" shingles.
No. 4	16" (Fivex) 18" (Perfections)	.40" .45"	14/14 or 20/20 14/14 or 18/18	2 bdls. 2 bdls.	A utility grade for undercoursing on double-coursed sidewall applications or for interior accent walls.
No. 1 or No. 2	16" (Fivex) 18" (Perfections) 24" (Royals)	.40" .45" .50"	33/33 28/28 13/14	1 carton 1 carton 4 bdls.	Same specifications as above for No. 1 and No. 2 grades but machine trimmed for exactly parallel edges with butts sawn at precise right angles. For sidewall application where tightly fitting joints are desired. Also available with smooth sanded face.

* All weights are APPROXIMATE.

Table 40-G. *Roof Coverage of Shingles at Various Exposures.*

Slope	Maximum exposure recommended for roofs:								
	No. 1			No. 2			No. 3		
	16"	18"	24"	16"	18"	24"	16"	18"	24"
3 In 12 to 4 In 12	3 3/4"	4 1/4"	5 3/4"	3 1/2"	4"	5 1/2"	3"	3 1/2"	5"
4 In 12 and Steeper	5"	5 1/2"	7 1/2"	4"	4 1/2"	6 1/2"	3 1/2"	4"	5 1/2"

Length and Thickness	Approximate coverage of one square (4 bundles) of shingles based on following weather exposures												
	3 1/2"	4"	4 1/2"	5"	5 1/2"	6"	6 1/2"	7"	7 1/2"	8"	8 1/2"	9"	9 1/2"
16" x 5 1/2"	70	80	90	100(a)	110	120	130	140	150(c)	160	170	180	190
18" x 5/2 1/4"	—	72 1/2	81 1/2	90 1/2	100(a)	109	118	127	136	145 1/2	154 1/2(c)	163 1/2	172 1/2
24" x 4/2"	—	—	—	—	—	80	86 1/2	93	100(a)	106 1/2	113	120	126 1/2
	10"	**10 1/2"**	**11"**	**11 1/2"**	**12"**	**12 1/2"**	**13"**	**13 1/2"**	**14"**	**14 1/2"**	**15"**	**15 1/2"**	**16"**
16"x 5 1/2"	200	210	220	230	240(b)	—	—	—	—	—	—	—	—
18" x 5/2 1/4"	181 1/2	191	200	209	218	227	236	245 1/2	254 1/2(b)	—	—	—	—
24" x 4/2"	133	140	146 1/2	153(c)	160	166 1/2	173	180	186 1/2	193	200	206 1/2	213(b)

* All weights and dimensions are APPROXIMATE.
(a) Maximum exposure recommended for roofs.
(b) Maximum exposure recommended for double-coursing No. 1 grades on sidewalls.
(c) Maximum exposure recommended for single-coursing No. 1 and No. 2 grades on sidewalls.

flashing is recommended. Fig. 40-38. Sheathing should be applied solidly above the eave line to cover a point at least 24" inside the interior wall line of the building. Fig. 40-20.

For 4-in-12 slopes, the eaves flashing is formed by applying a double layer of No. 15 asphalt-saturated felt to cover this section of solid sheathing. When the eave overhang requires the flashing to be wider than 36", the necessary horizontal joint between the felt strips is cemented and located outside the exterior wall line.

For slopes from 3 in 12 up to 4 in 12, or in areas subject to severe icing, eaves flashing may be formed as described for 4-in-12 slopes, except that the double layer of No. 15 asphalt-saturated underlayment is cemented. The eaves flashing is formed by applying a continuous layer of plastic asphalt cement, at the rate of 2 gals. per 100 sq. ft., to the surface of the underlayment starter course before the second layer of underlayment is applied.

Cement is also applied to the 19" underlying portion of each succeeding course which lies within the eaves flashing area, before placing the next course. It is important to apply the cement uniformly with a comb trowel, so that at no point does underlayment touch underlayment when the application is completed. The overlying sheet is pressed firmly into the entire cemented area. Fig. 40-21.

Flashing

If copper flashing is used with wood shingles, take special precautions. Fig. 40-39. Premature deterioration of the copper may occur when the metal and wood are in intimate contact in the presence of moisture.

Only the open method should be used to construct valley flashing. A closed valley is not recommended.

On slopes up to 12 in 12, metal valley sheets should be wide enough to extend at least 10" on each side of the valley center line. Fig. 40-46. On roofs of steeper slope, narrower sheets may be used extending on each side of the valley center line for a distance of at least 7". The open portion of the valley should be at least 4" wide, but valleys may begin 2" wide and increase at the rate of 1/2" per 8' of length as they descend.

In areas where the outside design temperature is 0 degrees F or colder, underlayment should be installed under metal valley sheets.

Application of Wood Shingles

The first course of shingles at the eaves should be doubled or tripled. It should project l" to 1½" beyond the eaves to provide a drip.

The second layer of shingles in the first course should be nailed over the first layer to provide a minimum sidelap of at least 1½" between joints. Fig. 40-47. If

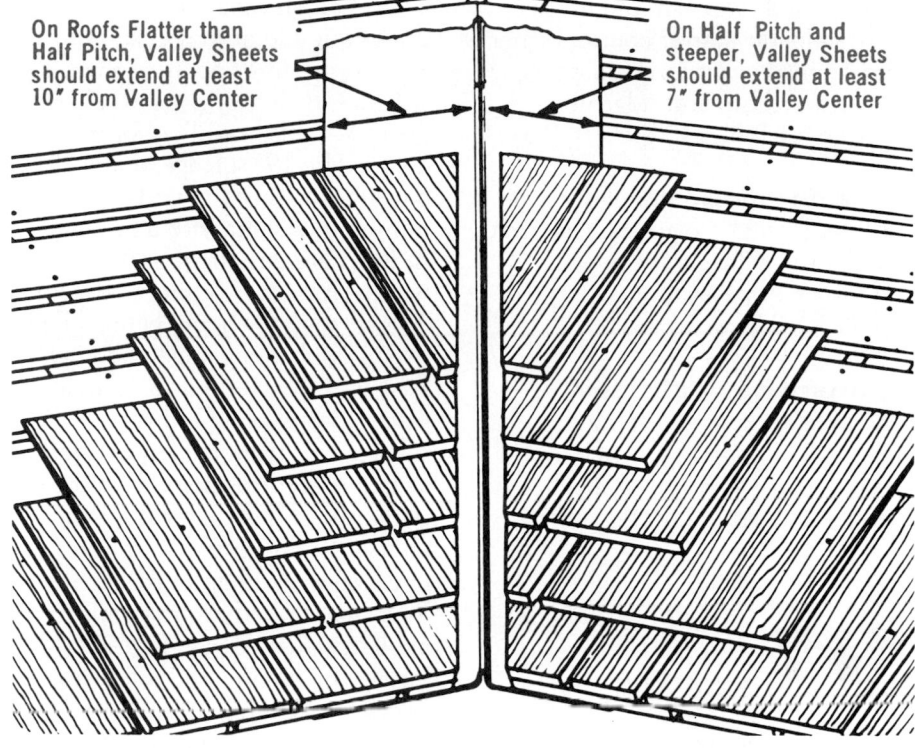

On Roofs Flatter than Half Pitch, Valley Sheets should extend at least 10" from Valley Center

On Half Pitch and steeper, Valley Sheets should extend at least 7" from Valley Center

40-46. *Open valley flashing construction with wood shingles.*

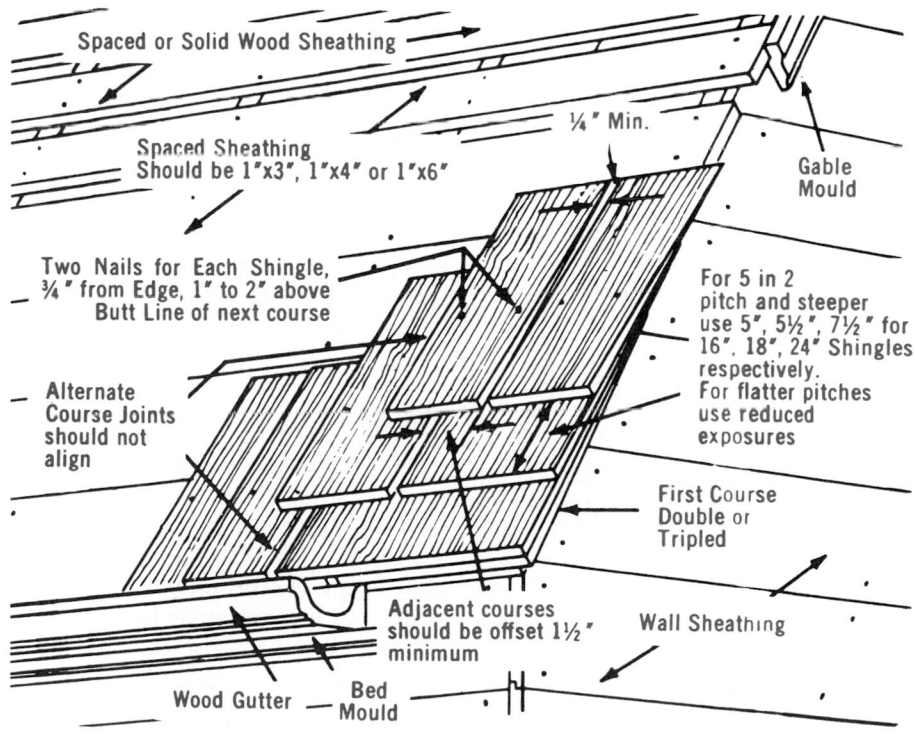

Spaced or Solid Wood Sheathing

Spaced Sheathing Should be 1"x3", 1"x4" or 1"x6"

¼" Min.

Two Nails for Each Shingle, ¾" from Edge, 1" to 2" above Butt Line of next course

Alternate Course Joints should not align

Gable Mould

For 5 in 2 pitch and steeper use 5", 5½", 7½" for 16", 18", 24" Shingles respectively. For flatter pitches use reduced exposures

First Course Double or Tripled

Adjacent courses should be offset 1½" minimum

Wall Sheathing

Wood Gutter — Bed Mould

40-47. *Details for applying wood shingles over spaced or solid sheathing.*

possible, joints should be "broken" by a greater margin. A triple layer of shingles in the first course provides additional insurance against leaks at the cornice. No. 3 grade shingles frequently are used for the starter course.

Shingles should be spaced at least ¼" apart to provide for expansion. Joints between shingles in any course should be separated not less than 1½" from joints in the adjacent course above or below. Joints in alternate courses should not be in direct alignment. When shingles are laid with the recommended exposure, triple coverage of the roof results. Fig. 40-47.

When the roof terminates in a valley, the shingles for the valley should be carefully cut to the proper miter at the exposed butts. These shingles should be nailed in place first so that the direction of shingle application is away from the valley. This permits valley shingles to be carefully selected and insures shingle joints will not break over the valley flashing.

Nailing. To insure that shingles will lie flat and give maximum service, only two nails should be used to secure each shingle. Nails should be placed not more than ¾" from the side edge of shingles, at a distance of not more than l" above the exposure line. Fig. 40-47. Nails should be driven flush but not so that the nailhead crushes the wood. Fig. 40-42a. The recommended nail sizes for the application of wood shingles are shown in Fig. 40-42b. As with shakes, the application of wood shingles can be speeded by the use of a shingler's or lather's hatchet. Fig. 40-41.

Hips and Ridges. Hips and ridges should be of the modified "Boston" type with protected nailing. Fig. 40-48. Nails at least two sizes larger than the nails used to apply the shingles are required.

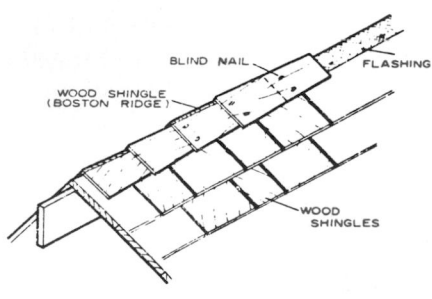

40-48. *Boston ridge with wood shingles.*

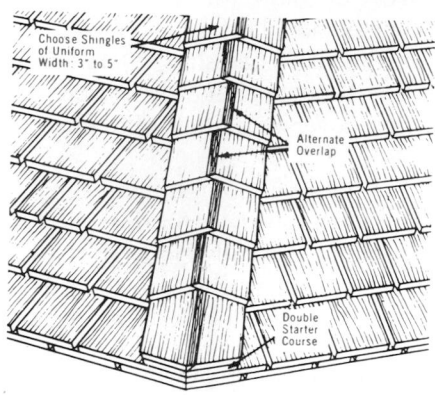

40-49. *Wood shingle hip and ridge construction.*

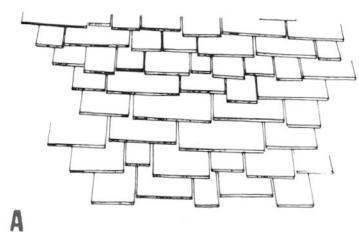

A

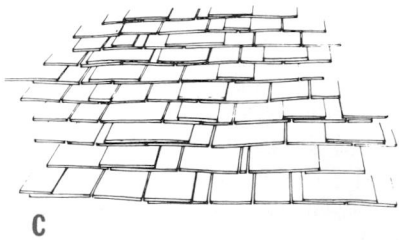

C

B

D

40-50. *Alternate application methods for wood shingles. A. Thatch. Shingles are positioned above and below a hypothetical course line, with deviation from the line not to exceed 1". B. Serrated. Courses are doubled every 3rd, 4th, 5th, or 6th course. Doubled courses can be laid butt-edge flush or with a slight overhang. C. Dutch weave. Shingles are doubled or superimposed at random throughout the roof area. D. Pyramid. Two extra shingles, narrow shingle over a wide one, are superimposed at random.*

Hips and ridges should begin with a double starter course. Either site-applied or preformed factory-constructed hip and ridge units may be used. Fig. 40-49.

Gable Rakes. Shingles should project 1" to 1½" over the rake. End shingles may be canted to eliminate drips as discussed in the application of wood shakes.

Alternate Application Methods. Several alternate methods of applying shingles, giving a different appearance to the roof, are illustrated in Fig. 40-50.

ROLL ROOFING

When economy is a factor in construction, the use of mineral-surfaced roll roofing might be considered. While this type of roofing will not be as attractive as an asphalt shingle roof and perhaps not as durable, it may cost up to 15% less than standard asphalt shingles. Roll roofing is excellent over old roofs as well as for new decks. The 19" selvage, double coverage rolls (65 pounds minimum weight with a mineral surface) are designed for flat decks with a slope of 1" or more per foot.

Roll roofing should be installed over a double coverage underlay. First nail the metal drip edges at eaves and rakes. Use the 19" selvage cut, trimmed out of a full sheet, as a starter strip. Save the remaining 17" strip for the last course. Nail the strip so that it overhangs eaves and rakes ¼" to ⅜". With galvanized roofing nails, apply the first course. Fig. 40-51. Apply the second and following courses with a full 19" overlap, leaving just the mineral surface exposed.

Next, lift the mineral surface of each course and apply a quick-setting lap cement to the underlying sheet to within ¼" of the exposed edge. Apply firm pressure over the entire cemented area, using a light roller or broom.

After you have finished the whole roof, check for any loose laps, and re-cement to insure complete bond. The ridge can be finished with a Boston-type covering or by 12" wide strips of the roll roofing, using at least 6" on each side.

BUILT-UP ROOFS

Built-up roof coverings are installed by roofing companies that specialize in this field. Fig. 40-52. Roofs of this type may have three, four, or five layers of roofer's felt, each mopped down with tar or asphalt. The final surface may be coated with asphalt and covered with gravel embedded in asphalt or

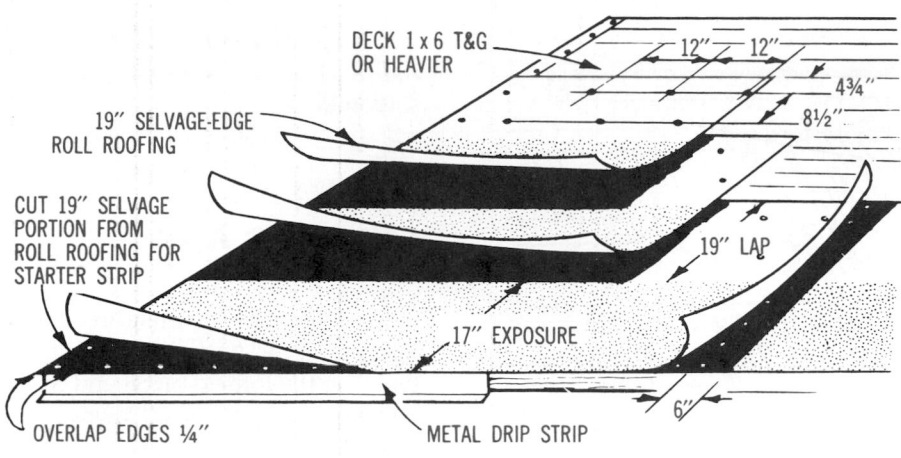

40-51. *Application details for roll roofing.*

40-52. *Preparing a roof deck for a built-up roof.*

tar, or covered with a cap sheet. For convenience, it is customary to refer to built-up roofs as 10-year, 15-year, or 20-year roofs, depending upon the method of application.

For example, a 15-year roof over a wood deck may have a base layer of 30-pound saturated roofer's felt laid dry, with edges lapped and held down with roofing nails. All nailing is done with either roofing

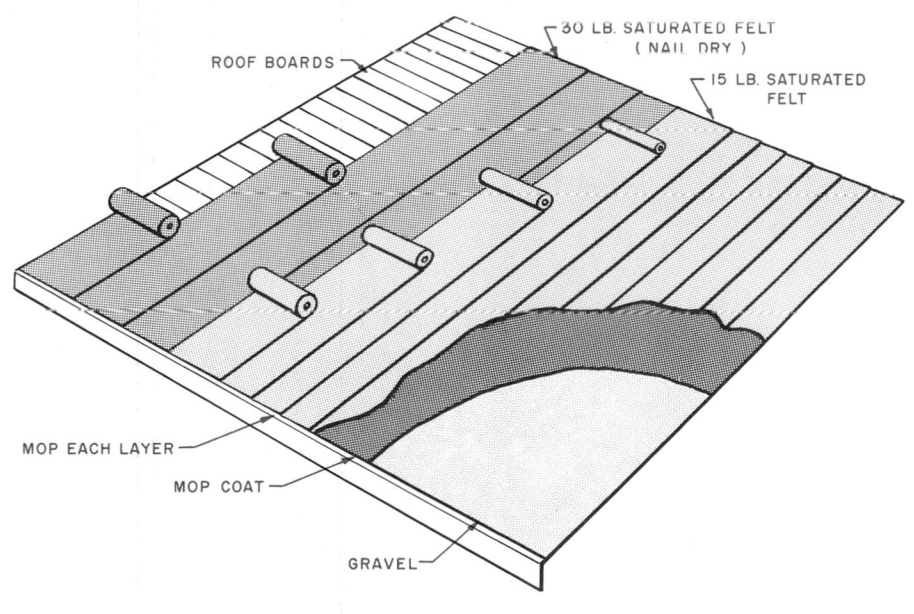

40-53. *Application details for a built-up roof.*

nails driven through flat tin caps or with 10-gauge roofing nails having heads of not less than ⅝" diameter. The dry sheet is intended to prevent tar or asphalt from entering the rafter spaces. Three layers of 15-pound saturated felt follow, each of which is mopped on with hot tar rather than being nailed. The final coat of tar or asphalt may be covered with roofing gravel or a cap sheet of roll roofing. Fig. 40-53.

The cornice or eave line of projecting roofs is usually finished with metal edging or flashing, which acts as a drip edge.

METAL ROOFING

Corrugated metal roofing comes in widths up to 4' and lengths up to 24' and therefore covers large areas quickly. It is ideal for utility buildings such as garages and sheds. It can be used on slopes as low as 4 in 12, or as low as 3 in 12 if a single panel will cover from eave to ridge.

Apply purlins across the roof rafters to support the roofing spacing according to roofing manufacturer's instructions. No sheathing is required. Set closure strips (they come with the roofing) at eave. Cut panels to length with tin snips, the length being the dimension from ridge to eave plus 2½". Nail through tops of ribs, using 1¾" screwshank nails with neoprene washers to prevent leaks. Next, set closure strips (inverted) at ridge and apply metal cap. Finally, flash at eaves as shown in Fig. 40-54.

Sheet-metal roofing must be laid over sheathing. The joints should be watertight, and the deck should be properly flashed where it joins with a wall. Nails should be of the same metal as that used on the roof, except with tin roofs, where

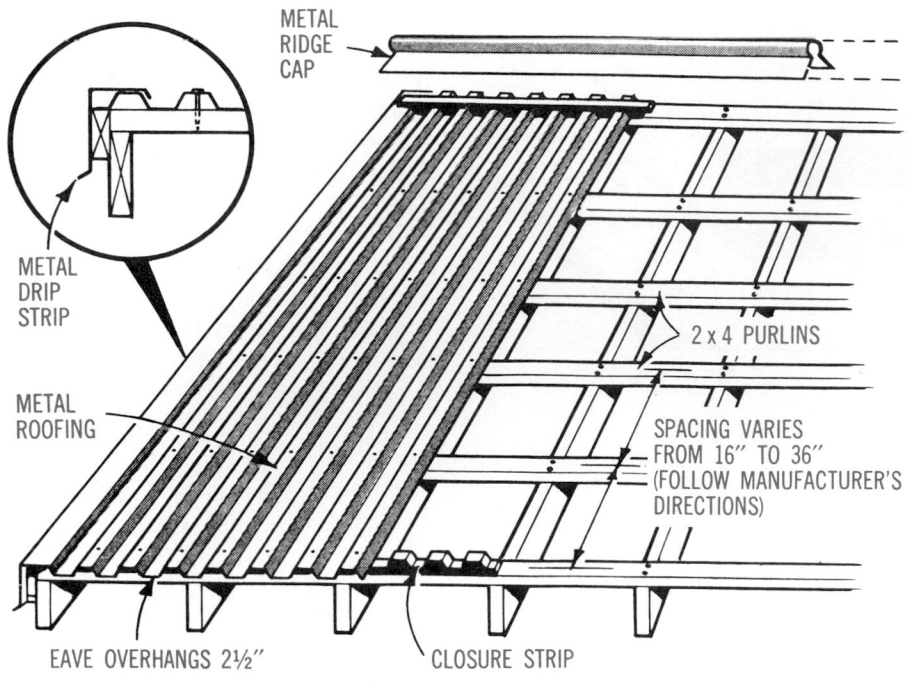

METAL RIDGE CAP

METAL DRIP STRIP

METAL ROOFING

2 x 4 PURLINS

SPACING VARIES FROM 16" TO 36" (FOLLOW MANUFACTURER'S DIRECTIONS)

EAVE OVERHANGS 2½"

CLOSURE STRIP

40-54a. *Installation details for corrugated metal roofing.*

40-54b. *Installing corrugated aluminum roofing.*

steel nails may be used. All exposed nailheads on tin roofs should be soldered.

GUTTERS AND DOWNSPOUTS

Various types of gutters are on the market. Fig. 40-55. The two general types are the formed metal and the half-round. Fig. 40-56a. Downspouts or leaders are rectangular or round, with the round leader being ordinarily used with the half-round gutter. Both the round and the rectangular leaders are usually corrugated for added strength. Fig. 40-56b. The corrugated patterns are less likely to burst when plugged with ice.

Wood gutters may be used in place of metal gutters and are usually fastened by means of rust-resistant screws or nails. Fig. 40-57. Nailing or spacing blocks are placed between the gutter and the fascia or frieze board about 16" on center. Wood gutters are given very little pitch because they usually are part of the architectural treatment. Joints in wood gutters are best made by dowels or splines. The joints are covered with heavy fabric tacked in place and covered with a mastic. It is recommended that 1 or 2 coats of water repellent containing a preservative be applied to the bare wood.

Hanging metal gutters are held with flat or wire metal hangers that are so installed that a pitch is formed for drainage. Fig. 40-58. Joints in metal gutters and downspouts should be soldered. Gutters should be mounted so that the shingle extension is over the center of the gutter. Hangers should be spaced 3' to 4' on center.

Another type of formed metal gutter has an extension or flashing strip that is fastened to the roof boards. Fig. 40-59. These gutters are usually made so that the back varies in height to allow a pitch for

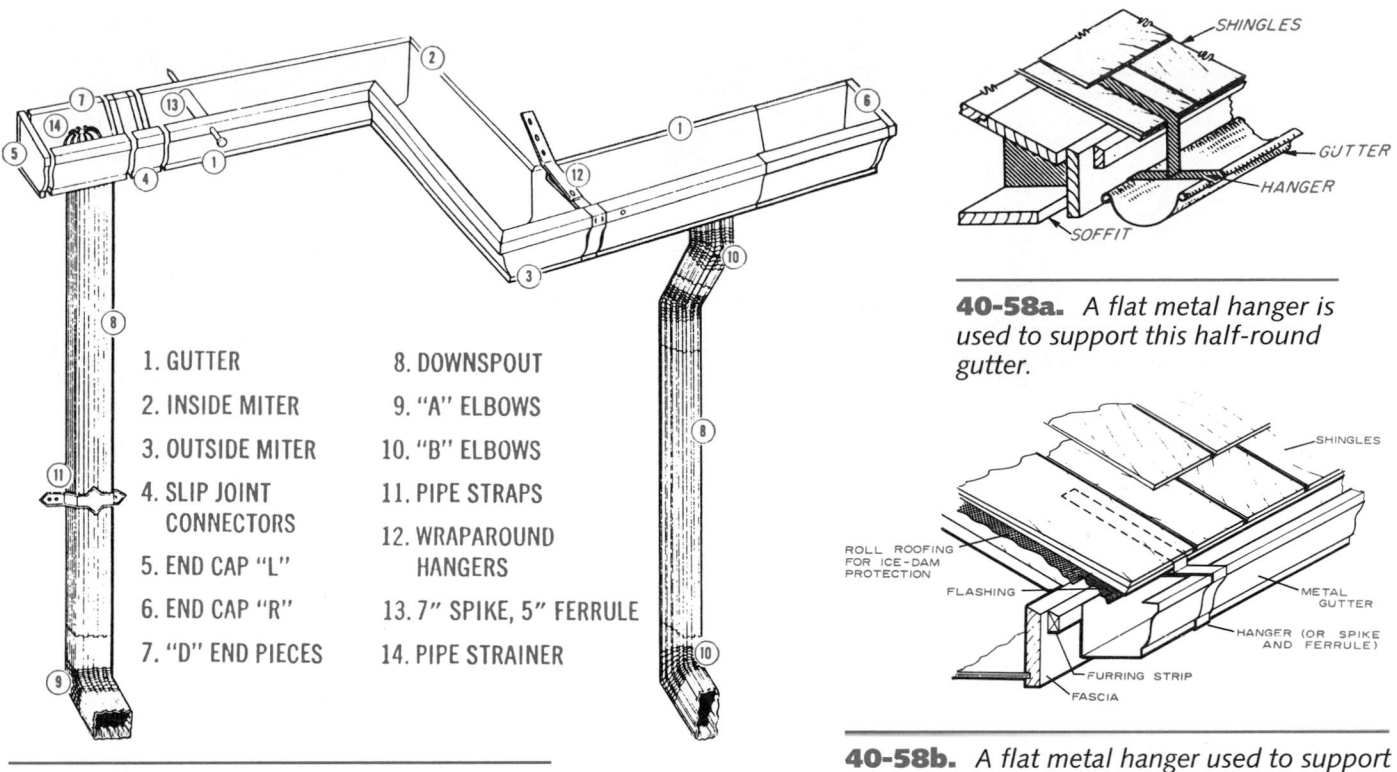

40-55. Parts of a formed metal gutter system.

1. GUTTER
2. INSIDE MITER
3. OUTSIDE MITER
4. SLIP JOINT CONNECTORS
5. END CAP "L"
6. END CAP "R"
7. "D" END PIECES

8. DOWNSPOUT
9. "A" ELBOWS
10. "B" ELBOWS
11. PIPE STRAPS
12. WRAPAROUND HANGERS
13. 7" SPIKE, 5" FERRULE
14. PIPE STRAINER

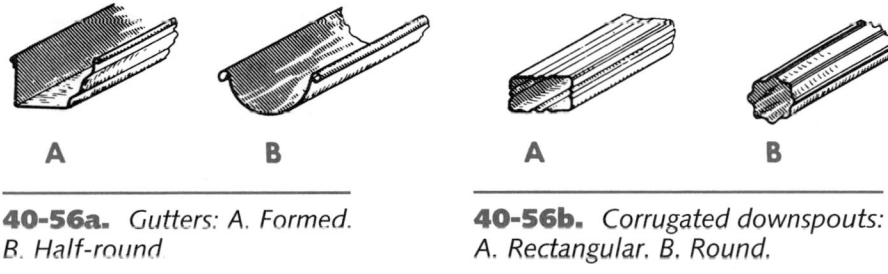

40-56a. Gutters: A. Formed. B. Half-round

40-56b. Corrugated downspouts: A. Rectangular. B. Round.

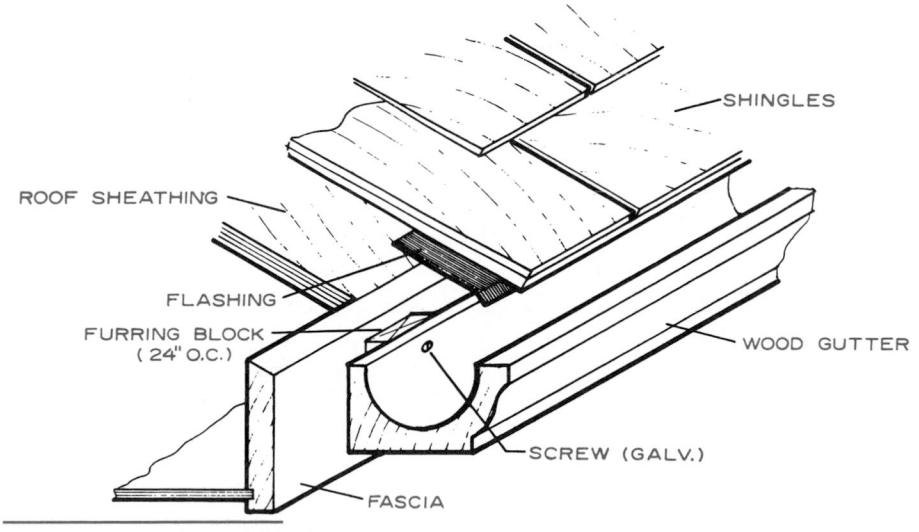

40-57. A wood gutter.

40-58a. A flat metal hanger is used to support this half-round gutter.

40-58b. A flat metal hanger used to support a formed gutter.

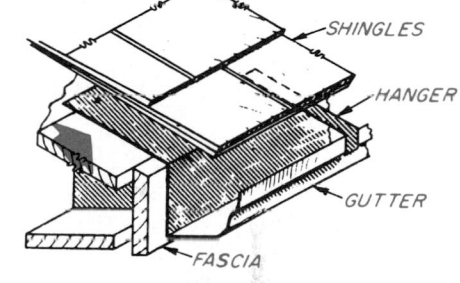

40-59. This formed metal gutter has an extension which also serves as a flashing strip. It is used to fasten the gutter to the roof boards.

drainage. Hangers are used at the outer rim to add stiffness.

Metal gutters are placed to drain toward the downspouts. With a slope of approximately 1" in 10', the maximum run between the high point and the downspout should not ordinarily exceed 25'. A gooseneck is used to bring the downspout in line with the wall. The form of this gooseneck will vary according to the extent of the cornice overhang.

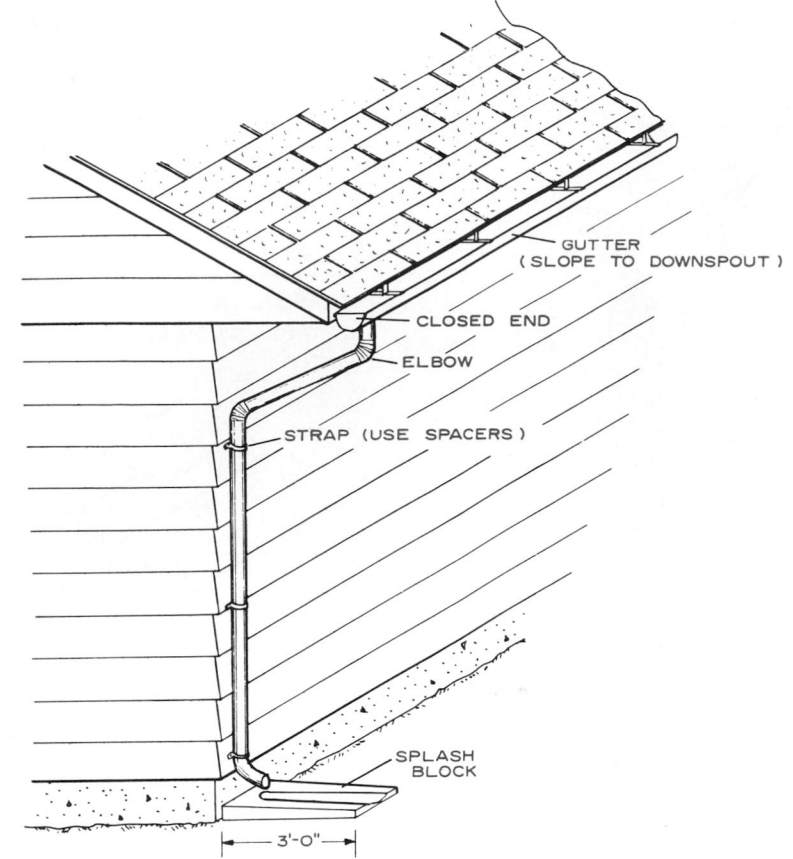

40-60. *A downspout installation.*

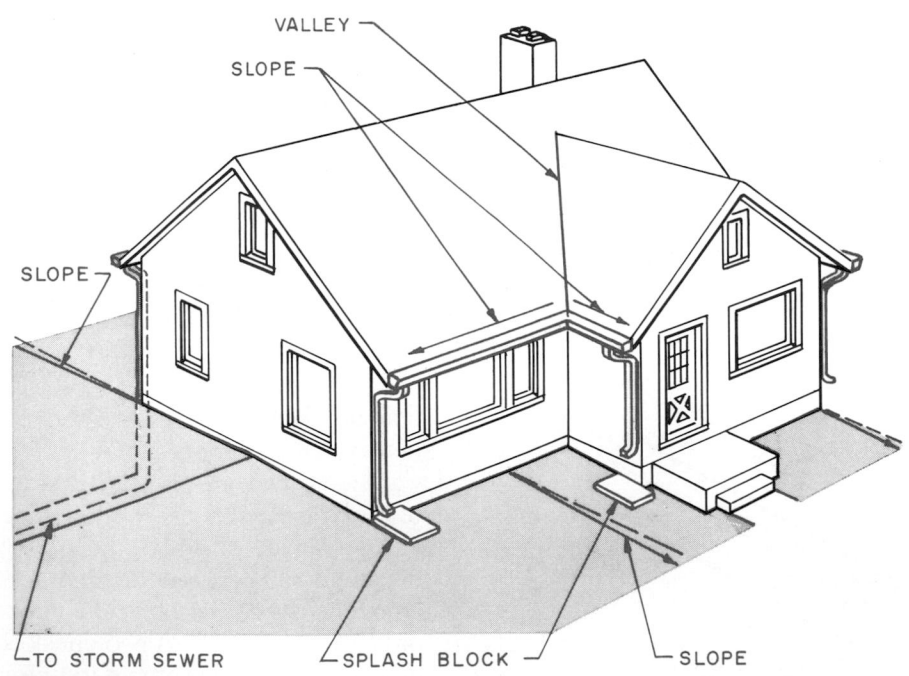

40-61. *All gutters are sloped toward the downspouts. The final grading should slope away from the building to insure proper drainage. Sometimes downspouts are connected to a storm sewer.*

Downspouts are fastened to the wall by means of leader straps or hooks. Fig. 40-60. Many patterns of straps are made to allow a space between the wall and the downspout. A minimum of two straps should be used in an 8' length of leader: one at the gooseneck and one at the bottom elbow. The elbow is used to lead the water to a splash block that carries the water away from the foundation. The minimum length of the splash block should be 3'. It is the practice, in some areas, to carry the water to a storm sewer by means of tile lines. Fig. 40-61. In final grading the slope should be such as to insure positive drainage of water away from the foundation walls.

ESTIMATING

Materials

To determine the number of shingles needed, the total area to be covered must be figured first. To figure the roof area without actually getting on the roof to measure the roof line, use Table 40-H. When the roof slope is known, this table may be used to figure the roof area from the plan. The plan area of the roofline (including the overhang) should be multiplied by the factor shown in the table opposite the rise of the roof, which is given in inches per horizontal foot. The result will be the total roof area.

For example, if a home is 70' long and 30' wide including the overhang, the area is 2,100 square feet. If the rise of the roof is 5½", multiply the area by 1.100 for a total roof area of 2,310 square feet. Use this total roof area for figuring the amounts of roofing materials, such as the felt underlayment or shingles, that will be needed.

One square of shingles covers 100 square feet of roof surface. To determine the number of squares needed to cover the roof, divide the total area by 100.

$$\frac{2310}{100} \times 23.1 \text{ squares of shingles}$$

A 10% waste and cutting factor must be added to this amount.

$$23.1 \times 0.10 = 2.31$$
$$23.1 + 2.31 = 25.41, \text{ or } 25 \text{ squares of shingles}$$

Another method of figuring the area of a plain gable roof is to multiply the length of the ridge by the length of a rafter. This will give you one-half the roof area. Multiply by 2 to obtain the total square feet of roof surface.

A similar method may be used to find the area of a hip roof. Multiply the length of the eaves by ½ the length of the common rafter at the end. Multiply this by 2 to obtain the area of both ends. To find the area of the sides, add the length of the eave to the length of the ridge and divide by 2. Multiply this by the length of the common rafter to obtain the area of one side of the roof. Multiply by 2 to find the number of square feet on both sides of the roof. Add this to the area of the two ends and divide the total area by 100 to get the number of squares.

The area of a plain hip roof running to a point at the top is obtained by multiplying the length of the eaves at one end by one-half the length of the rafter. This gives the area of one end of the roof. To obtain the total area, multiply by 4.

Be sure to subtract for openings in the roof such as the chimney, and where the dormer intersects the roof line so that the dormer area is not figured twice. Quantities of starter strips, eaves flashings, valley flashings, and ridge shingles all depend upon linear measurements along the hips, rakes, valleys, eaves, and ridge. Measurements for horizontal elements can be taken directly off the roof plan. The rakes, hips, and valleys run on a slope. The actual length of rakes, hips, and valleys must therefore be measured on the roof. The length of the rafters can also be figured as described in Unit 33.

The number of nails needed for asphalt roofing can be determined from Table 40-I. For the example,

Table 40-H. *Determining Roof Area from a Plan. When a roof area has to be figured from a plan only and the roof slope is known, the roof area may be computed from this table.*

Rise	Factor	Rise	Factor
3"	1.031	8"	1.202
3 1/2"	1.042	8 1/2"	1.225
4"	1.054	9"	1.250
4 1/2"	1.068	9 1/2"	1.275
5"	1.083	10"	1.302
5 1/2"	1.100	10 1/2"	1.329
6"	1.118	11"	1.357
6 1/2"	1.137	11 1/2"	1.385
7"	1.158	12"	1.414
7 1/2"	1.179		

Table 40-I. *Nail Requirements for Asphalt Roofing Products.*

Type of Roofing	Shingles Per Sq.	Nails Per Shingles	Length of Nails*	Nails Per Sq.	Pounds Per Sq. (approximate)		Labor Hours Per Sq.
					12 ga. by 7/16" head	11 ga. by 7/16" head	
Roll Roofing on new deck	—	—	1"	252**	0.73	1.12	1
Roll Roofing over old roof'g	—	—	1 3/4"	252**	1.13	1.78	1 1/4
19" Selvage over old shing	—	—	1 3/4"	181	0.83	1.07	1
3 Tab Sq. Butt on new deck	80	4	1 1/4"	336	1.22	1.44	1 1/2
3 Tab Sq. Butt reroofing	80	4	1 3/4"	504	2.38	3.01	1 5/6
Hex Strip on new deck	86	4	1 1/4"	361	1.28	1.68	1 1/2
Hex Strip reroofing	86	4	1 3/4"	361	1.65	2.03	2
Giant Amer.	226	2	1 1/4"	479	1.79	2.27	2 1/2
Giant Dutch Lap	113	2	1 1/4"	236	1.07	1.39	1 1/2
Individ. Hex	82	2	1 3/4"	172	0.79	1.03	1 1/2

(*) Length of nail should always be sufficient to penetrate at least 3/4" into sound wood. Nails should show little, if any, below underside of deck.
(**) This is the number of nails required when spaced 2" apart.

25 squares of three-tab square-butt shingles are required to cover the roof area. Read down the chart from the heading "Pounds per Square" to the line "3 Tab Square-Butt on New Deck." Using 11-gauge nails, 1.44 pounds are required for each square. The total number of pounds needed then would be 36.

25 (squares of shingles) × 1.44 (lbs. per square) = 36 lbs. of nails.

The number of nails required for wood shingles can be determined from the information on Table 40-J.

Labor

To figure the labor for installing the roof in the example, refer to Table 40-I. Read down the column headed "Labor Hours per Square" to the line "3 Tab Square-Butt on New Deck." Each square requires 1½ hours. Twenty-five squares would require 37½ hours.

25 (squares to be laid) × 1.5 (hours per square) = 37.5 hours

To figure the labor for laying wood shingles, use the information from Table 40-J.

Table 40-J. *Estimating Wood Shingles.*

Wood Shingles	Material Per 100 Square Feet of Surface			Nails Per 100 Square Feet		Labor Hours
Laid To Weather	Shingles per 100 Sq. Feet	Waste	Shingles per 100 Sq. Ft. with Waste	3d Nails	4d Nails	per 100 Square Feet
4"	900	10%	990	3 ³/₄ Lbs.	6 ¹/₂ lbs.	3 ³/₄
5"	720	10%	792	3 Lbs.	5 ¹/₄ Lbs.	3
6"	600	10%	660	2 ¹/₂ Lbs.	4 ¹/₄ Lbs.	2 ¹/₂

Note: Nails based on using 2 nails per shingle. Increase time factor 25% for hip roofs.

QUESTIONS

1. List several materials used for covering pitched roofs.

2. List several materials which are considered roofing accessories.

3. What is the minimum slope on main roofs for the application of wood asphalt and slate shingles?

4. What is the maximum slope recommended for built-up roofs?

5. Why is roof underlayment used under shingles?

6. What is flashing?

7. On roofs longer than 30', why are strip shingles started at the center and applied toward the ends?

8. List 3 variations for laying square-butt strip shingles.

9. When laying shingles on the ridge, in what direction should the exposed edge be laid?

10. What are the two methods used to construct valley flashing? Describe the difference.

11. What special precautions should be taken when laying strip shingles on a low-pitch roof?

12. What is the main advantage of interlocking shingles?

13. Which of these two— wood shakes or wood shingles —have been split?

14. What is considered the least expensive type of roofing?

15. How is the quality of a built-up roof designated?

16. What is the recommended slope for metal gutters?

17. Describe one method for determining the area of a plain gable roof. For determining the area of a plain hip roof.

ACTIVITIES

1. Math. If the pitch of a roof is ⁷/₂₄, what is the rise in a 14' run?

2. Math. If the slope of the roof is 5 in 12 and the rise is 5'6", what is the run?

3. Math. A rectangular house with a gable roof has outside dimensions of 26' by 44'. In addition there is an 18" overhang on all sides and the slope is 6 in 12. The roof covering consists of three-tab, square-butt asphalt shingles.

a. How many feet of drip edge will be needed for the eaves?

b. How many feet of drip edge will be needed for the rake?

c. Estimate how many squares of shingles will be needed. Include 10% for waste and trim.

4. Language Arts. As is mentioned in this unit, the terms slope and pitch "are often incorrectly used synonymously." In everyday terms, explain the difference between slope and pitch.

Ventilation

During cold weather, condensation of water vapor may occur in attic spaces and under flat roofs. Even when vapor barriers have been installed, some vapor will work into spaces around pipes and other inadequately protected areas and some through the vapor barrier itself. Although the amount may be unimportant if equally distributed, it may be sufficiently concentrated in cold spots to cause damage. While wood shingle and wood shake roofs do not resist vapor movement, such roofings as asphalt shingles and built-up roofs are highly resistant. The most practical method of removing the moisture is by adequately ventilating the roof spaces.

In addition to water condensation, a warm attic that is inadequately ventilated and insulated may cause formation of ice dams at the cornice. After a heavy snowfall, attic heat causes the snow on the roof to melt. Water running down the roof freezes on the colder surface of the cornice, often forming an ice dam at the gutter. The ice dam may cause water to back up at the eaves and leak into the wall and ceiling. Similar dams often form in roof valleys. Ventilation provides part of the answer to this problem. With a well-insulated ceiling and adequate ventilation, attic temperatures are low and melting of snow over the attic space will be greatly reduced.

Tight construction (including insulating windows and doors) and the use of humidifiers have also created potential moisture problems which must be resolved by adequate ventilation as well as the proper use of vapor barriers.

In hot weather, ventilation of attic and roof spaces allows hot air to escape, thereby lowering the temperature in these spaces. Insulation should be put between the ceiling joists located below the attic or roof space to further retard heat flow into the rooms below and to improve comfort conditions.

It is common practice to install louvered openings in the end walls of gable roofs for ventilation. Air movement through such openings depends primarily on wind direction and velocity. Little movement can be expected unless there is wind and one or more openings face the wind. More positive air movement can be obtained by providing openings in the soffit areas of the roof overhang in addition to openings at the gable ends or ridge.

Hip-roof houses are best ventilated by inlet ventilators in the soffit area and by outlet ventilators along the ridge. The differences in temperature between the attic and the outside will then create an air movement independent of the wind, and also a more positive movement when there is wind.

Where there is a crawl space under the house, ventilation is necessary to remove water vapor rising from the soil. Such vapor may otherwise condense on the wood below the floor and facilitate decay. A permanent vapor barrier on the soil of the crawl space greatly reduces the amount of ventilating area required.

AREA OF VENTILATORS

These are the FHA minimum requirements for ventilation of attics and foundations. Note that these are the *minimum* requirements. It is preferable to have more ventilation than called for by these standards.

Attic Area

Provide cross-ventilation for all spaces between roof and top-floor ceiling with corrosion-resistant 8-mesh screened louvers as follows:

➤ Roofs with slopes 2 in 12 or greater: $\frac{1}{300}$ of the horizontal projection of the roof area over each space. One-half the required ventilation shall be in the upper part of the ventilated space as near the high point of the roof as practicable. Use Table 41-A to find the square inches in $\frac{1}{300}$ of the ceiling area.

➤ Roofs with slopes less than 2 in 12: $\frac{1}{150}$ of the horizontal projection area over each space unless a complete continuous vapor barrier is provided. If the vapor barrier is provided, the requirement is $\frac{1}{300}$.

Foundation

Provide cross-ventilation by corrosion-resistant screened vents, 8 mesh per inch, as follows: 2 sq. ft. per 100 linear feet of foundation plus $\frac{1}{300}$ of the ground area.

Minimum—4 vents located at corners.

ROOF VENTILATION

Types of ventilators and minimum recommended sizes have been established for various types of roofs. Figs. 41-1, 41-2, and 41-3. The minimum area for attic or roof-space ventilators is based on the projected ceiling area of the rooms below. The ratios given in Figs. 41-1 to 41-3 are of *net* ventilator area to ceiling area. The actual ventilator area must be increased to allow for any restrictions such as louvers and wire cloth or screen. Table 41-B.

To obtain extra screen area without adding to the area of the vent, use a frame of required size to hold the screen away from the

Table 41-A. *Ventilation Guide. Use this table to figure the square inches of ventilation required to provide $\frac{1}{300}$ of the ceiling area. Find the ceiling length in the left-hand column. Read across to the column headed by the ceiling width. The number shown equals $\frac{1}{300}$ of the ceiling area in square inches. If there is no vapor barrier and the roof slope is less than 2 in 12, multiply this number by 2.*

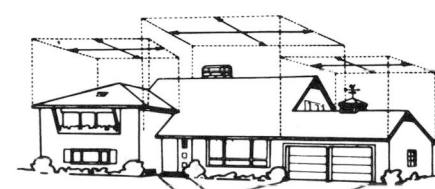

Length Feet	Width (In Feet)											
	20	22	24	26	28	30	32	34	36	38	40	42
20	192	211	230	250	269	288	307	326	346	365	384	403
22	211	232	253	275	296	317	338	359	380	401	422	444
24	230	253	276	300	323	346	369	392	415	438	461	484
26	250	275	300	324	349	374	399	424	449	474	499	524
28	269	296	323	349	376	403	430	457	484	511	538	564
30	288	317	346	374	403	432	461	490	518	547	576	605
32	307	338	369	399	430	461	492	522	553	584	614	645
34	326	359	392	424	457	490	522	555	588	620	653	685
36	346	380	415	449	484	518	553	588	622	657	691	726
38	365	401	438	474	511	547	584	620	657	693	730	766
40	384	422	461	499	538	576	614	653	691	730	768	806
42	403	444	484	524	564	605	645	685	726	766	806	847
44	422	465	507	549	591	634	676	718	760	803	845	887
46	442	486	530	574	618	662	707	751	795	839	883	927
48	461	507	553	599	645	691	737	783	829	876	922	968
50	480	528	576	624	672	720	768	816	864	912	960	1008

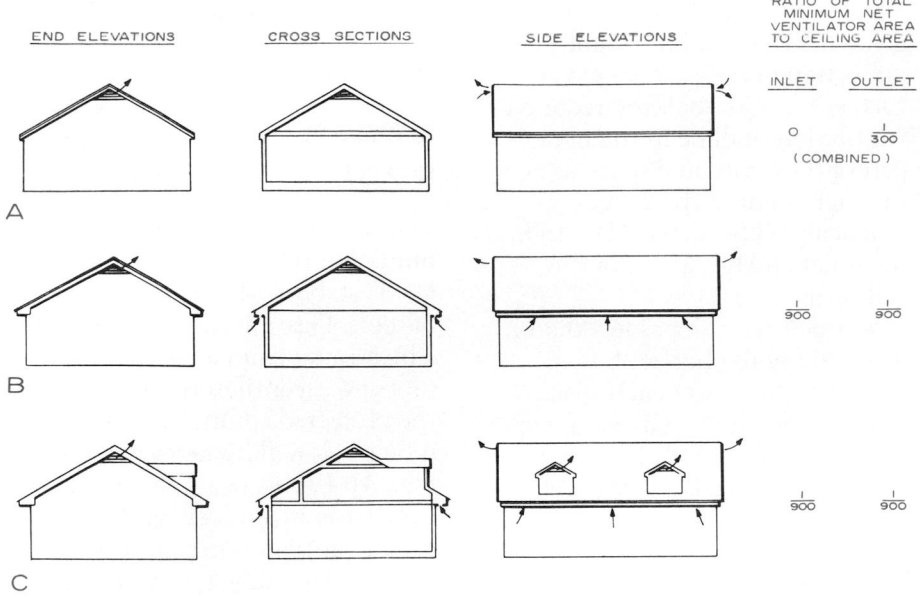

41-1. *Ventilating areas of gable roofs: A. End wall louver outlets. B. End wall louver outlets with soffit area inlets. C. End wall louver and dormer outlets with eave inlets.*

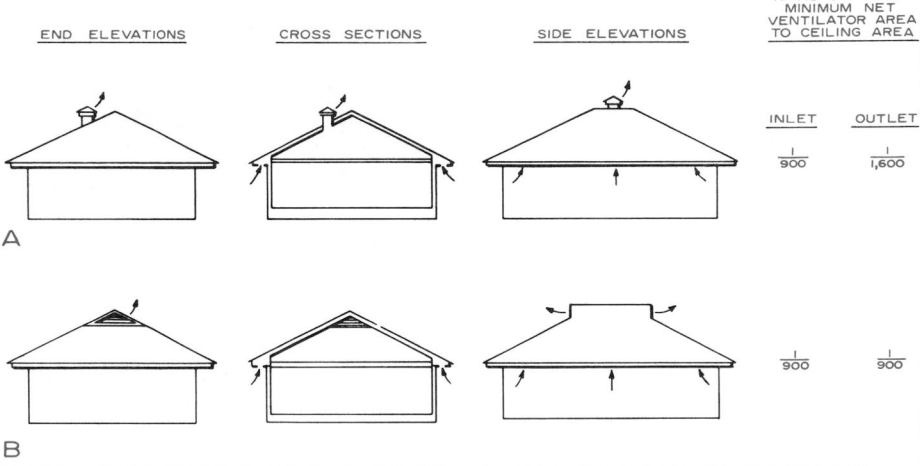

41-2. *Hip roof ventilation: A. Air inlet beneath the eaves and outlet vent near the ridge. B. Air inlet openings beneath the eaves and outlets in the small gable of a Dutch hip roof.*

Table 41-B. *Percentage of Increase Required for a Vent Opening When Vent Protection Material Is Used.*

Vent Protection	Increase in Total Area of Vent Opening Per Cent
¼- inch mesh	0
No. 8 mesh	25
No. 16 mesh	100
Louver + 1- inch mesh	100
Louver + No. 8 mesh	225
Louver + No. 16 mesh	300

the minimum total net area of the ventilators should be 4 square feet.

As previously explained, more positive air movement can be obtained if additional openings are provided in the soffit area. The minimum ventilation areas for this method are shown in B, Fig. 41-1.

Where there are rooms in the attic with sloping ceilings, the insulation should follow the roof slope and be so placed that there is a free opening of at least 1½" between the roof boards and the insulation for air movement. C, Fig. 41-1.

Hip Roofs

Hip roofs should have air inlet openings in the soffit area of the eaves and outlet openings at or near the peak. For minimum net areas of openings see A, Fig. 41-2. The most efficient type of inlet opening is the continuous slot, which should provide a free opening of not less than ¾". Fig. 41-4. The air outlet opening near the peak can be a continuous vent, a cupola, or several smaller roof ventilators located near the ridge. Fig. 41-5. The smaller roof ventilators can be located below the peak on the rear slope of the roof so that they will not be visible from the front of the house. Gabled extensions of a hip-roof house are sometimes used to provide efficient outlet ventilators. B, Fig. 41-2.

ventilator opening. Use as coarse a screen as conditions permit, not smaller than No. 16, because lint and dirt tend to clog fine-mesh screens. Screens should be installed in such a way that paint brushes will not easily contact the screen and close the mesh with paint.

Gable Roofs

Louvered openings are generally provided in the end walls of gable roofs. They should be as close to the ridge as possible. The net area for the openings should be ⅓₀₀ of the ceiling area. A, Fig. 41-1. For example, if the ceiling area equals 1,200 square feet,

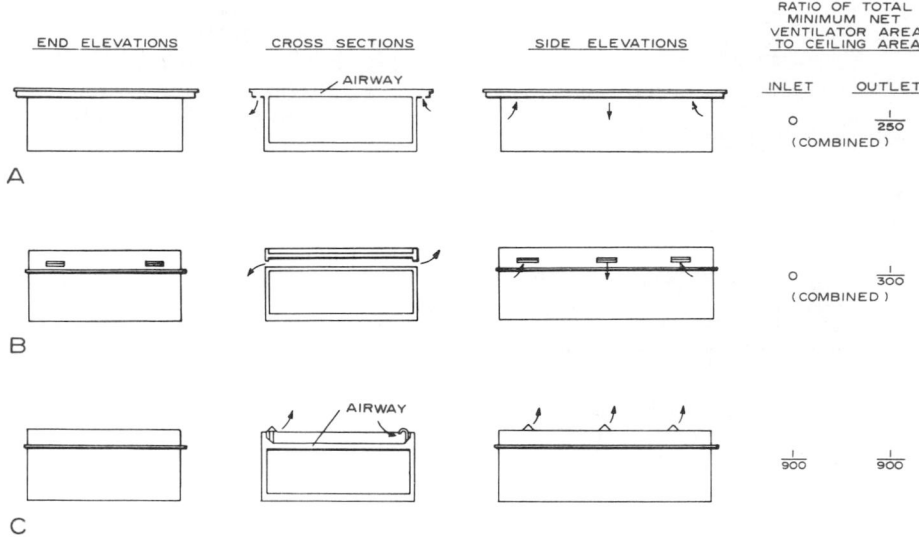

END ELEVATIONS	CROSS SECTIONS	SIDE ELEVATIONS	RATIO OF TOTAL MINIMUM NET VENTILATOR AREA TO CEILING AREA	
			INLET	OUTLET
A	AIRWAY		0	$\frac{1}{250}$ (COMBINED)
B			0	$\frac{1}{300}$ (COMBINED)
C	AIRWAY		$\frac{1}{900}$	$\frac{1}{900}$

41-3. *Flat roof ventilating area: A. Ventilator openings under the overhanging eaves where ceiling and roof joists are combined. B. Ventilating a roof with a parapet where roof and ceiling joists are separate. C. Ventilating a roof with a parapet where roof and ceiling joists are combined.*

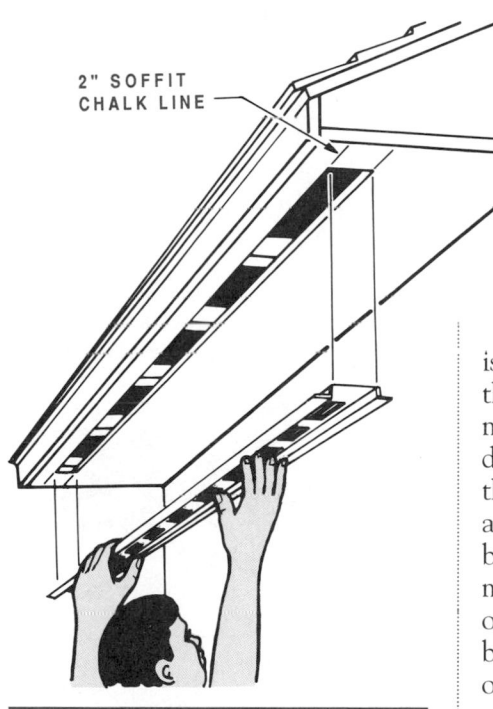

2" SOFFIT CHALK LINE

41-4. *Installing a continuous soffit vent.*

Flat Roofs

A greater ratio of ventilating area is required in some types of flat roofs than in pitched roofs because the air movement is less positive and is dependent upon wind. It is important that there be a clear open space above the ceiling insulation and below the roof sheathing for free air movement from inlet to outlet openings. Solid blocking should not be used for bridging or for bracing over bearing partitions if its use prevents air circulation.

Perhaps the most common type of flat or low-pitched roof is one in which the rafters extend beyond the wall, forming an overhang. A, Fig. 41-3. When soffits are used, this area can contain the combined inlet-outlet ventilators, preferably a continuous slot. When single ventilators are used, they should be distributed evenly along the overhang.

A parapet-type wall and flat roof combination may be constructed with the ceiling joists separate from the roof joists or combined. When members are separate, the space between can be used for an airway. B, Fig. 41-3. Inlet and outlet vents are then located as shown, or a series of outlet stack vents can be used along the centerline of the roof in combination with the inlet vents. When ceiling joists and flat rafters are combined in parapet construction, vents may be located as shown in C, Fig. 41-3. Wall inlet ventilators combined with center stack outlet vents are another option in this type of roof.

OUTLET VENTILATORS

Various styles of gable-end ventilators are available ready for installation. Fig. 41-6. Many are made with metal louvers and frames, while others may be made of wood or vinyl to fit the house design more closely. However, the most important considerations are to have sufficient net ventilating area and to locate ventilators as close to the ridge as possible.

One of the types commonly used fits the slope of the roof and is located near the ridge. A, Fig. 41-7. It can be made of wood or metal. In metal it is often adjustable to conform to the roof slope. A wood ventilator of this type is enclosed in a frame and placed in the rough opening much as a window frame. B, Fig. 41-7. Other forms of gable-end ventilators which might be used are also shown in Fig. 41-7.

Another system of attic ventilation can be used on houses with a wide roof overhang at the gable end. It consists of a series of

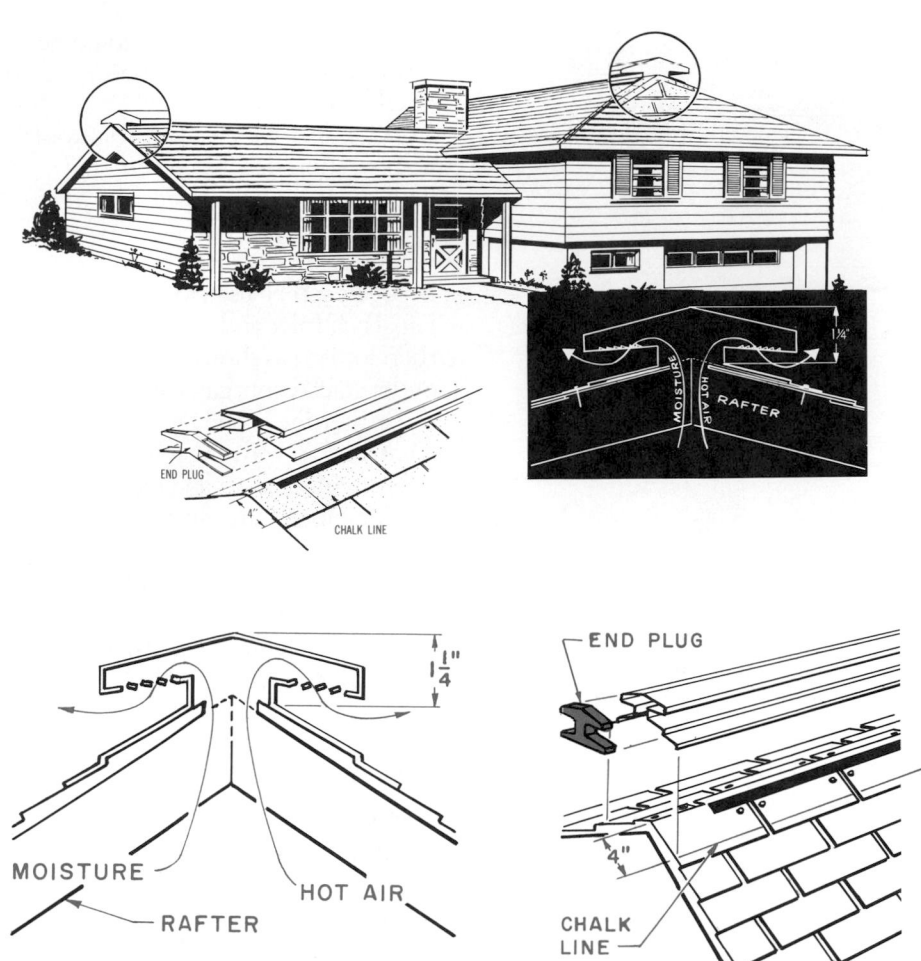

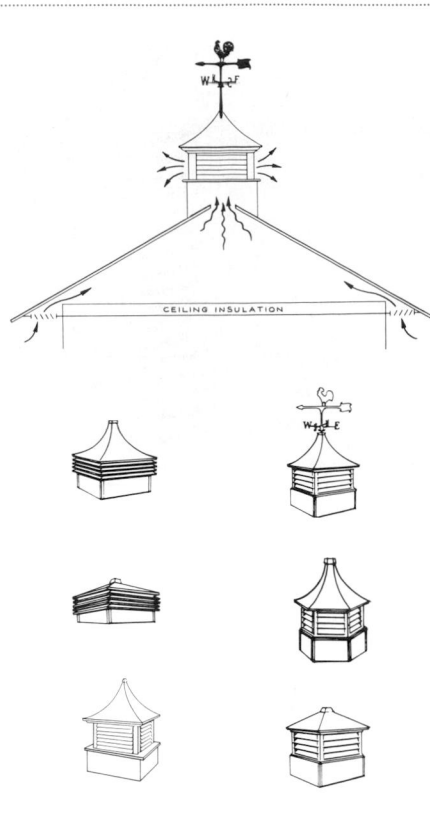

41-5a. *A continuous vent at the ridge.*

41-5c. *Cupolas are available in a variety of styles for venting at the ridge.*

41-5b. *Some continuous ridge vents can be capped with shingles. This helps the vent blend with the roof.*

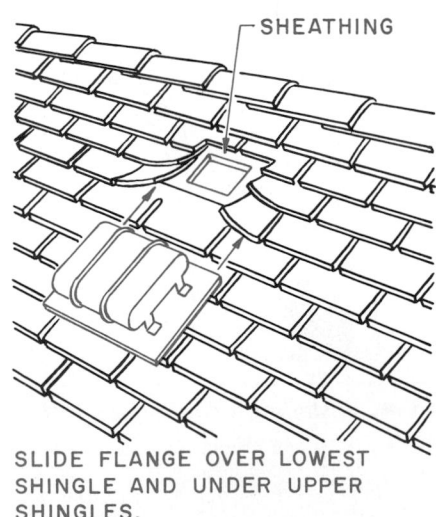

SHEATHING

SLIDE FLANGE OVER LOWEST SHINGLE AND UNDER UPPER SHINGLES.

41-5d. *Pitched roof ventilators are installed below the ridge on the rear slope of the roof.*

41-6a. *This vinyl gable-end louver is matched in color and finish to vinyl siding.*

41-6b. *This solid cedar gable vent complements wood siding.*

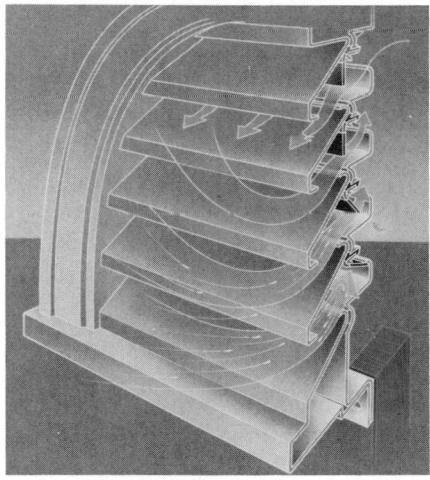

41-6c. *Some gable vents incorporate flexible flaps that reduce the chance for rain to enter the vent.*

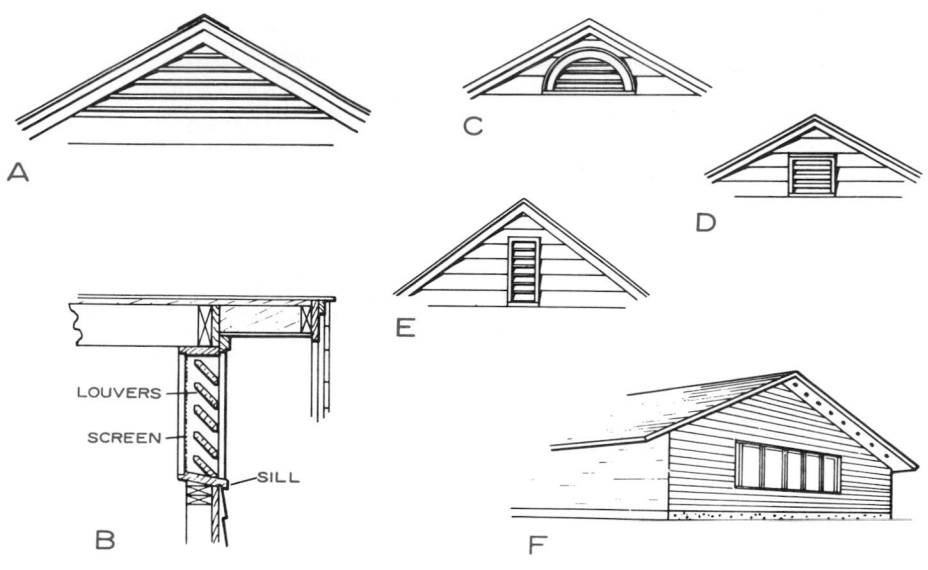

41-7. *A variety of outlet ventilators: A. Triangular. B. Typical ventilator cross-section. C. Half-circle. D. Square. E. Vertical. F. Soffit.*

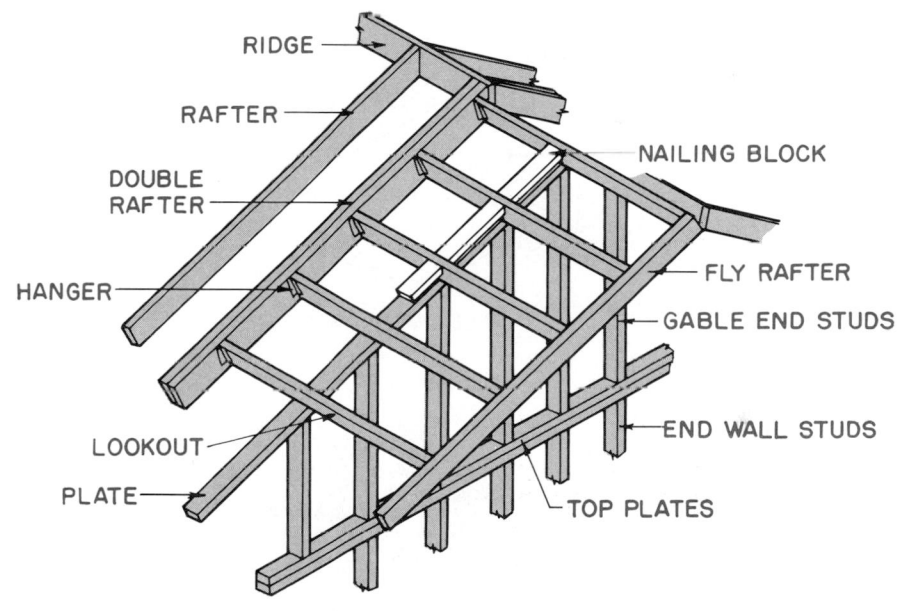

41-8. *The nailing blocks are laid out flat on the plate to allow airways into the attic.*

small vents or a continuous slot located on the underside of the soffit areas. F, Fig. 41-7. Several large openings located near the ridge might also be used. This system is especially desirable on low-pitched roofs where standard wall ventilators may not be suitable.

It is important that the roof framing at the wall line does not block off ventilation spaces to the attic area. Ventilation space might be provided by the use of a "ladder" frame extension. A flat nailing block used at the wall line will provide airways into the attic. Fig. 41-8. This can also be adapted to narrower rake sections, providing ventilating areas to the attic.

INLET VENTILATORS

Small, well-distributed ventilators or a continuous slot in the soffit provide inlet ventilation. These small louvered and screened vents can be obtained in most lumberyards or hardware stores and are simple to install.

Only small sections need to be cut out of the soffit. These can be sawed out before the soffit is applied. It is more desirable to use a number of smaller well-distributed ventilators than several large ones. A, Fig. 41-9. Any blocking which might be required between rafters at the wall line should be installed so as to provide an airway into the attic area.

A continuous screened slot is often desirable. It should be located near the outer edge of the soffit near the fascia. B, Fig. 41-9. Locating the slot in this area will minimize the chances of snow entering. This type may also be used on the extension of flat roofs.

CRAWL-SPACE VENTILATION AND SOIL COVER

The crawl space below the floor of a basementless house and under porches should be ventilated and protected from ground moisture by the use of a soil cover. Fig. 41-10. The soil cover should be a vapor barrier such as plastic film, roll roofing, or asphalt-laminated paper. Such protection will minimize the effect of ground moisture on the wood framing members. High moisture content and humidity encourage staining and decay of untreated members.

Where there is a partial basement open to a crawl-space area, no wall vents are required if there is some type of operable window. The use of a soil cover in the crawl space is still important, however.

For crawl spaces with no basement area provide at least four foundation wall vents near corners of the building. The total free (net) area of the ventilators should be equal to $\frac{1}{160}$ of the ground area when no soil cover is used. Thus, for a ground area of 1,200 square feet, a total net ventilating area of about 8 square feet is required, or 2 square feet for each of four ventilators. A greater number of smaller ventilators having the same net ratio would also provide satisfactory ventilation.

When a vapor-barrier ground cover is used, the required

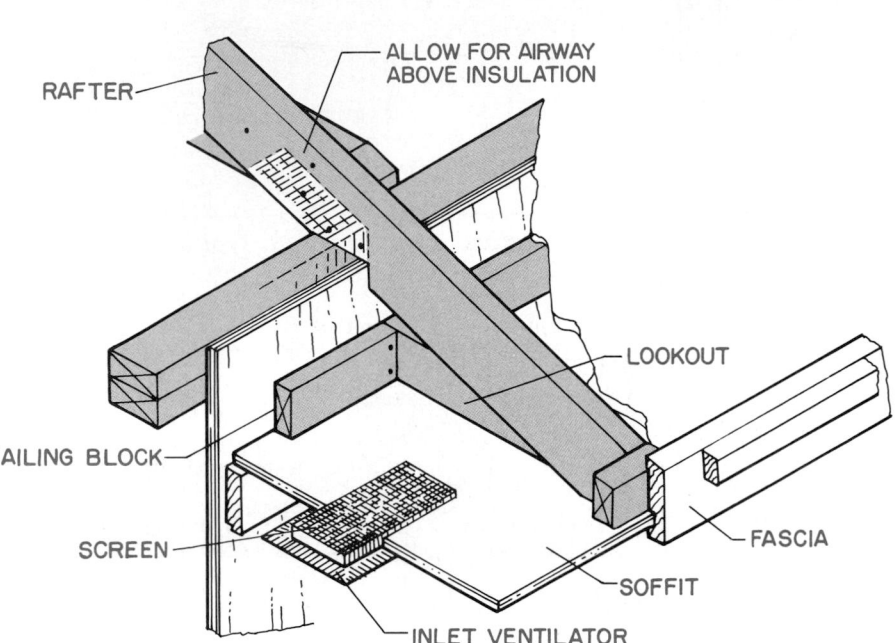

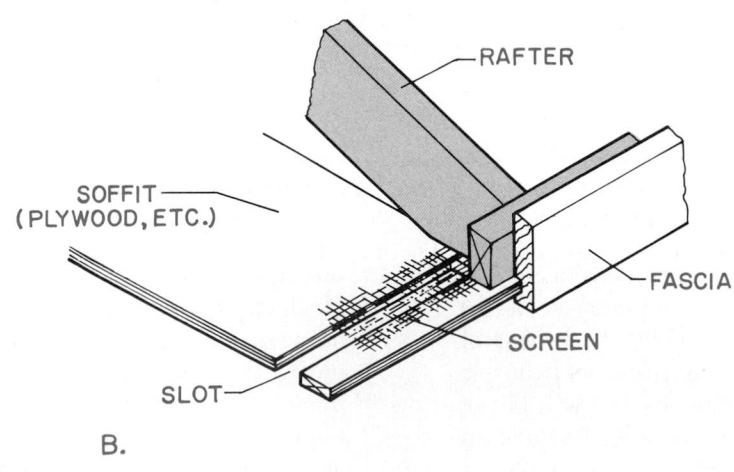

41-9. *Inlet soffit ventilators: A. A small insert ventilator. B. A slot ventilator.*

ventilating area is ¹⁄₁₆₀₀ of the ground area. For the 1,200-square-foot house, this would be 0.75 square foot. This area should be divided between two small ventilators located on opposite sides of the crawl space. Vents should be covered with a corrosion-resistant screen of No. 8 mesh. Fig. 41-10.

The use of a ground cover is recommended under all conditions. It not only protects wood framing members from ground moisture but also allows the use of small, inconspicuous ventilators.

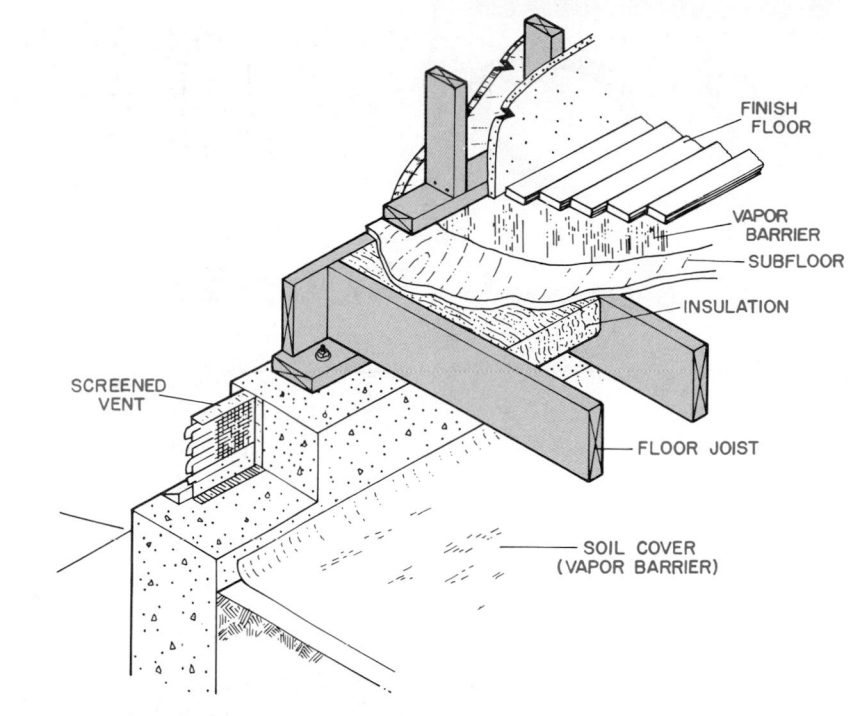

41-10. *A ventilated crawl space with vapor barrier.*

QUESTIONS

1. What is the most practical method of removing the moisture in a home?

2. What is meant by an ice dam?

3. What is the minimum net ventilator area required for a gable-roof home with an area of 1,950 square feet?

4. Why is a greater ratio of ventilating area required in flat roofs than in pitched roofs?

5. Why is the use of ground cover recommended in crawl-space areas?

ACTIVITIES

1. Language Arts. This unit mentions that "In recent years there have been remarkable changes in the methods and materials used in house construction." Compare the construction of a typical ranch home in the 1940s to a typical ranch today. Pick four major areas where there have been changes. You might, for example, compare windows, ventilation systems, building drainage, and exterior siding. Do research in your local library. You might also talk to a builder who may have knowledge of houses built in the 1940s, those built during the ensuing years, and those built at the present. Use the text material in this unit for information on present-day methods. Write down your findings in a three-paragraph comparison essay.

2. Math. For a rectangular house with outside dimensions of 34' by 46', polyethylene film is to be used as the vapor barrier for the walls, the attic, and the crawl space. If the house has 8' walls, how many square feet of film are needed?

3. Math. A gable roof house with 1,250 square feet of floor has 6 square feet of vent space in the gable ends and 2.5 square feet of vent space in the soffit. Is this adequate ventilation for the attic? If it is, how much excess is there? If it is not, how much more is required?

42

Roof Trim

The architectural style of a house is often evident from the type and variety of trim surrounding the roof. This trim can take a variety of forms, including molding along the gables, decorative cuts made in exposed rafter tails, and various types of soffit construction. Fig. 42-1.

The rafter-end overhangs of a roof are called the *eaves*. For example, on a hip roof, all four edges—the sides and ends—of the roof have eaves. A gable roof, however, has eaves only on the side-wall edges. The gable-end (end-wall) edges are called *rakes*. The exterior finish at and just below the eaves is called the *cornice*.

The cornice work may be done as soon as the roof has been framed. It may also, with the exception of the fascia, be done after the roofing has been applied. In most geographical areas, workers will put on the roof covering first to protect the structure from the weather. The rake molding on a gable roof,

42-1a. *The trim on a house should be consistent with the style of the house.*

42-1b. *These rafter tails were shaped with a jigsaw and a router.*

42-1c. *This trim accentuates the gable.*

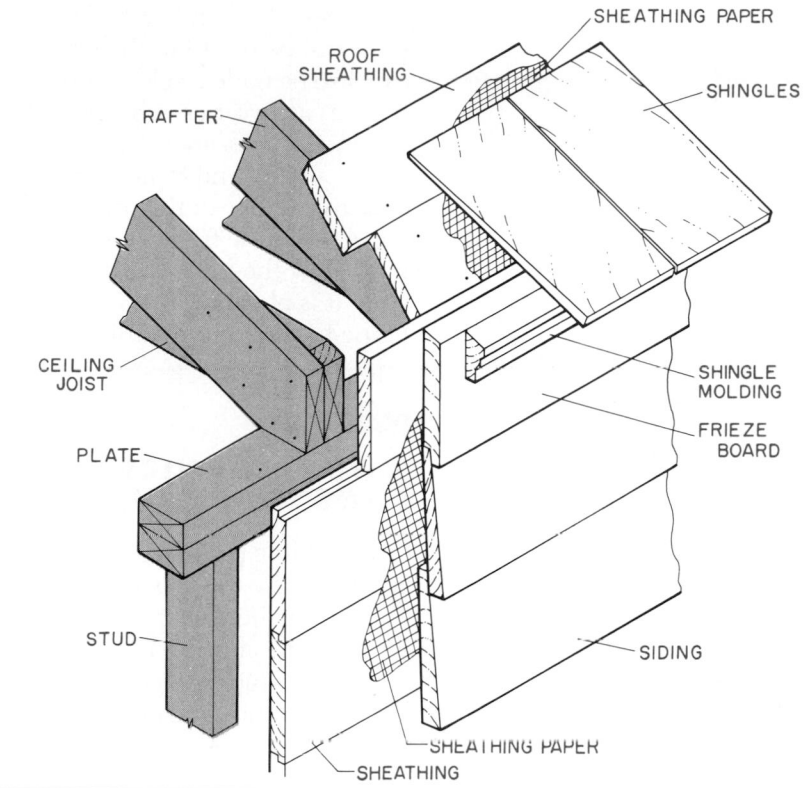

42-2. *A closed cornice.*

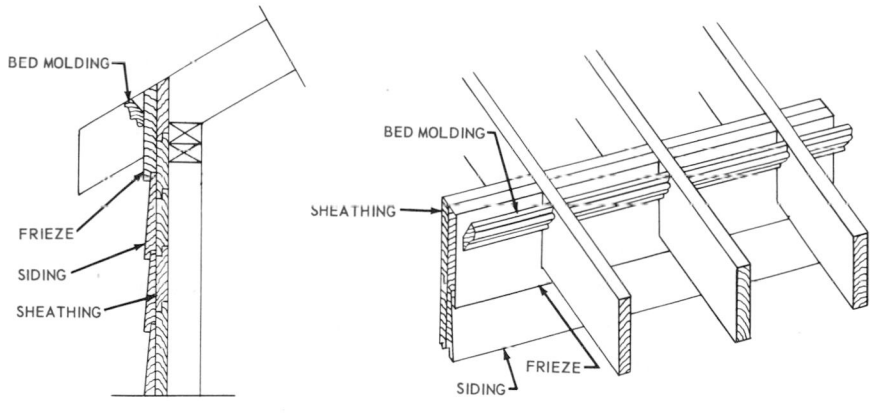

42-3. *Simplest type of open cornice.*

however, must be installed before the roofing.

TYPES OF CORNICES

The type of cornice required for a particular structure is shown on the wall sections of the house plans, and there are usually cornice detail drawings as well. Basically, there are three types of cornices:

➤ Closed.
➤ Open.
➤ Box.

A roof with no rafter overhang normally has a closed cornice. Fig. 42-2. This cornice consists of a single strip called a *frieze*. The frieze is beveled on its upper edge to fit close under the overhang of the eaves and rabbeted on its lower edge to overlap the upper edge of the top siding course. If trim is used, it usually consists of molding installed as shown in Fig. 42-2. Molding trim in this position is called *crown* or *shingle molding*.

A roof with a rafter overhang may have either an open cornice or a box cornice. The simplest type of open cornice consists of only a frieze, which must be notched to fit around the rafters. Fig. 42-3. If trim is used, it usually consists of molding cut to fit between the rafters. Molding in this position is called *bed molding*.

Another type of open cornice consists of a frieze and a fascia. Fig. 42-4. A *fascia* is a strip nailed to the tail plumb cuts of the rafters. Shingle molding can be attached to the top of the fascia, but it is seldom used.

With a box cornice, the rafter overhang is entirely boxed in by the roof covering, the fascia, and a bottom strip called a *plancier*, or

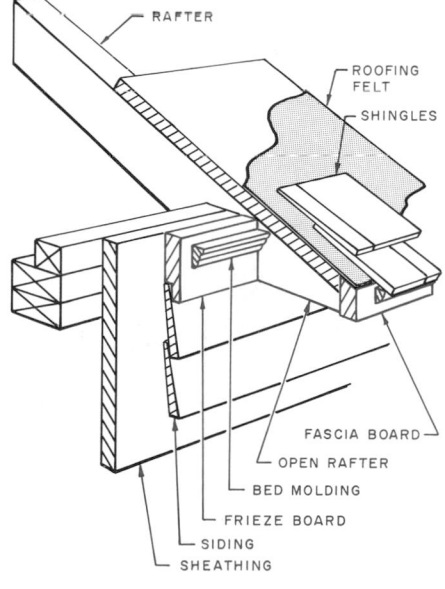

42-4a. *An open cornice with a fascia board.*

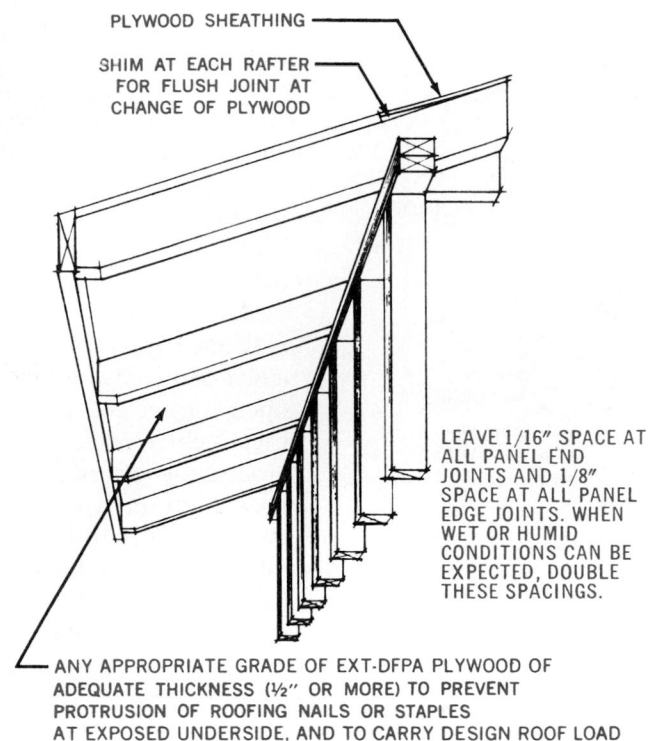

PLYWOOD SHEATHING

SHIM AT EACH RAFTER
FOR FLUSH JOINT AT
CHANGE OF PLYWOOD

LEAVE 1/16" SPACE AT
ALL PANEL END
JOINTS AND 1/8"
SPACE AT ALL PANEL
EDGE JOINTS. WHEN
WET OR HUMID
CONDITIONS CAN BE
EXPECTED, DOUBLE
THESE SPACINGS.

ANY APPROPRIATE GRADE OF EXT-DFPA PLYWOOD OF
ADEQUATE THICKNESS (½" OR MORE) TO PREVENT
PROTRUSION OF ROOFING NAILS OR STAPLES
AT EXPOSED UNDERSIDE, AND TO CARRY DESIGN ROOF LOAD

42-4b. *An open cornice, sometimes referred to as an open soffit, with plywood sheathing.*

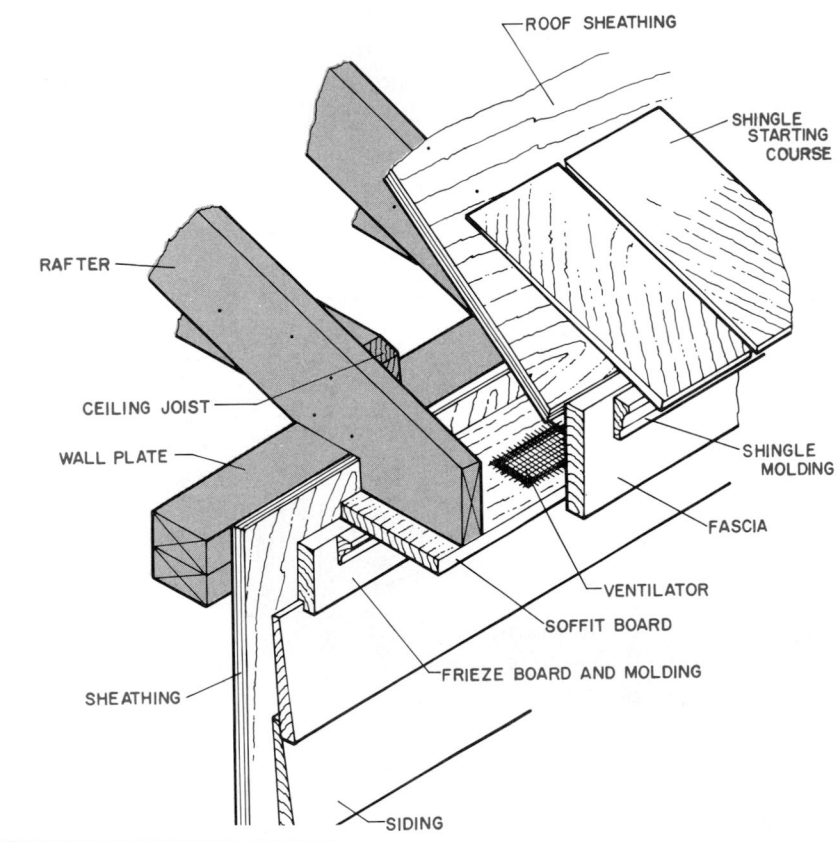

ROOF SHEATHING

SHINGLE
STARTING
COURSE

RAFTER

CEILING JOIST

WALL PLATE

SHINGLE
MOLDING

FASCIA

VENTILATOR

SOFFIT BOARD

FRIEZE BOARD AND MOLDING

SHEATHING

SIDING

42-5. *A narrow box cornice.*

soffit. Figs. 42-5 and 42-6. The soffit can be nailed to the rafters. It can also be nailed to lookouts. The *lookouts* are a series of horizontal members which are nailed to the rafters and extend from the rafter ends to the face of the sheathing. Fig. 42-6b. The frieze, if any, is set just below the lookouts. If trim is used, it is placed at the intersection of the frieze and the soffit.

WOOD CORNICE CONSTRUCTION

If building paper is used on the sidewalls, the top course of paper must be applied before beginning work on the cornice. For an open or a box cornice the paper must be slit to fit around the rafters.

Open Cornice

One method of constructing an open cornice is to measure the distance between the rafter at either the top or bottom edge. Fig. 42-7. Cut material to this length, making sure that both ends are cut square. Do this for each rafter spacing. Nail the material in position, as shown at A in Fig. 42-8. The nails can be driven through the side of the rafter into the end of the block on one side. Nails will have to be toenailed on the other side, as the block installed previously gets in the way for nailing. Fig. 42-9.

If vents are needed, determine their location and bore the necessary holes. Staple or tack a piece of window screen on the back of the vent openings. Fig. 42-7.

If tongued and grooved material is to be used on the roof, nail the material on the rafters with the good surface down since it will be visible from below. Fig. 42-10. Remove the groove from the starter board. Bevel the edge if desired. Place the starter board in position along the top of the

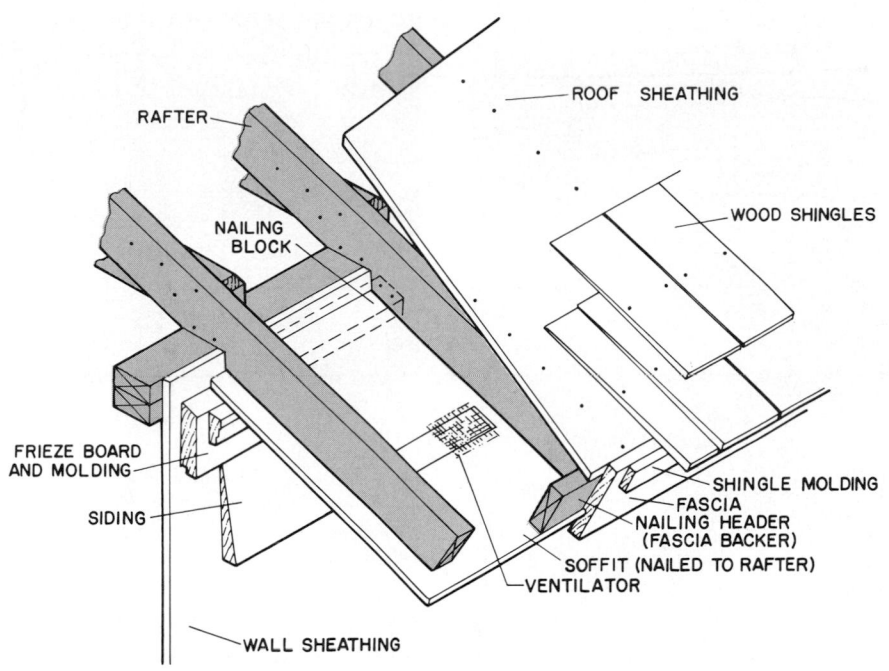

42-6a. *A box cornice with a sloping soffit.*

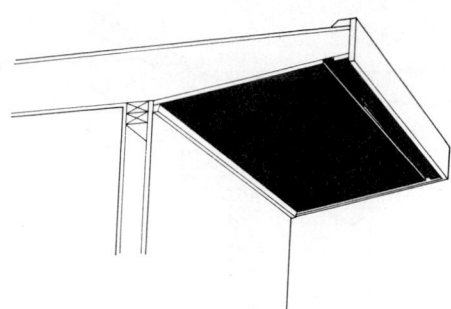

42-6c. *The box cornice on this flat roof overhang has a tapered soffit.*

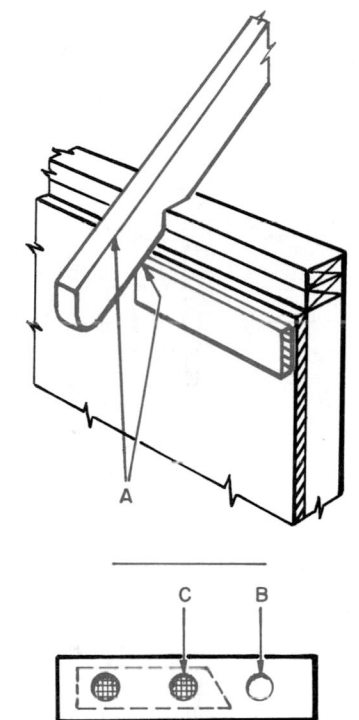

42-7. *Determining the length of blocking needed for an open cornice. Measuring may be done at either the top or bottom edge of the rafter, as shown by the arrows at A. For ventilation, the blocking should be drilled as shown at B and then screening stapled behind the holes as shown at C.*

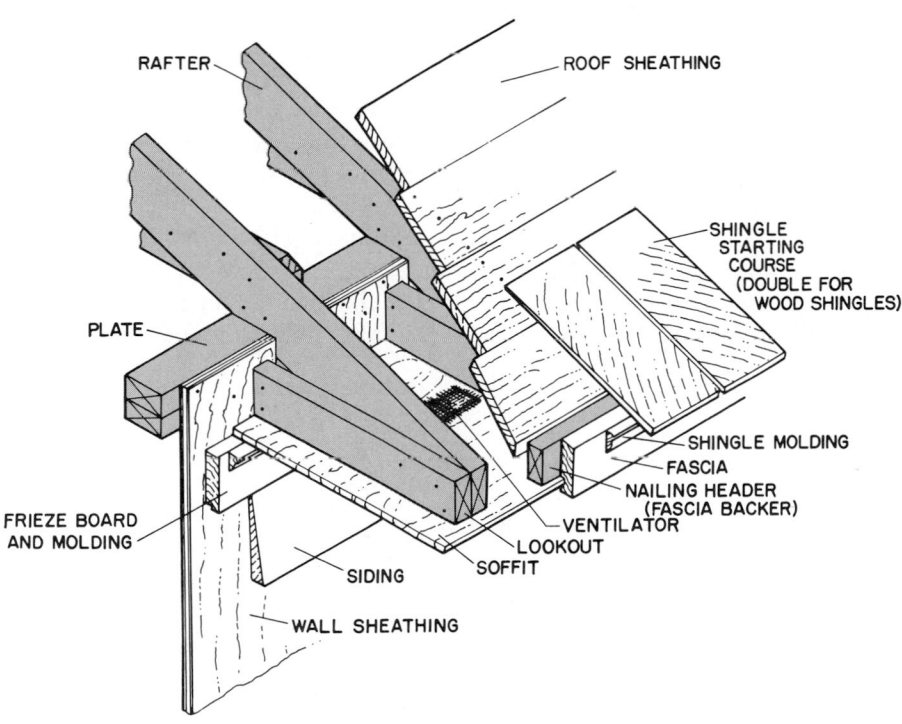

42-6b. *A box cornice with a flat soffit. Note that the soffit is nailed to lookouts.*

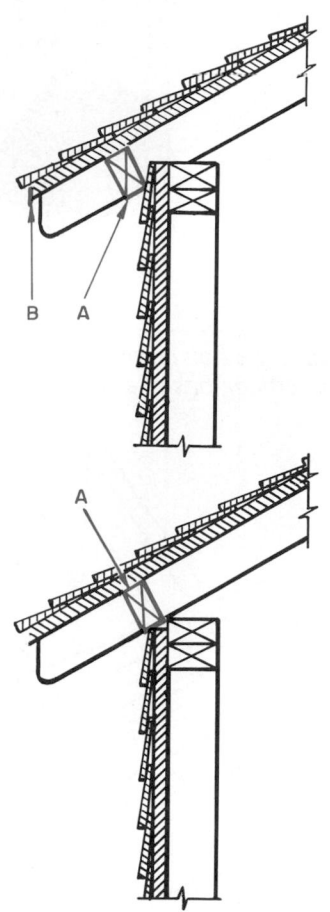

42-8. *The location of the blocking used in the open cornice is determined by the bird's-mouth in the rafter as shown at A in both drawings. Notice that the roof board at B in the first drawing has been beveled on the edge to conform to the roof pitch.*

42-9. *Nailing the blocking in place on an open cornice. Notice the vent holes which have been drilled in some of the blocks.*

42-10. *This open cornice was extended to serve as a roof for the porch area. Notice that the roof board material needs to be carefully selected and applied because it is clearly visible from below.*

rafter tail and align it before nailing it in place. B, Fig. 42-8. The type of sheathing used above the blocking will depend on the kind of roof covering. Plywood or lumber sheathing may be chosen.

All joints in the construction of an open cornice should be planed smooth and fitted together tightly. All moldings must be mitered for joining on outside corners and mitered or coped (see Unit 54) for joining on inside corners. Care should be taken in this type of cornice construction because the workmanship is readily visible from the ground.

Box Cornice

Before adding a box cornice, check the plumb cuts on the rafter tails to make certain they are all in line. This can be done by stretching a line along the top ends

42-11. *Cutting off the rafter tails after the rafters have been nailed in place.*

of the rafters from one corner of the building to the other. Many carpenters do not make the plumb cut on the rafter tails when the rafter is cut. Instead, the rafters are nailed in place with the tails projecting beyond the exterior wall at various lengths. Then the point at which the tails are to be cut off is determined, and a chalk line is snapped along the top edge of the rafter tails. The plumb line is drawn down the side of each rafter from this line. Each rafter tail is then cut off along this plumb line. Fig. 42-11.

Lookouts.

1. Use a piece of 1" × 4" material to serve as a ledger. Nail it temporarily against the exterior wall tight up under the rafters and aligned with the inside edge of the first rafter. Fig. 42-12. With a straightedge against the side of the rafter, make a line on the surface of the ledger. Place an *x* on the side of the line away from the underside of the rafter to indicate the location of the lookout. Do this along the entire length of the building.

2. Determine the length of the lookouts. Measure on a level line from the plumb cut on the rafter tail to the wall of the building. Subtract ¾" from this measurement to allow for the thickness of the nominal 1" × 4" ledger to which the lookouts will be nailed. Subtract another ¾" to make sure that the lookouts do not project beyond the end of the rafters. Otherwise, if there is any deviation in the alignment of the exterior wall, such as a slight bow or crooked stud, the lookout may extend beyond the end of the rafter tail. This will interfere later with the proper installation and alignment of the fascia board.

3. After the lookouts have been cut to length, remove the ledger from its temporary nailing and nail the lookouts to the ledger over the Xs. Nail through the back of the ledger into the end of the lookout with two 8d coated nails. Nail the last lookout into the end of the strip. Fig. 42-13. The lookouts may be made from either 2 × 4s or 1 × 4s. If 1 × 4s are used, place a 2 × 4 for additional nailing surface wherever the soffit pieces must be joined. Fig. 42-14.

4. Locate the position of the ledger on the exterior wall by leveling from the rafter tail in toward the wall and placing a mark on the sheathing. Point B, Fig. 42-15. Do this at each end of the building. Then snap a chalk line along the full length of the building on the sheathing.

5. Place bottom edge of ledger on this line. Nail it to studs through sheathing. Nail each lookout to side of rafter tail, except end lookout, which is nailed under rafter. Level each lookout as it is nailed.

Fascia Board. Lay out, rip (if necessary), and groove the fascia board. The groove is made in the

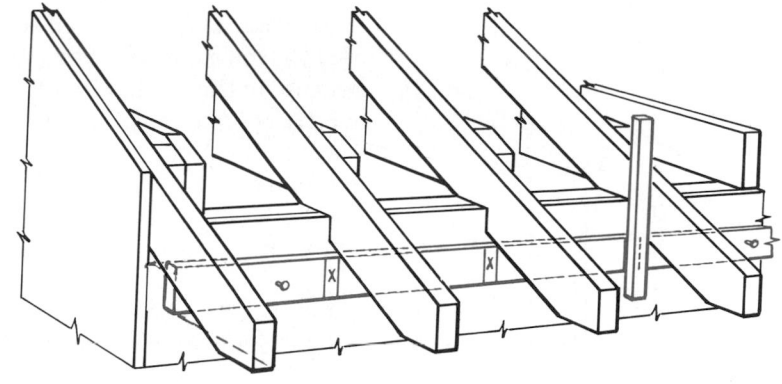

42-12. *Temporarily nail the ledger strip up under the rafters. Then mark the location of the lookouts.*

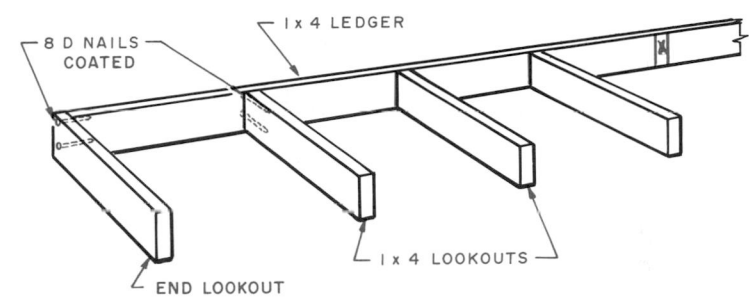

42-13. *The lookouts are nailed to the ledger strip next to the line and over the X made earlier. Note that the end lookout is nailed into the end of the ledger strip. This means that the end lookout has to be of the same thickness as the rafter and longer than the rest of the lookouts. It will have to be cut to fit under the rafter tail.*

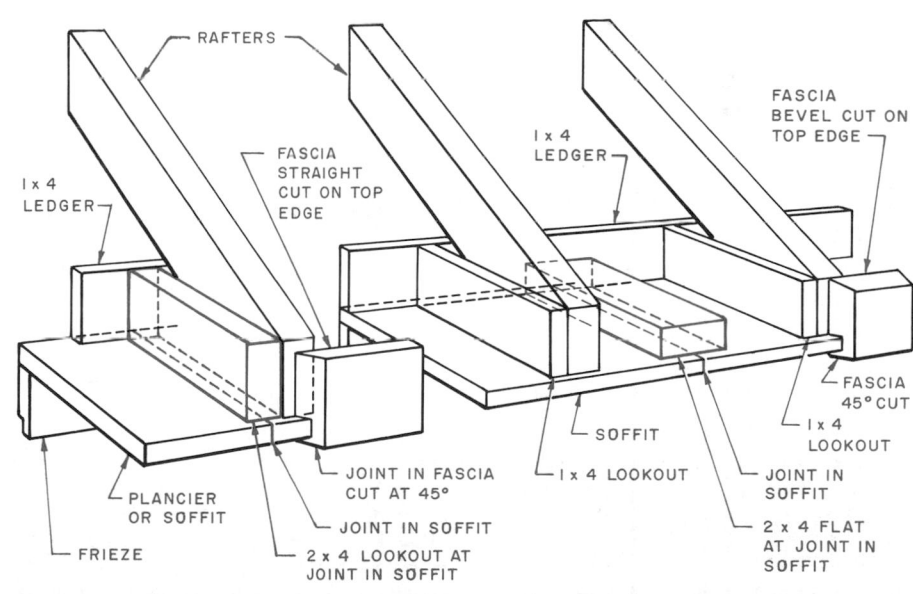

42-14. *The soffit material must be supported wherever it is joined together. If possible, the joints are usually located under a lookout. However, rather than cut the soffit off, nail a 2 × 4 laid flat from the ledger strip to the fascia over the soffit joint.*

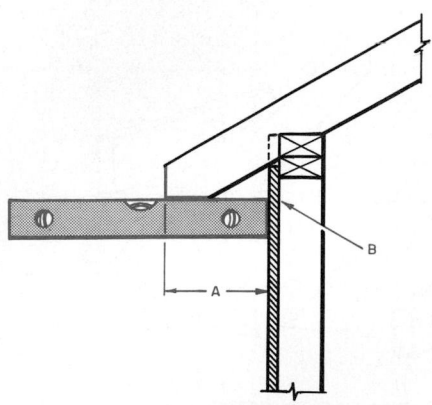

42-15. *To locate the position of the ledger strip on the side wall of the building (point B), level a line in from the rafter tail as shown at A. The rafters are usually cut off before the ledger strip is located on the building. However, in some cases, point B is located on the building first. The cutoff line on the bottom of the rafter tail is then marked by leveling out from point B.*

Soffit. Several materials may be used for the soffit on a box cornice. Because of the popularity of wide overhangs, materials which are available in large sheets are frequently used. These include plywood, gypsum board, and hardboard.

Plywood. This is one of the most popular materials for a box cornice. It simplifies construction and presents a smooth, attractive surface. Plywood also has the advantage of matching other wood surfaces when a stained wood grain finish is desirable.

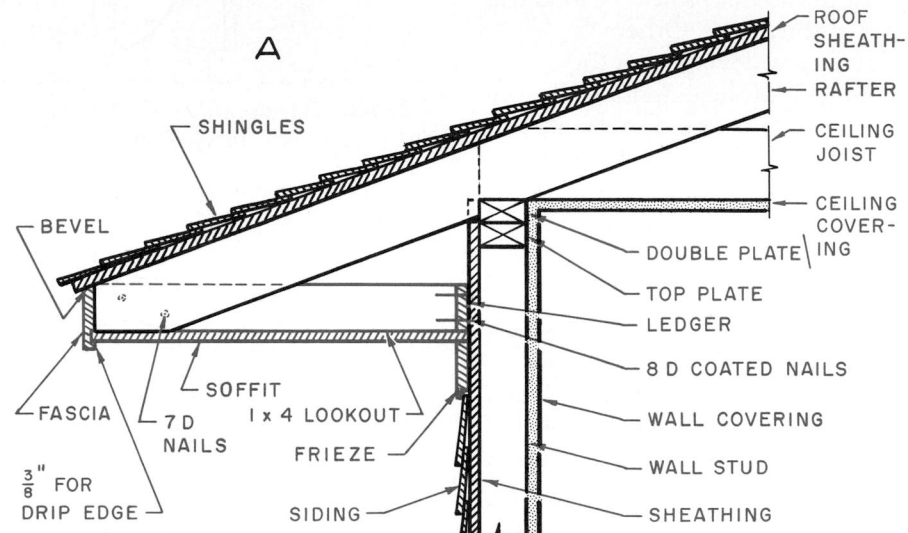

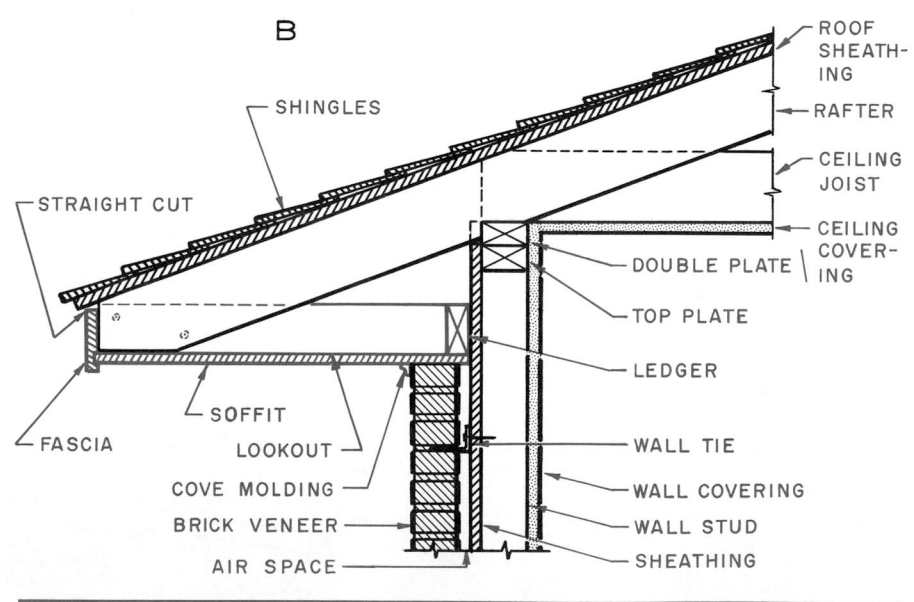

42-16. *The fascia board may be nailed to the ends of the rafters using either of the methods shown here. Bevel the top edge of the fascia board to conform to the roof pitch, as at A. Or rip the fascia board to width so that the outside top corner is in line with the top edge of the rafter, as at B. In either case, when the roof sheathing is applied it must lie flat. Notice also that the top edge of the groove in the fascia must be in line with the bottom edge of the lookout for proper installation of the soffit material.*

fascia board to receive the soffit. It should be cut about ⅜" up from the bottom edge of the fascia. This is done to provide a drip edge which prevents water from backing up into the groove.

Nail the fascia board in position along the ends of the rafter tails with the top of the groove even with the bottom edge of the lookouts. Fig. 42-16. If the fascia board must be spliced, it should be done with the joint on the end of a rafter tail, and the joint should be mitered. Fig. 42-17. The top edge of the fascia board may be beveled to the same angle as the pitch of the roof. If it is not, make certain that the fascia board is installed with its top outer edge in line with the top surface of the roof sheathing. Fig. 42-16. Make certain that the fascia is straight along its length. If necessary, straighten the fascia by driving shims between the rafter tail ends and the inside of the fascia board.

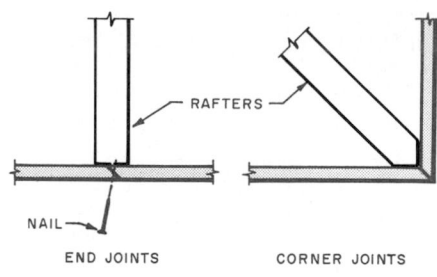

42-17. *On a hip roof the fascia is mitered at the corner on the end of the hip rafter. On any roof where the fascia must be joined, join it on a rafter end. Miter the joint as shown.*

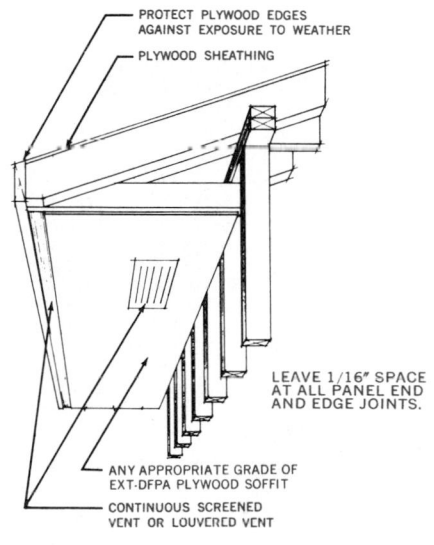

42-18. *Plywood is frequently used for soffit material on a box soffit, but certain precautions should be taken, as shown here.*

The recommended spans for box soffits are shown in Table 42-A. Exterior plywood should be used wherever the underside of the roof deck is exposed to the weather. Fig. 42-18.

To install plywood soffit, rip the soffit to width and slip the outer edge into the fascia groove. Then push the inside edge up against the lookouts and ledger strip. Nail the soffit securely to the ledger and to each lookout with 4d nails. The

nails should be spaced about 6" apart. If the soffit has to be made up of several pieces, join it under a lookout. If this is not possible, a 2 × 4 can be laid flat, toenailed into the ledger, and face-nailed through the fascia. The two pieces of soffit can then be joined under the center of the flat side of the 2 × 4. This will give adequate nail backing for the joint. Fig. 42-14.

Hardboard. Hardboard panels are frequently used for soffits on the undersides of eaves and the ceilings of porches, breezeways, and carports. If the hardboard does not have a factory-applied primer, the

panel should be conditioned prior to use. Follow the manufacturer's recommendations included in each product bundle. The soffit framing must provide continuous support at the edges, ends of panels, and joints.

The installation of hardboard soffits is similar to plywood soffit installation. Fasten the panels with 5d galvanized box, siding, or sinker nails. Space the nails 4" on center around edges and approximately 6" on center at intermediate supports. Never nail closer than ⅜" to the edge. Fig. 42-19a. Metal moldings are available for use in the

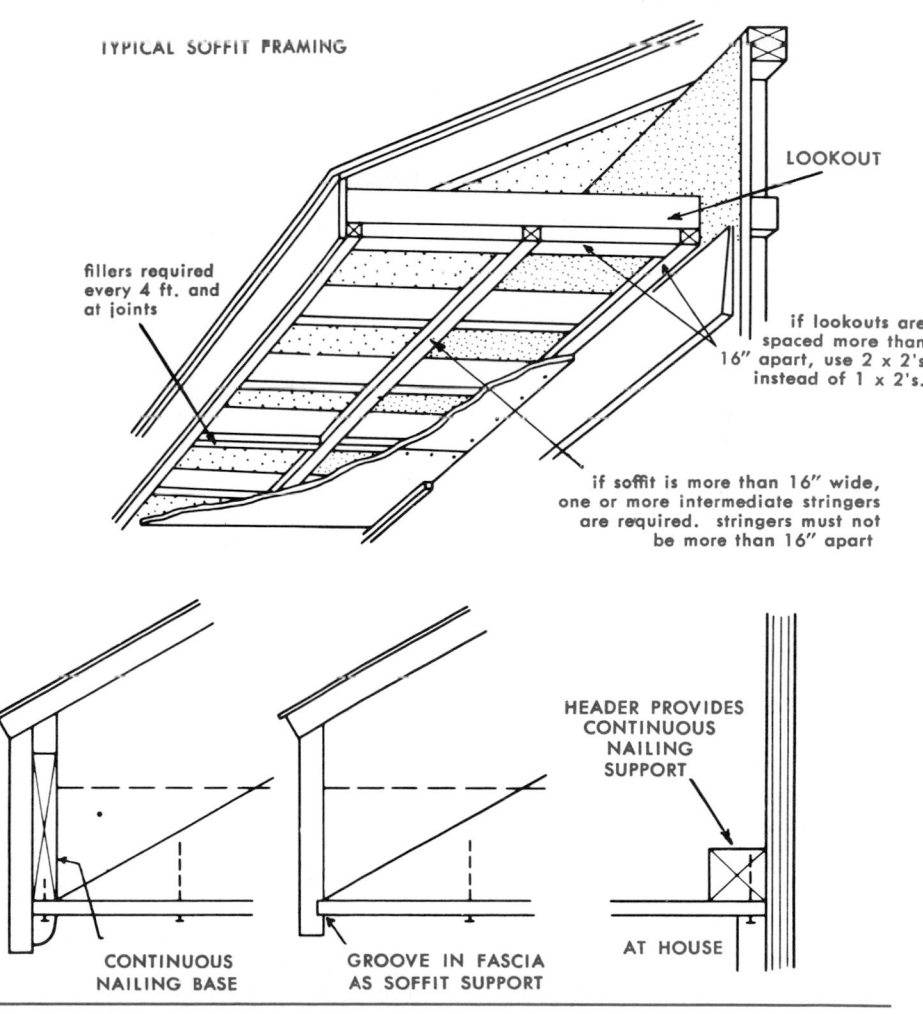

42-19a. *Hardboard soffits should be supported as shown. Nail them 4" on center around the edges and 6" on center at the intermediate supports.*

Table 42-A. *Soffit Support Spacing. This table indicates the maximum spacing of supports for various thicknesses of box (closed) plywood soffits. It also gives the correct nail sizes and spacing to be used.*

Exterior plywood soffits (closed)/ (Plywood continues over two or more spans; grain of face plys across supports)

Plywood Thickness (inch)	Closed Soffits			Nail		Nail Spacing (inches)	
	Group	Max. Spacing of Supports c. to c. (inches)	Size	Type		Panel Edges	Intermediate (each support)
3/8	1, 2, 3, or 4	24	6d	Non-corrosive type (galv. or alum.)		6 (or one nail each support)	12
5/8		48	8d	Box or casing			12

Use plywood with these typical APA grade trademarks.

Sanded Grades
A-C
GROUP 2
EXTERIOR
PS 1-74 000
(APA)

Specialty Panels
303 SIDING 16 oc
GROUP 3
EXTERIOR
PS 1-74 000
(APA)

M.D. OVERLAY
GROUP 1
EXTERIOR
PS 1-74 000
(APA)

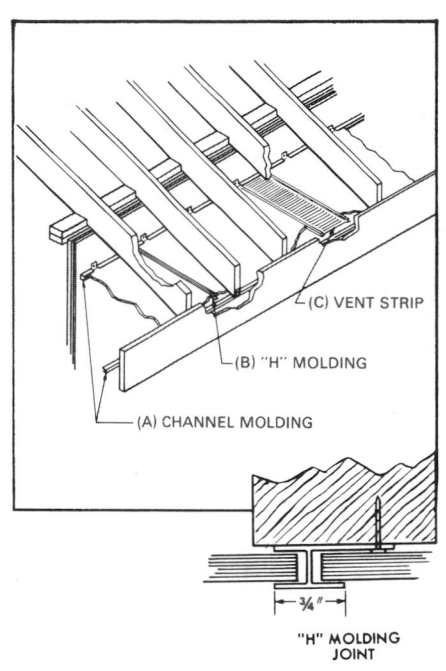

42-19b. *The channel molding (A) is attached to the exterior sidewall and to the inside of the fascia board to support the hardboard soffit. The H molding (B) is a divider strip. If desired, a vent strip (C) may be used in place of or in addition to the H molding.*

(C) VENT STRIP
(B) "H" MOLDING
(A) CHANNEL MOLDING

3/4"
"H" MOLDING JOINT

installation of hardboard soffit material. With these moldings, there are no exposed nailheads on soffits 2' or less in width. Fig. 42-19b.

METAL CORNICE CONSTRUCTION

Metal cornice material may be used for box cornices on most roofs, entryways, porches, and carport ceilings. This aluminum system requires little maintenance, is self-ventilating and self-supporting, and will not rust. It is entirely prefinished. Fig. 42-20. The ribbed soffit material may be nonperforated or it may be perforated to give approximately 8% open area. It comes in coils usually 50' long and of various widths. Fig. 42-21a.

Installation

It is important to plan the sequence of operation. The soffit material is pulled from coils and fed between the fascia and frieze runner guides into its proper position. Therefore one end of a soffit run cannot be closed off with enclosures, fascia runners, or

42-20. *An aluminum soffit.*

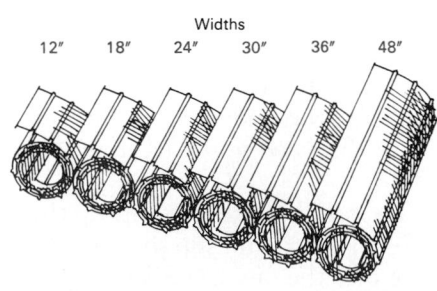

Widths
12" 18" 24" 30" 36" 48"

42-21a. *Aluminum soffit material is available in 50' coils, perforated or nonperforated, in various widths.*

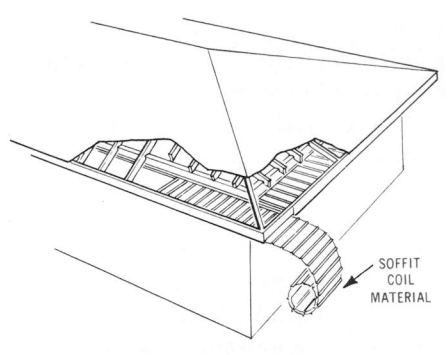

42-21b. *Aluminum soffit material is pulled from coils and fed into the fascia and frieze runner guides.*

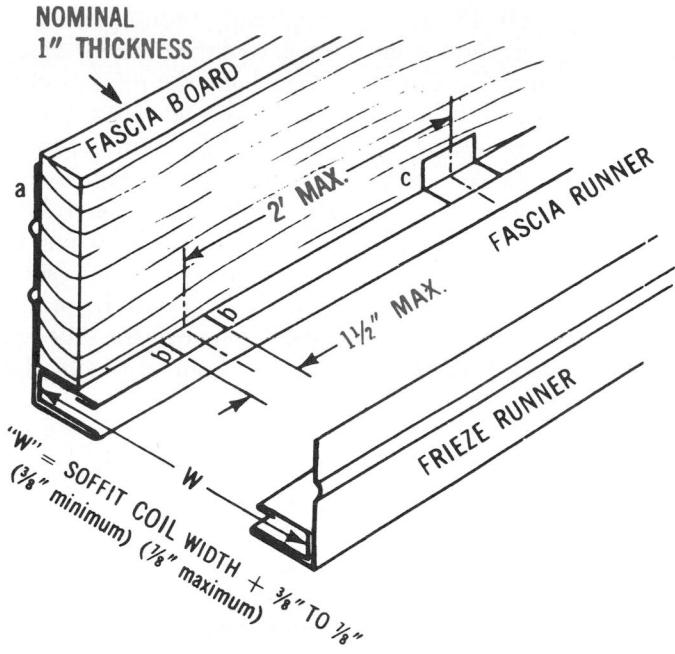

42-22. *The fascia runner is attached to the fascia board by notching (b) and then bending the tab up (c). This will hold the fascia runner in tightly against the fascia board at the bottom.*

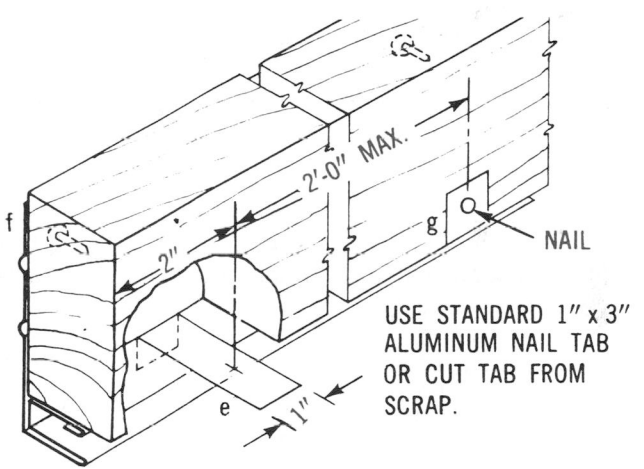

42-23. *When the fascia board is thicker than 1", special tabs about 1" wide are inserted (e), bent, and nailed (g). To provide for expansion and extraction, allow 1/16" minimum spacing between the fascia channels at lap joints. Do not secure the fascias to each other by nails, pop rivets, or screws. The tabs will hold the fascia runner in tightly against the bottom of the fascia board.*

extensions of frieze runners until the respective runs of soffit material are in place. Fig. 42-21b. To illustrate metal cornice construction, this section describes the installation procedure for a box cornice on a hip roof.

Fascia Runners. Hang the fascia level, using a chalk line for alignment. Do not force the aluminum or metal fascia to conform to the wood to which it is being attached.

Secure the top edge of the fascia runner to the fascia with 1½" spiral-shank aluminum nails. Place the nails no more than 2' apart along the length of the fascia.

Make two cuts 1" to 1½" apart and about ⅝" deep into the top flange of the runner's guide. Fig. 42-22 at B. While holding the fascia runner flush against the outside face of the fascia board, bend the 1" to 1½" tab up against the inside face of the fascia board. Fig. 42-22 at C. When bending the tab, make sure that the top flange of the runner's guide is still straight. If not, straighten as necessary. Cut and bend as many of these tabs as necessary to hold the fascia runner in place. Space the tabs not more than 2' apart.

If the fascia board is thicker than

1", the runner will not be wide enough for a tab. In that case, cut some nailing tabs from scrap material about 1" wide. Insert the nailing tabs into the slot between the fascia and channel runner. Fig.

42-23 at E. Secure the fascia runner as described previously. Bend the tabs up against the inside of the fascia board. Secure with a 1½" spiral-shank aluminum nail. Refer to Fig. 42-23 at G.

Be sure to allow for expansion and contraction between the fascia channels at the lap joints. Do not secure the channels to each other by nailing or any other fastening device and do not nail along the bottom edge of fascia runners. If this is done, it will cause buckling on the face when the aluminum expands.

Cutting and Fitting Fascia and Frieze Runners. A 1¼" notch is made in the fascia and frieze runners for end lap joints. To make lap cuts, use a pair of snips to cut the bottom flange of the runner through to the back of the runner. Fig. 42-24a. Then cut through both thicknesses of the runner groove back, removing piece A. On the

top flange of the runner, cut to the inside of the runner groove back. Now bend the piece back and forth until it breaks off as shown at B in Fig. 42-24b. Trim the rough edges and reshape the flanges as necessary. To make end cuts, cut through flanges a, b, and c to the runner groove back as shown in Fig. 42-25. Bend the piece back and forth until the groove back breaks. Trim off rough edges as necessary.

If the metal soffit system is to be used on a home which is of brick veneer, block out at the exterior wall above the brick line to permit the frieze runner to be installed flush with the top edge of the brick. Fig. 42-26. (Note in the detail B that a quarter-round frieze

runner may also be used for this installation with a slightly different method of blocking.)

Where overhangs exceed the width of the soffit material available, a double channel runner can be used so that two pieces of soffit can be installed. Fig. 42-27.

Trimming the corners of a horizontal soffit is slightly different from a sloping soffit. In the case of a horizontal soffit such as would be used on a hip roof, miter corner trim is available and is installed as shown in Fig. 42-28a. For a sloping soffit such as the end of a gable, another type of corner trim is available and can be installed as shown in Fig. 42-28b.

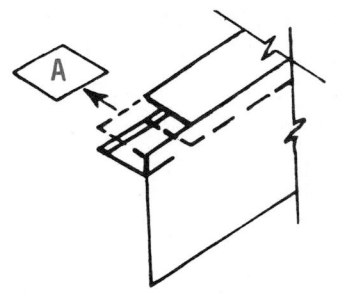

42-24a. *Cutting a notch for end lap joints. On the bottom flange of the runner make a cut through to the back of the runner. Then cut through both thicknesses along the back edge of the runner groove back and remove piece A.*

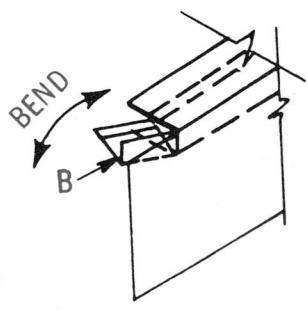

42-24b. *On the top flange of the runner, cut to the inside of the runner groove back and bend piece B back and forth until it breaks.*

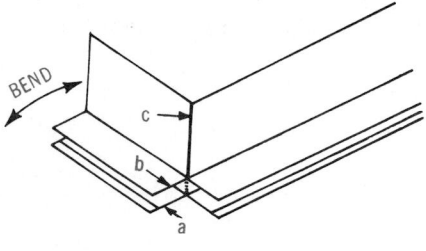

42-25. *To cut the material to length, cut through the flanges at a and b and then bend the piece back and forth at c until the back breaks.*

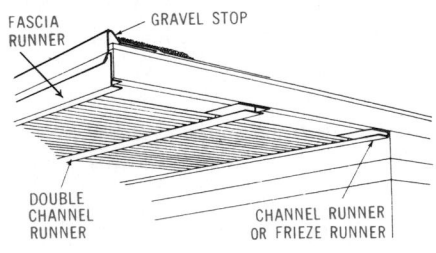

42-27. *On a flat roof installation where the overhang is wider than 48", a double-channel runner (H molding) may be used to support two widths of the soffit coil material.*

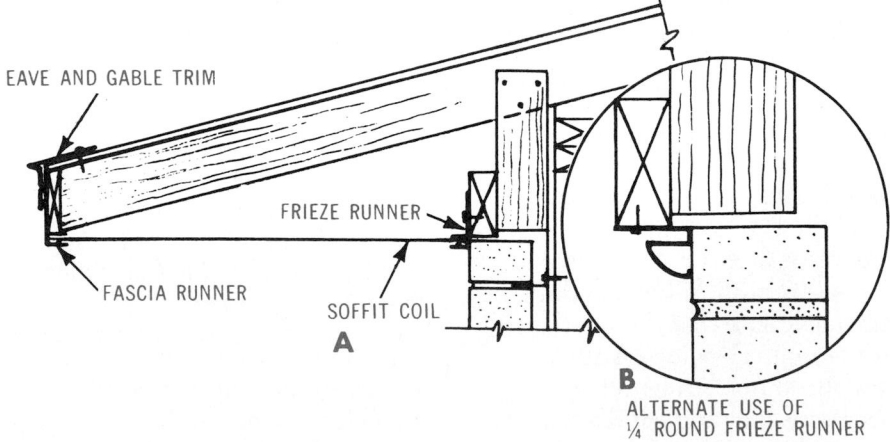

42-26. *On a brick veneer exterior wall, a frieze runner may be nailed to blocking material to bring it out flush with the wall (A). Or a quarter-round frieze runner can be used and blocked out (B).*

Cutting and Fitting Quarter-round Frieze Molding. End closures are made by cutting away the area shown by the dotted line on the flanges in Fig. 42-29. Bend the flange down over the end and cut the rounded contour with double action snips to complete the closure. Corners are fitted by mitering in the usual manner. End-laps are made by cutting away the area shown by the broken lines in Fig. 42-30 and shoving the ends together. Fig. 42-31. On the gable fascia trim, the end laps are made by notching. Fig. 42-32.

Installation Sequence.

1. Fascia and frieze runners are available in a variety of sizes. Fig. 42-33. Select the correct size for

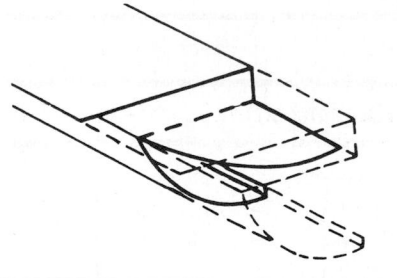

42-29. *To make an end closure on a quarter-round frieze molding, notch as shown. Bend the tab down, then cut the tab to conform to the profile of the quarter-round.*

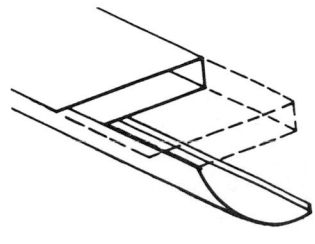

42-30. *When making an end lap, notch the piece as shown. With tin snips, cut away the dotted line area.*

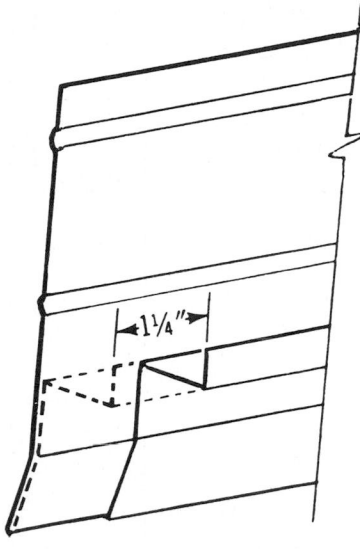

42-32. *Notch the gable fascia trim for end laps as shown by the broken lines.*

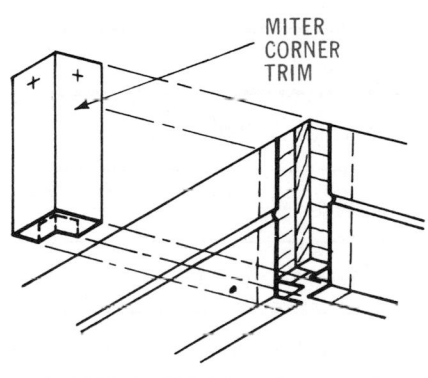

42-28a. *On a horizontal soffit a special miter corner trim can be used to enclose the corner.*

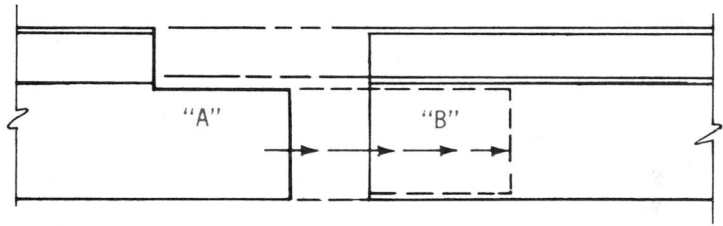

42-31. *When joining two pieces of quarter-round end to end, the pieces can be cut and telescoped as shown. Part A will fit over B, and the frieze runner will butt together with the cove overlapping.*

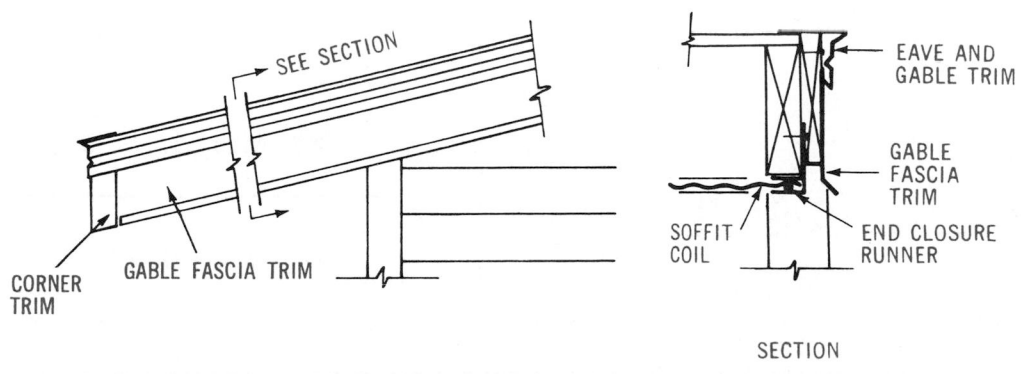

42-28b. *On a sloping soffit for a gable, special corner trim can be applied as shown here.*

Part Name		Part Description
Straight Fascia and Frieze Runners (Prenotched)		
1″ Leg	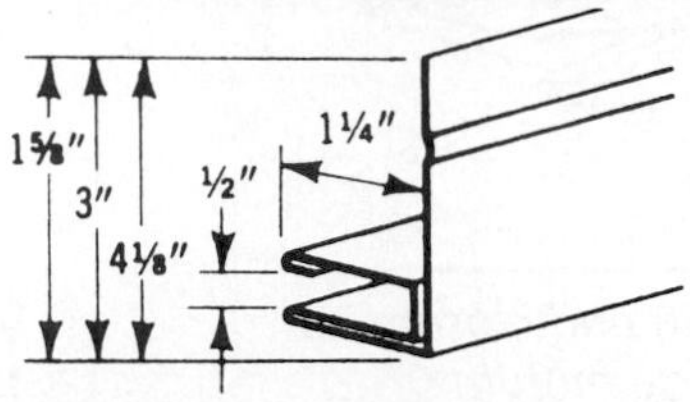	1⅝″ wide x 121¼″ long
3″ Leg		3″ wide x 121¼″ long
4″ Leg		4⅛″ wide x 121¼″ long
6″ Leg	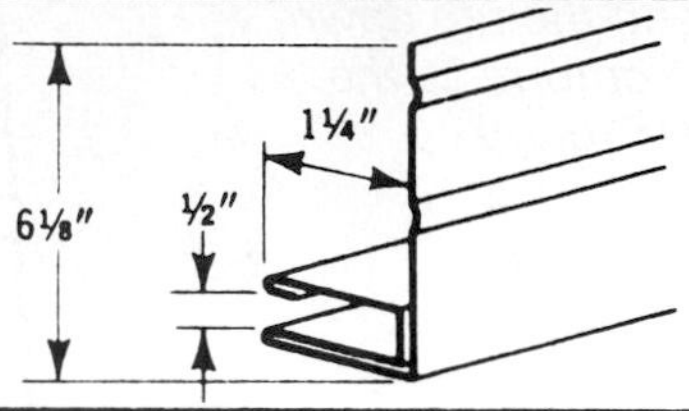	6⅛″ wide x 121¼″ long
8″ Leg	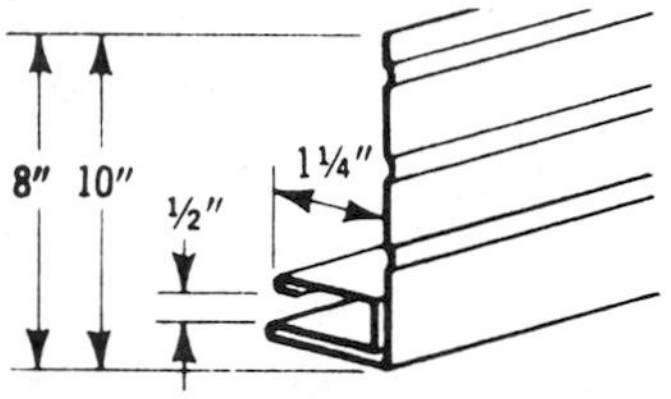	8″ wide x 121¼″ long
10″ Leg		10″ wide x 121¼″ long
Sloping Fascia and Frieze Runners, Type #1 (Prenotched)		
3″ Leg	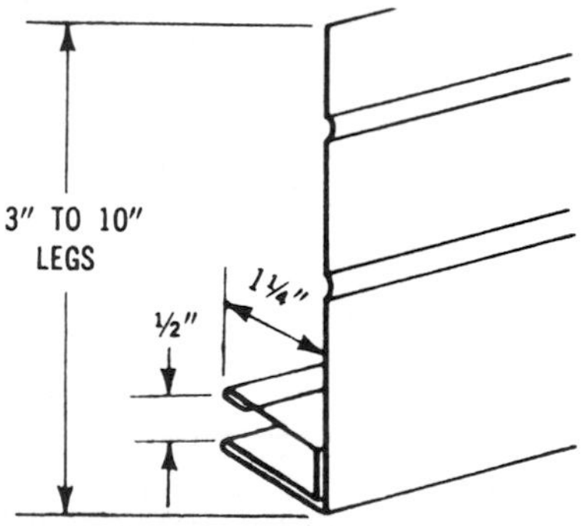	3″ wide x 121¼″ long
4″ Leg		4⅛″ wide x 121¼″ long
6″ Leg		6⅛″ wide x 121¼″ long
8″ Leg		8″ wide x 121¼″ long
10″ Leg		10″ wide x 121¼″ long
Sloping Fascia and Frieze Runners, Type #2 (Prenotched)		
3″ Leg	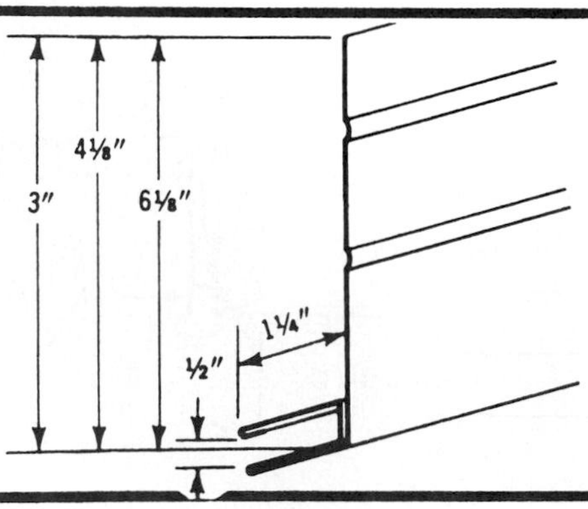	3″ wide x 121¼″ long
4″ Leg		4⅛″ wide x 121¼″ long
6″ Leg		6⅛″ wide x 121¼″ long

42-33. *Fascia and frieze runners are available either straight or sloping, in a variety of sizes.*

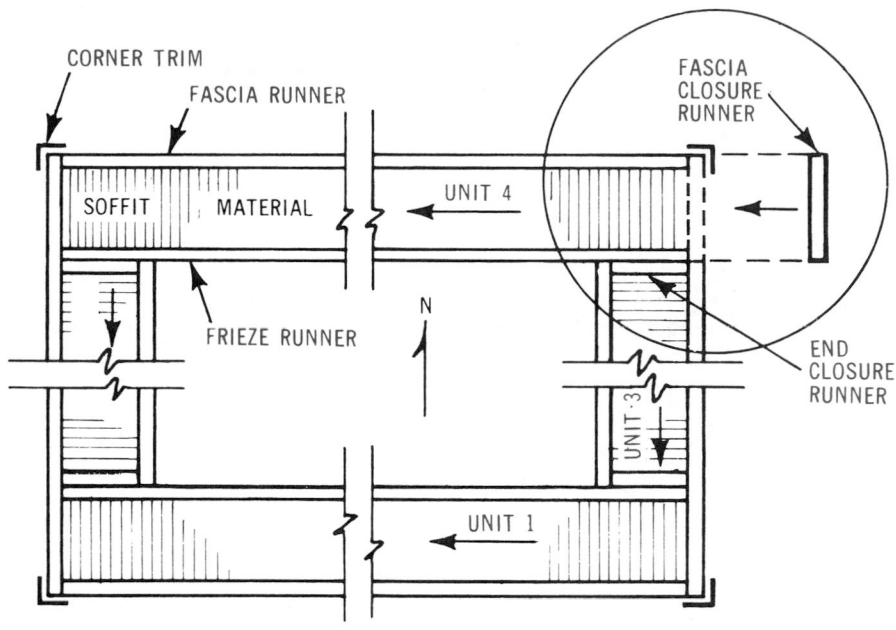

42-34. *This diagram shows the soffit of a hip roof from below. The arrows indicate the direction and sequence in which to pull the soffit coil into place.*

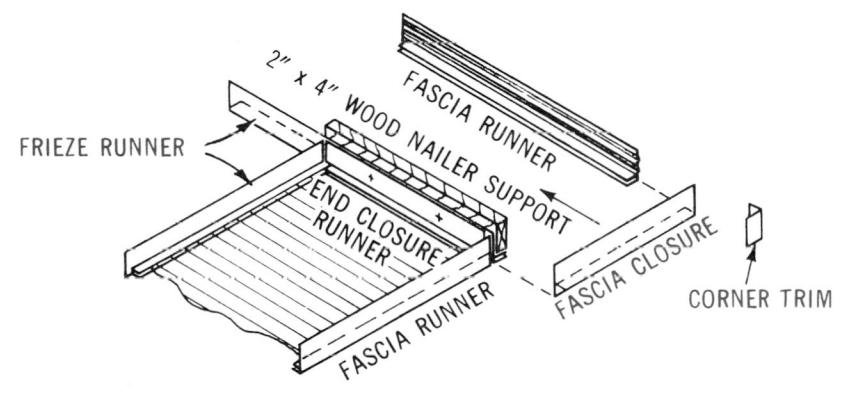

42-35a. *A corner assembly of the soffit on a hip roof showing the method of end and fascia closures.*

the job and apply the fascia and frieze runners for Unit 1 as shown in Fig. 42-34.

2. Pull the soffit coil into place in the direction of the arrow as shown in Fig. 42-34 for Unit 1.

3. Install end closure runners to Units 2 and 3 where they intersect with Unit 1. Fig. 42-35a.

4. Install the fascia and frieze runners of Units 2 and 3. Fig. 42-34. Note that you must leave out one section of fascia runner equal to the soffit width to allow Unit 4 to be installed later.

5. Pull in the soffit coil for Units 2 and 3. Fig. 42-34.

6. Apply end closure runners to

Units 2 and 3 where they intersect with Unit 4. Fig. 42-34.

7. Apply the fascia and frieze runners of Unit 4 and pull in the soffit coil.

8. Install the fascia closure runner referred to in Step 4. Figs. 42-34 and 42-35a.

9. Apply the corner trim angles or mitered corner trim. Fig. 42-35b.

10. Use a spline tool to apply a polyethylene spline along all sides and ends of the soffit sheet. Fig. 42-36.

RAKE OR GABLE-END FINISH

The extension of a gable roof beyond the end wall is called the *rake section*. This detail may be classed as being:

➤ A closed rake with little projection.

➤ A boxed or open extension varying from 6" to 2' or more.

When the rake extension is only 6" to 8", the fascia and soffit can be nailed to a series of short lookout blocks. A, Fig. 42-37. In addition, the fascia is further secured by nailing through the projecting roof sheathing. A frieze board and appropriate moldings complete the construction.

In a moderate overhang of up to 20", both the extending sheathing and a *fly rafter* aid in supporting the rake section. B, Fig. 42-37. The fly rafter extends from the ridge board to the nailing header which connects the ends of the rafters. The roof sheathing boards or the plywood should extend from inner rafters to the end of the gable projection to provide rigidity and strength.

The roof sheathing is nailed to the fly rafter and to the lookout blocks which aid in supporting the rake section and also serve as a

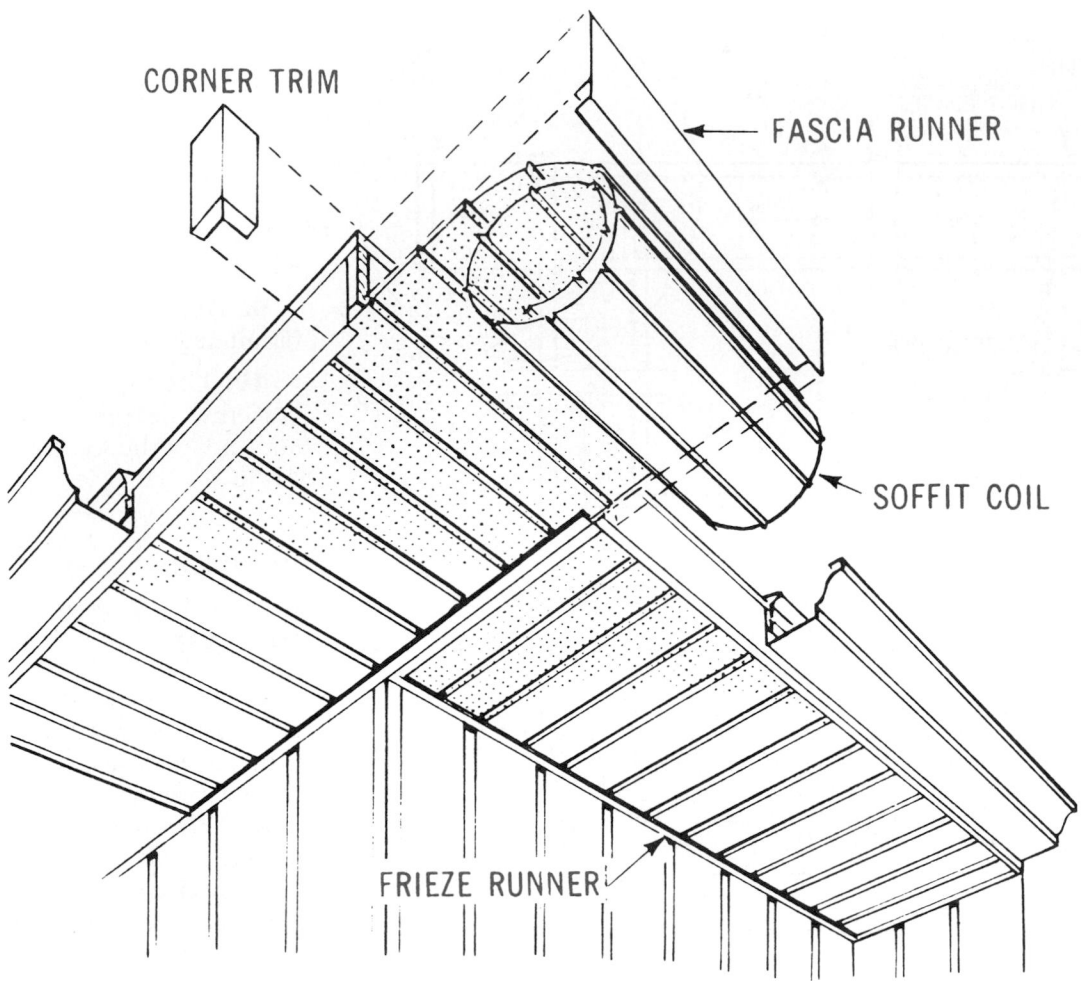

42-35b. *After all of the soffit coils have been pulled into place, the last soffit to be pulled in must be closed off by installing the fascia runner and the corner trim.*

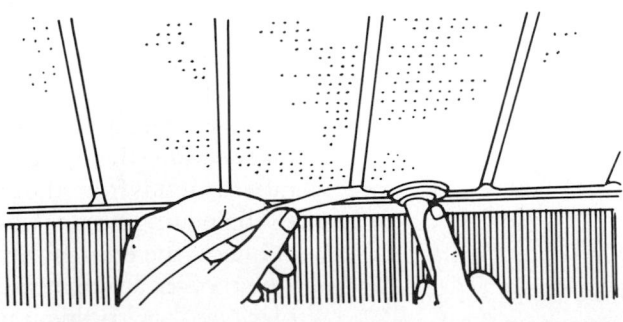

42-36. *Use the spline tool to insert the polyethylene spline along all sides and ends of the soffit sheet.*

nailing area for the soffit. Additional nailing blocks against the sheathing are sometimes required for thinner soffit materials.

Wide gable extensions (2' or more) require rigid framing to resist roof loads and prevent deflection of the rake section. This is usually accomplished by a series of *purlins* or lookout members nailed to a fly rafter at the outside edge and supported by the end wall and a doubled interior rafter. Fig. 42-38. This framing is often called a "ladder" and may be constructed in place or on the ground or other convenient area and hoisted in place.

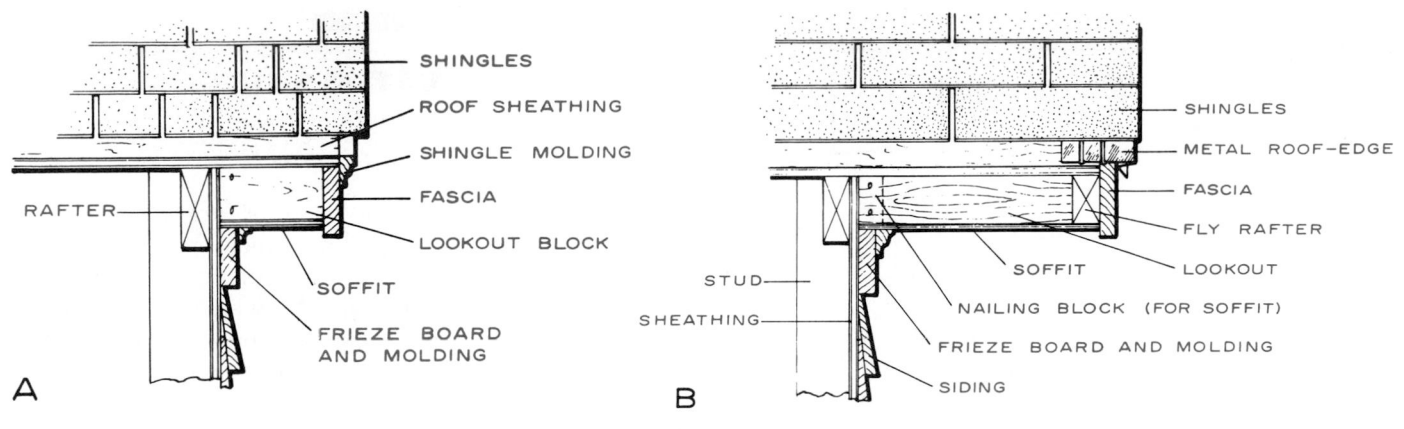

42-37. *Normal gable-end extensions: A. Narrow overhang. B. Moderate overhang.*

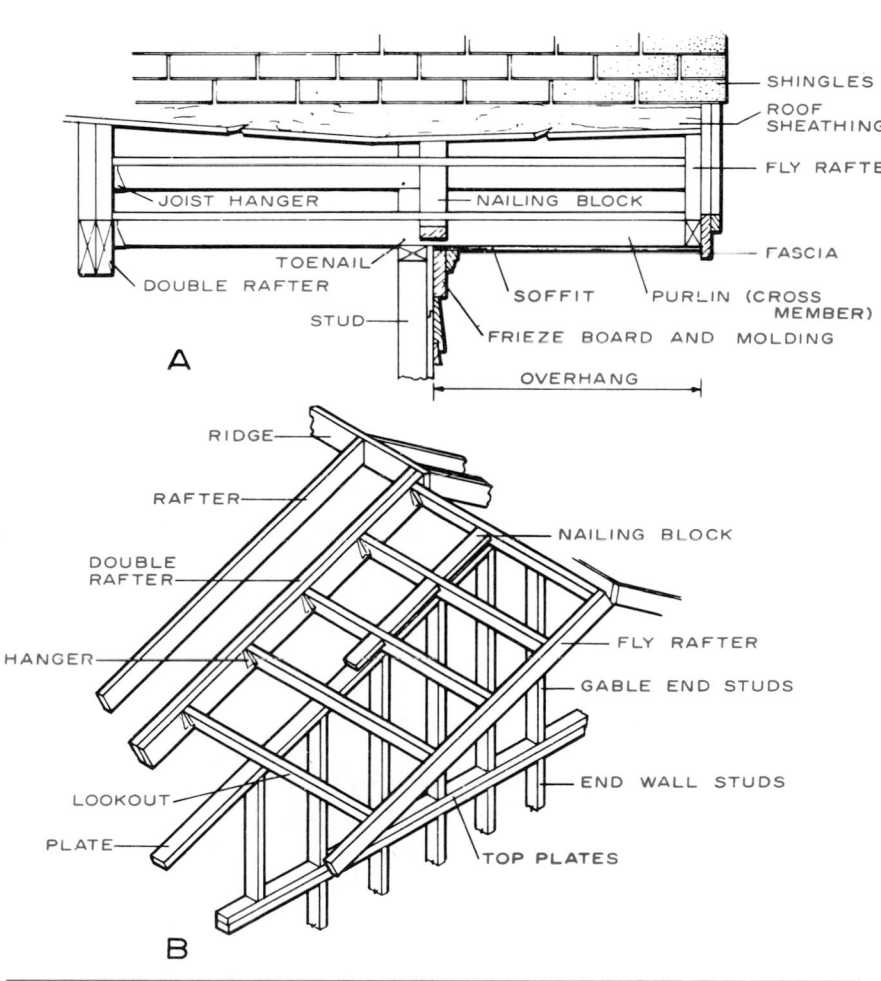

42-38. *Wide gable-end extension: A. Wide overhang. B. Ladder framing for a wide overhang.*

When ladder framing is preassembled, it is usually made up with a header rafter on the inside and a fly rafter on the outside. Each is nailed to the ends of the lookouts which bear on the gable-end wall. When the header is the same size as the rafter, be sure to provide a notch for the wall plates the same as for the regular rafters. In moderate width overhangs, nailing the header and fly rafter to the lookouts with supplemental toenailing is usually sufficiently strong to eliminate the need for the metal hangers shown in B, Fig. 42-38. The header rafters can be face-nailed directly to the end rafters with 12d nails spaced 16" to 20" apart.

Other details of soffits, fascia, frieze board, and moldings can be similar to those used for a wide gable overhang. Lookouts should be spaced 16" to 24" apart, depending on the thickness of the soffit material.

A closed rake has no extension beyond the end wall other than the frieze board and moldings. Some additional protection and overhang can be provided by using a 2" × 3" or 2" × 4" fascia block over the sheathing. Fig. 42-39. This member acts as a frieze board, as the siding can be butted against it. The fascia, often 1" × 6", serves as a trim

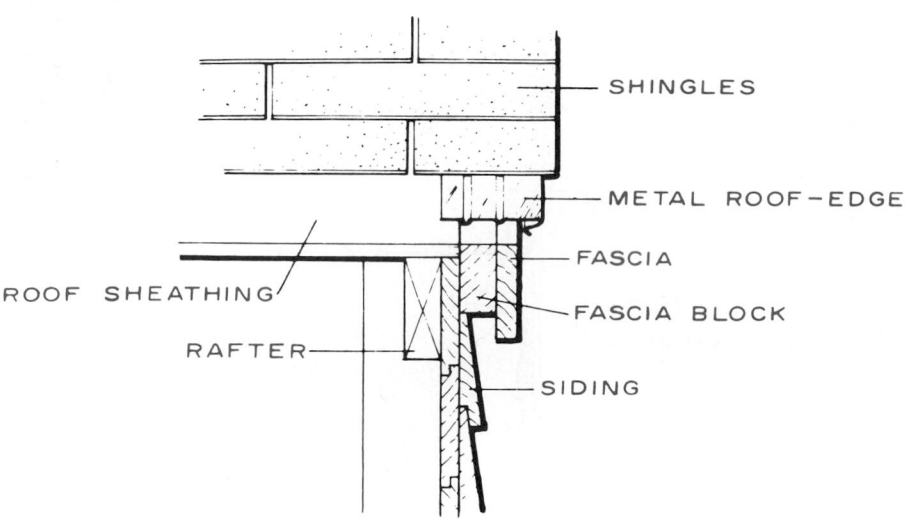

SHINGLES

METAL ROOF-EDGE

FASCIA

FASCIA BLOCK

ROOF SHEATHING

RAFTER

SIDING

42-39. *Closed rake.*

member. Metal roof edging is often used along the rake section as flashing.

CORNICE RETURN

The cornice return is the end finish of the cornice on a gable roof. On hip roofs and flat roofs, the cornice is usually continuous around the entire house. On a gable roof, however, it must be terminated or joined with the gable ends. The method selected depends to a great extent on the type of cornice and the projection of the gable roof beyond the end wall.

A narrow box cornice, often used in houses with Cape Cod or Colonial details, has a boxed return when the rake section has some projection. A, Fig. 42-40. The fascia board and shingle molding of the cornice are carried around the corner of the rake projection.

When a wide box cornice has no horizontal lookout members, the soffit of the gable-end overhang is at the same slope and coincides with the cornice soffit. B, Fig. 42-40. This is a simple system and is often used when there are wide

overhangs at both sides and ends of the house.

A closed rake (a gable end with little projection) may be used with a narrow box cornice or a closed cornice. In this type, the frieze board of the gable end, into which the siding butts, joins the frieze board or fascia of the cornice. C, Fig. 42-40.

While closed rakes and cornices with little overhang are lower in cost, the extra material and labor required for good gable and cornice overhangs are usually justified. Better sidewall protection and lower paint maintenance costs are only two of the benefits derived from good roof extensions.

GUTTERS

Wooden gutters are either built into the cornice or prefabricated and attached on the job site. They were once used extensively, but are now almost obsolete. Most modern gutters are of prefabricated metal, equipped with metal straps for attaching to the roof boards. See Unit 40.

ESTIMATING

Material

The materials for the cornice are strictly linear measure. All moldings and lumber or other materials which are attached to the house can be figured by determining the perimeter of the house. This includes material for ledger strips, frieze boards, and bed moldings. The amount of soffit material required is also determined by figuring the perimeter of the house and referring to the specifications of house plans for the width and thickness of the material required. The amount of material required for the fascia board and any crown molding attached to the fascia is figured by determining the perimeter of the house at the rafter ends. The linear footage for rake moldings is figured in the same way as the length of the gable-end rafter. (See Unit 33.) The amount of material necessary for the lookouts may be determined by multiplying the projection by the number of rafters.

Labor

It is possible to give a general estimate of the cost for installing a cornice. The rate of installation varies with the type of cornice.

➤ For a closed cornice, it is estimated that workers can install 20 linear feet per hour.

➤ For an open cornice, 12 linear feet per hour.

➤ For a box cornice, 10 linear feet per hour.

A house with an open cornice and a 148' perimeter would take about 12 hours and 20 minutes: 148' ÷ 12 = 12⅓ hours, or 12 hours and 20 minutes. In order to find the approximate cost of installing a cornice, multiply the estimated hours of labor by the cost per hour.

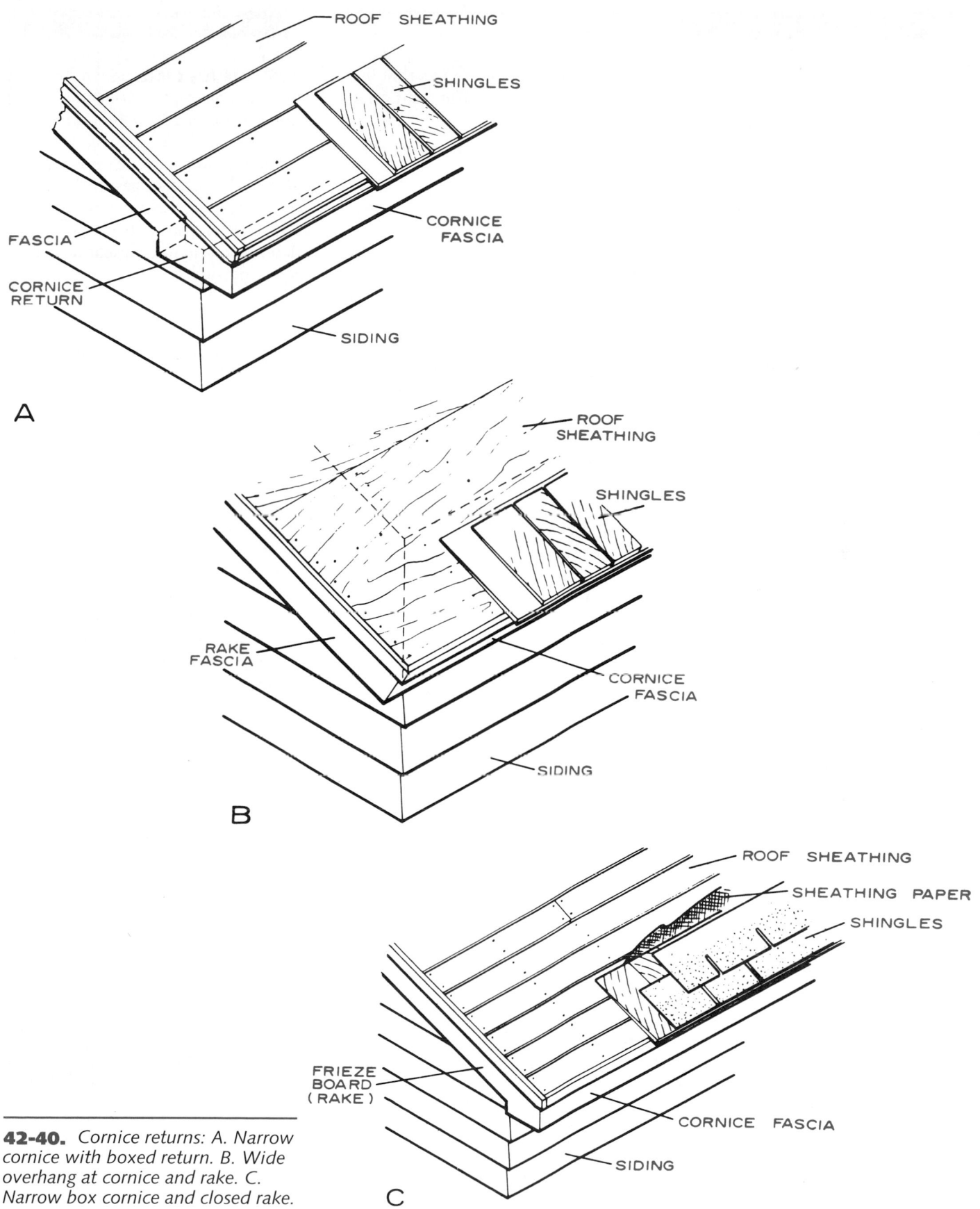

42-40. *Cornice returns: A. Narrow cornice with boxed return. B. Wide overhang at cornice and rake. C. Narrow box cornice and closed rake.*

1. List several types of cornices.

2. When constructing a box cornice, what procedure is used to ensure alignment of the plumb cuts on the rafter tails?

3. What is a fascia?

4. List three materials that are commonly used for the soffit on a closed cornice.

5. What is a cornice return?

1. Math. A rectangular house with a gable roof has outside dimensions of 26' by 44' and a roof slope of 7 in 12. It has a 12" overhang on the gable ends and 18" on the other edges. If the house has a box cornice with a flat soffit on the eave edges, determine the total linear feet of fascia needed.

THE SCHOOL-TO-WORK CONNECTION

When an architect designs a house, he or she will typically have very specific ideas for every part of the house. All the construction details will be drawn out, dimensioned, and specified. This is because the architect wants all the details to form a visually cohesive whole. Each house the architect designs represents a different set of problems to solve. The construction details are frequently different each time.

Most single-family houses, however, are not designed by architects. Oftentimes it is the builder who is most responsible for the design of the house. He or she may work out an original design for the house. Another option is for the builder to purchase stock home plans and simply adapt them for a particular project. Construction details are typically based on what the builder is familiar with.

1. Conduct an informal survey of roofs where you live. Visit a neighborhood and list the various types of roof types you see. As you look at the roofs, make cross-section sketches of the roof trim details at the gable ends and at the eaves. Try to guess at what dimensions the various trim elements are. Do you notice any details that repeat from house to house? Start a file titled "Roof Details." Keep your sketches in it.

43

Windows and Skylights

Windows and skylights are usually fully assembled at the factory. Window units often come with the sash fitted and weather-stripped, the frame assembled, and the exterior casing in place. Fig. 43-1. (For information on skylights, see pages 528 to 529.) Standard combination storms and screens or separate units can also be included. All wood components are treated with a water-repellent preservative at the factory to provide protection before and after they are placed in the walls.

Besides letting in light and air, windows are an important part of the architectural design. Fig. 43-2. Generally the glass area of a room should be not less than 10% of the floor area. The window area that can be opened for ventilation should be not less than 4% of the floor area unless a complete air conditioning system is used.

There should be a balance of fixed picture windows and operating windows. An operating window can always be closed to seal out unpleasant weather or opened to a cooling breeze, but a fixed window cannot be opened. Local climate and prevailing winds determine the best window placement and the degree of ventilation required.

The type of window specified in the plans will vary with the room requirements. Not every room will need the same size and type of window. In bedrooms, light and ventilation are a necessity, but privacy and wall space for furniture are also important factors. A row of narrow operating windows placed high on two walls of the room will provide light and ventilation as well as privacy and wall space. In the kitchen, windows should provide good ventilation of cooking odors.

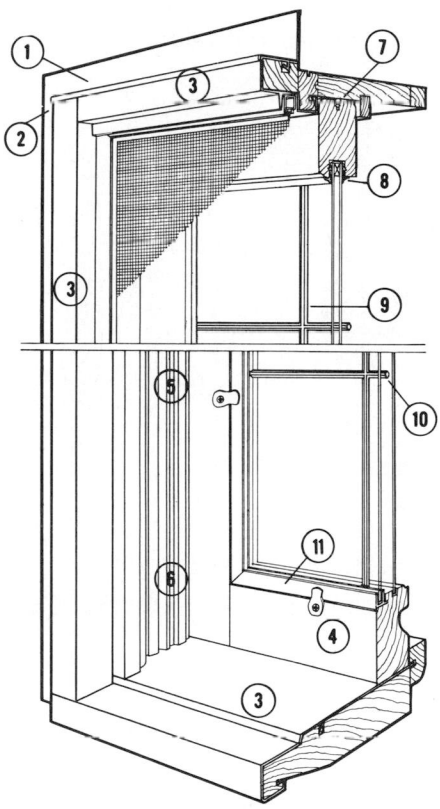

43-1. *Parts of an assembled double-hung window: 1. Head flashing. 2. Blind stops. 3. Casing. 4. Sash. 5. Counterbalancing unit. 6. Tracks. 7. Weather stripping. 8. Glazing. 9. Grill (installed on the inside when insulation glass is used). 10. Grill (installed between the glass when storm panels are used). 11. Storm panel.*

43-2a. *Windows can dramatically affect the exterior look of a house.*

43-2b. *Windows are often an important element of interior design.*

43-2c. *The type of wood trim applied to a window can affect its look.*

For the area over the sink and other hard-to-reach spots, a casement window or awning type that opens with a crank or lever action would be a good choice. The living areas are an ideal location for large picture windows which allow scenic views.

The window style and size should be such that it is convenient to look through the window whether a person is seated or standing. Eye-level (seated and standing) height charts for various window types are shown in Fig. 43-3.

ENERGY EFFICIENCY

As the costs of heating and cooling a house have climbed, window manufacturers have greatly improved the energy efficiency of windows. This is important, because 20% to 30% of the heat lost from an average house is lost through the windows. This can happen due to air leaking around the window or by heat being radiated through the glass. In hot climates, cool indoor air can be lost in the same ways.

Various parts of the window have been significantly improved in terms of energy efficiency. Improved weather stripping has reduced the amount of heat that escapes around the window sash. Improved construction techniques strengthen the sash and frame. This keeps them from distorting over time, which would cause air leakage. But many of the most dramatic changes have involved improvements in the glass.

High-Performance Glass

In many areas of the country, new houses are required by building codes to have insulating glass windows. These windows (sometimes called double-glazed windows) are used for both stationary and movable sash. The windows have two or more sheets of glass with an air space between the sheets. The edges are hermetically sealed to trap air between the sheets. This trapped air is what "insulates" the window. This type of window has more resistance to heat loss than one with a single thickness of glass, and is generally used without a storm sash. Fig. 43-4.

Low-E Glazing. Many window manufacturers offer low-emissivity glazing (called low-e glazing). "Low-emissivity" means that the

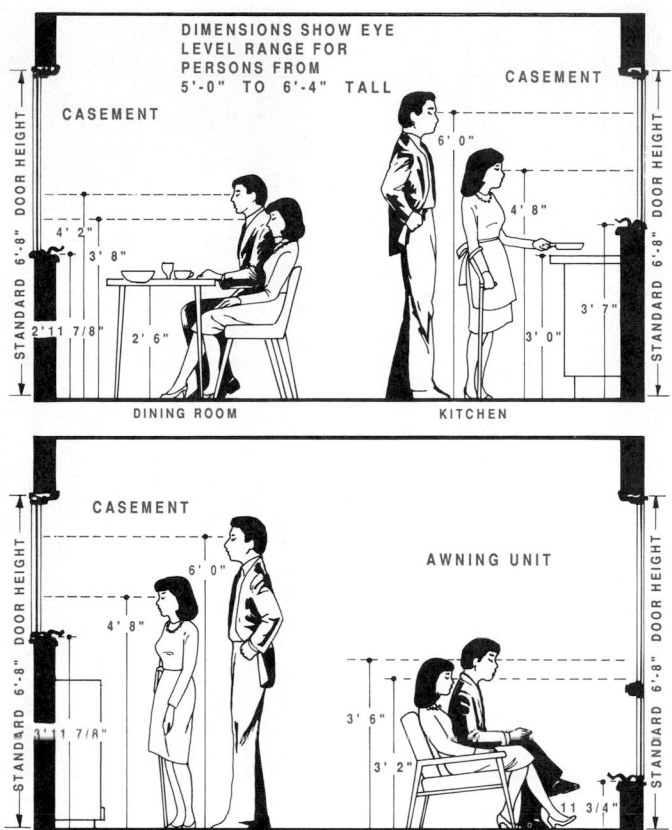

43-5a. *The low-e coating on insulating glass does not affect visability.*

43-3. *Recommended window heights for various rooms. Note that the header height of the window is standard and corresponds to the 6'8" door height. The sill height, however, will vary with the style and size window to be installed.*

43-5b. *Windows with low-e glazing come in many styles.*

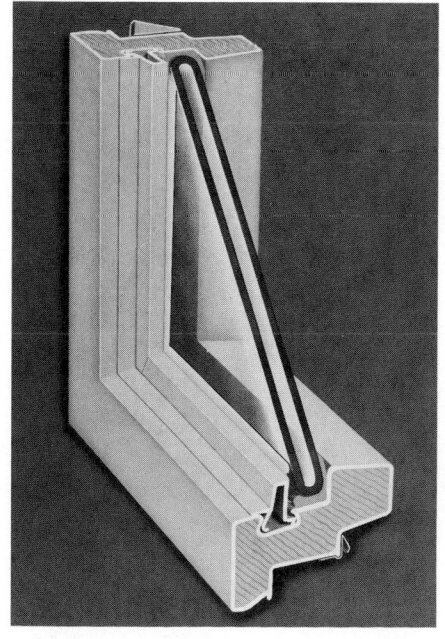

43-4. *Insulating glass.*

glass radiates less heat to the outdoors than does regular glass.

There are two versions of low-e glazing. One features a very thin (2-mil) sheet of coated polyester film that is stretched between the layers of insulating glass. This clear sheet is located in the airspace, and does not affect views through the glass. Another type of low-e glazing features a low-emissivity coating that is applied directly to the glass during manufacture. This coating is applied to one of the glass surfaces facing the airspace. Low-e glass can be helpful in climates where heating or cooling is necessary. Fig. 43-5.

Triple Glazing. In climates that are particularly cold, windows are sometimes triple glazed. This

means that instead of having insulating glass with two sheets of glass separated by an airspace, there are three sheets of glass. This adds another airspace, which improves the energy efficiency of the window. Triple-glazing can be expensive, however, so it is important to balance this cost against the cost of the energy saved. Fig. 43-6.

Argon Glazing. Argon is a colorless gas that is sometimes used to replace the air in double-glazed or triple-glazed windows. Because it is more dense than air, it insulates better. One of the concerns about

43-6. *Triple glazing has two insulating air spaces. This triple glazing is mounted in a one-piece PVC frame.*

this type of glazing is that the argon gas might leak out over time. This would reduce the performance of the glass. Some manufacturers take particular care to prevent this from happening.

TYPES OF WINDOWS

These are the principal types of windows. Fig. 43-7.

- ➤ Double-hung.
- ➤ Casement.
- ➤ Stationary (fixed).
- ➤ Awning.
- ➤ Hopper.
- ➤ Horizontal-sliding.
- ➤ Jalousie.

Glass blocks are sometimes used for admitting light in places where transparency or ventilation is not required. Fig. 43-8.

All the basic types of windows can have sashes and frames made either of metal, wood, or vinyl. Most windows used in residential construction are made of wood. In some wood windows, all the wood components are covered with a

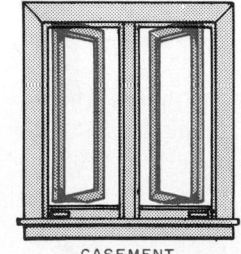

CASEMENT

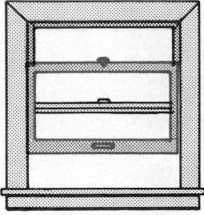

DOUBLE HUNG

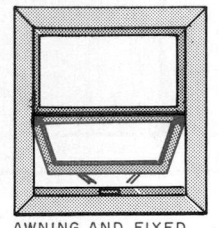

AWNING AND FIXED

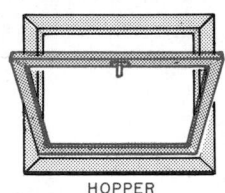

HOPPER

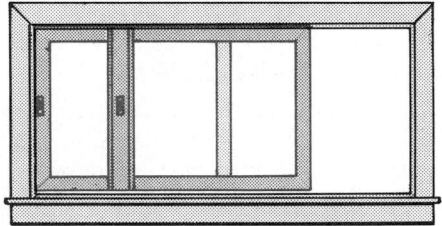

SLIDING

43-7. *Five of the basic window styles.*

43-8. *Glass blocks can be used to admit light where ventilation is not required.*

43-9. *To make this vinyl window, fiberglass strands were combined with polyester resin.*

durable vinyl layer. This protects the wood so that it never needs painting. Windows with structural vinyl sashes and frames are easy to maintain and have good thermal performance. Fig. 43-9.

Heat loss through metal frames and sash is much greater than through similar wood units. On the other hand, metal frames and sash require less maintenance. They also can be made more narrow and thus allow larger glass areas.

Wooden window frames and sash should be made from a clear grade of all-heartwood stock of a decay-resistant wood species or from wood which has been given a preservative treatment. Species commonly used include ponderosa and other pines, cedar, cypress, redwood, and spruce. Metal window frames and sash are made of aluminum or steel.

Window jambs (sides and tops of the frames) must be the same width as the wall section, including the exterior sheathing and the interior finished wall covering. Jambs are made of nominal 1" lumber; jamb liners are used to adapt the window unit to various wall thicknesses. Fig. 43-10. Sills (bottoms of frame) are made from nominal 2" lumber and are sloped at about 3 in 12 for good drainage. D, Fig. 43-11. Sash are normally 1⅜" thick, and wood combination storm and screen windows are usually 1⅛" thick.

Double-hung Windows

The double-hung window is perhaps the most familiar window type. It consists of an upper and a lower sash that slide vertically in separate grooves in the side jambs or in full-width metal weather stripping. Fig. 43-12. This type of window provides a maximum face opening for ventilation of one-half the total window area. Each sash is provided with springs, balances, or compression weather stripping to hold it in place in any position. Compression weather stripping, for example, prevents air infiltration, provides tension, and acts as a counterbalance. Several types allow the sash to be removed or pivoted away for easy cleaning, painting, or repair.

Sash may be divided into a number of compartments, or lights, by small wood members called muntins. A ranch-type house may provide the best appearance with top and bottom sash divided into two horizontal lights. A Colonial or Cape Cod house usually has each sash divided into six or eight lights. Some manufacturers provide preassembled dividers which snap in place over a single light, dividing it into six or eight lights. This simplifies painting and other maintenance. Fig. 43-13.

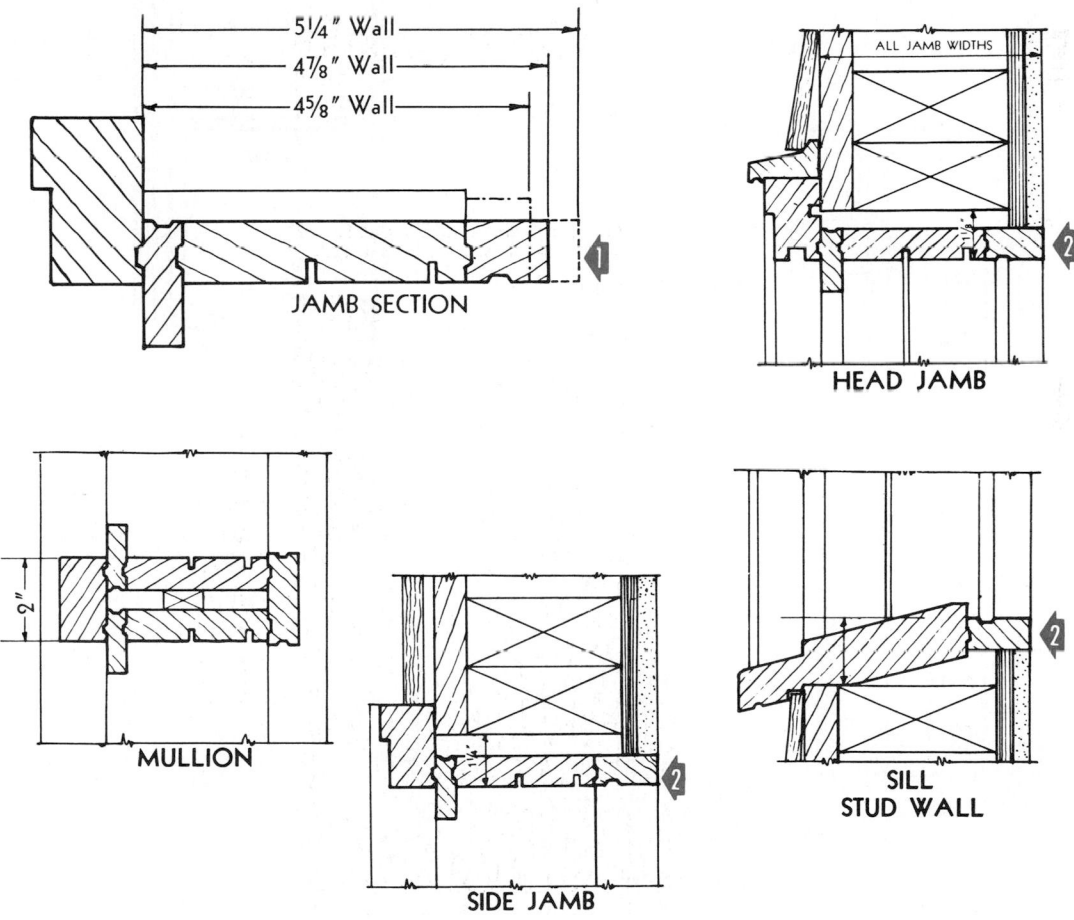

43-10. *Some manufacturers include a jamb liner that can be repositioned and adapted to various wall thicknesses as shown at arrow No. 1 in the jamb section. The jamb liner is shown at the No. 2 arrows with the window installed in a framed wall with lath and plaster.*

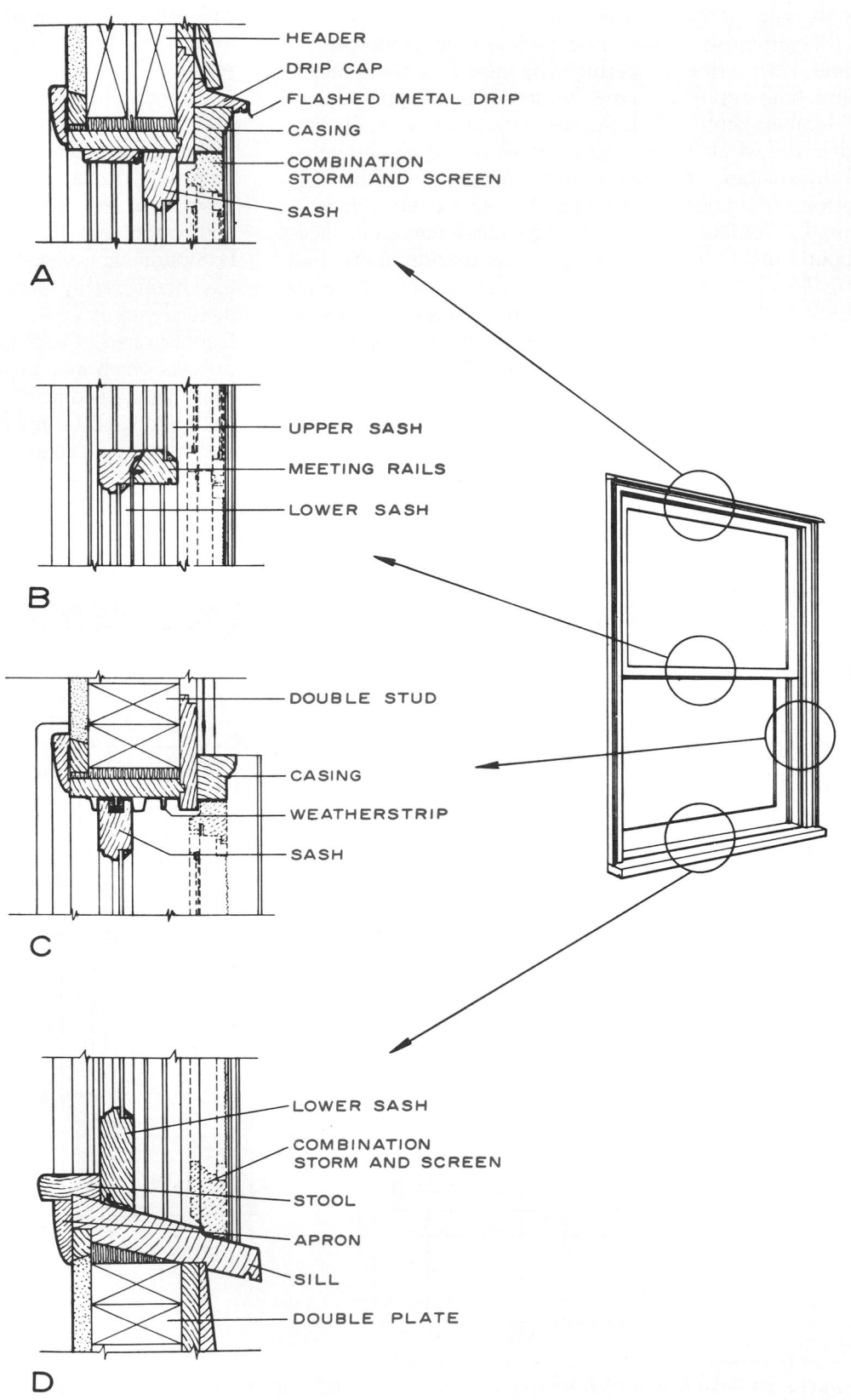

43-11. *Double-hung window. Cross-section: A. Head jamb. B. Meeting rails. C. Side jamb. D. Sill.*

A

HEADER
DRIP CAP
FLASHED METAL DRIP
CASING
COMBINATION STORM AND SCREEN
SASH

B

UPPER SASH
MEETING RAILS
LOWER SASH

C

DOUBLE STUD
CASING
WEATHERSTRIP
SASH

D

LOWER SASH
COMBINATION STORM AND SCREEN
STOOL
APRON
SILL
DOUBLE PLATE

43-12. *An aluminum double-hung window.*

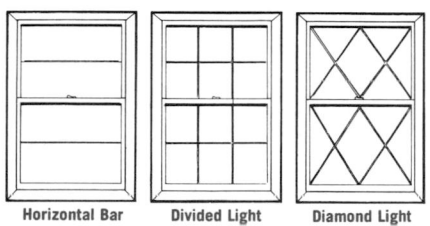

Horizontal Bar   Divided Light   Diamond Light

43-13. *Preassembled dividers of various styles for subdividing window lights are easily snapped into place.*

Hardware for double-hung windows includes the sash lifts (for opening the window) that are fastened to the bottom rail, although they are sometimes eliminated by providing a finger groove in the rail. Other hardware consists of sash locks or fasteners located at the meeting rails. They not only lock the window, but also draw the sash together to provide a "windtight" fit.

Double-hung windows can be arranged in a number of ways—as a single unit, doubled (or mullion) type, or in groups of three or more. One or two double-hung windows on each side of a large stationary insulated window are often used to effect a window wall. Such large openings must be framed with headers large enough to carry roof loads.

Casement Windows

Casement windows have side-hinged sash, usually designed to swing outward because this type can be made more weathertight than the type that swings inward. Fig. 43-14. Screens are located inside these outward-swinging windows, and winter protection is obtained with a storm sash or by using insulated glass in the sash. One advantage of the casement window over the double-hung type is that the entire window area can be opened for ventilation.

Weather stripping is also provided for this type of window, and units are usually received from the factory entirely assembled with hardware in place. Closing hardware consists of a rotary operator, a hinge assembly, and a sash lock. Fig. 43-15.

As in the double-hung units, casement sash can be used in a number of ways—as a pair or in combinations of two or more pairs. Style variations are achieved by divided lights. For example, snap-in muntins provide a small multiple-pane appearance for traditional styling.

Stationary Windows

Stationary windows, used alone or in combination with other types of windows, usually consist of a wood sash with a large single light of insulated glass. They are designed for providing light, as well

43-14a. *Wood casement window.*

43-14b. *An attractive window wall made up of casement windows with fixed units above.*

as for attractive appearance, and are fastened permanently into the frame. Fig. 43-16. Because of their size (sometimes 6 to 8 feet in width) and because of the thickness of the insulating glass, a

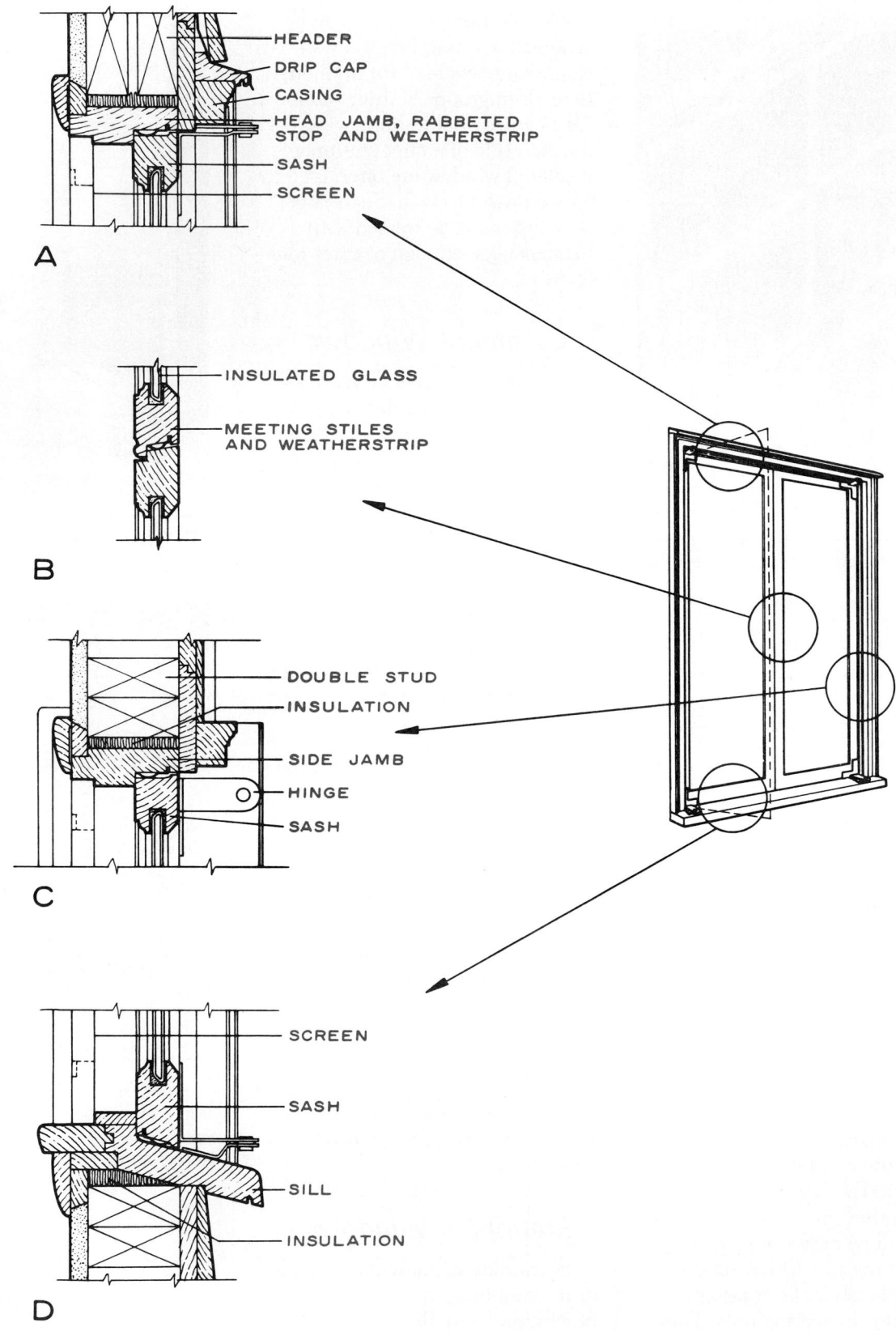

A

HEADER
DRIP CAP
CASING
HEAD JAMB, RABBETED STOP AND WEATHERSTRIP
SASH
SCREEN

B

INSULATED GLASS
MEETING STILES AND WEATHERSTRIP

C

DOUBLE STUD
INSULATION
SIDE JAMB
HINGE
SASH

D

SCREEN
SASH
SILL
INSULATION

43-14c. *Casement window. Cross sections: A. Head jamb. B. Meeting stiles. C. Side jamb. D. Sill.*

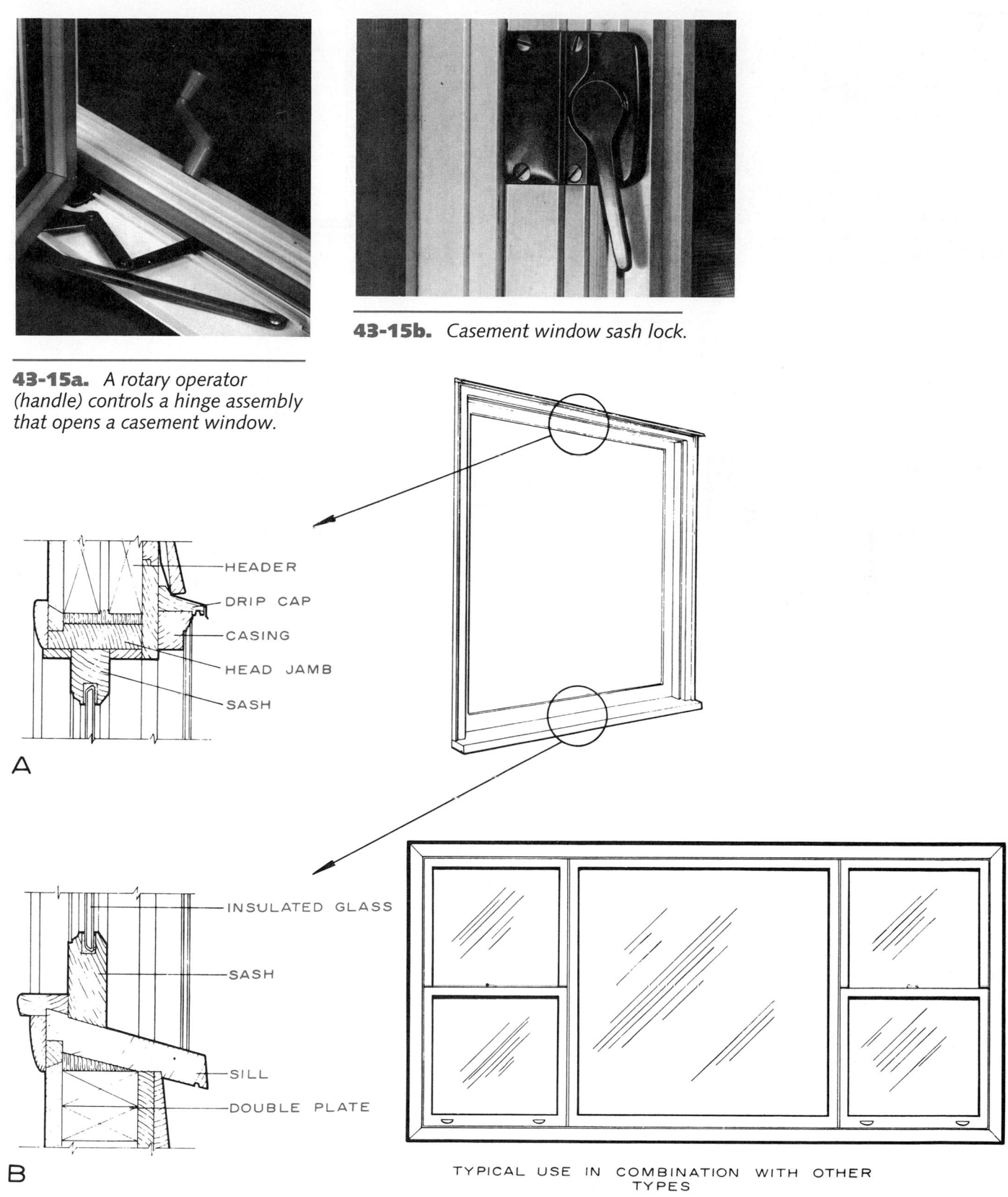

43-15b. *Casement window sash lock.*

43-15a. *A rotary operator (handle) controls a hinge assembly that opens a casement window.*

HEADER

DRIP CAP

CASING

HEAD JAMB

SASH

A

INSULATED GLASS

SASH

SILL

DOUBLE PLATE

B

TYPICAL USE IN COMBINATION WITH OTHER TYPES

43-16a. *Stationary window. Cross-sections: A. Head jamb. B. Sill.*

43-16b. *The two-story window wall on this house was made with large and small stationary windows.*

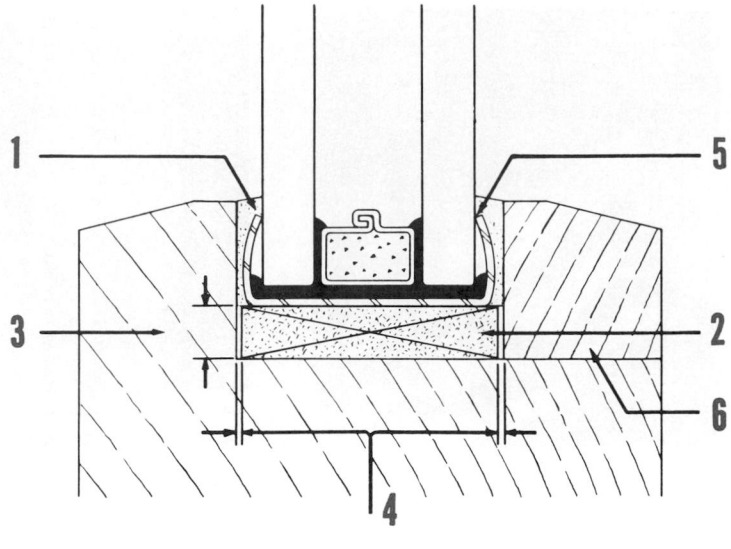

WOOD SASH

43-17a. *Puttying (glazing) of a metal edge insulating glass unit: 1. Glazing compound. 2. Setting blocks (two, treated wood, 4" long, located ¼ of the width in from each end of the unit). 3. Edge clearance (⅛", ³⁄₁₆", or ¼" at all edges, depending on the size; distribute proportionately). 4. Lateral clearance (a minimum of ¹⁄₁₆" for glazing compound). 5. Edge coverage (cover the channel with glazing compound for uniform appearance and maximum edge insulation). 6. Glazing stop (must not bear on the unit).*

43-16c. *Stationary windows come in many shapes. This one is called a round-top window.*

1¾" thick sash is usually used to provide strength.

Stationary windows may also be installed without a sash. The glass is set directly into rabbeted frame members and held in place with stops. As with the window-sash units, back puttying and face puttying of the glass (with or without a stop) will assure moisture-resistance. Fig. 43-17.

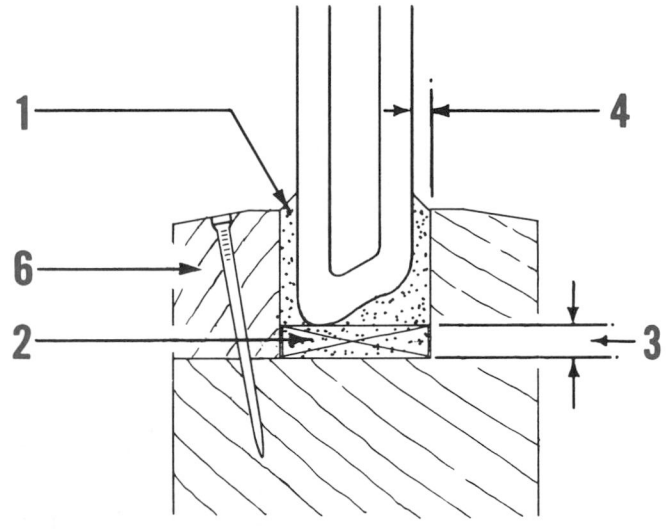

WOOD SASH

43-17b. *Glazing insulating glass with a glass edge: 1. Glazing compound. 2. Setting blocks (two, treated wood, 2" to 3" long, located ¼ of the width in from each end of the unit). 3. Edge clearance (allow ⅛" at all edges, and distribute proportionately). 4. Lateral clearance (a minimum of ¹⁄₁₆" for glazing compound). 5. Glazing stop (do not allow to bear on the unit).*

Awning and Hopper Windows

Awning window units have a frame in which one or more

operative sash are installed. Fig. 43-18. They often are made up for a large window wall and consist of three or more units in width and height.

Sash of the awning type are made to swing outward at the bottom. A similar unit, the hopper type, is one in which the top of the sash swings inward. Both types provide protection from rain when open.

Jambs are usually 1⅛" or more thick because they are rabbeted, while the sill is at least 1⁵⁄₁₆" thick when two or more sash are used in a complete frame. Each sash may also be provided with an individual

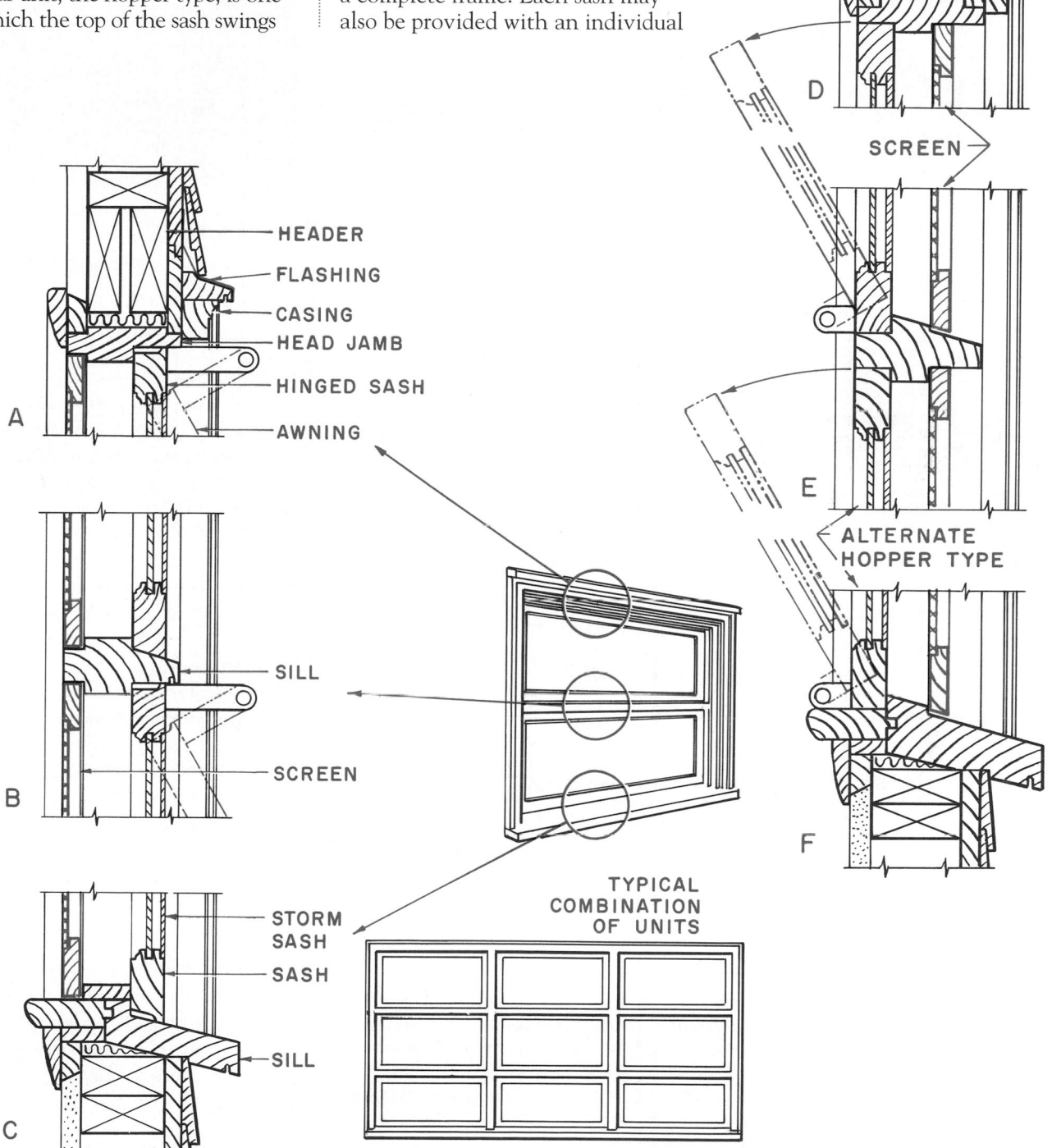

43-18. *Awning window cross sections: A. Head jamb. B. Horizontal mullion. C. Sill. Hopper window cross-sections: D. Head jamb. E. Horizontal mullion. F. Sill.*

VERTICAL SECTION

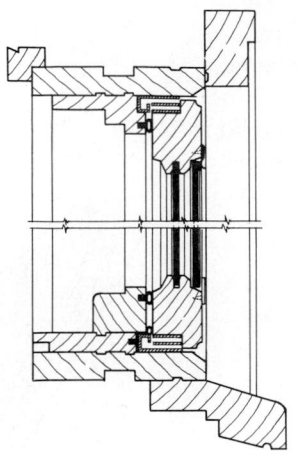

MULLION SECTION

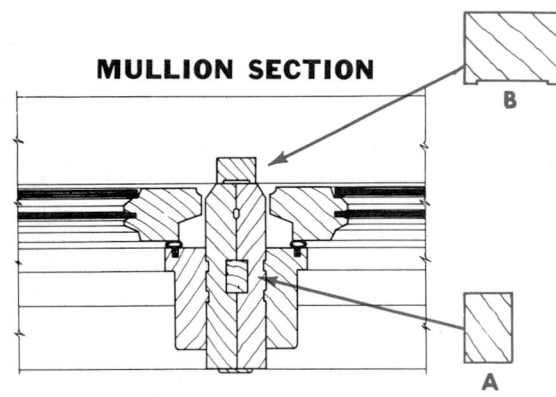

B

A

HORIZONTAL SECTION

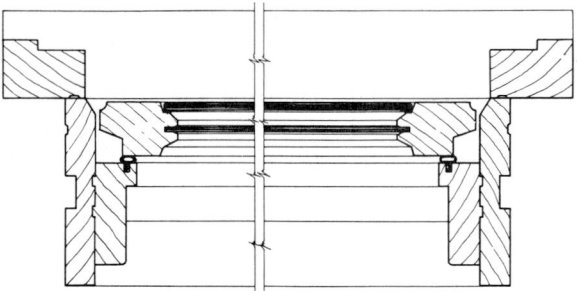

43-19a. *In the cross-section of the mullion, notice the spline, A, inserted in the groove provided in the side jambs. This aligns the window units when they are used in combination. A mullion strip, B, is then installed on the front edge for trim. In the vertical section, notice that the head and sill jambs also contain grooves in which a spline may be inserted to enable stacking these window units for other possible combinations.*

43-19b. *A window wall of hopper windows with stationary windows above.*

frame so that any combination in width and height can be used. Awning or hopper window units may consist of a combination of one or more fixed sash with the remainder being the operable type. Fig. 43-19. Operable sash are provided with hinges, pivots, and sash supporting arms. There are three types of operating hardware available for awning windows: the standard push bar, the lever lock, and the rotary gear. Fig. 43-20. Weather stripping and storm sash and screens are usually provided. The storm sash is eliminated when the windows are glazed with insulated glass.

Horizontal-Sliding Window Units

Horizontal-sliding windows appear similar to casement sash. However, the sash (in pairs) slide horizontally in separate tracks or guides located on the sill and head jamb. Fig. 43-21. Multiple window openings consist of two or more single units and may be used when a window-wall effect is desired. Fig. 43-22. As in most modern window units of all types, weather stripping,

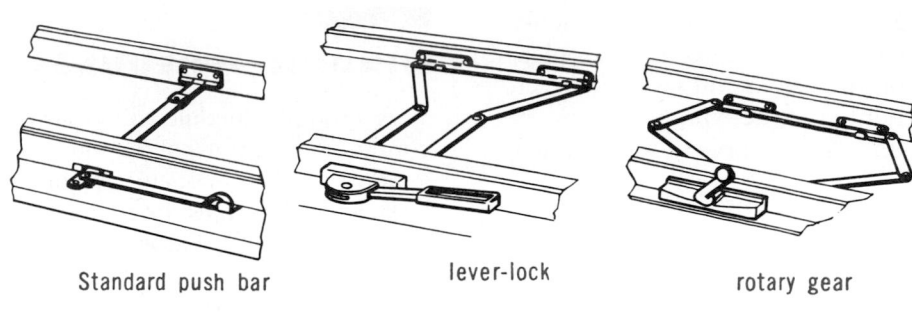

Standard push bar   lever-lock   rotary gear

43-20. *The three types of operating hardware for awning windows.*

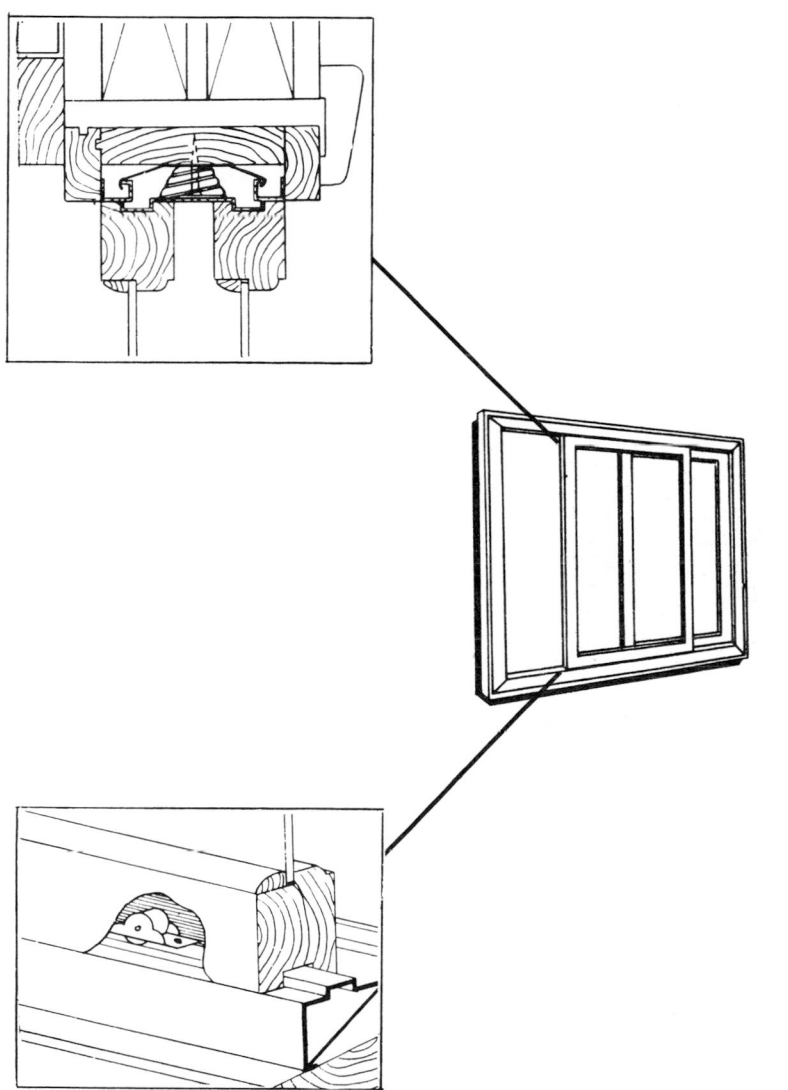

43-21. *A horizontal-sliding window unit. Note the spring-loaded track at the top of the sash. This provides a weathertight seal and also permits lifting the sash out of the window frame. In the sill section notice that the sash travels on a nylon roller for easy operation.*

43-22. *A window wall of horizontal-sliding window units.*

water-repellent preservative treatments, and sometimes hardware are included in these fully factory-assembled units.

Jalousie Windows

Jalousie windows consist of a series of small, horizontal glass pieces that are held by an end frame of metal. They usually open outward. Fig. 43-23. The sash can be metal or wood, and the window is opened by a handcrank similar to one on a casement window. Because of the difficulty in sealing their individual pieces of glass against air infiltration, jalousie windows are rarely used in cold climates. They are, however, quite common in warm climates because they open fully for good ventilation.

Metal Sash

Metal sash are available in units made of aluminum or steel, and the principal types are casement (Fig. 43-24), double-hung (Fig. 43-25),

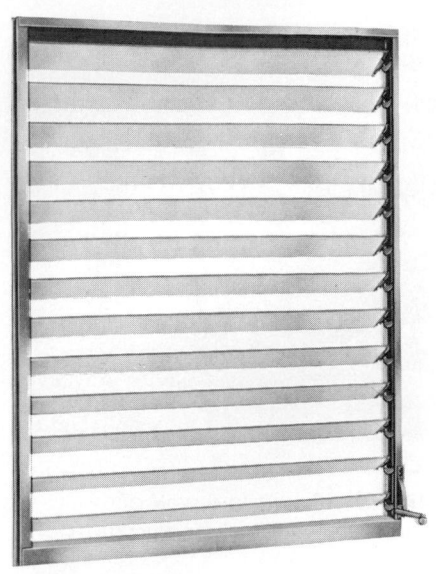

43-23. A jalousie window.

Moisture-laden air inside a house can condense into water droplets on the cold metal sash. However, neither of these problems are important factors in warm climates.

A window schedule will usually contain descriptions of the various windows, plus sash openings, glass sizes, and sometimes the rough opening sizes. The location of each

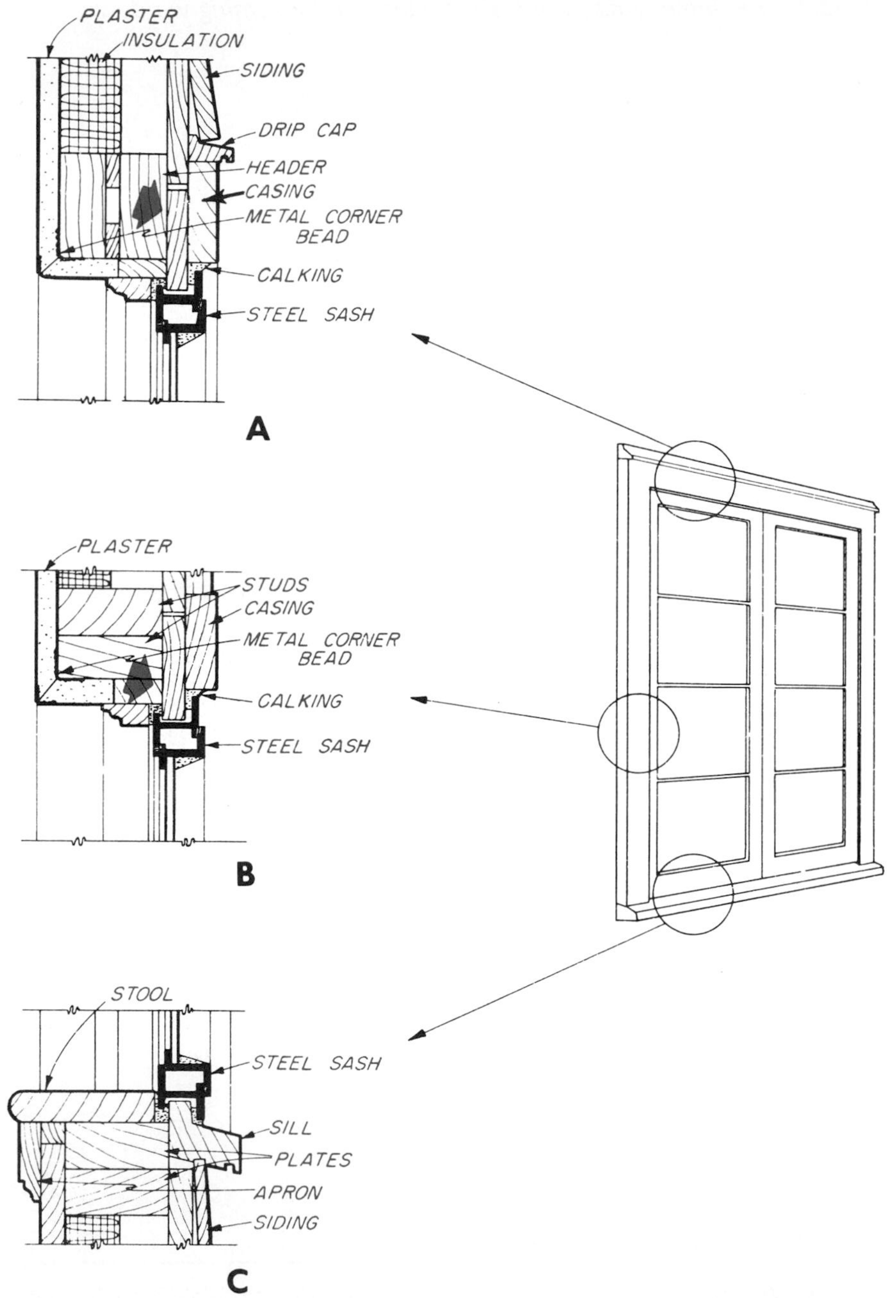

sliding, and stationary. Lights in the sash are divided in various patterns. The aluminum sash and frames are generally made of solid extruded aluminum alloy, welded at the joints. Steel sash are made of rolled shapes about ⅛" thick, most parts being Z-shaped or T-shaped, with welded butt joints. Steel sash should be treated to make them rust-resistant. Hardware, such as hinges, latches, and operators, is special and provided with the window. Screens should be ordered with the windows.

Actual details for installation vary according to the method of manufacture. It is common practice in frame construction to use a wood buck in the window opening to hold the metal frame. Fig. 43-24. The space between the metal and the wood is filled with caulking compound.

Because metal sash conducts heat away from the interior of the house, it is rarely used in cold climates. Another problem with using this type of sash in cold climates is condensation.

A — PLASTER, INSULATION, SIDING, DRIP CAP, HEADER, CASING, METAL CORNER BEAD, CALKING, STEEL SASH

B — PLASTER, STUDS, CASING, METAL CORNER BEAD, CALKING, STEEL SASH

C — STOOL, STEEL SASH, SILL, PLATES, APRON, SIDING

43-24. Metal casement sash. Cross-sections: A. Head jamb. B. Side jamb. C. Sill. The arrows indicate the wood buck which holds the metal frame in place.

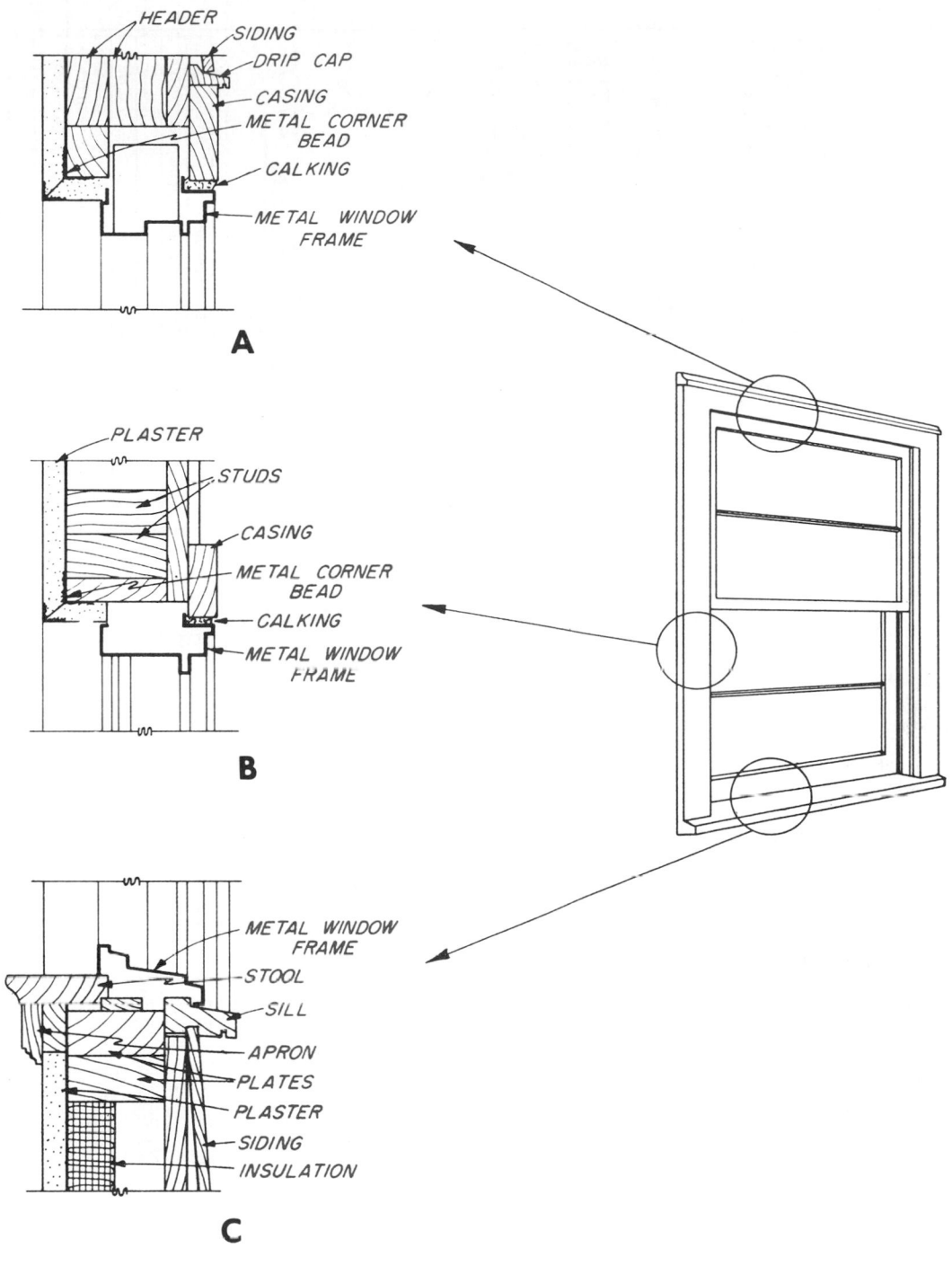

43-25. *Double-hung metal window. Cross-sections: A. Head jamb. B. Side jamb. C. Sill.*

window in a house is found by matching the number of the window in the window schedule with the corresponding number on the house plan. Fig. 43-26.

Figuring Rough Opening Sizes

When the rough opening size is not provided, it will have to be figured by the builder or obtained

from the window manufacturer's catalog. Tables showing glass size, sash size, and rough opening size for windows from various manufacturers are available from suppliers. In this book, typical

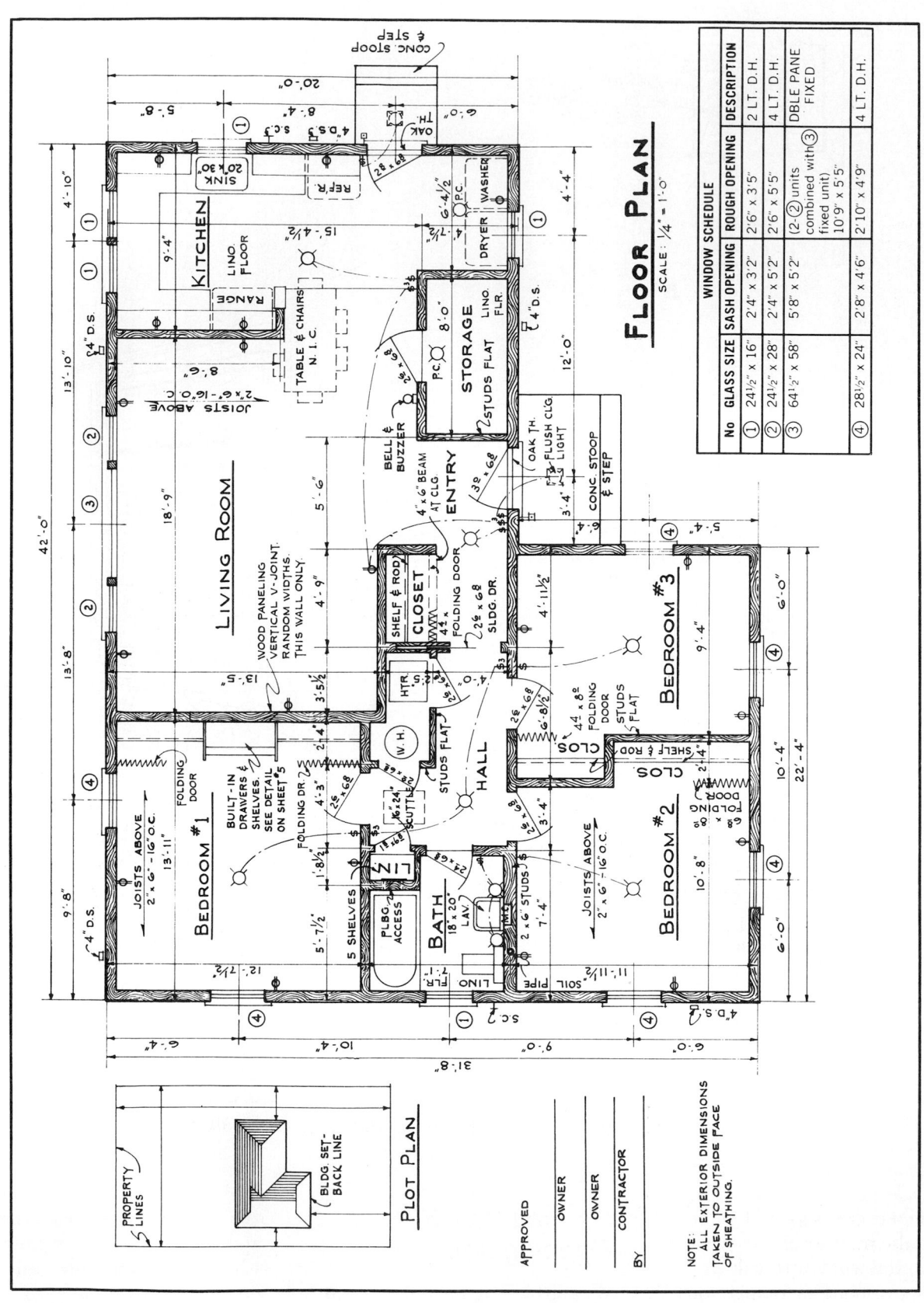

WINDOW SCHEDULE

No	GLASS SIZE	SASH OPENING	ROUGH OPENING	DESCRIPTION
①	24½" x 16"	2'4" x 3'2"	2'6" x 3'5"	2 LT. D.H.
②	24½" x 28"	2'4" x 5'2"	2'6" x 5'5"	4 LT. D.H.
③	64½" x 58"	5'8" x 5'2"	(2-②) units combined with ③ fixed unit) 10'9" x 5'5"	DBLE PANE FIXED
④	28½" x 24"	2'8" x 4'6"	2'10" x 4'9"	4 LT. D.H.

FLOOR PLAN

SCALE: ¼" = 1'-0"

43-26. *House plan with a window schedule.*

openings for double-hung windows are shown in Unit 30, "Wall Framing."

The rough opening size can also be figured if the glass size is known. Make the rough opening at least 6" wider and 10" higher than the window glass size. In specifying a window, the width of the glass is always given first, then the height, then the number of pieces of glass (or lights) and the window style. For example, 28½" × 24", 2 lights D.H. means that the glass itself is 28½" wide and 24" high and that there are two pieces of glass in a double-hung unit.

To figure the rough opening width, add 6" to the given width: 28½" + 6" = 34½", or 2' 10½". To obtain the rough opening height, add the upper and lower glass height together, and then add another 10": 24" + 24" + 10" = 58", or 4' 10". These allowances are fairly standard and provide for the weights, springs, balances, room for plumbing and squaring, and for the normal adjustments. However, when the window manufacturer is known, use his recommended rough opening sizes.

The rough opening sizes vary slightly among manufacturers, as can be seen by comparing sample tables from two typical manufacturers' catalogs designating the sizes of standard units. Fig. 43-27. The window schedule in Fig. 43-26 indicates a glass size of 28½" × 24" for window No. 4. In Fig. 43-26a, read the width of the glass size across the top (28½") and then follow down that column to the glass length (24"). The window is designated 2846, which is the manufacturer's catalog number. Note: in the case of this particular manufacturer, the number is also the sash opening. Window 2846 has a sash opening width of 2'8" and a length of 4'6". The rough opening given on this chart is 2'10" × 4'9" for a framed wall. (The unit

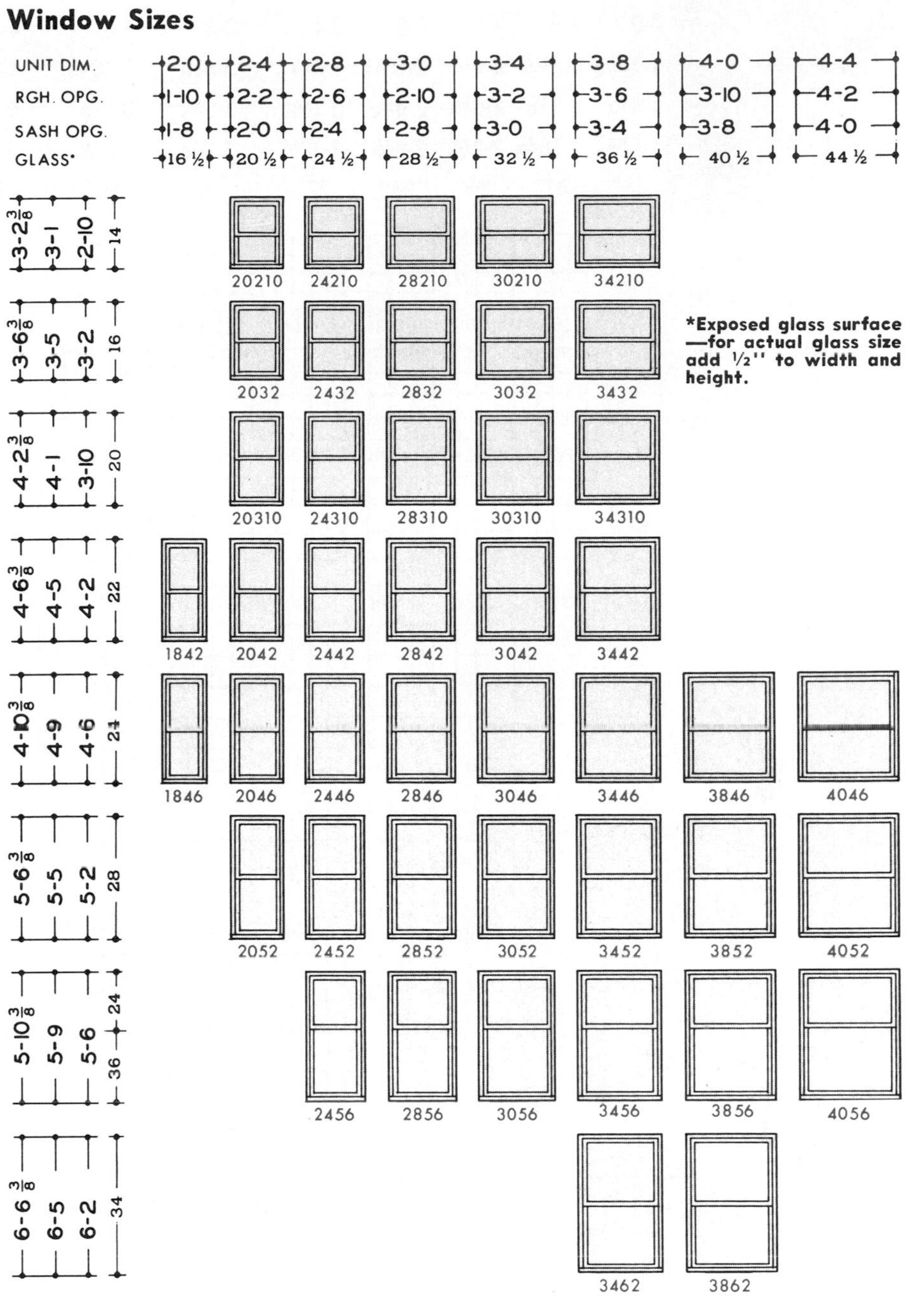

Window Sizes

UNIT DIM.	2-0	2-4	2-8	3-0	3-4	3-8	4-0	4-4
RGH. OPG.	1-10	2-2	2-6	2-10	3-2	3-6	3-10	4-2
SASH OPG.	1-8	2-0	2-4	2-8	3-0	3-4	3-8	4-0
GLASS*	16 ½	20 ½	24 ½	28 ½	32 ½	36 ½	40 ½	44 ½

*Exposed glass surface —for actual glass size add ½" to width and height.

43-27a. A manufacturer's table for double-hung windows.

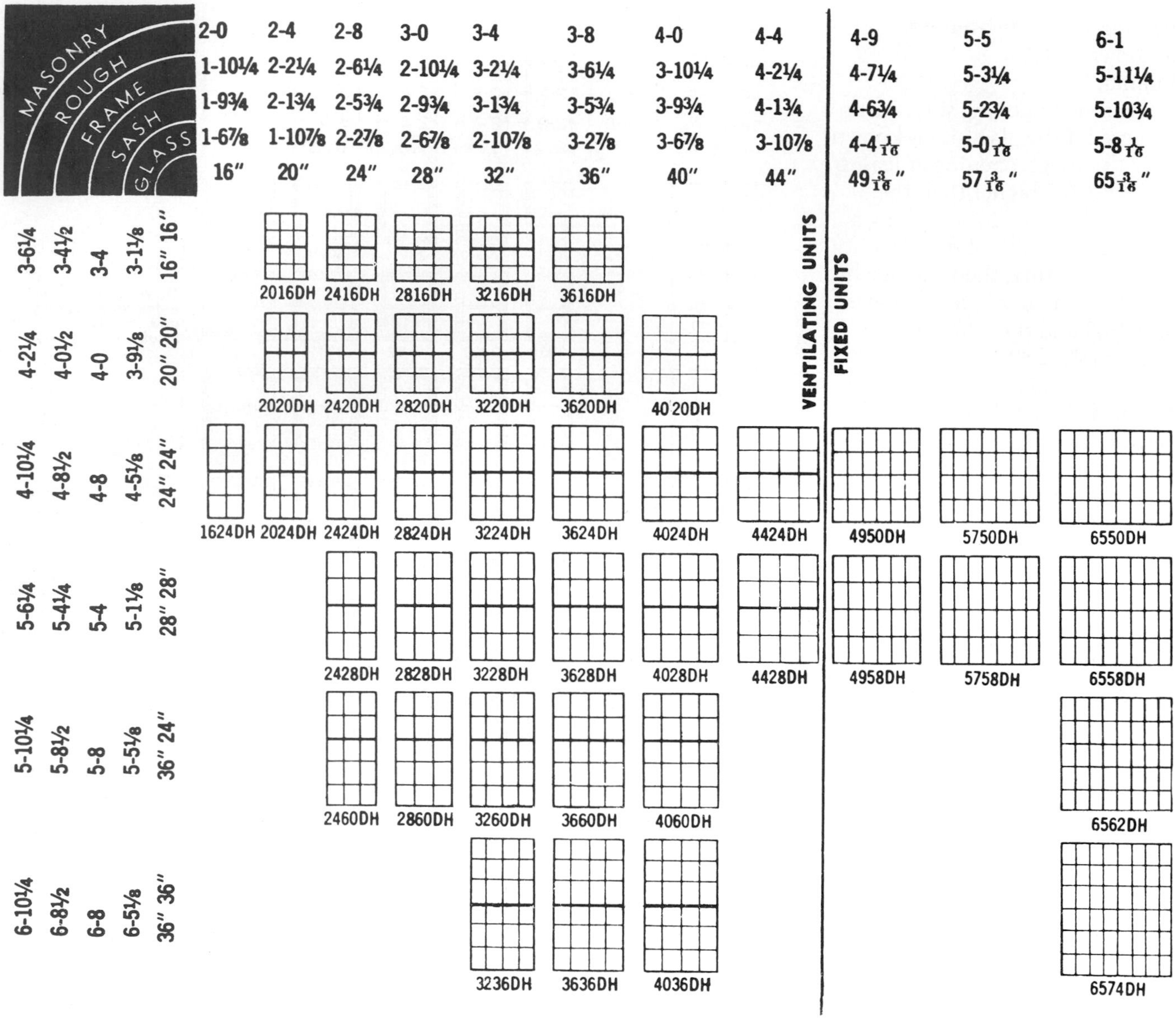
MASONRY
ROUGH
FRAME
SASH
GLASS
2-0 2-4 2-8 3-0 3-4 3-8 4-0 4-4 4-9 5-5 6-1
1-10¼ 2-2¼ 2-6¼ 2-10¼ 3-2¼ 3-6¼ 3-10¼ 4-2¼ 4-7¼ 5-3¼ 5-11¼
1-9¾ 2-1¾ 2-5¾ 2-9¾ 3-1¾ 3-5¾ 3-9¾ 4-1¾ 4-6¾ 5-2¾ 5-10¾
1-6⅞ 1-10⅞ 2-2⅞ 2-6⅞ 2-10⅞ 3-2⅞ 3-6⅞ 3-10⅞ 4-4 1/16 5-0 1/16 5-8 1/16
16" 20" 24" 28" 32" 36" 40" 44" 49 3/16" 57 3/16" 65 3/16"
VENTILATING UNITS
FIXED UNITS
3-6¼ 3-4½ 3-4 3-1⅛ 16" 16"
2016DH 2416DH 2816DH 3216DH 3616DH
4-2¼ 4-0½ 4-0 3-9⅛ 20" 20"
2020DH 2420DH 2820DH 3220DH 3620DH 40 20DH
4-10¼ 4-8½ 4-8 4-5⅛ 24" 24"
1624DH 2024DH 2424DH 2824DH 3224DH 3624DH 4024DH 4424DH 4950DH 5750DH 6550DH
5-6¼ 5-4¼ 5-4 5-1⅛ 28" 28"
2428DH 2828DH 3228DH 3628DH 4028DH 4428DH 4958DH 5758DH 6558DH
5-10¼ 5-8½ 5-8 5-5⅛ 36" 24"
2460DH 2860DH 3260DH 3660DH 4060DH 6562DH
6-10¼ 6-8½ 6-8 6-5⅛ 36" 36"
3236DH 3636DH 4036DH 6574DH

43-27b. *Another example of a table for double-hung windows.*

size, which is the masonry opening for a brick veneer wall, is also given on these tables.) The rough opening figured earlier (2'10½" × 4'10") is larger than the manufacturer's recommended opening. Using the method for figuring a rough opening will insure getting the window unit into the opening, but it may require additional blocking or shimming. Therefore, it is always best to use the specific manufacturer's recommendations for a rough opening size.

Figuring Rough Openings for Combination Units. Many times, window units of various styles and sizes are combined to make up larger units for a particular room and use. These combined units are separated only by vertical piers called mullion strips. Fig. 43-28. Therefore, the rough opening for the combined unit will be less than the total of the rough openings for the units if they were used individually.

In the house plan in Fig. 43-26, note the window schedule on the plan calls for a combination unit in the living room consisting of two window units No. 2 and one window unit No. 3. If this unit is to be made up to look like C in Fig. 43-28, figure the width of the multiple opening by adding the individual sash openings to the

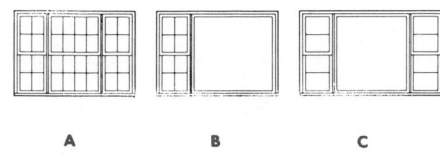

43-28. *Typical combinations for contemporary or traditional treatment with grills and mullions.*

width of the mullions, plus 2" for the overall rough opening. In this example the sash opening for the No. 2 unit in the window schedule is 2'4". The sash opening for the No. 3 unit is 5'8". Figs. 43-26 and 43-29. Since there are two No. 2 units, add 2'4" twice to the 5'8": 2'4" + 2'4" + 5'8" = 9'16", or 10'4". There are two mullions in our example. If each mullion is 1½" wide, the total mullion width would be 3". Add this to the sash width and then add 2" for the rough opening: 10'4" + 3" + 2" = 10'9". Note that this is the rough opening width listed for the combination window unit (No. 3) in the window schedule. Fig. 43-26. The rough opening height is figured the same way for combination units as for individual units.

INSTALLATION

Window frames are generally assembled in a mill. The preassembled window frame is easily installed, but care should be taken. Regardless of the quality of the window purchased, it is only as good as its installation. Before actually installing a window, apply a primer coat of paint to all wood members to prevent undue warpage.

The general procedure for the installation of a window frame is very similar regardless of style or manufacturer. Fig. 43-30. However, always refer to the manufacturer's instructions for any specific recommendations. For example, some manufacturers recommend that the sash be removed from the frame to prevent breakage and provide easier handling of the unit. Others specify not only that the sash be left in the frame but also that diagonal braces and, in some cases, reinforcing blocks be left in place to insure that the frame remains square and in proper alignment.

When a siding material is applied over sheathing, the windows are installed first and the siding applied later. Strips of 15-pound asphalt felt should be put over the sheathing around the openings. Fig. 43-31.

Place the frame in the opening from the outside, allowing the

PICTURE WINDOWS

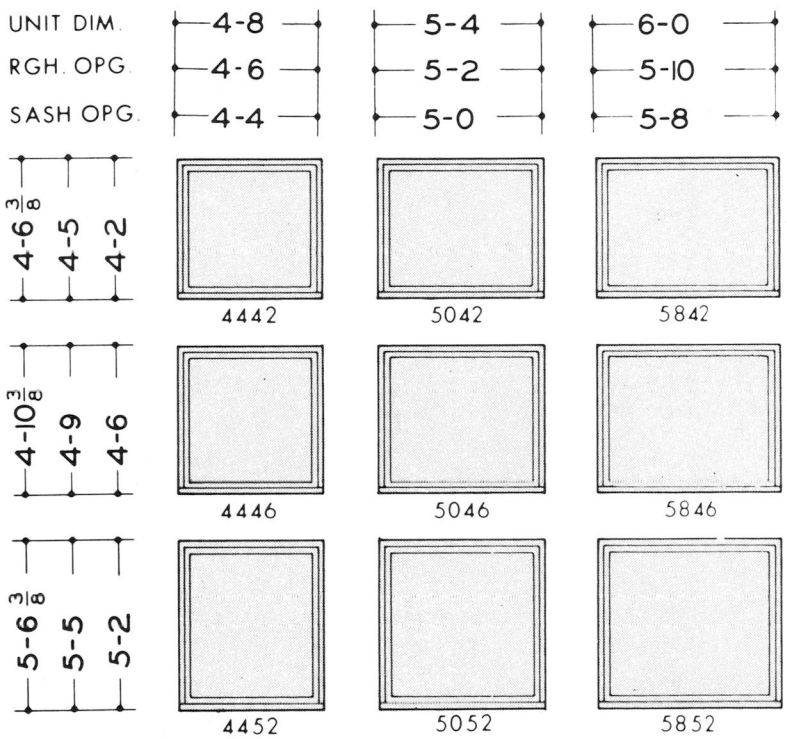

UNIT NO.	1" GLASS RABBET	1" GLASS SIZE
4442	49 x 46½	48½ x 46
5042	57 x 46½	56½ x 46⅛
5842	65 x 46½	64½ x 46
4446	49 x 50½	48½ x 50
5046	57 x 50½	56½ x 50
5846	65 x 50½	64½ x 50
4452	49 x 58½	48½ x 58
5052	57 x 58½	56½ x 58⅛
5852	65 x 58½	64½ x 58

43-29. *A manufacturer's table for stationary windows.*

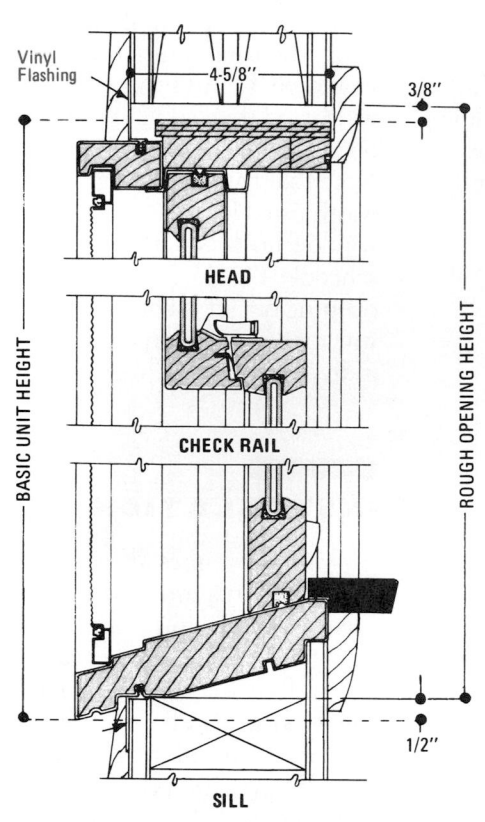

Vinyl Flashing

4-5/8"

3/8"

HEAD

BASIC UNIT HEIGHT

ROUGH OPENING HEIGHT

CHECK RAIL

1/2"

SILL

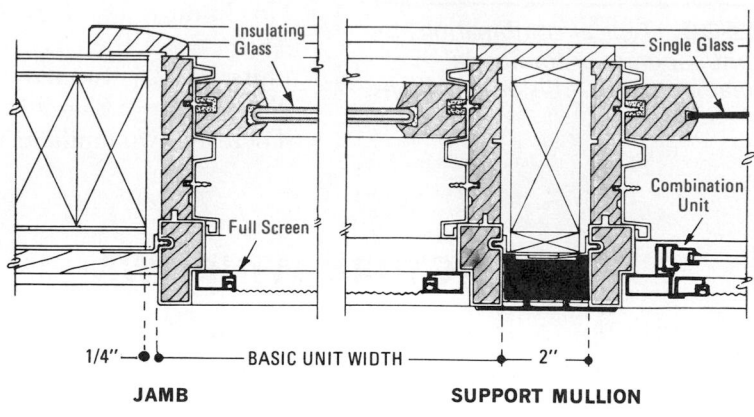

Insulating Glass

Single Glass

Full Screen

Combination Unit

1/4"

BASIC UNIT WIDTH

2"

JAMB

SUPPORT MULLION

BRICK VENEER AND SOLID MASONRY INSTALLATION DETAILS

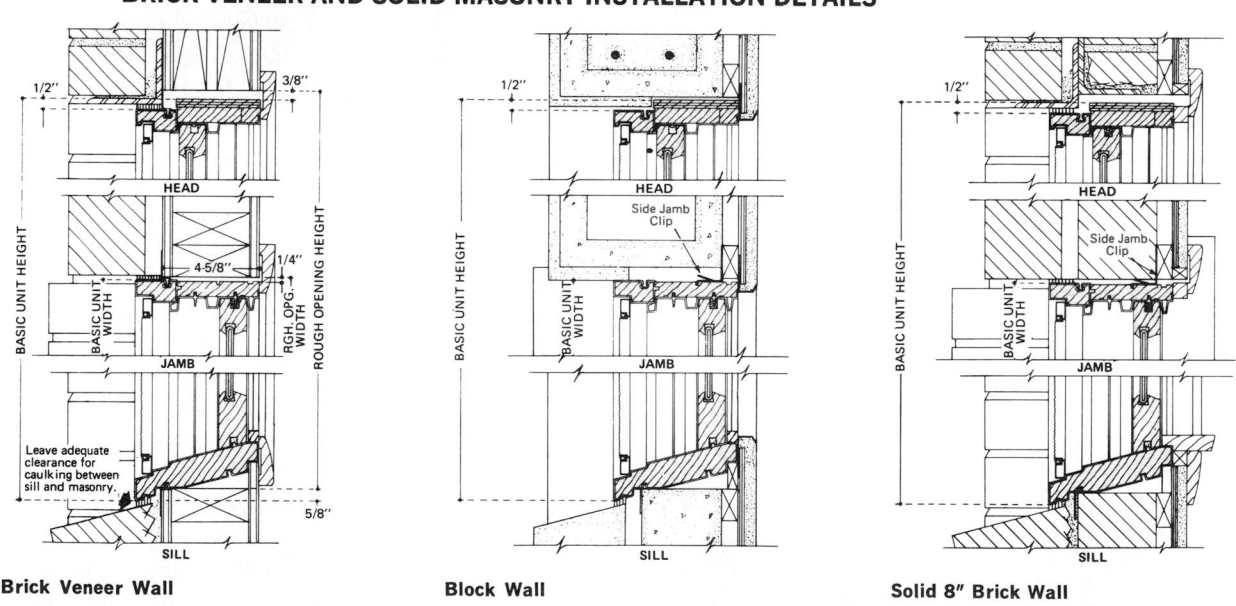

1/2"

3/8"

HEAD

BASIC UNIT HEIGHT

BASIC UNIT WIDTH

4-5/8"

1/4"

RGH. OPG. WIDTH

ROUGH OPENING HEIGHT

JAMB

Leave adequate clearance for caulking between sill and masonry.

5/8"

SILL

Brick Veneer Wall

1/2"

HEAD

Side Jamb Clip

BASIC UNIT HEIGHT

BASIC UNIT WIDTH

JAMB

SILL

Block Wall

1/2"

HEAD

Side Jamb Clip

BASIC UNIT HEIGHT

BASIC UNIT WIDTH

JAMB

SILL

Solid 8" Brick Wall

43-30a. *Installation details for double-hung windows.*

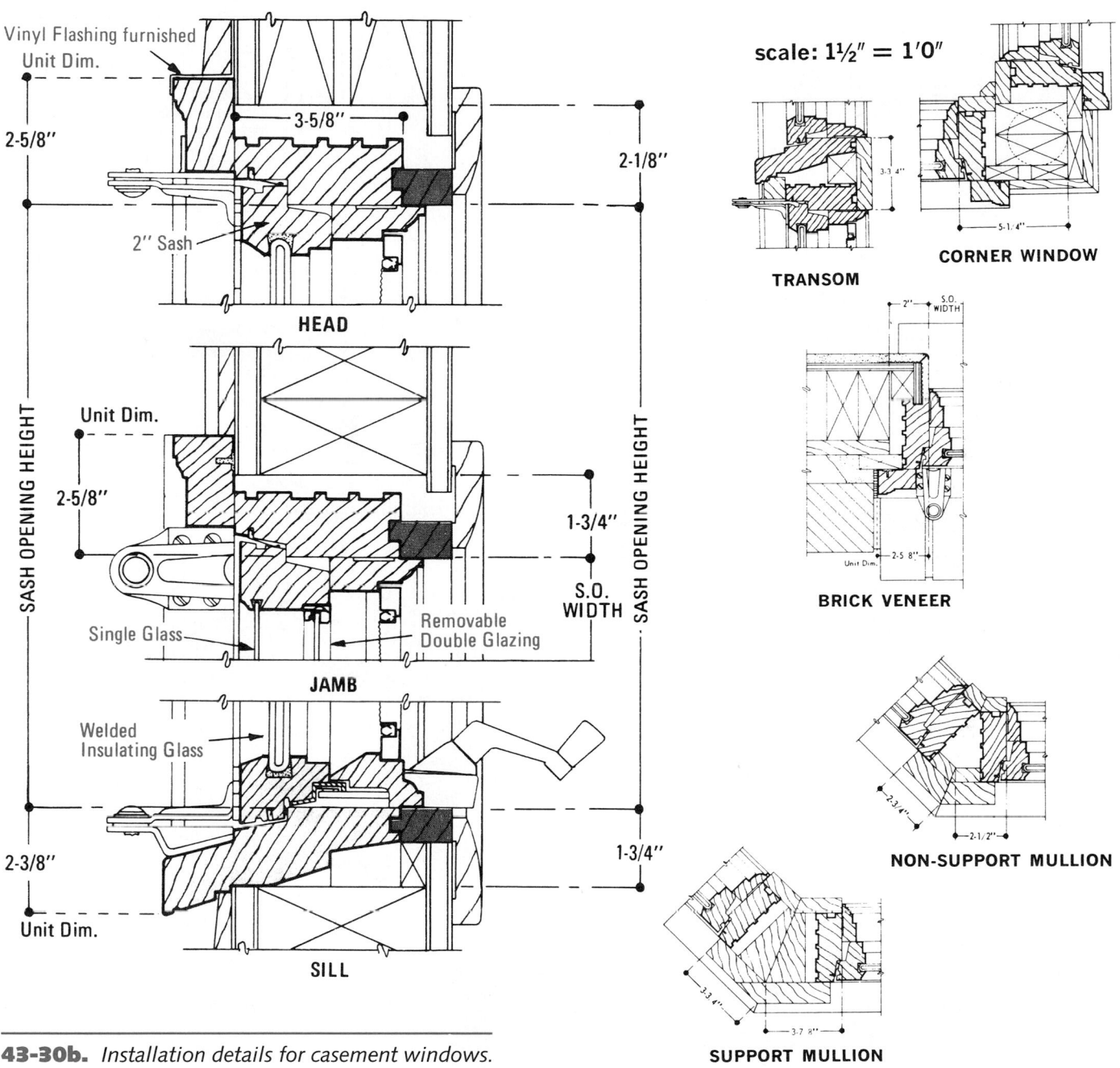

scale: $1\frac{1}{2}'' = 1'0''$

Vinyl Flashing furnished
Unit Dim.

2-5/8''

3-5/8''

2-1/8''

2'' Sash

HEAD

TRANSOM

CORNER WINDOW

Unit Dim.

2-5/8''

SASH OPENING HEIGHT

1-3/4''

S.O.
WIDTH

SASH OPENING HEIGHT

Single Glass

Removable
Double Glazing

JAMB

2''   S.O.
WIDTH

Unit Dim.

2-5 8''

BRICK VENEER

Welded
Insulating Glass

2-3/8''

1-3/4''

Unit Dim.

SILL

2-3 4''

2-1/2''

NON-SUPPORT MULLION

3-3 4''

3-7 8''

SUPPORT MULLION

43-30b. *Installation details for casement windows.*

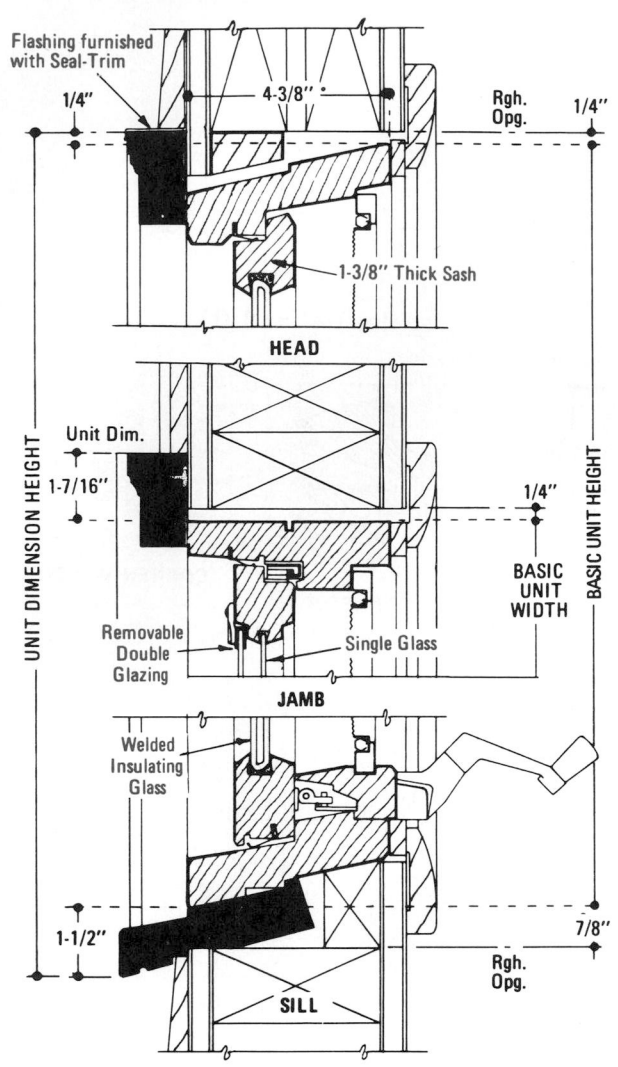

Flashing furnished with Seal-Trim

1/4"

4-3/8"

Rgh. Opg.

1/4"

1-3/8" Thick Sash

HEAD

UNIT DIMENSION HEIGHT

Unit Dim.

1-7/16"

1/4"

BASIC UNIT WIDTH

BASIC UNIT HEIGHT

Removable Double Glazing

Single Glass

JAMB

Welded Insulating Glass

1-1/2"

7/8"

Rgh. Opg.

SILL

Details: typical combinations

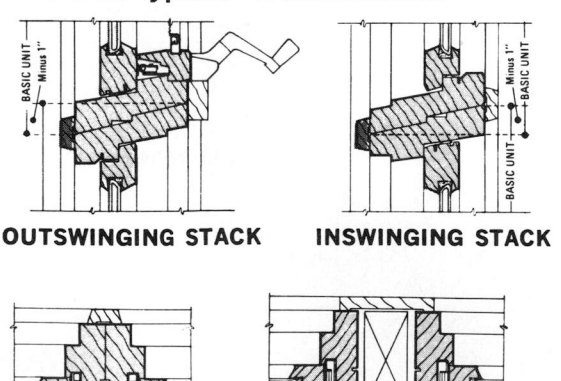

BASIC UNIT

Minus 1"

Minus 1"

BASIC UNIT

OUTSWINGING STACK

INSWINGING STACK

BASIC UNIT

BASIC UNIT

MULLION

BASIC UNIT

2-1/8"

BASIC UNIT

SUPPORT MULLION

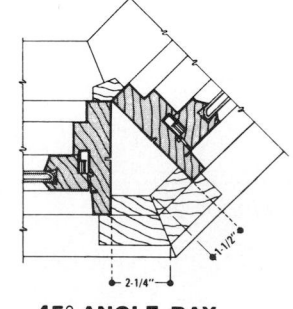

1-1/2"

2-1/4"

45° ANGLE BAY

43-30c. *Installation details for awning windows.*

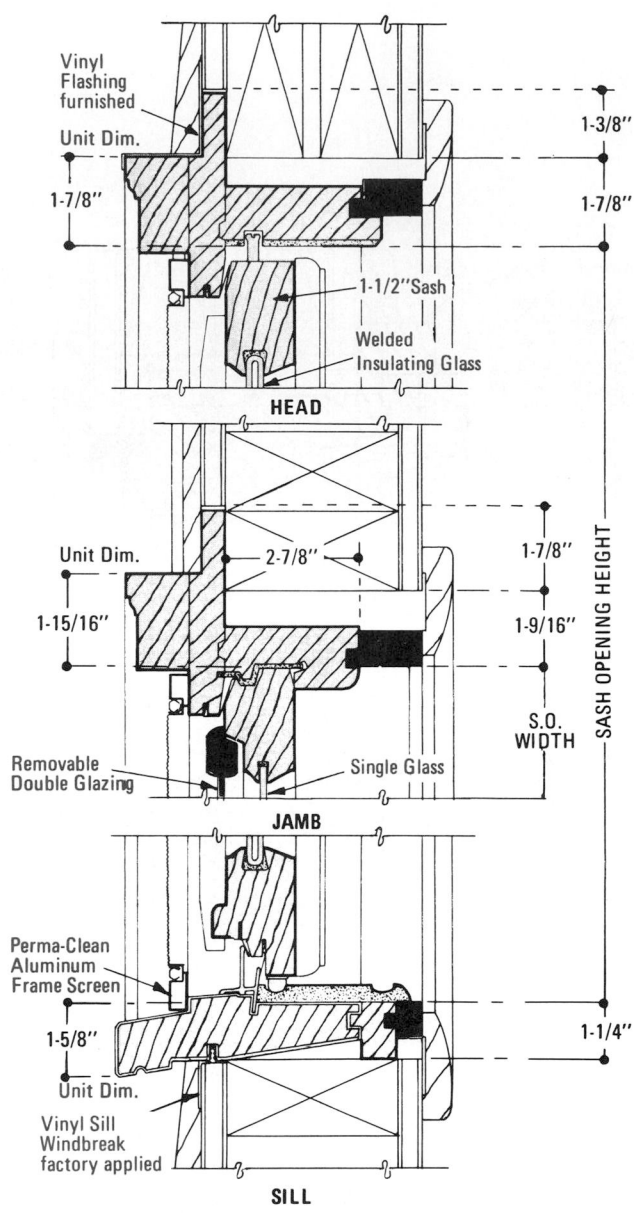

Vinyl Flashing furnished

Unit Dim.

1-7/8"

1-3/8"

1-7/8"

1-1/2"Sash

Welded Insulating Glass

HEAD

Unit Dim.

1-15/16"

2-7/8"

1-7/8"

1-9/16"

S.O. WIDTH

SASH OPENING HEIGHT

Removable Double Glazing

Single Glass

JAMB

Perma-Clean Aluminum Frame Screen

1-5/8"

Unit Dim.

Vinyl Sill Windbreak factory applied

1-1/4"

SILL

43-30d. *Installation details for horizontal-sliding windows.*

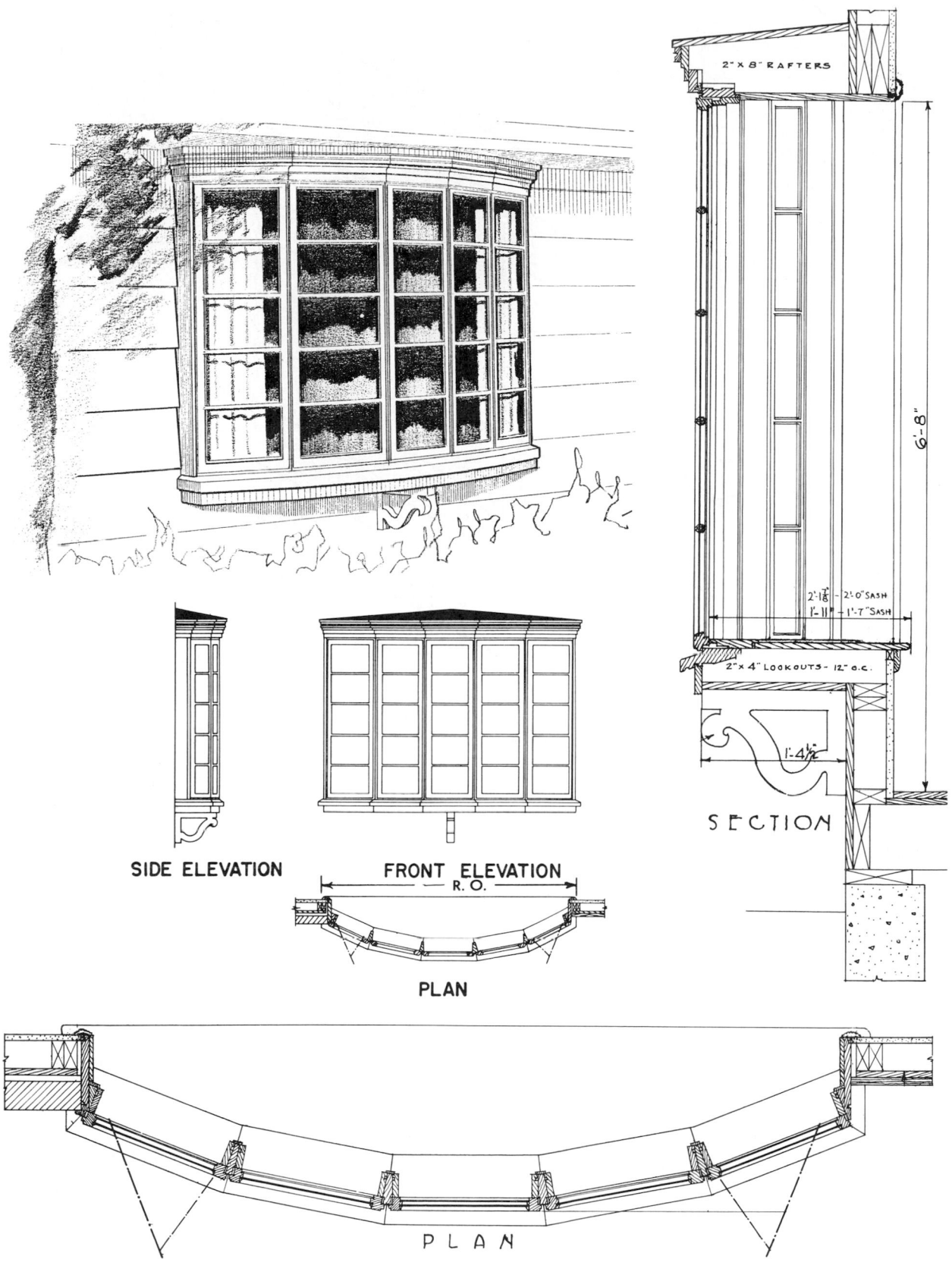

2" X 8" RAFTERS

6'-8"

2'-1⅛" – 2'-0" SASH
1'-11" – 1'-7" SASH

2" x 4" LOOKOUTS - 12" o.c.

1'-4½"

SECTION

SIDE ELEVATION

FRONT ELEVATION
R. O.

PLAN

PLAN

43-30e. *Installation details for a casement bow window.*

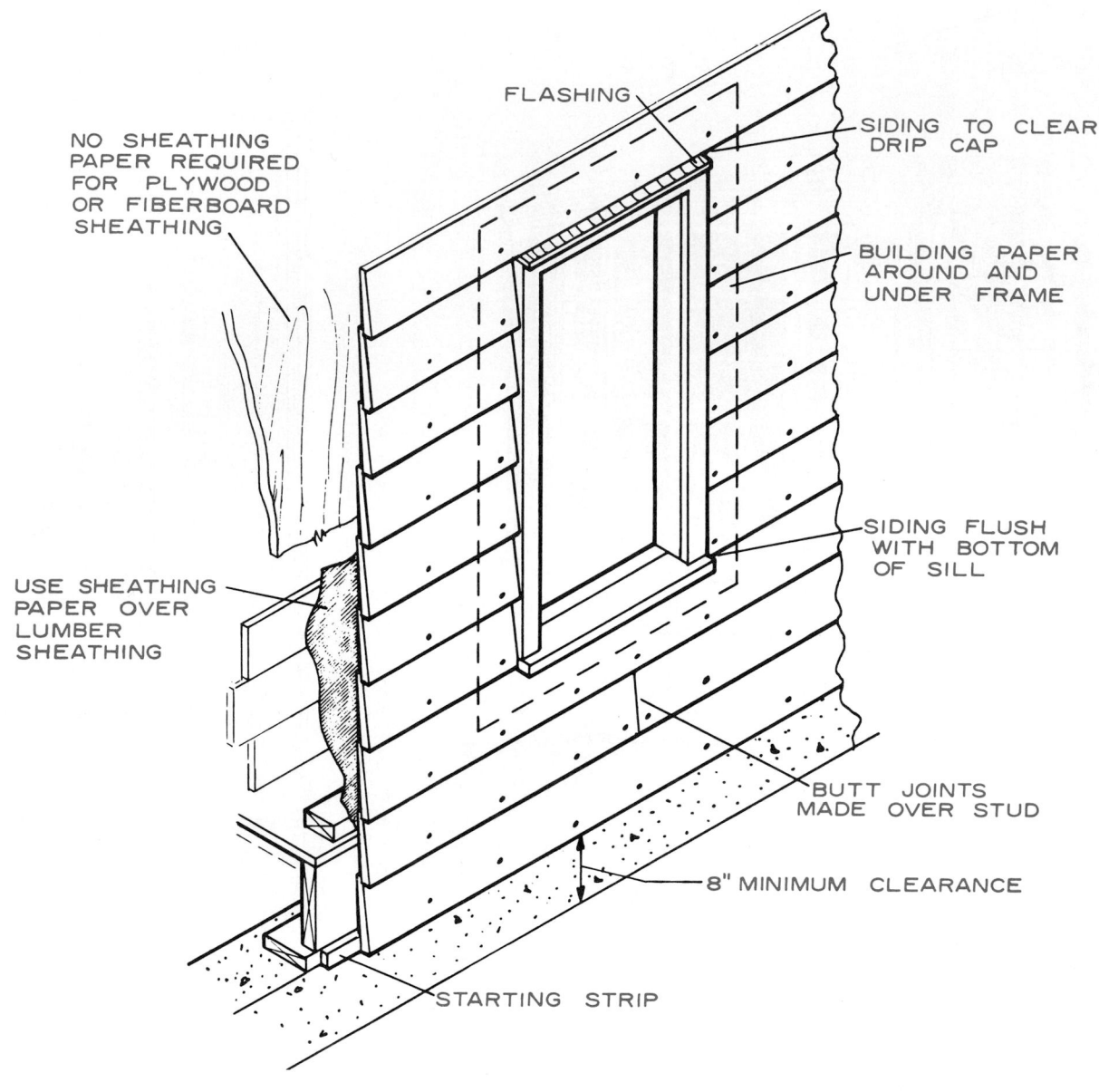

NO SHEATHING PAPER REQUIRED FOR PLYWOOD OR FIBERBOARD SHEATHING

FLASHING

SIDING TO CLEAR DRIP CAP

BUILDING PAPER AROUND AND UNDER FRAME

SIDING FLUSH WITH BOTTOM OF SILL

USE SHEATHING PAPER OVER LUMBER SHEATHING

BUTT JOINTS MADE OVER STUD

8" MINIMUM CLEARANCE

STARTING STRIP

43-31. *Window frame installation details for a framed wall with horizontal lap siding.*

subsill to rest on the rough frame at the bottom, and hold the unit up tightly against the building. Fig. 43-32a. Level and plumb the window frame, then wedge with shingles and tack in place. Fig. 43-32b. Check the sill and jamb with the level and square. Fig. 43-32c-e. When everything is in order, use 16d galvanized casing nails through the outside casings; or, if blind stops are provided, use 8d common nails. Fig. 43-32f-i. (When window frames are furnished with blind stops for installation, the sheathing should be installed 1½"back from the window rough openings. Figs. 43-33 and 43-34.) The nails should be spaced about 12" apart. They should penetrate the sheathing and/or the trimmer studs and the header over the window. While nailing, open and close the sash to

see that it works freely. The side and head casings are fastened in the same manner.

Basement Windows

Basement window units are made of wood, plastic, or metal. Fig. 43-35. In most cases, the sash is removed from the frame. The frame is set into the concrete forms for a poured wall, and the wall is

43-32a. *Install the window frame in the rough opening.*

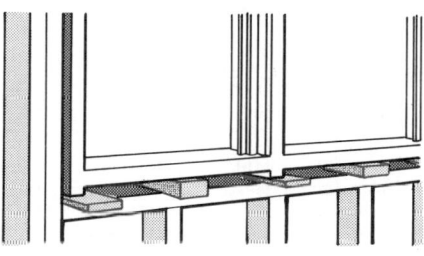

43-32b. *Shim under the raised jamb legs and at the center of long sills and mullions.*

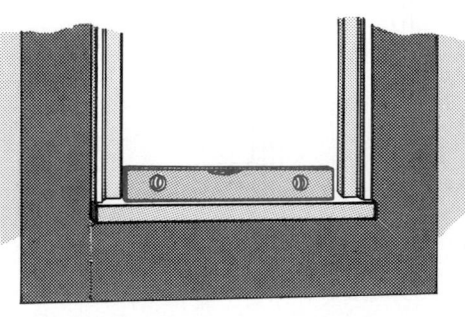

43-32c. *Level the sill by adjusting shims as necessary.*

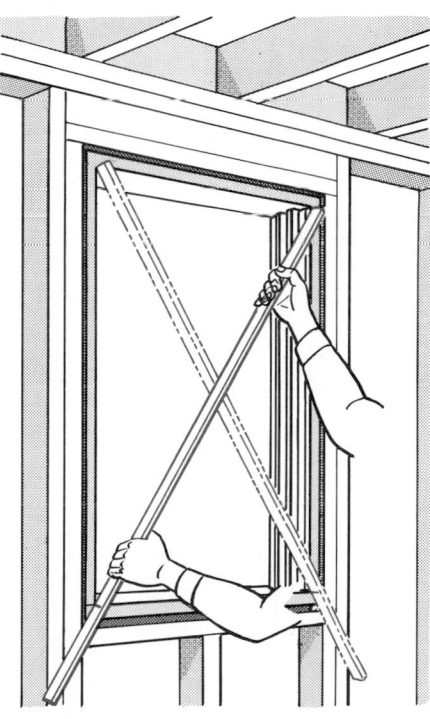

43-32d. *When the diagonal measurements are equal, the unit is square.*

43-32e. *Shim the tops of the jambs and recheck the diagonals.*

43-32f. *Measure the distance between the side jambs to be sure they are equidistant at all points.*

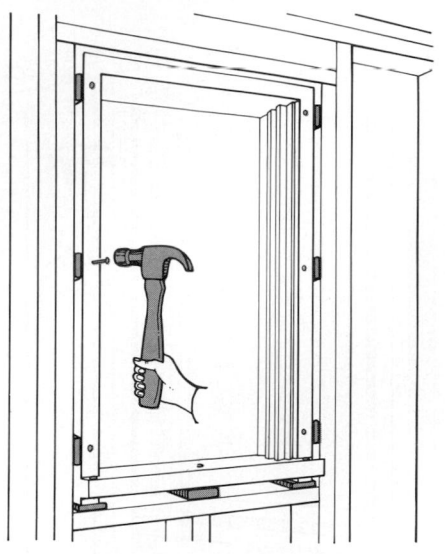

43-32g. *Nail the side jambs through the shims.*

43-32h. *Install the sash. If the unit is out of square, the meeting rails will not be parallel.*

43-32i. *Pack insulation between the jambs and the trimmer studs or use expanding foam to seal the gaps.*

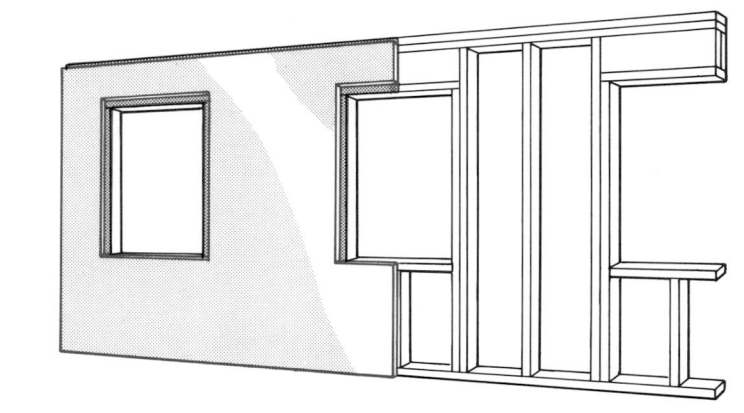

43-33a. *To accommodate the installation of a window unit with wood blind stops, the sheathing is nailed 1½" back from the rough opening.*

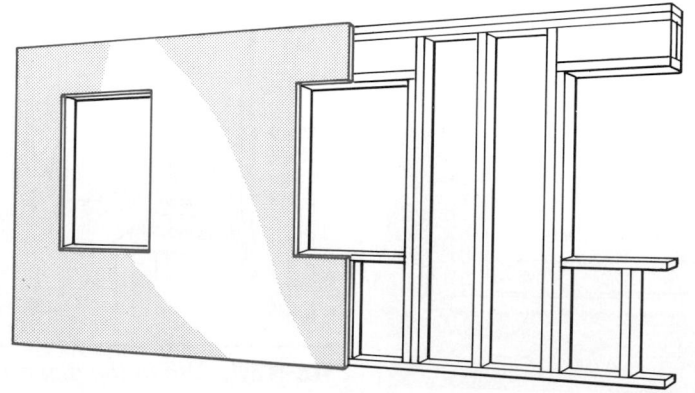

43-33b. *For the installation of windows that are nailed in place through the casing, the sheathing is nailed even with the inside of the rough opening.*

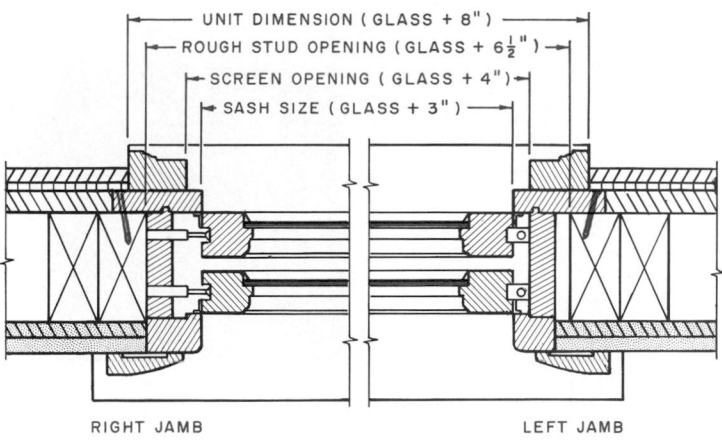

UNIT DIMENSION (GLASS + 8")
ROUGH STUD OPENING (GLASS + 6½")
SCREEN OPENING (GLASS + 4")
SASH SIZE (GLASS + 3")

RIGHT JAMB   LEFT JAMB

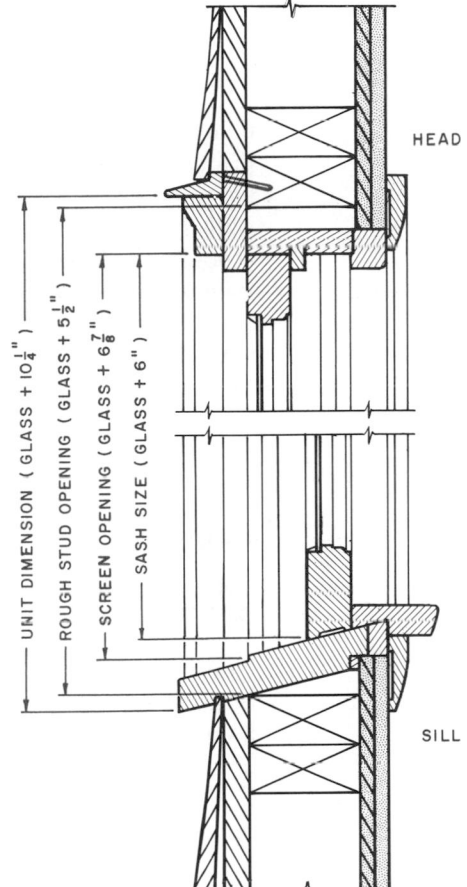

HEAD

UNIT DIMENSION (GLASS + 10¼")
ROUGH STUD OPENING (GLASS + 5½")
SCREEN OPENING (GLASS + 6⅞")
SASH SIZE (GLASS + 6")

SILL

43-34a. *Installation details for a double-hung window showing nailing through the blind stops.*

43-34b. *Some window units are available with a vinyl covering to eliminate painting. A vinyl anchorage flange and windbreak then serve as a blind stop (see arrows).*

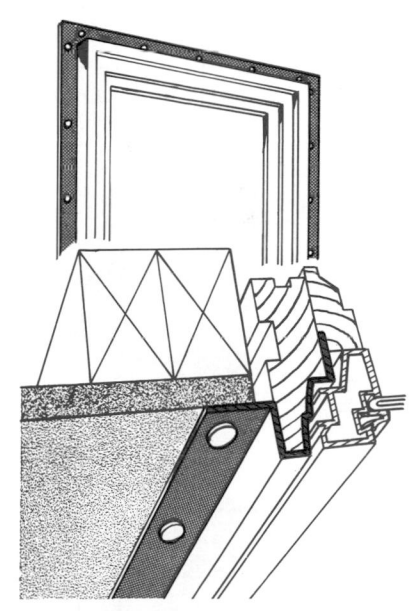

43-34c. *The window is installed with 1¾" galvanized nails through the vinyl anchoring flange. The outside wall covering is applied over this flange. With this method, there are no exposed nails on the exterior of the window.*

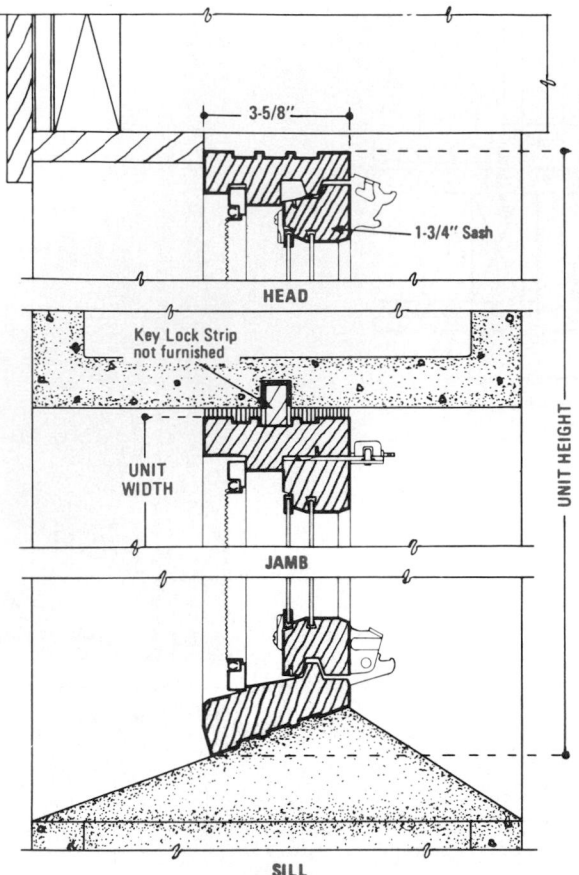

HEAD

3-5/8"

1-3/4" Sash

Key Lock Strip
not furnished

UNIT WIDTH

JAMB

UNIT HEIGHT

SILL

Typical basement installation in concrete block wall.

43-35a. *Installation details for a wood basement window unit.*

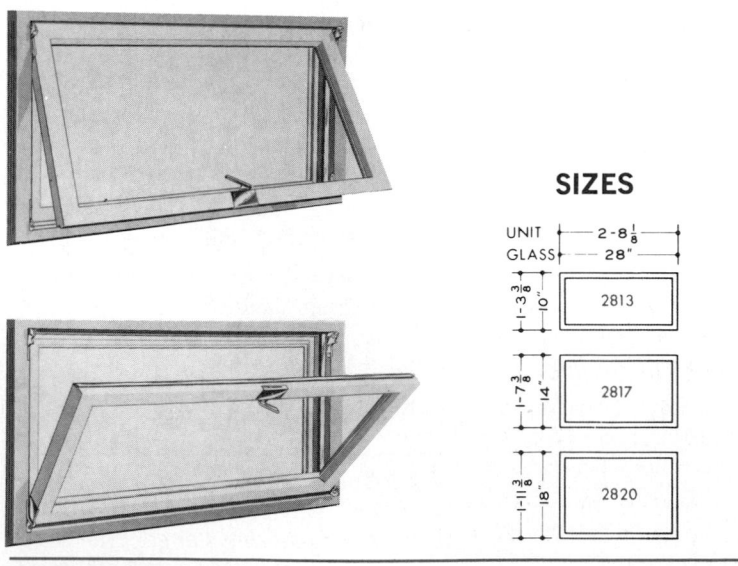

SIZES

UNIT	2-8⅛
GLASS	28"

1-3⅜ / 10"	2813
1-7⅜ / 14"	2817
1-11⅜ / 18"	2820

43-35b. *Some wood basement window units are dual hinged so that they may be opened from either the top or the bottom. The insert shows typical sizes of wood basement window units.*

43-36. *The frame of a basement window is usually cast into the foundation.*

poured with the window frame in place. Fig. 43-36. If the windows are to be set into a concrete block wall, special blocks are available to accommodate the various types of frames. The floor framing is then constructed on the foundation wall with the window frames already set in place. The sills are usually installed later.

WINDOW SCREENS AND STORM PANELS

Window screens and storms may be an integral part of the window frame, or they may be separate units of wood, metal, or plastic. Figs. 43-37 and 43-38. For double-hung windows, separate units are designed so that the screens and storm panels may be stored within the unit. In this type the lower sash is usually the only one that is screened. The unit is provided with three tracks; the upper window remains in the upper position, the lower window may be slid up out of the way and the screen brought down for warm weather. For cold weather the screen is stored in the upper position, and the storm panel is lowered.

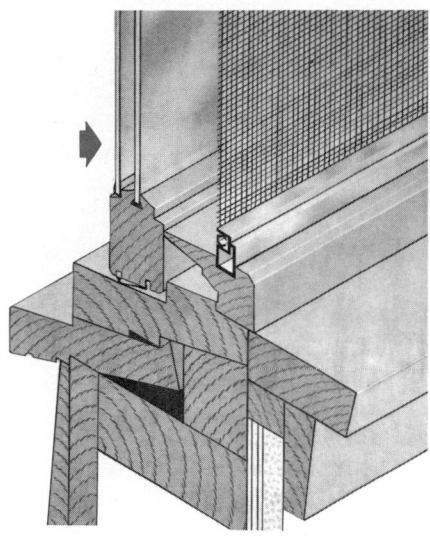

43-37. *If insulating glass is not used, a storm panel (arrow) can be installed as part of the window frame on most window styles.*

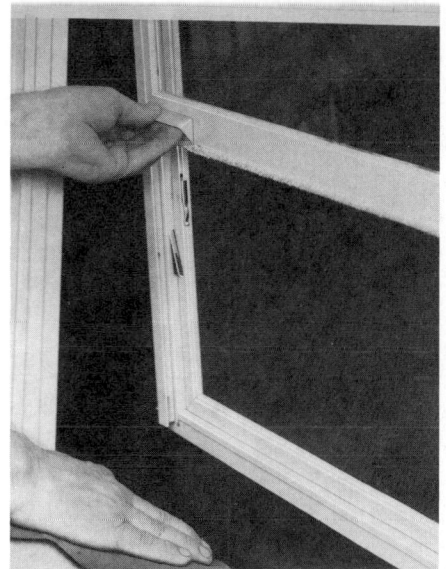

43-38. *Some combinations of screen and storm sash can be released to allow cleaning of the sill.*

Casement, awning, hopper, and sliding window units have the storm panel set into a rabbet in the outside of the window sash. The screen is a separate insert which is installed for the summer months. Screens used with double-hung,

43-39. *Screens for casement windows that open out are installed on the inside.*

sliding, and hopper windows are installed on the outside. For casement and awning type windows that open out, the screen is installed on the inside with a projecting handle for opening and closing the window sash. Fig. 43-39.

WINDOW CONDENSATION

Condensation (formation of moisture) on windows is the result of improved heating systems, more insulation, and houses that are tightly built. Homes today do not breathe through the many small openings that existed before the extensive use of storm sash, weather stripping, insulation, and automatic heating systems. All of these improvements are fuel savers and add to people's comfort, but they do promote annoying and damaging condensation and steps should be taken to prevent it.

Condensation on the inside window surfaces results from differences in outside and inside temperatures and from the humidity conditions inside the home. Warm, humid air in the interior of the home, when temperatures are cold outside, reaches the dew-point necessary to condensation. Keeping the relative humidity within the home at a point lower than necessary for condensation to occur is the most effective way of preventing condensation on windows. The recommended indoor relative humidity for various outside temperatures is shown in Table 43-A. These maximum safe humidities for the home are not only better for the windows, but they will also improve paint performance and insulation and will eliminate problems with structural members.

Fog on the lower corners of windows now and then is not serious. However, *excessive* condensation, condensation that blocks entire windows with fog or frost and produces water droplets, can stain woodwork and in some cases, even damage the wallpaper or plaster. Condensation on

Table 43-A. *Recommended Indoor Relative Humidity for Various Outside Temperatures. (With relative humidity conditions as shown in this table there will be no condensation.)*

Outside temperature as shown	Inside temperature 70°F
Below -20°F	Relative humidity not over 15%
-20 to -10°F	Relative humidity not over 20%
-10 to -0°F	Relative humidity not over 25%
-0 to 10°F	Relative humidity not over 30%
10 to 20°F	Relative humidity not over 35%
Above 20°F	Relative humidity not over 40%

It is important to prevent excess humidity

43-40. *This skylight has flat glazing. The one-piece flashing fits under shingles at the top and sides of the unit, and over shingles at the bottom.*

windows is easily seen and can be removed. More serious is excessive moisture in the walls and insulation, where it cannot be seen. High humidity resulting in condensation can contribute greatly to the deterioration of a house and to the discomfort of its occupants.

ESTIMATING

The cost of the individual window unit will depend on the quality, the style of the window, the glass to be installed in the unit, the material from which the unit is made, and whether or not it has a factory-applied finish. To determine an accurate cost, submit a complete list of the windows that are to be installed to the supplier for pricing.

Labor

The labor required for installing and setting windows will vary considerably, depending on the size and style of the unit. The approximate time can be estimated as follows:
- For a window that contains 10 square feet or less of glass area, figure 1 hour of labor.
- For windows containing up to 20 square feet of glass area, allow an additional half hour.

- For anything over 20 square feet, figure about 2 hours.

These estimates do not include the interior trim, just the preparation of the opening and the actual installation of the window unit.

SKYLIGHTS

Skylights are installed on either pitched or flat roofs to provide ventilation and light. There are many kinds of skylights, though most of them are rectangular. There are two basic types:
- Fixed skylights.
- Ventilating skylights.

Fixed skylights cannot be opened. They are generally less expensive and easier to install. Ventilating skylights swing open on hinges. They can allow heated air to escape the house in hot weather. They can also funnel cooling breezes into the house.

The glazing in a skylight may be glass or plastic, and is either flat or domed. Fig. 43-40. Most skylights are double glazed to reduce heat loss. To further reduce heat loss, some skylights include triple glazing or high-performance glazing with a low-e coating.

Some skylights are complete units, ready to set on the roof. Others must rest on a lumber curb

43-41. *A wood curb is often used to raise a skylight above the level of the roof.*

that lifts the skylight above the level of the roof. Fig. 43-41.

Because skylights are often high in a ceiling, they can be difficult to reach. Some skylights can be fitted with small motors controlled electronically from below. The units can be opened and closed with ease. Other skylights can be opened and closed with extending poles. Fig. 43-42.

43-42. *This ventilating skylight can be opened and closed from below with a telescoping hand crank.*

Installing a Skylight

In new construction, skylights are often installed when the rest of the windows are installed. This type of installation is fairly straightforward. Skylights are also very popular in remodeling projects. They are very effective at bringing light into a dark attic that is being converted to living space.

Installing a skylight in an existing roof is more difficult than installing one in a new roof. The installation sequence shown in Fig. 43-43 shows the basic steps.

It is also possible to install a skylight in a roof with tile roofing. In such cases, flexible lead step flashing is often used to seal the skylight against leakage. Fig. 43-44.

43-43a. *Hand tools, less than $50 worth of incidental materials, and basic carpentry knowledge are all that is needed to install a skylight.*

43-43b. *After framing, drive a common nail through at a corner of the opening to locate the skylight position on the roof.*

43-43c. *Skylight is held in position by shimming and nailing the liner to the framing with galvanized finish nails.*

43-43d. *The completed skylight. Note that the flashing extends over the shingles below the skylight.*

43-44. *Flexible step flashing is often used to install skylights in a tile roof.*

1. What are the principal types of windows?

2. How many panes does a casement window have?

3. What is the main purpose of a stationary window?

4. What is a jalousie window?

5. Where is a window schedule usually found?

6. What information is contained in a window schedule?

7. What type of window installation requires that the sheathing be installed 1½" back from the window rough opening?

8. Why are basement windows the first windows to be installed in a house?

9. What is insulating glass, and why is it used in windows?

10. What is low-e glass?

11. Name the two basic types of skylights.

12. What type of flashing is used to install a skylight in a tile roof?

ACTIVITIES

1. Math. The glass area of a room should be at least what percent of the floor area? Refer to Fig. 43-26. Use the window schedule to determine if Bedroom #1 and the Living Room meet the guidelines.

2. Language Arts. You should understand that good health is important in effective job performance. You should make every effort to avoid foods and practices that can harm your health. As part of being health-conscious, you should also be aware of the advantages of regular exercise. Good health, combined with good grooming, can help make you a more effective employee. In a brief essay, identify healthful habits that will contribute to effective performance.

THE SCHOOL-TO-WORK CONNECTION

The style, shape, size, and location of windows and skylights have a big effect on the way a house looks. They can also add considerable expense to the construction of a house.

To reduce costs, builders typically prefer to work with "stock" windows. These windows are in standard sizes kept in stock by the manufacturer. The alternative to stock windows is custom windows. Custom windows are sometimes required, for example, in remodeling projects where old windows are being replaced.

1. Imagine that you work for a builder who has an upcoming remodeling project. You have been asked to locate a manufacturer for a window with the following description:
1. double-hung
2. double glazed
3. no muntins
4. vinyl cladding
5. fits into standard 2 x 4 wall
6. fits into rough opening 34" wide by 48" tall

See if you can find a source of stock windows that fit this description. You will have to consult the latest catalogs from window manufacturers. One way to do this is to write letters to several manufacturers whose advertisements can be found in home repair and remodeling magazines. These magazines can be found in your local library. Another way to locate catalogs is to consult a reference book called *Sweet's Catalog*. It can be found in the reference section of many public libraries.

2. A skylight can be installed in any pitched roof to improve ventilation and add daylight. Small skylights that fit between existing rafters will eliminate the need for special framing. To install larger skylights, however, you'll have to remove part of at least one rafter. You will then need to reinforce roof framing on either side of the hole. Call the building department in your town to find out if a permit is required for installing a skylight in an existing roof. Does the need for a permit depend on the size of the skylight?

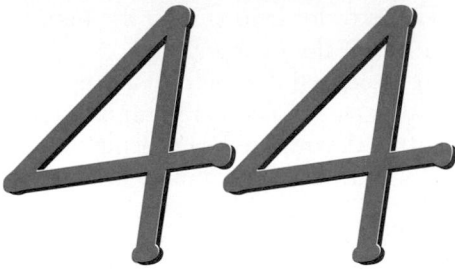
Exterior Doors and Frames

Exterior doors are made from wood or metal and are available in many styles. Fig. 44-1. Metal doors usually have cores of rigid insulation. This greatly reduces the amount of heat lost through the door. Care should be taken to select a door that is correct for the

44-1a. *Energy-efficient steel exterior doors are insulated with rigid foam. Wood stops hold the glazing in place.*

44-1c. *A hand-carved wood door.*

44-1b. *A door with sidelights.*

44-1d. *A hinged patio door with one fixed sidelight.*

architectural style of the house. The exterior trim around the main entrance door can vary in architectural design from a simple casing to a molded or plain pilaster with a decorative head casing. Decorative designs should always be in keeping with the architecture of the house. Many combinations of door and entry designs for every kind of house are available along with millwork items which are adaptable to many styles. Figs. 44-2 and 44-3.

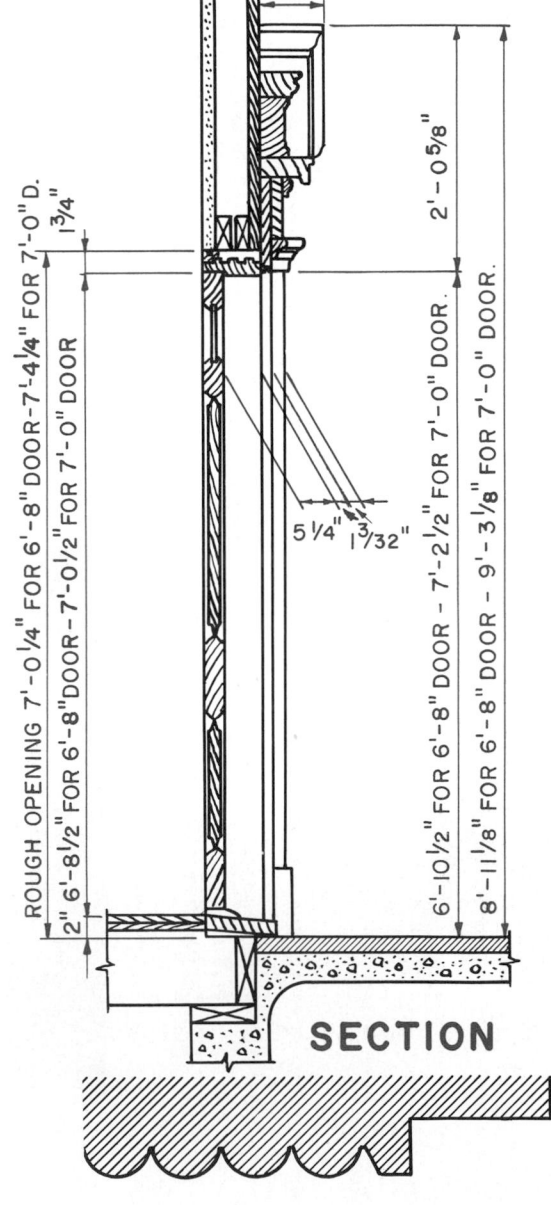

44-2. *Construction details for a decorative doorframe.*

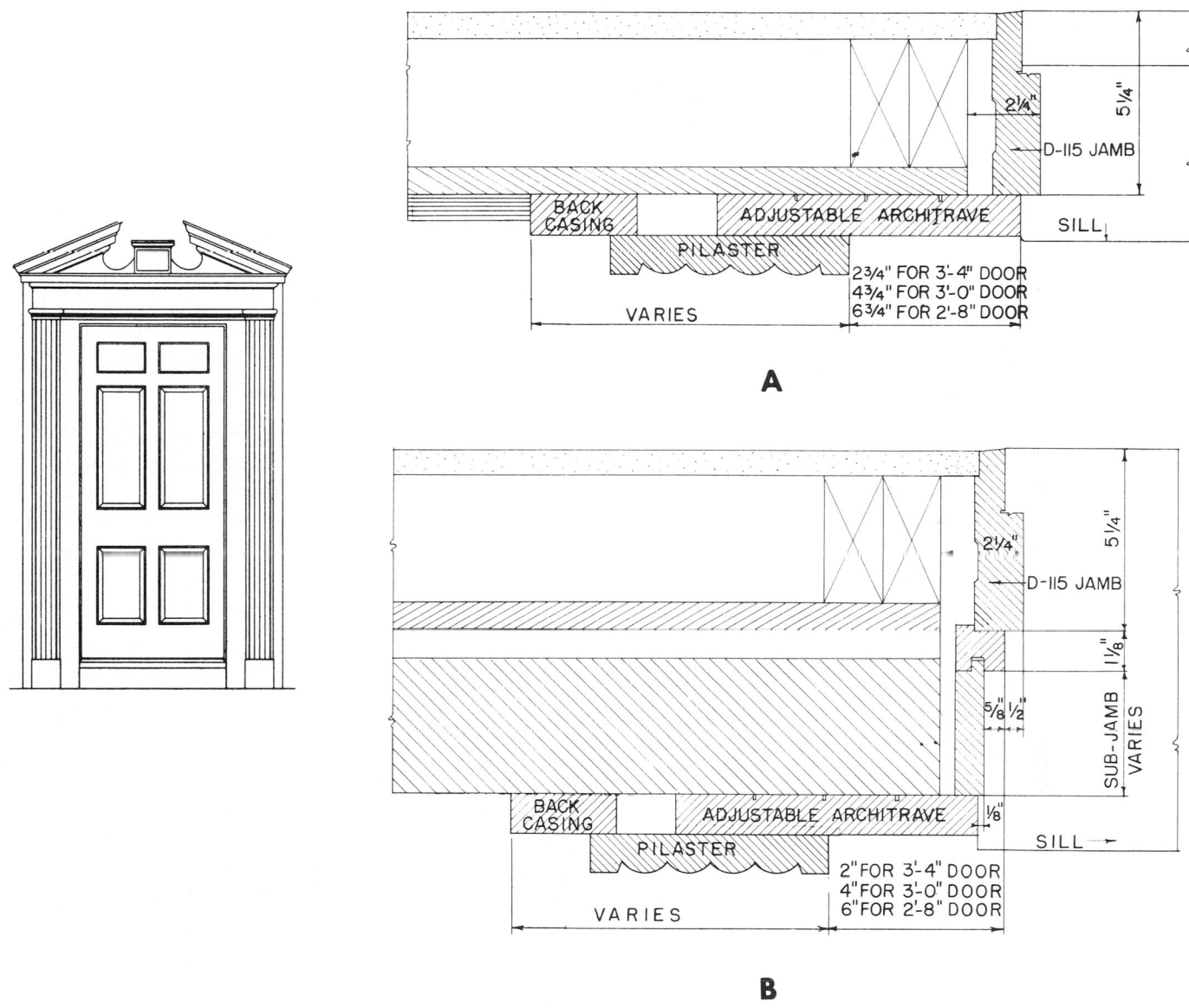

A

23/4" FOR 3'-4" DOOR
43/4" FOR 3'-0" DOOR
63/4" FOR 2'-8" DOOR

B

2" FOR 3'-4" DOOR
4" FOR 3'-0" DOOR
6" FOR 2'-8" DOOR

44-3. *The doorframe moldings shown in Fig. 44-2 are adaptable to wood or masonry construction: A. Detail of the stud wall frame construction. B. Detail of the brick veneer and masonry wall frame construction. Note that the moldings are designed to be adjusted to different door sizes.*

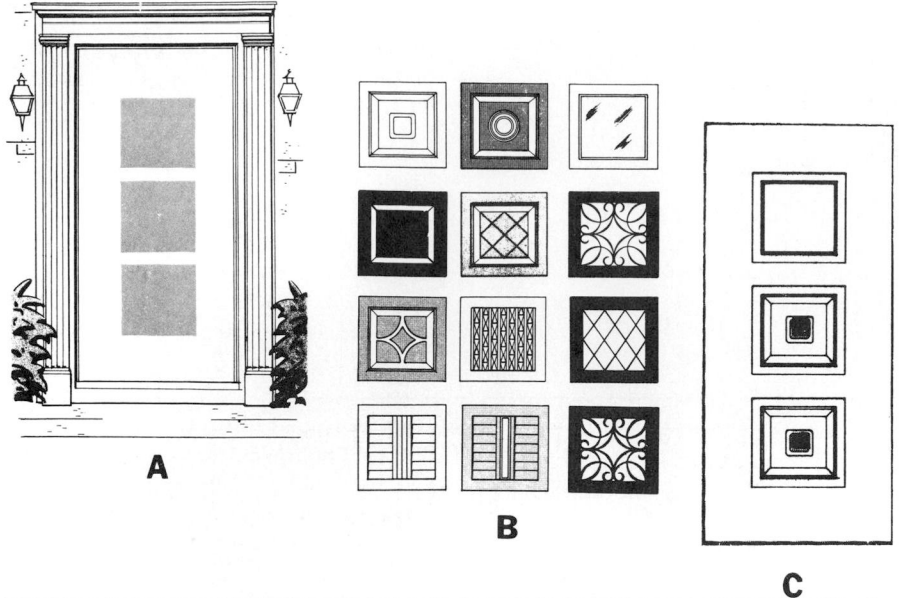

44-4. *Flush doors can be individually styled by selecting from a variety of insert panels. The panels in B can be mounted on the shaded areas of the door at A. C shows one possibility.*

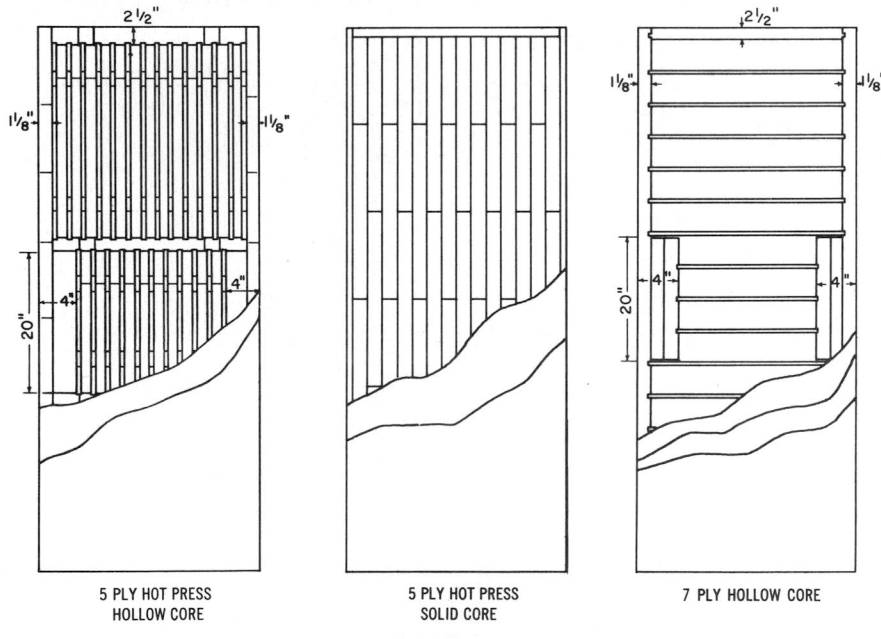

5 PLY HOT PRESS
HOLLOW CORE

5 PLY HOT PRESS
SOLID CORE

7 PLY HOLLOW CORE

44-5. *The core construction of a flush door will vary considerably with the manufacturer. The construction details shown here are an example of the techniques used by one manufacturer. Note the built-up areas at the edges near the center for installation of the lock set.*

TYPES OF EXTERIOR DOORS

Flush Doors

Flush doors are made with plywood or other suitable facing applied over light framework onto a core of suitable thickness. Fig. 44-4. There are two types of cores: hollow and solid. Fig. 44-5. Solid core construction is woodblock or particle board and is generally preferred for exterior doors. Solid core construction minimizes warping.

Panel Doors

Panel doors consist of stiles (solid wood vertical members), rails (solid cross-members), and panels (thinner parts filling spaces between the stiles and the rails). Fig. 44-6. Many types with various wood or glass panels are available. Fig. 44-7.

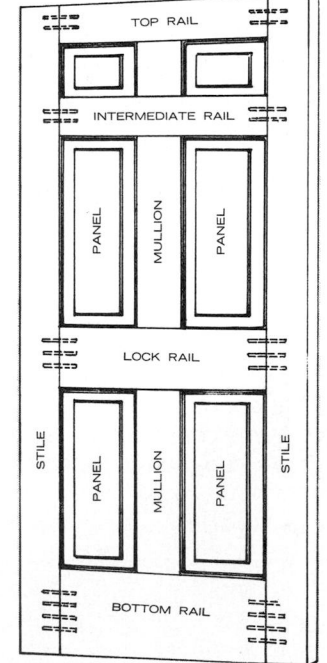

TOP RAIL

INTERMEDIATE RAIL

PANEL · MULLION · PANEL

LOCK RAIL

STILE · PANEL · MULLION · PANEL · STILE

BOTTOM RAIL

44-6. *Parts of a six-panel door.*

44-7. *Panel doors are available in many styles.*

44-8. *Glazed red oak doors, with two sidelights.*

Glazed Doors

Glazed doors consist of stiles and rails with a space divided into lights by bars called muntins. These may be used wherever daylight is needed in the area near the door. For a house with an entry hall that has no windows, it is usually desirable to have glass in the main door. The glass portion is often decorative. Fig. 44-8.

44-9. *French doors.*

French Doors

French doors are hung in pairs, and are usually fully glazed. They can swing into the room or out on hinges that are located at the edges of the door opening. Molding with a T-shaped profile is attached to the edge of one of the doors. This provides a stop against which the other door closes. This type of door often leads to a deck or patio.

Because both doors meet in the middle of the door opening, it can be difficult to seal them against the weather. Fig. 44-9.

Sliding Glass Doors

Sliding glass doors are available with either wood or metal frames. Fig. 44-10. The glass may be 1", ⅝", or ¼" thick insulating plate glass, depending on the local climate. These units are available in various combinations of stationary or operating doors in widths from 30" to 120". The door operation may be specified as right- or left-hand sliding (as viewed from the outside). Fig. 44-11. Snap-in muntins can be added to create a traditional appearance.

44-10. *A wood sliding glass door with regular muntins.*

WOOD DOOR SIZES

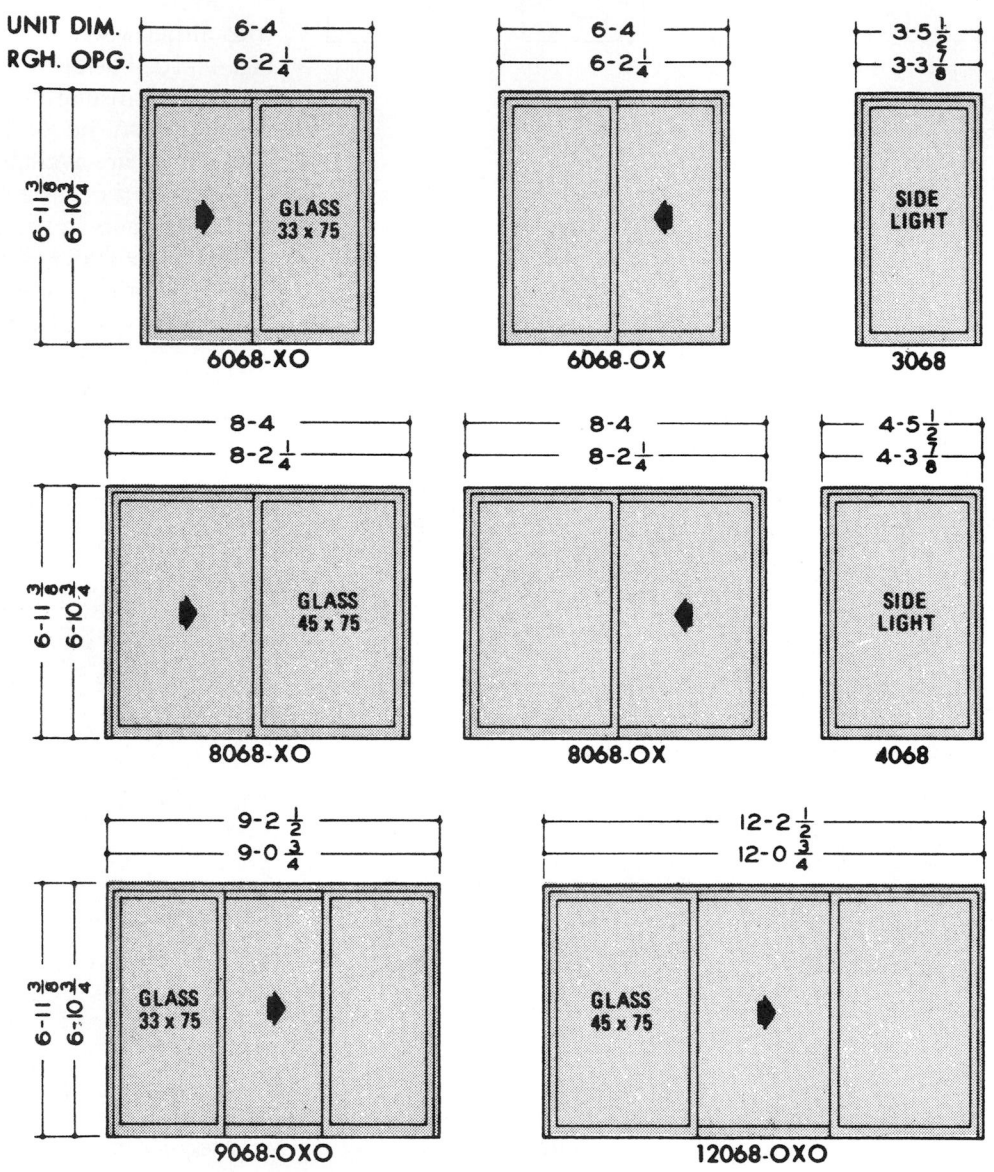

UNIT DIM. 6-4
RGH. OPG. 6-2¼

GLASS
33 x 75

6-11 3/8
6-10 3/4

6068-XO

6-4
6-2¼

6068-OX

3-5½
3-3⅞

SIDE
LIGHT

3068

8-4
8-2¼

GLASS
45 x 75

6-11 3/8
6-10 3/4

8068-XO

8-4
8-2¼

8068-OX

4-5½
4-3⅞

SIDE
LIGHT

4068

9-2½
9-0¾

GLASS
33 x 75

6-11 3/8
6-10 3/4

9068-OXO

12-2½
12-0¾

GLASS
45 x 75

12068-OXO

NUMBERING SYSTEM

44-11a. *A page from a manufacturer's catalog illustrating wood sliding glass doors.*

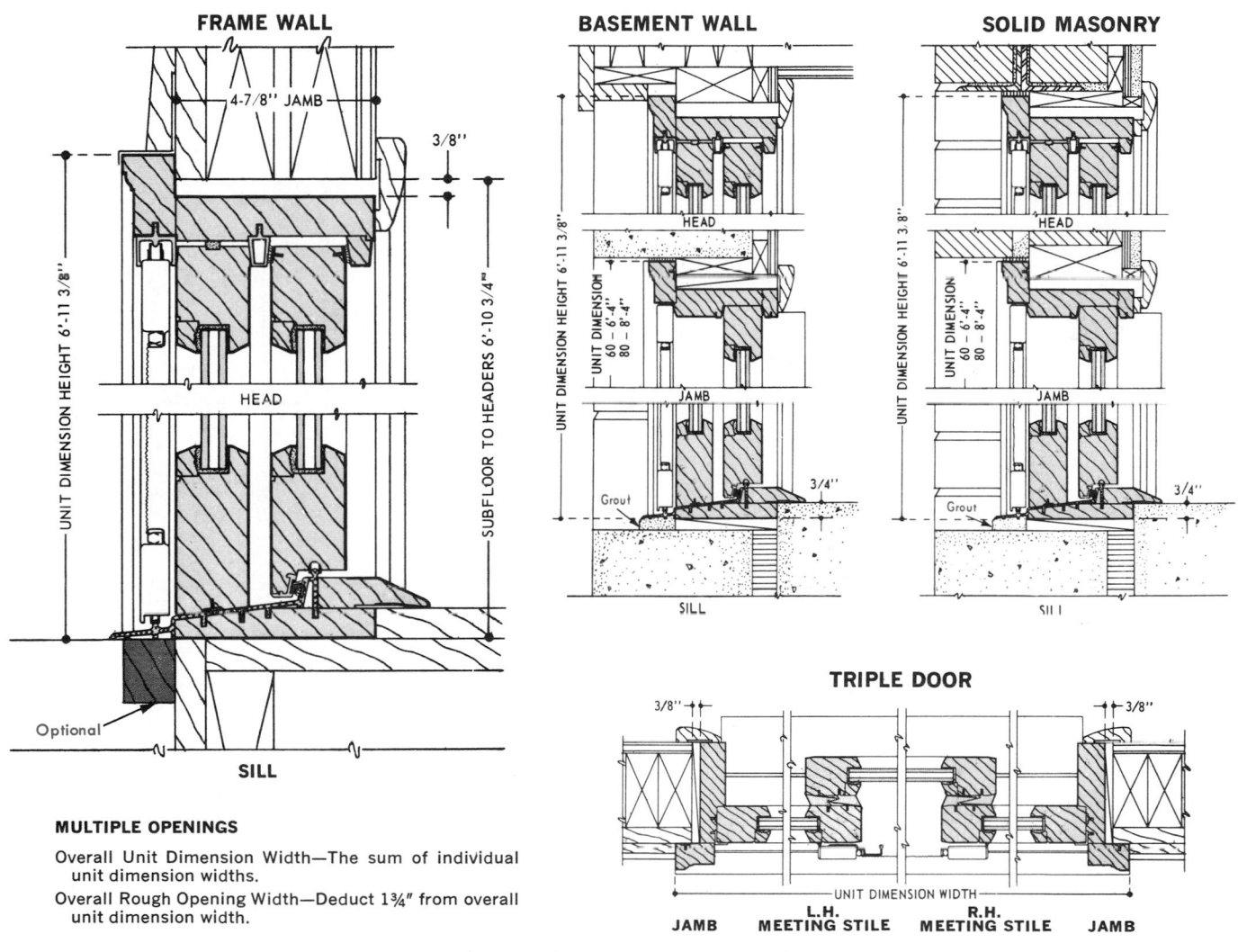

FRAME WALL

4-7/8'' JAMB

3/8''

UNIT DIMENSION HEIGHT 6'-11 3/8''

SUBFLOOR TO HEADERS 6'-10 3/4''

HEAD

Optional

SILL

MULTIPLE OPENINGS

Overall Unit Dimension Width—The sum of individual unit dimension widths.

Overall Rough Opening Width—Deduct 1¾" from overall unit dimension width.

BASEMENT WALL

UNIT DIMENSION HEIGHT 6'-11 3/8''

UNIT DIMENSION 60 – 6'-4'' 80 – 8'-4''

HEAD

JAMB

Grout

3/4''

SILL

SOLID MASONRY

UNIT DIMENSION HEIGHT 6'-11 3/8''

UNIT DIMENSION 60 – 6'-4'' 80 – 8'-4''

HEAD

JAMB

Grout

3/4''

SILL

TRIPLE DOOR

3/8''

3/8''

UNIT DIMENSION WIDTH

JAMB

L.H. MEETING STILE

R.H. MEETING STILE

JAMB

44-11b. *Construction details for wood sliding glass doors for various installations. Always consult the manufacturer's construction details for the specific door to be installed.*

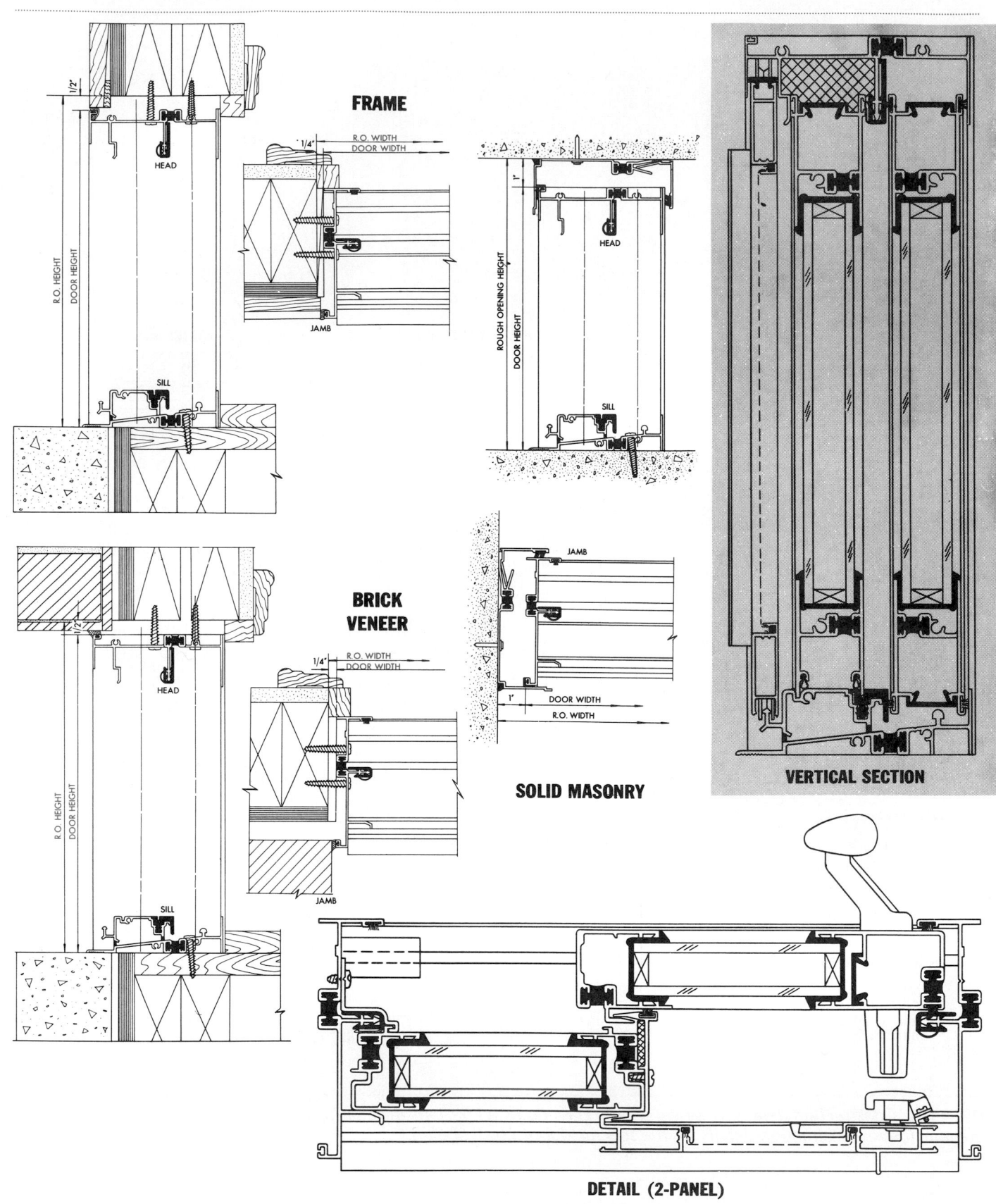

FRAME

HEAD

R.O. HEIGHT
DOOR HEIGHT

1/2"

JAMB

SILL

R.O. WIDTH
DOOR WIDTH
1/4"

BRICK VENEER

HEAD

R.O. HEIGHT
DOOR HEIGHT

1/2"

SILL

JAMB

R.O. WIDTH
DOOR WIDTH
1/4"

HEAD

ROUGH OPENING HEIGHT
DOOR HEIGHT

1"

SILL

JAMB

1"
DOOR WIDTH
R.O. WIDTH

SOLID MASONRY

VERTICAL SECTION

DETAIL (2-PANEL)

44-11c. *Construction details for aluminum sliding glass doors.*

44-12. *Aluminum prehung combination doors.*

A doorframe surrounds a door to conceal or beautify structural building parts. The doorframe consists of the doorjamb, the sill, interior trim, exterior trim, and other molding, depending on the architectural design of the building. Figs. 44-13 and 44-14.

The *doorjamb* is the part of the frame which fits inside the masonry opening or rough frame opening. Jambs may be wood or metal. Wood has been the traditional material, but steel and aluminum have gained in popularity and are not uncommon in residential building. The jamb has three parts: the two side jambs and the head jamb across the top. Exterior doorjambs have a stop as part of the jamb. The stop is the portion of

Combination Doors

Combination storm and screen doors of wood or metal are available in several styles. Fig. 44-12. Panels which include screen and storm inserts are normally located in the upper portion of the door. Some types have self-storing features similar to window combination units. Heat loss through metal combination doors is greater than through similar wood doors. Weather-stripping an exterior door will reduce both air infiltration and frosting of the glass on the storm door during cold weather.

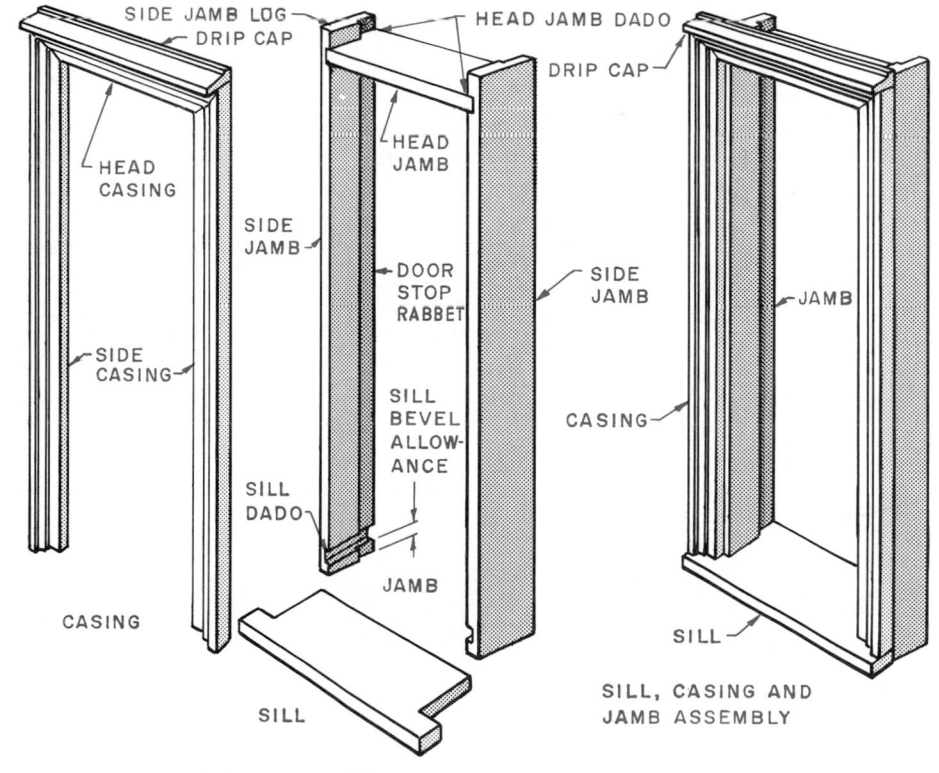

44-13a. *Parts of a doorframe.*

44-13b. *Doorframe installed in brick-veneer construction.*

the jamb which the face of the door closes against. The jamb is 1⅛" thick with a ½" rabbet serving as a stop.

Wood jambs are manufactured in two standard widths: 5¼" for lath and plaster and 4½" for dry wall. Jambs may easily be cut to fit walls of less thickness. If the jamb is not wide enough, strips of wood are nailed on the edges to form an extension. Jambs may also be custom-made to any size to accommodate various wall thicknesses.

Standard metal jambs are available in the following widths for lath and plaster, concrete block, brick veneer, etc.: 4¾", 5¾", 6¾", and 8¾". For dry-wall construction the common widths available are 5½" and 5⅝".

The *sill* is the bottom member in the doorframe. It is usually made of oak for wear resistance. When softer wood is used for the sill, a metal nosing and wear strips are included.

The brick mold or outside casings are designed and installed to serve as stops for the screen or combination door, which is 1⅛"

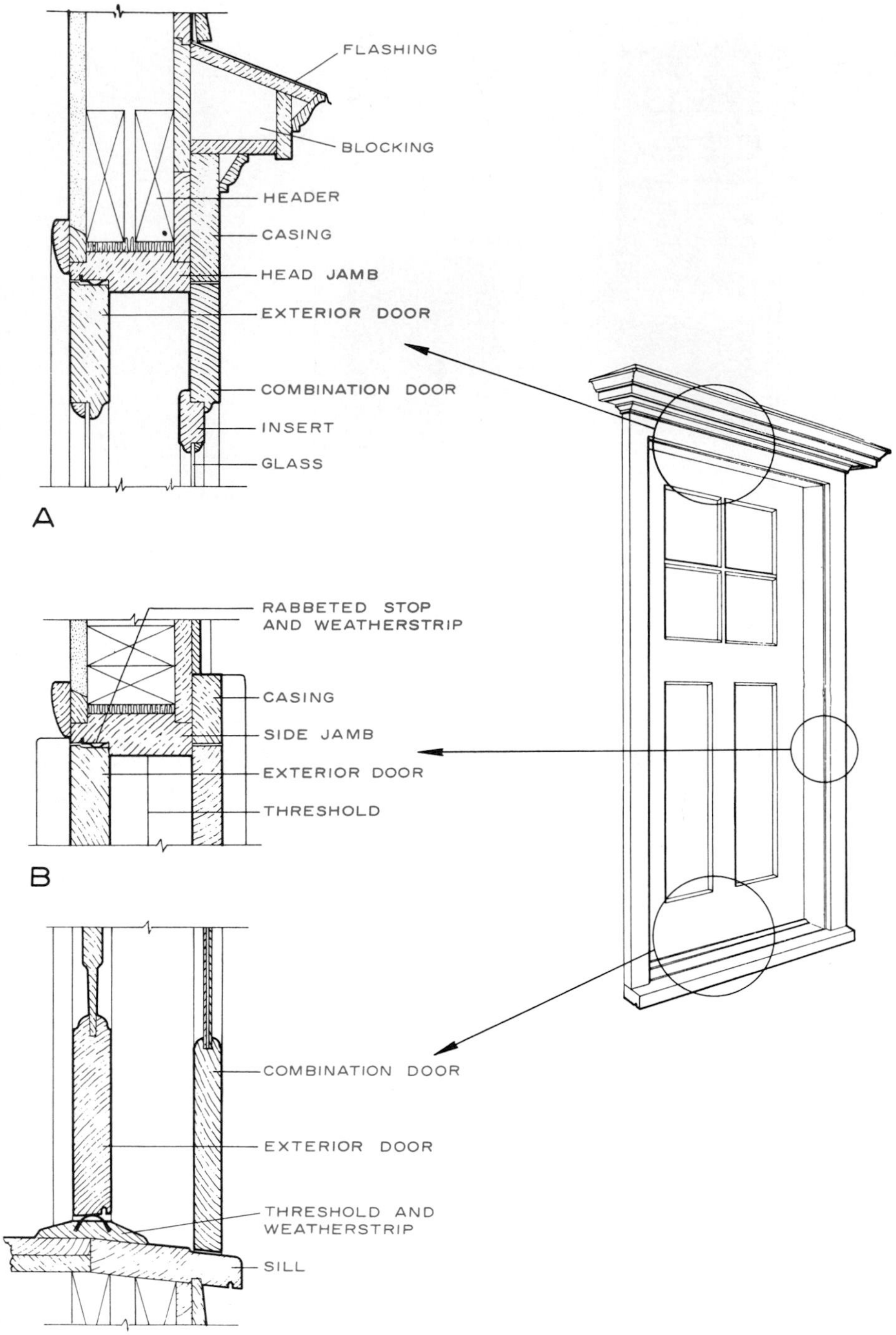

A

FLASHING
BLOCKING
HEADER
CASING
HEAD JAMB
EXTERIOR DOOR
COMBINATION DOOR
INSERT
GLASS

B

RABBETED STOP AND WEATHERSTRIP
CASING
SIDE JAMB
EXTERIOR DOOR
THRESHOLD

COMBINATION DOOR
EXTERIOR DOOR
THRESHOLD AND WEATHERSTRIP
SILL

44-14. *Cross sections of an exterior door and frame: A. Head jamb. B. Side jamb. C. Sill.*

thick. The stops are provided for by the edge of the jamb and the exterior casing thickness.

Doorframes may be purchased knocked down (K.D.) or preassembled with just the exterior casing or brick mold applied. In

some cases, they come preassembled with the door hung in the opening. Fig. 44-15. When the doorframe is assembled on the job, nail the side jambs to the head jamb and sill with 10d casing nails. Then nail the casings to the front

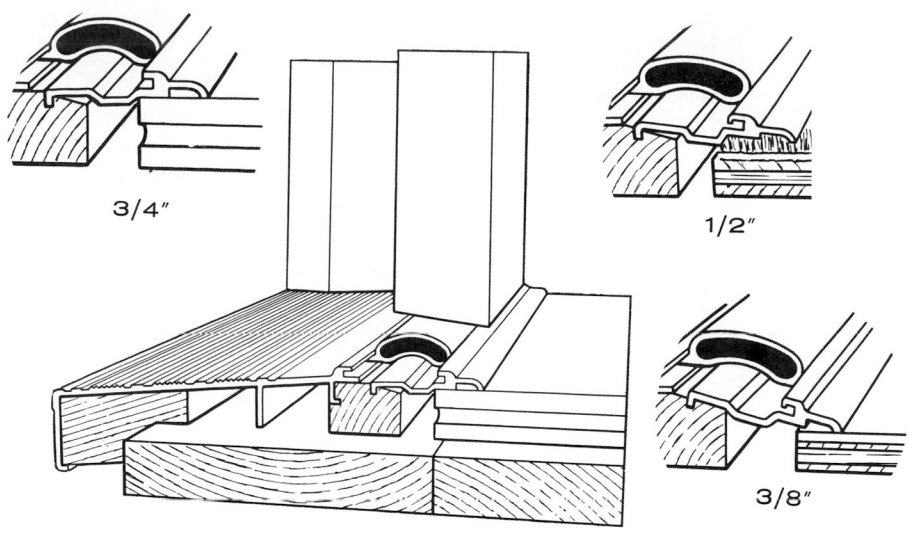

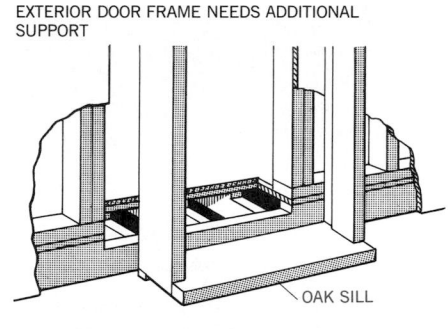

OAK SILL

FLOOR MUST BE NOTCHED OUT FOR SILL

44-17. *Close-up view of the floor framing trimmed out to receive the doorframe.*

44-15. *Preassembled door frames offer many conveniences for the worker. This one features a sill which is adjustable to eliminate trimming the floor joists.*

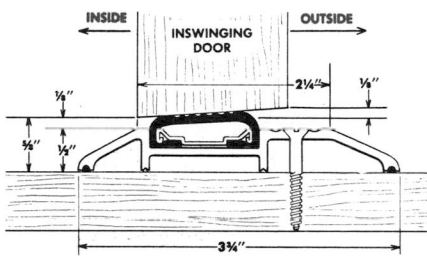

44-16a. *A metal threshold with a vinyl insert.*

44-16b. *Installing a metal threshold.*

edges of the jambs with 10d casing nails spaced 16" on center.

Exterior doors are 1¾" thick and not less than 6'8" high. The main entrance door is 3' wide, and the side or rear service door is 2'8" wide. A hardwood or metal threshold covers the joint between the sill and the finished floor. Fig. 44-16.

Installing the Exterior Doorframe

Before installing the exterior doorframe, prepare the rough opening to receive the frame. (The opening should be somewhat larger each way—3" wider and 2" higher—than the size of the door.) The sill should rest firmly on the floor framing, which commonly must be cut out to accommodate the sill. Fig. 44-17. The subfloor, floor joists, and stringer or header joist must be cut to a depth which will place the top of the sill even with the finished floor surface. Fig. 44-18.

Line the rough opening with a strip of 15-pound asphalt felt, 10" or 12" wide, as when installing windows. The assembled frame is then set into the opening. Set the sill of the assembled doorframe on the trimmed-out area in the floor framing, tip the frame into place, and brace it to keep it from falling out during adjustment. Fig. 44-19.

An outside doorframe is plumbed in the rough opening with wood shingles used as wedges. These are inserted at intervals up the side jambs, between the jambs and the trimmer studs. Check the sill with a level, and wedge it up as necessary. Insert the side jamb wedges. Drive the lower wedges on each side alternately until the space between the side jamb and the trimmer stud is exactly the same on both sides. Then drive a 16d casing nail through the side casing and into the trimmer studs on each side, near the bottom of the casing, to hold the sill in position. Drive the nails in only partway. Do not drive any nails all the way in until all the nails have been placed and a final check has been made for level and plumb.

Next place the level against one of the side jambs and adjust the remaining wedges on that side until the jamb is perfectly true and plumb. Repeat the same procedure on the other side. Make a final check for level and plumb. Fasten the frame in place with 16d casing nails driven through the casings into the trimmer studs and the door header. Nails are placed ¾" from the outer edges of the casings and

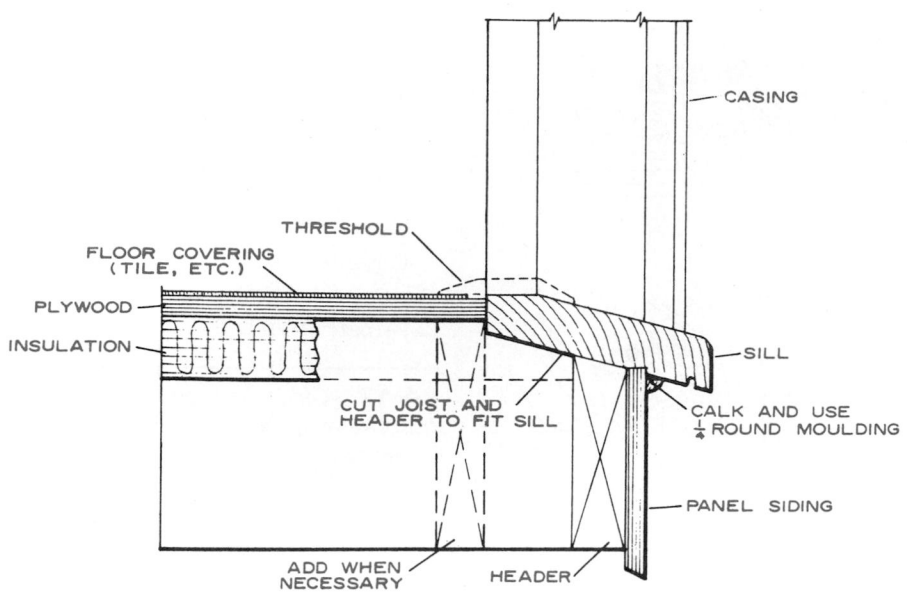

44-18. *The top of the doorframe sill should be set even with the surface of the finish floor.*

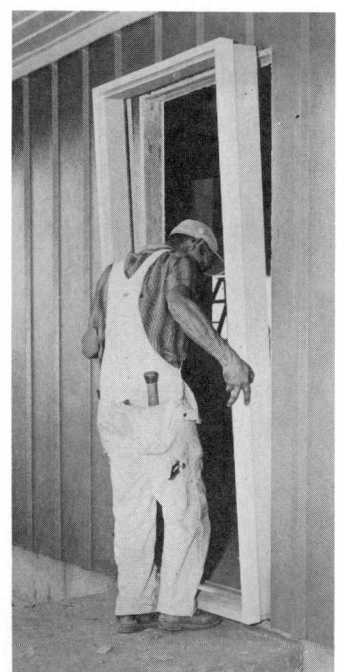

44-19. *Installing an exterior doorframe.*

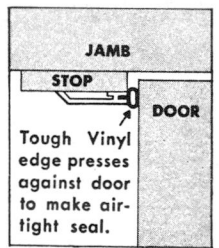
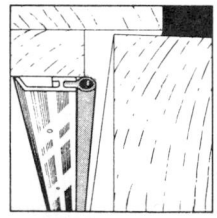

44-20. *There are many kinds of weather stripping available to reduce air infiltration. Shown here are two types: one for the head and side of the door and a second for installation on the door bottom.*

spaced about 16" on center. Set all nails with a nail set.

After the finish flooring is in place, a hardwood or metal threshold with a plastic weather strip covers the joint between the floor and the sill. Fig. 44-18. Thresholds are installed under exterior doors to close the space allowed for clearance. Weather stripping should be installed around exterior door openings to reduce drafts. Fig. 44-20.

HANDLING THE DOOR AT THE JOB SITE

A door is an important part of the building and has many functions. It guards the building and its possessions, insures privacy, protects against the elements, and lends beauty, refinement, and character to the building. A door is a high-grade precision-made item of cabinetwork and should be treated as such. Proper care and finishing of a door will insure maximum service and satisfaction.

Doors should not be delivered to the building site until after the plaster or concrete is dry. Then the doors should be:

➤ Stored under cover in a clean, dry, well-ventilated building, not in damp, moist, or freshly plastered areas.

➤ Stored on edge on a level surface.

➤ Sealed immediately on the top and bottom edges if they are to be stored at the job site for more than one week.

➤ Handled with clean gloves; bare hands leave finger marks and soil stains.

➤ Handled carefully. When moving doors, carry them. Do not drag a door except on the bottom end, and then only if it is protected by scuff strip or skid shoes. Do not drag one door across another.

➤ Conditioned to the average

moisture content of the locality before hanging.

➤ Finished as soon as the doors are hung in the opening.

➤ Kept away from abnormal heat, dryness, or humidity. Sudden changes, such as forced heat to dry out a building, should be avoided.

➤ Straight. Before hanging, warp or bow can usually be eliminated by laying (or piling) the door (or doors) flat under weight. Bow or warp is due to stress forces in the door, usually caused by unequal moisture conditions on the two sides of the door. Improper installation of hinges can also be the cause. When moisture differential is the cause, the door will usually straighten when the moisture equalizes. When improper installation is the cause, hinges should be adjusted.

DETERMINING THE HAND OF A DOOR

A door is designated as having right-hand or left-hand swing. The hand of a door is determined by the location of the hinges when the door is viewed from the outside. For example, if the hinges are on the right when the door is viewed from the outside, the door is considered a right-hand door. Fig. 44-21. In general, the outside of a door is the side from which the hinges are not visible when the door is closed. However, the outside of a closet door is the room side.

FITTING A DOOR

The first step in fitting a door is to determine from the floor plan which edge of the door is the hinge edge and which is the lock edge. Mark both door edges and the corresponding jambs accordingly.

Carefully measure the height of

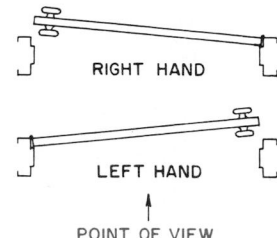
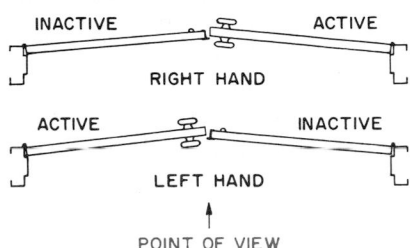

44-21. *Determining the hand of a door.*

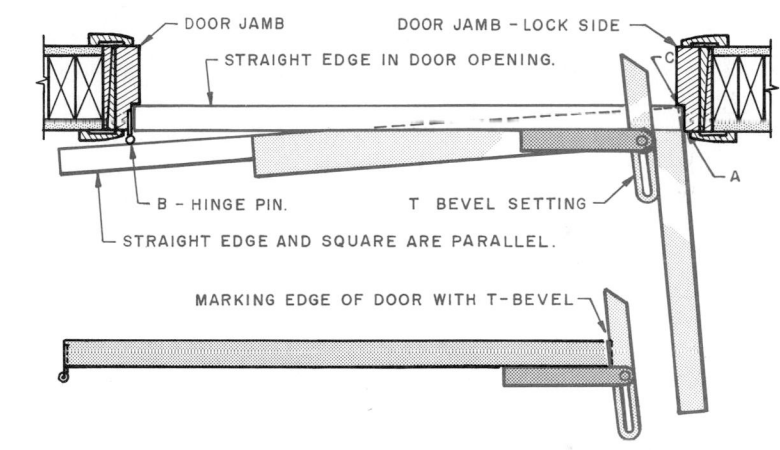

44-22. *Laying out the bevel for the lock edge of a door.*

the finished opening on both side jambs and the width of the opening at top and bottom. The finished opening should be perfectly rectangular, but it may not be. Regardless of the shape of the opening, the job is to fit the door accurately to the opening. A well-fitted door, when hung, should conform to the shape of the finished opening, less a clearance allowance of ⅟₁₆" at the sides and on top. For an exterior door with a sill and no threshold, the bottom clearance should be ⅟₁₆" above the sill. For a door with a threshold, the bottom clearance should be ⅛" above the threshold. The sill and threshold, if

any, should be set in place before the door is hung. Lay out the measured dimensions of the finished opening, less allowances, on the door.

Check the doorjambs for trueness and transfer any irregularities to the door lines. Plane the door edges to the lines, setting the door in the opening frequently to check the fit. The lock edge of a door must be beveled so that the inside edge will clear the jamb (at point A in Fig. 44-22) when the door is opened. The bevel required for this clearance is laid out by drawing a line from the point where the hinge pin will be located (B in Fig. 44-22) to the door's other side at the point where it intersects with the door stop (point C). Then place a T bevel on the face of the door and set the blade so that it is parallel to line AC. Fig. 44-22. As shown in the illustration, this can be easily done by placing the blade against the inside edge of the framing square. Plane the edge as necessary, checking frequently with the T bevel to determine the correct angle. When all the planing has been completed, use a piece of sandpaper to form a slight radius on all edges to remove the sharpness.

As an aid in fitting the door, a door jack similar to the one shown in Fig. 44-23 should be constructed. The jack will hold the doors upright for planing edges and for the installation of hardware. Commercially made holders are also available. Fig. 44-24.

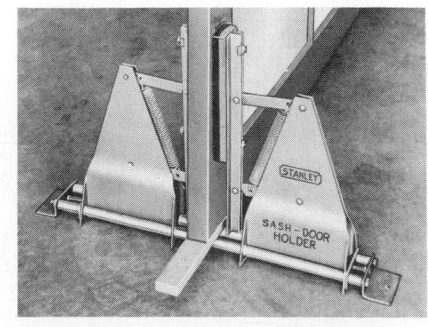

44-24. A commercially made sash and door holder.

HANGING A DOOR

The hinge most frequently used for hanging doors on a residential building is the loose-pin butt mortise hinge. Fig. 44-25. This has two rectangular leaves pivoted on a pin which is called a loose pin because it can be removed. The hinge is called a mortise hinge because the leaves are mortised into gains cut in the edge of the door and in the hinge jamb of the doorframe.

After the door has been properly fitted, the first step in hanging it is to lay out the locations of the hinges on the edge of the door and the hinge jamb. Exterior doors usually have three hinges. The following distances may be specified: the vertical distance between the top of the door and the top of the top hinge, and the vertical distance between the top of the finish floor and the bottom of the bottom hinge. If these distances are not specified, the distances customarily used are those shown in Fig. 44-26. The middle hinge is located midway between the other two. The size of a loose-pin butt mortise hinge is designated by the length of a leaf in inches. For an exterior door a 3½" or 4" hinge is recommended.

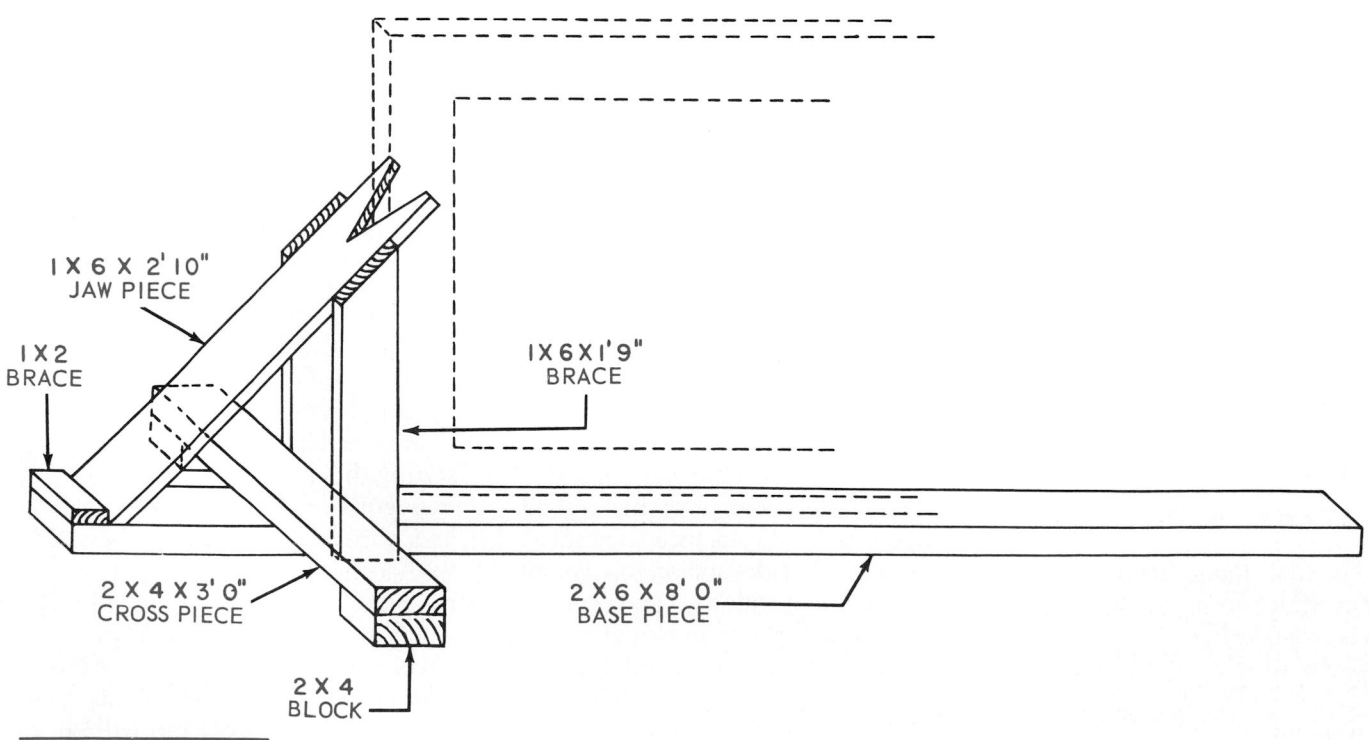

1 X 6 X 2' 10"
JAW PIECE

1 X 2
BRACE

1 X 6 X 1' 9"
BRACE

2 X 4 X 3' 0"
CROSS PIECE

2 X 6 X 8' 0"
BASE PIECE

2 X 4
BLOCK

44-23. A door jack.

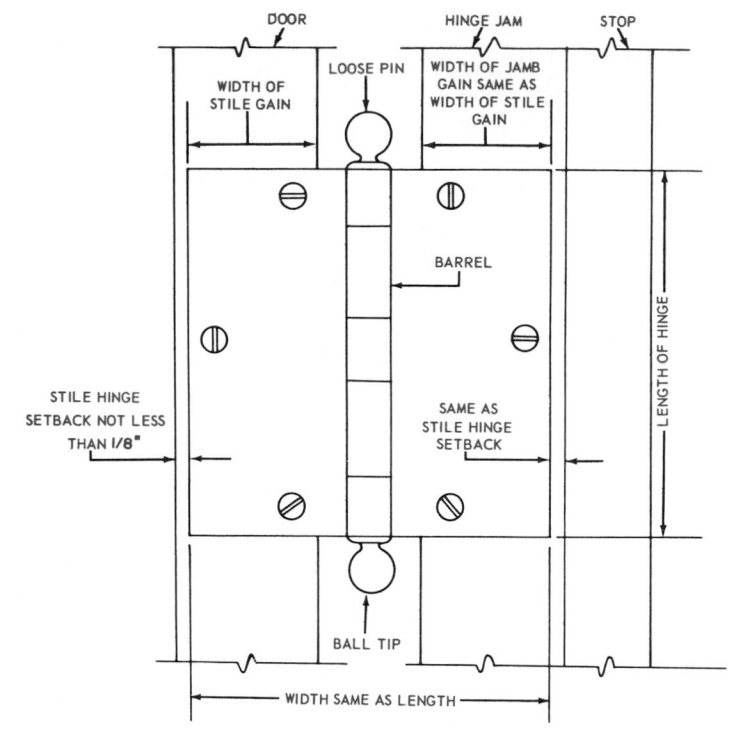

44-25. *A loose-pin butt mortise hinge.*

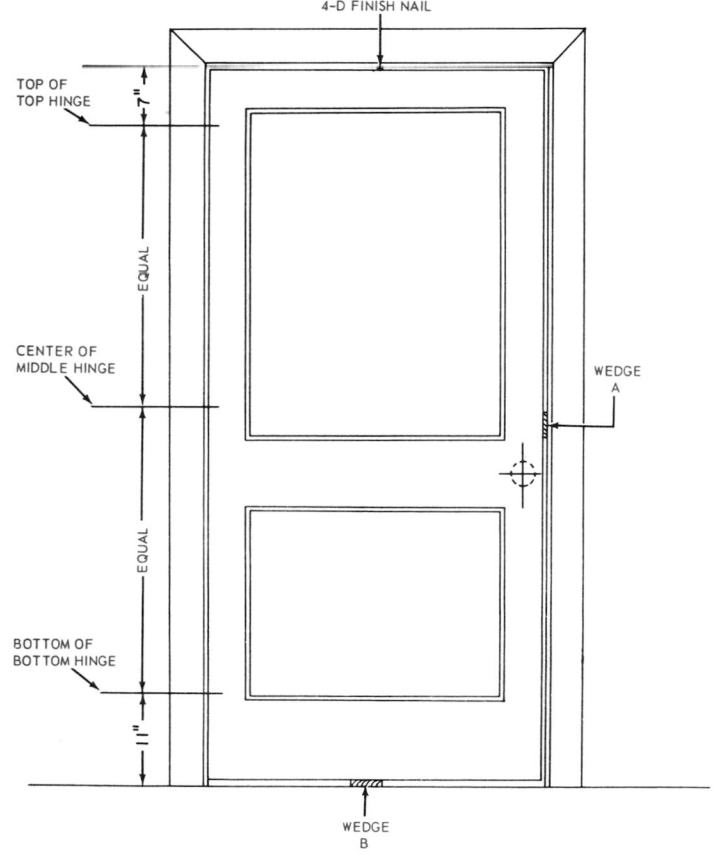

44-26. *Distances commonly used in laying out hinge locations on the door and door jamb.*

Set the door in the frame and force the hinge edge of the door against the hinge jamb with the wedge marked A in Fig. 44-26. Then insert a 4d finish nail between the top of the door and the head jamb and force the top of the door up against the nail with the wedge marked B in Fig. 44-26. Since a 4d finish nail has a diameter of 1/16" (which is the standard top clearance for a door), the door is now at the correct height.

Measure out the distance from the top of the door to the top of the top hinge and from the floor up to the bottom of the bottom hinge. Mark these locations with a 1/2" chisel or a knife. If a chisel is used, hold it so that the bevel of the chisel is toward the location of the hinge. For example, when marking the bottom hinge, the bevel on the chisel should be held up, and when marking the top hinge, the bevel on the chisel should be held down. Hold the chisel with the cutting edge in a level position so that it is in contact with both the jamb and the edge of the door. Apply pressure and make a small cut into both surfaces to mark the position of the hinge.

When marking for the center hinge, remember that the location line is to the center of the hinge; if a 4" hinge is used, measure 2" on one side of the location line and mark this point with a chisel. To help avoid mistakes it is best to pencil a small X on the side of the chisel mark where the gain for the hinge will be cut.

Remove the door from the opening. Place the door in a door jack and lay out the outlines of the gains on the edge of the door using a hinge leaf or a hinge butt gauge as a marker. Fig. 44-27. The door-edge hinge setback, shown in Fig. 44-25, should not be less than 1/8". It is usually made about 1/4". Fig. 44-28. Clearances for doors of

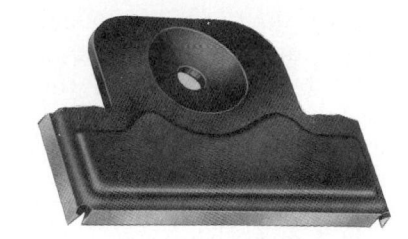

44-27. *A hinge butt gauge.*

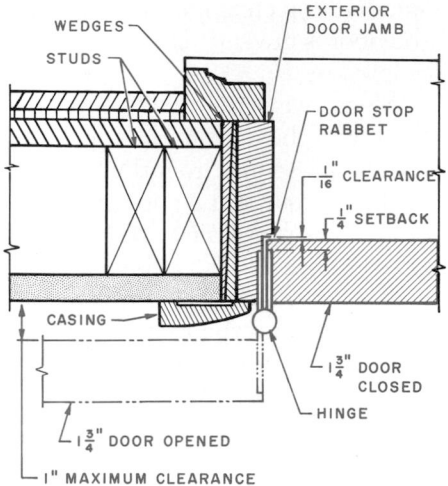

44-28. *The door hinge should be set back sufficiently to allow the door to clear the casing when the door is swung wide open. With a 1¾" exterior door and 4" butt hinges, the maximum clearance is 1", as specified in Table 44-A.*

various thicknesses are shown in Table 44-A. Lay out gains of exactly the same size on the hinge jamb. Chisel out the gains to a depth equal to the thickness of the hinge leaf.

Separate the leaves on the hinges by removing the loose pins. Screw the leaves into the gains on the door and the jamb. Make sure that the leaf in which the pin will be inserted is in the up position when the door is hung in place. Hang the door in place, insert the loose pins, and check the clearances at the side jambs. If the clearance along the hinge jamb is

too large (more than ¹⁄₁₆") and that along the lock jamb is too small (less than ¹⁄₁₆") extract the pins from the hinges and remove the door. Then remove the hinge leaves from the gains and slightly deepen the gains. If the clearance along the hinge jamb is too small and that along the lock jamb is too large, the gains are too deep. This can be corrected by shimming up the leaves with strips of cardboard placed in the gains under the hinges.

Hinge Butt Routing

A special template is available for hinge butt routing. Fig. 44-29a. The metal template may be adjusted for most common hinge spacings, and it is easily mounted on the door by driving six nails to hold the templates securely on the door. This template guides the router so that the hinge mortises

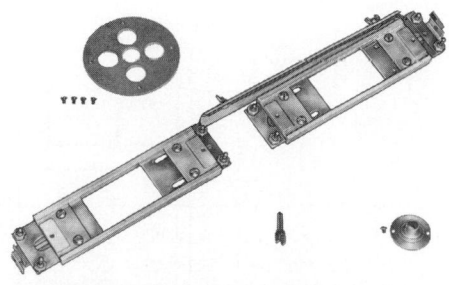

44-29a. *A door- and jamb-butt template and router accessories.*

44-29b. *Hinge butt routing with a door and jamb template.*

Table 44-A. *Trim Clearances for Wood and Metal Doors.*
The following table gives the clearances for trim of regular stock size butt hinges for wood or hollow metal doors. The clearance is estimated on butt hinges set back ¹⁄₄" for doors up to 2 ¹⁄₄" and ³⁄₈" for doors 2 ¹⁄₂" to 3" in thickness. Where trim presents a specific problem in determining the proper width of the butt hinges for a door, take twice the thickness of the door, plus the thickness of the trim and deduct ¹⁄₂" for doors up to 2 ¹⁄₄" in thickness, and ³⁄₄" for doors 2 ¹⁄₂" to 3" in thickness.

Thickness of Door (Inches)	Size of Butt Hinge (Inches)	Maximum Clearance (Inches)
1 ³⁄₈	3 x 3	³⁄₄
	3 ¹⁄₂ x 3 ¹⁄₂	1 ¹⁄₄
	4 x 4	1 ³⁄₄
1 ⁹⁄₁₆	4 x 4	1 ³⁄₈
	4 ¹⁄₂ x 4 ¹⁄₂	1 ⁷⁄₈
	5 x 5	2 ³⁄₈
	6 x 6	3 ³⁄₈
1 ³⁄₄	4 x 4	1
	4 ¹⁄₂ x 4 ¹⁄₂	1 ¹⁄₂
	5 x 5	2
	6 x 6	3
1 ⁷⁄₈	4 ¹⁄₂ x 4 ¹⁄₂	1 ¹⁄₄
	5 x 5	1 ³⁄₄
	6 x 6	2 ³⁄₄
2	4 ¹⁄₂ x 4 ¹⁄₂	1
	5 x 5	1 ¹⁄₂
	6 x 6	2 ¹⁄₂
2 ¹⁄₄	5 x 5	1
	6 x 6	2
	6 x 8	4
2 ¹⁄₂	5 x 5	³⁄₄
	6 x 6	1 ³⁄₄
	6 x 8	3 ³⁄₄

44-29c. *Round corner butt hinges save time when installed with the hinge butt router and door and jamb template.*

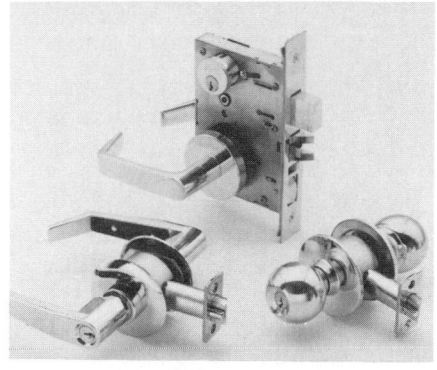

44-30. *Three different types of lock sets. From left to right: a lever set, a mortise lock set, and a cylindrical lock set.*

44-32a. *A deadbolt is sometimes used in combination with a lock set to increase security.*

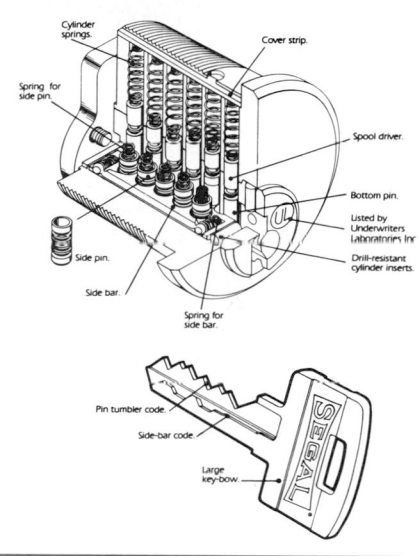

44-32b. *Parts of a deadbolt lock cylinder.*

are cut quickly and accurately to size and location. Fig. 44-29b. After the gains or mortises are cut on the door, the template guide can be transferred to the doorjamb for cutting the hinge mortises to match those on the door. Because the bits leave a radius at the corner of the cut, it is necessary to chisel the corners square for the hinges. It is also possible to purchase hinges designed with round corners. Fig. 44-29c.

INSTALLING A LOCK SET

Lock sets come in many styles, from very simple to ornate. Fig. 44-30. Some are mounted in the center of the door with large

decorative plates (escutcheons) behind the knob. Fig. 44-31. Sometimes a separate deadbolt is installed in a door to increase security. A deadbolt can have a separate key from the lockset, or it can have a matching key. Fig. 44-32. The installation instructions for lock sets, particularly the number and size of the holes to be bored in the door, will vary with the manufacturer. Always refer to the instructions which accompany the specific lock set to be installed. The general procedure for installing a lock set is as follows:

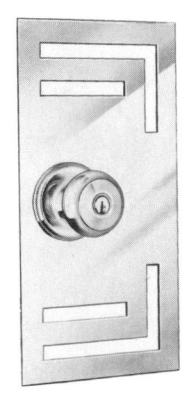
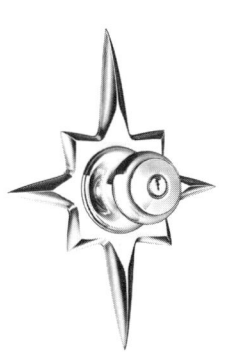

44-31. *A decorative touch is added to the front entrance door by choosing from the wide selection of ornamental escutcheons which are available. The escutcheons not only add beauty to the entrance but also provide protection against finger marks and scratches. When replacing old or damaged locks, the decorative escutcheons may be used to hide unsightly scars and holes.*

1. Open the door to a convenient working position and place wedges under the bottom near the outer edge to hold the door steady. Some carpenters prefer to remove the door for this operation. In such cases, the door is placed on padded sawhorses to prevent damage to the finish.

2. Measure up 36" from the floor to locate the height of the lock set.

3. Fold and apply the template (which comes with the lock set) to the edge of the door bevel. Fig. 44-33. Mark the center of the door edge and the center of the hole on the door face through the guides on the template. Fig. 44-34. If a boring jig is used, no template is needed. Fig. 44-35.

4. Bore a hole of the recommended diameter in the face of the door. It is recommended that the holes be bored from both sides to prevent splitting. Bore the hole on one side until the point of the bit breaks through and then complete from the other side. Fig. 44-36.

5. Bore a hole of the recommended diameter in the center of the door edge for the latch.

6. Insert the latch in the hole in the door edge. Keep the faceplate parallel to the edge of the door and mark with a sharp pencil around the faceplate. Fig. 44-37. A marking tool may also be used to mark the position of the faceplate. Fig. 44-38.

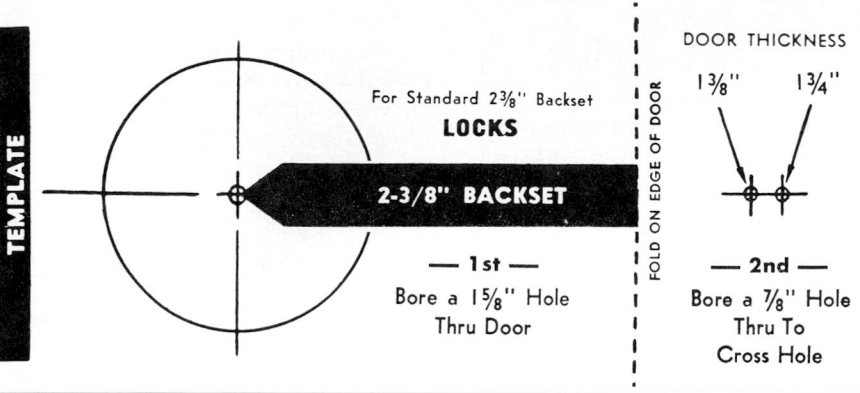

44-33. *A typical template for locating the center of the holes to be bored for a lock set.*

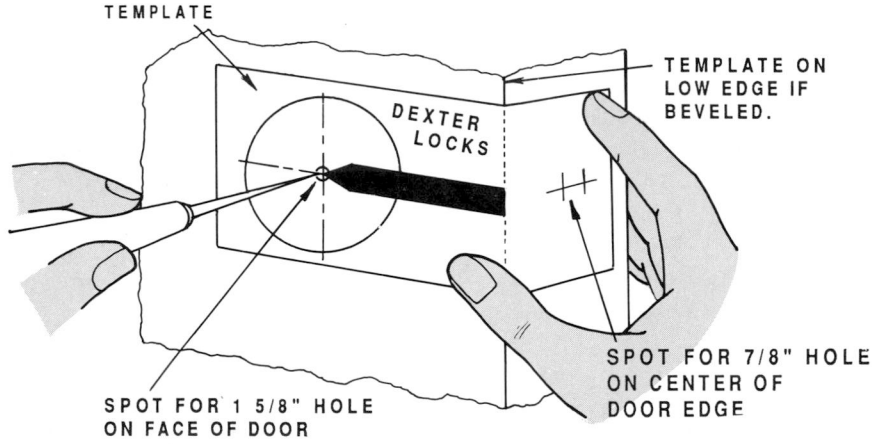

44-34. *Hold the template on the dotted line and place on the door edge. Mark the door through the template with an awl or nail.*

44-35. *When a boring jig is available, it is not necessary to use the template for marking the door previous to boring the holes for the lock set. The jig, when properly adjusted and clamped in position on the door, insures an accurate and rapid boring of the door.*

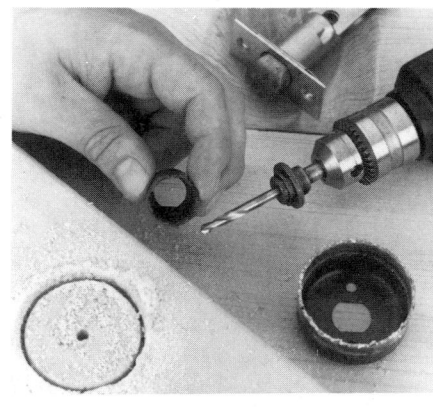

44-36. *A 1⅝" hole saw is used to bore a hole for the lock set. A ⅞" hole saw is used for the latch.*

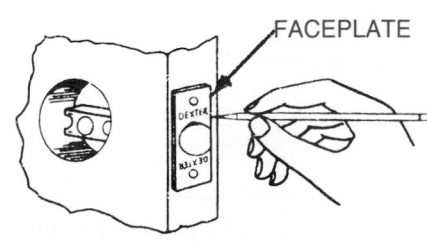

44-37. *Marking around the faceplate.*

44-38. *When a marking tool is available, it is not necessary to mark around the faceplate as shown in Fig. 44-37. The marking tool is inserted in the hole bored in the edge of the door. It is aligned parallel with the edge of the door and then given a sharp blow with a hammer to outline the area to be chiseled out for the latch faceplate.*

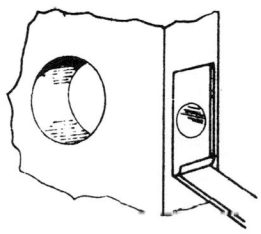

44-39. *Chisel out the marked area. The latch faceplate should mount flush with the edge of the door.*

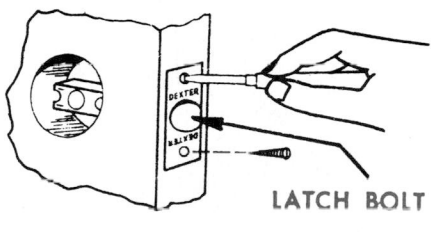

LATCH BOLT

44-40. *Installing the latch.*

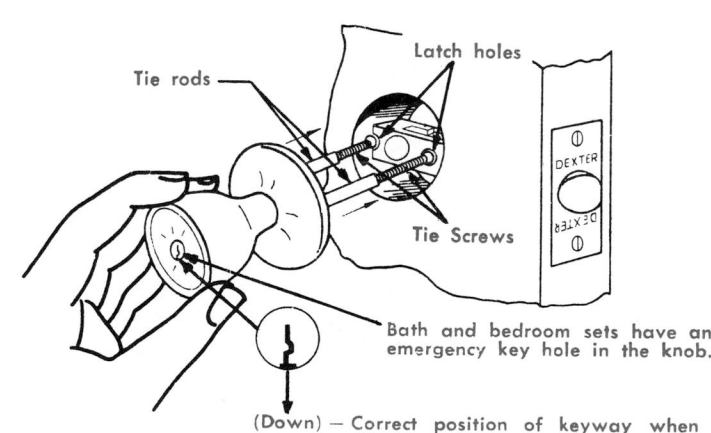

Tie rods — Latch holes — Tie Screws — DEXTER

Bath and bedroom sets have an emergency key hole in the knob.

(Down) — Correct position of keyway when installing keylock sets.

44-41. *Installing the exterior trim assembly. Tie rods and tie screws must go through the holes in the latch.*

7. Remove the latch. Chisel out the marked area so that the latch faceplate will be mounted flush with the edge of the door. Fig. 44-39.

8. Install the latch with the curved surface of the latch facing in the direction of the door closing. Insert and tighten the screws. Fig. 44-40.

9. Install the exterior knob by inserting the knob with the spindle into the latch. Make certain that the stems are positioned correctly through the latch holes and pressed flush against the door. Fig. 44-41.

10. Install the interior knob by placing it over the stem and aligning the screw guides with the stems. Push the assembly flush with the door, insert the screws, and tighten until the lock set is firm. Fig. 44-42.

11. Locate the strike on the doorjamb opposite the faceplate of the latch. To locate the strike, place it over the latch in the door. Then carefully close the door against the stops. The strike plate will hang on the latch in the clearance area between the door edge and the jamb. Push the strike plate in against the latch and, with a pencil, mark the top edge of the strike plate on the jamb. Then hold the pencil against the door edge

and draw a line down the face of the strike plate.

12. Open the door and hold the strike against the doorjamb just under the line previously marked. Make sure that the line marked on the face of the strike is aligned with the edge of the jamb. Mark around the strike and chisel out the marked area so that the strike will mount flush with the surface of the jamb.

13. Make a clearance hole for the latch bolt by drilling a $15/16$" hole $1/2$" deep in the doorjamb on the center line of the screws from top to bottom. Install the strike and tighten the screws. Fig. 44-43.

SCREW GUIDES — SCREW HOLES

44-42. *Installing the interior knob.*

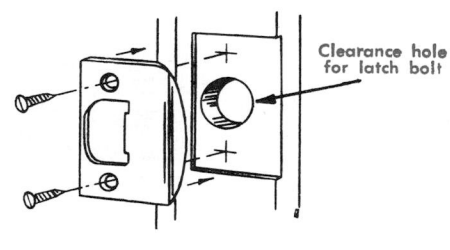

Clearance hole for latch bolt

44-43. *Installing the strike on the doorjamb.*

GARAGE DOORS

There are many types and sizes of garage doors. Fig. 44-44. The standard single door is 9' wide and 6½' or 7' high. Double doors are usually 16' × 6½' or 7'. Table 44-B. There are many architectural styles available to match the style of the home. To give the door a distinctive custom look, it can be trimmed at any time with easily mounted moldings, rosettes, or monogram plates. Fig. 44-45.

The various types of doors and hardware, with complete instructions for their installation, can be obtained from local suppliers. Figs.44-46 and 44-47. The three most commonly used doors are the hinged, the overhead swing, and the overhead sectional. Fig. 44-48. Occasionally, folding sliding doors are used.

Hinged doors open outward and are held in position with door holders. These doors are the least

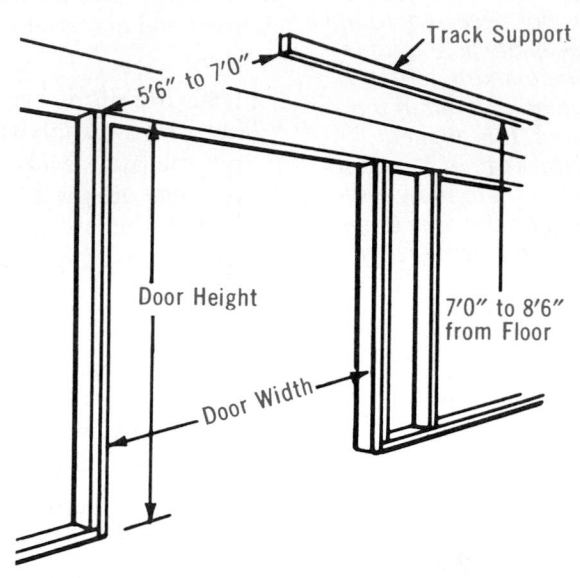

44-46a. *One manufacturer's specifications for framing a garage door opening.*

44-44. *A garage door (overhead sectional type).*

44-45. *Panels for trimming garage doors come in many styles.*

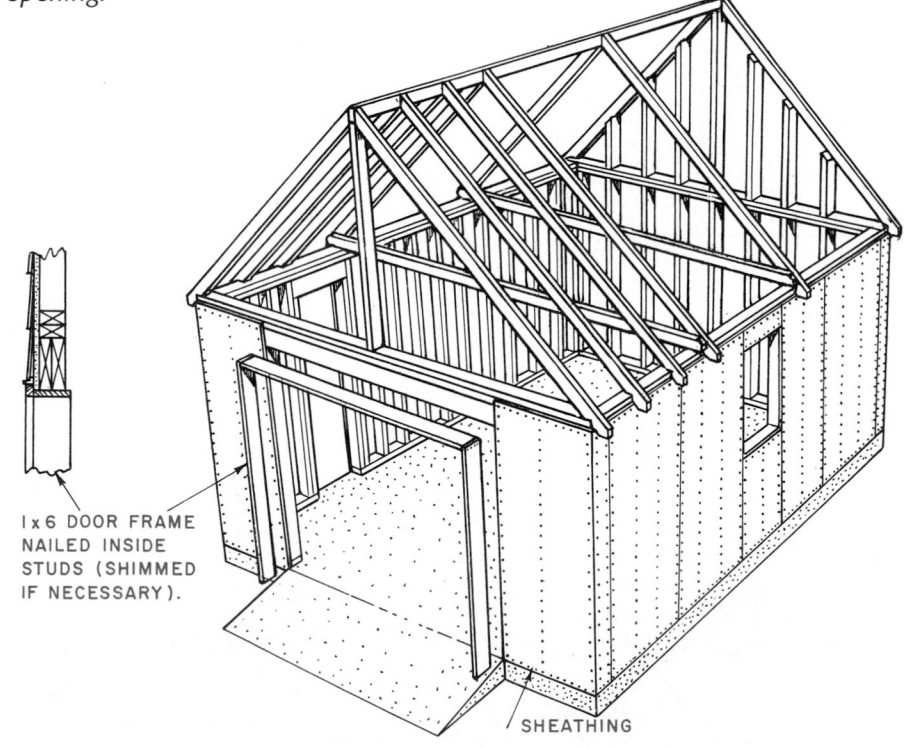

44-46b. *Finished doorjamb assembled and ready for installation.*

expensive and the easiest to install. However, when the door is standing open, it has no protection from rain and snow.

Sliding folding doors are hung from a track above the door. If the track is hung on the outside, the doors are subject to weathering. If the track is hung on the inside, the

Table 44-B. *Garage Door Sizes.*

Stock Heights	Stock Widths
6' 6"	7' 0"
6' 8"	8' 0"
6' 9"	9' 0"
7' 0"	10' 0"
	16' 0"
	18' 0"

Various combinations of height and width are available.

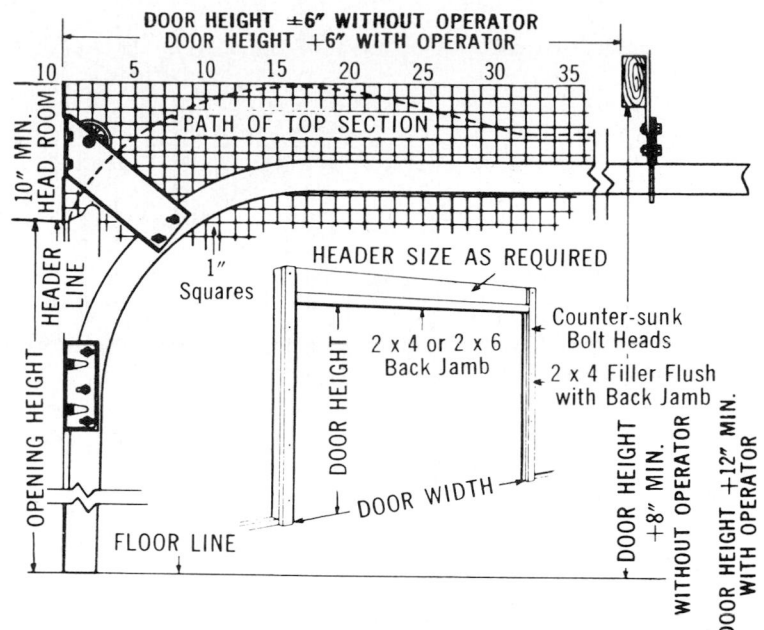

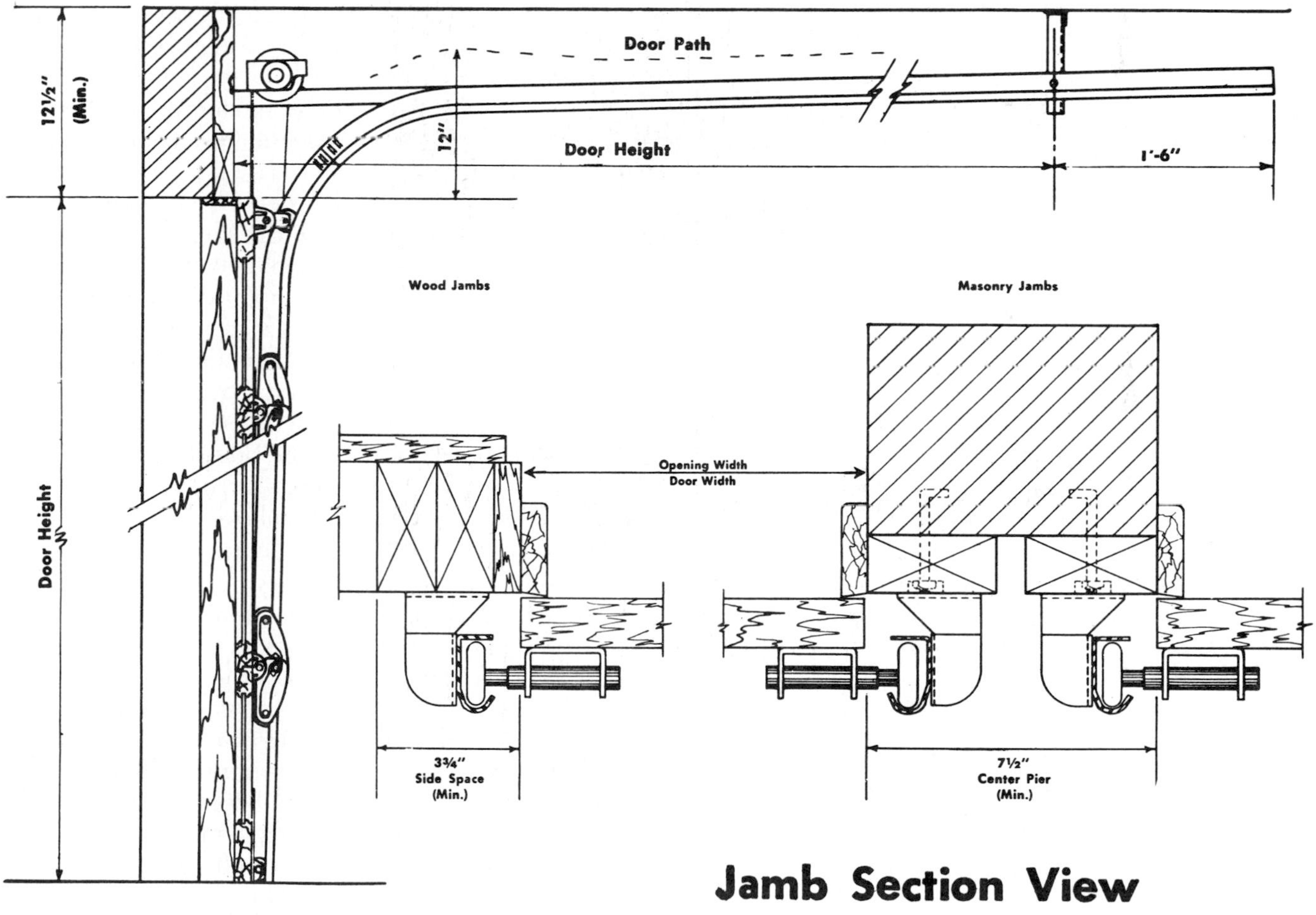

Jamb Section View

44-47. *Installation details for garage doors vary. Here are two manufacturers' instructions for installing a sectional overhead door.*

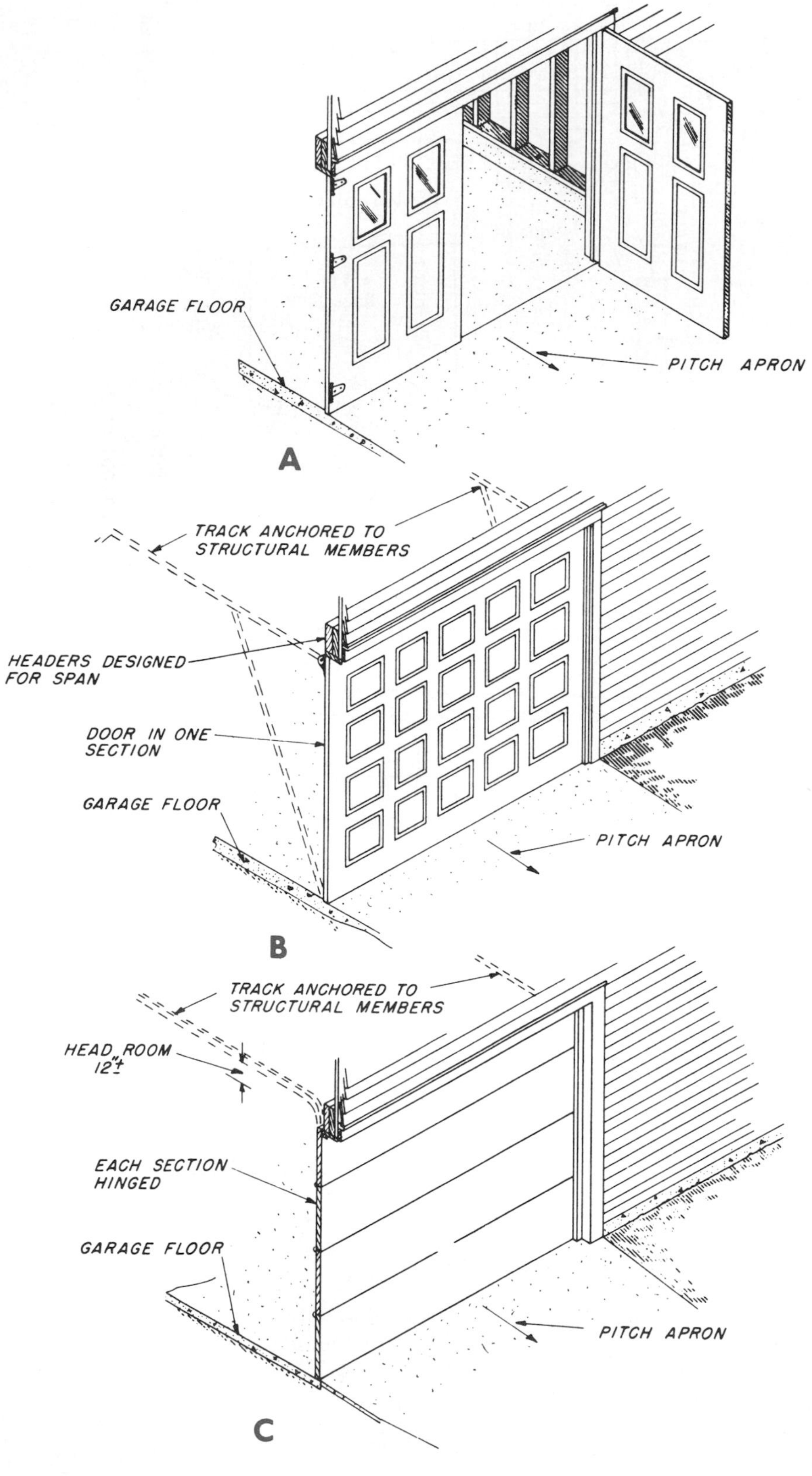

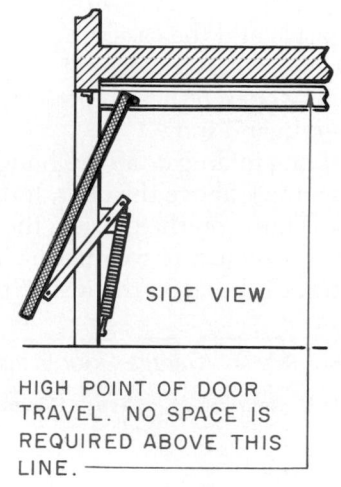

SIDE VIEW

HIGH POINT OF DOOR TRAVEL. NO SPACE IS REQUIRED ABOVE THIS LINE.

44-49. *The swing door must be moved outward slightly at the bottom as it is opened.*

GARAGE FLOOR

PITCH APRON

A

TRACK ANCHORED TO STRUCTURAL MEMBERS

HEADERS DESIGNED FOR SPAN

DOOR IN ONE SECTION

GARAGE FLOOR

PITCH APRON

B

TRACK ANCHORED TO STRUCTURAL MEMBERS

HEAD ROOM 12"±

EACH SECTION HINGED

GARAGE FLOOR

PITCH APRON

C

44-48. *Types of garage doors: A. Hinged. B. Overhead swing. C. Overhead sectional.*

---

doors can fold against one another in several thicknesses, or the track can be curved along the inside wall.

Overhead doors are made in two types: as a single-section (swing) door and as four or five sections hinged together. The swing-up door with the single section operates on a pivot principle with the track mounted on the ceiling and rollers located at the center and top of the door. Fig. 44-49. The sectional overhead door has rollers at each section fitted into a track at the side of the door and the ceiling. It requires more headroom above the opening than the swing door. However, it is by far the most widely used for residential building. Clearance required above the top of the sectional overhead doors is usually about 12". However, low-headroom brackets are available when such clearance is not possible.

Overhead doors are well protected from rain and wind, and snow and ice offer no particular problem. They are somewhat more difficult to install and more expensive than the hinged doors.

The overhead door has a pair of

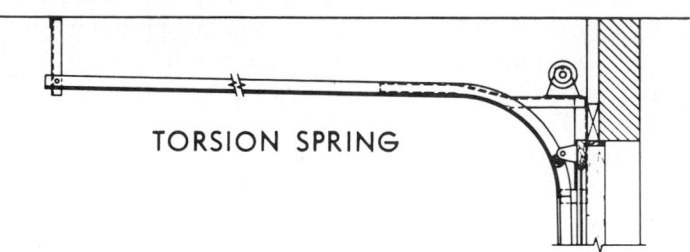

44-50. *This garage door is counterbalanced with a torsion spring.*

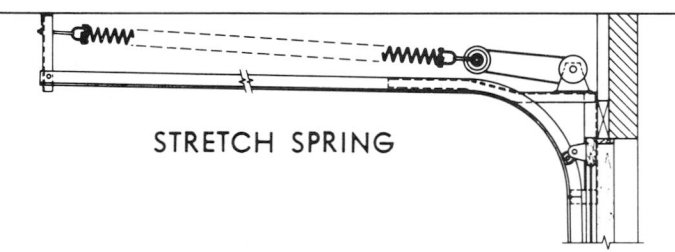

44-51. *This garage door is counterbalanced with a stretch spring.*

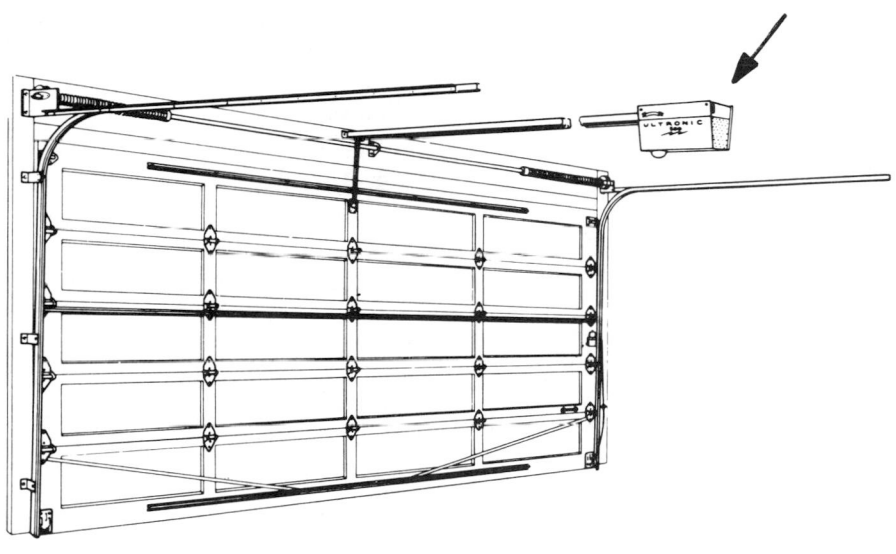

44-52. *An electric garage-door opener.*

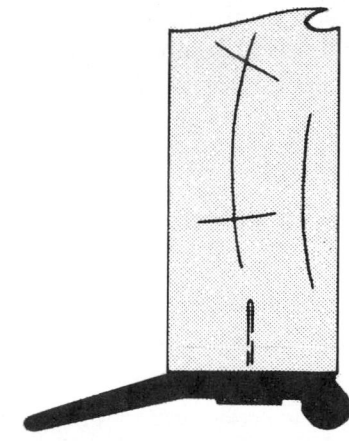

44-53. *Weather stripping should be applied to the bottom rail of a garage door.*

counterbalance springs mounted on it to help support the weight of the door so that it may be easily opened. These counterbalance springs are of two types: torsion and stretch. Figs. 44-50 and 44-51.

Power door operators are also available. These are electronically controlled by a wall-mounted button within the home or garage or by a portable battery-powered transmitter inside the car. Electric door operators can be installed during construction, or they can be added by the homeowner later. Fig. 44-52.

The bottom edge of a garage door should be scribed and cut to conform to the garage floor. An application of weather stripping is recommended for the bottom rail. It seals any minor irregularities in the floor and acts as a cushion in closing. Fig. 44-53.

The header beam over garage doors should be designed for the snow load which might be imposed on the roof. In wide openings, this may be a steel I-beam or a built-up wood section. For spans of 8' or 9', two doubled 2 × 10s of structural-grade Douglas fir or similar species are commonly used when only snow loads must be considered. If floor loads are also imposed on the header, a steel I-beam or wide-flange beam is usually selected.

ESTIMATING

The cost of the materials for an exterior door and frame depends on the style and trim. An accurate price should be obtained from the local supplier. The installation time required for an exterior doorframe will depend on how ornate the frame is. The conventional exterior frame and brick mold with an oak sill requires approximately two hours to assemble and install. It will require one extra hour to hang the door and half an hour to install the lock set. Combination storm and screen doors require approximately one hour for installation. A 9' × 7' garage door requires approximately 3½ hours and a 16' × 7' garage door about 5½ hours for assembly and installation. Radio-controlled garage door operators take about 2 hours to install.

QUESTIONS

1. List five kinds of exterior doors.

2. Name the parts of the doorframe.

3. What is the standard thickness of an exterior door?

4. What is the minimum width door recommended for a main entrance?

5. When the exterior doorframe is set into the opening, how far above the subfloor must the sill project?

6. When a door is fitted to the jamb, why is the lock edge of the door beveled?

7. What are the three types of garage doors most commonly used?

ACTIVITIES

1. Math. One way to check the squareness of a rectangle is to measure its diagonals. If a rectangular door is 3' by 6'8", what is the length of either diagonal?

2. Social Studies. Research the development of the door. What are some types of doors, other than the panel door on hinges?

3. Social Studies. We live in a democratic society. In our society, everyone is urged to develop their skills to the fullest. By doing this, they will be able to participate as more active members of society. In developing your skills, you also can develop some of the qualities of leadership.

All of us have known leaders. You may have noticed that all leaders have certain characteristics. For example, good leaders are good communicators. They are also able to concentrate their attention on a single project. They are determined. They are able to instill confidence in others. Of course, these qualities are more apparent in some people than in others. However, all of us can develop leadership skills. One way of developing such skills is by joining student clubs. Club membership provides an opportunity to practice effective communication. It also offers you practice in teamwork and the other skills needed to work within a group. Throughout your life, you will be given many opportunities for leadership. Now is the time to develop the skills you will need. Explore club membership in your school. What opportunities exist for joining a club?

4. Language Arts. In any job you take, you must be willing to demonstrate dependability. Dependability involves several things. It means, for example, that you will be attentive to the job. It also means that you will carry out a work task thoroughly. Dependability also requires that you be punctual, or on time for work. Identify the traits and work habits of a person who is dependable and punctual.

UNIT 45

Exterior Walls: Siding and Brick Veneer

The exterior wall covering of a house should be selected with great care. It has a tremendous effect on the overall appearance of the home, as well as on the ease of maintenance. A homebuilder today can select from a wide variety of siding materials, including solid wood, plywood, steel, aluminum, and vinyl. In addition, brick veneer is often specified where durability is of primary concern. Fig. 45-1.

A wide variety of exterior coverings is possible because changing any one of the following factors can produce a new kind of covering:

➤ Material used. Wood products used include solid wood and such manufactured wood materials as plywood, hardboard, and particle board. Masonry, either solid or veneer, may be of brick, stone, or stucco. Asphalt materials are also used for siding in two forms: as rolled products and as shingles. Common metals used are aluminum and steel, both of which are usually prefinished. Vinyl plastic is also a popular, easy-care exterior wall material.

➤ Shape and form. Some of the common shapes and forms in which exterior wall covering material is manufactured are bevel and drop siding, vertical tongued and grooved material, large panels, boards and battens, shingles and shakes, and rolled material.

➤ Surface treatment. Siding can be smooth or rough sawn, plywoods and hardboards can be textured, overlays of fiber and/or plastics can be added, and materials can be prefinished with paints, enamels,

45-1. *This house combines brick and vinyl siding.*

45-2. *Building materials dealers provide their customers with readily accessible displays from which siding selections are made. Each wing of this display holds eight siding samples.*

45-3. *The horizontal lines of wood siding are often used as an architectural feature.*

plastics, and other finishes. Most building supply dealers display samples of the wide variety of materials available. Fig. 45-2.

With the exception of solid wood and manufactured wood materials, most exterior wall coverings are applied either by bricklayers or masons or by specialty siding contractors.

WOOD SIDING

One of the materials most characteristic of the exteriors of North American houses is wood siding. Fig. 45-3. The essential properties required for wood siding are good painting characteristics, easy working qualities, and freedom from warp. These properties are present to a high degree in the cedars, eastern white pine, sugar pine, western white pine, cypress, and redwood. They are present to a good degree in western hemlock, ponderosa pine, spruce, and yellow poplar and to a fair degree in Douglas fir, western larch, and southern yellow pine.

Exterior siding materials should be select grade and should be free from knots, pitch pockets, and waney edges. The moisture content at the time of application should be the same that it would attain in service. This is about 12%, except in the dry southwestern United States, where the moisture content should average about 9%.

Wood siding is made in many shapes and sizes and with various edge treatments. The common types are:
➤ Bevel.
➤ Drop.
➤ Board.

Some types, such as bevel siding, must be installed horizontally. Others, such as board siding, may be installed either horizontally (clapboard) or vertically (board and batten). Fig. 45-4.

Vertical siding is commonly applied to the gable ends of houses, over entrances, and sometimes on large wall areas. It may consist of plain-surfaced matched boards, patterned matched boards, or square-edge boards covered at the joint with a batten strip. Fig. 45-4.

Matched vertical siding should preferably be not more than 8" wide. It should be fastened with two 8d nails not more than 4' apart. Backer blocks placed between studs provide a good nailing base. The bottom of the boards should be undercut to form a water drip.

Bevel siding. Plain bevel siding is made in nominal 4", 5", and 6" widths with $^{7}/_{16}$" butts, in 6", 8", and 10" widths with $^{9}/_{16}$" butts, and in 6", 8", 10", 12" widths with $^{11}/_{16}$" butts. Fig. 45-4. The top edge is $^{3}/_{16}$" for all sizes. Bevel siding is generally furnished in random lengths varying from 4' to 16'.

Drop siding. Drop siding is generally $^{3}/_{4}$" thick, has a flat back, and is made in a variety of patterns with either matched or shiplap edges. Fig. 45-4. All patterns of drop siding may be applied horizontally. Some patterns may also be applied vertically; for example, at the gable ends of a house.

Drop siding is designed to be applied directly to the studs. It thereby serves as both sheathing and exterior wall covering. It is widely used in this manner in farm structures, sheds, and garages in all parts of North America, and for houses in mild climates. When drop siding is used over and in contact with other material such as sheathing or sheathing paper, water may work through the joints and be held between the sheathing and the siding. This condition can lead to paint failures and decay. Such conditions are not common when the sidewalls are protected by a good roof overhang. When drop siding is applied vertically, it

	Board	Channel Rustic (Board and Gap)	Drop T&G Patterns / Shiplap Patterns	Bevel Plain / Rabbeted Edge
Patterns	Board and Batten / Board on board / Board Clapboard			
	Available surfaced or rough textured		Available in 13 different patterns. Some T&G (as shown), others shiplapped.	Plain Bevel may be used with smooth face exposed or sawn face exposed for textured effect.
Application And Nailing	Recommended 1" minimum overlap. Use 10d Siding nails as shown.	May be applied horizontally or vertically. Has ½" lap and 1¼" channel when installed. Use 8d Siding nails as shown for 6" widths. Wider widths nail twice per bearing.	6d Finish nails for T&G, 8d Siding nails for shiplap.	Recommend 1" minimum overlap on plain bevel siding. Use 6d Siding nails as shown.
Available Grades *Most commonly used	No. 1 Common* / No. 2 Common* / No. 3 Common / Or / Select Merchantable* / Construction* / Standard	No. 1 Common* / No. 2 Common* / No. 3 Common / Or / C&Btr*, D*, E	No. 1 Common* / No. 2 Common* / No. 3 Common / Or / C&Btr*, D*, E	All species except WRC & IWP / B&Btr*, C*, D / **WRC** / Clear-VG-All Heart* / A*, B*, Rustic* / **IWP** / Supreme*, Choice*, Quality
Seasoning	Shipped 15% moisture content or less when specified.	Shipped 15% moisture content or less when specified.	Shipped 15% moisture content or less when specified.	Usually shipped at 12% or less moisture content.

45-4. *Siding use guide. IWP = Idaho white pine. WRC = Western red cedar. The other letters stand for grades.*

	Bungalow	Dolly Varden	Log Cabin	Tongue & Groove
	Plain / Rabbeted Edge 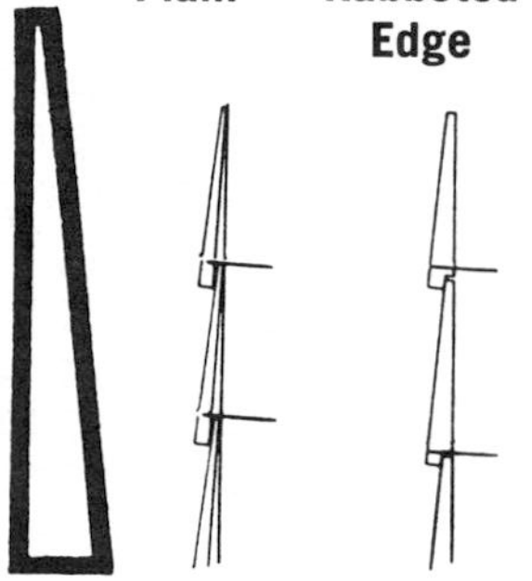	Rabbeted Edge 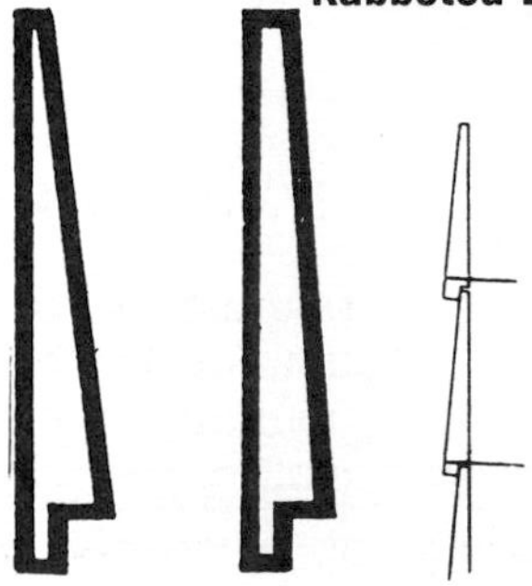	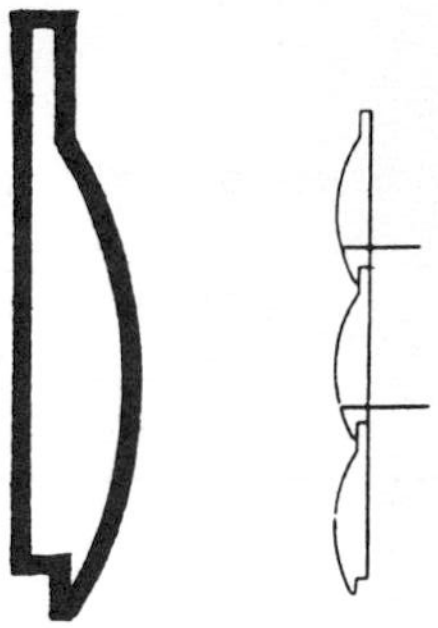	Plain 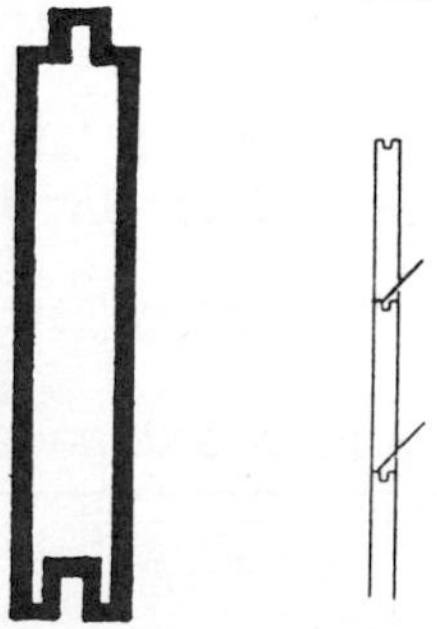
Patterns	(illustrations)	(illustrations)	(illustrations)	(illustrations)
	Thicker and wider than Bevel Siding. Sometimes called "Colonial." Plain bungalow may be used with smooth face exposed for textured effect.	Thicker than Bevel Siding. Rabbeted edge.	1½" at thickest point.	Available in smooth surface or rough surface.
Application And Nailing	Same as for Bevel siding, but use 8d Siding nails.	Same as for Rabbeted Bevel Siding but use 8d Siding nails.	Nail 1½" up from lower edge of piece. Use 10d Casing nails.	Use 6d Finish nails as shown for 6" widths or less. Wider widths, face nail twice per bearing with 8d Siding nails.
Available Grades *Most commonly used	see Bevel Siding Grades	all species except IWP B&Btr*, C*, D IWP Supreme* Choice* Quality	No. 1 Common* No. 2 Common* No. 3 Common	No. 1 Common* No. 2 Common* No. 3 Common Or C&Btr*, D*, E
Seasoning	Usually shipped at 12% or less moisture content.	Usually shipped at 12% or less moisture content.	Shipped 15% moisture content or less when specified.	Shipped 15% moisture content or less when specified.

45-4. (cont.) Siding use guide. IWP = Idaho white pine. WRC = Western red cedar. The other letters stand for grades.

should also be protected by a wide overhanging roof. Otherwise, water flowing down the face of the siding is let into the joint and held there.

Board siding. Square-edge or clapboard siding made of $^{25}/_{32}$" board is occasionally selected for architectural effect. In this case wide boards are generally used. Some of this siding is also beveled at the top of the back when used as clapboard siding. This allows the boards to lie rather close to the sheathing, thus providing solid nailing. Fig. 45-4.

In board and batten siding, when wide square-edged boards are used, they are subject to considerable expansion and contraction because of their width. The batten strips covering the joints should be nailed to only one siding board so that the adjacent board can swell and shrink without splitting the boards or the batten strip. Fig. 45-4.

INSTALLATION OF WOOD SIDING

Before application, exterior wood siding should be treated with a water repellent. This will improve finish performance no matter what type of finish is used.

Some siding is pretreated (or preprimed) by the lumber mill. If this has been done, mill instructions accompanying the siding should be followed carefully.

If the siding has not been pretreated, a water repellent is most easily and effectively applied before the siding is put in place. This may be done either by dipping or by brushing the water repellent on the face, back, ends, and edges of each piece. If the siding is stacked to dry after such treatment, stickers (strips of wood) placed between tiers also should be treated with a water repellent. Many

45-5. Boards that have been cut to length should have the fresh cut ends treated with a water repellent.

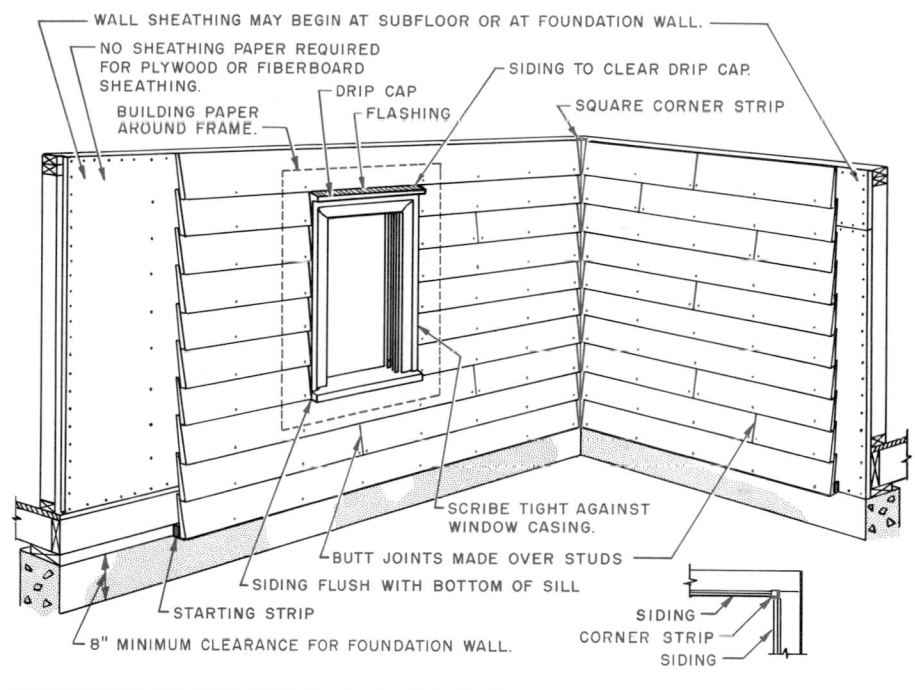

45-6. An exterior wall with wood sheathing and lap siding.

boards will be cut to length as the siding is put in place. Freshly cut surfaces also should receive a liberal treatment with a water repellent. Fig. 45-5.

The siding may be nailed into the sheathing at 24" intervals. Nails should penetrate at least 1½" into the studs. Fig. 45-6.

Housewrap is often applied to the sheathing before the siding is installed. Fig. 45-7.

For matched horizontal siding, the weather exposure (that part of the siding which will not be overlapped by another piece of siding) is predetermined by its machined edge treatment. In these applications, each succeeding course is installed up tight against the preceding course. Since the spacing is predetermined, it is not necessary to lay out the spacing, as it is for plain or bungalow siding.

Laying out the Spacing of Vertical Siding

When laying out board and batten siding, measure the length of the wall on which the siding is to be installed and carefully lay out the spacing of the boards and battens. The spacing will have to be increased or decreased between the boards so that the widths of the underboards will appear to be the same. The underboards are then cut accurately to length and installed according to this layout. Care should be taken that the boards are plumb as they are installed.

When all the underboards are in place, the battens or the overboards (for board on board siding) are installed. Again, make sure that these members are also plumb. The installation of the overboards is much more critical because they will give the wall its finished appearance.

Laying out the Spacing of Plain Bevel or Bungalow Siding

The spacing for plain bevel or bungalow siding should be carefully laid out before the first board is applied. Fig. 45-7. Siding starts with the bottom course of boards at the foundation. Fig. 45-8. Sometimes the siding is started on a water table, which is a projecting member at the top of the foundation to throw off water. Fig. 45-9. Each succeeding course of bevel siding overlaps the upper edge of the previous course.

Determine the number of courses by measuring the distance

45-7. *A housewrap is often applied to the sheathing before siding the house. It reduces air infiltration.*

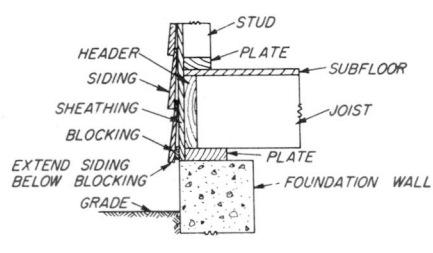

45-8. *The beginning courses of siding at the foundation wall.*

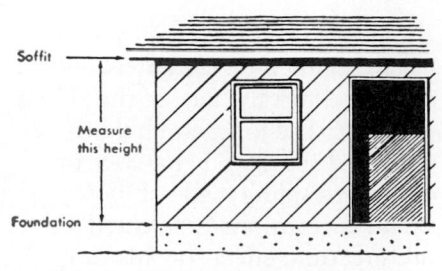

45-10. *Measuring the vertical distance to be covered by the siding.*

from at least 1" below the bottom plate to the underside of the soffit and dividing that height by the maximum weather exposure of the siding. Fig. 45-10. To determine the maximum exposure, deduct the minimum overlap, or head lap, from the overall width (dressed dimensions) of the siding. The minimum head lap is l" for 4" and 6" widths and 1¼" for widths over 6". The dressed dimensions for various sidings can be found in Table 45-A.

For example, if a nominal 10" bevel siding is used, the actual or dressed width is 9¼". Table 45-A. On 10" plain bevel siding, a minimum overlap of 1¼" is

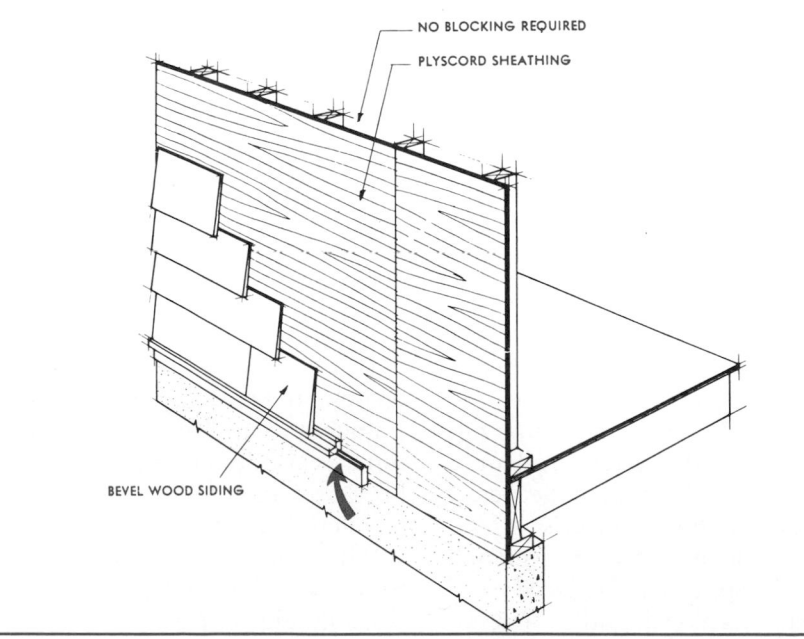

45-9. *Bevel siding started on a water table (see arrow) at the foundation.*

Table 45-A. *Nominal and Dressed Dimensions for Wood Siding.*

Product Description		Nominal Size		Dressed Dimensions		
		Thickness (In.)	Width (In.)	Thickness (In.)	Width (In.)	Lengths (Ft.)`
Rustic and Drop Siding	(D&M) If $3/8$" or $1/2$" T & G specified, same over-all widths apply.	$5/8$ 1	4 5 6 8 10	$9/16$ $23/32$	$3\,1/8$ $4\,1/8$ $5\,1/8$ $6\,7/8$ $8\,7/8$	Same
	(Shiplapped, $3/8$ in. lap)	$5/8$ 1	4 5 6	$9/16$ $23/32$	3 4 5	Same
	(Shiplapped, $1/2$ in. lap)	$5/8$ 1	4 5 6 8 10 12	$9/16$ $23/32$	$2\,7/8$ $3\,7/8$ $4\,7/8$ $6\,5/8$ $8\,5/8$ $10\,5/8$	Same
Ceiling and Partition	(S2S & CM)	$3/8$ $1/2$ $5/8$ $3/4$	3 4 5 6	$5/16$ $7/16$ $9/16$ $11/16$	$2\,1/8$ $3\,1/8$ $4\,1/8$ $5\,1/8$	Same
Bevel Siding Grades	Bevel Siding Western Red Cedar Bevel Siding available in $1/2$", $5/8$", $3/4$" nominal thickness. Corresponding thick edge is $15/32$", $9/16$" and $3/4$".	$1/2$ $9/16$ $5/8$ $3/4$ 1	4 5 6 8 10 12	$7/16$ butt, $3/16$ tip $15/32$ butt, $3/16$ tip $9/16$ butt, $3/16$ tip $11/16$ butt, $3/16$ tip $3/4$ butt, $3/16$ tip	$3\,1/2$ $4\,1/2$ $5\,1/2$ $7\,1/4$ $9\,1/4$ $11\,1/4$	Same
	Wide Bevel Siding (Colonial or Bungalow)	$3/4$	8 10 12	$11/16$ butt, $3/16$ tip	$7\,1/4$ $9\,1/4$ $11\,1/4$	Same
Finish and Boards S-Dry	S1S, S2S, S1S2E	$3/8$ $1/2$ $5/8$ $3/4$ 1 $1\,1/4$ $1\,1/2$ $1\,3/4$ 2 $2\,1/2$ 3 $3\,1/2$ 4	2 3 4 5 6 7 8 and wider nominal	$5/16$ $7/16$ $9/16$ $5/8$ $3/4$ 1 $1\,1/4$ $1\,3/8$ $1\,1/2$ 2 $2\,1/2$ 3 $3\,1/2$	$1\,1/2$ $2\,1/2$ $3\,1/2$ $4\,1/2$ $5\,1/2$ $6\,1/2$ $3/4$ off	3' and longer. In Superior grade, 3% of 3' and 4' and 7% of 5' and 6' are permitted. In Prime grade, 20% of 3' to 6' is permitted.
Factory and Shop Lumber	S2S*	1 (4/4) $1\,1/4$ (5/4) $1\,1/2$ (6/4) $1\,3/4$ (7/4) 2 (8/4) $2\,1/2$ (10/4) 3 (12/4) 4 (16/4)	5 and wider (4" and wider in 4/4 No. 1 Shop and 4/4 No. 2 Shop)	$25/32$ (4/4) $1\,5/32$ (5/4) $1\,13/32$ (6/4) $1\,19/32$ (7/4) $1\,13/16$ (8/4) $2\,3/8$ (10/4) $2\,3/4$ (12/4) $3\,3/4$ (16/4)	(See Rough Sizes Below)	6 ft. and longer in multiples of 1'

* These thicknesses also apply to Tongue & Grove (T&G). See coverage estimator table for T&G widths.

Minimum Rough Sizes. Thicknesses and Widths Dry or Unseasoned All Lumber (S1E, S2E, S1S, S2S). 80% of the pieces in a shipment shall be at least 1/8" thicker than the standard surfaced size, the remaining 20% at least 3/32" thicker than the surfaced size. Widths shall be at least 1/8" wider than standard surfaced widths. When specified to be full sawn, lumber may not be manufactured to a size less than the size specified.

required. Therefore the maximum exposed surface of a 10" piece of siding would be 8" ($9\,1/4$" - $1\,1/4$" = 8"). With a pair of dividers set at 8", make a trial layout on the sidewall beginning at the bottom and "walking off" this exposure dimension. The bottom of the board that passes over the top of the first-floor windows should coincide with the top of the window cap. Fig. 45-11. If the bottom of this board does not line up, adjust the spacing for each board to something slightly less than 8". (NOTE: Eight inches is the maximum exposure. Do not adjust it to a greater width.) Continue to modify the spacing, if at all possible, until the bottom edge of this piece of siding is even with the tops of the windows and doors. The location on the foundation wall for the bottom edge of the first piece of siding may also be adjusted slightly as an aid in making this alignment.

The board spacing should be such that the maximum exposure will not be exceeded. This may mean that the boards will have less than the maximum exposure.

Application of Plain Bevel or Bungalow Siding

The application of the first course of siding determines the level and uniformity of all succeeding courses. To insure the proper application of the first course, proceed as follows:

1. Measure down with a tape from the top of the top plate if possible. If not, measure from the underside of the soffit to a point at least 1" below the bottom plate. This point will usually be on the foundation. Make a mark on the foundation and record this measurement. Fig. 45-12, point A.

2. Repeat Step 1 along the sidewall at about 2' intervals using the same measured length each time. B, Fig. 45-12.

3. Snap a chalk line horizontally along the marks. With bevel, bungalow, or Anzac patterns, nail a furring strip about ⅜" above this line to provide support for the starting course. Fig. 45-13. The bottom edge of the first course of siding will be positioned along the chalk line. Fig. 45-12, line C.

4. Begin the application by placing the butt edge of the siding

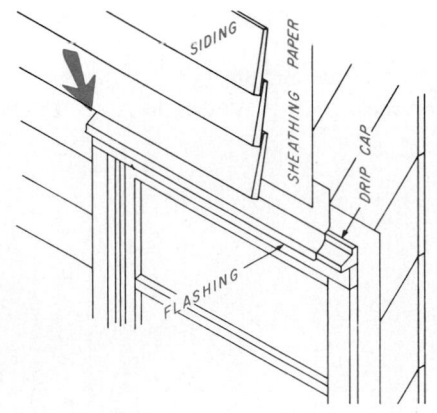

45-11. *Plan the courses of siding so that the bottom edge of the course running across the top of the window will be in alignment with the drip cap.*

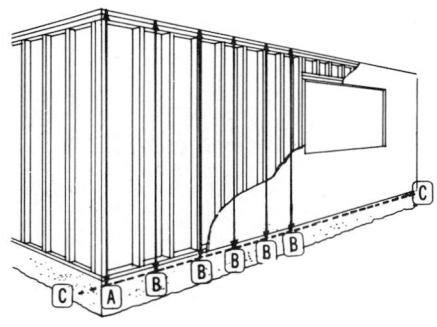

45-12. *Locating the first course of siding on an exterior wall.*

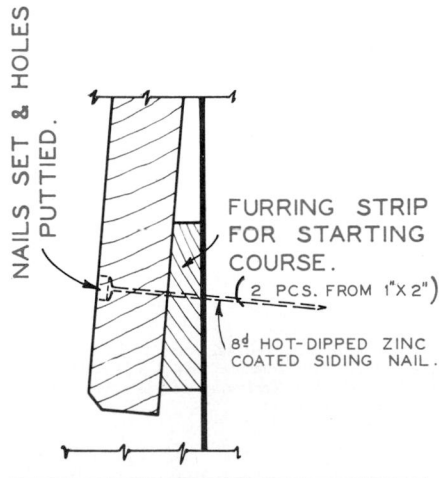

45-13. *The furring strip may be ripped at an angle to provide support along its full width. Notice that two furring strips were ripped from one piece of 1" × 2" stock.*

along the chalk line. Start the first piece of siding at the end of the sidewall and work toward the other end. The first course is nailed to the bottom plate at points just below each stud. This will mark the nailing locations for the succeeding courses. Fig. 45-14.

5. The amount of overlap is measured along the top of the siding course to be lapped. Snap a chalk line along this mark to locate the butt edge of the second course. Fig. 45-15, line D.

6. The second course is also started at the end of the sidewall. Align the siding horizontally along the chalk line and nail at each studbearing. E, Fig. 45-15. Use only one nail per bearing. Never nail through both courses of siding. F, Fig. 45-15. Tap the nail head flush with the siding surface. The siding courses should fit snug, not tight.

7. Repeat Steps 5 and 6 for the application of successive courses. Make certain that the vertical butt joints between boards are staggered along the sidewall and that they fall on studs, as shown at G in Fig. 45-16.

The siding should be carefully fitted and be in close contact with the adjacent piece. Some carpenters fit the boards so tightly that they have to spring the boards in place. Tight-fitting butt joints are obtained by cutting the closure board of each course approximately ¹⁄₁₆" too long. Bow the piece slightly to get the ends in position, and then snap it into place. Fig. 45-17. This assures a tight joint. Loosefitting joints allow water to get behind the siding. The water can cause paint deterioration around the joints and also set up conditions conducive to decay at the ends of boards.

Siding that passes under a window sill should be cut to fit the groove provided in the bottom of the sill. Fig. 45-18a. Siding

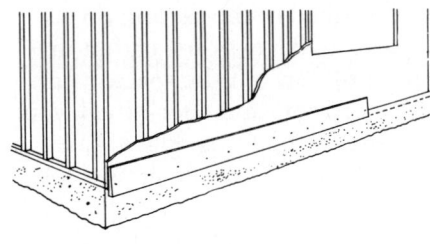

45-14. *Applying the first piece of siding with one nail below each stud location.*

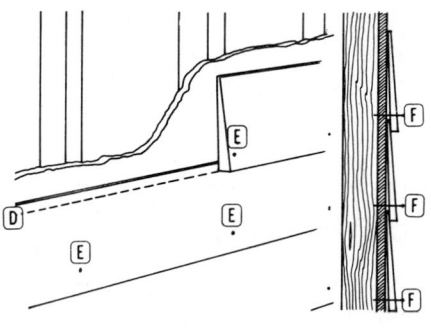

45-15. *Snap a chalk line along the top edge of the siding to locate the butt edge of the succeeding courses.*

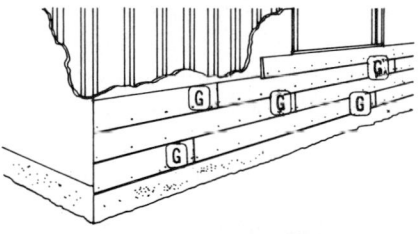

45-16. *Apply successive courses, making sure that all the vertical butt joints are staggered and that they fall on studs.*

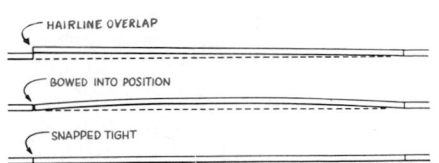

HAIRLINE OVERLAP

BOWED INTO POSITION

SNAPPED TIGHT

45-17. *To fit siding tightly, cut it about 1/16" too long, bow it into position, and then snap it tight.*

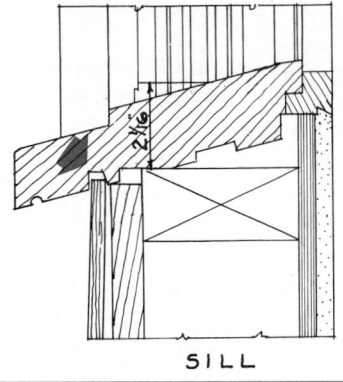

SILL

45-18a. *Bevel siding under window sills should fit in the groove provided.*

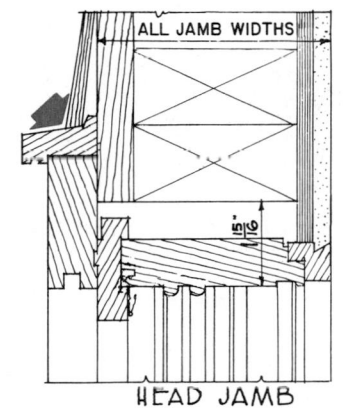

ALL JAMB WIDTHS

HEAD JAMB

45-18b. *Siding over doors and windows should rest on the drip cap.*

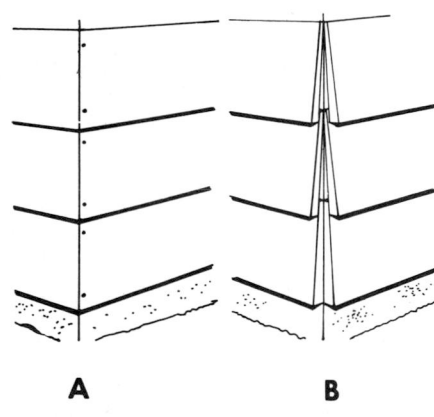

A   B

45-19. *Finishing an outside corner: A. Mitered corners. B. Siding installed and ready for metal corners.*

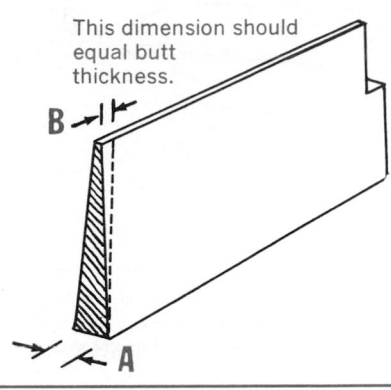

This dimension should equal butt thickness.

B

A

45-20. *Mitering of bevel siding corners must be done carefully to obtain a good joint. To lay out and cut the joint, measure the butt thickness at A. Measure back along the top edge a distance at B equal to the butt thickness shown at A. Then connect these two points as shown by the dotted line. With the saw blade set at about a 47° angle, make the cut beginning at the butt end.*

installed over doors and windows should be set on the drip cap. Fig. 45-18b.

8. Trim the last course of siding to fit under the eaves and apply a molding if required.

9. Outside corners may be mitered, covered with corner boards, or capped with metal corners. Fig. 45-19. For mitered corners the siding is cut to length and mitered before application. Fig. 45-20. Corner boards are installed before siding application. The siding is then cut to length and butted against the corner boards. If metal corners are used, the siding is cut off even with the outside corner of the building. The metal corners are applied after the siding is in place.

Inside corners are cut before application and butted against a square wood corner strip approximately 1⅛" × 1⅛" in size. Fig. 45-21.

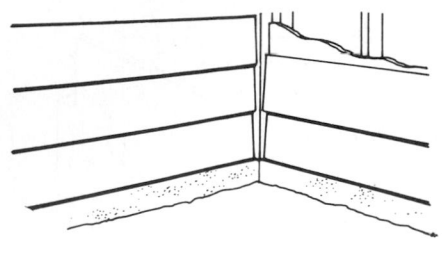

45-21. *Bevel siding at an inside corner. The bevel siding is butted against a square wood corner strip.*

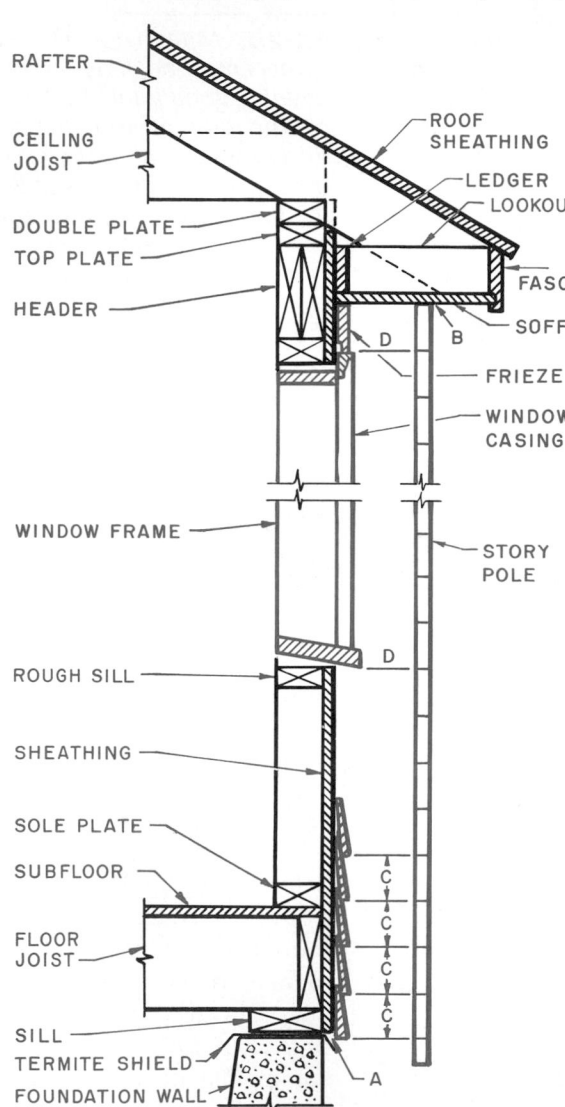

RAFTER

CEILING JOIST

DOUBLE PLATE
TOP PLATE

HEADER

ROOF SHEATHING

LEDGER
LOOKOUT

FASCIA

SOFFIT

FRIEZE

WINDOW CASING

WINDOW FRAME

STORY POLE

ROUGH SILL

SHEATHING

SOLE PLATE

SUBFLOOR

FLOOR JOIST

SILL
TERMITE SHIELD
FOUNDATION WALL

45-22. *The story pole should extend from the underside of the soffit to the bottom edge of the first piece of siding as shown from A to B. Hold the story pole in position against the building. Lay out the spacing on the story pole as shown at C. Check to be certain that the bottom edge of the piece of siding over the window is even with the top of the window as shown at D.*

Using a Story Pole

You may prepare a story pole when installing horizontal siding to insure accuracy and increase efficiency. Select a straight piece of 1" × 2" stock for the siding story pole. Place it under the soffit against a dominant wall of the house, usually the front, and mark the total height. Determine the number of courses and the spacing as described in the section on spacing of bevel siding earlier in this unit. Lay out the spacing on the story pole and check the layout against the building. Fig. 45-22.

Hold the story pole in position up against the soffit. Transfer the marks from the story pole to the house on all corners and on all window and door casings. Fig. 45-23. Make sure that the bottom marks are clearly visible on the foundation. Snap a chalk line on the bottom marks around the perimeter of the house. Then install the siding as described previously, beginning with Step 4.

Using a Siding Gauge, or "Preacher"

A siding gauge, or "preacher," is a small hardwood block used for accurately marking siding pieces to fit between two window casings or a window and a door casing. If corner boards are used at the corners, it may also be used for marking siding between a corner board and a window or door casing. To make a siding gauge, select a piece of ⅜" or ½" hardwood long enough to accommodate the width of siding used and proceed as follows:

45-23. *Transferring the marks of the story pole to the house.*

1. Center the siding on the block of hardwood material. A, Fig. 45-24.

2. Lay out the width of the siding plus ¼" for clearance. B, Fig. 45-24.

3. Lay out the thickness of the siding plus approximately ⅝". C, Fig. 45-24.

4. Allow about 1" around all of the inside cuts. D, Fig. 45-24.

5. Cut off the corners as shown at E in Fig. 45-24.

Fig. 45-25 illustrates how to use the preacher for marking siding between a corner board and a window casing. Cut the end of the siding to fit against the corner board on the spacing mark. A, Fig. 45-25. Align the other end of the siding with the spacing mark on the window casing. B, Fig. 45-25. Place the preacher over the siding and hold it tight against the casing. Holding a pencil against the edge of the preacher, draw a line along the face of the siding. C, Fig. 45-25. Cut the siding to finish length, position it on the marks, and nail it in place.

Siding Nails and Nailing

Good nails and nailing practices are a must for the proper application of wood siding. Nails should be long enough to penetrate into studs (or studs and wood sheathing combined) at least 1½". When this much penetration is not possible, threaded nails are recommended for increased holding power. Do not nail siding only to composition or pressed fiber sheathing. The nails must penetrate the studs. Nail locations and recommended nail sizes are shown in Fig. 45-4 in the "Application and Nailing" section. However, the following data about nails will be very helpful in the selection and use of the right nail for the application.

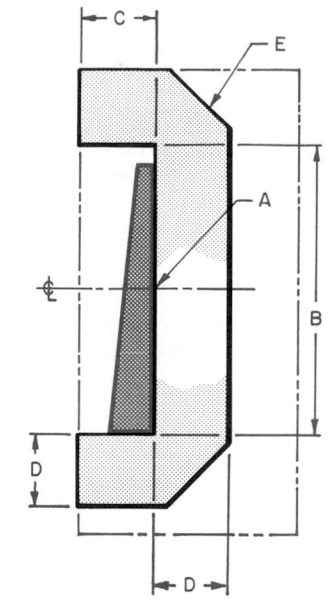

45-24. *Laying out a siding gauge, or "preacher".*

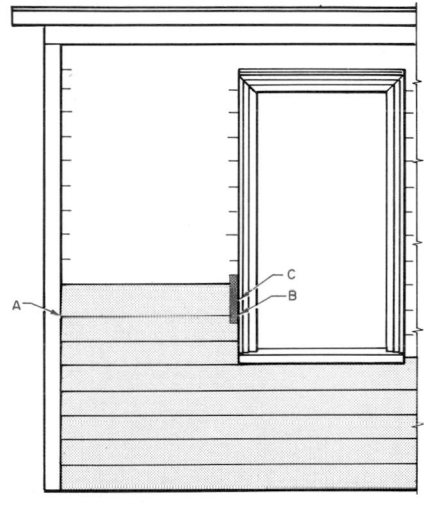

45-25. *Using the preacher to mark the length of a piece of siding.*

Nail Requirements. The following characteristics are essential for nails used on wood siding. Such nails:

➤ Should be rust-resistant, preferably rust proof.

➤ Must not cause the siding to discolor or stain.

➤ Should not cause splitting, even when driven near the end or edge of siding.

➤ Should have adequate strength to avoid the need for predrilling.

➤ Should be able to be driven easily and rapidly.

➤ Should not emerge or "pop" at any time after being driven flush with the siding.

➤ Should not cause an unsightly visible pattern on the sidewall.

Two types of nails which have these characteristics are:

➤ High-tensile strength aluminum nails.

➤ Galvanized nails.

High-tensile strength aluminum nails are corrosion-resistant and will not discolor or deteriorate the wood siding. They are economical when the nail count per pound is considered, although they are somewhat more expensive than the common galvanized nail. Table 45-B.

There are two kinds of galvanized nails: the mechanically plated and the hot-dipped. Mechanical plating is a process which provides a nail with a uniform coating, giving it outstanding corrosion resistance. With nails that are hot-dipped, the degree of coating protection varies.

Nail Design. The design of a nail influences the ease with which it can be driven and its holding power. Fig. 45-26. Nail design includes the head, shank, and point. The basic types of nail heads are illustrated in Fig. 45-27. Nail shanks may be smooth or threaded. Nails that are smooth shanked will loosen under extreme temperature changes. Increased holding power may be obtained by using a ring-threaded or spiral-threaded nail shank. The commonly used nail points include:

➤ Blunt—reduces splitting.

➤ Diamond—most widely used.

➤ Needle—tops in holding but tendency to cause splitting.

Table 45-B. *Nail Size Specification.*
A comparison of aluminum and hot-dipped galvanized nails.

Size	Length (Inches)		Siding Nails (Count per lb.)		Approx. lbs. Per 1,000 B.F. of Siding	
	*	**	*	**	*	**
6d	1 7/8"	2"	566	194	2	6
7d	2 1/8"	2 1/4"	468	172	2 1/2	6 1/2
8d	2 3/8"	2 1/2"	319	123	4	9
10d	2 7/8"	3"	215	103	5 1/2	11

* Aluminum   ** Hot-dipped galvanized

For the best possible holding power with the least splitting, a blunt or medium diamond point and a blunt or medium needle point with a ring-threaded shank are recommended.

Nailing Recommendations.
When nailing mitered corners or when nailing near the end of a piece, predrill the nail hole or blunt the nail point to avoid splitting the wood. With lapped siding, in order to prevent splitting and to allow expansion clearance, nail just above the lap and not through the tip of the undercourse. Fig. 45-28.

Specific nailing recommendations for standard siding patterns are shown in Figs. 45-4 and 45-29. All

45-26. *Choosing the proper nail will ensure proper siding performance.*

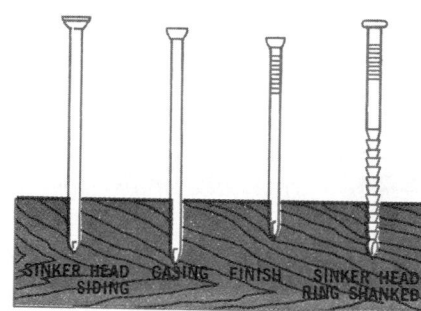

45-27. *Nails used for the application of siding.*

45-28. *Correct nailing procedure for lapped siding.*

recommendations refer to nailing at every stud, if siding courses are laid up horizontally. If siding is installed vertically, use 2 × 4 blocking between studs. Fig. 45-30. The blocking should be placed at top and bottom, and intermediately, at not more than 24" on center.

Bevel and bungalow siding. Face-nail with one nail per bearing only. Use 8d siding nails for ¾" thicknesses. Use 6d nails for thinner pieces. When applying plain bevel and bungalow siding, drive the nails so that the shank just clears the tip of the preceding course. For rabbeted bevel and bungalow siding, set each course to allow an expansion clearance of ⅛". Drive the nails about 1" from the lower edge of the course.

Shiplap and rustic siding. Face-nail with two siding nails per bearing for patterns wider than 6". Space each nail about halfway between the center and the edge of a piece. For narrower courses, one nail per bearing is enough. Drive the nail 1" from the overlapping edge. Use 8d siding nails for 1" thicknesses, 6d for thinner pieces.

Tongue-and-groove siding. Siding 4" or 6" wide should be blind-nailed through the tongue with 6d finish nails. Use one nail per bearing. For wider patterns, facenail with two 8d siding nails per bearing.

Board and batten siding. Space the underboards about ½" apart and fasten with one 8d siding nail per bearing, driven through the center of the piece. Fasten batten strips with one 10d siding nail per bearing, driven through the center of each piece so that the nail shank passes between the underboards. Variations of the board and batten with recommended nailing procedures are shown in Fig. 45-31.

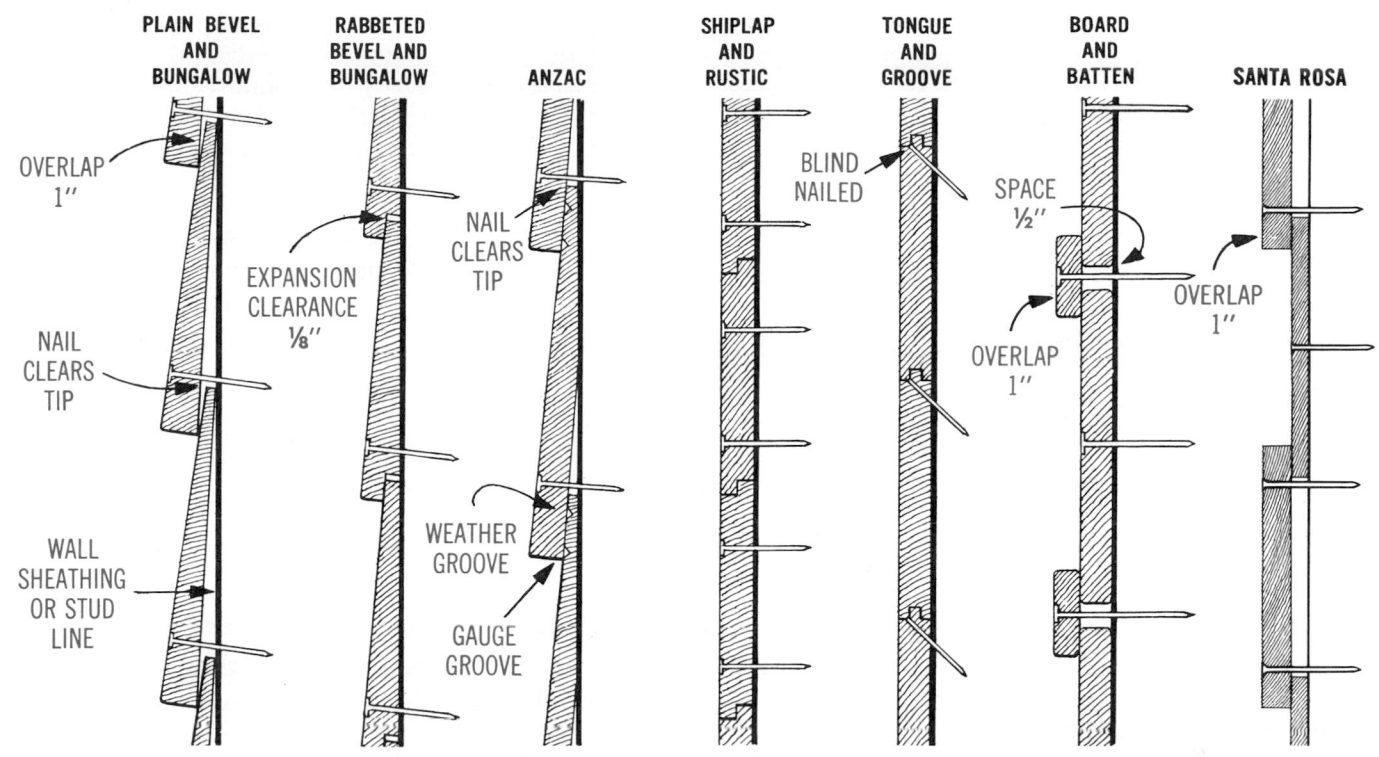

PLAIN BEVEL AND BUNGALOW

OVERLAP 1"

NAIL CLEARS TIP

WALL SHEATHING OR STUD LINE

RABBETED BEVEL AND BUNGALOW

EXPANSION CLEARANCE ⅛"

ANZAC

NAIL CLEARS TIP

WEATHER GROOVE

GAUGE GROOVE

SHIPLAP AND RUSTIC

TONGUE AND GROOVE

BLIND NAILED

BOARD AND BATTEN

SPACE ½"

OVERLAP 1"

SANTA ROSA

OVERLAP 1"

45-29a. *Suggested nailing methods for typical siding patterns.*

45-29b. *Installing Santa Rosa pattern siding.*

45-31a. *Red cedar board and batten siding has been installed on the exterior of this house.*

STUD

BLOCKING

45-30. *To provide backing when applying vertical siding, put 2" x 4" blocks between the studs at no more than 24" on center.*

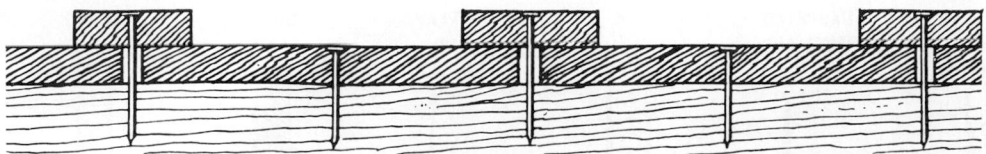

STANDARD BOARD AND BATTEN: One 8d siding nail is driven midway between edges of the underboard, at each bearing. Then apply batten strips and nail with one 10d siding nail at each bearing so that shank passes through space between underboards.

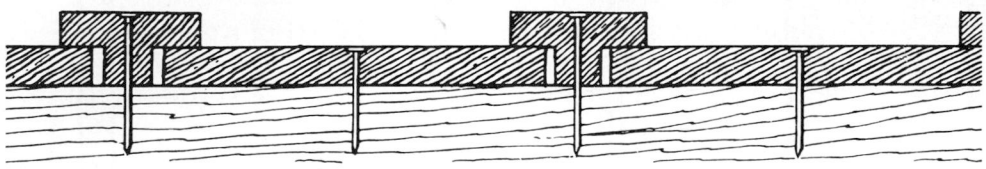

SPECIAL BATTENS: A T-shaped batten or standard batten nailed over a vertical nailing strip, is nailed exactly the same as the standard method; however, in this case an exceptionally good bearing is provided while driving nail through the batten.

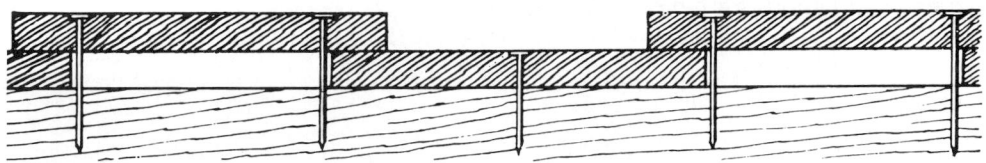

BOARD ON BOARD: Apply underboards first, spacing them to allow 1 ½-inch overlap by outer boards at both edges. Use standard nailing for underboards, one 8d siding nail per bearing. Outer boards must be nailed twice per bearing to insure proper fastening. Nails, having some free length, do not hold outer boards so rigidly as to cause splitting if there is "movement" from humidity changes. Drive 10d siding nails so that shanks clear edges of underboard approximately ¼-inch. This provides sufficient bearing for nailing, while allowing clearance to enable underboard to expand slightly.

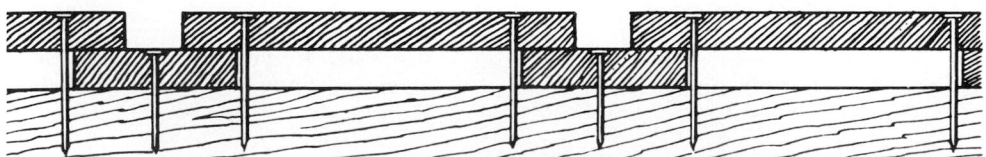

REVERSE BATTEN: Nailing is similar to board on board. Drive one 8d nail per bearing through center of under strip, and two 10d siding nails per bearing through outer boards.

45-31b. *Nailing details for various board and batten applications.*

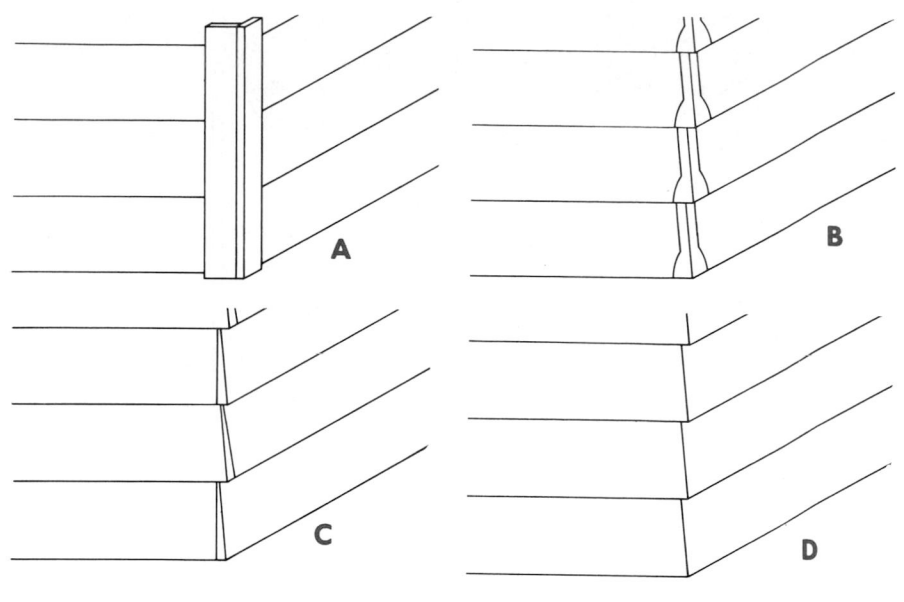

45-32. *Methods of treating bevel siding on an outside corner: A. Corner boards. B. Metal corners. C. Alternately lapped corners. D. Mitered corners.*

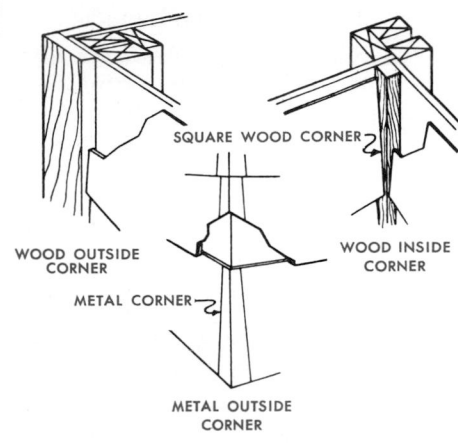

45-33. *Lap siding corner details.*

Exterior Corner Treatment

Wood siding is commonly joined at the exterior corners by corner boards, mitered corners, metal corners, or alternately lapped corners. Fig. 45-32. The method of finishing the wood siding at exterior corners is influenced somewhat by overall house design.

Corner boards are used with bevel or drop siding and are generally made of nominal 1" or 1¼" material, depending upon the thickness of the siding. The boards may be plain or molded, depending on the architectural treatment of the house.

The corner boards and the window and door trim may be applied to the sheathing, with the siding fitted tightly against the narrow edge of the corner boards and against the trim. When this method is used, the joints between the siding and the corner boards or trim should be calked or treated with a water repellent. Sometimes corner boards and trim around windows and doors are applied over the siding, a method that minimizes the entrance of water into the ends of the siding. This method works better for panel siding than for bevel siding. Fig. 45-33.

Mitered corners, sometimes used with the thicker patterns, should be cut in a miter box and must fit tightly and smoothly for the full depth of the miter. To maintain a tight fit at the miter, it is important that the siding be properly seasoned before delivery and protected from rain when stored at the site. The ends should be set in white lead when the siding is applied, and the exposed faces should be primed immediately after it is applied. Nail mitered ends to the corner posts, not to each other.

Metal corners are made of light-gauge metals, such as aluminum or galvanized iron, and are used with bevel siding as a substitute for mitered corners. Fig. 45-33. They can be purchased at most lumberyards. The application of metal corners takes less experience than is required to make good mitered corners or to fit siding to corner boards.

Alternately lapped corners are fitted so that every other piece of siding has the end exposed. Fig. 45-32.

Interior Corner Treatment

Interior corners of siding are butted against a corner strip of nominal 1" or 1¼" material, depending upon the thickness of the siding. Fig. 45-33.

Preventing Outside Moisture Problems

Poor construction detailing may enable water to seep into the siding, eventually causing paint or finish deterioration. Poor construction may also result in inadequate insulation, causing discomfort and high heating bills. To avoid these problems take the following precautions at the points where trouble may occur:

Careful Fitting. With any siding pattern, good joints are essential. Accurate cutting of pieces is the only way to insure the proper fit.

Bevel courses should have at least 1" lap to prevent wind-driven rain from working up between courses.

Gutter joints and downspouts are other areas which must be carefully fitted.

Caulking. The sealing of all joints helps provide protection against rain, snow, fog, and wind. It is particularly important at the butt joints of short length siding laid vertically. Use a nonhardening caulking compound.

Flashing. Flashing is necessary to drain away water at places where horizontal surfaces meet the siding. These places include the areas over door and window frames and around dormers. Figs. 45-34 and 45-35. Where siding returns against a roof, the siding should not be fitted tight against the shingles, but should have a clearance of 2". Windblown water working into the back of the siding is a potential cause of paint failure. Siding cannot dry out quickly where there is a tight fit. Fig. 45-35.

Flashing should be anchored tightly. It should extend well under the siding and sufficiently over edges and ends of wellsloped water tables to prevent water from running in behind siding or jambs. A bead of caulking should be laid under the flashing to help seal out moisture. Fig. 45-36.

Foundation Lines. The lowest edge of the siding should be at least 8" above ground level. Fig. 45-37. Water (often present at the base of a foundation due to landscaping) and high humidity can cause finish difficulties and structural problems as well.

It is particularly important that the end grain at the bottom of vertical siding be given a water repellent treatment. The use of a drip cap at the lower edge of the

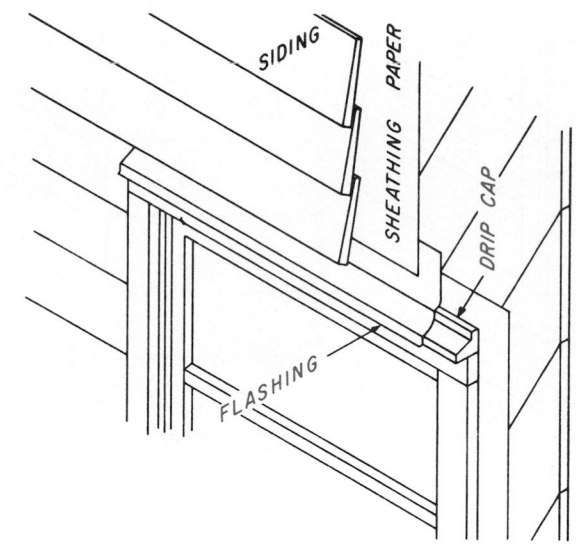

45-34. *Flashing should be used above windows and doors.*

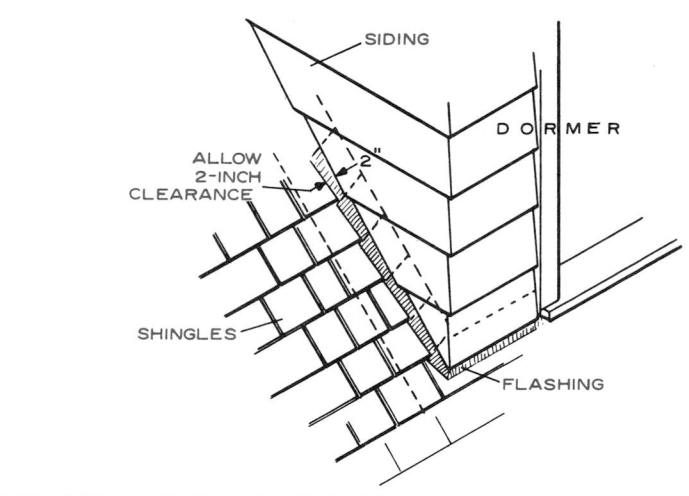

45-35. *Flashing should be used around dormers at the intersection of the siding and the roof.*

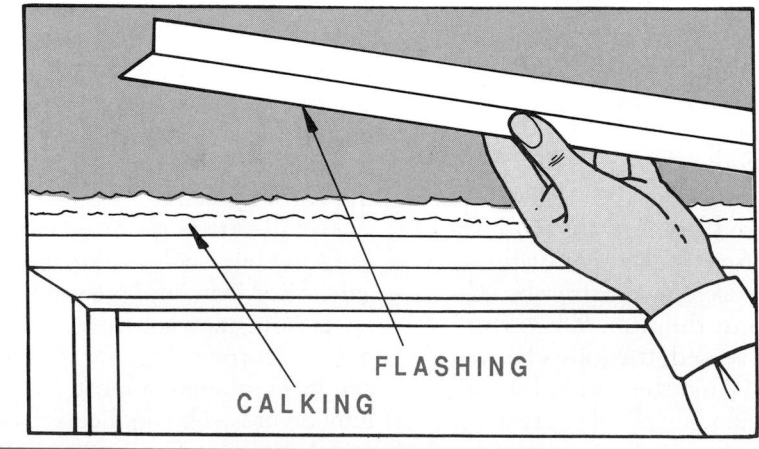

45-36. *Caulking should be used under the flashing.*

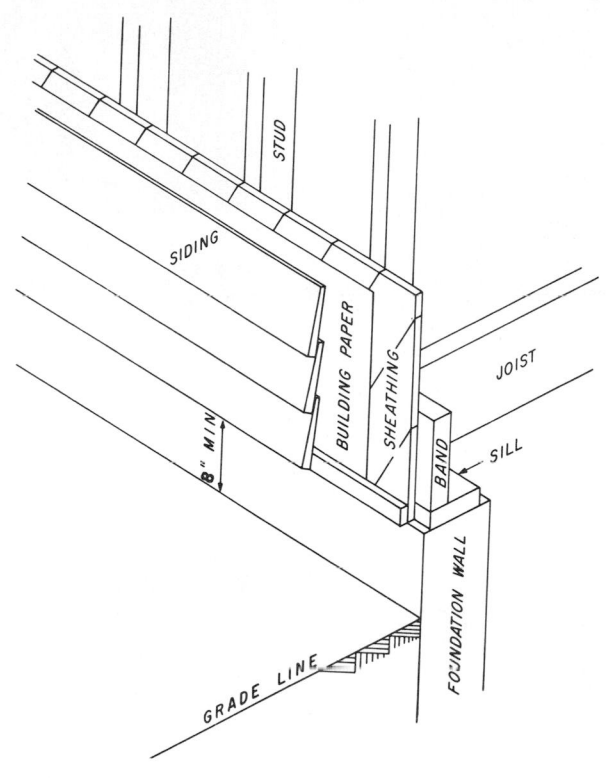

45-37. *Exterior siding should begin at least 8" above the grade line.*

siding will help direct water away from the foundation.

PLYWOOD AND OTHER COMPOSITION MATERIALS

Plywood Siding

Plywood sheets are often used in gable ends, sometimes around windows and porches, and occasionally as overall exterior wall covering. Figs. 45-38 and 45-39. Plywood siding comes in many grades and surface textures, providing almost unlimited freedom of design for all types of construction. Fig. 45-40. For best results with painted surfaces, specify "medium-density overlaid" plywood. This grade has a resin-impregnated fiber surface that is heat-fused to the panel faces. It takes paint well and holds it longer. Sheet siding can be applied directly to studs, thus eliminating the need for

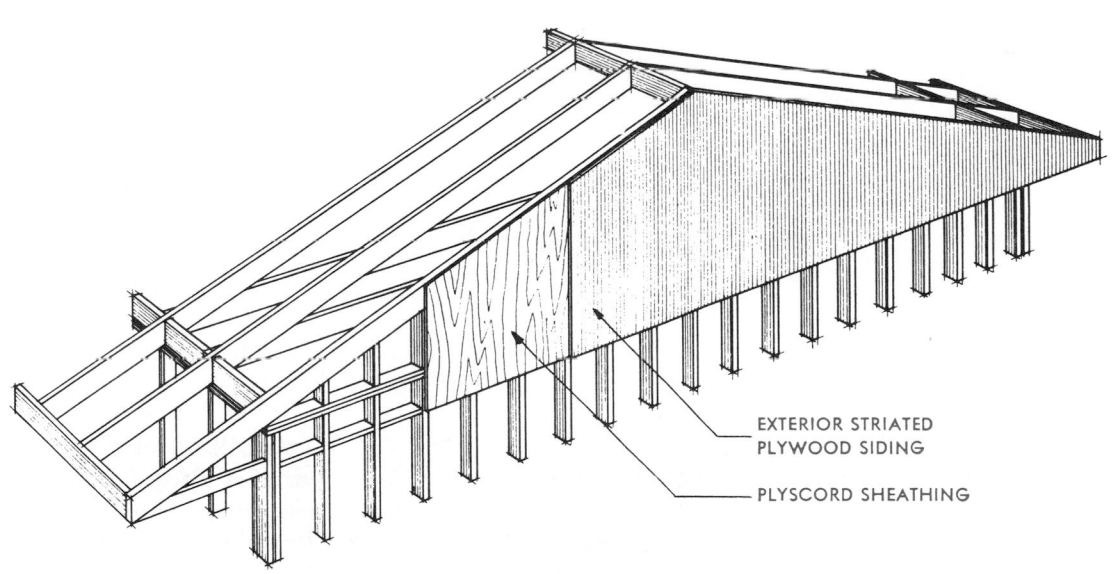

EXTERIOR STRIATED PLYWOOD SIDING

PLYSCORD SHEATHING

NOTE: PROVIDE ADEQUATE ATTIC VENTILATION THROUGH GABLE END OR SOFFIT OF ROOF OVERHANG

45-38. *Plywood used as an exterior covering for a gable.*

T-1-11 *on gable blends with frame or masonry walls*

T-1-11 *used on carport storagewall*

45-39. *Plywood paneling used in conjunction with stone veneer.*

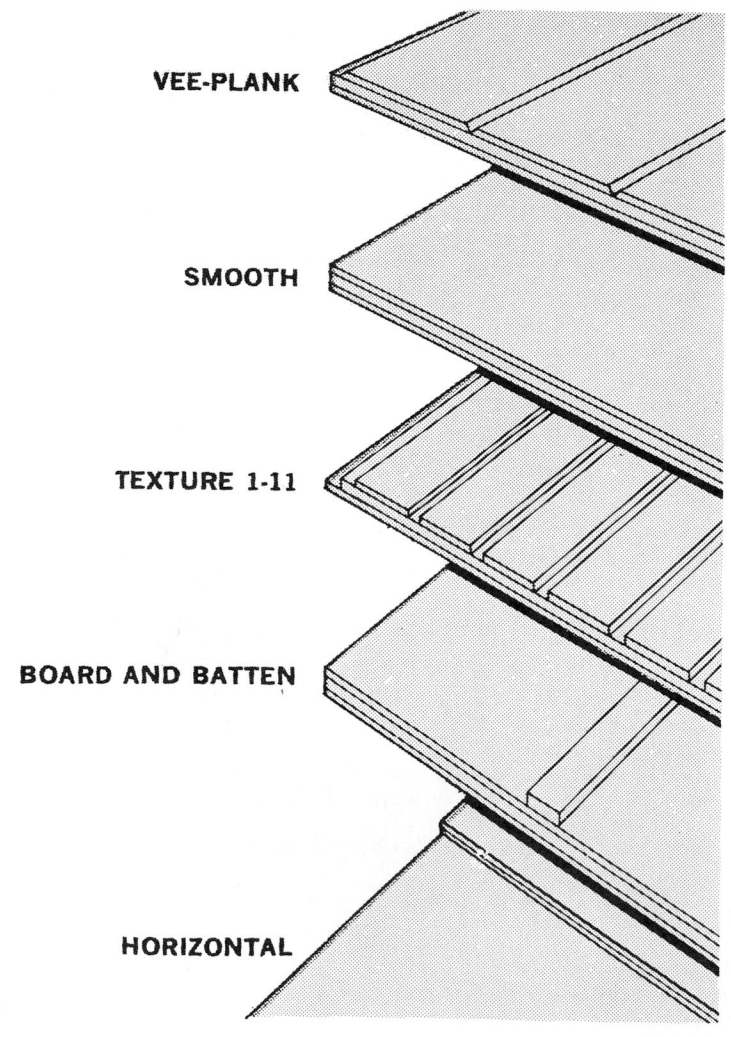

VEE-PLANK

SMOOTH

TEXTURE 1-11

BOARD AND BATTEN

HORIZONTAL

45-40. *Five of many plywood siding styles available.*

45-41. *Applying a plywood siding panel.*

sheathing. Fig. 45-41 and Table 45-C.

Plywood siding is strong. Tests conducted by United States Forests Products Laboratory at Madison, Wisconsin, proved that plywood as thin as ¼", when nailed directly to studs, provides more than twice the relative rigidity and more than three times the relative strength of 1" × 8" lumber sheathing nailed horizontally to studs.

Plywood siding can be applied horizontally or vertically. The joints can be battens, V-grooves, or flush joints. Sometimes plywood is installed as lap siding. Figs. 45-42 and 45-43.

Plywood panel (sheet) siding and plywood lap siding come in 8' standard and 12', 14', and 16' special lengths. Lap siding may be 12", 16", or 24" wide. Plywood siding will cover large areas and cut installation time. The wide exposure of the lap siding or the use of panel siding is in keeping with the style of the modern ranch home.

Application of Plywood Panel Siding. Plywood panel siding is normally installed vertically but may be installed horizontally. All edges of panel siding should be backed with framing members or blocking. Fig. 45-44. To prevent staining of the siding, galvanized, aluminum, or other noncorrosive nails are

Table 45-C. *Plywood Siding Details.*
Plywood siding direct to studs (Plywood continuous over two or more spans)/Recommedations apply to all species groups.

Panel Siding Mimimum Plywood Thickness (Inch)			Maximum Stud Spacing c. to c. (Inches)	Nail Size & Type[1]	Nail Spacing (Inches) Panel Edges	Intermediate
$^3/_8$			16	6d (non-corrosive	6	12
$^1/_2$			24	6d siding or	6	12
$^5/_8$			24	8d casing (galv. or	6	12
T 1-11 ($^5/_8$)			16	8d alum.))	6[2]	12

Lap or Bevel Siding[3]						
Typical Width (Inches)	Min. Lap Siding Thickness (Inch)	Min. Bevel Butt Thickness (Inch)				
12, 16 or 24	$^3/_8$	$^9/_{16}$	16	6d (non-corrosive	One nail per stud along bottom edge	4" at vertical joint: 8" at studs if siding wider than 12"
	$^1/_2$		20	8d siding or casing		
	$^5/_8$		24	8d (galv. or alum.))		

(1) Nails through battens must penetrate studs at least 1".
(2) Use single nail on shiplap edges slant-driven to catch both edges. Can nail to 3/8" from panel edge, but do not set nails. Nails may be set if placed on both sides of joint instead of slant-driven.
(3) Minimum head-lap 1 1/2".

Look for these typical APA grade-trademarks.

M.D. OVERLAY
GROUP 1 **APA**
EXTERIOR
PS 1-74 000

Sanded Grades
A-C
GROUP 2 **APA**
EXTERIOR
PS 1-74 000

Specialty Panels
303 SIDING 16 oc
GROUP 3 **APA**
EXTERIOR
PS 1-74 000

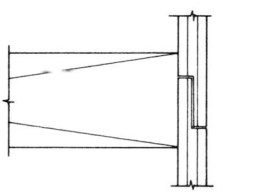
Shiplap—Horizontal or Vertical Joint

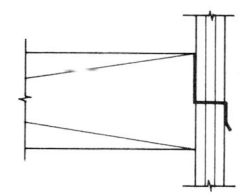
Flashed—Horizontal Joint galv. or alum. flashing

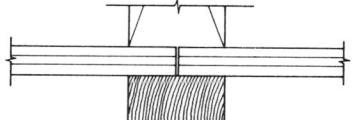
Batten (panel only)—Vertical Joint

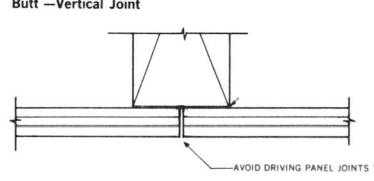
Butt —Vertical Joint

AVOID DRIVING PANEL JOINTS TIGHT

Note:
When finish is paint, prime all panel edges prior to application. Otherwise treat edges with water repellants or caulk joints. Building paper may be omitted under panel sidings; also under lapped and bevelled siding when plywood sheathing is used. Joints may occur away from studs when plywood or board sheathing is used.

Plywood panel siding

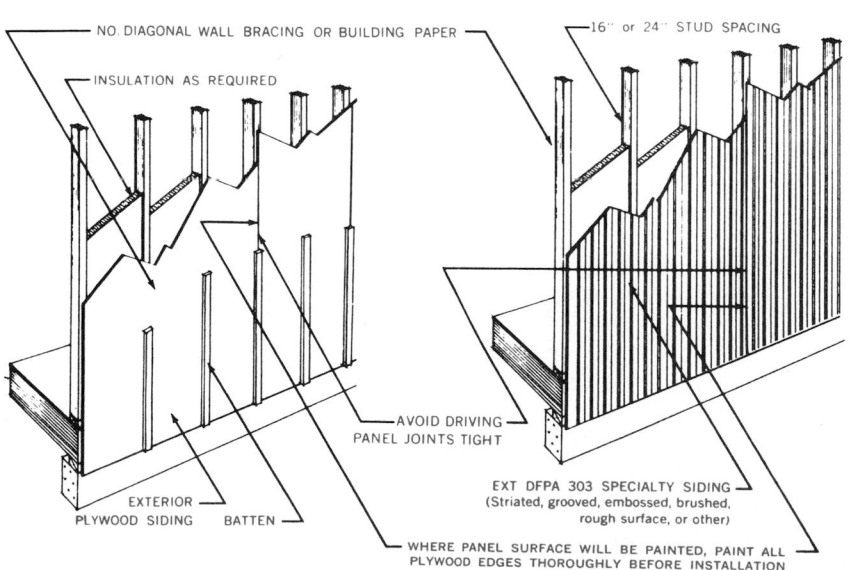

NO. DIAGONAL WALL BRACING OR BUILDING PAPER
INSULATION AS REQUIRED
16" or 24" STUD SPACING
AVOID DRIVING PANEL JOINTS TIGHT
EXTERIOR PLYWOOD SIDING   BATTEN
EXT DFPA 303 SPECIALTY SIDING (Striated, grooved, embossed, brushed, rough surface, or other)
WHERE PANEL SURFACE WILL BE PAINTED, PAINT ALL PLYWOOD EDGES THOROUGHLY BEFORE INSTALLATION

45-42. *Plywood siding.*
Consult Table 45-C.

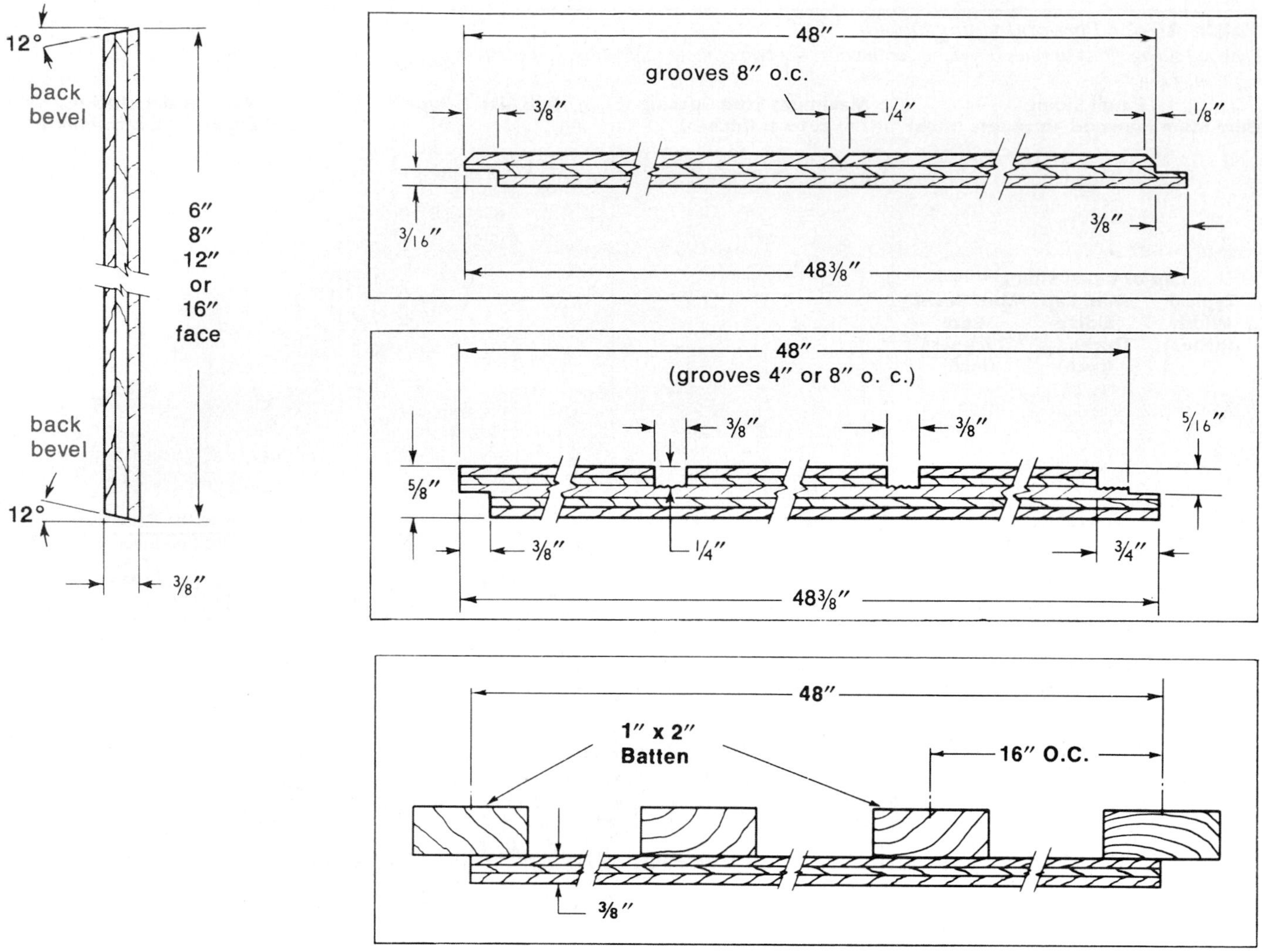

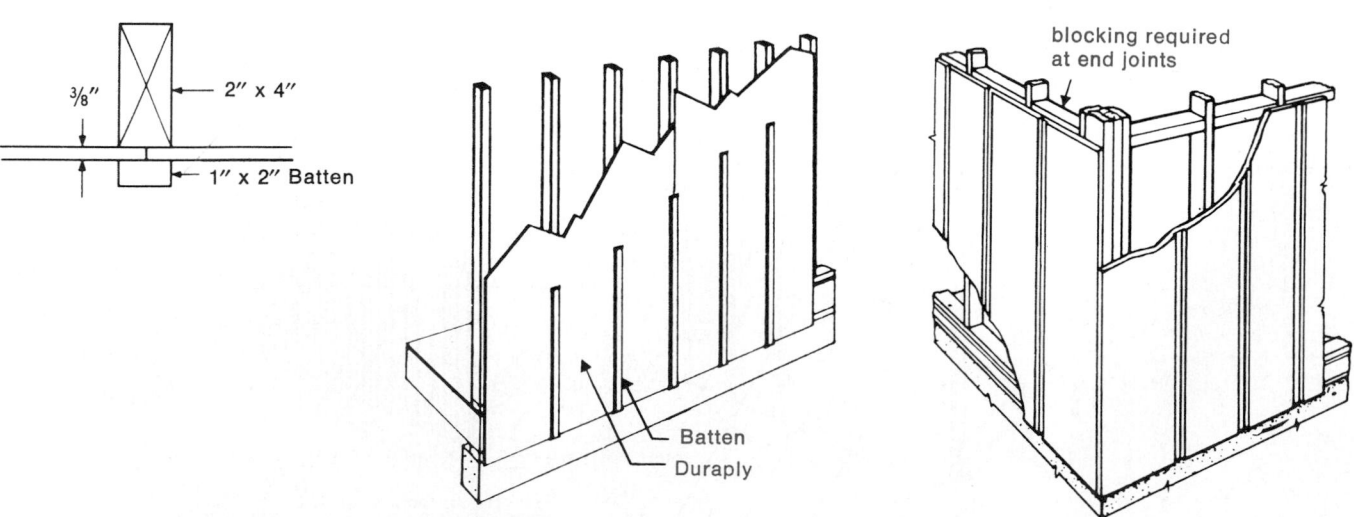

12°

back
bevel

6″
8″
12″
or
16″
face

back
bevel

12°

3/8″

48″

grooves 8″ o.c.

3/8″   ¼″   ⅛″

3/16″   3/8″

48⅜″

48″
(grooves 4″ or 8″ o. c.)

3/8″   3/8″   5/16″

5/8″

3/8″   ¼″   ¾″

48⅜″

48″

1″ x 2″
Batten   16″ O.C.

3/8″

45-43. *Details for plywood panel siding.*

3/8″   2″ x 4″

1″ x 2″ Batten

blocking required
at end joints

Batten

Duraply

45-44. *Siding details for board and batten and for panel siding.*

Table 45-D. *Framing and Nailing Schedule for Plywood Panel Siding.*

Framing and Nailing Schedule						
Panel Siding Thickness	5/16"	3/8"	1/2" grooved	1/2" flat	5/8" grooved	5/8" flat
Single-Wall Construction						
Maximum Stud Spacing	—	16" o.c.	16" o.c.	24" o.c.	16" o.c.	24" o.c.
Nail Size	—	6d	8d	8d	8d	8d
Over 3/8" Sheathing						
Maximum Stud Spacing	24"	24"	24"	24"	24"	24"
Nail Size	6d	6d	6d	6d	8d	8d
Approximate Nail Spacing*						
Edges	6"	6"	6"	6"	6"	6"
Intermediate Members	12"	12"	12"	12"	12"	12"

* Use non-corrosive casing, siding, or box nails.

Plywood lap or bevel siding

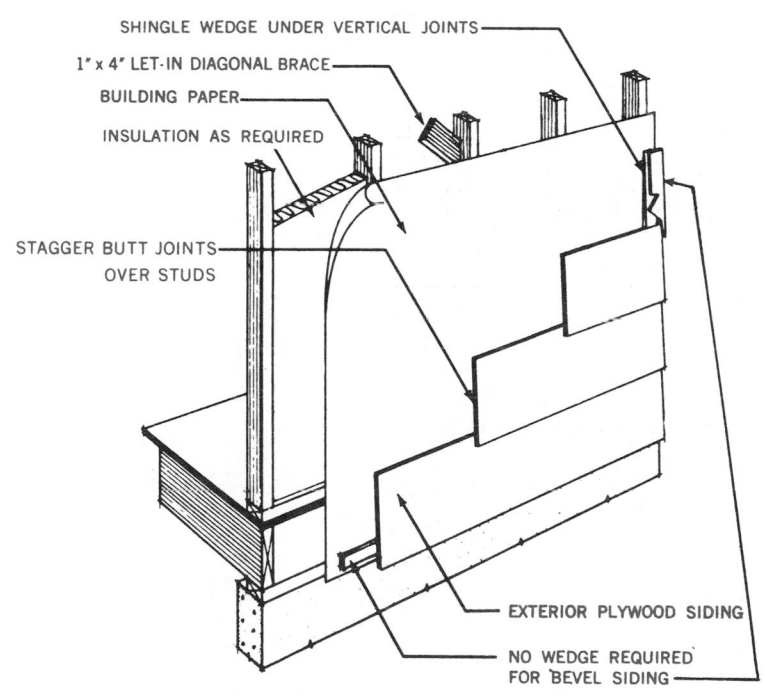

SHINGLE WEDGE UNDER VERTICAL JOINTS

1" x 4" LET-IN DIAGONAL BRACE

BUILDING PAPER

INSULATION AS REQUIRED

STAGGER BUTT JOINTS OVER STUDS

EXTERIOR PLYWOOD SIDING

NO WEDGE REQUIRED FOR BEVEL SIDING

45-45. *Plywood lap siding applied to an exterior wall without sheathing.*

recommended. Table 45-D.

To apply panel siding follow these suggestions:

➤ Single wall construction with plywood paneling less than 1/2" thick will permit a maximum stud spacing of 16" on center when no building paper, corner bracing, or sheathing is used. When sheathing is used, the maximum stud spacing may be increased to 24" on center. No building paper or corner bracing is required.

➤ Nail 6" on center on panel edges and 12" on center at intermediate supports. Fig. 45-42.

Application of Plywood Lap Siding. To apply lap plywood siding, follow these suggestions:

➤ In single wall construction the maximum stud spacing is 16" on center, and "let in" corner bracing must be installed to meet FHA requirements. Install building paper between the siding and the studs. Fig. 45-45. The minimum head lap is 2". Wedges are installed at butt ends and at corners. When sheathing is used, corner bracing is not required and the maximum stud spacing is 24" on center. The minimum head lap for 12" widths or less is 1". For widths over 12" use a 1½" head lap.

➤ Use a 3/8" thick starter strip for the first course. Fig. 45-46.

➤ Coat the edges of the siding with a primer before application.

➤ Vertical joints should be staggered. These joints must be centered over studs with a tapered wedge at least 1⅝" wide behind the joint. Fig. 45-46.

➤ Use 8d noncorrosive casing or box nails. Insert one nail at each stud on the bottom edge of the siding. At all vertical joints nail 4" on center for siding 12" wide or less. Nail 8" on center for siding 16" wide or more. All nails should be placed ¼" back from the edge of the plywood. Fig. 45-47. Set and putty all casing nails. Box nails are driven flush.

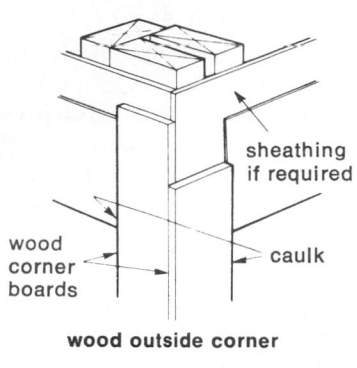

wood corner boards

sheathing if required

caulk

wood outside corner

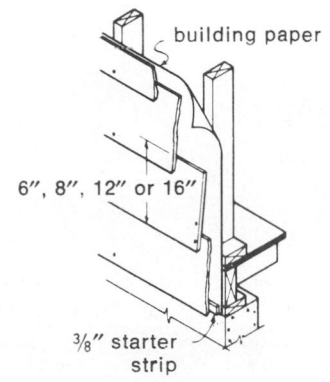

building paper

6", 8", 12" or 16"

³⁄₈" starter strip

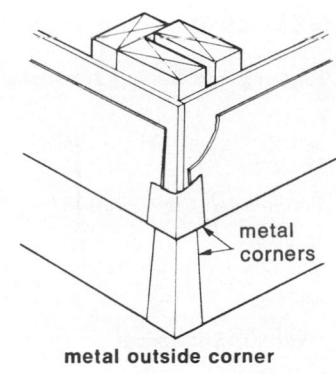

metal corners

metal outside corner

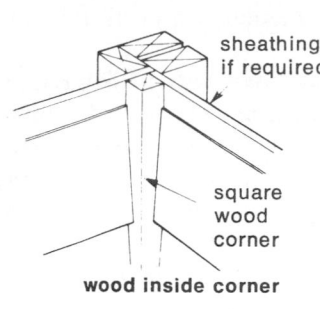

sheathing if required

square wood corner

wood inside corner

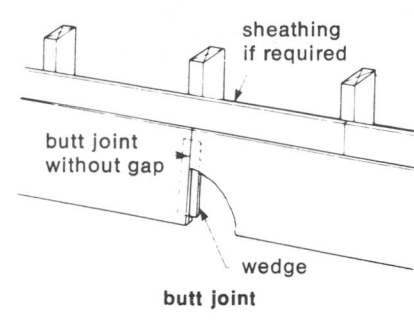

sheathing if required

butt joint without gap

wedge

butt joint

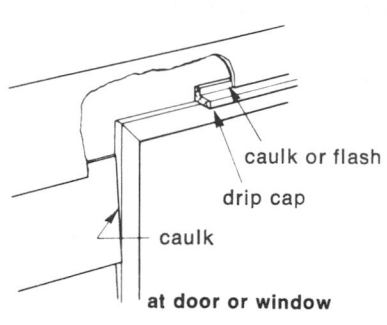

caulk or flash

drip cap

caulk

at door or window

45-46. *Typical plywood lap siding details.*

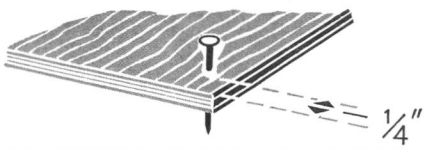

¼"

45-47. *Nails for lap siding should be placed ¼" back from the edge of the plywood.*

Hardboard Siding

Hardboard sidings are available in a variety of forms, including lap, panel, and shingle. Figs. 45-48, 45-49, and 45-50.

They are impregnated with a baked-on tempering compound. This process produces tough, dense, grainless sidings that will not split or splinter and are highly resistant to denting. Panel surfaces are completely free of imperfections.

Hardboards are available unprimed or factory primed.

45-48. *These hardboard siding panels are 16" wide. Patterns from left to right: V-side, channel, drop (smooth) and drop (textured).*

Factory-primed siding can be exposed to the weather prior to application of the finishing coats.

Application of Hardboard Siding. Hardboard siding may be applied over sheathed walls with studs spaced not more than 24" on center or over unsheathed

45-49. *Hardboard lap siding. This pattern has a beaded edge.*

45-50. *Hardboard shingle-style siding.*

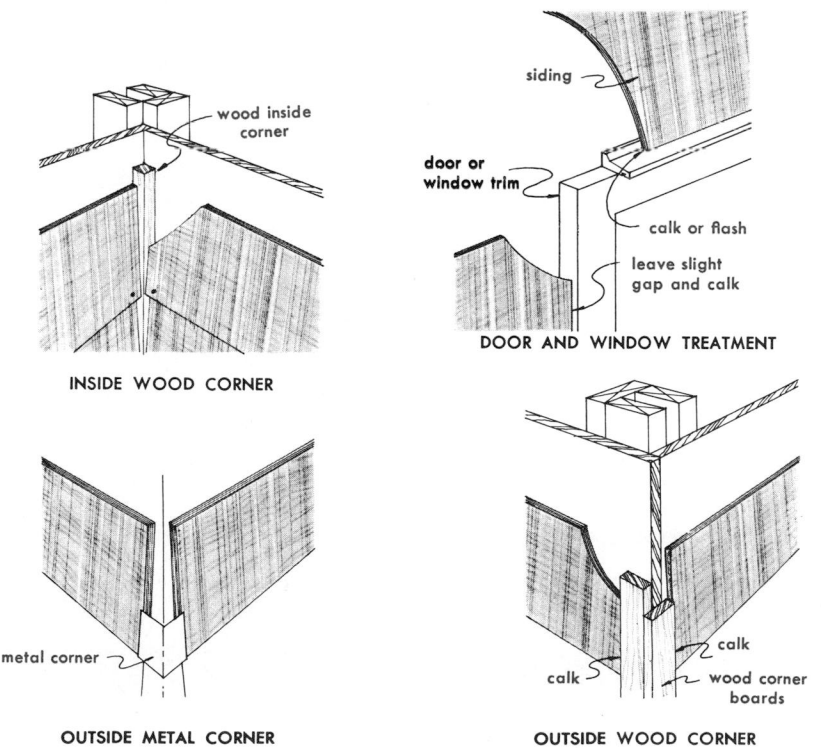

45-51. *Hardboard lap siding application details.*

JOINT DETAIL

STUD

NAIL INTO EACH EDGE OF PRECEDING SIDING COURSE AT BUTT JOINT

BUTT JOINT

NAILS

1" MIN. LAP

½"

NAIL THRU BOTH COURSES

LAP DETAILS

GUIDE LINES

12" LAP WITH 11" EXPOSURE
9" LAP WITH 8" EXPOSURE

45-52. *Corner treatment for hardboard lap siding.*

wood inside corner

INSIDE WOOD CORNER

metal corner

OUTSIDE METAL CORNER

siding

door or window trim

calk or flash

leave slight gap and calk

DOOR AND WINDOW TREATMENT

calk

calk

wood corner boards

OUTSIDE WOOD CORNER

walls with studs spaced not more than 16" on center. The lowest edge of the siding should be at least 8" above the finished grade level.

When hardboard siding is applied directly to studs or over wood sheathing, moisture-resistant building paper or felt (non-vapor-barrier) should be laid directly under the siding.

As in all frame construction, a vapor barrier must be used in all insulated buildings and in uninsulated buildings located in areas where the average January temperature is below 40°F. The vapor barrier is installed next to the heated wall. The installed vapor barrier must be continuous, with tight joints and with any breaks or tears repaired.

When applying hardboard siding, use rustproof siding nails. Nail only at stud locations and on special members around doors and windows. Nails must be kept back ½" from the ends and edges of the siding pieces. Fig. 45-51.

At inside corners, siding should be butted (with approximately 1/16" space) against a 1⅛" × 1⅛" wood corner member. Outside corners may be 1⅛" wood corner boards, or metal corners may be used. Fig. 45-52. Caulking should be applied wherever the siding butts against corner boards, windows, and door casings. Fig. 45-52.

Installing flat panels. Flat panels are installed vertically. All joints and panel edges should fall on the center of framing members. If it is necessary to make a joint with a panel that has been field cut and the shiplap joint removed, use a butt joint. Butter the edges with caulking and bring to light contact. Do not force or spring panels into place. Leave a slight space where siding butts against window or door trim and caulk. Fig. 45-53.

Installing lap siding. Start the application by fastening a wood starter strip (⅜" × 1⅜") along the bottom edge of the sill. Fig. 45-54. Level and install the first course of siding with the bottom edge at least ⅛" below the starter strip. Fasten the first course by nailing 1½" from drip edge of siding and ½" from butt end.

Install subsequent siding courses using a minimum overlap of 1". Fig. 45-51. Butt joints should occur only at stud locations. Factory-primed ends should be used for all

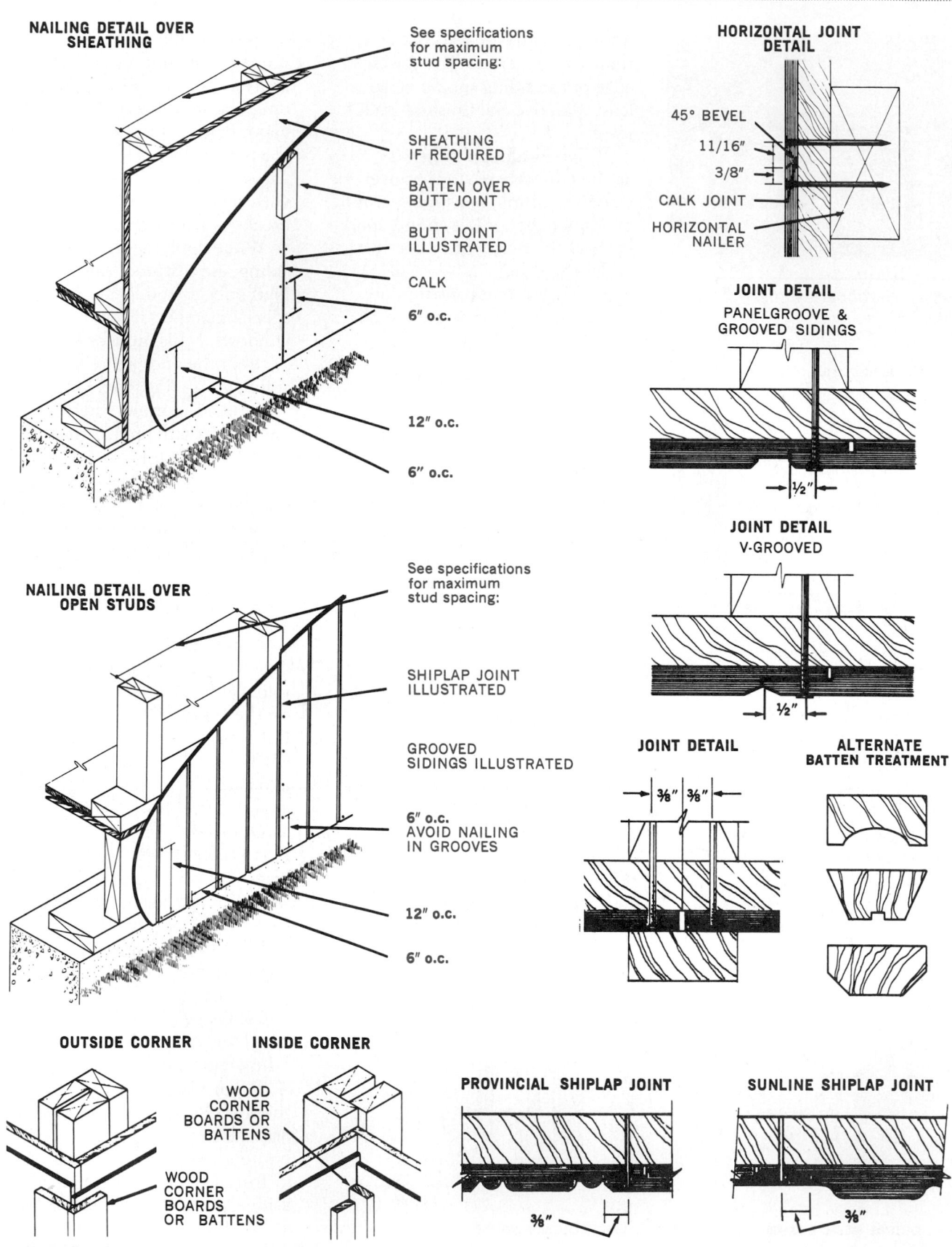

NAILING DETAIL OVER SHEATHING

See specifications for maximum stud spacing:

SHEATHING IF REQUIRED

BATTEN OVER BUTT JOINT

BUTT JOINT ILLUSTRATED

CALK

6" o.c.

12" o.c.

6" o.c.

NAILING DETAIL OVER OPEN STUDS

See specifications for maximum stud spacing:

SHIPLAP JOINT ILLUSTRATED

GROOVED SIDINGS ILLUSTRATED

6" o.c. AVOID NAILING IN GROOVES

12" o.c.

6" o.c.

HORIZONTAL JOINT DETAIL

45° BEVEL

11/16"

3/8"

CALK JOINT

HORIZONTAL NAILER

JOINT DETAIL
PANELGROOVE & GROOVED SIDINGS

½"

JOINT DETAIL
V-GROOVED

½"

JOINT DETAIL

⅜" ⅜"

ALTERNATE BATTEN TREATMENT

OUTSIDE CORNER   **INSIDE CORNER**

WOOD CORNER BOARDS OR BATTENS

WOOD CORNER BOARDS OR BATTENS

PROVINCIAL SHIPLAP JOINT

⅜"

SUNLINE SHIPLAP JOINT

⅜"

45-53. Hardboard panel siding details.

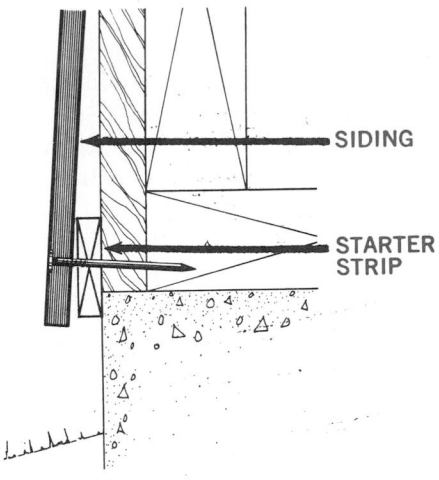

45-54. *Use a ³⁄₈" x 1³⁄₈" starter strip when applying hardboard lap siding.*

vertical butt joints which will not be covered. Adjacent siding pieces should just touch at butt joints, or a ¹⁄₁₆" space may be left and filled with a butyl caulk. Never force or spring siding into place.

WOOD SHINGLES AND SHAKES

Wood shingles and shakes are widely used for wall coverings, and a large selection is available. Fig. 45-55. Decorative shingles are sometimes mixed with standard shingles. Fig. 45-56. Wall shingles come in lengths of 16", 18", and 24". They may be prefinished or finished after installation. Handsplit shakes come in lengths of 18", 24", and 32".

Shingles

Shingles are usually separated into four grades. The first grade is composed of clear shingles, all heart, all edge grain. The second grade consists of shingles with clear butts and allows defects in that part of the shingle that will normally be

45-55. *Shingle siding is often seen on houses with traditional styling.*

45-56. *Decorative shingles can be combined with standard shingles. On this house, the interruption of horizontal lines adds interest to the siding.*

covered in use. The third grade includes shingles that have defects other than permitted in the second grade. The fourth grade is a utility grade for undercoursing on double-coursed sidewall applications or for interior accent walls.

Shingles are made in random widths. In the No. 1 grade, they vary from 3" to 14", with only a small proportion of the narrow width permitted. Shingles cut uniformly to widths of 4", 5", or 6" are also obtainable. They are known as dimension or rebutted-and-rejointed shingles. These are shingles with edges machine-trimmed so as to be exactly parallel, and with butts retrimmed at precise 90° angles. Dimension shingles are applied with tight-fitting joints to give a strong horizontal line. They are available with the natural "sawed" face or with one face sanded smooth. These shingles may be applied either single or doublecoursed.

Application of Shingles.

There are two basic ways to apply shingles: single-course and double-course. In single-coursing, shingles are applied much as in roof construction, but greater weather exposures are permitted. Shingle walls have two layers of shingles at every point, whereas shingle roofs have three-ply construction. To obtain architectural effect with deep bold shadow lines, shingles are frequently laid in double courses. Double-coursing allows for the application of shingles at extended weather exposures over undercoursing-grade shingles which are less expensive. When double-coursed, shingles should be tripled at the foundation line (by using a double underlay). Fig. 45-57. When the wall is single-coursed, the shingles should be doubled at the foundation line. For recommended exposures see Table 45-E.

The spacing for the shingle courses is determined the same way as described for bevel siding. When shingles are applied over fiberboard or gypsum sheathing, horizontal 1" × 4" nailing strips should first be nailed to the studs. Fig. 45-58. The on-center spacing of these strips should be the same distance as the weather exposure chosen for the shingles, to provide a good base for nailing. Shingles may be staggered for rustic effect. Fig. 45-59.

Shingles should be applied with rust-resistant nails. At least ¼" space should be allowed between shingles of the same course. It is frequently recommended that no shingle should be laid that is more than 8" in width. Shingles wider than this should be sawed or split and nailed as two shingles.

For double-coursing, each outer course shingle should be secured with two 5d (1¾") small head, rust-resistant nails driven about two inches above the butts, ¾" in from each side. Additional nails should be driven about four inches apart across the face of the shingle. Single-coursing involves the same number of nails, but they can be shorter (3d, 1¼") and should be blind-nailed not more than 1" above the butt line of the next course. Never drive the nail so hard that its head crushes the wood.

Outside corners should be constructed with an alternate overlap of shingles between successive courses. Inside corners may be mitered over a metal flashing. They may also be made by nailing an S4S strip, 1½" or 2" square, in the corner,

Table 45-E. *Wood Shingle Exposure and Coverage Table. The thickness dimension represents the total thickness of a number of shingles. For example, 5/2" means that 5 shingles, measured across the thickest portion, when green, measure 2 full inches.*

Length and Thickness	Approximate coverage of one square (4 bundles) of shingles based on following weather exposures												
	3 1/2"	4"	4 1/2"	5"	5 1/2"	6"	6 1/2"	7"	7 1/2"	8"	8 1/2"	9"	9 1/2"
16" x 5/2"	70	80	90	100(a)	110	120	130	140	150(b)	160	170	180	190
18" x 5/2 1/4"	—	72 1/2	81 1/2	90 1/2	100(a)	109	118	127	136	145 1/2	154 1/2(b)	163 1/2	172 1/2
24" x 4/2"	—	—	—	—	—	80	86 1/2	93	100(a)	106 1/2	113	120	126 1/2
	10"	**10 1/2"**	**11"**	**11 1/2"**	**12"**	**12 1/2"**	**13"**	**13 1/2"**	**14"**	**14 1/2"**	**15"**	**15 1/2"**	**16"**
16" x 5/2"	200	210	220	230	240(c)	—	—	—	—	—	—	—	—
18" x 5/2 1/4"	181 1/2	191	200	209	218	227	236	245 1/2	254 1/2	—	—	—	—
24" x 4/2"	133	140	146 1/2	153(b)	160	166 1/2	173	180	186 1/2	193	200	206 1/2	213(c)

(a) Maximum exposure recommended for roofs.
(b) Maximum exposure recommended for single-coursing on sidewalls.
(c) Maximum exposure recommended for double-coursing on sidewalls.

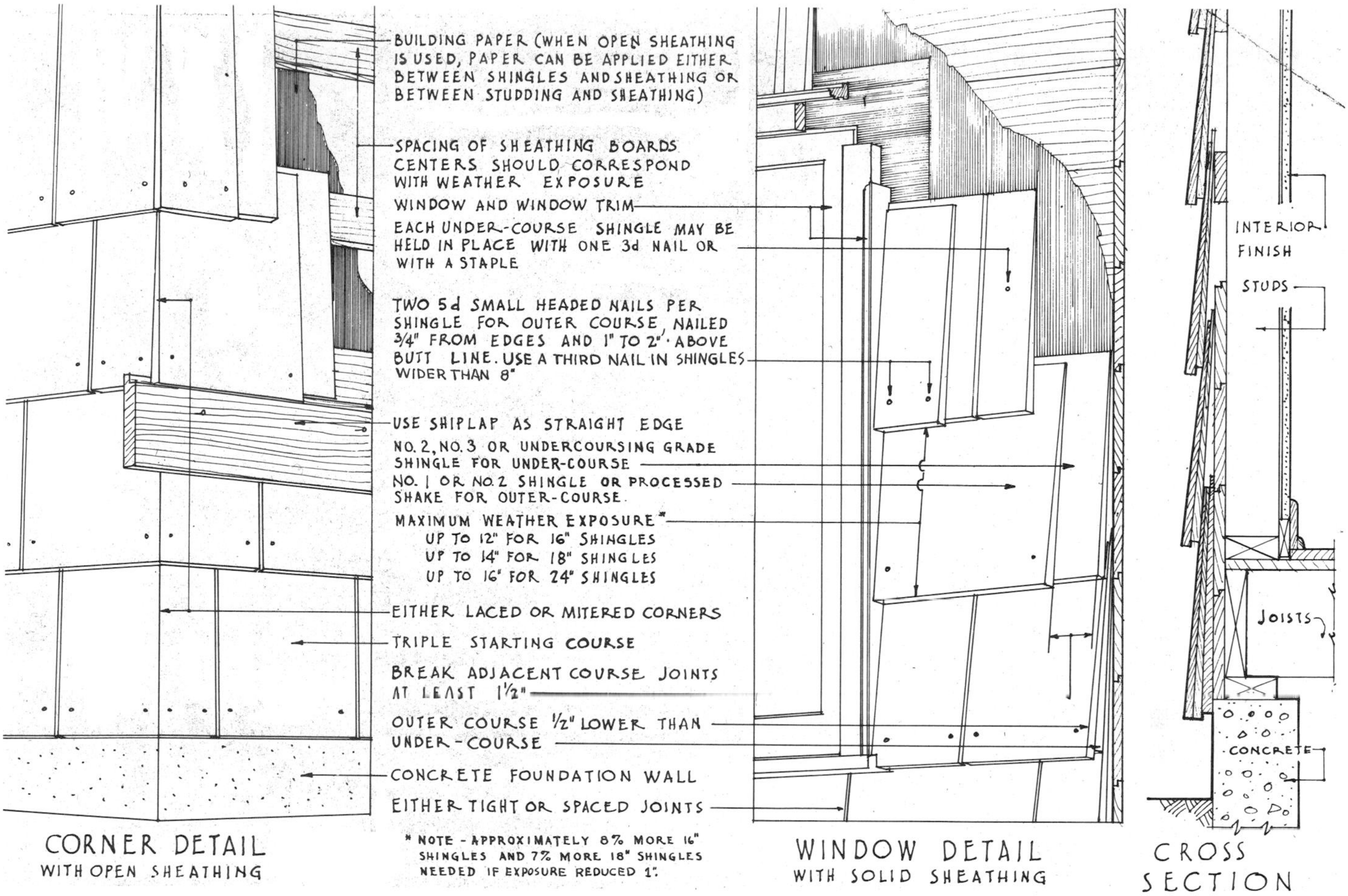

BUILDING PAPER (WHEN OPEN SHEATHING IS USED, PAPER CAN BE APPLIED EITHER BETWEEN SHINGLES AND SHEATHING OR BETWEEN STUDDING AND SHEATHING)
SPACING OF SHEATHING BOARDS CENTERS SHOULD CORRESPOND WITH WEATHER EXPOSURE
WINDOW AND WINDOW TRIM
EACH UNDER-COURSE SHINGLE MAY BE HELD IN PLACE WITH ONE 3d NAIL OR WITH A STAPLE
TWO 5d SMALL HEADED NAILS PER SHINGLE FOR OUTER COURSE, NAILED 3/4" FROM EDGES AND 1" TO 2" ABOVE BUTT LINE. USE A THIRD NAIL IN SHINGLES WIDER THAN 8"
USE SHIPLAP AS STRAIGHT EDGE
NO. 2, NO. 3 OR UNDERCOURSING GRADE SHINGLE FOR UNDER-COURSE
NO. 1 OR NO. 2 SHINGLE OR PROCESSED SHAKE FOR OUTER-COURSE
MAXIMUM WEATHER EXPOSURE*
UP TO 12" FOR 16" SHINGLES
UP TO 14" FOR 18" SHINGLES
UP TO 16" FOR 24" SHINGLES
EITHER LACED OR MITERED CORNERS
TRIPLE STARTING COURSE
BREAK ADJACENT COURSE JOINTS AT LEAST 1 1/2"
OUTER COURSE 1/2" LOWER THAN UNDER-COURSE
CONCRETE FOUNDATION WALL
EITHER TIGHT OR SPACED JOINTS
INTERIOR FINISH
STUDS
JOISTS
CONCRETE
CORNER DETAIL
WITH OPEN SHEATHING
* NOTE - APPROXIMATELY 8% MORE 16" SHINGLES AND 7% MORE 18" SHINGLES NEEDED IF EXPOSURE REDUCED 1".
WINDOW DETAIL
WITH SOLID SHEATHING
CROSS SECTION

45-57. *Double-course shingle sidewall detail.*

SHINGLES
SHEATHING PAPER
NAILER
FLASHING
SHEATHING

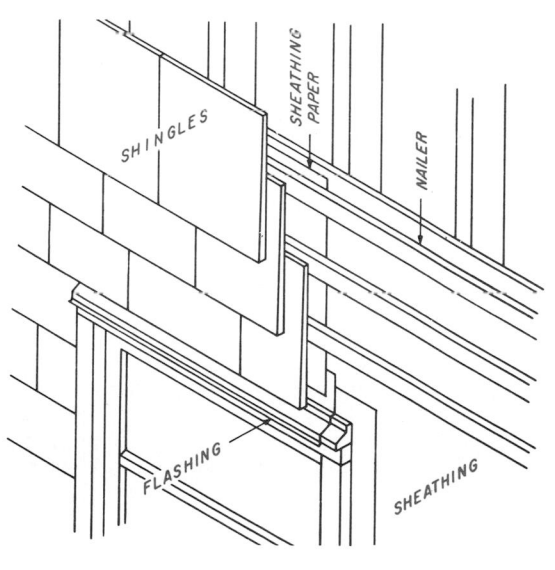

45-58. *The application of wood shingles over non-wood sheathing. Note the use of the nailing strip.*

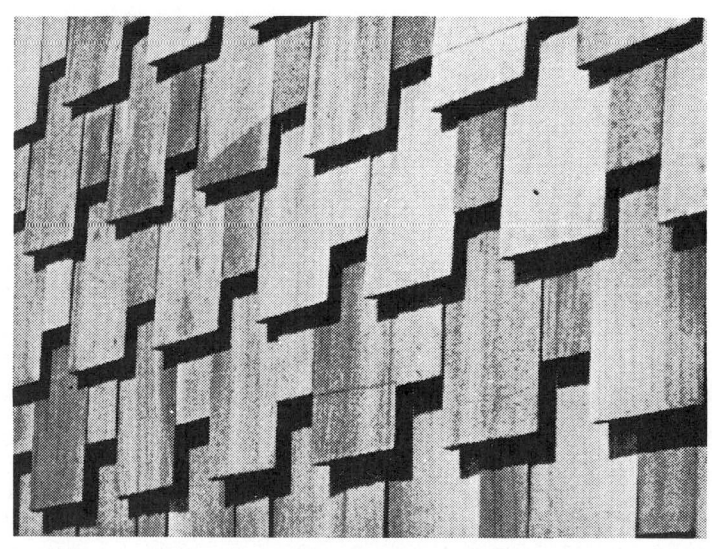

45-59. *Staggered shingles give a rustic appearance.*

after which the shingles of each course are jointed to the strip.

Shakes

There are three kinds of shakes:
➤ Handsplit-and-resawn.
➤ Tapersplit.
➤ Straightsplit.
The handsplit-and-resawn shakes have split faces and sawn backs. Cedar logs are first cut into desired lengths. Blanks or boards of proper thickness are split and then run diagonally through a bandsaw to produce two tapered shakes from each blank.

Tapersplit shakes are produced largely by hand, using a sharp-bladed steel froe and a wooden mallet. The natural shingle-like taper is achieved by reversing the block end-for-end with each split.

Straightsplit shakes are produced in the same manner as tapersplit shakes except that by splitting from the same end of the block the shakes acquire the same thickness throughout. Fig. 45-60.

Application of Shakes. Maximum recommended weather exposure with single-course application is 8½" for 18" shakes, 11½" for 24" shakes, and 15" for 32" shakes. Table 45-F. The nailing normally is concealed in single-

45-60. Using a froe to split shakes in the 1800s. Today, tapersplit and straightsplit shakes are still produced largely by hand.

course applications; that is, the nailing is done at points slightly above (about 1") the butt line of the course to follow.

Double-course application requires an underlay of shakes or regular cedar shingles. With handsplit-resawn or with taper-split shakes, the maximum weather exposure is 14" for 18" shakes and 20" for 24"shakes. If straightsplit shakes are used, the exposure may be 16" for 18" shakes and 22" for 24" shakes. Butt-nailing of shakes is required with double-course application.

Use rust-resistant nails, preferably hotdipped zinc-coated. The 6d size normally is adequate, but longer nails may be required, depending on the thickness of the shakes and the weather exposure. Do not drive nailheads into the shake surface. The methods for constructing the corners when applying shakes are shown in Fig. 45-61.

Table 45-F. Wood Shake Exposure and Coverage Table.

	Approximate sq. ft. coverage of one square of handsplit shakes based on these weather exposures											
	5 ½"	6 ½"	7"	7 ½"	8"	8 ½"	10"	11 ½"	13"	14"	15"	16"
18" x ½" to ¾" Handsplit-and-Resawn	55[a]	65	70	75[b]	80	85[d]	—	—	—	140[f]	—	—
18" x ¾" to 1 ¼" Handsplit-and-Resawn	55[a]	65	70	75[b]	80	85[d]	—	—	—	140[f]	—	—
24" x ⅜" Handsplit	—	65	70	75[c]	80	85	100[e]	115[d]	—	—	—	—
24" x ½" to ¾" Handsplit-and-Resawn	—	65	70	75[a]	80	85	100[b]	115[d]	—	—	—	—
24" x ¾" to 1 ¼" Handsplit-and-Resawn	—	65	70	75[a]	80	85	100[b]	115[d]	—	—	—	—
32" x ¾" to 1 ¼" Handsplit-and-Resawn	—	—	—	—	—	—	110[a]	115	130[b]	140	150[d]	—
24" x ½" to ⅝" Tapersplit	—	65	70	75[a]	80	85	100[b]	115[d]	—	—	—	—
18" x ⅜" True-Edge Straightsplit	—	—	—	—	—	—	—	—	—	100	106	112[f]
18" x ⅜" Straightsplit	65[a]	75	80	90	95	100[d]	—	—	—	—	—	—
24" x ⅜" Straightsplit	—	65	70	75[a]	80	85	100	115[d]	—	—	—	—
15" Starter-Finish Course	Use supplementary with shakes applied not over 10" weather exposure.											

(a) Recommended maximum weather exposure for 3-ply roof construction.
(b) Recommended maximum weather exposure for 2-ply roof construction.
(c) Recommended maximum weather exposure for roof pitches of 4/12 to 8/12.
(d) Recommended maximum weather exposure for single-coursed wall construction.
(e) Recommended maximum weather exposure for roof pitches of 8/12 or steeper.
(f) Recommended maximum weather exposure for double-coursed wall construction.

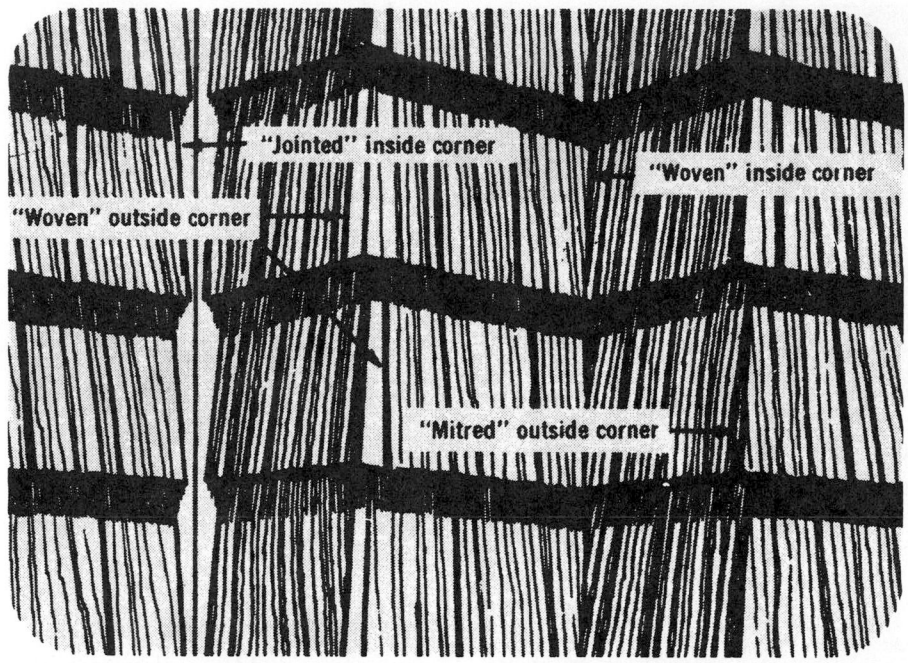

45-61. Wood shake corner treatment.

"Jointed" inside corner

"Woven" inside corner

"Woven" outside corner

"Mitred" outside corner

Finishing Wood Shingles and Shakes

Red cedar shingles and shakes are well equipped by nature to endure without any protective finish or stain. In this state, the wood will eventually weather to a silver or dark gray. The speed of change and final shade depend mainly on atmosphere and climate.

Bleaching agents may be applied, in which case the wood will turn an antique silver gray. So-called natural finishes, which are lightly pigmented and maintain the original appearance of the wood, are available commercially. Stains, whether heavy or semitransparent, are readily "absorbed" by cedar, and it also takes paint well. Quality finishes are strongly recommended because they will prove most economical on a long-term basis.

45-62. Shingle panels cover as much as 14 sq. ft. at a time.

PANELIZED SHINGLES

Wood shingles are generally installed one by one. However, some manufacturers provide a hybrid shingle product that allows groups of shingles to be installed at once. Fig. 45-62. The shingles are applied at the factory to a plywood backing. The resulting panel is then nailed in place. Shingle exposures are 4" or 5". Each panel covers 14 sq. ft. at a time.

45-63. The stucco exterior of this house provides a durable finish.

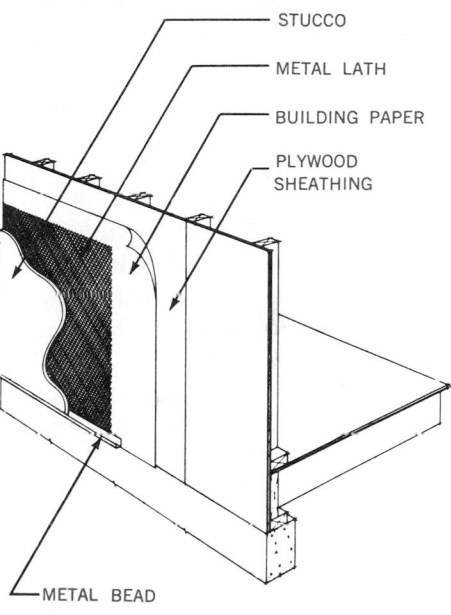

STUCCO

METAL LATH

BUILDING PAPER

PLYWOOD SHEATHING

METAL BEAD

45-64. Stucco applied as an exterior covering over plywood sheathing.

STUCCO SIDEWALL FINISH

Stucco when properly used makes a good wall finish. Fig. 45-63. It may be a natural cement color or colored as desired. If stucco is to be applied on houses more than one story high, balloon framing should be used in the outside walls. With platform framing, shrinkage of the joists and sills of the platform may cause an unsightly bulge or break in the stucco at that point.

Stucco is applied over lath. Fig. 45-64. Three acceptable types of lath are:

► Zinc-coated or galvanized metal, with large openings (1.8 pounds per square yard) or small openings (3.4 pounds per square yard).

► Galvanized woven-wire fabric. This material may be 18-gauge wire with 1" maximum mesh, 17-gauge wire with 1½" maximum mesh, or 16-gauge wire with a 2" maximum mesh.

► Galvanized welded-wire fabric. This may be made of 16-gauge wire with 2" × 2" mesh and waterproof paper backing, or it may be 18-gauge wire with 1" × 1" mesh but no paper backing.

The lath should be kept at least ¼" away from the sheathing so that the stucco can be forced through the lath and embedded completely. Galvanized furring nails, metal furring strips, or self-furring lath are available for this spacing. Nails should penetrate the wood at least ¾". Where fiberboard or gypsum sheathing is used, the length of the nail should be such that at least ¾" penetrates into the wood stud.

Stucco Plaster

The plaster should be one part portland cement, three parts sand, and hydrated lime equal to 10% of the cement by volume. It should be applied in three coats to a total thickness of 1". The first coat should be forced through the lath and worked so as to embed the lath at all points. Keep fresh stucco shaded and wet for three days. Do not apply stucco when the temperature is below 40°F. It sets very slowly, and there may be a freezing hazard before it has set.

Portland-cement stucco that has been commercially prepared may also be used. It should be applied according to the manufacturer's instructions.

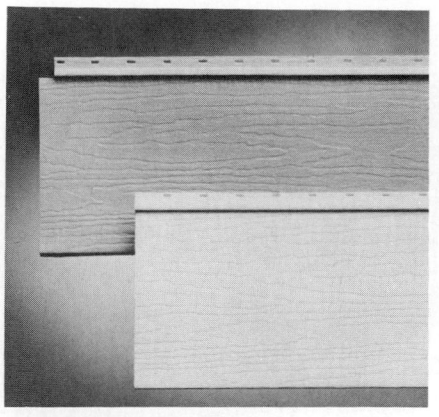

45-65a. *The nailing flanges at the top of these lengths of steel siding are used to secure the siding to the sheathing.*

45-65b. *This vinyl siding comes in wide panels to speed installation. Note how the top and bottom edges interlock to form a tight seal.*

METAL AND VINYL SIDING

There are many kinds of metal and vinyl sidings that can be applied over sheathing. Metal siding, either aluminum or steel, has a baked-on finish that requires little maintenance or care. Solid vinyl siding in various colors and textures is also available. Standard hand tools may be used to apply these siding materials. Fig. 45-65.

Application of Metal and Vinyl Siding

The interlocking joints of the pieces of siding and the accessory items vary with the manufacturer. Before starting, inspect and plan the job in accordance with the manufacturer's instructions for the material to be applied. Be sure to use the nail recommended to avoid corrosion and stains. Drive the nails firm and snug, but never so tight as to cause waves in the siding.

The general procedure for the application of metal or plastic siding is as follows:

1. Lay out the courses on the sidewalls of the building the same way as for wood bevel siding, or use a story pole. Fig. 45-22.

2. Run a chalk line for the starter strip around the house. Install the starter strip. A, Fig. 45-66. All nails should be driven so that the head is only slightly flush to the material. Do not drive the nails hard enough to bind the material tightly.

3. Nail the inside corner posts 12" on center before the rest of the siding is applied. The bottom of the corner posts should be aligned with the chalk line. The siding later fits into channels on both sides. B, Fig. 45-66.

4. Nail the outside corner posts 12" on center before the siding is applied. C, Fig. 45-66. Here also, siding fits into channels on the sides. Fill the cavity behind a wide corner post with a backer board or wood strips. To close in the open lower end of a wide corner post, cut a piece of "J" channel to the proper length (about 6⅛"). Miter it and nail it to the wall so that the bottom end of the corner post will fit over it.

5. Attach the door and window trim along the sides of the doors and windows. The gables are also

45-66a. *The letters identify typical siding accessories. Figure 45-66b shows details of these accessories.*

trimmed with this accessory. The same trim is used at the base of a wall intersecting a sloping roof, as on a breezeway. D, Fig. 45-66b.

6. Install undersill and general purpose trim under windows and at the tops of walls against soffit moldings, furring where necessary to preserve alignment with the adjacent panels. This may also be used inverted to lock lower cut edges of siding-courses which are located above the level of the starter strip, such as at porch floors and cellar bulkheads. E, Fig. 45-66.

7. Place the first siding panel in the starter strip and lock it securely. Fig. 45-67. Backerboards, if used, are dropped into place. Nail the panel and install succeeding courses similarly. Nails must never be driven so tightly as to cause distortion of the siding.

Allowance should be made for expansion and contraction by leaving a ¼" space at joints, channels, and corner posts. Field-cut end joints may be made with a razor knife, hack saw, or tin snips. On the end to be overlapped, cuts should be made according to the manufacturer's instructions. For best appearance, overlap the siding away from areas of greatest traffic. Stagger end laps a minimum of 24"

and in such a way that one is not directly above another unless separated by three courses. The end of the uncut panel should lap over the end of the cut panel.

8. Cut and fit the siding as necessary around windows and doors.

9. Attach window head flashing or window and door trim above the windows and doors as application reaches these levels, furring out where necessary for alignment with adjacent panels. See F, Fig. 45-66.

10. Trim the last course of siding to fit under the eaves. Install

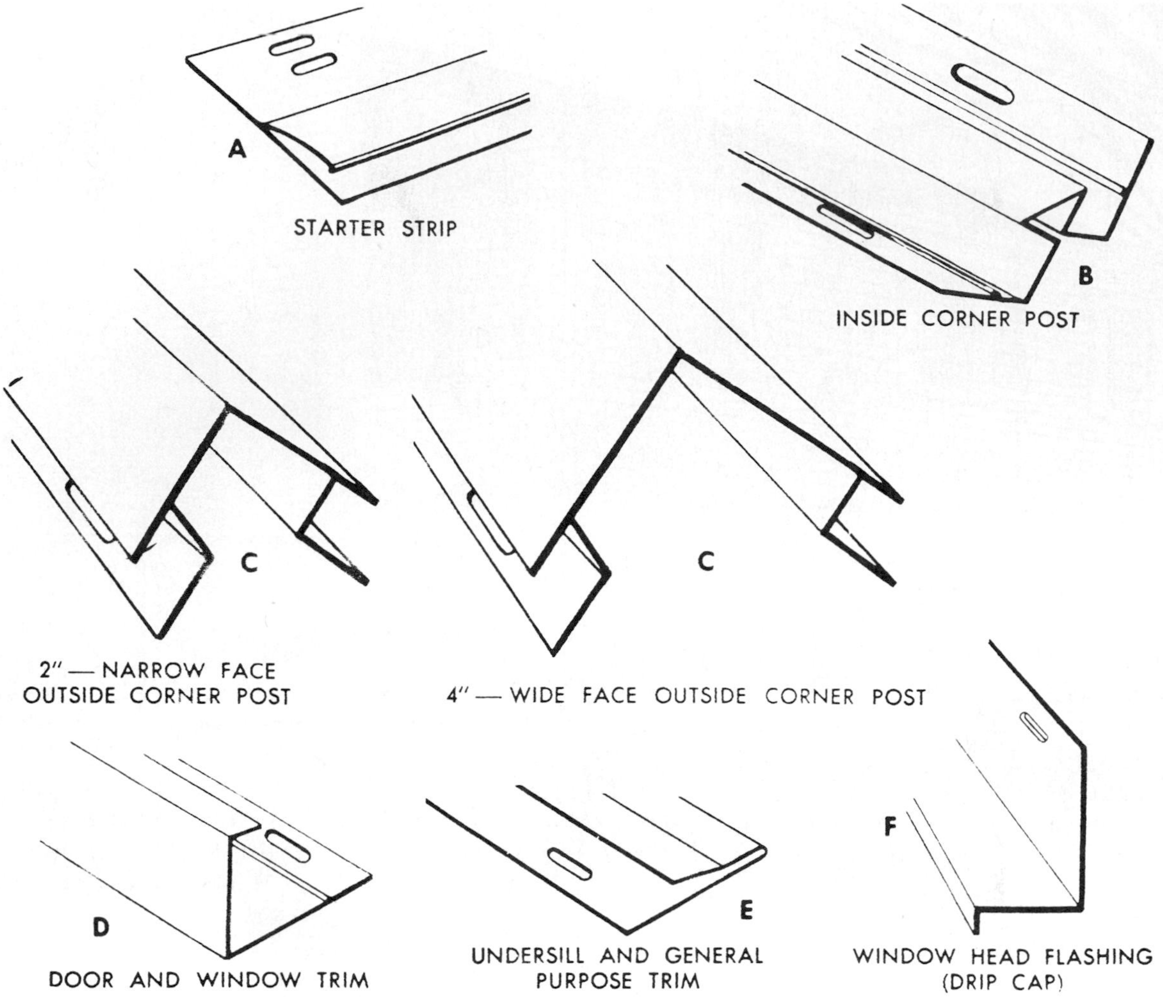

A

STARTER STRIP

B

INSIDE CORNER POST

C

2" — NARROW FACE
OUTSIDE CORNER POST

C

4" — WIDE FACE OUTSIDE CORNER POST

D

DOOR AND WINDOW TRIM

E

UNDERSILL AND GENERAL
PURPOSE TRIM

F

WINDOW HEAD FLASHING
(DRIP CAP)

45-66b. *Typical siding accessories. These are for vinyl, but manufacturers of aluminum siding offer similar accessories for the application of their particular product. Figure 45-66a shows how these accessories are used.*

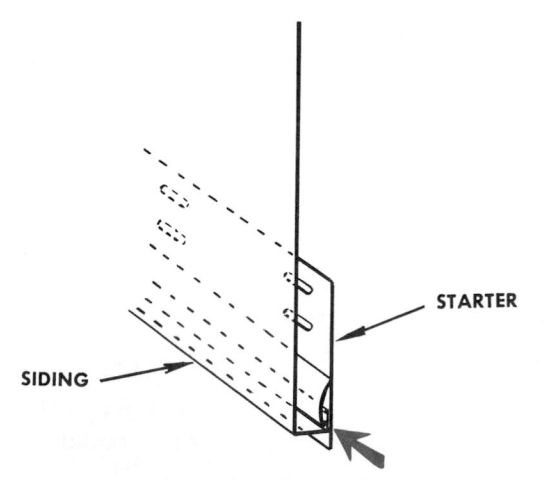

STARTER

SIDING

45-67. *Secure the bottom edge of the first piece of siding in the starter strip before nailing the top edge.*

45-68a. *Brick construction and carefully detailed woodwork were combined in this new house in Virginia.*

45-68b. *Thomas Jefferson, third president of the United States, designed and built his own house in the late 1700s. The brick construction of the house is an example of the durability of this material.*

45-69. *High-quality brick construction requires properly trained masons. This student placed first in a national masonry competition.*

45-68c. *This house in Illinois features very detailed curved brickwork.*

undersill and general purpose trim, furring where necessary to maintain proper panel angle. Engage the top of the panel with undersill and general purpose trim and lock at lower edge of panel as usual. Nail to secure when necessary.

11. To complete the gables, install windows and door trim above the windows at the gable ends. Cut the siding to the proper angle and install.

12. Caulk where required.

13. Finish by washing down the siding to remove fingerprints and soil. Clean up all scrap material around the house.

MASONRY VENEER

Brick or stone veneer is often used for part or all of the wall covering over wood frame walls. Although relatively high in initial cost, brick is frequently used in residential construction because of the low maintenance needs and long life of the material. Fig. 45-68. It is a material that can fit into a variety of architectural styles. Brick

construction is more prevalent in some areas of the country than in others.

Brick veneer wall coverings are applied by skilled brick masons. A brick mason may also work with other materials, such as stone, marble, and cement block. The majority of the work comes in laying brick walls, but brick masons also do ornamental brick work such as planters, walkways, and fireplaces. Fig. 45-69.

Brick and stone can also be used as structural materials, rather than as veneer over wood frame walls. In this unit, however, the discussion will be limited to veneer wall construction. For more on structural masonry walls, see *Residential Masonry*, by John Feirer and Gilbert Hutchings.

Tools

The basic brick mason's tool is the brick trowel. The trowel has a steel blade and a wood handle. The end of the blade is called the "toe" or "point." The wide portion is called the "heel." Fig. 45-70. Trowels are available in many sizes. However, short, wide trowels are most comfortable to use because the weight is nearer the handle. This puts less strain on the mason's wrist.

A good quality level is another important tool for the brick mason. It should have horizontal and vertical leveling vials that read from both sides of the level. The edges should be metal to withstand punishment on the job site. Fig. 45-71.

A mason's rule is important for measuring the height and spacing of brick courses as they are laid. A folding rule is preferred over a tape measure because the tape can be rendered useless by frequent contact with mortar. Two versions of folding rules are available. The standard mason's rule is white. It is used for measuring standard or modular brick. An oversized mason's rule is yellow. It is easier to use when oversized bricks are measured. Fig. 45-72.

A brick hammer is used for splitting and rough-breaking bricks. It has a hickory handle. The head has a chisel end and a square face. Fig. 45-73.

Materials

Brick is produced in factories by crushing clay and shale, tempering it with water, forming it into

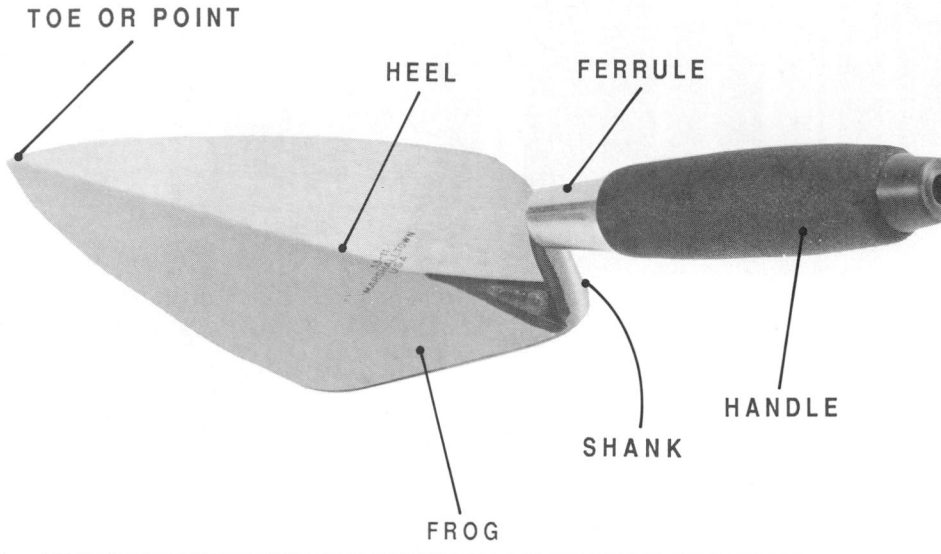

45-70. *This brick trowel has a PVC handgrip over a wood handle.*

TOE OR POINT

HEEL

FERRULE

HANDLE

SHANK

FROG

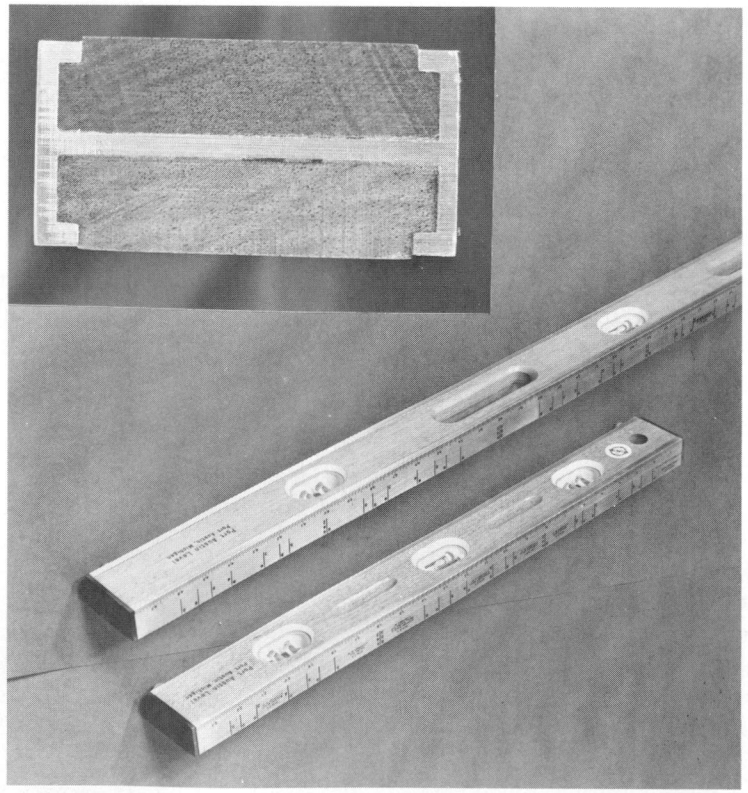

45-71. *A mason's level.*

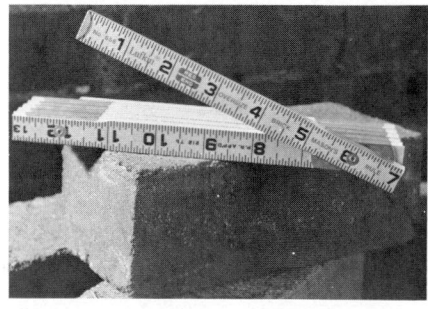

45-72. *A mason's rule. The front side of the rule reads in feet and inches. The back side of the rule is marked with brick coursing dimensions.*

45-73. *These brick mason's hammers have carbide chisel ends.*

bricks, and then drying the bricks in large kilns (ovens). The tempered material is formed in three basic ways:

➤ By extruding the material through dies and slicing the extruded ribbon of material into individual bricks.

➤ By placing the material into individual molds.

➤ By "dry-pressing" the material under high pressure.

Building brick is a strong, general-purpose brick. Its coloration varies from brick to brick, and the size of each brick is somewhat inconsistent.

Facing brick is used primarily for exterior surfaces. Because the manufacturing process is carefully controlled, the resulting brick is consistent in size, texture, and color.

Fire brick is usually pale yellow or buff in color. It is used specifically for lining fireplaces and other heating units.

Sizes of Bricks. For many years, only three sizes of bricks were available: standard, Roman, and Norman. Today there are hundreds of shapes, sizes, and types of brick.

All brick can be classified into two groups: modular and nonmodular. A modular unit is identified by a nominal size that includes an allowance for the thickness of a standard mortar joint. The actual dimension of a modular brick is therefore smaller than the nominal dimension, just as the actual dimension of a 2" × 4" stud is smaller than the nominal dimension. For example, the actual size of the Roman brick in Fig. 45-74 is 1½" thick by 3¾" wide by 11½" long. The actual dimensions of bricks will vary slightly depending on where and how they were made.

Mortar and Mortar Joints. The proper mortar will bond the

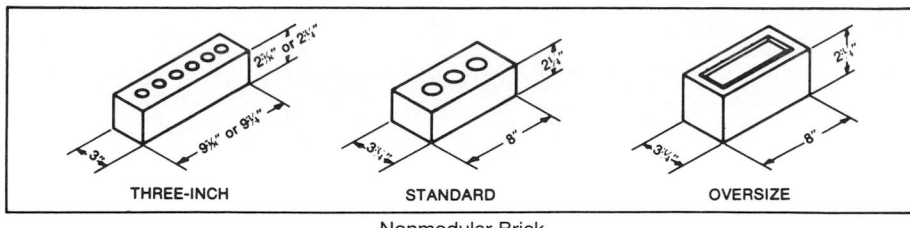

Nonmodular Brick
(Actual Dimensions)

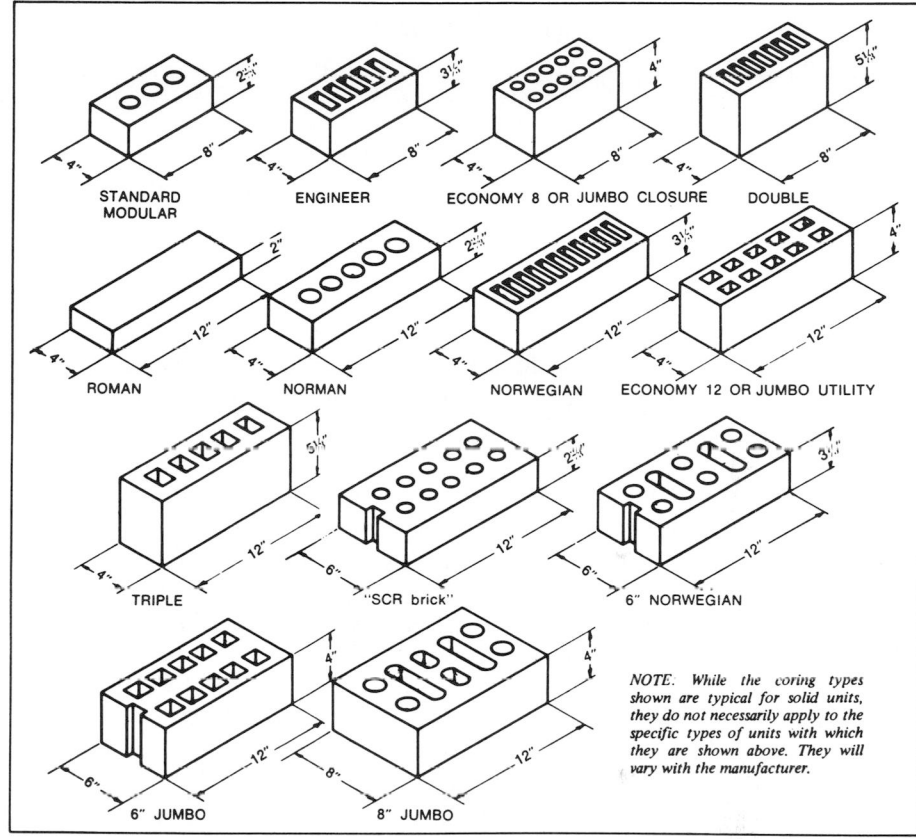

NOTE. While the coring types shown are typical for solid units, they do not necessarily apply to the specific types of units with which they are shown above. They will vary with the manufacturer.

Modular Brick
(Nominal Dimensions)

45-74. *Modular and nonmodular sizes of bricks.*

bricks into a strong, waterproof wall. The weakest part of any brick wall will be the mortar if it is not properly mixed and applied. Different types of mortar are needed in various situations:

➤ Type M is suitable for general use and is recommended specifically for masonry below grade and in contact with earth. This could include foundations, retaining walls, and walkways.

➤ Type S is suitable for general use. It is recommended where high resistance to lateral (sideways) force is required.

➤ Type N is suitable for general use in exposed masonry above grade. It is recommended specifically for exterior walls subjected to severe weather exposure conditions. This is the mortar usually used for brick veneer walls.

➤ Type O is recommended for load-bearing walls made with solid units when the masonry will not be subjected to freezing and thawing in the presence of moisture.

Table 45-G. *Mortar Proportions by Volume.*

| Type | Portland Cement-Lime Mortars | | |
	Portland Cement	Hydrated Lime or Lime Putty	Sand
M	1	1/4	3
S	1	1/2	4 1/2
N	1	1	6
O	1	2	9

| Type | Masonry Cement Mortars | | |
	Portland Cement	Masonry Cement Type II	Sand
M	1	1	6
S	1/2	1	4 1/2
N	—	1	3
O	—	1 (Type I or II)	3

45-75b. *Properly raked concave mortar joints.*

Mixing proportions for these basic types of mortar are found in Table 45-G. Measurements should be made carefully. A common mistake is to add too much sand. Various colorants may be added to mortar to change its color.

There are three standard joint thicknesses: ¼", ⅜", and ½". Properly finished mortar joints help to create a strong, tight bond between the mortar and the brick. This is particularly important when the wall will be exposed to the weather.

After several courses of brick have been laid, the joints can be tooled with a trowel or with various kinds of jointers. A jointer is a simple metal bar with a shaped end. It is run between the bricks to pack mortar into the joints and give them a particular shape. The shape of the joints can have a significant impact on how a wall looks. Fig. 45-75.

Concave joints and V-joints resist rain well and are recommended for walls exposed to

heavy rains and high winds. They are formed with a jointer. Weathered joints are somewhat compacted and shed water readily. They are formed with a trowel. Rough-cut joints made with a trowel are easy to make, but not always watertight. The struck joint is made with a trowel, but does not readily shed water. A raked joint produces deep shadow lines, but is difficult to make weathertight.

Construction Details for Brick Veneer

A brick veneer wall must be supported on a foundation as well as tied into the framework of the house. Fig. 45-76. The foundation is provided simply by forming a "shelf" into the main house foundation. This is done when the main foundation is installed. The first course of brick will be a leveling course intended to make up for any irregularities in the foundation. Subsequent courses should be checked frequently for level and plumb. Fig. 45-77.

The veneer wall is tied to the frame of the house with corrugated galvanized metal anchors nailed with 8d galvanized nails. The ties are nailed through the sheathing and into the studs, and embedded

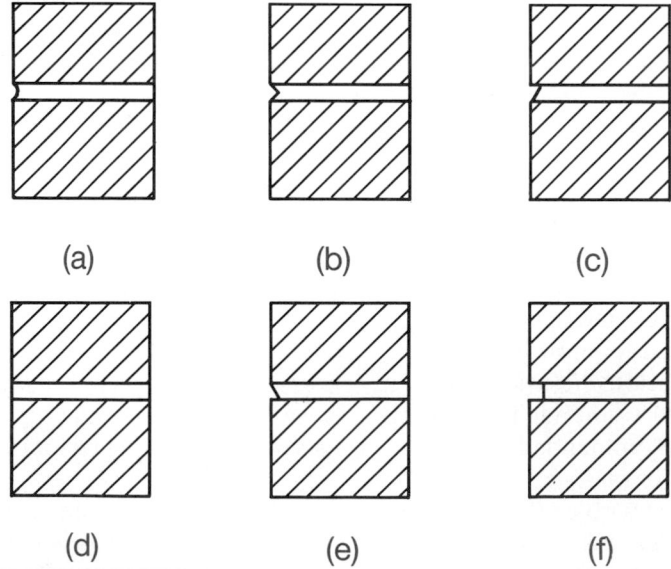

45-75a. *Mortar joints. (a) Concave. (b) V-shaped. (c) Weathered. (d) Rough cut or flush. (e) Struck. (f) Raked.*

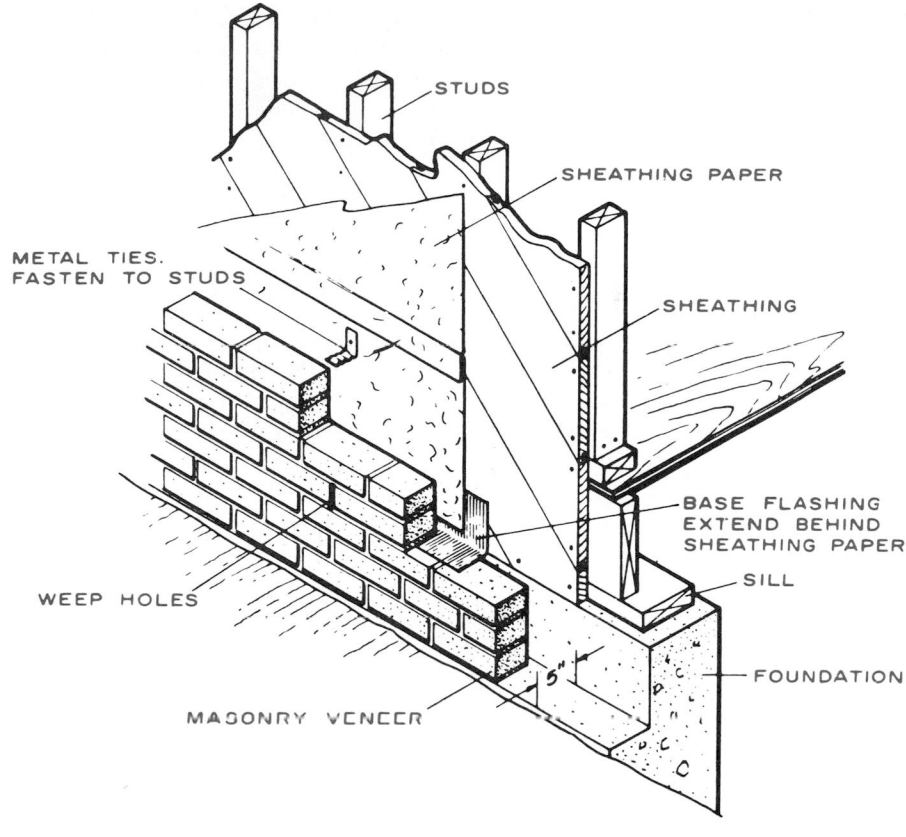

45-76a. Details of brick masonry veneer construction with a concrete foundation wall.

45-76b. Foundation preparations for brick veneer.

in the mortar as the wall goes up. The ties should be at least 22 gauge, ⅞" wide, and 6" long. Ties should be embedded 2" into the mortar joint. Check local codes for the spacing of ties. Generally, however, there should be one tie for every 2 sq. ft. of wall area.

Weep holes are left in the wall at intervals of 18" to 24" so moisture that might accumulate behind the veneer can escape to the outside. These holes are located in the lowest mortar joints above grade. Weep holes may be formed by selectively leaving out head joints, by mortaring short lengths of small-diameter plastic tubing into the wall, or by forming the hole with a removable metal rod.

All materials expand and contract as the temperature changes. This movement can produce forces great enough to crack masonry. Expansion joints should be installed in the wall to relieve these stresses. Local codes and local practice determine the location of expansion joints.

Repairing an Existing Wall

Over time, the mortar joints in a brick veneer wall may need repair. This may be due to the use of poor-quality mortar in the original wall, to mechanical damage, or simply to age. To repair the joints, the loose and damaged mortar should first be removed from the joints. New mortar can then be pushed into the joints. This is called *tuckpointing*. The repaired joints may then be tooled to match surrounding joints. Fig. 45-78.

45-77. When laying bricks, a leveled string line helps the mason to keep the courses straight. The storypole helps to keep each course at the proper height.

45-78. Tuckpointing damaged mortar joints. New mortar is pressed into the joints and later tooled to match surrounding joints.

45-79. *This house has two-panel louvered shutters which add to the architectural effect. They also provide the homeowner with an opportunity to brighten the home with additional color when decorating.*

SHUTTERS AND BLINDS

Shutters, or blinds, are used on today's homes more for architectural effect than for any functional purpose. Fig. 45-79. Historically they were intended as a means of protection from enemy attack or the weather. Shutters are particularly popular with the New England style Cape Cod home, on which they are usually installed adjacent to double-hung windows.

Shutters are made from wood, nylon, vinyl, or aluminum. They are available in a variety of sizes and styles to enhance the architectural effect desired. Table 45-H. When shutters are installed for a functional purpose, they are hinged to the window trim or doorjamb and will close and lock over the opening. Shutters used only as decoration are woodscrewed or held with special clips after the siding is applied and finished. Fig. 45-80.

ESTIMATING

Material

To determine the amount of siding necessary for the exterior of a home, it is first necessary to figure the amount of wall area to be covered. This is done by multiplying the perimeter of the house by the wall height and subtracting window and door openings. For a gable roof, the gable area must also be figured and added to the sidewall area.

Wood Bevel Siding. To figure the amount of wood bevel siding needed to cover the exterior of a house, first determine the area to be covered. Then consider the difference between the nominal and dressed dimensions of the siding material, the amount of lap, and the allowance for trimming and waste.

For example, a house 46' long and 26' wide has a perimeter of 144'. $(2 \times 46) + (2 \times 26) = 144$. With 8' sidewalls, the total area to be covered would be 1152 sq. ft. $(144 \times 8 = 1152)$. If the window and door openings equal 250 sq. ft.,

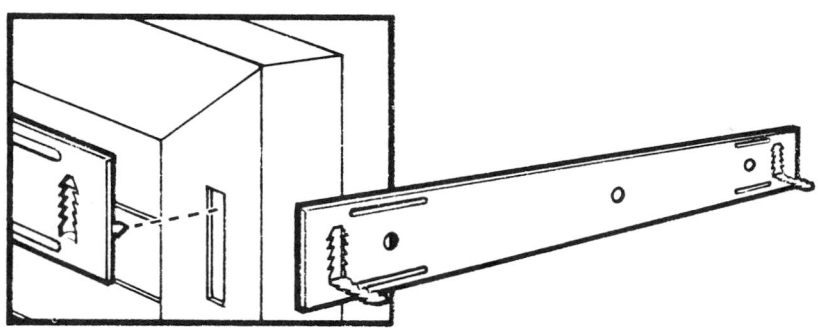

45-80. *Shutter mounting bracket. This mounting bracket is fastened to the wall. The projection on the mounting bracket snaps into a plastic insert at the rear of the shutter. With this mounting system, the shutter can be easily removed for cleaning or painting.*

Table 45-H. *Shutter Sizes. The sizes will vary with the manufacturer and the material from which the shutter or blind is made.*

1 1/8" Thick			
Widths (Pair)			
2'0"			2"10"
2'4"			3'0"
2'6"			3'4"
2'7"			3'8"
2'8"			4'0"
Heights			
1'3"	2'5"	3'7"	5'3"
1'7"	2'7"	3'11"	5'7"
1'9"	2'11"	4'3"	5'11"
1'11"	3'1"	4'7"	6'3"
2'1"	3'3"	4'11"	6'7"
2'3"			6'11"

the total area to be sided then would be 902 sq. ft. (1152 - 250 = 902).

The dressed width of the siding and the amount of lap are accounted for by the area factor. To find the area factor refer to Table 45-I. For example, if 1" × 10" bevel siding is to be used, the chart shows that the area factor is 1.21. Multiply this factor by the area to be covered:

$$902 \times 1.21 = 1091.42$$

Add five percent of this amount for the trim and waste. Five percent of 1091.42 sq. ft., is 54.57 sq. ft. Added to the original 1091.42 sq. ft., this yields a rounded total of 1146 sq. ft. of siding.

Shingles. To determine the number of shingles necessary to cover the exterior sidewall of a house, the area to be covered plus trim and waste allowance must be figured as for bevel siding. For single coursing, one square (4 bundles) of 16" shingles with a 7½" exposure will cover 150 sq. ft. of area. Table 45-E. Use the previous example of 902 sq. ft. After adding 5 percent to this number for the waste and cutting factor divide by 150.

$$902 \times 0.05 = 45.1$$
$$902 + 45.1 = 947.1$$

$$\frac{947.1 \text{ (area to be covered)}}{150 \text{ (area covered by 1 square of shingles)}} = 6.31 \text{ or } 6\frac{1}{2} \text{ squares}$$

Since there are 4 bundles in a square, 26 bundles will be required to shingle the house in the example. Shakes would be estimated the same way.

Vinyl and Metal Siding. Most manufacturers of vinyl and metal siding indicate the number of pieces of a given size siding required to cover one square

(100 sq. ft., or a wall area 10' × 10'). For example, 12 pieces of 8" siding will cover one square.

Figure the area to be covered (see "Wood Bevel Siding"). Divide this total area by 100 to find the number of squares. Multiply the number of squares by 12 (the number of pieces needed to cover one square). For the house in the previous example, the number of pieces would be calculated as follows:

$$\frac{947.1}{100} = 9.471$$
$$9.471 \times 12 = 113.65, \text{ or } 114 \text{ pieces}$$

Nails. To determine the number of nails necessary, refer to the chart in Fig. 45-76. For example, bevel siding ¾" × 10" (nominal 1" × 10") would require ½ (0.5) pound of nails per 100 square feet. Since we have 902 square feet, divide by 100 to find how many hundreds of square feet there are in the area to be covered.

$$\frac{902}{100} = 9.02$$

Multiply this by the weight of nails required per 100 square feet.

$$9.02 \times 0.5 = 4.51 \text{ (pounds of nails for the siding)}$$

Labor

Again using ¾" × 10" bevel siding, refer to Table 45-J. The chart indicates that a worker can apply 55 board feet per hour. If the house to be covered contains 1146 square feet, divide this by 55 to get the total number of hours necessary: 20.8.

Table 45-I. *Coverage Estimator.*

		Nominal Size	Width		Area Factor*
			Dress	Face	
Shiplap		1 x 6	5 $^{7}/_{16}$	4 $^{15}/_{16}$	1.22
		1 x 8	7 $^{1}/_{8}$	8 $^{5}/_{8}$	1.21
		1 x 10	9 $^{1}/_{8}$	6 $^{5}/_{8}$	1.16
		1 x 12	11 $^{1}/_{8}$	10 $^{5}/_{8}$	1.13
Tongue and Groove		1 x 4	3 $^{7}/_{16}$	3 $^{3}/_{16}$	1.26
		1 x 6	5 $^{7}/_{16}$	5 $^{3}/_{16}$	1.16
		1 x 8	7 $^{1}/_{8}$	6 $^{7}/_{8}$	1.16
		1 x 10	9 $^{1}/_{8}$	8 $^{7}/_{8}$	1.13
		1 x 12	11 $^{1}/_{8}$	10 $^{7}/_{8}$	1.10
S4S		1 x 4	3 $^{1}/_{2}$	3 $^{1}/_{2}$	1.14
		1 x 6	5 $^{1}/_{2}$	5 $^{1}/_{2}$	1.09
		1 x 8	7 $^{1}/_{4}$	7 $^{1}/_{4}$	1.10
		1 x 10	9 $^{1}/_{4}$	9 $^{1}/_{4}$	1.08
		1 x 12	11 $^{1}/_{4}$	11 $^{1}/_{4}$	1.07
Paneling Patterns		1 x 6	5 $^{7}/_{16}$	5 $^{1}/_{16}$	1.19
		1 x 8	7 $^{1}/_{8}$	6 $^{3}/_{4}$	1.19
		1 x 10	9 $^{1}/_{8}$	8 $^{3}/_{4}$	1.14
		1 x 12	11 $^{1}/_{8}$	10 $^{3}/_{4}$	1.12
Bevel Siding		1 x 4	3 $^{1}/_{2}$	3 $^{1}/_{2}$	1.60
		1 x 6	5 $^{1}/_{2}$	5 $^{1}/_{2}$	1.33
		1 x 8	7 $^{1}/_{4}$	7 $^{1}/_{4}$	1.28
		1 x 10	9 $^{1}/_{4}$	9 $^{1}/_{4}$	1.21
		1 x 12	11 $^{1}/_{4}$	11 $^{1}/_{4}$	1.17

* Allowance for trim and waste should be added

Table 45-J. *Estimating Drop or Bevel Siding.*

BEVEL SIDING		
Size	Nails (Per 100 Sq. Ft.)	Labor (Board Feet Per Hour)
$^1/_2$ x 4	1 $^1/_2$ Pounds	30
$^1/_2$ x 5	1 $^1/_2$ Pounds	40
$^1/_2$ x 6	1 Pound	45
$^1/_2$ x 8	$^3/_4$ Pound	50
$^5/_8$ x 8	$^3/_4$ Pound	50
$^3/_4$ x 8	$^3/_4$ Pound	50
$^5/_8$ x 10	$^1/_2$ Pound	55
$^3/_4$ x 10	$^1/_2$ Pound	55
$^3/_4$ x 12	$^1/_2$ Pound	55

DROP SIDING		
Size	Nails (Per 100 Sq. Ft.)	Labor (Board Feet Per Hour)
1 x 6	2 $^1/_2$ Pounds	50
1 x 8	2 Pounds	55

QUESTIONS

1. What factors are combined to produce the wide variety of exterior wall coverings?

2. What type of wood siding serves as both sheathing and exterior wall coverings?

3. What is the maximum exposure for a piece of 8" bevel siding?

4. What is the advantage of using a story pole when installing bevel siding?

5. What is the purpose of a "preacher"?

6. List several requirements for nails used on wood siding.

7. List several precautions that should be taken to prevent outside moisture problems.

8. When installing plywood siding, what type of surface should be specified?

9. List several advantages of hardboard siding.

10. What are the two methods of shingle sidewall application?

11. When using shingles as a sidewall covering, under what conditions must nailing strips be used?

12. What are the three kinds of shakes available?

13. When stucco is used as a sidewall finish, what holds it in place?

14. When installing metal and plastic siding, why aren't the nails driven in tightly?

15. When making a lap joint on metal or plastic siding, in which direction should the overlap be made?

16. Name four important tools for installing brick masonry.

17. What are the three basic kinds of brick used in residential construction?

18. What is a modular brick?

19. What is Type N mortar used for?

ACTIVITIES

1. Language Arts. If you were to build a home with a wood exterior, what type of wood siding would you choose? Find a home that uses the type of wood siding that you have chosen. In a short descriptive paragraph, describe in detail the appearance of the home. Conclude your paragraph with a statement that clarifies the reasons for your preference.

2. Language Arts. Research the use of wood shakes in the Colonial era. Why were shakes such a popular exterior wall covering at that time? Explain this in a brief essay.

3. Math. The measurement from the top of the foundation to the top of the window on the outside of a garage is 6'6". Bevel siding of 8" nominal width is to be applied. Refer to the guideline for overlap of courses requiring that the butt of the course just above the window be at the top of the window.

Determine the number of courses required to the top of the window.

SECTION

VII Completing the Interior

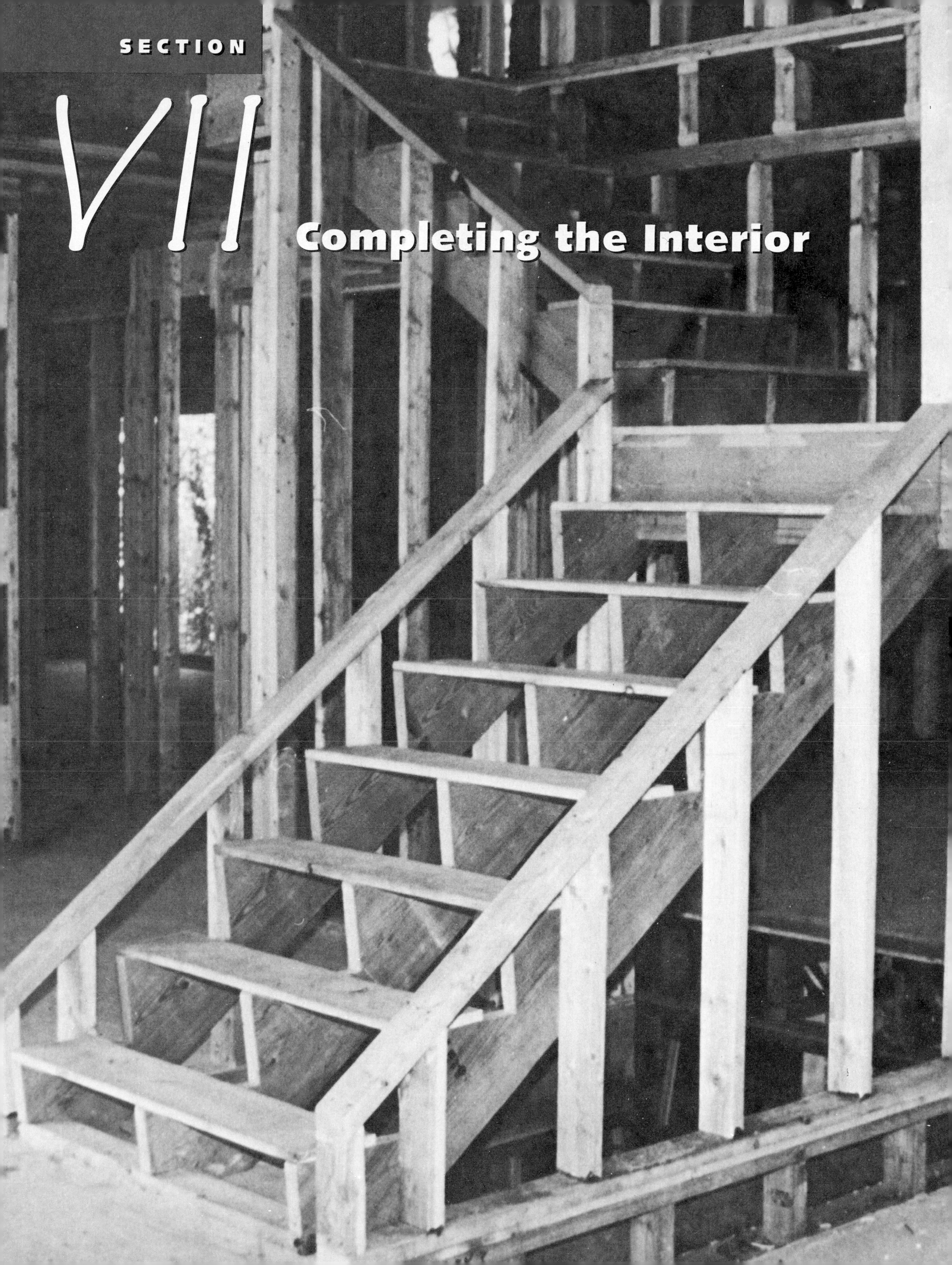

46

Thermal Insulation, Radiant Barriers, and Vapor Barriers

Insulation is the property of material which slows down the transmission of energy in the form of heat, sound, or electricity. In construction, insulation is usually thought of in relation to heat transmission, although sound is an equally important item to consider. (Sound insulation is discussed in Unit 47.) Most building materials—and even the air space between studs—have some heat insulation properties. However, by themselves they are not sufficient for modern homes that must have heating, air conditioning, and other climate control equipment. Insulation materials are products that are used in addition to ordinary building materials for the specific purpose of retarding the passage of heat. Insulation keeps homes warmer in the winter and cooler in the summer.

Better and more efficiently insulated homes are being built by contractors to please quality-conscious buyers. Upgrading of insulation beyond the minimum standards pays good dividends in the form of increased comfort, reduced heating and air conditioning costs, and smaller, less expensive furnaces, cooling equipment, and duct work. Maximum insulation also makes electric heating feasible. In warm climates, the use of insulation with air conditioning is justified because operating costs are reduced and units of smaller capacity are required.

INSULATING MATERIALS

Insulation is manufactured in a variety of forms and types, each with advantages for specific uses. Fig. 46-1. Materials commonly used for insulation may be grouped into the following general classes:
➤ Flexible (blanket and batt).
➤ Loose fill.
➤ Reflective.
➤ Rigid (structural and nonstructural).
➤ Miscellaneous types.

Flexible Insulation

Flexible insulation is manufactured in two forms: *blanket* and *batt*. In both cases, the material ranges in insulating value from R-3.4 to R-38. The thickness ranges from $1\frac{1}{8}$" to 13". Blanket insulation is furnished in rolls or packages. It comes in widths suited to 16" and 24" stud and joist spacing. A, Fig. 46-1b. These pieces can be easily cut to length to fit various size openings. Fig. 46-2. The body of the blanket is most commonly made of fiberglass. Most blanket insulation is covered with paper or other sheet material with tabs on the sides for fastening to studs or joists. One covering sheet serves as a vapor barrier to resist movement of water vapor and should always face the warm side of the wall. Aluminum foil, asphalt, and plastic-laminated paper are common barrier materials.

46-1a. *Rigid insulation applied to the outside of a house prior to installation of the siding.*

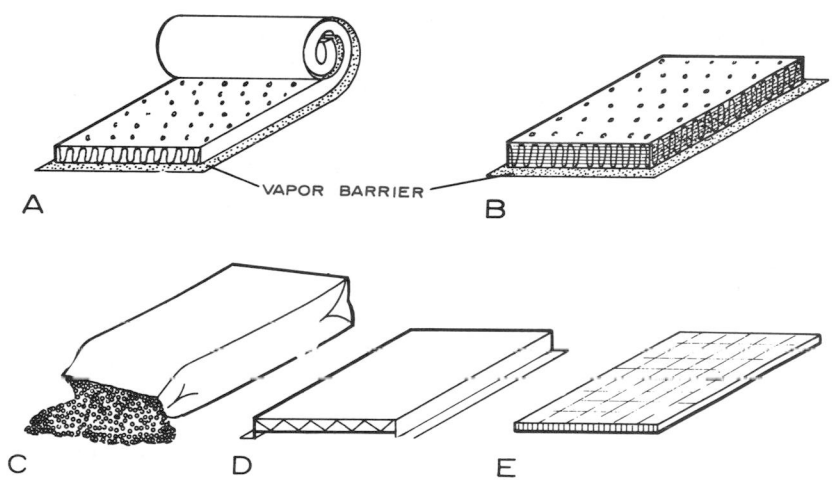

46-1b. *Types of insulation: A. Blanket. B. Batt. C. Loose fill. D. One type of reflective insulation. E. Rigid insulation.*

46-2. *To cut insulation, place it on a piece of scrap plywood or 2 x 4, compress the material with one hand, and cut it with a sharp knife. When cutting faced insulation, keep the facing up.*

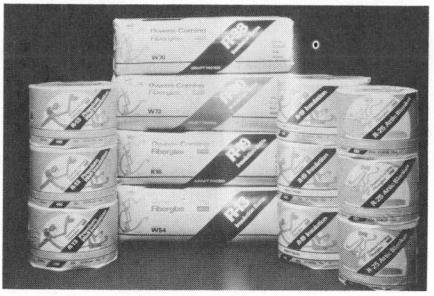

46-3. *Fiberglass insulation in rolls and batts is the most common insulation used in residential construction.*

46-4. *Installing 4" batt insulation. Note that the vapor barrier is placed so that it faces the warm side of the wall. Sometimes an additional thin sheet of plastic is added to completely seal the wall. This should always be done when insulation without a vapor barrier is used.*

Batt insulation is also made of fibrous material. B, Fig. 46-1b and Fig. 46-3. It is supplied with or without a vapor barrier. Fig. 46-4. One friction-type fiberglass batt is supplied without a covering and is designed to remain in place without the normal fastening methods.

Loose Fill Insulation

Loose fill insulation is usually supplied in bags or bales and placed by pouring, blowing, or packing by hand. C, Fig. 46-1b. Materials used include rock and glass wool, wood pulp products, and vermiculite.

Fill insulation is best used between first-floor ceiling joists in unheated attics. It is also used in sidewalls of existing houses that were not insulated during construction. Where no vapor barrier was installed during construction, suitable paint coatings, as described later in this unit, should be used for vapor barriers.

Reflective Insulation

Most materials reflect some radiant heat. Radiant heat is heat that flows through air in a direct line from a warm surface to a cooler one. Materials high in reflective properties include aluminum foil, sheet metal with tin coating, and paper products coated with a reflective oxide composition.

Reflective insulations are equally effective whether the reflective surface faces the warm or cold side. However, the reflective surface must face an air space at least ¾" deep. Where a reflective surface contacts another material, the reflective properties are lost and the material has little or no insulating value.

Sometimes, reflective insulation of foil is applied to blanket insulation and to the stud-surface side of gypsum lath. The type of reflective insulation shown in D, Fig. 46-1b has air spaces between the reflective surfaces. Metal foil suitably mounted on some supporting base also makes an excellent vapor barrier.

Rigid Insulation

Rigid insulation is manufactured in sheets and other forms. E, Fig. 46-1. These thin foam panels pack more R-value into a smaller space than most other types of insulation. There are several kinds of rigid insulation:

➤ Expanded polystyrene (EPS). The polystyrene is formed into beads that puff up when exposed to steam. The beads are then molded into blocks of insulation from which sheets are sliced at the factory. R-3.6 to R-4.2 per inch.

➤ Extruded polystyrene (XEPS). This material is similar to EPS, but has better compressive strength for use as foundation insulation. R-5 per inch.

➤ Polyurethane and polyisocyanurate. These materials are often faced with foil laminates to slow the loss of Freon blowing agent used in their manufacture. R-5.6 per inch.

➤ Phenolic foam. Though not as widely available as the other rigid insulations, this material has a relatively low flammability rating. R-8 per inch.

Rigid insulation may be structural or nonstructural. Structural insulating boards, in densities ranging from 15 to 31 pounds per cubic foot, are used as building boards, roof decking, sheathing, and wallboard. While they have moderately good insulating properties, their primary purpose is structural.

Roof insulation is nonstructural and serves mainly to provide thermal resistance to heat flow. It is called slab or block insulation and is manufactured in rigid units ½" to 3" thick and usually 2' × 4' in size.

In house construction, the most common forms of rigid insulation are for sheathing.

Miscellaneous Types

There are several other kinds of insulation. Sometimes lightweight vermiculite and perlite aggregates are used in plaster to increase its thermal resistance.

Foamed-in-place insulation includes sprayed and foam types. Sprayed insulation is usually inorganic fibrous material blown against a clean surface which has been primed with an adhesive coating. It is often left exposed for acoustical purposes.

Expanded polystyrene and urethane plastic foams may be molded or foamed in place. Urethane insulation may also be applied by spraying. Polystyrene and urethane in board form can be obtained in thicknesses from ½" to 2".

INSULATING VALUES

The thermal properties of most building materials are known, and the rate of heat flow, or coefficient of transmission, for most combinations of construction can be calculated. This coefficient, or U-value, is a measure of heat transmission between air on the warm side and air on the cold side of the construction unit. It is defined as the amount of heat (in Btu's) transmitted in 1 hour, through 1 square foot of surface, for each degree Fahrenheit difference in temperature between the inside and outside air. (One Btu, or British thermal unit, is the amount of heat which will raise the temperature of 1 pound of water 1 degree Fahrenheit.)

The insulating value of a wall will vary with different types of construction, with materials used in construction, and with different types and thicknesses of insulation. Comparisons of U-values may be used to evaluate different combinations of materials and insulation based on overall heat loss, potential fuel savings, influence on comfort, and installation costs. The amount of insulation required to obtain a desired *U*-value can be determined for any type of construction.

Table 26-A provides some comparison of the individual insulating values of various building materials. These are expressed as *k* values, or heat conductivity. Heat conductivity is defined as the amount of heat (in Btu's) that will pass in 1 hour through 1 square foot of material 1 inch thick per 1°F temperature difference between faces of the material. Simply expressed, *k* represents heat loss. The lower this numerical value, the better the insulating qualities.

Building materials are also rated on their resistance or *R* value, which is merely another expression of insulating value. Table 46-A. The *R* value is usually expressed as the total resistance of the wall or of a thick insulating blanket or batt, whereas *k* is the rating per inch of thickness. R = ¼. Thus, if the *k* value of 1 inch of insulation is 0.25, the resistance, *R*, is ¹⁄₀.₂₅, or 4.0. If there are 3 inches of this insulation, the *R* value is 3 × 4.0, or 12.0.

Climate must also be taken into consideration when choosing building materials, insulation, and heating and cooling equipment. The map in Fig. 46-5 shows the average winter low temperatures found in different areas of the United States. Such data is used in determining the size of heating plant required after calculating heat loss. This information is also useful in figuring the amount of

Table 46-A. *Thermal Properties of Various Building Materials per Inch of Thickness.*

Material	Thermal Conductivity K	Thermal Resistance R	Efficiency as insulator Percent
Wood	0.80	1.25	100.0
Air Space[1]	1.03	0.97	77.6
Cinder Block	3.6	0.28	22.4
Common Brick	5.0	0.20	16.0
Face Brick	9.0	0.11	8.9
Concrete (Sand and Gravel)	12.0	0.08	6.4
Stone (Lime or Sand)	12.5	0.08	6.4
Steel	312.0	0.0032	0.25
Aluminum	1416.0	0.00070	0.06

1 Thermal properties are for air in a space and apply for air spaces ranging from 3/4 to 4 inches in thickness

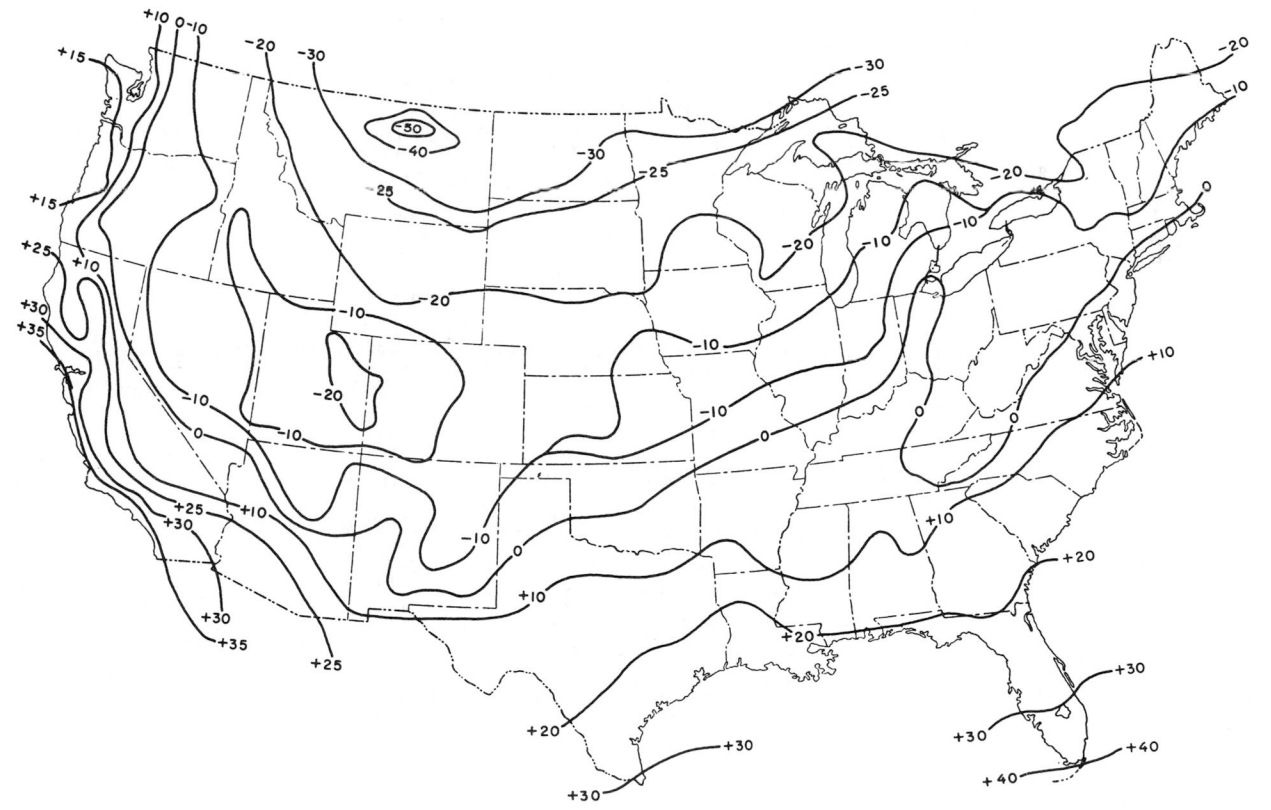

46-5. *This map of the United States indicates the lowest temperatures occurring in each zone during an average winter.*

insulation needed for walls, ceilings, and floors.

ACCEPTABLE COMFORT LEVELS

The amount of insulation necessary to provide indoor climate comfort can be determined accurately. The thermal properties of all common building materials are known, and the *U*-value for any combination of construction and insulation can be calculated.

Studies by heating engineers of home heating and air conditioning requirements have resulted in a number of *U*-value design standards recommended for new construction.

These standards are based on the geographical location of the structure and on the cost and type of fuel used.

The most widely used recommendations are in the *All-Weather Comfort Standard*, developed cooperatively by electric power suppliers, equipment makers, and material manufacturers, and in the supplementary performance standards created by the National Mineral Wool Insulation Association. Basically, these standards establish three degrees of comfort which may be attained by varying the amounts of insulation installed in ceilings, walls, and floors of homes.

► The *Maximum Comfort Standards* specify required amounts of insulation for houses in the coldest sections of the country and for energy-saving houses in any location.

► The *Moderate Comfort Standards* are for houses in the midsection of the country.

► The *Minimum Comfort Standards* apply to all homes as the minimum recommendations of many building codes.

In recent years, the need to conserve energy has caused insulation standards to be raised. Fig. 46-6. Table 46-B shows the currently recommended *U*-values. Shown on the table are the installed insulation requirements in terms of resistance units, or *R* numbers, which will provide the desired *U*-value in the building. This system of specifying insulation by total thermal resistance, instead of thickness, stems from the fact that insulating materials vary in density, type of surface, and heat conductivity.

In choosing the best, good, or minimum insulation standards in any climate zone, it should be remembered that comfort and operating economy are dual

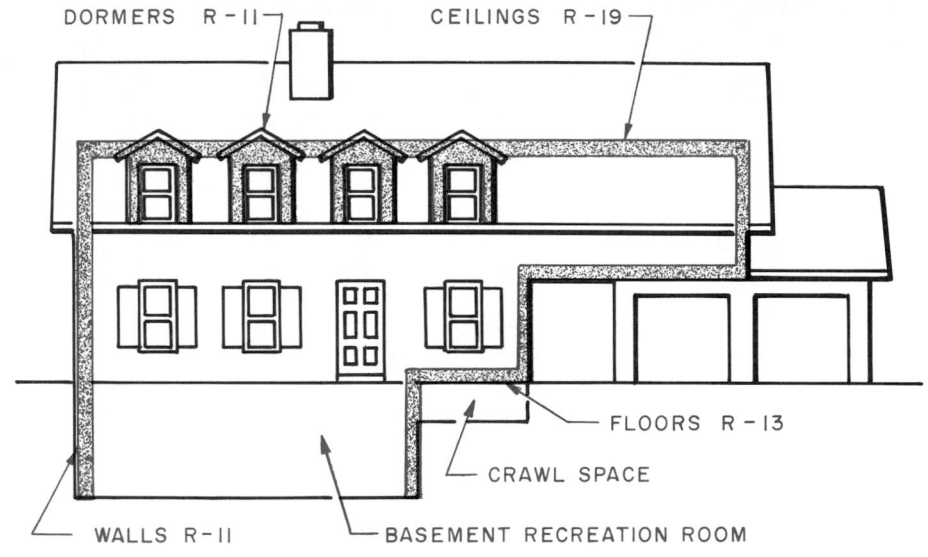

46-6. *Minimum insulation standards included in many local codes and recommended by many utilities.*

Table 46-B. *U-Values and Insulation Requirements.*

Maximum Comfort Standard		
	U-Value	**Insulation "R" Number**
Ceilings	0.02	R38-42
Walls	0.05	R19
Floors over unheated spaces	0.05	R22
Moderate Comfort Standard		
	U-Value	**Insulation "R" Number**
Ceilings	0.03	R30-33
Walls	0.05	R19
Floors over unheated spaces	0.05	R19-22
Minimum Comfort Standard		
	U-Value	**Insulation "R" Number**
Ceilings	0.05	R19
Walls	0.07	R11
Floors over unheated spaces	0.07	R13

benefits of insulation. Insulating for maximum comfort automatically provides maximum economy of operation, and reduces initial costs of heating and cooling equipment to a minimum.

WHERE TO INSULATE

To reduce heat loss from the house during cold weather in most climates, all walls, ceilings, roofs, and floors that separate heated from unheated spaces should be insulated. Fig. 46-7.

In houses with unheated crawl spaces, insulation should be placed between the floor joists or around the wall perimeter. If flexible insulation is used, it should be well supported between joists by slats and a galvanized wire mesh or by a rigid board. The vapor barrier should be installed toward the subflooring. Fig. 46-8. Press-fit or friction insulation fits tightly between joists and requires only a small amount of support to hold it in place. Reflective insulation is often used for crawl spaces, but only one dead-air space (between the insulation and the subflooring) should be assumed in calculating heat loss when the crawl space is ventilated. A ground cover of roll roofing or plastic film such as polyethylene should be placed on the soil of crawl spaces to decrease the moisture content of the space as well as of the wood members.

In 1½-story houses, insulation should be placed along all walls, floors, and ceilings that are adjacent to unheated areas. Fig. 46-9. These include stairways, dwarf (knee) walls, and dormers. Provisions should be made for ventilation of the unheated areas.

Where attic space is unheated and a stairway is included, insulation should be installed around the stairway as well as in the first-floor ceiling. Fig. 46-10.

The door leading to the attic should be weather stripped to prevent heat loss. Walls adjoining an unheated garage or porch should also be insulated.

In houses with flat or low-pitched roofs, insulation should be used in the ceiling area with sufficient space allowed above for

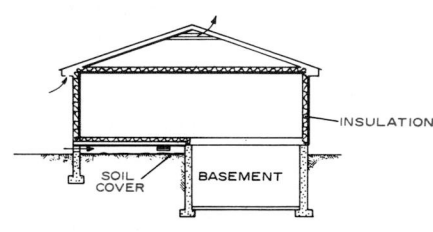

46-7. *A conventional one-story house is insulated in walls, floors over unheated crawl spaces, and ceilings.*

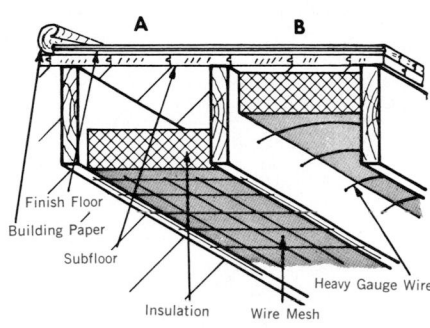

46-8. *Methods of installing insulation between floor joists: A. Wire mesh is stapled to the edges of the joists. B. Pieces of heavy-gauge wire pointed at each end are wedged between the joists to support the insulation.*

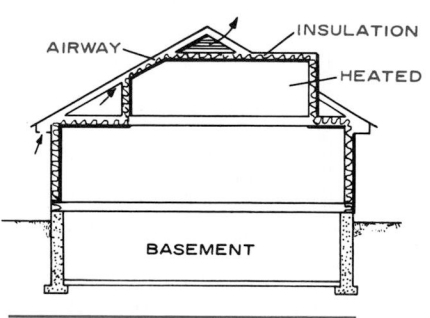

46-9a. *Insulating a 1½-story house.*

unobstructed ventilation between the joists. Insulation should be used along the perimeter of houses built on slabs. A vapor barrier should be included under the slab. Fig. 46-11.

In the summer, outside surfaces exposed to the direct rays of the sun may attain temperatures of 50°F or more above shade

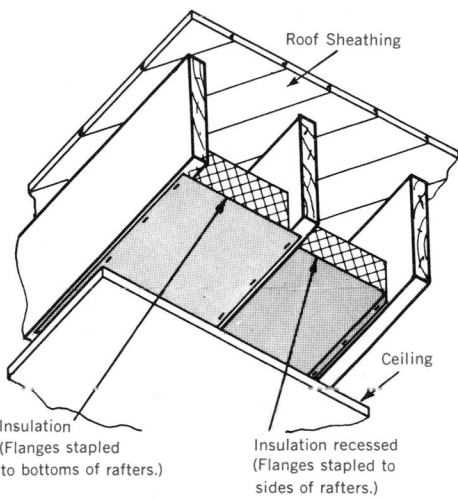

46-9b. *Methods of installing flexible insulation between rafters. Regardless of method, it is important that a space be provided between the insulation and the roof sheathing to permit air circulation.*

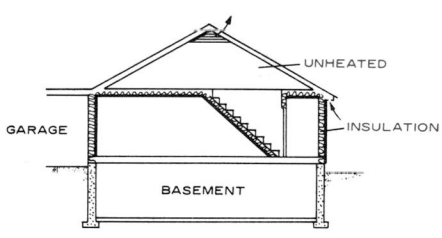

46-10. *Insulating unheated attic space.*

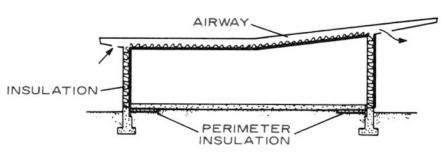

46-11. *When insulating a flat roof, leave an air space for ventilation. For houses built on slabs, use perimeter insulation under the slab.*

temperatures and, of course, tend to transfer this heat toward the inside of the house. Insulation in the walls and in attic areas retards the flow of heat, improving summer comfort conditions.

Where air conditioning systems are used, insulation should be placed in all exposed ceilings and walls in the same manner as when insulating against cold-weather heat loss. Shading of glass against direct rays of the sun and the use of insulated glass will aid in reducing the air conditioning load.

Ventilation of attic and roof spaces is an important addition to insulation. Without ventilation, an attic space may become very hot and hold the heat for many hours. (See Unit 41, "Ventilation.") Obviously, more heat will be transmitted through the ceiling when the attic temperature is 150°F than if it is 100° to 120°F. Ventilation methods suggested for protection against cold-weather condensation apply equally well to protection against excessive hot-weather roof temperatures.

The use of storm windows or insulated glass will greatly reduce heat loss. Almost twice as much

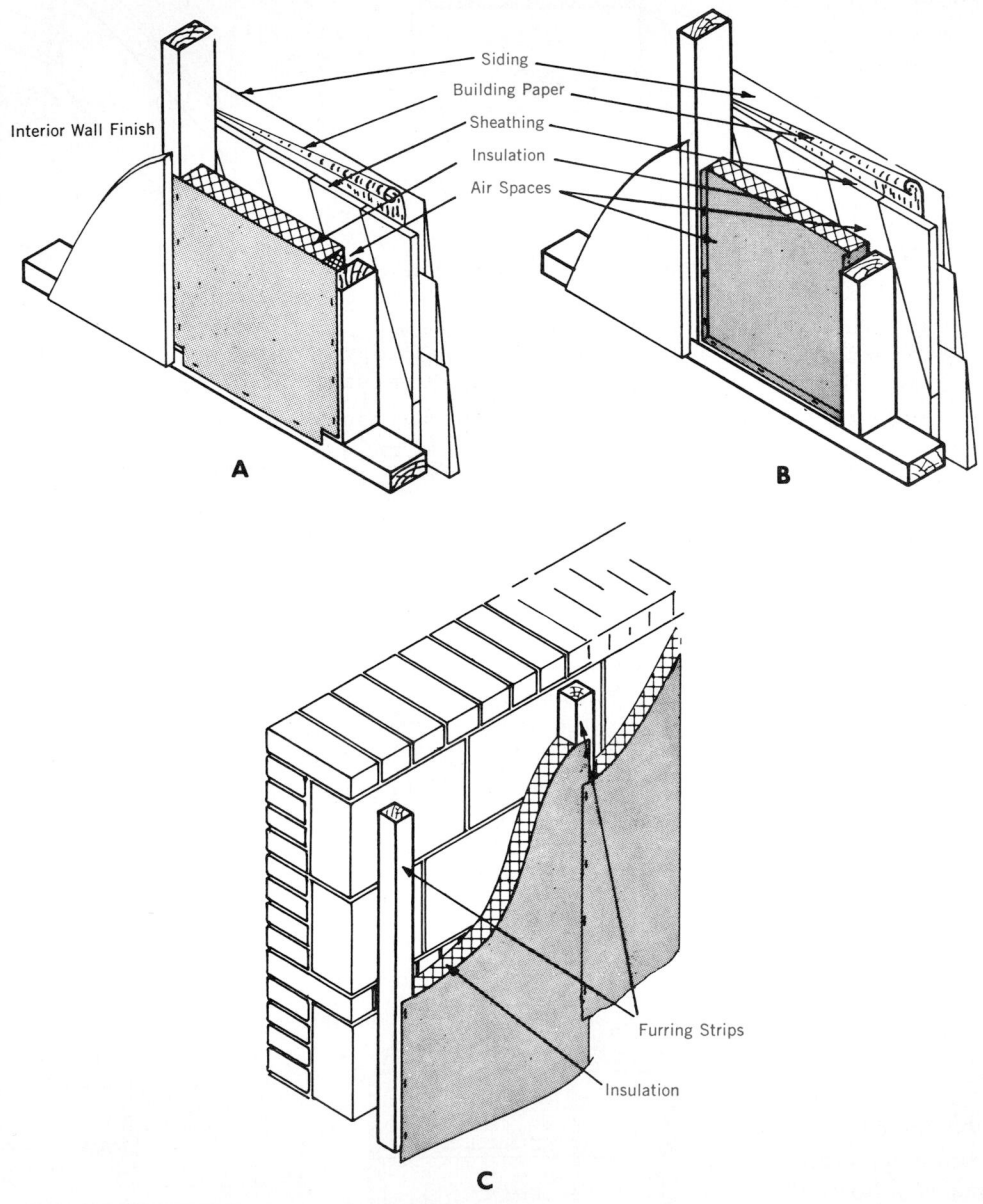

46-12. *Methods of installing wall insulation: A. The insulation flange is stapled to the inside edge of the stud. B. The insulation is recessed to provide an air space of at least ¾" on each side. C. Insulation on masonry walls is stapled to furring strips which have been nailed to the masonry on 16" centers.*

heat loss occurs through a single glass as through a window glazed with insulated glass or protected by a storm sash. Furthermore, double glass will normally prevent surface condensation and frost from forming on inner glass surfaces in winter. When excessive condensation persists, paint failures or even decay of the sash rail or other parts can occur.

HOW TO INSTALL INSULATION

Flexible Insulation

Blanket or batt insulation with a vapor barrier should be placed between framing members so that the tabs of the barrier lap the edge of the studs as well as the top and bottom plates. This method is not often popular with the contractor because it is more difficult to apply the drywall. However, it assures a minimum amount of vapor loss compared to the loss when tabs are stapled to the sides of the studs. Fig. 46-12. A hand stapler is commonly used to fasten the insulation and the barriers in place. Fig. 46-13.

46-13. *Installing batt insulation with a hand stapler following the method shown in B, Fig. 46-12.*

The installation of insulation is a job in which good craftsmanship pays off in money saved for the homeowner. When installing

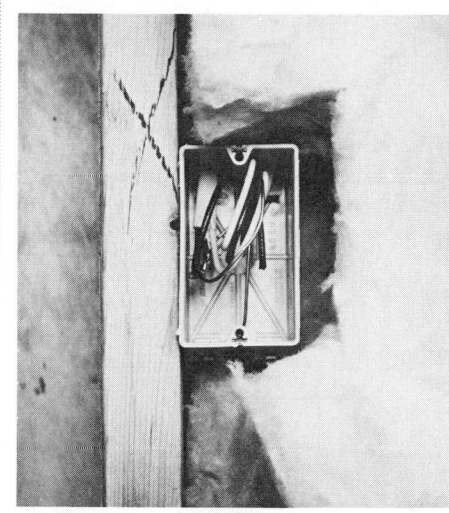

46-14. *This shows a poor insulation job. The gap between the insulation and the electrical box will allow heat to escape easily.*

flexible insulation, it is of prime importance to make sure that the insulation properly fills all the wall cavities. There should be no gaps between the insulation and the framing, and no gaps around electrical boxes. Any gaps form a ready passage through which heat can escape. Fig. 46-14.

To protect the head and sole plate as well as the headers over openings, it is good practice to use narrow strips of vapor barrier material along the top and bottom of the wall. A, Fig. 46-15. Ordinarily, these areas are not covered too well by the barrier on the blanket or batt.

For insulation without a barrier (press-fit or friction type), a plastic film vapor barrier such as 4-mil polyethylene is commonly used to envelop the entire exposed wall and ceiling. B, Fig. 46-15. It covers the openings as well as window and door headers and edge studs. This

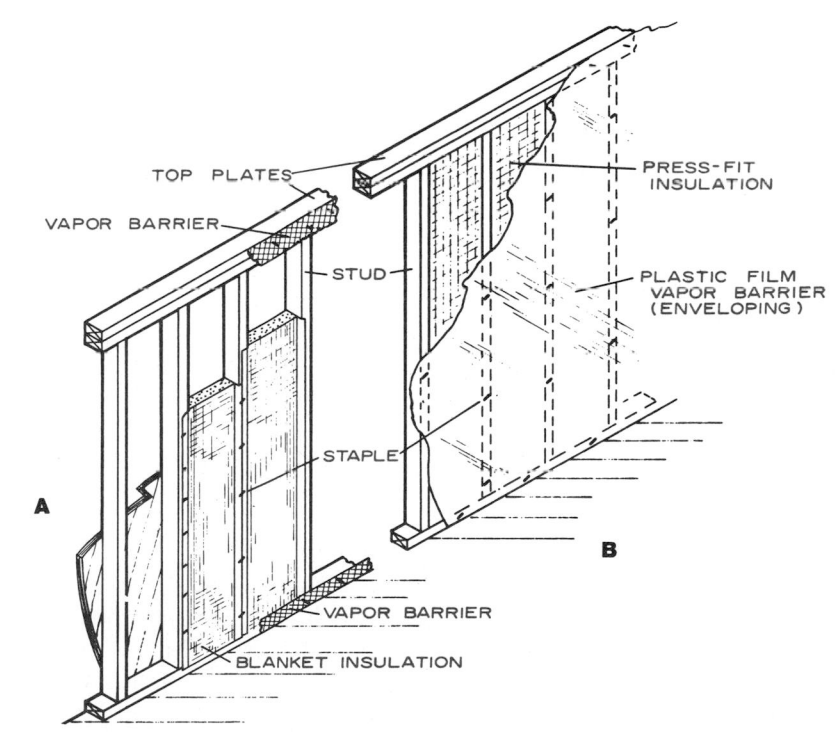

46-15. *Insulating a frame wall: A. Blanket insulation installed with a vapor barrier at the plates. B. Press-fit insulation installed with a plastic film vapor barrier.*

system is one of the best from the standpoint of resistance to vapor movement. Furthermore, it does not have the installation inconveniences encountered when tabs of the insulation are stapled over the edges of the studs. After the drywall is installed or plastering is completed, the film is trimmed around the window and door openings.

Reflective Insulation

Reflective insulation, in single-sheet form with two reflective surfaces, should be placed to divide the space formed by the framing members into two approximately equal spaces. For example, insulation between studs should be placed so as to leave an equal amount of air space on each side of the insulation. Some reflective insulations include air spaces and are furnished with nailing tabs. This type is fastened to the studs in such a way as to provide at least a ¾" space on each side of the reflective surfaces.

Loose Fill Insulation

Loose fill insulation is commonly used in ceiling areas and is poured or blown into place. Fig. 46-16. A vapor barrier should be used on the warm side (the bottom, in case of ceiling joists) before insulation is placed. A leveling board will give a constant insulation thickness. Fig. 46-16.

Thick batt insulation is also used in ceiling areas. Fig. 46-17. Batt and fill insulation can be combined to obtain the desired thickness. The vapor barrier is placed against the back of the ceiling finish. Ceiling insulation 6" or more thick greatly reduces heat loss in the winter and also provides summertime protection.

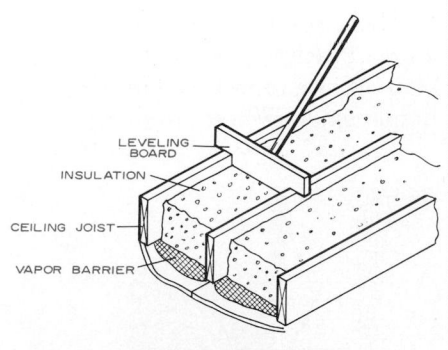

46-16. Installing loose fill insulation in a ceiling. Note the use of the leveling board.

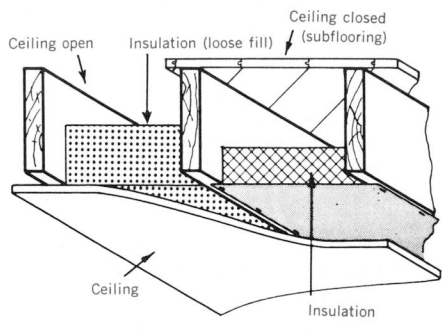

46-17. Loose fill or batt insulation may be installed in a ceiling under an unheated attic.

PRECAUTIONS IN INSULATING

Areas over door and window frames and along side and head jambs also require insulation. Fig. 46-18. Because these areas are filled with small sections of insulation, a vapor barrier must be used around the opening as well as over the header above the openings. Enveloping the entire wall eliminates the need for this type of vapor barrier installation.

In 1½-and 2-story houses and in basements, the area at the joist header at outside walls should be insulated and protected with a vapor barrier. Fig. 46-19.

Insulation should be placed behind electrical outlet boxes and other utility connections in

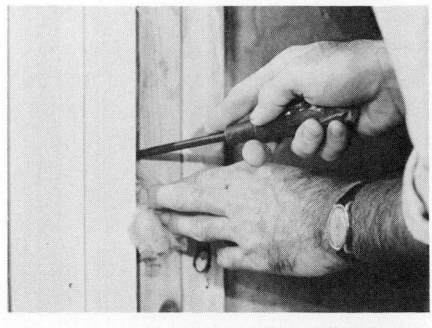

46-18a. Fill all cracks by forcing pieces of insulation into the voids between windows or door jambs and trimmer studs.

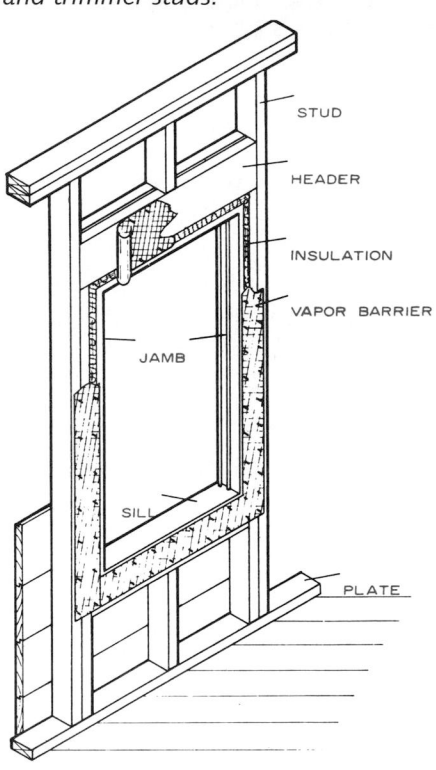

46-18b. A vapor barrier should be applied over the insulation around openings.

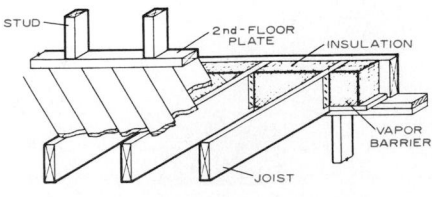

46-19. A vapor barrier and insulation should be installed in the joist space at outside walls.

46-20a. *As much insulation as possible should be pushed behind the electrical wiring, outlet boxes, and pipes in exposed walls. Doing so will minimize condensation on cold surfaces.*

46-20b. *Cover these items with additional insulation to completely fill the space between studs.*

exposed walls to minimize condensation. Fig. 46-20a and b.

Radiant Barriers

Increasing the energy efficiency of your home is one way to save on monthly cooling bills. Installing radiant barriers in a home's attic can reduce summer heat gain and decrease cooling energy usage.

Radiant barriers are a relatively new technology. They are particularly effective in hot climates.

They usually consist of a thin sheet or coating of a highly reflective material, usually aluminum. This is applied to one or both sides of an underlying material called a substrate. These substrate materials are commercially available. They can be constructed out of kraft paper, plastic films, cardboard, plywood sheathing, and air infiltration barrier material. Some of these products are fiber reinforced to increase their durability and ease of handling.

To effectively reduce indoor heat loss and summer heat gain, radiant barriers must have at least one reflective surface. This is usually a sheet or coating of aluminum. Some radiant barriers have a reflective coating on both sides. Both types are efficient. However, if a one-sided radiant barrier is used, the reflective surface must face the open air space in the attic. For example, assume that a one-sided radiant barrier is laid on top of the insulation in an attic with the reflective side facing down and touching the insulation. In this case, the radiant barrier will lose most of its effectiveness for reducing heating and cooling loads.

Radiant Barrier Installation.
Radiant barriers may be installed in attics in two different configurations: the attic floor application and the roof application. The simplest method—the attic floor application—involves placing the radiant barrier directly on top of existing attic insulation, with the reflective side up. Another way to install a radiant barrier is to attach it near the roof. The roof application has several variations. One variation is to attach the radiant barrier to the bottom surfaces of the attic truss chords or rafter framing. Another method, primarily for new construction, drapes the radiant barrier over the rafter tops before the roof deck is applied. Another variation attaches the radiant barrier directly to the underside of the roof deck.

How Radiant Barriers Work.
All materials emit energy by thermal radiation. The amount of energy emitted depends on the surface temperature and a property called the "emissivity." Emissivity determines the efficiency of a radiant barrier and is measured as a number between 0 and 1. The higher the emissivity, the greater the emitted radiation. A material property closely related to emissivity is reflectivity. Reflectivity measures how much radiant heat is reflected by a material, which is recorded as a number between 0 and 1 or as a percentage between 0 and 100%. A material with a high reflectivity has a low emissivity, and vice versa. To perform properly, radiant barrier materials must have high reflectivity (usually 0.9 or 90%, or more), a low emissivity (usually 0.1 or less), and face an open air space.

For example, on a sunny day, a roof absorbs solar energy. This heats the roof sheathing and causes the underside of the sheathing and the roof framing to radiate heat downward toward the attic floor. Placing a radiant barrier on the attic floor will reflect much of the heat radiated from the hot roof back toward the roof. Because the heat is reflected, the top surface of the insulation is cooler. Thus the amount of heat that moves through the insulation into the rooms below the ceiling is reduced. Under the same conditions, a roof-mounted radiant barrier will reduce the amount of radiation reaching the insulation. Because the radiant barrier reduces the amount of radiation striking the top of the insulation, the insulation surface temperature is lower. The heat flow through the insulation is reduced.

Radiant barriers can also reduce indoor heat losses through the ceiling in the winter. Radiant barriers reduce the amount of energy radiated from the top surface of the insulation. However, they can also reduce beneficial heat gains caused by solar heating of the roof. The net benefits of radiant barriers for reducing winter heat losses are still being studied.

Effectiveness of Radiant Barriers. Savings on heating and cooling bills from installing radiant barriers will vary. Expected savings will depend on the type of radiant barrier application, the size of the house, the type of house, the amount of insulation in the attic, effectiveness of attic ventilation, the color of the roof, the thermostat settings, the tightness of the building envelope, weather conditions, the efficiency of the heating and cooling equipment, and fuel prices.

The decision to install radiant barriers in your home should not rest solely on potential savings. The decision should also consider several important non-energy factors. These conditions include:
➤ the potential for moisture condensation.
➤ attic ventilation.
➤ the effect of radiant barriers on roof temperatures.
➤ fire ratings.
Condensation of moisture can be a concern when a radiant barrier is installed on the attic floor directly on top of conventional insulation. During the winter, water vapor from the interior of a house may move into the attic. In most cases, this water vapor will not cause problems because attic ventilation will carry excess vapor away.

During cold weather, a radiant barrier on top of the insulation could cause water vapor to condense on the barrier's underside.

Condensation of large amounts of water could lead to the following problems:
➤ The existing insulation could become wet and lose some of its insulating value.
➤ Water spots could appear on the ceiling.
➤ Under severe conditions, the ceiling framing could rot.

Using perforated or naturally permeable radiant barriers would lessen potential moisture condensation problems and reduce the potential for problems. Additional precautions include avoiding high indoor relative humidities, sealing cracks and air leaks in the ceiling, using a vapor retarder below the attic insulation, and providing for adequate attic ventilation.

The fire ratings of radiant barriers are also important. To meet the fire code, a radiant barrier must be rated either Class A by the National Fire Protection Association or Class I by the Uniform Building Code. These ratings are either printed on the product or listed on data sheets provided by the manufacturer.

VAPOR BARRIERS

Some discussion of vapor barriers has been included previously because vapor barriers are usually a part of flexible insulation. However, further information is given in the following paragraphs.

Most building materials are permeable to water vapor. This presents problems because considerable water vapor is generated in a house from cooking, dishwashing, laundering, bathing, humidifiers, and other sources. During cold weather, this vapor may pass through wall and ceiling materials and condense in the wall or attic space. Subsequently, in severe cases, it may damage the exterior paint and interior finish, or even promote decay in structural members. For protection, a material highly resistant to vapor transmission, called a *vapor barrier* should be used on the warm side of a wall or below the insulation in an attic space.

Among the effective vapor barrier materials are asphalt laminated papers, aluminum foil, and plastic films. Most blanket and batt insulations are provided with a vapor barrier on one side, some of them with paper-backed aluminum foil. Foil-backed gypsum lath or gypsum boards are also available and serve as excellent vapor barriers.

The effectiveness of vapor barriers is rated by their perm values. (1 perm = 1 grain of vapor transmission per square foot, per hour, for each inch of mercury vapor pressure difference.) Low perm values indicate high resistance to vapor transmission. The perm values of vapor barriers vary, but ordinarily it is good practice to use barriers which have values less than ¼ (0.25) perm. Although a value of ½ perm is considered adequate, aging reduces the effectiveness of some materials.

To obtain a positive seal against vapor transmission, wall-height rolls of plastic film vapor barriers should be applied over studs, plates, and window and door headers. This system, called "enveloping," is used over insulation having no vapor barrier or to insure excellent protection when used over any type of insulation. The plastic should be fitted tightly around outlet boxes and sealed if necessary. Fig 46-20c.

46-20c. *Staple the plastic film vapor barrier to the wood so the insulation is completely sealed.*

A ribbon of sealing compound around an outlet or switch box will minimize vapor loss at this area. Cold air returns in outside walls should consist of metal ducts to prevent vapor loss and subsequent paint problems.

Paint coatings on plaster may be very effective as vapor barriers if materials are properly chosen and applied. They do not, however, offer protection during construction, and moisture may cause paint blisters on exterior paint before the interior paint can be applied. This is most likely to happen in buildings that are constructed during periods when outdoor temperatures are 25°F or more below inside temperatures. Paint coatings cannot be considered a substitute for the membrane types of vapor barriers. However, they do provide some protection for houses where other types of vapor barriers were not installed during construction.

Of the various types of paint, one coat of aluminum primer followed by two decorative coats of flat wall or oil paint is quite effective. For rough plaster or for buildings in very cold climates, two coats of the aluminum primer may be necessary. A primer and sealer

of the pigmented type, followed by decorative finish coats or two coats of rubber-base paint, are also effective in retarding vapor transmission.

No type of vapor barrier can be considered 100% resistive, and some vapor leakage into the wall may be expected. Therefore the flow of vapor to the outside should not be impeded by materials of relatively high vapor resistance on the cold side of the vapor barrier. For example, sheathing paper should be of a type that is waterproof, but not highly vapor resistant. This also applies to "permanent" outer coverings or siding. The vapor barrier itself should have a low perm value to prevent the passage of moisture to the cold side of the barrier. This will reduce the danger of condensation on cold surfaces within the wall.

ESTIMATING

Materials

To determine the amount of insulation required for a home, the area to be insulated must first be figured. Using the house plan in Fig. 46-21, round off the outside dimensions of the home to a width of 28' and a length of 52'. The perimeter of the house is 160'. $(2 \times 28) + (2 \times 52) = 160$. If the wall height is 8', the walls will contain 1,280 square feet of area $(8 \times 160 = 1,280)$. This includes the window and door openings, which equal about 150 square feet. Subtract the area of the openings from the total area of 1,280 square feet $(1,280 - 150 = 1,130)$. The total wall area to be insulated is 1,130 square feet.

Figure the number of insulating batts required by using Table 46-C. Read down the left column under the size batt to be used, in this case 15" × 48". Read across to the number of batts per 100 square feet. The chart indicates 20 batts will cover 100 square feet, but only 95 square feet of wall area (5% waste allowance).

$$\frac{1130 \text{ (total area to be insulated)}}{95 \text{ (sq. ft. of wall space covered by 20 batts)}} = \text{approx. } 11.89$$

$11.89 \times 20 = 238 \text{ batts.}$

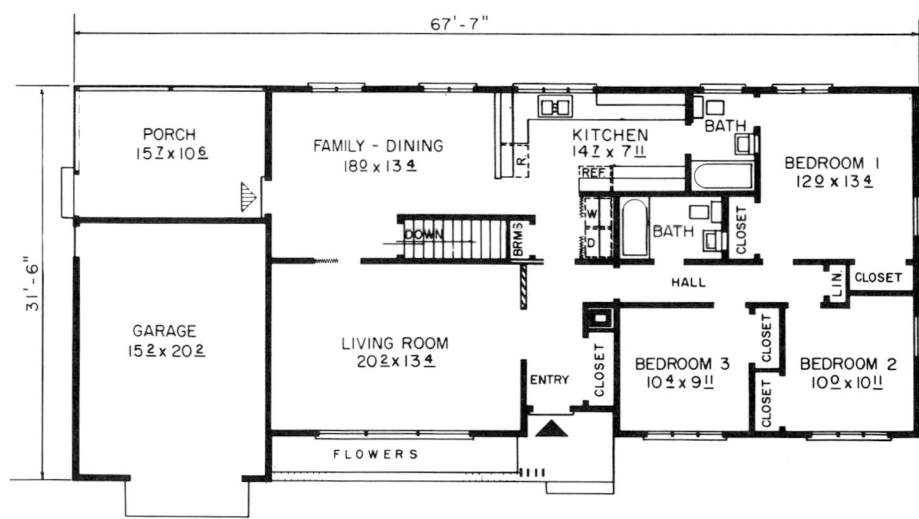

46-21. *Estimate the amount of insulation required to insulate the outside walls and the ceiling of this house.*

Table 46-C. *Estimating Insulation Batts.*

Insulation (Batts)		Material		Staples	Labor
Size	Sq. Ft.	Number of Batts Per 100 Sq. Ft.	Number of Sq. Ft. for 100 Sq. Ft. Wall	Per 100 Sq. Ft.	Sq. Ft. Per Hour
15 x 24	2.5	40	95	160	80
15 x 48	5.0	20	95	160	85
19 x 24	3.7	32	96	160	90
19 x 48	6.33	16	95	160	95
23 x 24	3.84	26	95	160	90
23 x 48	7.67	13	100	160	100

Note: Glass, Mineral or Rock Wool batts with paper back roll insulation or strip insulation. Studding or joist excluded. Batts stapled @ 6" O.C.

Table 46-D. *Estimating Loose Fill Insulation.*

Insulation (Loose Fill)	Material Number of Sq. Ft. Covered per Cubic Foot Density					Labor Sq. Ft. per Hour
Fill Thickness	6 Pounds	7 Pounds	8 Pounds	9 Pounds	10 Pounds	
1"	21.2	18.0	15.9	14.1	13.0	110
2"	10.6	9.1	8.0	7.1	6.4	100
3"	7.1	6.1	5.3	4.7	4.2	90
4"	5.3	4.6	4.0	3.5	3.2	85

(Since 11.89 is an approximate number, round off the total number of batts to 238 to make certain there will be enough batts.)

The number of staples required to install the insulation batts can also be figured by referring to Table 46-C. For 15" × 48" batts, 160 staples are needed for installing 100 square feet of insulation.

$$\frac{1130 \text{ (total area to be insulated)}}{100 \text{ (sq. ft. installed per 160 staples)}} = 11.3$$

11.3 x 160 = 1808 staples.

The ceiling area must also be insulated. Figure the area of the ceiling by multiplying the width times the length. Calculate the number of insulating batts needed in the same way as described for the walls, using Table 46-C. If loose fill insulation is specified, refer to Table 46-D.

Labor

The time required to insulate a house is estimated by dividing the total area to be insulated by the number of square feet insulated in one hour.

For example, Table 46-C under the column headed "Labor" indicates that 85 square feet of 15" × 48" insulation batts can be installed each hour. The total amount of time required to install the insulation batts is estimated as follows:

$$\frac{1130 \text{ (total area to be insulated)}}{85 \text{ (sq.ft. insulated per hour)}} = 13.29, \text{ or } 13\frac{1}{3} \text{ hours}$$

1. What is insulation?

2. List several types of commercial insulating materials.

3. List some of the materials used for loose fill insulation.

4. What is a Btu?

5. To reduce heat loss, what areas in a structure should be insulated?

6. When installing flexible insulation, to what should the tabs be fastened?

7. When discussing vapor barriers, what is meant by "enveloping"?

ACTIVITIES

1. Math. A rectangular house with outside dimensions 26' by 44' is to be insulated. For the 8' exterior walls, 4" thick batts 15" by 48" are to be used. If the area of the doors and windows is 15% of the floor area, how many batts will be needed?

2. Social Studies. Prior to the advent of modern insulation, how did homeowners in the 1600s, 1700s, 1800s, and early 1900s keep homes warm in the winter and cooler in the summer? Be specific in describing the materials used and how they were used.

3. Language Arts. In any team effort, organization is important. Proper leadership helps organize a construction project. One way to develop leadership skills is by joining a club. In your school, there probably are many clubs. Each club brings together people with an interest in one activity. There are, for example, technology and vocational education clubs. There are two national organizations of such clubs. These two organizations are the Technology Student Association (TSA) and the Vocational Industrial Clubs of America (VICA). Each seeks to develop an understanding of technology. Write a brief essay on the goals of each of these clubs.

4. Language Arts. The development of leadership skills will help you throughout life. Such skills will be valuable to you in any career you choose. The development of leadership skills will help you improve consumer understanding. It will also help you make good use of your leisure time and recognize high standards of achievement. Taking part in the activities of a club can help you develop leadership skills. Participation in club activities will help you in many ways. It can help you prepare for effective citizenship. This will help prepare you for effective participation in our democratic society. Club membership also will help you learn to conduct a meeting according to the rules of parliamentary procedure. Write a brief essay on the other benefits that might be gained from club membership.

THE SCHOOL-TO-WORK CONNECTION

A number of agencies conduct basic research in energy efficiency. In many cases, an agency will add you to its mailing list.

1. In the reference section of your local public library (and possibly even in your school library) you will find an encyclopedia or directory of organizations. Identify at least five organizations that might have information about energy-efficient construction. Write to each organization and ask to be put on their mailing list. Also ask for their publications list. This list is typically free. Start a file titled "Energy Efficiency." Add everything you gather to that file for future reference.

2. If you have access to the Internet or to a commercial online service, see if you can locate a discussion group or forum concerned with energy efficiency. Report to your class about what you find.

Sound Insulation

Sound insulation was once more important in apartments, motels, and hotels than in private homes. However, the use of household appliances, television, radio, and stereo systems has increased the noise levels in homes. House designs now often include a family room or "active" living room as well as a "quiet" living room. These rooms should be isolated from the remainder of the house. Sound insulation between the bedroom area and the living area is usually needed, as is isolation of the bathrooms and lavatories. Insulation against outdoor sounds is also desirable. Thus sound control has become a vital part of house design and construction.

HOW SOUND TRAVELS

Sound is transmitted by waves. Noises inside a house, such as loud conversation or a barking dog, create sound waves which radiate outward from the source through the air until they strike a wall, floor, or ceiling. These surfaces vibrate as a result of the fluctuating pressure of the sound waves. Because the surface vibrates, it conducts sound to the other side in varying degrees, depending on the construction. Fig. 47-1.

The resistance of a building element, such as a wall, to the passage of airborne sound is rated

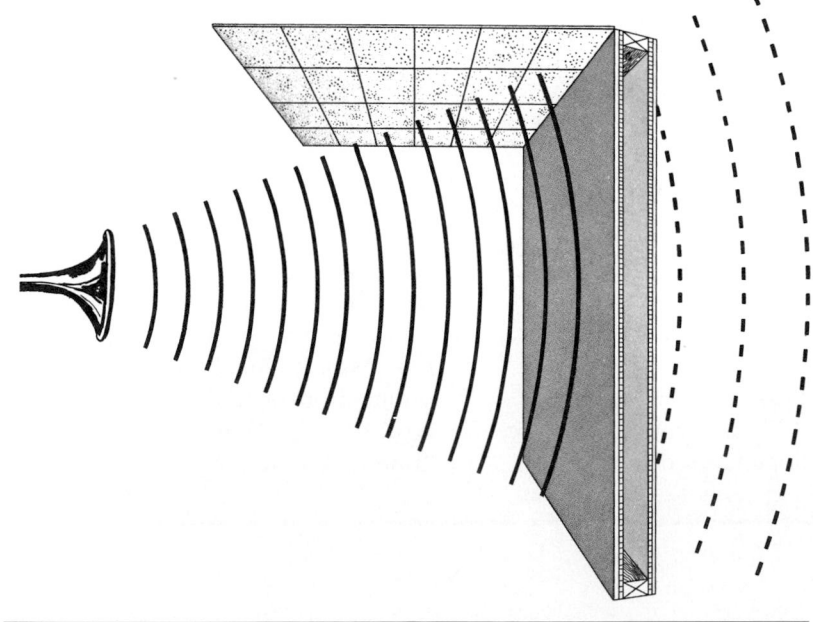

47-1. A wall will conduct sound to the other side in varying degrees, depending on its construction.

SOUND TRANSMISSION CLASS						
25 Normal speech can be understood quite easily	**30** Loud speech can be understood fairly well	**35** Loud speech audible but not intelligible	**42** Loud speech audible as a murmur	**45** Must strain to hear loud speech	**48** Some loud speech barely audible	**50** Loud speech not audible

47-2. *STC numbers have been adopted by acoustical engineers as a measure of the ability of structural assemblies to reduce airborne noise. The higher the number, the more effective the sound barrier.*

by its Sound Transmission Class (STC). The higher the number, the better the sound barrier. The approximate effectiveness of walls with varying STC numbers is shown in Fig. 47-2 and Table 47-A. Most authorities agree that a floor or wall in a multi-occupancy residence should have an STC rating of at least 45, while 50 is considered premium construction. Below 40, privacy and comfort may be impaired because loud speech can be heard as a murmur.

Sound travels readily through the air and also through some materials. When airborne sound strikes a conventional wall, the studs act as sound conductors unless they are separated in some way from the covering material.

Flanking Paths

Faulty construction, such as poorly fitted doors, can allow sound to get around a material without actually going through it. This type of sound transmission follows what is called a "flanking" path. Heating ducts, wiring chases, and plumbing runs can also allow sound to travel freely through the air within wall and ceiling assemblies. In fact, even a hole of 1 square inch in a wall rated at STC 50 can reduce that wall's performance to STC 30. Plumbers, electricians, and others who regularly cut holes in framing should keep this fact in mind as they work.

SOUND INSULATION IN WALL CONSTRUCTION

Thick walls of dense materials such as masonry can stop sound. In a wood-frame house, however, an interior masonry wall results in increased costs and in structural problems created by heavy walls. To economically provide a satisfactory sound-resistant wall has been a problem. At one time, sound-resistant frame construction for the home involved much higher costs because it usually meant double walls or suspended ceilings. However, a relatively simple system has been developed using sound-deadening insulating board along with a gypsum board outer covering. This provides good sound control at only slight additional cost. A number of combinations, providing different STC ratings, are possible with this system.

Table 47-A. *Partition Selector Guide. This table should be used only as a general guide to the partition performance required to meet specific control needs. Note that it does not incorporate the effects of interconnecting ducts, wiring, and plumbing.*

Location	Degree of Privacy	STC Requirement	Example of Wall Construction Needed
Rural (20 decibels background noise level)	High	60 or over	Solid dense masonry min. 12" thick.
	Moderate	50 to 60	3 5/8" metal studs, 2 layers of 5/8" fire-stop each side, 1 1/2" fiberglass insulation in cavity.
	Low	45 to 50	Double solid partition.
Suburban (30 decibels background noise level)	High	55 or over	Triple solid partition.
	Moderate	45 to 55	2" x 4" wood studs, resilient channel one side, 5/8" firestop both sides, 1 1/2" fiberglass insulation in cavity.
	Low	40 to 45	2" x 4" wood studs, resilient channel one side, 5/8" firestop both sides.
City (40 decibels background noise level)	High	45 or over	2 1/2" x 3" gypsum ribs, 2 1/2" steel track, 1/2" sound deadening board both sides, 5/8" firestop each side.
	Moderate	40 to 45	2" x 4" wood studs, 2 layers 5/8" firestop each side.
	Low	35 to 40	2" x 4" wood studs, 2 layers 5/8" firestop one side, 1 layer 5/8" firestop other side.

As Fig. 47-2 showed, a wall should have an STC rating of 45 or more to provide sufficient resistance to airborne sound. Gypsum wallboard or lath and plaster are commonly used for partition walls. A and B, Fig. 47-3. However, an STC rating of 45 cannot be obtained with this construction. An 8" concrete block wall has the minimum rating, but this construction is not always practical in a wood-frame house. C, Fig. 47-3.

In construction of a partition wall, its cost as related to the STC rating should be considered. Good STC ratings can be obtained in a wood-frame wall by using the combination of materials shown in D and E of Fig. 47-3. One-half inch of sound-deadening board nailed to the studs, followed by a lamination of ½" gypsum wallboard, will provide an STC value of 46 at a relatively low cost. Fig. 47-4. A slightly better rating can be

WALL DETAIL	DESCRIPTION	STC RATING
A	½" GYPSUM WALLBOARD	32
	⅝" GYPSUM WALLBOARD	37
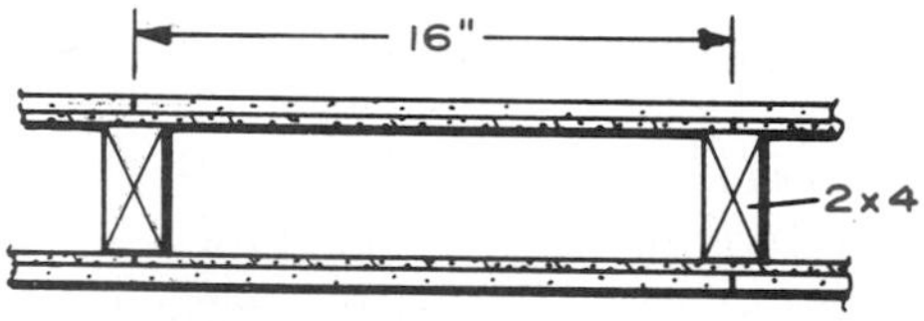 B	⅜" GYPSUM LATH (NAILED) PLUS ½" GYPSUM PLASTER WITH WHITECOAT FINISH (EACH SIDE)	39
 C	8" CONCRETE BLOCK	45
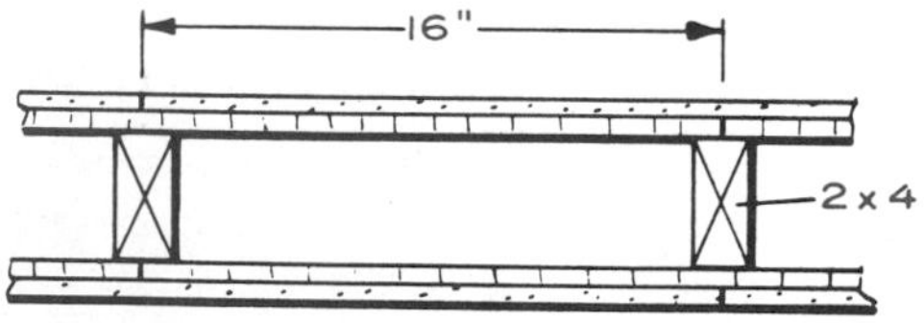 D	½" SOUND DEADENING BOARD (NAILED) ½" GYPSUM WALLBOARD (LAMINATED) (EACH SIDE)	46
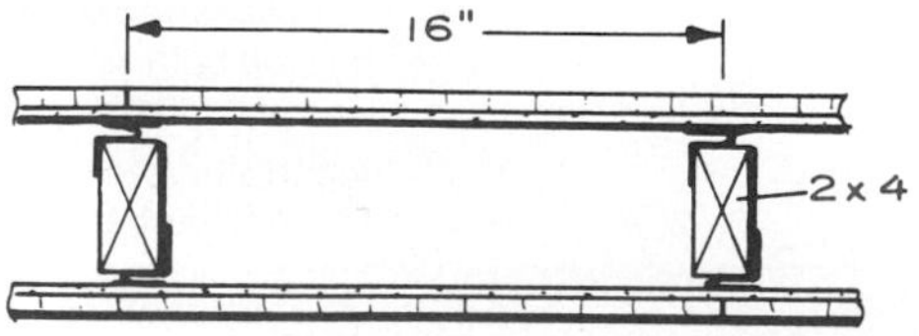 E	RESILIENT CLIPS TO ⅜" GYPSUM BACKER BOARD ½" FIBERBOARD (LAMINATED) (EACH SIDE)	52

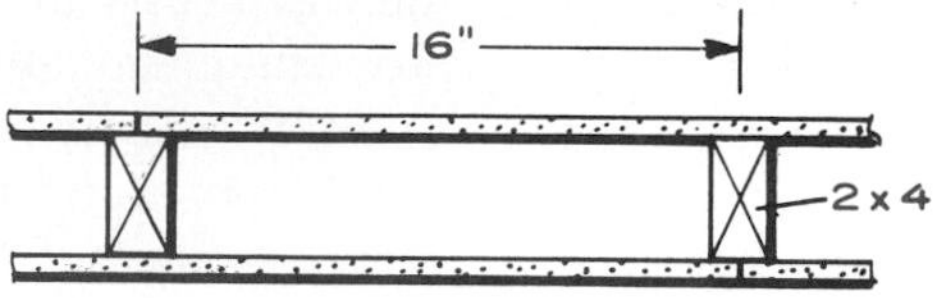

47-3. *Sound insulation of single walls.*

47-4. *Gypsum wallboard installed over a sound-deadening board will help assure quiet living.*

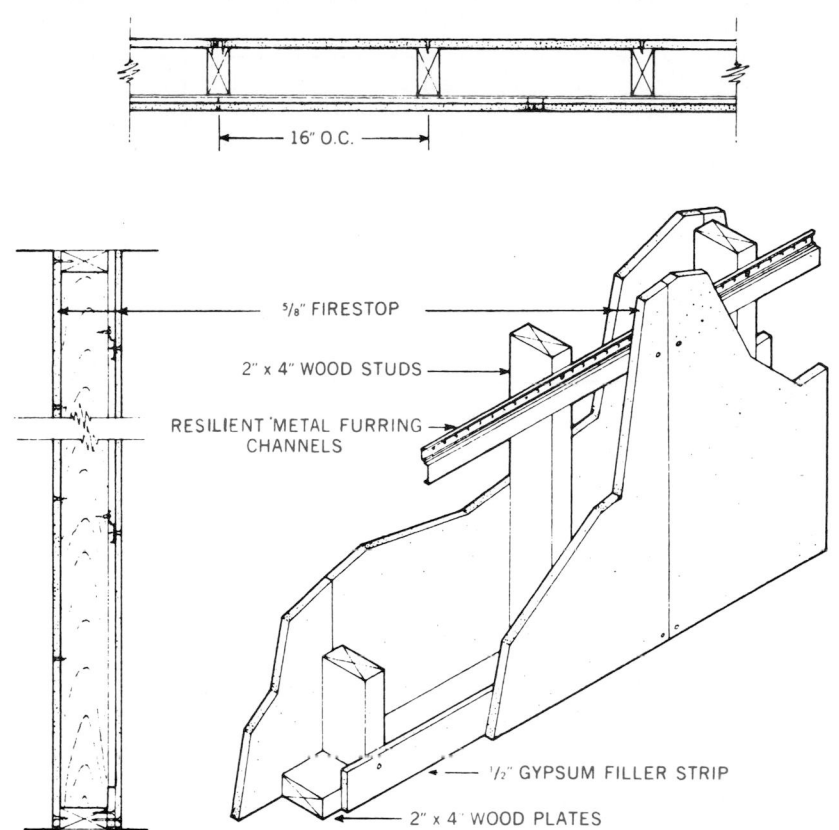

5/8" FIRESTOP

2" x 4" WOOD STUDS

RESILIENT METAL FURRING CHANNELS

16" O.C.

1/2" GYPSUM FILLER STRIP

2" x 4" WOOD PLATES

47-5. *Sound transmission can be reduced by fastening the interior wall covering to resilient metal furring channels.*

obtained by using ⅝" gypsum wallboard rather than ½". A very satisfactory STC rating of 52 can be obtained by using resilient clips to fasten ⅜" gypsum backer boards to the studs, followed by adhesive-laminated ½" fiberboard. E, Fig. 47-3. This method further isolates the wall covering from the framing.

A similar isolation system consists of resilient channels nailed horizontally to 2" × 4" studs spaced 16" on center. The channels are spaced 24" apart vertically, and ⅝" gypsum wallboard is screwed to the channels. An STC rating of 44 is thus obtained at a moderately low cost. Fig. 47-5.

A double wall, which may consist of 2" × 6" or wider plate and staggered 2" × 4" studs, is sometimes constructed for sound control. One-half-inch gypsum wallboard on each side of this wall results in an STC value of 45. A, Fig. 47-6. Two layers of ⅝" gypsum wallboard add little, if any, additional sound-transfer

resistance. B, Fig. 47-6. However, when 1½" blanket insulation is added to double wall construction, the STC rating increases to 49. C, Fig. 47-6. This insulation may be installed as shown or placed between studs on a single wall. A single wall with 3½" of insulation is low in cost and will resist sound transfer much better than an open stud space.

The use of ½" sound-deadening board and a lamination of gypsum wallboard in the double wall will result in an STC rating of 50. D, Fig. 47-6. The addition of blanket insulation to this combination will likely provide an even higher value, perhaps 53 or 54. This system, with single-wall construction, might also be used to insulate exterior walls against street noises.

SOUND INSULATION IN FLOOR-CEILING CONSTRUCTION

Sound insulation between an upper floor and the ceiling of a lower story involves not only resistance to airborne sounds but also to impact noises. Impact noise results when an object strikes or slides along a wall or floor surface. Footsteps, dropped objects, and furniture being moved all cause impact noise. It may also be caused by the vibration of a dishwasher, food disposal apparatus, or other equipment. In all instances, the floor is set into vibration by the impact or contact, and sound is radiated from both sides of the floor.

The impact noise passed through a floor system is summarized by

WALL DETAIL	DESCRIPTION	STC RATING
A 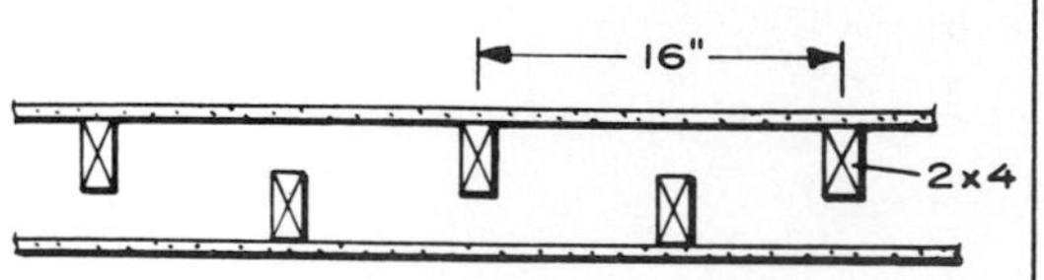	1/2" GYPSUM WALLBOARD	45
B 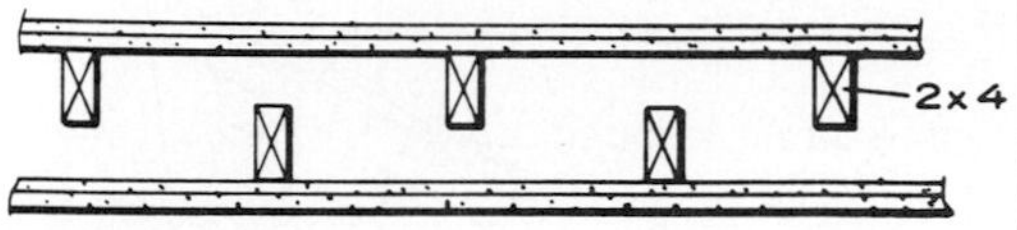	5/8" GYPSUM WALLBOARD (DOUBLE LAYER EACH SIDE)	45
C 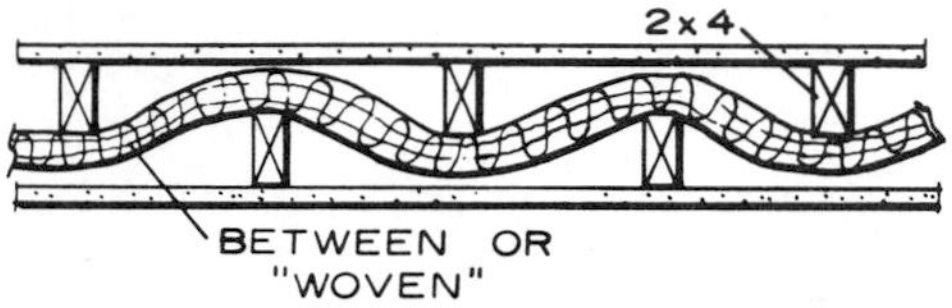	1/2" GYPSUM WALLBOARD 1 1/2" FIBROUS INSULATION	49
D 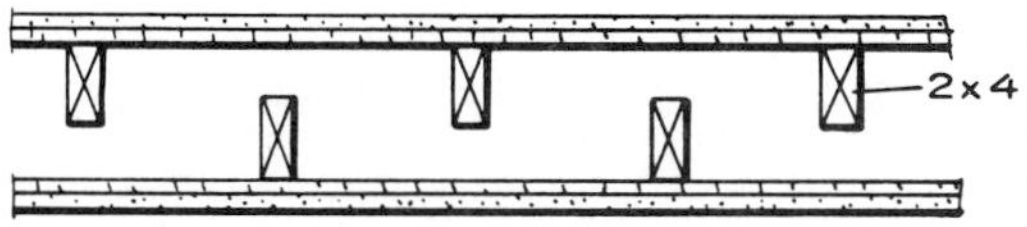	1/2" SOUND DEADENING BOARD (NAILED) 1/2" GYPSUM WALLBOARD (LAMINATED)	50

47-6. *Sound insulation of double walls.*

Impact Noise Ratings (INR). Another type of rating, called the Impact Insulation Class (IIC), is sometimes used instead because IIC figures are easier to determine.

The higher the INR, the better the impact sound reduction. For example, an INR of -5 is better than -10, and +5 is better than 0.

INR performance standards for floors are based on criteria established by the FHA. Those criteria range from -8 to +5, depending on location. Figure 47-7 shows STC and approximate INR (decibel) values for several types of floor construction. A minimum floor assembly with tongued and grooved floor and 3/8" gypsum board ceiling has an STC value of 30 and an approximate INR value of -18. A, Fig. 47-7. This is improved somewhat by the construction shown in part B, and still further by the combination of materials in part C.

The value of isolating the ceiling joists from a gypsum lath and plaster ceiling by means of spring clips is illustrated in Fig. 47-8, part A. An STC rating of 52 and an approximate INR value of -2 result.

Foam rubber padding and carpeting improve both the STC and the INR values. The STC rating increases from 31 to 45 and the approximate INR from -17 to + 5. B and C, Fig. 47-8. The ratings can probably be further improved by using an isolated ceiling finish with spring clips. The use of sound-deadening board and a

DETAIL	DESCRIPTION	ESTIMATED VALUES	
		STC RATING	APPROX. INR
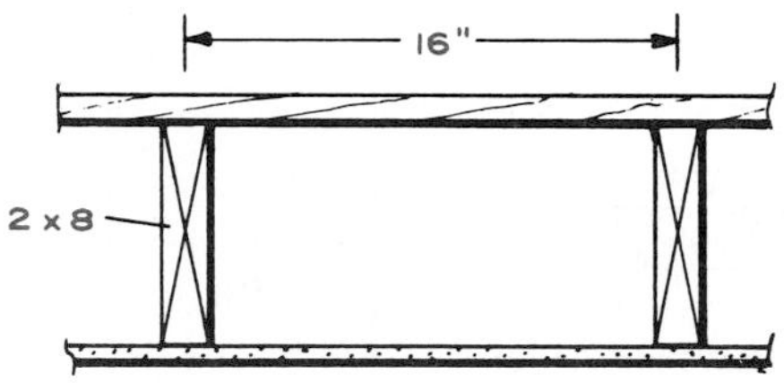 A	FLOOR 7/8" T. & G. FLOORING CEILING 3/8" GYPSUM BOARD	30	-18
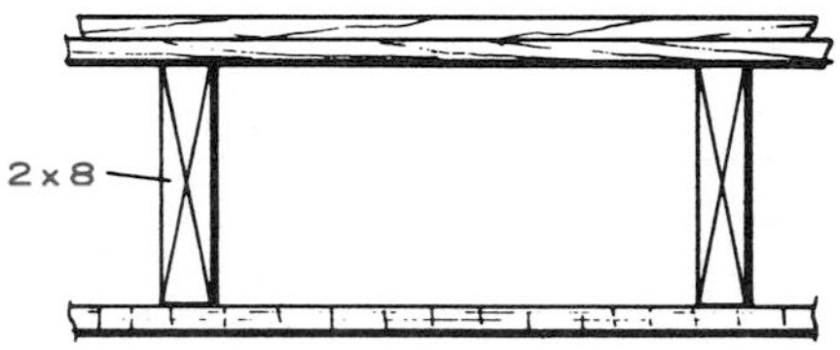 B	FLOOR 3/4" SUBFLOOR 3/4" FINISH FLOOR CEILING 3/4" FIBERBOARD	42	-12
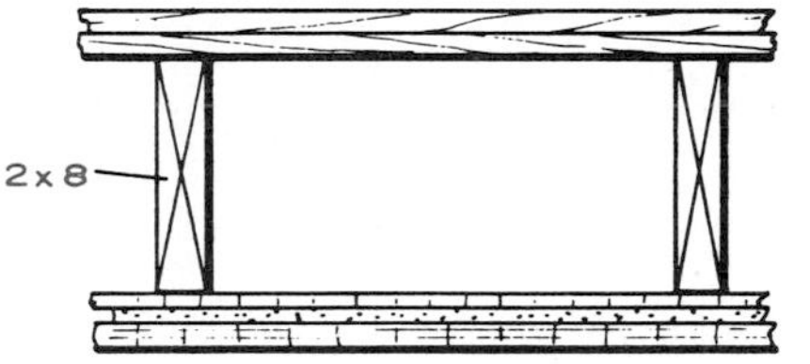 C	FLOOR 3/4" SUBFLOOR 3/4" FINISH FLOOR CEILING 1/2" FIBERBOARD LATH 1/2" GYPSUM PLASTER 3/4" FIBERBOARD	45	-4

47-7. *STC and INR values in floor-ceiling combination using 2" x 8" joists.*

lamination of gypsum board for the ceiling would also improve resistance to sound transfer.

An economical construction similar to (but an improvement over) the one shown in part C of Fig. 47-8 has an STC value of 48 and an approximate INR of + 18. It consists of the following: (1) a pad and carpet over 5/8" tongued and grooved plywood underlayment, (2) 3" fiberglass insulating batts between joists, (3) resilient channels spaced 24" apart across the bottom of the joists, and (4) 5/8" gypsum boards screwed to the bottom of the channels and finished with taped joints.

The use of separate floor joists with staggered ceiling joists below provides reasonable values, but adds a good deal to construction costs. Separate joists with insulation between and a sound-deadening board between subfloor and finish provide an STC rating of 53 and an approximate INR value of -3. Other combinations are illustrated in Fig. 47-9.

A new sound-insulation product was introduced to residential construction relatively recently. When placed beneath a floor surface, sound-resistant matting reduces the transmission of impact sounds. The material can be used beneath hardwood flooring, ceramic tile, and other common finish floors. Because of its open, compression-resistant structure, the material dampens the transmission of sound. Fig. 47-10.

DETAIL	DESCRIPTION	ESTIMATED VALUES	
		STC RATING	APPROX. INR
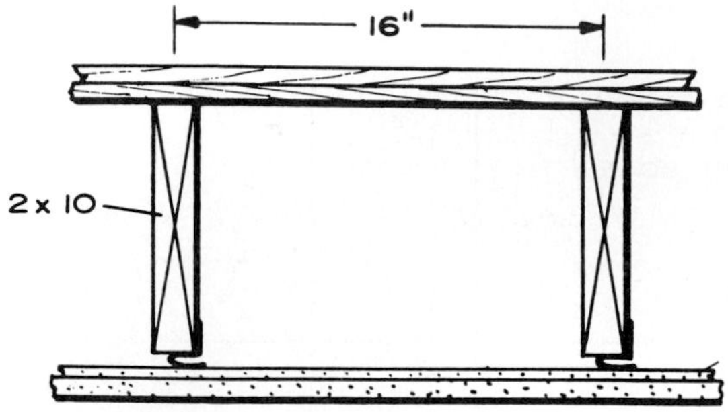 **A**	**FLOOR** 3/4" SUBFLOOR (BUILDING PAPER) 3/4" FINISH FLOOR **CEILING** GYPSUM LATH AND SPRING CLIPS 1/2" GYPSUM PLASTER	52	-2
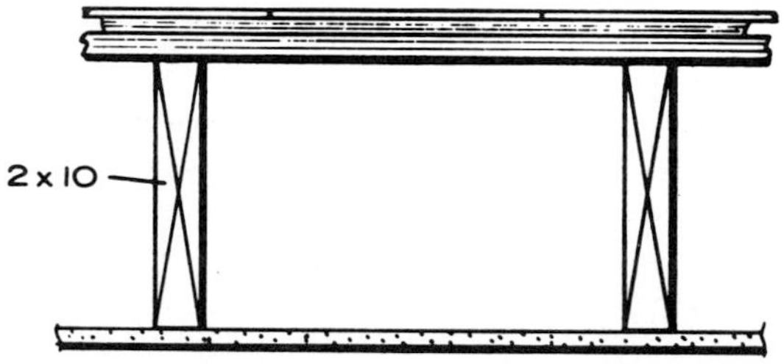 **B**	**FLOOR** 5/8" PLYWOOD SUBFLOOR 1/2" PLYWOOD UNDERLAYMENT 1/8" VINYL-ASBESTOS TILE **CEILING** 1/2" GYPSUM WALLBOARD	31	-17
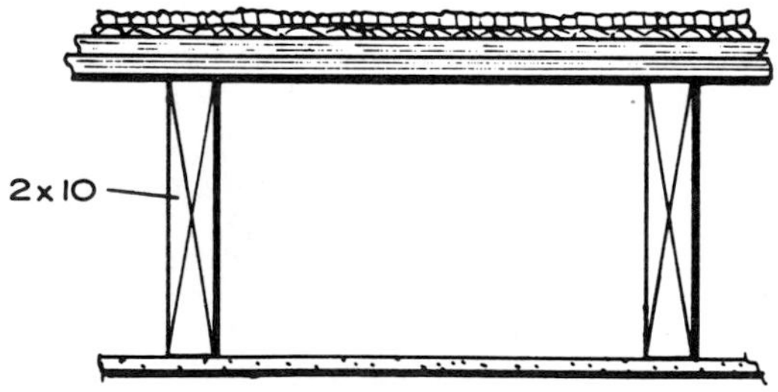 **C**	**FLOOR** 5/8" PLYWOOD SUBFLOOR 1/2" PLYWOOD UNDERLAYMENT FOAM RUBBER PAD 3/8" NYLON CARPET **CEILING** 1/2" GYPSUM WALLBOARD	45	+5

47-8. STC and INR values in floor-ceiling combinations using 2" x 10" joists.

Floor on sleepers

Weight lbs./sq. ft.	Floor	STC	INR	Test No.
10.9	.075" sheet vinyl on ⅝" T&G plywood underlayment	52	-2	L-224-5&6
11.7	44 oz. Carpet on 40 oz. hair pad on ⅝" T&G Plywood underlayment	52	+27	L-224-7&8
13.0	25/32" wood strip flooring nailed sleepers	53	0	L-224-9&10

Note: Flooring is fastened to sleepers on ½" insulation board over a ½" plywood subfloor on wood joists with insulation between. ⅝" gypsum board ceiling with taped joints is screwed to resilient channels.

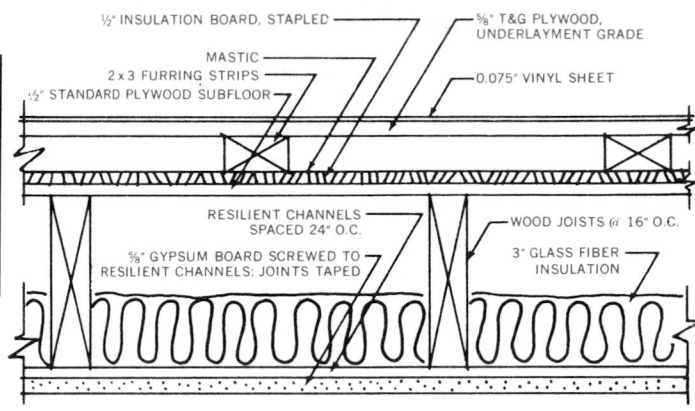

Separate ceiling joists

Weight lbs./sq. ft.	Floor	STC	INR	Test No.
11.0	25/32" hardwood strip flooring on ½" plywood subfloor	53	-6	L-224-12&13
10.7	44 oz. Carpet on 40 oz. hair pad on 1⅛" plywood subfloor (2-4-1 T&G)	51	+29	L-224-14&15

Note: Conventional wood joist floor system with finish floor applied directly on plywood. Separate 2 × 4 ceiling joists, with insulation, and ⅝" gypsum board ceiling with taped joints nailed directly to joists.

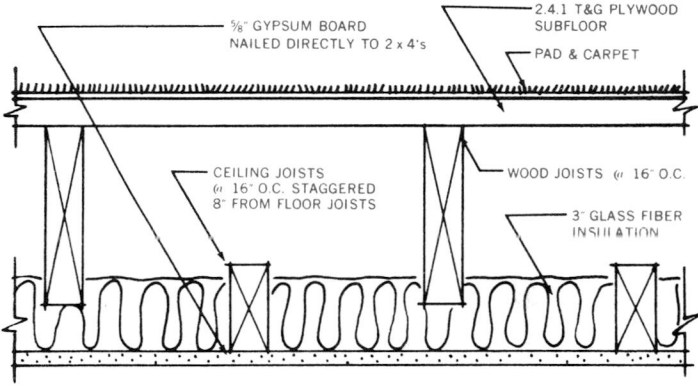

47-9. *Two of the sound-resistant floor-ceiling combinations that can be obtained with plywood construction.*

47-10. *The open, resilient structure of sound-resistant matting dampens sound transmission through floors.*

SOUND ABSORPTION

Design of the "quiet" house can include another system of sound insulation, namely, sound absorption. Sound-absorbing materials do not necessarily have resistance to airborne sounds, but they can minimize the amount of noise by stopping the reflection of sound back into a room. Perhaps the most commonly used sound-absorbing material is acoustic tile or panels. Fig. 47-11. Numerous tiny sound traps on the surfaces may consist of tiny drilled or punched holes, fissured surfaces, or a combination of both. Wood fiber or similar materials are used in the manufacture of the tile and panels, which are usually processed to provide some fire resistance.

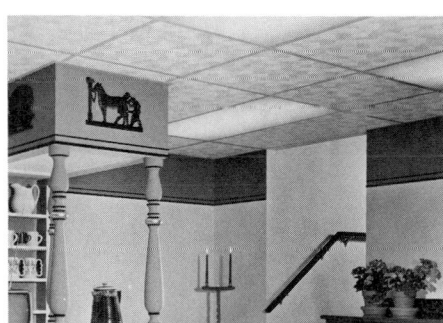

47-11. *A suspended-ceiling system with acoustical panel inserts will serve to absorb sound.*

Acoustic tile and panels are most often used in the ceiling and other areas, such as above a wall wainscoting, where they are not subject to excessive mechanical damage. Paint or other finishes which fill or cover the tiny holes or fissures for trapping sound will greatly reduce its efficiency.

1. How does sound travel?

2. What does STC stand for?

3. What do the higher numbers of STC indicate?

4. Why does an 8" concrete block wall have a lower STC rating compared to traditional methods of wood-frame wall construction?

5. What is impact noise?

6. What does INR stand for?

7. Which is considered better, an INR of -5 or an INR of +5?

8. What is the most commonly used sound-absorbing material in house construction?

ACTIVITIES

1. Science. A group of four is needed for the following activity. The goal is to estimate STC numbers in several settings. Refer to Table 47-A.

a. As a group, select ten settings to test. Include a standard frame wall in a home, a cement block wall, a wall between a living room and a bedroom, and a floor between a basement and a first floor.

b. In teams of two, assign STC numbers independently. Stand, for example, on the opposite side of a wall and talk in a normal or loud voice. Have the team member on the other side of the wall assign an STC number. Then, ask your team member to speak, while you assign the STC number.

c. Compare your ratings with those of the other team in your group. If there is a large difference (plus or minus 10 STC numbers), repeat the test together to determine why.

2. Language Arts. Walk around your home or apartment. Sit in each room and listen. Which room in your home or apartment is the most quiet? Why? How is this room insulated? Which room seems to be the noisiest? Why? Write down your observations in a descriptive paragraph.

3. Language Arts. Taking part in group activities will also help you develop your social skills. These are the skills that help you get along with others. In any career you choose, it will be important for you to be able to speak clearly and write clearly and precisely. In a short essay, discuss the need for teamwork and cooperation on a work project. Discuss also the problems that can result from unclear communication.

4. Language Arts. In your work, you may have set some personal goals for yourself. For example, you may have set for yourself a goal of accomplishing so much work in a single class session. Proper management can help you reach personal goals on the job. In a brief essay, list some ways in which proper management of your time and resources can assist you in reaching personal goals.

THE SCHOOL-TO-WORK CONNECTION

Some houses have a design that does not allow for a basement, so mechanical equipment has to be located near living areas. When the equipment operates, it may make sounds that are audible in adjacent rooms. Enclosing mechanical equipment in sound-resistant construction is one way to keep noise to a minimum. For safety reasons, however, building codes are very strict about the way this can be done.

1. As an architect, you have been hired to design a house for a steeply sloping lot. You have determined that a split-level house without a basement will be the most efficient design for this situation. Your clients decide that they want the master bedroom on the lower level. They also say that they don't want to hear noise from the furnace, which must also be on that level. You promise to put the furnace in a room by itself. Consult your local building codes. List any restrictions regarding this type of room.

Plaster and Drywall

Before plaster and drywall are applied, insulation should be in place. Wiring, heating ducts, and other utilities should be roughed in.

Plaster, applied over some type of lath, is a traditional wall and ceiling finish. When applied properly, it leaves a smooth, dense surface. It can be given a wide variety of textures, or it can serve as a base for paneling or wallpaper. Because it is applied as a wet material, it must dry before other work can continue. This can be inconvenient when the pace of construction is quick. However, many builders and homeowners feel the inconvenience is worthwhile.

Drywall (also known as gypsum wallboard or gypsum board) has become the most widespread interior wall and ceiling finish in residential construction. It can be applied quickly and efficiently, and does not require drying time before other work can progress. As with plaster, drywall is versatile enough to serve as a substrate for other finish materials or to stand alone with a painted finish.

However, when drywall is used as a wall finish, the framing lumber must have a low moisture content to prevent nail pops. These result when framing members dry out, causing the nail head to form small humps on the surface of the drywall. It is also very important when applying single-layer drywall finish that the studs be in alignment. Otherwise, the wall may have a wavy, uneven appearance. Since there are advantages to both plaster and drywall finishes, all factors should be considered along with the initial cost and the future maintenance that may be required.

PLASTER

A plaster finish requires a base upon which the plaster is applied. This base, or *lath*, is fastened to the framing members. It must have bonding qualities so that plaster adheres, or is keyed, to it. The most commonly used types of lath are the following:

➤ Gypsum.
➤ Metal.

Wood lath was once used as a base for plaster. Slender strips of split or sawn wood were nailed over the studs to completely cover the wall cavities. Plaster was then applied over the lath. This technique is not much used today, but remodelers frequently encounter wood lath under plaster as they cut into old walls.

Gypsum Lath

One of the most common types of plaster base used on sidewalls and ceilings is gypsum lath. This lath has paper faces with a gypsum filler. It comes in 16" × 48" boards and is applied horizontally across the framing members. Fig. 48-1. For stud or joist spacing of 16" on center, a ⅜" thickness is used. For

48-1. *Installing gypsum board lath.*

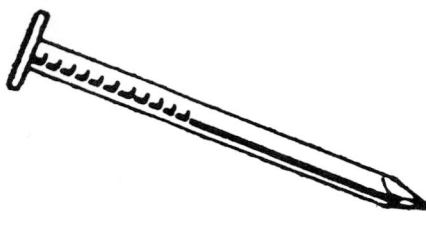

48-2. *A gypsum-lathing nail.*

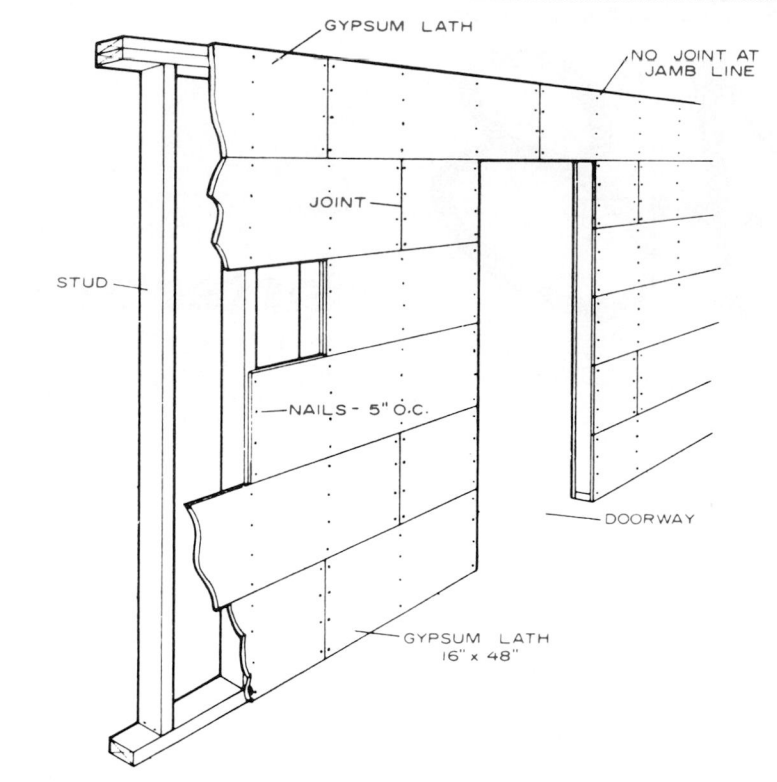

48-3. *Gypsum board lath is nailed horizontally. Note that the joints are broken and that there is no joint at the jamb line in the doorway.*

24" spacing, the thickness should be ½".

This material can be obtained with a foil back that serves as a vapor barrier. If the foil faces an air space, it also has reflective insulating value. Gypsum lath may also be obtained with perforations, which improve the bond and increase the time the plaster remains intact when exposed to fire. The building codes in some cities require these perforations. A waterproof facing is provided on one type of gypsum board for use as a ceramic tile base when the tile is applied with an adhesive.

Installing Gypsum Lath.
Vertical joints should be made over the center of studs or joists and nailed with 12- or 13-gauge gypsum-lathing nails 1½" long with ⅜" flat heads. Fig. 48-2. The nails should be spaced 5" on center, or

four nails for the 16" height, and used at each stud or joist crossing. Some manufacturers specify ring-shank nails with a slightly greater spacing. Joints over heads of openings should not occur at the jamb lines. Fig. 48-3. Gypsum lath may also be used in constructions where metal studs are used for framing. The lath is secured to the studs by the use of special clips or tapping screws. Fig. 48-4.

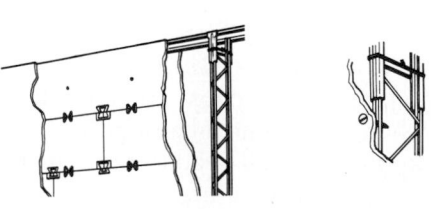

48-4. *Gypsum lath installed on metal studs with special clips and tapping screws.*

Metal Lath

Another type of plaster base is made of sheet metal. The metal is slit and expanded in various forms, such as diamond mesh, flat ribbed, and wire lath, to create innumerable openings for the keying of plaster. Fig. 48-5. Metal lath is usually 27" × 96" in size and galvanized or painted to resist rusting. Metal lath is usually

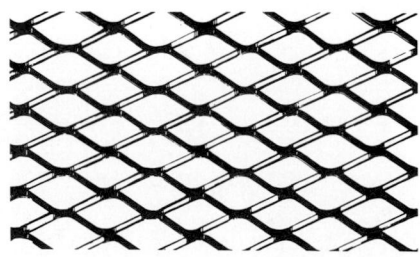

48-5. *Diamond mesh metal lath.*

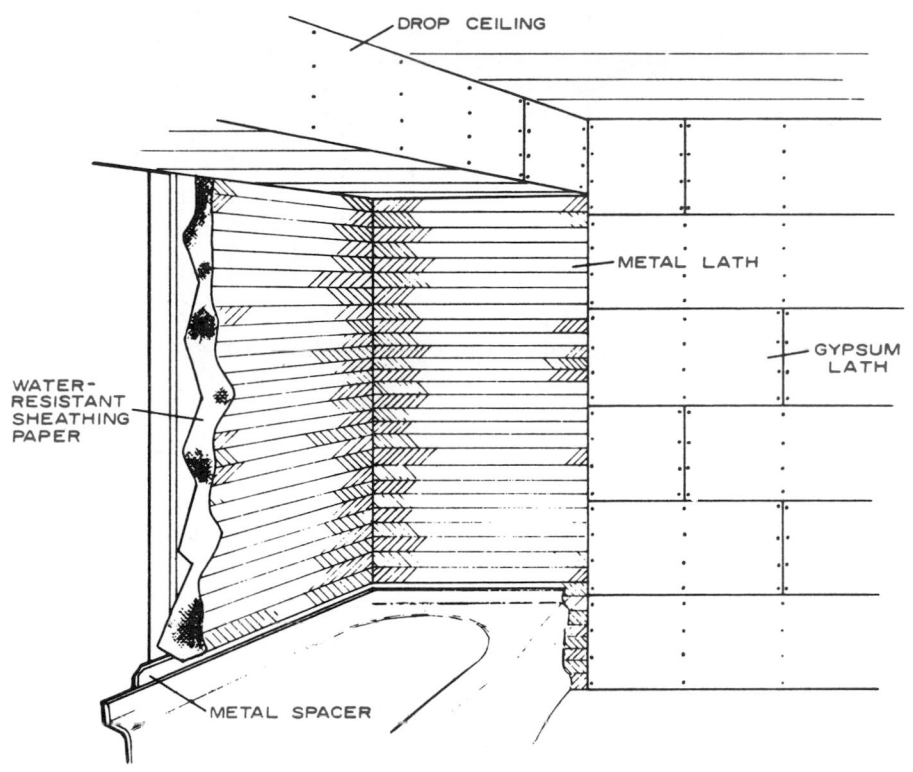

48-6. Metal lath used as a plaster base around a tub recess.

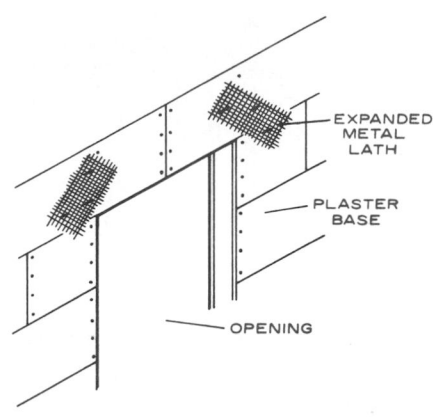

48-8. Expanded metal lath is used to help minimize plaster cracks.

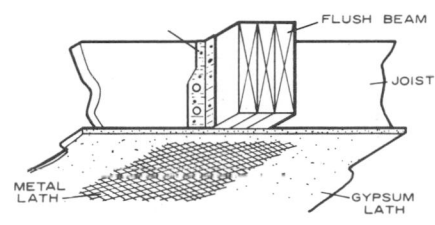

48-9. Metal lath used under a flush ceiling beam.

installed on studs or joists spaced 16" on center. The minimum weights to be installed on studs or joists spaced 16" on center are as follows:

➤ For walls—2.5 lbs. per sq. yd.

➤ For ceilings—3.4 lbs. per sq. yd. (if rib metal lath is used—2.75 lbs. per sq. yd.)

Metal lath is often used as a plaster base around tub recesses and other bath and kitchen areas. Fig. 48-6. It is also used when ceramic tile is applied over a plaster base. For these uses, the metal lath must be backed with water-resistant sheathing paper placed over the framing.

Installing Metal Lath. Metal lath is applied horizontally over the waterproof backing with side and end joints lapped. It is nailed with No. 11 or No. 12 roofing nails long enough to provide about 1½"

48-7. A No. 11 or No. 12 roofing nail is used to apply metal lath.

penetration into the framing member or blocking. Fig. 48-7.

Plaster Reinforcing

Because some drying usually takes place in wood framing members after a house is completed, some shrinkage can be expected. This in turn may cause plaster cracks to develop around openings and in corners. To minimize this cracking, expanded metal lath is used in certain key positions over the plaster base as reinforcement. Strips of expanded metal lath about 10" × 20" should

be placed diagonally across the upper corners of all window and door openings and tacked in place. Fig. 48-8.

Metal lath should also be installed under flush ceiling beams to prevent plaster cracks. Fig. 48-9. On wood drop beams extending below the ceiling line, the metal lath is applied with self-furring nails to provide space for keying of the plaster.

Corner beads of expanded metal lath or perforated metal should be installed on all exterior corners. They should be applied plumb and level. The bead acts as a leveling edge when walls are plastered and reinforces the corner against damage, such as from moving furniture. Fig. 48-10.

Inside corners at the intersection of walls and ceilings should also be reinforced. A cornerite of metal lath or wire fabric is tacked lightly

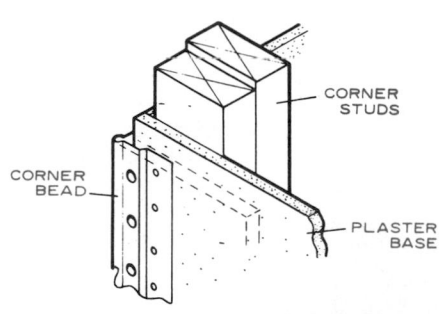

48-10. _A corner bead is installed at outside corners to serve as a leveling edge when the plaster is applied._

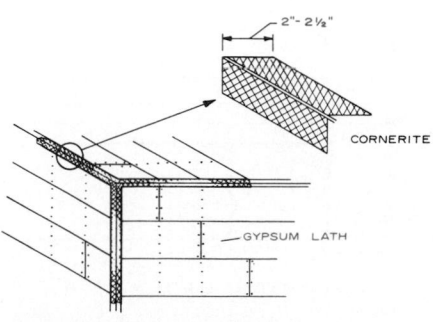

48-11. _A cornerite is installed at inside corners for reinforcement and to minimize plaster cracks._

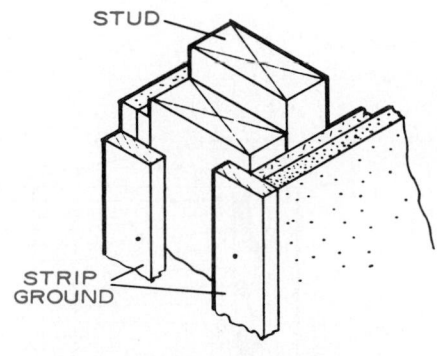

48-13. _Narrow strip grounds are sometimes used around interior openings._

in place in these areas. Cornerites provide a key width of 2" to 2½" at each side for plaster. Fig. 48-11.

Plaster Grounds

Plaster grounds are strips of wood used as guides or strike-off edges when plastering. They are located around window and door openings and at the base of the walls. Grounds around interior door openings are often full-width pieces nailed to the door sides over the studs and to the underside of the header. They are 5" in width, which coincides with standard jamb widths for interior walls with a plaster finish. Fig. 48-12. Narrow strip grounds might also be used around these interior openings. Fig. 48-13. These grounds are removed after plaster has dried.

The frames for window and exterior door openings are normally in place before plaster is applied. Thus the inside edges of the side and head jambs serve as grounds. The edge of the window sill may also be used as a ground, or a narrow ground strip ⅞" thick and 1" wide may be nailed to the edge of the 2" × 4" sill. The ⅞" × 1" grounds might also be used around window and door openings. Fig. 48-14. These are normally left in place and are covered by the casing.

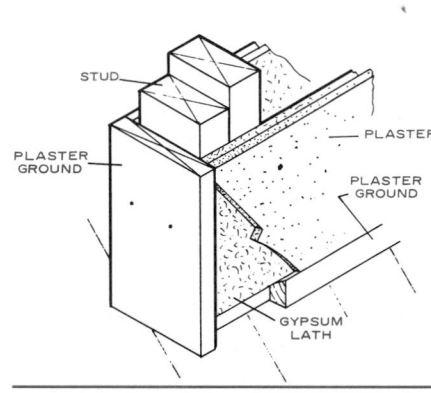

48-12. _A one-piece plaster ground whose width is equal to the finished wall thickness is applied to the trimmer studs and header. Do not drive the nails home. Nails will be pulled and the grounds removed after the plaster is dry._

A similar narrow ground, or screed, is used at the bottom of a wall for controlling the thickness of the plaster and providing an even surface for the baseboard and molding. Fig. 48-12. These strips are also left in place after the plaster has been applied.

Plaster Materials and Methods of Application

Plaster for interior finishing is made from combinations of sand, lime or prepared plaster, and water. Waterproof finishes for walls are

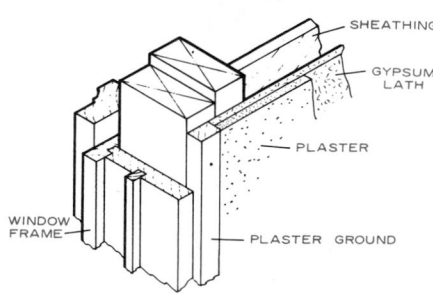

48-14. _When narrow ⅞" x 1" plaster grounds are used around a window or door opening, they remain in place and are eventually covered by the casing._

available and should be used in bathrooms, especially in shower and tub recesses when tile is not used, and sometimes on the kitchen wainscot.

Plaster should be applied in three-coat or in two-coat double-up work. The minimum thickness over ⅜" gypsum or insulating lath should be about ⅜".

Three-coat work is used on metal lath and is usually at least ¾" thick. The first plaster coat over metal lath is called the scratch coat. It is scratched, after a slight set has occurred, to insure a good bond for the second coat. The second coat is called the brown or leveling coat, and leveling is done during its application. The third coat is the finish coat. Fig. 48-15.

Double-up work, combining the scratch and brown coat, is used on

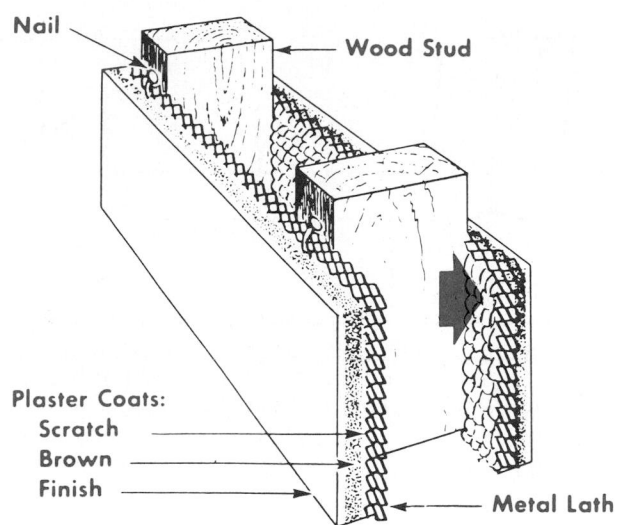

Nail — Wood Stud

Plaster Coats:
Scratch
Brown
Finish

Metal Lath

48-15. *A cross-section of plaster on metal lath showing the buildup of the various coats. Notice how the plaster is keyed to the metal lath in the area indicated by the arrow.*

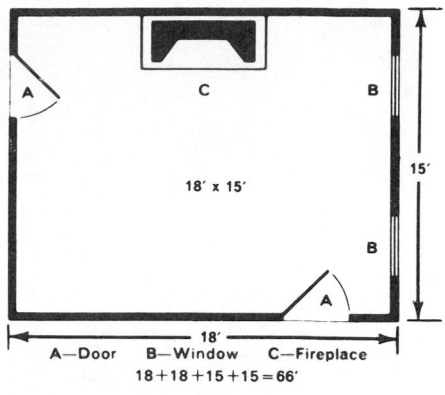

18' x 15'

A—Door   B—Window   C—Fireplace
18+18+15+15 = 66'

48-16. *Sample room for estimating purposes.*

gypsum or insulating lath. Leveling and plumbing of the walls and ceilings are done during application.

The final or finish coats are of two general types: the sand-float and the putty finish. In the sand-float finish, lime is mixed with sand, which results in a textured finish. The texture depends on the coarseness of the sand. Putty finish, used without sand, is smooth. This type is common in kitchens and bathrooms where a gloss paint or enamel finish is used, and in other rooms where a smooth finish is desired. Because of its durability, keene's cement is often used as a finish plaster in bathrooms.

Plastering should not be done in freezing weather without a source of constant heat. In normal construction, the heating unit is in place before plastering is started.

Insulating plaster, consisting of a vermiculite, perlite, or other aggregate with the plaster mix, may also be used for the finish coat.

Estimating Lath and Plaster

Gypsum lath is packaged in bundles of eight 24" × 48" pieces. A standard lath bundle therefore contains 64 square feet. To determine the number of bundles required, divide 64 into the total area to be covered. For example, suppose that the wall and ceiling area of the room in Fig. 48-16 is to be finished with lath and plaster. The total wall and ceiling area equals 686 square feet (416 + 270 = 686). Divide the number of square feet to be covered by the number of square feet in a bundle of gypsum lath (64) for a total of 10.7, or 11 bundles of gypsum lath.

A plasterer calculates the cost of a job by the number of square yards to be covered. Convert the square feet in the room to square yards by dividing by 9 (1 square yard equals 9 square feet). In our example, 686 ÷ 9 equals approximately 76 square yards.

Estimating Adhesive and Nails

To estimate the amount of nails required for installing the gypsum lath in the previous example, figure that five pounds are required to install 100 square feet of rock lath. Since approximately 700 square feet (686 actual square feet) of rock lath are to be installed, 35 pounds of nails are required.

DRYWALL

Drywall is so called because it requires little if any water for application. It can be used wherever excessive moisture is not a problem. Special moisture-resistant drywall, sometimes called M-R board, should be used in bathrooms. Fire-resistant drywall is also available. It should be used in garages and wherever a fire-rated wall is required. In addition to these kinds of drywall, another drywall product is available. It is made by mixing gypsum with wood fiber recycled from wastepaper. The fibers strengthen the gypsum core and improve nail-holding. As with the other kinds of drywall, the gypsum is sandwiched between paper faces. Fig. 48-17.

48-17. *Drywall being applied. The use of an electric "screw gun" speeds application, and screws hold better than nails.*

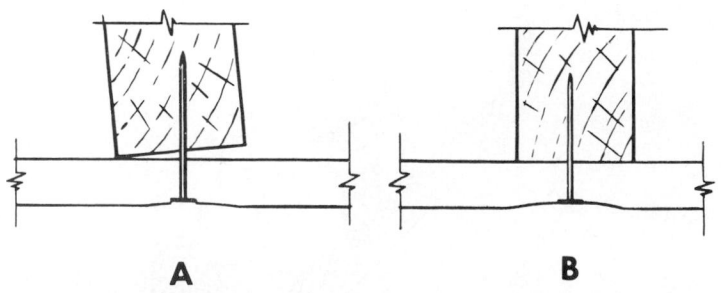

48-18. *A. A framing member has not been properly squared with the plate. This increases the possibility of puncturing the gypsum board paper with the nailhead. There is also the danger of a reverse twisting of the stud as it dries out, in which case the board will be loosely nailed and a "pop" will occur. B. The twisted stud has been squared before the application of the wallboard.*

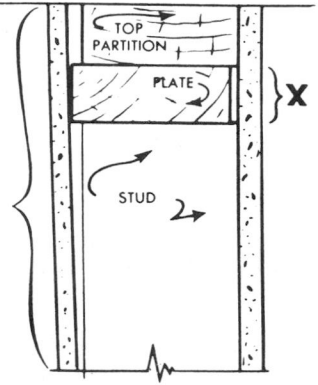

48-19a. *Improperly aligned studs, joists, or headers will result in the nailheads puncturing the paper or cracking the board.*

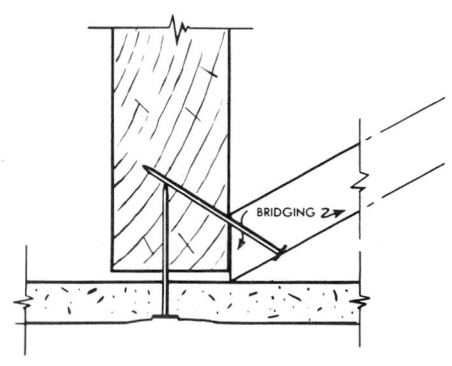

48-19b. *Protrusions, such as the bridging shown here, will puncture the face paper of wallboard. The bridging, which projects beyond the edge of the joists, also prevents the back of the board from being brought into contact with the nailing surface.*

When sheet material such as drywall is used, the studs and ceiling joists must be in alignment to provide a smooth, even surface. Figs. 48-18 and 48-19. If ceiling joists are uneven, a "strongback" may be used to align the joists. Fig. 48-20.

Drywall is a sheet material made up of gypsum filler faced with paper. These sheets are normally 4' wide and 8' long, but may be obtained in lengths up to 16'. The edges along the length are tapered and, on some types, the ends are tapered also. Tapering allows for a filled and taped joint.

Some drywall has a foil back which serves as a vapor barrier on exterior walls. Prefinished drywall is also available for single-layer application in new construction. A thickness of ½" is recommended. For two-ply laminated applications, two ⅜" thick sheets are used. The

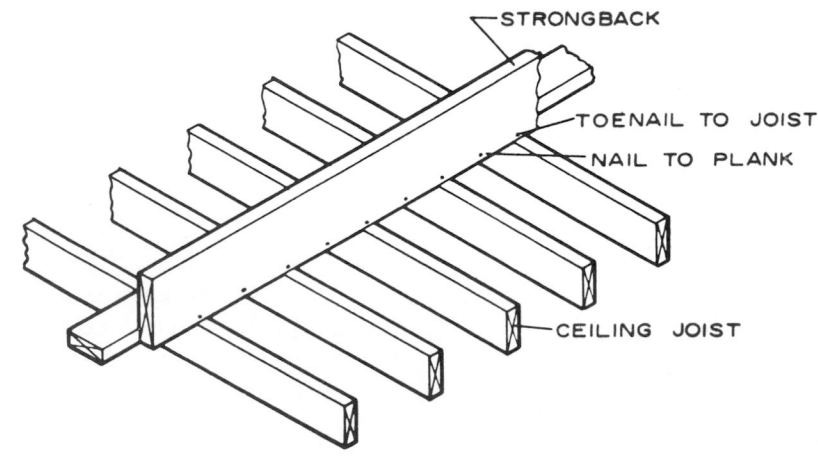

48-20. *A strongback used to align the joists.*

Table 48-A. *Maximum Framing Spacing Recommended for Various Thicknesses of Drywall.*

Installation long direction of sheet	Minimum thickness	Maximum spacing of supports (on center) Walls	Ceilings
Parallel to framing members	3/8"	16"	—
	1/2"	24"	16"
	5/8"	24"	16"
	3/8"	16"	16"
Right angles to framing members	1/2"	24"	24"
	5/8"	24"	24"

maximum spacing of framing members for various thicknesses of drywall is shown in Table 48-A.

Installing Drywall on Walls

Drywall may be applied with nails, screws, or adhesive. Fig. 48-21. The nails must have flat thin heads for flush driving without damage to the surface of the board. Fig. 48-22. Drywall ½" thick should be applied with a 5d nail (1⅝" long). For ⅜" thick material, use a 4d nail (1⅜" long). Table 48-B. When ring shank nails are used, a nail about ⅛" shorter will provide adequate holding power. Special screws will help prevent a bulging surface, sometimes referred to as a "nail pop," caused by the drying out of the framing members.

Nail pops are greatly reduced if the moisture content of the framing members is less than 15% when the drywall is applied. When framing members have a high moisture content, it is good practice to let them approach

Table 48-B. *Attaching Gypsum Wallboard*

NAIL ATTACHMENT: Nails for the attachment of single layer 3/8, 1/2 and 5/8-inch gypsum board comply with the "Performance Standards for Nails for Application of Gypsum Wallboard," as adopted and published by the Gypsum Association. Other nails may be used provided they have immediate and delayed holding power with penetration into wood frame not exceeding 7/8-inch; tear-through resistance and dimpling characteristics; and meet the dimensional requirements of nails so described under this performance standard.

Gypsum Board Product	Type Frame	Application Condition
1/2", 3/8" and 1/4" Wallboard	Wood	Direct to framing
1/2" and 3/8" Gypsum Backing Board	Wood	Direct to framing
5/8" Gypsum Wallboard	Wood	Direct to framing
3/8" and 1/4" Gypsum Wallboard	Wood	Over existing surfaces
5/8" Gypsum Wallboard with special core for increased fire resistance	Wood	Direct to wood frame
1/2" Gypsum Wallboard with special core for increased fire resistance	Wood	Direct to framing
5/8" Gypsum Wallboard	Steel	Direct to framing
5/8" Gypsum Backing Board with special core for increased fire resistance	Nailing Channel	Direct to framing
Woodgrained Gypsum Wallboard	Wood	Direct to framing/Over existing surfaces
Vinyl-coated Woodgrained	Wood	Direct to framing/Over existing surfaces
Gypsum Wallboard	Wood	Direct to framing/Over existing surfaces
Vinyl-Coated Gypsum Wallboard	Wood	Direct to framing

SCREW ATTACHMENT: Designed to provide positive mechanical attachment of single layer gypsum wallboard.

Gypsum Board Product	Type Frame	Application Condition
5/8", 1/2" and 3/8" Gypsum Wallboard/ 1/2" and 3/8" Gypsum Backing Board	Wood	Direct to framing
5/8", 1/2" and 3/8" Gypsum Wallboard/ 1/2" and 3/8" Gypsum Backing Board	Metal Stud and/or Drywall Furring Channel	Direct to framing
5/8", 1/2" and 3/8" Gypsum Wallboard	Metal Stud and/or Drywall Furring Channel	Permanent or temporary face layer attachment with double wall installation
5/8" Gypsum Wallboard	Metal Stud and/or Drywall Furring Channel	Direct to framing

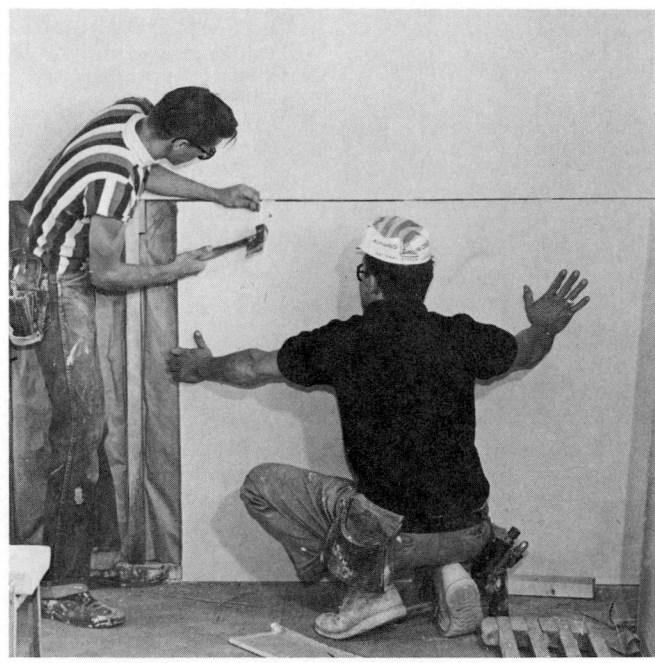

48-21a. *Applying gypsum wallboard with nails.*

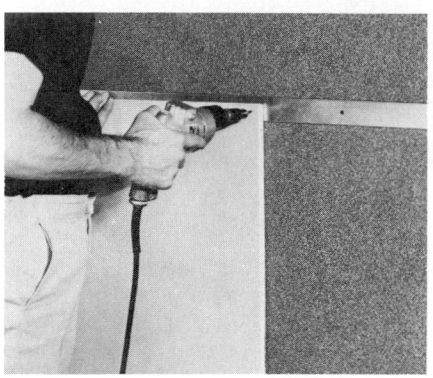

48-21b. *Applying drywall with screws.*

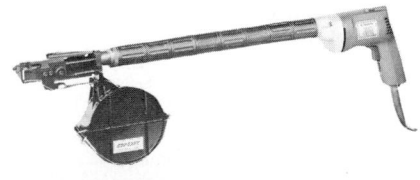

48-21c. *This electric drill has been fitted with an extension drive and a self-feeding screw attachment. It can be used to apply screws to drywall ceilings without requiring scaffolding.*

48-21d. *Applying drywall with an adhesive.*

moisture equilibrium before application of the drywall.

Nails should be spaced 6" to 8" on the sidewalls and 5" to 7" on the ceiling, with a minimum edge distance of ⅜". Nail spacing is the same for horizontal and vertical application. Fig. 48-23.

For studs or joists 16" on center, screws should be spaced not more than 12" apart on ceilings and 16"

apart on sidewalls. For studs 24" on center, screws must not be spaced further than 12" apart.

Horizontal application is best adapted to rooms in which full-length sheets can be applied because this reduces the number of vertical joints. Any joints necessary should be made at windows or doors. When this is not possible, the end joints should be staggered and centered on the framing members.

Horizontal nailing blocks between studs are not normally required when the studs are 16" on center and the drywall is ⅜" or thicker. However, if the spacing is greater or additional support at the joint is required, nailing blocks may be used. Fig. 48-23B.

In single-layer application, the 4' wide gypsum sheets are installed vertically or horizontally on the walls after the ceiling has been covered. When the sheets are applied vertically, they cover three stud spaces if the studs are spaced 16" on center and two if the studs are spaced 24" on center. The edges of the drywall should be centered on studs and should make a very light contact with each other.

The laminated, two-ply method of gypsum application is begun by applying an undercourse of ⅜" material vertically. To reduce sound transmission between rooms, sound-deadening panels are sometimes used as an undercourse. Fig. 48-24. The finish ⅜" sheet is usually in room-size lengths. It is applied horizontally with an adhesive. Be certain to follow the manufacturer's recommendations when applying the adhesive. Nails used in the application of the finish drywall should be driven with the head below the surface. The domed head of the hammer will form a small dimple in the drywall. Do not use a nail set. Care should be taken to avoid breaking the paper face of the drywall when nailing.

FASTENER	SPACING	QUANTITY REQUIRED
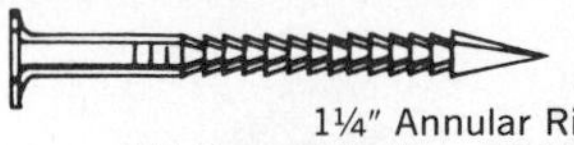 1¼" Annular Ring Nail—12½ gauge; ¼" dia. head with a slight taper to a small fillet at shank; bright finish; medium diamond point.	7" c. to c. on ceilings—8" c. to c. on walls	5¼ lbs./1000 sq. ft. approx. 325 nails/lb.
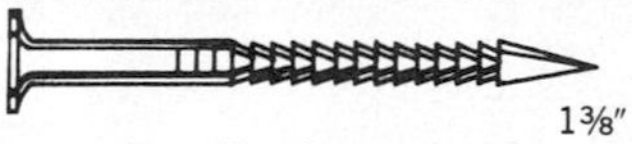 1⅜" Annular Ring Nail (Specification same as above except for length)	7" c. to c. on ceilings—8" c. to c. on walls	5¼ lbs./sq. ft., approx. 321 nails/lb.
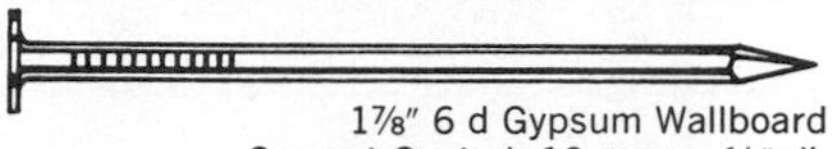 1⅞" 6 d Gypsum Wallboard Nail— Cement Coated, 13 gauge, ¼" dia. head	7" c. to c. on ceilings—8" c. to c. on walls	6¼ lbs./1000 sq. ft., approx. 275 nails/lb.
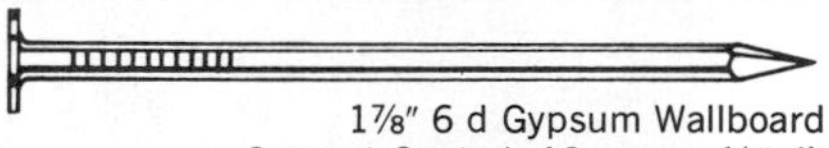 1⅞" 6 d Gypsum Wallboard Nail— Cement Coated, 13 gauge, ¼" dia. head	6" c. to c. on ceilings—7" c. to c. on walls	6¾ lbs./1000 sq. ft. approx. 278 nails/lb.
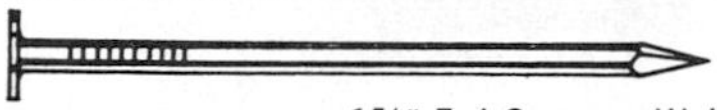 1⅝" 5 d Gypsum Wallboard Nail— Cement Coated, 13½ gauge, 15/64" dia. head	6" c. to c. on ceilings—7" c. to c. on walls	5¼ lbs./1000 sq. ft. approx. 366 nails/lb.
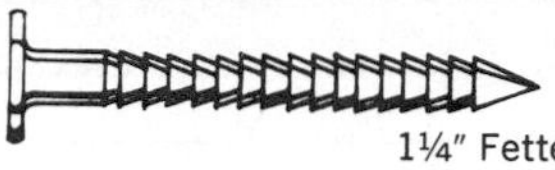 1¼" Fetter Annular Ring Nail— 11 gauge; 5/16" dia. head	6" c. to c. on ceilings	6 lbs./1000 sq. ft. approx. 315 nails/lb.
 1⅛" Matching Color Nail (Steel)	8" c.to c. on walls	1½ lbs./1000 sq. ft. approx. 1,008 nails/lb.
 1⅞" Matching Color Nail (Steel)	8" c. to c. on walls	4½ lbs./1000 sq. ft. approx. 349 nails/lb.
 1⅛" Matching Color Nail (Brass)	8" c. to c. on walls	1¾ lbs./1000 sq. ft. approx. 901 nails/lb.
 1¼" Drywall Screw— Type W	Framing spaced 16" c. to c. 12" c. to c. on ceilings—16" c. to c. on walls Framing spaced 24" c. to c. 12" c. to c. on ceilings—12" c. to c. on walls	Approx. 1000 screws/1000 sq. ft.
 1" Drywall Screw—Type S	12" c. to c. on walls and ceilings	Approx. 875 screws/1000 sq. ft.
 1⅝" Drywall Screw—Type S	16" c. to c. on walls and ceilings when installed permanently without laminating adhesive; or as required for temporary mechanical attachment while laminating adhesive dries	Varies depending on 2 layer system used.
 1" Drywall Screw—Type S	12" c. to c. in field of board and 8" c. to c. staggered at vertical joints on walls— 12" c. to c. on ceilings	Approx. 1100 screws/1000 sq. ft.

48-22. *Recommended gypsum wallboard fasteners for various applications.*

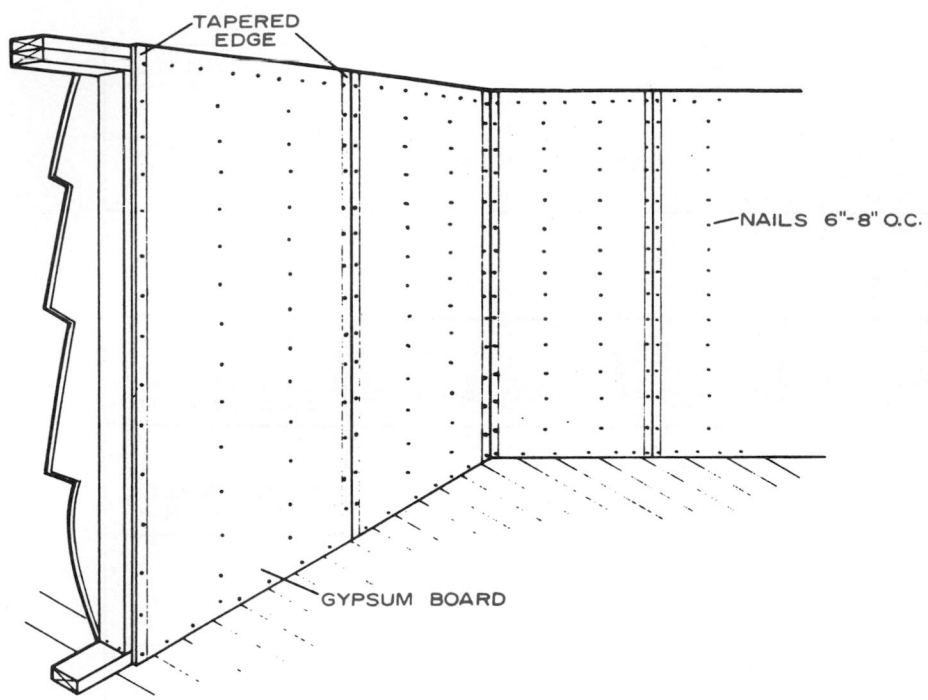

48-23a. *Drywall (gypsum board) applied vertically.*

48-24. *Installing gypsum board horizontally over the sound-deadening panels, which were applied vertically. Openings in the sound-deadening board for electrical outlets, heating vents, etc., must be caulked carefully, since even a small hole will destroy the sound-deadening effectiveness of the wall.*

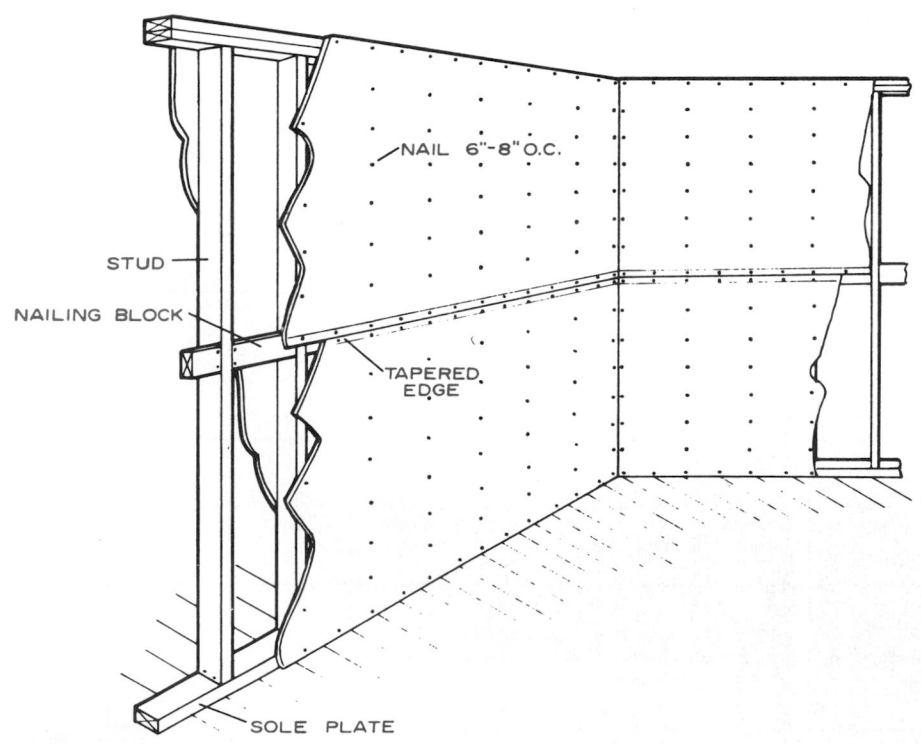

48-23b. *Drywall installed horizontally.*

Double Nailing System. A nail pop is caused by a movement of either the drywall or the nail head in relation to the other. These pops may be prevented if the drywall is held tightly against the framing by the head of the nail at all times. The double nailing system incorporates a second nail in close proximity (2") to the first to insure that the drywall is nailed tight. The drywall is first nailed to each framing member with nails spaced approximately 12" on center. This places five nails per 4' width into each framing member. The drywall is then nailed around its perimeter. The top and bottom are fastened with one nail at each framing member. At the ends of the drywall, nails are spaced 7" on

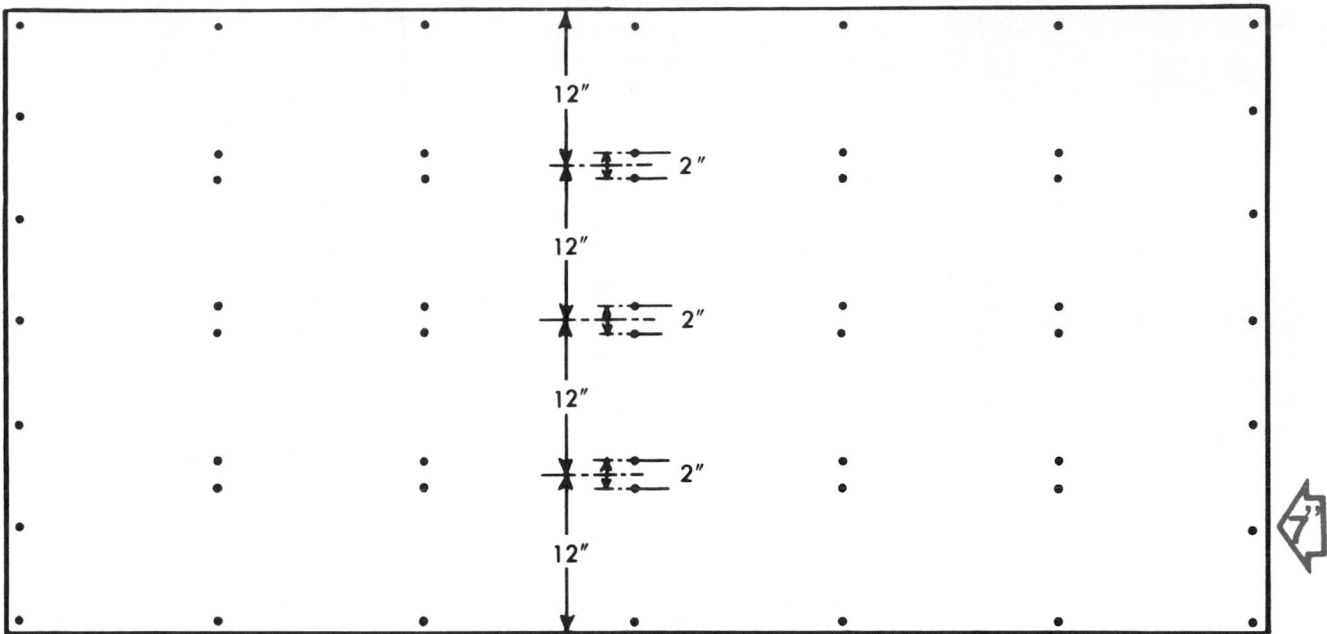

48-25. *The double nailing system for installing gypsum wallboard. Note that the nails are spaced 7" on center at the panel ends.*

center. Additional nails are then spaced approximately 2" from each nail on the inner area of the drywall. Fig. 48-25.

As the second nail in each group of two nails is driven home, the worker can watch for any movement between the drywall and the head of the first nail driven. Movement indicates that the first nail is not holding the drywall tight and that it should be given additional blows with the hammer. Always begin nailing at the center of the drywall and work toward the ends, making sure to hold the drywall tight against the framing member.

Cutting Drywall. Drywall may be cut to size by sawing. Another method is to score the finished side with a razor knife. Snap the drywall over a straight edge. Fig. 48-26. To complete the separation, score the back of the board with a sharp knife and snap the board forward toward the face side for a clean,

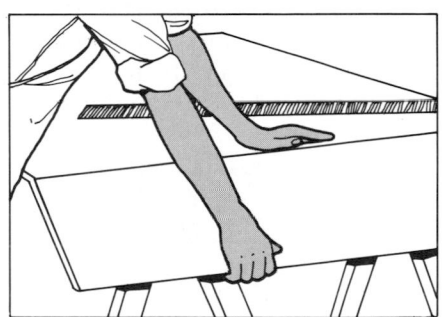

48-26. *Break the gypsum core by placing the scored line of the sheet over the edge of the table or bench and snapping down. Hold the sheet firmly on the table and support the cutoff with your other hand.*

straight joint break. Fig. 48-27.

Small cutouts for electrical outlets and other openings are made with a keyhole saw or a saber saw. To mark the location of the electrical outlet cutouts, hold the panel in place against the wall. With a wood block to protect the drywall, tap around the outlet with

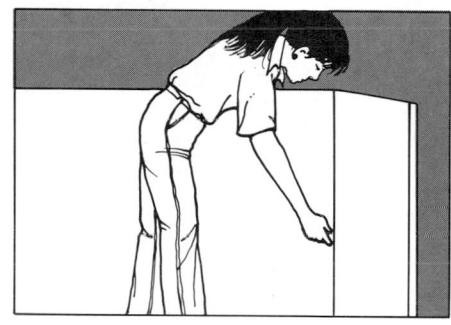

48-27. *Complete the separation by scoring the back paper of the board with a sharp knife. Then snap the board forward toward the face side.*

a hammer. An indentation of the outlet box will be made on the back of the drywall to use as a guide for cutting.

Some workers prefer to use a router for making cutouts in drywall panels. The small routers are made especially for this task. The bit can be plunged into the

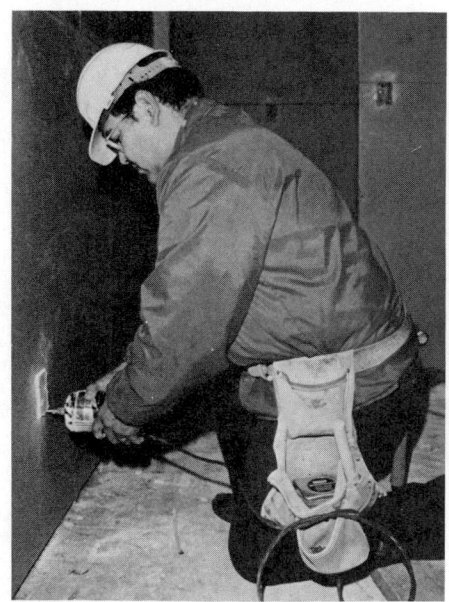

48-28. Holes for electrical boxes can be cut with a drywall router.

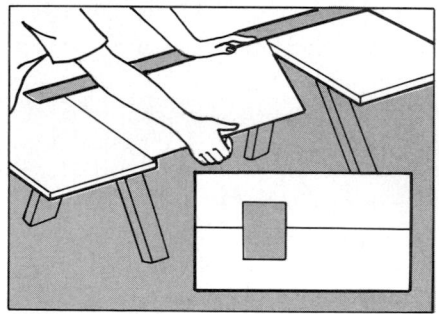

48-29. Making a cutout for a door or window. Make two saw cuts to the correct depth. Then score and snap.

drywall, and follows the contours of the electrical box. Fig. 48-28.

When notching drywall for door or window openings, make two saw cuts to the correct depth. The final cut is made by scoring and snapping, the same as when cutting the sheet to size. Fig. 48-29. The cut edges of drywall may be smoothed with coarse sandpaper wrapped around a wood block.

Joint Treatment. The joints between the panels are made smooth by applying joint

compound, perforated tape, and additional coats of joint compound, and then sanding the surface level with the wall surface. Fig. 48-30. Joint compound can be purchased in either premixed or powder form. The powder is mixed with water to a soft putty consistency that can be easily applied.

Use a 5" wide spackling knife or a mechanical applicator to fill the joints with the compound. Fig. 48-31. Press the tape into the recess with a wide, flat knife until the joint compound is forced through the perforations in the tape. Fig. 48-32. Next cover the tape with additional compound, feathering the outer edges. Fig. 48-33. After the compound has dried, sand the joint lightly and then apply a second coat, again feathering the edges. Sometimes a steel trowel is used to apply the second coat. For best results, a third coat is applied and the edges are feathered beyond the second coat. After the joint compound is completely dry, sand the joint smooth and even with the wall surface.

To tape interior corners, fold the tape down the center to form a right angle. Fig. 48-34. Apply the compound in the corner and press the tape in place. Then finish the corner with joint compound and sand smooth when dry. Apply a second coat if necessary and sand it smooth, flat, and even with the wall surface. The same procedure is followed for interior corners between a wall and ceiling, or a molding of some type is installed. Fig. 48-35. To hide hammer indentations, fill them with joint compound and sand them smooth when they are dry. Usually a second coat is necessary. Figs. 48-36 and 48-37.

Outside corners are given a slightly different treatment. Metal corner bead should be nailed along the entire length of the corner.

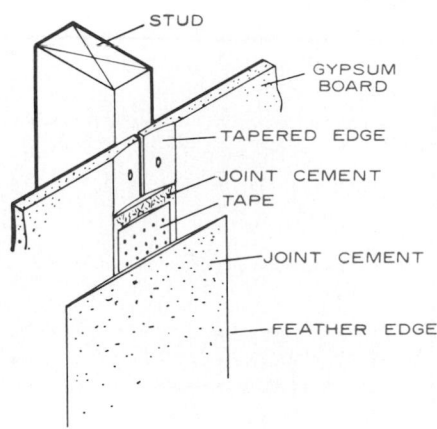

48-30. The tapered edge of the gypsum board is filled with joint cement and taped. Additional joint cement is then applied and feathered out to provide a smooth surface.

48-31a. Applying joint cement with a wide spackling knife.

48-31b. Applying joint compound with a mechanical applicator.

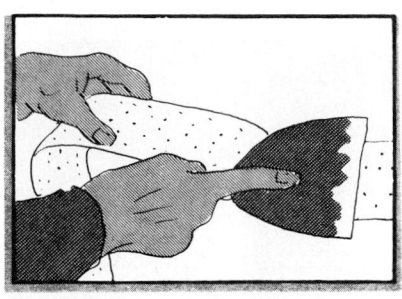

48-32. Press the perforated tape into the cement, forcing the excess cement from under the tape.

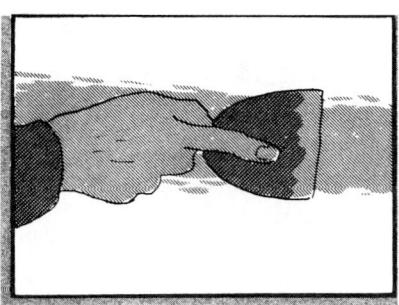

48-33. Spread a thin coat of cement over the tape. If necessary, follow with a second and third coat after each preceding coat has dried.

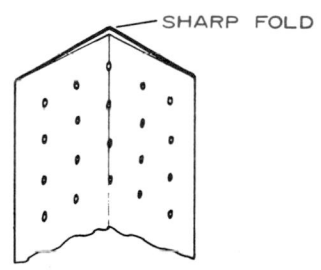

48-34. Fold the perforated tape down the center to form a right angle when taping interior corners.

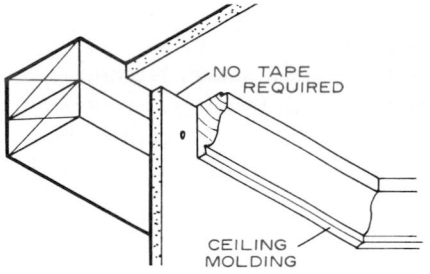

48-35. When a molding is installed between the wall and the ceiling, it is not necessary to tape the joint.

48-36. Filling the nail dimples with joint cement. Repeat the second and third coats of cement, if necessary, and sand smooth.

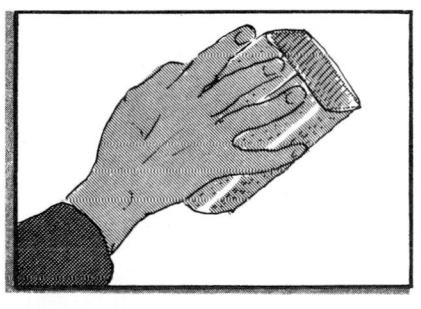

48-37. Sanding the joints and nail dimples after the joint is completely dried. This is the last step in preparing the gypsum board for a decorative treatment.

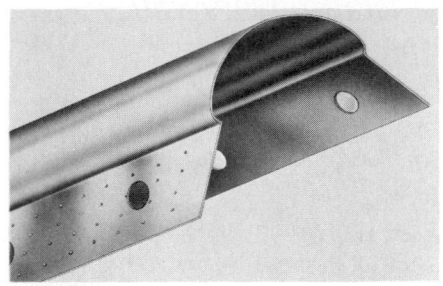

48-38. Curved bullnose corner bead.

This is a galvanized metal angle that reinforces the corner. The angle is usually 90 degrees. Some corner beads, called bullnose beads, have a curved surface. When this kind of corner bead is eventually mudded with joint compound and sanded, the corner will look curved. Fig. 48-38.

Temperature and humidity have a direct effect on the drying time of joint treatment products. Very little can be done to alter temperature and humidity under job conditions. However, care should be taken to note the average differences in drying time under different atmospheric conditions so that problems may be minimized. Joint treatment products must be thoroughly dry before successive coats and/or final decorations are applied. In all cases, a well-ventilated area assists in proper drying of these materials. Table 48-C indicates the average drying periods for joint treatment products under different temperature and humidity conditions.

Table 48-C. *Drying Time for Joint Compounds.*

Relative Humidity Temp. °F.	0	20%	40%	50%	60%	70%	80%	90%	98%
40	28H	34H	44H	2D	2 1/2D	3 1/2D	4 1/2D	9D	37D
60	13H	16H	20H	24H	29H	38H	2 1/2D	4 1/2D	18D
80	6H	8H	10H	12H	13 1/2H	19 1/2H	27H	49H	9D
100	3H	4H	5H	6H	8H	10H	14H	26H	5D

H = Hours   D = Days (24 hours)

Installing Drywall on the Ceiling

Drywall applied to the ceiling is nailed to ceiling joists or to the bottom chord of a truss. Nails are spaced 5" to 7" apart and dimpled in the same manner as when applying drywall to sidewalls. During installation, the drywall can be held in place with one or two braces about 1" longer than the height of the ceiling Fig. 48-39. Joints should be staggered and centered over framing members. Fig. 48-40. Joint treatment is the same for the ceiling as for the walls.

48-40. *Installing gypsum board on the ceiling. Note the staggering of the end joints.*

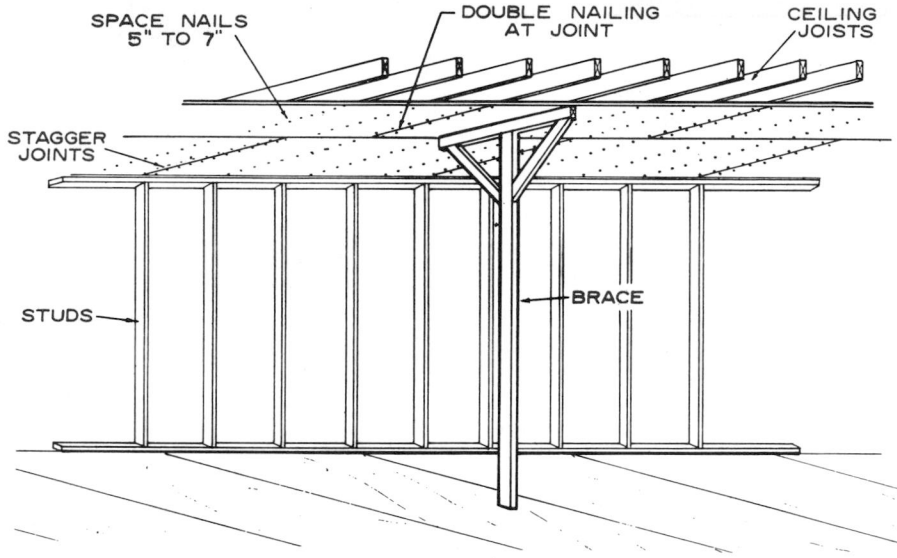

48-39. *Drywall ceiling installation details. A brace is used to hold the material in position for nailing.*

QUESTIONS

1. What materials are most frequently used as a plaster base?

2. Why is plaster reinforced at certain key positions?

3. What material is used for plaster reinforcing?

4. What are plaster grounds?

5. What are the ingredients of plaster?

6. What two plaster coats are combined when they are applied on gypsum or insulating lath?

7. When plastering, what is the difference between a sand-float and a putty finish?

8. When applying drywall, what is meant by double nailing?

9. Describe how drywall is held in place on a ceiling during application.

ACTIVITIES

1. Social Studies. Research interior wall coverings in the homes of the wealthy in Great Britain during the eighteenth century. How were the walls and ceiling covers constructed? Compare their quality with the quality and durability of ceiling and wall coverings used in today's homes.

2. Math. A 12' by 13' bedroom has an 8' ceiling. Find the area of the ceiling. Estimate the number of 4' by 8' panels of gypsum board needed to drywall the ceiling. Include 5% for trim and waste.

Wood Paneling

The texture and warmth of wood make it popular as a wall or ceiling finish indoors. It is particularly popular with homeowners because wood is easier to install than some other finishes, and requires only common tools. Wood paneling is often used in remodeling projects because it quickly covers imperfections in other wall surfaces.

Wood paneling can be installed directly over studs, over drywall and plaster, and even over masonry surfaces such as concrete block and brick. Though it is usually installed vertically, it can also be installed horizontally or at any angle. The basic types of paneling are plywood, hardboard, and solid wood strip paneling. All of these can be painted or stained. Some paneling is even prefinished.

PLYWOOD PANELING

Plywood paneling comes in thicknesses from ¼" to ¾". The sheet size is generally 4' × 8', but 4' × 10' panels are commonly available. Some types are narrower than 4' to make them easier to handle. Plywood paneling is available in a wide variety of textures and patterns, including saw-textured, relief grain, embossed, and grooved. To further increase the choices available, plywood paneling is available in a wide variety of veneers, including domestic and tropical hardwoods. Fig. 49-1.

Storing Plywood Paneling

Paneling should be stored in a dry location. It should be stacked flat on the floor, ideally with stickers between sheets to encourage air circulation. If panels must be stored on edge, they should rest on a long edge. Panels should be delivered to the room in which they will be installed 48 hours before installation. This allows them to acclimate to the temperature and humidity of the room.

49-1a. *The indentations of age can be felt as well as seen in this antiqued plywood paneling used as an accent wall.*

49-1b. *A pecan plywood paneling with darkly stained grooves was used to accent this living room wall.*

Installing Plywood Paneling

On exterior masonry walls above or below grade, be sure the wall is properly waterproofed before the studding or furring is applied. Where extreme humidity may cause condensation on the inside of the exterior masonry wall, apply a vapor barrier, paper, or film to prevent moisture penetration to the panel. Fig. 49-2.

Furring strips must be used on masonry and plaster walls. Paneling may be applied directly to furring strips or studs. However, for additional strength, fire resistance, and sound deadening, ⅜" or ½" gypsum wall board (drywall) is recommended as a backing behind plywood paneling. Plywood sheathing can also be used for application to the studs as a backing under finish paneling.

Applying Furring Strips to Masonry Walls. On masonry walls, apply furring strips horizontally every 16". Fig. 49-3.

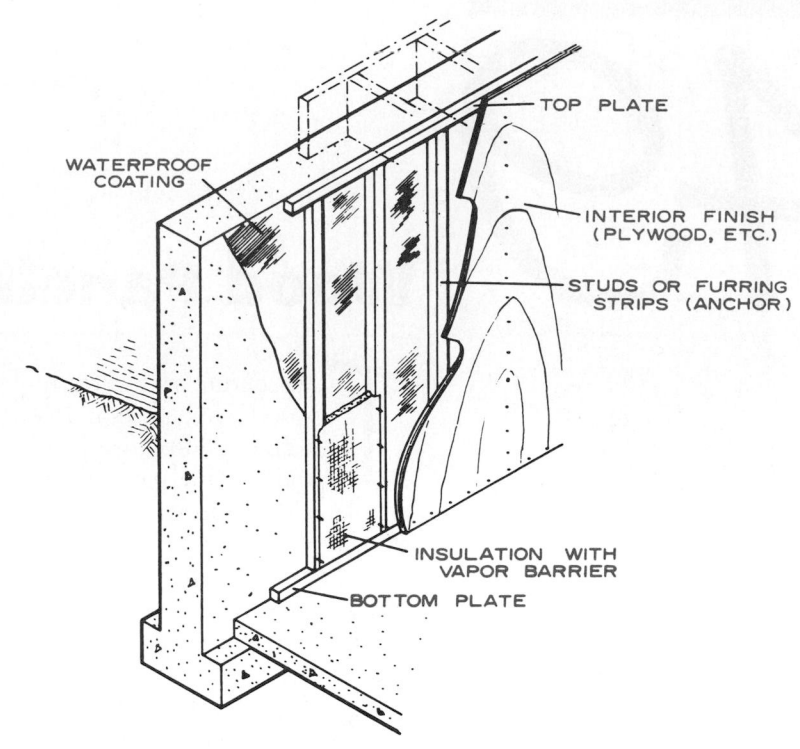

49-2a. *Plywood paneling applied to furring strips on a basement wall. A waterproof coating has been applied to the cement. Insulation with a vapor barrier has been installed between the furring strips.*

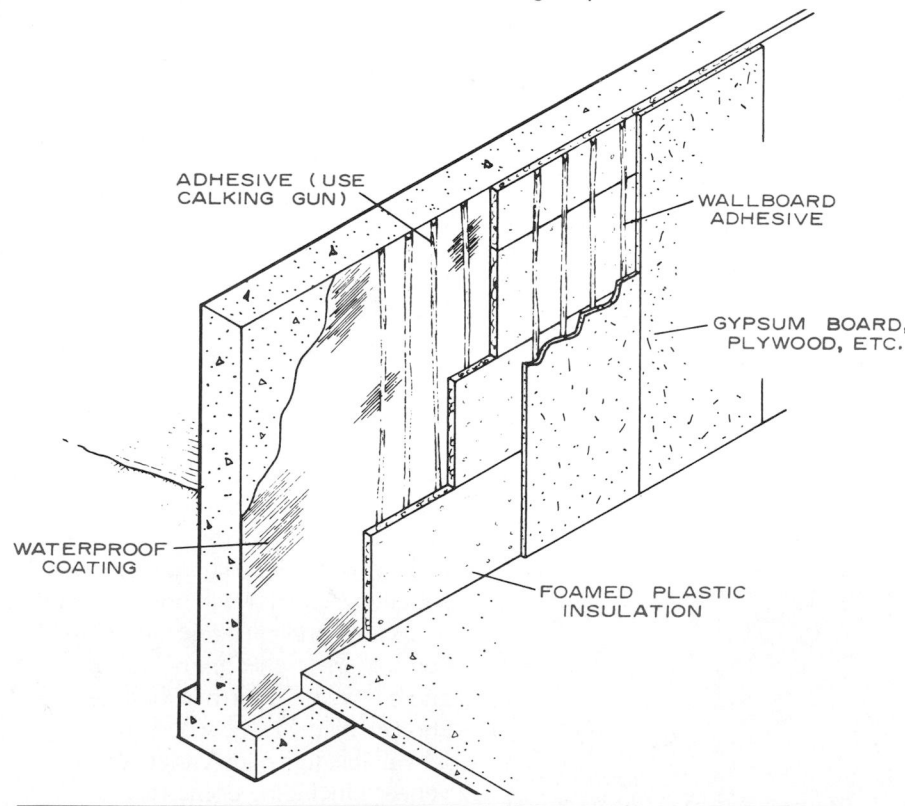

49-2b. *Basement paneling applied to a foamed plastic insulation with wallboard adhesive.*

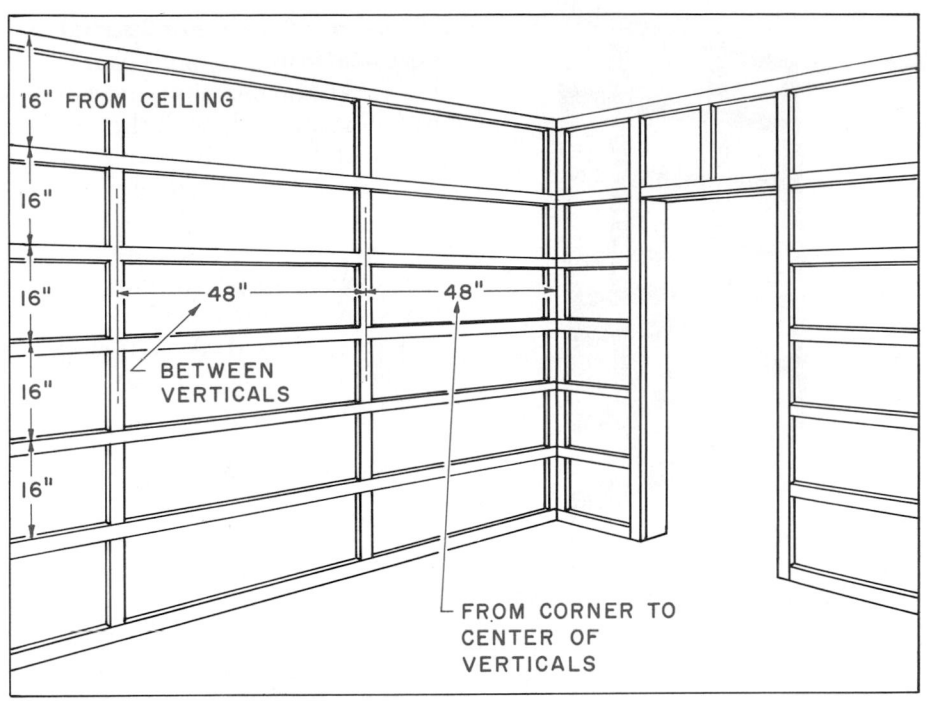

49-3. *Correct placement of furring strips in preparation for paneling.*

16" FROM CEILING
16"
16"
16"
16"
48"
BETWEEN VERTICALS
48"
FROM CORNER TO CENTER OF VERTICALS

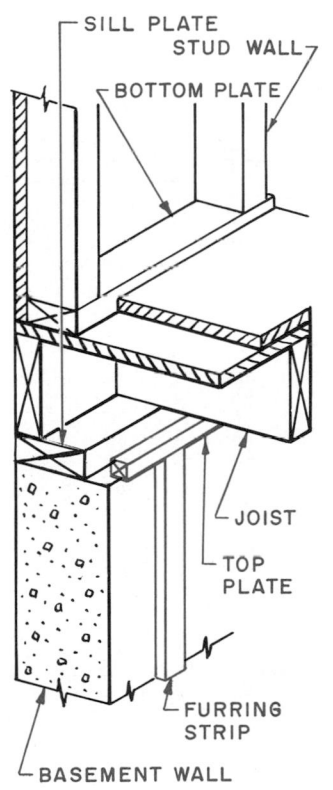

SILL PLATE
STUD WALL
BOTTOM PLATE
JOIST
TOP PLATE
FURRING STRIP
BASEMENT WALL

49-4a. *When the wall to be furred runs at right angles to the joists, nail the top plate (top furring strip) to the underside of the joists.*

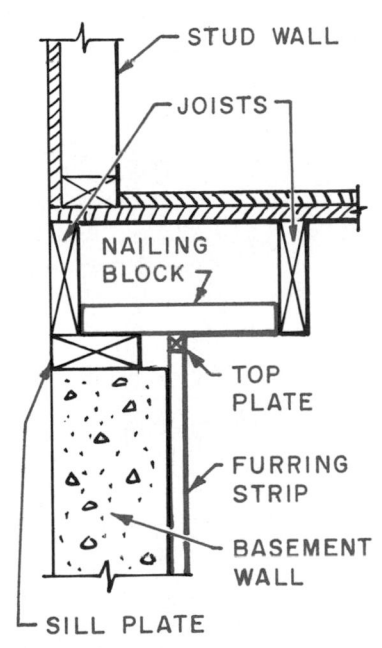

STUD WALL
JOISTS
NAILING BLOCK
TOP PLATE
FURRING STRIP
BASEMENT WALL
SILL PLATE

49-4b. *When the wall to be furred runs parallel to the joists, install a nailing block to which the top plate can be nailed.*

49-5. *Wood shingles are used as shims behind furring.*

Allow a clearance of at least ¼" between the top furring strip and the ceiling and between the bottom furring strip and the floor. The top furring strip is nailed to the bottom edge of the ceiling joists or to a nailing block. Fig. 49-4. Insert vertical strips every 48" to support the panel edges. Fig. 49-3. The furring strips are attached to the masonry walls with masonry nails, screws, nails driven into shields or wood dowels, nail anchors, adhesive anchors, or bolt anchors. Uneven furring strips can be leveled by placing shims in the low spots and driving a nail through the furring strip and the shims to hold them in place. Fig. 49-5.

Applying Furring Strips to Plaster Walls. If the paneling is to be applied on a plaster wall, the furring strips should be nailed horizontally to the studs, starting at the floor line and continuing up the wall every 16". Nail vertical strips every 48" to support the panel edges. The furring strips are shimmed as necessary with wood shingles to obtain a flush surface.

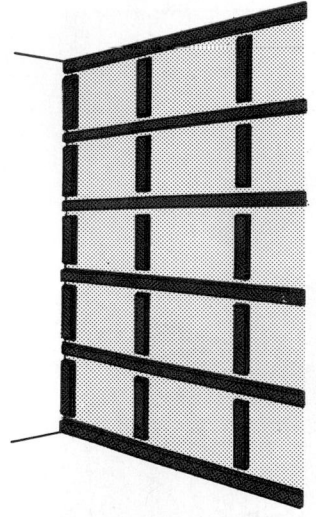

49-6a. *A wall over 8' high must have a horizontal furring strip positioned so that the top of an 8' panel wil be aligned with the center of the furring strip at that point.*

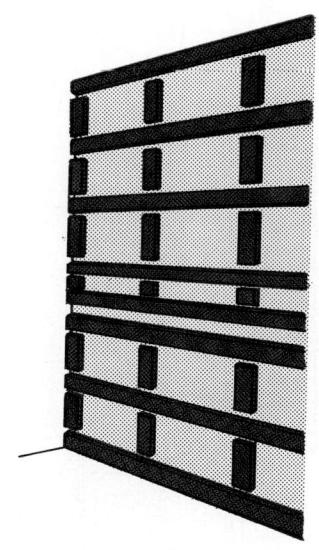

49-7. *An extra furring strip is nailed horizontally at the wainscot height.*

Furring Strips for Special Applications. For walls over 8' high, additional furring strips are nailed horizontally with the center of one of the strips 8' from the floor and another at the ceiling. Fig. 49-6.

When wainscoting is installed, nail an extra strip horizontally at the wainscot height. This is usually about 32", since three 32" pieces can be cut from a full 8' panel (96"). Fig. 49-7.

Laying Out the Job. Set up the panels around the room to plan their sequence. Arrange them so that the natural color variations form a pleasing pattern. Fig. 49-8. For most interiors, it is practical to start paneling from one corner and work around the room. After deciding in which corner to start

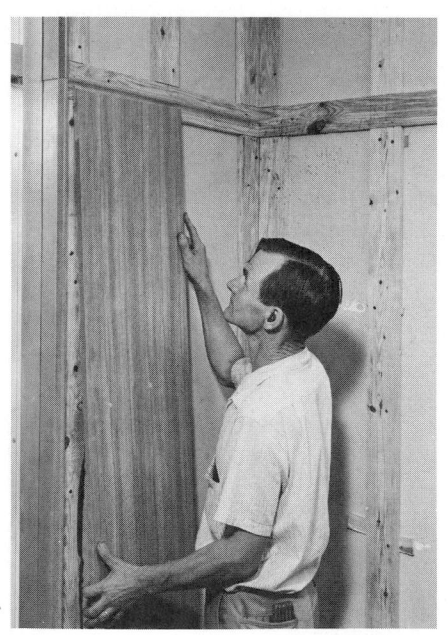

49-6b. *Installing paneling on a wall over 8' high.*

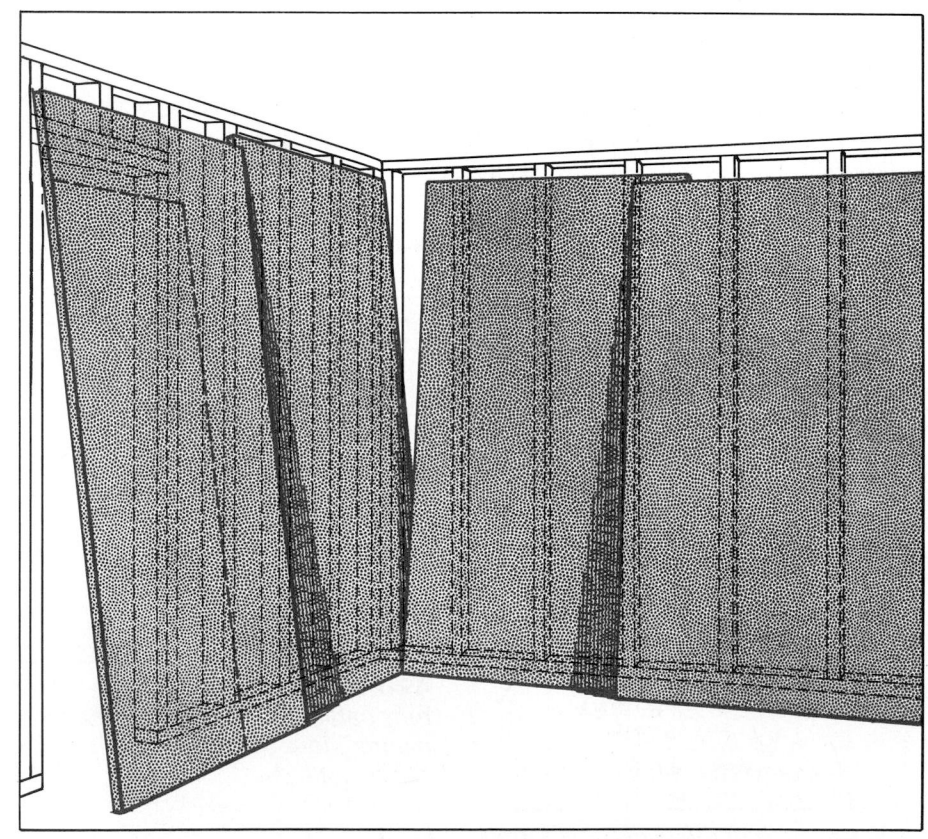

49-8. *Arrange the panels around the room to show the best pattern of color variations in both daylight and artificial light.*

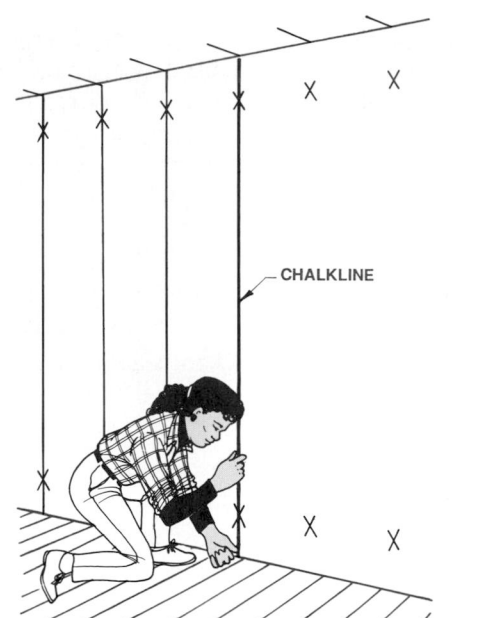

49-9. *Snapping a chalk line on the wall to indicate the center of each wall stud.*

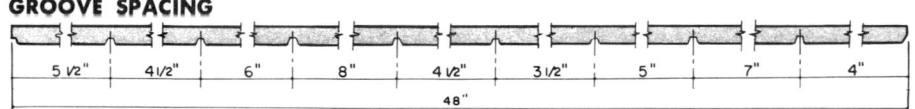

GROOVE SPACING

5 1/2" | 4 1/2" | 6" | 8" | 4 1/2" | 3 1/2" | 5" | 7" | 4"

48"

49-10. *A typical groove spacing for plywood paneling. The groove locations appear to be randomly spaced. However, when the dimensions are added together, the grooves fall on 16" and 24" centers. In this way, the panel can be nailed through the grooves to the studs.*

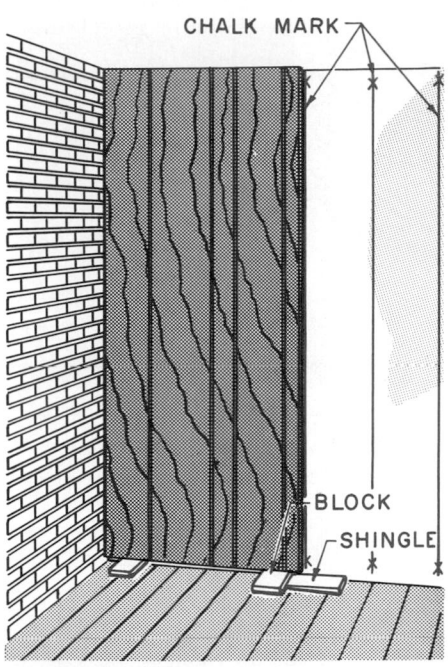

49-11. *Set the first panel in position, making certain that the edge is plumb.*

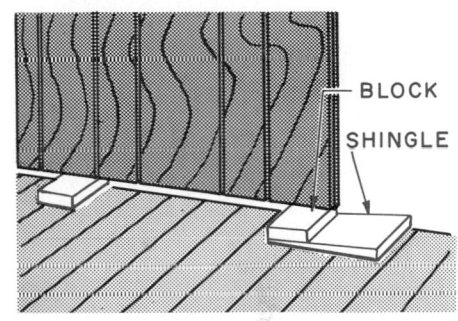

49-12. *Use a block and a shingle to position the panel at the correct height.*

the paneling, stack the panels in the correct sequence so that as the job proceeds, the panels may be removed from the stack in the proper order.

Installing Panels. Accurately measure the height of the wall in several places. The panels should be cut so that they have a 1/4" clearance at top and bottom. If the location of the studs is not visible, locate them and mark the center of each stud with a chalk line. Also lightly mark the stud center locations on the floor and ceiling to serve as a guide when nailing each panel in position. Fig. 49-9. If the panel has grooves, these will usually be spaced to line up with the studs. Fig. 49-10.

Place the first panel in position and butt it to the adjacent wall in the corner. Make sure the panel is perfectly plumb and the outer edge is directly over the chalk line which marks the center of the stud. Fig. 49-11. If this edge does not fall directly on the stud, cut the other edge of the panel so that it will. In most cases, the corner where the paneling begins is irregular. There may be a fireplace, concrete blocks, or uneven plaster. Scribe the panel with a small compass to insure a perfect fit. Position the panel at the proper height by setting it on a block and shimming it with a shingle to allow for 1/4" clearance at the top and bottom. Fig. 49-12. When the panel is set perfectly plumb and at the correct height,

set the compass for the amount to be cut off and scribe the line as shown in Fig. 49-13. Cut the panel along this line to fit the irregular wall.

Set the panel back in place against the wall to which it has been scribed and block the panel up as previously to the correct height. Fasten the panel to the wall. It may be applied with nails or adhesive; this will be discussed later. Butt the second panel to the

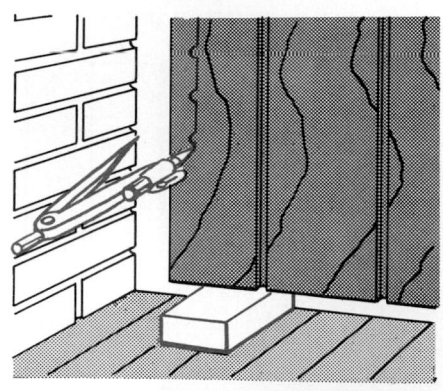

49-13. *Scribing the panel edge to fit the adjacent wall.*

49-14. *The panel edges must meet on the center of a stud or furring strip.*

first. With the first panel properly positioned on the studs, the edges of the remaining 4' panels will also land on stud centers, assuming that the stud spacing is uniform across the wall surface. Fig. 49-14. When paneling is being applied over a backer board with adhesive, the panel edges do not need to meet on a stud.

Fastening Panels with Nails. The nailing patterns for plywood paneling depend on the spacing of supports and the thickness of the panel. Table 49-A. Finishing nails or casing nails are generally used. Countersink the nails $\frac{1}{32}$" below the surface. These holes can be filled later with a putty stick to match the color of the panel. Colored nails which blend with the wood finish eliminate the need for countersinking and puttying. When nailing is complete, the paneling should be inspected carefully to ensure that all nails are set properly and that the paneling is tight against the wall beneath. Fig. 49-15.

Plywood panels 16¼" wide are available with a groove at one edge and a tongue on the other. The panel is attached to the wall with a metal clip which slips into the groove and is nailed to the stud or furring strip. The tongue on the next panel is then placed in the groove of the first, which covers up the nailing clip. This method of applying plywood paneling provides secure and completely invisible nailing.

49-15. *Inspecting a plywood panel installation. This paneling has been applied directly to the studs and is ready for door installation and trimming.*

Fastening Panels with Adhesive. Panel adhesive or other adhesives may be used instead of nails. Be sure to follow the manufacturer's instructions. After the panels are properly cut and fitted, the adhesive is applied to the studs, furring strips or backing. Fig. 49-16. Apply the adhesive in continuous $\frac{1}{8}$" wide beads or in intermittent beads 3" apart to all stud or furring strip surfaces. Apply a continuous $\frac{1}{8}$" wide bead at the corners and around cutouts. Position the panel and press it firmly against the adhesive. Place three or four

Table 49-A. *Nailing Recommendations for Interior Plywood Paneling.*

Plywood Thickness (In.)	Maximum Support Spacing (In.)	Nail Size (Use casing or finishing nails)	Nail Spacing (In.)	
			Panel Edges	**Intermediate**
$\frac{1}{4}$	16(a)	4d	6	12
$\frac{5}{16}$	16(b)	6d	6	12
$\frac{3}{8}$, $\frac{11}{32}$	24	6d	6	12
$\frac{1}{2}$, $\frac{15}{32}$	24	6d	6	12
$\frac{5}{8}$, $\frac{19}{32}$	24	8d	6	12
$\frac{3}{4}$	24	8d	6	12

(a) Can be 20 inches if face grain of paneling is across supports.
(b) Can be 24 inches if face grain of paneling is across supports.

49-16a. *Applying adhesive to the edges of the studs or furring strips.*

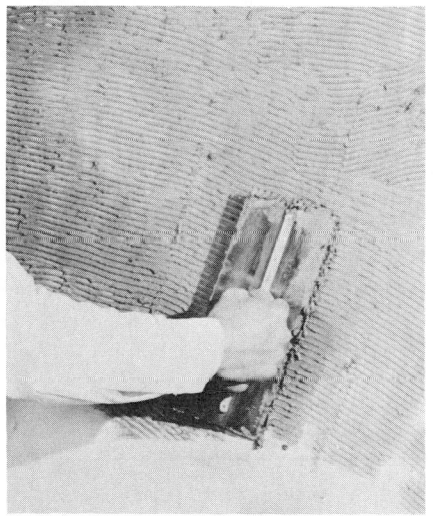

49-16b. *Applying adhesive to backer board.*

49-17. *After the panel has been nailed at the top for hinge action, pull the panel out from the wall and block it in this position to allow the adhesive to partially set.*

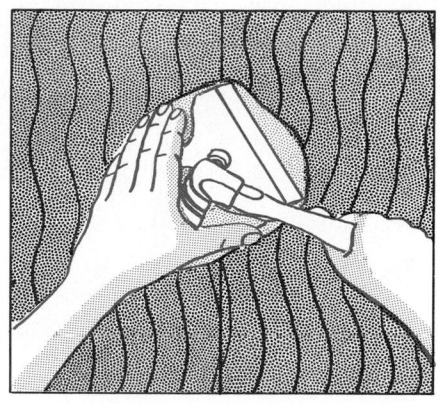

49-18. *Tapping the panel with a softwood block to press it firmly into place. You may put a cloth under the block to further protect the paneling.*

finishing nails across the top of the panel to hold it in place.

Pull the bottom of the panel 8" to 10" away from the wall, allowing the nails at the top to serve as a hinge. Hold the panel out with a spacer block for 8 to 10 minutes to allow the adhesive to dry. Fig. 49-17. Remove the spacer block and reposition the panel to fit perfectly. Place a clean block of softwood against the panel and tap the block with a hammer or rubber mallet to obtain a full surface contact. Fig. 49-18.

If a panel is not flush with the stud or furring strip surfaces, small finishing nails may be needed to hold the panel in position until the adhesive acquires full strength.

Cutting Plywood Panels.

When cutting panels with a crosscut hand saw or table saw, cut with the face side up. If a portable circular saw or saber saw is used, cut with the face side down. Never use a ripsaw, since this will tear the veneer on the edge of the panel. The best blade to use in a portable circular saw or a table saw is a plywood-cutting blade.

When cutting the panel for

49-19. *Cutting an opening for an electrical outlet box.*

outlets, locate the opening by chalking the edges of the outlet box and carefully fitting the panel loosely over the chalked box. Strike the face of the panel sharply several times with the heel of your hand to transfer the box outline to the back of the panel. Drill pilot holes in the corners from the back side; then cut out the outlet hole from the front side with a keyhole saw. Fig. 49-19. If a saber saw is used, a plunge cut can be made to eliminate the drilling of the pilot holes at the corners.

Moldings. There are several styles of wood and metal moldings for wood paneling. Pine moldings are sometimes used. They can be stained to harmonize with the prefinished paneling. Prefinished moldings to match the panel finish are also available.

Accurate measurements are essential for a good, professional-looking molding job. Measure along the ceiling line for the cove or crown molding. Measure along the floor for the exact length of the base and shoe molding. Do not assume that the ceiling and floor are the same length. Wood moldings should be scribed, mitered at 45 degrees, or coped as described in Unit 54, "Interior Trim." Construction details showing the use of various metal and wood moldings at corners, doors, windows, floors, and ceilings are illustrated in Fig. 49-20.

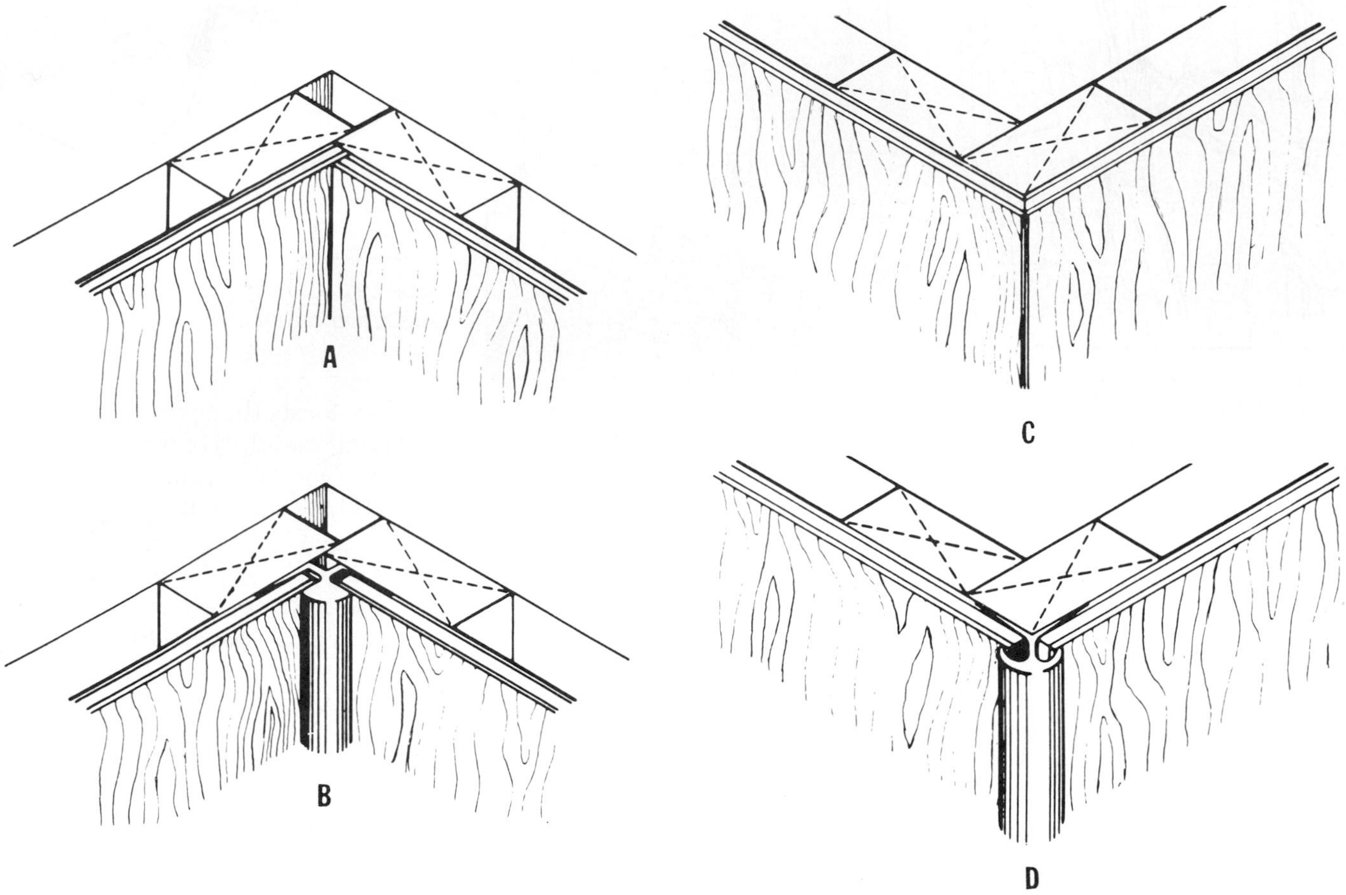

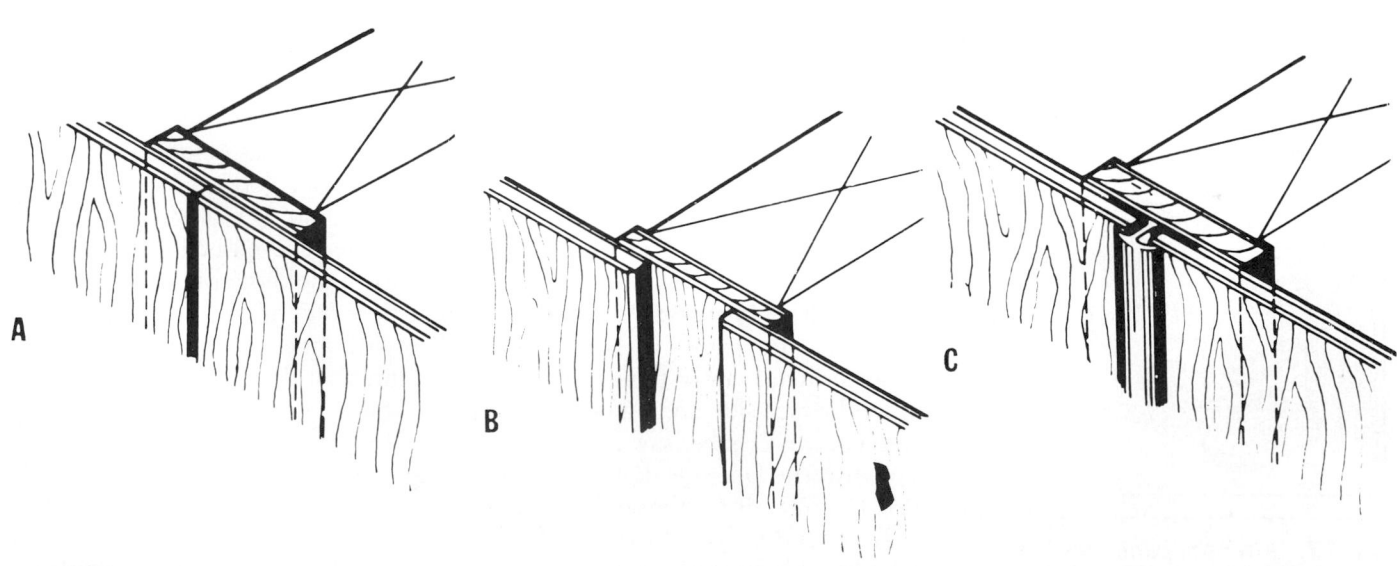

49-20a. Corner details: A. An inside corner with the first panel butted into the corner and the second panel scribed to the face of the first. B. An inside corner trimmed with a veneer-faced aluminum molding. C. An outside corner mitered. D. An outside corner trimmed with a veneer-faced aluminum molding.

49-20b. Joint details between panels: A. Shallow V-joint. B. Wide joint using ¼" x 2½" furring strips of matching or contrasting paneling. If a prefinished furring strip is not used, the strip should be finished before the panels are installed. C. Veneer-faced aluminum molding installed as a divider strip between panels.

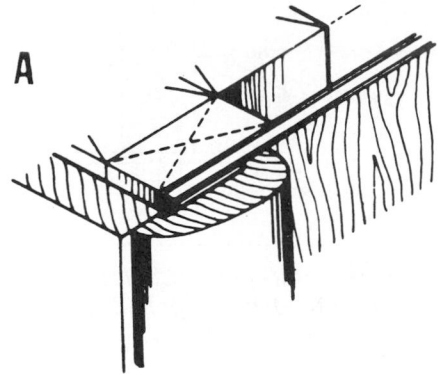

A

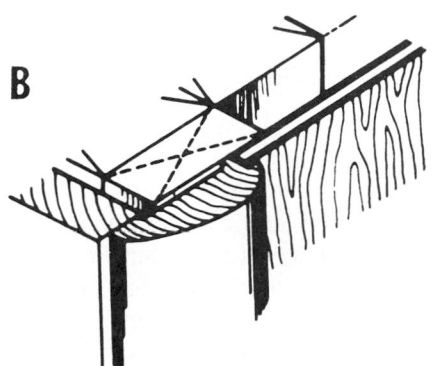

B

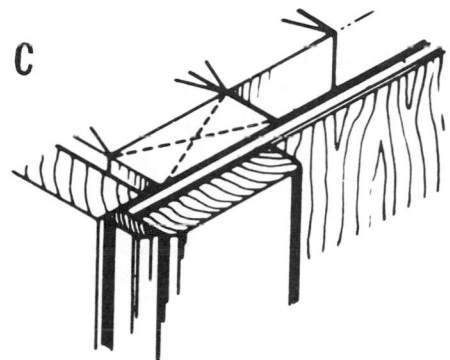

C

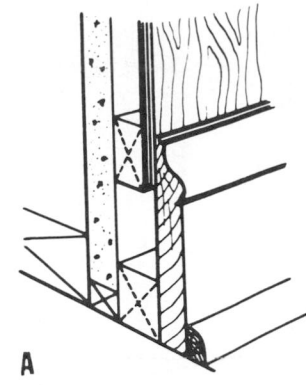

A

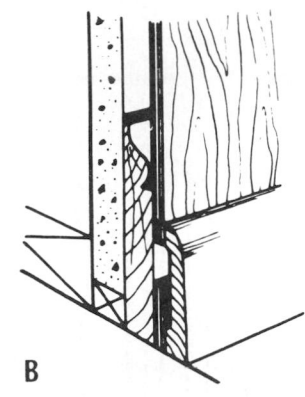

B

49-20d. *Base installation details: A. This method is used for installing wainscoting when it is desirable to gain a few inches of wall height. The panel is held up off the floor, and a piece of thicker furring is attached to the wall at the floor. The base is then nailed at the top and bottom to the two furring strips. B. This method is frequently used in remodeling. The walls are furred out, and the thickness of the old base is used as the bottom furring strip. The new base is then nailed to the face of the plywood paneling. This same method may be employed for new construction by using a furring strip at the floor line.*

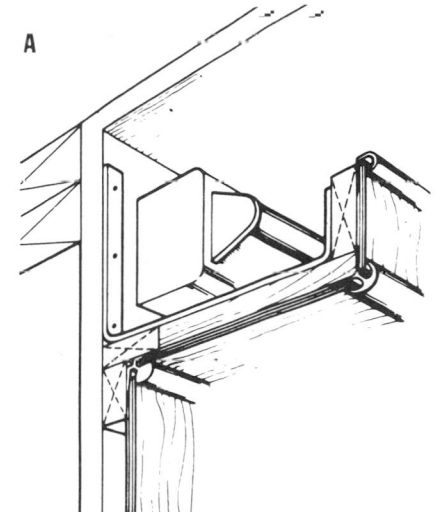

A

49-20c. *Window and door trimming details: A. Casing installed over paneling on furring strips. B. Rabbeted casing installed over plywood on furring strips. C. Quarter-round molding installed at the jamb to cover the joint between the plywood and the square-edge casing.*

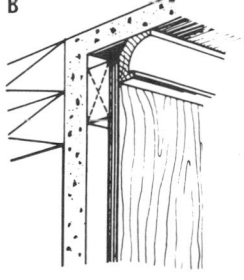

B

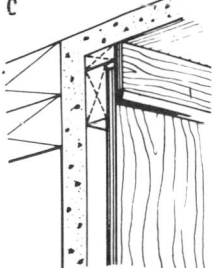

C

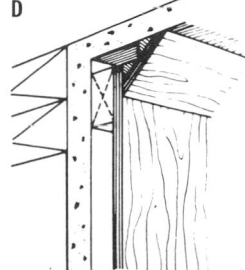

D

49-20e. *Plywood installation details at the ceiling: A. Cove lighting framed and covered with plywood paneling. Note the use of the veneer-faced aluminum cap and inside and outside corner moldings. B. Crown molding. C. A strip of prefinished paneling cut from leftover pieces and scribed to the ceiling with a quarter-round attached at the bottom edge. D. A strip of prefinished paneling ripped at 45° and installed at the ceiling line.*

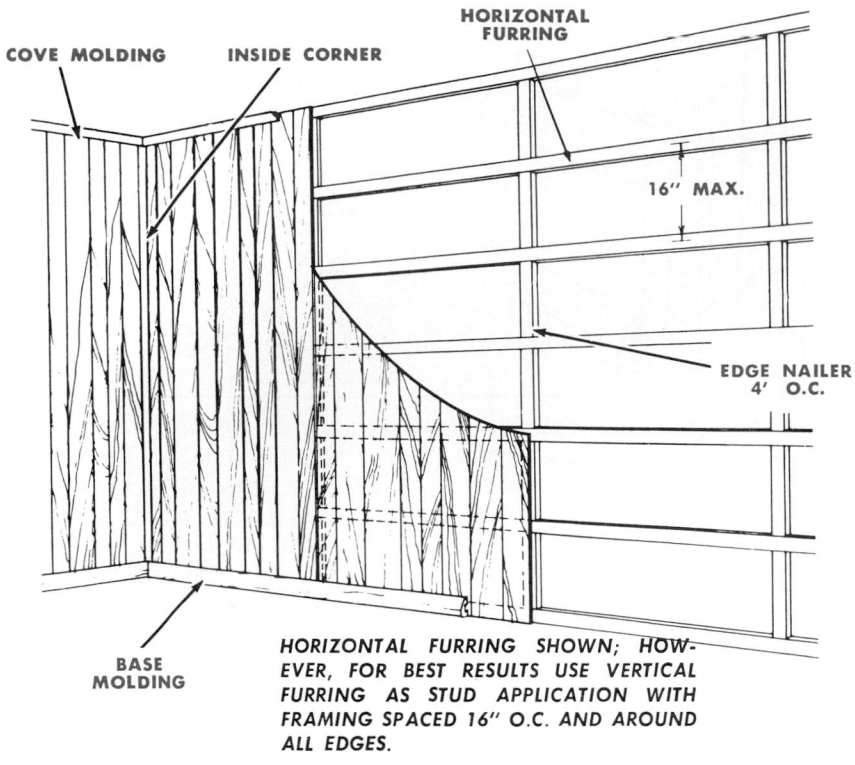

49-21. Horizontal furring details for hardboard paneling installation.

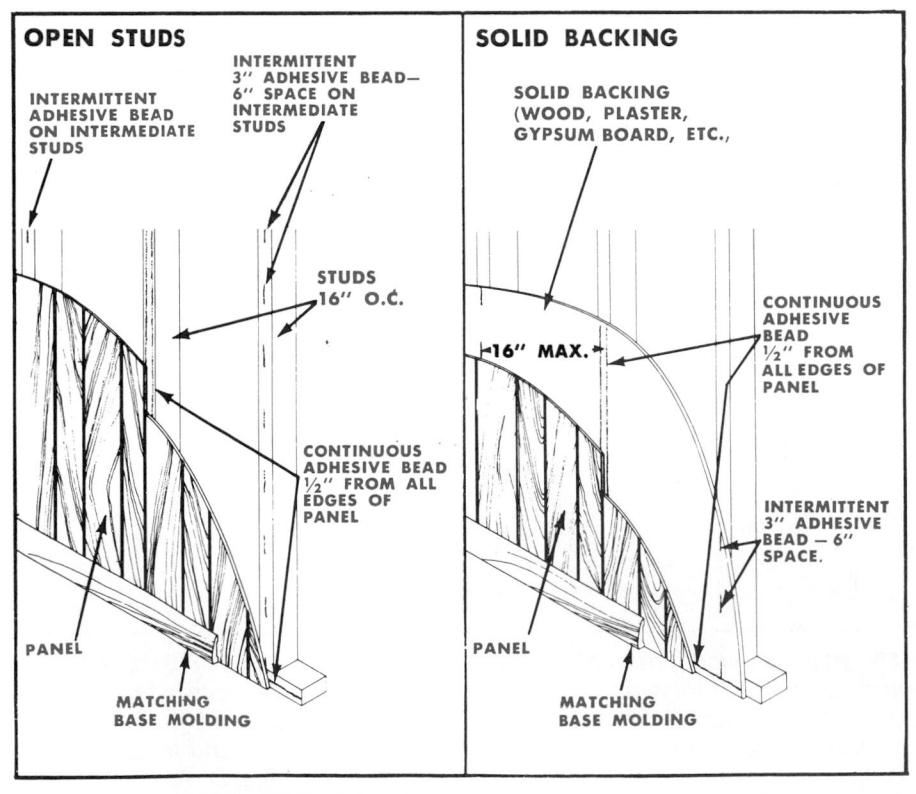

49-22a. Installation details for hardboard applied with an adhesive.

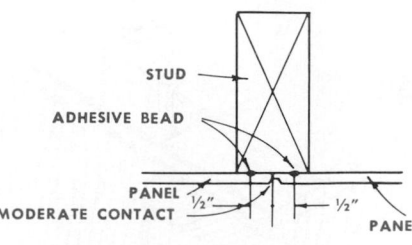

49-22b. Butt joint installation detail for hardboard applied with an adhesive.

Hardboard

Hardboard paneling is applied in the same manner as plywood. Hardboard should be at least ¼" thick when applied over open framing spaced 16" on center. It should be at least ⁷⁄₁₆" thick for framing spaced 24" on center. When ⅛" hardboard is used, a rigid backing of some type is required. For best results, vertical furring should be used with hardboard paneling. However, horizontal furring can be applied 16" on center over studs spaced 48" on center. Fig. 49-21.

The paneling may be nailed or applied with an adhesive. Fig. 49-22. Nails should penetrate into the studs at least ¾" and should be spaced 4" on center at all joints and along the edges. At all intermediate supports, nail 8" on center. Nails around the perimeter of the panel should be ¼" from the edge. Fig. 49-23. Wood or metal moldings are used as trim and are applied in the same manner as over plywood. Fig. 49-24.

Solid Wood Paneling

Many kinds of wood are made into paneling. For example, a rustic or informal look can be obtained with knotty pine, white pocket Douglas fir, sound wormy chestnut, and pecky cypress. The panels can be cut plain or with a tongue and groove. Fig. 49-25. These may be

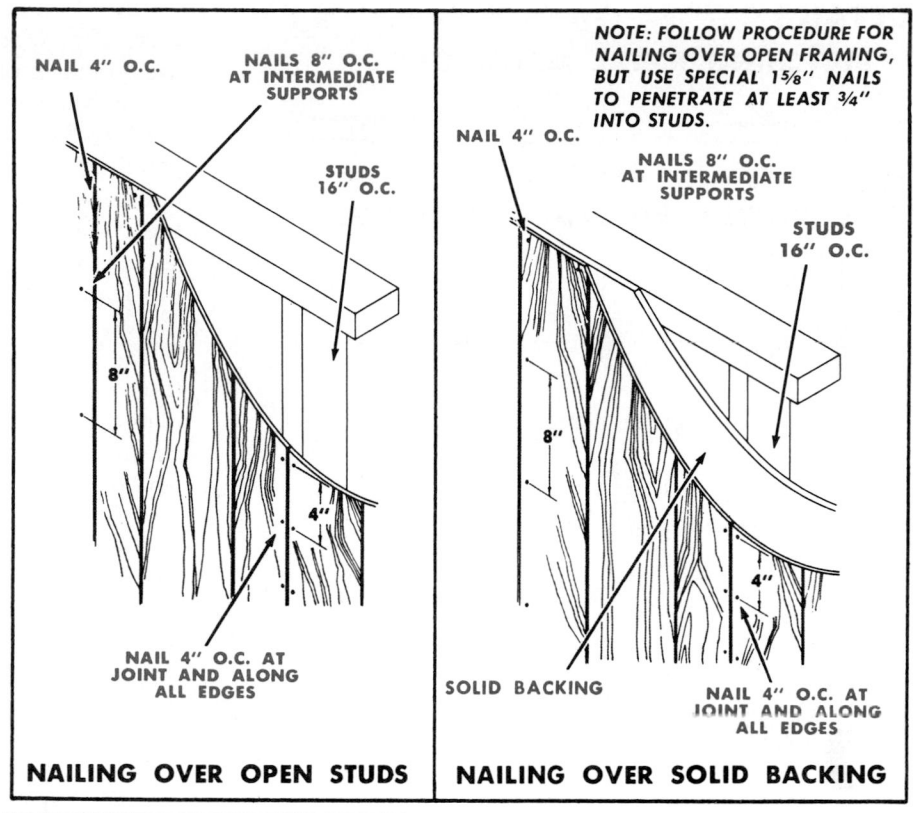

49-23. *Hardboard nailing details.*

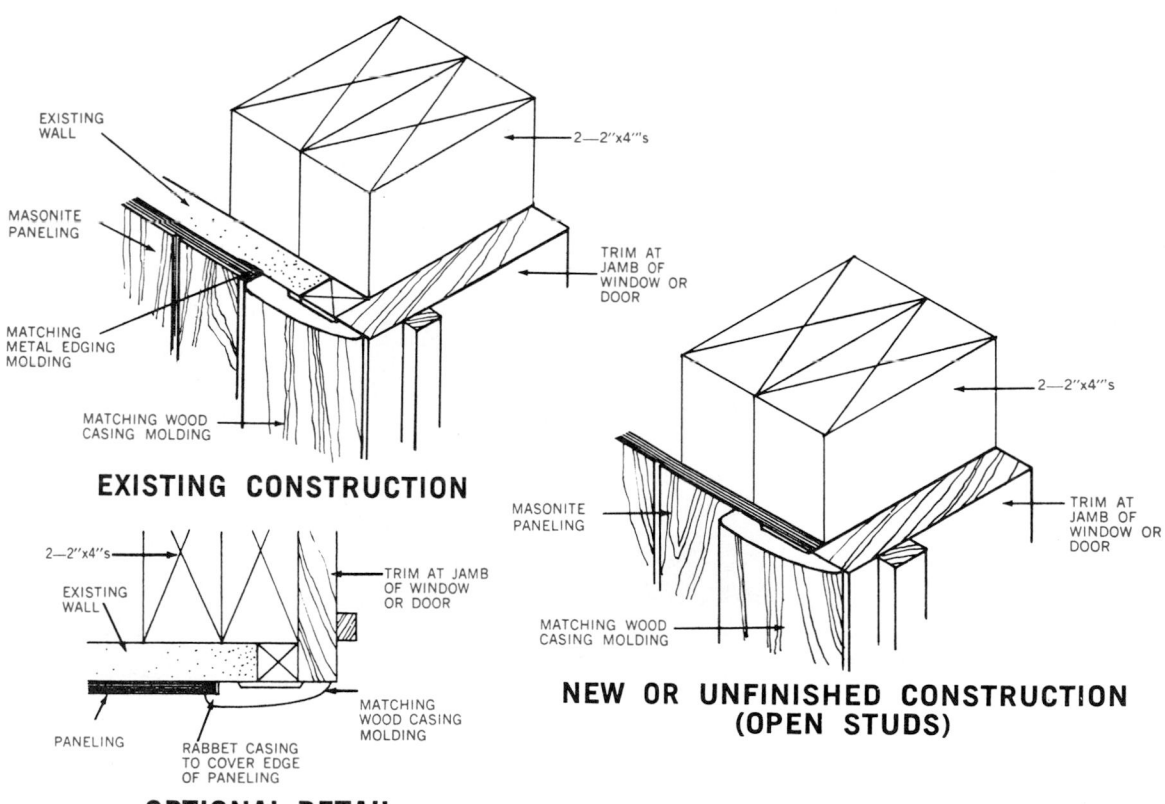

EXISTING CONSTRUCTION

OPTIONAL DETAIL

NEW OR UNFINISHED CONSTRUCTION (OPEN STUDS)

49-24a. *Window and door trim details.*

TRIM DETAILS
MATCHING METAL MOLDINGS

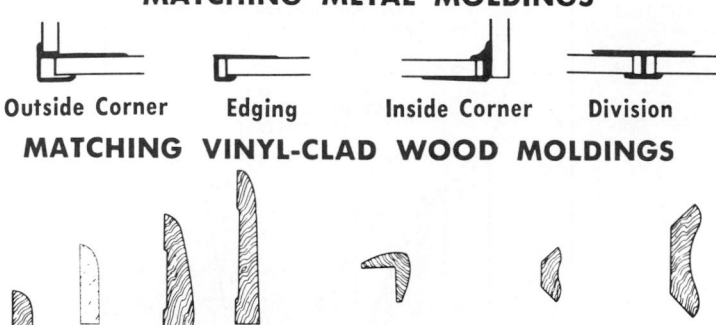

Outside Corner Edging Inside Corner Division

MATCHING VINYL-CLAD WOOD MOLDINGS

Shoe Stop Casing Base Outside Corner Inside Corner Cove

49-24b. *Metal and wood moldings in different styles for various applications are made to match prefinished paneling.*

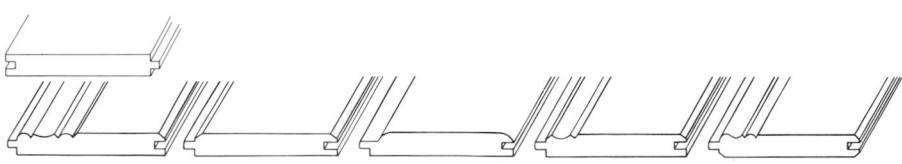

49-25a. *Six popular tongue-and-groove paneling patterns. Most retail lumberyards carry two or three patterns of these in stock.*

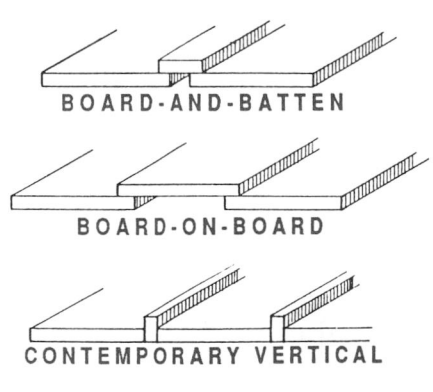

BOARD-AND-BATTEN

BOARD-ON-BOARD

CONTEMPORARY VERTICAL

49-25b. *Installation patterns for plain lumber paneling.*

49-25c. *An attractive board-on-board paneling installation.*

finished natural or stained and varnished. Wood paneling may be used to cover one or more walls or partial walls of a room.

Only thoroughly seasoned wood paneling should be used. The moisture content should be near the average it reaches in service, about 8% in most areas. However, in the dry southwestern United States, it should be about 6%, and in the southern and coastal areas of the country, about 11%. Allow the material to reach correct moisture content by storing it in the area in which it will be installed in such a way that air may circulate around all surfaces of the boards. Wood paneling on the inside of an exterior wall should be installed over a vapor barrier and insulation.

Wood paneling should not be too wide; a nominal 8" is recommended for most parts of the country. Boards wider than 8" should not be used except when they have a long tongue or matched edge. The boards may be applied horizontally or vertically.

Installation of Vertical Wood Paneling. For paneling that is to be installed vertically, adequate blocking should be installed between the studs to provide nailing support. The blocking should not be more than 24" o.c. Fig. 49-26.

A common practice when installing wood paneling is to nail a 1" × 8" board at the floor line. The 1" × 4" baseboard is then face-nailed to the 1" × 8" board. Fig. 49-27. The ends of the vertical paneling will rest on the top edge of the 1" × 4" base. This is a much cleaner application than resting the paneling ends on the floor and applying the base to the face of the paneling.

Plumb and scribe the first piece of paneling to the wall. Undercut the edge about 5 degrees to insure a snug fit against the wall. Fig. 49-28.

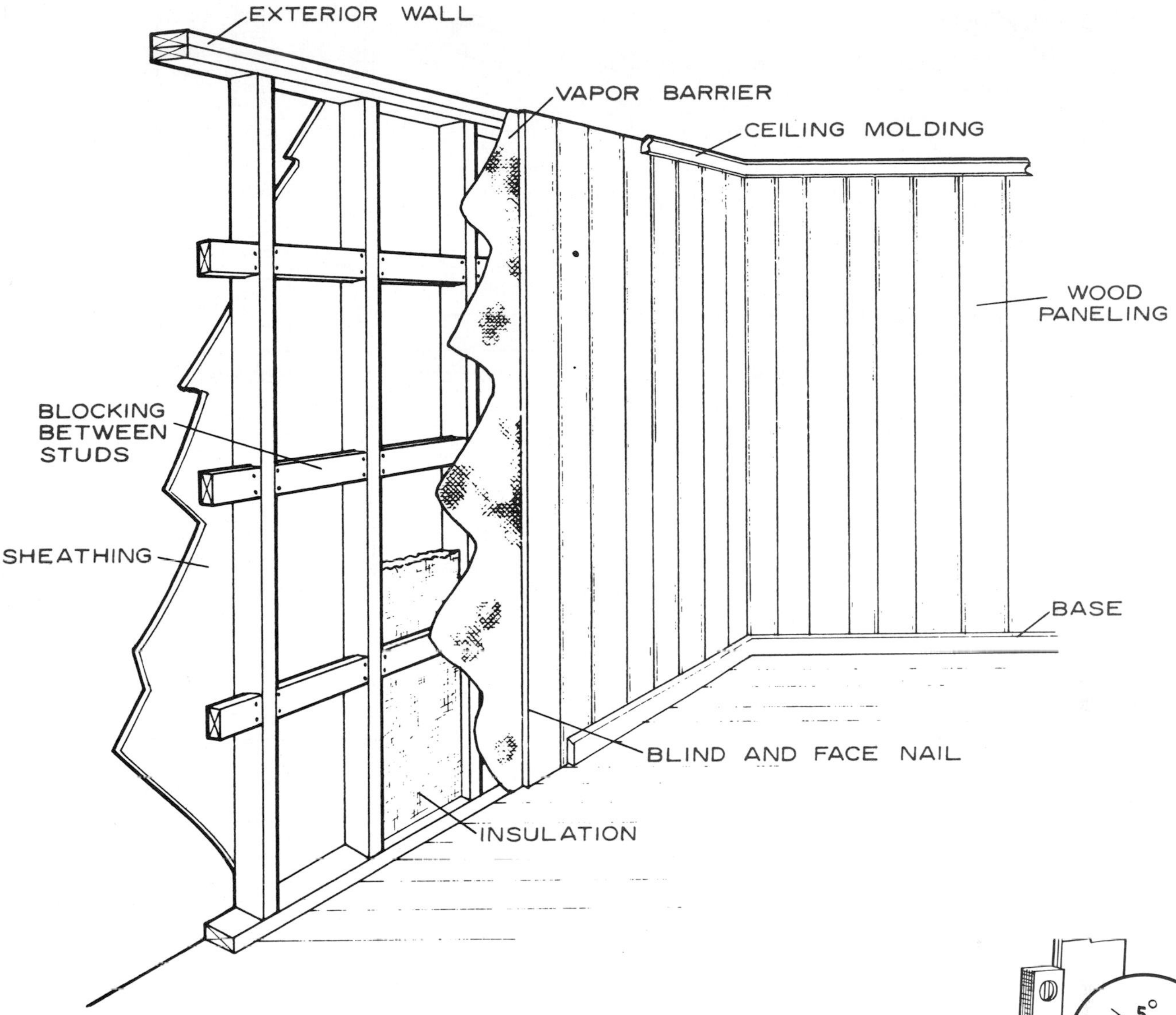

EXTERIOR WALL

VAPOR BARRIER

CEILING MOLDING

WOOD PANELING

BLOCKING BETWEEN STUDS

SHEATHING

BASE

BLIND AND FACE NAIL

INSULATION

49-26. *Installation details for vertical wood paneling.*

Blind-nail all paneling in place using 5d or 6d casing or finishing nails. Fig. 49-29. Continue to install the pieces of paneling, checking for plumb periodically. If necessary, adjust slightly on each added panel until the pieces are again in plumb. The tongue and groove is used for the adjustment. Fig. 49-30.

On the last piece of paneling to be installed on a wall, the edge that is to fit into the corner should be

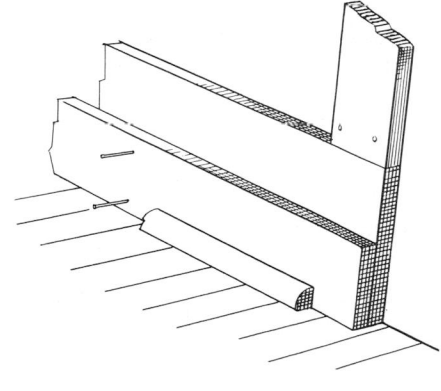

49-27. *The baseboard is nailed to a 1" x 8" furring strip at the floorline.*

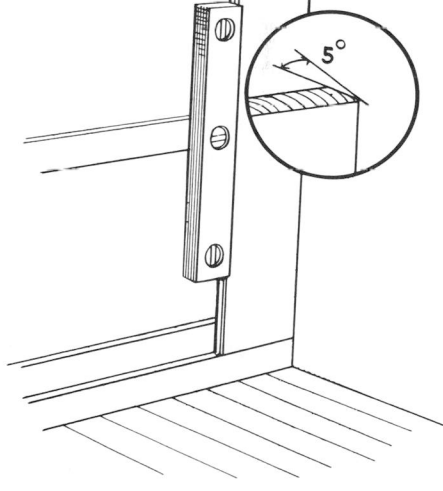

5°

49-28. *The first piece of paneling to be installed is scribed in a plumb position to the adjacent wall and undercut about 5° to provide a tight joint in the corner.*

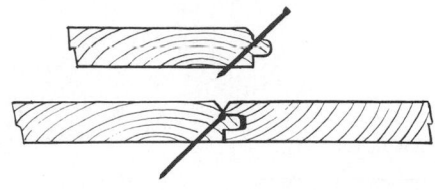

49-29. Blind-nailing details for lumber paneling.

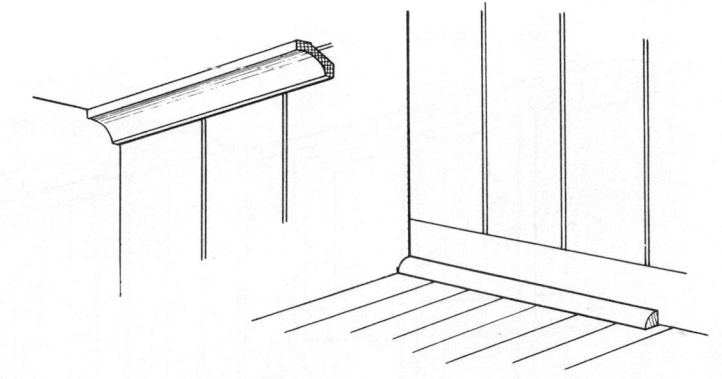

49-32. Apply cove or crown molding at the intersection of wall and ceiling and a base shoe at the floor.

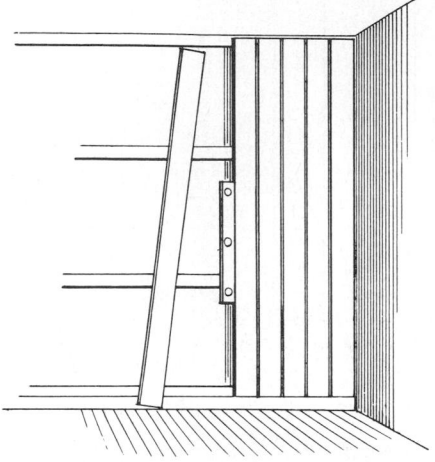

49-30. Periodically check the paneling for plumb as the installation progresses.

scribed and undercut at about a 5-degree angle. The groove of the panel can then be slipped over the tongue of the preceding piece and the panel snapped into place. Fig. 49-31. Apply a cove or a crown molding at the ceiling and wall intersection and a base shoe at the floor. Fig. 49-32. If necessary, install quarter-round trim in the corners.

Installation of Horizontal Wood Paneling. Horizontal paneling, while not as common as vertical paneling, has some advantages. This method of application requires fewer pieces to shape and install, and it is therefore much faster to apply. It also gives the room the appearance of being longer or larger with a lower ceiling.

Apply vertical nailing strips 18" on center as shown in Fig. 49-33. Horizontal paneling may also be nailed directly to the studs. Begin the paneling at the floor line, making certain that the first piece is installed level. Undercut the ends slightly to provide a tight joint at the inside corners. Outside corners should be mitered. Fig. 49-34. Blind-nail all the paneling as described for the vertical application, checking periodically to make certain the paneling remains level.

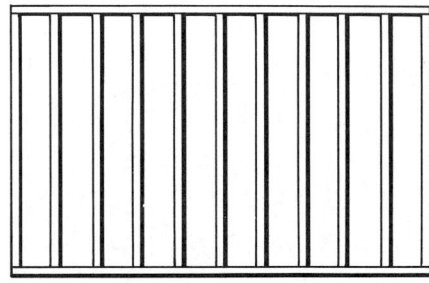

49-33. When applying wood paneling horizontally, apply the nailing strips vertically 18" on center. Begin the measurement at the wall on the end strips.

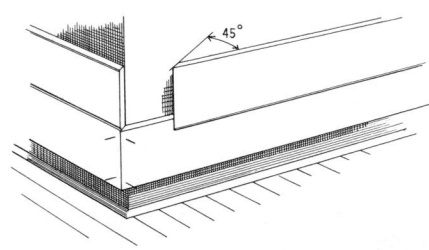

49-34. Wood paneling applied horizontally is mitered at outside corners. In this installation, instead of a baseboard, a "reveal" is shown.

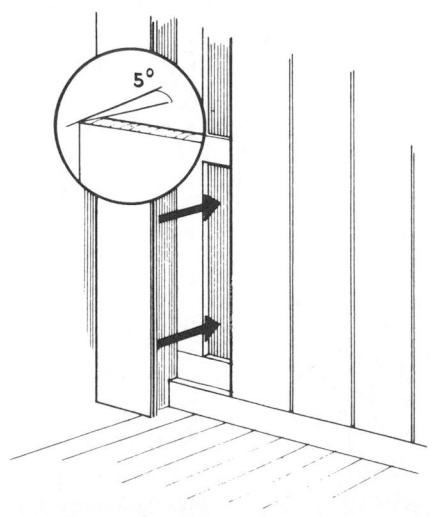

49-31. Scribe and undercut the last piece of paneling to insure a tight fit against the adjacent wall.

If no molding is to be used at the ceiling, undercut the last panel edge at a 5-degree angle to insure a snug fit against the ceiling line. When desired, apply cove or crown moldings at the ceiling and wall joints and apply base shoe at the floor. If necessary, quarter-round trim may be installed in the corners.

Installing Wood Paneling in a Herringbone Pattern. The herringbone style of application is very interesting, but it is also the most demanding in craftsmanship. Fig. 49-35. Apply vertical nailing strips so that the space between them is evenly divided. For example, if the wall is 12' long, space the strips 18" on center as shown in Fig. 49-36. When laying out, begin the actual measurement from the adjacent wall next to the end strip and measure to the center of the other strips. Make sure that each strip is plumb.

Install the baseboard as shown in Fig. 49-37. Then, using a long level, draw a plumb line at the center of every other nailing strip as shown at a, b, and c in Fig. 49-36. For a 12' wall, these lines should be as close as possible to 36" apart. Saw two pieces of paneling in the shape of a triangle with the tongue on the long edge, as shown in Fig. 49-38. Install them with the vertical joint on one of the plumb lines. Extreme care should be taken to make the paneling butt even with the baseboard. A molding strip will be applied later at the vertical joint.

In the same manner, measure and cut to length the second pieces to be installed. Install each paneling piece all the way across the wall, building toward the top. Use the play in the tongue and groove to keep the panels aligned at the "V" (along the vertical joint). After all the pieces have been applied, install the cove or

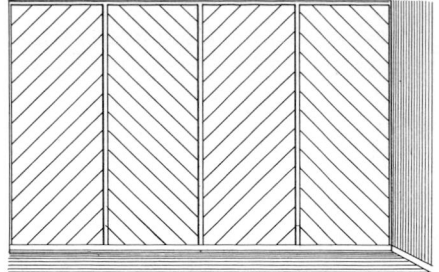

49-35. Wood paneling applied in a herringbone style.

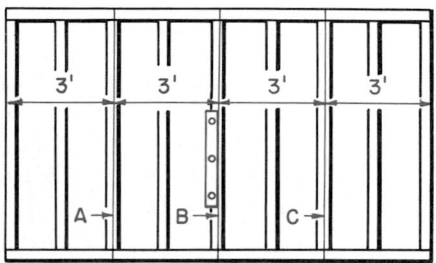

49-36. Locating the furring strips on a 12' wall for a herringbone application.

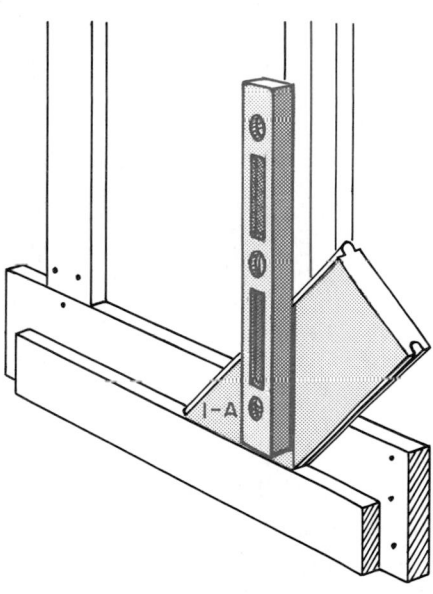

49-37. Laying out the first piece of paneling (A). Baseboard installation is necessary to provide backing for nailing the paneling in place.

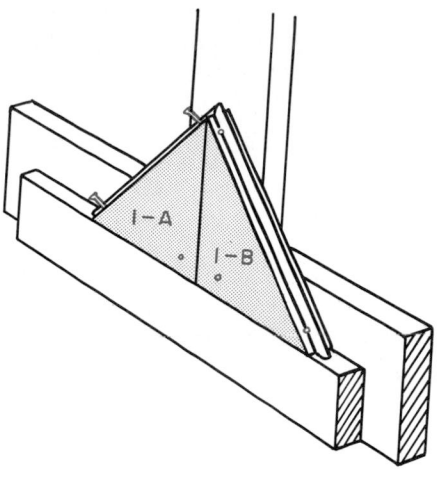

49-38. Lay out and cut the second piece (1B) before nailing the first piece (1A) in place.

crown molding at the ceiling. Next apply the molding at the butt joint of the paneling. This molding should stop at the baseboard and butt into the cove or crown molding at the ceiling. Fig. 49-39. A cove or quarter-round may be used at the corners and a base shoe at the floor if necessary. Table 49-B provides a quick means of figuring wall area. This chart tells the square feet of area per wall length. To find the total area to be covered, add up the areas of all the walls.

Determining the Amount of Sheet Paneling

Figure the perimeter of the room to be paneled. Convert the perimeter into the number of panels needed by using the conversion table in Table 49-C. For example, the room in Fig. 49-40 has a perimeter of 66'. The conversion table indicates that 17 panels are required. Should the perimeter fall between figures, use the next higher number.

Table 49-B. *Determining Wall Areas. Wall areas can be determined by using this table. The left-hand column shows ceiling heights. The top row represents wall lengths. For example, a wall 8' high and 16' long has an area of 128 square feet.*

Ceiling Height	6	8	10	12	14	16	18	20	22	24	26	28	30
7'6"	45	60	75	90	105	120	135	150	165	180	195	210	225
8'0"	48	64	80	96	112	128	144	160	176	192	208	224	240
8'6"	51	68	85	102	119	136	153	170	187	204	221	238	255
9'0"	54	72	90	108	126	144	162	180	198	216	234	252	270
9'6"	57	76	95	114	133	152	171	190	209	228	247	266	285
10'0"	60	80	100	120	140	160	180	200	220	240	260	280	300

Note: Square feet of area per wall length.

Table 49-C. *Determining Panels per Room. Find the perimeter of the room in the left-hand column. Follow across to the right-hand column headed "Panels Needed" to determine the number of panels for a room with a given perimeter. For example, a room with a perimeter of 60' would require 15 panels.*

Conversion Table

Perimeter	Panels needed
20'	5
24'	6
28'	7
32'	8
60'	15
64'	16
66'	17
68'	17
72'	18
92'	23

If the ceiling height is more than 8' (the standard length of a panel), determine the additional height. For example, if the room in Fig. 49-40 has a 10' ceiling, 2' of additional height are required. Use 10' panels if they are available, or cut 2' pieces from an 8' panel. Four 2' pieces can be cut from each 8' panel. Since 17 panels are required to go around the room, 4¼ (or, rounded off, 5) additional panels will be required. (17 ÷ 4 = 4¼.) This makes a total of 22 panels. Deduct for areas such as doors, windows, and fireplaces. For estimating purposes, deduct ⅔ of a

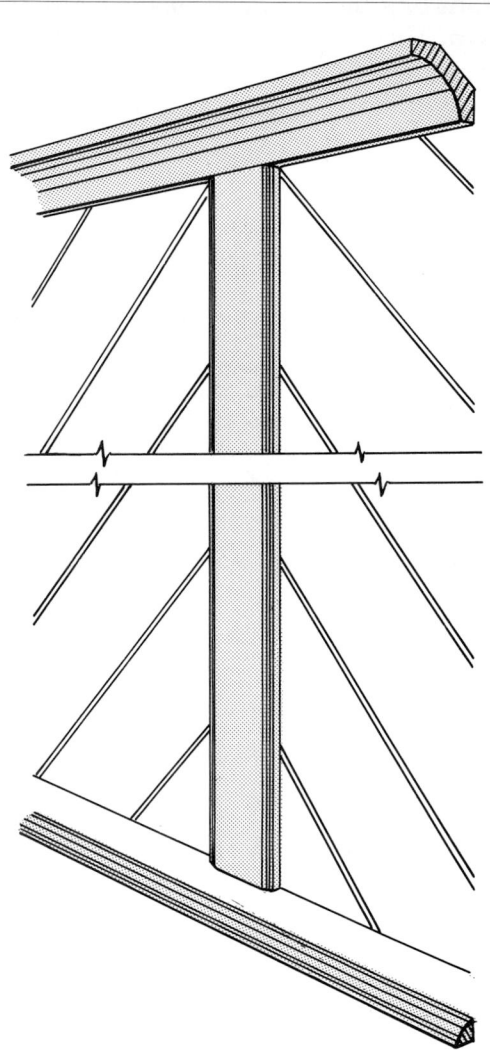

49-39. *Apply a molding strip at the vertical joint of the paneling. The molding should extend from the top of the baseboard to the underside of the ceiling molding.*

panel for a door and ½ for a window or fireplace. Subtract the total deductions from the number of panels originally determined and round off the remainder to the next higher number. Our example for an 8' ceiling showed 17 panels minus 2⅚ panels for doors, windows, and a fireplace, or a net of 14⅙ panels. Therefore it will be necessary to order 15 panels. For a room with a 10' ceiling, an additional 4¼ panels are necessary. A total of 18⁵⁄₁₂ panels are needed. (14⅙ + 4¼ = 18⁵⁄₁₂.) Round off this number to 19. This same system can be used for estimating all standard 4' wide wall covering materials.

Estimating Wood Paneling

To determine the amount of wood paneling required to panel a room, first figure the wall area to be covered. Using the room in Fig. 49-40 as an example, with a perimeter of 66' and a ceiling height of 8', the wall area is 528 sq. ft. Subtract the window, door, and fireplace areas. Assuming that these areas total 112 sq. ft., subtract this from the wall area. A total of 416 sq. ft. is to be covered by wood paneling (528 - 112 = 416).

If tongue-and-groove paneling is to be installed, multiply the total area to be covered by the area factor. Table 49-D. Add an allowance for trim and waste, usually 5%. The area factor for tongue-and-groove 1" × 8" paneling is 1.16. The room in our example contains 416 sq. ft. Multiplying 416 × 1.16 equals 482.56, or 483 board feet of paneling. To this is added a trim and waste factor of 5%, or 24 more board feet. (483 × 0.05 = 24.15, or 24.) The total amount required is then 507 board feet (483 + 24 = 507). Multiply this figure by the cost per board foot to determine the total cost of the paneling to be installed.

Table 49-D. *Coverage Estimator. For most installations, an allowance of 5% will be adequate for trim and waste. Sometimes, rather than add 5%, the area of the doors and windows is not subtracted but is used as a trim and waste allowance.*

		Nominal Size	Width Dress	Width Face	Area Factor*
Shiplap		1 x 6	5 ⁷⁄₁₆	4 ¹⁵⁄₁₆	1.22
		1 x 8	7 ¹⁄₈	6 ⁵⁄₈	1.21
		1 x 10	9 ¹⁄₈	8 ⁵⁄₈	1.16
		1 x 12	11 ¹⁄₈	10 ⁵⁄₈	1.13
Tongue and Groove		1 x 4	3 ⁷⁄₁₆	3 ³⁄₁₆	1.26
		1 x 6	5 ⁷⁄₁₆	5 ³⁄₁₆	1.16
		1 x 8	7 ¹⁄₈	6 ⁷⁄₈	1.16
		1 x 10	9 ¹⁄₈	8 ⁷⁄₈	1.13
		1 x 12	11 ¹⁄₈	10 ⁷⁄₈	1.10
S4S		1 x 4	3 ¹⁄₂	3 ¹⁄₂	1.14
		1 x 6	5 ¹⁄₂	5 ¹⁄₂	1.09
		1 x 8	7 ¹⁄₄	7 ¹⁄₄	1.10
		1 x 10	9 ¹⁄₄	9 ¹⁄₄	1.08
		1 x 12	11 ¹⁄₄	11 ¹⁄₄	1.07
Paneling Patterns		1 x 6	5 ⁷⁄₁₆	5 ¹⁄₁₆	1.19
		1 x 8	7 ¹⁄₈	6 ³⁄₄	1.19
		1 x 10	9 ¹⁄₈	8 ³⁄₄	1.14
		1 x 12	11 ¹⁄₈	10 ³⁄₄	1.12
Bevel Siding		1 x 4	3 ¹⁄₂	3 ¹⁄₂	1.60
		1 x 6	5 ¹⁄₂	5 ¹⁄₂	1.33
		1 x 8	7 ¹⁄₄	7 ¹⁄₄	1.28
		1 x 10	9 ¹⁄₄	9 ¹⁄₄	1.21
		1 x 12	11 ¹⁄₄	11 ¹⁄₄	1.17

* Allowance for trim and waste should be added.

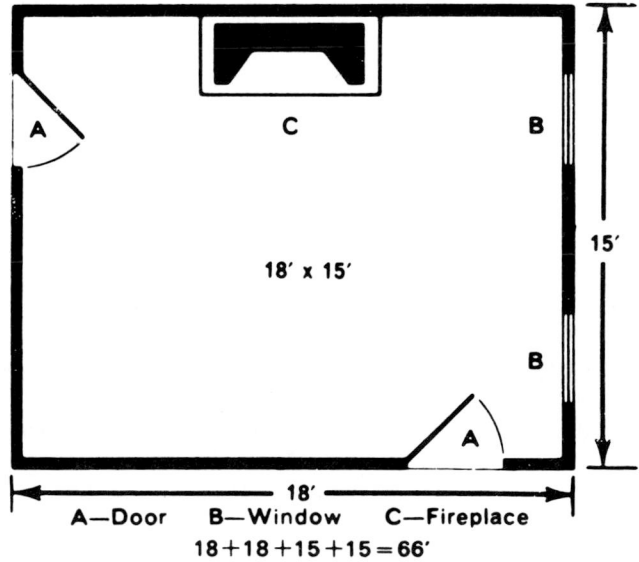

18' x 15'

15'

18'

A—Door   B—Window   C—Fireplace
18 + 18 + 15 + 15 = 66'

49-40. *The perimeter of a room is calculated by adding the lengths of the four walls together.*

QUESTIONS

1. Name the three basic types of wood paneling.

2. What technique is used to install wood paneling over masonry surfaces?

3. When installing plywood or hardboard paneling, what should be done with the edges that do not fall directly over a stud?

4. What types of nails are most often used to fasten wood paneling?

5. When cutting a plywood or hardboard panel with a table saw, which side of the panel should face up?

6. When cutting plywood or hardboard paneling with a portable circular saw or a table saw, what type of saw blade should be used?

7. Describe how the location for the outlet box cutout on a plywood panel is determined.

8. What recommended nominal width for wood paneling is used in most parts of the country?

9. Which method of wood paneling installation will give a room the appearance of being longer or larger and having a lower ceiling?

ACTIVITIES

1. Math. Using the placement of furring strips given in Fig. 49-3, determine how many linear feet of furring material are needed to panel a wall 8' by 10'.

2. Language Arts. In any job you take, you should have a good understanding of your own abilities. Not every aspect of a job may be appealing to you. For example, some parts of the job may be more attractive than others. To be effective, though, you should also recognize the importance of learning to accept criticism. If the criticism is deserved, you should be willing to put it to good use. You might, for example, use it to improve your job performance. Identify those characteristics of a person who is able to accept criticism—and benefit from that criticism. Express your thoughts in a brief essay.

THE SCHOOL-TO-WORK CONNECTION

Installing paneling in a basement presents a number of challenges that are not present in other areas of the house. Exposed posts and beams are usually in the way. They shouldn't be altered, moved, or eliminated without the advice of a structural engineer. That means they have to be concealed. This is often done by using the same paneling used on the walls.

Beams are usually made of wood, but may be steel or a combination of steel and wood. Newer houses generally have steel posts called lally columns. A lally column is essentially a steel tube that can be adjusted to various heights. It is sometimes filled with concrete. You can install nails or screws in wood posts and beams, but it is usually too much trouble to drill into steel.

1. Your job is to install paneling. Make some sketches showing two different ways that you could cover a lally column with 1/4" plywood paneling. Assume that the top of the column goes through a finished drywall ceiling. Show a section view and an elevation view. Label the type and dimension of all materials. Identify the type and size of any fastener you would use.

2. Consult Fig. 29-4a. Use sketches to explain how you would conceal the wood post and girder with solid 1 x 6 tongue-and-groove paneling. Assume that the ceiling will be 1/2" drywall. Label the type and dimension of all materials, the type and size of any fasteners, and the type of any adhesive you would use.

Wood and Vinyl Flooring

Finish flooring is the final wearing surface applied to a floor. Many materials are used as finish flooring, each one having properties suited to a particular usage. Durability and ease of cleaning are essential in all cases. Specific service requirements may call for special properties such as resistance to hard wear, comfort to users, and attractive appearance.

Hardwoods are available as strip flooring in a variety of widths and thicknesses and as random-width planks, parquetry, and block flooring. A wide variety of other flooring materials is available. Among these, vinyl flooring is the most common. Vinyl flooring, sometimes called resilient flooring, can be purchased in sheet or tile form. When a finish floor other than wood is to be installed on a subfloor of wood boards, an underlayment is required. This is usually plywood.

HARDWOOD STRIP FLOORING

Strip flooring is the most widely used type of hardwood flooring. Practically all species are produced in this form. As the name implies, it consists of flooring pieces cut in narrow strips. Fig. 50-1.

The most common hardwoods for strip flooring are oak, maple, beech, birch, and pecan. Oak, the most plentiful, is the most popular by far. It constitutes about 80% of the residential hardwood flooring in the United States.

Despite its extensive usage, strip flooring should not be considered commonplace. Its popularity is due to its high quality. No two hardwood floors are exactly alike. Each has individuality of character and beauty

50-1. *Hardwood strip flooring can be used throughout a house.*

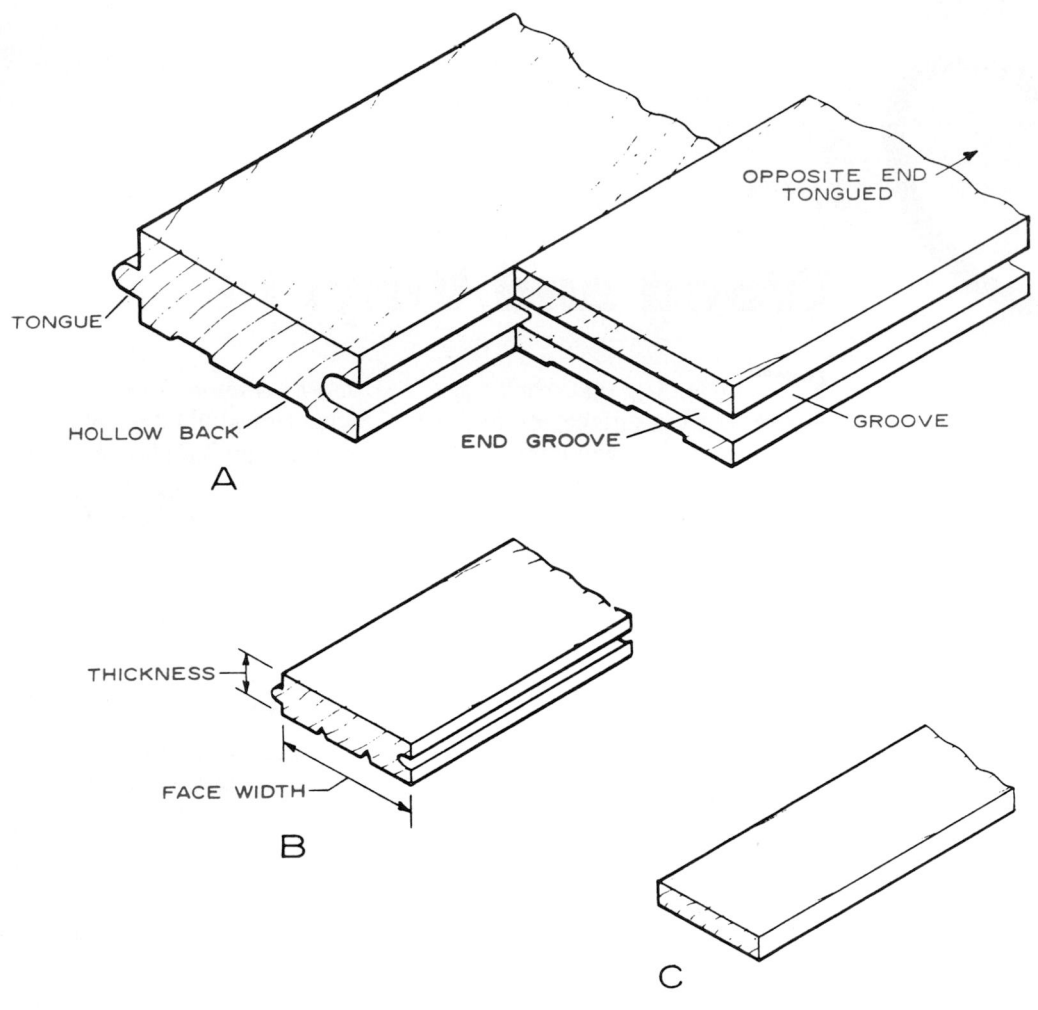

TONGUE

HOLLOW BACK

A

OPPOSITE END
TONGUED

END GROOVE

GROOVE

THICKNESS

FACE WIDTH

B

C

50-2. *Strip flooring. A. Side- and end-matched. B. Side-matched. C. Square-edged.*

of grain. Most floors of this type are composed of strips of uniform width. Interesting patterns are formed by use of stock selected for variations in color or other natural irregularities. Attractive designs also may be achieved with strips of random widths. Most hardwood strip flooring today is tongued and grooved at the factory so that each piece joins the next one snugly when laid. Fig. 50-2.

Sizes

Strip flooring of oak, maple, beech, birch, and pecan is manufactured in a variety of sizes, ranging in width from 1" to 2¼"

and in thickness from $^{5}/_{16}$" to $^{33}/_{32}$". The standard thicknesses for tongued and grooved strip flooring are ½", ⅜", and $^{25}/_{32}$". Since strips of these thicknesses are the most commonly chosen for homes, they are produced in greatest volume and are available at lower cost than special thicknesses. The $^{25}/_{32}$" strips, used the most, are manufactured in four widths: 1½", 2", 2¼", and 3¼". Most popular is the 2¼".

Square-edge oak strip flooring is $^{5}/_{16}$" thick and comes in widths of 1", 1⅛", 1½", and 2". Square-edge maple, beech, birch, and pecan strip flooring comes in two thicknesses: $^{25}/_{32}$" and $^{33}/_{32}$". Widths of 2½" and 3½" are available in

each thickness. The length of the strips in a bundle of flooring varies, but average lengths are specified for each grade. Some strips may be as long as 16 feet.

Grading

Through two major trade associations, the principal American producers of hardwood strip flooring have adopted uniform grading rules and regulations for commercial practice. Approved by the Bureau of Standards of the U.S. Department of Commerce, these rules and regulations are enforced rigidly, in part by the organizations themselves. The two organizations are the National Oak Flooring Manufacturers' Association, with headquarters at Memphis, Tennessee, and the Maple Flooring Manufacturers' Association, Northbrook, Illinois. Every bundle of flooring produced by a member of either association is identified as to grade and is guaranteed to meet all established specifications. Usually the manufacturer's name and a mill mark or identification are stated on each bundle.

The hardwood flooring grades in Canada are identical to those for the United States.

There are no official grading rules for plank, parquet, and block flooring. Generally the different grades correspond to those of strip flooring. Hardwood strip flooring grades are based principally on appearance. Since all regular grades have adequate strength, durability, and resistance to wear, these qualities are not factors. Chiefly considered are such characteristics as knots, streaks, pin wormholes and, in some cases, sapwood and variations in color. Slight imperfections in processing also are factors.

Oak. Oak is classified into two grades of quarter-sawn stock and four grades plain-sawn. In descending order the quarter-sawn grades are: Clear and Select. Plain-sawn grades are: Clear, Select, No. 1 Common, and No. 2 Common.

Clear Grade Oak has the best appearance and the most uniform color. Limited small character marks are permissible. Red oak and white oak ordinarily are separated, but that does not affect their grading. In most cases the average length of strip flooring pieces is greater in the higher grades.

Maple, Beech, Birch. Rules governing the grading of maple, beech, and birch are virtually identical for all three species.

Neither sapwood nor varying natural color is considered a defect in standard grades. These standard grades are first, second, and third, with first being the highest. Fig. 50-3. Each of these grades also is available in a special grade selected for uniformity of color.

Pecan. Pecan is generally available in three standard grades: first, second, and third. All grades allow natural color variation. The first grade offers the best appearance, while the third grade has a rustic appearance. As with the other woods, pecan is available in several mixes of the basic grades.

STORAGE AND DELIVERY

Certified hardwood flooring is kiln-dried at the factory to a low moisture content. However, moisture content later equalizes itself to the moisture conditions in the area where the flooring is used. The flooring must be protected from the elements during storage and delivery to guard against excessive shrinkage or expansion, which may cause cracks or buckling after the floor has been laid. Manufacturers who ship hardwood flooring in closed boxcars recommend the following precautions in handling:

➤ Do not unload, truck, or transfer hardwood flooring in rain or snow. Cover it with tarpaulin if the atmosphere is foggy or damp.

➤ Flooring should be stored in airy, well-ventilated buildings, preferably with weathertight windows that will admit sunlight.

➤ Do not pile flooring on storage floors that are less than 18" from the ground and which do not have good air circulation underneath.

➤ Do not store or lay flooring in

50-3a. *Typical first grade MFMA (Maple Flooring Manufacturers' Association) maple flooring.*

50-3b. *Typical second grade MFMA maple flooring.*

50-3c. *Typical third grade MFMA maple flooring.*

a cold or damp building. Wait until the plaster and concrete work have dried thoroughly and all but the final woodwork and trim have been installed.

➤ Especially in winter construction, the building in which the flooring is to be used should first be heated to 70 degrees F. Then the flooring should be stored in the building at least four or five days before being laid. This permits the flooring to reach a moisture content equivalent to that of the building.

INSTALLATION

Installation of the finish flooring should be the last construction operation in a house. All plumbing, electrical wiring, and plastering should be completed before the application of the finish floor is begun. Only the final interior trim work should remain.

Before laying the flooring, the bundles should be opened and the flooring spread out and exposed to warm, dry air for at least 24 hours, preferably 48 hours. Moisture content of the flooring should be 6% for the dry Southwest, 10% for southern and coastal areas, and 7% for the remainder of North America.

Preparing the Subfloor

Strip flooring can be laid over a plywood subfloor or over a board subfloor. The plywood should be of exterior grade at least ½" thick (⅝" or thicker is preferable). Nailing should be 6" on center along each joist. A space of ⅛" should be allowed at the end of each panel, and ¼" along panel edges, unless otherwise recommended by the plywood manufacturer. The National Oak Flooring Manufacturers Association does

not recommend nonveneered panel products (such as particleboard) for subfloors under wood flooring.

Board subfloors should be graded #1 or #2 pine or the equivalent. The boards should be square-edged, not T&G, and no wider than 6". They should be laid diagonally across the joists with ¼" expansion space between each board. All butt joints must be fully supported by a joist or blocking. Proper nailing is important to keep boards from squeaking later. At every bearing point, each board should be nailed with two 10d common nails. Some builders prefer ring shank nails.

Just before installation of the finish flooring is to begin, the subfloors should be examined carefully and any defects corrected. Raised nails, for instance, should be driven down and loose or warped boards replaced. The subfloors should be swept thoroughly and scraped if necessary to remove all

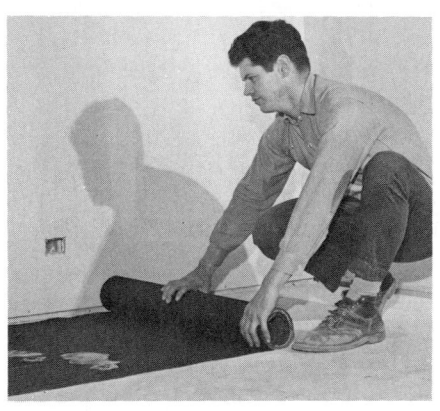

50-4. *Laying the asphalt building paper over the subfloor in preparation for the finish floor. NOTE: The building paper will cover up the nails in the subfloor which indicate the location of the floor joists. It is therefore advisable to mark the location of the floor joists on the walls before laying the building paper. Later chalk lines may be snapped on the building paper to indicate the location of the floor joists below for nailing the strip flooring.*

plaster, mortar, or other foreign materials. These precautions must be taken if the finish flooring is to be laid properly.

The last operation before actual installation of the finish flooring should be the application of 15 lb. asphalt building paper over the subflooring. Fig. 50-4. The paper will protect the finish floor and the interior of the home from dust, cold, and moisture which might seep through the floor seams. In the area directly over the heating plant, it is advisable to lay double-weight building paper or standard insulating board. This will protect the finish floor from excessive heat, which might shrink the boards.

Where to Start

Before the actual laying of strip flooring begins, the floor plans of the house should be studied. Careful consideration must be given to the area of the house in which the installation will begin. Strip flooring should be laid so that there is an uninterrupted flow from one room through the hall to the other rooms. Plan the job to eliminate having to align in the hall the courses of strip flooring from two rooms.

For example, in Fig. 50-5 if the courses from bedrooms 1 and 2 are laid through the doorways and into the hall, it is very unlikely that they will line up. Therefore it is best to start the first strip of flooring against the wall indicated by arrow A in bedroom 3. Fig. 50-5. Work across the bedroom and through the door into the hall. Continue along the hall wall into the living room.

Work the courses across the hall and the first few courses of the living room together. As the courses approach the rear wall of the hall, work through the doorways into bedrooms 1 and 2, and complete the laying of the

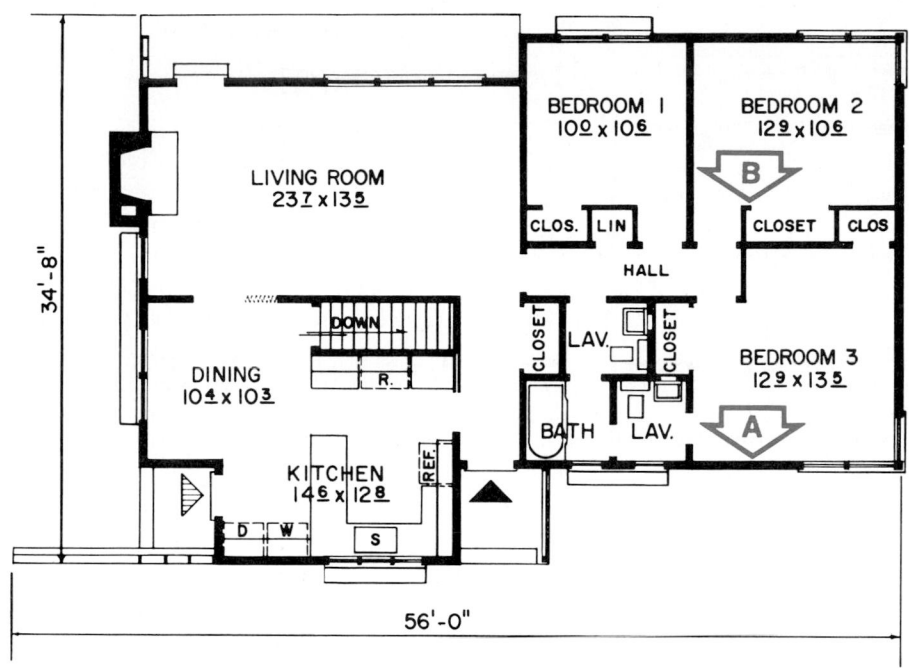

50-5. *The first piece of strip flooring should be laid at the wall indicated by arrow A above. At arrow B a piece of strip flooring is reversed as shown in Fig. 50-4. This will permit blind-nailing into the closet area.*

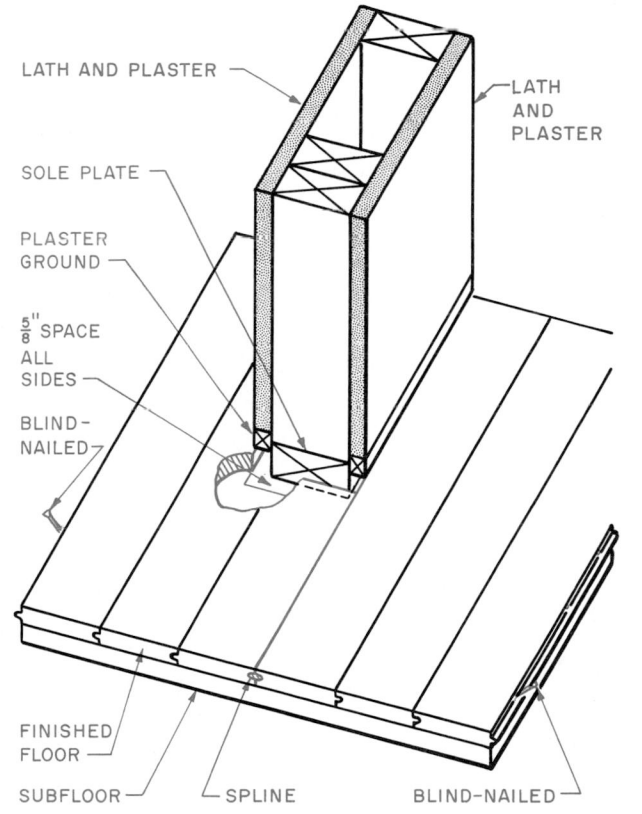

LATH AND PLASTER

LATH AND PLASTER

SOLE PLATE

PLASTER GROUND

$\frac{5}{8}$" SPACE ALL SIDES

BLIND-NAILED

FINISHED FLOOR

SUBFLOOR

SPLINE

BLIND-NAILED

50-6. *A spline is inserted between the two pieces of flooring at the wall line indicated by arrow B in Fig. 50-5.*

bedroom floors. Then return to the living room and finish laying the living room floor, working toward the rear of the house.

In working in this manner the closets in bedrooms 1 and 2 will require placing the grooves of two strips together, with a spline between the grooves. The tongues can then be blind-nailed on each piece. This will permit the courses of strip flooring in the closet to be blind-nailed as well as the pieces which will go across the bedroom floor toward the back wall. Fig. 50-6.

In a split-level, as shown in Fig. 50-7, the first strip of flooring is laid against the back wall of bedroom 1. The floor is laid through the door, across the hall, and into the two front bedrooms. The living room is done separately, and should be started at its front wall and laid in the direction of the arrow across the floor toward the dining room. If hardwood flooring is to be laid in the dining room, continue through the archway and to the rear wall of the house. If another type of flooring is to be used in the dining room, the strip flooring should terminate at the wall of the dining room. Fig. 50-7, line A.

When different floor coverings are laid in adjoining rooms and a doorway connects the two rooms, the hardwood flooring should terminate under the center of the door when the door is closed. The second type of flooring should begin at this point. In this way, when the door is closed, only the flooring of the room in which the individual is standing may be seen. When finish floors of different materials come together in an archway between two rooms, the hardwood floor is usually laid through the archway and even with the wall line of the adjacent room.

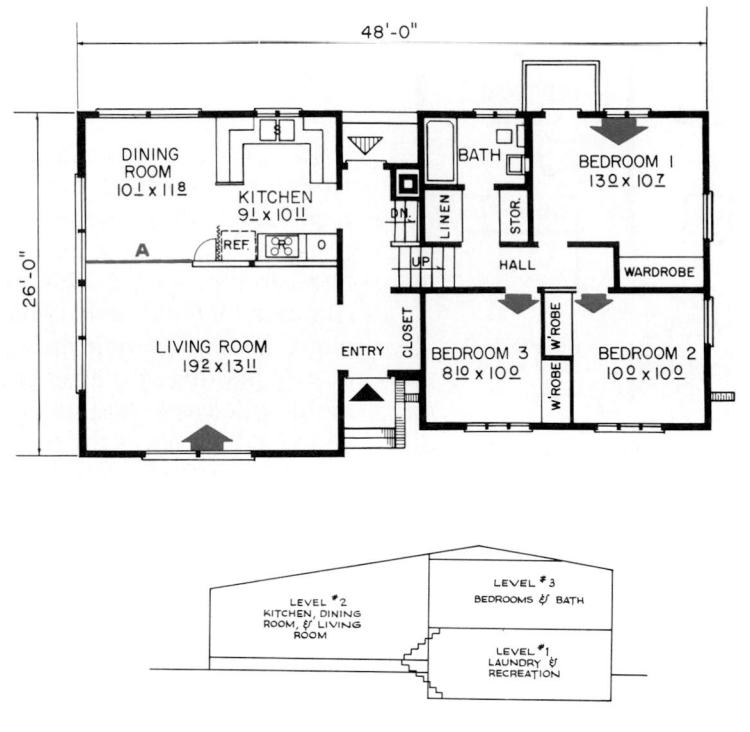

50-7. *In a split-level home, laying strip flooring is simplified. Each level is done independently, which eliminates many of the problems of lining up courses in several rooms.*

Arrangement of Flooring Pieces

In most houses strip flooring presents the most attractive appearance when laid lengthwise of the room's longest dimension. In some cases, however, it is considered acceptable to lay the flooring crosswise. This is true only if the rooms are sufficiently wide. Wood-strip flooring is usually laid at right angles to the direction of the joists under the largest room on that story. Fig. 50-8. Since interior thresholds are omitted today, the flooring should run continuously between adjoining rooms.

Proper placing of the strips of flooring calls for the use of the shorter lengths in closets and in the general floor area. The longer pieces should be used at entrances and doorways and for starting and finishing in a room. This arrangement results in maximum attractiveness of the floor as a whole. Care should be taken to stagger the end joints of the flooring pieces so that several of them are not grouped closely together. Fig. 50-9.

50-9. *Laying out the strip flooring in preparation for cutting the end pieces so that the joints are staggered.*

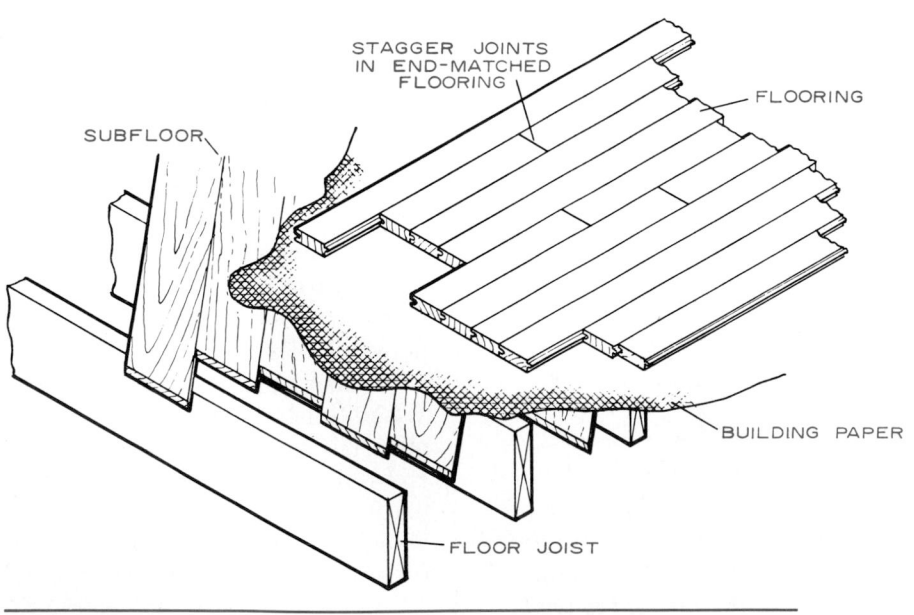

50-8. *Strip flooring should be laid at right angles to the floor joists.*

Table 50-A. *Nail Schedule. Tongued and grooved flooring must be blind nailed.*

Flooring Nominal Size, Inches	Size of Fasteners	Spacing of Fasteners
³/₄ x 1 ¹/₂	2" machine driven fasteners; 7d or 8d screw or cut nail.	10" - 12"* apart
³/₄ x 2 ¹/₄	2" machine driven fasteners; 7d or 8d screw or cut nail.	10" - 12"* apart
³/₄ x 3 ¹/₄	2" machine driven fasteners; 7d or 8d screw or cut nail.	10" - 12"* apart
³/₄ x 3" to 8" plank	2" machine driven fasteners; 7d or 8d screw or cut nail.	8" apart into and between joists.
Following flooring must be laid on a subfloor.		
¹/₂ x 1 ¹/₂	1 ¹/₂" machine driven fasteners; 5d screw, cut steel or wire casing nail.	10" apart
¹/₂ x 2	1 ¹/₂" machine driven fasteners; 5d screw, cut steel or wire casing nail.	10" apart
³/₈ x 1 ¹/₂	1 ¹/₄" machine driven fasteners; 4d bright wire casing nails.	8" apart
³/₈ x 2	1 ¹/₄" machine driven fasteners; 4d bright wire casing nails.	8" apart
Square-edge flooring as follows, face-nailed through top face.		
⁵/₁₆ x 1 ¹/₂	1", 15-gauge fully barbed flooring brad.	2 nails every 7 inches.
⁵/₁₆ x 2	1", 15-gauge fully barbed flooring brad.	2 nails every 7 inches.
⁵/₁₆ x 1 ¹/₃	1", 15-gauge fully barbed flooring brad.	1 nail every 5 inches on alternate sides of strip.

* If subfloor is 1/2 inch plywood, fasten into each joist, with additional fastening between joists.

50-11. *To line up the first course of flooring, stretch a string or snap a chalk line about 8" from the wall. The first course is face-nailed.*

Importance of Adequate Nailing

Adequate nailing is absolutely essential in the finish floor as well as the subfloor. Insufficient nailing may result in loose or squeaky flooring, one of the most annoying deficiencies a house may develop. The building paper should be chalklined at the joists as a guide in nailing the strip flooring. Tongue-and-groove flooring should be blind-nailed. The nails should be driven at an angle of about 45 or 50 degrees at the point where the tongue leaves the shoulder. Square-edge flooring should be face-nailed. It is recommended that nail heads be countersunk. Table 50-A includes information about the types of nails and the spacing commonly used. Figure 50-10 shows three types of flooring nails.

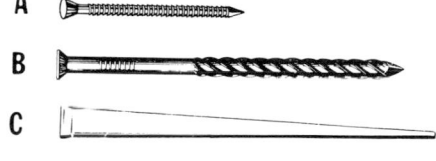

50-10. *Flooring nails: A. Barbed. B. Screw. C. Cut steel.*

Laying Strip Flooring over Subflooring

Cover the subfloor with building paper. Stretch a string the length of the room between two nails placed about 8" from a side wall. Many walls are not perfectly true. By lining up the first courses of flooring at a uniform distance from the string rather than from the wall itself, a straighter course is assured. Fig. 50-11.

Place a long piece of flooring with the groove edge about ¹/₂" to ⁵/₈" from a side wall and the groove end nearest an end wall. The ¹/₂" to ⁵/₈" space is for expansion. It will be hidden by shoe molding. Face-nail the flooring piece near the end. Fig. 50-12. Measure as you nail toward the other end, maintaining the same fixed distance from the guide string. Fig. 50-11. Do likewise in lining up succeeding pieces in the course. Drive one nail at each joist crossing, or every 10" to 12" if the joists run parallel to the flooring.

Observe nailing recommendations of the flooring manufacturer. For example, with flooring ²⁵/₃₂" thick and 1¹/₂" or more wide, 7d or 8d screw nails or cut steel nails are best. If steel wire flooring nails are used, they should be 8d, preferably cement coated.

After face-nailing the first course, toenail the pieces through the tongue edge, following the same spacing. Fig. 50-13. Drive the nail at the point where the tongue of the flooring leaves the shoulder, at an angle of about 45 or 50 degrees. Fig. 50-14. Each nail should be driven down to the point where another blow or two might

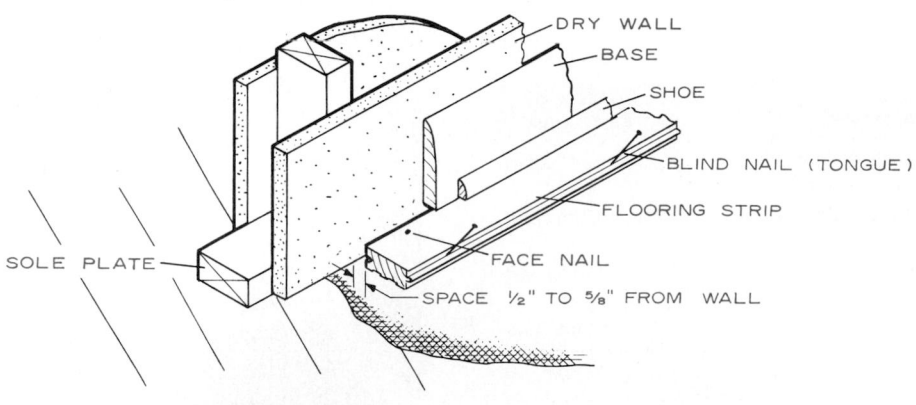

50-12. *Cross-section of a wall showing the first piece of strip flooring nailed in place. NOTE: With lath and plaster walls, sometimes the ground is kept off the subfloor about ⅞", and the edge of the first piece of strip flooring is set about even with the wall line. The flooring is then allowed to expand under the ground.*

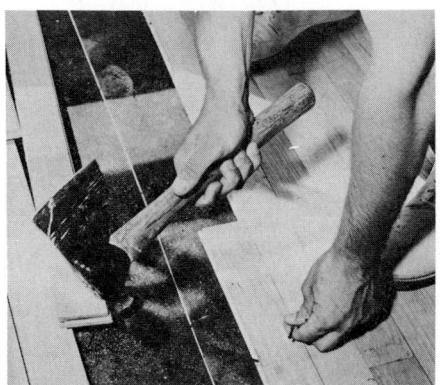

50-13. *Succeeding courses are toenailed into the flooring at the point where the tongue leaves the shoulder.*

50-14. *Strip flooring is nailed in place with the nail driven at about a 50° angle to the floor.*

cause the hammer to damage the edge of the strip. Use a nail set to drive the nail the rest of the way home. Fig. 50-15. The best nailing procedure is to stand on the strip, with toes in line with the outer edge, and strike the nail from a stooping position which will bring the hammer head square against the nail.

Fit the groove edges of pieces in each succeeding course with the tongues of those in the preceding course. Fit the groove end of each piece in a course with the tongue end of the previous pieces.

When a piece of flooring cannot be readily found to fit the remaining space in a course, cut one to size. Lay a piece down in reversed position from that in which it will be nailed. Draw a line at the point where it should be sawed. Fig. 50-16. Be sure the piece is reversed for this marking so that the tongue end will be cut off. The groove end is needed for joining with the tongue end of the previous piece.

Stagger the joints of neighboring pieces so that they will not be grouped closely. Fig. 50-17. A joint should not be closer than 6" to another in a previous course. To provide for this, arrange several pieces in their approximate positions in succeeding courses before they are nailed. After nailing three or four courses, place a piece of scrap flooring at intervals against the tongue edges of pieces in the last course. Strike the scrap piece a couple of good hammer blows. This drives the nailed flooring pieces up tightly. Fig. 50-18. Chisels and screwdrivers should never be used to lever floor boards into place. These tools are not designed to take lateral loads and could snap suddenly under stress. Instead, use a prybar or make the device shown in Fig. 50-19.

To fit flooring around a jutting door frame, place it flush against

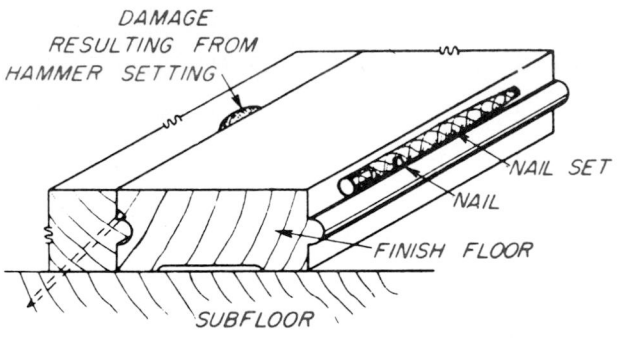

50-15. *When setting nails in strip flooring, many workers place the nail set on top of the nail as shown here. The nail set is struck with a sharp blow against its side. This sets the nail and at the same time tends to drive the piece of flooring up tightly against the piece previously laid.*

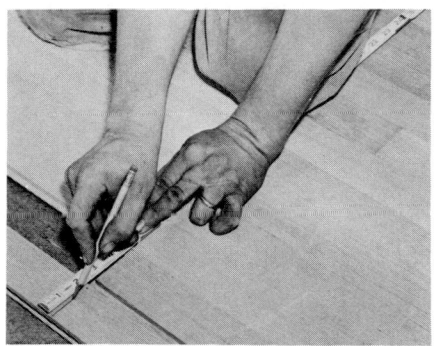

50-16. *When fitting a piece of flooring to the remaining space in a course, place it in reverse position for marking so that the tongue end is cut off. The groove end is needed for joining with the tongue of the previous piece.*

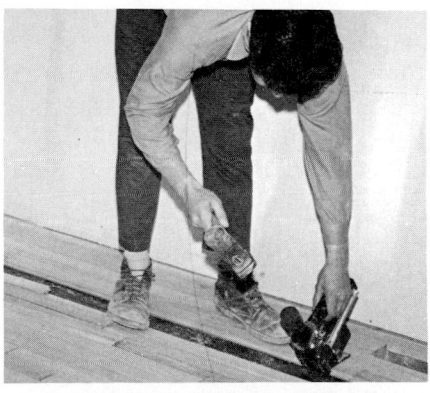

50-17a. *When installing strip flooring, it is customary for two people to work together in the room. One person nails the flooring in place, while the second works ahead laying out pieces, staggering joints, and cutting the end pieces to length. Notice in this picture that the man laying the flooring is using a nailing machine rather than nailing by hand as shown in Fig. 50-13.*

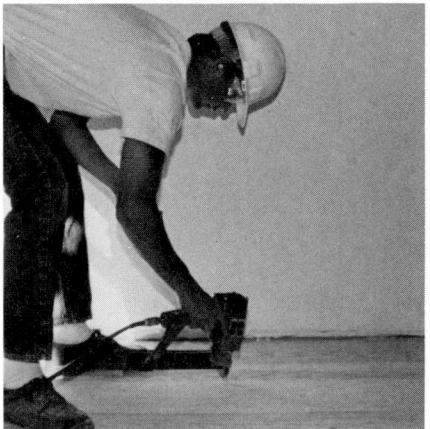

50-17b. *Pneumatic nailers can also be used to install strip flooring.*

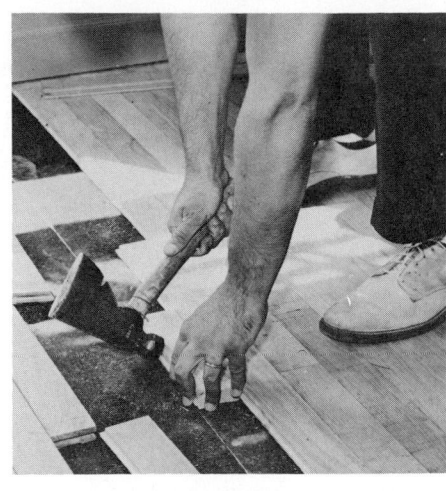

50-18. *After nailing three or four courses, place a piece of scrap flooring along the tongue edge of the flooring already laid. Drive the flooring up tight with two or three sharp hammer blows.*

the frame. Fig. 50-20. Measure the gap between the face of the previous piece and the groove edge of the piece to be nailed. Where the jutting begins, draw a straight line on the flooring to the same distance as the width of the gap. Fig. 50-20. Do the same on the other side of the door frame. Draw a straight line connecting the ends of these lines. Cut the flooring along the lines.

On reaching the opposite side of the room, you will find there is no space between the wall and the flooring to permit toenailing of the last two courses. Therefore just fit the pieces in. Face-nail the last few courses, at the same time pulling the flooring up tightly by exerting pressure against it with a crowbar driven into the subflooring. Fig. 50-21. Protect molding with cardboard or a piece of scrap lumber. After the last course, if the remaining space is too large to be covered by the shoe molding, rip pieces of flooring to the proper width and insert them in the spaces. Face-nail these strips. If they are very narrow, drill holes for the nails to prevent splitting.

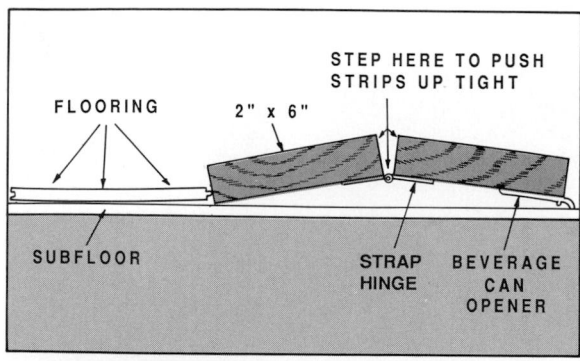

50-19. *A device for pushing floorboards together.*

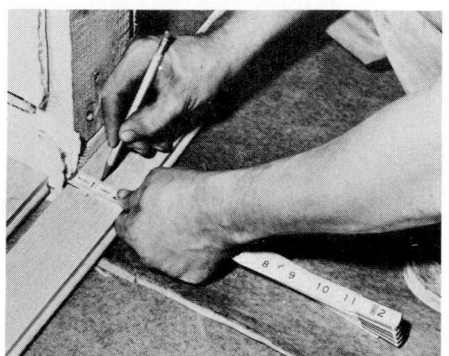

50-20. *The flooring should be fitted around a doorframe or other projection. Place the strip tight against the frame, measure the gap between the face edge of the previous piece and the groove edge of the piece to be nailed. Mark this distance, and the width of the frame, on the flooring and notch it out.*

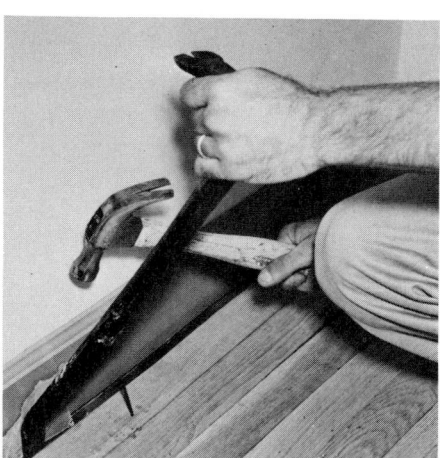

50-21. *When laying out the last few courses in the room, there will not be enough space to swing a hammer for toenailing. Therefore these courses are face-nailed. Place the last few courses in position, and pull the flooring up tightly when nailing. When prying the pieces with the crowbar, put something behind the crowbar to protect the plaster. A piece of paper is used here. However, a scrap piece of flooring or other piece of wood is better, particularly if it is a little longer and will span between the studs in the wall so that the plaster is not punctured.*

Laying Strip Flooring over Concrete

Before installing wood strip flooring over concrete, the slab should be tested for excessive moisture. Tape a 1' square of clear polyethylene to the slab. Use duct tape to seal the edges. Leave the plastic in place for 24 hours. At the end of this time, check the plastic for signs of moisture. If you do not see water droplets or a moisture fog beneath the plastic, the slab is dry enough for the installation of a wood floor.

Installing a Vapor Barrier

It is very important to ensure that moisture will be kept away from the wood flooring. Proper installation of a vapor barrier directly over the slab is the first step in doing this. Asphalt felt building paper or polyethylene plastic can be used as a vapor barrier.

To use asphalt felt, sweep the slab clean. Then apply cut-back asphalt mastic to the slab with a notched trowel. Cut-back mastic is mastic that has been thinned slightly with an appropriate solvent. About two hours after spreading the mastic, roll out strips of 15-lb. asphalt felt over the entire slab and lap the edges 4". Spread a second layer of mastic over the felt, then roll out a second layer of felt on top of it. Both layers of felt should run in the same direction, but the rows should be offset. Fig. 50-22.

To use a polyethylene plastic vapor barrier, sweep the slab clean. Then spread cut-back mastic over the slab with a notched trowel. After the mastic has dried, spread 4 mil to 6 mil polyethylene over the slab and use a weighted floor roller to press it into the mastic.

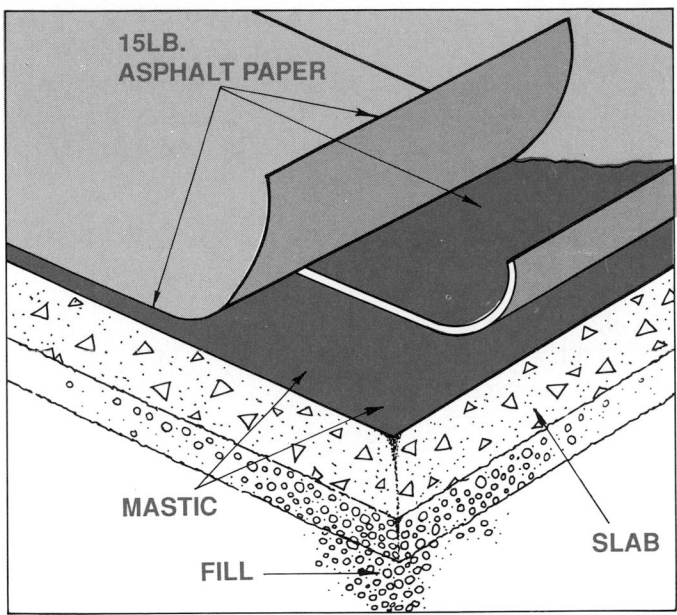

50-22. An asphalt paper vapor barrier.

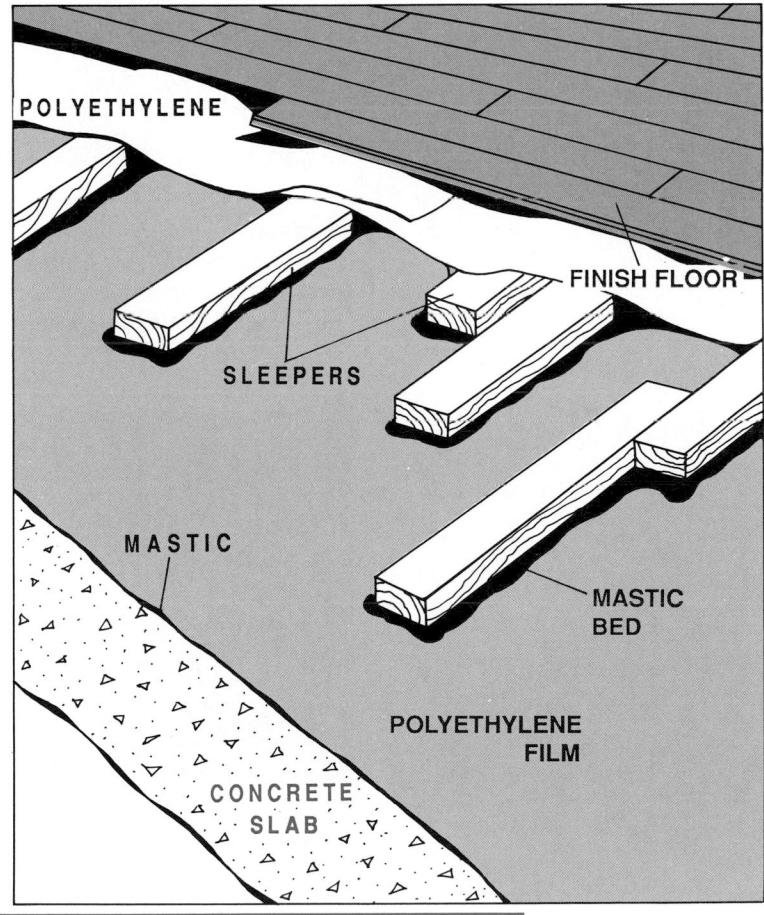

50-23. Strip flooring over concrete and sleepers.

With either type of vapor barrier in place, you can begin to install the strip flooring system. There are two methods used to install strip flooring over concrete: the sleeper method and the plywood method.

Flooring over Sleepers

1. Snap chalk lines 12" apart at right angles to the direction the flooring will run. Cover the lines with rivers of adhesive about 4" wide. The adhesive can be an asphalt mastic applied hot or cold.

2. Embed 2" × 4" sleepers in the mastic. The sleepers should be treated with a preservative other than creosote, which could stain the finished floor. Lap the ends of sleepers at least 4". Leave ¾" between the ends of sleepers and the walls. It is not necessary to nail the sleepers in place. Fig. 50-23.

3. After the mastic has cured, spread a 4 mil or 6 mil polyethylene vapor barrier over the sleepers. Lap all edges. This second vapor barrier adds another layer of moisture protection to the system.

4. Install the strip flooring at right angles to the sleepers. Fig. 50-24. Two adjoining courses of flooring should not have joints on the same sleeper. Where a flooring board runs over a lapped sleeper joint, the board should be nailed into both sleepers. Provide at least

50-24. The strip flooring is laid over the sleepers at right angles.

½" of clearance between flooring and the walls to allow for expansion.

Flooring over Plywood

1. Lay ¾" thicker exterior grade plywood over the vapor barrier. The end joints should be staggered 4'. Fig. 50-25.

2. When all the plywood is in place, fasten sheets to the slab with concrete nails or powder-actuated fasteners. Use at least nine nails per panel. To ensure that the panels stay flat, nail them at the center first, then work toward the edges. To allow for expansion, leave a gap of about ⅜" between each panel and a gap of ¾" at the walls.

3. Install the strip flooring as you would over a standard plywood subfloor.

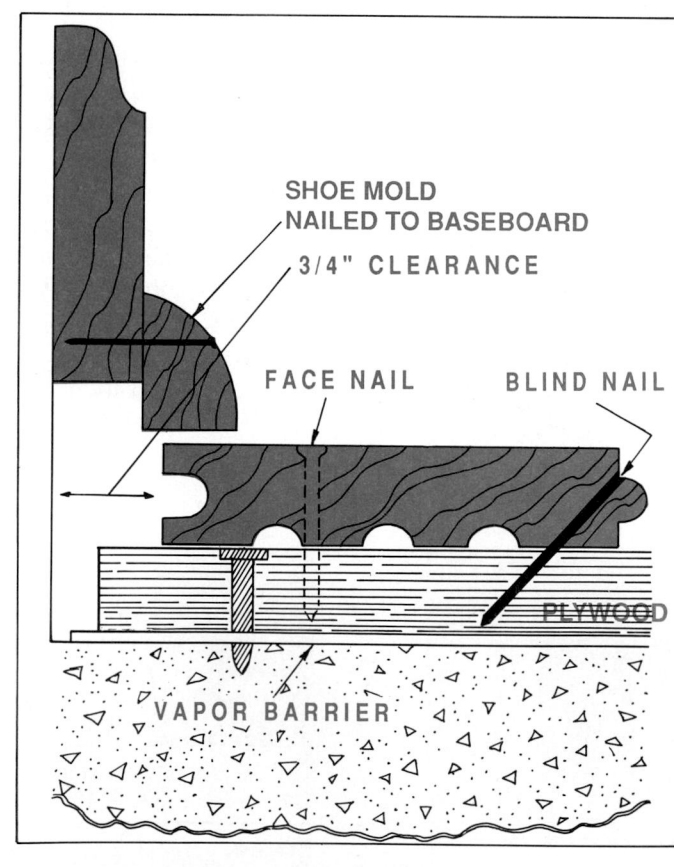

50-25. *Strip flooring over concrete and plywood.*

FINISHING

Sanding

Although certified unfinished hardwood flooring is smoothly surfaced at the factory, scratches and other slight marks caused by handling usually show after the floor has been laid. These may be removed by sanding or scraping. The work is often done by a specialist in that line. An electrically operated sanding machine generally is used for this work, since sanding or scraping by hand is laborious and time-consuming. Fig. 50-26. For fine floors, most manufacturers advise at least four sandings, starting with No. 2 sandpaper and graduating down to No ½, No. 0, and No. 00. A final

---

buffing with No. 00 or No. 000 sandpaper assures an even smoother surface. Many authorities say that best results are obtained when the final traverse is made by hand.

Stain

It is important that the first coat of stain or other finish be applied the same day as the last sanding. Otherwise the wood grain will have risen, and the finish consequently will be slightly rough. Stain is not used if the finish is to retain the natural color of the wood. If stain is used, it is applied first, before wood filler or other finishes. It should be put on evenly, preferably with a brush 3" or 4" wide.

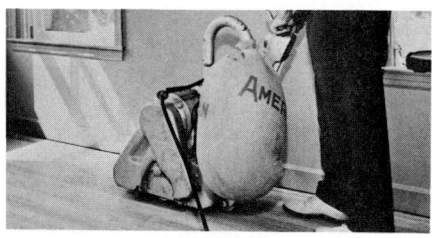

50-26a. *Although flooring is sanded at the mill, additional sanding is required after the floor is laid for a good finishing job.*

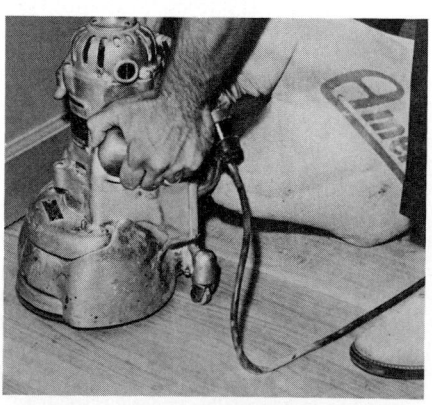

50-26b. *A small power sander called an edger is used for sanding floors near walls, in closets, and in other small areas where the floor machine is inefficient.*

Wood Filler

Paste wood filler customarily is used to fill the minute surface crevices in oak and other hardwoods with large pores. It gives the floor the perfectly smooth surface required for a lustrous appearance. Filler is applied after stains and sometimes after floor seals, but always before other finishing materials. It should be allowed to dry 24 hours before the next operation is begun. Wood filler may be colorless, or it may contain pigment to bring out the grain of the wood. For residential oak flooring, wood filler is always recommended.

Types of Finish

A finish for hardwood floors ideally should have the following qualities:
- ➤ Attractive appearance.
- ➤ Durability.
- ➤ Ease of maintenance.
- ➤ Capacity for being retouched in worn spots without revealing a patched appearance.

Safety. In recent years, a number of traditional finishes have been replaced by modern synthetic finishes. Varnish, for example, has given way to polyurethane. Another change in the area of floor finishes is the increased concern with safety and environmental factors.

Many of the new finishes contain chemicals and solvents that are hazardous to installers. It is very important, therefore, for anyone applying a floor finish to follow the manufacturer's instructions carefully. In general, these instructions call for plenty of ventilation and the use of a respirator while applying a floor finish.

In some parts of the country, particularly in large metropolitan areas, restrictions have been imposed on the use of solvents containing volatile organic

50-27. *There are several finishing materials available for hardwood floors. However, most hardwood flooring producers recommend a floor seal. Floor seal is a tough wear-resistant finish that can be mopped on easily with a longhandled lamb's wool or sponge applicator or a clean string mop. The floor should first be swept and dusted.*

compounds (VOCs). Many floor finishes contain such solvents, so manufacturers have been reformulating their products to reduce or eliminate them.

Penetrating Floor Seal. Floor seal is used for residential as well as heavy duty flooring. It differs from other finishes in this important respect: rather than forming a surface coating, it penetrates the wood fibers, sealing them together. In effect it becomes a part of the wood itself. It wears only as the wood wears, does not chip or scratch, and is practically immune to ordinary stains and spots. While it does not provide as shiny an appearance as other finishes, it has the advantage of being easily retouched. Worn spots may be refinished without presenting a patched appearance. Floor seals are available either with or without color.

It is difficult to give specific directions for applying floor seal because directions of different manufacturers vary widely. Generally it is applied across the grain first, then smoothed out in

50-28. *After the floor seal has dried completely, buff the floor lightly with a pad of fine steel wool on the polishing machine. Wax may also be polished with the machine pictured here by detaching the steel wool pad and attaching a brush provided with the machine.*

the direction of the grain. A wide brush, a squeegee, or a wool applicator may be used. Fig. 50-27. After a period of 15 minutes to 2 hours, depending on specific directions of the manufacturer, the excess seal should be wiped off with clean cloths or a rubber squeegee.

For best results the floor then should be buffed with No. 2 steel wool. An electric buffer makes this task relatively simple. Fig. 50-28. If a power buffer is not available, a sanding machine equipped with steel wool pads may be used, or the buffing may be done by hand. Although one application of seal sometimes is sufficient, a second coat frequently is recommended for new floors or floors just sanded. Floor seal is a complete finish in itself. However, it may also be used as a base for a surface finish such as varnish.

Urethane Finishes. A number of floor finishes are included in the general category of urethanes. These are durable finishes that cure to a hard film. They are relatively impervious to moisture.

Moisture-cured urethanes are the hardest and most moisture-resistant floor finishes. They offer a glossy look that resists abrasion. These urethanes cure by reacting with humidity in the air. The proper amount of humidity is critical, however. This makes these finishes difficult to apply. It is recommended that only professional floor finishers install them.

Oil-modified urethanes (sometimes called polyurethanes) are easier to apply than moisture-cured urethanes. They provide a durable coating that is available with a gloss, semigloss, or matte finish. This product is widely available and can be applied by a nonprofessional.

Water-based urethanes are fairly new to the market. The solid portions of the product are suspended primarily in water, rather than in a volatile solvent. Water-based urethanes are durable, but require more coats to build up a thickness comparable to other urethanes.

Acid-Curing Finishes. These finishes are similar to urethanes in durability. They provide a tough, relatively elastic finish. However, they should be installed only by a professional because they contain formaldehyde.

Other Finishes. Varnishes were once used extensively to finish floors, but are seldom used now. They have been replaced by synthetic finishes that are easier to install and more durable.

Natural oil finishes can be used on a floor, though they require considerable time to fully cure. Oils are less durable than other finishes, but are easy to repair. Linseed oil and tung oil are common products.

Though shellac finishes are thought by some to result in floors of great beauty, a shellac finish is difficult to maintain. Such a finish water-spots easily and does not hold up against common household solvents. Because of this, it is not recommended for floors.

Wax

All hardwood floors should be waxed after the finish has dried thoroughly. In some cases two or three coats are recommended for best results. Wax not only imparts a lustrous sheen to a floor, but forms a protective film that prevents dirt from penetrating the wood pores. When wax becomes dirty, it is easily removed and new wax applied.

Hardwood floor wax is available in paste or liquid form. The liquid is known as rubbing wax. Considered about equal in performance, both forms are applied in much the same manner. Usually the wax is mopped on with a cloth, then polished after an interval of 15 to 30 minutes with a soft cloth, a weighted floor brush, or an electric polisher. The latter is preferred, for it eliminates a great deal of labor and does the job equally well, if not better. Some electric polishers apply the wax and polish it in the same operation. Power-driven polishing machines, as well as sanding and buffing machines helpful in the earlier finishing steps, can usually be rented.

Prefinished Hardwood Flooring

When hardwood flooring is purchased in unfinished form, sanding and other finishing operations are performed after the floor has been installed. Some manufacturers produce flooring which is completely prefinished at the factory. It is ready for use immediately after being laid. All species and types of hardwood flooring may not be readily available in this form. However, a manufacturer equipped to make factory-finished flooring usually can furnish it in any species and type ordinarily produced unfinished.

OTHER TYPES OF HARDWOOD FLOORING

Plank Flooring

One of the oldest types of hardwood floors, plank flooring, dates back to the handicraft era. In its crude early form it was widely used in medieval Europe, and it later became a popular flooring for American colonial homes. Its use has been increasing in homes, clubs, and other buildings where an atmosphere of rugged informality is desired. Colonial plank flooring derived much of its charm from its rough effects and interesting irregularities, which were unintentional. This charm is retained in modern plank flooring even though it is now a precision-made product.

50-29. *A plank floor. Planks are fastened with screws, which are then covered with plugs.*

Oak is preferred for plank floors. Production of planks ordinarily is confined to that species, but they can also be obtained in solid walnut and East Indian teak, as well as in various veneers. The planks usually come in random widths. Generally the pieces are tongued and grooved, with square or matched ends, but sometimes they are produced with square edges and ends. Frequently the edges of planks are beveled to reproduce the effect of the large cracks which characterize early hand-hewn plank floors. The wood pegs by which the old plank floors were fastened also are simulated. This is done by gluing wood plugs in holes on top of the countersunk screws which actually fasten the planks to the subfloor. Fig. 50-29.

Pattern or Parquet Flooring

Pattern floors, also known as parquet and design floors, appeared as early as the 14th century in Europe. While today, as then, they are the most elaborate and expensive type of hardwood flooring, they have been simplified to a great extent. Early pattern floors presented bizarre effects which would be incompatible with present architectural styles. Today's parquetry uses squares, rectangles, and herringbone patterns to achieve an almost infinite variety of effects. Fig. 50-30. Literally hundreds of designs are available, many featuring various species or different shades of the same species. Most parquet flooring is of oak, although it also is produced in maple, beech, birch, walnut, mahogany, East Indian teak, and ebonized wood. The latter consists of dyed white maple or holly. Parquetry is manufactured in short lengths of individual pieces. Each piece must be cut to exact dimensions so that it will match

Fountainebleau

Woodstone

Herringbone

Marie Antoinette

50-30a. *Parquet flooring comes in a variety of patterns.*

50-30b. *Decorative parquet borders.*

Unit 50 • Wood and Vinyl Flooring 665

50-30c. *A parquet floor.*

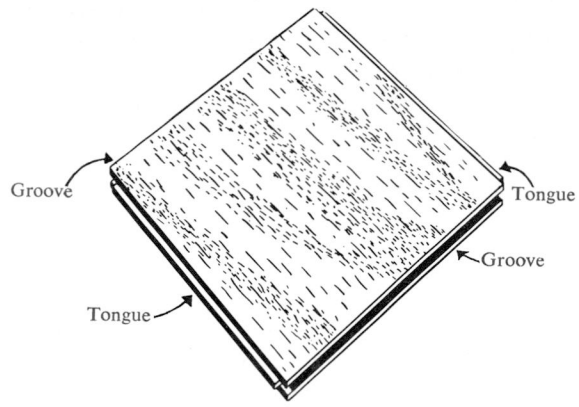

50-31a. *Wood block flooring. Note the tongue and groove locations.*

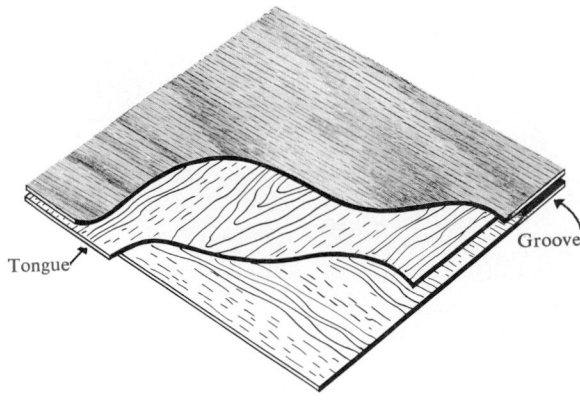

50-31b. *Laminated block flooring.*

perfectly the dimensions of another piece, or multiples thereof. Customarily tongued and grooved and end-matched, the pieces are laid separately, either by nailing or setting in mastic.

Block Flooring

Block flooring is really a form of parquetry, since it constitutes a definite pattern. It differs from conventional parquetry in that the pieces are assembled into square or rectangular blocks at the factory. They are held together by various means on the back, sides, or ends with matching tongue-and-groove edges. Fig. 50-31. These prefabricated blocks are laid as units, either in mastic or by nailing.

Installing Plank, Block, and Parquet Flooring

Each piece in plank flooring, in addition to being blind-nailed, should be face-nailed or screwed about every 30 inches. The ends of each piece also should be fastened to the subfloor with countersunk screws. Wood plugs glued in the plank conceal screwheads and lend a decorative effect.

Parquet flooring, including prefabricated blocks, may be nailed over a wood subfloor or old finish floor, or it may be laid in mastic over concrete. Preferably the subfloor should cross the joists at right angles rather than on a diagonal. When the subfloor is installed before the type of finish flooring has been decided upon, it is best to lay it at a 60 degree angle. This "compromise" will make it adaptable to any type of flooring.

ESTIMATING

To estimate the quantity of wood flooring needed, it is first necessary to detemine the number of square feet of floor space to be covered. The number of square feet is figured by multiplying the length of the room times the width of the room. Any offsets or closets may be figured separately by multiplying their length times their width and adding the product to the total number of square feet in the main room. For example, if the room is 10' by 12', the room contains 120 sq. ft. of floor area (10 × 12 = 120). If the closet is 2' wide by 8' long, the closet contains a total of 16 sq. ft. The main room and closet contain 136 sq. ft. of floor area (120 + 16 = 136).

Strip Flooring

To determine the amount of strip flooring needed, refer to Table 50-B. Under the section entitled strip flooring read across on the line for the size flooring to be used. If $^{25}/_{32}$" × 2$^1/_4$" strip flooring is selected, it will take 138.3 board feet to lay 100 square feet of floor area. In the sample room described earlier, there are 136 square feet of floor space; 188.09 board feet of strip flooring will be required.

136 (sq. ft. of floor space) = 1.36 (floor area in hundreds of sq. ft.)

1.36 × 138.3 (board ft. per 100 sq. ft.)= 188.09 board ft.

Material Cost. To figure the cost of the material, multiply the cost per board foot times the total number of board feet required for the job. Standard sizes, counts, and weights of wood flooring are given in Table 50-C. Table 50-B also has information for determining the number of nails necessary. Read across on the line for the size strip flooring used to the heading "Nails." The chart shows it will take 3 pounds of nails to lay 100 square feet of 2$^1/_4$" strip flooring. The floor in the example contains 136 square feet and will require a little over 4 pounds of nails.

$$\frac{1.36 \text{ (sq. ft. of floor area)}}{100} = 1.36 \text{ (floor area in hundreds of sq. ft.)}$$

1.36 × 3 (lbs. of nails per 100 sq. ft.) = 4.08 lbs.

Multiply the cost per pound times the number of pounds required to find the cost of the nails.

Labor Cost. To figure the labor for laying the floor in the example, refer to the column headed "Labor" in Table 50-B. The table shows

that a worker can lay 100 square feet of $^{25}/_{32}$" × 2$^1/_4$" strip flooring in 3 hours. By using the table, you can determine that the room in the example will require 4.08 hours to lay.

$$\frac{136 \text{ (sq. ft. of floor area)}}{100} = 1.36 \text{ (floor area in hundreds of sq. ft.)}$$

1.36 × 3 (hrs. of labor per 100 sq. ft.) = 4.08 hrs.

Multiply this figure by the hourly rate to determine total labor cost. If it is desirable to determine the cost for sanding and finishing, this may be figured in the same way.

RESILIENT FLOORING

Resilient flooring refers to a broad group of flooring products made of synthetic materials. The most common type of resilient flooring is vinyl. Vinyl floors are often used in kitchens, bathrooms, and recreation rooms because they are durable, stain-resistant, and relatively inexpensive.

Vinyl flooring comes in two forms. Sheet vinyl comes in large rolls 12' wide. Fig. 50-32. It is typically installed by flooring professionals in new construction. Vinyl tiles are usually 9" or 12" square. Fig. 50-33. Their size makes

Table 50-B. *Estimating Strip Flooring.*

Strip Flooring Size	Material		Nails per 100 Sq. Ft.	Labor Hours per 100 Sq. Ft.		
	Bd. Ft. per 100 Sq. Ft.	1000 Bd. Ft. will lay Sq. Ft.		Laying	Sanding*	Finishing*
$^{25}/_{32}$ x 1 $^1/_2$	155.0	645.0	3.7 Pounds	3.7 Hours	1.3 Hours	2.6 Hours
$^{25}/_{32}$ x 2	142.5	701.8	3.0 Pounds	3.4 Hours	1.3 Hours	2.6 Hours
$^{25}/_{32}$ x 2 $^1/_4$	138.3	723.0	3.0 Pounds	3.0 Hours	1.3 Hours	2.6 Hours
$^{25}/_{32}$ x 3 $^1/_4$	129.0	775.2	2.3 Pounds	2.6 Hours	1.3 Hours	2.6 Hours
$^3/_8$ x 1 $^1/_2$	138.3	723.0	3.7 Pounds	3.7 Hours	1.3 Hours	2.6 Hours
$^3/_8$ x 2	130.0	769.0	3.0 Pounds	3.4 Hours	1.3 Hours	2.6 Hours
$^1/_2$ x 1 $^1/_2$	138.3	723.0	3.7 Pounds	3.7 Hours	1.3 Hours	2.6 Hours
$^1/_2$ x 2	130.0	769.2	3.0 Pounds	3.4 Hours	1.3 Hours	2.6 Hours

* Sanding and finishing times are averages.

them easy to work with, which makes them popular with nonprofessionals. Sheet vinyl and vinyl tiles are usually applied to a wood subfloor with mastic. Vinyl floors can be laid over almost any solid, dry surface, including wood and concrete.

Table 50-C. *Standard Sizes, Counts, and Weights of Wood Flooring.*

OAK			
Nominal	**Actual**	**Counted**	**Wts. M Ft.**
Tongued and Grooved-End Matched			
$^{25}/_{32}$ x 3 $^{1}/_{4}$ in.	$^{25}/_{32}$ x 3 $^{1}/_{4}$ in.	1 x 4 in.	2300 lbs.
$^{25}/_{32}$ x 2 $^{1}/_{4}$ in.	$^{25}/_{32}$ x 2 $^{1}/_{4}$ in.	1 x 3 in.	2100 lbs.
$^{25}/_{32}$ x 2 in.	$^{25}/_{32}$ x 2 in.	1 x 2 $^{3}/_{4}$ in.	2000 lbs.
$^{25}/_{32}$ x 1 $^{1}/_{2}$ in.	$^{25}/_{32}$ x 1 $^{1}/_{2}$ in.	1 x 2 $^{1}/_{4}$ in.	1900 lbs.
$^{3}/_{8}$ x 2 in.	$^{11}/_{32}$ x 2 in.	1 x 2 $^{1}/_{2}$ in.	1000 lbs.
$^{3}/_{8}$ x 1 $^{1}/_{2}$ in.	$^{11}/_{32}$ x 1 $^{1}/_{2}$ in.	1 x 2 in.	1000 lbs.
$^{1}/_{2}$ x 2 in.	$^{15}/_{32}$ x 2 in.	1 x 2 $^{1}/_{2}$ in.	1350 lbs.
$^{1}/_{2}$ x 1 $^{1}/_{2}$ in.	$^{15}/_{32}$ x 1 $^{1}/_{2}$ in.	1 x 2 in.	1300 lbs.
Square Edge			
$^{5}/_{16}$ x 2 in.	$^{5}/_{16}$ x 2 in.	face count	1200 lbs.
$^{5}/_{16}$ x 1 $^{1}/_{2}$ in.	$^{5}/_{16}$ x 1 $^{1}/_{2}$ in.	face count	1200 lbs.
BEECH, BIRCH, HARD MAPLE AND PECAN			
Nominal	**Actual**	**Counted**	**Wts. M Ft.**
Tongued and Grooved-End Matched			
$^{25}/_{32}$ x 3 $^{1}/_{4}$ in.	$^{25}/_{32}$ x 3 $^{1}/_{4}$ in.	1 x 4 in.	2300 lbs.
$^{25}/_{32}$ x 2 $^{1}/_{4}$ in.	$^{25}/_{32}$ x 2 $^{1}/_{4}$ in.	1 x 3 in.	2100 lbs.
$^{25}/_{32}$ x 2 in.	$^{25}/_{32}$ x 2 in.	1 x 2 $^{3}/_{4}$ in.	2000 lbs.
$^{25}/_{32}$ x 1 $^{1}/_{2}$ in.	$^{25}/_{32}$ x 1 $^{1}/_{2}$ in.	1 x 2 $^{1}/_{4}$ in.	1900 lbs.
$^{3}/_{8}$ x 2 in.	$^{11}/_{32}$ x 2 in.	1 x 2 $^{1}/_{2}$ in.	1000 lbs.
$^{3}/_{8}$ x 1 $^{1}/_{2}$ in.	$^{11}/_{32}$ x 1 $^{1}/_{2}$ in.	1 x 2 in.	1000 lbs.
$^{1}/_{2}$ x 2 in.	$^{15}/_{32}$ x 2 in.	1 x 2 $^{1}/_{2}$ in.	1350 lbs.
$^{1}/_{2}$ x 1 $^{1}/_{2}$ in.	$^{15}/_{32}$ x 1 $^{1}/_{2}$ in.	1 x 2 in.	1300 lbs.
Special Thicknesses (T and G, End Matched)			
$^{17}/_{16}$ x 3 $^{1}/_{4}$ in.	$^{33}/_{32}$ x 3 $^{1}/_{4}$ in.	1 $^{1}/_{4}$ x 4 in.	2400 lbs.
$^{17}/_{16}$ x 2 $^{1}/_{4}$ in.	$^{33}/_{32}$ x 2 $^{1}/_{4}$ in.	1 $^{1}/_{4}$ x 3 in.	2250 lbs.
$^{17}/_{16}$ x 2 in.	$^{33}/_{32}$ x 2 in.	1 $^{1}/_{4}$ x 2 $^{3}/_{4}$ in.	2400 lbs.
Jointed Flooring — i.e., Square Edge			
$^{25}/_{32}$ x 2 $^{1}/_{2}$ in.	$^{25}/_{32}$ x 2 $^{1}/_{2}$ in.	1 x 3 $^{1}/_{4}$ in.	2250 lbs.
$^{25}/_{32}$ x 3 $^{1}/_{4}$ in.	$^{25}/_{32}$ x 3 $^{1}/_{4}$ in.	1 x 4 in.	2400 lbs.
$^{25}/_{32}$ x 3 $^{1}/_{2}$ in.	$^{25}/_{32}$ x 3 $^{1}/_{2}$ in.	1 x 4 $^{1}/_{4}$ in.	2500 lbs.
$^{17}/_{16}$ x 2 $^{1}/_{2}$ in.	$^{33}/_{32}$ x 2 $^{1}/_{2}$ in.	1 $^{1}/_{4}$ x 3 $^{1}/_{4}$ in.	2500 lbs.
$^{17}/_{16}$ x 3 $^{1}/_{2}$ in.	$^{33}/_{32}$ x 3 $^{1}/_{2}$ in.	1 $^{1}/_{4}$ x 4 $^{1}/_{4}$ in.	2600 lbs.

"Nominal size" is the term ordinarily used in referring to hardwood flooring sizes. In all cases the nominal and the actual widths are the same. In some instances, however, the nominal thickness is 1/32-inch greater. Nominal sizes probably have their origin in the sizes in which flooring actually was made years ago. Their continued use is a matter of convenience in the trade.

"Actual size" is the thickness and face width to which the flooring measures after it has been processed at the mill. It does not include the width of the tongue in side-matched flooring.

"Counted size" is the size used in determining the board feet in a shipment. In arriving at the counted size, pieces which are 1-inch or less in thickness are considered to be 1-inch flooring. Allowance is made over and above the actual face width for flooring which is tongued and grooved at the sides. In 25/32-inch flooring and thicker, the extra allowance is 3/4-inch, while in other sizes the allowance is 1/2-inch. Thus a piece of side-matched flooring which measured 25/32-inch x 2 1/4 inches in actual or face width is referred to as 3 inches in counted width.

50-32. *A sheet vinyl floor is often used in kitchens.*

50-33. *These 12" x 12" floor tiles look as if two sizes of tiles were used.*

Installing a Sheet Vinyl Floor

Following are the basic steps in installing a sheet vinyl floor:

1. A wood subfloor should be covered with plywood underlayment prior to the installation of sheet vinyl flooring. Underlayment should be at least ¼" thick and have a smooth, sanded surface. Nails or staples should be 6" apart in the field and 4" apart at the edges. The joints between underlayment panels should be staggered and butted together. Any gaps larger than ¹⁄₃₂" should be filled with latex patching compound and sanded flush, if necessary.

2. Sweep the floor thoroughly to remove any dust and debris. Check to ensure that nails or staples are flush with the surface of the underlayment. One way to check this quickly is to run a wide-blade putty knife over the floor. You will hear a metallic "ring" when the blade hits protruding fasteners. Set protruding fasteners as necessary.

3. Measure the room and determine if the sheet vinyl will require seaming. Because of the width of vinyl sheet goods, it is often possible to avoid a seam. If a seam is required, snap a chalkline where it will fall. Then snap two parallel lines about 8" away and on either side of the first line. These chalklines identify the width of the seam area.

4. Unroll the flooring and cut as many pieces as needed to cover the floor. Each piece should be about 3" longer than the length of the room. A razor knife works well for cutting vinyl flooring. Flooring that is cold will be more difficult to work with than flooring that is at room temperature.

5. Spread mastic with a notched trowel over one-half of the area to be covered by a single length of vinyl, but keep mastic out of the seam area. Place the flooring in the wet mastic and roll it smooth with a weighted floor roller. One edge should overlap the center seam line by about 1".

6. Lift the second half of the vinyl. Apply mastic to the underlayment beneath it. Lower this vinyl into the mastic and roll it smooth. Trim the ends of the vinyl to final length.

7. Repeat the procedures above with the next strip of vinyl. With adjoining lengths of vinyl flooring in place, there will be a 16" wide "dry zone" beneath the overlapping edges.

8. Cut through the overlapping edges with a razor knife. Guide the cut with a steel straightedge. Lift each edge of the flooring, apply mastic to the underlayment, and roll the seam smooth.

Installing a Vinyl Tile Floor

Vinyl tile can be laid directly over wood flooring or over a plywood floor. Fig. 50-34. If a hardwood floor is to be used in one room and the adjacent room is to have a tile floor, a base is required for the tile so that the floors will be exactly the same height. In other

words, the thickness of the base floor plus the thickness of the tile should equal the thickness of the finish floor in an adjacent room. Fig. 50-35. Some kinds of tile require an underfelt that must be applied over the floor before the tiles are installed. Figures 50-36 through 50-56 and the accompanying text describe how to install 9" × 9" vinyl tile. The same general procedure applies to other types and sizes of tile.

1. Prepare the surface on which the tile will be laid. The appearance of the finished floor will depend a great deal on the condition of the subfloor. Make sure the floor is smooth and completely free of wax, paint, varnish, grease, or oil. Holes or cracks in concrete subfloors should be filled with crack filler. Plane down high spots and renail

50-34. *Plywood is frequently used as an underlayment for a vinyl tile floor.*

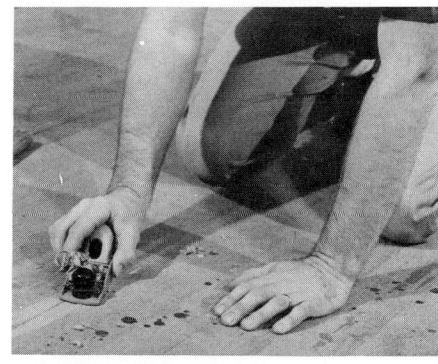

50-36. *Planing down high spots.*

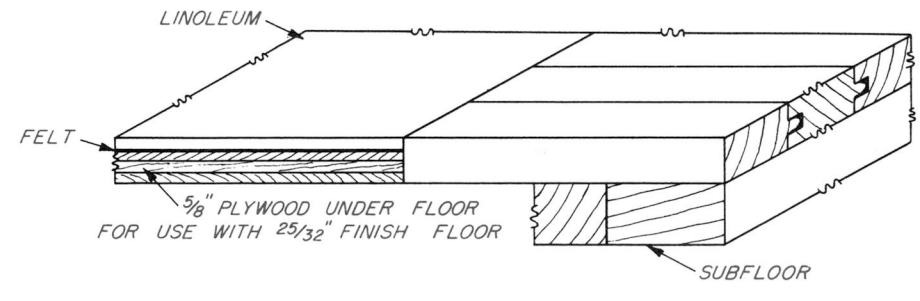

50-35. *The underlayment, in this case plywood, is usually thinner than the hardwood floor to compensate for the thickness of the tile or linoleum.*

50-37. *Covering the old floor with underlayment.*

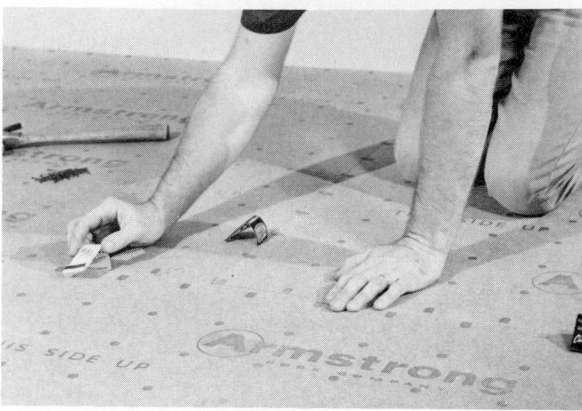

50-38. *Allow a distance equal to the thickness of a matchbook between the panels of underlayment.*

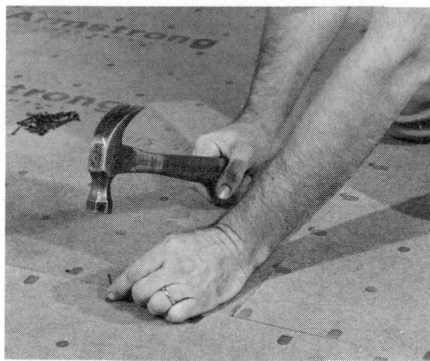

50-39. *Nailing the underlayment.*

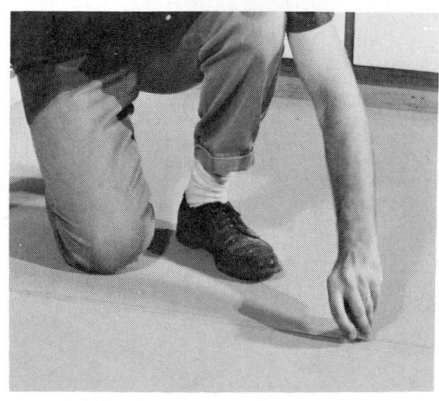

50-40. *Snapping a chalk line down the middle of the room.*

50-41. *Using a framing square to draw a perpendicular from the centerline.*

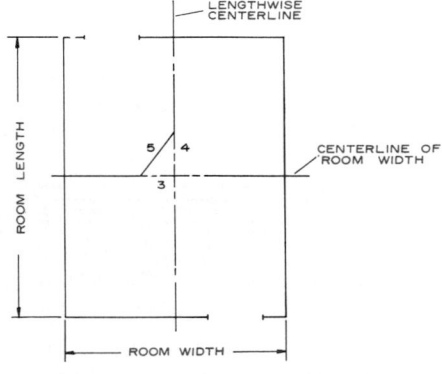

50-42. *The two lines must be exactly perpendicular.*

loose boards of wood floors. Fig. 50-36.

2. If a wood subfloor is only a single layer or if it is a double-layer floor and the boards are in bad condition, the old floor should be covered with an underlayment. Fig. 50-37.

3. Allow a little less than $\frac{1}{32}$", or the thickness of a paper matchbook, between each panel of underlayment or plywood to allow for expansion. Stagger the joints as shown. Fig. 50-38.

4. Nail the underlayment or plywood with coated or ring-shank nails at least every four inches along all edges and over the entire face of the panels. Fig. 50-39. Most manufacturers of underlayment provide a nailing guide in the form of lines or dots stenciled on the surface to indicate the nail locations.

5. Find the center points of the two end walls of the room. Connect these points with a chalk line and snap a line down the middle of the room. Fig. 50-40.

6. Locate the midpoint of this line. Use a framing square to draw a perpendicular line from this point. Fig. 50-41. If a square is not available, a tile may be used with one edge on the center line to establish the perpendicular.

7. The center lines should be at an exact 90-degree angle (right angle) to each other. This can be assured by constructing a 3' × 4' × 5' right triangle from the two lines and a diagonal. Fig. 50-42. In a large room, a 6' × 8' × 10' triangle can be used.

8. Along the perpendicular line, strike a chalk line which extends to both of the side walls. Along the chalk lines, lay one test row of uncemented tile from the center point to one side wall and to one end wall. Fig 50-43.

9. The uncemented tiles are placed along the line with the edge

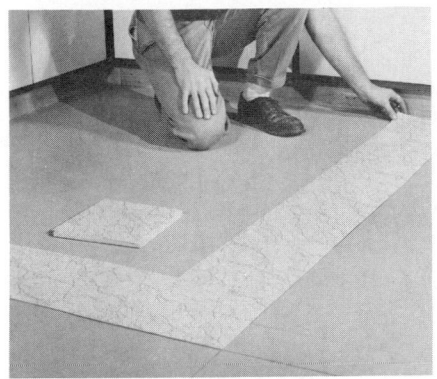

50-43. *Placing test rows of uncemented tile along the chalk lines.*

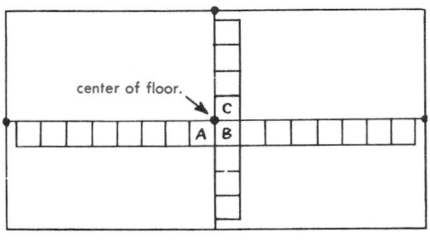

50-44. *Layout for an even number of tiles.*

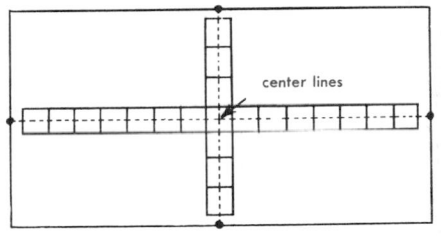

50-45. *Layout for an odd number of tiles.*

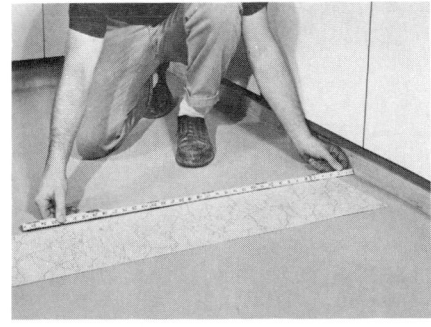

50-46. *Measuring the border space.*

of the tiles exactly on the line. The rows may be shifted by moving one tile at a time until the border space at the end of each of the rows is equal. Count the tiles in each row. If there is an even number of tiles, those at the center of each row (tiles A, B, and C) should meet exactly on the center lines. Fig. 50-44.

10. If there is an odd number of tiles, the center lines on the floor will bisect the tiles. Fig. 50-45.

11. Border tiles should not be less than half a tile wide. Measure the distance between the wall and the last tile. Fig. 50-46. If the distance is less than 2" or more than 8", move the center line parallel to that wall 4½" closer to the wall.

12. Locate the new center line with the chalk line and snap it. Fig. 50-47. Moving the center line closer to the wall creates wider borders. For example, if the borders are 1½" wide, moving the center line 4½" closer to one wall will take away the 1½" border plus 3" from the next tile. The border tile on that side will then be 6" wide. On the opposite side, 4½" will be gained. The border will thus become 6" wide (4½" + 1½"). Since the line is moved 4½", half the size of one tile, the border tile remains uniform on both sides.

13. Choose the correct adhesive for the tile. Spread a thin coat over one-fourth of the room. Do not cover the chalk lines. The adhesive may be troweled or brushed on, depending on the type of tile to be laid and the adhesive used. Fig. 50-48.

14. Allow the adhesive to dry about 15 minutes. Then test it for proper tackiness by touching lightly with the thumb. Fig. 50-49. It should feel tacky but not stick to the thumb. If it sticks to the thumb, allow more drying time.

15. For an even number of tiles,

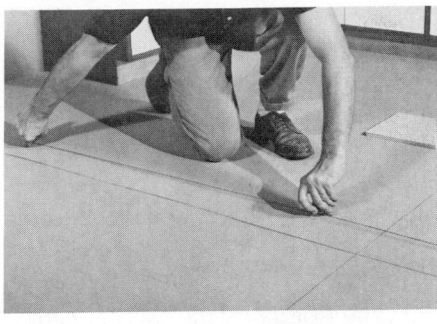

50-47. *Relocating the center line.*

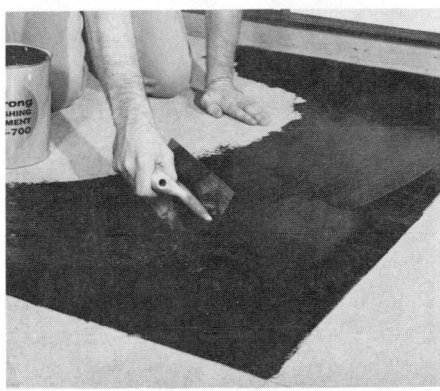

50-48. *Spreading the adhesive.*

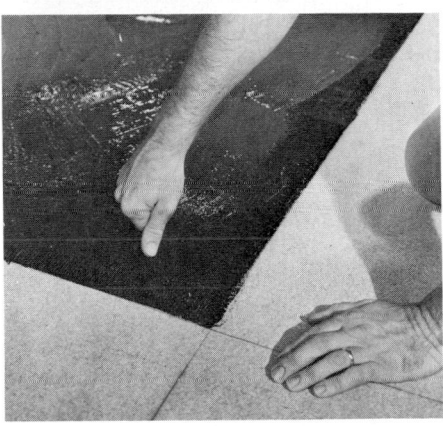

50-49. *Testing the adhesive for proper tackiness.*

50-50a. *Installing the tiles.*

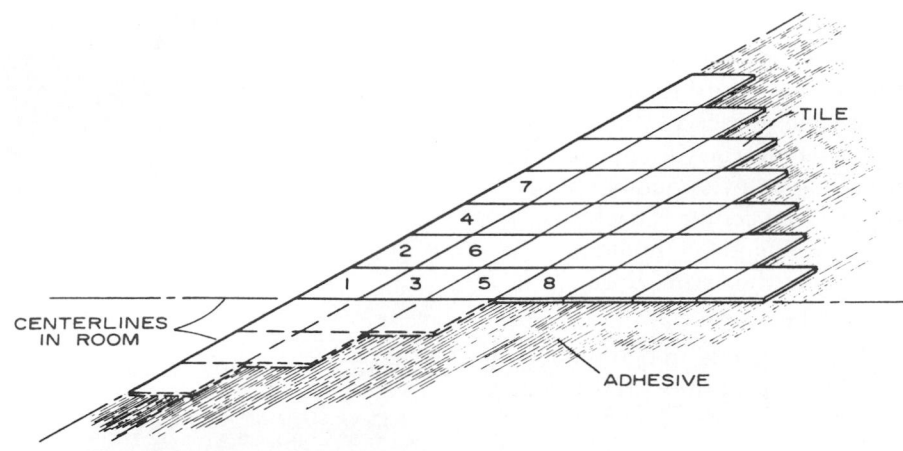

50-50b. *Diagram of installation sequence.*

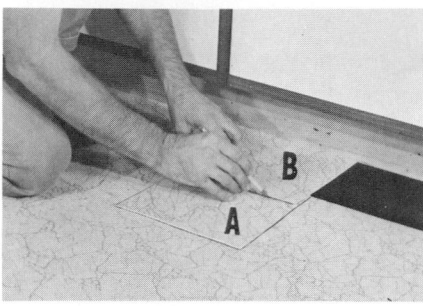

50-51. *Marking a border tile to be cut.*

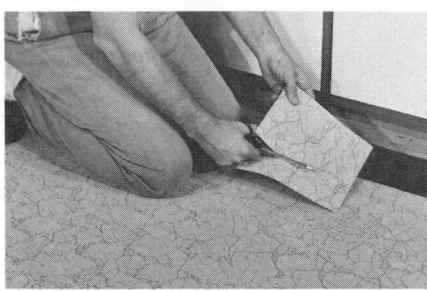

50-52. *Cutting the border tile to the correct size.*

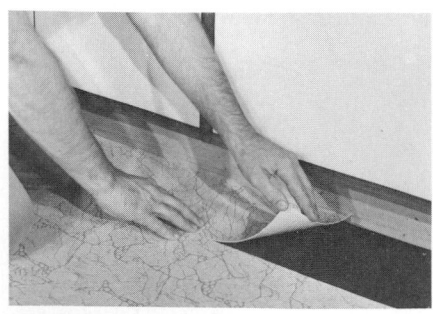

50-53. *Installing border tile.*

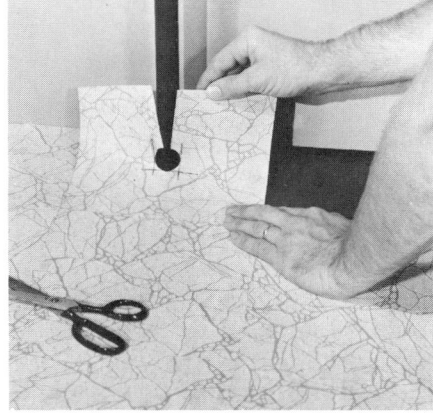

50-54. *Fitting tile around a pipe.*

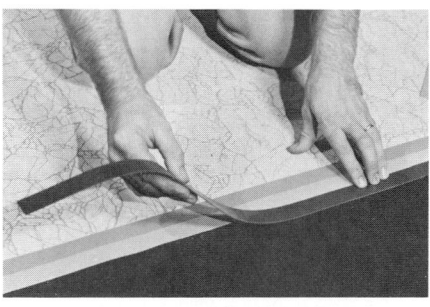

50-55. *Installing vinyl strips.*

start at one inside corner and lay the first tile exactly in line with the marked center lines. For an odd number of tiles, center the first tile over the intersection of the center lines. The second tile can be laid adjacent to the first on one side. The third tile is laid adjacent to the first on the other side. Continue laying tiles along the center line and filling in between until the entire section is covered. Fig. 50-50. The remaining three sections can be covered in the same way. Do not slide tiles into position. Some kinds of tile require only pressing in place; others should be rolled after installation for better adherence.

16. To fit border tiles, place a loose tile (A) exactly over the last tile in the row. Take another tile (B) and place it against the wall, overlapping tile A. Mark tile A with a pencil along the edge of B. Fig. 50-51.

17. With household shears, tin-snips, or a knife, cut tile A along the pencil mark. Fig. 50-52.

18. The cut portion of tile A will fit exactly into the border space. Fig. 50-53. Place the hand-cut edge against the wall. Repeat this procedure until the border area is completely covered. A clearance of ⅛" to ¼" should be allowed at all sides for expansion. This space is covered with a cove base of the same resilient material as the tile or with a standard wood base. Wood base is usually lower in cost than the resilient cove base, but installation costs are somewhat greater. When installing vinyl tile, each quarter of the room should be rolled with a linoleum roller or other smooth roller as it is completed.

19. To cut around pipes or other obstructions in a room, first make a paper pattern to fit the space exactly. Then trace the

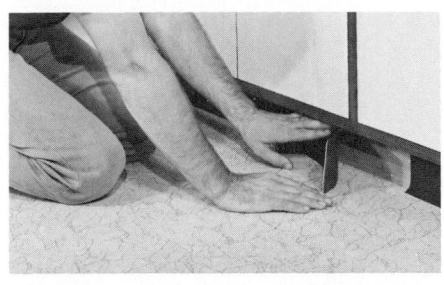

50-56. *Applying vinyl cove base.*

50-57. *A basement recreation room. Vinyl floor tiles, feature strips in three different colors, and a vinyl cove base create an attractive custom-designed floor.*

outline onto the tile and cut along the outline. Some tile can be cut with scissors. Fig. 50-54.

20. Feature strips in solid colors can be used to create an unusual effect. Several colors can be combined to provide a room with individuality and an interesting complement to the room's decor. Spread the adhesive, allow it to dry, and lay the feature strips in place. Fig. 50-55.

21. Vinyl cove base can be installed along the walls of the room. After cutting the proper lengths to fit into place, apply the adhesive to the back of the vinyl cove base and press the material against the wall. Fig. 50-56. This completes the floor installation. Fig. 50-57.

Estimating

Estimating the amount of sheet vinyl needed is simply a matter of determining the square footage of floor to be covered. Additional flooring will be needed to account for wastage, seams, and pattern matching. This will depend on the type of flooring and the pattern. The manufacturer or distributor should be consulted.

Tables 50-D and 50-E can be used to determine quantities for vinyl tiles and other resilient tile products.

Table 50-D. *Estimating Resilient Flooring.*

Resilient Flooring	Labor Hours Per 100 Sq. Ft.						Material Mastic
Type	4 x 4	6 x 6	9 x 9	6 x 12	12 x 12	9 x 18	Per 100 Sq. Ft.
Rubber Tile	5.0	3.3	2.2	2.2	1.8	1.3	0.75 Gallon
Asphalt Tile		3.3	2.0	2.0	1.3	1.3	0.75 Gallon
Linotile		7.0	6.4		5.7		1.50 Gallon
Plastic Tile			2.4				1.35 Gallon
Cork Tile		6.0	3.5		2.5		1.50 Gallon

Table 50-E. *Estimating Vinyl Floor Tile.*

ESTIMATING FLOOR TILE

Sq. Ft.	Number of Tiles 9" x 9"	Number of Tiles 12" x 12"	Number of Tiles 6" x 6"	Number of Tiles 9" x 18"
1	2	1	4	1
2	4	2	8	2
3	6	3	12	3
4	8	4	16	4
5	9	5	20	5
6	11	6	24	6
7	13	7	28	7
8	15	8	32	8
9	16	9	36	8
10	18	10	40	9
20	36	20	80	18
30	54	30	120	27
40	72	40	160	36
50	89	50	200	45
60	107	60	240	54
70	125	70	280	63
80	143	80	320	72
90	160	90	360	80
100	178	100	400	90
200	356	200	800	178
300	534	300	1200	267
400	712	400	1600	356
500	890	500	2000	445
Labor per 100 Sq. Ft.	2 Hours	1.3 Hours	3.3 Hours	1.3 Hours

FLOORING ADHESIVES

Type and Uses	Approximate Coverage in Sq. Ft.
Primer — For treating on-or-below-grade concrete subfloors before installing asphalt tile	250 to 350
Asphalt Cement — For installing asphalt tile over primed concrete subfloors in direct contact with the ground	200
Emulsion Adhesive — Adhesive used for installing asphalt tile over lining felt	130 to 150
Lining Paste — For cementing lining felt to wood subfloors	160
Floor and Wall Size — Used to prime chalky or dusty suspended concrete subfloors before installing resilient tiles other than asphalt	130 to 150
Waterproof Cement — Recommended for installing linoleum tile, rubber, and cork tile over any type of suspended subfloor in areas where surface moisture is a problem	130 to 150

TILE WASTE ALLOWANCES

1 to 50 Sq. Ft.	14%
50 to 100 Sq. Ft.	10%
100 to 200 Sq. Ft.	8%
200 to 300 Sq. Ft.	7%
300 to 1000 Sq. Ft.	5%
Over 1000 Sq. Ft.	3%

To find the number of tiles needed for an area not shown in the table, such as the number of 9" x 9" tile needed for 850 sq. ft., add the number of tiles for 50 sq. ft. to the number of tiles needed for 800 sq. ft. The result will then be 1513, to which must be added 5% for waste. (See table). Total 1589.

1. What is finish flooring?

2. What are some of the finish flooring materials?

3. What are the most common hardwoods used for wood strip flooring?

4. What wood species is used most often for wood strip flooring?

5. What is the most popular thickness and width of strip flooring?

6. Who enforces the grading rules and regulations for hardwood flooring?

7. What are the grades of oak strip flooring?

8. What is the last operation before actual installation of finish flooring?

9. What factors must be taken into consideration when deciding what area of the house to begin the installation?

10. When two different floor coverings are used in adjoining rooms, they should terminate under the center of the door when the door is closed. Why?

11. What kind and size of nails are recommended for laying strip flooring?

12. How is strip flooring installed over concrete?

13. What are some other types of hardwood flooring besides strip flooring?

14. What thickness of underlayment is used for vinyl floors?

ACTIVITIES

1. Social Studies. The text discusses various wood floorings oak, maple, beech, birch, and pecan. What climate is most suitable for the growth of these trees? Where in the United States would you find the most abundant growth of each of these trees? Is there one area of the United States where the most predominant tree growth occurs? If so, why?

2. Math. Standard 9" by 9" asphalt tiles are to be used on a rectangular 14'6" by 24'3" floor.

a. Compute the area of the floor in square feet.

b. Estimate the number of tiles needed, using Table 50-E. Allow the noted percentage for waste and trim.

3. Language Arts. You should have some understanding of personal loans. Your ability to obtain a loan is based on your credit worthiness. Your credit worthiness reflects your ability to repay a loan. Several factors influence your credit worthiness. These factors include your job, your income, and your past record of repaying your debts.

Obtain a bank loan application from a bank. Identify those questions on the loan application that directly relate to the applicant's credit worthiness. In a brief essay, state why the bank would be interested in such information.

THE SCHOOL-TO-WORK CONNECTION

Many types of durable synthetic finishes for floors are now available. Some of these finishes, however, must be applied with great care because of the potential health hazards associated with breathing their vapors.

1. If you were hired by a wood flooring contractor to apply finishes, what safety gear would you need? Write a short description of your safety plan. Describe the gear you will need (by brand and model number) and explain why. Then list a specific mail-order or local source for this equipment. Note how much each piece costs.

2. A potential client for your floor finishing business calls you and says he read something about a "Swedish" finish. He wonders if it's better than polyurethane. Find the answers to this question, using construction and remodeling magazines or the Internet. Write a letter to your client explaining what you found out and how you found it.

51

Ceramic Tile

Ceramic tile has become an increasingly useful and popular interior finish material in residential construction. It can be used throughout the house to provide durable, colorful, and easy-to-clean surfaces that complement the design of the house. Though found primarily in the kitchen and bathrooms, ceramic tile can be used elsewhere as well, including mudrooms, entry halls, decorative stair risers, and exterior patios. Fig. 51-1. It is available in a wide variety of shapes, sizes, and colors.

51-1a. *The ceramic tile in this kitchen is used on floors, countertops, and backsplashes. Note the trim tile along the edges of the countertops.*

Fig. 51-2. In new construction, tile is usually installed by tile contractors or tilesetters.

Ceramic tile is sometimes made from pure clay. However, most tile is a mixture of clay and other materials including ground shale or gypsum, talc, vermiculite, and sand. The tile is baked at high temperatures to form a relatively hard material that can be installed with a variety of adhesives, including mortar. Tile can have either a glazed or unglazed face.

The earliest known use of ceramic tiles with colored glazes dates to 4000 B.C. At that time, the Egyptians used tile only for their most important structures. The American tile industry dates to 1647, when sporadic production of roofing and paving tile began in the colonies. During the 1700s, local production of small quantities of floor and decorative wall tile began, usually in connection with pottery manufacturing. In 1853, the first mass-produced American tile was produced in Bennington, Vermont. Today, nearly 500 million square feet of tile are installed each year in the United States.

51-1b. *Ceramic tile can be used throughout the bathroom. The water-resistant and durable surfaces can be easily cleaned.*

51-2. *Ceramic tiles come in a wide variety of patterns, shapes, sizes, and colors.*

BASIC TILE MANUFACTURE

Custom lots of ceramic tile are still made by hand, but most tile is made in highly automated factories. Commonly, it is made from a combination of pure clay or pure gypsum, and other ingredients that extend the clay and control shrinkage of the tile. After the clay had been refined and mixed with water and these additives, it is shaped into a bisque, which is the body of the tile. To form the bisque, the clay mixture may be extruded, die-pressed, cut from a sheet, or formed by hand. Most commercial tile is made by the dust-press method. This means that the ingredients are mixed with so little water that only high pressure can bond them together.

Once the tile bisque has been formed, it is allowed to dry somewhat before being fired in a kiln at a temperature that usually ranges from 1900° to 2200°. The temperature and length of firing determine the water permeability of the bisque. (The glaze itself is waterproof.)

Types of Tile

The basic types of tile are divided according to the water permeability of the bisque after firing. Highly permeable tiles are the *least* waterproof because they absorb the most water. Mildly permeable tiles are more waterproof because they absorb less water. From most permeable to least permeable, these are the four types of tile:

- ➤ Nonvitreous tile.
- ➤ Semi-vitreous tile.
- ➤ Vitreous tile.
- ➤ Impervious tile.

The permeability of a tile bisque is important because it determines the best use of the tile. Tiles that will be exposed to water, for example, should be less permeable. To approximately test the permeability of a tile, turn it over and put a drop of water on the unglazed (back) portion of the tile. If the drop is absorbed immediately, that indicates a tile towards the nonvitreous side of the scale. If the drop sits on top of the tile, that indicates a tile that is towards the impervious side of the scale.

Categories by Location. In addition to the four basic types listed above, tile is often roughly categorized by where it is used.
Wall tile is generally a

nonvitreous tile with a relatively soft glaze. The softness of the glaze makes the tile unsuitable for floors. The tile is usually about ¼" thick, and is commonly made in 4¼" square size.

Floor tile can be any kind of tile (from nonvitreous to impermeable, glazed or unglazed) that is strong enough to hold up in use on the floor. A floor tile can, of course, be used on walls. Floor tile is made in a variety of shapes and sizes.

Categories by Use. Another way to categorize tile is to describe it by how it will be used. Using this method, all tile is either *field* or *trim tile*. Trim tile is specially shaped to form a border around a tile installation. The shape is typically bullnosed, but it may also be radiused to form more of a curve or ridged to form a pattern. Trim tile is glazed on one or more edges. Fig. 51-3.

Field tile is all the tile within the borders formed by the trim tile. Field tile is flat. It is glazed on the top surface only. Fig. 51-la.

Other Categories. Finally, tile can also be categorized by combinations of characteristics that make it more suitable or less suitable for certain applications. The following names are

51-3. *The edges of this trim tile are formed to provide non-slip ridges. The tiles are intended for use as stair treads.*

commonly used for certain kinds of tile used in residential construction.

Paver Tiles. These are at least ½" thick and intended for use on floors. They may be glazed or unglazed, and may be made by hand or by machine. Machine-made paver tiles are usually semi-vitreous or vitreous. They range in size from 4" by 6" to 12" square. Machine-made pavers may be up to ⅝" thick. Handmade pavers are generally nonvitreous. They have a slightly uneven surface. They range in size from 4" square to 24" square, and in thickness from ½" to 2". Handmade, unglazed pavers are commonly known as Mexican tiles or Mediterranean tiles.

Quarry Tile. This is generally semi-vitreous or vitreous clay tile that is unglazed. The tiles range in thickness from ½" to ¾", and in shape from square to hexagonal. Quarry tile is excellent for use on floors because of its density.

Mosaic Tile. This is considered to be any tile that is 2" square or smaller. It is usually vitreous, and ranges in thickness from 3⁄32" to ¼". Fig. 51-4.

51-4. *Mosaic tile used on a countertop and backsplash.*

51-5. *The lugs on the edges of these tiles ensure the proper spacing of the tiles. The lugs will later be covered with grout.*

Lugged Tile. This is any kind of tile that has spacing "lugs" built into the sides of the tile. When the tiles are placed edge-to-edge, the lugs automatically determine the proper spacing. Fig. 51-5.

ADHESIVES

Until the 1950s, tile was adhered with cement mortar. Since that time, cement mortar has been largely replaced by organic adhesives (mastics), dry-set mortars, and latex-Portland cement mortars. These are easier to use and allow the tile to set faster. Epoxy adhesives were developed in the 1960s.

All adhesives should be applied so that the material completely covers the back of the tile. This will ensure proper adhesion. A full bed of adhesive also helps to support the tile, preventing breakage caused by point loads on unsupported tile. Some adhesives are specially formulated to improve contact with the tile. Fig. 51-6.

All adhesives are applied with a notched trowel. The adhesive is troweled onto the substrate. It is then "combed" out evenly with the

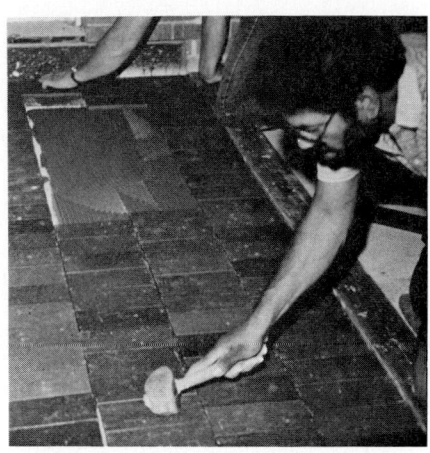

51-6. Tile should be set so that the adhesive (mortar, in this case) is in full contact with the tile.

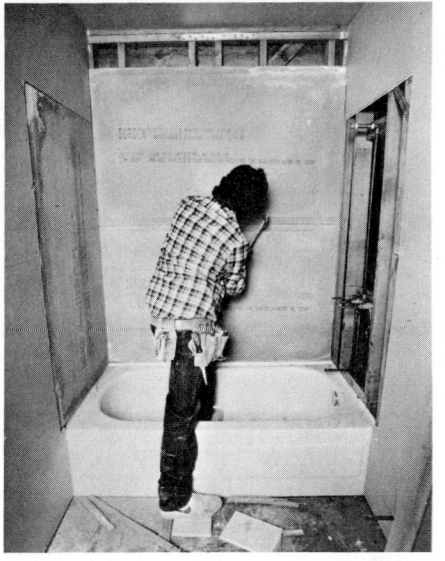

51-7. Backer board provides an excellent substrate for ceramic tile. Here it is being nailed to the framing surrounding a tub/shower.

51-8. Mastic is often used to adhere tile to drywall. Drywall used in tub areas should be of a special moisture-resistant type.

notched trowel. This evenly distributes the adhesive and ensures proper coverage. Figs. 51-6 and 51-8.

Mortar. Many people do not think of mortar strictly as an adhesive, but it is a very effective adhesive. The traditional mortar for ceramic tile installations was made from Portland cement, sand, and lime. Today, dry-set mortar (sometimes called *thinset* mortar) is more common. It consists of a mixture of Portland cement, sand, and certain additives that improve the ability of the mix to bond with the tiles. Dry-set mortar may be mixed with plain water, with a latex- or acrylic-modified liquid, or with epoxy resins.

Water-mixed dry-set mortar has a high bond strength and high compressive strength. It is relatively inexpensive and easy to use. The material is usually applied to masonry setting beds or to tile backer board (a factory-made Portland cement panel reinforced with fiberglass). Fig. 51-7.

Dry-set mortar mixed with a latex- or acrylic-modified liquid instead of water provides better adhesion, density, and impact strength than dry-set mixed only

with water. It is also more flexible and more resistant to frost damage. It can be applied to most surfaces except steel. Some companies, however, do not recommend application directly to plywood.

Epoxy dry-set mortar has a very high bond strength and resistance to impact, but is relatively expensive. Like latex and acrylic mortars, epoxy dry-set is fairly flexible. It can be applied to almost any surface, including plastic laminate, steel, and plywood.

Mastic. Mastic is an organic adhesive that comes ready-mixed. It is the least expensive and easiest to use of all the adhesives. Because mastic grips the tile even before it is fully cured, mastic is often used for setting wall tiles. Mastic is used for applying tiles to standard drywall, moisture-resistant drywall, or plywood. Fig. 51-8.

However, mastic does not have the strength or flexibility of mortar. It should not be used where it will be exposed to considerable heat, as in a fireplace hearth. Some

tilesetters prefer not to use mastic for tile installations that will be exposed to water, such as in a shower area.

GROUT

Once the tiles have been attached to a substrate with mortar or mastic, the spaces between the tiles must be filled in with grout. Grout is a form of mortar. It can be mixed either with water, or with latex- or acrylic-modified liquids. This prevents moisture and dirt from getting between the tiles. Grout comes in a wide array of colors. Tile distributors usually have cured samples of grouts in various colors so clients can compare the colors to the tile being selected. Fig. 51-9.

Tile grout comes in two forms: plain and sanded. Plain grout is a cement mixed with additives to give it a smooth, creamy consistency. It is generally used

51-9. *A manufacturer's sample kit of grout.*

when the spaces between tiles are less than 1/16" wide. Sanded grout is simply plain grout to which sand has been added. This improves its strength. Sanded grout is used for joints wider than 1/16".

MEMBRANES

Properly installed, ceramic tile is a durable and water-resistant surface finish. However, where the installation will be exposed to considerable amounts of water, such as in a bathroom, it is possible for the water to penetrate the installation. If this happens, the substrate will eventually rot. To prevent this, a waterproofing membrane should be installed beneath the tile. A membrane is any kind of flexible, waterproof sheet material that can be used between a tile installation and the substrate. Tar paper is one of the most common waterproofing membranes used beneath ceramic tile. It is nailed or stapled in place. Its edges may be sealed with asphalt adhesive. Other products, such as chlorinated polyethylene (CPE) may be used where more durability is required. CPE is a flexible material 30 mils thick. It comes in large rolls. It is attached directly to the substrate with dry-set mortar. A

51-10. *A waterproof membrane should be applied to substrates that might be exposed to water. This CPE membrane is being rolled into adhesive.*

roller is used to ensure a proper bond. Fig. 51-10.

TOOLS FOR CUTTING AND SETTING TILE

Cutting and setting tile does not require a large number of expensive tools. The tools shown in Fig. 51-11 are some of the basic tools that are used. Not all of them will be required for every installation.

1. *Portable snap cutter.* This is used to cut tiles in a straight line. The tile is placed on the bed of the tool (beneath the two rails) and against the guide. While lifting the long handle of the tool, pull it

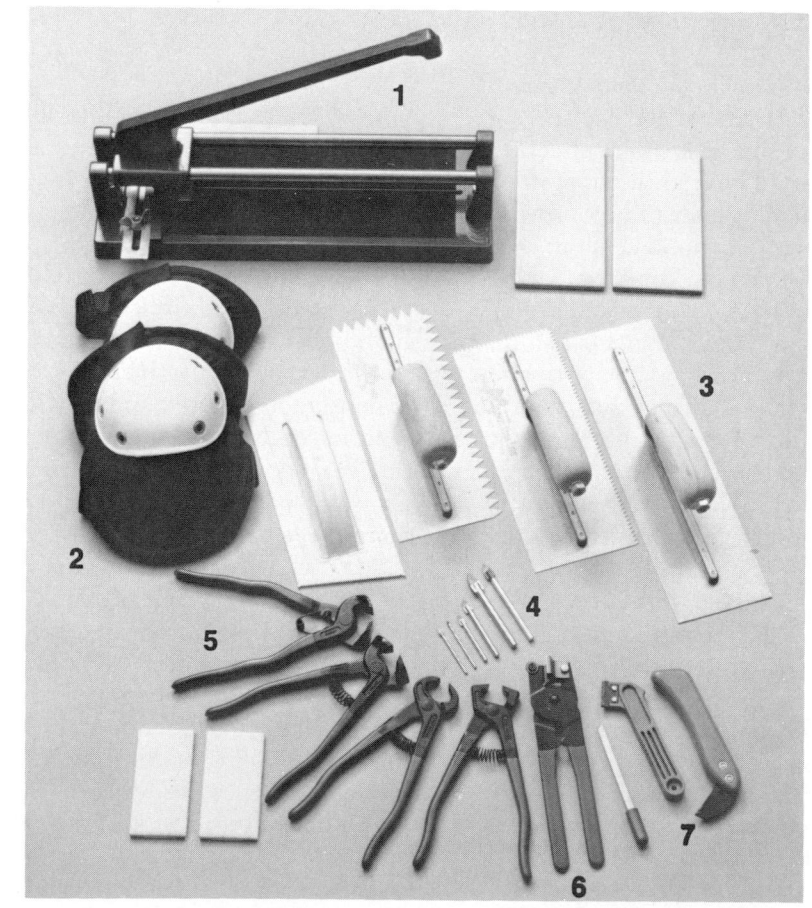

51-11. *Tools used in tilesetting: 1. snap cutters; 2. kneepads; 3. notched trowels; 4. tile drill bits; 5. nippers; 6. hand-held snap cutters; 7. laminate cutters.*

towards you. This forces a small scoring wheel against the tile and draws it across the tile's surface. The tile may then be snapped apart at the scored line.

2. *Knee pads.* These pads help to protect the tilesetter's knees from injury during long hours of setting floor tiles. Fig. 51-11.

3. *Trowels.* A tilesetter uses a variety of flat and notched trowels. These have steel blades. Trowels with notched edges are used to spread adhesive. The size of the notch gauges the depth of the adhesive. Fig. 51-11.

4. *Tile bits.* These carbide-tipped drill bits are used for cutting holes near the center of a ceramic tile. This is sometimes needed when water supply pipes must pass through a tile. Fig. 51-11. Carbide-tipped hole saws may also be used.

5. *Nippers and nibblers.* These tools look something like pliers or small nail pullers, but have straight, hardened edges. They are used to cut shapes in tile by "nibbling" away at the edges of a tile. Fig. 51-11.

6. *Hand-held snap cutter.* Like the cutter shown at number 1 in the photo, this tool cuts tiles in a straight line. It is more portable than the larger version. It is used where accuracy of the cut is less important. Fig. 51-11.

7. *Laminate cutters.* This tool is not strictly a tilesetter's tool. However, a tilesetter may have to cut plastic laminate in order to install the tile. Laminate cutters often have a sharpened carbide tip that scores the laminate so it can be snapped into two pieces. Fig. 51-11.

Other tools used by tilesetters include levels, straightedges, and grouting trowels. A grouting trowel has a cushioned working surface that allows the tilesetter to spread grout over the tiles without

51-12. *Grout is first troweled onto the floor. Then it is spread around with the grouting trowel. This forces grout into the gaps between tiles.*

damaging them. Fig. 51-12.

A wet saw can also be used to cut tile, particularly when large quantities must be cut with a high degree of accuracy. The tool is essentially a small radial-arm saw fitted with a diamond blade, a water pump, and a moisture-proof motor. The pump sprays a continuous stream of water on the blade during the cut. This lubricates and cools the blade. The result is an exceptionally smooth cut. Wet saws can be rented for periodic use. Standard power saws should never be used to wet-cut ceramic tile.

INSTALLING CERAMIC TILE

There are many methods for installing tile. Each installation will require a different combination of tile, adhesive, grout, and setting methods, depending on circumstances. The proper methods and materials will depend on several main factors, including structural loads expected, the stiffness of the substrate (the surface on which tiles will be laid), and the condition of the substrate.

The stiffness of the floor or wall is a particularly important factor to consider. Depending on its distance between supports, the substrate may flex more than the tile can handle. In such cases, additional supports beneath the substrate can be added (more joists in a floor, for example), or additional layers of substrate can be added (perhaps an additional layer of plywood). In some cases, a special material called an *isolation membrane* must be applied to the substrate before the adhesive is applied. This membrane reduces the chance that movement in the substrate will be transmitted to the tile.

The texture and condition of the substrate will also affect the type of installation. For example, a smooth subfloor in good condition can be a base for many installation methods. However, loose or uneven surfaces will require repair, or must be covered with another layer of material.

Thick-bed Installations

Using this method, tiles are applied over a mortar setting bed that is ¾" to 1¾" thick. After the setting bed has cured, tiles are applied to it with dry-set adhesive. Many tilesetters prefer this method, and use it whenever they can. The method allows for accurate slopes and planes in the finished tile

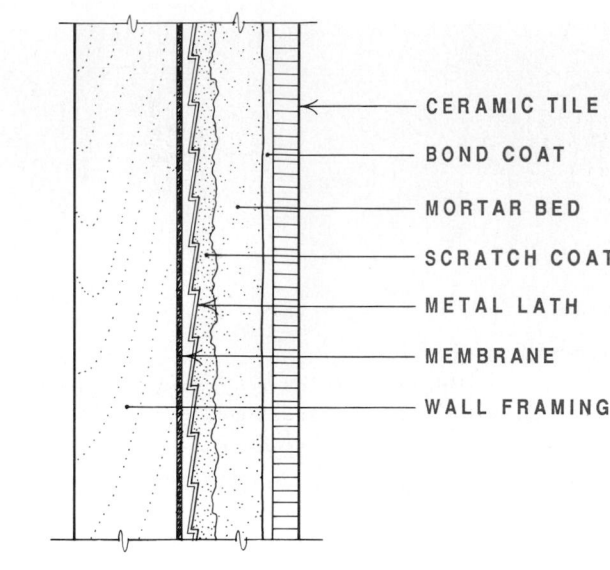

51-13. *Thick-bed installation over wood-frame walls.*

CERAMIC TILE
BOND COAT
MORTAR BED
SCRATCH COAT
METAL LATH
MEMBRANE
WALL FRAMING

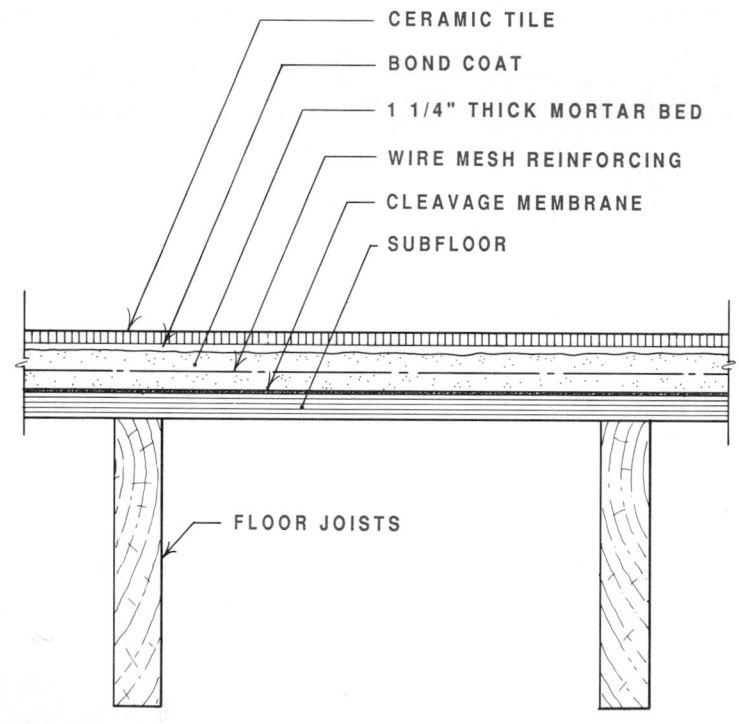

CERAMIC TILE
BOND COAT
1 1/4" THICK MORTAR BED
WIRE MESH REINFORCING
CLEAVAGE MEMBRANE
SUBFLOOR
FLOOR JOISTS

51-14. *Thick-bed installation over floors.*

work. It is structurally strong, is not affected by prolonged contact with water, and can be used to level uneven substrates. A waterproof membrane should be placed beneath the setting bed.

A thick-bed installation should be applied to metal lath. The mortar is generally applied in three layers, otherwise it would not stay in place. The layers include a scratch coat, a bed, and a bond coat. Typical thick-bed installations are shown in Figs. 51-13 and 51-14.

Thin-set Installations

Thin-set installations get their name because the tiles are adhered directly to the substrate with a thin layer of adhesive. The adhesive may be mastic or dry-set mortar. Thickness of the adhesive ranges from approximately $\frac{1}{32}$" to $\frac{1}{8}$" in thickness.

The advantages of thin-set installations are that they are less costly, relatively lightweight, easier to install, and quicker to install. Also, the overall installation is thinner as compared to thick-bed methods. One limitation of the thin-set method, however, is that the substrate must be very flat and very well prepared. Surfaces cannot be as easily sloped as the surface of thick-bed installations.

A thin-set installation is appropriate over a concrete slab. The photo sequence shows a typical installation of this type. Figs. 51-15a-h.

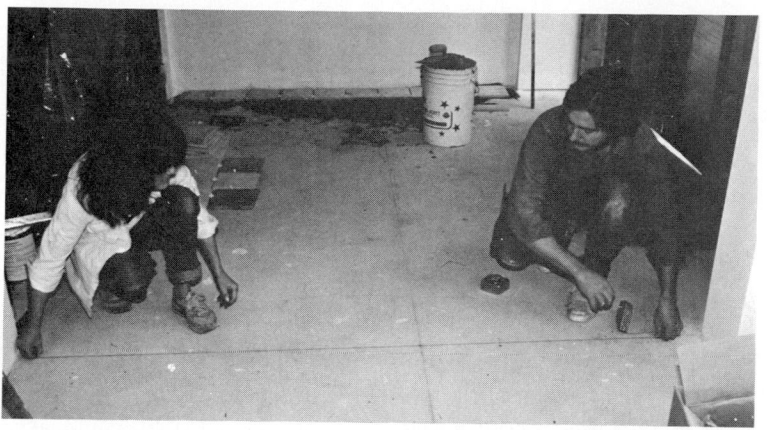

51-15a. *Using chalklines to snap out a layout on the subfloor.*

51-15f. *Sometimes additional adhesive must be applied to the tile. This is called "back buttering."*

51-15b. *Test fitting tiles on the layout. Note the spacers between tiles.*

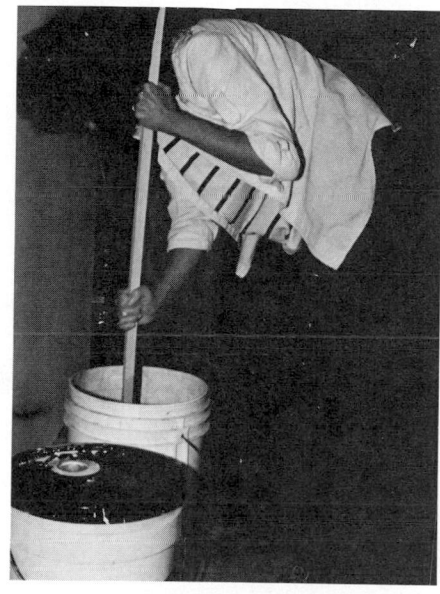

51-15d. *Mixing the adhesive.*

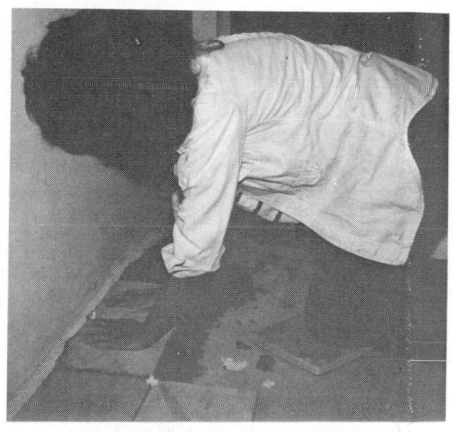

51-15g. *Pressing tiles into the adhesive.*

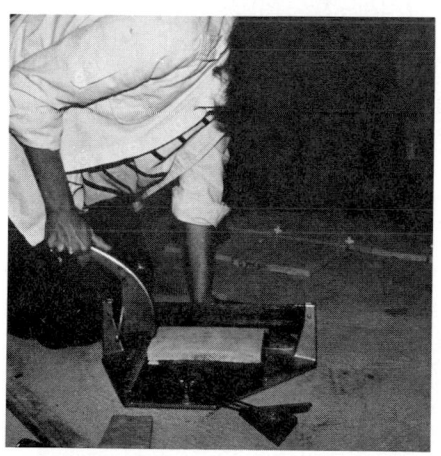

51-15c. *Using a snap cutter to cut tiles. It is often easier to make any cuts before spreading adhesive on the subfloor.*

51-15e. *Spreading adhesive with a trowel.*

51-15h. *Installing field tiles.*

1. Name five areas of the house in which ceramic tile is often used.

2. What is a bisque?

3. Tile is sometimes classified according to its moisture permeability. Name the four basic types of tile using this method.

4. Why is it important to know the permeability of a specific tile?

5. How is wall tile different from floor tile?

6. What is field tile?

7. What is the purpose of lugs on the side of a tile?

8. Name the three types of dry-set mortar.

9. Why is sand added to grout?

10. Describe how to use a portable snap cutter.

11. How does the stiffness of a floor affect the decision about what tilesetting methods to use?

ACTIVITIES

1. Social Studies. Ceramic tile has been used for thousands of years. Using the resources of your local library, research the manufacture of ceramic tile in ancient times. What were the principal uses of tile in ancient times? Do those uses differ at all from the main uses for ceramic tile today? Present your research in a short essay.

2. Language Arts. Human relationships will be very important in your career. In most jobs, you will probably be working with other people. Your success on the job will depend greatly on your ability to get along with other members of your work team. To get along with others, you will need to exercise self-control and cooperation. What personal work habits and attitudes will aid you in developing self-control? What work habits and attitudes will help you develop a spirit of cooperation? Express your thoughts in a brief essay.

THE SCHOOL-TO-WORK CONNECTION

When laying out the design of a tiled surface, it is crucial to consider not only the size of the tile itself, but also the width of the grout line. Grout line width is a particularly important factor to consider if the installation will include a lot of tiles. This is because seemingly small differences in the grout line accumulate with each course of tile. If you don't take this into account when laying out the job, you may find that the last tiles won't fit into place.

1. Visit a store that sells ceramic tile; take along a notepad. Ask the salesperson to show you tiles that would be suitable for a bathroom floor. Pick a tile that you like and measure its exact dimensions. How do these dimensions compare to the nominal size of the tile? Find out from the salesperson what width of grout line would be appropriate for this tile, and what type of grout would be suitable.

Stairs

There are two general types of stairs: principal and service. The principal stairs are designed to provide ease and comfort and are often made a feature of house design. Fig. 52-1a, b, c. The service stairs lead to the basement or attic. They are usually somewhat steeper and constructed of less expensive materials.

Stairs may be built on the job or assembled from units built in a mill. All parts for a finish stairway can be purchased from a lumberyard as stock mill items. Stairways may have a straight, continuous run with or without an intermediate platform. They may also consist of two or more runs at angles to each other. Usually there is a platform at the angle. The turn may also be made by radiating treads called winders.

Winders are not often used because they are not as safe as platforms. In fact, many building codes prohibit certain types of winders. Fig. 52-2. The stairway for most homes is a straight, continuous run, although a stairway with a landing or platform is sometimes used to conserve space. Fig. 52-3. Details for stair building are shown in the stairwell section of most house plans.

52-1a. *A stair often serves as the focal point of a house.*

52-1b. *This stair was built from a stock collection of parts.*

52-1c. *This straight stair features an ornamental balustrade.*

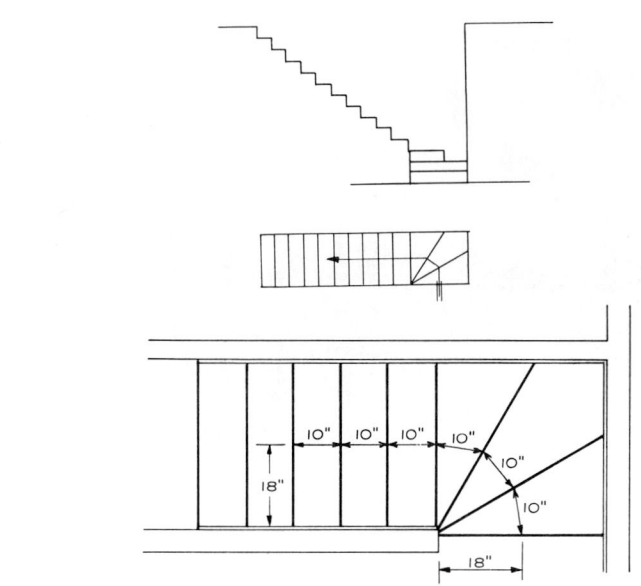

52-2. *A stairway with winders. At the inner corner where all the winders meet, there is very little if any tread to support one's foot. This makes this type of winder rather dangerous, and it is not often used.*

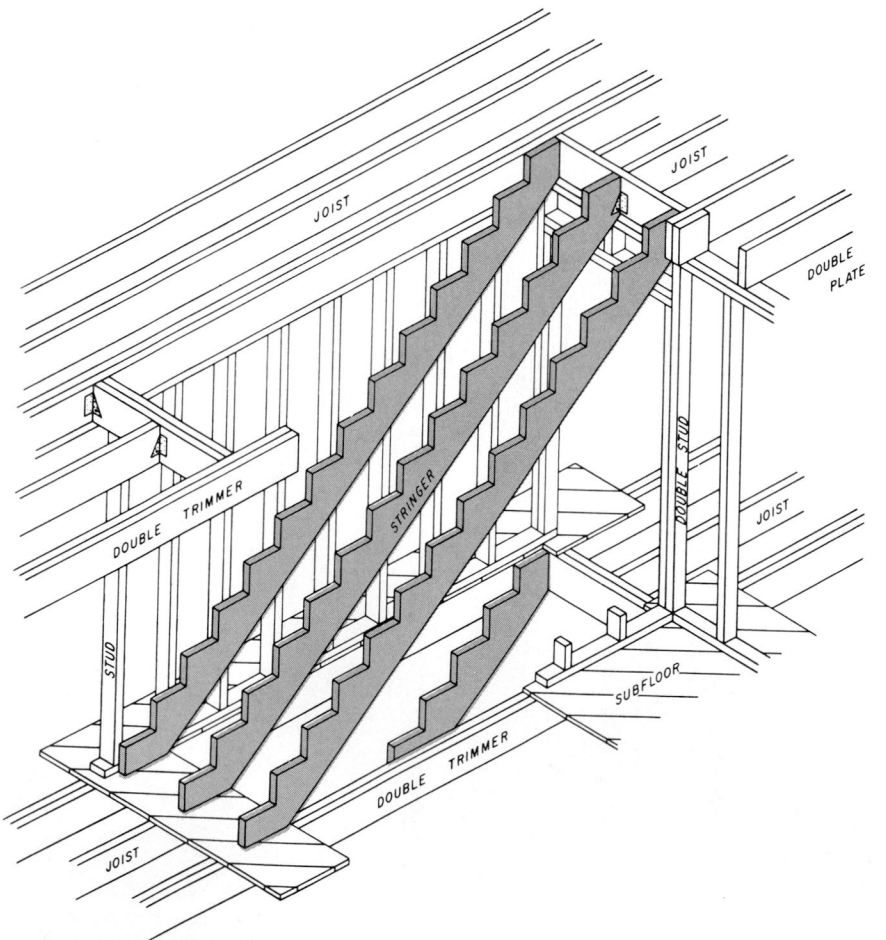

52-3a. *Framing for an interior straight continuous stairway.*

There are many different kinds of stairs, but all have two main parts in common: the treads people walk on and the stringers which support the treads. The simplest stairway has a pair of straight-edged stringers and a series of plank treads. Fig. 52-4. It is called a cleat stairway because the treads are supported by cleats nailed to the stringers. A complete stairway includes two or more sawtooth-edged stringers, a series of treads, and a series of risers. Fig. 52-5. The stringers shown in Fig. 52-5 are cut out of solid pieces (usually 2" × 12"), and are therefore called cutout or sawed stringers. In some stairways the treads and risers are supported on triangular stair blocks nailed to the upper edges of straight-edged stringers. Fig. 52-6.

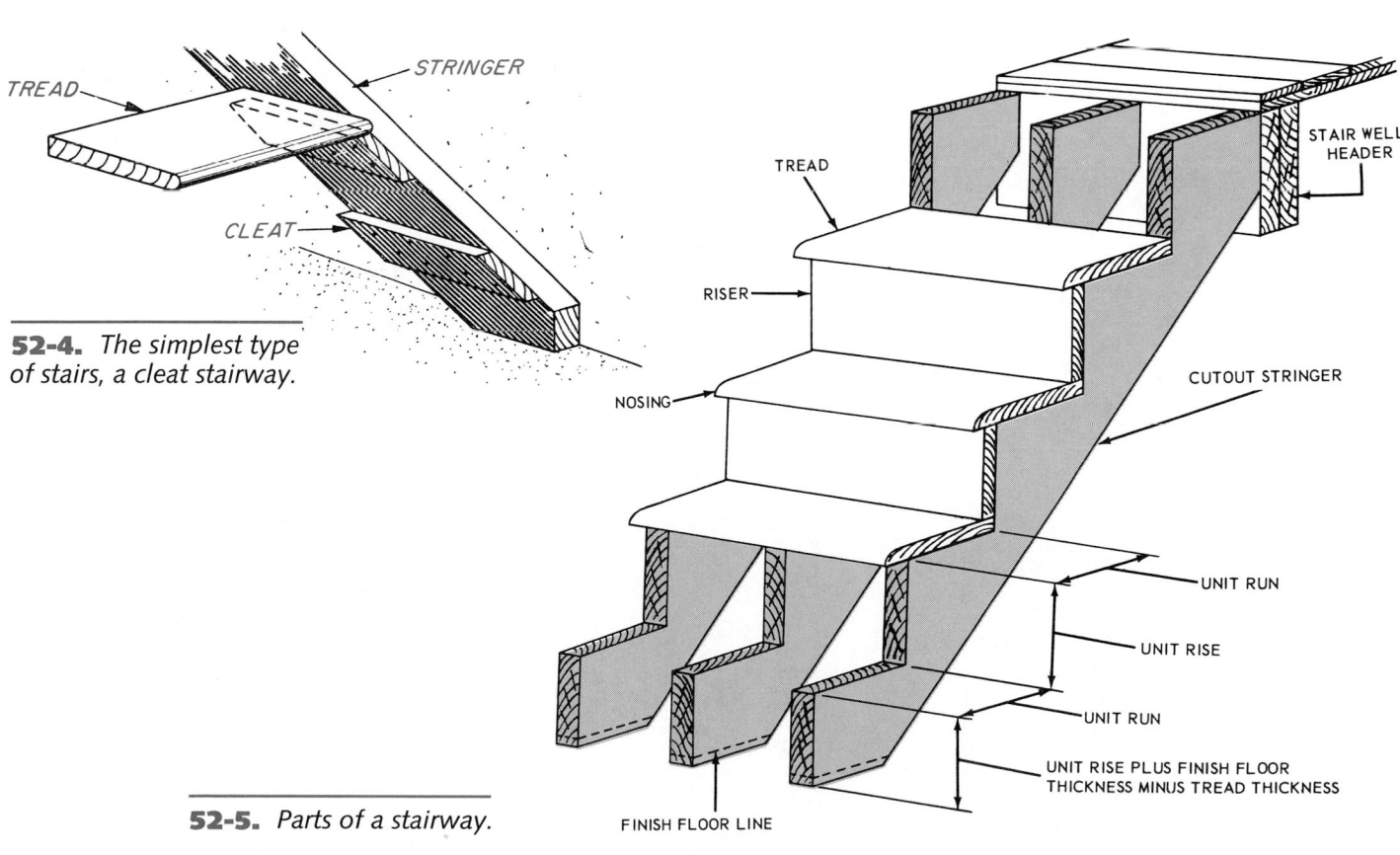

52-3b. *Framing for an interior stairway with a platform.*

COMMON STAIR PARTS AND TERMS

Stringer. Sometimes called a *string*, *carriage*, or *horse*. One of the inclined sides of a stair which supports the treads and risers. Open (plain) stringers can be either rough or finish stock and are cut to follow the lines of the treads and risers. Closed stringers have parallel sides, with the risers and treads housed into them. The term also applies to any similar member, whether a support or not, such as finish stock placed outside the carriage on open stairs and next to the walls on closed stairs. Figs. 52-3, 52-6, and 52-7 show various kinds of stringers.

Riser. The vertical face of one step. Fig. 52-8.

Tread. The horizontal face of one step. Fig. 52-8.

52-4. *The simplest type of stairs, a cleat stairway.*

52-5. *Parts of a stairway.*

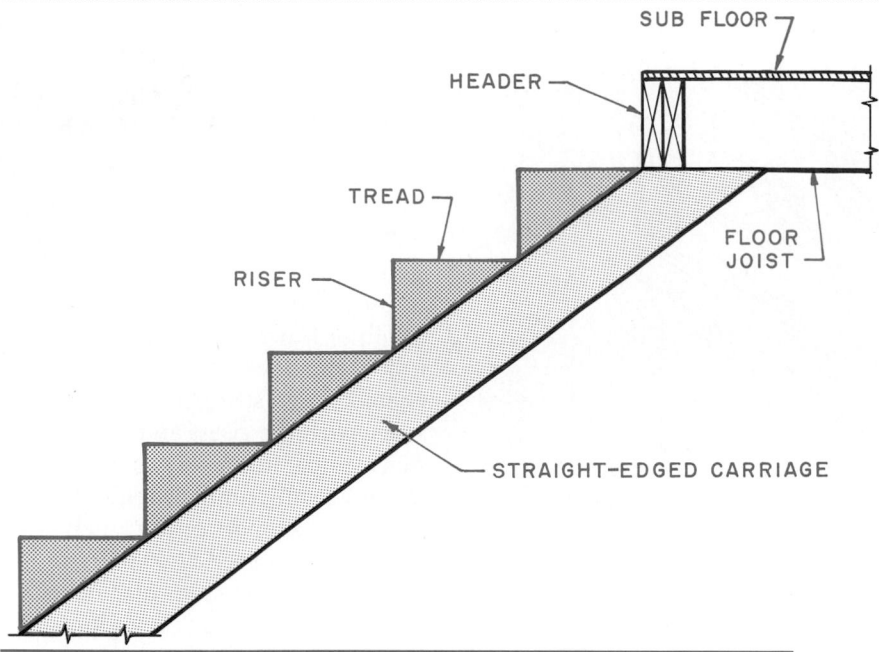

52-6. *A built-up stringer made up of a straight-edged carriage with triangular blocks attached.*

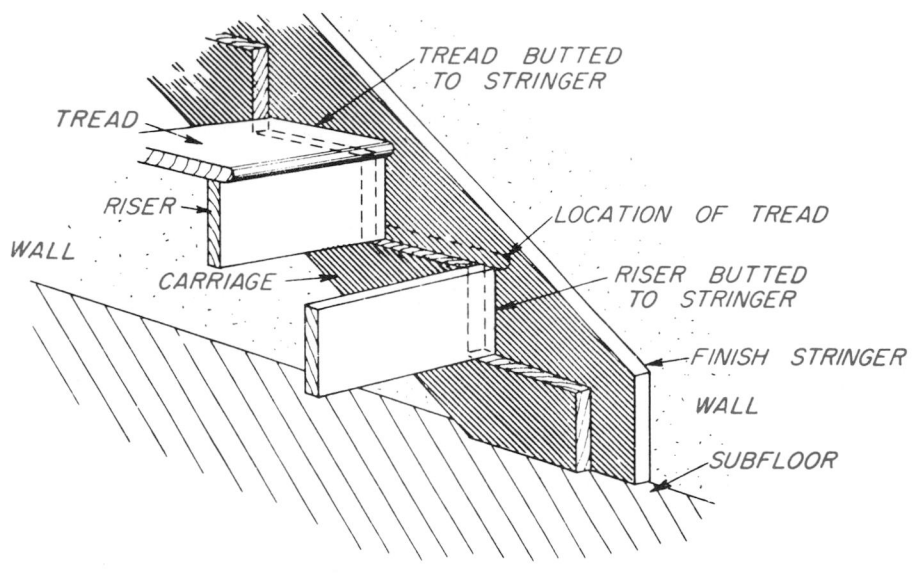

52-7. *A finished wall stringer and carriage.*

Winders. Radiating or wedge-shaped treads at turns of stairs. Fig. 52-9.

Nosing. The projection of tread beyond the face of the riser. Fig. 52-8.

Railing. The protection on the open side of a run of stairs. Fig. 52-8.

Newel. The main post of the railing at the start of the stairs and the stiffening post at angles or platforms. Fig. 52-8.

Handrail. The top finishing piece on the railing to be grasped by the hand when going up or down the stairs. Fig. 52-8.

Balusters. The vertical members supporting the handrail on open stairs. Fig. 52-8. For closed stairs where there is no railing, the handrail is attached to the wall with brackets.

Platform. The intermediate area between two parts of a flight of stairs. Fig. 52-10, arrow 1.

Landing. The floor at the top or bottom of each story where the flight of stairs ends or begins. Fig. 52-10, arrow 2.

Total rise. The total vertical distance from one floor to the next.

Total run. The total horizontal length of the stairs.

FRAMING A STAIRWELL

When large openings are made in floors, such as for stairwells, one or more joists must be cut. The location of openings in the floor determines the method of framing. When the length of the stairway is parallel to the joists, the opening is framed as shown in Fig. 52-11. When the stairway is arranged so that the opening is perpendicular to the length of the joists, the framing should follow the details shown in Fig. 52-12. Fig. 52-13 shows typical framing for a stair

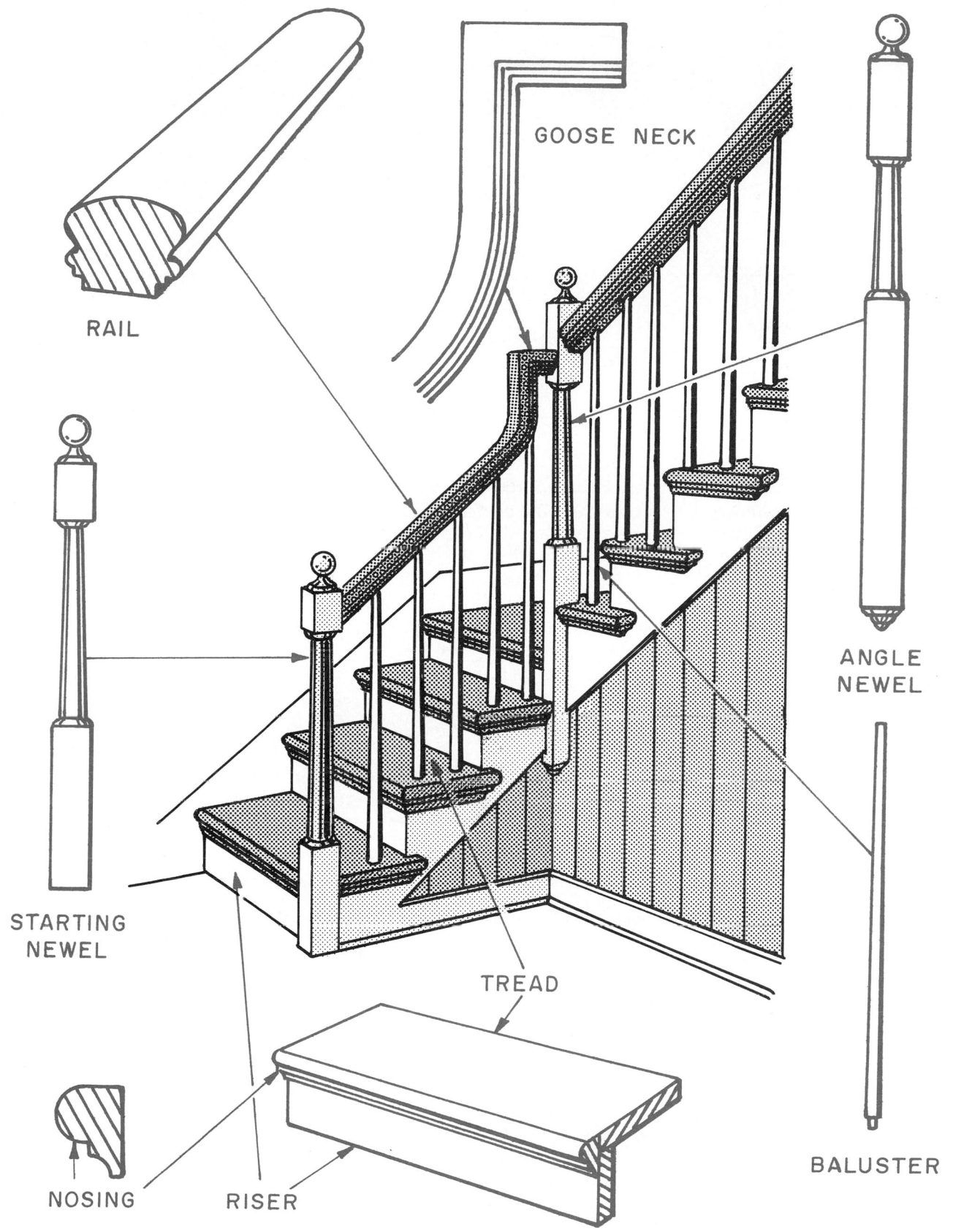

RAIL

GOOSE NECK

ANGLE
NEWEL

STARTING
NEWEL

TREAD

BALUSTER

NOSING

RISER

52-8. *The parts of this finished stairway can be purchased from a lumberyard as stock mill items.*

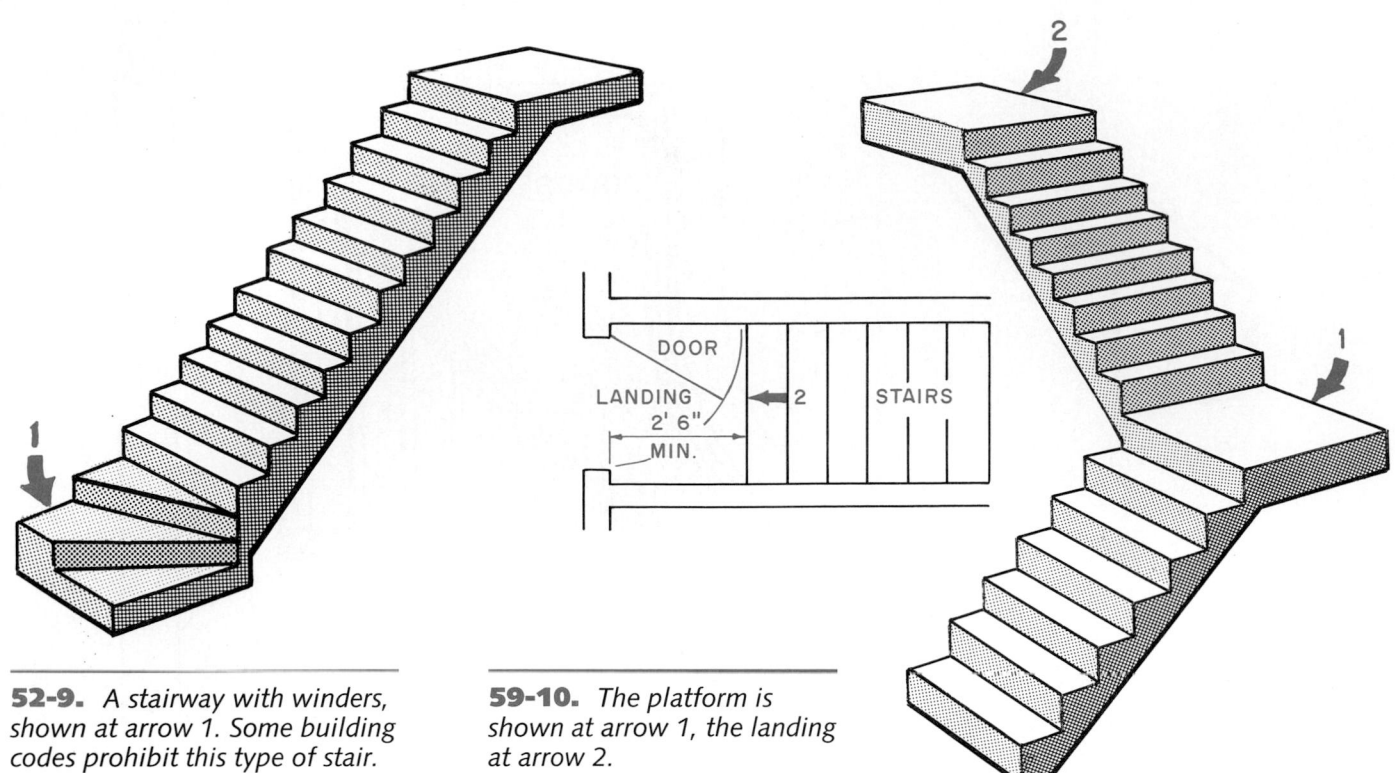

52-9. A stairway with winders, shown at arrow 1. Some building codes prohibit this type of stair.

59-10. The platform is shown at arrow 1, the landing at arrow 2.

DOOR

LANDING

2' 6"
MIN.

2

STAIRS

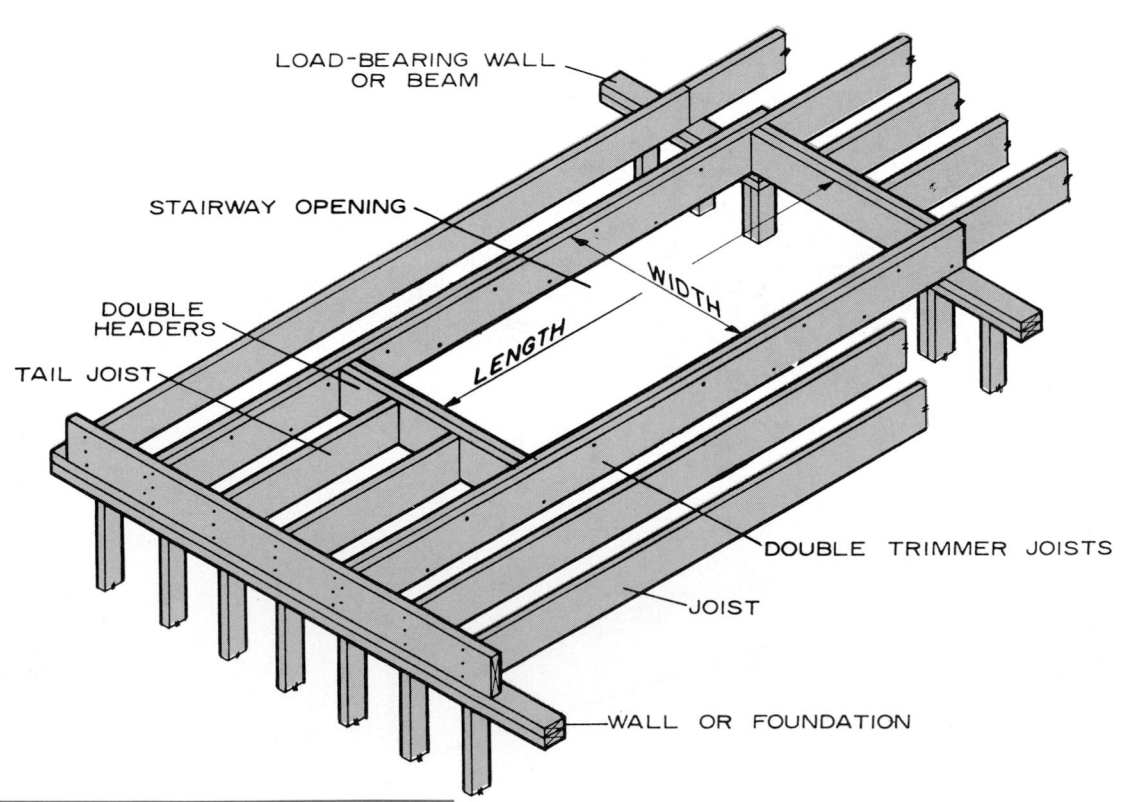

LOAD-BEARING WALL OR BEAM

STAIRWAY OPENING

WIDTH

LENGTH

DOUBLE HEADERS

TAIL JOIST

DOUBLE TRIMMER JOISTS

JOIST

WALL OR FOUNDATION

52-11. A stairwell framed parallel to the joists.

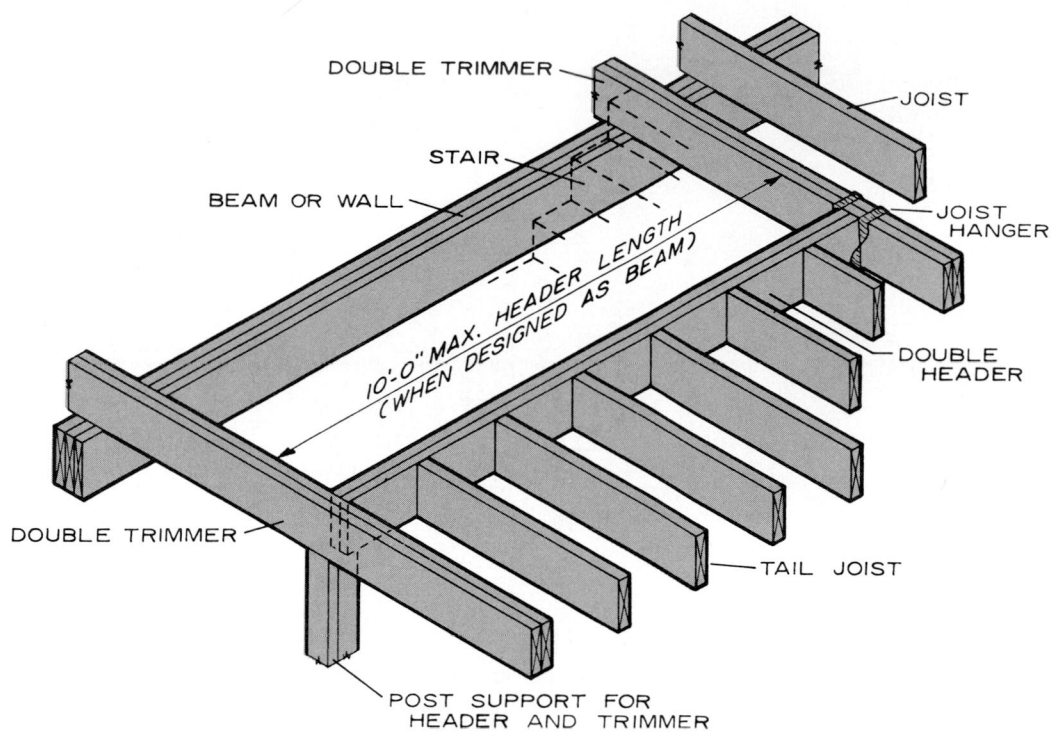

52-12. *A stairwell framed perpendicular to the joists.*

DOUBLE TRIMMER

STAIR

BEAM OR WALL

10'-0" MAX. HEADER LENGTH (WHEN DESIGNED AS BEAM)

JOIST

JOIST HANGER

DOUBLE HEADER

DOUBLE TRIMMER

TAIL JOIST

POST SUPPORT FOR HEADER AND TRIMMER

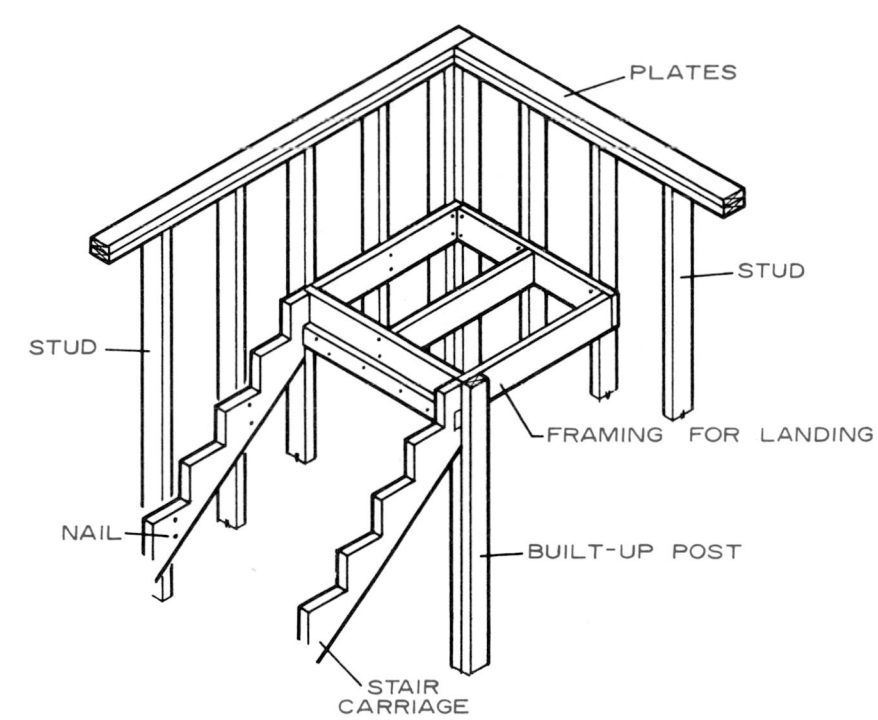

52-13. *Framing for a landing.*

PLATES

STUD

STUD

FRAMING FOR LANDING

NAIL

BUILT-UP POST

STAIR CARRIAGE

landing. Nailing and framing of stairwell openings should comply with the principles explained in Unit 29, "Floor Framing."

DESIGNING A STAIRWAY

Building codes tightly regulate the dimensions and design of stairs—and for good reason. A surprising number of people are killed falling down stairs. Some estimates have put the number of serious injuries in stair falls at *two million* per year in the United States alone. Before beginning a stair construction project, be sure to review the codes that apply in your area.

In addition to being designed and built to be as safe as possible, a good set of stairs will also allow adequate headroom and space for the passage of furniture.

There are five important considerations when designing the stairway:

- The stair width.
- The headroom.
- The relationship between the height of the riser and the width of the tread.
- The shape and location of handrails and guardrails.
- The spacing of balusters.

Stair Width

Staircases must be wide enough to allow two people to pass comfortably on the stairs and to permit furniture to be carried up or down. The minimum width for a main stair is generally 3 feet; however, 3½ feet is better. Fig. 52-14.

The width needed for the passage of furniture varies. Stairs which are open on one side, including open-well stairs, are best for moving large pieces of furniture. The furniture can usually be raised up over the handrails and newel posts.

Headroom

Headroom is the distance or clearance above a stair. It is measured from the outside edge of the nosing to the lowest point of the soffit or ceiling directly

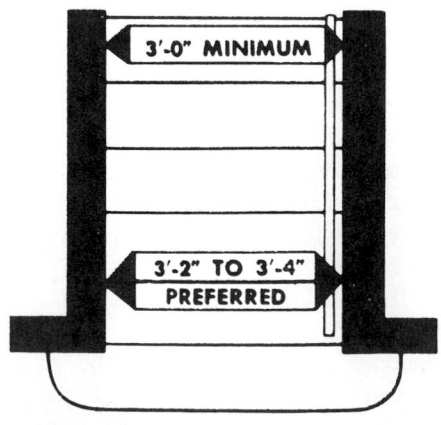

52-14. *The stair width should be adequate. Three feet is acceptable, but wider stairs are preferred.*

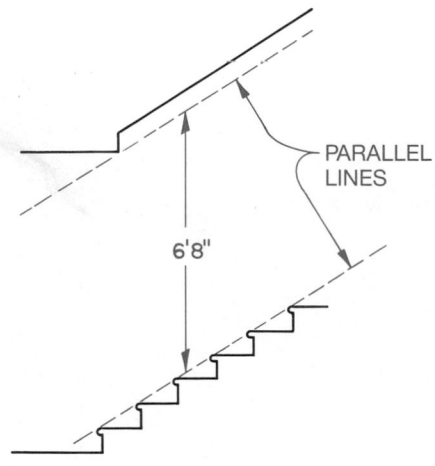

52-15. *Headroom should be a minimum of 6'8" for a main stair.*

overhead. If two or more flights of stairs are arranged one above the other in the same stairwell (for example, cellar stairs under, or attic stairs over, the main staircase), getting enough headroom beneath the upper stair is a planning problem and must be carefully considered. Although the minimum required by code is 6'8", this is usually not enough for the main stairway. It has been found from studies of the dimensions of the average man or woman that headroom may vary with the steepness of the stairs, but should generally be between 7'4" and 7'7". This allows for the arm to be swung up over the head without hitting anything. Fig. 52-15.

Riser and Tread Relationship

It is very important that the stairway be built with the proper rise and run. The relationship between the height of the riser and the width of the tread determines the ease with which the stairs may be ascended or descended. If the combination of run and rise is too great, the steps are tiring. There is a strain on the leg muscles and the heart. If the combination is too

short, the foot may kick the riser at each step. Fig. 52-16.

Building codes generally allow a minimum riser height of 4" and a maximum of about 8". Some codes allow treads as small as 9" wide. There are no maximum dimensions for treads. Safety research, however, indicates that the ideal riser is 7" high and the ideal tread is 11" wide.

Whatever riser/tread relationship is decided upon, the height and width of each step must be uniform. Most building codes allow a variation of no more than $\frac{3}{16}$" in the height of adjacent steps. Warped or poorly secured treads make uniformity difficult to achieve, and become a tripping hazard.

Treads should have a slip-resistant surface. Materials such as polished stone or glazed tile can be dangerous on a stair and should be avoided.

Handrails and Guardrails

One of the most important features of a good stair is a properly designed and installed handrail. A solid, easily grasped handrail can prevent a stair user from suffering

52-16. A stairway should be built with the proper rise and run: A. Stairway with a tread too wide and riser too short. B. Stairway with a tread too narrow and the riser too high. C. Stairway with a correct tread width (11") and the correct height (7").

serious injury in the event of a fall.

Fingers should be able to curl around and under the handrail. Handrails are most graspable when they are made from metal tubing or solid wood stock with a simple round profile. The diameter of a handrail should be 1½" to 2". Handrails with a larger diameter, or those with a rectangular shape, are more difficult to grasp.

A handrail should be between 30" and 38" high. The height is measured vertically from the upper edge of the nosing to the top of the handrail.

Guardrails at stair landings provide protection similar to that of a good handrail. Commercial building codes call for guardrails to be 42" to 44" high. Residential codes are less stringent. They require guardrails to be between 30" and 38" high.

Balusters

Balusters are the vertical members that support the handrail and guardrail. Their purpose is to prevent anyone, particularly children, from slipping under the railings and falling off the stair. The standard requirement is that a 6" diameter sphere should not be able to pass between balusters. Some codes, however, have recently reduced the sphere diameter to 4".

LAYING OUT A STAIRWAY

The first step in stairway layout is to determine the *unit rise* and *unit run* per step. Fig. 52-17. The unit rise (height of one riser) is calculated on the basis of the total rise of the stairway, and the fact that the unit rise for stairs should be about 7".

The total rise is the vertical distance between the lower finish

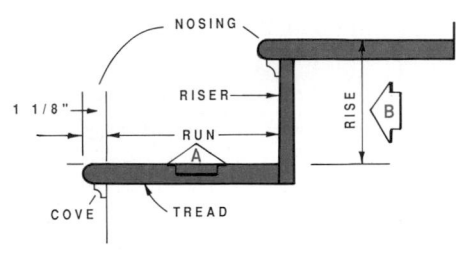

52-17. The unit run (arrow A) is the distance from the face of one riser to the face of the next riser. It does not include the nosing. The unit rise (arrow B) is the distance from the top of one tread to the top of the next tread.

floor level and the upper finish floor level. It is given on the elevations and wall sections. The actual distance, however, may vary slightly from the specified distance. Measure the actual distance. If both the lower and the upper floor are to be covered with finish flooring of the same thickness, the vertical distance between the subfloor levels will be the same as the vertical distance between the finish floor levels. However, you may be measuring up from a finish floor (a concrete basement floor, for example) to a floor which will be covered with finish flooring. In this case, you must add the thickness of the upper floor finish flooring to the vertical distance between the lower finish floor and the upper subfloor.

Let's assume that the total rise, or vertical distance between finish floors, is 8' 11". The unit rise can be determined from the total rise as follows:

➤ The total rise is 107" (8' 11" = 107").

➤ A permissible unit rise is anything near 7". Divide 107" by 7".

➤ The result (disregarding any fraction) is the total number of risers in the stairway. In this case, the total is 15 risers (107 ÷ 7 = 15).

➤ To get the unit rise, divide

the total rise by the number of risers. The unit rise in this case is 7⅛" (107 ÷ 15 = 7.13, or 7⅛).

The unit run is equal to the width of a tread, less the width of the nosing. Fig. 52-17. It is calculated on the basis of the unit rise and a rule, discussed earlier, that the sum of one riser and one tread should equal between 17" and 18". Subtract the unit rise from this sum. Let's assume that the sum of one riser and one tread should be 17½". If the unit rise is 7⅛", the unit run will be 10⅜" (17½" - 7⅛" = 10⅜").

You now have all the information you need to lay out, cut, and install a cutout stringer except the total run of the stairway. The total run is equal to the unit run times the number of treads in the stairway. The total number of treads depends on the manner in which the upper end of the stairway is anchored to the upper landing. Three common types of anchorage are shown in Fig. 52-18.

In A, Fig. 52-18, there is a complete tread at the top of the stairway. This means that the number of treads in the stairway is the same as the number of risers. If there are 15 risers and the unit run is 10⅜", the total run of the stairway is 12' 11⅝" (15 × 10⅜ = 155⅝", or 12' 11⅝").

In B, Fig. 52-18, there is only part of a tread at the top of the stairway. In this case, the number of complete treads is one less than the number of risers, or 14. The total run of the stairway is 14 × 10⅜, plus the run of the partial tread at the top. This run may be shown in detail. If not, you will have to estimate it as closely as possible. Let's assume it's about 7". The total run, then, is 12' 8¼" (14 × 10⅜ = 145¼"; 145¼" + 7" = 152¼", or 12' 8¼").

In C, Fig. 52-18, there is no tread at the top of the stairway. The upper finish flooring serves as a top tread. In this case the number

of treads is one less than the number of risers, or 14. The total run is 12' 1¼" (14 × 10⅜ = 145¼", or 12' 1¼").

After you have calculated the total run of the stairway, drop a plumb bob from the stairwell header to the floor below. Measure off along the floor the total run, starting at the plumb bob. You have now located the anchoring point for the lower end of the stairway. Some standard stair layouts can be found in the chart in Fig. 52-19.

STRINGERS

The treads and risers are supported by stringers, or carriages, that are solidly fixed in place, level and true, upon the framework of the building. The stringers may be cut or routed to fit the outline of the treads and risers. A third stringer should be installed in the middle of the stairs when the treads are less than 1⅛" thick or the stairs are more than 2' 6" wide.

In some cases, rough stringers with rough treads nailed across them are used during the construction period. These are installed for the convenience of the workers until wall finish is applied. When the wall finish is completed, the temporary stairway is removed and finished stairs, which usually have been made in a mill, are erected or built in place.

For a housed stringer, the wall stringer is routed out to the exact profile of the tread, riser, and nosing, with sufficient space at the back to take the wedges. Fig. 52-20 (page 696). The top of the riser is rabbeted to fit into a groove in the bottom front of the tread. The back of the tread is rabbeted into a groove in the bottom of the next riser. The wall stringer is spiked to the inside of the wall. The treads and risers are fitted together and

forced into the wall stringer housing, where they are set tight by driving and gluing wood wedges behind them. Fig. 52-21 (page 697). The wall stringer thus shows above the profiles of the treads and risers as a finish against the wall. It is often made continuous with the baseboard of the upper and lower landing.

If the outside stringer (stair carriage) is an open stringer, it is cut out to fit risers and treads and nailed against the finish stringer. The edges of the risers are mitered with the corresponding edges of the stringer. The nosing of the tread is returned upon its outside edge along the face of the stringer. Fig. 52-22 (page 697). Another method would be to butt the stringer to the riser and cover the joint with an inexpensive stair bracket.

Figure 52-23 (page 697) shows a finish stringer nailed in position on the wall and a rough carriage nailed in place against the stringer. If there are walls on both sides of the staircase, the other stringer and carriage are nailed in the same way. The risers are nailed to the riser cuts of the carriage on each side and butted against the stringers. The treads are nailed to the tread cuts of the carriage and butted against the stringers. This is the least expensive of the types described and perhaps the best type of construction to use when the treads and risers are to be nailed to the carriages.

Another method of fitting the treads and risers to wall stringers is shown in Fig. 52-24 (page 698). The finish stringers are laid out with the same rise and run as the stair carriages, but they are cut out in reverse. The risers are butted and nailed from the back to the riser cuts of the wall stringers, and the assembled stringers and risers are laid over the carriage. The treads are butted to the stringers and nailed to the risers. Sometimes the treads are allowed to run

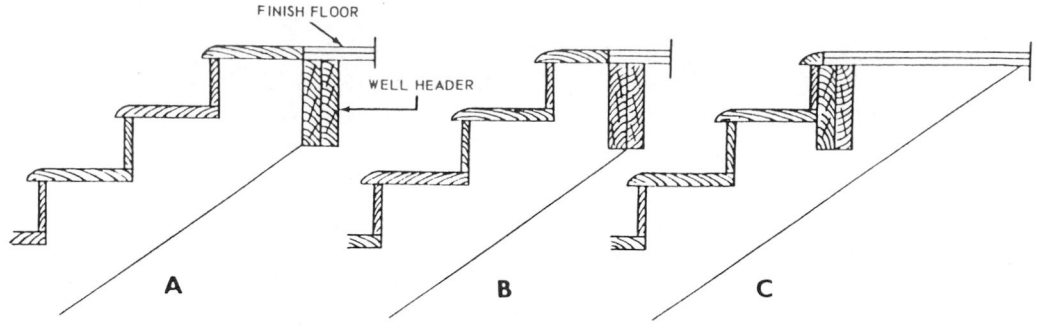

FINISH FLOOR

WELL HEADER

A   B   C

52-18. *Three methods of anchoring the upper end of a stringer.*

Stair With Landing

This type is easier to climb, safer, and reduces the length of space required. The landing provides a resting point and a logical place to have a right angle turn. Landing near bottom with quarter-turn is basis of calling this type "dog-legged" or "platform" stairs.

Height Floor to Floor H	Number of Risers	Height of Risers R	Width of Tread T	Run Number of Risers	Run L	Run Number of Risers	Run L2
8'0"	13	7⅜" +	10"	11	8'4" + W	2	0'10" + W
8'6"	14	7⁵/₁₆" −	10"	12	9'2" + W	2	0'10" + W
9'0"	15	7³/₁₆" +	10"	13	10'0" + W	2	0'10" + W
9'6"	16	7⅛"	10"	14	10'10" + W	2	0'10" + W

Straight Stairs

Simplest and least costly; requires a long hallway which may sometimes be a disadvantage. May have walls on both sides (closed string) or may have open balustrade on one side (open string).

Height Floor to Floor H	Number of Risers	Height of Risers R	Width of Treads T	Total Run L	Minimum Head Rm. Y	Well Opening U
8'0"	12	8"	9"	8'3"	6'6"	8'1"
	13	7⅜" +	9½"	9'6"	6'6"	9'2½"
	13	7⅜" +	10"	10'0"	6'6"	9'8½"
8'6"	13	7⅞" −	9"	9'0"	6'6"	8'3"
	14	7⁵/₁₆" −	9½"	10'3½"	6'6"	9'4"
	14	7⁵/₁₆" −	10"	10'10"	6'6"	9'10"
9'0"	14	7¹¹/₁₆" +	9"	9'9"	6'6"	8'5"
	15	7³/₁₆" +	9½"	11'1"	6'6"	9'6½"
	15	7³/₁₆" +	10"	11'8"	6'6"	9'11½"
9'6"	15	7⅝" −	9"	10'6"	6'6"	8'6½"
	16	7⅛"	9½"	11'10½"	6'6"	9'7"
	16	7⅛"	10"	12'6"	6'6"	10'1"

Note: Dimensions shown under well opening "U" are based on 6'6" minimum headroom. If headroom is increased well opening also increases.

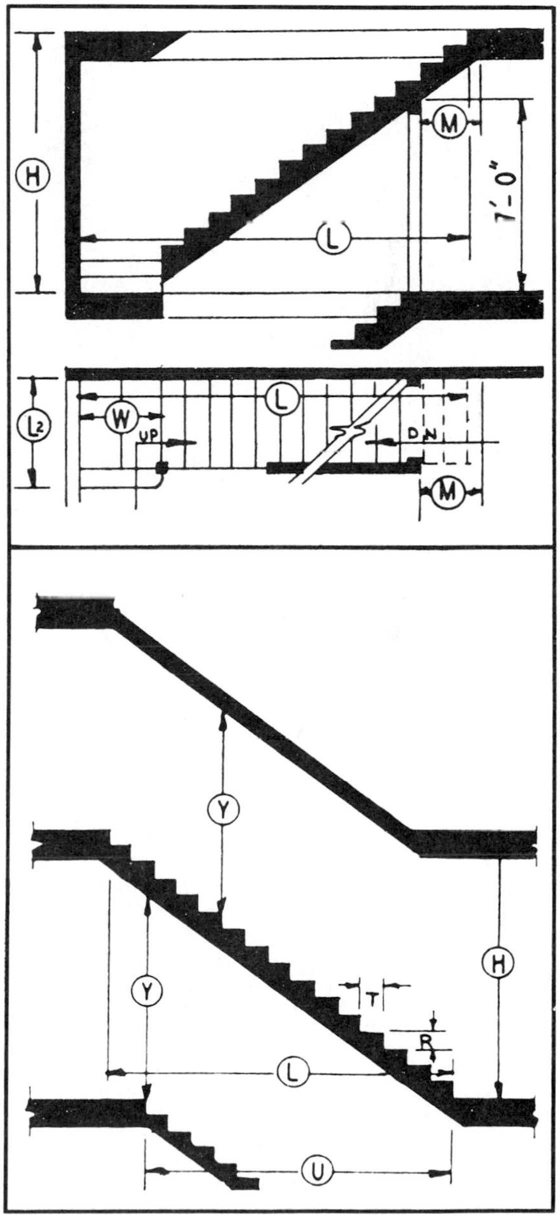

52-19. *Layout dimensions for some standard stairways.*

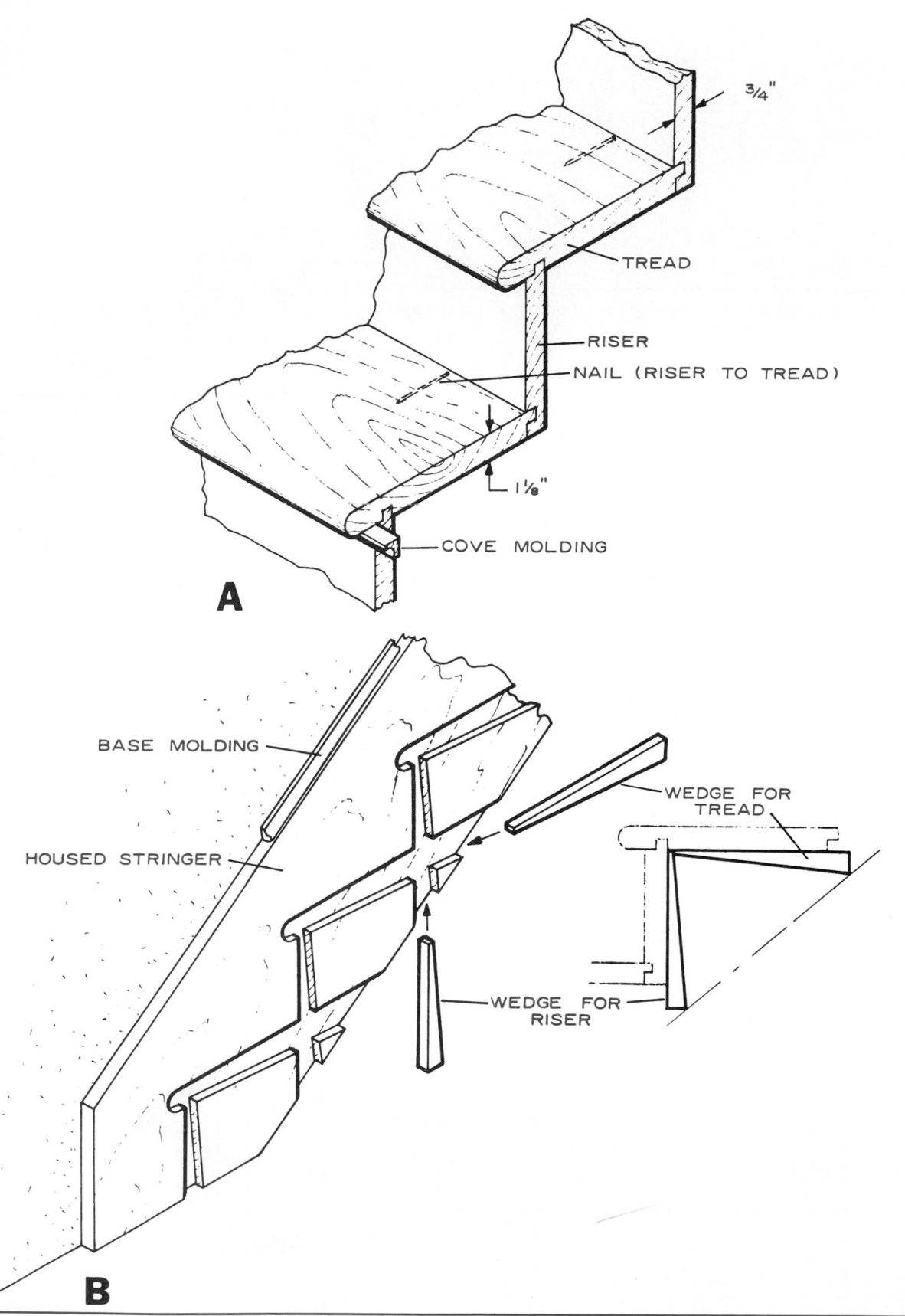

3/4"

TREAD

RISER

NAIL (RISER TO TREAD)

1⅛"

COVE MOLDING

A

BASE MOLDING

HOUSED STRINGER

WEDGE FOR TREAD

WEDGE FOR RISER

B

52-20. *Parts of stairs: A. Risers and treads rabbeted and grooved for installation in a housed stringer. B. A housed stringer.*

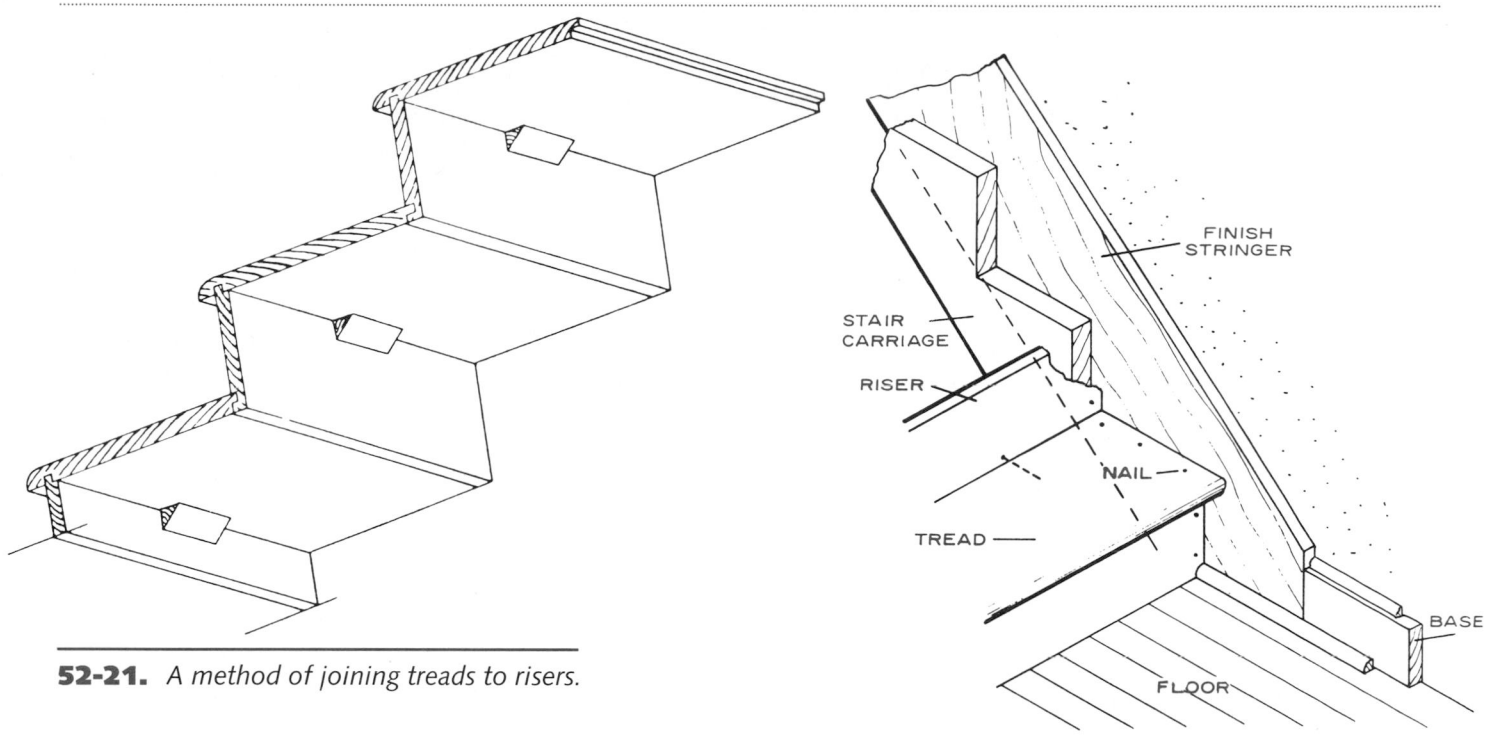

52-21. A method of joining treads to risers.

52-23. A finish stringer and a rough carriage nailed in place.

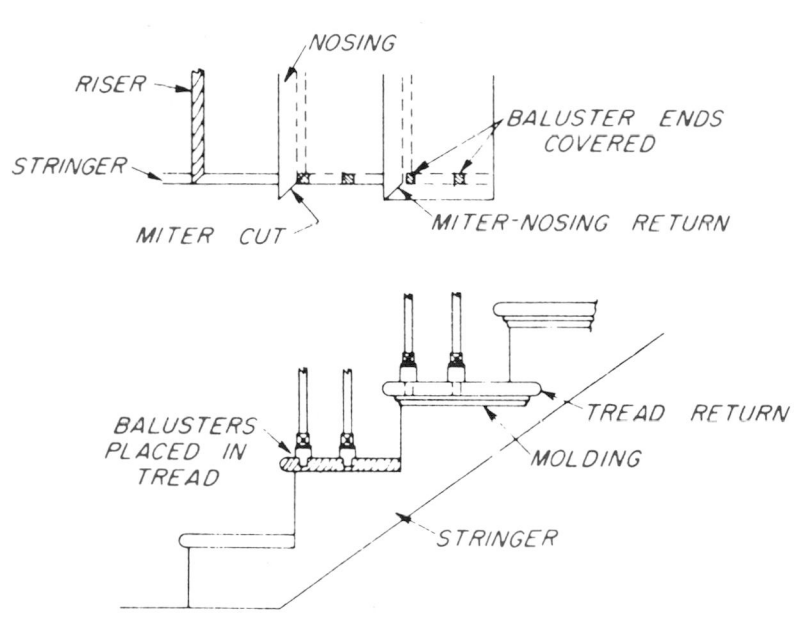

52-22. An open stringer with the risers mitered to the stringer. The balusters are set into the treads and trimmed with a nosing return and a molding.

underneath the tread cut of the stringer. This makes it necessary to notch the tread at the nosing to fit around the finish stringer. Fig. 52-24.

Laying Out a Cutout Stringer

Cutout stringers for main stairways are usually made from 2" × 12" stock. To lay out a cutout stringer, you must first determine how long a piece of stock you will need. Using the example from "Laying Out a Stairway," let's assume that the method of upper-end anchorage is the one shown in C, Fig. 52-18. In that case the total run of the stairway is 12' 1¼". The total rise in the example is 8' 11". On the framing square twelfth scale, measure the distance between a little over $12\frac{1}{12}$" on the blade and $8\frac{11}{12}$" on the tongue. You'll find that it comes to just about 15". Therefore you'll need a

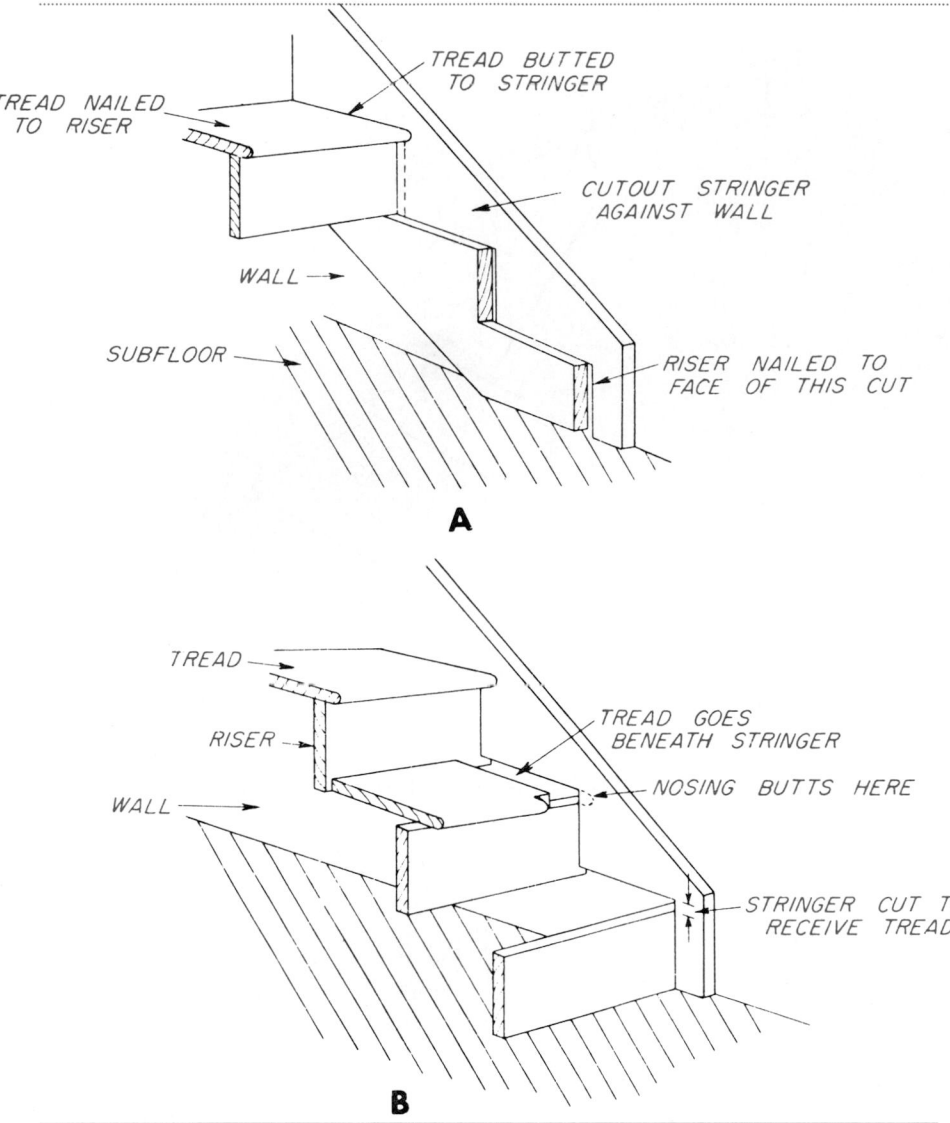

TREAD NAILED TO RISER

TREAD BUTTED TO STRINGER

CUTOUT STRINGER AGAINST WALL

WALL →

SUBFLOOR →

RISER NAILED TO FACE OF THIS CUT

A

TREAD →

RISER →

WALL →

TREAD GOES BENEATH STRINGER

NOSING BUTTS HERE

STRINGER CUT TO RECEIVE TREAD

B

52-24. *In this method the stringer is cut out in reverse of the carriage. In A, the riser fits between the stringer and the carriage. The treads butt against the stringer. In B, both the tread and the riser are fitted between the stringer and carriage, with the tread nosing notched and butted to the stringer.*

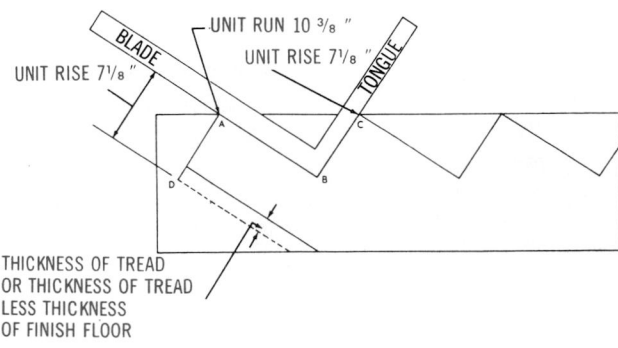

UNIT RISE 7⅛ "
BLADE
UNIT RUN 10 ⅜ "
UNIT RISE 7⅛ "
TONGUE

THICKNESS OF TREAD OR THICKNESS OF TREAD LESS THICKNESS OF FINISH FLOOR

52-25. *Laying out the lower end of a cutout stringer.*

piece of stock at least 15' long. It is better to allow about 4' more for waste and for the part that extends beyond the header at the upper end. Select or cut a piece about 19' long. Proceed to lay out the stringer from the lower end as follows:

Set the framing square to the unit run and unit rise as shown in Fig. 52-25. Draw the line AB along the blade and the line BC along the tongue. AB indicates the first tread, BC the second riser. Reverse the square and draw line AD from A, perpendicular to AB, and equal in length to the unit rise.

Line AD indicates the first riser. The first riser has to be shortened, a process which is called dropping the stringer. Fig. 52-26. As you can see, in the completed stairway the unit rise is measured from the top of one tread to the top of the next. Let's assume that the bottom of the stairway is to be anchored on a finished floor, such as a concrete basement floor. If AD were cut to the unit rise, when the first tread was put on, the height of the first step would be the unit rise plus the thickness of the tread. To make the height of the first step equal to the unit rise, you must shorten AD by the thickness of a tread.

If the bottom of the stringer is to be anchored on a subfloor to which finish flooring will be applied, shorten AD by the thickness of a tread less the thickness of the finish flooring. When you have shortened AD as required, proceed to step off the unit run and unit rise as many times as the stairway has treads—in this case, 14.

Finish the layout at the upper end as shown in Fig. 52-27. You are going to anchor the upper end by the method shown in C, Fig. 52-18, in which the stringer fits around the well header and extends beyond it to end level with the upper edges of the floor joists. Lay out the line AB, which indicates

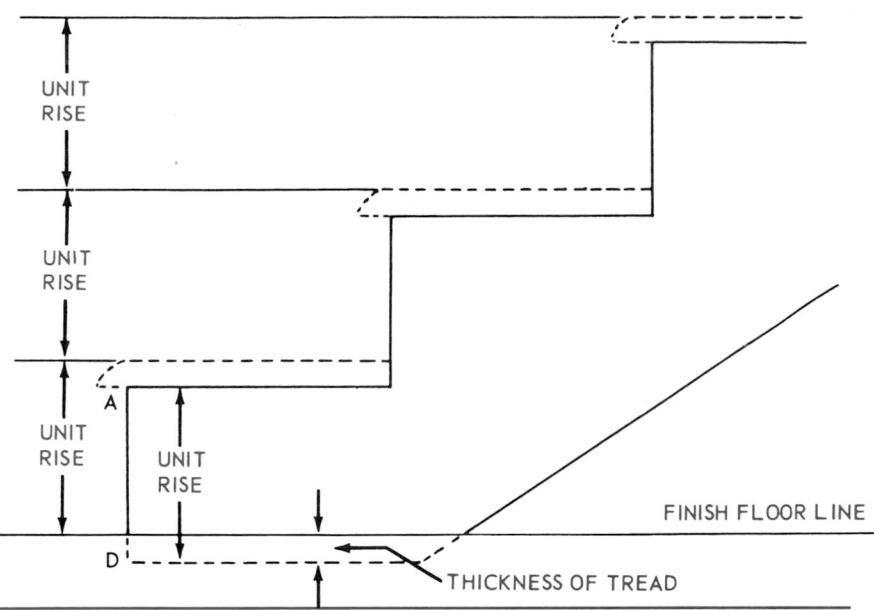

52-26. *Dropping the stringer to compensate for the thickness of the first tread keeps the unit rise uniform.*

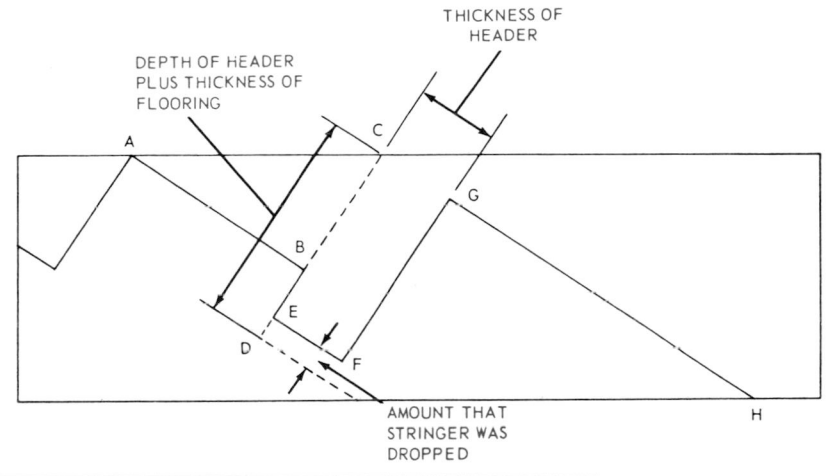

52-27. *Laying out the upper end of a cutout stringer.*

the last of the treads. Lay out the dotted line BC, which indicates the face of the well header. Extend BC down to D, so that BC plus BD will equal the depth of the header plus the thickness of the flooring.

To make the stringer fit close up under the lower edge of the header, you must shorten BD by the amount the stringer was dropped, as was shown in Fig. 52-26. Draw EF equal in length to the thickness of the header. From F draw FG equal in length to the depth of the header, and from G draw GH. When the stringer is set in place, the edge indicated by GH will lie close up under the subflooring, level with the upper edges of the joists.

Carefully cut out the first stringer, set it in position, and check it. Then use this as a pattern for cutting one or two more.

Installing Stringers

Methods used in framing stairways and securing stringers vary in different areas of the country. Regardless of method, the object of the stair builder should be the installation of a structurally strong, safe stairway. A few suggested ways of securing stringers are shown in Fig. 52-28. In A, the upper rough stringer is notched to fit the stairwell header. The stringers are hung by means of a metal supporting strap. B, Fig. 52-28, shows the stringer notched out for the stairwell header and supported by a ledger strip. This method will slightly reduce the headroom underneath.

The method shown in C, Fig. 52-28, requires a larger well "opening" and is not used too often, yet it offers the full bearing of the rough stringer against the stairwell header. The support is a ledger strip. In D, Fig. 52-28, a piece of plywood sheathing is used as a bearing surface and ledger. The stringers are secured by nailing from the back. This method would apply most often at a platform where the headers are usually of less depth than the floor joists. It also affords full headroom underneath.

In E, Fig. 52-28, the stair carriages are framed to a header or trimmer with metal brackets. Another method of installing stringers is to cut the top stair tread deeper to permit the stringer to pass under the header. Then attach the stringer to a special framing member between the floor joists as shown in F, Fig. 52-28. Note also in this illustration that the stringer has been cut off at the bottom to allow for the thickness of the first tread.

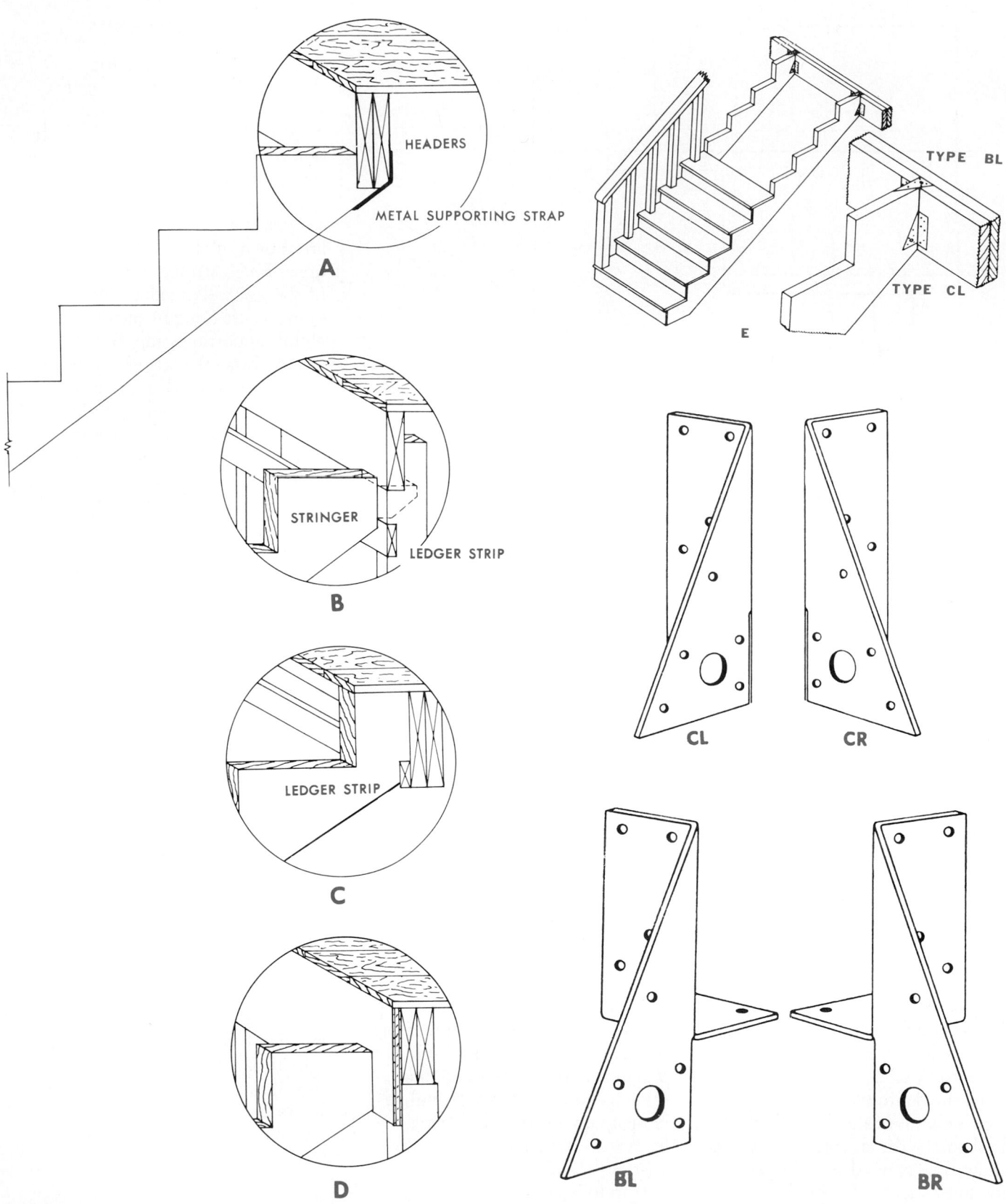

52-28. *Methods of securing stringers.*

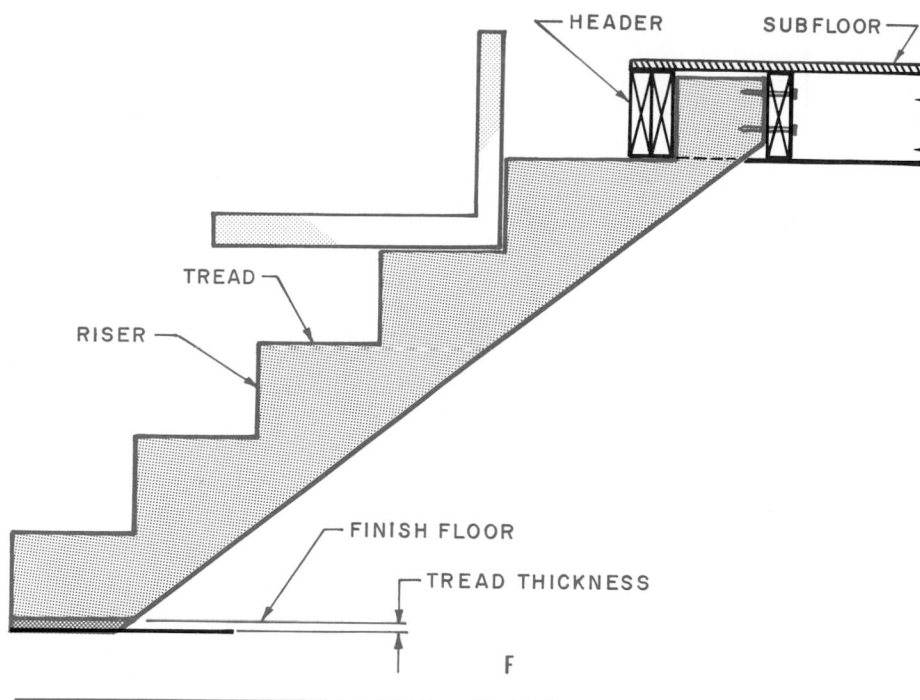

52-28. (cont.) Methods ot securing stringers.

Erecting the Stairway

The rough stringers are the first stairway members erected—except when a side of the stairway butts against a wall, in which case the wall (finish) stringer must be nailed on first. Temporarily nail the rough stringers in position. Check each stringer for plumb by holding the carpenter's level vertically against a riser cut. Then check the stringers for levelness with each other by setting the carpenter's level across the stringers on the tread cuts.

A stringer which lies against a trimmer joist should be spiked to the joist with at least three 16d nails. A stringer which is installed as shown at C in Fig. 52-28 and is not adjacent to a joist (a center stringer in a three-stringer stairway, for example) should be toenailed to the well header with 10d nails, three to each side of the stringer. The bottom of a stringer which is anchored on subflooring should be toenailed with 10d nails, four to each side if possible, driven into the subflooring and if possible into a joist below.

After the stringers are mounted to the wall and treads and risers cut to length, nail the bottom riser to each stringer with two 6d, 8d, or 10d nails, depending on the thickness of the stock.

The first tread, if 1 1/16" thick, is then nailed to each stringer with two 10d finish nails and to the riser below with at least two 10d finish nails. Proceed up the stair in this same manner. If 1 5/8" thick treads are used, a 12d finish nail may be required. Use three nails at each stringer, but eliminate nailing to the riser below. All finish nails should be set.

RAILING

All stairways should have a continuous handrail extending from one floor to the next. For closed stairways, the rail is attached to the wall with suitable metal brackets. The rail should be set 30" to 38" above the tread at the riser line and 30" to 38" above the floor on a landing. Handrails and balusters are used for open stairs and for open spaces around stairs. The handrails end against newel posts.

Stairs should be laid out so that stock parts may be used for newels, rails, balusters, and goosenecks. Fig. 52-8. These parts may be very plain or elaborate, but they should be in keeping with the style of the house. The balusters are doweled or dovetailed into the treads and in some cases are covered by a return nosing. Fig. 52-29. For the dovetail method, a strip called a nosing return is cut off the end of the tread, as shown in the upper (plan) view of Fig. 52-29. Dovetails are shaped on the lower ends of the balusters, and dovetail recesses of corresponding size are cut in the end section of the tread. The dovetails on the balusters are glued into the recesses in the tread, and the nosing return is then nailed back in place.

Newel posts should be firmly anchored. Where half-newels are attached to a wall, blocking should be provided at the time the wall is framed.

BASEMENT STAIRS

Basement stairs may be built either with or without riser boards. Cutout stringers are probably the most widely used supports for the treads, but in some cases the stringer is not cut out and the tread

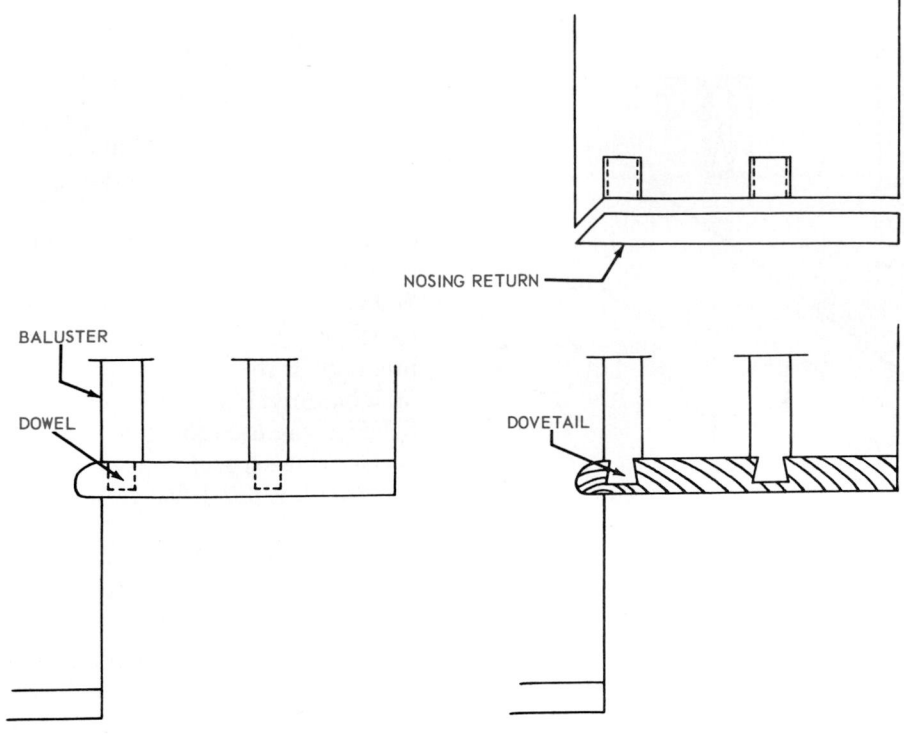

BALUSTER
DOWEL
NOSING RETURN
DOVETAIL

52-29. *Balusters are attached to the treads with either dowels or dovetails.*

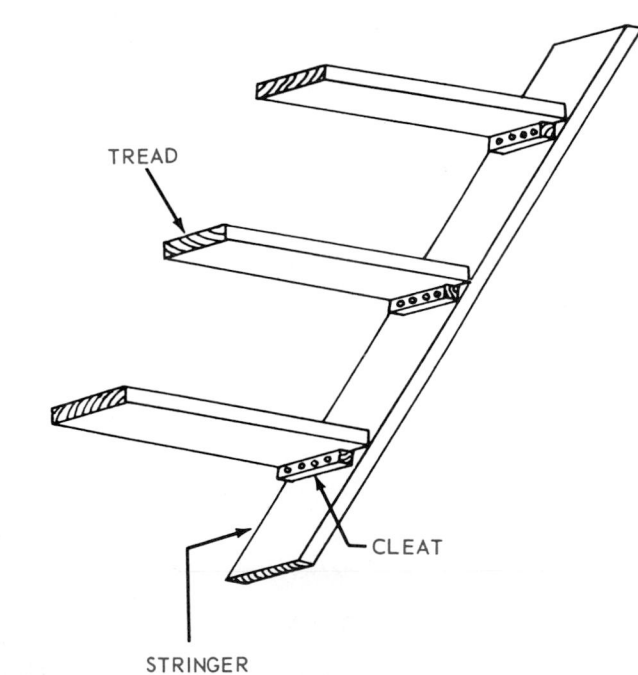

TREAD
CLEAT
STRINGER

52-30. *Cleat stairs are often installed in basements.*

is fastened to the stringers by cleats. Fig. 52-30. The lower end of a basement stairway is usually anchored against a kicker plate which has been bolted to the concrete. Fig. 52-31.

Laying Out and Framing a Cleat Stairway

A cleat stairway is inexpensive to build, it does not require risers, and the treads are usually made of softwood. First determine the total rise and run. Divide the rise by 7. If this does not result in even spacing, adjust the divisor until equal spacings are obtained. Try to keep this spacing between 6½" and 7½".

For the first tread position use the determined riser height *minus the thickness of the tread* and measure up the stringer at 90° from the bottom cut to establish point A. Fig. 52-32. Set the T bevel to the angle formed by the front edge of the stringer and the bottom cut as shown at B in Fig. 52-32. Slide the T bevel up the stringer until the tongue of the T bevel is at point A. Fig. 52-32. Mark a line across the stringer at this point.

Measure up from line A using the riser height and establish point C. Position the T bevel on the new point and mark another line across the stringer. Continue this operation until all tread positions are located. These lines locate the bottom of the tread and the top edge of the cleat.

Cut the cleats from 1" × 2" stock and nail the cleats in position below the line. Place the stringers in the stairwell and fasten them in place. Cut the treads to length. Starting with the bottom tread, work up, placing each tread in position and nailing securely.

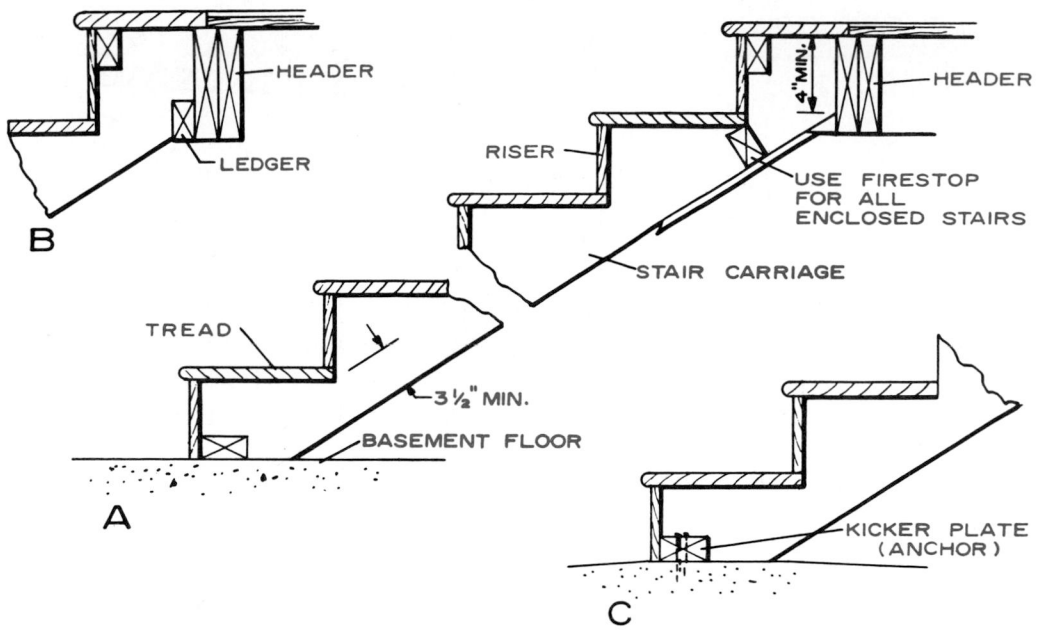

52-31. Basement stairs: A. Carriage details. B. Ledger for carriage. C. Kicker plate. The lower end of the stringer should be anchored against a kicker plate which has been bolted to the concrete floor.

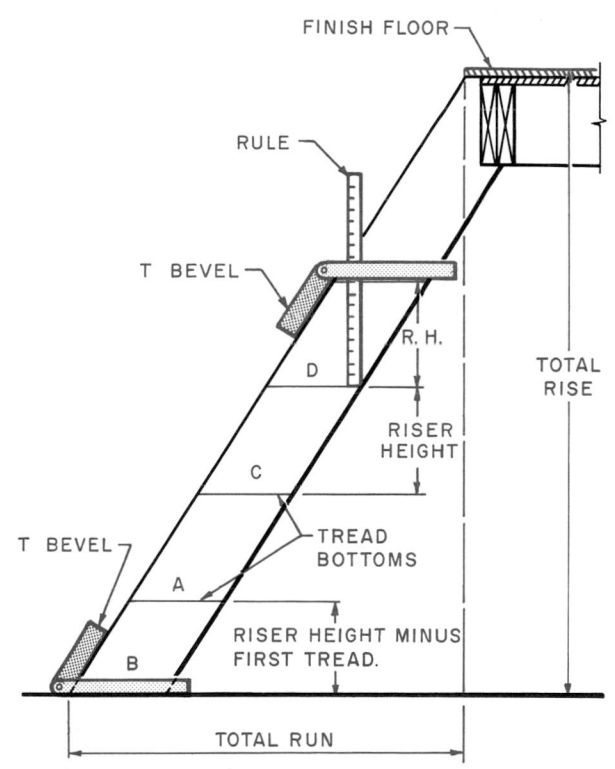

52-32. Laying out a cleat stairway. Note that the distance from A to C is the same as the distance from C to D and is equal to the riser height. The distance between the floor and line A, however, is less than the riser height to allow for the thickness of the first tread.

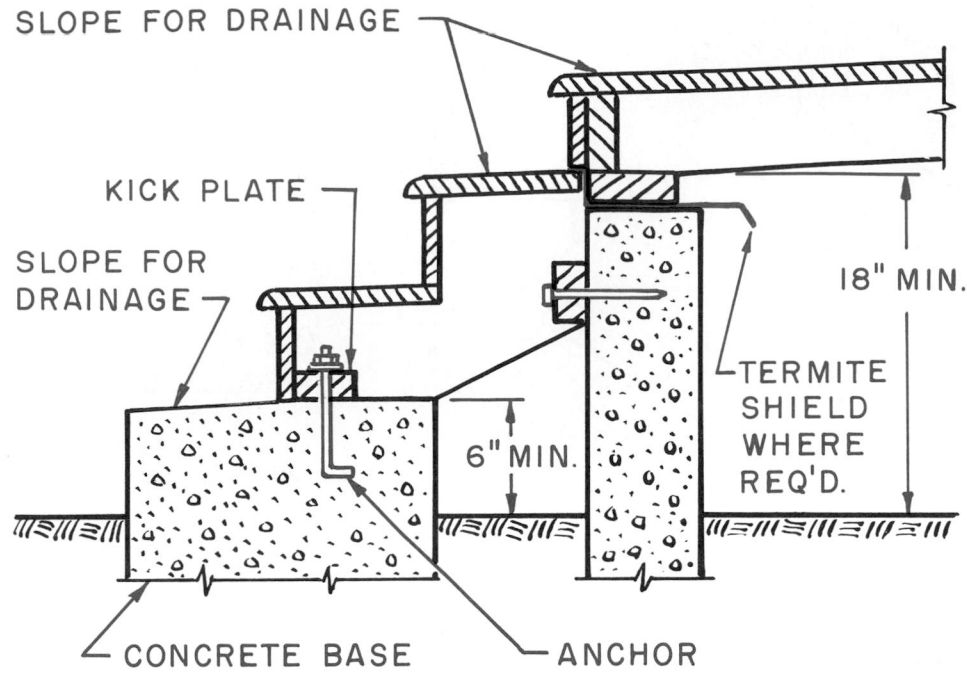

SLOPE FOR DRAINAGE

KICK PLATE

SLOPE FOR DRAINAGE

18" MIN.

TERMITE SHIELD WHERE REQ'D.

6" MIN.

CONCRETE BASE

ANCHOR

52-33. *Exterior steps of wood should have a bottom step of concrete. The stringer should be secured to the bottom step against a kick plate which has been bolted to the concrete.*

EXTERIOR STAIRS

Proportioning of risers and treads in laying out porch steps or approaches to terraces should be as carefully considered as the design of interior stairways. Similar riser-to-tread ratios can be used. However, the riser used in principal exterior steps should be between 6" and 7". The need for a good support or foundation for outside steps is often overlooked. If wood steps are used, the bottom step should be concrete. Fig. 52-33. If the steps are located over backfill or disturbed ground, the foundation should be carried down to undisturbed ground.

METAL SPIRAL STAIRWAYS

The standardized spiral stairway system provides unlimited versatility in design. These stairs are adaptable for use in all types of buildings, from a modest cottage to the most elegant residence, and are suitable for interior or exterior installation. Fig. 52-34.

Standardized construction provides a light, simple, strong, and durable stairway, meeting code requirements for design and carrying capacities. The basic stair structure is steel. To this can be added various types of treads, handrails, and railings.

The stairways are simple to install. No welding is necessary. Handrails are attached to balusters with adjustable brackets. The stairs are shipped knocked down for easy handling at the job site. All of the parts are matched and marked, and

52-34. *Note the use of wood on the balusters and the wood treads on this spiral stairway.*

52-35. *Disappearing stairs. When the stairs are in the stored position, the plywood door is barely noticeable.*

the manufacturer furnishes complete shop drawings and installation instructions.

DISAPPEARING STAIRS

When attics are used primarily for storage and space for a fixed stairway is not available, hinged or disappearing stairs are often used. Disappearing stairways may be purchased ready to install. They operate through an opening in the ceiling and swing up into the attic space, out of the way, when not in use. Fig. 52-35. Where such stairs are installed, the attic floor should be designed for regular floor loading.

ESTIMATING

Materials

To estimate the materials for a stairway, either precut or cut on the job, a complete material bill must first be made. The cost of the items can then be totaled to determine the material cost for the stairway.

Labor

Labor costs can be only roughly estimated because of the many variables which will affect the construction time. For example, for an open stairway less than 12' long and 42" wide, construction time is estimated at 8¾ hours. This includes roughcutting the stringers and framing and installing the stringers, treads, and risers. Add about 3 more hours if there is a turn in the stairway involving a platform or landing. If a handrail is to be installed, add 1 more hour; for an open stairway, add 2½ hours for the installation of the newel posts, rails, and balusters.

For assembling a precut stairway no longer than 12' and less than 42" wide, 6 hours are required. If this stairway has a turn including a platform, add about 3 more hours. A handrail takes 1 hour, and for an open stairway with newel posts, rails, and balusters, add 2½ more hours. A folding stairway which has been prefabricated will take approximately 2 hours to install.

It must be understood that these are very rough approximations. They depend on the species of wood, the style of the stairway, and the worker's experience.

1. What are the two general types of stairs?

2. What are the two main parts of a stairway?

3. What is the difference between a landing and a platform?

4. When designing a stairway, what are five important considerations?

5. The total rise of a stairway is the vertical distance between what two points?

6. When laying out a stringer for a basement stairway, what is subtracted from the bottom of the stringer?

7. After the stair stringers are installed and the other parts are cut to length, what is the next piece to be installed?

ACTIVITIES

1. Language Arts. In a paragraph, describe the construction of the staircase shown in Fig. 52-8 using the following terms: winders, nosing, risers, railing, open and closed stringers.

2. Social Studies. Evaluate the riser-tread relationship of a staircase in your school. Decide whether the staircase is too steep, just right, or too flat. Draw the staircase if you wish.

3. Math. A set of straight stairs is needed where the total rise is 7' 10". The risers are to be a minimum of 7". Use the guidelines in this unit to:

a. determine the number of risers.

b. determine the size of each riser.

c. determine the total run if the top of the stairs is as in Fig. 52-18.

Compare your answers with those of a friend. Discuss the differences.

4. Language Arts. When we clear a tract of land for a construction project, we alter a part of our natural environment. In many cases the construction project destroys the natural habitat of a variety of plants and animals. When the habitat is not destroyed, it is often greatly altered. Partly as a result of the widespread building to accomodate human growth, many plants and animals have become extinct. Therefore, the possible effects of a proposed construction project should be weighed carefully before the decision is made to begin building. By making responsible decisions, we can help preserve the environment. We can prepare sites and build structures that will do as little harm as possible to the environment and still provide for our needs. Identify a local construction project. Prepare a brief report on how the environment was affected by the construction project. Point out ways in which damage to the environment might have been lessened at this project.

THE SCHOOL-TO-WORK CONNECTION

Building codes are strict when it comes to stair construction. This is partly because small variations in details such as step height can make a big difference in the safety of the stair.

1. You have been asked to submit a bid for turning the attic of a one-story home into a home office. The existing attic stair is a pull-down unit located in a hallway ceiling. The building codes will not allow this to serve as a stair to living space. You can't find any other location that would be suitable for a stairway. The only option seems to be an exterior stair. Contact your local building department. Find out what local codes govern the construction of this stair. Report to your class on whether or not this stair can be built.

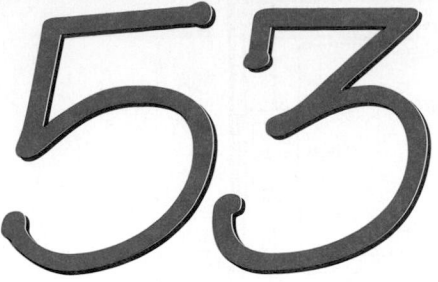

Cabinets and Built-Ins

Kitchen cabinets, wardrobes, linen closets, china cases, and similar pieces of millwork are installed at the same time as the interior trim. This work is usually done after the finish floor is in place. The kitchen normally contains more millwork than all other rooms combined, in the form of wall and base cabinets, broom closets, and other storage centers.

Kitchen design concepts have changed radically in recent years. Today's kitchen is often combined with the family room to create a center for casual everyday living or informal entertaining. Most important, today's kitchens are more beautiful, functional, efficient, and convenient.

Cabinet construction has also become more varied. Two basic types of cabinet construction are now available: face-frame cabinetry and frameless cabinetry. Fig. 53-1.

53-1a. *A kitchen with traditional-style face frame cabinetry.*

53-1b. *This kitchen features European-style (frameless) cabinetry. This cabinet construction method does not require the use of a face frame.*

KITCHEN FLOOR PLANS

There are five basic layouts commonly used in kitchen design:

- ➤ U-shape.
- ➤ L-shape.
- ➤ Parallel wall, or Pullman.
- ➤ Sidewall.
- ➤ Island.

The U-shape kitchen, with the sink at the bottom of the U and the range and refrigerator on opposite sides, is very efficient. Fig. 53-2a. The L-shape, also very popular, has the sink and range on one leg and the refrigerator on the other. Sometimes the dining space is located in the opposite corner. Fig. 53-2b. The parallel wall, or Pullman, kitchen plan is often used where there is limited space. It can be quite efficient with proper arrangement of sink, range, and

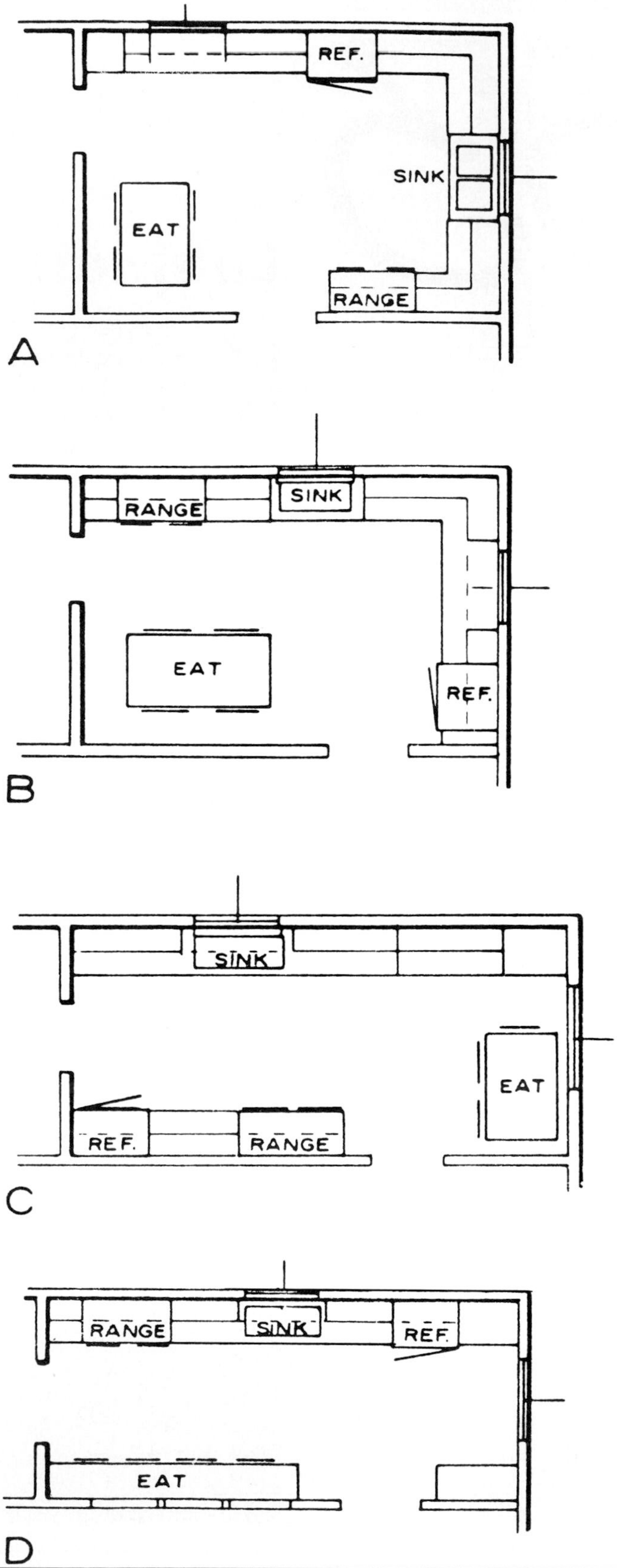

A

B

C

D

53-2. *Five of the most popular kitchen layouts: A. U-shape. B. L-shape. C. Parallel wall. D. Side-wall. E. Island.*

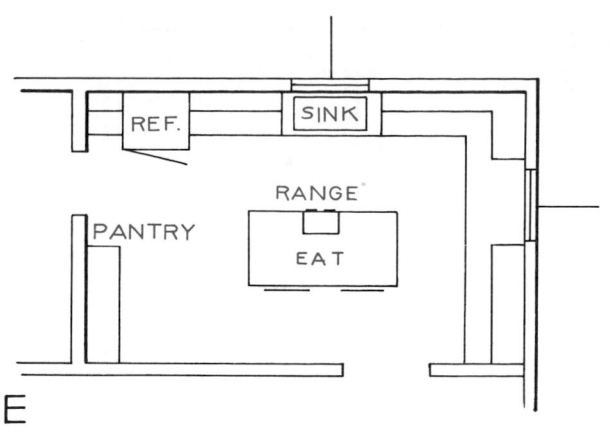

53-2. *(cont.) Five of the most popular kitchen layouts: A. U-shape. B. L-shape. C. Parallel wall. D. Side-wall. E. Island.*

refrigerator. Fig. 53-2c. The sidewall kitchen is usually preferred for small apartments. The cabinets, sink, range, and refrigerator are all located along one wall. With this design, counter space is somewhat limited when kitchens are small. Fig. 53-2d. The island kitchen features a cabinet "island" that is separate from the main cabinet runs in the rest of the kitchen. A range is usually placed in the island, along with storage for pans. Fig. 53-2e. This layout sometimes makes it difficult to provide a ventilating fan for the range. To solve this problem, some ranges have built-in downdraft fans that exhaust air outdoors through ducts in the floor.

KITCHEN WORK CENTERS

When planning a kitchen layout, three work centers must be kept in mind: the food preparation center, the cooking center, and the cleanup center. Fig. 53-3. All equipment, storage space, and surface work areas for each activity should be located in their respective work centers. The food

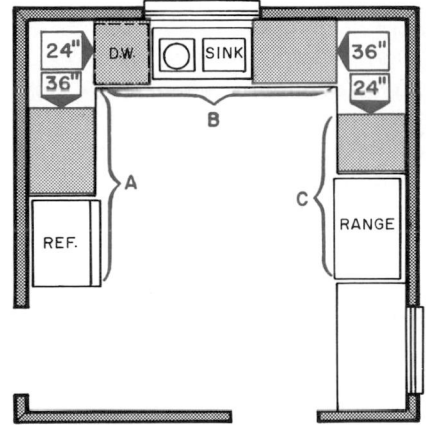

53-3. *The three basic work centers: A. Food preparation. B. Cleanup. C. Cooking and serving. The minimum counter space for each area is shown by the arrows.*

preparation center should be planned around the refrigerator and food storage area. Fig. 53-4. Ideally, the cleanup center (sink and dishwasher) should be located between the food preparation center and the cooking center. Figs. 53-5 and 53-6. Whenever possible, counter space should be continuous between work centers.

Arrange the work centers in a logical sequence, with the flow of materials in the same direction as

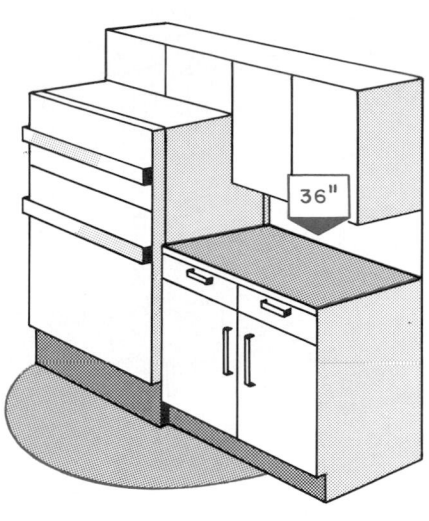

53-4. *The food preparation center is adjacent to the refrigerator and requires a minimum of 36" of counter space.*

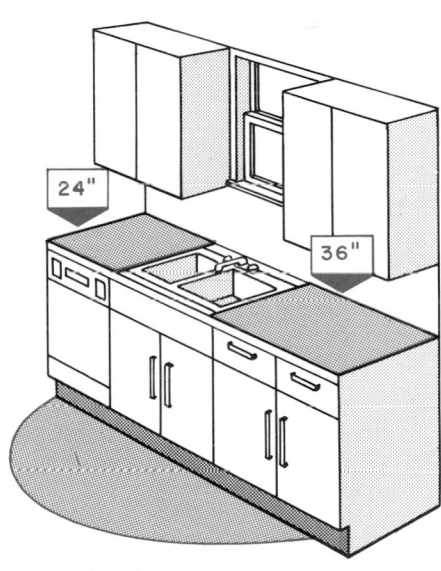

53-5. *The clean-up center includes the dishwasher and the sink and should provide at least 60" of counter space. If a dishwasher is not provided, the counter space to the left of the sink should be increased to 30", making a total counter top requirement of 66".*

53-6. The cooking and serving center requires a minimum of 24" of counter space.

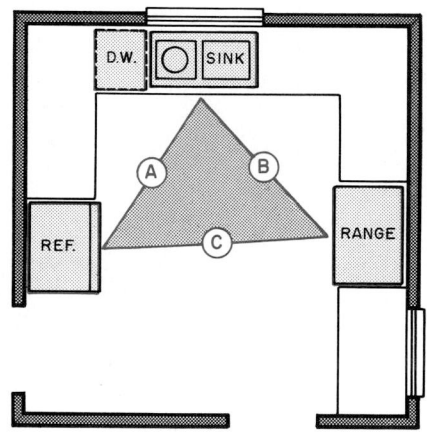

53-7. The work triangle has a major appliance for one of the work centers at each point. The distance at A should be from 4' to 7'; at B, 4' to 6'; at C, 4' to 9'. The minimum total is 12' and the maximum is 22'. Ideally, the perimeter of the triangle should be 15' to 20'.

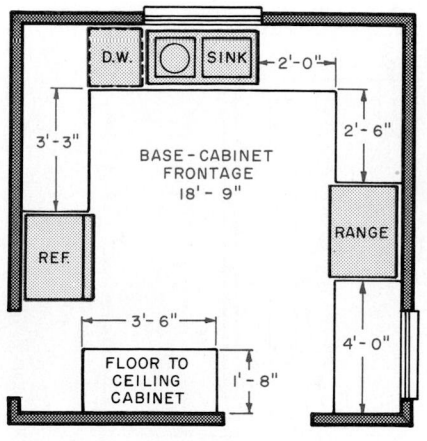

53-8. To determine the number of base cabinets required, measure the base-cabinet frontage. For a 1,000 sq. ft. home, there should be a minimum of 6', although 10' or more is preferred. For a home of 1,000 to 1,400 sq. ft., 6' of base cabinet is minimum and 12' or more is preferred. For homes over 1,400 sq. ft., the minimum is 10', and 14' or more is preferred.

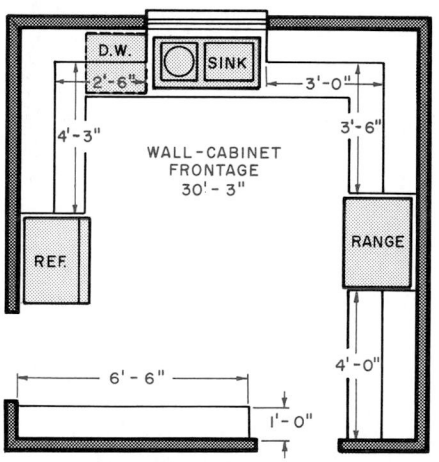

53-9. The number of wall cabinets required is determined by measuring the wall-cabinet frontage. For a home with 1,000 sq. ft., a minimum of 6' of wall cabinet frontage is required; 10' or more is preferred. For a home of 1,000 to 1,400 sq. ft., the minimum is 8' and 12' or more is preferred. For a home over 1,400 sq. ft., 10' is the minimum and 14' or more is preferred.

when preparing a typical meal. Most people work from right to left. Therefore, whenever possible, the work centers and equipment are arranged accordingly. A work triangle is developed among the work centers. Fig. 53-7. The three sides of the triangle should add up to at least 12'. The ideal total is 15' to 20'.

Ample storage in a kitchen is a necessity. A good rule of thumb is to allow 6 sq. ft. of storage cabinet shelf space for every member of the family, then add 12 sq ft. of storage for staple items used in the kitchen. Of course, this rule can be used only when the size of the family is known. Normally the base and wall cabinet needs are determined by the size of the home. Figs. 53-8 and 53-9.

KITCHEN CABINET DIMENSIONS

Base and wall units should be designed and installed to a standard height and depth. There are also standard clearances for wall cabinets over appliances and work centers. Fig. 53-10. While the limits for counter height range from 30" to 38", the standard height is 36". Wall cabinets vary in height. Depending on the type of installation at the counter, they may be anywhere from 12" to 33" high. The usual height is 30". The 12" wall cabinets are usually placed over refrigerators. When a range or sink is located under them, wall cabinets should not be more than 21" high. The tops of wall cabinets should all be at the same height. Wall cabinets may be hung free or under a 12" soffit (drop ceiling) or storage cabinet. Figs. 53-11 and 53-12. The important thing is to place the cabinets, counters, and shelves at heights designed for working efficiency, convenience, and comfort. Fig. 53-13.

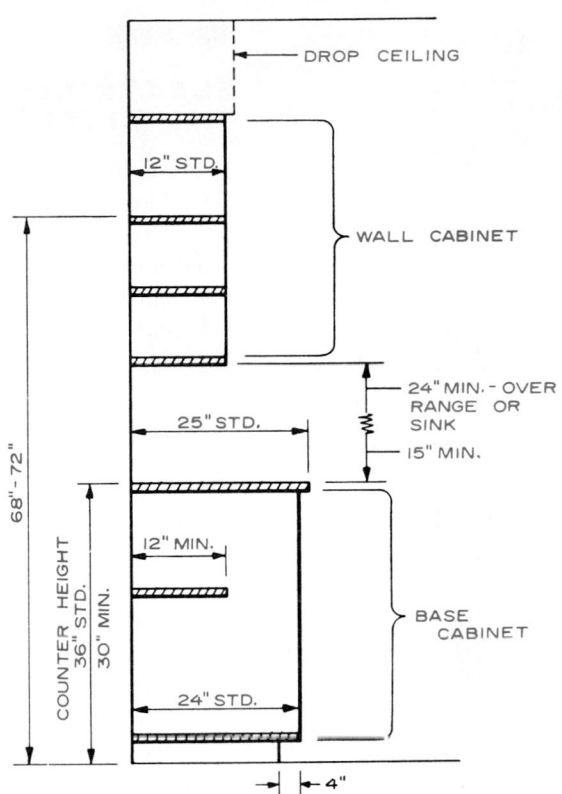

53-10a. *Minimum and standard dimensions for kitchen cabinets.*

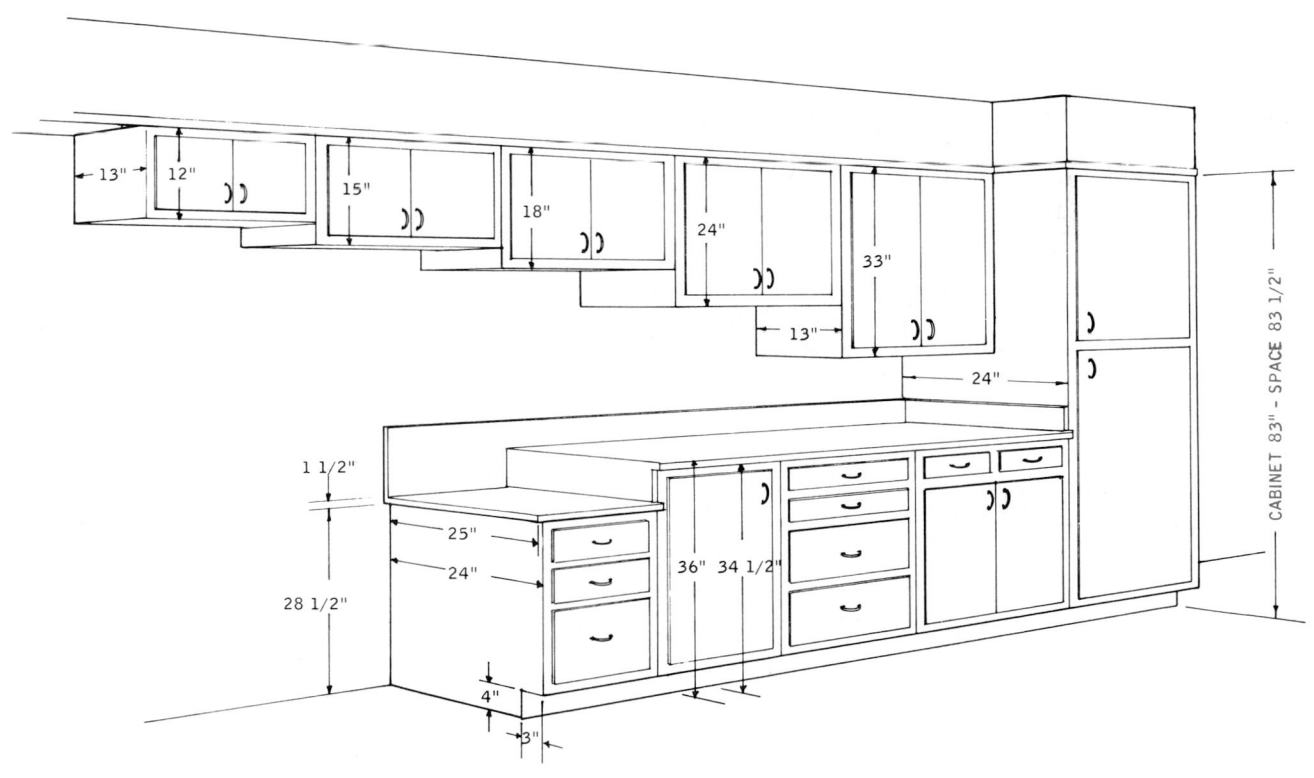

53-10b. *Typical kitchen cabinet dimensions.*

53-11. *These wall cabinets are hung free with the tops aligned.*

53-12. *These wall cabinets are installed under a soffit (drop ceiling).*

ELECTRICITY IN THE KITCHEN

Good lighting is important. A light source for each work center should be provided, as well as general overall lighting operated by a conveniently located switch. Adequate wiring must also be provided, with separate circuits for the electric range, water heater, dishwasher, and any other appliances which require heavy-duty circuits. Each work center should have at least one double convenience outlet. These should not all be on one circuit, and they must conform to local codes. Some building codes require that the outlets in kitchens and bathrooms be protected by a ground-fault circuit interrupter (GFCI). This device is a fast-acting circuit breaker that cuts power to an outlet when it detects conditions that could lead to an electrical shock. Proper ventilation should also be provided in the form of an exhaust fan and hood to control cooking odors and grease. Fig. 53-14. The electrical work is usually handled by an electrical contractor. The electrical contractor's work is coordinated with the builder's.

KITCHEN CABINET CONSTRUCTION

There are four basic ways in which kitchen cabinets are obtained. A cabinetmaker may build the cabinets on the job site, piece by piece, from the plans supplied by the architect. The second method is to purchase knocked-down kitchen cabinets which have been produced in a mill. The cabinetmaker assembles the parts on the job site and installs the cabinets as a unit. The third method is to purchase prebuilt

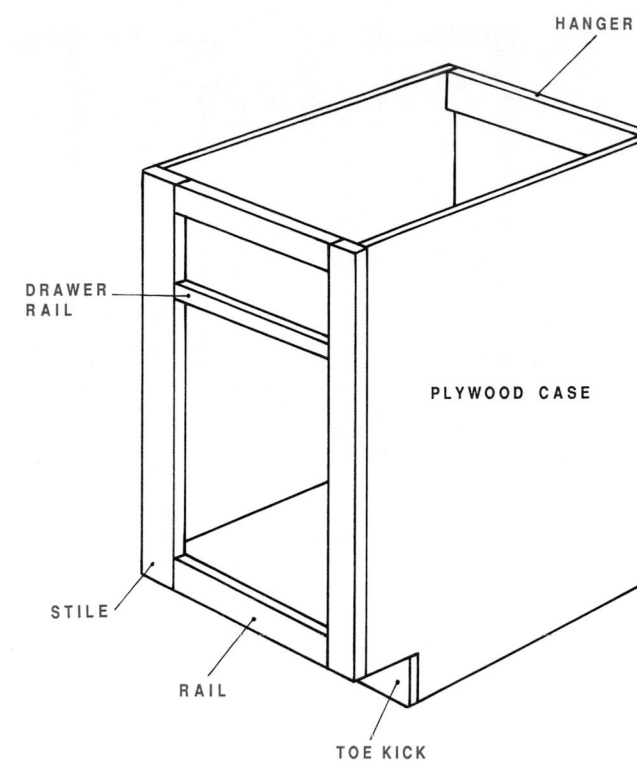

53-15b. *The base unit of a typical face frame cabinet.*

HANGER

DRAWER RAIL

PLYWOOD CASE

STILE

RAIL

TOE KICK

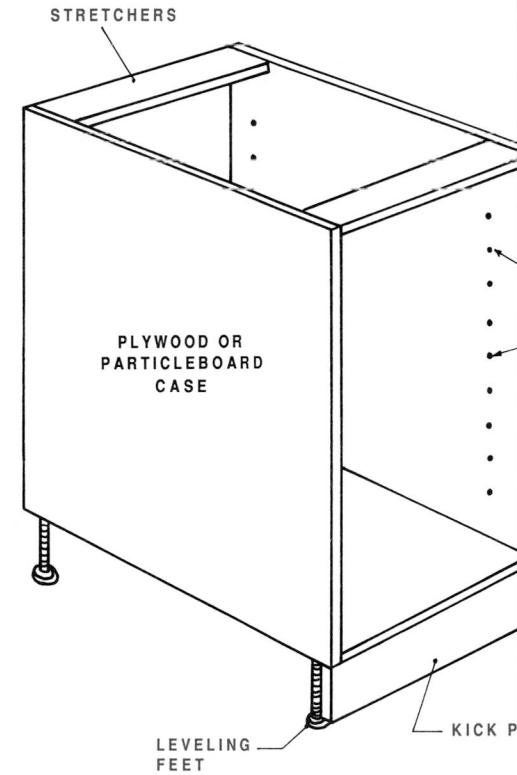

53-15c. *The base unit of a frameless cabinet.*

STRETCHERS

PLYWOOD OR PARTICLEBOARD CASE

LEVELING FEET

KICK P

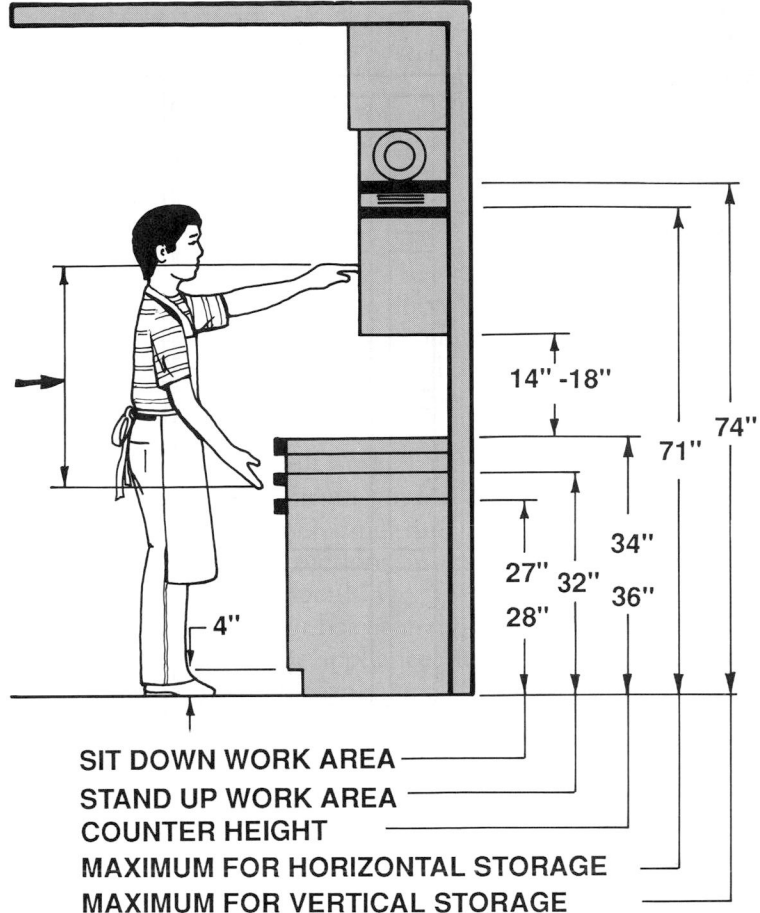

14" -18"

74"

71"

34"

27" 32" 36"

28"

4"

SIT DOWN WORK AREA
STAND UP WORK AREA
COUNTER HEIGHT
MAXIMUM FOR HORIZONTAL STORAGE
MAXIMUM FOR VERTICAL STORAGE

53-13. *Cabinets should be designed so that the height of the counters and shelves is convenient and comfortable. For example, counter tops should be 34" to 36" high. The most comfortable reach is from 30" to 60" above the floor, as shown by the arrow.*

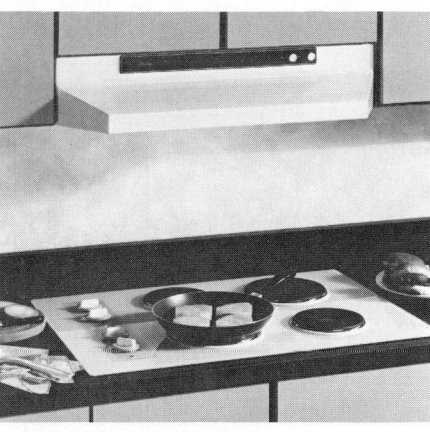

53-14a. *This cooking surface has an exhaust hood and fan to help eliminate cooking odors.*

kitchen cabinets that have been mass-produced in shops or factories. The fourth method is for a cabinetmaker to build custom cabinets in a shop. He or she then brings them to the house and installs them. More information about how cabinets are built and construction details are available in *Cabinetmaking and Millwork* by John L. Feirer. Construction details for cabinet construction are shown in Fig. 53-15.

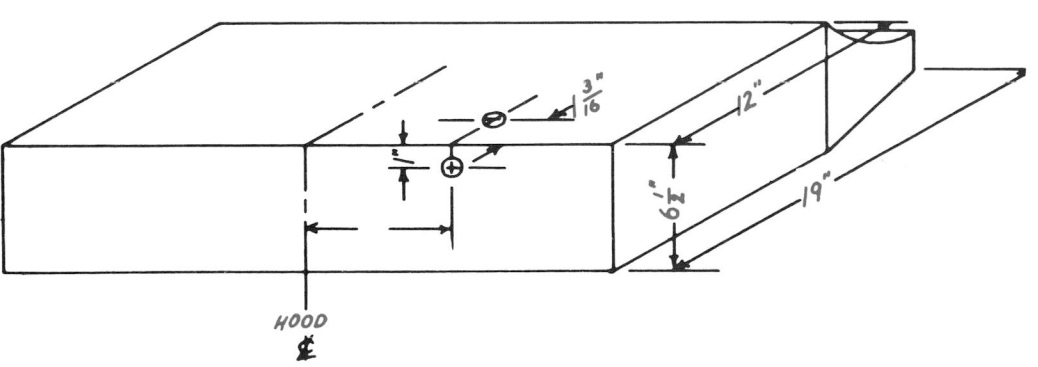

3"/16

12"

6 1/2"

19"

HOOD

53-14b. *When installing a range hood, the specifications for installation are available from the manufacturer. The drawing here was taken from a typical manufacturer's catalog.*

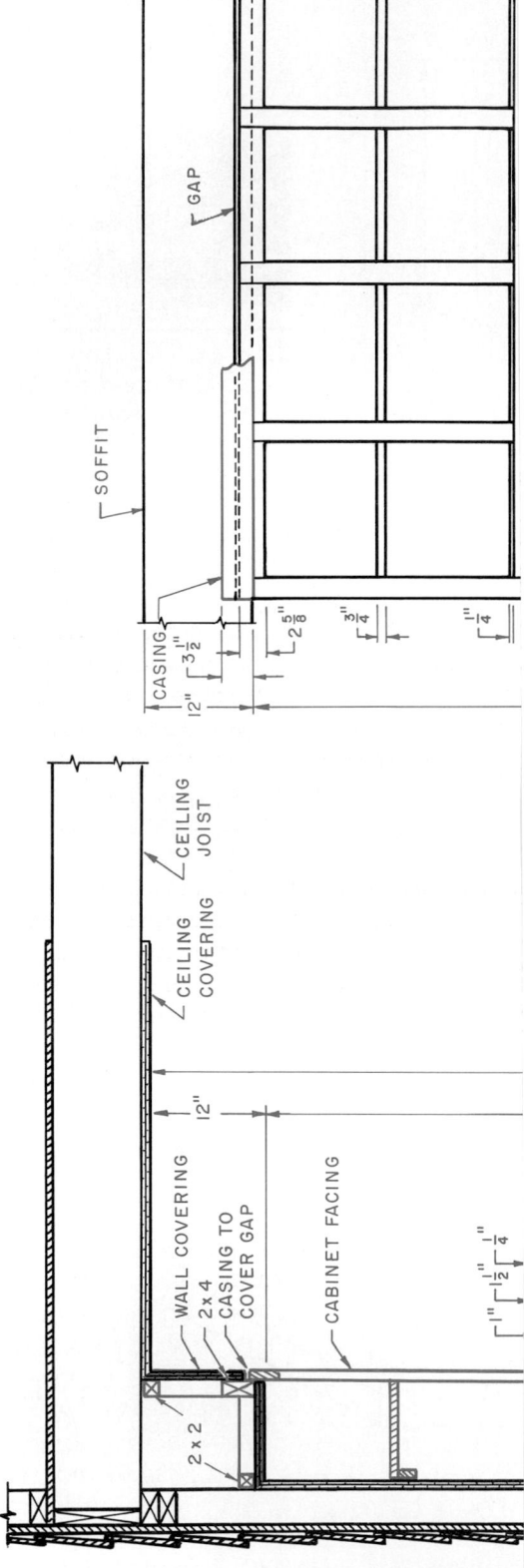

CEILING JOIST

CEILING COVERING

WALL COVERING

2 x 4 CASING TO COVER GAP

CABINET FACING

2 x 2

12"

$1\frac{1}{4}"$

$1\frac{1}{2}"$

$1\frac{1}{4}"$

SOFFIT

GAP

CASING

12"

$3\frac{1}{2}"$

$2\frac{5}{8}"$

$3\frac{3}{4}"$

$1\frac{1}{4}"$

53-15a. Construction details for job site kitchen cabinet

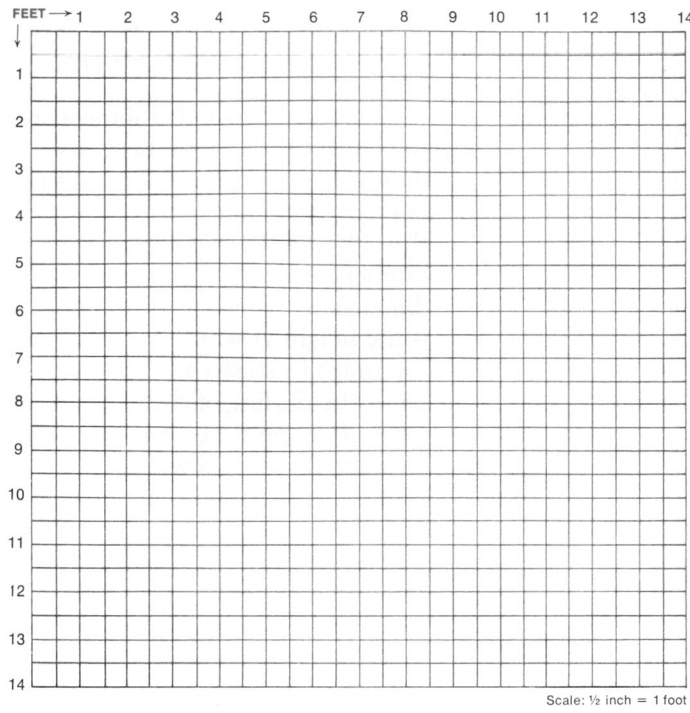

FEET → 1 2 3 4 5 6 7 8 9 10 11 12 13 14

Scale: ½ inch = 1 foot

53-16. *Graph paper, similar to that shown here, is usually provided in the catalog of factory-built cabinets as an aid in planning.*

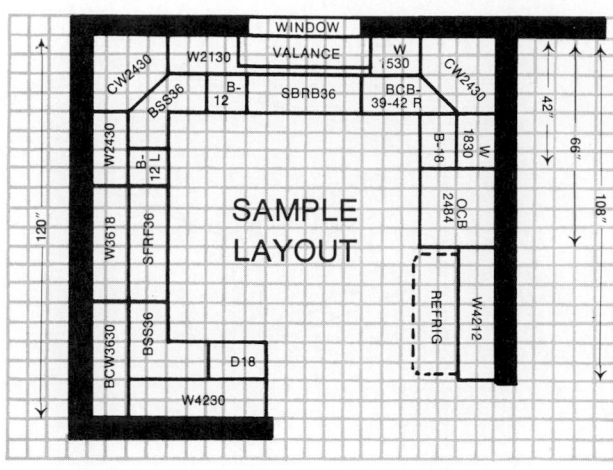

WINDOW
VALANCE
W 530
CW2430
W2130
CW2430
BSS36
B-12
SBRB36
BCB-39-42 R
W2430
B-12 L
B-18
W 1830
W3618
SFRF36
SAMPLE LAYOUT
OCB 2484
BCW3630
BSS36
REFRIG
W4212
D-18
W4230
120"
42"
66"
108"

53-18. *The cabinets for this kitchen layout were taken from the manufacturer's catalog shown in Fig. 53-19.*

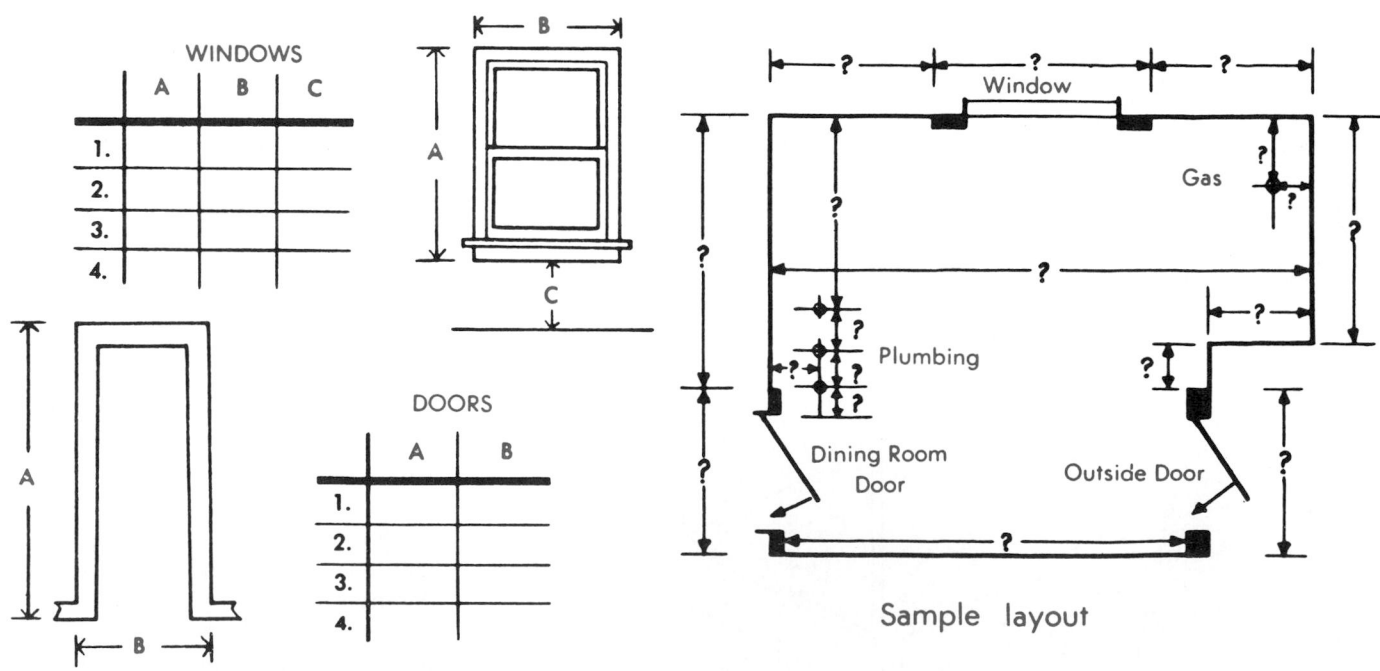

WINDOWS

	A	B	C
1.			
2.			
3.			
4.			

DOORS

	A	B
1.		
2.		
3.		
4.		

Window

Gas

Plumbing

Dining Room Door

Outside Door

Sample layout

53-17. *When drawing a room to scale, be sure to include all the necessary information.*

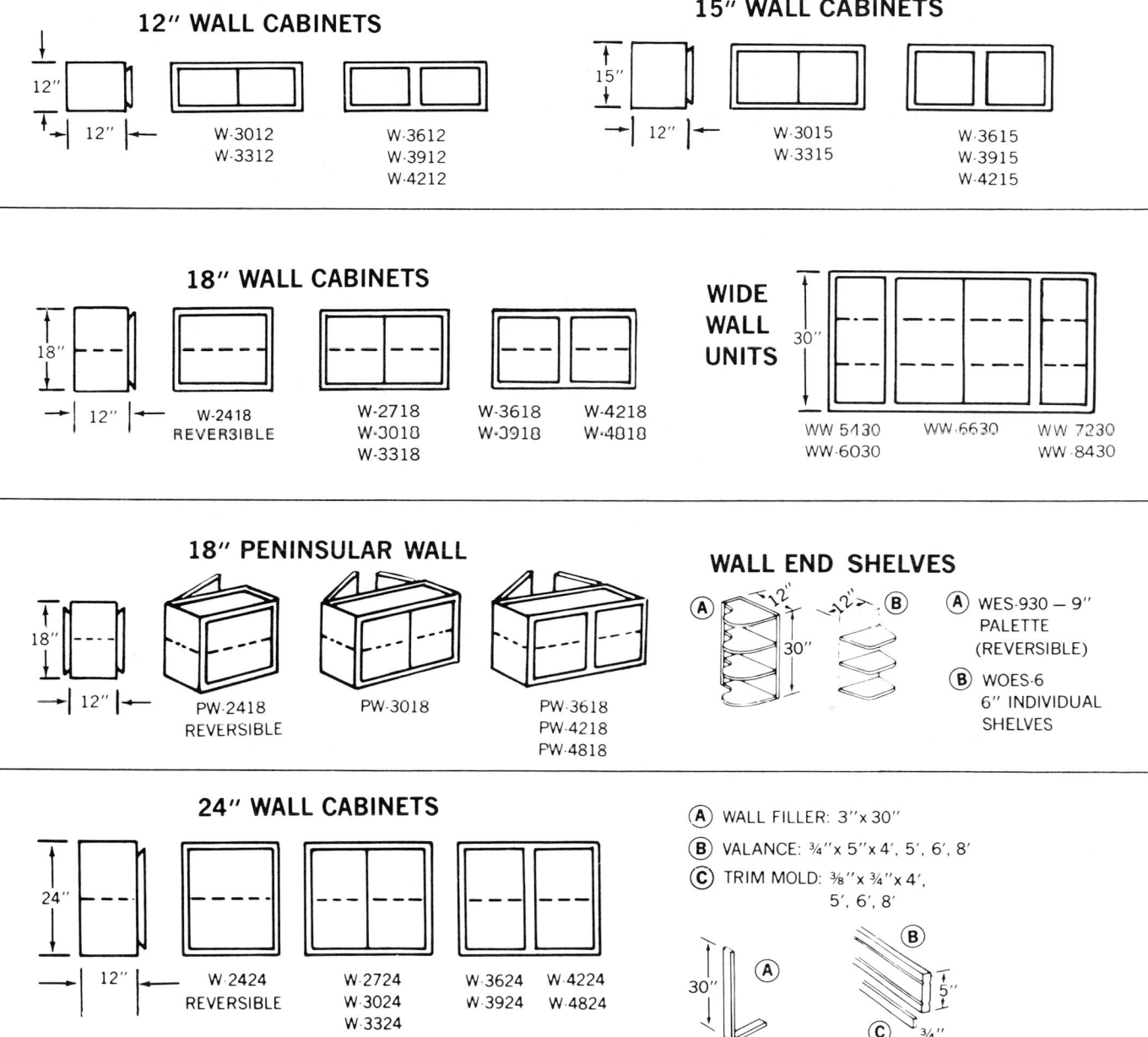

12" WALL CABINETS

12"

12"

W-3012
W-3312

W-3612
W-3912
W-4212

15" WALL CABINETS

15"

12"

W-3015
W-3315

W-3615
W-3915
W-4215

18" WALL CABINETS

18"

12"

W-2418
REVERSIBLE

W-2718
W-3018
W-3318

W-3618
W-3918

W-4218
W-4818

WIDE WALL UNITS

30"

WW-5430
WW-6030

WW-6630

WW-7230
WW-8430

18" PENINSULAR WALL

18"

12"

PW-2418
REVERSIBLE

PW-3018

PW-3618
PW-4218
PW-4818

WALL END SHELVES

Ⓐ 12" 12" Ⓑ

30"

Ⓐ WES-930 – 9"
PALETTE
(REVERSIBLE)

Ⓑ WOES-6
6" INDIVIDUAL
SHELVES

24" WALL CABINETS

24"

12"

W-2424
REVERSIBLE

W-2724
W-3024
W-3324

W-3624
W-3924

W-4224
W-4824

Ⓐ WALL FILLER: 3" x 30"

Ⓑ VALANCE: ¾" x 5" x 4', 5', 6', 8'

Ⓒ TRIM MOLD: ⅜" x ¾" x 4',
5', 6', 8'

30" Ⓐ

Ⓑ

5"

Ⓒ ¾"

53-19. *A manufacturer's catalog of kitchen cabinets showing stock numbers and cabinet dimensions available.*

30" BLIND CORNER WALL

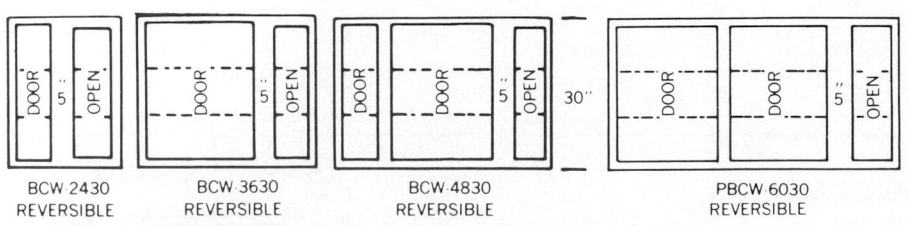

BCW-2430
REVERSIBLE

BCW-3630
REVERSIBLE

BCW-4830
REVERSIBLE

PBCW-6030
REVERSIBLE

FOR BCW—3" FILLER MUST BE USED FOR CLEARANCE

30" PENINSULAR BLIND CORNER WALL

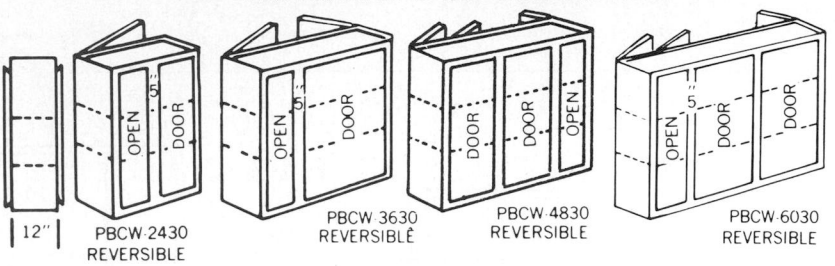

12"

PBCW-2430
REVERSIBLE

PBCW-3630
REVERSIBLE

PBCW-4830
REVERSIBLE

PBCW-6030
REVERSIBLE

FOR PBCW—3" FILLER MUST BE USED FOR CLEARANCE

30" WALL CABINETS

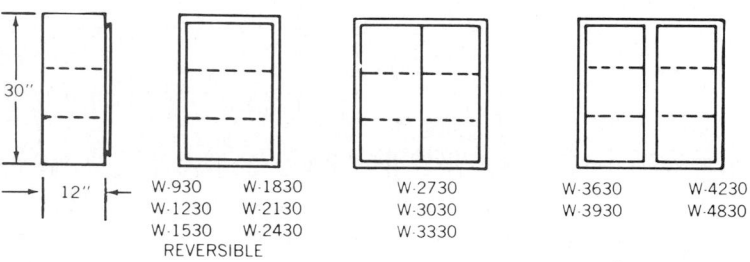

W-930	W-1830	W-2730	W-3630	W-4230
W-1230	W-2130	W-3030	W-3930	W-4830
W-1530	W-2430	W-3330		
	REVERSIBLE			

30" PENINSULAR WALL

PW-1830
PW-2430
REVERSIBLE

PW-3030

PW-3630
PW-4230
PW-4830

CORNER WALL — LAZY SUSAN

CW-2430
REVERSIBLE

L. OR R.
CW-2430 L.S.

VARIWALL UNITS

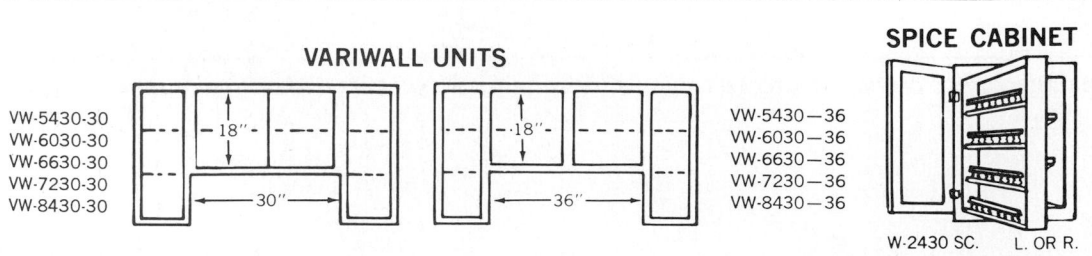

VW-5430-30
VW-6030-30
VW-6630-30
VW-7230-30
VW-8430-30

VW-5430—36
VW-6030—36
VW-6630—36
VW-7230—36
VW-8430—36

SPICE CABINET

W-2430 SC.   L. OR R.

53-19. *(cont.) A manufacturer's catalog of kitchen cabinets showing stock numbers and cabinet dimensions available.*

BASE CABINETS

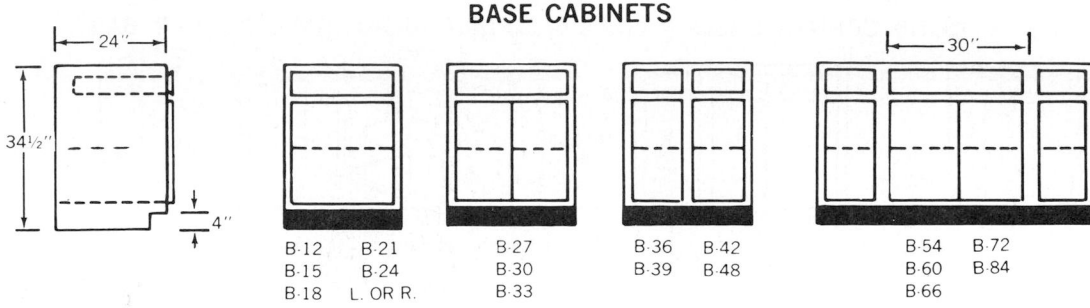

24″
34½″
4″

B-12   B-21
B-15   B-24
B-18   L. OR R.

B-27
B-30
B-33

B-36   B-42
B-39   B-48

30″

B-54   B-72
B-60   B-84
B-66

SINK OR RANGE BASE

30″
or 36″ (Specify)

TRAY BASE

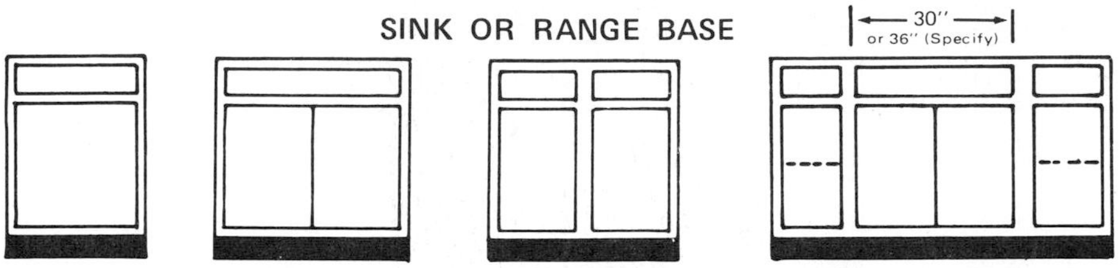

SBRB-24
L. OR R.

SBRB-27
SBRB-30
SBRB-33

SBRB-36   BRB-42
SBRB-39   BRB-48

SBRB-54-30   SBRB-72-36
SBRB-60-30   SBRB-84-36
SBRB-66-36

TB-9
L. OR R.

DRAWER BASE

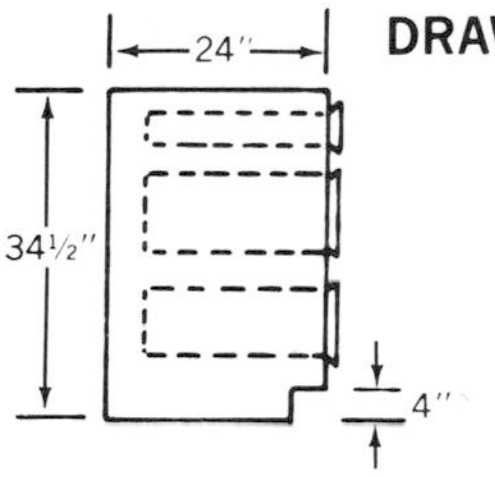

24″
34½″
4″

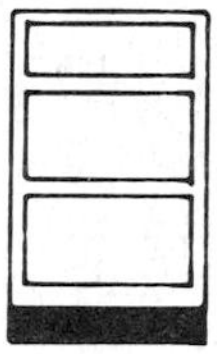

D-15   D-18-CB
D-18   D-18-VBCB
D-21   D-18-BDCB
D-24   D-18-VB
D-18-BDVBCB   D-18-BBBD
D-18-BDVB

MIXER BASE

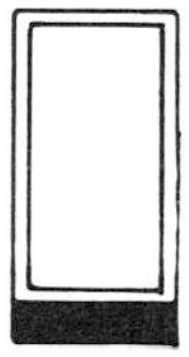

MB-18
L. OR R.

DESK 27

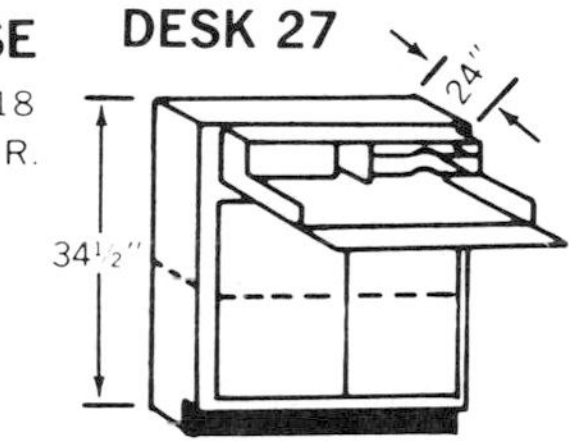

24″
34½″

SINK OR RANGE FRONT

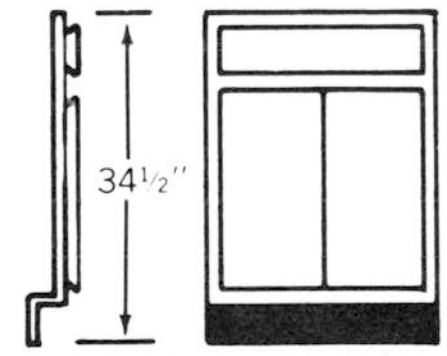

34½″

SFRF-30

CAN
TRIM
2½″
EACH
SIDE

SFRF-36
SFRF-42
SFRF-48

SWING SHELF

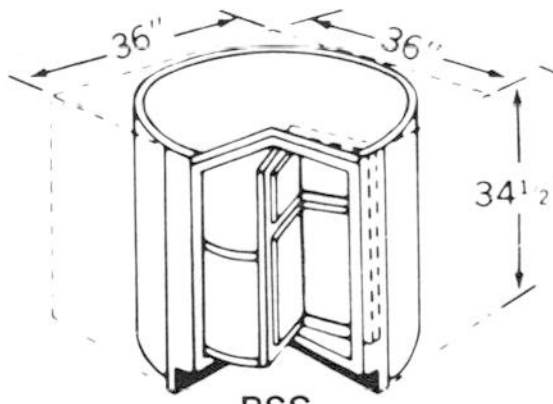

36″   36″

34½″

BSS

LAZY SUSAN

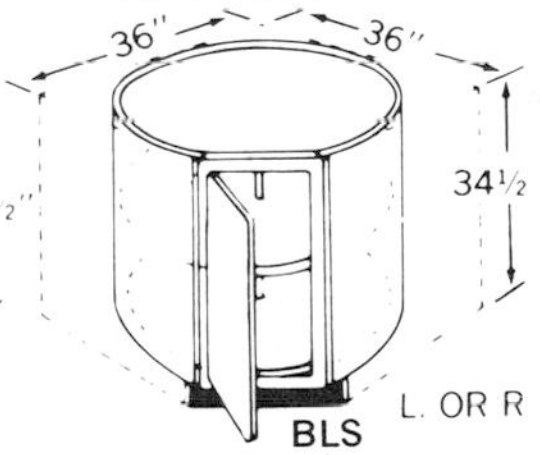

36″   36″

34½″

BLS
L. OR R

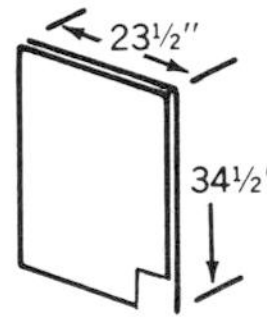

(D)

RANGE FRONT (RF)

23½″
34½″

13½″   30″

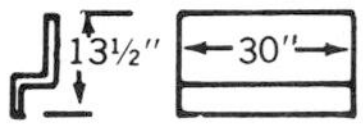

CAN BE TRIMMED IN
HEIGHT & WIDTH

END PANEL (EP)-24
L. OR R.

(D) CORNER BASE FILLER:
3″x 3″x 34½″

(E) BASE FILLER: 3″x 34½″

(E) OVEN FILLER: 3″x 84″

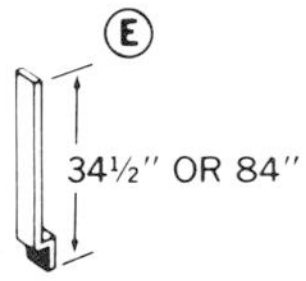

(E)

34½″ OR 84″

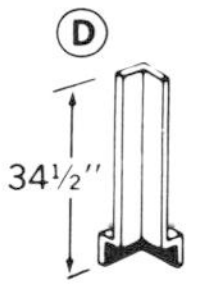

(D)

34½″

OPEN END SHELF-12

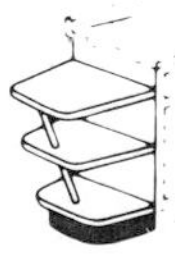

PENINSULAR BASE

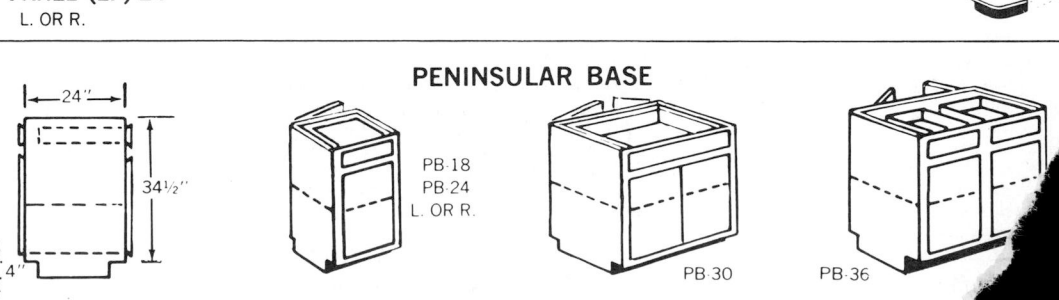

24″
34½″
4″

PB-18
PB-24
L. OR R.

PB-30

PB-36

BLIND CORNER BASES

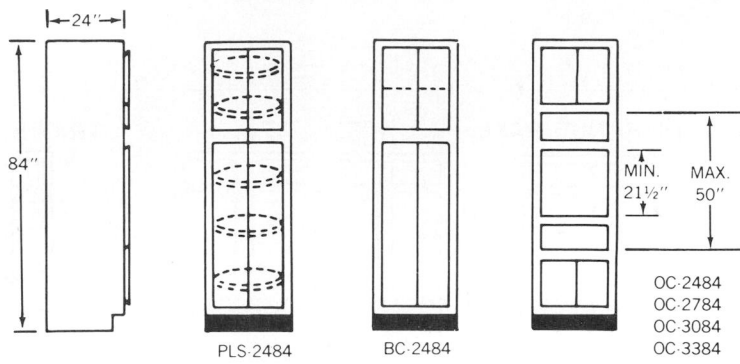

BCB·36
BCB·48
L. OR R.

BCB·60
L. OR R.

PENINSULAR BLIND CORNER BASE

PBCB·36
PBCB·48 L. OR R.

PBCB·60
L. OR R.

(FOR BCB·PBCB — 3" FILLER MUST BE USED FOR CLEARANCE)

24"

84"

MIN.
21½"

MAX.
50"

PLS·2484   BC·2484

OC·2484
OC·2784
OC·3084
OC·3384

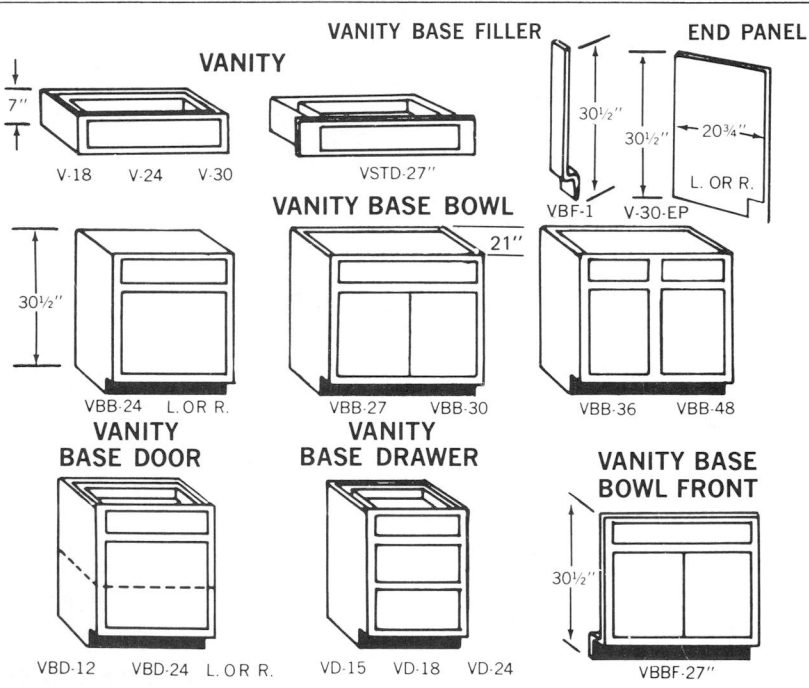

VANITY BASE FILLER   END PANEL

VANITY

7"

V·18   V·24   V·30

VSTD·27"

30½"   30½"   20¾"

L. OR R.

VBF·1   V·30·EP

VANITY BASE BOWL

21"

30½"

VBB·24   L. OR R.   VBB·27   VBB·30   VBB·36   VBB·48

VANITY BASE DOOR

VBD·12   VBD·24   L. OR R.

VANITY BASE DRAWER

VD·15   VD·18   VD·24

VANITY BASE BOWL FRONT

30½"

VBBF·27"

B—Base Cabinet	**LS**—Lazy Susan	**SFRF**—Sink or Range Front
BB—Bread Board (for BD-18 only)	**MB**—Mixer Base	**TB**—Tray Base
BC—Broom Cabinet	**OC**—Oven Cabinet	**VB**—Vegetable Bin
BCB—Blind Corner Base	**PW**—Peninsular Wall Cabinet	**V**—Vanity
BCW—Blind Corner Wall Cabinet	**PB**—Peninsular Base	**VBB**—Vanity Base Bowl
BD—Bread Drawer	**PBCB**—Peninsular Blind Corner Base	**VBBF**—Vanity Base Bowl Front
BLS—Base Lazy Susan		**VBD**—Vanity Base Door
BOES—Base Open End Shelf	**PBCW**—Peninsular Blind Corner Wall Cabinet	**VBF**—Vanity Base Filler
BSS—Base Swing Shelf	**PLS**—Pantry Lazy Susan	**VBD**—Vanity Base Drawer
CB—Chop Block (for D-18-CB only)	**RB**—Range Base	**VSTD**—Vanity Single Tray Drawer
	RFP—Range Front Panel	**VW**—Vari Wall
CW—Corner Wall Cabinet	**SBRB**—Sink or Range Base	**W**—Wall Cabinet
D—Drawer Base	**SC**—Spice Cabinet	**WES**—Wall End Shelf
EP—End Panel	**SF**—Sink Front	**WOES**—Wall Open End Shelf
		WW—Wide Wall

...ufacturer's catalog of kitchen cabinets showing stock numbers and cabinet dimensions available.

...ompleting the Interior

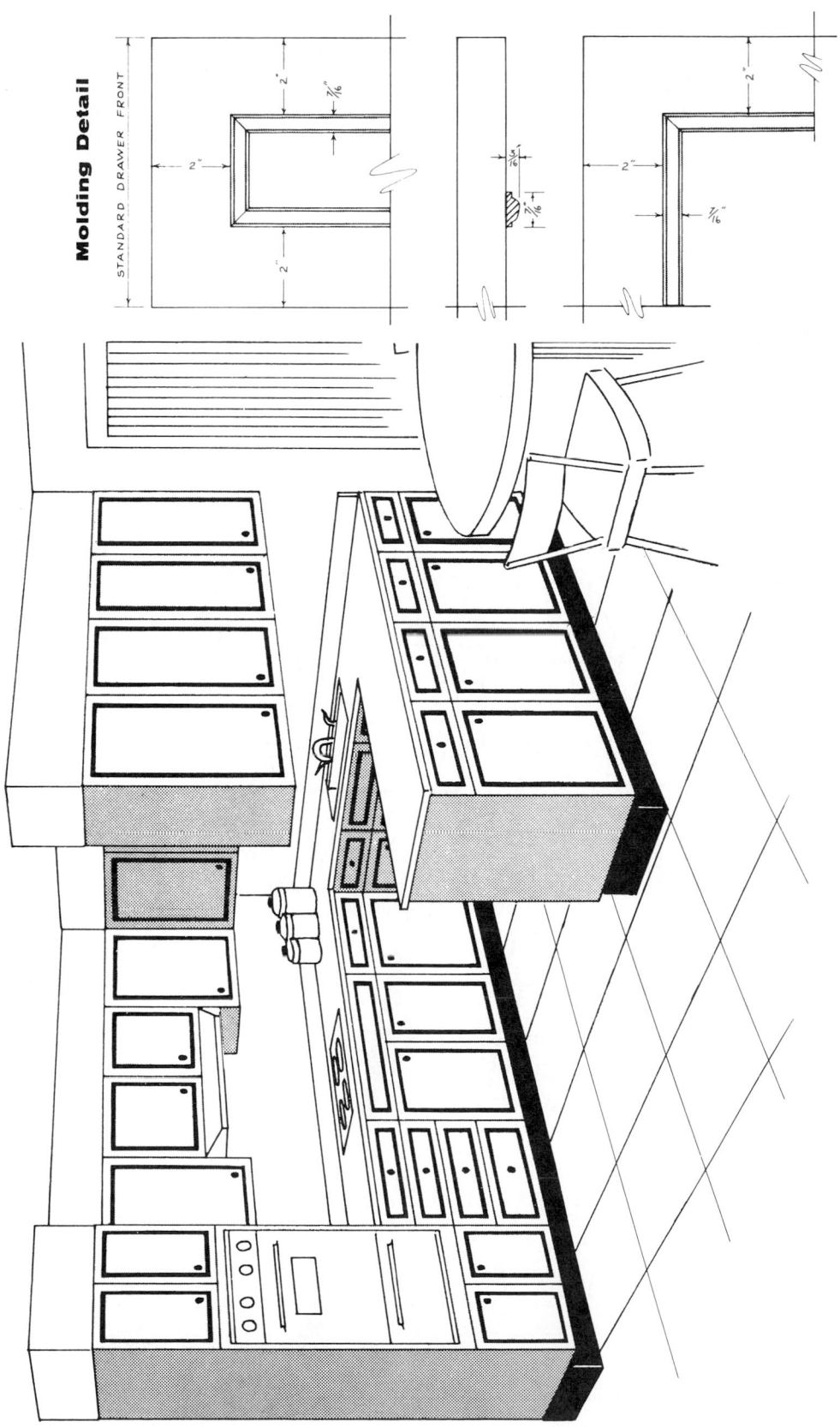

53-20a. *The style of many cabinets can be changed by the application of various wood moldings to the drawers and door fronts.*

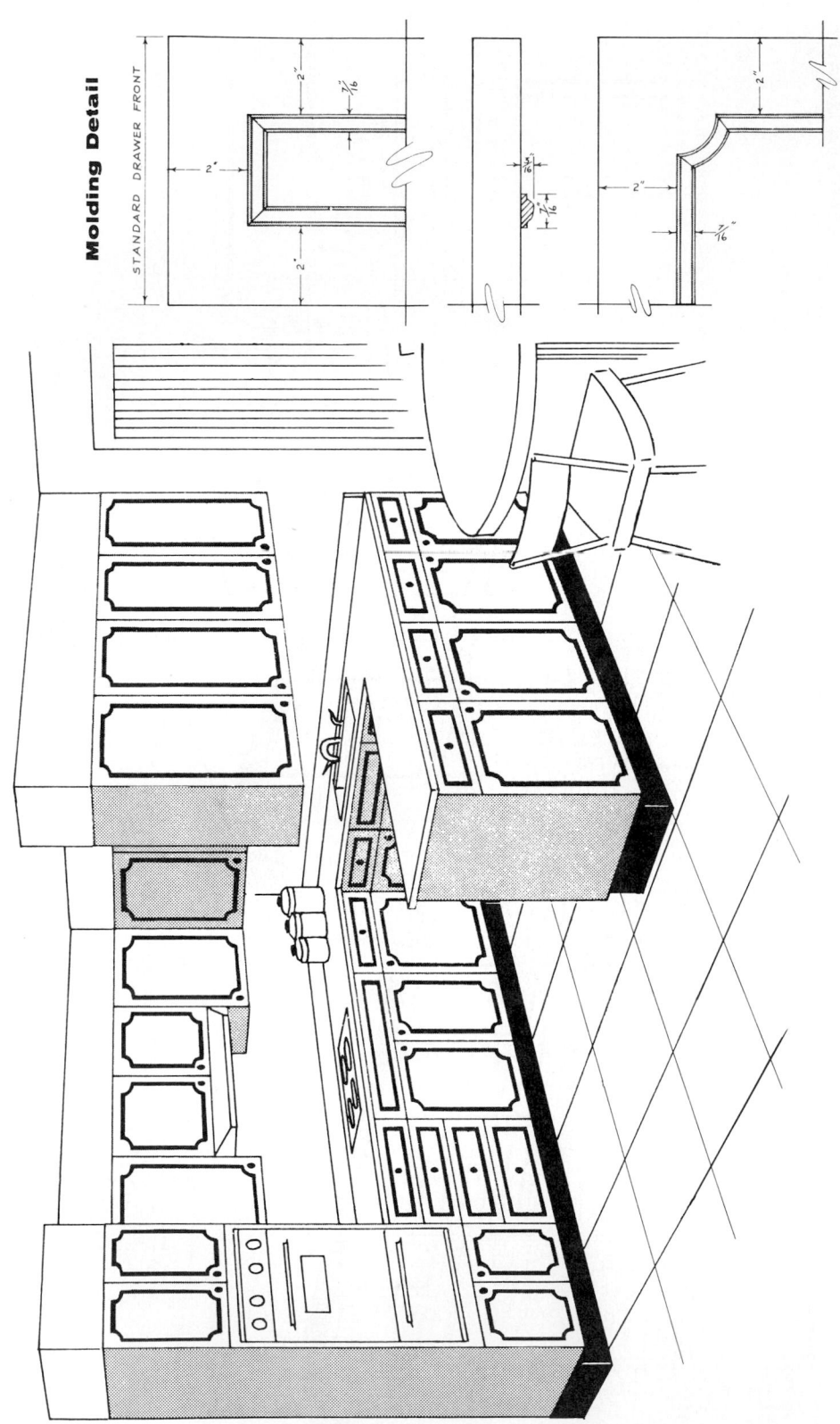

53-20b. *Notice the different look of these cabinets compared to those shown in Fig. 53-20a. It was done by changing the style of the molding on the door and drawer fronts.*

cabinets, always indicate whether the door is to be hinged on the right or the left side. Also provide the manufacturer with the size of the sink and the opening needed for built-ins such as the oven, dishwasher, and refrigerator. Be sure also to include the style of the cabinet and the finish desired. Fig. 53-20.

Installing Factory-Built Cabinets

Factory-built cabinets may be installed in either of two ways. Some cabinetmakers prefer to install the base cabinets first and then build platforms which rest on top of the base cabinets. The wall cabinets are set onto the platforms and held in place for installation. Other cabinetmakers prefer to install the wall cabinets first. This is sometimes more convenient because it allows the workers to stand up close to the wall when working on the wall cabinets, rather than having to reach over and climb onto the base cabinets during installation. With both procedures, the same precautions must be taken when installing the cabinets to insure that they are properly aligned and installed plumb and level.

Wall Cabinets. It is imperative that the wall cabinet be mounted securely and that it will easily bear normal heavy loads. The wall cabinets are attached to the wall with wood screws or toggle bolts through the upper and lower back rail, through the wall covering, and into each stud. Fig. 53-21. The wood screws should be at least a #9 or #10 round head and long enough to go through the ¾" back rail and the wall covering and extend at least 1" into the studding. A minimum of four screws should be used for each cabinet. Never rely on nails for hanging wall cabinets,

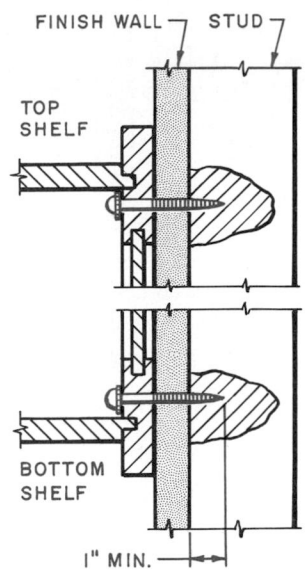

53-21. *Attaching upper cabinets to the wall with wood screws. The screws should penetrate the stud by at least 1".*

or on screws driven only into plaster. These will not hold securely.

Locate and mark the wall studs on the wall. Then mark the location of the bottom of the wall cabinet on the wall. The most common distance between a counter top and the bottom of an upper cabinet is 18" to accommodate taller electrical appliances.

Align the tops of the wall cabinets 7' from the floor. Start the installation from the corner and work toward windows and doorways. Place each of the cabinets in position and brace them so that the cabinets are held securely. Fig. 53-22. Make certain the cabinet is against the wall and up tight against the soffit. If there is no soffit, be sure the tops of the cabinets are properly aligned.

By measuring, determine where the back cabinet rails cross over the exact center of the studs. Drill through the cabinet rail only with the shank diameter drill (the screw

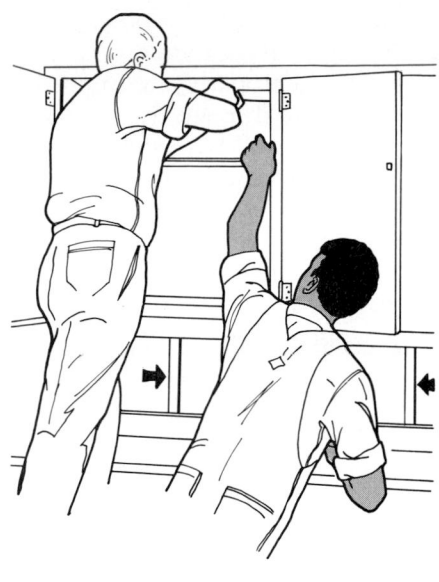

53-22a. *Support the cabinet on wood strips as shown at arrows. One worker holds the front of the unit while the second fastens the cabinet to the studs.*

53-22b. *When two or more narrow wall cabinets are placed side by side, it is better to fasten them together on the floor and mount them on the wall as one unit. Make certain that the joining forces of the stiles are flush and that the tops and bottoms of the cabinets are aligned before drilling.*

should slip through this hole freely). With the cabinet in position and properly aligned, drill the pilot hole through the shank hole and the wall covering into the stud. Drill the pilot hole to a depth which will accommodate the length of the screw.

For proper installation, each wall cabinet should be fastened with at least two screws in the upper rail and two in the lower rail. If it is impossible to screw directly into studs or wood blocking, toggle bolts or wall anchors may be used to fasten the cabinets to the plaster or drywall instead. Fig. 53-23. Should the cabinet span two studs, as shown in Fig. 53-24a, it is logical to secure at these points. However, if the cabinet spans only one stud, as shown in Fig. 53-24b, fasten wood screws into the stud and $3/16" \times 3\frac{1}{2}"$ toggle bolts into the plaster. Drill a hole through the back rail and the plaster just large enough for a slip fit of the folded leaves of the toggle. Then use a washer large enough to cover the resulting hole.

Uneven walls sometimes make it difficult to obtain proper alignment and get a snug fit. If the walls are out of plumb, the cabinet should be shimmed. Fig. 53-25. If material for scribing is provided on the back of the cabinet, the cabinet should be held in place, scribed, and cut to fit the irregular wall surface. When a high spot in the plaster occurs at the center of the cabinet, take care when securing the cabinet to the wall that stress is not placed on the front framing members of the cabinet. Such stress may cause a checking and breaking of the glued joints. This can be avoided by shimming out the ends of the cabinets equal to the high spot in the plaster.

If the cabinets are to be fastened together through the ends for additional strength and for a tight fit between the facings of the cabinets, use bolts or #10 wood screws of sufficient length. Once again,

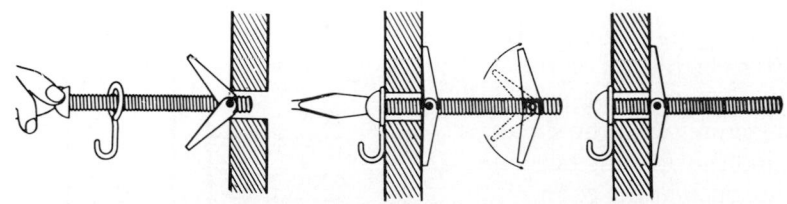

53-23a. *The holes that are drilled to receive toggle bolts must be drilled large enough to accept the wings. When the installation is complete, the wings form a perfect 90° angle with the wall, allowing the entire length of the wings to come in contact with the interior wall surface.*

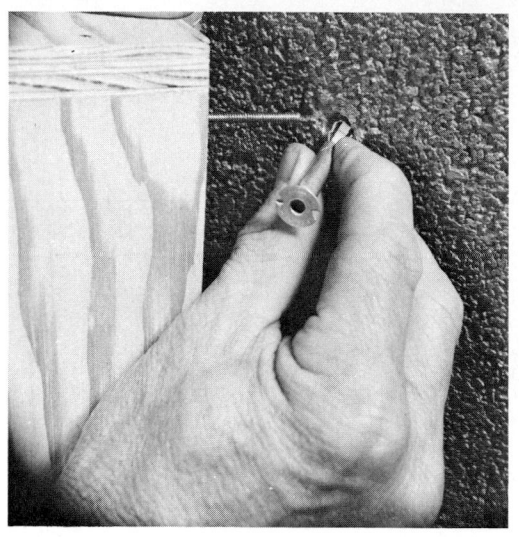

53-23b. *Using a hollow wall anchor to install wall cabinets.*

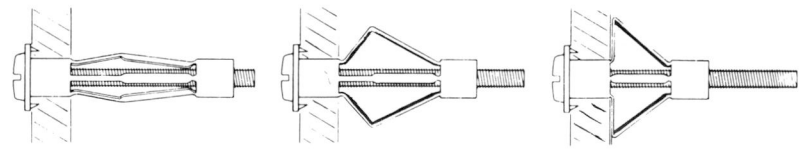

53-23c. *As the anchor is inserted in the opening and the screw is tightened, the legs of the fastener expand and are drawn up tightly against the inside of the wall. The advantage of this system is that once the anchor has been set, the screw may be removed as often as necessary.*

caution is needed when drawing the cabinets together because of the resulting strain on the facing joints. However, if the cabinets are properly aligned to the wall and fit snugly at the junction between the cabinets, there should be no problem.

Base Cabinets. Before installing the base cabinets, clean the walls. On remodeling jobs, remove any moldings such as quarter rounds and baseboards. Set the base cabinets loosely into their respective positions and check the measurements with the plans. Begin setting the cabinets at the corners or side wall. Fig. 53-26. If they fit snugly to the wall at the back and are level, they may be

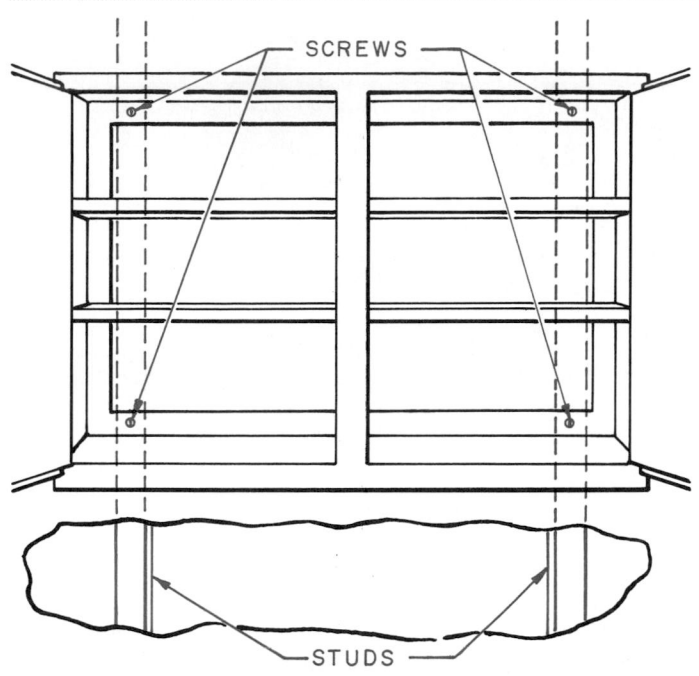

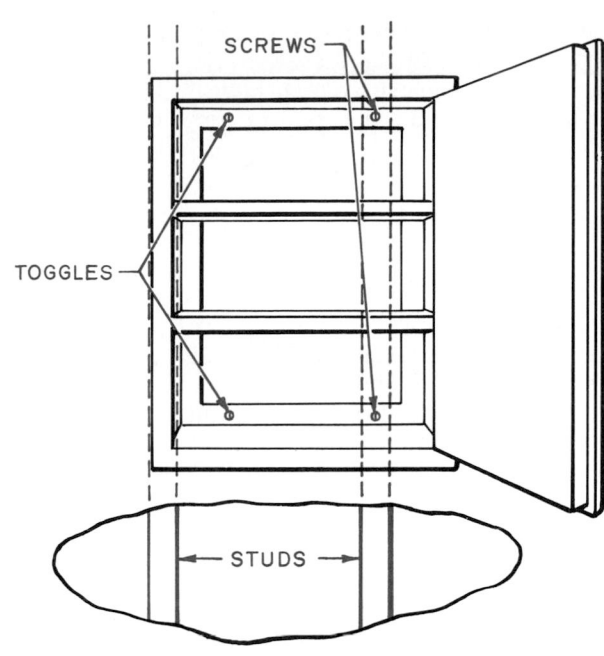

53-24a. *When the cabinet spans two studs, use wood screws.*

53-24b. *When the cabinet spans only one stud, a toggle bolt or hollow wall fastener is needed to install the wall cabinet securely.*

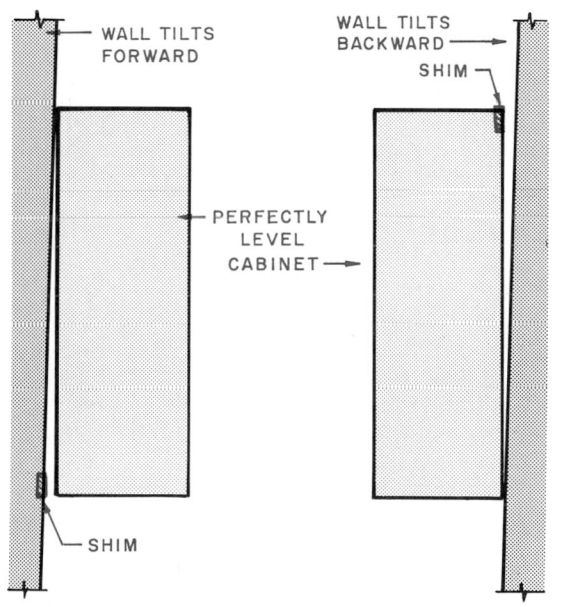

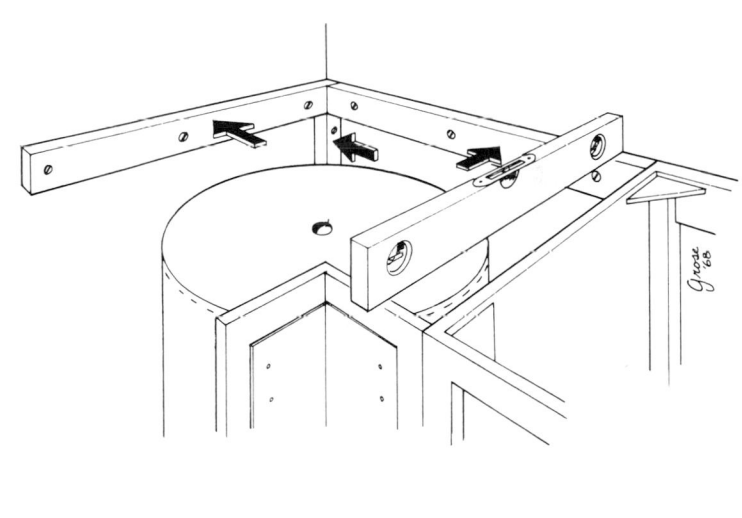

53-25. *If scribing the cabinet to the wall is not possible, place wood shims behind the wall cabinet so that it can be pulled up tightly against the wall in a plumb and level position.*

53-26. *When installing a revolving corner base, nail or screw 1" x 2" strips to the wall as shown at the arrows. The strips provide a level platform for the counter top to rest on.*

fastened together with one or two evenly spaced #10 wood screws or ¼" bolts through the panels just behind the front stiles. Fig. 53-27.

If a sink front is included in the assembly, the opening should be carefully checked and the facing under the sink should be properly fitted between the adjoining base cabinets. Secure this facing on the inside with wood screws through a ¾" × ¾" wood cleat or angle irons.

Sometimes the floor and/or wall is uneven and the cabinets do not set plumb and level and tightly against the wall. In that case, they must be shimmed or scribed and trimmed. Fig. 53-28. To trim a cabinet to fit the floor, scribe it or measure the distance A and mark the end panel as shown at B in Fig. 53-28. Cut the end panel along this line to fit the floor. Fig. 53-29. When the wall is uneven, the rear of the cabinet may be scribed to fit the wall if the end panel is exposed. If the end panel is not exposed, the cabinet may be shimmed and securely wood screwed through the wall covering and into the stud.

BATHROOM CABINETS

Bathroom cabinets, like kitchen cabinets, are obtained in three basic ways. They may be constructed on the job site; purchased knocked-down, then assembled and installed as a unit; or purchased prebuilt and ready to install from factories which mass-produce cabinets. Factory-built bathroom cabinets are installed in the same manner as described earlier in the discussion of kitchen cabinets. Fig. 53-30. Bathroom cabinets differ from kitchen cabinets slightly in size. They are usually 30" high and 21" deep. The drawer opening is usually made 4" deep, rather than 5" as in the case

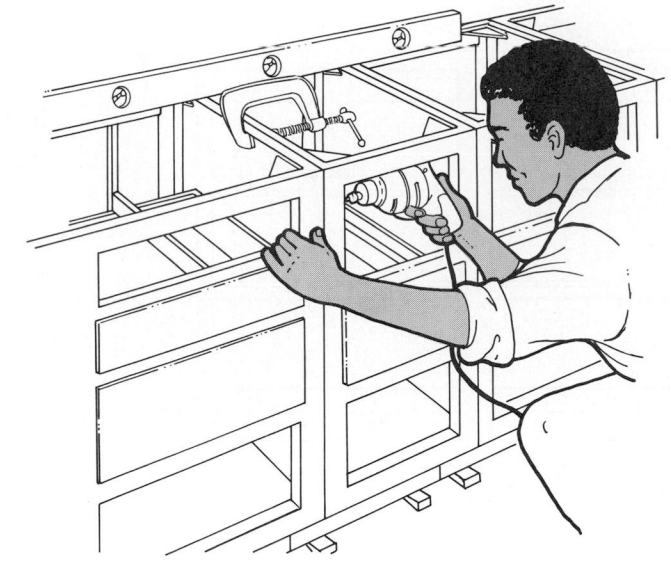

53-27. When more than one cabinet is installed, the cabinets should be fastened together with 1/4" bolts or #10 wood screws to unify the construction.

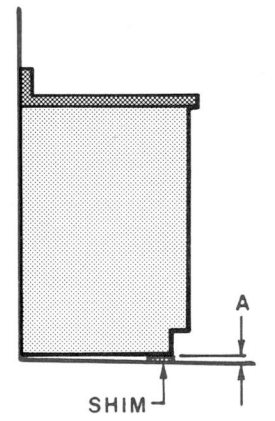

SHIM

A

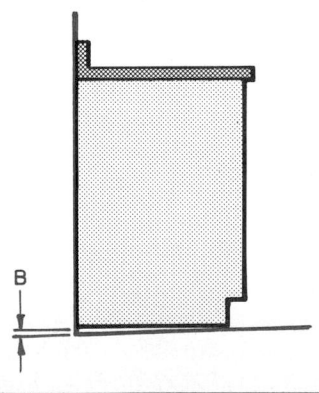

B

53-28. To make the base cabinet set plumb and level, it can be shimmed as shown at A or scribed as shown at B. If the cabinet is scribed, it should be cut off as shown in Fig. 53-29.

53-29. Cutting off the scribed base to fit the floor.

53-30. A bathroom cabinet.

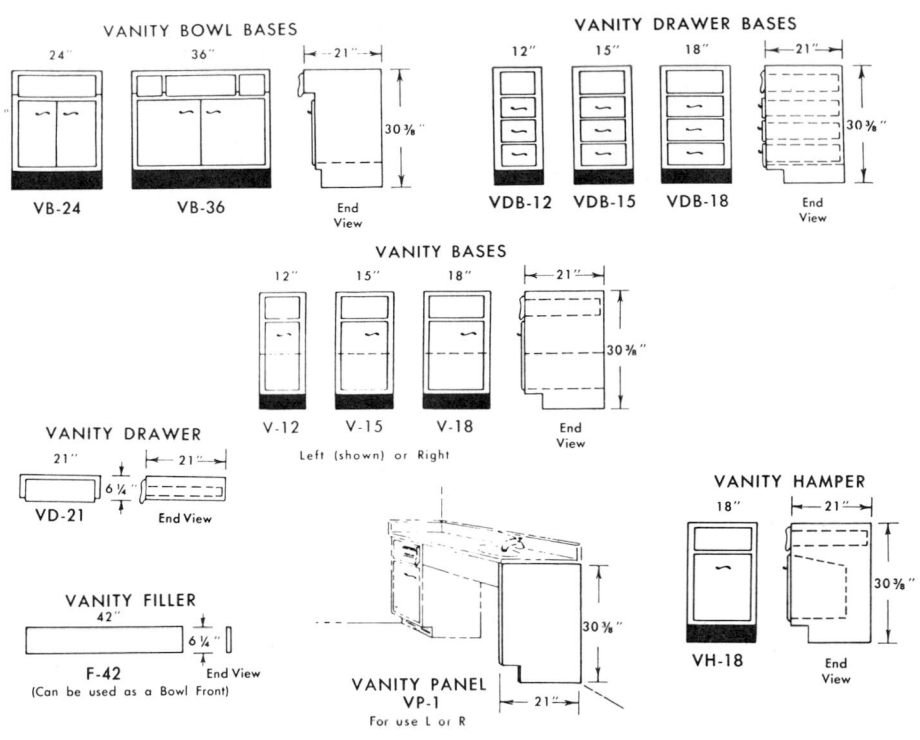

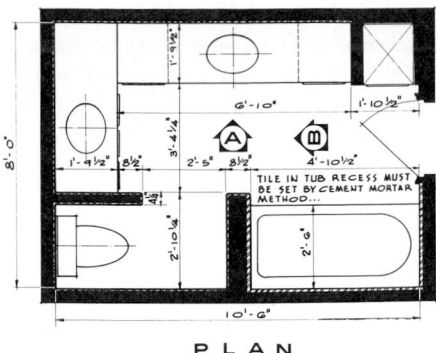

PLAN

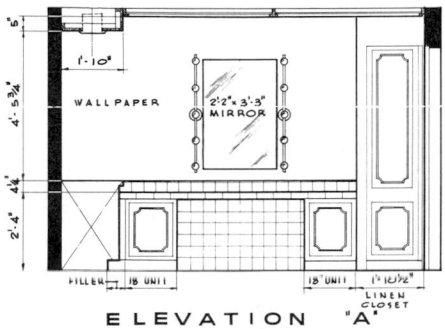

ELEVATION "A"

53-31a. *A typical selection of manufactured bathroom cabinets.*

53-31b. *Factory-built cabinets in a large bathroom with a dual lavatory installation.*

of the kitchen cabinet. Fig. 53-31. See *Cabinetmaking and Millwork* by John L. Feirer for additional information and construction details.

COUNTER TOPS

Counter tops for kitchen cabinets, bathroom vanities, built-in desks, and room dividers are often covered with plastic laminate or ceramic tile. Therefore the cabinetmaker or finish carpenter should have some knowledge of these materials. The installation of plastic laminate will be described here. The installation of ceramic tile is discussed in Unit 51.

Common trade names for plastic laminates are Formica® and Wilsonart®. They are available in widths of 24", 30", 36", 48", and 60". The common lengths are 60", 72", 84", 96", 120", and 144". Most manufacturers provide enough extra material in the stock sizes for one or two saw cuts to be made. For example, two 12" widths can usually be cut from a 24" width. Plastic laminates are sold by the

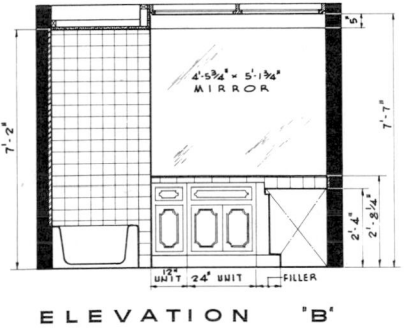

ELEVATION "B"

53-31c. *The layout of an attractive bathroom with factory-built cabinets installed.*

square foot, and the standard grade for counter tops is 1/16" thick.

A plastic laminate is quite thin and brittle, so it must be fastened or adhered to a core. Common core materials are plywood and particle board. These should be ¾" thick with no defects or voids in the surface. For most job site applications, the laminate is adhered to the core with a contact cement. Other adhesives such as casein, polyvinyl, urea, and other slow setting glues can be used, but the laminate must be clamped to the core long enough to allow the glue to cure.

Cutting the Laminate to Size

Plastic laminates may be sawed, routed, filed, drilled, and otherwise worked and fitted. The tools used may be hand- or power-operated. Since decorative laminate dulls tools more quickly than wood, the tools must be sharpened often. Dull tools may cause chipping. Whenever possible, carbide-tipped cutting tools should be used. Plastic laminate may also be sized by cutting it with special shears or by scoring the plastic with a scratch awl or a carbide-tipped scoring tool. Strips of laminate 1/16" to 4" wide can be cut with a laminate slitter. This tool is similar to a router. It can repeatedly and accurately cut strips of laminate for countertop edging. Figs. 53-32b and 53-32c. When using the scoring method, score a cutting line deeply on the decorative side of the plastic with a scratch awl. Place a straightedge along the scored line. Bend evenly and upward only. Fig. 53-32a. Do not try to tear the laminate. This method will not give as clean an edge as those methods previously mentioned. Therefore allow at least a half-inch oversize on all surface dimensions so that the edge may be trimmed back even with the edge of the core stock.

Measure the area to be covered. Allow 1/4" oversize on all edges unless the scored method of cutting is used. Cut the laminate to size. If there are any seams to be made, dress the edges smooth and straight until they fit together perfectly. Undercut the two edges slightly to allow a closer fit at the surface.

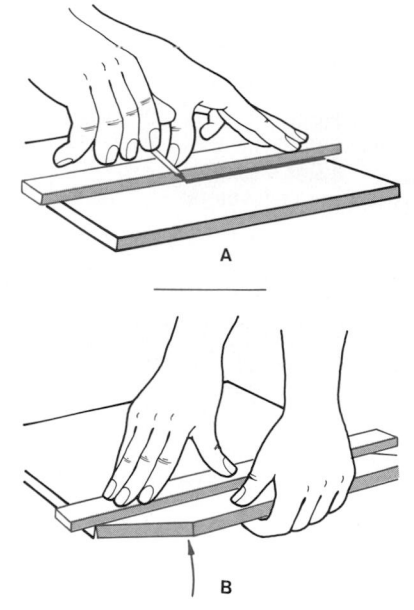

53-32a. Cutting plastic laminate: A. Score the face side of the laminate, using a straightedge as a guide. B. With the straightedge placed along the scribed line, bend the laminate up to break it off.

These edges may be dressed with a block plane and touched up with a fine abrasive paper or a file.

Preparation of the Surface for Installation

For best results, all materials should be at room temperature (70° F) or higher before installation. The core should have a smooth, sound surface. Make certain the surface is clean, dry, and free of oil, grease, or wax. Fill holes and cracks with a spackling compound and then sand smooth and even with the surface. Dust all surfaces.

Applying the Adhesive

The adhesive is applied to both the back of the plastic laminate and the top of the core. (NOTE: If the edge trim is plastic laminate,

53-32b. A laminate slitter.

53-32c. A laminate slitter allows strips of laminate to be cut with speed and accuracy.

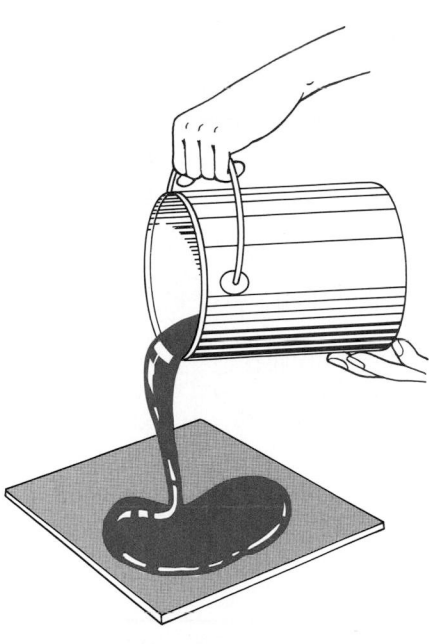

53-33. *Pouring the contact adhesive onto the surface to be covered.*

53-34a. *Spreading contact adhesive with a roller.*

53-34b. *Spreading contact adhesive with a notched spreader.*

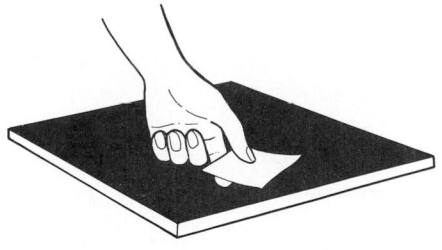

53-35. *Testing contact adhesive to make sure it is completely dry.*

apply the edge trim first. Coat and bond the top surface after the edge trim is bonded and trimmed.) Stir the adhesive thoroughly from the bottom of the can and pour it onto the core surface and the back of the laminate. Fig. 53-33. Spread the adhesive evenly, using a roller or a spreader with a notched edge. Fig. 53-34. If a spreader is used, the notched edge should be held at a 45° angle to the surface of the plastic laminate. Hold the spreader at 90° to the surface of the core material. A brush may also be used to apply adhesive and is recommended when adhesive is applied to vertical surfaces or edges, or whenever the use of a spreader is impractical. With a brush, both surfaces will need at least two coats. Be sure to allow the adhesive adequate drying time between coats.

To make certain that enough adhesive has been applied, look across the surface into the light after the adhesive is completely dry. There should be a glossy film. Dull spots after drying indicate that more adhesive should be applied to these areas. Let the adhesive dry according to the label directions on the can. Test dryness of the adhesive by pressing a piece of wrapping paper lightly against it and pulling it away. Fig. 53-35. If the adhesive sticks to the paper, more drying time is needed. If, for any reason, bonding of the plastic laminate to the core is not completed within two hours, the

adhesive should be reactivated by applying another thin coat to both the back of the laminate and the core.

Bonding and Finishing

If the edge trim is plastic laminate, install it first. If the edge trim is metal, install it after the top surface has been bonded in place. Fig. 53-36. The plastic laminate edge trim is carefully positioned so that its bottom edge is flush with the bottom edge of the core. The top edge of the trim will extend about ¼" or more above the top of the core surface. Press the edge trim in place by sliding a soft wood block along it. Tap the wood block with a hammer to complete the bond. Fig. 53-37. Carefully trim off excess material and file until the edge trim is flush with the top of the core surface. Fig. 53-38. Be sure the edge trim is bonded and completely trimmed before coating the top surface.

Apply adhesive to the top surface. *Use extreme care in aligning the plastic laminate with the core because bonding is immediate upon contact.* Place several dowel rods or strips of scrap plastic laminate with the smooth side down on top of the core. Fig. 53-39. Align the plastic laminate with the core so that an equal amount of laminate hangs over all edges. Now gently slip the center piece of plastic scrap or dowel rod from beneath the plastic laminate, leaving the others in place. The two adhesive surfaces will come in contact with each other. Press to make the bond. Remove the other scraps one at a time, working from the center toward the ends. Be careful not to jar the work as you move the scraps because the two pieces will bond immediately.

With a small roller, roll the surface from the center toward the edges in all directions. Fig. 53-40. If

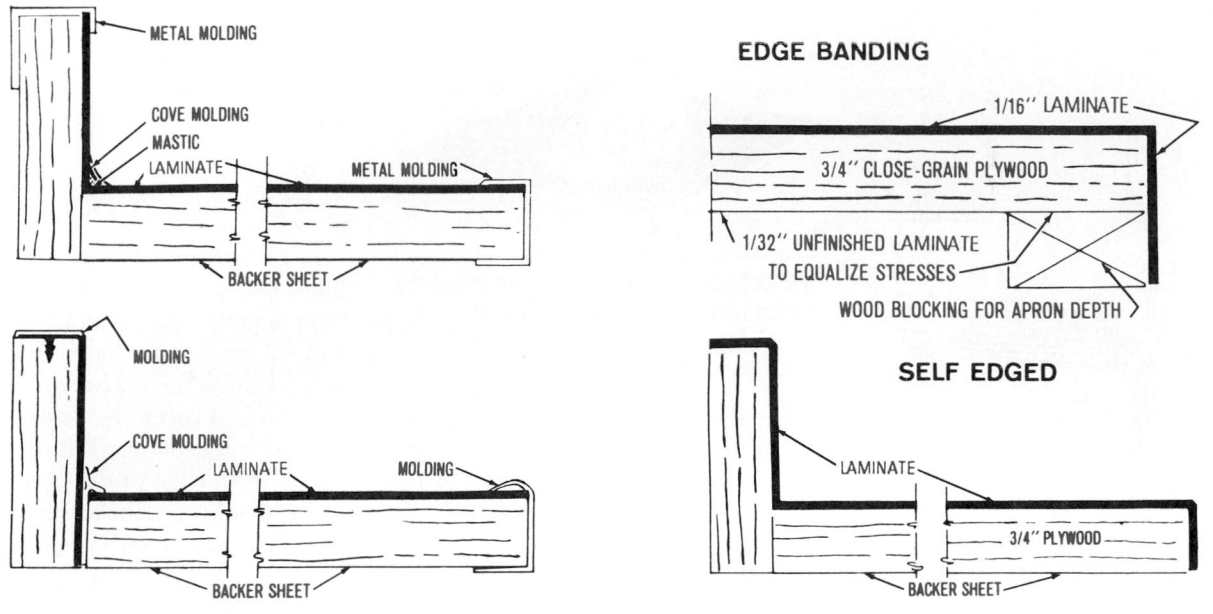

EDGE BANDING

1/16" LAMINATE

3/4" CLOSE-GRAIN PLYWOOD

1/32" UNFINISHED LAMINATE TO EQUALIZE STRESSES

WOOD BLOCKING FOR APRON DEPTH

SELF EDGED

LAMINATE

3/4" PLYWOOD

BACKER SHEET

METAL MOLDING

COVE MOLDING

MASTIC

LAMINATE

METAL MOLDING

BACKER SHEET

MOLDING

COVE MOLDING

LAMINATE

MOLDING

BACKER SHEET

53-36. *Cross-sections of job-site fabricated counter tops. They can be trimmed with metal molding or with plastic laminate which has been cut from the same material used on the surface.*

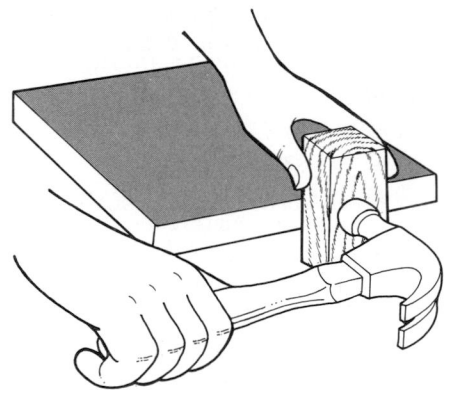

53-37. *Complete the bond between the plastic laminate and the core by sliding a soft wood block along the trim, tapping it with a hammer.*

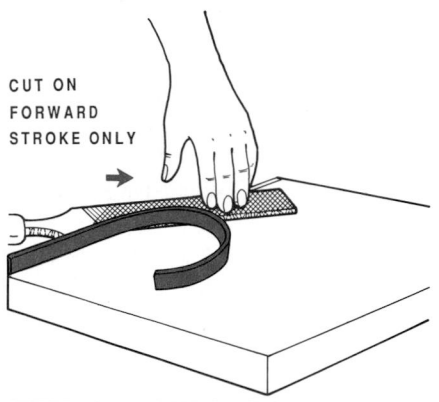

CUT ON FORWARD STROKE ONLY

53-38a. *Carefully file the excess material until the edge trim is flush with the top surface. Be sure to cut on the forward stroke only, to avoid chipping the edges of the laminate.*

53-38b. *An electric trimmer for plastic laminate.*

a roller is not available, use a block of soft wood. Place this on the center and work toward the edges, tapping sharply with a hammer. Tap or roll the entire surface to insure a complete bond. Use a hand plane or plastic laminate trimmer to remove the excess plastic laminate which overhangs the edges of the core. File the edges

smooth with a flat mill file at a 20° or 30° angle to the edge. Fig. 53-41. Use long, smooth downward strokes. If using metal or wood edge trim, file the laminate flush with the edge of the core. Then file a 45° bevel on the edge of the laminate to allow for expansion under the metal or wood edge trim. To butt seams, cut the seam as

53-39. Use scraps of plastic laminate to support the surface sheet of plastic laminate while aligning it with the core for bonding.

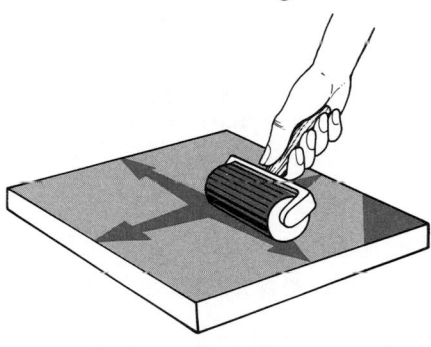

53-40. With a small roller, roll the surface of the plastic laminate from the center toward the edges in all directions to complete the bond.

FILE ON THE DOWNWARD STROKE ONLY

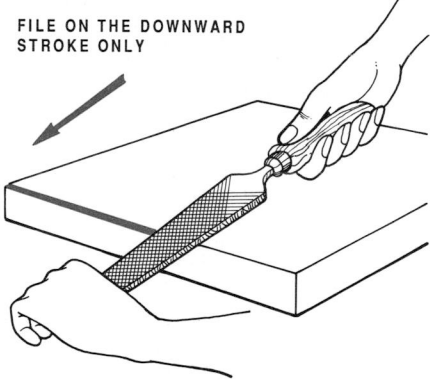

53-41. File the edges of the surface laminate smooth on the downward stroke only, to avoid lifting and tearing the edge of the surface material.

previously described. Apply one piece at a time along the predetermined seam line marked on the core surface. Position and adhere the laminate accurately to insure that the seam will be neat.

To insure a good plastic laminate job be sure that:
➤ The core and the back of the laminate are completely covered with glossy adhesive films.
➤ Both films are dry.
➤ Both adhesive films are brought into firm contact by rolling or tapping to complete the bond.

Preformed Plastic Laminate Counter Tops

Preformed counter tops, ready for installation, can be bought in slabs or custom made. Fig. 53-42. The premade slab counter top is generally available in 8', 10', and 12' lengths. The choice of patterns and colors is extensive. For an exposed end of the slab, premade end pieces are available.

The counter top is made to the exact measurements. For an L- or U-shaped kitchen, the custom counter top is made up as a single unit whenever possible. If it is impossible to get an assembled counter into the kitchen for

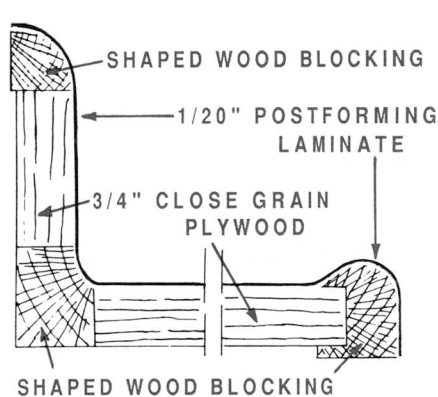

SHAPED WOOD BLOCKING
1/20" POSTFORMING LAMINATE
3/4" CLOSE GRAIN PLYWOOD
SHAPED WOOD BLOCKING

53-42. A cross-section of a premade plastic laminate counter top.

installation, it can be made in sections and held together at the corners with draw bolts.

INSTALLING A PREMADE COUNTER TOP

Set the counter on the cabinets so that the front face of the counter (nearest the user) is 2⅛" from the desired final position. (This dimension may vary with the make of laminate trimmer.) For example, if the counter is to overhang the cabinet by 1", then the top should be pulled out 3⅛". Clamp the counter securely in position. Use a laminate trimmer to fit the counter top to the wall. Fig. 53-43. Place the trimmer on the top edge of the backsplash and move the tool from left to right while keeping the wall guide bracket in contact with the wall. This will trim the rear edge of the plastic laminate. At the same time, the contour of the wall is duplicated on the trimmed edge of the laminate. This trimming operation will create a gap 2⅛" wide between the wall and the trimmed edge so that, when the clamps are removed from the counter top, the counter top can be

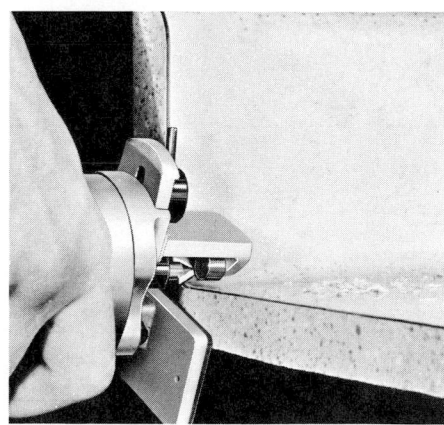

53-43. Using a laminate trimmer to trim the end piece on a preformed counter top.

pushed back snug against the wall.

If a trimmer is not available, the top edge of the backsplash on the preformed top will have to be hand-filed to fit the contour of the wall. After the top is secured to the cabinets, apply a small bead of caulking compound at the joint between the wall and the back top edge of the backsplash.

The counter top is fastened in place by driving wood screws through cleats on the underside of the cabinet up into the bottom of the counter top. Be careful to drill the correct size pilot hole and take special pains not to drill through the top. Be sure to use the correct length wood screw so that it does not penetrate the plastic laminate when the counter top is pulled down snug against the top of the cabinets.

Installing the Sink

Lay out the sink opening by positioning the sink rim upright on the counter top. Carefully trace around the outside bottom edge of the rim. Allow an additional 2" of space between the cutout and cabinet partitions or other parts to provide room for attaching the clips. Fig. 53-44. Cut out the opening with a saber saw or an electric hand circular saw. Use a

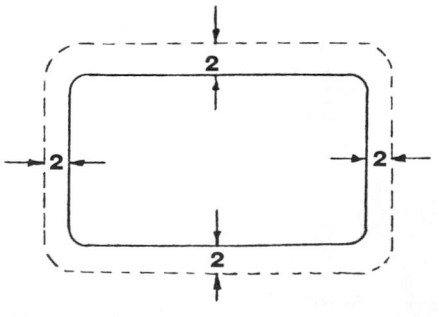

53-44. Allow at least 2" between the edge of the cutout and any cabinet partitions or other cabinet parts to provide room for attaching the clips used to install the sink.

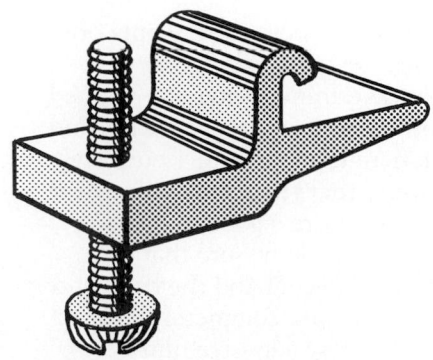

53-45. A clip used to fasten the sink. Two of these clamps should be placed at each corner, with the remaining clamps at equidistant points around the sink.

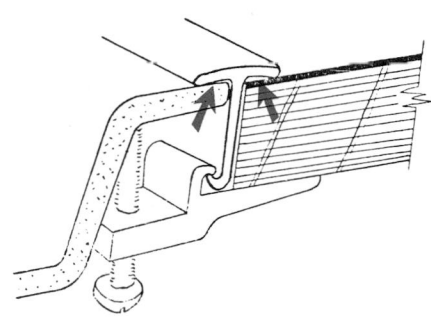

53-46. Apply caulking under the molding on both sides, as shown at the arrows. Use a screwdriver or special wrench to draw up the clamp screws. Wipe off the excess caulking compound that squeezes out.

saber saw for the corners.

The sink may be held in place with a one-piece, preformed sink frame. Another method is to fasten the sink with clips which attach to the bottom of the rim or, in the case of the self-rim type, to the bottom of the sink. Fig. 53-45. Apply caulking to the underside of the sink frame molding. Fig. 53-46. When installing a self-rim sink, place a bead of caulking around the underside of the sink at the edge so that, when the sink is pulled down against the top, it will seal properly.

LINEN CLOSETS

Built-in storage areas, such as a linen closet, reduce the amount of furniture required. A linen closet may be simply a series of shelves behind a flush or panel door, or it may consist of an open cabinet with doors and drawers built directly into a corner or wall area. Linen closets are usually located in hallways near the bedroom and bath. Adjustable shelves are very practical because of the large variety of sizes stored. If the shelves are not adjustable and are supported by cleats which are nailed to the wall, do not fasten the shelves to the cleats. The shelves can then be removed for convenience when painting and decorating. See *Cabinetmaking and Millwork* by John L. Feirer for additional information and construction details.

CHINA CASES

Another millwork item often found in a formal or traditional dining room is the china cabinet. It is usually designed to fit into a corner of the room. Sometimes a pair of cabinets is installed in two corners of the room. A corner cabinet often has glazed doors above and single or double paneled doors below. Fig. 53-47. Generally it is 7' or more high and about 3' wide across the front, with a drop ceiling above. Shelves are installed in both the upper and lower cabinet.

China cases or storage shelves in dining rooms of contemporary homes may be built in place by the contractor, or prefab cabinets can be installed. A row of cabinets or shelves installed between dining room and kitchen may act as a room divider and serve as a storage area for both rooms. Factory-built cabinets can be fitted with accessories which are available from the manufacturer. These cabinets and accessories are combined to form freestanding or built-in pieces such as bars, hutches, sideboards and barbecues. Many different arrangements can be assembled for use throughout the entire home. Fig. 53-48. For additional information on designing and building built-in cabinets, see *Cabinetmaking and Millwork* by John L. Feirer.

53-47. *A built-in corner cabinet.*

53-48b. *Manufactured cabinets installed in a dining area.*

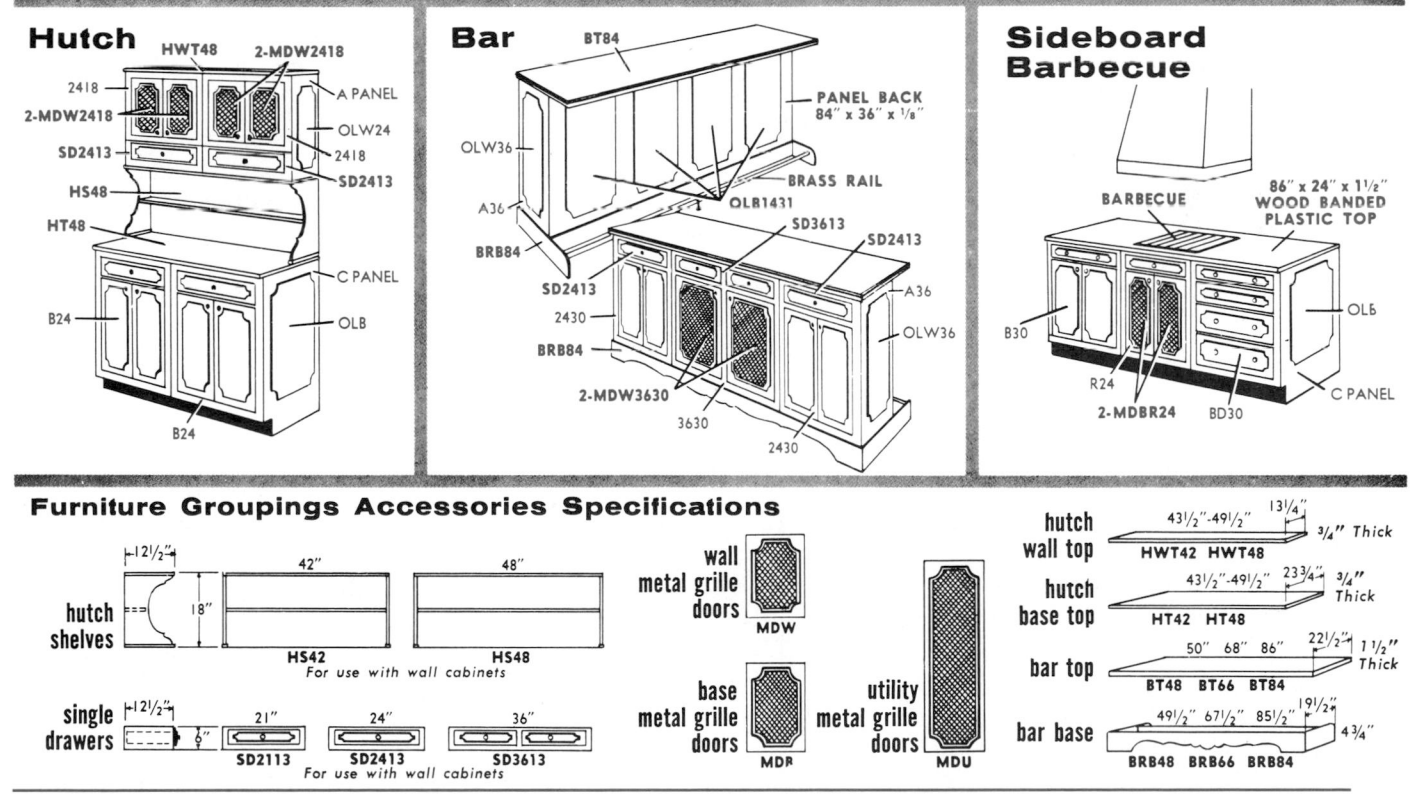

53-48a. *Details of accessories to be used with standard manufactured base cabinets for developing free-standing pieces of furniture.*

53-48c. *Manufactured cabinets in a child's bedroom.*

53-50b. *Full-extension drawer slides such as the one shown here can support up to 150 lbs. per pair.*

CABINET HARDWARE

To perform properly over a long period of time, a cabinet must be fitted with good-quality hardware. Door hinges and drawer slides are particularly important. The quality and expense of hinges and slides vary widely. Some cabinet manufacturers will offer several different grades of hardware for use with any of their cabinets. Other manufacturers will offer one grade of hardware with each grade of cabinet.

Drawer Slides

Drawers may be mounted inside a cabinet on one slide or on two slides.

The single slide is mounted beneath the centerline of the drawer. It can only be used on cabinetry that has a face frame because the front of the slide must be supported. It is generally attached to the inside surface of the face frame. To keep the drawer from tipping side to side, small rollers or plastic guides are mounted to the face frame on either side of the drawer opening.

53-49. *A center-mounted hardwood drawer slide.*

In manufactured cabinetry the center slide is always made of metal, but wood slides are available. Fig. 53-49.

Double slides are more secure than single slides because they support both sides of the drawer. Fig. 53-50. They can be used on face-frame cabinets or on frameless cabinets. They are available in versions that can extend the drawer either partially or fully away from the cabinet. Full-extension slides are most useful because they

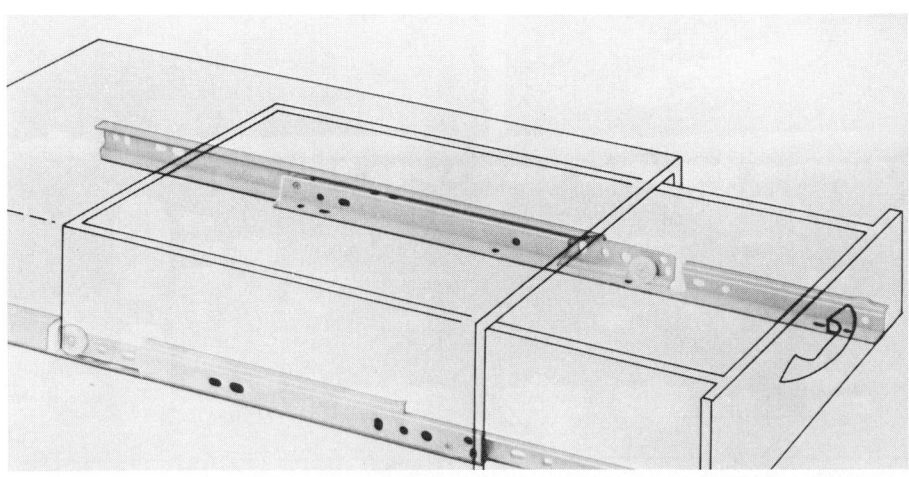

53-50a. *Side-mounted drawer slides.*

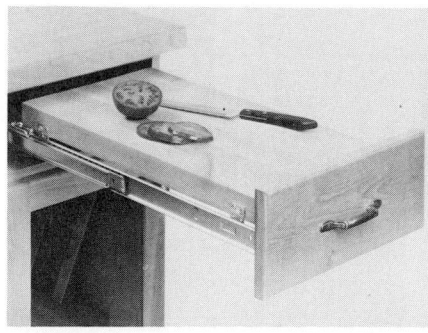

53-51. *A cutting board supported by full-extension drawer slides.*

allow complete access to the back of the drawer. Some full-extension slides can be used for cutting boards and other accessories. Fig. 53-51.

Drawer Hinges

Hinges come in a great variety of styles and configurations. There are three basic types:
- ➤ Barrel hinges.
- ➤ Knife hinges.
- ➤ Cup hinges.

Barrel hinges are the most common type of hinge used on cabinetry in the United States. Each hinge consists of two plates connected with a pin. One plate is screwed to the face frame and the other is screwed to the cabinet door. Some barrel hinges have an L-shaped plate that wraps around the face frame. Barrel hinges are visible from the outside of the cabinet, and come in many styles and finishes. Fig. 53-52.

Knife hinges have two leaves. Instead of being connected with a pin, they are connected with a simple spring mechanism. When the cabinet door is closed, the knife hinge will hold it against the face frame without requiring a separate latch. One leaf of a knife hinge is screwed to the face frame, while the other is inserted into a small slot cut into the door. Screws hold the leaf in the slot. Fig. 53-53.

Cup hinges (sometimes called concealed cup hinges or

53-52a. *The large plate of this barrel hinge wraps around the cabinet face frame.*

53-52b. *Barrel hinges are visible from the exterior of the cabinet.*

53-53. *A knife hinge with a self-closing spring.*

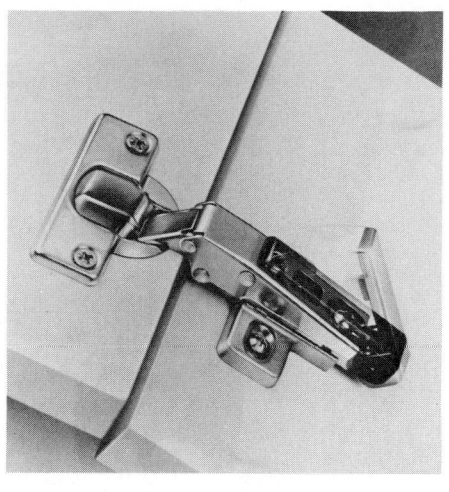

53-54a. *A cup hinge. This model has a metal cap that covers the hinge adjusting screws.*

53-54b. *The cup hinges on this door allow the door to swing open wide.*

European-style hinges) were devised for use on frameless cabinetry. Each hinge consists of a metal cup connected to a mounting flange by way of a pivoting mechanism. Fig. 53-54a. The cup is inserted into a 35mm diameter hole bored into the door. The mounting flange is screwed to the inside wall of the cabinet. Fig. 53-54b. There are several

53-55. *The clean lines of this cabinetry are made possible by concealed cup hinges and frameless casework.*

53-56a. *Shelf for microwave oven.*

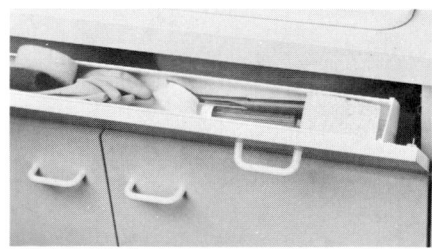

53-56b. *Pull-out storage tray beneath sink.*

53-56c. *Pull-out storage shelves.*

advantages to using cup hinges. They can be adjusted simply by turning one or more screws on the hinge. They are quite strong, and they can be installed quickly. Because the hinge is mounted to the inside of the cabinet, it is not visible from the outside of the cabinet. Fig. 53-55.

CABINET ACCESSORIES

Most cabinets may be made more useful with the addition of various accessories such as spice racks, drawer organizers, and slide-out storage trays. A selection of such accessories is shown in Fig. 53-56.

If any accessories are required, they should be specified at the time the cabinets are ordered. The manufacturer of the cabinets will supply and install them. Many

accessories are also available for installation after the cabinets have been installed. These are particularly useful when remodeling an existing kitchen.

53-56d. *Spice rack.*

53-56e. *Recycling bins.*

Materials

Cabinets are of three types: prefab, K.D. (knocked-down), and built on the job site. The prefab cabinet costs are found by selecting cabinets for the building, listing them with the identifying stock number, and pricing them according to current price lists. Knocked-down cabinets would be priced in much the same manner. Job-site built cabinets will require a complete bill of materials with pricing for each item. The estimate must include all items required for a complete installation, such as counter tops, hardware, drawers (if they are special drawers), glass, shelves, any special grill work, and any other items needed.

Counter tops are priced according to type. The preformed slab counter top is sold by the linear foot, and current prices would be available from a local dealer. Counter tops to be built on the job site would require that materials be itemized. The list would include core material, plastic laminate, adhesive, moldings, and any other items that might be required for a complete installation.

Labor

The time required to install prefab cabinets will vary with the complexity of the kitchen layout and the variety of cabinets to be installed. The approximate labor cost can be determined by totaling the installation time for the selected cabinets and multiplying this by the hourly rate. The approximate times for installing various cabinets and counter tops are listed in Tables 53-A and 53-B.

Table 53-A. *Approximate Installation Times for Factory-Built Cabinets.*

Type of Cabinet	Approximate Installation Time (Hours)
Base cabinet containing one door and one drawer	$1/2$
Base cabinet containing two doors and two drawers	$3/4$
Base corner cabinet	1
Broom closet	1
Drawer cabinet — four drawers	$1/2$
Oven cabinet	$1\ 1/4$
Sink cabinet	$1\ 1/2$
Wall cabinet — two doors (refrigerator cabinet)	$1/2$
Wall cabinet — two doors (standard height)	$1/2$
China case — corner unit with 36" front	2
Bathroom vanity — up to 84" long	2

Table 53-B. *Approximate Installation Times for Preformed Counter Tops.*

Counter Tops	Approximate Installation Time (Hours)
Preformed plastic laminate counter top	$3/4$ (per linear ft.)
25"-wide plastic laminate counter top with a 4" back splash and self edge.	1 (per linear ft.)
Preformed plastic laminate mitered corner (L- or U-shaped kitchen)	1
End cap on a preformed plastic laminate top	$1/3$

QUESTIONS

1. What are the five basic layouts commonly used in kitchen design?

2. List the kitchen work centers.

3. What is the standard height of the kitchen cabinet base unit?

4. When measuring along the kitchen wall for the installation of factory-built cabinets, how high off the floor are the dimensions taken?

5. Why are the dimensions taken at some point above the floor?

6. When installing factory-built base cabinets in a kitchen, which cabinets are installed first?

7. Other than ceramic tile, what is the most widely used material for kitchen cabinet counter top surfaces?

8. Name two basic mounting locations for drawer slides.

9. There are three types of cabinet hinges. Name two of them and tell how they are mounted.

ACTIVITIES

1. Social Studies. Assume that you are living in the United States in the 1820s, prior to the Industrial Revolution. You have an unlimited amount of money to use in building your own home. Design your own kitchen. Make it as modern as possible. Be careful not to place something in your kitchen that has not been developed yet.

2. Math. In a kitchen the range and sink are on adjacent walls. The refrigerator is on the wall opposite the sink. The distance from sink to range is 5'. The distance from sink to refrigerator is 8'6". The distance from range to refrigerator is 7'.

a. Sketch a possible arrangement of these work areas.

b. Discuss with a friend the strong and weak points of your plan.

3. Language Arts. You may have identified a career. However, you may wonder how you will be able to pay for the education or training you will need. For advice, you should consult your school guidance counselor. Many organizations offer scholarships, loans, and work-study programs. Individual states provide financial aid programs. The Federal government also provides several kinds of financial assistance to students.

Student loans are also available through banks and other private lenders. You should be able to identify the various types of financial institutions. A *commercial bank* offers the widest variety of loans.

Loans are also available from a *savings and loan institution*. Savings and loan institutions, however, often specialize in making loans for home mortgages.

Prepare a brief report in which you compare the services offered by banks with those offered by savings and loans.

THE SCHOOL-TO-WORK CONNECTION

The central position of most stairs makes the area under the stairs a particularly useful location for general storage.

1. Your client has three teenage children. Two of them are on baseball teams and the other one plays hockey. All three of them own in-line skates. However, the house you are remodeling for the family is short on storage space.

One stair in the house looks like the one shown in Fig. 52-28. Its treads are 10" wide and the risers are 7" high. The distance between the lowest riser and a wall to the right of the stairs is approximately 8'. Draw a sketch of this stair to scale. Then sketch custom cabinetry that would make good storage for sports gear. You will need the dimensions of the sporting gear.

54

Interior Trim and Interior Doors

One of the best ways to add character and individuality to a home is to detail the interior with trim. Careful trim carpentry is one of the hallmarks of high-quality building construction. Trim can be used in many places in the home.

It is most often used around doors, windows, and along walls and ceilings. The trim can be traditional or contemporary. Fig. 54-1. Standard patterns and shapes are readily available from local lumber dealers, allowing the development of many interesting designs with maximum economy. Fig. 54-2. However, special trim and trim accessories are also available. Fig. 54-3. Wood

moldings can also be used to create interesting effects over an entire wall. Figs. 54-4, 54-5, and 54-6.

MATERIALS

Interior doors, trim, and other millwork may be painted or given a natural finish with stain, varnish, or other nonpigmented material. The paint or natural finish desired for the woodwork in various rooms often determines the species of wood to be used. Woodwork to be painted should be smooth, close-grained, and free from pitch streaks. Some species having these qualities in a high degree include ponderosa pine, northern white pine, redwood, and spruce. When hardness and resistance to hard usage are additional requirements,

54-1a. *This room is accented by decorative door and window casing, ceiling trim, baseboard trim, and wainscoting.*

54-1b. *When corner blocks are used, baseboards may be cut with butt joints, instead of miter joints.*

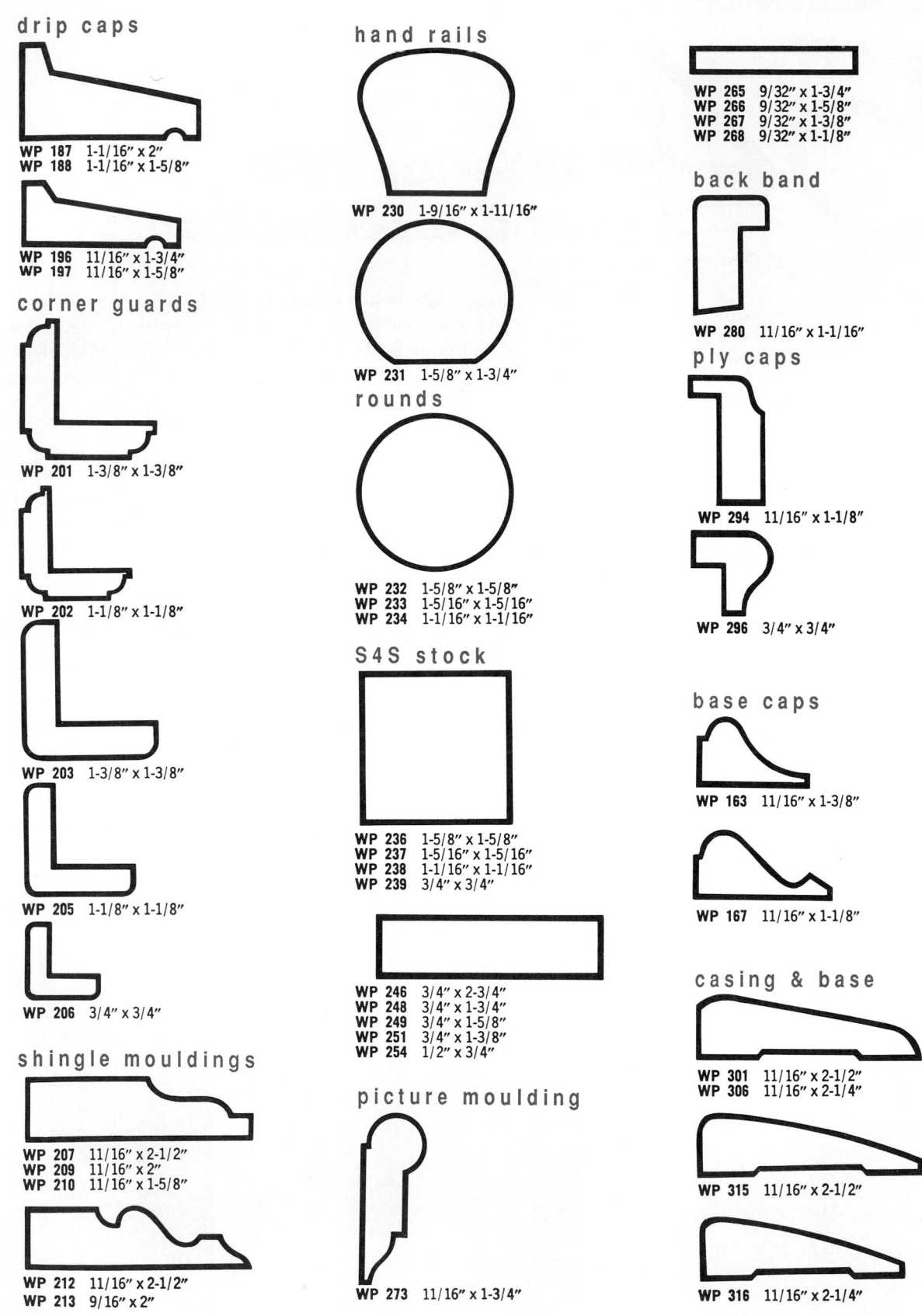

drip caps

WP 187 1-1/16" x 2"
WP 188 1-1/16" x 1-5/8"

WP 196 11/16" x 1-3/4"
WP 197 11/16" x 1-5/8"

corner guards

WP 201 1-3/8" x 1-3/8"

WP 202 1-1/8" x 1-1/8"

WP 203 1-3/8" x 1-3/8"

WP 205 1-1/8" x 1-1/8"

WP 206 3/4" x 3/4"

shingle mouldings

WP 207 11/16" x 2-1/2"
WP 209 11/16" x 2"
WP 210 11/16" x 1-5/8"

WP 212 11/16" x 2-1/2"
WP 213 9/16" x 2"

hand rails

WP 230 1-9/16" x 1-11/16"

WP 231 1-5/8" x 1-3/4"

rounds

WP 232 1-5/8" x 1-5/8"
WP 233 1-5/16" x 1-5/16"
WP 234 1-1/16" x 1-1/16"

S4S stock

WP 236 1-5/8" x 1-5/8"
WP 237 1-5/16" x 1-5/16"
WP 238 1-1/16" x 1-1/16"
WP 239 3/4" x 3/4"

WP 246 3/4" x 2-3/4"
WP 248 3/4" x 1-3/4"
WP 249 3/4" x 1-5/8"
WP 251 3/4" x 1-3/8"
WP 254 1/2" x 3/4"

picture moulding

WP 273 11/16" x 1-3/4"

WP 265 9/32" x 1-3/4"
WP 266 9/32" x 1-5/8"
WP 267 9/32" x 1-3/8"
WP 268 9/32" x 1-1/8"

back band

WP 280 11/16" x 1-1/16"

ply caps

WP 294 11/16" x 1-1/8"

WP 296 3/4" x 3/4"

base caps

WP 163 11/16" x 1-3/8"

WP 167 11/16" x 1-1/8"

casing & base

WP 301 11/16" x 2-1/2"
WP 306 11/16" x 2-1/4"

WP 315 11/16" x 2-1/2"

WP 316 11/16" x 2-1/4"

54-2. *A variety of wood molding styles.*

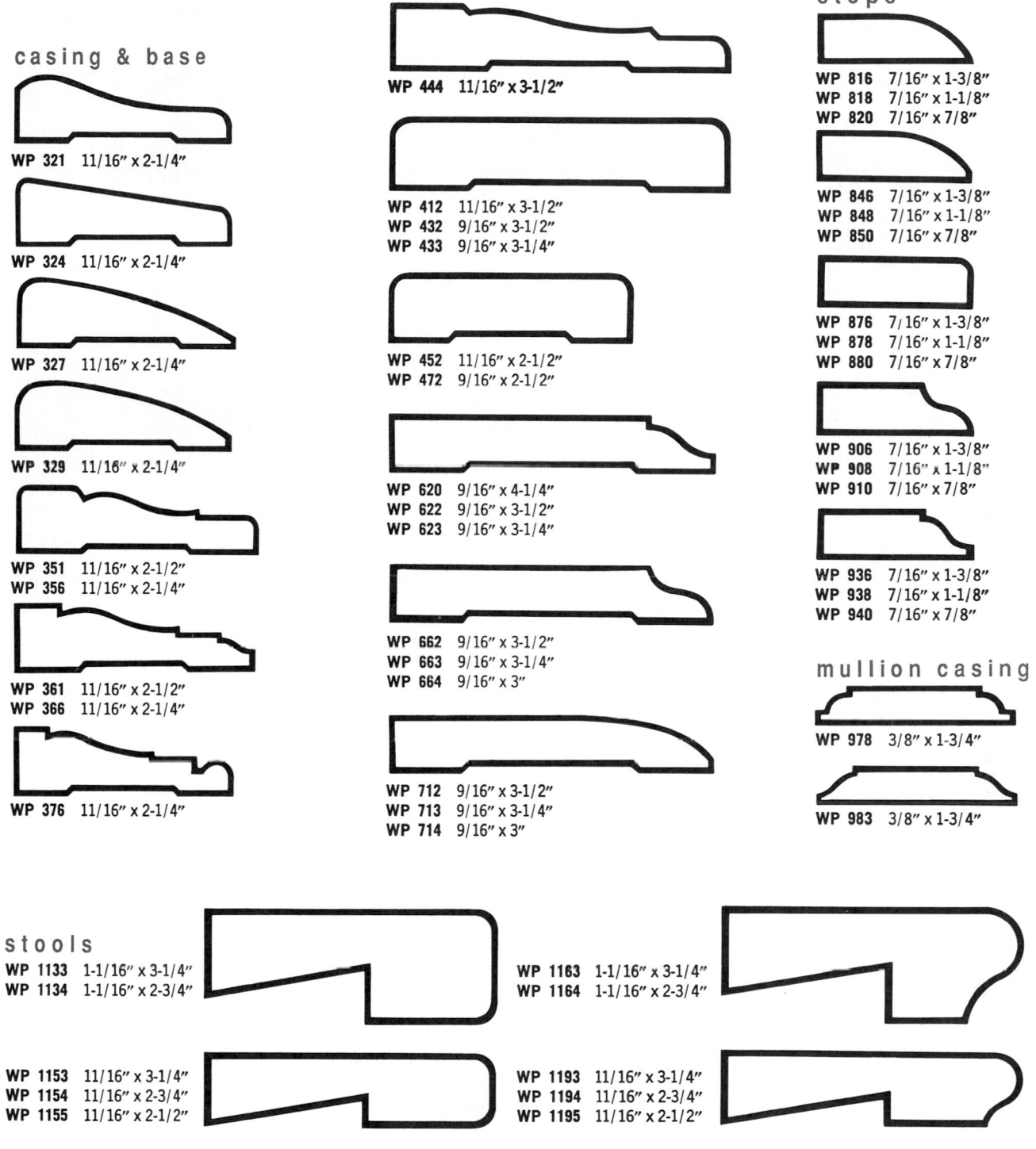

casing & base

WP 321 11/16" x 2-1/4"

WP 324 11/16" x 2-1/4"

WP 327 11/16" x 2-1/4"

WP 329 11/16" x 2-1/4"

WP 351 11/16" x 2-1/2"
WP 356 11/16" x 2-1/4"

WP 361 11/16" x 2-1/2"
WP 366 11/16" x 2-1/4"

WP 376 11/16" x 2-1/4"

WP 444 11/16" x 3-1/2"

WP 412 11/16" x 3-1/2"
WP 432 9/16" x 3-1/2"
WP 433 9/16" x 3-1/4"

WP 452 11/16" x 2-1/2"
WP 472 9/16" x 2-1/2"

WP 620 9/16" x 4-1/4"
WP 622 9/16" x 3-1/2"
WP 623 9/16" x 3-1/4"

WP 662 9/16" x 3-1/2"
WP 663 9/16" x 3-1/4"
WP 664 9/16" x 3"

WP 712 9/16" x 3-1/2"
WP 713 9/16" x 3-1/4"
WP 714 9/16" x 3"

stops

WP 816 7/16" x 1-3/8"
WP 818 7/16" x 1-1/8"
WP 820 7/16" x 7/8"

WP 846 7/16" x 1-3/8"
WP 848 7/16" x 1-1/8"
WP 850 7/16" x 7/8"

WP 876 7/16" x 1-3/8"
WP 878 7/16" x 1-1/8"
WP 880 7/16" x 7/8"

WP 906 7/16" x 1-3/8"
WP 908 7/16" x 1-1/8"
WP 910 7/16" x 7/8"

WP 936 7/16" x 1-3/8"
WP 938 7/16" x 1-1/8"
WP 940 7/16" x 7/8"

mullion casing

WP 978 3/8" x 1-3/4"

WP 983 3/8" x 1-3/4"

stools
WP 1133 1-1/16" x 3-1/4"
WP 1134 1-1/16" x 2-3/4"

WP 1153 11/16" x 3-1/4"
WP 1154 11/16" x 2-3/4"
WP 1155 11/16" x 2-1/2"

WP 1163 1-1/16" x 3-1/4"
WP 1164 1-1/16" x 2-3/4"

WP 1193 11/16" x 3-1/4"
WP 1194 11/16" x 2-3/4"
WP 1195 11/16" x 2-1/2"

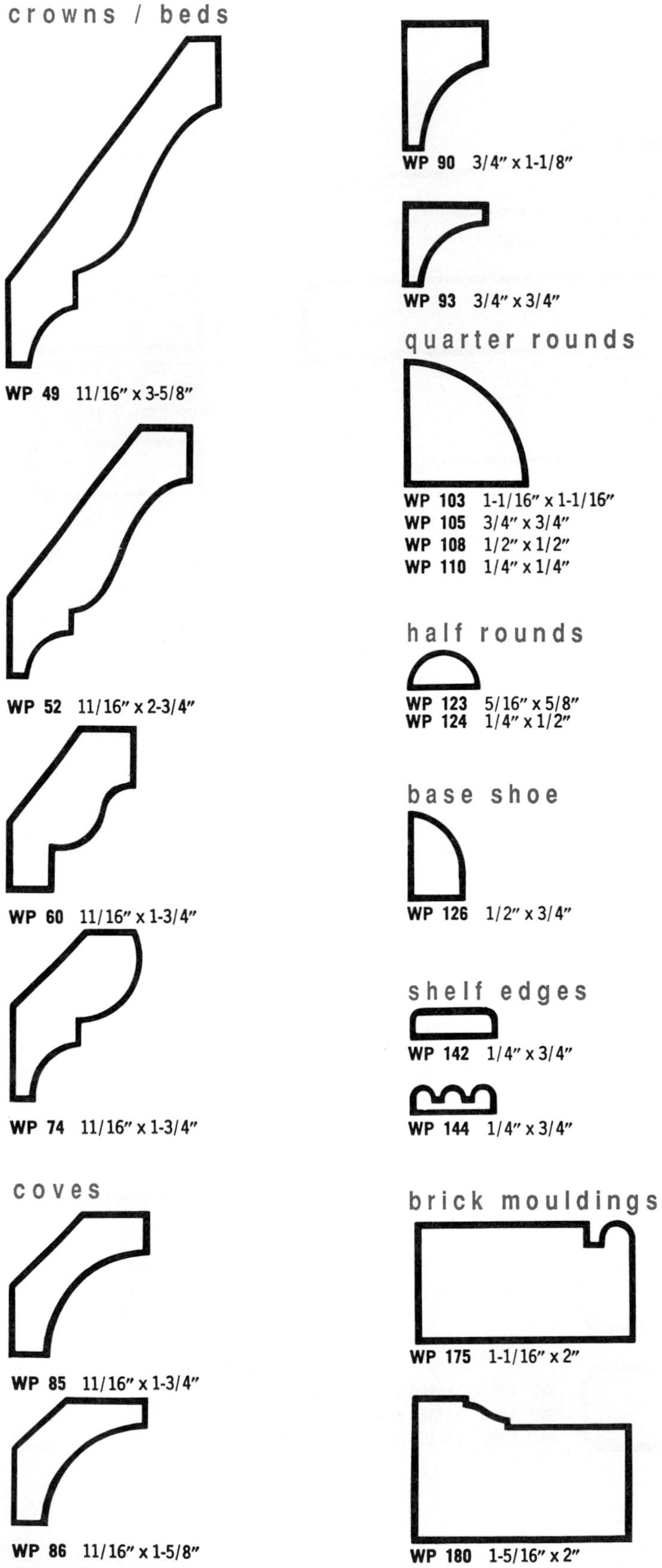

crowns / beds

WP 49 11/16" x 3-5/8"

WP 52 11/16" x 2-3/4"

WP 60 11/16" x 1-3/4"

WP 74 11/16" x 1-3/4"

coves

WP 85 11/16" x 1-3/4"

WP 86 11/16" x 1-5/8"

WP 90 3/4" x 1-1/8"

WP 93 3/4" x 3/4"

quarter rounds

WP 103 1-1/16" x 1-1/16"
WP 105 3/4" x 3/4"
WP 108 1/2" x 1/2"
WP 110 1/4" x 1/4"

half rounds

WP 123 5/16" x 5/8"
WP 124 1/4" x 1/2"

base shoe

WP 126 1/2" x 3/4"

shelf edges

WP 142 1/4" x 3/4"

WP 144 1/4" x 3/4"

brick mouldings

WP 175 1-1/16" x 2"

WP 180 1-5/16" x 2"

54-2. *(cont.) A variety of wood molding styles.*

54-3a. *Specialty trim includes rosettes, corner blocks, and baseboards with unusual profiles.*

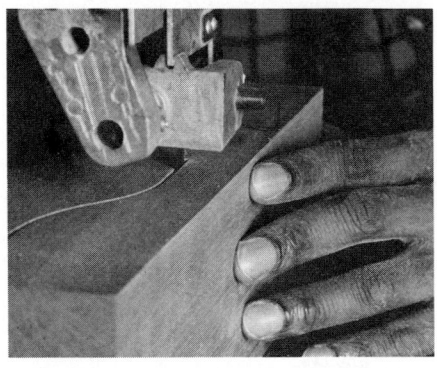

54-3b. *Some specialty trim is custom made. These blocks are being cut on a band saw.*

species such as birch or yellow poplar may be used.

When the finish is to be natural, a pleasing figure, hardness, and uniform color are usually desirable. Species with these qualities include ash, birch, cherry, maple, oak, and walnut. Some require staining for best appearance.

The recommended moisture content for interior trim varies from 6 to 11 percent, depending on climate. The average moisture content for various parts of the United States is shown in Fig. 54-7.

Most trim used in residential construction is solid hardwood or softwood, but other materials are increasingly used as well. Some manufacturers offer finger-jointed ponderosa pine stock that has been

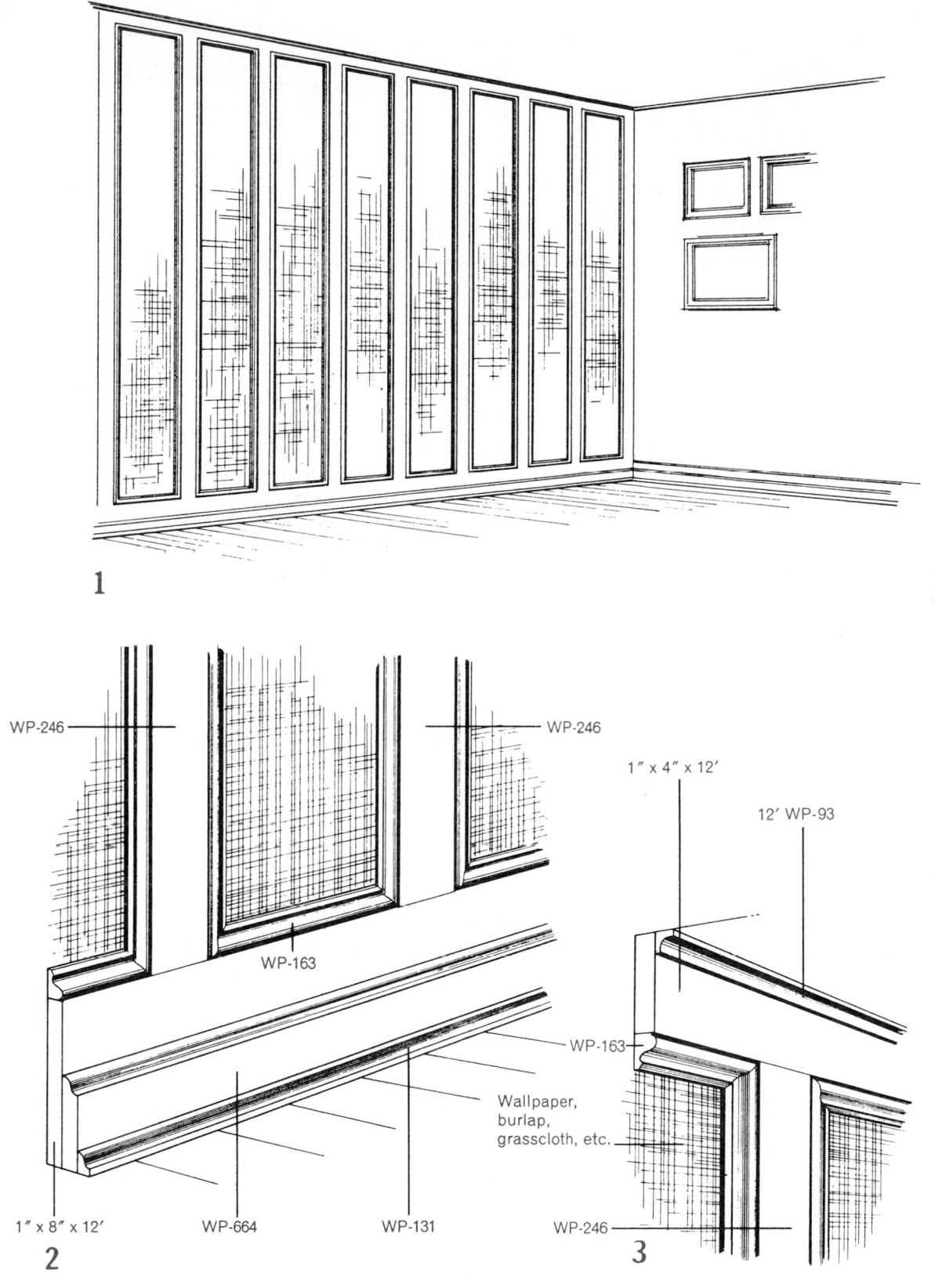

54-4. *Wood moldings used with wallpaper or fabric: 1. A wall enriched with moldings in a traditional design. 2. Base detail. 3. Ceiling detail.*

1 Spanish Wall & Divider

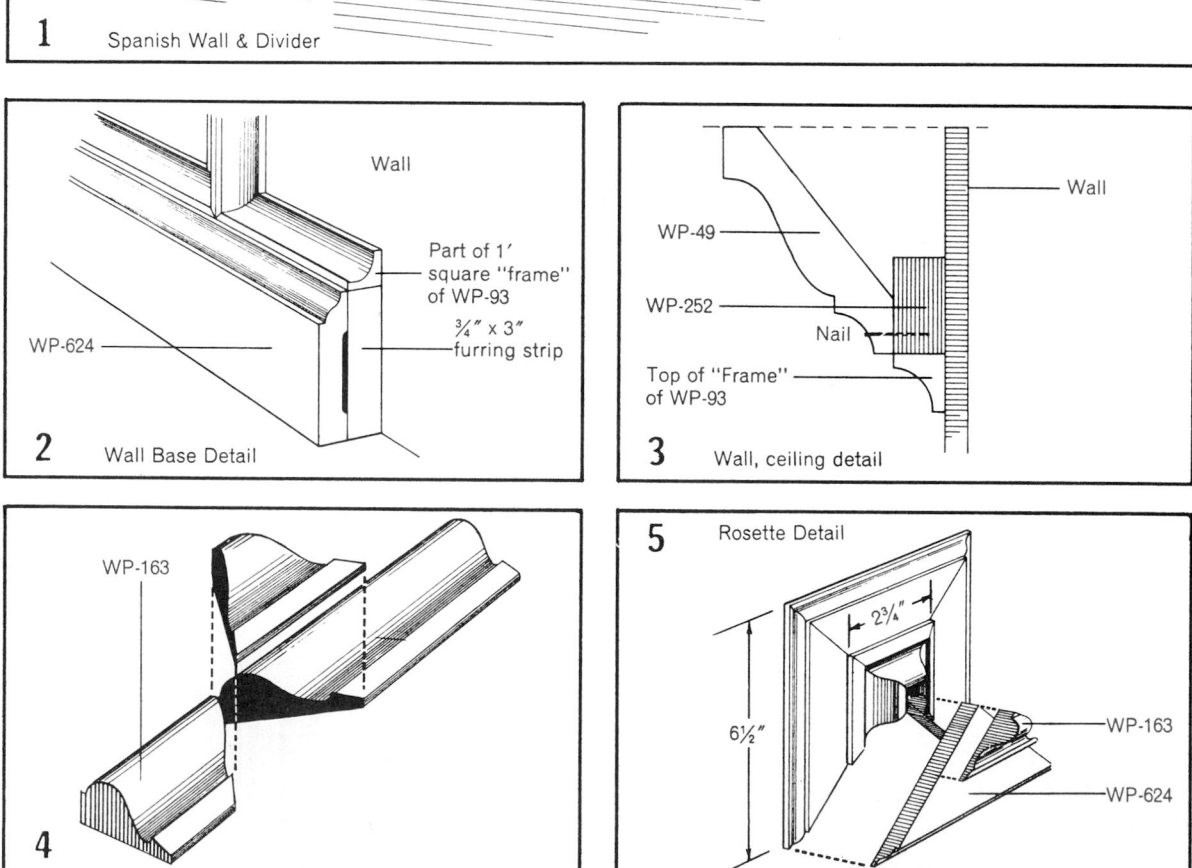

Wall

Part of 1'
square "frame"
of WP-93

¾" x 3"
furring strip

WP-624

2 Wall Base Detail

WP-49

WP-252

Nail

Wall

Top of "Frame"
of WP-93

3 Wall, ceiling detail

WP-163

4

5 Rosette Detail

2¾"

6½"

WP-163

WP-624

54-5a. *Moldings and woodwork are used to give this wall and room divider a Spanish motif: 1. Spanish wall and divider. 2. Wall base detail. 3. Wall, ceiling detail. 4. Cutting miters in the molding to make the rosettes. 5. Rosette detail.*

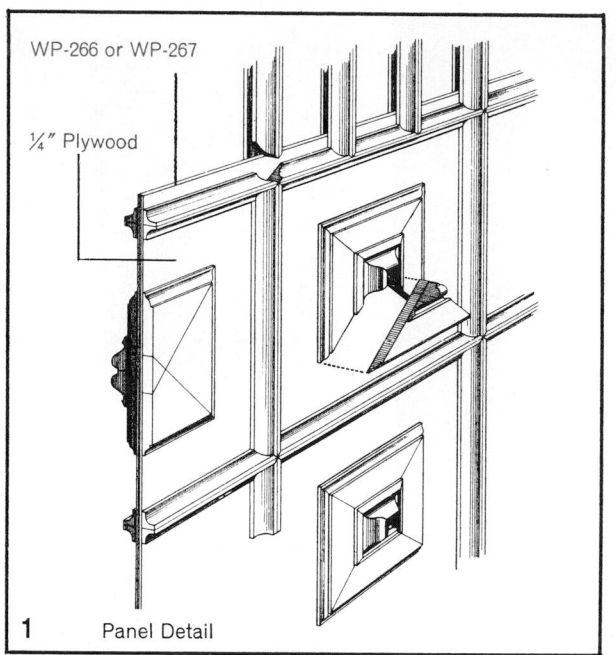

1 Panel Detail

WP-266 or WP-267

¼" Plywood

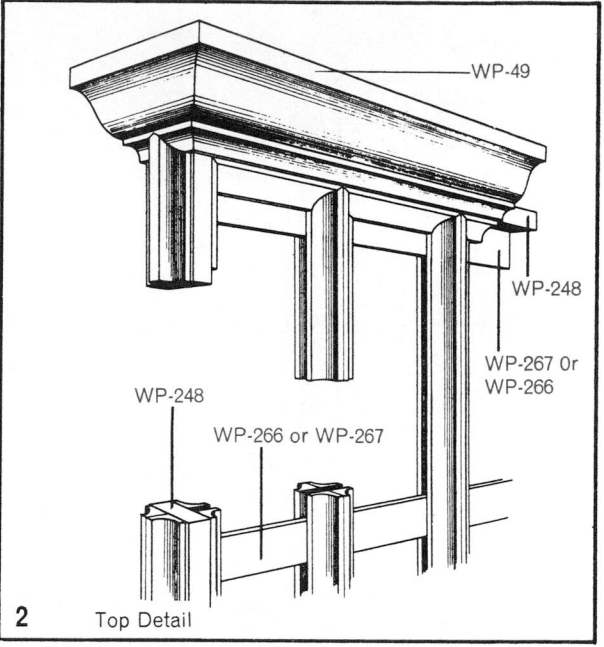

2 Top Detail

WP-49

WP-248

WP-267 Or WP-266

WP-248

WP-266 or WP-267

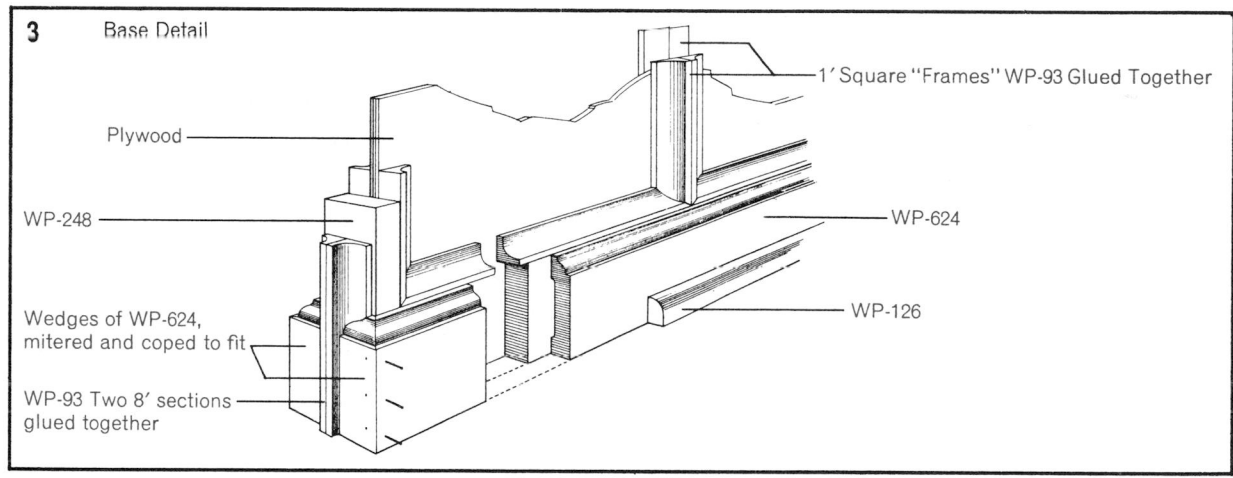

3 Base Detail

1' Square "Frames" WP-93 Glued Together

Plywood

WP-248

WP-624

Wedges of WP-624, mitered and coped to fit

WP-126

WP-93 Two 8' sections glued together

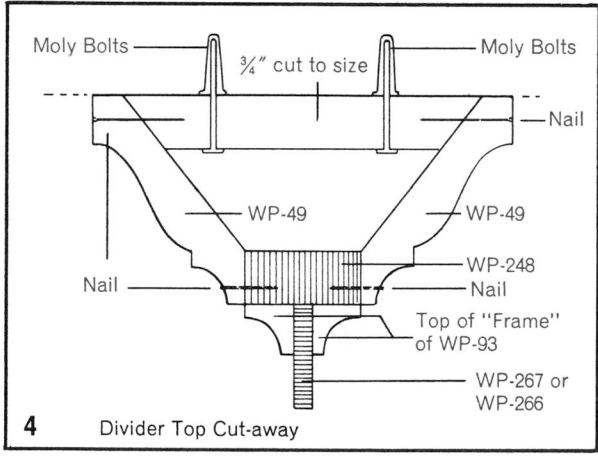

Moly Bolts

¾" cut to size

Moly Bolts

Nail

WP-49

WP-49

WP-248

Nail

Nail

Top of "Frame" of WP-93

WP-267 or WP-266

4 Divider Top Cut-away

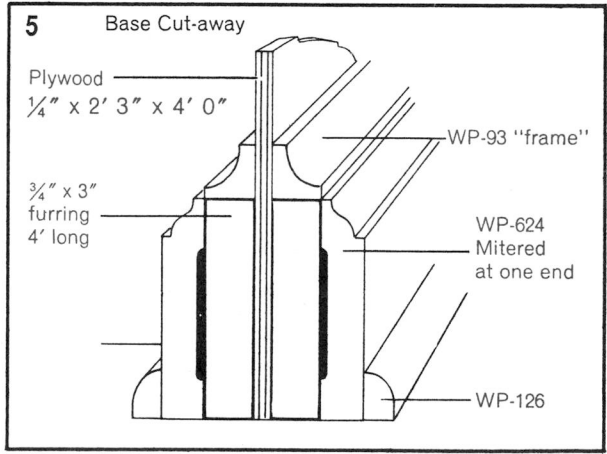

5 Base Cut-away

Plywood
¼" x 2' 3" x 4' 0"

WP-93 "frame"

¾" x 3" furring 4' long

WP-624 Mitered at one end

WP-126

54-5b. *Details for the room divider shown in Fig. 54-5a: 1. Panel details. 2. Top detail. 3. Base detail. 4. Top cutaway. 5. Base cutaway.*

54-6. Wood moldings added to an ordinary room divider will give a room a new focal point and added interest.

54-8. Finger-jointed pine window casing with a red oak veneer.

54-9a. The ceiling trim in this room is a synthetic product.

54-9b. Detail of the dentil molding shown in Fig. 54-9a.

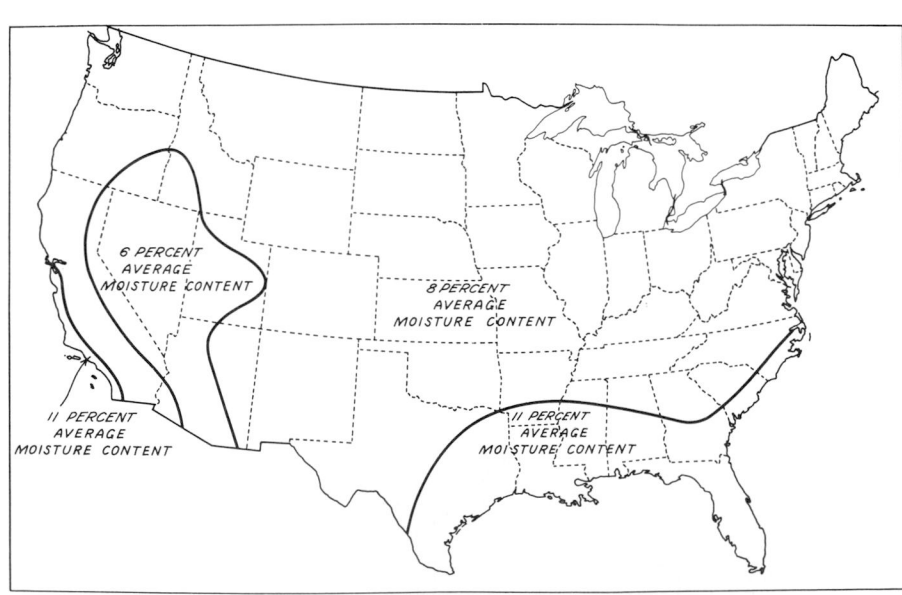

54-7. Recommended average moisture content for interior wood trim in various parts of the United States. In Canada the recommended moisture contents are as follows: Vancouver, 11%; Saskatoon, 7%; Ottawa, 8%; Halifax, 9%. (These cities represent four major geographical areas.)

veneered with one of several hardwoods. This allows the use of short lengths of pine that would otherwise become scrap. The trim can be finished as if it were solid oak. Fig. 54-8.

Other manufacturers produce trim made from synthetic materials. These materials can be cut and nailed with standard tools and techniques. They are usually painted. Fig. 54-9.

INTERIOR DOOR AND WINDOW TRIM

After interior wall covering has been applied and the finish floor laid, all floor and wall surfaces should be scraped clean and free of any irregularities. Mark the location of all wall studs lightly on the floor or wall. Usually the marks are placed on the floor because the interior wall covering may be a finished surface.

Door and window frames are usually trimmed first to allow other trim such as base moldings or wall moldings to be properly fitted between the door and window casings. Cabinets, built-in bookcases, fireplace mantels, and other millwork items are also installed at this time.

Doorframes

Rough openings in the stud walls for interior doors are usually framed out to be 3" more than the door height and 2½" more than the door width. This provides room for plumbing and leveling the frame in the opening. Interior doorframes are made up of two side jambs and a head jamb and include stop moldings which the door closes against. One-piece jambs are the most common. Fig. 54-10. They may be obtained in 5¼" widths for plaster walls and 4½" widths for walls with ½" dry-wall finish. Two- and three-piece adjustable jambs are also available. Fig. 54-11. Their chief advantage is in being adaptable to different wall thicknesses.

Some manufacturers produce interior doorframes with the door fitted and prehung, ready for installation. Application of the casing completes the job. When used with two- or three-piece jambs, casings are installed at the factory. Figs. 54-12 and 54-13.

Doorframe Installation.

When the frames and doors are not assembled and prefitted, the side jambs should be nailed through the notch into the head jamb with three 7d or 8d coated nails. Fig. 54-10. Cut a spreader to a length exactly equal to the distance

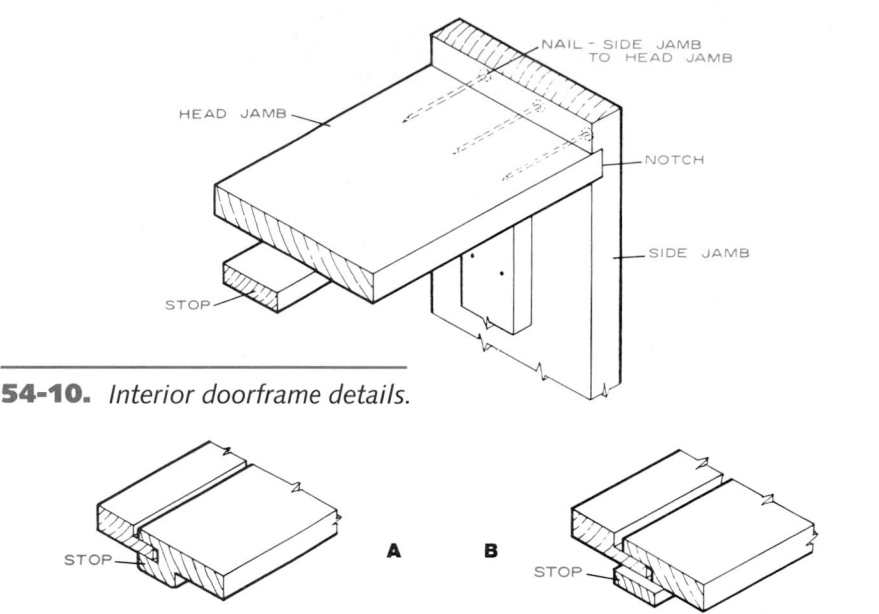

54-10. *Interior doorframe details.*

54-11. *Adjustable doorjambs: A. Two-piece adjustable jamb. B. Three-piece adjustable jamb. Two- and three-piece adjustable doorjambs adapt to various wall thicknesses.*

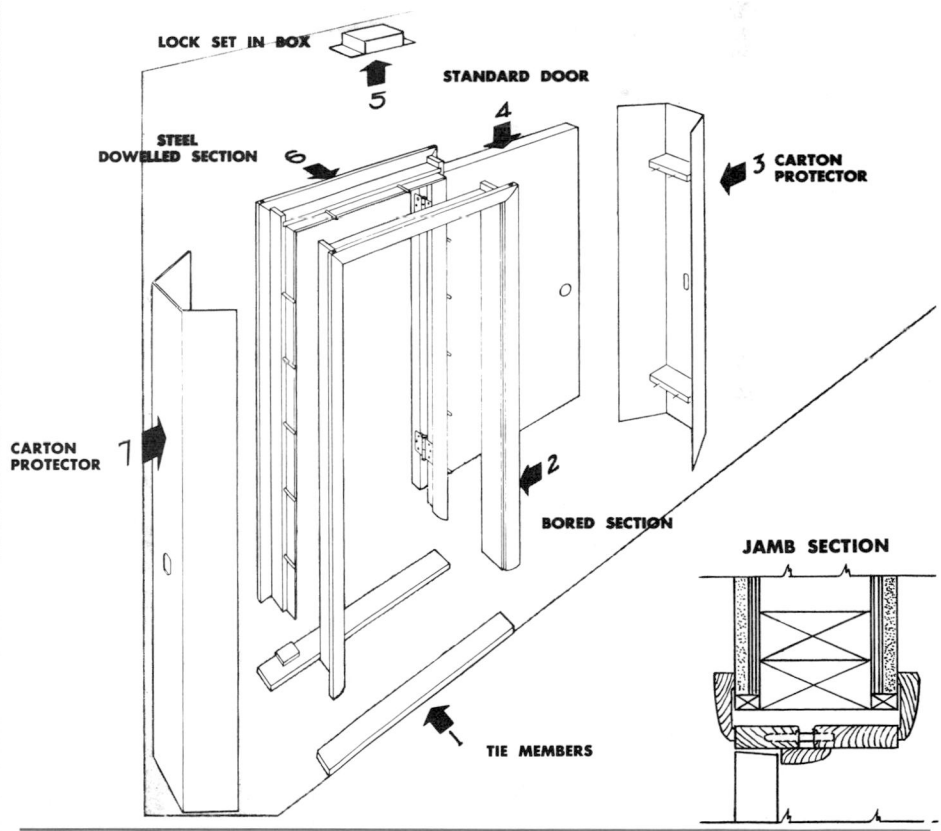

54-12a. *This prehung door has a two-piece jamb with pins for alignment behind the doorstop. The jamb can be adjusted to slight variations in wall thickness. However, when ordering a prehung door unit, be sure to specify the wall thickness. The manufacturer of this unit recommends a 2" allowance in width and height over the nominal door size for the rough stud opening. The height is figured from the finished floor.*

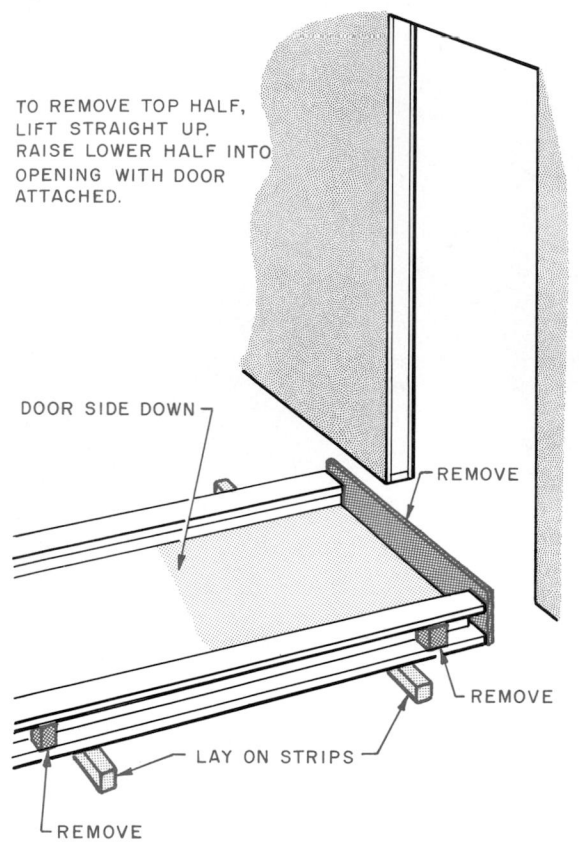

TO REMOVE TOP HALF,
LIFT STRAIGHT UP.
RAISE LOWER HALF INTO
OPENING WITH DOOR
ATTACHED.

DOOR SIDE DOWN

REMOVE

REMOVE

LAY ON STRIPS

REMOVE

54-12b. *Details for installing the door unit shown in Fig. 54-12a.*

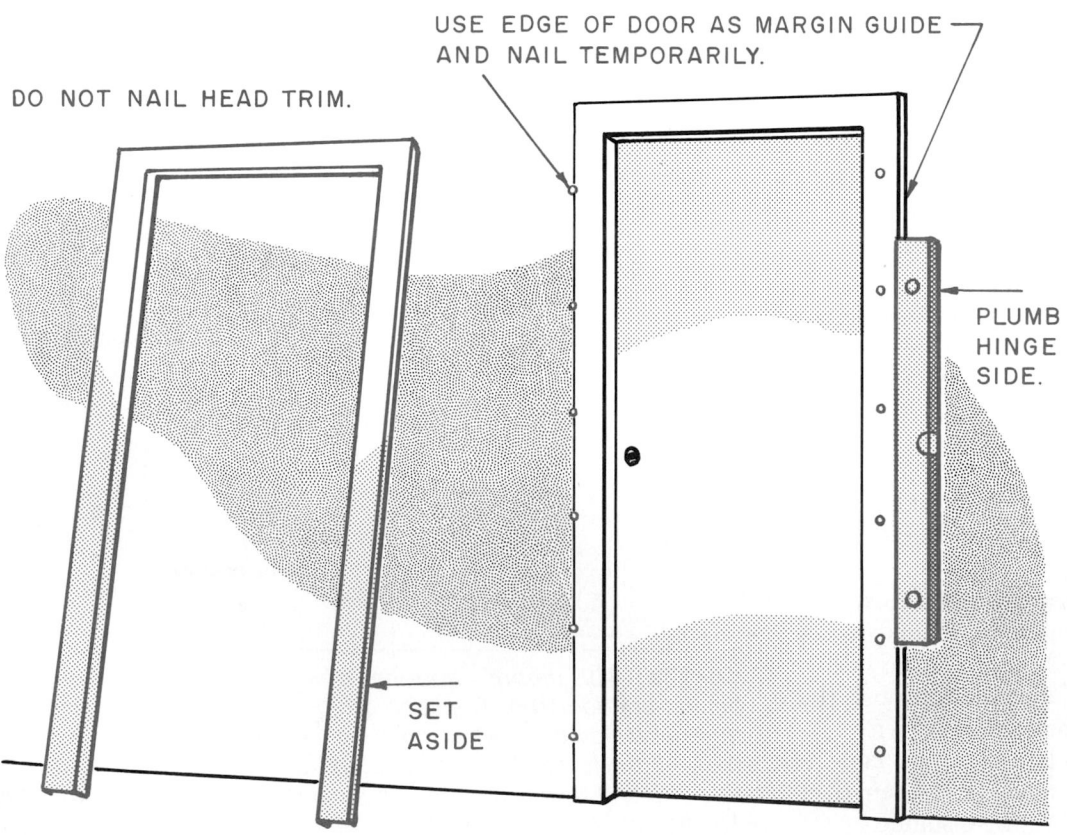

DO NOT NAIL HEAD TRIM.

USE EDGE OF DOOR AS MARGIN GUIDE
AND NAIL TEMPORARILY.

PLUMB
HINGE
SIDE.

SET
ASIDE

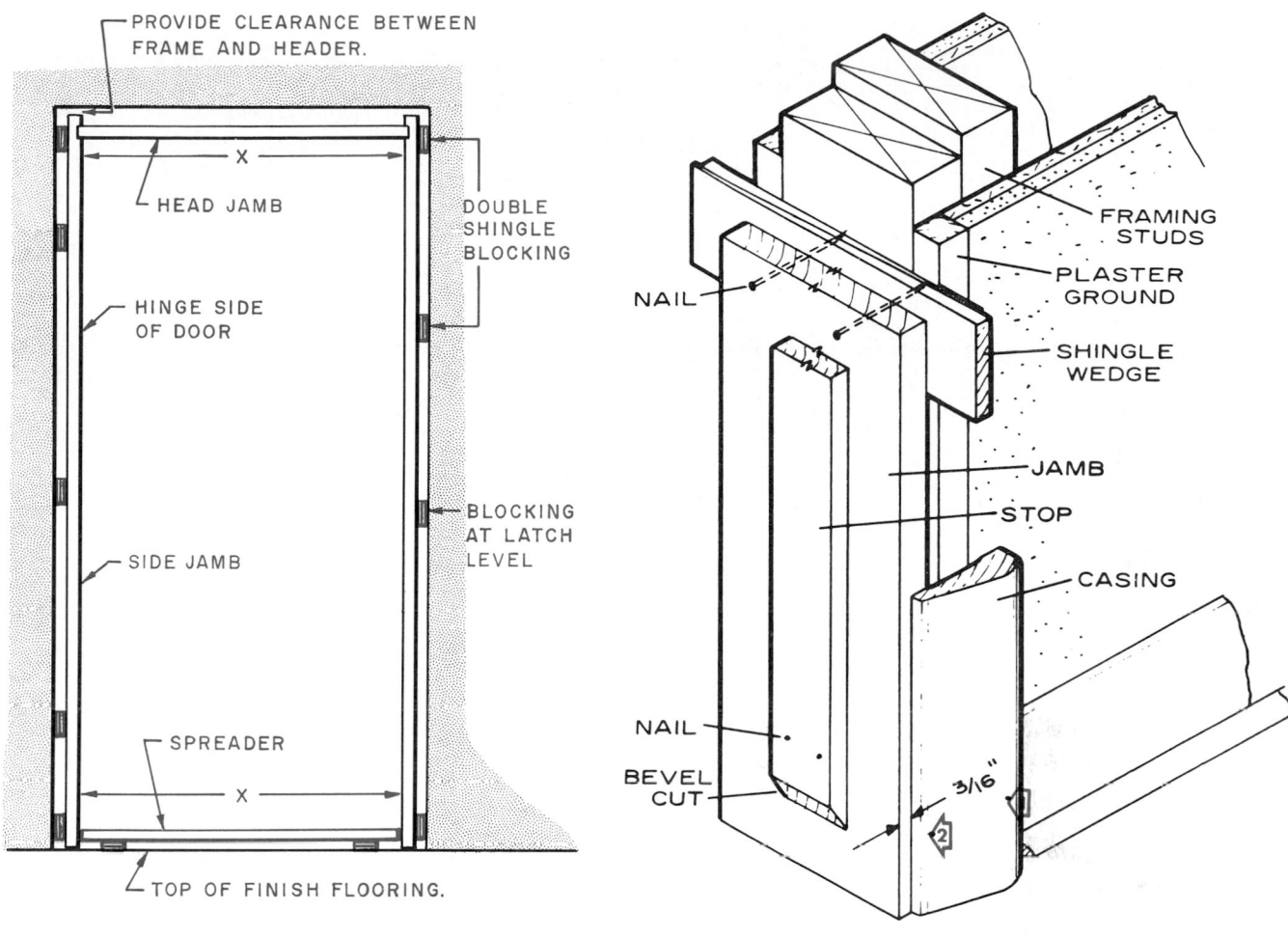

54-14. Cut the spreader equal to the distance (X) between the side jambs just below the head jamb. Place the spreader at the floorline to hold the side jambs parallel.

54-15. Doorframe and trim installation details. Use a 6d or 7d finish nail at arrow 1 to nail through the casing into the wall stud. At arrow 2, use a 4d or 5d finish nail to fasten the casing to the jamb.

between the jambs at the head jamb. Fig. 54-14.

The assembled frame is fastened in the rough opening by shingle wedges placed between the side jamb and the stud. Fig. 54-15. One jamb, usually the hinge jamb, is plumbed using four or five sets of shingle wedges for the height of the frame. Two 8d finishing nails are installed at each wedged area, one driven so the doorstop will cover it. Fig. 54-15.

Place the spreader in position at the floor line. Fig. 54-14. Fasten the opposite side jamb in place with shingle wedges and finishing

nails, using the first jamb as a guide in keeping a uniform width. This can be done by using a second precut spreader as a gauge, checking several points, or by carefully measuring at various points along the height of the doorframe between the side jambs.

Door Trim

Door trim, or *casing*, is nailed around interior door openings and is also used to finish the room side of windows and exterior doorframes. The most commonly used casings vary in width from

2¼" to 3½", depending on the style. Thicknesses vary from ½" to ¾", although ¹¹⁄₁₆" is standard in many of the narrow-line patterns. Two of the more common patterns are shown in Fig. 54-16.

Door Trim Installation.
Casings are nailed to both the jamb and the framing studs or header, allowing about a ³⁄₁₆" edge distance from the face of the jamb. Fig. 54-15. Finish or casing nails either 6d or 7d, depending on the thickness of the casing, are used to nail into the stud. Arrow 1, Fig. 54-15. Fourpenny or 5d finishing

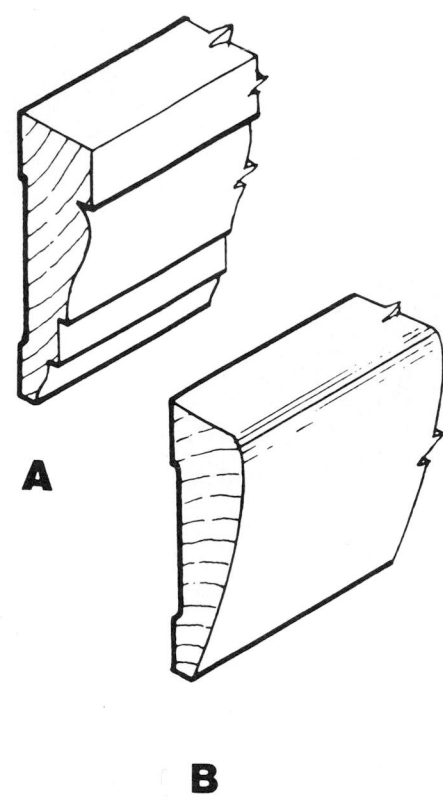

A

B

54-16. *Two common casings used for interior trim: A. Colonial. B. Ranch casing (sometimes called clamshell).*

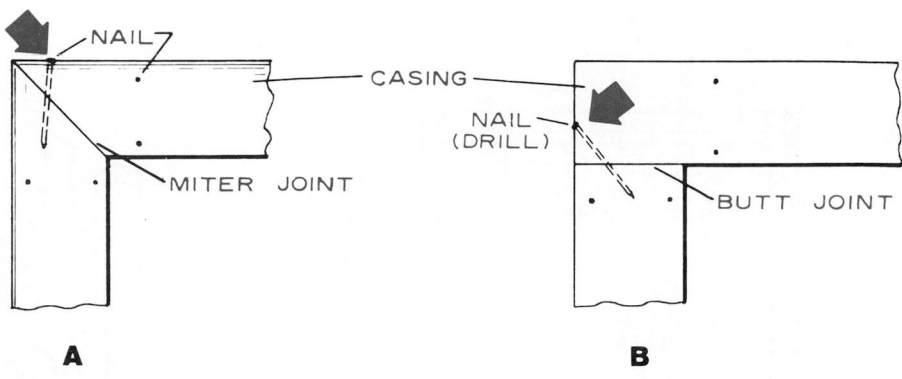

A **B**

54-17a. *A. Molding casing must have a mitered joint at the corner. B. Square-edge casing may be joined with a butt joint. In both cases, the joints may be reinforced by nailing at the arrows.*

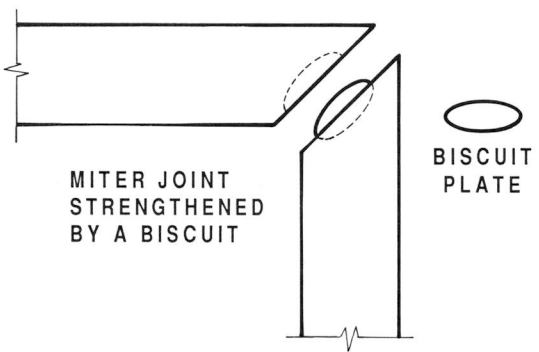

MITER JOINT
STRENGTHENED
BY A BISCUIT

BISCUIT
PLATE

54-17b. *Any joint can be strengthened with a wood biscuit that is glued in place. A slot for the biscuit is cut by a biscuit joiner machine.*

54-17c. *A biscuit joiner machine.*

nails or 1½" brads are used to fasten the thinner edge of the casing to the jamb. Arrow 2, Fig. 54-15. With hardwood, it is advisable to predrill to prevent splitting. Nails in the casing are located in pairs and spaced about 16" apart along the full height of the opening and at the head jamb. Fig. 54-15.

Casing with a molded shape must have mitered corner joints. A, Fig. 54-17. When casing is square-edged, a butt joint may be made at the junction of the side and head casing. B, Fig. 54-17. If the moisture content of the casing is well above the recommended amount, a mitered joint may open slightly at the outer edge as the material dries. This can be minimized by installing a small glued spline at the corner of the

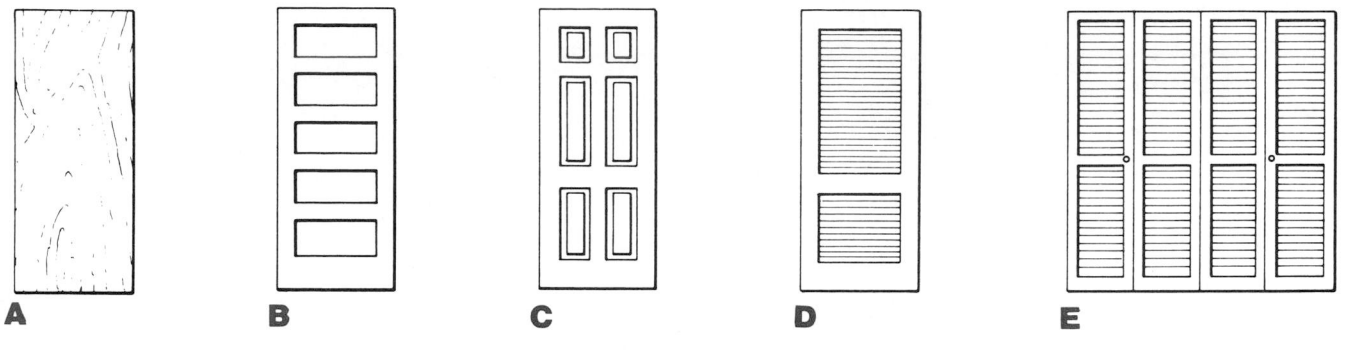

54-18. *Interior doors: A. Flush. B. Panel (5-cross). C. Panel (Colonial). D. Louvered. E. Folding (louvered).*

mitered joint. Actually, use of a spline joint under any moisture condition is considered good practice. Some prefitted jamb, door, and casing units are provided with splined joints. Nailing into the joint after drilling will aid in retaining a close fit.

Many trim carpenters prefer to use biscuit joints, which are similar to spline joints. A biscuit joiner machine is used to cut a shallow groove in both pieces to be joined. Fig. 54-18. A small, semicircular wood spline, called a "biscuit," is inserted into the groove and glued in place. The biscuit is made of compressed beech and has grooves pressed into it that hold the glue. When the joint is brought together, the biscuit absorbs moisture from the glue and expands slightly, forming a tight joint. Biscuits are supplied by various manufacturers. They are available in three standard sizes. Table 54-A.

Table 54-A. *Standard Sizes of Biscuit Joints.*

Biscuit Size	Dimension of Groove*
#0	$5/8$" wide x 1 $3/4$" long
#10	$3/4$" wide x 2 $1/8$" long
#20	1" wide x 2 $1/2$" long

* Lengths are approximate.

The door opening is now complete except for fitting and securing the hardware and nailing the stops in proper position.

Interior Doors

As in exterior door styles, the two general interior types are the flush and the panel. Bifold and sliding door units might be flush or louvered. Most standard interior doors are $1\frac{3}{8}$" thick. Folding and sliding doors are usually $1\frac{1}{8}$" thick.

The flush interior door is usually made up of a hollow core of light framework faced with thin plywood or hardboard. A, Fig. 54-18. Plywood-faced flush doors may be obtained in gum, birch, oak, mahogany, and woods of other species, most of which are suitable for natural finish. Nonselected grades are usually painted, as are hardboard-faced doors.

The panel door consists of solid stiles (vertical side members), rails (crosspieces), and panels of various types. The five-cross panel and the Colonial panel doors are perhaps the most common of this style. B and C, Fig. 54-18. The louvered door is also popular and is commonly used for closets because it provides some ventilation. D, Fig. 54-18. Sliding or folding doors are installed in openings for

wardrobes. These are usually flush or louvered. E, Fig. 54-18.

Common *minimum* widths for single interior doors are as follows:

➤ Bedrooms and other habitable rooms—2'6".

➤ Bathrooms—2'4".

➤ Small closets and linen closets—2'.

These sizes can vary a great deal. Sliding doors or folding door units, used for wardrobes, may be 6' or more in width. However, in most cases, the jamb, stop, and casing parts are still used to frame and finish the opening. The standard interior door height is 6'8".

Hinged doors should open or swing in the direction of natural entry, against a blank wall whenever possible. They should not be obstructed by other swinging doors. Doors should never be hinged to swing into a hallway. The door swing is designated as either right or left hand. A right-hand door is one in which the latch is on the right when a person faces a closed door on the hinge side. A left-hand door is one in which the latch is on the left when a person faces a closed door on the hinge side. Fig. 54-19.

Interior Door Installation. Interior doors are normally hung with two $3\frac{1}{2}$" $\times$ $3\frac{1}{2}$" loose-pin butt

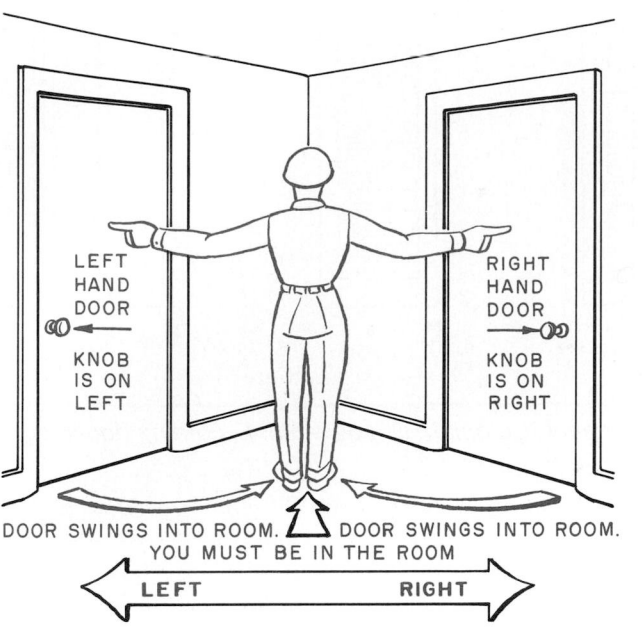

54-19. *Determining the hand of a door. When standing at the hinge side of the door, with the door closed, the knob is on the left for a left-hand door. For a right-hand door, the knob is on the right.*

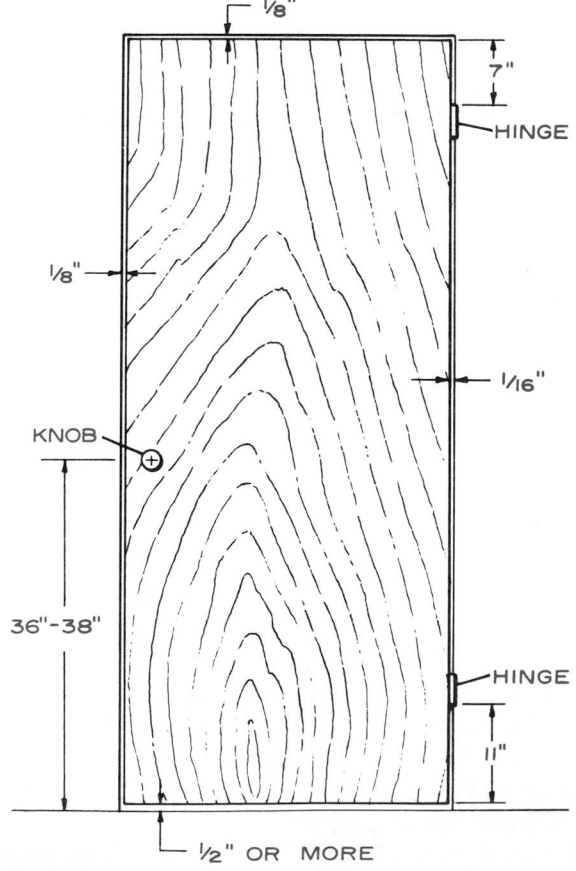

54-20. *Door clearance.*

hinges. The door is fitted into the opening with the clearances shown in Fig. 54-20. The clearance and location of hinges, lock set, and doorknob may vary somewhat, but the dimensions in Fig. 54-20 are generally accepted and conform to most millwork standards. The edge of the lock stile should be beveled slightly to permit the door to clear the jamb when swung open. See "Fitting a Door" in Unit 44. If the door is to swing across heavy carpeting, the bottom clearance should be increased.

When fitting doors, the stops are usually temporarily nailed in place until the door has been hung. Stops for doors in single piece jambs are generally ⁷⁄₁₆" thick and may be ¾" to 2¼" wide. They are installed with mitered joints at the junction of the side and head jambs. A 45° bevel cut at the bottom of the stop, about l" to 1½" above the finished floor line, will eliminate a dirt pocket and make cleaning or refinishing the floor easier. Fig. 54-15. Review "Fitting a Door" and "Hanging a Door," Unit 44.

Door Hardware

Hardware for doors is made in a number of finishes. Brass, bronze, and nickel are perhaps the most common. There are three kinds of door sets:

➤ Entry locks for exterior doors.

➤ Bathroom sets (inside lock control with safety slot for opening from the outside).

➤ Passage set (without lock). Fig. 54-21.

Hinges. Use two or three hinges for interior doors. Three hinges reduce the possibility of warpage and are useful on doors that lead to unheated attics or on wider and heavier doors.

Loose-pin butt hinges should be used. They must be the proper size for the door they will support. For

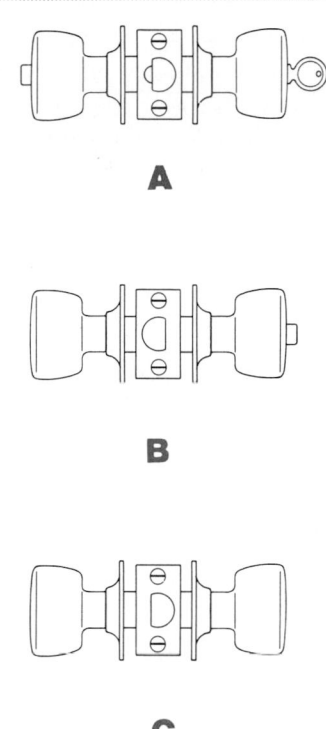

A

B

C

54-21. *Door sets: A. Exterior lock. Push button locks the outside knob, and a key is needed to unlock it. B. Bathroom or privacy door lock. Push button locks the outside knob. An emergency key may be used to unlock the door from the outside. C. Passage door lock. Neither knob locks.*

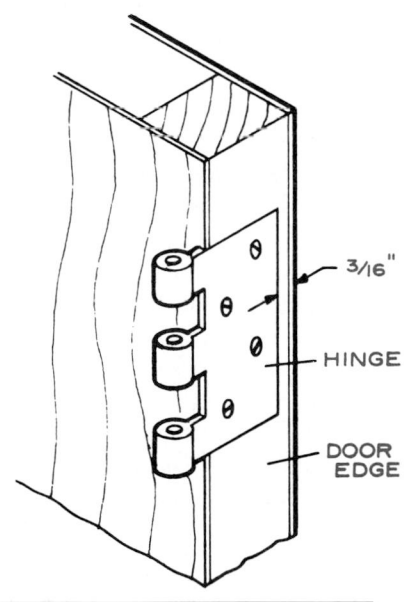

54-22. *Installation of the door hinge.*

$1\frac{3}{8}$" interior doors, choose $3\frac{1}{2}$" butts. After the door is fitted to the framed opening, with the proper clearances, hinge halves are fitted to the door. They are routed into the door edge with a back distance of about $\frac{3}{16}$". Fig. 54-22.

Locks. Types of door locks differ with regard to installation, cost, and the amount of labor required to set them. Follow the installation instructions supplied with the lock set. Some types require drilling of the edge and face of the door and routing of the edge to accommodate the lock set and faceplate. A, Fig. 54-23. A more common bored type is much easier to install. It requires only one hole drilled in the edge and one in the face of the door. B, Fig. 54-23. Boring jigs and faceplate markers are available to provide accurate installation. Locks should be installed so that the doorknob is 36" to 38" above the floor line. Most sets come with paper templates marking the location of the lock and size of the holes to be drilled. See "Installing a Lock Set," Unit 44.

Strike Plate. The strike plate, which is routed into the doorjamb, holds the door in place by contact

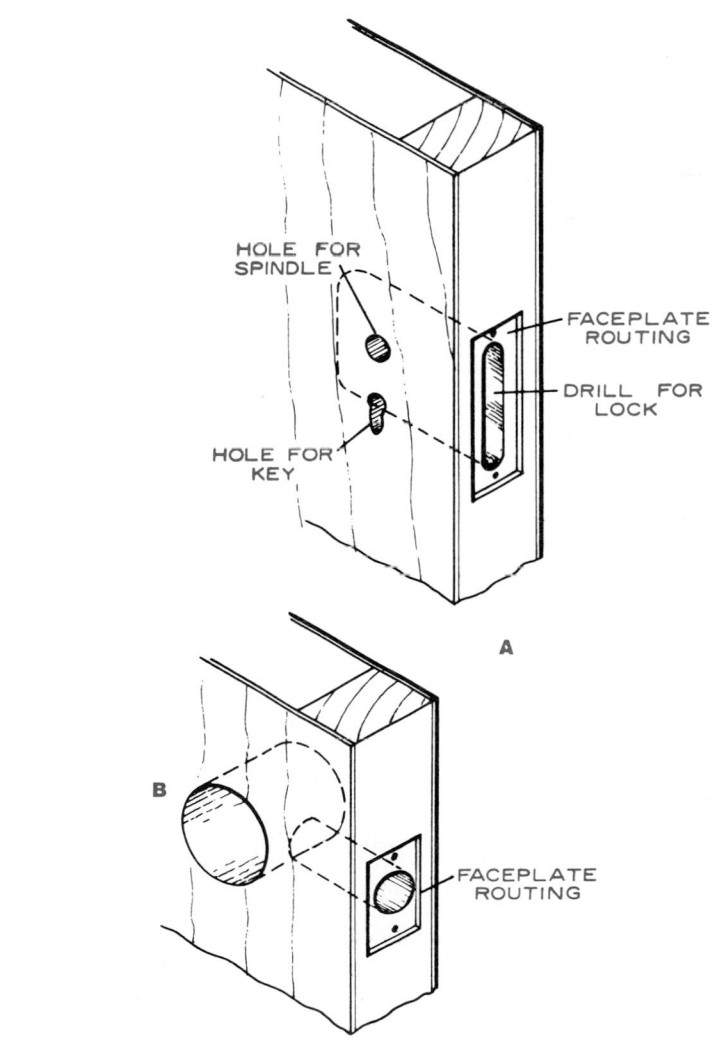

54-23. *Installation of lock set: A. Mortise lock. B. Bored lock.*

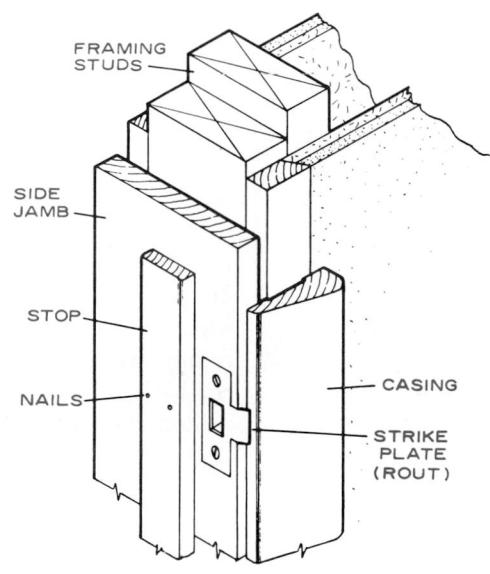

54-24. *Installation of the strike plate.*

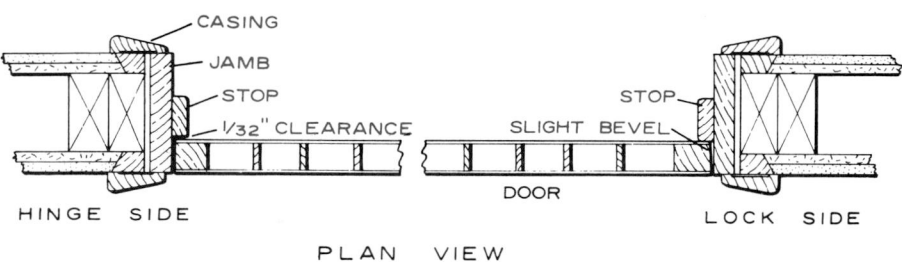

54-25. *Doorstop installation details.*

54-26. *Sliding bypass doors used on a storage wall.*

54-27. *Hanging the sliding door in the track. Note that the track is concealed behind a piece of trim mounted below the head jamb.*

with the latch. Fig. 54-24. When the door is latched, its face should be flush with the edge of the jamb. Review "Installing a Lock Set," Unit 44.

Doorstops

The stops which have been set temporarily during fitting of the door and installation of the hardware may now be permanently nailed in place. Finish nails or brads, 1½" long, should be used. The stop at the lock side should be nailed first, setting it tight against the door face when the door is latched. Space the nails 16" apart in pairs. Fig. 54-24.

The stop behind the hinge side is nailed next. A 1/32" clearance from the door face should be allowed to prevent scraping as the door is opened. Fig. 54-25. The head-jamb stop is then nailed in place. Remember that when door and trim are painted, some of the clearances will be taken up.

Sliding Doors

The bypass sliding door is designed for closets and storage walls. It requires no open swinging area, thus permitting a more effective and varied arrangement of furniture. No valuable floor space is lost due to door swing. Full access to the storage area is obtained by sliding the doors right or left. Fig. 54-26.

Sliding doors are usually installed in a standard doorframe. The track is mounted below the head jamb and then hidden from view with a piece of trim. Fig. 54-27. Standard size interior doors, 1⅜" thick, 6'8" or 7'0" high, and any width, may be used. Most sliding door hardware will also adapt to ¾" or 1⅛" door thicknesses. Fig. 54-28. The door rollers are adjustable so that the door may be plumbed and aligned

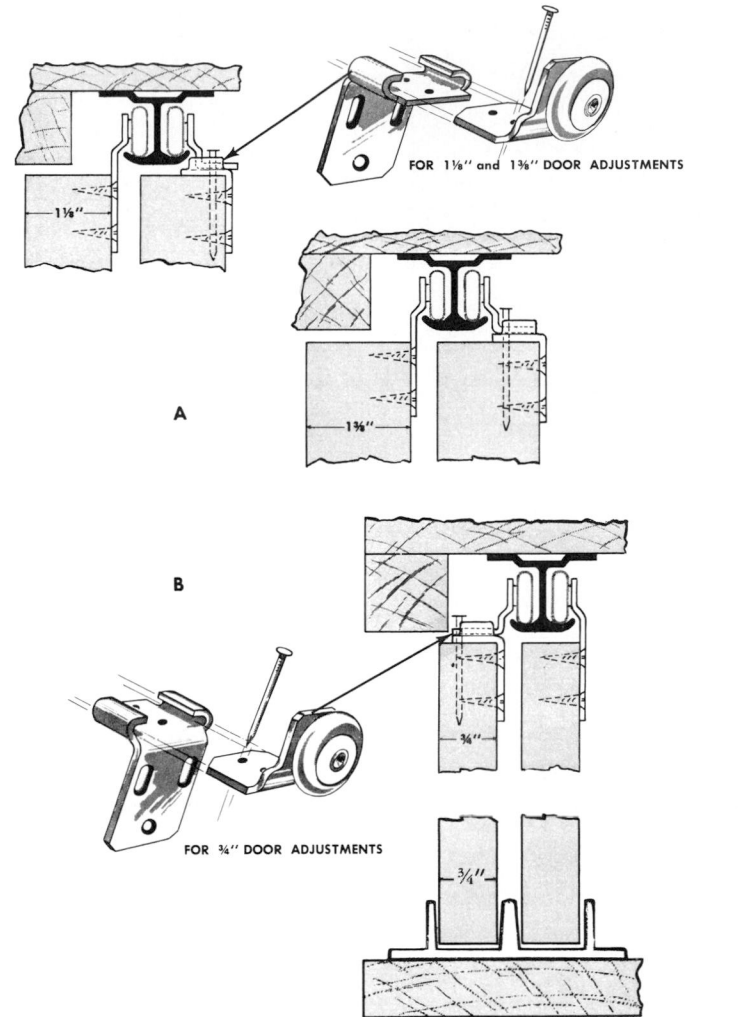

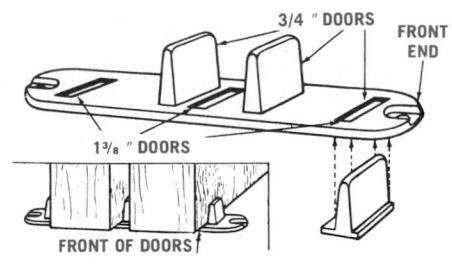

54-30. *The door guide on the floor is also adjustable. The plastic guides may be inserted in different slots of the metal plate to accommodate various door thicknesses.*

54-28. *Adjustable sliding door hardware: A. The bracket, when attached to the roller, is turned away from the roller. The nail may be inserted in either of two positions, making the roller adaptable to either 1⅛" or 1⅜" door thicknesses. B. When it is in position for a ¾" door thickness, the bracket is turned so that it is installed almost directly under the roller.*

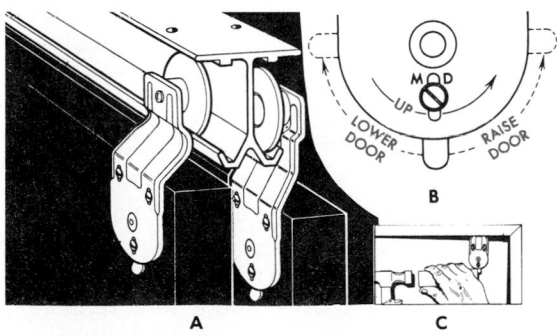

54-29. *Sliding door hardware is designed to permit aligning the doors with the opening without repositioning the hangers: A. The doors are mounted on the hangers and installed on the track. B. Details for adjusting the hangers when aligning the door. C. Tapping the adjustment with a block of wood and a hammer to make the alignment.*

with the opening. Fig. 54-29. The doors are guided at the bottom by a small guide which is mounted on the floor where the doors overlap at the center of the opening. Fig. 54-30. Rough opening sizes differ slightly from one manufacturer to another. Be sure to consult the specifications provided with each particular door unit.

Bifold Doors

Bifold doors may be used to enclose a closet area, storage wall, or laundry area. The doors may be wood, metal, or coated with plastic. They come in a large variety of styles to match the architecture of the home. Fig. 54-31.

The bifold unit has the advantage of opening up so that the entire opening is exposed at one time. With sliding bypass doors, the entire opening is accessible, but only half is exposed at one time. Fig. 54-32.

The doors are available in 6'8", 7'6", and 8'0" heights and in widths of 3', 4', 5', and 6'. These are four-panel units and, if desired, the tracks may be cut in half and a two-panel unit installed. For example, two panels of the 3'0" size could be used for a 1'6" linen closet opening.

54-31a. *These wood bifold doors match other doors in the house.*

54-31b. *Folding doors used to conceal a storage area.*

54-31c. *Wood louvered bifold doors used on a storage cabinet in a dining area.*

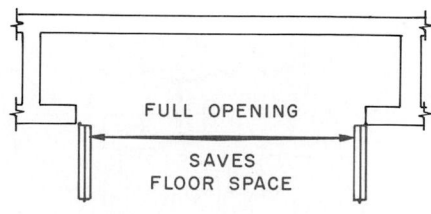

54-32. *A bifold door unit opens up to expose the entire opening.*

The bifold door is installed in a conventional doorframe. The frame may be trimmed with door casing to match the trim in the remainder of the house or, if desired, the jamb may be finished the same as the walls. Fig. 54-33. The rough opening is framed in the same way as for the conventional swinging door. The finish opening size, however, may vary with the manufacturer. Table 54-B.

To install a bifold door, install the top track first. Fasten the lower track to the floor, directly under the top track. Install the doors by inserting the bottom pivot into the bottom track socket. Insert the upper pivot into the top track socket. Adjust the panels to the opening by adjusting the track sockets. To make the tops of the panels even, raise or lower the panels by adjusting the lower pivot pin. Fig. 54-34.

Folding Doors

A folding door may be used as a room divider or to close off a laundry area, closet, or storage wall. Figs. 54-35 and 57-36. Folding doors are made from wood, reinforced vinyl, or plastic-coated wood. Wood folding doors, when closed, look like paneling. Folding doors made of a metal framework and covered with fabric or vinyl-coated materials are also available. These are called accordion-fold doors.

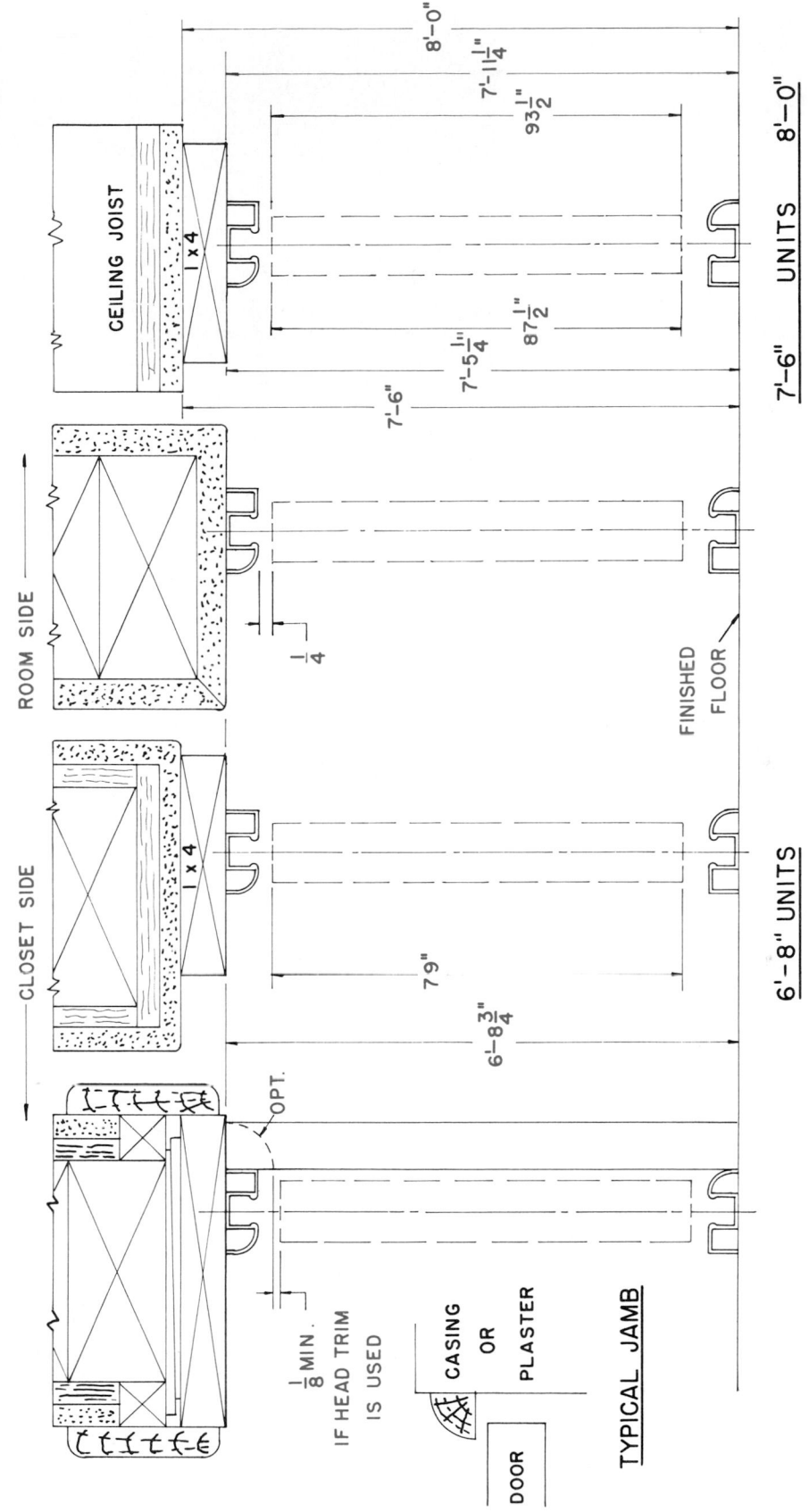

54-33. *Various header construction and trim details for a bifold door.*

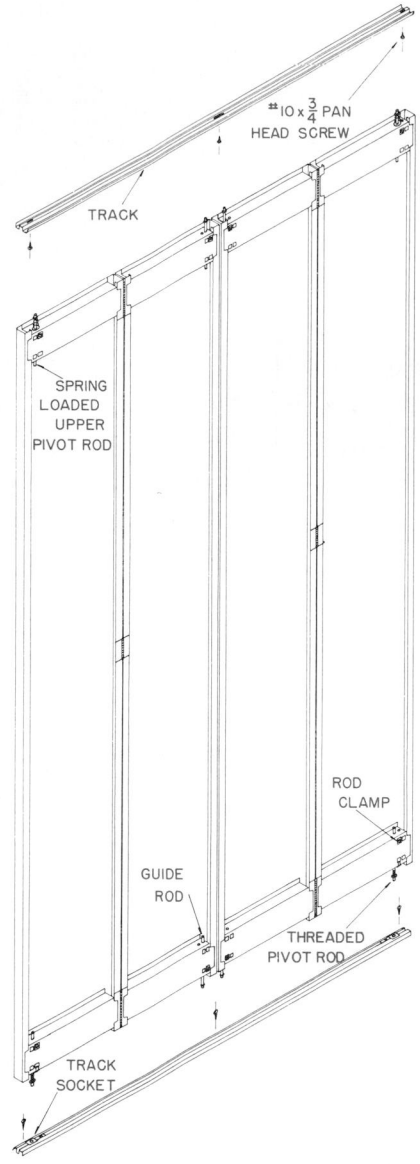

54-34. *Installation details for a bifold door unit. The track at the top is hidden by the matching wood molding.*

54-35. *Wood folding doors installed in a closet.*

Table 54-B. *A Typical Manufacturer's Specifications for Bifold Doors.*

TWO-PANEL UNITS*					
				Finished Heights	
Size	Door Width	Opening Width	6'8" Units	7'6" Units	8' Units
1' 6"	17 1/2"	18 1/2"	6' 8 3/4"	7' 5 1/4"	7' 11 1/4"
2' 0"	23 1/2"	24 1/2"	6' 8 3/4"	7' 5 1/4"	7' 11 1/4"
2' 6"	29 1/2"	30 1/2"	6' 8 3/4"	7' 5 1/4"	7' 11 1/4"
3' 0"	35 1/2"	36 1/2"	6' 8 3/4"	7' 5 1/4"	7' 11 1/4"
FOUR-PANEL UNITS*					
				Finished Heights	
Size	Door Width	Opening Width	6'8" Units	7'6" Units	8' Units
3' 0"	35"	36"	6' 8 3/4"	7' 5 1/4"	7' 11 1/4"
4' 0"	47"	48"	6' 8 3/4"	7' 5 1/4"	7' 11 1/4"
5' 0"	59"	60"	6' 8 3/4"	7' 5 1/4"	7' 11 1/4"
6' 0"	71"	72"	6' 8 3/4"	7' 5 1/4"	7' 11 1/4"

* Note: 2-panel units may be made on the job by cutting 4-panel unit tracks in half.

Folding doors are both convenient and attractive. They fold right inside their own doorway so that full advantage can be taken of every square foot of living space. The doors are hung on nylon rollers that glide smoothly in an aluminum track. The track at the top is concealed with beveled matching wood molding installed on each side. There is no exposed hardware to detract from the beauty of the door. Fig. 54-35.

Folding doors come from the factory already assembled. They are shipped complete in a package containing the door, hardware, latch fittings, and installation instructions. Standard or stock doors are available 6'8" high and 2'4", 2'8", 3', or 4' wide.

The folding door is installed in a standard doorframe. It may be trimmed in a conventional manner, or plaster jambs may be used. Fig. 54-37. A plaster channel is also available. This channel is installed before plastering. The track is mounted after the plaster is applied, eliminating the need for the wood head molding normally used. Fig. 54-38. Folding doors may also be installed to fit into a wall

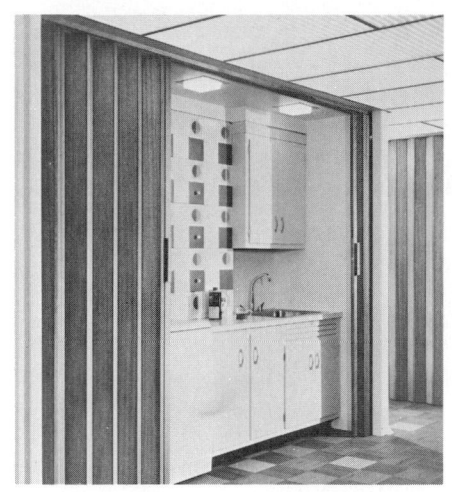

54-36. *A laundry area can be concealed by folding doors.*

cavity when opened. The cavity must be at least 7½" wide. Fig. 54-39.

Sliding Pocket Doors

The pocket type sliding door, in which the door slides into the wall, is often installed in places where the door is seldom closed. When the door stands open, it is out of the way. It is also convenient where there is minimum space for clearance of a swinging door. Fig. 54-40.

The unit can be bought complete with hardware, door, and trim. Universal sliding door hardware that will fit all door sizes can also be purchased. Fig. 54-41. Standard widths are 2'0", 2'4", 2'6", 2'8", and 3'0". Any style of door with a thickness of 1⅜" can be installed in the pocket to match the style of the other doors in the home.

When the opening for the door pocket unit is roughed in, the manufacturer should be consulted for specifications. The rough opening is usually 6'11½" or 7' high and twice the door width plus 2" or 2½". The wall header above the pocket must be adequate to support

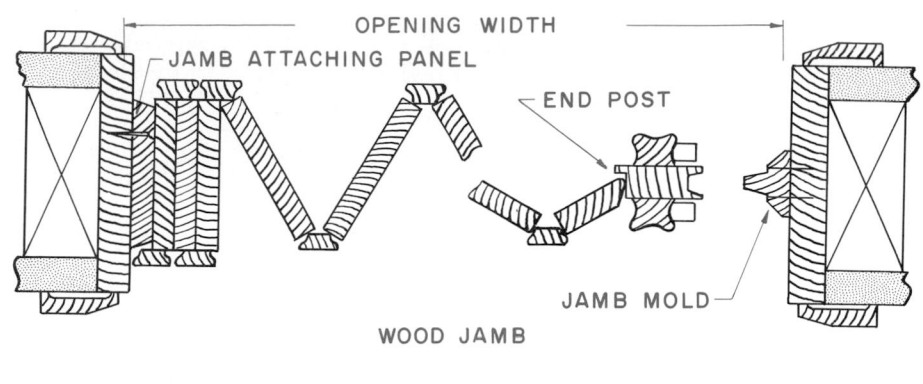

WOOD JAMB

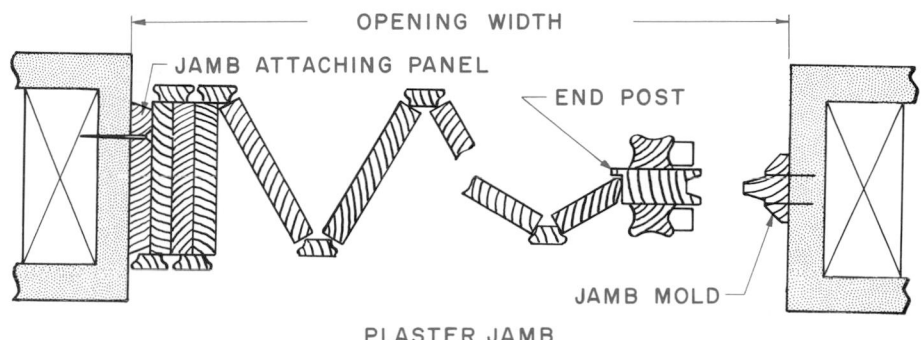

PLASTER JAMB

54-37. *Jamb sections showing the door installed with a wood jamb or a plaster jamb.*

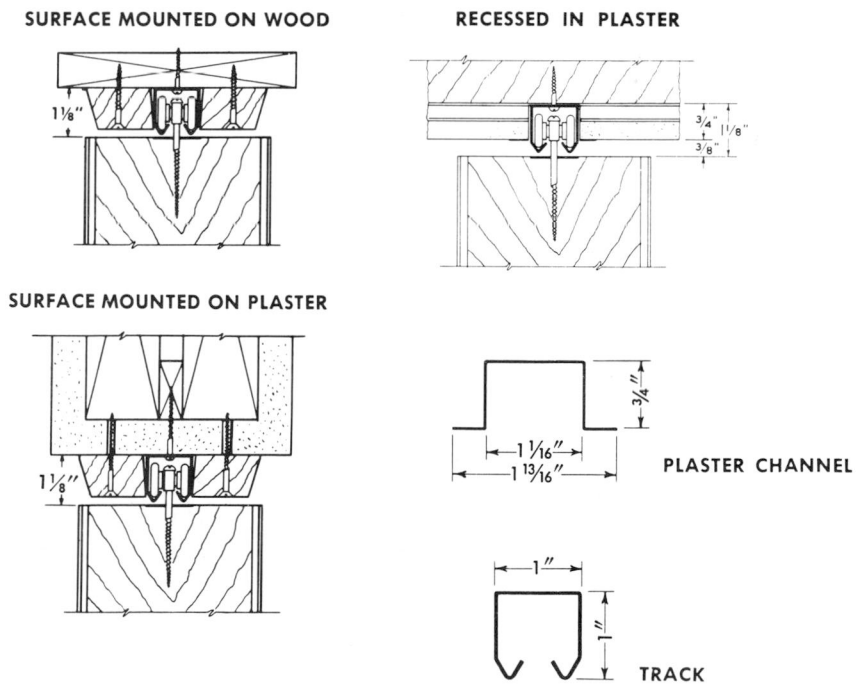

54-38. *Head sections of folding doors showing the track installation details for a channel mounted on wood, plaster, or recessed in plaster.*

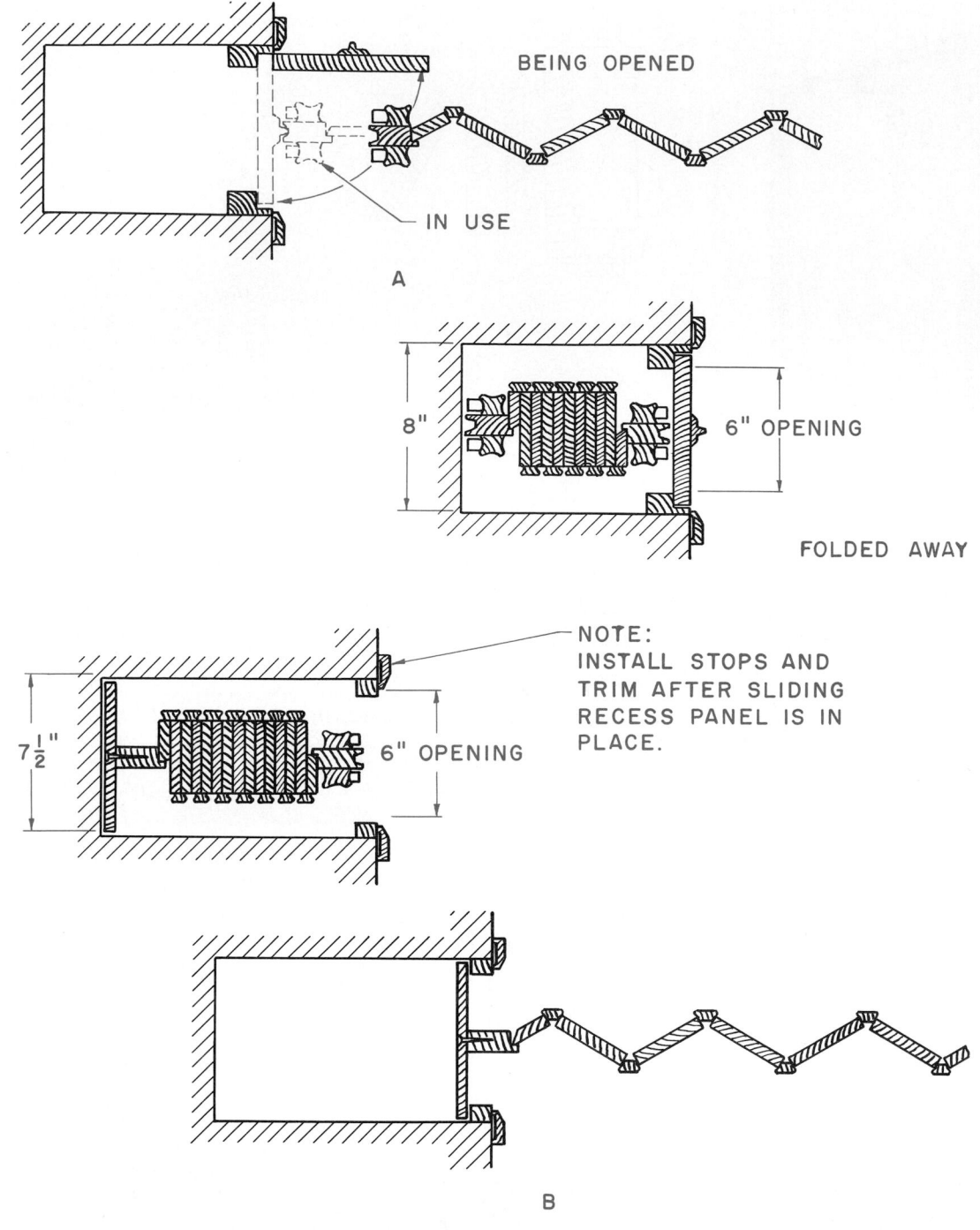

BEING OPENED

IN USE

A

8"

6" OPENING

FOLDED AWAY

NOTE:
INSTALL STOPS AND
TRIM AFTER SLIDING
RECESS PANEL IS IN
PLACE.

$7\frac{1}{2}$"

6" OPENING

B

54-39. *A. Hinged recessed door. The door can be stacked into the recessed area and the panel closed to cover the end of the door. B. Sliding recessed panel. When the door is in use, the panel travels forward and covers the opening of the recessed area.*

54-40a. *Sliding pocket door without wall covering.*

54-40b. *Sliding pocket door unit after wall covering is applied.*

54-41. *Metal-reinforced universal sliding door hardware. The hangers can be adjusted to align the door to the opening after the trim is installed.*

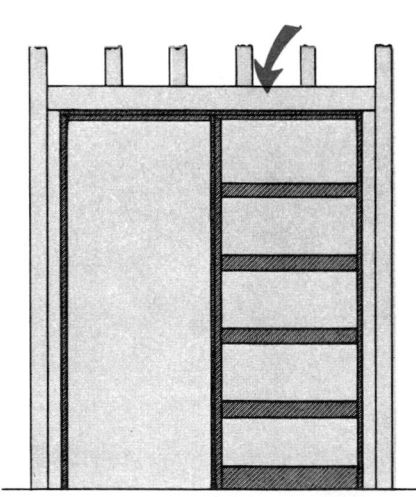

54-42. *A sliding pocket door frame installed in the rough opening. The wall header (arrow) must span the entire opening, which includes the pocket and the doorway.*

any weight on the wall and the structural frame of the building so that there is no weight on the pocket. Fig. 54-42.

The sliding door pocket frame comes complete and ready for installation into the rough wall opening. Install the pocket in the opening with 8d finish nails through shingle wedges at the head and the side jambs to level and plumb the unit. Fig. 54-43. After the wall covering has been applied, hang the door and install the stops. Fig. 54-44. Special care should be taken to use the correct nails when applying the wall covering. If the nails are too long and project through the frame slats into the opening, they may either scratch the surface of the door when it is slid into the pocket or prohibit it

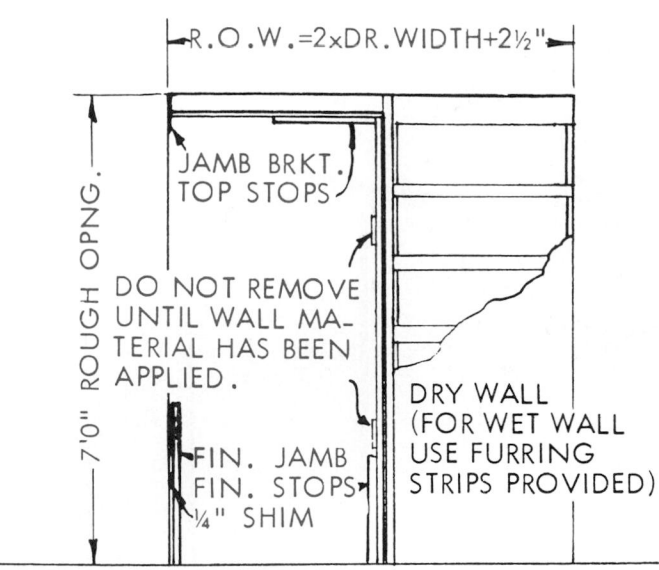

54-43. *Installing the pocket in the rough opening. Use shingle wedges at the head and side jambs to level and plumb the unit. Care should be taken to keep the jambs straight.*

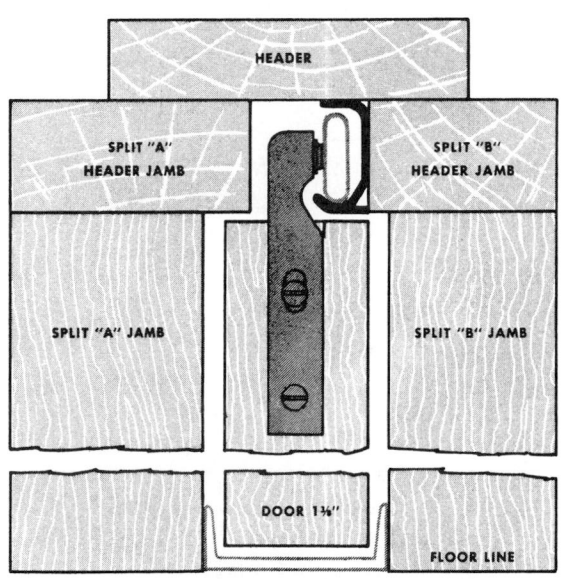

← End view of sliding door hardware assembly

← Top view of jambs showing heavy metal reinforcing

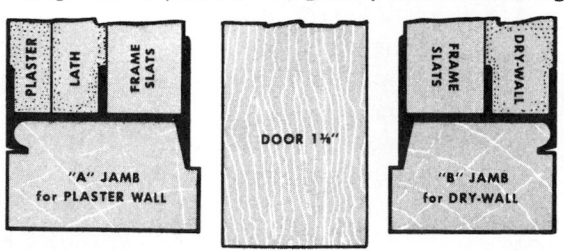

54-44. *Sliding door pocket frames are available for wet wall ("A" jamb) and drywall ("B") jamb.*

from entering the pocket. The same care in nail selection should be taken when installing the door casing and base molding.

Cafe Doors

The cafe door will add charm to the home and is adaptable to many uses. It may be installed in the kitchen, dining area, family room, or recreation room. Cafe doors swing from either direction and always freely return to the closed position. The hinges also permit the doors to be left open. Fig. 54-45. These doors are normally hung in pairs and come in a large variety of sizes. Fig. 54-46. They are installed with the door tops slightly below eye level to enable someone using the door to see anyone coming from the other side.

54-45. *The hinges on a cafe door will permit the door to stand in the open position or freely return to the closed position.*

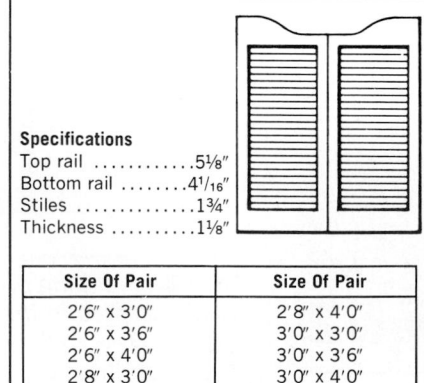

Specifications
Top rail ....5⅛″
Bottom rail ....4¹/₁₆″
Stiles ....1¾″
Thickness ....1⅛″

Size Of Pair	Size Of Pair
2′6″ x 3′0″	2′8″ x 4′0″
2′6″ x 3′6″	3′0″ x 3′0″
2′6″ x 4′0″	3′0″ x 3′6″
2′8″ x 3′0″	3′0″ x 4′0″
2′8″ x 3′6″	

54-46a. *One manufacturer's specifications for standard cafe door sizes.*

FOR JAMB OPENING WIDTHS
2'6", 2'8" and 3'0"

DOOR SIZES
1 1/8" THICK
2'5 1/8" x 3'7 1/2"
2'7 1/8" x 3'7 1/2"
2'11 1/8" x 3'7 1/2"

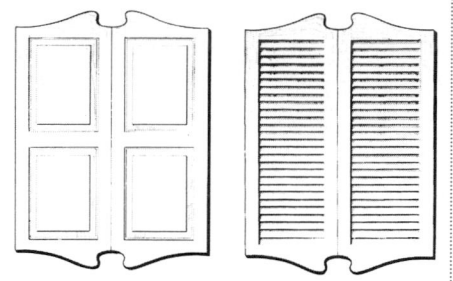

54-46b. *Another manufacturer's specifications for standard cafe door sizes, showing different door styles.*

wood window trim:
➤ With a stool and apron. Fig. 54-48.
➤ With complete casing trim. Fig. 54-49. Metal casing is sometimes used in place of wood trim around the window opening. Fig. 54-50.

Window Stool Installation.
The stool is normally the first piece of window trim to be installed. It is

Window Trim

Casing for window trim should be of the same pattern as that selected for door casing. Other trim parts consist of sash stops, the stool, and the apron. Fig. 54-47. The stool is the horizontal trim member that laps the window sill and extends beyond the casing. The apron serves as a finish member below the stool. There are two common methods of installing

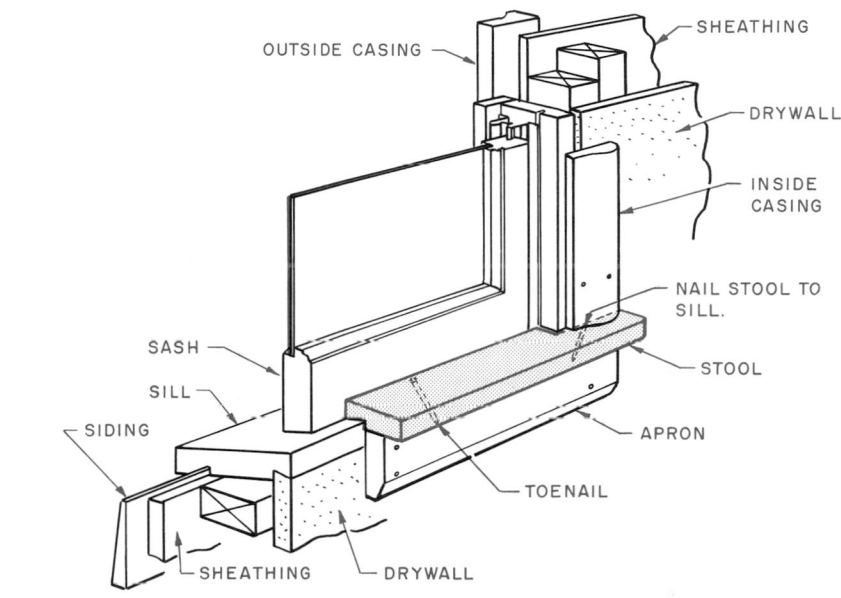

54-48. *Window trim installed with a stool and apron.*

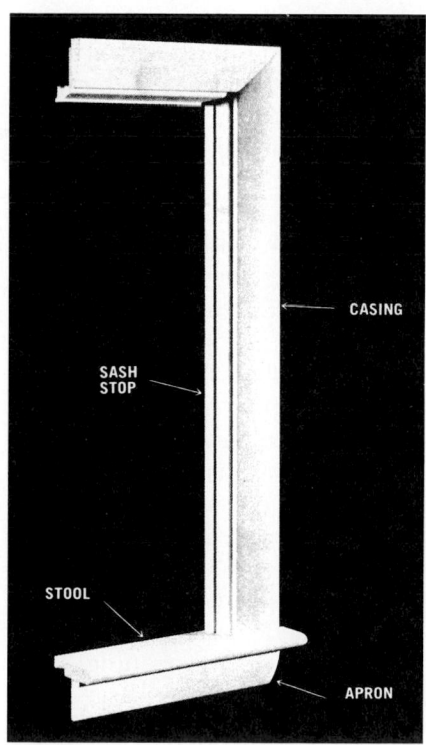

54-47. *Window trim parts.*

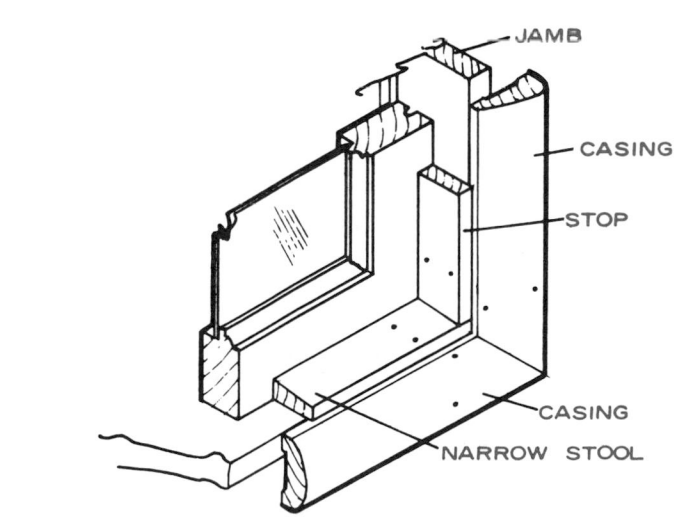

54-49. *A window trimmed with casing at the bottom instead of a stool and apron.*

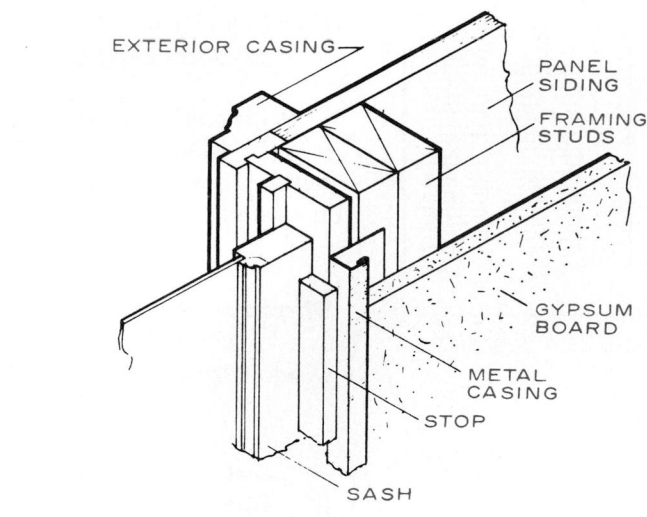

54-50. *A window installed with metal casing.*

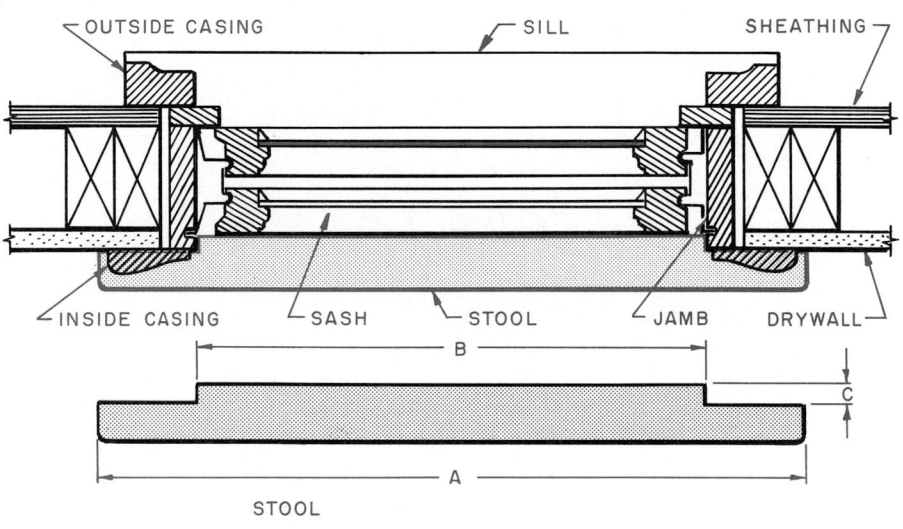

54-51. *Installation details for a window stool.*

notched out between the jambs so that the forward edge contacts the lower sash rail. Fig. 54-51.

The upper part of Fig. 54-51 shows a plan view of a stool in place. The lower view shows the stool laid out and cut, ready for installation. The distance A, the overall length of the stool, is equal to: the width of the finished opening, plus twice the width of the side casing, plus twice the

amount that each end of the stool extends beyond the outer edge of the side casing. Distance B is equal to the width of the finished opening.

Distance C is equal to the horizontal distance measured along the face of the side jamb between the inside edge of the side jamb and the inside face of the lower sash. An allowance of about $\frac{1}{32}$" should be deducted for clearance

between the sash and the stool. Lay out this width from the outside edge of the stool. If the stool is held in place (centered) against the inside edge of the window jamb, the distance between the front edge of the stool and the lower sash, dimension C, can be set on a scriber. The distance along the wall can then be scribed onto the top of the stool. Cut out the notch at each corner of the stool on the layout lines.

The stool is blind-nailed at the ends with 8d finish nails so that the casing at the sides will cover the nailheads. With hardwood, predrilling is usually required to prevent splitting. The stool should also be nailed at the center to the sill, and to the apron when it is installed. Toenailing may be substituted for face-nailing to the sill. Fig. 54-48.

Window Casing Installation.
The casing is applied after the stool is installed. It is nailed as described for the doorframes (Fig. 54-15) except that on some window types the inner edge is flush with the inner face of the jambs so that the stop covers the joint. Fig. 54-48. When stops are to be installed, they are fitted like the interior door stops and placed against the lower sash so that the sash can slide freely. A 4d casing nail or $1\frac{1}{2}$" brad should be used. Place nails in pairs spaced about 12" apart. When the window is made with channel-type weather stripping, it includes full-width metal subjambs in which the upper and lower sash slide, replacing the parting strip. In this case, the stops are located against the subjambs instead of the sash to provide a small amount of pressure.

When metal casing is used as trim around window openings, it is applied to the sill as well as at the sides and head of the frame. Consequently, the jambs and sill of the frame are not as deep as when wood casing is used. The stops are also narrower by the thickness of the wall covering. The metal casing is installed flush with the inside edge of the window jamb. Fig. 54-50. This type of trim is installed at the same time as the wall covering.

Window Apron Installation.
Cut the apron to a length equal to the outer width of the casing line. The ends of the apron should be cut with a coping saw to appear as though they had been returned, or a return may be cut and nailed in place. Fig. 54-52. The apron is attached to the framing sill below with 8d finish nails. Fig. 54-48.

When casing is used instead of a stool and apron to finish the bottom of the window frame, a narrow stool or stop may be needed on some window types. Miter the side casings at the bottom corners and apply the bottom casing in the same way as the side and head casings of the window. Fig. 54-49. When this method is used to trim a window, the casings can be cut to finished length with miters on each end. The four pieces of mitered casing are then laid face down on a clean, smooth surface and fastened together with ¼" × 5" corrugated fasteners from the back. The assembled casing, much like a picture frame, is then nailed as a unit to the window jambs and studs as described earlier.

Other types of windows, such as the awning, hopper, or casement, are trimmed about the same as the double-hung window. Casings of the same types are used for trimming these units.

Interior Shutters

Movable interior shutters were popular in the great mansions of New Orleans and in many of the finer homes of America from 1700 to the early part of the 19th century. The use of shutters has once again become popular. Fig. 54-53. They are found in the traditional interior, the provincial (country style) setting, and in the modern home, studio, or office. Shutters offer better control of light, air, visibility, and privacy than most other types of window treatment. They also make ideal

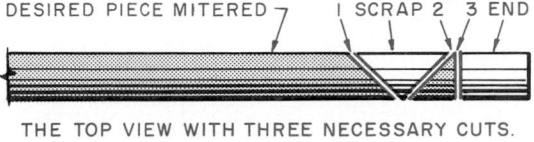

54-52. *The ends of the window apron should be coped to match the profile of the molding or mitered with a return nailed in place.*

BATHROOM

KITCHEN

BEDROOM

ARCHED WINDOW

LIVING ROOM

BAR

54-53. *Louvered shutters may be used throughout the home. They allow light and air to pass through, yet assure complete privacy and freedom from drafts.*

foldaway partitions or room separators that distinguish one living area from another.

To determine the size of the louver to be installed in a window, measure the width between the inside edges of the jamb or casing, depending on where you wish to hinge the shutters. Measure the height of the opening from the top of the sill to the inside edge of the top jamb or casing. If a cross rail is desired, it will be located at the approximate center of the shutter, referred to as the break. Fig. 54-54.

Installing Moveable Interior Shutters. When installing movable shutters on a double-hung window, a hinge strip replaces the sash stop. Fig. 54-55. The strip should be ¾" wide and have a depth equal to the distance from the front of the jamb to the sash. Mount the shutter to these strips with ¾" flush door hinges.

On casings that are reasonably flat, the shutter may be applied directly with a ¾" flush door hinge. The hinge should be set no more than 1" back from the inside edge of the casing. Fig. 54-56.

Another method of hanging shutters to casings that are reasonably flat is shown in Fig. 54-57. In this installation the hinges are applied in reverse so that the shutter will not cover the casing.

When there are no obstructions in back of the shutter, loose-pin butt hinges may be applied directly to the jamb. Fig. 54-58.

If the window jamb is other than wood and the wall is not cased, or if the casing has been removed, apply a hanging strip to the wall and use either loose-pin butt hinges or ¾" flush door hinges. Fig. 54-59.

When a casing is at least ¾" thick, the shutter may be applied directly to the casing with either type hinge. Fig. 54-60.

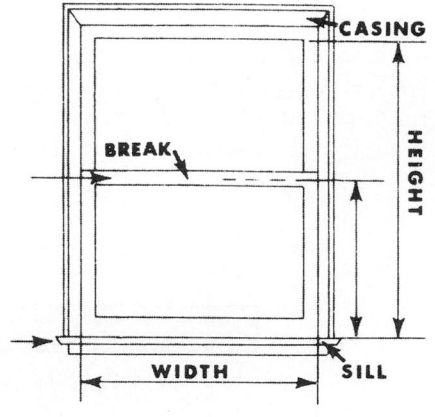

54-54. *Measuring a window for shutters.*

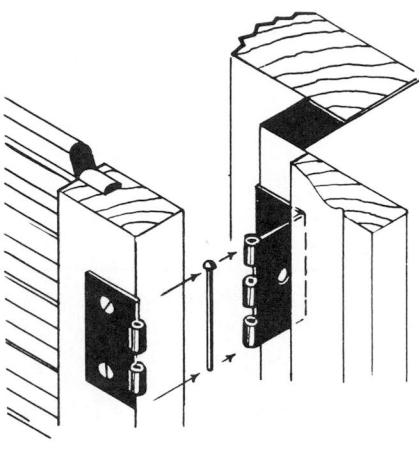

54-55. *A hinge strip installed on a double-hung window.*

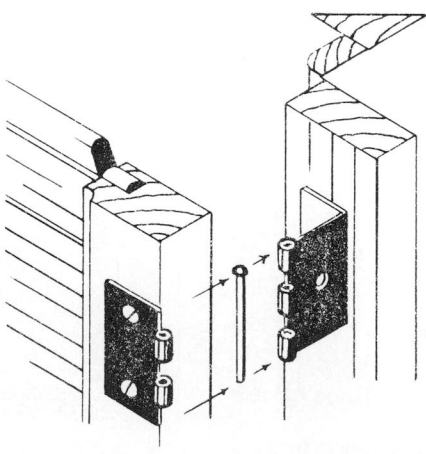

54-56. *When the window casings are flat, the hinge may be mounted directly on the casing.*

54-57. *The hinge is sometimes reversed on a flat casing so that the shutter will not cover the casing.*

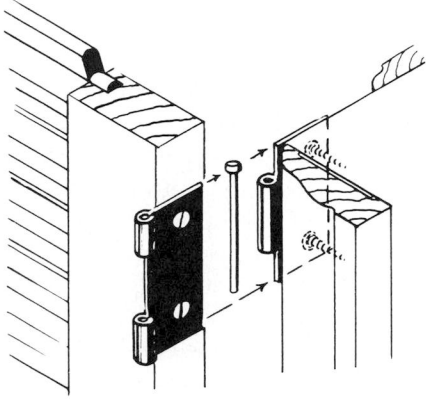

54-58. *A loose-pin butt hinge is used on a wide jamb.*

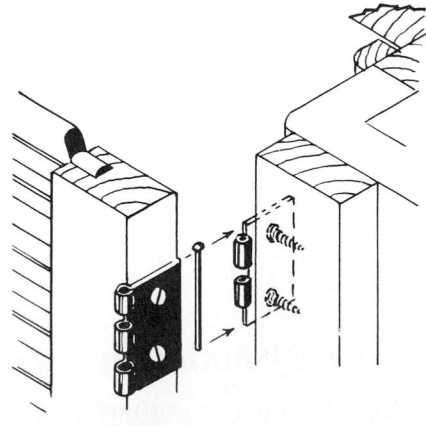

54-59. *A wood hinge strip is applied to the wall if the window jamb is not wood.*

54-60. *On a thick casing, the hinge may be applied directly to the edge.*

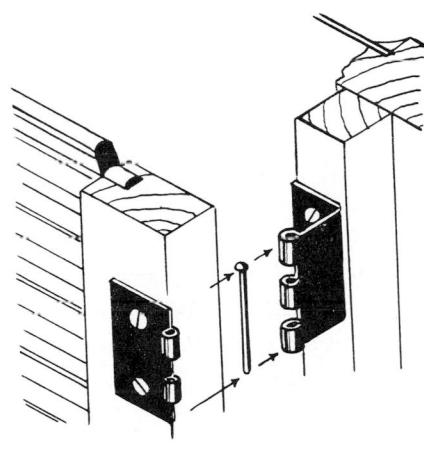

54-61. *Louvers applied to French doors or casement windows must be furred out to provide sufficient operating clearance for hardware.*

On French doors or casement windows, install a framing strip, ¾" wide × 1" deep, to the sash. Fig. 54-61. The shutter may then be installed with ¾" flush door hinges. Shutter and frame should overlap each side and top and bottom outside the glass area by ¾" to leave room for the hinges and operating clearance for louvers.

BASE, CEILING, AND WALL MOLDING

Installing Base Molding

Base molding is usually about the last trim to be installed. It must be installed after all the doors are trimmed and the cabinets are in place. Also, it usually butts wall openings such as warm and cold air registers. The base molding serves as a finish between the finished wall and floor. It is made in a number of sizes and shapes. Fig. 54-62.

Base molding may have several parts. Two-piece base consists of a baseboard topped with a small base cap. A, Fig. 54-62. When the wall covering is not straight and true, the small base cap molding will conform more closely to the variations than will a wider base alone. A common size for two-piece base is ⅝" × 3¼" or wider. One-piece base varies in size from ⁷⁄₁₆" × 2¼" to ½" × 3¼" and wider.

Most baseboards are finished with a base shoe, ½" × ¾" in size. B and C, Fig. 54-62. Base molding without the shoe is sometimes placed at the wall-floor junction, especially when carpeting is installed. Although a baseboard is desirable at the wall-floor junction to serve as a protective "bumper," wood trim is sometimes eliminated entirely.

Square-edged baseboards should be installed with a butt joint at inside corners and a miter joint at outside corners. Molded baseboards are also mitered at outside corners but they are coped at inside corners. Fig. 54-63. These methods

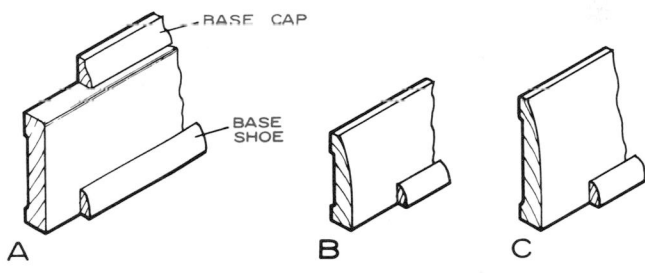

54-62. *Base moldings: A. Two-piece baseboard with a square-edged base and a base cap. B. Narrow ranch base. C. Wide ranch base.*

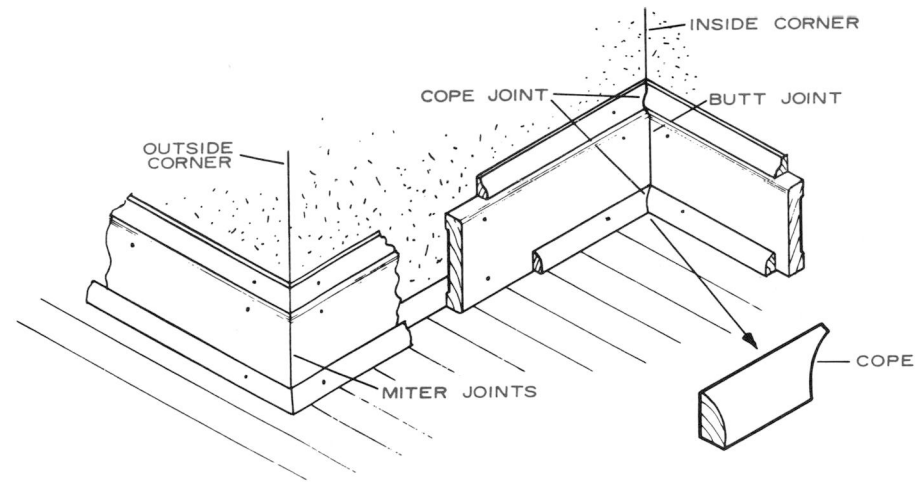

54-63. *Base molding installation details.*

of joining are necessary to provide tight joints because the walls at corner baseboard locations may not be perfectly vertical. When cutting molding to fit between walls, always cut it a little long so that the molding can be bowed slightly and sprung into place. When it is necessary to use more than one

length of molding along a wall, join the pieces on a wall stud with a lap miter joint. Fig. 54-64. The baseboard is secured to each stud with two 8d finishing nails.

When the face of the base shoe projects beyond the face of the molding to which it butts, the end of the base shoe should be returned

onto itself. The return is cut at 45° on the end of the shoe molding. This return will eliminate dirt pockets and give a better appearance. Fig. 54-65. The base shoe should be nailed into the subfloor and not into the baseboard itself. Thus, if there is a small amount of joint shrinkage, no opening will occur under the shoe. Fig. 54-66.

Scribing a Butt Joint. To butt join a piece of square-edged baseboard to another piece already in place at an inside corner, set the piece to be joined in position on the floor. Bring the end against or near the face of the piece already installed. Then scribe a line parallel to the installed piece on the face of the piece to be joined. Fig. 54-67. Be careful to hold the legs of the scriber at right angles to the reference surface (the baseboard which has already been installed). This will insure a parallel line. Follow the same procedure when putting ends of moldings against the side of door casings or wall registers.

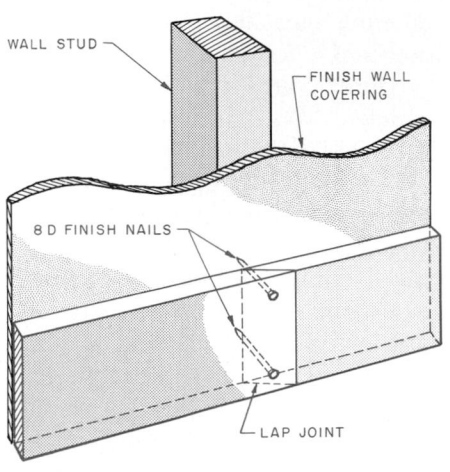

54-64. When several pieces of molding are needed to provide sufficient length, they should be joined with a lap miter joint on a wall stud. Use two 8d finish nails. The bottom nails should be close enough to the floorline to be covered by the base shoe molding.

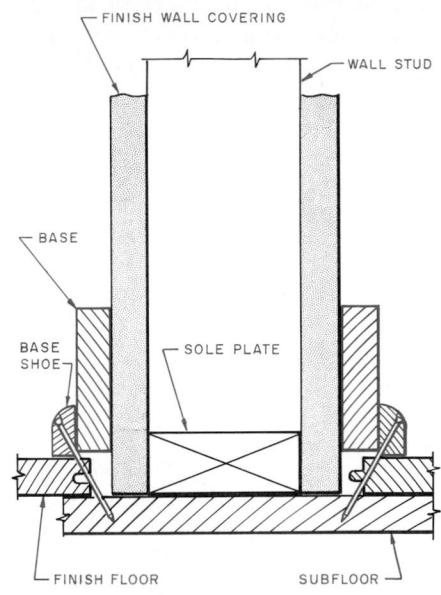

54-66. Base shoe installation details. The nail is driven through the base shoe and the finished floor into the subfloor.

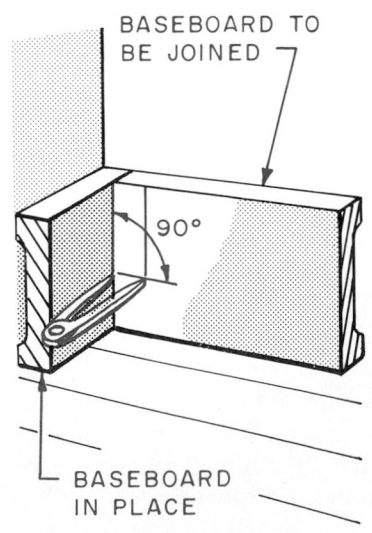

54-67. When an inside corner is butt-jointed, it must be scribed to insure a good tight joint.

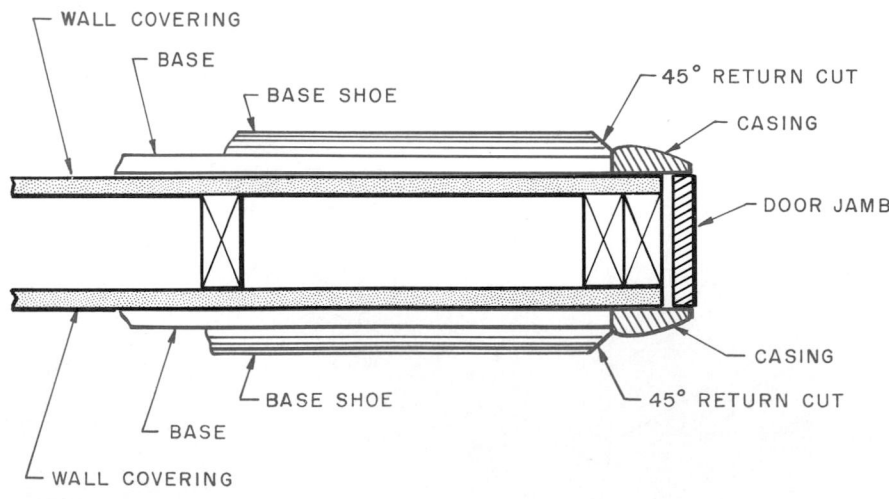

54-65. When the face of the base shoe projects beyond the face of the molding it abuts, a 45° return cut should be made on the base shoe.

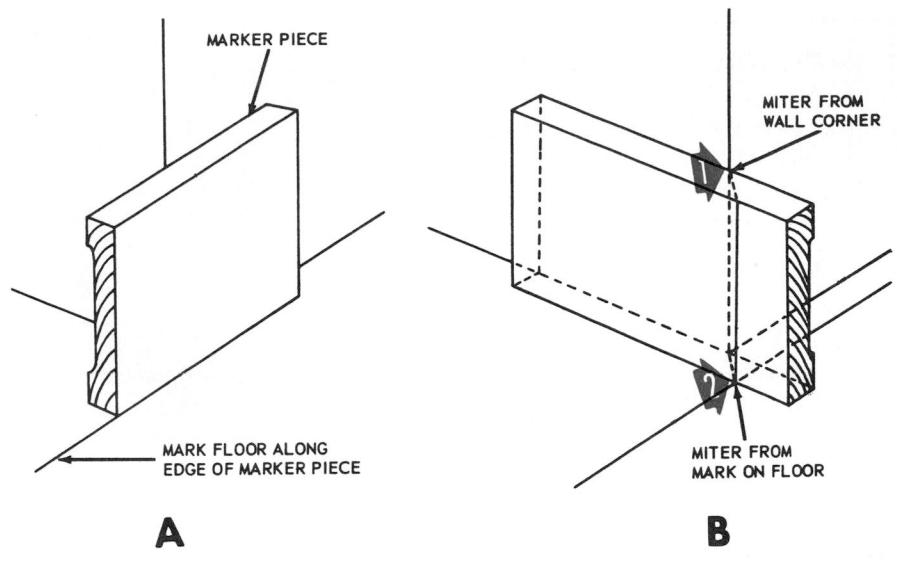

MARKER PIECE

MITER FROM
WALL CORNER

MARK FLOOR ALONG
EDGE OF MARKER PIECE

MITER FROM
MARK ON FLOOR

A

B

54-68. *Laying out a miter joint at an inside corner.*

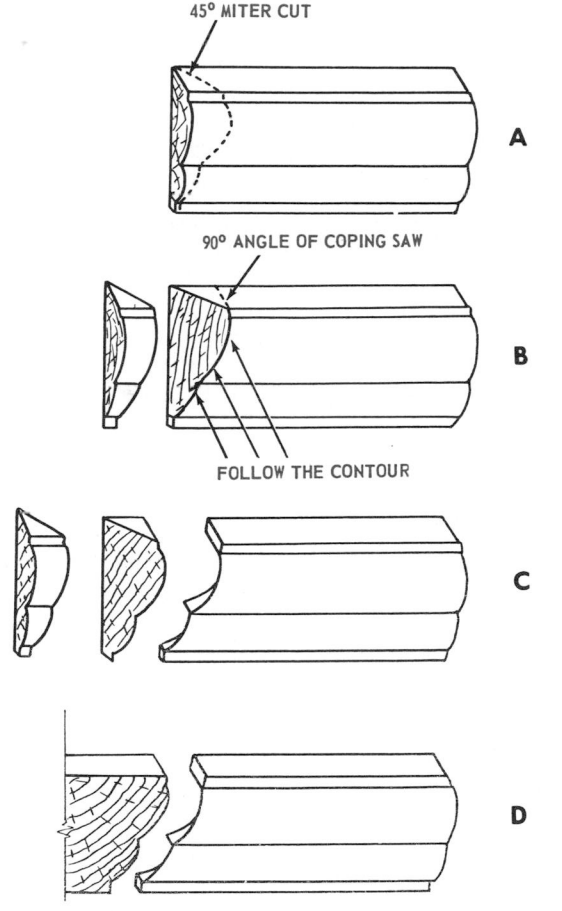

45° MITER CUT

A

90° ANGLE OF COPING SAW

B

FOLLOW THE CONTOUR

C

D

54-69a. *Coping a joint: A. Make a 45° miter cut. B. Set the coping saw at 90° to the back edge. C. Make the cut, following the contour line created by the 45° cut. D. The coped end of the molding will fit tightly against the face of the other member.*

Mitering a Joint. When miter joining an outside corner, set a marker piece of baseboard across the wall corner. A, Fig. 54-68. Mark a line on the floor along the edge of the piece. Set the piece to be mitered in place. Mark the place where the wall corner intersects the top edge and the point where the mark on the floor intersects the bottom edge. B, Fig. 54-68. Draw a 45° line across the top edge from the point marked at arrow 1 and draw a 45° line across the bottom edge from the point shown at arrow 2 in Fig. 54-68. Connect these lines with a line drawn across the face of the board and cut along the line.

Coping a Joint. Inside corner joints between molding trim members are usually made by cutting the end of one member to fit against the face of the other. Shaping the end of the butting member to fit the face of the other member is called coping. Fig. 54-63. To cope a molding, miter the end at 45° the same way as if the molding were to have a plain mitered inside corner joint. A, Fig. 54-69a. Then set the coping saw on the line at the top of the miter cut. Hold the saw at 90° to the back of the molding and saw along the face contour line created by the 45° miter cut. B and C, Fig. 54-69a. The end profile of the coped member will match the face of the other member. D, Fig. 54-69a. The result is a good, tight joint. It will not open up when the molding is nailed in place, and it is not likely to open up as the wood shrinks after installation. Fig. 54-69b.

Base Molding Installation Sequence. When applying base moldings in a room, the installation sequence should be carefully planned before starting the job to save time in making necessary and difficult cuts. The drawing in Fig. 54-70 shows the

54-69b. *Coping molding.*

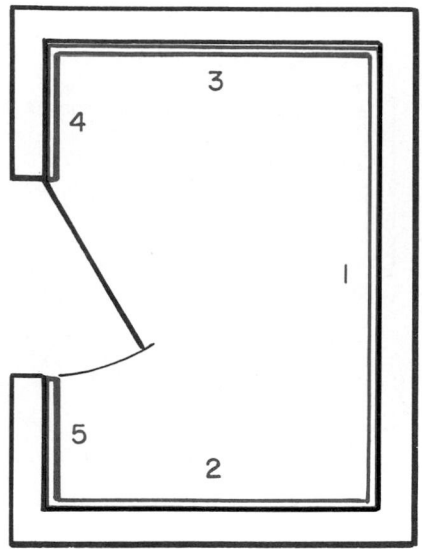

54-70. *An outline of a room with one door. Can you figure the best sequence for cutting and installing base molding in this room?*

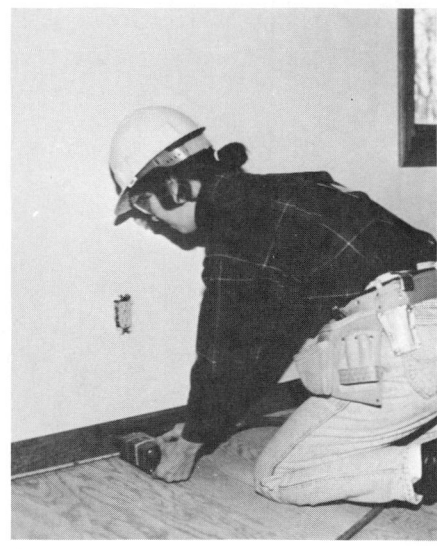

54-71. *Installing baseboard.*

outline of a room with one door. Here is one suggested sequence for installing the molding: Cut and fit a piece of molding to go along the wall marked 1, scribing each end to fit walls 2 and 3. Install molding on the walls marked 2 and 3. The molding for these walls should have one end coped to fit the molding on wall 1. Cope the joint first. Then measure and mark the piece and cut it to finish length. Cope one end of the moldings for walls 4 and 5 to fit against the face of the moldings for walls 2 and 3. Cut the other end to fit against the door casing.

Another approach to trimming this same room (Fig. 54-70) is to begin at the right and work around the room in a counterclockwise direction. The first piece is cut to fit along wall 5 between the door casing and the end wall. The piece of molding on wall 2 is coped on one end to fit against the molding on wall 5. It is then measured, marked, and cut to length so that the other end fits against wall 1.

The first end of wall molding 1 is coped to fit against piece 2, then measured, marked, and cut to length. This procedure is continued for walls 3 and 4.

A right-handed person will find in working around the room counterclockwise that the coping of the molding will be much easier. This is true for most molding shapes because the sawing is started at the top of the molding, where it is lighter and where most moldings are shaped and have a narrow edge. This narrow edge is weak and, if the cut is started at the bottom, the molding may break as the cut is finished.

The work of installing baseboard can be made more comfortable if the trim carpenter uses kneepads. These handy devices protect the knees from injury caused by continual contact with hard floors. Fig. 54-71.

Ceiling Molding

Moldings are sometimes used at the junction of wall and ceiling for architectural effect or to terminate dry wall or wood paneling. Fig. 54-72. A cut-back edge at the top of the molding will partially conceal any unevenness of the plaster and make painting easier when molding and ceiling are different colors. B, Fig. 54-72. For gypsum drywall construction a small simple molding might be preferred. C, Fig. 54-72.

Cut and fit ceiling molding in the same way as described for base moldings. This will help insure tight joints and retain a good fit if there are minor moisture changes. To secure the molding, a finish nail should be driven through the molding and into the upper wall plates. For large moldings, if possible, also drive a nail through the molding into each ceiling joist.

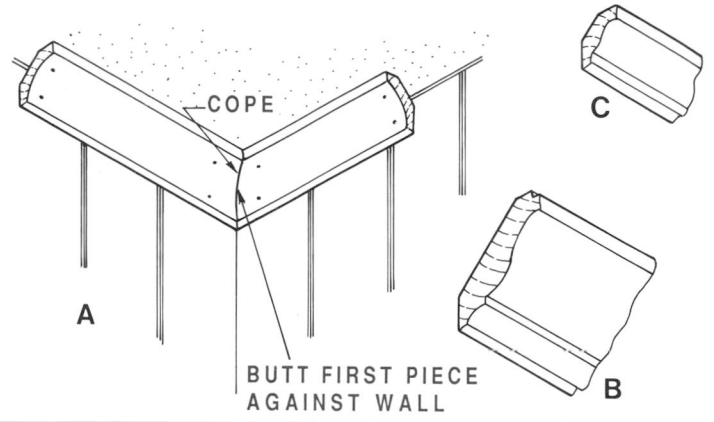

54-72. *Ceiling moldings: A. Installation details at an inside corner. B. Crown molding with a cut-back edge. C. A small crown molding.*

Wall Molding

Wall molding, sometimes called dado molding or chair rail, consists of strips of molding which run along the walls at 3' to 4' above the floor. This type of molding serves to protect the finished wall from the backs of chairs. It may also serve as trim between two different wall finishes. For example, a wall may be painted below the molding and wallpapered above. Regular casing, base, band, and cap moldings may be used as wall moldings. This allows a wide range

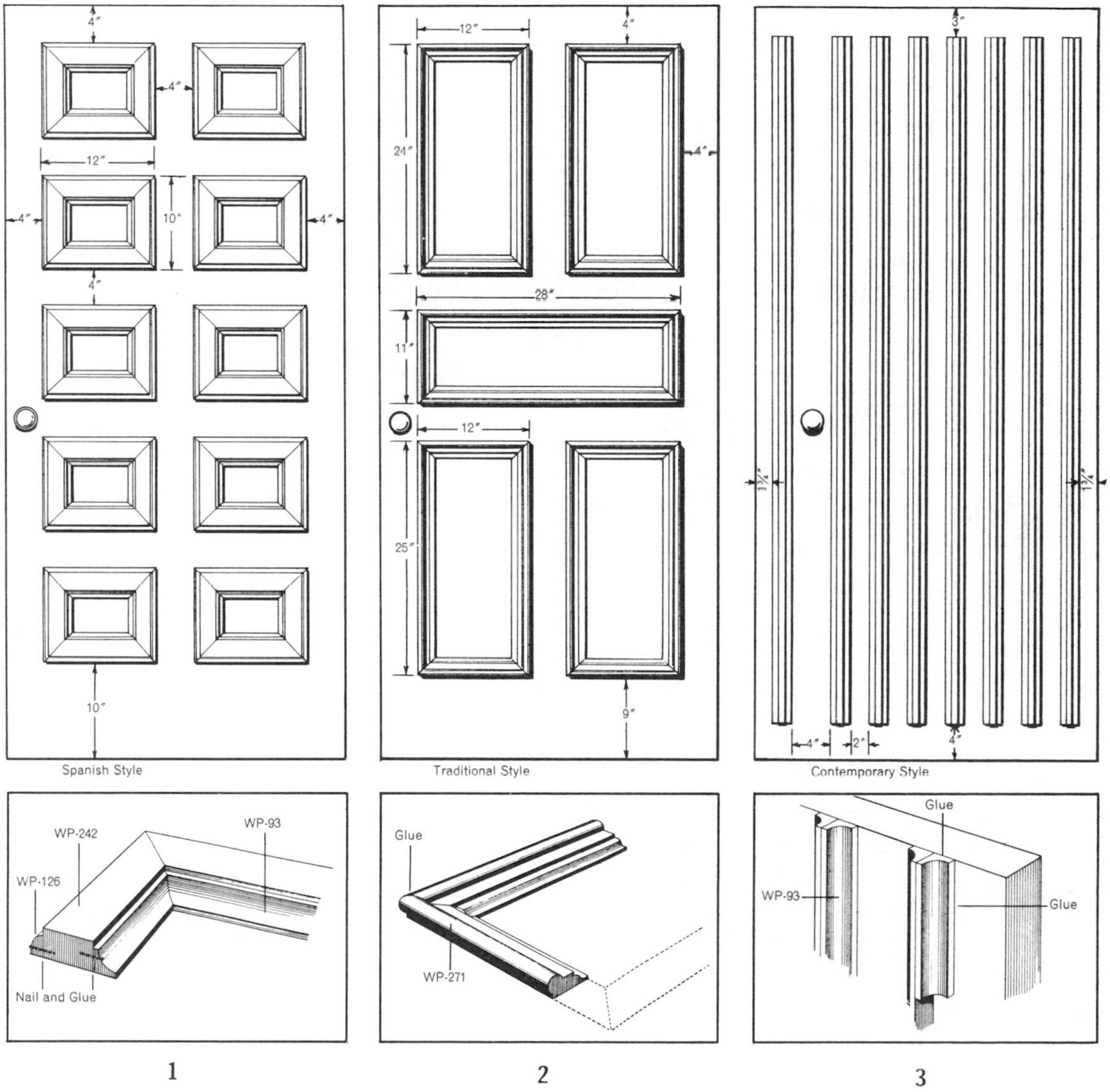

Spanish Style

Traditional Style

Contemporary Style

1

2

3

54-73. *Details for applying molding to a flush door: 1. Spanish style. 2. Traditional. 3. Contemporary.*

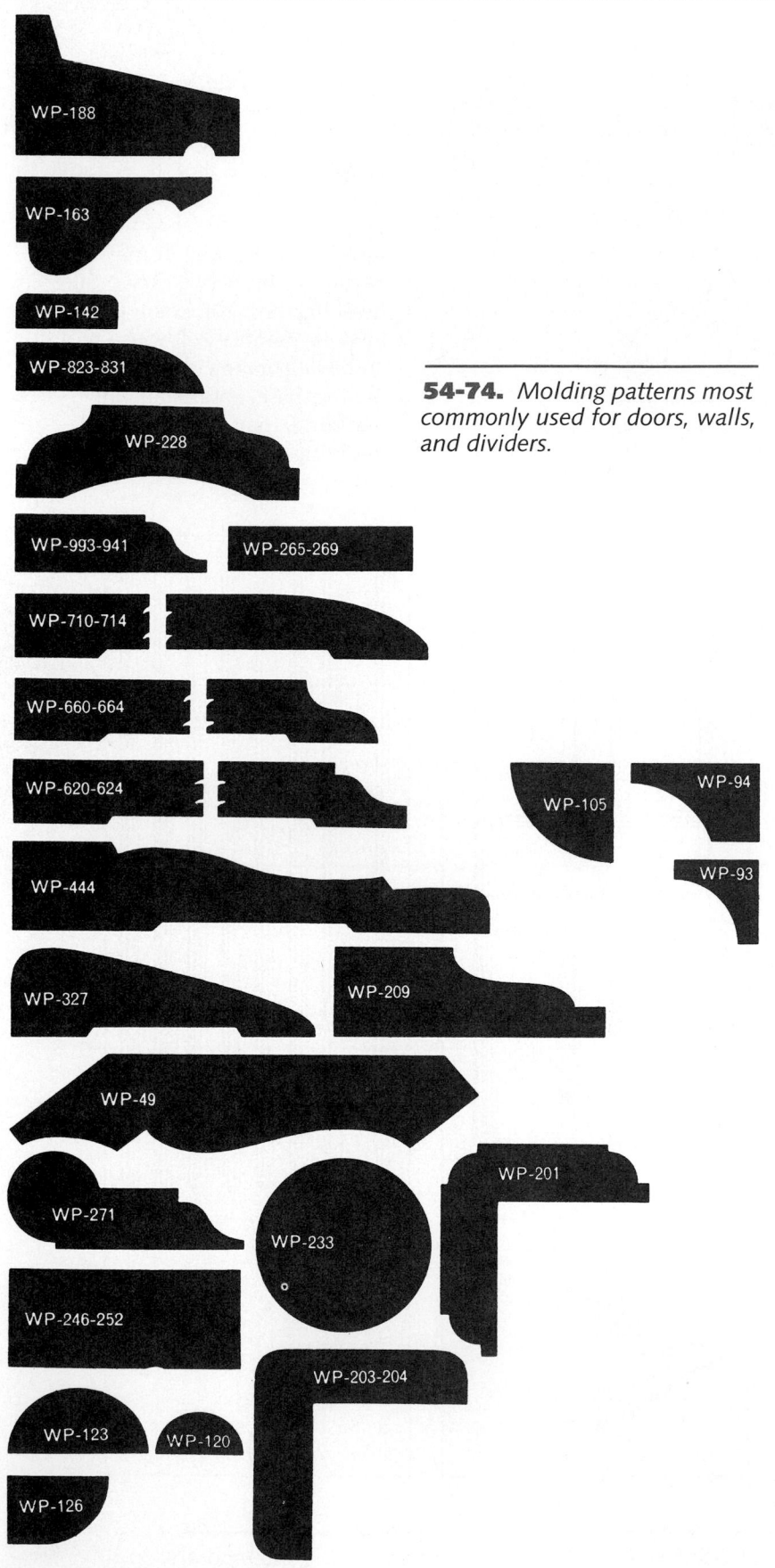

54-74. *Molding patterns most commonly used for doors, walls, and dividers.*

WP-188
WP-163
WP-142
WP-823-831
WP-228
WP-993-941
WP-265-269
WP-710-714
WP-660-664
WP-620-624
WP-444
WP-105
WP-94
WP-93
WP-327
WP-209
WP-49
WP-271
WP-233
WP-201
WP-246-252
WP-203-204
WP-123
WP-120
WP-126

of choices with an almost unlimited selection of thicknesses and widths. Wall moldings are installed in the same manner as base moldings.

Applying Molding to a Flush Door

The style of a flush door can be varied by the application of different moldings. A Spanish-style door is shown in Part 1 of Fig. 54-73. This door is trimmed with two molding patterns used in conjunction with a screen stock. Make a jig with the inside dimensions equal to the outside dimensions of the frame (12" × 10"). Cut the molding to length with mitered ends and assemble them in the jig.

Other moldings applied to a flush door can give it a contemporary or a traditional style. Parts 2 and 3, Fig. 54-73. Silhouettes of the various molding styles and their pattern numbers are shown in Fig. 54-74. Review the sections on cutting and coping moldings in this unit before cutting the moldings to size for the applications shown here or applications of your own design.

Trimming a Clothes Closet

Base and shoe moldings of the same pattern used in the adjoining room are installed at the floor line of clothes closets. These moldings are cut, fit, and installed in the same manner as the base moldings in the room.

A piece of wood molding or a piece of 1" × 3" clear stock may be used as a hook strip and a shelf support in which the closet pole is installed. Many times a piece of wood base turned upside down (with the square edge up) is used as a hook strip. Locate the height of the hook strip, usually about 66" above the finished floor line. Fig. 54-75. Level a line at this point on each wall of the closet. Cut and fit the molding in the same manner as the base molding.

Lay out and bore holes for the clothes pole. On one side, make a cut down from the top to remove the stock above the hole. Point A, Fig. 54-75. This will allow the pole to be inserted into the other hole and then slipped into the slot. Install the molding as you would base molding.

Cut the shelf to length and set it on top of the hook strip. The shelf is usually not nailed in order to make cleaning and painting easier.

Metal adjustable shelving is available prefinished in a variety of colors and wood grains. Also available are wall plates and brackets for mounting and a rod which adjusts to various lengths and fits into the wall plates. Fig. 54-76. Another accessory for clothes closets is a clothes hanger bar which attaches to the front

edge of a wood shelf. This unit, which will reinforce and trim the front edge of the shelf, comes in varying lengths up to 14'. Fig. 54-77.

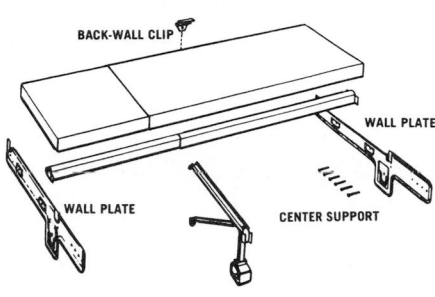

54-76. *Prefinished adjustable shelving, wall plates, brackets, and clothes rods made from metal are available for closet installations.*

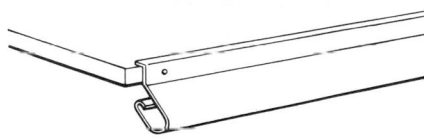

54-77. *A metal clothes hanger bar attaches to the front edge of the closet shelf.*

ESTIMATING

Materials

The cost of interior trim such as doorframes, doors, and moldings varies a great deal with wood species and styles. For example, pine casing used as trim for door and window frames may cost only half as much as some hardwood trim. However, some types of interior panel doors made of pine may cost twice as much as a mahogany flush door. Choice of materials should be based both on cost and utility. Such details are covered in the building plans and specifications.

Labor

To figure the total labor time, multiply the estimated labor rate by the number of windows, doors, or the total amount of molding to be installed. Table 54-C. This will give the total number of hours required for interior trimming. To obtain the total labor cost, multiply the total number of hours by the labor cost per hour.

For example, if ceiling molding were to be installed in a room 22' × 15', the total amount of molding to be installed would be 74' (22' + 22' for the side walls and 15' + 15' for the end walls). The total labor cost is then figured as follows:

$$\frac{74 \text{ (total amount of ceiling molding to be installed)}}{40 \text{ (linear feet of ceiling molding installed per hour)}} = \begin{array}{l} 1.85 \text{ (hours} \\ \text{to install} \\ \text{the ceiling} \\ \text{molding)} \end{array}$$

Multiply this by the rate per hour to obtain the total labor cost.

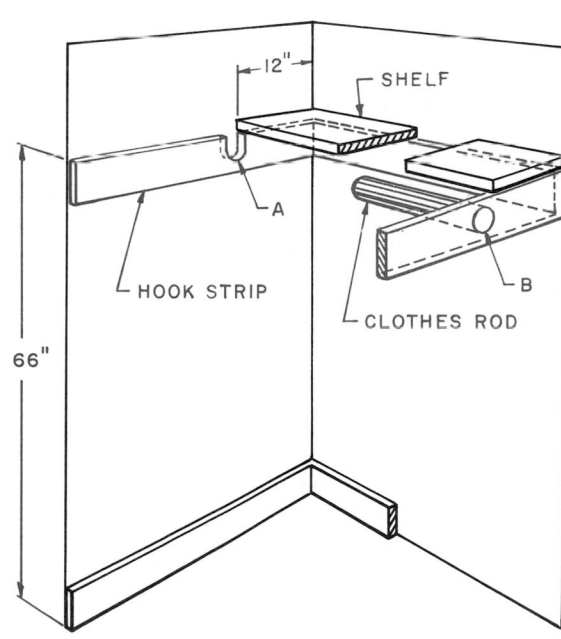

54-75. *Installation details for trimming a clothes closet.*

Table 54-C. *Interior Trim Labor Estimates.*

Item	Estimated Labor Rate
Window and casement units (includes window installation and casement trim)	2.8 hrs. each
Interior Doors (including jambs and trim)	4 hrs. each
Prehung Doors	$1/2$ hr. each
Shutters	1 hr. each
Ceiling and Wall molding	40 linear ft. per hr.
Base (softwood—add 25% for hardwood) One-Piece Base Two-Piece Base	20 linear ft. per hr. 15 linear ft. per hr.

QUESTIONS

1. What are the most common uses of wood or plastic moldings in the home?

2. What work must be completed before trimming interior doors and windows in a home?

3. What is the main advantage of a two- or three-piece doorjamb?

4. What is the standard thickness of interior doors?

5. What is the standard height of an interior door?

6. What is the advantage of a bifold door over a sliding door for a closet installation?

7. What are the two common methods of installing window trim?

8. What is the first piece of window trim to be installed?

9. How is the length of the window apron determined?

10. Why is base molding about the last trim to be installed?

11. What is the standard height for a clothes closet shelf?

ACTIVITIES

1. Language Arts. Look for molding accents in your home or apartment. List at least four ways that molding is used there. In your inventory of moldings, try to identify the moldings by type as shown in Fig. 54-2.

2. Science. Find out why there are recommended average moisture contents for interior wood trim. Why do the percentages vary according to climate? Talk to a builder or building code supervisor to find out. Determine what the recommendations for your area are.

3. Language Arts. Fig. 54-70. Based on this figure and the text information, describe how you would cut and install base molding for this room. Begin your paragraph with an exact description of where you would begin. Use transitional words such as "first," "second," "next," and "meanwhile," in your instructional paragraph.

4. Math. In preparing to cope an inside corner joint, a 45° miter cut is made first. Discuss with a friend which way the miter cut should be made.

5. Language Arts. Good money management is essential in any career. Once you get a job, the first thing you may want to do is to open a checking account. Regarding checking account fees, there are two general types of checking accounts. In one, the checking account holder is charged a certain amount for every check that he or she writes. In the other, the person is charged a flat fee, regardless of the number of checks that he or she writes. Obtain from a bank the basic information on checking acccounts. Evaluate this information. Then prepare a short written report on the advantages and disadvantages of each type of checking account.

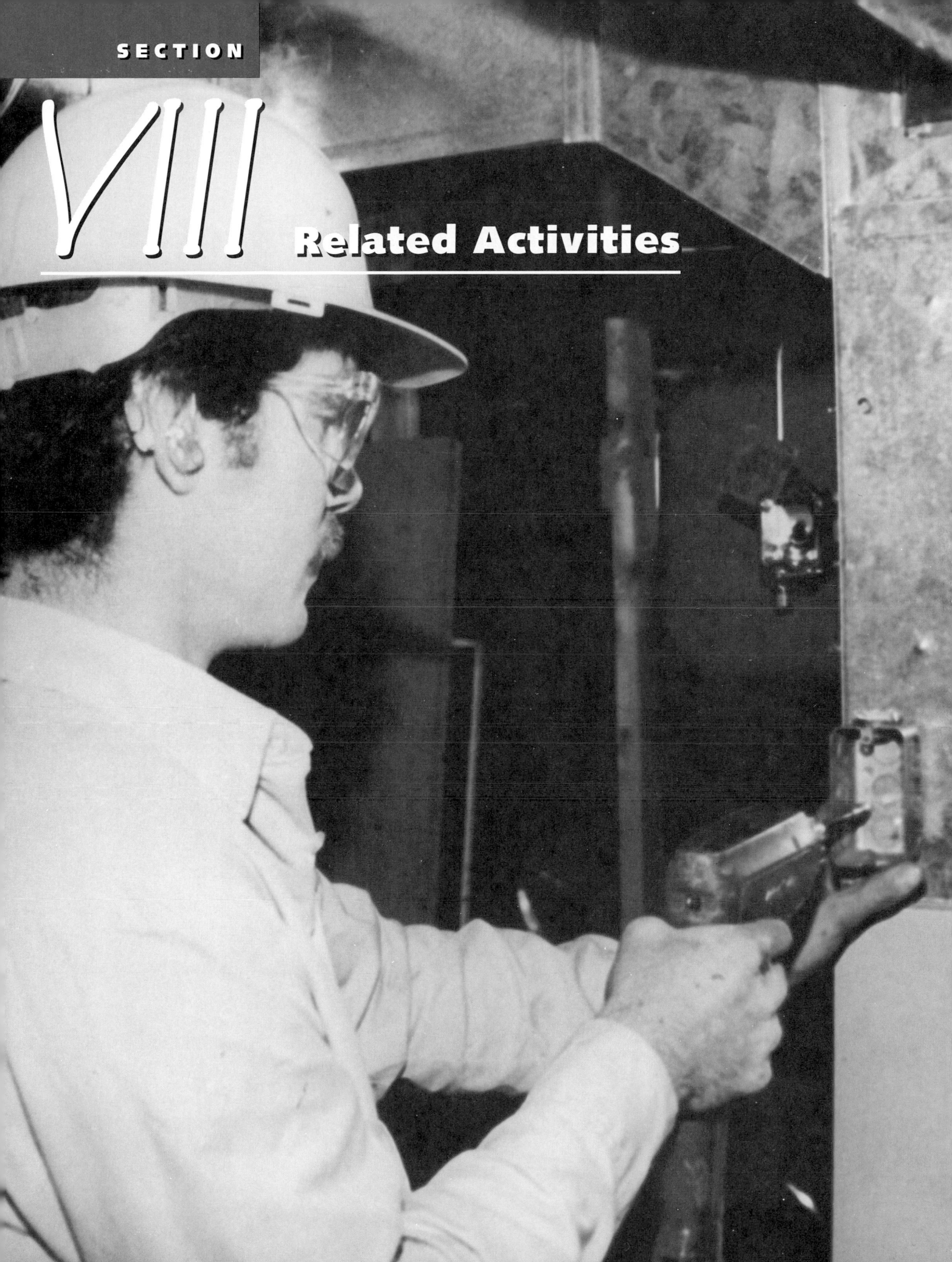

SECTION

VIII

Related Activities

55 Chimneys and Fireplaces

Proper construction of chimneys and fireplaces is essential for safe, efficient operation. Local codes vary, so be sure to consult and follow them. It is recommended that chimneys and fireplaces be designed and the construction supervised by someone experienced in this field of work. The chimney and the fireplace must be carefully built in order to be free of fire hazards. It is desirable to have them in harmony with the architectural style of the house. Fireplaces may be made of solid masonry, or they may consist of a prefabricated firebox. A woodstove is sometimes vented into a solid masonry fireplace. Fig. 55-1.

55-1a. *A prefabricated firebox with a tile and wood surround.*

55-1b. *A wood stove vented into a solid masonry chimney and firebox.*

CHIMNEYS

All fireplaces and fuel-burning equipment such as stoves and furnaces require some type of chimney. Fig. 55-2. Chimneys are generally constructed of masonry units supported on a suitable foundation. Lightweight, prefabricated chimneys that do not require masonry protection or concrete foundations are now accepted for certain uses by fire underwriters. Make certain, however, that they are approved and listed by Underwriters' Laboratories, Inc. The chimney must

55-1c. *A prefabricated firebox and a stone chimney.*

be designed and built so that it produces sufficient draft to supply an adequate quantity of fresh air to the fire and to expel smoke and harmful gases given off by the fire or fuel-burning equipment.

The greater the difference in temperature between chimney gases and outside atmosphere, the better the draft. Thus an interior chimney will have better draft because the masonry retains heat longer.

Chimney Construction

Flue Size. The flue is the passage in the chimney through which the air, gases, and smoke travel. Proper construction of the flue is important. Its size (area), height, shape, tightness, and smoothness determine the effectiveness of the chimney in producing adequate draft and in expelling smoke and gases.

Follow the manufacturer's specifications for fuel-burning equipment. These specifications usually include the requirements for equipment supplied by the manufacturer.

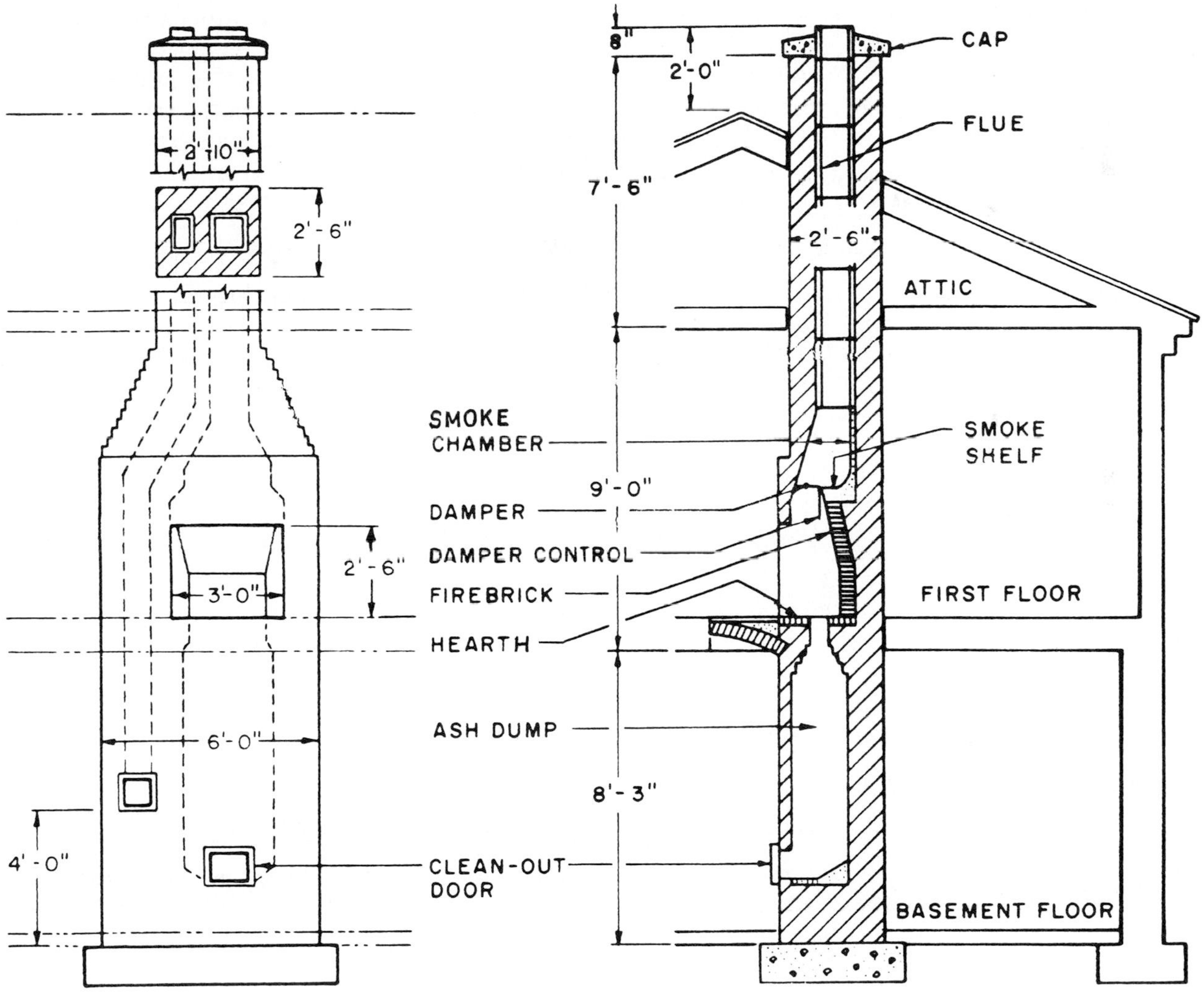

55-2. *This chimney is designed to serve the house-heating unit and one fireplace.*

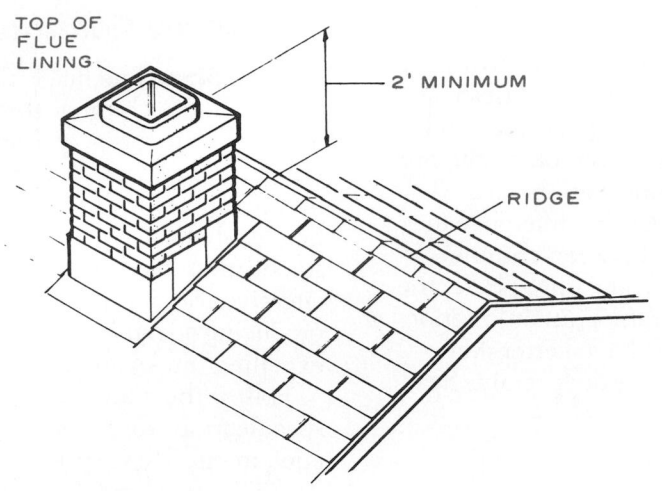

55-3. *The top of the flue lining should be at least 2' above the ridge line.*

Chimney Height. The height of the chimney is also an important factor in providing sufficient draft. The height of a chimney above the roofline usually depends upon its location in relation to the ridge. The top of the extending flue liners should not be less than 3' above flat roofs and at least 2' above a roof ridge or any raised part of a roof within 10' of the chimney. Fig. 55-3. A hood should be provided if a chimney cannot be built high enough above a ridge to prevent trouble from irregular air currents caused by wind being deflected from the roof. The open ends of the hood should be parallel to the ridge. C, Fig. 55-4.

In addition, some codes call for either one of the following restrictions:

➤ The top of the chimney must be above the height of any operable window within 20 ft., or

➤ The top of the chimney must be at least 35 ft. below the highest portion of any operable window within 20 ft.

These two restrictions help to prevent any smoke from being pulled back into the house.

Chimney Foundations. The chimney is usually the heaviest part of a building. It must rest on a solid foundation to prevent uneven settling of the building.

Concrete footings must be designed to distribute the load over an area wide enough to avoid exceeding the safe loadbearing capacity of the soil. The footings should extend at least 6" beyond the chimney on all sides and should be 8" thick for one-story houses and 12" thick for two-story houses having basements.

Chimneys in frame buildings should usually be built from the ground up. They may also rest on the building foundation or basement walls if the walls are of solid masonry 12" thick and have adequate footings. For houses with basements, the footings for the walls and fireplace are usually poured together and at the same elevation. If there is no basement, footings for an exterior chimney are poured on solid ground below the frostline.

Mortar. Brickwork around chimney flues and fireplaces should be laid with cement mortar. It is more resistant to the action of heat and flue gases than lime mortar.

Flue sections should be joined with refractory cement. All the joints in the flue should be tooled smooth. All bricks and blocks should be laid with full, push-filled

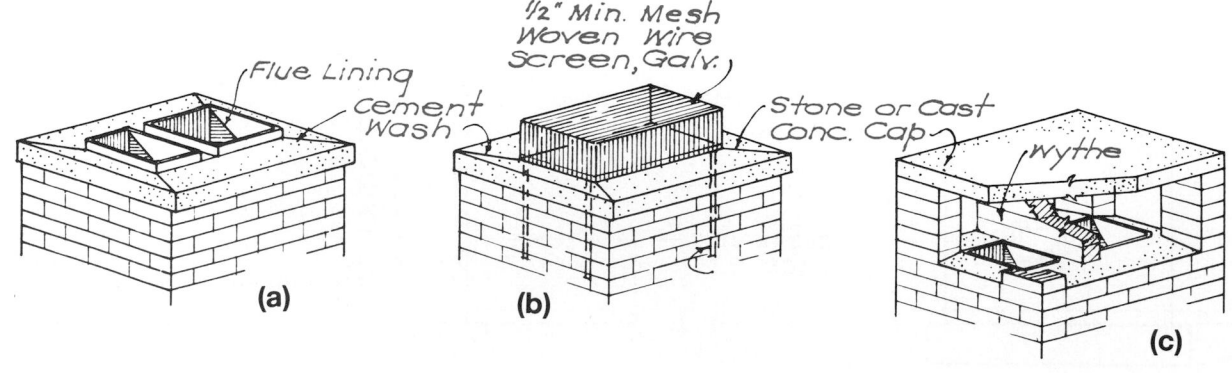

55-4. *Chimney top construction: A. Standard chimney top. B. Spark arrester or bird screen. C. Hood to keep out the rain.*

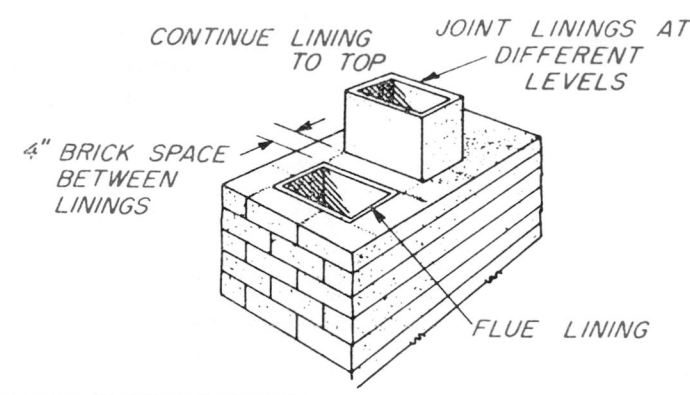

55-5. *Flues should be 4" apart.*

mortar joints. There should be no gaps anywhere in the mortar joints. A *push-filled joint* is one created by pushing the brick into a thick bed of mortar and then striking off the excess mortar that squeezes out.

Flue Lining. The size of the chimney depends on the number of flues, the presence of a fireplace, and the design of the house. The house design may include a room-wide brick or stone fireplace wall which extends through the roof. While only two or three flues may be required for heating units and fireplaces, several "false" flues may be added at the top for appearance. Each fireplace should have a separate flue and flues must be separated by a 4" wide brick spacer (wythe) between them. Fig. 55-5.

Chimneys are sometimes built without flue lining to reduce cost, but those with lined flues are safer and more efficient. Lined flues are recommended for brick chimneys. When the flue is not lined, mortar and bricks directly exposed to the action of flue gases disintegrate. This disintegration plus that caused by temperature changes can open cracks in the masonry. This will reduce the draft and increase the fire hazard.

Flue lining can be omitted if the chimney walls are made of reinforced concrete at least 6" thick or of unreinforced concrete or brick at least 8" thick. However, the cost of the extra brick or masonry and the labor involved are most likely greater than the cost of flue lining. Furthermore, a well-installed flue lining will result in a safer chimney.

Rectangular fireclay flue linings or round vitrified (glazed) tile can normally be used in all chimneys. Vitrified tile or a stainless steel lining is usually required for gas-burning equipment. Local codes outline specific requirements.

Rectangular flue lining is made in 2' lengths and in sizes of 8" × 8", 8" × 12", 12" × 12", 12" × 16", and up to 20" × 20". Wall thicknesses of the flue linings vary with the size of the flue. The smaller sizes have a ⅝" thick wall. The larger sizes vary from ¾" to 1⅜" in thickness.

Vitrified tiles, 8" in diameter, are most commonly used for the flues of heating units. Larger sizes are also available. This tile has a bell joint.

Each length of lining should be set in cement mortar with the joint struck smooth on the inside. The brick should then be laid around it. If the lining is slipped down after several courses of brick have been laid, the joints cannot be filled and leakage will occur. In masonry chimneys with walls less than 8" thick, there should be space between the lining and the chimney walls. This space should not be filled with mortar. Use only enough mortar to make good joints and to hold the flue lining in position.

Unless it rests on solid masonry at the bottom of the flue, the lower section of lining must be supported on at least three sides by brick courses projecting to the inside surface of the lining. The lining should extend to a point at least 8" below the smoke pipe thimble. Fig. 55-6. In fireplaces, the flue liner should start at the top of the throat and extend to the top of the chimney.

Flues should be as nearly vertical as possible. If a change in direction is necessary, the angle should never exceed 45°. An angle of 30° or less is better because sharp turns set up

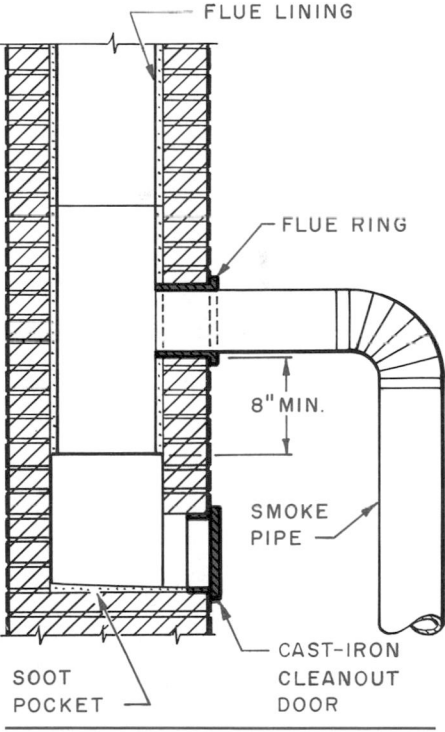

55-6. *Flue lining should extend at least 8" below the smoke pipe thimble. Note also the soot pocket and the cast-iron cleanout access door.*

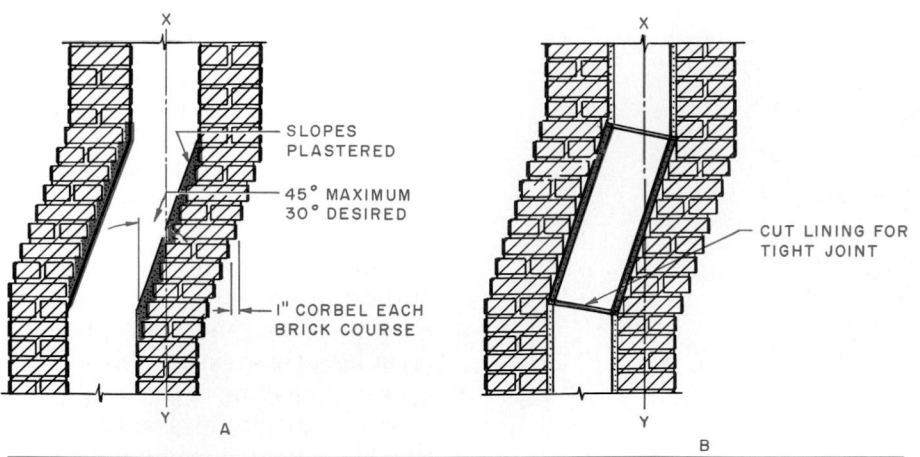

55-7. *Offsetting a chimney. For structural safety, the amount of offset must be limited. The centerline of the upper flue (XY) should not fall beyond the center of the lower-flue wall. A. Start to offset the left wall of an unlined flue two brick courses higher than the right wall so that the area of the sloping section will not be reduced after plastering. B. Method of cutting a flue lining to make a tight joint.*

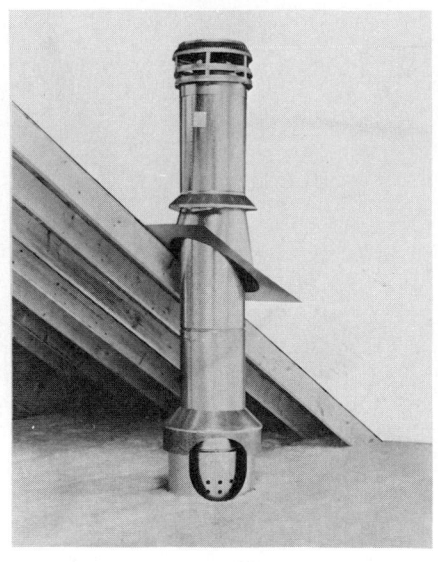

55-9. *An insulated metal chimney.*

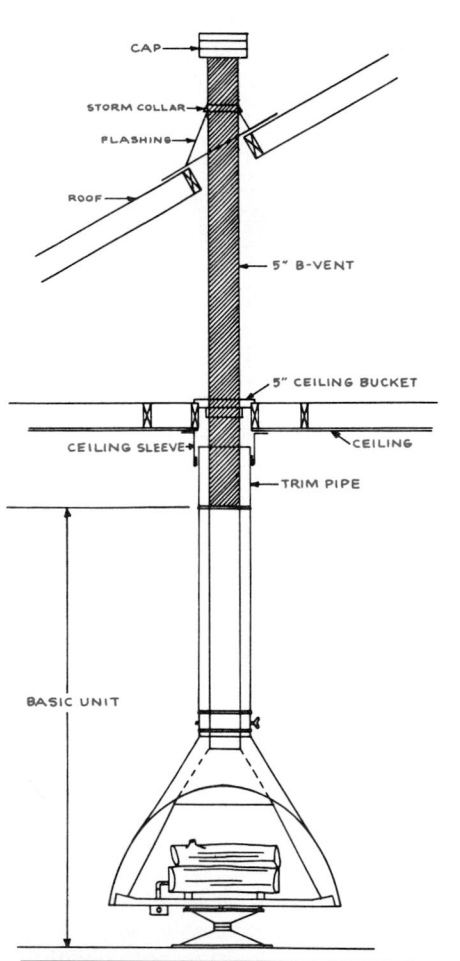

55-8. *Metal flues are frequently used for factory-built fireplaces.*

eddies (irregular air currents) which affect the motion of smoke and gases. Where a flue does change directions, the lining joints should be made tight by mitering or cutting equally the ends of the adjoining sections. Fig. 55-7. Cut the lining before it is built into the chimney. If cut after, it may break and fall out of place. To cut the lining, stuff a sack of damp sand into it and then tap a sharp chisel with a light hammer along the desired line of cut.

When laying lining and brick, draw a tight-fitting bag of straw up the flue as the work progresses to catch material that might fall and block the flue.

Metal Flues. Gas-fired house heaters and built-in metal fireplaces can be connected to metal flues instead of to a masonry chimney. Fig. 55-8. The flues should be made of corrosion-resistant metal not lighter than 20 gauge. They should comply with the recommendations of Underwriters' Laboratories, Inc. The flues must extend through the roof.

Metal flues sometimes consist of several layers of metal with an airspace between each layer. This allows air to circulate around each layer and cool it. These flues are sometimes called "air-insulated" or "triple wall" flues. Fig. 55-9. This type of flue system is often housed in a wood-framed chimney that matches the architectural style of the house. Fig. 55-10.

Chimney Walls. Walls of chimneys that have lined flues and are not more than 30' high should be at least 4" thick if made of brick or reinforced concrete and at least 12" thick if made of stone. A minimum thickness of 8" is recommended for the exterior wall of a chimney exposed to the weather.

The flue sizes are made to conform to the width and length of a brick so that full-length bricks can be used to enclose the flue lining. Thus an 8" × 8" flue lining (about 8½" × 8½" in outside dimensions) with the minimum 4" thickness of surrounding masonry will use six standard bricks for each course. Fig. 55-11a. An 8" × 12"

55-10. *Prefabricated metal chimneys are often contained in wood-framed chimney surrounds that match the style of the house.*

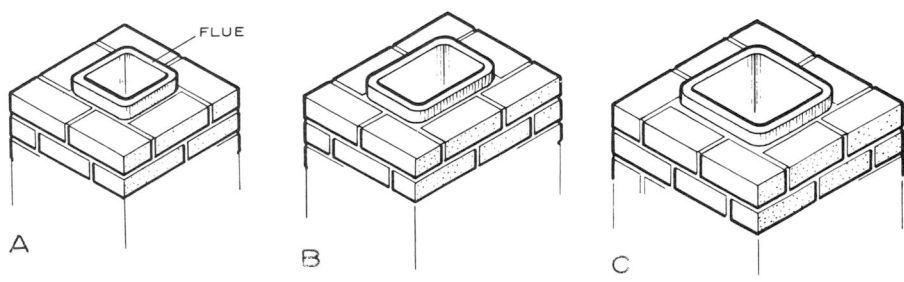

55-11. *Brick and flue combinations: A. 8" x 8" flue lining. B. 8" x 12" flue lining. C. 12" x 12" flue lining.*

flue lining (8½" × 13" in outside dimensions) will be enclosed by seven bricks at each course. Fig. 55-11b. A 12" × 12" flue (13" × 13" in outside dimensions) will be enclosed by eight bricks, and so on. Fig. 55-11c.

Brick chimneys that extend through the roof may sway enough in heavy winds to open up mortar joints at the roof line. Openings to the flue at that point are dangerous because sparks from the flue may start fires in the woodwork or roofing. A good practice is to make the upper walls 8" thick by starting to offset the bricks at least 6" below the underside of roof joists or rafters. Fig. 55-12.

Chimneys may contain more than one flue. Building codes generally require a separate flue for each fireplace, furnace, or boiler. If a chimney contains three or more lined flues, each group of two flues

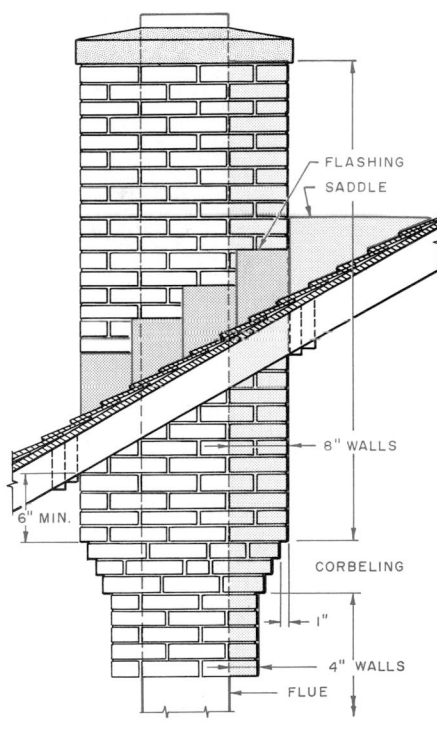

55-12. *Corbeling a chimney (offsetting the bricks) to provide 8" walls for the section above the roofline.*

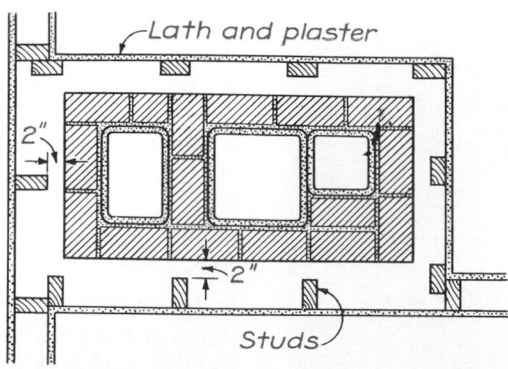

55-13a. *A three-flue chimney. The walls between the flues are bonded by staggering the joints of successive courses. Wood framing should be at least 2" from the masonry.*

55-13b. *Ceiling joists and other framing should not touch the chimney.*

must be separated from the other flues by brick divisions, or wythes. Fig. 55-13. Two flues grouped together without a dividing wall should have the lining joints staggered at least 7", and the joints must be completely filled with mortar. If a chimney contains two or more unlined flues, the flues must be separated by a well-bonded wythe at least 8" thick.

Soot Pocket and Cleanout.

A soot pocket and cleanout are recommended for each flue. Fig.

55-6. Deep soot pockets permit the accumulation of too much soot, which may catch fire. Therefore the pocket should be only deep enough to permit the installation of a cleanout door below the smoke pipe connection. The lower part of the chimney from the bottom of the soot pocket to the base of the chimney is filled with solid masonry.

The cleanout door should be made of cast iron. It should fit snugly and be kept tightly closed to keep air out. A cleanout should

serve only one flue. If two or more flues are connected to the same cleanout, air drawn from one to another will affect the draft in all the flues.

Smoke Pipe. No range, stove, fireplace, or other equipment should be connected to the flue for the central heating unit. In fact, as stated previously, each unit should be connected to a separate flue. If there are two or more connections to the same flue, fires may occur from sparks passing into one flue opening and out through another flue opening.

Smoke pipes connect a stove, furnace, or metal fireplace to a flue. They must be correctly installed and connected to the chimney for safe operation. A smoke pipe should enter the chimney horizontally and should not extend into the flue. Fig. 55-6. The hole in the chimney wall should be lined with fireclay, or metal thimbles should be tightly built into the masonry. Metal thimbles or flue rings are available in diameters of 6", 7", 8", 10", and 12", and in lengths of 4½", 6", 9", and 12". To make an airtight connection where the pipe enters the wall, install a closely fitting collar and apply boiler putty, good cement mortar, or stiff clay.

A smoke pipe should never be closer than 9" to woodwork or other combustible material. If it is less than 18" from woodwork or other combustible material, cover at least that half of the pipe nearest the woodwork with fire-resistant material. Commercial fireproof pipe covering is available.

If a smoke pipe must pass through a wood partition, the woodwork has to be protected. Either cut an opening in the partition and insert a galvanized-iron, double-wall ventilating shield at least 12" larger than the pipe, or install at least 4" of brickwork or

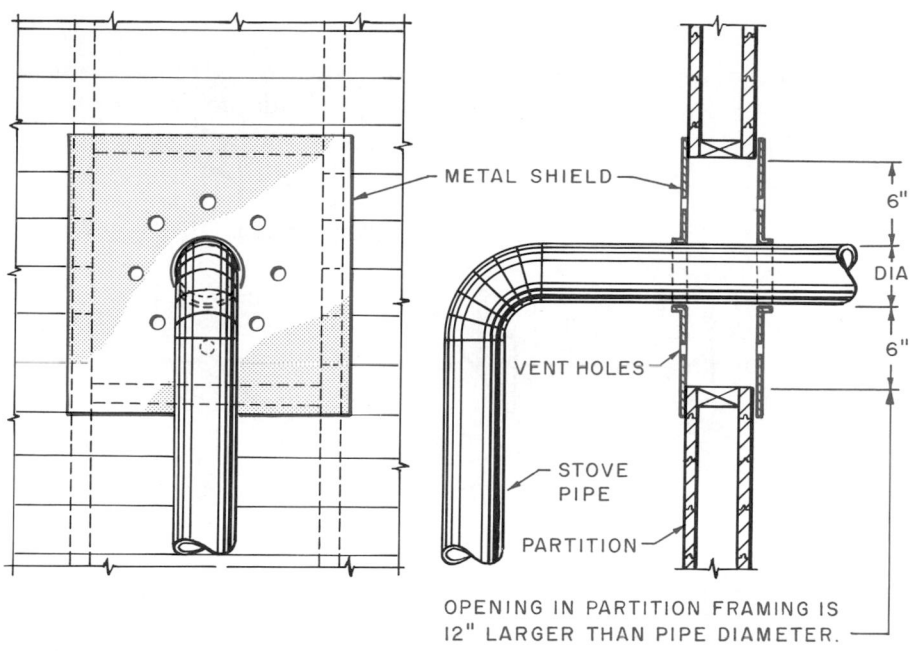

METAL SHIELD

VENT HOLES

STOVE PIPE

PARTITION

6"

DIA

6"

OPENING IN PARTITION FRAMING IS 12" LARGER THAN PIPE DIAMETER.

55-14. A wood partition must be protected when a smoke pipe passes through it.

other incombustible material around the pipe. Fig. 55-14.

Smoke pipes should never pass through floors, closets, or concealed spaces or enter the chimney in the attic.

Insulation. No wood should be in contact with the chimney. Leave

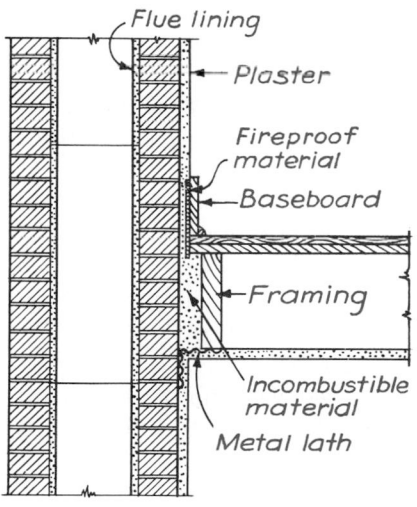

Flue lining

Plaster

Fireproof material

Baseboard

Framing

Incombustible material

Metal lath

55-15. Wood floor joists and the baseboard must be insulated at a chimney.

a 2" space between the chimney walls and all wooden beams or joists. Fig. 55-13. Solid masonry walls 8" thick can be within ½" of the chimney masonry.

Fill the space between wall and floor framing with porous, nonmetallic, incombustible material, such as loose cinders. Fig. 55-15. Do not use brickwork, mortar, or concrete. Place the filling before the floor is laid. It not only forms a firestop but also prevents the accumulation of shavings or other combustible

material. Flooring and subflooring can be laid within ¾" of the masonry.

A coat of cement plaster should be applied to chimney walls that will be surrounded by wood partitions or other combustible materials. Wood studding, furring, or lathing should be at least 2" from chimney walls. Plaster is sometimes applied directly to the masonry, or to metal lath laid over the masonry. However, this is not recommended because settlement of the chimney may crack the plaster.

Sometimes baseboards are fastened to plaster that is in direct contact with the chimney wall. In that case, install a layer of fireproof material at least ⅛" thick between the baseboard and the plaster. Fig. 55-15.

Roof Connection. Where the chimney passes through the roof, a 2" clearance between the wood framing and the masonry is required for fire protection. This clearance will also permit expansion due to temperature changes, settlement, and slight movement during heavy winds.

Chimneys must be flashed and counterflashed to make the junction with the roof watertight. Fig. 55-16. When the chimney is located on the slope of a roof, a saddle (sometimes called a cricket) is built high enough to shed water

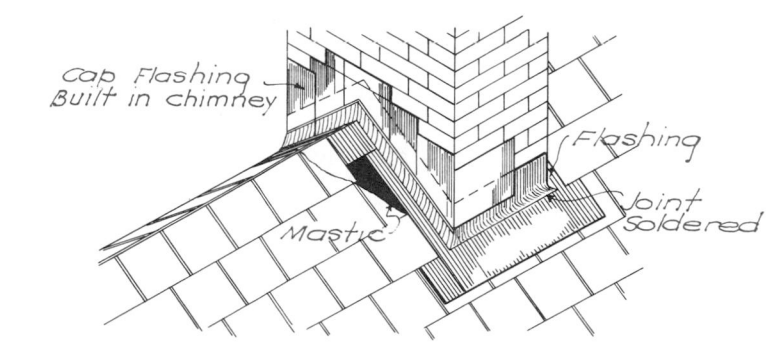

Cap Flashing Built in chimney

Flashing

Joint Soldered

Mastic

55-16. Flashing at a chimney located on a ridge.

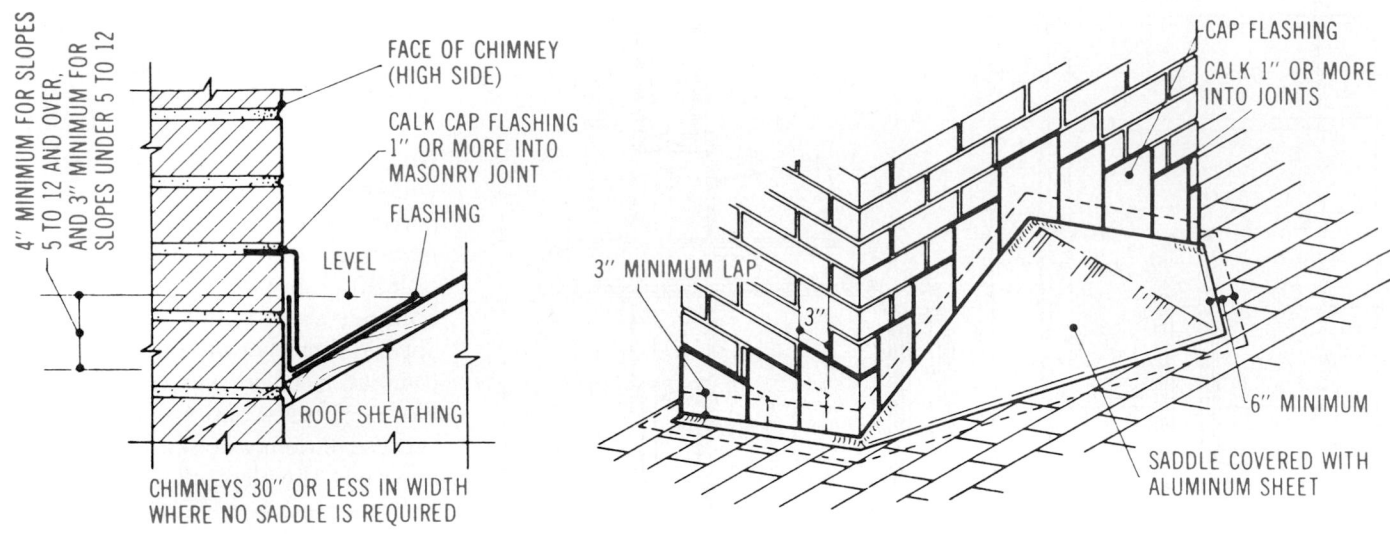

55-17. *Flashing a chimney that projects through a sloping roof.*

around the chimney. Fig. 55-17. Corrosion-resistant metal, such as copper, aluminum, zinc, or lead, should be used for flashing. Galvanized or tinned sheet steel will require occasional painting.

Chimney Top Construction

To prevent moisture from entering between the brick and flue lining, a concrete cap is usually poured over the top course of brick. Precast or stone caps with a cement wash are also used. The flue lining extends at least 4" above the cap or top course of brick and is surrounded by at least 2" of cement mortar. The mortar is finished with a straight or concave slope to direct air currents upward at the top of the flue and to drain water from the top of the chimney. Fig. 55-4a and 55-18.

Hoods are used to keep rain out of chimneys and to prevent downdraft due to nearby buildings, trees, or other objects. Common types are the arched brick hood and the flat stone or cast concrete cap. If the hood covers more than one

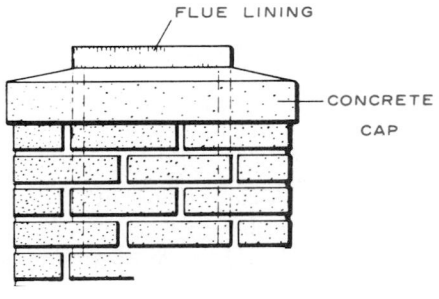

55-18. *A chimney cap.*

flue, it should be divided by wythes so that each flue has a separate section. The area of the hood opening for each flue must be larger than the area of the flue. Fig. 55-4c.

Spark arresters are recommended when burning fuels that give off sparks, such as sawdust, or when burning paper or other trash. Fig. 55-4b. Spark arresters may be required when chimneys are on or near combustible roofs, woodland, lumber, or other combustible material. They are not recommended when burning soft coal because they may become plugged with soot.

Spark arresters do not entirely eliminate the discharge of sparks.

However, if properly built and installed, they greatly reduce the hazard. They should be made of rust-resistant material and should have screen openings not larger than ⅝" nor smaller than ⁵⁄₁₆". They should completely enclose the flue discharge area and must be securely fastened to the top of the chimney.

Prefabricated Chimneys

Many new types of lightweight chimneys that require no masonry protection nor concrete footings are available. If a heating system is such that this type of chimney can be used, the following precautions should be observed.

➤ Make sure the model has been tested and listed by the Underwriters' Laboratories, Inc.

➤ Install the chimney in strict accordance with the manufacturer's instructions.

➤ Make sure the unit conforms to the local building code.

FIREPLACES

A fireplace is a luxury except in mild climates or in locations where other heating systems are not available. Since an ordinary fireplace has an efficiency of only about 10%, its value as a heating unit is low compared to its decorative value and to the cheerful and homelike atmosphere it creates. The heating efficiency of a fireplace can be materially increased by the use of a factory-made metal unit that is incorporated in the fireplace structure. This unit allows air to be heated and circulated throughout a room, separate from the direct heat of the fire.

Design

Varied fireplace designs are possible. Figs. 55-19 and 55-20. A fireplace should harmonize in detail and proportion with the room in which it is located, but safety and utility should not be sacrificed for appearance. A fireplace should not be located near doors.

Fireplace openings are usually made from 2' to 6' wide. The kind of fuel to be used will determine the width. For example, if cordwood (4' long) is to be cut in half and burned, an opening 30" wide is desirable. However, if coal is to be burned, a narrower opening can be used.

The height of the opening can range from 18" for an opening 2' wide to 28" for one that is 6' wide. The higher the opening, the more chance of a smoky fireplace.

In general, the wider the opening, the greater the depth. A shallow opening throws out relatively more heat than a deep one, but holds smaller pieces of wood. The choice, then, is between a deeper opening that holds larger,

55-19. A fireplace installed and trimmed becomes an attractive and functional part of the home.

longer-burning logs and a shallower one that takes smaller pieces of wood but throws out more heat. In small fireplaces, a depth of 12" may permit good draft. However, a minimum depth of 16" is recommended to lessen the danger of firebrands falling out on the floor. Suitable screens should be placed in front of all fireplaces to minimize the danger from brands and sparks.

Because of the reduced flue height, second-floor fireplaces are usually made smaller than first-floor ones.

Construction

The construction of a typical fireplace and recommended dimensions for essential parts or areas of fireplaces of various sizes are shown in Fig. 55-21.

Footings. Foundation and footing construction for chimneys with fireplaces is similar to that for chimneys without fireplaces. Be sure the footings rest on good firm soil below the frostline.

Hearth. The hearth consists of two parts: the front, or finish, hearth and the back hearth, under the fire. Because the back hearth must withstand intense heat, it is built of heat-resistant materials, such as firebrick. The front hearth is simply a precaution against flying sparks. While it must be noncombustible, it need not resist intense prolonged heat.

The fireplace hearth should project far enough in front of the fireplace opening to minimize the chance that any sparks could ignite the nearby floor:

➤ If the fireplace opening is less than 6' in area, the hearth should extend at least 16" in front of the opening. In width, the hearth should extend at least 8" on either side of the fireplace opening. In other words, the hearth should be at least 16" wider than the fireplace opening.

➤ If the fireplace opening is 6' in area or larger, the hearth should extend 20" in front of the opening. In width, the hearth should extend at least 12" to either side of the fireplace opening. In other words, it should be at least 24" wider than the fireplace opening.

The hearth can be flush with the floor so that sweepings can be brushed into the fireplace, or it can be raised. Raising the hearth to various levels and extending its length as desired is presently common practice, especially in contemporary design. If there is a basement, a convenient ash dump can be built under the back of the hearth. Fig. 55-22.

In buildings with wooden floors, the hearth in front of the fireplace should be supported by masonry trimmer arches or other fire-resistant construction. Fig. 55-23.

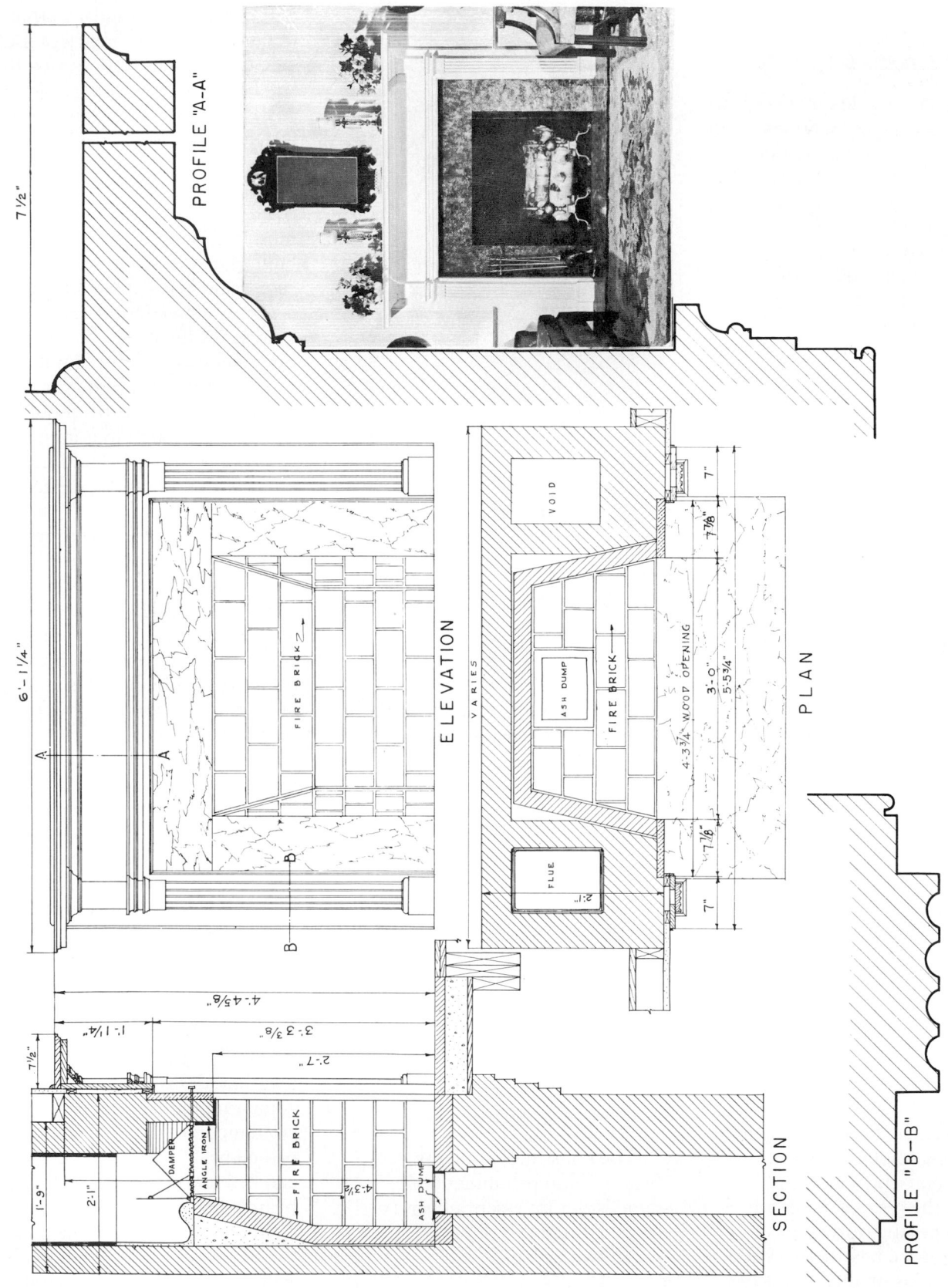

55-20a. *Construction details for a fireplace mantle available as a precut millwork item.*

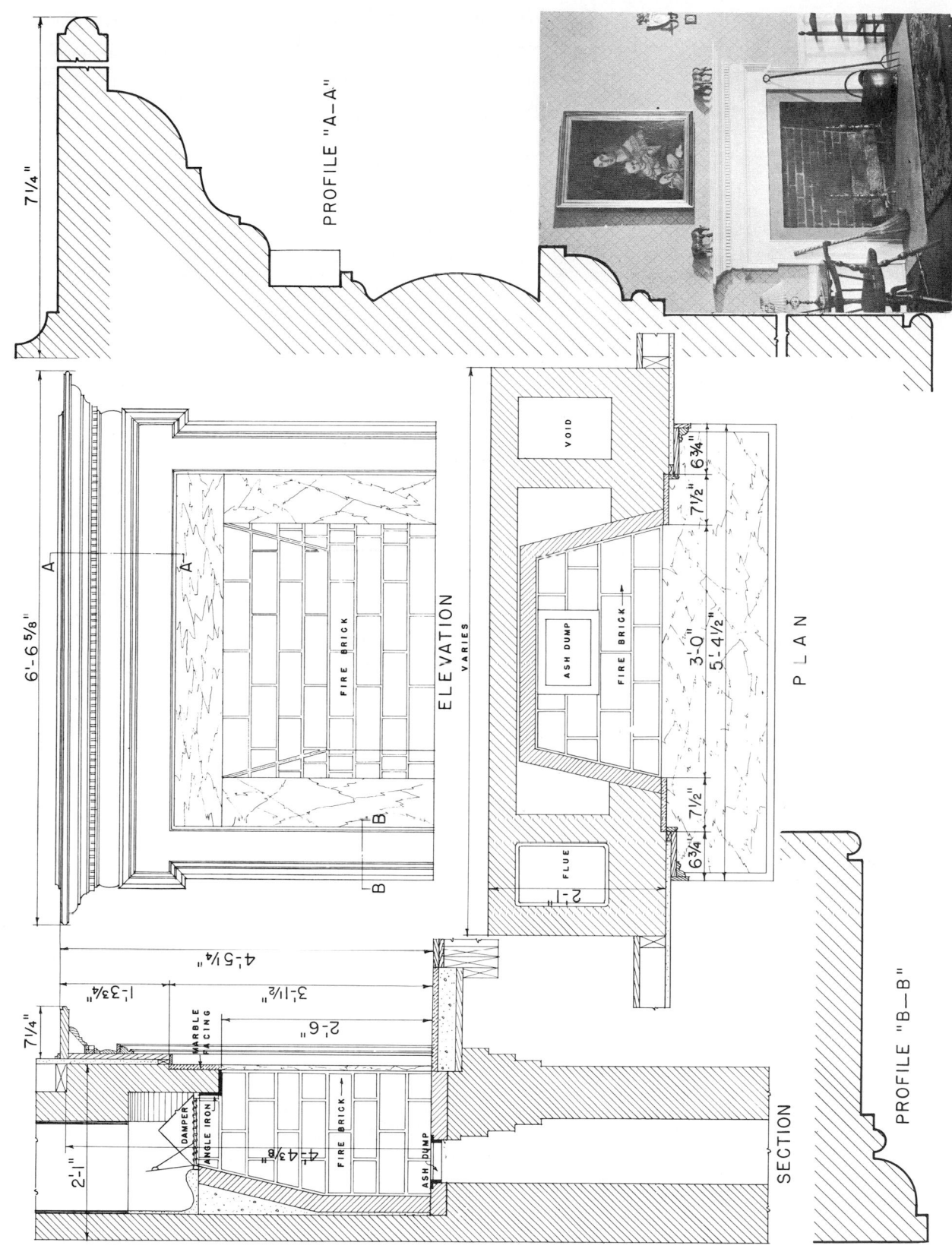

PROFILE "A–A"

7¼"

6'-6⅝"

A

A'

ELEVATION
VARIES

FIRE BRICK

B

B'

PLAN

VOID

ASH DUMP

FIRE BRICK

FLUE

2'-1"

7½"   6¾"

3'-0"

5'-4½"

7½"   6¾"

SECTION

7¼"

1'-3¾"

4'-5¼"

3'-1½"

2'-6"

MARBLE FACING

DAMPER

ANGLE IRON

FIRE BRICK

ASH DUMP

4'-4⅜"

2'-1"

PROFILE "B–B"

55-20b. *Another typical construction detail for a fireplace mantle available as a precut millwork item.*

Recommended Dimensions For Fireplaces And Size of Flue Lining Required

Size of fireplace opening		Depth	Minimum width of back wall	Height of vertical back wall	Height of inclined back wall	Size of flue lining required	
Width w Inches	Height h Inches	d Inches	c Inches	a Inches	b Inches	Standard rectangular (outside dimensions) Inches	Standard round (inside diameter) Inches
24	24	16–18	14	14	16	8½ x 8½	10
28	24	16–18	14	14	16	8½ x 8½	10
30	28–30	16–18	16	14	18	8½ x 13	10
36	28–30	16–18	22	14	18	8½ x 13	12
42	28–32	16–18	28	14	18	13 x 13	12
48	32	18–20	32	14	24	13 x 13	15
54	36	18–20	36	14	28	13 x 18	15
60	36	18–20	44	14	28	13 x 18	15
54	40	20–22	36	17	29	13 x 18	15
60	40	20–22	42	17	30	18 x 18	18
66	40	20–22	44	17	30	18 x 18	18
72	40	22–28	51	17	30	18 x 18	18

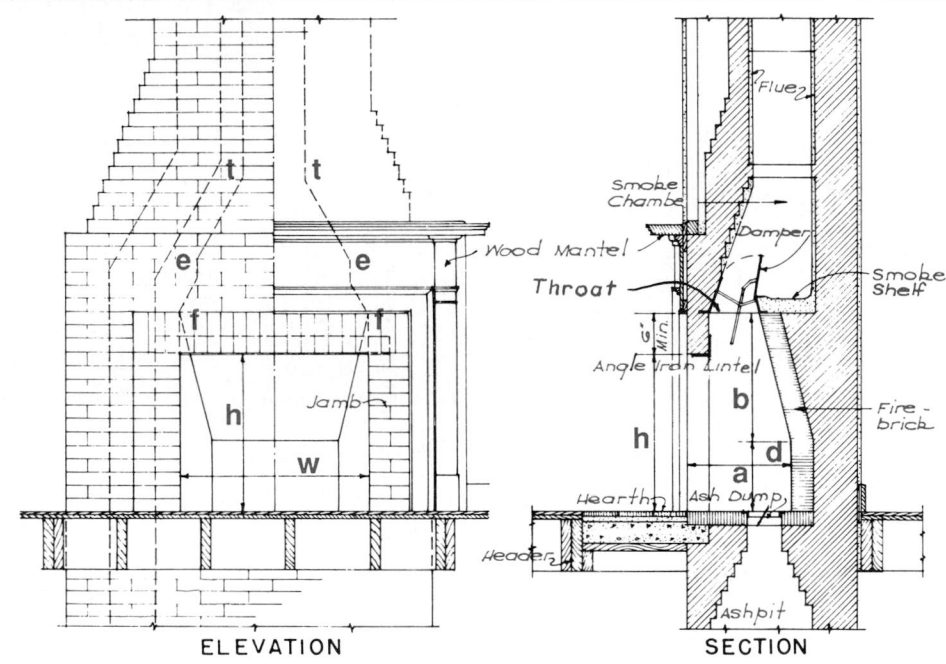

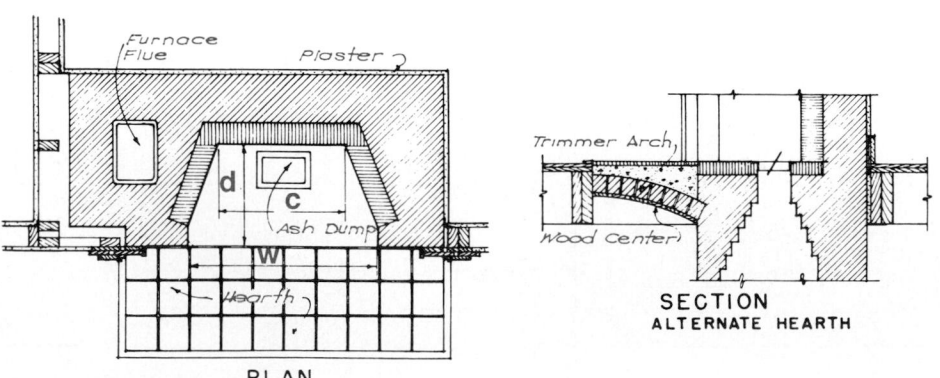

55-21. *Fireplace construction details.*

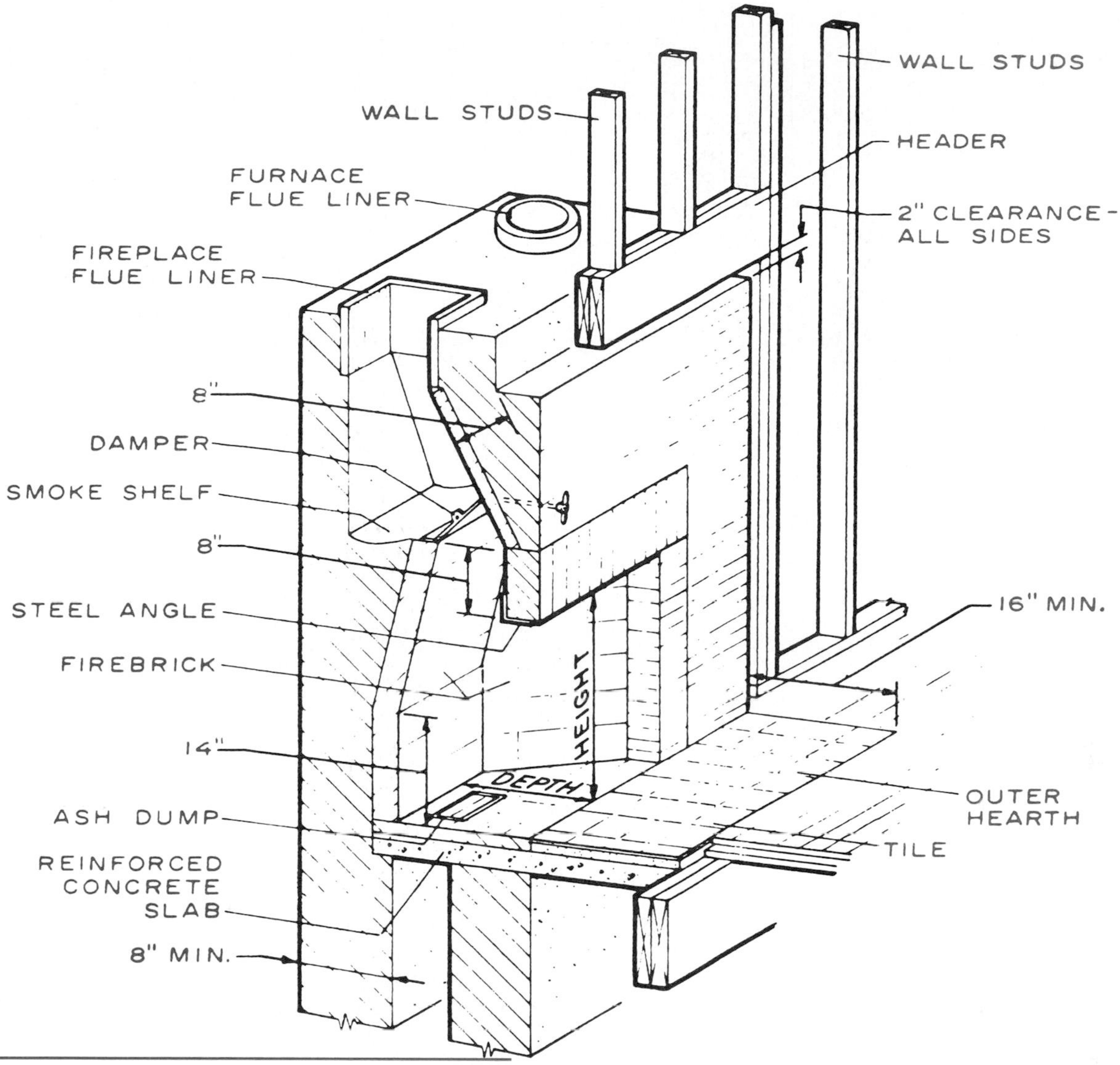

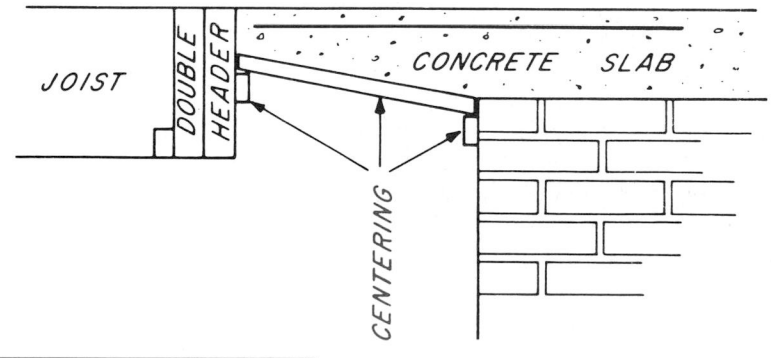

WALL STUDS

FURNACE FLUE LINER

FIREPLACE FLUE LINER

8"

DAMPER

SMOKE SHELF

8"

STEEL ANGLE

FIREBRICK

14"

ASH DUMP

REINFORCED CONCRETE SLAB

8" MIN.

HEIGHT

DEPTH

WALL STUDS

HEADER

2" CLEARANCE-ALL SIDES

16" MIN.

OUTER HEARTH

TILE

55-22. *Fireplace construction and framing details.*

JOIST

DOUBLE HEADER

CONCRETE SLAB

CENTERING

55-23. *Hearth centering detail.*

Wood centering under the arches used during construction of the hearth and hearth extension must be removed when construction is completed. Figure 55-24 shows the recommended method of installing floor framing around the hearth.

Walls. Building codes generally require that the back and sides of fireplaces be constructed of solid masonry or reinforced concrete at least 8" thick. They also generally require that they be lined with firebrick or other approved noncombustible material not less than 2" thick or with steel lining

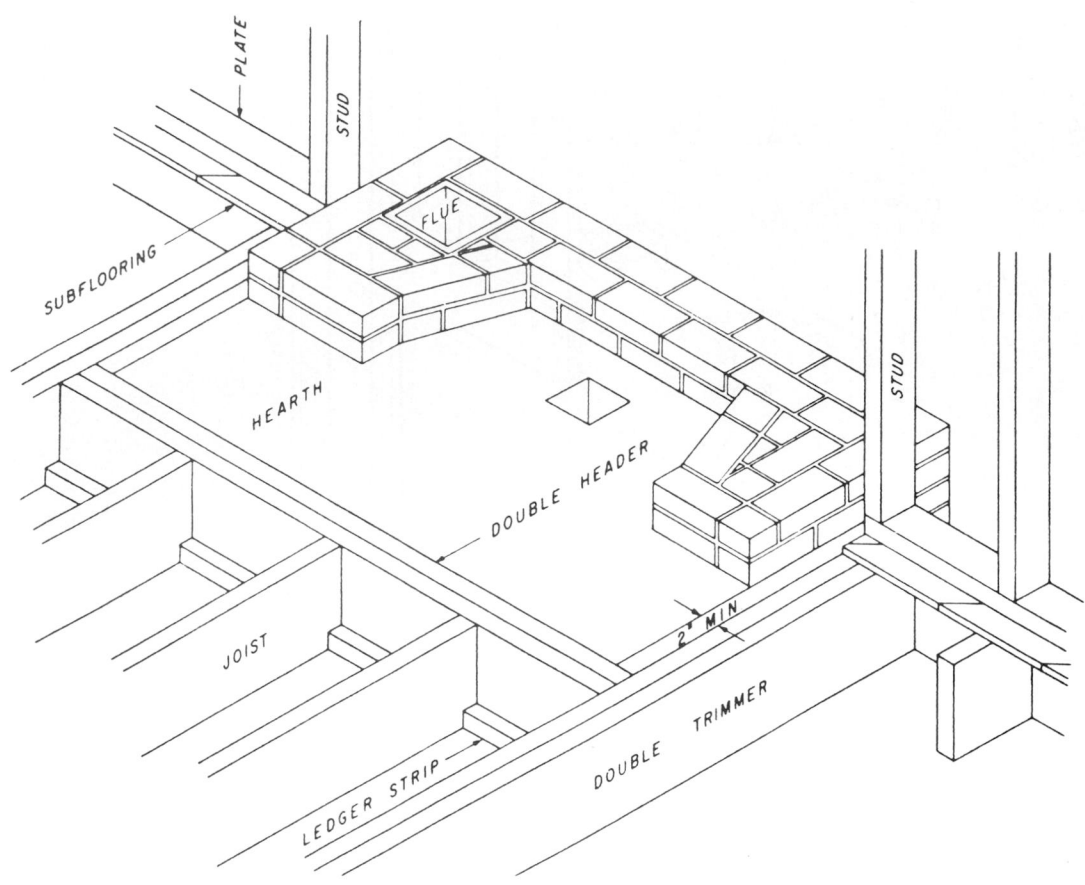

55-24. *Floor framing details around a fireplace.*

not less than ¼" thick. Such lining may be omitted when the walls are of solid masonry or reinforced concrete at least 12" thick.

Jambs. The jambs of the fireplace should be wide enough to provide stability and to present a pleasing appearance. For a fireplace opening 3' wide or less, the jambs can be 12" wide if a wood mantel will be used or 16" wide if they will be of exposed masonry. For wider fireplace openings, or if the fireplace is in a large room, the jambs should be proportionately wider. Fireplace jambs are frequently faced with ornamental brick or tile. Fig. 55-21.

No woodwork should be placed within 6" of the fireplace opening. Woodwork above and projecting more than 1½" from the fireplace opening should be placed at least 12" above the top of the fireplace opening. The mantel height above the opening can also be figured by adding 6" to the width of the mantel. Fig. 55-25.

Lintels. A lintel must be installed across the top of the fireplace opening to support the masonry. For fireplace openings 4' wide or less, ½" × 3" flat steel bars, 3½" × 3½" × ¼" angle irons, or specially designed damper frames may be used. Wider openings will require heavier lintels.

If a masonry arch is used over the opening, the fireplace jambs must be heavy enough to resist the thrust of the arch.

Throat. Proper construction of the throat area is essential for a satisfactory fireplace. Fig. 55-21, f-f. The sides of the fireplace must be vertical up to the throat, which should be 6" to 8" or more above the bottom of the lintel. The area of the throat must be not less than that of the flue. The length must be equal to the width of the fireplace opening, and the width of the throat will depend on the width of the damper frame (if a damper is installed). Five inches above the throat (at e-e in Fig. 55-21) the sidewalls should start sloping inward to meet the flue (at t-t in Fig. 55-21).

Damper. A damper consists of a cast iron frame with a hinged lid that opens or closes to vary the

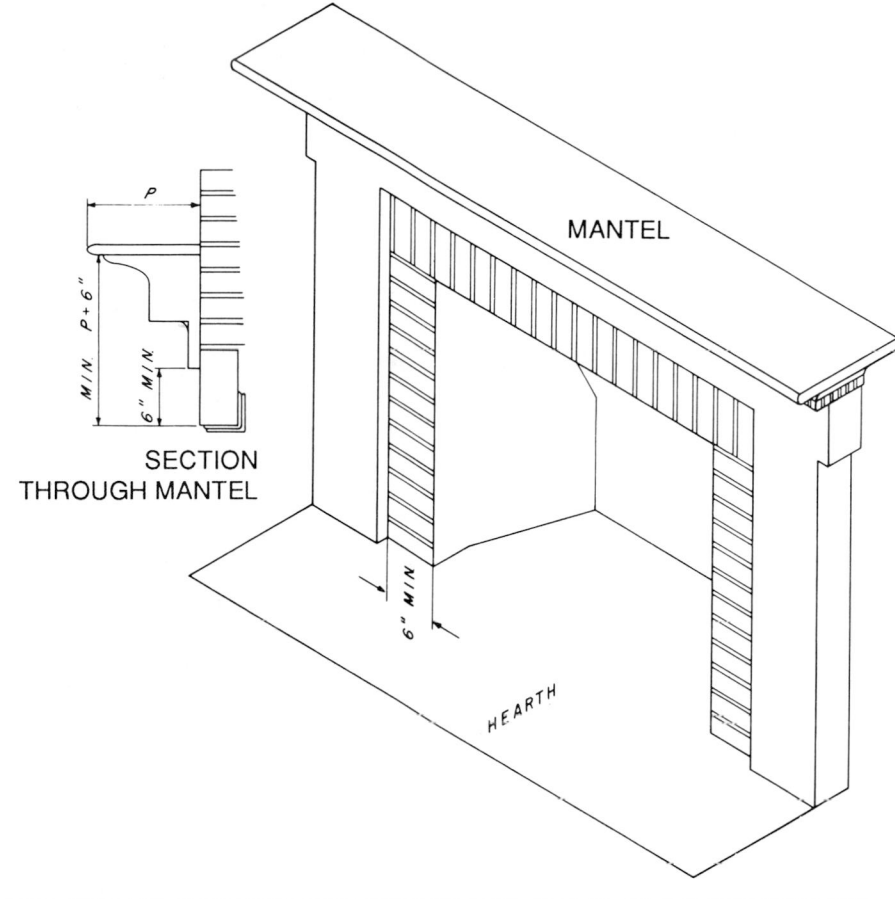

SECTION
THROUGH MANTEL

MANTEL

HEARTH

55-25. *Trim clearance around a fireplace opening. The mantel should be 6" plus the width of the mantel above the top of the fireplace opening.*

throat opening. Dampers are not always installed, but they are recommended, especially in cold climates.

With a well-designed, properly installed damper, you can:

➤ Regulate the draft.

➤ Close the fireplace flue to prevent loss of heat from the room when there is no fire in the fireplace. In the summer, the flue should be closed to prevent loss of cool air from the air-conditioning system.

➤ Adjust the throat opening according to the type of fire and thus reduce heat loss. For example, a roaring pine fire may require a full throat opening, but a slow-burning hardwood log fire may require an opening of only 1" or 2". Closing the damper to the opening

will reduce loss of heat up the chimney.

➤ Close or partially close the flue to prevent loss of heat from the main heating system. When air heated by a furnace goes up a chimney, an excessive amount of fuel may be wasted.

➤ Close the flue in the summer to prevent insects from entering the house through the chimney.

Dampers of various designs are on the market. Some support the masonry over fireplace openings, thus replacing ordinary lintels. It is important that the full damper opening equal the area of the flue.

Smoke shelf and chamber. A smoke shelf prevents downdraft. Fig. 55-21. It is made by setting the brickwork at the top of the throat

back to the line of the flue wall for the full length of the throat. Depth of the shelf may be 6" to 12" or more, depending on the depth of the fireplace. The smoke shelf is concave to retain any slight amount of rain that may enter.

The smoke chamber is the area from the top of the throat (e-e in Fig. 55-21) to the bottom of the flue (t-t in Fig. 55-21). As stated under "Throat," the sidewalls should slope inward to meet the flue. The smoke shelf and the smoke chamber walls should be plastered with cement mortar at least ½" thick.

Fireplace flue. Proper proportion between the area of the fireplace opening, area of the flue, and height of the flue is essential for satisfactory operation of the fireplace. The area of a lined flue 22' high should be at least 1/12 of the area of the fireplace opening. The area of an unlined flue or a flue less than 22' high should be 1/10 of the area of the fireplace opening.

The table in Fig. 55-21 lists dimensions of fireplace openings and indicates the size of flue lining required. Flue construction principles given under "Chimneys" apply also to fireplace flues.

Fireplaces with two or more openings require much larger flues than the conventional fireplace. Fig. 55-26. For example, a fireplace with two open adjacent faces would require a 12" × 16" flue for an opening 34" wide by 20" deep by 30" high. A, Fig. 55-26. Local building regulations usually cover the proper sizes for these types of fireplaces.

Modified Fireplaces

Modified fireplaces are manufactured fireplace units. They are made of heavy metal and are designed to be set in place and concealed by the usual brickwork

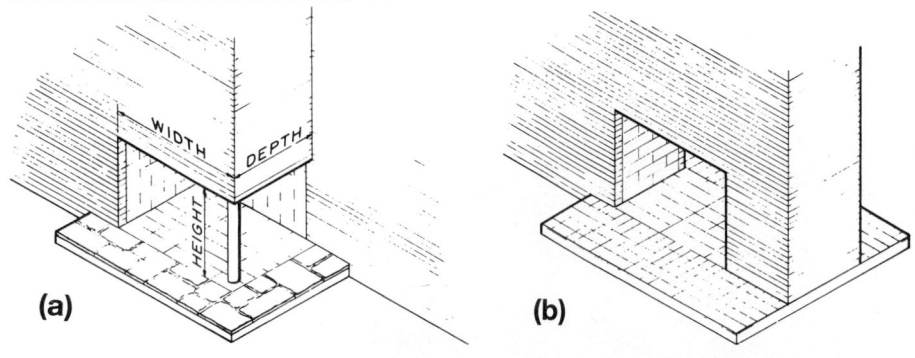

(a)   **(b)**

55-26. *Dual-opening fireplaces: A. Adjacent opening. B. Through fireplace.*

55-27a. *Modified fireplace. Air is drawn through inlet "a" from the room being heated. The air is heated upon contact with the metal and discharged through outlet "b". The inlets and outlets are connected to registers that may be located at the front, as shown, at the ends of the fireplace, or even in an adjacent or second-story room.*

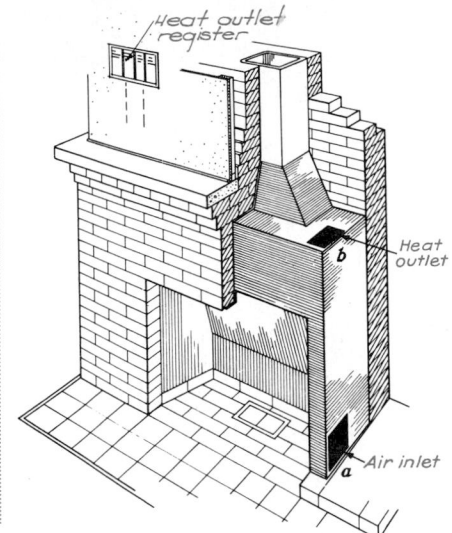

or other construction. Fig. 55-27. They contain all the essential fireplace parts: firebox, damper, throat, and smoke shelf and chamber. In the completed installation, only grilles show. Fig. 55-27a.

These fireplace units are available in a variety of styles for

55-27c. *A finished modified fireplace with contemporary styling. This unit is of the type shown at the right in Fig. 55-27b.*

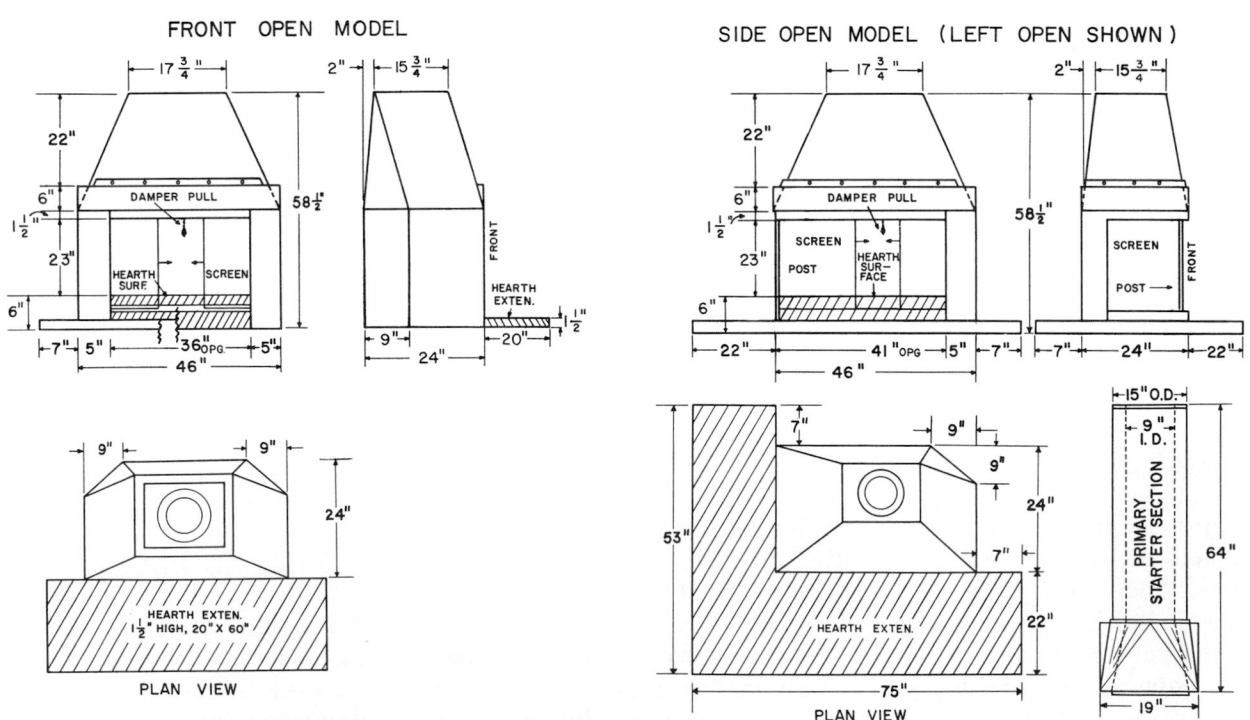

55-27b. *Manufacturer's details of two modified fireplace units.*

55-27d. *A finished modified fireplace with traditional styling. This unit is of the type shown at the left in Fig. 55-27b.*

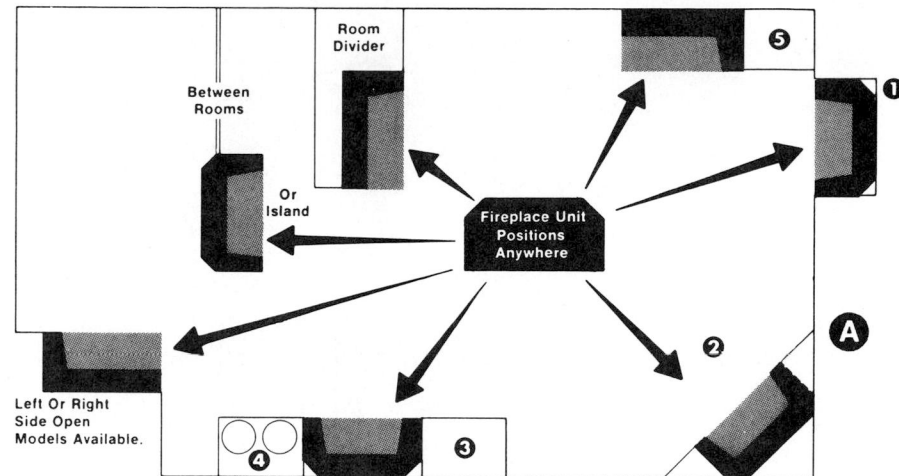

1. In Outside Chase, Breezeway, Garage, Or in Unused Attic If On Upper Floor.
2. Position In Corner And Save Additional Floor Space.
3. Built-In Bookcases Or Storage Space.
4. Venting From Other Units.
5. Log Storage, Etc.

55-28. *The modified fireplace system can be built into or out from any wall, used as part of a room divider, or placed into any corner.*

different room locations. Fig. 55-28. Multilevel installations are also possible through the use of chimney offsets, elbows, and various types of roof terminations. Figs. 55-29 and 55-30.

Modified fireplaces offer two advantages:

➤ The correctly designed and proportioned firebox provides a ready-made form for the masonry. This reduces the chance of faulty construction and assures a smokeless fireplace.

➤ When properly installed, the better designed units heat more efficiently than ordinary fireplaces. They circulate heat into the cold corners of rooms and can deliver heated air through ducts to upper or adjoining rooms.

Even a well-designed modified fireplace unit will not operate properly if the chimney is inadequate. Therefore, when a conventional masonry chimney is used, proper chimney construction is as important for a modified unit as it is for ordinary fireplaces.

The modified fireplace system is easy to handle. Factory-built components are quickly installed for a complete operating fireplace, hearth to chimney top.

Framing required to enclose modified fireplace units is not complicated. However, proper clearances should be observed. The manufacturer of the fireplace unit you select will have specific framing instructions. For an indication of the type of framing required, see Fig. 55-31.

Freestanding Fireplaces

Freestanding fireplace units, with all the parts needed for a complete fireplace-to-chimney installation, are also available. Figs. 55-32 and 55-33.

Such units offer these features:

➤ Wide selection of styles, shapes, and colors.

➤ Pretested design that is highly efficient in operation.

➤ Easy and versatile installation. They can be installed freestanding or flush against a wall in practically any part of a house.

➤ Light weight.

➤ Lower cost than comparable masonry units.

The basic part of the freestanding fireplace is a specially insulated metal firebox shell. Since it is light in weight, the fireplace can be set directly on the floor without the heavy footing required for masonry fireplaces.

Outdoor Fireplaces

Outdoor fireplaces range from simple makeshift units to elaborate structures designed to harmonize with and enhance the look of the house and the landscape.

Built-in features, such as ovens, grills, storage compartments, sinks, and benches add to the appearance and convenience of fireplaces. Many homes now include backyard picnic and cooking facilities. Fig. 55-34.

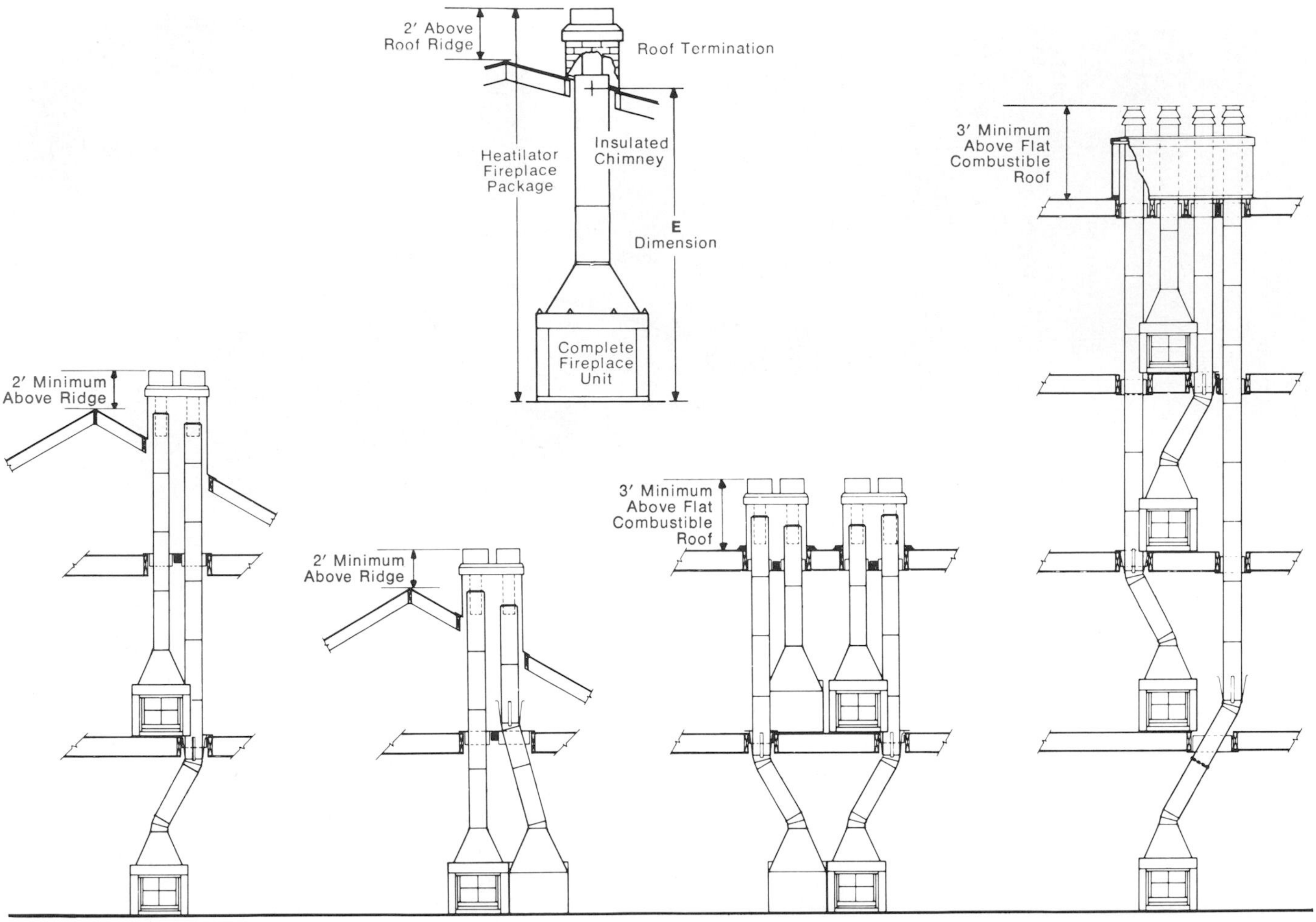

2' Above
Roof Ridge

Roof Termination

Heatilator
Fireplace
Package

Insulated
Chimney

E
Dimension

Complete
Fireplace
Unit

3' Minimum
Above Flat
Combustible
Roof

2' Minimum
Above Ridge

2' Minimum
Above Ridge

3' Minimum
Above Flat
Combustible
Roof

55-29. *Single and multi-unit applications. Chimney components are offset for venting around upper-floor fireplaces.*

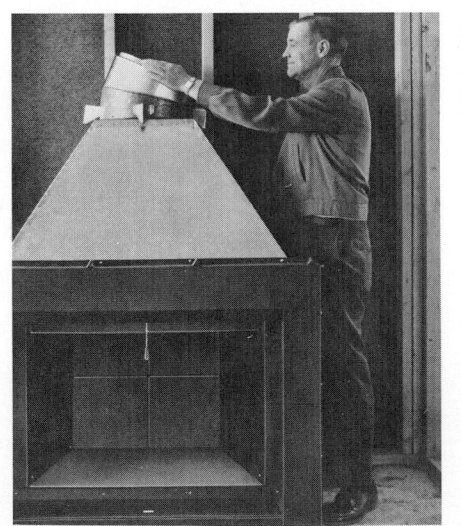

55-30a. *For installations requiring an inclined chimney, install the offset starter first. It allows for a 15° or 30° incline of the chimney to left, right, or rear of the fireplace.*

55-30b. *Installing the starter section.*

55-30c. *Installing the offset return. This is secured to the wood members of the framed opening. These members must then carry the weight of the vertical chimney.*

55-31a. *Framing for a modified fireplace (sometimes called a "zero-clearance" fireplace).*

55-32a. *A freestanding fireplace.*

55-32b. *A freestanding fireplace unit installed in a colonial setting.*

55-31b. *A fireplace framed with headers ready for the application of the interior wall covering.*

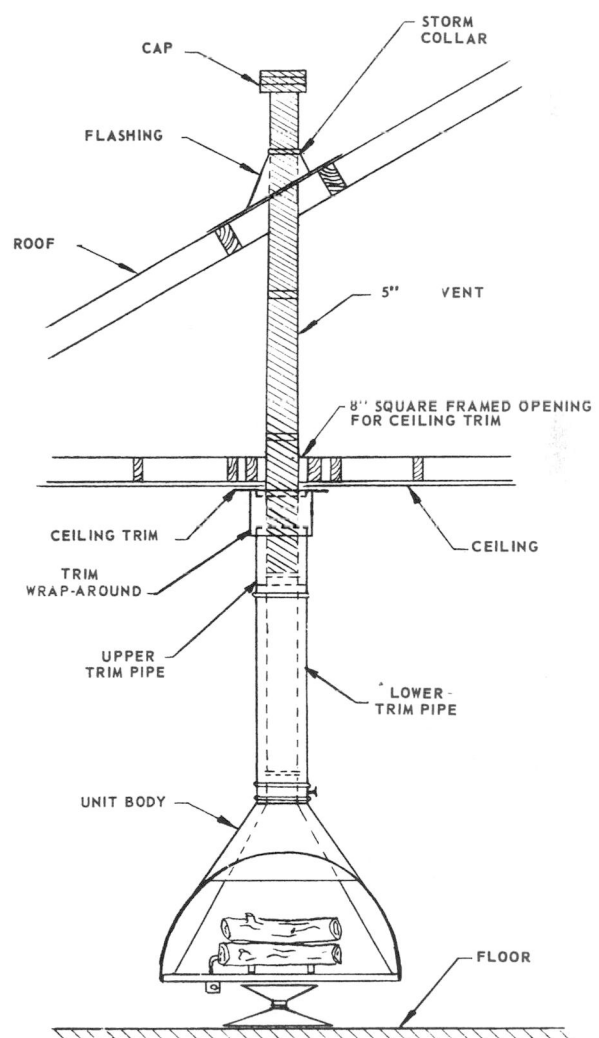

55-33. *Installation details for a freestanding fireplace.*

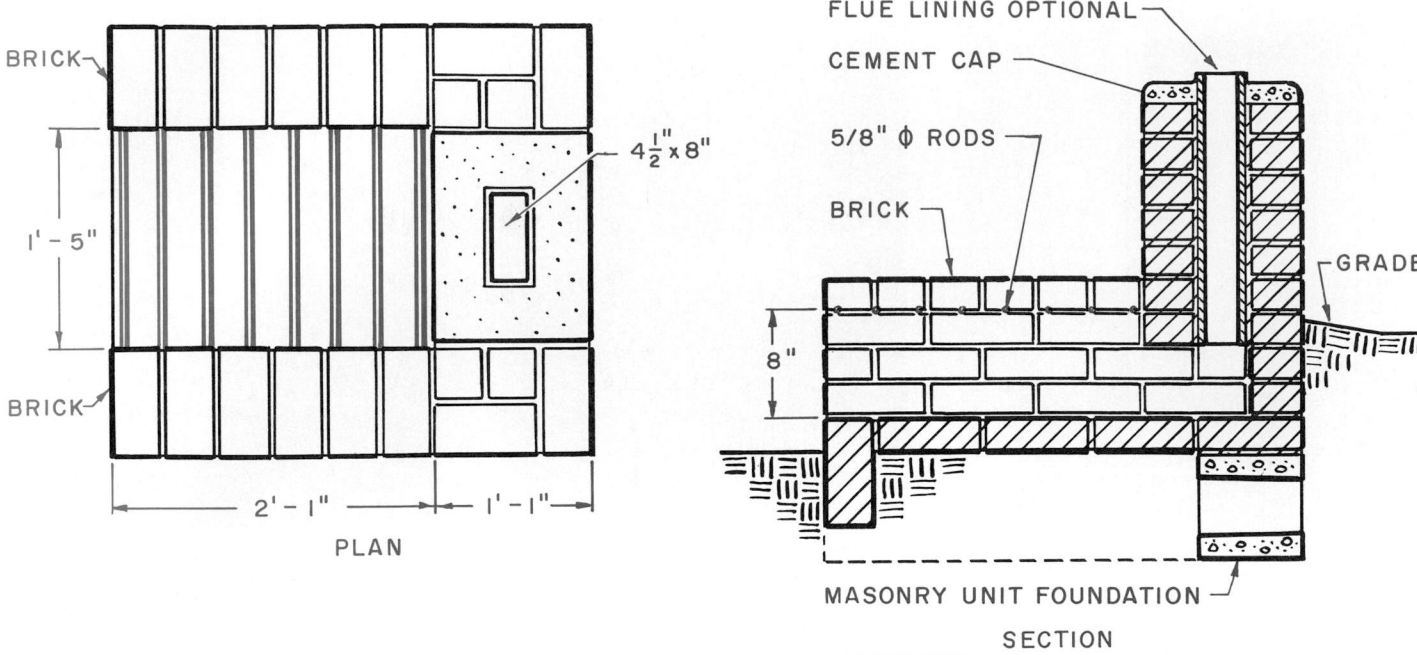

PLAN

FLUE LINING OPTIONAL
CEMENT CAP
5/8" ⌀ RODS
BRICK
8"
GRADE
MASONRY UNIT FOUNDATION
SECTION

BRICK
1'-5"
BRICK
$4\frac{1}{2}$"x8"
2'-1"
1'-1"

55-34. *An outdoor fireplace, such as this one, can be attractive and convenient.*

QUESTIONS

1. Why will a chimney at the interior of the house have a better draft than a chimney built on an exterior wall?

2. What is a flue?

3. What are two important factors that affect the draft of a chimney?

4. Why is cement mortar rather than lime mortar used around chimney flues and fireplaces?

5. Does the size of the chimney depend on the number of flues?

6. How much space should there be between the chimney walls and wood framing members of the house?

7. What is the purpose of a concrete cap on a chimney?

8. What is the purpose of a smoke shelf in a fireplace?

9. What is the difference between a modified fireplace and a freestanding fireplace?

ACTIVITIES

1. Social Studies. The early 1970s saw a rebirth in the use of wood-burning stoves. Lately, however, there has been controversy over the use of wood-burning stoves because they pollute the air. Find out what the controversy is all about. Research this topic by using the *Reader's Guide to Periodical Literature* or your library's computerized periodical research system.

2. Language Arts. Assume you are building your first home. You would like the contractor to include a fireplace. You live in another city. Write a letter to the contractor in which you specifically describe the type of fireplace, its location, and its appearance. In your letter, incorporate the following terms: fire brick, flue, mantel, and hearth. Don't forget to include the type of fireplace—either prefabricated, modified, or masonry.

3. Language Arts. In any job, you will be called upon to make choices regarding products and services. In making such a choice, you will need to make comparisons and judgements. For example, you will need to compare products and services. Clearly, cost and quality would be your first considerations. Identify other factors that would need to be considered. Among them might be the reliability of the supplier, the availability of the product or service, guarantees, and credit terms. Write a brief essay in which you outline the basic steps in evaluating a product or service with a view to buying that product or service. Discuss the various factors you would need to consider to arrive at a judgement on which product or service to buy.

UNIT

56

Protection against Decay and Insect Damage

Wood used under conditions where it will always be dry, or even where it is wetted briefly and rapidly dried, will not decay. However, all wood and wood products in construction use are subject to decay if kept wet for long periods under temperature conditions favorable to the growth of decay organisms. Most of the wood used in a house is not subjected to such conditions. There are places where water can work into the structure, but such places can be protected by proper design and construction, by use of suitable materials, and in some cases by using treated material.

Wood is also subject to attack by termites and some other insects. There are over fifty species of termites in the United States. Termites can be grouped into two main classes: subterranean and dry-wood. Subterranean termites account for about 95% of all termite damage. Fig. 56-1. Buildings may be fully protected against subterranean termites by employing fairly inexpensive protection measures during construction.

Since 1966 the Formosan subterranean termite has been discovered in several locations in the southern United States. It is a serious pest because its colonies

56-1. Line A marks the northern limit of damage by subterranean termites in the United States. Line B marks the northern limit of damage by dry-wood termites.

contain large numbers of the worker caste and cause damage rapidly. Though presently in localized areas, it could spread. Controls are similar to those for other subterranean species.

Dry-wood termites are found principally in Florida, southern California, the Gulf Coast states, and in Hawaii. They are more difficult to control, but the damage is less serious than that caused by subterranean termites.

Wood has proved itself through the years to be an excellent building material. Damage from decay and termites has been small in proportion to the total value of wood in homes, but it has been a troublesome problem to many homeowners. With changes in design and use of new building materials, it is important to note the basic safeguards which protect buildings against both decay and termites.

DECAY

Wood decay is caused by certain fungi that can utilize wood for food. These fungi, like the higher plants, require air, warmth, food, and moisture for growth. Early stages of decay caused by these fungi may be accompanied by a discoloration of the wood. Paint also may become discolored where the underlying wood is rotting. Advanced decay is easily recognized because the wood has by then undergone definite changes in properties and appearance. In advanced stages of building decay, the affected wood generally is brown and crumbly, but sometimes may be rather white and spongy. These changes may not be apparent on the surface. The loss of sound wood inside, however, is often indicated by sunken areas on the surface or by a hollow sound when the wood is tapped with a

hammer. Where the surrounding atmosphere is very damp, the decay fungus may grow out on the surface, appearing as white or brownish growths in patches or strands or in special cases as vinelike structures.

Fungi grow most rapidly at temperatures of about 70° to 85° F. Elevated temperatures such as those used in kiln-drying of lumber kill fungi. Low temperatures, even far below zero, merely cause them to remain dormant.

Moisture requirements of fungi are within definite limits. Wood-destroying fungi cannot grow in dry wood. A moisture content of 20% or less is safe. Moisture contents greater than this are practically never reached in wood that is sheltered against rain and protected, if necessary, against wetting by condensation or fog. Decay can be permanently stopped by simply taking measures to dry out the infected wood and to keep it dry. Brown crumbly decay, in the dry condition, is sometimes called *dry rot*, but this is a misnomer. Such wood must be damp if rotting is to occur.

The presence of mold or of fungus stains should serve as a warning that conditions are or have been suitable for decay fungi. Heavily molded or stained lumber, therefore, should be examined for evidence of decay. Such discolored wood is not entirely satisfactory for exterior millwork because it has greater water absorptiveness than bright wood.

The natural decay resistance of all common native species of wood lies in the heartwood. The sapwood of all species, when untreated, has low resistance to decay and usually has a short life under decay-producing conditions. Of the wood species commonly used in house construction, the heartwood of bald cypress, redwood, and the cedars is classified as being highest

in decay resistance. All-heartwood, quality lumber is becoming more and more difficult to obtain, however, as increasing amounts of timber are cut from the smaller trees of second-growth stands. In general, when substantial decay resistance is needed in loadbearing members that are difficult and expensive to replace, preservative-treated wood is recommended.

Safeguards against Decay

Except for special cases of wetting by condensation or fog, a dry piece of wood, when placed off the ground under a tight roof with wide overhang, will stay dry and never decay. This principle of "umbrella protection," when applied to houses of proper design and construction, is a good precaution. The use of dry lumber in designs that will keep the wood dry is the simplest way to avoid decay in buildings.

Lumber. Construction lumber that is green or partially seasoned may be infected with one or more of the staining, molding, or decay fungi and should be avoided. Such wood may contribute to serious decay in both the substructure and exterior parts of buildings. If wet lumber must be used, or if wetting occurs during construction, the wood should not be fully enclosed or painted until thoroughly dried.

Design Details. Untreated wood should not come in contact with the soil. Foundation walls should have a clearance of at least 8" above the exterior finish grade. Floor construction should have a clearance of 18" or more from the bottom of the joists to the ground in basementless spaces. Fig. 56-2. The foundation should be accessible at all points for inspection. Porches that prevent

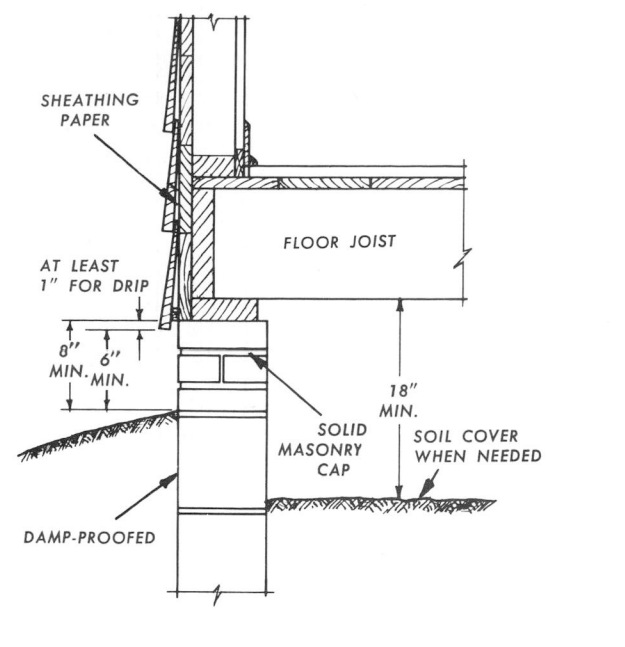

SHEATHING PAPER

FLOOR JOIST

AT LEAST 1" FOR DRIP

8" MIN. 6" MIN.

18" MIN.

SOLID MASONRY CAP

SOIL COVER WHEN NEEDED

DAMP-PROOFED

56-2. *Clearance between the wood members of a structure and the soil.*

access should be isolated from the soil by concrete or from the building itself by metal barriers or aprons. Fig. 56-3.

Steps and stair carriages, posts, wallplates, and sills should be insulated from the ground with concrete or masonry. Figs. 56-4 and 56-5. Sill plates and other wood in contact with concrete near the ground should be protected by a moistureproof membrane, such as heavy roll roofing or 6-mil polyethylene. Girder and joist openings in masonry walls should be big enough to assure an air space around the ends of these members. Fig. 56-6.

Surfaces like steps, porches, door and window frames, roofs, and other projections should be sloped to promote runoff of water. Fig. 56-7. Noncorroding flashing should

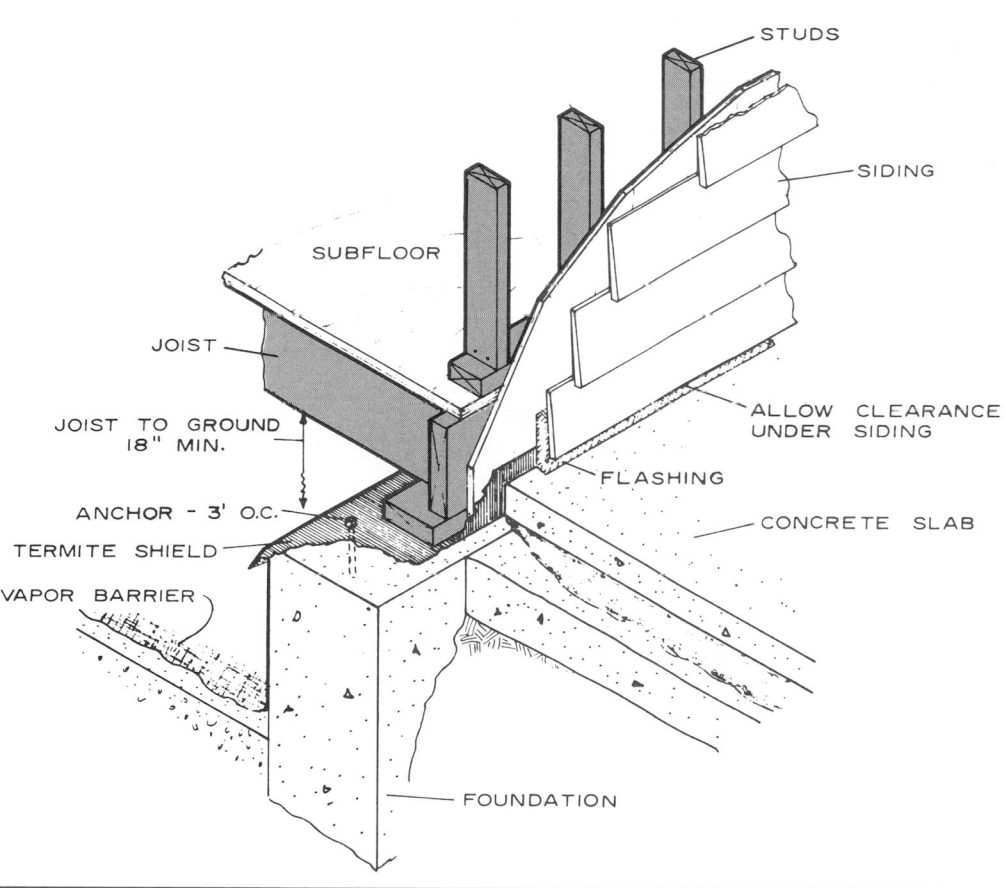

STUDS

SIDING

SUBFLOOR

JOIST

JOIST TO GROUND 18" MIN.

ANCHOR - 3' O.C.

TERMITE SHIELD

VAPOR BARRIER

ALLOW CLEARANCE UNDER SIDING

FLASHING

CONCRETE SLAB

FOUNDATION

56-3. *Metal flashing is used to protect the wood where the porch slab is connected. Note also the termite shield between the foundation wall and sill, and the vapor barrier in the crawl space.*

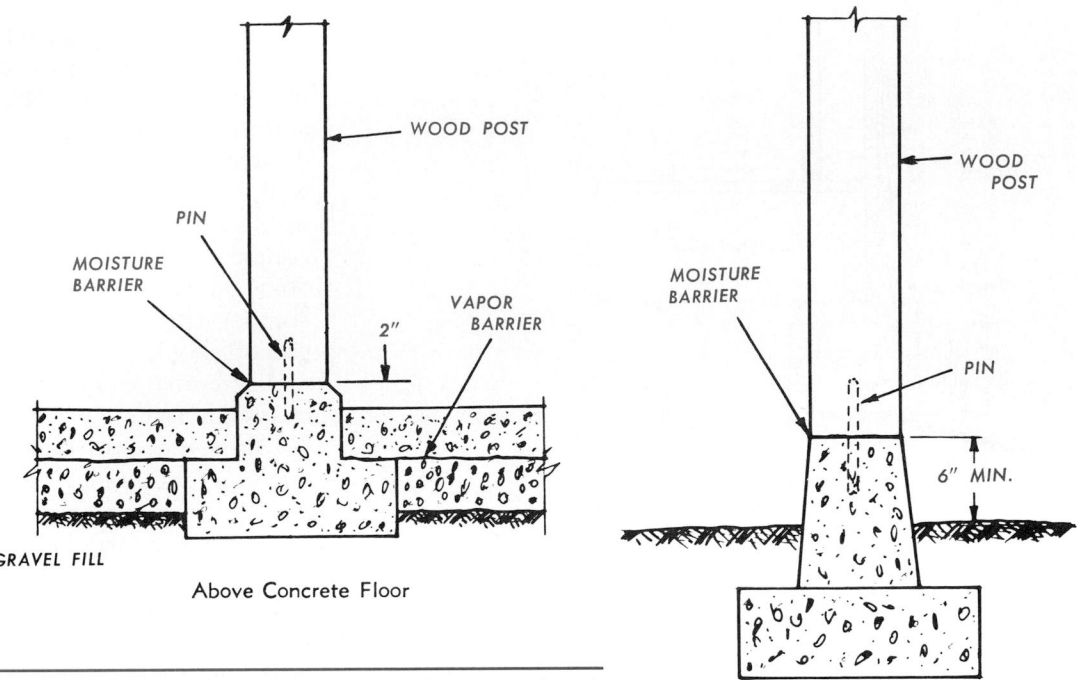

56-4. Wood posts should be insulated from the ground with concrete or masonry.

Above Concrete Floor

Above Earth Floor

56-5. Exterior wood steps should be at least 6" off the ground and supported on a concrete footing.

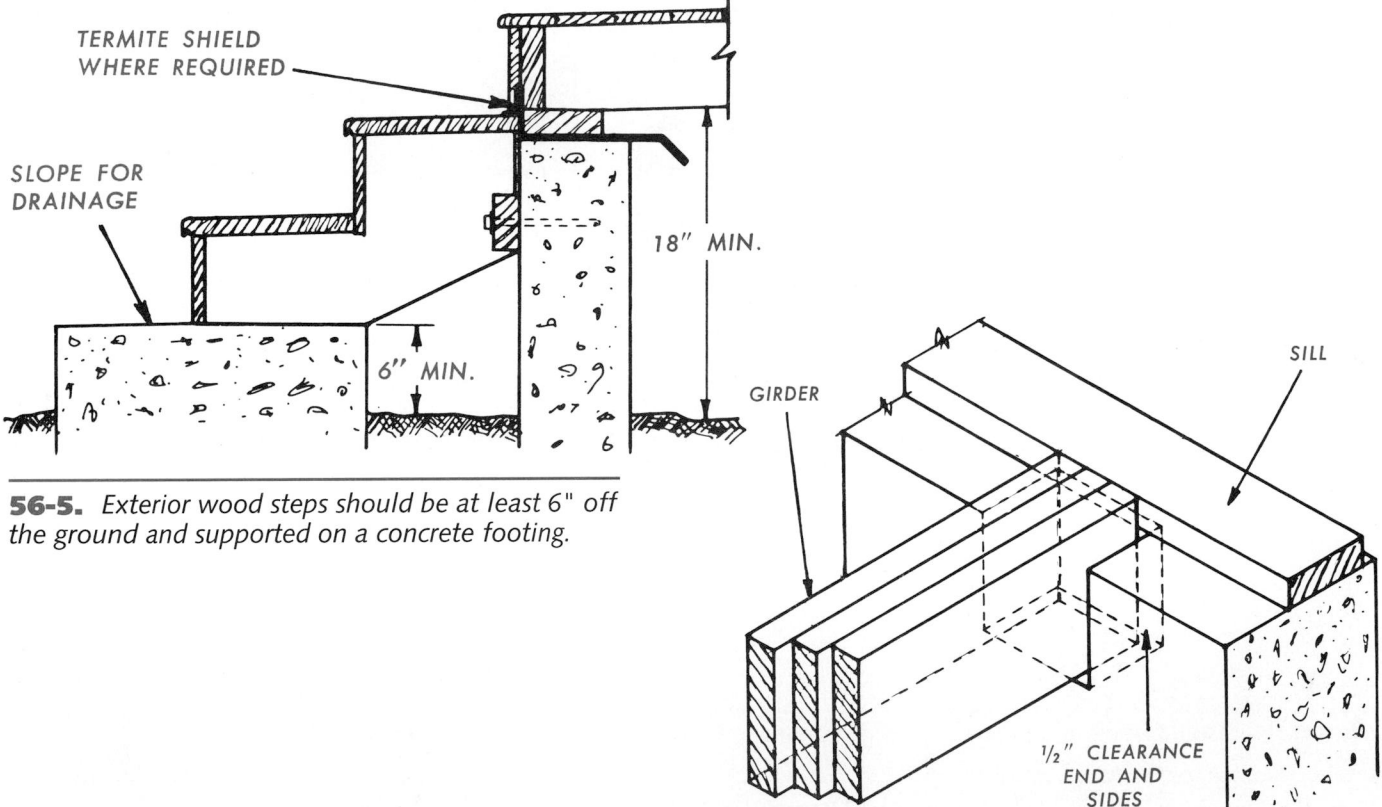

56-6. Girder and joist openings in masonry walls should be large enough to allow air circulation around the ends of these members.

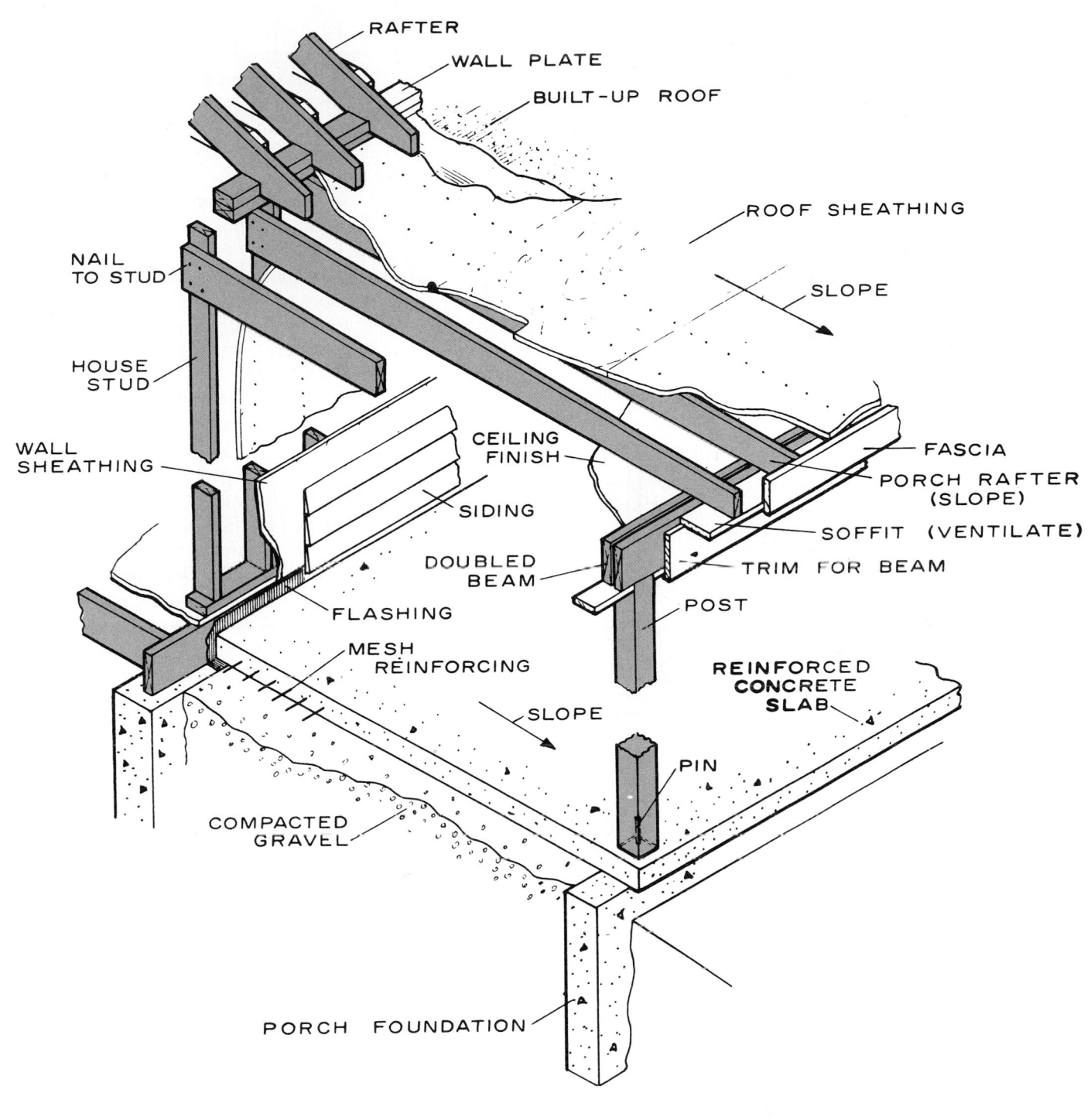

RAFTER

WALL PLATE

BUILT-UP ROOF

ROOF SHEATHING

SLOPE

NAIL TO STUD

HOUSE STUD

WALL SHEATHING

CEILING FINISH

SIDING

DOUBLED BEAM

FLASHING

MESH REINFORCING

SLOPE

FASCIA

PORCH RAFTER (SLOPE)

SOFFIT (VENTILATE)

TRIM FOR BEAM

POST

REINFORCED CONCRETE SLAB

PIN

COMPACTED GRAVEL

PORCH FOUNDATION

56-7. *Roofs and porches should slope away from the building to promote runoff of water.*

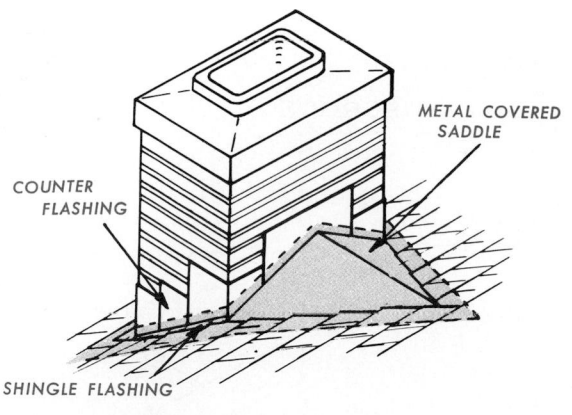

56-8. *Flashing should be installed at the chimney to prevent water seepage.*

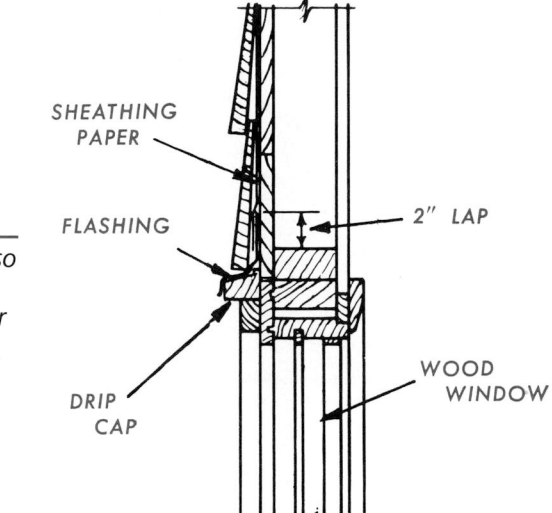

56-9. *Flashing should also be installed over windows and doors to prevent water seepage.*

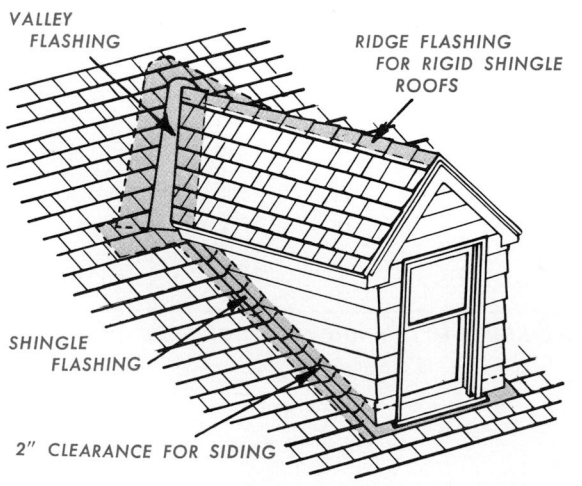

56-10. *Flashing should be provided on a roof at intersections with walls and other roofs.*

be used around chimneys, windows, doors, or other places where water might seep in. Figs. 56-8 through 56-11. Roofs with considerable overhang give added protection to the siding and other parts of the house. Gutters and downspouts should be placed and maintained to divert water away from the building. Porch columns and screen rails should be shimmed above the floor to allow quick drying, or posts should slightly overhang raised concrete bases. Fig. 56-12.

Wood Preservatives. Exterior steps, rails, and porch floors exposed to rain need protection from decay, particularly in warm, damp climates. Wood may be treated by the pressure method, in which it is impregnated with toxic chemicals at elevated pressures and temperatures. Pressure treatment of the wood provides a high degree of protection against decay and termite attack. One of the following classes of preservatives is commonly used:

➤ Creosote and creosote solutions.

➤ Oilborne preservatives.

➤ Waterborne preservatives.

➤ Water-repellent preservatives.

Where the chance of decay is relatively small or where pressure-treated wood is not readily obtainable, on-the-job application of water-repellent preservatives by brushing, dipping, or soaking has been found worthwhile. Preservatives used for non-pressure-treated wood are of two types:

➤ Water-repellent preservative—a solution of light petroleum solvent containing water-repellent materials and a minimum of 5% by weight of pentachlorophenol, meeting the standards of the National Woodwork Manufacturers' Association. This treatment can be painted.

➤ Oilborne preservative—a solution of heavier petroleum

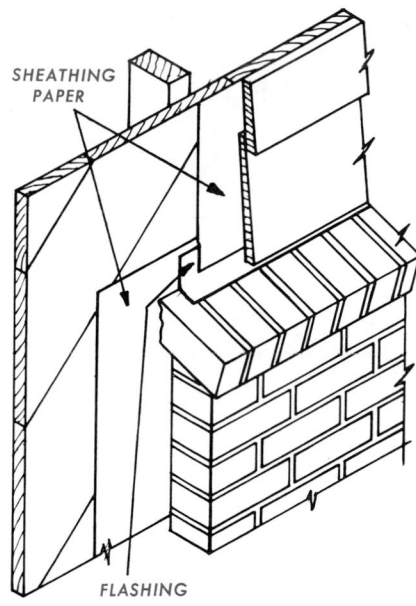

Brick Veneer and Wood Siding

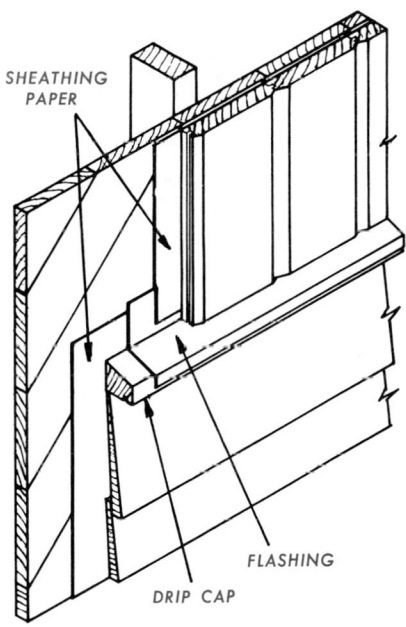

Horizontal and Vertical Wood Siding

56-11. *There should be flashing at a break in an exterior wall.*

solvent containing 5% by weight of pentachlorophenol meeting the American Wood-Preservers' Association standards. This treatment is not recommended for painting.

The wood should be dried, cut to final dimensions, and then brushed, dipped, or soaked. Soaking is the best of these nonpressure methods, and the ends of the boards should be soaked for at least 3 minutes. It is important to protect the end grain of wood at joints, for this area absorbs water easily and is the most common infection point. The edges of porch flooring should be coated with thick white lead or other durable coating as the porch is laid.

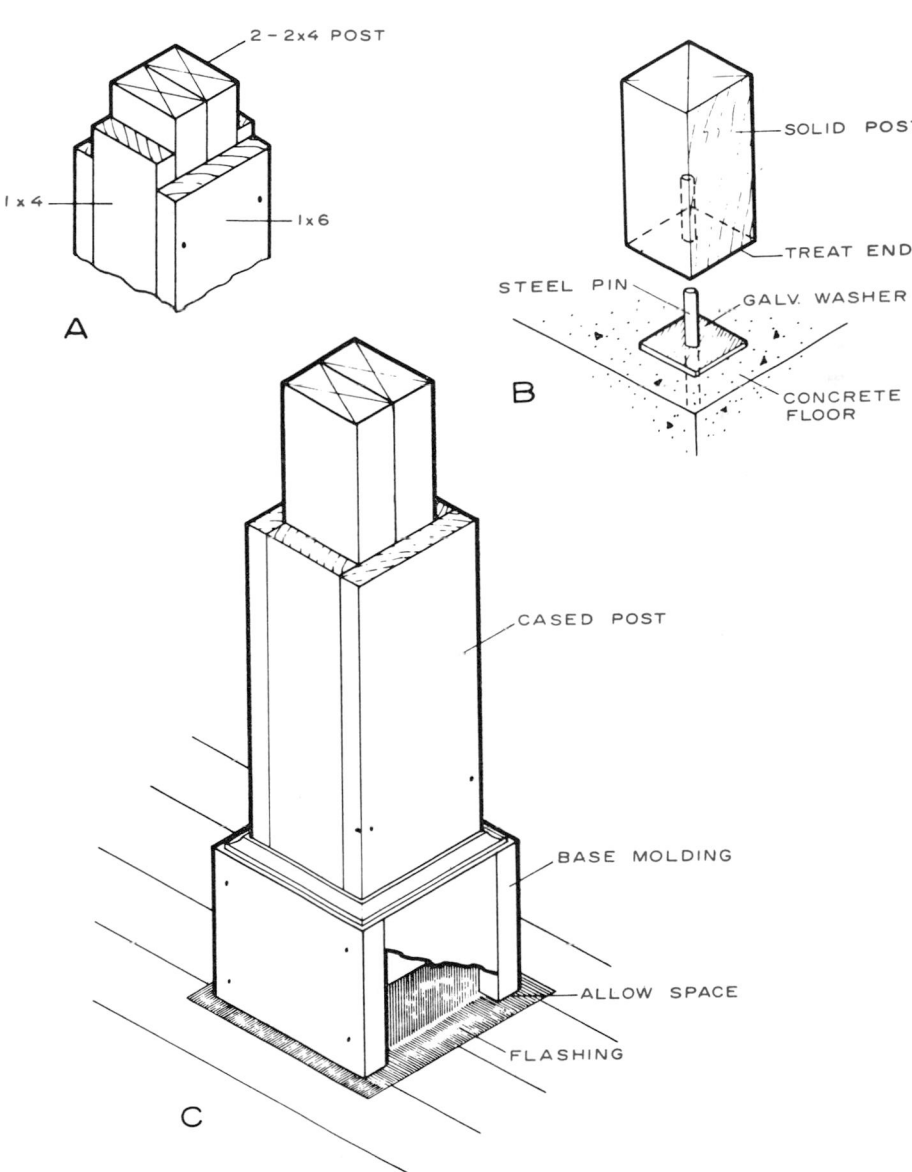

56-12. *Wood post details: A. Cased post. B. Post pinned to a concrete floor. Note the use of the galvanized washer as a spacer. C. Flashing at the base of a post. Note that the base molding is not set down tightly on the flashing.*

Water Vapor From the Soil. Crawl spaces of houses built on poorly drained sites may be subjected to high humidity. During the winter when the sills and outer joists are cold, moisture condenses on them and, in time, the wood absorbs so much moisture that it is susceptible to attack by fungi. Unless this moisture dries out before temperatures favorable for fungus growth are reached, considerable decay may result. However, this decay may progress so slowly that no weakening of the wood becomes apparent for a few years. Placing a layer of 45-pound or heavier roll roofing or a 6-mil sheet of polyethylene over the soil to keep the vapor from getting into the crawl space would prevent such decay. This might be recommended for all sites where, during the cold months, the soil is wet enough to be compressed in the hand. Fig. 56-3.

If the floor is uninsulated, there is an advantage in closing the foundation vents during the coldest months from the standpoint of fuel savings. However, unless the crawl space is used as a heat plenum chamber, insulation is usually located between floor joists. The vents could then remain open. Crawl-space vents can be very small when soil covers are used; only 10% of the area required without covers. (See Unit 41, "Ventilation.")

Water From Household Activities. Water vapor is given off during cooking, washing, and other household activities. This vapor can pass through walls and ceilings during very cold weather and condense on sheathing, studs, and rafters, causing condensation problems. A vapor barrier of an approved type is needed on the warm side of walls. It is also important that the attic space be ventilated as discussed in Unit 41, "Ventilation."

Leaking pipes should be fixed immediately to prevent damage to the house, as well as to guard against possible decay.

Water Supplied by the Fungus Itself. In the warmer coastal areas principally, some substructure decay is caused by a fungus that provides its own needed moisture by conducting it through a vinelike structure from moist ground to the wood. The total damage caused by this water-conducting fungus is not large, but in individual instances it tends to be unusually severe. Preventive and remedial measures depend on getting the soil dry and avoiding untreated wood "bridges," such as posts, between ground and sills or beams.

TERMITES

Subterranean Termites

Subterranean termites are the most destructive of the insects that infest wood in houses. The chance of infestation is great enough to justify preventive measures in the design and construction of buildings in areas where termites are common. Fig. 56-13.

Subterranean termites are common throughout the southern two-thirds of the United States and in Hawaii except in mountainous and extremely dry areas.

Subterranean termites thrive in moist, warm soil containing an abundant supply of food in the form of wood or other cellulosic material. In their search for additional food (wood), they build earthlike shelter tubes over foundation walls, in cracks in the walls, or on pipes or supports leading from the soil to the house. These flattened tubes are from ¼"

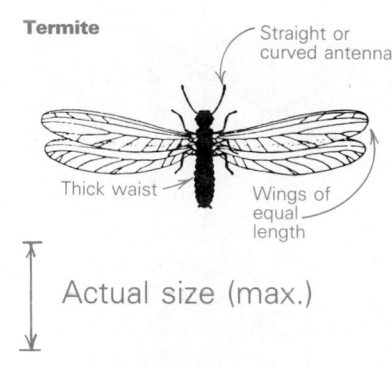

Termite
Straight or curved antenna
Thick waist
Wings of equal length
Actual size (max.)

56-13. *A termite. Termites are the most destructive insect pest in the United States.*

to ½" or more in width. They serve to protect the termites in their travels between food and shelter.

Since subterranean termites eat the interior of the wood, they may cause much damage before they are discovered. They honeycomb the wood with tunnels that are separated by thin layers of sound wood. Decay fungi, on the other hand, soften the wood and eventually cause it to shrink, crack, and crumble without producing anything like these continuous tunnels. When both decay fungi and subterranean termites are present in the same wood, even the layers between the termite tunnels will be softened.

Dry-Wood Termites

Dry-wood termites fly directly to the wood and bore into it instead of building tunnels from the ground as do the subterranean termites. Dry-wood termites are common in the tropics. They have also been found in the United States in a narrow strip along the Atlantic Coast from Cape Henry, Virginia, to the Florida Keys, and westward along the coast of the Gulf of Mexico to the Pacific Coast as far as northern California. Fig. 56-1. They may infest structural timber and other woodwork in buildings, and also furniture, particularly where the surface is not adequately protected by paint or other finishes.

Dry-wood termites cut across the grain of the wood and excavate broad pockets, or chambers. These chambers are connected by tunnels about the diameter of the termite's body. Dry-wood termites destroy both springwood and the usually harder summerwood, whereas subterranean termites principally attack springwood. Dry-wood termites remain hidden in the wood and are seldom seen, except when they make dispersal flights.

Safeguards against Termites

The best time to provide protection against termites is during the planning and construction of the building. Remove all woody debris, like stumps and discarded form boards, from the soil at the building site before and after construction. Steps should also be taken to keep the soil under the house as dry as possible.

The foundation should be made impervious to subterranean termites to prevent them from crawling up through hidden cracks to the wood in the building above. Figs. 56-14 and 56-15. Properly reinforced concrete makes the best foundation. Unit-construction walls or piers capped with at least 4" of reinforced concrete are also satisfactory.

The heartwood of foundation-grade redwood, particularly when painted, is more resistant to attack than most other native commercial species. No wood member of the house structure should be in contact with the soil.

The best protection against subterranean termites is chemical treatment of the soil near the foundation or under an entire slab

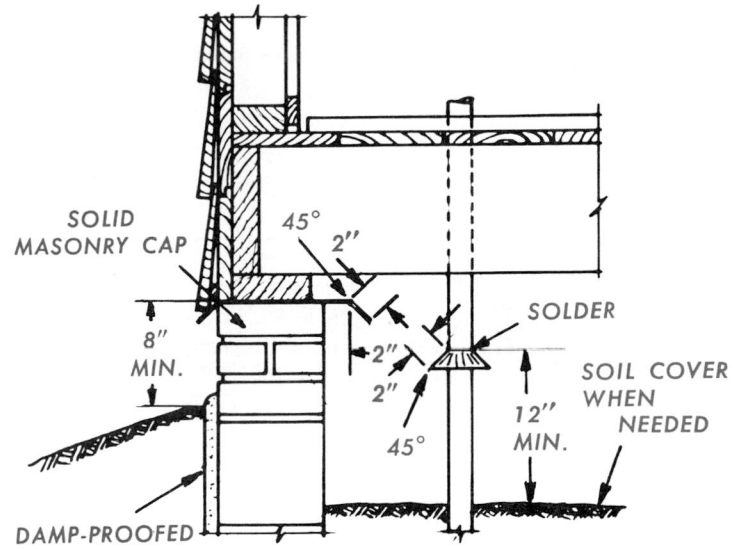

(a) At Exterior Wall

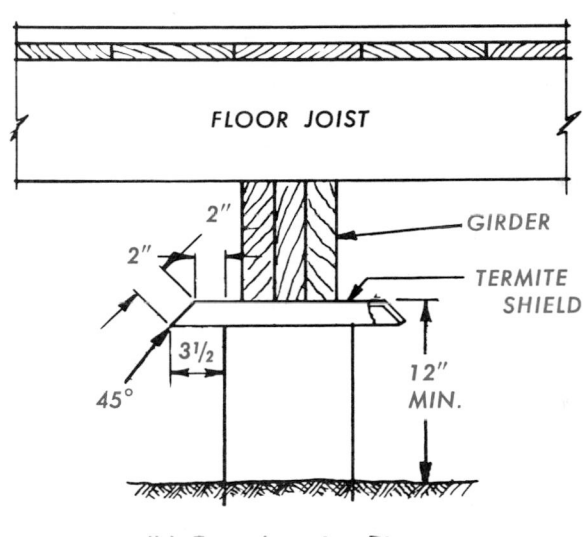

(b) Over Interior Pier

56-14. *Termite shields: Note in (a) the installation of the termite shield on the pipe that goes up through the flooring.*

foundation. The rate of application is 4 gallons per 10 linear feet at the edge and along expansion joints of slabs or along a foundation. For brick or hollow-block foundations, the rate is 4 gallons per 10 linear feet for each foot of depth to the footing. One to 1½ gallons of emulsion per 10 square feet of surface area is recommended for overall treatment before pouring

concrete slab foundations. Fig. 56-16. Any wood used in such places as wall extensions, decorative fences, and gates should be pressure-treated with a good preservative.

In regions where dry-wood termites are present, the following measures should be taken to prevent damage.

➤ All lumber, particularly secondhand material, should be

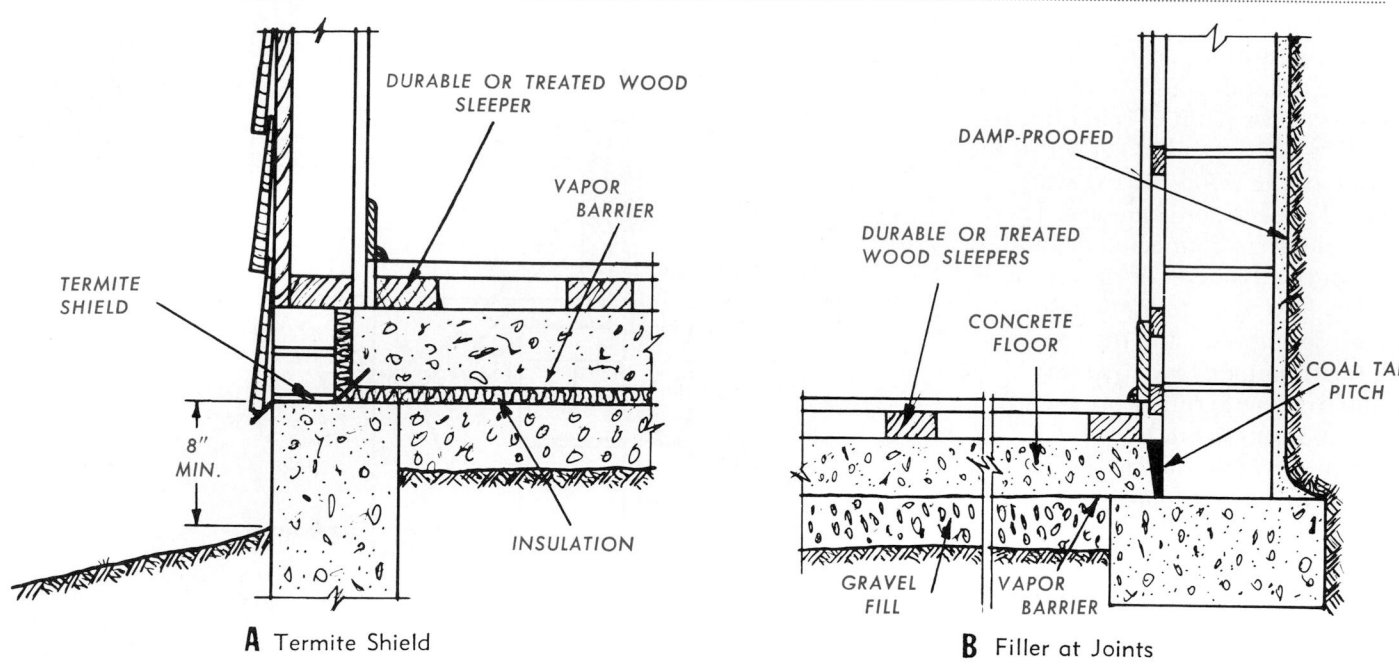

A Termite Shield

DURABLE OR TREATED WOOD SLEEPER

VAPOR BARRIER

TERMITE SHIELD

8" MIN.

INSULATION

B Filler at Joints

DAMP-PROOFED

DURABLE OR TREATED WOOD SLEEPERS

CONCRETE FLOOR

COAL TAR PITCH

GRAVEL FILL

VAPOR BARRIER

56-15. *Termite barriers on concrete slab-on-ground construction: A. Termite shield at the exterior wall. B. The use of a coal-tar pitch filler at the joint between the concrete floor and the cement block wall.*

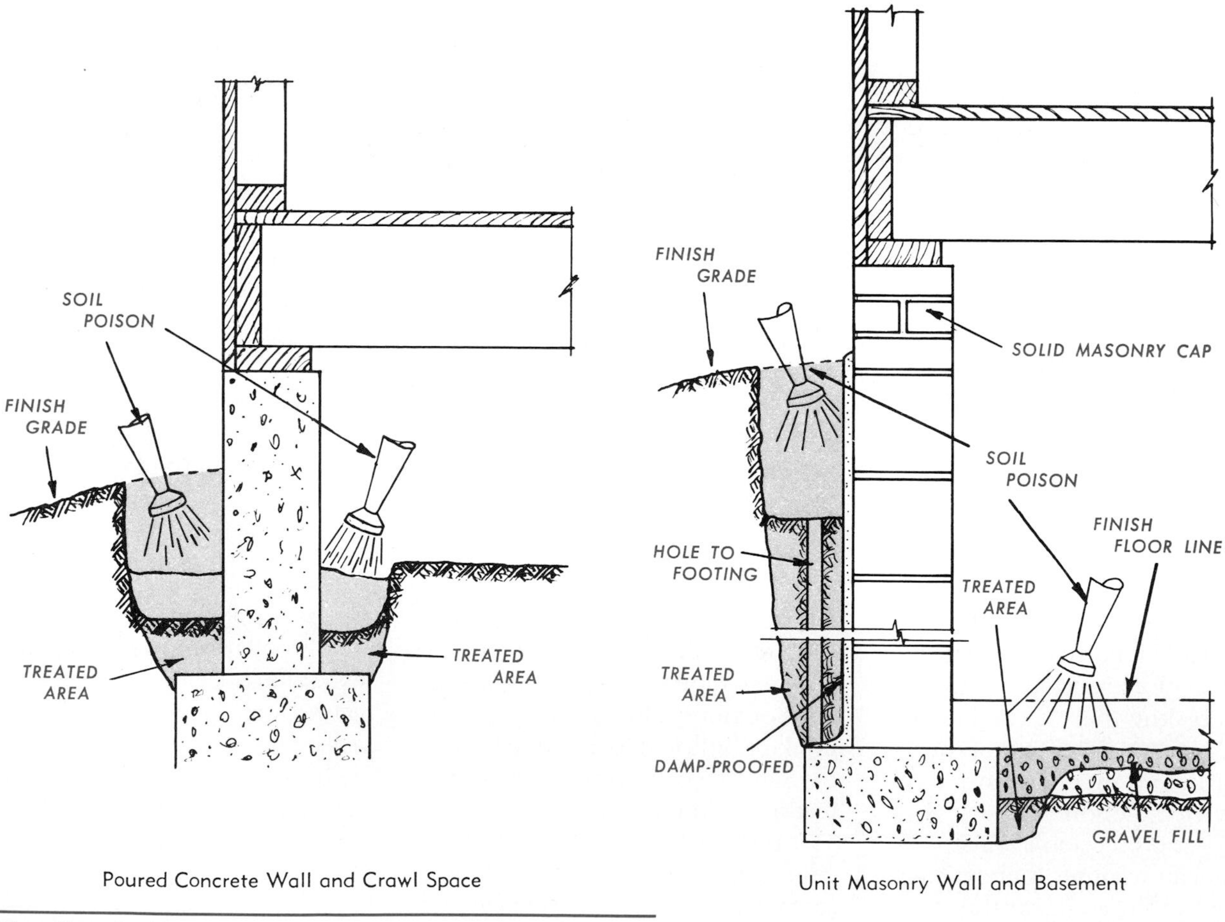

SOIL POISON

FINISH GRADE

TREATED AREA

TREATED AREA

Poured Concrete Wall and Crawl Space

FINISH GRADE

SOLID MASONRY CAP

SOIL POISON

FINISH FLOOR LINE

HOLE TO FOOTING

TREATED AREA

TREATED AREA

DAMP-PROOFED

GRAVEL FILL

Unit Masonry Wall and Basement

56-16. *Chemical treatment of the soil for termite protection.*

carefully inspected before use. If infected, discard the piece.

➤ All doors, windows (especially attic windows), and other ventilation openings should be screened with metal wire with not less than 20 meshes to the inch.

➤ Preservative treatment can be used to prevent attack in construction timber and lumber.

➤ Several coats of house paint will provide considerable protection to exterior woodwork in buildings. All cracks, crevices, and joints between exterior wood members should be filled with a mastic caulking or plastic wood before painting.

Handling Pesticides

Pesticides used improperly can be injurious to people, animals, and plants. Follow the directions and heed all precautions on the labels.

Store pesticides in original containers, out of reach of children and pets and away from food.

Apply pesticides selectively and carefully. Do not apply a pesticide when there is danger of drift to other areas. Avoid prolonged inhalation of a pesticide spray or dust. When applying a pesticide, it is advisable that you be fully clothed.

After handling a pesticide, do not eat, drink, or smoke until you have washed. In case a pesticide is swallowed or gets in the eyes, follow the first aid treatment given on the label, and get prompt medical attention. If the pesticide is spilled on skin or clothing, remove clothing immediately and wash skin thoroughly.

Dispose of empty pesticide containers by wrapping them in several layers of newspaper and placing them in the trash can. Do this only if local ordinances allow.

It is difficult to remove all traces of a herbicide (weed killer) from equipment. Therefore, to prevent injury to desirable plants, do not

use the same equipment for insecticides and fungicides that you use for a herbicide.

NOTE: Registrations of pesticides are under constant review by the U. S. Department of Agriculture. Use only pesticides that bear the USDA registration number and carry directions for home and garden use.

OTHER WOOD-INFESTING INSECTS

Carpenter Ants

Carpenter ants are primarily a problem in the Northeast, Midwest, and Northwest, though they can be found throughout the United States. These insects nest in the ground as well as in dead trees, firewood, and houses. They do not, however, eat wood. Instead, they eat plant juices, other insects, honey, and particles of food found inside a house. The damage they cause to a house comes from the irregular tunnels they create in wood. These tunnels serve as their nest. Fig. 56-17.

Controlling carpenter ants can be difficult. To be most effective, chemical treatment must be applied to the nest itself. A 2' to

10' band of chemical treatment applied to the area surrounding a house will discourage carpenter ants from entering, but it will not remove ants already nesting inside.

Beetles

Two types of beetles commonly infest wood. The powderpost beetle is the most common of the two. It is second only to termites in the amount of damage caused. The second type of beetle is a deathwatch beetle.

Powderpost beetles attack hardwoods only. They prefer ash, oak, mahogany, hickory, maple, and walnut. Most of the infestation occurs in sapwood. Beetles commonly enter the house via already infested wood. This can include firewood, roughsawn timbers, and barn wood. One common sign of a powderpost beetle infestation is a tiny pile of fine, flour-like powder. This material is pushed out of infested wood as the beetles emerge. The greatest beetle activity is in wood with a moisture content between 10% and 20%. Fig. 56-18.

There are several methods for controlling a powderpost beetle infestation:

➤ The infested wood can be removed and replaced.

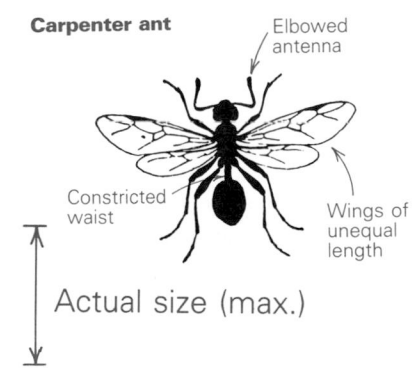

56-17. *Carpenter ant. These insects do not eat wood, but they do burrow through it to create nests.*

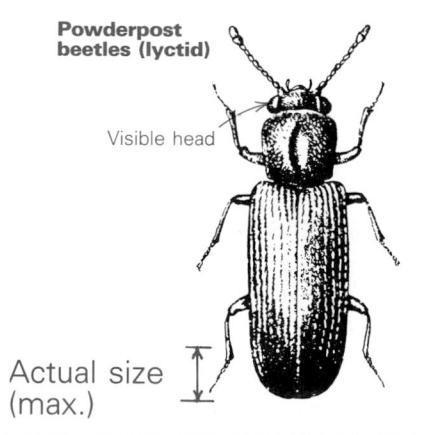

56-18. *Powderpost beetle.*

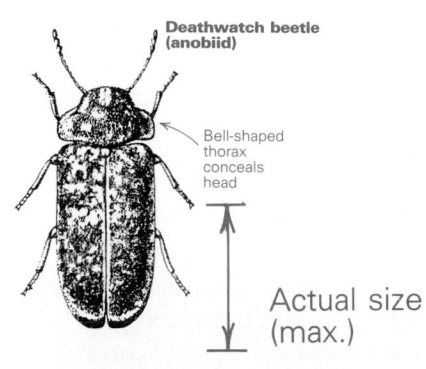

Deathwatch beetle
(anobiid)

Bell-shaped
thorax
conceals
head

Actual size
(max.)

56-19. *Deathwatch beetle.*

➤ The wood may be professionally fumigated. The most effective chemical is methyl bromide. Fumigation will kill existing beetles, but will not prevent reinfestation.

➤ The surface of the infested wood may be treated with an insecticide. Beetles are killed upon coming in contact with the chemical. This treatment will not kill beetles deep within the wood, however.

Deathwatch beetles are considerably larger than powderpost beetles, but do less damage overall. Fig. 56-19. These insects infest the sapwood of both hardwood and softwood. They are most likely to be found in wood with a high moisture content, such as that found in unheated housing and damp crawl spaces.

Treatment is similar to that required for powderpost beetles. In addition, it is very important to cut off the supply of moisture.

QUESTIONS

1. What causes decay in wood?

2. What are the two main classes of termites?

3. Below what moisture content is wood safe from decay?

4. What is the simplest way to avoid decay in buildings?

5. List several ways water may get into a structure.

6. Which of the two classes of termites is more destructive?

7. When is the best time to provide protection against termites?

ACTIVITIES

1. Math. A rectangular house with outside dimensions of 32' by 40' has 6' of backfill along the hollow block foundation wall. The house is to be protected against termites.

a. Determine the perimeter of the house.

b. Determine the number of gallons of emulsion needed.

2. Social Studies. Which states in the United States suffer from the worst insect infestations? What precautions must homeowners in these states take to guard against damage to their houses? Are any special building materials used in these homes to help prevent home decay?

3. Language Arts. You may discover, after you have found a job, that you do not like that job. You may discover this one month, one year or ten years after you start the job. Consider the steps you would take to terminate your employment. Remember that you would need to give your employer adequate notice. Remember also that you probably will be seeking a recommendation from that employer for future employment with another business. Before leaving one job, you would also need to be sure that you would be able to obtain another job.

Write a brief essay discussing the main steps in terminating employment. Discuss the means you would use to secure new employment. Mention the various resources you would have in doing that, such as friends who might be able to tell you of jobs. Mention also the role of employment agencies and job-finding services. Remember that you are terminating one job to find another that will be more satisfying.

THE SCHOOL-TO-WORK CONNECTION

Wood-destroying organisms cause considerable damage to houses.

1. Assume that you are about to repair a decayed floor. What skills would you like your helper to have? Write a "help wanted" ad. Use as few words as possible.

57

Scheduling

Two types of scheduling are needed in building a home: activity scheduling and material scheduling. It is the responsibility of the general contractor to set up these schedules and make sure they function smoothly. Naturally the size of the building project will have a great deal to do with the complexity of the scheduling. Figs. 57-1 and 57-2. A contractor who is building only a few houses with perhaps two or three workers often works part-time

57-1. *In a building project of this size a special crew is responsible for each phase of construction. For example, one crew puts in the footings and the foundation wall. A second crew does the floor framing. Another crew does the wall framing, etc. Supervisors who are directly responsible to the general contractor coordinate material deliveries and scheduling of the various work crews.*

57-2. *Many large homes are built by contractors with a work force of only two or three people.*

key to successful construction management. That is why some builders use graphical methods to keep track of what has to happen. Bar charts and flow diagrams are the most common graphical methods for tracking a project. Both of these can be done with pencil and paper. However, computer software now makes the job much easier.

MATERIAL SCHEDULING

Material scheduling must be coordinated by the lumber supply dealer who works with the general contractor. Since each general contractor operates in a slightly different manner, the lumber supplier must adapt the material schedule to the contractor's wishes. Naturally, the material deliveries vary depending on the type and size of the project, the number of people working on it, and the time set for completing the project. Fig. 57-3.

Generally, material deliveries are made as follows:

➤ The first load includes all items needed to complete the house up to and including the subfloor.

➤ The second load includes wall framing and ceiling joists.

➤ Third load—roof framing materials. If roof trusses are used, these will be shipped to the site on a special truck. This truck sometimes has a crane to lift trusses into position.

➤ Fourth load—exterior doors, windows, exterior trim, and siding as necessary. After the building has been enclosed with doors and windows and can be locked up, the interior wall finish is applied. If the walls are plastered, adequate drying time must be allowed before additional material shipments are made.

as part of the crew on the job site. The rest of the time is spent in coordinating the delivery of materials and the work of the subcontractors. Larger contractors spend all their time on these matters.

It is very important that each subcontractor's work is done at the correct time so as not to delay the overall construction progress. The more subcontractors used by the general contractor, the fewer will be the general subcontractor's responsibilities in coordinating material scheduling, since subcontractors arrange for their own materials. One of the most common faults of small general contractors is that they try to do too many specialized jobs themselves such as tile setting or concrete work. Most small general contractors are former carpenters. They should concentrate on this aspect of the building project.

The general contractor should always subcontract those jobs that require special equipment and skill. Plumbers, heating and air-conditioning specialists, and electricians have the knowledge and skill to do their work efficiently. In many areas of the country the amount of specialized work of this type that the general contractor can do is limited by local building codes and trade union regulations. Most of the following jobs normally are subcontracted: surveying, excavating, concrete and masonry work, plumbing, electrical work, termite control, climate control, heating, air-conditioning, sheetmetal work, interior wall finishing (except wood wall paneling), painting and decorating, ceramic tile, floor covering, and landscaping.

Scheduling is important, but keeping track of the schedule is the

57-3. *General contractors who work on a building project such as that shown in Fig. 57-1 buy large quantities of materials from a single source to obtain a better price. These materials are then delivered to a central receiving area for redistribution at the job site.*

➤ Fifth load—hardwood flooring and underlay materials.

➤ Sixth load—interior doors, trim, and built-in cabinet materials.

Materials to be delivered to the job site are stacked on the truck in the sequence in which they are to be used. In this way, after the materials are unloaded, those materials needed first will be on top of the pile.

It is the lumber supplier's responsibility to check on any missing materials and send the additional items needed to complete a job. Often some materials are left over, and these can be returned to the supplier for credit. The supplier keeps a running tally of the cost of materials shipped to the job site as well as any credits for returns. The general contractor is expected to pay for these materials on some time schedule, such as every week or month.

JOB SCHEDULING

To keep the building progressing at a smooth rate, the general contractor also has the responsibility of scheduling the jobs. Whenever it is necessary to have a subcontractor come in, the general contractor must arrange the time. Careful scheduling can minimize the frustrations of undue delays caused by subcontractors whose work needs to be done before other progress can be made.

The following is a list of steps in house construction. It is the general contractor's responsibility to see that these steps are carried out.

1. Survey. The job site is surveyed and the abstract brought up to date so that application for title insurance can be made.

2. Permit. A building permit is obtained from proper authorities so that work can begin.

3. Excavation. The excavator brings in power equipment and strips the topsoil away, piling it in one corner of the lot for future use. If the building will have a basement, it is excavated at this time.

4. Temporary power. The electrical company is contacted to arrange for a power pole to be set in place on the building site and a hookup made. The electricity is needed for operating power tools.

5. Temporary water. On some job sites the plumber makes the temporary water hookup, which must be coordinated with the city utilities. Sometimes a power-driven water pump for a well is used. In existing neighborhoods, water can be obtained from a neighbor. In this case, the permanent hookup for water to the building is not made until the foundation walls have been installed.

6. Foundation. Footings and foundation walls are installed by the concrete and masonry subcontractor. Fig. 57-4.

7. Soil treatment. In areas that require it, a termite control

57-4. *Pouring a concrete foundation wall. Note that forms are well braced to keep them aligned while the concrete is being placed.*

specialist will treat the soil at the base of the foundation wall and the footings.

8. Plumbing. Pipelines for plumbing are installed in the subsoil by the plumbing contractor.

9. Backfill. At this point the general contractor must make certain decisions concerning how the foundation walls are to be braced to permit backfilling. Backfilling cannot be done unless the foundation walls are braced or unless the building is framed to provide plenty of weight to the foundation. Even when the walls and roof have been framed, the foundation must be braced to some extent before backfilling. Whether to backfill immediately after the foundation is in or to wait until after the framing is completed is the general contractor's choice.

If backfilling is delayed until framing is completed, the workers have the inconvenience of working around a foundation with a large excavation. This is unsafe and can lead to injuries because the carpenters normally have to use planking to carry materials over the excavation into the building. On the other hand, if backfilling is done before construction, extra time and costs are involved in bracing the foundation securely so that it does not cave in. Before any backfilling can be completed, the exterior walls of the foundation must be moisture-proofed.

10. Framing. The carpenters can now do the floor, wall, and roof framing.

11. Masonry. Chimneys and fireplaces are built by the masonry contractor after the rough framing is completed.

12. Mechanicals. At this point in construction, a variety of activities may be carried out simultaneously, or at least in rapid succession. These include plumbing, heating, and electrical work. All of these mechanical subcontractors must work in two stages; namely, the "rough-in" and the "finish" work.

For example, when the rough framing is complete, the electrician comes in to do the rough wiring, including installing the outlet boxes and feeding all the wires through the framing. This is the rough-in portion of the work. Later after the interior walls are all completed, the electrician comes back to install the switches, outlets, and fixtures. This is also true of the plumber and the heating and air-conditioning workers. (The plumber will install bathtubs with the rough-in, since tubs are a built-in feature of the house.)

13. Windows and doors. While the mechanical subcontractors are doing the rough-in work, the carpenters install exterior doors, windows, and special framing. Fig. 57-5.

14. Insulation. After all rough-in work is done, insulation is installed in the walls and as necessary in the ceiling. Fig. 57-6.

15. Interior and exterior finishes. Most interiors of homes are finished either with gypsum drywall or with plaster. If plastering

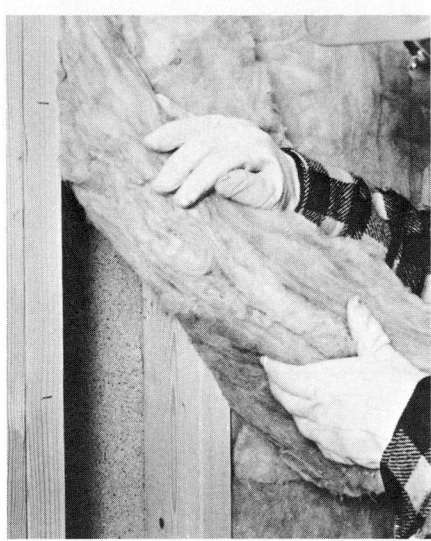

57-6. *Installing insulation. The installer is wearing gloves. Goggles also should be worn.*

57-5. *Ripping 2 x 4s into 2 x 2s for construction of the kitchen cabinet soffits.*

A. Architectural rendering. *This three-bedroom home with double garage attached is shown in construction sequence.*

B. Floor plan. *Color coding of floor plan: Red—Bathroom fixtures; Kitchen appliances; Chimney. Yellow—Floor covering; Exterior wall insulation. Green—Direction of door swings; Names of rooms; Heat registers. Blue—Electrical outlets.*

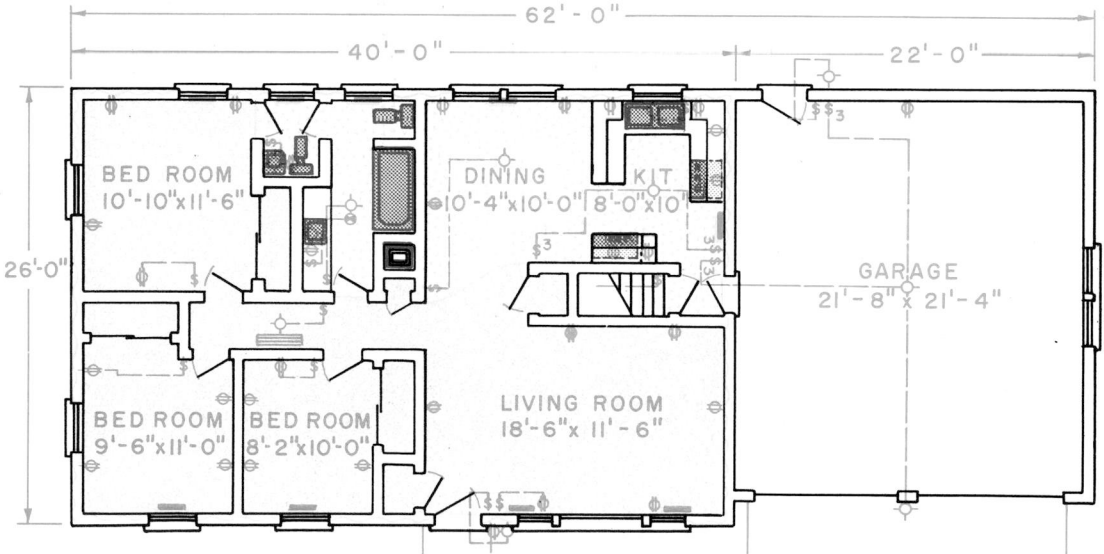

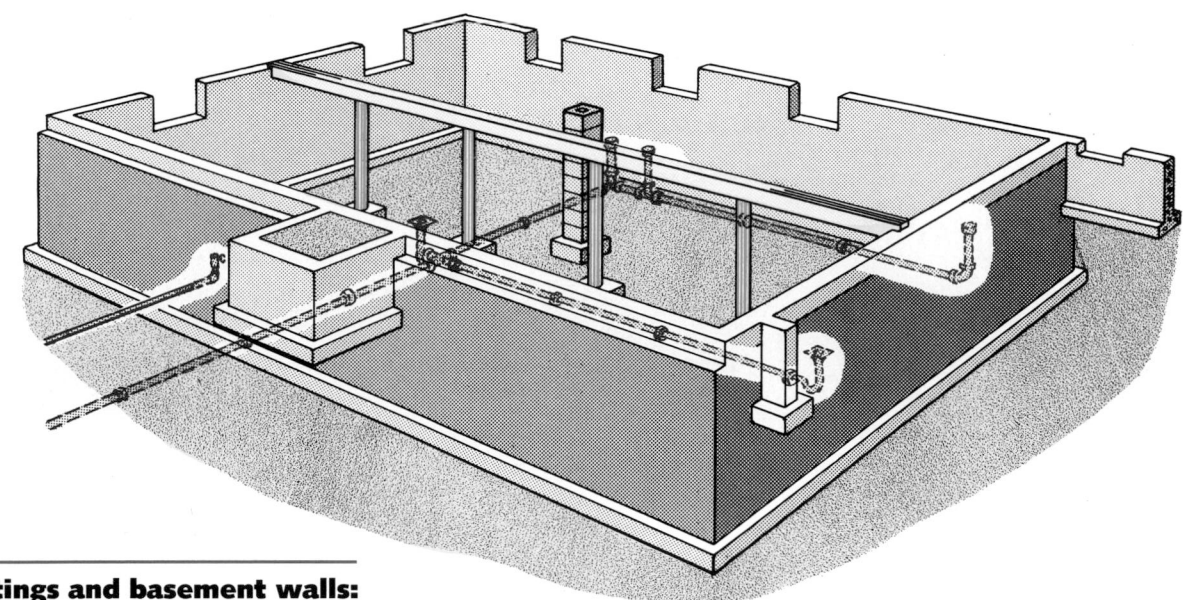

C. Footings and basement walls:

➤ The basement is excavated and then the footings are placed.

➤ The foundation walls are either poured or constructed of concrete block. (The fill around the basement is omitted here to show the footings and walls.)

➤ The supporting columns and the center beam are installed.

➤ The exterior surface of the walls is moisture-proofed up to the finish grade level.

➤ The rough plumbing is installed.

➤ The front porch excavation is filled with sand, ready for the porch and basement floors to be placed.

D. First floor construction:

➤ The rough grading is shown leveled off four inches below the finished grade line.

➤ The joists are installed. Notice the double joists at the stairwell and under inside partition walls.

➤ The double joists are separated with solid bridging. Metal or wood bridging is installed midway between the ends of other joists and the supporting beam.

➤ The plywood subfloor is laid.

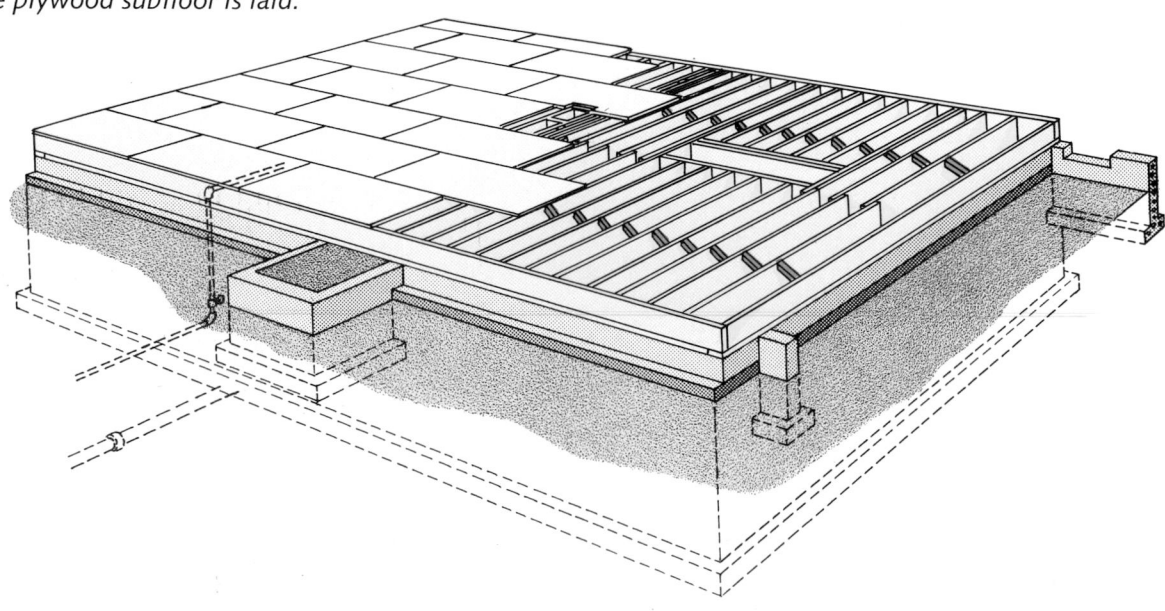

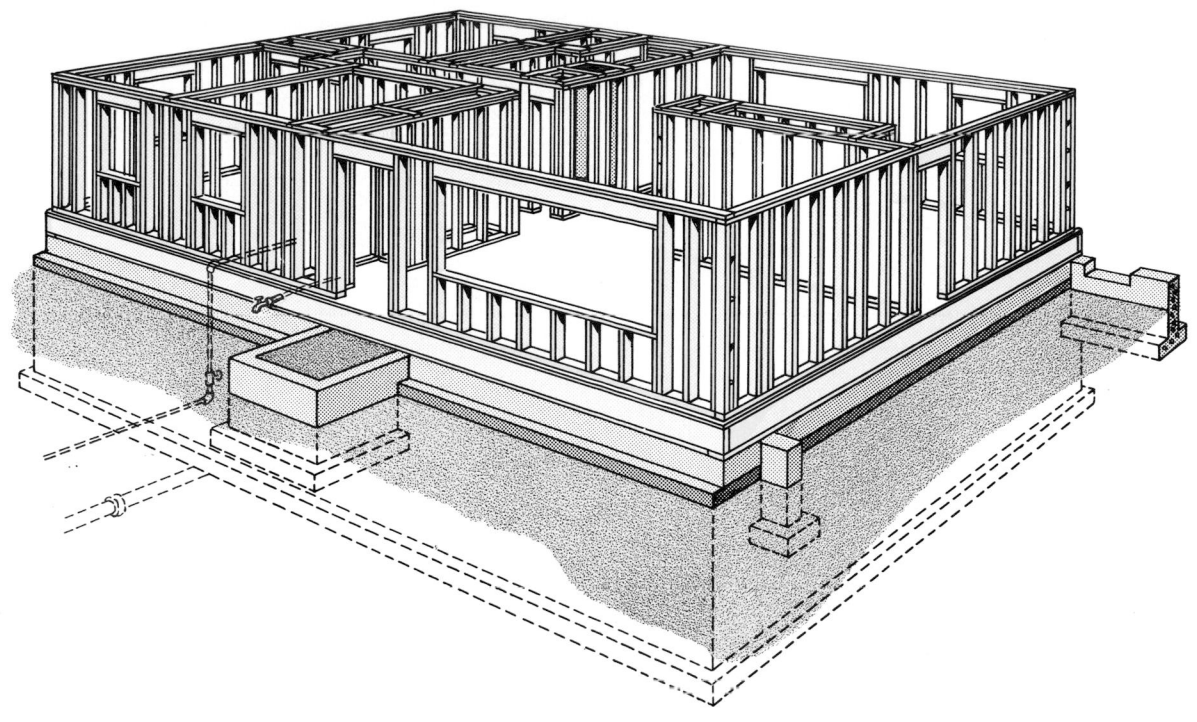

E. Wall framing. *Wall framing is completed. The chimney is built up to the level of the ceiling joists and is not completed.*

F. Complete framing. *Cutaway view of the house showing finished plumbing and heating. The basement plumbing is shown complete with the installation of laundry tubs and the placement of the washer and dryer. However, the actual placement of the fixtures and appliances would not be done until the house has been closed in.*

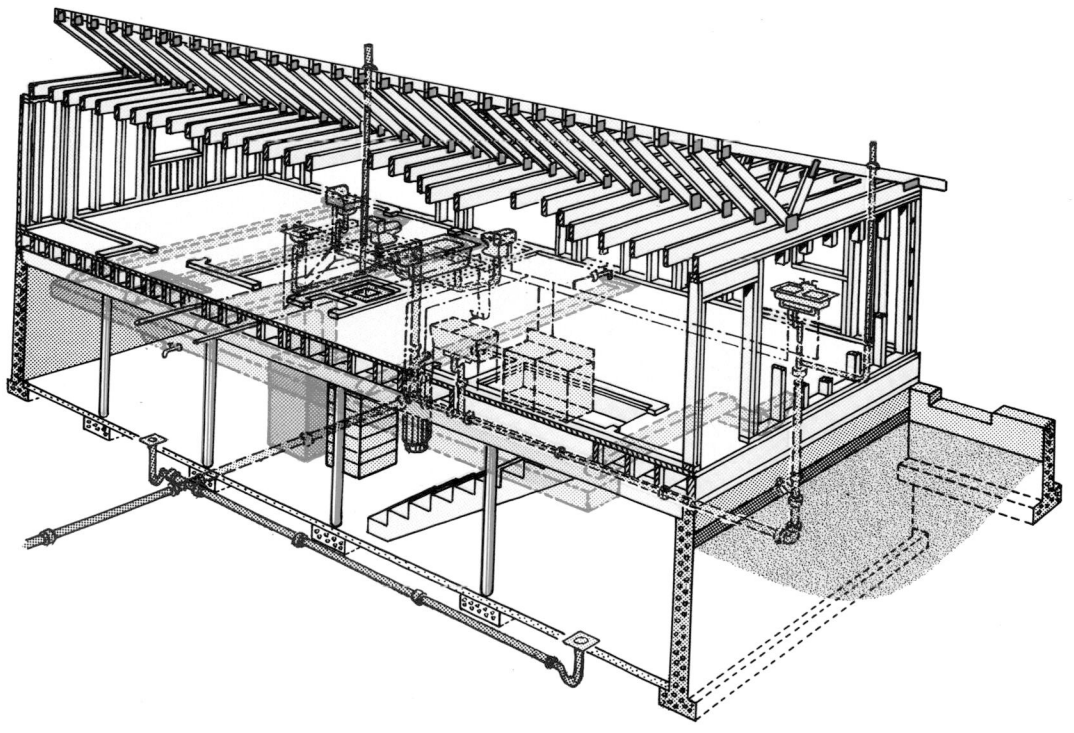

CUT - AWAY VIEW

1. 2. 3. 4. 5. 6. 7. 8. 9. 10. 11.

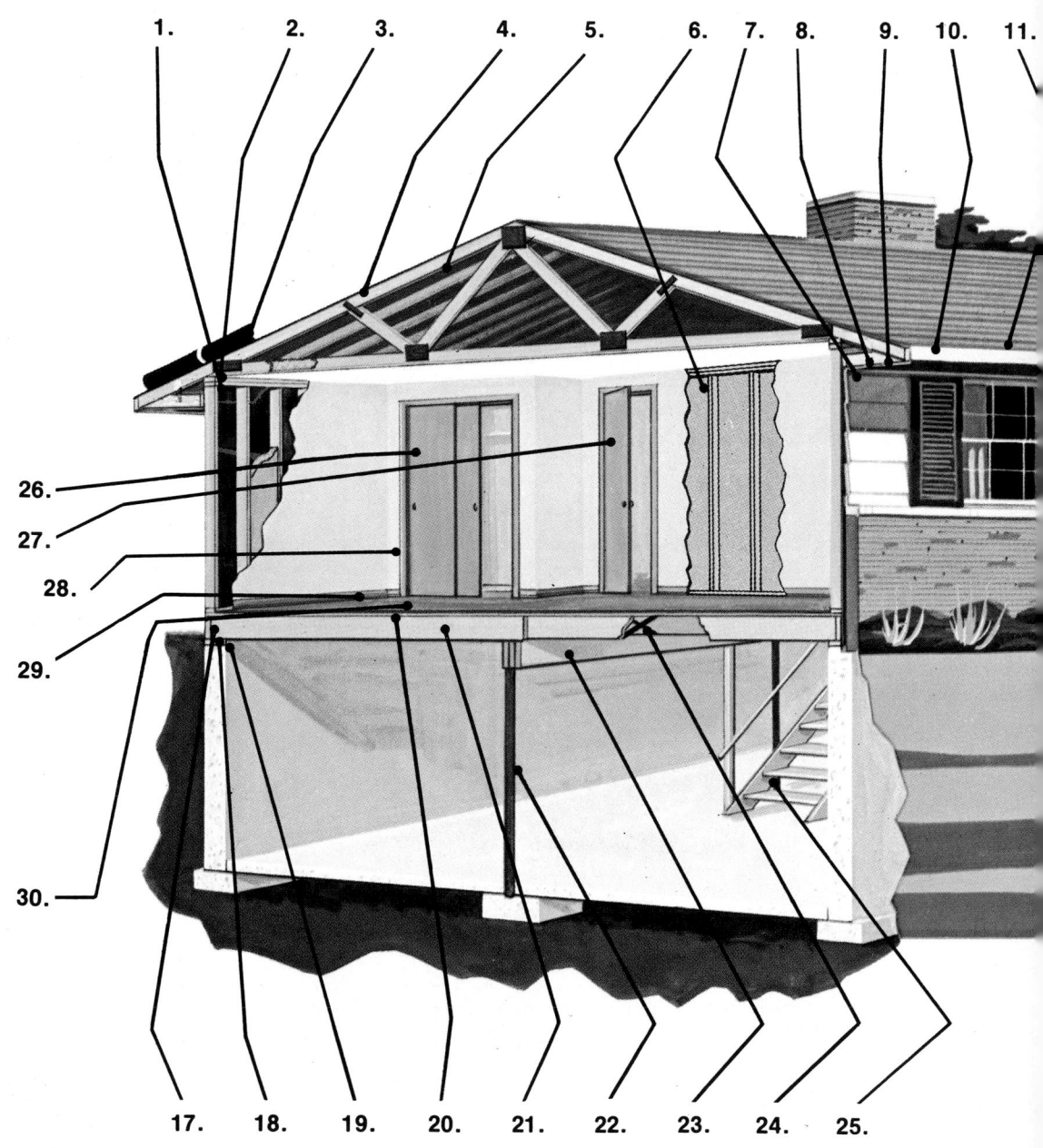

26.
27.
28.
29.
30.

17. 18. 19. 20. 21. 22. 23. 24. 25.

814 D

OF FINISHED HOME

12. **13.** **14.** **15.** **16.**

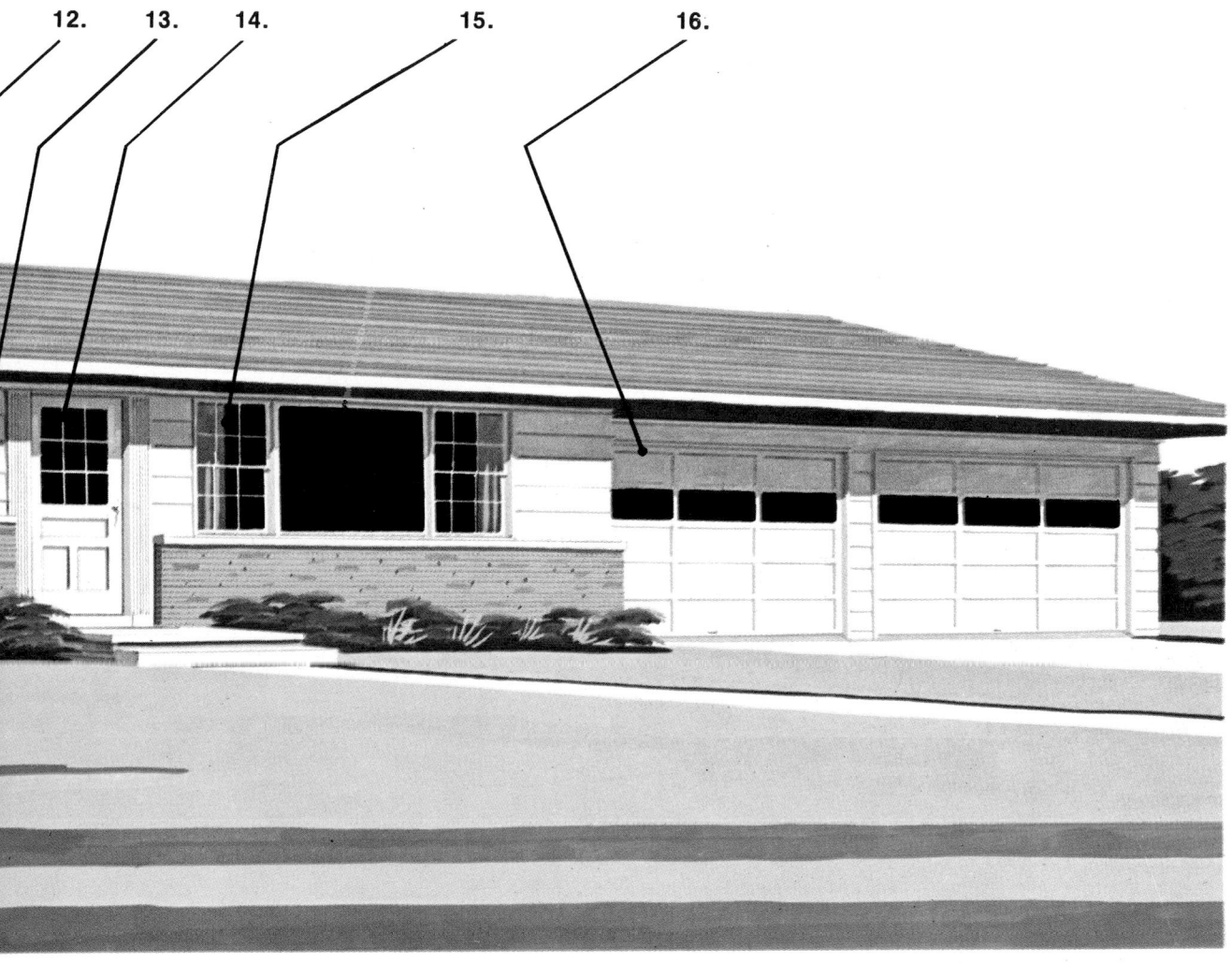

G. Cutaway view of finished home: *1. Exterior wall panels with 1/2" sheathing applied. 2. 2 x 4 tie plate—loose. 3. # 235 asphalt shingles with felt underlay. 4. 1/2" plywood roof decking. 5. Trusses 24" O.C. (16" optional). 6.Interior partition panels. 7. 3/4" frieze board. 8. 3/8" soffit material. 9. 2" continuous vent strip. 10. 5/4 x 6 fascia. 11. Metal roof edge. 12. Shutters. 13. 1/2" x 12" siding. 14. Front and rear doors installed and weatherstripped. 15. Double-hung, removable sash windows, installed in panels. 16. Garage doors. 17. 2 x 8 or 2 x 10 ribbon. 18. 2 x 8 plate. 19. Insulating sill sealer. 20. 1/2" plywood deck. 21. 2 x 8 or 2 x 10 joists. 22. Steel posts. 23. Beam, 3-2 x 10. 24. Metal bridging. 25. Precut stairs. 26. Bypass or bifold doors, semi-prehung. 27. Passage doors, prehung. 28. Door casing. 29. Base and shoe molding. 30. Finish floor, oak and tile underlayment.*

H. House exterior. *The house is shown closed in with:*

➤ *The doors and windows installed.*

➤ *The sheathing on the exterior walls.*

➤ *The masonry wall completed.*

➤ *The siding applied to the left of the front door.*

➤ *The concrete work all completed.*

➤ *The chimney finished.*

I. *This cutaway of the garage shows its construction. The exterior of the garage has not been completed.*

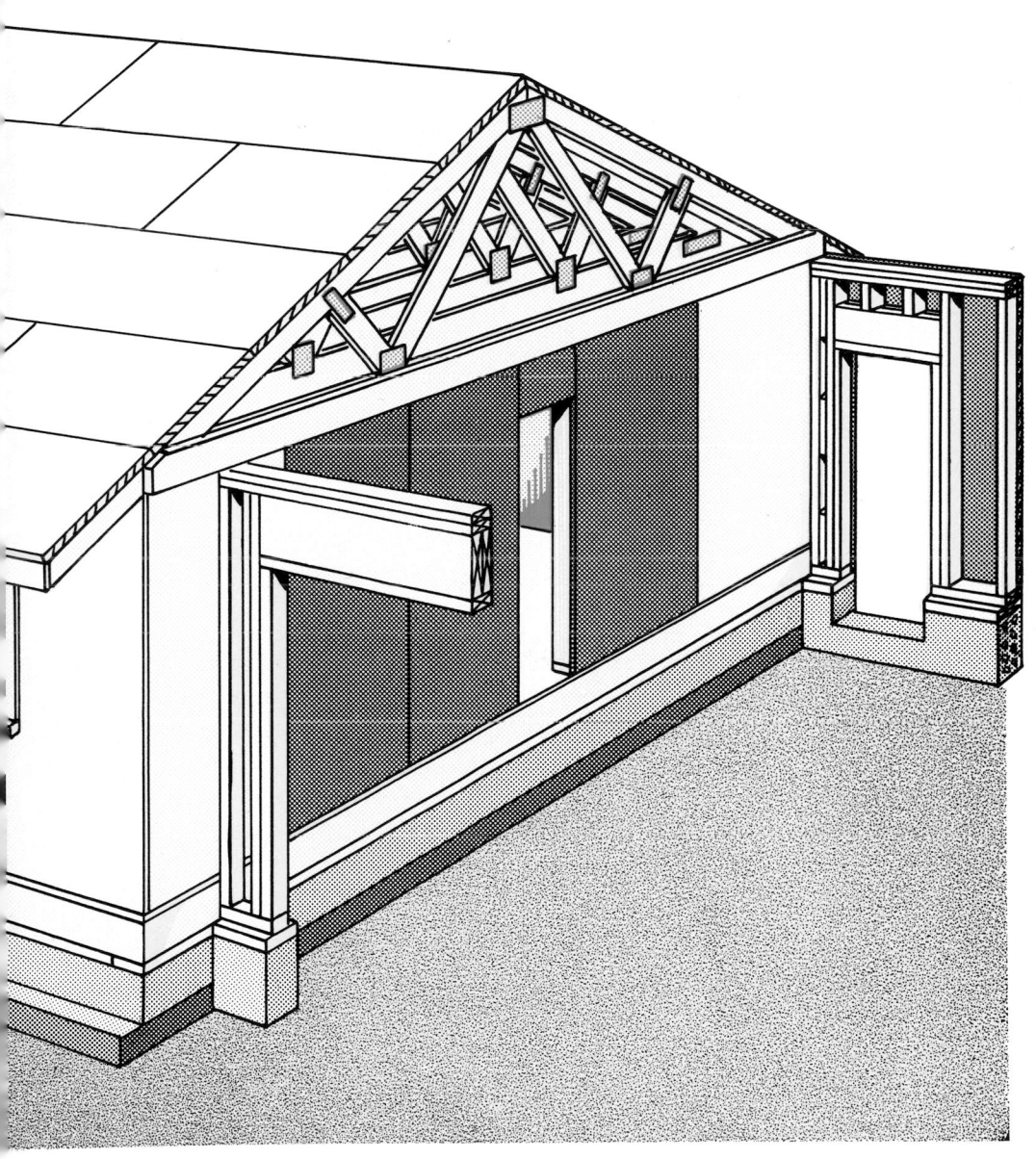

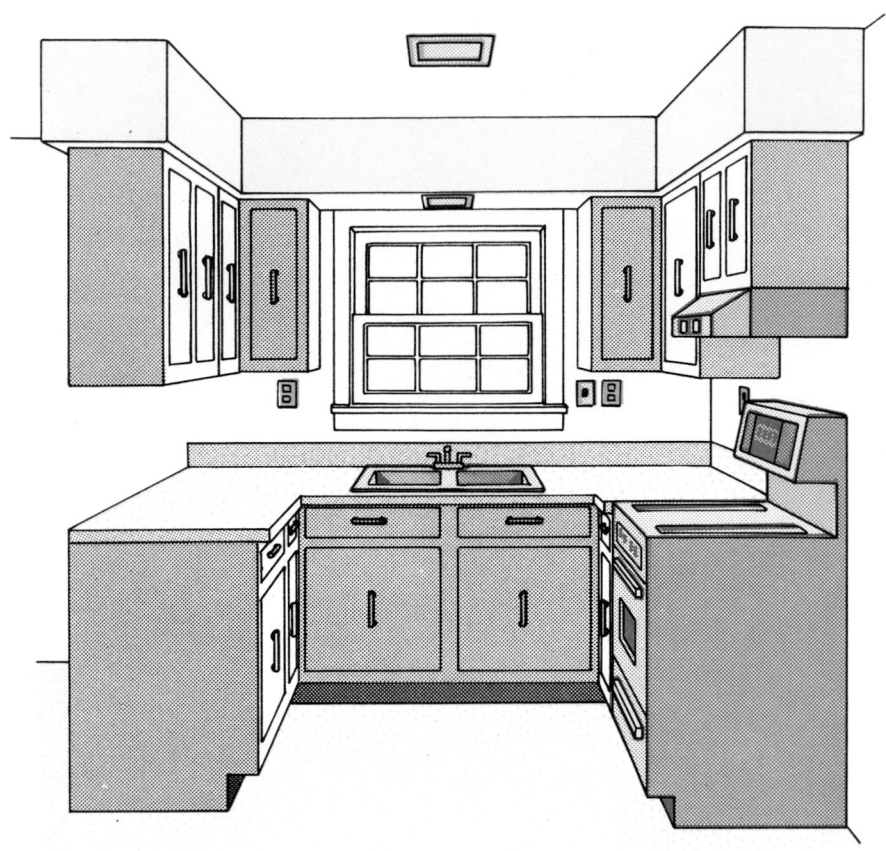

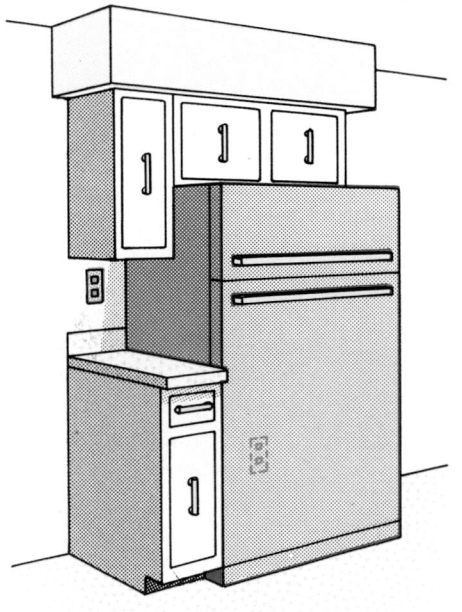

J. U-shaped kitchen:

➤ The sink, range, and range hood are shown in red.

➤ The counter appliance outlets and the lights are in blue.

➤ The floor covering (including matching counter covering), the door handles, drawer pulls, and the soffit are in yellow.

➤ The dining room floor covering is carpet, to contrast with the kitchen floor.

K. Refrigerator wall.

The refrigerator is in red. There is an appliance outlet over the small counter, as well as the usual outlet behind the refrigerator.

is specified, this should be done immediately. At the same time, carpenters can work on the exterior of the building installing siding, exterior trim, and the garage door.

Normally, plaster is applied in two stages, the rough coat and the finish coat. Plenty of time must be allowed for drying between stages and after the finish coat. Often a week or ten days must be allowed before proceeding with any interior work. If gypsum drywall is installed, the drying period is much shorter since the only wet application is taping the joints and covering nailheads.

16. Slabs. If the house has a basement, the concrete floor is poured after the rough plumbing is installed. However, this is done before the finish interior work. Concrete, too, must dry out thoroughly. The garage floor is put in anytime after the backfill is completed. Often this is done at the same time as the basement floor. The concrete is delivered to the site by special trucks. Fig. 57-7. Concrete driveways and sidewalks, however, are installed at the very last stages of the building construction, after finish grading.

17. Finish carpentry. At this stage the carpenters are ready to do the interior finishing, provided the plaster and concrete are thoroughly dry. If lumber is delivered and stored in a house where there is high humidity due to wet plaster and concrete, the wood absorbs the

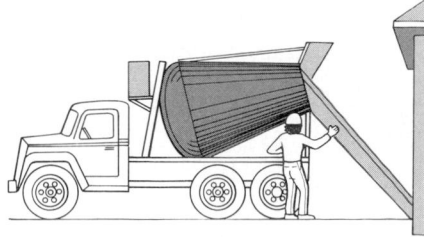

57-7. *Pouring the garage floor.*

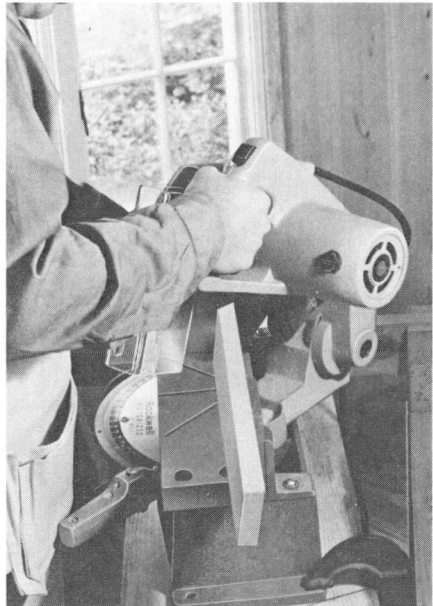

57-8. *Installing moldings. The finish floor has been laid and the wood paneling has already been installed.*

moisture and swells. Later it will dry out and show large cracks.

In completing the interior, the first job is to install underlayment, then flooring, wood paneling, and finally the finish flooring. The interior frames, doors, and cabinets are next installed. Finally the interior moldings are applied, including the base, shoe, ceiling, and window trim. Fig. 57-8.

18. Exterior painting. As carpenters are working on the inside of the house, painters can be finishing the exterior. The ideal arrangement is for the painters to work closely behind the carpenters on the exterior so that the wood is properly sealed. If exterior trim has been preprimed at the factory, this schedule is not so critical.

19. Grading. While the carpenters are completing the interior of the house, the exterior grading can be done and all flat concrete work such as sidewalks and driveways can be installed.

20. Landscaping. The final step in completing the exterior of the house is the landscaping.

21. Interior painting. When the carpenters have completed the interior of the house, the painting can be done.

22. Tile and floor coverings. After the paint is dry, the wall tile, floor tile, and linoleum are installed.

23. Finish electrical. At this point the electricians can return to install switches, outlets, and fixtures.

24. Finish plumbing. The plumbing fixtures can now be installed by the plumbing contractor.

25. Wood flooring. One of the last jobs on the interior of the house is to finish the wood flooring. Many homes are completely covered by carpeting and require no floor finishing. Carpets are often laid directly over a good plywood or particle board base. However, if hardwood floors are used, floor sanding should be done after the interior painting to remove any paint drops or spillage. The actual finishing is done as one of the last jobs so that traffic will not raise dust when the floor finish is drying. Hardwood flooring can be purchased prefinished, which greatly simplifies this part of the job.

26. Carpeting. After the wood floors are finished, carpeting is installed.

27. Cleanup. The general contractor is responsible for the final cleanup. A good contractor will make sure that the windows are washed and all waste materials removed from the job site.

28. Punch list. After the entire house has been completed, the general contractor walks through the house with the new owner.

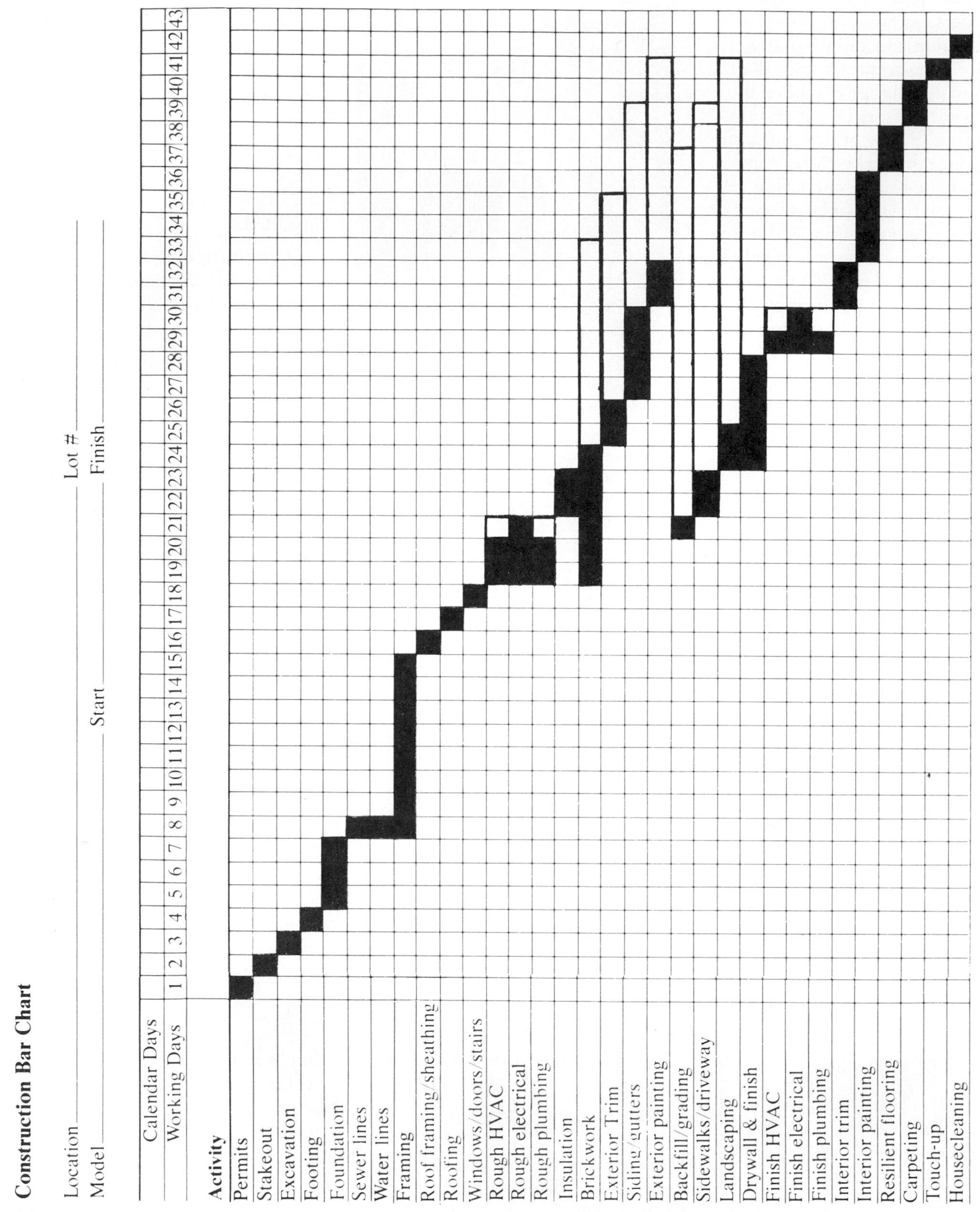
Construction Bar Chart
Location
Lot #
Model
Start
Finish
Calendar Days
Working Days
1 2 3 4 5 6 7 8 9 10 11 12 13 14 15 16 17 18 19 20 21 22 23 24 25 26 27 28 29 30 31 32 33 34 35 36 37 38 39 40 41 42 43
Activity
Permits
Stakeout
Excavation
Footing
Foundation
Sewer lines
Water lines
Framing
Roof framing/sheathing
Roofing
Windows/doors/stairs
Rough HVAC
Rough electrical
Rough plumbing
Insulation
Brickwork
Exterior Trim
Siding/gutters
Exterior painting
Backfill/grading
Sidewalks/driveway
Landscaping
Drywall & finish
Finish HVAC
Finish electrical
Finish plumbing
Interior trim
Interior painting
Resilient flooring
Carpeting
Touch-up
Housecleaning

57-9. *A bar chart shows the duration of tasks and arranges them in chronological order.*

This is a chance for the owner to make sure everything has been done to his or her satisfaction. Often the owner will spot such things as scuffed paint, cracked woodwork, or light fixtures that don't work properly. The contractor then makes a list, called a "**punch list.**" This lists all the items that must be completed before the house is acceptable to the owner.

Building Inspections

Throughout the many stages of building a home, a variety of inspections are done by the local building inspector. Frequently, the contractor must obtain not only a general building permit but also special permits for plumbing, heating, electrical, and roofing work. These building permits specify when inspections must be made before further building can be done. The inspectors check to see that local building codes are being followed. If they are not, the inspector can require the

contractor to make the necessary changes before further work can be done. The final inspection is made before a certificate of occupancy is issued.

KEEPING TRACK OF THE SCHEDULE

Once the contractor knows what tasks have to be performed, he or she must determine *when* they will be performed. This requires that the contractor allot a certain amount of time to each task. For example, forming the foundation might take three days, and pouring it might take one day. Once a duration of time has been identified for each task, there are two common graphical methods for keeping track of everything. One is a simple bar chart. The other uses work flow diagrams. Software available for both methods can be run on a computer.

Bar Chart Method

A bar chart is the easiest way to keep track of the scheduling for a job. It shows how long each task will take, and shows when the task will start and end. The bar chart has a calendar format that plots the entire job over time. Fig. 57-9.

Simple versions of the bar chart can be used to track small jobs such as the addition of a bedroom to a house. Expanded versions can track the construction of an entire house. The value of a bar chart is in its ability to show a comprehensive view of the entire project. However, its simplicity can also be a liability. A bar chart cannot show complicated interrelations between the various jobs. That is why it is used primarily as a general planning tool.

Critical Path Method

The critical path method (CPM) of scheduling was designed to pick up where bar charts leave off. A CPM schedule shows the interrelationships between various tasks. Thus its value is in highlighting potential problems in the schedule. Fig. 57-10.

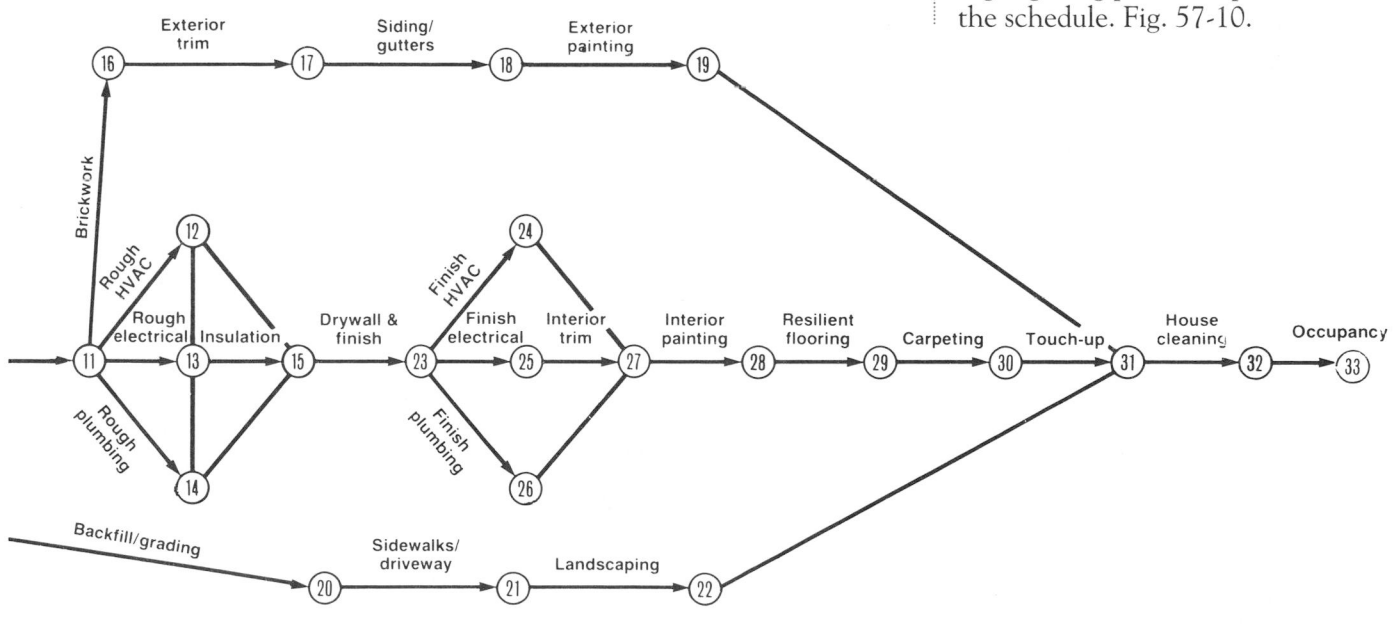

57-10. A CPM diagram arranges tasks by their relationship to each other.

To draw out a CPM schedule, list all the work that has to be done. The list of activities in "Job Scheduling" earlier in this unit is an example. The following three questions should be answered for each activity:

➤ What activities will precede this activity? All tasks have a logical order in which they will be performed. For example, the drywall must be installed before it can be painted.

➤ What activities cannot start until this activity is complete? For example, rough plumbing cannot be installed until the framing is in place.

➤ What activities can be conducted simultaneously? The job moves quickly when various trades are working at the same time. For example, electricians can be working while the site is being finish graded.

Once these questions have been answered, the various tasks can be plotted on a CPM diagram. The arrows on the diagram indicate tasks. The boxes, called *nodes*, represent events. Where arrows are in line with other arrows, that indicates that each task (the event) must end before the next task can begin. Parallel arrows represent tasks that can be conducted simultaneously.

QUESTIONS

1. What are the two types of scheduling needed when building a home?

2. Why should the general contractor subcontract those jobs that require special skills and equipment?

3. List several jobs that are normally subcontracted.

4. What factors control the material deliveries?

5. How are missing or extra materials handled?

6. Why is job scheduling so important?

7. If you were the contractor, at what stage of the construction would you backfill? Why?

8. What kinds of jobs will the carpenters be doing while the mechanical subcontractors are doing their rough-in work?

9. Why must the interior trim work be delayed until the plaster and concrete are thoroughly dry?

10. Who is responsible for the final cleanup?

11. How does the contractor know when certain inspections are to be made by the local building inspectors?

ACTIVITIES

1. Math. To complete a project, six subprojects (A, B, C, D, E, F) need to be completed. Some of the subprojects require more time than others. Some must be done before others can be completed, just as in home construction. The following list gives the six subprojects, the number of days required to complete them, and the other subprojects, if any, that must be completed first. The list is: A, three days; B, four days; C, two days, A&B; D, five days, C; E, three days, C; F, two days, D&E. Determine the minimum number of days to complete the total project. Hint: Draw a diagram using arrows to indicate the order in which the subprojects must be completed.

2. Language Arts. The business administration division is responsible for business and financial operations. Administrators are responsible for marketing, deciding which jobs to accept, and signing contracts and other legal documents. They also deal with personnel matters. In personnel management, the administration must be aware of any problems caused by job-related stress. On-the-job stress can result, in part, from tight deadlines, inadequate help, and equipment problems. Managers should be alert to ways of minimizing such stress. In a brief essay, identify several factors that can contribute to on-the-job stress. Then discuss some ways in which management might reduce on-the-job stress.

3. Science. There are a number of computer programs available for scheduling the various aspects of a job. Some of these programs are more detailed than others. By ordering the project's tasks in a certain sequence and by drawing relationships between different jobs, these programs can help keep a project on schedule. If your school has a computer lab, check to see if one of these scheduling programs might be available in the lab. If such a program is available, check to see if you can obtain instruction on its use.

UNIT

58

Plumbing, Electrical, and Heating, Ventilating and Air-Conditioning (HVAC) Systems

PLUMBING

Plumbing is one of the mechanical trades. The work is done by subcontractors who hire certified craftspeople to do the actual work. Fig. 58-1. Plumbers must possess a wide variety of skills. They must know how to use many types of tools and equipment. The required skills include woodworking, metalworking, welding, brazing, soldering, caulking, and threading. Their tools include wrenches, reamers, drills, braces and bits, hammers, chisels, and saws. Plumbers also must be able to use power tools such as portable drills, reciprocating saws, and nailers. They use gas-oxyacetylene and propane torches for welding, brazing, and soldering. It is the plumber's job to install the piping system for water and drainage—including all of the fixtures. The plumber must know the sizes of fixtures so that the pipe lines will be in the correct location for the size of each fixture. Fig. 58-2.

Specifications for installing plumbing systems are outlined in the Uniform Plumbing Code

58-1. *Plumbing is an important part of any kitchen installation. The stainless steel double-sink with a drain board is of top quality. It includes a spray head and a separate faucet for purified water.*

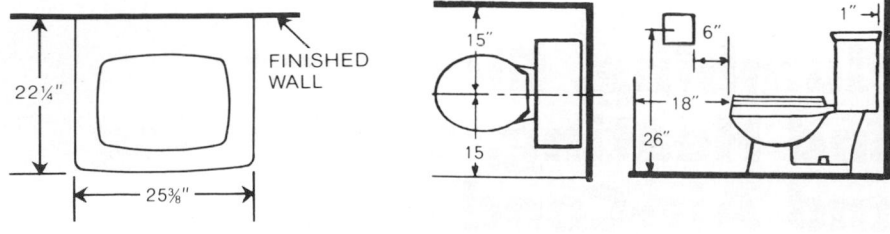

58-2. *Location of fixtures in a bathroom.*

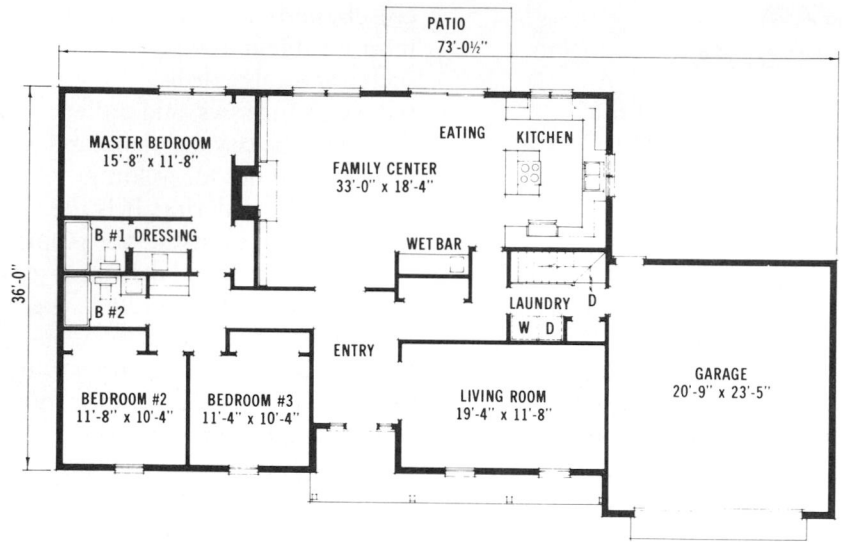

58-3. *The floor plan shows the location of the bathrooms, kitchen, and laundry.*

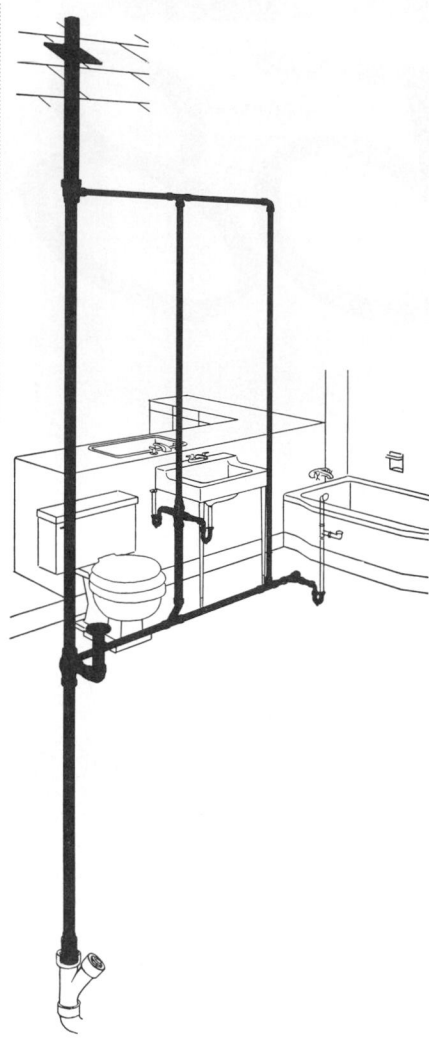

58-4. *A schematic drawing showing the rough-in plumbing with the finished fixtures set in place. In this installation, the plumbing is installed back to back on a partition wall. The kitchen sink is on one side, with the bathroom fixtures on the other side.*

(UPC), plus the local code. Usually the subcontractors must obtain a separate building permit for this work. The plumbing installation must be checked by a plumbing inspector at two stages of construction—the "rough-in" stage and the finish stage.

It is the architect's job to plan the number, type, and location of the plumbing fixtures and hardware. The architect develops the floor plans, elevations, and specifications showing and listing the location and various parts of the plumbing system. Fig. 58-3. Sometimes a separate basement and floor plan is produced to show the actual location of piping. However, this is usually the plumber's responsibility. The plumbing fixture schedule may

specify the type and quality of the fixtures, including the names of manufacturers.

Plumbing System

Residential plumbing brings fresh water into the house (the water supply system) and removes waste water and wastes (waste disposal system). Fig. 58-4. A service main is used to bring the water into the house from the public water system. A water meter is located just outside or inside the basement wall or utility to record the amount of water used. Sometimes the fresh-water pipes are joined to a water pump that supplies the water from an underground well. The water in a

house is under pressure so that it flows evenly through the house as needed for drinking, cooking, washing, bathing, showering, and humidifying. Waste water and other wastes flow out of the house to a public sewage system or to a private septic tank. All fixtures in a home must be vented to allow air to flow in and out. This helps reduce odors and keeps the pressure in the system even.

Plumbing Costs

The plumbing system in a house is the most expensive of all the mechanical systems. For example, the type and quality of the fixtures and hardware (such as water faucets and handles) help determine the total cost. Fig. 58-5. Most modern homes have more than one bathroom, one or more kitchen sinks, and washing and drying appliances, including a sink or tub in the basement or utility room. Fig. 58-6. In addition, the water system is connected to the hot water heater, water softener, water purifier, and humidifier, as well as to some types of furnaces. Water must also be piped to the outside of the house for sprinkling and washing. Some homes have a built-in spa. These appliances require special enclosures and proper venting. Fig. 58-7.

Framing for Plumbing

A major problem for carpenters when framing up a building is to provide adequate space for water and waste piping. Pipes in walls usually extend from the basement or ground floor through walls to the top floor with vents through the roof. All pipes must be installed without weakening the structure. Building codes specify the limits for cutting holes and notches in joists and studs so that the structure will remain strong. Fig. 58-8.

Special framing is needed to add support for heavy items such as

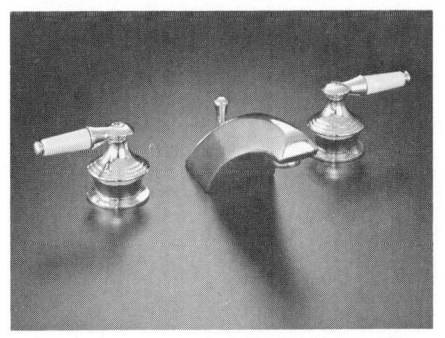

58-5. *Special plumbing hardware adds to the cost of the total system.*

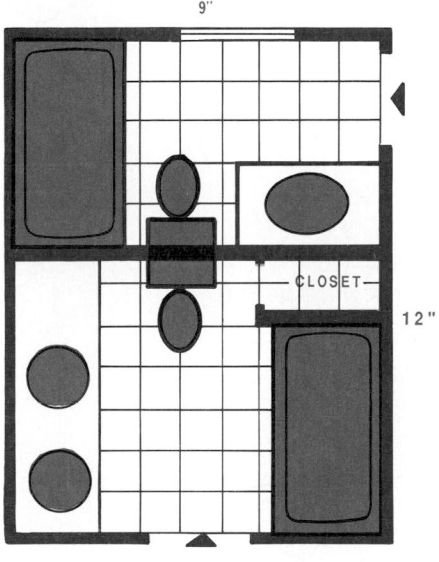

58-6. *Many homes have the two bathrooms back-to-back to simplify the plumbing and reduce cost.*

58-7. *An enclosed spa requires cooperation between the plumber and carpenter.*

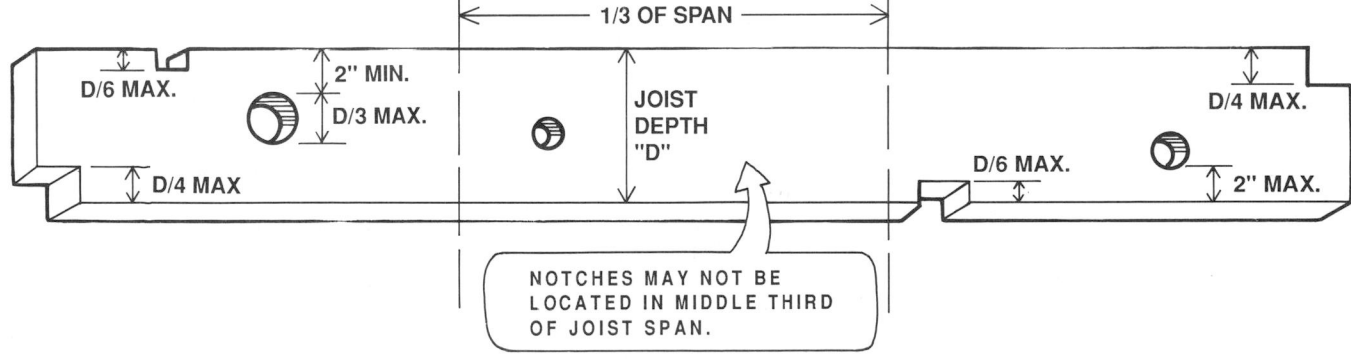

HOLES & NOTCHES IN WOOD JOISTS

58-8. *Location of holes and notches in wood joists as specified by UPC.*

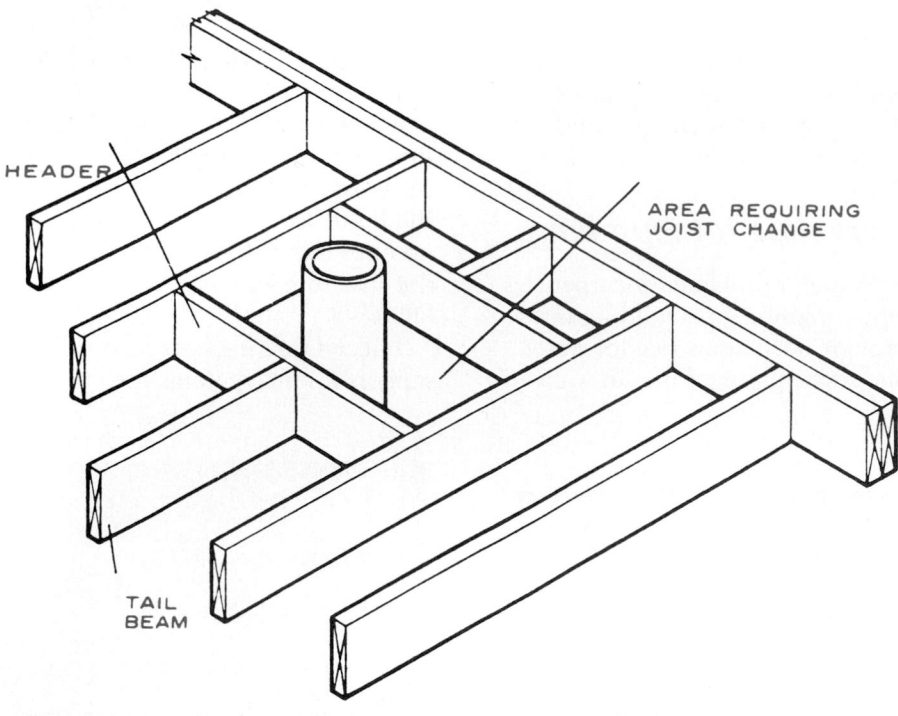

58-9. *Headers are used to support joists that must be cut.*

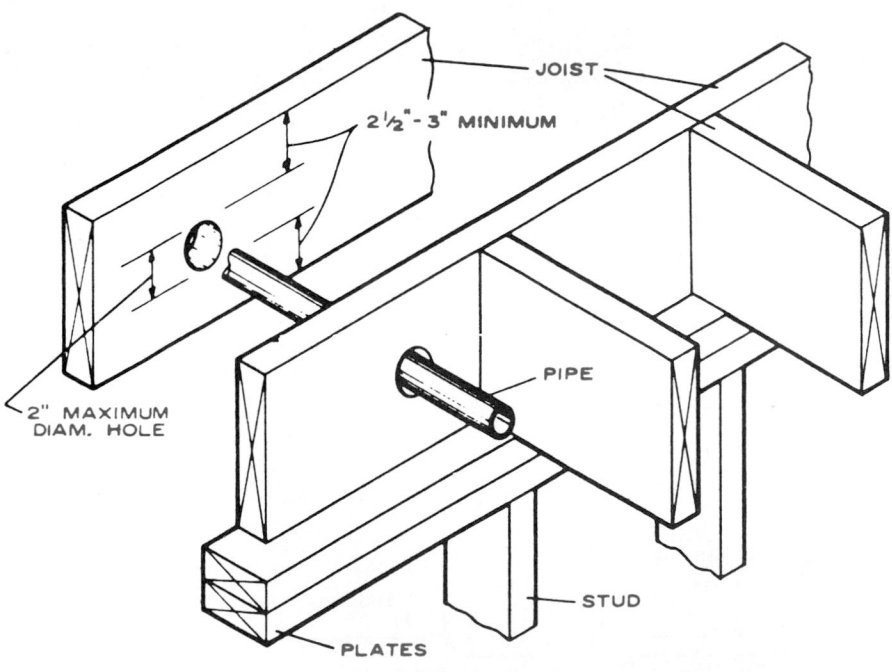

58-10. *Do not weaken the joists by cutting or boring too large a hole.*

bathtubs. For details of this framing, see page 339 in Unit 30 ("Wall Framing").

Cutting Floor Joists. Floor joists should be cut, notched, or drilled only where they will not be greatly weakened. While it is best to avoid cutting, alterations are sometimes required. Joists should then be reinforced by nailing a 2" × 6" scab to each side of the altered member, using 12d nails. An additional joist adjacent to the cut joist can also be used.

Notching the top or bottom of the joist should be done only in the end quarter of the span. The notch should not be more than one-sixth the depth of the joist. Thus for a nominal 2" × 8" joist, 12' long, the notch should not be more than 3' from the end support and about 1⅔" deep. When a joist would require greater alteration, headers and tail beams can be used instead. Fig. 58-9. Proper planning will reduce the need for altering joists.

When necessary, holes may be bored in joists if the diameters are no greater than 2" and the edges of the holes are not less than 2½" from the top or bottom edges. Fig. 58-10. This usually limits a 2"-diameter hole to joists of nominal 2" × 8" size and larger.

Bathroom Wall Covering. When a complete, prefabricated shower or combination shower and tub is installed in the bathroom instead of a tub, special wall finishes are not required. Fig. 58-11a, b, and c. When a tub is used, however, some type of waterproof wall covering is normally required around it to protect the wall. There are several types of finish, including coated hardboard paneling and various ceramic, plastic, and similar tiles. Fig. 58-12.

Plastic-surfaced hardboard materials are applied in sheet form.

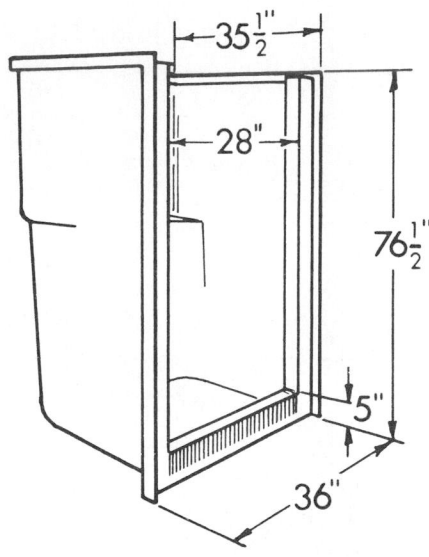

58-11a. *A shower cove bathing module made from plastic reinforced with fiberglass. Bathing modules are available in white and in several colors.*

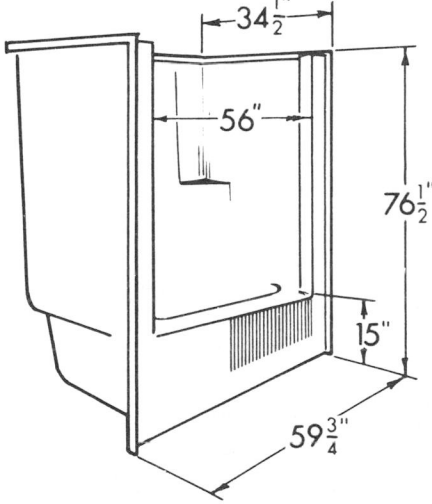

58-11b. *A bath and shower bathing module. This module includes a bathtub and walled alcove. The tub has a flat rim for seating or to accommodate a shower door. The unit is plastic reinforced with fiberglass.*

58-11c. *A tub and shower of plastic comes in three parts for easy installation.*

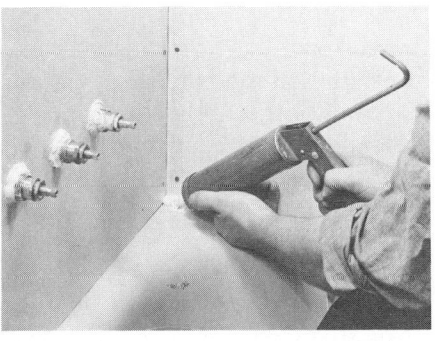

58-12. *Moisture-resistant drywall installed in a tub alcove. Corners and fittings must be caulked.*

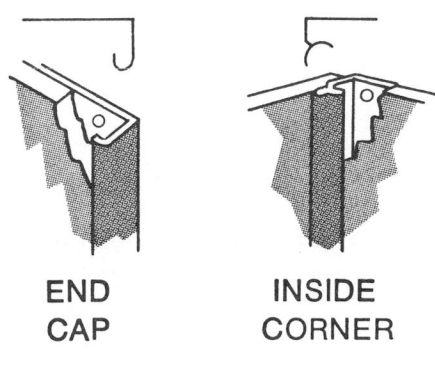

END CAP

INSIDE CORNER

58-13. *Inside corner molding and end cap.*

They are fastened with an adhesive or nails as described under "Installing Gypsum Board" or "Hardboard." The method of application depends on the nature of the material. Moldings are placed on inside corners, on tub edges at the joints, and as end caps. Fig. 58-13. Several types of caulking sealants are also available which will provide excellent results.

Ceramic, plastic, and metal tile are installed over water-resistant gypsum board. The adhesive is spread with a serrated trowel, and the tiles are pressed into place. A grout cement is inserted in the joints of the tile after the adhesive has set. The plastic, metal, or ceramic type of wall covering around the tub area is usually installed by subcontractors specializing in this craft.

Materials for Plumbing

Pipe and tubing used in plumbing systems are made of several different materials and are joined in different ways. Most fresh water systems have copper piping, while modern waste systems are usually of plastic.

➤ *Copper tubing* is joined with fittings that slide over the tubing. The joints are soldered (sweat joint) to seal the tubing and fittings together. The solder that was formerly used was a combination of lead and tin. Since lead is a health hazard in water, this solder must *not* be used. The Drinking Water Act Amendments that became law in 1988 specify that lead-free materials must be used for sealing the joints. Fig. 58-14.

➤ *Galvanized steel pipe* was the material commonly used in freshwater systems in older homes. Fittings joined the pipes. There were threads on the outside of the pipe and on the inside of the fitting. The joints were sealed using

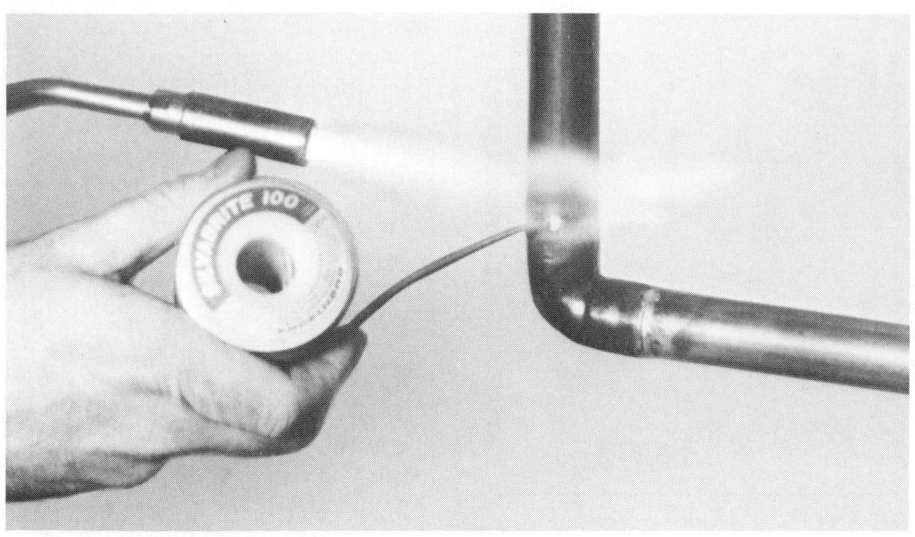

58-14. *Use a non-lead solder that is a combination of tin, copper and silver to make a tight joint, with the heat supplied by a propane torch.*

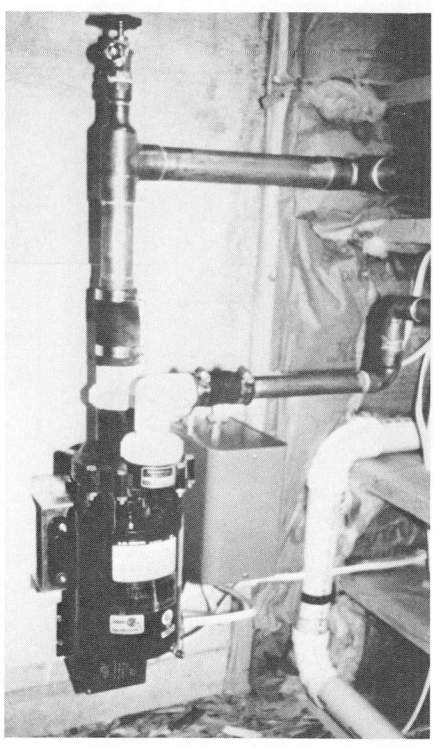

58-15. *Some plastic pipes are also clamped together at the joints. Pipe for drainage, waste, and ventilation can be made of ABS or PVC plastics.*

a compound called *pipe dope*.

➤ *Cast iron soil pipe* is used primarily for waste drainage systems. One end of the cast iron pipe (the bell end) is flared. The other end (the spigot end) fits into the flared end. The joints are sealed using various compounds.

➤ *Plastic pipe* is used both for the water and drainage systems because plastics are cheaper and easier to install. Most waste systems are of plastic. Two types of plastic water supply piping are in use in residential construction. These are slowly replacing copper pipe. Some of the common kinds of plastic piping include the following:

Chlorinated Polyvinyl Chloride (CPVC). This buff-colored rigid thermoplastic piping is already widely used throughout the residential construction industry. It is lightweight, easy to handle, and resists fracture in freezing conditions. Connections are typically threaded and/or solvent welded.

Polybutylene (PB). Newer on the market than CPVC, PB is typically gray or blue in appearance. It is flexible and thereby permits greater installation freedom than rigid piping materials. Joints and fittings are typically connected by mechanical means.

DWV Piping. Plastics in residential DWV systems were used in Europe as early as the 1930s, while their commercial application in the U.S. began in the 1960s. Approximately 75-80% of all new residential DWV is plastic.

Acrylonitrile-Butadiene-Styrene (ABS). The now-familiar, black or gray DWV material is inexpensive. It has good resistance to chemical attack. It is typically joined using a one-step chemical solvent.

Polyvinyl Chloride (PVC). This material appears in the field as tan, ivory, beige, gray or white. It has considerably lower thermal expansion characteristics than ABS. This makes long pipe runs easier to control. It is joined by applying a two-step primer/solvent to typical connections. Fig. 58-15.

The Plumber as Carpenter

Most plumbers want to cut their own holes and notches for fitting the rough plumbing into the structure. It is important that the plumber work closely with the carpenter so that the work will be neat and not weaken the joists or studs. Holes should be smooth and clean cut—just large enough for the pipe. Notches in the studs and joists should be square or rectangular in shape. They should be just large enough for the pipe to fit. After the pipes have been installed, the notches should be reinforced by adding a strip of metal across the outside of the notch.

58-16. *This home office needs at least four outlets for the two lamps, the computer, and the fax machine. Other electrical devices such as an electric pencil sharpener and desk clock need electrical service. At least two double receptacles each on a separate circuit are needed.*

ELECTRICAL SYSTEM

The materials and methods used to wire a house are controlled by local and national codes. Most local codes follow the provisions found in the current edition of the *National Electrical Code (NEC)*. The wiring plans for the home are done by the architect with both present and future needs carefully considered. Fig. 58-16. The wiring plans use symbols to indicate the type of electrical devices to install at each location. Fig. 58-17. Carpenters must know how to read these prints so they can help plan the openings. Fig. 58-18. The job of actually wiring a home must be performed by a licensed electrician working for a mechanical subcontractor. The carpenter must work closely with the electrician to make sure the structural parts of

SYMBOL	SWITCH
S SINGLE POLE	ON / OFF
S₃ THREE-WAY	
S_D DIMMER	

OUTLET SYMBOL	FIXTURE
◯ OR ⊖ CEILING LIGHT	
⊸◯ OR ⊖ WALL MOUNTED LIGHT	
◯ OR ⊖ PS PS PULL SWITCH	
FLOOD LIGHT	
▭ OR ▭ FLUORESCENT LIGHT	

58-17. *Symbols and pictorial illustrations of the various devices used in electrical systems.*

SYMBOL	RECEPTACLE
⊖ SINGLE	
⊖ DUPLEX	
⊖WP WEATHERPROOF	
⊖ SPLIT WIRED	EACH RECEPTACLE ON A DIFFERENT CIRCUIT
⊖R RANGE	
D = DRYER DW = DISHWASHER WH = WATER HEATER ⬤ SPECIAL PURPOSE	

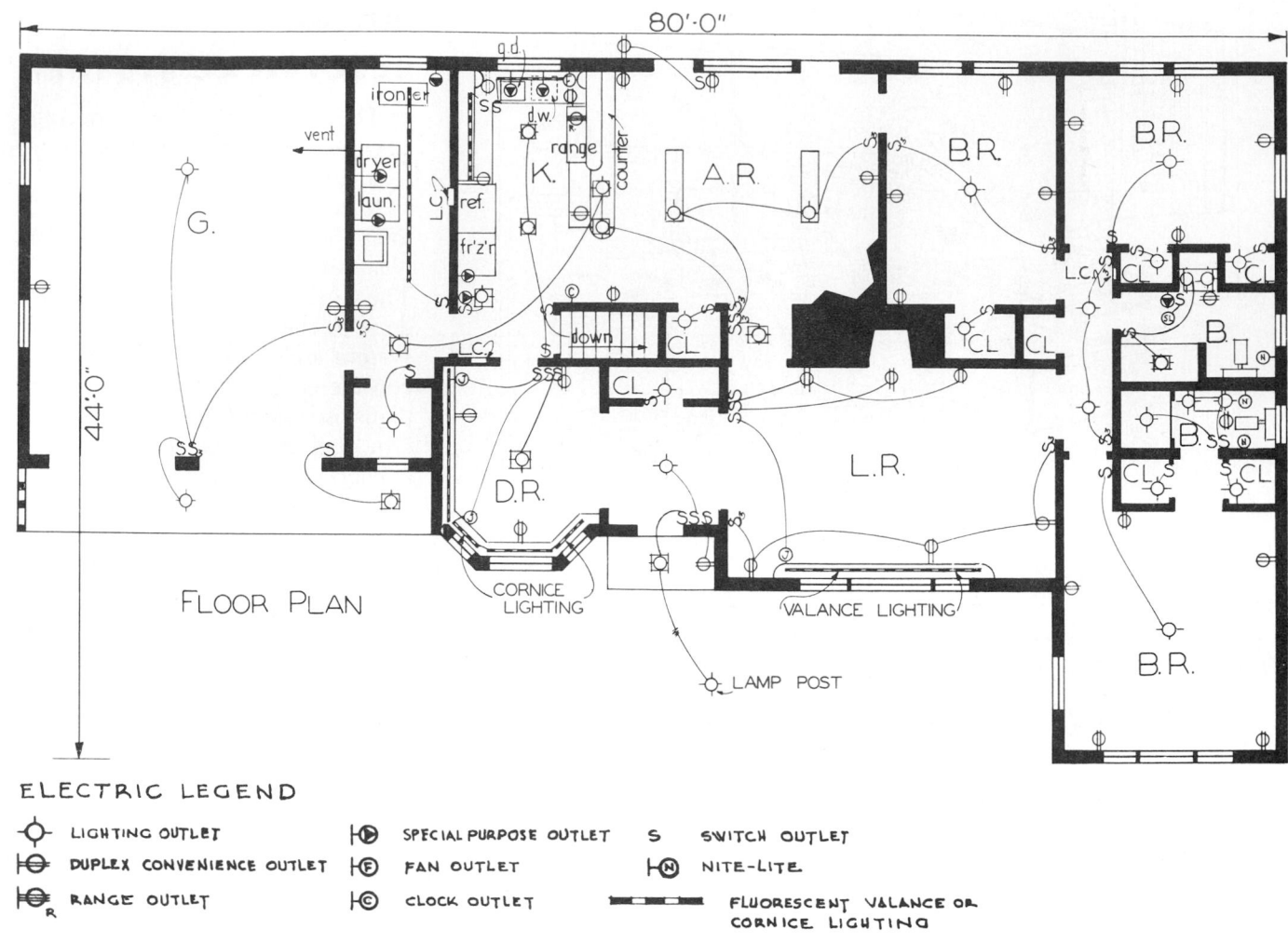

80'-0"

44'-0"

G.

iron'er

dryer

vent

laun.

L.C.

ref.

fr'z'r

K.

range

counter

d.w.

q.d.

SS

L.C.2

down

CL

CL

CL

D.R.

CORNICE
LIGHTING

A.R.

B.R.

B.R.

L.C.

CL

CL

B.

L.C.

B.

CL

CL

L.R.

VALANCE LIGHTING

LAMP POST

B.R.

FLOOR PLAN

ELECTRIC LEGEND

-O- LIGHTING OUTLET

-⊖- DUPLEX CONVENIENCE OUTLET

-⊖-R RANGE OUTLET

-▶ SPECIAL PURPOSE OUTLET

-(F) FAN OUTLET

-(C) CLOCK OUTLET

S SWITCH OUTLET

-(N) NITE-LITE

▬▭▬ FLUORESCENT VALANCE OR
CORNICE LIGHTING

58-18. *A floor plan showing the electrical system. The electrician uses this plan to locate and install the various outlet (junction) boxes and the necessary wiring.*

the home are not weakened when openings for wire are made in the framing members. For example, holes will weaken floor joists more if they are drilled towards the lower edge. Carpenters must be safety conscious when electricians are working in the home to avoid contact with "live" wires.

Electrical System

All power comes into a building through the *service entrance wires.* These may be overhead wires or an underground cable. The wires run first to the watt-hour meter, which records the amount of electricity

used. Fig. 58-19. From the meter, the wires run to a master switch and/or a distribution (service) panel that contains both a master switch and the circuit breakers for the various circuits. The master switch turns off all power in the home. Most houses must have at least a 100-150 ampere service. The distribution panel with circuit breakers provides the way of distributing the electricity through the various circuits needed to operate all the electrical devices in a house. There are three basic kinds of circuits:

➤ The *appliance circuits* must be wired with No. 12 wire protected by a 20-ampere circuit breaker.

These circuits are needed in the kitchen for the dishwasher, refrigerator, and small appliances.

➤ The *general-purpose circuits* (several of them) are 110- to 120-volt circuits with 20-ampere circuit breakers to use for lighting, TVs, VCRs, computers, and many small appliances.

➤ The third type are *special-purpose circuits.* These are designed to supply the heavy electrical needs of stoves, air conditioners, and furnaces. A separate circuit is provided for each of these heavy users of electricity. Most operate on 220- to 240-volt 50-ampere service.

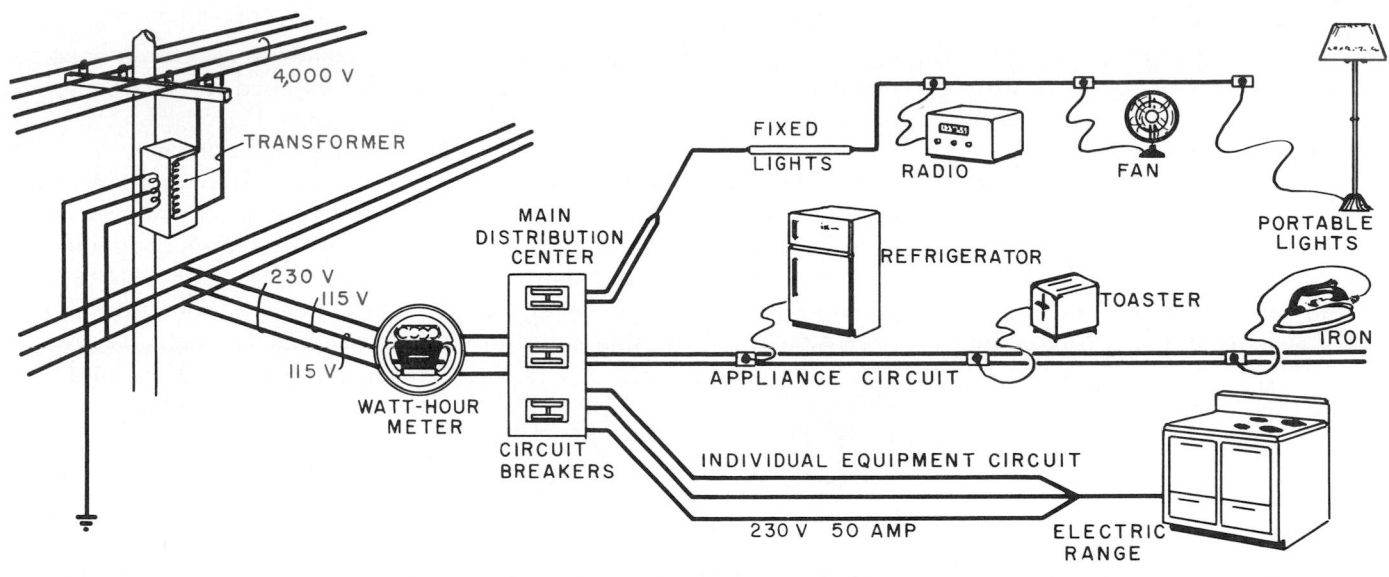

58-19. *A pictorial drawing of the electrical service to the house and the inside circuits. Note that the average voltage to the house is 115 and 230 volts. The minimum is 110 and 220 volts. The maximum is 120 and 240 volts.*

Kinds of Wiring Systems

Several different kinds of wiring are allowed by the NEC (National Electrical Code). All modern homes use two- and three-wire systems, with two or three wires providing the electricity and the third or fourth wire used for grounding.

➤ *Nonmetallic sheathed cable wiring* is the most common, the simplest to install, and the least expensive. It can be used for both open (exposed) and closed wiring. The cable consists of two or three wires with rubber- and/or thermoplastic-covered wires for the electricity and a bare copper wire for grounding. The individual wires are grouped together. They are covered with woven-fabric braid that is moisture-proof and flame-retardant. This is then covered with plastic. Its flat shape and gray or ivory color make it ideal for house wiring. Most people call this "Romex," which is a trade name for one brand of this cable. Fig. 58-20. Only one small hole is needed in the structural parts of the house to

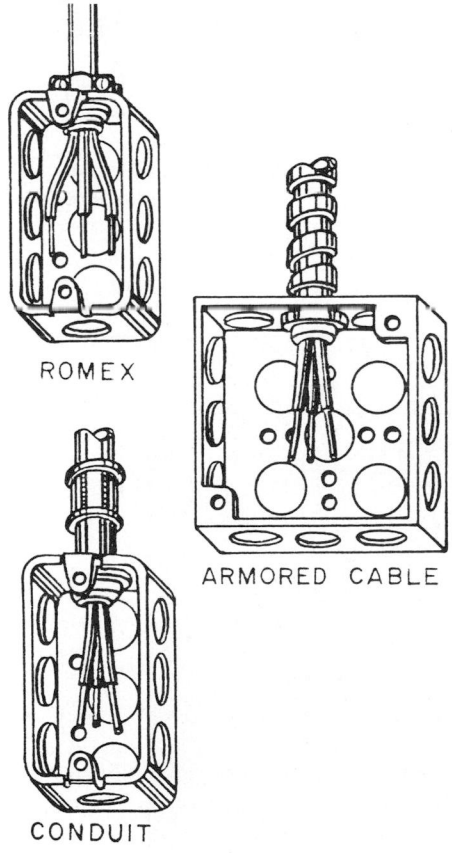

ROMEX

ARMORED CABLE

CONDUIT

58-20. *Three kinds of wiring used between the circuit breakers and the outlet (junction) boxes.*

run the wires from the distribution panel to the outlet (junction) boxes. No support is needed other than staples to hold the wires. The outlet boxes are of metal or heavy plastic. They are available in various sizes and in the shapes needed for switches, receptacles (convenience outlets), ceiling lamps, and appliances.

➤ The second type of wiring is the *armored cable* commonly called BX. With a flexible metal exterior, this system costs more and requires more labor to install.

➤ The third type is *metal conduit*, through which the wires are run. The thin metal conduit can be bent around corners. Often this system is specified for basement and garage wiring. The rigid metal conduit is not usually used in homes, but it is specified for fireproof buildings. This conduit cannot be bent and needs various connectors to assemble the system.

Wiring the House

Wiring a house is done in two stages, the "rough-in" stage and the "finish" wiring stage. The rough-in wiring is done after the exterior of the house has been completed and before the insulation and interior walls are installed. The electrician first installs the electrical meter and distribution panel, connecting them to the outside wiring. Fig. 58-21. Usually the meter is installed somewhere on the outside of the house. The distribution panel is usually placed in the basement or a service room on the first floor. Holes are drilled in the framing to run the wires for the various circuits in the distribution panel to the outlet boxes that have been attached to the studs and ceiling joists. Fig. 58-22. The wires are attached to the circuit breakers but left exposed at the various outlet boxes. Fig. 58-23.

All wiring is done with the master switch off or disconnected. The electrician knows how to wire many different kinds of circuits. For example, the general-purpose circuits are used for lighting and electrical devices such as a radio, fan, computer, TV, VCR, and portable lamp. The simplest circuit has a single-pole switch that controls a lamp. Fig. 58-24. Most receptacles (convenience outlets) are wired direct to the circuit breakers. Fig. 58-25. Lamps and other devices can be controlled by two three-way switches so that the electricity can be turned on and off from two locations. Fig. 58-26. After the rough-in wiring is completed, a building or electrical inspector must approve the wiring system for the first time. The carpenter and other craftspersons

58-21. Circuit breakers in a distribution panel. It is important to record each circuit by writing it on the card on the inside of the door.

58-23. Nonmetallic sheathed cable is run into the box and left exposed until the interior is completed. Note the crayon mark on the stud used to establish where the box is to be attached.

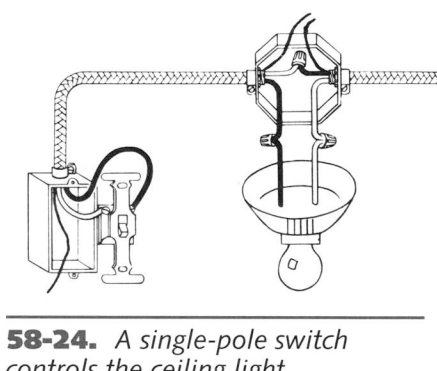

58-24. A single-pole switch controls the ceiling light.

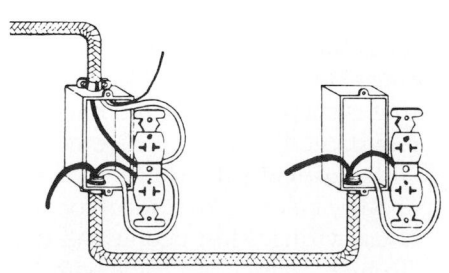

58-25. Receptacles (convenience outlets) wired directly to the circuit breakers.

58-22. Drilling or boring holes in joists for the electrical rough-in. Care must be exercised to limit the number and size of holes.

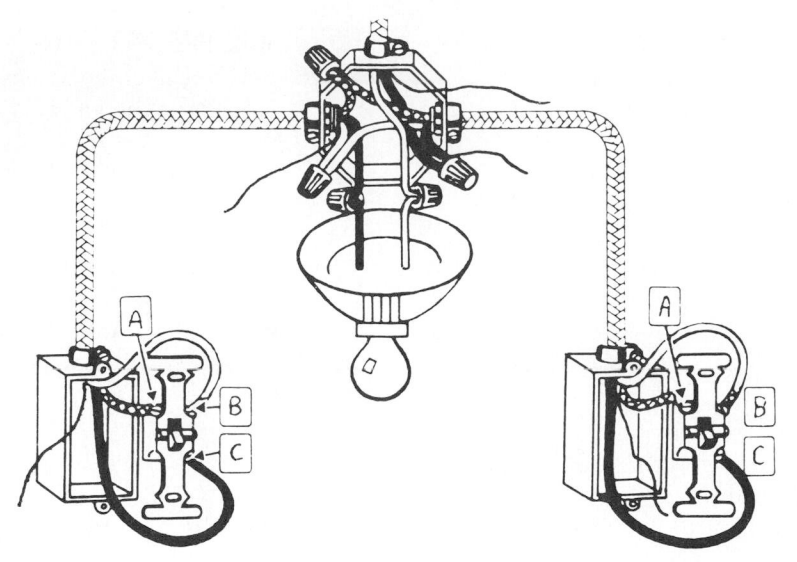

58-26. This circuit requires nonmetallic sheathed cable with three wires plus the ground wire. The terminals marked A and B are light-colored points to which the red and white wires must be connected. Terminal C is the dark-colored (brass screw) point to which the black wire is connected. The extra wire is uninsulated wire that must be grounded.

58-27. Installing drywall. Note the rough-in electrical wiring running through the studs and top plate.

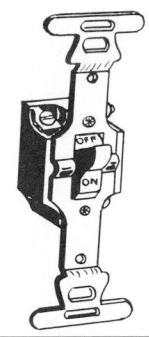

58-28a. A typical toggle switch. The ears on the ends of the straps are a convenience in mounting the switch.

58-28b. Approved receptacles and an adaptor. (1) Duplex receptacle with parallel blade openings and a U-shaped ground opening. (2) Single receptacle. (3) An adaptor for converting a two-wire system without ground to take a two-wire system with ground.

then install the insulation and complete the interior walls. Fig. 58-27.

The electrician comes back to finish the job, including installing switches, receptacles (convenience outlets), lamps, and other devices both inside and outside the house. Fig. 58-28. Often this involves joining two or more wires in the outlet boxes. The electrician strips the wires, twists them together, and then twists on an electrical wire nut. A simpler way is to hold the striped wires together, slip over an electrical connector, and squeeze together with a special pliers. Outlet covers must be attached over all switches and receptacles. After the wiring has been completed, the inspector returns to check and approve the installation.

58-29a. *This experimental house was built to test the suitability of plastics in various parts of housing.*

58-29b. *This experimental flooring system shows how water lines and electrical lines might one day be distributed throughout a house.*

58-29c. *A prototype baseboard electrical raceway was installed in the experimental house shown in Fig. 58-29a.*

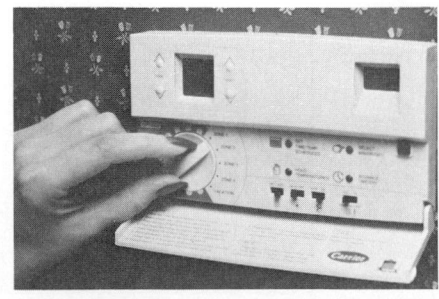

58-30. *A programmable electronic thermostat.*

HEATING, VENTILATING, AND AIR-CONDITIONING (HVAC) SYSTEMS

Without effective temperature control, houses in many parts of the country would be either too hot or too cold. Considerable research has been conducted to make heating and cooling systems more energy efficient. Related systems, such as plumbing and electrical systems, are becoming more efficient, as well. This is due partly to the research being devoted to improving construction materials and techniques. Fig. 58-29.

One aim of this research is to improve the energy efficiency of houses. Oil supplies are dwindling. As the oil supply is reduced, the availability of home heating oil is also reduced. The cost of heating a house increases. At the same time, the oil burned by electrical utility companies to generate electricity costs more. This raises the cost to the consumer. The result is that architects, builders, manufacturers, and homeowners are thinking more about how to conserve energy resources.

One way to conserve resources is to install heating, ventilating, and air conditioning (HVAC) systems that get more energy from less fuel. Most new HVAC systems are far more efficient than older systems. The thermostats controlling the systems are also more efficient. Many of them can be programmed to turn on the heat only at certain times of the day. Fig. 58-30.

Heating, ventilation, and air conditioning needs vary from region to region. This is due partly

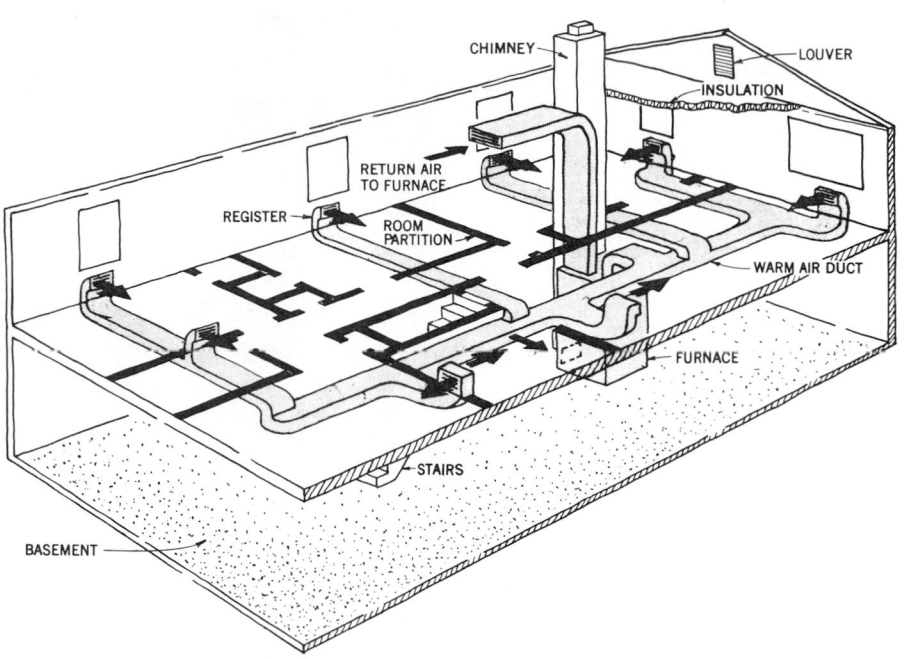

58-31. *Forced hot-air systems are the most popular heating systems. Most installations have a cold-air return in each room (except the bathroom and the kitchen). When the basement is heated, additional ducts should deliver hot air near the basement floor along the outside walls.*

58-32a. *A gas-fired hot-air furnace.*

58-32b. *The inside of the furnace shown in Fig. 58-32a.*

to climate and partly to the availability of resources. In the eastern United States, for example, the most common home heating system is the oil-fired furnace. This heats air, which is then distributed to the house through ducts. This is called an oil forced-air system. It is popular because oil is relatively inexpensive when compared to heating a house with electricity. In the Northwest, however, the reverse is true. With oil less available, electricity is relatively inexpensive. This is because the Northwest gets much of its electricity from hydroelectric sources. Thus, many homes are heated with electricity.

Forced Hot-air Heating

Forced hot-air systems consist of a furnace, ducts, and registers. A blower in the furnace circulates warm air to various rooms through supply ducts and registers. Return air registers and ducts carry the cooled room air back to the furnace. There, it is reheated and recirculated. Hot air systems are commonly fueled with oil, electricity, or natural gas. Fig. 58-31.

Forced hot-air systems respond quickly to changes in outdoor temperatures. They can be used in houses with or without basements. The furnace need not be located below the rooms to be heated. Fig. 58-32. Some systems can be adapted for cooling by the addition of cooling coils. Combination heating and cooling systems may be installed. These allow the same ducts to be used for both heating and cooling. A *heat pump* is a device that can heat or cool the air in a house. It is particularly useful in mild climates that do not experience extremely cold temperatures. The heat pump is connected to standard duct systems. Fig. 58-33.

The warmed air is usually filtered through replaceable or washable filters. These can easily be removed by the homeowner. They should be inspected on a regular basis during the heating season. Clogged filters reduce the

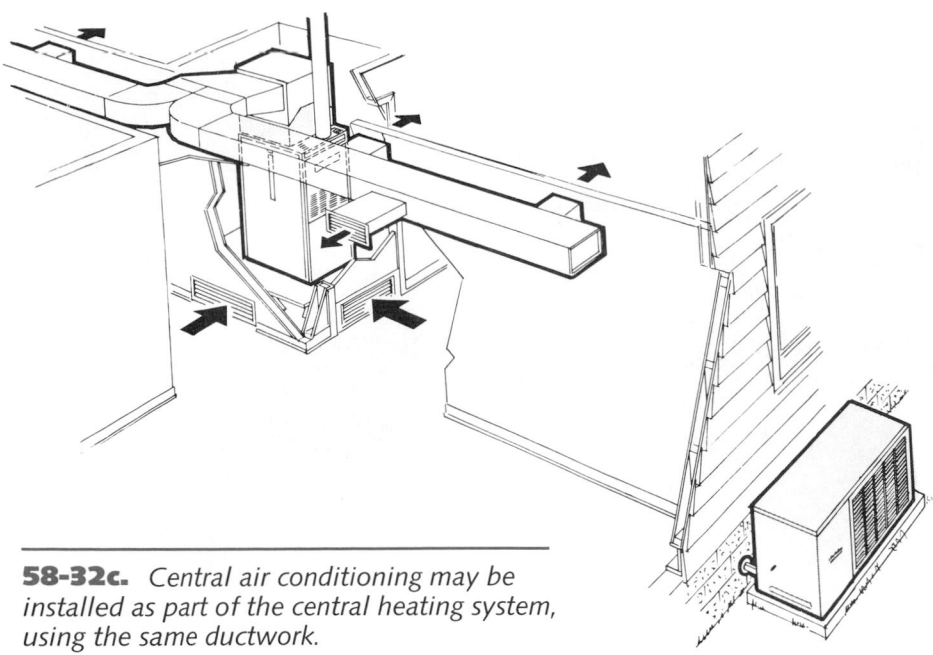

58-32c. *Central air conditioning may be installed as part of the central heating system, using the same ductwork.*

58-34a. *A clogged furnace filter should be replaced.*

58-34b. *This homeowner is removing the cells from an electronic air cleaner. The cells should be cleaned frequently to maintain the efficiency of the system.*

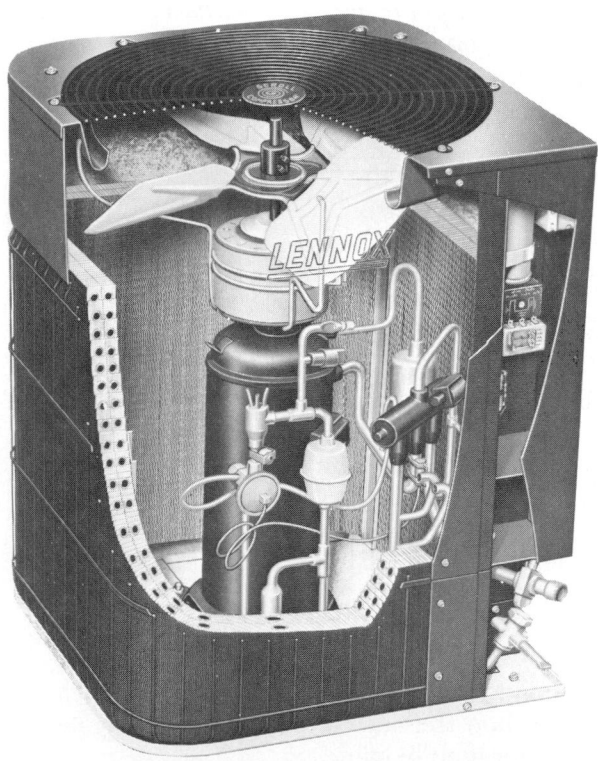

58-33. *A cutaway view of a heat pump. Heat pumps can both heat and cool a house.*

effectiveness of the heating system. Fig. 58-34a. Electronic air cleaners can be installed in some heating systems. They are better able to remove pollen, fine dust, and other irritants that normally pass through standard filters. The part within the electronic air cleaner that actually removes contaminants is called a *cell*. It should be cleaned periodically by the homeowner. Fig. 58-34b.

A humidifier is sometimes added to a hot-air system. A *humidifier* adds moisture to the house and counteracts the drying effects of hot air.

58-35a. *Installing fiberglass heating ducts.*

58-35b. *Installing metal heating ducts.*

58-36. *Perimeter loop heating systems are often used in basementless houses built on a concrete slab.*

Distribution of Heated Air.

The proper distribution of air in a hot-air system is important for the comfort of the homeowner. The ducting system should be designed by an HVAC specialist. Generally, however, the ducts are planned to move air as directly as possible to various areas of the house. The ducts may be made of sheet metal panels, rigid fiberglass panels, or flexible fiberglass tubes. Fig. 58-35.

The ducts are connected to outlet grills that are usually located along the outside walls. Outlets should be low in the wall, in the baseboard, or in the floor. High-wall or ceiling outlets are sometimes used when the system is designed primarily for cooling. However, ceiling outlets may cause drafts.

In addition to one or more outlets in each room, there is usually a return air register in each room. They are usually located in the part of the room opposite from the hot-air outlets. As air within the room cools, it sinks towards the floor level and flows into the return air registers. The cooled air is then returned to the furnace. There, it is reheated and recirculated to the house.

One problem encountered by HVAC contractors is finding space within the house to run the ducts.

To solve this problem, ducts are generally run over the ceiling joists in the attic and beneath the floor joists in the basement. In houses with a slab foundation, cylindrical ducts are sometimes located within the slab. This requires that they be put into place after the foundation formwork is complete. Fig. 58-36.

Hot Water and Steam Heating.

Hot water systems (sometimes called *hydronic systems*) and steam systems consist of a boiler, pipes, and room heating units (convectors or radiators). Hot water or steam generated in the boiler is circulated through the pipes to the convectors or radiators. There, the heat is transferred to the room. Fig. 58-37.

Boilers are made of steel or cast iron. They are designed for electricity, coal, natural gas, or oil. A few boilers designed for use in remote areas can use wood as the basic fuel. One problem with any system based on a boiler is that corrosive water can reduce the life of a boiler. This problem can be minimized by treating the water with chemicals. Boilers should be inspected at the beginning of each heating season. Fig. 58-38.

Radiators are set on the floor, mounted on the wall, or mounted

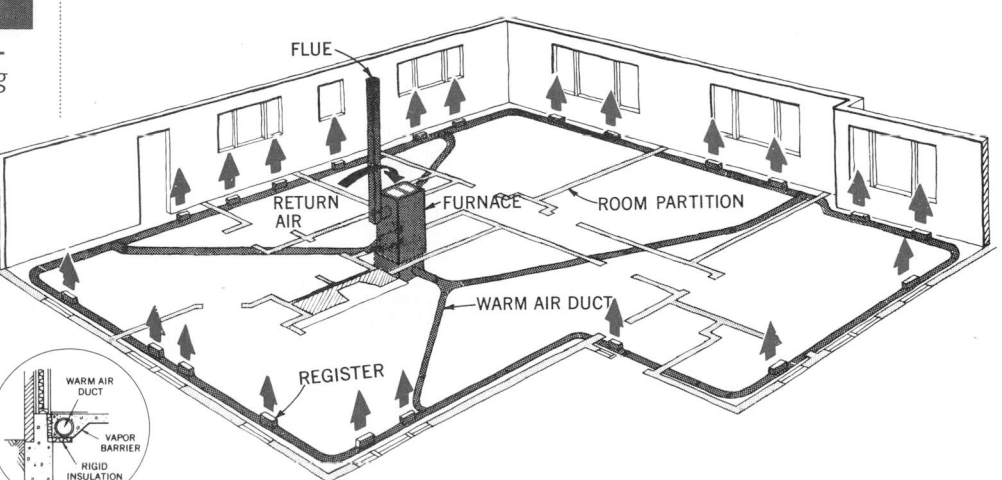

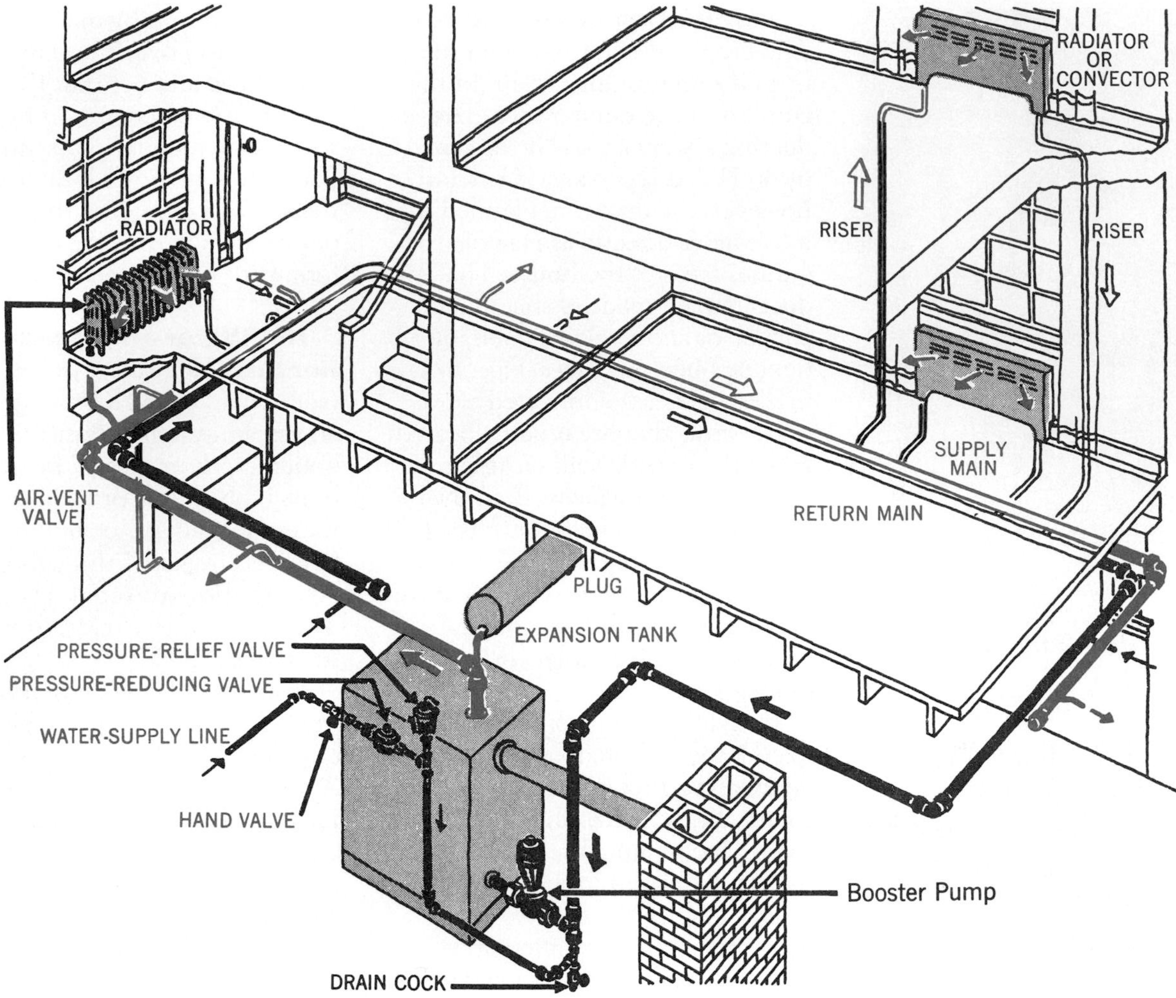

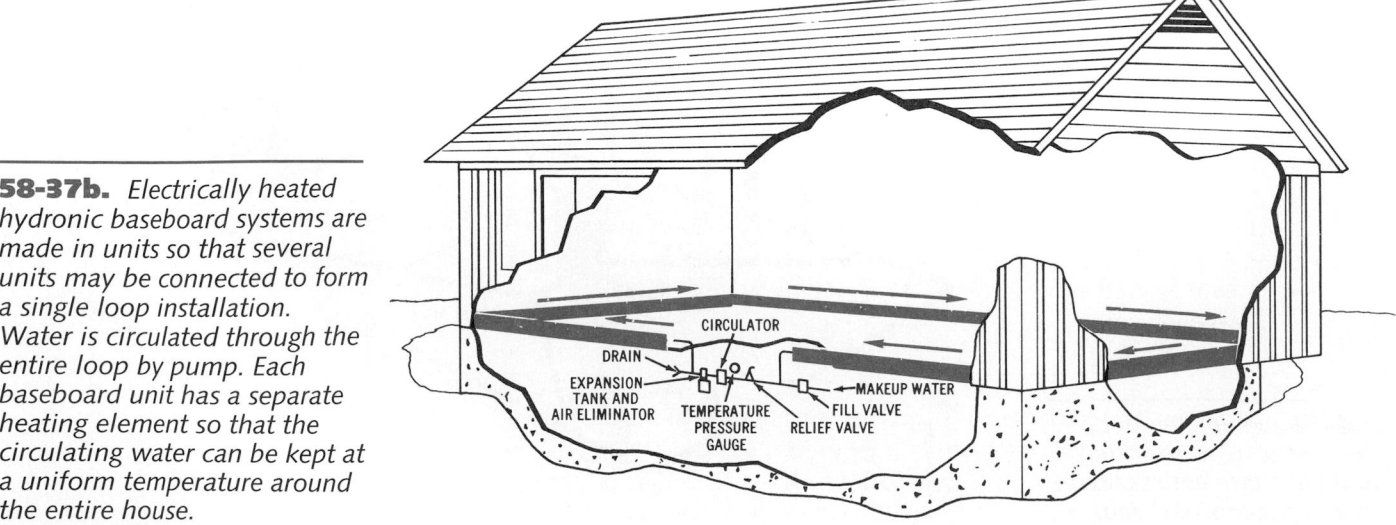

58-37a. *Two-pipe, forced hot-water systems have two supply pipes or mains. One supplies the hot water to the room heating units and the other returns the cooled water to the boiler.*

Labels in upper diagram:
RADIATOR OR CONVECTOR
RISER
RISER
RADIATOR
RETURN MAIN
SUPPLY MAIN
AIR-VENT VALVE
PLUG
EXPANSION TANK
PRESSURE-RELIEF VALVE
PRESSURE-REDUCING VALVE
WATER-SUPPLY LINE
HAND VALVE
Booster Pump
DRAIN COCK

58-37b. *Electrically heated hydronic baseboard systems are made in units so that several units may be connected to form a single loop installation. Water is circulated through the entire loop by pump. Each baseboard unit has a separate heating element so that the circulating water can be kept at a uniform temperature around the entire house.*

Labels in lower diagram:
CIRCULATOR
DRAIN
EXPANSION TANK AND AIR ELIMINATOR
TEMPERATURE PRESSURE GAUGE
FILL VALVE
RELIEF VALVE
MAKEUP WATER

58-38. *Boilers used in hydronic heating systems should get a yearly safety and efficiency inspection by a qualified service technician.*

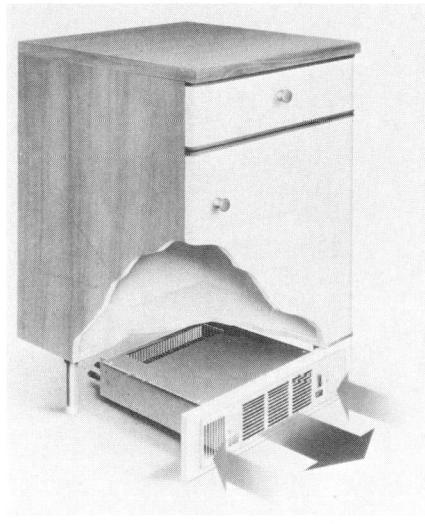

58-39. *This low-profile hydronic convector can be located in the kickspace of kitchen cabinetry. Intake air is indicated by the two small arrows. Heated air is indicated by the large arrow.*

in the wall. They may be partially or completely enclosed within a cabinet. The cabinet must have openings at the top and bottom so air can circulate around the radiator. Baseboard radiators can be used where a low profile is desirable.

Convectors usually consist of finned tubes enclosed in a housing that has openings at the top and bottom. Hot water or steam circulates through the tubes. The fins maximize the transfer of heat to the surrounding air. Low-profile convectors can be placed in locations that would otherwise be obstructed. Fig. 58-39.

Distribution of Heated Water. In a typical hot water system, a smaller pump circulates the hot water through pipes to the room radiators or convectors. In a one-pipe system, one pipe serves both for supply and return. The pipe makes a complete circuit from the boiler to the various rooms and back again. A two-pipe system uses one pipe to carry the heated water to the room heating units and one pipe to return the cooled water to the boiler.

Radiant Heat

Radiant heating systems can combine elements of hot-air and hydronic systems. They can be fueled by electricity, oil, natural gas, or the sun. What the systems have in common is the way heat is transferred. In hot-air systems and standard hydronic systems, heat is transferred to the air. The air then warms those in the house. In radiant systems, heat is transferred to a material, which then radiates the heat to people. In other words, hot-air systems heat air, while radiant systems heat objects.

In radiant systems, the heating coils or cables are buried within ceilings, floors, or walls. No registers, ducts, or return-air grills are required. In addition, the systems are very quiet in operation.

Electric Radiant Heat. Many types and designs of electric radiant heating are available. Ceiling heat may be provided with electric heating cable laid back and forth on the ceiling surface. It is covered with plaster or a second layer of drywall. Radiant panel units can

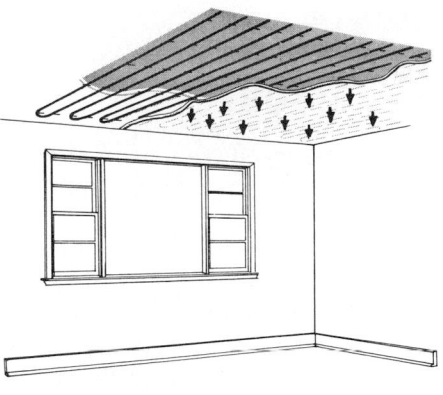

58-40. *Electric heating cable installed in the ceiling.*

58-41. *Installing a radiant floor heating system. Concrete is poured over a network of hot water distribution tubing.*

also be placed directly on the finished surface of the ceiling. Fig. 58-40. Ceiling heat is generally controlled by a thermostat located in each room.

Hot-Water Radiant Heat. In a radiant hot-water system, heated water is circulated through continuous coils of polyethylene tubing. The tubing is embedded in a masonry floor. As the heated water circulates, it conducts its heat to the masonry. The floor then radiates heat to the room's occupants. Fig. 58-41.

VENTILATING THE HOUSE

The energy efficiency of modern houses has increased considerably over the last fifteen years. Heating and cooling systems have become more efficient as well. Two types of ventilation systems—whole house ventilators and heat recovery ventilators—tackle the problem of ventilation in very different ways.

Heat Recovery Ventilators

In most older homes, fresh air leaks into the house through cracks around windows, doors, and foundations. The result is a complete air exchange about once every hour. Unfortunately, all this air must be heated in the winter. One of the main goals when building an energy-efficient house is to minimize the amount of cold air that can enter the house in the winter. This movement of air is called *infiltration*. Builders reduce air infiltration by building "tight" houses. This means that there are few gaps in the house that can let in cold air. This also means that fresh air cannot get in, either. Moisture and indoor pollutants such as formaldehyde, tobacco fumes, and combustion by-products can build to unhealthy levels in a tight house. The solution to this combination of problems is a device called a *heat recovery ventilator (HRV)*. Heat recovery ventilators are sometimes called air-to-air heat exchangers or energy recovery ventilators. Fig. 58-42.

An HRV removes the heat from stale indoor air before exhausting the air outdoors. At the same time, that heat is transferred to fresh air being brought into the house. To accomplish this, a fan within the HRV pulls in fresh air from

58-42a. *The inside of a heat recovery ventilator.*

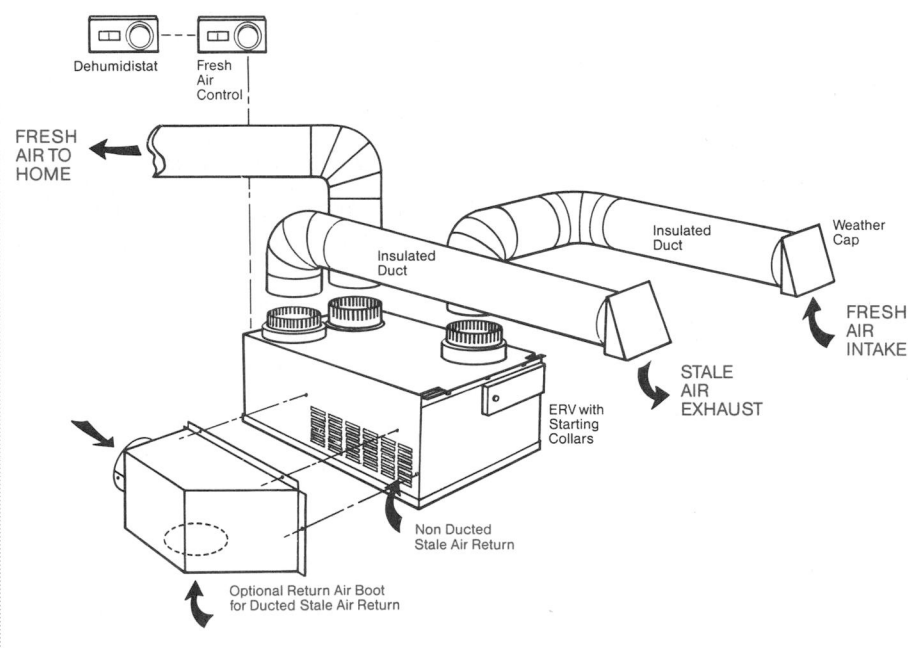

58-42b. *A heat recovery ventilation system. The heat from the stale indoor air is transferred to fresh incoming outdoor air.*

outdoors through ducts. A second fan removes stale air from inside the house through a separate set of ducts. Both sets of ducts meet at the HRV. There, heat is transferred from one airstream to the other. Each airstream is kept separate. By using heat from the outgoing air to warm the incoming air, less energy is required to raise the temperature of the incoming air. A heat recovery ventilation system is usually a separate system from the regular heating system.

Whole House Ventilation

Even in a tight, energy-efficient house, summertime air conditioning can be a significant expense. In some parts of the country, a house may be cooled somewhat by mechanical ventilation instead of air conditioning. In such systems, a large fan is mounted in the highest ceiling in the house. The fan draws relatively cool air into the house through open windows while exhausting hot air into the attic, where vents release it to the outside. The system requires no ducts. Fig. 58-43.

Some whole-house ventilating fans are designed to be mounted on top of ceiling joists. This eliminates the need to cut joists for installation. However, the unit should be isolated from the house framing by mounting it on rubber pads. This minimizes any noise and vibration that might otherwise be transmitted through the framing. Some fans have variable speed controls.

58-43a. *Ventilating fans are ideal for pulling the cool evening air in to reduce interior temperature quickly. A. The fan may be mounted horizontally for a low roof installation. B. The fan may be mounted vertically with a suction box installation.*

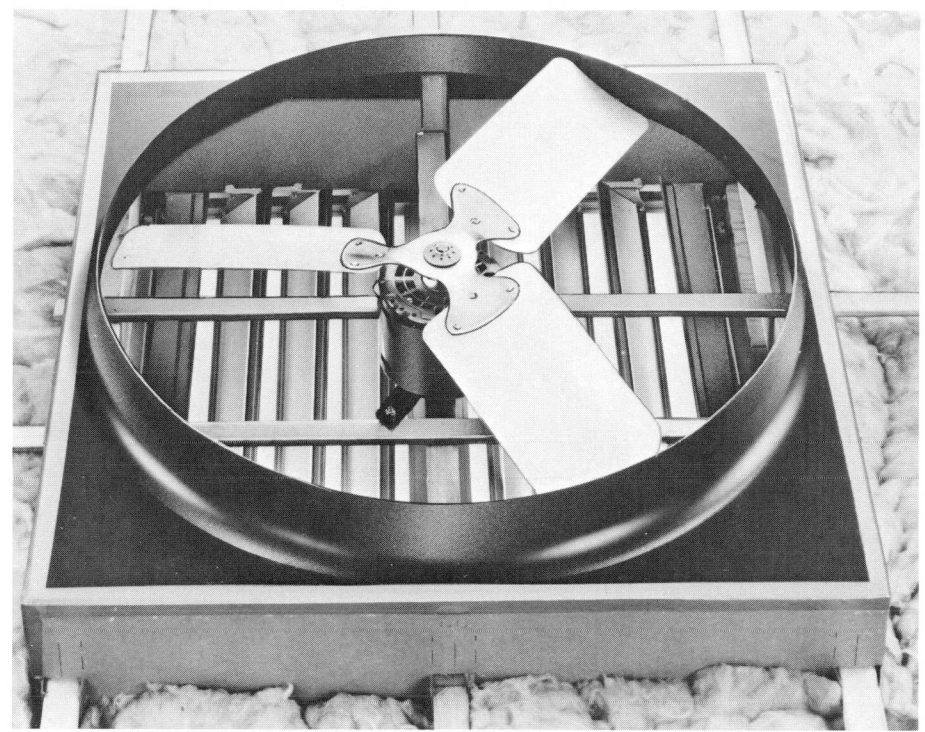

58-43b. *This whole house fan is mounted to the ceiling joists. Louvers beneath the fan blades can be closed when the fan is not operating.*

QUESTIONS

1. Why is solder with lead not allowed by the government?

2. What are the three basic kinds of circuits?

3. Why is it important to improve the energy-efficiency of houses?

4. Describe the operation of a forced hot-air heating system.

5. What is a heat pump?

6. What are the basic parts of a hydronic heating system?

7. What is an HRV? Describe its basic operation.

ACTIVITIES

1. Language Arts. Work can challenge our skills. Because a job may cause us to stretch our energies, there is dignity in performing a task well. It is important to take pride in the work you are doing. A sense of pride will prompt you to pay greater attention to the work at hand. This will cause you to pay attention to small details that might otherwise be overlooked. A sense of pride also will prompt you to explore more effective ways of completing a task. Write a brief essay, discussing other benefits of taking pride in your work.

Interior and Exterior Painting

Paints have been used for thousands of years to decorate and protect surfaces. Paint is now the most widely used finish on the exteriors and interiors of homes. Proper application of the material can prolong the life of a home and improve its appearance. Different effects and levels of protection can be obtained through the use of different kinds of paints. Outside surfaces require paints that will offer protection against weathering and moisture. Interior paints have various purposes:

➤ They make surfaces easy to clean.

➤ They impart wear resistance.

➤ They seal surfaces from moisture and vapor penetration.

➤ They complement or enhance a desired decorating effect.

This unit is divided into three sections. The first two (interior painting and exterior painting) cover tools and techniques. The third section discusses how to identify and solve paint problems.

INTERIOR PAINTING

Many different kinds of interior paints are available. The most popular are the latex paints because they are easy to apply and dry quickly. For a high-gloss or semigloss finish, a good-quality enamel is better. Flat alkyd wall paints are also very popular because they are easy to apply, washable, and good for one-coat hiding. These paints are made from alkyds combined with special oils. They are excellent for covering almost any interior surface, including plaster, wood, wallboard, metal, or wallpaper.

DRYWALL AND PLASTER

Most plaster and drywall surfaces are finished with two coats of either flat, alkyd or latex paint. An initial treatment with size or sealer will improve holdout (reduce penetration of succeeding coats). Thus less paint will be needed for good coverage.

Kitchen and bathroom walls, which are exposed to high humidity and receive more wear, are best finished with one application of undercoater and two coats of semigloss enamel. This type of finish wears well, is easy to clean, and resists moisture.

Planning the Painting

On no other surface is skillful application of paint so important as it is for flat work on plaster walls and ceilings. Because paint must be distributed in a uniform film, extra care in brushing is necessary. Interior surfaces are normally under longer and closer observation than are exterior surfaces. Hence, the brushing on, smoothing out, and leveling off of the paint must be done with particular care.

Indoor painting will be easier and faster if you:
- Select the paint product best suited for the job.
- Follow directions on the can.
- Use good-quality brushes or rollers.
- Protect floors and furniture.
- Prepare the surface properly.
- Paint at comfortable temperatures in a dry, well-ventilated room.
- Wipe up spatters and spills immediately.
- Clean brushes, rollers, and other tools as soon as you finish using them.
- Wear rubber gloves when cleaning brushes and rollers. The gloves will protect your hands and make cleaning up faster.

Supplies and Equipment. Besides the paint, brushes, and rollers, it will be necessary to check and assemble other items you may need for preparing the surface, protecting floors and furniture, mixing the paint, and cleaning up. Fig. 59-1.

Brushes. Good quality brushes are expensive, but worth the money. With a good brush you will get better results with less effort. A 3" or 4" brush is recommended for walls with trim 1½" or 2" wide and for "cutting in" corners and edges. (This will be explained later.) Bristles should be 5"–7" long and dense, with flagged—not square-cut—ends. Fig. 59-2.

Rollers and Pans. Rollers are easier and faster than brushes for painting large flat areas. Tray-fed rollers are the most popular. Short-nap roller covers are suitable for most paints and surfaces, but lambswool is used for flat finishes on rough or imperfect surfaces. Fig. 59-3.

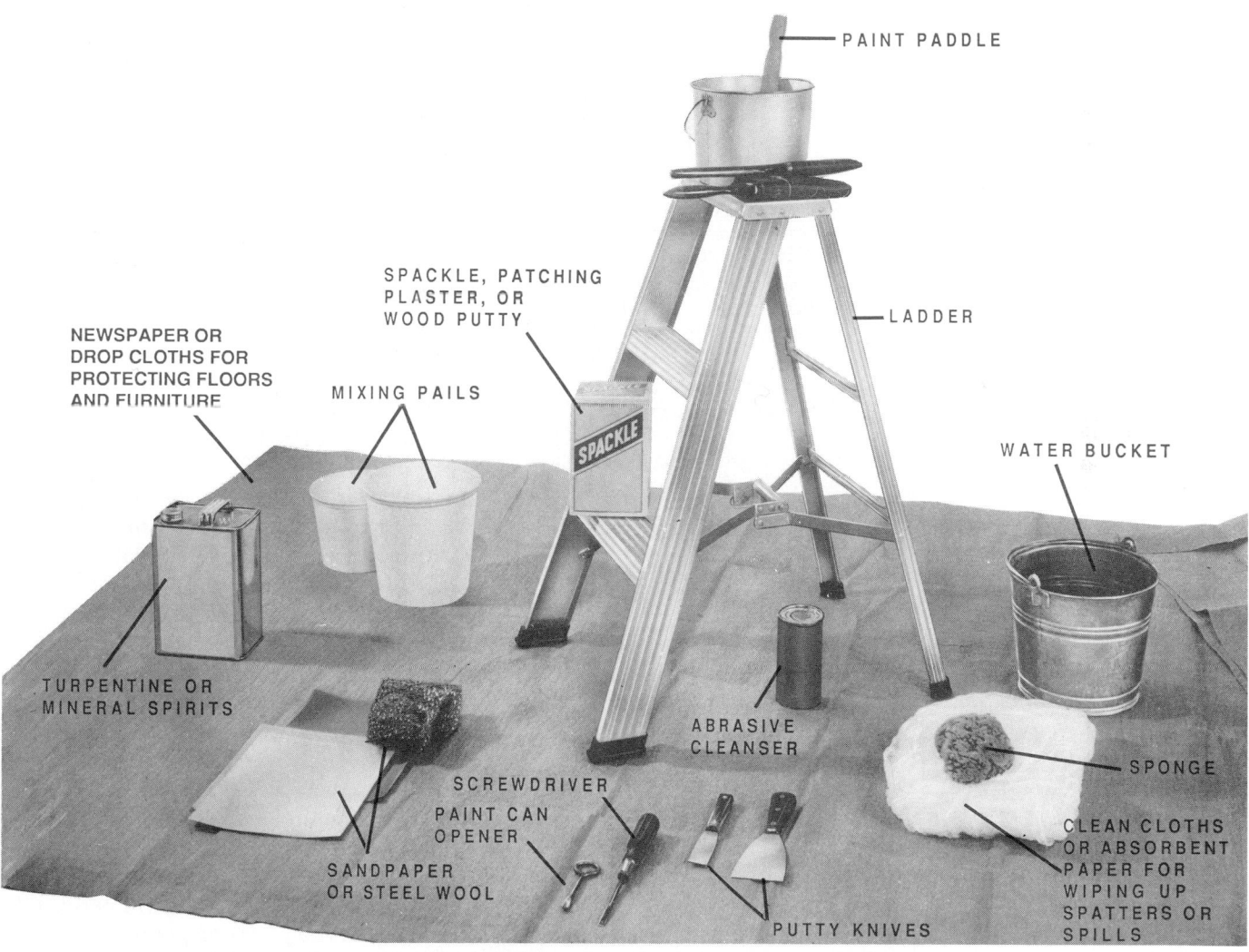

PAINT PADDLE

SPACKLE, PATCHING PLASTER, OR WOOD PUTTY

LADDER

NEWSPAPER OR DROP CLOTHS FOR PROTECTING FLOORS AND FURNITURE

MIXING PAILS

WATER BUCKET

TURPENTINE OR MINERAL SPIRITS

ABRASIVE CLEANSER

SPONGE

SCREWDRIVER

PAINT CAN OPENER

SANDPAPER OR STEEL WOOL

PUTTY KNIVES

CLEAN CLOTHS OR ABSORBENT PAPER FOR WIPING UP SPATTERS OR SPILLS

59-1. *These items are among the supplies and equipment needed for interior painting.*

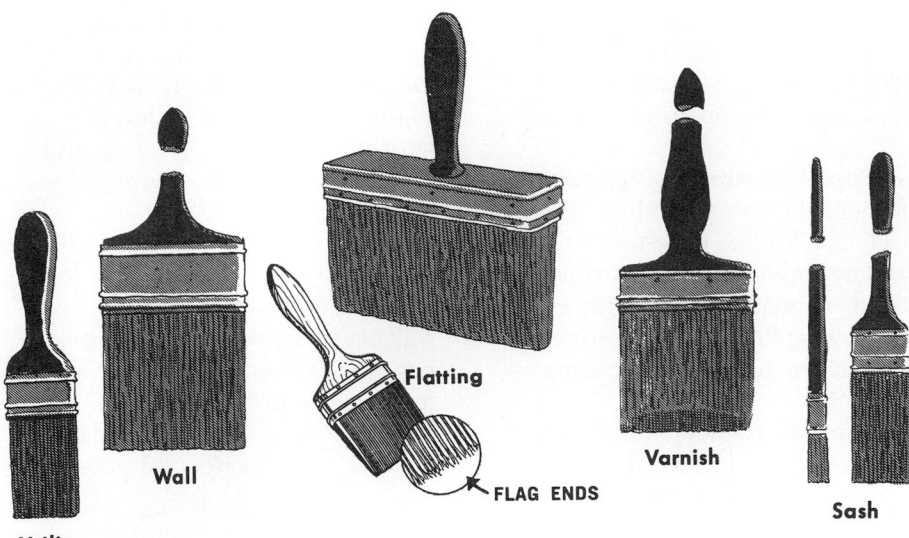

59-2a. *Common kinds of brushes.*

59-2b. *Wall brushes.*

59-2c. *The angular sash brush is good for "cutting in" around windows.*

59-3a. *A roller and tray. The small shelf attached to the tray edge is for holding the "cutting in" brush used ahead of the rolling.*

59-3b. *Roller covers come with naps of various lengths. Shown in this photo (from top to bottom): 1¼", 1", ¾", and ½". Longer naps are best for surfaces with a rough texture. Shorter naps are best for smooth surfaces.*

Preparation. Good preparation will make the painting job much easier and faster. If there is furniture in the home and the floors have been finished, be sure to protect these. Remove pictures, accessories, lamps, and small pieces of furniture from the room. Cover the floors and all the remaining furniture with newspapers or drop cloths. Roll up the rug and see that it is fully covered.

Remove hardware and switch plates. It is easier to take these items off before you start than to try to paint around them, and a more professional job is the result. Switch plates, door knobs, lock plates, and handles can be removed easily with a screwdriver. If there is a ceiling fixture, lower the canopy so that you can paint under it.

Start with a clean surface. A thorough dusting of the surfaces to be painted is usually enough. However, kitchen walls or badly soiled or glossy surfaces should be washed to remove dirt and grease and to dull the surface. Wash from the bottom up with an abrasive cleanser or a solution of trisodium phosphate. Rinse with clean, warm water. On new construction, the walls do not have to be washed.

Fill small cracks. Fine cracks in walls or nail holes in wood trim can be filled with spackling compound. Mix with water to a firm paste, or use ready-mixed material.

Press the paste into the cracks with a spatula or putty knife. Fig. 59-4. Force material into tiny cracks or corners with your fingers. When dry, the patched areas can be sandpapered smooth.

Patching plaster is best for filling large cracks. On cracks ¹⁄₁₆" wide or more, undercut to an inverted V-shape for anchorage. Fig. 59-5. Wet the edges of the old plaster so that the new plaster will bond. Mix the patching plaster according to directions and fill the cracks. Remove the excess and

59-4. Putty all cracks. Be sure to leave a little build-up on the surface to allow for shrinkage when drying. Sand to a smooth surface.

59-5. A large crack should be undercut with the putty knife to ensure good holding power for the fill material.

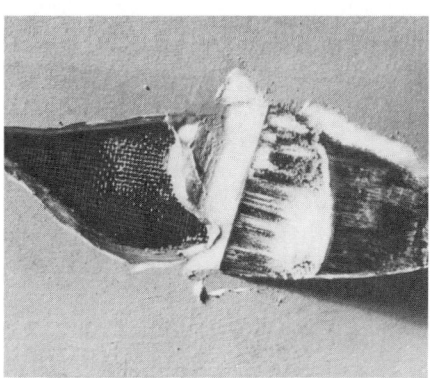

59-6. Large holes should have a piece of screen or hardware cloth tacked in place to support the plaster fill material.

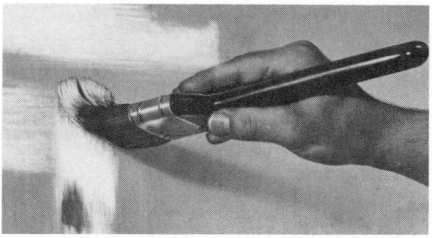

59-7. Patched areas should be spot-primed before applying the finish coat.

59-8. There are many sizes and shapes of scrapers for cleaning surfaces before finishing.

59-9. An electric heat gun can be used to remove old paint.

smooth the surface with a putty knife.

When filling large holes or broken areas, clean out the old plaster and tack a piece of wire screen or hardware cloth to the lath to anchor the plaster. Fig. 59-6. Fill the hole and smooth the plaster level with the surface. If shrinkage occurs in drying, a second filling may be necessary. Large cracks or holes in plaster should be repaired a day or two before painting to allow for adequate drying time.

Plaster that can be scratched with the fingernail is not thoroughly dry. When the plaster is dry and smooth, patched areas should be spot-primed with the same paint that will be used as a finish coat or with an appropriate primer. Fig. 59-7. To determine whether you should use a primer or some of the same paint as the finish coat, check the directions on the label of the container.

If old paint has peeled, the loose flakes can be removed by scraping. Fig. 59-8. Paint can also be removed with a heat gun. This is an electrical tool that produces hot air at temperatures that range from 250 degrees F to over 1,000 degrees F. The heated air softens paint so that it can be easily removed. Fig. 59-9.

When the loose paint has been removed, the remaining surface should be sanded smooth. Spot-prime the bare surfaces before painting. Vulnerable areas such as window sills will benefit from an extra overall coat of primer. Consult label directions for an appropriate primer.

Painting a Room

When the room is in order, the equipment is at hand, and the surfaces have been properly prepared, you are ready for the actual painting. Always start with the ceiling, then do the walls, and finish with the wood trim and the doors.

Be sure to check the label directions for any specific instructions about the method of application. This is especially important today because of the large variety of paint products on the market.

Even if the paint has been mechanically shaken, it should be well mixed just before using. Stir rapidly, working pigment up from the bottom of the can. Professional painters often buy paint in 5-gallon pails. Mechanical mixers can be used to mix large volumes of paint. Special paddles driven by an electric drill can also be used. Fig. 59-10.

When painting walls and ceilings, it is often a good idea to protect windows and other areas from being splattered with paint. This is called "masking off." Standard masking tape in various widths can be used. This tape

sometimes leaves behind a sticky residue when the tape is removed. Instead, painter's masking tape should be used. This tape is very easy to remove and will not mar glass or painted surfaces. To mask off large areas quickly, masking rolls can be used. This product combines painter's masking tape with continuous lengths of either plastic or paper. Fig. 59-11.

Ceiling. If you plan to paint both the walls and the ceiling, start with the ceiling. A single stepladder will do, but two stepladders holding a long plank will allow you to cover more area quickly, comfortably, and safely. Use a strong plank and be sure the ladder legs are firmly placed on the floor. Fig. 59-12.

You can use either a roller or a brush, but most people find a roller

easier and faster. In either case you will need a small brush to get into the corners between the ceiling and the wall. Fig. 59-13. Paint in two- or three-foot strips across the shortest dimension of the ceiling. In this way the next strip can be painted before the last edge is dry. Joining on a dry edge sometimes leaves a lap mark that will show later. Light strokes help to eliminate lap marks.

Walls. When painting a room, "cut in" the edges by painting a narrow strip at the ceiling line, around the doors and windows, and along baseboards. Then fill in the large areas with a brush or roller. Use a small brush for cutting in and a large brush or roller for filling in. Finish an entire unit—that is, one complete wall—before going on to another large area.

When using a brush, dip the bristles only one-third their length into the paint. Tap the brush gently against the inside edge of the can to release dripping paint. Starting at the ceiling line, paint down in three-foot strips, brushing from the unpainted into the painted areas.

Flat paint should be applied in wide overlapping arcs. When a few square feet have been covered, "lay off" with parallel upward strokes. Fig. 59-14.

59-10a. A heavy-duty paint mixer.

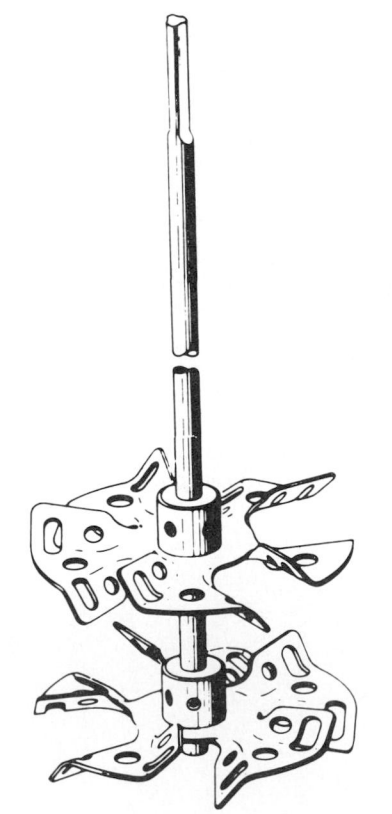

59-10b. Paint mixing paddles for use on an electric drill.

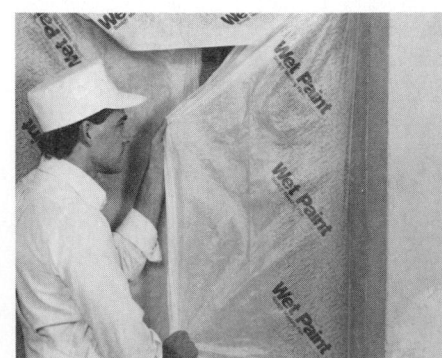

59-11. Masking rolls can be used to mask off large areas quickly.

59-12. *A platform made of two stepladders and a plank means less moving around and makes the job go quickly.*

59-15. *An extension can be inserted in the handle of many rollers to eliminate the need for ladders or scaffolding. Ceilings and floors can also be painted in this manner.*

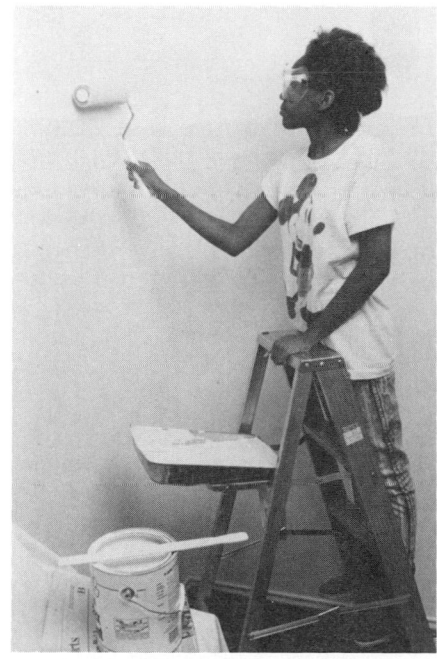

59-13. *When using the roller, cut in next to the walls with a small brush. Then start in the corner and roll a short distance, overlapping each stroke slightly.*

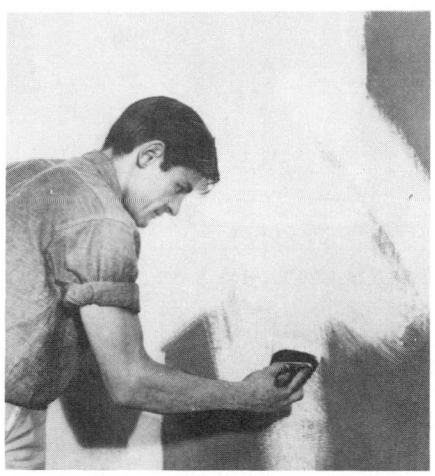

59-14. *When brushing on flat paint, start at the ceiling and paint down in wide, overlapping arcs. Then "lay off" with parallel upward strokes.*

When using a roller, pour a little paint into the deep end of the tray. Work the paint into the roller by moving it back and forth in the tray until the paint is evenly distributed around the roller. Start in the corner and roll a short distance, overlapping each stroke slightly. Move the roller across the wall in slow, smooth strokes, working first in one direction and then in another. Quick strokes and heavy uneven pressure may cause bubbles or spatters. Apply paint from top to bottom as recommended for brushing. Fig. 59-15.

Interior wall and ceiling paint can also be sprayed. This is done with spray guns which are attached by hose to air compressors and pressurized with "paint pots." If the interior of a house will be sprayed, the painter should carefully mask off windows, electrical outlets, and other features that should not be painted. Sometimes paint may be

59-16. *Interior wall paint is usually applied by spray gun or by rollers.*

59-17. *When applying enamels, lay on the material across the grain. Brush it lightly in the direction of the grain to level off the surface.*

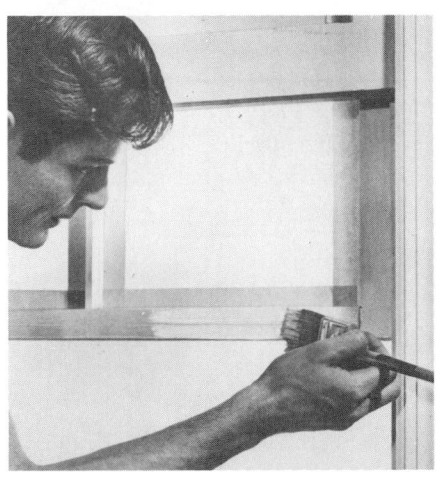

59-18. *Move the sash up and down as necessary so that all parts of the wood frame are painted and protected from moisture.*

59-19. *When painting a panel door, paint the panels first. Then brush in the rails and stiles.*

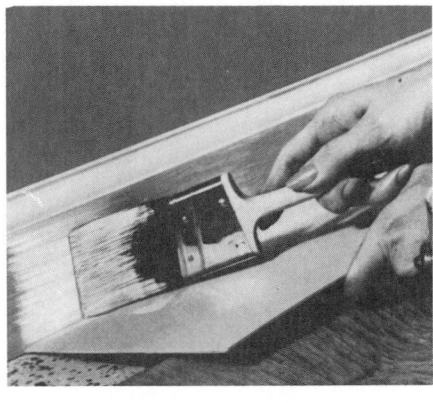

59-20. *When painting the baseboard, use a guard to keep the paint off the floor and to keep the brush clean. Tools used in latex or water-thinned paints can be washed under the faucet.*

applied to a room with spray guns, rollers, and brushes, depending on the circumstances. Fig. 59-16.

Trim. Never paint the woodwork until the walls are dry. Use a 1½" sash brush for windows and a 2" brush for other parts of the trim. Enamels and semigloss or gloss paints flow on more generously and with less pressure than flat paints. Completing a small area at a time, brush on the paint with horizontal strokes. Level off with even, vertical strokes. Work quickly and never go back to touch up a spot that has started to set. Fig. 59-17.

When painting window sash, make the job easier by placing masking tape along the edges of the window panes before painting. When the paint is dry, the tape can be pulled off, leaving a clean, sharp edge. Spatters on the glass can be wiped off when wet or removed with a razor blade later.

Adjust a double-hung window so that you can paint the lower part of the upper sash. Then raise the upper sash almost to the top to finish painting it. The lower sash is painted next. With the window open slightly at the top and bottom, it can be finished easily. Fig. 59-18. Paint the recessed part of the window frame next, then the frame, and finally the window sill.

The procedure for painting sliding doors and windows is the same as for double-hung windows

except that the door or sash is moved from left to right rather than up and down.

When painting a door, paint the jambs and casing first. Then paint the edges of the door itself. If the door is paneled, paint the panel molding first, starting at the top. Fig. 59-19. Keep a clean cloth handy to wipe off any paint that gets on the area surrounding the panels. Paint the remainder of the door last, starting at the top.

Paint the baseboard last. A

cardboard, metal, or plastic guard held flush against the bottom edge of the baseboard will protect the floor and prevent the brush from picking up dirt. Fig. 59-20. Do not let the paper or drop cloth touch the baseboard before the paint is dry.

Cleaning Brushes and Rollers. Consult the container label for the proper cleaning solvent. Tools used in latex or water-thinned paints can be washed in warm, soapy water immediately after use. Rinse well under a faucet and allow to dry before storing. Fig. 59-21. It is a good idea to rinse out the brush or roller cover in soapy water before, and occasionally during, painting. Rinse well and squeeze out excess water before using again.

Tools used for most other finishing materials except lacquer should be washed in turpentine or mineral spirits. Wipe off as much paint as possible, then immerse in a generous amount of the correct solvent. Fig. 59-22. Work the solvent well into the roller cover or brush until it is clean. Wipe and wash again in soap and water. Rinse in clear water and allow to dry. Wrap brushes in heavy paper

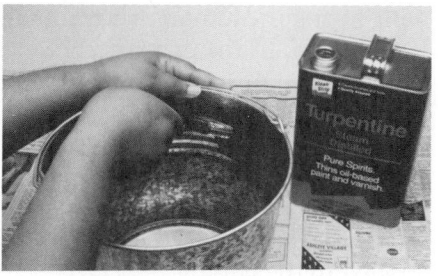

59-22. *Depending on the paint used, some brushes will have to be cleaned with turpentine or mineral spirits.*

and hang or lay them in a dry, cool place. Roller covers should be stored on end so that the nap of the cover is not flattened.

Estimating Materials

To figure the cost of materials more accurately, the painting needs should be figured on a room-to-room basis. To determine the amount of paint for a room, first find the wall area. The area of one wall is found by multiplying the length of the wall by the ceiling height. If the entire room is to be painted, multiply the perimeter of

the room by the ceiling height.

As an example, see bedroom 4 in the floor plan shown in Fig. 59-23. Assume that the ceiling height is 8' and that the entire room is to be painted. The end walls are each 10' long and front wall and closet wall are each 14' long. The perimeter of the room is therefore 48 linear feet $(10 + 10 + 14 + 14)$. Multiply this figure by the room height to obtain the total wall area, 384 square feet $(48 \times 8 = 384)$.

Paint will cover 650 to 750 square feet per gallon. Two coats would require enough paint to cover 768 square feet of wall area $(2 \times 384 = 768)$, or about one gallon. One coat of primer will also be required. This, of course, will take just half the amount required for two coats of wall finish, or two quarts of primer.

The end walls of the closet, each about 2', and the entrance to the room, another 2', are also factors which must be considered. Since a different paint will be used for the windows, doors, and other trim, these areas must be subtracted from the total paint requirement. According to the chart in

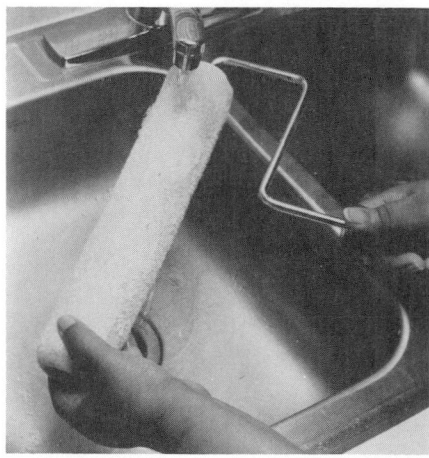

59-21. *Tools used in latex or water-thinned paints can be washed under the faucet.*

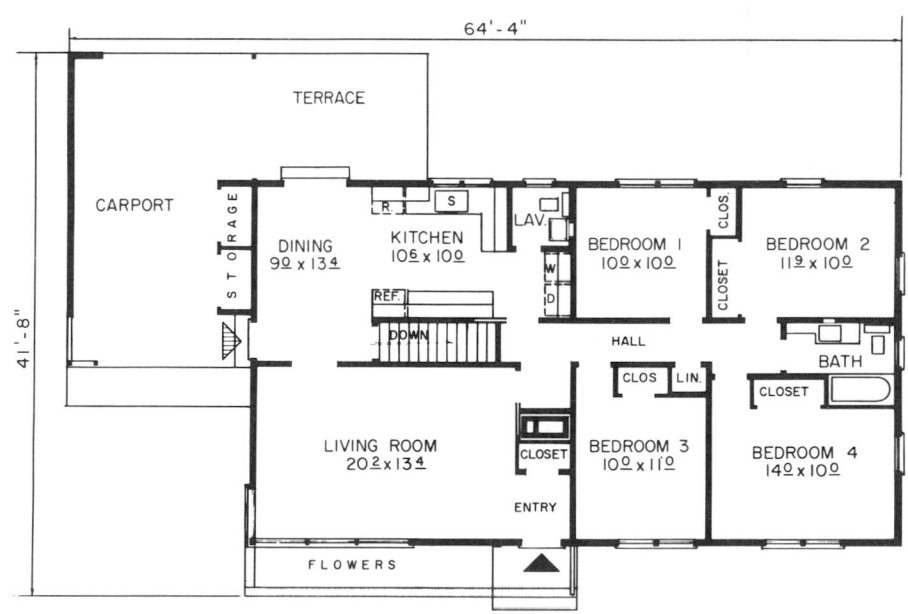

59-23. *Floor plan.*

Table 59-A, one-half pint of paint is subtracted for each door and window. The room has three windows and one door. The total to be subtracted is thus four half-pints of paint, or one quart. In the case of this particular room, the material to be subtracted will more than offset the additional wall area in the closet and passageway. Thus the paint requirement for the room remains the same.

To determine the amount of enamel needed for the trim, consult Table 59-A. Each window and frame requires one-fourth pint, and each doorframe and door one-half pint. The closet door, which is equal to two doors, plus the passage door will require 1½ pints of paint. The windows will require ¾ pint, making a total of 2¼ pints (¾ + 1½ = 2¼). The trim will take one coat of primer (2¼ pints) and two coats of finish (4½ pints). Since most paint is sold in quart cans, it will be necessary to buy 2 quarts of primer and 3 quarts of finish. This will also provide enough extra material for painting the baseboard, with some left over to allow for future touch-ups by the homeowner.

To determine the amount of paint needed for the ceiling, calculate the area of the ceiling by multiplying the length of the room by its width. In the example, the bedroom ceiling area is 140 square feet (10 × 14 = 140). A gallon of paint will cover 650 square feet. Since 140 is roughly ¼ of 650, the ceiling will require ¼ of a gallon (1 quart) of paint for each coat applied to the ceiling.

The wall and ceiling areas may also be determined from Table 59-B. Using the earlier example, bedroom number 4 measures 10' × 14'. Fig. 59-23. In the left-hand column of Table 59-B, headed "Lineal Feet per Wall," read down to number 14 for the length of the room. Read across to the column headed "10" for the width of the room. The table shows that the total wall area is 384 square feet, and the total ceiling area is 140 square feet, which agrees with the figures arrived at earlier.

Labor

To estimate labor for interior painting, use Table 59-C to determine the number of hours required. For example, the time needed to apply one coat of paint to one window is about ¾ of an hour. If there are ten windows and two coats of paint are to be applied, the total time will be 15 hours.

$$\tfrac{10}{1} \times \tfrac{3}{4} = \tfrac{30}{4} \times \tfrac{2}{1} = 15$$

Multiply this figure by the cost per hour to find the total labor cost.

EXTERIOR PAINTING

The exterior of a house can be painted as soon as the siding and roofing are complete and the windows and doors are in place. This means that painting is one of the last jobs to be completed when a new house is being built. The most important function of paint is to keep excess moisture out of the wood. Paint has other functions as well. In the summer, white and light-colored paints reflect heat away from the house. Fig. 59-24. The reflectivity of colors varies considerably. Table 59-D.

Architecture is influenced by the colors chosen for siding and trim. Painting can bring out the best points of styling and line in the home. A home may be kept looking new if a regular paint program, using quality materials, is maintained. A good quality house paint that is properly applied over

Table 59-A. *Approximate Paint Requirements for Interiors and Exteriors. On interior work, for rough, sand-finished walls or unpainted wallboard, add 50% to quantities: for each door or window deduct 1/2 pint of materials for walls. For trim, add 1/8 to 1/5 of the amount required for the body. For exterior blinds 1/2 gallon will cover 12 to 14 blinds, one coat.*

Distance Around the Room	Ceiling Height 8 Feet	Ceiling Height 8 ½ Feet	Ceiling Height 9 Feet	Ceiling Height 9 ½ Feet	Paint for Ceiling	Finish for Floors	For each Door or Window
30 Feet	⅝ Gallon	⅝ Gallon	¾ Gallon	¾ Gallon	1 Pint	1 Pint	
35 Feet	¾ Gallon	¾ Gallon	¾ Gallon	⅞ Gallon	1 Quart	1 Pint	Each Window and
40 Feet	⅞ Gallon	⅞ Gallon	⅞ Gallon	1 Gallon	1 Quart	1 Quart	Frame Requires
45 Feet	⅞ Gallon	1 Gallon	1 Gallon	1 ⅛ Gallons	3 Pints	1 Quart	¼ Pint.
50 Feet	1 Gallon	1 ⅛ Gallons	1 ⅛ Gallons	1 ¼ Gallons	3 Pints	1 Quart	
55 Feet	1 ⅛ Gallons	1 ⅛ Gallons	1 ¼ Gallons	1 ¼ Gallons	2 Quarts	3 Pints	Each Door and
60 Feet	1 ¼ Gallons	1 ¼ Gallons	1 ⅜ Gallons	1 ⅜ Gallons	2 Quarts	3 Pints	Frame Requires
70 Feet	1 ⅜ Gallons	1 ½ Gallons	1 ½ Gallons	1 ⅝ Gallons	3 Quarts	2 Quarts	½ Pint.
80 Feet	1 ½ Gallons	1 ⅝ Gallons	1 ¾ Gallons	1 ⅞ Gallons	1 Gallon	5 Pints	

Table 59-B. *Wall and Ceiling Areas for Rooms of Various Sizes.*

Square Feet — 4 Walls and Ceiling

Linear Ft. Per Wall*	6	8	10	12	14	16	18	20	22	24	26	28	30
6	C 36 / W 192	C 48 / W 224	C 60 / W 256	C 72 / W 288	C 84 / W 320	C 96 / W 352	C 108 / W 384	C 120 / W 416	C 132 / W 448	C 144 / W 480	C 156 / W 512	C 168 / W 544	C 180 / W 576
8	C 48 / W 224	C 64 / W 256	C 80 / W 288	C 96 / W 320	C 112 / W 352	C 128 / W 384	C 144 / W 416	C 160 / W 448	C 176 / W 480	C 182 / W 512	C 198 / W 544	C 224 / W 576	C 240 / W 608
10	C 60 / W 256	C 80 / W 288	C 100 / W 320	C 120 / W 352	C 140 / W 384	C 160 / W 416	C 180 / W 448	C 200 / W 480	C 220 / W 512	C 240 / W 544	C 260 / W 576	C 280 / W 608	C 300 / W 640
12	C 72 / W 288	C 96 / W 320	C 120 / W 352	C 144 / W 384	C 168 / W 416	C 192 / W 448	C 216 / W 480	C 240 / W 512	C 264 / W 544	C 288 / W 576	C 312 / W 608	C 336 / W 640	C 360 / W 672
14	C 84 / W 320	C 112 / W352	C 140 / W384	C 168 / W 416	C 196 / W 448	C 224 / W 480	C 252 / W 512	C 280 / W 544	C 308 / W 576	C 336 / W 608	C 364 / W 640	C 392 / W 672	C 420 / W 704
16	C 96 / W 352	C 128 / W 384	C 160 / W 416	C 192 / W 448	C 224 / W 480	C 256 / W 512	C 288 / W 544	C 320 / W 576	C 352 / W 608	C 384 / w 640	C 416 / W 672	C 448 / W 704	C 480 / W 736
18	C 108 / W 384	C 144 / W 416	C 180 / W 448	C 216 / W 480	C 252 / W 512	C 288 / W 544	C 324 / W 576	C 360 / W 608	C 396 / W 640	C 432 / W 672	C 468 / W 704	C 504 / W 736	C 540 / W 768
20	C 120 / W 416	C 160 / W 448	C 200 / W 480	C 240 / W 512	C 280 / W 544	C 320 / W 576	C 360 / W 608	C 400 / W 640	C 440 / W 672	C 480 / W 704	C 520 / W 736	C 560 / W 768	C 600 / W 800
22	C 132 / W 448	C 176 / W 480	C 220 / W 512	C 264 / W 544	C 308 / W 576	C 352 / W 608	C 396 / W 640	C 440 / W 672	C 484 / W 704	C 528 / W 736	C 572 / W 768	C 616 / W 800	C 660 / W 832
24	C 144 / W 480	C 182 / W 512	C 240 / W 544	C 288 / W 576	C 336 / W 608	C 384 / W 640	C 432 / W 672	C 480 / W 704	C 528 / W 736	C 576 / W 768	C 624 / W 800	C 672 / W 832	C 720 / W 864
26	C 156 / W 512	C 198 / W 544	C 260 / W 576	C 312 / W 608	C 364 / W 640	C 416 / W 672	C 468 / W 704	C 520 / W 736	C 572 / W 768	C 624 / W 800	C 676 / W 832	C 728 / W 864	C 780 / W 896
28	C 168 / W 544	C 224 / W 576	C 280 / W 608	C 336 / W 640	C 392 / W 672	C 448 / W 704	C 504 / W 736	C 560 / W 768	C 616 / W 800	C 672 / W 832	C 728 / W 864	C 784 / W 896	C 840 / W 928
30	C 180 / W 576	C 240 / W 608	C 300 / W 640	C 360 / W 672	C 420 / W 704	C 480 / W 736	C 540 / W 768	C 600 / W 800	C 660 / W 832	C 720 / W 864	C 780 / W 896	C 840 / W 928	C 900 / W 960

*Based on wall height of 8'. C=Ceiling Area. W=Wall Area= 4 Walls.

Table 59-C. *Interior Painting. Use this table to estimate labor time for interior painting.*

Preparation of Trim (including sanding & spackling)	115 linear ft. per hr.
Molding (chair rails & other trim up to six inches wide)	150 linear ft. per hr.
Windows (including sash, trim, sills, & apron)	Each coat $3/4$ hr. per window
Paneled Door (including door & trim)	Each coat $3/4$ hr. per door
Flush Door (including door & trim)	Each coat $1/2$ hr. per door
Finishing Walls & Ceiling Brush Roller	150 sq. ft. per hr. 300 sq. ft. per hr.

Note. No allowance for preparatory work or for setting up scaffolding is included in the above figures.

Table 59-D. *Light Reflectivity of Colors.*

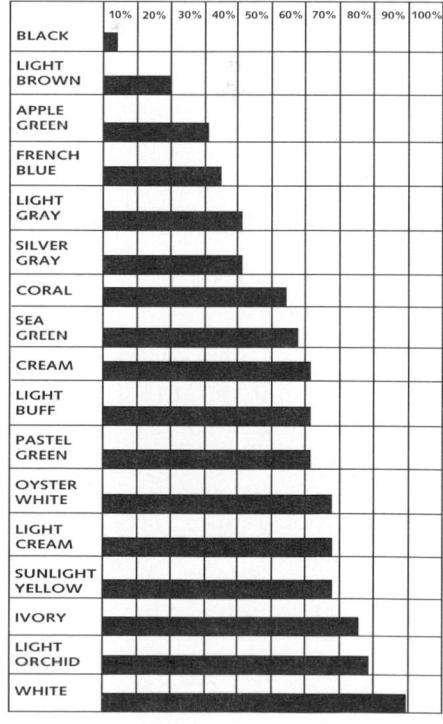

59-24. *This white house will reflect 90 percent of the sun's rays, reducing heat gain in hot weather.*

seasoned wood on a well-built house should last at least four to five years before repainting is needed.

Today the painter can choose from a wide variety of paints. Some are made to give specific service, but no one kind of house paint on the market has all desired characteristics. Paints should be chosen on the basis of the conditions to which they will be exposed and the area in which they will be used.

PAINTABILITY OF WOODS

While all woods can be painted, some take paint better than others. The painting characteristics of woods are determined by four factors:

➤ Kind of grain.
➤ Species.
➤ Density and texture.
➤ Grade.

Species

Tests have shown that cedar and cypress hold paint best. Northern white pine, western white pine, and sugar pine are almost as good. Serious flaking of paint occurs sooner on southern yellow pine, Douglas fir, and western larch. Western yellow pine, white fir, and hemlock fall between the latter two groups.

Density and Texture

Summerwood is the dense, dark-colored portion of the wood. Because its cells have thick walls and small cavities, summerwood does not hold paint as well as the more porous, light springwood. Boards are heavy or light depending on how much summerwood they contain. Thus the relative weight or "heft" of softwood boards roughly indicates their ability to hold paint. In boards which have many annual growth rings per inch, the summerwood may be confined to narrow bands, making the boards moderately heavy. This kind of

board holds paint better than one of equal weight in which summerwood is present in wide bands.

Grade

Select grades hold paint better than lower grades which contain troublesome defects such as knots and pitch pockets. The knots of yellow and white pines cause more trouble than the sound knots of such woods as cedar, hemlock, white fir, and larch.

Kind of Grain

Edge-grained or quartersawed boards hold paint much better than flat-grained or plain-sawed boards because they are cut so that the bands of summerwood are very narrow. Flat-grained boards hold paint better on the bark side than on the pith side.

EXTERIOR PAINTS

Some manufacturers print the composition of their paint on the label, but no quality standards apply throughout the industry. Many manufacturers make several different-quality paints of the same kind. They put their own brand name on the best and sell the other kinds under a different label. Because the cost of paint is such a small portion of the total cost of painting a home, it is wise to insist on only top-grade, brand-name paints. Buying inexpensive or off-brand paint is likely to be more expensive over a period of years.

Oil-based Paint

Exterior paints were made primarily with various pigmented vegetable oils until the 1920s. Only one vegetable oil (linseed oil) is still used extensively as a base for paint. Linseed oil is also used as one component of another type of oil-base paint, called alkyd paint. Oil-based paints are not as popular as water-based (latex) paints because cleanup after painting is more difficult, but they are still quite useful.

One characteristic of an oil-based paint is its ability to penetrate existing painted finishes. This is due to the linseed oil. Because of this penetration, oil-based paints are often used when painting older houses. The paint can help to bind the old layers of paint to the new layer. Another characteristic of oil-based paints is that they are less flexible than latex paints. This is an advantage where a tough, stable surface is required. However, some painters feel that the greater flexibility of latex paints allows them to last longer.

Oil-based paints usually contain zinc oxide. This material helps control mildew. It also stabilizes the color of the paint.

Latex Paint

The latex family of paints is made by mixing and emulsifying chemicals in water instead of dissolving them in such solvents as mineral spirits or turpentine. Many different kinds of resins are used in making latex paints, and these are being improved constantly. Latex paints were first developed for interior use, but are now available for exterior painting. Their prime advantages are:
➤ Ease of application, even on damp surfaces.
➤ Rapid drying.
➤ Easy cleanup. Tools can be washed clean with water before paint dries.
➤ Transmission of water vapor, making blistering uncommon.
Latex paints should not be applied if the temperature is below 40° F,

nor should they be applied to a chalky paint surface.

Paints and Enamels for Metal

There are many kinds of metal primers, enamels, and paints designed to prevent corrosion of iron and steel. These should be used in painting metal downspouts, gutters, and other metal parts around the home. There is a special metal primer for use over new metal or rusted metal as a rust-inhibiting prime coat. A high-gloss rust-inhibitive enamel is used over this primer.

THINNERS AND SOLVENTS

Thinners and solvents are needed for mixing paint to the correct consistency and for cleanup. Commonly used thinners and solvents include:
➤ Mineral spirits, a colorless liquid made from petroleum. It is used as a solvent or thinner.
➤ Turpentine, made from the resin drippings of pine trees. It is used as a solvent and thinner for varnish, paint, and enamel.
➤ Linseed oil, a yellowish oil pressed from flaxseed. It is available raw or boiled. Boiling improves the drying quality. Linseed oil is added to paints, fillers, and stains.
Check the manufacturer's recommendations on the label to determine the correct thinners or solvents for each material being used.

METHODS OF PAINTING

Paints are available for a one-coat, two-coat, or three-coat system of house painting. A one-coat

white house paint should be used only for painting over a previously painted light-colored surface that is in very good condition. It is not intended for use on new wood. The paint should not be tinted or mixed with other paints unless so stated on the label.

For maximum appearance and durability, the two- or three-coat system is best. As a rule, it is best to apply one prime coat and two finish coats. About as much paint is used when applying a primer and a single finish coat as when applying a primer and two finish coats because more thinner is used in the three-coat process.

The first coat should be a good primer or undercoat. Most paint manufacturers provide a zinc-free house paint primer or undercoat for use with their house paints. Usually it is wise to choose a primer and finish paint of the same brand.

Manufacturers also make paints for wood trim, screen frames, shutters, and similar areas. An undercoat of gray or other neutral color is used as a primer for trim or for dark-colored house paints. Fig. 59-25.

59-25. Special paint is available for screen frames.

59-26. *Select at least two brushes: one for cutting in and trim work and the second for large flat areas. A paint roller and tray will also be helpful for doing stucco or brick work. They can also sometimes be used for large flat areas such as the soffit.*

Equipment and Supplies

You will need the following materials and equipment to do your painting easily and efficiently:

➤ Stepladder.
➤ Extension ladder.
➤ Drop cloths.
➤ Caulking gun.
➤ Sandpaper, steel wool, wire brush, scraper.
➤ Hammer, nail set, putty, putty knife.
➤ Pot hook.
➤ Solvents for cleaning brushes and other equipment.
➤ Cleaning cloths.
➤ Mixing pails.
➤ Brushes. Fig. 59-26.

Be sure to use plenty of drop cloths to protect the shrubs and walks. Make certain that the ladder is tall enough to reach the highest parts of the house easily. Finally, make sure you have the tools and materials necessary for preparing the surfaces for painting. The paint job will last longer and look better if the surface is clean, sound, and well prepared.

Preparing the Surface

When painting outdoor surfaces, all construction should be completed first. During construction make sure that only dry lumber is used. Green wood causes poor paint adhesion. Sap in the wood will also cause problems because it does not permit the primer to penetrate and form a good bond with the wood.

To be sure you get all the wear, protection, and beauty the paint can offer, surfaces to be painted must be properly prepared. Usually, the following steps can be combined with the application of the primer. Always avoid painting in full sun.

Place the drop cloths under the area you are about to paint. Cover sidewalks as well as shrubs. Adequate protection before you begin painting will save a lot of clean-up time.

Take the equipment you need to the area in which you will be working. Keep your ladder trips to a minimum. Take up primer and brushes, scraper, wire brush, sandpaper, and whatever else you need and can carry safely. Fig. 59-27.

Just before you apply paint, clean off the dust and dirt with a sturdy cloth or a stiff brush. This will prevent a dust streak in the new paint. Fig. 59-28. Use a nail set and hammer to sink nailheads below the surface of the wood. Fig. 59-29. Seal any knots or pitch spots with shellac to avoid brown discoloration later. Fig. 59-30.

Look for scaling and flaking paint. Where old paint is damaged, scrape to the original surface with a broad knife and wire brush. Smooth all rough areas and remove rust marks with sandpaper or steel wool. Fig. 59-31.

There may be areas, especially under the eaves or on the trim, where the old paint is "shiny." Roughen these with sandpaper or a

59-27. *Use a good ladder and eliminate as many trips up and down the ladder as possible.*

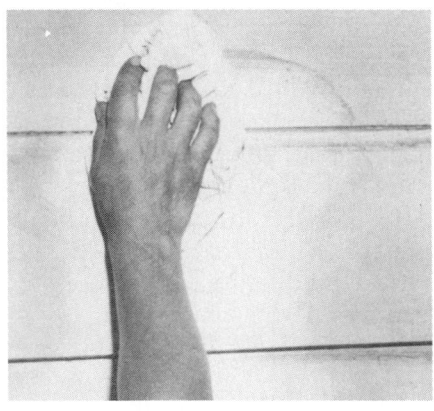

59-28. *Always clean the surface of old work before applying a new coat of paint to obtain maximum paint adhesion.*

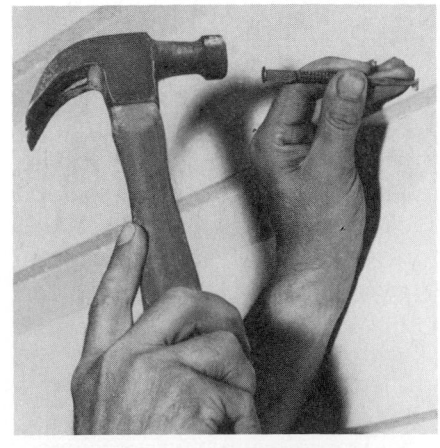

59-29. *Set all exposed nails and putty the heads to eliminate rust spotting.*

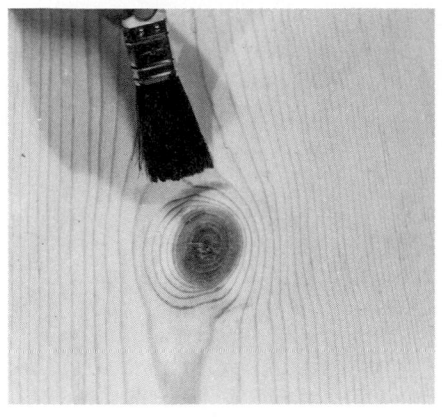

59-30. *Knots must be sealed to avoid discoloration of the finish paint surface.*

59-31. *When repainting an old surface, scrape off all the loose paint and feather the edges with sandpaper.*

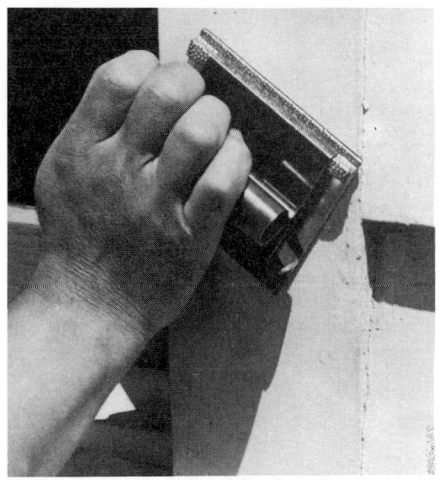

59-32. *Be sure to sand all shiny surfaces to eliminate gloss and improve the adhesion of the new paint.*

59-33. *Clean all galvanized metal surfaces and wipe with galvo-prep or use a special galvanized paint to insure proper adhesion. For aluminum surfaces, use the material recommended by the paint dealer.*

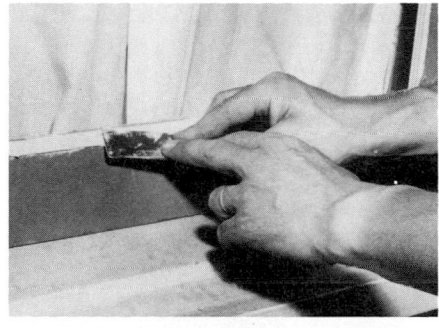

59-34. *Remove all loose or dry putty and then replace with fresh putty before applying the finish coat.*

59-35. *Caulk around the window and door moldings to weatherproof the house.*

wire brush. Fig. 59-32. Paint does not adhere very well to slick, shiny surfaces.

Clean and prime the gutters and downspouts. Remove the rust and peeling paint by scraping or wire brushing. Wash any protected areas and areas under the eaves with water. A strong stream from a garden hose does the best job. Apply the primer after the surface is dry. Fig. 59-33.

After priming and before applying the finish coat, remove loose or dry putty around windows and replace it with fresh putty. Fig. 59-34. For a smoother surface, cracks and nail holes in siding can also be filled with putty or caulk.

Caulk around the door and window frames where necessary. Tightly caulked joints help to weatherproof the house and prevent moisture damage. Fig. 59-35.

Applying the Finish Coat

Before applying the finish coat, check the prime coat. It must be hard and dry. Also check to see that all nails have been countersunk, the holes puttied, and that the windows, doors, and cracks have been caulked and filled. For best results, inspect the label of the material being used for any special instructions from the manufacturer. Use quality materials and have everything ready before you begin.

Paint a side of the house just after the sun has passed over it. Morning dew or water from a brief shower should be wiped off and an hour of warm sunshine should follow before any painting is done. After many hours of hard rain, several days may be needed for drying.

Even though the paint dealer has mixed the paint mechanically, mix it again just before and during painting. Stir the contents of the can from bottom up, and "box" the

59-36a. Stir the contents of the can from the bottom up.

59-36b. After the paint has been mixed, it should be "boxed." To box paint, pour it back and forth from one container to another.

59-37. Work the paint into the brush by dipping it about 2" into the paint and then tapping off the excess against the inside of the can.

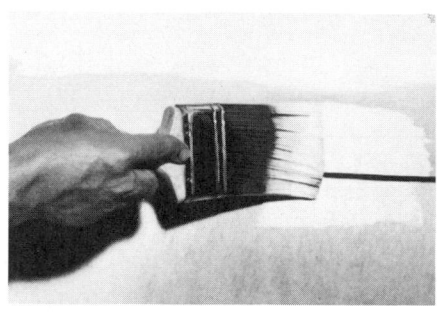

59-38. Deposit the paint onto the siding in two or three areas from the full brush.

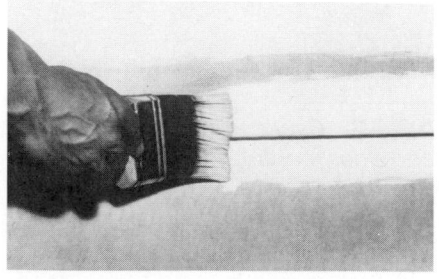

59-39. After the paint has been deposited as shown in Fig. 59-38, brush it out. Be sure to coat the under edge of a beveled siding.

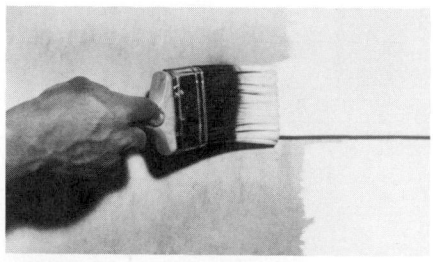

59-40. "Feather" the ends of your brush strokes so that areas can be joined without showing lap streaks.

59-41. Always start at the top and work down. This will keep paint from dripping onto the freshly painted area.

59-42. A deep nap roller works best for applying paint to a textured or rough surface such as a brick wall.

paint by pouring from one can into another. Fig. 59-36.

Work the paint into the brush by dipping it about two inches into the paint and tapping the excess off against the inside of the can. Fig. 59-37. Repeat several times. Apply the paint generously along the joint of the siding, distributing it evenly as you brush. Fig. 59-38. Brush the paint out well, taking care to coat the under edge of the clapboard. Fig. 59-39. "Feather" the ends of your brush strokes to assure smoothness where one painted area joins another. Do not bear down too hard on the brush. Fig. 59-40.

Start at the top of the house and work down to prevent drips and splatters from spoiling previously painted areas. This will mean doing gutters and eaves first if they are to match the siding color. Fig. 59-41.

Always paint with the grain, in horizontal strips. Paint under the eaves as you go. After the peak of the house is painted, start at the corner and work across. It makes no difference whether you work from the left or right but, before you move or shorten the ladder, finish an entire area about four or five feet square.

If you are using a roller, pour a small amount of paint into the well of a roller tray. Work the paint into the roller by rolling it in the well. Be sure the entire roller surface is covered. Remove excess paint by rolling over the ribbed portion of the tray. Apply the paint in even strokes, with light pressure. Roll first in one direction, then over-roll in the other. Fig. 59-42.

Exterior paint can also be sprayed using a compressor, a paint pot and a spray gun. Spray application tends to deposit a layer of paint on top of the wood. To ensure proper adhesion on relatively rough surfaces (such as plywood siding), the fresh paint should be "rolled in." Immediately after a portion of the house has been spray painted, a paint roller is

passed over the area to push the paint into the surface.

Whether the trim is finished in the same or in a contrasting color or product, it is usually painted last. Shutters should be painted separately and then installed when the rest of the job is completed.

Paint windows with a narrow sash brush. Paint the mullions first, then the crossrails, and then the vertical stiles. Do casing, sash, and trim last. Move the sash up and down before it is dry to prevent sticking. Fig. 59-43.

On a panel door, first paint the molding and then the panels. Do the crossrails next and finally the stiles. For flush doors, paint across from top to bottom. Do the edges last with a sash brush.

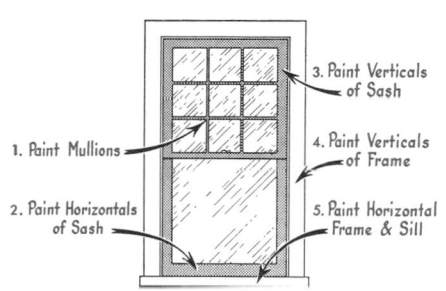

painting windows

1. Paint Mullions
2. Paint Horizontals of Sash
3. Paint Verticals of Sash
4. Paint Verticals of Frame
5. Paint Horizontal Frame & Sill

59-43a. *When painting windows, use the sequence shown above.*

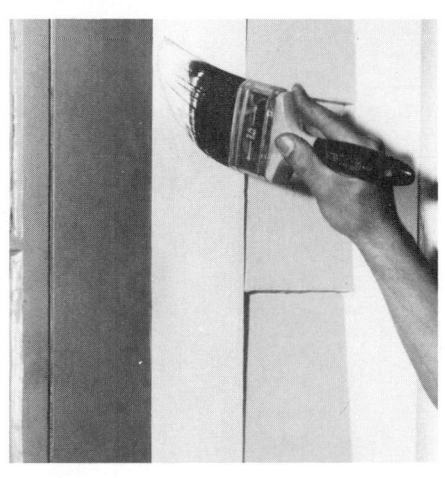

59-43b. *Paint window trim last.*

CLEANUP

Protect your tools and equipment with proper cleanup. Clean all equipment immediately after use, especially brushes and rollers.

When using oil paints, clean the brushes by working the solvent into the bristles with your fingers. Squeeze out as much paint and solvent as possible. Repeat this operation until the paint disappears. Fig. 59-44. Give the brushes a final rinse in clear solvent. Wash them in soapy water, rinse, and let dry.

To clean a roller cover, disassemble it and submerge the cover in a solvent. When most of the paint has been worked out, you can wash the cover in a mild detergent solution and rinse in clear water. Remove the paint from the roller frame with the proper solvent.

When using water-thinned paints, follow these same procedures for cleaning brushes and rollers, but substitute soapy water for the paint solvent. Rinse with clear water and allow to dry thoroughly before storing.

Pick up the drop cloths, allow them to dry if damp, and fold them

59-44. *Use the proper solvent for each material and clean brushes thoroughly.*

59-45. *Do a complete job by cleaning up the areas thoroughly when you are finished.*

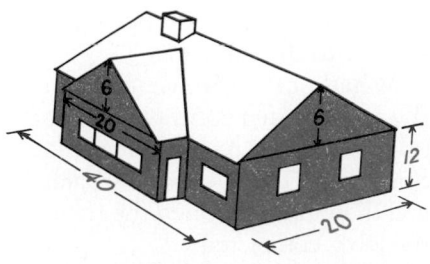

59-46. *Determine the number of gallons of undercoat and finish coat required to paint this house.*

for storage. If any paint did fall on walks, scrub it out with a solvent and a stiff brush. Fig. 59-45. Do not use solvents on shrubs because they may damage the plants. It is better to cut off the spotted portions. Spatters from water-thinned paints can be scrubbed off with soapy water if it is done before the paint has dried.

ESTIMATING

Materials

To estimate the amount of paint needed for the exterior of a house, find the number of square feet to be covered. Divide this figure by the number of square feet covered by one gallon of paint.

To determine the area to be covered, figure the siding area below the roofline by measuring the total distance around the house and multiplying this figure by the height. In the example in Fig. 59-46, the total perimeter is 120'; 80' (front and back) + 40' (two ends) = 120'. Multiply this by the height to determine the total area: 12' × 120' = 1,440 sq. ft.

For gables, multiply the height of the gable from the eaves by half the width of the gable. Do this for each gable. In the example, 6' (gable height) × 10' (½ the gable width) × 3 (number of gables) = 180 sq. ft.

Add the area for each gable to the siding area below the roofline. The total area to be painted thus is 1,440 sq. ft. (siding area below the

roofline) + 180 sq. ft. (area of the gables), or 1,620 sq. ft. Divide the total number of square feet by 450 to find how many gallons of undercoat will be needed. Divide by 500 to find the number of gallons required for each finish coat.

Table 59-E gives a simpler method of determining the amount of paint required. Figure the distance around the house. Take the longest length dimension and the greatest width dimension of the house. Double each of these, and add them together. For example, the house in Fig. 59-47 has a greatest length dimension of 60' 10". Double this and the result is 121' 8". The greatest width dimension is 45' 6". Doubled, this is 91'. Add the 91' to the 121' 8". The result is 212' 8", or roughly 213'. NOTE: When using the largest width and length dimensions of a house, it is not necessary to be concerned about offsets or L-shaped houses because the perimeter would be the same. However, in the case of a U-shaped house, double the amount of indentation and add it to the doubled width and length dimensions.

Figure the average height of the house. In the example, the average height for the house is 12'.

Refer to the column headed

Table 59-E. *Approximate Paint Requirements for Exteriors. The amounts shown in this table are general estimates. Actual requirements will vary considerably depending on thickness of coat, application to porous or nonporous surface, and other factors.*

Distance around the House	Average Height 12 Feet	Average Height 15 Feet	Average Height 18 Feet	Average Height 21 Feet	Average Height 24 Feet
60 Feet	1 Galllon	1 ¼ Gallons	1 ½ Gallons	1 ¾ Gallon	2 Gallons
76 Feet	1 ¼ Gallons	1 ½ Gallons	2 Gallons	2 ¼ Gallons	2 ½ Gallons
92 Feet	1 ½ Gallons	2 Gallons	2 ½ Gallons	2 ¾ Gallons	3 Gallons
108 Feet	1 ¾ Gallons	2 ¼ Gallons	2 ¾ Gallons	3 ¼ Gallons	3 ¾ Gallons
124 Feet	2 Gallons	2 ½ Gallons	3 ¼ Gallons	3 ¾ Gallons	4 ¼ Gallons
140 Feet	2 ½ Gallons	3 Gallons	3 ½ Gallons	4 Gallons	4 ½ Gallons
156 Feet	2 ¾ Gallons	3 ¼ Gallons	4 Gallons	4 ½ Gallons	5 ¼ Gallons
172 Feet	3 Gallons	3 ¾ Gallons	4 ½ Gallons	5 Gallons	5 ¾ Gallons

Table 59-F. *Exterior Painting. Use this table to estimate labor time for exterior painting.*

Preparation of Siding & Trim (sanding & puttying)	175 sq. ft. per hr.
Preparation of Trim Only (brick veneer or masonry construction	100 sq. ft. per hr.
Brushing Windows and Door Frames	175 linear ft. per hr.
Brushing wood siding	175 sq. ft. per hr.
Brushing asbestos shingles siding	75 sq. ft. per hr.
Brushing wood shingle siding	150 sq. ft. per hr.

Note: No allowance for preparatory work or for setting up scaffolding is included in the above figures.

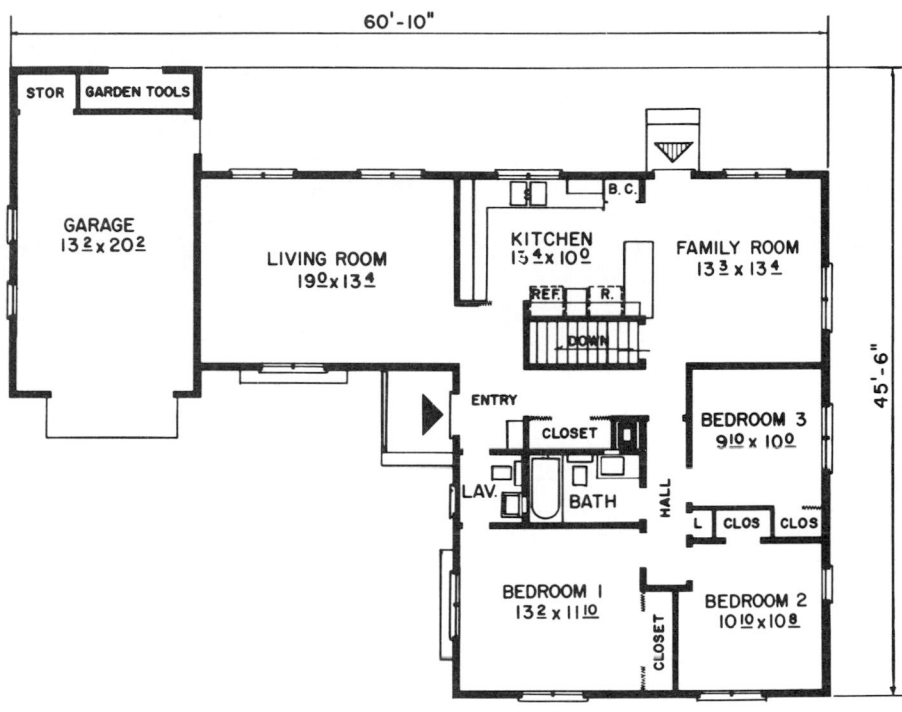

59-47. *To figure the perimeter of most homes, double the greatest length and width dimensions and add them together. In this example, the perimeter is about 213'.*

Labor

To estimate labor for exterior painting, use the chart in Table 59-F to determine the number of hours required. Then multiply this number by the cost per hour to find the total labor cost.

PAINT PROBLEMS

Condensed water vapor, in the form of free water or ice, can collect behind the siding of a building. This excess moisture may absorb chemicals from the wood and then stain the siding as it runs out over the surface. In some cases, the siding is thoroughly wetted. There is a loss of paint adhesion, and water-filled blisters form under the paint film.

Protection of exterior walls against moisture from both inside and outside sources is very important. There are a number of effective methods for preventing condensation.

A vapor barrier will protect outside walls and paint from moisture coming from within the home. Such barriers should be carefully applied to provide a complete envelope, preventing water vapor from entering enclosed wall spaces where condensation may occur. The goal of vapor protection is to make the warm side of the wall as vapor-tight as possible, and the cold side permeable enough to permit passage of water vapor to the outside.

Dull-surfaced asphalt- or tar-saturated sheet products, commonly used as sheathing papers, are water-repellent but not vapor-proof. They adequately serve as cold-side, vapor-resistant materials.

Good warm-side barriers are available in many forms. Some insulation is made with a vapor

"Distance around the House" in Table 59-E. The distance around the house in our example is 213', but this distance is not listed. However, 92' and 124' are listed. These two figures add up to 216'. These two figures add up to 216'.

Read across opposite 92' to the column headed "Average Height, 12'." One and one-half gallons of paint are required. Read across opposite 124'. Two gallons are required for an average height of 12'. Therefore the house in the

example will require a total of 3½ gallons of paint for each coat.

One coat of primer and two finish coats for the house in Fig. 59-47 will require 3½ gallons of primer and 7 gallons of finish coat. For trim, add ⅛ to ⅓ of the amount required for one coat. For exterior shutters, ½ gallon will cover 12 to 14 shutters with one coat.

barrier on one face. Polyethylene films and certain other plastic sheet materials also are satisfactory.

In homes built without vapor barriers, good vapor protection can be achieved by applying two coats of a low-permeability paint system to inside walls and ceilings. However, such measures do not provide complete protection. Paints of this type are intended to supplement the action of vapor barriers in new homes.

Improper paint application can also cause problems. Described here are some of the paint problems resulting from poor construction techniques or improper paint application. The recommended corrective procedures are also given.

Cracking and Alligatoring

This problem is created in two ways. The previous paint film may have been applied in several heavy coats without sufficient drying time between coats, or the undercoater may not be compatible with the finish coat. Fig. 59-48. This problem can be corrected by:

1. Sanding smooth the cracked or alligatored surface.

2. Applying one coat of undercoater and one top coat of a recommended house paint according to label directions.

Checking

Checking is caused by plywood veneer cracking from expansion and contraction as it weathers and ages. Fig. 50-49. This problem can be corrected by:

1. Sanding the surface smooth.

2. Spot priming the exposed bare wood and cracks with an exterior undercoater, if the cracked area is not extensive.

59-48. *Cracking and alligatoring.*

59-49. *Checking of plywood veneer.*

3. Filling the primed cracks with caulk.

4. Applying a top coat of recommended house paint. NOTE: Should this problem be extensive, the best procedure is to replace the plywood. To prevent checking on new plywood, sand the surface smooth and apply one coat of latex wood primer and two coats of latex house paint according to label directions.

Localized Peeling

This problem is caused when moisture that was trapped in siding is drawn from the wood by the sun's heat and pushes the paint from the surface. Fig. 59-50.

59-50. *Localized peeling.*

Peeling can be corrected by:

1. Locating and eliminating sources of moisture. Is the area near a bathroom or a kitchen? Is there seepage or leakage from eaves, roofs, or plumbing?

2. Scraping off the old paint. Either scrape down to the wood on the entire board or scrape off the old paint from the peeling area and for about 12" around the area.

3. Sanding the surface to fresh wood and spot priming with a recommended undercoater.

4. Sealing all seams, holes, and cracks against moisture with caulk.

5. Applying a top coat of recommended house paint according to label directions.

Flaking

This problem is caused by the siding alternately swelling and shrinking as the moisture from

59-53. *Top coat peeling.*

behind the siding is absorbed and then evaporates. Brittle paint film cracks under the strain and pulls away from the wood. Fig. 59-51. This problem can be corrected by:

1. Locating and eliminating sources of moisture. Is the affected area near a bathroom or kitchen? Is there seepage or leakage from eaves, roofs, or plumbing?

2. Scraping off the old flaking paint on the board to expose the wood or scraping off the old paint around the flaking area to about 12" away from this condition.

3. Sanding the surface to fresh wood and spot priming with a recommended undercoater.

4. Sealing all seams, holes, and cracks against moisture entry with caulk.

5. Applying a top coat of recommended house paint according to the label directions.

Mildew

Mildew thrives in high humidity and high temperature. Fig. 59-52. If left on the surface and painted over, it will grow through the new coat of paint. This problem can be corrected by:

1. Scrubbing the entire surface with a solution of ⅓ cup of trisodium phosphate (TSP), ½ cup of household bleach, and four quarts of warm water.

59-52. *Mildew.*

2. Applying one coat of wood undercoater. NOTE: Mildew-resistant additive may be added to an undercoat if mildew conditions are severe and an oil base top coat is used. The additive should not be put in the finish coat.

3. Applying one top coat of mildew- and fume-resistant latex house paint.

Top Coat Peeling

This problem is usually found on overhanging horizontal surfaces and other areas protected from weather. Fig. 59-53. It is due to the poor adhesion of a previous coat of paint from buildup of "salt" deposits which are not washed away by rain. This problem can be corrected by:

1. Sanding the surface thoroughly to remove all peeling paint.

2. Washing the sanded surface with a solution of ⅓ cup trisodium phosphate to one gallon of water. Rinse well and allow to dry.

3. Applying two coats of house paint undercoater, or one coat of undercoater and one top coat of a recommended house paint according to label directions.

Redwood and Cedar Staining

This problem is caused by moisture in the siding dissolving coloring matter in the wood. Colored water escapes onto the paint through breaks in the paint film and drips from underneath the overlapping board. The stain is deposited as the water dries. This problem can be corrected by:

1. Locating and eliminating the sources of moisture before painting.

2. Washing stained surface with a mixture of 50% denatured alcohol and 50% clean water.

3. Allowing the surface to dry for 48 hours, then applying two coats of the recommended house paint according to label directions.

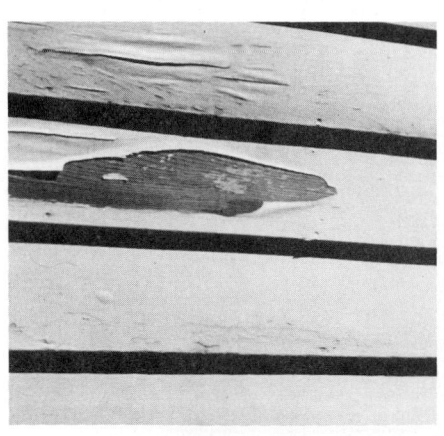

59-54. *Blistering.*

Blistering

This problem is caused when moisture trapped in the siding is drawn from the wood by the sun's heat and pushes paint from the surface. Fig. 59-54. It can be corrected by:

1. Locating and eliminating the sources of moisture.

2. Scraping off the old paint on the blistered surface for an area of about 12" away from the blister condition.

3. Sanding the surface to fresh wood and spot priming with a recommended undercoater.

4. Sealing all seams, holes, and cracks against moisture entry with a caulk.

5. Applying a top coat of recommended house paint according to label directions.

Nailhead Staining

This problem is caused when excessive moisture results in rusting of uncoated steel nails used in construction. Fig. 59-55. It can be corrected by:

1. Locating and eliminating the sources of moisture.

2. Sanding or wire brushing the stained paint and removing the rust

59-55. *Nailhead staining.*

down to the bright metal of the nailhead.

3. Countersinking the nailhead ⅛" below the surface of the siding. Immediately spot prime the countersunk nailhead with a recommended house paint undercoater.

4. Filling primed, countersunk holes with caulk. Apply two top coats of recommended house paint according to label directions.

QUESTIONS

1. Why are wood, dry wall, and plaster surfaces painted?

2. What is the most popular kind of interior paint?

3. Make a list of things that should be done to make the job easier when painting indoors.

4. What are some things that can be done in preparation for painting indoors?

5. When painting a room, what area should be done first?

6. What is meant by "cutting in"?

7. When should the woodwork be painted?

8. How often should a house be repainted if a good-quality house paint has been properly applied?

9. What are the four characteristics of wood that affect its paintability?

10. What are thinners and solvents used for?

11. What is meant by "boxing" the paint?

12. What is the sequence for painting a panel door?

13. What is the major cause of paint problems?

14. What is the purpose of a vapor barrier?

15. What are some of the paint problems which may develop as a result of factors other than improper construction techniques?

ACTIVITIES

1. Social Studies. Paint has had various uses throughout history. For example, it has been used to protect and to decorate. It has also been used to make objects seem larger and/or smaller than they really are. Research the various uses of paint. Research also the use of dark and light colors to alter the viewer's perception of an object's size.

2. Social Studies. What effect did the introduction of latex paint have on the painting industry and interior decoration? Contrast painting procedures as they were before the introduction of latex paint with painting procedures after its introduction.

Special Construction Activities

Building Architectural Models

Building a model is an excellent way to convert a drawing into a three-dimensional object that can be used to visualize the overall appearance of the project. Fig. 60-1. There are two basic types of models that are used: the *architectural* and the *structural* model. Figs. 60-2 and 60-3.

The architectural model is designed primarily to show the exterior of a building. It is often constructed of solid materials, thin balsa wood, illustrating paper, and other kinds of simple materials. It is usually built to a scale of ¼" = 1' for homes, and to a scale of ⅛" = 1' for larger buildings. However, this kind of model is of primary interest to architects, builders, and home purchasers who need to determine exterior appearance.

A structural model on the other hand is built to the exact structure of the building, but to a smaller scale. Framing members of pine or some other soft wood are cut to scale and assembled exactly the same as a house. Nothing, of

60-1a. *This architectural model was made from parts contained in a house design kit.*

60-1b. *Compare this photograph of the completed home to the model in Fig. 60-1a.*

60-2. *Architectural model.*

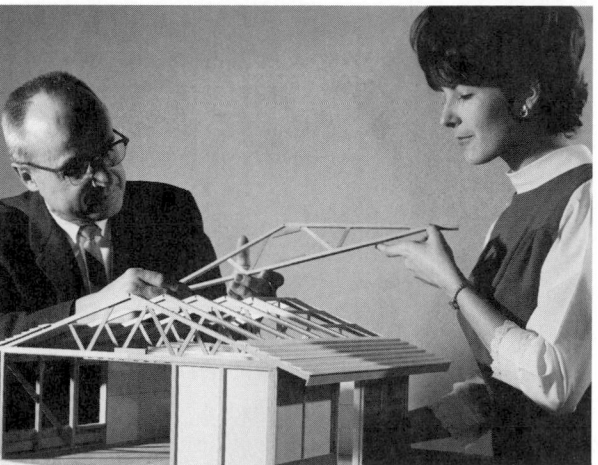

60-3. *Structural model.*

course, replaces the experience of actually cutting, fitting, and nailing full size 2 × 4s and other structural members to produce a house. Yet, much can be learned about building construction methods by building a structural model. This is an excellent way to study working drawings, to learn the names and parts, and to get some idea of the way to construct a wood-frame building. It is particularly useful when space does not permit the construction of a full-sized building. Builders sometimes use structural models to examine potential structural problems. It is much easier (and less expensive) to solve these problems on a model than on the job site.

HOUSE PLANS

Any standard set of house plans can be used to build a structural model. The plans can be followed as though they were being used for full-sized construction.

SCALE

The best scale for a structural model is 1½" = 1', or one-eighth as large as a full-size house. For example, if the real home measures 24' × 40', the miniature house would be 3' × 5'. Framing members are cut to the *nominal*, or *name*, size. For example, 2 × 4s will measure ¼" × ½", and a 2 × 6 will measure ¼" × ¾". An architect's scale can be used for most of the measuring and layout.

MATERIALS

A wide variety of materials can be used in constructing the model. These include:

Lumber. Structural members such as the joists, studs, plates, and so forth, should be referred to by their trade name (nominal size) such as 2 × 4s, or 2 × 6s rather than by the scale dimensions.

The structural parts can be cut from basswood, redwood, yellow poplar, or pine of softer variety. Woods such as Douglas fir can be used for larger members such as the foundation walls or footing. The woods used for structural model constructions should be the type that do not split easily. For parts that require a good deal of shaping, balsa wood is also useful. The lumber can be secured from the mill ends or shorts available at a lumberyard, or from waste stock found around any building project.

Plywood and other board materials. Plywood, particle board, or hardboard can be used for the base of the model.

Veneer. Veneer can be used for exterior and interior walls. Heavy illustration board can also be used.

Nails. Nails and other metal fasteners should be used in proportion to the size of the model. The nails for most of the house framing should be ½", 19- or 20-gauge wire nails. For spiking together joists, headers, and other large members, use ¾" No. 18 wire nails. Use ½" nails or staples for attaching shingles. A variety of common adhesives can be used instead of nails to fasten model parts together. White or yellow glue works well on most wood parts.

Other materials. A wide variety of common household items and other materials may be needed, including plaster of paris or rigid foam plastic for a foundation, materials like sponges for shrubbery, and sandpaper for shingles.

TOOLS FOR MODEL BUILDING

The tools needed for model building are relatively simple and easy to obtain. They include the following:

➤ Framing square.
➤ Razor knife.
➤ Pencil.

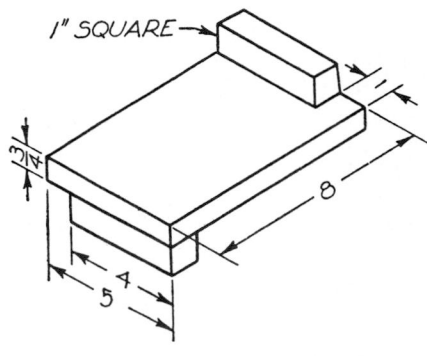

60-4. *Bench hook for holding structural model parts for sawing.*

➤ Eight-ounce magnetized or upholstery hammer; seven-ounce magnetized hammer to drive nails.
➤ Long-nosed pliers.
➤ Hacksaw or dovetail saw to cut scale model materials.
➤ Chisels for trimming rafters, bases, and other fine work.
➤ T square, triangle, and architectural scale.
➤ Sandpaper and masking tape.
➤ Bench hook, used for holding stock while sawing. Fig. 60-4.
➤ Brad awl.
➤ Stapler.
➤ Miter box for cutting angles for such pieces as rafters and bases. Fig. 60-5.

JIGS

Simple jigs can be made for supporting framing members 16" on center for floor and wall framing. Another method of doing floor and wall framing is to make a scale drawing of each section; namely, wall, front elevation, back elevation, right elevation, and left elevation. Fasten this to a piece of

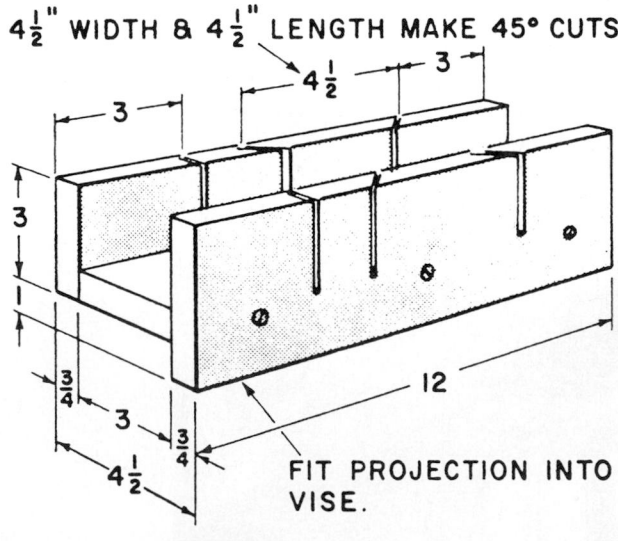

60-5. *Miter box for cutting angles.*

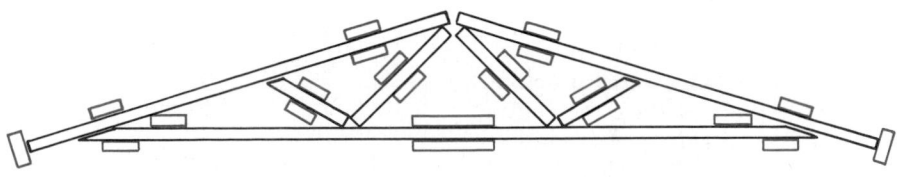

60-6. *This jig can be used to construct model-sized trusses.*

plywood to use as a guide in assembling the section.

A simple jig can also be made for holding the parts for making roof trusses. Fig. 60-6. Use a fast-acting glue to help hold the parts together while nailing.

CONSTRUCTION PRACTICES

Model Base

A model base can be made of ¾" plywood or particle board that is cut to lot size. Fig. 60-7. A slightly lighter base can be made by utilizing ¼" plywood with a 1" × 2" framework underneath. Diagonal bracing is necessary to give it rigidity. The base should be at least several inches wider and longer than the width and length of the house. If just a portion of the house will be modeled, the base should be big enough to hold it and have several inches of room to spare in all directions.

Foundation

Carefully lay out on the model base the outline for the foundation of the home. If there is a basement, make sure that the foundation wall is the same height above the model base (grade) as it would be in actual construction. If the house has no basement, a ¼" piece of plywood can represent the concrete slab.

The foundation walls can be made of rigid plastic foam or molding plaster. The foundation can also be made of wood scaled to the correct thickness and to the height above grade as indicated in the working drawing. Fig. 60-7. Make the termite shield of thin aluminum or copper foil.

Floor Framing

If the house plans call for a basement, the first step is to install a "steel" beam to support the floor framing. This beam can be made of several layers of thin wood that are glued and nailed together and painted an orange color to resemble the steel I-beam.

Now build the sill plate, the floor joists, and the box sill to complete the floor framing just as it would be done in full-sized construction. Cover the framing with thin veneer to serve as the subfloor. If you wish to expose part of the floor framing, cut a free-form opening in the veneer. Install bridging between the floor joists at the exposed sections.

Wall Framing

Construct each wall section according to a plan. Using a jig on a tabletop will facilitate spacing of studs and locating and framing of window and door openings.

Nail the first top plate solidly to the studding. The second top plate should be nailed to the ceiling joists or roof trusses. Exterior sheathing can cover the crack between the two top plates. This arrangement will permit the removal of the entire roof section so that the interior of the home can be easily seen.

Nail the wall sections to the subfloor, one at a time. Make sure that the walls are plumb and that the corners are tight. Now build the interior walls. Fig. 60-8.

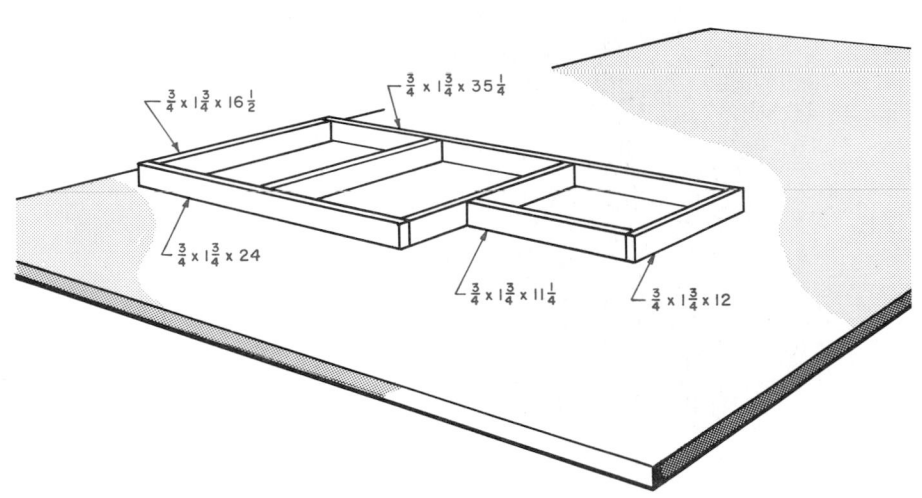

60-7. *Base and foundation of the model.*

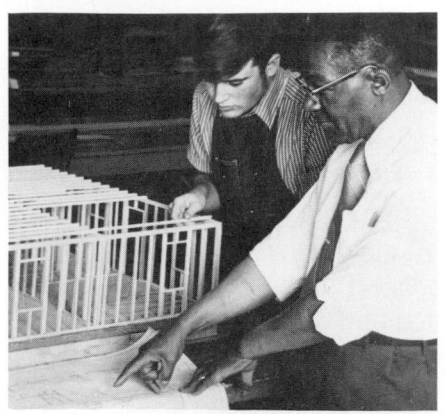

60-8. *Wall framing.*

60-9a. *Roof framing.*

60-9b. *A sectional model showing standard construction. Note the use of various materials to simulate actual building materials such as brick, roofing, steel beams, etc.*

Roof Framing

Build the roof by starting with a second top plate, adding the ceiling joists, and then the roof framing members or roof trusses. Fasten these all together to comprise one unit that can be removed when necessary. Fig. 60-9.

Exterior Wall

Complete at least the front of the model by adding the exterior wall, consisting of the sheathing, building paper, and exterior wall. The sheathing can be made of veneer or heavy construction paper. The building paper can be plain, thin black paper and the wall material can be made of thin balsa sheets. Wood siding can also be made from thin balsa wood.

Roof Covering

A thin veneer can be used for the roof sheathing. Many other materials can be used for the roof itself. For example, sandpaper might be used or miniature wood shingles can be cut. Only a small portion of the roof should be completed. On a gable or hip roof, for example, most of the front slope should be covered while the roof frame remains exposed.

Chimneys and Other Details

Chimneys and other details of brick or cement can be made of molding plaster.

Millwork

It is extremely difficult to build in miniature the millwork, such as doors and windows. In some cases, clear plastics can be used for windows and the framing can be painted on. Doors can be made of thin plywood.

Completing the Interior

The interior of the home can be completed in small details to show some of the construction materials. For example, drywall construction can be made by fastening a section of construction board to part of the interior. Several kinds of materials can be used to simulate the finished flooring.

LANDSCAPING

The main purpose in constructing the structural model is to gain experience in framing a house and building a roof. Therefore it is not necessary to add every exterior detail unless you wish a model for display purposes. Many kinds of materials can be used for landscaping. Grass areas, for example, can be made from green flocking, and the walls, driveways, and other items with

60-10. *Full-size mock up. Standard-sized materials are used, including such mill items as windows.*

various kinds of masking tape. Trees and shrubs can be made of wire and foam rubber. The creative model maker will find uses for many common household items to complete the model.

FULL-SCALE PARTS OF A BUILDING

To gain experience in working with full-size materials, it may be desirable to construct a full-size section of a house, wall, or roof. Fig. 60-10. Standard house plans can be followed.

QUESTIONS

1. What is the difference between an architectural and a structural model?

2. When building a structural model, why is a ⅛ scale recommended?

3. What are some of the materials that might be used for the foundation wall in a structural model?

4. What can be done to permit the removal of the entire roof section of the structural model?

5. What are some of the benefits gained from building a structural model?

ACTIVITIES

1. Math. A structural model for a rectangular house with outside dimensions 32' by 60' is to be built to a scale of 1½" = 1'.

a. What are the outside dimensions of the model?

b. The floor joists are 2" by 10" by 18'. What are the dimensions of the floor joist in the model?

c. After the model has been constructed, the opening for the garage door is measured as 9¾" by 22½". What are the dimensions of the actual garage door opening?

2. Science. This unit addresses constructing scale-model buildings from an architectural or structural standpoint. Investigate passive solar system construction.

Construct two scale-model passive solar absorber/storage systems from small paper drinking or pill cups. Paint one a light color (if not already light in color). Paint the other one a dark color. Place both system models in direct sunlight. Use your sense of touch to determine which model is a better

absorber/storage passive solar system. Explain where such a system should be located in a building.

3. Language Arts. Management is essential if any project is to be completed. Effective management identifies clear goals. It also works towards reaching those goals. The manager, then, often sets the goals for the entire work team. A work team may have supervisors on various levels. On a sheet of paper, draw a diagram of the last work team to which you belonged. Identify the various levels of management and the tasks for which individuals at each management level were responsible.

Construction Systems

Some important construction techniques are not commonly used in the standard house. Some of these techniques meet regional needs, such as the need for special construction along seacoasts and in seismic zones. Others are useful primarily for cluster housing, such as apartments. Still others are too new to be in common use yet.

COASTAL HIGH-HAZARD CONSTRUCTION

Building in coastal high-hazard areas involves special problems. Houses must be protected against tides, storm surges, wind-generated waves, and high winds. Special care must be taken to assure that houses have sound foundations. Sand is the most common soil in most coastal areas. It does not provide a good base for building unless special techniques are used. In some areas, clay is under the sand. Generally, clay soils are a better base for building than sandy soils. Before deciding on what kind of construction to use, it is a good idea to take boring samples.

Foundation Systems

Several types of foundations are suitable for elevated residential housing in coastal high-hazard areas. Wood pile is the most common foundation. Fig. 61-1.

A pile is a round or rectangular post driven into the soil. Wood piles must always be treated to minimize decay and damage from fungus and marine borers. Concrete or steel piles can also be used, but these are much more expensive.

The effectiveness of a pile foundation depends, in part, on the method of inserting the pile into the ground. The best way is to use a pile driver. A less desirable method is a technique known as *jetting*. Jetting involves shooting a high-pressure stream of water through a pipe advanced alongside the pile. The water blows a hole in the sand into which the pile is driven until the required depth is reached. If precast concrete piles or steel piles are used for the foundation, a regular pile driver is required.

61-1. *For protection against flooding, houses may be built on wood piles.*

Another foundation consists of wood posts resting on some kind of spread footing. Wood posts are satisfactory for areas where there is less danger of wind and flooding. In some areas, it is common to use reinforced masonry piers for elevated residential structures. A good place for pier construction is far enough away from the beach so that flood waters will not greatly affect the pier. Bracing of the foundation piers can be very effective in minimizing storm damage.

Floors

Once the required elevation is obtained, the framing must be attached. Primary floor beams spanning the supports should be parallel to the flow of water. If joists are used, cross bridging is necessary for added support. Subflooring must be waterproof plywood or either 1" × 4" or 1" × 6" boards placed diagonally.

Walls

The most commonly used studs are 2 × 4s, 16 inches on center. However, 2 × 6s will permit 50 percent thicker insulation for cold weather areas. Wood frame walls should be braced to resist wind forces. Plywood is the normal wall sheathing used for exterior walls to add structural strength.

Anchorage

Anchorage is one of the most critical building requirements in coastal areas. Metal anchors or clips should be installed to attach all parts together wherever possible. These mechanical fasteners greatly strengthen the total building. Some methods for anchoring the foundation and floor framing are shown in Fig. 61-2.

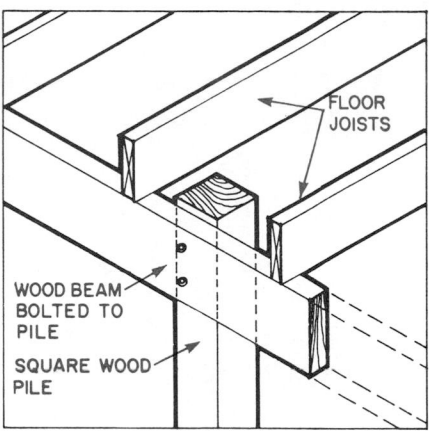
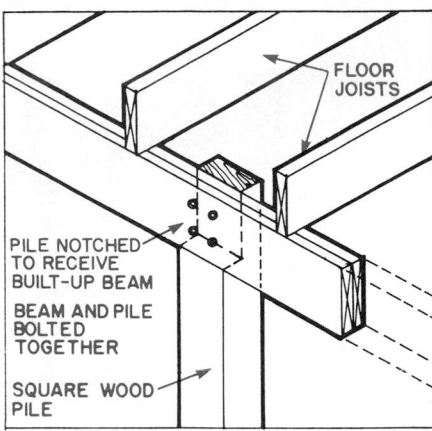
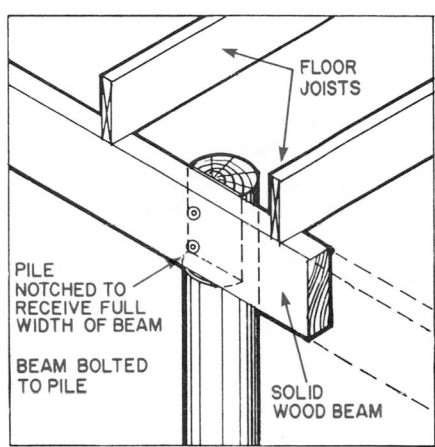
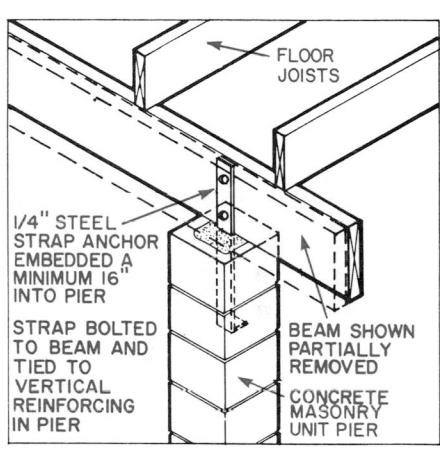
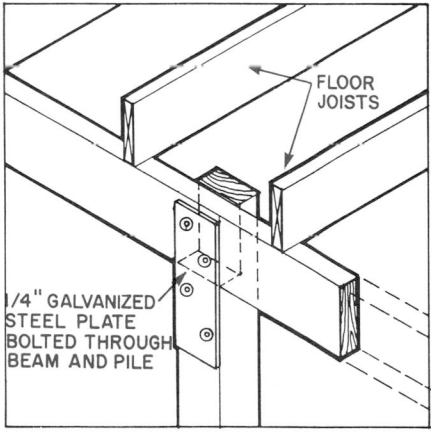
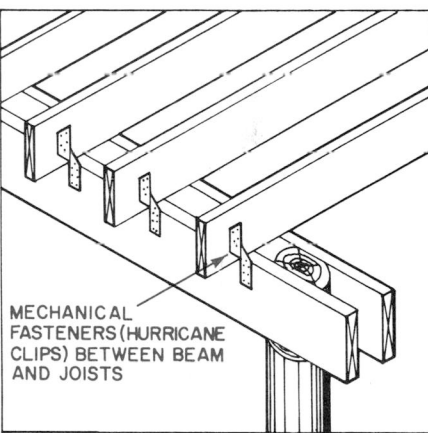

61-2. Floor framing may be anchored to piles in a variety of ways.

61-3. *A great many people live in some type of cluster housing.*

CLUSTER HOUSING

Cluster housing includes apartments, condominiums, cooperatives, town houses, and other types of row housing. Fig. 61-3. If wood is the primary building material, construction of these units is similar to that of single homes, with two major exceptions—fire control and sound control.

Fire Control

Building codes for cluster housing generally require that the walls and floors between apartments be built to resist fire for a specific time. The walls between apartments, for example, may be required to have a fire resistance rating of one hour. The fire resistance rating depends on framing techniques and on the materials used in the wall.

Fire stops are one important way of resisting the spread of flames. Fire stops block the flow of air upward inside walls and horizontally between enclosed floor joists. By blocking air flow, they slow down the spread of flames. Structural elements, such as top

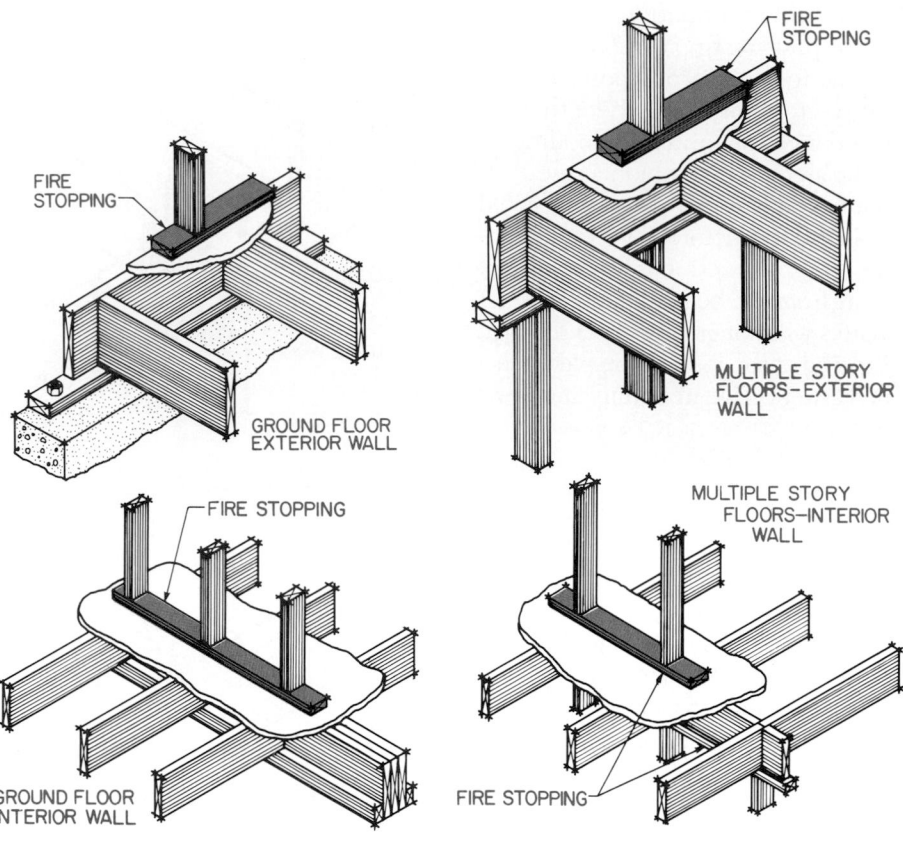

61-4. *Typical wood fire stops used in cluster housing.*

and bottom plates, function as fire blocks. Fig. 61-4. Nonstructural fire stops may also be nailed between studs or between floor joists.

Normal wood-and-panel assembly will meet the required fire resistance rating if the proper building materials are used. Each material and assembly is rated in tests performed by the Underwriters' Laboratories (UL). For example, a wall built of one layer of ⅝" type X gypsum board nailed to wood studs on 16" centers has a fire resistance rating of one hour. (Type X gypsum board is a gypsum board with a special fire-resistant core.) The fire resistance rating of the wall could be increased by using a double thickness of gypsum board, by using a mineral wool insulation in the

wall, and by many other means. Fig. 61-5 shows a typical fire-rated assembly. The *UL Fire Resistance Directory* lists the ratings of many materials and assemblies. It is the architect's responsibility to design buildings using these UL ratings to meet the local building codes.

Sound Control

In a well-built apartment building, sound should not travel easily from one unit to another. There are several methods for retarding the movement of sound.

Increasing Mass. Heavier materials block sound better than light materials. Therefore, adding another layer of gypsum wall board will make a wall more soundproof.

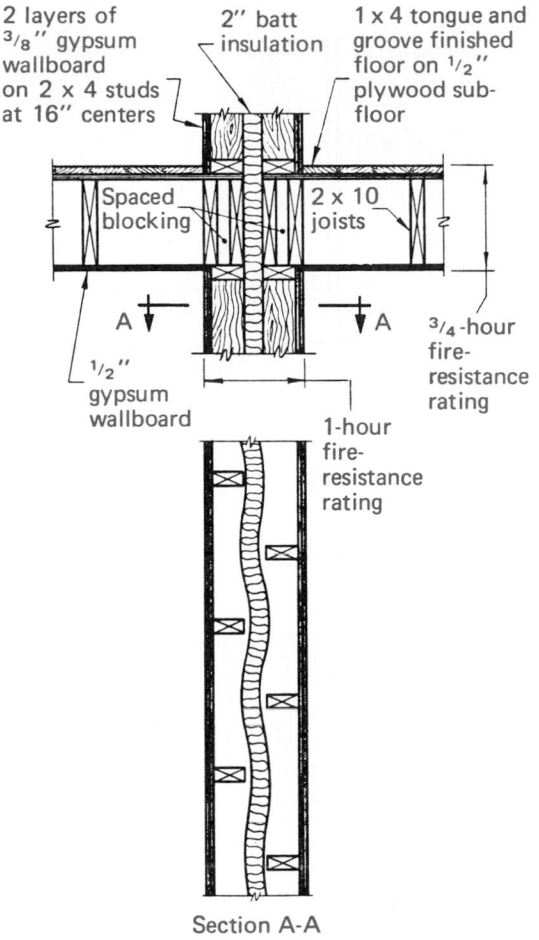

Section A-A

61-5. *A typical wall and floor design to provide for an adequate fire resistance rating.*

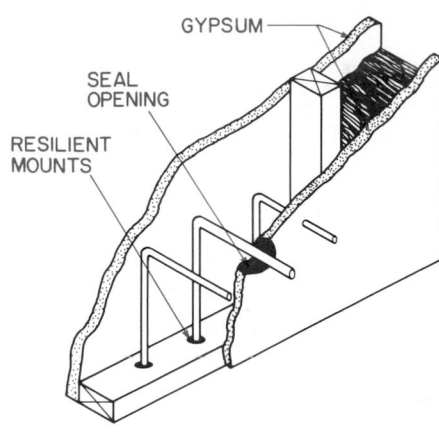

61-6. *Isolating pipes from surrounding structures with resilient mounts will reduce sound transmission.*

As a general rule, every doubling of the weight of the wall increases sound transmission loss by an additional 5 to 6 decibels.

Breaking Vibration Paths.

Another efficient way of controlling sound transmission is to break the vibration path. This can be done by staggering the studs. The wall of one unit is then attached to one set of studs, and the wall of the other unit to another set of studs. Another approach is to use metal studs. They are more resilient than wood studs and reduce the transmission vibration between one wall and the other. With wood studs, metal clips can be placed between the gypsum board and the studs to break the vibration path.

Absorbing Sound in the Wall.

Sound transmission can be decreased by filling the wall cavity with sound-absorbing material such as building insulation. Insulation is a good way to absorb sound without adding significant weight or mass to the partition.

Absorbing Sound in the Unit.

Another method of reducing sound transmission is to add sound-absorbing material in the unit itself. For example, rugs could be placed on the floor, or soundproof ceiling tile can be added to the ceiling.

Other Methods of Sound Control.

Some other ways to reduce the passage of sound include:

➤ Installing an air seal around the perimeter of the wall to create a proper acoustical seal.

➤ Reducing the window area by using fewer and smaller windows.

➤ Installing electrical items (including telephone bells and other wiring) on a well-insulated interior wall—never on a party wall.

➤ Insulating the plumbing from the adjacent structure so that the pipes will not carry noise. Fig. 61-6.

➤ Installing furnace ducts so that noise cannot be transmitted through the heating and ventilating system.

PERMANENT WOOD FOUNDATION

The permanent wood foundation system provides a way to build a foundation easily and quickly. It can be installed in less than a day by a small crew. Wet and freezing weather does not delay construction. Components can be fabricated in a factory, so the cost is low. Once in place, wood frame basement walls are easy to finish. Board or paneling can be nailed directly to the studs. The walls will not crack, and the basement will not smell damp or musty. The cost of construction is less than a comparable foundation of poured concrete or concrete block.

Materials

All lumber and plywood in the foundation must be pressure-treated to the standards of the American Wood Preservers Institute for full protection against termites and decay. The fasteners must be silicon, bronze, copper, or stainless steel. Hot-dipped, zinc-coated steel nails meet certain construction requirements.

Procedure

The first step in building a wood foundation is to provide footings. A layer of gravel, coarse sand, or crushed stone is required. A wood footing plate on top of this distributes the load. Fig. 61-7. The wall panels fabricated in a factory consist of the footing plate, bottom and top plates, studs, and plywood. Fig. 61-8. The footing plate is set in on one end of the bottom plate and extends out over the other end. Thus, the bottom plate of each panel overlaps the footing plate of an adjoining panel. The design also permits the interlocking of panels at the corners. The panels are set in place by a screw and the corners are solidly fitted together. The poured concrete subfloor consists of a layer of concrete that covers the treated sill and keeps the wall studs from moving.

If the exterior is to be brick veneered, a wood knee wall will provide a base for the brick. The knee wall must rest on an oversize treated sill. With an adequate crew

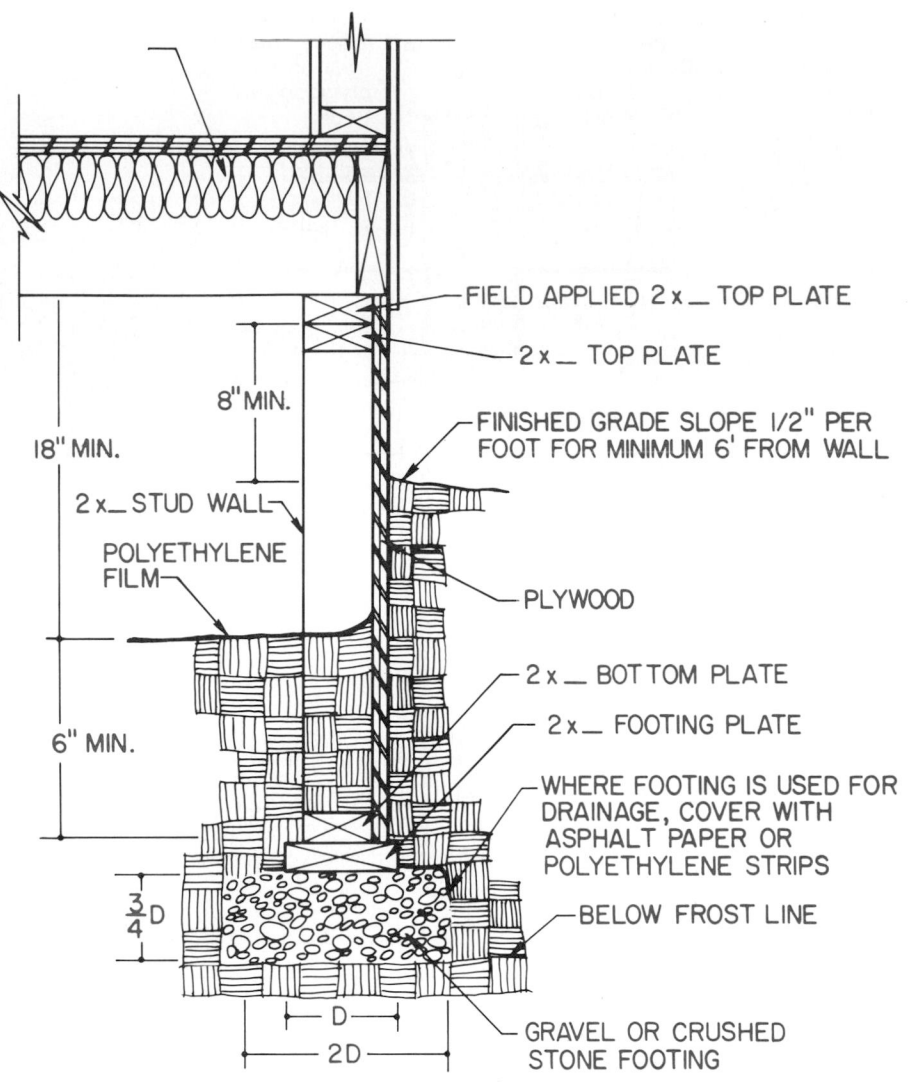

61-7. A wood foundation. Note the gravel footing and the footing plate to distribute the load.

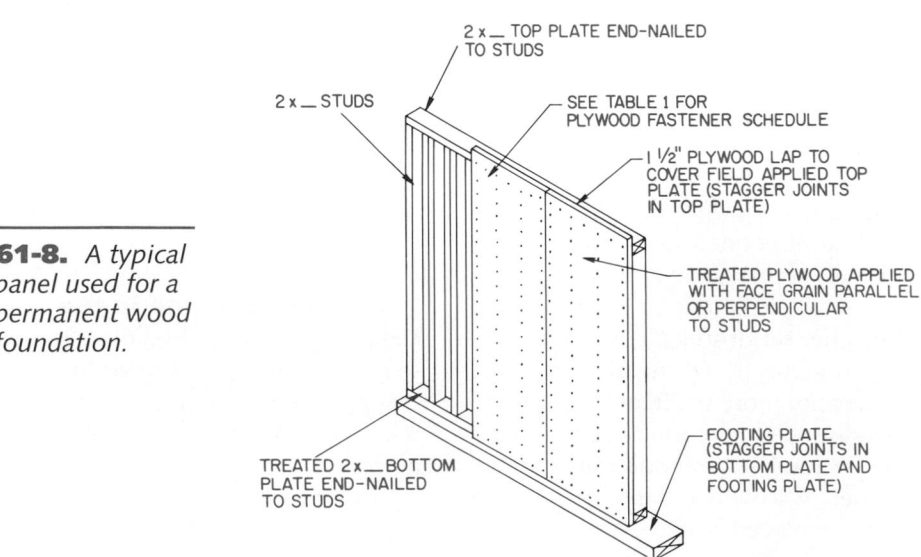

61-8. A typical panel used for a permanent wood foundation.

61-9. *This is how the permanent wood foundation looks when assembled.*

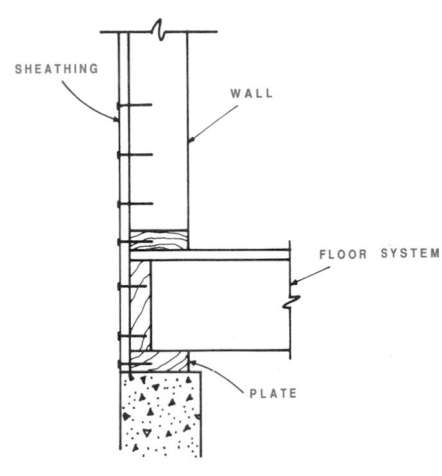

61-11. *In seismic areas, nails should penetrate all elements of the structure.*

and prefabricated panels, the foundation can be assembled in less than two hours. Fig. 61-9. Detailed directions and technical information concerning the permanent wood foundation can be obtained from the National Forest Products Association.

CONSTRUCTION IN SEISMIC ZONES

In the United States, a large portion of the population lives in areas that are subject to earthquake activity. This includes the entire West Coast (particularly the coast of California), Alaska, and Hawaii, as well as parts of the Midwest and the East Coast. The concerns for safety and loss of property are reflected in the building codes of those areas. Fig. 61-10.

Most of the materials used for standard construction can be used for earthquake-resistant construction. However, houses in seismically active areas are built so that the connections between all the materials are stronger. This reduces the chances that structural connections will fail during an earthquake.

The basic concept of earthquake-resistant construction is simple. First, build a strong foundation. Then make sure each successive structural member above the foundation is tied to it. For example, the foundation plate is bolted to the foundation, joists are strapped to the plate, walls are strapped to the joists, and rafters are strapped to the walls. In some cases, the walls are fastened directly to the foundation.

Properly nailed connections are only part of the solution.

61-10. *The results of improper construction in an earthquake-prone area.*

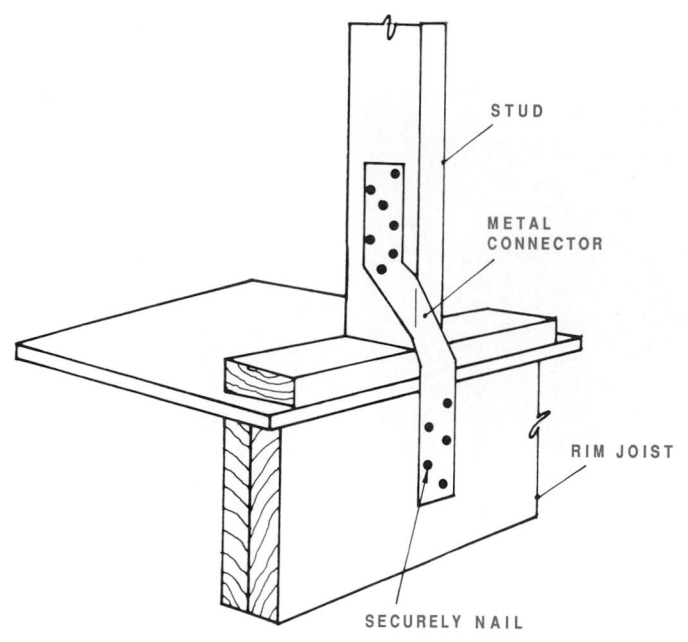

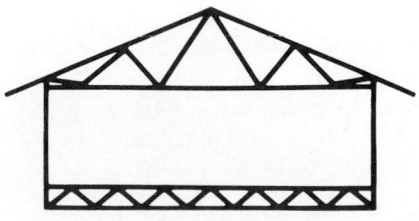

61-13. *A truss frame.*

61-12. *Metal connectors are used to reinforce all structural joints. This ties the frame of the house into the foundation.*

Fig. 61-11. Metal framing straps and connectors of various types are used to reinforce nailed connections. Fig. 61-12. As in areas of the country that experience high winds, it is important in seismic zones to provide secure connections between the walls and the roof structure.

TRUSS-FRAMED SYSTEM

The truss-framed system (TFS) of construction consists of a roof truss, floor truss, and wall studs fastened together in a single rigid unit. Fig. 61-13. The frames are placed 24" on center to form the skeleton of the building. This method saves about 30 percent of the lumber used in the traditionally built home, where wall studs are placed 16" on center. The truss frames are manufactured in a factory and then shipped to the construction site. Frames for the entire house can be erected in less than three hours by a small crew. The house can then be covered with wall sheathing and roofing to form a shell so that the completely enclosed structure is ready in one day. This is important during cold weather because it enables electricians, plumbers, and other contractors to finish the house under shelter.

Once the trusses are erected and the sheathing and roofing installed, the interior can be completed in a variety of designs. Since the inside is one large open space, different room arrangements are possible with the same exterior shell. It is easy to install the wiring and plumbing in the truss-framed house. Strength is another advantage of the truss-framed system. The system is used in hurricane country where disaster-resistant features are important. The system greatly increases the probability that the home will withstand hurricane forces. The truss-frame system can be used for any house with rectangular subdivisions, including L-shaped, U-shaped, and H-shaped designs. The system can be used for both single-story and two-story construction. The roof may be of any type found on conventional homes.

1. Describe two methods of installing piles for a home in a coastal region.

2. Why might it sometimes be preferable to use 2 × 6s instead of 2 × 4s as studs for exterior walls?

3. In what two ways does the construction of cluster housing differ from single home construction?

4. How does type-X gypsum board differ from regular gypsum board?

5. What features of an apartment building help assure that sound does not travel easily from one unit to another?

6. What are some of the advantages of a permanent wood foundation?

7. What are some of the advantages of using a truss-frame system?

ACTIVITIES

1. Social Studies. Research the type of houses that are found along the east and west coasts of the United States. What types of homes seem the most common? Why? Relate your findings to the information presented in this unit.

2. Science. Obtain at least fourteen large wooden match sticks with the lighting ends removed.

Glue four of the sticks together to form a square "pile" two matches wide by two matches thick. Glue two matches together to form a "beam" one match wide and two match-widths thick. Repeat the gluing process to fashion two "piles" and two "beams."

Anchor one of the "beams" to a "pile" without notching. Anchor the other "beam" to the other "pile" with a notch. Simulate the bolting process with a paper stapler.

Using destructive testing methods, determine which special construction technique is stronger.

3. Language Arts. Dependability and punctuality are important in any job. By being dependable and on time in the completion of work assignments, you signal that you are capable of assuming more responsibility. You also signal your willingness to accept this responsibility. Dependability and punctuality can, then, lead to promotion in your work. Promotion can lead to increased earnings. Write a brief essay on dependability and punctuality. Be sure to touch on ways in which dependability and punctuality can be demonstrated on the job.

4. Language Arts. In any work environment, you probably will be working with other people. Though these people may not have job responsibilities identical to yours, these other people will be in the workplace. This will mean that a spirit of cooperation is easier if you have a good understanding of yourself and others. To understand yourself and others you need to have a knowledge of your abilities. Such a knowledge will help you understand the ways in which cooperation with others can aid in the completion of a task on which you may all be working. Write a brief essay in which you discuss the attitudes that will help you gain a better understanding of others. Identify also those attitudes that will work against a spirit of teamwork and cooperation.

THE SCHOOL-TO-WORK CONNECTION

Many homes have been destroyed and much property has been damaged by earthquakes and violent weather. Building codes sometimes change in the aftermath of such natural disasters.

1. Build a research file about special construction techniques. First, contact your local building department to ask if there are any special building codes that help houses resist earthquake or storm damage. Photocopy the appropriate pages of the code. Write to a manufacturer of roofing shingles. Ask if there are shingles for use in high-wind areas. If so, get a brochure describing them and add it to your file.

62

Remodeling and Renovation

The market for new housing is large. Many people, however, purchase a house that already exists, rather than build a new one. This is partly because the supply of existing housing is huge. It is also because buying a house that already exists allows a family to move in quickly. An existing house, however, does not always make an exact fit with the needs of its new owners. Repairs have to be made, or spaces must be enlarged. Fig. 62-1.

Many builders of new homes, in fact, incorporate remodeling work into their activities. The homebuilding industry is a very cyclical one. It is affected by changes in interest rates and other aspects of the economy. When the demand for new construction falls off temporarily, remodeling work generally picks up. This is because families who cannot afford to buy a new house decide to improve the house they are already in.

An older house can sometimes

62-1b. *A common remodeling project is the installation of new siding.*

62-1a. *Repairing or remodeling an existing house can extend its life and increase its value.*

62-1c. *All kinds of buildings can be remodeled. The U.S. Capitol was enlarged in the 1850s. The original dome was replaced by a larger one, shown under construction here.*

be a good buy for someone who wants to fix it up. Some houses, however, need extensive and expensive repairs to put them in good shape. Time can take its toll on even the best-built houses. Older houses did not have all the benefits of modern building technology. It is not easy to judge the condition of an older house. A first glance is often deceiving. Sometimes a home that looks run-down may be in better condition than one that has just been patched up and painted. To determine whether it is cost-effective to renovate an older home, a thorough inspection must be conducted. Table 62-A.

Table 62-A. *Inspection Checklist.*

HOUSE EXTERIOR

I. Site Plan

A. House Orientation
  1. North-South
  2. East-West
B. Trees and Shrubs
  1. Provide windbreak
  2. Provide shade
  3. Allow south sunlight
C. House Location
  1. On hill
  2. Protected by trees
  3. In open plain

II. House Appearance

A. Yard
  1. Clean, well kept
  2. In need of landscaping
  3. Unkept, messy
B. House
  1. Well-maintained appearance
  2. Needs paint
  3. Needs roof
  4. Broken windows

III. Electrical

A. Service from pole
  1. 2-wire 110V/120V
  2. 3-wire 220V/240V

IV. Siding

A. Type
  1. Wood
  2. Stucco
  3. Masonry
  4. Aluminum or vinyl
  5. Other
B. Condition
  1. Satisfactory
  2. Repairs needed

V. Roof

A. Type
  1. Asphalt shingles
  2. Metal
  3. Rolled asphalt
  4. Other

B. Condition
  1. Satisfactory
  2. Repairs needed
C. Chimney
  1. Satisfactory condition
  2. Repairs needed
D. Flashing
  1. Satisfactory condition
  2. Repairs needed
E. Eaves and Downspouts
  1. Type
  2. Condition

VI. Exterior Foundation

A. Type
  1. Stone
  2. Stone capped with mortar
  3. Cement block
  4. Other
B. Condition
  1. Satisfactory condition
  2. Repairs needed

HOUSE INTERIOR

I. Basement

A. Floor
  1. Stone
  2. Cement
  3. Dirt
B. Walls
  1. Stone
  2. Block
  3. Cement
C. Condition
  1. Wet or damp
  2. Dry - no sign of moisture
D. Joists, Sillplate and Header
  1. Good condition, straight joists, no cracks
  2. Rotting wood, insect infestation, sagging wood
E. Heating System
  1. Type
  2. Appearance
  3. Original or new
  4. Type of fuel

II. Insulation

A. Type
B. Location (how many?)
  1. Wall
  2. Ceiling
  3. Floor

III. Electrical

A. Service Entrance
  1. 60 amperes
  2. 100 amperes
  3. 200 amperes
  4. Fuse box
  5. Circuit breakers
B. Branch Circuits (how many?)
  1. Area lighting circuits
  2. Appliance circuits
  3. Electric range/dryer/ hot water heater circuit

IV. Plumbing

A. Sewage System
  1. City sewer
  2. Septic tank
  3. Other
B. Septic Tank (if appropriate)
  1. Concrete
  2. Metal
  3. Size (500, 800, 1000 gal.)
C. Supply Lines
  1. City water
  2. Well (dug or drilled)
  3. Flow rate
D. Water Lines
  1. Copper
  2. Galvanized iron

  3. PVC plastic
  4. Other
E. Hot Water Tank
  1. Gas
  2. Electric
  3. Fuel oil
  4. Age and condition
  5. Size
F. Well Pump
  1. Type
  2. Condition

V. Room layout

A. Traffic flow
  1. Satisfactory
  2. Changes needed
B. Kitchen
  1. Modern/convenient
  2. Changes needed
C. Interior Walls
  1. Type (plaster, paneled, sheetrock)
  2. Condition

GENERAL INSPECTION

If you know what to look for, you can conduct much of the inspection yourself. Be sure to wear old clothes so you can check the attic and crawl spaces. Equip yourself with flashlight, pocketknife, pen, notepaper, and tape measure. As you inspect the house, remember that old homes are often not very energy efficient. Look for any flaws that waste heat. Fig. 62-2.

BUILDING SITE

Before entering, inspect the house from the outside. Walk around the house several times, checking the surrounding site, exterior walls, roof, windows, and doors. Locate the north and south exposures of the house. Ideally, the south side should have the most window space. The north side should be protected by a windbreak such as vegetation, a garage, or a hill. Trees on the south side should be deciduous, providing shade in the summer and allowing sunlight to enter in the winter. Trees on the north side should be evergreen, providing a windbreak during the winter.

Exterior Walls

Inspect exterior siding to see if it needs to be replaced or if it has been replaced. Houses with wood siding should be checked for peeling paint. Peeling paint or bare wood in random areas around a house indicates a moisture problem coming from inside the house. Paint peeling away from another layer of paint indicates that different kinds of paint have been used on the same surface. In either case, the old paint must be completely removed or new siding must be attached.

Check the wood trim around the eaves and soffit to make sure there is no dry rot due to ice damage, leaky eaves, troughs, insects, or mildew. In older homes, it takes much longer to repair and paint the trim than the main body of the house.

Aluminum or vinyl siding is often put on an older home over the original wood siding. Sometimes this is done to cover a paint-peeling problem caused by excessive moisture inside the house. Moisture finds its way into the wood siding and forces the paint off as it escapes. Sealing the wood siding with metal or vinyl siding captures this moisture in the wall spaces. The trapped moisture eventually causes dry rot or insulation damage. For this reason, unvented aluminum, vinyl, or composition siding should not be installed on a house that has inadequate vapor barriers.

Roof

Foundation settling in an older home will often show up in a swayback or leaning roof ridge. Fig. 62-3. If the roof ridge is not straight, make a note to check the basement walls, support columns, and joists. Roof shingles must lie flat and intact. Old roof shingles often curl and lose their granular surface. They can also curl under and break. Sometimes too many asphalt shingles have been placed over each other. There should not be more than two depths of shingles on a roof. Check the roof for large amounts of black tar. This indicates there have been roof leaks. Sometimes these roof leaks will cause the roof boards to rot. Check the chimney for loose mortar or broken bricks. Make sure that the metal flashing is in good condition.

Windows and Doors

Check to see that doors and windows are snug and well-fitted. Make sure also that they have storm doors and windows. Poorly fitted doors and windows, and those without storms, are a major cause of energy loss. Entrance doors

Chimney crack

No cap on chimney

Loose flashing

Loose shingles

Snow blown into open windward louvres

Lack of roof protection at edges

Ice dam caused by poor insulation and soffit ventilation

Too many openable windows

Air leakage through light fixture into roof

Open door

Window crack

Crack in door frame

Crack at door sill

62-2. An older home often needs insulation and other repairs to make it more energy efficient.

62-3. *The roof often indicates serious problems in a house's foundation.*

should also be protected by an overhang. Wood frame windows are best for energy savings. Aluminum frames can cause considerable heat loss in the winter. Be sure to check the window operation by raising and lowering double-hung windows and by cranking open casement windows.

Basement

Check the basement or crawl space, floors, and walls for damp spots. Mustiness indicates that moisture may be finding its way into the living space. Flooding in a basement will eventually undermine the foundation. Cracks on the inside of a foundation wall often indicate that the wall is being pushed in from the outside. Check the structural members for termites and dry rot. Also, make sure the floors are level.

Attic Vents

There should be at least two gable vents. If there is little or no attic ventilation, check the attic ceiling and rafters for condensation stains or dark colors. Look carefully for any signs of leaks. Check also to see what kinds of insulation have been installed in the house.

Interior Walls and Ceilings

Most older homes have plastered walls. These should be checked for cracks. Drywall or gypsum board is the surface material used instead of plaster in buildings today. Examine the walls and ceilings carefully for signs of leaks.

Check the insulation in the walls and determine if any must be added.

Common residential construction techniques years ago involved post-and-beam and balloon framing. The old post-and-beam construction is the most difficult to insulate. Balloon frame houses are not common any more.

Professional Assistance

You may need some professional help in making your inspection. A commercial termite inspection will often uncover damage that the untrained person will overlook. If there has been extensive damage due to termites, marine borers, or dry rot, repairs to the house may be very costly.

The heating system, plumbing, and electrical wiring should be looked at closely by someone who knows these systems. Problems with these systems often develop in

older houses. They, too, can mean costly repairs.

Plans for Remodeling

After a house has been examined and found fit for remodeling, plans for improvement can be made. The types of improvements to be made depend on the condition of the house and the needs of the owner. A serious problem that needs repair—such as a leaky roof—will probably deserve first attention. Work that will make the home more energy efficient should be considered. The homeowner may also want to make changes that will provide more space, add modern conveniences, or improve the appearance of the house.

Types of Remodeling

There are two general types of remodeling. One involves making changes to the exterior or interior without adding to the size of the structure. Fig. 62-4. The other involves making additions that increase the size of the structure. Fig. 62-5.

Most projects fall into the first category. A few typical specific remodeling projects are listed below:

➤ Changing the layout. It may be important to alter the interior layout of the home. Fig. 62-6. Large rooms can be made by removing walls between small rooms. A large room may be divided into smaller rooms by adding a wall. Doors can be relocated to change traffic patterns.

➤ Replacing windows. Old windows may be replaced with new ones to make the house weather tight. The number, size, or arrangement of windows can be changed to make the house more attractive.

➤ Adding closets. If a house

62-4a. *This house, typical of the 1950s, will be remodeled without adding floor space.*

62-4b. *This same house—with a stunning, contemporary exterior.*

62-4c. *The old kitchen.*

62-4d. *The remodeled kitchen.*

does not have enough closet space, the homeowner may need to add some.

➤ Remodeling the kitchen. Appliances such as a modern range and a dishwasher can be built into an old kitchen. Old, wornout cabinets and counters may need to

62-5a. *The foundation and rough floor for an addition to a house.*

62-5b. *Working on the rough exterior.*

62-5c. *The completed addition.*

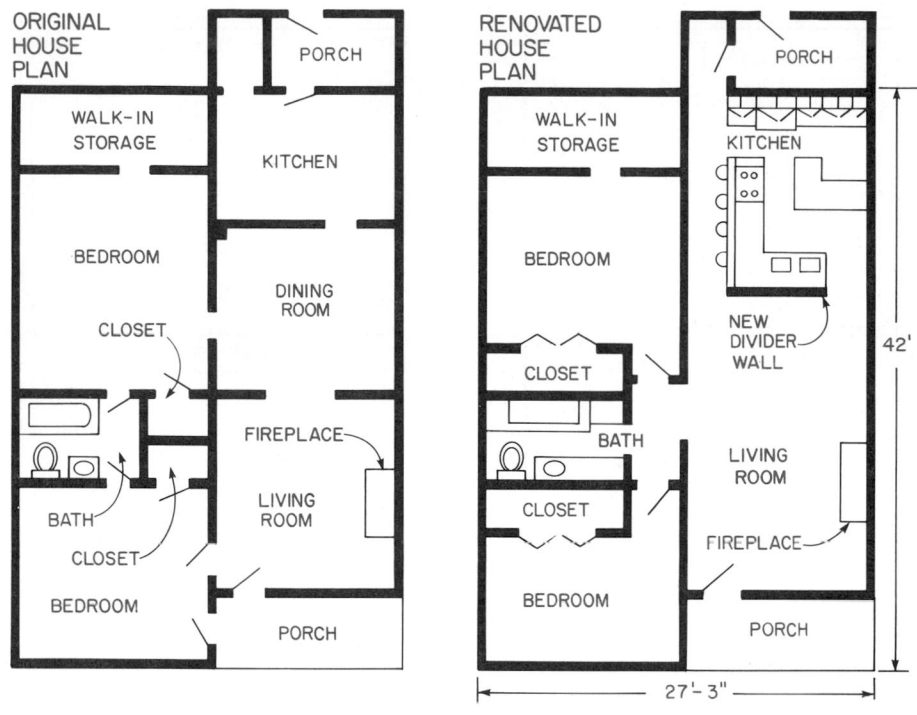

62-6. *A house's floor plan can be changed to meet a new owner's needs.*

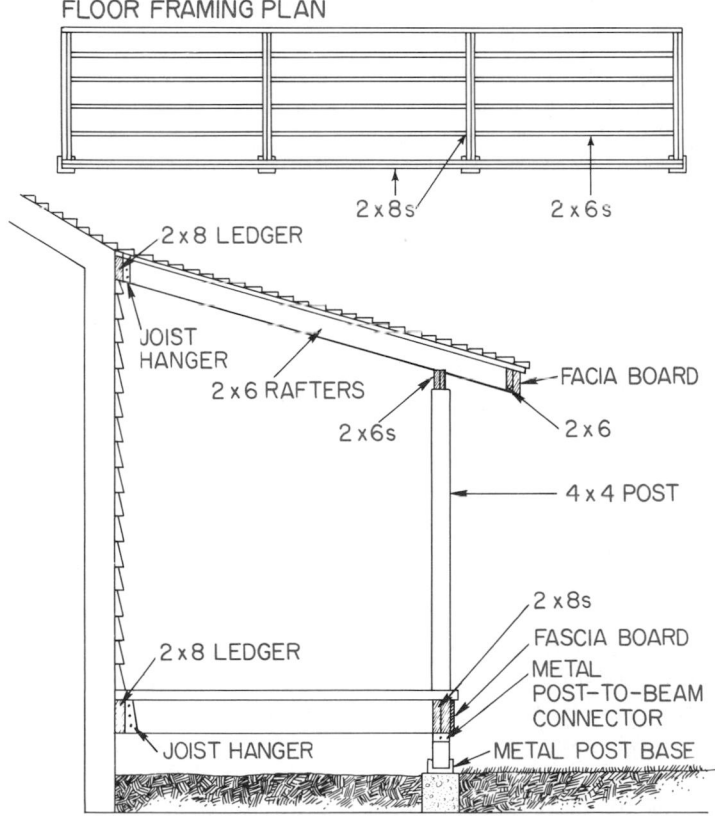

62-7. *The addition of a porch may be desirable.*

be replaced. So may the sinks and plumbing. Kitchen remodeling in an older house is often necessary and often costly. (The same is true in the case of bathroom remodeling.)

➤ Adding a room within an existing structure. An attic, basement, or garage may have space for an additional room. For a room in the attic, it may be necessary to add a dormer. Sometimes a garage can be converted into a room, particularly if the garage is attached to the house. An unfinished basement is one of the best places for expansion. The homeowner should check local building codes, however, to make sure the minimum ceiling height does not exceed the height of the basement. A new entrance to the basement can improve its appearance. A possible problem with a room in the basement is the lack of natural light.

➤ Adding a porch or a deck. Many older homes have no porch or deck. Adding one can improve the appearance of a house and make it more comfortable as well. Fig. 62-7.

THE VALUE OF REMODELING

Before remodeling a house, the homeowner should consider the cost of the project. That figure should be compared to the amount that the project will add to the resale value of the house. Generally speaking, the more that can be recovered in resale, the better the investment.

➤ Adding a room. Adding a room can be a better investment than buying a larger house. Adding a room can allow the homeowner to maintain a low mortgage rate. An attractive addition designed in the same style as the house can increase its resale value by quite a lot. Generally speaking, 55 to 60 percent of the cost of a room addition can be recaptured in the resale of the house. A room addition is a good investment, provided it does not make the house much larger than other homes in the area. If a house is much larger than those around it, its owner will have a hard time selling it for its true value.

➤ Kitchen remodeling. A major remodeling would include new cabinets, counter tops, flooring, appliances, and decorating. Since the kitchen can be a major concern of the homemaker, remodeling it can add greatly to the value of the house. As much as 75 to 80 percent of remodeling costs can be recovered in resale. Remodeling the kitchen, therefore, is a good investment, even if the home is sold soon afterwards.

➤ Bathroom remodeling. This involves new walls, floors, and fixtures. The remodeled bath will not only beautify but also update a home. However, in the short term, only about 30 percent of the cost will be recaptured in resale.

➤ Adding a full bath. A full bath includes a tub and shower, toilet, vanity, sink, and medicine cabinet. An extra bath is an important addition, particularly when there are three bedrooms and only one existing bath. It is a very strong selling feature. From 80 to 100 percent of the cost can be recaptured when selling the home. Fig. 62-8.

➤ Windows and doors. New windows and doors can improve the insulation of a home and reduce heating and air conditioning costs. They can also increase the security of the home. This improvement is an excellent investment for someone planning to keep a home. However, only 25 to 30 percent of the cost will be

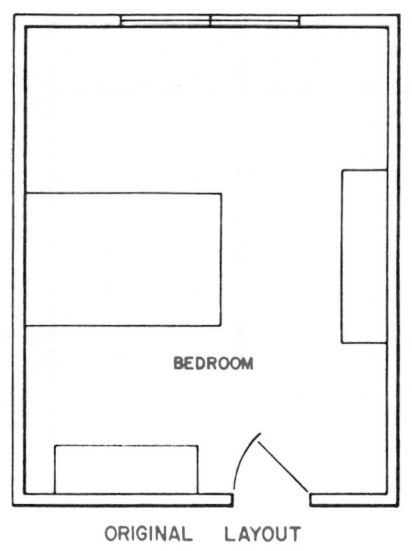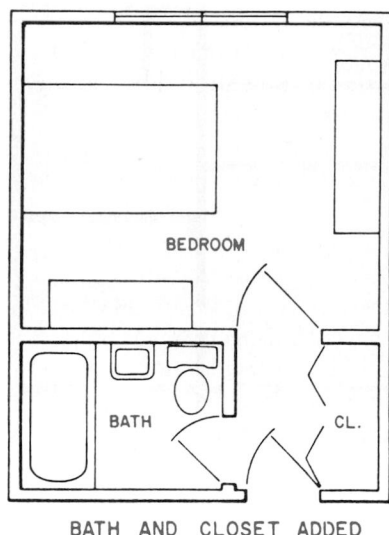

ORIGINAL LAYOUT BATH AND CLOSET ADDED

62-8. *A private bath can add to parents' comfort.*

recovered if the house is sold in a very short time.

➤ Siding. Siding usually includes added insulation plus aluminum or plastic siding. Siding will improve the appearance of a house, make it more maintenance free and increase its energy efficiency. This is a good investment even in the short term since up to 70 percent can be recovered.

➤ Insulation. Adding insulation to levels of R-42 in the attic and R-19 in the walls will improve energy efficiency. Such a project will pay for itself in three to five years. It is a good investment for anyone planning to live in the home for four to five years or more. However, in the shorter term, only about 50 percent will be recovered in the sale price.

➤ Patio and deck. A patio or a deck can be added to the house to improve its appearance and livability. They are of greater value in climates where they can be used more often. They can be good investments in the sun belt states. In colder climates only about 40 to 50 percent of the cost can be recaptured.

ADDING A ROOM

Three steps are necessary when adding a room to an existing house.

1. Do the necessary research to make sure the addition is practical.

2. Do the design to make sure that the addition is going to blend with the existing structure.

3. Do the actual construction.

Research

Check the building codes to be sure the addition will meet the site requirements for your property. The building code will tell you how close the house can be to the property line and how high the building can be. Check the utility lines. They must be available to the addition, and the new construction must not be built over them.

Consider your family's needs carefully during this initial stage. Be sure that the proposed addition will meet all the needs for which it is intended.

Consider the layout of the existing house when planning a

new room. In general, when adding to a home, dens should be near the living room or master bedroom. Family rooms should be placed by the kitchen or dining area. Bedrooms should be off by themselves, not close to the family room. Avoid awkward floor plans, such as a bedroom that opens onto a kitchen or dining area.

It is also important to check structural aspects of your home such as the foundation, framing, roof, and drainage system. You will need to consider such factors in your design plan. After all of these steps are taken, you are ready to do the designing of the addition.

Design

If a set of plans for the house itself is available, they should be used as the basis for the room addition. Determine the scale of the existing plan. Then use squared paper that will fit the same scale. Attach the squared paper to the existing plans where the addition is to take place. Draw to scale a floor plan of the addition, indicating the location of windows, doors, and all other structural details. Once the floor plan is complete, you must design the roof line and the elevation. The roof line should be influenced by the current roof line of your house. The shape (hip, gable, shed) and the pitch of the roof should either duplicate the present roof or harmonize with it. Fig. 62-9. The elevations will show the windows, doors, and other external features. Determine whether the house will be built with the conventional framing pattern or with panelized wall construction. Finally, using the completed design, develop a bill of materials.

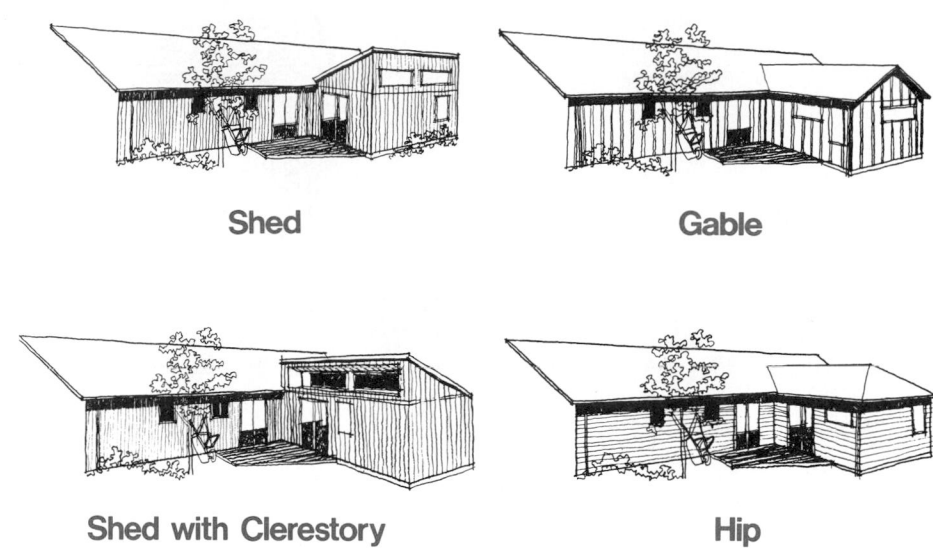

Shed

Gable

Shed with Clerestory

Hip

62-9. *Make sure that the addition follows the same roof line as the home itself.*

Construction

The first step after the plans are approved is to get the necessary building permit. Then the foundation should be planned. It may be slab-on-ground, crawl space, or full basement. The masonry and construction work is done in much the same way as in building a new home. Fig. 62-10.

REMODELING TECHNIQUES

Before doing any remodeling, make a thorough review of the structure. Make sure that you have carefully planned for the work to be done and that the new materials needed will be available. For example, before you begin to remove a wall, be sure to check the location of utilities such as heating, wiring, and plumbing. You could run into a problem that would require moving those lines before remodeling could proceed.

Before beginning any remodeling, review the units in this book on new construction. For windows and doors to be replaced, reread Units 43, 44, and 54.

Demolition Process

The major difference between new construction and remodeling is the demolition. In demolition, the construction process is reversed. Materials are removed, one piece at a time, until the rebuilding can begin. The general procedure is to remove first all hardware, then the trim, then the millwork, such as doors, windows, and flooring, and finally the wall covering and structural parts. If utilities must be removed and replaced, other subcontractors will become involved.

Be sure to consider whether the old materials can be reused. If any original material, such as the trim, can be used again, then demolition must be done with special care. In removing trim around a window or door, for example, start at one corner to lift the trim away from the wall. When the trim is loose, tap it back with a soft-faced mallet.

62-10. *This addition has one wall up even before construction starts. The extension of the existing roof can be done with conventional 2 x 6 rafters. The glass wall opening to the deck makes the project ideal for indoor/outdoor living.*

This will usually expose the finishing nails. These can be then removed one at a time with a hammer or heavy pliers. By using this technique, you will not crack the trim as you pull it away from the frame.

Replacing Windows

Doors and windows are often replaced to increase the energy efficiency of a house and improve its appearance. Before you begin, measure carefully the width and height of the opening of the door or window. Find out if you can obtain replacements that will fit into the existing opening.

Removing Old Windows. The basic procedures for removing all types of windows are about the same. Since double-hung windows are most common, they will be used as an illustration. Fig. 62-11. Run a razor blade around the casing (trim) to make a clean break from the paint or wallpaper. Remove the inside stops around the window with a pry bar or wide chisel. Remove the interior casing around the window. Raise the lower sash and remove the apron and stool. Now check carefully to see how the window unit is held in place. In older windows, the jambs are nailed directly into the studs. In newer types that were installed as a total unit, the window is held in place by nails driven into the outside casing. If the older type is being removed, drive the nails through the jamb using a nail set and hammer.

Sometimes it may be necessary to chisel the wood around the head and pull the nail out with a hammer or pliers. It may also be necessary to use a thin hacksaw blade to cut thin nails between the jamb and studs. If the nails are in the exterior casing, drive them through with a nail set and hammer or remove them from the outside. Now remove the window unit from the outside of the house.

Installing a Window. Select the correct size and kind of window. Often a different style is selected. Make sure the unit will fit the existing opening. Install the window unit from the outside, and nail it in place. Figs. 62-12. Caulk around the outside of the unit. From the inside, place insulation

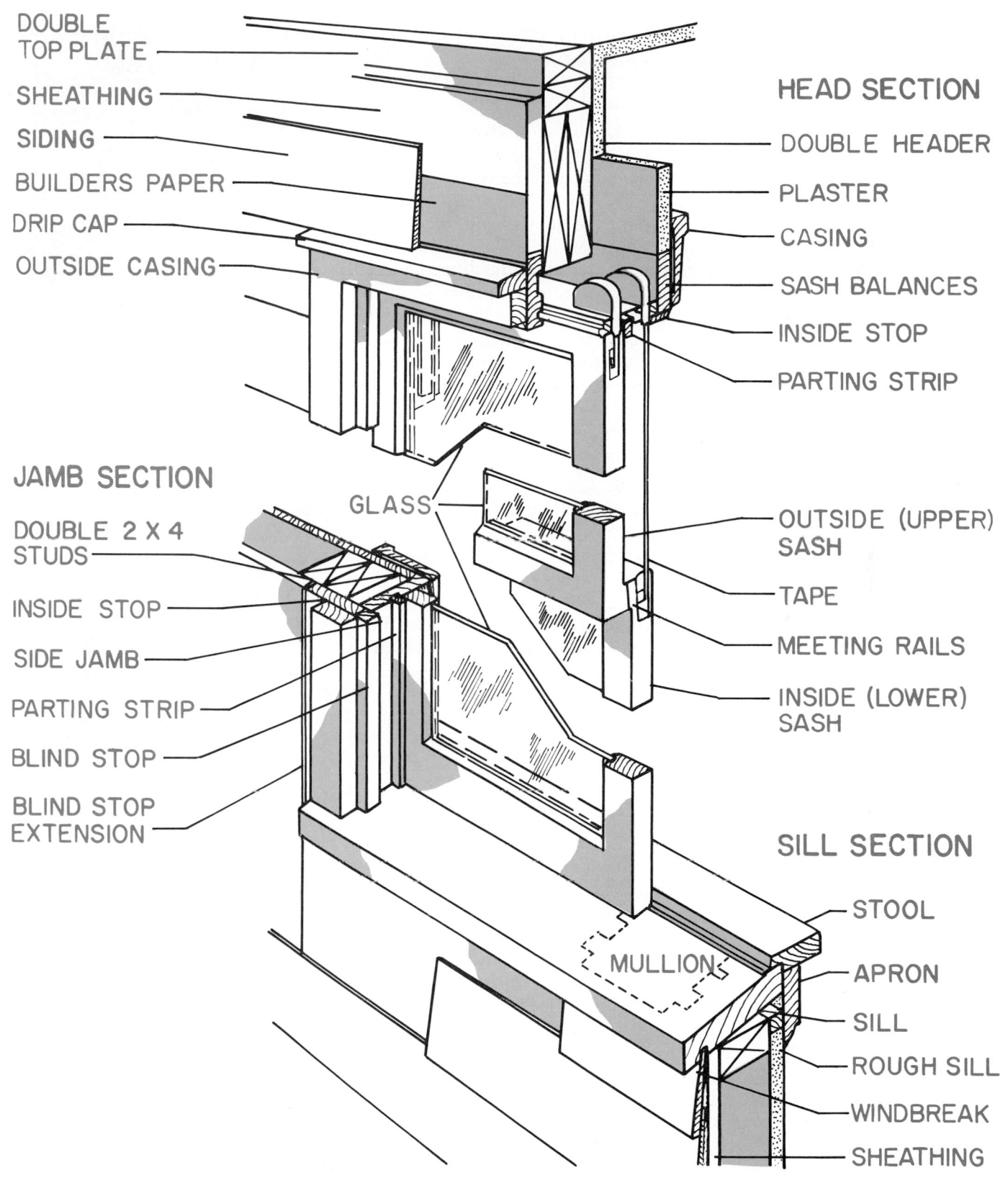

DOUBLE TOP PLATE

SHEATHING

SIDING

BUILDERS PAPER

DRIP CAP

OUTSIDE CASING

HEAD SECTION

DOUBLE HEADER

PLASTER

CASING

SASH BALANCES

INSIDE STOP

PARTING STRIP

JAMB SECTION

DOUBLE 2 X 4 STUDS

INSIDE STOP

SIDE JAMB

PARTING STRIP

BLIND STOP

BLIND STOP EXTENSION

GLASS

OUTSIDE (UPPER) SASH

TAPE

MEETING RAILS

INSIDE (LOWER) SASH

MULLION

SILL SECTION

STOOL

APRON

SILL

ROUGH SILL

WINDBREAK

SHEATHING

62-11. *Parts of a double-hung window. There are two sash that slide up and down in the grooves of the frame. The sash can be opened from either the top or the bottom. In some types, the sash can be removed for cleaning. Balances at the sides support the sash and make them easier to raise.*

62-12. *Cordless drills are very useful in window installation.*

around the window between the jambs and the rough opening. Then add the inside trim (casing).

Replacing Doors

There are two common ways of replacing old doors. You can replace the door only using the existing door frame, or you can replace the entire door and frame with a prehung door. Some prehung doors are designed to fit into the existing door frame.

Fitting and Hanging a Wood Door.

1. Remove the old door.

2. Check jambs and stop; they should be square and plumb. Before trimming a door to proper height, measure the inside of the jamb from floor to header. Do not go by the measurements of the door being replaced, as they may not be accurate. Measure both the height and width in several places, as the jamb may be out of square. Allow

room at the bottom for the sill or carpet. No more than ¾" should be trimmed from the width with a maximum of ⅜" from each side.

3. Use a fine tooth saw for trimming the door to proper height, across the grain of the stiles. A wood plane can be used for minor trimming to width. Otherwise a circular saw can be used to achieve the desired bevel. The best rule is to allow approximately 3/16" clearance under perfectly dry conditions. (Weatherstripping may require more trimming, depending upon the type used, but do not trim for weatherstripping until the door is hung and operational.)

4. Use three hinges on doors less than 7' high, four on doors over 7'. Position the top hinge 7" from the top and the bottom hinge 11" from the bottom. Use a sharp wood chisel (or a special tool made for this purpose) to cut insets for the hinges in the door stile and door jamb. Fig. 62-13. Check frequently that the hinges are installed in a straight line to prevent binding. Hang the door on its hinges and make final trim adjustments for a precise fit before installing the lockset.

5. When installing a lockset, follow the manufacturer's instructions and use the template provided for drilling and cutting holes. Fig. 62-14. Bore from one side of the door until the point of the hole saw protrudes from the opposite side. Then reverse the procedure and complete boring the holes from the other side. Fig. 62-15. Bore the holes from the edge of the door. Fig. 62-16. Use a sharp wood chisel to cut away wood. Leave at least 1" of solid wood in the stile behind the lockset to maintain the strength of the door. Take care in installing the striker plate accurately.

62-13. *Cutting the gains for hinges.*

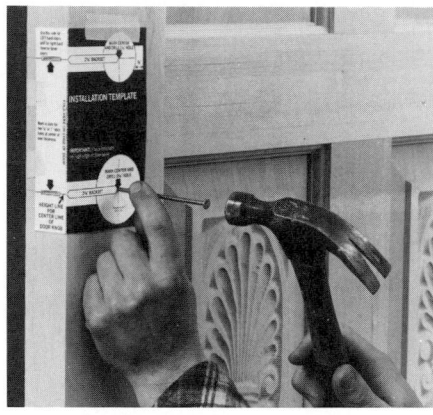

62-14. *Marking the location for the lockset.*

62-15. *Boring holes for the lockset.*

62-16. *Boring holes from the edge of the door.*

Installing a Prehung Door.
Prehung door units come in many sizes and styles. Indoor units are all-wood construction. Exterior door units may have a wood frame with a steel door that has an insulated core. When selecting the unit, consider its type, size, and design. Consider also the swing of the door and the kind of hardware needed. To install a prehung door, remove the casing, the old door and the door frame. (Some units are designed to fit into the old door frame, so check for this before buying the door.) Replace with a prehung door following the instructions in Unit 54.

Installing a New Door in an Existing Wall

Before beginning the job, check the following:
➤ Will it be an interior or exterior door?
➤ Will the door be installed in a bearing or non-bearing wall? All outside walls are bearing walls and one or more inside walls may be also. Usually if only one or two studs need to be removed, it will not be necessary to shore up the wall. However, shoring will always be necessary if a double-hung door is installed.
➤ What size will the door be?

Check Unit 54 for door sizes. The door opening is determined by the overall size of the door frame and the location of the studs. Usually the smallest rough opening must be 4" wider and 2" to 4" higher than the door frame size.
➤ Where are the utilities such as wiring, plumbing, or heating ducts? Avoid cutting a door where plumbing and heating ducts might be located. A single electrical wire running through the area can be moved. An electrical outlet will present a greater problem.
➤ Where are the studs in the wall? You can locate the studs in several different ways. The simplest method is to use a magnetic or electronic stud finder. You can also check carefully for taped wall joints or nails in the trim to help locate the studs. Still another method is to measure either 16" or 24" from the corner of the room and tap the surface with the handle of a hammer until you hear a solid sound. Whenever possible, the door opening should start from one side of a stud so that not more than two studs will have to be removed to install a single door.

Cutting the Opening for the Door.
1. Carefully mark the outline of the rough opening on one wall. If an outside door is to be installed, start the job on the inside wall. Check the lines with a plumb and level.

2. IF THERE IS ANY DANGER THAT AN ELECTRICAL WIRE RUNS THROUGH THIS AREA, TURN OFF THE APPROPRIATE CIRCUIT. Cut an inspection opening near the middle of the outline. An 8" × 8" opening is about the right size. Mark this opening and drill a starting hole at each corner. Use a wallboard saw to cut the drywall at an angle so that the opening can be closed, if

necessary, by replacing the original drywall or cutting a new piece to fit. If the wall is insulated, remove as much as possible.

3. Inspect the interior by shining a light into the opening to observe the location of the studs or any electrical wires. Another method is to use a stiff wire (a straightened wire coat hanger will do) to "fish" around the opening to locate the studs and any electric wire. If necessary, move the rough opening to the right or left a few inches so that one side of the rough opening will be next to a stud.

4. Drill starting holes in the upper corners and just above the floor trim for the rough opening.

5. Cut the drywall with a drywall saw, a portable saber saw, or a reciprocating saw. If electricity is needed, use a long extension cord plugged into a live circuit. It is a good idea to use a metal cutting saw blade on power saws. Cut along a straight line from corner to corner. If you hit a stud, tip the power saw slightly. When the cut is complete, remove the drywall in large sections, exposing the studs. Use a hand saw to cut the section of the floor trim and sole plate, including the base board and shoe. Check to see if an electric wire runs through the opening. When necessary, this wire can be spliced and run over the door frame to complete the circuit.

6. Now cut open the opposite wall in a similar manner.

7. Cut off and remove parts of the studs. This is best done by first cutting through the center of each stud. Then cut and remove each section of the studs for the opening.

8. To install an exterior door, the finished floor and subfloor must be notched out. Sometimes the joists must also be notched so that the sill will be even with the finished floor.

9. Rough in the opening and hang the door. (See Units 44 and 54.)

Changing Partitions

Often rooms are not the right size and it may be necessary to remove some partitions. This is not difficult if the partition is a non-bearing wall and if plumbing, electrical, and heating utilities are not involved.

All outside walls and usually the center interior partition parallel to the long side of the structure are bearing walls. To determine whether a wall is load-bearing, check the direction of the floor and ceiling joists. Partitions parallel to the joists are usually non-bearing walls. Fig. 62-17. However, the wall may support a second floor load, so that must be checked. In most house construction, when the second floor joists are perpendicular to the partition, the joists require support. The walls, therefore, are load bearing. An exception occurs when trusses are used instead of the traditional roof framing. If the trusses span the total width of the building, then all interior partitions are non-load

62-18. *The center partition will be load-bearing. Note how the joists are spliced over the girder.*

bearing. If joists are spliced over a girder, then the wall below and often the wall above are bearing walls. Fig. 62-18. The same is true for ceiling joists.

Removing Part or All of a Bearing Wall. To change partitions or to cut a large opening to a new room addition, it is often necessary to remove part or all of a bearing wall. Any load-bearing wall must be shored up (temporarily supported) before it can be removed. If it is an outside wall,

then shoring is needed only on the inside. If the bearing wall is on the inside, then shoring is needed on both sides of the wall. If a bearing wall is to be removed from the second floor, it is a good practice to start the shoring at the basement level. Before deciding on the shoring to use, review these definitions:

➤ Brace or bracing is a piece of wood or other material that helps to hold the total unit in place and resists weight or pressure.

➤ Shore is a prop placed against or beneath an object to support it.

➤ Shore head is a horizontal, heavy wood beam placed across a shore or shores.

➤ Shoring is a temporary support that is used for many purposes such as the removal of a bearing wall.

➤ Beam bottom or mudsill is a heavy wood beam or plank of wood which supports the shore or shores.

➤ Stringer is a heavy wood beam placed across the top of several shores as a horizontal support.

➤ Wedge is a tapered piece of wood or metal used to tighten the shoring.

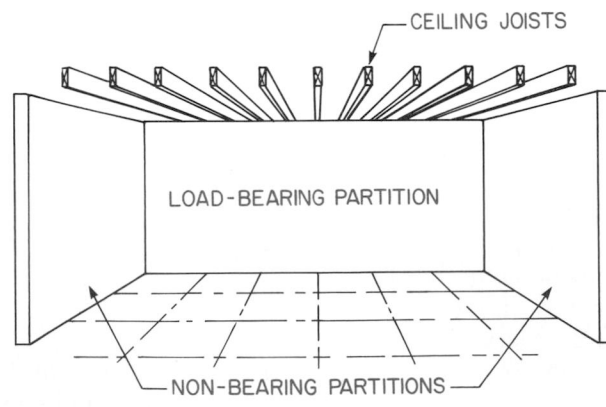

62-17. *Load bearing and nonbearing partitions. A second-floor load may place a load on any partition.*

There are several kinds of shoring that can be used:

➤ A temporary wall (called falsework) built ½" to 1" less than the ceiling height. Wedges are used to "block in place" the temporary wall so that it will give firm support to the ceiling. Fig. 62-19.

➤ A T-shore using wedges. Fig. 62-20.

➤ Jack posts (house jacks) between the shore head and the beam bottom or mudsill. Fig. 62-21.

➤ A patented shore device (adjustable) instead of house jacks. Fig. 62-22.

➤ Steel posts between the shore head and the beam bottom or mudsill.

Erect the shoring. Make sure the shoring is supported by several joists. At times, such as when cutting an opening in the outside end wall of the house, the shoring may be parallel to the joists. In such cases, place heavy plywood on the floor so that the weight is distributed over several joists. To protect the finished floor and ceiling, place scraps of rugs or towels over and under the shoring. Locate the shoring about 2' away from the wall so that you can work between the shoring and wall. Use wedges or adjust the shoring to bring the unit to full height for solid support.

Once the shoring is in place, remove the wall as you would a non-bearing wall.

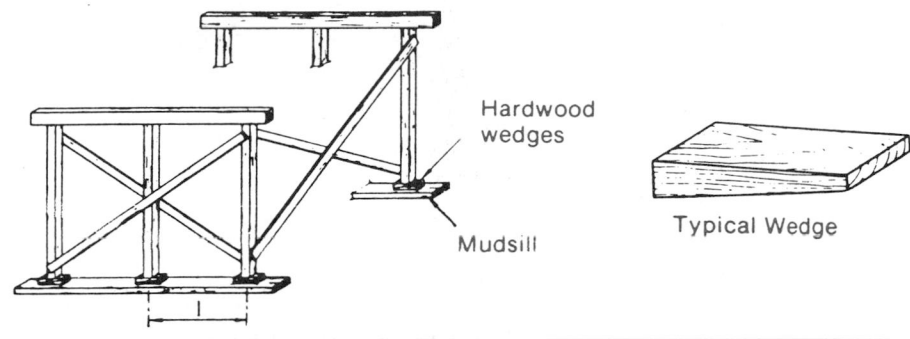

62-19. If an inside bearing wall is to be removed, use two temporary walls to support both sides. If there is a door in the wall, it is a good idea to brace the two temporary walls together.

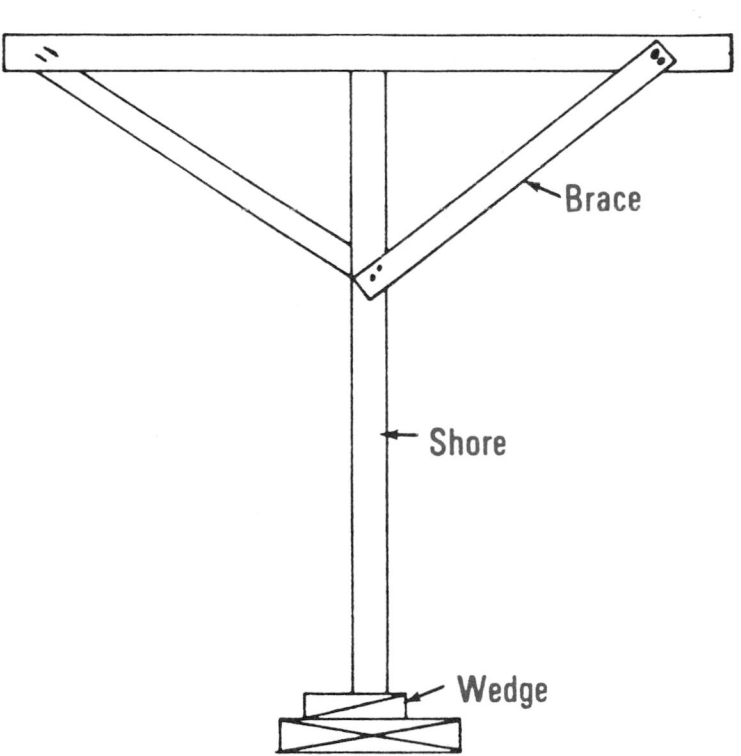

62-20. A T-shore can be used when cutting a small opening or for supporting large sheets of drywall or panel that are attached to the ceiling after the wall is removed.

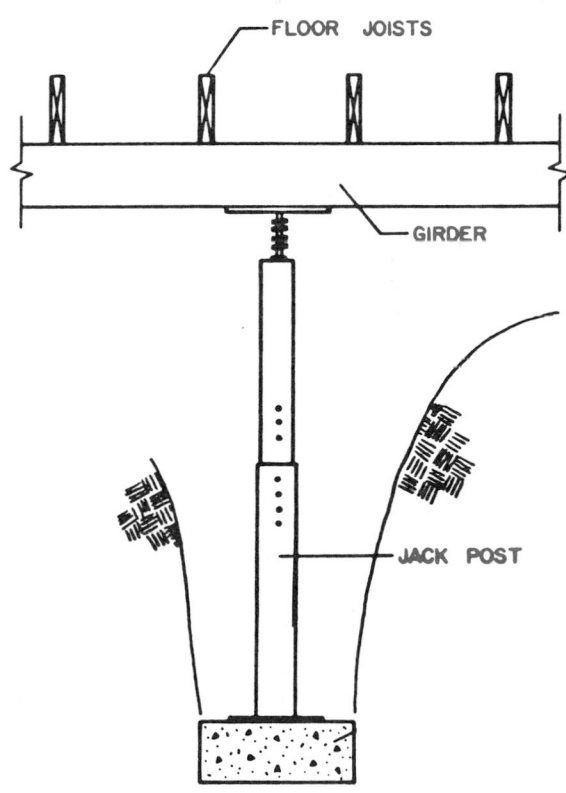

62-21. Jack posts can be used for temporary shoring. In an old house they can also be used to prop up a sagging floor.

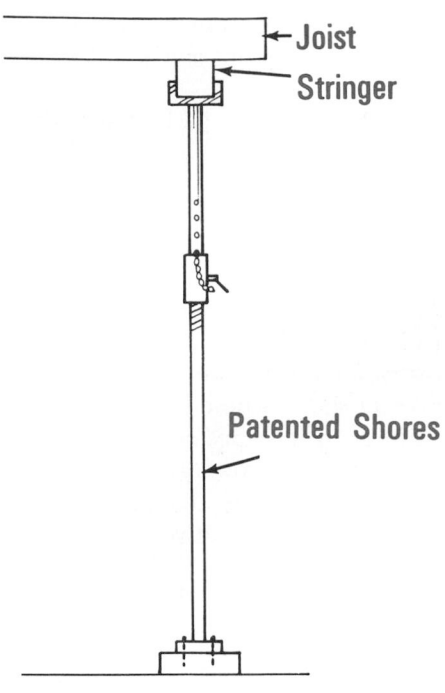

Joist
Stringer
Patented Shores

62-22. *Patented shores can be purchased or rented for remodeling.*

To take out a bearing wall, carefully remove the trim around any doors and along the flooring and ceiling. Remove the hardware and then the door. Remove the door frame. Then remove the drywall from both sides of the wall.

The correct way to remove the structural wall depends on how the wall was assembled. If the studs are nailed through the top plate and toenailed through the sole plate, use a pry bar or nail remover to take out the lower nails. Then pull the stud out from the top plate. If the wall was preassembled before erection using a nailing machine, the best approach is not to try to save the studs. Cut across the middle of each stud and remove each piece, one at a time. However, if a reciprocating saw with a metal cutting blade is available, cut the studs just below the top plate and just above the sole plate and remove the major portion of the studs, which then can be reused.

After the studs are removed, pry loose the sole plate and remove the top plate. If the ends are tied to the side walls, cut them flush with the wall. After the wall is removed, the ceiling, walls, and floor will require repair where the partition intersected them.

REPAIRS

There are hundreds of major and minor repair jobs that need to be done to keep a housing unit in good condition. Smaller repairs can be done by the home owner using one of the many books on home repair. Some major repairs, such as those described here, can be done by a general carpenter. Other major repairs and improvements are best left to skilled specialists. Such jobs include reroofing, installing new siding (usually of metal or plastic), replacing gutters and downspouts, and installing insulation.

Repairing Roof Leaks

When a leak develops, it must be repaired immediately. Even a small leak will cause damage such as discoloration of the ceiling and walls or stains on the finish flooring. If the leak is left unattended, the ceiling and wall will become so damp that parts or all of both will need to be replaced.

Locating a Roof Leak. It is very difficult to locate the point of leakage from the wet spot that appears on the ceiling. This is because the water will follow the rafters or trusses before dripping down on the ceiling or wall. If the attic is heavily insulated, the leakage can continue for some time before it appears on the inside of the house. It is also very difficult to locate the hole from the top of the roof.

If the rafters or trusses are exposed, the best method is to locate the holes from inside the attic on a very bright day. Even a small hole will be visible. Its location should be marked by pushing a small nail or wire through to the roof surface. Leaks can also be detected during a rain storm using a bright flashlight to check the attic. First, watch where the water starts to drip on the ceiling and then work back to where the leak starts. The rafter or truss will be wet up to the place where the leak begins.

Repairing Shingle Roofs. Make the repairs following the directions and the detailed steps shown in Fig. 62-23.

➤ Wood Shingles. If the shingle is cracked, it is better to repair the crack than replace the shingle. If the crack is small (¼" or less), pull out loose splinters so that only the large, solid pieces remain. Check the roofing material under the shingles to determine where the nails should go. Sometimes shingles are nailed to wood slats spaced 4" or 5" apart (Fig. 1). Sometimes they are nailed to wood sheathing. After the loose splinters are removed, butt the solid pieces tightly together and nail the split shingle together with galvanized roofing nails (Fig. 2). Do not drive the heads of the nails into the shingle and damage its surface. Cover the crack fully with asphalt roofing cement. Apply a dab of cement over the nailheads (Fig. 3).

If the crack is wide, add a sheet metal patch. To do this, drive a square piece of sheet metal up under the cracked shingle (Fig. 4). Make sure that the top of the sheet metal goes beyond the upper edge of the crack. Now complete the job as described above for the small crack.

If shingles are damaged beyond repair, replace them. This can be

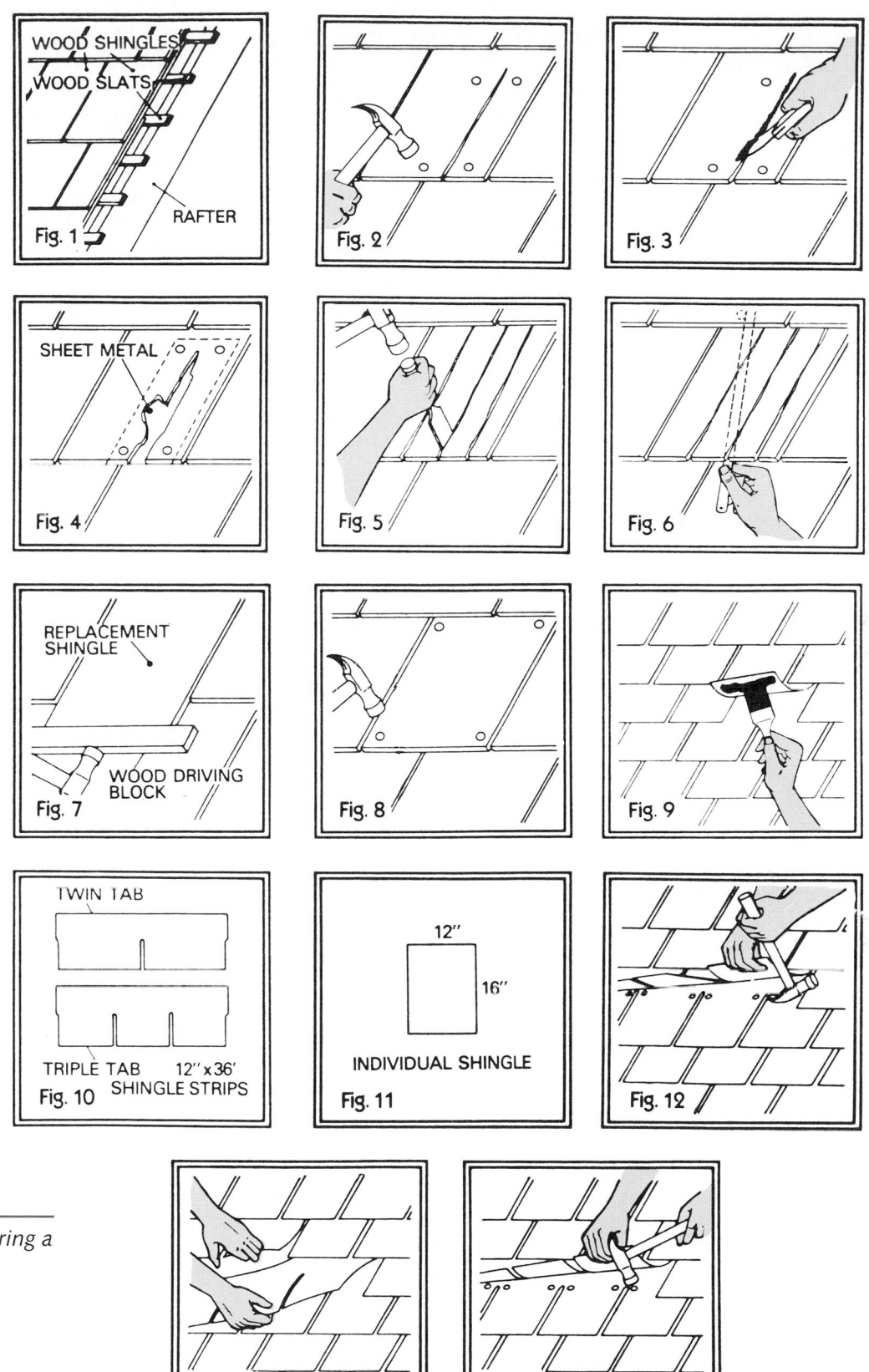

62-23. *Repairing a shingled roof.*

Fig. 1 — WOOD SHINGLES, WOOD SLATS, RAFTER

Fig. 2

Fig. 3

Fig. 4 — SHEET METAL

Fig. 5

Fig. 6

Fig. 7 — REPLACEMENT SHINGLE, WOOD DRIVING BLOCK

Fig. 8

Fig. 9

Fig. 10 — TWIN TAB, TRIPLE TAB, 12" x 36" SHINGLE STRIPS

Fig. 11 — 12", 16", INDIVIDUAL SHINGLE

Fig. 12

Fig. 13

Fig. 14

more tricky than repairing a cracked shingle. Using a screwdriver or chisel, cut the damaged shingle into smaller pieces that can be removed by pulling with your fingers (Fig. 5). Remove the damaged shingle. Using a hacksaw blade, cut the nails off flush with the wood slats or sheathing (Fig. 6). Since shingles overlap, you may have to pry up the shingle above to get at all the nails. Take care not to crack the good shingle. Measure the empty space and cut a replacement shingle to fit the space. Using a block of wood and hammer, drive the replacement shingle into place (Fig. 7). Nail the new shingle in place with galvanized roofing nails (Fig. 8). Apply a dab of asphalt cement to cover the nailheads.

➤ Asphalt Shingles. Locate the damaged area and examine the condition. If the shingle does not need replacing, simply raise the damaged or torn shingle and apply an ample amount of asphalt cement to the underside (Fig. 9). Press the shingle firmly into place and nail it down with broad-headed, galvanized or aluminum roofing nails. (Always remember to apply asphalt cement to the nailheads.)

If the shingle needs replacing, select a strip the same as the piece to be replaced. Your asphalt roofing will usually come in shingle strips (Fig. 10). Some roofing is in single, separate shingles (Fig. 11). Raise the shingles above the damaged one. Pull the nails from the damaged shingles with the claw hammer (Fig. 12). If nails cannot be reached with a hammer, cut them off with a hacksaw blade. Remove the damaged shingle, and slip the new shingle into place (Fig. 13). Nail the new shingle in place with roofing nails, placing two nails in each tab (Fig. 14). The shingle should be "blind nailed." This means that the nails should be

covered by the upper shingles when they are lowered into place. Apply a dab of asphalt cement over the nailheads and lower the upper shingles into place.

Repairing Siding

Make the repairs following the directions and the detailed steps shown in Fig. 62-24.

➤ Warped Boards (or Wood Shingles). Use screws, rather than nails, to straighten a warped board. First, drill guide holes for the screws into the thicker portion of the board (Fig. 1). Then drill the larger holes to countersink the screws. Pull the warped board into line by tightening the screws into the sheathing (Fig. 2). Cover the head of each screw with putty.

➤ Split Boards (or Wood Shingles). First, cut a piece of building paper to slip underneath the split board or shingle. Make it wide enough to fit between the in-place nails. Butt the two halves of the split shingle tightly together. Then nail both halves into place with galvanized or aluminum roofing nails. Countersink the nailheads and cover them with putty.

➤ Damaged Wood Shingles. First, using the chisel and hammer, splinter the shingle into small, slender pieces (Fig. 3). Carefully remove the splintered pieces so as not to damage the remaining shingles. Pull the exposed nails with a claw hammer. Examine the building paper underneath and patch any tears or cuts with asphalt cement (Fig. 4). Slip the new shingle into position (Fig. 5). Nail the shingle in place with galvanized or aluminum shingle nails (Fig. 6).

➤ Damaged Wood Siding. Instead of replacing the entire siding board, it is easier to cut out the damaged portion. Using the square, mark the board for cut lines

(Fig. 7). Pry up the bottom edge of the board and insert wedges underneath (Fig. 8). Using the saw, cut out the damaged portion of the siding (Fig. 9). Make the cut carefully. Don't damage siding boards above or below. Splinter the damaged portion into smaller pieces, using the hammer and chisel. Remove the pieces with a pry bar or chisel. Remove the remaining nails with the claw hammer.

Examine the building paper underneath. Patch any tears or cuts with asphalt cement. (Use asphalt cement sparingly, as too much will prevent "breathing" of the exterior.)

Measure the damaged board opening, mark the saw cut lines, and cut the replacement board to fit the opening. Slip the new board into position and drive it into place with the hammer. Hammer against a small wood block to avoid damaging the board (Fig. 10). Nail the board in place with galvanized siding nails, using the existing nailing pattern.

➤ Damaged Asphalt Shingles. Remove the damaged shingle by simply shattering it with the hammer. If the shingle is not brittle enough to shatter, splinter it into pieces. Remove the shingle pieces and the exposed nails. Drill the nail holes in the new shingle at its lower edge. Position the holes as they were in the old shingle. Patch any tears or cuts in the exposed building paper with asphalt cement (Fig. 4). Slip the new shingle into position (Fig. 5) and nail it in place with galvanized or aluminum shingle nails (Fig. 6).

Repairing Drywall

Gypsum drywall is the most common interior wall surface now used in residential construction. It is inexpensive and easy to install. Another advantage is that drywall

62-24. *Repairing siding.*

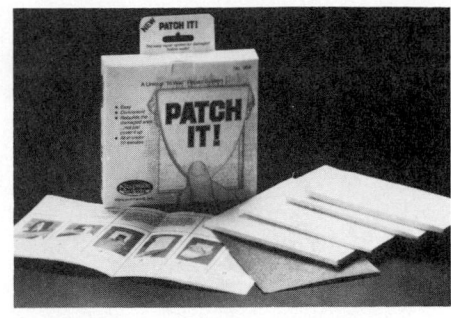

62-25. *A patching kit for drywall repairs.*

can be patched relatively easily. This is a particular advantage during remodeling, when such things as electrical outlets may have to be moved.

Commercially manufactured patching kits are available for drywall. Fig. 62-25. The photos in Fig. 62-26 show a sequence for patching a hole.

INSTALLING SUSPENDED CEILINGS

Suspended ceilings consist of panels held in place by a grid system at a desired distance from the existing ceiling structure. Fig. 62-27. The panels are made of fiberglass or plastic and are 24" × 48" or smaller. The grid system which supports these panels includes main runners, cross tees, and wall molding. Main runners are usually 12' long and are spaced 2' or 4' on center. Cross tees are installed at right angles to the main runners. There are many types of suspended ceiling grid components. Two kinds are shown in Fig. 62-28.

The suspended ceiling reduces noise in two ways. It absorbs a large amount of the noise striking its surface. Also, because of its suspension, it does not transmit the sound vibrations into the framing above as readily as materials

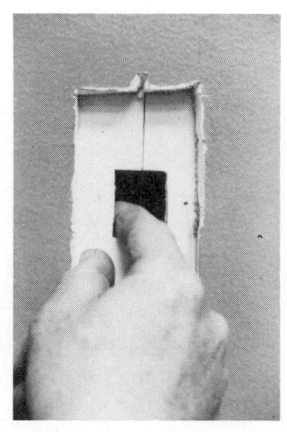

62-26. *Repairing drywall. An adhesive-coated backing board is inserted into the wall and pulled against the backside of the drywall. A filler panel is then adhered to the backing board and the gaps are spackled.*

62-27. *A suspended ceiling system with 2' x 4' drop-in panels. The embossed swirl design gives the effect of a notch-troweled plaster ceiling.*

applied directly to framing.

A suspended ceiling is easily and quickly installed. It conveniently covers up bare joists, exposed pipes, and wiring and it may be used to lower a high ceiling. Accessibility to unsightly valves, switches and controls hidden by the suspended ceiling is no problem because the panel in question can merely be slid to one side.

The first step when installing a suspended ceiling is to determine the ceiling height. Sometimes, such as for a basement ceiling, it is desirable that the ceiling be as high as possible to provide maximum headroom. Care should be taken, however, to keep the top edges of

the grid system at least 2" to 2½" below the bottom of the framing. This space is necessary for the insertion of the ceiling panels after the grid system is in place.

Mark or snap a level chalk line on each wall of the room, ¾" (the width of the wall molding) above the intended height. This permits the wall molding to be installed below the chalk line and eliminates any undesirable marks on the wall below the ceiling level after installation is completed. To insure a level ceiling, check these lines carefully with a carpenter's level.

Determining Room Layout

First determine the direction of the main runners. In most cases, the main runners should be installed perpendicular to the ceiling joists and parallel to the long wall.

Determine where the first main runner will be placed. To locate the distance of the first main runner from the long wall, proceed as follows:

1. Measure the length of one of the short walls and convert to inches.

2. Divide this figure by 48".

3. Take the number of inches left over (if any), and add 48" to it.

4. Divide this figure by 2.

You now have the distance that the first main runner should be placed from the long wall. This also will be the size of the long wall border panel. Example:

Short wall = 10'4" = 124"
Divide: 124 ÷ 48 = 2,
            remainder 28
Add: 28" + 48" = 76"
Divide: 76 ÷ 2 = 38", the
            distance of main
            runner and long
            wall border panel size

Slide Lock

A. Main runner with splicer attached

B. Cross tees—2-foot—4-foot

C. Wall molding

Custom Grid

A. Main runner with splicer attached

B. Cross tees—2-foot—4-foot

C. Wall molding

62-28. *Two of the many types of suspended ceiling grid components.*

NOTE: When using 24" × 24" ceiling panels, divide by 24" and add 24" instead of 48".

Measure out this exact distance (in the example, 38") on both short walls from the long wall. Fasten reference string A at the ceiling height line and stretch it between the two points. The first main runner will eventually be placed along this string. Fig. 62-29.

To determine the short wall border panel size and the location of cross tees, follow these steps:

1. Measure the length of one of the long walls and convert to inches.

2. Divide this figure by 24".

3. Take the number of inches left over (if any), and add 24" to it.

4. Divide this figure by 2.

Example:

Long wall = 18'8" = 224"
Divide: 224 ÷ 24 = 9,
             remainder 8
Add: 8" + 24" = 32"
Divide: 32 ÷ 2 = 16" Distance
             of first cross tee and
             short wall border
             panel size

Measure out this exact distance (in the example, 16") on both long walls from the short walls. Fasten a second reference string, B, at the ceiling height line between these two points. Fig. 62-29. The first row of cross tees will be installed in line with this string.

Since walls are seldom perfectly straight, it is imperative that the second reference string be perpendicular to the first. When stretching this string, make certain that it is exactly at a 90° angle.

Installing Wall Molding

Fasten the metal molding to the walls, making certain that the top of the molding is in line with the level chalk mark. Fig. 62-30a. If the molding cannot be nailed directly to the wall, hang a suspended main runner in place of the regular wall molding. For inside corners, lap one piece of molding over the other. Outside corners are formed by mitering the two wall moldings or by overlapping. Fig. 62-30b. If the molding is to be nailed to a cinderblock wall, use concrete stud nails. Drive the nail between the mortar joint and the edge of the cinder block.

Installing Main Runners

To insure that the short wall border panels are of equal size, the main runners must be accurately cut. To cut a main runner, follow these steps.

1. Subtract the short wall border measurement from 24". (In the example this measurement was 16"; 16" from 24" equals 8".)

2. Add 6" to remaining inches (6" + 8" = 14").

3. Cut the main runner by this amount. (In the example, the main runner is cut 14" from the end.) A, Fig. 62-31. NOTE: Be sure that a cross tee tab falls directly above

Main Runners

Cross Tees

Long Wall

38"

Joists

90°

Reference String "B"

16"

Reference String "A"

Short Wall

62-29. *Layout details for a 10'4" x 18' 8" suspended ceiling using 24" x 48" panels.*

reference string B. Figs. 62-29 and 62-31.

The main runners are suspended from the joists by hanger wires. To find the location of the first hanger wire, rest the cut end of the runner on the wall molding and directly above reference string A. See B, Fig. 62-31. Directly above any hole near the uncut end of the main runner, fasten the first hanger wire to the existing ceiling structure. Run the wire through the hole in

62-30a. *Nailing the wall molding*

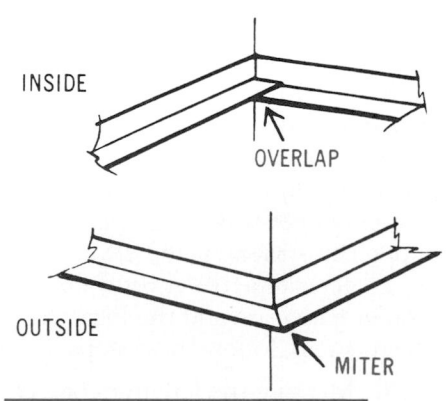

INSIDE

OVERLAP

OUTSIDE

MITER

62-30b. *Wall molding corner details.*

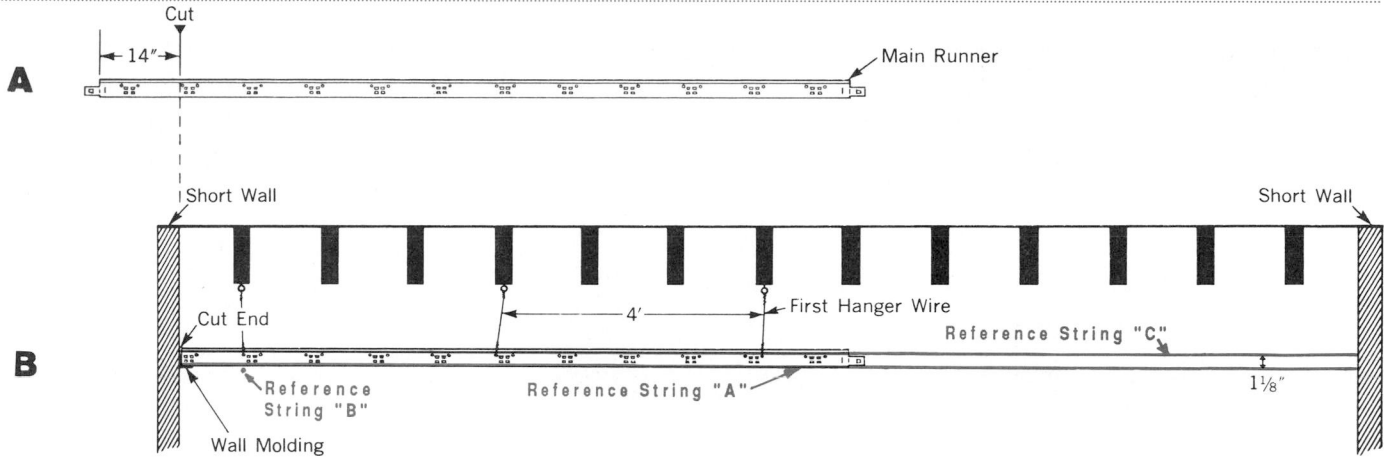

62-31. *Laying out the main runner for the room. Fig. 62-29. A. Fourteen inches should be cut from the end of the main runner. This end will rest on the wall molding. B. Suspend the main runner from the joists with wire. Use a string pulled taut to align the main runner. Make certain that the cross tee tab connection is located directly above the reference string B. This is essential so that a cross tee will be properly located to provide support for the border tile.*

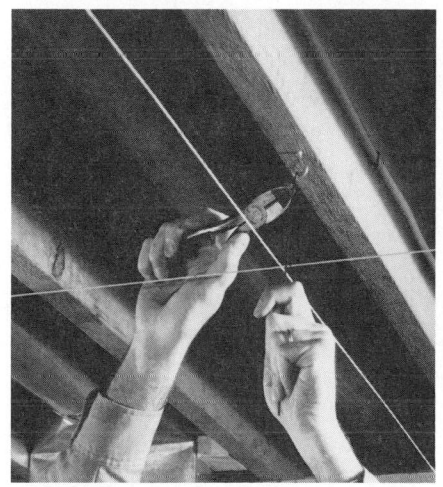

62-32. *The hanger wires are attached to the joists at 4' intervals.*

the main runner, but do not attach it permanently. Install the other hanger wires for this runner at 4' intervals.

Attach wires to the ceiling structure at each main runner location. Place them in line with the wires attached to the first main runner. Figs. 62-31 and 62-32.

To insure that all main runners will be perfectly level, follow these steps:

1. Stretch a string across all hanger wires in the direction of the main runner. Attach each reference string so that it is in line with the holes in the runner to which the hanger wires will be attached. Fig. 62-31, string C. For the system shown in Fig. 62-31, these holes should be located 1⅛" above the bottom edge of the runners. Thus string C is 1⅛" above string A. This string must be kept very tight.

2. Make sharp 90° bends where the wires come across the string. The best method is to clamp pliers horizontally to the wire so that the bottom of the pliers is at string level. With the other hand, firmly bend the wire tightly against the bottom of the pliers.

Install the remaining runners that go perpendicular to the joists. Measure each new main runner individually. After cutting a main runner, two of the holes on the runner should be directly above reference string B. Insert a hanger wire into one of these holes. Let one end of the main runner rest on the wall molding and support the other end with a hanger wire.

If the grid is uneven, fasten additional hanger wires as needed

62-33. *Fastening the main runner of the metal framework to the hanger wires.*

to the holes in the main runners. Bend the wire at the top of the hole, insert it through the hole, and wrap any excess wire around itself. Fig. 62-33. More than one runner may be needed to reach the opposite wall. For longer lengths, connect the main runners by inserting the end tabs into precut holes and bending them over.

62-34. *Installing the cross tees between the main runners.*

62-35. *Lay the ceiling panels into the grid formed by the main runners and the cross tees.*

Installing Ceiling Panels

Drop-in panels are installed by resting these units on the flanges of cross tees and main runners. Fig. 62-35. Exercise care when handling ceiling panels to avoid marring the surface. Handle the panels by the edges, keeping the fingers off the finished side of the board as much as possible.

Attaching Cross Tees to Main Runners

The first set of cross tees will be installed directly above reference string B. Figs. 62-29 and 62-31. Follow these steps:

1. Measure the distance from the long wall to reference string A. (In the example, this is 38".)

2. Cut the cross tee to this length and install it.

3. Complete the installation of cross tees above reference string B. Working in the same direction, install the balance of the cross tees in rows across the room. Fig. 62-34. The tees may be 2' or 4' apart.

Depending on the spacing of the main runners, the cross tees may be 24" or 48" long. If the cross tees are 48" long and 24" apart, and 24" × 24" ceiling panels are to be installed, attach 24" cross tees between the 48" cross tees, parallel to the runners.

Cutting the Panels

Measure and cut each of the border panels individually. A panel is cut face up, with a coping saw or a very sharp fiberboard knife.

62-36. *Translucent panels used with recessed lighting fixtures.*

Ceiling Light Fixtures for Use with Suspended Ceilings

Standard ceiling fixtures and chandeliers may be used with a suspended ceiling. Recessed lighting can also be conveniently installed at any point. Simply install any one of several styles of translucent panels in place of a ceiling tile. Fig. 62-36.

Fluorescent lighting fixtures can be suspended from the wood framing between floor joists. Special mounting brackets can also be obtained for attaching the fixture directly to the suspended grid. Some fluorescent fixtures are designed to fit flush against the ceiling surface. Fig. 62-37.

ESTIMATING

To determine the materials necessary to install a suspended ceiling, measure the room carefully. Draw the room outline on a piece of graph paper, with each square representing 2' × 2'. Select the desired grid pattern either for 2' × 4' or 2' × 2' panels. Draw in the main runners perpendicular to the joists and space them either 2' or 4' apart. Be sure to keep the border panels equal on both sides and as large as possible. Draw in the cross tees so that the border panels at the room ends are equal and as large as possible.

For a 2' × 2' pattern, the main runners may be spaced 4' on center with 4' cross tees spaced 2' apart. A 2' cross tee is then inserted between the 4' cross tees. Another pattern for 2' × 2' panels would be to space the main runners 2' apart and to use 2' cross tees also spaced 2' on center.

For 2' × 4' panels, the main runners may be spaced 4' on center, with the cross tees spaced 2' on center. Another method is to space the cross tees 4' on center and the main runners 2' on center.

The wall angle is available in 12' lengths. Measure the perimeter of the room and divide by 12 to determine the number of pieces of wall angle. Add one piece for any portion of a piece.

The main tees (main runners) are also available in 12' lengths. Determine the number of 12' main tees required from the layout. If main tees longer than 12' are required, they may be extended by splicing two or more tees together.

Count the number of 2' cross tees in the layout. When determining the number of 2' cross tees for border panels, no more than two border tees may be cut from any one 2' cross tee. If 4' cross tees are required, count the number shown in the layout. In determining 4' cross tees for border panels, no more than two border tees may be cut from any one 4' cross tee.

Count the number of lighting panels required. The remaining panels are the ceiling panels needed. The border panels are counted as whole panels.

62-37. *A fluorescent lighting fixture hung from the grid system. Special mounting brackets permit the fluorescent lighting fixture to be installed anywhere on the grid system of a suspended ceiling.*

1. What features of a house should you examine during an inspection to see if the house is worth remodeling?

2. What does a leaning roof ridge often indicate about a house?

3. In what three areas of a home can living space often be added without increasing the size of the structure?

4. What two types of remodeling generally prove to be the best investments when a house is resold?

5. What are the three general steps in adding a room to a house?

6. What is the major difference between remodeling and new construction?

7. Why are old doors and windows often replaced?

8. What are two different ways for replacing an old door?

9. Is it necessary to use shoring when installing a single door in an existing wall?

10. How do you determine the difference between a bearing and a non-bearing wall?

11. Briefly explain the process of removing a non-bearing wall.

12. Name three devices that can be used to shore up a bearing wall.

13. Why is the chalk line snapped above the location of the wall moldings for suspended ceilings?

14. Calculate the width of the border tile for a ceiling using 24" × 24" ceiling panels. The room measures 14'6" × 23'4".

15. List some of the lighting systems that can be used with a suspended ceiling.

ACTIVITIES

1. Math. Jose and Sylvia own a home that is thirty-five years old. They plan extensive remodeling and renovation. Their tentative plans include the following with estimated costs: a. room addition ($15,000), b. new windows ($3,500), c. remodeling one bathroom ($1,500), d. installing a new bathroom ($4,000), e. completely remodeling the kitchen ($8,000), f. adding insulation to the attic and sidewalls ($1,200), g. building a patio and deck ($4,500), and h. new shingles for the roof which currently has two layers ($2,400).

a. What is the total estimated cost for the changes?

b. How much of this could be recovered if they sell the house in the next few years? Give a range of dollar amounts.

2. Social Studies. One of the most impressive homes in the United States is the White House in Washington, D.C. What major renovations have been made to this famous building? How much did these renovations cost? What presidents were serving in office at the time these renovations were taking place? What was the most extensive piece of remodeling that took place? How much did that cost?

3. Science. This unit explains several different procedures for remodeling and renovation. The unit also identifies several areas for change (kitchen, bath, porch, etc.) In addition to the stated items for kitchen/bath remodeling, it is often necessary to replace the plumbing pipes as well in older homes with lead or galvanized pipes.

Prepare a table identifying three materials used for plumbing pipes. Include qualifiers in the table for rust prevention, cost, purity of the drinking water, ease of installation, and availability.

4. Language Arts. Leadership requires management skills. The application of these skills will depend on the situation. For example, management skills on the job site may differ in their application from management skills in the office. Management skills in a formal meeting also will be different. If you conduct a formal meeting, you will want to make sure that the meeting is properly organized. An organized meeting requires that everyone who wishes to speak be given the opportunity to speak one at a time and without interruption. These are two of the basic principles of parliamentary procedure set forth in *Robert's Rules of Order*. Obtain a copy of this book from your school or local library. Then write a brief essay, outlining the important rules this book sets forth for the conduct of formal meetings.

Manufactured Housing

For hundreds of years, the only method of building homes was to construct them stick by stick on the site. However, many houses today are built as *manufactured (industrialized) housing*. Fig. 63-1. This means that houses are built in whole or in part on factory assembly lines. One of the reasons for the growth of this industry is that this method of construction is very efficient. Few materials are wasted. Delays caused by weather are minimized. In some cases, there are also considerable cost savings.

This building method reduces the construction process to a series of relatively simple steps. Thus, it requires fewer carpenters and other skilled workers. In spite of this trend, carpentry will continue to be the single largest skilled trade in North America.

HISTORY OF INDUSTRIALIZED HOUSING

Industrialization was introduced to home building in the 1950s when prefabricated trusses became common. Builders and lumber dealers could assemble trusses on a

63-1a. *Many of the components of this handsome post-and-beam cedar home were made in a factory.*

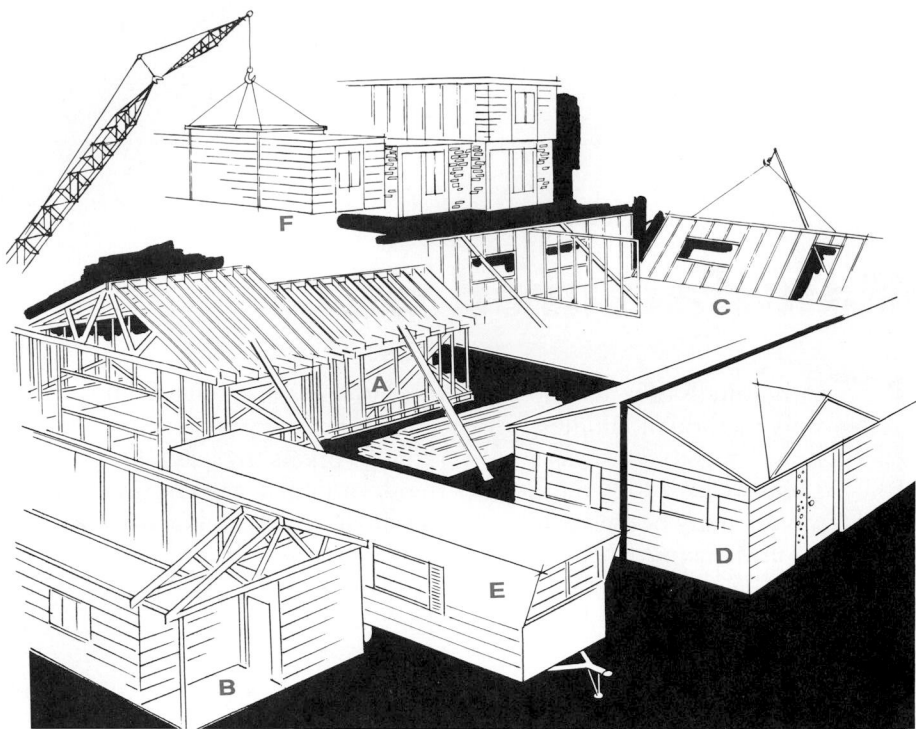

63-1b. *Some of the ways to produce housing: A. Custom "stick-by-stick method." B. Precut with prefabricated parts. C. Panelized. D. Sectional housing. E. Mobile homes. F. Modular units.*

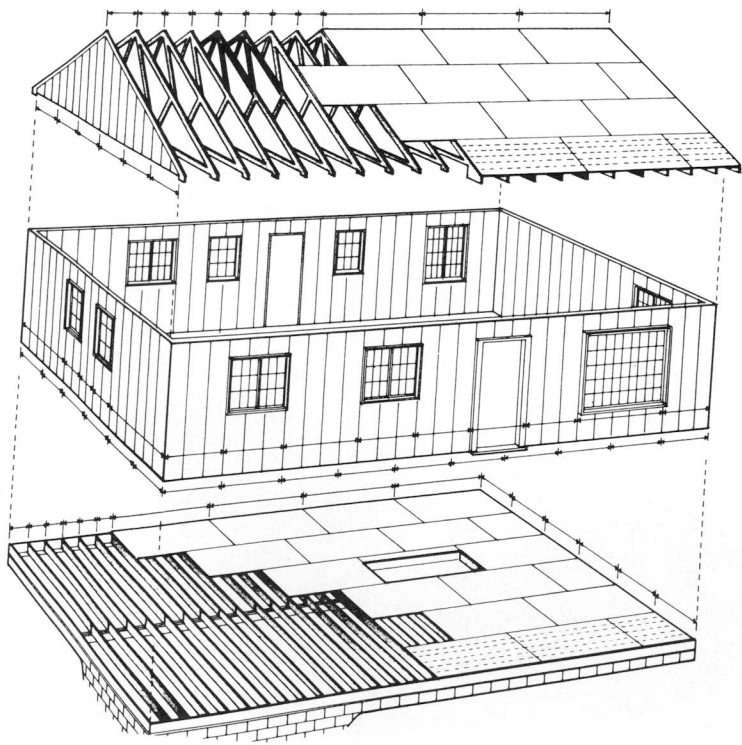

63-2. *The Unicom Method of house construction utilizes lumber framing members in modular sizes to eliminate waste.*

simple jig with hammers, nails, and some adhesive. Later, trusses were produced in large quantities in manufacturing plants. The same idea has been used in developing prehung doors, prefinished paneling, and many other items that speed home-building on site.

The next step in industrialization was the development of factory-built panels. These panels were used along with prefabricated roof trusses or flat roof panels to speed the building of the house shell. In this way the house could become enclosed in a short period of time and be completed in inclement weather.

The *Unicom Method* of house construction, developed by the National Lumber Manufacturers Association, is another method of promoting industrialized housing. Fig. 63-2. All dimensions are based on multiples of 4". The importance of using the modular planning grid as a design control is emphasized. Fig. 63-3.

An important advantage of the Unicom Method is that the wall, floor and roof elements are not tied to any fixed panel size. A designer need not adhere to a fixed four-foot or larger increment. With this system, a complete house is divided into basic horizontal and vertical elements at regular modular intervals. Fig. 63-4.

Although the elements are shown as sliced planes without thickness, allowance is made for wall thickness and tolerance variables based on fixed, not imaginary, module lines at the outside faces of the exterior wall studs. Complete exterior walls and partitions may have many overall thickness variables. These will depend upon whether or not they are load-bearing and which covering materials are used with them. Floor and roof construction elements vary in thickness,

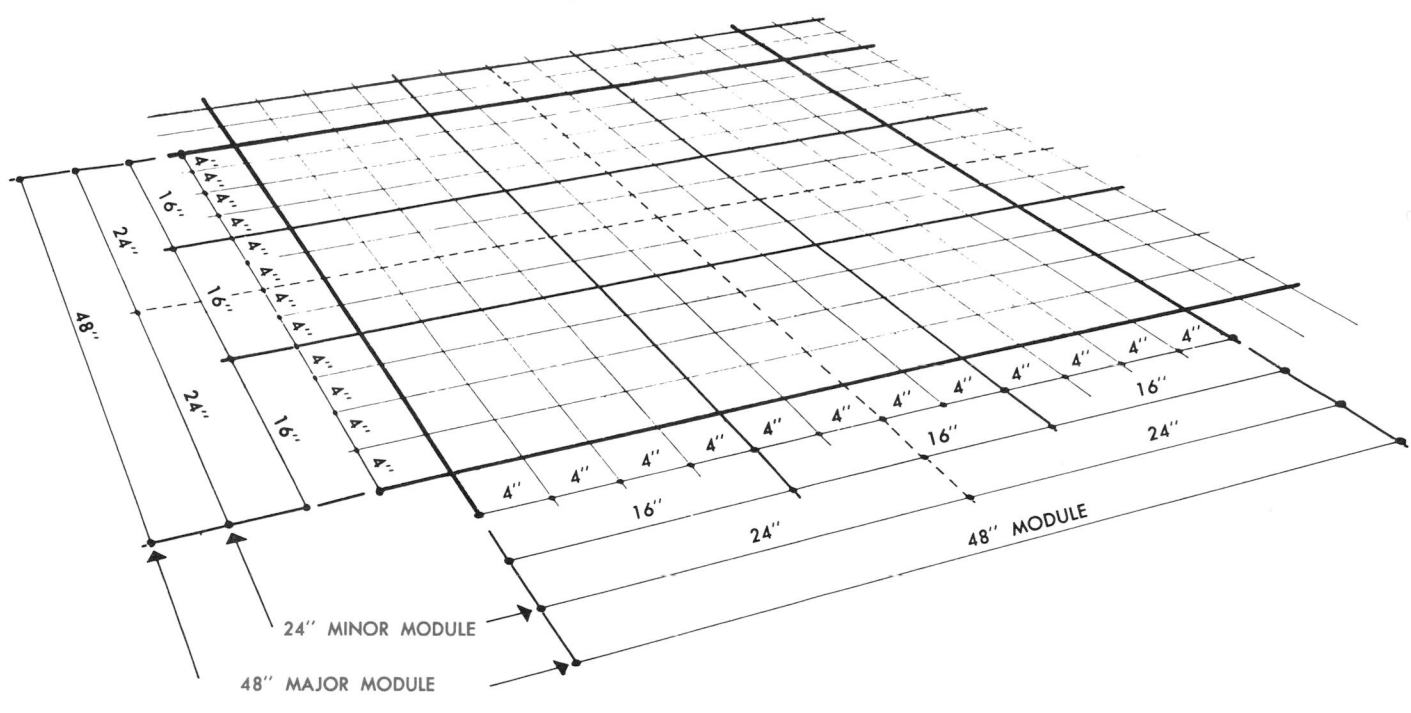

63-3. *Structures can be built with components or by conventional framing using this layout.*

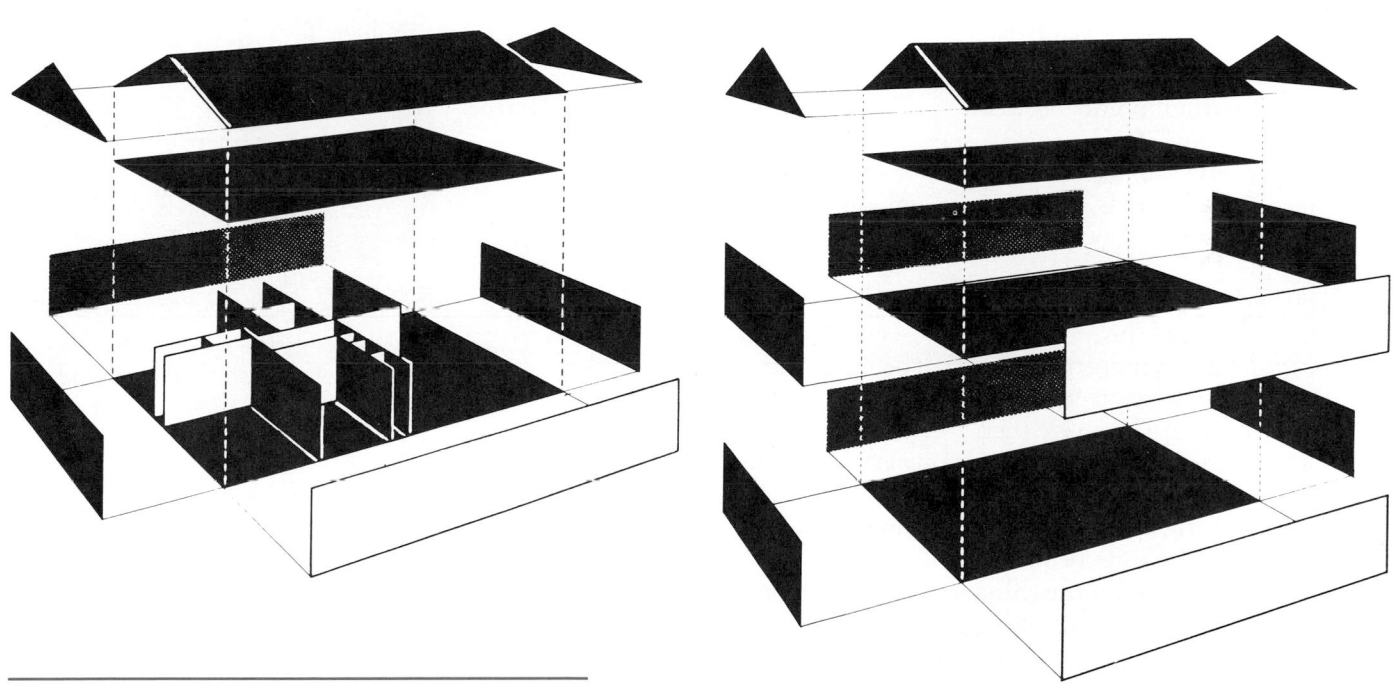

63-4. *The basic planes for modular construction.*

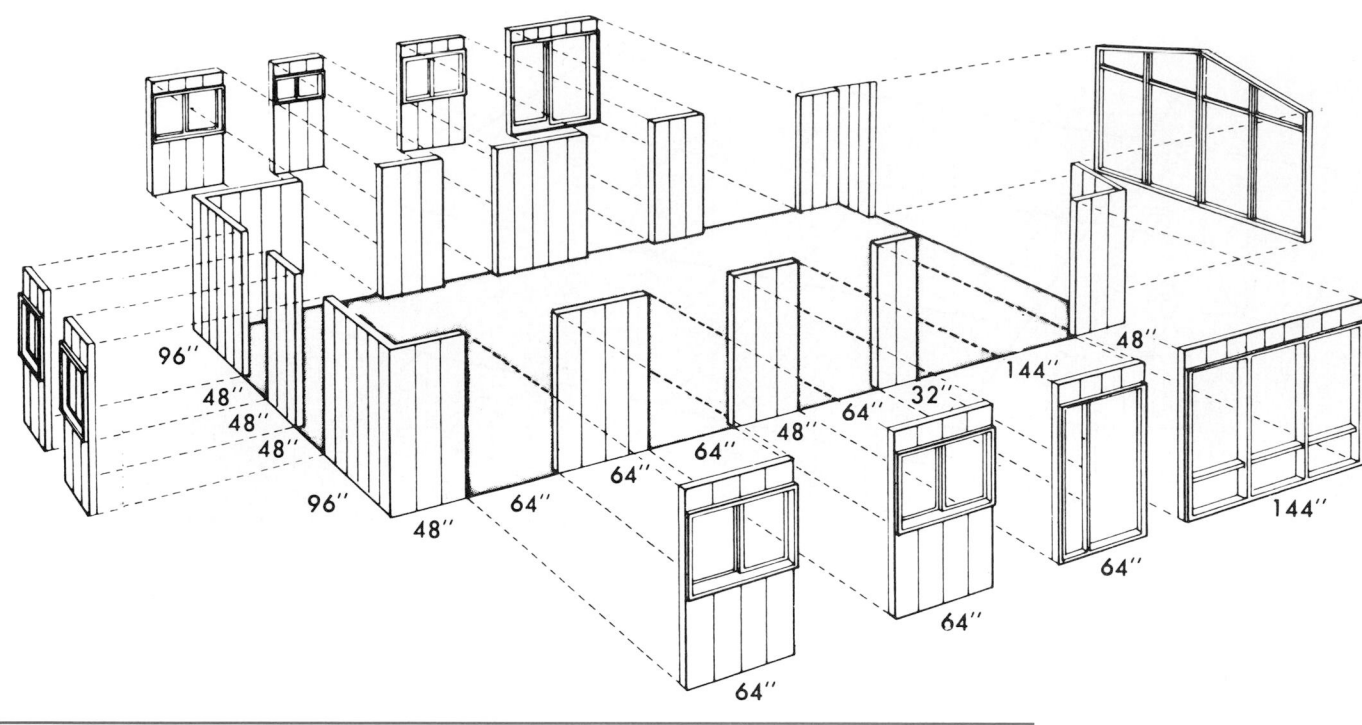

63-5. Note how the various units are all standard multiples of 4", such as 32", 48", etc.

depending upon their structural requirements, type of framing, and finishing.

The exterior wall units are separated at natural points between solid partitions and window and door units. Many prefabricated units such as wall panels, trusses, and prehung doors can be used. Fig. 63-5.

In the early 1960s, panels became the heart of the *prefabricated housing* industry. All parts of the house were precut and prefit at the factory. They were then moved to the site and assembled. However, prefabricated houses consisted of only the shell. They included none of the interior such as wiring, plumbing, and heating. Since the shell of the house amounted to only 25-35% of its cost, there was little difference in cost between the panelized house and a custom house built "stick by stick." During this period, mobile homes began to develop into more sophisticated housing.

Another type of all-factory-built house is the *sectional* house. It is built on an assembly line and is completely finished on the inside. Fig. 63-6. It is moved by sections to the site and then assembled. The sectional house differs from modules in that all the sections are designed for a single home. They may not be exactly the same. It is really a complete home built in sections in a factory so that it can be moved to the building site.

The most completely industrialized housing units are *modules* (modular units). With the modular boxlike system, complete units of the structure are built, shipped to the site, and assembled with other units. The units are completely finished including rugs, draperies, and even furniture. In one motel built with modules, the beds were made and the towels hung in the bathroom before the motel was assembled. For small houses, a single module may be used; for larger houses, several modules.

63-6a. A sectional home being put together on an assembly line.

Fig. 63-7. The same modular technique can be applied to building apartment houses, motels, and commercial buildings.

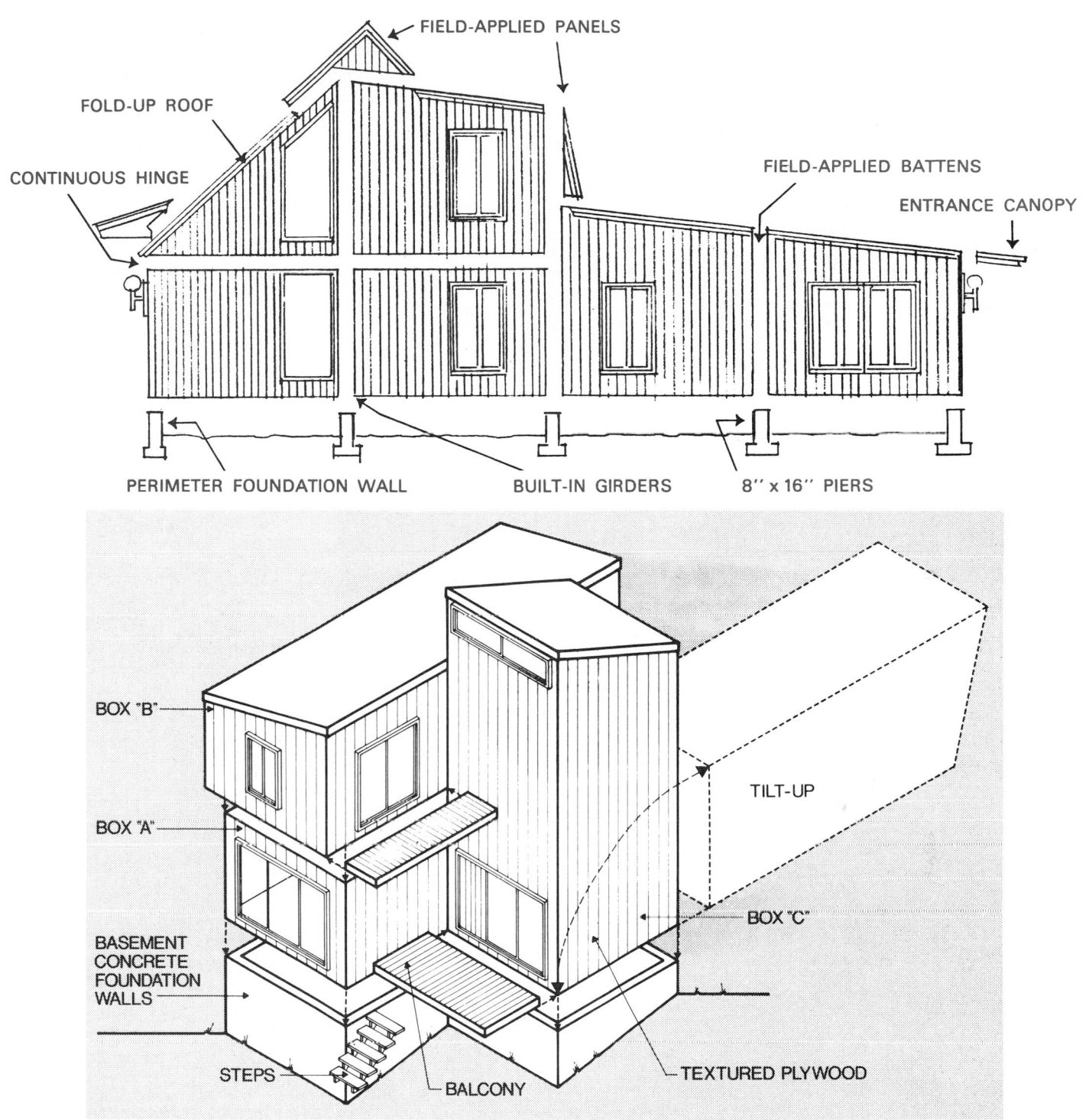

FIELD-APPLIED PANELS

FOLD-UP ROOF

FIELD-APPLIED BATTENS

CONTINUOUS HINGE

ENTRANCE CANOPY

PERIMETER FOUNDATION WALL

BUILT-IN GIRDERS

8″ x 16″ PIERS

BOX "B"

BOX "A"

TILT-UP

BOX "C"

BASEMENT CONCRETE FOUNDATION WALLS

STEPS

BALCONY

TEXTURED PLYWOOD

63-6b. *Certain building parts are added at the site to make the sectional home appear more like a conventional house.*

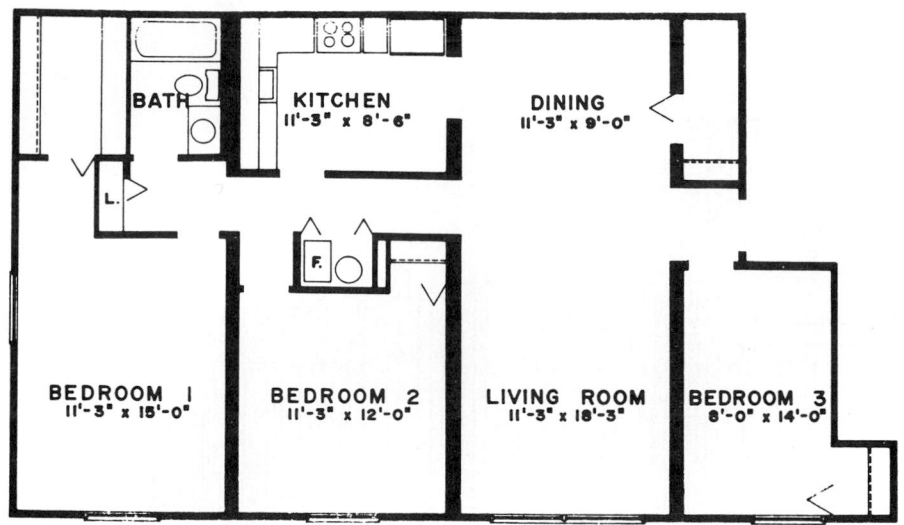

63-7a. *The floor plan for one apartment unit. Note that it is designed with standard width and length modules for easy assembly. Each module is limited to an overall width of 12' for easy transport.*

63-7b. *This attractive apartment house was assembled from modular units.*

TYPES OF MANUFACTURED HOUSING

Definitions

To understand the different types of manufactured homes and recreational vehicles, it is important to learn the definitions.

Panelized home. This is a home assembled from various wall, roof, and floor panels. Individual panels are assembled in a factory. They are then trucked to the building site, where they are assembled. Smaller panels are generally 4' by 8'. These can be installed by hand. Larger panels may be the length of an entire exterior wall. These must be installed with a crane.

Mobile home. This is a transportable structure, exceeding either 8 body feet in width or 32 body feet in length, built on a chassis, and designed to be used as a dwelling. It may or may not have a permanent foundation when connected to the required utilities.

Double-width mobile home. This is a mobile home consisting of two sections combined horizontally at the site but retaining their individual chassis for possible future movement.

Expandable mobile home. This is a mobile home with one or more room sections that fold, collapse, or telescope into the principal unit when being transported. The sections can be expanded at the site to provide additional living area.

Modular unit. This is a factory-built, transportable building unit designed to be used by itself or to be incorporated with similar units at a building site. Modular structures can be used for residential, commercial, educational, or industrial purposes.

Sectional home. This is a dwelling made of two or more units that are put on a foundation and joined to make a single house.

Mobile homes, double-wides, sectionals, and modules are transported to their sites by trucks, the movements of which are controlled by state highway regulations. They also are shipped on railroad flatcars.

Mobile Homes

Mobile homes come completely furnished with major appliances, drapes, lamps, carpeting, furniture, and everything else necessary for living. The home is centrally heated by gas, oil, or electric furnace. Mobile homes are available in widths from 8' to 14' and in lengths from 35' to 70'. The width of a mobile home is limited by what each state will permit to pass on the highway. Many states limit this to a 12' width, while other states allow homes 14' wide. By using a double-width mobile home, widths from 16' to 28' are possible.

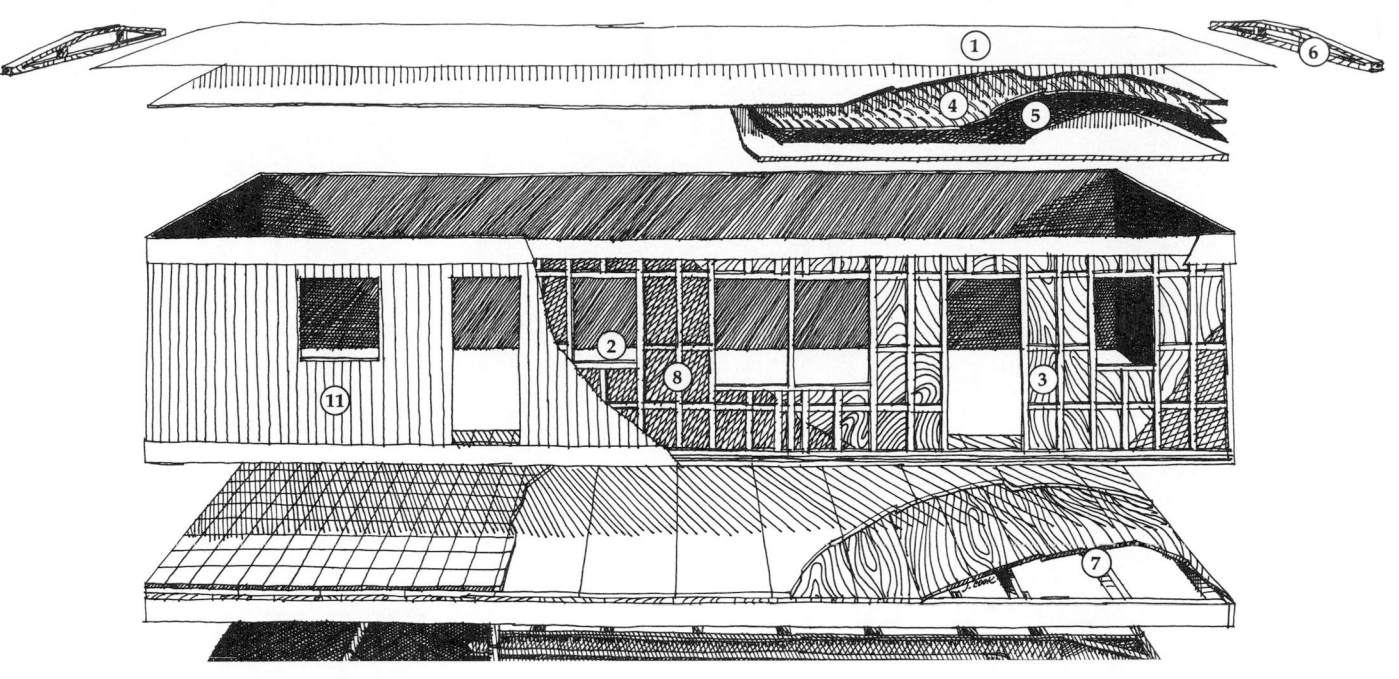

63-8. *Construction features of this mobile home include: 1. Galvanized, raised steel roof. 2. Ventilating window in bath. 3. Sturdy 4" sidewall construction. 4. & 5. Double fiberglass insulation with double vapor barrier in roof. 6. Truss-type, built-up roof rafters. 7. Sturdy, reinforced floor joists overlaid with ⅝" plywood or manufactured board, glued and mechanically secured. 8. 1½" high-density fiberglass insulation in sidewalls and floor. 9. Electrical, heating, and plumbing systems. 10. Basement-type frame, with enclosed plumbing system. 11. Prefinished, lifetime aluminum siding.*

Manufacture of Mobile Homes. Mobile homes are built on an assembly line. They differ from standard housing in that lighter materials are generally used for framing. Items such as built-ins and cabinets are on a smaller scale. Typical framing is 2" × 2", rather than the standard 2" × 4". A great deal of plastic and metal is used.

Mobile homes have five major parts:

➤ Frame.
➤ Floor assembly.
➤ Wall assembly.
➤ Roof assembly.
➤ Interior. Fig. 63-8.

The base, or frame, for mobile homes is a heavy steel chassis equipped with a single, double, or triple axis depending on length.

63-9. *Heavy metal frames are used in constructing a mobile home.*

Fig. 63-9. This is moved into place on the assembly line.

Next the floor framing is built. Fig. 63-10. Heating ducts, rough plumbing, and wiring are installed

63-10. *Two-by-six (2" x 6") floor joists, 16" on center, are joined and bolted to the frame to make a solid no-sag floor.*

63-11. *Plumbing is installed in the floor assembly.*

63-12. *A sidewall section before insulation is installed.*

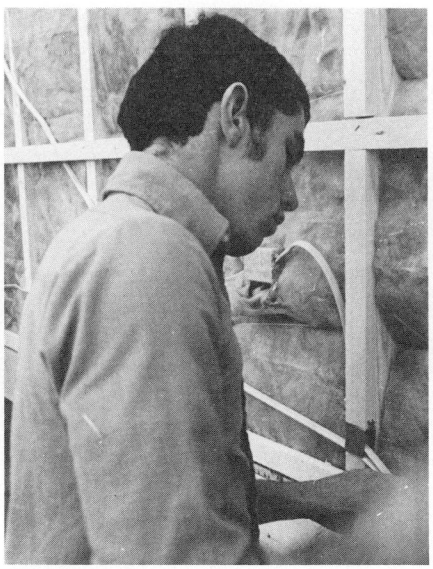

63-13a. *Wiring is run through the sidewalls.*

63-13b. *Sheets of aluminum siding being installed.*

63-13c. *The windows are also stapled into position.*

63-14. *Appliances and furniture are moved into the mobile home to complete it.*

in the floor assembly frame. Fig. 63-11. The frame is insulated and covered with tongue-and-groove plywood particleboard sheets. Another layer of insulation is usually installed over the plywood. When the floor is completed, the necessary heavy mechanical items such as the furnace and hot-water heater are installed.

Next the wall frames are assembled on jigs and lifted into place. Fig. 63-12. The necessary wiring, plumbing, and insulation are installed. The exterior shell is completed. Fig. 63-13. The roof assembly is attached to the frame of the house. The interior is then completed with cabinets, partitions, appliances, furniture, rugs, and all other installed items. Fig. 63-14.

The completed mobile home is moved off the assembly line ready to be trucked to the site. Most mobile homes are moved to the site by heavy-duty trucks and placed on a simple foundation. The necessary mechanical connections are made and the house is ready for use.

Most of the workers in mobile home factories do only one job, such as stapling wall assemblies together or wiring electrical circuits. Therefore few highly skilled workers are needed.

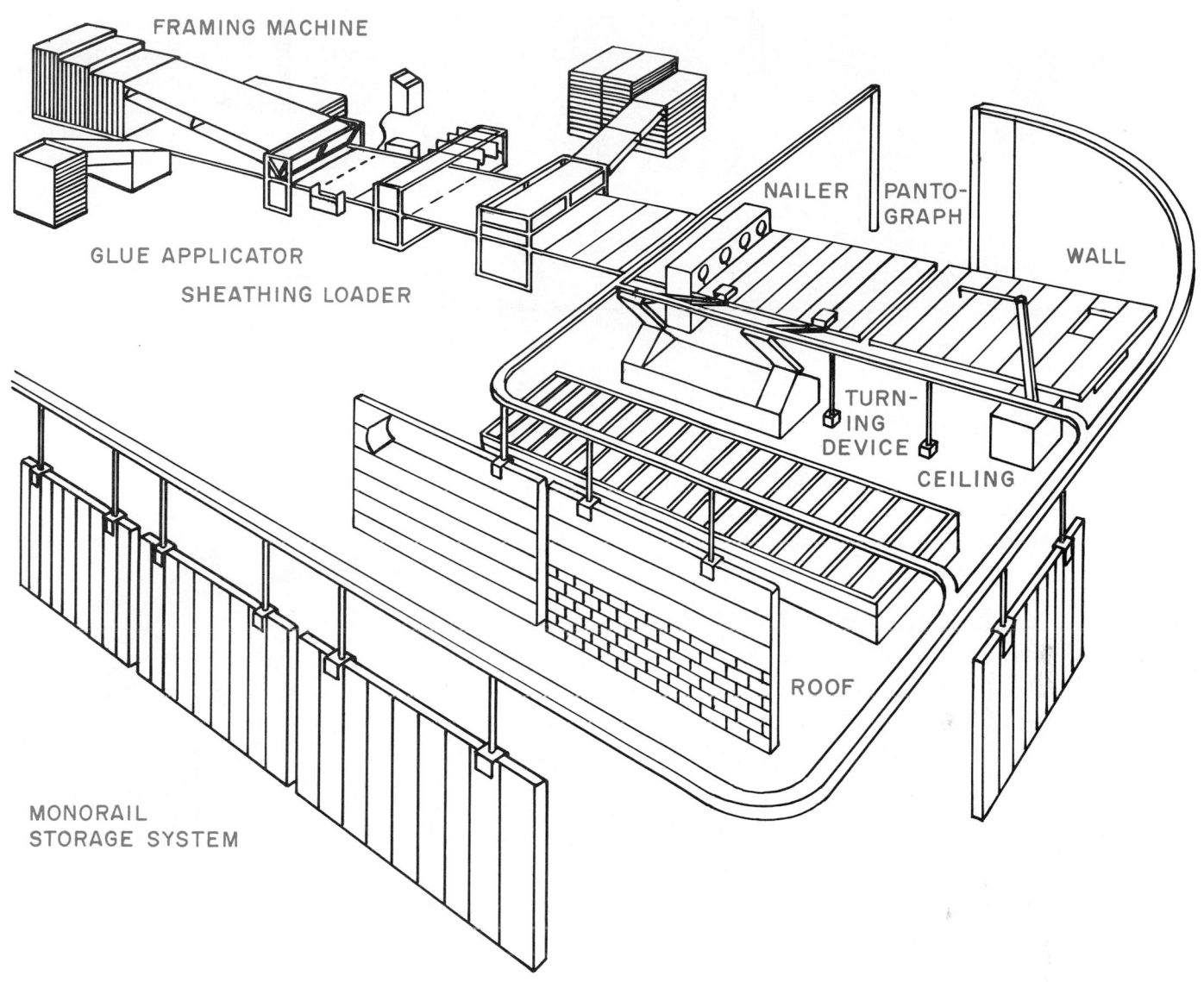

FRAMING MACHINE

GLUE APPLICATOR

SHEATHING LOADER

NAILER PANTO-
GRAPH

WALL

TURN-
ING
DEVICE

CEILING

ROOF

MONORAIL
STORAGE SYSTEM

63-15a. *An assembly line section in a modular home factory.*

Modular Housing

The manufacture of modular housing differs from that of mobile homes. Standard-size materials are used in its construction. Thus, the complete modular unit has at least the same strength as a house built "stick by stick." In fact, with modern industrial techniques the modular unit is stronger, better insulated, and more nearly soundproof than a house built by the traditional method.

Factories that produce modular housing use a great deal of heavy-duty equipment for cutting, assembling, nailing, stapling, and moving the units along an assembly line. Fig. 63-15. Modules produced on any assembly line are identical in size and shape for a particular model. Fig. 63-16. Several modules can be assembled on site. Details are added to give them a wide variety of appearances.

Hybrid Housing

Various types of assembly processes are required for building the different kinds of manufactured homes. Some manufacturers combine processes to maximize the advantages of each type and minimize the disadvantages. For example, manufactured wall panels may be combined with modular construction. Fig. 63-17.

The kitchen and the bathrooms are the most complicated rooms of

a house. These are sometimes assembled into modular units in a factory. The units are then trucked to a building site and set on a foundation. Wall panels are added to the modular units to form the rest of the house. The advantage of this system is that it offers an almost infinite variety of floor plans and house styles. However, it makes good use of the efficiency of factory construction.

63-15b. *A section of an assembly line on which wall panels are being assembled.*

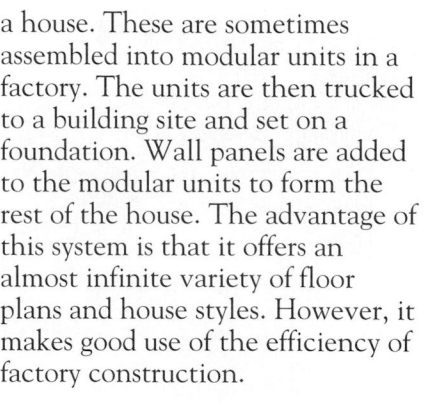

63-16a. *This 12' by 22' modular unit weighs approximately 13 tons, and contains all the electrical, cooling, heating, and plumbing facilities for the home in Fig. 63-17. It is placed on its own foundation.*

63-16b. *Insulated wall panels are combined with the modular units to complete the house. The 4' by 8' panels are coated with Portland cement plaster after installation. This serves as the final exterior surface.*

63-16c. *The wall panels can be fabricated with openings of various size. A modular core unit is shown in the background.*

63-17. *Hybrid housing offers the advantages of factory construction and versatile design. This house was made with modular units and panelized units.*

1. What part of the house was first prefabricated?

2. What is the basic unit of measurement in the Unicom Method?

3. What is the difference between a sectional house and a modular house?

4. What controls the width of mobile homes? Explain.

5. How do mobile homes differ from modules in construction?

ACTIVITIES

1. Math. Suppose that mobile homes are available in widths from 8' to 14' in 1' differences and in lengths from 32' to 70' in 2' differences.

a. Find the area in square feet of the smallest and the largest possible.

b. How many times more area does the largest one have than the smallest?

2. Math. Start with a 48" by 48" module.

a. What is the area in square feet of this module?

b. Double both dimensions of the beginning module. What is the area now? How many times larger is it?

c. Triple both dimensions of the beginning module. What is the area now? How many times larger is it?

d. Multiply one dimension by 6 and the other by 10. What is the area now? How many times larger is it?

3. Language Arts. If possible, walk through a recreational vehicle at a dealership. Take note of how appliances, furniture, and housing features such as cabinets are miniaturized to utilize maximum use of a little space. Write down your observations in a journal entry.

4. Social Studies. The manufacture of modular housing differs from that of mobile homes. Standard-size materials are used in its construction; so the complete modular unit is at least the same strength as a house built "stick by stick." In fact, with modern industrial techniques the modular unit is stronger, better insulated, and more nearly soundproof than a house built by the traditional method. If this statement is true, why doesn't every home builder use modular housing construction? Talk to a contractor. Why do people still build homes in the conventional way?

5. Language Arts. Most products will require servicing at some time. There are, however, levels of servicing. Some servicing is to be done only by factory-authorized technicians. Other servicing can be done by the user of the tool. Obtain the instruction manual for one of the power tools in common use on a construction site. Find out what levels of service you would be able to perform on the tool. If the tool is in need of servicing, perform this servicing. Then write a brief report on the service procedures you would be allowed to perform on the tool. Identify also those service procedures that are to be performed only by a factory-authorized technician.

THE SCHOOL-TO-WORK CONNECTION

Some manufacturers assemble wall framing panels that are then trucked to the jobsite. The builder lifts the panels into place on the subfloor, nails them into place, and sheaths and insulates the panels. Other manufacturers build wall panels that are almost complete. The wall delivered to the site has been framed, sheathed, and sided. Windows may even be in place, and the siding might be prefinished.

1. You are a builder who wants to know about the advantages (and disadvantages) of panelized framing. Use your local library to locate the names of manufacturers who specialize in panelized systems. Write to several and ask for a description of their systems. Start a file titled "Panelized Framing." Add whatever information you get to this file.

Appendix A: Finishes

Type of Finish	Preparation of Surface	Sealers and Primers	Application of Finish	Characteristics
General Use (Lumber, Boards, Planks and Paneling)				
Stains	Sand or scrape wood to flat, clean surface; for some hardwoods, fill pores with filler before sanding; if new wood, should already be flat and clean.	One coat of sealer often brushed into softwoods before finishing to reduce depth of penetration between springwood and summerwood; also used to reduce prominence of grain; no primers required for stains and most clear finishes.		
—Water Stains			Water stains are brushed onto surface; one coat is usually sufficient.	Easy to apply; water can raise wood grain making sanding necessary after stain has dried; fabric dyes in water are typical water stain.
—Spirit Stains			Spirit stains are brushed onto wood rapidly and evenly; one coat is usually sufficient.	Quick drying, so apply evenly; little time to restroke spots; little tendency to raise wood grain.
—Oil Stains			Oil stains are brushed onto wood, all strokes made along the grain; one coat is usually sufficient; sometimes used under varnishes.	Penetrate well; do not raise grain; dry slowly so easy to distribute evenly.
Clear Finishes				
—Waxes			Two coats of paste wax can be applied over shellac in methanol sealer; surface damage repaired by spot cleaning with mineral spirits and applying more wax.	Low-gloss finish; rarely used because of excellent performance of synthetic varnishes; great refinish problems if wax allowed to penetrate wood.
—Synthetic Varnishes (such as polyurethane)			Three coats of synthetic varnish brushed onto surface (two coats if filler used); can be polished with wax but not necessary.	Varying gloss finishes, synthetics give hard, tough finish, resistant to oil, water, and alcohol; dries quickly by reaction with moisture in air.
—Shellacs			Two coats of shellac are brushed onto surface (used as methanol solution); patched in spots using methanol remover and applying more shellac.	Brittle finish; water spots easily; not recommended because synthetic varnishes do better job.
—Boiled Linseed Oil			Two coats of boiled linseed oil are spread evenly onto surface using brush or rag; 24-hour drying period is required between coats.	Seldom used; long drying time required, so surface susceptible to marking.

(Continued on next page)

Type of Finish	Preparation of Surface	Sealers and Primers	Application of Finish	Characteristics
Paints				
—Alkyd Enamels	Sand or dust wood to ensure good paint adhesion.	Apply alkyd or oil-based primer with good enamel holdout for an enamel undercoat.	Two coats of alkyd-based enamel are brushed or rolled onto surface.	High- or semi-gloss finish; resistant to solvents; good color retention; optimum results using enamel undercoater.
—Latexes		Recommend application of latex primer; not absolutely necessary.	Two coats of latex are brushed or rolled onto surface; may be used without primer but primer recommended.	Full range of glosses available; high- or semi-gloss recommended for kitchens and bathrooms; fast drying; little yellowing; easy clean-up with water; no solvent vapor; spot touch-up without patch effect; reduced fire hazard.
			Plywood	
Stains	Hardwood and softwood plywood are usually factory sanded on face to be finished; require no surface preparation other than filling and sanding surface blemishes.	Priming and edge sealing not necessary; sealer will subdue grain contrast if dark stain preferred.	One coat of combined wax and stain is applied; after a few minutes wipe with rag to desired shade, then apply a coat of self-polishing wax and buff surface. Stains can be used alone as described under General Use.	Wood penetrates wood making surface unsuitable for refinishing.
Clear Finishes				
—Synthetic Varnishes	Fill nail holes with tinted filler, sand smooth, and spot prime.	Apply coat of sealer.	Brush two coats of varnish onto prepared surface; semi-gloss varnish often applied over flat varnish.	
—Blond Finish			Apply one coat of interior white undercoat (thinned so grain shows through) under one coat of flat synthetic varnish.	Easy and inexpensive; offers features of synthetic varnishes.
—Waxes			Wax systems commercially available but not recommended; if used, follow manufacturer's instructions closely.	Not recommended because wax imbedded in wood fibers cannot be removed; this wax will interfere with alternative refinishing.
Paints				
—Alkyd Enamels	Sand or scrape wood to smooth, clean surface.	Apply one coat of enamel undercoat.	Apply either one coat of undercoater tinted to finish color and one coat of alkyd enamel or two coats of alkyd enamel (for better gloss).	Good washable finish; checking and cracking may become problem.
—Latexes		Apply one coat of latex-based check-retardant primer.	Apply two coats of latex paint.	Primer effectively eliminates cracking and checking on new wood.

Type of Finish	Preparation of Surface	Sealers and Primers	Application of Finish	Characteristics
Particleboard				
Stains	Surfaces available smooth or porous depending on type of particleboard; porous surfaces must be filled and sanded; some boards available with resin-impregnated fibrous sheet applied in factory.	A primer or sealer may be necessary to isolate additives from the finish; finish a scrap to determine if primer or sealer is needed.	Apply stains as described under General Use.	Interesting decorative effects can be achieved with stains or clear finishes; shape and color contrast of wood particles is emphasized.
Clear Finishes			Apply any clear finish as described under General Use.	
Paints			Apply alkyd or latex paints as described under General Use.	Paint is most common finish for particleboard.
Hardboard				
Paints —Alkyd Enamels —Latexes	Nailheads should be countersunk and puttied, or treated with anti-corrosive primer; surface should be smooth and clean.	Apply one coat of primer unless hardboard has been factory primed.	Apply alkyd enamels or latexes as described under General Use.	Hardboard is usually painted because it has no grain, or natural characteristics to be emphasized.
Floors (Hardwood and Softwood)				
Pigmented Stains	Sand floor with power sander, first cut across the grain and successive cuts with the grain; after sanding, vacuum off dust; apply finish as soon as possible; some hardwoods, such as oak, require filler before sanding.	Not required unless sealer used alone as finish for industrial occupancies.	One coat of stain (oil stain if synthetic varnish is used) is brushed onto surface.	Stains change color of the wood and emphasize grain; often used under varnish.

(Continued on next page)

Type of Finish	Preparation of Surface	Sealers and Primers	Application of Finish	Characteristics
Floors (Hardwood and Softwood)				
Clear Finishes				
—Synthetic Varnishes (Polyure-thane)			Two coats of synthetic varnish are brushed onto stained or filled floor; bubbles should be removed by brushing back area lightly.	Varying degrees of gloss; extremely wear-resistant; no wax needed for protection; difficult to spot refinish.
—Floor Sealers			Apply sealer across grain as a spray or with a brush; buff with steel wool and vacuum off dust; apply second coat of sealer with the grain; sealed floor may be waxed or varnished for greater gloss.	Inexpensive; provides protection against water damage and warping in industrial occupancies.
—Shellac			Three coats of shellac are applied by brush, following wood grain.	Easily repaired; water staining becomes chronic problem, so shellac not recommended.
Paints				
—Alkyd Floor or Deck Enamels		Sealer may be required for softwood floors unless enamel is self-sealing.	Three coats of floor or deck enamel brushed onto surface.	Good wear resistance; wide color range; softwood and hardwood floors are easily painted.

Exterior Finishes

Type of Finish	Preparation of Surface	Sealers and Primers	Application of Finish	Characteristics
General Use (Lumber, Siding and Panel Products)				
Penetrating Finishes —Preservatives			Brush one coat of water-repellent preservative onto surface.	Imparts mildew and decay resistance; some protection from ultraviolet light destruction depending on pigment content; easy to maintain.
			Brush a solution of fungicide onto surface; best method is to add fungicide to finish.	May tend to leach out with rain.
—Stains	Sand or scrape wood to flat, clean surface; if new wood, no preparation required.	None required.	Bruch latex or oil-based stain onto surface; working area should be small enough to maintain a wet edge; one or two coats applied according to manufacturer's recommendations.	Easy to apply; attractive finish for even rough surfaces; easy to maintain; choice of semi-transparent or opaque finish.
—Madison Formula*			Brush one coat of Madison Formula onto new wood.	Semi-transparent oil-based stain intended for western red cedar; imparts water repellency and mildew and decay resistance; contains wax which leads to refinish problems.
—Oil			One coat of oil, applied by brush.	Not recommended; oil remains tacky on surface, collecting insects and dirt.
Surface Finishes —Solvent-Based Paints (Including Alkyds)	Sand or scrape off badly deteriorated finish; if new wood, no preparation is required.	Apply knot sealer or shellac to knots and pitch streaks; apply oil-based primer to new wood.	Painting should be done in dry weather with temperatures above 45° F; paint following sun around house, staying one side behind sun; apply one or two coats (depending on color) by brush.	Alkyd paints overcome blistering and excessive chalking associated with traditional oil-based paints; only white traditional oil-based paint is recommended; alkyd paints are recommended if color is required; alkyd trim paints should be used above masonry; solvent-based paints with other synthetic resins are available.
—Latex Paints		Apply knot sealer or shellac to knots and pitch streaks; apply oil-based primer as undercoat or special latex primer over previous coats of oil-based paints.	Follow application instructions above for solvent-based paints; apply two coats of latex paint by brush over primer.	Easy to apply; adhere well to damp surface; dry rapidly; easy equipment clean-up; chalk-resistant; slower to erode than oil-based paints; thinner surface film, therefore less leveling off of surface irregularities.

(Continued on next page)

Type of Finish	Preparation of Surface	Sealers and Primers	Application of Finish	Characteristics
General Use (Lumber, Siding and Panel Products)				
Synthetic Varnishes	For refinishing scrape off loose flaking materials, sand area, wash wood surface and stain bleached areas to match the rest of the wood; if new wood, no preparation required.	None required.	Three coats of synthetic varnish are applied by brush to new wood; fewer coats required for refinishing.	Refinishing required about every two years; finish allows penetration of ultraviolet light which degrades film and wood surface; results in darkening of wood color.
Shingles and Shakes (Western Red Cedar)				
Penetrating Finishes				
—Stains			Immersing shingles or shakes in stain (semi-transparent or opaque) is best technique; refinishing done with a brush.	Rough surface of shingles and shakes readily absorbs stain.
—Madison Formula*	Same as for General Use.	None required.	Apply as for other pigmented stains.	Madison Formula specifically formulated for western red cedar.*
—Preservatives			Pentachlorophenol (5% to 10% solution) may be added to stain; alternatively, wood may be pressure treated with preservatives.	Preservatives desired but not absolutely necessary for western red cedar.
Surface Finishes				
—Alkyd Paints	None required.	None required.	Two coats of specially formulated shingle and shake alkyd paint applied by brush.	Flat finish; covers all but extreme surface irregularities.
—Latex Paints		Specially formulated sealer required; factory primed shingles and shakes are available.	Two coats of latex paint applied by brush.	Covers all but extreme surface irregularities.

* Pour 1 gallon of mineral spirits into an open-top 5-gallon can. Heat 1 pound of paraffin and 2 ounces of zinc stearate in the top of a double boiler and stir until the mixture is uniform. Pour this into the mineral spirits, stirring vigorously. This should be done outside to avoid the risk of fire. Add 1/2 gallon of pentachlorophenol concentrate 10:1 and 3 gallons of boiled linseed oil to the cooled solution. Stir in 1 pint of burnt sienna color-in-oil and one pint of raw umber color-in-oil until the mixture is uniform. One gallon covers 400-500 square feet on a smooth surface and 200-250 square feet on a sawn-textured surface.

Appendix B: Metric Construction

Congress has stated that, "The metric system of measurement is the preferred system of weights and measures for United States trade and commerce." The Congress also requires that "all Federal agencies use the metric system to the extent economically feasible in procurements, grants and other business-related activities except to the extent that such use is impractical or is likely to cause significant inefficiencies." All American companies involved in internal trade use the metric system. However, the construction industry has been slow to convert.

In the United States, almost a million individual concerns are involved in the construction industry. These include manufacturers, contractors, architects, building supply companies, hardware stores, and many others. In the concrete block industry alone, there are over 160 different manufacturers. Total metric conversion will require that all of these concerns agree to go metric at the same time. Fig. B-1.

TABLE A. *SI Base Units.*

Unit	Quantity	Symbol
metre	length	m
second	time	s
kilogram[1]	mass	kg
degree Celsius[2]	temperature	°C
ampere	electric current	A
candela	luminous intensity	cd
mole	amount of substance	mol

[1] The kilogram, not the gram, is the base unit of mass.
[2] The Kelvin, symbol K, is used in scientific work instead of the degree Celsius. On the Kelvin scale, 0 K is equivalent to absolute zero, not the freezing point of water.

TABLE B. *Common SI Derived Units.*

Unit	Quantity	Symbol
square millimetre	area	mm²
square centimetre		cm²
square metre		m²
cubic centimetre	capacity	cm³
cubic decimetre		dm³
cubic metre		m³
litre (1 l = 1 dm³)	volume	L
metre per second	speed, linear	m/s
kilometre per hour		km/h
revolution per second*	speed, rotational	r/s
revolution per minute*		r/min
joule	energy and work	J
newton	force	N
pascal	pressure, stress	Pa
watt	power	W
newton metre	torque	N•m
volt	electrical potential	V
ohm	electrical resistance	Ω
hertz	frequency	Hz

* Technically, these are not SI derived units. They are included here for easier reference.

Fig. B-1. *Houses in all other English-speaking countries are designed and built to metric standards. In the United States, the construction industry has been slow to convert.*

THE SI SYSTEM

Let us look at the measuring system used by most of the world.

This is the updated metric system of units called *SI*, which stands for Systéme International d'Unités. It consists of seven *base* units, Table A, plus many derived units, Table

B. A *derived* unit is a unit that originates from one or more of the base units.

Only three base units are in common daily use. They are the

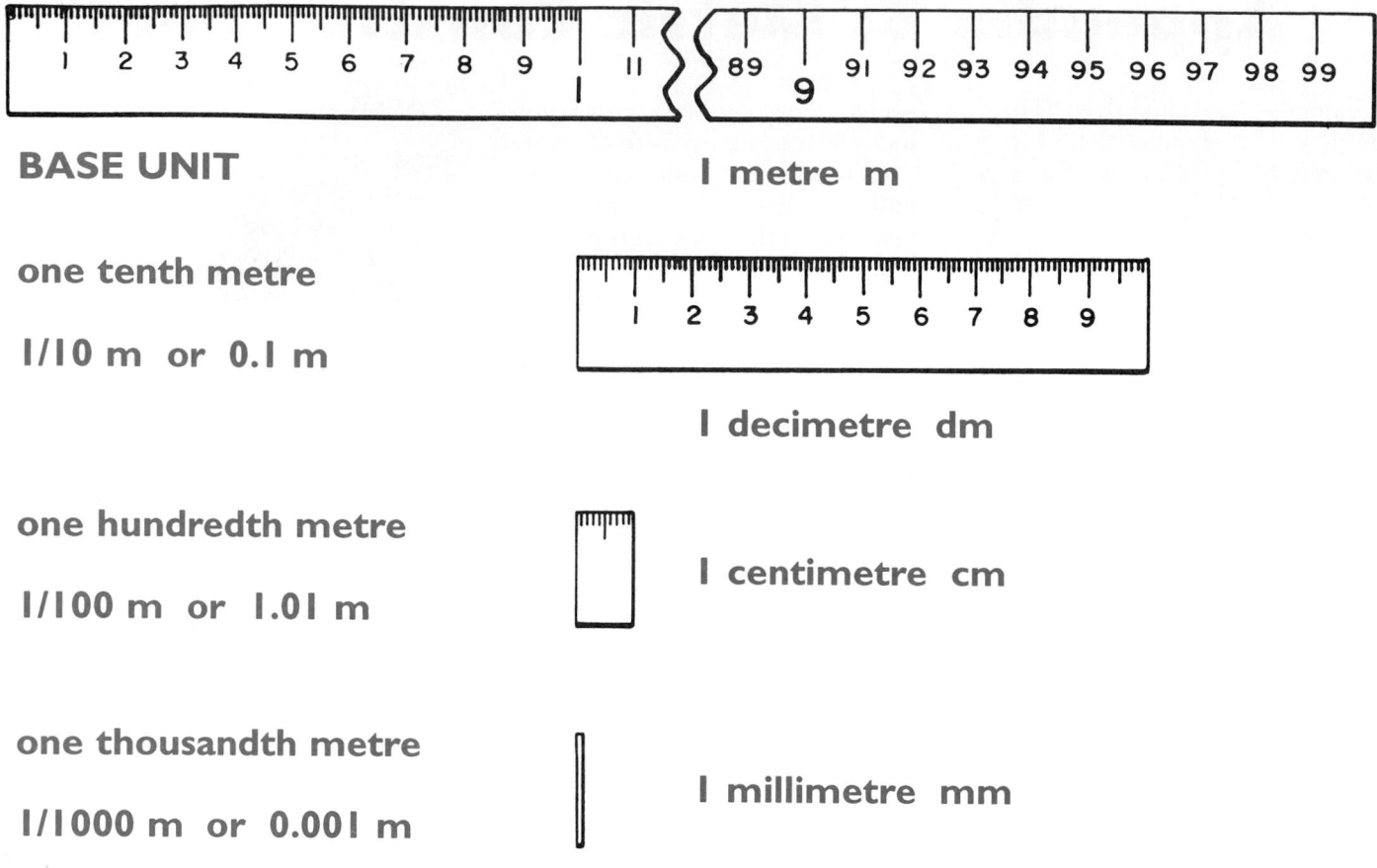

BASE UNIT   I metre m

one tenth metre

1/10 m or 0.1 m

                                       I decimetre dm

one hundredth metre

1/100 m or 1.01 m   I centimetre cm

one thousandth metre

1/1000 m or 0.001 m   I millimetre mm

Fig. B-2.   *The unit of length is the metre. It is divided into decimetres, centimetres, and millimetres. Industry will use the millimetre as the common unit of length.*

TABLE C. *Prefixes Used with SI Metric Units.*

Multiple or Submultiple	Prefix	Symbol	Pronunciation*	Means
$1\ 000\ 000\ 000 = 10^9$	giga	G**	jig'a (a as in about)	One billion times
$1\ 000\ 000 = 10^6$	mega	M**	as in <u>mega</u>phone	One million times
$1\ 000 = 10^3$	kilo	k**	as in <u>kilo</u>watt	One thousand times
$100 = 10^2$	hecto	h	heck'toe	One hundred times
$10 = 10^1$	deka	da	deck'a a (a as in about)	Ten times
Base unit $1 = 10^0$		**		
$0.1 = 10^{-1}$	deci	d	as in <u>deci</u>mal	One tenth of
$0.01 = 10^{-2}$	centi	c**	as in <u>centi</u>pede	One hundredth of
$0.001 = 10^{-3}$	milli	m**	as in <u>mili</u>tary	One thousandth of
$0.000\ 001 = 10^{-6}$	micro	μ**	as in <u>micro</u>phone	One millionth of
$0\ 000\ 000\ 001 = 10^{-9}$	nano	n**	nan'oh (an as in ant)	One billionth of

*The first syllable of every prefix is accented to make sure that the prefix will keep identity. For example, the preferred pronunciation of kilometre places the accent on the first syllable, not the second.

**Most commonly used and preferred prefixes. Centimetre is used mainly for measuring the body, clothing, sporting goods, and some household articles.

metre, kilogram, and degrees Celsius. The *metre*, the unit of length, is slightly longer than a yard. The *kilogram*, the unit of mass (weight), is a little more than two pounds. The unit of temperature is *degrees Celsius*.

In addition to these three base units, a number of derived units are commonly used in construction. Some of the derived units, such as the square metre (m²), cubic metre (m³), and the litre (L), do not have special names. They are designated by symbols that are lowercase letters. Others, such as the newton (N), pascal (Pa), joule (J), and watt (W), have a capital letter for their symbol because they are named after famous people.

The metric system is a decimal system, like our monetary system. This means that all units larger and smaller than the base unit are based on multiples of 10. There are 100 centimetres (cm) and 1000 millimetres (mm) in 1 metre (m). There are 1000 metres in 1

kilometre (km), which is used to measure long distances. The three most common prefixes are *kilo*, meaning 1000 times; *centi*, meaning 1/100 times; and *milli*, meaning 1/1000 times. These prefixes are used for all units, not just units of length. For example, 1/1000 of a litre is 1 millilitre (1 mL). Table C.

Common Base Units

The three base units commonly used in construction are the three units commonly used elsewhere—metre, kilogram, and degrees Celsius.

Length. The base unit of length, the metre (m), is about 39.37", 10 percent longer than a yard. A metre is divided into 10 equal parts called decimetres, 100 equal parts called centimetres, and 1000 equal parts called millimetres. Fig. B-2. One inch is about 2.5 centimetres, or about 25

millimetres. Construction dimensions are shown in metres and millimetres. Fig. B-3.

Mass (Weight). The mass of a kilogram is approximately 2.2 pounds. Think of a kilogram as being slightly more than 2 pounds. A kilogram is divided into 1000 grams. A gram is a very small unit. There are about 28 grams in 1 ounce. Five hundred grams, or 0.5 kilogram, is a little more than a pound (about 10 percent more). Materials such as cement, lime, and mortar will be sold by the kilogram. For example, a metric bag of cement has a mass of 40 kilograms.

Temperature. Temperatures are measured in degrees Celsius (°C). On this scale water freezes at 0° and boils at 100°C. Your normal body temperature is about 37°C. Ten degrees Celsius is equivalent to 50 degrees Fahrenheit. For every 9-degree increase in Fahrenheit temperature above 50 degrees, add 5 degrees to the Celsius

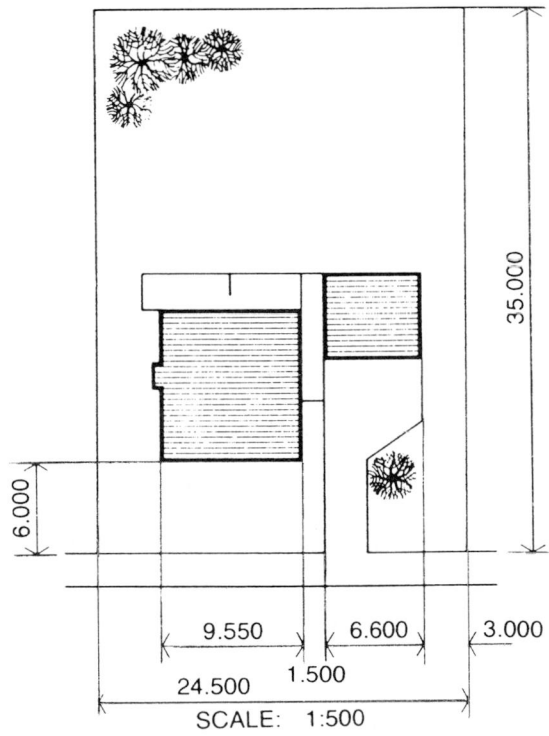

Fig. B-3a. *Example of a metric site plan. Note: Dimensions are in metres.*

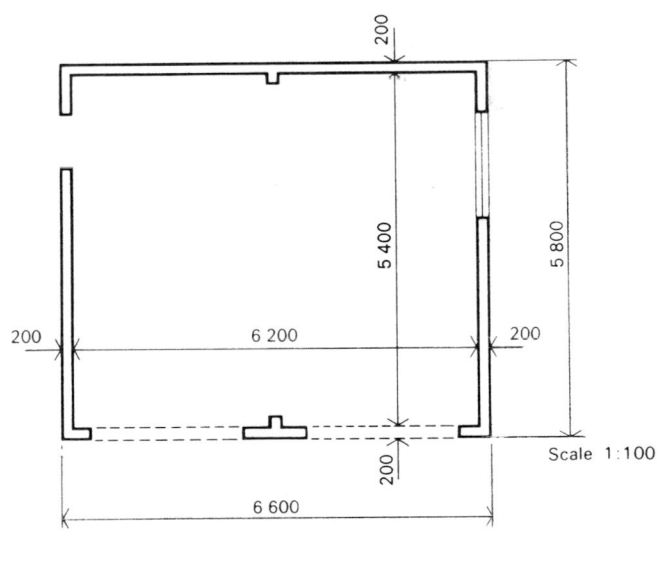

Fig. B-3b. *Example from metric house plans. Note: Dimensions are in millimetres.*

temperature to find the approximate equivalent temperature. For example, a good working temperature for a woodworking plant might be 20°C, which is equal to 68°F.

Derived Units

There are many derived units in the metric system. Some do not have special names, while others are named for famous scientists. Units such as the newton (N), joule (J), pascal (Pa), and watt (W) use uppercase letters for their symbols. For other units, the symbols are lowercase letters. Note that these letters are symbols and not abbreviations.

Frequently used derived units *without special names* are the following:

➤ Square metre (m²). The square metre is based on the metre and is about 20 percent larger than the square yard. The area covered by finishing materials will be specified in square metres. Panel material may be quoted and sold by its area in square metres plus its thickness in millimetres. Small areas such as plot plans will be shown in square metres. Fig. B-4.

➤ Cubic metre (m³). The base unit of volume is the cubic metre. This is a large unit, about 30 percent larger than the cubic yard. A cube that measures one decimetre (¹/₁₀ of a metre, or 10 centimetres) on each side is called a cubic decimetre (dm³). A cubic decimetre, when used as a unit of liquid capacity, is called a litre.

➤ Litre (L). The litre, a unit of liquid capacity, is slightly larger than the quart (about 5 percent more). It is the unit used for liquids such as finishing materials. Since most finishing materials are normally packaged in 5-gallon, 1-gallon, and 1-quart sizes, the metric quantities will be the number of litres close to those sizes. For example, the gallon may be replaced by the 3-litre (0.8 gal) or 4-litre (1.06 gal) size. The coverage of a litre of paint will be just a little more than that of a quart since the litre is slightly larger.

➤ Metres per second (m/s). Speed in the metric system is given in metres per second. Most machine speeds, however, are shown in metres per minute (m/min).

➤ Kilograms per cubic metre (kg/m³). Density is measured in kilograms per cubic metre. The density of sand for example is about 1700 kg/m³. Fig. B-5.

Commonly used derived units *with special names* are the following:

➤ Newton (N). The unit of force in the metric system is the newton. The force of gravity on a 1-kg mass is 9.8 N at sea level and 1.6 N on the moon. The force of gravity on a person with a mass of 100 kg (220 lb) is 980 N on earth and 160 N on the moon.

➤ Pascal (Pa). The unit of pressure is the pascal. Because one pascal is a very small amount, pressure is normally measured in kilopascals (kPa). One pound per square inch (psi) is equal to about 7 kPa. For example, if the air pressure specified for spraying is 60 psi, the metric equivalent is about 420 kPa. The strength of concrete is given in megapascals (MPa).

➤ Joule (J). The joule is the unit of energy or work. It is a very small unit; therefore, the kilojoule (kJ) is used most often. One kilojoule is about

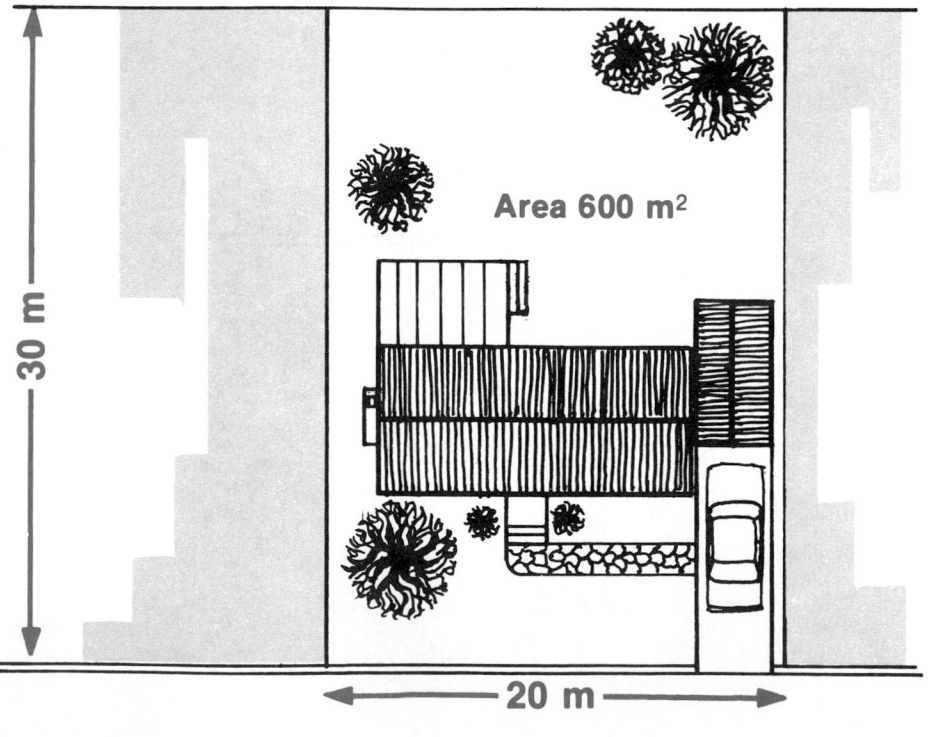

Area 600 m²

30 m

20 m

Fig. B-4. *This plot plan is 20 m wide and 30 m deep. Therefore, the area of the plot is found by multiplying 20 m by 30 m, which equals 600 m².*

equal to 1 British Thermal Unit (Btu) in the customary system.

➤ Watt (W). The unit for all power in the metric system, not just electricity, is the watt. However, the kilowatt (kW) is a more common unit. A small electric lamp may consume 100 watts per hour (W/h). One horsepower (hp) is equal to about three-quarters of a kW. Therefore, a 2-hp motor on a concrete mixer is listed as a 1.5-kW motor in metric units. The common units used in construction are shown in Table D and Table E.

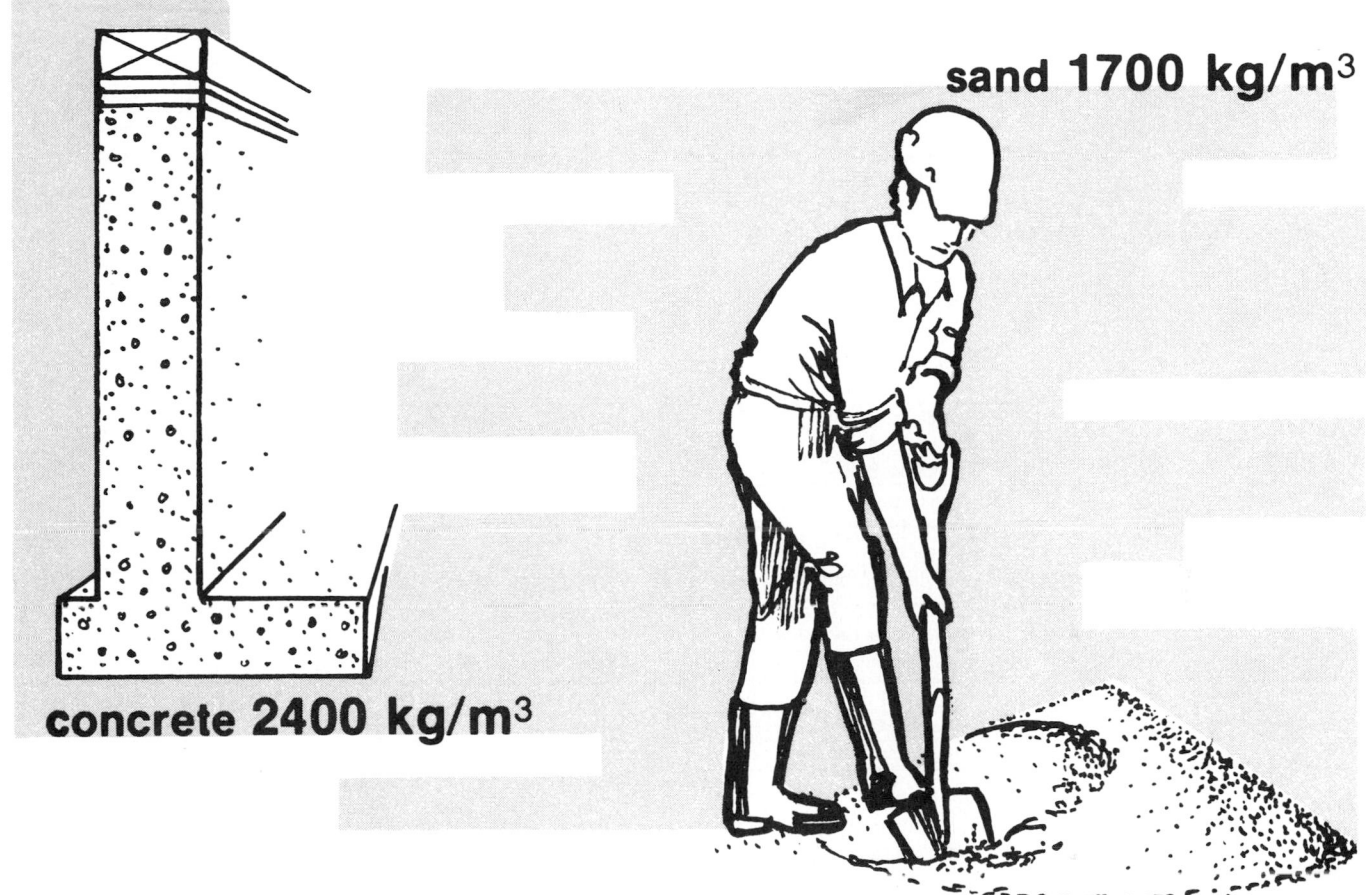

sand 1700 kg/m³

concrete 2400 kg/m³

Fig. B-5. *A cubic yard of sand weighs 2861 pounds. A cubic metre of sand, which is 30 percent larger than a yard, is equal to 3740 pounds.*

TABLE D. *A Customary-to-Metric Comparison of Common Construction Units.*

Units	Customary	Metric (SI)
Length	1ft	= 0.304 8 m
Area	1ft²	= 0.092 903 m²
Weight	1lb	= 0.453 592 kg
Volume	1ft³	= 0.028 317 m³
Volume (liquid)	1 gal	= 3.785 41 L
Mass per Unit Area	1 lb/ft²	= 4.882 43 kg/m²
Temperature Interval	1°F	= 0.555 556 K
Equivalent Temperature	$5/9\ t_f - 32 + 273.15$	$= t_k$
U-Values	1 Btu/(ft² • h • °F)	= 5.678 26 W/(m²• K)
Heat Flow	1 Btu/(ft² • h)	= 3.154 59 W/m²
R-Values	1 (ft² • h • °F)/Btu	= 0.176 109 (m² • K)/W
Heat Flow Rate	1 Btu/h	= 0.293 071 W
Tons of Refrigeration	1 Ton (12,000 Btu/h)	= 3.517 kW

TABLE E. *A Conversion Table of Common Metric Units.*

Quantity	Metric Unit and Symbol	Conversion Factors (approximate)	
		Customary to Metric Units	Metric to Customary Units
Length	millimetre (mm) centimetre (cm)	1 in. = 25.4 mm* 1 in. = 2.54 cm* 1 ft = 30.5 cm	1 mm = 0.0394 in. 1 cm = 0.394 in.
	metre (m) kilometre (km)	1 yd = 0.914 m 1 mi = 1.61 km	1 m = 3.28 ft 1 km = 0.62 mi
Weight (Mass)	gram (g) kilogram (kg) metric ton or tonne (t)	1 oz = 28.3 g 1 lb = 454 g 1 long ton = 1.02 t	1 g = 0.0353 oz 1 kg = 2.2 lb 1 t = 0.98 long ton
Area	square centimetre (cm²) square metre (m²)	1 in.² = 6.45 cm² 1 ft² = 929 cm² 1 yd² = 0.836 m²	1 cm² = 0.155 in² 1 m² = 10.8 ft² 1 m² = 1.2 yd²
	hectare (ha) square kilometre (km²)	1 acre = 0.405 ha 1 m² = 2.59 km²	1 ha = 2.47 acres 1 km² = 0.386 m²
Volume	cubic centimetre (cm³) cubic metre (m³)	1 in.³ = 16.4 cm³ 1 ft³ = 28 300 cm³ 1 yd³ = 0.765 m³	1 cm³ = 0.061 in.³ 1 m³ = 35.3 ft³ 1 m³ = 1.31 yd³
Volume (liquids and gross)	millilitre (ml) liter (L or l) kilolitre (kl)	1 fl oz = 29.6 ml 1 liq qt = 0.946 liter 1 gal = 3.79 liters	1 ml = 0.033 8 fl oz 1 liter = 1.057 liq qt 1 kl = 264 gal
Time Interval	second (s) minute (min) hour (h)		
Speed	metre per minute (m/min)	1 ft/min = 0.305 m/min	1 m/min = 3.28 ft/min
Pressure	kilopascal (kPa)	1 psi = 6.89 kPa	1 kPa = 0.145 psi
Energy	kilojoule (kJ)	1 Btu = 1.06 kJ	1 kJ = 0.948 Btu
Power	kilowatt (kW)	1 hp = 0.746 kW	1 kW = 1.34 hp
Temperature	degree Celsius (°C)	°C = 5/9 (°F-32)	°F = 9/5 °C + 32
*Accurate	47-13 Conversion of metric units to customary units and the reverse.		

USING THE METRIC SYTEM

When using SI, take care to conform to proper SI style. Use symbols only with numerical symbols and never with longhand names, i.e., 15 A, 15 amperes, or fifteen A. Write numbers of less than one with a zero to the left of the decimal marker, i.e., 0.5 mm.

Some other rules to follow when writing in SI are:

1. Always leave a space between a numerical symbol and the SI symbol, i.e., 38 mm, not 38mm.

2. Never use a period after a unit symbol except at the end of a sentence. (Symbols are never pluralized.)

3. Symbols start with upper case only if their units are named after someone. Capitalize only the first letter of the symbol, e.g., Hz for hertz.

4. Write fractions in decimal form wherever possible.

5. Express angles in decimalized degrees rather than in minutes and seconds.

6. With the exception of the degree Celsius, do not capitalize unit names unless they occur at the start of a sentence.

7. Do not use hyphens between units and prefixes, between complex units, or between prefixes and unit symbols.

8. When writing compound units involving division in symbol form, use the solidus (/) to indicate division. It stands for the word "per," e.g., 4/min (not r.p.m.) for revolutions per minute.

9. Use only one prefix with a unit at any one time.

On construction drawings certain style variations and standards apply. Whole numbers from one through nine may be written without a decimal marker and zero to the right of the number. Dimensions are expressed only in millimetres or metres. Whenever possible, only one unit is used for any particular drawing. Unit symbols may be omitted, providing the drawing carries a note identifying the unit of measure to be applied. If both metres and millimetres must appear on the same drawing, and it is desired to omit the unit symbols, all dimensions in metres must be carried three places beyond the decimal marker, e.g., 12.600. Whole numbers then indicate millimetres, e.g., 1200. If it is necessary, however, to specify item sizes (such as floor coverings or vapor barriers) in decimalized millimetre dimensions, the unit symbol must appear. Likewise, the unit symbol is used after all other notations and dimensions, e.g., 5.400 m², 2.6 mm.

There are three major steps involved in converting to the metric system:

1. Changing from measuring in the customary system to measuring with the metric system only.

2. Developing metric standards for materials based on metric modules.

3. Producing standard-sized materials based on the metric modules developed.

The first step is called a *soft* conversion because no physical changes take place. You simply measure existing materials using the metric system. An example would be to measure the thickness of a 7-⁵/₈" concrete block as 193.7 millimetres (mm). The thickness of the block has not changed; only the measurement has been converted. To convert from inches to millimetres you multiply: 1" = 25.4 mm.

The second and third conversion steps, which are very complex, are called *hard* conversion. Before an *all-metric* house can be built, it will be necessary to have metric standards for all its building materials. Such materials include brick, dimensioned lumber, panel stock, roofing materials, windows, doors, kitchen cabinets, appliances, and everything else used in its construction. In developing these standards, full millimetre metric modules of convenient sizes will be used. The basic module for building construction will be 100 mm. All measurements will be multiples and submultiples of 100 m. For example, lumber will be produced in widths of 25, 50, and 75 mm. Other house measurements will be 300, 600, 900, and 1200 mm. Panel stock will measure 1200 x 2400 mm.

When metric standards are available, companies must then produce materials based on metric modules. Only after such a change takes place will it be possible to build a completely metric house or building.

MODULE SIZES FOR HOME AND BUILDING CONSTRUCTION

The conversion to metric units for home and building construction

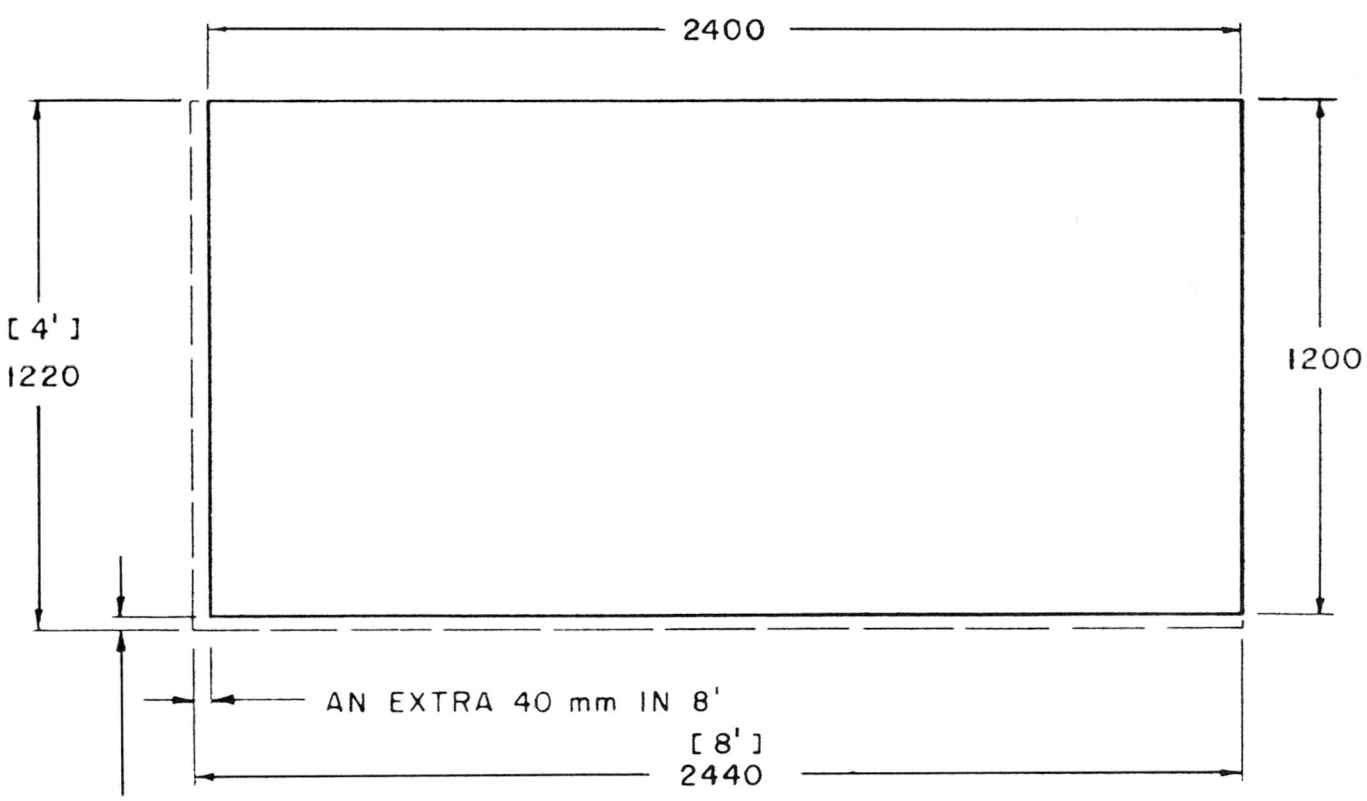

Fig. B-6. *The metric house will be built on a module of 100 mm. Therefore the sheets of panel stock will measure 1200 x 2400 mm.*

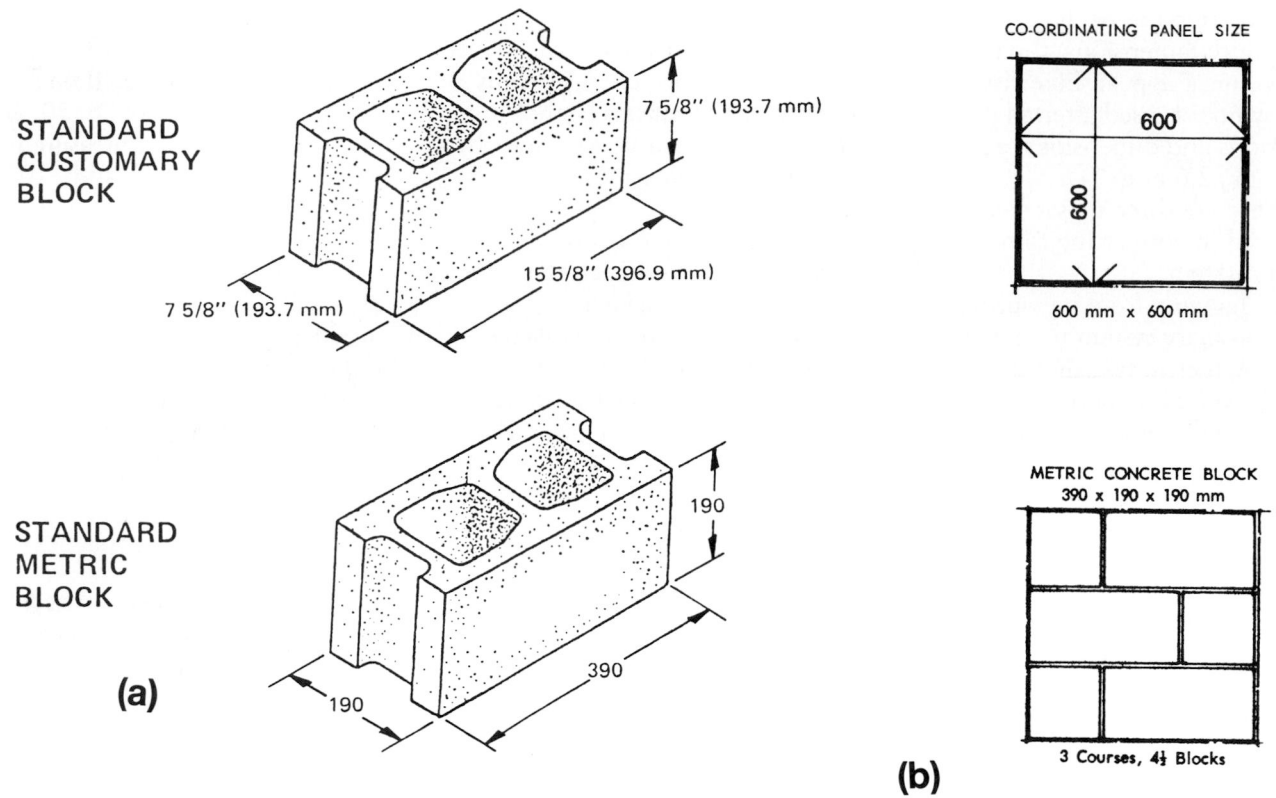

STANDARD CUSTOMARY BLOCK

7 5/8" (193.7 mm)

15 5/8" (396.9 mm)

7 5/8" (193.7 mm)

STANDARD METRIC BLOCK

(a)

190

390

190

CO-ORDINATING PANEL SIZE

600

600

600 mm x 600 mm

METRIC CONCRETE BLOCK
390 x 190 x 190 mm

3 Courses, 4½ Blocks

(b)

Fig. B-7. *(a) A metric-sized block will be about ⅛" smaller in thickness and height and about ¼" shorter than a block made to customary size. (b) Four and one-half metric blocks will make a wall measuring 600 x 600 mm.*

is more complicated than in any other area of woodworking. Most homes in the United States are designed and built to a standard module of 4". The design and materials used are thus based on multiples of 4". This allows everything to fit together easily. Typical measurements in home construction include 4", 8", 12", 16", 24", and 48". In framing a house, for example, studs are placed 16" or 24" apart to take a sheet of panel material that measures exactly 48" wide. Normally, walls are made 8' (96" or 24 x 4") high so that a 4' x 8' panel can be used without being cut.

In the metric system, the recommended standard is a building module of 100 mm, which is slightly smaller than 4". Commonly used multiples of this

standard are 300, 600, 900, and 1200 mm. All standard building products must be produced to the 100-mm module before it is possible to build an all-metric home. For example, using this metric module, the standard panel size for plywood, particleboard, and other sheet stock must be 1200 x 2400 mm. This sheet size is ¾" narrower and 1-½" shorter than the customary 4' x 8' sheet. Fig. B-6.

A customary concrete block has a nominal size of 8" x 8" x 16". The actual size of that block is 7-⅝" x 7-⅝" x 15-⅝" to allow ⅜" for mortar. Metric blocks would be made to a nominal size of 200 x 200 x 400 mm. Their actual size would be 190 x 190 x 390 mm to allow for 10 mm of mortar. The metric size is only slightly smaller than the customary block. Fig. B-7.

To determine the number of metric-sized blocks needed to build a wall, use the following equation:

wall area in mm²

$3600 \text{ mm}^2 \times 4.5 = $ total number of blocks needed

This formula is based on 4-½ blocks equaling a wall area of 600 x 600 mm. Both metric concrete blocks and bricks will be sized to fit the 600 x 600 mm coordinating panel size. This size is equal to one-eighth of a metric panel (1200 x 2400 mm).

A standard customary-sized brick has actual dimensions of 3-⅝" x 2-¼" x 7-⅝", which allows for ⅜" of mortar. The standard metric brick will allow for a 10-mm mortar joint and will measure 90 x 67 x 190 mm. Fig. B-8. The 67-mm dimension is rounded off so that 9 courses equal 600 mm, the preferred module size.

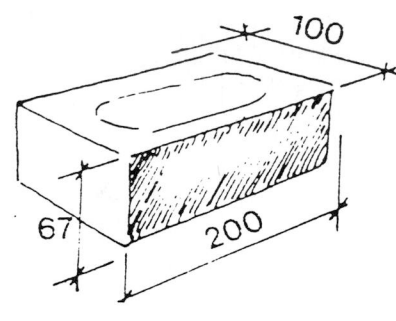

Fig. B-8. *The nominal dimensions shown for the metric brick include a 10-mm mortar allowance.*

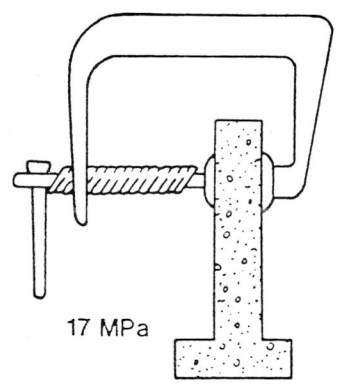

Fig. B-9. *A foundation wall must have a compression strength of 17 MPa (equal to 2465 psi) after 28 days.*

In masonry work, the only hard conversion will be in the size of bags of cement and other loose masonry materials. The bags will have a mass (weight) of 40 kg (88 lb), which is smaller than the U.S. customary standard 94-lb bag, and slightly larger than the Canadian imperial standard 80-lb bag. Other changes will be from customary to metric terms. For example, a concrete foundation wall must have a compressive strength at 28 days of 17 MPa. Fig. B-9. Garage floors and exterior steps require the greater strength of 21 MPa.

Concrete for a foundation must not be placed if the temperature is less than 10°C or more than 27°C. The density of concrete averages about 2400 kg/m³, bulk cement about 1400 kg/m³, and dry sand about 1700 kg/m³. In masonry work, it is well to remember the 10-20-30 metric rule, which is as follows:

➤ A *metre* is about 10 percent longer than a yard.

➤ A *square metre* is about 20 percent larger than a square yard.

➤ A *cubic metre* is about 30 percent larger than a cubic yard.

DIMENSIONAL COORDINATION

One advantage of going metric is that it will give the construction industry an opportunity to rethink the size of each product and the number of sizes needed. When the construction industry went metric in other English-speaking countries, the number of sizes of doors, windows, and other millwork items was greatly reduced.

When the industry goes metric, its efficiency will be greatly improved if all products are dimensionally coordinated. *Dimensional coordination* means that everyone connected with the construction industry will use the same dimension language. They will also manufacture all components to fit together in the space allotted to them. The internationally accepted basic module for metric buildings is 100 mm, which is slightly less than 4". Using this module, studs will be placed either 400 or 600 mm on center. Plywood and other panel stock will be manufactured to be 1200 x 2400 mm in size. Ceiling heights will be from 2400 to 3000 mm. The base for kitchen counters will be 600 mm wide and 900 mm high. To use dimensional coordination effectively, all manufacturers of building products must base all sizes on the same module. Obviously, this cannot be done unless there is agreement among all people involved.

BUILDING A METRIC HOUSE

A metric house could be built in the United States today by following these steps:

1. Design the house to metric dimensions based on the 100-mm module using joists, studs, rafters, and trusses spaced at 400 mm or 600 mm on center.

2. Use panel stock of metric size (1200 mm x 2400 mm).

3. Convert all other customary materials, such as bricks, cement blocks, doors, windows, and other materials, to metric dimensions using a soft conversion. Include all metric sizes on the plans.

4. Use rules, squares, and other measuring tools in metric units.

5. Acquaint the builder, owner, and others involved in the project with the metric system.

Before an all-metric home can be economically produced, the following must take place:

➤ There must be nationwide agreement on the 100-mm module and the multiples and submultiples that will be used.

➤ Each trade organization must establish a series of metric sizes in which all materials will be produced, based on the 100-mm module.

➤ Architectural standards must be revised to reflect hard metric conversion.

➤ Building codes must be revised to reflect hard metric conversion.

➤ Metric materials must be tested to make sure they meet current safety standards.

➤ All metric materials must be produced and be available at the same time.

➤ Everyone involved in building construction from the architect to the carpenter must understand the metric system.

➤ Metric measuring tools, including rules and squares, must be available.

When all of these steps have been completed, a metric house could be constructed with a substantial saving in time and money. Fig. B-10. In other countries that have gone metric, including Canada, Australia, New Zealand, and Great Britain, the government has passed laws requiring the building construction industry to make a hard conversion to metric.

Fig. B-10. *The apprentices shown here are competing in a contest that allows them to show their skills in framing a house. The framing of a metric house requires the same skills as those needed to frame a house using the customary system.*

Appendix C: Math and Science Concepts

This appendix provides an overview of some major concepts in math and science that apply to carpentry and building construction. The tables referred to in the various examples are at the end of this appendix.

ANGLES

Angles are commonly given in degrees or fractions of a degree. One degree is divided into 60 equal parts called minutes. Each minute is divided into 60 seconds.
1° = 60 minutes
1 minute = 60 seconds

A straight angle contains 180°.

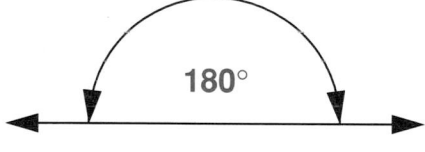

A right angle contains 90°. (Note the symbol for right angle.)

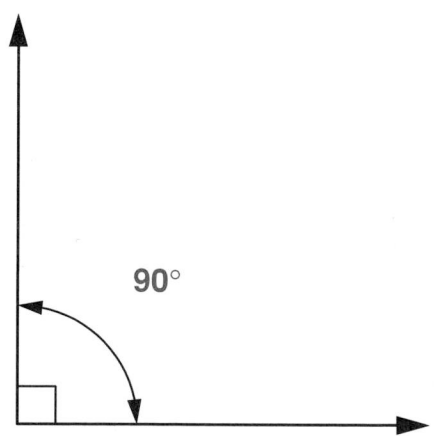

An acute angle contains less than 90°.

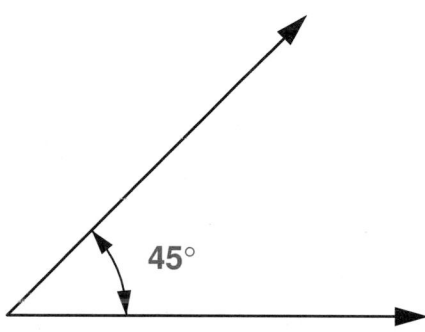

An obtuse angle contains more than 90° but less than 180°.

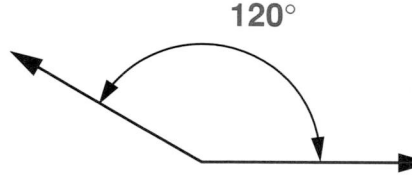

Two angles are complementary if their angles total 90°.

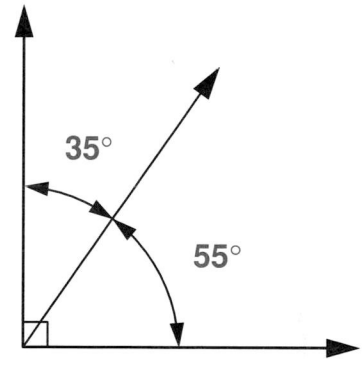

Two angles are supplementary if their angles total 180°.

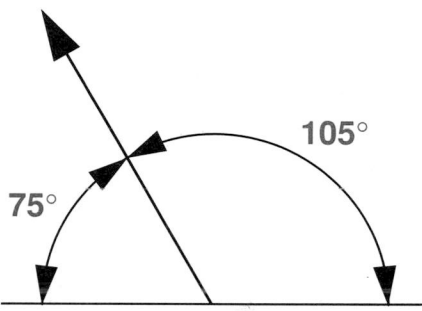

Lines are said to be parallel if they are always the same distance apart and in the same plane.

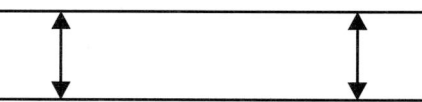

When two straight lines cross, note how the adjacent angles total 180° and how the opposite angles are always equal.

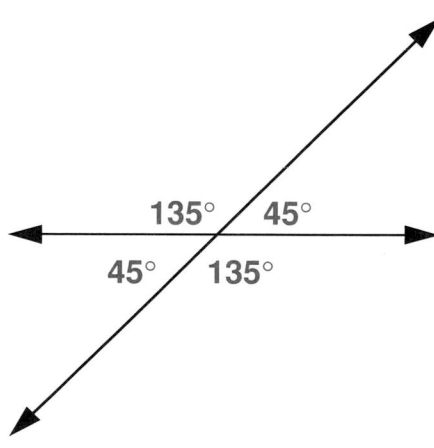

If all four angles are 90°, the two lines are perpendicular to each other.

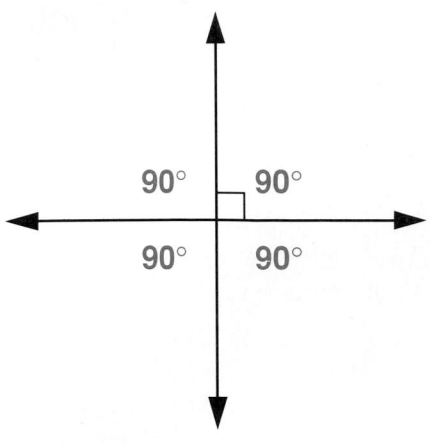

POLYGONS

A polygon is a closed figure with straight sides. It is classified by the number of sides.

In a regular polygon all sides are equal in length and all angles are equal.

3 Sides = Triangle

4 Sides = Square

5 Sides = Pentagon

6 Sides = Hexagon

7 Sides = Heptagon

8 Sides = Octagon

9 Sides = Nonagon

10 Sides = Decagon

12 Sides = Dodecagon

TRIANGLES

A closed three-sided figure is called a triangle. All triangles have a total of 180° in the sum of the angles.

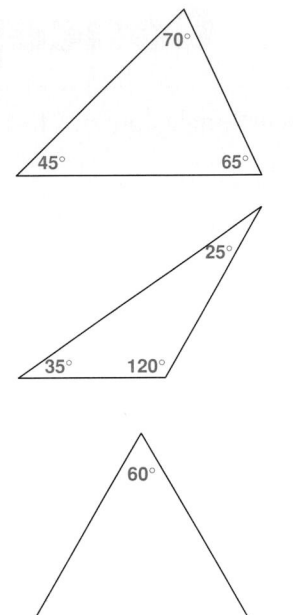

There is always a 90° angle in a right triangle.

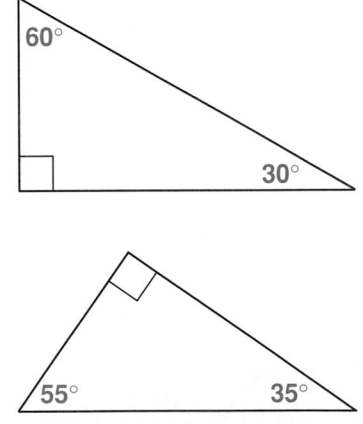

An isosceles triangle has two equal sides and two equal angles.

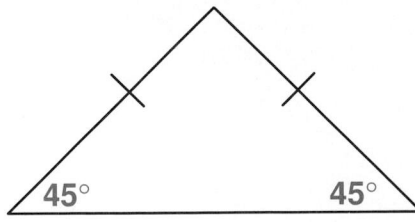

An equilateral triangle has three equal sides and three equal angles.

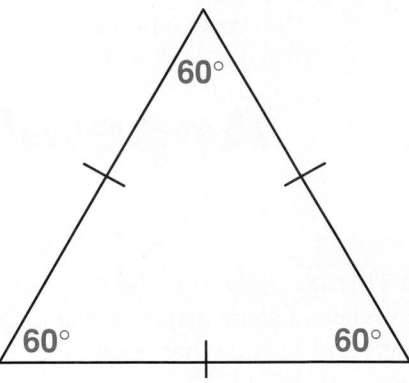

A scalene triangle has three sides of different lengths and three angles of different sizes.

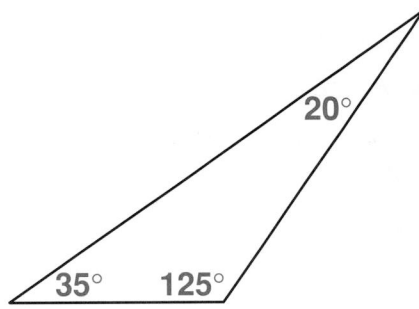

RECTANGLES

A rectangle is a four-sided shape with four right angles.

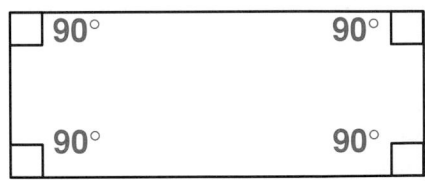

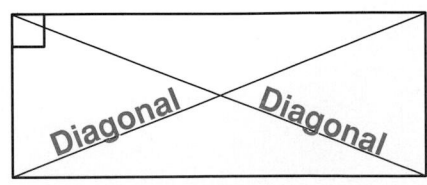

Diagonals of a rectangle are always equal. A diagonal divides a rectangle into two equal right triangles.

PERIMETER

The perimeter of a polygon is the total of the length of all the sides.

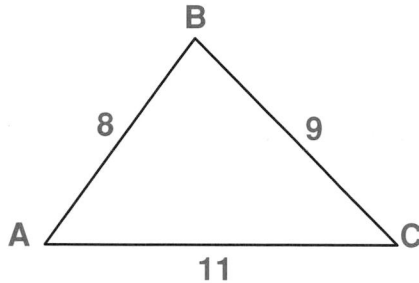

The perimeter of this triangle is:
8 + 9 + 11 = 28

The perimeter of this rectangle is:
P = 2 (length + width)
P = 2 (45.6 + 27.9)
P = 2 (73.5)
Perimeter = 147

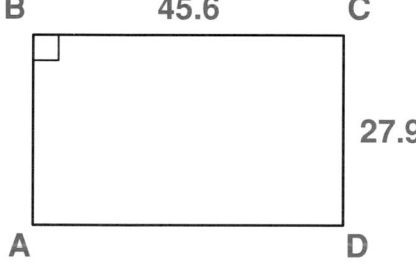

AREA

Area of a square
Area = 8^2
Area = 64 ft²

Area = S²

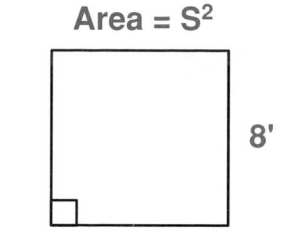

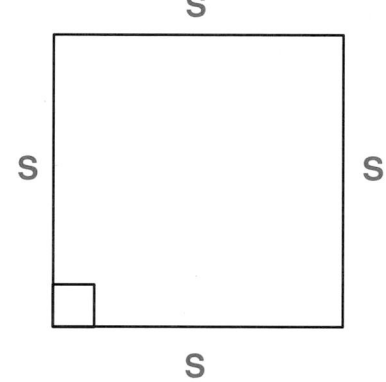

Area of a rectangle
Area = L x W
Area = 12 x 9
Area = 108 ft²

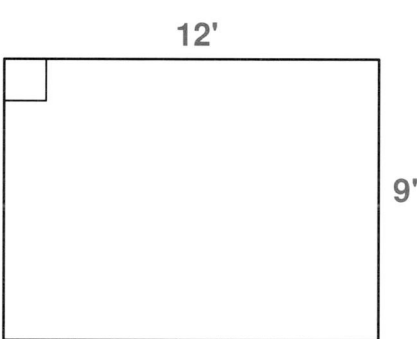

Area of a triangle
A = ½ BH

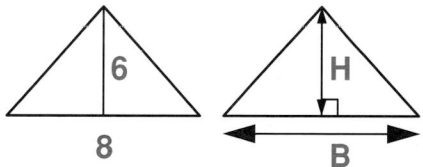

A = ½ x B x H
A = ½ x 8 x 6
A = 24 ft²

A = ½ x B x H
A = ½ x 12" x 5"
A = 30 in²

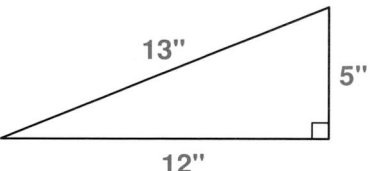

Area of shaded triangle:
A = ½ x BH
A = ½ 3' 6" x 4' 9"
A = ½ x 3.5 x 4.75
A = 8.3125 sq. ft.

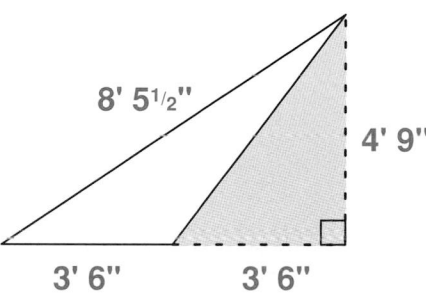

Area of a circle
π = 3.1416
A = π R²
A = 3.1416 x 4²
A = 3.1416 x 16
A = 50.2656 in²

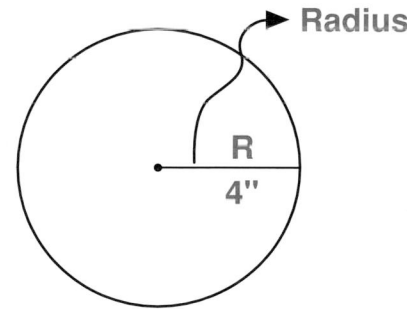

THE PYTHAGOREAN THEOREM

The Pythagorean theorem states that the square of the hypotenuse of a *right triangle* equals the sum of the squares of the other two sides. The hypotenuse is defined as the side opposite the 90° angle.

$A^2 + B^2 = C^2$

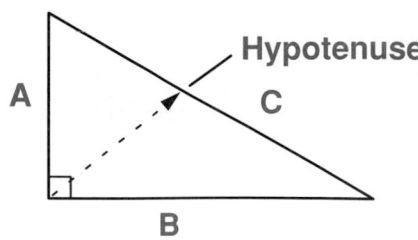

$C^2 = 6^2 + 8^2$
$C^2 = 36 + 64$
$C^2 = 100$
$C = \sqrt{100}$
$C = 10'$

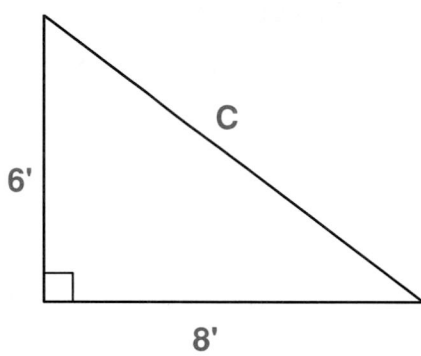

$C^2 = 8^2 + 11^2$
$C^2 = 64 + 121$
$C^2 = 185$
$C = \sqrt{185}$
$C = 13.601'$

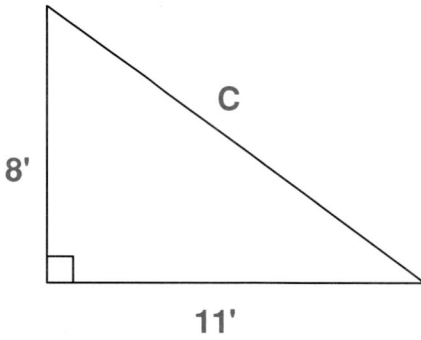

$A^2 + B^2 = C^2$
$A^2 + 6^2 = 9^2$
$A^2 + 36 = 81$
$A^2 = 81 - 36$
$A^2 = 45$
$A = \sqrt{45}$
$A = 6.708'$

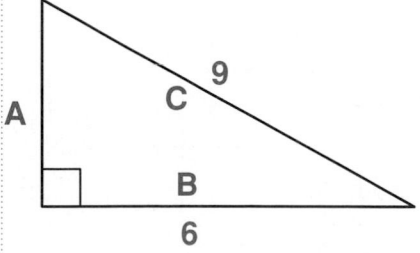

What is the length of the diagonal of this rectangle (floor of house)?
$36^2 + 28^2 = C^2$
$1296 + 784 = C^2$
$2080 = C^2$
$\sqrt{2080} = C$
$45.607' = C$

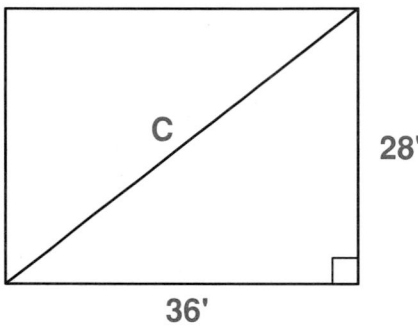

What is 12' 9⅞" in decimal feet? To find what part of a foot, in decimal form, 9⅞" is, simply look on Table A for 9⅞". Add that figure to 12'.
$12' + .8229' = 12.8229'$
$12.8229' = 12'\ 9\frac{7}{8}"$

What is 4.2292 feet in feet and inches?
To find what .2292 is, look on Table A to find the closest number and add the inches to 4'.
$4' + 2\frac{3}{4}" = 4'\ 2\frac{3}{4}"$
26.9072 ft = approximately (within ¹⁄₃₂") 26' 10⅞"

Find the diagonal of this rectangular building using the Pythagorean theorem.

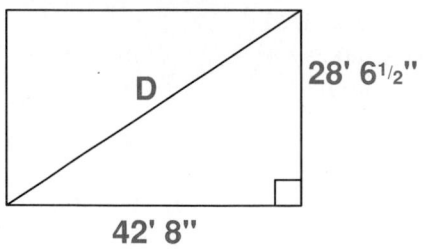

Diagonal² (D):
$= (42'\ 8")^2 + (28'\ 6\frac{1}{2}")^2$
42' 8" = 42.6667'
28' 6½" = 28.5417
$D^2 = 42.6667^2 + 28.5417^2$
$D^2 = 1820.4472 + 814.6286$
$D = \sqrt{2635.0758}$
$D = 51.3330$
$D = 51'\ 4"$

Using Table A and the Pythagorean theorem, find the diagonal of this rectangular house?

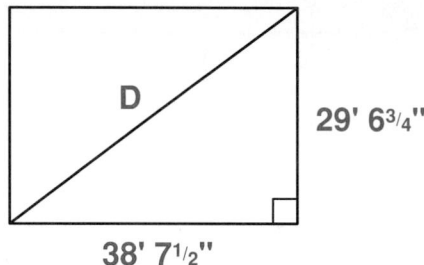

38' 7½" = 38.6250
29' 6¾" = 29.5625
$D^2 = 38.6250^2 + 29.5625^2$
$D^2 = 1491.8906 + 873.9414$
$D = \sqrt{2365.8320}$
$D = 48.6398'$
$D = 48'\ 7\frac{11}{16}"$

CIRCLES

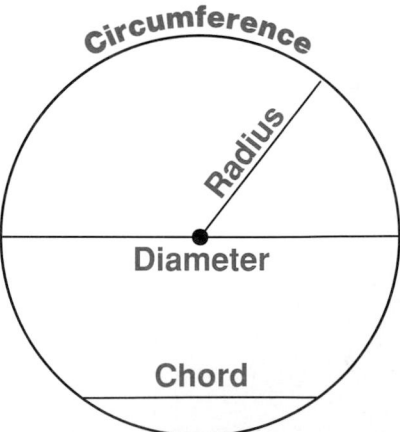

- The radius of a circle is a straight line from the center of a point on the circumference.
- The diameter is a straight line through the center with its ends on the circumference.

- A chord is a straight line having each end on the circumference.

π = 3.1416
R = 7
D = 14

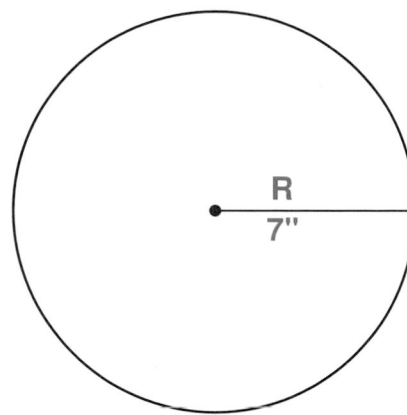

Circumference = 2πR
Circumference = 2 x 3.1416 x 7
Circumference = 43.9824"
  or
Circumference = πD
Circumference = 3.1416 x 14
Circumference = 43.9824"

Area of a circle = pi times the radius squared
A = πR²
A = 3.1416 x 4²
A = 3.1416 x 16
A = 50.2656 in²

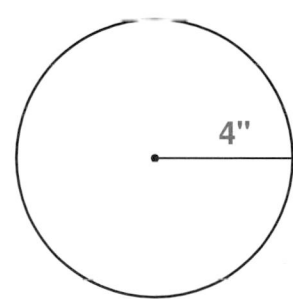

Area of a circle is also equal to the circumference times one-half the radius.
A = C x ¹/₂R

Surface Area of a rectangular prism is always in squares.

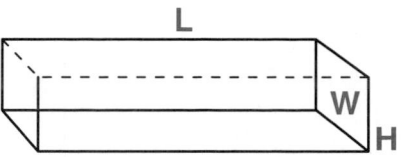

Surface Area = 2(LW + WH x LH)

Surface Area
= 2(10 x 8 + 8 x 5 + 10 x 5)
SA = 2(80 + 40 + 50)
SA = 2(170)
SA = 340 in²

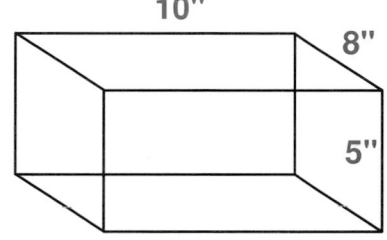

VOLUME OF A RECTANGULAR

Volume = Length x Width x Height

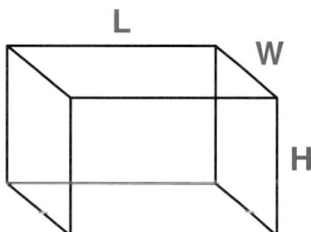

Volume is always in cubes.
  = 6 x 4 x 2
  = 48 in³

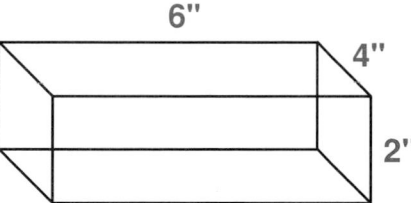

Volume = L x W x H
Volume = 40 x 3 x .333
Volume = 39.96 ft³ (cubic ft)

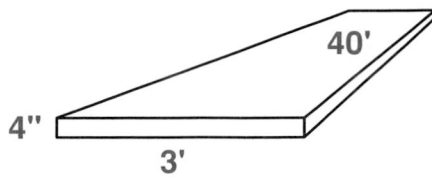

If this concrete is for a sidewalk its volume will need to be converted to cubic yards. Concrete is generally sold by the cubic yard.
1 cubic yard = 27 cubic feet
39.96 ft³ ÷ 27 = 1.48 yd³

Math does not have to be a difficult subject. Using a calculator with sine, cosine, and tangent keys, you can easily solve many construction and manufacturing problems. The following are trigonometric functions. They can be applied to many problems in the field of construction and manufacturing.

FINDING ANGLES AND MEASUREMENTS

There are ways to find angles and measurements with only limited input. Try these various formulas to find the unknown. It's not as hard as it might seem. Using a math calculator is the easiest way to find the various "functions," but you may also use trigonometric tables. Refer to Table B.

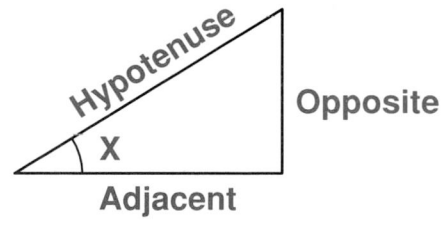

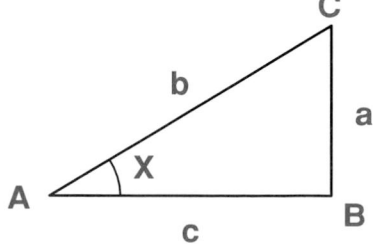

$$\text{SINE } x = \frac{\text{opposite side}}{\text{hypotenuse}}$$

$$\text{COS } x = \frac{\text{adjacent side}}{\text{hypotenuse}}$$

$$\text{TAN } x = \frac{\text{opposite side}}{\text{adjacent side}}$$

$$\text{CSC } x = \frac{\text{hypotenuse}}{\text{opposite side}}$$

$$\text{SCC } x = \frac{\text{hypotenuse}}{\text{adjacent side}}$$

$$\text{COT } x = \frac{\text{adjacent side}}{\text{opposite side}}$$

$$\text{SINE } 43° = \frac{\text{opposite side}}{\text{hypotenuse}}$$

a = 15 x SINE 43°
a = 15 x .6820
a = 10.23" (See Table B)
a = $10^{15}/_{64}$"

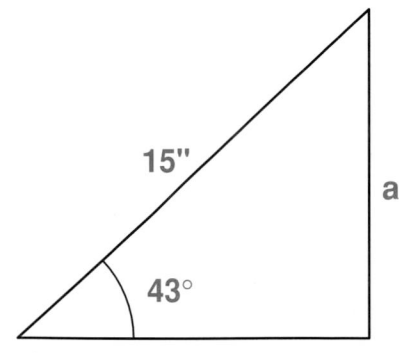

$$\text{TAN } 27 = \frac{\text{opposite side}}{\text{adjacent side}}$$

Opposite side
= Adjacent side x TAN 27
a = 7 x TAN 27
a = 7 x .5095
a = 3.5666" (See Table B)
a = $3^9/_{16}$"

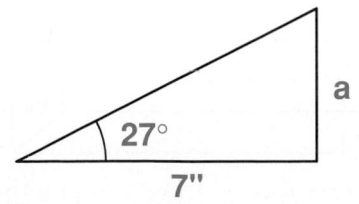

The Pythagorean Theorem
Hypotenuse^2 = Sum of the squares
of the two legs
a^2 = Hypotenuse^2 - 8^2

a = $\sqrt{10^2 - 8^2}$
a = $\sqrt{100-64}$
a = $\sqrt{36}$
a = 6"

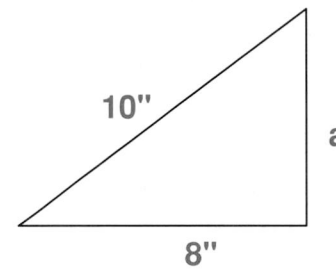

b = 5.5 x COS 44°
b = 5.5 x .7193
b = 3.9562 (See Table B)
b = $3^{61}/_{64}$"

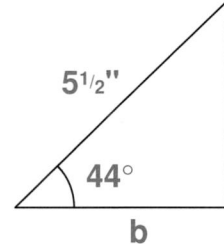

b = 3.125 x COT 11°
b = 3.125 x 5.1446
b = 16.0769 (See Table B)
b = $16^5/_{64}$"

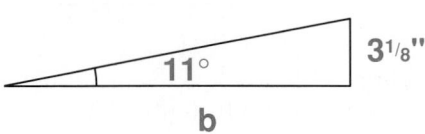

c = $\sqrt{40^2 + 32^2}$
c = $\sqrt{1600 + 1024}$
c = $\sqrt{2624}$
c = 51.2250
c = 51' 2$^{11}/_{16}$"

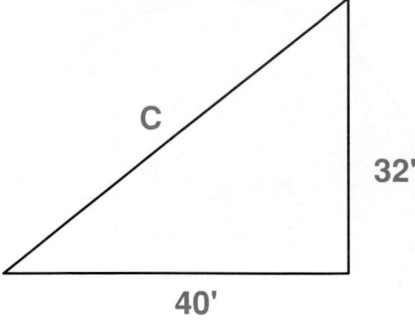

c = 8' 2" x CSC 45°
c = 8.1667 x 1.4142
c = 11.5493'
c = 11' 6$^9/_{16}$"

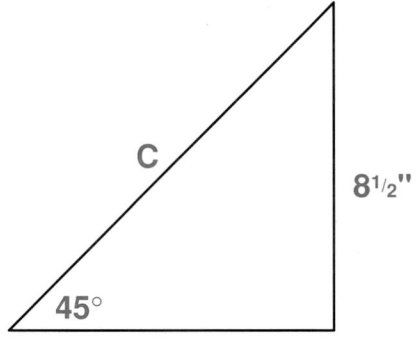

c = 16 x SEC 22°
c = 16 x 1.0785
c = 17.2560'
c = 17' 3$^1/_{16}$"

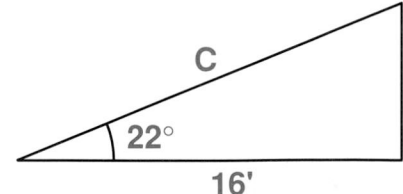

$SIN\ A\ =\ \dfrac{4.5}{6.5}$

$SIN\ A\ =\ .6923$ (See Table B)
$SIN\ A\ =\ 44°$

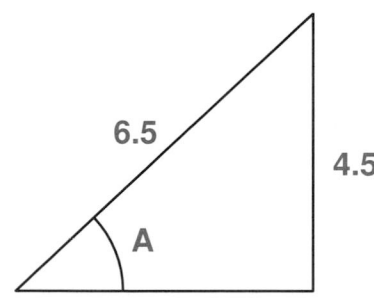

$COS\ A = \dfrac{8}{8.5}$

$COS\ A = .9412$ (See Table B)
$COS\ A = 20°$

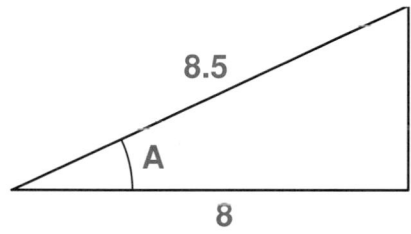

$TAN\ A = \dfrac{6'\ 7\frac{1}{2}''}{12'\ 5\frac{1}{2}''}$ (See Table A)

$TAN\ A = \dfrac{6.6250}{12.4583}$

$TAN\ A = .5318$ (See Table B)
$TAN\ A = 28°$

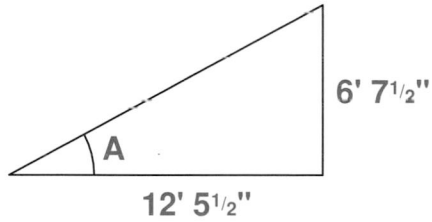

$A = 90° - 64°$
$A = 26°$
(26° is the complementary angle of 64°)

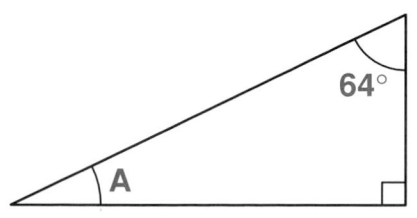

RATIOS AND PROPORTIONS

A ratio is the comparison of two numbers. Often ratios are used to show how large one object is when compared to another. A ratio is a comparison of two numbers by division.

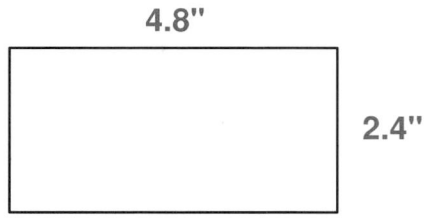

In the rectangle the ratio of the length to width is 4.8:2.4. Ratios can be written as fractions $\dfrac{4.8}{2.4}$

(Divide both by 2.4.)
4.8:2.4 and 2:1 are equivalent ratios.

What is a ratio equivalent of 4:5?
$^4/_5 = ^4/_5 \times ^3/_3$
$^4/_5 = ^{12}/_{15}$
(Multiply or divide numerator and denominator by the same number.)
12:15 is equivalent to $^4/_5$

A proportion is a statement that has two ratios that are equal.
3:4 = 15:?
$^3/_4 = 15/?$ (Multiply top number and bottom number by 5.)
$^3/_4 = ^{15}/_{20}$

PERCENT

The symbol % means "per hundred."
Thus, 22% means "22 out of 100" or $^{22}/_{100}$, or .22.

Examples
Express 19% as a decimal.
1% = .01
Therefore 19 x .01 = .19
19% = .19

Express .07 as a percent.
.07 = 7 x .01
.07 = 7 x 1%
.07 = 7%

To find the percent of a number, multiply the number by the percent.
22% of 49
22% of 49 = .22 x 49
22% of 49 = 10.78

170% of 28
170% of 28 = 1.70 x 28
170% of 28 = 47.6

25% of a number = 11
What is the number?
1% of the number:
= $^{11}/_{25}$ (11 ÷ 25 = .44)
100% of the number:
= $^{11}/_{25}$ x 100
The number = 44

Some common percents are easier to use as fractions.
25%	–	$^1/_4$
50%	=	$^1/_2$
75%	=	$^3/_4$
33.3%	=	$^1/_3$
66.6%	=	$^2/_3$
20%	=	$^1/_5$
40%	=	$^2/_5$
60%	=	$^3/_5$
80%	=	$^4/_5$
12.5%	=	$^1/_8$
37.5%	=	$^3/_8$
62.5%	=	$^5/_8$
87.5%	=	$^7/_8$

PULLEYS

Pulleys are used to make lifting easier. Imagine standing on a roof and pulling up materials. Now imagine standing on the ground and using a pulley to lift those materials. To raise the load shown in this illustration the effort must be greater than the load.

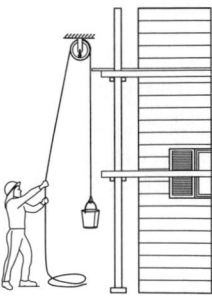

By using more than one pulley you can create a mechanical advantage. A greater advantage is created by using more pulleys. By counting the number of ropes between the top and bottom sets of pulleys you can determine the mechanical advantage.

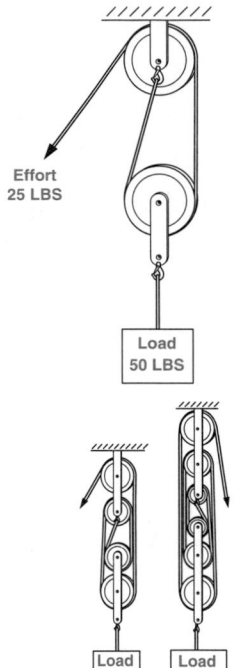

Triangles are used frequently in carpentry. Used together, triangulation can make a structure very strong and rigid.

Note the number of triangles in this roof structure.

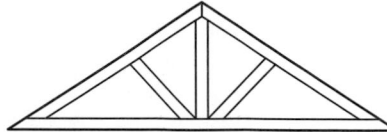

Note that a wall becomes much more stable by adding triangulation.

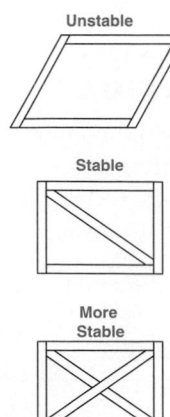

LEVERS

The lever is the most commonly used mechanism in carpentry. It can be used to move a heavy load with little effort or to increase or amplify movement. There are three classes (types) of levers. The class is determined by the location of the pivot in relation to the load.

First-Class Lever

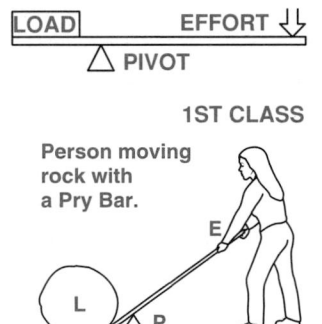

Second-Class Lever

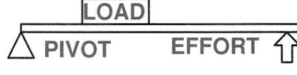

Third-Class Lever

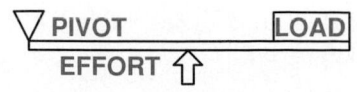

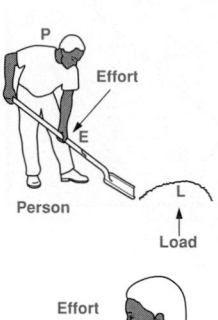

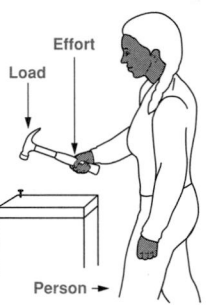

The effort of the force on a lever is determined by the distance of the force from the pivot. It is written as:

Movement = Force X Distance from Pivot

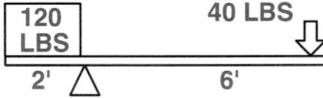

The mechanical advantage of this lever is determined by dividing the load by the effort.

$$MA = \frac{load}{effort}$$

$$MA = {}^{120}/_{40} = {}^{3}/_{1}$$
$$MA = 3 \text{ to } 1$$

TABLE A. *Table of Decimal Equivalents.*

DECIMALS OF A FOOT

FRACTION	DECIMAL	FRACTION	DECIMAL	FRACTION	DECIMAL
1/16	0.0052	4-1/16	0.3385	8-1/16	0.6719
1/8	0.0104	4-1/8	0.3438	8-1/8	0.6771
3/16	0.0156	4-3/16	0.3490	8-3/16	0.6823
1/4	0.0208	4-1/4	0.3542	8-1/4	0.6875
5/16	0.0260	4-5/16	0.3594	8-5/16	0.6927
3/8	0.0313	4-3/8	0.3646	8-3/8	0.6979
7/16	0.0365	4-7/16	0.3698	8-7/16	0.7031
1/2	0.0417	4-1/2	0.3750	8-1/2	0.7083
9/16	0.0469	4-9/16	0.3802	8-9/16	0.7135
5/8	0.0521	4-5/8	0.3854	8-5/8	0.7188
11/16	0.0573	4-11/16	0.3906	8-11/16	0.7240
3/4	0.0625	4-3/4	0.3958	8-3/4	0.7292
13/16	0.0677	4-13/16	0.4010	8-13/16	0.7344
7/8	0.0729	4-7/8	0.4063	8-7/8	0.7396
15/16	0.0781	4-15/16	0.4115	8-15/16	0.7448
1-	0.0833	5-	0.4167	9-	0.7500
1-1/16	0.0885	5-1/16	0.4219	9-1/16	0.7552
1-1/8	0.0938	5-1/8	0.4271	9-1/8	0.7604
1-3/16	0.0990	5-3/16	0.4323	9-3/16	0.7656
1-1/4	0.1042	5-1/4	0.4375	9-1/4	0.7708
1-5/16	0.1094	5-5/16	0.4427	9-5/16	0.7760
1-3/8	0.1146	5-3/8	0.4479	9-3/8	0.7813
1-7/16	0.1198	5-7/16	0.4531	9-7/16	0.7865
1-1/2	0.1250	5-1/2	0.4583	9-1/2	0.7917
1-9/16	0.1302	5-9/16	0.4635	9-9/16	0.7969
1-5/8	0.1354	5-5/8	0.4688	9-5/8	0.8021
1-11/16	0.1406	5-11/16	0.4740	9-11/16	0.8073
1 3/4	0.1458	5 3/4	0.4792	9-3/4	0.8125
1-13/16	0.1510	5-13/16	0.4844	9-13/16	0.8177
1-7/8	0.1563	5-7/8	0.4896	9-7/8	0.8229
1-15/16	0.1615	5-15/16	0.4948	9-15/16	0.8281
2-	0.1667	6-	0.5000	10-	0.8333
2-1/16	0.1719	6-1/16	0.5052	10-1/16	0.8385
2-1/8	0.1771	6-1/8	0.5104	10-1/8	0.8438
2-3/16	0.1823	6-3/16	0.5156	10-3/16	0.8490
2-1/4	0.1875	6-1/4	0.5208	10-1/4	0.8542
2-5/16	0.1927	6-5/16	0.5260	10-5/16	0.8594
2-3/8	0.1979	6-3/8	0.5313	10-3/8	0.8646
2-7/16	0.2031	6-7/16	0.5365	10-7/16	0.8698
2-1/2	0.2083	6-1/2	0.5417	10-1/2	0.8750
2-9/16	0.2135	6-9/16	0.5469	10-9/16	0.8802
2-5/8	0.2188	6-5/8	0.5521	10-5/8	0.8854
2-11/16	0.2240	6-11/16	0.5573	10-11/16	0.8906
2-3/4	0.2292	6-3/4	0.5625	10-3/4	0.8958
2-13/16	0.2344	6-13/16	0.5677	10-13/16	0.9010
2-7/8	0.2396	6-7/8	0.5729	10-7/8	0.9063
2-15/16	0.2448	6-15/16	0.5781	10-15/16	0.9115
3-	0.2500	7-	0.5833	11-	0.9167
3-1/16	0.2552	7-1/16	0.5885	11-1/16	0.9219
3-1/8	0.2604	7-1/8	0.5938	11-1/8	0.9271
3-3/16	0.2656	7-3/16	0.5990	11-3/16	0.9323
3-1/4	0.2708	7-1/4	0.6042	11-1/4	0.9375
3-5/16	0.2760	7-5/16	0.6094	11-5/16	0.9427
3-3/8	0.2813	7-3/8	0.6146	11-3/8	0.9479
3-7/16	0.2865	7-7/16	0.6198	11-7/16	0.9531
3-1/2	0.2917	7-1/2	0.6250	11-1/2	0.9583
3-9/16	0.2969	7-9/16	0.6302	11-9/16	0.9635
3-5/8	0.3021	7-5/8	0.6354	11-5/8	0.9688
3-11/16	0.3073	7-11/16	0.6406	11-11/16	0.9740
3-3/4	0.3125	7-3/4	0.6458	11-3/4	0.9792
3-13/16	0.3177	7-13/16	0.6510	11-13/16	0.9844
3-7/8	0.3229	7-7/8	0.6563	11-7/8	0.9896
3-15/16	0.3281	7-15/16	0.6615	11-15/16	0.9948
4-	0.3333	8-	0.6667	12-	1.0000

TABLE B. *Table of Trigonometric Tables.*

θ	SIN θ	COS θ	TAN θ	CSC θ	SEC θ	COT θ
0°	0.0000	1.0000	0.0000	—	1.0000	—
1°	0.0175	0.9998	0.0175	57.299	1.0002	57.290
2°	0.0349	0.9994	0.0349	28.654	1.0006	28.636
3°	0.0523	0.9986	0.0524	19.107	1.0014	19.081
4°	0.0698	0.9976	0.0699	14.336	1.0024	14.301
5°	0.0872	0.9962	0.0875	11.474	1.0038	11.4301
6°	0.1045	0.9945	0.1051	9.5668	1.0055	9.5144
7°	0.1219	0.9925	0.1228	8.2055	1.0075	8.1443
8°	0.1392	0.9903	0.1405	7.1853	1.0098	7.1154
9°	0.1564	0.9877	0.1584	6.3925	1.0125	6.3138
10°	0.1736	0.9848	0.1763	5.7588	1.0154	5.6713
11°	0.1908	0.9816	0.1944	5.2408	1.0187	5.1446
12°	0.2079	0.9781	0.2126	4.8097	1.0223	4.7046
13°	0.2250	0.9744	0.2309	4.4454	1.0263	4.3315
14°	0.2419	0.9703	0.2493	4.1336	1.0306	4.0108
15°	0.2588	0.9659	0.2679	3.8637	1.0353	3.7321
16°	0.2756	0.9613	0.2867	3.6280	1.0403	3.4874
17°	0.2924	0.9563	0.3057	3.4203	1.0457	3.2709
18°	0.3090	0.9511	0.3249	3.2361	1.0515	3.0777
19°	0.3256	0.9455	0.3443	3.0716	1.0567	2.9042
20°	0.3420	0.9397	0.3640	2.9238	1.0642	2.7475
21°	0.3584	0.9336	0.3839	2.7904	1.0711	2.6051
22°	0.3746	0.9272	0.4040	2.6695	1.0785	2.4751
23°	0.3907	0.9205	0.4245	2.5593	1.0864	2.3559
24°	0.4067	0.9135	0.4452	2.4586	1.0946	2.2460
25°	0.4226	0.9063	0.4663	2.3662	1.1043	2.1445
26°	0.4384	0.8988	0.4877	2.2812	1.1126	2.0503
27°	0.4540	0.8910	0.5095	2.2027	1.1223	1.9626
28°	0.4695	0.8829	0.5317	2.1301	1.1326	1.8807
29°	0.4848	0.8746	0.5543	2.0627	1.1434	1.8041
30°	0.5000	0.8660	0.5774	2.0000	1.1547	1.7321
31°	0.5150	0.8572	0.6009	1.9416	1.1666	1.6643
32°	0.5299	0.8480	0.6249	1.8871	1.1792	1.6003
33°	0.5446	0.8387	0.6494	1.8361	1.1924	1.5399
34°	0.5592	0.8290	0.6745	1.7883	1.2062	1.4826
35°	0.5736	0.8192	0.7002	1.7434	1.2208	1.4281
36°	0.5878	0.8090	0.7265	1.7013	1.2361	1.3764
37°	0.6018	0.7986	0.7536	1.6616	1.2521	1.3270
38°	0.6157	0.7880	0.7813	1.6243	1.2690	1.2799
39°	0.6293	0.7771	0.8098	1.5890	1.2868	1.2349
40°	0.6428	0.7660	0.8391	1.5557	1.3054	1.1918
41°	0.6561	0.7547	0.8693	1.5243	1.3250	1.1504
42°	0.6691	0.7431	0.9004	1.4945	1.3456	1.1106
43°	0.6820	0.7314	0.9325	1.4663	1.3678	1.0724
44°	0.6947	0.7193	0.9657	1.4396	1.3902	1.0355
45°	0.7071	0.7071	1.0000	1.4142	1.4142	1.0000
46°	0.7193	0.6947	1.0355	1.3902	1.4396	0.9657
47°	0.7314	0.6820	1.0724	1.3673	1.4663	0.9325
48°	0.7431	0.6691	1.1106	1.3456	1.4945	0.9004
49°	0.7547	0.6561	1.1504	1.3250	1.5243	0.8693
50°	0.7660	0.6428	1.1918	1.3054	1.5557	0.8391
51°	0.7771	0.6293	1.2349	1.2868	1.5890	0.8098
52°	0.7880	0.6157	1.2799	1.2690	1.6243	0.7813
53°	0.7986	0.6018	1.3270	1.2521	1.6616	0.7536
54°	0.8090	0.5878	1.3764	1.2361	1.7013	0.7265
55°	0.8192	0.5736	1.4281	1.2208	1.7434	0.7002
56°	0.8290	0.5592	1.4826	1.2062	1.7883	0.6745
57°	0.8387	0.5446	1.5399	1.1924	1.8361	0.6494
58°	0.8480	0.5299	1.6003	1.1792	1.8871	0.6249
59°	0.8572	0.5150	1.6643	1.1666	1.9416	0.6009
60°	0.8660	0.5000	1.7321	1.1547	2.0000	0.5774
61°	0.8746	0.4848	1.8041	1.1434	2.0627	0.5543
62°	0.8829	0.4695	1.8807	1.1326	2.1301	0.5317
63°	0.8901	0.4540	1.9626	1.1223	2.2027	0.5095
64°	0.8988	0.4384	2.0503	1.1126	2.2812	0.4877
65°	0.9063	0.4226	2.1445	1.1034	2.3662	0.4663
66°	0.9135	0.4067	2.2460	1.0946	2.4586	0.4452
67°	0.9205	0.3907	2.3559	1.0864	2.5593	0.4245
68°	0.9272	0.3746	2.4751	1.0785	2.6695	0.4040
69°	0.9336	0.3584	2.6051	1.0711	2.7904	0.3839
70°	0.9397	0.3420	2.7475	1.0642	2.9238	0.3640
71°	0.9455	0.3256	2.9042	1.0576	3.0716	0.3443
72°	0.9511	0.3090	3.0777	1.0515	3.2361	0.3249
73°	0.9563	0.2924	3.2709	1.0457	3.4203	0.3057
74°	0.9613	0.2756	3.4874	1.0403	3.6280	0.2867
75°	0.9659	0.2588	3.7321	1.0353	3.8637	0.2679
76°	0.9703	0.2419	4.0108	1.0306	4.1336	0.2493
77°	0.9744	0.2250	4.3315	1.0263	4.4454	0.2309
78°	0.9781	0.2079	4.7046	1.0223	4.8097	0.2126
79°	0.9816	0.1908	5.1446	1.0187	5.2408	0.1944
80°	0.9848	0.1736	5.6713	1.0154	5.7588	0.1763
81°	0.9877	0.1564	6.3138	1.0125	6.3925	0.1584
82°	0.9903	0.1392	7.1154	1.0098	7.1953	0.1405
83°	0.9925	0.1219	8.1443	1.0075	8.2055	0.1228
84°	0.9945	0.1045	9.5144	1.0055	9.5668	0.1051
85°	0.9962	0.0872	11.4301	1.0038	11.474	0.0875
86°	0.9976	0.0698	14.301	1.0024	14.336	0.0699
87°	0.9986	0.0523	19.081	1.0014	19.107	0.0524
88°	0.9994	0.0349	28.636	1.0006	28.654	0.0349
89°	0.9998	0.0175	57.290	1.0002	57.299	0.0175
90°	1.0000	0.0000	—	1.0000	—	0.0000

Appendix D: Employability Skills

To be successful in any job you must do your job well. This is true even if you are self employed, as many in the building trades are. Doing your job well includes being on time for work. It also includes having a mastery of the job skills needed. Your mastery of these skills will, in large part, depend on several factors.

FOCUS YOUR ENERGIES ON THE JOB

As an employee, you must be focused on the job at hand. This means that you must be attentive to what you are doing. You will do a better job if your attention is undivided. Being intent on the job at hand also means not disturbing others who are working. Fig. D-1.

EARN THE TRUST OF YOUR EMPLOYER

To be valued by an employer, an employee must earn the employer's trust. He or she does this by doing a good job. Doing a good job means completing the work on time and in the manner specified. Dependability is also important, as are safe work practices. The employer must know that he or she can count on you to stay late or come in early to get the job done. The employer must be able to count on you to work safely.

Fig. D-1. *Many of the tasks in building construction are repetitive. Because of this, it is especially important to keep your attention focused on the job at hand. This is necessary to ensure that quality work is done at every stage.*

Fig. D-2. *There is an old saying in carpentry, "Measure twice, cut once." Accuracy and precision are two of the characteristics of quality work habits.*

HAVE GOOD JOB SKILLS

Having good job skills relates directly to the job at hand. As an employee, you must be able to perform the assigned task to the employer's expectations. This means that you must have the knowledge and training needed to complete the job. He or she must also have the confidence that the job will be done correctly the first time. To complete the job in the minimum amount of time, you will need good organization skills. This means that you must be able to order and arrange information and material. Fig. D-2.

BE RESPONSIBLE FOR COMPANY RESOURCES

It is also important to manage company resources well. In any company, the major resources include employees, materials, and money. A fourth vital resource is time. An employer will trust an employee who is careful with the company resources. A good employee does not waste time, the company's materials or money, or the energies of his or her coworkers.

The most important resources in any company are its employees. A good employee manages the resources of the company carefully. In most companies, the main resources are materials and employees. This means that both money and employee time should be managed well. An essential part of this is that projects are well planned. It means that money is not spent unnecessarily. It also means that time is not wasted. Projects must be carefully planned, with each stage well organized. Such planning will help avoid delay and needless expense. Fig. D-3.

BE A TEAM PLAYER

Most people need to work with others in the workplace. The people with whom you work are known as your coworkers. They are fellow members of your work team. Even those individuals who may seem to work alone often depend on outside resources.

Being a team player can also help develop leadership. Fig. D-4.

DEVELOP GOOD COMMUNICATION SKILLS

Good communication skills are important. Information on developing these skills is presented on the following two pages.

Fig. D-3. *Various jobs require different types and levels of training. The operation of heavy machinery demands a keen sense of safe work practices on the part of the operator.*

Fig. D-4. *You may be required to use a variety of hand tools. To develop proficiency with these tools, you must be willing to take instruction on their careful use. You must also be able to accept suggestions for improvement.*

Appendix E: Communication Skills

Good communication skills are needed in almost every job. Good communication skills are especially important in the building trades. Here, an error in communicating or understanding information can have serious consequences.

THE NEED TO COMMUNICATE

It is the rare individual who works without the need to communicate with others. Almost everyone has to communicate with his or her fellow workers several times a day. Such communication can, of course, involve relatively unimportant information. It can also relate to serious matters. Communication with your coworkers is a necessary part of every job in the building trades. Because of this, it is important that you have good communication skills.

VERBAL SKILLS

All who work in the building trades need the same general communication skills. They need to be able to communicate clearly. They need to be able to listen well. Some individuals, however, will need these skills in a greater degree than others. This is because they will have a greater need to rely on such skills in their jobs. The need for communication skills can

depend on job responsibilities. For example, a worksite supervisor would generally have a need for a greater range of communication skills.

Regardless of your job, you must be able to tell your coworkers the information they need to do their jobs. If necessary, you must also be able to offer them clear instruction on work procedures.

WRITING SKILLS

Depending on your job, you may need to prepare written instructions or reports for others. Work of this sort is usually done by those immediately supervising a worksite. For very large construction projects, the preparation of such reports may be done by those overseeing the general project. Small builders and contractors have to communicate with clients by means of written bids. Fig. E-1.

ABILITY TO READ PLANS

You may need to refer to plans, such as building plans. The number and type of plans you will need to refer to will depend on your job. In any case, you must be able to read and understand the plans that you work with. This will require that you have a knowledge of the symbols and conventions used in technical drawing.

Fig. E-1. *This estimator is preparing an on-site evaluation of damage. This will help him in his work with a team that will prepare a bid for the replacement of the earthquake-damaged overpass in the background. For this job, excellent communication skills are essential.*

LISTENING SKILLS

Having good communication skills also means that you must be a good listener. As well as being able to communicate clearly with others, you must be able to understand what they are telling you. This means that you must be able to listen well. It also means that you must be able to read and understand written instructions (such as those on plans and drawings). You must also be able to ask clearly worded questions when you do not understand something.

The proper practice of most job skills depends on a set routine. Most jobs move in a certain sequence. That sequence has usually been arrived at through trial and error. In other words, most jobs are done in a certain way because over time it has been found that such a way is the most effective way of doing a job.

To learn any job, you need to be able to receive instruction. This means that you must be attentive. Much of what you may learn will be demonstrated to you.

COMPREHENSION

Some of the necessary information, however, may be presented to you in instruction manuals or information sheets. To use these effectively, you must be able to read and understand the information presented in them. Remember that much of this information will be technical. For example, you may need to consult material safety data sheets and tool manuals. You may also need to check safety and product specification sheets.

SKILLS IN ANALYZING INFORMATION

In some jobs, you will need to gather information. You may need to do this to achieve a certain goal. For example, you may be asked to buy a new circular saw. To decide which saw to buy you will need to practice certain decision-making skills. Many of these skills involve communication and your ability to evaluate information. Fig. E-2. You may need to evaluate various test reports on circular saws. You will need to compare the various saws regarding price, quality, and manufacturers' reputation. You will then need to compare the return policies of each retailer. Such a job

will require you to make accurate comparisons. This is only an example. The same general procedures could apply to the purchase of building materials and to many other aspects of building construction.

Research into tools, techniques, and materials has been considerably broadened by use of the computer. Subjects can be researched by logging onto the Internet or various on-line services.

NUMERICAL COMMUNICATION

Depending on your job, you may be involved in communicating with others by numbers. For example, you may need to provide a subcontractor with the number of cubic yards of concrete that need to be placed. You may need to order from a building supplier enough drywall to cover walls with a certain square footage. For both of these jobs you will need to work with math formulas. These math formulas will provide the information that you will need to communicate with the supplier.

INTERPERSONAL SKILLS

It has been observed that 90 percent of all communication is nonverbal. This means that people also communicate by what is sometimes called "body language." Interpersonal skills relate not only to your verbal communication skills but also to the way in which you act with people. Much of your success on a job will depend on your ability to maintain good communication with all members of your work team. This work team includes not only those on the job site but also all of those others you need to deal with to get your job

done. These others might include subcontractors and building suppliers. It might also include clients who hire your company to do work for them. This will mean that you must be able to work effectively with a number of different personality types. Fig. E-3.

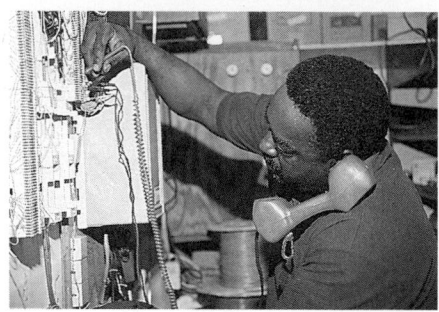

Fig. E-2. *Not every problem can be solved on the job site. Often, a technical representative from the manufacturer must be consulted. The technician shown here is obtaining the data he needs to consult with such a technical representative. In recording this data, the technician needs to work carefully and accurately.*

Fig. E-3. *Customers will require precise information regarding the materials they plan to purchase. To inform customers of material specifications, you will need good communication skills. You will need to communicate clearly not only with customers—to whom you sell the product—but also with the sales representative who sells you the product.*

Glossary*

Abrasives. Substances rubbed on wood to smooth the surface before or between applications of finish coats. Flint, garnet, aluminum oxide, and silicon carbide are common abrasives.

Adhesive. A material capable of holding other materials together by surface attachment. Glues, cements, pastes, and mucilage are some of the common adhesives.

Air-dried lumber. Lumber that has been dried by being stored in yards or sheds for any length of time. For North America as a whole, the minimum moisture content of thoroughly air-dried lumber is 12 to 15%, and the average is higher.

Airway. A space between roof insulation and roof boards for movement of air.

Alligatoring. Coarse checking pattern characterized by a slipping of the new paint coating over the old coating to the extent that the old coating can be seen through the fissures.

American lumber standards. Provisions or rules for softwood lumber, dealing with recognized classifications, nomenclature, sizes, descriptions, amounts, shipping provisions, basic grades, grade marking, and inspection. These are not commercial rules. Rather, these standards serve as a guide or basic example for the grading rules of various lumber manufacturers' associations. A purchaser must follow the rules of the various associations.

Anchor bolts. Bolts to secure a wooden sill plate to a concrete or masonry floor or wall.

Annual growth ring. The layer of wood grown by a tree in one year. It is comprised of springwood and summerwood.

Annular. Ring-shaped. Often used to describe annual growth rings of a tree.

Apron. The flat part of the inside trim of a window. It is placed against the wall directly beneath the window stool.

Arbor. A shaft or spindle on which a tool is mounted.

Areaway. An open subsurface space next to a building. It is used to admit light or air or permit access to a basement.

---

* Some of the terms in this glossary have several meanings, but only the definitions which pertain to woodworking or closely related fields are included here.

Asphalt. A brown to black bituminous substance. Most native asphalt is a residue from evaporated petroleum. It is insoluble in water but soluble in gasoline, and it melts when heated. Asphalt is used widely in building for such items as waterproof roof coverings of many types, exterior wall coverings, and flooring tile.

Astragal. A molding, attached to one of a pair of swinging doors, against which the other door strikes.

Attic ventilators. Openings in the roof or in gables for the purpose of allowing air to circulate. Also, mechanical devices with power-driven fans to force the circulation of air.

Backband. A simple molding sometimes used around the outer edge of plain rectangular casing as a decorative feature.

Backfill. The replacement of earth into a trench or pier excavation around and against a basement foundation.

Balanced construction. A method of constructing manufactured wood products so that moisture content changes will be uniformly distributed and therefore will not cause warping. An example would be symmetrical construction of plywood in which the grain direction of each ply is perpendicular to that of adjacent plies.

Balloon framing. (See **Framing, balloon.**)

Balusters. Usually small vertical members in a railing used between a top rail and the stair treads or a bottom rail. Also called banisters.

Balustrade. A railing made up of balusters, top rail, and sometimes bottom rail, used on the edge of stairs, balconies, and porches.

Banisters. (See **Balusters.**)

Bark. The outer layer of a tree, made up of a thin, living, inner part (phloem) and a corky outer part which is dry, dead tissue.

Base, baseboard. A board placed along the bottom of a wall next to the floor.

Base molding. A strip of wood used to trim the upper edge of a baseboard.

Base shoe or shoe mold. A strip of wood next to the floor on interior baseboard. Also called a carpet strip.

Battens. Narrow pieces of wood used to cover joints.

Batter boards. A pair of horizontal boards nailed to posts set at the corners of an excavation. They indicate the proper level and serve as a fastening place for stretched cord to show the outlines of foundation walls.

Bay window. Any window space projecting outward from the walls of a building. The bay may be square or polygonal in plan.

Beam. A long, heavy piece of lumber or metal. When used in construction, it is placed horizontally and is usually supported at the ends; it in turn supports a load which is laid across it.

Bearing partition. A partition that supports any vertical load in addition to its own weight.

Bearing wall. A wall that supports any vertical load in addition to its own weight.

Bed molding. A molding in an angle, as between the overhanging cornice, or eaves, of a building and the sidewalls.

Belt course. A horizontal board carried at the same level across or around a building. It is usually made of a flat member and a molding.

Bending. The amount of deflection of a piece of lumber when a load is applied. If a certain type of lumber tends to split easily when bent, it is said to have poor bending strength. (Not to be confused with **Stiffness.**)

Benzene (benzol). A material derived from coal tar and widely used as a solvent. Also used for cleaning after painting and other finishing operations.

Benzine. A liquid obtained from petroleum. Used in dyeing, painting, and as a cleansing agent.

Bevel. An angular surface across an edge of a piece of stock.

Bevel siding (lap siding). A type of finish siding used on the exterior of a house. It is usually manufactured by resawing a dry, squared, surfaced board diagonally to produce two wedge-shaped pieces.

Bird's-eye. Small, localized area in wood where the fibers are indented and otherwise contorted to form small circular or elliptical figures which look somewhat like birds' eyes. Common in sugar maple and used for decorative purposes; rare in other hardwood species.

Bleaching. A method of lightening the color of wood by applying chemicals.

Bleeding. Seeping of a stain or lower coat through the top coat, spoiling the appearance of the top coat.

Blend. Mixture, as of two pigments, to obtain a desired color.

Blind-nailing. Nailing in such a way that the nailheads are not visible on the surface.

Blinds (shutters). Lightweight, louvered or flush, wood or nonwood covers located at each side of a window. Some are made to close over windows to shut out light or give protection from the weather. Others are fastened to the wall and used as a decoration.

Blind stop. A rectangular molding, usually ¾ by 1⅜ inches or more in width, used in the assembly of a window frame. Serves as a stop for storm and screen or combination windows and to resist air infiltration.

Blisters. Cloudy or milky-looking raised spots on finished surfaces.

Blue stain. A bluish or grayish discoloration of the sapwood. It is caused by the growth of certain moldlike fungi on the surface and in the interior of a piece, and it is made possible by the same conditions that favor the growth of other fungi.

Board. Lumber less than 2" thick and 1" or more wide.

Board foot. A unit of lumber equal to the volume of a board 1' square and 1" thick.

Bodied linseed oil. Linseed oil that has been thickened by suitable processing with heat or chemicals. Bodied oils vary greatly in viscosity. Some are little thicker than raw linseed oil; others are almost jellylike.

Boiled linseed oil. Linseed oil to which enough lead, manganese, or cobalt salts have been added to make the oil harden more rapidly when spread in thin coatings.

Bolster. A short horizontal timber or steel beam on top of a column to support and decrease the span of beams or girders.

Bolts, anchor. (See **Anchor bolts.**)

Bond. A joining or adhering, as of two surfaces. Also, a substance which causes such a joining to take place.

Boston ridge. Applying asphalt or wood shingles at the ridge or at the hips of a roof as a finish.

Bow. (Rhymes with low.) The distortion in a board that is no longer flat lengthwise, but has remained flat across its faces.

Brace. (1) An inclined piece of framing lumber applied to the wall or floor to stiffen a structure. (See also **Let-in brace** and **Cut-in brace.**) (2) A hand tool.

Brick veneer. A facing of brick laid against and fastened to the sheathing of a frame wall or tile wall.

Bridging. Small wood or metal members inserted in a diagonal position between the floor joists. They brace the joists and spread the loads.

British thermal unit (Btu). The amount of heat needed to raise the temperature of 1 pound of water 1°F when it is at or near 39.2°F. The Btu is used to measure the amount of heat just as the inch or foot is used to measure length or as the minute or hour is used to measure time. There are approximately 13,000 Btu in a pound of coal, 141,000 Btu in a gallon of oil, and 1,000 Btu in a cubic foot of natural gas.

Buck. Assembly of the framing that constitutes a rough door or window opening.

Building code. A collection of legal requirements designed to protect the safety, health, morals, and general welfare of those in and around buildings.

Building paper. A general term for papers, felts, and similar sheet materials used in buildings, without reference to their properties or uses.

Built-up roof. A roofing composed of three to five layers of asphalt felt laminated with coal tar, pitch, or asphalt. The top is finished with crushed slag or gravel. Generally used on flat or low-pitched roofs.

Burl. (1) A hard, woody outgrowth on a tree, more or less rounded in form, usually resulting from the entwined growth of a cluster of buds. Burls are the source of highly figured veneers used for ornamental purposes. (2) A localized distortion of the grain, found both in lumber and in veneer. Generally rounded in outline, it is usually the result of an overgrowth of dead branch stubs. Diameter may vary from ½" to several inches. A burl often includes one or more clusters, each usually having a core or pith but little end grain surrounding it.

Butt joint. The junction where the ends of two pieces meet in a square-cut joint.

C. Represents the conductance of a material and is used to show the amount of heat (Btu) that will pass per hour through 1 square foot of a homogeneous or nonhomogeneous material or a combination of materials for the thickness or type under consideration for a difference in temperature of 1°F between the two surfaces. It differs from *k* value in that the *k* value represents conductance *per inch* of thickness. **C** value is the total conductance and is usually used for materials which are not uniform throughout, such as hollow concrete block. The average **C** value of an 8-inch hollow concrete block is 0.90.

Cabinet. A shop- or job-built unit for kitchens or other rooms. Often includes combinations of drawers, doors, and the like.

Cambium. A layer of tissue, one cell thick, between the bark and the wood of a tree. It divides to form new wood and bark cells.

Cant strip. A triangular-shaped piece of lumber used at the junction of a flat deck and a wall to prevent cracking of the roofing which is applied over it.

Cap. The upper member of a column, pilaster, door cornice, molding, and the like.

Carpet strip. (See **Base shoe.**)

Carriage. The supporting member for stair treads. Usually a 2" plank notched to receive the treads; sometimes termed a "rough horse."

Casein glue. An adhesive substance composed of casein (the curd of milk), lime, and sodium salt. It comes as dry powder to which water is added.

Casement. A window sash which opens on hinges fastened to a vertical side of the frame. Windows with such sash are called casement windows.

Cell. A general term for the tiny, usually microscopic, units of which wood is composed. Wood fibers, vessel segments, and other elements of diverse structure all are composed of cells.

Cellulose. (1) The principal substance in the framework or walls of wood cells. (2) An organic substance obtained from the cotton plant and used as raw material in the manufacture of paints and other materials.

Cement, Keene's. (See **Keene's cement.**)

Center-matched. Joint between two pieces of lumber. It consists of a groove in the edge of one piece and a tongue in the other. More commonly known as a tongue-and-groove joint.

Chamfer. A beveled surface cut on the corner of a piece of wood.

Check. A lengthwise crack or separation of the wood, usually extending across the rings of annual growth. This defect commonly results from stresses set up in wood during seasoning.

Checking. Cracks or fissures that appear with age in many exterior paint coatings. Superficial at first, they may in time penetrate the coating entirely.

Checkrails. Meeting rails sufficiently thicker than a window to fill the opening between the top and bottom sash made by the parting stop in the frame of doublehung windows. The checkrails are usually beveled.

Clamp. A device that holds things together; often used to hold pieces together while the glue dries.

Clapboard. A type of siding. It consists of narrow boards which are usually thicker at one edge than the other.

Cleat. A strip of material, such as wood, fastened to another piece to strengthen it or to furnish a grip.

CM. (See **Center-matched.**)

Cold-setting resin glue. A resin-base glue that comes in powder form and is mixed with water.

Collar beam. A beam connecting pairs of opposite roof rafters. It helps stiffen the roof structure.

Column. A vertical support (often square, rectangular, or cylindrical), as for roofs or ceilings.

Combination doors or windows. Doors or windows with self-storing or removable glass and screen inserts. The need for handling a different unit each season is thus eliminated.

Compreg. Wood in which the cell walls have been impregnated with synthetic resin and compressed. This process reduces swelling and shrinking and increases density and strength.

Concrete. A combination of cement and sand, broken stone, or gravel. It is used for foundations, building construction, walks, and many other purposes.

Condensation. In a building, beads or drops of water—and frequently frost in extremely cold weather—that accumulate on the inside of the exterior covering of the building. Condensation occurs when warm, moisture-laden air from the interior reaches a point where the temperature no longer permits the air to sustain the moisture it holds. Use of louvers or attic ventilators will reduce moisture condensation in attics. A vapor barrier under the gypsum lath or dry wall on exposed walls will reduce condensation.

Conduit, electrical. A pipe, usually metal, in which wire is installed.

Conifer. A cone-bearing tree. (See also **Softwood.**)

Construction, dry-wall. (See **Dry-wall construction.**)

Construction, frame. (See **Frame construction.**)

Coped joint. (See **Scribing.**)

Corbel out. To build out one or more courses of brick or stone from the face of a wall in order to form a support for timbers.

Core. In plywood, the center of the panel. It may be either veneer or lumber.

Corner bead. A strip of formed sheet metal, sometimes combined with a strip of metal lath, placed on corners before plastering to reinforce them. Also, a strip of wood finish three-quarters round or angular placed over a plastered corner for protection.

Corner block. A large triangular piece of wood or metal used for added strength at the corners of frames or where legs and rails join.

Corner boards. Boards used as trim for the external corners of a house or other frame structure and against which the ends of the siding are finished.

Corner braces. Diagonal braces at the corners of a frame structure to stiffen and strengthen the wall.

Cornerite. Metal lath cut into strips and bent to a right angle. Used in interior corners of walls and ceilings on lath to prevent cracks in plastering.

Cornice. (1) Overhang of a pitched roof at the eave line, usually consisting of a fascia board, a soffit for a closed cornice, and appropriate moldings. (2) A decorative member, usually molded, placed at or near the top of a wall.

Cornice return. That portion of the cornice that returns on the gable end of a house.

Counterboring. Enlarging a hole so that the head of a screw or bolt inserted in it can be completely covered.

Counterflashing. A flashing usually used on chimneys at the roofline to cover shingle flashing and to prevent moisture entry.

Countersinking. (1) Removing stock around the end of a hole so that heads of screws or bolts can be brought flush with the surface. (2) To sink a nail or screw even with or below the surface.

Courses. Alternate layers or thicknesses of material, as in a masonry wall or shingles on a roof.

Cove molding. A molding with a concave face; used as trim or to finish interior corners.

Crawl space. A shallow space between the floor of a house and the ground in no-basement construction.

Cricket. A small drainage-diverting roof structure of single or double slope placed at the junction of larger surfaces that meet at an angle, such as above a chimney. Also called a **saddle.**

Crook. In a board, a defect in which the edges do not form a straight line from end to end.

Crossbands. Layers of wood placed with their grains at right angles to each other to minimize shrinking and swelling. Also, in plywood of five or more plies, a layer of veneer whose grain direction is at right angles to that of the face plies.

Cross break. A crack or separation of wood cells across the grain of a board. Such defects may be caused by unequal shrinkage or by external forces.

Cross-bridging. Diagonal bracing between adjacent floor joists, placed near the center of the joist span to prevent joists from twisting.

Cross grain. (See **Grain.**)

Cup. Distortion or warping of a board so that it is no longer flat across its width.

Cut-in brace. Nominal 2"-thick members, usually 2 x 4s, cut in between each stud diagonally.

d. (See **Penny.**)

Dado. A rectangular groove across the grain in a board.

Dado joint. (See **Joint.**)

D & M. (See **Dressed and matched.**)

Dead load. The weight of the walls, permanent partitions, framing, floors, roofs, and all other permanent stationary construction in a building.

Decay. Disintegration of wood or other substance through the action of fungi or bacteria.

Deciduous. Trees which annually lose their leaves.

Deck paint. An enamel with a high degree of resistance to mechanical wear; designed for use on such surfaces as porch floors.

Defect. Any imperfection occurring in or on wood that may lower its quality.

Density. The mass or true quantity of wood (or any substance) in a unit of a given size. For instance, a board foot of white oak, a heavy hardwood, would have greater density than a board foot of a lighter wood such as ponderosa pine.

Dewpoint. Temperature at which a vapor begins to condense. Applies especially to moisture in the air.

Dimension. (See **Lumber.**)

Dimensional stabilization. Reduction in swelling and shrinkage of wood through special treatment which minimizes the moisture content changes in wood resulting from changes in relative humidity.

Dimension stock. Hardwood stock processed to a point where the maximum waste remains at the dimension mill and the maximum utility is delivered to the user. It is stock of specified thickness, width, and length. According to specifications, it may be solid or glued up; rough or surfaced; semifabricated or completely fabricated. Today it is commonly known as hardwood dimension lumber.

Direct nailing. (See **Face-nailing.**)

Dolly Varden siding. Beveled wood siding that is rabbeted on the bottom edge.

Doorjamb. The surrounding case into which and out of which a door closes and opens. It consists of two upright pieces, called side jambs, and a horizontal head jamb. Exterior doorjambs also have thresholds.

Dormer. A projection in a sloping roof, the framing of which forms a vertical wall suitable for windows or other openings.

Dovetail joint. (See **Joint.**)

Dowel. A small wooden pin used to strengthen a joint.

Downspout. A pipe, usually metal, for carrying rainwater from roof gutters.

Dressed and matched (tongued and grooved). Boards matched in such a way that there is a groove on one edge and a corresponding tongue on the other.

Dressed size. (See **Lumber.**)

Drier. A solution added to drying oils in paint to quicken the drying.

Drip. (1) A member of a cornice or other horizontal exterior-finish course that has a projection beyond the other parts for throwing off water. (2) A groove in the underside of a sill or drip cap to cause water to drop off on the outer edge instead of drawing back and running down the face of the building.

Drip cap. A molding place above the exterior of a door or window frame, causing water to drip beyond the outside of the frame.

Drop siding. Exterior wall covering, usually 3/4" thick and 6" wide, machined into patterns. Drop siding has tongue-and-groove or shiplap joints, and is heavier and stronger than bevel siding.

Drying lumber. (See **Kiln drying.**)

Drying oil. An oil which, when a thin film of it is exposed to the air, takes on oxygen and becomes hard, tough, and elastic. Drying oils are used in the manufacture of paints and varnishes. Linseed oil is a common drying oil.

Dry rot. A term loosely applied to any crumbly decay of wood, but especially to that which, when in an advanced stage, allows the wood to be crushed easily to a dry

powder. The term does not accurately describe decay, since fungi which cause the rot require considerable moisture for growth.

Dry-wall construction. A type of construction in which the interior wall finish is applied in a dry condition, generally in the form of sheet materials or wood paneling, as contrasted to plaster.

Ducts. Pipes which carry air from a furnace or an air conditioner to the rooms of a building. Usually they are round or rectangular and made of metal, although they may be made of asbestos and composition materials.

Earlywood. (See **Spring-wood.**)

Eaves. The overhang of a roof projecting over the walls.

Eave trough. (See **Gutter.**)

Edge-grained. (See **Grain.**)

Edge-matched. Lumber that has been worked with a tongue on one edge of each piece and a groove on the opposite edge. Also, lumber that has been rabbeted on both edges of each piece. In either case, the purpose is to provide a close joint when fitting two pieces together.

Empty-cell process. A method of obtaining deep penetration of a wood preservative with a relatively low net retention of the preservative. Surplus preservative is removed from the wood cells by vacuum.

Enamel. A kind of paint in which the vehicle is a drying oil or combination of drying oil and resin. The paint dries to an even, hard finish. Usually it leaves a glossy surface, but the addition of a flatting agent can reduce the glossiness.

Equilibrium moisture content. The moisture content at which wood neither gains nor loses moisture when surrounded by air at a given relative humidity and temperature.

Evaporate. To pass off in vapor; to change a liquid into vapor or gas.

Expansion joint. A bituminous fiber strip used to separate blocks or units of concrete to prevent cracking due to expansion caused by temperature changes. Also used on concrete slabs.

Extractives. Substances in wood, not part of the cellular structure, that can be removed by water, ether, benzene, or other solvents that do not react chemically with wood components.

Face-nailing. To nail perpendicular to the surface or to the junction of the pieces joined. Also termed **direct** nailing.

Factory and shop lumber. (See **Lumber.**)

Fascia. A flat member, as on a cornice or an eave. Often, the board of the cornice to which the gutter for rainwater is fastened.

FHA. Federal Housing Administration, established in 1934. Writes mortgage and loan insurance to help improve housing standards, to promote the use of sound financing methods, and to help keep the mortgage market steady. All loans insured under FHA programs are made by private FHA-approved lenders. FHA itself does not lend money or build houses.

Fiber. In wood, a comparatively long, narrow, tapering wood cell, closed at both ends. Also called **tracheid.**

Fiber-saturation point. The point in the drying or wetting of wood at which the cell walls are saturated but the cell cavities are free from water. It is usually taken as approximately 23 to 30% moisture content, based on weight when oven-dry.

Figure. The pattern produced in a wood surface by annual growth rings, rays, knots, irregular coloration, and deviations from regular grain such as interlocked and wavy grain.

Filler, wood. A heavily pigmented preparation used for filling and leveling off the pores in open-grained woods.

Finish. (1) Wood products to be used in joinery, such as doors and stairs, and other fine work required to complete a building, especially the interior. (2) The process of adding stains, filler, and other materials to protect and beautify the surface of wood.

Fire-resistive. In the absence of a specific ruling by the authority having jurisdiction, this term applies to construction materials that are not combustible in the temperatures of ordinary fires and that will withstand such fires without serious impairment of their usefulness for at least 1 hour.

Fire-retardant chemical. A chemical preparation used to reduce flammability or to retard the spread of flame.

Firestop. A solid, tight partition placed to prevent the spread of fire and smoke through a building. In a frame wall, this will usually consist of a 2 x 4 cross blocking between studs.

Flagstone (flagging or flags.) Flat stones, from 1 to 4 inches thick, used for rustic walks, steps, floors, and the like.

Flakes. (See **Rays.**)

Flat-grained. (See **Grain.**)

Flat paint. An interior paint with a high proportion of pigment. It dries to a flat, or lusterless, finish.

Flatting oil. A special liquid used with pigment-oil paste to produce a flat paint. It is clear, consisting primarily of thickened drying oils and turpentine.

Flitch. (1) Portion of a log sawed on two or more sides and intended for manufacture into lumber or veneer. (2) The term is also applied to the sheets of veneer laid together in sequence of cutting.

Flue. The opening in a chimney through which smoke can pass.

Flue lining. Fireclay or terra-cotta pipe, round or square, usually made in all of the ordinary flue sizes and in 2' lengths. It is used for the inner lining of chimneys, with brick or masonry work around the outside. Flue lining in chimneys runs from about a foot below the flue connection to the top of the chimney.

Flush. Even, or in the same plane (with reference to adjacent surfaces of two structural pieces).

Fly rafter. End rafter of the gable overhang supported by roof sheathing and lookouts.

FNMA. (Fannie Mae). Federal National Mortgage Association. Formerly a governmental agency, now a profit motivated public corporation dealing in the national secondary mortgage market. Buys when money is tight, releases when money is freer, thus serving to stabilize the market. Not to be confused with GNMA (Ginny Mae), Government National Mortgage Association, the special assistance mortgage loan service remaining under FHA.

Footing. A masonry section, usually concrete, in a rectangular form wider than the bottom of the foundation wall or pier it supports.

Foundation. The part of a building or wall which supports the superstructure.

Frame. (1) The surrounding or enclosing woodwork, as around windows or doors. (2) The skeleton of a building; that is, the rough structure of a building, including interior and exterior walls, floor, roof, and ceilings.

Frame construction. Construction in which the structural parts are of wood or depend on a wood frame for support. (See also **Framing, balloon and platform.**)

Framing. The rough structure of a building, including interior and exterior walls, floor, roof, and ceilings.

Framing, balloon. A system of framing a building in which all vertical structural elements of the bearing walls and partitions consist of single pieces. These pieces extend from the top of the foundation sill plate to the roofplate, and all floor joists are fastened to them.

Framing, platform. A system of framing a building in which floor joists of each story rest on the top plates of the story below (or on the foundation sill for the first story). The bearing walls and partitions rest on the subfloor of each story.

Frieze. (1) A horizontal, often decorative, member of a cornice, set flat against a wall. (2) More broadly, any sculptured or ornamental band in a house or on furniture.

Frostline. The depth of frost penetration in soil. This depth varies in different parts of the country. Footings should be placed below this line to prevent movement.

Full-cell process. A process for impregnating wood with preservatives or chemicals. In this process a vacuum is formed to remove air from the wood before adding the preservative.

Fungicide. A chemical that is poisonous to fungi.

Fungi, wood. Microscopic plants that live in damp wood and cause mold, stain, and decay.

Furring. Narrow strips of board nailed on walls and ceilings to form a level surface on which to fasten other materials.

Gable. A vertical, triangular part of a building, contained between the slopes of a double-sloped roof. Also, a similar part of a building, even though not triangular. Under a single-sloped roof, that vertical part of the building above the lowest elevation of the roof and below the ridge of the roof.

Gable end. An end wall having a gable.

Gain. A notch or mortise, as in a beam or a wall, for a joist, girder, or similar member.

Girder. A large or principal beam of wood or steel used to support concentrated loads at isolated points along its length.

Glazing compound. Calking compound used especially for holding window glass in place because it remains soft underneath the surface.

Gloss. A shiny, lustrous finish which reflects light. The term also refers to paint or enamel that dries to a high sheen or luster, usually with a hard, smooth coat.

Gloss enamel. A finishing material made of varnish and pigments. Such an enamel forms a hard coating with a smooth surface and high gloss.

Glue. An adhesive, commonly used in joining wood parts. (See also **Casein, Cold-setting resin.**)

Glue block. A small piece of wood used to strengthen and support two pieces of wood joined at an angle.

Glue joint. (See **Joint.**)

Grade. The designation of quality, as of logs or plywood.

Grain. The direction, size, arrangement, appearance, or quality of the fibers in wood or lumber. The following terms describe wood with specific types of grain.

Close-grained wood. Woods with narrow, inconspicuous annual rings. The term is sometimes used for wood having small and closely spaced pores.

Coarse-grained wood. Wood with wide, conspicuous annual rings, indicating considerable difference between springwood and summerwood. The term is sometimes used for wood with large pores such as oak, ash, chestnut, and walnut.

Cross-grained wood. Wood in which the fibers deviate from a line parallel to the sides of the piece. Cross grain may be either diagonal or spiral grain, or a combination of the two.

Curly-grained wood. Wood in which the fibers are distorted so that they have a curled appearance, as in "bird's-eye" wood.

Diagonal-grained wood. Wood in which the annual rings are at an angle with the axis of the piece. This effect is produced by sawing at an angle to the bark of the tree or log. A form of cross grain.

Edge-grained lumber. Lumber that has been sawed so that the wide surfaces extend approximately at right angles to the annual growth rings. Lumber is considered edge grained when the rings form an angle of 45 to 90° with the wide surface of the piece.

Flat-grained lumber. Lumber that has been sawed in a plane approximately perpendicular to a radius of the log. Lumber is considered flat grained when the annual growth rings make an angle of less than 45° with the surface of the piece.

Open-grained wood. Common term for woods with large pores such as oak, ash, chestnut, and walnut. Also known as "coarse textured."

Plain-sawed lumber. Another term for flat-grained lumber.

Quarter-sawed lumber. Another term for edge-grained lumber.

Spiral-grained wood. Wood in which the fibers take a spiral course about the trunk of a tree instead of the normal vertical course. The spiral may extend in a right-hand or left-hand direction around the tree trunk. Spiral grain is a form of cross grain.

Straight-grained wood. Wood in which the fibers run parallel to the axis of the piece.

Vertical-grained lumber. Another term for edge-grained lumber.

Wavy-grained wood. Wood in which the fibers collectively take the form of waves or undulations.

Green. Freshly sawed lumber, or lumber that has had no intentional drying; unseasoned.

Groove. A long, hollow channel, cut by a tool, into which a piece fits or in which it works. Carpenters have given special names to certain forms of grooves, such as dadoes and housings.

Ground cover. (See Soil cover.)

Grounds. Guides used around openings and at the floorline to strike off plaster. They can consist of narrow strips of wood or of wide subjambs at interior doorways. They provide a level plaster line for installation of casing and other trim.

Grout. Mortar made of such consistency (by adding water) that it will just flow into the joints and cavities of the masonry work and fill them solid.

Growth ring. (See Annual growth ring.)

Gum. A sticky substance obtained from the sap of certain trees and plants, and used in making varnishes and paints.

Gusset. A triangular or trapezoidal piece of wood or metal fastened to the exterior of a joint to strengthen it. Most commonly used on wood trusses.

Gutter (eave trough). A shallow channel or conduit of metal or wood set below and along the eaves of a house to catch and carry off rainwater from the roof.

Gypsum plaster. Gypsum made to be used with sand and water for base-coat plaster.

Hardboard. A synthetic product made by converting wood chips into wood fiber which is then formed into panels under heat and pressure.

Hardwood. In forestry, the wood of trees that have broad leaves, in contrast to the wood of cone-bearing trees, which is called softwood. In this sense the term has no reference to the actual hardness of the wood.

Hardwood dimension lumber. (See Dimension stock.)

Header. (1) In framing, a piece of timber, usually a short joist, which supports tail beams and is framed between trimmer joists. (2) A piece of timber over door or window openings to support roof framing members.

Hearth. The floor of a fireplace, usually made of brick, tile, or stone.

Heartwood. In a tree, the wood extending from the pith to the sapwood, the cells of which no longer help in the life processes of the tree. Heartwood may be infiltrated with gums, resins, and other materials that usually make it darker and more decay-resistant than sapwood.

Heel (of a rafter). The end, or foot, that rests on the wall plate.

Hip. The external angle formed by the meeting of two sloping sides of a roof.

Hip rafter. A rafter that extends from the wall plate to the ridge of the roof and forms the angle of a hip roof.

Hip roof. A roof which slopes up toward the center from all sides, requiring a hip rafter at each corner.

Honeycombing. Checks, often not visible at the surface, that occur in the interior of a piece of wood, usually along the wood rays.

Housing. A groove cut at any angle with the grain and partway across the piece. Housings are used for framing stair risers and treads.

HUD. U.S. Department of Housing and Urban Development. A major federal agency; contains Federal Housing Administration.

Humidifier. A device designed to discharge water vapor for the purpose of increasing or maintaining the relative humidity in a room or a house.

Humidity. The dampness of the air. *Absolute Humidity* is the percentage of water vapor, by weight, in a given volume of air. *Relative humidity* is the ratio of the amount of vapor in the air to the greatest amount possible at that temperature.

I-beam. A steel beam which, when seen in cross section, resembles the letter I. Used for long spans, as basement beams, or over wide wall openings when wall and roof loads are imposed on the opening.

IIC. Impact Insulation Class. A system used in the Federal Housing Administration's recommended criteria for impact sound insulation.

Impreg. Wood in which the cell walls have been impregnated with synthetic resin so as to reduce greatly its swelling and shrinking. Impreg is not compressed (see also **Compreg**).

Impregnate. To saturate, fill,

or permeate one substance with another, as wood with chemicals.

Inflammable. Easily set on fire.

Inlay. A decoration in which the design is set into the surface.

INR. Impact Noise Rating. A single-figure rating which provides an estimate of the impact sound-insulating performance of a floor-ceiling assembly.

Insulation. Any material which resists the transfer of electricity, heat, or sound. For example, thermal insulation is placed in the walls, ceilings, or floors of a home to reduce the rate of heat flow.

Insulation board (fiberboard). A low-density board made of wood, sugar cane, cornstalks, or similar material. It is dried and usually pressed to a thickness of $\frac{1}{2}$" or $\frac{25}{32}$".

Interior finish. Material used to cover the interior framed areas, or materials for walls and ceilings.

Jack rafter. A short rafter; often, a rafter placed between the top plate and a hip rafter or from a valley rafter to a ridge board.

Jamb. The surrounding case for a door or window. It consists of two upright pieces, called side jambs, and a head jamb, fitted together and rabbeted.

Jig. A device that simplifies a hand or machine operation, usually by guiding a tool or serving as a template.

Joint. The junction of two pieces, as of wood or veneer. Specific types of joints:

Butt joint. A square-cut joint

where the ends of two pieces meet.

Dado joint. A joint in which one piece is grooved to receive the piece which forms the other part of the joint.

Dovetail joint. A joint in which one piece has dovetail-shaped pins or tenons which fit into corresponding openings on the other piece.

Glue joint. A joint held together with glue.

Lap joint. A joint composed of two pieces, one overlapping the other.

Mortise-and-tenon joint. A joint made by cutting a hole or mortise in one piece, and a tenon, or piece to fit the hole, in the other.

Scarf joint. A joint made by fastening together two wedge-shaped pieces which have been cut to correspond to one another.

Joint cement. A powder that is usually mixed with water and used for joint treatment in gypsum-wallboard finish. Often called "spackle."

Jointing. (1) Smoothing and straightening the edge of a board. A jointer is a machine which does this automatically. (2) Grinding or filing the teeth or knives of power tools to the correct height. Circular saws are jointed so that there are no high or low teeth. Knives of planers and jointers are jointed so that each knife makes the same depth of cut as all others.

Joist. One of a series of parallel beams which support floor and ceiling loads and which are supported in turn by larger beams, girders, or bearing walls.

k. The amount of heat (Btu) transferred in 1 hour through 1 square foot of a homogeneous material 1 inch thick for a difference in temperature of 1°F. For example, the average **k** for mineral wool blankets is 0.27. This means that for a one-inch thickness there is a heat transfer of 0.27 Btu per hour per square foot for each degree difference in temperature between its two surfaces. (See also **C.**)

Keene's cement. A white finish plaster that produces an extremely durable wall. Because of its density, it excels for use in bathrooms and kitchens and is also widely used for the finish coat in auditoriums, public buildings, and other places where walls may be subjected to unusually hard wear or abuse.

Kerf. The cut made by a saw.

Key. A small piece of wood inserted in one or both parts of a joint to align it and hold it firmly together.

Kiln-dried lumber. Lumber that has been kiln-dried, often to a moisture content of 6 to 12%. Common varieties of softwood lumber, such as framing lumber, are dried to a somewhat higher moisture content.

Kiln drying. Artificial drying of lumber in a specially designed furnace or heated chamber called a kiln.

Knot. A hard, irregular lump formed at the point where a branch grows out from the trunk or a large limb of a tree. As it appears on the sawed surface, a knot is merely a section of the entire knot, its shape depending on the direction of the cut.

Knurled. Having a surface covered with small knobs or beads, as a nail which may have such a surface for greater holding power.

Lacquer. A varnish-type solution used for finishing wood, metal, porcelain, and similar materials. Lacquers dry quickly and leave a tough, durable, flexible, light-weight film. They should not be used over oil-base paints because they contain solvents that will cut such paints. There are several types of lacquers. Cellulose lacquers have a base of nitrocellulose or pyroxylin; others have a resin base.

Laminate. To form a product by bonding together two or more layers of materials. Also, the product so formed, such as a plastic laminate.

Laminated wood. A product made by bonding layers of veneer or lumber with an adhesive so that the grain of all layers is generally parallel.

Laminate, paper-base. A multilayer panel made by compressing sheets of resin-impregnated paper together into a solid mass.

Landing. A platform between flights of stairs or at the termination of a flight of stairs.

Lap joint. (See **Joint.**)

Lap siding. (See **Bevel siding.**)

Lath. A building material of wood, metal, gypsum, or insulating board that is fastened to the frame of a building to act as a plaster base.

Lattice. A framework of crossed wood or metal strips.

Layout. A full-sized drawing showing arrangement and structural features.

Leader. (See **Downspout.**)

Ledger strip. A strip of lumber nailed along the bottom of the side of a girder on which joists rest.

Let-in brace. Nominal 1"-thick boards applied into notched studs diagonally.

Level. (1) A term describing the position of a line or plane which is parallel to the surface of still water. (2) An instrument or tool used in testing for horizontal and vertical surfaces and in determining differences of elevation.

Light. In builder's terminology, space in a window sash for a single pane of glass; also, a pane of glass.

Lignin. The second most abundant component of wood. It is located principally in the thin cementing layer between the wood cells. The chemical structure of lignin is not definitely known.

Linear measure. Measurement along a line.

Linseed oil. Yellowish drying oil made from flaxseed, widely used as a vehicle for lead-based paints. It is soluble in ether, benzene, and turpentine. (See also **Bodied linseed oil** and **Boiled linseed oil.**)

Lintel. A horizontal structural member, usually made of stone, wood, or metal, which supports the load over an opening; a header.

Live load. All loads on a building except dead and lateral loads.

Log. A section of tree trunk suitable in length for sawing into commercial lumber.

Lookout. The end of a rafter, or a construction which projects beyond the sides of a house to support the eaves.

Louver. An opening with a series of horizontal slats so arranged as to permit ventilation but to exclude rain, sunlight, or vision. (See also **Attic ventilators.**)

Lumber. The product of the sawmill and planing mill not further manufactured than by sawing, resawing, passing lengthwise through a standard planing machine, crosscutting to length, and matching. Types of lumber:

Board. Yard lumber less than 2" thick and 1" or more wide.

Dimension. Lumber at least 2" but less than 5" thick, and 2" or more wide. Includes joists, rafters, studding, planks, and small timbers. (See also **Dimension stock.**)

Dressed size. The dimension of lumber after shrinking and being surfaced with a planing machine. Usually this size is ⅜" or ½" less than the nominal or rough size. For example, a 2" x 4" stud actually meaures 1½" by 3½" under American lumber standards for softwood lumber.

Factory and shop lumber. Lumber intended to be cut up for use in further manufacture.

Matched lumber. Lumber that is edge-dressed and shaped to make a close tongue-and-groove joint.

Nominal size. As applied to lumber, the rough-sawed commercial size by which it is known and sold.

Patterned lumber. Lumber that is shaped to a pattern or to a molded form in addition to being dressed, matched, or shiplapped, or any combination of these.

Rough lumber. Lumber as it comes from the saw.

Shiplapped lumber. Lumber that is edge-dressed to make a lap joint.

Structural lumber. Lumber that is 2" or more thick and 4" or more wide; intended for use where strength is required. The grading of structural lumber is based on the strength of the piece and its use.

Structural timbers. Pieces of wood of relatively large size (with a cross section greater than 4" x 6"), the strength of which is the controlling element in their selection and use. Framing for buildings, and crossarms for posts are examples of structural timbers.

Yard lumber. Lumber of all sizes and patterns, intended for general building purposes.

Mantel. The shelf above a fireplace. Originally it referred to the beam or lintel which supports the arch above the fireplace opening. Used also in referring to the entire finish around a fireplace.

Manufactured home. A home whose major components are made in a factory. It may be assembled at the factory or on the site.

Masonry. Anything constructed of stone, brick, concrete, hollow tile, concrete blocks, gypsum blocks, or similar materials, or a combination of them.

Mastic. A pasty material used as a cement (as for setting tile) or a protective coating (as for thermal insulation or waterproofing).

Matched lumber. (See **Lumber.**)

Meeting rails. Rails sufficiently thicker than a window to fill the opening between the top and bottom sash made by the parting stop in the frame of double-hung windows. They are usually beveled.

Metal lath. Sheets of metal slit and drawn out to form openings. Used as a plaster base for walls and ceilings and as reinforcing over other plaster bases.

Millwork. Generally, all wood materials manufactured in millwork plants and planing mills. Includes such items as inside and outside doors, window and door frames, blinds, mantels, panel work, stairways, moldings, and interior trim. Does not include flooring, ceiling, or siding.

Miter. The joint formed by two abutting pieces meeting at an angle.

Mobile home. Complete factory-made home, constructed on a chassis and wheels for instant mobility.

Modular unit. A factory-built, transportable building unit designed to be used by itself or with other, similar units. It is built with standard-size materials.

Modulus of elasticity. A measure of the stiffness of a board.

Moisture content of wood. The amount of water contained in the wood, usually expressed as a percentage of the weight of oven-dry wood.

Molded plywood. (See **Plywood.**)

Molding (moulding). In building construction, a strip of wood, often decorative, such as that on the top of a baseboard or around windows and doors.

Mortise. The slot which is to receive a tenon; or, any hole cut into or through a piece by a chisel or mortiser. Generally of rectangular shape.

Mortise-and-tenon joint. (See **Joint.**)

Mullion. The vertical bar between the windows in a frame which holds two or more windows.

Muntin. A small member which divides the glass or openings of sash or doors.

Naptha. Any of several volatile, flammable liquids obtained by distilling certain materials containing carbon. Naphtha is used as a solvent or thinner in varnish and as a fuel. Petroleum naphtha is also known as benzine.

Natural finish. A transparent finish, usually a drying oil, sealer, or varnish, applied to wood for protection against soiling or weathering. Such a finish should not seriously change the original color of the wood or obscure its grain pattern.

Naval stores. A term applied to the oils, resins, tars, and pitches derived from oleoresin found in conifers, especially in pine trees.

Newel. The chief post at the foot of a staircase. Also, the central support of a winding flight of stairs.

Nominal-size lumber. (See **Lumber.**)

Nonbearing partition. A partition which extends from floor to ceiling but which supports no load other than its own weight.

Nonbearing wall. A wall supporting no load other than its own weight.

Nosing. (1) The part of a stair tread which projects over the riser; any similar projection. (2) A term applied to the rounded edge of a board.

Notch. A crosswise rabbet at the end of a board.

O.C. (on center). The measurement of spacing for studs, rafters, joists, and similar members in a building from the center of one member to the center of the next.

O.G. (ogee). In building construction, a molding with a profile in the form of the letter S; having the outline of a reversed curve.

Oil paint. A paint in which the vehicle is oil.

Oil varnish. A varnish consisting of a hard resin combined with a drying oil and a drier thinned with a volatile solvent. After application, the solvent dries first by evaporation; then the oil dries by oxidation.

Outrigger. An extension of a rafter beyond the wall line. Usually a smaller member nailed to a larger rafter to form a cornice or roof overhand.

Oven-dry wood. Wood dried to constant weight in an oven at temperatures above that of boiling water (usually 101 to 105°C or 214°F).

Oxidation. The process of combining with oxygen.

Paint. A combination of pigments with suitable thinners or oils to provide decorative and protective coatings.

Panel. (l) A large, thin board or sheet of lumber, plywood, or other material. (2) A thin board with all its edges inserted in a groove of a surrounding frame of thick material. (3) A section of floor, wall, ceiling, or roof, usually prefabricated and of large size, handled as a single unit in the operations of assembly and erection.

Panel siding. Large sheets of plywood or hardboard which may serve as both sheathing and siding.

Paper-base laminate. (See **Laminate, paper-base.**)

Paper, building. (See **Building paper.**)

Paper, sheathing. (See **Sheathing paper.**)

Papreg. Any of various products made by impregnating sheets of specially manufactured high-strength paper with synthetic resin and laminating them to form a dense, moisture-resistant product.

Particleboard. A board composed of wood chips held together with adhesive.

Parting stop or strip. A small wood piece used in the side and head jambs of double-hung windows to separate upper and lower sash.

Partition. That which subdivides space within a building; especially, an interior wall. (See also **Bearing partition** and **Nonbearing partition.**)

Patterned lumber. (See **Lumber.**)

Penny. As applied to nails, it originally indicated the price per hundred. The term now serves as a measure of nail length and is abbreviated by the letter d.

Perm. A measure of water vapor movement through a

material, such as a vapor barrier. One perm equals one grain of vapor transmission per square foot, per hour, for each inch of mercury difference in vapor pressure.

Piers. Masonry supports, independent of the main foundation.

Pigment. A substance which gives color, as in paint, enamel, dye, or lacquer. It is in the form of fine, powdery particles which are held in suspension, not dissolved, in the vehicle.

Piles. Long posts driven into the soil in swampy locations or wherever it is difficult to secure a firm foundation. Other timbers or the footing courses of masonry are then laid on these posts.

Pitch. The incline of a roof. It is the ratio of the total rise to the total width of a house. For example, an 8' rise and a 24' width make a ⅓ pitch roof.

Pitch pocket. An opening in a piece of lumber, parallel to the annual growth rings, which contains or has contained solid or liquid pitch.

Pitch streak. A well-defined accumulation of pitch visible as a more or less regular streak in the wood of certain conifers.

Pith. The small, soft core of a tree trunk, branch, twig, or log.

Plain-sawed. (See **Grain.**)

Plan (of a building). The representation of a horizontal section of a building, showing such parts as walls, doors, windows, stairs, chimneys, and columns.

Plank. A broad board, usually more than 1" thick; especially, one laid with its wide dimension horizontal and used as a bearing surface.

Plaster. A mixture of lime, sand, and water, used to cover outside and inside wall surfaces.

Plaster grounds. (See **Grounds.**)

Plasticizing wood. Softening wood by hot water, steam, or chemical treatment to make it easier to mold.

Plate. *Sill plate:* a horizontal member anchored to a masonry wall. *Sole plate:* bottom horizontal member of a frame wall. *Top plate:* top horizontal member of a frame wall supporting ceiling joists, rafters, or other members.

Plate cut. (See **Seat cut.**)

Platform framing. (See **Framing, platform.**)

Plough (plow). To cut a groove in the same direction as the grain of the wood.

Plumb. Exactly perpendicular; vertical.

Plumb cut. Any vertical cut; especially one at the top end of a rafter.

Ply. A term used to denote a layer or thickness, as of building or roofing paper, or a layer of wood in plywood.

Plywood. A wood product made by fastening together layers of veneer or a combination of veneer layers and a lumber core. The layers are joined with an adhesive. Adjoining plies are usually laid with grains at right angles to each other, and almost always an odd number of plies are used.

Molded plywood. Plywood made to some desired shape other than perfectly flat. Often this shaping is done at the time the layers are glued together.

Two ways of molding plywood are (1) by applying fluid pressure and (2) with curved forms.

Porch. A floor extending beyond the exterior walls of a building. It may be covered and enclosed or open.

Pores. Openings on the surface of a piece of wood. These openings result when vessels in the wood are severed during sawing. (See also **Vessels.**)

Porous woods. Another name for hardwoods, which frequently have vessels or pores large enough to be seen without magnification.

Post. A timber set on end to support a wall, girder, or other structural member.

Preservative. Any substance that, for a reasonable length of time, is effective in preventing the development and action of wood-rotting fungi, borers of various kinds, and insects that cause deterioration in wood.

Primer. The first coat of paint in a job that consists of two or more coats; also, the paint used for such a coat.

Purlin. In a roof, a horizontal timber which supports rafters, or one that supports the roof sheathing directly.

Putty. A soft, pliable type of cement, having nearly the consistency of dough. Used in sealing glass in sash, filling small holes and crevices in wood, and for similar purposes.

Pumice. An extremely light and porous material used in powder form to smooth and polish surfaces.

Quarter-round. A molding which, in profile, appears as a quarter-circle.

Quarter-sawed. (See **Grain.**)

R. Resistance to thermal conductivity. R = 1/k or 1/C.

Rabbet. A rectangular groove cut in the corner of a board.

Radial. Extending out from the center, as the rays in a tree.

Radiant heating. (1) A method of heating consisting of a forced hot water system with pipes placed in the floor, wall, or ceiling. (2) A method of heating with electrically heated panels.

Rafter. One of a series of structural members of a roof, designed to support roof loads. The rafters of a flat roof are sometimes called roof joists. (See also **Hip, Jack, and Valley Rafters.**)

Rail. (1) A horizontal bar or timber extending from one post or support to another, such as a guard or barrier in a fence or staircase. (2) The horizontal members of the framework of a sash, door, blind, or any paneled assembly.

Raised grain. A roughened condition of the surface of dressed lumber in which the hard summerwood is raised above the softer springwood but not torn loose from it.

Rake. The inclined edge of a gable roof. (The trim member is a rake molding.)

Rate of growth. The rate at which a tree has increased its amount of wood. This is measured radially in the trunk or in lumber cut from the trunk. The rate is determined from the number of annual growth rings per inch.

Raw linseed oil. The crude product processed from flaxseed, usually without much further treatment.

Rays. In wood, strips of cells extending radially within a tree. They vary in height from a few cells in some species to 4" or more in oak. The rays serve chiefly to store food and transport it horizontally in the tree.

Reflective insulation. Sheet material of which one or both surfaces will conduct comparatively little heat. When used with the surfaces facing air spaces, such material reduces the heat radiation across the air space.

Reinforcing. Steel rods or metal fabric placed in concrete slabs, beams, or columns to increase their strength.

Relative humidity. (See **Humidity.**)

Resawing. Sawing lumber again after the first sawing; specifically, sawing into boards or dimension lumber.

Resin. A sticky material obtained from the sap of certain trees and plants (natural resin) or made synthetically from coal-tar products and other organic substances (synthetic resin). Resins are widely used in making varnishes and paints.

Resorcinol glue. A glue that is high in both wet and dry strength and resistant to high temperatures. It is used for gluing lumber or assembly joints that must withstand severe service conditions.

Ribbon. A narrow board let into the studding to add support to joists.

Ridge. The horizontal line at the junction of the top edges of two sloping roof surfaces. The rafters of both slopes are nailed to a board at the ridge.

Ridge board. The board placed on edge at the ridge of the roof to support the upper ends of the rafters.

Ripping. Sawing wood along the grain.

Rise. (1) In a roof, the vertical distance between the top of the double plate and the center of the ridge board. (2) In stairs, the vertical distance from the top of one stair tread to the top of the next.

Riser. Each of the vertical boards closing the spaces between the treads of stairways.

Roll roofing. Roofing material composed of fiber and saturated with asphalt and supplied in 36" rolls containing 108 square feet. It is generally furnished in weights of 45 to 90 pounds per roll.

Roof. The covering or upper part of a building.

Roofing. Material put on a roof to protect it from wind and water.

Roof sheathing. Boards or sheet material, fastened to the roof rafters, on which the shingles or other roof covering is laid.

Rosin. A hard resin used in making certain varnishes.

Rotary cutting. A way of cutting veneer from a log. The log is fastened in a large lathe and a sharp knife cuts the veneer, much as paper is unwrapped from a roll.

Rough lumber. (See **Lumber.**)

Rout. To gouge out or make a furrow in, as in wood.

RPM. Revolutions per minute.

Rubber-emulsion paint. Paint with a vehicle of fine droplets of natural or synthetic rubber dispersed in water.

Rubbing compound. An abrasive material used to produce a smoothly finished wood surface.

Run. (1) In reference to roofs, the horizontal distance that underlies the slope of the roof from a wall to the ridge. (2) Referring to stairways, the width of a step, measured from the face of one riser to the face of the next, and not including the nosing; also, the horizontal distance covered by a flight of steps.

S1E. Surfaced one edge.

S1S. Surfaced one side.

S2S. Surfaced two sides.

S4S. Surfaced four sides.

S1S1E. Surfaced one side, one edge.

S1S2E. Surfaced one side, two edges.

Saddle. Two sloping surfaces meeting in a horizontal ridge, used between the back side of a chimney or other vertical surface and a sloping roof. Also called a **cricket.**

Sag. An unevenness or irregularity in a coat of paint, varnish, or lacquer. It results if too much of the liquid is allowed to collect in one spot or area.

Sand float finish. Lime mixed with sand, resulting in a textured finish.

Sanding. Rubbing sandpaper or similar abrasive over a surface before applying a finish.

Sandwich construction. (See **Structural sandwich construction.**)

Sap. Most of the fluids in a tree. Certain secretions and excretions, such as oleoresin, are excepted.

Sapwood. The living wood, usually of pale color, near the outside of the tree. Generally, the sapwood is more susceptible to decay than the heartwood.

Sash. The framework which holds the glass in a window.

Sash balance. A device, usually operated by a spring or tensioned weather stripping designed to counterbalance double-hung window sash.

Saturated felt. A felt which is impregnated with tar or asphalt.

Sawing. See terms listed under **Grain** for explanation of certain sawing methods.

Scab. A short piece of wood or plywood fastened to two abutting timbers to splice them together.

Scaffold. A temporary structure or platform for workers to sit or stand on when working at a height above the floor or ground.

Scale. A proportion between two sets of dimensions, as between those of a drawing and its original. For example, the scale of a drawing may be expressed as $\frac{1}{4}$" = 1'.

Scarfing. A joint between two pieces of wood which allows them to be spliced lengthwise.

Scarf joint. (See **Joint.**)

Scotia. A hollow molding used as a part of a cornice, and often under the nosing of a stair tread.

Scratch coat. The first coat of plaster, which is scratched to form a bond for the second coat.

Screed. A small strip of wood, usually the thickness of the plaster coat, used as a guide for plastering.

Scribing. (1) The marking of a piece of wood to provide for the fitting of one of its surfaces to the irregular surface of another. (2) Fitting woodwork to an irregular surface. In moldings, cutting the end of one piece to fit the molded face of the other at an interior angle to replace a miter joint. Such a joint is called a coped joint.

Sealer. A finishing material, either clear or pigmented, that is usually applied directly over uncoated wood. It prevents subsequent coats of paint or varnish from seeping into the wood.

Seasoning. Removing moisture from green wood in order to improve its serviceability.

Seat cut (plate cut). The cut at the bottom end of a rafter to allow it to fit on the plate.

Second growth. New timber that has grown after the removal, whether by cutting, fire, or other agent, of all or a large part of the previous stand.

Section. A drawing showing the kind, arrangement, and proportion of the various parts of a structure. It shows how the structure would appear n cut through by a plane.

Semigloss paint or enamel. A paint or enamel made so that its coating, when dry, has some luster but is not very glossy.

Shake. (1) In lumber, a separation or crack along the grain, the greater part of which occurs between the rings of annual growth. (2) A handsplit shingle, usually edge-grained.

Sheathing. The material, usually wood boards, plywood, or wallboard, placed over exterior studding or rafters of a structure.

Sheathing paper. A building material, generally paper or felt, used in wall and roof construction to retard the passage of air and sometimes moisture.

Sheet-metal work. All components of a house employing sheet metal, such as flashing, gutters, and downspouts.

Shellac. A transparent coating made by dissolving lac in alcohol; used commonly in wood finishing. Lac is a resinous substance secreted by a tropical insect.

Shingles. A covering applied in overlapping layers, as for the roof or sides of a building. Shingles can be made of wood, asphalt, asbestos, tile, or slate, among other materials. They are cut fairly small.

Shingle stain. A very thin oil paint, intended for coloring rough-surfaced wood, such as shingles, without forming a coating of significant thickness or gloss.

Shiplap. (See **Lumber.**)

Shrinkage. A decrease in volume, as of molten metal when it solidifies, or in wood when it dries.

Shutters. (See **Blinds.**)

Siding. The finish covering of the outside wall of a frame building. It may be made of horizontal weatherboards, vertical boards and battens, shingles, or other material. (See also specific kinds, such as **Bevel siding.**)

Sill. (1) The lowest member of the frame of a structure, resting on the foundation and supporting the uprights of the frame. (2) The member forming the lower side of an opening, as a door sill or a window sill.

Sill plate. (See **Plate.**)

Sizing. (1) Working material to the desired size. (2) A coating of glue, shellac, or other material applied to a surface to prepare it for paint or other finish.

Sleeper. Usually, a wood member embedded in concrete, as in a floor, that serves to support and to fasten subfloor or flooring.

Slope. The incline of a roof, expressed as inches of rise per foot of run.

Soffit. The underside of a staircase, cornice, beam, arch, or a similar member of a building; relatively small in area as compared with ceilings.

Softwood. One of the botanical groups of trees that, in most cases, have needlelike or scalelike growths rather than broad leaves. (These trees are known as conifers.) The term *softwood* also applies to the wood produced by such trees. In this sense it has no reference to the actual softness of the wood.

Soil cover (ground cover). A light covering of plastic film, roll roofing, or similar material used over the soil in crawl spaces of buildings to minimize moisture permeation of the area.

Soil stack. A general term for the vertical main of a system of soil, waste, or vent piping.

Sole or sole plate. (See **Plate.**)

Solid bridging. A solid member placed between adjacent floor joists near the center of the span to prevent joists from twisting.

Soluble. Capable of being dissolved.

Solvent. A liquid in which things can be dissolved. Also, more loosely, a liquid in which tiny particles of a substance can be dispersed in suspension, without actually dissolving. Solvents commonly used in wood finishing include turpentine, alcohol, and petroleum and coal-tar distillates. The solvent in a finishing material usually evaporates, leaving the pigment or other necessary ingredients dry on the finished surface.

Sound deadening. Construction intended to prevent the passage of sound.

Span. The distance between structural supports such as walls, columns, piers, beams, girders, and trusses.

Spar varnish. A varnish consisting mainly of drying oil and the harder types of resins. It is waterproof and strongly resistant to the damaging effect of moisture and sunlight.

Specifications. The written or printed directions regarding construction details for a building.

Specific gravity. A measure of the relative density of a substance. For woods it is expressed as the ratio of the weight of a body to the weight of an equal volume of water at 4°C or other specified temperature.

Splash block. A small masonry block laid with the top close to the ground surface to receive drainage from downspouts and to carry it away from the building.

Spline. A thin strip of wood used to reinforce joints. Also known as a "feather" or "tongue."

Springwood. The portion of a tree's wood that is formed during the early part of the season's growth, as indicated by the annual growth rings. It is usually less dense and weaker than **summerwood.**

Square. As a unit of measure, one hundred square feet. Usually applied to roofing material.

Sidewall coverings are often packed to cover 100 square feet and are sold on that basis.

Stain. (1) A discoloration in wood. It may be caused by microorganisms, metal, or chemicals. (2) Materials that are used in coloring wood. (See also **Shingle stain.**)

STC. Sound Transmission Class. A measure of a building element's resistance to the passage of airborne sound.

Steam bending. The process of forming curved wood members by steaming or boiling the wood and bending it to a desired shape.

Stickers. Wood strips or boards used to separate the layers of lumber in a pile and thus permit air to circulate between layers.

Stiffness. The resistance of a piece of wood to bending.

Stile. An upright framing member in a panel door.

Stool. The flat, narrow shelf which forms the top member of the interior trim at the bottom of a window.

Storm sash (storm window). An extra window usually placed on the outside of an existing window as additional protection against cold weather.

Story. That part of a building which is between any floor and the floor or roof next above.

Strength. In a broad sense, all the properties that enable wood to resist forces or bear loads. In a more restricted sense, the term may apply to any one of these properties. In that case the property under consideration should be specified; for instance, "strength in compression parallel to grain."

Stress-grade lumber. Structural lumber that has been graded and stamped with information to indicate the specific load it will support.

String, stringer. A timber or other support for cross members in floors or ceilings. In stairs, the support on which the stair treads rest.

Strip flooring. Wood flooring consisting of narrow, matched strips.

Structural sandwich construction. A construction in which layers of relatively high-strength facing materials are tightly bonded to, and act integrally with, a low-density core material.

Structural timbers. (See **Lumber.**)

Stucco. Most commonly refers to an outside plaster made with portland cement as its base.

Stud. One of a series of slender wood or metal vertical structural members placed as supporting elements in walls and partitions, usually 16" on center. (Plural: studs or studding.)

Subfloor. Boards or sheet material laid on joists, and over which a finish floor is to be laid.

Summerwood. That portion of wood formed after the springwood formation has ceased. It is usually denser and stronger than **springwood**.

Suspended ceiling. A ceiling system supported by hanging it from the overhead structural framing.

Tack rag. A piece of cheesecloth or cotton rag moistened with thinned varnish. It is used to pick up small particles of dust.

Tacky. Not quite dry; sticky.

T & G. Tongued and grooved.

Tail beam. A relatively short beam or joist supported in a wall on one end and by a header on the other.

Taper. A gradual and uniform decrease in size, as of a round or rectangular piece or hole.

Template. A full-sized pattern from which structural layouts are made. Templates may be of paper, cardboard, plywood, or metal.

Termites. Insects that resemble ants in size, general appearance, and habit of living in colonies. Hence, they are frequently called "white ants." About 56 species of termites are known in the United States. The two major species, classified from the manner in which they attack wood, are (1) ground-inhabiting or subterranean termites, the most common, and (2) drywood termites, found in the United States chiefly along the extreme southern border and the Gulf of Mexico.

Termite shield. A shield, usually of noncorrodible metal, placed in or on a foundation wall or other mass of masonry, or around pipes, to prevent passage of termites.

Terneplate. Sheet iron or steel coated with an alloy of lead and tin.

Texture. A term often used interchangeably with grain. Sometimes refers to the density of a wood and the degree of contrast between springwood and summerwood. Texture often refers to the finer structure of wood (see **Grain**) rather than to the annual rings.

Thermosetting glues and resins. Glues and resins that are cured with heat and do not soften when subjected later to high temperatures.

Thinner. A volatile liquid added to finishing material to make it flow more easily and smoothly.

Threshold. A strip of wood or metal beveled on each edge and used above the finished floor under outside doors.

Tie beam. A beam so situated that it holds the principal rafters of a roof together and prevents them from thrusting the plate out of line.

Timber. (See **Lumber.**)

Tint. A color produced by adding white pigment or paint to a colored pigment or paint, with the amount of white greater than the amount of colored pigment.

Toenailing. To drive a nail so that it enters the first surface diagonally. It usually penetrates the second member at a slant also.

Tongue. A projecting edge, as on a board, that fits into a groove of another piece.

Tongued and grooved. (See **Dressed and matched.**)

Top plate. (See **Plate.**)

Tracheids. Elongated cells that constitute the greater part of the structure of softwoods and are also present in some hardwoods. Tracheids are frequently referred to as fibers.

Transom. A transverse structural member, such as a lintel, or the horizontal crossbar in a window.

Tread. The horizontal board in a stairway; the part on which a person walks.

Trim. Finish materials, such as moldings, applied around openings (window trim, door trim) or where walls join the floor or ceiling of a room (baseboard, cornice, and other moldings).

Trimmer. A beam or joist to which a header is nailed in framing, as for a chimney or a stairway.

Truss. An assembly of members, such as beams, bars, and rods, combined to form a rigid framework. Often used in roof construction.

Tung oil. A yellow drying oil obtained from the seed pods of tung trees and widely used in water-resistant varnishes, lacquers, and high-gloss paints.

Turpentine. A volatile oil used as a thinner in paints and as a solvent in varnishes.

Twist. A wood defect characterized by a turning or winding of the edges of a board so that the four corners of any face are no longer in the same plane.

U-value. The total or overall Btu of heat transmitted in 1 hour per square foot of area per 1°F temperature difference between the air on one side of the material and the air on the other side.

Undercoat. A coating applied prior to the final or top coat of a paint job.

Underlayment. A material placed under finish coverings, such as flooring or shingles, to provide a smooth, even surface for applying the finish.

Valley. The internal angle formed by the meeting of two sloping sides of a roof.

Valley rafter. A rafter which runs from a wall plate to the ridge, along the valley of a roof. It is usually made of doubled 2"-thick members.

Vapor barrier. Material used to prevent vapor or moisture from getting into walls and condensing. There are two common types of vapor barriers: membrane and paint. The vapor barrier must be a part of the warm side of the wall.

Varnish. A thickened preparation of drying oil or drying oil and resin. When applied to a surface, it leaves a hard, glossy, transparent coating. It may also be mixed with pigments to make enamels. Clear varnish is a slightly yellow, semitransparent liquid.

Vehicle. The liquid portion of a finishing material. It consists of the binder (nonvolatile) and thinners (volatile).

Veneer. A thin layer or sheet of wood; usually one that has beauty or value and is intended to be overlaid on an inferior surface.

Rotary-cut veneer. Veneer cut in a lathe which rotates a log against a knife.

Sawed veneer. Veneer produced by sawing.

Sliced veneer. Veneer that is sliced off a log, bolt, or flitch with a knife.

Vermiculite. A mineral closely related to mica. When heated, it expands to form lightweight material with insulation quality. Used as bulk insulation and also as aggregate in insulating and acoustical plaster and in insulating concrete floors.

Vessels. Wood cells of comparatively large diameter that have open ends and are set one above the other so that they resemble tubes. The cells themselves are sometimes called vessels, and so are the tubelike structures they form. The openings of the vessels on the surface of a piece of wood are usually referred to as pores.

Virgin growth. The original growth of trees on a piece of land. (To be distinguished from **Second growth.**)

Volatile thinner. A liquid that evaporates readily and is used to thin or reduce the consistency of finishes without altering the relative volumes of pigments and nonvolatile vehicles.

Wainscoting. Matched boarding or panel work covering the lower portion of a wall.

Wallboard. Large, rigid sheets of wood pulp, gypsum, or similar materials that may be fastened to the frame of a building, usually to form the interior walls.

Wane. A defect in lumber in which there is bark or a lack of wood at a corner or edge.

Warp. A variation from a true or plane surface, as in a piece of lumber. Warp includes bow, crook, cup, twist, and any combination thereof.

Water paint. A paint in which the vehicle is a water emulsion.

Water repellent. A liquid designed to penetrate into wood to make it resist water.

Water stain. A colored dye that is soluble in water.

Wax. A fatty material obtained from the honeycombs of bees or from similar plant, animal, or mineral substances. Used for providing an attractive, protective coating, as for wood. Waxes may be used by themselves or combined with other ingredients to make certain paints, varnishes, and paint removers.

Weathering. The mechanical or chemical disintegration and discoloration of a wood surface resulting from exposure to light, action of dust and sand carried by winds, alternate shrinking and swelling brought about by changes in the weather, or a combination of these causes. Weathering does not include decay.

Weather stripping. Narrow strips of material, such as metal, installed around doors and windows to retard passage of air, water, moisture, or dust.

Whalers. The lumber used to stiffen concrete forms, either vertical or horizontal.

Wind. (Rhymes with kind.) The defect of a board which appears slightly twisted, or which rests on two diagonally opposite corners when it is laid on a flat surface.

Wood filler. (See **Filler, wood.**)

Wood fungi. (See **Fungi, wood.**)

Wood rays. (See **Rays.**)

Wood substance. The solid material of which wood is composed. Usually (but not always) this term refers to the extractive-free solid substance of which the cell walls are composed.

Workability. The ease with which wood can be smoothly cut and shaped with hand or machine tools.

Yard lumber. (See **Lumber.**)

Index

Nails
for air nailers, 170
roofing, 450-451
siding, 565-568
Nail set, 116
National Bureau of Standards (NBS), 65
National Concrete Masonry Association, 258
National Hardwood Lumber Association, 62
National Lumber Manufacturers' Association, 69, 900
National Mineral Wool Insulation Association, 600
National Oak Flooring Manufacturers' Association, 653-654
National Woodwork Manufacturers' Association, 804
Newel, 688
Nibbler, 681
Nipper, 681
Nonbearing walls, 252, 282, 336
Northeastern Lumber Manufacturers' Association, 66
Northern Hardwood and Pine Manufacturers Association, 66
Nosing of stair tread, 688
Notch for wood beam, 241
Notes in construction drawings, 33
No. 1 common lumber grade, 62

Oak, 653
Open cornice, 481-484
Open-end wrench, 119
Openings
floor, 294-295
in wall framing, 322-323
Optical level, 217-221
Oriented-strand board, 84-85
Oriented-strand board sheathing, 438-439

OSHA. *See* Federal Occupational Safety and Health Act
Outfeed table of jointer, 191-192, 197
Outlet ventilators, 475-477
Overhang, roof, 376, 385-386, 398

Paint, 815, 838-858
Panel doors, 534
Paneling
hardboard, 642
plywood, 633-641
solid wood, 642-647
Panelized shingles, 583
Paper, building, 355-356
Parliamentary procedures, 609, 898
Parquet flooring, 665-666
Particleboard, 88-90
Partition
changing, 886-888
corner post, 328
cross, 291
wall, 336
Passive solar energy system, 49-51
Patching block walls, 256
Patio, 880
Pattern flooring, 665-666
Pecan, 653
Pedestal footings, 232
Perforated hardboard, 86
Permanent wood foundation, 869-871
Perm values of vapor barriers, 606
Pesticides, 809
Photovoltaic panel, 53-54
Piers, 21, 232, 297, 298
Pilasters, 245, 261
Pipe-screed strips, 273
Pipe wrench, 119
Pitch (lumber defect), 62
Pitch of roof, 367, 445
Pitch-pocket (lumber defect), 62
Plain-sawn lumber, 57-58
Plancier, 481
Planer blade, 130

Planes, 113-114
Planing on jointer, 193-195
Plank flooring, 664-665
Planking, 439-440, 443
Plans, 11, 12, 31
Plaster
for stucco, 584
wall and ceiling finish, 619-623, 814
Plate
rafter, 336-337
sill, 291
sole, 319-322
strike (door), 755-756
top, 323-324
Plate joiners, 201-203
Platform-frame construction, 277, 290-291, 317, 358
Platform of stairs, 688
Pliers, 120
Plumb and level lines of rafter, 368, 383
Plumb bob, 217, 220
Plumb bob and line
general discussion, 111
used in wall framing, 334
Plumbing
general discussion, 814-815, 819-824
lines, 266, 291, 814
of wall framing, 340
stack vents, 339
wall sections, 334-335
Plunge cutting, 184
Ply, 77
Plywood
blade, 130
general discussion, 74-81
paneling, 633-641
roof sheathing, 435-438
siding, 571, 579
soffit, 486-487
subfloor, 307-308
wall sheathing, 351-352, 354

Credits

Abbey Floors / Ann Garvin, 104 (bottom right)

Acorn Manufacturing Co., Inc., 735 (middle center)

AEG Power Tool Corp., 159 (upper left), 185 (top)

ALCOA Building Products, 476 (bottom left), 477 (top left), 488 (middle right), 555

Amana Refrigeration, Inc., 713 (top right)

American Concrete Institute, Rocky Mountain Chapter, 271 (top right)

American Plywood Association, 74 (left, right), 305 (bottom), 620 (bottom left), 783 (top)

Anderson Corp., 500 (bottom right), 501 (bottom right)

Arco Solar, Inc., 10 (top left), 53 (top right, center right)

Arnold & Brown, 46H (bottom), 937 (bottom), 940 (top)

Art MacDillo's / Gary Skillestad, 927, 928, 929, 930, 931, 932, 933, 934

Artist Blacksmith Association of North America, 686 (top left)

Vincent Babak, 98 (top left), 152, 164, 172 (top right), 202 (top left), 208 (bottom center), 216 (bottom), 312 (top, bottom left), 331 (bottom), 661 (top, bottom left), 682 (top left, top right)

BASF Corporation-Fibers Division, 617 (bottom left)

Bayou Park Corp. / Peter Serebrenik, 11 (bottom right)

Roger B. Bean, 4 (bottom), 5 (bottom left), 105 (bottom), 365, 457 (left), 832 (top right), 874 (top), 884 (top left)

Benchmark Doors, 531 (bottom left)

Benjamin Moore & Co., 840 (middle left, bottom left, bottom

right), 841 (top left, middle left, bottom left, top right), 843 (top left, bottom right), 844 (top center, bottom left, top right), 850 (top left, top right, middle right, bottom), 851 (middle left, bottom left, top right, middle right), 852 (middle center, bottom center, top right, middle right, bottom right), 853 (bottom left), 854 (top left)

Jeffrey Bellantuono, 420 (bottom), 424, 430 (top center), 431 (top left), 709 (top left)

Bennett Industries, Inc., 535 (bottom left), 758 (top left)

Benson Woodworking Co., Inc., 283 (top, bottom right)

Better Homes & Gardens, 583 (top right)

Black & Decker, 104 (top middle), 124 (bottom left), 158 (middle left, middle right), 160 (bottom right), 174, 180 (bottom left), 548 (top right)

Boise Cascade, 57 (top)

Bosch, 158 (bottom right), 159 (lower left), 176 (center left), 183 (center left)

Robert Bosh Power Tool Corp., 123 (bottom left), 189 (bottom left), 730, (bottom right)

Bostik Tile and Flooring Group, 680 (top left)

The Brinkman Group Ltd., 366 (bottom)

Bruce Hardwood Floors, 651, 664, 666 (top)

Bureau of Labor Statistics, 3

Burnham, 835 (top left)

Dick Burrows, 135 (top left)

CalComp Inc., 16 (bottom left)

Calculated Industries, Inc., 375 (bottom left)

California Redwood Association, 644 (bottom right)